BUSINESS LAW AND THE REGULATION OF BUSINESS

THIRD EDITION

Len Young Smith
Chairman of the Department of Business Law
Northwestern University (Retired)
Member of the Illinois Bar

Richard A. Mann
Professor of Business Law
The University of North Carolina at Chapel Hill
Member of the North Carolina Bar

Barry S. Roberts
Professor of Business Law
The University of North Carolina at Chapel Hill
Member of the North Carolina and Pennsylvania Bars

West Publishing Company
St. Paul   New York   Los Angeles   San Francisco

Copy Editor: Mary Hough
Cover Design: Pete Thiel ·
Composition: Carlisle Communications
Indexing: Northwind Editorial Services
Proofreading: Lynn Reichel

A STUDENT STUDY GUIDE

A study guide containing outlines and summaries of major topics plus review questions for additional practice is available with this text. If you cannot locate a copy of the study guide in your bookstore, please ask your bookstore manager to order a copy for you under the title *Study Guide to Accompany Business Law and the Regulation of Business, Third Edition.*

COPYRIGHT ©1984, 1987   By WEST PUBLISHING COMPANY
COPYRIGHT ©1990   By WEST PUBLISHING COMPANY
                        50 W. Kellogg Boulevard
                        P.O. Box 64526
                        St. Paul, MN 55164-1003

Printed in the United States of America

97 96 95 94 93 92 91 90   8 7 6 5 4 3 2 1

Library of Congress Cataloging-in-Publication Data

Smith, Len Young, 1901–
    Business law and the regulation of business / Len Young Smith,
Richard A. Mann, Barry S. Roberts.—3rd ed.
        p.   cm.
    ISBN 0–314–67278–8
    1. Commercial law—United States. 2. Trade regulation—United
States. I. Mann, Richard A. II. Roberts, Barry S. III. Title.
KF889.S54 1990
346.73'07—dc20
[347.3067]   89-22716
                                                                  CIP

ABOUT THE AUTHORS

Len Young Smith received an A.B., an M.A., and a J.D. from Northwestern University. He was a member of the Illinois State Board of Law Examiners for forty years, and served as President of the Board for over thirty years. He served on the National Conference of Bar Examiners for over thirty years, and chaired the conference from 1955 to 1956. He is also a former editor of *The Bar Examiner*. Len Smith is a member of the Illinois Bar, Who's Who in American Law, and Who's Who in the World. He is a co-author of *Smith and Roberson's Business Law, Seventh Edition*, as well as *Essentials of Business Law, Third Edition*.

Richard A. Mann received a B.S. in Mathematics from the University of North Carolina at Chapel Hill and a J.D. from Yale Law School. He is currently Professor of Business Law at the University of North Carolina. Richard Mann is a past president of the Southeastern Regional Business Law Association. He is a member of Who's Who in American Law, Outstanding Young Men of America, and the North Carolina Bar.

Professor Mann has written extensively on a number of legal topics including bankruptcy, sales, secured transactions, real property, insurance law, and business associations. He has received the *American Business Law Journal's* award for both the best article (1984) and the best comment (1979). He has served as a reviewer and staff editor for the *American Business Law Journal*. He teaches in several executive education programs and is a founder, managing director, and instructor in the Carolina CPA Review. He is a co-author of *Smith and Roberson's Business Law, Seventh Edition*, as well as *Essentials of Business Law, Third Edition*.

Barry S. Roberts received a B.S. in Business Administration from Pennsylvania State University, a J.D. from the University of Pennsylvania, and an LL.M. from Harvard Law School. He served as a judicial clerk for the Pennsylvania Supreme Court prior to practicing law in Pittsburgh. Barry Roberts is currently Professor of Business Law at the School of Business Administration, University of North Carolina at Chapel Hill. He is a member of Who's Who in American Law, Outstanding Young Men of America, and the North Carolina Bar.

Professor Roberts has written numerous articles on such topics as antitrust, products liability, constitutional law, banking law, employment law, and business associations. He has been a reviewer and staff editor for the *American Business Law Journal*. Professor Roberts is a founder, managing director, and instructor in the Carolina CPA Review. He is a co-author of *Smith and Roberson's Business Law, Seventh Edition*, as well as *Essentials of Business Law, Third Edition*.

CONTENTS IN BRIEF

CONTENTS

LAW IN THE NEWS ARTICLES

TABLE OF CASES

PREFACE

The third edition of *Business Law and the Regulation of Business* is in the tradition of accuracy, comprehensiveness, and authoritativeness long associated with *Smith and Roberson's Business Law*. This text covers all the material presented in the current edition of Smith and Roberson in a less technical, but none-theless authoritative manner. It covers the material succinctly, yet in depth sufficient to be easily comprehended by today's students.

This text is designed for use in Business Law and Legal Environment courses generally offered in universities, colleges, and schools of business and commerce. By reason of the broad coverage and variety of the material this volume may be readily adapted to specially designed courses in Business Law by assigning and emphasizing different combinations of the subject matter. All topics included in the CPA exam are covered by the text.

Greater emphasis has been placed upon the regulatory environment of Business Law: The first six chapters are devoted to introductory coverage of the legal environment of business; Part Nine (Chapters 40 to 46) thoroughly addresses the area of government regulation of business; and each of the parts opens with an introductory discussion of the public policy, social issues, and business ethics pertaining to that part. A new chapter—International Business Law—has been added.

From long classroom experience we are of the opinion that fundamental legal principles can be more effectively learned from text and case materials having at least a degree of human interest. To accomplish this objective a large number of recent cases have been included. Landmark cases, on the other hand, have not been neglected. All of the cases have the facts and decision summarized for clarity and the opinion edited to preserve the language of the court. The cases are also integrated into the chapters. The edited portion of the case begins with the judge's name. In addition, Law in the News has been updated to provide the student with recent news articles that discuss the implications of the legal principles covered in the text.

To improve readability, all unnecessary "legalese" has been eliminated while essential legal terms are printed in boldface and clearly defined, explained, and illustrated. The text has been enriched by numerous illustrative hypothetical and case examples to help students relate material to real life experiences.

Strong classroom tested problems appear at the end of the chapters to test the student's understanding of major concepts. We have used the problems and consider them excellent stimulants to classroom discussion.

Students have found the problems helpful in enabling them to apply the basic rules of law to factual situations, many of which are taken from reported court decisions. The problems serve as a springboard for discussion and readily suggest other and related problems to the inquiring, analytical mind. We have added discussion questions to the end of all chapters to provide another opportunity for the students to examine their comprehension of the material.

A new feature has been added to Part Two—Contracts, Part Three—Sales, and Chapters 40, 41, 42, and 45 of Part Nine—Regulation of Business: Computer Research Problems. These additional problems are based on cases appearing in LEGAL CLERK, which is an interactive software package that introduces students to the basics of computer-aided research and amplifies the principles of business law covered in those chapters. Access to LEGAL CLERK provides the student the opportunity to review the legal principles relating to the facts of the problem and to read an edited version of the court's decision in the case upon which the facts are based. In these chapters, the principal cases that appear in LEGAL CLERK and the Computer Research Problems are identified with a logo indicating which of the three versions of LEGAL CLERK contains that case:

 Uniform Commercial Code Article 2 Sales-Version 1.0

 Government Regulation and The Legal Environment of Business Version 1.0

 Contracts-Version 1.0

We have used approximately 150 classroom tested figures, charts, and diagrams. The diagrams help the student conceptualize the many abstract concepts in the law; the charts not only summarize prior discussions but also aid in pointing out relationships between different legal rules. In addition, each chapter ends with a chapter summary which is an annotated outline summarizing the entire chapter, including the key terms.

Classroom use and study of this book should provide for the student the following benefits and skills:

1. Perception and appreciation of the scope, extent, and importance of the law
2. Basic knowledge of the fundamental concepts, principles, and rules of law that apply to business transactions
3. Acquisition of knowledge of the function and operation of courts and governmental administrative agencies
4. Ability to recognize the possibility of potential legal problems which may arise in a doubtful or complicated situation, and the necessity of consulting a lawyer and obtaining competent professional legal advice
5. Development of analytical skills and reasoning power

We express our gratitude to the following professors for their helpful comments:

William Dennis Ames   David Cooper
Indiana University of Pennsylvania   *Fullerton College*

Gary A. Hanson
Pepperdine University

Debbie L. Mescon
Salisbury State University

Clay Hipp
New Mexico State University

Robert L. Peace
North Carolina State University

Susan S. Jarvis, J.D.
Pan American University

Daniel L. Reynolds
Middle Tennessee State University

Logan Langwith
College of St. Thomas

Stanley E. Stettz
Lafayette College

Stephen M. Maple, LL.W.
University of Indianapolis

John G. Williams (Attorney at Law)
Northwestern State University

We also are grateful to those who provided us with comments regarding earlier editions of the book:

John R. Jozwiak
Loyola University of Chicago

Darwin H. Mueller
Tacoma Community College

Jack E. Karns
East Carolina University

Dorothy L. Steele
Montclair State College

Douglas E. McClelland
Montana State University

Raymond Wyrsch
Catholic University

D. Lynn Morison
Michigan State University

Joseph Zavaglia, Jr.
Brookdale Community College

We express our thanks and appreciation to Carol Courts and Karen Beck for typing the manuscript, and to Lynn Reichel for assistance in proofing the galleys. For their support we extend our thanks to Helen T. Smith, Karlene Fogelin Knebel, and Joanne Erwick Roberts. And we are grateful to Richard Fenton, Mélina Brown-Hall, and Nancy Hill-Whilton of West Publishing Company for their invaluable assistance and cooperation in connection with the preparation of this text.

Len Young Smith
Richard A. Mann
Barry S. Roberts

SUPPLEMENTAL MATERIALS

The **Study Guide** provides for each chapter a brief statement of purpose, chapter checkpoints, study tips, chapter outlines, key term definitions, true/false and multiple choice questions, and short essays. Each part has optional integrated questions and a sample test bank of 20 cumulative test questions. The study guide also includes a CPA exam business law review.

The **Instructor's Manual** contains: chapter outlines; teaching notes; answers to problems and questions; discussion questions and answers; key terms; recommendations for transparency masters and acetates; and Part Openers which provide suggested research and outside activities for students.

The Test Bank is bound in a separate volume and includes true/false, multiple choice, short essay, and challenge test questions.

Computerized Testing—WesTest contains the complete test bank on disk and allows professors the ability to generate a variety of tests using floppy diskettes for either IBM PC's and compatibles or for Apple II family microcomputers. This is available to qualified adopters.

190 Transparency Masters and 52 two-color **Acetates** highlight text illustrations.

Legal CLERK Software (Computerized Legal Research Package) is West's new software package that introduces students to computerized legal research. It's intended to help schools meet AACSB recommendations for using microcomputers in business law courses. The complete package includes copyable disks, a Student User's Guide, and an Instructor's Guide. CLERK is available to qualified adopters

West's Book of Legal Forms by McNutt offers 40 sample business forms.

Library of Cases the full text of all cases upon which end of chapter problems have been based are on computer disk.

PART 1
THE LEGAL ENVIRONMENT OF BUSINESS

1
INTRODUCTION TO LAW

2
THE JUDICIAL SYSTEM

3
CONSTITUTIONAL AND ADMINISTRATIVE LAW

4
CRIMINAL LAW

5
INTENTIONAL TORTS

6
NEGLIGENCE AND STRICT LIABILITY

Law concerns the relations of individuals with one another as they affect the social and economic order. It is both the product of civilization and the means by which civilization is maintained. As such, law reflects the social, economic, political, religious, and moral philosophy of society. Judge Learned Hand, in *The Spirit of Liberty*, captured the absolute importance of law when he stated: "Without it we cannot live; only with it can we insure the future which by right is ours. The best of man's hopes are enmeshed in its success; when it fails we must fail; the measure in which it can reconcile our passions, our wills, our conflicts, is the measure of our opportunity to find ourselves."

One of the essential roles that law performs is that of social control. As the legal philosopher Roscoe Pound observed in *An Introduction to the Philosophy of Law:*

> For the purpose of understanding the law of today, . . . I am content to think of law as a social institution to satisfy social wants—the claims and demands and expectations involved in the existence of civilized society—by giving effect to as much as we may with the least sacrifice, so far as such wants may be satisfied or such claims given effect by an ordering of human conduct through politically organized society. For the present purposes, I am content to see in legal history the record of a continually wider recognizing and satisfying of human wants or claims or desires through social control; a more embracing and more effective secur-

ing of social interests; a continually more complete and effective elimination of waste and precluding of friction in human enjoyment of the goods of existence.

In this textbook we are primarily concerned with law as an agency of social control over economic activity. As we discuss in Chapter 1, law in this country arises in four different ways: constitutions, legislation, court decisions, and actions by administrative agencies. Together these sources of law form an intricate network that governs, regulates, and facilitates the conduct of business affairs. We refer to this network as the *legal environment of business.*

In Part 1 we deal with that portion of the legal environment of business that affects *all* economic activity. Chapters 1 and 2 provide an introduction to our legal system by briefly examining its nature, structure, origins, processes, and purposes. Chapter 3 covers constitutional law as it applies to business. Constitutional law involves the allocation of power to government and the preservation of individual liberty against governmental action. Consequently, you should understand constitutional law to appreciate the basic legal system of the United States. Moreover, a number of public policy issues affecting business have constitutional dimensions. For example, to what extent should commercial speech such as advertising be protected by the First Amendment? When do the activities of private corporations become "state action" and therefore subject to the constitutionally imposed requirements of due process?

Chapter 3 also addresses the law determining the powers and procedures of administrative agencies. This chapter provides the background for understanding the operation of these agencies (such as the Federal Trade Commission, the National Labor Relations Board, the Occupational Safety and Health Administration, and the Securities and Exchange Commission), which today play a dominant role in regulating business and protecting society.

Chapter 4 discusses the criminal law, which is of great importance in protecting the state and the individual. Many public policy issues involve the application of criminal law to the conduct of business. For example, should a corporation be held criminally liable for the conduct of its employees? Should punishment of criminal offenses by business be limited to fines, or should management also be imprisoned?

Finally, Chapters 5 and 6 deal with the law of torts. The following passage is quoted in *Torts*, 5th ed., by Prosser and Keeton:

> Arising out of the various and ever-increasing clashes of the activities of persons living in a common society, carrying on business in competition with fellow members of that society, owning property which may in any of a thousand ways affect the persons or property of others—in short, doing all the things that constitute modern living—there must of necessity be losses, or injuries of many kinds sustained as a result of the activities of others. The purpose of the law of torts is to adjust these losses, and to afford compensation for injuries sustained by one person as the result of the conduct of another. Wright, "Introduction to the Law of Torts," 1944, 8 *Camb. L.J.* 238.

In adjusting these losses the courts inevitably make decisions that affect public policy. For example, if the courts impose liability for injuries caused by defective products, then the manufacturer's cost of paying these claims will increase the price of the product to all customers.

We encourage you to think about these and other relevant policy, social, and ethical issues as you read the chapters in this text. As we stated earlier, the law reflects the social, economic, political, religious, and moral philosophy of society. Consequently, your understanding and appreciation of the law will be enhanced by considering the public policy behind the law as well as the social implications of the law.

1 INTRODUCTION TO LAW

Law is an instrument of social control. Its function is to regulate, within certain limitations, human conduct and human relations. Accordingly, the laws of the United States affect and influence the life of every American citizen. At the same time, the laws of each State affect and influence the life of each of its citizens as well as a large number of noncitizens. The rights and duties of all individuals, as well as the safety and security of all people and their property, depend on the law.

The law is pervasive. It interacts with and influences the political, economic, and social systems of every civilized society. It permits, forbids, and/or regulates practically every known human activity and affects all persons either directly or indirectly. Law, in part, is prohibitory: certain acts must not be committed. One must not steal; one must not murder. Law is, in part, mandatory: certain acts must be done, or be done in a prescribed way; taxes must be paid; corporations must make and file certain reports with State authorities; traffic must keep to the right. Finally, law is permissive: one may or may not enter into a contract; one may or may not dispose of one's estate by will.

Because the law is so highly interrelated, you will find it helpful in studying the different areas of business law first to consider law as a whole. This will enable you not only to understand better each specific area of law but also to understand its relationship to other areas of law.

NATURE OF LAW

The law has evolved slowly and it will continue to change. It is not a pure science based on unchanging and universal truths. Rather, it is a continuous striving to attain a workable set of rules that balance the individual and group rights of a society.

Definition of Law

A fundamental but difficult question regarding law is, What is it? Numerous philosophers and jurists (legal scholars) have attempted to define it. The American jurists and Supreme Court Justices Oliver Wendell Holmes and Benjamin Cardozo defined law as predictions of the way that a court will decide specific legal questions. The English jurist Blackstone, on the other hand, defined law as "a rule of civil conduct prescribed by the supreme power in a state, commanding what is right, and prohibiting what is wrong."

Because of its great complexity, many legal scholars have attempted to explain the law by outlining its essential characteristics. Roscoe Pound, a distinguished American jurist and former dean of the Harvard Law School, described law as having multiple meanings:

First, we may mean the legal order, that is, the régime of ordering human activities and relations through systematic application of the force of politically organized society, or through social pressure in such a society backed by such force.

We use the term "law" in this sense when we speak of "respect for law" or for the "end of law."

Second, we may mean the aggregate of laws or legal precepts; the body of authoritative grounds of judicial and administrative action established in such a society. We may mean the body of received and established materials on which judicial and administrative determinations proceed. We use the term in this sense when we speak of "systems of law" or of "justice according to law."

Third, we may mean what Mr. Justice Cardozo has happily styled "the judicial process." We may mean the process of determining controversies, whether as it actually takes place, or as the public, the jurists, and the practitioners in the courts hold it ought to take place.

Functions of Law

At a general level the primary function of law is to maintain stability in the social, political, and economic system while at the same time permitting change. The law accomplishes this basic function by performing a number of specific functions, among them dispute resolution, protection of property, and preservation of the state.

Disputes inevitably arise in a society as complex and interdependent as ours. Disputes may involve criminal matters, such as theft, or noncriminal matters, such as an automobile accident. Because disputes threaten the stability of society, the law has established an elaborate and evolving set of rules to resolve disputes. In addition, the legal system has instituted societal remedies, usually administered by the courts, in place of private remedies such as revenge.

The recognition of private ownership of property is fundamental to our economic system, based as it is upon the exchange of goods and services among privately held units of consumption. Therefore, a crucial function of law is not only to protect the owner's use of property but also to assist in making voluntary agreements (called contracts) regarding exchanges of property and services. Accordingly, a significant portion of law, as well as this text, involves property and its disposition, including the law of property, contracts, sales, commercial paper, and business associations.

A third essential function of the law is preservation of the state. In our system, law ensures that changes in the political structure and leadership are brought about by political action, such as elections, legislation, and referenda, rather than by revolution, sedition, and rebellion.

Legal Sanctions

A primary function of the legal system is to make sure that legal rules are enforced. **Sanctions** are the means by which the law enforces the decisions of the courts. Laws without sanctions would be ineffectual and unenforceable.

An example of a sanction in a civil (noncriminal) case is the seizure and sale of the debtor's property if the debtor fails to pay the court-ordered obligation called a judgment. Moreover, under certain circumstances the court may enforce its orders by finding an offender in contempt of court and sentencing him to jail until he obeys the court's order. In criminal cases, the principal sanctions are the imposition of a fine, imprisonment, and capital punishment.

Law and Morals

Although the law is greatly affected by moral concepts, morals and law are not the same. They may be considered as two intersecting circles (see Figure 1–1). The shaded area common to both circles includes the vast body of ideas that are both moral and legal. For instance, "Thou shall not kill" and "Thou shall not steal" are both moral precepts and legal constraints.

On the other hand, the part of the legal circle not intersecting the morality circle (the lightly shaded portion) includes many rules of law that are completely unrelated to morals, such as the rules that you must drive on the right side of the road and that you must register before you can vote. Likewise, the part of the morality circle not intersecting the legal circle includes moral precepts not enforced by law,

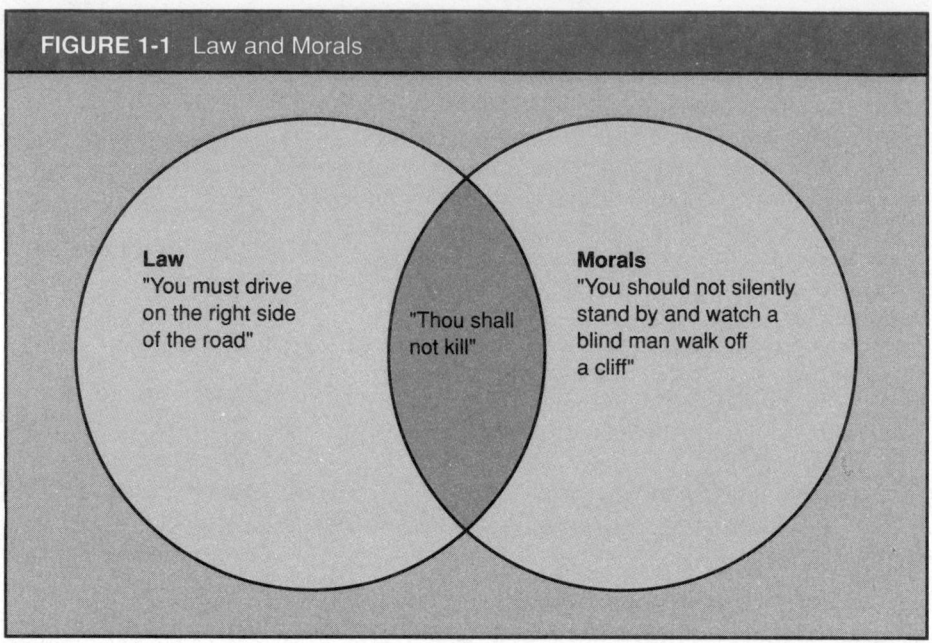

FIGURE 1-1   Law and Morals

such as you should not silently stand by and watch a blind man walk off a cliff or you should not foreclose a poor widow's mortgage.

Law and Justice

Law and justice represent separate and distinct concepts. Without law, however, it is difficult to have justice. Although there are at least as many definitions of justice as there are of law, justice may be defined as fair, equitable, and impartial treatment of competing interests and desires of individuals and groups with due regard for the common good.

On the other hand, law is no guarantee of justice. Some of history's most monstrous acts have been committed pursuant to "law." For example, recall the actions of Nazi Germany during the 1930s and 1940s. Moreover, totalitarian societies have often carefully shaped a formal legal system around the atrocities they have caused to be committed.

CLASSIFICATION OF LAW

Because the law is vast, it is helpful to classify it into categories. This can be done in a number

of ways, but the most useful categories are (1) substantive and procedural, (2) public and private, and (3) civil and criminal (see Figure 1–2).

Basic to understanding these classifications are the terms *right* and *duty*. A **right** is the capacity of a person, with the aid of the law, to require another person or persons to perform, or to refrain from performing, a certain act. Thus, if A sells and delivers goods to B for the agreed price of $500 payable at a certain date, A has the capability, with the aid of the courts, of enforcing the payment by B of the $500. A **duty** is the obligation imposed by law upon a person by which he is required to perform a certain act or to refrain from performing a certain act. Duty and right are correlatives: there can be no right in one person without a corresponding duty resting upon some other person, or in some cases upon all other persons.

Substantive and Procedural Law

Substantive law creates, defines, and regulates legal rights and obligations. Thus, the rules of contract law that determine when a

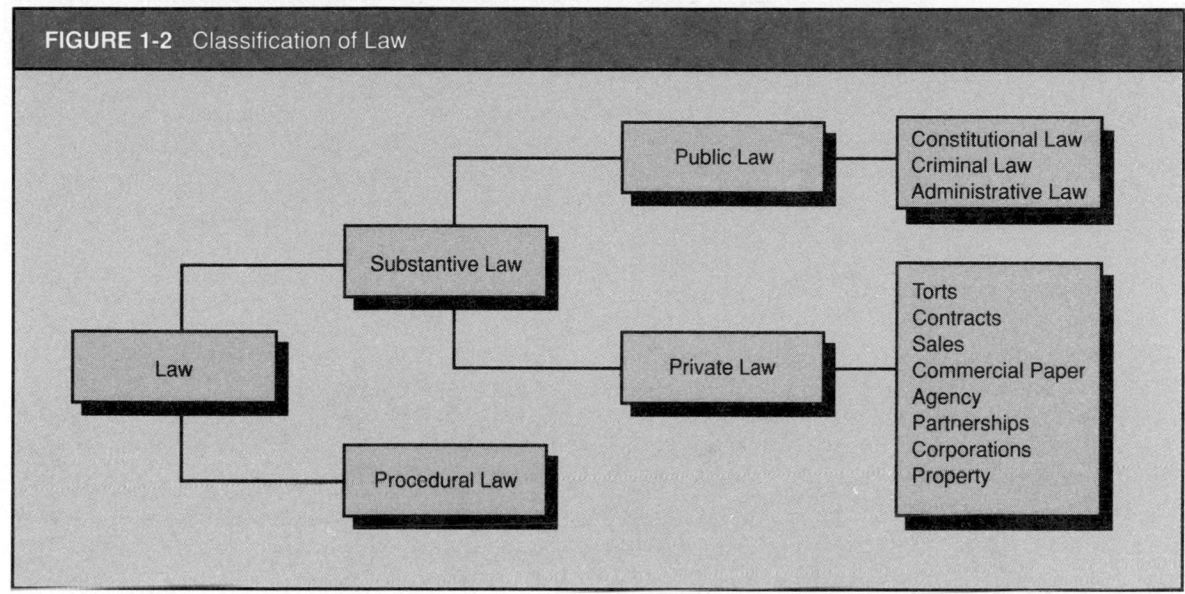

FIGURE 1-2 Classification of Law

binding contract is formed are rules of substantive law. On the other hand, **procedural law** sets forth the rules for enforcing those rights that exist by reason of the substantive law. Thus procedural law defines the method by which to obtain a remedy in court.

Public and Private Law

Public law is that branch of substantive law that deals with the government's rights and powers and its relationship to individuals or groups. Public law consists of constitutional, administrative, and criminal law. **Private law** is that part of substantive law governing individuals and legal entities (such as corporations) in their relationships with one another. Business law is primarily private law.

Civil and Criminal Law

The **civil law** defines duties the violation of which constitutes a wrong against the party injured by the violation. In contrast, the **criminal law** establishes duties the violation of which is a wrong against the whole community. Civil law is a part of private law, whereas criminal law is a part of public law. In a civil

action the injured party **sues** to recover *compensation* for the damage and injury sustained as a result of the **defendant's** wrongful conduct. The party bringing a civil action (the **plaintiff**) has the burden of proof, which the plaintiff must sustain by a **preponderance** (greater weight) **of the evidence.** The purpose of the civil law is to compensate the injured party, not to punish the wrongdoer as in the case of criminal law. The principal forms of relief afforded by the civil law are a judgment for money damages and a decree ordering the defendant to specifically perform a certain act or to desist from specified conduct.

A crime is any act or omission prohibited by public law in the interest of protection of the public and made punishable by the government in a judicial proceeding brought (**prosecuted**) by it. The government must prove criminal guilt **beyond a reasonable doubt,** which is a significantly higher burden of proof than that required in a civil action. Crimes are prohibited and punished on the ground of public policy, which may include the protection and safeguarding of government, human life, or private property. Additional purposes of the criminal law include deterrence and rehabilitation. See Figure 1–3 for a comparison of civil with criminal law.

FIGURE 1-3   Comparison of Civil and Criminal Law

	Civil Law	Criminal Law
Commencement of action	Aggrieved individual (plaintiff) sues	State or Federal government prosecutes
Purpose	Compensation Deterrence	Punishment Deterrence Rehabilitation Preservation of peace
Burden of proof	Preponderance of the evidence	Beyond a reasonable doubt
Principal sanctions	Monetary damages Equitable remedies	Capital punishment Imprisonment Fines

SOURCES OF LAW

The sources of law in the American legal system are the Federal and State constitutions, Federal treaties, interstate compacts, Federal and State statutes, the ordinances of countless local municipal governments, Federal and State executive orders, the rules and regulations of Federal and State administrative agencies, and an ever-increasing volume of reported Federal and State court decisions.

The *supreme law* of the land is the United States Constitution. The Constitution also provides that statutes and treaties made under the authority of the United States shall be the supreme law of the land. Federal legislation and treaties are, therefore, paramount to State constitutions and statutes. Federal legislation is of great significance as a source of law. The importance and complexity of new bills enacted at each congressional session result from the interplay of tremendous economic and social forces within this nation. Other Federal actions having the force of law are executive orders by the president and rules and regulations set by Federal administrative officials, agencies, and commissions. The Federal courts also contribute considerably to the body of law in the United States.

The same pattern exists in every State. The paramount law of each State is contained in its written constitution. Subordinate to this are the statutes enacted by its legislature and the case law developed by its judiciary. Likewise, rules and regulations of State administrative agencies have the force of law, as do executive orders issued by the governor. In addition, cities, towns, and villages have limited legislative powers within their respective municipal areas to pass ordinances and resolutions.

Constitutional Law

A **constitution**—the fundamental law of a particular level of government—serves a number of critical functions. It establishes the governmental structure and allocates power among the levels of government, thereby defining political relationships. One of the fundamental principles on which our government is founded is that of separation of powers. As incorporated into our Constitution this means that there are three distinct and independent branches of government—the Federal judiciary, the Congress, and the executive branch.

A constitution also restricts the powers of government and specifies the rights and liberties of the people. For example, the Constitution of the United States not only specifically states what rights and authority are vested in the national government but also specifically enumerates certain rights and liberties of the people. Moreover, the Ninth Amendment to the U.S. Constitution makes it clear that this enumeration of rights does not in any way deny or limit other rights that are retained by the people.

All other law in the United States is subordinate to the Federal Constitution. No law, Federal or State, is valid if it violates the Federal Constitution. Under the principle of **judicial review,** the Supreme Court of the United States determines the constitutionality of *all* laws.

Judicial Law

The American legal system is a **common law system** first developed in England. It relies heavily on the judiciary as a source of law and on the **adversary system** for settling disputes. In an adversary system the parties, not the court, must initiate and conduct litigation. This approach is based on the belief that the truth is more likely to emerge from the investigation and presentation of evidence by two opposing parties, both motivated by self interest, than from judicial investigation motivated only by official duty. The common law system is also used in other English-speaking countries, including England, Canada, and Australia.

In distinct contrast to the common law system are **civil law systems** (as opposed to civil or noncriminal law), which are based on Roman law. These systems depend on comprehensive legislative enactments (called codes) and the **inquisitorial system** of determining disputes. In the inquisitorial approach, the judiciary initiates litigation, investigates pertinent facts, and conducts the presentation of evidence. The civil law system prevails in most of Europe, Scotland, the state of Louisiana, the province of Quebec, Mexico, and South America.

Common Law The courts in common law systems have developed a body of law that serves as precedent for determination of later controversies. This law is called case law, judge-made law, or common law. In this sense, common law is distinguished from other sources of law, such as legislation and administrative rulings.

In order to evolve in a stable and predictable manner, the common law has developed by application of *stare decisis*. Under the principle of **stare decisis** ("to stand by the decisions"), rules of law announced and applied by courts in prior decisions are later adhered to and relied on in deciding cases of a similar nature. Judicial decisions thus have two uses: first, to determine with finality the case being decided; and second, to indicate how similar cases will be decided if and when they arise.

Stare decisis does not, however, preclude correction of erroneous decisions or judicial choice among conflicting precedents. Thus, the doctrine allows sufficient flexibility for the common law to change. The strength of the common law is its ability to adapt to change without losing its sense of direction. As Justice Cardozo said: "The inn that shelters for the night is not the journey's end. The law, like the traveler, must be ready for the morrow. It must have a principle of growth."

Equity As the common law developed in England, it became overly rigid and beset with technicalities. As a consequence, in many cases no remedies were provided because the judges insisted that a claim must fall within one of the recognized forms of action. Moreover, courts of common law could provide only limited remedies; the principal type of relief obtainable was a money judgment. Consequently, individuals who could not obtain adequate relief from monetary awards began to petition the king directly for justice. He, in turn, came to delegate these petitions to his chancellor.

Gradually, there evolved what was in effect a new and supplementary system of needed judicial relief for those who could not receive adequate remedies through the common law. This new system, called **equity,** was administered by a court of chancery presided over by the chancellor. The chancellor, deciding cases

LAW IN THE NEWS

The Lawyering of America

We are now seeing the glimmers of a new legal crisis in America. It arises from the clamor over liability insurance and a vague unease that lawyers are exercising too much influence. The United States now has more lawyers (an estimated 675,000 of them in 1985) per capita than any other major nation. Since 1950, their numbers have grown twice as fast as the population. But our sense that lawyers are meddling too much sits awkwardly with the great American faith in law as a remedy for almost any ill. Or, as one book a few years ago put it, "Sue the B*st*rds."

The key to understanding this confusion—if not entirely dispelling it—is to grasp a basic truth. Lawyers and law firms are businesses, and their business is conflict. Creative lawyering often means exploiting or creating conflicts. Just as companies develop new products, so lawyers search for new legal theories on which to sue. Rights of action are lawyers' markets. But their economic self-interest—their legal innovations—may subvert their social usefulness. The civil-justice system's essential purpose is to resolve conflict, not to excite it.

It's often a pretense that lawyers represent other people's grievances rather than their own economic interests. There are thousands of cases where lawyers, not their supposed clients, are the main aggressors. In the early 1980s, for example, many new "high technology" companies sold stock to the public. Many of these admittedly speculative stocks subsequently collapsed. Now there are dozens of suits against these companies, their officers, accountants and insurance companies alleging that investors were misled. But the suits have been brought by a few law firms on a contingency-fee basis. The lawyers—who typically take 30 percent or more of a settlement or damages—stand to win the most.

Of course, a rising tide of lawsuits is not the only reason for more lawyers. Greater government regulation, complicated tax rules and expanding international business have all contributed. But the growth of lawsuits also has a big multiplier effect. It requires defense lawyers and lawyers to advise people and companies how to avoid being sued. Consider the evidence of more litigation:

■ Since 1970, membership of the Association of Trial Lawyers of America has nearly tripled, to 60,000. (In the same period, all lawyers rose 90 percent.) To belong, half a lawyer's work must be representing people in personal-injury cases.
■ The number of product-liability cases filed in federal courts has risen from 1,579 in 1975 to 10,745 in 1984. Although most cases are settled before trial, the volume of jury awards in product-liability and medical-malpractice suits roughly tripled between 1975 and 1984, says Jury Verdict Research Inc.
■ Since the mid-1970s, suits against officers and directors of public corporations—from sharehold-

on "equity and good conscience," provided relief in many instances in which the common law judges refused to act or where the remedy at law was inadequate. Thus, there grew up, side by side, two systems of law administered by different tribunals, the common law courts and courts of equity.

An important difference between law and equity is that the chancellor could order a defendant to do or refrain from doing a specific act. If the defendant did not comply with this order, called a **decree,** he could be held in contempt of court and punished by fine or imprisonment. This power of compulsion available in a court of equity opened the door to many needed remedies not available in a court of common law.

While courts of equity in some cases recognized rights that were enforceable at common law, they provided more effective remedies. For example, for breach of a land contract the buyer could obtain a decree of **specific performance** in a court of equity. The defendant seller would be commanded to perform his part of the contract by transferring title to the land. Another powerful and effective remedy available only in the courts of equity was the **injunction,** a court order requiring a party to

ers, employees, customers and others—have more than doubled, according to The Wyatt Co., a Chicago actuarial firm. Many of these cases are contingency-fee cases.

To be fair, the liability-insurance mess—complaints from doctors, cities, consulting engineers, day-care centers and others that insurance is too costly or unavailable—is not entirely the doing of lawyers. The insurance industry bears much of the blame. A few years ago companies lowered premiums to compete for business. They expected to earn lush profits by investing premium income at high interest rates. Declining interest rates wrecked that gamble and, combined with steep insurance losses, triggered premium increases and coverage cutbacks. But the insurers' blunder only mitigates the role of the lawyers.

Side Effects

If courts adopt expansive liability doctrines, then the costs—not just insurance—will be huge. The gravest danger is becoming a precautionary society. Unintended side effects are already emerging. The threat of suits has driven some drug companies from manufacturing vaccines; consulting engineers now refuse to work on hazardous sites for fear of suits. Companies are losing outside directors for lack of liability coverage. As attorney Peter Huber argues, courts deal poorly with the full social effects of products, like vaccines, whose public benefits overwhelm the risks. Courts see only mistakes. "Beneficiaries of risk-reducing products . . . do not litigate," he writes.

Stating the problem is easier than solving it. Lawsuits are an important discipline on corporate and individual irresponsibility. They do compensate victims. There is no neat dividing line between too much or too little liability. But we can impose self-restraint on the legal system by treating lawyers for what they are—businesses. We need legal rules with proper economic incentives. In damage suits, the losing side should always pay the other side's legal fees. This would deter weak suits by reducing the pressure for expedient settlements that are less than the cost of litigation. And a losing defense would ultimately pay if its delays run up the other side's costs.

These common-sense ideas strike many lawyers as radical. They aren't. One inevitable complaint is that having losers pay would make it tougher for people of modest means to bring legitimate cases to court. This is nonsense. The reality is that the contingency-fee lawyer is already financing these cases. Strong cases would be more attractive under this system, because—aside from the contingency fee—the lawyer would also recover costs. But weak cases would be less attractive (the losing contingency-fee lawyer would pay the other side's legal fees), and they should be. The system exists to settle conflicts, not to generate lawyer caseloads. In a subtle way, commercial interests of lawyers now corrupt the law.

So let the lawyers grumble. If the current insurance mess leads to any good, it will be renewed political interest in our legal system. And that is as it should be. To paraphrase an old cliché: law is sometimes too important to be left to lawyers.

By Robert J. Samuelson from *Newsweek*. March 10, 1986. © 1986, Newsweek, Inc. All Rights Reserved. Reprinted by Permission.

do or refrain from doing a specified act. Another remedy in courts of equity not available elsewhere was the remedy of **reformation,** where, upon the ground of mutual mistake, an action could be brought to reform or change the language of a written agreement to conform to the actual intention of the contracting parties. An action for **rescission** of a contract, which allowed a party to invalidate a contract under certain circumstances, was another remedy.

Although courts of equity provided remedies not available in courts of law, they granted them only at their discretion, not as a matter of right. This discretion was exercised according to the general legal principles, or **maxims,** formulated by equity courts over the years.

In nearly every jurisdiction in the United States there has been a union of courts of common law and equity into a single court that administers both systems of law. Vestiges of the old division continue, however. For example, the right to a trial by jury applies only to actions at law and, under Federal law and in almost every State, not to suits filed in equity.

Restatements of Law   The common law of the United States results from the independent decisions of the State and Federal courts. The rapid increase in the number of decisions by these courts led to the establishment of the American Law Institute (ALI) in 1923. The ALI is composed of a distinguished group of lawyers, judges, and law teachers who set out to prepare ''an orderly restatement of the general common law of the United States, including in that term not only the law developed solely by judicial decision, but also the law that has grown from the application by the courts of statutes that were generally enacted and were in force for many years.''

The Restatements cover many of the important areas of the common law, including torts, contracts, agency, property, and trusts. Although not law by themselves, they are highly persuasive, and courts have frequently used them to support their opinions. The Restatements are regarded as the authoritative statement of the common law of the United States. Because they provide a concise and clear statement of much of the common law, relevant portions of the Restatements are frequently relied on in this book.

Legislative Law

Since the end of the nineteenth century, legislation has become the primary source of new law and ordered social change in the United States. The annual volume of legislative law is enormous. Justice Felix Frankfurter's remarks to the New York City Bar in 1947 are even more appropriate today:

> . . . Inevitably the work of the Supreme Court reflects the great shift in the center of gravity of law-making. Broadly speaking, the number of cases disposed of by opinions has not changed from term to term. But even as late as 1875 more than 40 percent of the controversies before the Court were common-law litigation, fifty years later only 5 percent, while today cases not resting on statutes are reduced almost to zero. It is therefore accurate to say that courts have ceased to be the primary makers of law in the sense in which they ''legislated'' the common law. It is certainly true of the Supreme Court that almost every case has a statute at its heart or close to it.

This emphasis on legislative or statutory law has occurred because common law, which develops evolutionarily and haphazardly, is not well suited for making drastic or comprehensive changes. Moreover, although courts tend to be hesitant about overruling prior decisions, legislatures commonly repeal prior enactments. In addition, legislatures are independent and able to choose the issues they wish to address, but courts may deal only with those issues presented by actual cases. As a result, legislatures are better equipped to make the dramatic, sweeping, and relatively rapid changes in the law that are needed to respond to technological, social, and economic innovations.

Some business law topics, such as contracts, agency, property, and trusts, remain governed principally by the common law. But most areas of commercial law have become largely statutory, including partnerships, corporations, sales, commercial paper, secured transactions, insurance, securities regulation, antitrust, and bankruptcy. Because most States enacted their own statutes dealing with these branches of commercial law, a great diversity developed among the States and hampered the conduct of commerce on a national scale. The increased need for greater uniformity brought about the codification of large parts of business or commercial law.

The most successful example is the **Uniform Commercial Code** (UCC), which was prepared under the joint sponsorship and direction of the National Conference of Commissioners on Uniform State Laws and the American Law Institute. The Code is set forth in the appendix of this book. All fifty States (although Louisiana has adopted only Articles 1, 3, 4, 5, 7, and 8), the District of Columbia, and the Virgin Islands have adopted the Uniform Commercial Code. The underlying purposes and policies of the Code are:

1. to simplify, clarify, and modernize the law governing commercial transactions;
2. to permit the continued expansion of commercial practices through custom, usage, and agreement of the parties; and
3. to make uniform the law among the various jurisdictions.

Other uniform laws include the Uniform Partnership Act, the Uniform Limited Partnership Act, the Model Business Corporation Act, and the Uniform Probate Code.

Treaties   A **treaty** is an agreement between or among independent nations. The United States Constitution authorizes the president to enter into treaties with the advice and consent of the Senate "providing two thirds of the Senators present concur."

Treaties may be entered into only by the Federal government and not by the States. Examples of treaties include NATO and SALT I. A treaty signed by the president and approved by the Senate has the legal force of a Federal statute. Accordingly, a Federal treaty may supersede a prior Federal statute, while a Federal statute may supersede a prior treaty. As with any statute, treaties are subordinate to the Federal Constitution and subject to judicial review.

Executive Orders   In addition to executive functions, the president of the United States also has authority to issue laws, which are called **executive orders.** This authority typically derives from specific delegation by Federal legislation. An executive order may be amended, revoked, or superseded by a subsequent executive order. An example of an executive order is the one issued by President Johnson in 1965 prohibiting discrimination by Federal contractors on the basis of race, color, sex, religion, or national origin in employment on any work performed by the contractor during the period of the Federal contract.

The governors of the States enjoy comparable authority to issue executive orders.

Administrative Law

Administrative law is the branch of public law that deals with the various regulatory functions and activities of the government in its executive capacity as performed, supervised, and regulated by public officials, departments, boards, and commissions. It also involves controversies arising between individuals and these public officials and agencies. Administrative functions and activities in general concern matters of public health, safety, and welfare including the establishment and maintenance of military forces, police, citizenship and naturalization, taxation, the coinage of money, elections, environmental protection, the regulation of transportation, interstate highways, waterways, television, radio, and trade and commerce.

Because of the increasing complexity of the social, economic, and industrial life of the nation, the scope of administrative law has expanded enormously. Justice Jackson stated that "the rise of administrative bodies has been the most significant legal trend of the last century, and perhaps more values today are affected by their decisions than by those of all the courts, review of administrative decisions apart." This is evidenced by the great increase in the number and activities of Federal government boards, commissions, and other agencies. Certainly, agencies create more legal rules and decide more controversies than all the legislatures and courts combined.

LEGAL ANALYSIS

Decisions in State trial courts are not generally reported or published. The weight of the precedent set by a trial court is not sufficient to warrant permanent reporting. Except in New York and a few other States where selected opinions of trial courts are published, decisions in trial courts are simply filed in the office of the clerk of the court, where they are available for public inspection. Decisions of State courts of appeals are published in volumes called "reports," which are numbered consecutively. Most State court decisions are found in the State reports of that State. In addition, State reports are published in a regional reporter, published by West Publishing Company, called the National Reporter System, composed of the following: Atlantic (A. or A.2d); South Eastern (S.E. or S.E.2d); South Western (S.W. or S.W.2d); New York Supplement (N.Y.S. or N.Y.S.2d); North Western (N.W. or N.W.2d); North Eastern (N.E. or N.E.2d); Southern (So. or So.2d); and Pacific (P. or P.2d). After they are published, these opinions or "cases" are referred to ("cited") by giving the name of the case, the volume, name, and page of the official State report, if any, in which it is published; the volume, name, and page of the particular set and series of the National Reporter System; and the volume, name, and page of any other selected case series. For instance, the case of *Lefkowitz v. Great Minneapolis Surplus Store, Inc.*, 251 Minn. 188, 86 N.W.2d 689 (1957), indicates that the opinion in this case may be found in Volume 251 of the official Minnesota Reports at page 188; and in Volume 86 of the Northwestern Reporter, Second Series, at page 689.

The decisions of courts in the Federal system are found in a number of reports. Federal District Court opinions appear in the Federal Supplement (F.Supp.). Decisions of the U.S. Court of Appeals are found in the Federal Reporter (Fed. or F.2d), while the U.S. Supreme Court's opinions are published in the United States Supreme Court Reports (U.S.), Supreme Court Reporter (S.Ct.), and Lawyers Edition (L.Ed.).

In reading the title of a case, such as "Jones v. Brown," the "v." or "vs." means versus or against. In the trial court, Jones is the *plaintiff,* the person who filed the suit, and Brown is the *defendant,* the person against whom the suit was brought. When the case is appealed, some, but not all, courts of appeals or appellate courts place the name of the party who appeals, or the **appellant,** first, so that "Jones v. Brown" in the trial court becomes, if Brown loses and is the appellant, "Brown v. Jones" in the appellate court. Therefore, it is not always possible to determine from the title itself who was the plaintiff and who was the defendant. You must carefully read the facts of each case and clearly identify each party in your mind in order to understand the discussion by the appellate court. In a criminal case the caption in the trial court will first designate the prosecuting governmental unit and then will indicate the defendant, as in "State v. Jones" or "Commonwealth v. Brown."

Study of the reported cases requires an understanding and application of legal analysis. Normally, the reported opinion in a case sets forth (a) the essential facts, the nature of the action, the parties, what happened to bring about the controversy, what happened in the

lower court, and what pleadings are material to the issues; (b) the issues of law or fact; (c) the legal principles involved; (d) the application of these principles; and (e) the decision.

A serviceable method of analyzing and briefing cases after a careful reading and comprehension of the opinion is for students to write in their own language a brief containing the following:

1. the facts of the case
2. the issue or question involved
3. the decision of the court
4. the reasons for the decision

The following excerpt from Professor Karl Llewellyn's *The Bramble Bush* contains a number of useful suggestions for reading cases:

The first thing to do with an opinion, then, is read it. The next thing is to get clear the actual decision, the judgment rendered. Who won, the plaintiff or defendant? And watch your step here. You are after in first instance the plaintiff and defendant *below,* in the trial court. In order to follow through what happened you must therefore first know the outcome *below;* else you do not see what was appealed from, nor by whom. You now follow through in order to see exactly what *further* judgment has been rendered on appeal. The stage is then cleared of form—although of course you do not yet know all that these forms mean, that they imply. You can turn now to what you want peculiarly to know. Given the actual judgments below and above as your indispensable framework—what has the case decided, and what can you derive from it as to what will be decided later?

You will be looking, in the opinion, or in the preliminary matter plus the opinion, for the following: a statement of the facts the court assumes; a statement of the precise way the question has come before the court—which includes what the plaintiff wanted below, and what the defendant did about it, the judgment below, and what the trial court did that is complained of; then the outcome on appeal, the judgment; and, finally the reasons this court gives for doing what it did. This does not look so bad. But it is much worse than it looks.

For all our cases are decided, all our opinions are written, all our predictions, all our arguments are made, on certain four assumptions. They are the first presuppositions of our study. They must be rutted into you till you can juggle with them standing on your head and in your sleep.

1. *The court must decide the dispute that is before it.* It cannot refuse because the job is hard, or dubious, or dangerous.

2. *The court can decide* only *the particular dispute which is before it.* When it speaks to that question it speaks ex cathedra, with authority, with finality, with an almost magic power. When it speaks to the question before it, it announces *law,* and if what it announces is new, it legislates, it *makes* the law. But when it speaks to any other question at all, it says mere words, which no man needs to follow. Are such words worthless? They are not. We know them as judicial *dicta;* when they are wholly off the point at issue we call them *obiter dicta*—words dropped along the road, wayside remarks. Yet even wayside remarks shed light on the remarker. They may be very useful in the future to him, or to us. But he will not feel bound to them, as to his ex cathedra utterance. They came not hallowed by a Delphic frenzy. He may be slow to change them; but not so slow as in the other case.

3. *The court can decide the particular dispute only according to a* general *rule which covers a whole class*

of like disputes. Our legal theory does not admit of single decisions standing on their own. If judges are free, are indeed forced, to decide new cases for which there is no rule, they must at least make a new rule as they decide. So far, good. But how wide, or how narrow, is the general rule in this particular case? That is a troublesome matter. The practice of our case-law, however, is I think fairly stated thus: it pays to be suspicious of general rules which look too wide; it pays to go slow in feeling *certain* that a wide rule has been laid down at all, or that, if seemingly laid down, it will be followed. For there is a fourth accepted canon:

4. *Everything, everything, everything, big or small, a judge may say in an opinion, is to be read with primary reference to the particular dispute, the particular question before him.* You are not to think that the words mean what they might if they stood alone. You are to have your eye on the case in hand, and to learn how to interpret all that has been said *merely* as a reason for deciding *that* case *that* way.

By way of example, the following edited case of *Caldwell v. Bechtel, Inc.* is presented and then briefed using the suggested format.

CALDWELL v. BECHTEL, INC.
United States Court of Appeals, District of Columbia Circuit, 1980.
631 F.2d 989.

Opinion: MacKinnon, J. We are here concerned with a claim for damages by a worker who allegedly contracted silicosis while he was mucking in a tunnel under construction as part of the metropolitan subway system [WMATA]. The basic issue is whether a consultant engineering firm owed the worker a duty to protect him against unreasonable risk of harm.

* * *

In attempting to convince the court that it owes no duty of reasonable care to protect appellant's safety, Bechtel argues that by its contract with WMATA it assumed duties only to WMATA. Appellant has not brought action, however, for breach of contract but rather seeks damages for an asserted breach of the duty of reasonable care. Unlike contractual duties, which are imposed by agreement of the parties to a contract, a duty of due care under tort law is based primarily upon social policy. The law imposes upon individuals certain expectations of conduct, such as the expectancy that their actions will not cause foreseeable injury to another. These societal expectations, as formed through the common law, comprise the concept of duty.

Society's expectations, and the concomitant duties imposed, vary in response to the activity engaged in by the defendant. If defendant is driving a car, he will be held to exercise the degree of care normally exercised by a reasonable person in like circumstances. Or if defendant is engaged in the practice of his profession, he will be held to exercise a degree of care consistent with his superior knowledge and skill. Hence, when defendant Bechtel engaged in consulting engineering services, the company was required to observe a standard of care ordinarily adhered to by one providing such services, possessing such skill and expertise.

A secondary but equally important principle involved in a determination of duty is to whom the duty is owed. The answer to this question is usually framed in terms of the foreseeable plaintiff, in other words, one who might foreseeably be injured by defendant's conduct. This secondary principle also serves to distinguish tort law from contract law. While in contract law, only one to whom the contract specifies that a duty be rendered will have a cause of action for its breach, in tort law, society, not the contract, specifies to whom the duty is owed, and this has traditionally been the foreseeable plaintiff.

It is important to keep these differences between contract and tort duties in mind when examining whether Bechtel's undertaking of contractual duties to WMATA created a duty of reasonable care toward Caldwell. Dean Prosser expressed the relationship in this terse fashion:

> [B]y entering into a contract with A, the defendant may place himself in such a relation toward B that the law will impose upon him an obligation, sounding in tort and not in contract, to act in such a way that B will not be injured. The incidental fact of the existence of the contract with A does not negative the responsibility of the actor when he enters upon a course of affirmative conduct which may be expected to affect the interests of another person.

* * *

Analyzing the common law, Prosser noted that courts have found a duty to act for the protection of another when certain relationships exist, such as carrier—passenger, innkeeper—guest, shipper—seaman, employer—employee, shopkeeper—visitor, host—social guest, jailor—prisoner, and school—pupil. These holdings suggest that courts have been eroding the general rule that there is no duty to act to help another in distress, by creating exceptions based upon a relationship between the actors.

* * *

We find that case law provides many such analogous situations from which the principles deserving of application to this case may be culled. The foregoing concepts of duty converge in this case, as the facts include both the WMATA-Bechtel contractual relationship from which it was foreseeable that a negligent undertaking by Bechtel might injure the appellant, and a special relationship established between Bechtel and the appellant because of Bechtel's superior skills, knowledge of the dangerous condition, and ability to protect appellant.

* * *

We reverse the summary judgment of the district court, and hold that as a matter of law, on the record as we are required to view it at this time, Bechtel owed Caldwell a duty of due care to take reasonable steps to protect him from the foreseeable risk of harm to his health posed by the excessive concentration of silica dust in the Metro tunnels. We remand so that Caldwell will have an opportunity to prove, if he can, the other elements of his negligence action.

BRIEF OF CALDWELL v. BECHTEL, INC.

I. Facts: Caldwell was a laborer who now suffers from silicosis. He claims that he contracted the disease while he was working in a tunnel under construction as part of the Washington Metropolitan Area Transportation Authority (WMATA). He brought this action for damages against Bechtel, Inc., a consultant engineering firm under contract with WMATA for the project.

II. Issue: Did Bechtel breach a duty of due care owed to Caldwell to take reasonable steps to protect him from the foreseeable risk of harm to his health posed by the excessive concentration of silica dust in the subway tunnels?

III. Decision: In favor of Caldwell. Summary judgment reversed and case remanded to the district court.

IV. Reasons: Caldwell has not brought an action for breach of contract as Bechtel seems to believe. Rather, he seeks damages for an alleged breach of the duty of reasonable care. Unlike contractual duties, which are imposed by agreement of the parties to a contract, a duty of due care under tort law is based primarily on social policy. That is, the law imposes upon individuals the expectation that their actions will not cause foreseeable injury to another. These societal expectations comprise the concept of duty—a concept that varies in response to the activity engaged in by the individual. Moreover, the duty is owed to anyone who might foreseeably be injured by the conduct of the actor in question. In contrast, under contract law, a duty is owed only to those parties specified in the contract. Here, by entering into a contract with WMATA, Bechtel placed itself in such a relation toward Caldwell that the law will impose upon it an obligation in tort, and not in contract, to act in such a way that Caldwell would not be injured.

CHAPTER SUMMARY

Nature of Law	**Definition of Law** "a rule of civil conduct by the supreme power in a state, commanding what is right, and prohibiting what is wrong" (Blackstone) **Functions of Law** to maintain stability in the social, political, and economic system through dispute resolution, protection of property, and the preservation of the state while at the same time permitting ordered change **Legal Sanctions** means of enforcing decisions of courts **Law and Morals** are different but overlapping: law has sanctions while morals do not **Law and Justice** are separate and distinct concepts; justice is the fair, equitable, and impartial treatment of competing interests with due regard for the common good

Classification of Law	**Substantive and Procedural** ■ *Substantive Law* law creating rights and duties ■ *Procedural Law* rules for enforcing substantive law **Public and Private** ■ *Public Law* law dealing with the relationship between government and individuals ■ *Private Law* law governing the relationships among individuals and legal entities **Civil and Criminal** ■ *Civil Law* law dealing with the rights and duties of individuals and legal entities among themselves ■ *Criminal Law* law establishing duties, which, if violated, constitute a wrong against the entire community

Sources of Law	**Constitutional Law** fundamental law of a government establishing its powers and limitations **Judicial Law** ■ *Common Law* body of law developed by the courts that serves as precedent for determination of later controversies ■ *Equity* body of law based upon principles distinct from common law and providing remedies not available at law **Legislative Law** statutes adopted by legislative bodies ■ *Treaties* agreements between or among independent nations ■ *Executive Orders* laws issued by the president or the governor of a State **Administrative Law** law dealing with the establishment, duties, and powers of agencies in the executive branch of government

QUESTIONS

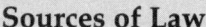

1. Identify and describe the basic functions of law.
2. Distinguish between law and justice.
3. Distinguish between law and morals.
4. Define and discuss substantive and procedural law.
5. Distinguish between public law and private law.
6. Distinguish between civil and criminal law.
7. Identify and describe the sources of law.
8. Distinguish between law and equity.
9. Explain the principle of *stare decisis*.
10. Identify and define five remedies available in equity.

2 THE JUDICIAL SYSTEM

As we discussed in Chapter 1, substantive law sets forth the rights and duties of individuals and other legal entities, whereas procedural law determines how these rights are asserted. Procedural law attempts to accomplish two competing objectives—to be fair and impartial and to operate efficiently. The judicial process in the United States represents a balance between these two objectives as well as a commitment to the adversary system.

In the first part of this chapter, we describe the structure and function of the Federal and State court systems. The second part deals with jurisdiction, and the final section covers the procedure in civil lawsuits.

THE COURT SYSTEM

Courts are impartial tribunals (seats of judgment) established by governmental bodies to settle disputes. A court may render a binding decision only when it has jurisdiction over the dispute and the parties to that dispute; that is, when it has a right to hear and make a judgment in a case. The United States has a dual court system: the Federal government has its own independent system, as does each of the fifty States and the District of Columbia.

The Federal Courts

Article III of the United States Constitution states that the judicial power of the United States shall be vested in one Supreme Court and such lower courts as Congress may establish. Congress has established a Federal court system consisting of a number of special courts, district courts, courts of appeals, and the Supreme Court. Judges in the Federal court system are appointed for life by the president, subject to confirmation by the Senate. The structure of the Federal court system is illustrated in Figure 2–1.

District Courts The district courts are trial courts of general jurisdiction in the Federal system; they can hear and decide most legal controversies. Most Federal cases begin in the district court, and it is here that issues of fact are decided. The district court is generally presided over by *one* judge, although in certain cases three judges preside. In a few cases, an appeal from a judgment or decree of a district court is taken directly to the Supreme Court. In most cases, however, appeals go to the Circuit Court of Appeals of the appropriate circuit, the decision of which is in most cases final.

Congress has established judicial districts, each of which is located entirely in a particular State. All States have at least one district, while certain States contain more than one district. For instance, New York has four districts, Illinois has three, and Wisconsin has two, while a number of less populated States each make up a single district (see Figure 2–2).

Courts of Appeals Congress has established twelve judicial circuits (eleven numbered circuits plus the D.C. circuit), each having a court known as the Court of Appeals, which primarily hears appeals from the district courts located within its circuit (see Figure 2–2). In addition, they review orders of certain administrative agencies. Congress has also established the U.S. Court of Appeals for the Federal Circuit, which we discuss below under

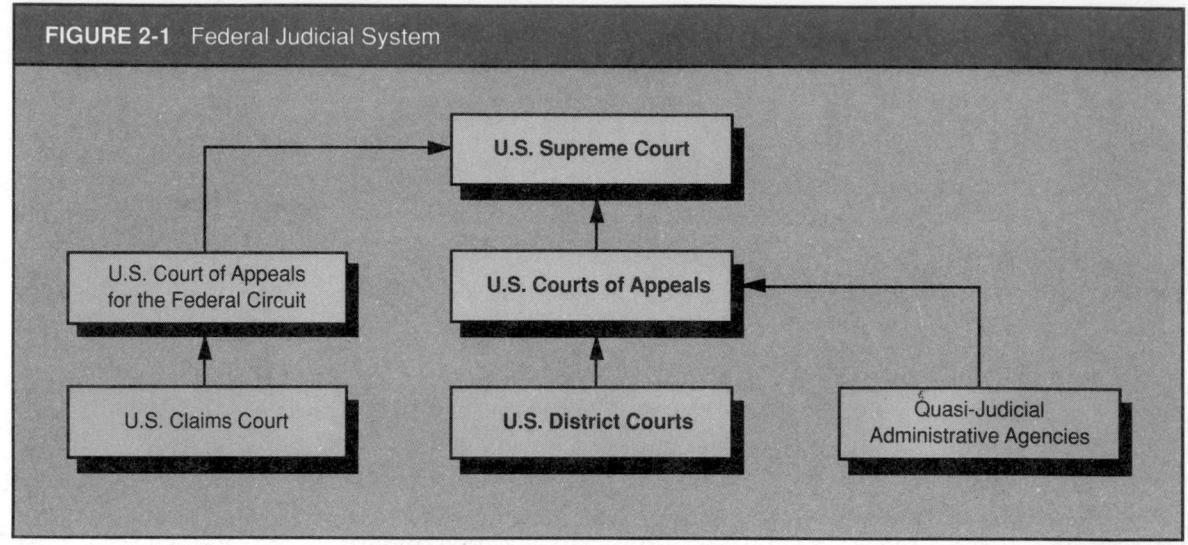

FIGURE 2-1 Federal Judicial System

"Special Courts." The United States Courts of Appeals generally hear cases in panels of *three* judges, although in some instances all judges of the circuit will sit *en banc* to decide a case.

The Courts of Appeals exercise no original jurisdiction (the right to hear a case first), being solely courts of review. Accordingly, they do *not* hear witnesses. Their function is to examine the record of a case on appeal and to determine whether the trial court committed prejudicial error (error substantially affecting the appellant's rights and duties). If so, the appellate court will **reverse** or **modify** the judgment of the lower court and if necessary **remand** or send it back to the lower court for further proceeding. If there is no prejudicial error, the appellate court will **affirm** the decision of the lower court.

The Supreme Court   The nation's highest tribunal is the United States Supreme Court, which consists of nine justices (a Chief Justice and eight Associate Justices) who sit as a group in Washington, D.C. Although the United States Supreme Court has original jurisdiction in certain types of cases, the Court's principal function is to review decisions of the Federal Courts of Appeals and, in some instances, those of the highest State courts or other tribunals. Cases reach the Supreme Court under its appellate jurisdiction by one of two routes. A relatively few come by way of **appeal by right.** The Court must hear these cases if one of the parties requests the review. In 1988 Congress enacted legislation that almost completely eliminated the right to appeal to the U.S. Supreme Court.

The second way in which a decision of a lower court may be reviewed by the Supreme Court is by the discretionary **writ of *certiorari,*** which requires a lower court to produce the records of a case it has tried. The great majority of cases reaching the Supreme Court come to it by means of writs of *certiorari.* The Court grants writs when there is a Federal question of substantial importance or a conflict in the decisions of the U.S. Circuit Courts of Appeals and if four justices vote to hear the case. Only a small percentage of the petitions to the Supreme Court for review by *certiorari* are granted, however, as the Court uses the writ as a device to choose which cases it wishes to hear. The following case describes some of the criteria the Supreme Court uses in deciding whether to grant review by *certiorari* as well as explaining the effect of a denial.

Special Courts   The special courts in the Federal judicial system include the U.S. Claims Court, the U.S. Bankruptcy Courts, the Tax Court, and the U.S. Court of Appeals for the Federal Circuit. These courts have jurisdiction

FIGURE 2-2   District and Circuit Courts of the United States

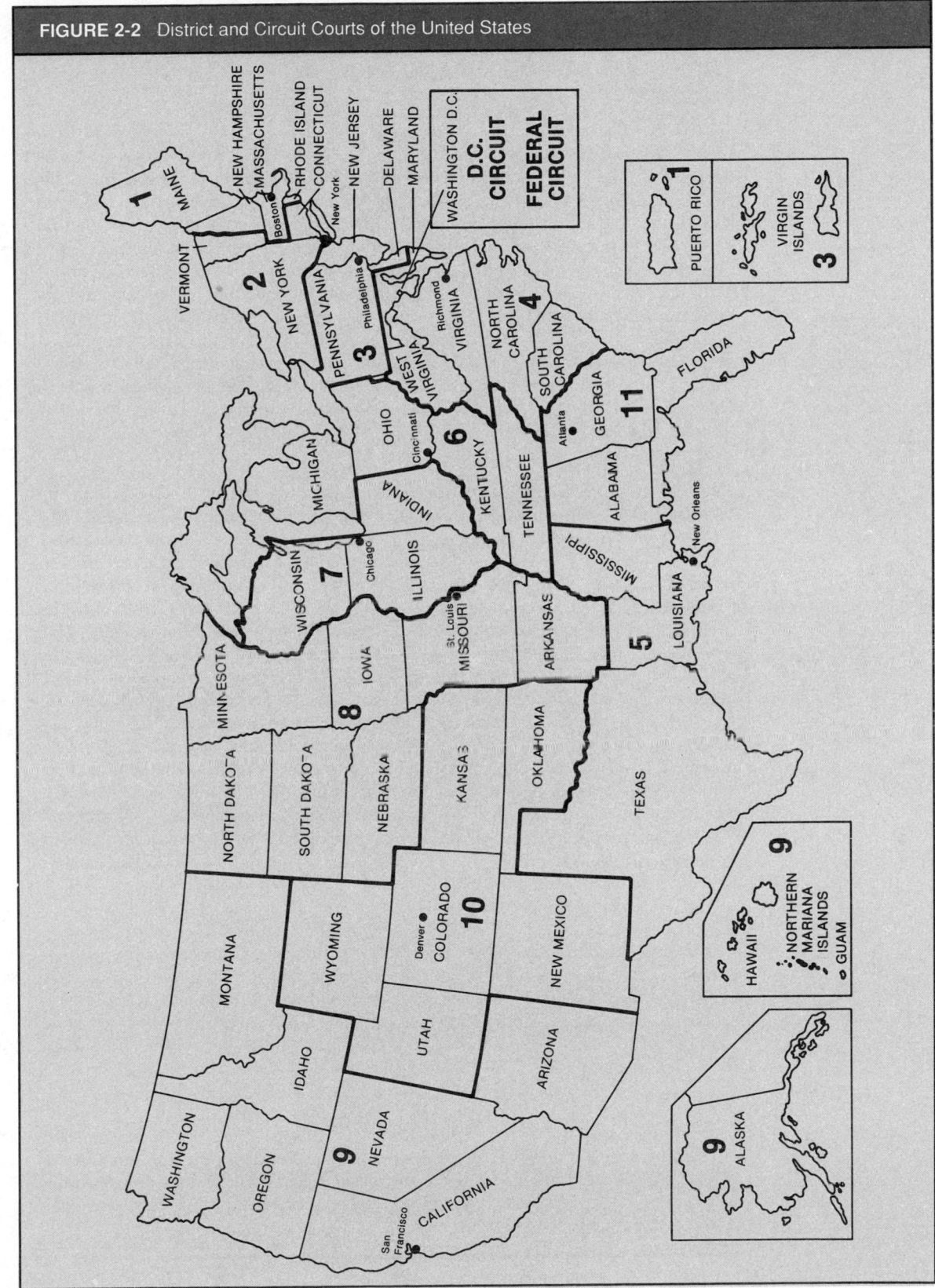

MARYLAND v. BALTIMORE RADIO SHOW, INC.
Supreme Court of the United States, 1950.
338 U.S. 912, 70 S.Ct. 252, 94 L.Ed. 562.

Facts: Eugene James was arrested for the brutal slaying of a young girl who was dragged from her bicycle and stabbed to death in Baltimore. On the night of his arrest, Baltimore Radio Show broadcasted over much of Maryland a sensational and devastating account disclosing that James had confessed to the crime, that he had a long criminal record, and that he returned to the scene with the police and dug up the knife he had used. As a result, the Criminal Court of Baltimore found Baltimore Radio Show guilty of contempt for obstructing justice because its broadcast had prevented James from exercising his right to an impartial jury trial. The Maryland Court of Appeals, however, reversed this contempt conviction based on its interpretations of the U.S. Supreme Court's recent decisions concerning freedom of speech and the press. The State of Maryland then asked the U.S. Supreme Court to issue a writ of *certiorari* to review the decision of the Maryland Court of Appeals.

Decision: *Certiorari* denied.

Opinion: Frankfurter, J.   This Court now declines to review the decision of the Maryland Court of Appeals. The sole significance of such denial of a petition for writ of certiorari need not be elucidated to those versed in the Court's procedures. It simply means that fewer than four members of the Court deemed it desirable to review a decision of the lower court as a matter "of sound judicial discretion." [Citation.] A variety of considerations underlie denials of the writ, and as to the same petition different reasons may lead different Justices to the same result. This is especially true of petitions for review on writ of certiorari to a State court. Narrowly technical reasons may lead to denials. Review may be sought too late; the judgment of the lower court may not be final; it may not be the judgment of a State court of last resort; the decision may be supportable as a matter of State law, not subject to review by this Court, even though the State court also passed on issues of federal law. A decision may satisfy all these technical requirements and yet may commend itself for review to fewer than four members of the Court. Pertinent considerations of judicial policy here come into play. A case may raise an important question but the record may be cloudy. It may be desirable to have different aspects of an issue further illumined by the lower courts. Wise adjudication has its own time for ripening.

* * *

Inasmuch, therefore, as all that a denial of a petition for a writ of certiorari means is that fewer than four members of the Court thought it should be granted, this Court has rigorously insisted that such a denial carries with it no implication whatever regarding the Court's views on the merits of a case which it has declined to review. The Court has said this again and again; again and again the admonition has to be repeated.

* * *

It becomes necessary to say that denial of this petition carries no support whatever for concluding that either the majority or the dissent in the court below correctly interpreted the scope of our decisions in [citation]. It does not carry any implication that either, or neither, opinion below correctly applied those decisions to the facts in the case at bar.

over particular areas. The U.S. Claims Court hears claims against the United States. The U.S. Bankruptcy Courts hear and decide certain matters under the Federal Bankruptcy Act, subject to review by the U.S. District Court. The Tax Court has jurisdiction over certain cases involving Federal taxes. The U.S. Court of Appeals for the Federal Circuit reviews decisions of the Claims Court, the Patent and Trademark Office, the United States Court of International Trade, and the Merit Systems Protection Board.

State Courts

Each of the fifty States and the District of Columbia has its own independent court system. In most States, judges are elected by the voters for a stated term. State courts have general jurisdiction—they can hear and decide all cases arising under the common law and under the statutes of the State, as well as most cases arising under Federal law. Although the structure of State court systems varies from State to State, Figure 2-3 shows a typical system.

Inferior Trial Courts At the bottom of the State court system are the inferior trial courts, which decide the least serious criminal and civil matters. Usually inferior trial courts do not keep a complete written record of the trial proceedings. Minor criminal cases such as traffic offenses are heard in inferior trial courts, which are referred to as justice of the peace courts, municipal courts, or traffic courts. These courts also conduct preliminary hearings in the more serious criminal cases.

Small claims courts are inferior trial courts which hear civil cases involving a limited amount of money. Usually there are no jury trials in small claims courts, the procedure is informal, and typically neither side employs an attorney. Appeal from small claims court is taken to the trial court of general jurisdiction, where a new trial (called a trial *de novo*) is begun and in which the small claims court's decision is given no weight.

Trial Courts Each State has trial courts of general jurisdiction, which may be called county, district, superior, circuit, or common pleas court. (In New York the trial court is called the Supreme Court.) These courts do not have a dollar limitation on their jurisdiction in civil cases and hear all criminal cases other than minor offenses. Their **general jurisdiction** extends to all cases arising under the common law and statutes of the State, as well as most cases arising under Federal law. Unlike

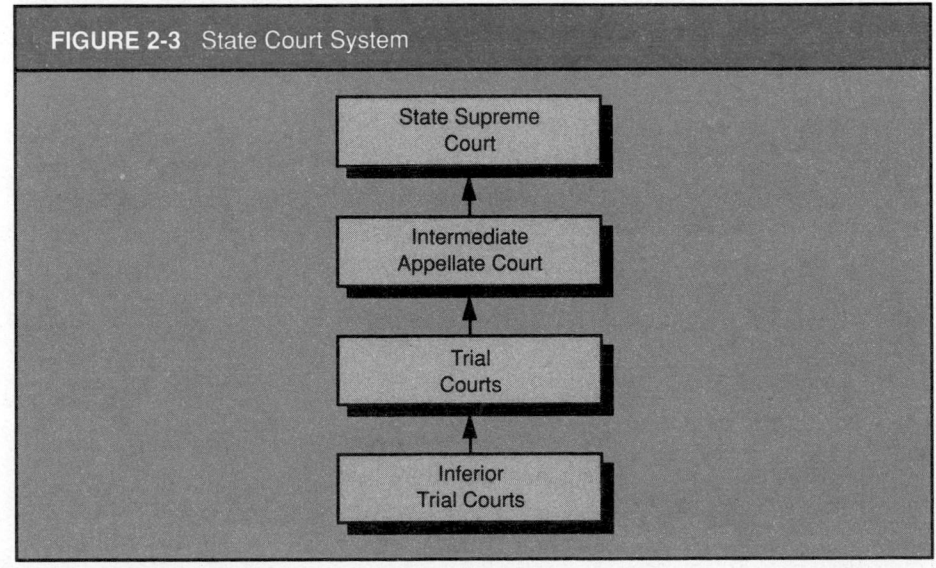

FIGURE 2-3 State Court System

the inferior trial courts, trial courts of general jurisdiction maintain formal records of their proceedings as procedural safeguards.

Appellate Courts　At the summit of the State court system is the State's court of last resort, a reviewing court generally called the Supreme Court of the State. Except for those cases in which review by the U.S. Supreme Court is available, the decision of the highest State tribunal is final. In most States, the large volume of cases in which review is sought has necessitated the creation of intermediate appellate courts. Review by such a court is usually by right. Further review is in most cases a matter of the highest court's discretion.

JURISDICTION

Jurisdiction simply means the power or authority of a court to hear and decide a given case. To proceed with a lawsuit, a court must have two kinds of jurisdiction. The first is jurisdiction over the subject matter of the lawsuit. Where a court lacks jurisdiction over the subject matter of a case, any action it takes in the case will not have legal effect.

The second kind of jurisdiction is over the parties to a lawsuit. A court usually may obtain jurisdiction over the defendant in a lawsuit if the defendant lives or is present in the court's territory or the transaction giving rise to the case has a substantial connection to the court's territory. The court obtains jurisdiction over the plaintiff when the plaintiff voluntarily submits to the court's power through filing a complaint with the court.

A valid exercise of jurisdiction also requires that the parties to the dispute be given fair notice and a reasonable opportunity to be heard. This overriding limitation is imposed on the Federal and State courts by the U.S. Constitution.

Subject Matter Jurisdiction

Subject matter jurisdiction refers to the authority of a particular court to judge a controversy of a particular kind. Federal courts have *limited* subject matter jurisdiction. State courts have jurisdiction over *all* matters that have not been exclusively given to the Federal courts or expressly taken away by the Constitution or Congress.

Exclusive Federal Jurisdiction　The Federal Courts have **exclusive jurisdiction** over Federal criminal prosecutions, admiralty, bankruptcy, antitrust, patent, trademark and copyright cases, suits against the United States, and cases arising under certain Federal statutes that expressly provide for exclusive Federal jurisdiction.

Concurrent Federal Jurisdiction　All instances of Federal jurisdiction other than exclusive are **concurrent jurisdiction;** this means that they may be heard by either State or Federal courts. Federal concurrent jurisdiction may be classified into two basic categories. The first arises when the Federal courts do not have exclusive jurisdiction over a Federal question. A **Federal question** is any case arising under the Constitution, statutes, or treaties of the United States.

The second type of concurrent Federal jurisdiction occurs in a civil suit where there is diversity of citizenship and the amount in controversy exceeds $50,000. **Diversity of citizenship** exists: (1) when the plaintiffs are citizens of a State or States different from the State or States of which the defendants are citizens; (2) when a foreign country brings an action against citizens of the United States; *or* (3) when the controversy is between citizens of the United States and citizens of a foreign country. The citizenship of an individual litigant (party in a lawsuit) is the State of the individual's residence or domicile, whereas that of a corporate litigant is both the State of incorporation and the State where its principal place of business is located. For example, if the amount in controversy exceeds $50,000, then diversity of citizenship jurisdiction would be satisfied if A, a citizen of California, sues B, a citizen of Idaho. If, however, W, a citizen of Virginia, and X, a citizen of North Carolina, sue Y, a citizen of Georgia, and Z, a citizen of North Carolina, there is *not* diversity of citizenship, because both X, a plaintiff, and Z, a defendant, are citizens of North Carolina.

As the next case explains, the jurisdictional requirement is satisfied if the amount claimed is made in good faith, unless it is clear to a legal certainty that the claim does not exceed the required amount.

When a Federal district court hears a case solely under diversity of citizenship jurisdiction, no Federal question is involved, and accordingly the Federal courts must apply State law.

In any case involving concurrent jurisdiction, the plaintiff has the choice of bringing the action in either an appropriate Federal court or State court. If the plaintiff brings the case in a State court, however, the defendant usually may have it removed (shifted) to a Federal court for the district in which the State court is located.

DEUTSCH v. HEWES STREET REALTY CORP.
United States Court of Appeals, Second Circuit, 1966.
359 F.2d 96.

Facts: Mariana Deutsch worked as a knitwear mender and attended a school for beauticians. The sink in her apartment collapsed on her foot, fracturing her big toe and making it painful for her to stand. She claims that as a consequence of the injury she was compelled to abandon her plans to become a beautician because that job requires standing for long periods of time. She also asserts that she was unable to work at her current job for a month. She filed a tort claim against Hewes Street Realty for negligence in failing properly to maintain the sink. She brought the suit in Federal district court, claiming damages of $25,000. Her medical expenses and actual loss of salary were less than $1,500; the rest of her alleged damages were for loss of future earnings as a beautician. Hewes Street moved to dismiss the suit on the basis that Deutsch's claim fell short of the jurisdictional requirement which then was $10,000 and therefore the Federal court lacked subject matter jurisdiction over her claim. The district court dismissed the suit and Deutsch appeals.

Decision: District court's dismissal reversed.

Opinion: Waterman, J.   One cannot underestimate the difficulties involved in developing clear and just rules to assist the district courts in determining whether an amount in controversy in a case exceeds $10,000. The problem is especially difficult because the major considerations tug in precisely opposite directions. On the one hand, with mounting federal case loads, as Chief Judge Lumbard recently has stated, "it has become doubly important that the district courts take measures to discover those suits which ought never to have been brought in the federal court and to dismiss them when the court is convinced to a legal certainty that the plaintiff cannot recover an amount in excess of $10,000." [Citation.] On the other hand, we must not permit a preliminary jurisdictional determination regarding recoverable damages to deprive a plaintiff unfairly of a federal court trial of a case on its merits. The Supreme Court has struck the balance between these considerations thus: "The rule governing dismissal for want of jurisdiction in cases brought in the federal court is that, unless the law gives a different rule, the sum claimed by the plaintiff controls if the claim is apparently made in good faith. It must appear to a legal certainty that the claim is really for less than the jurisdictional amount to justify dismissal." [Citation.]

* * *

Of course district courts are not restricted by the rule adopted here from looking further than the plaintiff's complaint in deciding whether a controversy involves recoverable sums in excess of $10,000. For example, dismissal will be proper when, under applicable law, the damages claimed are not recoverable, [citation], or when the damages claimed, even though recoverable, cannot as a matter of law exceed $10,000. [Citation]. Furthermore, flagrant cases may arise in which, even though the complaint demands unliquidated damages in excess of $10,000, dismissal is proper because the district court can justifiably conclude that the amount demanded was inflated solely in order to gain access to the federal courts. * * *

In the present case there is no independent evidence tending to establish that appellant's claim was inflated solely in order to gain access to the federal courts. * * *

Here we have a rather uncomplicated tort case in which appellant seeks unliquidated damages for the alleged impairment of her earning capacity, and the amount she demands seems far in excess of any likely verdict she can obtain. Nevertheless, under applicable New York tort law it appears that one who seriously has been preparing oneself for a change from a present vocation to a more remunerative one may, if the injury has impaired or frustrated the likelihood of success in the new vocation, recover nonspeculative damages for this damage factor based upon the loss of future probabilities of earning capacity. [Citations.]

Though it may seem unlikely that plaintiff will be able to substantiate that she should recover damages in excess of $10,000, on this record it is not clear to a legal certainty that she cannot do so; we ought not affirmatively decide more than that. Accordingly, we reverse the district court order dismissing the plaintiffs' actions and remand for further proceedings below.

Exclusive State Jurisdiction   The State courts have exclusive jurisdiction over *all other matters*. All matters not granted in the Constitution or not exercised by Congress are solely within the jurisdiction of the States. Accordingly, exclusive State jurisdiction would include cases involving diversity of citizenship but where the amount in controversy is $50,000 or less. In addition, the State courts have exclusive jurisdiction over all cases to which the Federal judicial power does not reach, including, but by no means limited to, property, torts, contract, agency, commercial transactions, and most crimes.

The jurisdiction of the Federal and State courts is illustrated in Figure 2–4.

Stare Decisis in the Dual Court System   The doctrine of *stare decisis* presents certain problems when there are two parallel court systems. As a consequence, in the United States *stare decisis* works approximately as follows (see also Figure 2–5):

1. The United States Supreme Court has never held itself to be rigidly bound by its own decisions, and lower Federal courts and State courts have followed that course in respect to their own decisions.

2. A decision of the U.S. Supreme Court on Federal questions is binding on all other courts, Federal or State.

3. Although a decision of a Federal court other than the Supreme Court may be persuasive in a State court on a Federal question, it is nevertheless not binding.

4. A decision of a State court may be persuasive in the Federal courts, but it is not binding except where Federal jurisdiction is based on diversity of citizenship. In such a case, the Federal courts must apply local State law as determined by the highest State tribunal and not by a trial or intermediate appellate court.

5. Decisions of the Federal courts (other than the U.S. Supreme Court) are not binding on other Federal courts of coordinate rank or inferior rank, unless the latter owe obedience

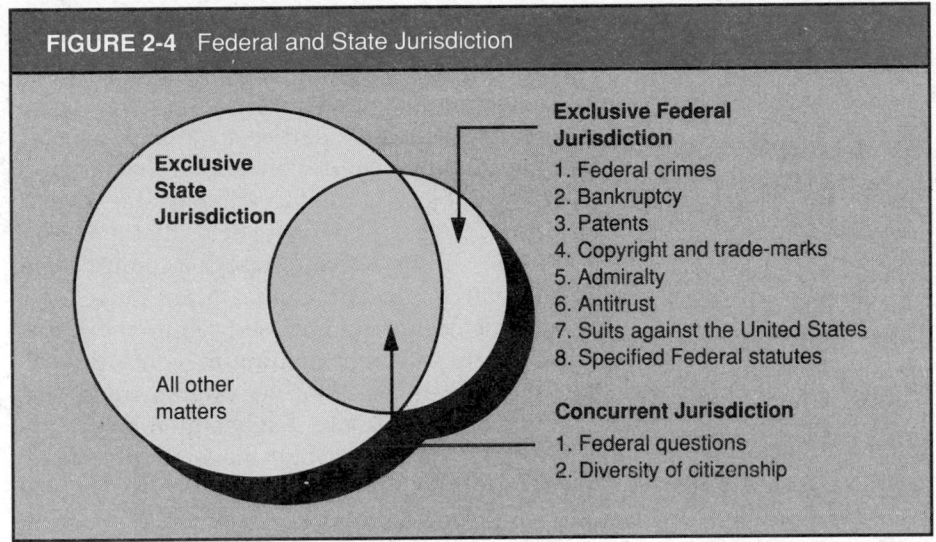

FIGURE 2-4   Federal and State Jurisdiction

to the deciding court. For example, a decision of the Fifth Circuit Court of Appeals binds district courts in the fifth circuit but no other Federal court.

6. A decision of a State court is binding on all courts inferior to it in its jurisdiction. Thus, the decision of the supreme court in a State binds all other courts in that State.

7. A decision of a State court is not binding on courts in another State except where the latter courts are required to apply the law of the first State as determined by the highest court in that State. For example, if a North Carolina court is required to apply Virginia law, it must follow decisions of the Virginia Supreme Court.

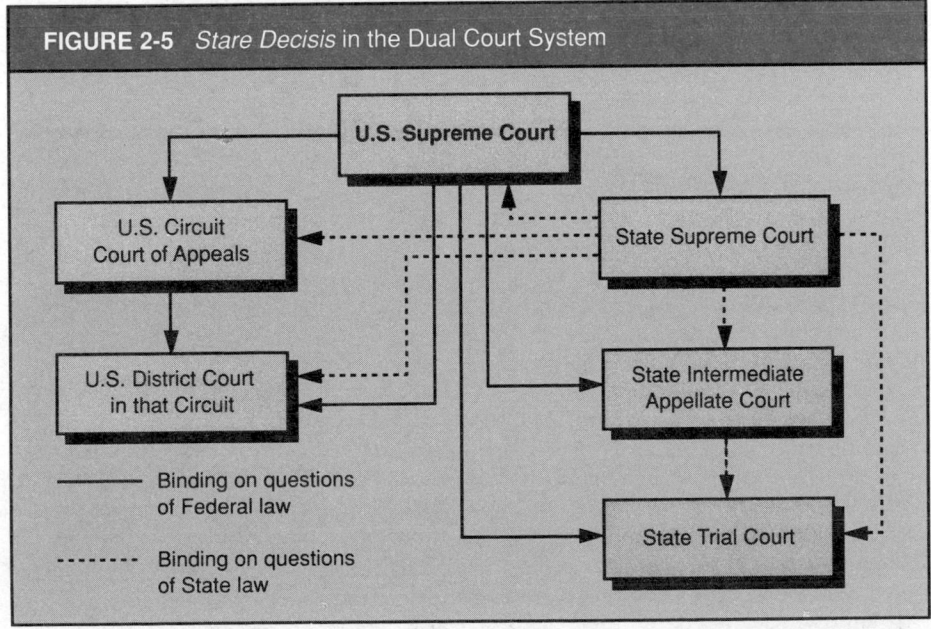

FIGURE 2-5   *Stare Decisis* in the Dual Court System

Jurisdiction over the Parties

The second essential type of jurisdiction a court must have is the power of a court to bind the parties involved in the dispute. This type of jurisdiction is called **jurisdiction over the parties,** and its requirements may be met in any of three ways: (1) *in personam* jurisdiction, (2) *in rem* jurisdiction, or (3) attachment jurisdiction. In addition, the exercise of jurisdiction must satisfy the constitutionally imposed requirements of reasonable notification and a reasonable opportunity to be heard. This means that the courts must exercise jurisdictional power in a manner consistent with the principle of "due process" of law as we discuss more fully in Chapter 3.

In Personam Jurisdiction   *In personam* jurisdiction or personal jurisdiction is jurisdiction of a court over the parties to a lawsuit in contrast to jurisdiction over their property. A court obtains *in personam* jurisdiction over a person either (1) by serving process on the party within the State in which the court is located, or (2) by reasonable notification to a party outside the State in those instances where a "long-arm statute" applies. To *serve process* means to deliver a summons, which is an order to respond to a complaint lodged against a party. (The terms *summons* and *complaint* are more fully explained later in this chapter.)

Personal jurisdiction may be obtained by personally serving a person within a State if that person is domiciled in that State. Personal jurisdiction may also arise from a party's consent. For example, parties to a contract may agree that any dispute concerning that contract will be subject to the jurisdiction of a specific court. Some courts have held that personal service within a State upon a nonresident temporarily present in that State must meet the constitutionally imposed requirement that there are sufficient minimum contacts with that State so as "not to offend traditional notions of fair play and substantial justice."

In addition, most States have adopted *long-arm statutes* to expand their jurisdictional reach. These statutes typically allow courts to obtain jurisdiction over nonresident defendants under the following conditions, as long as the exercise of jurisdiction does not offend traditional notions of fair play and substantial justice: if the defendant (1) has committed a tort (civil wrong) within the State, (2) owns property within the State if that property is the subject matter of the lawsuit, (3) has entered into a contract within the State, or (4) has transacted business within the State if that business is the subject matter of the lawsuit. *Tavoularis v. Womer* illustrates the factors courts consider in determining whether a State may extend its jurisdiction beyond its territorial borders through the use of a long-arm statute.

TAVOULARIS v. WOMER
Supreme Court of New Hampshire, 1983.
462 A.2d 110.

Facts: Mark Womer and Brian Perry were members of the United States Navy and were stationed in Newport, Rhode Island. On April 10, 1978, Womer allowed Perry to borrow his automobile so that Perry could visit his family in New Hampshire. Later that day, while operating Womer's vehicle, Perry was involved in an accident in Manchester, New Hampshire. As a result of the accident, Tzannetos Tavoularis was injured. Tavoularis brought this action against Womer in a New Hampshire superior court, contending that Womer was negligent in lending the automobile to Perry when he knew or should have known that Perry did not have a valid driver's license. Womer sought to dismiss the action on the ground that the New Hampshire courts lacked jurisdiction over him, citing the following facts: (1) he lived and worked in Georgia; (2) he had no relatives in New Hampshire; (3) he neither owned property nor possessed investments in New Hampshire; and (4) he had never conducted business in New Hampshire. The court found that Womer "authorized the use of the highways of New Hampshire" by Perry, constituting sufficient "minimum contacts" to invoke the long-arm statute. Womer then brought this appeal.

Decision: Judgment affirmed.

Opinion: **King, C. J.** The long-arm statute provides that any person who "in person or through an agent . . . commits a tortious act within this state . . . submits himself . . . to the jurisdiction of the courts of this state as to any cause of action arising from or growing out of the [tortious] act[ ]. . . ." [Citation.] * * *

A number of courts in States with similar statutory language have held that the use of the term "tortious act" or "tortious conduct" in a long-arm statute does not preclude the exercise of jursidiction over a nonresident when only the alleged injury occurred within the forum. [Citations.] An essential part of the reasoning of these courts has been that their long-arm statutes must be interpreted expansively in order to effectuate the legislative intent of providing a convenient forum so that resident plaintiffs may recover for their injuries from nonresident defendants. [Citations.]

* * *

Because the long-arm statute must be construed in its broadest legal sense to give effect to the legislative intent, and in light of our decision in [citation], we hold that the fact that only the alleged injury occurred within the State does not preclude New Hampshire courts from subjecting a nonresident to their jurisdiction under the long-arm statute.

Having determined that the defendant's conduct falls within the purview of [the long arm statute], we must now determine whether the exercise of jurisdiction over the defendant comports with constitutional due process. [Citation.]

In order to subject a defendant to a personal judgment, the defendant must have certain "minimum contacts" with a State such that the maintenance of a suit does not offend "traditional notions of fair play and substantial justice." [Citation.] In [citation], the United States Supreme Court stated that the "minimum contacts" requirement is both a protection against inconvenient or distant litigation and a consequence of territorial limitations on the power of the states. [Citations.]

* * *

* * * Since [citation], many courts have upheld the exercise of jurisdiction over a nonresident defendant when the cause of action arose from a tort, even though only the injury occurred within the forum state, when the defendant engaged in an activity outside the state that had reasonably foreseeable consequences within the forum state. [Citations.]

It is insufficient for purposes of due process, however, if the fact that the injury occurred in the forum state was "fortuitous." [Citation.] * * *

We believe that the defendant's conduct and connection with New Hampshire in this case were such that he reasonably should have anticipated being brought into court here. Taking the plaintiff's pleadings and all reasonable inferences therefrom as true, [citation], it was reasonably foreseeable that the defendant would be sued in New Hampshire for negligently entrusting an automobile to Perry. The fact that the injury occurred in New Hampshire was not "fortuitous," because he specifically authorized Perry to drive in New Hampshire. For these reasons, we hold that the defendant had sufficient "minimum contacts" with this State for the constitutional exercise of jurisdiction by our courts.

In Rem Jurisdiction Courts in a State have the jurisdiction to adjudicate claims to property situated within the State if the plaintiff gives reasonable notice and an opportunity to be heard to those persons who have an interest in the property. Such jurisdiction over property is called *in rem* **jurisdiction** from the Latin word *res*, which means "thing." For example, if A and B are involved in a lawsuit over property located in Kansas, then an appropriate court in Kansas would have *in rem* jurisdiction to adjudicate claims over this property as long as both parties are given notice of the lawsuit and a reasonable opportunity to contest the claim.

Attachment Jurisdiction Attachment jurisdiction, or *quasi in rem* **jurisdiction,** like *in rem* jurisdiction, is jurisdiction over property rather than over a person. But attachment jurisdiction is invoked by seizing the defendant's property located within the State to obtain payment of a claim against the defendant that is *unrelated* to the property seized. The basis of jurisdiction, therefore, is the State's connection with the property; it does not depend on any connection between the State and the defendant. Attachment jurisdiction differs from *in rem* jurisdiction in that the purpose of *in rem* jurisdiction is to resolve conflicting claims to the property; in attachment jurisdiction both parties accept that the property is owned by the defendant, but the plaintiff seeks to seize it to obtain payment for his claim against the defendant. For example, A, a resident of Ohio, has obtained a valid judgment in the amount of $20,000 against B, a citizen of Kentucky. A can attach B's automobile, which is located in Ohio, to satisfy his court judgment against B.

In attachment jurisdiction, however, as with all forms of jurisdiction, the State must have sufficient, minimum contacts with the controversy so that due process will not be violated. In the preceding example, the fact that A was a resident of Ohio satisfies this requirement. But if the automobile had been located in West Virginia, it is doubtful that a court in West Virginia could constitutionally assert attachment jurisdiction over B's automobile.

Venue **Venue,** which is often confused with jurisdiction, deals with the location where a lawsuit *should* be brought. The purpose of venue is to regulate the distribution of cases within a specific court system and to identify a convenient forum. In the Federal court system, venue determines the district or districts in a given State in which suit may be brought. State rules of venue typically require that a suit be initiated in the county where one of the defendants lives. In matters involving real estate, most venue rules require that a suit be initiated in the county where the property is situated. A defendant may, however, object to the venue for various reasons. For instance, a defendant may object to venue based on the principle of *forum non-conveniens*. This basically means that the presentation of the case in that court will create a hardship on the defendant or on relevant witnesses because of the great distance the individuals must travel.

CIVIL PROCEDURE

Civil disputes that enter the judicial system must follow the rules of civil procedure. These rules are designed to resolve the dispute in a just, prompt, and inexpensive way.

To acquaint you with civil procedure, we shall carry a hypothetical action through the trial court to the highest court of review in the State. Although there are technical differences in trial and appellate procedure among the States, the following illustration will give you a general understanding of the trial and appeal of cases.

Assume that Pam Pederson, a pedestrian, while crossing a street in Chicago, is struck by an automobile driven by David Dryden. Pederson suffers serious personal injuries, incurs heavy medical and hospital expenses, and is unable to work for several months. She desires that Dryden pay her for the loss and damages she sustained. Attempts at settlement failing, Pederson brings an action at law against Dryden. Thus Pederson is the plaintiff and Dryden the defendant. Each is represented by a lawyer. Let us follow the progress of the case.

The Pleadings

The purpose of **pleadings** is to give notice and to establish the issues of fact and law presented and disputed. An "issue of fact" is a dispute between the parties regarding the events that gave rise to the lawsuit. In contrast, an "issue of law" is a dispute between the parties as to what legal rules apply to these facts. Issues of fact are decided by the jury, whereas issues of law are decided by the court. A lawsuit begins when Pederson, the plaintiff, files with the clerk of the trial court a **complaint** against Dryden, which contains (1) a statement of the claim and supporting facts showing that she is entitled to relief, and (2) a demand for that relief. Pederson's complaint alleges that while exercising due and reasonable care for her own safety, she was struck by Dryden's automobile, which was negligently being driven by Dryden, causing personal injuries and damages of $50,000, for which Pederson requests judgment.

The county sheriff or a deputy sheriff serves a summons and a copy of the complaint on Dryden, the defendant, commanding him to file his appearance and answer with the clerk of the court within a specific time, usually thirty days from the date the summons was served. The **summons** has the important function of notifying the defendant that a suit has been brought against him. Proper service of the summons establishes the court's jurisdiction over the person of the defendant.

At this point Dryden, the defendant, has several options. If he fails to respond at all, a **default judgment** will be entered against the defendant for the relief requested in the complaint. He may make **pretrial motions** contesting the court's jurisdiction over him or asserting that the action is barred by the statute of limitations, which requires suits to be brought within a specified time. Dryden may also move, or request, that the complaint be made more definite and certain, or he may instead move that the complaint be dismissed for failure to state a claim on which relief may be granted. Such a motion is sometimes called a **demurrer;** it essentially asserts that even if all of Pederson's allegations are true, she would still not be entitled to the relief she seeks, and therefore there is no need for a trial of the facts. The court rules on this motion as a matter of law. If it rules in favor of the defendant, the plaintiff may appeal the ruling.

If he does not make any pretrial motions, or if they are denied, Dryden will respond to the complaint by filing an **answer,** which may contain denials, admissions, affirmative defenses, and counterclaims. Dryden might answer the complaint by denying its allegations of negligence and stating that he was driving his car at a low speed and with reasonable care (a **denial**) when his car struck Pederson (an **admission**), who had dashed across the street in front of his car without looking in any direction to see whether cars or other vehicles were approaching; that, accordingly, Pederson's injuries were caused by her own negligence (an **affirmative defense**), and therefore she should not be permitted to recover any damages. Dryden might further state that Pederson caused damage to his car and request a judgment for $2,000 (a **counterclaim**). These pleadings create an issue of fact about whether Dryden or Pederson, or both, failed to exercise due and reasonable care under the circumstances and were thus negligent and liable for their carelessness.

If the defendant counterclaims, the plaintiff must respond by a **reply,** which may also contain admissions, denials, or affirmative defenses.

After the pleadings, either party may move for **judgment on the pleadings,** which requests the judge to rule as a matter of law whether the facts as alleged in the pleadings of the nonmoving party are sufficient to grant the requested relief.

Pretrial Procedure

In preparation for trial and even before completion of the pleadings stage, each party has the right to obtain relevant evidence, or facts that may lead to evidence, from the other party. This procedure is known as **discovery.** It includes (1) pretrial *depositions* consisting of sworn testimony of the opposing party or other witnesses taken out of court; (2) sworn answers by the opposing party to *written interrogatories*, or questions; (3) *production* of documents and physical objects in the possession of the opposing party; (4) *examination* by a physician of the physical or mental condition of the opposing party, as needed; and (5) admissions of facts set forth in a *request for admissions* submitted to the opposing party. By using discovery properly, each party may become fully informed of the relevant evidence and avoid surprise at the trial. Another purpose of this procedure is to encourage and help settlements by giving both parties as much relevant information as possible.

Also furthering these objectives is the **pretrial conference** between the judge and the attorneys representing the parties. The basic purposes of the conference are (1) to simplify the issues in dispute by amending the pleadings, admitting or stipulating facts, and limiting the number of expert witnesses; and (2) to encourage settlement of the dispute without trial. If no settlement occurs, then the judge will enter an order containing all of the amendments, stipulations, admissions, and other matters agreed to during the pretrial conference. The order supersedes the pleadings and controls the trial.

The evidence disclosed by discovery may be so clear that a trial to determine the facts becomes unnecessary. If this is so, either party may move for a summary judgment, which requests the judge to rule that, because there are no issues of fact to be determined by trial, as a matter of law that party should prevail. A **summary judgment** is a final binding determination on the merits made by the judge before a trial. The following case involving the famous actress Shirley MacLaine explains the rules courts use to determine whether to grant summary judgment.

PARKER v. TWENTIETH CENTURY-FOX FILM CORP.
Supreme Court of California, 1970.
3 Cal.3d 176, 89 Cal.Rptr. 737, 474 P.2d 689.

Facts: Shirley MacLaine Parker, a well-known actress, contracted with Twentieth Century-Fox Film Corporation in August 1965 to play the female lead in Fox's upcoming production of "Bloomer Girl," a motion picture musical that was to be filmed in California. Fox agreed to pay Parker $750,000 for fourteen weeks of her services. Fox decided to cancel its plans for "Bloomer Girl" before production had begun, and, instead, offered Parker the female lead in another film, "Big Country, Big Man," a dramatic western to be filmed in Australia. The compensation offered was identical, but Parker's right to approve the director and screenplay would have been eliminated or altered by the "Big Country" proposal. She refused to accept and brought suit to recover the $750,000 for Fox's breach of the "Bloomer Girl" contract. Fox's sole defense in its answer was that it owed no money to Parker because she had deliberately failed to mitigate or reduce her damages by unreasonably refusing to accept the "Big Country" lead. Parker filed a motion for summary judgment. Fox, in opposition to the motion, claimed, in effect, only that the "Big Country" offer was not employment different or inferior to that under the "Bloomer Girl" contract. The trial court granted Parker a summary judgment and Fox appealed.

Decision: Summary judgment affirmed.

Opinion: Burke, J.   The familiar rules are that the matter to be determined by the trial court on a motion for summary judgment is whether facts have been presented which give rise to a triable factual issue. The court may not pass upon the issue itself. Summary judgment is proper only if the affidavits or declarations in support of the moving party would be sufficient to sustain a judgment in his favor and his opponent does not by affidavit show facts sufficient to present a triable issue of fact. The affidavits of the moving party are strictly construed, and doubts as to the propriety of summary judgment should be resolved against granting the motion. Such summary procedure is drastic and should be used with caution so that it does not become a substitute for the open trial method of determining facts. The moving party cannot depend upon allegations in his own pleadings to cure deficient affidavits, nor can his adversary rely upon his own pleadings in lieu or in support of affidavits in opposition to a motion; however, a party can rely on his adversary's pleadings to establish facts not contained in his own affidavits. [Citations.] Also, the court may consider facts stipulated to by the parties and facts which are properly the subject of judicial notice. [Citations.]

As stated, defendant's sole defense to this action which resulted from its deliberate breach of contract is that in rejecting defendant's substitute offer of employment plaintiff unreasonably refused to mitigate damages.

The general rule is that the measure of recovery by a wrongfully discharged employee is the amount of salary agreed upon for the period of service, less the amount which the employer affirmatively proves the employee has earned or with reasonable effort might have earned from other employment. [Citations.] However, before projected earnings from other employment opportunities not sought or accepted by the discharged employee can be applied in mitigation, the employer must show that the other employment was comparable, or substantially similar, to that of which the employee has been deprived; the employee's rejection of or failure to seek other available employment of a different or inferior kind may not be resorted to in order to mitigate damages. [Citations.]

* * *

Applying the foregoing rules to the record in the present case, with all intendments in favor of the party opposing the summary judgment motion—here, defendant—it is clear that the trial court correctly ruled that plaintiff's failure to accept defendant's tendered substitute employment could not be applied in mitigation of damages because the offer of the "Big Country" lead was of employment both different and inferior, and that no factual dispute was presented on that issue. The mere circumstance that "Bloomer Girl" was to be a musical review calling upon plaintiff's talents as a dancer as well as an actress, and was to be produced in the City of Los Angeles, whereas, "Big Country" was a straight dramatic role in a "Western Type" story taking place in an opal mine in Australia, demonstrates the difference in kind between the two employments; the female lead as a dramatic actress in a western style motion picture can by no stretch of imagination be considered the equivalent of or substantially similar to the lead in a song-and-dance production.

Additionally, the substitute "Big Country" offer proposed to eliminate or impair the director and screenplay approvals accorded to plaintiff under the original "Bloomer Girl" contract *   *   * and thus constituted an offer of inferior employment. No expertise or judicial notice is required in order to hold that the deprivation or infringement of an employee's rights held under an original employment contract converts the available "other employment" relied upon by the employer to mitigate damages, into inferior employment which the employee need not seek or accept. [Citation.]

---

* * *

In view of the determination that defendant failed to present any facts showing the existence of a factual issue with respect to its sole defense—plaintiff's rejection of its substitute employment offer in mitigation of damages—we need not consider plaintiff's further contention that for various reasons, including the provisions of the original contract, plaintiff was excused from attempting to mitigate damages.

Trial

In all Federal cases at common law involving more than twenty dollars, the United States Constitution guarantees the right to a jury trial. In addition, nearly every State constitution provides a similar right. Under Federal law and in almost all States, jury trials are *not* available in equity cases. Even in cases where a jury trial is available, the parties may waive (choose not to have) a trial by jury. When a trial is conducted without a jury, the judge serves as the fact finder and will make separate findings of fact and conclusions of law. When a trial is conducted *with* a jury, the judge determines issues of law and the jury determines questions of fact.

Assuming a timely demand for a jury has been made, the trial begins by selection of a jury. The jury selection process involves an examination by the parties' attorneys (or in some courts by the judge) of the potential jurors called **voir dire.** Each party has an unlimited number of **challenges for cause,** which allow a party to prevent a prospective juror from serving if the juror is biased or cannot be fair and impartial. In addition, each party has a limited number of **peremptory challenges** for which no cause is required to disqualify a prospective juror.

After the jury has been selected, both attorneys make an **opening statement** about the facts that they expect to prove in the trial. The plaintiff and plaintiff's witnesses then testify on **direct examination** by the plaintiff's attorney. Each is subject to **cross-examination** by the defendant's attorney. Pederson has her witnesses testify that the traffic light at the street intersection where she was struck was green for traffic in the direction in which she was crossing but changed to yellow when she

was about one-third of the way across the street.

During the trial the judge rules on the admission and exclusion of evidence. If the judge does not allow certain evidence to be introduced or certain testimony to be given, the attorney must make an **offer of proof** to preserve for review on appeal the question of its admissibility. The offer of proof is not regarded as evidence, and the offer, which consists of oral statements of counsel or witnesses for the record to show the evidence that the judge has ruled inadmissible, is not heard by the jury.

After cross-examination, followed by redirect examination of each of her witnesses, Pederson rests her case. At this time Dryden may move for a directed verdict in his favor. A **directed verdict** is a final binding determination on the merits made by the judge after a trial has begun but before the jury renders a judgment. If the judge concludes that the evidence introduced by Pederson, which is assumed to be true, would not be sufficient for the jury to find in favor of the plaintiff, then the judge will grant the directed verdict in favor of the defendant.

If the judge denies the motion for a directed verdict, however, the defendant then has the opportunity to present evidence. Dryden and his witnesses testify that he was driving his car at a low speed when it struck Pederson and that Dryden at the time had the green light at the intersection. After the defendant has presented his evidence and both parties have rested (concluded), then each party may move for a directed verdict. By this motion the party contends that the evidence is so clear that reasonable persons could not differ about the outcome of the case. If the judge grants the motion for a directed verdict, he takes the case away from the jury and enters a judgment for the party making the motion.

If these motions are denied, then Pederson's attorney makes a closing argument to the jury, reviewing the evidence and urging a verdict in favor of Pederson. Then the defendant's attorney makes a closing argument, summarizing the evidence in the light most favorable to Dryden. Pederson's attorney is permitted to make a short argument in rebuttal.

The attorneys have previously given written **jury instructions** on the applicable law to the trial judge, who gives those which he approves to the jury and denies those which he considers incorrect. The judge may also give the jury instructions of his own. These instructions (called "charges" in some States) advise the jury of the particular rules of law that apply to the facts as the jury determines from the evidence. The jury then retires to the jury room to deliberate and to reach its **verdict** in favor of one party or the other. If the jury finds the issues in favor of Dryden, its verdict is that he is not liable. If, however, it finds the issues for Pederson and against Dryden, its verdict will be that the defendant is liable and will specify the amount of the plaintiff's damages. In this case the jury found that Pederson's damages were $35,000. On returning to the jury box, the foreman either announces the verdict or hands it in written form to the clerk to give to the judge, who reads the verdict in open court. In some jurisdictions, a **special verdict** is used, by which the jury makes specific written findings on each factual issue. The judge then applies the law to these findings and renders a judgment.

The unsuccessful party may then file a written motion for a new trial or for judgment notwithstanding the verdict. A **motion for a new trial** may be granted if (1) the judge committed prejudicial error during the trial, (2) the verdict is against the weight of the evidence, (3) the damages are excessive, or (4) the trial was not fair. The judge has the discretion to grant a motion for a new trial (on grounds 1, 3, or 4 above) even if the verdict is supported by substantial evidence. On the other hand, the motion for judgment notwithstanding the verdict (also called a judgment n.o.v.) must be denied if there is any

substantial evidence supporting the verdict. This motion is similar to a motion for a directed verdict, only it is made after the jury's verdict. To grant the **motion for judgment notwithstanding the verdict,** the judge must decide that the evidence is so clear that reasonable people could not differ as to the outcome of the case.

If these motions are denied, the judge enters judgment on the verdict for $35,000 in favor of the plaintiff.

If Dryden does not appeal, or if the reviewing court affirms the judgment if he does appeal, and Dryden does not pay the judgment, the task of enforcement remains. Pederson requests the clerk to issue a *writ of execution* demanding payment of the judgment, which is served by the sheriff on the defendant. If the writ is returned "unsatisfied," that is, if Dryden still does not pay, Pederson may post bond or other security and order a levy on and sale of specific nonexempt property belonging to the defendant, which is then seized by the sheriff, advertised for sale, and sold at a public sale under the writ of execution. If the sale does not produce enough money to pay the judgment, Pederson's attorney may begin another proceeding in an attempt to locate money or other property belonging to Dryden. Pederson's attorney may also proceed by *garnishment* against Dryden's employer to collect from his wages or a bank in which he has an account in an attempt to collect the judgment.

Appeal

The purpose of an appeal is to determine whether the trial court committed prejudicial error. As a general rule only errors of law are reviewed by an appellate court. Errors of law include the judge's decisions to admit or exclude evidence; the judge's instructions to the jury; and the judge's actions in denying or granting a motion for a demurrer, a summary judgment, a directed verdict, or a judgment notwithstanding the verdict. Errors of fact will only be reversed if they are so clearly erroneous that they are considered to be an error of law.

Let us assume that Dryden directs his attorney to appeal. The attorney files a notice of appeal with the clerk of the trial court within the prescribed time. Later Dryden, the party appealing or appellant, files in the reviewing court the record on appeal, which contains the pleadings, a transcript of the testimony, rulings by the judge on motions made by the parties, arguments of counsel, jury instructions, the verdict, posttrial motions, and the judgment from which the appeal is taken. In States where there is an intermediate court of appeals, it will usually be the reviewing court. In States where there are no intermediate courts of appeal, a party may appeal directly from the trial court to the State supreme court.

Dryden, as appellant, is required to prepare a condensation of the record, known as an abstract, or pertinent excerpts from the record, which he files with the reviewing court together with a **brief** and argument. His brief contains a statement of the facts, the issues, the rulings by the trial court that Dryden contends are erroneous and prejudicial, grounds for reversal of the judgment, a statement of the applicable law, and arguments on his behalf. Pederson, the appellee, files an answering brief and argument. Dryden may, but is not required to, file a reply brief. The case is now ready to be considered by the reviewing court.

The appellate court does not hear any evidence. It decides the case on the record, abstracts, and briefs. After **oral argument** by the attorneys, if the court elects to hear one, the court takes the case under advisement, or begins deliberations. The appellate court then makes a decision based on majority rule. The court prepares a written opinion containing the reasons for its decision, the rules of law that apply, and its judgment. The judgment may affirm the judgment of the trial court, or if the court finds that reversible error was committed, the judgment may be reversed or modified or returned to the lower court (remanded) for a new trial. In some instances the appellate court will affirm the lower court's decision in part and will reverse it in part. The losing party may file a petition for rehearing, which is usually denied.

If the reviewing court is an intermediate appellate court, the party losing in that court may decide to seek a reversal of its judgment by filing within a prescribed time a notice of appeal, if the appeal is by right, or a petition for leave to appeal to the State supreme court, if the appeal is by discretion. This petition corresponds to a petition for a writ of *certiorari* in the United States Supreme Court. The party winning in the appellate court may file an answer to the petition for leave to appeal. If the petition is granted, or if the appeal is by right, the record is certified to the higher court, and each party files a new brief and argument in the supreme court. The supreme court may hear oral argument or simply review the record; it then takes the case under advisement. If the supreme court concludes that the judgment of the appellate court is correct, it affirms. If it decides otherwise, it reverses the judgment of the appellate court and enters a reversal or an order of remand. The unsuccessful party may again file a petition for a rehearing, which is likely to be denied. Barring the remote possibility of an application for still further review by the United States Supreme Court, the case has either reached its termination or, on remand, is about to start its second journey through the courts, beginning as originally in the trial court.

The various stages in civil procedure are illustrated in Figure 2–6.

ALTERNATIVE DISPUTE RESOLUTION

Litigation is complex, time-consuming, and expensive. Consequently, several nonjudicial methods of dealing with disputes have developed. The most important of these alternatives to litigation is arbitration. Others include negotiation, conciliation, and mediation. Alternate dispute resolution mechanisms have developed in an attempt to overcome some of the disadvantages of litigation. In addition to being complex, time-consuming, and expensive, court adjudications involve long delays, lack special expertise in substantive areas, provide a limited range of remedies, are structured such that one party takes all with little opportunity for compromise, and often cause personal dislike between the parties.

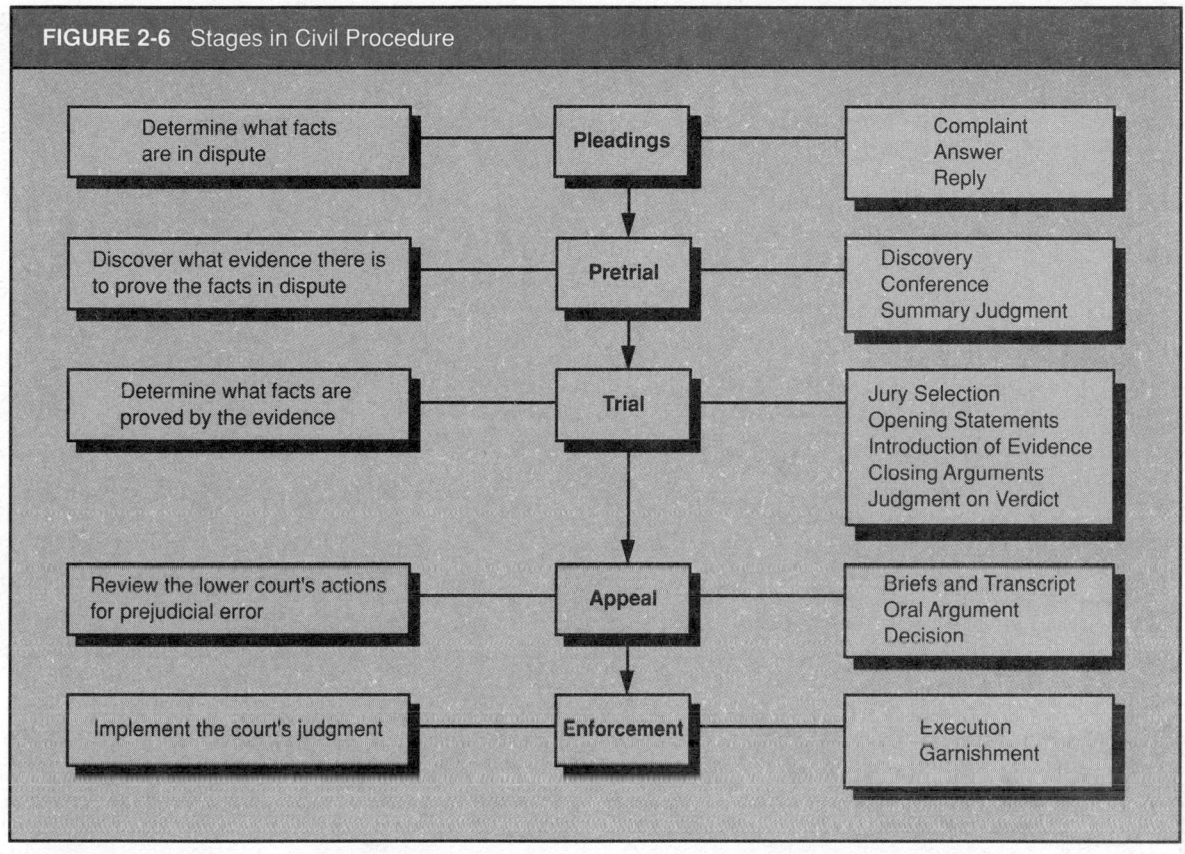

FIGURE 2-6   Stages in Civil Procedure

Determine what facts are in dispute	**Pleadings**	Complaint / Answer / Reply
Discover what evidence there is to prove the facts in dispute	**Pretrial**	Discovery / Conference / Summary Judgment
Determine what facts are proved by the evidence	**Trial**	Jury Selection / Opening Statements / Introduction of Evidence / Closing Arguments / Judgment on Verdict
Review the lower court's actions for prejudicial error	**Appeal**	Briefs and Transcript / Oral Argument / Decision
Implement the court's judgment	**Enforcement**	Execution / Garnishment

Alternative dispute resolution methods are especially suitable where privacy, speed, preservation of continuing relations, and control over the process—including the flexibility to compromise—are important to the parties. Nevertheless, the disadvantages and limitations of using alternative dispute mechanisms may make court adjudication more appropriate. Except for arbitration, only courts can compel participation and provide a binding resolution. In addition, only courts can establish precedents and create public duties. Furthermore, the courts provide greater due process protections and uniformity of outcome. Finally, the courts are independent of the parties and publicly funded. See Law in the News on page 40.

Arbitration

In **arbitration** the parties select a third person or persons (the arbitrator) who render(s) a binding decision after hearing arguments and reviewing evidence. Because the presentation of the case is less formal and the rules of evidence are more relaxed, arbitration usually takes less time and costs less than litigation. Moreover, in many arbitration cases the parties are able to select an arbitrator with special expertise concerning the subject of the dispute. Thus, the quality of the arbitrator's decision may be higher than that available through the court system. In addition, arbitration is normally conducted in private, thus avoiding unwanted publicity. Arbitration is commonly used in commercial and labor management disputes.

There are two basic types of arbitration—consensual, which is by far the most common, and compulsory. **Consensual arbitration** occurs whenever the parties to a dispute agree to submit the controversy to arbitration. They may do this in advance by agreeing in their contract that disputes arising out of their contract will be resolved by arbitration. Or they

FIGURE 2-7 Comparison of Adjudication, Arbitration, and Mediation/Conciliation

	Court Adjudication	Arbitration	Mediation/Conciliation
Advantages	Binding	Binding	Preserves relations
	Public norms	Parties control	Parties control
	Precedents	process	process
	Uniformity	Privacy	Privacy
	Publicly funded	Special expertise	Flexible
	Compels participation	Speedy resolution	
Disadvantages	Expensive	No public norms	Not binding
	Time-consuming	No precedent	Lacks finality
	Long delays	No uniformity	No compelled
	Limited remedies		participation
	Lacks special expertise		No precedent
	No compromise		No uniformity
	Disrupts relationships		
	Publicity		

Source: Adapted from Table 4 of *Report of the Ad Hoc Panel on Dispute Resolution and Public Policy*, prepared by the National Institute for Disute Resolution.

may do so after a dispute arises by then agreeing to submit the dispute to arbitration. In either instance, such agreements are enforceable under the U.S. Arbitration Act and statutes in over forty States. In **compulsory arbitration,** which is relatively infrequent, a Federal or State statute requires arbitration for specific types of disputes, such as those involving public employees like police officers or fire fighters.

The decision of the arbitrators, called an **award,** is binding on the parties. Nevertheless, it is subject to limited judicial review for such matters as illegality, fraud or other misconduct, lack of due process, or excess of the arbitrators' powers. Historically, the courts were unfriendly to arbitration; however, as the following case illustrates, the courts have dramatically changed their attitude and now favor arbitration.

La STELLA v. GARCIA ESTATES, INC.
Supreme Court of New Jersey, 1975.
66 N.J. 297, 331 A.2d 1.

Facts: La Stella leased property from Garcia for use as a golf course. A few years later, Garcia refused to allow La Stella to exercise the renewal option, so La Stella filed suit to compel renewal of the lease. The court submitted the issue to an arbitration proceeding as stipulated under the contract. The arbitration clause provided that all disputes arising under the lease would be settled by arbitration; that the landlord and tenant would each choose an arbitrator and the two arbitrators thus chosen would select a third arbitrator; and that the findings and award of the three arbitrators thus chosen would be final and binding on the parties.

   The arbitrators reached a majority decision (two to one) in La Stella's favor. Garcia appealed, claiming that under the common law the panel's decision must be unanimous to be binding. The appellate court reversed the arbitrators' decision. La Stella appealed to the Supreme Court.

Decision: Judgment of appellate court reversed.

Opinion: **Jacobs, J.**   We granted certification on the plaintiff's application in order to reconsider the subject and, after hearing oral argument, we are satisfied that the single issue of merit calling for present consideration and determination is whether the common law rule should not now be abandoned in favor of a rule that a majority determination is sufficient unless otherwise directed by the agreement to arbitrate.

* * *

The common law unanimity rule was in all likelihood a subordinate incident of the judicial hostility to arbitrations; it was generally adopted by the various state courts without discussion of its origin or validity * * *

Since the enactment of the United States Arbitration Act the federal courts have appropriately given it broad interpretative sweep. [Citations.] * * * There would appear to be little reason to doubt that under the Supreme Court's holding in [citation] and the broad interpretative principles set forth in [citation] and its succeeding cases, an arbitration agreement enforceable under the United States Arbitration Act will be construed by the federal courts as permitting a majority determination in the absence of a contrary direction in the agreement to arbitrate.

Two years before the federal statute was adopted, New Jersey enacted its current arbitration act. [Citation.] It provided, as did the federal statute, that agreements to arbitrate future as well as existing disputes shall be "valid, enforceable and irrevocable, except upon such grounds as exist at law or in equity for the revocation of a contract." * * *

Our cases since the enactment of the 1923 statute repeatedly stress that arbitration is now "looked upon favorably by the courts" and "every intendment is indulged in favor of an award." [Citations.]

* * *

* * * we do know that in modern times arbitration agreements generally contemplate that majority awards are to be binding; this is particularly true where, as here, the agreement provides that each party shall designate a single arbitrator and that the two arbitrators shall select the third, sometimes referred to as "the 'neutral' arbitrator." [Citation.]

Parties ordinarily agree to arbitrate because they consider that arbitration is much more expeditious and much less costly than court litigation. However, they are aware that only an effective and final arbitration will serve their interests and that insistence on unanimity among several arbitrators may well entail successive proceedings with additional cost and additional delay. While they are at liberty to insist on unanimity, the pertinent values strongly suggest that when their agreement is silent on the subject, unanimity should not be required. This is in effect what the Supreme Court concluded under the 1925 Federal Arbitration Act [citation] and what we now consider may fairly be concluded under our 1923 State Arbitration Act [citation.]

* * * Whatever validity the common law rule may originally have had, it is clear to us that it has no proper place in current times. This Court has not hesitated to reject common law doctrines which have outlived their usefulness and which no longer serve justice or the interests of society. [Citations.] We now explicitly overrule the common law doctrine adhered to in [citation] in favor of a rule that a majority award is sufficient unless otherwise directed by the agreement to arbitrate.

LAW IN THE NEWS

Novel Effort to Settle Asbestos Claims Fails As Lawsuits Multiply
Many Victims Sickened, Died While Companies Clashed Over How to Pay Claims

Back to the Legal Crapshoot

Joseph Kremenic, a strapping six-footer who spent most of his life working in a shipyard, dreamed of a quiet retirement on his farm in East Texas. In 1980, his dreams were shattered by a chilling diagnosis: asbestosis, a respiratory disease that slowly suffocates its victims.

Some sick co-workers were going to court and winning judgments against asbestos concerns. But Mr. Kremenic's claim got stuck in a clogged court. So in 1986, he took his case to a new agency set up by asbestos companies and their insurers that promised victims speedy settlements.

His settlement demands went unanswered for two years. Mr. Kremenic died in March, his claim still unresolved. "I wonder, Will it ever come to an end?" Margaret Kremenic, his widow, says. "I'm inclined to go to a jury, after all this time, all the suffering."

That's precisely what the asbestos and insurance companies had hoped to avoid three years ago when they pledged to lay down their arms and pay victims. The Asbestos Claims Facility was an experiment designed to mix cost savings with compassion. Companies wanted out of the courts, where they were spending huge sums to defend themselves. Victims wanted compensation, without the anguish of fighting for it and, in some cases, dying without it.

The experiment failed.

A Deluge of Claims

Seven of the facility's biggest members have pulled out of the organization in recent months, citing disagreements over settling claims. The departing companies were responsible for providing more than 60% of the facility's claims budget. Among them are Eagle-Picher Industries Inc.,

Owens-Illinois Inc., and Owens-Corning Fiberglass Corp. The remaining members have agreed to dissolve the facility, though they say they may form a new, smaller claims agency.

The Asbestos Claims Facility fell apart just as the flood of claims turned into a deluge. Some 63,000 claims, seeking billions in damages, are pending; new ones are pouring in at a rate of 1,300 a month, triple the rate of a few years ago. Asbestos litigation threatens to overwhelm courts in some areas. Nevertheless, asbestos producers and victims now have no choice but to rely on the courts to referee their disputes. And that is likely to mean more delay and bigger legal bills for both sides.

"It puts us back to square one," says Fred Baron, a plaintiffs' lawyer in Dallas who represents thousands of asbestos victims. "We're back to the old system of fierce litigation and huge litigation costs."

Bitter History

The history of asbestos litigation is a long and bitter one. The fiber was used widely as insulation for a century, until asbestos exposure was linked to cancer. The first lawsuit against an asbestos producer was filed in the 1950s, but plaintiffs didn't begin to win big until the 1980s. That's when juries, outraged by evidence that indicated the companies knew of the fiber's dangers long before alerting workers, began awarding millions of dollars in damages. Eventually, Manville Corp. and a half-dozen other concerns were forced to seek the protection of Chapter 11 bankruptcy proceedings.

But court was a crapshoot for both sides. Some victims won huge awards or managed to wring sizable settlements from asbestos producers; others got little or nothing. The only ones for whom the dice were always hot were the lawyers. Producers had retained 1,100 law firms around the U.S. to defend them by the mid-1980s; thousands more lawyers specialized in representing victims.

Asbestos producers found themselves battling not only victims but also their own insurers as lawsuits multiplied. Some insurance companies reread the fine print in their policies and decided they weren't liable for the billions of dollars the asbestos concerns demanded to cover claims. Those disputes also ended up in court.

Declaring a Truce

As it was first conceived, the Asbestos Claims Facility was supposed to represent a truce among all the combatants. Its founders envisioned a one-stop settlement shop for claims, a system that would offer a faster, less costly and more orderly way to resolve claims than in court. The facility even had the support of some of the most prominent plaintiffs' lawyers in the U.S., who promised their cooperation if the asbestos concerns and the insurers settled their differences.

"What might have been . . . would have been wonderful," says Harry Wellington, who, as then dean of Yale Law School, helped organize the facility. "And it probably would have been advantageous to everybody."

Fifty companies joined, among them some of the biggest names in the asbestos and insurance industries: Aetna Life & Casualty Co.; National Gypsum Co; Lloyd's of London; and U.S. Gypsum Co. Under terms, every member agreed to pay a portion of each claim based on the percentage it had historically paid, regardless of whether the claimant had been exposed to its product.

The facility succeeded in meeting some of its goals. Companies' legal bills dropped, in part because the number of law firms representing asbestos concerns was reduced to 55. Since it opened, the facility says, it has settled or tried 21,000 claims, paying out "substantially more" than $500 million to victims.

But ties to the plaintiffs' bar quickly became strained. Then members started to clash. Some wanted to settle claims quickly. Others, especially those that had limited insurance, wanted to delay. Further, some companies chafed at making payments to victims who hadn't been exposed to their products. The arguments got more and more heated as certain members edged closer to insolvency.

'Tyranny of the Minority'

Owens-Illinois, Louisiana-Pacific Corp.'s Fibreboard unit and Pittsburgh-Corning Corp. led a dissident faction that sought to delay payouts. Though a minority, the group often prevailed, by sheer force of its representatives' personalities, according to other board members and facility executives.

"It was tyranny of the minority," recalls Lawrence Fitzpatrick, the facility's acting chief executive. "They managed to wear everyone down."

Complicating the situation was a sudden surge in new and, in the view of some members, questionable claims. Most of the early victims had worked directly with asbestos, fabricating or installing it. In recent years, thousands who had less exposure to the fiber—steelworkers and rubber workers, to name a few—also have sought compensation.

The claims sparked more dispute. Some members felt that the original formula for splitting the cost of claims among members didn't reflect their liability in the new cases.

Logjam of Claims

The result was a logjam of claims. Victims found themselves waiting months, even years, before their settlement demands were answered. Some never heard from the facility at all before dying of asbestos-related diseases.

R. Bruce Ryan, an industrial electrician from Steubenville, Ohio, was one of them. After years of exposure to asbestos, Mr. Ryan developed mesothelioma, an invariably fatal cancer of the lining of the lung. Thomas White, his lawyer, says the facility never responded to Mr. Ryan's first settlement demand of $750,000, made in June 1986.

A year later, and by then seriously ill, Mr. Ryan made a second settlement demand for $1.5 million. Mr. Ryan died last summer at age 49. "They never responded, even to say yes, no or maybe," Mr. White says. (The facility concedes it didn't handle the claim in a "timely" way.)

The facility also outraged many by taking a hard line on the types of injuries for which it would offer settlements. It refused to settle cases filed by workers whose lungs had been scarred by asbestos exposure but who weren't yet disabled. Because some victims had won court awards for such injuries, others viewed the ruling as a declaration of war.

Fighting Back

It was as if the facility said, "We don't care what the law is. We don't care what the history is,'" says Gene Locks, a plaintiffs' lawyer in Philadelphia. (The facility admits the ruling was "unreasonable." It now allows victims who show early signs of disease to file claims, though they still don't get paid until they are disabled.)

Victims fought back—in court. In some jurisdictions, their plight caught the attention of sympathetic judges. To heighten pressure on the facility to settle claims, some judges scheduled dozens of asbestos lawsuits for trial each month, knowing the facility couldn't risk taking so many cases to trial simultaneously.

The tactic seemed to work, further encouraging lawyers to race to the courthouse. In retrospect, Mr. Fitzpatrick concedes, the facility's tough stance on settling cases undermined its mission to move the asbestos fray out of the courts. "It's a philosophy that shoots you in the foot in the long term," he says.

Bullying Claims Adjusters

Internal strife at the facility further heightened tension. "If I come in with 1,000 cases settled," Mr. Fitzpatrick, the facility's third chief executive, says, "half the board would say, 'Why didn't you settle 2,000?' The other half would say 'What, are you crazy? You shouldn't settle more than 500.' "

Mr. Fitzpatrick also says some directors tried to bully claims adjusters into disapproving large settlements. In some cases, he says, directors threatened to fire adjusters if they wouldn't comply. The meddling got so disruptive that the board eventually had to pass a resolution ordering directors to leave the staff alone.

Several asbestos producers announced they would drop out of the facility late last year. In February, Eagle-Picher quit, but, unlike the others, it refused to pay on pending claims. It says only about one-third of the $63.1 million it paid to settle claims through the facility last year was covered by insurance. The company says it believes it can settle claims for less money by negotiating directly with victims and their lawyers.

The remaining members are trying to form a new settlement organization, but without the support of such big concerns and former members as Eagle-Picher and Owens-Corning Fiberglas, it is unlikely to have a significant impact.

Living Down a Disaster

The facility's collapse is a blow not just to those involved in the asbestos fray. It is also dismaying news for chemical manufacturers and others who face a rising tide of personal-injury lawsuits over exposure to toxic substances. Those companies had looked to the facility as a model for resolving mass tort claims.

The failure also is a setback for the alternative dispute resolution movement, which advocates resolving cases out of court. Early on, proponents had hailed the facility as proof that the litigation explosion could be controlled. Eric Green, a Boston University law professor who advises companies on alternative dispute resolution, says: "We're going to be living down this disaster for a long time."

By Cynthia F. Mitchell and Paul M. Barrett. Reprinted by permission of the *Wall Street Journal*, © Dow Jones & Company, Inc. 1988. All Rights Reserved.

Conciliation and Mediation

Conciliation is a nonbinding, informal process in which a third party (the conciliator) selected by the disputing parties attempts to help them reach a mutually acceptable agreement. The functions of the conciliator include improving communications, explaining issues, scheduling meetings, discussing differences of opinion, and when the parties are unwilling to meet, serving as an intermediary between them.

Mediation is a process in which a third party (the mediator) selected by the disputants helps them to reach a resolution of their disagreement. In addition to employing the techniques of conciliation to improve communications, the mediator, unlike the conciliator, proposes possible solutions for the parties to consider. Like the conciliator, the mediator does not have the power to render a binding decision.

CHAPTER 2 THE JUDICIAL SYSTEM

CHAPTER SUMMARY

The Court System	**Federal Courts**
	■ *District Courts* trial courts of general jurisdiction that can hear and decide most legal controversies in the Federal system
	■ *Courts of Appeals* hear appeals from the district courts and review orders of certain administrative agencies
	■ *The Supreme Court* nation's highest court whose principal function is to review decisions of the Federal Courts of Appeals and the highest State courts
	■ *Special Courts* have jurisdiction over cases in a particular area of Federal law and include the U.S. Claims Court, the Tax Court, the U.S. Bankruptcy Court, and the U.S. Court of Appeals for the Federal Circuit
	State Courts
	■ *Inferior Trial Courts* hear minor criminal cases such as traffic offenses, civil cases involving small amounts of money, and preliminary hearings in more serious criminal cases
	■ *Trial Courts* have general jurisdiction over civil and criminal cases
	■ *Appellate Courts* include one or two levels; the highest court's decisions are final except for those cases reviewed by the U.S. Supreme Court

Jurisdiction	**Subject Matter Jurisdiction** authority of a court to decide a particular kind of case
	■ *Exclusive Federal Jurisdiction* Federal courts have sole jurisdiction over Federal crimes, bankruptcy, antitrust, patent, trademark, copyright, and other specified cases
	■ *Concurrent Federal Jurisdiction* authority of more than one court to hear the same case; State and Federal courts have concurrent jurisdiction over (1) Federal question cases (cases arising under the Constitution, statutes, or treaties of the United States) which do not involve exclusive Federal jurisdiction and (2) diversity of citizenship cases involving more than $50,000
	■ *Exclusive State Jurisdiction* State courts have exclusive jurisdiction over all matters to which the Federal judicial power does not reach
	Jurisdiction Over the Parties the power of a court to bind the parties to a suit
	■ **In Personam** *Jurisdiction* jurisdiction based upon claims against a person in contrast to jurisdiction over his or her property
	■ **In Rem** *Jurisdiction* jurisdiction based on claims against property
	■ *Attachment Jurisdiction* jurisdiction over a person's property to obtain payment of a claim against a defendant not related to the property
	■ *Venue* location where a lawsuit should be brought

Civil Procedure	**The Pleadings** series of statements that give notice and establish the issues of fact and law presented and disputed
	■ *Complaint* initial pleading by the plaintiff stating his or her case
	■ *Summons* notice given to inform a person of a lawsuit against him or her
	■ *Answer* defendant's pleading in response to the plaintiff's complaint
	■ *Reply* plaintiff's pleading in response to the defendant's answer
	Pretrial Procedure discovers what evidence is available to prove the facts in dispute
	Trial determines what the facts are and the outcome of the case
	Appeal determines whether the trial court committed prejudicial error

Alternative Dispute Resolution	**Arbitration** a nonjudicial proceeding in which a neutral third party selected by the disputants renders a binding decision (award)
	Conciliation a nonbinding process in which a third party acts as an intermediary between the disputing parties
	Mediation a nonbinding process in which a third party acts as an intermediary between the disputing parties and proposes solutions for them to consider

QUESTIONS

1. List and describe the courts in the Federal court system and in a typical State court system.
2. Distinguish between appeal by right and writ of *certiorari*.
3. Distinguish between subject matter jurisdiction and jurisdiction over the parties.
4. Distinguish between exclusive and concurrent Federal jurisdiction. Identify the two types of Federal concurrent jurisdiction.
5. Define and describe a typical long-arm statute.
6. List and distinguish among the three types of jurisdiction over the parties.
7. Describe the purpose of pleadings.
8. List and explain the various stages of a civil proceeding.
9. Compare and contrast the following: demurrer, judgment on the pleadings, summary judgment, directed verdict, and judgment notwithstanding the verdict.
10. Compare and contrast litigation, arbitration, conciliation, and mediation.

3 CONSTITUTIONAL AND ADMINISTRATIVE LAW

We mentioned in Chapter 1 that public law is the branch of substantive law that deals with the government's rights and powers and its relationship to individuals or groups. Public law consists of constitutional law, administrative law, and criminal law. We discuss the first two in this chapter, and we cover criminal law in the next chapter.

Public law continues to increase in importance in the study of business. Significant areas of the regulation of business arise from public law. For example, bankruptcy, antitrust, employment law, and securities regulation are principally public law. Other areas of the law, such as products liability and warranties, unfair competition, and consumer protection, are also greatly affected by public law.

CONSTITUTIONAL LAW

You will recall from Chapter 1 that a constitution is the fundamental law of a particular level of government. It establishes the structure of government and defines political relationships within it. It also places restrictions on the powers of government and guarantees the rights and liberties of the people.

The Constitution of the United States was adopted on September 17, 1787, in Philadelphia by representatives of the thirteen newly created States. Its purpose is stated in the preamble:

> We the People of the United States, In Order to form a more perfect Union, establish Justice, insure domestic Tranquility, provide for the common defense, promote the general Welfare, and secure the Blessings of Liberty to ourselves and our Posterity, do ordain and establish this Constitution for the United States of America.

Although the framers of the U.S. Constitution stated precisely what rights and authority were vested in the new national government, they considered it unnecessary to list those liberties the people kept to themselves. Nonetheless, at the time of its adoption, all the representatives at the convention were agreed that the Constitution would contain a Bill of Rights that should guarantee protection of individuals from oppression by the newly formed Federal government. The Bill of Rights, which consists of the first ten amendments to the Constitution, was adopted on December 15, 1791.

We are concerned in this chapter with constitutional law as it applies to business and commerce. We begin by surveying some of the basic principles of constitutional law, and then we examine the allocation of power between the Federal and State governments with respect to the regulation of business. Finally, we discuss the constitutional restrictions imposed on the power of government to regulate business.

BASIC PRINCIPLES

A number of concepts are basic to constitutional law in the United States. These fundamental principles apply to both the power of and the limitations on government. These principles are (1) Federal supremacy and preemption, (2) judicial review, (3) separation of powers, and (4) state action.

Federal Supremacy and Preemption

All other law in the United States, whether case law, statutory law, or administrative law, is subject to the Federal Constitution, which is the **supreme law** of the land. Accordingly, no law, Federal or State, is valid if it violates the Federal Constitution. In the landmark case of *McCulloch v. Maryland*, 17 U.S. (4 Wheat.) 316 (1819), Chief Justice Marshall stated, "This great principle is, that the Constitution and the laws made in pursuance thereof are supreme; that they control the Constitution and laws of the respective states, and cannot be controlled by them."

Whenever Congress enacts legislation within its constitutional powers, any conflicting State legislation is **preempted** (overridden) by the Federal action. Even if a State regulation is not obviously in conflict, it must still give way if Congress has clearly intended that its action should preempt the State legislation. In such a situation, nonconflicting State legislation would be prohibited. This intent may be specifically stated in the legislation or inferred from the scope of the legislation, the need for uniformity, or the danger of conflict between coexisting Federal and State regulation.

When Congress has *not* intended to displace all State legislation, then nonconflicting State legislation is permitted. *Silkwood v. Kerr-McGee Corporation* illustrates this point. Where Congress has not acted, the fact that Congress has the power to act does not prevent the States from acting. Until Congress exercises its power to preempt, State regulation is *not* forbidden.

SILKWOOD v. KERR-McGEE CORPORATION
Supreme Court of the United States, 1984.
464 U.S. 238, 104 S.Ct. 615, 78 L.Ed.2d 443.

Facts: Karen Silkwood was a laboratory analyst for Kerr-McGee Corporation at its Cimmaron plant in Oklahoma. The plant made plutonium fuel pins for use as reactor fuel in nuclear power plants. Accordingly, the plant was subject to licensing and extensive Federal regulation by the Nuclear Regulatory Commission (NRC), pursuant to the Atomic Energy Act, which preempts Oklahoma's regulation of the safety aspects of nuclear energy. During a three-day work period in 1974, Silkwood was contaminated by plutonium at the plant. After high levels of contamination were detected on her when she arrived at work on the third day, Kerr-McGee ordered a decontamination squad to Silkwood's apartment, resulting in the unavoidable destruction of many of her personal belongings. Silkwood was sent to the Los Alamos Scientific Laboratory to determine the extent of the contamination in her body's vital organs. A week later she returned to work but died that night in an unrelated automobile accident. Her father, as administrator of her estate, filed a claim against Kerr-McGee under Oklahoma tort law for Karen's personal injuries and property damage resulting from her contamination. On the basis of the jury's verdict, the trial court awarded Silkwood $505,000 ($500,000 for personal injuries and $5,000 for property damage) plus punitive damages of $10,000,000. The appellate court held that because Federal statutes regulate nuclear energy punitive damages may not be awarded. Silkwood appeals.

Decision: Judgment of appellate court reversed.

Opinion: **White, J.** As we recently observed in *Pacific Gas & Electric Co.* v. *State Energy Resources Conservation & Development Comm'n*, [citation], state law can be preempted in either of two general ways. If Congress evidences an intent to occupy a given field, any state law falling within that field is preempted. [Citations.] If Congress has not entirely displaced state regulation over the matter in question, state law is still preempted to the extent it actually conflicts with federal law, that is, when it is impossible to comply with both state and federal law, [citation], or where the state law stands as an obstacle to the accomplishment of the full purposes and objectives of Congress, [citation]. Kerr-McGee contends that the award in this case is invalid under either analysis. We consider each of these contentions in turn.

In *Pacific Gas & Electric*, an examination of the statutory scheme and legislative history of the Atomic Energy Act convinced us that "Congress . . . intended that the federal government regulate the radiological safety aspects involved . . . in the construction and operation of a nuclear plant." [Citation.] Thus, we concluded that "the federal government has occupied the entire field of nuclear safety concerns, except the limited powers expressly ceded to the states." [Citation.]

Kerr-McGee argues that our ruling in *Pacific Gas & Electric* is dispositive of the issue in this case. Noting that "regulation can be as effectively asserted through an award of damages as through some form of preventive relief," [citation], Kerr-McGee submits that because the state-authorized award of punitive damages in this case punishes and deters conduct related to radiation hazards, it falls within the prohibited field. However, a review of the same legislative history which prompted our holding in *Pacific Gas & Electric*, coupled with an examination of Congress' actions with respect to other portions of the Atomic Energy Act, convinces us that the preempted field does not extend as far as Kerr-McGee would have it.

* * *

Congress' decision to prohibit the states from regulating the safety aspects of nuclear development was premised on its belief that the Commission was more qualified to determine what type of safety standards should be enacted in this complex area. As Congress was informed by the AEC, the 1959 legislation provided for continued federal control over the more hazardous materials because "the technical safety considerations are of such complexity that it is not likely that any State would be prepared to deal with them during the foreseeable future." [Citation.] If there were nothing more, this concern over the states' inability to formulate effective standards and the foreclosure of the states from conditioning the operation of nuclear plants on compliance with state-imposed safety standards arguably would disallow resort to state-law remedies by those suffering injuries from radiation in a nuclear plant. There is, however, ample evidence that Congress had no intention of forbidding the states from providing such remedies.

Indeed, there is no indication that Congress even seriously considered precluding the use of such remedies either when it enacted the Atomic Energy Act in 1954 and or when it amended it in 1959. This silence takes on added significance in light of Congress' failure to provide any federal remedy for persons injured by such conduct. It is difficult to believe that Congress would, without comment, remove all means of judicial recourse for those injured by illegal conduct. [Citation.]More importantly, the only congressional discussion concerning the relationship between the Atomic Energy Act and state tort remedies indicates that Congress assumed that such remedies would be available. After the 1954 law was enacted, private companies contemplating entry into the nuclear industry expressed concern over potentially bankrupting state-law suits arising out of a nuclear incident. As a result, in 1957 Congress passed the Price-Anderson Act, an amendment to the Atomic Energy Act. [Citation.] That Act established an indemnification scheme under which operators of licensed nuclear facilities could be required to obtain up to $60 million in private financial protection against such suits. The government would then provide indemnification for the next $500 million of liability, and the resulting $560 million would be the limit of liability for any one nuclear incident.

Although the Price-Anderson Act does not apply to the present situation, the discussion preceding its enactment and subsequent amendment indicates that Congress assumed that persons injured by nuclear accidents were free to utilize existing state tort law remedies.

* * *

The belief that the NRC's exclusive authority to set safety standards did not foreclose the use of state tort remedies was reaffirmed when the Price-Anderson Act was amended in 1966. The 1966 amendment was designed to respond to concerns about the adequacy of state law remedies.

* * *

* * * Indeed, the entire discussion surrounding the 1966 amendment was premised on the assumption that state remedies were available notwithstanding the NRC's exclusive regulatory authority. For example, the Committee rejected a suggestion that it adopt a federal tort to replace existing state remedies, noting that such displacement of state remedies would engender great opposition. [Citation.] If other provisions of the Atomic Energy Act already precluded the states from providing remedies to its citizens, there would have been no need for such concerns. Other comments made throughout the discussion were similarly based on the assumption that state remedies were available.

* * *

In sum, it is clear that in enacting and amending the Price-Anderson Act, Congress assumed that state-law remedies, in whatever form they might take, were available to those injured by nuclear incidents. This was so even though it was well aware of the NRC's exclusive authority to regulate safety matters. No doubt there is tension between the conclusion that safety regulation is the exclusive concern of the federal law and the conclusion that a state may nevertheless award damages based on its own law of liability. But as we understand what was done over the years in the legislation concerning nuclear energy, Congress intended to stand by both concepts and to tolerate whatever tension there was between them. We can do no less. It may be that the award of damages based on the state law of negligence or strict liability is regulatory in the sense that a nuclear plant will be threatened with damages liability if it does not conform to state standards, but that regulatory consequence was something that Congress was quite willing to accept.

We do not suggest that there could never be an instance in which the federal law would preempt the recovery of damages based on state law. But insofar as damages for radiation injuries are concerned, preemption should not be judged on the basis that the federal government has so completely occupied the field of safety that state remedies are foreclosed but on whether there is an irreconcilable conflict between the federal and state standards or whether the imposition of a state standard in a damages action would frustrate the objectives of the federal law. We perceive no such conflict or frustration in the circumstances of this case.

* * *

We conclude that the award of punitive damages in this case is not preempted by federal law.

Judicial Review

Judicial review describes the process by which the courts examine governmental actions to determine whether they conform to the U.S. Constitution. Judicial review extends to legislation, acts of the executive branch, and the decisions of inferior courts. Judicial review includes actions of both the Federal and State governments and applies the same standards of constitutionality to both governments. The U.S. Supreme Court is the final authority on the constitutionality of any Federal and State law.[1] Alexander Hamilton forcefully expressed the idea of judicial review: "The interpretation of the laws is the proper and peculiar province of the courts. A constitution is, in fact, and must be regarded by the judges, a fundamental law. It therefore belongs to them to ascertain its meaning as well as the meaning of any particular act or proceeding from the legislative body. If there should happen to be an irreconcilable variance between the two, that which has the superior obligation and validity ought of course to be preferred; or, in other words, the Constitution ought to be preferred to the statute, the intention of the people to the intention of their agents." *The Federalist*, No. 78, Lodge Ed., pp. 485–86.

Separation of Powers

Another basic principle on which our government is founded is that of **separation of powers.** In our Constitution this means that there are three distinct and independent branches of government—the executive, legislative, and judicial branches.[2] The purpose of the doctrine of separation of powers is to prevent any branch of government from gaining too much power. The doctrine also permits each branch to function without interference from any other branch. Basically, the legislative branch is granted the power to make the law, the executive branch to enforce the law, and the judicial branch to interpret the law. The separation of power is not complete, however. For example, the executive branch has veto power over legislation enacted by Congress; the legislative branch has the power to reject a great number of executive appointments; and the judicial branch may declare both legislative and executive actions unconstitutional. Nevertheless, our government generally operates under a three-branch scheme providing for separation of powers with checks and balances on the power of each branch. See Law in the News on page 54.

State Action

Most of the protections provided by the U.S. Constitution and its amendments apply only to governmental action, referred to as **state action.** Only the Thirteenth Amendment, which abolishes slavery or involuntary servitude, applies to the actions of private individuals. "State action" includes any actions of the Federal and State governments and their subdivisions, such as city or county governments and agencies.

In addition, if "private" individuals or entities engage in public functions, their actions may be considered state action subject to constitutional limitations. For example, in *Marsh v. Alabama*, 326 U.S. 501 (1946), it was held that a company town was subject to the First Amendment because the State had allowed the company to exercise all of the public functions and activities that usually were conducted by a town government. Since that case, the Supreme Court has been less willing to find state action based upon private entities performing public functions, now limiting it to those functions "traditionally exclusively reserved to the State." *Jackson v. Metropolitan Edison Co.* illustrates this trend.

POWERS OF GOVERNMENT

The U.S. Constitution created a Federal government of enumerated powers. Moreover, as the Tenth Amendment declares, "the powers not delegated to the United States by the Constitution, nor prohibited by it to the States, are reserved to the States respectively, or to the people." Consequently, legislation enacted by Congress must be based on a specific power granted to the Federal government by the Constitution.

In this part of the chapter, we examine the sources and extent of the powers of the Federal

JACKSON v. METROPOLITAN EDISON CO.
Supreme Court of the United States, 1974.
419 U.S. 345, 95 S.Ct. 449, 42 L.Ed.2d 477.

Facts: Metropolitan Edison Company is a privately owned and operated Pennsylvania corporation subject to extensive regulation by the Pennsylvania Public Utility Commission. Under a provision of its general tariff filed with the commission, Edison had the right to discontinue electric service to any customer on reasonable notice of nonpayment of bills. Catherine Jackson had been receiving electricity from Metropolitan Edison when her account was terminated in 1970 because of her delinquency in payments. Edison later opened a new account for her residence in the name of James Dodson, another occupant of Jackson's residence. In August 1971, Dodson moved away and no further payments were made to the account. Finally, in October 1971, Edison disconnected Jackson's service without any prior notice. Jackson brought suit claiming that her electric service could not be terminated without notice and a hearing. She further argued that such action, allowed by a provision of Edison's tariff filed with the commission, constituted "state action" depriving her of property in violation of the Fourteenth Amendment's guarantee of due process of law. The trial court dismissed the case and the appellate court affirmed the dismissal. Jackson appeals to the U.S. Supreme Court.

Decision: Judgment for defendant Metropolitan Edison Company affirmed.

Opinion: Rehnquist, J.   The Due Process Clause of the 14th Amendment provides "nor shall any State deprive any person of life, liberty or property, without due process of law." In 1883, this Court in the Civil Rights Cases [citation] affirmed the essential dichotomy set forth in [the Fourteenth Amendment] between deprivation by the State, subject to scrutiny under its provisions, and private conduct, "however discriminatory or wrongful," against which the Fourteenth Amendment offers no shield. [Citation.]

   * * * While the principle that private action is immune from the restrictions of the Fourteenth Amendment is well established and easily stated, the question whether particular conduct is "private," on the one hand, or "state action," on the other, frequently admits of no easy answer. [Citations.]

   Here the action complained of was taken by a utility company which is privately owned and operated, but which in many particulars of its business is subject to extensive state regulation. The mere fact that a business is subject to state regulation does not by itself convert its action into that of the State for purposes of the Fourteenth Amendment. [Citation.] Nor does the fact that the regulation is extensive and detailed, as in the case of most public utilities, do so. [Citation.] It may well be that acts of a heavily regulated utility with at least something of a governmentally protected monopoly will more readily be found to be "state" acts than will the acts of an entity lacking these characteristics. But the inquiry must be whether there is a sufficiently close nexus between the State and the challenged action of the regulated entity so that the action of the latter may be fairly treated as that of the State itself. [Citation.] * * *

* * *

   All of petitioner's arguments taken together show no more than that Metropolitan was a heavily regulated privately owned utility, enjoying at least a partial monopoly in the providing of electrical service within its territory, and that it elected to terminate service to petitioner in a manner which the Pennsylvania Public Utility Commission found permissible under state law. Under our decisions this is not sufficient to connect the State of Pennsylvania with respondent's action so as to make the latter's conduct attributable to the State for purposes of the Fourteenth Amendment.

government—as well as the power of the States—to regulate business and commerce.

Federal Commerce Power

The U.S. Constitution provides in part that "the Congress shall have Power . . . To regulate Commerce with foreign Nations, and among the several States . . ."[3] This commerce clause has two important effects: (1) it is a broad source of **commerce power** for the Federal government to regulate the economy, and (2) it operates as a restriction on State regulations that obstruct or unduly burden interstate commerce. We discuss the first of these effects below and discuss the second effect in the next section.

The U.S. Supreme Court interprets the commerce clause as granting virtually complete power to Congress to regulate the economy and business. A court may invalidate legislation enacted under the commerce clause for only two reasons: (1) if it is clear that the activity regulated by the legislation does not affect interstate commerce, or (2) if it is clear that there is no reasonable connection between the regulatory means selected and the stated ends. For example, activities that are carried on solely in one State, such as the practice of law or real estate brokerage agreements, are subject to Federal antitrust laws under the power granted by the commerce clause provided that (1) the local activity substantially affects interstate commerce, or (2) the local activity is in the flow of commerce.

The following civil rights case illustrates the operation of this test.

KATZENBACH v. McCLUNG
Supreme Court of the United States, 1964.
379 U.S. 294, 85 S.Ct. 377, 13 L.Ed.2d 290.

Facts: The McClungs own Ollie's Barbecue, a restaurant located a few blocks from the interstate highway in Birmingham, Alabama, with dining accommodations for whites only and take-out service for blacks. In the year preceding the passage of the Civil Rights Act of 1964, the restaurant had purchased a substantial portion of the food it served from outside the State. The restaurant has refused to serve blacks since its original opening in 1927 and asserts that if it were required to serve blacks it would lose much of its business. The trial court issued an injunction restraining the enforcement of the Civil Rights Act against Ollie's Barbecue. Appeal was taken directly to the U.S. Supreme Court.

Decision: Decree of trial court reversed.

Opinion: Clark, J. This case was argued with No. 515, *Heart of Atlanta Motel v. United States,* decided this date, [citation], in which we upheld the constitutional validity of Title II of the Civil Rights Act of 1964 against an attack by hotels, motels, and like establishments. This complaint for injunctive relief against appellants attacks the constitutionality of the Act as applied to a restaurant. * * *

* * *

Section 201 (a) of Title II commands that all persons shall be entitled to the full and equal enjoyment of the goods and services of any place of public accommodation without discrimination or segregation on the ground of race, color, religion, or national origin; and § 201 (b) defines establishments as places of public accommodation if their operations affect commerce or segregation by them is supported by state action. Sections 201(b)(2) and (c) place any "restaurant . . . principally engaged in selling food for consumption on the premises" under the Act "if . . . it serves or offers to serve interstate travelers or a substantial portion of the food which it serves . . . has moved in commerce."

Ollie's Barbecue admits that it is covered by these provisions of the Act. The Government makes no contention that the discrimination at the restaurant was supported by the State of Alabama. There is no claim that interstate travelers frequented the restaurant. The sole question, therefore, narrows down to whether Title II, as applied to a restaurant annually receiving about $70,000 worth of food which has moved in commerce, is a valid exercise of the power of Congress.   * * *

* * *

Articles I, § 8, cl. 3, confers upon Congress the power "[t]o regulate Commerce . . . among the several States" and Clause 18 of the same Article grants it the power "[t]o make all Laws which shall be necessary and proper for carrying into Execution the foregoing Powers. . . ." * * *

This Court has held time and again that this power extends to activities of retail establishments, including restaurants, which directly or indirectly burden or obstruct interstate commerce. * * *

* * *

Here * * * Congress has determined for itself that refusals of service to Negroes have imposed burdens both upon the interstate flow of food and upon the movement of products generally. Of course, the mere fact that Congress has said when particular activity shall be deemed to affect commerce does not preclude further examination by this Court. But where we find that the legislators, in light of the facts and testimony before them, have a rational basis for finding a chosen regulatory scheme necessary to the protection of commerce, our investigation is at an end. * * *

* * *

Confronted as we are with the facts laid before Congress, we must conclude that it had a rational basis for finding that racial discrimination in restaurants had a direct and adverse effect on the free flow of interstate commerce. Insofar as the sections of the Act here relevant are concerned, §§ 201(b)(2) and (c), Congress prohibited discrimination only in those establishments having a close tie to interstate commerce, *i.e.*, those, like the McClungs', serving food that has come from out of the State. We think in so doing that Congress acted well within its power to protect and foster commerce in extending the coverage of Title II only to those restaurants offering to serve interstate travelers or serving food, a substantial portion of which has moved in interstate commerce.

* * *

The power of Congress in this field is broad and sweeping; where it keeps within its sphere and violates no express constitutional limitation it has been the rule of

> this Court, going back almost to the founding days of the Republic, not to interfere. The Civil Rights Act of 1964, as here applied, we find to be plainly appropriate in the resolution of what the Congress found to be a national commercial problem of the first magnitude. We find it in no violation of any express limitations of the Constitution and we therefore declare it valid.

Because of the broad and permissive interpretation of the commerce power, Congress currently regulates a vast range of activities. Many of the activities discussed in the text are regulated by the Federal government based on the commerce power, including: Federal crimes, consumer warranties, consumer credit transactions, electronic fund transfers, trademarks, unfair trade practices, consumer transactions, residential real estate transactions, consumer safety, employee safety, labor relations, civil rights in employment, and transactions in securities.

State Regulation of Commerce

The commerce clause, as we previously discussed, specifically grants to Congress the power to regulate commerce among the States. In addition to acting as a broad source of Federal power, the commerce clause also implicitly restricts the States' power to regulate activities if the result obstructs or unduly burdens interstate commerce.

Regulations   The Supreme Court ultimately decides the extent of permissible State regulation affecting interstate commerce. In doing so, the Court weighs and balances several factors: (1) the necessity and importance of the State regulation, (2) the burden it imposes on interstate commerce, and (3) the extent to which it discriminates against interstate commerce in favor of local concerns. The application of these factors involves case-by-case analysis by the courts.

Taxation   The commerce clause in conjunction with the import-export clause also limits the power of the State to tax. The import-export clause provides: "No State shall, without the Consent of the Congress, lay any Imposts or Duties on Imports or Exports."[4] Together, the commerce clause and the import-export clause exempt or immunize from State taxation goods that have entered the stream of commerce, whether they are interstate or foreign and whether as imports or exports. The purpose of this immunity is to protect goods in commerce from both discriminatory and cumulative State taxes. Once the goods enter the stream of interstate or foreign commerce, the power of the State to tax ceases and does not resume until the goods are delivered to the purchaser or the owner terminates the movement of the goods through interstate or foreign commerce.

Federal Fiscal Powers

The Federal government exerts a dominating influence over the national economy through its control of financial matters. Much of this impact results from the exercise of its regulatory powers under the commerce clause, as previously discussed. In addition, a substantial portion of its influence derives from powers arising independently of the commerce clause. These include (1) the power to tax and spend, (2) the power to borrow and coin money, and (3) the power of eminent domain.

Taxation and Spending   The Federal government's power to tax, although extremely broad, has three major limitations: (1) direct taxes other than income taxes must be apportioned among the States,[5] (2) all custom duties and excise taxes must be uniform throughout the United States,[3] and (3) no duties may be levied on exports from any State.[6]

Besides raising revenues, taxes also have regulatory and socioeconomic effects. For example, import taxes and custom duties can

LAW IN THE NEWS

Limits on the Presidency
The Court Upholds the Special Prosecutor

The Supreme Court rarely speaks with one voice anymore, particularly on controversial issues. But it came close to full harmony last week when Chief Justice William H. Rehnquist delivered its resounding 7-to-1 affirmation of the Ethics in Government Act. The decision was a blow to the White House, which has strongly opposed the Watergate-era law permitting independent counsels to investigate suspected crimes by administration officials. The fact that the opinion was written by one of the president's staunchest allies on the court made it only more devastating. The ruling cleared the way for pending investigations of more than a half dozen top Reagan aides. And it bolstered those who reject the Reagan vision of strong presidential power unchecked by Congress.

The decision will have immediate consequences. In the investigation that gave rise to the case, prosecutor Alexia Morrison can now resume her probe of former Justice Department official Theodore Olson. He challenged the Ethics Act by refusing to cooperate with an inquiry into his alleged misleading of Congress. The ruling also gives new force to pending convictions of former White House aides Michael Deaver (for perjury) and Lyn Nofziger (illegal lobbying). Both cases would have been dropped if the law were struck down; now both men are expected to appeal. And U.S. District Court Judge Gerhard Gesell can now press ahead with trials of John Poindexter, Oliver North and others indicted by Lawrence Walsh in the Iran-contra affair. Special counsel James C. McKay's coming report on Edwin Meese III is expected to exonerate the attorney general of any illegality. But even so, supporters of the Ethics Act say, it is important that the inquiry was independent of the White House. "An administration investigation of administration officials cannot be credible," says Arthur Liman, counsel to the Senate Iran-contra committee. "And without that credibility, there can be no confidence in government."

At the heart of the case is a dispute about how, in the broadest sense, the Constitution should be read. The act's conservative opponents, buoyed

protect domestic industry from foreign competition. Graduated or progressive tax rates and exemptions may further social policies of redistributing wealth. Tax credits encourage investment in favored enterprises to the disadvantage of unfavored businesses. Even though a tax does more than just raise revenue, it will be upheld "so long as the motive of Congress and the effect of its legislative action are to secure revenue for the benefit of the general government. . . ." *J. W. Hampton Co. v. United States*, 276 U.S. 394 (1928).

The Constitution authorizes the Federal government to pay debts and spend for the common defense and general welfare of the United States.[3] The spending power of Congress is extremely broad and will be upheld so long as it does not violate a specific constitutional limita-

tion on Federal power. Moreover, the power to spend is an important way in which the Federal government regulates the economy. In some cases this is accomplished directly because the level and type of government expenditure significantly impact economic cycles and activity. More indirectly, governmental expenditures may have as a condition that the recipients engage in or refrain from certain conduct. For instance, under an executive order issued in 1965, many contractors who enter into contracts with the Federal government must comply with affirmative action requirements in their employment practices. Whether directly or indirectly, the power of the Federal government to spend money represents an important regulatory force in the economy and significantly affects the general welfare of the United States.

by high-court rulings in other recent separation-of-powers cases, argue for a stark interpretation. Executive, legislative and judicial branches are, in this view, very neatly defined. They do not, and must not, overlap; power to execute laws belongs to the president alone. Critics are troubled by the act's call for three-branch cooperation (among Congress, the attorney general and three judges) in appointing prosecutors. They feel, as Justice Antonin Scalia said in his agitated dissent, that Congress has usurped the president's rightful control over law enforcement.

Pragmatic View

Those who support the act take a more flexible view of the Constitution. "Our system of government is not made up of three rigidly insulated governing bodies," says Prof. Paul Gewirtz of Yale University. "It is a system of overlapping functions." Rehnquist's opinion paid homage to this messy but workable system. "[We] have never held," he wrote, "that the Constitution requires that the three branches of Government 'operate with absolute independence'." The ruling also approved of the many careful ways in which the Ethics Act mandates cooperation among the branches, both in appointing the prosecutor and in permitting the executive to dismiss him if necessary. In Gewirtz's view, the credit belongs to the

congressmen who wrote the act. "[They] considered the competing concerns of the different branches and came up with a balanced compromise." And according to the high court, that balancing does nothing to violate the separation of powers.

Among the most striking features of the decision was the unifying role played by Justice Rehnquist. Harvard law professor Laurence Tribe says "the chief justice acted as chief justice," siding not with his conservative allies but with the consensus view. Many court watchers hope to see more of this statesmanship, which strengthens the bench by bolstering its authority. But most observers are reluctant to place bets on either Rehnquist or new justice Anthony Kennedy, a critical swing vote, who for undisclosed reasons took no part in last week's ruling. If anything, the justices' other actions this term—especially their vote to reconsider a major 1976 civil-rights ruling—suggest an emerging conservative majority. In the end, the special-prosecutor decision decides this case and nothing but this case, whatever tantalizing hints it may offer about the future of the Rehnquist court.

—Tamar Jacoby

Borrowing and Coining Money The Constitution provides: "The Congress shall have Power . . . To borrow money on the credit of the United States. . . ."[3] The broad extent of this grant of power is shown by the current size of the Federal deficit. The Constitution also provides: "The Congress shall have Power . . . to coin Money, regulate the Value thereof, and of foreign Coin. . . ."[3] The power to borrow and the power to coin money together have enabled the Federal government to establish a national banking system, the Federal Reserve System, and specialized Federal lending programs such as the Federal Land Bank. Through these and other institutions and agencies, the Federal government wields extensive control over national fiscal and monetary policies and exerts considerable influence over interest

rates, the money supply, and foreign exchange rates.

Eminent Domain The government's power to take private property for public use, known as the power of **eminent domain,** is recognized as one of the inherent powers of government in the Federal Constitution and in the constitutions of the States. At the same time, however, the power is carefully limited. The Fifth Amendment to the Federal Constitution provides: "nor shall private property be taken for public use, without just compensation."[7] This amendment applies to the States through the Fourteenth Amendment,[8] which we discuss later. Moreover, similar or identical provisions are found in the constitutions of the States. There is, therefore, a direct constitutional prohibition against taking private property without just compensation and an implicit prohibition against taking private property for other than public use. Under both Federal and State constitutions, the individual is entitled to due process of law in connection with the taking. Eminent domain is discussed further in Chapter 50.

LIMITATIONS ON GOVERNMENT

The U.S. Constitution specifies certain powers that are granted to the Federal government. Other unspecified powers have been reserved to the States. The Constitution and its amendments, however, impose limits on all these powers. In this part of the chapter, we discuss those limitations most applicable to business: (1) the contract clause, (2) the First Amendment, (3) due process, and (4) equal protection.

None of these restrictions operates as an absolute limitation, but instead triggers review or scrutiny by the courts to determine whether the governmental power exercised encroaches impermissibly upon the interest protected by the Constitution. The U.S. Supreme Court has used different levels of scrutiny depending on the interest affected and the nature of the governmental action. Although the differentiation among levels of scrutiny has been most fully developed in the area of equal protection, it also occurs in other areas, including substantive due process and protection of free speech.

The least rigorous level of scrutiny is the **rational relationship test,** which requires that the legislation conceivably bear some rational relationship to a legitimate governmental interest furthered by the legislation. The most exacting level of scrutiny is the **strict scrutiny test,** which requires that the legislation be necessary to promote a compelling governmental interest. Finally, under the **intermediate test,** the legislation must have a substantial relationship to an important governmental objective. These standards will be more fully explained below (also see Figure 3–1).

Contract Clause

The Constitution provides: ''No State shall . . . pass any . . . Law impairing the Obligation of Contracts. . . .''[4] The Supreme Court has used the **contract clause** to restrict States from retroactively modifying public charters and private contracts. For example, the contract clause protects the charter of a corporation formed under a State incorporation statute against modification.

Incorporation and other enabling statutes commonly reserve to the State the power to prescribe such regulations, provisions, and limitations as it shall deem advisable and to amend, repeal, or modify the statute at its pleasure. Because such reservations are actually written into the contract between the State and the other party, any amendment or modification does not impair the obligation of con-

FIGURE 3-1	Limitations Upon Government		
Test/Interest	**Equal Protection**	**Substantive Due Process**	**Free Speech**
Strict Scrutiny	Fundamental Rights Suspect Classifications	Fundamental Rights	Protected Noncommercial Speech
Intermediate	Gender Legitimacy Citizenship		Commercial Speech
Rational Relationship	Economic Regulation	Economic Regulation	

tract because it was expressly permitted by the contract or charter.

Moreover, the Supreme Court has held that the contract clause does *not* preclude the States from exercising eminent domain or their police powers. As the Supreme Court ruled, "No legislature can bargain away the public health or the public morals." *Stone v. Mississippi,* 101 U.S. 814 (1880).

Because State enabling statutes typically provide for amendment and because States retain their police powers, the contract clause had seemed to lose most of its significance. Two decisions in the late 1970s, however, suggested that the Supreme Court was reviving the contract clause. In *United States Trust Company v. New Jersey,* 431 U.S. 1 (1977), the Supreme Court held that New Jersey could not retroactively alter a statutory covenant relied on by bond purchasers. In the following year, the Supreme Court invalidated a Minnesota statute that required certain private employers to pay a pension funding charge if they terminated a pension plan or closed a Minnesota office even though such charge was inconsistent with the employers' obligations under their private pension plans. *Allied Structural Steel Co. v. Spannus,* 438 U.S. 234 (1978). Since these two decisions, however, the Court has generally been unwilling to use the contract clause to invalidate State economic regulation, at least with respect to private contracts, where the legislation reasonably promotes a significant and legitimate public purpose that justifies the impairment of the contractual obligation.

First Amendment

The First Amendment states:

> Congress shall make no law respecting an establishment of religion, or prohibiting the free exercise thereof; or abridging the freedom of speech, or of the press; or the right of the people peaceably to assemble, and to petition the Government for a redress of grievances.

The First Amendment's protection of free speech is not absolute. Some forms of speech, such as obscenity, receive no protection. Most forms of speech, however, are protected by strict or exacting scrutiny to determine whether a compelling and legitimate state interest exists. If so, then to achieve this purpose, the legislature must use means that are the least restrictive of free speech. One of the most important justifications for the First Amendment is that "the best test of truth is the power of the thought to get itself accepted in the competition of the market." *Abrams v. United States*, 250 U.S. 616 (1919) (dissenting opinion). To promote this competition of ideas, the First Amendment's guarantee of free speech applies not only to individuals but also to corporations. Accordingly, corporations may not be prohibited from speaking out on political issues.

The First Amendment is the constitutional source of many of the civil and political rights enjoyed in the United States. Accordingly, it gives rise to a wide range of issues, far too broad for us to address fully in this text. We will examine the application of the First Amendment's guarantee of free speech to (1) commercial speech and (2) defamation.

Commercial Speech Commercial speech is expression related to the economic interests of the speaker and his audience, such as advertisements of a product or service. Within the past decade, U.S. Supreme Court decisions have eliminated the doctrine that commercial speech is wholly outside the protection of the First Amendment. Instead the Court has established the principle that speech that does no more than propose a commercial transaction is entitled to a "lesser degree" of constitutional protection. Protection is accorded commercial speech because of interest in the communication by the advertiser, consumer, and general public. Advertising and other such messages provide important information for the proper and efficient distribution of resources in our free market system. At the same time, commercial speech is less valuable and less vulnerable than other varieties of speech and therefore does not merit complete First Amendment protection.

In commercial speech cases, a four-part analysis has developed. First, the court must determine whether the expression is protected by the First Amendment. For commercial speech to come within that provision, it at least must concern lawful activity and not be misleading. Second, the court must determine whether the asserted governmental interest is substantial. If both inquiries yield positive answers, then, third, the court must determine whether the regulation directly advances the governmental interest asserted, and, fourth, whether it is not more extensive than is necessary to serve that interest.

Because the constitutional protection extended to commercial speech is based on the informational function of advertising, governments may regulate or suppress commercial messages that do not accurately inform the public about lawful activity. "The government may ban forms of communication more likely to deceive the public than to inform it, or commercial speech related to illegal activity." *Central Hudson Gas and Electric Corp. v. Public Service Commission*, 447 U.S. 557 (1980). Therefore, governmental regulation of false and misleading advertising is permissible under the First Amendment.

Defamation   **Defamation** is a civil wrong or tort consisting of a false communication that injures a person's reputation by disgracing and diminishing the respect in which the person is held. An example would be the publication of a statement that a person had committed a crime or had a loathsome disease. (Defamation is also discussed in Chapter 5.)

Because defamation involves a communication, the protection extended to speech by the First Amendment applies. But the Supreme Court has ruled in *New York Times Co. v. Sullivan*, 376 U.S. 254 (1964), that a public official who is defamed in regard to his conduct, fitness, or role as public official may *not* recover in an action of defamation unless the statement was made with *actual malice*, which requires proof that the defendant had knowledge of the falsity of the communication or acted in reckless disregard of its truth or falsity. This restriction on the right to recover for defamation is based on "a profound national commitment to the principle that debate on public issues should be uninhibited, robust

and wide-open, and that it may well include vehement, caustic and sometimes unpleasantly sharp attacks on government and public officials." The communication may deal with the official's qualifications for and performance in office, which would likely include most aspects of his character and public conduct.

In addition, the Supreme Court has extended the same rule to candidates for public office and public figures. The Court, however, has not precisely defined the term *public figure*. Examples of persons held to be public figures include a well-known football coach of a State university and a retired army general who takes a prominent and controversial position regarding racial segregation. The Court has explained:

> For the most part [public figures are] those who attain this status [by assuming] roles of especial prominence in the affairs of society. Some occupy positions of such persuasive power and influence that they are deemed public figures for all purposes. More commonly, those classed as public figure have thrust themselves to the forefront of particular public controversies in order to influence the resolution of the issues involved. *Gertz v. Robert Welch, Inc.*, 418 U.S. 323 (1974).

Thus, the public official or public figure must prove that the defendant published the defamatory and false comment about him with knowledge or in reckless disregard of the comment's falsity and its defamatory character.

Due Process

The Fifth[7] and Fourteenth Amendments[8] respectively prohibit the Federal and State governments from depriving any person of life, liberty, or property without due process of law. Due process has two different aspects: *substantive* due process and *procedural* due process. As we discussed in Chapter 1, substantive law creates, defines, or regulates legal rights, whereas procedural law establishes the rules for enforcing rights created by the substantive law. Accordingly, **substantive due process** concerns the compatibility of a law or governmental action with fundamental constitutional rights such as free speech. In contrast, **procedural due process** involves the review of the decision-making process that enforces substantive laws and results in depriving a person of life, liberty, or property.

Substantive Due Process Substantive due process involves a court's determination of whether a particular governmental action is compatible with individual liberties. From 1885 until 1937, the Supreme Court viewed substantive due process as authorizing it to act as a "super legislature" and enabling it to invalidate any law it considered unwise. Since 1937, the Court has abandoned this approach and no longer overturns legislation affecting economic and social interests, so long as the legislation is rationally related to legitimate governmental objectives.

Where fundamental rights of individuals under the Constitution are affected, however, the Court will carefully scrutinize the legislation to determine that it is necessary to promote a compelling or overriding state interest. Included among the fundamental rights that trigger the strict scrutiny standard of substantive due process are (1) the First Amendment rights of freedom of speech, religion, press, peaceful assembly, and petition; (2) the right to engage in interstate travel; (3) the right to vote; (4) the right to privacy; and (5) the right to marry.

Procedural Due Process Procedural due process pertains to the governmental decision-making process that results in depriving a person of life, liberty, or property. As the Supreme Court has interpreted procedural due process, the government is required to provide persons with a fair procedure if, but only if, the person is faced with deprivation of life, liberty, or property. When governmental action adversely affects an individual but does not deny life, liberty, or property, the government is not required to give the person any hearing at all.

Liberty, for the purposes of procedural due process, generally includes the ability of individuals to engage in freedom of action and choice regarding their personal lives. Any significant physical restraint is a deprivation of liberty that requires procedural safeguards.

The most important and common example is criminal proceedings, which we discuss in Chapter 4. Civil proceedings that result in depriving a person of freedom of action are also subject to the requirements of procedural due process. Liberty also includes an individual's right to engage in the fundamental rights described above.

Property, for the purposes of procedural due process, includes not only all forms of real and personal property but also certain benefits (entitlements) conferred by government, such as social security payments and food stamps. If a person is hired by the government and is assured continued employment or dismissal only for specified reasons, then there must be a fair procedure to discharge the employee. On the other hand, if the employment is terminable at any time by the government, there is no property interest in the employee and, therefore, no requirement of procedural due process applies to a dismissal of the employee.

When applicable, procedural due process requires that the procedure be fair and impartial in the resolution of the factual and legal basis for the governmental actions that result in the deprivation of life, liberty, or property. The Supreme Court generally considers three factors in determining which procedures are required: (1) the importance of the individual interest involved; (2) the adequacy of the existing procedural protections and the probable value, if any, of additional safeguards; and (3) the governmental interest in fiscal and administrative efficiency. Different situations will call for various types of procedures as the following case illustrates. See case on page 60.

Equal Protection

The Fourteenth Amendment provides that "nor shall any State . . . deny to any person within its jurisdiction the equal protection of the laws." Although this amendment applies only to the actions of State governments, the Supreme Court has interpreted the due process clause of the Fifth Amendment to subject Federal actions to the same standards of review. Basically, the guarantee of **equal protection** requires that similarly situated persons be treated similarly by governmental actions.

BOARD OF CURATORS OF THE UNIVERSITY OF MISSOURI v. HOROWITZ

Supreme Court of the United States, 1978.
435 U.S. 78, 98 S.Ct. 948, 55 L.Ed.2d 124.

Facts: In the fall of 1971, Miss Horowitz was admitted as an advanced medical student at the University of Missouri-Kansas City. During the spring of 1972, several faculty members expressed dissatisfaction with Miss Horowitz's clinical performance, noting that it was below that of her peers, that she was erratic in attendance at her clinical sessions, and that she lacked a critical concern for personal hygiene. Upon the recommendation of the school's Council on Evaluation, she was advanced to her second and final year on a probationary basis. After subsequent unfavorable reviews during her second year and a negative evaluation of her performance by seven practicing physicians, the council recommended that Miss Horowitz be dismissed from the school for her failure to meet academic standards. The decision was approved by the dean and later affirmed by the provost after an appeal by Miss Horowitz. She brought suit against the school's Board of Curators, claiming that her dismissal violated her right to procedural due process under the Fourteenth Amendment and deprived her of "liberty" by substantially impairing her opportunities to continue her medical education or to return to employment in a medically related field. The trial court found for the defendant but the appellate court reversed. The Board of Curators appeals.

Decision: Judgment of appellate court reversed.

Opinion: Rehnquist, J. To be entitled to the procedural protections of the Fourteenth Amendment, respondent must in a case such as this demonstrate that her dismissal from the school deprived her of either a "liberty" or a "property" interest. * * *

* * *

We need not decide, however, whether respondent's dismissal deprived her of a liberty interest in pursuing a medical career. Nor need we decide whether respondent's dismissal infringed any other interest constitutionally protected against deprivation without procedural due process. Assuming the existence of a liberty or property interest, respondent has been awarded at least as much due process as the Fourteenth Amendment requires. The school fully informed respondent of the faculty's dissatisfaction with her clinical progress and the danger that this posed to timely graduation and continued enrollment. The ultimate decision to dismiss respondent was careful and deliberate. These procedures were sufficient under the Due Process Clause of the Fourteenth Amendment. We agree with the District Court that respondent

> was afforded full procedural due process by the (school). In fact, the Court is of the opinion, and so finds, that the school went beyond (constitutionally required) procedural due process by affording (respondent) the opportunity to be examined by seven independent physicians in order to be absolutely certain that their grading of the (respondent) in her medical skills was correct [citation].

> In *Goss v. Lopez*, [citation], we held that due process requires, in connection with the suspension of a student from public school for disciplinary reasons, "that the student be given oral or written notice of the charges against him and, if he denies

them, an explanation of the evidence the authorities have and an opportunity to present his side of the story." [Citation.] The Court of Appeals apparently read *Goss* as requiring some type of formal hearing at which respondent could defend her academic ability and performance. All that *Goss* required was an "informal give-and-take" between the student and the administrative body dismissing him that would, at least, give the student "the opportunity to characterize his conduct and put it in what he deems the proper context." [Citation.] But we have frequently emphasized that "[t]he very nature of due process negates any concept of inflexible procedures universally applicable to every imaginable situation." [Citation.] The need for flexibility is well illustrated by the significant difference between the failure of a student to meet academic standards and the violation by a student of valid rules of conduct. This difference calls for far less stringent procedural requirements in the case of an academic dismissal.

* * *

* * * A school is an academic institution, not a courtroom or administrative hearing room. In *Goss*, this Court felt that suspensions of students for disciplinary reasons have a sufficient resemblance to traditional judicial and administrative factfinding to call for a "hearing" before the relevant school authority. While recognizing that school authorities must be afforded the necessary tools to maintain discipline, the Court concluded:

> [I]t would be a strange disciplinary system in an educational institution if no communication was sought by the disciplinarian with the student in an effort to inform him of his dereliction and to let him tell his side of the story in order to make sure that an injustice is not done.

* * *

> [R]equiring effective notice and informal hearing permitting the student to give his version of the events will provide a meaningful hedge against erroneous action. At least the disciplinarian will be alerted to the existence of disputes about facts and arguments about cause and effect. [Citation.]

Even in the context of a school disciplinary proceeding, however, the Court stopped short of requiring a *formal* hearing since "further formalizing the suspension process and escalating its formality and adversary nature may not only make it too costly as a regular disciplinary tool but also destroy its effectiveness as a part of the teaching process." [Citation.]

Academic evaluations of a student, in contrast to disciplinary determinations, bear little resemblance to the judicial and administrative factfinding proceedings to which we have traditionally attached a full-hearing requirement. In *Goss*, the school's decision to suspend the students rested on factual conclusions that the individual students had participated in demonstrations that had disrupted classes, attacked a police officer, or caused physical damage to school property. The requirement of a hearing, where the student could present his side of the factual issue, could under such circumstances "provide a meaningful hedge against erroneous action." [Citation.] The decision to dismiss respondent, by comparison, rested on the academic judgment of school officials that she did not have the necessary clinical ability to perform adequately as a medical doctor and was making insufficient progress toward that goal. Such a judgment is by its nature more subjective and evaluative than the typical factual questions presented in the average disciplinary decision. Like the decision of an individual professor as to the proper grade for a student in his course, the determination whether to dismiss a student for academic reasons requires an expert evaluation of cumulative information and is not readily adapted to the procedural tools of judicial or administrative decisionmaking.

Under such circumstances, we decline to ignore the historic judgment of educators and thereby formalize the academic dismissal process by requiring a hearing. The educational process is not by nature adversary; instead it centers around a continuing relationship between faculty and students, "one in which the teacher must occupy many roles—educator, adviser, friend, and, at times, parent-substitute." [Citation.] This is especially true as one advances through the varying regimes of the educational system, and the instruction becomes both more individualized and more specialized.

Since 1937, when the Supreme Court abandoned substantive due process as a critical check on legislation, the equal protection guarantee has become the most important constitutional concept protecting individual rights.

When governmental action involves classification of people, the equal protection guarantee comes into play. In determining whether legislation satisfies the equal protection guarantee, the Supreme Court uses one of three standards of review: (1) the rational relationship test, (2) the strict scrutiny test, or (3) the intermediate test.

Rational Relationship Test The rational relationship test applies to economic legislation and simply requires that it is *conceivable* that the legislation bears some rational relationship to a legitimate governmental interest furthered by the legislation. Under this standard of review, the legislature is permitted to attack part of the evil to which the legislation is addressed. Moreover, there is a strong presumption that the legislation is constitutional. Therefore, the courts will overturn the legislation *only* if clear and convincing evidence shows that there is *no* reasonable basis justifying the legislation.

Strict Scrutiny Test The strict scrutiny test is far more exacting than the rational relationship test. Under this test, the courts do not defer to the legislature; rather they independently determine whether the classification is constitutionally permissible. This determination requires that the legislature's classification is necessary to promote a compelling or overriding governmental interest.

The strict scrutiny test is applied when the legislation affects fundamental rights or involves suspect classifications. Fundamental rights include most of the provisions of the Bill of Rights. Suspect classifications include those made on the basis of race or national origin. A classic and important example of strict scrutiny applied to classifications based upon race is the 1954 school desegregation case of *Brown v. Board of Education of Topeka* in which the Supreme Court ruled that segregated public school systems violated the equal protection guarantee. Subsequently, the Court has invalidated segregation in public beaches, municipal golf courses, buses, parks, public golf courses, and courtroom seating.

Another important example of strict scrutiny is the "one person, one vote" rule based upon the fundamental right to vote. Chief Justice Warren formulated the rule as follows:

Legislators represent people, not trees or acres. . . . And, if a State should provide that the votes of citizens in one part of the State should be given two times, or five times, or ten times the weight of votes of citizens in another part of the State, it could hardly be contended that the right to vote of those residing in the disfavored areas had not been effectively diluted . . . the Equal Protection Clause requires that the seats in both houses of a bicameral state legislature must be apportioned on a population basis. *Reynolds v. Sims*, 377 U.S. 533 (1964).

BROWN v. BOARD OF EDUCATION OF TOPEKA
Supreme Court of the United States, 1954.
347 U.S. 483, 74 S.Ct. 686, 98 L.Ed. 873.

Facts: These are consolidated cases from Kansas, South Carolina, Virginia, and Delaware, each with a different set of facts and local conditions but also presenting a common legal question. Minors of the black race, through their legal representatives, sought court orders to obtain admission to the public schools in their community on a nonsegregated basis. They had been denied admission to schools attended by white children under laws requiring or permitting segregation according to race. This Court had previously upheld such laws under the "separate but equal" doctrine, which provides that there is equality of treatment of the races through substantially equal, even though separate, facilities. There were findings by the lower courts that the white schools and the black schools involved had been or were being equalized with respect to buildings, curricula, qualifications and salaries of teachers, and other "tangible" factors. The black minors contended, however, that segregated public schools are not and cannot be made "equal," and that hence they have been deprived of the equal protection of the laws guaranteed by the Fourteenth Amendment. In each case, except the Delaware case, a three-judge panel denied relief to the plaintiffs.

Decision: Judgment for plaintiffs.

Opinion: **Warren, C. J.** In the first cases in this Court construing the Fourteenth Amendment, decided shortly after its adoption, the Court interpreted it as proscribing all state-imposed discriminations against the Negro race. The doctrine of "separate but equal" did not make its appearance in this Court until 1896 in the case of *Plessy v. Ferguson*, involving not education but transportation. American courts have since labored with the doctrine for over half a century. In this Court, there have been six cases involving the "separate but equal" doctrine in the field of public education. * * * In none of these cases was it necessary to reexamine the doctrine to grant relief to the Negro plaintiff. And in *Sweatt v. Painter*, [citation], the Court expressly reserved decision on the question whether *Plessy v. Ferguson* should be held inapplicable to public education.

In the instant cases, that question is directly presented. Here, unlike *Sweatt v. Painter*, there are findings below that the Negro and white schools involved have been equalized, or are being equalized, with respect to buildings, curricula, qualifications and salaries of teachers, and other "tangible" factors. Our decision, therefore, cannot turn on merely a comparison of these tangible factors in the Negro and white schools involved in each of the cases. We must look instead to the effect of segregation itself on public education.

* * *

Today, education is perhaps the most important function of state and local governments. Compulsory school attendance laws and the great expenditures for education both demonstrate our recognition of the importance of education to our democratic society. It is required in the performance of our most basic public responsibilities, even service in the armed forces. It is the very foundation of good citizenship. Today it is a principal instrument in awakening the child to cultural values, in preparing him for later professional training, and in helping him to adjust normally to his environment. In these days, it is doubtful that any child may reasonably be expected to succeed in life if he is denied the opportunity of an education. Such an opportunity, where the state has undertaken to provide it, is a right which must be made available to all on equal terms.

We come then to the question presented: Does segregation of children in public schools solely on the basis of race, even though the physical facilities and other "tangible" factors may be equal, deprive the children of the minority group of equal educational opportunities? We believe that it does.

In *Sweatt v. Painter*, [citation], in finding that a segregated law school for Negroes could not provide them equal educational opportunities, this Court relied in large part on "those qualities which are incapable of objective measurement but which make for greatness in a law school." In *McLaurin v. Oklahoma State Regents*, [citation], the Court in requiring that a Negro admitted to a white graduate school be treated like all other students, again resorted to intangible considerations: "* * * his ability to study, to engage in discussions and exchange views with other students, and, in general, to learn his profession." Such considerations apply with added force to children in grade and high schools. To separate them from others of similar age and qualifications solely because of their race generates a feeling of inferiority as to their status in the community that may affect their hearts and minds in a way unlikely ever to be undone. The effect of this separation on their educational opportunities was well stated by a finding in the Kansas case by a court which nevertheless felt compelled to rule against the Negro plaintiffs:

"Segregation of white and colored children in public schools has a detrimental effect upon the colored children. The impact is greater when it has the sanction of the law, for the policy of separating the races is usually interpreted as denoting the inferiority of the Negro group. A sense of inferiority affects the motivation of a child to learn. Segregation with the sanction of law, therefore, has a tendency to (retard) the educational and mental development of Negro children and to deprive them of some of the benefits they would receive in a racial(ly) integrated school system."

Whatever may have been the extent of psychological knowledge at the time of *Plessy v. Ferguson*, this finding is amply supported by modern authority. Any language in *Plessy v. Ferguson* contrary to this finding is rejected.

We conclude that in the field of public education the doctrine of "separate but equal" has no place. Separate educational facilities are inherently unequal. Therefore, we hold that the plaintiffs and others similarly situated for whom the actions have been brought are, by reason of the segregation complained of, deprived of the equal protection of the laws guaranteed by the Fourteenth Amendment. This disposition makes unnecessary any discussion whether such segregation also violates the Due Process Clause of the Fourteenth Amendment.

Intermediate Test   The intermediate test applies to legislation based on gender, legitimacy, and usually alienage (citizenship). Under this test, the legislation must have a substantial relationship to an important governmental objective. The intermediate standard eliminates the strong presumption of constitutionality adhered to by the rational relationship test. For example, in *Orr v. Orr*, 440 U.S. 268 (1979), the Court invalidated an Alabama law that al-lowed courts to grant alimony awards only from husbands to wives and not from wives to husbands. Similarly, in *Reed v. Reed*, 404 U.S. 71 (1971), an Idaho statute gave preference to males over females in qualifying for selection as administrators of estates. The Court invalidated the statute because the preference did not bear a fair and substantial relationship to any legitimate objective of the legislation. On the other hand, not all legislation based upon

LAW IN THE NEWS

Court Refuses to Close 1954 Brown Case

DENVER—A federal appeals court refused to close the landmark 1954 Brown vs. Board of Education desegregation case, saying the school board in Topeka, Kan., has failed to carry out fully the U.S. Supreme Court's mandate.

In an opinion published Friday but not made available until Monday, the 10th U.S. Circuit Court of Appeals reversed a ruling from 1986 that could have closed the case that paved the way for nationwide school desegregation.

The court noted that neither Topeka's school district nor community are resisting desegregation. But the court added that "for the most part, the Topeka school district has exercised a form of benign neglect."

The court sent the case back to U.S. District Court in Kansas, saying Judge Richard Rogers of Topeka had erred in requiring the plaintiffs to prove intentional discriminatory conduct. It also reversed a lower court ruling that the school district had not violated Title VI of the Civil Rights Act of 1964.

Parents of 17 schoolchildren in Topeka had reopened the case in 1979, saying the district had not done enough to eliminate segregation. Included in the group was Linda Brown Buckner, whose maiden name provided the title for the 1954 ruling.

On Monday, one of their attorneys said the ruling vindicated their contentions. "We won," Rich Jones said. "We feel that 10 years of work was not in vain."

The Topeka School Board said its attorneys were reviewing the decision.

Board Chairman Curtis Hartenberger said at a news conference: "I have been told the findings relate primarily to student, faculty and staff assignment and that Judge Rogers' findings of equality of education, curriculum, facilities, transportation and extracurricular activities were not contested."

The Associated Press. Used by permission of The Associated Press.

gender is invalid. For example, the Court has upheld a California statutory rape law, which imposed penalties only upon males, as well as the Federal military selective service act, which exempted women from registering for the draft.

ADMINISTRATIVE LAW

Administrative law is the branch of public law that governs the powers and procedures of administrative agencies, as well as judicial review of agency action. **Administrative agencies** are governmental entities—other than courts and legislatures—having authority to affect the rights of private parties through their operations. Administrative agencies are referred to by various names such as commission, board, department, agency, administration, government corporation, bureau, or office. These agencies regulate a vast array of important matters

of national safety, welfare, and convenience. For instance, Federal administrative agencies are charged with responsibility for national security, citizenship and naturalization, law enforcement, taxation, currency, elections, environmental protection, consumer protection, regulation of transportation, telecommunications, labor relations, trade, commerce, and securities markets, as well as providing health and social services.

Because of the increasing complexity of the social, economic, and industrial life of the nation, the scope of administrative law has expanded enormously. In 1952 Justice Jackson observed that "the rise of administrative bodies has been the most significant legal trend of the last century, and perhaps more values today are affected by their decisions than by those of all the courts, review of administrative decisions apart." *Federal Trade Commission v. Ruberoid Co.*, 343 U.S. 470 (1952). This observation is even more apt today, as evidenced by the great increase in the number and activities of Federal government boards, commissions, and other agencies. Certainly, agencies create more legal rules and adjudicate more controversies than all the legislatures and all the courts combined.

State agencies also play a significant role in the functioning of our society. Among the more important boards and commissions in the States are those supervising and regulating banking, insurance, communications, transportation, public utilities, pollution control, and workers' compensation.

Much of Federal, State, and local law in this country is established by the countless administrative agencies. These agencies, which many label the "fourth branch of government," possess tremendous power and have long been criticized as being "in reality miniature independent governments . . . [which are] a haphazard deposit of irresponsible agencies. . . ." (*1937 Presidential Task Force Report.*) A 1979 article in *Fortune* magazine stated:

> In recent years, economists have joined the chorus of criticism, and have blamed excessive regulation for the nation's baffling troubles with innovation, productivity, shortages, unemployment, and inflation. The total cost of complying with government regulation, variously estimated at $50 billion to $150 billion a year, is now in the same league as industry's outlays on new plant and equipment.

Despite these criticisms of administrative regulations, it is clear that these agencies play a significant and necessary role in our society. Administrative agencies serve the important function of relieving legislatures from the impossible burden of fashioning legislation that deals with every detail of the specific problem addressed. As a result, Congress can enact legislation, such as the Federal Trade Commission Act, which prohibits unfair and deceptive trade practices, without having to define this phrase or anticipate all the particular problems that may arise. Instead, Congress created an agency—in this example, the Federal Trade Commission—to which it could delegate the power to issue rules, regulations, and guidelines to carry out the statutory mandate. In

addition, the establishment of separate, specialized bodies enables administrative agencies to be staffed by individuals with expertise in the field being regulated. Administrative agencies can thus develop the knowledge and devote the time necessary to provide continuous and flexible solutions to evolving regulatory problems.

OPERATION OF ADMINISTRATIVE AGENCIES

Most administrative agencies perform three basic functions: (1) make rules, (2) enforce the law, and (3) adjudicate controversies. The term **administrative process** refers to the entire set of activities in which administrative agencies engage while carrying out their rulemaking, enforcement, and adjudicative functions. Administrative agencies exercise powers that have been allocated by the Constitution to the three separate branches of government. More specifically, agencies exercise legislative power when they make rules, executive power when they enforce the statute and their rules, and judicial power when they adjudicate disputes. This concentration of power has raised questions regarding the propriety of having the same persons who establish the rules also act as prosecutor and judge in determining whether the rules have been violated. To address this issue and bring about other procedural reforms, the Administrative Procedure Act (APA) was enacted in 1946.

Rulemaking

Rulemaking is the process by which an administrative agency promulgates rules of law. Under the APA a **rule** is "the whole or part of an agency statement of general or particular applicability and future effect designed to implement, interpret, or process law or policy." Once promulgated, rules are applicable to all parties. Moreover, the process of rulemaking puts all parties on notice that the impending rule is being considered and provides concerned individuals with an opportunity to be heard.

Legislative rules, often called regulations, are in effect "administrative statutes." Legislative rules have the force of law if they are constitutional, within the power granted to the agency by the legislature, and issued according to proper procedure.

To be constitutional, regulations must not violate any provisions of the U.S. Constitution, such as due process or equal protection. In addition, they may not involve an unconstitutional delegation of legislative power from the legislature to the agency. To be constitutionally permissible, the statute granting power to an agency must establish reasonable standards guiding the agency in implementing the statute. This requirement has been met by statutory language such as "to prohibit unfair methods of competition," "fair and equitable," "public interest, convenience, and necessity," and other equally broad expressions. In any event, agencies may not exceed the actual authority granted by the enabling statute.

Most legislative rules must be promulgated in accordance with the rulemaking procedures of the APA, which require that the agency provide:

1. prior notice of a proposed rule, usually by publication in the *Federal Register;*
2. an opportunity for interested parties to participate in the rulemaking; and
3. publication of a final draft containing a concise general statement of its basis and purpose at least thirty days before the rule's effective date.

In some instances the enabling statute requires that certain rules be made only after the opportunity for an agency hearing. This "formal" rulemaking procedure is far more complex than the "informal" procedures and is governed by the same provisions of the APA as is an adjudication, discussed below. In formal rulemaking, the agency must base its rules upon consideration of the record of the trial-like agency hearing and include a statement of "findings and conclusions, and the reasons or basis therefore, on all the material issues of fact, law, or discretion presented on the record."

Distinguished from legislative rulemaking, which has the force of law, are interpretative and procedural rules. **Interpretative rules** are statements issued by the agency that explain how the agency construes its governing statute. For instance, the Securities and Exchange Commission "renders administrative interpretations of the law and regulations thereunder to members of the public, prospective registrants and others, to help them decide legal questions about the application of the law and the regulations to particular situations and to aid them in complying with the law. This advice, for example, might include an informal expression of opinion about whether the offering of a particular security is subject to the registration requirements of the law and, if so, advice as to compliance with the disclosure requirements of the applicable registration form." *The Work of the SEC* (1980). These interpretative rules, however, which are exempt from the APA requirements just discussed, are *not* law in that they are not automatically binding on private parties regulated by the agency or on the courts, although they are given substantial weight. As the Supreme Court has stated, "the weight of such [an interpretative rule] in a particular case will depend upon the thoroughness evident in its consideration, the validity of its reasoning, its consistency with earlier and later pronouncements, and all those factors which give it power to persuade. . . ."

Procedural rules, which are also exempt from the APA, establish rules of conduct for practice before the agency, identify an agency's organization, and describe its method of operation. For example, the Securities and Exchange Commission's Rules of Practice deal with such matters as who may appear before the commission; business hours, notice of proceedings and hearings; settlements, agreements, and conferences; presentation of evidence and taking of depositions and interrogatories; and review of hearings.

Enforcement

Agencies are also charged with investigating conduct to determine whether the statute or the agency's legislative rules have been violated. In carrying out this executive function, the agencies have traditionally been accorded great discretion to compel the disclosure of information, subject to constitutional limitations. For example, the following explains some of the investigating and enforcement functions of the Securities and Exchange Commission:

It is the duty of the Commission under the laws it administers to investigate complaints or other indications of possible law violations in securities transactions, most of which arise under the Securities Act of 1933 and the Securities Exchange Act of 1934. Investigation and enforcement work is conducted by the Commission's Regional Offices and the Division of Enforcement.

Most of the Commission's investigations are conducted privately, the facts being developed to the fullest extent possible through informal inquiry, interviewing of witnesses, examination of brokerage records and other documents, reviewing and trading data, and similar means. The Commission however, is empowered to issue subpoenas requiring sworn testimony and the production of books, records and other documents pertinent to the subject matter under investigation; in the event of refusal to respond to a subpoena, the Commission may apply to a Federal court for an order compelling obedience thereto.

Inquiries and complaints of investors and the general public provide one of the primary sources of leads for detection of law violations in securities transactions. Another is the surprise inspections by Regional Offices of the books and records of brokers and dealers to determine whether their business practices conform to the prescribed rules. Still another is the conduct of inquiries into market fluctuations in particular stocks which appear not to be the result of known developments affecting the issuing company or of general market trends. *The Work of the SEC* (1980).

Adjudication

After concluding an investigation, the agency may use informal or formal methods to resolve the matter. Informal procedures, which include advising, negotiating, and settling, constitute the great preponderance of administra-

tive adjudication. For example, under its procedural rules, the Internal Revenue Service answers inquiries from individuals and organizations "whenever appropriate in the interest of sound tax administration, as to their status for tax purposes and as to the tax effects of their acts or transactions." The IRS responses take the form of countless rulings, determination letters, opinion letters, and information letters. Similarly, the Securities and Exchange Commission issues thousands of "no action" letters, which advise private parties whether the SEC staff would *not* recommend that the commission take any enforcement action against the party seeking the advice.

The formal procedure by which an agency resolves a matter (called adjudication) involves finding facts, applying legal rules to the facts, and formulating orders. An **order** "means the whole or a part of the final disposition, whether affirmative, negative, injunctive or declaratory in form, of an agency." Adjudication is in essence an administrative trial.

The procedures employed by the various administrative agencies to adjudicate cases are nearly as varied as the agencies themselves. Nevertheless, the APA does establish certain standards that must be followed by those Federal agencies covered by the act. Notice must be given of the hearing. The APA also requires that the agency give all interested parties the opportunity to submit and consider "facts, arguments, offers of settlement, or proposals of adjustment." If no settlement is reached, then a hearing must be held.

The hearing is presided over by an administrative law judge and is prosecuted by the agency. There are more than twice as many administrative law judges as there are Federal judges. Juries are never used. Thus, the agency serves as both the prosecutor and decision maker. In order to reduce this conflict of interest, the APA provides for the separation of functions between those engaged in investigation and prosecution and those involved in decision making.

Oral and documentary evidence may be introduced by either party. All sanctions, rules, and orders must be based upon "consideration of the whole record or those parts cited by a party and supported by and in accordance with the reliable, probative, and substantial evidence." All decisions must include a statement of findings of fact and conclusions of law and the reasons or basis for them as well as a statement of the appropriate rule, order, sanction, or relief.

If authorized by law and within the jurisdiction delegated to an agency, it may impose in its orders sanctions such as penalties; fines; seizing property; assessing damages, restitution, compensation, or fees; and requiring, revoking, or suspending a license. In most instances orders are final unless appealed, and failure to comply with an order is subject to a statutory penalty.

Although administrative adjudications mirror to a large extent the procedures of judicial trials, there are many differences between the two. "Agency hearings tend to produce evidence of general conditions as distinguished from facts relating solely to the respondent. Administrative agencies more consciously formulate policy by adjudicating (and rulemaking) than do courts. Consequently, administrative adjudications may require that the administrative law judge consider more consciously the impact of his decision upon the public interest as well as upon the particular respondent. . . . Even more important is the fact that an administrative hearing is tried to an *administrative law judge* and never to a *jury*. Since many of the rules governing the admission of proof in judicial trials are designed to protect the jury from unreliable and possibly confusing evidence, the rules need not be applied with the same vigor in proceedings solely before an administrative law judge. The administrative judge decides both the facts and the law to be applied." *McCormick on Evidence*, 3d ed., Section 350, p. 1005.

LIMITS ON ADMINISTRATIVE AGENCIES

A most important and fundamental part of administrative law is the limits imposed by judicial review upon the activities of administrative agencies. Courts, however, are not supposed to substitute their judgment on matters of policy for the agency's judgment. Additional limitations arise from the legislature and the executive branch, which, unlike the judiciary, may address the wisdom and the correctness of an agency's decision or action.

Judicial Review

Judicial review acts as a control or check on a particular rule or order of an administrative agency. In exercising judicial review the court may either compel agency action unlawfully withheld or set aside impermissible agency action. In conducting a review, the court decides all relevant questions of law, interprets constitutional and statutory provisions, and determines the meaning or applicability of the terms of an agency action.

The scope of judicial review of administrative agencies is limited to determining whether the agency has (1) exceeded its authority, (2) properly interpreted the applicable law, (3) violated any constitutional provision, (4) acted contrary to the procedural requirements of the law, (5) acted arbitrarily, capriciously, or in abuse of discretion, or (6) reached conclusions that are not supported by substantial evidence. The courts, thus, essentially review questions of law and are severely restricted in their scrutiny of questions of fact or policy. In making these determinations the court must review the whole record and may set aside agency action only if the error is prejudicial. See case on page 70.

Legislative Control

The legislature may exercise control over administrative agencies in various ways. Through its budgetary power, it may greatly restrict or expand an agency's operations. Congress may amend the enabling statute to increase, modify, or decrease the agency's authority. Even more drastically, it may completely eliminate an agency. Or Congress may establish general guidelines governing agency action, as it did by enacting the Administrative Procedure Act. Moreover, it may reverse or change an agency rule or decision by specific legislation. In addi-

AMERICAN TEXTILE MANUFACTURERS INSTITUTE INC. v. DONOVAN
Supreme Court of the United States, 1981.
452 U.S. 490, 101 S.Ct. 2478, 69 L.Ed.2d 185.

Facts: Cotton dust is an airborne particle by-product of the preparation and manufacture of cotton products. Exposure to cotton dust causes a condition known as byssinosis, most seriously manifested as "brown lung disease." In 1978, following the completion of an extensive record on the matter, the Occupational Safety and Health Administration (OSHA) issued a standard limiting exposure to cotton dust in the workplace. The American Textile Manufacturers Institute, representing the cotton industry, challenged the new standard, maintaining that the Occupational Safety and Health Act of 1970 requires OSHA to demonstrate a reasonable relationship between the costs and benefits associated with its standards. Respondents, the Secretary of Labor and two labor organizations, contended that Congress balanced costs and benefits in the act itself, and that OSHA is charged with enacting the most protective standard possible to eliminate significant health risks, subject only to economic and technological feasibility. The Court of Appeals ruled in favor of OSHA. The institute then brought this appeal.

Decision: Judgment for OSHA affirmed.

Opinion: **Brennan, J.** The principal question presented in this case is whether the Occupational Safety and Health Act requires the Secretary, in promulgating a standard [citation] to determine that the costs of the standard bear a reasonable relationship to its benefits.

* * *

The starting point of our analysis is the language of the statute itself. [Citations.] Section 6(b)(5) of the Act provides:

The secretary, in promulgating standards dealing with toxic materials or harmful physical agents under this subsection, shall set the standard which most adequately assures, *to the extent feasible*, on the basis of the best available evidence, that no employee will suffer material impairment of health or functional capacity even if such employee has regular exposure to the hazard dealt with by such standard for the period of his working life.

Although their interpretations differ, all parties agree that the phrase "to the extent feasible" contains the critical language in § 6(b)(5) for purposes of this case.

* * *

Thus, § 6(b)(5) directs the Secretary to issue the standard that "most adequately assures . . . that no employee will suffer material impairment of health," limited only by the extent to which this is "capable of being done." In effect then, as the Court of Appeals held, Congress itself defined the basic relationship between costs and benefits, by placing the "benefit" of worker health above all other considerations save those making attainment of this "benefit" unachievable. Any standard based on a balancing of costs and benefits by the Secretary that strikes a different balance than that struck by Congress would be inconsistent with the command set forth in § 6(b)(5). Thus, cost-benefit analysis by OSHA is not required by the statute because feasibility analysis is. [Citation.]

* * *

Section 6(f) of the Act provides that "[t]he determinations of the Secretary shall be conclusive if supported by substantial evidence in the record considered as a whole." [Citation.] Petitioners contend that the Secretary's determination that the Cotton Dust Standard is "economically feasible" is not supported by substantial evidence in the record considered as a whole. In particular, they claim (1) that OSHA underestimated the financial costs necessary to meet the Standard's requirements; and (2) that OSHA incorrectly found that the Standard would not threaten the economic viability of the cotton industry.

In statutes with provisions virtually identical to § 6(f) of the Act, we have defined substantial evidence as "such relevant evidence as a reasonable mind might accept as adequate to support a conclusion." [Citation.] The reviewing court must take into account contradictory evidence in the record, [citation], but "the possibility of drawing two inconsistent conclusions from the evidence does not prevent an administrative agency's finding from being supported by substantial evidence," [citation].

* * *

The Court of Appeals found that the agency "explained the economic impact it projected for the textile industry," and that OSHA has "substantial support in the record for its . . . findings of economic feasibility for the textile industry." [Citation.] On the basis of the whole record, we cannot conclude that the Court of Appeals "misapprehended or grossly misapplied" the substantial evidence test.

* * *

When Congress passed the Occupational Safety and Health Act in 1970, it chose to place pre-eminent value on assuring employees a safe and healthful working environment, limited only by the feasibility of achieving such an environment. We must measure the validity of the Secretary's actions against the requirements of that Act. For "[t]he judicial function does not extend to substantive revision of regulatory policy. That function lies elsewhere—in Congressional and Executive oversight or amendatory legislation." [Citations.]

tion, each house of Congress has oversight committees that review the operations of administrative agencies. Finally, the Senate has the power of confirmation over some high-level appointments to administrative agencies.

Control by Executive Branch

The president has significant control over administrative agencies housed within the executive branch by virtue of his power to appoint and remove the chief administrators of these agencies. With respect to independent agencies, the president has less control because commissioners serve for a fixed term that is staggered with the president's term of office. Nevertheless, his power to appoint the chairman and to fill vacancies confers considerable control, as does his power to remove commissioners for statutorily defined cause. The president's central role in the budgeting process of agencies also enables him to exert great control over agency policy and operations. Even more extreme is the president's power to impound monies appropriated to an agency by Congress. In addition, the president may radically alter, combine, or even abolish agencies of the executive branch unless disapproved by either house of Congress within a prescribed time.

CHAPTER SUMMARY

CONSTITUTIONAL LAW

Basic Principles	**Federal Supremacy** all law in the United States is subject to the U.S. Constitution **Federal Preemption** right of Federal government to regulate matters within its power to the exclusion of the States **Judicial Review** examination of governmental actions to determine whether they conform to the U.S. Constitution **Separation of Powers** allocation of powers among executive, legislative, and judicial branches of government **State Action** actions of governments to which constitutional provisions apply

Powers of Government	**Federal Commerce Power** exclusive power of Federal government to regulate commerce with other nations and among the States
	State Regulation of Commerce the commerce clause of the Constitution restricts the States' power to regulate activities if the result obstructs interstate commerce
	Federal Fiscal Powers
	  ■ *Taxation and Spending* the Constitution grants Congress broad powers to tax and spend which is an important way the Federal government regulates the economy
	  ■ *Borrowing and Coining Money* enables the Federal government to establish a national banking system and control national fiscal and monetary policy
	  ■ *Eminent Domain* the government's power to take private property for public use with the payment of just compensation

Limitations upon Government	**Contract Clause** restricts States from retroactively modifying contracts
	Freedom of Speech First Amendment protects most speech by utilizing a strict scrutiny standard
	  ■ *Commercial Speech* expression related to the economic interests of the speaker and its audience, which receives a lesser degree of protection
	  ■ *Defamation* a tort consisting of a false communication that injures a person's reputation, which receives limited constitutional protection
	Due Process Fifth and Fourteenth Amendments prohibit the Federal and State governments from depriving any person of life, liberty, or property without due process of law
	  ■ *Substantive Due Process* determination of whether a particular governmental action is compatible with individual liberties
	  ■ *Procedural Due Process* requires the governmental decision-making process to be fair and impartial if it deprives a person of life, liberty, or property

Equal Protection   requires that similarly situated persons be treated similarly by governmental actions
- *Rational Relationship Test*   a standard of review used to determine whether economic legislation satisfies the equal protection guarantee
- *Strict Scrutiny Test*   exacting standard of review applicable to legislation affecting a fundamental right or involving a suspect classification
- *Intermediate Test*   standard of review applicable to legislation based on gender, legitimacy, and citizenship

ADMINISTRATIVE LAW

Operation of Administrative Agencies	**Rulemaking** process by which an administrative agency promulgates rules of law **Enforcement** process by which agencies determine whether their rules have been violated **Adjudication** formal methods by which an agency resolves disputes

Limits on Administrative Agencies	**Judicial Review** acts as a control or check by a court on a particular rule or order of an administrative agency **Legislative Control** control over the agency's budget and enabling statute **Control by Executive Branch** includes the president's power to appoint members of the agency

QUESTIONS

1. List and distinguish the basic principles of constitutional law.
2. Explain the two effects of the commerce clause.
3. Distinguish the three levels of scrutiny used by the courts to determine the constitutionality of governmental action.
4. Explain the difference between substantive and procedural due process.
5. List and explain the three basic functions of administrative agencies.

PROBLEMS

1. In May, Patricia Allen left her automobile on the shoulder of a road in the city of Erewhon after the car stopped running. A member of the Erewhon city police department found the car later that day and placed on the car a sticker stating that unless the car were moved, it would be towed. When after a week the car had not been removed, the police department authorized Baldwin Auto Wrecking Co. to tow it away and to store it on its property. Allen was told by a friend that her car was at Baldwin's. Allen asked Baldwin to allow her to take possession of her car, but Baldwin refused to relinquish the car until the $70 towing fee was paid. Allen could not afford to pay the fee, and the car remained at Baldwin's for six weeks. At that time, Baldwin requested the police department for a permit to dispose of the automobile. After the police department tried unsuccessfully to telephone Allen, the department issued the permit. In late July, Baldwin destroyed the automobile. Allen brings an action against the city and Baldwin for damages for loss of the vehicle, arguing that she was denied due process. Decision?

2. In 1967 large oil reserves were discovered in the Prudhoe Bay area of Alaska. As a result the State revenues increased from $124 million in 1969 to $3.7 billion in 1981. In 1980 the State legislature enacted a dividend program that would distribute annually a portion of these earnings to the State's adult residents. Under the plan, each citizen eighteen years of age or older receives one unit for each year of residency subsequent to 1959, the year Alaska became a State. Crawford, a resident since 1978, brings suit challenging the dividend distribution plan as violative of the equal protection guarantee. Decision?

3. Maryland enacted a statute prohibiting any producer or refiner of petroleum products from operating retail service stations within the State. The statute also required that any producer or refiner discontinue operating its company-owned retail service stations. Approximately 3,800 retail service stations in Maryland sell over twenty different brands of gasoline. No petroleum products are produced or refined in Maryland, however, and only 5 percent of the total number of retailers are operated by a producer or refiner. Maryland enacted the statute because a survey conducted by the State Comptroller indicated that gasoline stations operated by producers or refiners had received preferential treatment during periods of gasoline shortage. Seven major producers and refiners brought an action challenging the statute on the ground that it discriminates against interstate commerce in violation of the commerce clause of the United States Constitution. Decision?

4. The Federal Aviation Act of 1958 provides that "The United States of America is declared to possess and exercise complete and exclusive national sovereignty in the airspace of the United States." The city of Orion adopted an ordinance that makes it unlawful for jet aircraft to take off from its airport between 11 P.M. of one day and 7 A.M. of the next day. The Jordan Airlines, Inc., is adversely affected by this ordinance and brings suit challenging it under the supremacy clause of the United States Constitution. Decision?

5. The Public Service Commission of State X issued a regulation completely banning all advertising that "promotes the use of electricity" by any electric utility company in State X. The commission issued the regulation in order to conserve energy. Central Electric Corporation of State X challenges the order in the State courts, arguing that the commission had restrained commercial speech in violation of the First Amendment. Decision?

6. E-Z-Rest Motel is a motel with 216 rooms located in the center of a large city in State Y. It is readily accessible from two interstate highways and three major state highways. The motel solicits patronage from outside State Y through various national advertising media, including magazines of national circulation. It accepts convention trade from outside State Y, and approximately 75 percent of its registered guests are from out of State Y. An action under the Federal Civil Rights Act of 1964 has been brought against E-Z-Rest Motel alleging that the motel discriminates on the basis of race and color. The motel contends that the statute cannot be applied to it because it is not engaged in interstate commerce. Decision?

7. State Z enacted a Private Pension Benefits Protection Act requiring private employers with 100 or more employees to pay a pension funding charge on terminating a pension plan or closing an office in State Z. Acme Steel Company closed its offices in State Z, whereupon the State assessed the company $185,000 under the vesting provisions of the act. Acme challenged the constitutionality of the act under the contract clause (Article I, Section 10) of the U.S. Constitution. Decision?

8. In 1942 Congress passed the Emergency Price Control Act in the interest of national defense and security. The stated purpose of the act was "to stabilize prices and to prevent speculative, unwarranted and abnormal increases in prices and rents. . . ." The act established the Office of Price Administration, which was authorized to establish maximum prices and rents that were to be "generally fair and equitable and [were to] effectuate the purposes of this Act." Stark was convicted for selling beef at prices in excess of those set by the agency. Stark appeals on the ground that the act was an unconstitutional delegation to the agency of the legislative power of Congress to control prices. Decision?

9. A State statute empowered public school principals to suspend students for up to ten days without any notice or hearing. A student who was suspended for ten days challenges the constitutionality of his suspension on the grounds that he was denied due process. Decision?

10. Iowa enacted a statute prohibiting the use of sixty-five-foot double trailer truck combinations. All of the other States in the midwest and west permit such trucks to be used on their roads. Consolidated Freightways is adversely affected by this statute and brings suit against Iowa, alleging that the statute violated the commerce clause. Decision?

ENDNOTES

1. U.S. Constitution, Article III, Sections 1 and 2.
2. U.S. Constitution, Article I, Section 1, Article II, Section 1, and Article III, Section 1.
3. U.S. Constitution, Article I, Section 8.
4. U.S. Constitution, Article I, Section 10.
5. U.S. Constitution, Amendment XVI.
6. U.S. Constitution, Article I, Section 9.
7. U.S. Constitution, Amendment V.
8. U.S. Constitution, Amendment XIV.

4 CRIMINAL LAW

As we discussed in Chapter 1, the civil law defines duties the violation of which constitutes a wrong against the injured party. In contrast, the criminal law establishes duties the violation of which is a wrong against the whole community. Civil law is a part of private law, whereas criminal law is a part of public law. In a civil action, the injured party sues to recover compensation for the damage and injury that he has sustained as a result of the defendant's wrongful conduct. The party bringing a civil action (the plaintiff) has the burden of proof, which he must sustain by a preponderance (greater weight) of the evidence. The purpose of the civil law is to compensate the aggrieved party. Criminal law, on the other hand, is designed to prevent harm to society by declaring what conduct is criminal and establishing punishment for such conduct. In a criminal case, the defendant is prosecuted by the government. The government must prove the defendant's guilt **beyond a reasonable doubt,** which is a significantly higher burden of proof than that required in a civil action. Moreover, under our legal system, guilt is never presumed. Indeed, the law presumes the innocence of the accused, and this presumption is not affected by the defendant's failure to testify in her own defense. The government still has the burden of affirmatively proving the guilt of the accused beyond a reasonable doubt.

Of course, the same conduct may, and often does, constitute both a crime and a tort, which is a civil wrong. (We discuss torts in Chapters 5 and 6.) But an act may be criminal without being tortious, and by the same token, an act may be a tort but not a crime.

In this chapter we cover the general principles of criminal law as well as the definitions of particular crimes under the following headings: (1) nature of crimes, (2) offenses against property, (3) criminal defenses, and (4) criminal procedure.

NATURE OF CRIMES

A **crime** is any act or omission forbidden by public law in the interest of protecting society and made punishable by the government in a judicial proceeding brought by it. Punishment for criminal conduct includes fines, imprisonment, and death. Recently, some States and the Federal government have enacted victim indemnification statutes establishing funds, financed by criminal fines, to provide indemnification in limited amounts to victims of criminal activity. Crimes are prohibited and punished on grounds of public policy, which may include the protection and safeguarding of government (as in treason), human life (as in murder), or private property (as in larceny). Additional purposes of the criminal law include deterrence, rehabilitation, and retribution.

Within recent times the scope of the criminal law has increased greatly. Traditional crimes have been expanded by a great number of regulations and laws to which are attached criminal penalties. These pertain to nearly every phase of modern living. Typical examples in the field of business law are those laws concerning the licensing and conduct of a business, antitrust laws, and the laws governing the sales of securities.

Historically, both criminal law and civil law were primarily common law. Today, however, criminal law is almost exclusively statutory. All States have enacted comprehensive criminal law statutes (or codes) covering most, if not all, of the common law crimes. Moreover, these statutes have made the number of crimes defined in criminal law far greater than the number of crimes defined under common law. Some codes expressly limit crimes to those included in the codes, thus abolishing common law crimes. Furthermore, because there are no Federal common law crimes, all Federal crimes are statutory.

Essential Elements

In general, a crime consists of two elements: (1) the wrongful or overt act **(actus reus),** and (2) the **criminal** or **mental intent (mens rea).** For example, to support a larceny conviction it is not enough to show that the defendant stole another's goods; it must also be established that he intended to steal the goods. Conversely, criminal intent without an overt act is not a crime. For instance, Ann says to herself that she ought to rob the neighborhood grocery store and then really "live it up." Without more, Ann has committed no crime.

Actus reus refers to the nonmental elements of a crime, including the physical act that must be performed, the consequences of that act, and the circumstances under which it must be performed. The *actus reus* required for specific crimes will be discussed later in this chapter. *Mens rea,* or mental fault, refers to the mental element of a crime. Most common law and statutory crimes require **subjective fault,** which includes both those consequences a person desires to cause as well as those consequences he knows, or should know, are virtually certain to result from his conduct. Thus, if Arthur shoots his rifle at Donna, who is seemingly out of gunshot range, with the desire to kill Donna, and in fact does kill her, Arthur had the required criminal intent to kill Donna. Likewise, if Benjamin, desiring to poison Paula, places a toxic chemical in the water cooler in Paula's office and unwittingly poisons Gail and Ram, Benjamin will be found to have intended to kill Gail and Ram, regardless of Benjamin's feelings toward Gail and Ram.

Some statutory crimes require a lesser degree of mental fault, called objective fault. **Objective fault** involves a gross deviation from the standard of care that a reasonable person would observe under the circumstances. Criminal statutes refer to objective fault by such terms as *carelessness* or *negligence*. Examples of crimes requiring objective fault are involuntary manslaughter (negligently causing the death of another), carelessly driving an automobile, and, in some States, issuing a bad check.

Many regulatory statutes have totally dispensed with the mental element of a crime. These statutes impose criminal liability without fault. **Liability without fault** makes it a crime for a person to do a specified act or to bring about a certain result without regard to the care exercised by that person. Statutory crimes imposing liability without fault include bigamy and statutory rape. Other examples are the sale of adulterated food, narcotics without a prescription, and alcoholic beverages to a minor. Most of these crimes involve regulatory statutes dealing with health and safety, and impose only fines for violations (see Figure 4–1).

Classification

Historically, crimes were classified *mala in se* (wrongs in themselves or morally wrong, such as murder) or *mala prohibita* (not morally wrong but declared wrongful by law, such as the requirement to drive on the right side of the road).

From the standpoint of the seriousness of the offense, crimes are also classified as a (1) **felony** or serious crime (any crime punishable by death or imprisonment in the penitentiary), or (2) **misdemeanor** or less serious crime (any crime punishable by a fine or imprisonment in a local jail). Federal law includes another category known as (3) **petty crime** (any misdemeanor punishable by fine or imprisonment of six months or less).

FIGURE 4-1 Degrees of Mental Fault

Type	Fault Required	Examples
Subjective Fault	Purposeful Malicious Knowing	Larceny Embezzlement
Objective Fault	Negligent Careless	Careless driving Bad check (some States)
Liability without Fault	None	Sale of alcohol to a minor Sale of adulterated food Bigamy

White-Collar Crime

An additional classification of crime is white-collar crime, which has been defined in various ways. The Justice Department defines it as nonviolent crime involving deceit, corruption, or breach of trust. It has also been defined as "crimes in the [corporate] suites," which includes crimes committed by individuals—such as embezzlement and forgery—as well as crimes committed on behalf of a corporation—such as commercial bribery, product safety and health crimes, false advertising, and antitrust violations. A less precise definition is crime "committed by a person of respectability and high social status in the course of his occupation," while a more narrow definition is fraud or deceit practiced through misrepresentation to gain an unfair advantage. Regardless of the definition of white-collar crime, it is clear that such crime costs society billions of dollars; estimates range from $40 billion to over $200 billion per year. Historically, prosecution of white-collar crime was deemphasized because it was not considered violent. Now, however, many contend that white-collar crime often inflicts violence but does so impersonally. For example, unsafe products cause injury and death to consumers, while unsafe working conditions cause injury and death to employees.

For a recent case involving white-collar crime, see Law in the News on page 78.

Liability of the Employer Vicarious liability is liability imposed upon one person for the acts of another person. An employer is vicariously liable for the authorized criminal acts of its employees if the employer directed, participated in, or approved of the act. For example, if an employer directs its vice-president of marketing to fix prices with its company's competitors, and the employee does so, both the employer and employee have criminally violated the Sherman Antitrust Act. On the other hand, an employer is ordinarily not liable for the unauthorized criminal acts of his employees. As previously discussed, most crimes require mental fault, and this element is not present so far as criminal responsibility of the employer is concerned where the act of the employee was not authorized.

An employer may, however, be subject to criminal penalty for the unauthorized act of a managerial person acting in the scope of employment. Moreover, an employer may be criminally liable under liability without fault statutes for certain unauthorized acts of its employees, whether the employee is managerial or not. For example, many States have statutes that punish "every person who by himself or his employee or agent sells anything at short weight," or "whoever sells liquor to a minor and any sale by an employee shall be deemed the act of the employer as well." The leading case on executive criminal liability without fault is *United States v. Park*, 421 U.S.

LAW IN THE NEWS

Two Former Executives of Beech-Nut Guilty in Phony Juice Case

Two former top executives of the Beech-Nut Nutrition Corporation were found guilty yesterday of violating Federal laws by intentionally distributing phony apple juice intended for babies.

After five days of deliberations, the verdict was returned by a jury in Federal District Court in Brooklyn that had heard testimony since mid-November. Among the Government witnesses was a Beech-Nut chemist who called the bogus product, which had been labeled as pure fruit juice, "a chemical cocktail."

Thomas H. Roche, the lead Government prosecutor on the case, praised the verdict as an important victory for the consumer. He likened the actions of the convicted defendants to "a hand reaching out from a store shelf and taking money out of the pockets of consumers."

The 1986 indictment charged that Beech-Nut, the two executives and other defendants had intentionally shipped adulterated and misbranded juice to 20 states, Puerto Rico, the Virgin Islands and five foreign countries with the intent to defraud and mislead.

It charged that the product Beech-Nut had been marketing as 100 percent apple juice was actually made from beet sugar, cane sugar, corn syrup and other ingredients, with little if any apple juice in the mixture.

During the trial, Mr. Roche, an assistant United States attorney, told the jury, "This case is a story of corporate greed and irresponsibility." He said the defendants' "main concern was making money for Beech-Nut, even if it meant selling a phony product."

Niels L. Hoyvald, 54 years old, who was president and chief executive of Beech-Nut at the time of the indictment in November 1986, was found guilty of some 350 counts of violating the Food, Drug and Cosmetic Act. Each count carries a possible three-year prison term and a $10,000 fine.

The jury could not reach a verdict on about 80 other counts against Mr. Hoyvald involving purported violations of the Federal act, as well as one count of conspiracy and 18 counts of mail fraud. Judge Thomas C. Platt declared a mistrial on those charges, which carry maximum five-year prison terms. The Government, if it wishes, could seek a new trial on those counts.

John F. Lavery, 56, former vice president for manufacturing at the Beech-Nut plant in Canajoharie, N.Y., about 45 miles west of Albany, was found guilty on 448 counts, including the conspiracy and mail fraud charges.

Both Brendan V. Sullivan Jr., who represented Mr. Hoyvald, and Steven Kimelman, who represented Mr. Lavery, declined to comment on the verdict but said they would appeal the convictions.

Last November Beech-Nut, the nation's second-largest maker of baby food products after the Gerber Products Company, pleaded guilty to Federal charges that it had sold phony apple juice and agreed to pay a $2 million fine. Government officials said they believed the fine was at least six times as great as any paid under the Food, Drug and Cosmetic Act, which became law in 1938.

Beech-Nut also agreed to pay $140,000 in investigative costs to the Food and Drug Administration. Beech-Nut, a subsidiary of Nestlé S.A. of Switzerland, is based in Fort Washington, Pa.

In the court proceedings last November, the company pleaded guilty to 215 counts charging

658 (1975). John Park, chief executive officer of Acme Markets, a retail supermarket food chain with over 36,000 employees, 874 stores, 12 general warehouses, and 4 special warehouses, was convicted of violating the Federal Food and Drug Act. The allegations were based on rodent infestation of Acme's warehouses. In 1970, the FDA informed Acme of rodent infestation in its Philadelphia warehouse and gave notice that the situation must be corrected. In 1971 an FDA inspection discovered unsanitary conditions in Acme's Baltimore warehouse. The FDA notified Park by letter of these findings. After receiving the

that it shipped mislabeled products purporting to be apple juice with intent to defraud and mislead the public. As part of the plea agreement, 145 other counts, including conspiracy and mail fraud, were dismissed.

At the same time, two other defendants, both suppliers of the bogus apple juice concentrate used by Beech-Nut, pleaded guilty. They were Zeev Kaplansky, president of the Universal Juice Inc., and Raymond H. Wells, owner of the defunct Food Complex Company.

Prosecutors said the improperly labeled juice cost about 20 percent less to make than the genuine product.

Earlier last year Beech-Nut settled a class-action suit against it involving the phony apple juice for $7.5 million. The settlement, which was approved in Federal District Court in Philadelphia, provided $2.5 million in Beech-Nut and affiliated products to certain retailers and a $5 million cash fund for consumers who purchased the misrepresented juice.

At the trial the Government introduced evidence to show that from 1978 until June 1982, Beech-Nut bought adulterated and misbranded apple juice concentrate from Universal Juice and Food Complex and used this in its apple juice and mixed apple juice products that it distributed to 20 states, the Caribbean and other markets.

Prosecutors said that Mr. Lavery knew of the purchase of the bogus concentrate as early as 1978 and that Mr. Hoyvald, who became president of Beech-Nut in April 1981, knew of the use of the adulterated concentrate the previous January while he was still senior vice president in charge of marketing.

A key prosecution witness was Jerome LiCari, who was director of the Beech-Nut research and development department until he left the company in 1982.

Mr. LiCari said he tried unsuccessfully to get the company to stop using the concentrate in ques-

tion, which it was able to purchase at a price 20 to 25 percent below the price of competing apple juice concentrates. He said that in 1983 he sent an anonymous letter about the situation to the Food and Drug Administration, signing the letter "Johnny Appleseed."

Mr. Hoyvald, who testified in his own defense, said he first learned of the situation on June 25, 1982, from a private investigator for the Processed Apples Institute.

Mr. Sullivan, Mr. Hoyvald's lawyer, told the jury that adulterated concentrate was an industry-wide problem and that there were no reliable scientific tests until after 1982 that could identify the components of the concentrate. He said his client had been taken in by "unscrupulous suppliers."

After June 25, 1982, when he became aware of a problem, Mr. Hoyvald, acting in good faith, sought and acted upon the legal advice of a number of lawyers, and thus should not be convicted, Mr. Sullivan told the jury.

But Mr. Roche, who is on the staff of the United States Attorney's Office for the Eastern District of New York, said that Mr. Hoyvald, after that date, was trying to stall to give the company time to distribute the bogus apple juice.

The prosecutor said the company saved about $750,000 by buying the adulterated concentrate and avoided a loss of about $3 million by selling the bogus juice.

Author's Update: On March 30, 1989 the U.S. Court of Appeals for the Second Circuit overturned the convictions of Neils Hoyvald and John Lavery for violation of the Federal Food, Drug and Cosmetic Act on the ground that the district court that tried the case was not the proper court to hear the case. The court, however, affirmed Mr. Lavery's conviction on charges of mail fraud and conspiracy.
By Leonard Buder

1971 letter, Park met with the vice-president for legal affairs, who informed him that the situation was being corrected. When the FDA reinspected the Baltimore facility in March 1972, it again found continued rodent contamination, despite some improvement in sanitary conditions. The FDA charged both Acme, which

pleaded guilty, and Park. In upholding the conviction of Park, the U.S. Supreme Court ruled that under the "Federal Food and Drug Act of 1906 knowledge and intent were not required to be proved in prosecutions under its criminal provisions, and that responsible corporate agents could be subjected to the liability thereby imposed." The Court stated that the jury had found that Park had authority and responsibility to deal with the situation, but he had failed to do so.

Liability of the Corporation   Historically, corporations were not held criminally liable, because under the traditional view a corporation could not possess the requisite criminal intent and, therefore, was incapable of committing a crime. The dramatic growth in size and importance of corporations has brought about a change in this view. Under the modern approach, a corporation may be liable for violation of statutes imposing liability without fault. In addition, a corporation may be liable where the offense is perpetrated by a high corporate officer or the board of directors. The American Law Institute's proposed Model Penal Code provides that a corporation may be convicted of a criminal offense for the conduct of its employees if

1. the legislative purpose of the statute defining the offense is to impose liability on corporations and the conduct is within the scope of the agent's office or employment;
2. the offense consists of an omission to discharge a specific, affirmative duty imposed upon corporations by law; or
3. the offense was authorized, requested, commanded, performed, or recklessly tolerated by the board of directors or by a high managerial agent of the corporation.

Punishment of a corporation for crimes is necessarily by fine and not imprisonment. Nonetheless, individuals bearing responsibility for the criminal act face either or both fines and imprisonment. A recent Cook County, Illinois, case demonstrates this possibility and puts businesses and their officers on notice that they may be criminally liable for unsafe business practices. In what many consider a landmark case, three corporate officials of Film Recovery Systems, Inc., were convicted of murder and face a minimum twenty-year prison term, while the company and its parent company were found guilty of involuntary manslaughter. The case involved the death of a Film Recovery employee from acute cyanide poisoning. The court found that (1) the condi-

tions at the company facility were "totally unsafe"; and (2) the company officials knew of the danger and knew that employees were becoming ill but the company did nothing to alleviate the situation.

Computer Crime   One special type of white-collar crime is computer crime. **Computer crime** includes the use of a computer to steal money or services, to remove personal or business information, and to tamper with information. Computer crimes can be broken down into five general categories: (1) theft of computer hardware, software, or secrets; (2) unauthorized use of computer services; (3) theft of money by computer; (4) vandalism of computer hardware or software; and (5) theft of computer data.

Detection of crimes involving computers is extremely difficult. In addition, computer crimes often are not reported because businesses do not want to give the impression that their security is lax. Nonetheless, losses due to computer crimes are estimated to be in the tens of billions of dollars. Moreover, with the ever-increasing societal dependence upon computers, this type of crime will in all likelihood continue to increase.

Already, computer crimes have become commonplace. Examples abound: employees of Hitachi and Mitsubishi were indicted for attempting to steal IBM trade secrets. Software piracy (the unauthorized copying of copyrighted software) is now so widespread that it is estimated that two out of every three copies of software are illegally obtained. A computer consultant hired by Security Pacific Bank wrongfully transferred $10 million dollars from the bank to his own Swiss bank account. Six employees stole TRW's credit-rating data and offered to repair poor credit ratings for a fee. Disgruntled or discharged employees have used computer programs called "logic bombs" to destroy software.

As a consequence, enterprises are spending large sums of money to increase computer security. In addition, approximately twenty States have enacted computer crime laws. Despite numerous attempts, the Federal government has not passed comprehensive legislation prohibiting computer crime. The absence of comprehensive Federal legislation has been explained on three grounds: (1) computer crime is not unique and can be addressed under existing criminal law statutes, (2) State legislation can deal with the problem, and (3) writing effective legislation is difficult. In 1984, however, Congress enacted specific legislation (the Counterfeit Access Device and Computer Fraud and Abuse Act) making unauthorized access to a computer a Federal crime.

Racketeering Influenced and Corrupt Organizations Act The Racketeering Influenced and Corrupt Organizations Act (*RICO*) was enacted in 1970 with the stated purpose of terminating the infiltration by organized crime into legitimate business. The act subjects enterprises that engage in a pattern of racketeering to severe civil and criminal penalties. A pattern of racketeering is defined as the commission of two or more predicate acts within a period of ten years. A "predicate act" is any of several criminal offenses listed in RICO. Included are nine major categories of State crimes and twenty-six Federal crimes, such as murder, kidnapping, arson, extortion, drug dealing, securities fraud, mail fraud, and bribery. The most controversial issue concerning RICO is its application to businesses that are not engaged in organized crime but that do meet the "pattern of racketeering" test under the act. Criminal conviction under the law may result in a prison term up to twenty years plus a fine up to $25,000 per violation. In addition, individuals harmed by RICO violations may invoke the statute's civil remedies, which include treble damage and attorney's fees.

OFFENSES AGAINST PROPERTY

Offenses against property greatly affect businesses and amount to losses in the hundreds of billions of dollars each year. In this section we cover the following crimes against property: (1) larceny, (2) embezzlement, (3) false pretenses, (4) robbery, (5) extortion and bribery, (6) burglary, (7) forgery, and (8) bad checks.

Larceny

The crime of **larceny** is the (1) trespassory (2) taking and (3) carrying away of (4) personal property (5) of another (6) with the intent to deprive the victim permanently of the goods. All six elements must be present for the crime to exist. Thus, if Barbara pays Larry $5,000 for an automobile that Larry agrees to deliver the following week, and Larry does not do so, Larry is *not* guilty of larceny because he has not trespassed on Barbara's property. Larry has not taken anything from Barbara; he has simply refused to turn over the automobile to her. Larceny applies only when a person takes personal property from another without the other's consent. Here Barbara voluntarily paid the money to Larry. Larry has not committed larceny but has obtained the $5,000 by false pretenses (which is discussed later). Likewise, if Carol takes Dan's 1968 automobile without Dan's permission, intending to use it for a joyride and then to return it to Dan, Carol has not committed larceny because she did not intend to deprive Dan permanently of the automobile. On the other hand, if Carol left Dan's 1968 car in a junkyard after the joyride, Carol would most likely be held to have committed a larceny because of the high risk that Dan would be permanently deprived of the car. The case on page 82 deals with the question of whether persons may be convicted of larceny for shoplifting if they are arrested before leaving the store.

Embezzlement

Embezzlement is the improper taking of another's property by one who was in lawful possession of it. This statutory crime was first enacted in response to a 1799 English case in which a bank employee was found not guilty of larceny for taking money given to him for deposit in the bank because the money had been voluntarily handed to him. Thus, embezzlement is a crime intended to prevent individuals who are lawfully in possession of property of another from taking the property for their own use. The key distinction between larceny and embezzlement, therefore,

PEOPLE v. OLIVO
Court of Appeals of New York, 1981.
52 N.Y.2d 309, 438 N.Y.S.2d 242, 420 N.E.2d 40.

Facts: Olivo was in the hardware area of a department store. A security guard saw him look around, take a set of wrenches, and conceal it in his clothing. Olivo looked around once more and proceeded to head toward an exit, passing several cash registers. The guard stopped him short of the exit. Olivo testified at trial that he was waiting in line at a cashier with the tools under his arm when he was seized by the guard. A jury found him guilty of larceny. Olivo then brought this appeal, maintaining that larceny is not legally established unless the defendant leaves a place of business without paying for merchandise in his possession.

Decision: Judgment affirmed.

Opinion: **Cooke, C. J.**   Larceny at common law was defined as a trespassory taking and carrying away of the property of another with intent to steal it. The early common-law courts apparently viewed larceny as defending society against breach of the peace, rather than protecting individual property rights, and therefore placed heavy emphasis upon the requirement of a *trespassory taking* [citation].

Thus, a person such as a bailee who had rightfully obtained possession of property from its owner could not be guilty of larceny [citation]. The result was that the crime of larceny was quite narrow in scope.

Gradually, the courts began to expand the reach of the offense, initially by subtle alterations in the common-law concept of possession [citation]. Thus, for instance, it became a general rule that goods entrusted to an employee were not deemed to be in his possession, but were only considered to be in his custody, so long as he remained on the employer's premises [citation]. And, in the case of [citation], it was held that a shop owner retained legal possession of merchandise being examined by a prospective customer until the actual sale was made. In these situations, the employee and the customer would not have been guilty of larceny if they had first obtained lawful possession of the property from the owner. By holding that they had not acquired possession, but merely custody, the court was able to sustain a larceny conviction.

As the reach of larceny expanded, the intent element of the crime became of increasing importance, while the requirement of a trespassory taking became less significant. As a result, the bar against convicting a person who had initially obtained lawful possession of property faded. . . .

Later cases went even further, often ignoring the fact that a defendant had initially obtained possession lawfully, and instead focused upon his later intent. The crime of larceny then encompassed, not only situations where the defendant initially obtained property by a trespassory taking, but many situations where an individual, possessing the requisite intent, exercised control over property inconsistent with the continued rights of the owner. During this evolutionary process, the purpose served by the crime of larceny obviously shifted from protecting society's peace to general protection of property rights.

Modern penal statutes generally have incorporated these developments under a unified definition of larceny [citation]. Case law, too, now tends to focus upon the actor's intent and the exercise of dominion and control over the property [citation]. Indeed, this court has recognized, in construing the New York Penal Law, that the *"ancient* common-law concepts of larceny" no longer strictly apply [citation].

This evolution is particularly relevant to thefts occurring in modern self-service stores. In stores of that type, customers are impliedly invited to examine, try on, and carry about the merchandise on display. Thus in a sense, the owner has consented to the customer's possession of the goods for a limited purpose. That the owner has consented to that possession does not, however, preclude a conviction for larceny. If the customer exercises dominion and control wholly inconsistent with the continued rights of the owner, and the other elements of the crime are present, a larceny has occurred. Such conduct on the part of a customer satisfies the "taking" element of the crime.

It is this element that forms the core of the controversy. . . . The defendant argue[s], in essence, that the crime is not established, as a matter of law, unless there is evidence that the customer departed the shop without paying for the merchandise.

Although this court has not addressed the issue, case law from other jurisdictions seems unanimous in holding that a shoplifter need not leave the store to be guilty of larceny. This is because a shopper may treat merchandise in a manner inconsistent with the owner's continued rights—and in a manner not in accord with that of prospective purchaser—without actually walking out of the store. Indeed, depending upon the circumstances of each case, a variety of conduct may be sufficient to allow the trier of fact to find a taking. . . .

In many cases, it will be particularly relevant that defendant concealed the goods under clothing or in a container. Such conduct is not generally expected in a self-service store and may in a proper case be deemed an exercise of dominion and control inconsistent with the store's continued rights. Other furtive or unusual behavior on the part of the defendant should also be weighed. Thus, if the defendant surveys the area while secreting the merchandise or abandoned his or her own property in exchange for the concealed goods, this may evince larcenous rather than innocent behavior. Relevant too is the customer's proximity to or movement towards one of the store's exits. Certainly it is highly probative of guilt that the customer was in possession of secreted goods just a few short steps from the door or moving in that direction. Finally, possession of a known shoplifting device actually used to conceal merchandise, such as a specially designed outer garment or false bottomed carrying case, would be all but decisive.

is whether the thief is in lawful possession of the property. In both there is a misuse of the property of another, but in larceny the thief unlawfully possesses the property, whereas in embezzlement the thief lawfully possesses the property.

A second distinction between larceny and embezzlement is that unlike larceny, embezzlement does not require the intent to permanently deprive the owner of his property. Nonetheless, in order to constitute an embezzlement, there must be a serious act of interference with the owner's rights to the property.

False Pretenses

Obtaining property by false pretenses, like embezzlement, is a statutory crime enacted to close a loophole in the requirements of larceny. **False pretenses** is the crime of obtaining title to property of another by means of materially false representations of fact, with knowledge of their falsity, and made with the intent to defraud. Larceny does not cover this situation because the victim voluntarily transfers the property to the thief. For example, a con artist who goes door to door and collects money by saying he is selling stereo equipment, when indeed he is not, is committing the crime of false pretenses. The test of deception is *subjective;* if the victim is actually deceived, the test is satisfied even though a reasonable person would not have been deceived by the defendant's lies. Therefore, gullibility or lack of due care on the part of the victim is no defense.

Robbery

Under the common law as well as most statutes, **robbery** is a larceny with the additional elements that: (1) the property is taken from the victim or in the immediate presence of the victim, and (2) it is accomplished through either force or threat of force. The defendant's force or threat of force need not be against the person from whom the property is taken. For example, a robber threatens Sam that unless Sam opens up his employer's safe, the robber will shoot Maria. Moreover, the victim's presence may be actual or constructive. *Constructive presence* means that the victim is prevented from being present by the defendant's actual or threatened force. For example, if the robber knocks the victim unconscious or ties her up, the victim is considered constructively present.

Extortion and Bribery

Although extortion and bribery are frequently confused, they are two distinct crimes. **Extortion,** or blackmail as it is sometimes called, is generally held to be the making of threats for the purpose of obtaining money or property. For example, Lindsey tells Jason that unless Jason pays her $10,000 she will tell Jason's customers that Jason was once arrested for embezzling. Lindsey has committed the crime of extortion. In a few jurisdictions, however, the crime of extortion occurs only if the defendant actually causes the victim to relinquish money or property.

Bribery, on the other hand, is the offer of money or property to a public official to influence the official's decision. The crime of bribery is committed when the illegal offer is made, whether accepted or not. Thus, if Andrea offered Edward, the mayor of Allentown, a 20 percent interest in Andrea's planned real estate development if Edward would use his influence to have the development proposal approved, Andrea would be guilty of criminal bribery. In contrast, if Edward had threatened Andrea that unless he received a 20 percent interest in Andrea's development he would use his influence to prevent the approval of the development, Edward would be guilty of criminal extortion. Bribery of foreign officials is covered in the Foreign Corrupt Practices Act discussed in Chapter 43.

Some jurisdictions have gone beyond the general bribery law and have adopted statutes that make **commercial bribery** illegal. Commercial bribery is the use of bribery to acquire new business, obtain secret information or processes, or obtain kickbacks.

Burglary

At common law, **burglary** was defined as breaking and entering a dwelling house at night with the intent to commit a felony. Of these elements, the three that caused the greatest degree of confusion were (1) breaking, (2) entering, and (3) dwelling house. Breaking required that the defendant had to create the breach or opening; the opening could not have been created by the resident. Therefore, persons would not be guilty of common law burglary if they entered another's home in the night through an *open* window to steal jewelry. Moreover, the crime of burglary would not be committed even if the defendant had to open the window further in order to climb into the house. On the other hand, the common law was extremely lenient with respect to entry and required only that any part of the defendant's body enter the house, regardless of the length of the entry. For example, Kathy punches in a window of a dwelling house at night to gain entry and steal a television. When she reaches her hand in the broken window, she triggers the burglar alarm and flees. Kathy has committed a burglary. Finally, the dwelling house of another means that it is someone's residence regardless of whether the tenant is present at the time of the burglary.

Modern statutes are very different from the common law definition. Many of them simply require that there be (1) an entry (2) into a building (3) with the intent to commit a felony in the building. Thus, these statutory definitions omit three elements of the common law crime—the building need not be a dwelling house, the entry need not be at night, and the entry need not be a technical breaking. The modern statutes vary so greatly it is impossible to generalize, except that most of the statutes include some, but not all, of the common law elements.

Forgery

Forgery is the intentional falsification or false making of a document with the intent to defraud. Accordingly, if William prepares a false certificate of title to a stolen automobile, he is guilty of forgery. Likewise, if an individual alters some receipts in order to increase her income tax deductions, she has committed the crime of forgery.

Bad Checks

A statutory crime that has some relation to both forgery and false pretenses is the passing of **bad checks**—that is, writing a check when there is not enough money in the account to cover the check. All jurisdictions have now enacted laws making it a crime to issue bad checks; however, these statutes vary greatly from jurisdiction to jurisdiction. Most jurisdictions simply require that the check be issued; they do not require that the issuer receive anything in return for the check. Also, most jurisdictions require that defendants issue a check with knowledge that they do not have enough money to cover the check. A few jurisdictions require only that there be insufficient funds. The Model Penal Code requires that the check be dishonored (not paid) and that the maker fail to pay the check within ten days.

CRIMINAL DEFENSES

Even though a defendant is found to have committed a criminal act, he will not be convicted if he has a valid defense. Most criminal law defenses are valid against both crimes against the person and crimes against property. The one exception to this rule is that the defense of person or property serves only as a defense to crimes against the person.

Defense of Person or Property

Individuals may use reasonable force to protect themselves, other individuals, and their property. These defenses enable a person to commit without any criminal liability what would otherwise be considered the crime of assault, battery, manslaughter, or murder.

Self-Defense   An individual need not submit to force or violence against his person but may use force to protect himself. **Self-defense** entitles individuals to use *reasonable* force to protect themselves against an attack if they reasonably believe that they are in immediate danger of unlawful bodily harm and that the use of force is necessary to protect them from such harm. Accordingly, even though individuals act on the mistaken belief that they are defending themselves against an unlawful attack, so long as the belief is based on reasonable grounds, they are entitled to the same defense as if the attack had been as they believed. Individuals who act in self-defense have a complete defense against any crime based on them causing physical harm to the aggressor.

What constitutes "reasonable force" has given rise to a great deal of litigation and considerable commentary. As a general rule, persons may use *nondeadly* force to protect themselves against unlawful bodily harm and *deadly* force to protect themselves against an attack threatening death or serious bodily harm. Thus, Alan may not shoot Betty in order to protect himself against a punch in the mouth. On the other hand, if Betty attacked Alan with a knife, Alan could properly defend himself by shooting Betty, even if Betty's knife was in fact plastic, so long as Alan reasonably believed it to be real. A minority of States and the Model Penal Code require persons to retreat before using deadly force provided that they can safely do so. The objective of this rule is to protect human life even though it requires the avoidance of confrontation. Most States, however, do not require retreat, based on the view that a person should not be forced to take "cowardly" action against a criminal aggressor. Moreover, even in the jurisdictions following the minority rule, retreat is not required before persons may reasonably use deadly force in their own home.

Defense of Another   Generally, an individual has a complete defense against criminal prosecution if he uses reasonable force in defense of another provided he reasonably believes the other to be in immediate danger of unlawful bodily harm and that use of such force is necessary to prevent this harm. Most States permit this defense to be used by an individual in defense of *any* other person, even a stranger, although some States limit its use to the defense of individuals who have some defined relationship to the person who intervened. Moreover, some States limit the rule's application by permitting the defense only when the original victim had the right of self-defense. In other words, these States place the intervenor in the shoes of the party whom he is assisting.

Defense of Property   Individuals also have the right to use reasonable force to protect their property. Under the majority rule, deadly force is *never* reasonable to protect property because life is deemed more important than the protection of property. For this reason, individuals cannot use a deadly mechanical device, such as a spring gun, to protect their property.

Incapacity

Under some circumstances, an individual is declared incapable of forming criminal intent.

Thus, even though that person commits a criminal act, he will not be held liable because of the lack of criminal intent. In these situations, the person has a complete criminal defense based on incapacity.

Insanity   The extent to which insanity should be a defense to criminal conduct has long troubled the legal system. Although it is difficult to conceive how any "sane" person could commit a brutal murder or a rape, it is not in that sense that the term **criminally insane** is used. The criminal law defense of insanity is directed at those for whom criminal sanctions are not appropriate. Those who are found "not guilty by reason of insanity" are generally not allowed to go free but are typically committed to a mental institution for treatment.

The traditional and most common test for insanity is the **M'Naghten test.** Under this test, as in the case that follows, defendants are *not* criminally responsible for their conduct if, at the time of committing the act, they did not understand the nature and quality of the act or they could not distinguish between right or wrong. For example, if Alex axed Betty, believing that Betty was a tree trunk that he was splitting for firewood, Alex would be found to be not guilty by reason of insanity.

STATE v. CRENSHAW
Supreme Court of Washington, 1983.
98 Wash.2d 789, 659 P.2d 488.

Facts: Rodney Crenshaw and his wife, Karen, were on their honeymoon in Canada. Crenshaw became involved in a brawl and was deported. He secured a motel room in Blaine, Washington, where his wife joined him two days later. He immediately sensed that his wife had been unfaithful. He beat her unconscious and stabbed her twenty-four times, inflicting a fatal wound. Crenshaw then procured an ax and decapitated his wife. After placing the body and head in his wife's car, he cleaned the room of blood and fingerprints and departed. Crenshaw disposed of the body in a remote area twenty-five miles away and subsequently told his story to two hitchhikers some 200 miles from the scene of the crime. Crenshaw was arrested and voluntarily confessed to the crime. He pleaded not guilty and not guilty by reason of insanity to the charge of first degree murder, contending that as a follower of the Muscovite religious faith, he was bound to kill his wife if she committed adultery. Crenshaw also had a history of mental problems. Crenshaw was found guilty by a jury of first degree murder. He then brought this appeal, maintaining that the trial court erred in instructing the jury on the insanity defense.

Decision: Judgment affirmed because there was no reversible error committed by the trial court.

Opinion: Brachtenbach, J.   Insanity is an affirmative defense the defendant must establish by a preponderance of the evidence. [Citation.] Sanity is presumed, even with a history of prior institutional commitments from which the individual was released upon sufficient recovery.

The insanity defense is not available to all who are mentally deficient or deranged; legal insanity has a different meaning and a different purpose than the concept of medical insanity. [Citation.] A verdict of not guilty by reason of insanity completely absolves a defendant of any criminal responsibility. Therefore, "the defense is available only to those persons who have lost contact with reality so completely that they are beyond any of the influences of the criminal law." [Citation.]

Petitioner assigned error to insanity defense instruction 10 which reads:

* * *

For a defendant to be found not guilty by reason of insanity you must find that, as a result of mental disease or defect, the defendant's mind was affected to such an extent that the defendant was unable to perceive the nature and quality of the acts with which the defendant is charged or was unable to tell right from wrong with reference to the particular acts with which defendant is charged.

What is meant by the terms "right and wrong" refers to knowledge of a person at the time of committing an act that he was acting contrary to the law.

[Citation.] But for the last paragraph, this instruction tracks the language of [citation], which is the *M'Naghten* test as codified in [Washington State]. Petitioner contends, however, that the trial court erred in defining "right and wrong" as legal right and wrong rather than in the moral sense.

We find this instruction was not reversible error on three, alternative grounds: (1) The *M'Naghten* opinion amply supports the "legal" wrong definition as used in this case, (2) under these facts, "moral" wrong and "legal" wrong are synonymous, therefore the "legal" wrong definition did not alter the meaning of the test, and (3) because Crenshaw failed to prove other elements of the insanity defense, any error in the definition of wrong was harmless.

* * *

Such an interpretation is consistent with Washington's strict application of *M'Naghten*. This court's view has been that "when *M'Naghten* is used, all who might possibly be deterred from the commission of criminal acts are included within the sanctions of the criminal law." [Citation.]

[O]nly those persons "who have lost contact with reality so completely that they are beyond any of the influences of the criminal law," may have the benefit of the insanity defense in a criminal case.

* * *

Alternatively, the statement in instruction 10 may be approved because, in this case, legal wrong is synonymous with moral wrong. . . .

[I]n discussing the term "moral" wrong, it is important to note that it is society's morals, and not the individual's morals, that are the standard for judging moral wrong under *M'Naghten*. If wrong meant moral wrong judged by the individual's own conscience, this would seriously undermine the criminal law, for it would allow one who violated the law to be excused from criminal responsibility solely because, in his own conscience, his act was not morally wrong. [Citations.] . . .

* * *

We conclude that Crenshaw knew his acts were morally wrong from society's viewpoint and also knew his acts were illegal. His personal belief that it was his duty to kill his wife for her alleged infidelity cannot serve to exculpate him from legal responsibility for his acts.

* * *

We also find that, under any definition of wrong, Crenshaw did not qualify for the insanity defense under *M'Naghten;* therefore, any alleged error in that definition must be viewed as harmless. . . . Here, any error is harmless for two alternate reasons. First, Crenshaw failed to prove an essential element of the defense because he did not prove his alleged delusions stemmed from a mental defect; second, he did not prove by a preponderance of the evidence that he was legally insane at the time of the crime.

In addition to an incapacity to know right from wrong, *M'Naghten* requires that such incapacity stem from a mental disease or defect. [Citation.] Assuming, arguendo, that Crenshaw did not know right from wrong, he failed to prove that a mental defect was the cause of this inability.

Some States have added another test to the *M'Naghten* test—the **irresistible impulse** test. Under this test, a defendant is freed of criminal responsibility if he had a mental disease that prevented him from controlling his conduct, even though he understood the nature of his act and that it was wrong. For example, Aaron killed Betsy, although he knew it to be illegal and wrong, because he believed God's messenger had ordered him to do so. Under the irresistible impulse test, Aaron would be not guilty by reason of insanity.

A third test of insanity has been accepted by some States and incorporated into the American Law Institute's Model Penal Code:

1. A person is not responsible for criminal conduct if at the time of such conduct as a result of mental disease or defect he lacks substantial capacity either to appreciate the criminality (wrongfulness) of his conduct or to conform his conduct to the requirements of law.
2. As used in this article, the terms "mental disease or defect" do not include an abnormality manifested only by repeated criminal or otherwise antisocial conduct. Section 4.01.

This test differs from the other two tests in that it requires only a substantial lack of capacity, whereas the others require a complete impairment of capacity or self-control. This test was universally adopted by the United States Courts of Appeals.

In 1984 Congress adopted the Comprehensive Crime Control Act, which governs the use of the insanity defense in Federal criminal cases. The act rejects the Model Penal Code's formulation and adopts a variant of the *M'Naghten* test. It also places the burden on the defendant to prove his insanity by clear and convincing evidence.

Another significant development in the area of the insanity defense is the guilty but mentally ill verdict. Before the adoption by some States of this verdict, the jury was limited to verdicts of guilty, not guilty, or not guilty by reason of insanity. The new guilty but mentally ill verdict applies to lesser degrees of mental illness and permits the court to sentence the defendant as if he had been found guilty. The key distinction is that after sentencing the defendant undergoes a psychiatric examination to determine whether he is in need of psychiatric treatment, in which case he is transferred to a mental hospital. Once placed in a mental hospital the defendant remains there until (1) his sentence expires, or (2) he regains his sanity, at which point he will serve the remainder of his sentence in prison.

Infancy   Under the common law and most modern statutes, a child under the age of seven is conclusively presumed to be incapable of committing a crime. From the ages of seven to fourteen, there is a rebuttable presumption that the child is incapable of committing a crime. Above the age of fourteen, there is a rebuttable presumption that the child is capable of committing a crime. The common law defense of infancy has been rendered moot, however, by the enactment of juvenile court acts, which require that all individuals below a certain age—varying among States between fourteen and eighteen—be brought before a juvenile, and not a criminal, court. Juvenile courts are not criminal in nature; rather they attempt to deal with the welfare of the youth and decide if the youth is a delinquent.

Intoxication   The great majority of the States follow what is commonly known as the voluntary/involuntary test, which makes voluntary intoxication *not* a defense. Thus, if Andy commits a burglary while so intoxicated as not to know what he is doing, Andy would *not* be guilty of criminal burglary if he involuntarily drank the alcohol because Jose forced him to against his free will. On the other hand, if Andy had drunk the liquor voluntarily, he would not have the defense of intoxication.

Other Defenses

In addition to those defenses already discussed, criminal liability is not imposed if duress, mistake of fact, or entrapment are present.

Duress   A person who is threatened with immediate, serious bodily harm to himself or another unless he engages in criminal activity has the valid defense of **duress** to criminal conduct other than murder. For example, Ann threatens to kill Ben if Ben does not assist her

in committing larceny. Ben complies. Ben would not be guilty of the larceny because of duress. If Ann threatens Ben with death unless Ben kills Carol, however, Ben would *not* be relieved of the crime of homicide, although the crime may be reduced from murder to manslaughter. The Model Penal Code has rejected the "murder limitation" and relieves a person of all criminal responsibility if "a person of reasonable firmness would have been unable to resist."

Mistake of Fact   If a person reasonably believes the facts to be such that his conduct would not constitute a crime, then the law will treat the facts as he reasonably believed. Accordingly, an honest and reasonable mistake of fact will justify the defendant's conduct. For example, if Ann gets into a car that she reasonably believes to be hers—the car is the same color, model, and year as hers, is parked in the same parking lot, and is started by her key—she will be relieved of criminal responsibility for taking Ben's automobile.

Entrapment   The defense of **entrapment** arises when a law enforcement official induces a person to commit a crime when that person would not have done so otherwise. The rationale behind the rule is to prevent law enforcement officials from provoking crime and from engaging in reprehensible conduct. The doctrine is aimed only at government officials and agents and does not apply to private individuals. For example, if Paul, a police officer, entices Robert to commit a robbery, Robert would possess the valid defense of entrapment; if Paul were a private citizen, Robert would be guilty of criminal robbery.

CRIMINAL PROCEDURE

Each of the States and the Federal government has procedures for initiating and coordinating criminal prosecutions. In addition, the first ten amendments to the U.S. Constitution (the Bill of Rights) guarantee many defenses and rights of an accused. The First Amendment guarantees freedom of speech, religion, and association. The Fourth Amendment prohibits unreasonable searches and seizures to obtain incriminating evidence. The Fifth Amendment requires indictment for capital crimes by a grand jury, prevents double jeopardy, protects against self-incrimination, and prohibits deprivation of life or liberty without due process of law. The Sixth Amendment requires a speedy and public trial by jury, and that the accused be informed of the nature of the accusation, be confronted with the witnesses who testify against him, be given the power to obtain witnesses in his favor, and have the right to competent counsel for his defense. The Eighth Amendment prohibits excessive bail, excessive fines, and cruel or unusual punishment (see Figure 4–2).

Most State constitutions have similar provisions protecting the rights of accused persons. In addition, the Fourteenth Amendment prohibits State governments from denying any person of life, liberty, or property without due process of law. Moreover, the U.S. Supreme Court has held that most constitutional protections just discussed apply to the States

through operation of the Fourteenth Amendment.

We will first discuss the steps in a criminal prosecution; then we will focus on the major constitutional protections for the accused in our system of criminal justice.

Steps in Criminal Prosecution

Although the particulars of criminal procedure vary from State to State, the following provides a basic overview. After arrest, the accused is booked and appears before a magistrate, commissioner, or justice of the peace, where formal notice of the charges is given, he is given advice of his rights, and bail is set. Next, a **preliminary hearing** is held to determine whether there is probable cause to believe the defendant is the one who committed the crime. The defendant is entitled to be represented by counsel.

For less serious crimes, prosecution begins by issuing a warrant, which is served on the accused together with an "information" of the

---

FIGURE 4-2 Constitutional Protection for the Criminal Defendant

Amendment	Protection Conferred
First	Freedom of speech Freedom of religion Freedom of association
Fourth	Freedom from unreasonable search and seizure
Fifth	Right to due process Right to indictment by grand jury for capital crimes* Freedom from double jeopardy Freedom from self-incrimination
Sixth	Right to speedy, public trial by jury Right to be informed of accusations Right to confront witnesses Right to present witnesses Right to competent counsel
Eighth	Freedom from excessive bail Freedom from cruel and unusual punishment

*This right has *not* been applied to the States through the Fourteenth Amendment.

charge at the time of his arrest. Serious crimes are prosecuted by an **indictment** or "true bill" after being presented to a grand jury, which determines whether a criminal action should be brought. A grand jury consists of not less than sixteen and not more than twenty-three people. If there is sufficient evidence, the grand jury "indicts" the accused. **Information,** which is used in most misdemeanor cases and some felony cases, is a formal accusation of a crime brought by a prosecuting officer and not a grand jury.

At the **arraignment,** the accused is informed of the charge against him and he enters his plea. The arraignment must be held promptly after the indictment or information has been filed. If his plea is "not guilty," he must stand trial. He is entitled to a jury trial, but if he chooses, he may have his guilt or innocence determined by the court sitting without a jury, which is called a "bench trial."

The trial begins with the selection of the jury and the opening statements by the prosecutor and the attorney for the defense. The prosecution presents evidence first; then the defendant presents his. At the conclusion of the testimony, closing statements are made and the jury is instructed as to the applicable law and retires to arrive at a verdict. In most States the verdict must be unanimous. If the verdict is "not guilty," the matter ends there. The State has no right to appeal from an acquittal; and the accused, having been placed in "jeopardy," cannot be tried a second time for the same offense. If the verdict is "guilty" and a judgment is entered, the defendant has further recourse. He may make a motion for a new trial, asserting that prejudicial error occurred at the trial, thus requiring a retrial of the case. Or he may assert that the evidence was insufficient to establish guilt beyond a reasonable doubt and ask for his discharge. Proof **beyond a reasonable doubt** means that the evidence must be entirely or fully convincing, it must be sufficient to a moral certainty. The defendent may appeal to a reviewing court, alleging error by the trial court and asking for either his discharge or a remandment of the case for a new trial.

Fourth Amendment

The Fourth Amendment protects all individuals against unreasonable searches and seizures. This amendment is designed to protect the privacy and security of individuals against arbitrary invasions by government officials. Although the Fourth Amendment directly applies only to the Federal government, the Fourteenth Amendment makes it applicable to the States.

When there is a violation of the Fourth Amendment, the general rule prohibits the introduction of the illegally seized evidence. The purpose of this **exclusionary rule** is to discourage illegal police conduct and to protect individual liberty, not to hinder the search for the truth. Nonetheless, in recent years the Supreme Court, as shown in *United States v. Leon,* has limited the exclusionary rule.

UNITED STATES v. LEON
Supreme Court of the United States, 1984.
468 U.S. 897, 104 S.Ct. 3405, 82 L.Ed.2d 677.

Facts: Officer Cyril Rombach of the Burbank Police Department, an experienced and well-trained narcotics officer, applied for a warrant to search several residences and automobiles for cocaine, methaqualone, and other narcotics. Rombach supported his application with information given to another police officer by a confidential informant of unproven reliability. He also based the warrant application on his own observations made during an extensive investigation—known drug offenders visiting the residences and leaving with small packages as well as a suspicious trip to Miami by two of the suspects. A state superior court judge issued a search warrant to Rombach based on this information. Rombach's searches netted large quantities of drugs and other evidence, which produced indictments of several suspects on charges of conspiracy to possess and distribute cocaine. The defendants moved to suppress the evidence on the grounds that the search warrant was defective in that Rombach had failed to establish the informant's credibility and that the information provided by the informant about the suspect's criminal activity was fatally stale. The district court declared that the searches lacked probable cause, that the warrant was invalid, and that the obtained evidence must be excluded from the prosecution's case under the Fourth Amendment's exclusionary rule. The Court of Appeals for the Ninth Circuit affirmed.

Decision: Judgments of the district court and Court of Appeals reversed.

Opinion: **White, J.**   The Fourth Amendment contains no provision expressly precluding the use of evidence obtained in violation of its commands, and an examination of its origin and purposes makes clear that the use of fruits of a past unlawful search or seizure "work[s] no new Fourth Amendment wrong." [Citation.] The wrong condemned by the Amendment is "fully accomplished" by the unlawful search or seizure itself, and the exclusionary rule is neither intended nor able to "cure the invasion of the defendant's rights which he has already suffered." [Citation.] The rule thus operates as "a judicially created remedy designed to safeguard Fourth Amendment rights generally through its deterrent effect, rather than a personal constitutional right of the person aggrieved." [Citation.]

Whether the exclusionary sanction is appropriately imposed in a particular case, our decisions make clear, is "an issue separate from the question whether the Fourth Amendment rights of the party seeking to invoke the rule were violated by police conduct." [Citation.] Only the former question is currently before us, and it must be resolved by weighing the costs and benefits of preventing the use in the prosecution's case-in-chief of inherently trustworthy tangible evidence obtained in reliance on a search warrant issued by a detached and neutral magistrate that ultimately is found to be defective.

The substantial social costs exacted by the exclusionary rule for the vindication of Fourth Amendment rights have long been a source of concern. "Our cases have consistently recognized that unbending application of the exclusionary sanction to enforce ideals of governmental rectitude would impede unacceptably the truth-finding functions of judge and jury." [Citation.] An objectionable collateral consequence of this interference with the criminal justice system's truth-finding function is that some guilty defendants may go free or receive reduced sentences as a result of favorable plea bargains. Particularly when law enforcement officers have acted in objective good faith or their transgressions have been minor, the magnitude of the benefit conferred on such guilty defendants offends basic concepts of the criminal justice system. [Citation.] Indiscriminate application of the exclusionary rule, therefore, may well "generat[e] disrespect for the law and the administration of justice." [Citation.] Accordingly, "[a]s with any remedial device, the application of the rule has been restricted to those areas where its remedial objectives are thought most efficaciously served." [Citation.]

Close attention to those remedial objectives has characterized our recent decisions concerning the scope of the Fourth Amendment exclusionary rule. The Court has, to be sure, not seriously questioned, "in the absence of a more efficacious sanction, the continued application of the rule to suppress evidence from the [prosecution's] case where a Fourth Amendment violation has been substantial and deliberate. . . ." [Citation.] Nevertheless, the balancing approach that has evolved in various contexts including criminal trials—"forcefully suggest[s] that the exclusionary rule be more generally modified to permit the introduction of evidence obtained in the reasonable good-faith belief that a search or seizure was in accord with the Fourth Amendment." [Citation.]

* * *

As yet, we have not recognized any form of good-faith exception to the Fourth Amendment exclusionary rule. But the balancing approach that has evolved during the years of experience with the rule provides strong support for the modification currently urged upon us. As we discuss below, our evaluation of the costs and benefits of suppressing reliable physical evidence seized by officers reasonably relying on a warrant issued by a detached and neutral magistrate leads to the conclusion that such evidence should be admissible in the prosecution's case-in-chief.

Because a search warrant "provides the detached scrutiny of a neutral magistrate, which is a more reliable safeguard against improper searches than the hurried judgment of a law enforcement officer 'engaged in the often competitive enterprise of ferreting out crime,' " [citations], we have expressed a strong preference for warrants and declared that "in a doubtful or marginal case a search under a warrant may be sustainable where without one it would fail." [Citations.] Reasonable minds frequently may differ on the question whether a particular affidavit establishes probable cause, and we have thus concluded that the preference for warrants is most appropriately effectuated by according "great deference" to a magistrate's determination. [Citations.]

Deference to the magistrate, however, is not boundless.

* * *

If exclusion of evidence obtained pursuant to a subsequently invalidated warrant is to have any deterrent effect, therefore, it must alter the behavior of individual law enforcement officers or the policies of their departments. One could argue that applying the exclusionary rule in cases where the police failed to demonstrate probable cause in the warrant application deters future inadequate presentations or "magistrate shopping" and thus promotes the ends of the Fourth Amendment. Suppressing evidence obtained pursuant to a technically defective warrant supported by probable cause also might encourage officers to scrutinize more closely the form of the warrant and to point out suspected judicial errors. We find such arguments speculative and conclude that suppression of evidence obtained pursuant to a warrant should be ordered only on a case-by-case basis and only in those unusual cases in which exclusion will further the purposes of the exclusionary rule.

We have frequently questioned whether the exclusionary rule can have any deterrent effect when the offending officers acted in the objectively reasonable belief that their conduct did not violate the Fourth Amendment.

As indicated in *Leon*, to obtain a search warrant of a particular person, place, or thing, the law enforcement official must demonstrate to a magistrate that he has probable cause to believe that the search will reveal evidence of criminal activity. **Probable cause** means that "the apparent facts set out in the affidavit [of the requesting authority] are such that a rea-

sonably discreet and prudent man would be led to believe that there was a commission of the offense charged. . . ." *Dumbra v. United States*, 268 U.S. 435 (1925).

Even though the Fourth Amendment requires that a search and seizure generally be made after a valid search warrant has been obtained, in some instances a search warrant is not necessary. For example, it has been held that a warrant is not necessary where (1) there is hot pursuit of a fugitive, (2) voluntary consent is given, (3) an emergency requires such action, (4) there has been a lawful arrest, (5) evidence of a crime is in plain view of the law enforcement officer, or (6) delay would present a significant obstacle to the investigation.

Fifth Amendment

The Fifth Amendment protects persons against self-incrimination, double jeopardy, and being charged with a capital or infamous crime except by grand jury indictment.

The prohibitions against self-incrimination and double jeopardy, but not the grand jury clause, also apply to the States through the due process clause of the Fourteenth Amendment.

The privilege against self-incrimination extends only to testimonial evidence and not to physical evidence. The Fifth Amendment "privilege protects an accused only from being compelled to testify against himself, or otherwise provide the State with evidence of a testimonial or communicative nature." *Schmerber v. California*, 384 U.S. 757 (1966). Therefore, a person can be forced to stand in a lineup for identification purposes, provide a handwriting sample, or take a blood test. Most significantly, the Fifth Amendment does not protect business records—it applies only to papers of individuals. Moreover, the Fifth Amendment does not prohibit examination of an individual's business records as long as the individual is not compelled to testify against himself.

The Fifth Amendment and the Fourteenth Amendment also guarantee due process of law, which is basically the requirement of a fair trial. All persons are entitled to have charges or complaints against them, whether in civil or criminal proceedings, made publicly and in writing and to be given the opportunity to defend against them. In criminal prosecutions, it includes the right to counsel, to confront and cross-examine adverse witnesses, to testify in one's own behalf if desired, to produce witnesses and offer other evidence, and to be free from any and all prejudicial conduct and statements.

Sixth Amendment

The Sixth Amendment provides that the Federal government shall provide the accused with a speedy and public trial by an impartial jury, inform him of the nature and cause of the accusation, confront him with the witnesses against him, have compulsory process for obtaining witnesses in his favor, and have the assistance of counsel for his defense. The Fourteenth Amendment extends these guarantees to the States.

The Supreme Court has explained the purpose of guaranteeing the right to a trial by jury as follows: "[T]he purpose of trial by jury is to prevent oppression by the Government by providing a safeguard against the corrupt or overzealous prosecutor and against the compliant, biased, or eccentric judge. . . . [T]he essential factors of a jury trial obviously lie in the interposition between the accused and his accuser of the common sense judgment of a group of laymen." *Apodaca v. Oregon*, 406 U.S. 404 (1972). Nevertheless, a defendant may give up his right to a jury trial.

Historically, juries consisted of twelve jurors, but in the Federal courts and in the courts of certain States, the number has been reduced to six. The Supreme Court has held that the use of a six-member jury in a criminal case does not violate a defendant's right to a jury trial under the Sixth Amendment. The Supreme Court recognized that there was no observable difference between the results reached by a jury of twelve or by a jury of six, nor was there any evidence to suggest that a jury of twelve is more advantageous to a defendant. The jury needs only to be large enough "to promote group deliberation, free from outside attempts at intimidation, and to provide a fair possibility for obtaining a representative cross section of the community." Moreover, State court jury verdicts need not be unanimous provided the vote is sufficient to assure adequate deliberations. Thus, the Supreme Court has upheld jury votes of 11–1, 10–2, and 9–3 but rejected as insufficient a 5–1 vote.

CHAPTER SUMMARY

Nature of Crimes	**Definition** any act or omission forbidden by public law

Nature of Crimes

Definition   any act or omission forbidden by public law

Essential Elements

- ■ *Actus Reus*   wrongful or overt act
- ■ *Mens Rea*   criminal intent

Classification

- ■ *Felonies*   serious crimes
- ■ *Misdemeanors*   less serious crimes
- ■ *Petty Crimes*   misdemeanors punishable by imprisonment of 6 months or less

White-Collar Crime   nonviolent crime involving deceit, corruption, or breach of trust

- ■ *Liability of an Employer*   vicariously liable for acts of his or her employees if the employer directed, participated in, or approved of the acts
- ■ *Liability of a Corporation*   under certain circumstances may be convicted of crimes and punished by fines
- ■ *Computer Crime*   use of a computer to commit a crime
- ■ *RICO*   Federal law intended to stop organized crime from infiltrating legitimate businesses

Offenses against Property

Larceny   trespassory taking and carrying away of personal property of another with the intent to deprive the victim permanently of the property

Embezzlement   taking of another's property by a person who was in lawful possession of the property

False Pretenses   obtaining title to property of another by means of materially false representations of fact, with knowledge of their falsity, and made with intent to defraud

Robbery   committing larceny with the use of force or threat of force

Extortion   the making of threats to obtain money or property

Bribery   offering money or property to a public official to influence the official's decision

Burglary   under most modern statutes, an entry into a building with the intent to commit a felony

Forgery   intentional falsification of a document in order to defraud

Bad Checks   knowingly issuing a check without sufficient funds to cover the check

Criminal Defenses

Defense of Person or Property

- ■ *Self-Defense*   right to use reasonable force to protect oneself if he reasonably believes that he is in immediate danger
- ■ *Defense of Another*   right to use reasonable force in defense of another provided she reasonably believes the other to be in immediate danger
- ■ *Defense of Property*   right to use reasonable but not deadly force to protect property

Incapacity
- ■ *Insanity* traditional test is the *M'Naghten* test: a person is not criminally liable if at the time of committing the act he could not distinguish right from wrong
- ■ *Infancy* a child under the age of seven is conclusively presumed to be incapable of committing a crime; between seven and fourteen there is a rebuttable presumption that the child is incapable; and over fourteen there is a rebuttable presumption of capability
- ■ *Intoxication* most states permit involuntary intoxication as a defense

Other Defenses
- ■ *Duress* coercion by threat of serious bodily harm is a defense to criminal conduct other than murder
- ■ *Mistake of Fact* honest and reasonable belief that conduct is not criminal is a defense
- ■ *Entrapment* inducement by a law enforcement official to commit a crime is a defense

Criminal Procedure	**Steps in Criminal Prosecution** generally include arrest, booking, formal notice of charges, preliminary hearing to determine probable cause, indictment or information, arraignment, and trial
	Fourth Amendment protects individuals against unreasonable searches and seizures
	Fifth Amendment protects persons against self-incrimination, double jeopardy, and being charged with a capital crime except by grand jury indictment
	Sixth Amendment provides the accused with the right to a speedy and public trial, the opportunity to confront witnesses, process for obtaining witnesses, and the right to counsel

QUESTIONS

1. Discuss criminal intent and the various degrees of mental fault.
2. List and define the eight offenses against property.
3. Identify the significant features of white-collar crimes.
4. List and explain the constitutional amendments affecting criminal procedure.
5. Discuss the defense of criminal insanity and the various tests employed.

PROBLEMS

1. Sam said to Carol, "Kim is going to sell me a good used car next Monday and then I'll deliver it to you in exchange for your microcomputer, but I'd like to have the computer now." Relying on this statement, Carol delivered the computer to Sam. Sam knew Kim had no car, would have none in the future, and had no such arrangement with Kim. The appointed time of exchange passed, and Sam failed to deliver the car to Carol. Has a crime been committed? Discuss.

2. Sara, a lawyer, drew a deed for Robert by which Robert was to convey land to Rick. The deed was correct in every detail. Robert examined and verbally approved it but did not sign it. Sara erased Rick's name and substituted her own. Robert signed the deed with all required legal formalities without noticing the change. Was Sara guilty of forgery? Discuss.

3. Ann took Bonnie's watch before Bonnie was aware of the theft. Bonnie discovered her loss immediately and pursued Ann. Ann pointed a loaded pistol at Bonnie, who, in fear of being shot, allowed Ann to escape. Was Ann guilty of robbery? Of any other crime?

4. Jones and Wilson were on trial, separately, for larceny of a $1,000 bearer bond (payable to the holder of the bond not a named individual) issued by Brown, Inc. The Commonwealth's evidence showed that the owner of the bond had dropped it accidentally in the street enclosed in an envelope bearing his name and

address; that Jones found the envelope with the bond in it; that Jones could neither read nor write; that Jones presented the envelope and bond to Wilson, an educated man, and asked Wilson what he should do with it; that Wilson told Jones that the finder of lost property becomes the owner of it; that Wilson told Jones that the bond was worth $100 but that the money could only be collected at the issuer's home office; that Jones then handed the bond to Wilson, who redeemed it at the corporation's home office and received $1,000; that Wilson gave Jones $100 of the proceeds. What rulings?

5. Truck drivers for a hauling company, while loading a desk, found a $100 bill that fell out of the desk. They agreed to get it exchanged for small bills and divide the proceeds. En route to a bank, one of them changed his mind and refused to proceed with the scheme, whereupon the other pulled a knife and demanded the bill. A police officer intervened. It turned out that the bill was counterfeit money. What crimes have been committed?

6. William was judged legally insane and committed as an inmate of a State hospital. Six months after his commitment he escaped and met his friend Roberta. After Roberta and William had several drinks of hard liquor, they rode to a liquor store in a car driven by William. In accordance with a previous plan William waited in the car while Roberta held up the proprietor of the liquor store. William and Roberta were later apprehended and are now being prosecuted for robbery. William pleaded not guilty by reason of insanity and intoxication and on the further ground that he did not enter the building or receive any part of the stolen property. Discuss and decide.

7. Peter, an undercover police agent, was trying to locate a laboratory where it was believed that methamphetamine or "speed"—a controlled substance—was being manufactured illegally. Peter went to Mary's home and said that he represented a large organization that was interested in obtaining methamphetamine. Peter offered to supply a necessary ingredient for the manufacture of the drug, which was very difficult to obtain, in return for one-half of the drug produced. Mary agreed and processed the chemical given to her by Peter in Peter's presence. Later Peter returned with a search warrant and arrested Mary. Mary was charged with various narcotics law violations. Mary asserted the defense of entrapment. Decision?

8. The police obtained a search warrant based on an affidavit that contained the following allegations: (a) Donald was seen crossing a State line on four occasions during a five-day period and going to a particular apartment; (b) telephone records disclosed that the apartment had two telephones; (c) Donald had a reputation as a bookmaker and as an associate of gamblers; and (d) the FBI was informed by a "confidential reliable informant" that Donald was conducting gambling operations. When a search was made based on the warrant, evidence was obtained that resulted in Donald's conviction of violating certain gambling laws. Donald challenged the constitutionality of the search warrant. Decision?

9. A national bank was robbed by a man with a small strip of tape on each side of his face. An indictment was returned against David. David was then arrested, and counsel appointed to represent him. Two weeks later, without notice to David's lawyer, an FBI agent arranged to have the two bank employees observe a lineup, including David and five or six other prisoners. Each person in the lineup wore strips of tape, as had the robber, and each was directed to repeat the words "Put the money in the bag," as had the robber. Both of the bank employees identified David as the robber. At David's trial he was again identified by the two, in the courtroom, and the prior lineup identification was elicited on cross-examination by David's counsel. David's counsel moved the court either to grant a judgment of acquittal or alternatively to strike the courtroom identifications on the grounds that the lineup had violated David's Fifth Amendment privilege against self-incrimination and his Sixth Amendment right to counsel. Decision?

10. Waronek owned and operated a trucking rig, transporting goods for L.T.L. Perishables, Inc., of St. Paul, Minnesota. He accepted an offer to haul a trailer load of beef from Illini Beef Packers, Inc., in Joslin, Illinois, to Midtown Packing Company in New York City. After his truck was loaded with ninety-five forequarters and ninety-five hindquarters of beef in Joslin, Waronek drove north to his home in Watertown, Wisconsin, rather than east to New York. While in Watertown, he asked employees of the Royal Meat Company to butcher and prepare four hindquarters of beef—two for himself and two for his friends. He also offered to sell ten hindquarters to one employee of the company at an alarmingly reduced rate. The suspicious employee contacted the authorities, who told him to proceed with the deal. When Waronek arrived in New York with his load short nineteen hindquarters, Waronek telephoned L.T.L. Perishables in St. Paul. He notified them "that he was short nineteen hindquarters, that he knew where the beef went, and that he would make good on it out of future settlements." L.T.L. told him to contact the New York police but he failed to do so. Shortly thereafter, he was arrested by the Federal Bureau of Investigation and indicted for the embezzlement of goods moving in interstate commerce. Decision?

5 INTENTIONAL TORTS

All forms of civil liability are either (1) voluntarily assumed, as by contract, or (2) involuntarily imposed by law. Tort liability is of the second type. **Tort** law gives persons relief from civil wrongs or injuries to their person, property, and economic interests. Thus, the law of torts reallocates losses caused by human misconduct. In general, a tort is committed when (1) a duty owing by one person to another (2) is breached and (3) proximately causes (4) injury or damage to the owner of a legally protected interest.

Each person is legally responsible for the damages that are proximately caused by his tortious conduct. Moreover, as we discuss in Chapter 28, businesses that employ agents to conduct their business activities are also liable for the torts committed by their agents in the course of employment. The tort liability of employers makes the study of tort law essential to business managers.

In a tort action, the injured party *sues* to recover *compensation* for the damage and injury sustained as a result of the defendant's wrongful conduct. The purpose of tort law is to compensate the injured party, not to punish the wrongdoer as in the case of criminal law.

Of course, the same conduct may, and often does, constitute both a crime and a tort. An example is an assault and battery committed by A against B. For the commission of this crime, the State may take appropriate action against A. In addition, A has violated B's right to be secure in his person, and so has committed a tort against B. B, regardless of the criminal action by the State against A, may bring a civil tort action against A for damages. But an act may be criminal without being tortious; by the same token, an act may be a tort but not a crime. The closest that tort law comes to an implementation of the objectives of the criminal law is in certain cases where courts may award exemplary or **punitive damages.** Where the defendant's tortious conduct has been intentional and deliberate, showing malice or a fraudulent or evil motive, many courts permit a jury to award damages over and above the amount necessary to compensate the plaintiff. The allowance of punitive damages is designed to punish and make an example of the defendant and thus deter others from similar conduct.[1]

Harms or injuries may be inflicted (1) intentionally, (2) negligently, or (3) without fault (strict liability). We discuss intentional torts in this chapter and cover negligence and strict liability in Chapter 6.

Tort law is primarily common law, and as we mentioned in Chapter 1, the Restatements, prepared by the American Law Institute, give an orderly presentation of many important areas of the common law, including torts. Although they are not law by themselves, they are highly persuasive in the courts. The first Restatement of Torts was adopted by the American Law Institute from 1934 to 1939. Since then, it has served as a vital force in shaping the law of torts. Between 1965 and 1978 the institute adopted a revised edition of the Restatement of Torts, which takes the place of the First Restatement. The revised Restatement will be referred to simply as the Restatement.

INTENT

Intent, as used in tort law, does not require a hostile or evil motive. Rather, it means that the actor desires to cause the consequences of his act *or* that he believes the consequences are substantially (almost) certain to result from it.[2] The following examples should help you understand the definition of intent: (1) If Mark fires a gun in the middle of the Mojave Desert, he intends to fire the gun, but when the bullet hits Steven, who is in the desert without Mark's knowledge, Mark does not intend that result. (2) Mark throws a bomb into Steven's office in order to kill Steven. Mark knows that Carol is in Steven's office and that the bomb is substantially certain to injure Carol, although Mark has no desire to do so. Mark is, nonetheless, liable to Carol for any injury caused Carol. Mark's intent to injure Steven is *transferred* to Carol.

Infants (persons who have not reached the age of majority) are held liable for their intentional torts. The infant's age and knowledge, however, are critical in determining whether the infant had sufficient intelligence to form the required intent. Incompetents, like infants, are generally held liable for their intentional torts.

INJURY OR DAMAGE TO THE PERSON

The most common intentional torts involve an interference with personal rights. They include battery, assault, false imprisonment, infliction of emotional distress, defamation, and invasion of privacy. We discuss these torts in that order.

Battery

Battery is an intentional infliction of harmful or offensive bodily contact. It may cause serious injury, as a gunshot wound or a blow on the head with a club. Or it may cause little or no physical injury, such as knocking a hat off of a person's head or flicking a glove in another's face, as shown in *Fisher v. Carrousel Motor Hotel*. Bodily contact is offensive if it would offend a reasonable person's sense of dignity. Bodily contact may be accomplished by the use of objects, such as Gustav's throwing a rock at Hester with the intention of hitting her. If the rock hits Hester or any other person, Gustav has committed a battery.

FISHER v. CARROUSEL MOTOR HOTEL, INC.
Supreme Court of Texas, 1967.
424 S.W.2d 627.

Facts: Fisher, a black man, attended a business meeting held at the Carrousel Motor Hotel. The meeting included a buffet luncheon. While he stood in the buffet line, a hotel employee approached Fisher and snatched the plate from his hand, shouting that no Negro could be served in the hotel. Fisher was not actually touched by the employee nor was he in apprehension of physical injury, but he was highly embarrassed by the incident, which occurred in the presence of his business associates. He brought an action for battery against Carrousel based on the employee's conduct, seeking to recover actual damages for his humiliation and indignity plus punitive damages.

Decision: Judgment for Fisher.

Opinion: Greenhill, J. Under the facts of this case, we have no difficulty in holding that the intentional grabbing of plaintiff's plate constituted a battery. The intentional snatching of an object from one's hand is as clearly an offensive invasion of his person as would be an actual contact with the body. "To constitute an assault and battery, it is not necessary to touch the plaintiff's body or even his clothing; knocking or snatching anything from plaintiff's hand or touching anything connected with his person, when done in an offensive manner, is sufficient." [Citation.]

Such holding is not unique to the jurisprudence of this State. In [citation] the defendant was held to have committed "an assault or trespass upon the person" by snatching a book from the plaintiff's hand. The jury findings in that case were that the defendant "dispossessed plaintiff of the book" and caused her to suffer "humiliation and indignity."

The rationale for holding an offensive contact with such an object to be a battery is explained in 1 Restatement of Torts 2d § 18 (Comment p. 31) as follows.

"Since the essence of the plaintiff's grievance consists in the offense to the dignity involved in the unpermitted and intentional invasion of the inviolability of his person and not in any physical harm done to his body, it is not necessary that the plaintiff's actual body be disturbed. Unpermitted and intentional contacts with anything so connected with the body as to be customarily regarded as part of the other's person and therefore as partaking of its inviolability is actionable as an offensive contact with his person. There are some things such as clothing or a cane or, indeed, anything directly grasped by the hand which are so intimately connected with one's body as to be universally regarded as part of the person."

We hold, therefore, that the forceful dispossession of plaintiff Fisher's plate in an offensive manner was sufficient to constitute a battery. * * *

Damages for mental suffering are recoverable without the necessity for showing actual physical injury in a case of willful battery because the basis of that action is the unpermitted and intentional invasion of the plaintiff's person and not the actual harm done to the plaintiff's body. Restatement of Torts 2d § 18. Personal indignity is the essence of an action for battery; and consequently the defendant is liable not only for contacts which do actual physical harm, but also for those which are offensive and insulting. [Citations]. We hold, therefore, that plaintiff was entitled to actual damages for mental suffering due to the willful battery, even in the absence of any physical injury.

Assault

Assault is intentional conduct by one person directed at another that places him in apprehension of immediate bodily harm or offensive contact. It is usually committed immediately before a battery, but if the intended battery fails, the assault remains. Assault is essentially a mental rather than a physical intrusion. Accordingly, damages for it may include compensation for fright and humiliation. The person in danger of immediate bodily harm must have *knowledge* of the danger and be apprehensive of its imminent threat to his safety. For example, Ada aims a loaded gun at Bryan's back but is subdued by Charles before Bryan becomes aware of the danger. Ada has not committed an assault on Bryan.

False Imprisonment

The tort of **false imprisonment** or *false arrest* is the intentional confining of a person against her will within fixed boundaries if the person is conscious of the confinement or harmed by it. The restraint may be brought about by physical force, the threat of physical force, or by force directed against a person's property. As in the *Peterson* case, merely obstructing a person's freedom of movement is not false imprisonment so long as there is a reasonable alternative exit available.

Merchants occasionally have a problem with potential liability for false imprisonment when they seek to question a suspected shoplifter. If the merchant detains an innocent person, she may face a lawsuit for false imprisonment. Most States have statutes protecting the merchant, provided she detains the suspect in a reasonable manner, for not more than a reasonable time, and with probable cause.

PETERSON v. SORLIEN
Supreme Court of Minnesota, 1980.
299 N.W.2d 123.

Facts: Susan Jungclaus Peterson was a twenty-one-year-old student at Moorehead State College who had lived most of her life on her family farm in Minnesota. A dean's list student during her first year, her academic performance declined after she became deeply involved in an international religious cult organization known locally as The Way of Minnesota, Inc. The cult demanded an enormous psychological and monetary commitment from Susan. Near the end of her junior year, her parents became alarmed by the changes in Susan's physical and mental well-being and concluded that she had been "reduced to a condition of psychological bondage by The Way." They sought help from Kathy Mills, a self-styled "deprogrammer" of minds brainwashed by cults.

On May 24, 1976, Norman Jungclaus, Susan's father, picked up Susan from Moorehead State. Instead of returning home, they went to the residence of Veronica Morgel, where Kathy Mills attempted to deprogram Susan. For the first few days of her stay, Susan was unwilling to discuss her involvement. She lay curled in a fetal position in her bedroom, plugging her ears and hysterically screaming and crying while her father pleaded with her to listen. By the third day, however, Susan's demeanor changed completely. She became friendly and vivacious and communicated with her father. Susan also went roller skating and played softball at a nearby park over the following weekend. She spent the next week in Columbus, Ohio, with a former cult member who had shared her experiences of the previous week. While in Columbus, she spoke daily by telephone with her fiance, a member of The Way, who begged her to return to the cult. Susan expressed the desire to get her fiance out of the organization, but a meeting between them could not be arranged outside the presence of other members of The Way. Her parents attempted to persuade Susan to sign an agreement releasing them from liability for their actions but Susan refused. After nearly sixteen days of "deprogramming" Susan left the Morgel residence and returned to her fiance and The Way. Upon the direction of The Way ministry, she brought this action against her parents for false imprisonment. Susan appealed from the trial court's judgment in favor of her parents.

Decision: Judgment for Mr. and Mrs. Jungclaus affirmed.

Opinion: Sheran, C. J.   * * * this case marks the emergence of a new cultural phenomenon: youth-oriented religious or pseudo-religious groups which utilize the techniques of what has been termed "coercive persuasion" or "mind control" to cultivate an uncritical and devoted following. Commentators have used the term "coercive persuasion," originally coined to identify the experience of American prisoners of war during the Korean conflict to describe the cult-induction process. * * * Coercive persuasion is fostered through the creation of a controlled environment that heightens the susceptibility of a subject to suggestion and manipulation through sensory deprivation, physiological depletion, cognitive dissonance, peer pressure, and a clear assertion of authority and dominion. The aftermath of indoctrination is a severe impairment of autonomy and the ability to think independently, which induces a subject's unyielding compliance and the rupture of past connections, affiliations and associations. [Citation.] One psychologist characterized the process of cult indoctrination as "psychological kidnapping." [Citation.]

The period in question began on Monday, May 24, 1976, and ceased on Wednesday, June 9, 1976, a period of 16 days. The record clearly demonstrates that Susan willingly remained in the company of defendants for at least 13 of those days. * * * Had Susan desired, manifold opportunities existed for her to alert the authorities of her allegedly unlawful detention * * * At no time during the 13-day period did she complain of her treatment or suggest that defendants were holding her against her will. If one is aware of a reasonable means of escape that does not present a danger of bodily or material harm, a restriction is not total and complete and does not constitute unlawful imprisonment. Damages may not be assessed for any period of detention to which one freely consents. [Citations.]

* * *

* * * the behavior Susan manifested during the initial three days at issue must be considered in light of her actions in the remainder of the period. Because, it is argued, the cult conditioning process induces dramatic and non-consensual change giving rise to a new temporary identity on the part of the individuals whose consent is under examination, Susan's volitional capacity prior to treatment may well have been impaired. Following her readjustment, the evidence suggests that Susan was a different person, "like her old self." As such, the question of Susan's consent becomes a function of time. We therefore deem Susan's subsequent affirmation of defendants' actions dispositive.

* * *

* * * The facts in this case support the conclusion that plaintiff only regained her volitional capacity to consent after engaging in the first three days of the deprogramming process. As such, we hold that when parents, or their agents, acting under the conviction that the judgmental capacity of their adult child is impaired, seek to extricate that child from what they reasonably believe to be a religious or psuedo-religious cult, and the child at some juncture assents to the actions in question, limitations upon the child's mobility do not constitute meaningful deprivations of personal liberty sufficient to support a judgment for false imprisonment. * * *

Infliction of Emotional Distress

One of the more recently recognized torts is that of intentional **infliction of emotional distress.** One who by extreme and outrageous conduct intentionally or recklessly causes severe emotional distress to another is liable for such emotional distress as well as any resulting bodily harm.[3] As in *Agis v. Howard Johnson*, damages may be recovered for severe emotional distress even in the absence of any physical injury.

This cause of action does not protect a person from abusive language or rudeness but rather from atrocious, intolerable conduct beyond all bounds of decency. Examples of this tort include leading to a person's home, when he is present, a noisy demonstrating mob

AGIS v. HOWARD JOHNSON COMPANY

Supreme Judicial Court of Massachusetts, 1976.
371 Mass. 140, 355 N.E.2d 315.

Facts: Debra Agis was a waitress in a restaurant owned by the Howard Johnson
Company. On May 23, 1975, Roger Dionne, manager of the restaurant, called a
meeting of all waitresses at which he informed them that "there was some stealing
going on." Dionne also stated that the identity of the party or parties responsible
was not known and that he would begin firing all waitresses in alphabetical order
until the guilty party or parties were detected. He then fired Debra Agis, who
allegedly "became greatly upset, began to cry, sustained emotional distress, mental
anguish, and loss of wages and earnings." Mrs. Agis brought this complaint against
the Howard Johnson Company and Roger Dionne, alleging that the defendants
acted recklessly and outrageously, intending to cause emotional distress and
anguish. The defendants argued that damages for emotional distress are not
recoverable unless physical injury occurs as a result of the distress. The judge
dismissed the complaint, and Mrs. Agis appealed.

Decision: Judgment dismissing the complaint reversed.

Opinion: **Quirico, J.**   Our discussion of whether a cause of action exists for the
intentional or reckless infliction of severe emotional distress without resulting
bodily injury starts with our decision in *George v. Jordan Marsh Co.*, [citation.] While
in that case we found it unnecessary to address the precise question raised here, we
did summarize the history of actions for emotional distress and concluded that the
law of the Commonwealth should be, and is, "that one who, without a privilege to
do so, by extreme and outrageous conduct intentionally causes severe emotional
distress to another, with bodily harm resulting from such distress, is subject to
liability. . . ." [Citation.] The question whether such liability should be extended to
cases in which there is no resulting bodily injury was "left until it arises," and that
question has arisen here.

   In the *George* case, we discussed in depth the policy considerations underlying
the recognition of a cause of action for intentional infliction of severe emotional
distress with resulting physical injury, and we concluded that the difficulties
presented in allowing such an action were outweighed by the unfair and illogical
consequences of the denial of recognition of such an independent tort. In so doing,
we examined the persuasive authority then recognizing such a cause of action, and
we placed considerable reliance on the Restatement (Second) of Torts § 46 (1965).
Our examination of the policies underlying the extension of that cause of action to
cases where there has been no bodily injury, and our review of the judicial
precedent and the Restatement in this regard, lead us to conclude that such
extension is both warranted and desirable. [Citation.]

   The most often cited argument for refusing to extend the cause of action for
intentional or reckless infliction of emotional distress to cases where there has been
no physical injury is the difficulty of proof and the danger of fraudulent or frivolous
claims. There has been a concern that "mental anguish, standing alone, is too
subtle and speculative to be measured by any known legal standard," that "mental
anguish and its consequences are so intangible and peculiar and vary so much with
the individual that they cannot reasonably be anticipated," that a wide door might
"be opened not only to fictitious claims but to litigation over trivialities and mere
bad manners as well," and that there can be no objective measurement of the extent
or the existence of emotional distress. [Citation.]

While we are not unconcerned with these problems, we believe that "the problems presented are not . . . insuperable" and that "administrative difficulties do not justify the denial of relief for serious invasions of mental and emotional tranquility. . . ." [Citation.] "That some claims may be spurious should not compel those who administer justice to shut their eyes to serious wrongs and let them go without being brought to account. It is the function of courts and juries to determine whether claims are valid or false. This responsibility should not be shunned merely because the task may be difficult to perform." [Citations.]

Furthermore, the distinction between the difficulty which juries may encounter in determining liability and assessing damages where no physical injury occurs and their performance of that same task where there has been resulting physical harm may be greatly overstated. "The jury is ordinarily in a better position . . . to determine whether outrageous conduct results in mental distress than whether that distress in turn results in physical injury. From their own experience jurors are aware of the extent and character of the disagreeable emotions that may result from the defendant's conduct, but a difficult medical question is presented when it must be determined if emotional distress resulted in physical injury. . . . Greater proof that mental suffering occurred is found in the defendant's conduct designed to bring it about than in physical injury that may or may not have resulted therefrom."

* * *

In light of what we have said, we hold that one who, by extreme and outrageous conduct and without privilege, causes severe emotional distress to another is subject to liability for such emotional distress even though no bodily harm may result. However, in order for a plaintiff to prevail in a case for liability under this tort, four elements must be established. It must be shown (1) that the actor intended to inflict emotional distress or that he knew or should have known that emotional distress was the likely result of his conduct, Restatement (Second) of Torts § 46, comment i (1965); [citations]; (2) that the conduct was "extreme and outrageous," was "beyond all possible bounds of decency" and was "utterly intolerable in a civilized community," Restatement (Second) of Torts § 46, comment d (1965) [citation]; (3) that the actions of the defendant were the cause of the plaintiff's distress, [citations]; and (4) that the emotional distress sustained by the plaintiff was "severe" and of a nature "that no reasonable man could be expected to endure it." Restatement (Second) of Torts § 46, comment j (1965). [Citation.] These requirements are "aimed at limiting frivolous suits and avoiding litigation in situations where only bad manners and mere hurt feelings are involved," [citation], and we believe they are a "realistic safeguard against false claims. . . ." [Citation.]

Testing the plaintiff Debra Agis's complaint by the rules stated above, we hold that she makes out a cause of action and that her complaint is therefore legally sufficient.

yelling threats to lynch him unless he leaves town, or placing a rattlesnake in another's bed as a practical joke.

Defamation

The tort of **defamation** is a false communication that injures a person's reputation by dis-gracing him and diminishing the respect in which he is held. An example would be the publication of a statement that a person had committed a crime or had a loathsome disease.

If the defamatory communication is hand-written, typewritten, printed, pictorial, or in any other form with similar communicative power, such as television or radio, it is designated **libel.** If it is spoken or oral, it is designated **slander.** In either case it must be communicated to a person or persons other than the one who is defamed. This is referred to as its *publication.* Thus, if Maurice writes a defamatory letter about Pierre's character that he hands or mails to Pierre, this is not a publication because it is intended only for Pierre.

A new and significant trend affecting business has been the bringing of defamation suits against former employers by discharged employees. It has been reported that such suits comprise approximately one-third of all defamation lawsuits. The following case demonstrates the consequences of failing to be careful in discharging an employee.

FRANK B. HALL & CO., INC. v. BUCK
Court of Appeals of Texas, Fourteenth District, 1984.
678 S.W.2d 612.

Facts: On June 1, 1976, Larry W. Buck, an established salesman in the insurance business, began working for Frank B. Hall & Co. In the course of the ensuing months, Buck brought several major accounts to Hall and produced substantial commission income for the firm. In October 1976 Mendel Kaliff, then president of Frank B. Hall & Co. of Texas, informed Buck that his salary and benefits were being reduced because of his failure to generate sufficient income for the firm. On March 31, 1977, Kaliff and Lester Eckert, Hall's office manager, fired Buck. Buck was unable to procure subsequent employment with another insurance firm. He hired an investigator, Lloyd Barber, to discover the true reasons for his dismissal and for his inability to find other employment.

Barber contacted Kaliff, Eckert, and Virginia Hilley, a Hall employee, and told them he was an investigator and was seeking information about Buck's employment with the firm. Barber conducted tape-recorded interviews with the three in September and October of 1977. Kaliff accused Buck of being disruptive, untrustworthy, paranoid, hostile, untruthful, and of padding his expense account. Eckert referred to Buck as "a zero" and a "classical sociopath" who was ruthless, irrational, and disliked by other employees. Hilley stated that Buck could have been charged with theft for certain materials he brought with him from his former employer to Hall. Buck sued Hall for damages for defamation and was awarded over $1.9 million by a jury—$605,000 for actual damages and $1,300,000 for punitive damages. Hall then brought this appeal.

Decision: Judgment for Buck affirmed.

Opinion: Junell, J. Any act wherein the defamatory matter is intentionally or negligently communicated to a third person is a publication. In the case of slander, the act is usually the speaking of the words. Restatement (Second) Torts § 577 comment a (1977). There is ample support in the record to show that these individuals intentionally communicated disparaging remarks to a third person. The jury was instructed that "Publication means to communicate defamatory words to some third person in such a way that he understands the words to be defamatory. A statement is not published if it was authorized, invited or procured by Buck and if Buck knew in advance the contents of the invited communication." In response to special issues, the jury found that the slanderous statements were made and published to Barber.

Hall argues that Buck could and should have expected Hall's employees to give their opinion of Buck when requested to do so. Hall is correct in stating that a

PART 1   THE LEGAL ENVIRONMENT OF BUSINESS

plaintiff may not recover for a publication to which he has consented, or which he has authorized, procured or invited, [citation]; and it may be true that Buck could assume that Hall's employees would give their opinion when asked they do so. However, there is nothing in the record to indicate that Buck knew Hall's employees would defame him when Barber made the inquiries. The accusations made by Kaliff, Eckert and Hilley were not mere expressions of opinion but were false and derogatory statements of fact.

* * *

A defamer cannot escape liability by showing that, although he desired to defame the plaintiff, he did not desire to defame him to the person to whom he in fact intentionally published the defamatory communication. The publication is complete although the publisher is mistaken as to the identity of the person to whom the publication is made. Restatement (Second) of Torts § 577 comment 1 (1977). Likewise, communication to an agent of the person defamed is a publication, unless the communication is invited by the person defamed or his agent. Restatement s 577 comment e. We have already determined that the evidence is sufficient to show that Buck did not know what Kaliff, Eckert or Hilley would say and that he did not procure the defamatory statements to create a lawsuit. Thus, the fact that Barber may have been acting at Buck's request is not fatal to Buck's cause of action. There is absolutely no proof that Barber induced Kaliff, Eckert or Hilley to make any of the defamatory comments.

* * *

When an ambiguity exists, a fact issue is presented. The court, by submission of proper fact issues, should let the jury render its verdict on whether the statements were fairly susceptible to the construction placed thereon by the plaintiff. [Citation.] Here, the jury found (1) Eckert made a statement calculated to convey that Buck had been terminated because of serious misconduct; (2) the statement was slanderous or libelous; (3) the statement was made with malice; (4) the statement was published; and (5) damage directly resulted from the statement. The jury also found the statements were not substantially true. The jury thus determined that these statements, which were capable of a defamatory meaning, were understood as such by Barber.

* * *

We hold that the evidence supports the award of actual damages and the amount awarded is not manifestly unjust. Furthermore, in responding to the issue on exemplary damages, the jury was instructed that exemplary damages must be based on a finding that Hall "acted with ill will, bad intent, malice or gross disregard to the rights of Buck." Although there is no fixed ratio between exemplary and actual damages, exemplary damages must be reasonably apportioned to the actual damages sustained. [Citation.] Because of the actual damages [$605,000] and the abundant evidence of malice, we hold that the award of punitive damages [$1,300,000] was not unreasonable. . . .

Truth and privilege are complete defenses to defamation. In most States, **truth** is a complete defense no matter what the purpose or intent in publishing the defamation. **Privilege** is an immunity from tort liability granted when the defendant's conduct furthers a societal interest of greater importance than the injury inflicted upon the plaintiff. There are three kinds of privileges that apply to defamation: absolute, conditional, and constitutional.

As with the defense of truth, **absolute privilege** protects the defendant regardless of his motive or intent. Absolute privilege has been confined to those few situations where public policy clearly favors complete freedom of speech and includes: (1) statements made during a judicial proceeding; (2) statements made by members of Congress on the floor of Congress; (3) statements made by certain executive officers while performing their governmental duty; and (4) statements made between spouses when they are alone.

Qualified or **conditional privilege** depends on proper use of the privilege. A person has conditional privilege to publish defamatory matter to protect his own legitimate interests, or in some cases the interests of another. Conditional privilege also extends to many cases where the publisher and the recipient have a common interest, as with letters of reference. Conditional privilege, however, is forfeited by the publisher if she acts in an excessive manner, without probable cause, or for an improper purpose.

The First Amendment to the U.S. Constitution guarantees freedom of speech and freedom of the press. The courts have applied these rights to the law of defamation by extending a form of **constitutional privilege** to comment about public officials or public figures so long as it is done without *malice*. For these purposes, "malice" is not ill will but proof of the publisher's knowledge of falsity or reckless disregard of the truth.[4] Thus, under constitutional privilege the public official or public figure must prove that the defendant published the defamatory and false comment with knowledge or in reckless disregard of the comment's falsity and its defamatory character. In a defamation suit brought by a private person (one who is not a public official and is not a public figure) against a member of the news media, the plaintiff must prove that the defendant published the defamatory and false comment with malice *or* negligence. Where a private person brings suit against a defendant who is *not* a member of the news media, it is currently unresolved whether the plaintiff

must prove anything beyond the fact that a defamatory statement had been made. See Law in the News on page 110.

Invasion of Privacy

The invasion of a person's right to privacy actually consists of four distinct torts: (1) appropriation of a person's name or likeness; (2) unreasonable intrusion on the seclusion of another; (3) unreasonable public disclosure of private facts; (4) unreasonable publicity that places another in a false light in the public eye.

It is entirely possible and not uncommon for a person's right of privacy to be invaded in such a way that two or more of these related torts are committed. For example, Bart forces his way into Cindy's hospital room, takes a photograph of Cindy, and publishes it to promote Bart's cure for Cindy's illness along with false statements about Cindy that would be highly objectionable to a reasonable person. Cindy would be entitled to recover on any or all of the four torts comprising invasion of privacy.

Appropriation Appropriation is the use of another person's name or likeness for one's own benefit, as for example in promoting or advertising a product or service.[5] The tort of appropriation seeks to protect the individual's right to the exclusive use of his identity and is also known as the "right of publicity." In the example above, Bart's use of Cindy's photograph to promote Bart's business constitutes the tort of appropriation. The following case involving Johnny Carson also is an example of appropriation.

Intrusion Intrusion is the unreasonable and highly offensive interference with the solitude or seclusion of another.[6] Such unreasonable interference includes improper entry into another's dwelling, unauthorized eavesdropping on another's private conversations, and unauthorized examination of another's private papers and records. The intrusion must be offensive or objectionable to a reasonable person and must involve private matters. Thus, there is no liability if the defendant examines public

CARSON v. HERE'S JOHNNY PORTABLE TOILETS, INC.
United States Court of Appeals, Sixth Circuit, 1983.
698 F.2d 831.

Facts: Plaintiff, John W. Carson, is the host and star of "The Tonight Show," a well-known television program broadcast by the National Broadcasting Company. Carson also appears as an entertainer in night clubs and theaters around the country. From the time he began hosting "The Tonight Show" in 1962, he has been introduced on the show each night with the phrase "Here's Johnny." The phrase "Here's Johnny" is generally associated with Carson by a substantial segment of the television viewing public. In 1967 Carson began authorizing use of this phrase by outside business ventures.

Defendant, Here's Johnny Portable Toilets, Inc., is a Michigan corporation engaged in the business of renting and selling "Here's Johnny" portable toilets. Defendant's founder was aware at the time he formed the corporation that "Here's Johnny" was the introductory slogan for Carson on "The Tonight Show." He indicated that he coupled the phrase with a second one, "The World's Foremost Commodian," to make "a good play on a phrase." Carson brought suit for invasion of privacy. The trial court dismissed Carson's claim and he appealed.

Decision: Judgment of trial court reversed.

Opinion: **Brown, J.** In an influential article, Dean Prosser delineated four distinct types of the right of privacy: (1) intrusion upon one's seclusion or solitude, (2) public disclosure of embarrassing private facts, (3) publicity which places one in a false light, and (4) appropriation of one's name or likeness for the defendant's advantage. Prosser, *Privacy*, 48 Calif.L.Rev. 383, 389 (1964). This fourth type has become known as the "right of publicity." [Citations.] Henceforth we will refer to Prosser's last, or fourth, category as the "right of publicity."

* * *

The right of publicity has developed to protect the commercial interest of celebrities in their identities. The theory of the right is that a celebrity's identity can be valuable in the promotion of products, and the celebrity has an interest that may be protected from the unauthorized commercial exploitation of that identity. In [citation], we stated: "The famous have an exclusive legal right during life to control and profit from the commercial use of their name and personality." [Citation.]

The district court dismissed appellants' claim based on the right of publicity because appellee does not use Carson's name or likeness. [Citation.] It held that it "would not be prudent to allow recovery for a right of publicity claim which does not more specifically identify Johnny Carson." [Citation.] We believe that, on the contrary, the district court's conception of the right of publicity is too narrow. The right of publicity, as we have stated, is that a celebrity has a protected pecuniary interest in the commercial exploitation of his identity. If the celebrity's identity is commercially exploited, there has been an invasion of his right whether or not his "name or likeness" is used. Carson's identity may be exploited even if his name, John W. Carson, or his picture is not used.

In *Motschenbacher v. R. J. Reynolds Tobbaco Co.*, [citation], the court held that the unauthorized use of a picture of a distinctive race car of a well known professional race car driver, whose name or likeness were not used, violated his right of publicity. * * *

> In *Ali v. Playgirl, Inc.*, [citation], Muhammad Ali, former heavyweight champion, sued Playgirl magazine under the New York "right of privacy" statute and also alleged a violation of his common law right of publicity. The magazine published a drawing of a nude, black male sitting on a stool in a corner of a boxing ring with hands taped and arms outstretched on the ropes. The district court concluded that Ali's right of publicity was invaded because the drawing sufficiently identified him in spite of the fact that the drawing was captioned "Mystery Man." The district court found that the identification of Ali was made certain because of an accompanying verse that identified the figure as "The Greatest." The district court took judicial notice of the fact that "Ali has regularly claimed that appellation for himself." [Citation.]
>
> * * *
>
> In this case, Earl Braxton, president and owner of Here's Johnny Portable Toilets, Inc., admitted that he knew that the phrase "Here's Johnny" had been used for years to introduce Carson. * * *
>
> * * *
>
> * * * It is our view that, under the existing authorities, a celebrity's legal right of publicity is invaded whenever his identity is intentionally appropriated for commercial purposes. * * * It is not fatal to appellant's claim that appellee did not use his "name." Indeed, there would have been no violation of his right of publicity even if appellee had used his name, such as "J. William Carson Portable Toilet" or the "John William Carson Portable Toilet" or the "J. W. Carson Portable Toilet." The reason is that, though literally using appellant's "name," the appellee would not have appropriated Carson's identity as a celebrity. Here there was an appropriation of Carson's identity without using his "name."

records or observes the plaintiff in a public place. This form of invasion of privacy is committed once the intrusion occurs—publicity is not required.

Public Disclosure of Private Facts   The law of privacy imposes liability for offensive *publicity* given to private information about another, or **public disclosure of private facts.** As with intrusion, this tort applies only to private, not public, information about an individual, but unlike intrusion it requires publicity. The publicity required differs in degree from "publication" as used in the law of defamation. Under this tort the private facts must be communicated to the public at large or become public knowledge, whereas publication of a defamatory statement need only be made to a single third party. Thus Kathy, a creditor of Gary, will not invade Gary's privacy by writing a letter to Gary's employer informing the employer of Gary's failure to pay the debt, but Kathy would be liable if she posted in the window of her store a statement that Gary will not pay a debt owed to Kathy. Also unlike defamation, this tort applies to truthful private information if the matter published would be offensive and objectionable to a reasonable person of ordinary sensibilities.

False Light   This invasion of privacy imposes liability for highly offensive *publicity* placing another in a **false light** if the defendant *knew* that the matter publicized was false or acted in *reckless disregard* of the truth.[7] For example, Edgar includes Jason's name and photograph in a public "rogues' gallery" of convicted criminals. Jason has never been convicted of any crime. Edgar is liable to Jason for placing him in a false light.

Taking the Peril Out of Parody
In Falwell v. Flynt, the First Amendment Won

No one ever accused *Hustler* of good taste. Even so, it would require a tough hide not to be offended by the ad parody that it first ran in 1983. Taking off on a Campari Liqueur campaign that featured celebrities reminiscing about their "first time"—with the drink, that is—*Hustler* ran a spoof that portrayed the Rev. Jerry Falwell as a drunkard whose first sexual encounter was a tryst with his mother in an outhouse. Outrageous? Yes. Funny? Hardly. Plausible? No. But just in case, small print at the foot of the page warned the less discerning reader, "Ad parody—not to be taken seriously."

Falwell took it very seriously. He sued the X-rated magazine and Publisher Larry Flynt for $45 million, charging them with invasion of privacy, libel and intentional infliction of emotional distress. In 1984 his privacy claim was thrown out by a federal judge, and a jury found no libel, believing no reasonable person could think that the spoof was being presented as factual. But the jury agreed with Falwell's complaint about emotional distress and awarded the televangelist $200,000. Despite the novelty of the verdict, an appeal court upheld the judgment. The jury's award to Falwell set off alarm bells among journalists, political cartoonists, comedians—anyone who might poke fun at public figures.

They can rest easier now. Last week the U.S. Supreme Court unanimously rejected Falwell's argument in terms that decisively reaffirmed First Amendment protections. Falwell had argued that "outrageous" parody like *Hustler's* should not be given the protection that more conventional satire and cartooning deserved. But while acknowledging that the ad was "gross and repugnant in the eyes of most," Chief Justice William Rehnquist

said for the court that to define and penalize the outrageous would require some very fine judgments, allowing jurors to award damages on the basis of their personal taste or "their dislike of a particular expression." Protecting vulgar parody may not be a pretty task, said Rehnquist, but it has to be done to give the First Amendment "breathing space."

The decision should also discourage a trend that has led plaintiffs who feel offended by the media to try to collect damages for injury—to their right of privacy, for instance, or their feelings—when they cannot make the more difficult case for libel. But the court said last week that even when public figures claim emotional injury, they still must meet the complex "actual malice" standard devised for libel in the landmark 1964 decision *New York Times Co. v. Sullivan*. In that case, the court said that a public figure must show that a publication knew its statements were false or had recklessly disregarded the possibility that they might be. Shot through as it was with unstinting references to *Sullivan*, last week's ruling should dampen speculation that the justices might be ready to reconsider that decision.

Falwell, of course, was none too happy. The court, he said, had "given the green light to Larry Flynt and his like to print what they wish about any public figure at any time with no fear of reprisal." Flynt, always a blunt instrument, has put it more inelegantly: "I think that the First Amendment gives me the right to be offensive." And, to protect more important things, it does.

By Richard Lacayo. Reported by Anne Constable/Washington Copyright 1988, Time, Inc. Reprinted by permission.

As with defamation, the matter must be untrue, but unlike defamation it must be "publicized," not merely "published." Although the matter must be objectionable to a reasonable person, it need not be defamatory. In many instances, the same facts will give rise to both an action for defamation and false light.

Defenses *Absolute*, *conditional*, and *constitutional* privilege apply to the same extent to the torts of disclosure of private facts and false light as they do to defamation.

The following case deals with both public disclosure of private facts and false light as well as with constitutional privilege.

KINSEY v. MACUR
Court of Appeals of California, First District, 1980.
107 Cal.App.3d 265, 165 Cal.Rptr. 608.

Facts: Bill Kinsey was charged with murdering his wife while working for the Peace Corps in Tanzania. After waiting six months in jail he was acquitted at a trial that attracted wide publicity. Five years later, while a graduate student at Stanford University, Kinsey had a brief affair with Mary Macur. He abruptly ended the affair by telling Macur he would no longer be seeing her because another woman, Sally Allen, was coming from England to live with him. A few months later, Kinsey and Allen moved to Africa and were subsequently married. Soon after Bill ended their affair, Macur began a letter writing campaign designed to expose Bill and his mistreatment of her. Macur sent several letters to both Bill and Sally Kinsey, their former spouses, their parents, their neighbors, their parents' neighbors, members of Bill's dissertation committee, other faculty, and the president of Stanford University. The letters contained statements accusing Bill of murdering his first wife, spending six months in jail for the crime, being a rapist, and other questionable behavior. The Kinseys brought an action for invasion of privacy, seeking damages and a permanent injunction. Macur appeals from the trial court's judgment in favor of Kinsey.

Decision: Judgment for Kinsey affirmed.

Opinion: **Miller, J.** Courts now recognize four separate torts within the broad designation of "invasion of privacy": (1) the commercial appropriation of the plaintiff's name or likeness * * *; (2) intrusion upon the plaintiff's physical solitude or seclusion; (3) public disclosure of true embarrassing private facts concerning the plaintiff; and (4) publicity which places the plaintiff in a false light in the public eye. (Prosser, Law of Torts (4th ed., 1971) § 117, pp. 804–814.) In the present case, only the latter two forms of invasion of privacy are alleged.

As discussed in [citation], the concept of a legal right to privacy was first suggested in a now famous Harvard Law Review article by Warren and Brandeis, *The Right to Privacy* (1890) 4 Harv.L.Rev. 193. While they had difficulty tracing a common law basis for the right, Warren and Brandeis expressed the belief that it was mass exposure to the public gaze and not just backyard gossip which provided the raison d'être for the tort.

Subsequently, in discussing the right of privacy in the area of public disclosure of embarrassing private facts, Prosser stated: "The disclosure of the private facts must be a public disclosure, and not a private one; there must be, in other words, publicity." [Citation.]

Thus, except in cases involving physical intrusion, the tort must be accompanied by publicity in the sense of communication to the public in general or to a large number of persons as distinguished from one individual or a few. [Citation.] "The gravamen of the tort is unwarranted publication of intimate details of plaintiff's private life. [Citations.] The interest to be protected is individual freedom from the wrongful publicizing of private affairs and activities which are outside the realm of legitimate public concern. [Citations.]

Appellant first contends that her mailing of letters to "perhaps twenty [people] at most" was insufficient publicity to justify a finding that respondent's privacy had been invaded. Since these mailings were ostensibly to only a small select group of people, appellant argues that the requirement of mass exposure to the public as opposed to a few people has not been satisfied. Appellant's contention misstates the applicable law.

* * *

In the instant case, appellant, in her professed attempts to "tell the whole world what a bastard he is," sought to reach a large group of people whom she knew had nothing in common except the possible acquaintance of Bill Kinsey. * * * recipients of appellant Macur's letters comprised a diverse group of people living in several states and totally unconnected either socially or professionally. Recipients of her letters included the Kinseys, their former spouses, their parents, their neighbors, their parents' neighbors, members of Bill Kinsey's dissertation committee, other faculty and the President of Stanford University. Since this court believes these recipients adequately reflect "mass exposure" we decline to yield to appellant's claim of insufficient publicity. To do so, we conclude, would only emasculate the legal remedy available to individuals for the invasion of their privacy by another individual.

As the Supreme Court noted: "Men fear exposure not only to those closest to them; much of the outrage underlying the asserted right to privacy is a reaction to exposure to persons known only through business or other secondary relationships. The claim is not so much of total secrecy as it is the right to *define* one's circle of intimacy. . . ." [Citation.]

Under this standard, appellant clearly has violated Bill Kinsey's right of privacy. While it may be true that there is little to admire in Kinsey's treatment of appellant, this does not justify the harassment of Kinsey and his wife which followed.

* * *

Appellant next contends that, even if respondent's privacy had been invaded, the invasion was privileged since Kinsey was a public figure. This status, she contends, was achieved "by virtue of his entry into the Peace Corps and through his trial for the murder of his first wife." Given this "public figure" status, she asserts that she may exercise her constitutional privilege to disseminate critical material if done without malice. [Citation.] We disagree.

Contrary to appellant's assertion that "the definition of 'public figure' for the purposes of the qualified privilege to publish is not clearly defined," the United States Supreme Court opinion in the leading case of *Gertz v. Robert Welch, Inc.* [citation] is particularly instructive: "Hypothetically, it may be possible for someone to become a public figure through no purposeful action of his own, but the instances of truly involuntary public figures must be exceedingly rare. For the most part those who attain this status have assumed roles of especial prominence in the affairs of society. Some occupy positions of such persuasive power and influence that they are deemed public figures for all purposes. More commonly, those classified as public figures have thrust themselves to the forefront of particular public controversies in order to influence the resolution of the issues involved. In either event, they invite attention and comment." [Citation.]

Additionally, *Gertz* cautioned against lightly assuming ". . . that a citizen's participation in community and professional affairs rendered him a public figure for all purposes. . . . It is preferable to reduce the public-figure question to a more meaningful context by looking to the nature and extent of an individual's participation in the particular controversy. . . ." [Citation.]

> Under this standard, it is difficult to see how respondent could become a public figure simply because of his participation in the Peace Corps or his employment with the United Nations.
>
> With respect to Kinsey's notoriety by virtue of his trial, respondent was involuntarily thrust into the public limelight through the unfortunate death of his first wife. Offered the opportunity to be released on bail, he declined in favor of waiting some six months in jail for his trial at which time he was acquitted.

INTERFERENCE WITH PROPERTY RIGHTS

In addition to protecting against intentional interference with the person, the law also provides protection against invasions of a person's interests in property. Intentional interference with property rights includes the torts of (1) trespass to real property, (2) nuisance, (3) trespass to personal property, and (4) conversion.

Real Property

Real property is land and anything attached to it, such as buildings, trees, and minerals. The law protects the rights of the possessor of land to its exclusive use and quiet enjoyment.

Trespass   A person is liable for **trespass to real property** if he intentionally (1) enters or remains on land in the possession of another, (2) causes a thing or a third person to do so, or (3) fails to remove from the land a thing that he is under a duty to remove. Liability exists even though no actual damage is done to the land.

It is no defense that the intruder acted on the mistaken belief of law or fact that he was not trespassing. If the intruder intended to be on the particular property, it is irrelevant that he reasonably believed that he owned the land or had permission to enter on the land.[8] An intruder is not liable if his presence on the land of another is not caused by his own actions. For example, if Shirley is thrown onto Roy's land by Jimmy, Shirley is not liable to Roy for trespass, although Jimmy is.

A trespass may be committed on, beneath, or above the surface of the land, although the law regards the upper air, above the prescribed minimum altitude of flight, as a public highway. There is no trespass unless the aircraft enters into the lower reaches of the air space and substantially interferes with the landowner's use and enjoyment.

Nuisance   A **nuisance** is a nontrespassory invasion of another's interest in the private use and enjoyment of land. In contrast to trespass, nuisance does not require interference with another's right to exclusive possession of land, but rather imposes liability for significant and unreasonable harm to another's use or enjoyment of land. Examples of nuisances include the emission of unpleasant odors, smoke, dust, or gas, as well as the pollution of a stream, pond, or underground water supply.

Personal Property

Personal property is any type of property other than an interest in land. The law protects a number of interests in the possession of personal property, including an interest in the property's physical condition and usability, an interest in the retention of possession, and an interest in the property's availability for future use.

Trespass   **Trespass to personal property** consists of the intentional dispossession or unauthorized use of the personal property of another. The interference with the right to exclusive use and possession may be direct or indirect, but liability is limited to instances in which the trespasser (1) dispossesses the other of the property, (2) substantially impairs the condition, quality, or value of the property, or (3) deprives the possessor of the use of the property for a substantial time.[9] For example, Albert parks his car in front of his house. Later,

Ronald pushes Albert's car around the corner. Albert subsequently looks for his car but cannot find it for several hours. Ronald is liable to Albert for trespass.

Conversion   **Conversion** is the intentional exercise of dominion or control over another's personal property that so seriously interferes with the other's right of control as justly to require the payment of full value for the property. Conversion may consist of the intentional destruction of the personal property or the use of the property in an unauthorized manner. For example, Barbara entrusts an automobile to Ken, a dealer, for sale. Ken drives the car 8,000 miles on his own business. Ken is liable to Barbara for conversion. On the other hand, in the example above in which Ronald pushed Albert's car around the corner, Ronald would *not* be liable to Albert for conversion.

A major distinction between trespass to personal property and conversion is the measure of damages. In trespass, the possessor recovers damages for the actual harm to the property or for the loss of possession. In conversion, the possessor recovers the full value of the property, and the convertor takes possession of it on payment of the judgment.

INTERFERENCE WITH ECONOMIC INTERESTS

A third set of interests protected by the law against intentional interference is economic interests. The following are covered under this heading: (1) interference with contractual relations, (2) disparagement, and (3) fraudulent misrepresentation.

Interference with Contractual Relations

Interference with contractual relations consists of the intentional and improper interference with the performance of a contract by inducing one of the parties not to perform the contract.[10] (Contracts are discussed extensively in Part 2 of this text.) The injured party may recover the economic loss resulting from the breach of the contract. Similar liability is imposed for intentional and improper interfer-

ence with another's prospective contractual relation.

In either case, the rule applies whenever a person acts with the purpose or motive of interfering with another's contract or with the knowledge that such interference is substantially certain to occur as a natural consequence of her actions. The interference may be by prevention through the use of physical force or by threats. Frequently, it is accomplished by inducement, such as the offer of a better contract. For instance, Calvin may offer Becky, an employee of Fran, a yearly salary of $5,000 per year more than the contractual arrangement between Becky and Fran. If Calvin is aware of the contract between Becky and Fran and that his offer to Becky interferes with that contract, then Calvin is liable to Fran for intentional interference with contractual relations. If the employment contract between Becky and Fran was at will (that is, of no definite duration), however, there would be no tort, for Fran had no legal right to have the relation continued. Another example is *Pennzoil Company v. Texaco Inc.* in which a jury found Texaco liable in the amount of $10.53 billion for tortiously interfering with a merger agreement that Pennzoil had entered into with Getty Oil. See Law in the News on page 176.

Disparagement

The tort of **disparagement** or injurious falsehood imposes liability for the publication of a false statement that results in harm to another's monetary interests if the publisher knows that the statement is false or acts in reckless disregard of its truth or falsity.[11] This tort most commonly involves intentionally false statements casting doubt on the right of ownership or quality of another's property or products. Thus Simon, while contemplating the purchase of a stock of merchandise that belongs to Marie, reads an advertisement in a newspaper in which Ernst falsely asserts he owns the merchandise. Ernst has disparaged Marie's property in the goods. Absolute, conditional, and constitutional privilege apply to the same extent to the tort of disparagement as they do to defamation.

Fraudulent Misrepresentation

One who intentionally makes a misrepresentation of fact for the purpose of inducing another to act is liable for monetary loss caused by justifiable reliance on the misrepresentation. For example, Smith misrepresents to Jones that a tract of land in Texas is located in an area where drilling for oil had recently commenced. Smith made this statement knowing it was not true. In reliance upon the statement, Jones purchased the land from Smith. Smith is liable to Jones for **fraudulent misrepresentation.** Although intentional, or fraudulent, misrepresentation is a tort action, it is closely connected with contractual negotiations and is discussed in Chapter 9.

DEFENSES TO INTENTIONAL TORTS

Even though the defendant has intentionally invaded the interests of the plaintiff, the de-fendant will not be liable if such conduct was privileged. A defendant's conduct is privileged if it furthers an interest of such social importance that the law grants immunity from tort liability for damage to others. Examples of privilege include self-defense, defense of property, and defense of others. In addition, the plaintiff's consent to the defendant's conduct is a defense to intentional torts.

CONSENT

If a person consents to conduct resulting in damage or harm done to his own person, property, or economic interests, there is generally no liability for the intentional infliction of injury. **Consent** to an act is the willingness that it shall occur and negates its wrongfulness. It may be shown expressly or impliedly, by words or by conduct. For example, Lorenzo states that he wishes to kiss Wanda. Although Wanda does not wish Lorenzo to do so, she does not object or resist by word or act. Lorenzo kisses Wanda. Lorenzo is not liable to

---

FIGURE 5-1   Intentional Torts

Interest Protected	Tort
Person	
Freedom from contact	Battery
Freedom from apprehension	Assault
Freedom of movement	False imprisonment
Freedom from distress	Infliction of emotional distress
Reputation	Defamation
Privacy	Appropriation
	Intrusion
	Public disclosure of private facts
Property	
Real	Trespass
	Nuisance
Personal	Trespass
	Conversion
Economic	
Contracts	Interference with contractual rights
Good will	Disparagement
Freedom from deception	Fraudulent misrepresentation

Wanda for battery because Wanda has impliedly consented to Lorenzo's conduct.

Consent must be given by an individual with capacity to do so. Consent given by a minor, mental incompetent, or intoxicated individual is invalid if he is not capable of understanding the nature, extent, or probable consequences of the conduct to which he has consented.

Exceeding Consent

The defendant's privilege is limited to the conduct to which the plaintiff consents. For example, Vincent consents to an exploratory operation by Michelle, a surgeon, but refuses to have any further operation performed. While Vincent is under ether, Michelle discovers a condition indicating that an operation is needed and proceeds to operate. Michelle is liable to Vincent, even though the operation is properly and successfully performed, because Michelle exceeded the consent given.

By agreeing to participate in a game, a person consents to encounter such bodily contact and limitations on freedom of movement as is permitted by or general to the game. Such consent does not, however, extend to intentional acts of violence or restrictions beyond the rules and usages of the game. Thus, if Guy participates in a game of ice hockey, he does not consent to an intentional attack by Stanley, another player, wielding his hockey stick as a weapon.

Consent to a Criminal Act

The jurisdictions are divided whether consent to criminal conduct is a valid defense to an intentional tort. If conduct is made criminal in order to protect a certain class of persons, however, the consent of members of that class will *not* be effective as a defense to a tort action. For example, a statute makes it a crime to sell alcoholic beverages to a person who is intoxicated. Dwight sells liquor to Mark in violation of the statute. Mark consumes the liquor and suffers physical injury from it. Mark's consent in purchasing the liquor does not bar his suit against Dwight.

PRIVILEGE

In this section we deal with that form of privilege entitling an individual to injure another's person without that person's consent. These privileges are created by law to enable an individual to protect himself, others, or his property against tortious interference. By virtue of these privileges an individual may inflict or impose what would otherwise constitute battery, assault, or false imprisonment. In this section we cover the following privileges: (1) self-defense, (2) defense of others, and (3) defense of property.

Self-Defense

The law permits an individual to take appropriate action to prevent harm to herself where time does not allow resort to the law. A person is privileged to use reasonable force, not intended or likely to cause death or serious bodily harm, to defend herself against a threatened harmful or offensive contact or confinement.[12] The privilege of self-defense exists whether or not the danger actually exists, provided that the defendant reasonably believed self-defense was necessary. The reasonableness of the defendant's actions is based on what a person of average courage would have thought under the circumstances.

Self-defense is warranted even if the defendant reasonably believed that she could avoid the threatened contact or confinement by retreating. The defendant is not privileged to retaliate, however, because revenge is not self-defense. To protect herself from offensive or nonserious bodily contact, the defendant is limited to reasonable force, which is proportionate in extent to the harm from which the defendant is seeking to protect herself.

The defendant is privileged to defend by the use of force intended or likely to cause death or serious bodily harm if she reasonably believes that the plaintiff is about to inflict death, serious bodily harm, or ravishment on the defendant. Most States limit the right to use deadly force in self-defense to those situations in which the defendant does not have a completely safe means of escape. If the defendant, however, has the slightest reasonable doubt about the safety of her escape, she may stand her ground. A person may also stand her ground and use deadly force if the attack occurs in her own residence, even though a reasonable means of escape exists.

Defense of Others

An individual is privileged to defend third persons from harmful or offensive contact to the same extent that he is privileged to protect himself, provided that the defendant correctly or reasonably believes that the third person possesses the privilege of self-defense and that the defendant's intervention is necessary for the safety of the third person.[13] For example, Allan sees Bob about to strike Allan's friend Carol. Bob is, in fact, privileged to do so to repel Carol's attack. Allan has no reason to suspect that Carol is the aggressor and intercedes to assist Carol. Allan is privileged to use reasonable force to assist Carol against Bob.

Defense of Property

A possessor of property is permitted to use reasonable force, not intended or likely to cause death or serious bodily harm, to protect his real and personal property. Such force can be employed only if the possessor reasonably believes that the intrusion can only be terminated or prevented by use of force and the intruder has disregarded requests to cease. For example, Wayne sees Sandra walking across his vacant lot. Wayne is not privileged to use even the mildest of force to eject Sandra until Wayne has requested Sandra to leave and Sandra has disregarded the warning. Once reasonable force has been used, the defendant may use such greater force as is necessary to protect himself and his property. The intruder is not entitled to invoke the privilege of self-defense.

A person may not through indirect means, such as mechanical devices, employ deadly force to protect his property unless he would, if present, have been privileged to employ such force. This applies to spring guns, electrified fences, and other traps that are intended or likely to cause death or serious bodily harm.

KATKO v. BRINEY
Supreme Court of Iowa, 1971.
183 N.W.2d 657.

Facts: The Brineys (defendants) owned a large farm on which was located an abandoned farmhouse. For a ten-year period the house had been the subject of several trespassings and house breakings. In an attempt to stop the intrusions, Briney boarded up the windows and doors and posted "no trespassing" signs. After one break-in, however, Briney set a spring gun in a bedroom. It was placed over the bedroom window so that the gun could not be seen from outside, and no warning of its presence was posted. The gun was set to hit an intruder in the legs. Briney loaded the gun with a live shell, but he claimed that he did not intend to injure anyone.

Katko (plaintiff) and a friend, McDonough, had broken into the abandoned farmhouse on an earlier occasion to steal old bottles and fruit jars for their antique collection. They returned for a second time after the spring gun had been set, and Katko was seriously wounded in the leg when the gun discharged as he entered the bedroom. He then brought this action for damages. The defendants appeal from a judgment in favor of Katko for $20,000 actual and $10,000 punitive damages.

Decision: Judgment for Katko affirmed.

Opinion: Moore, C. J.   The main thrust of defendants' defense in the trial court and on this appeal is that "the law permits use of a spring gun in a dwelling or warehouse for the purpose of preventing the unlawful entry of a burglar or thief." * * *

"* * * the law has always placed a higher value upon human safety than upon mere rights in property, it is the accepted rule that there is no privilege to use any force calculated to cause death or serious bodily injury to repel the threat to land or chattels, unless there is also such a threat to the defendant's personal safety as to justify a self-defense. * * * spring guns and other man-killing devices are not justifiable against a mere trespasser, or even a petty thief. They are privileged only against those upon whom the landowner, if he were present in person would be free to inflict injury of the same kind."

Restatement of Torts, Section 85 * * * states: "The value of human life and limb, not only to the individual concerned but also to society, so outweighs the interest of a possessor of land in excluding it from those whom he is not willing to admit thereto that a possessor of land has, as is stated in § 79, no privilege to use force intended or likely to cause death or serious harm against another whom the possessor sees about to enter his premises or meddle with his chattel, unless the intrusion threatens death or serious bodily harm to the occupiers or users of the premises. * * *

CHAPTER SUMMARY

INTENT

Injury or Damage to the Person	**Battery** intentional infliction of harmful or offensive bodily contact **Assault** intentional infliction of apprehension of immediate bodily harm or offensive contact **False Imprisonment** intentional confining of a person against her will **Infliction of Emotional Distress** extreme and outrageous conduct intentionally or recklessly causing severe emotional distress **Defamation** false communication that injures a person's reputation 　■ *Libel* written defamation 　■ *Slander* spoken defamation **Invasion of Privacy** 　■ *Appropriation* unauthorized use of a person's name or likeness 　■ *Intrusion* unreasonable and offensive interference with the seclusion of another 　■ *Public Disclosure of Private Facts* offensive publicity of private information 　■ *False Light* offensive and false publicity about another
Interference with Property Rights	**Real Property** land and anything attached to it 　■ *Trespass* wrongful entering on land of another 　■ *Nuisance* a nontrespassory interference with another's use and enjoyment of land

	Personal Property any property other than land ■ *Trespass* an intentional taking or use of another's personal property ■ *Conversion* intentional exercise of control over another's personal property

Interference with Economic Interests	Interference with Contractual Relations intentionally causing one of the parties to a contract not to perform Disparagement publication of false statements about another's property or products Fraudulent Misrepresentation a false statement made with knowledge of its falsity intended to induce another to act

DEFENSES TO INTENTIONAL TORTS

Consent	Definition voluntary and knowing willingness that an act shall occur Effect negates wrongfulness of an otherwise tortious act

Privilege	Self-defense action taken to prevent harm to oneself Defense of Others action taken to prevent harm to another Defense of Property action taken to protect real or personal property

QUESTIONS

1. Identify and define the torts that protect against intentional interference with personal rights.
2. Explain the application of the various privileges to defamation suits and how they are affected by whether the plaintiff is a (a) public figure, (b) public official, or (c) private person.
3. Distinguish the four torts comprising invasion of privacy.
4. Distinguish by example among interference with contractual relations, disparagement, and fraudulent misrepresentation.
5. Identify and describe the defenses to intentional torts.

PROBLEMS

1. The Penguin intentionally hits Batman with his umbrella. Batman, stunned by the blow, falls backwards, knocking Robin down. Robin's leg is broken in the fall, and he cried out, "Holy broken bat bones! My leg is broken." Who, if anyone, has liability to Robin? Why?

2. For the purpose of frightening Kure, Bob comes up behind Kure in the desert and sounds a buzzer that is an excellent imitation of a rattlesnake. Kure, believing that he is about to be bitten, is frightened but suffers no bodily harm. May Kure recover from Bob for (a) the tort of assault? (b) the tort of intentional infliction of mental distress?

3. Ralph kisses Edith while she is asleep but does not waken or harm her. Edith sues Ralph for battery. Decision?

4. Claude, a creditor, seeking to collect a debt, calls on Dianne and demands payment in a rude and insolent manner. When Dianne says that she cannot pay, Claude calls Dianne a deadbeat and says that he will never trust Dianne again. Is Claude liable to Dianne? If so, for what tort?

5. Lana, a ten-year-old child, is run over by a car negligently driven by Mitchell. Lana, at the time of the accident, was acting reasonably and without negligence. Clark, a newspaper reporter, photographs Lana while she is lying in the street in great pain. Two years later, Perry, the publisher of a newspaper, prints Clark's picture of Lana in his newspaper as a lead to an article concerning the

negligence of children. The caption under the picture reads: "They ask to be killed." Lana, who has recovered from the accident, brings suit against Clark and Perry. What result?

6. In 1963 the *Saturday Evening Post* featured an article entitled "The Story of a College Football Fix," characterized in the subtitle as "A Shocking Report of How Wally Butts and Bear Bryant Rigged a Game Last Fall." Butts was athletic director of the University of Georgia, and Bryant was head coach of the University of Alabama. The article was based on a claim by one George Burnett that he had accidentally overheard a long distance telephone conversation between Butts and Bryant in the course of which Butts divulged information on plays Georgia would use in the upcoming game against Alabama. The writer assigned to the story by the *Post* was not a football expert and did not interview either Butts or Bryant, nor did he personally see the notes Burnett had made of the telephone conversation. Butts admitted that he had a long distance telephone conversation with Bryant but denied that any advance information on prospective football plays was given. Butts brought a libel suit against the *Post*. Decision?

7. Joan is a patient confined in a hospital with a rare disease that is of great interest to the public. Carol, a television reporter, requests Joan to consent to an interview. Joan refuses, but Carol, nonetheless, enters Joan's room over her objection and photographs her. Joan brings a suit against Carol. Decision?

8. Owner has a place on his land where he piles trash. The pile has been there for a period of three months. John, a neighbor of Owner, without Owner's consent or knowledge, throws trash onto the trashpile. Owner learns that John has done this and sues him. What tort, if any, has John committed?

9. Chris leaves her car parked in front of a store. There are no signs that say Chris cannot park there. The store owner, however, needs the car moved to enable a delivery truck to unload. He releases the brake and pushes Chris's car three or four feet, doing no harm to the car. Chris returns and sees that her car has been moved and is very angry. She threatens to sue the store owner for trespass to her personal property. Can she recover?

10. Carr borrowed John's brand-new Ford for the purpose of going to the store. He told John he would be right back. Carr then decided, however, to go to the beach while he had the car. Can John recover from Carr the value of the automobile? If so, for what tort?

11. Marcia Samms, a respectable married woman, claimed that David Eccles had repeatedly and persistently called her at various hours, including late at night, from May to December, soliciting her to have illicit sexual relations with him. She also claimed that on one occasion Eccles came over to her residence to again solicit sex and indecently exposed himself to her. Mrs. Samms had never encouraged Eccles but had continuously repulsed his "insulting, indecent, and obscene" proposals. She brought suit against Eccles, claiming she suffered great anxiety and fear for her personal safety and severe emotional distress, demanding actual and punitive damages. Decision?

12. National Bond and Investment Company sent two of its employees to repossess Whithorn's car after he failed to complete the payments. The two repossessors located Whithorn while he was driving his car. They followed him and hailed him down in order to make the repossession. Whithorn refused to abandon his car and demanded evidence of their authority. The two repossessors became impatient and called a wrecker. They ordered the driver of the wrecker to hook Whithorn's car and move it down the street while Whithorn was still inside the vehicle. Whithorn started the car and tried to escape, but the wrecker lifted the car off the road and progressed seventy-five to one hundred feet until Whithorn managed to stall the wrecker. Whithorn sued National Bond for false imprisonment. Decision?

13. In March 1975 William Proxmire, a United States senator from Wisconsin, initiated the "Golden Fleece of the Month Award" to publicize what he believed to be wasteful government spending. The second of these awards was given to the Federal agencies that had for seven years funded Dr. Hutchinson's research on stress levels in animals. The award was made in a speech Proxmire gave in the Senate; the text was also incorporated into an advance press release that was sent to 275 members of the national news media. Proxmire also referred to the research again in two subsequent newsletters sent to 100,000 constituents and during a television interview. Hutchinson then brought this action alleging defamation resulting in personal and economic injury. Decision?

ENDNOTES

1. Restatement, Second, Torts, Section 908, Punitive Damages.

2. Restatement, Second, Torts, Section 8A, Intent.

3. Restatement, Second, Torts, Section 46(1), Outrageous Conduct Causing Severe Emotional Distress.

4. Restatement, Second, Torts, Section 580A, Defamation of Public Official or Public Figure.

5. Restatement, Second, Torts, Section 652C, Appropriation of Name or Likeness.

6. Restatement, Second, Torts, Section 652B, Intrusion upon Seclusion.

7. Restatement, Second, Torts, Section 652E, Publicity Placing Person in False Light.

8. Restatement, Second, Torts, Section 164, Intrusions Under Mistake.

9. Restatement, Second, Torts, Section 218, Liability to Person in Possession.

10. Restatement, Second, Torts, Section 766, Intentional Interference with Performance of Contract by Third Person.

11. Restatement, Second, Torts, Section 623A, Liability for Publication of Injurious Falsehood—General Principle.

12. Restatement, Second, Torts, Section 63(1), Self-Defense by Force Not Threatening Death or Serious Bodily Harm.

13. Restatement, Second, Torts, Section 76, Defense of Third Person.

6 NEGLIGENCE AND STRICT LIABILITY

Negligence involves conduct that creates an unreasonable risk of harm, whereas intentional torts deal with conduct that has a substantial certainty of causing harm. The basis of liability for negligence is the failure to exercise reasonable care under the circumstances for the safety of another person or his property, which proximately causes injury to such person or damage to his property, or both. Thus, if the driver of an automobile intentionally runs down a person, she has committed the intentional tort of battery. If, on the other hand, the driver hits and injures a person while driving unreasonably for the safety of others, she is negligent.

Strict liability is not based on the negligence or intent of the defendant but rather on the nature of the activity in which he is engaging. Under this doctrine, defendants who engage in certain activities, such as keeping animals or maintaining abnormally dangerous conditions, are held liable for injuries they caused even though they exercise the utmost care. The law imposes this liability in order to bring about a just reallocation of loss, given that the defendant engaged in the activity for his own benefit and is in a better position to manage the risk by insurance or otherwise. Both negligence and strict liability are the subject matter of this chapter.

NEGLIGENCE

The Restatement defines **negligence** as "conduct which falls below the standard established by law for the protection of others against unreasonable risk of harm." The stan-

dard established by law is the conduct of a **reasonable man** acting prudently and with due care under the circumstances.

A person is not liable for injury caused to another by an unavoidable accident—an occurrence that was not intended and could not have been prevented by the exercise of reasonable care. Thus, no liability results from the loss of control of an automobile because the driver is suddenly and unforeseeably stricken with a heart attack, stroke, or fainting spell. If the driver, however, had warning of the imminent heart attack or other infirmity, it would be negligent for him to drive at all.

An action for negligence consists of four elements, each of which must be proved by the plaintiff:

1. that a legal duty required the defendant to conform to the standard of conduct established for the protection of others;
2. that the defendant failed to conform to the required standard of conduct;
3. that the injury and harm sustained by the plaintiff were proximately caused by the defendant's failure to conform to the required standard of conduct; and
4. that the injury and harm are protected against negligent interference.

We discuss the first two elements under the heading "Duty of Care," the third under "Proximate Cause," and the last under "Injury."

DUTY OF CARE

The duty of care imposed by law is measured by the degree of carefulness that a reasonable man would exercise in a given situation.

Reasonable Man Standard

The reasonable man is a fictitious individual who is always careful and prudent and never negligent. What the judge or jury determines that a reasonable man would have done in the light of the facts brought out by the evidence in a particular case sets the standard of conduct for that case. The **reasonable man standard** is thus *external* and *objective.*

Children   The standard of conduct to which a child must conform to avoid being negligent is that of a reasonable person of like age, intelligence, and experience under like circumstances. The law applies an individualized test because children do not have the judgment, intelligence, knowledge, and experience of an adult. Moreover, children as a general rule do not engage in activities entailing high risk to others, and their conduct does not involve the same magnitude of harm. A child who engages in an adult activity, however, such as flying an airplane or driving a boat or car, is held to the standard of care applicable to adults.

Physical Disability   If a person is ill or otherwise physically disabled, the standard of conduct to which he must conform to avoid being negligent is that of a reasonable man under like disability. Thus a blind man must act as a reasonable man who is blind.

Mental Deficiency   The law makes no allowance for the insanity or other mental deficiency of the defendant in a negligence case, and he is held to the standard of conduct of a reasonable man who is *not* mentally deficient even though it is, in fact, beyond his capacity to conform to the standard.

Superior Skill or Knowledge   Persons who are qualified and who practice a profession or trade that requires special skill and expertise are required to use the same care and skill normally possessed by members of their profession or trade. This standard applies to such professionals as physicians, surgeons, dentists, attorneys, pharmacists, architects, accountants, and engineers and to such skilled trades as airline pilots, electricians, carpenters, and plumbers. If a member of a profession or skilled trade possesses greater skill than that common to the profession or trade, she is required to exercise that skill.

Emergencies   In determining whether a defendant's conduct is reasonable, the fact that he was at the time confronted with an emergency is taken into consideration.[1] An **emergency** is a sudden, unexpected event that calls for immediate action and does not permit time for deliberation. The standard is still that of a reasonable man under the circumstances—the emergency is simply part of the circumstances. An emergency is not helpful to a defendant, however, if his own negligent or tortious conduct created the emergency.

Violation of Statute   The reasonable man standard of conduct may be established by legislation. Some statutes expressly impose civil liability on violators. Without such a provision, courts may adopt the requirements of the statute as the standard of conduct if the statute is intended to protect a class of persons that includes the plaintiff against the particular hazard and kind of harm that resulted.[2] If the statute is found to apply, the great majority of the courts hold that an unexcused violation is **negligence** *per se;* that is, it is conclusive on the issue of negligent conduct. In a minority of States, the violation is considered merely evidence of negligence. In either event, the plaintiff must also prove legal causation and injury.

For example, a statute enacted to protect employees from injuries requires that all factory elevators be equipped with specified safety devices. Arthur, an employee in Leonard's factory, and Marian, a business visitor to the factory, are injured when the elevator falls because of the failure to install the safety devices. The court may adopt the statute as a standard of conduct as to Arthur, and hold Leonard negligent *per se* to Arthur, but not as to Marian, because Arthur, and not Marian, is within the class of persons intended to be protected by the statute. Marian would have to establish that a reasonable person in the position of Leonard under the circumstances would have installed the safety device.

WALZ v. HUDSON
Supreme Court of South Dakota, 1982.
327 N.W.2d 120.

Facts: Larry VanEgdom, in an intoxicated state, bought alcoholic beverages from the Hudson Municipal Liquor Store in Hudson, South Dakota. Immediately following the purchase, VanEgdom, while driving a car, struck and killed Guy William Ludwig, who was stopped on his motorcycle at a stop sign. Lela Walz, as special administrator of Ludwig's estate, brought an action against the city of Hudson, which operated the liquor store, for the wrongful death of Ludwig. Walz alleged that the store employee was negligent in selling intoxicating beverages to VanEgdom when he knew or could have observed that VanEgdom was drunk. The trial court dismissed the action and Walz appealed.

Decision: Trial court's dismissal reversed.

Opinion: Fosheim, C. J.   Appellant urges that we overrule our decision in *Griffin v. Sebek,* [citation], thus affording her a cause of action against appellee.

In *Griffin* the plaintiffs brought a negligence action against defendants, licensed tavernkeepers, seeking damages for personal injury resulting from defendants' unlawful sale of alcoholic beverages. Our decision, affirming the trial court's order granting defendants' motion to dismiss for failure to state a claim, said the issue was whether, in the absence of a dram shop act, "the common law now authorizes or should be liberalized to afford a remedy." We determined that no such cause of action exists in South Dakota and declined to expand the common law to afford a remedy. We also did not extend SDCL 35–4–78(2) to impose a civil liability duty. [SDCL 35–4–78(2) reads: No licensee shall sell any alcoholic beverage, except low-point beer . . . (t)o any person who is intoxicated at the time, or who is known to the seller to be an habitual drunkard. A violation of this section is a Class 1 misdemeanor.] We take judicial notice that since *Griffin* was decided, alcohol has been involved in 50.8% of this state's traffic fatalities from 1976 to 1981; in 1981 alone 62% of South Dakota's traffic fatalities were alcohol-related. [Citation.] This tragic waste of life prompts us to review our conclusions in *Griffin.* If the Legislature does not concur with our application of SDCL 35–4–78(2), as now announced, it is the prerogative of the Legislature to so assert. We fully realize this decision, while hopefully helpful, certainly cannot resolve the problems of alcohol-related deaths or injuries.

Negligence is the breach of a legal duty imposed by statute or common law. [Citation.] Griffin recognized that a liquor licensee is not liable at common law for damages resulting from a patron's intoxication. The common law is in force in South Dakota except where it conflicts with federal or state constitutions and laws. [Citation.] SDCL 35–4–78(2) makes it a crime to sell intoxicating beverages to one in Mr. VanEgdom's inebriated state and violation of a statute is negligence as a matter of law if the statute "was intended to protect the class of persons in which plaintiffs are included against risk of the type of harm which has in fact occurred." [Citations.]

The reason for this rule is that the statute or ordinance becomes the standard of care or conduct to which the reasonably prudent person is held. Failure to follow the statute involved constitutes a breach of the legal duty imposed and fixed by such statute. Since negligence is a breach of a legal duty, the violator of a statute is then negligent as a matter of law.

> * * *
>
> We believe that statute [SDCL 35–4–78(2)] was enacted to include the protection of the class of people in Mr. Ludwig's position from the risk of being killed or injured "as a result of the drunkenness to which the particular sale of alcoholic liquor contributes." [Citation.] Since SDCL 35–4–78(2) must be liberally construed "with a view to effect its objects and to promote justice," [citations], we conclude that SDCL 35–4–78(2) establishes a standard of care or conduct, a breach of which is negligence as a matter of law. [Citation.] It follows that such negligence must be a proximate cause of any resulting injury and defenses, such as contributory negligence, are available when appropriate.

Duty to Act

Except in special circumstances, no one is required to aid another in peril. For example, Adolf, an adult standing along the edge of a steep cliff, observes a baby carriage with a crying infant in it slowly heading toward the edge and certain doom. Adolf could easily prevent the baby's fall at no risk to his own safety. Nonetheless, Adolf does nothing, and the baby falls to its death. Adolf is under no legal duty to act and therefore incurs no liability for failing to do so.[3] Special relations between the parties may exist, however, that impose a duty on the defendant to aid or protect the other. Thus, if Adolf were the baby's parent or babysitter, Adolf would be under a duty to act and would therefore be liable for not taking action.

A duty to act is also imposed on those whose conduct, whether tortious or innocent, has injured another and left him helpless and in danger of further harm. For example, Alice drives her car into Frank, who is rendered unconscious. Alice leaves Frank lying in the middle of the road, where he is run over by a second car driven by Rebecca. Alice is liable to Frank for the additional injuries inflicted by Rebecca. Moreover, a person incurs a duty to exercise care by voluntarily coming to the assistance of another in need of aid. In such instance, the actor is liable if his failure to exercise reasonable care increases the risk of harm, causes harm, or leaves the other in a worse position. For example, Ann finds Ben drunk and stumbling along a dark sidewalk. Ann leads Ben halfway up a steep and un-guarded stairway, where she abandons Ben. Ben attempts to climb the stairs but trips and falls, suffering serious injury. Ann is liable to Ben for having left him in a worse position.

Special Duties of Possessors of Land

The duty of a possessor of land to persons who come on the land depends on whether that person is a trespasser, a licensee, or an invitee.

Duty to Trespassers   A **trespasser** is a person who enters or remains on the land of another without permission or privilege to do so. The lawful possessor of the land is *not* liable to trespassers for her failure to maintain the land in a reasonably safe condition. Nonetheless, the lawful possessor is not free to inflict intentional injury on him. Moreover, some courts have held that the lawful possessor is required to exercise reasonable care for the safety of the trespasser on discovery of his presence on the land.

The law, however, extends greater protection to a child who trespasses by imposing on a possessor of land the liability for physical harm caused by artificial conditions upon the land if:

1. the place where the condition exists is one the possessor knows or has reason to know that children are likely to trespass;
2. the condition involves an unreasonable risk of death or serious bodily harm to children;
3. the children do not realize the risk involved;
4. the burden of eliminating the danger is slight compared with the risk to children involved; and

LAW IN THE NEWS

Torts Are Taking Over for Morality

In a series of highly publicized cases, prosecutors are charging women with crimes, ranging from child abuse to homicide, if they take illegal drugs during pregnancy and then give birth to damaged babies. This has upset civil libertarians, who warn of "prenatal police patrols," in the words of Lynn Paltrow, head of the American Civil Liberties Union's Reproductive Freedom Project.

The civil libertarians seem to be winning this round. In the most recent of these cases, an Illinois grand jury last month declined to indict 24-year-old Melanie Green for manslaughter and delivering a dangerous drug to a minor in the death of her daughter two days after birth. The grand jury's decision seemed to stem from the logical stumbling-block in the way of finding that a crime has been committed when the victim is not yet in legal existence.

Thousands of Babies

The civil libertarian position has a certain appeal: What if police started arresting women for having a glass of wine or putting on a few extra pounds during pregnancy? But prosecutors, along with increasing numbers of judges, legislatures and a large segment of the public, don't see the drug epidemic in terms of legal niceties or slippery slopes down which the best of us might be pushed. They see victims: Thousands of babies born undersized, brain-damaged or dead because their mothers spent their pregnancies behind lines of cocaine. Currently 11% of the babies born in this country show symptoms of their mothers' drug use, estimates the Association for Perinatal Addiction Research.

The idea that a drug-using mother should be legally liable if her infant is born damaged or deformed may be a novel one in the criminal system, but it is old hat in the tort system. Talk to Aaron Levine, a plaintiffs' personal-injury lawyer

in Washington. In 1987 he won a key ruling from the District of Columbia Court of Appeals, allowing an injured 15-year-old girl to sue her mother for negligence in driving the family car into a tree. The District of Columbia thus did away with the time-honored legal doctrine called parental immunity.

Under this doctrine, children were barred from bringing tort suits against their parents. There were a lot of reasons for this, the chief being that the family should in some ways be beyond the reaches of the legal system and the state. But during the past two decades, some 30 states have dropped or severely restricted parental immunity. Mr. Levine's court victory simply follows a trend.

Mr. Levine says the ruling in his case set a clear precedent for negligence suits by drug- or alcohol-damaged children against their drug- or alcohol-using mothers, or even suits over transmitting AIDS. In fact, he says, the only thing that has so far prevented a flood of such suits is no funds to tap from the defendant and no insurance policy. "Let's face it," says Mr. Levine. "Most addicts are not too financially secure."

Other draconian measures that prosecutors, judges and legislatures are trying these days in the wars against drugs and gangs have their precedents in recent tort-law developments. Judges are starting to haul parents into court to pay restitution to the victims of crimes committed by their delinquent children. Logically, legalistically, this makes no sense; the parents didn't commit a crime.

Last year the California Legislature passed the Street Terrorism Enforcement and Prevention Act, which makes it a crime for parents to fail to supervise their children. The first to be arrested under the new law, just a few weeks ago, was Gloria Williams in Los Angeles, whose 17-year-old son, an alleged member of the Crips, is suspected of participating in the gang rape of a 12-year-old

5. the possessor fails to exercise reasonable care to eliminate the danger or otherwise to protect the children.

The Restatement provides the following illustration: "A has on his land a small artificial

pond full of goldfish. A's land adjoins a nursery in which children from two to five years of age are left by their parents for the day, and such children are, as A knows, in the habit of trespassing on A's land and going near the pond. A could easily prevent this by

CHAPTER 6 NEGLIGENCE AND STRICT LIABILITY

127

girl. The mother's offense appears to have been cultivating a Ma Barker image and using gang paraphernalia as a form of punk interior decoration.

In the past few decades, to ensure a source of compensation for victims, virtually all states have paved the way in tort law by enacting statutes that hold parents financially responsible, usually up to stated monetary limits, for the damage their delinquent minor children cause.

A court in New Mexico ruled in 1982 that parents even had to pay for damage done by their 17-year-old daughter while she was living with her boyfriend. The laws are a kind of precursor to a 1985 Wisconsin statute that makes parents financially responsible for raising the offspring of their unwed teenage daughters.

It can be argued that such laws, coupled with the current trend of giving young people all the "rights" of adults (sex, abortion, free speech at school and so forth), encourage them to act in ways that combine the worst features of adults and children, doing adult-level damage with the certain knowledge that Mom and Dad, not they, will pay up.

Parental immunity began to fall by the wayside a decade or so ago when another concept became more important to lawyers and judges: the parental insurance policy. As the tort system came to be viewed less as a justice system than as a compensation system, it came to seem unfair that someone injured in an accident could collect large amounts of money from a negligent stranger, while someone injured in a similar accident with a negligent family member got nothing.

Family members might have a natural disinclination to take each other to court, but homeowners' insurance has made it easier. Dog bites, cat bites, icy steps and puddles of water on the bathroom floor have set sibling against sibling, grown son against aging sire. Insurance companies have responded by writing family exclusions into policies, although such exclusions themselves have been challenged as contrary to public policy.

Insurers worry about collusion—the likelihood that the policyholder will freely admit negligence in order to benefit an injured family member. But even worse may be the next step down the litigation line, the suit by the grown child claiming psychic injury from the way he was raised. So far, courts still allow parents discretion in rearing and supervising their children, but that circle of discretion is steadily shrinking. "I don't know which is more troublesome, the insincere suit between parents and children or the sincere suit," says Walter Olson, a fellow at the Manhattan Institute who is writing a book about the litigation explosion.

Words Are Corrupted

In our age, the tort system has replaced the moral system. We don't know any longer how to use words like "good" and "evil" and "right" and "wrong." We have no place in our vocabularies for the word "vice," which perfectly describes conduct that degrades those who indulge in it and the environment around them. We hear a lot about the pregnancy police from civil libertarians but not one word about the sheer malignancy of letting one's baby be born brain-damaged because it feels so good to get high. And what kind of mother lets her son grow up to be a gang-rapist?

While we have no words of moral condemnation in our vocabularies, we still have words like "victim" and "compensation," borrowed from the tort system, that can serve as stand-ins. This is why the new draconian remedies are so popular (48% of the population supports holding pregnant alcohol users and smokers legally responsible for damage to their offspring, according to a Gallup survey commissioned by Hippocrates magazine). The problem is that these words themselves are fast being corrupted. "Victim" is coming to mean anyone with a beef, and "compensation" someone else's pot of gold.

By Charlotte Low Allen
Reprinted by permission of the *Wall Street Journal*, © Dow Jones & Company, Inc. 1989. All Rights Reserved.

closing and locking his gate. A does not do so. B, a child three years of age, trespasses, enters the pond to catch goldfish, and is drowned. A is subject to liability for the death of B."

Duty to Licensees A **licensee** is a person who is privileged to enter or remain on land only by virtue of the consent of the lawful possessor. Licensees include members of the possessor's household and *social guests.* A licensee, however, will become a trespasser if he enters a portion of the land to which he is not invited or remains on the land after his invitation has expired.

The possessor owes a higher duty of care to licensees than to trespassers. The possessor must warn the licensee of dangerous activities and conditions of which the possessor has knowledge and the licensee does not and is not likely to discover.[4] If he is not warned, the licensee may recover if the activity or dangerous condition resulted from the possessor's failure to exercise reasonable care to protect him from the danger. To illustrate: Henry invites a friend, Anne, to his place in the country at eight o'clock on a winter evening. Henry knows that a bridge in his driveway is in a dangerous condition that is not noticeable in the dark. Henry does not inform Anne of this fact. The bridge gives way under Anne's car, causing serious harm to Anne. Henry is liable to Anne.

Duty to Invitees   An **invitee** is either a *public invitee* or a *business visitor.* A person is a public invitee if she enters on land that is open to the public, such as a public park, beach, or swimming pool or a governmental facility where business with the public is transacted openly, such as a post office or an office of the recorder of deeds. A business visitor is a person who enters on the premises to engage in private business with the possessor of the land, such as one who enters a store or a worker who enters a residence to make repairs.

The duty of the possessor of land to invitees with respect to the condition of the premises is to exercise reasonable care to protect them against dangerous conditions they are unlikely to discover. This liability extends not only to those conditions the possessor actually knows of but also to those conditions of which he *should* reasonably know.[5] For example, David's store has a large glass front door that is well lighted and plainly visible. Maxine, a customer, mistakes the glass for an open doorway and walks into the glass, injuring herself. David is not liable to Maxine. If, on the other hand, the glass was difficult to see and it was foreseeable that a person might mistake the glass for an open doorway, then David would be liable to Maxine if Maxine crashed into the glass while exercising reasonable care.

These three kinds of duties are illustrated in Figure 6–1.

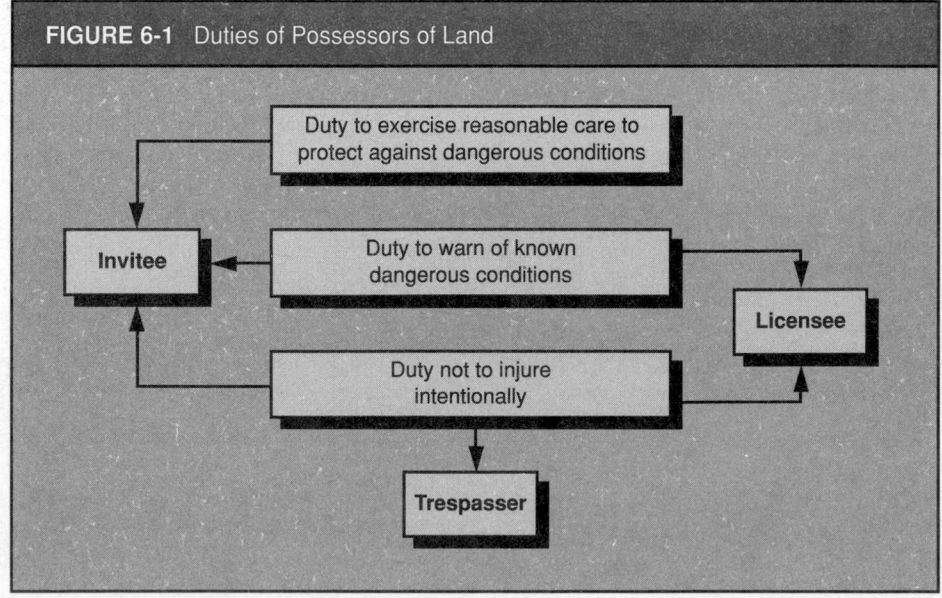

FIGURE 6-1   Duties of Possessors of Land

YANIA v. BIGAN

Supreme Court of Pennsylvania, 1959.
397 Pa. 316, 155 A.2d 343.

Facts: Joseph Yania and Boyd Ross visited a coal strip-mining operation owned by John Bigan to discuss a business matter with Bigan. On Bigan's property there were several cuts and trenches he had dug to remove the coal underneath. While there, Bigan asked the two men to help him pump water from one of these cuts in the earth. This particular cut contained water eight to ten feet in depth with side walls or embankments sixteen to eighteen feet in height. The two men agreed, and the process began with Ross and Bigan entering the cut and standing at the point where the pump was located. Yania stood at the top of one of the cut's side walls. Apparently, Bigan taunted Yania into jumping into the water from the top of the side wall—a height of sixteen to eighteen feet. As a result, Yania drowned. His widow brought a negligence action against Bigan. She claims that Bigan was negligent "(1) by urging, enticing, taunting and inveigling Yania to jump into the water; (2) by failing to warn Yania of a dangerous condition on the land. . . ; [and] (3) by failing to go to Yania's rescue after he jumped into the water." The trial court dismissed the action and Yania's widow appeals.

Decision: Judgment for Bigan.

Opinion: Jones, J. * * * The complaint does not allege that Yania slipped or that he was pushed or that Bigan made any *physical* impact upon Yania. On the contrary, the only inference deducible from the facts alleged in the complaint is that Bigan, by the employment of cajolery and inveiglement, caused such a *mental* impact on Yania that the latter was deprived of his volition and freedom of choice and placed under a compulsion to jump into the water. Had Yania been a child of tender years or a person mentally deficient then it is conceivable that taunting and enticement could constitute actionable negligence if it resulted in harm. However, to contend that such conduct directed to an adult in full possession of all his mental faculties constitutes actionable negligence is not only without precedent but completely without merit. * * *

* * * Yania was a business invitee in that he entered upon the land for a common business purpose for the mutual benefit of Bigan and himself (Restatement, Torts, § 332; *Parsons v. Drake*, 347 Pa. 247, 250, 32 A.2d 27). As possessor of the land, Bigan would become subject to liability to Yania for any physical harm caused by any artificial or natural condition upon the land (1) if, and only if, Bigan knew or could have discovered the condition which, if known to him he should have realized involved an unreasonable risk of harm to Yania, (2) if Bigan had no reason to believe Yania would discover the condition or realize the risk of harm and (3) if he invited or permitted Yania to enter upon the land without exercising reasonable care to make the condition reasonably safe or give adequate warning to enable him to avoid the harm. [Citations.] The inapplicability of this rule of liability to the instant facts is readily apparent.

The *only* condition on Bigan's land which could possibly have contributed in any manner to Yania's death was the water-filled cut with its high embankment. Of this condition there was neither concealment nor failure to warn, but, on the contrary, the complaint specifically avers that Bigan not only requested Yania and Boyd to assist him in starting the pump to remove the water from the cut but "led" them to the cut itself. If this cut possessed any potentiality of danger, such a condition was as obvious and apparent to Yania as to Bigan, both coal strip-mine operators. Under the circumstances herein depicted Bigan could not be held liable in this respect.

Lastly, it is urged that Bigan failed to take the necessary steps to rescue Yania from the water. The mere fact that Bigan saw Yania in a position of peril in the water imposed upon him no legal, although a moral, obligation or duty to go to his rescue unless Bigan was legally responsible, in whole or in part, for placing Yania in the perilous position. Restatement, Torts, § 314. [Citations.] * * * The complaint does not aver any facts which impose upon Bigan legal responsibility for placing Yania in the dangerous position in the water and, absent such legal responsibility, the law imposes on Bigan no duty of rescue.

Res Ipsa Loquitur

A rule has developed that permits the jury to infer *both* negligent conduct and causation from the mere occurrence of certain types of events. This rule is called *res ipsa loquitur,* which means "the thing speaks for itself," and it applies when the event is of a kind that ordinarily does not occur in the absence of negligence and other possible causes are sufficiently eliminated by the evidence.[6] For example, Camille rents a room in Leo's motel. During the night a large piece of plaster falls from the ceiling and injures Camille. In the absence of other evidence, the jury may infer that the harm resulted from Leo's negligence in permitting the plaster to become defective. Leo is permitted, however, to introduce evidence to contradict the inference of negligence. The following case involving the New York Mets explains the requirements of *res ipsa loquitur.*

UZDAVINES v. METROPOLITAN BASEBALL CLUB, INC.
Civil Court of the City of New York, Queens County, 1982.
115 Misc.2d 343, 454 N.Y.S.2d 238.

Facts: A foul ball struck Marie Uzdavines on the head while she was watching the Metropolitan Baseball Club ("The Mets") play the Philadelphia Phillies at "The Mets" home stadium in New York. The ball came through a hole in a screen designed to protect spectators sitting behind home plate. The screen contained several holes that had been repaired with baling wire, a lighter weight wire than that used in the original screen. Although the manager of the stadium makes no formal inspections of the screen, his employees do try to repair the holes as they find them. Weather conditions, rust deterioration, and baseballs hitting the screen are the chief causes of these holes. The owner of the stadium, the city of New York, leases the stadium to "The Mets" and replaces the entire screen every two years. Uzdavines sued "The Mets" for negligence under the doctrine of *res ipsa loquitur.* "The Mets" appeal from a jury verdict in favor of Uzdavines.

Decision: Judgment for Uzdavines.

Opinion: Hentel, J. Defendant's motion to set aside the verdict fixing defendant's liability under the doctrine of *res ipsa loquitur* presents an issue of apparent first impression under this particular set of facts. The court must undertake an analysis of the duty owed to plaintiff by defendant, and once having established that, seek to determine whether this duty supports a finding of *"exclusive control"* under the *res ipsa loquitur* doctrine. Only an affirmative answer to this query will support the jury's finding of liability. Fortunately, guidance is furnished as to the duty of care owed to baseball game spectators by our state's highest court.

In *Akins v. Glens Falls City School Dist.*, [citation],* * * the Court of Appeals chose to adopt the majority rule and set it forth as follows:

> We hold that, in the exercise of reasonable care, the proprietor of a ball park need only provide screening for the area of the field behind home plate where the danger of being struck by a ball is the greatest * * * In * * * providing adequate protection in the most dangerous area of the field for those spectators who wish to avail themselves of it, a proprietor fulfills its duty of reasonable care under such circumstances. [Citation.]

* * *

The Court adopts the position that professional sports teams charging admission to assigned seats cannot shirk responsibility for personal injury, nor deny a duty to keep structures free from defects. They must be held to a standard of reasonable care at a minimum. [Citation.]

The Court believes that a duty has clearly been imposed on "the Mets" via the *Akins* decision. It is equally well-settled that even where one has no duty to plaintiff, but assumes a duty and chooses to perform, he is then under an affirmative duty to use reasonable care to see that the instrumentality provided, or acts done, are safe for the purpose for which they were to be used. [Citation.]

The testimony reveals that "the Mets", through its responsible employees, did notice and repair holes which developed in the safety screen in the ordinary course of events. The law requires that such repairs be done in a non-negligent manner. Thus, the Court finds that "the Mets" had a duty to provide protected seating, consonant to its duty to use reasonable care; and to keep the people seated in the area behind home plate free from foreseeable danger, because of the duty imposed upon it as *primary user* of the ball field, the benefits obtained by it from its use, and the reliance of the public on the safety of seats behind home plate, generally.

* * *

The more complex question before the Court involves whether there is a legal basis for a verdict of negligence under the theory of *res ipsa loquitur.*

* * *

The elements of *res ipsa loquitur*, having been set forth many times by our courts, are well known:

(1) the event must be of a kind which ordinarily does not occur in the absence of someone's negligence;
(2) it must be caused by an agency or instrumentality within the *exclusive control* of the defendant; (*emphasis added*)
(3) it must not be due to any voluntary action or contribution on the part of the plaintiff; and
(4) evidence as to the true explanation of the event must be more readily accessible to the defendant than to plaintiff. [Citation.]

There is no question that requirements (1), (3), and (4) have been met by plaintiff. The words "*exclusive control*", however, have been the subject of much interpretation. The trend evident to this court is that "*The requirement of exclusive possession and control is not an absolutely rigid concept.*" [Citation.]

* * *

"Reliance on *res ipsa* would not require plaintiff to establish exclusive control over the (instrumentality) but merely a degree of domination sufficient to identify defendant with probability as the party responsible for plaintiff's injuries * * * " [Citation.]

* * *

The Court finds that defendant, by its own testimony, has admitted either exclusive or at least joint control of the safety screen in fact as interpreted under the law. Both "the Mets" and the City of New York owed an independent duty to a spectator, and indeed a heightened duty arising out of the dangers reasonably to be anticipated from extending an invitation to the public to sit in the most dangerous area of the stadium. This duty mandates that "the Mets" exercise strict control of the screen, assuring the public that they may rely on the implied safety of sitting in that area.

Considering all the circumstances, the indicia of sole, joint, or concurrent dominion or control over the safety nets to qualify for the application of the *res ipsa* doctrine are compelling: * * *

Accordingly, on this record, the jury was free to conclude logically that defendant was at all times under a duty to maintain and control the protective screening for the safety of plaintiff who has purchased a ticket seating her behind the safety screen, thereby causing her to rely on its protection; and the injury from a foul ball was an accident that would not have occurred in the absence of defendant's negligence.

Thus, the Court denies defendant's motion to set aside the jury's verdict under the doctrine of *res ipsa loquitur.*

PROXIMATE CAUSE

One of the requirements of imposing liability for the negligent conduct of a defendant is that the conduct not only caused injury to the plaintiff but was also the proximate cause of the injury. Most simply expressed, proximate cause consists of the judicially imposed limitations on a person's liability for the consequences of his negligence. As a matter of social policy, legal responsibility has not been permitted to follow all the consequences of a negligent act. Responsibility has been limited—to a greater extent than with intentional torts—to those persons and results that are closely connected with the negligent conduct.

Causation in Fact

To support a finding that the defendant's negligence was the proximate cause of the plain-tiff's injury, it is first necessary to show that the defendant's conduct was the *actual cause* of the injury. A widely applied test for causation in fact is the **but for rule:** A person's conduct is a cause of an event if the event would not have occurred *but for* the person's negligent conduct. Under this test, an act or omission to act is *not* a cause of an event if that event would have occurred regardless of the act or omission. For instance, Arnold fails to erect a barrier around an excavation. Doyle is driving a truck when its accelerator becomes stuck. Arnold's negligence is not a cause in fact of Doyle's death if the runaway truck would have crashed through the barrier even if it had been erected. Similarly, failure to install a proper fire escape to a hotel is not the cause in fact of the death of a person who is suffocated by the smoke while sleeping in bed.

The "but for" test, however, is not useful where there are two or more forces actively operating, each of which is sufficient to bring about the harm in question. For example, Jay accidentally stabs Mary with a knife while Carlos negligently fractures Mary's skull with a rock. Either wound would be fatal, and Mary dies from both. Under the "but for" test, either Jay or Carlos, or both, could argue that Mary would have died from the wound inflicted by the other and therefore he is not liable. The **substantial factor test** addresses this problem by stating that negligent conduct is a legal cause of harm to another if the conduct is a substantial factor in bringing about the harm.[7] Under this test the conduct of both Jay and Carlos would be found to be a cause in fact of Mary's death.

Limitations on Causation In Fact

As a matter of policy, the law imposes limitations on the causal connection between the defendant's negligence and the plaintiff's injury. Two of the factors that are taken into consideration in determining such limitations are (a) unforeseeable consequences, and (b) superseding causes.

Unforeseeable Consequences The liability of a negligent defendant for unforeseeable consequences has proved to be troublesome and controversial. The Restatement and a majority of the courts have adopted the following position. Even if the defendant's negligent conduct is a cause in fact of harm to the plaintiff, the defendant is *not* liable to the plaintiff *unless* the defendant could have reasonably anticipated injuring the plaintiff or a class of persons of which the plaintiff is a member.[8] Proximate cause involves a recognition of the risk of harm to the plaintiff individually or to a class of persons of which the plaintiff is a member.

For example, A, while negligently driving an automobile, collides with a car carrying dynamite. A is unaware of the contents of the other car and had no reason to know about it. The collision causes the dynamite to explode, shattering glass in a building a block away. The shattered glass injures B, who is inside the building. The explosion also injures C, who is walking on the sidewalk near the collision. A would be liable to C because A should have realized that his negligent driving might result in a collision that would endanger pedestrians nearby, and the fact that the actual harm resulted in an unforeseeable manner does not affect his liability. B, however, was beyond the zone of danger, and A is therefore not liable to B. A's negligent driving is not deemed to be the "proximate cause" of B's injury because, looking back from the harm to A's negligence, it appears highly extraordinary that A's conduct should have brought about the harm to B.

PALSGRAF v. LONG ISLAND RAILROAD CO.
Court of Appeals of New York, 1928.
248 N.Y. 339, 162 N.E. 99.

Facts: Palsgraf was on the railroad station platform buying a ticket when a train stopped at the station. As it began to depart, two men ran to catch it. After the first was safely aboard, the second jumped onto the moving car. When he started to fall, a guard on the train reached to grab him and another guard on the platform pushed the man from behind. They helped the man to regain his balance, but in the process they knocked a small package out of his arm. The package, which contained fireworks, fell onto the rails and exploded. The shock from the explosion knocked over a scale resting on the other end of the platform, and it landed on Mrs. Palsgraf. She then brought an action against the railroad to recover for the injuries she sustained. The railroad appeals from the trial and appellate courts' decisions in favor of Palsgraf.

Decision: Judgment for Palsgraf reversed.

Opinion: Cardozo, C. J.   The conduct of the defendant's guard, if a wrong in its relation to the holder of the package, was not a wrong in its relation to the plaintiff, standing far away. Relatively to her it was not negligence at all. Nothing in the situation gave notice that the falling package had in it the potency of peril to persons thus removed. Negligence is not actionable unless it involves the invasion of a legally protected interest, the violation of a right. "Proof of negligence in the air, so to speak, will not do." [Citations.] "Negligence is the absence of care, according to the circumstances." [Citations.]

* * *

If no hazard was apparent to the eye of ordinary vigilance, an act innocent and harmless, at least to outward seeming, with reference to her, did not take to itself the quality of a tort because it happened to be wrong, though apparently not one involving the risk of bodily insecurity, with reference to some one else. "In every instance, before negligence can be predicated of a given act, back of the act must be sought and found a duty to the individual complaining, the observance of which would have averted or avoided the injury." [Citations.]

* * *

A different conclusion will involve us, and swiftly too, in a maze of contradictions. A guard stumbles over a package which has been left upon a platform. It seems to be a bundle of newspapers. It turns out to be a can of dynamite. To the eye of ordinary vigilance, the bundle is abandoned waste, which may be kicked or trod on with impunity. Is a passenger at the other end of the platform protected by the law against the unsuspected hazard concealed beneath the waste? If not, is the result to be any different, so far as the distant passenger is concerned, when the guard stumbles over a valise which a truckman or a porter has left upon the walk? The passenger far away, if the victim of a wrong at all, has a cause of action, not derivative, but original and primary. His claim to be protected against invasion of his bodily security is neither greater nor less because the act resulting in the invasion is a wrong to another far removed. In this case, the rights that are said to have been violated, the interests said to have been invaded, are not even of the same order. The man was not injured in his person nor even put in danger. The purpose of the act, as well as its effect was to make his person safe. If there was wrong to him at all, which may very well be doubted, it was a wrong to a property interest only, the safety of his package. Out of this wrong to property, which threatened injury to nothing else, there has passed, we are told, to the plaintiff by derivation or succession a right of action for the invasion of an interest of another order, the right to bodily security. The diversity of interests emphasizes the futility of the effort to build the plaintiff's right upon the basis of a wrong to some one else.* * * One who jostles one's neighbor in a crowd does not invade the rights of others standing at the outer fringe when the unintended contact casts a bomb upon the ground. The wrongdoer as to them is the man who carries the bomb, not the one who explodes it without suspicion of the danger.

Superseding Cause   A **superseding cause** is an *intervening* event or act that occurs after the defendant's negligent conduct and relieves him of liability for harm to the plaintiff caused in fact by both the defendant's negligence and the intervening event or act.[9] For example, Gerald negligently runs down a cow, which is left lying stunned in the road. Several minutes later the cow regains consciousness, takes fright, and charges into Tina, a bystander. The cow's conduct is an intervening, but *not* a superseding, cause of harm to Tina because it is a normal consequence of the situation caused by Gerald's negligence. Therefore, Gerald is liable to Tina.

In contrast, William negligently leaves an excavation in a public sidewalk into which Jack intentionally hurls Jill. William is not liable to Jill because Jack's conduct is a superseding cause that relieves William of liability.

PETITION OF KINSMAN TRANSIT CO.
United States Court of Appeals, Second Circuit, 1964.
338 F.2d 708.

Facts: The *MacGilvray Shiras* was a ship owned by the Kinsman Transit Company. During the winter months when Lake Erie was frozen, the ship and others moored at docks on the Buffalo River. As oftentimes happened, one night an ice jam disintegrated upstream, sending large chunks of ice downward. Chunks of ice began to pile up against the *Shiras*, which at that time was without power and manned only by a shipman. The ship broke loose when a negligently constructed "deadman" to which one mooring cable was attached pulled out of the ground. The "deadman" was operated by Continental Grain Company. The ship began moving down the S-shaped river stern first and struck another ship, the *Tewksbury*. The *Tewksbury* also broke loose from its mooring, and the two ships floated down the river together. Although the crew manning the Michigan Avenue Bridge downstream had been notified of the runaway ships, they failed to raise the bridge in time to avoid a collision because of a mixup in the shift changeover. As a result, both ships crashed into the bridge and were wedged against the bank of the river. The two vessels substantially dammed the flow of the river, causing ice and water to back up and flood installations as far as three miles upstream. The injured parties brought this action for damages against Kinsman, Continental, and the city of Buffalo. The trial court found the three defendants liable and they appeal from that decree.

Decision: Decree of trial court affirmed as to liability.

Opinion: **Friendly, J.** The very statement of the case suggests the need for considering *Palsgraf v. Long Island RR.*, [citation], and the closely related problem of liability for unforeseeable consequences.

* * *

We see little similarity between the Palsgraf case and the situation before us. The point of Palsgraf was that the appearance of the newspaper-wrapped package gave no notice that its dislodgement could do any harm save to itself and those nearby, and this by impact, perhaps with consequent breakage, and not by explosion. In contrast, a ship insecurely moored in a fast flowing river is a known danger not only to herself but to the owners of all other ships and structures down river, and to persons upon them. No one would dream of saying that a shipowner who "knowingly and wilfully" failed to secure his ship at a pier on such a river "would not have threatened" persons and owners of property downstream in some manner. The shipowner and the wharfinger in this case having thus owed a duty of care to all within the reach of the ship's known destructive power, the impossibility of advance identification of the particular person who would be hurt is without legal consequence. [Citations.] Similarly the foreseeable consequences of the City's failure to raise the bridge were not limited to the Shiras and the Tewksbury. Collision plainly created a danger that the bridge towers might fall onto adjoining property, and the crash of two uncontrolled lake vessels, one 425 feet and the other 525 feet long, into a bridge over a swift ice-ridden stream, with a channel only 177 feet wide, could well result in a partial damming that would flood property upstream.

* * *

All the claimants here met the Palsgraf requirement of being persons to whom the actors owed a "duty of care," * * *. But this does not dispose of the alternative argument that the manner in which several of the claimants were harmed, particularly by flood damage, was unforeseeable and that recovery for this may not be had—whether the argument is put in the forthright form that unforeseeable damages are not recoverable or is concealed under a formula of lack of "proximate cause."

So as far as concerns the City, the argument lacks factual support. Although the obvious risks from not raising the bridge were damage to itself and to the vessels, the danger of a fall of the bridge and of flooding would not have been unforeseeable under the circumstances to anyone who gave them thought. And the same can be said as to the failure of Kinsman's shipkeeper to ready the anchors after the danger had become apparent.* * *

Continental's position on the facts is stronger. It was indeed foreseeable that the improper construction and lack of inspection of the "deadman" might cause a ship to break loose and damage persons and property on or near the river—that was what made Continental's conduct negligent. With the aid of hindsight one can also say that a prudent man, carefully pondering the problem, would have realized that the danger of this would be greatest under such water conditions as developed during the night of January 21, 1959, and that if a vessel should break loose under those circumstances, events might transpire as they did. But such *post hoc* step by step analysis would render "foreseeable" almost anything that has in fact occurred; if the argument relied upon has legal validity, it ought not be circumvented by characterizing as foreseeable what almost no one would in fact have foreseen at the time.

* * *

Foreseeability of danger is necessary to render conduct negligent; where as here the damage was caused by just those forces whose existence required the exercise of greater care than what was taken—the current, the ice, and the physical mass of the Shiras, the incurring of consequences other and greater than foreseen does not make the conduct less culpable or provide a reasoned basis for insulation. [Citation.] The oft encountered argument that failure to limit liability to foreseeable consequences may subject the defendant to a loss wholly out of proportion to his fault seems scarcely consistent with the universally accepted rule that the defendant takes the plaintiff as he finds him and will be responsible for the full extent of the injury even though a latent susceptibility of the plaintiff renders this far more serious than could reasonably have been anticipated. [Citation.]

The weight of authority in this country rejects the limitation of damages to consequences foreseeable at the time of the negligent conduct when the consequences are "direct," and the damage, although other and greater than expectable, is of the same general sort that was risked.

* * *

Here it is surely more equitable that the losses from the operator's negligent failure to raise the Michigan Avenue Bridge should be ratably borne by Buffalo's taxpayers than left with the innocent victims of the flooding; yet the mind is also repelled by a solution that would impose liability solely on the City and exonerate the persons whose negligent acts of commision and omission were the precipitating force of the collision with the bridge and its sequelae. We go only so far as to hold that where, as here, the damages resulted from the same physical forces whose existence required the exercise of greater care than was displayed and were of the same general sort that was expectable, unforeseeability of the exact developments and of the extent of the loss will not limit liability. Other fact situations can be dealt with when they arise.

INJURY

The plaintiff must prove that the defendant's negligent conduct caused harm to a legally protected interest. Certain interests receive little or no protection from negligent interference, while others receive full protection. The extent of protection for a particular interest is determined by the courts as a matter of law on the basis of social policy and expediency. For example, negligent conduct that is the proximate cause of harmful contact with the person of another is actionable. Thus, if Bob negligently runs into Julie, a pedestrian, who is carefully crossing the street, Bob is liable for physical injuries sustained by Julie as a result of the collision. On the other hand, if Bob's careless conduct causes only offensive contact with Julie's person, Bob is not liable.

The courts have traditionally been reluctant to allow recovery for negligently inflicted emotional distress. This view has gradually changed during this century, and the majority of courts now hold a person liable for negligently causing emotional distress if bodily harm results from the distress. If the defendant's conduct merely results in emotional disturbance without bodily harm, however, the defendant is not liable.

DEFENSES

Although a plaintiff has established by the preponderance of the evidence all the required elements of a negligence action, he may nevertheless be denied recovery if the defendant proves a valid defense. As a general rule, any defense to an intentional tort is also available in an action in negligence. In addition, there are defenses available in negligence cases that are not defenses to intentional torts.

Contributory Negligence

Contributory negligence is defined as conduct on the part of the *plaintiff* that falls below the standard to which he should conform for his own protection and that is a legal cause of the plaintiff's harm.[10] If negligence of the plaintiff together with negligence of the defendant proximately caused the injury and damage sustained by the plaintiff, he cannot recover *any* damages from the defendant. It does not matter whether the plaintiff's contributory negligence was slight or extensive.

Notwithstanding the contributory negligence of the plaintiff, if the defendant had a **last clear chance** to avoid injury to him but did not avail himself of such chance, the contributory negligence of the plaintiff does not bar his recovery of damages. For example, Kenneth negligently stops his car on the highway. Susan, who is driving along, sees Kenneth's car in sufficient time to stop. Susan, however, negligently puts her foot on the accelerator instead of the brake and runs into Kenneth's car. Because Susan had the last clear chance to stop her car before striking Kenneth's car, Kenneth's contributory negligence does not bar his recovery from Susan.

Comparative Negligence

The harshness of the contributory negligence doctrine has caused the great majority of States to reject the all-or-nothing rule of contributory negligence and to substitute the doctrine of **comparative negligence.** Under comparative negligence, damages are divided between the parties in proportion to the degree of fault or negligence found against them. For instance, Matthew negligently drives his automobile into Nancy, who is crossing against the light. Nancy sustains damages in the amount of $10,000 and sues Matthew. If the trier of fact (the jury or judge, depending on the case) determines that Matthew's negligence contributed 70 percent to Nancy's injury and that Nancy's contributory negligence contributed 30 percent of her injury, then Nancy would recover $7,000.

Most States that have adopted the doctrine of comparative negligence have enacted statutes that do not permit the plaintiff any recovery if her contributory negligence was as great as or greater than that of the defendant. Thus, in the example above, if the trier of fact determined that Matthew's negligence contributed 40 percent to Nancy's injury and Nancy's contributory negligence contributed 60 percent to her injury, then Nancy would not recover anything from Matthew.

Assumption of Risk

A plaintiff who has *voluntarily* and *knowingly* assumed the risk of harm arising from the negligent or reckless conduct of the defendant cannot recover from such harm. Basically, **assumption of risk** is the plaintiff's express or implied consent to encounter a known danger. Thus a spectator entering a baseball park may be regarded as consenting that the players may proceed with the game without taking precautions to protect him from being hit by the ball. The following case involves both contributory negligence and assumption of risk.

FALGOUT v. WARDLAW
Court of Appeal of Louisiana, Second Circuit, 1982.
423 So.2d 707.

Facts: Carolyn Falgout accompanied William Wardlaw as a social guest to Wardlaw's brother's camp. After both parties had consumed intoxicating beverages, Falgout walked onto a pier that was then only partially completed. Wardlaw had requested that she not go on the pier. Falgout said "don't tell me what to do," and proceeded to walk on the pier. Wardlaw then asked her not to walk past the completed portion of the pier. She ignored his warnings and walked to the pier's end. When returning to the shore, her shoe got caught between the boards. She fell, hanging by her foot, with her head and arms in the water. Wardlaw rescued Falgout, who had seriously injured her knee and leg. She sued Wardlaw for negligence. Falgout appeals from the trial court's judgment for Wardlaw.

Decision: Judgment for defendant affirmed.

Opinion: **Marvin, J.:** As a defense to * * * liability, [plaintiff] fault in some circumstances may encompass either or both assumption of the risk and contributory negligence * * *

Knowledge is the mainstay of assumption of risk and is imputed to a plaintiff, not because he was in a position to make observations, but only when he actually made the observations and it is found that plaintiff should reasonably have known that a particular risk existed. [Citation.] Assumption of risk is a subjective inquiry. [Citation.]

Contributory negligence is conduct which falls below the reasonable man standard and is determined by objective inquiry on a case to case basis. As a defense to liability, it is applied only where the policy considerations imposing the liability on the defendant in the first place are not present, such as where the defendant's conduct is not ultra hazardous, not abnormally dangerous, is not that of a manufacturer whose product causes injury, and is not commercial in the sense that it is designed to render a profit. Where these policy considerations are not present, [plaintiff] fault includes contributory negligence. [Citation.] Some circumstances which may not constitute assumption of risk, may constitute contributory negligence. [Citation.]

Here Ms. Falgout was told by her host not to go on the pier and, after she was on it, she was effectively told not to walk on the area where the decking boards were widely spaced. She had knowledge and, having traversed the pier to its end, she admittedly observed the variance in spacing of the decking. She was returning to the safer area where the decking was more closely and uniformly spaced when her foot or shoe got caught. The trial court's conclusions that she *saw* and *understood* the risk are supported by competent evidence which the trial court could believe. We find no error in the ultimate conclusion that Ms. Falgout assumed the risk because she *observed* and she was effectively told of the risk. Under these circumstances she should reasonably have known of the existence of the particular risk of getting her foot or her shoe caught in the wider spacing. [Citation.]

These circumstances also constitute contributory negligence. [Citation.] The defendants here were not engaged in an ultra hazardous or abnormally dangerous activity and were not engaged in a commercial enterprise. While the Wardlaw brothers manufactured or constructed the partially completed pier, they cannot be deemed to have been manufacturers of a product to gain a profit. The policy considerations or factors which impose strict liability to which contributory negligence is not a defense are sorely lacking and, in such circumstances, contributory negligence is encompassed in the defense of [plaintiff] fault. [Citation.]

STRICT LIABILITY

In some instances a person may be held liable for injuries he has caused even though he has not acted intentionally or negligently. Such liability is called strict liability, absolute liability, or liability without fault. The courts have determined that certain types of otherwise socially desirable activities pose sufficiently high risks of harm regardless of how carefully they are conducted, and therefore those who carry on these activities should bear the cost of all harm they cause. The doctrine of strict liability is *not* based on any particular fault of the defendant, but rather on the nature of the activity in which he is engaging. In effect, strict liability makes those who conduct these activ-ities insurers of all who may be harmed by the activity.

ACTIVITIES GIVING RISE TO STRICT LIABILITY

The activities that give rise to strict liability are: (1) maintaining abnormally dangerous conditions, (2) keeping animals, and (3) selling defective, unreasonably dangerous products.

Abnormally Dangerous Activities

Strict liability is imposed for harm resulting from extraordinary, unusual, abnormal, or exceptional activities, as determined in light of the place, time, and manner in which the activity is conducted. Activities to which the

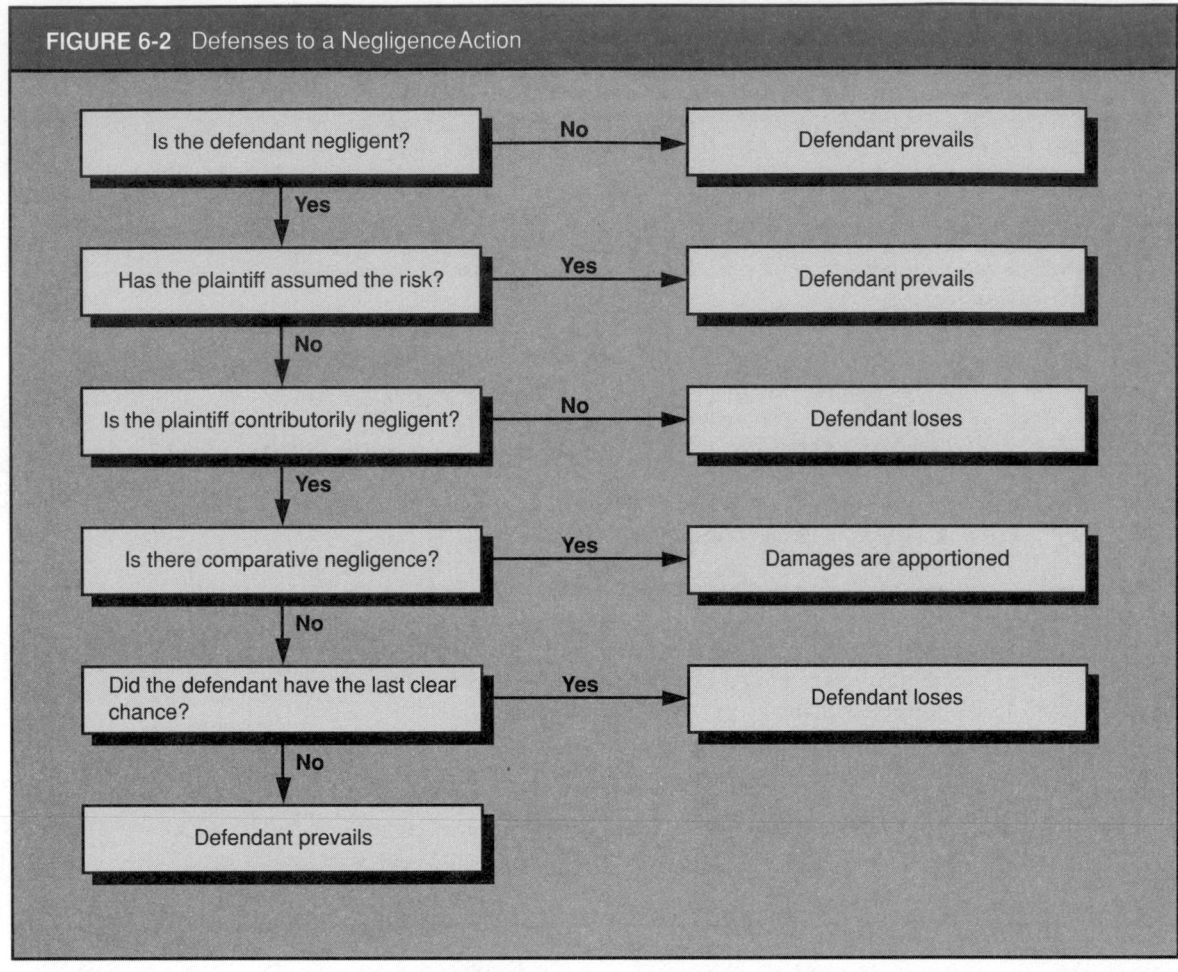

FIGURE 6-2 Defenses to a Negligence Action

rule has been applied include collecting water in such quantity and location as to make it dangerous; storing explosives or flammable liquids in large quantities; blasting or pile driving; crop dusting; drilling for or refining oil in populated areas; and emitting noxious gases or fumes into a settled community. On the other hand, courts have refused to apply the rule where the activity is a "natural" use of the land, such as drilling for oil in the oil fields of Texas, collecting water in a stock watering tank, and transmitting gas through a gas pipe or electricity in electric wiring.

Whether strict liability is imposed for abnormally dangerous activities is determined by considering a number of factors, including:

1. whether the activity involves a high degree of risk of harm;

2. whether the gravity of the harm is likely to be great;
3. whether the activity is a matter of common usage;
4. whether the activity is inappropriate to the place where it is carried on; and
5. the value of the activity to the community.

Keeping of Animals

Strict liability for harm caused by animals existed at common law and continues today with some modification. As a general rule, those who possess animals for their own purposes do so at their peril and must protect against harm to people and property.

Trespassing Animals Keepers of animals are generally held liable for any damage done if their animals trespass on the property of another. There are three exceptions to this rule: (1) keepers of cats and dogs are liable only for negligence; (2) keepers of animals are not strictly liable for animals straying from a highway on which they are being lawfully driven, although the owner may be liable for negligence if he fails to control them properly; and (3) in some western States keepers of farm animals, typically cattle, are not strictly liable for harm caused by their trespassing animals that are allowed to graze freely.

Nontrespassing Animals Keepers of wild animals are strictly liable for harm caused by such animals, whether or not they are trespassing. **Wild animals** are defined as those that in the particular region are known to be likely to inflict serious damage and that cannot be considered safe no matter how domesticated. Animals included in this category are bears, lions, elephants, monkeys, tigers, deer, and raccoons.

Domestic animals are those animals that are traditionally devoted to the service of mankind and that as a class are considered safe. Examples of domestic animals are dogs, cats, horses, cattle, and sheep. Keepers of domestic animals are liable if they knew, or should have known, of the animal's dangerous propensity.[11] As in the next case, the dangerous propensity of the animal must be the cause of the harm. For example, a keeper is not liable for a dog that bites a human merely because he knows that the dog has a propensity to engage in combat with other dogs. On the other hand, if a person's 150-pound sheep dog has a propensity to jump enthusiastically on visitors, the animal's keeper would be liable for any damage done by the dog's playfulness.

ALLEN v. WHITEHEAD
Supreme Court of Alabama, 1982.
423 So.2d 835.

Facts: Two-year-old David Allen was bitten by Joseph Whitehead's dog while he was playing on the porch at the Allen residence. Allen suffered facial cuts, a severed muscle in his left eye, a hole in his left ear, and scarring over his forehead. He sued Whitehead, claiming that, as owner, Whitehead is responsible for his dog's actions. Whitehead admitted that (1) the dog was large, mean looking, and frequently barked at neighbors; (2) the dog was allowed to roam wild; and (3) the dog frequently chased and barked at cars. He stated, however, that (1) the dog was friendly and often played with his and neighbors' children; (2) he had not received previous complaints about the dog; (3) the dog was neither aggressive nor threatening; and (4) the dog had never bitten anyone before this incident. The court granted a summary judgment in favor of Whitehead.

Decision: Summary judgment for Whitehead affirmed.

Opinion: Per Curiam This Court in *Kershaw v. McKown*, [citation], reiterated the common law rule that the owner of a dog is not liable for acts of the dog unless the owner had knowledge of the vicious propensities of the dog that resulted in the injury complained of. In *McCullar v. Williams*, [citation], the Court stated, ''[p]revious knowledge of the animal's vicious habits must be alleged and proved,'' although positive proof is not always necessary. [Citation.] This Court held in *Owen v. Hampson*, [citation], that the common law rule was still applicable in Alabama: * * * that previous knowledge of the animal's dangerous propensity, whether it be shown by positive proof or inferred from the circumstances, must be alleged and proved.

* * *

[Plaintiff] Allen asserts that there is a genuine issue of material fact relating to the alleged vicious propensities of the dog and the knowledge of appellee [Whitehead] as to such propensities. * * *

* * * we hold as a matter of law that evidence that a dog was large and mean looking, chased and barked at cars, and frequently barked at neighbors is not sufficient to present an issue of fact as to the dangerous propensities of such an animal.

* * *

* * * In his treatise, Professor Prosser has also stated that notice of the character of the animal "must extend to the trait or propensity which caused the damage." [Citation.] Accordingly, notice of an animal's playful character is not notice that it will viciously attack and bite a person. Liability is limited to the particular risk known to the defendant.

In *Owen v. Hampson*, [citation], the defendant's dog ran out and overturned plaintiff's motorcycle while plaintiff was riding on a public street. This Court stated that the law makes no distinction between an animal dangerous from playfulness and one dangerous from viciousness, but places on the owner a burden of restraint when he knows of the animal's dangerous propensities. [Citation.] The crucial issue remains whether the owner knows or has reason to know of the animal's dangerous propensities. This is not a case where the plaintiff was knocked down or injured in a manner traditionally associated with an overly friendly dog. The claim and the evidence is that David was attacked and bitten. Knowledge of an animal's playfulness would not provide sufficient notice that the dog would be likely to act in the harmful manner alleged in this incident.

Products Liability

A recent and important trend in the law is the imposition of a limited form of strict liability on manufacturers and merchants who sell goods in a *defective condition* unreasonably dangerous to the user or consumer.[12] Liability is imposed regardless of the seller's due care and applies to all merchant sellers. We cover this topic in Chapter 19.

DEFENSES

Contributory Negligence

Because the strict liability of one who carries on an abnormally dangerous activity, keeps animals, or sells products is not based on his negligence, the ordinary contributory negligence of the plaintiff is *not* a defense to such liability. The law in imposing strict liability places the full responsibility for preventing harm on the defendant. For example, Sharon negligently fails to observe a sign on a highway warning of a blasting operation conducted by Nick. As a result Sharon is injured by these operations. Sharon may nonetheless recover from Nick.

Comparative Negligence

Despite the rationale that disallows contributory negligence as a defense to strict liability, the great majority of States apply the doctrine of comparative negligence to products liability.

Assumption of Risk

Voluntary assumption of risk *is* a defense to an action based on strict liability. If the owner of an automobile knowingly and voluntarily parks the vehicle in a blasting zone, he may not recover for harm to his automobile. The assumption of risk, however, must be voluntary. If blasting operations are established, the possessor of nearby land is not required to move away and may recover for harm suffered.

CHAPTER SUMMARY

NEGLIGENCE

Duty of Care	**Definition of Negligence** conduct which falls below the standard established by law for the protection of others against unreasonable risk of harm **Reasonable Man Standard** degree of carefulness that a reasonable person would exercise in a given situation ■ *Children* must conform to conduct of a reasonable person of like age, intelligence, and experience ■ *Physical Disability* disabled person's conduct must conform to that of a reasonable person under like disability ■ *Mental Deficiency* mentally deficient person is held to reasonable man standard ■ *Superior Skill or Knowledge* professionals must exercise same care and skill normally possessed by members of their profession ■ *Emergencies* the reasonable man standard applies but the emergency is considered part of the circumstances ■ *Violation of Statute* if the statute applies, the violation is negligence *per se* **Duty of Affirmative Action** except in special circumstances, no one is required to aid another in peril **Special Duties of Possessors of Land** ■ *Duty to Trespassers* not to injure intentionally ■ *Duty to Licensees* to warn of known dangerous conditions licensees are unlikely to discover ■ *Duty to Invitees* to exercise reasonable care to protect invitees against dangerous conditions possessor should know of but invitees are unlikely to discover **Res Ipsa Loquitur** permits the jury to infer both negligent conduct and causation

Proximate Cause	**Causation in Fact** the defendant's conduct was the actual cause of, or a substantial factor in causing, the injury **Limitations upon Causation in Fact** ■ *Unforeseeable Consequences* no liability if defendant could not have reasonably anticipated the consequences ■ *Superseding Cause* an intervening act that relieves the defendant of liability

Injury	**Harm to Legally Protected Interest** plaintiff bears the burden of proof

Defenses to Negligence	Contributory Negligence failure of a plaintiff to exercise reasonable care for his own protection which prevents plaintiff from recovering anything Comparative Negligence damages are divided between the parties in proportion to their degree of negligence Assumption of Risk plaintiff's express or implied consent to encounter a known danger

STRICT LIABILITY

Activities Giving Rise to Strict Liability	Definition of Strict Liability liability for non-intentional and non-negligent conduct Abnormally Dangerous Activities as determined in light of the place, time, and manner in which activity is conducted Keeping of Animals for wild animals and usually for trespassing domestic animals Products Liability imposed upon manufacturers and merchants who sell goods in a defective condition unreasonably dangerous to the user or consumer

Defenses to Strict Liability	Contributory Negligence is *not* a defense to strict liability Comparative Negligence most States apply this doctrine to products liability cases Assumption of Risk is a defense to an action based upon strict liability

QUESTIONS

1. List and briefly describe the four required elements of an action for negligence.
2. Explain the duty of care that is imposed upon (a) adults, (b) children, (c) persons with a physical disability, (d) persons with a mental deficiency, (e) persons with superior knowledge, and (f) persons acting in an emergency.
3. Define trespassers, licensees, and invitees. Discuss the duties owed by possessors of land to each of these.
4. Identify the defenses that are available to a tort action in negligence. Identify those that are available in a tort action in strict liability.
5. Identify and discuss those activities giving rise to a tort action in strict liability.

PROBLEMS

1. A statute that requires railroads to fence their tracks is construed as intended solely to prevent injuries to animals straying onto the right-of-way. B & A Railroad Company fails to fence its tracks.

Two of Calvin's cows wander onto the track. Nellie is hit by a train. Elsie is poisoned by weeds growing beside the track. For which cows, if any, is B & A Railroad Company liable to Calvin? Why?

2. Martha invites John to come to lunch. Martha knows that her private road is dangerous to travel, having been guttered by recent rains. She doesn't warn John of the condition, reasonably believing that he will notice the gutters and exercise sufficient care. John's attention, while driving over, is diverted from the road by the screaming of his child, who has been stung by a bee. He fails to notice the condition of the road, hits a gutter, and skids into a tree. If John is not contributorily negligent, is Martha liable to John?

3. Nathan is run over by a car and left lying in the street. Sam, seeing Nathan's helpless state, takes him in his car for the purpose of taking him to the hospital. Sam drives negligently into a ditch, causing additional injury to Nathan. Is Sam liable to Nathan?

4. Vance was served liquor while he was an intoxicated patron of the Clear Air Force Station Non-Commissioned Officers' Club. He later injured himself as a result of his intoxication. An Alaska State statute makes it a crime to give or to sell liquor to intoxicated persons. Vance has brought an action

seeking damages for the injuries suffered. He argues that the United States was negligent *per se* by its employee's violation of the statute. Decision?

5. A statute requires all vessels traveling on the Great Lakes to provide lifeboats. One of Winston Steamship Company's boats is sent out of port without a lifeboat. Perry, a sailor, falls overboard in a storm so heavy that had there been a lifeboat it could not have been launched. Perry drowns. Is Winston liable to Perry's estate?

6. Lionel is negligently driving an automobile at excessive speed. Reginald's negligently driven car crosses the center line of the highway and scrapes the side of Lionel's car, damaging its fenders. As a result, Lionel loses control of his car, which goes into the ditch, wrecking the car and causing personal injuries to Lionel. What can Lionel recover?

7. (a) Ellen, the owner of a baseball park, is under a duty to the entering public to provide a reasonably sufficient number of screened seats to protect those who desire it against the risk of being hit by batted balls. Ellen fails to do so. Frank, a customer entering the park is unable to find a screened seat and, although fully aware of the risk, sits in an unscreened seat. Frank is struck and injured by a batted ball. Is Ellen liable?

(b) Gretchen, Frank's wife, has just arrived from Germany and is viewing baseball for the first time. Without asking any questions, she follows Frank to a seat. After the batted ball hits Frank, it caroms into Gretchen, injuring her. Is Ellen liable to Gretchen?

8. CC Railroad is negligent in failing to give warning of the approach of its train to a crossing and thereby endangers Larry, a blind man who is about to cross. Mildred, a bystander, in a reasonable effort to save Larry, rushes onto the track to push Larry out of danger. Although Mildred acts as carefully as possible, she is struck and injured by the train.

(a) Can Mildred recover from Larry?
(b) Can Mildred recover from CC Railroad?

9. An unidentified man was held up by two thugs in an alley in Manhattan. When the thieves departed with his possessions, the man quickly gave chase. He had almost caught one when the thief managed to force his way into an empty taxicab stopped at a traffic light. The cab was owned by the Peerless Transport Company. The thief pointed his gun at the driver's head and ordered him to drive on. The driver started to follow the directions while closely pursued by a posse of good citizens, but then suddenly jammed on the brakes and jumped out of the car to safety. The thief also jumped out, but the car traveled on, injuring Mrs. Cordas and her two children. The Cordases then brought an

action for damages, claiming that the cab driver was negligent in jumping to safety and leaving the moving vehicle uncontrolled. Decision?

10. Timothy keeps a pet chimpanzee that is thoroughly tamed and accustomed to playing with its owner's children. The chimpanzee escapes, despite every precaution to keep it on the owner's premises. It approaches a group of children. Wanda, the mother of one of the children, erroneously thinking the chimpanzee is about to attack the children, rushes to her child's assistance. In her hurry and excitement, she stumbles and falls, breaking her leg. Can Wanda recover for her personal injuries?

11. Hawkins slipped and fell on a puddle of water just inside of the automatic door to the H. E. Butt Grocery Company's store. The water had been tracked into the store by customers and blown through the door by a strong wind. The store manager was aware of the puddle and had mopped it up several times earlier in the day. Still, no signs had been placed to warn store patrons of the danger. Hawkins brought an action to recover damages for injuries sustained in the fall. Decision?

12. Escola, a waitress, was injured when a bottle of Coca Cola exploded in her hand while she was putting it into the restaurant's cooler. The bottle came from a shipment that had remained under the counter for thirty-six hours after being delivered by the bottling company. The bottler had subjected the bottle to the method of testing for defects commonly used in the industry, and there is no evidence that Escola or anyone else did anything to damage the bottle between its delivery and the explosion. Escola brought an action against the bottler for damages. Since she is unable to show any specific acts of negligence on its part, she seeks to rely on the doctrine of *res ipsa loquitur*. Decision?

13. Hunn injured herself when she slipped and fell on a loose plank while walking down some steps that the hotel had repaired the day before. The night before, while entering the hotel, she had noticed that the steps were dangerous, and although she knew from her earlier stays at the hotel that another exit was available, she chose that morning to leave via the dangerous steps. The hotel was aware of the hazard, as one of three other guests who had fallen that night had reported his accident to the desk clerk then on duty. Still, there were no cautionary signs on the steps to warn of the danger, and they were not roped off or otherwise excluded from use. Hunn brought an action against the hotel for injuries she sustained as a result of her fall. Decision?

14. Fredericks, a hotel owner, had a dog named "Sport" that he had trained as a watch-dog. When

Vincent Zarek, a guest at the hotel, leaned over to pet the dog, it bit him. Although Sport had never bitten anyone before, Fredericks was aware of the dog's violent tendencies and, therefore, did not allow it to roam around the hotel alone. Vincent brought an action for injuries sustained when the dog bit him. Decision?

ENDNOTES

1. Restatement, Second, Torts, Section 296, Emergency.

2. Restatement, Second, Torts, Section 286, When Standard of Conduct Defined by Legislation or Regulation Will Be Adopted.

3. Restatement, Second, Torts, Section 314, Duty to Act for Protection of Others.

4. Restatement, Second, Torts, Section 342, Dangerous Conditions Known to Possessor.

5. Restatement, Second, Torts, Section 343, Dangerous Conditions Known to or Discoverable by Possessor.

6. Restatement, Second, Torts, Section 328D, Res Ipsa Loquitur.

7. Restatement, Second, Torts, Section 432, Negligent Conduct as Necessary Antecedent of Harm.

8. Restatement, Second, Torts, Section 435, Foreseeability of Harm or Manner of Its Occurrence.

9. Restatement, Second, Torts, Section 442, Considerations Important in Determining Whether an Intervening Force is a Superseding Cause.

10. Restatement, Second, Torts, Section 463, Contributory Negligence Defined.

11. Restatement, Second, Torts, Section 509, Harm Done by Abnormally Dangerous Domestic Animals.

12. Restatement, Second, Torts, Section 402A, Special Liability of Seller of Product for Physical Harm to User or Consumer.

PART 2
CONTRACTS

Contract law, like the law as a whole, is not static. It has undergone—and is still under-going—enormous changes. In the nineteenth century almost total freedom in forming con-tracts was the rule. As the noted legal scholar Samuel Williston wrote, "Economic writers adopted the same line of thought. Adam Smith, Ricardo, Bentham and John Stuart Mill successfully insisted on freedom of bargaining as the fundamental and indispensable requi-site of progress; and imposed their theories on the educational thought of their times with a thoroughness not common in economic spec-ulation." "Freedom of Contract," 6 *Cornell L.Q.* 365, 366 (1921). Although there was great free-dom in forming contracts, there were also many technicalities involved. Contract liability was imposed only when the parties complied strictly with the required formalities. Once properly formed, however, a contract bound the parties tightly. It was enforced according to its terms, and neither party would be lightly excused from performing it.

This view was consistent with the philoso-phy of governmental *laissez-faire* that was dominant at the time. As Professor Fried-mann in *Law in a Changing Society* explained it, "[t]he idea that the state on behalf of the community should intervene to dictate or alter terms of contracts in the public interest, is, on the whole, alien to the classical theory of common-law contract." Consequently, the watchword of the day was *caveat emptor*—let the buyer beware. The following excerpt fur-ther describes the nineteenth-century doc-trines as well as outlining the social forces and policies that brought about their decline:

The general principle that the buyer should and could look after himself had its roots in the idea that a system of robust trading was a good system in which the final outcome with respect to resource allocation and income distribution

was desirable. This attitude was itself supported by three ideas. The value judgment was wide-spread that if a fool and his money were soon parted then that was no more than was to be expected and was 'right': just as a tone-deaf person could not expect a career as a profes-sional musician, so a fool could not expect to engage in other than foolhardy actions. The second idea which consolidated the *caveat emp-tor* approach was the Adam Smith argument that a free market led to the best resource use. The third idea, running parallel to the second, was that if a buyer and seller made a 'contract' then, save for such cases as overt fraud, that contract was sacred.

If contracts, voluntarily entered into, were not going to be supported by the courts, then it was believed that fewer people would trade and so there would be less benefit from specialization and division of labour. This whole system of ideas seemed to be interlocking whole—and what is more a sensible way of running society, for it was also consistent with the notion of individual free-dom and individual responsibility.

This system of values thus gave a low priority to consumer protection. The rising role of con-sumer protection law is an example of the point that—whatever lawyers claim—the law is not an immutable system but manmade. Changes in the law are largely the result of men perceiv-ing the world differently from hitherto.

At least four reasons may be found for the rise of consumer protection law and the associated consumer lobbies. First, *caveat emptor* makes much sense in a primitive society where there is little trade but much self-reliance within the family and the village and what trade there is concerns goods such as farm produce where both buyer and seller might be equally knowl-edgeable. The buyer at the occasional fair or market would indeed be expected to take care, since he might never see the itinerant seller again. In many cases, the value of the sale would in any event be less than the likely transaction costs of going to court.

The twentieth-century consumer lives in a very different world. A far greater proportion of the family consumption of goods and services is bought and the average consumer is at some disadvantage compared to the retailer and manufacturer of electrical goods, consumer durables, and so forth—*that is, information is asymmetrically distributed.* This means that the concept of a bargain struck between equals is quite inappropriate and so, as in the case of monopoly legislation, attempts are made to defend the weaker party against any unfortunate outcomes of the bargains into which he freely enters—because he may have entered them innocently. It should be said that in many trivial transactions the costs of going to court far outweigh the losses and so many breaches of the letter or the spirit of the law go unpunished. The disgruntled shopper simply takes his business elsewhere in future.

If one reason for the attack on *caveat emptor* is because the world is more complex, and the distribution of information and bargaining power unequal, a second reason is that free market systems have come to be seen, at least technically, as not necessarily leading to the optimal use of resources. A third reason is that the value judgment implicit in the 'devil take the hindmost' attitude to the parting of a fool from his money is now much less widely held. People are commonly seen as the products of their own history and environment rather than as responsible in any direct sense for their own foolhardiness. J. M. Oliver, *Law and Economics*, 82–83 (1979).

As a result of these forces, contract law has experienced tremendous changes during this century. As we discuss in the next ten chapters, many of the formalities of contract formation have been relaxed. Today contractual obligations are usually recognized whenever the parties clearly intend to be bound. In addition, an increasing number of promises are now enforced in certain circumstances even though they do not comply strictly with the basic requirements of a contract. Although, in the past, contract liability was absolute and there were few, if any, escapes from liability once assumed, presently the law allows a party to be excused from contractual duties where fraud, duress, undue influence, mistake, unconscionability (unfairness), or impossibility is present. The nineteenth century's narrow view of contract damages has been expanded to grant equitable remedies and restitution for breach of contract. The older doctrine of privity of contract, which sharply restricted which parties could enforce contract rights, has given way to the current view that permits intended third-party beneficiaries to sue in their own right. Earlier contract theory did not require good faith and fair dealing among contracting parties who dealt at arm's length. Today the duty of good faith is imposed on parties to a contract, and the doctrine of unconscionability protects against grossly unfair dealings.

In brief, the twentieth century has left its mark on contract law by limiting the absolute freedom of contract and, at the same time, by relaxing the requirements of contract formation. The external, objective, and formal contract model of the nineteenth century has been replaced by one that is more individualized, subjective, and informal. Accordingly, we can say that now it is considerably easier both to get into a contract and to get out of one.

7 INTRODUCTION TO CONTRACTS

Every business enterprise, whether large or small, must enter into contracts with its employees, its suppliers of goods and services, and its customers in order to conduct its business operations. Thus contract law is an important subject for the business manager. Contract law is also basic to fields of law treated in other parts of this book, such as agency, sales of personal property, commercial paper, and secured transactions.

Even the most common transaction may involve many contracts. In a typical contract for the sale of land, the seller promises to transfer title, or right of ownership, to the land, and the buyer promises to pay an agreed-upon purchase price. In addition, the seller may promise to pay certain taxes, and the buyer may promise to assume a mortgage on the property or to pay the purchase price to a creditor of the seller. The buyer may pay part of the purchase price with a check, which is a contract containing the buyer's written order to his bank to pay a sum certain in money to the seller. If the parties have lawyers, they very likely have contracts with them. If the seller deposits the proceeds of the sale in a bank, he enters into a contract with the bank. If the buyer rents the property, he enters into a contract with the tenant. When one of the parties leaves his car in a parking lot to attend to any of these matters, he assumes a contractual relationship with the owner of the lot. In short, nearly every business transaction is based on contract and the expectations created by the agreed-upon promises. It is, therefore, essential that you know the legal requirements for making a promise or set of promises binding.

DEVELOPMENT OF THE LAW OF CONTRACTS

Common Law

Contracts are primarily governed by State common law. An orderly presentation of this law is found in the Restatements of the Law of Contracts. The first Restatement was adopted on May 6, 1932, by the American Law Institute. On May 17, 1979, the Institute adopted a revised edition of the Restatement—the Restatement, Second, Contracts—which will be referred to as the Restatement. For more than fifty years the Restatements have been regarded as a valuable authoritative reference work and have been extensively relied on and quoted in reported judicial opinions.

The Uniform Commercial Code

The sale of personal property is a large part of commercial activity. Article 2 of the Uniform Commercial Code (the Code or UCC) governs such sales in all States except Louisiana. A **sale** is a contract involving the transfer of title to goods from seller to buyer for a price.[1] The Code essentially defines **goods** as tangible personal property.[2] **Personal property** is any property other than an interest in land. For example, the purchase of a television set, an automobile, or a textbook is a sale of goods. All such transactions are governed by Article 2 of the Code, but, where general contract law has not been specifically modified by the Code, the common law of contracts continues to apply.[3]

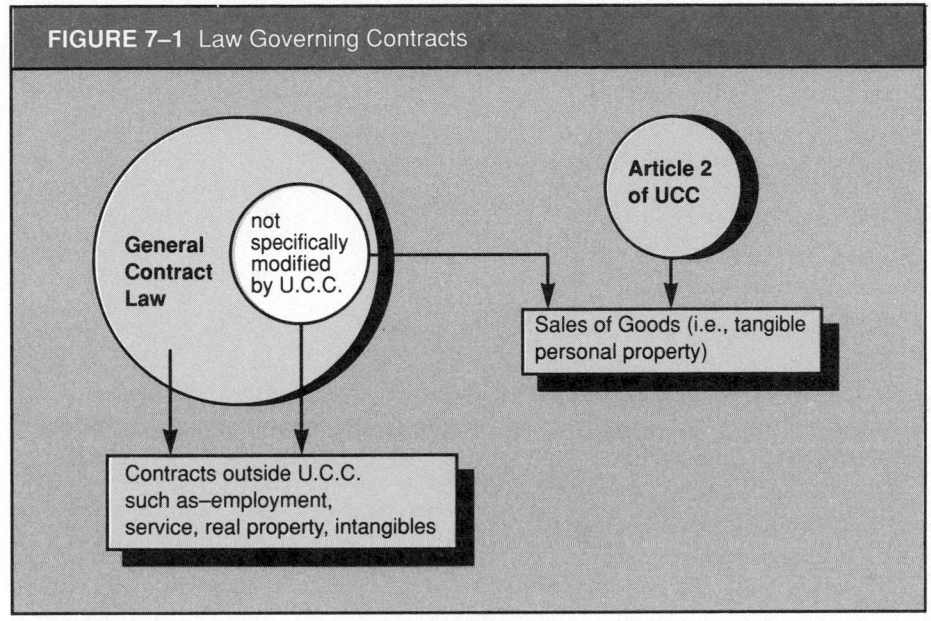

FIGURE 7–1 Law Governing Contracts

In other words, the law of sales is a specialized part of the general law of contracts, and the law of contracts governs unless specifically displaced by the Code.

Prior to the UCC, sales of personal property were governed by State laws, which varied from State to State. Since such sales are an important part of commercial activity, and since much of that activity takes place across State lines, the diversity of laws created difficulties. The Code has been successful in bringing uniformity to the commercial laws of forty-nine of the fifty States.

Types of Contracts Outside the Code

General contract law governs all contracts outside the scope of the Code. Such contracts play a significant role in commercial activities. For example, the Code does *not* apply to employment contracts, service contracts (as in the next case), insurance contracts, contracts involving **real property** (land and anything attached to it, including buildings), and contracts for the sale of intangibles such as patents and copyrights. These transactions continue to be governed by general contract law. See Figure 7–1 for a summary of what law governs contracts.

OSTERHOLT v. ST. CHARLES DRILLING CO.
United States District Court, E.D. Missouri, 1980.
500 F.Supp. 529.

Facts: St. Charles Drilling Co. contracted with Osterholt to install a well and water system that would produce a specified quantity of water. The water system failed to meet its warranted capacity and Osterholt sued for breach of contract.

Decision: Judgment for plaintiff.

Opinion: Filippine, J. The parties have not addressed the possibility that the Uniform Commercial Code, as adopted by Illinois, governs this case. The Court has given strong consideration to that possibility, but has concluded that the contract at issue was primarily a service contract, with a sale of goods incidental thereto, rather than vice versa. [Citation.] At least one Illinois appellate court has adopted a "predominant factor in the contract" test, [citation] to determine the applicability of the U.C.C. [Citation.] *Bonebrake v. Cox* [citation] involved a contract to sell and install specified items of used equipment in a bowling alley that had been damaged by fire. The Court held that the contract fell within the (Iowa) Uniform Commercial Code, rejecting the decision below that because the contract was "mixed" (for goods and services), the U.C.C. did not govern. The Court held that the U.C.C. did apply because the items to be installed fell within the U.C.C.'s definition of "goods" and because the language of the contract was essentially that of a sales contract. The Court formulated the following general test of the U.C.C.'s applicability: "The test for inclusion or exclusion is not whether [contracts] are mixed, but, granting that they are mixed, whether their predominant factor, their thrust, their purpose, reasonably stated, is the rendition of service, with goods incidentally involved (e.g., contract with artist for painting) or is a transaction of sale, with labor incidentally involved (e.g., installation of a water heater in a bathroom)." [Citation.] The Seventh Circuit, in a case governed by Illinois law, approved the *Bonebrake* test and held that a contract for the construction of a one-million-gallon water tank fell within the U.C.C. [Citation.]

This Court finds that the transaction between the parties in the instant case falls on the "service" side of the *Bonebrake* test, for two reasons: with two exceptions discussed below, the parties had no agreement specifying the various component parts of the "water system" which were to be installed. The defendant was not bound to use specified items of "goods" in the water system. Neither party has suggested that the estimate sheet . . . prepared by defendant the day before the contract was signed, was a part of the parties' contract. Essentially, defendant undertook to install a "water system" of indefinite description but with a certain warranted capacity, rather than to install a detailed list of specific "goods." Therefore, not only was the contract essentially for defendant's services, but the component parts did not become identified to the contract until they were actually installed on plaintiff's property, and thus it is doubtful that they fell within the definition of "goods" contained in [U.C.C.] 2–105.

Secondly, the language of the instant contract is unmistakably that of service rather than of sale. Defendant is identified as the "contractor," and the contract acknowledges "an express mechanics lien . . . to secure the amount of contract or repairs."

Thus, the Court concludes that the U.C.C. does not, strictly speaking, govern this case.

DEFINITION OF CONTRACT

Put simply, a **contract** is a binding agreement that the courts will enforce. The Restatement more precisely defines a contract as "a promise or a set of promises for the breach of which the law gives a remedy, or the performance of which the law in some way recognizes a duty."[4] A promise is a manifestation or demonstration of the intention to act or refrain from acting in a specified manner.[5] Those promises that meet *all* of the essential requirements of a binding contract are contractual and will be enforced. All other promises are *not* contractual, and usually no legal remedy is available for a **breach** (a failure to perform properly) of these promises. Thus, a promise may be contractual and therefore binding or noncontractual. In other words, all contracts are promises, but not all promises are contracts (see Figure 7–2).

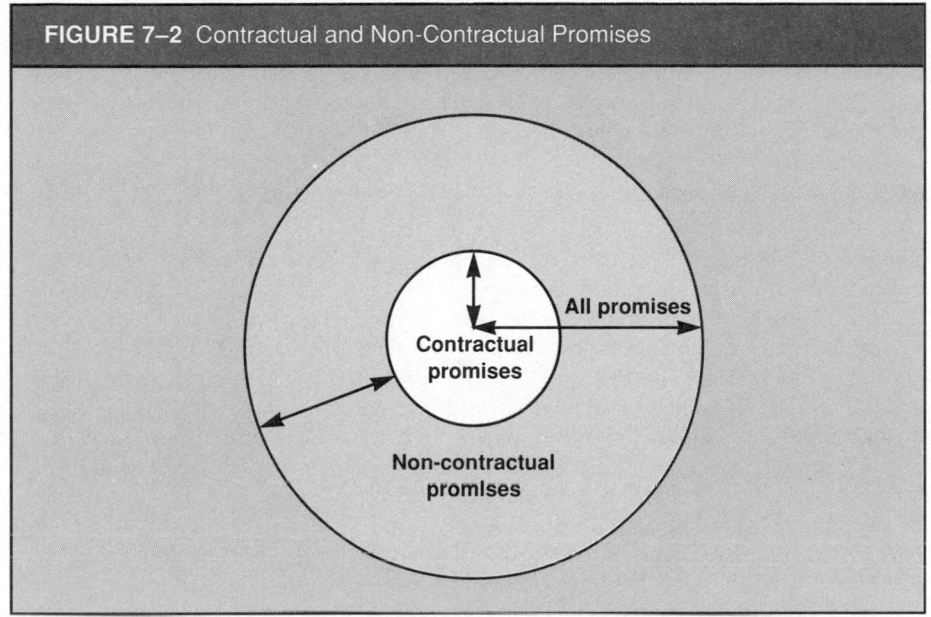

FIGURE 7–2 Contractual and Non-Contractual Promises

All promises

Contractual promises

Non-contractual promises

For example, a contract must have a lawful purpose to be binding. If Andy promises to pay Brenda $5,000 in return for Brenda's promise to burn down Carl's factory, neither promise is contractual and neither is binding because they are for an illegal purpose. As a result, the law will not provide a remedy to Brenda for Andy's failure to fulfill his promise. The law will also not provide a remedy to Andy for Brenda's failure to perform her promise.

ESSENTIALS OF A CONTRACT

The four essential ingredients of a contract are the following:

1. Manifestation of mutual assent
2. Consideration
3. Legality of object
4. Capacity of the parties

In addition, in a limited number of instances, a contract must be in writing to be enforceable, although in most cases an oral contract is binding and enforceable. As the following case shows, if all of these essentials are present, the promise is contractual and legally binding. If any of them is lacking, the promise is noncontractual. We consider these essentials separately in succeeding chapters.

STEINBERG v. CHICAGO MEDICAL SCHOOL
Illinois Court of Appeals, 1976.
41 Ill.App.3d 804, 354 N.E.2d 586.

Facts: Robert Steinberg applied for admission to the Chicago Medical School as a first-year student and paid an application fee of $15. The school, a private educational institution, rejected his application. Steinberg brought an action against the school, claiming that it did not evaluate his and other applications according to the academic entrance criteria printed in the school's bulletin. Instead, he argues, the school based its decisions primarily on nonacademic considerations, such as the applicant's family relationship to the school's faculty and members of its board of trustees and the ability of the applicant or his family to donate large sums of money to the school. Steinberg asserts that by evaluating his application according to these unpublished criteria, the school breached the contract it had created when it accepted his application fee. The trial court granted the defendant's motion to dismiss and Steinberg appeals.

Decision: Trial court's dismissal reversed and case remanded.

Opinion: Dempsey, J.   A contract is an agreement between competent parties, based upon a consideration sufficient in law, to do or not do a particular thing. It is a promise or a set of promises for the breach of which the law gives a remedy, or the performance of which the law in some way recognizes as a duty. [Citation.] A contract's essential requirements are: competent parties, valid subject matter, legal consideration, mutuality of obligation and mutuality of agreement. Generally, parties may contract in any situation where there is no legal prohibition, since the law acts by restraint and not by conferring rights. [Citation.] However, it is basic contract law that in order for a contract to be binding the terms of the contract must be reasonably certain and definite. [Citation.]

A contract, in order to be legally binding, must be based on consideration. [Citation.] Consideration has been defined to consist of some right, interest, profit or benefit accruing to one party or some forbearance, disadvantage, detriment, loss or responsibility given, suffered, or undertaken by the other. [Citation.] Money is a valuable consideration and its transfer or payment or promises to pay it or the benefit from the right to its use, will support a contract.

In forming a contract, it is required that both parties assent to the same thing in the same sense [citation] and that their minds meet on the essential terms and conditions. [Citation.] Furthermore, the mutual consent essential to the formation of a contract, must be gathered from the language employed by the parties or manifested by their words or acts. The intention of the parties gives character to the transaction, and if either party contracts in good faith he is entitled to the benefit of his contract no matter what may have been the secret purpose or intention of the other party. [Citation.]

Steinberg contends that the Chicago Medical School's informational brochure constituted an invitation to make an offer; that his subsequent application and the submission of his $15 fee to the school amounted to an offer; that the school's voluntary reception of his fee constituted an acceptance and because of these events a contract was created between the school and himself. He contends that the school was duty bound under the terms of the contract to evaluate his application according to its stated standards and that the deviation from these standards not only breached the contract, but amounted to an arbitrary selection which constituted a violation of due process and equal protection. He concludes that such a breach did in fact take place each and every time during the past ten years that the school evaluated applicants according to their relationship to the school's faculty members or members of its board of trustees, or in accordance with their ability to make or pledge large sums of money to the school. Finally, he asserts that he is a member and a proper representative of the class that has been damaged by the school's practice.

The school counters that no contract came into being because informational brochures, such as its bulletin, do not constitute offers, but are construed by the courts to be general proposals to consider, examine and negotiate. The school points out that this doctrine has been specifically applied in Illinois to university informational publications.

* * *

> We agree with Steinberg's position. We believe that he and the school entered into an enforceable contract; that the school's obligation under the contract was stated in the school's bulletin in a definitive manner and that by accepting his application fee—a valuable consideration—the school bound itself to fulfill its promises. Steinberg accepted the school's promises in good faith and he was entitled to have his application judged according to the school's stated criteria.

CLASSIFICATION OF CONTRACTS

Contracts can be classified from various standpoints, such as their method of formation, their content, and their legal effect. The standard classifications are (1) express or implied contracts; (2) bilateral or unilateral contracts; (3) void, voidable, or unenforceable contracts; (4) executed or executory contracts; and (5) formal or informal contracts. These classifications are not mutually exclusive. For example, a contract may be express, bilateral, valid, and informal.

Express and Implied Contracts

Parties to a contract may indicate their assent either in words or by conduct implying such willingness. For instance, a woman might pick up an item at a drug store, show it to the clerk, and walk out. This is a perfectly valid contract. The clerk knows from the customer's conduct that she is buying the item at the specified price and wants it charged to her account. Her actions speak as effectively as words. A contract in which the parties manifest assent in words is called an **express contract;** a contract formed by conduct is an implied, or more precisely, an **implied in fact contract.** Both are contracts, equally enforceable. The difference between them is merely the manner in which assent is manifested.

RICHARDSON v. J. C. FLOOD CO.
District Court of Appeals, 1963.
190 A.2d 259.

Facts: Richardson hired J. C. Flood Company, a plumbing contractor, to correct a stoppage in the sewer line of her house. The plumbing company's "snake" device, used to clear the line leading to the main sewer, became caught in the underground line. To release it, the company excavated a portion of the sewer line in Richardson's backyard. In the process, the company discovered numerous leaks in a rusty, defective water pipe that ran parallel with the sewer line. To meet public regulations, the water pipe, of a type no longer approved for such service, had to be replaced then or later when the yard would have to be redug for that purpose. The plumbing company proceeded to repair the water pipe. Richardson inspected the company's work daily and did not object to the extra work involved in replacing the water pipe, but she refused to pay any part of the total bill after the company completed the entire operation. J. C. Flood Company then sued Richardson for the costs of labor and material it had furnished. Richardson argues that she only requested correction of a sewer obstruction but had never agreed to the replacement of the water pipe. Richardson appeals from a trial court judgment against her for costs of labor and materials.

Decision: Judgment for J. C. Flood Company affirmed.

> **Opinion: Myers, J.** Contracts for work to be done are either express or implied—*express* when their terms are stated by the parties, *implied* when arising from a mutual agreement and promise not set forth in words. Direct evidence is not essential to prove a contract which may be presumed from the acts and conduct of the parties as a reasonable man would view them under all the circumstances. The testimony was conflicting but we cannot say that the trial court was wrong in holding that the burden of proving its right to recover had been carried by appellee [J. C. Flood Co.].
>
> With respect to the costs of both jobs the record reveals that no testimony was offered by appellant [Richardson] to show that itemized amounts for labor and materials furnished by appellee were wrong or excessive and unreasonable or that the work performed was either unnecessary or unsatisfactory. Appellee produced testimony that the charges were fair and reasonable and that the work on both the sewer and the water lines was fully completed. We find no merit in appellant's claim of error that the evidence on the costs of labor and material was insufficient to support the finding on this point.

Bilateral and Unilateral Contracts

In the typical contractual transaction, each party makes at least one promise. For example, Adelle says to Byron, "If you promise to mow my lawn, I will pay you ten dollars," and Byron agrees to mow Adelle's lawn. Adelle and Byron have made mutual promises, each agreeing to do something in exchange for the promise of the other. When a contract is formed by the exchange of promises, each party is under a duty to the other. This kind of contract is called a **bilateral contract** because each party is both a **promisor** (a person making a promise) and a **promisee** (the person to whom a promise is made).

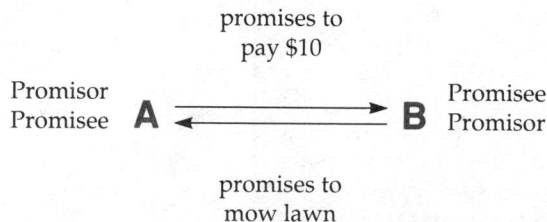

promises to
pay $10

Promisor
Promisee **A** ⇄ **B** Promisee
Promisor

promises to
mow lawn

But suppose that only one of the parties makes a promise. Adelle says to Byron, "If you will mow my lawn, I will pay you ten dollars." A contract will be formed when Byron has finished mowing the lawn and not before. At that time Adelle becomes contractually obligated to pay ten dollars to Byron. Adelle's offer was in exchange for Byron's act of mowing the lawn, and not for a promise of Byron to mow it. Byron was under no duty to mow the lawn. This is a **unilateral contract** because only *one* of the parties has made a promise.

promises to pay $10

Promisor **A** ⟶ **B** Promisee

Thus a bilateral contract results from the exchange of a promise for a return promise. A unilateral contract results from the exchange of a promise either for performing an act or for refraining from doing an act. Where it is not clear whether a unilateral or bilateral contract has been formed, the courts presume that the parties intended a bilateral contract. Thus, if Adelle says to Byron, "If you will mow my lawn, I will pay you ten dollars," and Byron replies "O.K., I will mow your lawn," a bilateral contract is formed.

Valid, Void, Voidable, and Unenforceable Contracts

By definition a **valid contract** is one that meets all of the requirements of a binding contract. It is an enforceable promise or agreement. Thus, a **void** contract is no contract at all. It is merely a promise or agreement that has no legal effect. An example of a void agreement is an agreement entered into by a person whom the courts have declared incompetent.

A **voidable** contract, on the other hand, is not wholly lacking in legal effect. It is a contract, but because of the manner in which it was formed or a lack of capacity of a party to it, the law permits one or more of the parties to avoid the legal duties created by the contract.[6] For instance, through intentional misrepresentation (*fraud*), Thomas induces Regina to enter into a contract. Regina may, upon discovery of the fraud, notify Thomas that by reason of the misrepresentation she will not perform her promise, and the law will support Regina. The contract induced by fraud is not void, but is voidable at the election of Regina, the defrauded party. Thomas, the fraudulent party, has no such election.

Although a contract may be neither void nor voidable, it may be unenforceable. An **unenforceable contract** is one for the breach of which the law does not provide a remedy.[7] For example, a contract may be unenforceable because of a failure to satisfy the requirements of the Statute of Frauds, which requires that certain kinds of contracts be in writing to be enforceable. Also, a party may not have the right to bring a lawsuit for breach of contract because of time limitations specified in the Statute of Limitations. After that period of time has passed, the contract is referred to as unenforceable, rather than void or voidable.

Executed and Executory Contracts

A contract that has been fully carried out by all of the parties is an **executed contract.** Strictly, an executed contract is no longer a contract because all duties under it have been performed, but it is useful to have a term for the completed contract. The term **executory contract** applies to contracts that are still partially or entirely unperformed by one or more of the parties.

Formal and Informal Contracts

A **formal contract** is legally binding because of its particular form or mode of expression. For example, at common law a promise under seal, a particular symbol that authenticates a document, is enforceable. (We discuss promises under seal in Chapter 10.) Another formal

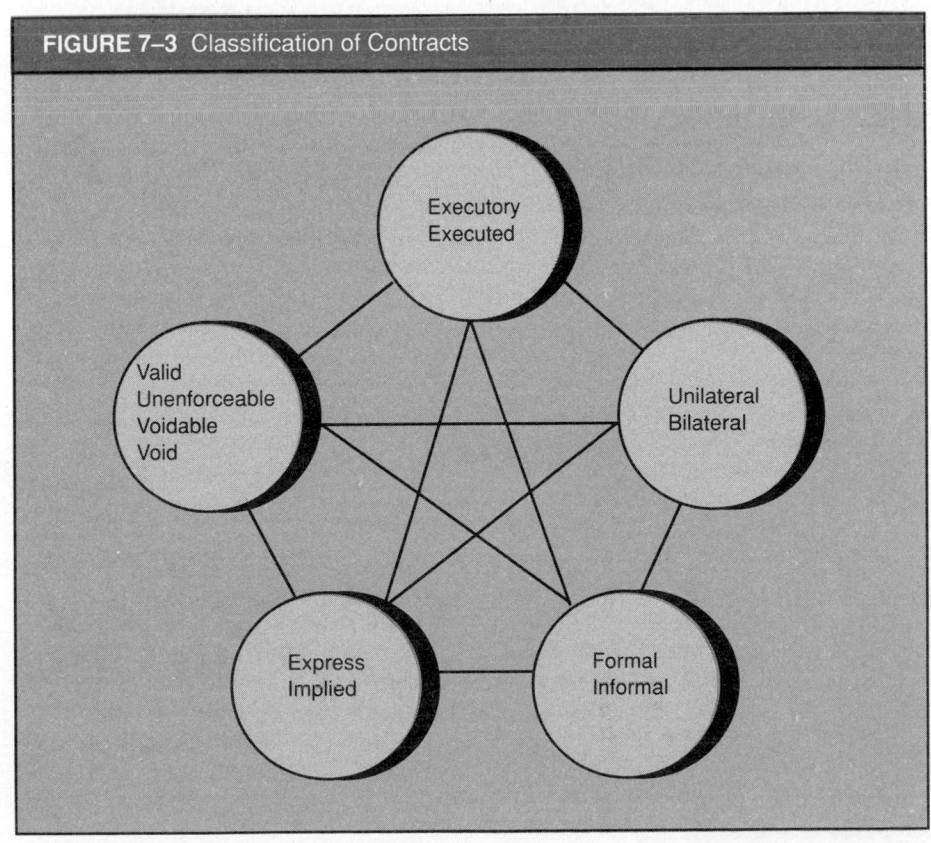

FIGURE 7–3 Classification of Contracts

contract is a negotiable instrument, such as a
check, which has certain legal attributes because of its special form. We cover negotiable
instruments in Chapters 22–26. A letter of
credit (a promise to honor drafts or other
demands for payment) is also a formal contract. Recognizances, formal acknowledgments of indebtedness made in court, are
another example of formal contracts. All other
contracts, whether oral or written, are **informal contracts** because they do not depend on
mere formality for their legal validity.

QUASI CONTRACTS

In addition to express and implied in fact
contracts, there are **implied in law** contracts or
quasi contracts, which were not included in
the previous classification of contracts for the

reason that a quasi (meaning "as if") contract
is not a contract at all.

A quasi contract is not a contract because it is
not based either on an express or an implied
promise. For example, Willard by mistake delivers to Roy a plain, unaddressed envelope
containing $100 intended for Lucia. Roy is
under no contractual obligation to return it,
but Willard is permitted to recover the $100
from Roy. The law imposes an obligation on
Roy in order to prevent his unjust enrichment
at the expense of Willard. The elements of
such a recovery are (1) a benefit conferred
upon the defendant (Roy) by the plaintiff
(Willard); (2) an appreciation or knowledge by
the defendant (Roy) of the benefit; and (3) an
acceptance or retention by the defendant (Roy)
of the benefit under circumstances making it
inequitable for the defendant (Roy) to retain
the benefit without payment of its value.

NURSING CARE SERVICES, INC. v. DOBOS
District Court of Appeals of Florida, Fourth District, 1980.
380 So.2d 516.

Facts: Mary Dobos was admitted to Boca Raton Community Hospital in serious
condition with an abdominal aneurysm. The hospital called upon Nursing Care
Services, Inc., to provide around-the-clock nursing services for Mrs. Dobos. She
received two weeks of in-hospital care, forty-eight hours of postrelease care, and
two weeks of at-home care. The total bill was $3,723.90. Mrs. Dobos refused to pay,
and Nursing Care Services, Inc., brought an action to recover. Mrs. Dobos
maintained that she was not obligated to render payment in that she never signed
a written contract nor did she orally agree to be liable for the services. The necessity
for the services, reasonableness of the fee, and competency of the nurses were
undisputed. After Mrs. Dobos admitted that she or her daughter authorized the
forty-eight hours of postrelease care, the trial court ordered compensation of $248
for that period. It did not allow payment of the balance, and Nursing Care Services,
Inc., appealed.

Decision: Remanded to trial court for entry of an amended final judgment for
Nursing Care Services, Inc. in the amount of $3,723.90 plus interest and court costs.

Opinion: Hurley, J.   We concur in the trial court's determination that the plaintiff failed to prove an express contract or a contract implied in fact. It is our view,
however, that the uncontradicted testimony, provided by plaintiff and defendant
alike, clearly established a contract implied in law which entitles the plaintiff to
recover.

Contracts implied in law, or as they are more commonly called, "quasi contracts,"
are obligations imposed by law on grounds of justice and equity. Their purpose is

to prevent unjust enrichment. Unlike express contracts or contracts implied in fact, quasi contracts do not rest upon the assent of the contracting parties. [Citation.]

One of the most common areas in which recovery on a contract implied in law is allowed is that of work performed or services rendered. The rationale is that the defendant would be unjustly enriched at the expense of the plaintiff if she were allowed to escape payment for services rendered or work performed. There is, however, an important limitation. Ordinarily liability is imposed to pay for services rendered by another only when the person for whose benefit they were rendered requested the services or knowingly and voluntarily accepted their benefits. [Citations.]

The law's concern that needless services not be foisted upon the unsuspecting has led to the formulation of the "officious intermeddler doctrine." It holds that where a person performs labor for another without the latter's request or implied consent, however beneficial such labor may be, he cannot recover therefor. [Citation.] A notable exception to this rule, however, is that of emergency aid:

A person who has supplied things or services to another, although acting without the other's knowledge or consent, is entitled to restitution therefor from the other if he acted unofficiously and with intent to charge therefor, and the things or services were necessary to prevent the other from suffering serious bodily harm or pain, and the person supplying them had no reason to know that the other would not consent to receiving them, if mentally competent, and it was impossible for the other to give consent or, because of extreme youth or mental impairment, the other's consent would have been immaterial. [Citation.]

In the case at bar it is unclear whether Mrs. Dobos, during the period of in-hospital care, understood or intended that compensation be paid. Her condition was grave. She had been placed in the hospital's intensive care unit and thereafter had tubes and other medical equipment attached to her body which necessitated special attention. She was alone, unable to cope and without family assistance. It is worthy of note that at no point during the litigation was there any question as to the propriety of the professional judgment that the patient required special nursing care. To the contrary, the record demonstrates that the in-hospital care was essential to Mrs. Dobos' health and safety. Given these circumstances it would be unconscionable to deny the plaintiff recovery for services which fall squarely within the emergency aid exception. [Citation.]

The third period of care is less difficult. It is unquestioned that during the at-home recuperation, Mrs. Dobos was fully aware of her circumstances and readily accepted the benefits conferred. Given such facts, we believe the rule set down in [Citation] must govern:

It is well settled that where services are rendered by one person for another which are knowingly and voluntarily accepted, the law presumes that such services are given and received in expectation of being paid for, and will imply a promise to pay what they are reasonably worth.

A patient's unannounced misconception that the cost of accepted services will be paid by an insurer or Medicare does not absolve her of responsibility to bear the cost of the services.

CHAPTER SUMMARY

Law of Contracts	**Definition of Contract** a binding agreement that the courts will enforce
	Common Law most contracts are primarily governed by State common law including contracts involving employment, services, insurance, real property (land and anything attached to it), patents, and copyrights
	Uniform Commercial Code Article 2 of the UCC governs the sales of goods
	  ■ *Sale* the transfer of ownership from seller to buyer
	  ■ *Goods* tangible personal property (personal property is all property other than an interest in land)

Classification of Contracts	**Express and Implied Contracts**
	  ■ *Express Contract* an agreement that is stated in words either in writing or orally
	  ■ *Implied in Fact Contract* contract where the agreement of the parties is inferred from their conduct
	Bilateral and Unilateral Contracts
	  ■ *Bilateral Contract* contract in which both parties exchange promises
	  ■ *Unilateral Contract* contract in which only one party makes a promise
	Void, Voidable, and Unenforceable Contracts
	  ■ *Void Agreement* no contract at all; without legal effect
	  ■ *Voidable Contract* contract capable of being made void
	  ■ *Unenforceable Contract* contract for the breach of which the law does not provide a remedy
	Executed and Executory
	  ■ *Executed Contract* contract that has been fully performed by all of the parties
	  ■ *Executory Contract* contract that has not been fully performed
	Formal and Informal Contracts
	  ■ *Formal Contract* agreement which is legally binding because of its particular form or mode of expression
	  ■ *Informal Conracts* all oral or written contracts other than formal contracts
	Quasi Contract an obligation not based upon contract that is imposed by law to avoid injustice; also called an *implied in law* contract

QUESTIONS

1. Distinguish between contracts that are covered by the UCC and those covered by common law.
2. Define the terms contract and breach.
3. List the essential elements of a contract.
4. Distinguish between express and implied contracts.
5. Distinguish between unilateral and bilateral contracts.
6. Explain the differences among void, voidable, and unenforceable agreements.
7. Distinguish between executed and executory contracts.
8. Distinguish between formal and informal contracts.

9. Explain how a quasi contract differs from a contract.

10. Identify the three elements of an enforceable quasi contract.

ENDNOTES

1. Uniform Commercial Code, Section 2—106(1), Definitions.

2. Uniform Commercial Code, Section 2—105(1), Definitions.

3. Uniform Commercial Code, Section 1—103, Supplementary General Principles of Law Applicable.

4. Restatement, Second, Contracts, Section 1, Contract Defined.

5. Restatement, Second, Contracts, Section 2(1), Promise; Promisor; Promisee; Beneficiary.

6. Restatement, Second, Contracts, Section 7, Voidable Contracts.

7. Restatement, Second, Contracts, Section 8, Unenforceable Contracts.

8 MUTUAL ASSENT

Although each of the four requirements for the formation of a contract is essential to its existence, mutual assent is so basic that frequently a contract is referred to as an agreement between the parties. When the contract is enforced, it is the agreement that is enforced. The agreement between the parties is the very core of the contract.[1]

A contractual agreement always involves either a promise exchanged for a promise (**bilateral contract**) or a promise exchanged for an act or forbearance to act (**unilateral contract**) as shown by what the parties communicate to one another. The way in which parties usually show mutual assent is by offer and acceptance.

To form a contract, the agreement must be objectively manifested. The important thing is what the parties indicate to one another by spoken or written words or by conduct. The law therefore applies an *objective* standard and is concerned only with the assent, agreement, or intention of a party as it reasonably appears from his words or actions. The law of contracts is not concerned with what a party may have actually thought or the meaning that he intended to convey, insofar as his subjective understanding or intention differed from the meaning objectively manifested. For example, if Joanne offers to sell to Bruce her Chevrolet automobile but intended to offer and believes that she is offering her Ford automobile, and Bruce accepts the offer, reasonably believing it was for the Chevrolet, a contract has been formed for the sale of the Chevrolet. Subjectively, there is no agreement as to the subject matter, but objectively there is a manifestation of agreement, and this is binding.

OFFER

An **offer** is a definite proposal or undertaking made by one person to another indicating a willingness to enter into a contract.[2] The person making the proposal is the **offeror.** The person to whom it is made is the **offeree.** When it is received, the offer confers on the offeree the power of acceptance, which is an expression of willingness to comply with the terms of the offer. The communication of an offer to an offeree does not of itself confer any rights or impose any duties on either of the parties. The offeror, by making an offer, has simply conferred upon the offeree a power to create a contract between the parties by duly accepting the offer. Until the offeree exercises this power, the outstanding offer creates neither rights nor liabilities.

ESSENTIALS OF AN OFFER

An offer need not take any particular form to have legal effect. To be effective, however, it must: (1) be communicated to the offeree; (2) manifest an intent to enter into a contract; and (3) be sufficiently definite and certain. If these essentials are present, an offer that has not terminated grants the offeree the power to form a contract by accepting the offer.

Communication

To have the mutual assent required to form a contract, the offeree must know about the offer, he cannot agree to something that he does not know about. In addition, the offer must be communicated by the offeror. For example, Oscar signs a letter containing an offer to Ellen and leaves it on top of the desk in his office. Later that day, Ellen, without prearrangement, goes to Oscar's office, discovers that he is away, notices the letter on his desk, reads it, and then writes on it an acceptance that she dates and signs. No contract is formed because the offer never became effective because it was never communicated by Oscar to Ellen.

Not only must the offer be communicated to the offeree, but the communication must also be made or authorized by the offeror. If Jones tells Black that she is going to offer $600 to White for a piano, and Black promptly informs White of Jones's intention, no offer has been made. There was no authorized communication of any offer by Jones to White. By the same token, if David should offer to sell to Lou his diamond ring, an acceptance of this offer by Tia would not be effective, as David made no offer to Tia.

An offer need not be stated or communicated by words. Conduct from which a reasonable person may infer a promise in return for either an act or a promise amounts to an offer.

An offer may be made to the general public. No person can accept such an offer, however, until and unless he knows that the offer exists. For example, if a person, without knowledge of the existence of an advertised reward for information leading to the return of a lost watch, gives information leading to the return, he is not entitled to the reward. His act was not an acceptance of the offer because he could not accept something of which he had no knowledge.

Intent

To have legal effect, an offer must further show an intent to enter into a contract. Some proposals lack such intent and are therefore not deemed offers. As a result, a purported acceptance does not bring about a contract but operates only as an offer.

Invitations Seeking Offers It is important to distinguish language that constitutes an offer from that which merely solicits or invites of-

fers. Communications between the parties in many cases take the form of preliminary negotiations. The parties are either requesting or supplying the terms of an offer that may or may not be given. A statement that may indicate a willingness to offer is not itself an offer. If Brown writes to Young, "Will you buy my automobile for $3,000?" and Young replies "Yes," there is no contract. Brown has not made an offer to sell her automobile to Young for $3,000. The offeror must manifest an intent to enter into a contract and not merely a willingness to enter into negotiation.

Merchants desire to sell their merchandise and thus are interested in informing potential customers about the goods, the terms of sale, and price. But if they make widespread promises to sell to each person on their mailing list, it is conceivable that the number of acceptances and resulting contracts might exceed their ability to perform. Consequently, a merchant might refrain from making offers by merely announcing that he has goods for sale, describing the goods, and quoting prices. He is inviting his customers and, in the case of published advertisements, the public, to make offers to him to buy the goods. His advertisements, circulars, quotation sheets, and display of merchandise are *not* offers because: (1) they do not contain a promise, and (2) they leave unexpressed many terms that would be necessary to the making of a contract. Accordingly, the responses are not acceptances because no offer to sell has been made.

Nonetheless, a seller is not free to advertise goods at one price and then raise the price once demand has been stimulated. Although as far as contract law is concerned no offer has been made, such conduct is prohibited by the Federal Trade Commission as well as legislation in most States. Moreover, in some circumstances a public announcement or advertisement may constitute an offer. This is so if the advertisement or announcement contains a definite promise of something in exchange for something else and confers a power of acceptance on a specified person or class of persons. The typical offer of a reward is an example of a definite offer as is the landmark *Lefkowitz* case, which follows.

LEFKOWITZ v. GREAT MINNEAPOLIS SURPLUS STORE, INC.
Supreme Court of Minnesota, 1957.
251 Minn. 188, 86 N.W.2d 689.

Facts: On April 6, 1956, Great Minneapolis Surplus Store published an advertisement in a Minneapolis newspaper reporting that "Saturday, 9:00 A.M. sharp; 3 brand new fur coats worth to $100; first come, first served, $1 each." Lefkowitz was the first to arrive at the store, but the store refused to sell him the fur coats because the "house rule" was that the offers were intended for women only and sales would not be made to men. The following week, Great Minneapolis published a similar advertisement for the sale of two mink scarves and a black lapin stole. Again Lefkowitz was the first to arrive at the store on Saturday morning, and once again the store refused to sell to him, this time because Lefkowitz knew of the house rule. This appeal is from a judgment awarding the plaintiff the sum of $138.50 as damages for breach of contract.

Decision: Judgment for Lefkowitz affirmed.

Opinion: Murphy, J. The defendant * * * relies upon authorities which hold that, where an advertiser publishes in a newspaper that he has a certain quantity or quality of goods which he wants to dispose of at certain prices and on certain terms, such advertisements are not offers which become contracts as soon as any person to whose notice they may come signifies his acceptance by notifying the other that he will take a certain quantity of them. Such advertisements have been construed as an invitation for an offer of sale on the terms stated, which offer, when received, may be accepted or rejected and which, therefore does not become a contract of sale until accepted by the seller; and until a contract has been so made, the seller may modify or revoke such prices or terms. [Citations.] * * *

On the facts before us we are concerned with whether the advertisement constituted an offer.

* * *

The test of whether a binding obligation may originate in advertisements addressed to the general public is "whether the facts show that some performance was promised in positive terms in return for something requested."

* * *

Whether in any individual instance a newspaper advertisement is an offer rather than an invitation to make an offer depends on the legal intention of the parties and the surrounding circumstances. [Citations.] We are of the view on the facts before us that the offer by the defendant of the sale * * * was clear, definite, and explicit, and left nothing open for negotiation. The plaintiff having successfully managed to be the first one to appear at the seller's place of business to be served, as requested by the advertisement, and having offered the stated purchase price of the article, he was entitled to performance on the part of the defendant. We think the trial court was correct in holding that there was in the conduct of the parties a sufficient mutuality of obligation to constitute a contract of sale.

Objective Standard for Intent An offer, as shown in the case that follows, is determined from the **objective manifestations** of the parties. This manifestation of intent of the parties is based upon what a reasonable person in the other's position would have believed.

CITY OF EVERETT v. ESTATE OF SUMSTAD
Supreme Court of Washington, 1981.
95 Wash.2d 853, 631 P.2d 366.

Facts: On August 12, 1978, Mr. and Mrs. Mitchell, the owners of a small secondhand store, attended Alexander's Auction, where they bought a used safe for $50. The safe, part of the Sumstad estate, contained a locked inside compartment. This fact was known to both the auctioneer and the Mitchells. Soon after the auction, the Mitchells had the compartment opened by a locksmith, who discovered $32,207 inside. The Everett Police Department impounded the money. The city of Everett brought an action against the Sumstad estate and the Mitchells to determine the owner of the money. Both parties moved for summary judgment. The trial court entered summary judgment for the estate, and the court of appeals affirmed. The Mitchells appealed.

Decision.   Case remanded to the trial court for entry of the summary judgment in favor of the Mitchells.

Opinion: Dolliver, J.   A sale is a consensual transaction. The subject matter which passes is to be determined by the intent of the parties as revealed by the terms of their agreement in light of the surrounding circumstances. [Citation.] The objective manifestation theory of contracts, which is followed in this state [citation] lays stress on the outward manifestation of assent made by each party to the other. The subjective intention of the parties is irrelevant.

> A contract has, strictly speaking, nothing to do with the personal, or individual, intent of the parties. A contract is an obligation attached by the mere force of law to certain acts of the parties, usually words, which ordinarily accompany and represent a known intent. If, however, it were proved by twenty bishops that either party, when he used the words, intended something else than the usual meaning which the law imposes upon them, he would still be held, unless there were some mutual mistake, or something else of the sort. [Citation.]

* * *

The inquiry, then, is into the outward manifestations of intent by a party to enter into a contract. We impute an intention corresponding to the reasonable meaning of a person's words and acts. [Citation.] If the offeror, judged by a reasonable standard manifests an intention to agree in regard to the matter in question, that agreement is established. [Citation.]

* * *

In the case before us, * * * the Mitchells were aware of the rule of the auction that all sales were final. Furthermore, the auctioneer made no statement reserving rights to any contents of the safe to the estate. Under these circumstances, we hold reasonable persons would conclude that the auctioneer manifested an objective intent to sell the safe and its contents and that the parties mutually assented to enter into that sale of the safe and the contents of the locked compartment.

Occasionally, a person exercises a sense of humor by speaking or writing words that, taken literally and without regard to context or surrounding circumstances, could be construed as an offer. The promise is intended as a joke, however, and the promisee as a reasonable man should understand it to be such. Therefore it is not an offer. It should not create a sense of reasonable expectancy in the mind of the person to whom it is made because he realizes or should realize that it is not made in earnest. There is no contractual intent on the part of the promisor, and the promisee is or reasonably ought to be aware of that fact. If, however, the intended jest is so successful that the promisee as a reasonable person under all the circumstances reasonably believes that it has been made as an offer, and so believing accepts, the objective standard applies, and the parties have entered into a contract.

A promise made under circumstances of obvious excitement or emotional strain is likewise not an offer. For example, Sara, after having her month-old Cadillac break down for the third time in two days, screams in disgust, "I will sell this car to anyone for ten dollars." Larry hears Sara and hands her a ten-dollar bill. Under the circumstances, Sara's statement was not an offer—if a reasonable person in Larry's position would not have considered it one.

Definiteness

The terms of a contract must be clear enough to provide a court with a reasonable basis for determining the existence of a breach and for giving an appropriate remedy.[3] It is a fundamental policy that contracts should be made by the parties and not by the courts; accordingly, remedies for breach must have a basis in the parties' contract. Recently, Pennzoil was awarded a 10.53 billion dollar verdict (subsequently settled for 3 billion dollars) in a lawsuit against Getty Oil Company involving whether a definite contract was formed or whether the parties merely "shook hands." See Law in the News on page 176.

Where the parties have intended to form a contract, the courts will attempt to find a basis for granting a remedy. Missing terms may be supplied by course of dealing, usage of trade, or by inference. Thus uncertainty as to incidental matters will seldom be fatal so long as the parties intend to form a contract. A court will nevertheless not rescue a contract in which the parties cover a term but leave it vague or indefinite.

Open Terms   With respect to agreements for the sale of goods, the Uniform Commercial Code provides standards by which omitted terms may be determined, provided the parties intended to enter into a binding contract.[4] The Restatement has adopted an approach similar to the Code's in supplying terms omitted in the parties' contract.[3, 5]

Under the Code and Restatement, an offer may leave open particulars of performance to be specified by one of the parties. Any such specification must be made in good faith and within limits set by commercial reasonableness.[6] **Good faith** is defined as honesty in fact in the conduct or transaction concerned.[7] **Commercial reasonableness** is a standard measured by the business judgment of reasonable persons familiar with the customary practices in the type of transaction involved and with regard to the facts and circumstances of the case.

For instance, the parties may enter into a contract for the sale of goods even though they have reached no agreement on the price. Thus, a contract for the sale of goods may contain an open price term. In such a case the price is a reasonable one at the time for delivery where the agreement (1) says nothing as to price; (2) provides that the parties shall agree later on the price and they fail to so agree; or (3) fixes the price in terms of some agreed market or other standard or as set by a third person or agency, and the price is not so set.[3,8] Whenever an agreement provides that the price is to be fixed by the seller or buyer, it must be fixed in good faith.

If the price is to be fixed otherwise than by agreement and is not so fixed through the fault of one of the parties, the other party has an option to treat the contract as cancelled or to fix a reasonable price in good faith for the goods. However, where the parties intend not to be bound unless the price is fixed or agreed upon as provided in the agreement, and it is not so fixed or agreed upon, the Code provides in accordance with the parties' intent that there is no contractual liability. In such case the seller must refund to the buyer any portion of the price received, and the buyer must return the goods to the seller or, if unable to do so, pay the reasonable value of the goods.[8]

The Code also provides missing terms in a number of other instances, such as where the contract fails to specify the time or place of delivery or payment.[4, 9]

Output, Requirements, and Exclusive Dealings

An agreement of a buyer to purchase the entire output of a seller's factory for a stated period, or an agreement of a seller to supply a buyer with all his requirements for certain goods used in his business, may appear to lack definiteness and mutuality of obligation. The exact quantity of goods is not specified; moreover, the seller may have some degree of control over his output and the buyer over his requirements. Under the Code and the Restatement, however, such agreements are enforceable by the application of an objective standard based on good faith of both parties. Thus the seller cannot operate her factory twenty-four hours a day and insist that the buyer take all of the output when she operated it only eight hours a day before the agreement was made. Nor can the buyer expand his business abnormally and insist that the seller supply all of his requirements.

A valid agreement between buyer and seller for exclusive dealing in goods, unless otherwise agreed, imposes an obligation on the seller to use her best efforts to supply the goods and on the buyer to use his best efforts to promote the sale of the goods.[10]

DURATION OF OFFERS

An offer confers upon the offeree a power of acceptance, which continues until the offer terminates. The ways in which an offer may be terminated, other than by acceptance, are (1) lapse of time, (2) revocation, (3) rejection, (4) counteroffer, (5) death or incompetency of the offeror or offeree, (6) destruction of the specific subject matter to which the offer relates, and (7) subsequent illegality of the type of contract contemplated by the offer.

Lapse of Time

The offeror may specify the time within which the offer is to be accepted, just as he may specify any other term or condition in the offer. Unless otherwise terminated, the offer remains open for the **specified** time period.

After the expiration of that time, the offer no longer exists and cannot be accepted. Any purported acceptance of an expired offer will only serve as a new offer.

If no time is stated in the offer within which the offeree may accept, the offer will terminate after a **reasonable** period of time. What is a reasonable period of time is a question of fact, depending on the nature of the contract proposed, the usages of business, and other circumstances of the case. For instance, an offer to sell a perishable good would be open for a shorter period of time than an offer to sell undeveloped real estate.

Revocation

Prior to its acceptance, the offeror generally may cancel or **revoke** an offer at any time. If the offeror originally promises that the offer will be open for thirty days, but after five days wishes to terminate it he may do so merely by giving the offeree notice—explicitly or implicitly, as in *Hoover Motors*, on page 168—that he is withdrawing the offer. This notice may be given by any means of communication and effectively terminates the offer when **received** by the offeree. An offer made to the general public is revoked only by giving publicity to the revocation equivalent to that given the offer.

Notice of revocation may be indirectly communicated to the offeree, as where he receives reliable information from a third person that the offeror has disposed of the property he has offered for sale or has otherwise placed himself in a position indicating an unwillingness or inability to perform the promise contained in the offer.[11] For example, Aaron offers to sell his portable television set to Ted and tells Ted that he has ten days in which to accept. One week later, Ted observes the television set in Celia's house and is informed that Celia purchased it from Aaron. The next day Ted sends to Aaron an acceptance of the offer. There is no contract because Aaron's offer was effectively revoked when Ted learned of Aaron's inability to sell the television set to Ted by reason of his having sold it to Celia.

Certain limitations, however, have been imposed on the offeror's power to revoke the

HOOVER MOTOR EXPRESS CO. v. CLEMENTS PAPER CO.
Supreme Court of Tennessee, 1951.
193 Tenn. 6, 241 S.W.2d 851.

Facts: On November 19, 1949, Hoover Motor Express Company sent to Clements Paper Company a written offer to purchase certain real estate. Some time in December, Clements authorized Williams to accept. Williams, however, attempted to bargain with Hoover to obtain a better deal, specifically that Clements would retain easements on the property. In a telephone conversation on January 13, 1950, Williams first told Hoover of his plan to obtain the easements. Hoover replied: "Well, I don't know if we are ready. We have not decided, we might not want to go through with it." On January 20 Clements sent a written acceptance of Hoover's offer. Hoover refused to sell, claiming it had revoked its offer through the January 13 phone conversation. Clements then brought suit to compel the sale or obtain damages. The trial court and Court of Appeals held in favor of Clements. Hoover appealed.

Decision: Judgment for Hoover.

Opinion: **Tomlinson J.** Although there is no Tennessee case deciding the point, in so far as we can find, the general rule is that express notice, in so many words, of withdrawal before acceptance of an offer of the character we have here is not required. * * * "It is sufficient to constitute a withdrawal that knowledge of acts by the offeror inconsistent with the continuance of the offer is brought home to the offeree."

The same principle is declared to be the law in the text of [citation] in this language: "it being sufficient that the person making the offer does some act inconsistent with it, as, for example, selling the property, and that the person to whom the offer was made has knowledge of such act."

Restatement of the Law of Contracts, Section 41, has this to say: "Revocation of an offer may be made by a communication from the offeror received by the offeree, which states or implies that the offeror no longer intends to enter into the proposed contract, if the communication is received by the offeree before he has exercised his power of creating a contract by acceptance of the offer."

* * *

Applying to the undisputed testimony as furnished by Williams the rule clearly stated in all the authorities from which we have above quoted—and we find none to the contrary—we think it must be concluded that Hoover's written offer of November 19 was withdrawn on January 13 * * * prior to [Clements'] attempted acceptance on January 20, and that the concurrent finding of the Chancellor and the Court of Appeals to the contrary is not supported by any material evidence. There can be no doubt as to it being a fact that on January 13 knowledge was brought home to Williams that Hoover no longer consented to the transaction. There was, therefore, no offer continuing up to the time of the attempted acceptance on January 20. * * *

offer at any time prior to its acceptance. These limitations apply to the following four situations.

Option Contracts An **option** is a contract by which the offeror is bound to hold open an offer for a specified period of time. It must comply with all of the requirements of a contract, including **consideration** being given to the offeror by the offeree. For example, if in consideration of $500 paid to Alan by Barry, Alan gives Barry an option to buy Blackacre at a price of $80,000, exercisable at any time within thirty days, Alan's offer is irrevocable. Alan is legally bound to keep the offer open for thirty days, and any communication by Alan to Barry of notice of withdrawal of the offer is ineffective. Barry is not bound to accept the offer, but the option contract entitles him to thirty days in which to consider acceptance.

Ryder v. Wescoat, which follows, deals with the question of whether an option holder has the right to accept an option within the prescribed period of time after he had previously rejected the optioned offer.

RYDER v. WESCOAT
Missouri Court of Appeals, 1976.
535 S.W.2d 269.

Facts: Ryder purchased from Wescoat an option to buy a 120-acre farm upon which Wescoat had an option to buy. Ryder's option was to run until September 1, which was far enough in advance of Wescoat's option to give Wescoat time to exercise his option. On August 20, Ryder informed Wescoat that he was going to "pass" on the 120-acre farm. Wescoat thereafter proceeded to talk to his bank about obtaining a mortgage to buy the land for himself and also talked to several subcontractors about doing some work on the land. None of these discussions, however, resulted in an agreement legally binding on Wescoat.

On August 30, Ryder delivered to Wescoat a contract to purchase the 120-acre farm along with a down payment. Wescoat refused to accept both the contract and the down payment. The trial court found in favor of Wescoat on the ground that Ryder rejected the option and thus relinquished his right to purchase. Ryder brings this appeal.

Decision: The judgment in favor of Wescoat reversed and the cause remanded with directions to enter a judgment for specific performance in favor of Ryder.

Opinion: Turnaje, J. No case has been [found] * * * involving this precise issue. However, text writers have dealt with the problem. In Simpson on Contracts, [citation] the author states:

> Where an offer is supported by a binding contract that the offeree's power of acceptance shall continue for a stated time, will a communicated rejection terminate the offeree's power to accept within the time? On principle, there is no reason why it should. The offeree has a contract right to accept within the time. . . . So an option holder may complete a contract by communicating his acceptance despite the fact that he has previously rejected the offer. Where, however, before the acceptance the offeror has materially changed his position in reliance on the communicated rejection, as by selling or contracting to sell the subject matter of the offer elsewhere, the subsequent acceptance will be inoperative. . . .

* * *

It must be kept in mind Ryder had purchased for a valuable consideration the right to purchase this farm. This removes this case from the rule applied in those cases where an offer has been made, but the offeree has not paid any consideration for the making of the offer. In those cases, it is uniformly held that a rejection of the offer terminates the offer. Likewise, the making of a counter-offer terminates the original offer and places it beyond the power of the offeree to thereafter accept the offer.

* * *

Since an option stands on a different footing from an offer which is made without consideration being paid therefor, and since it has been held that an option is irrevocable for the time stated, and that a counter-offer does not effect a rejection, it necessarily follows that a rejection standing alone would not end the rights of the option holder. This court adopts the rule . . . that a rejection of an option which has been purchased for a valuable consideration does not terminate the rights of the option holder unless the optionor has materially changed his position prior to a timely acceptance.

This rule fully protects the rights of both parties. It extends to the optionor the protection he requires in the event a rejection of the option is communicated to him and he thereafter changes his position in reliance thereon to his detriment. At the same time it protects the right of the option holder to have the opportunity to exercise his option for the full period for which he paid, absent the material change in position.

To apply this rule in this case, it must be held Ryder retained his right to exercise the option for the reason Wescoat has not shown any material change in his position between the time of the rejection and the later acceptance. The material change required by the rule . . . requires that a party must suffer a legal detriment or change his position for the worse and be prejudiced. [Citation.]

Wescoat did not show that he had suffered any detriment, had changed his position for the worse, or had been prejudiced by any action he took between the time of Ryder's rejection and acceptance. Wescoat talked about obtaining a loan, doing bulldozing and spreading lime on the farm, but actually took no action which obligated him to pay prior to Ryder exercising his option to purchase. In that situation, Wescoat did not materially change his position prior to the acceptance by Ryder, and Ryder's acceptance prior to September 1 was a valid exercise of his right to purchase the farm.

Firm Offers under the Code The Code provides that a *merchant* is bound to keep an offer to buy or sell **goods** open for a stated period not over three months, if the merchant gives assurance in a **signed writing** that it will be held open.[12] The Code, therefore, makes a merchant's **firm offer** (written promise not to revoke an offer for a stated period of time) enforceable even though no consideration is given the offeror for that promise. A **merchant** is defined as a person (1) who is a dealer in the goods, or (2) who by his occupation holds himself out as having knowledge or skill peculiar to the goods or practices involved, or (3) who employs an agent or broker whom he holds out as having such knowledge or skill.

Statutory Irrevocability Certain offers are made irrevocable by statute, such as bids made to the State, municipality, or other governmental body for the construction of a building or some public work. Another example is pre-incorporation stock subscription agreements, which are irrevocable for a period of six months under many State corporation statutes.

Irrevocable Offers of Unilateral Contracts Where the offer contemplates a **unilateral** contract, that is, a promise for an act, injustice to the offeree may result if revocation is permitted after the offeree has started to perform the act requested in the offer and has substantially but not completely finished it. Such an offer is not accepted and no contract is formed until the offeree has completed the requested act. By starting performance, the offeree does not bind himself to complete performance and historically did not bind the offeror to keep the offer open. Thus the offeror could revoke the offer at any time before the offeree's completion of performance. For example, Jordan offers Karlene $300 if Karlene will climb to the top of the flagpole in the center of campus. Karlene starts to climb, but when she is five feet from the top, Jordan yells to her, "I revoke."

The Restatement deals with this problem by providing that where the performance of the requested act necessarily requires time and effort to be expended by the offeree, the offeror is obligated not to revoke the offer for a reasonable time.[13] This obligation arises when the offeree begins the invited performance and the offeror's duty of performance is conditional on completion of the invited performance according to the terms of the offer. It is reasoned that the offeree's commencement of performance is equivalent to consideration being given to keep the offer open. If, however, the offeror does not know of the offeree's performance and has no adequate means of learning of it within a reasonable period of time, the offeree must exercise reasonable diligence to notify the offeror.[14]

Rejection

An offeree is at liberty to accept or reject the offer as he sees fit. If he decides not to accept it, he is not required to reject it. Just as the acceptance of an offer is a manifestation of the willingness of the offeree to accept, a **rejection** of an offer is a manifestation by the offeree of his unwillingness to accept. The power of acceptance is terminated by a communicated rejection. From the effective moment of rejection, which is the **receipt** of the rejection by the offeror, the offeree may no longer accept the offer. Rejection by the offeree may consist of express language or may be implied from language or conduct.

Counteroffer

A **counteroffer** is a counterproposal from the offeree to the offeror and indicates a willingness to contract with reference to the subject matter of the offer but on terms or conditions different from those contained in the original offer. It is not an unequivocal acceptance, and by indicating an unwillingness to agree to the terms of the offer, it operates as a rejection. See *Zeller v. First National Bank & Trust* below. To further illustrate, assume that Worthy writes Joanne a letter stating that he will sell to Joanne a secondhand color television set for $300. Joanne replies that she will pay Worthy $250 for the set. This is a counteroffer that, on **receipt** by Worthy, terminates the original offer. If Joanne in her reply states that she wishes to consider the $300 offer but is willing to pay $250 at once for the set, that is a counteroffer that does *not* terminate Worthy's original offer. In the first instance, after making the $250 counteroffer, Joanne may not accept the $300 offer. In the second instance she may do so, as the counteroffer was stated in such a manner as not to indicate an unwillingness to accept the original offer, and Joanne therefore did not terminate it.

ZELLER v. FIRST NATIONAL BANK & TRUST
Appellate Court of Illinois, First District, 1979.
79 Ill.App.3d 170, 34 Ill.Dec. 473, 398 N.E.2d 148.

Facts: On December 23, Wyman, a lawyer representing the First National Bank & Trust (defendant), wrote to Zeller (plaintiff) stating that he had been instructed to offer a building to Zeller for sale at a price of $240,000. Zeller had previously expressed an interest in purchasing the building for $240,000. The letter also set forth details concerning interest rates and loan fees.

   After receiving the letter, Zeller instructed his attorney, Jamma, to send Wyman a written counteroffer of $230,000 with varying interest and loan arrangements.

Jamma sent the written counteroffer as instructed on January 10. On the same day, Jamma telephoned Wyman and informed him of the counteroffer. Jamma then tried to telegraph acceptance of the original offer to Wyman. When Wyman refused to sell the property to him, Zeller brought this action to seek enforcement of the alleged contract. The trial court entered summary judgment against Zeller and he appeals.

Decision: Summary judgment for defendant affirmed.

Opinion: McNamara, J.   It is elementary that for a contract to exist, there must be an offer and acceptance. [Citations.] Moreover, to create a binding contract, an acceptance must comply strictly with the terms of the offer. An acceptance requesting modification or containing terms which vary from those offered constitutes a rejection of the original offer, and becomes a counterproposal which must be accepted by the original offeror before a valid contract is formed. [Citations.]

On December 23, 1977, Wyman offered to sell plaintiff the property for $240,000. In a telephone conversation with Wyman on January 10, 1978, plaintiff's attorney discussed the counter-offer of $230,000. This counter-offer, containing terms varying from the original offer, operated as a rejection and terminated plaintiff's power to accept Wyman's offer. There was no suggestion that Wyman, the offeror, assented to the price modification in plaintiff's counter-offer so as to create a contract. Once having rejected Wyman's offer, plaintiff could not revive the offer by later telegraphing acceptance. [Citation.]

Another common type of counteroffer is the **conditional acceptance.** A conditional acceptance claims to accept the offer but expressly makes the acceptance contingent on the offeror's assent to additional or different terms. Nonetheless, it is a counteroffer and generally terminates the original offer. A mere inquiry about the possibility of obtaining different or new terms, however, is not a counteroffer and does not terminate the original offer. The Code's treatment of acceptances containing terms that vary from the offer are discussed later in this chapter.

Death or Incompetency

The death or incompetency of either the offeror or the offeree ordinarily terminates an offer. On his death or incompetency the offeror no longer has the legal capacity to enter into a contract, and thus all outstanding offers are terminated. Death or incompetency of the offeree likewise terminates the offer, because an ordinary offer is not assignable and can be accepted only by the person to whom it was made. When the offeree dies or ceases to have legal capability to enter into a contract, there is, in effect, no one who can accept the offer. Therefore, the offer necessarily terminates.

The death or incompetency of the offeror or offeree, however, does *not* terminate an offer contained in an option.

Destruction of Subject Matter

Destruction of the specific subject matter of an offer terminates the offer. The impossibility of performance prevents a contract from being consummated and thus terminates all outstanding offers with respect to the destroyed property. Suppose that Sarah, owning a Buick, offers to sell the car to Barbara and allows Barbara five days in which to accept. Three days later the car is destroyed by fire. On the following day Barbara, in ignorance of the destruction of the car, notifies Sarah that she accepts Sarah's offer. There is no contract. Sarah's offer was terminated by the destruction of the car. Clearly, there can be no agreement made concerning a specific car no longer in existence.

Subsequent Illegality

One of the four essential ingredients of a contract, as we previously mentioned, is legality of purpose or subject matter. If performance of a valid contract is subsequently made illegal, the obligations of both parties under the contract are discharged. Illegality taking effect after the making of an offer but prior to acceptance has the same effect: the offer is legally terminated.

ACCEPTANCE OF OFFER

The acceptance of an offer is essential to the formation of a contract. Once an acceptance has been given, the contract is formed. **Acceptance** of an offer for a bilateral contract is some overt act by the offeree that manifests his assent to the terms of the offer, such as speaking or sending a letter, a telegram, or other explicit or implicit communication to the offeror. If the offer is for a unilateral contract, acceptance is the performance of the requested act with the intention of accepting. For example, if Joy publishes an offer of a reward to anyone who returns the diamond ring that she has lost (a unilateral contract offer), and Bob, with knowledge of the offer, finds and returns the ring to Joy, Bob has accepted the offer.

DEFINITENESS

An acceptance must be *positive* and *unequivocal*. It may not change any of the terms of the offer nor add to, subtract from, or qualify in any way the provisions of the offer. It must be the **mirror image** of the offer. Except as modified by the Code, any communication by the offeree that attempts to modify the offer is not an acceptance but a mere counteroffer.

The common law mirror image rule, by which the acceptance cannot vary or deviate from the terms of the offer, is modified by the Code. This modification is necessitated by the realities of modern business practices. A vast number of business transactions use standardized business forms. For example, a buyer sends to the seller on the buyer's order form a purchase order for one thousand dozen cotton shirts at $60 per dozen with delivery by October 1 at the buyer's place of business. On the reverse side of this standard form are twenty-five numbered paragraphs containing provisions generally favorable to the buyer. When

the seller receives the buyer's order, he sends to the buyer on his acceptance form an unequivocal acceptance of the offer. Despite the fact that the seller agrees to the buyer's quantity, price, and delivery terms on the back of his acceptance form, the seller has thirty-two numbered paragraphs generally favorable to himself and in significant conflict with buyer's form. Under the common law's *mirror image* rule, no contract would exist, for there has not been an unequivocal acceptance of all of the material terms of the buyer's offer.

The Code attempts to alleviate this **battle of the forms** problem by focusing on the intent of the parties. If the offeree definitely and seasonably expresses his acceptance of the offer and does not expressly make his acceptance conditional on the buyer's assent to the additional or different terms, a contract is formed. The issue then becomes whether the offeree's different or additional terms become part of the contract. If both offeror and offeree are merchants, additional terms will be part of the contract if they do not materially alter the agreement and are not objected to either in the offer itself or within a reasonable period of time. If both of the parties are not merchants or if the additional terms materially alter the offer, the additional terms are merely construed as proposals to the contract. Different terms proposed by the offeree will not become part of the contract unless accepted by the offeror.[15]

EFFECTIVE MOMENT

As we discussed previously, an offer, a revocation, a rejection, and a counteroffer are effective when they are *received*. An acceptance, as shown in the case of *Cushing v. Thomson* on page 174, is generally effective upon **dispatch** (see Figure 8–1). This is true unless the offer specifically provides otherwise or the offeree uses an unauthorized means of communication.

Authorized Means

Historically, an authorized means of communication was the means expressly authorized by the offeror in the offer, or if none was authorized, it was the means used by the

CUSHING v. THOMSON
Supreme Court of New Hampshire, 1978.
118 N.H. 292, 386 A.2d 805.

Facts: Cushing filed an application with the office of the Adjutant General of the State of New Hampshire for the use of the Portsmouth Armory to hold a dance on the evening of April 29, 1978. The application, made on behalf of the Portsmouth Area Clamshell Alliance, was received by the Adjutant General's office on or about March 30, 1978. On March 31 the Adjutant General mailed a signed contract after agreeing to rent the armory for the evening requested. The agreement required acceptance by the renter affixing his signature to the agreement and then returning the copy to the Adjutant General within five days after receipt. Cushing received the contract offer, signed it on behalf of the alliance, and mailed it on April 3. At 6:30 on the evening of April 4, Cushing received a telephone call from the Adjutant General revoking the rental offer. Cushing stated during the conversation that he had already signed and mailed the contract. The Adjutant General sent a written confirmation of the withdrawal on April 5. On April 6 the Adjutant General's office received by mail the signed contract dated April 3 and postmarked April 5. The trial court ruled that a binding contract existed and ordered the defendants to honor the contract.

Decision: Judgment for plaintiff affirmed.

Opinion: Per Curiam The issue presented is whether the trial court erred in determining that a binding contract existed. Neither party challenges the applicable law. "To establish a contract of this character . . . there must be . . . an offer and an acceptance thereof in accordance with its terms . . . . [W]hen the parties to such a contract are at a distance from one another and the offer is sent by mail . . . the reply accepting the offer may be sent through the same medium, and the contract will be complete when the acceptance is mailed . . . properly addressed to the party making the offer and beyond the acceptor's control." [Citation.] Withdrawal of the offer is ineffectual once the offer has been accepted by posting in the mail. [Citation.]

* * *

   Plaintiffs introduced the sworn affidavit of Mr. Cushing in which he stated that on April 3, he executed the contract and placed it in the outbox for mailing. Moreover plaintiff's counsel represented to the court that it was customary office practice for outgoing letters to be picked up from the outbox daily and put in the U.S. mail. * * * Thus the representation that it was customary office procedure for the letters to be sent out the same day that they are placed in the office outbox, together with the affidavit, supported the implied finding that the completed contract was mailed before the attempted revocation. [Citation.]

offeror. As in the above case of *Cushing v. Thomson*, if in reply to an offer by mail, the offeree places in the mail a letter of acceptance properly stamped and addressed to the offeror, a contract is formed at the time and place that the offeree mails the letter. This assumes, of course, that the offer at that time was open and had not been terminated by any of the methods previously discussed. The reason for this rule is that the offeror, by using the mail,

---

FIGURE 8–1 Offer and Acceptance

	Time Effective	Effect
Communications by Offeror		
Offer	Received by offeree	Creates power to form a contract
Revocation	Received by offeree	Terminates power
Communications by Offeree		
Rejection	Received by offeror	Terminates offer
Counter-offer	Received by offeror	Terminates offer
Acceptance	Sent by offeree	Forms a contract
Acceptance after prior rejection	Received by offeror	If received before rejection, forms a contract

---

impliedly authorized the offeree to use the same means of communication, and his mailing of an acceptance is an overt act of manifestation of assent. It is immaterial if the letter of acceptance goes astray in the mails and is never received.

The Restatement[16] and the Code[17] both now provide that where the language in the offer or the circumstances do not otherwise indicate, an offer to make a contract shall be construed as authorizing acceptance in any reasonable manner. Thus, an **authorized means** is any **reasonable** means of communication. These provisions are intended to allow flexibility of response and the ability to keep pace with new modes of communication.

Unauthorized Means

When the medium of communication used by the offeree is unauthorized, the traditional rule is that acceptance is effective when and if received by the offeror, provided that it is received within the time the authorized means would have arrived. The Restatement goes further by providing that if these conditions are met, then the effective time for the acceptance is the moment of dispatch.[18]

Stipulated Provisions in the Offer

If the offer specifically stipulates the means of communication to be used by the offeree, the acceptance must conform to that specification. Thus, if an offer states that acceptance must be made by registered mail, any purported acceptance not made by registered mail would be ineffective. Moreover, the rule that an acceptance is effective when dispatched or sent does not apply where the offer provides that the acceptance must be received by the offeror. If the offeror states that a reply must be received by a certain date or that he must hear from the offeree or uses other language indicating that the acceptance must be received by him, the effective moment of the acceptance is when it is received by the offeror and not when it is sent or dispatched by the offeree.

Acceptance Following a Prior Rejection

After dispatching a rejection, an acceptance is not effective when sent by the offeree, but only when and if **received** by the offeror prior to his receipt of the rejection. Thus, when an acceptance follows a prior rejection, the *first communication* received by the offeror is the effective

LAW IN THE NEWS

Pennzoil-Texaco Fight Is Question of Honor
Tradition Tested in $14 Billion Suit Over Buyout of Getty

Houston—J. Hugh Liedtke, one of the wiliest deal makers in the oil patch, was jubilant after making the biggest deal of his life. Standing in a sumptuous suite in New York's Pierre hotel, Mr. Liedtke, chairman of Pennzoil Co., shook hands and hoisted a glass of champagne with Gordon P. Getty, toasting an apparent decision by Getty Oil Co.'s board under which Pennzoil would assume management control of Getty Oil in a $5.3 billion leveraged buyout.

Forty-eight hours later, the party was over. Before Mr. Liedtke had the chance to complete a definitive contract, Mr. Getty made an abrupt about-face and agreed to sell the Getty family trust's 40.2% stake in Los Angeles-based Getty Oil to giant Texaco Inc. Within a day of that January 1984 agreement, Getty's board approved the company's sale to Texaco for about $10 billion. "They used to say that the oil business was built upon a handshake," Mr. Liedtke would soon tell Pennzoil shareholders. "Should it now require handcuffs?"

Next month, a state court jury here will begin hearing testimony on whether Mr. Liedtke had a contract with Getty Oil and whether Texaco induced Getty Oil to break it. Pennzoil, in its lawsuit against Texaco, is demanding a whopping $14 billion in damages, and a Delaware judge has said that Mr. Liedtke has a strong case.

But the suit represents much more than an opportunity for Pennzoil to reap a huge award for damages. It is one of the highest-stakes battles ever over the definition of a contract. And some veteran deal makers in oil, where a man's word was always considered as good as his signature, view such disputes these days as a final stand against an erosion of traditional oil patch values in an era of mega-mergers engineered by slick Wall Street lawyers and investment bankers.

"If we keep breaking these agreements, handshakes won't be worth a damn, say-sos won't be worth a damn, and contracts won't be worth a damn," says Michel T. Halbouty, a legendary Houston independent oil man. "Where is the morality in business anymore?"

Texaco lawyers view the talk of handshakes, etiquette and honor as a smoke screen put up by Pennzoil to mask its ineptitude in the transaction. Moreover, they dismiss the discussion of morality as the product of a bygone era.

"That stuff won't get you to first base in New York," says Richard B. Miller, Texaco's lead lawyer in the case. "The crux of the matter is that Pennzoil doesn't have a written agreement of any kind with Getty." Mr. Miller likens the validity of Pennzoil's agreement with Getty Oil to a scene from the 1940 movie "Boom Town," in which two oil men decide ownership of their company by flipping a coin.

Pennzoil's Mr. Liedtke has lived by the code of the oil patch for more than 30 years. He treasures his membership in the All-American Wildcatters, an industry group whose motto is, "My word is my bond."

"Texaco evidently thinks it is rich enough and strong enough and powerful enough to walk over people with callous disregard," Mr. Liedtke said in a deposition. Texaco, he added, "reminds me of the gorilla who sleeps where the gorilla wants to."

For a case that supposedly involves questions of honor and gentlemanliness, neither quality has been abundant in the proceedings so far. The only attempt to settle out of court took place in a meeting of Mr. Liedtke and Texaco Chairman John McKinley in Washington, D.C., during which Mr. Liedtke threatened to use all his "influence" on Capitol Hill unless Pennzoil was allowed to take part in the Getty transaction, according to a deposition given by Mr. McKinley. The Texaco chairman declined, but offered to sell Pennzoil part of Texaco's 35% interest in the bountiful Hueso oil field off the California coast, a Pennzoil official testified. But Mr. Liedtke, noting that *hueso* is Spanish for "bone," replied, "We're not interested in being thrown any bones," according to Pennzoil court documents.

Texaco, too, has played tough. After learning that a Pennzoil lawyer, Joe Jamail, had given a $10,000 campaign contribution to state court judge Anthony J. P. Ferris, who is presiding in the case, Texaco accused Mr. Jamail of impropriety and unsuccessfully moved to have the judge withdraw from the case. Another judge found no reason for Judge Ferris to withdraw.

Mr. Jamail, a personal-injury lawyer, says he intends to make an issue in the trial of Texaco's reputation for dealing heavy-handedly with suppliers and partners—an image the company has been working to correct. "The difference between Texaco's reputation and Hugh Liedtke's reputation is the difference between chicken manure and chicken salad," Mr. Jamail claims.

Contract law, which is taught to every first-year law student, is fraught with twists and turns, as this case demonstrates. Even though Mr. Liedtke never obtained any signed documents spelling out the agreement with Getty Oil, his lawyers are preparing to argue that a binding contract can be formed before all the papers are signed.

For one thing, Pennzoil says Getty's board, meeting in a marathon session to consider the proposed leveraged buyout, approved the bid in a 14–1 vote. Not so, says Texaco. Several former Getty directors said in depositions that the vote was on the price of the offer, not on whether to accept it.

Exactly what the board decided may never be known for certain, however. Getty Oil's counsel, Ralph Copley, destroyed his handwritten notes of the meeting a week later, three days after the litigation began. His were the only original minutes of the meeting. Mr. Copley says he often destroys such notes. The surviving minutes were edited three times on a word processor.

If any doubt existed over the board's action, Pennzoil also will argue, it disappeared the following morning, Jan. 4, when Getty Oil issued a news release proclaiming that it had reached an agreement in principle with Pennzoil on the buyout. In Los Angeles, an attorney for Mr. Getty in another case stood up in a courtroom and called the transaction "an agreement which has been entered into after extremely careful consideration." In New York, as Messrs. Liedtke and Getty toasted the agreement, they discussed plans to meet with and reassure Getty Oil employees.

Were these events tantamount to a contract? "The evidence is as strong as an acre of garlic,"

says Mr. Jamail, the Pennzoil lawyer. Texaco will counter that news releases and handshakes don't count as contracts and that the transaction was subject to a definitive agreement.

A Delaware judge's opinion last year seems to favor Pennzoil, however. "I am convinced that Pennzoil has demonstrated a likelihood that it will be able to establish . . . that a contract came into being," wrote the judge, ruling in an unsuccessful attempt by Pennzoil to block the Texaco-Getty Oil merger. The judge noted a wide body of law holding that "a binding contract can be formed despite material open issues."

But Pennzoil won't have an easy time proving that Texaco induced Getty Oil to break a contract, if one existed. The Delaware judge termed this issue "a close call." Indeed, Goldman, Sachs & Co., shopping to obtain the best deal for Getty Oil, invited a bid from Texaco during a break in the Getty board meeting. Two days later, when Texaco's chairman called a top executive of Getty to ask whether the company was still for sale, he was assured that, "The fat lady hasn't sung." Messrs. McKinley and Getty spent the night working out details of Texaco's better offer, and the rest is history.

Mr. Liedtke would be busy managing Getty Oil today instead of the court case if he had obtained a contract from Getty Oil in addition to the handshake from Mr. Getty. Some lawyers close to the case suggest that Pennzoil's longtime Houston law firm, Baker & Botts, simply didn't move quickly enough to put the agreement in writing after the Getty board meeting. Delays by Getty Oil lawyers also interfered with negotiations for a definitive agreement, lawyers on both sides agree. At one point after Texaco entered the picture, Getty Oil lawyers kept the Pennzoil legal team waiting an entire afternoon.

But as the trial nears, Texaco lawyers aren't underestimating Mr. Liedtke, a law graduate himself who personally structured the Pennzoil-Getty transaction and who has assumed a personal stake in the outcome of the litigation. Referring to Mr. Liedtke, Texaco's Mr. Miller says: "If you think a guy who graduated from Amherst, Harvard Business School and the University of Texas and who's been CEO of a major oil company for 20 years is a simple country boy—well, maybe he is. We'll find out."

By Brian Burrough, Staff Reporter of The Wall Street Journal. Reprinted by permission of The Wall Street Journal, © Dow Jones & Company, Inc. 1985. All Rights Reserved Worldwide.

PENNZOIL v. TEXACO: THE LONG ROAD TO SETTLEMENT

January 1984 (Washington, D.C.) Pennzoil offers to withdraw lawsuit in exchange for right to buy about 37% of Getty Oil from Texaco. Texaco refuses.

December 10, 1985 (Houston) After jury verdict [awarding Pennzoil 10.53 billion dollars], Texaco offers to sell 42% of Getty to Pennzoil. Pennzoil refuses claiming "they had decimated Getty."

Late December–early January 1986 (Tulsa, Okla., and Nashville, Tenn.) Talks on settlement involving transfer of assets to Pennzoil, shifting to possible purchase of Pennzoil assets by Texaco. On January 7, 1986, Pennzoil angrily rejects takeover bid from Texaco valued at about $83 a Pennzoil share, saying it never wanted to settle in that manner.

March–April 1986 (New York) Face-to-face talks between chairmen lead to offer involving sale of Getty assets to Pennzoil, eventually rejected as "same old picked-over bones."

July 1986 (Locations unknown) Low-level talks begin, lasting several weeks.

April 7–10, 1987 (Houston) Facing possible seizure of assets by Pennzoil, Texaco presents several proposals valued at about $2 billion. Pennzoil rejects all.

April 11, 1987 (White Plains, N.Y.) While discussing possible Chapter 11 filing, Texaco board receives letter from Pennzoil offering to settle for $4.1 billion. But Texaco instead files bankruptcy-law petition.

April–June 1987 (New York) Investment bankers discuss variety of settlement plans, narrowing differences to within several hundred million dollars, depending on value of various proposals.

Talks discontinued after SEC announces plan to file legal brief supporting one aspect of Texaco's appeal.

November 19, 1987 (New York) Pennzoil proposes that Texaco pay a nonrefundable $1.5 billion in exchange for a promise that it would cap its award at $5 billion even if the full judgment was sustained on appeal.

November 25, 1987 (Houston) Texaco offers Mr. Liedtke a nonrefundable payment of $370 million and a cap of $2.6 billion. Mr. Liedtke says no.

December 1, 1987 (White Plains) At a bankruptcy court hearing, creditors' committee discloses a base-cap settlement proposal that calls for Texaco to pay Pennzoil $1 billion in return for a promise from Pennzoil to cap its award at $3.5 billion. On December 6, Texaco management decides to go along with the numbers. But Pennzoil says no.

December 10, 1987 (Houston) Mr. Liedtke agrees to go along with a proposal by a shareholders' committee that Pennzoil and Texaco settle for a single sum of $3.001 billion. Creditors agree to those numbers December 14. Plan falls apart when Carl Icahn, a major shareholder, pulls out.

December 19, 1987 (New York) Texaco and Pennzoil sign an accord ending their four-year-old dispute in which Texaco agrees to pay its foe $3 billion.

March 23, 1988 (White Plains) Bankruptcy Court Judge Howard Schwartzberg confirms Texaco's plan of reorganization, allowing the company to emerge from bankruptcy proceedings on April 7.

Note: May not include all meetings or proposals; unknown details may have significantly affected value of some proposals. Reprinted by permission of The Wall Street Journal, © Dow Jones & Company, Inc. 1988. All Rights Reserved Worldwide.

one. For example, Carlos in New York sends by air mail to Paula in San Francisco an offer that is expressly stated to be open for one week. On the fourth day, Paula sends to Carlos by air mail a letter of rejection, which is delivered on the morning of the sixth day. At noon on the fifth day, Paula dispatches a telegram of acceptance that is received by Carlos before the close of business on that day. A contract was formed when Paula's telegram of acceptance was received by Carlos—it was the first communication received by Carlos.

Defective Acceptances

A late acceptance or defective acceptance does not create a contract. After the offer has expired, it cannot be accepted. A late or defective acceptance, however, does manifest a willingness on the part of the offeree to enter into a contract and therefore constitutes a new offer. In order to create a contract based on this offer, the original offeror must accept the new offer by manifesting his assent.

MODE OF ACCEPTANCE

Although a contract may be formed by conduct, the law will not generally force an offeree to respond to or reject an offer. In this section we will cover (1) silence as an acceptance, (2) conduct as a form of acceptance, and (3) auction sales.

Silence as Acceptance

An offeree is generally under no legal duty to reply to an offer. Silence or inaction is therefore *not* an acceptance of the offer. By custom, usage, or course of dealing, however, silence or inaction by the offeree may operate as an acceptance.

Salespeople employed by a manufacturing company or by a distributor to solicit orders for its merchandise from its customers frequently have no authority to bind their employer by contract. The order forms often recite that no contract is formed until the order of the buyer is accepted at the home office of the seller. On receipt of purchase orders, however, the law holds that the manufacturer or distributor is under a duty to notify the customer within a reasonable time of its nonacceptance in the event of its inability or unwillingness to ship the merchandise ordered. Silence or inaction by the soliciting company *is* treated as an acceptance of the order.

Furthermore, if an offeror sends unordered or unsolicited merchandise to a person with an offer stating that the goods are sent for examination, that the addressee may purchase the goods at a specified price, and that unless the goods are returned within a stated period of time the offer will be deemed to have been accepted, the offer is one for an inverted unilateral contract (i.e., an act for a promise). This practice led to abuse, however, which has prompted the Federal government as well as most States to enact statutes providing that in such cases the offeree-recipient of the goods may keep them as a gift and is under no obligation either to return them or to pay for them.

Contract Formed by Conduct

A contract may be formed by conduct. Thus there may be no definite offer and acceptance, or definite acceptance of an offer, yet a contract exists if both of the parties have acted in a manner that manifests a recognition by each of them of the existence of a contract. Recognition may result from the cumulative effect of a number of occurrences or events indicating the reliance of both parties on the existence of a contract. Thus it may be impossible to determine the exact moment when such a contract formed by conduct was made.

Auction Sales

The auctioneer at an auction sale does not make offers to sell the property being auctioned but invites offers to buy. The classic statement by the auctioneer is, "How much am I offered?" The persons attending the auction may make progressively higher bids for the property, and each bid or statement of a price or a figure is an offer to buy at that figure. If the bid is accepted, which is customarily indicated by the fall of the hammer in the hands of the auctioneer, a contract results. A bidder is free to withdraw his bid at any time prior to its acceptance. The auctioneer is likewise free to withdraw the goods from sale *unless* the sale is advertised or announced to be without reserve.

If the auction sale is advertised or announced in explicit terms to be **without reserve,** the auctioneer may not withdraw an article or lot put up for sale unless no bid is made within a reasonable time. Unless so advertised or announced, the sale is with reserve. Whether with or without reserve, a bidder may retract his bid at any time prior to acceptance by the auctioneer. Such retraction does not revive any previous bid.

Under the Code, if the auctioneer knowingly receives a bid by or on behalf of the seller, and notice has not been given that the seller reserves the right to bid at the auction sale, any such bid by or on behalf of the seller gives the bidder to whom the goods are sold an election either (1) to avoid the sale, or (2) to take the goods at the price of the last good faith bid.[19]

CHAPTER SUMMARY

OFFER

Essentials of an Offer	**Definition** indication of willingness to enter into a contract **Intent** determined by an objective standard of what a reasonable offeree would have believed **Communication** offeree must have knowledge of the offer and the offer must be made by the offeror to the offeree **Definiteness** offer's terms must be clear enough to provide a court with a basis for giving an appropriate remedy

Duration of Offers	**Lapse of Time** offer remains open for the time period specified or, if no time is stated, for a reasonable period of time
	Revocation generally, an offer may be terminated any time before it is accepted, subject to the following exceptions
	  ■ *Option Contracts* contract that binds offeror to keep an offer open for a specified period of time
	  ■ *Firm Offer* irrevocable offer to sell or buy goods by a merchant in a signed writing that gives assurance that it will not be terminated for up to three months
	  ■ *Statutory Irrevocability* offer made irrevocable by statute
	  ■ *Irrevocable Offer of Unilateral Contracts* a unilateral offer may not be revoked for a reasonable period of time after performance is begun
	Rejection refusal to accept an offer terminates the power of acceptance
	Counteroffer counterproposal to an offer terminates the original offer
	Death or Incompetency of either the offeror or the offeree terminates the offer
	Destruction of Subject Matter of an offer terminates the offer
	Subsequent Illegality of the subject matter of the offer terminates the offer

ACCEPTANCE

Requirements	**Definition** positive and unequivocal expression of a willingness to enter into a contract on the terms of the offer **Mirror Image Rule** except as modified by the Code, an acceptance cannot deviate from the terms of the offer

Effective Moment of Acceptance	**General Rule** acceptance effective upon dispatch unless the offer specifically provides otherwise or the offeree uses an unauthorized means of communication **Specific Provisions in the Offer** acceptance must conform to the specification

Authorized Means   Restatement and the Code provide that, unless the offer provides otherwise, acceptance is authorized to be in any reasonable manner
Unauthorized Means   acceptance effective when received, provided that it is received within the time the authorized means would have arrived
Acceptance Following a Prior Rejection   first communication received by the offeror is effective
Defective Acceptance   does not create a contract but serves as a new offer

Mode of Acceptance

Silence as Acceptance   not an acceptance unless it becomes one by custom, usage, or course of dealing
Contract Formed by Conduct   if both parties' conduct recognizes the existence of a contract
Auction Sales   auctioneer invites bids or offers which the auctioneer may accept or reject unless the auction is without reserve

QUESTIONS

1. Identify the three essentials of an offer and discuss briefly the requirements associated with each.
2. Identify and discuss briefly seven ways by which an offer may be terminated other than by acceptance.
3. Compare briefly the traditional and modern theories of definiteness of acceptance of an offer as shown by the common law "mirror image" rule and by the rule of the Uniform Commercial Code.
4. Discuss the four situations limiting an offeror's right to revoke her offer.
5. Explain the various rules that determine when an acceptance takes effect.

PROBLEMS

1. Ames, seeking business for his lawn maintenance firm, posted the following notice in the meeting room of the Antlers, a local lodge: "To the members of the Antlers—Special this month. I will resod your lawn for four dollars per square foot using Fairway brand sod. This offer expires July 15."

The notice also included Ames's name, address, and signature and specified that the acceptance was to be in writing.

Bates, a member of the Antlers, and Cramer, the janitor, read the notice and were interested. Bates wrote a letter to Ames saying he would accept the offer if Ames would use Putting Green brand sod. Ames received this letter July 14 and wrote to Bates saying he would not use Putting Green sod. Bates received Ames's letter on July 16 and promptly wrote Ames that he would accept Fairway sod. Cramer wrote to Ames on July 10 saying he accepted Ames's offer.

By July 15 Ames had found more profitable ventures and refused to resod either lawn at the specified price. Bates and Cramer brought an appropriate action against Ames for breach of contract. Decision as to the respective claims of Bates and Cramer?

2. Justin owned four speedboats named Porpoise, Priscilla, Providence, and Prudence. On April 2, Justin made written offers to sell the four boats in the order named for $4,200 each to Charles, Diane, Edward, and Fran respectively, allowing ten days for acceptance. In which, if any, of the following four situations was a contract formed?

(a) Five days later, Charles received notice from Justin that he had contracted to sell Porpoise to Mark. The next day, April 8, Charles notified Justin that he accepted Justin's offer.

(b) On the third day, April 5, Diane mailed a rejection to Justin that reached Justin on the morning of the fifth day. At 10 A.M., on the fourth day, Diane sent an acceptance by telegram to Justin, who received it at noon the same day.

(c) Edward, on April 3, replied that he was interested in buying Providence but declared the price asked appeared slightly excessive and wondered if, perhaps, Justin would be willing to sell the boat for $3,900. Five days later, having received no reply from Justin, Edward accepted Justin's offer by letter, and enclosed a certified check for $4,200.

(d) Fran was accidently killed in an automobile accident on April 9. The following day, the executor of her estate mailed an acceptance of Justin's offer to Justin.

3. Alpha Rolling Mill Corporation, by letter dated June 8, offered to sell Brooklyn Railroad Company 2,000 to 5,000 tons of fifty-pound iron rails on certain specified terms and added that, if the offer was accepted, Alpha Corporation would expect to be notified prior to June 20. Brooklyn Company, on June 16, by telegram, referring to Alpha Corporation's offer of June 8, directed Alpha Corporation to enter an order for 1,200 tons of fifty-pound iron rails on the terms specified. The same day, June 16, Brooklyn Company, by letter to Alpha Corporation, confirmed the telegram. On June 18 Alpha Corporation, by telegram, declined to fulfill the order. Brooklyn Company, on June 19, telegraphed Alpha Corporation: "Please enter an order for 2,000 tons rails as per your letter of the eighth. Please forward written contract. Reply." To Brooklyn Company's repeated inquiries whether the order for 2,000 tons of rails had been entered, Alpha denied the existence of any contract between Brooklyn Company and itself. Thereafter, Brooklyn Company sues Alpha Corporation for breach of contract. Decision?

4. On April 8 Crystal received a telephone call from Akers, a truck dealer, who told Crystal that a new model truck in which Crystal was interested would arrive in one week. Although Akers initially wanted $10,500, the conversation ended after Akers agreed to sell and Crystal to purchase the truck for $10,000, with $1,000 down payment and the balance on delivery. The next day, Crystal sent Akers a check for $1,000, which Akers promptly cashed.

One week later, when Crystal called Akers and inquired about the truck, Akers informed Crystal he had several prospects looking at the truck and would not sell for less than $10,500. The following day Akers sent Crystal a properly executed check for $1,000 with the following notation thereon: "Return of down payment on sale of truck."

After notifying Akers that she will not cash the check, Crystal sues Akers for damages. Decision?

5. On November 15, Gloria, Inc., a manufacturer of crystalware, mailed to Benny Buyer a letter stating that Gloria would sell to Buyer one hundred crystal "A" goblets at $100 per goblet and that "the offer would remain open for fifteen (15) days." On November 18 Gloria, noticing the sudden rise in the price of crystal "A" goblets, decided to withdraw his offer to Buyer and so notified Buyer. Buyer chose to ignore Gloria's letter of revocation and gleefully watched as the price of crystal "A" goblets continued to skyrocket. On November 30 Buyer mailed to Gloria a letter accepting Gloria's offer to sell the goblets. The letter was received by Gloria on December 4. Buyer demands delivery of the goblets. What result?

6. On May 1, Melforth Realty Company offered to sell Greenacre to Dallas, Inc., for $1,000,000. The offer was made by telegraph and stated that the offer would expire on May 15. Dallas decided to purchase the property and sent a registered letter to Melforth on May 10 accepting the offer. As a result of unexplained delays in the postal service, the letter was not received by Melforth until May 22. Melforth wishes to sell Greenacre to another buyer who is offering $1,200,000 for the tract of land. Has a contract resulted between Melforth and Dallas?

7. Rowe advertised in newspapers of wide circulation and otherwise made known that she would pay $5,000 for a complete set consisting of ten volumes of certain rare books. Ford, not knowing of the offer, gave Rowe all but one of the set of rare books as a Christmas present. Ford later learned of the offer, obtained the one remaining book, tendered it to Rowe, and demanded the $5,000. Rowe refused to pay. Is Ford entitled to the $5,000?

8. Scott, manufacturer of a carbonated beverage, entered into a contract with Otis, owner of a baseball park, whereby Otis rented to Scott a large signboard on top of the center field wall. The contract provided that Otis should letter the sign as desired by Scott and would change the lettering from time to time within forty-eight hours after receipt of written request from Scott. As directed by Scott, the signboard originally stated in large letters that Scott would pay $100 to any ball player hitting a home run over the sign.

In the first game of the season, Hume, the best hitter in the league, hit one home run over the sign. Scott immediately served written notice on Otis instructing Otis to replace the offer on the signboard with an offer to pay $50 to every pitcher who pitched a no-hit game in the park. A week after receipt of Scott's letter, Otis had not changed the wording on the sign, and on that day Perry, a pitcher for a scheduled game, pitched a no-hit game and Todd, one of his teammates, hit a home run over Scott's sign.

Scott refuses to pay any of the three players. What are the rights of Scott, Hume, Perry, and Todd?

9. Barney accepted Clark's offer to sell to him a portion of Clark's coin collection. Clark forgot that

her prized $20 gold piece at the time of the offer and acceptance was included in the portion that she offered to sell to Barney. Clark did not intend to include the gold piece in the sale. Barney, at the time of inspecting the offered portion of the collection, and prior to accepting the offer, saw the gold piece. Is Barney entitled to the $20 gold piece?

10. Small, admiring Jasper's watch, asked Jasper where and at what price he had purchased it. Jasper replied: "I bought it at West Watch Shop about two years ago for around $85, but I am not certain as to that." Small then said: "Those fellows at West are good people and always sell good watches. I'll buy that watch from you." Jasper replied: "It's a deal." The next morning Small telephoned Jasper and said he had changed his mind and did not wish to buy the watch.

Jasper sued Small for breach of contract. In defense, Small has pleaded that he made no enforceable contract with Jasper because (a) the parties did not agree on the price to be paid for the watch, and (b) the parties did not agree on the place and time of delivery of the watch to Small. Are either, or both, of these defenses good?

11. Jeff says to Brenda, "I offer to sell you my IBM PC for $900." Brenda replies, "If you do not hear otherwise from me by Thursday, I have accepted your offer." Jeff agrees and does not hear from Brenda by Thursday. Does a contract exist between Jeff and Brenda? Explain.

COMPUTER RESEARCH PROBLEMS

1. The Brewers contracted to purchase Dower House from McAfee. Then, several weeks before the May 7 settlement date for the purchase of the house, the two parties began to negotiate for the sale of certain items of furniture in the house. On April 30 McAfee sent the Brewers a letter containing a list of the furnishings to be purchased at specified prices; a payment schedule including a $3,000 payment due on acceptance; and a clause reading: "If the above is satisfactory please sign and return one copy with the first payment."

On June 3 the Brewers sent a letter to McAfee stating that enclosed was a $3,000 check; that the original contract had been misplaced and could another be furnished; that they planned to move into Dower House on June 12; and that they wished that the red desk be included in the contract. McAfee then sent a letter dated June 8 to the Brewers listing the items of furniture purchased.

The Brewers moved into Dower House in the middle of June. Soon after they moved in, they tried to contact McAfee at his office to tell him that there had been a misunderstanding relating to their purchase of the listed items. They then refused to pay him any more money, and he brought this action to recover the balance outstanding. Decision?

2. The Thoelkes were owners of real property located in Orange County, which the Morrisons agreed to purchase. The Morrisons signed a contract for the sale of that property and mailed it to the Thoelkes in Texas on November 26. The next day the Thoelkes executed the contract and placed it in the mail addressed to the Morrisons' attorney in Florida. After the executed contract was mailed but before it was received in Florida, the Thoelkes called the Morrisons' attorney in Florida and attempted to repudiate the contract. Decision?

3. On December 20, 1952, Lucy and Zehmer met while having drinks in a restaurant. During the course of their conversation, Lucy apparently offered to buy Zehmer's 471.6-acre farm for $50,000 cash. Although Zehmer claims that he thought the offer was made in jest, he wrote the following on the back of a pad: "We hereby agree to sell to W. O. Lucy the Ferguson Farm complete for $50,000, title satisfactory to buyer." Zehmer then signed the writing and induced his wife Ida to do the same. She claims, however, that she signed only after Zehmer assured her that it was only a joke. Finally, Zehmer claims that he was "high as a Georgia pine" at the time but admits that he was not too drunk to make a valid contract. Decision?

4. On July 31, Lee Calan Imports advertised a used Volvo station wagon for sale in the Chicago Sun-Times newspaper. As part of the information for the advertisement, Lee Calan Imports instructed the newspaper to print the price of the car as $1,795. However, due to a mistake made by the newspaper, without any fault on the part of Lee Calan Imports, the printed ad listed the price of the car as $1,095. After reading the ad and then examining the car, O'Brien told a Lee Calan Imports salesman that he wanted to purchase the car for the advertised price of $1,095. Calan Imports refuses to sell the car to O'Brien for $1,095. Is there a contract? If so, for what price?

5. On May 20 cattle rancher Oliver visits his neighbor Southworth, telling him "I know you're

interested in buying the land I'm selling." Southworth replies "Yes, I do want to buy that land,
especially since it adjoins my property." Although
the two men did not discuss the price, Oliver told
Southworth he would determine the value of the
property, and send that information to him so that
Southworth would have "notice" of what Oliver
"wanted for the land." On June 13, Southworth
called Oliver to ask if he still planned to sell the
land. Oliver answered "Yes, and I should have the
value of the land determined soon." On June 17
Oliver sent a letter to Southworth listing a price
quotation of $324,000. Southworth then responded
to Oliver by letter on June 21 stating that he accepted Oliver's offer. However, on June 24 Oliver
wrote back to Southworth saying "There has never
been a firm offer to sell, and there is no enforceable
contract between us." Oliver maintains that a price
quotation alone is not an offer. Southworth claims a
valid contract has been made. Who wins? Discuss.

ENDNOTES

1. Restatement, Second, Contracts, Section 3,
Agreement Defined; Bargain Defined.
2. Restatement, Second, Contracts, Section 24, Offer Defined.
3. Restatement, Second, Contracts, Section 33, Certainty.
4. Uniform Commercial Code, Section 2—204, Formation in General.
5. Restatement, Second, Contracts, Section 34, Certainty and Choice of Terms; Effect of Performance or
Reliance.

6. Uniform Commercial Code, Section 2—311, Options and Cooperation Respecting Performance.
7. Uniform Commercial Code, Section 1—201(19),
Good Faith.
8. Uniform Commercial Code, Section 2—305,
Open Price Term.
9. Uniform Commercial Code, Sections 2—308 and
2—310, Absence of Specified Place for Delivery;
Open Time for Payment or Running of Credit;
Authority to Ship Under Reservation.
10. Uniform Commercial Code, Section 2—306,
Output, Requirements and Exclusive Dealings.
11. Restatement, Second, Contracts, Section 43, Indirect Communication of Revocation.
12. Uniform Commercial Code, Section 2—205,
Firm Offers.
13. Restatement, Second, Contracts, Section 45,
Option Contract Created by Part Performance or
Tender.
14. Restatement, Second, Contracts, Section 54;
Uniform Commercial Code, Section 2—206(2), Acceptance by Performance; Necessity of Notification
to Offeror; Offer and Acceptance in Formation of
Contract.
15. Uniform Commercial Code, Section 2—207, Additional Terms in Acceptance or Confirmation.
16. Restatement, Second, Contracts, Section 30,
Form of Acceptance Invited.
17. Uniform Commerical Code, Section 2–206(1),
Offer and Acceptance in Formation of Contract.
18. Restatement, Second, Contracts, Section 67, Effect of Receipt of Acceptance Improperly Dipatched
19. Uniform Commercial Code, Section 2–328, Sale
by Auction.

9 CONDUCT INVALIDATING ASSENT

In Chapter 8 we considered one of the essential requirements of a contract, namely, the objective manifestation of mutual assent by each party to the other. This chapter deals with situations in which the manifested consent by one of the parties to the contract is not effective because it was not knowingly and voluntarily given. We consider five such situations in this chapter: duress, undue influence, fraud, nonfraudulent misrepresentation, and mistake.

DURESS

A person should not be held to an agreement that he has not entered into voluntarily. Ac-cordingly, the law will not enforce any contract induced by improper physical or mental coercion—**duress.** There are two basic types of duress. The first is called **physical duress** and occurs when a party is compelled to manifest assent to contract through actual physical force, such as pointing a gun at a person or taking a person's hand and compelling him to sign a written contract. This type of duress is extremely rare, but it renders the agreement **void,**[1] as in the case which follows.

The second type of duress involves the use of **improper threats** or acts, including economic and social coercion, to compel a person to enter into a contract. The threat may be

---

STATE v. ROLLINS
Supreme Court of Rhode Island, 1976.
116 R.I. 528, 359 A.2d 315.

Facts: Rollins and Marchetti, two inmates of the Adult Correctional Institution in Rhode Island, led a takeover of one of the prison's cellblocks. In the process, they locked Picard, a uniformed correctional officer, in one of the emptied cells. With the cellbock completely overrun and Picard a hostage, Rollins made several demands upon prison officials threatening possible bloodshed if the State police were called in. Travisano, the director of the Department of Corrections, out of fear for the safety of Officer Picard, agreed to meet all but two of the prisoners' list of nine demands. Picard was then released by the prisoners. Rollins and Marchetti were subsequently convicted of assault, extortion, and kidnapping and each sentenced to twenty years. They appeal, claiming that during the hostage negotiations, Travisano, acting in his capacity as director of the Department of Corrections, had promised them immunity from prosecution.

Decision: Judgment for the State affirmed.

Opinion: **Paolino, J.** We find no merit in any of the arguments made by defendants under this point. Promises extorted through violence and coercion are no promises at all; they are void from the beginning and unenforceable as a matter of public policy.

explicit or it may be inferred from words or conduct. This type of duress makes the contract **voidable** at the option of the coerced party.[2] For example, if Ellen, a landlord, induces Vijay, an infirm, bedridden tenant, to enter into a new lease on the same apartment at a greatly increased rent by wrongfully threatening to terminate Vijay's lease and evict him, Vijay can avoid the new lease by reason of duress exerted on him. The next case illustrates how economic duress renders a contract voidable.

 INTERNATIONAL UNDERWATER CONTRACTORS, INC. v. NEW ENGLAND TELEPHONE AND TELEGRAPH COMPANY
Appeals Court of Massachusetts, Suffolk, 1979.
8 Mass.App. 340, 393 N.E.2d 968.

Facts: International Underwater Contractors, Inc. (IUC), entered into a written contract with New England Telephone and Telegraph Company (NET) to assemble and install certain conduits under the Mystic River for a lump sum price of $149,680. Delays caused by NET forced IUC's work to be performed in the winter months instead of during the summer as originally bid, and as a result a major change had to be made in the system from that specified in the contract. NET repeatedly assured IUC that it would pay the cost if IUC would complete the work. The change cost IUC an additional $811,810.73; nevertheless, it signed a release settling the claim for a total sum of $575,000. IUC, which at the time was in financial trouble, now seeks to recover the balance due, arguing that the signed release is not binding because it was signed under economic duress. Summary judgment was entered in favor of NET.

Decision: Summary judgment reversed.

Opinion: **Brown, J.** A release signed under duress is not binding. [Citation.] "Coercion sufficient to avoid a contract need not, of course, consist of physical force or threats of it. Social or economic pressure illegally or immorally applied may be sufficient." [Citations.]

To show economic duress (1) a party "must show that he has been the victim of a wrongful or unlawful act or threat, and (2) such act or threat must be one which deprives the victim of his unfettered will." [Citation.] "As a direct result of these elements, the party threatened must be compelled to make a disproportionate exchange of values." [Citation.]

The elements of economic duress have also been described as follows: "(1) that one side involuntarily accepted the terms of another; (2) that circumstances permitted no other alternative; and (3) that said circumstances were the result of coercive acts of the opposite party." [Citations.] "Merely taking advantage of another's financial difficulty is not duress. Rather, the person alleging financial difficulty must allege that it was contributed to or caused by the one accused of coercion." [Citation.] Thus "(i)n order to substantiate the allegation of economic duress or business compulsion . . . (t)here must be a showing of acts on the part of the defendant which produced (the financial embarrassment). The assertion of duress resulted from defendant's wrongful and oppressive conduct and not by plaintiff's necessities." [Citation.]

* * * Here, if the plaintiff's allegations are true, the defendant's acts in (1) insisting on a deviation from the contract and repeatedly assuring the plaintiff that it would pay the additional cost, which was substantially greater than the original,

if the plaintiff would complete the work and (2) then refusing to make payments for almost a year caused the plaintiff's financial difficulties. Such acts could be considered "wrongful" acts and indications of bad faith.

* * *

The unequal bargaining power of the two parties (both in terms of their comparative size and resources as well as the financial difficulties into which the plaintiff had fallen, allegedly because of the defendant's acts) is a factor to be considered in determining whether the transaction involved duress. [Citations.] In addition, the disparity between not only the plaintiff's alleged costs ($811,816) but also the amount NET's engineers had recommended in November, 1974, to the board for settlement ($775,000) and the amount offered on a "take-it-or-leave-it" basis in December and accepted in settlement ($575,000) raises the possibility there may have been a disproportionate exchange of values and should be considered in determining whether the release was signed under duress. [Citation.]

The defendant argues that it did not have to settle the case but could have "exercised its lawful right to litigate the rights of the parties under the agreement" and that "(d)oing or threatening to do what a party has a legal right to do cannot form the basis of a claim of economic duress." [Citation.] However, if the assertions of the plaintiff are true, the defendant did more than assert a legal right, as its acts created the financial difficulties of the plaintiff, of which it then took advantage.

* * *

In summary, we are therefore unable to say as matter of law that the signing of the release was voluntary. Accordingly, it was error to enter summary judgment.

In the second and more common type of duress, the fact that the act or threat would not affect a person of average strength and intelligence is not important if it places the particular person in fear and induces an action against his will. The test is **subjective,** and the question is, did the threat actually induce assent on the part of the person claiming to be the victim of duress. Threats that would suffice to induce assent by one person may not suffice to induce assent by another. All circumstances must be considered, including the age, background, and relationship of the parties. The Restatement provides the following rationale:

> Persons of a weak or cowardly nature are the very ones that need protection; the courageous can usually protect themselves. Timid and inexperienced persons are particularly subject to threats, and it does not lie in the mouths of the unscrupulous to excuse their imposition on such persons on the ground of their victims' infirmities. Restatement, Section 175, Comment C.

Ordinarily, the acts or threats constituting duress are themselves crimes or torts. But this is not true in all cases. The acts need not be criminal or tortious in order to be *wrongful*; they merely need be contrary to public policy or morally reprehensible. For example, if the threat involves a breach of a contractual duty of good faith and fair dealing it is improper.[3]

Moreover, it has generally been held that contracts induced by threats of criminal prosecution are voidable, regardless of whether the coerced party had committed an unlawful act. Similarly, a threat of criminal prosecution of a close relative, as in *Great American Indemnity Co. v. Berryessa*, is also duress. To be distinguished are threats to resort to ordinary civil remedies in order to recover a debt due from another. It is not wrongful to threaten to bring a civil suit against an individual to recover a debt. What is prohibited is the use of a threat of criminal prosecution to induce the making of a contract.

GREAT AMERICAN INDEMNITY CO. v. BERRYESSA
Supreme Court of Utah, 1952.
122 Utah 243, 248 P.2d 367.

Facts: Frank Berryessa stole funds from his employer, the Eccles Hotel Company. His father, W. S. Berryessa, learned of his son's trouble and, thinking the amount involved was about $2000, gave the hotel a promissory note for $2,186 to cover the shortage. In return, the hotel agreed not to publicize the incident or notify the bonding company. (A bonding company is an insurer that is paid a premium for agreeing to reimburse an employer for thefts by an employee.) Before this note became due, however, the hotel discovered that Frank had actually misappropriated $6,865. The hotel then notified its bonding company, Great American Indemnity Company, to collect the entire loss. W. S. Berryessa claims that the agent for Great American told him that unless he paid them $2,000 in cash and signed a note for the remaining $4,865, Frank would be prosecuted. Berryessa agreed, signed the note, and gave the agent a cashier's check for $1,500 and a personal check for $500. He requested that the agent not cash the personal check for about a month. Subsequently, Great American sued Berryessa on the note. He defends against the note on the grounds of duress and counterclaims for the return of the $1,500 and the cancellation of the uncashed $500 check. The jury returned a verdict in favor of Berryessa.

Decision: Judgment for Berryessa on the $4,865 note affirmed. Judgment in favor of Berryessa on his counterclaim for the two checks reversed.

Opinion: Wade, J. It is well settled that a note given to suppress a criminal prosecution is against public policy and is not enforceable between the parties. * * *

In this case respondent relied on two separate defenses, duress and illegal consideration, either one of which is sufficient to nullify this note. So if the jury found that the note was the result of duress or that respondent signed the note because appellant promised to refrain from criminal prosecution of his son, either one would be sufficient to invalidate the note and would constitute a defense thereto. The uncashed check and the payment of $1,500 cash, present a different problem. Respondent had given the hotel a note for slightly over $2,000 to pay for the son's defalcations. At the time this note was given, there can be no question that no coercion was exercised against respondent and that his act was voluntary and at his own suggestion. There is nothing in the record to indicate that this note was given under duress or a promise to suppress prosecution.

UNDUE INFLUENCE

Undue influence is taking unfair advantage of a person by reason of a dominant position based on a relationship of trust and confidence. The law has traditionally scrutinized very carefully contracts between those in a relationship of trust and confidence that is likely to permit one party to exert *unfair persuasion* on the other. Examples are the relationships of guardian and ward, trustee and beneficiary, agent and principal, spouses, parent and child, attorney and client, physician and patient, and clergy and parishioner.

Where one party is under the domination of another, or because of the relationship between them is justified in assuming that the other party will not act in a manner inconsistent with his welfare, a transaction induced by unfair persuasion on the part of the dominant party is induced by undue influence and is **voidable.**[4] The ultimate question in undue influence cases is whether the transaction was induced by dominating the mind or emotions of a submissive party. The weakness or dependence of the person persuaded is a strong circumstance tending to show that persuasion may have been unfair. For example, Abigail, a person without business experience, has for years relied in business matters on the advice of Boris, who is experienced in business. Boris, without making any false representations of fact, induces Abigail to enter into a contract with Boris's confederate, Cassius, that is disadvantageous to Abigail, as both Boris and Cassius know. The transaction is voidable on the grounds of undue influence.

SCHANEMAN v. SCHANEMAN
Supreme Court of Nebraska, 1980.
206 Neb. 113, 291 N.W.2d 412.

Facts: Conrad Schaneman is a Russian immigrant who can neither read nor write the English language. In 1975 Conrad deeded (conveyed) a farm he owned to his eldest son, Laurence, for $23,500, which was the original purchase price of the property in 1945. The value of the farm in 1975 was between $145,000 and $160,000. At the time he executed the deed, Conrad was an eighty-two-year-old invalid, severely ill, and completely dependent on others for his personal needs. He weighed between 325 and 350 pounds, had difficulty breathing, could not walk more than fifteen feet, and needed a special jackhoist to get in and out of the bathtub. Conrad enjoyed a long-standing, confidential relationship with Laurence, who was his principal advisor and handled Conrad's business affairs. Laurence also obtained a power of attorney from Conrad and made himself a joint owner of Conrad's bank account and $20,000 certificate of deposit. Conrad brought this suit to cancel the deed, claiming it was the result of Laurence's undue influence. The district court found that the deed was executed as a result of undue influence, set aside the deed, and granted title to Conrad. Laurence appealed.

Decision: Judgment for Conrad Schaneman affirmed.

Opinion: Clark, J.   An examination of the evidence reflects, in our opinion, that from the fall of 1974 until the conservatorship proceedings were commenced, there existed between the defendant and Conrad a confidential relationship and that, during that period, Conrad relied on the defendant for advice in his business affairs.

   [A confidential] relationship exists between two persons if one has gained the confidence of the other and purports to act or advise with the other's interest in mind. [Citation.]
   In a confidential or fiduciary relationship in which confidence is rightfully reposed on one side and a resulting superiority and opportunity for influence is thereby created on the other, equity will scrutinize the transaction critically, especially where age, infirmity, and instability are involved, to see that no injustice has occurred. [Citation.]

Here the evidence reflects that, due to age and physical infirmities, Conrad was, for all intents and purposes, an invalid at the time of the conveyance. It further supports a finding that Conrad's mental acuity was impaired at times and that he sometimes suffered from disorientation and lapse of memory. Considering all the

> evidence, we find that, in March 1975, Conrad was subject to the influence of the defendant, who was acting in a confidential relationship; that the opportunity to exercise undue influence existed; that there was a disposition on the part of the defendant to exercise such undue influence; and that the conveyance appears to be the effect of such influence.

FRAUD

Another factor affecting the validity of consent manifested by a contracting party is fraud. Fraud prevents the assent from being knowingly given. There are two distinct types of fraud: fraud in the execution and fraud in the inducement.

Fraud in the Execution

Fraud in the execution, which is extremely rare, consists of a misrepresentation deceiving the defrauded person as to the very nature of the contract.[5] In this situation, the innocent party is entirely unaware that he is entering into a contract and has no intention of doing so. For example, Melody delivers a package to Ray, requests Ray to sign a receipt for it, holds out a simple printed form headed "Receipt," and indicates the line on which Ray is to sign. This line appears to Ray to be the bottom line of the form, but instead it is the bottom line of a promissory note cleverly concealed underneath the receipt. Ray signs where directed without knowing that he is signing a note. This is fraud in the execution. The note is **void** and of no legal effect. The reason is simply that, although the signature is genuine and appears to be a manifestation of assent to the terms of the note, there is no actual assent. The nature of Melody's fraud precluded consent to the signing of the note because it prevented Ray from reasonably knowing what he was signing.

Fraud in the Inducement

Fraud in the inducement, generally referred to as fraud or deceit, is an intentional misrepresentation of material fact by one party to the other, who consents to enter into a contract in reliance on the misrepresentation. For example, Alice, in offering to sell her dog to Bob, tells Bob that the dog won first prize in its class in the recent national dog show. In fact, the dog had not even been entered in the show. This statement induces Bob to accept the offer and pay a high price for the dog. There is a contract, but it is **voidable** by Bob because Alice's fraud induced his assent.

The requisite elements of fraud in the inducement are:

1. a false representation
2. of a fact
3. that is material
4. and made with knowledge of its falsity and the intention to deceive
5. that is justifiably relied on.

False Representation A basic element of fraud is a false representation or a **misrepresentation.** There must be some positive statement or conduct that misleads. As a general rule, silence alone does *not* amount to fraud. There is generally no obligation on the part of a seller to tell a purchaser everything he knows about the subject of the sale, although if there is a latent (hidden) defect of a substantial character, one that would not be discovered by an ordinary examination, the seller is obliged to reveal it.

There are other situations in which the law imposes a duty of disclosure. For example, a person may have a duty of disclosure because of prior representations innocently made that are later discovered to be untrue before entering into the contract. Thus, Jay makes a true statement of his financial condition, intending that its substance be published to Brown's subscribers. Brown summarizes the information and transmits the summary to Cindy, a subscriber. Shortly thereafter, Jay's financial condition becomes seriously impaired, but he does not disclose this to Brown. Cindy makes a contract to lend money to Jay. Jay's failure to disclose is equivalent to an assertion that his financial condition is not seriously impaired, and this assertion is a misrepresentation.

Another instance in which silence may constitute fraud is a transaction involving a fiduciary. A **fiduciary** is a person who owes a duty of trust, loyalty, and confidence to another. For example, an agent owes a fiduciary duty to his principal, as does a trustee to the beneficiary of the trust and a partner to her copartners. A fiduciary may not deal at *arm's length* but rather owes a duty to make full disclosure of all relevant facts when entering into a transaction with the other party to the relationship. In contrast, in most business transactions, the parties deal at arm's length: that is, on equal terms. Accordingly neither party is required to make disclosures to the other.

Active **concealment** can likewise form the basis for fraud, as where a seller puts heavy oil or grease in a car engine to conceal a knock. Truth may be suppressed by concealment quite as much as by active misrepresentation. An express denial of knowledge of a fact that a party knows to exist, or a statement of misleading half-truth, can be fraudulent. Such conduct is clearly more than mere silence and is considered the equivalent of a false representation.

Fact The basic element of fraud is the misrepresentation of a material fact; actionable fraud can rarely be based on what is merely a statement of opinion. A **fact** is an event that actually took place or a thing that actually exists. A representation is one of **opinion** if it expresses only the belief of the representor as to the existence of a fact or a judgment as to quality, value, authenticity, or other matters of judgment. The line between fact and opinion is not an easy one to draw and in close cases presents an issue for the jury. Suppose that Ellen induces Dan to purchase shares in a company unknown to Dan at a price of $100 per share by stating that she had paid $150 per share for them the preceding year, when in fact she had paid only $50 per share. This is a representation of a past event, definitely ascertainable, verifiable, and therefore fraudulent. If, on the other hand, Ellen said to Dan that the shares were "a good investment," she is merely stating her opinion, and in the usual case Dan ought to regard it as no more than that. Suppose, however, that Ellen said the company "had a good year last year," when in fact it failed to show a profit. Is this opinion or fact? It is difficult, if not impossible, to decide without additional evidence. The solution will often depend on the knowledgability of the person making the statement and the information available to the other party. If the representor is a professional broker advising a client, the courts are more likely to regard an untrue statement of opinion as actionable. It is the expression of opinion by one holding himself out as having **expert** knowledge, and the tendency is to grant relief to those who have sustained loss by reasonable reliance on expert evaluation, as in the next case.

VOKES v. ARTHUR MURRAY, INC.
Court of Appeal of Florida, 1968.
212 So.2d 906.

Facts: Mrs. Audrey E. Vokes, a widow of fifty-one years and without family, purchased fourteen separate dance courses from J. P. Davenport's Arthur Murray, Inc., school of dance. The fourteen courses totaled in the aggregate 2,302 hours of dancing lessons at a total cost to Mrs. Vokes of $31,090.45. Mrs. Vokes was induced continually to reapply for new courses by representations made by Mr. Davenport that her dancing ability was improving, that she was responding to instructions, that she had excellent potential, and that they were developing her into an accomplished dancer. In fact, she had no dancing ability or aptitude and had trouble "hearing the musical beat." Mrs. Vokes brought this action to have the contracts set aside. The plaintiff's complaint was dismissed for failure to state a cause of action and she now appeals.

Decision: Judgment reversed.

Opinion: Pierce, J. It is true that "generally a misrepresentation, to be actionable, must be one of fact rather than of opinion." [Citation.] But this rule has significant qualifications, applicable here. * * *

"A statement of a party having * * * superior knowledge may be regarded as a statement of fact although it would be considered as opinion if the parties were dealing on equal terms."

It could be reasonably supposed here that defendants had "superior knowledge" as to whether plaintiff had "dance potential" and as to whether she was noticeably improving in the art of terpsichore. And it would be a reasonable inference from the undenied averments of the complaint that the flowery elogiums heaped upon her by defendants as a prelude to her contracting for 1944 additional hours of instruction in order to attain the rank of the Bronze Standard, thence to the bracket of the Silver Standard, thence to the class of the Gold Bar Standard, and finally to the crowning plateau of a Life Member of the Studio, proceeded as much or more from the urge to "ring the cash register" as from any honest or realistic appraisal of her dancing prowess or a factual representation of her progress.

Even in contractual situations where a party to a transaction owes no duty to disclose facts within his knowledge or to answer inquiries respecting such facts, the law is if he undertakes to do so he must disclose the *whole truth*. [Citations.] From the face of the complaint, it should have been reasonably apparent to defendants that her vast outlay of cash for the many hundreds of additional hours of instruction was not justified by her slow and awkward progress, which she would have been made well aware of if they had spoken the "whole truth."

In addition, statements of **value,** such as "This is the best car in town for the money" or "This deluxe model will give you twice the wear of a cheaper model," are not grounds for the avoidance of a contract. Such exaggerations and commendations of articles offered for sale are to be expected from dealers who are merely **puffing** their wares with "sales talk."

Also to be distinguished from a representation of fact is a **prediction** of the future. Predictions are closely akin to opinions, as one cannot know with certainty what will happen in the future, and normally they are not regarded as factual statements. Likewise, promissory statements ordinarily do not constitute a basis of fraud, as a breach of promise does not necessarily indicate that the promise was fraudulently made. A promise that the promisor, at the time of making, had no intention of keeping is fraudulent as a misrepresentation of fact. Most courts take the position that the state of a person's mind, which is being misrepresented, "is as much a fact as the state of a person's digestion." *Edgigton v. Fitzmaurice,* 29 Ch.D. 459 (1885). If a dealer promises, "I will service this machine free for the next year," but at the time has no intention of doing so, his conduct is actionable if the other elements of fraud are present.

Misrepresentations of **law** are also generally distinguished from those of fact. Suppose that the seller of land induces a sale by misrepresenting that a certain zoning classification will permit the type of commercial activity contemplated by the purchaser or that the zoning ordinance is unconstitutional as applied to the property. Has he made a misrepresentation of fact? Practically all courts will agree that he has not. Rather, he has misrepresented the state of the law, and since everyone is presumed to know the law, the purchaser is not justified in relying on the seller's representation, and the sale is not fraudulent. There are, however, a few exceptions to this rule. If the seller occupies a fiduciary or confidential relationship with the purchaser, the latter will be able to avoid the transaction. A misrepresentation by one who is learned in the law, as a practicing attorney, may under certain circumstances be fraudulent.

Materiality   In addition to the requirement that the misrepresentation be one of fact, it is necessary that it be **material.** It must relate to something of sufficient substance to induce reliance. In the sale of a race horse, it may not be material whether the horse was ridden in its most recent race by a certain jockey, but its running time for the race probably would be. In determining the materiality of a representation, courts look to the impression made on the mind of the party to whom it was made. It is usually material if, but for the representation, he would not have entered into the transaction. Most courts deem the misrepresentation to be material if, to a substantial degree, it influenced the making of a decision, even though it was not the decisive factor. The following case and the situation in Law in the News on page 195 present unusual factual situations raising the question of when a seller is obligated to disclose.

REED v. KING

California Court of Appeals, 1983.
145 Cal.App.3d 261, 193 Cal.Rptr. 130.

Facts: Dorris Reed bought a house from Robert King for $76,000. King and his real estate agent knew that a woman and her four children had been murdered in the house ten years earlier and allegedly knew that the market value of the house had been materially affected by the event. They said nothing about the murders to Reed, and King asked a neighbor not to inform her of them. After the sale, neighbors told Reed about the murders and informed her that the house was consequently worth only $65,000. Reed brought an action against King and the real estate agent, alleging fraud and seeking rescission and damages. The complaint was dismissed and Reed appealed.

Decision: Judgment reversed.

Opinion: Blease, J.   Does Reed's pleading state a cause of action? Concealed within this question is the nettlesome problem of the duty of disclosure of blemishes on real property which are not physical defects or legal impairments to use.

Reed seeks to state a cause of action sounding in contract, i.e., rescission, or in tort, i.e., deceit. In either event her allegations must reveal a fraud. [Citation.] "The elements of actual fraud, whether as the basis of the remedy in contract or tort, may be stated as follows: There must be (1) a *false representation* or concealment of a material fact (or, in some cases, an opinion) susceptible of knowledge, (2) made with *knowledge* of its falsity or without sufficient knowledge on the subject to warrant a representation, (3) with the *intent* to induce the person to whom it is made to act upon it; and such person must (4) act in *reliance* upon the representation (5) to his *damage*." (Original italics.) [Citation.]

The trial court perceived the defect in Reed's complaint to be a failure to allege concealment of a material fact. . . .

Concealment is a term of art which includes mere nondisclosure when a party has a duty to disclose. [Citation.] Rest.2d Contracts, § 161; Rest.2d Torts, § 551; Reed's complaint reveals only nondisclosure despite the allegation King asked a neighbor to hold his peace. There is no allegation the attempt at suppression was a cause in fact of Reed's ignorance. (See Rest.2d Contracts, §§ 160, 162–164; Rest.2d Torts, § 550; Rest., Restitution, § 9.) Accordingly, the critical question is: does the seller have a duty to disclose here? Resolution of this question depends on the materiality of the fact of the murders.

In general, a seller of real property has a duty to disclose: "where the seller knows of facts *materially* affecting the value or desirability of the property which are known or accessible only to him and also knows that such facts are not known to, or within the reach of the diligent attention and observation of the buyer, the seller is under a duty to disclose them to the buyer. [Citation.] This broad statement of duty has led one commentator to conclude: "The ancient maxim *caveat emptor* ('let the buyer beware.') has little or no application to California real estate transactions." [Citation.]

Whether information "is of sufficient materiality to affect the value or desirability of the property . . . depends on the facts of the particular case." [Citation.] Materiality "is a question of law, and is part of the concept of right to rely or justifiable reliance." [Citation.] . . . Three considerations bear on this legal conclusion; the gravity of the harm inflicted by nondisclosure; the fairness of imposing a duty of discovery on the buyer as an alternative to compelling disclosure, and the impact on the stability of contracts if rescission is permitted.

Numerous cases have found nondisclosure of physical defects and legal impediments to use of real property are material. [Citation.] However, to our knowledge, no prior real estate sale case has faced an issue of nondisclosure of the kind presented here.

* * *

The murder of innocents is highly unusual in its potential for so disturbing buyers they may be unable to reside in a home where it has occurred. This fact may foreseeably deprive a buyer of the intended use of the purchase. Murder is not such a common occurrence that *buyers* should be charged with anticipating and discovering this disquieting possibility. Accordingly, the fact is not one for which a duty of inquiry and discovery can sensibly be imposed upon the buyer.

Reed alleges the fact of the murders has a quantifiable effect on the market value of the premises. We cannot say this allegation is inherently wrong and, in the pleading posture of the case, we assume it to be true. If information known or accessible only to the seller has a significant and measurable effect on market value and, as is alleged here, the seller is aware of this effect, we see no principled basis for making the duty to disclose turn upon the character of the information. Physical usefulness is not and never has been the sole criterion of valuation. . . .

Reputation and history can have a significant effect on the value of reality. "George Washington slept here" is worth something, however physically inconsequential that consideration may be. Ill-repute or "bad will" conversely may depress the value of property. . . .

Whether Reed will be able to prove her allegation the decade-old multiple murder has a significant effect on market value we cannot determine. If she is able to do so by competent evidence she is entitled to a favorable ruling on the issues of materiality and duty to disclose.

LAW IN THE NEWS

Realty and Reality
Must Toxic Dump Be Revealed?

William Jackson and his wife and family were ready to settle down in Gloucester Township, N.J. He says they told their real estate agent they wanted to keep their children far from poisonous chemicals but were shocked to discover—even after a favorable property inspection report—that they were sold a home near a toxic landfill.

They refused to move in, and the case has gone to court.

"It [toxic wastes on or near property] is a growing area of concern. We are getting an increasing number of reports or complaints" from people who own homes near such sites, said William North, counsel to the National Association of Realtors in Chicago.

Duty to 'Disclose Facts'

North said the duties of real estate agents and brokers are not always clear. For example, he asked, who should test the soil and decide when wastes are at a toxic level?

Last year California's First District Court of Appeal held that a real estate agent had a duty "to conduct a reasonably competent and diligent inspection" and "to disclose material facts" and "adverse factors" that the agent "should have known" [Citation].

Jackson said his home inspection report was enthusiastic. The couple put $1,000 down.

But they refused to move in after a neighbor told them about the nearby landfill operated by Gloucester Environmental Management Systems, or GEMS. The lending bank and several other plaintiffs sued the Jacksons for backing out of the deal. The Jacksons countersued, claiming that agents, inspectors and others failed to disclose information on the environmental hazard.

"Naturally, I'm very angry," Jackson said. "The banker used the state's money to defraud me." State officials are looking into how its mortgage money is spent, he said.

'Is It Fraud?'

The lawsuits have been consolidated and may plow new legal ground, said Jackson's lawyer, Arnold Feldman of Camden. He said the bank and others "knew or should have known" of the landfill. His complaint alleges that "material facts" were concealed [Citation].

Asks Feldman: "What is the duty of a seller in disclosing latent defects? Does the duty extend to latent property defects, and is it fraud for an appraiser to exclude a toxic waste dump from her appraisal when it is 1,000 feet from the property?"

By Cheryl Frank
Reprinted with permission from the April 1985 ABA Journal, The Lawyer's Magazine, published by the American Bar Association.

Knowledge of Falsity and Intention to Deceive To establish fraud, the misrepresentation must have been known by the one making it to be false and must be made with an intent to deceive. This element of fraud is called **scienter.** Knowledge of falsity can consist of (a) actual knowledge, (b) lack of belief in the statement's truthfulness, or (c) reckless indifference as to its truthfulness.

Justifiable Reliance A person is not entitled to relief unless he has **justifiably relied** on the misrepresentation to his detriment or injury. If the complaining party's decision was in no way influenced by the misrepresentation, he must abide by the terms of the contract. He is not deceived if he does not rely. Moreover, if the complaining party knew or should have known that the representation of the defendant was untrue, but still entered into the contract, he has not justifiably relied. For example, Paul, seeking to purchase a six-passenger car, was told by the salesman that a two-seat sports car was appropriate and took

Paul for a test drive. If Paul, nevertheless, relied on the salesman's statement, such reliance would not be justified, and Paul would not have been legally defrauded. Neverthe-less, as the following case shows, the courts will not demand that a party go to unreasonable lengths to verify a factual representation.

GIBSON v. HOME FOLKS MOBILE HOME PLAZA, INC.
United States District Court, S.D. Georgia, 1982.
533 F.Supp. 1211.

Facts: Plaintiff, Gibson, entered into negotiation with W. S. May, president of Home Folks Mobile Home Plaza, Inc., to buy Home Plaza Corporation. Plaintiff visited the mobile home park on several occasions, at which time he noted the occupancy, visually inspected the sewer and water systems, and asked May numerous questions concerning the condition of the business. Plaintiff, however, never requested to see the books, nor did May try to conceal them. May admits making the following representations to the plaintiff: (1) the water and sewer systems were in good condition and no major short-term expenditures would be needed; (2) the park realized a 40 percent profit on natural gas sold to tenants; and (3) usual park vacancy was 5 percent. Additionally, May gave plaintiff the park's accountant-prepared income statement, which showed a net income of $38,220 for the last eight months. Based on these figures, plaintiff projected an annual net profit of $57,331.20. Upon being asked whether this figure accurately represented income of the business for the last three years, May stated by letter that indeed it did.

Plaintiff purchased the park for $275,000. Shortly thereafter, plaintiff spent $5,384 repairing the well and septic systems. By the time plaintiff sold the park three years later, he had expended $7,531 on the wells and $8,125 on the septic systems. Furthermore, in the first year park occupancy was nowhere near 95 percent. Even after raising rent and the charges for natural gas, plaintiff still operated at a deficit.

Plaintiff sued defendant, alleging that May, on behalf of defendant, made false and fraudulent statements on which plaintiff relied when he purchased the park. Defendant moved for summary judgment.

Decision: Defendant's motion for summary judgment denied.

Opinion: Bowen, J. The elements of this cause of action [fraud], which plaintiff has alleged with the requisite specificity, [citation] are: "(1) false representation made by the defendant; (2) scienter; (3) an intention to induce the plaintiff to act or refrain from acting in reliance by the plaintiff; (4) justifiable reliance by the plaintiff; (5) damage to the plaintiff." [Citation.] Central to defendant's motion for summary judgment is the applicability *vel non* to the facts in this case of the fourth of these elements—"justifiable reliance by the plaintiff."

As a general rule, a defrauded party cannot state a claim of justifiable reliance upon the false representations of another, when such person, in the exercise of ordinary diligence, could have discovered the falsity of the representations before acting thereon. [Citation.] The scope of the defrauded party's duty to discover, as defined by the "ordinary," "reasonable," or "due," diligence standard, does not go so far as to require the exhaustion of all available means to ascertain the truth of the representations. [Citation.] Furthermore, as recognized by Georgia appellate courts, questions of whether the defrauded party "could have protected himself by the exercise of proper diligence are, except in plain and indisputable cases, questions for the jury." [Citation.]

* * * [P]ositive misrepresentations by words or acts are clearly actionable unless it appears as a matter of law that plaintiff was not justified in relying on them in the exercise of common prudence and diligence. [Citation.] A lack of diligence may appear as a matter of law where plaintiff blindly relies upon the representations of another without rhyme or reason. [Citation.] "Blind reliance exists where 'it cannot be said that the purchase originated in fraud so much as in the carelessness of the purchaser to exercise ordinary care for his own interest'." [Citations.] In a similar manner, a failure of due diligence by plaintiff may exist as a matter of law, where the alleged fraud consisted of defendant's silence on a particular matter and plaintiff could have discovered the existence of the unspoken fact by simple inspection.

Allegations of fraud also may not be actionable if it appears as a matter of law that the person relying on the fraud had an equal and ample opportunity to prevent the happening of the occurrence causing injury. * * * Finally, plaintiff's lack of diligence may exist as a matter of law where he clearly had notice of the allegedly misrepresented fact and yet proceeded with the sale. * * *

On review of the foregoing Georgia appellate decisions, it is apparent that the facts in the present case do not show, as a matter of law, that plaintiff failed to exercise common prudence and ordinary diligence before acting on the alleged misrepresentations. Certainly, this is not a case of "blind reliance." Plaintiff visited the park on several occasions and corresponded with and questioned Mr. May extensively about the operation of the park. [Citation.] ("[W]e are not aware of any rule of law, or decision of any court, that goes to the extent of saying that one who has been imposed upon by a deceitful and false statement can have no relief unless, before acting upon such a statement, he had exhausted all means at his command to ascertain its truth."). [Citation.] During the course of these discussions, plaintiff sought verification from Mr. May of several items, most notably the eight month income statement and the yearly projection therefrom. Such conduct cannot be termed blind reliance as a matter of law. [Citation.] The Georgia Court of Appeals has commented:

> [W]here the basis upon which the contract was entered upon lies in the existence or nonexistence of certain material facts, the verity of which must be ascertained from the statement of one acquainted with such facts, each of the contracting parties has a right to rely upon the truth of the other's statements with reference thereto, when such statements relate to matters apparently within the knowledge of the party asserting them; and to do this without checking up the statement with the declarations of other and different persons, in order, by such and investigation, to test their probable truth.

NONFRAUDULENT MISREPRESENTATION

At common law it was necessary for the injured party in a fraud action, whether seeking rescission or damages, to prove an intention by the defendant to deceive. Hence the necessity for showing knowledge of the falsity, or at least culpable ignorance. Today, a majority of courts permit a rescission for negligent or innocent (nonnegligent) misrepresentation, provided, of course, that all of the remaining elements of fraud are present. **Negligent misrepresentation** is a false representation that is made without due care in ascertaining its truthfulness. **Innocent misrepresentation** is a false representation made without knowledge of its falsity but with due care. Thus, a contract induced by negligent or innocent misrepresentation is **voidable.** Moreover, some courts also permit the recovery of damages for nonfraudulent misrepresentation.

MISTAKE

Mistake is an understanding or belief that is not in accord with existing fact. An elusive branch of the law is that concerned with the effect of "mistake" on the formation of a contract. Certain problems have been settled, but many have not. There is, however, one concept that runs through the cases and that will at least help to place the issues in a meaningful context as well as assist in predicting results. In Chapter 8, we gave attention to the standard by which the assent of the parties is to be tested. The courts favor an objective approach. A person is bound by the reasonable impressions he has created in the mind of the other party, even if this differs from her own subjective intention.

An illustration is an offer in language manifesting an intention different from that actually intended by the offeror: a mistake resulting from carelessness, inattention, or failure to double check. This occurs in the case of Sandra offering to sell her Chevrolet when she intended to offer her Ford automobile. If the offer is accepted before it is corrected, Sandra is bound by the intention that she manifested. In the absence of duress, fraud, or breach of fiduciary duty by the buyer, she has no legal remedy.

The problem is, how far can the objective theory be extended in mistake cases? At what point is there a lack of "real consent"? The law grants relief in a situation involving mistake only where there has been a **mutual mistake** of material fact by both parties to the contract. The law generally does not grant relief where there is merely a **unilateral mistake** of fact.

Existence or Identity of Subject Matter

Suppose Nancy offers to sell Sidney a certain boat, but unknown to both parties the boat has been destroyed. If Sidney accepts, is he entitled to damages on Nancy's failure to deliver the boat as promised? He is not. The Code provides that, where the contract requires for its performance goods identified when the contract is made, and the goods suffer casualty without fault of either party before the risk of loss passes to the buyer, then, if the loss is total, the contract is avoided.

The rationale of this rule is based on the presumed intention of the parties in ordinary transactions; that is, *no subject matter, no contract.* To be distinguished is the case in which the contract contemplates an assumption of the risk. For instance, a ship at sea may be sold "lost or not lost." In such case, the buyer is liable whether the ship was lost or not lost at the time of the making of the contract. There is no mistake; instead, there is a conscious allocation of risk.

Possibly the most famous decision involving mutual mistake is the 1864 English decision of *Raffles v. Wichelhaus,* 2 Hurlstone & Coltman 906 (1864), popularly known as the "Peerless Case." A contract of purchase was made for 125 bales of cotton to arrive on the *Peerless* from Bombay. It happened, however, that there were two ships by the name of *Peerless*, each sailing from Bombay, one in October and the other in December. The buyer had in mind the ship that sailed in October, while the seller reasonably believed the agreement referred to the *Peerless* sailing in December. Neither party was at fault, but both believed in good faith that a different ship was intended. The English court held that no contract existed. The Restatement is in accord.[6] There is no manifestation of mutual assent where the parties attach materially different meanings to their manifestations *and* neither party knows or has reason to know the meaning attached by the other. Nevertheless, if blame can be ascribed to either party, he will be held responsible. Thus, if the seller knew of the sailing from Bombay of two ships by the name of *Peerless*, then he would be at fault, and the contract would be for the ship sailing in October as the buyer expected. If *neither* is to blame or *both* are to blame, there is *no* contract at all.

STATE OF FLORIDA, DEPARTMENT OF STATE v. TREASURE SALVORS, INC.

United States Court of Appeals, Fifth Circuit, 1980.
621 F.2d 1340.

Facts: Beginning in 1971, Treasure Salvors and the State of Florida entered into a series of four annual contracts governing the salvage of the *Nuestra Senora de Atocha*. The *Atocha* is a Spanish galleon that sank in 1622, carrying a treasure now worth well over $250 million. Both parties had contracted under the impression that the seabed on which the *Atocha* lay was land owned by Florida. Treasure Salvors agreed to relinquish 25 percent of the items recovered in return for the right to salvage on State lands. In accordance with these contracts, Treasure Salvors delivered to Florida its share of the salvaged artifacts. In 1975 the United States Supreme Court held that the part of the continental shelf on which the *Atocha* was resting had *never* been owned by Florida. Treasure Salvors then brought suit to rescind the contracts and to recover the artifacts it had delivered to the State of Florida. The State appeals from a judgment in favor of Treasure Salvors.

Decision: Judgment for Treasure Salvors affirmed.

Opinion: **Johnson, J.**   Even the briefest of glances at these facts cannot help but invoke thoughts of the doctrine of mutual mistake and call to mind the seminal case of *Sherwood v. Walker*, [citation]. *Sherwood* involved the classic remedy, "replevin for a cow." Plaintiff had agreed to purchase Rose 2d of Aberlone from defendants for $80. When the plaintiff tendered the money, the sellers refused to accept it and declined to yield Rose. At trial the sellers introduced evidence establishing that at the time of the agreement both parties thought Rose was barren and could not breed. Only in the interim, between the agreement to sell and the buyer's tender of the funds, was it discovered that Rose was with calf. This mistake, sellers argued, went to the root of the parties' agreement. The Michigan Supreme Court agreed and allowed the sellers to avoid their contractual obligation.

The case at bar presents another example of mutual mistake. The parties entered into the salvage contracts under the mistaken assumption that the State of Florida owned the land. But for this belief, the Division of Archives and Treasure Salvors would not have executed the agreements. The trial court correctly held that the parties made a mutual mistake.

Nature of Subject Matter

If Florence contracts to purchase Henry's automobile under the belief that she can sell it at a profit to Edmund, she obviously is not excused from liability if she is mistaken in this belief. Nor can she rescind the agreement simply because she was mistaken as to her estimate of what the automobile was worth. These are the ordinary risks of business, and courts do not undertake to relieve against them. But suppose that the parties contract on the assumption that the automobile is a 1988 Cadillac with 15,000 miles of use, when in fact the engine is that of a cheaper model and has been run in excess of 50,000 miles? Here, a court would likely allow a rescission because of mutual mistake respecting a material fact. Another example of mutual mistake of fact was presented in a California case where a noted violinist purchased two violins from a collector for $8,000, the bill of sale reading: ". . . I have on this date sold to Mr. Efrem Zimbalist one Joseph Guarnerius violin and one Stradivarius violin dated 1717." Actually, unknown to either party, neither violin was genuine. Taken together they were worth no more than $300. The sale was **voidable** by the purchaser for mutual mistake.

The foregoing cases are to be contrasted with situations in which the parties are aware that they do not know the character or value of the item sold. For example, the Supreme Court of Wisconsin refused to set aside the sale of a stone for which the purchaser paid one dollar, but which was subsequently discovered to be an uncut diamond valued at $700. The parties did not know at the time of sale what the stone was and knew they did not know. Each consciously assumed the risk that the value might be more or less than the selling price.

A mistake unknown to the party making it, however, becomes voidable if the other party recognizes it as a mistake. For example, suppose a building contractor submits a bid for a job that is one-half of what it should be, because he made a serious error in his computations. If the other party knows that he made such an error, or reasonably should have known of it, he cannot, as a general rule, take advantage of the other's mistake and accept the offer. In one such case the plaintiff, in computing his bid on a city sewer project, by mistake omitted the cost of one item, the steel. Accordingly, his bid was substantially lower than the others. He bid $429,444.20; the next higher bid was $671,600. All other bids were even higher. An estimate made by the city engineers, undisclosed to the bidders prior to the submission of the bids, was $632,000. The plaintiff received a sympathetic ear from the Oregon Supreme Court, which stated in the course of its opinion: "It is our belief that although the plaintiff alone made the mistake, the City was aware of it. When it accepted the plaintiff's bid, with knowledge of the mistake, it sought to take an unconscionable advantage of an inadvertent error." *Rushlight Automatic Sprinkler Co. v. City of Portland*, 189 Or. 194, 219 P.2d 732 (1950). Some courts refer to a case of this type as one of **palpable unilateral mistake**, to distinguish it from the situation where the other had no suspicion nor any good reason to suspect that an error had been committed. In the latter type of case no judicial relief from the unilateral mistake is available.

Failure to Read Document

As a general proposition, a party is held to what she signs. Her signature authenticates the writing, and she cannot repudiate that which she has voluntarily approved. As a Louisiana court expressed it: "Signatures to obligations are not mere ornaments." Generally, one who assents to a writing is presumed to know its contents and cannot escape being bound by its terms merely by contending that

FIGURE 9–1 Conduct Invalidating Assent

Conduct	Effect
Duress by physical force	Void
Duress by improper threats	Voidable
Undue influence	Voidable
Fraud in the execution	Void
Fraud in the inducement	Voidable
Nonfraudulent misrepresentation	Voidable
Mutual mistake of fact	Voidable

she did not read them; her assent is deemed to cover unknown as well as known terms.[7] There are, however, instances where one is relieved of obligations to which one has apparently assented; namely, where the character of the writing was misrepresented by the other party or where the writing was such that a reasonable person would not think it contained contractual provisions. An example of the latter would be a coat-check stub containing in fine print a limitation of the proprietor's liability in case of loss or damage to the item checked. Ordinarily, stubs of this type are used for identification purposes only; hence, in the usual case one is not held to have assented to the limitation of proprietor liability merely by accepting the stub.

Mistake of Law

In the absence of fraud, one cannot obtain a release from contractual liability on the ground that one did not understand the legal effect of the contract. Courts will not grant relief from a mistake of law. By the majority view in this country, one paying money to another under a mistake of law cannot recover that money even though it was not legally due, provided the payee's claim was asserted in good faith. There are, however, some exceptions. Payments made by governmental agencies or payments made to a court or court official under mistake of law are recoverable. The general reluctance to grant relief for mistake of law has been subjected to serious criticism and has been changed by statute in some States. In these States, relief for mutual mistake of law is placed upon the same basis as mutual mistake of a material fact.

CHAPTER SUMMARY

Duress	**Physical Duress** coercion involving physical force renders the agreement void **Duress by Means of Improper Threats** improper threats or acts, including economic and social coercion, renders the contract voidable
Undue Influence	**Definition** taking unfair advantage of a person by reason of a dominant position based on a confidential relationship **Effect** renders a contract voidable

Fraud	**Fraud in the Execution** a misrepresentation that deceives the other party as to the nature of a document evidencing the contract renders the agreement void
	Fraud in the Inducement renders the agreement voidable if the following elements are present:
	  ■ *False Representation* positive statement or conduct that misleads
	  ■ *Fact* an event that took place or thing that exists
	  ■ *Materiality* of substantial importance
	  ■ *Knowledge of Falsity and Intention to Deceive* called *scienter* and includes (a) actual knowledge, (b) lack of belief in statement's truthfulness, or (c) reckless indifferences to its truthfulness
	  ■ *Justifiable Reliance* a defrauded party is reasonably influenced by the misrepresentation

Nonfraudulent Misrepresentation	**Negligent Misrepresentation** misrepresentation made without due care in ascertaining its truthfulness; renders agreement voidable **Innocent Misrepresentation** misrepresentation made without knowledge of its falsity but with due care; renders contract voidable

Mistake	**Definition** an understanding that is not in accord with existing fact **Mutual Mistake** both parties have a common but erroneous belief forming the basis of the contract; renders the contract voidable by either party **Existence or Identity of Subject Matter** if the subject matter of a contract does not exist, the contract is void **Nature of Subject Matter** a contract is voidable where both parties are mistaken as to the subject matter of the contract **Mistake of Law** in the absence of fraud, a party cannot obtain a release from contractual liability on the grounds of not understanding the contract's legal effect **Palpable Unilateral Mistake** erroneous belief by one party that is recognized by the other, may render the contract voidable

QUESTIONS

1. Identify the types of duress and discuss the legal effect of each.
2. Identify the types of fraud and the elements that must be shown to establish the existence of each.
3. Discuss undue influence and identify some of the situations giving rise to a confidential relationship.
4. Identify and discuss the situations involving voidable mistakes.
5. Define the two types of nonfraudulent misrepresentation.

PROBLEMS

1. Anita and Barry were negotiating, and Anita's attorney prepared a long and carefully drawn contract that was given to Barry for examination. Five days later and prior to its execution, Barry's eyes became so infected that it was impossible for him to read. Ten days thereafter and during the continuance of the illness Anita called on Barry and urged him to sign the contract, telling him that time was running out. Barry signed the contract despite the fact he was unable to read it. In a subsequent action by Anita, Barry claimed that the contract was not binding on him because it was impossible for him to read and he did not know what it contained prior to his signing it. Decision?

2. (a) William tells Carol that he paid $150,000 for his farm in 1983 and that he believes it is worth twice that at the present time. Relying on these statements, Carol buys the farm from William for $225,000. William did pay $150,000 for the farm in 1983, but its value has increased only slightly, and it is presently not worth $300,000. On discovering this, Carol offers to reconvey the farm to William and sues for the return of her $225,000. Result?
(b) Modify the facts in (a) by assuming that William had paid $100,000 for the property in 1983. What result?

3. On September 1 Adams in Portland, Oregon, wrote a letter to Brown in New York City offering to sell to Brown 1,000 tons of chromite at $48 per ton, to be shipped by *S.S. Malabar* sailing from Portland, Oregon, to New York City via the Panama Canal. Upon receiving the letter on September 5, Brown immediately mailed to Adams a letter stating that she accepted the offer. There were two ships by the name of *S.S. Malabar* sailing from Portland to New York City via the Panama Canal, one sailing in October and the other sailing in December. At the time of mailing her letter of acceptance Brown knew of both sailings and further knew that Adams knew only of the December sailing. Is there a contract? If so, to which *S.S. Malabar* does it relate?

4. Adler owes Perreault, a police captain, $500. Adler threatens Perreault that unless Perreault gives him a discharge from the debt, Adler will disclose the fact that Perreault has on several occasions become highly intoxicated and has been seen in the company of certain disreputable persons. Perreault,

induced by fear that such a disclosure would cost him his position or in any event lead to social disgrace, gives Adler a release, but subsequently sues to set it aside and recover on his claim. Decision?

5. Harris owned a farm that was worth about $600 an acre. By false representations of fact Harris induced Pringle to buy the farm at $1,500 an acre. Shortly after taking possession of the farm, Pringle discovered oil under the land. Harris, on learning this, sues to have the sale set aside on the ground that it was voidable because of fraud. Decision?

6. On February 2 Phillips induced Mallor to purchase from her fifty shares of stock in the XYZ Corporation for $10,000, representing that the actual book value of each share was $200. A certificate for fifty shares was delivered to Mallor. On February 16 Mallor discovered that the book value was only $50 per share on February 2. Thereafter, Mallor sues Phillips. Decision?

7. Dorothy mistakenly accused Fred's son, Steven, of negligently burning down Dorothy's barn. Fred believed that his son was guilty of the wrong, and that he, Fred, was personally liable for the damage, since Steven was only fifteen years old. Upon demand made by Dorothy, Fred paid Dorothy $2,500 for the damage to Dorothy's barn. After making this payment, Fred learned that his son had not caused the burning of Dorothy's barn and was in no way responsible for its burning. Fred then sued Dorothy to recover the $2,500 that he had paid her. Decision?

8. Jones, a farmer, found an odd-looking stone in his fields. He went to Smith, the town jeweler, and asked him what he thought it was. Smith said he did not know but thought it might be a ruby. Jones asked Smith what he would pay for it, and Smith said two hundred dollars; whereupon Jones sold it to Smith for $200. The stone turned out to be an uncut diamond worth $3,000. Jones brought an action against Smith to recover the stone. On trial, it was proved that Smith actually did not know the stone was a diamond when he bought it, but thought it might be a ruby. Decision?

9. Decedent, Joan Jones, a bedridden, lonely woman eighty-six years old, owned outright Greenacre, her ancestral estate. Biggers, her physician and friend, visited her weekly and was held in the highest regard by Joan. Joan was extremely fearful of pain and suffering and depended on Biggers to ease her anxiety and pain. Several months before her death, Joan deeded Greenacre to Biggers for $5,000. The fair market value of Greenacre at this time was $125,000. Joan was survived by two chil-

dren and six grandchildren. Decedent's children challenge the validity of the deed. Decision?

10. In February, Gardner, a school teacher with no experience in running a tavern, entered into a contract to purchase for $40,000 the Punjab Tavern from Meiling. The contract was contingent upon Gardner's obtaining a five-year lease for the tavern's premises and a liquor license from the State. Prior to the formation of the contract, Meiling had made no representations to Gardner concerning the gross income of the tavern. Approximately three months after the contract was signed, Gardner and Meiling met with an inspector from the Oregon Liquor Control Commission (OLCC) to discuss transfer of the liquor license. Meiling reported to the agent, in Gardner's presence, that the tavern's gross income figures for February, March, and April were $5,710, $4,918, and $5,009 respectively. The OLCC granted the required license, the transaction was closed, and Gardner took possession on June 10. After discovering that the tavern's income was very low, and that the tavern had very few female patrons, Gardner contacted Meiling's bookkeeping service and learned that the actual gross income for those three months had been approximately $1,400 to $2,000. Gardner then sued for rescission of the contract. Decision?

11. Dorothy and John Huffschneider listed their house and lot for sale with C. B. Property. The asking price was $165,000, and the owners told C. B. that the property contained 6.8 acres. Dean Olson, a salesman for C. B., advertised the property in local newspapers as consisting of six acres. James and Jean Holcomb signed a contract to purchase the property through Olson after first inspecting the property with Olson and being assured by Olson that the property was at least 6.6 acres. The Holcombs never asked for nor received a copy of the survey. In actuality, the lot was only 4.6 acres. The Holcombs now seek to rescind the contract. Decision?

12. Christine Boyd was designated as the beneficiary of a life insurance policy issued by Aetna Life Insurance Company on the life of Christine's husband, Jimmie Boyd. The policy insured against Jimmie's permanent total disability and also provided for a death benefit to be paid on Jimmie's death.

Several years after the policy was issued, Jimmie and Christine separated. Jimmie began to travel extensively, and therefore, Christine was unable to keep track of his whereabouts or his state of health. Jimmie, however, continued to pay the premiums on the policy until Christine tried to cash in the policy to alleviate her financial distress. A loan had previously been made on the policy, however, so that its cash surrender value, and thus the amount received by Christine, was only $4.19. Shortly thereafter, Christine learned that Jimmie had been permanently and totally disabled before the surrender of the policy. Aetna also was unaware of Jimmie's condition, and Christine requested the surrendered policy be reinstated and that the disability payments be made. Jimmie died soon thereafter, and Christine then requested that Aetna pay the death benefit. Decision?

COMPUTER RESEARCH PROBLEMS

1. Jane Francois married Victor H. Francois in 1984. At the time of the marriage, Victor was a fifty-year-old bachelor living with his elderly mother, and Jane was a thirty-year-old, twice-divorced mother of two. Victor had a relatively secure financial portfolio; Jane, on the other hand, brought no money or property to the marriage.

The marriage deteriorated quickly over the next couple of years, with disputes centered on financial matters. During this period, Jane systematically gained a joint interest in and took control of most of Victor's assets. Then, in September of 1987, Jane contracted Harold Monoson, an attorney, to draw up divorce papers. Victor was unaware of Jane's decision until he was taken to Monoson's office where Monoson presented for Victor's signature a "Property Settlement and Separation Agreement." Monoson told Victor that he would need an attorney, but Jane vetoed Victor's choice. Monoson then asked another lawyer, Gregory Ball, to come into the office. Ball read the agreement and strenuously advised Victor not to sign it because it would commit him to financial suicide. The agreement transferred most of Victor's remaining assets to Jane. Victor, however, signed it because Jane and Monoson persuaded him that it was the only way that his marriage could be saved. In October of 1988, Jane informed Victor that she had sold most of his former property and that she was leaving him permanently. Victor brought this action to have the agreement set aside as a result of undue influence. Decision?

2. Iverson owned Iverson Motor Company, an enterprise engaged in the repair as well as the sale of Oldsmobile, Rambler, and International Harvester Scout automobiles. 40 percent of the business's sales volume and net earnings came from the Oldsmobile franchise.

Whipp contracted to buy Iverson Motors, which Iverson said included the Oldsmobile franchise. After the sale, however, General Motors refused to transfer the franchise to Whipp. Whipp then returned the property to Iverson and brought this action seeking rescission of the contract. Decision?

3. On February 10, Mrs. Sunderhaus purchased a diamond ring from Perel & Lowenstein for $6990. She was told by the company's salesman that the ring was worth its purchase price, and she also received at that time a written guarantee from the company attesting to the diamond's value, style, and trade-in value. When Mrs. Sunderhaus went to trade the ring for another, however, she was told by two jewelers that the ring was valued at $3000 and $3500, respectively. Mrs. Sunderhaus knew little about the value of diamonds and claims to have relied on the oral representation of the Perel & Lowenstein's salesman and the written representation as to the ring's value. She seeks rescission of the contract or damages in the amount of the sales price over the ring's value. Decision?

4. Division West Chinchilla Ranch advertised on television that a five figure income could be earned by raising chinchillas with an investment of only $3.75 per animal per year and only 30 minutes of maintenance per day. The minimum investment was $2,150 for one male and six female chinchillas. Division West represented to plaintiffs that chinchilla ranching would be easy and that no experience was required to make ranching profitable. Plaintiffs, who had no experience raising chinchillas, each invested $2,150 or more to purchase Division's chinchillas and supplies. After three years without earning a profit, plaintiffs sue Division for fraud. Decision?

5. William Schmalz entered into an employment contract with Hardy Salt Company. The contract granted Schmalz six months' severance pay for involuntary termination but none for voluntary separation or termination for cause. Schmalz was asked to resign from his employment. He was informed that if he did not resign he would be fired for alleged misconduct. When Schmalz turned in his letter of resignation, he signed a release prohibiting him from suing his former employer as a consequence of his employment. Schmalz consulted an attorney before signing the release and upon signing it received $4,583.00 (one month's salary) in consideration. Schmalz now sues his former employer for the severance pay claiming that he signed the release under duress. Decision?

ENDNOTES

1. Restatement, Second, Contracts, Section 174, When Duress by Physical Compulsion Prevents Formation of a Contract.
2. Restatement, Second, Contracts, Section 175, When Duress by Threat Makes a Contract Voidable.
3. Restatement, Second, Contracts, Section 176, When a Threat Is Improper.
4. Restatement, Second, Contracts, Section 177, When Undue Influence Makes a Contract Voidable.
5. Restatement, Second, Contracts, Section 163, When a Misrepresentation Prevents Formation of a Contract.
6. Restatement, Second, Contracts, Section 20, Effect of Misunderstanding.
7. Restatement, Second, Contracts, Section 157, Effect of Fault of Party Seeking Relief.

10 CONSIDERATION

To be binding, a promise or agreement must satisfy the requirement of legally sufficient consideration. If there is no consideration, neither party can enforce the promise or agreement. The doctrine of consideration has been used to ensure that promises are enforced only where the parties have exchanged something of value in the eye of the law. **Gratuitous** (gift) **promises,** accordingly, are not legally enforceable.

Consideration, the inducement given to enter into a contract, is whatever is given in exchange for something else. It is present only when the parties intend an exchange, whether it is a promise exchanged for a promise, a promise exchanged for an act, or a promise exchanged for a forbearance to act.[1] Thus consideration has two basic elements: (1) legal sufficiency (something of value), and (2) bargained-for exchange. Both must be present to satisfy the requirement of consideration.

LEGAL SUFFICIENCY

The doctrine of consideration requires that the promises or performance of *both* parties be legally sufficient. If the consideration is not mutual, the agreement is not binding. To have **legal sufficiency,** the promise must be something of "value in the eye of the law," either a benefit to the promisor *or* a detriment to the promisee. In other words, has the promisor received something of legal value, or has the promisee given up something of legal value in return for the promise?

Definition

The definition of legal sufficiency is technical, and in certain cases its application produces an artificial result. To be legally sufficient, the consideration for the promise must be either a legal detriment to the promisee *or* a legal benefit to the promisor. Thus, a promise will not be enforced against the person who makes it unless the person who receives the promise also gives "consideration," which may consist of either a legal detriment to the promisee or a legal benefit to the promisor.

Legal detriment means (1) the doing (or undertaking to do) that which the promisee was under no prior legal obligation to do, *or* (2) the refraining from doing (or undertaking to refrain from doing) that which he was previously under no legal obligation to refrain from doing. **Legal benefit** means the obtaining by the promisor of that which he had no prior legal right to obtain.

Unilateral Contracts In a unilateral contract a promise is exchanged for an act or a forbearance to act. Since only one promise exists, one party, the person making the promise, is the **promisor** and the other party, the person receiving the promise, is the **promisee.** For example, A promises to pay B $500 if B paints A's house. B paints A's house.

Promise to
pay $500

(Promisor) **A** ⟷ **B** (Promisee)

Act of painting
house

A's promise is binding only if it is supported by consideration consisting of either a legal detriment to B, the promisee, or a legal benefit to A, the promisor. B's painting the house is a legal detriment to B, the promisee, because she was under no prior legal duty to paint A's house. Also, B's painting of A's house is a legal benefit to A, the promisor, because A had no prior legal right to have his house painted by B.

A unilateral contract may also consist of a promise exchanged for a forbearance. To illustrate, A negligently injures B, for which B may recover damages in a tort action. A promises to pay B $5,000 if B forbears from bringing suit. B accepts by not suing.

Promise to
pay $5,000

(Promisor) **A** ⇄ **B** (Promisee)

Forbearance
from suing

A's promise to pay B $5,000 is binding because it is supported by consideration; B, the promisee, has incurred a legal detriment by refraining from bringing suit, which he was under no prior legal obligation to refrain from doing. A, the promisor, has received a legal benefit because she had no prior legal right to B's forbearance from bringing suit.

To illustrate further, suppose that Andrew promises Bonnie, a high school graduate, that if Bonnie will attend and graduate from XYZ College, Andrew will pay to Bonnie the entire cost of her college education when she graduates. Bonnie enters XYZ College and duly graduates. The college education she received is an actual benefit to Bonnie, but legally she suffered a detriment in graduating from XYZ College because she gave up her freedom to attend any other college, or to not attend college at all, in consideration for Andrew's promise. Consequently, the consideration that Bonnie, the promisee, gave for Andrew's promise, although not actually detrimental, was legally detrimental to Bonnie. It is therefore legally sufficient, and Andrew's promise is enforceable by Bonnie. Furthermore, Andrew, the promisor, may have received no actual benefit from Bonnie's having obtained a college education at XYZ College, yet Andrew received a legal benefit in that he obtained from Bonnie something that he had no previous right to have—Bonnie's attendance at XYZ College and her graduation. Although this legal benefit may be of no value or usefulness to Andrew, nevertheless his promise allowed him to obtain a performance from her that he was not otherwise entitled to have. Thus, in this illustration the promisor (Andrew) received a legal benefit and the promisee (Bonnie) suffered a legal detriment, although *either* one of these by itself would satisfy the test of legal sufficiency.

Bilateral Contracts In a bilateral contract each party is *both* a promisor and a promisee. Thus, if A promises to purchase an automobile from B for $10,000 and B promises to sell the automobile to A for $10,000, the following relationship exists.

Promise to
(Promisor) pay $10,000 (Promisee)

A ⇄ **B**

(Promisee) *Promise to sell* *(Promisor)*
automobile

A's promise to pay B $10,000 is binding if that promise is supported by legal consideration, which may consist of either a legal detriment to B, the *promisee*, or a legal benefit to A, the *promisor*. B's promise to sell A the automobile is a legal detriment to B because he was under no prior legal duty to sell the automobile to A. Moreover, B's promise is also a legal benefit to A because A had no prior legal right to that automobile. Consequently, A's promise to pay $10,000 to B *is* supported by consideration and is binding.

Promise to
pay $10,000

(Promisor) **A** ⇄ **B** (Promisee)

Promise to
sell automobile
(Consideration for A's promise)

For **B's promise** to sell the automobile to A to be binding, it likewise must be supported by consideration, which may be either a legal detriment to A, the *promisee*, or a legal benefit to B, the *promisor*. A's promise to pay B $10,000 is a legal detriment to A because he was under no prior legal duty to pay $10,000 to B. At the same time, A's promise is also a legal benefit to B because B had no prior legal right to the $10,000. Thus, B's promise to sell the automobile *is* supported by consideration and is binding.

(Consideration for B's promise)
Promise to
pay $10,000

(Promisee) **A** ⟷ **B** (Promisor)

Promise to
sell automobile

To summarize, for *A's promise* to B to be binding, it must be supported by legally sufficient consideration, which requires that the promise or forbearance received from B in exchange provide either a legal benefit to *A (the promisor)* or a legal detriment to *B (the promisee)*. B's return promise to A must also be supported by consideration. In most cases where there is legal detriment to the promisee, there is also a legal benefit to the promisor. As the following case demonstrates, however, the presence of *either* one is sufficient.

 COLLINS v. PARSONS COLLEGE
Supreme Court of Iowa, 1973.
203 N.W.2d 594.

Facts: Ben Collins was a full professor with tenure at Wisconsin State University in 1966. In March of 1966 Parsons College, in order to lure Dr. Collins from Wisconsin State, offered him a written contract promising him the rank of full professor with tenure and a salary of $25,000 for the 1966–67 academic year. The contract further provided that the College would increase his salary by $1000 each year for the next five years. In return, Collins was to teach two trimesters of the academic year beginning in October 1966. In addition, the contract stipulated, by reference to the College's faculty bylaws, that tenured professors could only be dismissed for just cause and after written charges were filed with the Professional Problems Committee. The two parties signed the contract, and Collins resigned his position at Wisconsin State.

In February of 1968, the college tendered a different contract to Collins to cover the following year. This contract reduced his salary to $15,000 with no provision for annual increments, but left his rank of full professor intact. It also required that Collins waive any and all rights or claims existing under any previous employment contracts with the College. Collins refused to sign this new contract and Parsons College soon notified him that he would not be employed the following year. The College did not give any grounds for his dismissal nor file charges with the Problems Committee. As a result, Collins was forced to take a teaching position at the University of North Dakota at a substantially reduced salary. He sued to recover the difference between the salary Parsons College promised him until 1971 and the amount he earned. The trial court ruled in favor of Parsons College and Collins appeals.

Decision: Judgment reversed and remanded with directions.

Opinion: Uhlenhopp, J.   The question before us, then, becomes one of consideration. Collins did not promise to serve permanently or even until 1971, and so we have no promise from him in exchange for the promise of the college to employ him permanently at a specified salary with increments to 1971. Did he prove other consideration?

Collins points to his surrender of his tenured position at Wisconsin State University to accept his position, to the knowledge of Parsons College. The evidence shows that he had good academic credentials as well as experience in teaching, and evidently the college believed he would be a valuable addition and would lend stature to its staff. The college appeared eager to get him and was aware that he was surrendering a secure position to accept its offer. Once Collins left Wisconsin, he lost his tenure there. Did his surrender of that position constitute consideration for the agreement of Parsons College?

Courts are divided on such a question, some holding yes and some no. [Citations.] This court has adverted to the question but does not appear to have decided it squarely. [Citations.] Some courts hold the surrender of employment to take a new job constitutes consideration if the new employer is aware that the employee is giving up the other position. [Citations.] Generally consideration may, of course, consist of a detriment to the promisee. [Citations.] Consideration need not move to the promisor. * * *

After considering the question, we think the better rule to be that an employee who gives up other employment to accept an offer of a permanent job provides independent consideration—at least, when as here the employment surrendered was itself permanent and the new employer is aware of the facts. [Citations.]

The result is that the college agreed to employ Collins permanently and at the salary and increments promised to 1971, and that Collins provided consideration for the agreement of the college.

Adequacy

Legal sufficiency has nothing to do with **adequacy of consideration**. The items or actions that the parties agree to exchange do not need to have the same value. The law will regard the consideration as adequate if the parties have freely agreed to the exchange. The requirement of legally sufficient consideration is, therefore, *not* at all concerned with whether the bargain was good or bad or whether one party received disproportionately more or less than what he gave or promised in exchange for it. Such an inquiry might be relevant if a question of fraud, duress, or undue influence were involved. The requirement of legally sufficient consideration is simply: (1) that the parties have voluntarily agreed to an exchange; and (2) that with respect to each party the subject matter exchanged, or promised in exchange, either imposed a legal detriment on the promisee or conferred a legal benefit on the promisor.

Mutuality of Obligation

A contract is enforceable only if *both* parties to a contract give consideration. In a bilateral contract, each promise is the consideration for the other, and the parties are mutually obligated to perform their respective promises. The issue of whether both parties have made binding promises arises in the following situations: illusory promises, output and requirement contracts, exclusive dealing contracts, and conditional contracts.

Illusory Promises An **illusory promise** imposes no obligation on the promisor. Thus a promise to purchase such quantity of goods as the promisor may "desire" or "want" or "wish to buy" imposes no obligation to buy any goods, because its performance is entirely optional.[2] Thus, if Exxon offers to sell to Gasco as many barrels of oil as Gasco shall choose at $40 per barrel, there is no contract for lack of consideration. An offer containing such a promise, although accepted by the offeree, does not create a contract because the promise is illusory—performance is entirely optional by Gasco, and no constraint is placed on its freedom. It is not bound to do anything, nor can Exxon reasonably expect it to do anything. Thus, Gasco, by its promise, suffers no legal detriment and confers no legal benefit. Consequently, Gasco's promise does not provide legally sufficient consideration for Exxon's promise, and thus Exxon's promise is not binding.

Output and Requirement Contracts An agreement to sell the entire production of a particular seller is called an **output contract.** It gives the seller an assured market for her product. An agreement to purchase all the materials of a particular kind that the purchaser needs is called a **requirements contract.** It assures the buyer of a ready source of inventory or supplies. These contracts, when made, may or may not include an estimate of the quantity to be sold or purchased. Nevertheless, they are *not* illusory. The buyer under a requirements contract does not promise to buy as much as she desires to buy, but rather to buy as much as is *needed.* Similarly, under an output contract the seller promises to sell to the buyer the seller's entire production, not merely as much as the seller desires.

Furthermore, the Code[3] as well as the Restatement[4] impose a good-faith limitation on the quantity to be sold or purchased under an output or requirements contract. Thus an output or requirements contract means such actual output or requirements as may occur in good faith, except that no quantity unreasonably different from any stated estimate or, in the absence of a stated estimate, any normal prior output or requirements may be demanded. Therefore, after contracting with Smith to sell to Smith its entire output, Miles Company cannot increase its production from one eight-hour shift per day to three eight-hour shifts per day.

Exclusive Dealing Contracts Where a manufacturer of goods grants an exclusive franchise or license to a distributor to sell its products in a designated territory, unless otherwise agreed, an implied obligation is imposed on the manufacturer to use its best efforts to supply the goods and on the distributor to use her best efforts to promote their sale. The obligations that arise on acceptance of the **exclusive dealing** are sufficient consideration to bind both parties to the contract.

Conditional Contracts A **conditional contract** is an executory contract the performance of which depends upon the happening or not happening of a stated event. The fact that the obligation to perform a contract may not arise until a specified event occurs does not invalidate the contract. This is so even though the specified event may never occur. Mutuality of obligation still exists because neither party need perform if the event does not occur. This is also true where the obligation to perform terminates on the occurrence of a specified event.

Thus, if Joanne offers to pay Barry $8,000 for Barry's automobile provided that Joanne receives such amount as an inheritance from the estate of her deceased uncle, and Barry accepts the offer, the duty of Joanne to pay $8,000 to Barry is *conditioned* on her receiving $8,000 from her deceased uncle's estate. The consideration moving from Barry to Joanne is the promise to transfer title to the automobile. The consideration moving from Joanne to Barry is the promise of $8,000 subject to the condition. Although the contract is conditional, it is complete, definite, and certain. If, however, the stated condition is an event that could not possibly occur, then no contract would exist because the agreement would be illusory.

Preexisting Public Obligation

The law does not regard the performance of or promise to perform a preexisting legal duty, public or private, as either a legal detriment or a legal benefit.[5] A public duty is one that does not arise out of a contract but is imposed on members of society by force of the common law or by statute. Illustrations are found in the law of torts, such as the duty not to commit an assault, battery, false imprisonment, or defamation. The criminal law also imposes many public duties on everyone. Thus, if Norton promises to pay Holmes, the village ruffian, $100 not to abuse him physically, Norton's promise is unenforceable because Holmes is under a preexisting public obligation imposed by both tort and criminal law to refrain from such abuse.

Public officials, such as the mayor of a city, members of a city council, police (see *Denny v. Reppert* below), and firefighters, are under a preexisting obligation to perform their duties by virtue of their public office. If Smith's house catches fire and Smith telephones the chief of the city's fire department and promises him $500 if he will immediately send a fire truck and firefighters to Smith's house to put out the fire, and he does so, the promise is not enforceable. A public official is not allowed to gain privately by performing his duty.

Preexisting Contractual Obligation

The performance of, or promise to perform, a preexisting contractual duty, which is neither doubtful nor the subject of honest dispute, is also legally insufficient consideration, because the doing of what one is legally bound to do is neither a detriment to a promisee nor a benefit to the promisor. For example, if Anita employs Ben for one year at a salary of $1,000 per month, and at the end of six months promises Ben that in addition to the salary she will pay Ben $3,000 if Ben remains on the job for the remainder of the period originally agreed on, Anita's promise is not binding for lack of legally sufficient consideration. If Ben's duties were by agreement changed even to a small extent in nature or amount, Anita's promise would be binding.

The following case deals with both preexisting public and contractual obligations.

DENNY v. REPPERT
Court of Appeals of Kentucky, 1968.
432 S.W.2d 647.

Facts: In June three armed men entered and robbed the First State Bank of Eubank, Kentucky, of $30,000. Acting on information supplied by four employees of the bank, Denney, Buis, McCollum, and Snyder, three law enforcement officials apprehended the robbers. Two of the arresting officers, Godby and Simms, were State policemen and the third, Reppert, was a deputy sheriff in a neighboring county. Now all claim the reward for the apprehension and conviction of the bank robbers. The trial court held that only Reppert was entitled to the reward.

Decision: Judgment affirmed.

Opinion: **Myre**   The first question for determination is whether the employees of the robbed bank are eligible to receive or share in the reward? The great weight of authority answers in the negative. * * *

"To the general rule that, when a reward is offered to the general public for the performance of some specified act, such reward may be claimed by any person who performs such act, is the exception of agents, employees and public officials who are acting within the scope of their employment or official duties. * * * "

* * *

At the time of the robbery the claimants Murrell Denney, Joyce Buis, Rebecca McCollum, and Jewell Snyder were employees of the First State Bank of Eubank. They were under duty to protect and conserve the resources and moneys of the bank, and safeguard every interest of the institution furnishing them employment. Each of these employees exhibited great courage, and cool bravery, in a time of stress and danger. The community and the county have recompensed them in commendation, admiration and high praise, and the world looks on them as heroes. But in making known the robbery and assisting in acquainting the public and the officers with details of the crime and with identification of the robbers, they performed a duty to the bank and the public, for which they cannot claim a reward.

State Policemen Garret Godby, Johnny Simms and [deputy sheriff] Tilford Reppert made the arrest of the bank robbers and captured the stolen money. All participated in the prosecution. At the time of the arrest, it was the duty of the state policemen to apprehend the criminals. Under the law they cannot claim or share in the reward and they are interposing no claim to it.

This leaves * * * Tilford Reppert the sole eligible claimant. The record shows that at the time of the arrest he was a deputy sheriff in Rockcastle County, but the arrest and recovery of the stolen money took place in Pulaski County. He was out of his jurisdiction, and was thus under no legal duty to make the arrest, and is thus eligible to claim and receive the award.

* * *

It is manifest from the record that Tilford Reppert is the only claimant qualified and eligible to receive the reward. Therefore, it is the judgment of the circuit court that he is entitled to receive payment of the $1,500.00 reward now deposited with the Clerk of this Court.

Modification of a Preexisting Contract A modification of a contract occurs when the parties to the contract mutually agree to change one or more of its terms. Under the common law, a modification of an existing contract must be supported by mutual consideration to be enforceable. In other words, the modification must be supported by some new consideration beyond that which is already owing. For example, Diane and Fred agree that Diane shall put in a gravel driveway for Fred at a cost of $2,000. Subsequently, Fred agrees to pay an additional $1,000 if Diane will blacktop the driveway. Since Diane was not bound by the original contract to provide blacktopping, she would incur a legal detriment in doing so and is therefore entitled to the additional $1,000. Likewise, as in the following case, consideration may consist of the promisee refraining from exercising a legal right.

 BRENNER v. LITTLE RED SCHOOL HOUSE, LIMITED
Court of Appeals of North Carolina, 1982.
295 S.E.2d 607.

Facts: Plaintiff, Brenner, entered into a contract with the defendant, Little Red School House, Ltd., which stated that in return for a nonrefundable tuition of $1,080 Brenner's son could attend defendant's school for a year. When Brenner's ex-wife refused to enroll their son, plaintiff sought and received a verbal promise of a refund. Defendant now refuses to refund plaintiff's money for lack of consideration.

Decision: Judgment for Brenner.

Opinion: Arnold, J. Before a contract modification is effective there must be consideration to support it. [Citation.] Consideration can be found in benefit to the promisor or detriment to the promisee.

[T]here is a consideration if the promisee, in return for the promise, does anything legal which he is not bound to do, or refrains from doing anything which he has a right to do, whether there is any actual loss or detriment to him or actual benefit or not. [Citation.]

> The defendant argues that there was no consideration given by the plaintiff because the plaintiff as promisee suffered no detriment. But as the Supreme Court observed [in a prior case]:
>
> > [i]n return for the defendant's promise to refund the tuition paid, plaintiff would relinquish his right to have his child educated in defendant school. * * * It is well established that any benefit, right, or interest bestowed upon the promisor, or any forbearance, detriment, or loss undertaken by the promisee, is sufficient consideration to support a contract. [Citation.]
>
> The record shows that plaintiff was relinquishing the opportunity to have his child educated by the defendant when he testified "From the time * * * [the defendant] first told me that she would refund the tuition to me and from that point on. I did not expect the school to do anything else in regard to providing services or anything else on behalf of Russ Brenner." [Citation.] [Thus,] the record as quoted above shows sufficient consideration to support the modification in this case.

The Code has modified the common law rule by providing that a contract for the sale of goods can be effectively modified by the parties without new consideration, provided they intend to do so and act in good faith.[6] Moreover, the Restatement has moved toward this position by providing that a modification of an executory contract is binding if it is fair and equitable in light of the surrounding facts that were not anticipated by the parties when the contract was made.[7]

Settlement of an Undisputed Debt An **undisputed debt** is an uncontested obligation to pay a certain sum in money or to pay an amount that can be reduced to a certain sum in money. If the debtor has made an express promise to pay a specific sum of money, for example, $100, the debt is **liquidated** or certain in amount. If she has agreed to pay $3 per bushel for apples delivered, and fifty bushels of apples have been delivered, the debt is liquidated in the amount of $150.

Under the common law, the payment of a lesser sum of money than is owed in consideration of a promise to discharge a fully matured, undisputed debt is legally insufficient to support the promise of discharge. To illustrate, assume that Barbara owes Arnold $100, and in consideration of Barbara's paying Arnold $50, Arnold agrees to accept the lesser sum in full satisfaction of the debt. In a subsequent suit by Arnold against Barbara to recover the remaining $50, at common law Arnold is entitled to a judgment for $50 on the ground that Arnold's promise of discharge is not binding because Barbara's payment of $50 was no legal detriment to the promisee, Barbara, as she was under a **preexisting legal obligation** to pay that much and more. By the same token, the receipt of $50 was no legal benefit to the promisor, Arnold. Consequently, the consideration for Arnold's promise of discharge was legally insufficient, and Arnold is not bound by his promise. If, however, Arnold had accepted from Barbara any new or different consideration, such as the sum of $40 and a fountain pen worth $10 or less or even the fountain pen with no payment of money in full satisfaction of the $100 debt, the consideration moving from Barbara would be legally sufficient because Barbara was under no legal obligation to give a fountain pen to Arnold. In this example, consideration would also exist if Arnold had agreed to accept $50 *before* the debt became due, in full satisfaction of the debt. Barbara was under no legal obligation to pay any of the debt before its due date. Consequently, Barbara's early payment is a legal detriment to Barbara as well as a legal benefit to Arnold. The law is not concerned with the amount of the discount, because that is simply a question of adequacy. Likewise, Barbara's payment of a lesser amount on the due date at an agreed-upon different place of payment would be legally sufficient consideration.

Settlement of a Disputed Debt A **disputed debt** is an obligation whose existence or amount is contested. Implied contracts frequently create obligations to pay uncertain amounts. For example, where a person has requested professional services from a doctor or a dentist and no agreement was made about the amount of the fee to be charged, the doctor or dentist is entitled to receive from her patient a reasonable fee for the service performed. Because no definite amount was agreed on, the patient's obligation is uncertain or **unliquidated.** The patient has a legal obligation to pay the reasonable value of the services that were performed. When the doctor or dentist sends the patient a bill for her services, the amount stated in the bill is her estimate of the reasonable value of the services, but the debt does not in this manner become liquidated until and unless the patient agrees to pay the amount of the bill. If the patient honestly disputes the amount that is owing and offers in full settlement an amount less than the bill, acceptance of the lesser amount by the creditor discharges the debt. Thus, if Andy sends to Bess, an accountant, a check for $120 in payment of his debt to Bess for services rendered, which services Andy considered worthless but for which Bess billed Andy $600, Bess's acceptance (cashing) of the check releases Andy from any further liability. Andy has given up his right to dispute the billing further, and Bess has forfeited her right to further collection. Thus, there is mutuality of consideration.

For the giving up of a disputed claim to constitute legally sufficient consideration, the dispute must be *honest* and not frivolous. Where the dispute is based on contentions without merit or not made in good faith, giving up such contentions by the debtor is not a legal detriment.

FIEGE v. BOEHM
Court of Appeals of Maryland, 1956.
210 Md. 352, 123 A.2d 316.

Facts: Hilda Boehm, an unmarried typist, became pregnant while she was dating Louis Fiege. Boehm told Fiege that he was the father of her child and proposed an agreement to provide support for it. Before the child was born, Fiege agreed to pay all her medical and miscellaneous expenses; to compensate her for her loss of salary due to the child's birth; and to pay her $10 per week for child support until the child reached the age of twenty-one. In return, Boehm promised not to institute bastardy proceedings against him. Boehm had the child and three years later placed the child for adoption, claiming $2,895 total expenses to be paid by Fiege under the agreement. Fiege paid $480 of that sum, but ceased payments when blood tests revealed that the child could not have been his. Boehm instituted bastardy proceedings, but Fiege was acquitted, based largely on the evidence of the blood tests. Boehm then sued to recover the remainder of the expenses Fiege had agreed to pay under their previous agreement. Fiege claims that their "alleged" contract was not supported by consideration since Boehm's promise not to prosecute was not based on a valid claim. Defendant appeals from a verdict in favor of Boehm.

Decision: Judgment for Boehm affirmed.

Opinion: Delaplaine, J. Defendant contends that, even if he entered into the contract as alleged, it was not enforceable, because plaintiff's forbearance to prosecute was not based on a valid claim, and hence the contract was without consideration. * * *

Prosecutions for bastardy are treated in Maryland as criminal proceedings, but they are actually civil in purpose. * * * Accordingly a contract by the putative father of an illegitimate child to provide for its support upon condition that bastardy proceedings will not be instituted is a compromise of civil injuries resulting from a criminal act, and not a contract to compound a criminal prosecution, and if it is fair and reasonable, it is in accord with the Bastardy Act and the public policy of the State.

Of course, a contract of a putative father to provide for the support of his illegitimate child must be based, like any other contract, upon sufficient consideration.

* * *

We have thus adopted the rule that the surrender of, or forbearance to assert an invalid claim by one who has not an honest and reasonable belief in its possible validity is not sufficient consideration for a contract. Restatement, Contracts, sec. 76(b). We combine the subjective requisite that the claim be *bona fide* with the objective requisite that it must have a reasonable basis of support. Accordingly a promise not to prosecute a claim which is not founded in good faith does not of itself give a right of action on an agreement to pay for refraining from so acting, because a release from mere annoyance and unfounded litigation does not furnish valuable consideration.

* * *

In the case at bar there was no proof of fraud or unfairness. Assuming that the hematologists were accurate in their laboratory tests and findings, nevertheless plaintiff gave testimony which indicated that she made the charge of bastardy against defendant in good faith.

Substituted Contracts Distinguished A **substituted contract** occurs when the parties to a contract mutually agree to rescind or withdraw their original contract and enter into a new one. Substituted contracts are perfectly valid and effective to discharge the original contract and to impose obligations under the new contract. The rescission is binding in that each party, by giving up his rights under the original contract, has provided consideration to the other, as long as each party still has rights under the original contract.

BARGAINED-FOR EXCHANGE

The central idea behind consideration is that the parties have intentionally entered into a **bargained exchange** with each other and have each given to the other something in exchange for her promise or performance. Bargain, as used in this context, does not mean making an advantageous deal or buying something at a price less than its fair market value. As used in

the phrase "bargained-for exchange," it means simply that the parties have negotiated and mutually agreed upon the terms of what each party is giving to the other party in exchange for what he is receiving. Thus, a promise to give someone a birthday present is without consideration, because the promisor received nothing in exchange for her promise of a present.

Past Consideration

The element of exchange is absent where a promise is given for an act already done. Hence, **past consideration** is no consideration. A promise made on account of something that the promisee has already done is not enforceable. For example, Donna gives emergency care to Tim's adult son while the son is ill. Tim subsequently promises to reimburse Donna for her expenses. Tim's promise is not binding because there is no bargained-for exchange. Consideration is the inducement for a promise or performance. Therefore, unbargained-for past events are not consideration, despite their designation as "past consideration."

Moral Obligation

A promise made in order to satisfy a preexisting moral obligation is likewise unenforceable for lack of consideration. Instances involving such moral obligation include promises to pay for board and lodging previously furnished to a needy relative, promises to pay debts owed by a relative, and the promise made in the case below.

The Restatement, however, takes a position contrary to this case and provides that a promise following the rendering of emergency services is binding even though it is not supported by consideration.

The Restatement also provides for enforcement of a moral obligation when a person promises to pay for a mistakenly conferred benefit. For example, Pam hires Elizabeth to pave her driveway and Elizabeth mistakenly paves Chuck's driveway next door. Chuck subsequently promises to pay Pam $1,000 for the benefit conferred. Under the Restatement's view, Chuck's promise to pay $1,000 is binding.

Third Parties

Consideration to support a promise may be given to a person other than the promisor if the promisor bargains for that exchange. For example, A promises to pay B $15 if B delivers a specified book to C.

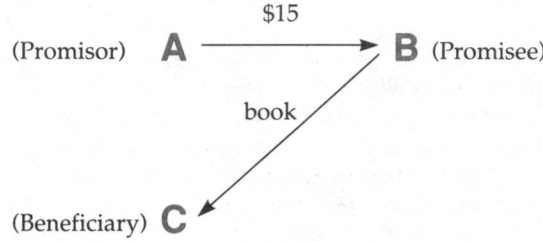

A's promise is binding because B incurred a legal detriment by delivering the book to C, as B was under no prior legal obligation to do so. A's promise to pay $15 is also consideration for B's promise to give C the book.

Conversely, consideration may be given by some person other than the promisee. For

---

 HARRINGTON v. TAYLOR
Supreme Court of North Carolina, 1945.
225 N.C. 690, 36 S.E.2d 227.

Facts: Taylor assaulted his wife, who then took refuge in Ms. Harrington's house. The next day, Mr. Taylor entered the house and began another assault on his wife. Taylor's wife knocked him down and, while he was lying on the floor, attempted to cut his head open or decapitate him with an axe. Harrington intervened to stop the bloodshed and was hit by the axe as it was descending. The axe fell upon her hand, mutilating it badly, but sparing Taylor his life. Afterwards, Taylor orally promised to compensate Harrington for her injury. He payed a small sum but nothing more. Harrington sued to enforce Taylor's promise. Judgment was entered in favor of Taylor and Harrington appeals.

Decision: Judgment for Taylor affirmed.

Opinion: Per Curiam The question presented is whether there was a consideration recognized by our law as sufficient to support the promise. The court is of the opinion that however much the defendant should be impelled by common gratitude to alleviate the plaintiff's misfortune, a humanitarian act of this kind, voluntarily performed, is not such consideration as would entitle her to recover at law.

example, A promises to pay B $25 in return for D's promise to give A a radio.

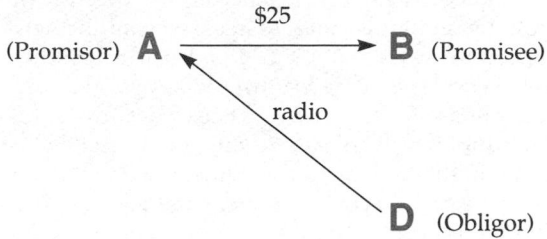

$25
(Promisor) **A** ———————→ **B** (Promisee)

radio

D (Obligor)

A's promise to pay $25 to B is consideration for D's promise to give A a radio and *vice versa*.

CONTRACTS WITHOUT CONSIDERATION

Certain transactions are enforceable even though they are not supported by consideration. These transactions include the following.

Promise to Pay Debt Barred by the Statute of Limitations

Every State has statutes stating that actions to enforce a debt must be brought within a prescribed period of time after the debt becomes due. Actions not begun within the specified time period will be dismissed. The time periods vary among the States and also with the nature of the claim. These statutes are known as **statutes of limitations.**

A new promise by the debtor to pay the debt renews the running of the statute of limitations for a second statutory period. This new promise requires no consideration. The following facts operate as a sufficient promise unless circumstances indicate otherwise: (1) a voluntary, unqualified admission that the debt is

owing; (2) a partial payment of the debt; or (3) a statement that the statute of limitations will not be pleaded as a defense.[8]

Promise to Pay Debt Discharged in Bankruptcy

A promise to pay a debt that has been discharged in bankruptcy is also enforceable without consideration. The Bankruptcy Act, however, imposes a number of requirements before a promise to pay a debt discharged in bankruptcy may be enforced. These requirements are discussed in Chapter 39.

Promissory Estoppel

A person may make a promise under circumstances that lead the promisor to expect that the promisee will act or refrain from acting based on the promise. If the promisee does take such action or forbearance, the promisor is estopped, or prohibited, from denying the promise. The basis of the promisor's liability is the doctrine of **promissory estoppel,** and consideration for the promise is not required. This does not mean that every promise given without consideration is binding simply because it is followed by a change of position on the part of the promisee. Liability is created by the change of position in justifiable reliance on the promise if injustice can be avoided only by the enforcement of the promise. For example, Ann promises Larry not to foreclose on a mortgage Ann owns on Larry's land for a period of six months. Larry then spends $100,000 on a building constructed on the land. Ann's promise not to foreclose is binding on her under the doctrine of promissory estoppel.

WHEELER v. WHITE
Supreme Court of Texas, 1965.
398 S.W.2d 93.

Facts: Wheeler wanted to construct a commercial building or shopping center on a tract of land he owned in Port Arthur, Texas. He entered into a contract with White whereby White was to obtain for Wheeler a $70,000 loan either procuring it from a third party or supplying it himself. White was to receive $5,000 for this service and a 5 percent commission on all rentals from tenants secured by him for the building. After the contract was signed, White urged Wheeler to proceed with the demolition of the buildings currently on the site so as to make way for the new structure. The buildings on the site were valued at $58,500 and had a monthly rental value of $400. White promised Wheeler that the loan would be available and emphasized that he would provide it himself if necessary. Wheeler destroyed the old buildings. White then refused to supply the loan. After trying unsuccessfully to obtain the loan himself, Wheeler brought this action against White, alleging that he was entitled to recover from White on the grounds of inducement and reliance. The complaint was dismissed, and Wheeler appealed.

Decision: Judgment dismissing complaint reversed, and case remanded for trial under theory of promissory estoppel.

Opinion: Smith, J. Where a promisee acts to his detriment in reasonable reliance upon an otherwise unenforceable promise, courts in other jurisdictions have recognized that the disappointed party may have a substantial and compelling claim for relief. The Restatement, Contracts, § 90, says:

> "A promise which the promisor should reasonably expect to induce action or forbearance of a definite and substantial character on the part of the promisee and which does induce such action or forbearance is binding if injustice can be avoided only by enforcement of the promise."

* * *

The binding thread which runs through the cases applying promissory estoppel is the existence of promises designedly made to influence the conduct of the promisee, tacitly encouraging the conduct, which conduct, although not necessarily constituting any actual performance of the contract itself, is something that must be done by the promisee before he could begin to perform, and was a fact known to the promisor. As to the argument that no new cause of action may be created by such a promise regardless of its established applicability as a defense, it has been answered that where one party has by his words or conduct made to the other a promise or assurance which was intended to affect the legal relations between them and to be acted on accordingly, then once the other party has taken him at his word and acted on it, the party who gave the promise cannot afterward be allowed to revert to the previous relationship as if no such promise had been made. This does not create a contract where none existed before, but only prevents a party from insisting upon his strict legal rights when it would be unjust to allow him to enforce them. [Citations.]

* * *

We agree with the reasoning announced in those jurisdictions that, in cases such as we have before us, where there is actually no contract, the promissory estoppel theory may be invoked, thereby supplying a remedy which will enable the injured party to be compensated for his foreseeable, definite and substantial reliance. Where the promisee has failed to bind the promisor to a legally sufficient contract, but where the promisee has acted in reliance upon a promise to his detriment, the promisee is to be allowed to recover no more than reliance damages measured by the detriment sustained. Since the promisee in such cases is partially responsible for his failure to bind the promisor to a legally sufficient contract, it is reasonable to conclude that all that is required to achieve justice is to put the promisee in the position he would have been in had he not acted in reliance upon the promise. [Citations.]

The most common application of the doctrine of promissory estoppel is to charitable subscriptions. Numerous churches, memorials, college buildings, stadiums, hospitals, and other structures used for religious, educational, or charitable purposes have been built with the assistance of contributions made through fulfillment of pledges or promises to contribute to particular worthwhile causes. Although the pledgor regards herself as making a gift for a charitable purpose and gift promises are generally not enforceable, the courts have generally enforced charitable subscription promises. Although various reasons and theories have been advanced in support of liability, the one most commonly accepted is that the subscription has induced a change of position by the promisee (the church, school, or charitable organization) in reliance on the promise. The Restatement, moreover, has relaxed the reliance requirement for charitable subscriptions so that actual reliance need not be shown; the probability of reliance is sufficient.[9]

Contracts under Seal

Under the common law, when a person desired to bind himself by bond, deed, or solemn promise, he executed his promise under seal. He did not have to sign the document. His delivery of a document to which he had affixed his seal was sufficient. No consideration for his promise was necessary. In some States a promise under seal is still binding without consideration.

Nevertheless, most States have abolished by statute the distinction between contracts under seal and written unsealed contracts. In these States, the seal is no longer recognized as a substitute for consideration. The Code has also adopted this position and specifically eliminates the use of seals in contracts for the sale of goods.

Other Promises That Require No Consideration

Renunciation   Under the Code any claim or right arising out of an alleged breach of contract can be discharged in whole or in part without consideration by a written waiver or renunciation signed and delivered by the aggrieved party.[10]

Firm Offer   Under the Code, a written offer signed by a merchant offeror to buy or sell goods is not revocable for lack of consideration during the time stated that it is open, not to exceed three months, or if no time is stated, for a reasonable time.[11]

CHAPTER SUMMARY

Consideration	Definition the inducement to enter into a contract Elements legal sufficiency and bargained-for exchange

Legal Sufficiency	Definition consists of either a benefit to the promisor or a detriment to the promisee ■ *Legal Benefit* obtaining something to which one had no prior legal right ■ *Legal Detriment* doing an act one is not legally obligated to do or not doing an act that one has a legal right to do

Adequacy   not required where the parties have freely agreed to the exchange

Mutuality of Obligation   a contract is legally binding only if both parties give consideration; the following, with the exception of illusory promises, are considered legally sufficient consideration

- ■ *Illusory Promise*   promise that imposes no obligation on the promisor
- ■ *Output Contract*   agreement to sell all of one's production
- ■ *Requirements Contract*   agreement to buy all of one's needs
- ■ *Exclusive Dealing Contract*   grant to a franchisee or licensee by a manufacturer of the sole right to sell goods in a defined market
- ■ *Conditional Contracts*   one where the obligations are contingent upon the occurrence of a stated event

Preexisting Public Obligation   public duties such as those imposed by tort or criminal law are neither a legal detriment nor a legal benefit

Preexisting Contractual Obligation   performance of a preexisting contractual duty is not consideration

- ■ *Modification of a Preexisting Contract*   under the common law a modification of a preexisting contract must be supported by mutual consideration; under the Code a contract can be modified without new consideration
- ■ *Settlement of an Undisputed Debt*   payment of a lesser sum of money to discharge an undisputed debt (one whose existence or amount are not contested) does not constitute legally sufficient consideration
- ■ *Settlement of a Disputed Debt*   payment of a lesser sum of money to discharge a disputed debt (one whose existence or amount is contested) is legally sufficient consideration
- ■ *Substituted Contracts*   the parties agree to rescind their original contract and to enter into a new one; rescission and new contract are supported by consideration

---

Bargained-For Exchange

Definition   a mutually agreed upon exchange

Past Consideration   an act done before the contract is made is not consideration

Moral Obligation   a promise made to satisfy a preexisting moral obligation is unenforceable for lack of consideration

Third Parties   consideration to support a promise may be given to a person other than the promisor or given by a person other than the promisee

---

Contracts Enforceable without Consideration

Promise to Pay Debt Barred by the Statute of Limitations   a new promise by the debtor to pay the debt renews the running of the statute for a second statutory period

Promise to Pay Debt Discharged in Bankruptcy   may be enforceable without consideration

Promissory Estoppel   doctrine that prohibits a party from denying his promise when the promisee takes action or forbearance to his detriment reasonably based upon the promise

Contracts under Seal   where still recognized, acts as a substitute for consideration

QUESTIONS

1. Define consideration and what is meant by legal sufficiency.
2. What is meant by mutuality of obligations? Do illusory promises, output contracts, requirements contracts, exclusive dealing contracts, or conditional contracts satisfy this requirement? Explain.
3. Explain whether preexisting public and contractual obligations satisfy the legal requirement of consideration.
4. Explain the concept of bargained-for exchange. Is this element present with past consideration, moral obligation, or third-party beneficiaries? Explain.
5. Identify and discuss those contracts that are enforceable even though they are not supported by consideration.

PROBLEMS

1. In consideration of $800 paid to him by Joyce, Hill gave Joyce a written option to purchase his house for $80,000 on or before April 1. Prior to April 1, Hill verbally agreed to extend the option until July 1. On May 18, Hill, known to Joyce, sold the house to Gray, who was ignorant of the unrecorded option. Joyce brought suit against Hill. Decision?

2. (a) Ann owed $500 to Barry for services Barry rendered to Ann. The debt was due June 30, 1989. In March 1990, the debt was still unpaid. Barry was in urgent need of ready cash and told Ann that if she would pay $150 of the debt at once, Barry would release her from the balance. Ann paid $150 and stated to Barry that all claims had been paid in full. In August 1990, Barry demanded the unpaid balance and subsequently sued Ann for $350. Decision?

(b) Modify the facts in (a) by assuming that Barry gave Ann a written receipt stating that all claims had been paid in full. Result?

(c) Modify the facts in (a) by assuming that Ann owed Barry the $500 on Ann's purchase of a motorcycle from Barry. Result?

3. (a) Judy orally promises her daughter, Liza, that she will give her a tract of land for her home. Liza, as intended by Judy, gives up her homestead and takes possession of the land. Liza lives there for six months and starts construction of a home. Is Judy bound to convey the real estate?

(b) Ralph, knowing that his son, Ed, desires to purchase a tract of land, promises to give him the $25,000 he needs for the purchase. Ed, relying on this promise, buys an option on the tract of land. Ralph now seeks to rescind his promise. Decision?

4. George owed Keith $800 on a personal loan. Neither the amount of the debt nor George's liability to pay the $800 was disputed. Keith had also rendered services as a carpenter to George without any agreement as to the price to be paid. When the work was completed, an honest and reasonable difference of opinion developed between George and Keith with respect to the value of Keith's services. Upon receiving Keith's bill for the carpentry services for $600, George mailed in a properly stamped and addressed envelope his check for $800 to Keith. In an accompanying letter, George stated that the enclosed check was in full settlement of both claims. Keith indorsed and cashed the check. Thereafter, Keith unsuccessfully sought to collect from George an alleged unpaid balance of $600. Keith then sued George for $600. Decision?

5. The Snyder Mfg. Co., being a large user of coal, entered into separate contracts with several coal companies, in each of which it was agreed that the coal company would supply coal during the year 1989 in such amounts as the manufacturing company might desire to order, at a price of $49 per ton. In February 1989, the Snyder Company ordered 1,000 tons of coal from Union Coal Company, one of the contracting parties. Union Coal Company delivered 500 tons of the order and then notified Snyder Company that no more deliveries would be made and that it denied any obligation under the contract. In an action by Union Coal to collect $49 per ton for the 500 tons of coal delivered, Snyder files a counterclaim, claiming damages of $1,500 for failure to deliver the additional 500 tons of the order and damages of $4,000 for breach of agreement to deliver coal during the balance of the year. Decision?

6. On February 5, Devon entered into a written agreement with Gordon whereby Gordon agreed to drill a well on Devon's property for the sum of $5,000 and to complete the well on or before April 15. Before entering into the contract, Gordon made test borings and had satisfied himself as to the character of the subsurface. After two days of drilling, Gordon struck hard rock. On February 17, Gordon removed his equipment and advised Devon that the project had proved unprofitable and that he would not continue. On March 17, Devon went to Gordon and told Gordon that he would assume the risk of the enterprise and would pay Gordon $100 for each day required to drill the well, as compen-

sation for labor, the use of Gordon's equipment, and Gordon's services in supervising the work, provided Gordon would furnish certain special equipment designed to cut through hard rock. Gordon said that the proposal was satisfactory. The work was continued by Gordon and completed in an additional fifty-eight days. Upon completion of the work, Devon failed to pay, and Gordon brought an action to recover $5,800. Devon answered that he had never become obligated to pay $100 a day and filed a counterclaim for damages in the amount of $500 for the month's delay based on an alleged breach of contract by Gordon. Decision?

7. Discuss and explain whether there is valid consideration for each of the following promises:

(a) A and B entered into a contract for the purchase and sale of goods. A subsequently promised to pay a higher price for the goods when B refused to deliver at the contract price.

(b) A promised in writing to pay a debt, which was due from B to C, on C's agreement to extend the time of payment for one year.

(c) A executed a promissory note to her son, B, solely in consideration of past services rendered to A by B, for which there had been no agreement or request to pay.

8. Alan purchased shoes from Barbara on open account. Barbara sent Alan a bill for $10,000. Alan wrote back that 200 pairs of the shoes were defective and offered to pay $6,000 and give Barbara his promissory note for $1,000. Barbara accepted the offer, and Alan sent his check for $6,000 and his note in accordance with the agreement. Barbara cashed the check, collected on the note, and one month later sued Alan for $3,000. Decision?

9. Nancy owed Sharon $1,500, but Sharon did not initiate a lawsuit to collect the debt within the time period prescribed by the statute of limitations. Nevertheless, Nancy promises Sharon that she will pay the barred debt. Thereafter, Nancy refuses to pay. Sharon brings suit to collect on this new promise. Decision?

10. Anthony lends money to Frank. Frank dies without having paid the loan. Frank's widow, Carol, promises Anthony to repay the loan. Upon Carol's refusal to pay the loan, Anthony brings suit against Carol for payment of the loan. Decision?

COMPUTER RESEARCH PROBLEMS

1. Jonnel Enterprises, Inc., contracted to construct a student dormitory at Clarion State College. On May 6, Jonnel entered into a written agreement with Graham and Long as electrical contractors to perform the electrical work and to supply materials for the dormitory. The contract price was $70,544.66. Graham and Long claim that they believed the May 6 agreement obligated them to perform the electrical work on only one wing of the building, but that three or four days after work was started, a second wing of the building was discovered. At that time Graham and Long informed Jonnel that they would not wire both wings of the building under the present contract, so a new contract was orally agreed upon by the parties. Under the new contract Graham and Long were obligated to wire both wings and were to be paid only $65,000, but they were relieved of the obligations to supply entrances and a heating system. Graham and Long resumed their work, and Jonnel made seven of the eight progress payments called for. When Jonnel did not pay the final payment, Graham and Long brought this action. Jonnel claims that the May 6 contract is controlling. Decision?

2. Baker entered into an oral agreement with Healey, the State distributor of Ballantine & Son's liquor products, that Ballantine would supply Baker with its products on demand and that Baker would have the exclusive agency for Ballantine within a certain area of Connecticut. Shortly thereafter the agreement was modified to give Baker the right to terminate at will. Eight months later, when Ballantine & Son's revoked its agency, Baker sued to enforce the oral agreement. Decision?

3. PLM, Inc. entered into an oral argeement with Quaintance Associates, an executive "headhunter" service, for the recruitment of qualified candidates to be employed by PLM. As agreed, PLM's obligation to pay Quaintance did not depend on PLM actually hiring a qualified candidate presented by Quaintance. After several months Quaintance sent a letter to PLM, admitting that it had so far failed to produce a suitable candidate, but included a bill for $9,806.61 covering fees and expenses. PLM responded that Quaintance's services were only worth $6,060.48, and that payment of the lesser amount was the only fair way to handle the dispute. Accordingly, PLM enclosed a check for $6,060.48, writing on the back of the check "IN FULL PAYMENT OF ANY CLAIMS QUAINTANCE HAS AGAINST PLM, INC." Quaintance cashed the check, and then sues PLM for the remaining $3,746.13. Decision?

4. Red Owl Stores told the Hoffman family that, upon the payment of approximately $18,000, a

grocery store franchise would be built for them in a
new location. Upon the advice of Red Owl, the
Hoffmans bought a small grocery store in their
hometown in order to get management experience.
After three months of operating at a profit, Red Owl
advised the Hoffmans to sell the small grocery,
assuring them that Red Owl would find them a
larger store elsewhere. Although selling at that
point would cost them much profit, the Hoffmans
followed Red Owl's directions. Additionally, to
raise the required money for the deal, the Hoffmans
sold their bakery business in their hometown. The
Hoffmans also sold their house, and moved to a
new home in the city where their new store was to
be located. Red Owl then informed the Hoffmans
that it would take $24,100, not $18,000, to complete
the deal. The family scrambled to find the additional
funds. However, when told by Red Owl that it
would now cost them $34,000 to get their new
franchise, the Hoffmans decided to sue instead.
Decision?

ENDNOTES

1. Restatement, Second, Contracts, Section 71, Requirement of Exchange; Types of Exchange.

2. Restatement, Second, Contracts, Section 77, Illusory and Alternative Promises.
3. Uniform Commercial Code, Section 2—306, Output, Requirements and Exclusive Dealings.
4. Restatement, Second, Contracts, Section 77,
Comment d.
5. Restatement, Second, Contracts, Section 73, Performance of Legal Duty.
6. Uniform Commercial Code, Section 2—209,
Modification, Rescission and Waiver.
7. Restatement, Second, Contracts, Section 89,
Modification of Executory Contract.
8. Restatement, Second, Contracts, Section 82,
Promise to Pay Indebtedness; Effect on the Statute
of Limitations.
9. Restatement, Second, Contracts, Section 90,
Promise Reasonably Inducing Action or Forbearance.
10. Uniform Commercial Code, Section 1—107,
Waiver or Renunciation of Claim or Right After
Breach.
11. Uniform Commercial Code, Section 2—205,
Firm Offers.

ILLEGAL BARGAINS

An essential requirement of a binding promise or agreement is that the objective is legal. When the formation or performance of an agreement is criminal, tortious, or otherwise contrary to public policy, the agreement is illegal and **unenforceable.** The law does *not* provide a remedy for the breach of an unenforceable agreement and thus "leaves the parties where it finds them." It is preferable to use the term "illegal bargain" or "illegal agreement" rather than "illegal contract," because the word "contract," by definition, denotes a legal and enforceable agreement. The illegal bargain is made unenforceable (1) to discourage the undesirable conduct in the future, and (2) to avoid the inappropriate use of the judicial process in carrying out the socially undesirable bargain.

In this chapter we discuss this subject in terms of agreements (a) in violation of a statute, and (b) contrary to public policy.

VIOLATIONS OF STATUTES

An agreement declared illegal by statute will not be enforced by the courts. For example, "wagering or gambling contracts" are specifically declared unenforceable in most States. Likewise, an agreement induced by criminal conduct will not be enforced. For example, if Alice enters into an agreement with Brent Co. through the bribing of Brent Co.'s purchasing agent, the agreement would be unenforceable.

Licensing Statutes

Every jurisdiction has laws requiring a **license** for those who engage in certain trades, profes-

sions, or businesses. Common examples are licensing statutes that apply to lawyers, doctors, dentists, accountants, brokers, plumbers, and contractors. Whether a person may recover for services rendered if he has failed to comply with a licensing requirement depends on the terms or type of licensing statute.

The statute itself may expressly provide that an unlicensed person engaged in a business or profession for which a license is required shall not recover for services rendered. Where there is no such statutory provision, the courts commonly distinguish between regulatory statutes and those that are enacted merely to raise revenue. If the statute is regulatory, a person cannot recover for professional services unless he has the required license as long as the public policy behind the regulatory purpose clearly outweighs the person's interest in being paid for his services.[1] If the law requiring a license is for revenue purposes only, however, agreements for such services are enforceable.

A **regulatory license** is a measure designed to protect the public against unqualified persons. Examples, as the case on page 225 demonstrates, are statutes prescribing standards for those who seek to practice law or medicine or those who operate as general building contractors or architects. A **revenue license,** on the other hand, does not seek to protect against the incompetent or unqualified, but simply seeks to raise money. An example is a statute requiring a license of plumbers but not establishing standards of competence for those who seek to follow the trade. The courts regard this as a taxing measure lacking any expression of legislative intent to prevent unlicensed plumbers from enforcing their business contracts.

BRADY v. FULGHUM
Supreme Court of North Carolina, 1983.
308 S.E.2d 327.

Facts: In February 1980, Brady contracted to construct a house for Fulghum for $106,850. Brady began construction on March 13, 1980. Neither during the negotiation of this contract nor when he began performance was Brady licensed as a general contractor as required by North Carolina law. Brady was awarded his builder's license on October 22, 1980, having passed the examination on his second attempt. At that time, he had completed two-thirds of the work on Fulghum's house. Fulghum paid Brady $104,000. Brady brought suit seeking an additional $2,850 on the original contract and $28,926 for "additions and changes" requested by Fulghum during construction. The trial court entered summary judgment in favor of Fulghum on the basis of the contractor's noncompliance with statutory licensing requirements. Brady then appealed to the North Carolina Court of Appeals, which affirmed, concluding that the contractor had not "substantially" complied with licensing requirements. Brady now appeals to the Supreme Court of North Carolina.

Decision: Summary judgment for Fulghum affirmed.

Opinion: **Exum, J.**   The legislature has provided a mechanism for certification of general construction contractors. [Citation.] This process * * * protects the public by insuring confidence and integrity within the construction industry. [Citation.] Although the statute does not expressly preclude an unlicensed contractor's suit against an owner for breach of contract, *Builders Supply v. Midyette* [citation] held the contractor may not recover on the contract or *in quantum meruit* when he has ignored the protective statute.

After *Midyette*, the Court of Appeals determined several cases, including the one at bar, in terms of whether the contractor had "substantially" complied with the licensing statutes.

* * *

A majority of the [Court of Appeals] concluded [in this case] that because [Brady] did not have a license at the time the contract was made and "was not licensed during at least 66 percent of the construction, which comprised the major portion of the work," plaintiff had not substantially complied with the licensing requirements of the statute. * * * [However] the division on the Court of Appeals in this case demonstrates that the doctrine of substantial compliance is sometimes difficult to apply. By generating skewed results, it leaves uncertain the rights of parties, which tends to promote litigation. We now reject the doctrine and end its application in this state.

Generally, contracts entered into by unlicensed construction contractors, in violation of a statute passed for the protection of the public, are unenforceable by the contractor. [Citation.] A majority of jurisdictions adhere to this interpretation. [Citation.] Reading these statutes as being designed to protect the public from irresponsible contractors, [citation] most state courts find "no legal remedy for that which is illegal itself." [Citation.] General contractors have been precluded from maintaining actions if they must rely on their illegal act to justify their recovery. [Citation.] The unenforceability of such contracts by the contractor stems directly from their conception in the contractor's illegal act.

The express language of the North Carolina licensing statute indicates that it is designed to insure competence within the construction industry. * * * (T)he legislature seeks to guarantee "skill, training and ability to accomplish such construction in a safe and workmanlike fashion." [Citation.] In tandem, these requirements "protect members of the general public without regard to the impact upon individual contractors." [Citation.]

In examining the licensing statute in question, we recognize the distinction between legislation designed to produce revenue and to protect the public. In the former situation, the legislature exercises its taxing authority. In the latter, it exercises its police power. Accordingly, when a legislature invokes its police power to provide statutory protection to the public from fraud, incompetence, and irresponsibility, as ours has done with the contractor licensing statutes, courts impose greater penalties on violators. [Citation.] Making contracts unenforceable by the violating contractor produces "a salutary effect in causing obedience to the licensing statute." [Citation.] These public policy considerations militate against permitting unlicensed general construction contractors to enforce their contracts.

* * *

In recognition of the essential illegality of an unlicensed contractor's entering into a construction contract for which a license is required and in order to give full effect to the legislative intent to furnish protection to the public by strict licensing requirements, we reject the doctrine of substantial compliance, cognizant that harsh consequences may sometimes fall on those who do contracting work without a license. [Citation.]

We do recognize the minority rule, adhered to by our Court of Appeals, is not without some support. California applies the doctrine of substantial compliance in certain cases to avoid unnecessarily harsh results on unlicensed contractors who perform well. [Citations.] * * *

We agree that the existence of a license at the time the contract is signed is determinative and attach "great weight to the significant moment of the entrance of the parties into the relationship." [Citation.] Accordingly, we adopt the rule that a contract illegally entered into by an unlicensed general construction contractor is unenforceable by the contractor. It cannot be validated by the contractor's subsequent procurement of a license. [Citation.] In this circumstance there can be no substantial compliance with the licensing statutes. Neither may the contractor recover for extras, additions or changes made during construction commenced pursuant to the contract. Such a contract is not, however, void. Others not regulated by the licensing statutes passed for their protection do not act illegally in becoming parties to such a contract. The policy underlying the licensing statutes would not be served by preventing enforcement by those for whose protection the statutes were passed. These parties may enforce the contract against the unlicensed contractor. [Citation.] Further, if a licensed contractor's license expires, for whatever reason, during construction, he may recover for only the work performed while he was duly licensed. If, in that situation, the contractor renews his license during construction, he may recover for work performed before expiration and after renewal. If, by virtue of these rules, harsh results fall upon unlicensed contractors who violate our statutes, the contractors themselves bear both the responsibility and the blame.

Plaintiff was unlicensed at the time he negotiated and contracted with defendants to construct their house. He illegally entered into the contract; it is, therefore, unenforceable by him. His subsequent procurement of a valid license cannot validate or make legal that which was illegal in its inception. * * *

Gambling Statutes

In a **wager** the parties stipulate that one shall win and the other lose depending on the outcome of an event in which their only "interest" is the possibility of such gain or loss.

All States have legislation on gambling, and U.S. courts generally refuse to recognize the enforceability of a gambling agreement. Thus, if Smith makes a bet with Brown on the outcome of a ball game, the agreement is unenforceable by either party. Some States, however, now permit certain kinds of regulated gambling; these include State-operated lotteries.

Usury Statutes

Historically, every State had a **usury law,** a statute establishing a maximum rate of permissible interest that may be contracted for between a lender and borrower of money. Recently, however, the trend is to limit or relax usury statutes. Maximum rates permitted vary greatly from State to State and among types of transactions. These statutes typically are general in their application, although certain types of transactions are exempted. For example, many States impose no limit on the rate of interest that may be charged on loans to corporations. Furthermore, some States permit the parties to contract for any rate of interest on loans made to individual proprietorships or partnerships for the purpose of carrying on a business.

In addition to the exceptions accorded certain designated types of borrowers, a number of States have exempted specific lenders. For example, the majority of States have enacted installment loan laws, which permit eligible lenders a higher return on installment loans than would otherwise be permitted under the applicable general interest statute. These **specific lender usury** statutes, which have all but eliminated the general usury statute, vary greatly but have generally included small consumer loans, corporate loans, loans by small lenders, real estate mortgages, and numerous other transactions.

General usury statutes have traditionally been interpreted to exempt credit terms granted by vendors under the judicially created time-price doctrine. The **time-price doctrine** provides that sellers may have two prices for their merchandise—a cash price and a credit or "time price," and that the credit price may exceed the cash price by more than the statutorily allowed interest on the cash price. Today, most States have rendered the time-price doctrine moot by adopting State retail installment sales acts, which apply specific usury statutes to specific consumer transactions and are beyond the scope of the general usury statutes.

For a transaction to be usurious, courts usually require evidence of the following factors: (a) a loan (b) of money (c) that is repayable absolutely and in all events (d) for which an interest charge is exacted in excess of the interest rate allowed by law. Transactions that are really loans may not be clothed with the trappings of a sale for the purpose of avoiding the usury laws.

Assuming that it is established that the arrangement is for a loan, certain expenses or charges are permitted in addition to the maximum legal interest. Payments made by a borrower to the lender for expenses incurred or for services rendered in good faith in making a loan or in obtaining security for its repayment are generally not included in determining whether the loan is usurious. Commonly permissible expenses by the lender include costs of examining title, investigating the credit rating of the borrower, drawing necessary documents, and inspecting the property. If not excessive, they are not considered in determining the rate of interest under the usury statutes. As shown in the case on page 228, however, payments made to the lender or from which he derives an advantage if they exceed the reasonable value of services actually rendered are considered.

The legal effect of a usurious loan varies from State to State. In a few States, the lender forfeits both principal and interest. In some jurisdictions, the lender can recover the principal but forfeits all interest. In other States, only that portion of interest exceeding the maximum permitted is forfeited. In several States, the amount forfeited is a multiple

ABRAMOWITZ v. BARNETT BANKS OF WEST ORLANDO
Florida Court of Appeals, 1981.
394 So.2d 1033.

Facts: Abramowitz obtained a one year-mortgage loan from Barnett Bank for $400,000 at 9 percent interest with a 1 percent "point" or service fee. The maximum lawful rate of interest on such a loan is 10 percent. The bank deducted the $4000 service fee from the loan proceeds, actually disbursing only $396,000 to Abramowitz. During the one-year term of his loan, Abramowitz was charged and he paid $36,347.78 in interest. He claims the loan was usurious since the $4000 "service fee" plus the $36,347 interest charge exceeded the 10 percent limit on total interest. Abramowitz appeals from a judgment denying him any relief.

Decision: Judgment reversed and the case remanded for imposition of damages against the bank in favor of Abramowitz.

Opinion: **Sharp, J.** A lender will not be allowed to impose any miscellaneous fees or service charges on the front end of a loan when that sum, added to the interest charged, exceeds the maximum legal rate of interest allowable. [Citations.] Application of such fees to pay the general overhead of a lender or the cost of participating out the loan are not sufficient to alter the characterization of these charges as interest. [Citation.]

It is also well established that a borrower can be charged the actual reasonable expenses of making a particular loan. [Citations.] However "bogus" charges for services not actually rendered will not be allowed to cloak the extraction of illegal interest. [Citation.]

The only basis to characterize the "service fee" in this case as something other than interest, is to allocate part of it as an "inspection" fee performed "in-house" by the bank's president. Such fees are usually paid to third-parties, and are documented on the mortgage loan closing statement. We are not prepared to say, however, that in all cases the inspection must be done by a third-person or that it must be documented on the closing statement, although that obviously is the better practice. The fact that Maynard himself performed the inspection does not flaw the charges although any charge for this "service is" inconsistent with his testimony that he did the inspection "in-house" to save the borrower money.

It is fundamental that the charges must be "reasonable." [Citations.] This loan was not a "construction" loan which requires more inspections to insure the lender's construction funds are being properly used as the building progresses. Rather, it was a loan on a completed building, and similar to a "take-out" loan for a permanent lender, only a final inspection fee is required. The only testimony in the record on this point established that $300 was the maximum a third party expert would have charged.

The conclusion thus follows inescapably that Abramowitz was charged in excess of 10% interest on this one year loan.

"Service Fee"	$ 4,000.00
Less "Reasonable Expenses"	− 300.00
"Hidden Interest"	$ 3,700.00
Principal of Loan	$ 400,000.00
Less Prepaid Interest	− 3,700.00
Actual Principal	$ 396,300.00

Maximum legal amount of interest collectible on this loan (10%) of actual principal	$ 39,630.00
Actual interest charged and billed	36,347.78
Plus "hidden interest"	+3,700.00
	$ 40,047.78
Amount of over-charge	$ 40,047.78
	−39,630.00
	$ 417.78

The lower court found there was no "corrupt" intent on the part of the bank to charge a usurious rate of interest because the bank did not deliberately charge more than 10%. It charged 9% on the loan plus 1% in points only. The difficulty here was that the 1% was taken up-front, resulting in a reduction in principal received, and an increase in the rate paid. [Citation.] The "intent" to exceed the legal rate of interest need not be to consciously decide to charge a borrower greater than the legal rate, when the lender consciously intends and does in fact make the charges which add up to usury. [Citations.]

In this case, the closing statement showing a 1% point or service fee was prepared by the bank; and it calculated and billed the borrower interest throughout the year. No errors were shown to have occurred in the billing. In fact during two quarters, the lender billed on a 360-day year basis, which for a 10% or maximum rate loan, was usurious in and of itself. [Citation.] We conclude the bank had the requisite intent to make the usurious charges. [Citation.]

(double or treble) of the interest charged. How the usurious interest already paid is disposed of also varies. Some States do not allow the borrower to recover any of the usurious interest paid; others allow a recovery of the usurious interest paid or a multiple of it.

VIOLATIONS OF PUBLIC POLICY

The reach of a statute may extend beyond its language. Sometimes the courts, by analogy, use the statute and the policy it embodies as a guide in determining the private contract rights of a person. In addition, the courts must frequently express the "public policy" of the State without significant help from statutory sources. This judicially declared public policy is very broad in scope, it often being said that agreements that have "a tendency to be injurious to the public or the public good" are contrary to public policy. For a discussion of public policy involved in the issue of surrogate motherhood (Baby M) see Law in the News on page 231. In the following sections we consider examples of agreements that (1) involve tor-

tious conduct, (2) restrain trade, (3) tend to obstruct the administration of justice, (4) tend to corrupt public officials or impair the legislative process, (5) excuse or exculpate a party from liability for his own negligence, or (6) are unconscionable.

Marvin v. Marvin provides a general overview of the nature and extent of public policy.

Tortious Conduct

An agreement that requires a person to commit a tort is an illegal agreement and thus is unenforceable.[2] The courts will not permit contract law to violate the law of torts. Any agreement attempting to do so is considered contrary to public policy. For example, Ada and Bernard enter into an agreement under which Ada promises Bernard that in return for $5,000 she will disparage the product of Bernard's competitor, Cone, in order to provide Bernard with a competitive advantage. Ada's promise is to commit the tort of disparagement and is unenforceable as contrary to public policy.

MARVIN v. MARVIN
Supreme Court of California, 1976.
18 Cal.3d 660, 134 Cal.Rpt. 815, 557 P.2d 106.

Facts: In 1964 Michelle Marvin and Lee Marvin began living together, holding themselves out to the general public as man and wife without actually being married. The two orally agreed that while they lived together they would share equally any and all property and earnings accumulated as a result of their individual and combined efforts. In addition, Michelle promised to render her services as "companion, homemaker, housekeeper and cook" to Lee. Shortly thereafter, she gave up her lucrative career as an entertainer in order to devote her full time to being Lee's companion, homemaker, housekeeper, and cook. In return he agreed to provide for all of her financial support and needs for the rest of her life. In 1970, Lee compelled Michelle to leave his household but continued to provide for her support. In late 1971, however, he refused to provide further support. Michelle sued to recover support payments and half of their accumulated property. Lee contends that their agreement is so closely related to the supposed "immoral" character of their relationship that its enforcement would violate public policy. The trial court granted Lee's motion for judgment on the pleadings.

Decision: Judgment on the pleadings in favor of defendant reversed.

Opinion: Tobriner, J. Defendant first and principally relies on the contention that the alleged contract is so closely related to the supposed "immoral" character of the relationship between plaintiff and himself that the enforcement of the contract would violate public policy. He points to cases asserting that a contract between nonmarital partners is unenforceable if it is "involved in" an illicit relationship [citations] or made in "contemplation" of such a relationship. [Citations.]

A review of the numerous California decisions concerning contracts between nonmarital partners, however, reveals that the courts have not employed such broad and uncertain standards to strike down contracts. The decisions instead disclose a narrower and more precise standard: a contract between nonmarital partners is unenforceable only *to the extent* that it *explicitly* rests upon the immoral and illicit consideration of meretricious sexual services.

* * *

In summary, we base our opinion on the principle that adults who voluntarily live together and engage in sexual relations are nonetheless as competent as any other persons to contract respecting their earnings and property rights. Of course, they cannot lawfully contract to pay for the performance of sexual services, for such a contract is, in essence, an agreement for prostitution and unlawful for that reason. But they may agree to pool their earnings and to hold all property acquired during the relationship in accord with the law governing community property; conversely they may agree that each partner's earnings and the property acquired from those earnings remains the separate property of the earning partner. So long as the agreement does not rest upon illicit meretricious consideration, the parties may order their economic affairs as they choose, and no policy precludes the courts from enforcing such agreements.

Baby M Meets Solomon's Sword
The New Jersey Supreme Court Says No to Surrogacy for Pay

Approaching the case of Baby M, the New Jersey Supreme Court might have wished for the sword of Solomon—not to divide the child, but to cut through the Gordian thicket of paradox, bad faith and conflicting feelings that has surrounded the matter from the start. As it turned out, in a unanimous ruling last week the court sliced the issue in a way that gave important concessions to both the parents, but cut to the quick the practice of surrogacy for pay.

The seven justices voided the 1985 contract by which Biochemist William Stern and his pediatrician wife Elizabeth had arranged to pay Mary Beth Whitehead $10,000 to bear a child fathered by him through artificial insemination. Under state adoption law and public policy, the court concluded, paying women to be surrogate mothers was "illegal, perhaps criminal, and potentially degrading to women." Wrote Chief Justice Robert Wilentz: "There are, in a civilized society, some things that money cannot buy."

Even so, the justices gave custody of 22-month-old Melissa Elizabeth to her father. The Sterns, the court decided, could provide a more stable home: "Their household and their personalities promise a much more likely foundation for Melissa to grow and thrive." Last November Whitehead divorced her first husband to marry Dean Gould, and the couple is now expecting a child of their own. But the justices also restored the parental rights of Whitehead-Gould, which the trial judge had terminated, and invalidated last year's adoption of Melissa by Elizabeth Stern. By instructing a lower court to decide the question of Whitehead-Gould's visitation rights, they also opened the way for her to maintain contact with her daughter for many years to come.

The court said surrogate arrangements would not be illegal if the mother were not paid and if the agreement allowed her to change her mind after the birth of the child. But in practice that concession may not amount to much. How many women would be likely to bear a child without compensa-tion? And how many infertile couples would be as willing to go through the process, faced with the possibility that the mother might renege? Though the ruling applies only to New Jersey, that state's supreme court is one of the nation's most influential, especially in matters of bioethics. "This ruling deals a death blow" to the practice, says Jeremy Rifkin of the National Coalition Against Surrogacy. About 27 states have considered legislation on surrogacy, ranging from regulation to outright prohibition. Last July Louisiana passed a law voiding surrogate contracts, and last week the Nebraska legislature voted to do the same.

Supporters of surrogacy have managed some lesser court victories in the past. Two years ago, for example, the Kentucky Supreme Court ruled that surrogate arrangements in themselves did not violate that state's public policy. "We're getting different decisions in different jurisdictions," says Michigan Attorney Noel Keane, one of the nation's chief surrogacy brokers and the man who helped arrange the birth of Baby M.

States that legalize the practice could become magnets for infertile couples from other states where commercial surrogacy is banned. And where the practice is prohibited entirely, say some, it will merely be driven underground. "There is so much infertility," observes Feminist Attorney Lynne Gold-Bikin. "Desperate people will resort to desperate methods."

Meanwhile, the once desperate people in the Baby M case are likely to find themselves tied together for some time by the common bond of the child they all claim. Whitehead-Gould declared herself "delighted to know my relationship with my daughter will continue for the rest of our lives." That prospect left the Sterns considerably less than delighted. They plan to try to block or limit the visits.

Common Law Restraint of Trade

A **restraint of trade** is any contract or agreement that eliminates or tends to eliminate competition or otherwise obstructs trade or commerce. One type of restraint is a **covenant not to compete,** which is an agreement to refrain from entering into a competing trade, profession, or business.

At early common law any restraint on an individual's right to engage in his trade or calling was illegal. Such restraints were viewed with disfavor because the courts believed that they would diminish the individual's means of earning a living, deprive the public of useful services, adversely affect competition, and otherwise be harmful to the welfare of the community. But this strict view has been modified so that **reasonable** restraints of trade are enforceable.[3]

Today, an agreement to refrain from a particular trade, profession, or business is enforceable if (1) the purpose of the restraint is to protect a property interest of the promisee, and (2) the restraint is no more extensive than is reasonably necessary to protect that interest. Restraints typically arise in two situations: (a) the sale of a business, and (b) employment contracts.[4]

Sale of a Business   As part of an agreement to sell a business, the seller frequently promises not to compete in the particular business in a *defined area* for a stated period of *time*. To protect the business's good will, an asset that the buyer has purchased, the buyer must be allowed to enforce such a covenant (promise) by the seller not to compete with the purchaser within reasonable limitations. Most litigation on this subject has involved the requirement that the restraint be no greater than is reasonably necessary. The reasonableness of the restraint depends on the geographic area covered and the time period for which the restraint is to be effective.

For example, the promise of a person selling a service station business in Detroit not to enter the service station business in Michigan for the next twenty-five years is unreasonable, both as to area and time. The business interest to be protected would not include the entire State, so it is not necessary to the protection of the purchaser that the seller be prevented from engaging in the service station business in the entire State or perhaps, for that matter, in the entire city of Detroit. Limiting the area to the neighborhood or within a radius of a few miles would probably be adequate protection.

The same type of inquiry must be made about time limitations. In the sale of a service station, twenty-five years would be unreasonable, but one year probably would not. Each case must be considered on its own facts, with the court determining what is reasonable under the particular circumstances.

HAYNES v. MONSON
Supreme Court of Minnesota, 1974.
301 Minn. 327, 224 N.W.2d 482.

Facts: Haynes sold Monson a business known as Haynes Bookkeeping and Tax Service located in Austin, Minnesota. As part of the sale, Haynes agreed not to engage in the business of bookkeeping, accounting, or tax practice within fifty miles of Austin for a period of five years. After working for Monson for eighteen months after the sale, Haynes opened a new office in Red Wing, a town 100 miles from Austin. He did not sell his Austin residence, however, nor did he disconnect his telephone service, and therefore, he was able to maintain contact with his former clients. Under this arrangement Haynes continued to furnish bookkeeping and tax service for forty-five residents of Austin and filed tax returns for them from his new office. Monson claims that Haynes breached their contract by violating his covenant not to compete. The trial court entered summary judgment dismissing the plaintiff's action.

Decision: Summary judgment for Monson affirmed.

Opinion: Scott, J. This court has construed covenants not to compete so as to effectuate the purpose for their inception, i.e., to protect purchasers of a going concern from an infringement upon their investment and the continuation of the business for a profit. To allow one to sell his business, with its accompanying customer lists and files, and then allow him to compete for the patronage of these former customers would be contrary to the covenant, and would frustrate the intent of the parties.

This court has long held that where the restraint is for a "just and honest purpose, for the protection of a legitimate interest of the party in whose favor it is imposed, reasonable as between the parties, and not injurious to the public," that restraint is valid. [Citations.] Under these standards, covenants, such as the one before us, should be strictly construed. [Citation.]

Furthermore, covenants with rather specific geographic and economic limitations have been enforced. [Citation.]

[Haynes] contends that the absence of the element of solicitation should be controlling. [Citation.] We, however, are of the opinion that when one has conducted a business in the same area for many years and has built a sizable clientele, active solicitation on his part is unnecessary to compete so as to defeat the covenant. Solicitation by mere reputation and past business practices is more than sufficient.

Employment Contracts Salespeople, management personnel, and other employees are frequently required to sign employment contracts prohibiting them from competing with their employers during the time of employment and for some additional stated period after termination. The same is also frequently true among professional partnerships or corporations, such as accountants, lawyers, investment brokers, stockbrokers, or doctors. The courts readily enforce a covenant not to compete during the period of employment. But the promise not to compete after termination of employment is subjected to an even stricter test of reasonableness than that applied to noncompetition promises included in a contract for the sale of a business. A court order enjoining (prohibiting) the former employee from competing in a described territory for a stated period of time is the usual way an employer seeks enforcement of an employee's promise not to compete. Before the courts will grant such injunctions, the employer must demonstrate the restriction is *necessary* to pro-

tect his legitimate interests, such as trade secrets or customer lists. Because the injunction may have the practical effect of placing the employee out of work, the courts must carefully balance the public policy favoring the employer's right to protect his business interests against the public policy favoring full opportunity for individuals to gain employment.

Thus, one court has held unreasonable a covenant in a contract that a travel agency employee after termination of her employment would not engage in a like business in any capacity in either of two named towns or within a radius of sixty miles of the towns for a period of two years. There was no indication that the employee had enough influence over customers to cause them to move their business to her new agency nor was it shown that any trade secrets were involved. In addition, some courts, as the following case indicates, instead of refusing to enforce an unreasonable restraint, will modify the restrictive covenant to make it reasonable under the circumstances.

BOB PAGAN FORD, INC. v. SMITH
Court of Appeals of Texas, Houston, First District, 1982.
638 S.W.2d 176.

Facts: The defendant, Charles Smith, was employed by plaintiff Bob Pagan Ford, Inc., under a written contract that prohibited defendant from selling automobiles or automobile parts in Galveston County, Texas, for a period of three years after terminating his employment. Several months after signing the contract, Smith voluntarily left the company to accept a position as auto salesman with a competing dealer. Plaintiff sued defendant to enforce the noncompetition clause of the contract. The trial court held in favor of the plaintiff, but limited the restrictive covenant to six months. Plaintiff appealed.

Decision: Judgment of the trial court affirmed.

Opinion: **Evans, C. J.**   Covenants against competition are not favored by our courts because of the public policy against restraints of trade and the hardships resulting from interference with a person's means of livelihood. [Citation.] Because such a covenant is in restraint of trade, its terms will not be enforced by the courts unless they are reasonable. [Citation.]

Whether a restrictive covenant is reasonable as to time and area is a question of law to be determined by the court, [citation], usually on the basis of whether the restriction imposes greater restraint on the employee than is reasonably necessary to protect the employer's business and goodwill. Thus, the trial court must examine the circumstances of each case to determine whether the restrictions sought to be imposed are greater than those required to protect the employer's interests, and whether they impose undue hardship upon the employee. [Citation.]

In determining whether a restrictive covenant is reasonable as to duration, the trial court is accorded considerable discretion, and it is appropriate for the court to consider whether the interests which the covenant was designed to protect are still outstanding and to balance those interests against the hardships which would be imposed upon the employee by enforcement of the restrictions. [Citation.] The proceeding is in equity, and the court may reduce the duration of the restrictive covenant to that which it considers reasonable under the circumstances. [Citation.] The record tends to support the trial court's determination that a full and liberal application of the contractual restrictions would impose a much more onerous burden on Smith than would, on balance, be required to protect the business and goodwill of Bob Pagan Ford. Thus, we hold that the trial court did not abuse its discretion in reducing the duration of the restrictive covenant.

Obstructing the Administration of Justice

Agreements that are harmful to the administration of justice are illegal and unenforceable. For example, a promise by an employer not to press criminal charges against an embezzling employee who restores the stolen funds is not enforceable. Similarly, a promise to conceal evidence or to give false testimony tends to obstruct the administration of justice and for that reason is illegal and unenforceable.

Corrupting Public Officials

Agreements that may adversely affect the public interest through the corruption of public officials or the impairment of the legislative process are unenforceable. Examples include using improper means to influence legislation, to secure some official action, or to procure a government contract. For example, an agreement to pay a public officer something extra for performing his official duty, such as a promise to a police officer for strictly enforcing the traffic laws on her beat, is illegal.

Exculpatory Clauses

Some contracts for services contain an **exculpatory clause** that excuses one party from liability for his own tortious conduct. The courts generally regard this type of clause with disfavor because it is public policy to discourage overreaching and to assure that wrongdoers will pay the damages caused by their negligence. Accordingly, an exculpatory clause on the reverse side of a parking lot claim check that attempts to relieve the parking lot operator of liability for negligently damaging the customer's automobile is unenforceable. On the other hand, the policy of freedom of contract is also a factor in determining the validity of contractual clauses exempting a party from liability for his negligence, and thus all such clauses are not held to be against public policy.

HENRIOULLE v. MARIN VENTURES, INC.
Supreme Court of California, 1978.
20 Cal.3d 512, 573 P.2d 465, 143 Cal.Rptr. 247.

Facts: Henrioulle was an unemployed widower with two children and received public assistance in the form of a rent subsidy. He entered into a lease agreement with Marin Ventures that provided "INDEMNIFICATION: Owner shall not be liable for any damage or injury to the tenant, or any other person, or to any property, occurring on the premises, or any part thereof, and Tenant agrees to hold Owner harmless for any claims for damages no matter how caused." Henrioulle fractured his wrist when he tripped over a rock on a common stairway in the apartment building. At the time of the accident, the landlord had been having difficulty keeping the common areas of the apartment building clean. Henrioulle appeals from the trial court's orders granting Marin Ventures a judgment not withstanding the jury's verdict and a new trial.

Decision: The orders of the trial court are reversed and the case is remanded with directions to enter a judgment for Henrioulle on the verdict.

Opinion: **Bird, C. J.** In *Tunkl v. Regents of the University of California* [citation], this court held invalid a clause in a hospital admission form which released the hospital from liability for future negligence. This court noted that although courts have made "diverse" interpretations of [California] Civil Code section 1668, which invalidates contracts which exempt one from responsibility for certain wilful or negligent acts, all the decisions were in accord that exculpatory clauses affecting the public interest are invalid. [Citation.]

In *Tunkl*, six criteria are used to identify the kind of agreement in which an exculpatory clause is invalid as contrary to public policy. "[1] It concerns a business of a type generally thought suitable for public regulation. [2] The party seeking exculpation is engaged in performing a service of great importance to the public, which is often a matter of practical necessity for some members of the public. [3] The party holds himself out as willing to perform this service for any member of the public who seeks it, or at least any member coming within certain established standards. [4] As a result of the essential nature of the service, in the economic setting of the transaction, the party invoking exculpation possesses a decisive advantage of bargaining strength against any member of the public who seeks his services. [5] In exercising a superior bargaining power the party confronts the public with a standardized adhesion contract of exculpation, and makes no provision whereby a purchaser may pay additional fees and obtain protection against negligence. [6] Finally, as a result of the transaction, the person or property of the purchaser is placed under the control of the seller, subject to the risk of carelessness by the seller or his agents." [Citation.]

The transaction before this court, a residential rental agreement, meets the *Tunkl* criteria.

* * *

In holding that exculpatory clauses in residential leases violate public policy, this court joins an increasing number of jurisdictions. [Citations.]

Unconscionable Contracts

The Uniform Commercial Code provides that every contract for the sale of goods may be scrutinized by the court to determine whether in its commercial setting, purpose, and effect it is **unconscionable** or unfair. The court may refuse to enforce an unconscionable contract or any part of the contract it finds to be unconscionable.

The Code denies or limits enforcement of an unconscionable contract for the sale of goods in the interest of fairness and decency and to correct harshness in contracts resulting from unequal bargaining positions of the parties.[5] The Restatement incorporates a provision that mirrors that of the Code.[6] Although the principle is not novel, its embodiment in a statute dealing with commercial transactions is novel.

The doctrine of unconscionability has been justified on the basis that it permits the courts to resolve issues of unfairness explicitly on that basis without recourse to formalistic rules or legal fictions. In policing contracts for fairness, the courts have again demonstrated their willingness to limit freedom of contract in order to protect the less advantaged from overreaching by dominant contracting parties. The doctrine of unconscionability has evolved through its application by the courts to include both procedural and substantive unconscionability. **Procedural unconscionability** involves scrutiny for the presence of "bargaining naughtiness." In other words, was the negotiation process fair, or were there procedural irregularities such as burying important terms of the agreement in fine print or obscuring the true

meaning of the contract with impenetrable legal jargon?

Substantive unconscionability deals with the actual terms of the contract and involves oppressive or grossly unfair provisions such as an exorbitant price or an unfair exclusion or limitation of contractual remedies. An all too common example is that involving a buyer in pressing need who is in an unequal bargaining position with a seller who has obtained an exorbitant price for his product or service. In one case, a price of $749 ($920 on time) for a vacuum cleaner that cost the seller $140 was held unconscionable. In another case, the buyers, welfare recipients, purchased by a time payment contract a home freezer unit for $900 that, when added to the time credit charges, credit life insurance, credit property insurance, and sales tax, amounted to $1,235. The purchase resulted from a visit to the buyer's home by a salesman representing Your Shop At Home Service, Inc., and the maximum retail value of the freezer unit at the time of purchase was $300. The court held the contract unconscionable and reformed it by reducing the price to the total payment ($620) made by the buyers. Another landmark case appears on page 237.

EFFECT OF ILLEGALITY

With few exceptions, illegal contracts are **unenforceable.** In most cases, neither party to an illegal agreement can sue the other for breach or recover for any performance rendered. It is often said that where parties are *in pari delicto* (in equal fault), a court will leave them where it finds them. The law will provide neither

WILLIAMS v. WALKER-THOMAS FURNITURE CO.
United States Court of Appeals, District of Columbia Circuit, 1965.
350 F.2d 445.

Facts: Between 1957 and 1962, Williams purchased a number of household items on credit from Walker-Thomas Furniture Co., a retail furniture store. Walker-Thomas retained the right in its contracts to repossess an item if Williams defaulted on an installment payment. Each contract also provided that each installment payment by Williams would be credited *pro rata* to all outstanding accounts or bills owed to Walker-Thomas. As a result of this provision, an unpaid balance would remain on every item purchased until the entire balance due on all items, whenever purchased, was paid in full. Williams defaulted on a monthly installment payment in 1962, and Walker-Thomas sought to repossess all the items that Williams had purchased since 1957. Williams claimed that the contracts were unconscionable and therefore unenforceable. The trial court granted judgment for Walker-Thomas and the District of Columbia Court of Appeals affirmed.

Decision: Judgment reversed and remanded to determine the possible unconscionability of the contracts.

Opinion: **Wright, C. J.**   Unconscionability has generally been recognized to include an absence of meaningful choice on the part of one of the parties together with contract terms which are unreasonably favorable to the other party. Whether a meaningful choice is present in a particular case can only be determined by consideration of all the circumstances surrounding the transaction. In many cases the meaningfulness of the choice is negated by a gross inequality of bargaining power. The manner in which the contract was entered is also relevant to this consideration. Did each party to the contract, considering his obvious education or lack of it, have a reasonable opportunity to understand the terms of the contract, or were the important terms hidden in a maze of fine print and minimized by deceptive sales practices? Ordinarily, one who signs an agreement without full knowledge of its terms might be held to assume the risk that he has entered a one-sided bargain. But when a party of little bargaining power, and hence little real choice, signs a commercially unreasonable contract with little or no knowledge of its terms, it is hardly likely that his consent, or even an objective manifestation of his consent, was ever given to all the terms. In such a case the usual rule that the terms of the agreement are not to be questioned should be abandoned and the court should consider whether the terms of the contract are so unfair that enforcement should be withheld.

In determining reasonableness or fairness, the primary concern must be with the terms of the contract considered in light of the circumstances existing when the contract was made. The test is not simple, nor can it be mechanically applied. The terms are to be considered "in the light of the general commercial background and the commercial needs of the particular trade or case." Corbin suggests the test as being whether the terms are "so extreme as to appear unconscionable according to the mores and business practices of the time and place." [Citation.] We think this formulation correctly states the test to be applied to those cases where no meaningful choice was exercised upon entering the contract.

Because the trial court and the appellate court did not feel that enforcement could be refused, no findings were made on the possible unconscionability of the contracts in these cases. Since the record is not sufficient for our deciding the issue as a matter of law, the cases must be remanded to the trial court for further proceedings.

with any remedy. This strict rule of unenforce-ability is subject to certain exceptions, however, which we discuss below.

Party Withdrawing before Performance

Under some circumstances a party to an illegal agreement may, before performance, withdraw from the transaction and recover whatever she has contributed. A common example is recovery of money left with a stakeholder for a wager before it is paid over to the winner, but the rule has also been applied to more serious misconduct.

Party Protected by Statute

Sometimes an agreement is illegal because it violates a statute designed to protect persons who by their actions take the position of one of the parties. For example, State "Blue Sky Laws" prohibiting the sale of unregistered securities are designed primarily to protect investors. In such case, even though there is an unlawful agreement, the statute usually expressly gives the purchaser a right to withdraw from the sale and recover the money paid.

Party Not Equally at Fault

Where one of the parties is less at fault than the other, he will be allowed to recover payments made or property transferred. For example, this exception would apply where one party is induced to enter into an illegal bargain through the fraud, duress, or undue influence of the other party.

CHAPTER SUMMARY

Violations of Statutes	**General Rule** agreements declared illegal by statute will not be enforced by the courts **Licensing Statutes** require formal authorization to engage in certain trades, professions, or businesses ■ *Regulatory License* licensing statute that is intended to protect the public against unqualified persons; an unlicensed person may not recover for services ■ *Revenue License* licensing statute that seeks to raise money; an unlicensed person may recover for services **Gambling Statutes** prohibit wagers which are agreements that one party will win or lose depending upon the outcome of an event in which the only interest is the gain or loss **Usury Statutes** establish a maximum rate of interest
Violations of Public Policy	**Tortious Conduct** an agreement that requires a person to commit a tort is unenforceable **Common Law Restraint of Trade** unreasonable restraints on trade are not enforceable ■ *Sale of a Business* the promise by a seller of a business not to compete in that particular business in a reasonable geographic area for a reasonable period of time is enforceable ■ *Employment Contracts* an employment contract prohibiting an employee from competing with his employer for a reasonable period following termination is enforceable provided the restriction is necessary to protect legitimate interests of the employer

Obstructing the Administration of Justice agreements which are harmful to the administration of justice are not enforceable

Corrupting Public Officials agreements which corrupt public officials are not enforceable

Exculpatory Clauses contractual provisions excusing a party from liability for his own tortious conduct are generally looked upon with disfavor by the courts

Unconscionable Contracts unfair or unduly harsh agreements are not enforceable

- *Procedural Unconscionability* unfair or irregular bargaining
- *Substantive Unconscionability* oppressive or grossly unfair contractual terms

Effect of Illegality

Unenforceability neither party may recover under an illegal agreement where both parties are *in pari delicto* (in equal fault)

Exceptions permits one party to recover payments

- *Party Withdrawing Before Performance*
- *Party Protected by Statute*
- *Party Not Equally at Fault*

QUESTIONS

1. Define unenforceable. Why are illegal agreements unenforceable? What are the major exceptions to this rule?
2. Identify and distinguish between the two types of licensing statutes.
3. Distinguish between general and specific usury laws.
4. Describe when a covenant not to compete will be enforced and discuss the two situations in which these types of covenants most frequently arise.
5. Distinguish between procedural and substantive unconscionability.

PROBLEMS

1. Johnson and Wilson were the principal shareholders in XYZ Corporation located in the city of Jonesville, Wisconsin. This corporation was engaged in the business of manufacturing paper novelties, which were sold over a wide area in the Midwest. The corporation was also in the business of binding books. Johnson purchased Wilson's shares of the XYZ Corporation and, in consideration thereof, Wilson agreed that for a period of two years he would not: (a) manufacture or sell in Wisconsin any paper novelties of any kind that would compete with those sold by the XYZ Corporation, or (b)

engage in the bookbinding business in the city of Jonesville. Discuss the validity and effect, if any, of this agreement.

2. Wilkins, a Texas resident licensed by that State as a certified public accountant, rendered service in his professional capacity in Louisiana to Coverton Cosmetics Company. He was not registered as a certified public accountant in Louisiana. His service under his contract with the cosmetics company was not the only occasion on which he had practiced his profession in that State. The company denied liability and refused to pay him, relying on a Louisiana statute declaring it unlawful for any person to perform or offer to perform services as a CPA for compensation until he has been registered by the designated agency of the State and holds an unrevoked registration card. The statute provides that a CPA certificate may be issued without examination to any applicant who holds a valid unrevoked certificate as a CPA under the laws of any other State. The statute provides further that rendering services of the kind performed by Wilkins, without registration, is a misdemeanor punishable by a fine or imprisonment in the county jail or by both fine and imprisonment. Wilkins brought action against Coverton, seeking to recover a fee in the amount of $1,500 as the reasonable value of his services. Decision?

3. Michael is interested in promoting the passage of a bill in the State legislature. He agrees with Christy, an attorney, to pay Christy for her services in writing the required bill, obtaining its introduc-

tion in the legislature, and making an argument for its passage before the legislative committee to which it will be referred. Christy renders these services. Subsequently, on Michael's refusal to pay Christy, Christy sues Michael for damages for breach of contract. Decision?

4. Anthony promises to pay McCarthy $10,000 if McCarthy reveals to the public that Washington is a communist. Washington is not a communist and never has been. McCarthy successfully persuades the media to report that Washington is a communist and now seeks to recover the $10,000 from Anthony, who refuses to pay. McCarthy initiates a lawsuit against Anthony. What result?

5. The Dear Corporation was engaged in the business of making and selling harvesting machines. It sold everything pertaining to the business to the HI Company, agreeing "not again to go into the manufacture of harvesting machines anywhere in the United States." The Dear Corporation had a national and international goodwill in its business. It now begins the manufacture of such machines contrary to its agreement. Should the court stop it from doing so? Explain.

6. Charles Leigh, engaged in the industrial laundry business in Central City, employed Tim Close, previously employed in the home laundry business, as a route salesman. Leigh rents linens and industrial uniforms to commercial customers; the soiled linens and uniforms are picked up at regular intervals by the route drivers and replaced with clean ones. Every employee is assigned a list of customers whom he or she services. The contract of employment stated that in consideration of being employed, on termination of the employment, Close would not "directly or indirectly engage in the linen supply business or any competitive business within Central City, Illinois, for a period of one year from the date when his employment under this contract ceases." On May 10 of the following year, Close's employment was terminated by Leigh for valid reasons. Close then accepted employment with Ajax Linen Service, a direct competitor of Leigh in Central City. He began soliciting former customers he had called on for Leigh and obtained some of them as customers for Ajax.

Leigh brings an action to enforce the provisions of the contract. Decision?

7. On July 5, 1988, Barbara and Kitty entered into a bet on the outcome of the 1988 presidential election. On January 28, 1989, Barbara, who bet on the winner, approached Kitty, seeking to collect the $3,000 Kitty had wagered. Kitty paid Barbara the wager and now seeks to recover the funds from Barbara. Result?

8. Carl, a salesman for Smith, comes to Benson's home and sells him a complete set of "gourmet cooking utensils" that are worth approximately $300. Benson, an eighty-year-old man, lives alone in a one-room efficiency apartment. Benson signs a contract to buy the utensils for $1,450 plus a credit charge of $145 and to make payment in ten equal monthly installments. Three weeks after Carl leaves with the signed contract, Benson decides he cannot afford the cooking utensils and has no use for them. What can Benson do? Explain.

9. Consider the same facts as in problem 8, but assume that the price was $350. Benson, nevertheless, wishes to avoid the contract based on the allegation that Carl befriended and tricked him into the purchase. Decision?

10. Adrian rents a bicycle from Barbara. The bicycle rental contract Adrian signed provides that Barbara is not liable for any injury to the renter caused by any defect in the bicycle or the negligence of Barbara. Adrian is injured when she is involved in an accident due to Barbara's improper maintenance of the bicycle. Adrian sues Barbara for her damage. Decision?

COMPUTER RESEARCH PROBLEMS

1. Merrill Lynch employed Post and Maney as account executives beginning on April 20, 1959, and May 15, 1961, respectively. Both men elected to be paid a salary and to participate in the firm's pension and profit-sharing plans rather than take a straight commission. Merrill Lynch terminated the employment of both Post and Maney on August 30, 1974. On September 4, 1974, both began working for Bache & Company, a competitor of Merrill Lynch. Merrill Lynch then informed them that all of their rights in the company-funded pension plan had been forfeited pursuant to a provision of the plan that permitted forfeiture in the event an employee directly or indirectly competed with the firm. Decision?

2. Tovar applied for the position of resident physician in Paxton Community Memorial Hospital. The hospital examined his background and licensing and assured him that he was qualified for the position. Relying upon the hospital's promise of permanent employment, Tovar resigned from his job and began work at the hospital. He was discharged two weeks later, however, because he did not hold a license to practice medicine in Illinois as required by State law. He had taken the examination but had never passed it. Tovar claims that the

hospital promised him a position of permanent employment and that by discharging him it breached their employment contract. Decision?

3. Carolyn Murphy, a welfare recipient with four minor children, responded to an advertisement which offered the opportunity to purchase televisions without a deposit or credit history. She entered into a rent-to-own contract for a twenty-five inch console color television set that required seventy-eight weekly payments of $16 (a total of $1,248 which was two and one half times the retail value of the set). Under the contract, the renter could terminate the agreement by returning the television and forfeiting any payments already made. After Murphy had paid $436 on the television she read a newspaper article critical of the lease plan. She stopped payment and sued the television company. The television company has attempted to take possession of the set. Decision?

4. Albert Bennett, an amateur cyclist, participated in a bicycle race conducted by the United States Cycling Federation. During the race Bennett was hit by an automobile. Bennett claims that employees of the Federation improperly allowed the car onto the course. The Federation claims that it cannot be held liable to Bennett because Bennett signed a release exculpating the Federation from responsibility for any personal injury resulting from his participation in the race. Decision?

ENDNOTES

1. Restatement, Second, Contracts, Section 181, Effect of Failure to Comply with Licensing or Similar Requirement.
2. Restatement, Second, Contracts, Section 192, Promise Involving Commission of a Tort.
3. Restatement, Second, Contracts, Section 186, Promise in Restraint of Trade.
4. Restatement, Second, Contracts, Section 187, Non-Ancillary Restraints on Competition, and Section 188, Ancillary Restraints on Competition.
5. Uniform Commercial Code, Section 2—302, Unconscionable Contract or Clause.
6. Restatement, Second, Contracts, Section 208, Unconscionable Contract or Term.

12 CONTRACTUAL CAPACITY

A binding promise or agreement requires that the parties to the agreement have contractual capacity. Everyone is regarded as having such capacity unless the law, for public policy reasons, holds that the individual lacks such capacity. We consider this essential ingredient of a contract by discussing those classes and conditions of persons who are legally limited in their capacity to contract: minors, incompetent persons, and intoxicated persons.

MINORS

A **minor,** also called an infant, is a person who has not attained the age of legal majority. At common law, a minor was an individual who had not reached the age of twenty-one years. Today the age of majority has been changed in nearly all jurisdictions by statute, usually to age eighteen. Almost without exception a minor's contract is **voidable** at his option.[1] Some States recognize special categories of contracts that either cannot be avoided (such as student loans or contracts for medical care) or have a lower age for capacity (such as bank accounts, marriage, and insurance contracts). Even an "emancipated" minor, one who because of marriage or other reasons is no longer subject to strict parental control, may nevertheless avoid contractual liability in most jurisdictions. Consequently, business people deal with minors at their peril.

Liability for Necessaries

Contractual immunity does not excuse a minor from an obligation to pay for necessaries, those things that suitably and reasonably supply his personal needs, such as food, shelter, medicine, and clothing. Even here, however, the minor is liable not for the agreed price but for the *reasonable* value of the items furnished. Recovery is based on quasi contract. Thus, if a clothier sells a minor a suit that the minor needs, the clothier can successfully sue the minor and recover the reasonable value of the suit. The clothier is limited to this amount even if it is much less than the agreed-upon selling price.

Determining what are necessaries is a difficult problem. In general, the States regard as **necessary** those things that the minor needs to maintain himself in his particular station in life. Items necessary for subsistence and health, such as food, lodging, clothing, medicine, and medical services, are obviously included. But other less essential items, such as textbooks, school instruction, and legal advice, may be included as well. Further, some States enlarge the concept of necessaries to include articles of property and services that a minor needs to earn the money required to provide the necessities of life for himself and his dependents. Moreover, many States limit necessaries to items that are not provided to the minor. Thus, if a minor's guardian provides her with an adequate wardrobe, a blouse the minor purchased would *not* be considered a necessity. In addition, a minor is not liable for anything on the ground that it is necessary unless it has been actually furnished to him and used or consumed by him. In other words, a minor may repudiate his executory contracts for necessaries and refuse to accept the clothing, lodging, or other necessaries.

The following is the leading case on the rights and obligations of minors for the purchase of "necessaries."

GASTONIA PERSONNEL CORP. v. ROGERS
Supreme Court of North Carolina, 1970.
276 N.C. 279, 172 S.E.2d 19.

Facts: Rogers was a nineteen-year-old (the age of majority then being twenty-one) high school graduate pursuing a civil engineering degree when he learned that his wife was expecting a child. As a result, he quit school and sought assistance from Gastonia Personnel Corporation in finding a job. Rogers signed a contract with the employment agency providing that he would pay the agency a service charge if it obtained suitable employment for him. The employment agency found him such a job, but Rogers refused to pay the service charge, asserting that he was a minor when he signed the contract. Gastonia sued to recover the agreed-upon service charge from Rogers. The trial court dismissed the plaintiff's claim and the Court of Appeals affirmed.

Decision: Judgment reversed and the case is remanded for a new trial in accordance with legal principles stated in the opinion.

Opinion: Bobbitt, C. J. Under the common law, persons, whether male or female, are classified and referred to as *infants* until they attain the age of twenty-one years. [Citations.]

"By the fifteenth century it seems to have been well settled that an infant's bargain was in general void at his election (that is, voidable), and also that he was liable for necessaries." [Citation.]

An early commentary on the common law, after the general statement that contracts made by persons (infants) before attaining the age of twenty-one "may be avoided," sets forth "some exceptions out of this generality," to wit: *"An infant may bind himselfe to pay for his necessary meat, drinke, apparell, necessary physicke, and such other necessaries,* and likewise for his good teaching or instruction, whereby he may profit himself afterwards." (Our italics.) [Citations.] * * * If the infant married, "necessaries" included necessary food and clothing for his wife and child. [Citation.]

In accordance with this ancient rule of the common law, this Court has held an infant's contract, unless for "necessaries" or unless authorized by statute, is voidable by the infant, at his election, and may be disaffirmed during infancy or upon attaining the age of twenty-one. [Citations.]

* * *

In general, our prior decisions are to the effect that the "necessaries" of an infant, his wife and child, include only such necessities of life as food, clothing, shelter, medical attention, etc. In our view, the concept of "necessities" should be enlarged to include such articles of property and such services as are reasonably necessary to enable the infant to earn the money required to provide the necessities of life for himself and those who are legally dependent upon him.

The evidence before us tends to show that defendant, when he contracted with plaintiff, was nineteen years of age, emancipated, married, a high school graduate, within "a quarter or 22 hours" of obtaining his degree in applied science, and capable of holding a job at a starting annual salary of $4,784.00. To hold, as a matter of law, that such a person cannot obligate himself to pay for services rendered him in obtaining employment suitable to his ability, education and specialized training, enabling him to provide the necessities of life for himself, his wife and his expected child, would place him and others similarly situated under a serious economic handicap.

In the effort to protect "older minors" from improvident or unfair contracts, the law should not deny to them the opportunity and right to obligate themselves for articles of property or services which are reasonably necessary to enable them to provide for the proper support of themselves and their dependents. The minor should be held liable for the reasonable value of articles of property or services received pursuant to such contract.

* * *

To establish liability, plaintiff must satisfy the jury by the greater weight of the evidence that defendant's contract with plaintiff was an appropriate and reasonable means for defendant to obtain suitable employment. If this issue is answered in plaintiff's favor, plaintiff must then establish by the greater weight of the evidence the reasonable value of the services received by defendant pursuant to the contract. Thus, plaintiff's recovery, if any, cannot exceed the reasonable value of its services to defendant.

Ordinarily, luxury items, such as cameras, tape recorders, stereo equipment, television sets, and motorboats, do not qualify as necessaries. Whether automobiles and trucks are necessaries has caused considerable controversy, but some courts have recognized that under certain circumstances an automobile may be a necessary where it is used by the minor for his business activities.

Liability on Contracts

A minor's contract is not entirely void and of no legal effect; rather, it is voidable at the minor's option. He has a power of avoidance. His exercise of this power is called a **disaffirmance**, and he is released from any liability on the contract. On the other hand, after the minor becomes of age, he may choose to adopt or ratify the contract, in which case he becomes bound by his **ratification.**

Disaffirmance   As we stated earlier, a minor's contract is voidable at his option; he thus has the power to avoid liability. He may exercise his power to disaffirm a contract through words or conduct showing an intention not to abide by it.

In general, a minor may disaffirm a contract at any time, either before or within a reasonable time after he becomes of age. In most States, what is a reasonable time depends upon such circumstances as the nature of the transaction, whether either party has caused the delay, and the extent to which either party has been injured by the delay. Some States, however, statutorily prescribe a time period, generally one year, in which the minor may disaffirm the contract.

A notable exception is that a sale of land by a minor cannot be disaffirmed until after he reaches his majority. But must he disaffirm immediately upon becoming an adult? In the case of a sale of land, there is a strong precedent that the minor may wait until the expiration of the period of the statute of limitations if there are no questions of fairness and equity involved. This is not the case with other types of contracts. There he must disaffirm either during his minority or within a reasonable time after reaching majority, the precise time period varying with the circumstances and local law.

Disaffirmance may be either *express* or *implied*. No particular form of words is essential, so long as it shows an intention not to be bound. This intention may be manifested by acts or by conduct. For example, a minor agrees to sell property to Andy and then sells the property to Betty. The sale to Betty constitutes a disaffirmance of the contract with Andy.

A troublesome yet important problem in this area pertains to the minor's duty upon disaffirmance. The courts do not agree on this question. The majority, as demonstrated in *Halbman v. Lemke*, hold that the minor must only return any property he has received from the other party, provided he has it in his possession at the time of disaffirmance. Nothing more is required. If the minor disaffirms the purchase of an automobile and the vehicle has been wrecked, he need only return the wrecked vehicle. Other States require at least the payment of a reasonable amount for the use of the property or the amount of its depreciation while in the hands of the minor. A few States, however, either by statute or court ruling, recognize a duty on the part of the minor to make *restitution;* that is, to return an equivalent of what has been received so that the seller will be in approximately the same position he would have occupied had the sale not occurred.

 ## HALBMAN v. LEMKE
Supreme Court of Wisconsin, 1980.
99 Wis.2d 241, 298 N.W.2d 562.

Facts: Halbman, a minor, purchased a 1968 Oldsmobile from Lemke for $1,250. Under the terms of the contract, Halbman would pay $1,000 down and the balance in $25 weekly installments. Upon making the down payment, Halbman received possession of the car, but Lemke retained the title until the balance was paid. After Halbman had made his first four payments, a connecting rod in the car's engine broke. Lemke denied responsibility, but offered to help Halbman repair it if Halbman would provide the parts. Halbman, however, placed the car in a garage where the repairs cost $637.40. Halbman never paid the repair bill.

Hoping to avoid any liability for the vehicle, Lemke transferred title to Halbman even though Halbman never paid the balance owed. Halbman returned the title with a letter disaffirming the contract and demanded return of the money paid. Lemke refused. Since the repair bill remained unpaid, the garage removed the car's engine and transmission and towed the body to Halbman's father's house. Vandalism during the period of storage rendered the car unsalvageable. Several times Halbman requested Lemke to remove the car. Lemke refused. Halbman sued Lemke for the return of his consideration, and Lemke countersued for the amount still owed on the contract. The trial court ruled in favor of Halbman, holding that when a minor disaffirms a contract he need only return the property in his possession without regard to use or depreciation.

Decision: Judgment for Halbman affirmed.

Opinion: Callou, J. The sole issue before us is whether the minor, having disaffirmed a contract for the purchase of an item which is not a necessity and having tendered the property back to the vendor, must make restitution to the vendor for damage to the property prior to the disaffirmance. Lemke argues that he should be entitled to recover for the damage to the vehicle up to the time of disaffirmance, which he claims equals the amount of the repair bill.

Neither party challenges the absolute right of a minor to disaffirm a contract for the purchase of items which are not necessities. That right, variously known as the doctrine of incapacity or the "infancy doctrine," is one of the oldest and most venerable of our common law traditions. [Citations.] Although the origins of the doctrine are somewhat obscure, it is generally recognized that its purpose is the protection of minors from foolishly squandering their wealth through improvident contracts with crafty adults who would take advantage of them in the marketplace.

[Citation.] Thus it is settled law in this state that a contract of a minor for items which are not necessities is * * * voidable at the minor's option. [Citations.]

Once there has been a disaffirmance, however, as in this case between a minor vendee and an adult vendor, unresolved problems arise regarding the rights and responsibilities of the parties relative to the disposition of the consideration exchanged on the contract. As a general rule a minor who disaffirms a contract is entitled to recover all consideration he has conferred incident to the transaction. [Citation.] In return the minor is expected to restore as much of the consideration as, at the time of disaffirmance, remains in the minor's possession. [Citations.] The minor's right to disaffirm is not contingent upon the return of the property, however, a disaffirmance is permitted even where such return cannot be made.

* * *

A minor, as we have stated, is under an enforceable duty to return to the vendor, upon disaffirmance, as much of the consideration as remains in his possession. When the contract is disaffirmed, title to that part of the purchased property which is retained by the minor revests in the vendor; it no longer belongs to the minor. [Citation.] The rationale for the rule is plain: a minor who disaffirms a purchase and recovers his purchase price should not also be permitted to profit by retaining the property purchased. The infancy doctrine is designed to protect the minor, sometimes at the expense of an innocent vendor, but it is not to be used to bilk merchants out of property as well as proceeds of the sale. Consequently, it is clear that, when the minor no longer possesses the property which was the subject matter of the contract, the rule requiring the return of property does not apply. The minor will not be required to give up what he does not have.

* * *

Here Lemke seeks restitution of the value of the depreciation by virtue of the damage to the vehicle prior to disaffirmance. Such a recovery would require Halbman to return more than that remaining in his possession. It seeks compensatory value for that which he cannot return. Where there is misrepresentation by a minor or willful destruction of property, the vendor may be able to recover damages in tort. [Citations.] But absent these factors, as in the present case, we believe that to require a disaffirming minor to make restitution for diminshed value is, in effect, to bind the minor to a part of the obligation which by law he is privileged to avoid.

Finally, can a minor disaffirm and recover property that he has sold to a buyer who in turn has sold it to a good faith purchaser for value? Traditionally, the minor could avoid the contract and recover the property, despite the fact that the third person gave value for it and had no notice of the minority. Thus, in the case of the sale of real estate, a minor's deed of conveyance may be taken back even against a good faith purchaser of the land who did not know of the minority. The Uniform Commercial Code, however, has changed this principle in connection with sales of goods. The Code provides that a person with voidable title (e.g., the person buying goods from a minor) has power to transfer valid title to a good faith purchaser for value.[2] For example, a minor sells his car to an individual who resells it to a used-car dealership, a good faith purchaser for value. The used-car dealer would acquire legal title even though he bought the car from a seller who had only voidable title.

PARRENT v. MIDWAY TOYOTA
Supreme Court of Montana, 1981.
626 P.2d 848.

Facts: A fifteen-year-old minor was employed by Midway Toyota, Inc., of Great Falls, Montana. On August 18, 1975, the minor, while engaged in lifting heavy objects, injured his lower back. In October 1975 he underwent surgery to remove a herniated disk. Midway Toyota paid him the appropriate amount of temporary total disability payments ($53.36 per week) from August 18, 1975, through November 15, 1976. In February 1977 a final settlement was reached for 150 weeks of permanent partial disability benefits totaling $6,136.40. Tom Mazurek represented Midway Toyota in the negotiations leading up to the agreement and negotiated directly with the minor and his mother, Hermoine Parrent. The final settlement agreement was signed by the minor only. Mrs. Parrent was present at the time and did not object to the signing, but neither she nor anyone else of "legal guardian status" cosigned the agreement. The minor later sought to disaffirm the agreement and reopen his workers' compensation case. The workers' compensation court denied his petition, holding that Mrs. Parrent "participated fully in consideration of the offered final settlement and . . . ratified and approved it on behalf of her ward . . . to the same legal effect as if she had actually signed [it]. . . ." The minor appeals.

Decision: Judgment for the minor setting aside the final compromise settlement.

Opinion: Harrison, J.   The [Montana statute] allows a minor to disaffirm his contract. Because the sixteen-year-old claimant signed the petition for final settlement in his own behalf, he alone was the contracting party.

Tom Mazurek chose to contract with the claimant; he must, therefore, be prepared to accept the consequences of claimant's disaffirmance of the petition. The person who deals with an infant does so at his own peril. [Citation.]

Defendant claims that the mother, Hermoine Parrent, was present at all times during the signing of the contract; that the mother approved of the contract; that there was no objection to the contract; that the adjuster negotiated with the mother and the claimant during the weeks prior to the signing of the contract and that after the contract was signed, the mother was still aware of the contract rights of claimant and did not object to the same. Because of this close relation and continuous awareness of the mother, the contract is enforceable. We disagree.

It is immaterial that Hermoine Parrent may have advised and counseled claimant with respect to his workers' compensation claim. The mother is the natural guardian of the minor claimant, but this relation only affects her right to the custody of the minor and does not enlarge her rights to the property of the minor. Claimant was the sole contracting party. He is the only party that bound himself legally to the contract. As a minor, he is entitled to disaffirm and rescind the final settlement.

* * *

It is the policy of the law to discourage adults from contracting with a minor. Tom Mazurek testified he knew claimant was a minor at the time claimant signed the petition for final settlement; yet, Mazurek was not discouraged from obtaining claimant's signature on the petition.

> The insurer, adjuster Mazurek and the Workers' Compensation Division have much greater expertise and knowledge in the area of workers' compensation law than have claimant and his mother. We are dismayed that these knowledgeable parties overlooked simple contract law. Defendant erred in not requiring claimant's legal guardian to sign the petition for final settlement on behalf of and in place of claimant himself.

Ratification Suppose that a minor makes a contract to buy property from an adult. The contract is voidable by the minor, and she can escape liability. But suppose that after reaching her majority, she promises to go through with the purchase. Her promise is binding, and the adult can recover for breach if she fails to carry out the terms of the contract. She has *expressly* ratified the contract entered into when she was a minor.

Ratification makes the contract binding *ab initio* (from the beginning). That is, the result is the same as if the contract had been valid and binding from the beginning. Ratification, once effected, is final and cannot be withdrawn.

Ratification must be in total; it must validate the entire contract. The minor can ratify the contract only as a whole, both as to burdens and benefits. He cannot, for example, ratify so as to retain the consideration he received and escape payment or other performance on his part, nor can he, as the following case shows, retain part of the contract and disaffirm another part.

LANGSTRAAT v. MIDWEST MUTUAL, INS. CO.
Supreme Court of Iowa, 1974.
217 N.W.2d 570.

Facts: Langstraat, age seventeen, owned a motorcycle that he insured against liability with Midwest Mutual Insurance Company. He signed a notice of rejection attached to the policy indicating that he did not desire to purchase uninsured motorists' coverage from the insurance company. Later he was involved in an accident with another motorcycle owned and operated by a party who was uninsured. Langstraat now seeks to recover from the insurance company, asserting that his rejection was not a valid rejection because he is a minor. The district court entered judgment in favor of Midwest Mutual.

Decision: Judgment for Midwest Mutual Insurance Company affirmed.

Opinion: LeGrand, J. The issue is clearly drawn. Defendant admits it issued a policy of insurance covering plaintiff's motorcycle. Plaintiff admits he signed the notice of rejection [regarding uninsured motorists coverage]. In reply to defendant's answer setting up the affirmative defense that plaintiff had rejected uninsured motorist coverage, plaintiff alleged his rejection was not a valid rejection * * * because of his minority.

This is not a case in which a minor seeks to disaffirm a contract. He may, of course, do so * * * [Citation.] Such a course, however, would leave plaintiff with *no* insurance. What he seeks here, by whatever name it is called, is to retain the benefits of the policy but to avoid the one provision which has become burdensome. There is no rule permitting such a selective choice.

Ratification need not be express; it may be *implied* from a person's conduct. Suppose that the minor, after attaining her majority, uses the property, undertakes to sell it to someone else, or performs some other act showing an intention to affirm the contract. She may not thereafter disaffirm the contract but is bound by it. Perhaps the most common form of implied ratification occurs when the minor, after attaining her majority, continues to use the property that she purchased as a minor. This use is obviously inconsistent with the nonexistence of the contract. Whether the contract is performed or still partly executory, the continued use of the property amounts to a ratification and prevents a disaffirmance by the minor. Simply keeping the goods for an unreasonable time after attaining majority has also been construed as a ratification. Although the courts are divided on this issue, payments by the minor upon reaching majority either on principal or interest or on the purchase price of goods have been held to amount to a ratification. Some courts require some additional evidence of an intention to abide by the contract, such as an express promise to that effect or the actual use of the subject matter of the contract.

Note that a minor has *no* power to ratify a contract while he remains a minor. A ratification *cannot* be based on words or conduct occurring while he is still underage, for his ratification at that time would be no more effective than his original contractual promise. The ratification must take place after the individual has acquired contractual capacity by attaining his majority.

Liability for Misrepresentation of Age

The States do not agree whether a minor who fraudulently misrepresents her age when entering into a contract has the power to disaffirm. Suppose a minor says that she is eighteen years of age (or twenty-one if that is the year of attaining majority) and actually looks that old or even older? By the prevailing view in this country, the minor may nevertheless disaffirm the contract. Some States, however, prohibit disaffirmance if a minor misrepresents her age and the adult, in good faith, reasonably relied on the misrepresentation. Other States, as indicated in *Halbman v. Lemke*, not following the majority rule either (a) require the minor to restore the other party to the position she occupied before making the contract, or (b) allow the defrauded party to recover damages against the minor in tort.

Liability for Tort Connected with Contract

It is well settled that minors are generally liable for their torts. There is, however, a doctrine in the law that if a tort and a contract are so connected or "interwoven" that to enforce the tort action the court must enforce the contract, the minor is not liable in tort. Thus, if a minor rents an automobile from an adult, he enters into a contractual relationship obliging him to exercise reasonable care and diligence to protect the property from injury. By negligently damaging the automobile, he breaches that contractual undertaking. But his contractual immunity protects him from an action by the adult based on the contract. Can the adult sue for damages on a tort theory? By the majority view he cannot. For, it is reasoned, a tort recovery would, in effect, be an enforcement of the contract and would defeat the protection that contract law gives the minor.

There is a different result, however, when the minor departs from the terms of the agreement, as by using a rental automobile for an unauthorized purpose and in so doing negligently causes damage to the automobile. In that event, most courts would hold that the tort is independent, and the adult can collect from the minor. This would not involve the breach of a contractual duty but rather the commission of a tort during the course of an activity that is a complete departure from the rental agreement.

INCOMPETENT PERSONS

In this section, we will discuss incompetent persons who are under court appointed guardianship and those who are not adjudicated incompetents.

Person under Guardianship

If a person is under **guardianship** by **court order,** her contracts are **void** and of no legal effect.[3] A *guardian* is appointed by a court, generally under the terms of a statute, to control and preserve the property of a person (the *ward*) with impaired capacity to manage her own property. Nonetheless, a party dealing with an individual under guardianship may be able to recover the fair value of any necessaries provided to the incompetent. Moreover, the contracts of the ward may be ratified by her guardian during the period of guardianship.

Mental Illness or Defect

Because a contract is a consensual transaction, the parties to a valid contract must have a certain level of mental capacity. If a person lacks such capacity, or is **mentally incompetent,** he may avoid liability under the agreement. A person who is lacking in sufficient mental capacity to enter into a contract is one unable to comprehend the subject of the contract, its nature, and its probable consequences.[4] He does not need to be proved permanently incompetent to avoid the contract, but his mental defect must be something more than a weakness of intellect or a lack of average intelligence. In short, a person is competent unless he, as in the following case, is unable to understand the nature and effect of his act.

As with minors and persons under guardianship, an incompetent person is liable for *necessaries* furnished on the principle of quasi contract, the amount of recovery being the reasonable value of the goods or services.

G.A.S. v. S.I.S.
Family Court of Delaware, New Castle County, 1978.
407 A.2d 253.

Facts: G.A.S. married his wife, S.I.S., on January 19, 1957. His mental health problems began in 1970 when he was hospitalized at the Delaware State Hospital for eight weeks. Similar illnesses occurred in 1972 and the early part of 1974, with G.A.S. suffering from such symptoms as paranoia and loss of a sense of reality. In early 1975 G.A.S. was still committed to the Delaware State Hospital, attending a regular job during the day and returning to the hospital at night. It was during this time that he entered into a separation agreement prepared by his wife's attorney. G.A.S., however, never spoke with the attorney about the contents of the agreement, nor did he read it prior to signing. Moreover, G.A.S. was not independently represented by counsel when he executed this agreement. G.A.S. brings this action to disaffirm the separation agreement.

Decision: Judgment for G.A.S. voiding the separation agreement.

Opinion: James, J. Only competent persons can make a contract, and where there is no capacity to understand or agree, there can be no contract. [Citations.]

Although petitioner was still under commitment to Delaware State Hospital at the time of execution of the separation agreement, he had not been judicially adjudicated mentally incompetent, and therefore the agreement is not void but may be voidable. [Citations.]

The mental incapacity sufficient to permit the cancellation of an agreement must render the afflicted individual incapable of understanding the nature and effect of the transaction. [Citation.] The court must determine whether his mental faculties have been impaired to such an extent that he is unable to properly, intelligently, and fairly protect and preserve his property rights. [Citation.]

At the time of the execution of the separation agreement not only was petitioner a diagnosed paranoid schizophrenic still receiving in-patient treatment, but he was also receiving significant amounts of "antipsychotic" medication. The only psychiatrist to testify, Dr. S., treated petitioner in February of 1978, and based his testimony upon direct knowledge of petitioner and a review of the existing medical records. Dr. S's opinion, based upon reasonable medical certainty, was that when petitioner executed the separation agreement on February 20, 1975, he would not have been fully able to understand or comprehend what he was signing nor the implications thereof.

* * *

Delaware courts have held that mental incapacity, resulting from the use of drugs, may furnish a ground for voiding a contract, [citation] however,

> [I]f no circumstances of unfairness, fraud, duress, or undue influence appear, the reasoning powers must be so impaired as to render the person actually incapable of comprehending and acting rationally in the particular transaction.

The facts of this case do not require this Court to make the extremely difficult decision as to whether petitioner was, in fact, incapable of comprehending and acting rationally in executing the separation agreement. For even if the mental weakness of the petitioner in this case did not rise to the level of contractual incapacity, such weakness is a circumstance that operates to make the separation agreement voidable when coupled with the evidence of lack of independent counsel, undue influence, and unfairness in the transaction that is present in this case.

Moreover, an incompetent person may *ratify* or *disaffirm* his **voidable** contracts when he becomes competent, or during a lucid period.

According to the predominant view in this country, an incompetent person's responsibility on disaffirmance varies somewhat from a minor's. If the contract is fair, and the competent party had no reason to suspect the incompetency of the other, the incompetent must restore the competent party to the *status quo* by a return of the consideration received by the incompetent or its equivalent in money.

INTOXICATED PERSONS

A person may *avoid* any contract that he enters into if the other party has reason to know that, because of intoxication, he is unable to understand the nature and consequences of his actions or unable to act in a reasonable manner.[5] Such contracts, as in the case that follows, are **voidable.** Although slight intoxication will not destroy one's contractual capacity, it is not essential that a person is so drunk that he is totally without reason or understanding.

 WILLIAMSON v. MATTHEWS
Supreme Court of Alabama, 1980.
379 So.2d 1245.

Facts: Williamson, her mortgage in default, was threatened with foreclosure on her home. She decided to sell the house. The Matthewses learned of this and contacted her about the matter. Williamson claims that she offered to sell her equity for $17,000, and that the Matthewses agreed to pay off the mortgage. The

Matthewses contend that the asking price was $1,700. On September 27, 1978, the parties signed a contract of sale, which stated the purchase price to be $1,800 ($100 increase regarding furniture in the house) plus the unpaid balance of the mortgage. The parties met again on October 10 to sign the deed. Later that day, Williamson, concerned that she had not received her full consideration contacted an attorney. On October 12 Williamson filed for injunctive relief, seeking to set aside the sale based upon inadequate consideration and mental weakness due to intoxication. Her petition was denied, and she appealed.

Decision: Judgment reversed and remanded.

Opinion: Per Curiam   Williamson contends that the "something else" in the case at bar is mental weakness, either due to some form of permanent mental incapacity or due to intoxication. . . . Williamson, however, is not contending that she was insane at the time of the contract, but rather is contending that she had a mental incapacity, which coupled with inadequacy of consideration requires the setting aside of the transaction.

Our rule in such a case is that a party cannot avoid, free from fraud or undue influence, a contract on the ground of mental incapacity, unless it be shown that the incapacity was of such a character that, at the time of execution, the person had no reasonable perception or understanding of the nature and terms of the contract. [Citation.]

Our rule regarding incapacity due to intoxication is much the same. The drunkenness of a party at the time of making a contract may render the contract voidable, but it does not render it void; and to render the contract voidable, it must be made to appear that the party was intoxicated to such a degree that he was, at the time of the contracting, incapable of exercising judgment, understanding the proposed engagement, and of knowing what he was about when he entered into the contract sought to be avoided. [Citation.] Proof merely that the party was drunk on the day the sale was executed does not per se show that he was without contractual capacity; there must be some evidence of a resultant condition indicative of that extreme impairment of the faculties which amounts to contractual incapacity. [Citation.]

The burden was therefore cast on Williamson to show, by clear and convincing evidence, that she was incapable, at the time of execution, of executing the contract for sale and of executing the deed. [Citation.]

We hold that Williamson met this burden.

* * *

Indulging the usual presumption due the trial court, we nevertheless hold that, under the facts of this case, it appears to us that Williamson was not, at the time of execution, capable of fully and completely understanding the nature and terms of the contract and of the deed. [Citation.] Williamson's contention that she was intoxicated supports this holding. Testimony was admitted from various witnesses to the effect that Williamson had a history of drinking, that she still had the problem at the time she executed the contract, and that she had in fact taken a couple of drinks before leaving for the meeting in attorney Arthur Cook's office. We do not hold that Williamson was so intoxicated as to render her incapable of contracting. However, numerous factors combine to warrant the conclusion that she was operating under diminished capacity. Testimony showed that Williamson's capacity to transact business was impaired, that she had a history of drinking, that she had been drinking the day she conducted negotiations, and that she had an apparent weakened will because she was pressured by the possibility of an impending foreclosure. Moreover, Williamson made complaint to an attorney only hours after the transaction. These factors are combined with a gross inadequacy of consideration. [The property was appraised twice, once at $16,500 and once at $19,500.]

The effect of intoxication on contractual capacity is generally the same as that given to contracts that are voidable because of incompetency. The options of *ratification* or *disaffirmance* remain, although the courts are even more strict with respect to the requirement of restitution on disaffirmance than they are in the area of an incompetent person's agreements. The rule is relaxed only where the person dealing with the intoxicated person fraudulently takes advantage of the intoxicated individual. As with incompetent persons, intoxicated persons are liable in quasi contract for necessaries furnished during their incapacity.

Figure 12–1 summarizes the effects of contracts made by persons with contractual incapacity.

FIGURE 12-1 Contractual Incapacity

Incapacity	Effect
Minority	Voidable
Mental illness or defect	Voidable
Guardianship for incompetency	Void
Intoxication	Voidable

CHAPTER SUMMARY

Minors	**Definition** a person who is under the age of majority (18 years)
	Liability for Necessaries a minor is liable for the reasonable value of necessary items (those needed to maintain a person's station in life)
	Liability on Contracts minor's contracts are voidable at the minor's option
	    ■ *Ratification* affirmation of the entire contract; may be done upon reaching majority
	    ■ *Disaffirmance* avoidance of the contract; may be done during minority and for a reasonable time after reaching majority
	Liability for Misrepresentation of Age prevailing view is that a minor may disaffirm the contract

	Liability for Tort Connected with Contract if a tort and a contract are so connected that to enforce the tort the court must enforce the contract, the minor is not liable in tort
Incompetent and Intoxicated Persons	**Person under Guardianship** contracts made by a person placed under guardianship by court order are void **Mental Illness or Defect** a contract entered into by a mentally incompetent person (one who is unable to understand the nature and consequences of his acts) is voidable **Intoxicated Persons** a contract entered into by an intoxicated person (one who cannot understand the nature and consequence of his actions) is voidable

QUESTIONS

1. Define a necessary and explain how it affects the contracts of a minor.
2. How and when may a minor ratify a contract?
3. What is the liability of a minor who disaffirms a contract?
4. Distinguish between the legal capacity of a person under guardianship and a mentally incompetent person who is not under guardianship.
5. What is the rule governing an intoxicated person's capacity to enter into a contract?

PROBLEMS

1. Mark, a minor, operates a one-man automobile repair shop. Rose, having heard of Mark's good work on other cars, takes her car to Mark's shop for a thorough engine overhaul. Mark, while overhauling Rose's engine, carelessly fits an unsuitable piston ring on one of the pistons, with the result that Rose's engine is seriously damaged. Mark offers to return the sum that Rose paid him for the work, but refuses to make good the damage. Rose sues Mark in tort for the damage to her engine. Decision?

2. (a) On March 20 Andy Small became seventeen years old, but he appeared to be at least eighteen (the age of majority). On April 1 he moved into a rooming house in Chicago and orally agreed to pay the landlady $300 a month for room and board, payable at the end of each month.
(b) On April 4 he went to Honest Hal's Car-feteria and signed a contract to buy a used car on time with a small down payment. He made no representation as to his age, but Honest Hal represented the car to

be in top condition, which it subsequently turned out not to be.
(c) On April 7 Andy sold and conveyed to Adam Smith a parcel of real estate that he owned.

On April 30 Andy refused to pay his landlady for his room and board for the month of April; he returned the car to Honest Hal and demanded a refund of his down payment; and he demanded that Adam Smith reconvey the land, although the purchase price, which Andy received in cash, had been spent in riotous living. Decisions as to each claim?

3. Jones, a minor, owned a 1989 automobile. She traded it to Stone for a 1990 car. Jones went on a three-week trip and found that the 1990 car was not as good as the 1989 car. She asked Stone to return the 1989 car but was told that it had been sold to Tate. Jones thereupon sued Tate for the return of the 1989 car. Decision?

4. On May 7 Roy, a minor, a resident of Smithton, purchased an automobile from Royal Motors, Inc., for $7,750 in cash. On the same day he bought a motor scooter from Marks, also a minor, for $750 and paid him in full. On June 5 two days before attaining his majority, Roy disaffirmed the contracts and offered to return the car and the motor scooter to the respective sellers. Royal Motors, Inc., and Marks each refused the offers. On June 16 Roy brought separate appropriate actions against Royal Motors, Inc., and Marks to recover the purchase price of the car and the motor scooter. By agreement on July 30, Royal Motors, Inc., accepted the automobile. Royal filed a counterclaim against Roy for the reasonable rental value of the car between June 5 and July 30. The car was not damaged during this period. Royal knew that Roy lived twenty-five miles from his place of employment in Smithton and that he would probably use the car, as he did, for transportation. De-

cision as to (a) Roy's action against Royal Motors, Inc., and its counterclaim against Roy; (b) Roy's action against Marks?

5. On October 1 George Jones, who was then a minor, entered into a contract with Johnson Motor Company, a dealer in automobiles, to buy a car for $7,600. He paid $1,100 down and agreed to make monthly payments thereafter of $325 each. Although he made the first payment on November 1, he failed to make any more payments. Jones was seventeen years old at the time he made the contract. He represented to the company that he was twenty-one years old because he was afraid that the company would not sell the car to him if it knew his real age. His appearance was that of a man of twenty-one years of age. On December 15 the company repossessed the car under the terms provided in the contract. At that time, the car had been damaged and was in need of repairs. On December 20 George Jones became of age and at once disaffirmed the contract and demanded the return of the $1,425 paid on the contract. When the company refused to do so, Jones brought an action to recover the $1,425, and the company set up a counterclaim for $1,500 for expenses to which it was put in repairing the car. Decision?

6. Rebecca entered into a written contract to sell certain real estate to Mary, a minor, for $80,000, payable $4,000 on the execution of the contract and $800 on the first day of each month thereafter until paid. Mary paid the $4,000 down payment and eight monthly installments before attaining her majority. Thereafter, Mary made two additional monthly payments and caused the contract to be recorded in the county where the real estate was located. Mary was then advised by her attorney that the contract was voidable. After being so advised, Mary immediately tendered the contract to Rebecca, together with a deed reconveying all of Mary's interest in the property to Rebecca. Also, Mary demanded that Rebecca return the money she had paid under the contract. Rebecca refused the tender and declined to repay any portion of the money paid to her by Mary. Mary then brought an action to cancel the contract and recover the amount paid to Rebecca. Decision?

7. Anita sold and delivered an automobile to Marvin, a minor. Marvin, during his minority, returned the automobile to Anita, saying that he disaffirmed the sale. Anita accepted the automobile and said she would return the purchase price to Marvin the next day. Later in the day, Marvin changed his mind, took the automobile without Anita's knowledge, and sold it to Chris. Anita had not returned the

purchase price when Marvin took the car. On what theory, if any, can Anita recover from Marvin? Explain.

8. Ira, who in 1989 had been found innocent of a criminal offense because of insanity, was released from the hospital for the criminally insane during the summer of 1990 and since that time has been a reputable and well-respected citizen and businessman. On February 1, 1991, Ira and Shirley entered into a contract in which Ira would sell his farm to Shirley for $100,000. Ira seeks to void the contract. Shirley insists that Ira is fully competent and has no right to avoid the contract. Who will prevail? Why?

9. Daniel, while under the influence of alcohol, agreed to sell his 1988 automobile to Belinda for $8,000. The next morning when Belinda went to Daniel's house with the $8,000 in cash, Daniel stated that he did not remember the transaction but "a deal is a deal." One week after completing the sale, Daniel decides that he wishes to avoid the contract. What result?

10. On June 11, 1964, Chagnon bought a 1959 Edsel from Keser for $995. Chagnon, who was then a twenty-year-old minor, obtained the contract by falsely advising Keser that he was over twenty-one years old, the age of majority. On September 25, 1964, two months and four days after his twenty-first birthday, Chagnon disaffirmed the contract and, ten days later, returned the Edsel to Keser. He then brought suit to recover the money he had paid for the automobile. Keser counterclaims that he suffered damages as the direct result of Chagnon's false representation as to his age. Decision?

COMPUTER RESEARCH PROBLEMS

1. Rose, a minor, bought a new Buick Riviera from Sheehan Buick. Seven months later, while still a minor, he attempted to disaffirm the purchase. Sheehan Buick refused to accept the return of the car or to refund the purchase price. Rose, at the time of the purchase, gave all the appearance of being of legal age. The car had been used by him to carry on his school, business, and social activities. Decision?

2. L. D. Robertson bought a pickup truck from King and Julian, doing business as the Julian Pontiac Company. Robertson, at the time of purchase was seventeen years old, living at home with his parents, and driving his father's truck around the county to different construction jobs. According to the sales contract, he traded in a passenger car for

the truck and was given $723 credit toward the truck's $1,743 purchase price, agreeing to pay the remainder in monthly installments. After he paid the first month's installment, the truck caught fire and was rendered useless. The insurance agent, upon finding that Robertson was a minor, refused to deal with him. Consequently, Robertson sued to exercise his right as a minor to rescind the contract and to recover the purchase price he had already paid ($723 credit for the car plus the one month's installment). The defendants argue that Robertson, even as a minor, cannot rescind the contract since it was for a necessary item. Decision?

3. Haydocy Pontiac sold Jennifer Lee an automobile for $1,552, of which $1,402 was financed with a note and security agreement. At the time of the sale Lee, age 20, represented to Haydocy that she was 21 years old, the age of majority, and capable of contracting. After receiving the car, Lee allowed John Roberts to take possession of it. Roberts took the car and has not returned. Lee has failed to make any further payments on the car. Haydocy has sued to recover on the note. Lee disaffirms the contract claiming that she was too young to enter into a valid contract. Decision?

4. Carol White ordered a $225.00 pair of contact lenses through an optometrist. White, an emancipated minor, paid $100.00 by check and agreed to pay the remaining $125.00 at a later time. The doctor ordered the lenses incurring an indebtedness of $110.00. After the lenses were ordered, White called to cancel her order and stopped payment on the $100.00 check. The lenses could be used by no one but White. The doctor sued White for the value of the lenses. Decision?

ENDNOTES

1. Restatement, Second, Contracts, Section 12, Capacity to Contract.
2. Uniform Commercial Code, Section 2—403, Power to Transfer.
3. Restatement, Second, Contracts, Section 13, Persons Affected by Guardianship.
4. Restatement, Second, Contracts, Section 15, Mental Illness or Defect.
5. Restatement, Second, Contracts, Section 16, Intoxicated Persons.

13 CONTRACTS IN WRITING

An **oral** contract, that is, one not in writing, is in every way as enforceable as a written contract unless otherwise provided by statute. Although most contracts do not need to be in writing to be enforceable, it is highly desirable that significant contracts be written. Written contracts avoid many problems inevitably involved in proving the terms of oral contracts. The process of setting down the contractual terms in a written document also tends to clarify the terms and bring to light a number of problems the parties might not otherwise foresee. Moreover, the terms of a written contract do not change over time, whereas the parties' recollections of the terms might.

When the parties do reduce their agreement to a complete and final written expression, the law (the parol evidence rule) honors this document by not allowing the parties to introduce any evidence in a lawsuit that would alter, modify, or vary the terms of the written contract. Nevertheless, the parties may differ as to the proper or intended meaning of language contained in the written agreement where such language is ambiguous or susceptible to different interpretations. To determine the proper meaning requires an interpretation, or construction, of the contract. The rules of construction permit the parties to introduce evidence to resolve ambiguity and to show the meaning of the language employed and the sense in which both parties used it.

In this chapter we examine (1) the types of contracts that must be in writing to be enforceable, (2) the parol evidence rule, and (3) the rules of contractual interpretation.

STATUTE OF FRAUDS

The **statute of frauds** requires that certain designated types of contracts be in a particular form to be enforceable. The original statute became law in 1677 when the English Parliament adopted "An Act for Prevention of Frauds and Perjuries," commonly referred to as the statute of frauds. From the early days of American history practically every State had and continues to have a statute of frauds patterned on the original English statute.

The statute of frauds has no relation whatever to any kind of fraud practiced in the making of contracts. The rules relating to such fraud are rules of common law and are discussed in Chapter 9. For example, Adam claims that Brenda fraudulently misrepresented a material fact and thereby induced Adam to make a certain contract. Adam cannot rely upon the statute of frauds in support of his claim. It has been frequently stated that the word "frauds" in the title of this statute is misleading. The purpose of the statute is to prevent fraud in the proof of certain oral contracts by perjured testimony in court. This purpose is accomplished by the requirement that certain contracts be proved by a signed writing. On the other hand, the statute does not prevent the performance of oral contracts if the parties are willing to perform. In brief, the statute relates only to the proof or evidence of a contract. It has nothing to do with the circumstances surrounding the making of a contract or with the validity of a contract.

CONTRACTS WITHIN THE STATUTE OF FRAUDS

Many more types of contracts are not subject to the statute of frauds than are subject to it. Most oral contracts, as previously indicated, are as enforceable and valid as a written contract. If, however, a given contract is subject to the statute of frauds, the contract is said to be *within* the statute, and to be enforceable it must comply with the requirements of the statute. All other types of contracts are said to be "not within" or "outside" the statute and need not comply with its requirements to be enforceable.

The following five kinds of contracts are within the original English statute and remain within most State statutes.[1] Compliance requires a writing signed by the party to be charged (the party seeking to avoid the contract).

1. Promises to answer for the duty of another,
2. Promises of an executor or administrator to answer personally for a duty of the decedent whose funds he is administering,
3. Agreements upon consideration of marriage,
4. Agreements for the sale of an interest in land, and
5. Agreements not to be performed within one year.

A sixth type of contract within the statute applied to contracts for the sale of goods. The Uniform Commercial Code now governs the enforceability of contracts of this kind.[2]

In addition to those contracts specified in the original statute, some modern statutes require that others be written. Examples are a contract to make a will, to authorize an agent to sell real estate, or to pay a commission to a real estate broker. Moreover, the UCC requires that a contract for the sale of securities[3] and contracts creating certain types of security interests be in writing.[4]

Suretyship Provision

The **suretyship** provision applies to a contractual promise by a **surety** (*promisor*) to a **creditor** (*promisee*) to perform the duties or obligations of a third person (**principal debtor**) if the principal debtor does not perform. Thus, if a mother tells a merchant to extend $1,000 worth of credit to her son and says, "If he doesn't pay, I will," the promise must be in writing to be enforceable. The factual situation can be reduced to the simple "If X doesn't pay, I will." The promise is said to be a **collateral promise,** in that the promisor is not the one who is primarily liable. The mother does not promise to pay in any event; her promise is to pay only if the one primarily obligated, the son, defaults.

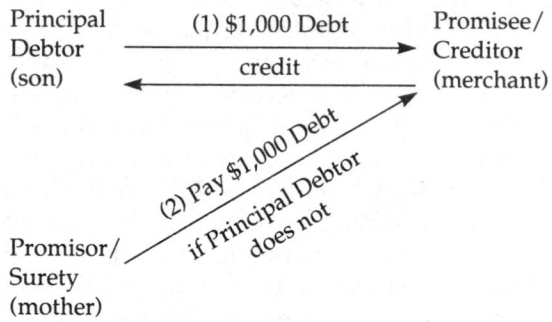

The rule applies only to cases where three parties and two contracts are involved. The primary contract is between the principal debtor and the creditor and creates the indebtedness. The collateral contract is made by the third person (surety) directly with the creditor, whereby she promises to pay the debt to the creditor in case the principal debtor (son) fails to do so. For a complete discussion of suretyship see Chapter 38.

Original Promise If the promisor makes an **original promise** by undertaking to become primarily liable, then the statute of frauds does not apply. For example, a father tells a merchant to deliver certain items to his daughter and says, "I will pay $400 for them." The father is not promising to answer for the debt of another, but rather he is making the debt his own. It is to the father, and to the father alone, that the merchant extends credit and may look for payment. The statute of frauds does not apply, and the promise may be oral.

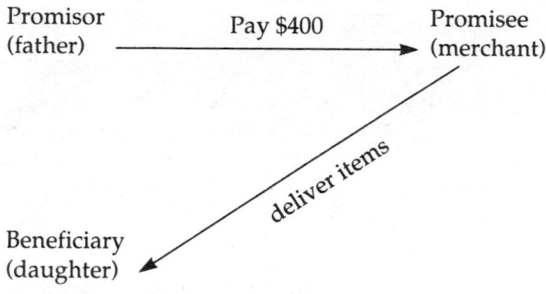

Promisor (father) — Pay $400 → Promisee (merchant)

deliver items

Beneficiary (daughter)

The following case further illustrates the distinction.

Main Purpose Doctrine   The courts have developed an exception to the suretyship provision based on the purpose or object of the promisor, called the "main purpose doctrine" or "leading object rule." Where the object of the promisor is to obtain an economic benefit that he did not previously have, the promise is *not* within the statute.[5] The expected benefit to the surety "must be such as to justify the conclusion that his main purpose in making the promise is to advance his own interest."[6]

SHANE QUADRI v. GOODYEAR SERVICE STORES
Court of Appeals of Indiana, Third District, 1980.
412 N.E.2d 315.

Facts: The defendant, Shane Quadri, contacted Don Hoffman, an employee of defendant Al J. Hoffman & Co., to procure car insurance. Later, Quadri's car was stolen on October 25 or 26, 1977. Quadri contacted Hoffman who arranged with Budget Rent-a-Car, a plaintiff in this case, for a rental car for Quadri until his car was recovered. Hoffman authorized Budget Rent-a-Car to bill the Hoffman Agency. Later, when the stolen car was recovered, Hoffman telephoned plaintiff, Goodyear, and arranged to have four new tires put on Quadri's car to replace those damaged during the theft. The plaintiffs (Budget and Goodyear) sued the defendants (Quadri and Hoffman) for payment for the car rental and tires. Judgment was entered in favor of Budget and Goodyear against the defendant Hoffman but in favor of Quadri.

Decision: Judgment for Budget and Goodyear against Hoffman and judgment for Quadri affirmed.

Opinion: **Hoffman, J.**   The Hoffman Agency's liability must be based on Don Hoffman's oral promises. The Hoffman Agency asserts that these promises are promises to pay the debts of Shane Quadri and are therefore made unenforceable by the Statute of Frauds. [Citation.]

The Hoffman Agency is correct in the theoretical statement of the law but errs in its application in this case. Although the statute makes unenforceable contracts to pay the debts of a third person, it does not affect the enforceability of oral contracts between two parties for the benefit of a third party. [Citation.] The statute therefore does not apply to original promises to pay for services rendered to a third person. [Citation.] The evidence in the present case is clear that Don Hoffman made original promises to both Budget and Goodyear that the Hoffman Agency would pay for goods and services rendered to Quadri.

* * *

The evidence discloses that Don Hoffman initiated the transactions with both Goodyear and Budget through a telephone call. Hoffman indicated that Quadri was insured and authorized the billing of the Hoffman Agency. Hoffman also gave both Goodyear and Budget a claim number to use in their records. Quadri merely went to Goodyear and Budget to obtain the benefits as negotiated by Hoffman. Although

Quadri's signature appears on the Budget rental agreement and the Goodyear invoice, both documents indicate that Don Hoffman authorized the transaction. Based on this evidence it cannot be said that the trial court erred in determining that credit was extended solely to the Hoffman Agency. Don Hoffman's oral promises are not within the Statute of Frauds.

The fact that the surety received consideration for his promise or that he might receive a slight and indirect advantage is insufficient to bring the promise within the main purpose doctrine.

Suppose that a supply company has refused to furnish materials on the credit of a building contractor. Faced with a possible slowdown in construction of his building, the owner of the land promises the supplier that if he will extend credit to the contractor, the owner will pay if the contractor does not. Here, the purpose of the promisor was to serve an economic interest of his own, even though the performance of the promise would discharge the duty of another. The intent to benefit the contractor was at most incidental, and courts will uphold oral promises of this type. Another application of the rule is provided in the following case.

STUART STUDIO, INC. v. NATIONAL SCHOOL OF HEAVY EQUIPMENT, INC.

Court of Appeals of North Carolina, 1975.
25 N.C.App. 544, 214 S.E.2d N.C. 192.

Facts: Stuart Studios, an art studio, prepared a new catalog for a school run by Gilbert and Donald Shaw. When the artwork was virtually finished, Gilbert Shaw requested Stuart Studios to purchase and supervise the printing of 25,000 catalogs. Shaw told the art studio that payment of the printing costs would be made within ten days after billing and that if the "National School would not pay the full total that he would stand good for the entire bill." Shaw was chairman of the board of directors of the school, and he owned 100 percent of its voting stock and 49 percent of its nonvoting stock. The school became bankrupt, and Stuart Studios was unable to recover the sum from the school. Stuart Studios then brought this action against Shaw on the basis of his promise to pay the bill. The trial court granted Shaw's motion for a directed verdict and Stuart Studios brought this appeal.

Decision: Judgment granting defendant's motion for directed verdict modified and remanded for trial on the issue of the liability of Shaw.

Opinion: Clark, J.   The North Carolina Statute of Frauds, a substantial prototype of the historic English statute [citation] contains the provision that "no action shall be brought * * * upon a special promise to answer the debt * * * of another person, unless the agreement upon which such action shall be brought, or some memorandum or note thereof, shall be in writing, and signed by the party charged therewith or some other person thereunto by him lawfully authorized." [Citations.]

The promise of Gilbert S. Shaw to stand good for the debt of National School of Heavy Equipment, Inc., to be incurred for the printing of catalogues was not in writing and was within the Statute of Frauds unless plaintiff has offered evidence to invoke the application of the "main purpose rule", which is a well-known exception to the rule requiring that such promises be evidenced by a written memorandum.

The "main purpose rule" is * * * as follows:

* * * [W]henever the main purpose and object of the promisor is not to answer for another, but to subserve some pecuniary or business purpose of his own, involving either a benefit to himself, or damage to the other contracting party, his promise is not within the statute, although it may be in form a promise to pay the debt of another, and although the performance of it may incidentally have the effect of extinguishing that liability. * * *

Shaw's personal and pecuniary interest in the transaction was evident; he was the founder of the School, owned 100% of the Class A voting stock and 49% of the Class B stock, was Chairman of the Board of Directors, and as an officer drew a monthly salary of $2,000. At this time, 6 March 1972, it is reasonable to assume that the School was facing financial difficulty; Shaw personally advanced $12,000 to the School during this period of financial distress. The School went into receivership in December 1972, and bankruptcy in March 1973. Apparently, Shaw sought, in a final effort to avoid the School's financial ruin, to attract new students through an advertising campaign, which included the production and circulation of new catalogues.

Burlington Industries v. Foil, [citation] a 1974 decision, culminates a line of cases which have developed the "main purpose rule" and prescribed its limitations. The *Foil* case holds that the benefit accruing to a party merely by virtue of his position as a stockholder, officer, or director is not alone such personal, immediate and pecuniary benefit as to invoke the main purpose rule, and that Foil's evidence failed to establish the required *direct interest* on the part of Foil.

In *Foil*, the Court cited with approval the cases of May v. Haynes, [citation] and Warren v. White, [citation.] In Warren v. White, defendant promisor was the principal investor and owned most of the capital stock, and during a period of financial difficulty advanced in excess of $20,000 to the corporation. In May v. Haynes, the defendant and his wife owned the entire capital stock of the corporation, and he was its president, managing officer and controlling stock-holder. In both of these cases it was held that the evidence was sufficient to invoke the main purpose rule and in doing so it is obvious that the significant, if not controlling, factor was the extent of the promisor's control over the corporation.

In this case the evidence offered by the plaintiff tends to show that Gilbert S. Shaw had a personal and direct interest in the School; and the evidence is clearly sufficient to raise an issue for jury determination.

Promise Made to Debtor   The statute has been interpreted *not* to include promises made to a *debtor*. For example, D owes a debt to C. S promises D to pay her debt. Since the promise of S was made to the debtor, not the creditor, the promise may be oral. (See diagram to the right.)

Executor-Administrator Provision

The executor-administrator provision applies to promises of an executor of a decedent's will,

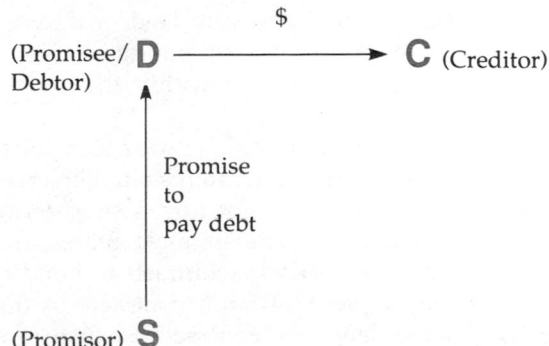

or the administrator of the estate if there is no will, to answer personally for a duty of the decedent.[7] An **executor** or **administrator** is a person appointed by a court to carry on the administration of the estate of a deceased person. If the will of a decedent nominates a certain person as executor, the court usually appoints that person. For a more detailed discussion of executors and administrators and their differences see Chapter 51. If an executor or administrator promises to answer personally for a duty of the decedent, the promise is unenforceable unless in writing. For example, Edgar, who is Donna's son and executor of Donna's will, recognizes that Donna's estate will not have enough funds to pay all of the decedent's debts. He orally promises Clark, one of Donna's creditors, that he will personally pay all of his mother's debts in full. Edgar's oral promise is not enforceable.

Marriage Provision

The notable feature of the marriage provision is that it does *not* apply to mutual promises to marry. The provision applies only if a promise to marry is made in consideration for some promise other than a mutual promise to marry.[8] Therefore, this provision covers the ordinary "marriage settlement," as for example, where a man promises a woman to convey title to a certain farm to her if she accepts his proposal of marriage.

Land Contract Provision

The land contract provision covers promises to transfer any **interest in land,** which includes any right, privilege, power, or immunity in real property.[9] Thus, all promises to transfer, buy, or pay for an interest in land, including ownership interests, leases, mortgages, options, and easements, are within the provision.

The land contract provision does not include contracts to transfer an interest in personal property. It also does not cover short-term leases, which by statute in most States are those for one year or less; contracts to build a building on a piece of land; contracts to do work on the land; or contracts to insure a building.

An oral contract for the transfer of an interest in land may be enforced if the party seeking enforcement has so changed his position in reasonable reliance on the contract that injustice can be prevented only by enforcing the contract.[10] In applying this **part performance** exception, most States require that the transferee have paid a portion or all of the purchase price *and* either have taken possession of the real estate or have started to make valuable improvements on the land. Payment of part or all of the price is not sufficient itself to take the contract outside of the statute under this exception. For example, Jane orally agrees to sell land to Jack for $30,000. With Jane's consent, Jack takes possession of the land, pays Jane $10,000, builds a house on the land, and occupies it. Several years later, Jane repudiates the contract. The courts will enforce the contract against Jane. On the other hand, courts will not enforce the promise unless equity so demands.

One-Year Provision

The statute requires that all contracts that **cannot** be fully performed within one year of the making of the contract be in writing.[11]

The Possibility Test The test to determine whether a contract can be performed within a year is whether it is *possible* for its performance to be completed within a year. The **possibility test** is not whether the agreement is likely to be performed within one year from the date it was formed nor whether the parties think that performance will be within the year. The enforceability of the contract does *not* depend on probabilities or on the actuality of subsequent events. For example, an oral contract between Alice and Bill for Alice to build a bridge, which should reasonably take three years, is enforceable if it is possible, although extremely unlikely and difficult, for Alice to perform the contract in one year. Similarly, if Alice agrees to employ Bill for life, the contract is not within the statute of frauds. It is possible that Bill may die within the year, in which case the contract would be completely performed. The contract is therefore one that is *fully performable* within a year. On the other hand, an oral contract to employ another person for thirteen months could not possibly be performed within a year and is unenforceable.

Computation of Time   The year runs from the time the *agreement is made*, not from the time when the performance is to begin. For example, on January 1, 1989, A hires B to work for eleven months starting on May 1, 1989, under the terms of an oral contract. That contract will be fully performed on March 31, 1990, which is more than one year after January 1, 1989, the date the contract was made. Consequently, it is *within* the statute of frauds and unenforceable because it is oral.

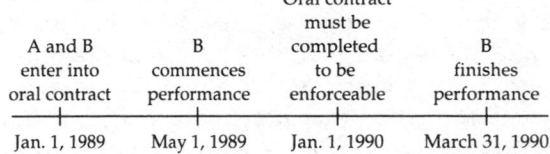

A and B enter into oral contract	B commences performance	Oral contract must be completed to be enforceable	B finishes performance
Jan. 1, 1989	May 1, 1989	Jan. 1, 1990	March 31, 1990

Similarly, a contract for a year's performance that is to begin three days after the date of the making of the contract is within the statute and, if oral, is unenforceable. If, however, the performance is to begin the following day or under the terms of the agreement *could* have begun the following day, it is not within the statute and need not be in writing.

 CO-OP DAIRY, INC. v. DEAN
Supreme Court of Arizona, 1968.
102 Ariz. 573, 435 P.2d 470.

Facts: Dean was hired on February 12, 1962, as a sales manager of the Co-op Dairy for a minimum period of one year with the dairy agreeing to pay his moving expenses. By February 26, 1962, Dean had signed a lease, moved his family from Oklahoma to Arizona, and reported for work. After he worked for a few days, he was fired. Dean then brought this action against the dairy for his salary for the year, less what he was paid. The dairy argues that enforcement of the oral contract is barred by the statute of frauds because the contract was not to be performed within one year. A jury verdict was entered in favor of Dean.

Decision: Judgment for Dean affirmed.

Opinion: **McFarland, J.**   One principle that generally has been upheld is that the words "not to be performed within one year" mean *"impossible to be performed within one year."*

"In its actual application, however, the courts have been perhaps even less friendly to this provision than to the other provisions of the statute. * * * In general, the cases indicate that there must not be the *slightest possibility* that it can be fully performed within one year. It makes no difference how long the agreed performance may be delayed or over how long a period it may in fact be continued. It makes no difference how long the parties expect performance to take, or how reasonable and accurate those expectations are, if the agreed performance can *possibly* be completed within one year." [Citations.]

* * *

We are inclined to agree with the court in Farmer v. Arabian American Oil Company, [citation] in which it said that the Statute of Frauds, applied to an employment contract, "is an anachronism in modern life and we are not disposed to expand its destructive force." We therefore hold that there was nothing to prevent Dean from turning over the moving details to his wife and going to work the next day. Had he done so, the Statute of Frauds would not be applicable. Though he did not do so, the mere fact that he could have done so takes the contract out of the Statute of Frauds.

Full Performance by One Party Where a contract has been fully performed by one party, most courts hold that the promise of the other party is enforceable even though by its terms its performance was not possible within the period of a year.[11] For example, Jane borrows $4,800 from Tom. Jane orally promises to pay Tom $4,800 in three annual installments of $1,600. Jane's promise is enforceable, notwithstanding the one-year provision, because Tom has fully performed by making the loan.

Sales of Goods

The English statute of frauds applied to contracts for the sale of goods and has been used as a prototype for the UCC, Article 2, statute of frauds provision.[2] The UCC provides that a contract for the sale of goods for the price of **$500 or more** is not enforceable unless there is some writing sufficient to indicate that a contract for sale has been made between the parties. **Goods** are movable personal property and include growing crops and unborn animals.[12]

A summary of the contracts within and the exceptions to the statute of frauds is provided in Figure 13–1.

Modification or Rescission of Contracts within the Statute of Frauds

Oral contracts modifying previously existing contracts are unenforceable if the resulting contract is within the statute of frauds. The reverse is also true: an oral modification of a prior contract is enforceable if the new contract is not within the statute of frauds.

Thus, examples of unenforceable oral contracts include an oral promise to guarantee additional duties of another, an oral agreement to substitute different land for that described in the original contract, and an oral agreement to extend an employee's contract for six months to a total of two years. On the other hand, an oral agreement to modify an employee's contract from two years to six months at a higher salary is not within the statute of frauds and is enforceable.

By extension, an oral rescission is effective and discharges all unperformed duties under the original contract. For example, Jones and Brown enter into a written contract of employment for a two-year term. Later they orally agree to rescind the contract. The oral agreement is effective and the written contract is rescinded. Where land has been transferred, however, an agreement to rescind the transac-

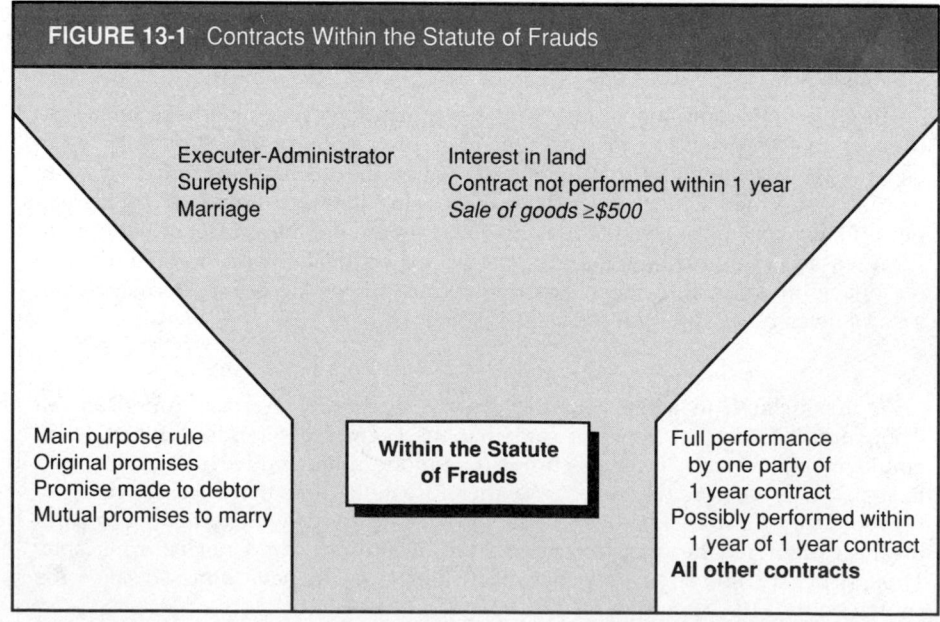

FIGURE 13-1 Contracts Within the Statute of Frauds

Executer-Administrator
Suretyship
Marriage

Interest in land
Contract not performed within 1 year
Sale of goods ≥$500

Main purpose rule
Original promises
Promise made to debtor
Mutual promises to marry

Within the Statute of Frauds

Full performance
by one party of
1 year contract
Possibly performed within
1 year of 1 year contract
All other contracts

tion is a contract to retransfer the land and is within the statute of frauds.

Under the UCC, if the parties enter into an oral contract to sell a motorcycle for $450 to be delivered to the buyer and later, prior to delivery, orally agree that the seller shall paint the motorcycle and install new tires and the buyer shall pay a price of $550, the modified contract is unenforceable. Conversely, if the parties have a written contract for the sale of 200 bushels of wheat at a price of $4 per bushel and later orally agree to decrease the quantity to 100 bushels at the same price per bushel, the agreement as modified is for a total price of $400 and thus is enforceable.[13]

Figure 13–2 summarizes the enforceability of modifications to contracts.

METHODS OF COMPLIANCE

The most common way to satisfy the statute of frauds is for the parties to enter into a written agreement; nevertheless, there are several other methods by which the parties may comply with the statutory requirements.

A Writing or Memorandum

The writing need not be in any specific form nor be an attempt by the parties to enter into a binding contract nor represent the entire agreement of the parties. The writing must merely comply with the requirements of the statute of frauds.

FIGURE 13-2 Modification of Contracts

Original Contract	Modification/ Rescission	New Contract	Result
2 year oral employment contract	*Oral:* Shorten contract by 1.5 years, increase salary	Employment contract for 6 months	Modification and new contract are binding, original contract was not binding
2 year written employment contract	*Oral:* Rescission of contract	None	Rescission of written employment contract is effective
Sale of land	*Oral:* Rescission of contract	Retransfer of land	Rescission of original contract must be in writing to be enforceable
$450 for motorcycle	*Oral:* $100 for new tires and paint job	$550 for motorcycle with new tires and paint job	Modification must be in writing to be enforceable
Written: $800 for 200 bushels of wheat ($4.00/ bushel)	*Oral:* Decrease contract by 100 bushels ($4.00/ bushel)	$400 for 100 bushels of wheat ($4.00/ bushel)	Modification and new contract are binding

General Contract Provisions The English statute of frauds and most modern statutes of frauds require that the agreement be in writing to be enforceable. The statute's purpose in requiring a writing is to make sure that the parties have actually entered into a contract. Therefore, the writing or memorandums must:

1. be signed by the party to be charged or by her agent;
2. specify the parties to the contract; and
3. specify with reasonable certainty the subject matter and the essential terms of the unperformed promises.

The note or memorandum may be formal or informal; all that is necessary is that it contain the required information and be signed by the party to be charged (the person seeking to avoid the contract). The "signature" may be by initials or even typewritten or printed so long as the party intended it to authenticate the writing. Furthermore, the "signature" need not be at the bottom of the page or at the customary place for a signature.

The memorandum may be such that the parties view it as having no legal significance whatever. For example, a personal letter between the parties, an interdepartmental communication, an advertisement, or the record books of a business may serve as a memorandum. The writing need not have been delivered to the party who seeks to take advantage of it, and it may even contain a repudiation of the oral agreement. For example, Sid and Gail enter into an oral agreement that Sid will sell Blackacre to Gail for $5,000. Sid subsequently receives a better offer and sends Gail a signed letter, which begins by reciting all the material terms of the oral agreement. The letter concludes: "Since my agreement to sell Blackacre to you for $5,000 was oral, I am not bound by my promise. I have since received a better offer and will accept that one." Sid's letter constitutes a sufficient memorandum for Gail to enforce Sid's promise to sell Blackacre. Because Gail did not sign the memorandum, however, the writing does not bind her. Thus a contract may be enforceable against only one of the parties.

The memorandum may consist of *several* papers or documents, none of which would be sufficient by itself. The several memoranda, however, must together satisfy all of the requirements of a writing to comply with the statute of frauds and must clearly indicate that they relate to the same transaction.[14]

UCC Provisions The statute of frauds provision under Article 2 (Sales) of the UCC is more liberal. For a sale of goods the Code, as evidenced in *Alice v. Robett Manufacturing Co.*, requires merely some writing (a) sufficient to indicate that a contract has been made between the parties; (b) signed by the party against whom enforcement is sought or by her authorized agent; and (c) specifying the **quantity** of goods to be sold.[2] The writing is sufficient even if it omits or incorrectly states a term agreed on, but where the quantity term is misstated the contract can be enforced only to the extent of the quantity stated in the writing.

 ALICE v. ROBETT MANUFACTURING CO.
United States District Court, District of Georgia, 1970.
328 F.Supp. 1377.

Facts: Alice solicited an offer from Robett Manufacturing Company to manufacture certain clothing that Alice intended to supply to the government. Alice contends that in a telephone conversation Robett made an oral offer that he immediately accepted. He then received the following letter from Robett, which, he claims confirmed their agreement:

Confirming our telephone conversation, we are pleased to offer the 3,500 shirts at $4.00 each and the trousers at $3.80 each with delivery approximately ninety days after receipt of order. We will try to cut this to sixty days if at all possible.

This, of course, as quoted f.o.b. Atlanta and the order will not be subject to cancellation, domestic pack only.

Thanking you for the opportunity to offer these garments, we are

Very truly yours,

ROBETT MANUFACTURING CO., INC.

Alice sued to enforce this agreement and Robett moved for summary judgment.

Decision: Summary judgment granted for Robett Manufacturing Company.

Opinion: **Smith, C. J.** In order to recover * * * [the] memorandum would have to satisfy the statute of frauds, since the alleged transaction involved a sale of goods for more than $500.

Under Georgia law prior to the adoption of the Uniform Commercial Code, a writing was not sufficient to comply with the requirements of the statute of frauds unless it contained *all* the terms of the agreement. [Citations.] It is clear, however, that Ga. Code [U.C.C., Section] 2–201 (1962) changes that rule of law.

The changed phraseology of this section is intended to make it clear that:

1. The required writing need not contain all the material terms of the contract and such material terms as are stated need not be precisely stated. All that is required is that the writing afford a basis for believing that the offered oral evidence rests on a real transaction. It may be written in lead pencil on a scratch pad. It need not indicate which party is the buyer and which the seller. The only term which must appear is the quantity term which need not be accurately stated but recovery is limited to the amount stated. The price, time, and place of payment or delivery, the general quality of the goods, or any particular warranties may all be omitted.

* * *

Only three definite and invariable requirements as to the memorandum are made by this subsection. First, it must evidence a contract for the sale of goods; second, it must be "signed," a word which includes any authentication which identifies the party to be charged; and third, it must specify a quantity. U.C.C. § 2–201, Comment 1.

The courts of other states have given effect to the changes which this Comment states were intended. [Citation.]

But it does not appear that the letter upon which the plaintiff must rely is a sufficient memorandum to satisfy even the minimal requirements of * * * § 2–201.

* * *

Although it is not signed, the defendant admits its authenticity. Nevertheless, it does not evidence a contract for the sale of goods but very clearly is only an offer.

As with general contracts, several related documents may satisfy the writing requirement. Moreover, the "signature" may be by initials or even typewritten or printed, so long as the party intended to authenticate the writing.

Other Methods of Compliance Under the UCC

An oral contract for the *sale of goods* is enforceable in the following instances.

Written Confirmation The Code provides relief to a merchant who, within a reasonable period of time after entering into the oral contract, confirms the agreement for the sale of goods by letter or signed writing to the other party if he too is a merchant. As between merchants, a written confirmation that is sufficient against the sender is also sufficient against the recipient of the confirmation unless the recipient gives written notice of his objection within ten days after receiving the confirmation.[2]

For example, Brown Co. and ATM Industries enter into an oral contract which provides that ATM will deliver 1,000 dozen shirts to Brown at $6 per shirt. Brown sends a letter to ATM acknowledging the agreement. The letter is signed by Brown's president, contains the quantity term but not the price, and is mailed to ATM's vice president for sales. Brown is bound by the contract once its authorized agent signed the letter, while ATM is bound by the oral contract ten days after receiving the letter if it does not object within that time period. Therefore, as further illustrated by the following case, merchants should examine written confirmations carefully and promptly to make certain that they are accurate.

THOMSON PRINTING MACHINERY CO. v. B. F. GOODRICH CO.
United States Court of Appeals, Seventh Circuit, 1983.
714 F.2d 744.

Facts: Thomson Printing Company is a buyer and seller of used machinery. On April 10, 1979, the president of the company, James Thomson, went to the surplus machinery department of B. F. Goodrich Company in Akron, Ohio, to examine some used equipment that was for sale. Thomson discussed the sale, including a price of $9,000, with Ingram Meyers, a Goodrich employee and agent. Four days later, on April 14, Thomson sent a purchase order to confirm the oral contract for purchase of the machinery and a partial payment of $1,000 to Goodrich in Akron. The purchase order contained Thomson Printing's name, address, and telephone number, as well as certain information about the purchase, but did not specifically mention Meyers or the surplus equipment department. Goodrich sent copies of the documents to a number of its divisions, but Meyers never learned of the confirmation until weeks later, by which time the equipment had been sold to another party. Thomson Printing brought suit against Goodrich for breach of contract. Goodrich claimed that no contract had existed and that at any rate the alleged oral contract could not be enforced because of the statute of frauds. The district court found the contract unenforceable, and Thomson Printing appealed.

Decision: District court's order granting judgment in favor of Goodrich reversed and the cause remanded for trial consistent with this opinion.

Opinion: **Cudahy, J.** A modern exception to the usual writing requirement is the "merchants" exception to the Uniform Commercial Code (U.C.C. § 2–201(2)), which provides:

> Between merchants if within a reasonable time a writing in confirmation of the contract and sufficient against the sender is received and the party receiving it has reason to know its contents, it satisfies the [writing requirement] against such party unless written notice of objection to its contents is given within 10 days after it is received.

We must emphasize that the only effect of this exception is to take away from a merchant who receives a writing in confirmation of a contract the Statute of Frauds defense if the merchant does not object. The sender must still persuade the trier of fact that a contract was in fact made orally, to which the written confirmation applies.

In the instant case, James Thomson sent a "writing in confirmation" to Goodrich four days after his meeting with Ingram Meyers, a Goodrich employee and agent. The purchase order contained Thomson Printing's name, address, telephone number and certain information about the machinery purchase. . . .

Goodrich argues, however, that Thomson's writing in confirmation cannot qualify for the 2–201(2) exception because it was not received by anyone at Goodrich who had reason to know its contents. Goodrich claims that Thomson erred in not specifically designating on the envelope, check or purchase order that the items were intended for Ingram Meyers or the surplus equipment department. Consequently, Goodrich contends, it was unable to "find a home" for the check and purchase order despite attempts to do so, in accordance with its regular procedures, by sending copies of the documents to several of its various divisions. Ingram Meyers testified that he never learned of the purchase order until weeks later when James Thomson called to arrange for removal of the machines. By then, however, the machines had long been sold to someone else.

We think Goodrich misreads the requirements of 2–201(2). First, the literal requirements of 2–201(2), as they apply here, are that a writing "is received" and that Goodrich "has reason to know its contents." There is no dispute that the purchase order and check were received by Goodrich, and there is at least no specific or express requirement that the "receipt" referred to in 2–201(2) be by any Goodrich agent in particular.

* * *

Even if we go beyond the literal requirements of 2–201(2) and read into the "receipt" requirement the "receipt of notice" rule of 1–201(27), we still think Thomson Printing satisfied the "merchants" exception. Section 1–201, the definitional section of the U.C.C., provides that notice received by an organization

is effective for a particular transaction . . . from the time when it would have been brought to [the attention of the individual conducting that transaction] if the organization had executed *due diligence*.

U.C.C. § 1–201(27) (emphasis supplied). The Official Comment states:

reason to know, knowledge, or a notification, although "received" for instance by a clerk in Department A of an organization, is effective for a transaction conducted in Department B only from the time when it was *or should have been* communicated to the individual conducting that transaction.

U.C.C. § 1–201(27), Official Comment.

Thus, the question comes down to whether Goodrich's mailroom, given the information it had, should have notified the surplus equipment manager, Ingram Meyers, of Thomson's confirmatory writing. At whatever point Meyers should have been so notified, then at that point Thomson's writing was effective even though Meyers did not see it. [Citations.]

* * *

One cannot say that Goodrich's mailroom procedures were reasonable as a matter of law: if Goodrich had exercised due diligence in handling Thomson Printing's purchase order and check, these items would have reasonably promptly come to Ingram Meyers' attention. First, the purchase order on its face should have alerted the mailroom that the documents referred to a purchase of used printing equipment. Since Goodrich had only one surplus machinery department, the

> documents "home" should not have been difficult to find. Second, even if the mailroom would have had difficulty in immediately identifying the kind of transaction involved, the purchase order had Thomson Printing's phone number printed on it and we think a "reasonable routine" in these particular circumstances would have involved at some point in the process a simple phone call to Thomson Printing. Thus, we think Goodrich's mailroom mishandled the confirmatory writings. This failure should not permit Goodrich to escape liability by pleading nonreceipt. [Citations.]

Admission   The Code permits an oral contract for the sale of goods to be enforced against a party who in his pleading, testimony, or otherwise in court admits that a contract was made, but limits enforcement to the quantity of goods he admits.[2] Moreover, some courts hold that a party, as in the Law in the News case at page 272, may implicitly admit the existence of a contract, such as by performing over a period of time.

Specially Manufactured Goods   The Code permits enforcement of an oral contract for goods specially manufactured for the buyer but only if evidence indicates that the goods were made for the buyer and the seller can show that he has made a *substantial beginning* of their manufacture before receiving any notice of repudiation.[2] If the goods, although manufactured on special order, may be readily resold in the ordinary course of the seller's business, this exception does not apply.

Delivery or Payment and Acceptance   Before the UCC was in force, delivery and acceptance of part of the goods or payment and acceptance of part of the price made enforceable the entire oral contract against the buyer who had received part delivery or against the seller who had received part payment. Under the Code, such "partial performance," as a substitute for the required written memorandum, validates the contract only for the goods that have been accepted or for which payment has been accepted.[2] To illustrate, Liz orally agrees to buy 1,000 watches from David for $15,000. David delivers 300 watches to Liz, who receives and accepts the watches. The oral contract is enforceable to the extent of 300 watches

($4,500)—those received and accepted—but is unenforceable to the extent of 700 watches ($10,500).

But what if the contract is indivisible, such as one for the sale of an automobile, so that if part payment is made there is only a choice between not enforcing the contract or enforcing the contract as a whole? Presently, there is a division of authority on this issue, although the better rule appears to be that such part payment and acceptance makes the entire contract enforceable.

A summary of methods of compliance with the statute of frauds is presented in Figure 13–3.

EFFECT OF NONCOMPLIANCE

The English statute provided that "no action shall be brought" on a contract to which the statute of frauds applied *and* that did not comply with its requirements. The Code states that the contract "is not enforceable by way of action or defense." Despite the difference in language, the basic legal effect is the same: a contracting party has a defense to an action by the other for enforcement of an oral contract that is within the statute and does not comply with its requirements. In short, the oral contract is **unenforceable.**

If Kirkland, a painter, and Riggsbee, a homeowner, make an oral contract under which Riggsbee is to give Kirkland a certain tract of land in return for the painting of Riggsbee's house, the contract is unenforceable under the statute of frauds. It is a contract for the sale of an interest in land. Either party can repudiate and has a defense to an action by the other to enforce the contract.

FIGURE 13-3 Methods of Compliance

Type of Contract	Applicable Method of Compliance					
	Written memos	Full performance by both parties	Written confirmation	Admission	Specially manufactured	Delivery or payment and acceptance
Executor—Administrator	•	•				
Suretyship	•	•				
Marriage	•	•				
Interest in Land	•	•				
One-year	•	•				
Sale of Goods ≥ $500	•	•	•	•	•	•

After *all* the promises of an oral contract have been *performed* by all the parties, the statute of frauds no longer applies. Accordingly, neither party may ask the court to rescind the executed oral contract on the basis that it did not meet the requirements of the statute of frauds.

If the painter has already performed a *part* of the work, is she completely without a remedy? Clearly, she cannot enforce the contract, but courts may still permit a recovery in quasi contract to prevent an unjust enrichment. The remedy of restitution allows the painter to recover damages equal to the amount of the benefit that she has conferred on the homeowner. Thus, all may not be lost to a party unable to enforce an oral contract. Despite this possibility, a contracting party should use the utmost care to comply with the statute in order to obtain the full benefit of the bargain that has been made.

PAROL EVIDENCE RULE

A contract reduced to writing and signed by the parties is frequently the result of many conversations, conferences, proposals, counterproposals, letters, and memoranda and sometimes is the product of negotiations conducted, or partly conducted, by agents of the parties. At some stage in the negotiations tentative agreements may have been reached on a certain point or points that were superseded (or so regarded by one of the parties) by subsequent negotiations. Offers may have been made and withdrawn, either expressly or by implication, or lost sight of in the give-and-take of negotiations. Ultimately a final draft of the written contract is prepared and signed by the parties. It may or may not include all of the points that were discussed and agreed upon in the course of the negotiations. By signing the agreement, however, the parties have declared it to be their contract, and the terms as contained in it represent the contract they have made. As a rule of substantive law, neither party is later permitted to show that the contract they made is different from the terms and provisions that appear in the written agreement. This rule is called the "parol evidence" rule.

THE RULE

When a contract is expressed in a writing that is intended to be the complete and final ex-

LAW IN THE NEWS

The Tripple Ripple Ice Cream Case
How Much Is a Handshake Agreement Worth These Days? Quite a Bit, McDonald's Learned, Much to Its Dismay.

In the autumn of 1970 McDonald's Corp. founder and Chairman Ray Kroc came up with what he thought was one great idea. Along with Big Macs and fries, he wanted to sell combinations of vanilla, chocolate and strawberry ice cream in special, slow-dripping cones. No such cone existed at the time, so Kroc contacted Tom Cummings, the son of an old friend, whose Central Ice Cream Co. produced ice cream pops for Chicago's zoo and hospitals, and asked him to design one.

Since no contract was ever written and signed, what happened next has been debated for over 15 years. According to Cummings, Kroc promised him that if Central's "Tripple Ripple" cone passed McDonald's taste test, the fast-food chain would carry it exclusively for 20 years. McDonald's claims there was no exclusive long-term agreement, and, accordingly, the chain phased out Tripple Ripple after it bombed with customers after several years on the menu. Central Ice Cream Co., which had borrowed heavily to upgrade for the production of the cones, headed into Chapter 11. Cummings sued, and after a decade and a half of dispute, Central Ice Cream finally won and now stands to collect $15.5 million in damages for breach of contract and fraud.

Central Ice Cream won because Kroc and McDonald's lost sight of a basic legal principle that can cost businessmen dearly if ignored: Many business contracts do not have to be written down to be enforceable. In much the same way that Texaco was found last year to have induced Getty Oil to break an oral agreement to merge with Pennzoil, and thus wound up being hit with $10.5 billion in trial court damages, McDonald's was found to have induced Central Ice Cream to invest in reliance on a promise that McDonald's disavowed.

"Often these kinds of disputes boil down to whether you believe Sam or Joe," says Klaus

---

pression of the rights and duties of the parties, parol evidence of **prior** oral or written negotiations or agreements of the parties or their **contemporaneous** oral agreements that **vary** or **change** the written contract are not admissible. The word *parol* means literally "speech" or "words." The term **parol evidence**, however, refers to any evidence, whether oral or in writing, that is outside the written contract and not incorporated into the contract either directly or by reference.

The parol evidence rule applies only to an **integrated contract,** that is, one in which the parties have assented to a certain writing or writings as the statement of the complete agreement or contract between them. When there is such an integration of a contract, parol evidence of any prior or contemporaneous agreement will not be permitted to vary, change, alter, or modify any of the terms or provisions of the written contract.[15]

The reason for the rule is that the parties, by reducing their entire agreement to writing, are regarded as having intended the writing that they signed to include the whole of their agreement. The terms and provisions contained in the writing are there because the parties intended them to be in their contract. Any provision not in the writing is regarded as having been omitted because the parties intended that it should not be a part of their contract. The rule, as shown in the following case, excluding evidence that would tend to change, alter, vary, or modify the terms of the

Eppler, a senior partner at Proskauer Rose Goetz & Mendelsohn and an authority on contract law. "But in each case there's always the issue of whether the type of oral contract involved is as enforceable as a written one would have been, and that differs from state to state."

Generally, oral or written short-term contracts worth only small sums of money are equally binding. Lawyers have to prove either that both parties agreed to the contract or that one party made an offer and the other party acted in reliance on it. But when contracts are worth more than $500, the Uniform Commercial Code, used in every state with minor variations, requires that agreements be in writing unless both parties admit that an oral contract existed. Moreover, the UCC holds that once a written agreement does exist, its terms supersede any past or future oral understandings on the matter.

In the Tripple Ripple case, it was up to Theodore Becker, Central Ice Cream's attorney, to prove that McDonald's admitted an oral contract existed. A Cook County, Ill. jury bought his argument. What swayed them? The fact that the two companies had been doing business for three years. "The law is full of a lot of mumbo jumbo about when your oral agreement qualifies as a contract," Becker says. "But in my experience, juries make their decisions based on whether they think bad faith was involved in the agreement." Stunned by a $52 million trial court award, McDonald's offered to settle for $15.5 million, which has been accepted. "We still believe in doing business by handshake agreements," says Shelby Yastrow, McDonald's vice president and general counsel, "but it worked against us in the Tripple Ripple case. This was an agreement between two men, and one of them, Ray Kroc, was seriously ill and then died before the trial was over. So it was tough for us to prove exactly what had and hadn't been agreed on."

Central's victory, like Pennzoil's early success, has understandably made corporations and lawyers more wary of oral agreements. Says Eppler, "I recently represented some Sperry directors during the tender offer for Sperry by Burroughs. Once the Sperry board agreed that it wouldn't oppose the offer and made a public announcement to that effect, I warned my clients that by so doing they had probably created an enforceable contract. They could then have gotten in trouble by talking to any other potential suitor."

So where does that leave the perplexed businessman? When it comes to oral contracts at least, the lesson should be clear: Think before you speak. Better yet, commit your agreement to paper.

by Jill Andresky
Reprinted by permission of *Forbes* magazine, August 25, 1986 © Forbes, Inc., 1986.

written agreement safeguards the contract as made by the parties. The rule applies to all integrated written contracts and deals with what terms are part of the contract. The rule differs from the statute of frauds, which governs what contracts must be in writing to be enforceable.

CONTINENTAL LIFE AND ACCIDENT CO. v. SONGER

Court of Appeals of Arizona, 1979.
124 Ariz. 294, 603 P.2d 921.

Facts: David and Nancy Songer sought to obtain medical insurance that would cover them during an upcoming trip to the island of Ponape. On August 13, 1973, David Songer submitted an application for insurance coverage and a $133 check for the first six months' premium to an agent of the Continental Life and Accident Company. The application provided that "the insurance applied for will not become effective until this application has been accepted by the Company at its

Home Office." The agent claims that he explained to the Songers that coverage
would begin as of the date of application if the application was later accepted by the
company. The Songers maintain that the agent assured them they were immediately covered unless and until the company notified them to the contrary. The
Songers left the country about a week after submitting the application and had been
gone for two months without hearing anything from Continental. Mary Songer's
mother, Mrs. Knowles, then learned that Continental was having trouble obtaining
Mrs. Songer's medical records, but this problem was resolved on October 24. On
October 30, Mrs. Songer was severely injured in a motor vehicle accident on
Ponape. On November 3, Continental rejected the Songers' insurance application
by means of a letter to Mrs. Knowles accompanied by a refund check dated October
29. The Songers brought an action to recover damages, including benefits allegedly
due under the insurance policy. The jury determined that the alleged statements of
Continental's agent formed an oral contract under which the Songers were
immediately covered by temporary insurance as of August 13. Continental appealed, contending that the jury was erroneously allowed to alter the written terms
of the application on the basis of inadmissible parol evidence.

Decision: Judgment for Songer reversed and case remanded for retrial barring
the oral representations of the agent.

Opinion: **Contreras, J.** We next consider, . . . whether an oral contract for
temporary insurance arose on the basis of the statements by Continental's agents
that a "binder", effective immediately, was created when the Songers submitted
the completed application. The oral representations made by Continental's agents
could only have been considered to establish a temporary contract if such evidence
did not violate the parol evidence rule. This rule, in essence, provides that "[i]n the
absence of fraud or mistake, parol evidence is inadmissible to change, alter or vary
the express terms in a written contract." [Citation.] The express terms of the health
insurance application filled out by the Songers specified that "the insurance applied
for will not become effective until this application has been accepted by the
Company at its Home Office." Appellees argue that, because this provision is
ambiguous, or was made so by the representations of Continental's agent, the parol
evidence rule does not apply to bar consideration of the representations. We
disagree.

It is well settled that parol evidence is admissible to clarify and explain a
document where an ambiguity exists on the face of the document or the language
admits of differing interpretations. [Citation.] The Songers contend that the
acceptance provision in their application was so uncertain that its meaning could
not be determined from the language of the document. Although the legal effect of
a given provision is dependent on the specific terms of the application and receipt
used in a particular transaction, this court has, in *Pawelczyk v. Allied Life Insurance
Co.*, [citation], a case factually similar to the instant case, provided some guidance
as to the interpretation of a similar provision in an application for life insurance.

* * *

In holding that the provision presented no ambiguity, the court [in *Pawelcyzk*]
stated: "Courts must give effect to agreements as they are written, however, and
ambiguities will not be found or created where they do not exist in order to avoid
a harsh result." [Citation.] The court in upholding the enforcement of the parol
evidence rule, concluded that:

. . . the [oral] representation in question would clearly vary the terms of the application and the contemplated contract of which it would form a part, and that its admission would be, therefore, in violation of the parol evidence rule. [Citations.]

It is our opinion that the same conclusion reached in *Pawelczyk* obtains in the instant case. The quoted language in the Songers' application for health insurance is too clear to admit of any doubt. The only difference between the application in *Pawelczyk* and the application of the Songers is that the *Pawelczyk* application requires that is (*sic*) be "approved" (at the home office), whereas the Songers' application requires that it be "accepted" (at the home office). This is a distinction without substantive difference. There could be no insurance in effect until the application was "accepted *by* the Company *at* its Home Office." [Citation.]

In view of our conclusion that there was no ambiguity in the application, the parol evidence rule necessarily bars consideration of the oral representations of the agent. The representation by Continental's agent that the insurance would take effect immediately upon completion of the application and payment of the premium clearly varies the terms of the application and the contemplated contract of which it would form a part. Therefore, admission and consideration of such representations as evidence of a contract would be in violation of the parol evidence rule. [Citations.]

SITUATIONS TO WHICH THE RULE DOES NOT APPLY

The parol evidence rule, in spite of its name, is not an exclusionary rule of evidence, nor is it a rule of construction or interpretation. It is a rule of substantive law that defines the limits of a contract. Bearing this in mind, as well as the reason underlying the rule, the rule does **not** apply to any of the following situations:

1. A contract that is *partly written* and partly oral; that is, the parties do not intend the writing to be their entire agreement.[16]
2. A clerical or *typographical error* that obviously does not represent the agreement of the parties.
3. The lack of *contractual capacity* of one of the parties, such as proof of minority, intoxication, or mental incompetency. Such evidence would not tend to vary, change, or alter any of the terms of the written agreement but rather would show that the written agreement was voidable or void.[16]
4. A *defense* of fraud, misrepresentation, duress, undue influence, mistake, or illegality. Evidence establishing any of these defenses would not claim to vary, change, or alter any of the terms of the written agreement but rather would show such agreement to be voidable, void, or unenforceable.[16]
5. A *condition precedent* agreed on orally at the time of the execution of the written agreement and to which the entire agreement was made subject. Such evidence does not tend to vary, alter, or change any of the terms of the agreement but rather shows whether the entire written agreement, unchanged and unaltered, ever became effective.[17]
6. A *subsequent mutual rescission* or *modification* of the written contract. Parol evidence of a later agreement does not tend to show that the integrated writing did not represent the contract between the parties at the time it was made.

For a summary of the parol evidence rule see Figure 13-4.

SUPPLEMENTAL EVIDENCE

Although a written agreement may not be contradicted by evidence of a prior agreement or of a contemporaneous agreement, under

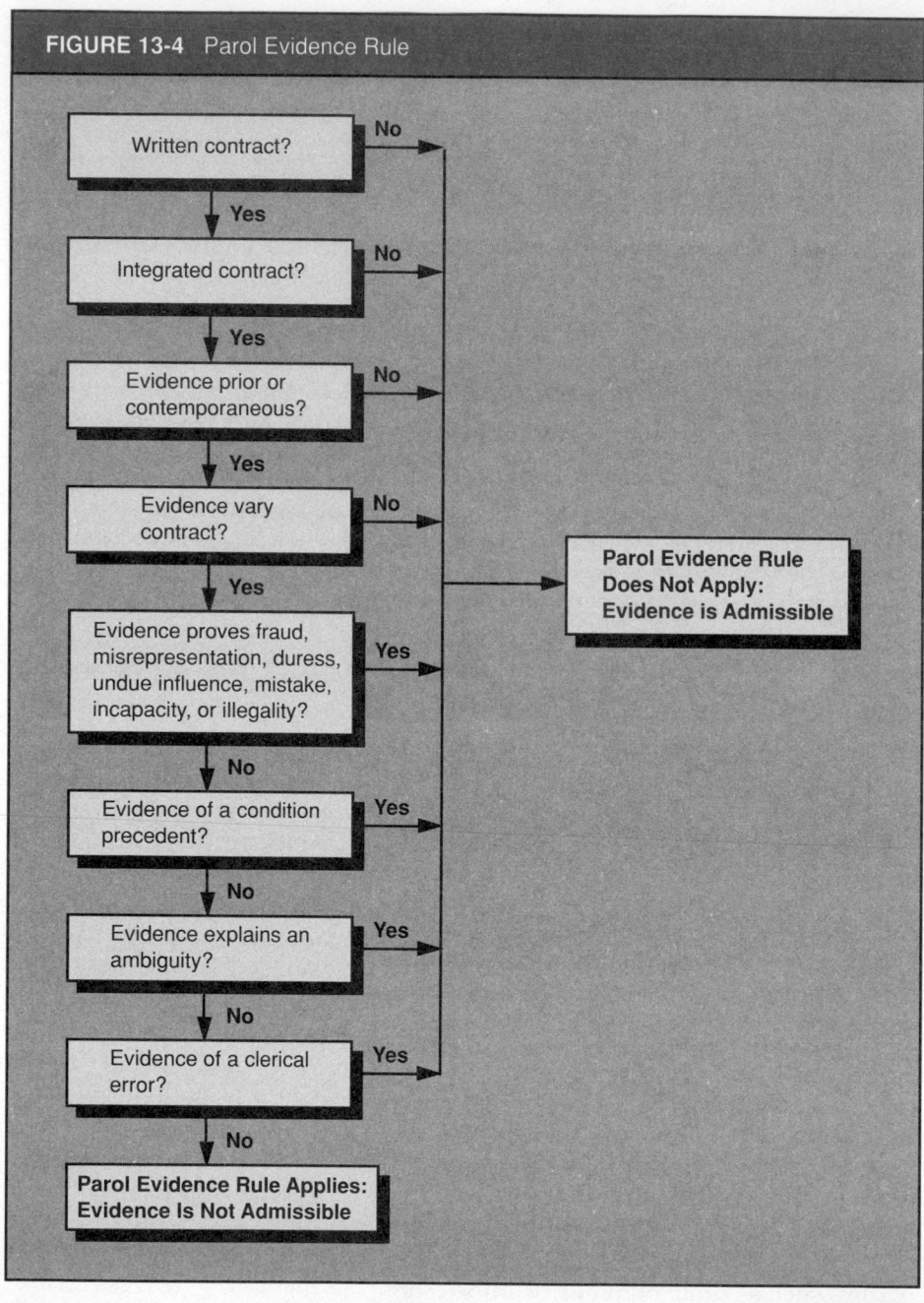

FIGURE 13-4   Parol Evidence Rule

the Restatement[18] and the Code,[19] a written contract may be explained or supplemented by (1) course of dealing between the parties, (2) usage of trade, (3) course of performance, or (4) evidence of consistent additional terms unless the writing was intended by the parties as a complete and exclusive statement of their agreement.

A **course of dealing** is a sequence of previous conduct between the parties to an agreement that may be fairly regarded as establishing a common basis of understanding for interpreting their expressions and other conduct.

A **usage of trade** is a practice or method of dealing regularly observed and followed in a place, vocation, or trade.

Course of performance refers to the manner and extent to which the respective parties to a contract have accepted successive tenders of performance by the other party without objection.

The Restatement[20] and the Code[19] permit *supplemental consistent evidence* to be introduced into a court proceeding. Such evidence is admissible only if it does not contradict a term or terms of the original agreement and would probably not have been included in the original contract.

INTERPRETATION OF CONTRACTS

Although the written words or language in which the parties embodied their agreement or contract may not be changed by parol evidence, the ascertainment (determination) of the meaning to be given to the written language is outside the scope of the parol evidence rule. The written words embody the terms of the contract. Words are but symbols, however. If their meaning is not clear, it may be made clear by the application of rules of interpretation or construction and by the use of extrinsic (external) evidence for this purpose where necessary.

The Restatement defines **interpretation** as the ascertainment of the meaning of a promise or agreement or a term of the promise or agreement.[21] Where the language in a contract is clear and unambiguous, extrinsic evidence tending to show a meaning different from that which the words clearly convey will not be accepted by a court. It is the function of the court to interpret and construe written contracts and documents. The court adopts rules of interpretation to apply a legal standard to the words contained in the agreement by which to determine their sense or meaning.

Among the rules [22] that aid interpretation are the following:

1. Words and other conduct are interpreted in the light of all the circumstances, and if the principal purpose of the parties is ascertainable, it is given great weight.

2. A writing is interpreted as a whole, and all writings that are part of the same transaction are interpreted together.

3. Unless a different intention is manifested, where language has a commonly accepted meaning, it is interpreted in accordance with that meaning.

4. Unless a different intention is manifested, technical terms and words of art are given their technical meanings.

5. Wherever reasonable, the manifestations of intention of the parties to a promise or agreement are interpreted as consistent with each other and with any relevant course of performance, course of dealing, or usage of trade.

6. An interpretation that gives a reasonable, lawful, and effective meaning to all the terms is preferred to an interpretation that leaves a part unreasonable, unlawful, or of no effect.

7. Specific terms and exact terms are given greater weight than general language.

8. Separately negotiated or added terms are given greater weight than standardized terms or other terms not separately negotiated.

9. Express terms, course of performance, course of dealing, and usage of trade are weighted in that order.

10. Where a term or promise has several possible meanings, it will be interpreted against the party who supplied the contract or the term.

Through the application of the parol evidence rule, where it is properly applicable, and the above rules of interpretation and construction, it may be observed that the law not only enforces a contract but in doing so exercises great care that the contract being enforced is the one the parties made and that the sense and meaning of the intentions of the parties are carefully ascertained and given effect.

CHAPTER SUMMARY

STATUTE OF FRAUDS

Contracts within the Statute of Frauds	**Rule** contracts within the statute of frauds must be in writing to be enforceable
	Suretyship Provision applies to promises to pay the debt of another
	   ◼ *Promise Must Be Collateral* promisor must be secondarily, not primarily, liable
	   ◼ *Main Purpose Doctrine* if primary object is to provide an economic benefit to the surety, then the promise is not within the statute
	Executor-Administrator Provision applies to promises to answer personally for a duty of the decedent
	Marriage Provision applies to promises made in consideration of marriage but not to mutual promises to marry
	Land Contract Provision applies to promises to transfer any right, privilege, power, or immunity in real property
	One-Year Provision applies to contracts that cannot be performed within one year
	   ◼ *The Possibility Test* the criterion is whether it is possible, not likely, for the agreement to be performed within one year
	   ◼ *Computation of Time* the year runs from the time the agreement is made
	   ◼ *Full Performance by One Party* makes the promise of the other party enforceable under majority view
	Sale of Goods a contract for the sale of goods for the price of $500 or more must be in writing to be enforceable
	Modification or Rescission of Contracts within the Statute of Frauds oral contracts modifying existing contracts are unenforceable if the resulting contract is within the statute of frauds

Methods of Compliance	**A Writing or Memorandum under General Contract Law** the writing or writings must:
	   ◼ be signed by the party to be charged or by her agent
	   ◼ specify the parties to the contract
	   ◼ specify the subject matter and essential terms
	A Writing under the UCC the writing or writings must:
	   ◼ be sufficient to indicate that a contract has been made between the parties
	   ◼ be signed by the party against whom enforcement is sought or by her authorized agent
	   ◼ specify the quantity of goods to be sold

Other Methods of Compliance under the UCC
- *Written Confirmation* between merchants, a written confirmation that is sufficient against the sender is also sufficient against the recipient unless the recipient gives written notice of his objection within ten days
- *Admission* an admission in pleadings, testimony, or otherwise in court makes the contract enforceable for the quantity of goods admitted
- *Specially Manufactured Goods* an oral contract for specially manufactured goods is enforceable
- *Delivery or Payment and Acceptance* validates the contract only for the goods that have been accepted or for which payment has been accepted

Effects of Noncompliance	**Oral Contract within Statute of Frauds** is unenforceable **Restitution** is available in quasi-contract for benefits conferred in reliance on the oral contract

PAROL EVIDENCE RULE AND INTERPRETATION OF CONTRACTS

Parol Evidence Rule	**Statement of Rule** when a contract is expressed in a writing that is intended to be the complete and final expression of the rights and duties of the parties, evidence of prior oral or written negotiations or agreements of the parties or their contemporaneous oral agreements that vary or change the written contract are not admissible **Situations to Which the Rule Does Not Apply** • a contract that is not an integrated document • correction of a typographical error • showing that a contract was void or voidable • showing whether a condition has in fact occurred • showing a subsequent mutual rescission or modification of the contract **Supplemental Evidence** may be admitted • *Course of Dealing* previous conduct between the parties • *Usage of Trade* practice engaged by the trade or industry • *Course of Performance* conduct between the parties concerning performance of the particular contract • *Supplemental Consistent Evidence*

Interpretation of Contracts	**Definition** the ascertainment of the meaning of a promise or agreement or a term of the promise or agreement
	Rules of Interpretation
	■ all the circumstances are considered and the principal purpose of the parties is given great weight
	■ a writing is interpreted as a whole
	■ commonly accepted meanings are used unless a different intention is intended
	■ wherever possible, the intentions of the parties are interpreted as consistent with each other and with course of performance, course of dealing, or usage of trade
	■ technical terms are given their technical meaning
	■ specific terms are given greater weight than general language
	■ separately negotiated terms are given greater weight then standardized terms or those not separately negotiated
	■ the order for interpretation is express terms, course of performance, course of dealing, and usage of trade
	■ where a term has several possible meanings, the term will be interpreted against the party who supplied the contract or term

QUESTIONS

1. Identify and discuss the five types of general contracts covered by the statute of frauds and the contracts covered by the UCC statute of frauds provision.
2. Describe the writing that is required to satisfy the general contract and UCC statute of frauds provisions.
3. Identify and discuss the other methods of complying with the UCC statute of frauds provision.
4. Explain the parol evidence rule and identify the situations to which the rules does not apply.
5. Discuss the rules that aid in the interpretation of a contract.

PROBLEMS

1. Rafferty was the principal shareholder in Continental Corporation, and as a result, he received the lion's share of Continental Corporation's dividends. Continental Corporation was anxious to close an important deal for iron ore products to use in its business. A written contract was on the desk of Stage Corporation for the sale of the iron ore to Continental Corporation. Stage Corporation, however, was cautious about signing the contract, and it was not until Rafferty called Stage Corporation on the telephone and stated that if Continental Corporation did not pay for the ore, he would pay, that Stage Corporation signed the contract. Business reverses struck Continental Corporation and it failed. Stage Corporation sues Rafferty. What defense, if any, has Rafferty? Decision?

2. Green was the owner of a large department store. On Wednesday, January 26, he talked to Smith and said, "I will hire you to act as sales manager in my store for one year at a salary of $18,000. You are to begin work next Monday." Smith accepted and started work on Monday January 31. At the end of three months, Green discharged Smith. On May 15, Smith brings an action against Green to recover the unpaid portion of the $18,000 salary. Decision?

3. Rowe was admitted to the hospital suffering from a critical illness. He was given emergency treatment and later underwent surgery. On at least four occasions Rowe's two sons discussed with the hospital the payment for services to be rendered by the hospital. The first of these four conversations took place the day after Rowe was admitted. The sons informed the treating physician that their father had no financial means but that they themselves would pay for such services. During the other conversations, the sons authorized whatever treatment their father needed, assuring the hospital that they would pay for the services. After Rowe's discharge, Dr. Peterson brought this action against the sons to recover the unpaid bill for the services rendered to their father. Decision?

4. Ames, Bell, Cain, and Dole each orally ordered color television sets from Marvel Electronics Company, which accepted the orders. Ames's set was to

be specially designed and encased in an ebony cabinet. Bell, Cain, and Dole ordered standard sets described as "Alpha Omega Theatre." The price of Ames's set was $1,800, and the sets ordered by Bell, Cain, and Dole were $700 each. Bell paid the company $75 to apply on his purchase; Ames, Cain, and Dole paid nothing. The next day, Marvel sent Ames, Bell, Cain, and Dole written confirmations captioned "Purchase Memorandum," numbered 12345, 12346, 12347, and 12348 respectively, containing the essential terms of the oral agreements. Each memorandum was sent in duplicate with the request that one copy be signed and returned to the company. None of the four purchasers returned a signed copy. Ames promptly sent the company a repudiation of the oral contract, which it received before beginning manufacture of the set for Ames or making commitments to carry out the contract. Cain sent the company a letter reading in part, "Referring to your Contract No. 12347, please be advised I have cancelled this contract. Yours truly, (Signed) Cain." The four television sets were duly tendered by Marvel to Ames, Bell, Cain, and Dole, all of whom refused to accept delivery. Marvel brings four separate actions against Ames, Bell, Cain, and Dole for breach of contract. Decide each claim.

5. Moriarity and Holmes enter into an oral contract by which Moriarity promises to sell and Holmes promises to buy Blackacre for $10,000. Moriarity repudiates the contract by writing a letter to Holmes in which she states accurately the terms of the bargain, but adds "our agreement was oral. It, therefore, is not binding upon me, and I shall not carry it out." Thereafter, Holmes sues Moriarity for specific performance of the contract. Moriarity interposes the defense of the statute of frauds, arguing that the contract is within the statute and hence unenforceable. Decision?

6. On March 1 Lucas called Craig on the telephone and offered to pay him $90,000 for a house and lot that Craig owned. Craig accepted the offer immediately on the telephone. Later in the same day, Lucas told Annabelle that if she would marry him, he would convey to her the property then owned by Craig that was the subject of the earlier agreement. On March 2 Lucas called Penelope and offered her $16,000 if she would work for him for the year commencing March 15, and she agreed. Lucas and Annabelle were married on June 25. By this time Craig had refused to convey the house to Lucas. Thereafter, Lucas renounced his promise to convey the property to Annabelle. Penelope, who had been working for Lucas, was discharged without cause on July 5; Annabelle left Lucas and instituted divorce proceedings in July.

What rights, if any, have (a) Lucas against Craig for his failure to convey the property; (b) Annabelle against Lucas for failure to convey the house to her; (c) Penelope against Lucas for discharging her before the end of the agreed term of employment?

7. Blair orally promises Clay to sell him five crops of potatoes to be grown on Blackacre, a farm in Idaho, and Clay promises to pay a stated price for them on delivery. Is the contract enforceable?

8. Rachel leased an apartment to Bertha for the term May 1, 1990, to April 30, 1991, at $250 a month "payable in advance on the first day of each and every month of said term." At the time the lease was signed, Bertha told Rachel that she received her salary on the tenth of the month, and that she would be unable to pay the rent before that date each month. Rachel replied that would be satisfactory. On June 2, Bertha not having paid the June rent, Rachel sued Bertha for the rent. At the trial, Bertha offered to prove the oral agreement as to the date of payment each month. Decision?

9. Ann bought a car from the Used Car Agency under a written contract. She purchased the same in reliance on Used's agent's oral representations that the car had never been in a wreck and could be driven at least 2,000 miles without adding oil. Thereafter, Ann discovered that the car had, in fact, been previously wrecked and rebuilt, that it used excessive quantities of oil, and that Used's agent was aware of these facts when the car was sold. Ann brings an action to rescind the contract and recover the purchase price. Used objects to the introduction of oral testimony concerning representations of its agent, contending that the written contract alone governed the rights of the parties. Decision on the objection?

10. In a contract drawn up by Goldberg Company, it agreed to sell and Edwards Contracting Company agreed to buy wood shingles at $650. After the shingles were delivered and used, Goldberg Company billed Edwards Company at $650 per bunch of 900 shingles. Edwards Company refused to pay because it thought the contract meant $650 per thousand shingles. Goldberg Company brought action to recover on the basis of $650 per bunch. The evidence showed that there was no applicable custom or usage in the trade and that each party held its belief in good faith. Decision?

11. Amos orally agrees to hire Elizabeth for an eight-month trial period. Elizabeth performs the job magnificently, and after several weeks Amos orally offers Elizabeth a six-month extension at a salary increase of 20 percent. Elizabeth accepts the offer. At the end of the eight-month trial period Amos discharges Elizabeth. Elizabeth brings suit against

Amos for breach of contract. Is Amos liable? Why?

COMPUTER RESEARCH PROBLEMS

1. Yokel, a grower of soybeans, had sold soybeans to Campbell Grain and Seed Company and other grain companies in the past. Campbell entered into an oral contract with Yokel to purchase soybeans from him. Promptly after entering into the oral contract, Campbell signed and mailed to Yokel a written confirmation of the oral agreement. Yokel received the written confirmation but did not sign it or object to its content. Campbell now brings this action against Yokel for breach of contract upon Yokel's failure to deliver the soybeans. The trial court ruled in favor of the defendant, Yokel, on the ground that the defendant is not a "merchant" within the meaning of the Code. Decision?

2. Presti claims that he reached an oral agreement with Wilson by telephone in October 1970 to buy a horse for $60,000. Presti asserts that he sent Wilson a bill of sale and a postdated check, which was retained by Wilson. Presti also claims that Wilson told him that he wished not to consummate the transaction until January 1, 1971, for tax reasons. The check was neither deposited nor negotiated. Wilson denies that he ever agreed to sell the horse or that he received the check and bill of sale from Presti. Presti's claim is supported by a copy of his check stub and by the affidavit of his executive assistant, who says that he monitored the telephone call and prepared and mailed both the bill of sale and the check. Wilson argues that the statute of frauds governs this transaction, and since there was no writing, the contract claim is barred. Decision?

3. Louie E. Brown worked for the Phelps Dodge Corporation under an oral contract for approximately twenty-three years. In 1967 he was suspended from work for unauthorized possession of company property. In 1968 Phelps Dodge fired Brown after discovering that he was using company property without permission and building a trailer on company time. Brown sued Phelps Dodge for benefits under an unemployment benefit plan. According to the plan, "in order to be eligible for unemployment benefits, a laid-off employee must: (1) Have completed 2 or more years of continuous service with the company, and (2) Have been laid off from work because the company had determined

that work was not available for him." The trial court held that the wording of the second condition was ambiguous and should be construed against Phelps Dodge, the party who chose the wording. A reading of the entire contract, however, indicates that the plan was not intended to apply to someone who was fired for cause. Decision?

4. Katz offered to purchase land from Joiner, and after negotiating the terms, Joiner accepted. On October 13, over the telephone, both parties agreed to extend the time period for completing and mailing the written contract until October 20. Although the original paperwork deadline in the offer was October 14, Katz stated he had inserted that provision "for my purpose only." All other provisions of the contract remained unchanged. Accordingly, Joiner completed the contract and mailed it on October 20. Immediately after, however, Joiner sends Katz a telegram stating that "I have signed and returned contract, but have changed my mind. Do not wish to sell property." Joiner now claims an oral modification of a contract within the statute of frauds is unenforceable. Katz counters that the modification is not material, and therefore does not affect the underlying contract. Decision?

5. When Mr. McClam died, he left the family farm, heavily mortgaged, to his wife and children. In order to save the farm from foreclosure, Mrs. McClam planned to use insurance proceeds and her savings to pay off the debts. She was unwilling to do so, however, unless she had full ownership of the property. Mrs. McClam wrote her daughter, stating that the daughter should deed over her interest in the family farm to her mother. Mrs. McClam promised that upon her death all the children would inherit the farm from their mother equally. The letter further explained that if foreclosure occurred, each child would receive very little, but if they complied with their mother's plan, each would eventually receive a valuable property interest upon her death. Finally, the letter stated that all the other children had agreed to this plan. The daughter also agreed. Years later, Mrs. McClam tries to convey the farm to her son Donald. The daughter challenges, arguing that the mother is contractually bound to convey the land equally to all children. Donald says this was an oral agreement to sell land, and is unenforceable. Daughter says the letter satisfies the statute of frauds, making the contract enforceable. Who gets the farm? Explain.

6. Butler Brothers Building Company sublet all of the work in a highway construction contract to Ganley Brothers, Inc. Soon thereafter, Ganley brought this action against Butler for fraud in the inducement of the contract. The contract, however, provided: "The contractor [Ganley] has examined the said contracts . . ., knows all the requirements, and is not relying upon any statement made by the company in respect thereto." Decision.

ENDNOTES

1. Restatement, Second, Contracts, Section 110, Classes of Contracts Covered.

2. Uniform Commercial Code, Section 2—201, Formal Requirements; Statute of Frauds.

3. Uniform Commercial Code, Section 8—319, Statute of Frauds.

4. Uniform Commercial Code, Section 9—203(1), Attachment and Enforceability of Security Interest; Proceeds; Formal Requisites.

5. Restatement, Second, Contracts, Section 116, Main Purpose; Advantage to Surety.

6. Restatement, Second, Contracts, Section 116, Comment b.

7. Restatement, Second, Contracts, Section 111, Contract of Executor or Administrator.

8. Restatement, Second, Contracts, Section 124, Contract Made Upon Consideration of Marriage.

9. Restatement, Second, Contracts, Section 125, Contract to Transfer, Buy, or Pay for an Interest in Land.

10. Restatement, Second, Contracts, Section 129, Action in Reliance, Specific Performance.

11. Restatement, Second, Contracts, Section 130, Contract Not to Be Performed Within a Year.

12. Uniform Commercial Code, Section 2—105(1), Definitions: Transferability; "Goods"; "Future" Goods; "Lot"; "Commercial Unit."

13. Uniform Commercial Code, Section 2—209, Modification, Rescission and Waiver.

14. Restatement, Second, Contracts, Section 132, Several Writings.

15. Restatement, Second, Contracts, Section 213, Effect of Integrated Agreement on Prior Agreements (Parol Evidence Rule).

16. Restatement, Second, Contracts, Section 214, Evidence of Prior or Contemporaneous Agreements and Negotiations.

17. Restatement, Second, Contracts, Section 217, Integrated Agreement Subject to Oral Requirement of a Condition.

18. Restatement, Second, Contracts, Section 216, Consistent Additional Terms.

19. Uniform Commercial Code, Section 2—102, Final Written Expression: Parol or Extrinsic Evidence.

20. Restatement, Second, Contracts, Section 212, Comment b.

21. Restatements, Second, Contracts, Section 200, Interpretation of Promise or Agreement.

22. Restatement, Second, Contracts, Section 201, Whose Meaning Prevails; Section 202, Rules in Aid of Interpretation; Section 203, Standards of Preference in Interpretation.

14 THIRD PARTIES TO CONTRACTS

In prior chapters we considered situations that essentially involved only two parties. In this chapter we deal with the rights and duties of third parties, namely, persons who are not parties to the contract but have a right to or obligation for its performance. These rights and duties arise either by (1) an assignment of the rights of a party to the contract; (2) a delegation of the duties of a party to the contract, or (3) the express terms of a contract entered into for the benefit of a third person. In an assignment or delegation, the third party's rights or duties arise *after* the contract is made, whereas in the third situation the third-party beneficiary's rights arise at the time the contract was formed. We consider these three situations in that order.

ASSIGNMENT OF RIGHTS AND DELEGATION OF DUTIES

It is important to distinguish between an *assignment* of rights and a *delegation* of duties. Every contract creates both rights and duties. For instance, A promises to sell to B an automobile for which B promises to pay $10,000 by monthly installments over the next three years. A's right under the contract is to receive payment from B, whereas A's duty is to deliver the automobile. B's right is to receive the automobile; his duty is to pay for the automobile.

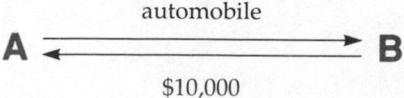

An **assignment of rights** is the voluntary transfer to a third party of the rights arising from the contract. In the above example, if A were to transfer his right under the contract (the installment payments due from B) to C for $8,500 in cash, this would constitute a valid assignment of rights. In this case, A would be the **assignor,** C would be the **assignee,** and B would be the **obligor.**

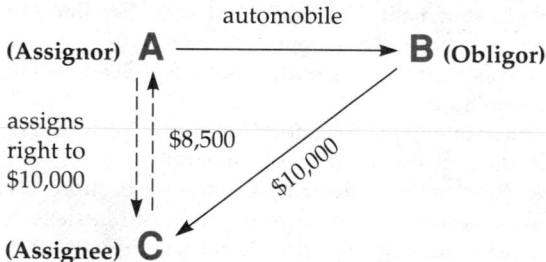

An effective assignment terminates the assignor's right to receive performance by the obligor. After an assignment *only* the assignee has a right to the obligor's performance.

On the other hand, if A and D agree that D should deliver the automobile to B, this would constitute a delegation, not an assignment, of duties between A and D. A **delegation of duties** is a transfer to a third party of a contractual obligation. In this instance, A would be the **delegator,** D would be the **delegatee,** and B would be the **obligee.**

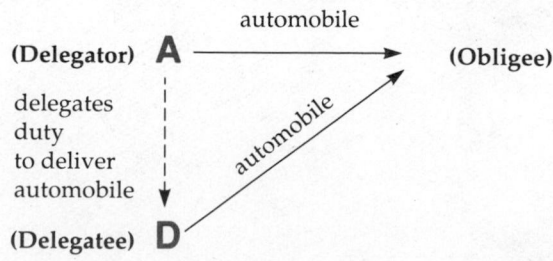

A delegation of duty does *not* extinguish the delegator's obligation to perform because A remains liable to B. When the delegatee accepts or **assumes** the delegated duty, **both** the delegator and delegatee are liable for performance of the contractual duty to the obligee.

ASSIGNMENT OF RIGHTS

At early common law, an assignment of a contractual right was not allowed. The law regarded the personal relationship between the parties to the contract as a vital part of the agreement. It could not be changed by one party any more than any other term of the contract. As commerce increased, the need to sell contract rights also increased. In response, courts of equity began to enforce assignments. Relief was allowed in equity so consistently that ultimately courts of law began to enforce assignments. Because this gave assignees an adequate remedy, courts of equity no longer were called upon to grant relief for assignments.

Requirements of an Assignment

The Restatement defines an assignment of a right as a manifestation of the assignor's intention to transfer it so that the assignor's right to performance by the obligor is distinguished in whole or in part and the assignee acquires the right to such performance.[1] No special form or particular words are necessary to create an assignment. Any words that fairly indicate an intention to make the assignee the owner of the right are sufficient, and the assignment, unless otherwise provided by statute, may be oral or written. For instance, Eve delivers to Harold a writing addressed to Mary stating "Pay Harold for his own use $1,000 out of the amount you owe me." This writing is a legally sufficient assignment.

Consideration is *not* required for an effective assignment. Consequently, gratuitous assignments are valid and enforceable. When the assignee gives value for the assignment, the assignee indicates his assent to the assignment as part of the bargained-for exchange. On the other hand, when the assignment is gratuitous, the assignee's assent is not always required. Any assignee who has not assented to an assignment, however, may disclaim the assignment within a reasonable time after learning of its existence and terms. No particular formality is required for the disclaimer, which renders the assignment inoperative from the beginning.

Revocability of Assignments When the assignee gives consideration in exchange for an assignment, there is a contract between the assignor and the assignee. Consequently, the assignor may not revoke the assignment without the assent of the assignee. A gratuitous assignment is revocable by the assignor and is terminated by the assignor's death, incapacity, or subsequent assignment of the right, *unless* an effective delivery of the assignment has been made by the assignor to the assignee, as in *Speelman v. Pascal*. Such delivery can be accomplished by transferring a deed or other document evidencing the right, such as a stock certificate or savings passbook. Delivery may also consist of physically delivering a signed, written assignment of the contract right.

SPEELMAN v. PASCAL
Court of Appeals of New York, 1961.
10 N.Y.2d 313, 178 N.E.2d 723.

Facts: In 1952 the estate of George Bernard Shaw granted to Gabriel Pascal Enterprises, Limited, the exclusive rights to produce a musical play and a motion picture based on Shaw's play *Pygmalion*. The agreement contained a provision terminating the license if Gabriel Pascal Enterprises did not arrange for well-known composers, such as Lerner and Loewe, to write the musical and produce it within a specified period of time. George Pascal, owner of 98 percent of the Gabriel Pascal

Enterprise's stock, attempted to meet these requirements but died in July 1954 before negotiations had been completed. In February 1954, however, while the license had two years yet to run, Pascal sent a letter to Kingman, his executive secretary, granting to her certain percentages of his share of the profits from the expected stage and screen productions of *Pygmalion*. Subsequently, Pascal's estate arranged for the writing and production of the highly successful *My Fair Lady*, based on Shaw's *Pygmalion*. Kingman then sued to enforce Pascal's gift assignment of the future royalties. The trial court entered judgment for Kingman.

Decision: Judgment for Kingman affirmed.

Opinion: **Desmond, C. J.** The only real question is as to whether the 1954 letter * * * operated to transfer to plaintiff an enforceable right to the described percentages of the royalties to accrue to Pascal on the production of a stage or film version of a musical play based on "Pygmalion." We see no reason why this letter does not have that effect. It is true that at the time of the delivery of the letter there was no musical stage or film play in existence but Pascal, who owned and was conducting negotiations to realize on the stage and film rights, could grant to another a share of the moneys to accrue from the use of those rights by others. There are many instances of courts enforcing assignments of rights to sums which were expected thereafter to become due to the assignor. * * * In every such case the question must be as to whether there was a completed delivery of a kind appropriate to the subject property. * * * In our present case there was nothing left for Pascal to do in order to make an irrevocable transfer to plaintiff of part of Pascal's right to receive royalties from the productions.

A gratuitous assignment is also made irrevocable if, before the attempted revocation, the donee-assignee receives payment of the claim from the obligor, obtains a judgment against the obligor, or obtains a new contract from the obligor. For example, Nancy owes Howard $50,000. Howard signs a written statement granting Paul a gratuitous assignment of his rights from Nancy. Howard dies prior to delivering to Paul the signed, written assignment of the contract right. The assignment is terminated and therefore ineffective. On the other hand, had Howard delivered the signed, written assignment to Paul before Howard died, the assignment would have been effective and irrevocable.

Partial Assignments A **partial assignment** is a transfer of a portion of the contractual rights to one or more assignees, as in the case above. Although at early common law, partial assignments were not enforceable, today partial assignments are permitted and are enforceable; however, the obligor may require all the parties entitled to the promised performance to litigate the matter in one action. This en-

sures that all parties are present and avoids the undue hardship of multiple lawsuits. For example, Jack owes Richard $2,500. Richard assigns $1,000 to Mildred. Neither Richard nor Mildred can maintain an action against Jack if Jack objects, unless the other is joined in the proceeding against Jack.

Rights That Are Assignable

As a general rule, most contract rights, including rights under an option contract, are assignable. So long as the assignment merely substitutes the assignee for the assignor and does not materially increase the burden or risk on the obligor, the assignment is effective and valid, as in the next case involving Billy Cunningham. The most common contractual right that may be assigned is the right to the payment of money such as interest due or an account receivable. The right to other property like land or goods is frequently assignable.

Rights That Are Not Assignable

In order to protect the obligor or the public interest, some contract rights are not assignable. These nonassignable contract rights include those that

MUNCHAK CORPORATION v. CUNNINGHAM
United States Court of Appeals, Fourth Circuit, 1972.
457 F.2d 721.

Facts: While under contract to play professional basketball for the Philadelphia 76ers, Billy Cunningham negotiated a three-year contract with the Carolina Cougars, another professional basketball team. The contract with the Cougars was to begin at the expiration of the contract with the 76ers. In addition to a signing bonus of $125,000, Cunningham was to receive under the new contract a salary of $100,000 for the first year, $110,000 for the second, and $120,000 for the third. The contract also stated that Cunningham "had special, exceptional and unique knowledge, skill and ability as a basketball player" and therefore that Cunningham agreed the Cougars could enjoin him from playing basketball for any other team for the term of the contract. In addition, the contract contained a clause prohibiting its assignment to another club without Cunningham's consent. In 1971 the ownership of the Cougars changed and Cunningham's contract was assigned to Munchak Corporation, the new owners, without his consent. When Cunningham refused to play for the Cougars, Munchak Corporation sought to enjoin his playing for any other team. Cunningham asserts that his contract was not assignable. The trial court denied injunctive relief and Munchak appealed.

Decision: Reversed and remanded for entry of an injunction restraining Cunningham from playing for any other team.

Opinion: Winter, J. We recognize that under North Carolina law the right to performance of a personal service contract requiring special skills and based upon the personal relationship between the parties cannot be assigned without the consent of the party rendering those services. [Citation.] But, as discussed in [citation], some of such contracts may be assigned when the character of the performance and the obligation will not be changed. To us it is inconceivable that the rendition of services by a professional basketball player to a professional basketball club could be affected by the personalities of successive corporate owners. Cf. *Washington Capitols Basketball Club, Inc. v. Barry*, [citation]. Indeed, Cunningham had met only Gardner of Southern Sports Club [owner of Cougars at the time of the original contract], and had not met, nor did he know, the other stockholders. If Gardner had sold all or part of his stock to another person, Cunningham could not seriously contend that his consent would be required.

   The policy against assignability of certain personal service contracts is to prohibit an assignment of a contract in which the obligor undertakes to serve only the original obligee. [Citations.] This contract is not of that type, since Cunningham was not obligated to perform differently for plaintiffs than he was obligated to perform for Southern Sports Club. We, therefore, see no reason to hold that the contract was not assignable under the facts here.

(a) materially increase the risk or burden upon the obligor, (b) transfer highly personal contract rights, (c) are validly prohibited by the contract, or (d) are prohibited by law.[2]

Assignments That Materially Increase the Risk or Burden An assignment is ineffective where performance by the obligor to the assignee would be materially different from performance to the assignor; that is, where the assignment would significantly change the nature or extent of the obligor's duty. Thus, an automobile liability insurance policy issued to Alex is not assignable by Alex to Betty. The risk assumed by the insurance company was liability for Alex's negligent operation of the automobile. Liability for operation of the same automobile by Betty would be an entirely different risk and one that the insurance company had not assumed. Similarly, Candice would not be allowed to assign her contractual right to have David paint her small, two bedroom house to Eunice, the owner of a twenty-five room mansion. Clearly, such an assignment would materially increase David's duty of performance. By comparison, the right to receive monthly payments under a contract may be assigned, for it costs no more to mail the check to the assignee than it does to mail it to the assignor.

Assignments of Personal Rights Where the rights under a contract are of a highly personal nature, they are not assignable. An extreme example of such a contract is an agreement of two persons to marry one another. The prospective groom obviously may not transfer the prospective bride's promise to marry to some third party. A more common example of contracts of a personal character is a contract for the personal services of one of the parties.

Express Prohibition Against Assignment At common law, the courts enforced contracts containing express prohibitions against an assignment of the rights created under it. Such prohibitions, however, are now strictly construed; most courts interpret a general prohibition against assignments as a mere promise not to assign. As a consequence, the prohibition, if violated, gives the obligor a right to damages for breach of the terms forbidding assignment but does *not* render the assignment ineffective.

The Restatement[3] and Article 2 of the Code[4] provide that, unless circumstances indicate the contrary, a contract term prohibiting assignment of the *contract* bars only the delegation to the assignee (delegatee) of the assignor's (delegator's) *duty* of performance and not the assignment of *rights*. Thus, Norman and Lucy contract for the sale of land by Lucy to Norman

for $30,000 and provide in their contract that Norman may not assign his rights under it. Norman pays Lucy $30,000 and thereby fully performs his obligations under the contract. Norman then assigns his rights to George. George is entitled to receive the land from Lucy (the obligor) despite the contractual prohibition of assignment.

Assignments Prohibited by Law Various Federal and State statutes, as well as public policy, prohibit or regulate the assignment of certain types of contract rights. For instance, assignments of future wages are subject to statutes. Some statutes prohibit them altogether; others require them to be in writing and subject to certain restrictions. An assignment that violates public policy will be unenforceable even in the absence of a prohibiting statute.

Rights of the Assignee

Obtains Rights of Assignor The general rule is that an assignee **stands in the shoes** of the assignor. He acquires the rights of the assignor but *no* new rights and takes the assigned right with all of the defenses, defects, and infirmities to which it would be subject in an action against the obligor by the assignor. Thus, in an action brought by the assignee against the obligor, the obligor may plead fraud, duress, undue influence, failure of consideration, breach of contract, or any other defense against the assignor arising out of the original contract. The obligor may assert rights of **setoff** or counterclaim arising out of entirely separate matters that he may have against the assignor, as long as they arose before he had notice of the assignment.

The Code permits the buyer under a contract of sale to agree as part of the contract that he will not assert against an assignee who takes an assignment for value and in good faith any claim or defense that the buyer may have against the seller.[5] Such a provision in an agreement gives greater marketability to the rights of the seller. The Federal Trade Commission, however, has invalidated such waiver of defense provisions in consumer credit transactions. This rule is discussed more fully in Chapter 24.

Notice

Notice   A valid assignment does not require that notice be given to the obligor. It is advisable, however, that such notice be given, because an assignee will lose his rights against the obligor if the obligor pays the assignor without notice of the assignment. It would be unfair to compel an obligor to pay a claim a second time when she has already paid it to the only person whom she knew to be entitled to receive payment. For example, Donald owes Gary $1,000 due on September 1. Gary assigns the debt to Paula on August 1, but neither Gary nor Paula informs Donald. On September 1, Donald pays Gary. Donald is fully discharged from his obligation while Gary is liable for $1,000 to Paula. On the other hand, if Paula had given notice of the assignment to Donald before September 1 and Donald had nevertheless paid Gary, Paula would then have the right to recover the $1,000 from either Donald or Gary. Furthermore, as already indicated, notice cuts off any defenses based on subsequent agreements between the obligor and assignor, as well as subsequent setoffs and counterclaims of the obligor that arise out of entirely separate matters.

Implied Warranties of Assignor

An **implied warranty** is an obligation imposed by law upon the transferor of property or contract rights. In the absence of an express intention to the contrary, an assignor who receives value makes the following implied warranties to the assignee with respect to the assigned right:

1. that he will do nothing to defeat or impair the assignment;
2. that the assigned right actually exists and is subject to no limitations or defenses other than those stated or apparent at the time of the assignment;
3. that any writing evidencing the right delivered to the assignee or exhibited to him as an inducement to accept the assignment is genuine and what it purports to be; and
4. that he has no knowledge of any fact that would impair the value of the assignment.

Thus, Eric has a right against Julia and assigns it for value to Gwen. Later Eric gives Julia a release. Gwen may recover damages from Eric.

The assignor is further bound by any specific **express warranties** he makes to the assignee about the right assigned. Unless explicitly stated, however, the assignor does *not* guarantee that the obligor will pay the assigned debt or otherwise perform.

Successive Assignments of the Same Right

The owner of a right could conceivably make successive assignments of the same claim to different persons. Although this action is morally and legally inappropriate, it raises the question of what rights successive assignees have. Assume that B owes A $1,000. On June 1, A for value assigns the debt to C. Thereafter, on June 15, A assigns it to D, who in good faith gives value and has no knowledge of the prior assignment by A to C. If the assignment is subject to Article 9, then its priority rules will control as discussed in Chapter 37. Otherwise, the priority is determined by the common law. The majority rule in the United States[6] is that the **first assignee in point of time** (C) prevails over later assignees. In England and in a minority of the States, the first assignee that notifies the obligor prevails.

The Restatement adopts a third view and provides that a prior assignee is entitled to the assigned right and its proceeds to the exclusion of a subsequent assignee, **except** where the prior assignment is revocable or voidable by the assignor or the subsequent assignee in good faith and without knowledge of the prior assignment gives value and obtains one of the following: (1) payment or satisfaction of the obligor's duty, (2) a judgment against the obligor, (3) a new contract with the obligor, or (4) possession of a writing of a type customarily accepted as a symbol or as evidence of the right assigned.

BOULEVARD NATIONAL BANK OF MIAMI v. AIR METAL INDUSTRIES
Supreme Court of Florida, 1965.
176 So.2d. 94.

Facts: Tompkins-Beckwith, as the contractor on a construction project, entered into a subcontract with a division of Air Metal Industries. Air Metal procured American Fire and Casualty Company to be surety on certain bonds in connection with contracts it was performing for Tompkins-Beckwith and others. As security for these bonds, on January 3, 1962, Air Metal executed an assignment to American Fire of all accounts receivable under the Tompkins-Beckwith subcontract. On November 26, 1962, Boulevard National Bank lent money to Air Metal. To secure the loans, Air Metal purported to assign to the bank certain accounts receivable it had under its subcontract with Tompkins-Beckwith.

In June 1963 Air Metal defaulted on various contracts bonded by American Fire. On July 1, 1963, American Fire served formal notice on Tompkins-Beckwith of Air Metal's assignment. Tompkins-Beckwith acknowledged the assignment and agreed to pay. In August 1963 Boulevard National Bank notified Tompkins-Beckwith of its assignment. Tompkins-Beckwith refused to recognize the bank's claim and, instead, paid all remaining funds that had accrued to Air Metal to American Fire. The bank then sued to enforce its claim under Air Metal's assignment. The trial court granted a summary judgment in favor of American Fire and Air Metal. The appellate court affirmed the summary judgment.

Decision: Summary judgment for American Fire and Air Metal affirmed.

Opinion: **Willis, J.**   The "question" * * * is whether the law of Florida requires recognition of the so-called "English" rule or "American" rule of priority between assignees of successive assignments of an account receivable or other similar chose in action. Stated in its simplest form, the American rule would give priority to the assignee first in point of time of assignment, while the English rule would give preference to the assignment of which the debtor was first given notice. Both rules presuppose the absence of any estoppel or other special equities in favor of or against either assignee. The English rule giving priority to the assignee first giving notice to the debtor is specifically qualified as applying "unless he takes a later assignment with notice of a previous one or without a valuable consideration". [Citations.]

* * *

The American rule for which petitioner contends is based upon the reasoning that an account or other chose in action may be assigned at will by the owner; that notice to the debtor is not essential to complete the assignment; and that when such assignment is made the property rights become vested in the assignee so that the assignor no longer has any interest in the account or chose which he may subsequently assign to another. [Citations.]

* * *

It is undoubted that the creditor of an account receivable or other similar chose in action arising out of contract may assign it to another so that the assignee may sue on it in his own name and make recovery. Formal requisites of such an assignment are not prescribed by statute and it may be accomplished by parol, by instrument in writing, or other mode, such as delivery of evidences of the debt, as may demonstrate an intent to transfer and an acceptance of it. * * *

It seems to be generally agreed that notice to a debtor of an assignment is necessary to impose on the debtor the duty of payment to the assignee, and that if before receiving such notice he pays the debt to the assignor, or to a subsequent assignee, he will be discharged from the debt. [Citation.] To regard the debtor as a total nonparticipant in the assignment by the creditor of his interests to another is to deny the obvious. An account receivable is only the right to receive payment of a debt which ultimately must be done by the act of the debtor. For the assignee to acquire the right to stand in the shoes of the assigning creditor he must acquire some "delivery" or "possession" of the debt constituting a means of clearly establishing his right to collect. The very nature of an account receivable renders "delivery" and "possession" matters very different and more difficult than in the case of tangible personalty and negotiable instruments which are readily capable of physical handling and holding. However, the very principles which render a sale of personal property with possession remaining in the vendor unexplained fraudulent and void as to creditors applies with equal urgency to choses in action which are the subject of assignment. It would seem to follow that the mere private dealing between the creditor and his assignee unaccompanied by any manifestations discernable to others having or considering the acquiring of an interest in the account would not meet the requirement of delivery and acceptance of possession which is essential to the consummation of the assignment. Proper notice to the debtor of the assignment is a manifestation of such delivery. It fixes the accountability of the debtor to the assignee instead of the assignor and enables all involved to deal more safely.

* * *

We thus find that the so-called English rule which the trial and appellate court approved and applied is harmonious with our jurisprudence, whereas the so-called American rule is not. * * *

DELEGATION OF DUTIES

As we indicated earlier, contractual **duties** are *not* assignable, but their performance may generally be *delegated* to a third person. For example, Helen has entered into a contract with Jack to deliver to Jack a specified amount of copper for $5,000. Helen may properly delegate the performance of this contract to Olivia. The courts, however, will examine a delegation more closely than an assignment because with a delegation the nondelegating party to the contract (the obligee) is being compelled to receive performance from a party with whom she has not dealt.

A delegation will not be permitted if (a) the nature of the duties are personal; (b) the per-formance is expressly made nondelegable; or (c) the delegation is prohibited by statute or public policy.[7] For example, a school teacher may not delegate her performance to another teacher, even if the substitute is equally competent, for this contract is personal in nature. On the other hand, where performance by a party involves no special skill and where no personal trust or confidence is involved, the party may delegate performance of his duty. The next case deals with this question.

Even when permitted, a delegation of a duty to a third person leaves the delegator bound to perform. If the delegator desires to be discharged of the duty, it may be possible for her to enter into an agreement obtaining the consent of the obligee to substitute a third person

MACKE COMPANY v. PIZZA OF GAITHERSBURG, INC.
Court of Appeals of Maryland, 1970.
259 Md. 479, 270 A.2d 645.

Facts: In 1966 Pizza of Gaithersburg and The Pizza Shops contracted with Virginia Coffee Service to have vending machines installed in each of their pizza establishments. One year later, The Macke Company purchased Virginia's assets and the vending machine contracts were assigned to Macke. When the Pizza Shops attempted to terminate their contracts for vending services, Macke brought suit for damages for breach of contract. The Pizza Shops argued that they had dealt with Macke before but had chosen Virginia because they preferred the way it conducted its business. They contended that since there was a material difference between the performance of Virginia and that of Macke, they were justified in refusing to recognize Virginia's delegation of its duties to Macke. Macke appealed from a judgment for the defendants.

Decision: Judgment reversed.

Opinion: **Singley, J.**   In the absence of a contrary provision—and there was none here—rights and duties under an executory bilateral contract may be assigned and delegated, subject to the exception that duties under a contract to provide personal services may never be delegated, nor rights be assigned under a contract where *delectus personae* [choice of person] was an ingredient of the bargain. [Citations.] *Crane Ice Cream Co. v. Terminal Freezing & Heating Co.* [citation], held that the right of an individual to purchase ice under a contract which by its terms reflected a knowledge of the individual's needs and reliance on his credit and responsibility could not be assigned to the corporation which purchased his business. In [citation], our predecessors held that an advertising agency could not delegate its duties under a contract which had been entered into by an advertiser who had relied on the agency's skill, judgment and taste.

The six machines were placed on the appellees' premises under a printed "Agreement-Contract" which identified the "customer," gave its place of business, described the vending machine, and * * *.

We cannot regard the agreements as contracts for personal services. They were either a license or concession granted Virginia by the appellees, or a lease of a portion of the appellees' premises, with Virginia agreeing to pay a percentage of gross sales as a license or concession fee or as rent, [citations], and were assignable by Virginia unless they imposed on Virginia duties of a personal or unique character which could not be delegated, [citation].

The appellees earnestly argue that they had dealt with Macke before and had chosen Virginia because they preferred the way it conducted its business. Specifically, they say that service was more personalized, since the president of Virginia kept the machines in working order, that commissions were paid in cash, and that Virginia permitted them to keep keys to the machines so that minor adjustments could be made when needed. Even if we assume all this to be true, the agreements with Virginia were silent as to the details of the working arrangements and contained only a provision requiring Virginia to "install * * * the above listed equipment and * * * maintain the equipment in good operating order and stocked with merchandise. "We think the Supreme Court of California put the problem of personal service in proper focus a century ago when it upheld the assignment of a contract to grade a San Francisco street:

All painters do not paint portraits like Sir Joshua Reynolds, nor landscapes like Claude Lorraine, nor do all writers write dramas like Shakespeare or fiction like Dickens. Rare genius and extraordinary skill are not transferable, and contracts for their employment are therefore personal, and cannot be assigned. But rare genius and extraordinary skill are not indispensable to the workmanlike digging down of a sand hill or the filling up of a depression to a given level, or the construction of brick sewers with manholes and covers, and contracts for such work are not personal, and may be assigned. [Citation.]

* * * Moreover, the difference between the service the Pizza Shops happened to be getting from Virginia and what they expected to get from Macke did not mount up to such a material change in the performance of obligations under the agreements as would justify the appellees' refusal to recognize the assignment, [citation].

* * *

* * * Modern authorities * * * hold that, absent provision to the contrary, a duty may be delegated, as distinguished from a right which can be assigned, and that the promisee cannot rescind, if the quality of the performance remains materially the same. * * *

As we see it, the delegation of duty by Virginia to Macke was entirely permissible under the terms of the agreements.

(the delegatee) in her place. This is a **novation** whereby the delegator is discharged and the third party becomes directly bound on his promise to the obligee.

A delegation authorizes a third party to perform the duty for the delegator. A delegatee becomes liable for performance only if he assents to perform the delegated duties. Thus, if Frank owes a duty to Grace, and Frank delegates that duty to Henry, Henry is not obligated to perform the duty to either Frank or Grace unless Henry agrees to do so. If Henry promises either Frank (the delegator) or Grace (the obligee) that he will perform Frank's duty, Henry is said to have **assumed the delegated duty** and becomes liable for nonperformance to both Frank and Grace. Accordingly, when there has been a delegation of duties *and* an assumption of the delegated duties, *both* the delegator and the delegatee are liable to the obligee for proper performance of the original contractual duty.

The question of whether the delegatee has assumed the delegated duties has frequently arisen when A and C agree to an assignment of A's *contract* with B. The common law rule is unclear because there is a division of authority among the jurisdictions. The Restatement[8] and the Code[9] clearly resolve this conflict by providing that, unless the language or circumstances indicate the contrary, an assignment of "the contract" or of "all my rights under the contract" or an assignment in similar general terms is an assignment of rights *and* a delegation of performance of the duties of the assignor, and its acceptance by the assignee constitutes a promise by her to perform those duties. For example, Cooper Oil Company has a contract to deliver oil to Halsey. Cooper makes a written assignment to Lowell Oil Company "of all Cooper's rights and duties under the contract." Lowell is under a duty to Halsey to deliver the oil called for by the contract, and Cooper is liable to Halsey if Lowell does not perform. You should also recall that the Restatement and the Code provide that a clause prohibiting an assignment of "the contract" is to be construed as barring only the delegation to the assignee (delegatee) of the assignor's (delegator's) performance, unless the circumstances indicate the contrary.

THIRD-PARTY BENEFICIARY CONTRACTS

A contract in which a party (the **promisor**) promises to render a certain performance not to the other party (the **promisee**) but to a third person (the **beneficiary**) is called a **third-party beneficiary contract.** The third person is not a party to the contract but is merely a beneficiary of the contract. Such contracts may be divided into two types: (1) intended beneficiary contracts and (2) incidental beneficiary contracts. An **intended beneficiary** is intended by the two parties to the contract (the promisor and promisee) to receive a benefit from the performance of their agreement. Accordingly, the courts generally enforce intended beneficiary third-party contracts. For example, A promises B to deliver an automobile to C if B promises to pay $10,000. C is the intended beneficiary.

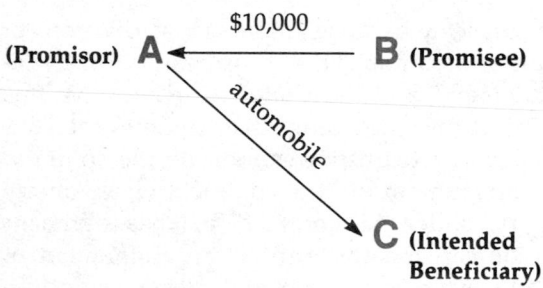

In an **incidental beneficiary** contract the third party is not intentionally to receive a benefit under the contract. Accordingly, no court will enforce the third party's right to the benefits of the contract. For example, A promises to purchase and deliver to B an automobile for $10,000. In all probability A would acquire the automobile from D. D would be an incidental beneficiary.

INTENDED BENEFICIARY

There are two types of intended beneficiaries: (1) donee beneficiaries and (2) creditor beneficiaries.

Donee Beneficiary

A third party is an **intended donee beneficiary** if the promisee's purpose in bargaining for and obtaining the agreement with the promisor was to make a gift to the beneficiary. The ordinary life insurance policy is an illustration of this type of intended beneficiary third-party contract. The insured (the promisee) makes a contract with an insurance company (the promisor), which promises, in consideration of premiums paid to it by the insured, to pay upon the death of the insured a stated sum of money to the named beneficiary, who is an *intended donee beneficiary.*

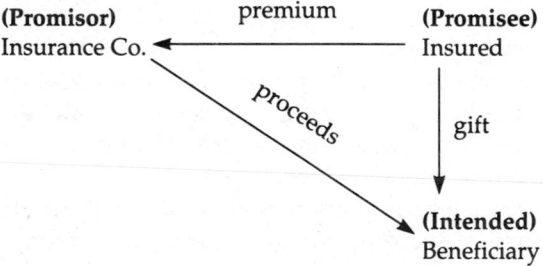

Creditor Beneficiary

A third person is an **intended creditor beneficiary** if the promisee intends the performance of the promise to satisfy a legal duty owed to the beneficiary, who is a creditor of the promisee. The contract involves consideration moving from the promisee to the promisor in exchange for the promisor's engaging to pay some debt or discharge some obligation of the promisee to the third person.

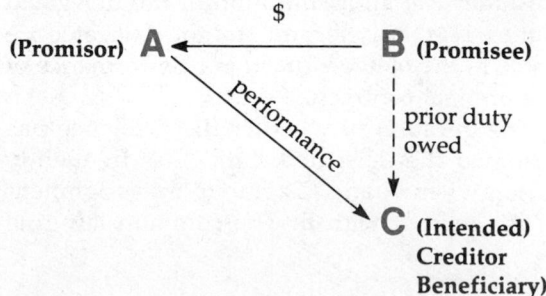

To illustrate: in the contract for the sale by Wesley of his business to Susan, she promises Wesley that she will pay all of his outstanding business debts, as listed in the contract. Wesley's creditors are creditor beneficiaries. Similarly, in the classic case of *Lawrence v. Fox*, 20 N.Y. 268 (1859), Holly loaned Fox $300 in consideration for Fox's promise to pay that sum to Lawrence, a creditor of Holly's. Fox failed to pay Lawrence, who sued Fox for the $300. The court held for Lawrence, who was permitted to recover as a third-party creditor beneficiary to the contract between Holly and Fox.

Rights of Intended Beneficiary

A contract for the benefit of an intended beneficiary confers upon that beneficiary rights that the beneficiary may enforce. Until these rights vest (take effect), however, the promisor and promisee may, by later agreement, vary or completely discharge these rights. There is considerable variation among the States as to when vesting takes place. Some States hold that vesting takes place immediately upon making the contract. In other States, vesting occurs when the third party learns of the contract and assents to it. In a third group of States, vesting requires the third party to change his position in reliance upon the promise made for his benefit. The Restatement has adopted the following position: If the contract between the promisor and promisee provides that its terms may not be varied without the consent of the beneficiary, such a provision will be upheld. If there is no such provision, the parties to the contract may rescind or vary the contract unless the intended beneficiary: (1) has brought an action on the promise, (2) has changed her position in reliance on it, or (3) has assented to the promise at the request of the promisor or promisee.

On the other hand, the promisor and promisee may provide that the benefits will *never* vest. For example, Mildred purchases an insurance policy on her own life, naming her husband as beneficiary. Her policy, as is common with such policies, reserves to Mildred the right to change the beneficiary or even to cancel the policy entirely.

An intended *donee* beneficiary may enforce the contract against the promisor only. He cannot maintain an action against the promisee, since the promisee was under no legal obligation to him. An intended *creditor* beneficiary, however, may sue either or both parties.

In an action by the intended beneficiary of a third party contract to enforce the promise, the promisor may assert any defense that would be available to him if the action had been brought by the promisee. The rights of the third party are based on the promisor's contract with the promisee. Thus, the absence of mutual assent or consideration, lack of capacity, fraud, mistake, and the like may be asserted by the promisor against the intended beneficiary.

BROWN v. NATIONAL SUPERMARKETS, INC.
Missouri Court of Appeals, Eastern District, Division Three, 1984.
679 S.W.2d 307.

Facts: Pauline Brown was shot and seriously injured by an unknown assailant in the parking lot of National Supermarkets. Pauline and George Brown brought a negligence action against National, Sentry Security Agency, and T. G. Watkins, a security guard and Sentry employee. The Browns maintained that the defendants have a legal duty to protect National's customers both in the store and in the parking lot and that this duty was breached. The defendants denied this allegation and were granted summary judgment by the trial court. The Browns appealed.

Decision: Trial court decision for summary judgment reversed and case remanded for action consistent with this opinion.

Opinion: Karohl, J.   The question as to Sentry and its employee is whether they assumed a duty to plaintiff if, as alleged, they contracted with National to provide protection National may owe to its patrons. The cases do not clearly establish whether a security company or security guard working for a business owner under contract have a duty to protect patrons from crime. It is the general rule that a private person has no duty to protect another from a deliberate criminal attack by a third person. [Citation.] We find that Sentry may or may not have assumed such a duty when it entered into the security contract. [Citation.] The existence of a duty will turn on the terms of the contract and the circumstances.

Plaintiffs allege in their amended petition that Sentry contracted with National to provide security against criminal activities for National *and its patrons* (our emphasis). In effect plaintiffs claim that the contract between National and Sentry is an attempt to perform National's previously established duty. The provisions of the contract are not in evidence. However, the National store manager testified by deposition that although he had never seen the contract he understood it to cover the area both inside and outside the store. T. G. Watkins, the security guard, stated in his deposition that he was never told to patrol the parking lot. As it is unclear whether the security company assumed any duty through the contract an issue of facts remain and summary judgment was error.

Plaintiffs may be third party beneficiaries to this contract. As such they may sue in tort or contract for any contract breach by Sentry or its employees.

Third party beneficiary is the nomenclature given to one who is not privy to a contract nor its consideration but to whom the law gives the right to maintain a cause of action for breach of contract. . . . Only those third parties for whose primary benefit the contracting parties intended to make the contract may maintain an action. . . . The intention of the parties is to be gleaned from the four corners of the contract, and if uncertain or ambiguous from the circumstances surrounding its execution.

[Citation.]

Privity of contract is no longer always necessary to maintain a suit for breach of contract. [Citation.]

[T]here are situations in which the making of the contract creates a relation between the defendant and the promise, which is sufficient to impose a tort duty of reasonable care . . .

. . . Where an agent or servant has accepted the control of property under a contract with his principal, and under circumstances where there is an obvious risk of harm to outsiders if he does not use reasonable care, the obligation of affirmative conduct has been imposed upon him.

W. Prosser, Law of Torts 623–624 (1971).

As a matter of law both National and Sentry *may* have a duty to protect National patrons from criminal assaults. Summary judgment was inappropriate because questions of fact remain.

INCIDENTAL BENEFICIARY

An incidental third-party beneficiary is a person whom the parties to a contract did not intend to benefit but who nevertheless would derive some benefit by its performance. For instance, a contract to raze an old, unsightly building and replace it with a costly, modern house would benefit the owner of the adjoining property by increasing his property's value. He would have no rights under the contract, however, as the benefit to him is unintended and incidental.

A third person who may be incidentally benefitted by the performance of a contract to which he is not a party has no rights under the contract. It was not the intention of either the promisee or the promisor that the third person benefit. Assume that for a stated consideration Charles promises Madeline that he will purchase and deliver to Madeline a new Sony television of the latest model. Madeline performs. Charles does not. Reiner, the local exclusive Sony dealer, has no rights under the contract, although performance by Charles would produce a sale from which Reiner would derive a benefit. Reiner is only an incidental beneficiary.

The following case further illustrates that incidental beneficiaries may not enforce contracts.

JACKSON, LEWIS, SCHNITZLER & KRUPMAN v. LOCAL 100, TRANSPORT WORKERS UNION OF AMERICA
Supreme Court, Special Term, Queens County, New York, 1981.
108 Misc.2d 458, 437 N.Y.S.2d 895.

Facts: On April 1, 1980, members of Local 100, Transport Workers Union of America (TWU), began an eleven-day mass transit strike that paralyzed the life and commerce of the city of New York. Jackson, Lewis, Schnitzler & Krupman, a Manhattan law firm, brought a class action suit against the TWU for the direct and foreseeable damages it suffered as a result of the union's illegal strike. The law firm sought to recover as a third-party beneficiary of the collective bargaining agreement between the union and New York City. The agreement contains a no-strike clause and states that the TWU agreed to cooperate with the city to provide a safe, efficient, and dependable mass transit system. The law firm argues that its members are a part of the general public that depends on the mass transit system to go to and from work. Therefore, they are in the class of persons for whose benefit the union has promised to provide dependable transportation service.

Decision: Judgment for the Transit Workers Union.

Opinion: Kassoff, J.   Plaintiffs * * * seek recovery as a third-party beneficiary of the collective bargaining agreement between defendant unions and the public employers. Plaintiffs particularly claim the benefit of the no-strike clauses contained in those agreements. Historically, New York has been in the vanguard of the development of the third-party beneficiary doctrine. The doctrine itself had its American genesis in *Lawrence v. Fox*, 20 N.Y. 268 [1859]. Subsequent cases have applied this principle to contracts where one of the parties was a governmental entity. [Citations.] Extensive research by the court has failed to disclose any New York case where a public sector union breached an explicit no-strike clause of a contract which explicitly referred to protecting the interests of those who utilize the public service. In this regard, the facts before the court are highly unusual.

The critical inquiry in third-party beneficiary claims is whether the contracting parties intended their contract to benefit third parties. The best evidence of such intent is language in the agreement to that effect. The TWU's agreement states one of its purposes is "[t]o assure to the people of the State of New York efficient, economic, sufficient and dependable transportation service * * * and to protect the interests of the public" (Agreement, Article 1A). The TWU has also agreed "to cooperate with the authorities in a joint effort to place and keep the transit system on a safe, efficient, economical operating basis" (Agreement, Article 4).

As a member of the public which depends on the public transit system and which employs dozens of persons who need the public transit system to get to and from work, plaintiffs argue that they are within the class of persons for whose benefit the TWU has promised to provide "dependable transportation service". [Citation.]

A person not a party to a contract may sue for damages resulting from non-performance if the contract demonstrates that its primary intent was to benefit that person. [Citations.] Such cannot be said to be the case here. Where, as here, the government agency contracts for services which it bears no obligation to provide to the public, no duty can be found against the promisor on behalf of the member of the public unless the contract clearly makes the promisor answerable to that person for the breach. This, the court does not find. [Citation.]

CHAPTER SUMMARY

Assignment of Rights	**Definition of Assignment** voluntary transfer to a third party of the rights arising from a contract so that the assignor's right to performance is extinguished
	■ *Assignor* party making an assignment
	■ *Assignee* party to whom contract rights are assigned
	■ *Obligor* party owing a duty to the assignor under the original contract
	Revocability of Assignment when the assignee gives consideration the assignor may not revoke the assignment
	Assignability most contract rights are assignable except:
	■ Assignments that materially increase the risk or burden upon the obligor
	■ Assignments of personal rights
	■ Assignments expressly forbidden by the contract
	■ Assignments prohibited by law
	Rights of Assignee assignee stands in the shoes of the assignor
	■ *Defenses of Obligor* may be asserted against the assignee
	■ *Implied Warranties* obligation imposed by law upon the assignor of a contract right
	■ *Express Warranty* explicitly made contractual promise regarding contract rights transferred
	■ *Successive Assignments* the majority rule is that the first assignee in point of time prevails over later assignees; minority rule is that the first assignee to notify the obligor prevails
Delegation of Duties	**Definition of Delegation** transfer to a third party of a contractual obligation
	■ *Delegator* party delegating his duty to a third party
	■ *Delagatee* third party to whom the delegator's duty is delegated
	■ *Obligee* party to whom a duty of performance is owed by the delegator and delegatee
	Delegability most contract duties may be delegated except:
	■ Duties that are personal
	■ Duties that are expressly nondelegable
	■ Duties whose delegation is prohibited by statute or public policy

Obligation of Delegator
- *Delegation*   delegator is still bound to perform original obligation
- *Novation*   contract substituting a new promisor for an existing promisor (who is no longer liable on the original contract and is not liable as a delegator) and to which the obligee is a party

Third-Party Beneficiary Contracts

Definition   a third-party beneficiary contract is one in which one party promises to render a performance to a third person (the beneficiary)

Intended Beneficiaries   third parties intended by the two contracting parties to receive a benefit from their contract
- *Donee Beneficiary*   a third party intended to receive a benefit from the agreement as a gift
- *Creditor Beneficiary*   a third person intended to receive a benefit from the agreement to satisfy a legal duty owed to him
- *Rights of Intended Beneficiaries*   an intended donee beneficiary may enforce the contract against the promisor; an intended creditor beneficiary may enforce the contract against either or both the promisor and the promisee

Incidental Beneficiary   third party whom the two parties to the contract have no intention of benefitting by their contract and who acquires no rights under the contract

QUESTIONS

1. Distinguish between an assignment of rights and a delegation of duties.
2. Identify (a) the requirements of an assignment of contract rights, and (b) those rights that are *not* assignable.
3. Identify those situations in which a delegation of duties is not permitted.
4. Distinguish between an intended beneficiary and an incidental beneficiary.
5. When do the rights of an intended beneficiary vest?

PROBLEMS

1. On December 1 Euphonia, a famous singer, contracted with Boito to sing at Boito's theater on December 31 for a fee of $25,000 to be paid immediately after the performance.
(a) Euphonia, for value received, assigns this fee to Carter.
(b) Euphonia, for value received, assigns this contract to sing to Dumont, an equally famous singer.
(c) Boito sells his theater to Edmund and assigns his contract with Euphonia to Edmund.
State the effect of each of these assignments.

2. The Smooth Paving Company entered into a paving contract with the city of Chicago. The contract contained the clause "contractor shall be liable for all damages to buildings resulting from the work performed." In the process of construction, one of the bulldozers of the Smooth Paving Company struck and broke a gas main, causing an explosion and a fire that destroyed the house of John Puff. Puff brought an appropriate action against the Smooth Paving Company to recover damages for the loss of his house. Decision?

3. Anne, who was unemployed, registered with the Speedy Employment Agency. A contract was then made under which Anne, in consideration of such position as the agency would obtain for Anne, agreed to pay the agency one-half of her first month's salary. The contract also contained an assignment by Anne to the agency of one-half of her first month's salary. Two weeks later, the agency obtained a permanent position for Anne with the Bostwick Co. at a monthly salary of $900. The agency also notified the Bostwick Co. of the assignment by Anne. At the end of the first month, the Bostwick Co. paid Anne her salary in full. Anne then quit and disappeared. The agency now sues the Bostwick Co. for $450 under the assignment. Decision?

4. Georgia purchased an option on Blackacre from Pamela for $1,000. The option contract contained a provision by which Georgia promised not to assign

the option contract without Pamela's permission. Georgia, without Pamela's permission, assigns the contract to Michael. Michael seeks to exercise the option, and Pamela refuses to sell Blackacre to him. Decision?

5. Julia contracts to sell to Hayden, an ice cream manufacturer, the amount of ice Hayden may need in his business for the ensuing three years to the extent of not more than 250 tons a week at a stated price per ton. Hayden makes a corresponding promise to Julia to buy such an amount of ice. Hayden sells his ice cream plant to Reed and assigns to Reed all Hayden's rights under the contract with Julia. On learning of the sale, Julia refused to furnish ice to Reed. Reed sues Julia for damages. Decision?

6. Brown enters into a written contract with Ideal Insurance Company under which, in consideration of the payment of the premiums, the insurance company promises to pay XYZ College the face amount of the policy, $100,000, on Brown's death. Brown pays the premiums until her death. Thereafter, XYZ College makes demand for the $100,000 of insurance company, which refuses to pay on the ground that XYZ College was not a party to the contract. Decision?

7. Grant and Debbie enter into a contract binding Grant personally to do some delicate cabinet work. Grant assigns his rights and delegates performance of his duties to Clarence.

(a) On being informed of this, Debbie agrees with Clarence, in consideration of Clarence's promise to do the work, that Debbie will accept Clarence's work, if properly done, instead of the performance promised by Grant. Later, without cause, Debbie refuses to allow Clarence to proceed with the work, though Clarence is ready to do so, and makes demand on Grant that Grant perform. Grant refuses. Can Clarence recover damages from Debbie? Can Debbie recover from Grant?

(b) Debbie refuses to permit Clarence to do the work, employs another carpenter, and brings an action against Grant, claiming as damages the difference between the contract price and the cost to employ the other carpenter. Decision?

8. Rebecca owes Lewis $2,500 due on November 1. On August 15 Lewis assigns this right for value received to Julia, who gives notice on September 10 of the assignment to Rebecca. On August 25 Lewis assigns the same right to Wayne, who in good faith gives value and has no prior knowledge of the assignment by Lewis to Julia. Wayne gives Rebecca notice of the assignment on August 30. What are the rights and obligations of Rebecca, Lewis, Julia, and Wayne?

9. Lisa hired Jay in the spring, as she had for many years, to set out in beds the flowers Lisa had grown in her greenhouses during the winter. The work was to be done in Lisa's absence for $300. Jay became ill the day after Lisa departed and requested his friend, Curtis, to set out the flowers, promising to pay Curtis $250 when he was paid. Curtis agreed. On completion of the planting, an agent of Lisa's, who had authority to dispense the money, paid Jay, and Jay paid Curtis. Within two days it became obvious that the planting was a disaster. Everything set out by Curtis had died of water rot, because he did not operate Lisa's automatic watering system properly.

May Lisa recover damages from Curtis? May Lisa recover damages from Jay, and, if so, does Jay have an action against Curtis?

10. Caleb, operator of a window-washing business, dictated a letter to his secretary addressed to Apartments, Inc., stating: "I will wash the windows of your apartment buildings at $4.10 per window to be paid on completion of the work." The secretary typed the letter, signed Caleb's name, and mailed it to Apartments, Inc. Apartments, Inc., replied: "Accept your offer."

Caleb wrote back: "I will wash them during the week starting July 10 and direct you to pay the money you will owe me to my son, Bernie. I am giving it to him as a wedding present." Caleb sent a signed copy of the letter to Bernie.

Caleb washed the windows during the time stated and demanded payment to him of $8,200 (2,000 windows at $4.10 each), informing Apartments, Inc., that he had changed his mind about having the money paid to Bernie.

What are the rights of the parties?

COMPUTER RESEARCH PROBLEMS

1. The International Association of Machinists (the union) was the bargaining agent for the employees of Powder Power Tool Corporation. On August 24, 1953, the union and the corporation executed a collective bargaining agreement providing for retroactively increased wage rates for the corporation's employees effective as of April 1, 1953. Three employees were working for Powder before and for several months after April 1, 1953, but were not employed by the corporation when the agreement was executed on August 24, 1953. They were paid to the time their employment terminated at the old wage scale. The three employees assigned their claims to Springer who brought this action against the corporation for the extra wages. Decision?

2. In March 1962 Adrian Saylor sold government bonds owned exclusively by him and with $6,450 of the proceeds opened a savings account in a bank in the name of "Mr. or Mrs. Adrian M. Saylor." In June 1963 Saylor deposited the additional sum of $2,132 of his own money in the account. There were no other deposits and no withdrawals prior to the death of Saylor in May 1964. Is the balance of the account on Saylor's death payable wholly to Adrian Saylor's estate, wholly to his widow, or half to each?

3. Linda King was found liable to Charlotte Clement as the result of an automobile accident. King, who was insolvent at the time, declared bankruptcy and directed her attorney, Prestwich, to list Clement as an unsecured creditor. The attorney failed to carry out this duty, and consequently King sued him for legal malpractice. When Clement pursued her judgment against King, she received a written assignment of King's legal malpractice claim against Prestwich. Clement has attempted to bring the claim, but Prestwich alleges that a claim for legal malpractice is not assignable. Decision?

4. Rensselaer Water Company contracted with the city of Rensselaer to provide water to the city for use in homes, public buildings, industry, and fire hydrants. During the term of the contract a building caught fire. The fire spread to a nearby warehouse and destroyed it and its contents. The water company knew of the fire but failed to supply adequate water pressure at the fire hydrant to extinguish the fire. The warehouse owner sued the water company for failure to fulfill its contract with the city. Decision?

ENDNOTES

1. Restatement, Second, Contracts, Section 317(1), Assignment of a Right.
2. Restatement, Second, Contracts, Section 317(2), Assignment of a Right; Uniform Commercial Code, Section 2—210(2), Assignment of Rights.
3. Restatement, Second, Contracts, Section 322, Contractual Prohibition of Assignment.
4. Uniform Commercial Code, Section 2—210(3), Delegation of Performance; Assignment of Rights.
5. Uniform Commercial Code, Section 9—206(1), Agreement Not to Assert Defenses Against Assignee.
6. Restatement, Second, Contracts, Section 342, Successive Assignees from the Same Assignor.
7. Restatement, Second, Contracts, Section 318, Delegation of Performance of Duty; Uniform Commercial Code, Section 2—210(1), Delegation of Performance; Assignment of Rights
8. Restatement, Second, Contracts, Section 328, Interpretation of Words of Assignment; Effect of Acceptance of Assignment.
9. Uniform Commercial Code, Section 2—210(4), Delegation of Performance; Assignment of Rights.

15 PERFORMANCE, BREACH, AND DISCHARGE

The subject of discharge of contracts concerns the termination of contractual duties. In earlier chapters we have seen how parties may become contractually bound by their promises. It is also important to know how a person may become unbound from a contract. When a contract is made, neither party intends that the duties created will exist forever. Contractual promises are made for a purpose, and the parties reasonably expect this purpose to be fulfilled by performance. But performance of a contractual duty is only one method of discharge.

Whatever causes a binding promise to cease to be binding is a discharge of the contract. In general, there are four kinds of discharge: (1) by performance of the parties, (2) by breach of one or both of the parties, (3) by agreement of the parties, and (4) by operation of law.

Moreover, many contractual promises are not absolute and unconditional promises to perform but rather are conditional promises. The obligation to perform conditional promises depends on the happening or nonhappening of a specific event. We shall discuss the subject of conditions briefly and then turn to the four kinds of discharge.

CONDITIONS

A **condition** is an event whose happening or nonhappening affects a duty of performance under a contract. Some conditions must be satisfied before any duty to perform arises; others terminate the duty to perform; still others either limit or modify the duty to perform. A condition is therefore the natural enemy of a promise. It is inserted in a contract to protect and benefit the promisor. The more conditions to which a promise is subject, the less content the promise has. A promise to pay $8,000 provided that such sum is realized from the sale of an automobile, provided the automobile is sold within sixty days, and provided that the automobile, which has been stolen, can be found, is clearly different from and worth considerably less than an unconditional promise by the same promisor to pay $8,000.

There is a fundamental difference between the breach or nonperformance of a promise and the failure or nonhappening of a condition. A breach of contract subjects the promisor to liability. It may or may not, depending on its materiality, excuse nonperformance by the other party, the promisee, of his duty under the contract. The happening or nonhappening of a condition, on the other hand, either prevents the promisee from acquiring a right or deprives him of a right, but subjects neither party to any liability.

Conditions may be either (1) express, (2) implied in fact, or (3) implied in law. They are also classified as (4) conditions concurrent, (5) conditions precedent, and (6) conditions subsequent.

Express Conditions

An **express condition** is explicitly set forth in language, usually preceded by such words as *provided that, on condition that, while, after, upon,* or *as soon as*. Although no particular form of words is necessary to create an express condition, the event to which the performance of the promise is made subject is in some manner clearly expressed. An illustration is the provision frequently found in building contracts that before the owner is required to pay, the builder shall furnish the architect's certificate stating that the building has been constructed according to the plans and specifications. The price is being paid for the building, not for the certificate, yet before the owner is obliged to pay, he must have both the building and the certificate. The duty of payment was made expressly conditional on the presentation of the certificate.

The parties to a contract may also agree that performance by one of them shall be to the **satisfaction** of the other, who will not be obligated to pay for it unless he is satisfied. This is an express condition to the duty to pay for the performance. It is a valid condition. Assume that tailor Ken contracts to make a suit of clothes to Dick's satisfaction, and that Dick promises to pay Ken $250 for the suit if he is satisfied with it when completed. Ken completes the suit using materials ordered by Dick. The suit fits Dick beautifully, but Dick tells Ken that he is not satisfied with it and refuses to accept or pay for it. Ken is not entitled to recover $250 or any amount from Dick because the express condition did not happen. This is so even if the dissatisfaction of Dick, although honest and sincere, is unreasonable. Where satisfaction relates to a matter of personal taste, opinion, or judgment, the law applies the **subjective satisfaction** standard, and the condition has not occurred if the promisor is actually dissatisfied. If the contract does not clearly indicate that satisfaction is subjective, or if the performance contracted for relates to mechanical fitness or utility, the law would assume an **objective satisfaction** standard. For example, the objective standard of satisfaction would be applied in the sale of a building or goods; it would be assumed that the satisfaction standard applies to the marketability, utility, or mechanical fitness of the item being sold. In such cases, the question would not be whether the promisor was actually satisfied with the performance by the other party, but whether as a reasonable man he ought to be satisfied.

Implied in Fact Conditions

Implied in fact conditions are similar to express conditions in that they are understood by the parties to be part of the agreement even though they are not stated in express language. They are necessarily inferred from the promise contained in the contract. Thus, if Edna, for $750, contracts to paint Sy's house any color desired by Sy, it is necessarily implied in fact that Sy will inform Edna of the desired color before Edna begins to paint. The notification of choice of color is an implied in fact condition, an operative event that must occur before Edna is subject to the duty of painting the house.

Implied in Law Conditions

An **implied in law condition** is imposed by law in order to accomplish a just and fair result. For example, Fernando contracts to sell a certain tract of land to Marie for $18,000, but the contract is silent as to the time of delivery of the deed and payment of the price. According to the law, the contract implies that payment and delivery of the deed are not independent of each other. The courts will treat the promises as mutually dependent and will therefore hold that a delivery or tender of the deed by Fernando to Marie is a condition to the duty of Marie to pay the price. Conversely, payment or tender of $18,000 by Marie to Fernando is a condition to the duty of Fernando to deliver the deed to Marie. If the contract specifies a sale on credit, however, giving Marie thirty days after delivery of the deed within which to pay the price, these conditions are not implied by law, because the parties by their contract have expressly made their respective duties of performance independent of each other.

Concurrent Conditions

Concurrent conditions are performances by two mutual promisors that are to take place at the same time. As we indicated in the section above, in the absence of agreement to the contrary, the law assumes that the respective performances under a contract are concurrent conditions. See *K & G Construction Co. v. Harris* on page 305 for an illustration of mutually dependent, concurrent conditions.

Condition Precedent

A **condition precedent** is an event that must occur before performance is due under a contract. In other words, the immediate duty of one party to perform is subject to the condition that some event must first occur. For instance, Steve is to deliver shoes to Nancy on June 1, and Nancy is to pay for the shoes on July 15. Steve's delivery of the shoes is a condition precedent to Nancy's performance. Similarly, if Rachel promises to buy Justin's land for $50,000, provided Rachel can obtain financing in the amount of $40,000 at 12 percent or less for thirty years within sixty days of signing the contract, Rachel's obtaining the specified financing is a condition precedent to her duty. If the condition is met, Rachel is bound to perform; if it does not occur, she is not bound to perform. Rachel, however, is under an implied in law duty to use her best efforts to obtain financing under these terms.

Condition Subsequent

A **condition subsequent** is an event that terminates an existing duty. Where goods are sold under terms of "sale or return," the buyer has the right to return the goods to the seller within a stated period but is under an immediate duty to pay the price unless credit has been agreed on. The duty to pay the price is terminated by a return of the goods, which operates as a condition subsequent.

DISCHARGE BY PERFORMANCE

Discharge by **performance** is undoubtedly the most frequent method of discharging a contractual duty. If a promisor exactly performs his duty under the contract, he is no longer subject to that duty.[1] Substantial but less than exact performance does not fully discharge a promisor, although under the common law, substantial performance by one party deprives

the other party of an excuse for nonperformance of his promise.

Where the contract is bilateral, the refusal or rejection of a **tender** or offer of performance by one party may be treated as a repudiation, excusing or discharging the tendering party from further duty of performance under the contract. A tender of payment of a debt past due does not discharge the debt if the creditor refuses to accept the tender; instead, further accumulation of interest on the debt will stop.

DISCHARGE BY BREACH

A **breach** of a contract is a wrongful failure to perform the terms of a contract.[1] Breach of contract always gives rise to a cause of action for damages by the aggrieved (injured) party. It may, however, have a more important effect. Because of the rule that one party need not perform unless the other party performs, an uncured (uncorrected) material breach by one party operates as an excuse for nonperformance by the other party and discharges the aggrieved party from any further duty under the contract. If the breach, on the other hand, is nonmaterial, the aggrieved party is not discharged from the contract, although she may recover money damages.

Material Breach

An unjustified failure to perform *substantially* the obligations promised in a contract is a **material breach.** The key is whether the aggrieved party obtained substantially what he bargained for or were his rights under the contract significantly impaired by the breach.[2] A material breach discharges the aggrieved party from his duty of performance. For instance, Joe orders a specially made, tailored suit from Peggy to be made of wool, but Peggy makes the suit of cotton instead. Peggy has materially breached the contract. Consequently, Joe is discharged from his duty to pay for the suit. Joe may also sue for money damages.

Although there are no clear-cut rules as to what constitutes a material breach, several basic principles can be applied. First, partial performance is a material breach of a contract if it omits some essential part of the contract. Second, the courts will consider a breach material if it is quantitatively or qualitatively serious. Third, an *intentional* breach of contract is generally held to be material. Fourth, a failure to perform a promise promptly is a material breach if time is of the essence; that is, if the parties have clearly indicated that a failure to perform by the stated time is material; otherwise, the aggrieved party may recover damages only for loss caused by the delay. Fifth, the parties to a contract may, within limits, specify what breaches are to be considered material.

K & G CONSTRUCTION CO. v. HARRIS

Court of Appeals of Maryland, 1960.
223 Md. 305, 164 A.2d 451.

Facts: K & G Construction Co. was the owner and general contractor for a housing subdivision project. Harris contracted with it to do excavating and earth-moving work on the project. Certain provisions of the contract stated that: (1) K & G was to make monthly progress payments to Harris; (2) no such payments were to be made until Harris obtained liability insurance; and (3) all of Harris's work on the project must be performed in a workmanlike manner. On August 9 a bulldozer operator, working for Harris, drove too close to one of K & G's houses, causing the collapse of a wall and other damage. When Harris and his insurance carrier denied liability and refused to pay for the damage, K & G refused to make the August monthly progress payment. Harris, nonetheless, continued to work on the project until mid-September when it ceased its operations due to K & G's refusal to make the progress payment. K & G had another excavator finish the job at an added cost of $450. It then sued Harris for the bulldozer damage, alleging negligence, and also for the $450 damages for breach of contract. Harris claims that K & G defaulted first, having no legal right to refuse the August progress payment. The trial court entered judgment for Harris and K & G appealed.

Decision: Judgment for Harris reversed and judgment entered in favor of K & G Construction Co. for $450.

Opinion: **Prescott, J.** The vital question, more tersely stated, remains: Did the contractor have a right, under the circumstances, to refuse to make the progress payment due on August 10, 1958?

The answer involves interesting and important principles of contract law. Promises and counter-promises made by the respective parties to a contract have certain relations to one another, which determine many of the rights and liabilities of the parties. Broadly speaking, they are (1) independent of each other or (2) mutually dependent, one upon the other. They are independent of each other if the parties intend that *performance* by each of them is in no way conditioned upon *performance* by the other. [Citation.] In other words, the parties exchange promises for promises, not the *performance* of promises for the *performance* of promises. [Citation.] A failure to perform an independent promise does not excuse non-performance on the part of the adversary party, but each is required to perform his promise, and, if one does not perform, he is liable to the adversary party for such non-performance. (Of course, if litigation ensues questions of set-off or recoupment frequently arise.) Promises are mutually dependent if the parties intend *performance* by one to be conditioned upon *performance* by the other, and, if they be mutually dependent, they may be (a) precedent, i.e., a promise that is to be performed before a corresponding promise on the part of the adversary party is to be performed, (b) subsequent, i.e., a corresponding promise that is not to be performed until the other party to the contract has performed a precedent covenant, or (c) concurrent, i.e., promises that are to be performed at the same time by each of the parties, who are respectively bound to perform each. [Citation.]

* * * The modern rule, which seems to be of almost universal application, is that there is a presumption that mutual promises in a contract are dependent and are to be so regarded, whenever possible. [Citations.] * * *

* * * It would, indeed present an unusual situation if we were to hold that a building contractor, who has obtained someone to do work for him and has agreed to pay each month for the work performed in the previous month, has to continue the monthly payments, irrespective of the degree of skill and care displayed in the performance of work, and his only recourse is by way of suit for ill-performance. If this were the law, it is conceivable, in fact, probable, that many contractors would become insolvent before they were able to complete their contracts. As was stated by [citation]: "Covenants are to be construed as dependent or independent according to the intention of the parties and the good sense of the case."

We hold that when the subcontractor's employee negligently damaged the contractor's wall, this constituted a breach of the subcontractor's promise to perform his work in a "workmanlike manner, and in accordance with the best practices." [Citations.] And there can be little doubt that the breach was material: the damage to the wall amounted to more than double the payment due on August 10. [Citation.] Corbin, [citation], says: "The failure of a contractor's (in our case, the subcontractor's) performance to constitute 'substantial' performance may justify the owner (in our case, the contractor) in refusing to make a progress payment . . . If the refusal to pay an installment is justified on the owner's (contractor's) part, the contractor (subcontractor) is not justified in abandoning work by reason of that refusal. His abandonment of the work will itself be a wrongful repudiation that goes to the essence, even if the defects in performance did not." [Citations.] Professor Corbin, in § 954, states further: "The unexcused failure of a contractor to render a promised performance when it is due is always a breach of contract. . . . Such failure may be of such great importance as to constitute what has been called herein a 'total' breach. . . . For a failure of performance constituting such a 'total' breach, an action for remedies that are appropriate thereto is at once maintainable. Yet the injured party is not required to bring such action. He has the option of treating the nonperformance as a 'partial' breach only. . . ." In permitting the subcontractor to proceed with work on the project after August 9, the contractor, obviously, treated the breach by the subcontractor as a partial one. As the promises were mutually dependent and the subcontractor had made a material breach in his performance, this justified the contractor in refusing to make the August 10 payment; hence, as the contractor was not in default, the subcontractor again breached the contract when he, on September 12, discontinued work on the project, which rendered him liable (by the express terms of the contract) to the contractor for his increased cost in having the excavating done—a stipulated amount of $450.

The Code greatly alters the common law doctrine of material breach by adopting what is known as the **perfect tender rule.** This rule, which we discuss more fully in Chapter 20, essentially provides that *any* deviation from the promised performance in a sales contract under the Code constitutes a material breach of the contract and discharges the aggrieved party of his duty of performance.

Substantial Performance

If a party substantially, but not completely, performs her obligations under a contract, the courts will generally allow that party to obtain the other party's performance less any damages caused by the partial performance. If no harm is caused, the breaching party will obtain the other party's full contractual performance. Thus, in the specially ordered suit illustration, if Peggy, the tailor, improperly used black buttons instead of blue, she would be permitted to collect from Joe the contract price of the suit less the damage, if any, caused to Joe by the substitution of the wrongly colored but-tons. The doctrine of **substantial performance** assumes particular importance in the construction industry in cases where a structure is built on the aggrieved party's land. Consider the following: Adam builds a $300,000 house for Betty but deviates from the specifications, causing Betty $10,000 in damages. If the courts considered this breach material, then Betty would not have to pay for the house that is now on her land. This would clearly be unjust, however. Therefore, because Adam's performance has been substantial, the courts would probably not deem the breach material. As a result, Adam would be able to collect $290,000 from Betty.

MAYOR & CITY OF DOUGLASVILLE v. HILDEBRAND
Court of Appeals of Georgia, 1985.
175 Ga.App. 434, 333 S.E.2d 674.

Facts: On August 20, 1981, Hildebrand entered into a written contract with the city of Douglasville whereby he was to serve as community development project engineer for three years at an "annual fee" of $19,000. This salary figure could be changed without affecting the other terms of the contract. One of the provisions for termination of the contract was written notice by either party to the other at any time at least ninety days prior to the intended date of termination. The contract listed a number of services and duties Hildebrand was to perform for the city, among them: (1) keeping the community development director (Hildebrand's supervisor) informed at all times of his whereabouts and how he could be contacted, and (2) attending meetings at which his presence was requested. On September 20, 1983, by which time Hildebrand's annual fee had risen to $1,915.83 per month, the city fired Hildebrand effective immediately, citing "certain material breaches . . . of the. . . agreement." Hildebrand sued the mayor and city for breach of his employment contract, seeking damages in the amount of $5,747.49 because of the city's failure to give him ninety days' notice prior to termination. The city contended that Hildebrand repeatedly violated the terms and conditions of the contract. The city specifically charged that he did not attend the necessary meetings although requested to do so and seldom if ever kept his supervisor informed of his whereabouts and how he could be contacted. The trial court granted summary judgment to Hildebrand, and the city appealed.

Decision: Judgment for Hildebrand affirmed.

Opinion: Beasley, J. Assuming the city could repudiate the contract without giving ninety days notice, the requirement for such termination must be based on a material breach, a substantial failure to perform. A breach which is "incidental and subordinate to the main purpose of the contract, and which may be compensated in damages, does not warrant a rescission . . ." or termination nor does "a mere breach of contract not so substantial and fundamental as to defeat the object of the parties in making the agreement." In order to trigger the right to rescission, "the act failed to be performed must go to the root of the contract. . . ." [Citation.]

* * *

Here there were broad conclusions in the affidavit for the city as to plaintiff's "continuous failure to comply" with the contractual terms. Since mere legal conclusions and allegations present no issue of fact on motion for summary judgment, [citation] we need consider only the two specific charges involving plaintiff's alleged noncompliance. Neither alone nor collectively do either rise to the level necessary to warrant termination, i.e., constituting noncompliance, so substantial and fundamental as to defeat the contract's object. That being true, the city was obliged to give plaintiff the ninety-day notice of termination to which it had agreed in the contract.

* * *

A wrongful discharge in violation of a contract right to continued employment gives an employee the right to recover damages. Even though there is a repudiation of the promise of future earnings, the injured party is not necessarily entitled to the sum for the complete contract term. [Citation.] "Where a contract of employment expressly empowers an employer to terminate the contract upon giving notice, recovery for wrongful breach is limited to the notice period." [Citation.] Here plaintiff is limited to 90 days, to his actual contractual loss, as a measure of liquidated damages.

Prevention of Performance

One party's substantial interference with or prevention of performance by the other generally constitutes a material breach that discharges the other party to the contract. For instance, Dale prevents an architect from giving a certificate that is a condition to Dale's liability to pay Lucy a certain sum of money. Dale may not use Lucy's failure to produce a certificate as an excuse for nonpayment. Likewise, if Maude has contracted to grow a certain crop for Harold, and after Maude has planted the seed, Harold plows the field and destroys the seedling plants, his interference with Maude's performance discharges Maude from her duty under the contract. It does not, however, discharge Harold from his duty under the contract.

Anticipatory Repudiation

A breach of contract is simply a failure to perform the terms of the contract. It is logically and physically impossible to fail to perform a duty before the date that performance is due.

A party, however, may announce before the due date that she will not perform, or she may commit an act that makes her unable to perform. Either of these acts is a repudiation of the contract, which notifies the other party that a breach is imminent. Such repudiation before the date fixed by the contract for performance is called an **anticipatory repudiation.** The courts, as shown in the leading case that follows, allow it to be treated as a breach and permit the nonrepudiating party to bring suit immediately as if it were a breach. Nonetheless, under the concept of election, the nonbreaching party may wait until the time of performance to see if the repudiator will retract his repudiation and perform his contractual duties. If the "repudiator" does perform, then there is a discharge by performance; if he does not perform, there is a material breach.

Material Alteration of Written Contract

An unauthorized alteration or change of *any* of the material terms or provisions of a written contract or document is a discharge of the

HOCHSTER v. De La TOUR
2 Ellis and Blackburn Reports.
678 (Q.B. 1853) (England).

Facts: On April 12, 1852, Hochster contracted with De La Tour to serve as a guide for De La Tour on his three-month trip to Europe, beginning on June 1 at an agreed-upon salary. On May 11 De La Tour notified Hochster that he would not need Hochster's services. He also refused to pay Hochster any compensation. Hochster brings this action to recover damages for breach of contract.

Decision: Judgment for Hochster.

Opinion: Lord Campbell, C. J. On this motion * * * the question arises, Whether, if there be an agreement between A. and B., whereby B. engages to employ A. on and from a future day for a given period of time, to travel with him into a foreign country as a [guide], and to start with him in that capacity on that day, A. being to receive a monthly salary during the continuance of such service, B. may, before the day, refuse to perform the agreement and break and renounce it, so as to entitle A. before the day to commence an action against B. to recover damages for breach of the agreement; A. having been ready and willing to perform it, till it was broken and renounced by B.

* * *

  If the plaintiff has no remedy for breach of the contract unless he treats the contract as in force, and acts upon it down to the 1st June, 1852, it follows that, till then, he must enter into no employment which will interfere with his promise "to start with the defendant on such travels on the day and year," and that he must then be properly equipped in all respects as a [guide] for a three months' tour on the continent of Europe. But it is surely much more rational, and more for the benefit of both parties, that, after the renunciation of the agreement by the defendant, the plaintiff should be at liberty to consider himself absolved from any future performance of it, retaining his right to sue for any damage he has suffered from the breach of it. Thus, instead of remaining idle and laying out money in preparations which must be useless, he is at liberty to seek service under another employer, which would go in mitigation of the damages to which he would otherwise be entitled for a breach of the contract. It seems strange that the defendant, after renouncing the contract, and absolutely declaring that he will never act under it, should be permitted to object that faith is given to his assertion, and that an opportunity is not left to him of changing his mind.

* * *

  The man who wrongfully renounces a contract into which he has deliberately entered cannot justly complain if he is immediately sued for a compensation in damage by the man whom he has injured: and it seems reasonable to allow an option to the injured party, either to sue immediately, or to wait till the time when the act was to be done, still holding it as prospectively binding for the exercise of this option, which may be advantageous to the innocent party, and cannot be prejudicial to the wrongdoer.

entire contract.[3] To be a discharge, the alteration must be material and fraudulent and must be the act of a party to the contract or someone acting on his behalf. An unauthorized change in the terms of a written contract by a person who is not a party to the contract does not discharge the contract.

DISCHARGE BY AGREEMENT OF THE PARTIES

The parties to a contract may by agreement discharge each other from performance under the contract. They may do this before breach by rescission, by substituted contract, or by novation. Liability after breach of contract may be discharged by an accord and satisfaction.

Mutual Rescission

A **rescission** is an agreement between the parties to terminate their respective duties under the contract. It is a contract to end a contract. All of the essentials of a contract must be present. Each party, as shown in the following case, furnishes consideration in giving up his rights under the contract in exchange for the other party's relinquishment of his rights under the contract.

WATTS CONSTRUCTION CO. v. CULLMAN COUNTY
Supreme Court of Alabama, 1980.
382 So.2d 520.

Facts: In May 1976 Watts was awarded a construction contract, based on its low bid, by the Cullman County Commission. The contract provided that it would not become effective until approved by the state director of the Farmers Home Administration. In September construction still had not been authorized, and Watts wrote to the County Commission requesting a 5 percent price increase to reflect seasonal and inflationary price increases. The County Commission countered with an offer of 3.5 percent. Watts then wrote the commission, insisting on a 5 percent increase and stating that if this was not agreeable, it was withdrawing its original bid. The commission obtained another company to perform the project, and on October 14, 1976, informed Watts that it had accepted the withdrawal of the bid. Watts sued for breach of contract. The trial court granted the county's motion for summary judgment.

Decision: The judgment entered in favor of Cullman County is affirmed.

Opinion: **Shores, J.**   Watts's letter of September 21 withdrawing his bid and the commission's letter of October 14 accepting that withdrawal effectively rescinded any contract that might have existed. Parties to a written contract may by mutual consent and without other consideration rescind the contract. [Citation.] Where the acts and conduct of one party inconsistent with the existence of a contract are acquiesced in by the other, such contract will be treated as abandoned or rescinded. [Citation.] Watts's demand for an increase in the contract price demonstrated his intention not to be bound by the original contract. The commission acquiesced in his desire not to be so bound, and the contract was rescinded. Once a party to a contract has repudiated or broken it, he cannot reinstate the contract by an offer to perform. [Citation.] Where the parties by mutual agreement rescinded a contract, one of the parties thereto cannot recover damages in an action for breach of contract. [Citation.] Where parties agree to rescind the contract, each gives up the provisions for its benefit, and the parties are then competent to contract with others. [Citation.]

A contract containing a provision that is contrary to or inconsistent with a provision in a prior contract between the same parties is a mutual rescission of the inconsistent provision in the prior contract. Whether the later contract completely supersedes and discharges all of the provisions of the prior contract is a matter of interpretation.

Substituted Contracts

A **substituted contract** occurs when the parties to a contract mutually agree to rescind their original contract and enter into a new one.[4] Substituted contracts are perfectly valid and effective to discharge the original contract and to impose obligations under the new contract.

Accord and Satisfaction

An *accord* is a contract between a promisee and promisor by which the promisee agrees to accept and the promisor agrees to give a substituted performance in *satisfaction* of an existing contractual duty.[5] Thus, if Dan owes Sara $500, and the parties agree that Dan will paint Sara's house in satisfaction of the debt, the agreement is an executory accord. The debt, however, is not discharged until Dan performs the accord by painting Sara's house; the $500 debt is then discharged by **accord and satisfaction.**

Novation

A **novation** is a substituted contract that involves an agreement among *three* parties to substitute a new promisee for the existing promisee or to replace the existing promisor with a new one.[6] A novation discharges the old obligation because it creates a new contract in which there is either a new promisee or a new promisor. Thus, if B owes A $500, and A, B, and C agree that C will pay the debt and B will be discharged, the novation is the substitution of the new debtor C for B. Alternatively, if the three parties agree that B will pay $500 to C instead of to A, the novation is the substitution of a new creditor C for A. In each instance the debt owed by B to A is discharged.

DISCHARGE BY OPERATION OF LAW

In this chapter we have considered various ways by which contractual duties may be discharged. In all of these cases, the discharge resulted from the action of one or both of the parties to the contract. In this section, we examine discharge brought about by the operation of law.

Subsequent Illegality

The performance of a contract that was legal when formed may become illegal or impractical because of a subsequently enacted law. In such a case, the duty of performance is discharged.[7] For example, Linda contracts to sell and deliver to Carlos ten cases of a certain whiskey each month for one year. A subsequent prohibition law makes the manufacture, transportation, or sale of intoxicating liquor unlawful. The duties in the contract that are still unperformed by Linda are discharged.

Impossibility

It may be impossible for a promisor to perform his contract because he is financially unable or because he personally lacks the capability or competence. This is *subjective* impossibility and does not excuse the promisor from liability for breach of contract. For example, the Christys entered into a written contract to purchase an apartment house from Pilkinton for $30,000. Pilkinton tendered a deed to the property and demanded payment of the unpaid balance of $29,000 due on the purchase price. As a result of a decline in Christy's used car business, the Christys did not possess and could not borrow the unpaid balance and, thus, asserted that it was impossible for them to perform their contract. Judgment for Pilkinton. There is an important distinction between objective impossibility, which amounts to saying, "the thing cannot be done," and subjective impossibility—"I cannot do it." The latter, which is well illustrated by a promisor's financial inability to pay, does not discharge the contractual duty. *Christy v. Pilkinton*, 224 Ark. 407, 273 S.W.2d 533 (1954).

As noted in *Christy v. Pilkinton*, performance may be impossible not because the particular promisor is unable to perform, but because no one is able to perform. This is **objective impossibility** and generally will be held to excuse the promisor or discharge his duty to perform. Thus, the death or illness of a person who has contracted to render personal services is a discharge of his contractual duty. Furthermore, if a jockey contracts to ride a certain horse in the Kentucky Derby and the horse dies prior to the derby, the contract is discharged. It is objectively impossible for this or any other jockey to perform the contract. Also, if Ken contracts to lease to Karlene a certain ballroom for a party on a scheduled future date, destruction of the ballroom by fire without Ken's fault before the scheduled event discharges the contract. Destruction of the subject matter or of the agreed-upon means of performance of a contract is excusable impossibility.

Where the purpose of a contract has been frustrated by unexpected circumstances that deprive the performance of the value attached to it by the parties, although performance is not impossible, the courts generally regard the frustration as a discharge. This rule developed from the so-called coronation cases. When Edward VII became king of England on the death of his mother Queen Victoria, impressive coronation ceremonies were planned, including a procession along a designated route through London. Owners and lessees of buildings along the route made contracts to permit the use of rooms on the day scheduled for the procession. The king became ill, and the procession did not take place. Consequently the rooms were not used. Numerous suits were filed, some by landowners seeking to hold the would-be viewers liable on their promises, and some by the would-be viewers seeking to recover money they had paid in advance for the rooms. The principle involved was novel, but from these cases evolved the **frustration of purpose** doctrine, under which a contract is discharged if supervening circumstances make impossible the fulfillment of a purpose that both parties had in mind, unless one of the parties contractually assumed that risk.

The Restatement[8] and the Code[9] conform to and expand this position by providing that performance need not be actually or literally impossible, but that **commercial impracticability** will excuse nonperformance. This does not mean mere hardship or that the cost of performance would be more than expected. A party will be discharged from performing his duty only when his performance is made impracticable by a supervening event. Moreover, the nonoccurrence of the subsequent event must have been a "basic assumption" made by both parties when entering into the contract.

 NORTHERN CORP. v. CHUGACH ELECTRICAL ASSOCIATION
Supreme Court of Alaska, 1974.
518 P.2d 76.

Facts: Northern Corporation entered into a contract with Chugach in August 1966 to repair and upgrade the upstream face of Cooper Lake Dam in Alaska. The contract required Northern to obtain rock from a quarry site at the opposite end of the lake and to transport the rock to the dam during the winter across the ice on the lake. In December 1966 Northern cleared the road on the ice to permit deeper freezing, but thereafter water overflowed on the ice preventing its use. Northern complained of unsafe conditions of the lake ice, but Chugach insisted on performance. In March 1967 one of Northern's loaded trucks broke through the ice and sank. Northern continued to encounter difficulties and ceased operations with the approval of Chugach. On January 8, 1968, Chugach notified Northern that it would be in default unless all rock was hauled by April 1. After two more trucks broke through the ice, causing the deaths of the drivers, Northern ceased operations and notified Chugach that it would make no more attempts to haul across the lake. Northern advised Chugach it considered the contract terminated for impossibility of performance and commenced suit to recover the cost incurred in attempting to complete the contract. The trial court found for Northern.

Decision: Judgment for Northern affirmed.

Opinion: Boochever, J. The focal question is whether the * * * contract was impossible of performance. The September 27, 1966 directive specified that the rock was to be transported "across Cooper Lake to the dam site when such lake is frozen to a sufficient depth to permit heavy vehicle traffic thereon," and * * * specified that the hauling to the dam site would be done during the winter of 1966–67. It is therefore clear that the parties contemplated that the rock would be transported across the frozen lake by truck. Northern's repeated efforts to perform the contract by this method during the winter of 1966–67 and subsequently in February 1968, culminating in the tragic loss of life, abundantly support the trial court's finding that the contract was impossible of performance by this method.

Chugach contends, however, that Northern was nevertheless bound to perform, and that it could have used means other than hauling by truck across the ice to transport the rock. The answer to Chugach's contention is that * * * the parties contemplated that the rock would be hauled by truck once the ice froze to a sufficient depth to support the weight of the vehicles. The specification of this particular method of performance presupposed the existence of ice frozen to the requisite depth. Since this expectation of the parties was never fulfilled, and since the provisions relating to the means of performance was clearly material, Northern's duty to perform was discharged by reason of impossibility.

There is an additional reason for our holding that Northern's duty to perform was discharged because of impossibility. It is true that in order for a defendant to prevail under the original common law doctrine of impossibility, he had to show that no one else could have performed the contract. However, this harsh rule has gradually been eroded, and the Restatement of Contracts has departed from the early common law rule by recognizing the principle of "commercial impracticability." Under this doctrine, a party is discharged from his contract obligations, even if it is technically possible to perform them, if the costs of performance would be so disproportionate to that reasonably contemplated by the parties as to make the contract totally impractical in a commercial sense. * * * Removed from the strictures of the common law, "impossibility" in its modern context has become a coat of many colors, including among its hues the point argued here—namely, impossibility predicated upon "commercial impracticability." This concept—which finds expression both in case law * * * and in other authorities* * * is grounded upon the assumption that in legal contemplation something is impracticable when it can only be done at an excessive and unreasonable cost. As stated in *Transatlantic Financing Corp. v. United States* [Citation.]

> * * * The doctrine ultimately represents the ever-shifting line, drawn by courts hopefully responsive to commercial practices and mores, at which the community's interest in having contracts enforced according to their terms is outweighed by the commercial senselessness of requiring performance. * * *

In the case before us the detailed opinion of the trial court clearly indicates that the appropriate standard was followed. There is ample evidence to support its findings that "[t]he ice haul method of transporting riprap ultimately selected was within the contemplation of the parties and was part of the basis of the agreement which ultimately resulted in amendment No. 1 in October 1966," and that that method was not commercially feasible within the financial parameters of the contract. We affirm the court's conclusion that the contract was impossible of performance.

Bankruptcy

Bankruptcy is a method of discharge of a contractual duty by operation of law available to a debtor who, by compliance with the requirements of the Bankruptcy Act, obtains an order of discharge by the bankruptcy court. It applies only to obligations that the act provides are dischargeable in bankruptcy. We treat the subject of bankruptcy in Chapter 39.

Statute of Limitations

At common law a plaintiff was not subject to any time limitation within which to bring an action. Now, however, all States have statutes providing such a limitation. Although the courts hold that the running of the period of the statute of limitations does not operate as a discharge, it does bar the remedy. The debt is not discharged, but the creditor cannot maintain an action against the debtor after the statute has run.

For a summary of discharge of contracts, see Figure 15–1.

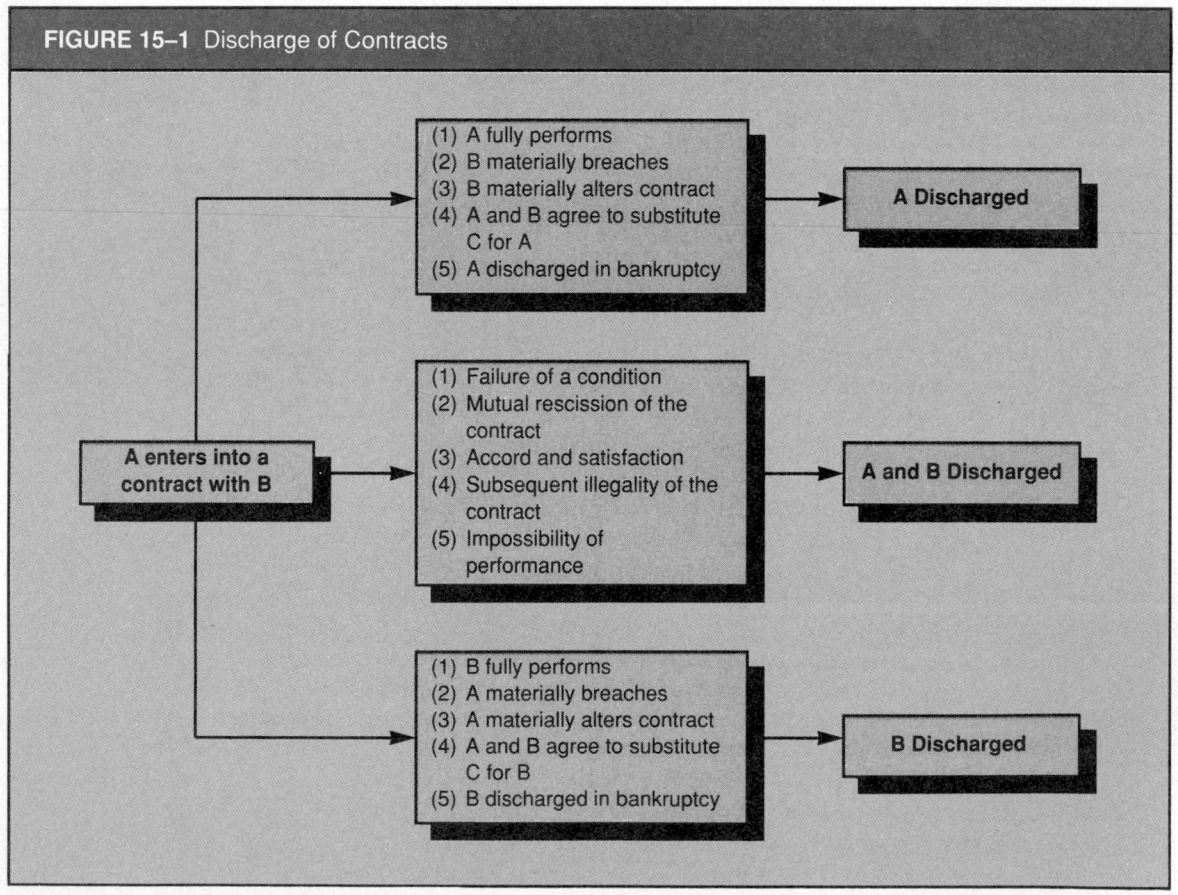

FIGURE 15–1 Discharge of Contracts

A enters into a contract with B

(1) A fully performs
(2) B materially breaches
(3) B materially alters contract
(4) A and B agree to substitute C for A
(5) A discharged in bankruptcy
→ **A Discharged**

(1) Failure of a condition
(2) Mutual rescission of the contract
(3) Accord and satisfaction
(4) Subsequent illegality of the contract
(5) Impossibility of performance
→ **A and B Discharged**

(1) B fully performs
(2) A materially breaches
(3) A materially alters contract
(4) A and B agree to substitute C for B
(5) B discharged in bankruptcy
→ **B Discharged**

CHAPTER SUMMARY

Conditions	**Definition of a Condition** an uncertain event whose happening or non-happening affects a duty of performance
	Express Condition contingency explicitly set forth in language
	■ *Satisfaction* express condition making performance contingent upon one of the party's approval of the other's performance
	■ *Subjective Satisfaction* approval based upon a party's honestly held opinion
	■ *Objective Satisfaction* approval based upon whether a reasonable person would be satisfied
	Implied in Fact Condition contingency understood but not expressed by the parties to be part of the agreement
	Implied in Law Condition contingency not contained in the language of the contract but imposed by law
	Concurrent Conditions conditions that are to take place at the same time
	Condition Precedent an event which must occur or not occur before performance is due
	Condition Subsequent an event which terminates a duty of performance

Discharge by Performance	**Discharge** termination of a contractual duty
	Performance fulfillment of a contractual obligation resulting in a discharge

Discharge by Breach	**Breach** a wrongful failure to perform the terms of a contract which gives rise to a right to damages by the injured party
	■ *Material Breach* nonperformance which significantly impairs the injured party's rights under the contract and discharges the injured party from any further duty under the contract
	■ *Substantial Performance* performance that is incomplete but that does not defeat the purpose of the contract; does not discharge the injured party but entitles him to damages
	■ *Perfect Tender Rule* standard under the UCC that performance must strictly comply with contractual duties and that any deviation discharges the injured party
	Prevention of Performance one party's substantial interference with or prevention of performance by the other; constitutes a material breach and discharges the other party to the contract
	Anticipatory Repudiation a breach of contract before performance is due which is treated as a breach allowing the nonrepudiating party to bring suit immediately
	Material Alteration a material and fraudulent alteration of a written contract discharges the entire contract

Discharge by Agreement of the Parties	**Mutual Rescission** an agreement between the parties to terminate their respective duties under the contract **Substituted Contract** an agreement between the parties to rescind their old contract and replace it with a new contract **Accord and Satisfaction** substituted performance under a contract (the accord) and the discharge of the prior contractual obligation by performance of the new duty (the satisfaction) **Novation** a substituted contract involving a new third-party promisor or promisee

Discharge by Operation of Law	**Subsequent Illegality** if performance becomes illegal or impractical as a result of a change in the law, the duty of performance is discharged
	Impossibility performance cannot be done
	  ■ *Subjective Impossibility* the promisor—but not all promisors—cannot perform; does not discharge the promisor
	  ■ *Objective Impossibility* no promisor is able to perform; generally discharges the promisor
	  ■ *Commercial Impracticability* where performance can only be accomplished under unforeseen and unjust hardship, the contract is discharged under the Code and Restatement
	Bankruptcy discharge available to a debtor who obtains an order of discharge by the bankruptcy court
	Statute of Limitations after the statute of limitations has run, the debt is not discharged but the creditor cannot maintain an action against the debtor

QUESTIONS

1. Identify and distinguish among the various types of conditions.
2. Distinguish between full performance and tender of performance.
3. Explain the difference between material breach and substantial performance. Explain how the UCC perfect tender rule differs from these rules.
4. Distinguish among a mutual rescission, substituted contract, accord and satisfaction, and novation.
5. Identify and discuss the ways discharge may be brought about by operation of law.

PROBLEMS

1. A-1 Roofing Co. entered into a written contract with Jaffe to put a new roof on the latter's residence for $900 with a specified type of roofing, and to complete the job without unreasonable delay. A-1 undertook the work within a week thereafter, and when all the roofing material was at the site and the labor 50 percent completed, the premises were totally destroyed by fire caused by lightning. A-1 submitted a bill to Jaffe for $600 for materials furnished and labor performed up to the time of the destruction of the premises. Jaffe refused to pay the bill, and A-1 sued Jaffe. Decision?

2. By contract dated January 5, Rebecca agreed to sell to Nancy and Nancy agreed to buy from Rebecca a certain parcel of land then zoned commercial. The specific intent of Nancy, which was known to Rebecca, was to erect a storage plant on the land. The contract stated that the agreement was conditioned on Nancy's ability to construct a storage plant on the land. The closing date for the transaction was set for April 1. On February 15 the city council rezoned the land from commercial to residential, which precluded the erection of the storage plant intended by Nancy. As the closing date drew near, Nancy made it known to Rebecca that she did not intend to go through with the purchase because the land could no longer be used as intended. On April 1 Rebecca tendered the deed to Nancy, who refused to pay Rebecca the agreed purchase price. Rebecca brought an action against Nancy for breach of contract. Decision?

3. The Perfection Produce Company entered into a written contract with Hiram Hodges for the pur-

chase of 200 tons of potatoes to be grown on Hodges's farm in Maine at a stipulated price per ton. The land would ordinarily produce 1,000 tons. Although the planting and cultivation were properly done, Hodges was able to deliver only 100 tons because an unprecedented drought caused a partial crop failure. Hodges sued the produce company to recover an unpaid balance of the agreed price for 100 tons of potatoes. The produce company, by an appropriate counterclaim against Hodges, sought damages for his failure to deliver the additional 100 tons. Decision?

4. On November 23 Sally agreed to sell to Bart her Pontiac automobile for $7,000, delivery and payment to be made on December 1. On November 26 Bart informed Sally that he wished to rescind the contract and would pay Sally $350 if Sally agreed. Sally agreed and took the $350 cash. On December 1 Bart tendered to Sally $6,650 and demanded that Sally deliver the automobile. Sally refused and Bart initiated a lawsuit. Decision?

5. Webster, Inc., dealt in automobile accessories at wholesale. Although manufacturing a few items in its own factory, among them windshield wipers, Webster, Inc., purchased most of its supplies from a large number of other manufacturers. In January Webster entered into a written contract to sell Hunter 2,000 windshield wipers for $1,900, delivery to be made June 1. In April Webster's factory burned to the ground, and Webster failed to make delivery on June 1. Hunter, forced to buy windshield wipers elsewhere at a higher price, brings an action against Webster for breach of contract. Decision?

6. Erwick Construction Company contracted to build a house for Charles. The specifications called for the use of Karlene Pipe for all plumbing. Erwick, nevertheless, got a better price on Boynton Pipe and substituted the equally good Boynton Pipe for Karlene Pipe. Charles's inspection discovered the change and Charles now refuses to make the final payment. The contract price was for $200,000 and the final payment is $20,000. Erwick now brings suit seeking the $20,000. Decision?

7. Green owed White $3,500, which was due and payable on June 1. White owed Brown $3,500, which was due and payable on August 1. On May 25 White received a letter signed by Green stating: "If you will cancel my debt to you, in the amount of $3,500, I will pay, on the due date, the debt you owe Brown, in the amount of $3,500." On May 28 Green received a letter signed by White stating: "I received your letter and agree to the proposals recited therein. You may consider your debt to me canceled as of the date of this letter." On June 1 White, needing money to pay his income taxes, made a demand upon Green to pay him the $3,500 due on that date. Is Green obligated to pay the money demanded by White?

8. By written contract, Ames agreed to build a house on Bowen's lot for $45,000, commencing within ninety days of the date of the contract. Prior to the date for beginning construction, Ames informed Bowen that he was repudiating the contract and would not perform. Bowen refused to accept the repudiation and demanded fulfillment of the contract. Eighty days after the date of the contract, Bowen entered into a new contract with Curd for $42,000. The next day, without knowledge or notice of Bowen's contract with Curd, Ames began construction. Bowen ordered Ames from the premises and refused to allow him to continue. Ames sued Bowen for damages. Decision?

9. Judy agreed in writing to work for Northern Enterprises, Inc. for three years as superintendent of Northern's manufacturing establishment and to devote herself entirely to the business, giving it her full time, attention, and skill, for which she was to receive $24,000 per annum, in monthly installments of $2,000. Judy worked and was paid for the first twelve months, when through no fault of her own or Northern's, she was arrested and imprisoned for one month. It became imperative for Northern to employ another, and it treated the contract with Judy as breached and abandoned, refusing to permit Judy to resume work on her release from jail. What rights, if any, does Judy have under the contract?

10. The Park Plaza Hotel awarded the valet and laundry concession to Larson for a three-year term. The contract contained the following provision: "It is distinctly understood and agreed that the services to be rendered by Larson shall meet with the approval of the Park Plaza Hotel, which shall be the sole judge of the sufficiency and propriety of the services." After seven months, the hotel gave a month's notice to discontinue services based on the failure of the services to meet its approval. Larson brought an action against the hotel, alleging that its dissatisfaction was unreasonable. The hotel defended on the ground that subjective or personal satisfaction may be the sole justification for termination of the contract. Decision?

11. Schlosser entered into an agreement to purchase a cooperative apartment from Flynn Company. The written agreement contained the following provision: "This entire agreement is conditioned on Purchaser's being approved for occupancy by the board of directors of the Cooperative. In the event approval of the Purchaser shall be denied, this agreement shall thereafter be of no further force

or effect." When Schlosser unilaterally revoked her "offer," Flynn sued for breach of contract. Schlosser claims the approval provision was a condition precedent to the existence of a binding contract and, thus, she was free to revoke. Decision?

COMPUTER RESEARCH PROBLEMS

1. Walker & Co. contracted to provide a sign for Harrison to place above his dry cleaning business. According to the contract, Harrison would lease the sign from Walker, making monthly payments for thirty-six months. In return, Walker agreed to maintain and service the sign at its own expense. Walker installed the sign in July 1953 and Harrison made the first rental payment. Shortly thereafter, someone hit the sign with a tomato. Harrison also claims he discovered rust on its chrome and little spider webs in its corners. Harrison repeatedly called Walker for the maintenance work promised under the contract, but Walker did not respond. Harrison then telegraphed Walker that due to Walker's failure to perform the maintenance services, he held Walker in material breach of the contract. Decision?

2. Barta entered into a written contract to buy the K&K Pharmacy, located in the local shopping center. Included in the contract was a provision stating that "this Agreement shall be contingent upon Buyer's ability to obtain a new lease from Landlord for the premises presently occupied by Seller. In the event Buyer is unable to obtain a lease satisfactory to Buyer, this Agreement shall be null and void." Barta planned to sell "high traffic" grocery items, such as bread, milk, and coffee in order to attract customers to his drugstore. However, a grocery store in the local shopping center had the exclusive right to sell grocery items there. Barta, therefore, could not obtain a leasing agreement meeting his approval. When Barta refused to close the sale, K&K Pharmacy sued him for breach of contract. Decision?

3. Victor Packing Co. contracted to supply Sun Maid Raisin Growers 1,800 tons of raisins from the current year's crop. After delivering 1,190 tons of raisins by August, Victor refused to supply any more. Although Victor had until the end of the crop season to ship the remaining 610 tons of raisins, Sun Maid treated Victor's repeated refusals to ship any more raisins as a repudiation of the contract. In order to prevent breaching its own contracts, Sun Maid went into the market place to "cover" and bought the raisins needed. Unfortunately, between the time Victor refused delivery and Sun Maid went into the market disastrous rains had caused the price of raisins to skyrocket. May Sun Maid recover from Victor the difference between the contract price and the market price before the end of the current crop year?

ENDNOTES

1. Restatement, Second, Contracts, Section 235, Effect of Performance as Discharge and of Non-Performance as Breach.
2. Restatement, Second, Contracts, Section 241, Circumstances Significant in Determining Whether a Failure Is Material.
3. Restatement, Second, Contracts, Section 286, Alteration of Writing.
4. Restatement, Second, Contracts, Section 279, Substituted Contract.
5. Restatement, Second, Contracts, Section 281, Accord and Satisfaction.
6. Restatement, Second, Contracts, Section 280, Novation.
7. Restatement, Second, Contracts, Section 264, Prevention by Governmental Regulation or Order.
8. Restatement, Second, Contracts, Section 261, Discharge by Supervening Impracticability.
9. Uniform Commercial Code, Section 2—615, Excuse by Failure of Presupposed Conditions.

16 REMEDIES

When one party to a contract breaches the contract by failing to perform his contractual duties, the law provides a remedy for the injured party. The primary objective of contract remedies is to compensate the injured party for the loss resulting from the breach, but it is impossible for any remedy to equal the promised performance. Even a decree of *specific performance* (a court order requiring the breaching party to perform his contractual duties) does not give the injured party what he was entitled to receive by the terms of the contract because the remedy comes at the end of a lawsuit many months or even years after the performance was due.

In this chapter we examine the most common remedies available for breach of contract: (1) monetary damages, (2) the equitable remedies of specific performance and injunction, and (3) restitution. Sales of goods are governed by Article 2 of the Uniform Commercial Code, which provides specialized remedies that we discuss in Chapter 21.

MONETARY DAMAGES

A judgment awarding monetary damages is the most common judicial remedy for breach of contract. The equitable remedies discussed in this chapter are discretionary and available only if monetary damages are not adequate.

Compensatory Damages

The right to recover **compensatory damages** for breach of contract is always available to the injured party.[1] As we previously mentioned, the purpose in allowing damages is to provide compensation to the injured party that will, to the extent possible, place him in as good a position as if the other party had performed under the contract. These damages are intended to protect the injured party's **expectation interest,** which is the value he expected to derive from the contract. Thus, the amount of damages is generally the loss of value to the injured party caused by the other party's failure to perform or by his deficient performance. Damages are not recoverable for loss beyond an amount that the injured party can establish with reasonable certainty.[2]

In general, the **loss of value** is the *difference between the value of the promised performance* of the breaching party *and the value of the actual performance* rendered by the breaching party.

Value of promised performance
– Value of actual performance
Loss of value

If no performance is rendered at all, then the loss of value is the value of the promised performance. If defective or partial performance is rendered, the loss of value is the difference between the value that full performance would have had and the value of the performance actually rendered. Thus, where there has been a breach of warranty, the injured party may recover the difference between the value of the goods if they had been as warranted and the value of the goods in their actual condition when received by the buyer. To illustrate, Jacob sells an automobile to Juliet and expressly warrants that it will get forty-five miles per gallon, but the automobile gets only twenty miles per gallon. The automobile would have been worth $8,000 if as warranted but is worth only $6,000 as delivered. Juliet would recover $2,000 in damages for loss of value.

The injured party may *also* recover for all other losses actually suffered, subject to the limitation of foreseeability discussed below. These damages include incidental and consequential damages. **Incidental damages** are damages that arise directly out of the breach, such as costs incurred to acquire the nondelivered performance from some other source. For example, Agnes employs Benton for nine months for $20,000 to supervise construction of a factory. Agnes fires Benton without cause after three weeks. Benton spends $350 in reasonable fees attempting to find comparable employment. Benton may recover $350 in incidental damages in addition to any other actual loss suffered. **Consequential damages** include lost profits and injury to person or property resulting from defective performance. Thus, if Tracy leases to Sean a defective machine that causes $4,000 in property damage and $12,000 in personal injuries, Sean may recover, in addition to damages for loss of value and incidental damages, $16,000 as consequential damages.

The recovery by the injured party, however, is reduced by any cost or loss she has avoided by not having to perform. For example, Clinton agrees to build a hotel for Debra for $1,250,000 by September 1. Clinton breaches by not completing construction until October 1. As a consequence, Debra loses revenues for one month in the amount of $10,000 but saves operating expenses of $6,000. Debra may recover damages for $4,000. Similarly, in a contract in which the injured party has not fully performed, the injured party's recovery is reduced by the value to the injured party of the performance promised by the injured party but not rendered. For example, Victor agrees to convey land to Joan in return for Joan's promise to work for Victor for two years. Joan repudiates the contract before Victor has conveyed the land to Joan. Victor's recovery for loss from Joan is reduced by the value to Victor of the land.

To summarize, the amount of **compensatory damages** an injured party may recover for breach of contract is computed as follows:

Loss of value
+ Incidental damages
+ Consequential damages
− Loss or cost avoided by injured party
Compensatory damages

Nominal Damages

An action to recover damages for breach of contract may be maintained even though the plaintiff has not sustained or cannot prove any injury or loss resulting from the breach.[1] In such case he will be permitted to recover **nominal damages**—a small sum fixed without regard to the amount of loss. Such a judgment may also include an award of court costs.

Reliance Damages

Instead of seeking compensatory damages, the injured party may seek reimbursement for loss caused by his reliance on the contract. The result of **reliance damages** is to place the injured party in as good a position as he would have been in had the contract *not been made*. Reliance damages include expenses incurred in preparing to perform, in actually performing, or in foregoing opportunities to enter into other contracts. An injured party may prefer damages for reliance to compensatory damages when he is unable to establish his lost profits with reasonable certainty or when the contract is itself unprofitable. For example, Donald agrees to sell his retail store to Gary. Gary spends $50,000 in acquiring inventory and fixtures. Donald then repudiates the contract, and Gary sells the inventory and fixtures for $35,000. Neither party can establish with reasonable certainty what profit Gary would have made. Gary may recover from Donald as damages the loss of $15,000 he sustained on the sale of the inventory and fixtures plus any other costs he incurred in entering into the contract.

Foreseeability of Damages

A contracting party is generally expected to consider those risks that are foreseeable at the time he entered into the contract. Therefore, compensatory or reliance damages are recoverable only for loss that the party in breach had reason to foresee as a *probable* result of a breach when the contract was made. The breaching party is not liable in the event of a breach for loss that was not foreseeable at the time of entering into the contract.[3] The test of **foreseeable damages** is an *objective* test based on what the breaching party had reason to foresee. Loss may be foreseeable as a probable result of a breach because it follows from the breach (a) in the ordinary course of events, or (b) as a result of special circumstances, beyond the ordinary course of events, that the party in breach had reason to know about.[3]

A leading case on the subject of foreseeability of damages is *Hadley v. Baxendale*, decided in England in 1854. In this case the plaintiffs operated a flour mill at Gloucester. Their mill was compelled to cease operating because of a broken crankshaft attached to the steam engine which furnished power to the mill. It was necessary to send the broken shaft to a foundry located at Greenwich so that a new shaft could be made. The plaintiffs delivered the broken shaft to the defendants, who were common carriers, for immediate transportation from Gloucester to Greenwich, but did not inform the defendants that operation of the mill had ceased because of the nonfunctioning crankshaft. The defendants received the shaft, collected the freight charges in advance, and promised the plaintiffs to deliver the shaft at Greenwich the following day. The defendants neglected to make prompt delivery as promised, and as a result the resumption of the operation of the mill was delayed for several days, causing the plaintiffs to lose profits which they otherwise would have received. The defendants contended that the loss of profits was too remote, and therefore unforeseeable, to be recoverable. In awarding damages to the plaintiffs, the jury was permitted to take into consideration the loss of these profits. The appellate court reversed the decision and ordered a new trial on the ground that the special circumstances which caused the loss of profits, namely, the continued stoppage of the mill while awaiting the return of the repaired crankshaft, had never been communicated by the plaintiffs to the defendants. A common carrier would not reasonably foresee that the plaintiff's mill would be shut down as a result of delay in transporting the broken crankshaft.

On the other hand, if the defendants in *Hadley v. Baxendale* had been informed that the shaft was necessary for the operation of the mill, or otherwise had reason to know this fact, they would be liable to the plaintiffs for loss of profit during the period of shutdown caused by their delay. Under these circumstances the loss would be the "foreseeable" and "natural" result of the breach in accordance with common experience. The plaintiffs' loss of profit would be the probable result of the defendants' delay in transporting the shaft and would be recoverable from the defendants.

But what if a plaintiff's expected profit should be extraordinarily large? The general rule, as stated above, is that the breaching party will be liable for such extraordinary loss only if he had reason to know of the special loss. In any event, the plaintiff may recover for any ordinary loss resulting from the breach. Thus, if Madeline breaches a contract with Jane, causing Jane, due to special circumstances, $10,000 in damages where ordinarily such a breach would only result in $6,000 in damages, Madeline would be liable to Jane for $6,000, not $10,000, so long as Madeline was unaware of the special circumstances causing Jane the unusually large loss.

Damages for Misrepresentation

Fraud   A party who has been induced to enter into a contract by fraud may recover damages in a tort action. The minority of States allow the injured party to recover only **"out-of-pocket"** damages equal to the difference between the value of what she has received and the value of what she has given for it. The great majority of States, however, permit the intentionally defrauded party to recover **"benefit-of-the-bargain"** damages that are equal to the difference between the value of what she has received and the value of the fraudulent party's performance as represented. The Restatement of Torts provides the fraudulently injured party with the option of either out-of-pocket or benefit-of-the-bargain damages.[4] To illustrate, Emily intentionally misrepresents the capabilities of a printing press and thereby induces Melissa to purchase the machine for $20,000. The value of the press as delivered is $14,000, but if the machine had performed as represented it would be worth $24,000. Under the out-of-pocket rule, Melissa would recover $6,000, whereas under the benefit-of-the-bargain rule she would recover $10,000.

Nonfraudulent Misrepresentation Where the misrepresentation is not fraudulent, the Restatement of Torts permits out-of-pocket damages but expressly excludes recovery of benefit-of-the-bargain damages.[5]

Punitive Damages

Punitive damages are monetary damages in addition to compensatory damages awarded to a plaintiff in certain situations involving willful, wanton, or malicious conduct. Their purpose is to punish the defendant and thus discourage him and others from similar wrongful conduct. The purpose of allowing contract damages, on the other hand, is to compensate the plaintiff for the loss he sustained because of the defendant's breach of contract. In a case where the plaintiff has established a breach of contract and evidence of loss or damage, the court will award him a judgment in an amount it deems sufficient to place him in the position where he would have been if the defendant had not breached the contract. Accordingly, the Restatement provides that punitive damages are *not* recoverable for a breach of contract unless the conduct constituting the breach is also a tort for which punitive damages are recoverable.[6]

Frank, a roofer, purchases disability insurance from Wholewide Insurance Co. While working at a job, Frank fell off a ladder and seriously injured his back. Frank was physically unable to continue working and filed a claim for total disability with Wholewide. Wholewide's claims adjuster refused to honor the claim despite the overwhelming medical

evidence Frank presented. Wholewide's adjuster called Frank a fraud and a malingerer in an attempt to have Frank settle the claim for 60 percent disability. Wholewide was aware that Frank's finances would not last very long without some recovery for disability. In a suit by Frank against Wholewide, many courts would award Frank punitive damages in addition to compensatory damages for his actual disability. The punitive damages award would be based upon the insurance company's tortious conduct in its bad-faith refusal to pay a legitimate claim.

Liquidated Damages

A contract may contain a **liquidated damages** provision by which the parties agree in advance to the damages to be paid in event of breach. Such a provision will be enforced if it amounts to a reasonable forecast of the loss that may result from the breach.[7] If, however, the sum agreed on as liquidated damages does not bear a reasonable relationship to the amount of probable loss, it is unenforceable as an invalid penalty. This is because the objective of contract remedies is compensatory, not punitive. The courts will look at the substance of the provision, the nature of the contract, and the extent of probable harm to the promisee that may reasonably be expected to be caused by a breach in order to determine whether the agreed amount is proper as liquidated damages or unenforceable as a penalty. It is immaterial what name or label the parties to the contract attach to the provision. If a liquidated damages provision is not enforceable, the injured party is nevertheless entitled to the ordinary remedies for breach of contract.

Mitigation of Damages

The doctrine of **mitigation of damages** requires the injured party to take reasonable action to lessen or mitigate the damages that he may sustain as a result of the breach of contract. The injured party may not recover damages for loss that he could have avoided without undue risk, burden, or humiliation.[8] Thus, where Earl is under a contract to manu-

FIELDS FOUNDATION, LTD. v. CHRISTENSEN
Court of Appeals of Wisconsin, 1981.
103 Wis.2d 465, 309 N.W.2d 125.

Facts: On June 2, 1977, Dr. Dennis Christensen became the medical director of the Midwest Medical Center, a clinic operated by the Fields Foundation in Madison, Wisconsin. His employment contract with Fields included a covenant not to compete and a liquidated damages clause. The covenant restricted Christensen from performing medical services similar to those provided by the center within fifty miles of Madison for two years after termination of his employment. The liquidated damages clause provided that Christensen pay Fields $2,000 for each day of his violation of the covenant. Christensen resigned from Fields in December 1979 and began a competing clinic in Madison. Fields brought an action against Christensen for damages for breach of contract. The trial court refused to enforce the liquidated damages clause, and Fields appealed.

Decision: Judgment affirmed.

Opinion: Gartzke, Presiding Judge.   The covenant not to compete requires that Christensen pay Fields $2,000 in liquidated damages for each day of its violation. The trial court refused to enforce the liquidated damages clause because it is penal. A liquidated damages clause is penal, and therefore unenforceable, if the stipulated damages are grossly in excess of the actual damages. [Citation.]

The trial court held that the clause is penal because the Center assumed in computing the $2,000 that it would lose all its income to Christensen's competition. The Center scheduled the same number of [procedures] after Christensen resigned as before, about 400 each month. Fields offered no evidence of actual damages suffered by the Center after Christensen's breach.

* * *

Fields contends that its actual damages are irrelevant to whether the clause is penal because a liquidated damages clause is an attempt to predetermine future damages "to the extent those damages are reasonably contemplated by the parties at the time of the contract." [Citation.] Here, however, the trial court considered the complete absence of harm from Christensen's breach, rather than merely the amount of Fields' damages.

The total absence of actual harm resulting from a breach may be considered in determining whether liquidated damages are penal rather than compensatory. A defendant against whom a liquidated damages clause is sought to be enforced "should be allowed to show that there has in fact been no injury at all." [Citation.] Even if the parties honestly but mistakenly believe that a breach will cause harm, a liquidated damages clause is unenforceable when no harm results. [Citation.]

facture goods for Karl and Karl repudiates the contract after Earl has begun performance, Earl will not be allowed to recover for losses he sustains by continuing to manufacture the goods, if to do so would increase the amount of damages. The amount of loss that could reasonably have been avoided is deducted from the amount that would otherwise be recoverable as damages. On the other hand, if the goods were almost completed when Karl repudiated the contract, the completion of the goods might reduce the damages, because the finished goods may be resalable whereas the unfinished goods may not.[9]

Similarly, a buyer who does not receive goods or services promised to him under a contract cannot recover damages resulting from his doing without such goods or services where it is possible for him to substitute goods or services that he can obtain elsewhere. Likewise, if Harvey contracts to work for Olivia for one year for a weekly salary and after two months is wrongfully discharged by Olivia, Harvey must use reasonable efforts to mitigate his damages by seeking other employment. If he cannot obtain other employment of the same general character, he is entitled to recover full pay for the contract period that he is unemployed. He is not obliged to accept a radically different type of employment or to accept work at a distant place. For example, a person employed as a school teacher or accountant who is wrongfully discharged is not obliged to accept employment as a chauffeur or truck driver. The next case involving Shirley MacLaine turns on whether acting in a western is equivalent employment to singing and dancing in a musical.

 PARKER v. TWENTIETH CENTURY-FOX FILM CORP.
Supreme Court of California, 1970.
3 Cal.3d 176, 89 Cal.Rptr. 737, 474 P.2d 689.

Facts: Shirley MacLaine Parker, a well-known actress, contracted with Twentieth Century-Fox Film Corporation in August 1965 to play the female lead in Fox's upcoming production of *Bloomer Girl*, a motion picture musical that was to be filmed in California. The contract provided that Fox would pay Parker a minimum "guaranteed compensation" of $750,000 for fourteen weeks of Parker's services, beginning May 23, 1966. By letter dated April 4, 1966, Fox notified Parker of its intention not to produce the film and, instead, offered to employ Parker in the female lead of another film entitled *Big Country, Big Man*, a dramatic western to be filmed in Australia. The compensation offered and most of the other provisions in the substitute contract were identical to the *Bloomer Girl* provisions, except that Parker's right to approve the director and screenplay would have been eliminated or reduced under the *Big Country* contract. Parker refused to accept and brought suit against Fox to recover $750,000 for breach of the *Bloomer Girl* contract. Fox contended that it owed no money to Parker because she had deliberately failed to mitigate or reduce her damages by unreasonably refusing to accept the *Big Country* lead. The trial court granted Parker a summary judgment. [The court's opinion with respect to the rules for determining whether to grant summary judgment appears in Chapter 2.]

Decision: Judgment for Parker affirmed.

Opinion: Burke, J. The general rule is that the measure of recovery by a wrongfully discharged employee is the amount of salary agreed upon for the period of service, less the amount which the employer affirmatively proves the employee has earned or with reasonable effort might have earned from other employment. [Citations.] However, before projected earnings from other employment opportunities not sought or accepted by the discharged employee can be applied in mitigation, the employer must show that the other employment was comparable, or substantially similar, to that of which the employee has been deprived; the employee's rejection of or failure to seek other available employment of a different or inferior kind may not be resorted to in order to mitigate damages. [Citations.]

In the present case defendant has raised no issue of *reasonableness of efforts* by plaintiff to obtain other employment; the sole issue is whether plaintiff's refusal of defendant's substitute offer of "Big Country" may be used in mitigation. Nor, if the "Big Country" offer was of employment different or inferior when compared with the original "Bloomer Girl" employment, is there an issue as to whether or not plaintiff acted reasonably in refusing the substitute offer. Despite defendant's arguments to the contrary, no case cited or which our research has discovered holds or suggests that reasonableness is an element of a wrongfully discharged employee's option to reject, or fail to seek, different or inferior employment lest the possible earnings therefrom be charged against him in mitigation of damages.

Applying the foregoing rules to the record in the present case, with all intendments in favor of the party opposing the summary judgment motion—here, defendant—it is clear that the trial court correctly ruled that plaintiff's failure to accept defendant's tendered substitute employment could not be applied in mitigation of damages because the offer of the "Big Country" lead was of employment both different and inferior, and that no factual dispute was presented on that issue. The mere circumstance that "Bloomer Girl" was to be a musical review calling upon plaintiff's talents as a dancer as well as an actress, and was to be produced in the City of Los Angeles, whereas "Big Country" was a straight dramatic role in a "Western Type" story taking place in an opal mine in Australia, demonstrates the difference in kind between the two employments; the female lead as a dramatic actress in a western style motion picture can by no stretch of imagination be considered the equivalent of or substantially similar to the lead in a song-and-dance production.

Additionally, the substitute "Big Country" offer proposed to eliminate or impair the director and screenplay approvals accorded to plaintiff under the original "Bloomer Girl" contract * * * and thus constituted an offer of inferior employment. No expertise or judicial notice is required in order to hold that the deprivation or infringement of an employee's rights held under an original employment contract converts the available "other employment" relied upon by the employer to mitigate damages, into inferior employment which the employee need not seek or accept. [Citation.]

REMEDIES IN EQUITY

The remedies of specific performance and injunction are forms of equitable relief that may be available as alternatives to damages as means of enforcing contracts. The remedies of specific performance and injunction are not a matter of right but rest largely in the discretion of the court. Consequently, they will not be granted where there is an adequate remedy at law; where it is impossible to enforce them, as where the seller has already transferred the subject matter of the contract to an innocent third person; where the contract is without consideration; where the consideration is grossly inadequate; or where the contract is tainted with fraud, duress, undue influence, or other defect. Also, the plaintiff must be ready and able to perform in full on his part. This can usually be shown by a tender of the full purchase price into court.

Another equitable remedy is **reformation,** which is a process whereby the court "rewrites" or "corrects" a written contract to make it conform to the true agreement of the parties. The purpose of reformation is *not* to make a new contract for the parties but rather to express adequately the contract they have made for themselves. The remedy of reformation is granted when the parties agree on a contract but write it down in a way that does not reflect their actual agreement. For example, Acme Insurance Co. and Bell agree that for good consideration Acme will issue an annuity paying $500 per month. Because of a clerical error, the annuity policy is issued for $50 per month. A court of equity, upon satisfactory proof of the mistake, will reform the policy to provide for the correct amount—$500 per month.

Specific Performance

As a general principle, a contract creates enforceable rights, courts will enforce contracts, and a remedy is the means of enforcing rights. These statements are substantially correct, but as to the vast majority of contracts they are not literally correct. Ordinarily, a contract will not be enforced by courts in the sense that they will require the breaching party literally to carry out his contractual obligations. The usual remedy for breach of contract, as we have seen, is an action at law for money damages by way of compensation for the loss. Suppose, for example, that Empire Coal Co. contracts to sell and deliver coal to Municipal Utility, Inc., and that Empire wrongfully refuses to deliver the coal to Municipal. No court will force Empire to deliver the coal, which can be bought elsewhere. If, however, Municipal suffers a loss by having to pay a higher price than the contract price, it has its remedy at law: an action against Empire for money damages to compensate Municipal for its loss. Cases, however, occasionally arise where an award of money damages is wholly inadequate as a remedy.[10] Since this is the only remedy a court of law can grant, the injured party is without an adequate remedy at law. In such a case, his remedy is a suit in equity for specific performance of the contract. See *Tamarind Lithography Workshop v. Sanders.*

TAMARIND LITHOGRAPHY WORKSHOP v. SANDERS
Court of Appeals of California, Second District, 1983.
143 Cal.App.3d 571, 193 Cal.Rptr. 409.

Facts: In 1969 Sanders agreed in writing to write, direct, and produce a motion picture on the subject of lithography for the Tamarind Lithography Workshop. After the completion of this film, *Four Stones for Kanemitsu*, litigation arose concerning the parties' rights and obligations under their 1969 agreement. Tamarind and Sanders resolved this dispute by a written settlement agreement, whereby Tamarind promised to provide Sanders a screen credit stating: "A Film by Terry Sanders." Tamarind did not comply with this agreement and failed to include a screen credit for Sanders in the prints it subsequently distributed. In the ensuing litigation, Sanders seeks damages for Tamarind's breach of the settlement agreement and specific performance to compel Tamarind's compliance with its obligation to provide a screen credit. The trial court denied Sander's request for specific performance.

Decision: Decision for Sanders granting specific performance.

Opinion: Stephens, J. The availability of the remedy of specific performance is premised upon well established requisites. These requisites include: A showing by plaintiff of (1) the inadequacy of his legal remedy; (2) an underlying contract that is both reasonable and supported by adequate consideration; (3) the existence of a mutuality of remedies; (4) contractual terms which are sufficiently definite to enable the court to know what it is to enforce; and (5) a substantial similarity of the requested performance to that promised in the contract. [Citation.]

It is manifest that the legal remedies available to Sanders for harm resulting from the future exhibition of the film are inadequate as a matter of law. The primary reasons are twofold: (1) that an accurate assessment of damages would be far too difficult and require much speculation, and (2) that any future exhibitions might be deemed to be a continuous breach of contract and thereby create the danger of an untold number of lawsuits.

There is no doubt that the exhibition of a film, which is favorably received by its critics and the public at large, can result in valuable advertising or publicity for the artists responsible for that film's making. Likewise, it is unquestionable that the nonappearance of an artist's name or likeness in the form of screen credit on a successful film can result in a loss of that valuable publicity. However, whether that loss of publicity is measurable dollar wise is quite another matter.

By its very nature, public acclaim is unique and very difficult, if not sometimes impossible, to quantify in monetary terms. Indeed, courts confronted with the dilemma of estimating damages in this area have been less than uniform in their disposition of same. Nevertheless, it is clear that any award of damages for the loss of publicity is contingent upon those damages being reasonably certain, specific, and unspeculative. [Citation.]

* * *

Accordingly, where the jury in the matter sub judice was fully apprised of the favorable recognition Sanders' film received from the Academy of Motion Picture Arts and Sciences, the Los Angeles International Film Festival, and public television, and further, where they were made privy to an assessment of the value of said exposure by three experts, it was reasonable for the jury to award monetary damages for that ascertainable loss of publicity. However, pecuniary compensation for Sanders' future harm is not a fully adequate remedy. [Citation.]

We return to the remaining requisites for Sanders' entitlement to specific performance. The need for our finding the contract to be reasonable and supported by adequate consideration is obviated by the jury's determination of respondent's [Tamarind's] breach of that contract. The requisite of mutuality of remedy has been satisfied in that Sanders had fully performed his obligations pursuant to the agreement (i.e., release of all claims of copyright to the film and dismissal of his then pending action against respondents). [Citation.] Similarly, we find the terms of the agreement sufficiently definite to permit enforcement of the respondent's performance as promised.

In the present case it should be obvious that specific performance through injunctive relief can remedy the dilemma posed by the somewhat ambiguous jury verdict. The injunction disposes of the problem of future damages, in that full compliance by Tamarind moots the issue. Of course, violation of the injunction by Tamarind would raise new problems, but the court has numerous options for dealing with the situation and should choose the one best suited to the particular violation.

Specific performance is the equitable remedy that compels the actual performance by the defaulting party of her contractual obligations. Ordinarily, as we have seen, in case of breach by the seller of her contract for the sale of personal property, the buyer has a sufficient remedy at law. Where, however, **personal property** contracted for is rare or *unique*, this remedy is inadequate. Examples are a famous painting or statue, an original manuscript or a rare edition of a book, a patent, a copyright, shares of stock in a closely held corporation, a relic, or an heirloom. Articles of this kind cannot be purchased elsewhere. Accordingly, on breach by the seller of her contract for the sale of any such article, money damages will not adequately or completely compensate the buyer. Consequently, in these cases, the buyer may avail himself of the equitable remedy of specific performance.

While it is only in exceptional circumstances that courts of equity will grant specific performance in connection with contracts for the sale of personal property, they will always grant it in case of breach of contract for the sale of **real property.** The reason for this is that any particular parcel of land is regarded as unique and as differing from any other parcel. Consequently, if the seller refuses to convey title to the real estate contracted for, the buyer may seek the aid of a court of equity to compel the seller to convey the title. As to real estate contracts, the remedy is mutual. Courts of equity will likewise compel the buyer to perform at the suit of the seller.

Courts of equity will not grant specific performance of contracts for personal services.[11] In the first place, there is the practical difficulty, if not impossibility, of enforcing a decree in any such case. In the second place, it is against the policy of the courts to force one person to work for or serve another against his will, even though he has contracted to do so. Such enforcement would probably amount to involuntary servitude. For example, if Carmen, an accomplished concert pianist, agrees to appear at a certain time and place to play a specified program for Rudolf, upon Carmen's refusal to appear, a court would not issue a decree of specific performance.

Injunctions

The **injunction,** as used as a contract remedy, is a formal court order enjoining (commanding) a person to refrain from doing a specific act or engaging in a specific conduct. A person who violates an injunctive order may be held guilty of contempt of court and fined or imprisoned until released by the court.

A court of equity, at its discretion, may grant an injunction against breach of a contractual duty where damages for a breach would be inadequate. For example, Clint enters into a written agreement to give Janice the right of first refusal on a tract of land owned by Clint. Clint, however, subsequently offers the land to Blake without first offering it to Janice. A court of equity may properly enjoin Clint from selling the land to Blake. Similarly, valid covenants not to compete may be enforced by an injunction.

An employee's promise of exclusive personal services may be enforced by an injunction against serving another employer as long as the probable result will not be to leave the employee without other reasonable means of making a living.[12] Suppose, for example, that Allan makes a contract with Marlene, a famous singer, under which Marlene agrees to sing at Allan's theater on certain dates for an agreed fee. Before the date of the first performance, Marlene makes a contract with Craig to sing for Craig at his theater on the same dates. Allan cannot obtain specific performance by Marlene of his contract, as already discussed. A court of equity will, however, on suit by Allan against Marlene, issue an injunction against Marlene ordering Marlene not to sing for Craig. This is the situation in *Madison Square Garden Corp., Ill. v. Carnera* on page 329. Where the services contracted for are *not* unusual or extraordinary in character, the injured party cannot obtain injunctive relief. His only remedy is an action at law for damages.

RESTITUTION

One of the remedies that may be available to a party to a contract is restitution. **Restitution** is a return to the aggrieved party of the consideration, or its value, that he gave to the other party. The purpose of restitution is to restore the injured party to the position he was in before the contract was made. Therefore, the party seeking restitution must return what he has received from the other party.

Restitution is available in several contractual situations: (1) as an alternative remedy for a party injured by breach, (2) for a party in default, (3) for a party who may not enforce the contract because of the Statute of Frauds, and (4) on rescission (avoidance) of a voidable contract.

MADISON SQUARE GARDEN CORP., ILL. v. CARNERA

Circuit Court of Appeals, Second Circuit, 1931.
52 F.2d 47.

Facts: Carnera (defendant) agreed with Madison Square Garden (plaintiff) to render services as a boxer in his next contest with the winner of the Schmeling-Stribling contest for the heavyweight championship title. The contract also provided that prior to the match Carnera would not engage in any major boxing contest without the permission of Madison Square Garden. Without obtaining such permission, Carnera contracted to engage in a major boxing contest with Sharkey. Madison Square Garden brought suit requesting an injunction against Carnera's performing his contract to box Sharkey. The trial court granted a preliminary injunction.

Decision: Order for Madison Square Garden affirmed.

Opinion: Chase, J.   The District Court has found on affidavits which adequately show it that the defendant's services are unique and extraordinary. A negative covenant in a contract for such personal services is enforceable by injunction where the damages for a breach are incapable of ascertainment. [Citations.]

The defendant points to what is claimed to be lack of consideration for his negative promise, in that the contract is inequitable and contains no agreement to employ him. It is true that there is no promise in so many words to employ the defendant to box in a contest with Stribling or Schmeling, but the agreement read as a whole binds the plaintiff to do just that, providing either Stribling or Schmeling becomes the contestant as the result of the match between them and can be induced to box the defendant. The defendant has agreed to "render services as a boxer" for the plaintiff exclusively, and the plaintiff has agreed to pay him a definite percentage of the gate receipts as his compensation for so doing. The promise to employ the defendant to enable him to earn the compensation agreed upon is implied to the same force and effect as though expressly stated. * * * [Citations.]

As we have seen, the contract is valid and enforceable. It contains a restrictive covenant which may be given effect. Whether a preliminary injunction shall be issued under such circumstances rests in the sound discretion of the court. [Citations.] The District Court, in its discretion, did issue the preliminary injunction and required the plaintiff as a condition upon its issuance to secure its own performance of the contract in suit with a bond for $25,000 and to give a bond in the sum of $35,000 to pay the defendant such damages as he may sustain by reason of the injunction. Such an order is clearly not an abuse of discretion.

Party Injured by Breach

A party is entitled to restitution if the other party totally breaches the contract by nonperformance or repudiation. For example, Benedict agrees to sell land to Beatrice for $60,000. Beatrice makes a partial payment of $15,000. Benedict wrongfully refuses to transfer title. As an alternative to damages or specific performance, Beatrice may recover the $15,000 in restitution.

Party in Default

Where a party, after having partly performed, commits a breach by nonperformance or repudiation that discharges the other party's duty to perform, the party in default is entitled to

---

FIGURE 16–1 Contract Remedies

Monetary	**Equitable**	**Restitution**
Compensatory	Specific performance	Return of consideration
Reliance	Injunctions	
Liquidated		

---

restitution for any benefit she has conferred in excess of the loss she has caused by her breach. For example, Nathan agrees to sell land to Lilly for $60,000, and Lilly makes a partial payment of $15,000. Lilly then repudiates the contract. Nathan sells the land to Murray in good faith for $55,000. Lilly may recover from Nathan in restitution the part payment of the $15,000 *less* the $5,000 damages Nathan sustained because of Lilly's breach, which equals $10,000.

Statute of Frauds

Parties to a contract that is unenforceable because of the Statute of Frauds may, nonetheless, have acted in reliance on the contract. In such a case, each party may recover in restitution the benefits conferred on the other in relying on their unenforceable contract. Thus, if Wilton makes an oral contract to furnish services to Rochelle that are not to be performed within a year, and Rochelle discharges Wilton after three months, Wilton may recover as restitution the value of the services rendered during the three months.

Voidable Contracts

A party who has rescinded or avoided a contract for lack of capacity, duress, undue influence, fraud, misrepresentation, or mistake is entitled to restitution for any benefit he has conferred on the party. For example, Samuel fraudulently induces Edith to sell land for $60,000. Samuel pays the purchase price, and Edith conveys the land. Edith then discovers the fraud. Edith may disaffirm the contract and recover the land as restitution. Generally, the party seeking restitution must return any benefit that he has received under the agreement; however, this is not always the case, as we discussed in Chapter 12, which dealt with contractual capacity.

Figure 16–1 summarizes the remedies for breach of contract.

LIMITATIONS ON REMEDIES

Election of Remedies

If a party is injured by a breach of contract and has more than one remedy available to him, his manifestation of a choice of one of them, such as bringing suit, does not prevent him from seeking another remedy unless the remedies are inconsistent and the other party materially changes his position in reliance on the manifestation. For example, a party who seeks specific performance, an injunction, or restitution may be entitled to incidental damages, such as delay in performance. Damages for total breach, however, are inconsistent with the remedies of specific performance, injunction, and restitution. Likewise, the remedy of specific performance or an injunction is inconsistent with that of restitution.

With respect to contracts for the sale of goods, the Code rejects any doctrine of election of remedies. Thus, the remedies it provides are essentially cumulative in nature and include all of the available remedies for breach. Whether one remedy prevents the use of another depends upon the facts of the individual case. In addition, the Code liberalizes the common law by not restricting a defrauded party to an election of remedies.[13] That is, he may both rescind the contract by restoring the status quo and, in addition, recover damages or obtain any other remedy available under the Code.

HEAD & SEEMAN, INC. v. GREGG
Court of Appeals of Wisconsin, 1981.
104 Wis.2d 156, 311 N.W.2d 667.

Facts: Bettye Gregg offered to purchase a house from Head & Seeman, Inc. (seller). She represented in writing that she had $15,000 to $20,000 of equity in another home that she would pay to the seller after she sold the other home. She knew that she did not have such equity. In reliance upon these intentionally fraudulent representations, the seller accepted Gregg's offer and the parties entered into a land contract. After taking occupancy, Gregg failed to make any of the contract payments. The seller's investigations then revealed the fraud. Head & Seeman then brought suit seeking rescission of the contract, return of the real estate, and restitution. Restitution was sought for the rental value for the five months of lost use of the property and the seller's out-of-pocket expenses made in reliance upon the bargain. Gregg contends that under the election of remedies doctrine the seller cannot both rescind the contract and recover damages for its breach. The trial court denied recovery for rental value and out-of-pocket expenses.

Decision: Order reversed.

Opinion: Voss, P. J.   The election of remedies doctrine is an equitable principle barring one from maintaining inconsistent theories or forms of relief. [Citation.] Its underlying purpose is to prevent double recovery for the same wrong. [Citations.] * * *

The classic application of the election of remedies doctrine is that a defrauded party has the election of either rescission or affirming the contract and seeking damages. [Citation.] The choice is forced with respect to alternative theories in a single lawsuit because of inconsistency of both rescinding and affirming the contract. [Citation.]

Thus, it superficially appears that if a claimant chooses to seek rescission, he may not sue for damages. But the word "damages," like the label "election of remedies," impedes rather than aids the inquiry into the types of relief appropriate in a given case. Rescission is always coupled with restitution: the parties return the money, property or other benefits so as to restore each other to the position they were in prior to the transaction. In the case of fraud or misrepresentation, the victim has the priority of restoration, and if a loss must be borne, the wrongdoer bears it. [Citation.]

This case presents a crucial question dealing with the nature of restitution. At issue is whether restitution to a rescinding fraud victim includes everything he has reasonably paid out or given up in the transaction or only includes what the other party has actually received.

* * *

Many * * * cases recognize that "disaffirmance" of damages [rescission] only rules out "expectation" damages—the benefit of the bargain—and distinguish restitutionary "damages."

Damages for restitution are different from damages for breach of contract; and the former are permissible to restore the plaintiff to his former position when rescission is granted because of fraud. [Citation.] Several other states allow the recovery of restitutionary damages along with rescission when fraud or misrepresentations is the cause of the claim. [Citations.] We believe that restitutionary damages conform with the purpose of rescission, which is to put the defrauded party back in as good a position as he occupied before entering the contract. Consequently, we hold that such damages may be awarded along with rescission.

[Citation.] In equity, the court makes the calculated adjustments necessary to do complete justice. If complete justice requires that damages be awarded with the rescission, the court will award them. [Citations.]

Two clear forms of restitutionary awards are recoverable when coupled with rescission: The first is "reasonable expenditures in reliance on the bargain." [Citations.] The second is the rent or use value of the real estate during the other's possession. [Citations.]

Even in situations where the buyer is defrauded and entitled to the rescission, he or she must ordinarily pay rental value to the seller. This provides *a fortiori* support for the above authorities. [Citations.]

In the instant case, plaintiff seeks rental value and incidental expenses as part of restitution, items clearly recoverable under the great weight of authority. We believe that [citation] recognized the position that rescission and restorative damages are consistent remedies which work together to restore the injured party to his precontract position. For this reason, restorative damages, which in this case is rent, should be allowed in addition to rescission. The two are not inconsistent remedies.

Loss of Power of Avoidance

A party with a power of avoidance for lack of capacity, duress, undue influence, fraud, misrepresentation, or mistake may lose that power if (1) she affirms the contract, (2) she delays unreasonably in exercising the power of disaffirmance, or (3) the rights of third parties intervene.

Affirmance   A party who has the power to avoid a contract for lack of capacity, duress, undue influence, fraud, misrepresentation, or mistake will lose that power by affirming the contract. Affirmance occurs where the party, with full knowledge of the facts, either declares his intention to proceed with the contract or takes some other action from which such intention may reasonably be inferred. Thus, suppose that Pam was induced to purchase a ring from Sally through Sally's fraudulent misrepresentation. If, after learning the truth, Pam undertakes to sell the ring to Janet or does something else that is consistent only with her ownership of the ring, she may no longer rescind the transaction. In the case of incapacity, duress, or undue influence, affirmance is effective only after the circumstances that made the contract voidable

cease to exist. Where there has been fraudulent misrepresentation, the defrauded party may affirm only after he knows of the misrepresentation, whereas if the misrepresentation is nonfraudulent or there is a mistake, only after he knows or should know of the misrepresentation or mistake.

Delay   The power of avoidance may be lost if the party who has the power does not rescind within a reasonable time. What is a reasonable time depends on all the circumstances, including the extent to which the delay enables the party with the power of avoidance to speculate at the other party's risk. To illustrate, a defrauded purchaser of stock cannot wait unduly to see if the market price or value of the stock appreciates sufficiently to justify retaining the stock. A reasonable time does not begin until the circumstances that made the contract voidable have ceased to exist.

Rights of Third Parties   The power of avoidance and the accompanying right to restitution are further limited by the intervening rights of third parties. If A transfers property to B in a transaction that is voidable by A, and B sells the property to C, a good faith purchaser for value, before A exercises her power of avoidance, A will lose the right to recover the property.

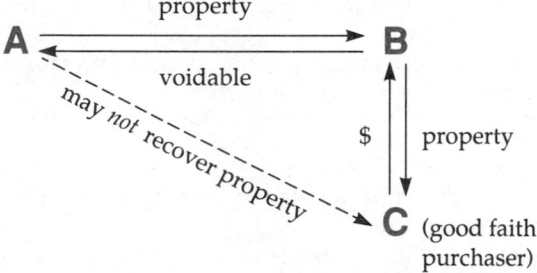

Thus, if a third party (C), who is a good faith purchaser for value, acquires an interest in the subject matter of the contract before A has elected to rescind, no rescission is permitted. Because the transaction is voidable, B acquires

a voidable title to the property. Upon a sale of the property by him to C, who is a purchaser in good faith and for value, C obtains good title and is allowed to retain the property. Since both A and C are innocent, the law will not disturb the title held by C, the good faith purchaser. In this case, as in all cases where rescission is not available, A's only recourse is against B.

The one notable exception to this rule is the situation involving a sale by a minor who subsequently wishes to avoid a transaction, *other than for a sale of goods*, from a good faith purchaser. Under this special rule, a good faith purchaser is deprived of the protection generally provided. Therefore, the third party in a transaction not involving goods is no more protected from the minor's disaffirmance than is the person dealing directly with the minor.

CHAPTER SUMMARY

Monetary Damages	**Compensatory Damages** contract damages placing the injured party in as good a position as if the other party had performed; equals loss of value plus incidental damages plus consequential damages minus loss avoided by injured party
	■ *Loss of Value* value of promised performance minus value of actual performance
	■ *Incidental Damages* damages arising directly out of a breach of contract
	■ *Consequential Damages* damages not arising directly out of a breach but as a foreseeable result of the breach
	Nominal Damages a small sum awarded where a contract has been breached but the loss is negligible or unproved
	Reliance Damages contract damages placing the injured party in as good a position as he would have been in had the contract not been made
	Foreseeable Damages loss that the party in breach had reason to know of when the contract was made
	Damages for Misrepresentation
	■ *Benefit-of-the-Bargain Damages* difference between the value of the fraudulent party's performance as represented and the value received
	■ *Out-of-Pocket Damages* difference between the value given and the value received
	Punitive Damages are generally not recoverable for breach of contract
	Liquidated Damages reasonable damages agreed to in advance by the parties to a contract
	Mitigation of Damages requirement that the injured party take reasonable steps to lessen or avoid damages

Remedies in Equity	Availability only where there is no adequate remedy at law
	 Types
	     ■ *Specific Performance* court decree ordering breaching party to render promised performance
	     ■ *Injunction* court order prohibiting a party from doing a specific act
	     ■ *Reformation* court order correcting a written contract to conform with the original intent of the contracting parties

Restitution	Definition of Restitution restoration of the injured party to the position she was in before the contract was made
	 Availability
	     ■ *Party Injured by Breach* if the other party totally breaches the contract by nonperformance or repudiation
	     ■ *Party in Default* for any benefit conferred in excess of the loss caused by the breach
	     ■ *Statute of Frauds* where a contract is unenforceable because of the Statute of Frauds, a party may recover the benefits conferred on the other party in reliance on the contract
	     ■ *Voidable Contracts* a party who has avoided a contract is entitled to restitution for any benefit conferred on the other party

Limitations on Remedies	Election of Remedies if remedies are inconsistent, a party injured by a breach of contract must elect which remedy to pursue
	 Loss of Power of Avoidance a party with the power to avoid a contract may lose that power by
	     ■ Affirming the contract
	     ■ Delaying unreasonably in exercising the power of avoidance
	     ■ Intervening rights of third parties

QUESTIONS

1. Explain how compensatory damages are computed.
2. Explain how reliance damages are computed.
3. Define (a) nominal damages, (b) incidental damages, (c) consequential damages, (d) foreseeability of damages, (e) punitive damages, (f) liquidated damages, and (g) mitigation of damages.
4. Discuss when the courts will grant equitable relief and define the various types of equitable relief.
5. Identify and discuss the situations in which restitution is available as a contractual remedy.

PROBLEMS

1. Edward contracted to buy 1,000 barrels of sugar from Marcia. Marcia failed to deliver, and because Edward could not buy any sugar in the market, he was forced to shut down his candy factory. (a) What damages is Edward entitled to recover? (b) Would it make any difference if Marcia had been told by Edward that he wanted the sugar to make candies for the Christmas trade and that he had accepted contracts for the delivery by certain dates?
2. Daniel agreed to erect an apartment building for Steven for $750,000, Daniel to suffer deduction of $1,000 per day for every day of delay. Daniel was

twenty days late in finishing the job, losing ten days because of a strike and ten days because the material suppliers were late in furnishing Daniel with materials. Daniel claims that he is entitled to payment in full (a) because the agreement as to $1,000 a day is a penalty; (b) because Steven had not shown that he has sustained any damage. Discuss each contention and decide.

3. Sharon contracted with Jane, a shirtmaker, for 1,000 shirts for men. Jane manufactured and delivered 500 shirts, for which Sharon paid. At the same time, Sharon notified Jane that she could not use or dispose of the other 500 shirts and directed Jane not to manufacture any more under the contract. Nevertheless, Jane made up the other 500 shirts and tendered them to Sharon. Sharon refused to accept the shirts. Jane then sued for the purchase price. Decision?

4. Stuart contracts to act in a comedy for Charlotte and to comply with all theater regulations for four seasons. Charlotte promises to pay Stuart $800 for each performance and to allow Stuart one benefit performance each season. It is expressly agreed that "Stuart shall not be employed in any other production for the period of the contract." Stuart and Charlotte, during the first year of the contract, had a terrible quarrel. Thereafter, Stuart signed a contract to perform in Elaine's production and ceased performing for Charlotte. Charlotte seeks (a) to prevent Stuart from performing for Elaine, and (b) to require Stuart to perform his contract with Charlotte. What result?

5. Louis leases a building to Pam for five years at a rental of $1,000 per month, commencing July 1, 1986. Pam is to deposit $10,000 as security for performance of all her promises in the lease, to be retained by Louis in case of any breach on Pam's part, otherwise to be applied in payment of rent for the last ten months of the term of the lease. Pam defaulted in the payment of rent for the months of May and June 1990. After proper notice to Pam of the termination of the lease for nonpayment of rent, Louis sued Pam for possession of the building and recovered a judgment for possession. Thereafter, Pam sues Louis to recover the $10,000 less the amount of rent due Louis for May and June 1990. Decision?

6. (a) Mary and Anne enter into a written agreement under which Mary agrees to sell and Anne agrees to buy for $10 per share 100 shares of the 300 shares outstanding of the capital stock of the Infinitesimal Steel Corporation, whose shares are not listed on any exchange and are closely held. Mary refused to deliver when tendered the $1,000, and Anne sues in equity for specific performance, tendering the $1,000. Decision?

(b) Modifying (a) above, assume that the subject matter of the agreement is stock of the United States Steel Corporation, which is traded on the New York Stock Exchange. Decision?

(c) Modifying (a) above, assume that the subject matter of the agreement is undeveloped farm land of little commercial value. Decision?

7. On March 1 Joseph sold to Sandra fifty acres of land in Oregon that Joseph at the time represented to be fine black loam, high, dry, and free of stumps. Sandra paid Joseph the agreed price of $40,000 and took from Joseph a deed to the land. Sandra subsequently discovered that the land was low, swampy, and not entirely free of stumps. Sandra, nevertheless, undertook to convert the greater part of the land into cranberry bogs. After one year of cranberry culture, Sandra became entirely dissatisfied, tendered the land back to Joseph, and demanded from Joseph the return of the $40,000. On Joseph's refusal to repay the money, Sandra brings an action at law against him to recover the $40,000. What judgment?

8. James contracts to make repairs to Betty's building in return for Betty's promise to pay $12,000 on completion of the repairs. After partially completing the repairs, James is unable to continue. Betty hires another builder, who completes the repairs for $5,000. The building's value to Betty has increased by $10,000 as a result of the repairs, but Betty has lost $500 in rents because of the delay caused by James's breach. James sues Betty. How much, if any, may James recover in restitution from Betty?

9. Linda induced Sally to enter into a purchase of a stereo amplifier by intentionally misrepresenting the power output to be sixty watts R.M.S. at rated distortion, when in fact it only delivered twenty watts. Sally paid $450 for the amplifier. Amplifiers producing twenty watts generally sell for $200. Amplifiers producing sixty watts generally sell for $550. Sally decides to keep the amp and sue for damages. How much may Sally recover in damages from Linda?

10. Virginia induced Charles to sell Charles's boat to Virginia by misrepresentation of material fact on which Charles reasonably relied. Virginia promptly sold the boat to Donald, who paid fair value for it and knew nothing concerning the transaction between Virginia and Charles. Upon discovering the misrepresentation, Charles seeks to recover the boat. What are Charles's rights against Virginia and Donald?

11. Felch was employed as a member of the faculty of Findlay College on a continuing basis. He was dismissed by action of the president and board of trustees without compliance with a contractual provision for dismissal that requires a hearing. Felch requested the court to enjoin Findlay College to continue Felch as a member of the faculty and to pay him the salary agreed upon. Decision?

COMPUTER RESEARCH PROBLEMS

1. Copenhaver, the owner of a laundry business, contracted with Berryman, the owner of a large apartment complex, to allow Copenhaver to own and operate the laundry facilities within the apartment complex. Berryman terminated the contract with Copenhaver when forty-seven months remained in the five-year contract. Within six months, Copenhaver placed the equipment into use in other locations. Copenhaver filed suit, claiming that he was entitled to conduct the laundry operations for an additional forty-seven months and, by such, would have earned a profit of $13,886.58, after deducting Berryman's share of the gross receipts and other operating expenses. Decision?

2. Billy Williams Builders and Developers entered into a contract with Hillerich under which Williams agreed to sell to Hillerich a certain lot and to construct on it a house according to submitted plans and specifications. The house built by Williams was defectively constructed. Hillerich brought suit for specific performance of the contract and for damages resulting from the defective construction and delay in performance. Williams argued that Hillerich was not entitled to have both specific performance and damages for breach of the contract because the remedies were inconsistent and Hillerich had to make an election between them. Decision?

3. Developers under a plan approved by the city of Rye had constructed six luxury cooperative apartment buildings and were to construct six more. In order to obtain certificates of occupancy for the six completed buildings, the developers were required to post a bond with the city to insure completion of the remaining buildings. The developers posted a $100,000 bond upon which the defendant, Public Service Mutual Insurance Company, as guarantor or surety, agreed to pay $200 for each day after April 1, 1971, that the remaining buildings were not completed. More than 500 days passed without completion of the buildings within the time limit. The city sued the developers and the insurance company to recover $100,000 on the bond. Decision?

4. Kerr Steamship Company sent a telegram to the Philippines through the Radio Corporation of America. The telegram contained instructions for loading cargo on one of Kerr's ships. The telegram was mislaid and never delivered. Consequently, the ship was improperly loaded and the cargo was lost. Kerr sued the Radio Corporation for $6,675.29 in profits lost on the cargo caused by the Radio Corporation's failure to deliver the telegram. Decision?

5. El Dorado Tire Company fired Bill Ballard, a sales executive. Ballard had a five year contract with El Dorado but was fired after only two years of employment. Ballard sued El Dorado for breach of contract. El Dorado claims that any damages due to breach of the contract should be mitigated because of Ballard's failure to seek other employment after he was fired. Decision?

ENDNOTES

1. Restatement, Second, Contracts, Section 346, Availability of Damages.
2. Restatement, Second, Contracts, Section 352, Uncertainty as a Limitation on Damages.
3. Restatement, Second, Contracts, Section 351, Unforeseeability and Related Limitations on Damages.
4. Restatement, Second, Torts, Section 549, Measure of Damages for Fraudulent Misrepresentation.
5. Restatement, Second, Torts, Sections 552B, Damages for Negligent Misrepresentation; 552C, Misrepresentation in Sale, Rental or Exchange Transaction.
6. Restatement, Second, Contracts, Section 355, Punitive Damages.
7. Restatement, Second, Contracts, Section 356(1), Liquidated Damages and Penalties.
8. Restatement, Second, Contracts, Section 350, Avoidability as a Limitation on Damages.
9. Uniform Commercial Code, Section 2—704, Seller's Right to Identify Goods to the Contract Notwithstanding Breach or to Salvage Unfinished Goods.
10. Restatement, Second, Contracts, Section 360, Factors Affecting Adequacy of Damages.
11. Restatement, Second, Contracts, Section 367(1), Contracts for Personal Service or Supervision.
12. Restatement, Second, Contracts, Section 367(2), Contracts for Personal Service or Supervision.
13. Uniform Commercial Code, Section 2—721, Remedies for Fraud.

PART 3
SALES

Part Three of the text deals with sales—the most common and important of all commercial transactions. In an exchange economy such as ours, sales are the essential means by which the various units of production exchange their outputs, thereby providing the opportunity for specialization and enhanced productivity. An advanced, complex, industrialized economy with highly coordinated manufacturing and distribution systems requires a reliable mechanism for assuring that *future* exchanges can be entered into today and fulfilled at a later time. The critical role of the law of sales is to establish a framework in which these present and future exchanges may take place in a predictable, certain, and orderly fashion with a minimum of transaction costs.

Until the early 1900s sales transactions were completely governed by general contract law. In 1906 the Uniform Sales Act was promulgated and eventually adopted by thirty-six States. By the end of the 1930s, however, dissatisfaction with this and other uniform commercial statutes brought about the development of the Uniform Commercial Code. Article 2 of the Code deals with transactions in sales. Nevertheless, the law of sales still remains in large measure a part of general contract law:

> The law of sales is a branch of the more general law of contracts. Therefore, rules of law applicable to contracts generally are applicable to contracts for the sale of goods unless those rules have been displaced by the Code. Nordstrom, *Law of Sales*, 80–81.

One of the most significant ways in which the Code has displaced common law is the Code's movement away from formalistic rules to an emphasis on the intent of the parties. Under the common law, parties intending to enter into a binding sale often discovered that they had not done so due to an inadvertent failure to comply with one or more formalities. Such an outcome is much less likely under the Code. The rules for contract formation have been greatly relaxed by the Code, and thus it is far easier for parties to form a binding sales contract. This approach achieves two important policies of sales law: to add predictability to the use of sales contracts by recognizing contracts where the parties intend to be bound, and to reduce the transaction costs of sales. It also promotes a third objective of modernizing the law governing business transactions. Accordingly, the Code not only responds more closely than the common law to the intention of the parties, but it also reflects the needs, practices, and usages of the marketplace. As Section 1-102 states, one of the underlying purposes and policies of the Code is "to permit the continued expansion of commercial practices through custom, usage and agreement of the parties."

The Code has also modified general contract law by providing that an agreement of the parties does not fail merely because it does not state all the material terms of the contract. The drafters of the Code realized that the parties may intentionally omit a term—such as price—in order to ensure themselves of a contract while at the same time not binding themselves to a specific price in a widely fluctuating market. The Code has explicitly adopted the policy of permitting the parties to a sales contract to use such "open terms" by systematically supplying its own terms to fill the omitted terms. The Code does so on the assumption that the parties intended to be bound by terms that are commercially reasonable.

To counterbalance the relaxed rules of contract formation, the Code has statutorily established two overriding regulatory requirements on all sales transactions—unconscionability and good faith. Under the doctrine of unconscionability, courts may invalidate a contract, or any part of a contract, that is so one-sided as to be unconscionable. This doctrine recognizes that the parties to a contract may not be of relatively equal bargaining power and, therefore, that the laissez-faire principle of freedom of contract must be modified to reflect this reality of the modern world. For example, although standardized contracts are widely used today, they are usually nonnegotiable and incomprehensible to the typical consumer. Therefore, the Code has provided the potent device of unconscionability to prevent oppression and unfair surprise.

The other policing device established by the Code is the obligation imposed on all parties to contracts formed under the Code to act in good faith. The significance of this provision to business ethics has been explained by Robert Summers:

> It is natural for two parties to assume that each will act in good faith toward the other throughout the course of their contractual dealings. Moreover, morals obligate them to act this way. Yet, in one sense their interests will remain essentially antagonistic, for each will be expecting to get something from the other on advantageous terms. And, in a given case, misunderstandings may arise, unforeseen events occur, expected gains disappear or dislikes develop which may motivate one party to act in bad faith. If, however, such a party is legally as well as morally obligated to act in good faith, he will be significantly less likely to break faith. Summers, " 'Good Faith' in General Contract Law and the Sales Provisions of the Uniform Commercial Code," 54 *Va. L. Rev.* 195 (1968).

The Uniform Commercial Code continues and expands upon the public policy of contract law to place the aggrieved party in as good a position as if the other party had fully performed. The Code accomplishes this by providing an impressive array of cumulative remedies for both the buyer and seller. At the same time, the Code deplores economic waste and requires commercially reasonable actions by the aggrieved party to mitigate damages.

Intertwined with the Code's enhanced remedies is its strengthened warranty provisions. As Professor Friedrich Kessler stated:

> Modern sales law, in its desire to protect the buyer and his expectations as to quality, is adopting the position that the seller is responsible for the qualities which the buyer is entitled to expect in the light of all surrounding circumstances, including the purchase price. . . . Indeed, the conviction is gaining ground that the function of warranty law is to establish a "subjective" equivalence between price and quality. Kessler, "The Protection of the Consumer Under Modern Sales Law," 74 *Yale L.J.* 262 (1964).

Since information is one-sided and frequently not available to the consumer, it is important to ensure a certain minimum level of quality and safety, an objective that has been greatly furthered by both the warranty provisions in sales law and strict liability in tort law.

While reading the five chapters in this part, you should consider the overall purpose and policy of the law governing sales: to provide a predictable, certain, and orderly system by which exchanges of goods may take place in a complex, highly interdependent exchange economy. General contract law supplies the greater part of this system, but Article 2 of the Code has refined it considerably by simplifying, clarifying, and modernizing the law governing sales transactions.

17 INTRODUCTION TO SALES

Of all business and legal transactions, the sale is without question the most common. The manufacture and distribution of goods involve numerous sales transactions, and practically everyone in our economy is a purchaser of both durable and consumable goods. Originally part of the Law Merchant, the law of sales was absorbed into the common law and codified in Article 2 of the Uniform Commercial Code, which has been adopted in all States—except Louisiana—plus the District of Columbia and the Virgin Islands.

In this chapter we discuss the nature and formation of sales contracts.

NATURE OF SALES CONTRACTS

The law of sales, which governs contracts involving the sale of goods, is a specialized branch of both the law of contracts (discussed in Chapters 7–16) and the law of personal property (discussed in Chapter 47). This relationship is illustrated by Figure 17–1. This section will cover the definition of a sales contract and the fundamental principles of Article 2 of the Code.

DEFINITION

The Code defines a **sale** as the transfer of title to goods from seller to buyer for a price.[1] The price can be money, other goods, real estate, or services. **Goods** are essentially defined as movable, tangible, personal property. For example, the sale of a bicycle, stereo set, or this textbook is considered a sale of goods. "Goods" also include the unborn young of animals, growing crops, and, if removed by the seller, timber, minerals, or a building attached to real property.[2]

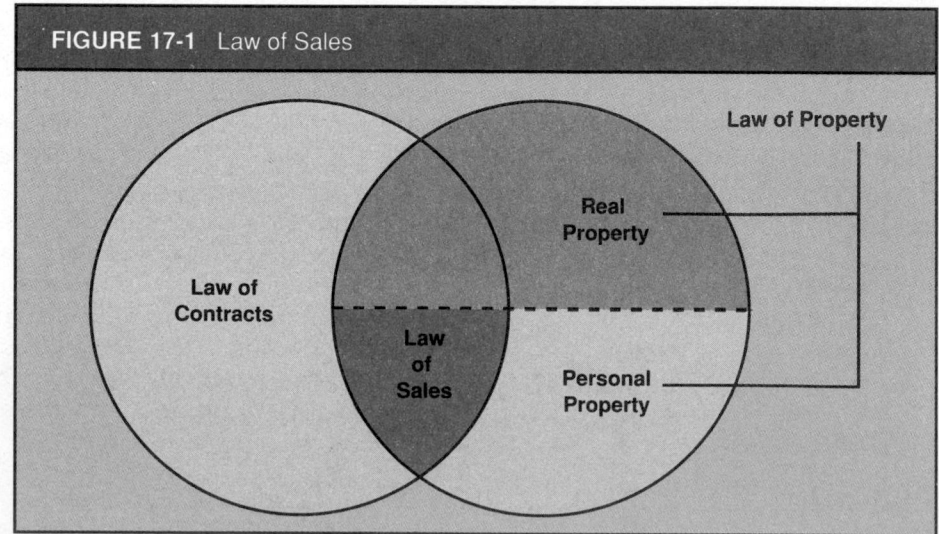

FIGURE 17-1 Law of Sales

Governing Law

Sales transactions are governed by Article 2 of the Code, but where general contract law has not been specifically modified by the Code, contract law continues to apply. In other words, the law of sales is a specialized part of the general law of contracts, and the law of contracts continues to govern unless specifically displaced by the Code.

General contract law also continues to govern all contracts outside the scope of the Code.

Transactions not within the scope of Article 2 include employment contracts, service contracts, insurance contracts, contracts involving real property, and contracts for the sale of intangibles such as stocks, bonds, patents, and copyrights. For an illustration of this relationship see Figure 7–1 and *Osterholt v. Charles Drilling Co.* in Chapter 7. The following case deals with the question of whether a contract containing both a sale of movable personal property and a service is a UCC contract or general contract.

COLORADO CARPET INSTALLATION, INC. v. PALERMO
Supreme Court of Colorado, 1983.
668 F.2d 1384.

Facts: In April 1980 Jack Duran, president of Colorado Carpet Installation, Inc., began negotiations with Fred and Zuma Palermo for the sale and installation of carpeting, carpet padding, tile, and vinyl floor covering in their home. Duran drew up a written proposal that referred to Colorado Carpet as "the seller" and to the Palermos as "the customer." The proposal listed the quantity, unit cost, and total price of each item to be installed. The total price of the job was $4,777.75. Although labor was expressly included in this figure, Duran estimated the total labor cost at $926. Mrs. Palermo orally accepted Duran's written proposal soon after he submitted it to her. After Colorado Carpet delivered the tile to the Palermo home, however, Mrs. Palermo had a disagreement with Colorado Carpet's tile man and arranged for another contractor to perform the job. Colorado Carpet brought an action against the Palermos for breach of contract. The trial court determined that the agreement between Colorado Carpet and the Palermos constituted a service contract for the performance of labor, not a contract for the sale of goods, and thus did not have to be in writing to be enforceable. The court of appeals reversed the decision, finding that the agreement was a contract for the sale of goods and was unenforceable under the "writing" requirement of the statute of frauds section of the Uniform Commercial Code.

Decision: Judgment of court of appeals affirmed.

Opinion: Quinn, J. We first address the court of appeals' determination that the contract was one for the sale of goods, rather than for the performance of labor or services. We conclude that the agreement in question involved a contract for the sale of goods as contemplated by [UCC] Section 2–201(1).

This section prohibits the enforcement of contracts "for the sale of goods for the price of $500 or more . . . unless there is some writing sufficient to indicate that a contract for sale has been made between the parties and signed by the party against whom enforcement is sought. . . ." By its terms, the statute applies only to contracts for the sale of goods, and not to contracts for labor or services. [Citations.] The Uniform Commercial Code defines "goods" to mean "all things (including specially manufactured goods) which are movable at the time of identification to the contract for sale other than the money in which the price is to be paid, investment securities . . . and things in action." [UCC] Section 2–105(1). [Citation.] * * *

In this case the subject of the contract involved "goods" because the carpeting and other materials were movable at the time that Colorado Carpet procured them for installation pursuant to the agreement. Since the agreement contemplated that title to the carpeting and other materials would pass to the Palermos, it constituted a "contract for sale." The scope of the contract, however, included not only the sale of goods but also the performance of labor or service. Thus, we must determine whether such a mixed contract qualified as a contract for the sale of goods or, instead, constituted a contract for labor or service outside the scope of [UCC] Section 2–201(1).

The performance of some labor or service frequently plays a role in sales transactions. "Goods," however, are not the less "goods" merely because labor or service may be essential to their ultimate use by the purchaser. The mere furnishing of some labor or service, in our view, should not determine the ultimate character of a contract for purposes of . . . the Uniform Commercial Code. Rather, the controlling criterion should be the primary purpose of the contract—that is, whether the circumstances underlying the formation of the agreement and the performance reasonably expected of the parties demonstrates the primary purpose of the contract as the sale of goods or, in contrast, the sale of labor or service.

* * *

This "primary purpose" test, we believe, is designed to promote one of the expressed statutory policies of the Uniform Commercial Code—"[t]o simplify, clarify, and modernize the law governing commercial transactions." [Citation.] Useful factors to consider in determining whether "goods" or "service" predominates include the following: the contractual language used by the parties [citations]; whether the agreement involves one overall price that includes both goods and labor or, instead, calls for separate and discrete billings for goods on the one hand and labor on the other [citations]; the ratio that the cost of goods bears to the overall contract price [citations]; and the nature and reasonableness of the purchaser's contractual expectations of acquiring a property interest in goods. . . .

Considering the contract under these guidelines, we are satisfied that, as a matter of law, its primary purpose was the sale of goods and not the sale of labor or service. The language in Colorado Carpet's proposal referred to the parties as "seller" and "customer." In addition, the agreement called for an overall contract price that included both the cost of goods and labor, and, as the trial evidence established, the charge for labor was slight in relation to the total contractual price. Finally, the carpeting and other materials were movable when Colorado Carpet procured them for the purpose of selling them to the Palermos.

Nonsales Transactions in Goods

A number of transactions that are not sales significantly affect goods. For example, a **bailment** is a transfer of the possession of personal property by the owner or rightful possessor **(bailor)** to another **(bailee)** for a determinable period of time *without* a transfer of title. For example, Arnold (the bailor) creates a bailment when he delivers his dirty laundry to the Bailey Laundry Company (the bailee) for cleaning. Other examples of bailments include delivery of goods to a repairman, a carrier, or a warehouseman. In contrast, transfer of title is essential to a sale, although transfer of possession is not.

A **lease** of goods is a contract whereby the owner of the goods (the **lessor**) agrees with another person (the **lessee**) that he will transfer to the lessee the possession and right to use the goods for a period of time in consideration of a specified payment. A lease of goods differs from a sale in that it does not involve a transfer of title to the goods.

A **gift** is a transfer of property from one person to another without consideration. The lack of any consideration is the basic distinction between a gift and a sale. A promise to make a gift is not binding. Because a gift involves no consideration or compensation, to be effective it must be completed by delivery of the gift. There must also be intent on the part of the maker (the **donor**) of the gift to make a present transfer, and there must be acceptance by the recipient (the **donee**) of the gift. In a sale, delivery of the property is not necessary to transfer title.

A sale is distinguished from a security interest in that a sale transfers to the buyer all of the ownership rights of the seller in the goods, whereas under a security agreement both the **creditor** and the **debtor** have ownership rights in the goods. A **security interest** is a grant of a right in personal property by a debtor to a creditor to secure payment or performance of an obligation. The right of the secured creditor in the goods is to take possession of the goods in the event of default by the debtor.

Although Article 2 governs sales, the drafters of the article have invited the courts to extend Code principles to nonsale transactions in goods. To date, a number of courts have accepted this invitation and have applied Code provisions by analogy to other transactions in goods not expressly included within the article, most frequently to leases and bailments. The Code has also greatly influenced the Restatement, Second, Contracts, which, as we discussed in Chapter 7, has great effect on all contracts. In these ways the policies and principles of the Code have been extended to nonsales transactions. In 1987 the drafters of the Code went further and approved **Article 2A** of the Uniform Commercial Code—Leases. This article is an analogue of Article 2 and adopts many of the rules contained in that article and applies them to leases of goods.

Figure 17–2 summarizes the various transactions in goods.

FUNDAMENTAL PRINCIPLES OF ARTICLE 2

The purpose of Article 2 is to modernize, clarify, simplify, and make uniform the law of sales. Furthermore, the article is to be interpreted according to these principles and not according to some abstraction such as the passage of title. The Code "is drawn to provide flexibility so that, since it is intended to be a semi-permanent piece of legislation, it will provide its own machinery for expansion of commercial practices. It is intended to make it possible for the law embodied in this Act to be

---

FIGURE 17–2 Transactions in Goods

	Transfer of Title	Transfer of Possession	Governing Law
Sale	Yes	Usually, but not necessarily	Article 2
Gift	Yes	Yes	Common Law
Bailment	No	Yes	Common Law
Lease	No	Yes	Common Law
Non-possessory Security Interest	No	No	Article 9

developed by the courts in the light of unforeseen and new circumstances and practices. However, the proper construction of the Act requires that its interpretation and application be limited to its reason." This open-ended drafting includes the following fundamental concepts.

Good Faith

All parties who enter into a contract or duty within the scope of the Code must perform their obligations in good faith. The Code defines **good faith** as "honesty in fact in the conduct or transaction concerned."[3] In the case of a merchant (defined below), good faith also requires the observance of reasonable commercial standards of fair dealing in the trade.[4] For instance, if the parties agree that the seller is to set the price term, the seller must establish the price in good faith.

Unconscionability

Every contract of sale may be scrutinized by the courts to determine whether in its commercial setting, purpose, and effect it is unconscionable. The reviewing court may refuse to enforce an unconscionable contract or any part of it found to be unconscionable.[5] The Code does not define *unconscionable*; however, the term is defined in the *New Webster's Dictionary* (Deluxe Encyclopedic Edition) as: "contrary to the dictates of conscience; unscrupulous or unprincipled; exceeding that which is reasonable or customary; inordinate, unjustifiable."

The Code denies or limits enforcement of an unconscionable contract for the sale of goods in the interest of fairness and decency and to correct harshness or oppression in contracts resulting from unequal bargaining position of the parties. Although the principle is not novel, its embodiment in a statute dealing with commercial transactions is.

The doctrine of unconscionability has been justified on the basis that it permits the courts to resolve issues of unfairness explicitly on that basis without recourse to formalistic rules or legal fictions. In policing contracts for fairness, the courts have again demonstrated their willingness to limit freedom of contract in order to protect the less advantaged from overreaching by dominant contracting parties. The doctrine of unconscionability has evolved through its application by the courts to include both procedural and substantive unconscionability. **Procedural unconscionability** involves scrutiny for the presence of "bargaining naughtiness." In other words, was the negotiation process fair, or were there procedural irregularities such as burying important terms of the agreement in fine print or obscuring the true meaning of the contract with impenetrable legal jargon?

Substantive unconscionability deals with the actual terms of the contract and looks for oppressive or grossly unfair provisions such as an exorbitant price or an unfair exclusion or limitation of contractual remedies. An all too common example is that involving a necessitous buyer in an unequal bargaining position with a seller who has obtained an exorbitant price for his product or service. In one case, a price of $749 ($920 on time) for a vacuum cleaner that cost the seller $140 was held unconscionable. In another case, the buyers, welfare recipients, purchased by time payment contract a home freezer unit for $900 plus time credit charges, credit life insurance, credit property insurance, and sales tax for a total price of $1,235. The purchase resulted from a visit to the buyer's home by a salesman representing Your Shop At Home Service, Inc., and the maximum retail value of the freezer unit at the time of purchase was $300. The court held the contract unconscionable and reformed it by changing the price to the total payment ($620) made by the buyers.

The case on page 345 illustrates the application of the doctrine of unconscionability, as does *Williams v. Walker-Thomas Furniture Co.* in Chapter 11.

Expansion of Commercial Practices

An underlying policy of the Code is "to permit the continued expansion of commercial practices through custom, usage and agreement of the parties."[6] In particular, the Code places great emphasis on course of dealings and usage of trade in interpreting agreements.

FRANK'S MAINTENANCE AND ENGINEERING, INC. v. C. A. ROBERTS CO.
Appellate Court of Illinois, First District, Fourth Division, 1980.
86 Ill.App.3d 980, 42 Ill.Dec. 25, 408 N.E.2d 403.

Facts: Frank's Maintenance and Engineering, Inc., orally ordered steel tubing from C. A. Roberts Co. for use in the manufacture of motorcycle front fork tubes. Since these front fork tubes bear the bulk of the weight of a motorcycle, the steel used must be of high quality. Roberts Co. sent an acknowledgment with conditions of sale including one that limited consequential damages and restricted remedies available upon breach by requiring claims for defective equipment to be promptly made upon receipt. The conditions were located on the back of the acknowledgment. The legend "conditions of sale on reverse side" was stamped over so that on first appearance it read "No conditions of sale on reverse side." Roberts delivered the order in December 1975. The steel had no visible defects; however, when Frank's Maintenance began using the steel in its manufacture in the summer of 1976, it discovered that the steel was pitted and cracked beyond repair. Frank's Maintenance informed Roberts Co. of the defects, revoked its acceptance of the steel, and sued for breach of warranty of merchantability. The trial court granted the defendant's motion for summary judgment.

Decision: Judgment reversed and remended for proceedings consistent with this opinion.

Opinion. Romiti, J. The Uniform Commercial Code [citation], provides that consequential damages may be limited or excluded unless the limitation or exclusion is unconscionable and such clauses have been upheld in many cases. [Citations.] The Code provides that such limitation is prima facie unconscionable where personal injuries are involved, but not where the loss is commercial. Nevertheless, the existence of a commercial setting is not of itself sufficient insulation against a charge of unconscionability. [Citation.] While under the Code [U.C.C. § 2–302], the question of the unconscionability of a clause is for the court to decide, the court before making this determination must give the parties a reasonable opportunity to present evidence as to its commercial setting, purpose and effect. Generally a full hearing on the issue is required. [Citations.]

Unconscionability can be either procedural or substantive or a combination of both. [Citations.] Procedural unconscionability consists of some impropriety during the process of forming the contract depriving a party of a meaningful choice. [Citation.] *Williams v. Walker-Thomas Furniture Co.* (1965), [Chapter 11]. Factors to be considered are all the circumstances surrounding the transaction including the manner in which the contract was entered into, whether each party had a reasonable opportunity to understand the terms of the contract, and whether important terms were hidden in a maze of fine print; both the conspicuousness of the clause and the negotiations relating to it are important, albeit not conclusive factors in determining the issue of unconscionability. [Citation.] To be a part of the bargain, a provision limiting the defendant's liability must, unless incorporated into the contract through prior course of dealings or trade usage, have been bargained for, brought to the purchaser's attention or be conspicuous. [Citation.] If not, the seller has no reasonable expectation that the remedy was being so restricted and the restriction cannot be said to be part of the agreement of the parties. [Citation.] Nor does the mere fact that both parties are businessmen justify the utilization of unfair surprise to the detriment of one of the parties since the

Code specifically provides for the recovery of consequential damages and an individual should be able to rely on their existence in the absence of being informed to the contrary either directly or constructively through prior course of dealings or trade usage. [Citation.] This requirement that the seller obtain the knowing assent of the buyer "does not detract from the freedom to contract, unless that phrase denotes the freedom to impose the onerous terms of one's carefully-drawn printed document on an unsuspecting contractual partner. Rather, freedom to contract is enhanced by a requirement that both parties be aware of the burdens they are assuming. The notion of free will has little meaning as applied to one who is ignorant of the consequences of his acts." [Citation.]

Substantive unconscionability concerns the question whether the terms themselves are commercially reasonable. [Citation.] While the Code permits the limitation of remedies, it must be remembered that it disfavors them [sic] and specifically provides for their deletion if they would act to deprive a contracting party of reasonable protection against a breach. [Citations.] The Code 1–106(1), specifically provides that the remedies provided by it shall be liberally construed to the end that the aggrieved party may be put in as good a position as if the other party had fully performed. [Citations.] And as specifically stated in [the comments to the U.C.C.], if the parties intend to conclude a contract for sale within the scope of the Uniform Commercial Code-Sales, they must accept the legal consequence that there be at least a fair quantum of remedy for breach of the obligations or duties outlined in the contract. Reasonable agreements which limit or modify remedies will be given effect but the parties are not free to shape their remedies in an unreasonable or unconscionable way. [Citations.] It is for this reason that courts have tended to strike down clauses barring the recovery of consequential damages or otherwise limiting recovery when the defect was latent. [Citations.]

In the present case, the evidence produced by the plaintiff discloses that the limiting clause was not conspicuous and was not known to the plaintiff at the time the contract was made. Indeed, the clause directing the plaintiff's attention to conditions on the reverse side of the acknowledgment was stamped over, indicating that legend was irrelevant. In addition, the plaintiff was directed to check to see if the order as acknowledged conformed to the terms of the order as the seller otherwise could not be responsible for mistakes in the execution of the order. Thus by implication plaintiff was informed that there was nothing else in the acknowledgment to be checked. Furthermore the defects in the steel allegedly were latent. Absent evidence produced by the defendants tending to refute this evidence or tending to show the paragraph had been negotiated by the parties and agreed to, or that prior contracts between the parties had established a consistently adhered to policy of excluding consequential damages, or whether a recognized trade practice, reasonable as applied to the plaintiff, had established such a policy [citation], we do not believe that the court could reasonably find the clause to be conscionable.

A **course of dealing** is a sequence of previous conduct between the parties that may fairly be regarded as establishing a common basis of understanding for interpreting their expressions and agreement.[7]

A **usage of trade** is a practice or method of dealing regularly observed and followed in a place, vocation, or trade.[8] To illustrate: Connie contracts to sell Ward 1,000 feet of San Domingo mahogany. By usage of dealers in mahogany, known to Connie and Ward, good figured mohagany of a certain density is known as San Domingo mahogany, though it does not come from San Domingo. Unless otherwise agreed, the usage is part of the contract.

Sales By and Between Merchants

A novel feature of the Code is the establishment of separate rules that apply to transactions between merchants or involving a merchant as a party. A **merchant** is defined as a person (1) who is a dealer in the goods, or (2) who by his occupation holds himself out as having knowledge or skill peculiar to the goods or practices involved, or (3) who employs an agent or broker whom he holds out as having such knowledge or skill.[9]

TERMINAL GRAIN CORP. v. FREEMAN
Supreme Court of South Dakota, 1978.
270 N.W.2d 806.

Facts: Terminal Grain Corporation brought an action against Glen Freeman, a farmer, to recover damages for breach of an oral contract to deliver grain. According to the company, Freeman orally agreed to two sales of wheat to Terminal Grain of 4,000 bushels each at $1.65½ a bushel and $1.71 a bushel, respectively. Dwayne Maher, merchandising manager of Terminal Grain, sent two written confirmations of the agreements to Freeman. Freeman never made any written objections to the confirmations. After the first transaction had occurred, the price of wheat rose to between $2.25 and $2.30 per bushel, and Freeman refused to deliver the remaining 4,000 bushels at the agreed upon price. Freeman denies entering into any agreement to sell the second 4,000 bushels of wheat to Terminal Grain but admits that he received the two written confirmations sent by Maher. Terminal Grain appeals from a judgment in favor of Freeman.

Decision: Judgment for Freeman affirmed.

Opinion: Hanson, J.   As a farmer, Freeman contends he is not a "merchant" within the contemplation of the above statute [U.C.C. § 2-201] and it, therefore, has no application to him. The term "merchant" is defined in [U.C.C. § 2-104] as meaning

> a person who deals in goods of the kind or otherwise by his occupation holds himself out as having knowledge or skill peculiar to the practices or goods involved in the transaction or to whom such knowledge or skill may be attributed by his employment of an agent or broker or other intermediary who by his occupation holds himself out as having such knowledge or skill.

In similar factual cases the courts which have considered whether or not a "farmer" is or may be considered a "merchant" under the above Uniform Commercial Code provisions are almost equally divided in their opinions. The courts in Illinois, Texas, Missouri, Ohio, and North Carolina have held farmers to be merchants under various facts and circumstances. . . .

On the other hand the courts in Iowa, New Mexico, Utah, Kansas, Arkansas, and Alabama have held that a farmer is not a merchant. . . .

In arriving at its conclusion that the defendant farmer/seller was not a "merchant" within the meaning of the Uniform Commercial Code, the Kansas Court [stated]:

> (T)he appellee neither "deals" in wheat, as that item is used in 2–104 nor does he by his occupation hold himself out as having knowledge or skill peculiar to the practices or goods involved in the transaction. The concept of professionalism is heavy in determining who is a merchant under the statute. The writers of the official UCC comment virtually equate professionals with merchants, the casual

or inexperienced buyer or seller is not to be held to the standard set for the professional in business. The defined term "between merchants," used in the exception proviso to the statute of frauds, contemplates the knowledge and skill of professionals on each side of the transaction. The transaction in question here was the sale of wheat. Appellee as a farmer undoubtedly had special knowledge or skill in raising wheat but we do not think this factor, coupled with annual sales of a wheat crop and purchases of seed wheat, qualified him as a merchant in that field. The parties' stipulation states appellee has sold only the products he raised. There is no indication any of these sales were other than cash sales to local grain elevators, where conceivably an expertise reaching professional status could be said to be involved. [Citation.]

We agree with the reasoning of the Kansas Court and with the other courts which hold the average farmer, like Freeman, with no particular knowledge or experience in selling, buying, or dealing in future commodity transactions, and who sells only the crops he raises to local elevators for cash or who places his grain in storage under one of the federal loan programs, is not a "merchant" within the purview of the exception provision to the Uniform Commercial Code statute of frauds. Through training and years of experience a farmer may well possess or acquire special knowledge, skills, and expertise in the production of grain crops but this does not make him a "professional," equal in the marketplace with a grain buying and selling company, whose officers, agents, and employees are constantly conversant with the daily fluctuations in the commodity market, the many factors affecting the market, and with its intricate practices and procedures.

Various sections of the Code contain special rules that apply solely to transactions between merchants or to transactions in which a merchant is a party. These rules exact a higher standard of conduct from merchants because of their knowledge of trade and commerce and because merchants as a class generally set the standards. The more significant of these merchant provisions are listed in Figure 17–3.

Liberal Administration of Remedies

The Code provides that its remedies shall be liberally administered in order to place the aggrieved party in as good a position as if the defaulting party had fully performed.[10] The Code does make it clear, however, that remedies are limited to compensation and may not include consequential or punitive damages, unless specifically provided by the Code. Nevertheless, the Code provides that even in cases where the Code does not expressly provide a remedy for a right or obligation, the courts should provide an appropriate remedy.

Freedom of Contract

Most of the Code's provisions are not mandatory but permit the parties to vary or displace them altogether. The effect of provisions of the Code may be varied by agreement, except as otherwise provided and except that the obligations of good faith, diligence, reasonableness, and care prescribed by the Code may not be disclaimed by agreement. The parties may by agreement determine the standards by which the performance of these obligations is to be measured, so long as these standards are not obviously unreasonable.[11] This approach of the Code not only maximizes freedom of contract but also permits the continued expansion of commercial practices through private agreement.

Validation and Preservation of Sales Contracts

One of the requirements of commercial law is the establishment of rules that determine

---

FIGURE 17-3 Selected Rules Applicable to Merchants

Merchant Rules	Chapter in Text Where Discussed
Good faith	17
Confirmation of oral contracts	13,17
Firm offers	8,17
Battle of the forms	8,17
Warranty of title	19
Warranty of merchantability	19
Sales on approval	18
Retention of possession of goods by seller	18
Entrusting of goods	18
Risk of loss	18
Duties after rightful rejection	20

---

when an agreement is valid. The Code's approach to this is to reduce formal requisites to the bare minimum and attempt to preserve agreements whenever the parties manifest an intent to enter into a contract.

FORMATION OF A SALES CONTRACT

The Code's basic approach to validation is to recognize contracts whenever the parties manifest such an *intent*. This is so whether or not the parties can identify a precise moment at which they formed the contract.[12]

As already noted, the law of sales is a subset of the general law of contracts and is governed by general contract law unless particular provisions of the Code displace the general law. Although the Code leaves the great majority of issues of contract formation to general contract law, it has modified the general law of contract formation in several significant respects. These modifications were made to modernize contract law, to relax the validation requirements of contract formation, and to promote fairness.

MANIFESTATION OF MUTUAL ASSENT

In order for a contract to exist there must be an objective manifestation of mutual assent: an offer and an acceptance. In this section we will examine the UCC rules that impact upon offers and acceptances.

Definiteness of an Offer

At common law, the terms of a contract were required to be definite and complete. The Code has rejected the strict approach of the common law by recognizing an agreement as valid, despite missing terms, if there is any reasonably certain basis for granting a remedy. Accordingly, the Code provides that even though one or more terms to a contract may have been omitted, the contract need not fail for indefiniteness.[13] The Code provides standards by which omitted essential terms may be ascertained and supplied, provided the parties intended to enter into a binding agreement. The more terms left open, however, the more likely the parties did not intend to enter into a binding contract.

Open Price The parties may enter into a contract for the sale of goods even though they have reached no agreement on the price. Under the Code, the price is a reasonable one at the time for delivery where the agreement: (1) says nothing as to price, (2) provides that the parties shall agree later as to the price and they fail to so agree, or (3) fixes the price in terms of some agreed market or other standard or as set by a third person or agency and the price is not so set.[14]

An agreement that the price is to be fixed by the seller or buyer means that it must be fixed in good faith. If the price is to be fixed other than by agreement and is not so fixed through the fault of one of the parties, the other party has an option to treat the contract as canceled or to fix a reasonable price in good faith for the goods. Where the parties intend not to be bound unless the price is fixed or agreed upon as provided in the agreement, and it is not so fixed or agreed upon, the Code, in accordance with the parties' intent, provides that there is no contract.[14]

Open Delivery Unless otherwise agreed, the place of delivery is the seller's place of business or if he has none his residence. Moreover, the delivery, if unspecified, must be made within a reasonable time period and in a single delivery.

Open Quantity: Output and Requirement Contracts An agreement of a buyer to purchase the entire output of a seller for a stated period, or an agreement of a seller to supply a buyer with all her requirements of certain goods used in her business operations, may appear to lack definiteness and mutuality of obligation. The exact quantity of goods is not specified, and the seller may have some degree of control over his output and the buyer over her requirements. Such agreements are enforceable, however, by the application of an objective standard based on the good faith of both parties, and the quantities may not be disproportionate to any stated estimate or the prior output or requirements.[15] For example, the seller cannot operate his factory twenty-four hours a day and insist that the buyer take all of the output when he operated the factory only eight hours a day at the time the agreement was made. Nor can the buyer triple the size of her business and insist that the seller supply all of her requirements.

Other Open Terms Where the parties do not agree, the Code further provides rules as to the terms of payment, duration, and the particulars of performance.

Irrevocable Offer

An **option** is a contract by which the offeror is bound to hold open an offer for a specified period of time. It must comply with all of the requirements of a contract, including consideration. Option contracts apply to all types of contracts, including sales of goods.

The Code has made certain offers—called **firm offers**—irrevocable without any consideration being given for the promise to keep the offer open. The Code provides that a merchant is bound to keep an offer open for a maximum of three months if the merchant gives assurance in a signed writing that it will be held open. The Code, therefore, makes a merchant's written promise not to revoke an offer for a stated period of time enforceable even though no consideration is given the merchant-offeror for that promise.[16]

For example, Ben's Brewery approached Flora Flooring, Inc., to replace the tile on Ben's floor. On June 6 Flora sent Ben a written, signed offer to provide and install the tile according to Ben's specifications for $26,000 and promised "that the offer would remain open until July 17." Flora is bound by her firm offer to keep the offer open until July 17. The result, however, would differ if Flora had merely stated that the "offer terminated on July 17" or that "the offer will terminate if not accepted on or before July 17." In both of these instances, because there is no assurance to keep the offer open, the offer is not a firm offer and thus is revocable by Flora at any time prior to Ben's acceptance.

Variant Acceptances

The common law **mirror image** rule, by which the acceptance cannot vary or deviate from the terms of the offer, has been modified by the Code. This modification is necessitated by the realities of modern business practices. A vast number of businesses use standardized business forms. For example, a buyer sends to the seller on the buyer's order form a purchase order for 1,000 dozen cotton shirts at $60 per dozen with delivery by October 1 at the buyer's place of business. On the reverse side of this standard form are twenty-five numbered paragraphs containing provisions generally favorable to the buyer. When the seller receives the buyer's order, he sends to the buyer an unequivocal acceptance of the offer on his acceptance form. Although the seller agrees to the buyer's quantity, price, and delivery terms, on the back of his acceptance form the seller has thirty-two numbered paragraphs generally favorable to himself and in significant conflict with the buyer's form. Under the common law's "mirror image" rule, no contract would exist, for there has not been an unequivocal acceptance of all of the material terms of the buyer's offer.

The Code addresses this **battle of the forms** problem by focusing on the intent of the parties. If the offeree expressly makes his acceptance conditioned upon assent to the additional or different terms, no contract is formed. If the offeree does not expressly make his acceptance conditional on the offeror's assent to the additional or different terms, a contract is formed. The issue then becomes whether the offeree's different or additional terms become part of the contract. If both offeror and offeree are merchants, **additional** terms will be part of the contract if they do not materially alter the agreement and are not objected to either in the offer itself or within a reasonable period of time. If neither of the parties are merchants, or if the terms materially alter the offer, then the additional terms are merely construed as proposals for addition to the contract. **Different** terms proposed by the offeree also will not become part of the contract unless specifically accepted by the offeror.[17] See Figure 17–4.

DORTON v. COLLINS & AIKMAN CORP.
United States Court of Appeals, Sixth Circuit, 1972.
453 F.2d 1161.

Dorton, as a representative for the Carpet Mart, purchased carpets from Collins & Aikman that were supposedly manufactured of 100 percent Kodel polyester fiber but were, in fact, made of cheaper and inferior fibers. Dorton then brought suit for compensatory and punitive damages against Collins & Aikman for its fraud, deceit, and misrepresentation in the sale of the carpets. Collins & Aikman moved for a stay pending arbitration, claiming that Dorton was bound to an arbitration agreement printed on the reverse side of Collins & Aikman's printed sales acknowledgment form. A provision printed on the face of the acknowledgment form stated that its acceptance was "subject to all of the terms and conditions on the face and reverse side thereof, including arbitration, all of which are accepted by buyer." Holding that there existed no binding arbitration agreement between the parties, the district court denied the stay. Collins & Aikman appeals.

Decision: Case remanded to district court for further findings of fact.

Opinion: Celebrezze, J.   Under the common law, an acceptance or a confirmation which contained terms additional to or different from those of the offer or oral agreement constituted a rejection of the offer or agreement and thus became a counter-offer. The terms of the counter-offer were said to have been accepted by the original offeror when he proceeded to perform under the contract without objecting to the counter-offer. Thus, a buyer was deemed to have accepted the seller's counter-offer if he took receipt of the goods and paid for them without objection.

Under Section 2–207 the result is different. This section of the Code recognizes that in current commercial transactions, the terms of the offer and those of the acceptance will seldom be identical. Rather, under the current "battle of the forms," each party typically has a printed form drafted by his attorney and containing as many terms as could be envisioned to favor that party in his sales transactions. Whereas under common law the disparity between the fine-print terms in the parties' forms would have prevented the consummation of a contract when these forms are exchanged, Section 2–207 recognizes that in many, but not all, cases the parties do not impart such significance to the terms on the printed forms. [Citation.] Subsection 2–207(1) therefore provides that "[a] definite and seasonable expression of acceptance or a written confirmation . . . operates as an acceptance even though it states terms additional to or different from those offered or agreed upon, unless acceptance is expressly made conditional on assent to the additional or different terms." Thus, under Subsection (1), a contract is recognized notwithstanding the fact that an acceptance or confirmation contains terms additional to or different from those of the offer or prior agreement, provided that the offeree's intent to accept the offer is definitely expressed, *see* Sections 2–204 and 2–206, and provided that the offeree's acceptance is not expressly conditioned on the offeror's assent to the additional or different terms. When a contract is recognized under Subsection (1), the additional terms are treated as "proposals for addition to the contract" under Subsection (2), which contains special provisions under which such additional terms are deemed to have been accepted when the transaction is between merchants. Conversely, when no contract is recognized under Subsection 2–207(1)—either because no definite expression of acceptance exists or, more specifically, because the offeree's acceptance is expressly conditioned on the offeror's assent to the additional or different terms—the entire transaction aborts at this point. If, however, the subsequent conduct of the parties—particularly, performance by both parties under what they apparently believe to be a contract—recognizes the existence of a contract, under Subsection 2–207(3) such conduct by both parties is sufficient to establish a contract, notwithstanding the fact that no contract would have been recognized on the basis of their writings alone. Subsection 2–207(3) further provides how the terms of contracts recognized thereunder shall be determined.

* * *

Assuming, for purposes of analysis, that the arbitration provision was an addition to the terms of The Carpet Mart's oral offers, we must next determine whether or not Collins & Aikman's acceptances were "expressly made conditional on assent to the additional . . . terms" therein, within the proviso of Subsection 2–207(1). * * * [T]he provision appearing on the face of Collins & Aikman's acknowledgment forms stated that the acceptances (or orders) were "subject to all

---

of the terms and conditions on the face and reverse side thereof, including arbitration, all of which are accepted by buyer." * * * Although Collins & Aikman's use of the words "subject to" suggests that the acceptances were conditional to some extent, we do not believe the acceptances were "expressly made conditional on [the buyer's] assent to the additional or different terms," as specifically required under the Subsection 2–207(1) proviso. In order to fall within this proviso, it is not enough that an acceptance is expressly conditional on additional or different terms; rather, an acceptance must be *expressly* conditional on the offeror's *assent* to those terms. Viewing the Subsection (1) proviso within the context of the rest of that Subsection and within the policies of Section 2–207 itself, we believe that it was intended to apply only to an acceptance which clearly reveals that the offeree is unwilling to proceed with the transaction unless he is assured of the offeror's assent to the additional or different terms therein.

* * *

Because Collins & Aikman's acceptances were not expressly conditional on the buyer's assent to the additional terms within the proviso of Subsection 2–207(1), a contract is recognized under Subsection (1), and the additional terms are treated as "proposals" for addition to the contract under Subsection 2–207(2). Since both Collins & Aikman and The Carpet Mart are clearly "merchants" as that term is defined in Subsection 2–104(1), the arbitration provision will be deemed to have been accepted by The Carpet Mart under Subsection 2–207(2) unless it materially altered the terms of The Carpet Mart's oral offers. [UCC § 2–207(2)(b)]. We believe that the question of whether the arbitration provision materially altered the oral offer under Subsection 2–207(2)(b) is one which can be resolved only by the District Court on further findings of fact in the present case. If the arbitration provision did in fact materially alter The Carpet Mart's offer, it could not become a part of the contract "unless expressly agreed to" by The Carpet Mart. [UCC § 2–207], Official Comment No. 3.

We therefore conclude that if on remand the District Court finds that Collins & Aikman's acknowledgments were in fact acceptances to the terms of The Carpet Mart's oral orders, contracts will be recognized under Subsection 2–207(1). The arbitration clause will then be viewed as a "proposal" under Subsection 2–207(2) which will be deemed to have been accepted by The Carpet Mart unless it materially altered the oral offers.

Manner of Acceptance

The Code provides that where the language in the offer or the circumstances do not otherwise clearly indicate, an offer to make a contract invites acceptance in any manner and by any medium reasonable in the circumstances.[18] The Code therefore allows flexibility of response and the ability to keep pace with new modes of communication.

An offer to buy goods for prompt or current shipment may be accepted either by a prompt promise to ship or by prompt shipment.[18] Acceptance by performance requires notice within a reasonable time, or the offer may be treated as lapsed.

Auctions

The Code provides that if an auction sale is advertised or announced in explicit terms to be *without reserve,* the auctioneer may not withdraw the article put up for sale unless no bid is made within a reasonable time. Unless the sale is advertised as being without reserve, the sale is *with reserve,* and the auctioneer may withdraw the goods at any time until he announces

FIGURE 17-4　Battle of the Forms

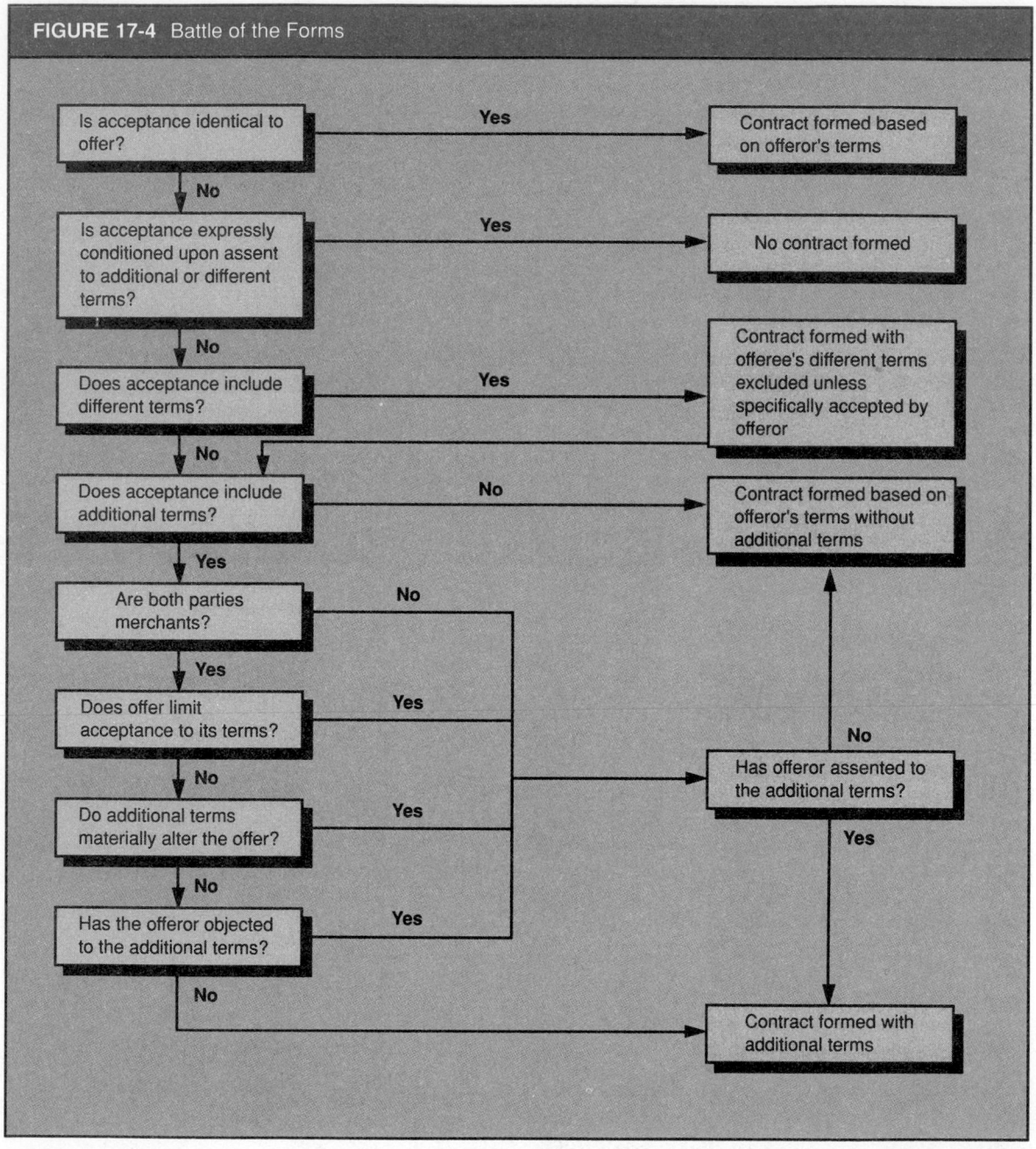

completion of the sale. Whether with or without reserve, a bidder may retract his bid at any time prior to acceptance by the auctioneer. Such a retraction, however, does not revive any previous bid.[19]

If the auctioneer knowingly receives a bid by or on behalf of the seller, and notice has not been given that the seller reserves the right to bid at the auction sale, the bidder to whom the goods are sold can either avoid the sale or take the goods at the price of the last good faith bid before the sale. For example, Adam advertises a sale of his household furniture without reserve. An article of furniture is put up for sale without a contrary announcement and Belle is the highest *bona fide* bidder. Adam, however, is dissatisfied with the bidding and accepts a higher, fictitious bid from an agent employed for that purpose. Adam is obligated to sell the article to Belle at the price Belle bid.

CONSIDERATION

The Code has abandoned the common law rule requiring that a modification of an existing contract be supported by consideration in order to be valid. The Code provides that a contract for the sale of goods can be effectively modified without new consideration, provided the modification is made in good faith.

In addition, (1) any claim of right arising out of an alleged breach of contract can be discharged in whole or in part without consideration by a written waiver or renunciation signed and delivered by the aggrieved party and (2) as previously noted, a firm offer is not revocable for lack of consideration.

FORM OF THE CONTRACT

Statute of Frauds

The original statute of frauds applied to contracts for the sale of goods and has been used as a prototype for the Article 2 statute of frauds provision. The Code provides that a contract for the sale of goods costing *$500 or more* is not enforceable unless there is some writing sufficient to evidence the existence of a contract between the parties.[20]

Modification of Contracts within the Statute of Frauds An agreement modifying a contract must be in writing if the resulting contract is within the statute of frauds.[21] Conversely, if a contract that was previously within the statute of frauds is modified so as to no longer fall within it, the modification is enforceable even if it is oral. Thus, if the parties enter into an oral contract to sell a dining room table for $450 to be delivered to the buyer and later, prior to delivery, *orally* agree that the seller shall stain the table and the buyer pay a price of $550, the modified contract is unenforceable. In contrast, if the parties have a written contract for

the sale of 150 bushels of wheat at a price of $4.50 per bushel and later orally agree to decrease the quantity to 100 bushels at the same price per bushel, the agreement, as modified, is enforceable. See Figure 13–2 in Chapter 13.

Written Compliance The statute of frauds compliance provisions under the Code are more liberal than the rules under general contract law. The Code requires merely some writing (1) sufficient to indicate that a contract has been made between the parties, (2) signed by the party against whom enforcement is sought or by her authorized agent or broker, and (3) including a term specifying the quantity. Whereas general contract law requires that all essential terms be included in the writing, under the Code a writing may be sufficient even if it omits or incorrectly states a term agreed upon. This is consistent with other provisions of the Code that contracts may be enforced even though material terms are omitted. Nevertheless, the contract is enforceable only to the extent of the quantity stated. Given proof that a contract was intended and a signed writing describing the goods, the quantity of goods, and the names of the parties, the court, under the Code, can supply omitted terms such as price and particulars of performance. Moreover, several related documents may satisfy the writing requirement.

Between merchants, a written confirmation, if sufficient against the sender, is also sufficient against the recipient of the confirmation unless the recipient gives written notice of her objection within ten days after receiving the confirmation.[20]

For example, Brown Co. and ATM Industries enter into an oral contract providing that ATM will deliver 1,000 dozen shirts to Brown at $6 per shirt. The next day Brown sends a letter signed by Brown's president to ATM confirming the agreement. The letter contains the quantity term but does not mention the price. Brown is bound by the contract when its authorized agent sent the letter, whereas ATM is bound by the oral contract ten days after receiving the letter unless it objects in writing within that time period. Therefore, as further illustrated by *Thomson Printing Machinery Co. v. B. F. Goodrich Co.* in Chapter 13, it is extremely important for merchants to examine written confirmations carefully and promptly to make certain that they are accurate. Where one or both of the parties is not a merchant, however, this rule does not apply.

Alternative Methods of Compliance A contract that does not satisfy the writing requirement but is otherwise valid is enforceable in the following instances.

The Code permits an oral contract for the sale of goods to be enforced against a party who in his pleading, testimony, or otherwise in courts **admits** that a contract was made, but the Code limits enforcement to the quantity of goods he admits.[20] This provision recognizes that the policy behind the statute of frauds does not apply when the party seeking to avoid the oral contract admits under oath the existence of the contract.

The Code also permits enforcement of an oral contract for goods **specially manufactured** for the buyer.[20] Nevertheless, if the goods are readily marketable in the ordinary course of the seller's business, even though they were manufactured on special order, the contract is not enforceable unless in writing.

Prior to the Code, in most States, delivery and acceptance of part of the goods or payment of part of the price and acceptance of the payment made the entire oral contract enforceable against the buyer who had received part delivery or against the seller who had received partial payment. Under the Code, such "partial performance" validates the contract only for the goods that have been **delivered and accepted** or for which **payment** has been **accepted**.[20] To illus-

trate, Debra orally agrees to buy 1,000 watches from Brian for $15,000. Brian delivers 300 watches to Debra, who receives and accepts the watches. The oral contract is enforceable to the extent of 300 watches ($4,500)—those received and accepted—but is unenforceable to the extent of 700 watches ($10,500).

But what if the contract is indivisible, such as one for the sale of an automobile, so that if part payment is made there is only a choice between not enforcing the contract or enforcing the contract as a whole? Presently, there is a division of authority on this issue, although the better rule appears to be that such part payment and acceptance makes the entire contract enforceable.

Parol Evidence

Contractual terms that are set forth in a writing intended by the parties as a final expression of their agreement may not be contradicted by evidence of any prior agreement or of a contemporaneous oral agreement, but under the Code the terms may be explained or supplemented by: (a) course of dealing, usage of trade, or course of performance; and (b) evidence of consistent additional terms, unless the writing was intended as the complete and exclusive statement of the terms of the agreement. Therefore, the Code slightly relaxes the common law parol evidence rule.

Seal

The Code makes seals inoperative with respect to contracts for the sale of goods or an offer to buy or sell goods.[22]

For a comparison of general contract and sale of goods, see Figure 17–5.

FIGURE 17-5 Contract Law Compared with Law of Sales

	Contract Law	Law of Sales
Definiteness	Contract must include all material terms.	Open terms permitted if parties intend to make a contract.
Counteroffers	Acceptance must be a mirror image of offer. Counteroffer and conditional acceptance are rejections.	Battle of Forms. See Figure 17-4.
Modification of Contract	Consideration is required.	Consideration is not required.
Irrevocable Offers	Options.	Options. Firm offers up to three months binding without consideration.
Statute of Frauds	Writing must include all material terms.	Writing must include quantity term. Specially manufactured goods. Confirmation by merchants. Delivery or payment and acceptance. Admissions.
Minor	Minor may disaffirm contract and recover property from a *bona fide* purchaser.	Minor may disaffirm contract but may not recover goods from a *bona fide* purchaser.

CHAPTER SUMMARY

Definitions	**Sale** transfer of title to goods from seller to buyer for a price
	■ *Governing Law* sales transactions are governed by Article 2 of the Code, but where general contract law has not been specifically modified by the Code, general contract law continues to apply
	■ *Transactions outside the Code* include employment contracts, service contracts, insurance contracts, contracts involving real property, and contracts for the sale of intangibles
	Goods movable personal property

Fundamental Principles	**Purpose** to modernize, clarify, simplify, and make uniform the law of sales
	Good Faith the Code requires all sales contracts to be performed in good faith, which means honesty in fact in the conduct or transaction concerned, but in the case of a merchant, it also includes the observance of reasonable commercial standards

Unconscionability   a court may refuse to enforce an unconscionable contract or any part of a contract found to be unconscionable
- *Procedural Unconscionability*   unfairness of the bargaining process
- *Substantive Unconscionability*   oppressive or grossly unfair contractual provisions

Expansion of Commercial Practices
- *Course of Dealing*   a sequence of previous conduct between the parties establishing a common basis for interpreting their agreement
- *Usage of Trade*   a practice or method of dealing regularly observed and followed in a place, vocation, or trade

Sales by and between Merchants   the Code establishes separate rules that apply to transactions between merchants or involving a merchant (a dealer in goods or a person who by his occupation holds himself out as having knowledge or skill peculiar to the goods or practices involved, or who employs an agent or broker whom he holds out as having such knowledge or skill)

Liberal Administration of Remedies

Freedom of Contract   most provisions of the Code may be varied by agreement

Validation and Preservation of Sales Contract   the Code reduces formal requisites to the bare minimum and attempts to preserve agreements whenever the parties manifest an intention to enter into a contract

FORMATION OF A SALES CONTRACT

| **Manifestation of Mutual Assent** | Definiteness of an Offer   the Code provides that a contract does not fail for indefiniteness even though one or more terms may have been omitted; the Code provides standards by which missing essential terms may be supplied
Irrevocable Offers
- *Firm Offer*   a signed writing by a merchant to hold open an offer for the purchase or sale of goods for a maximum of three months
- *Option*   a contract to hold open an offer
Variant Acceptances   the inclusion of different or additional terms in an acceptance is addressed by focusing on the intent of the parties
Manner of Acceptance   an acceptance can be made in any reasonable manner and is effective upon dispatch
Auctions
- *Auction without Reserve*   the auctioneer may not withdraw the article put up for sale unless no bids are made
- *Auction with Reserve*   the auctioneer may withdraw the article at any time prior to acceptance by the auctioneer |
| **Consideration** | Contractual Modifications   the Code provides that a contract for the sale of goods may be modified without new consideration if made in good faith
Firm Offers   are not revocable for lack of consideration |

Form of the Contract	**Statute of Frauds** sale of goods costing $500 or more must be in a signed writing to be enforceable
	■ *Written Compliance* the Code requires some writing or writings sufficient to indicate that a contract has been made between the parties, signed by the party against whom enforcement is sought or by her authorized agent or broker, and including a term specifying the quantity of goods
	■ *Alternative Methods of Compliance* written confirmation between merchants, admission, specially manufactured goods, and delivery or payment and acceptance
	Parol Evidence contractual terms that are set forth in a writing intended by the parties as a final expression of their agreement may not be contradicted by evidence of any prior agreement or of a contemporaneous oral agreement, but they may be explained or supplemented by course of dealing, usage of trade, course of performance, or consistent additional evidence

QUESTIONS

1. Distinguish a sale from other kinds of transactions that affect goods.
2. Identify and discuss the fundamental principles of Article 2.
3. Discuss the significant changes Article 2 has made in the need for an offer to include all material terms.
4. Distinguish between the common law's mirror image rule and the Code's provisions for dealing with variant acceptances.
5. Discuss (a) the Code's approach to the requirement that certain contracts must be in writing, and (b) the alternative methods of compliance.

PROBLEMS

1. Dickison orders 1,000 widgets at $5 per widget from International Widget to be delivered within sixty days. After the contract is consummated and signed, Dickison requests that International deliver the widgets within thirty days rather than sixty days. International agrees. Is the contractual modification binding?
2. In question 1, what affect, if any, would the following telegram have:

International Widget:

   In accordance with our agreement of this date you will deliver the 1,000 previously ordered widgets within thirty days. Thank you for your cooperation in this matter.

(signed) Dickison

3. Hicks, a San Francisco company, orders from U.S. Electronics, a New York company, 10,000 electronic units. Hicks's order form provides that any dispute would be resolved by an arbitration panel located in San Francisco. U.S. Electronics executes and delivers to Hicks its acknowledgment form accepting the order and containing the following provision: "All disputes will be resolved by the State courts of New York." A dispute arose concerning the workmanship of the parts, and Hicks wishes the case to be arbitrated in San Francisco. What result?
4. Would the result change in problem 3 if the U.S. Electronics form contained the following provisions:

(a) "The seller's acceptance of the purchase order to which this acknowledgment responds is expressly made conditional on the buyer's assent to any or different terms contained in this acknowledgment"?
(b) "The seller's acceptance of the purchase order is subject to the terms and conditions on the face and reverse side hereof and which the buyer accepts by accepting the goods described herein"?
(c) "The seller's terms govern this agreement—this acknowledgment merely constitutes a counteroffer"?

5. Reinfort executed a written contract with Bylinski to purchase an assorted collection of shoes for $3,000. A week before the agreed shipment date, Bylinski called Reinfort and said, "We cannot deliver at $3,000; unless you agree to pay $4,000, we will cancel the order." After considerable discussion, Reinfort agreed to pay $4,000 if Bylinski would ship as agreed in the contract. After the shoes had been delivered and accepted by Reinfort, Reinfort refused to pay $4,000 and insisted on paying only $3,000. Decision?

6. On November 23 Blackburn, a dress manufacturer, mailed to Conroy a written and signed offer to sell 1,000 sundresses at $50 per dress. The offer stated that "it would remain open for ten days and that it could not be withdrawn prior to that date."

Two days later, Blackburn, noting a sudden increase in the price of sundresses, changed his mind. Blackburn therefore sent Conroy a letter revoking the offer. The letter was sent on November 25 and received by Conroy on November 28.

Conroy chose to disregard the letter of November 25; instead, she happily continued to watch the price of sundresses rise. On December 1 Conroy sent a letter accepting the original offer. The letter, however, was not received by Blackburn until December 9, due to a delay in the mails.

Conroy has demanded delivery of the goods according to the terms of the offer of November 23, but Blackburn has refused. Decision?

7. Henry and Wilma, an elderly immigrant couple, agree to purchase from Harris a refrigerator with a fair market value of $450 for twenty-five monthly installments of $60 per month. Henry and Wilma now wish to void the contract, asserting that they did not realize the exorbitant price they were paying. Result?

8. The Courts Distributors needed 200 compact refrigerators on a rush basis. It contacted Eastinghouse Corporation, a manufacturer of refrigerators. Eastinghouse said it would take some time to quote a price on an order of that size. Courts replied, "Send the refrigerators immediately and bill us later." The refrigerators were delivered three days later, and the invoice ten days after that. The invoice price was $140,000. Courts believes that the wholesale market price of the refrigerators is only $120,000. Discuss.

COMPUTER RESEARCH PROBLEMS

1. While adjusting a television antenna beside his mobile home and underneath a high voltage electric transmission wire, Prince received an electric shock resulting in personal injury. He claims the high voltage electric current jumped from the transmission wire to the antenna. The wire, which carried some 7,200 volts of electricity, did not serve his mobile home but ran directly above it. Prince sued the Navarro County Electric Co-Op, the owner and operator of the wire, for breach of implied warranty of merchantability under the Uniform Commercial Code. He contends that the Code's implied warranty of merchantability extends to the container of a product—in this instance the

wiring—and that the escape of the current shows that the wiring was unfit for its purpose of transporting electricity. The electric company argues that the electricity passing through the transmission wire was not being sold to Prince and, therefore, there was no sale of goods to Prince. Decision?

2. HMT, already in the business of marketing agricultural products, decides to try its hand at marketing processing potatoes. Nine months before the potato harvest, HMT contracted to supply Bell Brand with 100,000 sacks of potatoes. At harvest time, Bell Brand would only accept 60,000 sacks. HMT sues for breach of contract. Bell Brand argues that custom and usage in marketing processing potatoes allows buyers to give *estimates* in contracts, not fixed quantities, since the contracts are established so far in advance. HMT responds that the quantity term in the contract was definite and unambiguous. Can custom and trade usage be used to interpret an unambiguous contract? Discuss.

3. Schreiner, a cotton farmer, agreed over the telephone to sell 150 bales of cotton to Loeb & Co. Schreiner had sold cotton to Loeb & Co. for the pasts five years. Written confirmation of the date, parties, price, and conditions was mailed to Schreiner, who neither signed nor returned it, nor responded to the confirmation in any way. Four months later, when the price of cotton had doubled, Loeb & Co. sought to enforce the contract. Is the contract enforceable?

4. American Sand & Gravel Inc. agreed to sell sand to Clark at a special discount if 20,000–25,000 tons were ordered. The discount price was 45¢ per ton, compared to the normal price of 55¢ per ton. Two years later, Clark orders, and receives, 1,600 tons of sand from American Sand & Gravel. Clark refuses to pay more than 45¢ per ton. American Sand & Gravel sues for the remaining 10¢ per ton. Decision?

ENDNOTES

1. Uniform Commercial Code, Section 2—106(1), Definitions: Sale.

2. Uniform Commercial Code, Section 2—105(1), Definitions: Goods.

3. Uniform Commercial Code, Section 1—201(19), General Definitions: Good Faith.

4. Uniform Commercial Code, Section 2—103(1)(b), Definitions and Index of Definitions.

5. Uniform Commercial Code, 2—302, Unconscionable Contract or Clause.

6. Uniform Commercial Code, Section 1—102(2), Purposes; Rules of Construction; Variation by Agreement.

7. Uniform Commercial Code, Section 1—205(1), Course of Dealing.

8. Uniform Commercial Code, Section 1—205(2), Usage of Trade.

9. Uniform Commercial Code, Section 2—104(1), Definitions: Merchant.

10. Uniform Commercial Code, Section 1—106, Remedies to Be Liberally Administered.

11. Uniform Commercial Code, Section 1—102(3), Purpose * * * Variation by Agreement.

12. Uniform Commercial Code, Section 2—204(2), Formation in General.

13. Uniform Commercial Code, Section 2—204(3), Formation in General.

14. Uniform Commercial Code, Section 2—305, Open Price Term.

15. Uniform Commercial Code, Section 2—306(1), Output, Requirements and Exclusive Dealings.

16. Uniform Commercial Code, Section 2—205, Firm Offers.

17. Uniform Commercial Code, Section 2—207, Additional Terms in Acceptance or Confirmation.

18. Uniform Commercial Code, Section 2—206, Offer and Acceptance in Formation of Contract.

19. Uniform Commercial Code, Section 2—328, Sale by Auction.

20. Uniform Commercial Code, Section 2—201, Formal Requirements; Statute of Frauds.

21. Uniform Commercial Code, Section 2—209(3).

22. Uniform Commercial Code, Section 2—203, Seals Inoperative.

18 TRANSFER OF TITLE AND RISK OF LOSS

Historically, the principle of title governed nearly every aspect of the rights and duties of the buyer and seller arising out of a sales contract. In an attempt to add greater precision and certainty to sales contracts, the Code has abandoned the common law's reliance on title. Instead, the Code approaches each legal issue arising out of a sales contract on its own merits and provides separate and specific rules to control various transactional situations. In this chapter we will cover the Code's approach to the transfer of title and other property rights, the passage of risk of loss, and the transfer of goods sold in bulk.

TRANSFER OF TITLE AND OTHER PROPERTY RIGHTS

In addition to de-emphasizing the significance of the passage of title, the Code makes use of other property rights in its transactional approach to the law of sales. These other property rights include special property as well as insurable interests and security interests. Nevertheless, the determination of who has title to the goods does retain some significance. In this section we explore these topics in addition to the circumstances under which the seller has the right or power to transfer title to the buyer.

PASSAGE OF TITLE

A sale of goods is defined as the transfer of title from the seller to the buyer for a consideration known as the price.[1] Transfer of title is, therefore, fundamental to the existence of a sale of goods.

Title passes when the parties *intend* it to pass as in *Meinhard-Commercial Corp. v. Hargo Woolen Mills.* In many cases, however, such intention is difficult to ascertain because of conflicting testimony or because the negotiation between the parties leading to formation of the contract involved no discussion or mention of title. Where the parties have no explicit agreement to transfer title, the Code provides rules that determine when title passes to the buyer.[2]

MEINHARD-COMMERCIAL CORP. v. HARGO WOOLEN MILLS
Supreme Court of New Hampshire, 1972.
112 N.H. 500, 300 A.2d 321.

Facts: Shabry Trading Company shipped twenty-four bales of card waste to Hargo, a manufacturer of woolen cloth. Although Shabry had supplied card waste to Hargo for many years, Hargo had not ordered the present shipment, nor did it wish to purchase it. Hargo intended to return the card waste, but Shabry, in order to avoid the cost of warehouse storage, offered to let Hargo retain possession of the bales with the option to buy as much as Hargo would give notice that it intended to use. Hargo agreed and accordingly marked and stored Shabry's card waste separately from its other goods. On one occasion Hargo notified Shabry that it would use eight bales of waste, and Shabry invoiced the goods to Hargo accordingly. The sixteen remaining bales were kept separately stored until a receiver appointed for Hargo took possession of them. Shabry claimed that it was the owner of the bales and requested their return. A master found in favor of the receiver and Shabry brought this appeal, taking exceptions to the ruling.

Decision: Exceptions of Shabry sustained and case remanded.

Opinion: **Grimes, J.**   The utilization of the concept of title in sales transactions is not novel, nor is the misconception and the misuse of it. Learned Hand has said: " '[T]itle' is a formal word for a purely conceptual notion; I do not know what it means and I question whether anybody does, except perhaps legal historians." [Citation.] Prior to the Uniform Commercial Code, the Uniform Sales Act accepted the common-law notion that title determination was the main solvent of sales problems. The U.C.C. deliberately deemphasizes this view. 2-101, Uniform Law Comments. The code supplants many title-determined issues with specific code provisions to determine the rights and duties of the buyer and seller, such as risk of loss (2-509, 2-510), insurable interest (2-501), suit of third parties (2-722), buyer's rights on seller's insolvency (2-709), and buyer's right to replevy identified goods (2-716). Despite its minimization of the title concept, the code does recognize situations where the lack of any other legal tool requires the courts to fall back on the eternal title question of mine or thine. The code therefore provides a catch-basin rule (2-401) that applies only when the more specific code provisions fail to deal with the issue. The case before us was decided below with resort to this catch-basin rule, the pertinent portion of which reads as follows: "Any retention or reservation by the seller of the title (property) in goods shipped or delivered to the buyer is limited in effect to a reservation of a security interest. *Subject to these provisions * * *,* title to goods passes from the seller to the buyer in any manner and on any conditions explicitly agreed on by the parties." 2-401(1) (emphasis added).

* * *

However, since 2-401 speaks only in terms of buyers and sellers, we believe it does not apply to the transaction between these parties. 2-103(1)(d) defines seller as "unless the context otherwise requires * * * (1)(d) 'Seller' means a person who sells or contracts to sell goods." A buyer is defined in 2-103(1)(a) as "unless the context otherwise requires * * *, (a) 'Buyer' means a person who buys or contracts to buy goods." To determine the meaning of these sections, we refer to the definition of sale and contract for sale in 2-106(1). " 'Contract for sale' includes both a present sale of goods and a contract to sell goods at a future time. A 'sale' consists in the passing of title from the seller to the buyer for a price. (See 2-401)." For 2-401(1) to apply, we must therefore first find that the transaction between the supplier, Shabry, and the manufacturer, Hargo, was a sale. [Citation.]

Whether this transaction was a sale or some other type of transaction is a question of the intent of the parties, which is a question for the trier of fact to determine. [Citation.] Under the code, there must still be a meeting of minds between the parties before there is a contract. [Citation.] The master found in the parties' requests for findings and rulings that the factual understanding between Hargo and Shabry contemplated no passage of title until Shabry was notified of Hargo's intention to use the goods and Shabry thereafter invoiced the goods to Hargo. The master also found that Hargo was never obligated to purchase and Shabry could have sold the goods to other buyers.

> Given these findings, it is clear that the parties' agreement concerning the delivered card waste created no contract for sale by the passage of title for a price. The parties showed no intent to pass title. No title may pass for a price without commitment of the buyer to pay the price. [Citations.] The mere fact that goods are delivered to the premises of a prospective buyer does not in and of itself create a sale, where neither party considered it a sale. [Citation.]
>
> * * *
>
> We find from the master's finding of the express terms of the parties' agreement, from the parties' course of dealing, and from the parties' course of performance, that the parties agreed only as to storage of the goods with Hargo for their mutual benefit. No sale was made until Shabry's offer was accepted by Hargo through notification of intent to use. No such acceptance occurred with respect to the sixteen bales at issue here.
>
> * * *
>
> We therefore hold that, since there was no sale, title to these goods cannot be determined by 2-401 and, since no other provisions of the code apply, the rights of the parties are determined by the law of contracts. *See* 2-102, 1-103.
>
> The master found the parties' stated intentions to be that title to these sixteen bales never passed to Hargo. We therefore hold that title remained in Shabry and that the receiver wrongfully withheld return of the sixteen bales to Shabry.

Physical Movement of the Goods

When delivery is to be made by moving the goods, title passes at the time and place the seller completes his performance with reference to delivery of the goods.[2] When and where delivery occurs depends upon whether the contract is a shipment contract or a destination contract.

Shipment Contract A **shipment contract** requires or authorizes the seller to send the goods to the buyer but does not require the seller to deliver them to a particular destination. Under a shipment contract **title** passes to the buyer at the time and place the seller delivers the goods to the carrier for shipment to the buyer.

Destination Contract

requires the seller to deliver the goods to a particular destination, and **title** passes to the buyer on tender of the goods at that destination. For example, under a destination contract specifying the destination as the buyer's place of business, title passes at the time the goods are tendered to the buyer at her place of business. **Tender** requires that the seller (1) put and hold conforming goods at the buyer's disposition, (2) give notice to the buyer that the goods are available, and (3) do so at a reasonable time and keep the goods available for a reasonable period of time.

No Movement of the Goods

When delivery is to be made without moving the goods, title passes: (a) on delivery of a document of title where the contract calls for delivery of such document (documents of title are documents that evidence a right to receive specified goods; they are discussed more fully in Chapter 48); or (b) at the time and place of contracting where the goods at that time have been identified by either the seller or the buyer as the goods to which the contract refers and no documents are to be delivered.[2] Where the goods are not identified at the time of contracting, title passes when the goods are identified.

For a summary of passage of title in the absence of an agreement by the parties, see Figure 18-1.

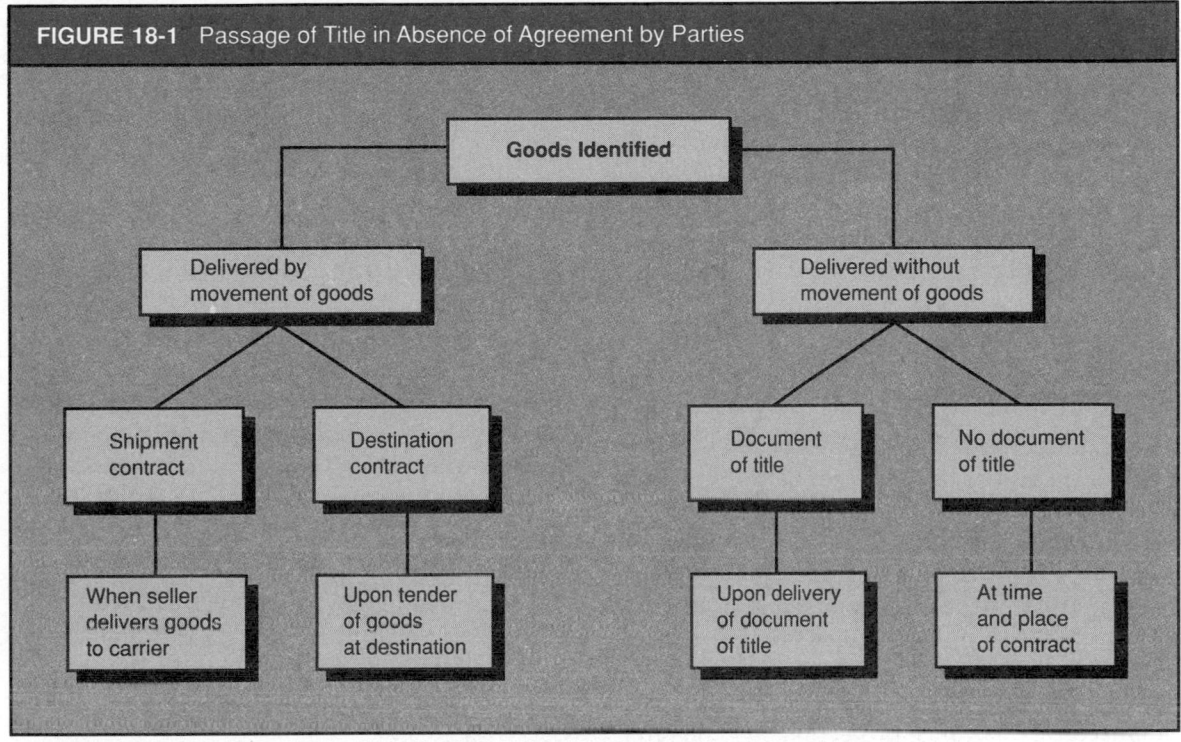

FIGURE 18-1   Passage of Title in Absence of Agreement by Parties

OTHER PROPERTY RIGHTS

Special Property

The Code created a new property interest in goods that did not exist at common law. It is a "special property" right that the buyer obtains by the **identification** of existing goods as goods to which the contract of sale refers.[3] After forming a contract, it is normal for the seller to take steps to obtain, manufacture, prepare, or select goods with which to fulfill her obligation under the contract. At some stage in the process, the seller will have identified the goods that she intends to ship, deliver, or hold for the buyer. These goods may or may not conform to the contract, but in either case the identification of goods to the contract immediately creates for the buyer a special property right in the goods identified. This Code-created interest gives the buyer an insurable interest in the goods, as well as a number of specific remedies that we discuss in Chapter 21.

Identification may be made by either the seller or the buyer and can be made at any time and in any manner agreed on by the parties. In the absence of explicit agreement, identification takes place as follows:

1. if the contract is for goods already existing and identified, when the contract is made;
2. if the contract is for crops to be grown within twelve months or the next normal harvest or for the offspring of animals to be born within twelve months, when the crops are planted or start growing or when the young animals are conceived; or
3. if the contract is for all other future goods, when the seller ships, marks, or otherwise designates the goods as those to which the contract refers.[3]

To further illustrate: Suppose Barringer contracts to purchase a particular Buick automobile from Stevenson's car lot. Identification occurs as soon as the contract is entered into. If, however, Barringer agreed to purchase a television set from Stevenson, who has his storeroom filled with such televisions, identification will not occur until either Barringer or

Stevenson selects a particular television to fulfill the contract.

If the goods are **fungible** (the equivalent of any other unit), identification of a share of undivided goods occurs when the contract is entered into. Thus, if Barringer agreed to purchase 1,000 gallons of gasoline from Stevenson, who owns a 5,000 gallon tank of gasoline, identification occurs as soon as the contract is formed.

Insurable Interest

For a contract or policy of insurance to be valid, the insured must have an **insurable interest** in the subject matter. At common law, only a person with title or a **lien** (a legal claim on property) could insure his interest in specific goods. The Code, as previously noted, extends this right to a buyer's interest in goods that have been identified as those to which the contract refers.[3] This interest enables the buyer to purchase insurance protection on goods that he does not presently own but that he will own when delivered by the seller.

So long as he has title to them or any security interest in them, the seller also has an insurable interest in the goods.[3] Nothing prevents both seller and buyer from simultaneously carrying insurance on goods in which they both have a property interest, whether it is title, a security interest, or a special property.

Security Interest

As indicated in Chapter 17, a security interest is defined in the Code as an interest in personal property or fixtures that ensures payment or performance of an obligation.[4] Any reservation by the seller of title to goods delivered to the buyer is limited in effect to a reservation of a security interest.[2] Security interests in goods are governed by Article 9 of the Code and are discussed in Chapter 37.

POWER TO TRANSFER TITLE

It is important to understand under what circumstances a seller has the right or power to transfer title or other property rights to a buyer. If the seller is the rightful owner of goods or is authorized to sell the goods for the rightful owner, then the seller has the **right** to transfer title. But when a seller possesses goods that he neither owns nor has authority to sell, then the sale is not rightful. In some situations, however, nonowner sellers may have the **power** to transfer good title to certain buyers. This section pertains to such sales by a person in possession of goods that he neither owns nor has authority to sell.

The rule of property law protecting existing ownership of goods is the starting point and background in any discussion of a sale of goods by a nonowner. It is elementary that a purchaser of goods obtains such title as his transferor had or had power to transfer, and the Code expressly states this.[5] Likewise, the purchaser of a limited interest in goods acquires rights only to the extent of the interest that he purchased. By the same token, no one can transfer what he does not have. A purported sale by a thief or finder or ordinary bailee of goods does not transfer title to the purchaser.

The reasons underlying the policy of the law in protecting existing ownership of goods are obvious. A person should not be required to retain possession at all times of all the goods that he owns in order to maintain his ownership of them. One of the valuable incidents of ownership of goods is the freedom of the owner to make a bailment of his goods as he pleases, and the mere possession of goods by a bailee does not authorize the bailee to sell them.

A policy of the law that conflicts with the policy protecting existing ownership is protection of the good faith purchaser based on the importance in trade and commerce of protecting the security of good faith transactions in goods. To encourage and make secure good faith acquisitions of goods, it is necessary that *bona fide* (good faith) purchasers for value under certain circumstances be protected. A **good faith purchaser** is defined as one who acts honestly, gives value, and takes the goods without notice or knowledge of any defect in the title of his transferor.

You should consider the problems presented in this section and the rules for their solution in the light of these two competing policies of the law. Both policies are sound, beneficial, and worthy of enforcement. One protects existing property rights; the other protects good faith transactions in the marketplace. In the area of sales of goods by a nonowner, these policies come into conflict. In every such conflict only one may prevail. Between these two innocent parties, the law must either protect existing ownership and defeat the interest of the *bona fide* purchaser for value, or vice versa.

Void and Voidable Title to Goods

A void title is no title. A person claiming ownership of goods by an agreement that is void obtains no title to the goods. Thus, a person who acquires goods by physical duress or from someone under guardianship or a thief or a finder of goods has no title to them and can transfer none.

A voidable title is one acquired under circumstances that permit the former owner to rescind the transfer and revest herself with title, as in the case of mistake, common duress, undue influence, fraud in the inducement, or sale by a person without contractual capacity (other than an individual under guardianship). In these situations, the buyer has acquired legal title to the goods of which he may be divested by action taken by the seller. If, however, the buyer should resell the goods to a *bona fide* purchaser for value and without notice of any infirmity in his title before the seller has rescinded the transfer of title, the right of rescission in the seller is cut off, and the *bona fide* purchaser acquires good title.

The distinction between a void and voidable title is, therefore, extremely important in determining the rights of *bona fide* purchasers of goods. The *bona fide* purchaser always believes that she is buying the goods from the owner or from one with authority to sell. Otherwise she would not be acting in good faith. In each situation, the party selling the goods appears to be the owner, whether his title is valid, void, or voidable. Between two innocent persons—the true owner who has done nothing wrong and the *bona fide* purchaser who has done nothing wrong—the law will not disturb the legal title but will rule in favor of the one who has it. Thus, where A transfers possession of goods to B under such circumstances that B acquires no title or a void title, and B thereafter sells the goods to C, a *bona fide* purchaser for value, B has nothing except possession to transfer to C. In a lawsuit between A and C involving the right to the goods, A will win because she has the legal title. C's only recourse is against B for breach of warranty of title which we discuss in Chapter 19. (See Figure 18–2.) If, however, B acquired a voidable title from A and resold the goods to C, in a suit between A and C over the goods, C would win. In this case, B had title, although it was voidable, which she transferred to the

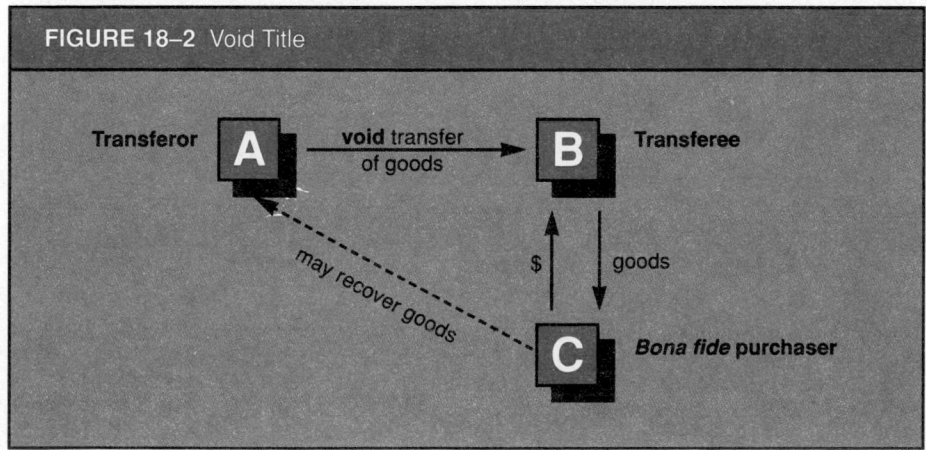

FIGURE 18–2 Void Title

Transferor   A $\xrightarrow{\text{\textbf{void} transfer of goods}}$ B   **Transferee**

may recover goods

$ goods

C   ***Bona fide*** **purchaser**

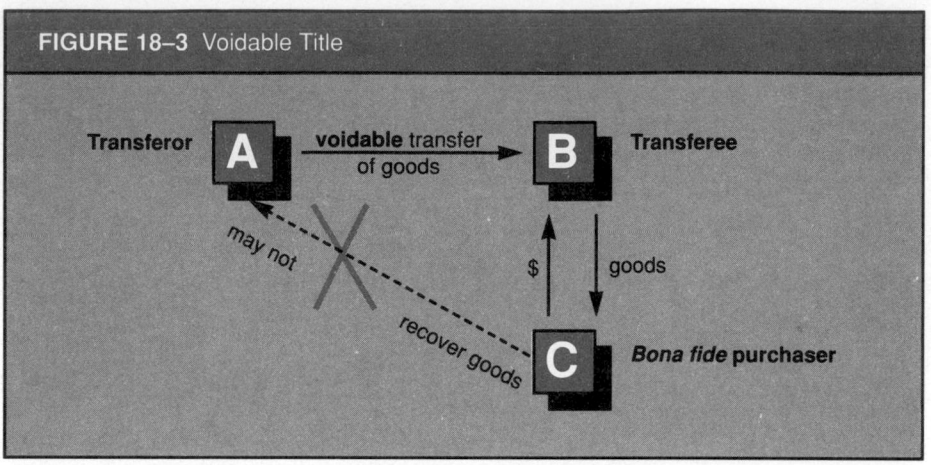

FIGURE 18–3 Voidable Title

bona fide purchaser. The title thus acquired by C will be protected. The voidable title in B is title until it has been avoided. After transfer to a bona fide purchaser, it may not be avoided.

(See Figure 18–3.) A's only recourse is against B for restitution or damages. The following case raises the issue whether the buyer was a bona fide purchaser for value.

LILES BROS. & SON v. WRIGHT
Tennessee Supreme Court, 1982.
638 S.W.2d 383.

Facts: On November 25, 1977, Tony Mangum purchased a new 580C backhoe and loader from Liles Bros. & Son for $20,561. Mangum paid for the equipment with one check dated November 25 for $3,000 and a second check dated December 2 for the balance. Mangum resold the equipment for $11,000 to Carl Wright, the operator of a septic tank service that required the use of heavy machinery. On December 2 Liles learned that Mangum's postdated check had bounced. Liles saw Mangum on December 6, and Mangum informed him that Wright might have the equipment. Liles contacted Wright and explained the situation to him, but Wright was uncooperative. Liles subsequently discovered the backhoe on Wright's property, but Wright refused to surrender it. On February 28, 1978, Liles brought an action against Wright, claiming that Wright was not a bona fide purchaser for value and sought possession of the equipment. The trial court ruled in favor of Liles, and the court of appeals held for Wright.

Decision: Judgment for Liles.

Opinion: Brock, J.   Contrary to the holding of the Court of Appeals, there appears to be ample proof in the record that Wright had reason to believe that the property was stolen or obtained in a fraudulent or devious manner. The defendant's actions should not allow him to claim the status of good faith purchaser for value.

Since 1975, Wright was engaged in the construction business operating as Carl's Septic Service. He required the use of heavy equipment including a backhoe and loader. Wright owned two backhoes and was familiar with their operation and value.

Furthermore, Wright was in the market for a new backhoe and had recently solicited quotations from local equipment dealers. . . .

The record indicates, therefore, that Wright had ample knowledge of the true market value of the equipment which he purchased.

Other factors which would tend to indicate that Wright had notice of suspicious dealing include: the bill of sale was a blank purchase order without any reference to the name of Mangum's company, its location, its phone number, or the type of merchandise it handled; unlike previous backhoe purchases that Wright had made, he did not receive any warranty papers which is standard on a new machine; and unlike other heavy equipment dealers, such as Liles who specialized in Case equipment and Hixson who specialized in Ford equipment, Mangum specifically told Wright that he could make him a good deal on any kind of equipment that he wanted. Wright also admitted that he knew quite a bit of equipment had recently been "stolen" in the western Tennessee and Kentucky area and he claimed he did not want to get involved in such dealings. Despite knowledge of the foregoing facts, Wright never inquired where Mangum's dealership or place of business was located. . . .

The court, therefore, holds that the defendant, Wright, is not a bona fide purchaser for value. He did not conduct himself honestly in his purchase of the backhoe, and he had ample information which would have led a reasonably prudent person either to refuse to buy the backhoe or to make a considerably more detailed investigation of the facts before purchasing. Furthermore, he attempted to secrete the property so that the serial number could not be obtained when the plaintiff tried to locate the backhoe in question.

[U.C.C.] § 1-201(19), defines "good faith" as "honesty in fact in the conduct or transaction concerned." A buyer is not considered a good faith purchaser if he had "notice of facts that would put a reasonably prudent man on inquiry."

If Wright was not a good faith purchaser of the backhoe, then he only has voidable title to the backhoe pursuant to [U.C.C.] § 2-403(1), and Liles Bros. has the right to possession of the backhoe, under a repossession action. [U.C.C.] § 2-403(1), states that "a person with voidable title has power to transfer a good title to a good faith purchaser for value. When goods have been delivered under a transaction of purchase, the purchaser has such power even though: . . . (b) delivery was in exchange for a check which was later dishonored." The statute in effect recognizes that a person such as Mangum who buys goods in exchange for a check which is later dishonored only obtains voidable title, but has power to pass good title to a good faith purchaser for value. Since Wright was not a good faith purchaser of value, he too only received voidable title. Therefore, the original seller, Liles Bros., has the right to rescind its sale with Mangum, the original purchaser, who only has voidable title and reclaim the backhoe from the third party, Wright, because he, too, only had voidable title.

The Code has enlarged this common law doctrine by providing that a good faith purchaser for value obtains valid title from one possessing voidable title even if that person's voidable title was obtained by (1) fraud as to that person's identity, (2) delivery of a subsequently dishonored check, (3) an agreement that the transaction was to be a cash sale and the sale price has not been paid, or (4) criminal fraud punishable as larceny.[5]

In addition, the Code has expanded the rights of *bona fide* purchasers with respect to sales by **minors**. The common law permitted a minor seller of goods to disaffirm the sale and to recover the goods from a third person who had purchased them in good faith from the party who acquired the goods from the minor. The Code changed this rule and does not permit a minor seller to prevail over a *bona fide* purchaser for value.[5]

Entrusting of Goods to a Merchant

Frequently, an owner of goods entrusts (transfers possession of) goods to a bailee for resale, repair, or some other use. In some instances, this entrusting is violated by the bailee selling the goods to a good faith purchaser. Although, the "true" owner has a right of recourse against the bailee for the value of the goods, what right, if any, should the true owner of the goods have against the good faith purchaser? Once again the law must balance the right of ownership against the rights of market transactions.

The Code takes the position of protecting good faith buyers of goods in the ordinary course of business from merchants who deal in goods of that kind, where the owner has entrusted possession of the goods to the merchant. Because the merchant who deals in goods of that kind is cloaked with the appearance of ownership or apparent authority to sell, the Code seeks to protect the innocent third-party purchaser. Any such **entrusting** of possession bestows on the merchant the power to transfer all rights of the entruster to a buyer in the ordinary course of business.[5] For

example, A brings his stereo for repair to B, who also sells both new and used stereo equipment. C purchases A's stereo from B in good faith and in the ordinary course of business. The Code protects the rights of C and defeats the rights of A. (See Figure 18–4.) A's only recourse is against B.

The Code, however, does not go so far as to protect the *bona fide* purchaser from a merchant to whom the goods have been entrusted by a thief or finder or by a completely unauthorized person. It merely grants the good faith buyer in the ordinary course of business the rights of the entruster.

The Code defines **buyer in ordinary course of business** as a person who in good faith and without knowledge that the sale to him is in violation of the ownership rights or security interest of another buys the goods in the ordinary course of business from a person in the business of selling goods of that kind, other than a pawnbroker.[6] The case on page 371 deals with the definition of a buyer in the ordinary course of business.

Where a buyer of goods to whom title has passed leaves the seller in possession of the goods, the buyer has "entrusted the goods" to the seller. If that seller is a merchant and resells and delivers the goods to a *bona fide* purchaser for value, this second buyer acquires good title to the goods. Thus, Dennis sells certain goods to Sylvia, who pays the price but allows possession to remain with Dennis. Dennis thereafter sells the same goods to Karen, a *bona fide*

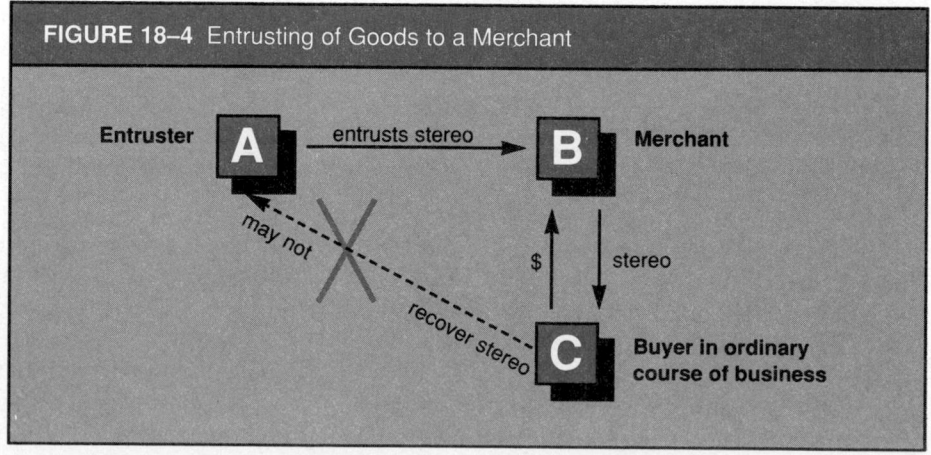

FIGURE 18–4 Entrusting of Goods to a Merchant

MATTEK v. MALOFSKY
Supreme Court of Wisconsin, 1969.
42 Wis.2d 16, 165 N.W.2d 406.

Facts: Mattek entrusted a car to Frankes, a used car dealer. Malofsky, another automobile dealer, subsequently purchased the car from Frankes without obtaining or inquiring about the certificate of title to the car. Although Frankes did not have to secure a certificate of title for cars held in stock or acquired for stock purposes, he did have a duty under State law to deliver the certificate on the subsequent sale to Malofsky. Mattek brought suit against Malofsky to recover the car. The trial court entered judgment for Mattek and Malofsky appeals.

Decision: Judgment for Mattek affirmed.

Opinion: **Hallows, C. J.**   Two issues are presented on this appeal. (1) Whether the provisions of [U.C.C.] 2–403 are applicable to sales between merchants; and (2) whether an automobile dealer who buys a used car from another automobile dealer, who has lawful possession of the car, without obtaining or inquiring about the certificate of title to the used car is a "buyer in the ordinary course of business" within the meaning of [U.C.C.] 2–403.

We think the provisions of [U.C.C.] 2–403 are applicable to sales between merchants. We come to this conclusion because the purpose of [U.C.C.] 2–403(2) and (3) is to protect a person from a third-party interest in goods purchased from the general inventory of a merchant regardless of that merchant's actual authority to sell those goods. This section does not expressly or by implication restrict such protection of a sale by a merchant to a member of the consumer public. If the policy of negotiability of goods held in the inventory of a merchant is to be promoted, it would seem to apply between merchants where merchants buy from one another in the ordinary course of business. The protection is afforded to "a buyer in the ordinary course of business," and by other provisions of the Uniform Commercial Code the term "buyer" includes a merchant.

In [U.C.C.] 1–201(9) a buyer in the ordinary course of business is defined as "a person who in good faith and without knowledge that the sale to him is in violation of the ownership rights or security interest of a third party in the goods buys in ordinary course from a person in the business of selling goods of that kind but does not include a pawn broker." Good faith is defined in [U.C.C.] 1–201(19) to mean "honesty in fact in the conduct or transaction concerned." This definition applies to a member of the consumer public only, because in [U.C.C.] 2–103(1)(b) " 'good faith' in the case of a merchant" is defined to mean "honesty in fact and the observance of reasonable commercial standards of fair dealing in the trade." In addition, [U.C.C.] 2–104(3), relating to the general standard applicable to transactions between merchants charges each merchant with the "knowledge or skill of merchants."

Consequently, a merchant may be a buyer in the ordinary course of business under [U.C.C.] 2–403 from another merchant if he meets four elements: (1) be honest in fact, (2) be without knowledge of any defects of title in the goods, (3) pay value, and (4) observe reasonable commercial standards. In the observance of reasonable commercial standards, however, a merchant is chargeable with the knowledge or skill of a merchant.

We think Malofsky was not the buyer in the ordinary course of business within the meaning of [U.C.C.] 2–403. Although the delivery of the automobile to Frankes, a used-car dealer, constituted an entrustment, Frankes, could by subsequent sale pass title to a buyer in the ordinary course of business. However, Malofsky as a merchant was not a buyer in the ordinary course of business because he was chargeable with the knowledge that the registration law, [citation], which provides that while a dealer need not apply for a certificate of title for a vehicle in stock or acquired for stock purposes, he shall upon the transfer of such vehicle give the transferee evidence of title, and in the case of a vehicle which has a certificate of title, the certificate of title shall be reassigned and delivered to the transferee. Malofsky should have known the used automobile had a certificate of title outstanding and that Frankes was required to give him such certificate of title. Under the standards set forth in [U.C.C.] 2–104(3) applicable to transactions between merchants, Malofsky is chargeable with this knowledge and his failure to procure a certificate of title or some evidence of title was reasonable as a matter of law. Evidence of custom or usage of automobile dealers contrary to the statute cannot be used to defeat the rights of a third party whatever the value of such evidence may be in adjusting disputes between dealers.

purchaser for value without notice of the prior sale to Sylvia. Karen takes delivery of the goods. Sylvia does not have any rights against Karen or to the goods. Sylvia's only remedy is against Dennis.

RISK OF LOSS

Risk of loss, as the term is used in the law of sales, addresses the allocation of loss between seller and buyer where the goods have been damaged, destroyed, or lost *without the fault* of either the seller or the buyer. If the loss is placed on the buyer, he is under a duty to pay the price for the goods even though they were damaged or he never received them. If placed on the seller, he has no right to recover the purchase price from the buyer, although he does have the right to the return of the damaged goods.

In determining who has the risk of loss, the Code provides definite rules for specific situations, a sharp departure from the common law concept of risk of loss, which was determined by ownership of the goods and depended on whether title had been transferred. In its transactional approach, the Code is necessarily detailed and for this reason is probably more understandable and meaningful than the common law's reliance on the abstract concept of title. The Code has adopted separate rules for determining the risk of loss in the absence of breach from those that apply where there has been a breach of the sales contract.

RISK OF LOSS WHERE THERE IS A BREACH

Where one party breaches, the Code places the risk of loss on the party who breaches the contract, even though this allocation differs from the passage of risk of loss in the absence of a breach. The Code also pursues a policy of placing the risk of loss on the nonbreaching party if he is in control of the goods, but only to the extent of his insurance coverage.

Breach by the Seller

If the seller ships goods to the buyer that do not conform to the contract, the risk of loss remains on the seller until the buyer has accepted the goods or the seller has remedied the defect.[7]

Where the buyer has accepted nonconforming goods, and thereafter by timely notice to the seller rightfully revokes his acceptance (discussed in Chapter 20), he may treat the risk of loss as resting on the seller from the beginning to the extent of any deficiency in the buyer's effective insurance coverage.[7] For example, Stuart delivers to Bernard nonconforming goods, which Bernard accepts. Subsequently, Bernard discovers a hidden defect in the goods and rightfully revokes his prior acceptance. If the goods are destroyed through no fault of either party, and Bernard has insured the goods for 60 percent of their fair market value of $10,000, then the insurance company will cover $6,000 of the loss and Stuart will bear the loss of $4,000. If the buyer's insurance coverage had been $10,000, then Stuart would not bear any of the loss.

Breach by the Buyer

Where conforming goods have been identified to a contract that the buyer repudiates or breaches before risk of loss has passed to him, the seller may treat the risk of loss as resting on the buyer "for a commercially reasonable time" to the extent of any deficiency in the seller's effective insurance coverage.[7] For example, Susan agrees to sell 40,000 pounds of plastic resin to Bella, F.O.B. Bella's factory, delivery by March 1. On February 1 Bella wrongfully repudiates the contract by telephoning Susan and telling her that she does not want the resin. Susan immediately seeks another buyer, but before she is able to locate one, and within a commercially reasonable time, the resin is destroyed by a fire through no fault of Susan's. The fair market value of the resin is $35,000. Susan's insurance covers only $15,000 of the loss. Bella is liable for $20,000.

RISK OF LOSS IN ABSENCE OF A BREACH

Where there is no breach, then the risk of loss may be allocated by the agreement of the parties. Where there is no breach and the parties have not otherwise agreed, then the Code places the risk of loss, for the most part, on the party who is more likely to have greater control over the goods, is more likely to insure the goods, or is better able to prevent the loss.

Agreement of the Parties

The parties, by agreement, may not only shift the allocation of risk of loss but also may divide the risk between them.[8] Such agreement is controlling. Thus, the parties may agree that a seller shall retain the risk of loss even though the buyer is in possession of the goods or has title to them. Furthermore, the agreement may provide that the buyer bears 60 percent of the risk and the seller bears 40 percent.

Trial Sales

Some sales are made on the understanding that the buyer can return the goods even though they conform to the contract. These trial sales permit the buyer to try the goods for a period of time in order to determine if she wishes to keep them or try to resell them. Under the Code, there are two types of trial sales: a sale on approval and a sale or return.

Sale on Approval In a **sale on approval,** possession of, but not title to, the goods is transferred to the buyer for a stated period of time or, if none is stated, for a reasonable time, during which period the buyer may use the goods to determine whether she wishes to accept them. Both title and risk of loss remain with the *seller* until "approval" or acceptance of the goods by the buyer.[9] Until acceptance by the buyer, the sale is a bailment with an option to purchase.

Use of the goods consistent with the purpose of approval by the buyer is not acceptance, but failure of the buyer within a reasonable period of time to notify the seller of her election to return the goods is an acceptance. The buyer's approval may also be manifested by exercising any dominion or control over the goods inconsistent with the seller's ownership. On approval, risk of loss and title pass to the buyer, who then becomes liable to the seller for the purchase price of the goods. If the buyer decides to return the goods and notifies the seller, the return is at the seller's risk and expense.

Sale or Return In a **sale or return,** the goods are sold and delivered to the buyer with an option to return them to the seller. The risk of loss is on the *buyer,* who also has title until she revests it in the seller by a return of the goods.

The return of the goods is at the buyer's risk and expense.

It is frequently difficult to determine from the facts of a particular transaction whether the parties intended a sale on approval or a sale or return. The consquences are drastically different with respect to transfer of title and risk of loss. Thus, the Code provides a neat, sensible, and easily applied test: unless otherwise agreed, if the goods are delivered primarily for the buyer's use, the transaction is a sale on approval; if they are delivered primarily for resale by the buyer, it is a sale or return.[10]

A **consignment** is a delivery of possession of personal property to an agent for sale by the agent. Under the Code, a sale on consignment is regarded as a sale or return. Therefore, creditors of the consignee (the agent who receives the merchandise for sale) prevail over the consignor and may obtain possession of the consigned goods, provided the consignee maintains a place of business where he deals in goods of the kind involved under a name other than the name of the consignor. Nevertheless, the consignor will prevail if she: (a) complies with applicable State law requiring a consignor's interest to be evidenced by a sign, or (b) establishes that the consignee is generally known by his creditors to be substantially engaged in selling the goods of others, or (c) complies with the filing provisions of Article 9 (Secured Transactions).[10]

Contracts Involving Carriers

Sales contracts frequently contain terms indicating the agreement of the parties as to delivery by a carrier. These terms designate whether the contract is a shipment contract or a destination contract and, by implication, when the risk of loss passes. If the contract does not require the seller to deliver the goods at a particular destination but merely to the carrier (a shipment contract), risk of loss passes to the buyer when the goods are delivered to the common carrier. If the seller is required to deliver them to a particular destination (a destination contract), risk of loss passes to the buyer at destination when the goods are tendered to the buyer.

Shipment Contracts   The initials **F.O.B.** mean "free on board"; **F.A.S.** means "free alongside." Under the Code, these are delivery terms even though used only in connection with the stated price.[11] When the contract provides that the sale is **F.O.B. place of shipment** or **F.A.S. port of shipment,** then the contract is a shipment contract. For example, Jackson, whose place of business is in New York, enters into a contract with Marshall, the buyer, who is located in San Francisco. The contract calls for delivery of the goods F.O.B. New York. This is a shipment contract.

The initials **C.I.F.** mean "cost, insurance, and freight"; **C. & F.** means simply "cost and freight." Under a C.I.F. contract, in consideration for an agreed unit price for the goods the seller pays all costs of transportation, insurance, and freight to destination. The amount of the agreed unit price of the goods will, of course, reflect these costs. The unit price in a C. & F. contract is less than in a C.I.F. contract because it does not include the cost of insurance. Under the Code, *both* C.I.F. and C. & F. contracts are regarded as shipment contracts, not destination contracts.

Under any of these shipment contracts, when the seller has *delivered* the goods to the carrier under a proper contract of shipment, title and risk of loss pass to the buyer.

Destination Contracts   Where the contract provides that the sale is **F.O.B. place of destination,** the seller must at his own expense and risk transport the goods to that place and there *tender* delivery of them to the buyer[11,12]. These are destination contracts. For example, if the buyer is in Boston and the seller in Chicago, a contract providing F.O.B. Boston is a destination contract under which the seller must tender the goods at the designated place in Boston at his own expense and risk.

Where the contract provides for delivery **ex-ship,** or "from the ship," it is a destination contract, and risk of loss does not pass to the buyer until the goods are unloaded from the carrier at destination.

Finally, where the contract contains the term **"no arrival, no sale,"** the title and risk of loss do not pass to the buyer until the seller makes a tender of the goods after their arrival at destination. The major significance of the "no arrival, no sale" term is that it excuses the seller from any liability to the buyer for failure of the goods to arrive, unless the seller has caused their nonarrival.

The following case deals with the question of when the risk of loss passes where the parties have no specific provision or any delivery term. As this case demonstrates, if it is unclear whether the contract is a destination or shipment contract, the law assumes that it is a shipment contract.

 ### PESTANA v. KARINOL
District Court of Appeals of Florida, Third District, 1979.
367 So.2d 1096.

Facts: Nahim Amar B. contracted with Karinol for the purchase of electronic watches. The contract contained no explicit provisions specifying who would bear the risk of loss while the watches were in the carrier's possession. Nor were there any F.O.B., F.A.S., or C. & F. terms in the contract. It did contain a notation specifying Chetumal, Mexico, as the destination. Karinol delivered the watches to its agent for delivery to Amar. Karinol's carrier obtained insurance for the two cartons of watches, naming Karinol as the insured. The goods were then shipped by air to Belize where they were to be shipped by truck to Chetumal. Upon their arrival in Belize, Amar paid Pestana the balance due on the contract. But when customs officials and an agent of Amar opened the cartons in Belize for customs clearance, they found the packages were empty.

Pestana, the executor of Amar's estate, contends that the "send to Chetumal, Mexico," notation made the contract a destination contract. Therefore, he argues, Karinol should bear the loss of the watches since its carrier had not yet tendered delivery of them in Chetumal. The plaintiff Pestana appeals from a verdict in favor of Karinol.

Decision: Judgment for Karinol affirmed.

Opinion: Hubbart, J. There are two types of sales contracts under Florida's Uniform Commercial Code wherein a carrier is used to transport the goods sold: a shipment contract and a destination contract. A shipment contract is considered the normal contract in which the seller is required to send the subject goods by carrier to the buyer but is not required to guarantee delivery thereof at a particular destination. Under a shipment contract, the seller, unless otherwise agreed, must: (1) put the goods sold in the possession of a carrier and make a contract for their transportation as may be reasonable having regard for the nature of the goods and other attendant circumstances, (2) obtain and promptly deliver or tender in due form any document necessary to enable the buyer to obtain possession of the goods or otherwise required by the agreement or by usage of the trade, and (3) promptly notify the buyer of the shipment. On a shipment contract, the risk of loss passes to the buyer when the goods sold are duly delivered to the carrier for shipment to the buyer. [Citations.]

A destination contract, on the other hand, is considered the variant contract in which the seller specifically agrees to deliver the goods sold to the buyer at a particular destination and to bear the risk of loss of the goods until tender of delivery. This can be accomplished by express provision in the sales contract to that effect or by the use of delivery terms such as F.O.B. (place of destination). Under a destination contract, the seller is required to tender delivery of the goods sold to the buyer at the place of destination. The risk of loss under such a contract passes to the buyer when the goods sold are duly tendered to the buyer at the place of destination while in the possession of the carrier so as to enable the buyer to take delivery. The parties must explicitly agree to a destination contract; otherwise the contract will be considered a shipment contract. [Citations.]

Where the risk of loss falls on the seller at the time of goods sold are lost or destroyed, the seller is liable in damages to the buyer for non-delivery unless the seller tenders a performance in replacement for the lost or destroyed goods. On the other hand, where the risk of loss falls on the buyer at the time the goods sold are lost or destroyed, the buyer is liable to the seller for the purchase price of the goods sold. [Citation.]

In the instant case, we deal with the normal shipment contract involving the sale of goods. The defendant Karinol pursuant to this contract agreed to send the goods sold, a shipment of watches, to the plaintiff's decedent in Chetumal, Mexico. There was no specific provision in the contract between the parties which allocated the risk of loss on the goods sold while in transit. In addition, there were no delivery terms such as F.O.B. Chetumal contained in the contract.

All agree that there is sufficient evidence that the defendant Karinol performed its obligations as a seller under the Uniform Commercial Code if this contract is considered a shipment contract. Karinol put the goods sold in the possession of a carrier and made a contract for the goods [sic] safe transportation to the plaintiff's decedent; Karinol also promptly notified the plaintiff's decedent of the shipment and tendered to said party the necessary documents to obtain possession of the goods sold.

The plaintiff Pestana contends, however, that the contract herein is a destination contract in which the risk of loss on the goods sold did not pass until delivery on such goods had been tendered to him at Chetumal, Mexico—an event which never occurred. He relies for this position on the notation at the bottom of the contract between the parties which provides that the goods were to be sent to Chetumal, Mexico. We cannot agree. A "send to" or "ship to" term is a part of every contract involving the sale of goods where carriage is contemplated and has no significance in determining whether the contract is a shipment or destination contract for risk of loss purposes. [Citations.] As such, the "send to" term contained in this contract cannot, without more, convert this into a destination contract.

It therefore follows that the risk of loss in this case shifted to the plaintiff's decedent as buyer when the defendant Karinol as seller duly delivered the goods to the defendant freight forwarder American under a reasonable contract of carriage for shipment to the plaintiff's decedent in Chetumal, Mexico. The defendant Karinol, its agent the defendant American, and its insurer the defendant Fidelity could not be held liable to the plaintiff in this action. The trial court properly entered judgment in favor of all the defendants herein.

Goods in Possession of Bailee

In some sales, the goods, at the time of the contract, are held by a bailee and are to be delivered without being moved. For instance, a seller may contract with a buyer to sell grain that is located in a grain elevator and that the buyer intends to leave in the same elevator. In such situations, the risk of loss passes to the buyer when one of the following occurs:

1. If a negotiable document of title (discussed in Chapter 48) is involved, when the buyer *receives* the document.

2. If a nonnegotiable document of title is used by the bailee as a receipt for storage of the seller's goods, when the document is *tendered* to the buyer, unless the buyer objects within a reasonable time.

3. If no documents of title are employed, either (a) when the seller *tenders* to the buyer written directions to the bailee to deliver the goods to the buyer, unless the buyer seasonably objects, or (b) when the bailee acknowledges the buyer's right to possession of the goods.[12]

All Other Sales

If the buyer possesses the goods when the contract is formed, risk of loss passes to the buyer at that time. All other sales not involving breach are covered by the Code's catchall provision. This provision applies to those instances in which the buyer picks up the goods at the seller's place of business or the goods are delivered by the seller using the seller's own transportation. In these cases, risk of loss depends on whether the seller is a merchant. If the seller is a **merchant,** risk of loss passes to the buyer on the buyer's *receipt* of the goods. If the seller is **not a merchant,** it passes on *tender* of the goods from the seller to the buyer.[12] The policy behind this rule is that so long as the merchant seller is making delivery at her place of business or with her own vehicle, she continues to control the goods and can be expected to insure them. The buyer, on the other hand, has no control over the goods and is not likely to have insurance on them.

Suppose Ted goes to Jack's furniture store, selects a particular set of dining room furniture, and pays Jack the agreed price of $800 for it on Jack's agreement to stain the set a darker color and deliver it. Jack stains the furniture and notifies Ted that he may pick up the furniture. That night it is accidentally destroyed by fire. Ted can recover the $800 payment from Jack. The risk of loss is on seller Jack because he is a merchant and the goods were not received by Ted but were only tendered to him.

On the other hand, suppose Debra, an accountant, having moved to a different city, contracts to sell her household furniture to Dwight for $3,000 by a written agreement signed by Dwight and notifies Dwight that the furniture is available for Dwight to pick up. Dwight delays picking up the furniture several days, and in the interim the furniture is stolen from Debra's residence through no fault of Debra's. Debra may recover the $3,000 purchase price from Dwight. The risk of loss is on buyer Dwight because seller Debra is not a merchant and tender is sufficient to transfer the risk of loss.

MARTIN v. MELLAND'S INC.
Supreme Court of North Dakota, 1979.
283 N.W.2d 76.

Facts: Martin entered into a written agreement with Melland's, a farm implement dealer, to purchase a truck and attached haystack mover. According to the contract, Martin was to trade in his old truck and haystack mover unit; to mail or bring the certificate of title to the old unit to Melland's within a week; and to retain the use and possession of the old unit until Melland's had the new one ready. The contract contained no provision allocating the risk of loss of the trade-in unit. After Martin mailed the certificate to Melland's, but while he still had possession of the trade-in unit itself, the unit was destroyed by fire. Martin then sued to compel Melland's to bear the loss of the trade-in, claiming that title had passed to Melland's before the destruction of the old unit. The district court dismissed the cause of action and Martin appeals.

Decision: Judgment for Melland's Inc. affirmed.

Opinion: **Erickstad, C. J.**   Thus the concept of title under the U.C.C. is of decreased importance. The official comment to Section 2–101 U.C.C. provides in part:

> The arrangement of the present Article is in terms of contract for sale and the various steps of its performance. The legal consequences are stated as following directly from the contract and action taken under it without resorting to the idea of when property or title passed or was to pass as being the determining factor. The purpose is to avoid making practical issues between practical men turn upon the location of an intangible something, the passing of which no man can prove by evidence and to substitute for such abstractions proof of words and actions of a tangible character.

[§ 2–401 U.C.C.], which the district court applied in this case, provides in relevant part:

> Each provision of this chapter with regard to the rights, obligations and remedies of the seller, the buyer, purchasers or other third parties applies irrespective of title to the goods except where the provision refers to such title. Insofar as situations are not covered by the other provisions of this chapter and matters concerning title become material the following rules apply * * *

[§ 2–509 U.C.C.], is an "other provision of this chapter" and is applicable to this case without regard to the location of title. Comment one to Section 2–509 U.C.C. provides that "the underlying theory of these sections of risk of loss is the adoption of the contractual approach rather than an arbitrary shifting of the risk with the 'property' in the goods."

The position that the Code has taken, divorcing the question of risk of loss from a determination of title, is summed up by Professor Nordstrom in his hornbook on sales:

> No longer is the question of title of any importance in determining whether a buyer or seller bears the risk of loss. It is true that the person with title will also (and incidentally) often bear the risk that the goods may be destroyed or lost; but the seller may have title and the buyer the risk, or the seller may have the risk and the buyer the title. In short, title is not a relevant consideration in deciding whether the risk has shifted to the buyer. [Citation.]

* * *

Thus, the question of this case is not answered by a determination of the location of title, but by the risk of loss provisions in [§ 2–509 U.C.C.]. Before addressing the risk of loss question in conjunction with [§2–509 U.C.C.], it is necessary to determine the posture of the parties with regard to the trade-in unit, *i.e.* who is the buyer and the seller and how are the responsibilities allocated. It is clear that a barter or trade-in is considered a sale and is therefore subject to the Uniform Commercial Code. [Citations.] It is also clear that the party who owns the trade-in is considered the seller. [§ 2–304 U.C.C.], provides that the "price can be made payable in money or otherwise. If it is payable in whole or in part in goods each party is a seller of the goods which he is to transfer." [Citations.]

Martin argues that he had already sold the trade-in unit to Melland's and, although he retained possession, he did so in the capacity of a bailee (apparently pursuant to [§ 2–509(2) U.C.C.]). White and Summers in their hornbook on the Uniform Commercial Code argue that the seller who retains possession should not be considered a bailee within Section 2–509.

* * *

The courts that have addressed this issue have agreed with White and Summers. [Citations.]

It is undisputed that the contract did not require or authorize shipment by carrier pursuant to Section [2–509(1)] therefore, the residue section, subsection 3, is applicable:

> In any case not within subsection 1 or 2, the risk of loss passes to the buyer on his receipt of the goods if the seller is a merchant; otherwise the risk passes to the buyer on tender of delivery.

Martin admits that he is not a merchant; therefore, it is necessary to determine if Martin tendered delivery of the trade-in unit to Melland's. Tender is defined [§ 2–503 U.C.C.] as follows:

> *Manner of seller's tender of delivery.*—1. Tender of delivery requires that the seller put and hold conforming goods at the buyer's disposition and give the buyer any notification reasonably necessary to enable him to take delivery. The manner, time and place for tender are determined by the agreement and this chapter, and in particular.
>
> a. tender must be at a reasonable hour, and if it is of goods they must be kept available for the period reasonably necessary to enable the buyer to take possession; but
>
> b. unless otherwise agreed the buyer must furnish facilities reasonably suited to the receipt of the goods.

It is clear that the trade-in unit was not tendered to Melland's in this case. The parties agreed that Martin would keep the old unit "until they had the new one ready."

* * *

We hold that Martin did not tender delivery of the trade-in truck and haystack mover to Melland's pursuant to [§ 2–509 U.C.C.]; consequently, Martin must bear the loss.

See Figure 18–5 for an illustration of risk of loss in the absence of breach.

SALES OF GOODS IN BULK

A sale of goods in bulk occurs when a merchant sells all or a major portion of his inventory all at once. Creditors have an obvious interest in such a disposal of the bulk of merchandise made not in the ordinary course of business. The danger to creditors is that the debtor may secretly liquidate all or a major part of his tangible assets by a bulk sale and conceal or divert the proceeds of the sale without paying his creditors. The central purpose of bulk sales law is to deal with two common forms of commercial fraud. These oc-

cur when (a) the merchant, owing debts, sells out his stock in trade to a friend for a low price, pays his creditors less than he owes them, and hopes to come back into the business through the back door some time in the future; and (b) the merchant, owing debts, sells out his stock in trade to anyone for any price, pockets the proceeds, and disappears without paying his creditors.

Article 6 of the Code applies to such sales and defines a **bulk transfer** as "any transfer in bulk and not in the ordinary course of the transferor's business of a major part of the materials, supplies, merchandise, or other inventory." The transfer of a substantial part of the equipment is a bulk transfer only if made in connection with a bulk transfer of inventory.

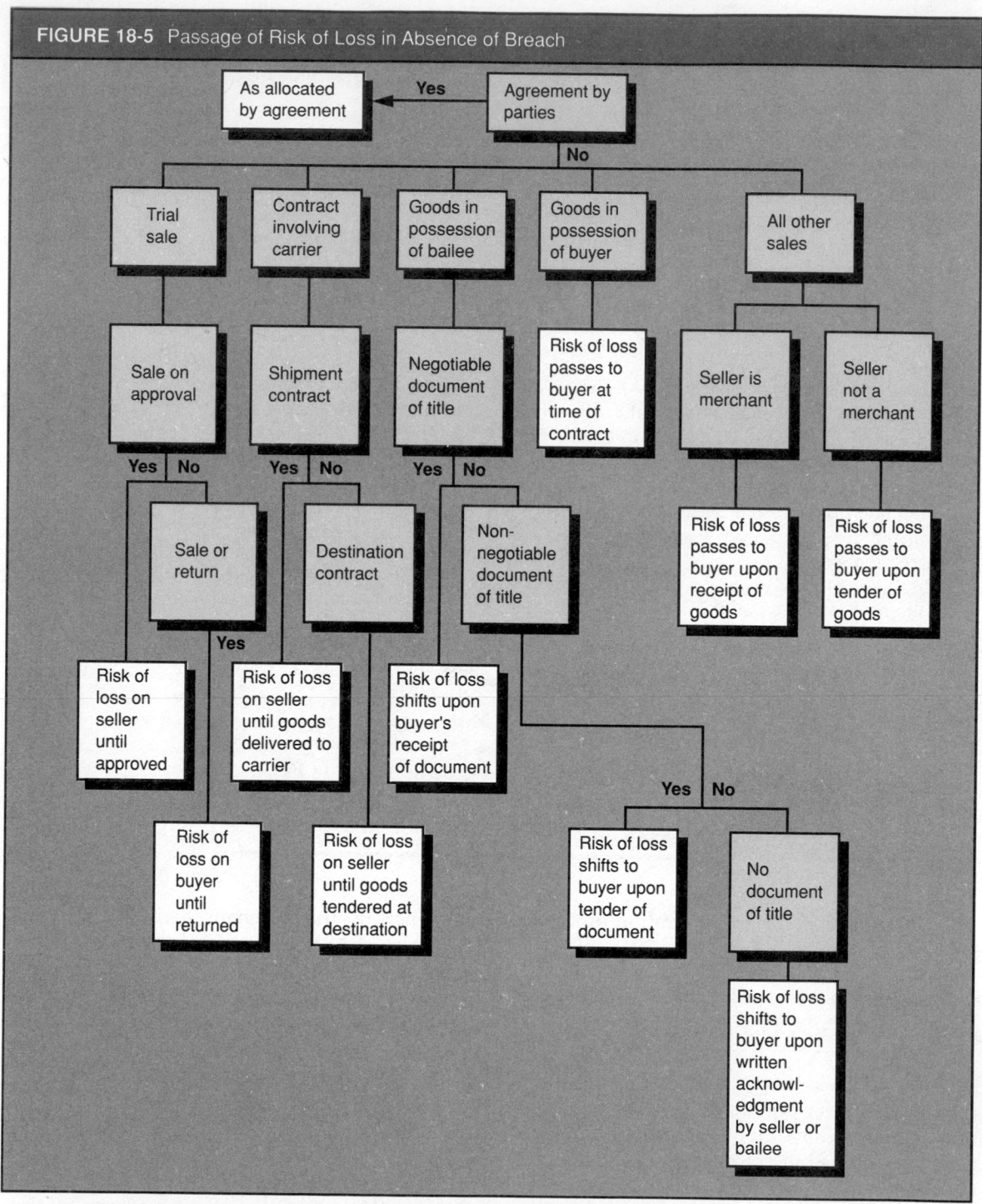

FIGURE 18-5 Passage of Risk of Loss in Absence of Breach

The enterprises subject to Article 6 of the Code are those whose principal business is the sale of merchandise from stock, including those who manufacture what they sell.

REQUIREMENTS OF ARTICLE 6

The Code provides that a bulk transfer of assets is ineffective against any creditor of the transferor, unless the following four requirements are met:

1. The transferor furnishes to the transferee a sworn list of his existing creditors, including those whose claims are disputed, stating names, business addresses, and amounts due and owing when known.[13]
2. The transferor and transferee prepare a schedule or list of the property being transferred.[13]
3. The transferee preserves the list of creditors and schedule of property for six months and permits inspection by any creditor of the transferor.[13]
4. The transferee gives the notice of the proposed transfer in bulk to each creditor of the transferor at least ten days before the transferee takes possession of the goods or makes payment for them.[14] This notice must specify: (a) that a bulk transfer is about to be made, (b) the names and business addresses of the transferor in bulk and transferee in bulk, and (c) whether all debts of the transferor in bulk are to be paid in full as a result of the transaction, and if so, the address to which creditors should send their bills.[15]

EXEMPTED BULK TRANSFERS

Certain transfers in bulk are exempt and need not comply with Article 6 of the Code:

1. Transfers by way of security
2. General assignments for the benefit of all the creditors of the transferor in bulk
3. Transfers in settlement or realization of a lien or security interest
4. Sales by executors, administrators, receivers, trustees in bankruptcy, or any public officer under judicial process
5. Sales in the course of proceedings for the dissolution or reorganization of a corporation in a court proceeding where notice is given to creditors
6. Transfers to a person who maintains a known place of business in the State who agrees to become bound to pay in full the debts of the transferor in bulk, gives public notice of that fact, and is solvent after becoming so bound
7. Transfers to a new business enterprise organized to take over and continue the business of the transferor in bulk, if public notice is given and the new enterprise assumes the debts of the transferor, who receives nothing from the transaction except an interest in the new enterprise that is subordinate to the claims of creditors
8. Transfers of property that is exempt from execution under exemption statutes

EFFECT OF FAILURE TO COMPLY WITH ARTICLE 6

The effect of a failure to comply with the requirements of Article 6 of the Code is that the goods in the possession of the transferee continue to be subject to the claims of unpaid creditors of the transferor. These creditors may proceed against the goods by levy or attachment and by sheriff's sale, or by causing the involuntary bankruptcy of the transferor and the appointment of a trustee in bankruptcy to take over the goods from the transferee.

Where the title of the transferee is subject to the defect of noncompliance with the Code, a *bona fide* purchaser of the goods from the transferee who pays value in good faith and takes the property without notice of such defect acquires the goods free of any claim of creditors of the transferor. A purchaser of the property from the transferee who pays no value or who takes them with notice of noncompliance acquires the goods subject to the claims of creditors of the transferor.

APPLICATION OF THE PROCEEDS

In the case of bulk transfers for which new consideration is payable, except those made at auction sales, the Code imposes in an optional section, a personal duty on the transferee to apply the new consideration to the payment of the debts of the transferor, and if it is insufficient to pay them in full, to make a proportional distribution to the creditors.[16]

In States that do not adopt the optional section of the Code, the transferee owes no duties to the creditors of the transferor. If there has been noncompliance with the Code, except for sales at auction, the creditors merely proceed to enforce their claims against the transferred property as though it belonged to the transferor. This is what is meant by the language of the Code that the bulk transfer "is ineffective against any creditor of the transferor." The transferee loses the property but does not assume any obligation to pay the debts of the transferor.

The optional section provides that the transferee may discharge her duty to pay the cred- itors of the transferor out of the proceeds by payment of the consideration into court within ten days after taking possession of the goods and by giving notice to all of the creditors that such payment has been made and that they should file their claims with the court.[16]

CHAPTER SUMMARY

TRANSFER OF TITLE AND OTHER PROPERTY RIGHTS

Passage of Title	**General Rule** title passes when the parties intend it to pass; where there is no specific agreement of the parties, the Code provides rules to determine when title passes **Physical Movement of the Goods** when delivery is to be made by moving the goods, title passes at the time and place where the seller completes his performance with reference to delivery **No Movement of the Goods** ■ *Document of Title* title passes upon the delivery of the document of title ■ *No Document of Title* title passes at the time and place of contracting where the goods at that time have been identified either by the seller or the buyer ■ *Goods Not Identified* title passes when the goods are identified to the contract
Other Property Rights	**Special Property Right** buyer obtains an insurable interest and specific remedies in the goods by the identification of existing goods as goods to which the contract of sale refers **Security Interest** an interest in personal property or fixtures that ensures payment or performance of an obligation
Power to Transfer Title	**General Rule** the purchaser of goods obtains such title as his transferor either has or had the power to transfer; however, to encourage and make secure good faith acquisitions of goods, it is necessary that certain third parties be protected under certain circumstances ■ *Good Faith Purchaser* one who acts honestly, gives value, and takes the goods without notice or knowledge of any defect in the title of his transferor ■ *Buyer in Ordinary Course of Business* person who buys in ordinary course of the seller's business, in good faith, and without knowledge that the sale to him is in violation of anyone's ownership rights **Void and Voidable Title to Goods** ■ *Void Title* no title can be transferred ■ *Voidable Title* the good faith purchaser acquires good title **Entrusting of Goods to a Merchant** buyers in the ordinary course of business from merchants acquire good title

RISK OF LOSS

General Rule	**Definition of Risk of Loss** allocation of loss between seller and buyer where the goods have been damaged, destroyed, or lost without the fault of either party
	Effect
	  ■ *On Buyer* he must pay the purchase price for the goods
	  ■ *On Seller* she has no right to recover payment but does have a right to the return of the damaged goods

Risk of Loss Where There Is a Breach	**Breach by the Seller** if the seller ships goods to the buyer that do not conform to the contract, the risk of loss remains on the seller until the buyer has accepted the goods or the seller has remedied the defect **Breach by the Buyer** the seller may treat the risk of loss as resting on the buyer for a commercially reasonable time to the extent of any deficiency in the seller's effective insurance coverage

Risk of Loss in Absence of a Breach	**Agreement of the Parties** the parties may by agreement allocate the risk of loss
	Trial Sales unless otherwise agreed, if the goods are delivered primarily for the buyer's use, the transaction is a sale on approval; if they are delivered primarily for resale by the buyer, it is a sale or return
	  ■ *Sale on Approval* risk of loss remains with the seller until "approval" or acceptance of the goods by the buyer
	  ■ *Sale or Return* the risk of loss is on the buyer until she returns the goods
	Contracts Involving Carriers
	  ■ *Shipment Contracts* seller bears the risk of loss and expense until the goods are delivered to the carrier for shipment; shipment terms include the following: F.O.B. (free on board) place of shipment, F.A.S. (free alongside) port of shipment, C.I.F. (cost, insurance, freight), C & F (cost and freight)
	  ■ *Destination Contracts* seller bears the risk of loss and expense until tender of the goods at a particular destination; destination terms include the following: F.O.B. place of destination, ex-ship (from the ship), no arrival, no sale (if goods do not arrive seller is excused from liability unless it is due to seller's fault)
	Goods in Possession of Bailee
	  ■ *Negotiable Document of Title* risk of loss shifts when buyer receives the document
	  ■ *Nonnegotiable Document of Title* risk of loss shifts to buyer upon tender of document
	  ■ *No Document of Title* risk of loss shifts to buyer when either the seller tenders to the buyer written directions for bailee to deliver the goods to the buyer or when the bailee acknowledges the buyer's rights to the goods
	All Other Sales
	  ■ *Merchant Seller* risk of loss passes to buyer on the buyer's receipt of the goods
	  ■ *Nonmerchant Seller* risk of loss passes to buyer upon tender of goods

SALE OF GOODS IN BULK

Bulk Sales	**Definition** a transfer not in the ordinary course of the transferor's business of a major part of his inventory to prevent commercial fraud

Requirements of Article 6	**Effect of Bulk Transfer** transfer is ineffective against any creditor of the transferor, unless certain requirements are met **Bona Fide Purchaser** good faith purchaser of the goods from the transferee acquires the goods free of any claim of creditors of the transferor

Exempted Bulk Transfers	Certain transfers in bulk are specifically exempted from Article 6

QUESTIONS

1. Explain the relative importance of title under the common law and Article 2.
2. Distinguish between a shipment and a destination contract. When does title and risk of loss pass under each?
3. When does the seller have a right or power to transfer title? When is the transfer void or voidable? By whom? Against whom?
4. Discuss the rules covering (a) risk of loss in the absence of a breach, and (b) risk of loss when there is a breach.
5. What is a bulk transfer? When is it effective?

PROBLEMS

1. Stein, a mechanic, and Beal, a life insurance agent, entered into a written contract for the sale of Stein's tractor to Beal for $2,800 cash. It was agreed that Stein would tune the motor on the tractor. Stein fulfilled this obligation and on the night of July 1 telephoned Beal that the tractor was ready to be picked up on making payment. Beal responded, "I'll be there in the morning with the money." On the next morning, however, Beal was approached by an insurance prospect and decided to get the tractor at a later date. On the night of July 2, the tractor was destroyed by fire of unknown origin. Neither Stein nor Beal had any fire insurance. Who must bear the loss?
2. Regan received a letter from Chase, the material portion of which stated: "Chase hereby places an order with you for fifty cases of Red Top tomatoes. Ship them C.O.D." As soon as he received the letter, Regan shipped the tomatoes to Chase. While en route, the railroad car carrying the tomatoes was wrecked. When Chase refused to pay for the tomatoes, Regan started an action to recover the purchase price. Chase defended on the ground that because the shipment was C.O.D., neither title to the tomatoes nor risk of loss passed until their delivery to Chase. Decision?
3. On May 10, the Adair Company, acting through Brown, entered into a contract with Clark for the installation of a milking machine at Clark's farm. Following the enumeration of the articles to be furnished, together with the price of each article, the written contract provided: "This machinery is subject to thirty days free trial and is to be installed about June 1." Within thirty days after installation, all the purchased machinery, except for the double utility unit, was destroyed by fire through no fault of Clark's. The Adair Company sued Clark to recover the value of the articles destroyed. Decision?
4. Brown contracted to buy sixty cases of Lovely Brand canned corn from Smith, a Toledo seller, at a contract price of $600. Based on the contract, Smith selected and set aside sixty cases of Lovely Brand canned corn and tagged them "For Brown." The contract required Smith to ship the corn to Brown via T Railroad, F.O.B. Toledo. Before Smith delivered the corn to the railroad, the sixty cases were stolen from Smith's warehouse.

(a) Who is liable for the loss of the sixty cases of corn, Brown or Smith?
(b) Suppose Smith had delivered the corn to the railroad in Toledo. After the corn was loaded on a freight car but before the train left the yard, the car

was broken open and its contents, including the corn, were stolen. Who is liable for the loss, Brown or Smith?

(c) Would your answer in question (b) be the same if this contract were F.O.B. Brown's warehouse, all other facts remaining the same?

5. Farber owned a quantity of corn that was stored in a corncrib located on Farber's farm. On March 12 Farber wrote a letter to Barber stating that he would sell to Barber all of the corn in this crib, which he estimated at between 900 and 1,000 bushels, for $3.60 per bushel. Barber received this letter on March 13 and on the same day immediately wrote and mailed a letter to Farber stating that he would buy the corn. The corncrib and contents were accidentally destroyed by a fire that broke out about 3:00 A.M. on March 14. What are the rights of the parties? What difference, if any, in result if Farber were a merchant?

6. Franco, a New York dealer, purchased twenty-five barrels of specially graded and packed apples from a producer at Hood River, Oregon. He afterward resold the apples to Harris under a contract that specified an agreed price on delivery at Harris's place of business in New York. The apples were shipped to Franco from Oregon but, through no fault of either Franco or Harris, were totally destroyed before reaching New York. Does any liability rest on Franco?

7. Smith was approached by a man who introduced himself as Brown of Brown and Co. Smith did not know Brown, but Smith asked Dun & Bradstreet for a credit report on Brown. He thereupon sold Brown some expensive gems and billed Brown & Co. "Brown" turned out to be a clever jewel thief, who later sold the gems to Brown & Co. for valuable consideration. Brown & Co. was unaware of "Brown's" transaction with Smith. Smith sued Brown & Co. for the return of the gems or the price billed to Brown & Co. Decision?

8. Charlotte, the owner of a new Cadillac automobile, agreed to loan the car to Ellen for the month of February while she (Charlotte) went to Florida for a winter vacation. It was understood that Ellen, who was a small-town Cadillac dealer, would merely place Charlotte's car in her showroom for exhibition and sales promotion purposes. While Charlotte was away, Ellen sold the car to Bob. When Charlotte returned from Florida, she sued to recover the car from Bob. Decision?

9. Steven offered to sell his used automobile to Benito for $2,600 cash. Benito agreed to buy the car, gave Steven a check for $2,600, and drove away in the car. The next day Benito sold the car for $3,000 to Jose, a *bona fide* purchaser. The bank returned Benito's $2,600 check to Steven because of insufficient funds in Benito's account. Steven brings an action against Jose to recover the automobile. What judgment?

10. Justin told Jennifer he wished to buy Jennifer's automobile. He drove the car for about ten minutes, returned to Jennifer, stated he wanted to take the automobile to show it to his wife, and then left with the automobile and never returned. Justin sold the automobile in another State to Thomas and gave him a bill of sale. Jennifer sued Thomas to recover the automobile. Decision?

11. On February 7 Pillsbury purchased 8,000 bushels of wheat from Landis. The wheat was being stored at the Greensville Grain Company. Pillsbury also intended to store the wheat with Greensville. On February 10 the wheat was destroyed. Landis demands payment for the wheat from Pillsbury. Who prevails? Who has title? Who has the risk of loss? Explain.

12. Johnson, who owns a hardware store, was indebted to Hutchinson, one of his suppliers. Johnson sold her business to Lockhart, one of Johnson's previous competitors. Lockhart combined the inventory from Johnson's store with his own and moved them to a new, larger store. Hutchinson claims that Lockhart must pay Johnson's debt because the sale of the business had been made without complying with the requirements of the bulk sales law. Decision?

13. Seller had manufactured 40,000 pounds of plastic resin pellets specially for the buyer, who agreed to accept them at the rate of 1,000 pounds per day upon his issuance of shipping instructions. Despite numerous requests by the seller, the buyer issued no such instructions. On August 18, the seller, after warehousing the goods for forty days, demanded by letter that the buyer issue instructions. The buyer agreed to issue them beginning August 20 but never did. On September 22 a fire destroyed the seller's plant containing the goods, which were not covered by insurance. Who bears the risk of loss? Why?

14. United Road Machinery Company, a dealer in heavy road equipment (including truck scales supplied by Thurman Scale Company), received a telephone call on July 21, from James Durham, an officer of Consolidated Coal Company, seeking to acquire truck scales for his coal mining operation. United and Consolidated entered into a twenty-four-month lease-purchase arrangement. United then notified Thurman that Consolidated would take possession of the scales directly. United paid for the scales and Consolidated took possession of them, but the latter never signed and returned the contract papers forwarded to it by United. Consol-

idated also never made any of the rental payments ($608/month) due under the lease. On September 20, Consolidated, through its officer Durham, sold the scales to Kentucky Mobile Homes for $8,500. Kentucky's president, Ethard Jasper, checked the county records prior to the purchase and found no lien or encumbrance on the title; likewise, he denied knowledge of the dispute between Consolidated and United. On September 22, Kentucky sold the scales to Clyde Jasper, individually, for $8,500. His search also failed to disclose any lien on the title to the scales, and he denied knowledge of the dispute between Consolidated and United. United brought suit to recover the scales from Jasper. Decision?

COMPUTER RESEARCH PROBLEMS

1. Porter, the owner of a collection of artworks, had a number of art transactions with Harold Von Maker who used, among other names, that of Peter Wertz. Porter permitted Von Maker to have temporarily a painting by Maurice Utrillo, *Chateau de Lion-sure-Mer*, and to hang it in his home until he decided whether to purchase it. A few months later, Porter sought the return of the Utrillo painting but was unable to reach Von Maker. Porter subsequently discovered that he was not dealing with Peter Wertz but with Harold Von Maker, a man with an extensive criminal record, including a conviction for defrauding the Chase Manhattan Bank. When Porter finally reached him, Von Maker claimed the Utrillo was on consignment with a client. Von Maker then agreed in writing either to return the painting to Porter within ninety days or to make compensation for it. At the time he entered this agreement, Von Maker had already sold the painting. He had used the real Peter Wertz, a delicatessen employee and acquaintance, to effect the sale of the Utrillo to Feigen for $20,000. Feigen, an art dealer, then sold the painting to Brenner, and it is now somewhere in Venezuela. Porter brought suit against Feigen and the others involved to recover possession of the Utrillo or its value. Decision?

2. Home Indemnity, an insurance company, paid one of its insureds after the theft of his car. The car reappeared in another State and was sold to Michael Schrier for $4,300 by a used car dealer. The dealer promised to give Mr. Schrier a certificate of title. One month later the car was seized by the police on behalf of Home Indemnity. Mr. Schrier sued for the return of the car and won. Home Indemnity seeks reversal of that decision and possession of the car. Decision?

3. Fred Lane sells boats, motors, and trailers. Lane sold a boat, motor, and trailer to John Willis in exchange for a check for $6,285.00. The check was not honored when Lane attempted to use the funds. Willis subsequently left the boat, motor, and trailer with John Garrett. Garrett sold the boat, motor, and trailer to Jimmy Honeycutt for $2,500.00. Honeycutt was surprised at how inexpensive the boat was considering its quality. He did not know where Garrett got the boat, but he had dealt with Garrett before and described him as a "sly businessman." Garrett did not sell boats but rather sold fishing tackle and provisions. Honeycutt also received a forged certificate for the boat on which he observed Garrett forge the purported owner's signature. Lane sues Honeycutt for return of the boat, motor, and trailer. Decision?

4. Mike Moses purchased a mobile home, including installation, from Gary Newman. Newman delivered the home to Moses' lot. Upon inspection of the home, Moses fiancée found a broken window and water pipe. Moses also had not received keys to the front door. Before Newman corrected these problems, a windstorm destroyed the home. Moses sued Newman for loss of the home. Decision?

ENDNOTES

1. Uniform Commercial Code, Section 2—106(1), Definitions: Contract; Agreement; Contract for Sale; Sale; Present Sale.

2. Uniform Commercial Code, Section 2—401, Passing of Title; Reservation for Security; Limited Application of This Section.

3. Uniform Commercial Code, Section 2—501, Insurable Interest in Goods; Manner of Identification of Goods.

4. Uniform Commercial Code, Section 1—201(37), Security Interest.

5. Uniform Commercial Code, Section 2—403, Power to Transfer; Good Faith Purchase of Goods, "Entrusting."

6. Uniform Commercial Code, Section 1—201(9), Buyer in Ordinary Course of Business.

7. Uniform Commercial Code, Section 2—510, Effect of Breach on Risk of Loss.

8. Uniform Commercial Code, Section 2—303, Allocations or Division of Risks.

9. Uniform Commercial Code, Section 2—327, Special Incidents of Sale on Approval and Sale or Return.

10. Uniform Commercial Code, Section 2—326, Sale on Approval and Sale or Return; Consignment Sales and Rights of Creditors.

11. Uniform Commercial Code, Section 2—319, F.O.B. and F.A.S. Terms.

12. Uniform Commercial Code, Section 2—509, Risk of Loss in the Absence of Breach.

13. Uniform Commercial Code, Section 6—104(1), Schedule of Property, List of Creditors.

14. Uniform Commercial Code, Section 6—105, Notice to Creditors.

15. Uniform Commercial Code, Section 6—107(1), The Notice.

16. Uniform Commercial Code, Section 6—106, Application of the Proceeds.

19 PRODUCTS LIABILITY: WARRANTIES AND STRICT LIABILITY

In this chapter we consider the liability of manufacturers and sellers of goods to buyers, users, consumers, and bystanders for damages caused by defective products. The rapid and expanding development of case law has established product liability as a separate and distinct field of law, combining and enforcing rules and principles of contracts, sales, negligence, strict liability, and statutory law.

One reason for the expansion of such liability has been the modern practice of sales. Today, retailers serve principally as a conduit of prepackaged goods in sealed containers that are widely advertised by the manufacturer or distributor. This has hastened the extension of product liability coverage to include manufacturers and other parties within the chain of distribution. The extension of product liability to manufacturers, however, has not noticeably lessened the liability of a seller to his immediate purchaser. Rather, it has broadened and extended the base of liability by the development and application of new principles of law.

Currently, the entire area of product liability has attracted a great deal of public attention. The cost of maintaining product liability insurance has skyrocketed, causing great concern in the business community. In response to the clamor over this insurance "crisis," nearly every State has either considered or is presently considering legislative solutions for the alleged explosion of product liability lawsuits and the size of the damages awarded in these suits. A frequent proposal has been the imposition of an upper dollar limit (cap) on recovery for noneconomic damages.

The liability of manufacturers and sellers of goods for a defective product, or its failure to perform adequately, may be based on one or more of the following: (1) negligence, (2) misrepresentation, (3) violation of statutory duty, (4) warranty, and (5) strict liability in tort. We covered the first three of these causes of actions in Chapters 6 and 9. In this chapter we explore the last two.

WARRANTIES

The concept of warranty as an obligation of the seller to the buyer concerning the title, quality, condition, or performability of goods sold or to be sold is an ancient one. Historically, the remedy of the buyer for breach of warranty was an action in tort for deceit. Today, however, the liability of a seller for breach of warranty is recognized as contractual, and it has been codified by the Uniform Commercial Code.

The liability of a seller for the quality of goods sold has long presented many legal problems. The traditional concept of *caveat emptor*—"let the buyer beware"—was premised on the principle that the buyer and seller were each attempting to obtain the best bargain possible. Because each had relatively equal bargaining power, the law did not interfere. Today, however, this is not the case; the consumer generally possesses far less bargaining power than the seller. Consequently, the law of sales has abandoned the doctrine of *caveat emptor* and employs warranties to protect the buyer.

A **warranty** creates a duty on the part of the seller to assure that the goods he sells will conform to certain qualities, characteristics, or conditions. A seller, however, is not required to warrant the goods, and in general he may, by appropriate words, disclaim (exclude) or modify a particular warranty or even all warranties. Moreover, he may carefully refrain from making an express warranty. But, he must act affirmatively and in the manner prescribed by the Code to effectively disclaim liability for implied warranties.

In this section we examine the various types of warranties, as well as the obstacles to a cause of action for breach of warranty.

TYPES OF WARRANTIES

A warranty may arise out of an affirmation of fact or promise to the buyer (an express warranty), the mere existence of a sale (a warranty of title), or the circumstances under which the sale is made (an implied warranty). In a contract for the sale of goods, it is possible to have both express and implied warranties as well as a warranty of title. All warranties are to be construed as consistent with each other and cumulative, unless such construction is unreasonable. If the seller breaches his warranty, the buyer may recover a judgment against the seller for damages. In addition, by timely notice, the buyer may reject or revoke acceptance of the goods.

Express Warranties

An **express warranty** is an explicit declaration by the seller about the quality, description, condition, or performability of the goods. The declaration may consist of **affirmations** or statements of **fact** or **promises.** For example, a statement made by the seller that a camera has automatic focus is an express warranty. The Code does not require that the affirmation by the seller be relied on by the buyer but only that it constitute a part of the **basis of the bargain.**[1] If affirmations are part of the buyer's assumption underlying the sale, then reliance by the buyer is presumed.

To create an express warranty, the seller does not need to have a specific intention to make a warranty or use formal words such as "warrant" or "guarantee." Moreover, it is not necessary that a seller have knowledge of the falsity of a statement made by her in order to be liable for breach of express warranty; the seller may be acting in good faith. To be liable for fraud, on the other hand, a person must make a misrepresentation of fact with knowledge of its falsity.

Affirmations of fact by the seller about the goods are frequently part of the **description** of the goods. If so, the seller expressly warrants that the goods will conform to the description. The use of a **sample** or model is another means of describing the goods, and the seller expressly warrants that the entire lot of goods sold will conform to the sample or model.

Statements or promises made by the seller to the buyer before the sale may be express warranties because they may form a part of the basis of the bargain just as much as statements made at the time of the sale. Therefore, statements in advertisements, catalogs, and the like may constitute an express warranty. Under the Code, statements or promises made by the seller after the contract of sale may become express warranties even though no new consideration is given.[2] Thus, a statement or promise of assurance concerning the goods made by the seller to the buyer at the time of delivery may be a binding modification of the prior contract of sale and held to be an express warranty basic to the bargain.

The Code further provides that a mere statement of the value of the goods or a statement purporting merely to be the seller's **opinion** of the goods does *not* create a warranty.[1] Such statements are not factual and do not deceive the ordinary buyer. They are accepted merely as opinions or as **puffery** (sales talk). If the seller genuinely believes that the goods are more valuable than the stated price, she probably would not sell them. A statement of **value,** however, may be an express warranty in situations where the seller states the price at which the goods were purchased from a former owner or where she gives market figures relating to sales of similar goods. These are affirmations of facts. They are statements of events and not mere opinions, and the seller is liable for breach of warranty if they are untrue.

Although a statement of opinion by the seller is not ordinarily a warranty, if the seller is an **expert** and gives her opinion as such, she may be liable for breach of warranty. Thus, if an art expert states that a certain painting is a genuine Rembrandt, and this becomes part of the basis of the bargain, then the expert warrants the accuracy of her professional opinion. A seller may also be liable if she misrepresents her opinion. A seller may say, "This car is in excellent mechanical condition," or "In my opinion, this car is in excellent mechanical condition." In the first instance, she has made an express warranty of the mechanical soundness of the car. In the second, she has made no warranty as to the mechanical soundness of the car but has warranted that she believes the car to be mechanically sound. Thus, if she knew at the time that the car was mechanically unsound, she has misrepresented her opinion as a factual matter. This is not only fraud but also a breach of warranty.

Warranty of Title

Under the Code's **warranty of title,** the seller implicitly warrants that (1) the title conveyed is good and its transfer rightful and (2) the goods have no security interest or other lien (a claim on property by another for payment of debt) of which the buyer had no knowledge at the time of contracting.[3]

For example, Steven acquires goods from Nancy in a transaction that is void and then sells the goods to Rachel. Nancy brings an action against Rachel and recovers the goods. Steven has breached the warranty of title because he did not have good title to the goods and his transfer of the goods to Rachel was not rightful. Accordingly, Steven is liable to Rachel for damages.

The Code does not label the warranty of title as an implied warranty, even though it arises out of the sale and not from any particular words or conduct. Instead, the Code has a separate disclaimer provision for warranty of title;[3] thus, the Code's general disclaimer provision for implied warranties does not apply. Nevertheless, a seller of goods does implicitly warrant title to those goods.

Implied Warranties

An implied warranty, unlike an express warranty, is not a specific affirmation or promise by the seller; it is not found in the language of the sales contract. Instead, it exists by operation of law. An **implied warranty** arises out of the circumstances under which the parties enter into their contract and depends on such factors as the type of contract or sale entered into, whether the seller is a merchant, the conduct of the parties, and the applicability of other statutes. Implied warranties have been developed by the law, not as something to which the parties have agreed but as a departure from the early rule of *caveat emptor.*

Merchantability At early common law, a seller was not held to any implied warranty concerning the quality of the goods. Under the Code, however, a **merchant seller** does make an implied warranty of the merchantability of goods that are of the kind in which he deals.[4] The implied warranty of **merchantability** is a warranty by the merchant seller that the goods are reasonably fit for the **ordinary** purposes for which they are manufactured and sold, and also that they are of fair, average quality. *Vlases v. Montgomery Ward and Company* provides an example.

The official Comments to the Code further provide that a contract for the sale of second-hand goods "involves only such obligation as is appropriate to such goods for that is their description." It has been held that "such obligation" includes an implied warranty of merchantability. In defining this warranty, the price, age, and condition of the goods are considered.

Fitness for Particular Purpose **Any** seller, whether or not he is a merchant, makes an implied warranty that the goods are reasonably **fit for the particular purpose** of the buyer, if at the time of contracting the seller had reason to know the buyer's particular purpose and that the buyer was relying on the seller's skill and judgment to select suitable goods.[5]

In contrast to the implied warranty of merchantability, the implied warranty of fitness for a particular purpose pertains to a specific purpose, rather than the ordinary purpose, of the goods. A particular purpose may be a specific use or may relate to a special situation in which the buyer intends to use the goods. Thus, if the seller has reason to know that the buyer is purchasing a pair of shoes for mountain climbing and that the buyer is relying on the seller's judgment to furnish suitable shoes for this purpose, a sale of shoes suitable only for ordinary walking purposes would be a breach of this implied warranty. Likewise, a buyer indicates to a seller that she needs a stamping machine to stamp 10,000 packages in an eight-hour pe-

riod and relies upon the seller to select an appropriate machine. By selecting a machine, the seller impliedly warranty that the machine selected will stamp 10,000 packages in an eight-hour period.

The buyer need not specifically inform the seller of her particular purpose. It is sufficient if the seller has reason to know it. For the implied warranty to exist, however, the buyer must rely on the seller's skill or judgment to select or furnish suitable goods.

Frequently, as in the case that follows, a seller's conduct may involve both the implied warranty of merchantability *and* the implied warranty of fitness for a particular purpose.

VLASES v. MONTGOMERY WARD & COMPANY, INC.
United States Court of Appeals, Third Circuit, 1967.
377 F.2d 846.

Facts: Vlases, a coal miner who had always raised small flocks of chickens, spent two years building a new two-story chicken coop large enough to house 4,000 chickens. After its completion, he purchased 2,200 one-day-old chicks from Montgomery Ward for the purpose of producing eggs for sale. He had selected them from Ward's catalogue, which stated that these chicks, hybrid Leghorns, were noted for their excellent egg production. Vlases had equipped the coop with brand new machinery and had taken further hygiene precautions for the chicks' health. Almost one month later, Vlases noticed that their feathers were beginning to fall off. A veterinarian's examination revealed signs of drug intoxication and hemorrhagic disease in a few of the chicks. Eight months later, it was determined that the chicks were suffering from visceral and ocular leukosis, or bird cancer, which reduced their egg-bearing capacity to zero. Avian leukosis may be transmitted either genetically or by unsanitary conditions. Subsequently, the disease infected the entire flock. Vlases then brought suit against Montgomery Ward for its breach of the implied warranties of merchantability and of fitness for a particular purpose. Ward claims that there was no way to detect the disease in the one-day-old chicks nor was there medication available to prevent this disease from occurring. Montgomery Ward brings this appeal from a judgment in favor of Vlases.

Decision: Judgment for Vlases affirmed.

Opinion: McLaughlin, J.   The two implied warranties before us are the implied warranty of merchantability, [U.C.C.] § 2-314, and the implied warranty of fitness for a particular purpose, [U.C.C.] § 2-315. Both of these are designed to protect the buyer of goods from bearing the burden of loss where merchandise, though not violating a promise expressly guaranteed, does not conform to the normal commercial standards or meeting the buyer's particular purpose, a condition upon which he had the right to rely.

Were it to be assumed that the sale of 2,000 chickens infected with avian leukosis transgressed the norm of acceptable goods under both warranties, appellant's [Ward's] position is that the action will not lie in a situation where the seller is unable to discover the defect or cure the damage if it could be ascertained. That theory does not eliminate the consequences imposed by the Code upon the seller of commercially inferior goods. It is without merit.

The fact that avian leukosis is nondetectable could be an important issue but only as bearing on the charge of negligence, which is no longer this suit. . . . The entire purpose behind the implied warranty sections of the Code is to hold the seller responsible when inferior goods are passed along to the unsuspecting buyer. What the Code requires is not evidence that the defects should or could have been uncovered by the seller but only that the goods upon delivery were not of a merchantable quality or fit for their particular purpose. If those requisite proofs are established the only exculpatory relief afforded by the Code is a showing that the implied warranties were modified or excluded by specific language under Section 2-316. Lack of skill or foresight on the part of the seller in discovering the product's flaw was never meant to bar liability. The gravamen here is not so much with what precautions were taken by the seller but rather with the quality of the goods contracted for by the buyer. Even a provision specifically disclaiming any warrant against avian leukosis would not necessarily call for the defendant's freedom from liability. Section 1-102(3) of the Code's General Provisions states that standards which are manifestly unreasonable may not be disclaimed and prevents the enforcement of unconscionable sales where, as in this instance, the goods exchanged are found to be totally worthless.

Appellant contends that plaintiff failed to meet the burden of proof that the chickens were delivered with avian leukosis and further asserts that the verdict is against the weight of the evidence. The argument advanced is founded on the fact that avian leukosis may be contracted in two ways, either inherited through the egg or acquired by reason of an unhealthy environment. Appellant urges that since the disease was first diagnosed when the chickens were nine months of age and since there was evidence indicating the existence of other maladies aside from leukosis, that plaintiff failed to show the presence of avian leukosis at delivery and also that the disease was the cause of the inability of the chicks to produce eggs and of their deaths. Upon consideration of all the trial testimony, appellant's argument must be rejected.

It was firmly established by the evidence that with reference to inherited as opposed to environmental leukosis, incidents of the latter are minimized where proper care and health standards are strictly observed. Testimony revealed that environmental infection will more than likely occur where the chicks are housed in a coop previously occupied by a diseased flock, where leukosis is present in nearby chickens or where the young chicks come in contact with contaminated equipment. On behalf of the plaintiff it was shown that the chicks were placed by him in a newly constructed coop with new equipment. There was no evidence that the disease was then present on the farm or had ever affected other chickens raised by Vlases. Plaintiff's expert witness, Dr. Frank A. Bartus, had examined the chickens six or seven months after the first diagnosis of the disease and testified that at that time "this disease [avian leukosis complex] was just running rampant through the whole flock." In the opinion of Dr. Bartus the leukosis found in plaintiff's chickens was transmitted through the egg. That opinion was based on the witness' expertise and factually supported by the consideration that ". . . he [Vlases] has raised chickens in the past, and the fact that he was a fairly good husbandry man, and the fact that he had a new coop I think are very important features in this case." . . .

OBSTACLES TO WARRANTY ACTIONS

Disclaimer or Modification of Warranties

The Code calls for a reasonable construction of words or conduct to **disclaim** (negate) or limit warranties.[6] In addition, it provides that remedies and recovery of damages for breach of warranty may be contractually limited.

The Code makes clear that the seller should not rely on a time-honored formula of words and expect to obtain a disclaimer that may go unnoticed by the buyer. To be effective, disclaimers should be positive, explicit, unequivocal, and conspicuous.

Express Exclusions A **warranty of title** may be excluded or modified only by specific language or by certain circumstances, including a judicial sale or sales by sheriffs, executors, or foreclosing lienors.[3] In the latter cases the seller is clearly offering to sell only such right or title as he or a third person might have in the goods, because it is apparent that the goods are not the property of the person selling them.

A seller can avoid making an **express warranty** by carefully refraining from making any promise or affirmation of fact relating to the goods, refraining from making a description of the goods, or refraining from using a sample or model in a sale. It may be possible that a seller can negate an express warranty by clear, specific, unambiguous language. The Code provides that words or conduct relevant to the creation of an express warranty and words or conduct negating or limiting a warranty shall be construed wherever reasonable as consistent with each other and that a negation or limitation has no effect if it is unreasonable.[6] Thus, seller and buyer make a written contract in which the seller warrants that a camera is free of defects. This express warranty nullifies another provision in the contract that attempts to disclaim liability for any repairs required by defects in the camera. The inconsistency between the two contractual provisions makes the disclaimer ineffective. Moreover, a general disclaimer attempting to negate "all express warranties" would be ineffective against the specific express warranty providing that the camera is free of all defects. Finally, oral warranties made before the execution of a written agreement that contains an express disclaimer are subject to the parol evidence rule. Thus, as discussed in Chapter 13, if the written contract is intended to be the final and *complete* statement of the agreement between the parties, parol evidence of warranties that *contradicts* the terms of the written contract is inadmissible.

To exclude or modify an **implied warranty of merchantability,** the language of disclaimer or modification must mention *merchantability* and, in the case of a writing, must be *conspicuous.*[6]

To exclude or to modify an **implied warranty of fitness** for the particular purpose of the buyer, the disclaimer must be in *writing* and conspicuous.[6]

All implied warranties, unless the circumstances indicate otherwise, are excluded by expressions like **"as is,"** "with all faults," or other language plainly calling the buyer's attention to the exclusion of warranties.[6] Implied warranties may also be excluded by course of dealing, course of performance, or usage of trade.

O'NEIL v. INTERNATIONAL HARVESTER CO.
Colorado Court of Appeals, 1978.
40 Colo.App. 369, 575 P.2d 862.

Facts: On August 22, 1975, O'Neil purchased a used diesel tractor-trailer combination from International Harvester. O'Neil claimed that International Harvester's salesman had told him that the truck had recently been overhauled and that it would be suitable for hauling logs in the mountains. The written installment contract signed by the parties provided that the truck was sold "AS IS WITHOUT WARRANTY OF ANY CHARACTER express or implied." O'Neil admitted that he had read the disclaimer clause but claimed that he understood it to mean that the tractor-trailer would be in the condition that International Harvester's salesman had promised.

O'Neil paid the $1,700 down payment, but he failed to make any of the monthly payments. He claimed that he refused to pay because his employee had many problems with the truck when he took it to the mountains. Delays resulting from those problems, O'Neil argued, had caused him to lose his permit to cut firewood and, therefore, the accompanying business. An International Harvester representative agreed to pay for one-half of the cost of certain repairs, but the several attempts made to fix the truck were unsuccessful. O'Neil then tried to return the truck and to rescind the sale, but International Harvester refused to cooperate. The trial court granted a summary judgment dismissing O'Neil's complaint against International Harvester.

Decision: Judgment dismissing O'Neil's claim for breach of implied warranty affirmed; judgment dismissing O'Neil's claim for breach of express warranty reversed and remanded.

Opinion: Roland, J.   O'Neil first contends that the trial court improperly granted summary judgment against him on his claim that the defendants breached an implied warranty of fitness for a particular purpose relative to the capability of the truck. In response, the defendants assert that summary judgment was proper because this warranty was effectively disclaimed in the contract. We agree with the defendants.

Pursuant to the Uniform Commercial Code, one way an implied warranty of fitness for a particular purpose can be excluded is by a conspicuous writing which states generally that there are no warranties extending beyond the description in the contract. § 2-316(2). O'Neil admits reading the warranty disclaimer provision. * * * And, we hold that the languae, "AS IS WITHOUT WARRANTY OF ANY CHARACTER expressed or implied" was sufficient to inform O'Neil that there was no implied warranty in effect for the truck. See § 2-316(2). [Citation.]

Even though express warranties are also included in the above quoted language, still O'Neil asserts that summary judgment was improvidently granted against him on his claim that International Harvester breached the express warranties. The defendants argue that the trial court's ruling was correct. We agree with O'Neil.

Section 2-316 provides that "[w]ords or conduct relevant to the creation of an express warranty *and* words or conduct tending to negate or limit warranty shall be construed wherever reasonable as consistent with each other. . . ." Here, the oral warranties relied upon by O'Neil are totally inconsistent with the warranty exclusion clause of the contract. Section 2-316 further provides that, under these circumstances (but subject to the provisions of the Code governing the admission of parol evidence), a provision limiting an express warranty is inoperative.

Turning to the applicable parol evidence rule as set forth in §2-202, one finds that:

Terms with respect to which the confirmatory memoranda of the parties agree or which are otherwise set forth in writing intended by the parties as a final expression of their agreement with respect to such terms as are included therein, may not be contradicted by evidence of any prior agreement or of a contemporaneous oral agreement. . . .

Various commentators have noted the difficulty in applying §§ 2-316 and 2-202 when, as here, the buyer alleges oral warranties by the seller, but the written contract contains both a warranty disclaimer clause and an "integration" provision. [Citations.] While the courts divide on whether testimony as to the oral warranties may be admitted under these circumstances, [citations] we do not reach that issue in this case.

Where, as here, the buyer alleges the existence of oral warranties prior to execution of the written contract, as well as conduct following the sale (such as a commitment to pay for certain repairs) which tends to show that warranties were in fact made, there is a material issue of fact for resolution. That issue is whether the parties intended the written contract to be a final expression of their agreement, and if not, what the terms actually agreed upon by the parties consisted of. Further, we hold that, under such circumstances, evidence of both oral warranties and the conduct of the parties subsequent to signing the contract is admissible for purpose of resolving this issue. Thus, entry of summary judgment on this issue was error. [Citations.]

Disclaimers that are viewed as being unconscionable will likewise be invalidated by the courts. The Code, as previously discussed in Chapter 17, permits a court to limit the application of any contract or provision of a contract that it finds unconscionable.[7]

Buyer's Examination or Refusal to Examine If the buyer inspects the goods, **implied warranties** do not apply to obvious defects that are apparent on examination. Moreover, there is no implied warranty on defects that an examination ought to have revealed, not only where the buyer has examined the goods as fully as she desired, but also where the buyer has *refused* to examine the goods.[6]

Federal Legislation Relating to Warranties of Consumer Goods To protect purchasers of **consumer goods** (defined as "tangible personal property normally used for personal, family, or household purposes"), Congress enacted the **Magnuson-Moss Warranty Act.** The purpose of the act is to prevent deception and to make sure consumer purchasers are adequately informed about warranties.

The Federal Trade Commission administrates and enforces the act. The commission's guidelines about the type of information that must be given in warranties of consumer products are aimed at providing the consumer with clear and useful information. More significantly, the act provides that a seller who makes a written warranty *cannot* disclaim *any* implied warranty. For a complete discussion of the act see Chapter 45.

For a summary of the types of warranties and the way in which they can be disclaimed, see Figure 19–1.

Privity of Contract

Because of the close association between warranties and contracts, a principle of law became established in the nineteenth century that a plaintiff could not recover for breach of warranty unless he was in a contractual relationship with the defendant. This relationship is known as **privity** of contract.

Under this rule, a warranty by seller Ingrid to buyer Sylvester, who resells the goods to purchaser Lyle under a similar warranty, gives Lyle no rights against Ingrid. There is no privity of contract between Ingrid and Lyle. In the event of breach of warranty, Lyle may recover only from his seller, Sylvester, who in turn may recover from Ingrid.

Horizontal privity pertains to noncontracting parties who are injured by the defective goods; this group would include users, consumers, and bystanders who are not the contracting purchaser. Horizontal privity determines who benefits from a warranty and may therefore sue for its breach.

The Code relaxes the requirement of horizontal privity of contract by permitting recovery on a seller's warranty to, at a minimum, members of the family or household of the buyer or guests in

---

FIGURE 19-1 Warranties

Type of Warranty	How Created	What is Warranted	How Disclaimed
Title	Seller contracts to sell goods	• Good title • Rightful transfer	• Specific language • Circumstances giving buyer reason to know that seller does not claim title
Express	• Affirmation of fact • Promise • Description • Sample	• Conform to affirmation • Conform to promise • Conform to description • Conform to sample	• Specific language
Merchantability	Merchant sells goods	• Fit for ordinary purpose • Adequately contained, packaged, and labeled	• Must mention "merchantability" • If in writing must be conspicuous • As-is sale • Buyer examination • Course of dealing, course of performance, usage of trade
Fitness for a particular purpose	Seller knows buyer is relying upon seller to select goods suitable for buyer's particular purpose	Fit for particular purpose	• No specific words necessary • In writing and conspicuous • As-is sale • Buyer examination • Course of dealing, course of performance, usage of trade

---

his home.[8] The Code provides three alternative sections from which the State may select. Alternative A, the least comprehensive and most widely adopted of these legislative alternatives, provides that a seller's warranty, whether express or implied, extends to any natural person who is in the family or household of the buyer or who is a guest in his home if it is reasonable to expect that such person may use, consume, or be affected by the goods and who is injured in person by breach of the warranty. Alternative B extends Alternative A to "any natural person who may reasonably be expected to use, consume or be affected by the goods." Alternative C further expands the coverage of the section to any person, not just natural persons, and to property damage as well as personal injury. A seller may not exclude or limit the operation of this section except for injury not to a person.

Nonetheless, the Code was not intended to establish outer boundaries for which third parties may recover for injuries caused by defective goods. Rather, it sets a minimum standard that the States may expand through case law. Most States have judicially accepted the Code's invitation to relax the requirements of horizontal privity and, for all practical purposes, have *eliminated* horizontal privity in warranty cases.

Vertical privity pertains to remote sellers within the chain of distribution, such as manufacturers and wholesalers, with whom the consumer purchaser has not dealt. Thus, vertical privity determines who is liable for breach of warranty. Although the Code adopts a neutral position regarding vertical privity, the courts in most States have *eliminated* the requirement of vertical privity in warranty actions.

Notice of Breach

When a buyer has accepted a tender of goods that are not as warranted by the seller, she is required to notify the seller of any breach of warranty, express or implied, as well as any other breach, within a reasonable time after she has discovered or should have discovered it. If the buyer fails to notify the seller of any breach within a reasonable time, she is barred from any remedy against the seller.[9]

The purpose of the reasonable notice requirement is (1) to enable the seller to cure the defect or to minimize the buyer's loss, (2) to provide the seller an opportunity to prepare for conflict resolution and litigation, and (3) to provide the seller with an end point to liability. In determining whether notice was provided in a reasonable period of time, the courts are much more sympathetic to a consumer's delay in acting than that of a commercial entity.

Plaintiff's Conduct

Because of the development of warranty liability in the law of sales and contracts, **contributory negligence** of the buyer is *no* defense to an action against the seller for breach of warranty. Contributory negligence is a tort concept and does not apply to contract actions.

If the buyer discovers a defect in the goods that may cause injury and nevertheless proceeds to make use of them, he will not be permitted to recover damages from the seller for loss or injuries caused by such use. This is not contributory negligence but **voluntary assumption** of a known risk.

STRICT LIABILITY IN TORT

The most recent and far-reaching development in the field of product liability is that of strict liability in tort. All but a very few States have now accepted the concept, which is embodied in **Section 402A** of the Restatement, Second, Torts. It imposes liability only on a person who is in the *business* of selling the product involved. It does not apply to an occasional seller who is not in the business of selling the product, such as a person who trades in his used car or who sells his lawn mower to a neighbor. It is similar in this respect to the implied warranty of merchantability, which applies only to sales by a merchant of goods of the type in which he deals.

NATURE OF STRICT LIABILITY IN TORT

Section 402A imposes **strict liability in tort** on merchant sellers for both personal injuries and property damage for selling the product in a **defective condition, unreasonably dangerous** to the user or consumer. Specifically, this section provides:

1. One who sells any product in a defective condition unreasonably dangerous to the user or consumer or to his property is subject to liability for physical harm thereby caused to the ultimate user or consumer, or to his property, if (a) the seller is engaged in the business of selling such a product, and (b) it is expected to and does reach the user or consumer without substantial change in the condition in which it is sold.

2. The rule stated in Subsection (1) applies although (a) the seller has exercised all possible care in the preparation and sale of his products, and (b) the user or consumer has not bought the product from or entered into any contractual relation with the seller.

We emphasize that negligence is *not* the basis of this liability; it applies even though the seller has exercised all possible care in the preparation and sale of his product. The seller is not an insurer of the goods that he manufactures or sells, however, and the essential requirements for this type of liability are (1) that the defendant sold the product in a defective condition; (2) that the defendant was engaged in the business of selling such a product; (3) that the defective condition made the product unreasonably dangerous to the user or consumer or to his property; (4) that the defect in the product existed at the time it left the hands of the defendant; (5) that the plaintiff sustained physical harm or property damage by use or consumption of the product; (6) that the defective condition was attributable to the defendant; and (7) that the defective condition was the proximate cause of the injury or damage. For an interesting case deciding whether a plaintiff must prove that the defendant's product caused his injury, see Law in the News at page 398.

Way Is Cleared for DES Damage Claims

ALBANY, April 4—New York State's highest court today issued the broadest guidelines of any state in the nation for women to recover damages from manufacturers of the drug DES, which has been linked to cancer, miscarriages and infertility.

Under the Court of Appeals ruling, New York becomes the only state in which companies that made the drug can be held liable, even if they can prove that they did not manufacture the DES that a plaintiff says caused her injury.

The drug manufacturers' responsibility would be based entirely on the national share of the DES market that they held. Three other states—California, Wisconsin and Washington—have adopted this market-share theory but have ruled that a company is not liable if it can prove it did not sell the DES that caused a plaintiff's injury.

$3 Billion in Claims

The New York decision clears the way for processing hundreds of cases filed in the state, with damage claims topping $3 billion.

DES was a drug used by about two million pregnant American women from 1941 to 1970; it was prescribed to avert miscarriage and to quell morning sickness. It has since been blamed for a variety of medical problems, which sometimes took 20 or 30 years to become apparent, in the daughters of the women who took it.

The court, acknowledging the immense network of product liability issues raised by the DES cases, said they presented an "unprecedented identification problem," because it is generally impossible for a plaintiff to trace her injury back to a specific company.

The court's decision today did not address the question of whether people outside New York State could sue here for damages from DES. Lower-court rulings have held that the "cause of action" must have taken place in New York, meaning that the drug was either purchased or taken in the state.

In a companion ruling, the court upheld the constitutionality of a state law, passed in 1986, that extends the statute of limitations for cases involving DES and four other toxic substances whose effects, lawyers for victims assert, take several years to become evident. They are asbestos, chlordane, tungsten carbide and polyvinylchloride.

But in outlining its market-share theory, the court made clear that it was dealing only with DES and not the four other substances. Under existing rulings, then, plaintiffs in cases involving the other substances would still have to prove that an individual manufacturer caused them harm.

The DES ruling was immediately praised by women who said they had suffered from use of the drug. Lawyers for a consortium of major drug manufacturers now facing a battery of lawsuits were sharply critical.

"We won, but we're now in a place we should have been 10 years ago," said Mindy Hymowitz, a member of the DES Cancer Daughter's Network

---

This liability is imposed by law as a matter of public policy and does not depend on contract, either express or implied. It does not require reliance by the injured user or consumer on any statements made by the manufacturer or seller. The liability is not limited to persons in a relationship of buyer and seller; thus neither vertical nor horizontal privity is required. No notice of defect is required to have been given by the injured user or consumer. The liability, furthermore, is generally not subject to disclaimer, exclusion, or modification by contractual agreement. The liability is strictly in tort and arises out of the common law. It is not governed by the provisions of the Uniform Commercial Code. The majority of courts considering the question, however, have held that Section 402A imposes liability only for injury to person and damage to property but not for commercial loss (such as loss of bargain or profits), which is recoverable in an action for breach of warranty.

and a plaintiff in a lawsuit against the manufacturer's consortium.

Miss Hymowitz, a New York City resident who had a radical hysterectomy in 1979 after doctors diagnosed vaginal cancer said she was glad the case would go forward but doubted that victory in a trial would bring her a sense of relief.

"I lost the ability to bear a child," she said. "No amount of money can replace that." Her mother took DES in 1954.

Lawyers for several companies that once manufactured DES said the court's decision could set what they described as an unfair precedent for liability cases.

Ruling Called Unique

"This is the only decision I am aware of in which someone who can absolutely prove they were not the party who manufactured the product which is alleged to have caused the damage can nevertheless be found liable for even a portion of the damages," said Jay P. Mayesh, a lawyer who represents the Upjohn Company of Kalamazoo, Mich.

But some company lawyers said they were pleased that the court, in adopting the market-share theory, had declined to embrace another legal theory under which a single manufacturer could be held liable for all damages arising from a woman's injury.

"At least they have carefully limited the liability here to the percentage that the company held of the market," said Theodore Mayer, who represents Merck & Company of Rahway, N.J.

Under the court's decision, a plaintiff who wins a lawsuit could recover damages from several manufacturers, with each company's share based on the national market share that it held when the plaintiff or the plaintiff's mother took the drug.

Only Those Sued Affected

For example, a woman who was awarded $1 million in a suit would collect $500,000 from a company with 50 percent of the market share, $250,000 from a company with 25 percent of the market, and so on.

The consortium of manufacturers now being sued in New York City represents the great majority of companies holding market shares, thus insuring that a victorious plaintiff would get most, but not all, of the money that a jury awards, said Aaron Twersky, a professor at Brooklyn Law School who is the author of a casebook on product liability cases.

Aside from Upjohn and Merck, the other companies sued in the case heard by the Court of Appeals case are Eli Lilly & Company, E. R. Squibb & Sons, the Abbott Company, the Boyle Company and the Rorer Company.

Chief Judge Sol Wachtler, who wrote the majority decision, strongly defended New York's course in going beyond other states on the liability issue.

"Because liability here is based on the overall risk produced, and not causation in a single case, there should be no exculpation of a defendant who, although a member of the market producing DES for pregnancy use, appears not to have caused a particular plaintiff's injury," Judge Wachtler wrote.

Although liability for personal injuries caused by defective goods is usually associated with sales of goods, this liability also exists on **leases** and **bailments** of defective goods. The extension of liability to lessors and bailors of goods is not surprising in view of the rationale developed by the courts in imposing strict liability in tort on manufacturers and sellers of products. The danger to which the public is exposed by defectively manufactured cars and trucks traveling on the highways is not greatly different from the hazards of defectively maintained cars and trucks leased to operators.

Defective Condition

In an action against a defendant manufacturer or seller to recover damages under the rule of strict liability in tort, the plaintiff must prove a defective condition in the product, but she is not required to prove how or why or in what manner the product became defective. In an action based on 402A liability, the reason or cause of the defect is not material. The plaintiff, however, must show that at the time she was injured the condition of the product was not substantially changed from what it was at the time it was sold by the defendant manufacturer or seller. In general, defects may arise through faulty manufacturing, through faulty product design, or through inadequate warning, labeling, packaging, or instructions.

Manufacturing Defect A **manufacturing defect** occurs when the product is not properly made; that is, it fails to meet its own manufacturing specifications. For instance, suppose a chair is manufactured with legs designed to be attached by four screws and glue. If the chair was produced without inserting the appropri-

ate screws, this would constitute a manufacturing defect.

Design Defect A product contains a **design defect** when it is produced as specified but is dangerous or hazardous because its design is inadequate. Design defects can result from a number of causes, including poor engineering, poor choice of materials, and poor packaging. An example of a design defect that received great notoriety was the Ford Pinto. A number of courts found the car to be inadequately designed because the fuel tank had been placed too close to its rear axle, causing the fuel tank to rupture when the car was hit from the rear. Another example involving an alleged design defect is provided in the following case.

HECKMAN v. FEDERAL PRESS CO.
United States Court of Appeals, Third Circuit, 1979.
587 F.2d 612.

Facts: Heckman, an employee of Clark Equipment Company, severely injured his left hand when he caught it in a power press that he was operating at work. The press was manufactured by Federal Press Company and sold to Clark in 1970. It could be operated either by hand controls that required the use of both hands away from the point of operation or by an optional foot pedal. When the foot pedal was used without a guard, nothing remained to keep the operator's hands from the point of operation. Federal Press did not provide safety appliances unless the customer requested them, but when it delivered the press to Clark with the optional pedal, it suggested that Clark install a guard. The press had a similar warning embossed on it. Clark did, in fact, purchase a guard for $100, but it was not mounted on the machine at the time of the injury nor was it believed to be an effective safety device.

Heckman argued that one type of guard, if installed, would have made the press safe in 95 percent of its customary uses. Federal, in turn, argued that the furnishing of guards was not customary in the industry; that the machine's many uses made it impracticable to design and install any one guard as standard equipment; that Clark's failure to obey Federal's warning was a superseding cause of the injury; and that State regulations placed responsibility for the safe operation of presses on employers and employees. The jury awarded Heckman $750,000 and Federal appeals.

Decision: The judgment as to Federal's liability is affirmed, but a new trial is granted due to reversible error in the award of damages.

Opinion: **Weis, J.** * * * In *Webb v. Zern*, [citation], Pennsylvania adopted the strict liability provisions of § 402A of the Restatement (Second) of Torts. Cases interpreting this section have held that lack of proper safety devices can constitute a defective design which may subject the manufacturer of machinery to liability. [Citations.]

We find the present case quite similar on its facts to *Capasso v. Minster Machine Co.*, [citation], which also discussed a power press injury. There, as here, a two button system provided protection in manual operation, but no guard was provided when the optional foot control pedal was used. The manufacturer failed to provide any proposals for a safety guard and a device of the customer's own design proved to be ineffective. We held that since the original purchase included the optional foot switch, its use did not as a matter of law constitute a "substantial change" in the machinery within the scope of § 402(A)(1)(b) absolving the manufacturer; nor did the use of the inadequate shield act as a superseding cause as a matter of law. [Citations.] We concluded that the issue of a defect in the press at delivery was for the jury.

Similarly here, plaintiff's expert maintained that the defendant should have provided safeguards to be used in connection with the foot pedal operation, and that effective implements were available at a reasonable cost. [Citation.]

Federal asserts that the bolster plate which Clark had installed blocked the operator's view of the machine's warning plate, and that this screening constituted a superseding cause insulating the manufacturer from liability. Thus, Federal's theory is that when Clark obscured the warning sign it effected a substantial change that became a superseding cause of the accident. But it cannot be said that as a matter of law the decreased visibility of the plaque was such a major departure from the original design of the machine as to cut off the manufacturer's obligations. [Citation.] Particularly is this so when the sign was addressed to a condition that was not latent. We are unwilling to accept the proposition that the warning plate in and of itself absolved Federal as a matter of law. As we observed in *Schell v. AMF, Inc.*, [citation]:

> [A]s a matter of policy, it is questionable whether a manufacturer which produces a machine without minimal available safeguards is entitled to escape liability by warning of a dangerous condition which could reasonably have been avoided by a better design.

In the circumstances here, the warning issue was for the jury as was the defense of assumption of the risk. [Citation.]

Federal also maintains that it was exculpated as a matter of law because regulations of the Pennsylvania Department of Labor and Industry requiring the use of point-of-operation devices placed the responsibility upon the employer and employee. We do not accept this premise. Whatever effect the regulations might have as between employer and employee does not extend to relieve the manufacturer of its liability under § 402A as a matter of law. If a manufacturer fails to provide reasonable safety devices for a product and thus creates an unreasonable risk of harm to the user, the fact that the manufacturer may expect the user to provide a protective appliance is not sufficient to preclude liability in most circumstances. [Citations.] The issue is one which should be decided by a jury in light of such matters as the feasibility of incorporating safety features during manufacture of the machine, the likelihood that users will not secure adequate devices, whether the machinery is of a standard make or built to the customer's specifications, the relative expertise of manufacturer and customer, the extent of risk to the user, and the seriousness of injury which may be anticipated.

Since lawsuits under Section 402A often are brought many years after the product is sold, advances in technology made after the sale frequently demonstrate that there are safer ways to design the product. This raises the question whether a manufacturer should be liable if it uses technology that is **state of the art** at the time but subsequently proves to be unsafe by future standards. In most States, either by common law or statute, the determination of adequate design is made in accordance with state of the art technology at the time the product was designed and not by standards at the time of litigation.

Inadequate Warning, Instructions, or Packaging A seller has a duty to provide adequate warning of possible danger, to provide appropriate directions for safe use, and to safely package the product. Nevertheless, inadequate and dangerous products, regardless of their warning, will be held to be defective, especially if there are superior alternative designs or manufacturing procedures.

Typically, warnings or instructions are needed to ensure that appropriately designed and manufactured products are properly used. Comment j to Section 402A provides that in

some instances, "in order to prevent the product from being unreasonably dangerous, the seller may be required to give directions or warning, on the container, as to its use." For example, in a number of cases, drug companies have been found liable for inadequately warning of the dangerous and not infrequent side effects of one of its drugs.

Almost any product may be used or misused in a manner that may cause physical harm. The blow of a poorly aimed hammer may crush a thumb. The inhaling of a feather may damage a lung. The use of a sled on a busy street may endanger the child using it. The excessive drinking of liquor is dangerous. Allowing children to play with firearms is also dangerous. These hazards arise when products are used in a way that they were not intended by the supplier to be used, and generally no duty is imposed on the manufacturer or seller to give warning against the possible dangers that might arise from such misuse of the product.

The duty to give a warning arises out of a foreseeable danger of physical harm arising out of the normal or probable use of the product and the likelihood that unless warned, the user or consumer will not ordinarily be aware of such danger or hazard.

TOUPS v. SEARS, ROEBUCK AND CO.
Supreme Court of Louisiana, 1987.
507 So.2d 809.

Facts: Shawn Toups, a three-year-old child, was injured when a hot water heater purchased from Sears, Roebuck and Co. exploded. The explosion was caused by leakage from overfilling a gasoline-powered lawn mower. The gasoline vapors were sucked into the air intake system of the water heater, resulting in a flashback explosion. Sears provided no precautionary warning of the danger involved in having gasoline appliances within fifteen feet of the water heater. The Toups brought a strict product liability action against Sears. The jury ruled in favor of Sears and the Toups appeal.

Decision: Judgment reversed and remanded.

Opinion: **Watson, J.** The jury apparently concluded that this hot water heater was not defective because it was a standard model similar to countless others on the market at the time. Because of erroneous trial rulings, the jury did not have the benefit of the manufacturer/vendor's knowledge of the hidden danger inherent in this hot water heater. The jury was unaware that precautionary warnings were not only needed but were subsequently added to later Sears' models and manuals, proving that they were feasible. In addition, the jury was not specifically asked about Sears' failure to warn its consumers of the danger involved in having gasoline appliances within fifteen feet of the hot water heater. [Citation.]

* * *

The jury was instructed at length about negligence and assumption of the risk and was charged: "A defense to liability in a case of this type may be assumption of the risk or contributory negligence."

The jury was also charged: "As a general rule, a seller or vendor of a product is not presumed to know of any latent defects in the product he sells."

In pertinent part, the interrogatories submitted to the jury only asked if the water heater was defective. No interrogatories were submitted to the jury on the issues of failure to warn or failure to adopt an alternative design.

Plaintiffs objected to the trial court's failure to submit a jury interrogatory on failure to warn and also objected to the jury being charged that a design is not defective if reasonable care is taken in its adoption.

"[I]n order to recover from a manufacturer, the plaintiff must prove that the harm resulted from the condition of the product, that the condition made the product unreasonably dangerous to normal use, and that the condition existed at the time the product left the manufacturer's control. The plaintiff need not prove negligence by the maker in its manufacture or processing, since the manufacturer may be liable even though it exercised all possible care in the preparation and sale of its product." [Citations.]

"Although a product is not unreasonably dangerous per se or flawed by a construction defect, it may still be an unreasonably dangerous product if the manufacturer fails to adequately warn about a danger related to the way the product is designed. A manufacturer is required to provide an adequate warning of any danger inherent in the normal use of its product which is not within the knowledge of or obvious to the ordinary user." [Citations.]

Even if the utility of a product outweighs its danger, if the product could feasibly be designed to be less hazardous, the manufacturer is liable. [Citation.]

A manufacturer is presumed to know of the defects in its product and is therefore required to protect persons against foreseeable risks of injury by adequate warnings.

In generally, remedial measures taken after an incident of negligent conduct are not admissible in evidence because such evidence would discourage people from taking steps to prevent future harm. [Citations.] Because of this exclusionary rule, the trial court here did not allow evidence of subsequent warnings added to Sears' water heaters and users' manuals.

The policy considerations which exclude evidence of remedial measures in negligence cases are not applicable where strict liability is involved. [Citations.]

In a strict product liability case, evidence of such remedial measures should be allowed insofar as they are relevant in establishing what the manufacturer knew or should have known at the time of the injury.

* * *

"Contributory negligence does not apply in strict products liability cases. The principle of comparative fault may be applied in some products cases . . ." [Citation.]

The trial court erred in instructing the jury that: "a seller or vendor of a product is not presumed to know of any latent defects in the product he sells." There was no question at trial that Sears, which marketed the product under its brand name, was a professional vendor, with the same responsibility as the manufacturer. In this factual context, the instruction, even though later corrected and qualified, was erroneous.

The phrase "duty to warn" can be misleading because it tends to focus attention on the reasonableness of defendants in failing to give a warning and strict liability should not focus on the question of fault. This is the basis for the distinction in [citation] between products which are "unreasonably dangerous per se" and those strict liability cases based on failure to warn of foreseeable dangers. In the latter, a balancing test is used to determine whether the manufacturer could have reasonably known of the danger and should have issued a warning. [Citation.] The simplistic jury charge that a design is not defective if reasonable care is taken in its adoption was inaccurate, it did not explain the balancing test required in failure to warn cases.

The jury interrogatories failed to inquire whether the hot water heater was defective for lack of a warning, a trial error which must have influenced the jury's verdict.

In sum, the numerous trial errors here resulted in a jury verdict that was clearly wrong. [Citations.] When Sears' prior knowledge is considered in conjunction with adoption of later warnings, the inescapable conclusion is a breach of the duty to warn.

* * *

For the foregoing reasons, the judgment of the court of appeal is reversed, and the matter is remanded to the court of appeal to fix the quantum of damages.

In addition to warning of dangers, the seller must provide adequate directions for the safe and efficient use of the product as well as adequate packaging of the product. Furthermore, whenever a deviation from the directions may give rise to a serious danger to the user, the seller must provide warning of this danger.

Unreasonably Dangerous

Section 402A liability only applies if the defective product is unreasonably dangerous to the user or consumer. A **unreasonably dangerous** product is one that contains a danger beyond that which would be contemplated by the ordinary consumer who purchases it with the common knowledge of its characteristics. Thus, Comment i to Section 402A states: "good whiskey is not unreasonably dangerous merely because it will make some people drunk, and is especially dangerous to alcoholics; but bad whiskey, containing a dangerous amount of fuel oil, is unreasonably dangerous. Good tobacco is not unreasonably dangerous merely because the effects of smoking may be harmful; but tobacco containing something like marijuana may be unreasonably dangerous. Good butter is not unreasonably dangerous merely because, if such be the case, it deposits cholesterol in the arteries and leads to heart attacks; but bad butter, contaminated with poisonous fish oil, is unreasonably dangerous." Most courts have left the question of what a consumer reasonably expects to find to the jury.

OBSTACLES TO RECOVERY

Disclaimers and Notice

Comment m to Section 402A provides that the basis of strict liability rests solely in tort and therefore is not subject to contractual defenses.

The comment specifically states that strict product liability is not governed by the Code, that it is not affected by contractual limitations or disclaimers, and that it is not subject to any requirement that notice be given to the seller by the injured party within a reasonable time. Nevertheless, most courts have *allowed* clear and specific disclaimers of Section 402A liability in *commercial* transactions between merchants of relatively equal economic power.

Privity

Horizontal Privity   The strict liability in tort of manufacturers and other sellers extends not only to buyers, users, and consumers, but also to injured bystanders.

Vertical Privity   The rule of strict liability in tort, as formulated in Section 402A, imposes liability on the seller for physical harm to the ultimate user or consumer of the defective product. Such liability extends to any seller who is engaged in the business of selling the product, including a wholesaler or distributor as well as the manufacturer and retailer.

The rule of strict liability in tort also applies to the manufacturer of a defective component part that is used in a larger product where no essential change has been made in it by the manufacturer of the finished product. Moreover, the manufacturer of a defective component is not excused from liability because the manufacturer of the finished product failed to discover the defect by testing or inspection. The manufacturer of the finished product is also liable for damages caused by a defective condition of the goods resulting exclusively from a defective component part.

Finally, a growing number of jurisdictions recognize the applicability of strict liability in tort to merchant sellers of used goods. One court has stated in a case involving the sale of a used automobile that "the safety of the general public demands that when a used motor vehicle, for example, is sold for use as a *serviceable motor vehicle* (and not as junk parts), absent special circumstances, the seller be responsible for safety defects whether known or unknown at the time of sale, present while the machine was under his control."

Plaintiff's Conduct

Contributory Negligence   At common law in an action based on negligence, contributory negligence of the plaintiff completely barred recovery. Contributory negligence generally is immaterial in an action based on strict liability in tort, although a few States have held contributory negligence to be a valid defense. The minority view, however, which totally bars the plaintiff from recovery, is contrary to the principle of strict liability and is contrary to Comment n to Section 402A.

Comparative Negligence   Many States have adopted the rule of comparative negligence in negligence actions. This rule diminishes the amount of a plaintiff's recovery in proportion to his fault. In response to the doctrinal difficulties and inequities of applying contributory negligence to strict liability in tort, a growing number of courts and legislatures have applied the principle of comparative negligence to strict liability in tort.

Voluntary Assumption of the Risk   Assumption of risk is a defense in an action based on strict liability in tort. The user or consumer who voluntarily uses the goods in an unusual, inappropriate, or improper manner for which they were not intended, and that under the circumstances is unreasonable, assumes the risk of injuries that result from such use. Thus, a person who drives an automobile after realizing that the brakes are not in working order or an employee who attempts to remove a foreign object from a high-speed roller press without shutting off the power have assumed the risk of their own injuries.

To establish such defense, the burden is on the defendant to show that (1) the plaintiff actually knew and appreciated the particular risk or danger created by the defect, (2) the plaintiff voluntarily encountered the risk while realizing the danger, and (3) the plaintiff's decision to encounter the known risk was unreasonable.

Misuse or Abuse of the Product   Closely connected to voluntary assumption of the risk is the valid defense of misuse or abuse of the product by the injured party. The major difference is that misuse or abuse includes actions that the injured party does not know to be dangerous, whereas assumption of the risk does not include such conduct. Instances of such misuse or abuse include standing on a rocking chair to change a light bulb or using a lawn mower to trim hedges.

The courts, however, have significantly limited this defense by requiring that the misuse or abuse not be foreseeable by the seller. If a use is foreseeable, then the seller must take measures to guard against it. Thus, a manufacturer has been held liable for injuries to a stevedore, who was injured while walking on cargo, for failing to package its cargo so as to avoid such injury. It was found foreseeable that stevedores would walk on the cargo.

Subsequent Alteration

Section 402A provides that liability only exists if the product reaches "the user or consumer without substantial change in the condition in which it is sold." Accordingly, most but not all courts would not hold a manufacturer liable for a faulty carburetor if the retailer had removed the part and made significant changes in it before reinserting it into the automobile.

KENNEDY v. CUSTOM ICE EQUIPMENT CO., INC.
Supreme Court of South Carolina, 1978.
271 S.C. 171, 246 S.E.2d 176.

Facts: Kennedy was fifteen years old and working his first job as an employee of Georgetown Ice Company. On his third day at work, he was instructed to empty ice storage bins that were fed by an overhead conveyor. The machinery had been designed and installed by Custom Ice Equipment Company. It was common for the ice to freeze and not fall out of the bins through the trap doors. Thus, it had to be physically dislodged. Georgetown had constructed a catwalk alongside the bins from which its employees would reach into them and break up the frozen ice with a garden hoe. Kennedy proceeded to dislodge the frozen ice with a hoe and was drawn into the conveyor by his left arm, which was then torn off. Kennedy brought suit against Custom for the amputation of his left arm, claiming strict liability in tort. Custom defends on the ground that Georgetown modified the conveyor when it constructed the catwalk, creating the defect and relieving Custom of liability. Custom appeals from a judgment in favor of Kennedy.

Judgment for Kennedy in the amount of $208,000 affirmed.

Opinion: Gregory, J.   The test of whether a product is defective when sold is whether the product is unreasonably dangerous to the consumer or user given the conditions and circumstances that will foreseeably attend the use of the product. Under this test, the jury could have determined that the construction of the catwalk by Georgetown was a foreseeable circumstance that required the incorporation of protective shields in the design of the conveyor. [Citation.]

The evidence created a factual question of whether respondent's injuries were proximately caused by a defect in the product as designed or by a defect created by an unforeseeable modification by a third party. [Citation.]

In Young v. Tide Craft, Inc., [citation], we held the question of proximate cause was improperly submitted to the jury where the only reasonable inference to be drawn from the evidence was that the product was not defective as designed. Since the evidence here is susceptible of the inference that the product was defective as designed, the trial judge did not err by submitting the question of proximate cause to the jury. [Citations.]

Statute of Repose

A number of lawsuits have been brought against manufacturers many years after the product had been first sold. In one case, a manufacturer was successfully sued twenty-two years after a defective water-meter was first purchased and fourteen years after it was installed in the plaintiff's home. In another case, Volkswagen of America was ordered to pay $1.8 million in damages for a missing door latch costing $.35. The accident occurred ten years after the car had been manufactured and nine years after Volkswagen had informed its dealers to repair the defect.

In response to this threat of continued liability, many States have adopted statutes of repose. These enactments limit the time period—typically between six to twelve years—for which a manufacturer is liable for injury caused by its product. After the statutory time period has elapsed, a manufacturer ceases to be liable for harm caused by its defective products.

Figure 19–2 compares strict liability in tort with the implied warranty of merchantability.

FIGURE 19-2 Products Liability

	Warranty of Merchantability	Strict Liability in Tort
Condition of goods	Not fit for ordinary purpose	Defective condition, unreasonably dangerous
Character of defendant	Seller who is a merchant with respect to the goods sold	Seller who is engaged in the business of selling such a product
Disclaimer	Permitted if: 1) specific 2) conspicuous 3) conscionable subject to Magnuson–Moss Act	None possible in consumer transaction; most courts allow in commercial transactions
Notice	Within reasonable time	None required
Causation	Required	Required
Protected Harm	Alt. A: To person of buyer, family, or guests in home Alt.B: To person of anyone reasonably to be expected to use product Alt. C: To person reasonably to be expected to use product or to his property	Physical harm to person or property of the ultimate user or consumer; Judicial trend towards including bystanders
Type of Transaction	Sales; some courts apply to leases* and bailments	Sales, leases, and bailments

* Article 2A, where adopted, applies to leases

CHAPTER SUMMARY

WARRANTIES

Types of Warranties	**Definition of Warranty** an obligation of the seller to the buyer concerning title, quality, characteristics, or condition of goods **Express Warranty** an affirmation of fact or promise about the goods or a description, including a sample, of the goods which becomes part of the basis of the bargain **Warranty of Title** the obligation of a seller to convey the right to ownership without any lien **Implied Warranty** a contractual obligation arising out of certain circumstances of the sale which is imposed by operation of law and is not found in the language of the sales contract ■ *Merchantability* warranty by a merchant seller that the goods are reasonably fit for the ordinary purpose for which they are manufactured or sold, and that they be of fair, average quality ■ *Fitness for Particular Purpose* warranty by any seller that the goods are reasonably fit for the particular purpose, if at the time of contracting, the seller had reason to know the buyer's particular purpose and that the buyer was relying on the seller's skill and judgment to furnish suitable goods
Obstacles to Warranty Actions	**Disclaimer of Warranties** a negation of a warranty ■ *Warranty of Title* may be excluded or modified by specific language or by certain circumstances, including judicial sale or a sale by a sheriff, executor, or foreclosing lienor ■ *Express Warranty* very difficult to disclaim ■ *Implied Warranty of Merchantability* the disclaimer must mention "merchantability" and, in the case of a writing, it must be conspicuous ■ *Implied Warranty of Fitness for a Particular Purpose* the disclaimer must be in writing and conspicuous ■ *Other Disclaimers of Implied Warranties* the implied warranties of merchantability and fitness for a particular purpose may also be disclaimed (1) by expressions like "as is," "with all fault," or other similar language; (2) by course of dealing, course of performance, or usage of trade; or (3) as to defects an examination ought to have revealed where the buyer has examined the goods or where the buyer has refused to examine the goods ■ *Federal Legislation Relating to Warranties of Consumer Goods* the Magnuson-Moss Warranty Act protects purchasers of consumer goods by providing that warranty information be clear and useful and that a seller who makes a written warranty cannot disclaim any implied warranty **Privity of Contract** a contractual relationship between parties that was necessary at common law to maintain a lawsuit ■ *Horizontal Privity* doctrine determining who benefits from a warranty and therefore may bring a cause of action; the Code provides three alternatives ■ *Vertical Privity* doctrine determining who in the chain of distribution is liable for a breach of warranty; the Code has not adopted a position on this

Notice of Breach if the buyer fails to notify the seller of any breach within a reasonable time, she is barred from any remedy against the seller
Plaintiff's Conduct
- *Contributory Negligence* is not a defense
- *Voluntary Assumption of the Risk* is a defense

STRICT LIABILITY IN TORT

Nature	**General Rule** imposes tort liability on merchant sellers for both personal injuries and property damage for selling a product in a defective condition, unreasonably dangerous to the user or consumer

Defective Condition
- *Manufacturing Defect* the product is not properly made by failing to meet its own manufacturing specifications
- *Design Defect* the product is made as designed, but the product is dangerous because the design is inadequate
- *Inadequate Warning or Instructions* failure to provide adequate warning of possible danger or to provide appropriate directions for use of a product

Unreasonably Dangerous contains a danger beyond that which would be contemplated by the ordinary consumer

Obstacles to Recovery	**Plaintiff's Conduct**

- *Contributory Negligence* not a defense in the majority of States
- *Comparative Negligence* most States have applied the rule of comparative negligence to strict liability in tort
- *Voluntary Assumption of the Risk* is a defense
- *Misuse or Abuse of the Product* is a defense

Subsequent Alteration liability only exists if the product reaches the user or consumer without substantial change in the condition in which it is sold
Statute of Repose limits the time period for which a manufacturer is liable for injury caused by its product
Other Defenses contractual defenses, such as privity, disclaimers, and notice, generally do not apply to tort liability

QUESTIONS

1. Identify and describe the types of warranties.
2. Discuss the various defenses that may be successfully raised to a warranty action.
3. Describe the elements of an action based upon strict liability in tort.
4. Discuss the obstacles to an action based upon strict liability in tort.
5. Compare strict liability in tort with the implied warranty of merchantability.

PROBLEMS

1. At the start of the social season, Aunt Lavinia purchased a hula skirt in Sadie's dress shop. The saleswoman told her: "This superior garment will do things for a person." Aunt Lavinia's houseguest, her niece, Florabelle, asked and obtained her aunt's permission to wear the skirt to a masquerade ball. In the midst of the festivity, where there was much dancing, drinking, and smoking, the long skirt brushed against a glimmering cigarette butt. Un-

known to Aunt Lavinia and Florabelle, its wearer, the garment was made of a fine unwoven fiber that is highly flammable. It burst into flames, and Florabelle suffered severe burns. Aunt Lavinia notified Sadie of the accident and of Florabelle's intention to recover from Sadie. Florabelle seeks to recover damages in action against Sadie, the proprietor of the dress shop, and Exotic Clothes, Inc., the manufacturer from which Sadie purchased the skirt. Decision?

2. The Talent Company, manufacturer of a widely advertised and expensive perfume, sold a quantity of this product to Young, a retail druggist. Dorothy and Bird visited the store of Young, and Dorothy, desiring to make a gift to Bird, purchased a bottle of this perfume from Young, asking for it by its trade name. Young wrapped up the bottle and handed it directly to Bird. The perfume contained an injurious foreign chemical substance that upon the first use of the perfume by Bird, severely burned her face and caused a permanent facial disfigurement. What are the rights of Bird, if any, against Dorothy, Young, and the Talent Company?

3. John Doe purchased a bottle of "Bleach-All," a well-known brand, from Roe's combination service station and grocery store. When John used the "Bleach-All," the clothes severely deteriorated due to an error made in mixing the chemicals during manufacture of "Bleach-All." John brings an action against Roe to recover damages. Decision?

4. A route salesman for Ideal Milk Company delivered a one-half gallon glass jug of milk to Allen's home. The next day when Allen grasped the milk container by its neck to take it out of his refrigerator, it shattered in his hand and caused serious injury. Allen paid Ideal on a monthly basis for the regular delivery of milk. Ideal's milk bottles each contained the legend "Property of Ideal—to be returned," and the route salesman would pick up the empty bottles when he delivered milk. Allen brought an action against Ideal Milk Company. Decision?

5. While Butler and his wife Wanda were browsing through Sloan's used car lot, Butler told Sloan that he was looking for a safe but cheap family car. Sloan said, "That old Cadillac hearse ain't hurt at all, and I'll sell it to you for $2,950." Butler said, "I'll have to take your word for it because I don't know a thing about cars." Butler asked Sloan whether he would guarantee the car, and Sloan replied, "I don't guarantee used cars." Then Sloan added, "But I have checked that Caddy over, and it will run another 10,000 miles without needing any repairs." Butler replied, "It has to because I won't have an extra dime for any repairs." Butler made a down payment of $400 and signed a printed form contract furnished by Sloan that contained a provision, "Seller does not warrant the condition or performance of any used automobile."

As Butler drove the car out of Sloan's lot, the left rear wheel fell off, and Butler lost control of the vehicle. It veered over an embankment, causing serious injuries to Wanda. What is Sloan's liability to Butler and Wanda?

6. John purchased for cash a Revenge automobile manufactured by Japanese Motors, Ltd., from an authorized franchise dealer in the United States. The dealer told John that the car had a "twenty-four months—24,000 miles warranty." Two days after John accepted delivery of the car, he received an eighty-page manual in fine print that stated, among other things, on page 72:

> The warranties herein are expressly in lieu of any other express or implied warranty, including any implied warranty of merchantability or fitness, and of any other obligation on the part of the company or the seller dealer.
>
> Japanese Motors, Ltd., and the selling dealer warrant to the owner each part of this vehicle to be free under use and service from defects in material and workmanship for a period of twenty-four months from the date of original retail delivery of first use or until it has been driven for 24,000 miles, whichever first occurs.

Within nine months after the purchase, John was forced to return the car for repairs to the dealer on thirty different occasions, and the car has been in the dealer's custody for over seventy days during these nine months. The dealer has been forced to make major repairs of the engine, transmission, and steering assembly. The car is now in the custody of the dealer for further major repairs, and John has demanded that it keep the car and refund his entire purchase price. The dealer has refused on the ground that it has not breached its contract and is willing to continue repairing the car during the remainder of the "twenty-four—twenty-four" period. What are the rights and liabilities of the dealer and John?

7. Fred Lyon of New York, while on vacation in California, rented a new model Home Run automobile from Hart's Drive-A-Car. The car was manufactured by the Ange Motor Company and was purchased by Hart's from Jammer, Inc., an automobile importer. Lyon was driving the car on a street in San Jose when, due to a defect in the steering mechanism, it suddenly became impossible to steer. The speed of the car at the time was thirty miles per hour, but before Lyon could bring it to a stop, the car jumped a low curb and struck Peter Wolf, who

was standing on the sidewalk, breaking both of his legs and causing other injuries. Wolf sues Hart's Drive-A-Car, the Ange Motors Company, Jammer, Inc., and Lyon. Decisions?

8. Plaintiff brings this cause of action against a manufacturer for the loss of one leg below the hip. The leg was lost when caught in the gears of a screw auger machine sold and installed by the defendant. Shortly before the accident, plaintiff's co-employees had removed a covering panel from the machine by use of sledgehammers and crowbars in order to do repair work. When finished, they replaced the panel with a single piece of cardboard instead of restoring the equipment to its original condition. The plaintiff stepped on the cardboard in the course of his work and fell, catching his leg in the moving parts. Decision?

9. The plaintiff, while driving a van manufactured by the defendant, was struck in the rear by another motor vehicle. Upon impact, the plaintiff's head was jarred backward against the rear window of the cab, causing the plaintiff serious injury. The van was not equipped with a headrest, and none was required at the time. Should the plaintiff prevail on a cause of action based upon strict liability in tort? Why?

10. Plaintiff, while dining at defendant's restaurant, ordered a chicken pot pie. While she was eating the food, she swallowed a sliver of chicken bone, which became lodged in her throat, causing her serious injury. Plaintiff brings a cause of action. Should she prevail? Why?

11. Salem Supply Co. sells new and used gardening equipment. Ben Buyer purchased a slightly used riding lawn mower for $1,500. The price was considerably less than comparable mowers. The sale was clearly indicated to be "as is." Two weeks after Ben purchased the mower, the police arrived at his house with Owen Owner, the true owner of the lawn mower, which was stolen from his yard, and reclaimed the mower. What recourse, if any, does Ben have?

12. Seigel, a seventy-three-year-old man, was injured at one of Giant Food's retail food stores when a bottle of Coca-Cola exploded as he was placing a six-pack of Coke into his shopping cart. The explosion caused him to lose his balance and fall, with injuries resulting. Seigel brought suit against Giant Food for damages allegedly caused by Giant's breach of its implied warranty of merchantability. The trial court granted judgment in favor of Giant, and Seigel brought this appeal. Decision?

13. Guarino and two others (plaintiffs) died of gas asphyxiation and five others were injured when they entered a sewer tunnel without masks to answer the cries for help of their crew leader, Rooney. Rooney had left the sewer shaft and entered the tunnel to fix a water leakage problem. Having corrected the problem, Rooney was returning to the shaft when he apparently was overcome by gas because of a defect in his oxygen mask manufactured by Mine Safety Appliance Company (defendant). Plaintiffs brought this action against the defendant for breach of warranty, and defendant raised the defense of plaintiffs' voluntary assumption of the risk. Decision?

14. Green Seed Company packaged, labeled, and marketed a quality tomato seed known as "Green's Pink Shipper" for commercial sale. Brown Seed Store, a retailer, purchased the seed from Green Seed and then sold it to Guy Jones. Jones was an individual engaged in the business of growing tomato seedlings for sale to commercial tomato growers. Williams purchased the seedlings from Jones and then transplanted and raised them in accordance with accepted farming methods. The plants, however, produced not the promised "Pink Shipper" tomatoes but rather an inferior variety that spoiled in the field. Williams then brought an action against Green Seed for $900, claiming that his crop damage had been caused by Green Seed's breach of an express warranty. Green Seed argued in defense that its warranty did not extend to remote purchasers and that the company did not receive notice of the claimed breach of warranty. Decision?

15. Shell Oil Company leased to Flying Tiger Line a gasoline tank truck with a movable ladder for refueling certain types of aircraft. Under the terms of the lease, Flying Tiger was to maintain the equipment in safe operating order, but Shell was obligated to make most of the repairs at Flying Tiger's request. Four years after the lease was entered into, Shell, at Flying Tiger's request, replaced the original ladder with a new one built by an undisclosed manufacturer. Both Flying Tiger and Shell inspected the new ladder. Two years later, however, Price, an aircraft mechanic employed by Flying Tiger, was seriously injured when the ladder's legs split while he was climbing onto an airplane wing. Decision?

COMPUTER RESEARCH PROBLEMS

1. Mrs. Embs went into Stamper's Cash Market to buy soft drinks for her children. She removed five bottles from an upright soft drink cooler, placed them in a carton, and then turned to move away from the display when a bottle of

Seven-Up in a carton at her feet exploded, cutting her leg. Apparently, several other bottles had exploded that same week: Stamper's Cash Market received its entire stock of Seven-Up from Arnold Lee Vice, the area distributor. Vice in turn received his entire stock of Seven-Up from Pepsi-Cola Bottling Co. Decision?

2. Catania wished to paint the exterior of his house. He went to Brown, a local paint store owner, and asked him to recommend a paint for the job. Catania told Brown that the exterior walls were stucco, and in a chalky, powdery condition. Brown suggested Pierce's shingle and shake paint. Brown then instructed Catania how to mix the paint, and to use a wire brush to prepare the surface. Five months later the paint began to peel, flake, and blister. Catania brings an action against Brown. Decision?

3. Robinson, a truck driver for a moving company, decided to buy a used truck from the company. Branch, the owner, told Robinson that the truck was being repaired, and that Robinson should wait and inspect the truck before signing the contract. Robinson, who had driven the truck before, felt that inspection was unnecessary. Again, Branch suggested Robinson wait to inspect the truck, and again Robinson declined. Branch then told Robinson he was buying the truck "as is." Robinson then signed the contract. After the fourth time that the truck broke down, Robinson sued. Decision?

4. Perfect Products manufactures balloons, which are then bought and resold by wholesale novelty distributors. Mego Corp. manufactures a doll called "Bubble Yum Baby." A balloon is inserted in the doll's mouth with a mouthpiece, and the doll's arm is pumped to inflate the balloon, simulating the blowing of a bubble. Mego Corp. used Perfect Products balloons in the dolls, bought through the independent distributors. Plaintiff's infant daughter dies after swallowing a balloon removed from the doll. Planintiff sues Perfect Products, and others, on a theory of strict liability. Decision?

5. Patient was injured when the footrest of an adjustable X-ray table collapsed, causing Patient to fall to the floor. G.E. manufactured the X-ray table and the footrest. At trial evidence was introduced that G.E. had manufactured for several years another model footrest complete with safety latches. However, there was no evidence that the footrest involved was manufactured defectively. The action is based on a theory of strict liability. Who wins? Why?

ENDNOTES

1. Uniform Commercial Code, Section 2—313, Express Warranties by Affirmation, Promise, Description, Sample.

2. Uniform Commercial Code, Section 2—209, Modification, Rescission and Waiver.

3. Uniform Commercial Code, Section 2—312, Warranty of Title and Against Infringement; Buyer's Obligation Against Infringement.

4. Uniform Commercial Code, Section 2—314, Implied Warranty: Merchantability; Usage of Trade.

5. Uniform Commercial Code, Section 2—315, Implied Warranty: Fitness for Particular Purpose.

6. Uniform Commercial Code, Section 2—316, Exclusion or Modification of Warranties.

7. Uniform Commercial Code, Section 2—302, Unconscionable Contract or Clause.

8. Uniform Commercial Code, Section 2—318, Third Party Beneficiaries of Warranties Express or Implied.

9. Uniform Commercial Code, Section 2—607, Effect of Acceptance; Notice of Breach; Burden of Establishing Breach After Acceptance; Notice of Claim or Litigation to Person Answerable Over.

20 PERFORMANCE

Performance is the carrying out of a contract's obligations according to its terms so that the obligations are discharged. The basic obligation of the seller in a contract for the sale of goods is to transfer and deliver the goods, and that of the buyer is to accept and pay for the goods in accordance with the contract. A contract of sale also requires that each party not impair the other party's expectation of having the contract performed. Although the essential purpose of a contract is actual performance, an important feature is a continuing sense of reliance and security that performance will occur when due. If either the willingness or ability of a party to perform is put in doubt after contracting but before the time for performance, the other party is threatened with the loss of a substantial part of what he has bargained for. Therefore, when reasonable grounds for insecurity arise regarding either party's performance, the other party may demand written assurance and suspend his own performance until he receives that assurance. If adequate assurance of performance is not received within a reasonable time, there is a breach of the contract.

The obligations of the parties are determined by their contractual agreement. Thus the contract of sale may expressly state whether the seller must deliver the goods before receiving payment of the price or whether the buyer must pay the price before receiving the goods. If the contract does not sufficiently cover the particulars of performance, these terms will be supplied by the Code, common law, course of dealings, usage of trade, and course of performance. In all events, both parties to the sales contract must perform their contractual obligations in good faith. As we discussed in Chap-

ter 17, good faith is defined as honesty in fact in the conduct or transaction. In the case of merchants, the Code imposes the additional requirement that the merchants observe reasonable commercial standards of fair dealing.

In this chapter, we examine the performance obligations of the seller and the buyer as well as the circumstances under which they may be excused from performance of their contractual obligations.

PERFORMANCE BY THE SELLER

Unless the parties have agreed otherwise, the Code is explicit in requiring performance or tender of performance by one party as a condition to performance by the other party.[1] Tender of conforming goods by the seller entitles him to acceptance of them by the buyer and to payment of the price according to the contract. Nonetheless, the rights of the parties may be otherwise fixed by the terms of the contract. For example, if the seller has agreed to sell goods on sixty or ninety days' credit, he is required to perform his part of the contract before the buyer performs.

Tender of delivery requires that the seller put and hold goods that conform to the contract at the buyer's disposition and that he give the buyer reasonable notification to enable him to take delivery.[2] Tender must also be made at a reasonable time and kept open for a reasonable period of time. For example, Jim agrees to sell Joan a stereo system composed of a turntable, a receiver, a tape deck, and two speakers. Each component is specified by manufacturer and model number, and delivery is to be at Jim's store. Jim obtains the ordered equipment in accordance with the contractual specifications and notifies Joan that she may pick up the system at her convenience. Jim has now tendered and thus performed his obligations under the sales contract: he holds goods that conform to the contract, he has placed them at the buyer's disposition, and he has notified the buyer of their readiness.

Time and Manner of Delivery

Tender must be at a *reasonable* time, and the goods tendered must be kept available for the period reasonably necessary to enable the buyer to take possession of them.[2] If no definite time for delivery is fixed by the terms of the contract, the seller is allowed a reasonable time after the making of the contract within which to deliver the goods to the buyer. Likewise, the buyer has a reasonable time within which to accept delivery. What length of time is reasonable depends on the facts and circumstances of each case. If the goods can be delivered immediately, a reasonable time would be very short. If the goods must be constructed or manufactured, however, a reasonable time would be longer and would depend on all the circumstances, including the usual length of time required to make the goods.

A contract is not performable piecemeal or in installments unless the parties specifically so agree. If not so specified, all of the goods called for by a contract must be tendered in a single delivery, and payment is due on such tender.[3]

Place of Tender

If the contract does not specify the place for delivery of the goods, the place for delivery is the **seller's place of business,** or if he has none, his residence. If the contract is for the sale of identified goods that the parties know at the time of making the contract are located elsewhere than the seller's place of business or residence, the *location* of the goods is then the place for delivery.[4] For example, Arnold, a boat builder in Chicago, contracts to sell to Susan a certain yacht, which both parties know is anchored at Milwaukee. The place of delivery would be Milwaukee. On the other hand, if the contract provides that Arnold shall overhaul the motor at Arnold's shipyard in Chi-

cago, Arnold would have to return the yacht to Chicago, and the place of delivery would be Arnold's Chicago shipyard.

As we discussed in Chapter 18, the parties frequently agree expressly on the place of delivery, typically by use of one of the various *delivery terms.* Such agreements determine the place where the seller must tender delivery of the goods.

Shipment Contracts   The delivery terms *F.O.B. place of shipment, F.A.S. seller's port, C.I.F.,* and *C. &. F.* are all shipment contracts. Under a **shipment contract,** the seller is required or authorized to send the goods to the buyer, but the contract does not obligate her to deliver them at a particular destination. In these cases, the seller's tender of performance occurs at the point of shipment, provided the seller meets certain specified conditions designed to protect the interests of the absent buyer.

Under a shipment contract, the seller is required to (1) deliver the goods to a carrier; (2) make a contract for their transportation that is reasonable according to the nature of the goods and other circumstances; (3) obtain and promptly deliver or tender to the buyer any document necessary to enable the buyer to obtain possession of the goods from the carrier; and (4) promptly notify the buyer of the shipment.[5]

The most complicated of these responsibilities is the seller's obligation to contract for proper shipment. For example, shipment of perishable goods might require the refrigeration of the goods; extremely valuable or fragile goods might require additional precautions for their safety. Failing to make a proper contract for transportation or failing to notify the buyer of the shipment is a ground for rejection *only* if material loss or delay results.

Destination Contracts   The delivery terms *F.O.B. city of buyer, ex-ship,* and *no arrival, no sale* are destination contracts. Since a **destination contract** requires the seller to *tender* delivery of conforming goods at a *specified destination,* the seller must place the goods at the buyer's disposition and give the buyer reasonable notice to enable him to take delivery. In addition, if the destination contract involves documents of title, the seller must tender the necessary documents.[2]

Goods Held by Bailee   Where goods are in the possession of a bailee and are to be delivered without being moved, in most instances the seller may either tender a document of title or obtain an acknowledgment by the bailee of the buyer's right to possess the goods.[2]

Goods Held by Seller   If the contract does not require delivery to the buyer and the goods are not held by a bailee, the seller's obligation is to tender the goods to the buyer at the seller's place of business.[4] The seller must hold the goods for the buyer's disposition and notify her that the goods are being held for her to pick up.

For a summary of performance by the seller, see Figure 20–1.

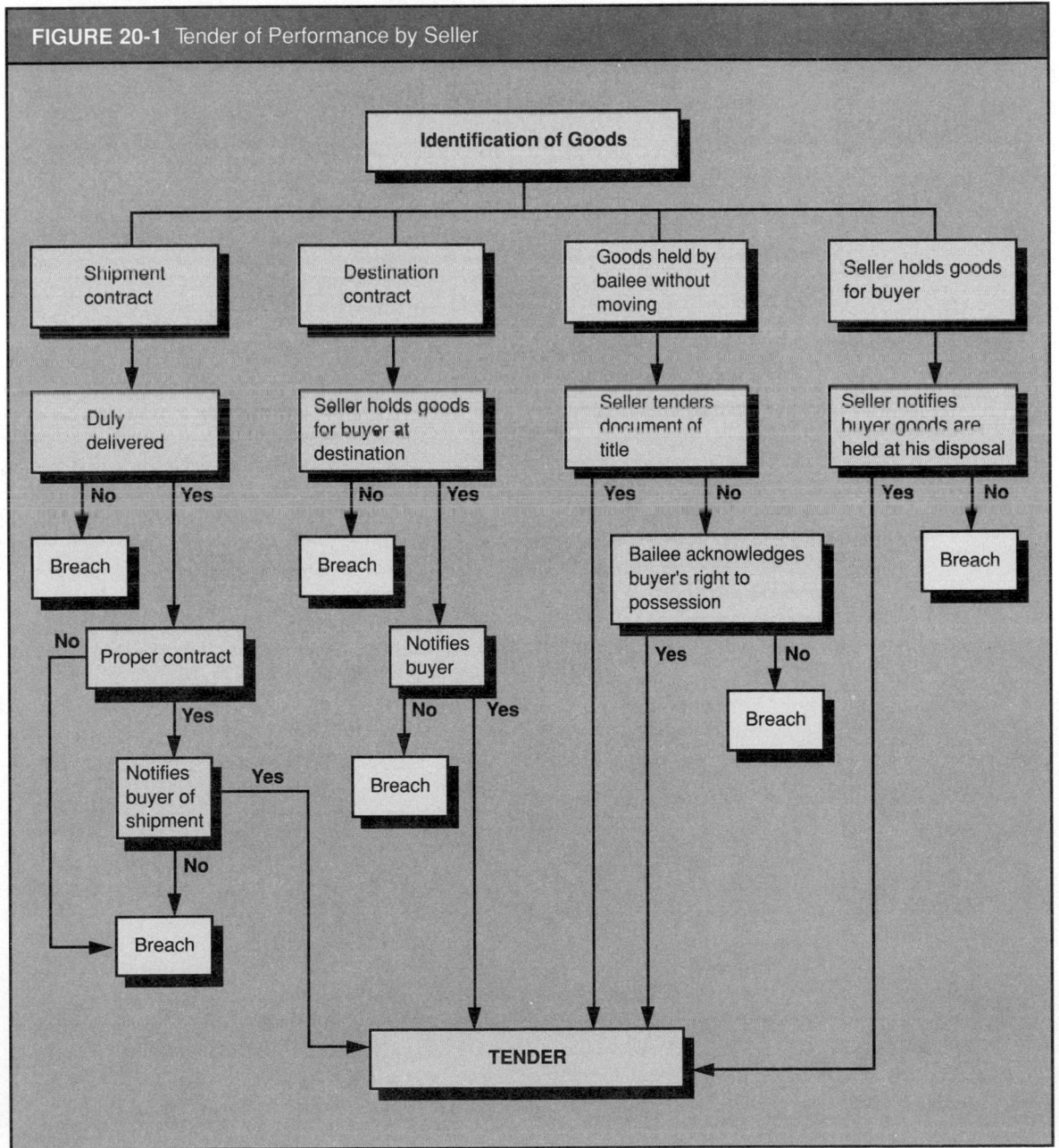

FIGURE 20-1 Tender of Performance by Seller

Quality of Tender

The Code's perfect tender rule requires that the seller's tender conform exactly to the requirements of the contract. There are, however, three basic qualifications of the buyer's right to reject the goods upon the seller's failure to comply with the perfect tender rule: (1) agreement between the parties limiting the buyer's right to reject nonconforming goods, (2) cure by the seller, and (3) installment contracts. In this section we discuss the perfect tender rule and the limitations imposed upon it.

Perfect Tender Rule The Code's **perfect tender rule** imposes on the seller the obligation that her tender of goods conform *exactly* to the requirements of the contract. The seller's tender cannot deviate in any way from the terms of the contract. If the goods or the tender of delivery fail in any respect to conform to the contract, the buyer may (1) reject the whole lot, (2) accept the whole lot, or (3) accept any commercial unit or units and reject the rest.[6] A commercial unit means such a unit of goods that by commercial usage is a single unit and which, if divided, would materially impair its character or value.[7]

Thus, a buyer may rightfully reject the delivery of 110 dozen shirts under an agreement calling for delivery of 100 dozen shirts. The size or extent of the breach does *not* affect the right to reject. The following case further illustrates the perfect tender rule.

 MOULTON CAVITY & MOLD INC. v. LYN-FLEX IND.
Supreme Court of Maine, 1979.
396 A.2d 1024.

Facts: Moulton Cavity & Mold Inc. agreed to manufacture twenty-six innersole molds to be purchased by Lyn-Flex. Moulton delivered the twenty-six molds to Lyn-Flex after Lyn-Flex allegedly approved the sample molds. Lyn-Flex rejected the molds, claiming that the molds did not satisfy the specifications exactly, and denied that it had ever approved the sample molds. Moulton then sued, contending that Lyn-Flex wrongfully rejected the molds. Lyn-Flex argues that the Code's perfect tender rule permitted its rejection of the imperfect molds, regardless of Moulton's substantial performance. Lyn-Flex appeals from a judgment entered by the trial court in favor of Moulton.

Decision: Judgment for Moulton reversed and a new trial ordered.

Opinion: Delahanty, J. In *Smith, Fitzmaurice Co. v. Harris*, [citation], a case decided under the common law, we recognized the then-settled rule that with respect to contracts for the sale of goods the buyer has the right to reject the seller's tender if in any way it fails to conform to the specifications of the contract. We held that "[t]he vendor has the duty to comply with his order in kind, quality and amount." [Citation.] Thus, in *Smith*, we ruled that a buyer who had contracted to purchase twelve dozen union suits could lawfully refuse a tender of sixteen dozen union suits. Various provisions of the Uniform Sales Act, enacted in Maine in 1923, codified the common-law approach. [Citation.] The so-called "perfect tender" rule came under considerable fire around the time the Uniform Commercial Code was drafted. No less an authority than Karl Llewellyn, recognized as the primum mobile of the Code's tender provisions, [citations], attacked the rule principally on the ground that it allowed a dishonest buyer to avoid an unfavorable contract on the basis of an insubstantial defect in the seller's tender. [Citation.] Although Llewellyn's views are represented in many Code sections governing tender, the

> basic tender provision, Section 2–601, represents a rejection of Llewellyn's approach and a continuation of the perfect tender policy developed by the common law and carried forward by the draftsmen of the Uniform Sales Act. [Citations.] Thus, Section 2–601 states that, with certain exceptions not here applicable, the buyer has the right to reject "if the goods or the tender of delivery fail *in any respect* to conform to the contract . . ." (emphasis supplied). Those few courts that have considered the question agree that the perfect tender rule has survived the enactment of the Code. [Citations.] We, too, are convinced of the soundness of this position.

Agreement between the Parties The parties may contractually agree to limit the operation of the perfect tender rule. For example, they may agree that the seller shall have the right to repair or replace any defective parts or goods. We discuss these contractual limitations in Chapter 21.

Cure by the Seller The Code recognizes two situations in which a seller may **cure** or correct a nonconforming tender of goods.[8] This relaxation of the seller's obligation to make a perfect tender gives the seller an opportunity to make a second delivery or a substitute tender. The first opportunity for cure occurs when the time for performance under the contract has not expired. The second opportunity for cure is available after the time for performance has expired, but only if the seller had reasonable grounds to believe that the nonconforming tender would be acceptable to the buyer with or without monetary adjustment.

Where the buyer refuses to accept a tender of goods that do not conform to the contract, the seller, by acting promptly and within the time allowed for performance, may make a proper tender or delivery of conforming goods and cure his defective tender or performance. Upon notice of the buyer's rightful rejection, the seller must first give the buyer reasonable notice of her intention to cure the defect and then must make a proper tender according to the original contract. This rule, which was recognized before the Code, is fair to both parties. It gives the seller the full contractual period in which to perform but does not cause

any harm to the buyer, who receives full performance within the time agreed to in the contract.

For example, Neal is to deliver to Jessica twenty-five blue shirts and fifty white shirts by October 15. On October 1 Neal delivers twenty-nine blue shirts and forty-six white shirts, which Jessica rejects as not conforming to the contract. Jessica notifies Neal of her rejection and the reasons for it. Neal has until October 15 to cure the defect by making a perfect tender provided he seasonably notifies Jessica of his intention to do so.

The Code also provides the seller an opportunity to cure a nonconforming tender that the seller had reasonable grounds to believe would be acceptable to the buyer with or without money allowance. If, on the buyer's notice of rejection, the seller seasonably notifies the buyer of his intention to cure, the seller is permitted a reasonable period of time to substitute a conforming tender. For example, Tim orders from Noel a model 110X television to be delivered on January 20. The 110X is unavailable, but Noel can obtain a model 110, which is last year's model of the same television and lists for 5 percent less than the 110X. On January 20 Noel delivers to Tim the 110 at a discount price of 10 percent less than the contract price for the 110X. Tim rejects the substituted television set. Noel promptly notifies Tim that she will obtain and deliver a model 110X. Noel will have a reasonable time beyond the January 20 deadline in which to deliver the 110X television set to Tim, because under these facts Noel had reasonable grounds to believe the model 110 would be acceptable with the money allowance. See also *Wilson v. Scampoli* below.

If the buyer refuses a tender of goods or rejects it as nonconforming without disclosing to the seller the nature of the defect, she may not assert such defect as an excuse for not accepting the goods or as a breach of contract by the seller if the defect is curable.[9]

 WILSON v. SCAMPOLI
District of Columbia Court of Appeals, 1967.
228 A.2d 848.

Facts: On November 4, 1965, Wilson purchased a color television set from Scampoli. When the set was delivered, installed, and turned on two days later, the picture had a reddish tinge. Scampoli's delivery man told Wilson's daughter, Mrs. Kolley, that he could not adjust the set but that a service representative would arrive in a couple of days to fix it. Mrs. Kolley then unplugged the set and did not use it.

On November 8 a service representative arrived but after an hour of work was unable to remove the red tinge from the picture. He told Mrs. Kolley that he would have to remove the chassis from the set and take it to his shop for a closer examination. Mrs. Kolley refused, demanding a brand-new set rather than a repaired one. She then requested that her purchase price be returned. Scampoli refused, but he repeated his offer to repair the set, or if unable to do so, to replace it. The trial court granted Wilson rescission and directed Scampoli to return the purchase price plus interest and costs.

Decision: Judgment of trial court reversed.

Opinion: Myers, J. [Scampoli] argues that he was always willing to comply with the terms of the sale either by correcting the malfunction by minor repairs or, in the event the set could not be made thereby properly operative, by replacement; that as he was denied the opportunity to try to correct the difficulty, he did not breach the contract of sale or any warranty thereunder, expressed or implied. [U.C.C.] 2–508 provides:

   (1) Where any tender or delivery by the seller is rejected because nonconforming and the time for performance has not yet expired, the seller may seasonably notify the buyer of his intention to cure and may then within the contract time make a conforming delivery.

   (2) Where the buyer rejects a nonconforming tender which the seller had reasonable grounds to believe would be acceptable with or without money allowance the seller may if he seasonably notifies the buyer have a further reasonable time to substitute a conforming tender.

A retail dealer would certainly expect and have reasonable grounds to believe that merchandise like color television sets, new and delivered as crated at the factory, would be acceptable as delivered and that, if defective in some way, he would have the right to substitute a conforming tender. The question then resolves itself to whether the dealer may conform his tender by adjustment or minor repair or whether he must conform by substituting brand new merchandise. The problem seems to be one of first impression in other jurisdictions adopting the Uniform Commercial Code as well as in the District of Columbia.

* * *

While these cases provide no mandate to require the buyer to accept patchwork goods or substantially repaired articles in lieu of flawless merchandise, they do indicate that minor repairs or reasonable adjustments are frequently the means by which an imperfect tender may be cured. In discussing the analogous question of defective title, it has been stated that:

The seller, then, should be able to cure [the defect] under subsection 2–508(2) in those cases in which he can do so without subjecting the buyer to any great inconvenience, risk, or loss. [Citations.]

Removal of a television chassis for a short period of time in order to determine the cause of color malfunction and ascertain the extent of adjustment or correction needed to effect full operational efficiency presents no great inconvenience to the buyer. In the instant case, [Scampoli's] expert witness testified that this was not infrequently necessary with new televisions. Should the set be defective in workmanship or parts, the loss would be upon the manufacturer who warranted it free from mechanical defect. Here the adamant refusal of Mrs. Kolley * * * to allow inspection essential to the determination of the cause of the excessive red tinge to the picture defeated any effort by the seller to provide timely repair or even replacement of the set if the difficulty could not be corrected. The cause of the defect might have been minor and easily adjusted or it may have been substantial and required replacement by another new set—but the seller was never given an adequate opportunity to make a determination.

We do not hold that appellant [Scampoli] has no liability to appellee [Wilson], but as he was denied access and a reasonable opportunity to repair, appellee has not shown a breach of warranty entitling him either to a brand new set or to rescission. We therefore reverse the judgment of the trial court granting rescission and directing the return of the purchase price of the set.

Installment Contracts Unless the parties have otherwise agreed, the buyer does not have to pay any part of the price of the goods until the entire quantity specified in the contract has been delivered or tendered to her. An **installment contract** is an instance in which the parties have otherwise agreed. It expressly provides for delivery of the goods in separate lots or installments and usually for payment of the price in installments. If the contract is silent about payment, the Code provides that the price, if it can be apportioned, may be demanded for each lot.[10]

The buyer may reject any nonconforming installment if the nonconformity *substantially* impairs the value of that *installment* and cannot be cured.[11] When, however, the installment does substantially impair the value of the installment but not the value of the entire contract and the seller gives adequate assurance of the installment's cure, then the buyer cannot reject the installment. Whenever the noncon-formity or default of one or more of the installments substantially impairs the value of the *whole contract*, the buyer can treat the breach as a breach of the whole contract.

PERFORMANCE BY THE BUYER

A buyer is obliged to accept conforming goods and to pay for them according to the contract terms. Payment or tender of payment by the buyer, unless otherwise agreed, is a condition of the seller's duty to tender and to complete any delivery. The buyer is not obliged to accept a tender or delivery of goods that do not conform to the contract. Upon determining that the tender or delivery is nonconforming, the buyer has three choices. He may (1) reject all of the goods, (2) accept all of the goods, or (3) accept any commercial unit or units of the goods and reject the rest. The buyer must pay at the contract rate for the commercial units he accepts.

Inspection

Unless otherwise agreed between the parties, the buyer has a right to inspect the goods before payment or acceptance.[12] This **inspection** enables him to satisfy himself that the goods tendered or delivered conform to the contract. If the contract requires payment before acceptance, such as where the contract provides for shipment C.O.D., payment must be made prior to inspection.[13] Payment, however, in such a case is not an acceptance of the goods.

The buyer is allowed a reasonable time to inspect the goods. He may lose the right to reject or revoke acceptance of nonconforming goods by failing to inspect them within a reasonable time. Although the expenses of inspection must be borne by the buyer, they may be recovered from the seller if the goods do not conform and are rejected.[12]

Rejection

Rejection is a manifestation by the buyer of his unwillingness to become owner of the goods. It must be made within a reasonable time after the goods have been tendered or delivered and is not effective unless the buyer seasonably notifies the seller.[14]

Rejection of the goods may be rightful or wrongful, depending on whether the goods tendered or delivered conform to the contract. The buyer's rejection of nonconforming goods or tender is rightful under the perfect tender rule.

After the buyer has rejected the goods, any exercise of ownership of the goods by her is not allowed. If the buyer possesses the rejected goods but has no security interest in them, she is obliged to hold them with reasonable care for a time sufficient to permit the seller to remove them. The buyer who is not a merchant is under no further obligation with regard to goods rightfully rejected.[14]

A merchant buyer of goods who has rightfully rejected them is obligated to follow reasonable instructions from the seller about disposing of the goods in her possession or con trol when the seller has no agent or business at the place of rejection.[15] If the merchant buyer receives no instructions from the seller within a reasonable time after notice of the rejection, and the rejected goods are perishable or threaten to decline in value speedily, she is obligated to make reasonable efforts to sell them for the seller's account. Otherwise, she may (1) store the goods for the seller's account, (2) reship them to the seller, or (3) resell them for the seller's account. Such action is not an acceptance of the goods.[16]

When the buyer sells the rejected goods, she is entitled to reimbursement from the seller or out of the proceeds for the reasonable expenses of caring for and selling them and a reasonable selling commission not to exceed 10 percent of the gross proceeds.[15]

CAN-KEY INDUSTRIES, INC. v. INDUSTRIAL LEASING CORP.
Supreme Court of Oregon, 1979.
286 Or. 173, 593 P.2d 1125.

Facts: Can-Key Industries, Inc., manufactured a turkey-hatching unit, which it sold to Industrial Leasing Corporation (ILC), which leased it to Rose-A-Linda Turkey Farms. ILC conditioned its obligation to pay on Rose-A-Linda's acceptance of the equipment. Rose-A-Linda indicated its dissatisfaction with the equipment, and ILC refused to perform its obligations under the contract. Can-Key then brought suit against ILC for breach of contract. It argued that Rose-A-Linda accepted the equipment, since it used it for fifteen months between March 1976 and May 1977. ILC contended that the equipment was unacceptable and asked that it be removed. It claimed that Can-Key refused and failed to instruct Rose-A-Linda to refrain from using the equipment. Therefore, ILC argued, Rose-A-Linda effectively rejected the turkey-hatching unit, relieving ILC of its contractual obligations. From a judgment for the plaintiff Can-Key, the defendant ILC appeals.

Decision: Judgment reversed.

Opinion: Howell, J.   The sole issue in this case is whether defendant "accepted" the equipment manufactured by plaintiff. The contract between plaintiff and defendant provided that defendant's obligation to pay would be conditioned upon acceptance of the equipment by its lessee. Consequently, the trial court could properly find that defendant accepted the equipment only if there is evidence that Rose-A-Linda, the lessee, accepted the equipment.

* * *

[U.C.C. § 2–606(1)] provides:

Acceptance of goods occurs when the buyer:

(a) After a reasonable opportunity to inspect the goods signifies to the seller that the goods are conforming or that he will take or retain them in spite of their nonconformity; or

(b) Fails to make an effective rejection as provided in subsection (1) of [U.C.C. § 2–602], but such acceptance does not occur until the buyer has had a reasonable opportunity to inspect them; or

(c) Does any act inconsistent with the seller's ownership; but if such act is wrongful as against the seller it is an acceptance only if ratified by him.

No contention is made that [U.C.C. § 2–606(1)(a)] is applicable in this case. There is absolutely no evidence that Rose-A-Linda ever signified that the turkey-hatching equipment was conforming or that it would retain the equipment in spite of its nonconformity. Plaintiff does contend, however, that the trial court could have found that there was an acceptance under the terms of [U.C.C. § 2–606(1)(b) or (c)]. The applicability of these subsections will be considered separately.

Plaintiff argues that the trial court "could have found" that defendant failed to make an effective rejection and that acceptance therefore occurred under the terms of [U.C.C. § 2–606(1)(b)]. Plaintiff notes that the equipment was first in use on March 3, 1976, and it was still in use as late as May 6, 1977. Plaintiff concludes that the trial court "could readily have found that 15 months was an unreasonable time to make a rejection."

Plaintiff's position can only be sustained if we ignore the uncontradicted testimony of Mr. Gibson, Rose-A-Linda's president. As noted above, Gibson testified that he twice notified plaintiff that the equipment was unacceptable and asked that it be removed.

* * *

In these particular circumstances, we hold that the uncontradicted testimony of Gibson is conclusive of the facts involved in this case. [Citation.] We further hold that Gibson's statements constituted an "effective rejection" as that term is used in [U.C.C. § 2–606(1)(b)]. Plaintiff's evidence that Rose-A-Linda accepted the equipment is therefore sufficient only if it shows that Rose-A-Linda performed acts inconsistent with the seller's ownership under the terms of [U.C.C. § 2–606(1)(c)].

What constitutes "any act inconsistent with the seller's ownership" has proved to be one of the trouble areas under Article 2 of the Uniform Commercial Code. Courts that have applied the provision have reached inconsistent results and commentators have termed the provision an "obstreperous" one. [Citations.] It has been suggested that "courts are first deciding upon the merits of the buyer's claim and then reasoning backwards to the determination of whether there has been an acceptance because of an inconsistent act." [Citation.]

A reasoned application of the section requires that the court recognize the existence of two competing policies. A buyer who verbally rejects goods should not in all cases be allowed to use the goods as if he were the owner and effectively "have it both ways." On the other hand, there are many cases in which use of the goods after rejection is not only reasonable in that it minimizes economic waste, but may be required under the buyer's statutory duty to mitigate consequential damages. [U.C.C. § 2–715(2)(a).] The court must consider both policies when defining the scope of "any act inconsistent with the seller's ownership."

* * *

Nearly all the evidence plaintiff relies upon to demonstrate that Rose-A-Linda performed acts inconsistent with plaintiff's ownership was provided by Gibson, Rose-A-Linda's president. Plaintiff did introduce testimony that Rose-A-Linda used the equipment in March and April of 1976, but it is clear from the record that these uses related to Rose-A-Linda's initial inspection of the equipment and plaintiff's effort to solve the "problems" with the equipment that it recognized in its April letter to Rose-A-Linda. Neither of these uses was inconsistent with plaintiff's ownership of the equipment. Rose-A-Linda's initial inspection cannot be considered inconsistent with plaintiff's ownership because [U.C.C. § 2–606(1)(b)] assures a buyer of goods a "reasonable opportunity to inspect them." Nor can the use of the equipment during April be considered inconsistent, because that use was approved by plaintiff, which was attempting to solve the problems with the equipment.

Plaintiff's primary reliance is on the modifications and alterations performed by Rose-A-Linda "after the equipment was installed and functioning." These acts all occurred after Gibson notified plaintiff that the equipment was unacceptable and asked that it be removed. The only testimony concerning these acts is Gibson's. That testimony shows that Rose-A-Linda employed the original developer of the equipment in an attempt to remedy the defects. It used the equipment four times during 1977. Three of those uses followed modifications or suggestions for modifications by the developer, and the final use was for the purpose of conducting a comparative test. Although the equipment apparently remains in Rose-A-Linda's possession, it has not been used since May of 1977.

We hold that this evidence does not demonstrate a use inconsistent with the seller's ownership under the terms of [U.C.C. § 2–606(1)(c)]. To hold otherwise would have the effect of penalizing Rose-A-Linda for its apparent good faith efforts to cure the defects in the equipment. We do not believe such a holding is compelled by the language of [U.C.C. § 2–606(1)(c)]. On the contrary, we think such a holding might be inconsistent with other provisions of the code, specifically the statutory duty to mitigate consequential damages and the statutory obligation of good faith. [U.C.C. §§ 2–715(2)(a), 1–203.]

It must be remembered that this transaction involved a newly developed product, the first of its kind manufactured by plaintiff. All parties to the transaction undoubtedly expected that the equipment would have some initial "bugs." After an initial test, Rose-A-Linda found the equipment unsatisfactory and notified plaintiff to that effect. Plaintiff then attempted to remedy the problems, and Rose-A-Linda again found the equipment unsatisfactory. Rose-A-Linda asked plaintiff to remove the equipment and plaintiff refused. Plaintiff did not instruct Rose-A-Linda to

> refrain from using the equipment, and plaintiff has not demonstrated that Rose-A-Linda's testing and modifications damaged the equipment in any way.
>
> * * * Viewing the evidence in the present case in a light most favorable to the plaintiff, we nevertheless conclude that, as a matter of law, Rose-A-Linda did not perform any act inconsistent with plaintiff's ownership within the meaning of [U.C.C. § 2–606(1)(c).]

Acceptance

Acceptance of goods means a willingness by the buyer to become the owner of the goods tendered or delivered to him by the seller. Acceptance of the goods precludes any rejection of the goods accepted. It includes overt acts or conduct that manifest such willingness. Acceptance may be indicated by express words, by the presumed intention of the buyer through his failure to act, or, as shown by the case that follows, by conduct of the buyer inconsistent with the seller's ownership of the goods. More specifically, acceptance occurs when the buyer, after a reasonable opportunity to inspect the goods, (1) signifies to the seller that the goods conform to the contract, (2) signifies to the seller that he will take the goods or retain them in spite of their nonconformity to the contract, or (3) fails to make an effective rejection of the goods.[17]

IMPORT TRADERS, INC. v. FREDERICK MANUFACTURING CORP.
Civil Court of the City of New York, Kings County, 1983
117 Misc.2d 305, 457 N.Y.S.2d 742.

Facts: Frederick Manufacturing Corp. ordered 500 dozen units of Import Traders' rubber pads for $2,580. The order indicated that the pads should be "as soft as possible." Import Traders delivered the rubber pads to Frederick Manufacturing on November 19, 1981. Frederick failed to inspect the goods upon delivery, even though the parties recognized that there might be a problem with the softness. Frederick finally complained about the nonconformity of the pads in April 1982, when Import Traders requested the contract price for the goods. Import Traders then sued Frederick to recover the contract price.

Decision: Judgment for Import Traders.

Opinion: Diamond, J. The remedies available to a seller for the breach of a sales contract, by a buyer, are provided in UCC § 2–703. In the present case, the seller has brought an action for the price pursuant to UCC § 2–709. The contract price may be recovered by seller when buyer accepts the goods. *UCC § 2–709(1)(a).* Acceptance occurred when buyer failed to make an effective rejection (UCC § 2–602(1)) after having had a reasonable opportunity to inspect the goods. *UCC § 2–606(1)(b).* Official Comment 1 to this section states, "Under this Article 'acceptance' as applied to goods means that the buyer takes particular goods which have been appropriated to the contract as his own, whether or not he is obligated to do so, and whether he does so by words, action or silence when it is time to speak." The goods were delivered to buyer in November, 1981 and it was not until April, 1982, when seller contacted buyer about payment, did buyer first complain about the non-conformity of the rubber pads. Buyer had a reasonable opportunity to inspect and reject the goods. It was his silence for five months that constituted the acceptance.

The acceptance of goods precludes their subsequent rejection. *UCC § 2–607(2).* Once accepted, return of the goods can only be made by way of revocation of acceptance. *UCC § 2–608.* "Revocation of acceptance must occur within a reasonable time after the buyer discovers or should have discovered the grounds for it. * * * It is not effective until the buyer notified the seller of it." *UCC § 2–608(2).* Although this assertion was not made by defendant, he failed to act within a reasonable time to revoke acceptance of the goods.

The buyer must pay at the contract rate for any goods accepted but may recover damages for any nonconformity of the goods, provided the buyer reasonably notifies the seller of any breach. For example, Nancy agrees to deliver to Paul 500 light bulbs of 100 watts each for $300 and 1,000 light bulbs of 60 watts each for $500. Nancy delivers on time, but the shipment contains only 400 of the 100-watt bulbs and 750 of the 60-watt bulbs. If Paul accepts the shipment, he must pay Nancy $240 for the 100-watt bulbs accepted and $375 for the 60-watt bulbs accepted less the amount of damages caused Paul by Nancy's nonconforming delivery.

Acceptance of any part of a commercial unit is acceptance of the entire unit.

Revocation of Acceptance

A buyer may have accepted goods that contain a defect because it was difficult to discover the defect by inspection or because the buyer reasonably assumed that the seller would correct the defect. In such an instance the buyer may revoke his acceptance of the goods if the uncorrected defect substantially impairs the value of the goods to him. **Revocation of acceptance** gives the buyer the same rights and duties with respect to the goods as if he had rejected them. More specifically, the buyer may revoke his acceptance of goods that do not conform to the contract if the nonconformity *substantially* impairs the value of the goods to him, provided that his acceptance was (1) premised on the reasonable assumption that the nonconformity would be cured by the seller, and it was not seasonably cured; or (2) made without discovery of the nonconformity, and such acceptance was reasonably induced by the difficulty of discovery before acceptance or by assurances of the seller.[18]

Revocation of acceptance is not effective until notification is given to the seller. This must be done within a reasonable time after the buyer discovers or should have discovered the grounds for revocation and before the goods have undergone any substantial change not caused by their own defects.

The following case further explains the right of revocation of acceptance.

McCULLOUGH v. BILL SWAD CHRYSLER-PLYMOUTH, INC.
Supreme Court of Ohio, 1983.
5 Ohio St. 3d 181, 449 N.E.2d 1289.

Facts: Deborah McCullough bought a new car from Bill Swad Chrylser-Plymouth, Inc. The car was protected by both a limited warranty and an extended warranty. McCullough immediately encountered problems with the automobile's brakes, transmission, and air conditioning, as well as a number of cosmetic defects.

She returned the car to Swad for repairs, but Swad did not fix the brakes properly or perform any of the cosmetic work. Moreover, new problems appeared with respect to the car's steering mechanism. McCullough returned the car twice more for repairs, but on each occasion, old problems persisted and new ones emerged. After the engine abruptly shut off on a short trip away from home and the brakes again failed on a more extensive excursion, McCullough presented Swad with a list of thirty-two of the car's defects and demanded their correction. When Swad failed to remedy more than a few of the problems, McCullough wrote a letter to Swad calling for rescission of the purchase agreement and a refund of the purchase price and offering to return the car upon receipt of shipping instructions from Swad. Swad did not respond to the letter, and McCullough brought an action against Swad. She continued to operate the vehicle until the time of trial, some five and one-half months (and 23,000 miles) later. The trial court entered judgment for McCullough in the amount of $9,376.82 and ordered the return of the automobile to Swad. The court of appeals affirmed and Swad appeals.

Decision: Judgment affirmed.

Opinion: Locher, J.   The case at bar essentially poses but a single question: Whether appellee, by continuing to operate the vehicle she had purchased from appellant after notifying the latter of her intent to rescind the purchase agreement, waived her right to revoke her initial acceptance. After having thoroughly reviewed both the relevant facts in the present cause and the applicable law, we find that appellee, despite her extensive use of the car following her revocation, in no way forfeited such right.

The ultimate disposition of the instant action is governed primarily by [U.C.C. 2–608] which provides, in pertinent part:

"(A) The buyer may revoke his acceptance of a lot or commercial unit whose nonconformity substantially impairs its value to him if he has accepted it:

"(1) on the reasonable assumption that its non-conformity would be cured and it has not been seasonally cured; . . .

* * *

"(B) Revocation of acceptance must occur within a reasonable time after the buyer discovers or should have discovered the ground for it and before any substantial change in condition of the goods which is not caused by their own defects. It it not effective until the buyer notifies the seller of it."

* * *

Appellant essentially argues that appellee's revocation of her initial acceptance of the automobile was ineffective as it did not comply with the mode prescribed for revocation in U.C.C. 2–608. Specifically, appellant asserts that appellee's continued operation of the vehicle after advising appellant of her revocation was inconsistent with her having relinquished ownership of the car, that the value of the automobile to appellee was not substantially impaired by its alleged nonconformities, and that the warranties furnished by appellant provided the sole legal remedy for alleviating the automobile's defects. Each of appellant's contentions must be rejected.

Although the legal question presented in appellant's first objection is a novel one for this bench, other state courts which have addressed the issue have held that whether continued use of goods after notification of revocation of their acceptance vitiates such revocation is solely dependent upon whether such use was reasonable. [Citations.] . . .

The genesis of the "reasonable use" test lies in the recognition that frequently a buyer, after revoking his earlier acceptance of a good, is constrained by exogenous circumstances—many of which the seller controls—to continue using the good until a suitable replacement may realistically be secured. Clearly, to penalize the buyer for a predicament not of his own creation would be patently unjust.

* * *

It is manifest that . . . appellee acted reasonably in continuing to operate her motor vehicle even after revocation of acceptance. First, the failure of the seller to advise the buyer, after the latter has revoked his acceptance of the goods, how the goods were to be returned entitles the buyer to retain possession of them. [Citations.] Appellant, in the case at bar, did not respond to appellee's request for instructions regarding the disposition of the vehicle. Failing to have done so, appellant can hardly be heard now to complain of appellee's continued use of the automobile.

Secondly, appellee, a young clerical secretary of limited financial resources, was scarcely in position to return the defective automobile and obtain a second in order to meet her business and personal needs. A most unreasonable obligation would be imposed upon appellee were she to be required, in effect, to secure a loan to purchase a second car while remaining liable for repayment of the first car loan.

* * *

Finally, it is apparent that appellant was not prejudiced by appellee's continued operation of the automobile. Had appellant retaken possession of the vehicle pursuant to appellee's notice of revocation, the automobile, which at the time had been driven only 12,000 miles, could easily have been resold. Indeed, the car was still marketable at the time of trial, as even then the odometer registered less than 35,000 miles. In any event, having failed to reassume ownership of the automobile when requested to do so, appellant alone must bear the loss for any diminution of the vehicle's resale value occurring between the two dates.

* * *

Appellant maintains, however, that even if appellee's continued operation of the automobile after revocation was reasonable, such use is "prima facie evidence" that the vehicle's nonconformities did not substantially impair its value to appellee, thus precluding availability of the remedy of revocation. Such an inference, though, may not be drawn. As stated earlier, external conditions beyond the buyer's immediate control often mandate continued use of an item even after revocation of its acceptance. Thus, it cannot seriously be contended that appellee, by continuing to operate the defective vehicle, intimated that its nonconformities did not substantially diminish its worth in her eyes.

We must similarly dismiss appellant's assertion that, as appellee's complaints primarily concerned cosmetic flaws, the defects were trivial. First, the chronic steering, transmission and brake problems which appellee experienced in operating the vehicle could hardly be deemed inconsequential. Moreover, even purely cosmetic defects, under the proper set of circumstances, can significantly affect the buyer's valuation of the good. [Citation.]

* * *

> Clearly, no error was committed in finding that the fears occasioned by the recurrent brake failings, steering malfunctions and other mechanical difficulties, as well as the utter frustration caused by the seemingly endless array of cosmetic flaws, constituted nonconformities giving rise to the remedy of revocation.

Obligation of Payment

The terms of the contract may expressly state the time and place that the buyer is obligated to pay for the goods. If so, these terms are controlling. Thus, if the buyer has agreed to pay for the goods in advance of delivery either to the seller or to a carrier, his duty to perform is not conditional on performance or a tender of performance by the seller. Where the sale is on credit, the buyer is not obligated to pay for the goods when he receives them. The credit provision in the contract will control the time of payment.

In the absence of agreement, payment is due at the time and place the buyer is to receive the goods, even though the place of shipment is the place of delivery.[19] This rule is understandable in view of the right of the buyer to inspect the goods before being obliged to pay for them in the absence of agreement to the contrary. Tender of payment in the form of a check in the ordinary course of business is sufficient unless the seller demands cash and allows the buyer a reasonable time within which to obtain it.

For a summary of performance by the buyer, see Figure 20–2.

EXCUSES FOR NONPERFORMANCE

Contracts for the sale of goods necessarily involve risks that future events may or may not occur. In some instances, the parties explicitly allocate these risks, but in most instances they do not. The Code contains three sections that allocate these risks when the parties fail to do so. Each provision, when applicable, relieves the parties from the obligation of full performance under the sales contract.

Casualty to Identified Goods

If goods are destroyed before an offer to sell or buy them is accepted, the offer is terminated by general contract law. But what if the goods are destroyed after the sales contract is formed? With one exception, the rules for the passage of risk of loss apply: if the contract is for goods that are *identified* when the contract was made, and these goods are totally lost or damaged without fault of either party and before the risk of loss passes to the buyer, the contract is avoided.[20] This means that the seller is no longer obligated to deliver and the buyer need not pay the price. Each party is excused from his performance obligation under the contract.

In the case of a partial destruction or deterioration of the goods, the buyer has the option to avoid the contract or to accept the goods with due allowance or deduction from the contract price for the deterioration or deficiency in quantity.[20] Thus, Erica agrees to sell to Henry a specific lot of wheat containing 1,000 bushels at a price of $4 per bushel. Without the fault of Erica or Henry, fire destroys 300 bushels of the wheat. Henry does not have to take the remaining 700 bushels of wheat, but he has the option to do so upon paying $2,800, the price of 700 bushels.

If the destruction or casualty to the goods, whether total or partial, occurs after risk of loss has passed to the buyer, the buyer must pay the entire contract price of the goods.

Nonhappening of Presupposed Condition

The ability to perform a contract for the sale of goods is subject to a number of possible hazards, such as strikes, lockouts, unforeseen shutdown of sources of supply, and loss of plant or machinery by fire or other casualty.

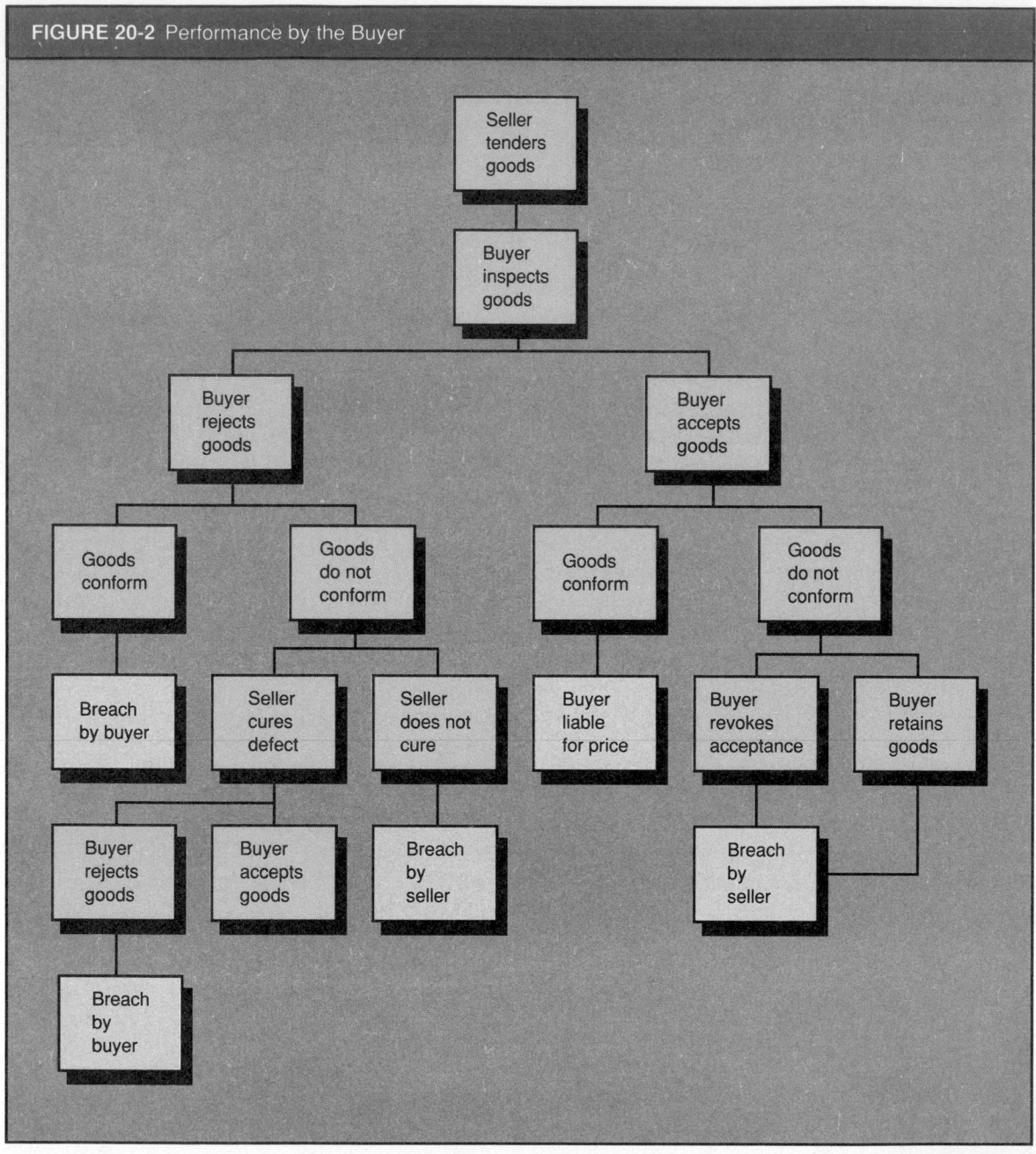

FIGURE 20-2 Performance by the Buyer

Ordinarily these do not operate as an excuse on the ground of impossibility of performance, unless the contract expressly so provides. Both parties may have understood at the time the contract was made, however, that its performance depended on the existence of certain facilities or that the purpose of the contract and the value of performance depended entirely on the happening of a specific future contemplated event. In such a case, the seller is excused from her duty of performance on the nonoccurrence of presupposed conditions that were a basic assumption of the contract, unless the seller has expressly assumed the risk.[21]

Central to the Code's approach to impossibility of performance is the concept of **commercial impracticability.** The Code excuses performance even when performance may not be actually or literally impossible, but where it is commercially impracticable. This, however, requires more than mere hardship or increased cost of performance. In order for a party to be discharged, performance must be rendered impracticable as a result of an unforeseen supervening event not within the contemplation of the parties at the time of contracting. Moreover, the nonoccurrence of the subsequent event must have been a "basic assumption" that both parties made when entering into the contract. See *Northern Corp. v. Chugach Electrical Association* in Chapter 15.

Increased production cost alone does not excuse performance by the seller, nor does a collapse of the market for the goods excuse the buyer. But, a contract for the sale of programs for a scheduled Superbowl that is called off, for the sale of tin horns for export that become subject to embargo, or for the production of goods at a designated factory that becomes damaged or destroyed by fire would be an excuse for nonperformance.

Although the seller may be relieved of her contractual duty by the nonhappening of presupposed conditions, if the contingency affects only part of the seller's capacity to perform, she must, to the extent of her remaining capacity, allocate delivery and production among her customers.[21]

Substituted Performance

The Code provides that where neither party is at fault and the agreed manner of delivery of the goods becomes commercially impracticable, for example, because of the failure of loading or unloading facilities, or the unavailability of an agreed type of carrier, a substituted manner of performance, if commercially reasonable, must be tendered and accepted.[22] Neither seller nor buyer is excused on the ground that delivery in the express manner provided in the contract is impossible where a practical alternative or substitute exists.

If the means or manner in which the buyer is to make payment becomes impossible because of subsequent governmental regulation, the seller may withhold or stop delivery of the goods unless the buyer provides payment that is commercially a substantial equivalent to that required by the contract. If delivery has already been made, payment as provided by the governmental regulation discharges the buyer unless the regulation is discriminatory, oppressive, or predatory.[22]

CHAPTER SUMMARY

Performance by the Seller	**Tender of Delivery** the seller makes available to the buyer goods conforming to the contract and so notifies the buyer
	▪ Buyer is obligated to accept conforming goods
	▪ Seller is entitled to receive payment of the contract price
	Time of Tender tender must be made at a reasonable time and kept open for a reasonable period of time
	Place of Tender if none is specified, place for delivery is the seller's place of business, or if he has none, his residence
	Quality of Tender
	▪ *Perfect Tender Rule* the seller's tender of performance must conform exactly to the contract
	▪ *Agreement by the Parties* the parties may contractually limit the operation of the perfect tender rule

- *Cure by the Seller*   when the time for performance under the contract has not expired or when the seller has shipped nonconforming goods in the belief that the nonconforming tender would be acceptable, a seller may cure or correct his nonconforming tender
- *Installment Contracts*   when the contract calls for the goods to be delivered in separate lots, the buyer may reject a nonconforming installment if it substantially impairs the value of that installment and cannot be cured, but if nonconformity or default of one or more of the installments substantially impairs the value of the whole contract, the buyer can treat the breach as a breach of the whole contract

Performance by the Buyer

Inspection   unless otherwise agreed, the buyer has a reasonable time to inspect the goods before payment or acceptance to determine whether they conform

Rejection   buyer's manifestation of unwillingness to become the owner of the goods; must be made within a reasonable time after the goods have been tendered or delivered and gives the buyer the right to (1) reject all of the goods, (2) accept all of the goods, or (3) accept any commercial unit(s) and reject the rest

Acceptance   buyer's express or implied manifestation of willingness to become the owner of the goods

Revocation of Acceptance   rescission of buyer's acceptance of the goods based upon the nonconformity of the goods if the nonconformity substantially impairs their value, provided that the acceptance was (1) premised on the assumption that the nonconformity would be cured by the seller and it was not, or (2) the nonconformity was an undiscovered hidden defect

Obligation of Payment   in the absence of an agreement, payment is due at the time and place the buyer is to receive the goods

Excuses for Nonperformance

Casualty to Identified Goods   if the contract is for goods that are identified when the contract was made, and those goods are totally lost or damaged without fault of either party and before the risk of loss has passed to the buyer, the contract is avoided

Nonhappening of Presupposed Condition   the seller is excused from the duty of performance on the nonoccurrence of presupposed conditions that were a basic assumption of the contract, unless the seller has expressly assumed the risk

Substituted Performance   where neither party is at fault and the agreed manner of delivery of goods becomes commercially impracticable, a substituted manner of performance must be tendered and accepted

QUESTIONS

1. Explain the requirements of tender of delivery with respect to time, manner, and place of delivery.
2. Explain the perfect tender rule and the three limitations upon it.
3. Explain when the buyer has the right to reject the goods and what obligations the buyer has upon rejection.
4. Discuss the buyer's right to revoke acceptance.
5. Identify and discuss the excuses for nonperformance.

PROBLEMS

1. Tammie contracted with Kristine to manufacture, sell, and deliver to Kristine and put in running order a certain machine. Tammie set up the machine and put it in running order. Kristine found it unsatisfactory and notified Tammie that she rejected the machine. She continued to use it for three months, but continually complained of its defective condition. At the end of the three months she notified Tammie to come and get it. Has Kristine lost her right (a) to reject the machine? (b) to revoke acceptance of the machine?

2. Smith, having contracted to sell to Beyer thirty tons of described fertilizer, shipped to Beyer by carrier thirty tons of fertilizer that he stated conformed to the contract. Nothing was stated in the contract as to time of payment, but Smith demanded payment as a condition of handing over the fertilizer to Beyer. Beyer refused to pay unless he was given the opportunity to inspect the fertilizer. Smith sues Beyer for breach of contract. Decision?

3. Benny and Sheree entered into a contract for the sale of 100 barrels of flour. No mention was made of any place of delivery. Thereafter, Sheree demanded that Benny deliver the flour at her place of business, and Benny demanded that Sheree come and take the flour from his place of business. Neither party acceded to the demand of the other. Has either one a right of action against the other?

4. Johnson, a manufacturer of air conditioning units, made a written contract with Maxwell to sell to Maxwell forty units at a price of $200 each and to deliver them at a certain apartment building owned by Maxwell for installation by Maxwell. On the arrival of Johnson's truck for delivery at the apartment building, Maxwell examined the units on the truck, counted only thirty units, and asked the driver if that was the total delivery. The driver replied that it was as far as he knew. Maxwell told the driver that she would not accept delivery of the units. The next day Johnson telephoned Maxwell and inquired why delivery was refused. Maxwell stated that the units on the truck were not what she ordered, that she ordered forty units, that only thirty were tendered, and that she was going to buy air conditioning units elsewhere. In an action by Johnson against Maxwell for breach of contract, Maxwell defends on the ground that the tender of thirty units was improper, as the contract called for delivery of forty units. Is this a valid defense?

5. Edwin sells a sofa to Jack for $800. Edwin and Jack both know that the sofa is in Edwin's warehouse located approximately ten miles from Jack's home. The contract did not specify the place of delivery, and Jack insists that the place of delivery is either his house or Edwin's store. Is Jack correct?

6. On November 4 Kim contracted to sell to Lynn 500 sacks of flour at $4 each to be delivered by December 12 to Lynn. On November 27 Kim shipped the flour. By December 5, when the car arrived, containing only 450 sacks, the market price of flour had fallen. Lynn refused to accept delivery or to pay. Kim shipped 50 more sacks of flour, which arrived December 10. Lynn refused delivery. Kim resold the flour for $3 per sack. What are Kim's rights against Lynn?

7. Farley and Trudy entered into a written contract whereby Farley agreed to sell and Trudy to buy 6,000 bushels of wheat at $3.75 per bushel, deliverable at the rate of 1,000 bushels a month commencing June 1, the price for each installment being payable ten days after delivery thereof. Farley delivered and received payment for the June installment. Farley defaulted by failing to deliver the July and August installments. By August 15 the market price of wheat had increased to $4 per bushel. Trudy thereupon entered into a contract with Albert to purchase 5,000 bushels of wheat at $4 per bushel deliverable over the ensuing four months. In late September the market price of wheat started to decline and by December 1 was $3.25 per bushel. Trudy brings an action against Farley for breach of contract. Decision?

8. Bain ordered from Marcum a carload of lumber, which he intended to use in the construction of small boats for the U.S. Navy pursuant to contract. The order specified that the lumber was to be free from knots, wormholes, and defects. The lumber was shipped, and immediately on receipt Bain looked into the door of the fully loaded car, ascer-

432

tained that there was a full carload of lumber, and acknowledged to Marcum that the carload had been received. On the same day, Bain moved the car to his private siding and sent to Marcum full payment in accordance with the terms of the order.

A day later, the car was moved to the work area and unloaded in the presence of the navy inspector, who refused to allow three-fourths of it to be used because of excessive knots and wormholes in the lumber. Bain then informed Marcum that he was rejecting the order and requested refund of the payment and directions on disposition of the lumber. Marcum replied that since Bain had accepted the order and unloaded it, he was not entitled to return of the purchase price. Bain thereupon brought an action against Marcum to recover the purchase price. Decision?

9. Plaintiff, a seller of milk, had for ten years bid on contracts to supply milk to defendant school district, and had supplied milk to other school districts in the area. On June 15, 1990, plaintiff contracted to supply defendant's requirements of milk for the school year 1990–1991 at a price of $.0759 per half pint. The price of raw milk delivered from the farm had been for years controlled by the U.S. Department of Agriculture. On June 15, 1990, the department's administrator for the New York-New Jersey area had mandated a price for raw milk of $8.03 per hundredweight. By December 1990 the mandated price had been raised to $9.31 a hundredweight, an increase of nearly 20 percent. If required to complete deliveries at the contract price, plaintiff would lose $7,350.55 on its contract with defendant and would face similar losses on contracts with two other school districts. Plaintiff sued for a judgment that its performance had become impracticable through unforeseen events, particularly unanticipated grain crop failures. Decision?

10. In April F. W. Lang Company purchased an ice cream freezer and refrigeration compressor unit from Fleet for $2,160. Although the parties agreed to a written installment contract providing for an $850 down payment and eighteen installment payments, Lang made only one $200 payment upon receipt of the goods. One year later, Lang moved to a new location and took the equipment along without notifying Fleet. Two years after the sale, Lang disconnected the compressor from the freezer and used it to operate an air conditioner. Lang continued to use the compressor for that purpose until the sheriff seized the equipment and returned it to Fleet pursuant to a court order. Fleet then sold the equipment for $500 in what both parties conceded was a fair sale. Lang then brought an action charging that the equipment was defective and unusable

for the intended purpose and sought to recover the down payment and expenses incurred in repairing the equipment. Fleet counterclaimed for the balance due under the installment contract less the proceeds from the sale. Decision?

COMPUTER RESEARCH PROBLEMS

1. On March 17, Peckham bought a new car from Larsen Chevrolet for $6,400.85. During the first one and one-half months after the purchase, Peckham discovered that the car's hood was dented, its gas tank contained no baffles, its emergency brake was inoperable, the car did not have a jack or a spare tire, and neither the clock nor the speedometer worked. Larsen claimed that Peckham knew of the defects at the time of the purchase. Peckham, on the other hand, claimed that despite his repeated efforts the defects were not repaired until June 11. Then, on July 15 the car's dashboard caught fire, leaving the car's interior damaged and the car itself inoperable. Peckham then returned to Larsen Chevrolet and told Larsen that he had to repair the car at his own expense or he, Peckham, would either rescind the contract or demand a new automobile. Peckham also claimed that at the end of their conversation he notified Larsen Chevrolet that he was electing to rescind the contract and demanded the return of the purchase price. Larsen denied having received that oral notification. On October 12, Peckham sent a written notice of rescission to Larsen. Decision?

2. Joc Oil bought a cargo of fuel oil for resale. The certificate from the foreign refinery stated the sulphur content of the oil was .5 percent. Joc Oil entered into a written contract with Con Ed for the sale of this oil. The contract specified a sulphur content of .5 percent. Joc Oil knew, however, that Con Ed was authorized to buy and burn oil of up to 1 percent sulphur content, and that Con Ed often bought and mixed oils of varying contents to stay within this limit. The oil under contract was delivered to Con Ed, but independent testing revealed a sulphur content of .92 percent. Con Ed promptly rejected the nonconforming shipment. Joc Oil immediately offered to substitute a conforming shipment of oil, although the time for performance had expired after the first shipment of oil. Con Ed refused to accept the substituted shipment. Joc Oil sues Con Ed for breach of contract. Judgment?

3. Plaintiff West German wine producer and exporter contracted to ship 620 cases of wine to the

defendant distributor in North Carolina. The contract was silent as to the shipment destination. During the next several months, defendant called repeatedly to find out the status of the shipment. Later, without notifying defendant, plaintiff delivered the wine to a shipping line in Rotterdam, destined for Wilmington, N.C. The ship, and the wine, were lost at sea en route to Wilmington. When defendant refused to pay on the contract, plaintiff sued. Decision?

ENDNOTES

1. Uniform Commercial Code, Section 2—507, Effect of Seller's Tender; Delivery on Condition.

2. Uniform Commercial Code, Section 2—503, Manner of Seller's Tender of Delivery.

3. Uniform Commercial Code, Section 2—307, Delivery in Single Lot or Several Lots.

4. Uniform Commercial Code, Section 2—308, Absence of Specified Place for Delivery.

5. Uniform Commercial Code, Section 2—504, Shipment by Seller.

6. Uniform Commercial Code, Section 2—601, Buyer's Rights on Improper Delivery.

7. Uniform Commercial Code, Section 2—105(6), Definitions: * * * "Commercial Unit".

8. Uniform Commercial Code, Section 2—508, Cure by Seller of Improper Tender or Delivery; Replacement.

9. Uniform Commercial Code, Section 2—605, Waiver of Buyer's Objections by Failure to Particularize.

10. Uniform Commercial Code, Section 2—307, Delivery in Single Lot or Several Lots.

11. Uniform Commercial Code, Section 2—612, "Installment Contract"; Breach.

12. Uniform Commercial Code, Section 2—513, Buyer's Right to Inspection of Goods.

13. Uniform Commercial Code, Section 2—512, Payment by Buyer Before Inspection.

14. Uniform Commercial Code, Section 2—602, Manner and Effect of Rightful Rejection.

15. Uniform Commercial Code, Section 2—603, Merchant Buyer's Duties as to Rightfully Rejected Goods.

16. Uniform Commercial Code, Section 2—604, Buyer's Options as to Salvage of Rightfully Rejected Goods.

17. Uniform Commercial Code, Section 2—606, What Constitutes Acceptance of Goods.

18. Uniform Commercial Code, Section 2—608, Revocation of Acceptance in Whole or in Part.

19. Uniform Commercial Code, Section 2—310, Open Time for Payment or Running of Credit; Authority to Ship Under Reservation.

20. Uniform Commercial Code, Section 2—613, Casualty to Identified Goods.

21. Uniform Commercial Code, Section 2—615, Excuse by Failure of Presupposed Conditions.

22. Uniform Commercial Code, Section 2—614, Substituted Performance.

21 REMEDIES

A contract for the sale of goods may be completely performed at one time or performed in stages, according to the agreement made. At any stage, one of the parties may breach or repudiate the contract or become insolvent. Breach is the failure of a party to perform his obligations under the contract. In a sales contract, breach may consist of the seller's delivering defective goods, too few goods, the wrong goods, or no goods. The buyer may breach by not accepting conforming goods or by failing to pay for conforming goods that he has accepted. Breach may occur when the goods are in the possession of the seller, in the possession of a bailee of the buyer, in transit to the buyer, or in the possession of the buyer.

Remedies, therefore, are necessary to address not only the type of breach of contract but also the factual situation with respect to the goods. Consequently, the Code provides separate and distinct remedies for the seller and for the buyer, each specifically keyed to the factual situation.

In all events, the purpose of the Code is to put the aggrieved party in as good a position as if the other party had fully performed. Therefore, the Code has provided that its remedies should be liberally administered to accomplish this purpose. Moreover, damages do not have to be "calculable with mathematical precision": they must be proved with "whatever definiteness and accuracy the facts permit, but no more." Finally, the Code has rejected the doctrine of election of remedies. Essentially, the Code provides that remedies for breach are cumulative. Whether one remedy bars another depends entirely on the facts of the individual case.

REMEDIES OF THE SELLER

When a buyer defaults in performing any of his contractual obligations, the seller has been deprived of the rights for which he bargained. The buyer's default may consist of any of the following acts: the buyer wrongfully rejects the goods; the buyer wrongfully revokes acceptance of the goods; the buyer fails to make a payment due on or before delivery; or the buyer repudiates (indicates that he does not intend to perform) the contract in whole or in part. The Code catalogs the seller's remedies for each of these defaults.[1] These remedies allow the seller to:

1. withhold delivery of the goods;
2. stop delivery of the goods by a carrier or other bailee;
3. identify conforming goods to the contract not already identified;
4. resell the goods and recover damages;
5. recover damages for nonacceptance of the goods or repudiation of the contract;
6. recover the price;
7. recover incidental damages;
8. cancel the contract; and
9. reclaim the goods on the buyer's insolvency.

It is useful to note that the first three and the ninth remedies indexed above are **goods oriented**—that is, they relate to the seller's exercising control over the goods. The fourth through seventh remedies are **money oriented** because they provide the seller with the opportunity to recover monetary damages. The eighth remedy is **obligation oriented** because it allows the seller to avoid his obligation under the contract.

Moreover, if the seller delivers goods on credit and the buyer fails to pay the price when due, the seller's sole remedy, unless the buyer is insolvent, is to sue for the unpaid price. If, however, the buyer received the goods on credit while insolvent, the seller may be able to reclaim the goods. Insolvency is defined by the Code to include both its equity meaning and its bankruptcy meaning.[2] The **equity** meaning of **insolvency** is the inability of a person to pay his debts in the ordinary course of business or as they become due. The **bankruptcy** meaning of **insolvency** is that total liabilities exceed the total value of all assets.

As noted, the Code's remedies are **cumulative.** Thus, by way of example, an aggrieved seller may (1) identify goods to the contract, *and* (2) withhold delivery, *and* (3) resell or recover damages for nonacceptance or recover the price, *and* (4) recover incidental damages, *and* (5) cancel the contract.

To Withhold Delivery of the Goods

A seller may withhold delivery of the goods to a buyer who has wrongfully rejected or revoked acceptance of the goods, who has failed to make a payment due on or before delivery, or who has repudiated the contract.[1] This right is essentially that of a seller to withhold or discontinue performance of her side of the contract because of the buyer's breach.

Where the contract calls for installments, any breach of an installment that impairs the value of the *whole* contract will permit the seller to withhold the entire undelivered balance of the goods. In addition, on discovery of the buyer's insolvency, the seller may refuse to deliver the goods except for cash, including payment for all goods previously delivered under the contract.[3]

To Stop Delivery of the Goods

An extension of the right to withhold delivery is the right of an aggrieved seller to stop delivery of the goods in transit to the buyer or in the possession of a bailee. The seller accomplishes this by timely notification to the carrier or other bailee to stop delivery of the goods. After this notification, the carrier or bailee must hold and deliver the goods according to the directions of the seller, who is liable to the carrier or bailee for any charges or damages incurred.[4]

If the seller discovers that the buyer is insolvent, then the seller may stop *any* delivery. If the buyer is not insolvent but repudiates or otherwise breaches the contract, the seller may stop carload, truckload, planeload, or larger shipments.

The right of the seller to stop delivery ceases when (1) the buyer receives the goods; or (2) the bailee of the goods, except a carrier, acknowledges to the buyer that he holds them for the buyer; or (3) the carrier acknowledges to the buyer that he holds them for the buyer by reshipment or as warehouser; or (4) a negotiable document of title covering the goods is negotiated to the buyer.[4]

To Identify Goods to the Contract

On a breach of the contract by the buyer, the seller may proceed to identify to the contract conforming goods in her possession or control that were not so identified at the time she learned of the breach.[5] Furthermore, the seller may resell any unfinished goods that have demonstrably been intended for fulfillment of the particular contract. The seller may either complete the manufacture of unfinished goods and identify them to the contract or cease their manufacture and resell the unfinished goods for scrap or salvage value.[5] In so deciding, the seller must exercise reasonable judgment to minimize her loss.

To Resell the Goods and Recover Damages

Under the same circumstances that permit the seller to withhold delivery of goods to the buyer (i.e., wrongful rejection or revocation, repudiation, or failure to make timely payment), the seller may resell the goods concerned or the undelivered balance of the goods. If the resale is made in good faith and in a commercially reasonable manner, the seller may recover from the buyer the **difference between the contract price and the resale price,** *together* with any incidental damages (discussed below), *less* expenses saved in consequence of the buyer's breach.[6] For example, Floyd agrees to sell goods to Beverly for a contract price of $8,000 due on delivery. Beverly wrongfully rejects the goods and refuses to pay Floyd anything. Floyd resells the goods in strict compliance with the Code for $6,000 and incurs incidental damages for sales commissions of $500 but saves $200 in transportation costs. Floyd would recover from Beverly the contract price ($8,000) minus the resale price ($6,000) plus incidental damages ($500) minus expenses saved ($200), which equals $2,300.

The resale may be a public or private sale, and the goods may be sold as a unit or in parcels. The goods resold must be identified as those related to the contract, but it is not necessary that the goods be in existence or that they have been identified to the contract before the buyer's breach.[6]

Where the resale is a private sale, the seller must give the buyer reasonable notice of his intention to resell. Where the resale is at a public sale, only identified goods can be sold, except where there is a recognized market for a public sale of future goods of the kind involved. The public sale must be made at a usual place or market for public sale if one is reasonably available. The seller must give the buyer reasonable notice of the time and place of the resale unless the goods are perishable or threaten to decline in value speedily. Prospective bidders at the sale must be given an opportunity for reasonable inspection of the goods before the sale. The seller may be a purchaser of the goods at the public sale.

The seller is not accountable to the buyer for any profit made on any resale of the goods. Moreover, a *bona fide* purchaser at a resale takes the goods free of any rights of the original buyer, even though the seller has failed to comply with one or more of the requirements of the Code in making the resale.[6]

To Recover Damages for Nonacceptance or Repudiation

In the event of the buyer's wrongful rejection or revocation, repudiation, or failure to make timely payment, the seller may recover damages from the buyer measured by the **difference between the unpaid contract price and the market price** at the time and place of tender of the goods, *plus* incidental damages, *less* expenses saved in consequence of the buyer's breach.[7] This remedy is an alternative to the remedy of reselling the goods.

For example, Joyce in Seattle agrees to sell goods to Maynard in Chicago for $20,000 F.O.B. Chicago, delivery on June 15. Maynard wrongfully rejects the goods. The market price would be ascertained as of June 15 in Chicago because F.O.B. Chicago is a destination contract in which the place of tender would be Chicago. The market price of the goods on June 15 in Chicago is $15,000. Joyce incurred $1,000 in incidental expenses while saving $500 in expenses. Joyce's recovery from Maynard would be the contract price ($20,000), minus the market price ($15,000), plus incidental damages ($1,000), minus expenses saved ($500), which equals $5,500.

If the difference between the contract price and the market price will not place the seller in as good a position as performance would have, then the measure of damages is the profit, including reasonable overhead, that the seller would have realized from full performance by the buyer, plus any incidental damages, less expenses saved in consequence of the buyer's breach.[7] For example, Green, an automobile dealer, enters into a contract to sell a large, fuel inefficient luxury car to Holland for $22,000. The price of gasoline increases 20 percent, and Holland repudiates. The market value of the car is still $22,000, but because Green cannot sell as many cars as he can obtain, Green's sales volume has decreased by one as a result of Holland's breach. Therefore, Green would be permitted to recover the profits he lost on the sale to Holland (computed as the contract price, minus what the car costs Green, plus an allocation of overhead), plus any incidental damages. The following case explains the computation of lost profits.

TERADYNE, INC. v. TELEDYNE INDUSTRIES, INC.
United States Court of Appeals, First Circuit, 1982.
676 F.2d 865.

Facts: Teledyne Industries, Inc., entered into a contract with Teradyne, Inc., to purchase a T-347A transistor test system for the list and fair market price of $98,400 less a discount of $984. After the system was packed for shipment, Teledyne cancelled the order, offering to purchase a Field Effects Transistor System for $65,000. Teradyne refused the offer. Teradyne then sold the T-347A to another purchaser pursuant to an order that was on hand prior to cancellation. Teradyne then sued Teledyne for breach of contract. Judgment was entered in favor of Teradyne for lost profits. Teledyne appealed.

Decision: Judgment vacated and remanded.

Opinion: Wyzanski, J.   The parties are agreed that § 2–708(2) applies to the case at bar. Inasmuch as this conclusion is not plain from the text, we explain the reasons why we concur in that agreement.

Section 2–708(2) applies only if the damages provided by § 2–708(1) are inadequate to put the seller in as good a position as performance would have done. Under § 2–708(1) the measure of damages is the difference between unpaid contract price and market price. Here the unpaid contract price was $97,416 and the market price was $98,400. Hence no damages would be recoverable under § 2–708(1). On the other hand, if the buyer had performed, the seller (1) would have had the proceeds of two contracts, one with the buyer Teledyne and the other with the "resale purchaser" and (2) *it seems* would have had in 1976–7 one more T-347A sale.

A literal reading of the last sentence of § 2–708(2)—providing for "due credit for payments or proceeds of resale"—would indicate that Teradyne recovers nothing because the proceeds of the resale exceeded the price set in the Teledyne-Teradyne contract. However, in light of the statutory history of the subsection, it is universally agreed that in a case where after the buyer's default a seller resells the goods, the proceeds of the resale are not to be credited to the buyer if the seller is a lost volume seller—that is, one who had there been no breach by the buyer, could and would have had the benefit of both the original contract and the resale contract.

Thus, despite the resale of the T-347A, Teradyne is entitled to recover from Teledyne what § 2–708(2) calls its expected "profit (including reasonable overhead)" on the broken Teledyne contract.

Teledyne not only "does not dispute that damages are to be calculated pursuant to § 2–708(2)" but concedes that the formula used in *Jericho Sash & Door Co. v. Building Erectors, Inc.*, [citation], for determining lost profit including overhead—that is, the formula under which direct costs of producing and selling manufactured goods are deducted from the contract price in order to arrive at "profit (including reasonable overhead)" as that term is used in § 2–708(2)—"is permissible provided all variable expenses are identified."

* * *

Teledyne's more significant objection to Teradyne's and the master's application of the Jericho formula in the case at bar is that neither of them made deductions on account of the wages paid to testers, shippers, installers, and other Teradyne employees who directly handled the T-347A, or on account of the fringe benefits amounting in the case of those and other employees to 12 per cent of wages. Teradyne gave as the reason for the omission of the wages of the testers, etc. that those wages would not have been affected if each of the testers, etc. handled one product more or less. However, the work of those employees entered as directly into producing and supplying the T-347A as did the work of a fabricator of a T-347A. Surely no one would regard as "reasonable overhead" within § 2–708(2) the wages of a fabricator of a T-347A even if his wages were the same whether he made one product more or less. We conclude that the wages of the testers, etc. likewise are not part of overhead and as a "direct cost" should have been deducted from the contract price. A fortiori fringe benefits amounting to 12 per cent of wages should also have been deducted as direct costs. Taken together we cannot view these omitted items as what Jericho called "relatively insignificant items." We, therefore, must vacate the district court's judgment. [Citations.] [We] remand this case so that with respect to the omitted direct labor costs specified above the parties may offer further evidence and the court may make findings "with whatever definiteness and accuracy the facts permit, but no more." [Citation.]

To Recover the Price

The Code permits the seller to recover the price plus incidental damages in three situations: (1) where the buyer has accepted the goods; (2) where conforming goods have been lost or damaged after the risk of loss has passed to the buyer; and (3) where the goods have been identified to the contract and there is no ready market available for their resale at a reasonable price.[8] For example, Kelly, in accordance with her agreement with Sally, prints 10,000 letterheads and envelopes with Sally's name and address on them. Sally wrongfully rejects the stationery, and Kelly is unable to resell them at a reasonable price. Kelly is entitled to recover the price plus incidental damages from Sally.

A seller who sues for the price must hold for the buyer any goods that have been identified to the contract and are still in her control. If resale becomes possible, the seller may resell the goods at any time before the collection of the judgment, and the net proceeds of such resale must be credited to the buyer. Payment of the judgment entitles the buyer to any goods not resold.[8]

To Recover Incidental Damages

In addition to recovering damages for the difference between the resale price and the contract price or recovering damages for non-acceptance or repudiation or recovering the price, the seller may also recover in the same action her incidental damages. **Incidental damages** are defined to include any commercially reasonable charges, expenses, or commissions incurred in stopping delivery; in the transportation, care, and custody of goods after the buyer's breach; in connection with return or resale of the goods; or otherwise resulting from the breach.[9]

To Cancel the Contract

Where the buyer wrongfully rejects or revokes acceptance of the goods or fails to make a payment due on or before delivery or repudiates the contract in whole or in part, the seller may cancel the part of the contract that concerns the goods directly affected. If the breach is of an installment contract and it substantially impairs the whole contract, the seller may cancel the entire contract.

The Code defines **cancellation** as putting an end to the contract by one party because of a breach by the other.[10] The obligation of the canceling party for any future performance under the contract is discharged, although he retains any remedy for breach of the whole contract or any unperformed balance. Thus, if the seller has the right to cancel, he may recover damages for breach without having to tender any further performance.

To Reclaim the Goods upon the Buyer's Insolvency

In addition to the right of an unpaid seller to withhold and stop delivery of the goods, he may reclaim them from an insolvent buyer by demand made to the buyer within ten days after the buyer has received the goods.[3] Moreover, where the buyer has committed fraud by misrepresentation of her solvency made to the seller in writing within three months prior to delivery of the goods, the ten-day limitation does not apply.

The seller's right to reclaim, however, is subject to the rights of a purchaser of the goods from the buyer in ordinary course of business or other good faith purchaser. If a seller successfully reclaims the goods from an insolvent buyer, he is excluded from all other remedies with respect to those goods.[3]

REMEDIES OF THE BUYER

There are basically three different ways in which a seller may default: he may repudiate; he may fail to deliver the goods without repudiation; or he may deliver or tender goods that do not conform to the contract. The Code provides remedies for each of these breaches.[11] Some remedies are available for all of these types of breaches, whereas others are available only for certain types. Moreover, some remedies must be triggered by certain actions taken by the buyer. For example, if the seller tenders nonconforming goods, the buyer may reject or accept them. If the buyer rejects them, he can choose from a number of remedies. On the other hand, if the buyer accepts the nonconforming goods and does not justifiably revoke his acceptance, he limits himself to recovering damages.

Where the seller fails to make delivery or repudiates, or the buyer rightfully rejects or justifiably revokes acceptance, the buyer may, with respect to any goods involved, or with respect to the whole if the breach goes to the whole contract, (1) cancel, *and* (2) recover payments made.

In addition, the buyer may (3) "cover" and obtain damages, *or* (4) recover damages for nondelivery. Where the seller fails to deliver or repudiates, the buyer, where appropriate, may also (5) recover identified goods if the seller is insolvent, *or* (6) "replevy" the goods, *or* (7) obtain specific performance. Moreover, on rightful rejection or justifiable revocation of acceptance, the buyer (8) has a security interest in the goods. Where the buyer has accepted goods and given notification to the seller of their nonconformity, the buyer may (9) recover damages for breach of warranty. Finally, in addition to the remedies listed above, the buyer may, where appropriate, (10) recover incidental damages, and (11) recover consequential damages.

It may be observed that the first remedy catalogued above is **obligation oriented;** the second through fourth and ninth through eleventh are **money oriented;** and the fifth through eighth are **goods oriented.**

To Cancel the Contract

Where the seller fails to make delivery or repudiates the contract or where the buyer rightfully rejects or justifiably revokes acceptance of goods tendered or delivered to him, the buyer may cancel the contract with respect to any goods involved, and if the breach by the seller concerns the whole contract, the buyer may cancel the entire contract.[11] The buyer must give the seller notice of his cancellation of the contract and is excused from further performance or tender on his part.

To Recover Payments Made

The buyer, on the seller's breach, may also recover as much of the price as he has paid.[11] For example, Jonas and Sheila enter into a contract for a sale of goods for a contract price of $3,000, and Sheila, the buyer, has made a down payment of $600. Jonas delivers nonconforming goods to Sheila, who rightfully rejects them. Sheila may cancel the contract and recover the $600 plus whatever other damages she may prove.

To Cover

On the seller's breach, the buyer may protect herself by obtaining **cover.** This means that the buyer may in good faith and without unreasonable delay proceed to purchase goods or make a contract to purchase goods in substitution for those due under the contract from the seller.[12] This right enables the buyer to assure herself of the needed goods.

On making a reasonable contract of cover, the buyer may recover from the seller the **difference between the cost of cover and the contract price,** *plus* any incidental and consequential damages, *less* expenses saved in consequence of the seller's breach.[12] For example, Phillip, whose factory is in Oakland, agrees to sell goods to Edith, in Atlanta, for $22,000 F.O.B. Oakland. Phillip fails to deliver and Edith covers by purchasing substitute goods for $25,000, incurring $700 in sales commissions. Edith suffered no other damages as a consequence of Phillip's breach. Shipping costs from Oakland to Atlanta for the goods are $1,300. Edith would recover the cost of cover ($25,000), less the contract price ($22,000), plus incidental damages ($700 in sales commissions), minus expenses saved ($1,300 in shipping costs Edith need not pay under the contract of cover), which equals $2,400.

The buyer is not required to obtain "cover," and his failure to do so does not bar him from any other remedy provided by the Code.[12] The buyer, however, may not recover consequential damages that he could have prevented by cover.[13]

 BIGELOW-SANFORD, INC. v. GUNNY CORP.
United States Court of Appeals, Fifth Circuit, Unit B, 1981.
649 F.2d 1060.

Facts: The plaintiff, Bigelow-Sanford, Inc., contracted with defendant Gunny Corp. for the purchase of 100,000 linear yards of jute at $.64 per yard. Gunny delivered 22,228 linear yards in January 1979. The February and March deliveries required under the contract were not made, and 8 rolls (each roll containing 66.7 linear yards) were delivered in April. With 72,265 linear yards undelivered, Gunny told Bigelow-Sanford that no more would be delivered. In mid-March Bigelow-Sanford then turned to the jute spot market to replace the balance of the order at a price of $1.21 per linear yard. Since several other companies had also defaulted on their jute contracts with Bigelow-Sanford, the plaintiff purchased a total of 164,503 linear yards on the spot market. Plaintiff sues defendant to recover losses sustained as a result of the breach of contract. Gunny appealed from a judgment in favor of Bigelow-Sanford.

Decision: Judgment for Bigelow-Sanford affirmed.

Opinion: Kravitch, J.   Gunny contends that appellee's [Bigelow-Sanford] alleged cover purchases should not have been used to measure damages in that they were not made in substitution for the contract purchases, were not made seasonably or in good faith and were not shown to be due to Gunny's breach. [W]e disagree. Again, we quote UCC § 2–711 providing in part for cover damages where the seller fails to make delivery or repudiates the contract:

"(1) Where the seller fails to make delivery or repudiates or the buyer rightfully rejects or justifiably revokes acceptance then with respect to any goods involved, and with respect to the whole if the breach goes to the whole contract (2–612), the buyer may cancel and whether or not he has done so may in addition to recovering so much of the price as has been paid.

(a) 'cover' and have damages under the next section as to all the goods affected whether or not they have been identified to the contract; or

(b) recover damages for nondelivery as provided in this Article (2–713)."

UCC § 2–712 defines cover:

"(1) After a breach within the preceding section the buyer may 'cover' by making in good faith and without unreasonable delay any reasonable purchase of or contract to purchase goods in substitution for those due from the seller.

"(2) The buyer may recover from the seller as damages the difference between the cost of cover and the contract price together with any incidental or consequential damages as hereinafter defined (2–715), but less expenses saved in consequence of the seller's breach.

"(3) Failure of the buyer to effect cover within this section does not bar him from any other remedy."

In addition, the purchaser may recover under 2–713:

"(1) Subject to the provisions of this Article with respect to proof of market price (2–723), the measure of damages for nondelivery or repudiation by the seller is the difference between the market price at the time when the buyer learned of the breach and the contract price together with any incidental and consequential damages provided in this Article (2–715), but less expenses saved in consequence of the seller's breach.

"(2) Market price is to be determined as of the place for tender or, in cases of rejection after arrival or revocation of acceptance, as of the place of arrival."

Most importantly, "whether a plaintiff has made his cover purchases in a reasonable manner poses a classic jury issue." [Citation.] The district court thus acted properly in submitting the question of cover damages to the jury, which found that Gunny had breached, appellee had covered, and had done so in good faith without unreasonable delay by making reasonable purchases, and was therefore entitled to damages under § 2–712. Gunny argues Bigelow is not entitled to such damages on the ground that it failed to make cover purchases without undue delay and that the jury should not have been permitted to average the cost of Bigelow's spot market purchases totalling 164,503 linear yards in order to arrive at the cost of cover for the 72,265 linear yards Gunny failed to deliver. Both arguments fail. Gunny notified Bigelow in February that no more jute would be forthcoming. Bigelow made its first spot market purchases in mid-March. Given that it is within the jury's province to decide the reasonableness of the manner in which cover purchases were made, we believe the jury could reasonably decide such purchases, made one month after the date the jury assigned to Gunny's breach, were made without undue delay. The same is true with respect to Gunny's second argument: Bigelow's spot market purchases were made to replace several vendors' shipments. Bigelow did not specifically allocate the spot market replacements to individual vendors' accounts, however, nor was there a requirement that they do so. The jury's method of averaging such costs and assigning them to Gunny in proportion to the amount of jute if [sic] failed to deliver would, therefore, seem not only fair but well within the jury's permissible bounds.

Gunny also argues that the court erroneously charged the jury regarding damages under both § § 2–712 and 2–713. We disagree. Whether Bigelow covered was a question of fact submitted to the jury. In the event that it had not, alternative damages were available to Bigelow under § 2–713. [Citation.] The jury found that Bigelow had covered and awarded damages under § 2–712; § 2–713 then became irrelevant. Since either was applicable until that time, the court's charge as to both sections was not error.

To Recover Damages for Nondelivery or Repudiation

If the seller repudiates the contract or fails to deliver the goods, or if the buyer rightfully rejects or justifiably revokes acceptance of the goods, the buyer is entitled to recover damages from the seller measured by the **difference between the market price** at the time when the buyer learned of the breach **and the contract price,** together *with* incidental and consequential damages, *less* expenses saved in consequence of the seller's breach.[14] This remedy is a complete alternative to the remedy of cover and is available only to the extent the buyer has not covered. As previously indicated, the buyer who elects this remedy may not recover those consequential damages that could have been avoided by cover.

The market price is to be determined as of the place for tender, or in the event that the buyer has rightfully rejected the goods or has justifiably revoked his acceptance of them, the market price is to be determined as of the place of arrival.[14] For example, Janet agrees to sell goods to Laura for $7,000 C.O.D., with delivery by November 15. Janet fails to deliver. As a consequence, Laura suffered incidental damages of $1,500 and consequential damages of $1,000. In the case of nondelivery or repudiation, market price is determined as of the place of tender. Since C.O.D. is a shipment contract, the place of tender would be the seller's city. Therefore, the market price must be determined in the seller's city and on November 15, when Laura learned of the breach. At this time and place the market price is $8,000. Laura would recover the market price ($8,000), minus the contract price ($7,000), plus incidental damages ($1,500), plus consequential damages ($1,000), less expenses saved ($0 in this example), which equals $3,500.

In the example above, if Janet had instead delivered nonconforming goods that Laura rejected, then the market price would be determined at Laura's place of business; if instead Janet repudiated the contract on November 1, then the market price would be determined on that date.

To Recover Identified Goods on the Seller's Insolvency

Where existing goods are identified to the contract of sale, the buyer acquires a **special property interest** in the goods.[15] This special property interest exists even though the goods are nonconforming and the buyer has the right to return or reject them. Identification of the goods to the contract may be made either by the buyer or by the seller.

The Code gives the buyer a right, which does not exist at common law, to recover from an insolvent seller the goods in which the buyer has a special property interest and for which he has paid a part or all of the price.[16] This right exists where the seller, who is in possession or control of the goods, becomes insolvent within ten days after receipt of the first installment of the price. To exercise it, the buyer must tender to the seller any unpaid portion of the price. If the special property interest exists by reason of an identification made by the buyer, he may recover the goods only if they conform to the contract for sale.

To Sue for Replevin

Replevin is a form of action at law to recover specific goods in the possession of a defendant that are being unlawfully withheld from the plaintiff. The buyer may maintain against the seller an action for replevin for goods that have been identified to the contract where the seller has repudiated or breached the contract, if (1) the buyer after a reasonable effort is unable to obtain cover for such goods, or (2) the goods have been shipped under reservation of a security interest in the seller and satisfaction of this security interest has been made or tendered.[17]

To Sue for Specific Performance

Specific performance is an equitable remedy compelling the party in breach to perform the contract according to its terms. At common law, specific performance is available only if the legal remedies are inadequate. For example, where the contract is for the purchase of a unique item such as a work of art, a famous racehorse, or an heirloom, money damages may not be an adequate remedy. In such a case, a court of equity has the discretion to order the seller specifically to deliver to the buyer the goods described in the contract on payment of the price.

The Code not only has continued the availability of specific performance but also has sought to further a more liberal attitude towards its use. Accordingly, it does not expressly require that the remedy at law be inadequate. Instead, the Code states that "specific performance may be decreed where the goods are unique or in other proper circumstances." In addition, the Code provides that a decree for specific performance may include terms and conditions as to payment of the price, damages, or other relief.[17]

To Enforce a Security Interest in the Goods

A buyer who has rightfully rejected or justifiably revoked acceptance of goods that remain in her possession or control has a security interest in these goods to the extent of any payment of the price that she has made and for any expenses reasonably incurred in their inspection, receipt, transportation, care, and custody. The buyer may hold such goods and resell them in the same manner as an aggrieved seller may resell goods.[11] In the event of resale, the buyer is required to account to the seller for any excess of the net proceeds of the resale over the amount of her security interest.[6]

To Recover Damages for Breach in Regard to Accepted Goods

Where the buyer has accepted nonconforming goods and has given timely notification to the seller of the breach of contract, the buyer is entitled to maintain an action at law to recover from the seller the damages resulting in the ordinary course of events from the seller's breach.[18] In the event of breach of warranty, the measure of damages is the **difference** at the time and place of acceptance **between the value** that the goods would have had if they had been **as warranted and the value of the goods that have been accepted,** unless special circumstances show proximate damages of a different amount.[18] In addition, incidental and consequential damages, where appropriate, may also be recovered.

The contract price of the goods does not figure in this computation, because the buyer is entitled to the benefit of his bargain, which is to receive goods that are as warranted. For example, Eleanor agrees to sell goods to Timothy for $1,000. The value of the goods accepted is $800, but if they had been as warranted, their value would have been $1,200. The buyer's damages for breach of warranty are $400, which he may deduct from any unpaid balance due on the purchase price on notice to the seller of his intention to do so.[19]

To Recover Incidental Damages

In addition to such remedies as covering, recovering damages for nondelivery or repudiation, or recovering damages for breach of warranty, the buyer may recover incidental damages. The buyer's incidental damages resulting from the seller's breach include expenses reasonably incurred in inspection, receipt, transportation, and care and custody of goods rightfully rejected; any commercially reasonable charges, expenses, or commissions in connection with obtaining cover; and any other reasonable expense connected to the delay or other breach.[13] For example, the buyer of a racehorse justifiably revokes acceptance because the horse does not conform to the contract. The buyer will be allowed to recover as incidental damages the cost of caring for the horse from the date the horse was delivered until it is returned to the seller.

To Recover Consequential Damages

In many cases, the remedies discussed above will not fully compensate the aggrieved buyer for her losses. For example, nonconforming goods that are accepted may explode and destroy the buyer's warehouse and its contents. Undelivered goods may have been the subject of a lucrative contract of resale, the profits from which are lost. The Code responds to this problem by providing the buyer with the opportunity to recover **consequential damages** resulting from the seller's breach, including (1) any loss resulting from the buyer's requirements and needs of which the seller at the time of contracting had reason to know and which could not reasonably be prevented by cover or otherwise; and (2) injury to person or property proximately resulting from any breach of warranty.[13]

An illustration of the first type of consequential damage is: Supreme Machine Co., a manufacturer, contracts to sell Allied Sales Inc., a dealer in used machinery, a used machine that Allied plans to resell. Supreme repudiates and Allied is unable to obtain a similar machine elsewhere. Allied's damages include the net profit that it would have made on resale of the machine. A buyer may not recover consequential damages he could have prevented by cover, however. For instance, Supreme Machine Co. contracts to sell Capitol Manufacturing Co. a used machine for $10,000 to be delivered at Capitol's factory by June 1. Supreme repudiates the contract on May 1. By reasonable efforts, Capitol could buy a similar machine from United Machinery Inc. for $11,000 in time to be delivered by June 1. Capitol fails to do so and loses a profit of $5,000 that it would have made from the resale of the machine. Capitol's damages do *not* include the loss of the $5,000 profit, but it can recover $1,000 from Supreme.

An example of the second type of consequential damage is: Federal Machine Co. sells a machine to Southern Manufacturing Co., warranting its suitability for Southern's purpose. The machine is not suitable for Southern's purpose and causes $10,000 in damage to Southern's property and $15,000 in personal injuries. Southern can recover the $25,000 consequential damages in addition to any other loss suffered.

BURRUS v. ITEK CORP.

Appellate Court of Illinois, Third District, 1977.
46 Ill.App.3d 350, 4 Ill.Dec. 793, 360 N.E.2d 1168.

Facts: Sherman Burrus, a job printer, purchased a printing press from the Itek Corporation for a price of $7,006.08. Before making the purchase, Burrus was assured by an Itek salesman, Mr. Nessel, that the press was appropriate for the type of printing Burrus was doing. Burrus encountered problems in operating the press almost continuously from the time he received it. Burrus, his employees, and Itek representatives spent many hours in an unsuccessful attempt to get the press to operate properly. Burrus requested that the press be replaced, but Itek refused. Burrus then brought an action against Itek for (1) damages for breach of the implied warranty of merchantability, and (2) consequential damages for losses resulting from the press's defective operation. The trial court awarded damages of $10,435 to Burrus, and Itek appealed.

Decision: Judgment for Burrus affirmed.

Opinion: Scott, J.   The Commercial Code of our state provides for the award of such damages [for breach of implied warranty of merchantability]. * * *

Following the language of the statute the first element of damages recoverable by plaintiff is the difference between the value of the goods accepted and the value they would have had as warranted. * * * The record clearly indicates that the cost of the press to the plaintiff including finance charges was $7,006.08. It is proper to include finance charges in arriving at the value of goods as warranted. [Citation.]

Since the defects complained of by the plaintiff were present at the time the press was installed we do not deem it unreasonable to accept the figure of $7,006.08 as its warranted value at a time some sixty plus days later. In examining the record we find testimony that the actual value of the defective press at time of acceptance was one sixth of its purchase price or the sum of $1,167. Subtracting this latter figure from the warranted value, to-wit, $7,006.08, we arrive at the figure of $5,839.08 as the amount to which the plaintiff is entitled as the result of the defendant's breach of implied warranty as to the press. It appears from the record and briefs submitted to the trial court by both parties that the trial court arrived at the figure of $5,833 as the first element of damages to be awarded to the plaintiff. In view of such slight discrepancy between the trial court's computation and the computation of this court, to-wit, a difference of $6.08, we unhesitatingly approve of and accept the trial court's computation. [U.C.C. §] 1–106, states:

"(1) The remedies provided by this Act shall be liberally administered to the end that the aggrieved party may be put in as good a position as if the other party had fully performed. . . ."

The committee comments to this section reject the doctrine that damages must be calculated to a mathematical certainty. Where the right of recovery exists the defendant cannot escape liability because the damages are difficult to prove. The best evidence which the subject will admit is receivable is nothing more than opinions of persons well informed on the subject under investigation. [Citation.] * * *

The second element of damages allowed by the trial court was consequential damages. Such recovery is authorized by [U.C.C. §] 2–715(2)(a), which provides:

"(2) Consequential damages resulting from the seller's breach include
    (a) any loss resulting from general or particular requirements and needs of which the seller at the time of contracting had reason to know and which could not reasonably be prevented by cover or otherwise; . . . ."

It is the defendant's contention that consequential damages are not recoverable in the instant case since the plaintiff elected to keep the press and continue to use it. In support of this contention the defendant cites the case of [citation]. In the first instance we question the defendant's allegation that the plaintiff elected to keep the press. As we interpret the record he had no choice in the matter in that the defendant refused to provide a replacement machine. It is true that the plaintiff in spite of many problems did continue to use the machine in an effort to maintain his business; however, we do not deem such continued usage as grounds for denying the recovery of consequential damages. [Citation.] The provisions of our Commercial Code relating to the recovery of consequential damages does not require any prior agreement on the part of the seller that he may be held liable for such damages. [Citation.]

Without making a further recital of the facts we can summarize the evidence adduced regarding consequential damages by stating that it was proved that the defendant's press did not increase the plaintiff's volume of printing, but on the contrary his output decreased. The plaintiff spent one thousand hours trying to get the machine to work properly and this time is in addition to that expended by Mr. Wiese and other employees who attempted to correct the press's defects. There is also evidence of a great loss of paper as the result of what in printing parlance is known as a "jam up." Lost profits are also a proper element to consider in determining consequential damages. [Citations.] Based upon the facts already recited it is obvious that the plaintiff suffered loss of profits. Mr. Wiese testified that at least $15.00 per hour should have been generated by the press if it operated properly, however, during the one thousand hours he operated the press one-third of his time was wasted and unproductive as the result of the press's defects.

The trial court entered a judgment for the plaintiff and against the defendant in the sum of $10,435. This total sum granted included consequential damages. We are of the opinion that the evidence adduced during the course of the trial well supports the trial court's granting of a total judgment in this amount.

A summary and classification of the remedies for breach available to both buyer and seller are given in Figure 21–1. This figure shows which remedies are available for each type of breach. It also points out the analogous remedies of seller and buyer.

CONTRACTUAL PROVISIONS AFFECTING REMEDIES

Within specified limits, the Code permits the parties to a sales contract to modify, exclude, or limit by agreement the remedies or damages that will be

---

FIGURE 21–1 Remedies for Breach

Buyer's Breach

1) B wrongfully rejects
2) B wrongfully revokes acceptance
3) B fails to make payment
4) B repudiates

Seller's Breach

1) B rightfully rejects
2) B justifiably revokes acceptance
3) S fails to deliver
4) S repudiates
5) B accepts non-conforming goods

Seller's Remedy

Buyer's Remedy

Obligation Oriented

	Seller's Remedy	Buyer's Remedy	
(1–4)	Cancel	Cancel	(1–4)

Goods Oriented

	Seller's Remedy	Buyer's Remedy	
(1–4)	Withhold delivery of goods	Recover payments made	(1–4)
(3)	Reclaim goods upon B's insolvency	Recover identified goods if S is insolvent	(3,4)
(1–4)	Stop delivery of goods by carrier or bailee	Have security interest	(1,2)
(1–4)	Identify conforming goods to contract		

Money Oriented

	Seller's Remedy	Buyer's Remedy	
(1–4)	Resell and recover damages	Cover and recover damages	(1–4)
(1–4)	Recover damages for non-acceptance	Recover damages for non-delivery	(1–4)
		Recover damages for breach of warranty	(5)

Specific Performance

	Seller's Remedy	Buyer's Remedy	
(1–4)	Recover price	Replevy goods	(3,4)
		Obtain specific performance	(3,4)

available for breach of that contract. Two basic types of contractual provisions affect remedies: (1) liquidation or limitation of damages, and (2) modification or limitation of remedy.

Liquidation or Limitation of Damages

The parties may provide for liquidated damages in their contract by specifying the amount or measure of damages that either party may recover in the event of a breach by the other party. The amount of such damages must be reasonable in light of the anticipated or actual loss resulting from a breach. A provision in a contract fixing unreasonably large liquidated damages is void as a penalty.[20]

To illustrate, Sterling Cabinetry Company contracts to build and install shelves and cabinets for an office building being constructed by Baron Construction Company. The contract price is $120,000, and the contract provides that Sterling would be liable for $100 per day for every day's delay beyond the completion date specified in the contract. The stipulated sum of $100 per day is reasonable and commensurate with the anticipated loss. Therefore, it is enforceable as liquidated damages. If, instead, the sum stipulated had been $5,000 per day, it would be unreasonably large and therefore void as a penalty.

Modification or Limitation of Remedy by Agreement

The contract between the seller and buyer may expressly provide for remedies in addition to or instead of those provided in the Code and may limit or change the measure of damages recoverable in the event of breach.[21] For instance, the contract may validly limit the remedy of the buyer to a return of the goods and a refund of the price, or to the replacement of nonconforming goods or parts.

A remedy provided by the contract, however, is deemed optional unless it is expressly agreed to be exclusive of other remedies, in which event it is the sole remedy. Moreover, where circumstances cause an exclusive or limited remedy to fail in its essential purpose, resort may be had to the remedies provided by the Code[21] as in the next case.

The contract may expressly limit or exclude consequential damages unless such limitation or exclusion would be unconscionable. Limitation of consequential damages for personal injuries resulting from breach of warranty in the sale of consumer goods is *prima facie* unconscionable, whereas limitation of such damages where the loss is commercial is not.[21] For example, Ace Motors, Inc., sells a pick-up truck to Brenda, a consumer. The contract of sale excludes liability for all consequential damages. The next day the truck explodes, causing serious personal injury to Brenda. Brenda would recover for her personal injuries unless Ace could prove that the exclusion of consequential damages was *not* unconscionable.

WILSON TRADING CORP. v. DAVID FERGUSON, LIMITED
Court of Appeals of New York, 1968.
23 N.Y.2d 398, 297 N.Y.S.2d 108, 244 N.E.2d 685.

Facts: Wilson Trading Corp. agreed to sell David Ferguson a specified quantity of yarn for use in making sweaters. The written contract provided that notice of defects, to be effective, had to be received by Wilson before knitting or within ten days of receipt of the yarn. When the knitted sweaters were washed, the color of the yarn "shaded" (i.e., variations in color from piece to piece appeared). David Ferguson immediately notified Wilson of the problem and refused to pay for the yarn, claiming that the defect made the sweaters unmarketable. Wilson brought suit against Ferguson. The trial court granted Wilson summary judgment for the contract price and the appellate court affirmed.

Decision: Order of appellate court reversed and Wilson's motion for summary judgment denied.

Opinion: **Jasen, J.** Subdivision (3) (par. [a]) of section 2–607 of the Uniform Commercial Code expressly provides that a buyer who accepts goods has a reasonable time after he discovers or should have discovered a breach to notify the seller of such breach. * * * Defendant's affidavits allege that a claim was made immediately upon discovery of the breach of warranty after the yarn was knitted and washed, and that this was the earliest possible moment at which the defects could reasonably be discovered in the normal manufacturing process. * * *

However, the Uniform Commercial Code allows the parties, within limits established by the code, to modify or exclude warranties and to limit remedies for breach of warranty. * * *

We are, therefore confronted with the effect to be given the time limitation provision in * * * the contract. * * *

Parties to a contract are given broad latitude within which to fashion their own remedies for breach of contract (Uniform Commercial Code, § 2–316 (subd. [4]; §§ 2–718–2–719). Nevertheless, it is clear from the official comments to section 2–719 of the Uniform Commercial Code that it is the very essence of a sales contract that at least minimum adequate remedies be available for its breach. "If the parties intend to conclude a contract for sale within this Article they must accept the legal consequence that there be at least a fair quantum of remedy for breach of the obligations or duties outlined in the contract. Thus any clause purporting to modify or limit the remedial provisions of this Article in an *unconscionable manner* is subject to deletion and in that event the remedies made available by this Article are applicable as if the stricken clause had never existed." [Citation.]

It follows that contractual limitations upon remedies are generally to be enforced unless unconscionable. * * *

However, it is unnecessary to decide the issue of whether the time limitation is unconscionable on this appeal for section 2–719 (subd. [2]) of the Uniform Commercial Code provides that the general remedy provisions of the code apply when "circumstances cause an exclusive or limited remedy to fail of its essential purpose". As explained by the official comments to this section: "where an apparently fair and reasonable clause because of circumstances fails in its purpose or operates to deprive either party of the substantial value of the bargain, it must give way to the general remedy provisions of this article." [Citation.] Here * * * the contract bars all claims for shade and other specified defects made after knitting and processing. Its effect is to eliminate any remedy for shade defects not reasonably discoverable within the time limitation period. It is true that parties may set by agreement any time not manifestly unreasonable whenever the code "requires any action to be taken within a reasonable time" [citation], but here the time provision eliminates all remedy for defects not discoverable before knitting and processing and section 2–719 (subd. [2]) of the Uniform Commercial Code therefore applies.

* * * The time limitation clause of the contract, therefore, insofar as it applies to defects not reasonably discoverable within the time limits established by the contract, must give way to the general code rule that a buyer has a reasonable time to notify the seller of breach of contract after he discovers or should have discovered the defect. [Citation.]

CHAPTER SUMMARY

Remedies of the Seller	**Buyer's Default** the seller's remedies are triggered by a buyer who has wrongfully rejected or revoked acceptance of the goods, who has failed to make payment due on or before delivery, or who has repudiated the contract
	To Withhold Delivery
	To Stop Delivery if the buyer is insolvent (unable to pay his debts as they become due or whose total liabilities exceed his total assets), the seller may stop any delivery; if the buyer repudiates or otherwise breaches, the seller may stop carload, truckload, planeload or larger shipments
	To Identify Goods
	To Resell the Goods the seller may resell the goods concerned or the undelivered balance of the goods and recover the difference between the contract price and the resale price, together with any incidental damages, less expenses saved
	  ■ *Type of Resale* may be public or private
	  ■ *Manner of Resale* must be made in good faith and in a commercially reasonable manner
	To Recover Damages for Nonacceptance or Repudiation
	  ■ *Market Price Differential* the seller may recover damages from the buyer measured by the difference between the unpaid contract price and the market price at the time and place of tender of the goods, plus incidental damages, less expenses saved
	  ■ *Lost Profit* in the alternative the seller may recover the lost profit, including reasonable overhead, plus incidental damages, less expenses saved
	To Recover the Price the seller may recover the price:
	  ■ where the buyer has accepted the goods
	  ■ where the goods have been lost or damaged after the risk of loss has passed to the buyer
	  ■ where the goods have been identified to the contract and there is no ready market available for their resale
	To Recover Incidental Damages incidental damages include any commercially reasonable charges, expenses, or commissions directly resulting from the breach
	To Cancel the Contract
	To Reclaim the Goods upon the Buyer's Insolvency an unpaid seller may reclaim goods from an insolvent buyer under certain circumstances

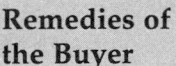**Remedies of the Buyer**	**Seller's Default** the buyer's remedies arise where the seller fails to make delivery or repudiates the contract, or where the buyer rightfully rejects or justifiably revokes acceptance of goods tendered or delivered **To Cancel the Contract** **To Recover Payments Made** **To Cover** the buyer may obtain cover by proceeding in good faith and without unreasonable delay to purchase substitute goods; the buyer may recover the difference between the cost of cover and the contract price, plus any incidental and consequential damages, less expenses saved

To Recover Damages for Nondelivery or Repudiation the buyer may recover the difference between the market price at the time when the buyer learned of the breach and the contract price, together with any incidental and consequential damages, less expenses saved

To Recover Identified Goods on the Seller's Insolvency for which he has paid all or part of the price

To Sue for Replevin the buyer may recover goods identified to the contract if (1) the buyer is unable to obtain cover, or (2) the goods have been shipped under reservation of a security interest in the seller

To Sue for Specific Performance the buyer may obtain specific performance where the goods are unique or in other proper circumstances

To Enforce a Security Interest a buyer who has rightfully rejected or justifiably revoked acceptance of goods that remain in her possession has a security interest in these goods to the extent of any payment that she has made

To Recover Damages for Breach in Regard to Accepted Goods the buyer may recover damages resulting in the ordinary course of events from the seller's breach; in the case of breach of warranty it is the difference between the value the goods would have had if they had been as warranted and the value of the nonconforming goods that have been accepted

To Recover Incidental Damages the buyer may recover incidental damages which include any commercially reasonable expenses connected with the delay or other breach

To Recover Consequential Damages the buyer may recover consequential damages resulting from the seller's breach, including (1) any loss resulting from the buyer's requirements and needs of which the seller at the time of contracting had reason to know and which could not reasonably be prevented by cover or otherwise, and (2) injury to person or property proximately resulting from any breach of warranty

Contractual Provisions Affecting Remedies

Liquidation or Limitation of Damages the parties may specify the amount or measure of damages that may be recovered in the event of a breach if the amount is reasonable

Modification or Limitation of Remedy by Agreement the contract between the parties may expressly provide for remedies in addition to those in the Code or it may limit or change the measure of damages recoverable for breach

QUESTIONS

1. Identify and discuss the goods oriented remedies of the seller and the buyer.
2. Identify and discuss the obligation oriented remedies of the seller and the buyer.
3. Identify and discuss the money oriented damages of the seller and the buyer.
4. Identify and discuss the "specific performance" remedies of the seller and buyer.
5. Describe the basic types of contractual provisions affecting remedies and the limitations the Code imposes upon these provisions.

PROBLEMS

1. Mae contracts to sell 1,000 bushels of wheat to Lloyd at $4 per bushel. Just before Mae was to deliver the wheat, Lloyd notified her that he would not receive or accept the wheat. Mae sold the wheat for $3.60 per bushel, the market price, and later sued Lloyd for the difference of $400. Lloyd claims he was not notified by Mae of the resale and hence is not liable. Decision?

2. On December 15, Judy wrote a letter to David stating that she would sell to David all of the mine-run coal that David might wish to buy during

the next calendar year for use at David's factory, delivered at the factory at a price of $40 per ton. David immediately replied by letter to Judy stating that he accepted the offer, that he would purchase all of his mine-run coal from Judy, and that he would need 200 tons of coal during the first week of January. During the months of January, February, and March, Judy delivered to David a total of 700 tons of coal, for all of which David made payment to Judy at the rate of $40 per ton. On April 10 David ordered 200 tons of mine-run coal from Judy, who replied to David on April 11 that she could not supply David with any more coal except at a price of $48 per ton delivered. David thereafter purchased elsewhere at the market price, namely $48 per ton, all of the requirements of his factory of mine-run coal for the remainder of the year, amounting to a total of 2,000 tons of coal. David now brings an action against Judy to recover damages at the rate of $8 per ton for the coal thus purchased, amounting to $16,000. Decision?

3. On January 10 Betty, of Emanon, Missouri, visited the showrooms of the Forte Piano Company in St. Louis and selected a piano. A sales memorandum of the transaction signed both by Betty and by the salesman of the Forte Piano Company read as follows: "Sold to Betty one new Andover piano, factory number 46832, price $3,300 to be shipped to the buyer at Emanon, Missouri, freight prepaid, before February 1. Prior to shipment seller will stain the case a darker color in accordance with buyer's directions and will make the tone more brilliant." On January 15 Betty repudiated the contract by letter to the Forte Piano Company. The company subsequently stained the case, made the tone more brilliant and offered to ship the piano to Betty on January 26. Betty persisted in her refusal to accept the piano. In an action by the Forte Piano Company against Betty to recover the contract price, what judgment?

4. Sims contracted in writing to sell Blake 100 electric motors at a price of $100 each, freight prepaid to Blake's warehouse. By the contract of sale, Sims expressly warranted that each motor would develop twenty-five brake horsepower. The contract provided that the motors would be delivered in lots of twenty-five per week beginning January 2, that Blake should pay for each lot of twenty-five motors as delivered, but that Blake was to have the right of inspection on delivery.

Immediately on delivery of the first lot of twenty-five motors on January 2, Blake forwarded Sims a check for $2,500, but on testing each of the twenty-five motors, Blake determined that none of them would develop more than fifteen brake horsepower. State all of the remedies available to Blake.

5. Henry and Mary entered into a written contract whereby Henry agreed to sell and Mary agreed to buy a certain automobile for $3,500. Henry drove the car to Mary's residence and properly parked it on the street in front of Mary's house, where he tendered it to Mary and requested payment of the price. Mary refused to take the car or pay the price. Henry informed Mary that he would hold her to the contract; but before Henry had time to enter the car and drive it away, a fire truck, answering a fire alarm and traveling at a high speed, crashed into the car and demolished it. Henry brings an action against Mary to recover the price of the car. Who is entitled to judgment? Would there be any difference in result if Henry were a dealer in automobiles?

6. Jane sells and delivers to Gerald on June 1 certain goods and receives from Gerald at the time of delivery Gerald's check in the amount of $900 for the goods. The following day Gerald is petitioned into bankruptcy, and the check is dishonored by Gerald's bank. On June 5, Jane serves notice on Gerald and the trustee in bankruptcy that she reclaims the goods. The trustee is in possession of the goods and refuses to deliver them to Jane. What are the rights of the parties?

7. The ABC Company, located in Chicago, contracted to sell a carload of television sets to Dodd in St. Louis, Missouri, on sixty days' credit. ABC Company shipped the carload to Dodd. On arrival of the car at St. Louis, Dodd paid the freight charges and reshipped the car to Hines of Little Rock, Arkansas, to whom he had previously contracted to sell the television sets. While the car was in transit to Little Rock, Dodd went bankrupt. ABC Company was informed of this at once and immediately telegraphed XYZ Railroad Company to withhold delivery of the television sets. What should the XYZ Railroad Company do?

8. Robert in Chicago entered into a contract to sell certain machines to Terry in New York. The machines were to be manufactured by Robert and shipped F.O.B. Chicago not later than March 25. On March 24, when Robert was about to ship the machines, he received a telegram from Terry wrongfully repudiating the contract. The machines cannot readily be resold for a reasonable price because they are a special kind used only in Terry's manufacturing processes. Robert sues Terry to recover the agreed price of the machines. What are the rights of the parties?

9. Calvin purchased a log home construction kit manufactured by Boone Homes, Inc., from an authorized dealer of Boone. The sales contract stated that Boone would repair or replace defective materials and that this was the exclusive remedy available against Boone. The dealer assembled the

house, which was defective in a number of respects. The knotholes in the logs caused the walls and ceiling to leak. A support beam was too small and therefore cracked, causing the floor to crack also. These defects could not be completely cured by repair. Calvin sues Boone for breach of warranty to recover damages for the loss in value. Decision?

10. Margaret contracted to buy a 1973 Rolls Royce Corniche from Paragon Motors, Inc. She paid a $3,000 deposit on the car. Only 100 Corniches are built each year. Paragon sold the car to Gluck. What remedy, if any, does Margaret have against Paragon?

11. Technical Textile agreed by written contract to manufacture and sell 20,000 pounds of yarn to Jagger Brothers at a price of $2.15 per pound. After Technical had manufactured, delivered, and been paid for 3,723 pounds of yarn, Jagger Brothers by letter informed Technical that it was repudiating the contract and that it would refuse any further yarn deliveries. On August 12, the date of the letter, the market price of yarn was $1.90 per pound.

Technical was awarded $4,069.25 in damages by the trial court, an amount equal to 16,277 times the difference between the contract price ($2.15) and the market price ($1.90) of the yarn on the repudiation date. Jagger Brothers appealed, contending that the proper measure of damages was the difference between the contract price and the cost of manufacture, and that, because no evidence was offered as to the cost of manufacture, Technical was entitled only to nominal damages. Decision?

COMPUTER RESEARCH PROBLEMS

1. Lee Oldsmobile sells Rolls-Royce automobiles. Mrs. Kaiden sent Lee a $5,000 deposit on a $29,500 1973 Rolls-Royce. Although Lee informed Mrs. Kaiden that the car would be delivered in November, the order form did not indicate the delivery date and contained a disclaimer for delay or failure to deliver due to circumstances beyond the dealer's control. On November 21 Mrs. Kaiden purchased another car from another dealer and cancelled her car from Lee. When Lee attempted to deliver a Rolls-Royce to Mrs. Kaiden on November 29, Mrs. Kaiden refused to accept delivery. Lee later sold the car for $26,495.00. Mrs. Kaiden sued Lee for her $5,000 deposit plus interest. Lee counterclaims, based on the terms of the contract, for liquidated damages of $5,000 (the amount of the deposit) as a result of Mrs. Kaiden's breach of contract. Decision?

2. Servebest contracted to sell Emessee 200,000 pounds of 50 percent lean beef trimmings for $105,000. Upon a substantial fall in the market price, Emessee refused to pay the contract price and informed Servebest that the contract was cancelled. Servebest sues Emessee for breach of contract including (a) damages for the difference between the contract price and the resale price of the trimmings and (b) for incidental damages. Decision?

3. Mrs. French was the highest bidder on eight antique guns at an auction held by Sotheby & Company. When Sotheby's billed Mrs. French $24,886.27 for the guns, she refused to pay. Sotheby's sued Mrs. French for the price of the guns. Decision?

ENDNOTES

1. Uniform Commercial Code, Section 2—703, Seller's Remedies in General.
2. Uniform Commercial Code, Section 1—201(23), General Definitions: Insolvent.
3. Uniform Commercial Code, Section 2—702, Seller's Remedies on Discovery of Buyer's Insolvency.
4. Uniform Commercial Code, Section 2—705, Seller's Stoppage of Delivery in Transit or Otherwise.
5. Uniform Commercial Code, Section 2—704, Seller's Right to Identify Goods to the Contract Notwithstanding Breach or to Salvage Unfinished Goods.
6. Uniform Commercial Code, Section 2—706, Seller's Resale Including Contract for Resale.
7. Uniform Commercial Code, Section 2—708, Seller's Damages for Non-Acceptance or Repudiation.
8. Uniform Commercial Code, Section 2—709, Action for the Price.
9. Uniform Commercial Code, Section 2—710, Seller's Incidental Damages.
10. Uniform Commercial Code, Sections 2—106, Definitions: "Termination"; "Cancellation"; 2—720, Effect of "Cancellation" or "Rescission" on Claims for Antecedent Breach.
11. Uniform Commercial Code, Section 2—711, Buyer's Remedies in General; Buyer's Security Interest in Rejected Goods.
12. Uniform Commercial Code, Section 2—712, "Cover"; Buyer's Procurement of Substitute Goods.

13. Uniform Commercial Code, Section 2—715, Buyer's Incidental and Consequential Damages.

14. Uniform Commercial Code, Section 2—713, Buyer's Damages for Non-Delivery or Repudiation.

15. Uniform Commercial Code, Section 2—501, Insurable Interest in Goods; Manner of Identification of Goods.

16. Uniform Commercial Code, Section 2—502, Buyer's Rights to Goods on Seller's Insolvency.

17. Uniform Commercial Code, Section 2—716, Buyer's Right to Specific Performance or Replevin.

18. Uniform Commercial Code, Section 2—714, Buyer's Damages for Breach in Regard to Accepted Goods.

19. Uniform Commercial Code, Section 2—717, Deduction of Damages From the Price.

20. Uniform Commercial Code, Section 2—718, Liquidation or Limitation of Damages; Deposits.

21. Uniform Commercial Code, Section 2—719, Contractual Modification or Limitation of Remedy.

PART 4
COMMERCIAL PAPER

Commercial paper includes checks, promissory notes, drafts, and certificates of deposit. These instruments, as they are commonly called, are crucial to the sale of goods and services as well as the financing of most businesses. The use of commercial paper has increased to such an extent that payments made with these instruments, particularly checks, far outnumber payments made with cash. In fact, currency is now primarily used for smaller transactions. Accordingly, the vital importance of commercial paper as a method of payment cannot be overstated:

> A reliable payment system is crucial to the economic growth and stability of the nation. The smooth functioning of markets for virtually every good and service is dependent upon the smooth functioning of banking and financial markets, which in turn is dependent upon the integrity of the nation's payment mechanism. History tells us—all too vividly—that fragility of a country's payment system can precipitate or intensify a general economic crisis. *Federal Reserve Bulletin*, September, 1984.

To accomplish these social and economic objectives, the payment system must be quick, sure, and efficient. The use of cash can never satisfy all of these requirements because (1) it is inconvenient to maintain large quantities of cash; (2) the risk of loss or theft is far too great; (3) the risk in sending cash is likewise too high, as is the cost of postage and insurance in shipping cash over long distances; and (4) the costs to the Federal government of maintaining an adequate supply of currency would be prohibitive. In addition, commer-

cial paper used for payment provides a convenient receipt as well as a record for accounting and tax purposes. Although commercial paper acts as a very close approximation of cash for the purpose of payment, it is not the exact equivalent of cash because, for example, commercial paper is more susceptible to forgery, it may be drawn on insufficient funds, payment may be stopped, or the instrument may be materially altered. Nevertheless, these risks (which are real but very infrequent—over 99 percent of all checks are paid), assume small proportions compared to the advantages that commercial paper provides for payment. Consequently, a major policy objective of the law of commercial paper and the bank collection process is to reduce these risks by increasing the safety, soundness, and operating efficiency of the entire payment system.

Because commercial paper plays a central role in the payment system, it is important that you are aware of the social and ethical issues arising out of the use of commercial paper. Many of these issues involve the relationship between customers and their bank. For instance, should a customer have the right to stop payment on a check? If so, under what conditions? At whose expense? How long should a stop payment order be effective? What effect do stop payment orders have on public confidence in the payment system? Who should bear the loss for forgeries: the bank or the customer? With the enormous volume of checks written daily, can a bank be expected to "know" the signatures of all of its customers? These are just some of the public policy questions concerning customer/bank relations that you should consider in studying this part of the text.

Equally important are the ethical issues concerning the forthrightness of banks in informing their customers of their rights as depositors. What obligations should a financial institution have to inform its customers of their rights? What responsibility should the customer have to inform himself of his rights? Should the State or Federal governments be involved in resolving these issues?

Closely related is the ethical question of what essential services financial institutions should provide and how much they should charge for their services. It has been argued that with the deregulation of the financial services industry, current customer service fees greatly favor large customers at heavy financial cost to lower income households. Should such unequal treatment be permitted? Who should be responsible for monitoring such developments?

Another significant ethical question that various legislative and administrative bodies are now addressing concerns the right of banks to "hold" deposited checks before making the funds available to their depositors. In order to determine the validity of checks, some banks had held checks for up to fifteen days before permitting customers to use the funds. The banks use the funds during this delay, but depositors cannot. Beginning on September 1, 1988, the Federal government restricted this time period to two days for a check drawn on a local bank and six days for checks drawn on a nonlocal bank. Effective September 1, 1990, the time period is reduced to one day for a local bank and four days for a nonlocal bank.

Overall, the current payment system has transformed the United States into a virtually cashless society. The advent and technological advances of computers make it likely that electronic fund transfer systems will bring about a checkless society in the foreseeable future. Such a system could increase the speed and efficiency of the payment system by eliminating the cumbersome process of moving paper. There are however, important, and to date, unanswered, questions about the safety of electronic fund transfer systems. Moreover, it is not yet clear how, if at all, such a system would be able to perform all of the various functions now accomplished by checks.

While studying Part Four, you should consider these and other social, ethical, and policy issues in order to determine the reasonableness, appropriateness, and above all, the fairness of the legal principles of commercial paper.

Modern business could not be conducted without the use of **commercial paper**—checks, drafts, promissory notes, and certificates of deposit. A tremendous number of transactions involve the writing of one or more checks. Drafts, of which checks are a specialized form, provide an important monetary and credit function in the business world, both inside and outside the banking system. Promissory notes serve an important business purpose, not only in areas of high finance, but also at the level of the small business person and consumer as well. In recent years, certificates of deposit have been increasingly used by individuals instead of savings accounts.

The various forms of commercial paper, commonly referred to as instruments, may or may not have the unique characteristic of negotiability, although the term "commercial paper" is usually used to refer to negotiable instruments. The way rights and obligations are acquired in commercial paper is important because of the huge volume of daily transactions in promissory notes, certificates of deposit, drafts, and checks.

NEGOTIABILITY

The law gives the quality of negotiability to commercial paper. The concept was devised by the law to meet the needs of traders, merchants, and business people who wanted promises and orders to pay money to circulate freely in the marketplace, not as money, but as a ready substitute for money in business transactions. **Negotiability,** therefore, is a legal concept that makes written instruments a readily accepted form of payment in substitution for money. The concept of negotiability applies not only to commercial paper, which is governed by *Article 3* of the Code, but also to documents of title (governed by Article 7 and discussed in Chapter 48) and investment securities (governed by Article 8 and discussed in Chapter 34).

The starting point for an understanding of negotiable instruments is to recognize that four or five centuries ago in England a contract right to the payment of money was not assignable. The reason was that a contractual promise ran to the promisee. Performance could be rendered to him and to no one else. This was a hardship on the owner of the right because it prevented him from selling or disposing of it. Eventually, the law permitted recovery on an assignment by the assignee against the obligor, although the assignee acquired no new rights but only those of his assignor.

An innocent assignee bringing an action against the obligor was subject to all defenses available to the obligor. Such an action would result in the same outcome regardless of whether it was brought by the assignee or assignor. Thus, a contract right became assignable but not very marketable, because merchants had no interest in buying into a possible lawsuit. This remains the law of assignments: the **assignee stands in the shoes of his assignor.**

With the flourishing of trade and commerce, it became essential to develop means to exchange contractual rights for money. For example, a merchant who sells goods for cash may use the cash to buy more goods for resale. If he makes a sale on credit in exchange for a promise to pay money, why shouldn't he be permitted to sell that promise to someone else for cash with which to carry on his business? One difficulty was that the buyer of the goods gave the seller only a promise to pay money to him. He was the only person to whom performance or payment was promised. If, however, the seller obtained from the buyer a promise in writing to pay money to anyone in possession (*bearer*) of the **instrument** (commercial paper) or to anyone the seller (*payee*) designated, then the duty of performance would run directly to the bearer of the paper or to the person to whom the payee ordered payment to be made. This is one of the essential distinctions between negotiable and nonnegotiable instruments. Although there are other formal requirements of a negotiable instrument, this particular one eliminates the limitations of a promise to pay money only to a named promisee.

Moreover, if the promise to pay were not subject to all of the defenses available against the assignor, then a transferee, such as the bearer or the person to whom the payee *ordered* payment to be made, would not only be more willing to acquire the promise but also would pay more for it. The law of negotiable instruments accordingly developed the concept of **holder in due course,** whereby certain good faith transferees who gave value acquired the right to be paid free of most of the defenses to which an assignee would be subject. Thus, by reason of this doctrine, such a transferee of a negotiable instrument could acquire *greater* rights than his transferor, whereas an assignee would acquire *only* the rights of his assignor.

With these basic innovations, negotiable instruments enabled merchants to sell their contractual rights more readily and thereby keep their capital working.

Negotiability invests commercial paper with a high degree of marketability and commercial utility. It allows commercial paper to be freely transferable and enforceable by a person with the rights of a holder in due course against any person obligated on the paper, subject only to a limited number of defenses. To illustrate, let it be assumed that George sells and delivers goods to Elaine for $500 on sixty days' credit and that, a few days later, George assigns this account to Marsha. Unless Elaine is duly notified of this assignment, she may safely pay the $500 to George on the due date without incurring any liability to Marsha, the assignee. Assume next that the goods were defective and that Elaine accordingly has a defense against George to the extent of $200. Assume also that Marsha duly notified Elaine of the assignment. The result is that Marsha can recover only $300 from Elaine and not $500, because Elaine's defense against George is equally available against George's assignee, Marsha. In other words, an assignee of contractual rights merely "steps into the shoes" of his assignor and hence acquires only the same rights as his assignor—and no more.

Assume instead, that on the sale by George to Elaine, Elaine executed and delivered her negotiable promissory note to George for $500 payable to George's order in sixty days, and that, a short time later, George duly negotiates (transfers) the note to Marsha. In the first place, Marsha is not required to notify Elaine that she has acquired the note from George. One who issues a negotiable instrument is held with knowledge that the instrument may be negotiated from hand to hand and is obligated to pay the holder of the instrument. In the second place, assuming that Marsha acquired the note in good faith, for value, and had no knowledge of Elaine's defense against George, Elaine's defense is not available against Marsha. Marsha, therefore, is entitled to hold Elaine at maturity for the full face amount of the note, namely, $500. In other words, Marsha, by the negotiation of the negotiable note to her, acquired greater rights than George had, since George, had he kept the note, could have recovered only $300 because Elaine could have successfully asserted the defense to the amount of $200 against George.

To have the full benefit of negotiability, commercial paper must not only meet the requirements of negotiability but also must be acquired by a "holder in due course." In this chapter we discuss the formal requirements instruments must satisfy to be negotiable. Chapter 23 deals with the manner in which a negotiable instrument must be transferred (negotiated) to preserve its advantages. Chapter 24 covers the requisites and rights of a holder in due course. Finally, Chapter 25 integrates these interrelated legal rules by examining the liability of all the parties to a negotiable instrument.

TYPES OF COMMERCIAL PAPER

There are four types of commercial paper: drafts, checks, notes, and certificates of deposit.[1] The first two each contain **orders** or directions to pay money; the last two contain **promises** to pay money.

Drafts

A **draft** involves three parties, each in a distinctly different capacity. One party, the **drawer,** *orders* a second party, the **drawee,** to pay a sum certain in money to a third party, the **payee**[1] (see Figure 22–1). The drawee is ordinarily a person or entity who is in possession of money belonging to the drawer or owes money to him. A sample draft is reproduced as Figure 22–2. The same party may appear in more than one capacity; for instance, the drawer may also be the payee.

Drafts may be either ''time'' or ''sight.'' A **time** draft is one payable at a specified future date, whereas a **sight** draft is payable on presentation to the drawee.

A form of time draft, known as a trade acceptance, is frequently used as a credit device in a commercial transaction. A **trade ac-**ceptance is a time draft drawn by the seller (drawer) on the buyer (drawee) and names the seller or some third party as the payee. For example, Ben Buyer wishes to purchase goods from Sam Seller. Seller needs cash immediately, but Buyer cannot pay for the goods until he has resold them. Therefore, Seller draws a draft on Buyer ordering Buyer to pay the amount of the purchase price to the order of Seller at a specified future date. Seller presents this draft to Buyer, who ''accepts'' it thereby agreeing to make payment according to its terms, and returns the accepted draft to Seller, who can then sell the draft to a third party.

A sight draft, sometimes called customer's draft, is used by the seller of goods who desires immediate payment for the goods upon delivery of a bill of lading (a document issued by a carrier evidencing receipt of goods shipped, which may also stipulate that the goods will be delivered to its holder). Upon shipment of the goods, the seller would obtain from the carrier an order bill of lading which he would attach to a customer's draft drawn on the buyer and would send to his local bank for handling. The local bank would send the paper to a bank located in the city where the goods were to be delivered. That bank would then notify the buyer upon arrival of the goods. In order to obtain the bill of lading and thus the goods, the buyer would pay the amount of the seller's draft, which would be forwarded to the seller's bank and there credited to his account.

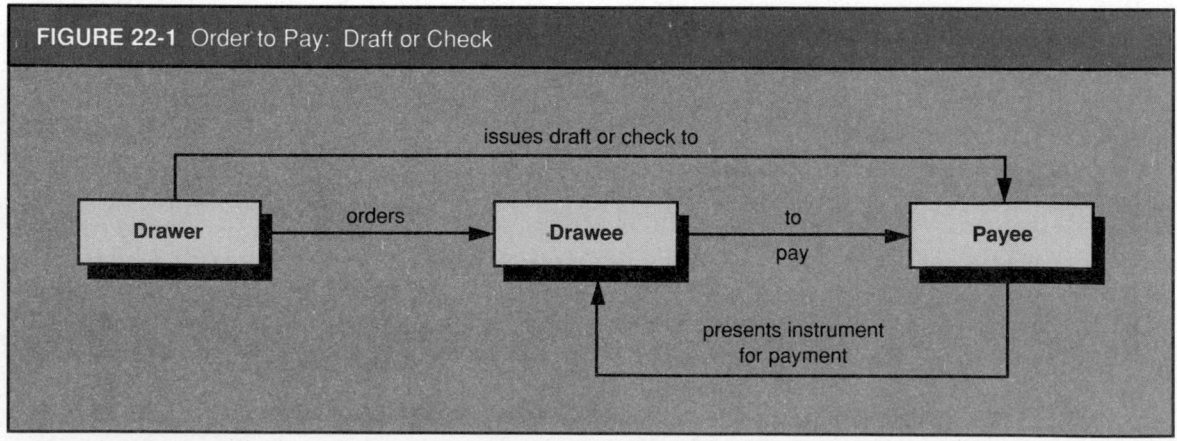

FIGURE 22-1 Order to Pay: Draft or Check

FIGURE 22-2 Draft

St. Louis, Missouri
May 1, 1990

Two years from date pay to the order of Perry Payee
$50,000 Fifty Thousand . . . Dollars

(Signed) Donald Drawer
DONALD DRAWER

To: DEBRA DRAWEE
50 Main St.
Louisville, Kentucky

Checks

A **check** is a specialized form of draft; namely, an order to pay money drawn on a **bank** and payable on **demand** (that is, upon the payee's or holder's request for payment).[1] Once again, there are parties involved in three distinct capacities: the **drawer,** who orders the **drawee,** a bank, to pay the **payee** on demand (see Figure 22–3). Checks are by far the most widely used form of commercial paper. Each year over ten billion checks are written for over five trillion dollars.

A *cashier's check* is a check drawn by a bank on itself to the order of a payee.

Notes

A **promissory note** is an instrument involving two parties in two capacities. One party, the **maker,** promises to pay to the order of a second party, the **payee,** a stated sum of money, either on demand or at a stated future date[1] (see Figure 22–4). The note may range from the simple, "I promise to pay $X to the order of Y," form to more complex legal instruments such as installment notes, collateral notes, mortgage notes, and judgment notes. Figure 22–5 is a note payable at a definite time—six months from the date of April 7, 1990—and hence is referred to as a **time note.**

FIGURE 22-3 Check

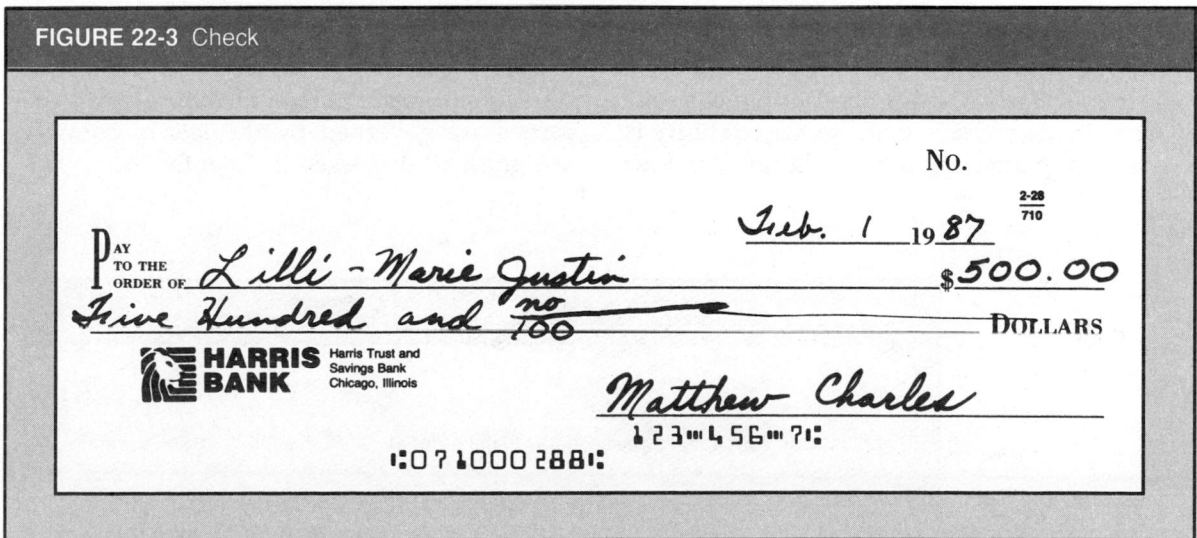

No.

$\frac{2\text{-}28}{710}$

Feb. 1 19 87

Pay to the order of *Lilli-Marie Justin* $500.00

Five Hundred and $\frac{no}{100}$ _____ DOLLARS

HARRIS BANK Harris Trust and Savings Bank Chicago, Illinois

Matthew Charles

123⋯456⋯7⦂

⦂071000288⦂

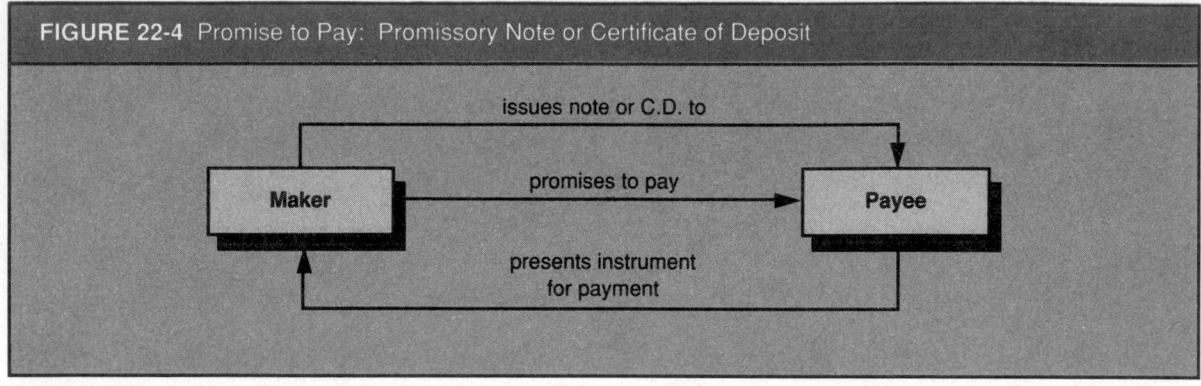

FIGURE 22-4 Promise to Pay: Promissory Note or Certificate of Deposit

A note payable upon the request or demand of the payee or holder is a **demand note.**

Certificates of Deposit

A **certificate of deposit,** or C.D. as it is frequently called, is a specialized form of *promise to pay money* given by a **bank.** It is a written acknowledgment by a bank of the receipt of money that it promises to repay on demand or at a stated future date, with interest at a stated rate.[1] The issuing party, the **maker,** which is always a bank, promises to pay a second party, the **payee,** who is named in the C.D. (see Figure 22–6).

FORM OF COMMERCIAL PAPER

To perform its function in the business community effectively, commercial paper must be capable of passing from hand to hand freely. This is made possible because **negotiability** is wholly a matter of form. Within the four corners of the instrument must be all the information required to determine whether it is negotiable. No reference to any other source is required or permitted. For this reason a **negotiable instrument** is called a "courier without luggage." In addition, indorsements *cannot* create or destroy negotiability.

In order to be negotiable, an instrument must

1. be in writing,
2. be signed,
3. contain a promise or order to pay,
4. be unconditional,
5. be for a sum certain in money,
6. contain no other promise or order,
7. be payable on demand or at a definite time, and
8. be payable to order or to bearer.[2]

If these requirements are not met, the instrument is not negotiable, and the rights of the parties are governed by the law of contract (assignment) discussed in Chapter 14.

FIGURE 22-5 Note

$10,000   Albany, N.Y.   April 7, 1990

Six months from date I promise to pay to the order of Pat Payee ten thousand dollars.

(signed) Matthew Maker

FIGURE 22-6 Certificate of Deposit

NEGOTIABLE CERTIFICATE OF DEPOSIT

The Mountain Bank

No. 13900   Mountain, N.Y.   June 1, 1990

THIS CERTIFIES THAT THERE HAS BEEN DEPOSITED with the undersigned the sum of $200,000.00

Two hundred thousand............................Dollars

Payable to the order of Pablo Payee on December 1, 1992 with interest only to maturity at the rate of TEN percent (10%) per annum upon surrender of this certificate properly indorsed.

The Mountain Bank

By (Signature) Malcolm Maker, Vice-President

Authorized Signature

FIRST STATE BANK AT GALLUP v. CLARK
Supreme Court of New Mexico, 1977.
91 N.M. 117, 570 P.2d 1144.

Facts: Horne executed a $100,000 note in favor of R. C. Clark. On the back of the instrument was a restriction stating that the note could not be transferred, pledged, or otherwise assigned without Horne's written consent. As part of the same transaction between Horne and Clark, Horne gave Clark a separate letter authorizing Clark to pledge the note as collateral for a loan of $50,000 that Clark intended to secure from First State Bank. Clark did secure the loan and pledged the note, which was accompanied by Horne's letter authorizing Clark to use the note as collateral. First State contacted Horne and verified the agreement between Horne and Clark as to using the note as collateral, but when First State later attempted to collect on the note, Horne refused to pay, and this suit was instituted. Summary judgment was granted for First State.

Decision: Judgment for First State Bank affirmed, even though the note in question is not a negotiable instrument.

Opinion: **Easley, J.** The issues raised on appeal include (1) whether the note was a negotiable instrument for purposes of Article 3 of the Uniform Commercial Code (U.C.C.) * * *. Article 3 of the U.C.C. defines a certain type of readily transferable instrument and lays down certain rules for the treatment of that instrument and rules concerning the rights, remedies and defenses of persons dealing with it.

In order to be a "negotiable instrument" for Article 3 purposes the paper must precisely meet the definition set out in § 3–104, since § 3–104 itself states that, to be a negotiable instrument, a writing "must" meet the definition therein set out.

Moreover, it is clear that in order to determine whether an instrument meets that definition *only the instrument itself* may be looked to, *not* other documents, even when other documents are referred to in the instrument. [Citations.] As [citation] points out * * *

The applicability of Article 3 must be determined from the instrument itself, without reference to other documents or oral agreements. The "four-corners test" is still applicable: the determination of negotiability under Article 3 must be made by inspecting only the instrument itself. . . .

This is clear from the mandatory language of U.C.C. § 3–104, and from the following language from the Official Comment to U.C.C. § 3–105 found under the heading "Purposes of Changes": "The section is intended to make it clear that, so far as negotiability is affected, the conditional or unconditional character of the promise or order is to be determined by what is expressed in the instrument itself. . . .

We recognize the Official Comments to the U.C.C. as persuasive, though they are not controlling authority. [Citation.]

Section 3–104 thus requires that, in order to be a negotiable instrument for Article 3 purposes, one must be able to ascertain without reference to other documents that the instrument:

(a) [is] signed by the maker or drawer; and (b) contain[s] an unconditional promise or order to pay a sum certain in money and no other promise, order, obligation or power given by the maker or drawer except as authorized by [Article 3]; and (c) [is] payable on demand or at a definite time; and (d) [is] payable to order or to bearer.

The note in question here failed to meet the requirements of § 3–104, since the promise to pay contained in the note was not unconditional. Moreover, the note was expressly drafted to be non-negotiable since it stated:

This note may not be transferred, pledged, or otherwise assigned without the written consent of M. S. Horne.

These words, even though they appeared on the back of the note, effectively cancelled any implication of negotiability provided by the words "Pay to the order of" on the face of the note. Notations and terms on the back of a note, made contemporaneously with the execution of the note and intended to be part of the note's contract of payment, constitute as much a part of the note as if they were incorporated on its face. [Citation.]

* * *

The whole purpose of the concept of a negotiable instrument under Article 3 is to declare that transferees in the ordinary course of business are only to be held liable for information appearing in the instrument itself and will not be expected to know of any limitations on negotiability or changes in terms, etc., contained in any separate documents. The whole idea of the facilitation of easy transfer of notes and instruments requires that a transferee be able to trust what the instrument says, and be able to determine the validity of the note and its negotiability from the language in the note itself. [Citation.]

* * *

Since the note in question is not negotiable for Article 3 purposes, First State cannot be a holder in due course under Article 3, and we need not discuss that issue.

Writing

The requirement that the instrument be a writing is broadly construed. Printing, type-writing, handwriting, or any other tangible expression is sufficient to satisfy the requirement.[3] Most negotiable instruments, of course, are written on paper, but this is not required. In one instance a check was reportedly written on a coconut.

Signed

A note or certificate of deposit must be signed by the maker; a draft or check must be signed by the drawer. As in the case of a writing, extreme latitude is granted in determining what constitutes a **signature**.[4] Any symbol executed or adopted by a party with the intention to validate a writing is sufficient. Moreover, it may consist of any word or mark used in place of a written signature, such as initials, an X, or a thumb print. It may be a trade name or assumed name. Even the location of the signature on the document is unimportant. Normally, a maker or drawer signs in the lower right-hand corner of the instrument, but this is not required. Negotiable instruments are frequently signed by an agent for his principal. For a discussion of the appropriate way in which an agent should sign a negotiable instrument, see Chapter 25.

Promise or Order to Pay

A negotiable instrument must contain a promise to pay money, in the case of a note or certificate of deposit, or an order to pay, in the case of a draft or check.

A **promise to pay** is an undertaking and must be more than the mere acknowledgment or recognition of an existing obligation.[5] The so-called due bill or I.O.U. is not a promise but a mere acknowledgment of indebtedness. Accordingly, an instrument stating "due Adam Brown $100" or "I.O.U., Adam Brown, $100" is not negotiable because it does not contain a promise to pay.

An **order to pay** is a direction or command to pay. It must be more than an authorization or request and must identify the person to pay

with reasonable certainty.[5] The usual way to express an order is by use of the word *pay*: "*Pay* to the order of John Jones" or "*Pay* bearer." The addition of words of courtesy, such as *please pay* or *kindly pay*, will not destroy negotiability. Nonetheless, caution should be exercised in employing words modifying the prototypically correct *Pay*. For example, it has been held that the use of the words "I wish you would pay" destroyed the negotiability of an instrument and rendered its transfer a contractual assignment.

Unconditional

The requirement that the promise or order be unconditional is to prevent the inclusion of any term that could reduce the promised obligation to pay. The payment and credit functions of negotiable instruments would be diminished by conditions limiting the promise. Costly and time-consuming investigations would become necessary to determine the degree of risk imposed by the condition. Moreover, if the person in possession of the instrument had to take an instrument subject to certain conditions, her risk factor would be substantial, and this would lead to limited transferability. Substitutes for money must be capable of rapid circulation at minimum risks.

The issue is whether there is an absolute promise to pay, one which is not subject to any contingencies or qualifications. Thus, an instrument would not be negotiable if it stated that "ABC Corp. promises to pay $100,000 to the order of Johnson provided the helicopter sold meets all contractual specifications." On the other hand, suppose when he delivered an instrument that provided "ABC Corp. promises to pay $100,000 to the order of Johnson," Meeker, the president of ABC Corp., stated that the money would be paid only if the helicopter met all contractual specifications. The instrument would nonetheless be negotiable because negotiability is determined solely by examining the instrument itself and is not affected by matters beyond the face of the instrument.

A promise or order is conditional if (a) the instrument states that it is subject to or governed by any other agreement, or (b) the instrument states that it is to be paid only out of a particular fund or source.[6]

Reference to Other Agreements The restriction against reference to another agreement is to enable any person to determine the right to payment provided by the instrument without having to look beyond its four corners. If such right is made subject to the terms of another agreement, the instrument is nonnegotiable.

A distinction is to be made between a mere recital of the *existence* of a separate agreement (this does not destroy negotiability) and a recital that makes the instrument *subject* to the terms of another agreement (this does destroy negotiability).

A statement in a note such as

This note is given in partial payment for a color TV set to be delivered two weeks from date in accordance with a contract of this date between the payee and the maker

does not impair negotiability. It merely is a description of the transaction giving rise to the note and describes the consideration. The promise is not made subject to any other agreement. Added words that *would* impair negotiability are:

and the seller is subject to all of the terms of said agreement.

The following case provides another example of words that render the instrument conditional and thus nonnegotiable.

HOLLY HILL ACRES, LIMITED v. CHARTER BANK OF GAINESVILLE
District Court of Appeals of Florida, Second District, 1975.
314 So.2d 209.

Facts: Holly Hill Acres, Ltd., executed and delivered a promissory note and a purchase money mortgage to Rogers and Blythe. The note provided that it was secured by a mortgage on certain real estate and that the terms of that mortgage "are by this reference made a part hereof." Rogers and Blythe then assigned the note to Charter Bank, and the bank now seeks to foreclose on the note and mortgage. Holly Hill Acres refuses to pay and claims that it was defrauded by Rogers and Blythe. Holly Hills appeals from a summary judgment entered in favor of plaintiff Charter Bank.

Decision: Summary judgment reversed and case remanded for further proceedings.

Opinion: Scheb, J. The note having incorporated the terms of the purchase money mortgage was not negotiable. * * *

The note, incorporating by reference the terms of the mortgage, did not contain the unconditional promise to pay required by [U.C.C.§] 3–104(1)(b).

Appellee [Charter] Bank [assignee of the note from Rogers and Blythe] relies upon Scott v. Taylor, [citation] as authority for the proposition that its note is negotiable. *Scott*, however, involved a note which stated: "this note secured by mortgage." Mere reference to a note being secured by mortgage is a common commercial practice and such reference in itself does not impede the negotiability of the note. There is, however, a significant difference in a note stating that it is "secured by a mortgage" from one which provides, "the terms of said mortgage are by this reference made a part hereof." In the former instance the note merely refers to a separate agreement which does not impede its negotiability, while in the latter instance the note is rendered nonnegotiable. *See* [U.C.C. §] 3–105(2)(a); [U.C.C. §] 3–119.

> As a general rule the assignee of a mortgage securing a non-negotiable note, even though a bona fide purchaser for value, takes subject to all defenses available as against the mortgagee [assignor]. [Citation.] Appellant [Holly Hill] raised the issue of fraud as between himself and other parties to the note, therefore, it was incumbent on the appellee Bank, as movant for a summary judgment, to prove the non-existence of any genuinely triable issue. [Citation.]

The Particular Fund Doctrine An order or promise to pay only out of a particular fund is conditional and destroys negotiability because payment depends on the existence and sufficiency of the particular fund. On the other hand, a promise or order to pay, coupled with a mere indication of a particular fund out of which reimbursement is to be made or a particular account to be debited with the amount, does not impair negotiability, because the drawer's or maker's general credit is relied on, and charging a particular account is merely a bookkeeping entry to be followed after payment. Thus, there is a difference between an instrument stating, "Sixty days after date pay to the order of John Jones $500, payment will be limited to the proceeds of the sale of the contents of freight car No. 1234," and one stating, "Sixty days after date pay to the order of John Jones $500 and charge to proceeds of sale of the contents of freight car No. 1234." In the first case, payment would be made only if the contents of the freight car were sold and then only to the extent of the proceeds. In the second case, the instrument contains an unqualified order to pay with merely bookkeeping instructions to the drawee of the draft.

Sum Certain in Money

The holder must be able to determine from the face of the instrument the amount that he is entitled to receive so that he can ascertain the present and future value of the instrument.

Money The term **money** means legal tender. It must be a medium of exchange authorized or adopted by a sovereign government as part of its currency.[7] Consequently, even though local custom may make gold dust or uncut diamonds a medium of exchange, an instrument payable in such commodities would be nonnegotiable because the government does not sanction these articles as legal tender. On the other hand, an instrument paying a sum certain in French francs, German marks, Italian lira, Japanese yen, or other foreign currency is negotiable.

Sum Certain The requirement that payment be of a "sum certain" must be considered from the point of view of the holder, not the maker or drawer. The holder must be assured of a determinable minimum payment, although provisions of the instrument may increase the amount of recovery under certain circumstances. Thus, a frequent provision of a note is that the maker will pay, in addition to the face amount and specified interest, costs of collection and attorney's fees on default in payment. Such a provision is designed to make the paper more attractive without lessening the certainty of the amount due and therefore does not destroy its negotiability.

An instrument payable with a stated rate of interest is an obligation for a sum certain. The rates may be different before and after default, or before and after a specified date.[8] If interest is payable "at the current rate" (which means the current banking rate), however, it is nonnegotiable because this is *not* a matter that can be determined without reference to any outside source. Thus, a variable rate mortgage, as discussed in Law in the News on page 468, is not a sum certain and therefore is a nonnegotiable instrument.

A sum payable is a sum certain even though it is payable in installments or with a fixed discount if paid before maturity or a fixed addition if paid after maturity. This is so be-

LAW IN THE NEWS

Variable-Rate Notes and the UCC
Some Want Code Amended to Make Notes Negotiable

Although it's common knowledge that the majority of new mortgages and outstanding loans have variable rates, many people don't know these variable-rate instruments are considered non-negotiable under the Uniform Commercial Code.

That means a holder of a variable-rate instrument is not a holder in due course and therefore has fewer rights and is subject to more legal defenses than someone who is a holder.

Recent litigation over the variable-rate instruments has involved mortgage companies, real estate owners, banks and borrowers.

For instance, if a homebuyer stops paying on his mortgage and a subsequent mortgage holder tries to foreclose on the property, the foreclosure proceeding can be tied up in court for several years with the borrower refusing to pay, saying the variable-rate note is non-negotiable.

Or a person who borrows from a bank may refuse to pay off the loan, claiming the builder breached the contract when he finished the job, by, for example, leaving a cracked concrete slab. If the bank were a holder in due course, the borrower couldn't assert a contract defense for nonpayment.

Gary Tillman of Alexandria, La., who has written widely on the topic, said the current non-negotiable status of variable-rate notes makes it harder to sell them in the secondary market. "Buyers want 'holder in due course' status on their notes," said Tillman.

Added Roger Warren, president of the Savings and Loan League of Connecticut: "Investors buying mortgages want to be able to receive their principal and interest without having to worry about legal problems, and these could arise with variable-rate notes." He said, however, that variable notes continue to be traded despite their murky legal status.

The issue has come up in the courts in the past few years, with most decisions so far holding the variable-rate instrument non-negotiable. In *Northern Trust Co. v. E. T. Clancy Export Corp.*, 612 F. Supp. 712 (N.D. Ill. 1985), the court held non-

cause it is always possible to make the necessary computations from the face of the instrument to determine the amount due at any given time.

No Other Promise or Order

A negotiable instrument must contain a promise or order to pay money, but it may not contain any other promise, order, obligation, or power given by the maker or drawer, except as specifically authorized under the Code.[2] Accordingly, if an instrument contains an order or promise to do an act in addition to the payment of money, it is not negotiable. For example, a promise to pay $100 "and a ton of coal" is nonnegotiable.

The UCC sets out a list of terms and provisions that may be included in instruments without affecting negotiability. Among these are: (1) a promise or power to maintain, protect, or increase collateral and to sell it in case of a default in payment of the instrument; (2) a term authorizing confession of judgment (written authority by the debtor to allow the holder to enter judgment against the debtor in favor of the holder) on the instrument if it is not paid when due; (3) a term purporting to waive the benefit of any law intended for the advantage or protection of any obligor; and (4) a term in a draft providing that the payee, by indorsing or cashing it, acknowledges full satisfaction of an obligation of the drawer.[9] It is important to note that the UCC does not render any of these negotiable a note providing interest at one-half percent above the Northern Trust's prime floating-interest rate.

In light of UCC § 3–106(1), the court reasoned a sum is uncertain and negotiability is destroyed when the interest computation requires looking off the face of the note to determine a particular bank's variable prime lending rate.

However, the same year, an Illinois state appellate court held the opposite in *Klehm v. Grecian Chalet, Ltd.*, 518 N.E.2d 187. In that case, the note required payment of interest at the "prime rate" plus 2¾ percent. It defined "prime rate" as "the minimum prime lending rate at either New York or Large Money Center Banks as published in the Wall Street Journal." The note also required quarterly adjustment of the rate.

That decision held that the "sum certain" requirement was satisfied. However, its precedential value is limited because the note in question specified a date on which the interest rate would change and most notes don't do that.

The Virginia Supreme Court also considered this question in 1987, with the Federal Home Loan Mortgage Corp. filing an amicus brief asking adjustable-rate mortgages (ARMs) to be deemed negotiable instruments.

"Without the ability to rely on negotiability of adjustable-rate mortgage notes," said the brief, "Freddie Mac would be concerned with borrower defenses related to the enforceability of adjustable-rate notes on grounds such as failure of consideration, borrower set-offs, and in some instances, defenses which arise in connection with faulty disclosure by mortgage loan originators, state usury law restrictions and state and federal truth-in-lending requirements."

Despite that plea, the court held variable-rate notes non-negotiable under UCC § 3–106. It added, however, that legislative action—such as that taken by Tennessee in amending its version of the UCC—is the proper solution to the problem.

This year, Warren's league tried to have Connecticut's law amended to specify that variable-rate notes are negotiable, but he said it proved to be more trouble than it was worth.

Warren thinks more states will address this problem through legislative action over the next few years. In fact, New York and Louisiana are considering doing so.

Tillman, however, believes the answer lies in amending the UCC to reflect current financial realities. He predicted the UCC's 13-member Permanent Editorial Board could amend the code's treatment of variable-rate notes as early as this summer.

—Nancy Blodgett
ABA Journal/August 1, 1988
Reprinted with permission from the August 1988 *ABA Journal*, The Lawyer's Magazine, a publication of the American Bar Association.

terms legal or effective; it merely provides that their inclusion will not affect negotiability.

Payable on Demand or at a Definite Time

A negotiable instrument must "be payable on demand or at a definite time."[2] This requirement, like the other formal requirements of negotiability, is designed to promote certainty in determining the present value of a negotiable instrument.

Demand paper always has been considered sufficiently certain as to time of payment to satisfy the requirements of negotiability, because it is the holder who makes the demand and thus sets the time for payment. An instrument payable upon demand means that the money owed under the instrument must be paid upon the holder's request. An instrument, such as a check in which no time for payment is stated, is payable on demand. An instrument qualifies as being payable on demand if it is payable "at sight" or "on presentation."[10]

Instruments payable at a definite time are called **time paper.** An instrument that by its terms is payable only on an act or event whose time of occurrence is uncertain is *not* payable at a definite time, even though the act or event has occurred. Examples include instruments providing for payment to the payee or order "thirty days after my marriage" or "when the payee is twenty-one years old." Such promises in otherwise negotiable instruments destroy their negotiability. The instruments are not payable at a definite time. Nor does the fact that the maker or drawer may marry or the payee becomes twenty-one years of age change the result. Negotiability is determined from the face of the instrument.

PP, INC. v. McGUIRE
United States District Court, District New Jersey, 1981.
509 F.Supp. 1079.

Facts: Sandra and Thomas McGuire entered into a purchase and sale agreement for "Becca's Boutique" with Pascal and Rebecca Tursi. The agreement provided that the McGuires would buy the store for $75,000, with a down payment of $10,000 and the balance of $65,000 to be paid at closing on October 5, 1979. The settlement clause stated that the sale was contingent upon the McGuires obtaining a Small Business Administration loan of $65,000. On September 4, 1979, Mrs. McGuire signed a promissory note in which the McGuires promised to pay to the order of the Tursis and the Green Mountain Inn the sum of $65,000. The note specified that interest payments of $541.66 would become due and payable on the fifth days of October, November, and December 1979. The entire balance of the note, with interest, would become due and payable at the option of the holder if any installment of interest was not paid according to that schedule.

The Tursis had for several months been negotiating with Parker Perry for the purchase of the Green Mountain Inn in Stowe, Vermont. On September 7, 1979, the Tursis delivered to Perry a $65,000 promissory note payable to the order of Green Mountain Inn, Inc. This note was secured by transfer to the Green Mountain Inn of the McGuires' note to the Tursis. Subsequently, Mrs. McGuire learned that her Small Business Administration loan had been disapproved. On December 5, 1979, the Tursis defaulted on their promissory note to the Green Mountain Inn. On June 11, 1980, PP, Inc., formerly Green Mountain Inn, Inc., brought an action against the McGuires to recover on the note held as security for the Tursis' promissory note. PP, Inc., moved for summary judgment.

Decision: PP, Inc.'s motion for summary judgment denied.

Opinion: Debevoise, J. If the McGuires' promissory note were a negotiable instrument and plaintiff were a holder in due course or a transferee from a holder in due course, see U.C.C. § 3–201, he would be entitled to recover on the instrument free of the claims and defenses asserted by the defendants.

* * *

It is not necessary, however, to decide whether plaintiff meets the requisites of a holder in due course because the note on which he sues is clearly not a negotiable instrument. For an instrument to be negotiable, it must satisfy each of the requirements outlined in U.C.C. § 3–104(1). It must (a) be signed by the maker or drawer; and

(b) contain an unconditional promise or order to pay a sum certain in money and no other promise, order, obligation, or power given by the maker or drawer except as authorized by this Article; and

(c) be payable on demand or at a definite time; and

(d) be payable to order or bearer.

* * *

The McGuires' note upon which plaintiff seeks to recover fails of negotiability because it is not, on its face, payable either on demand or at a definite time. The note calls for three installments of interest to be paid on "the 5th day of October, November, and December, 1979." It also contains an acceleration clause giving the holder the option of declaring the entire balance of principal, with interest, due and payable prior to maturity upon the makers' default on any installment of "principal or interest." Nowhere on the instrument's face, however, has a time for repayment of principal been specified.

Under U.C.C. § 3–109.

An instrument is payable at a definite time if by its terms it is payable

(a) on or before a stated date or at a fixed period after a stated date; or

(b) at a fixed period after sight; or

(c) at a definite time subject to any acceleration; or

(d) at a definite time subject to extension at the option of the holder, or to extension to a further definite time at the option of the maker or acceptor or automatically upon or after a specified act or event.

This promissory note clearly contains none of the provisions necessary to make it payable at a definite time.

An instrument may also be negotiable if it is payable on demand. "Instruments payable on demand include those payable at sight or on presentation and those in which no time for payment is stated." U.C.C. § 3–108. If the note had merely stated that the McGuires promised to pay the Tursis $65,000 at a given rate of interest, there can be no question that the note would have been payable on demand. [Citations.] Here, however, it is apparent from the face of the instrument that the parties did not intend for this note to be payable on demand, nor would any reasonable person so interpret it. Were the note payable on demand, for example, there would be no need for an acceleration clause. Moreover, no note payable on demand would specify a fixed amount of interest payable for the following three months and make no provision for interest thereafter. One can speculate that the parties intended the note to mature at a definite time approximately three months after the date it was signed. Exactly what time was intended, however, is impossible to ascertain from the face of the note. When a note is payable only at an indefinite time in the future, and parol evidence is required to supplement its terms, the note is not a negotiable instrument within the meaning of Article 3 of the Uniform Commercial Code. [Citations.]

The fact that the McGuires' promissory note is not a negotiable instrument within the meaning of Article 3 does not mean that it cannot be enforced as a contract. [Citation.] The assignee of a simple contract, however, takes the contract subject to all claims and defenses arising out of that contract. [Citation.] Plaintiff, therefore, is not entitled to automatic recovery on the McGuires' instrument on this motion for summary judgment.

As indicated in the preceding case, various types of provisions are regarded as fixing a definite time for payment of an instrument.[11] We discuss these provisions below.

"On or Before" Clauses An instrument is payable at a definite time if it is payable "on or before a stated date." The holder is thus as-sured that she will have her money by the maturity date at the latest, although she may receive it sooner. This right of anticipation enables the obligor, at his option, to pay before the stated maturity date (prepayment) and thereby stop the further accrual of interest or, if interest rates have gone down, to refinance at a lower rate of interest. Nevertheless, it constitutes sufficient certainty so as not to impair negotiability.

At a Fixed Period after a Stated Date Frequently, instruments are made payable at a fixed period after a stated date. For example, the instrument may be made payable "thirty days after date." This means it is payable thirty days after the date of issuance given on the instrument. Such an instrument is payable at a definite time, for its exact maturity date can be determined by simple arithmetic.

An undated instrument payable "thirty days after date" is not payable at a definite time, because the date of payment cannot be determined from its face. It is therefore nonnegotiable until a date is added.

At a Fixed Period after Sight This clause is frequently used in drafts. An instrument payable at a fixed period after sight is negotiable, for it means a fixed period after acceptance, and therefore a slight mathematical calculation makes the maturity date certain.

At a Definite Time Subject to Acceleration An instrument payable at a fixed time subject to acceleration by the holder satisfies the requirement of being payable at a definite time. Indeed, such an instrument would seem to have a more certain maturity date than a demand instrument because it at least states a definite maturity date. In addition, the acceleration may be upon the happening of some act or event.

At a Definite Time Subject to Extension A provision in an instrument granting the **holder** an option to extend the maturity of the instrument for an indefinite period does not impair its negotiability. A provision permitting the **obligor** of an instrument to extend the maturity date to a further *definite* time does not affect negotiability. For example, a provision in a note, payable one year from date, that the maker may extend the maturity date six months does not impair negotiability. If the obligor is given an option to extend the maturity of the instrument for an *indefinite* period of

time, however, his promise is illusory, and there is no certainty of time of payment. Such an instrument is nonnegotiable. If the obligor's right to extend is limited to a definite time, the extension clause is no more indefinite than an acceleration clause with a time limitation.

Payable to Order or to Bearer

A negotiable instrument must contain words indicating that the maker or drawer intends that it may pass into the hands of someone other than the payee. The "magic words" of negotiability are thus *to the order of* or *to bearer*, but other words that mean the same as these will also fulfill this requirement. The use of synonyms, however, only invites trouble.

This requirement should not be confused with the requirement that the instrument contain an order or promise to pay. An order to pay is a direction to a third party to pay the instrument as drawn. An "order instrument," on the other hand, pertains to the transferability of the instrument rather than specifying which party is to pay.

Payable to Order In addition to the eminently correct "Pay to the order of Jane Jones," the maker or drawer of **order paper** may state: "Pay to Jane Jones or her order"; or "Pay to Jane Jones or her assigns."[12] Moreover, in every instance the person to whose order the instrument is payable must be designated with reasonable certainty. Within this limitation a broad range of payees is possible, including an individual, the maker or drawer, the drawee, two or more payees, an office, an estate, a trust or fund, a partnership or unincorporated association, and a corporation.

Payable to Bearer An instrument fulfills the requirements of being **payable to bearer** if by its terms it does not designate a specific payee or is payable: (1) to bearer or the order of bearer; (2) to a specified person or "bearer;" or (3) to "cash" or to the order of "cash."[13] It should be noted, however, that an instrument made payable both to order and to bearer (that is, "pay to the order of Mildred Courts or bearer'') is payable to order. But if the words "or bearer" were handwritten or typewritten, then the instrument would be payable to bearer.

Moreover, it should be remembered that indorsements cannot create or destroy negotiability and that negotiability must be determined from the "face" of the instrument.

IN RE LEVINE
United States Bankruptcy Court, S.D. New York, 1982.
23 B.R. 410.

Facts: On September 2, 1976, Levine executed a mortgage bond under which she promised to pay the Mykoffs a preexisting obligation of $54,000. On October 14, 1979, the Mykoffs transferred the mortgage to Bankers Trust Co., indorsing the instrument with the words "Pay to the Order of Bankers Trust Company Without Recourse." The Lincoln First Bank, N.A., brought this action asserting that the Mykoffs' mortgage is a nonnegotiable instrument because it is not payable to order or bearer; thus it is subject to Lincoln's defense that the mortgage was not supported by consideration since antecedent debt is not consideration.

Decision: Judgment for Lincoln First Bank.

Opinion: Schwartzberg, B.J.   If the bond in question were a negotiable instrument, the lack of legal consideration supporting it would not affect Bankers Trust's secured status as assignee of the mortgage. New York's Uniform Commercial Code (U.C.C.) § 3–408 states in pertinent part:

"§ 3–408. Consideration
Want or failure of consideration is a defense as against any person not having the rights of a holder in due course (Section 3–305), except that no consideration is necessary for an instrument or obligation thereon given in payment of or as security for an antecedent obligation of any kind."

The use of the word "instrument" in the statute means a negotiable instrument. U.C.C. § 3–102(1)(e). Thus, an antecedent debt is sufficient consideration for the execution of a *negotiable instrument*, even if the holder of the instrument does not have the rights of a holder in due course. Here, the assignee does not have the rights of a holder in due course and therefore would ordinarily be subject to the defense of want or failure of consideration [U.C.C. § 3–306(c)]; however, if the bond is a negotiable instrument, U.C.C. § 3–408 would resolve any problem regarding the consideration. In light of the foregoing, it is crucial to determine the character of the mortgage bond which was endorsed over and assigned to Bankers Trust.

A negotiable instrument is one that meets the standards set out in U.C.C. § 3–104. It is § 3–104(1)(d) that is of concern here, a writing, to be negotiable, must "be payable to order or to bearer" [see U.C.C. § 3–110 and § 3–111]. The mortgage bond in question does not contain such language and therefore cannot be a negotiable instrument. In the case of *In re Deveson's Estate*, [citation], the court addressed the issue of whether an ordinary mortgage bond, payable to the obligee, his executors, administrators, or assigns, accompanied by real estate security, is a negotiable instrument. (This language is identical to that used in the subject mortgage bond). Citing the former Negotiable Instruments Law, § 20(4) (now incorporated in the U.C.C.), which was in accord with the U.C.C. requirement that the instrument be payable to order or bearer, the court concluded, "[t]hus, by statute, a mortgage bond, as in the instant case, becomes nonnegotiable." [Citation.] In *Enoch v. Brandon*, [citation], the court stated:

> "True, to become negotiable an instrument need not follow any precise language. . . But it 'must conform' to the definition specified in Section 20. [Section 20 of the N.I.L., now U.C.C. § 3–104]. In the face of a command so explicit, we must adhere to the design of the Legislature. . . . We turn, therefore, to the more serious question. The statute deals with the form of the instrument—with what a mere inspection of its face should disclose. It must contain an unconditional promise to pay a fixed sum, on demand, or at a fixed or determinable future time, to order or to bearer. Only if it fulfills these requirements is it negotiable."

The fact that the Mykoffs endorsed the bond with the words "payable to the order of Bankers Trust Company without recourse" does not change the inherent character of the bond. "[N]o intention, no agreement, may make negotiable an instrument which the statute declares to be nonnegotiable."

Accordingly, it must be concluded that the subject mortgage bond is not a negotiable instrument, and that U.C.C. § 3–408 cannot operate to excuse the lack of legal consideration. The bond which the Levines executed and gave to the Mykoffs, evidencing their promise to pay an antecedent debt is unenforceable, and therefore the accompanying mortgage falls with it. Since the assignee, Bankers Trust, holds an unenforceable bond and mortgage (its position can be no better than that of its assignor), its claim is rendered unsecured.

Terms and Omissions and Their Effect on Negotiability

The negotiability of an instrument may be questioned because of an omission of certain provisions or ambiguity of language. Problems may also arise in connection with interpretation of instruments whether or not negotiability is called into question. Accordingly, the Code contains rules of construction that apply to every instrument.[14]

Absence of Statement of Consideration Consideration is required to support a contract; however, as stated in *In re Levine*, the negotiability of an instrument is *not* affected by the omission of a statement of consideration.[9]

Absence of Statement of Where the Instrument Is Drawn or Payable To determine what law applies to the issuance and form of an instrument, the place of issue must be known. To determine the law applicable to matters of payment, the place of payment must be

known. But the omission of a statement of either of these on the face of the instrument does not affect its negotiability.[9]

Sealed Instruments The fact that an instrument is under seal has no effect on its negotiability, whatever other effect the seal might have under common law.[15]

Dating of the Instrument The negotiability of an instrument is not affected by the fact that it is *undated*, antedated, or postdated.[16]

If the instrument is *antedated*, that is, carries a date prior to its actual issue, the stated date controls. Hence, a note dated October 1, 1990, payable thirty days after date, and issued on November 1, 1990, is due and payable the day before its issue.

If the instrument is *postdated*, that is, it carries a date later than the day on which it was issued, the date stated on the instrument is conclusive. A demand instrument, therefore, by postdating becomes a time instrument. For example, if on January 2, 1990, the drawers issues a check and dates it January 21, 1990, the drawer's bank is not authorized to pay the instrument until January 21.

Incomplete Instruments Occasionally a party will sign a paper that is clearly intended to be an instrument but is incomplete in some necessary way, such as the omission of promise or order, designation of the payee, amount payable, or time for payment. Such an instrument is not negotiable until completed.[17]

Ambiguous Instruments Rather than commit the parties to the use of parol evidence to establish the interpretation of an instrument, the Code establishes rules to resolve common ambiguities.[14] This promotes negotiability by providing a degree of certainty to the holder.

Where it is doubtful whether the instrument is a draft or note, the holder may treat it as either and present it for payment to the drawee or the person signing it. For example, an instrument reading

> To X: On demand I promise to pay $500 to the order of Y.
>
> /s/Z

may be presented for payment to X as a draft or to Z as a note.

An instrument naming no drawee but stating

> On demand, pay $500 to the order of Y
>
> /s/Z

although in the form of a draft, may be treated as a note and presented to Z for payment.

If a printed form of note or draft is used and the party signing it inserts handwritten or typewritten language that is inconsistent with the printed words, the handwritten words control the typewritten and the printed words, and the typewritten words control the printed.

If the amount payable is set forth on the face of the instrument in both figures and words, and the amounts differ, the words control the figures. It is presumed that the maker or drawer would be more careful with words.

Figure 22–7 shows examples of nonnegotiable and negotiable instruments.

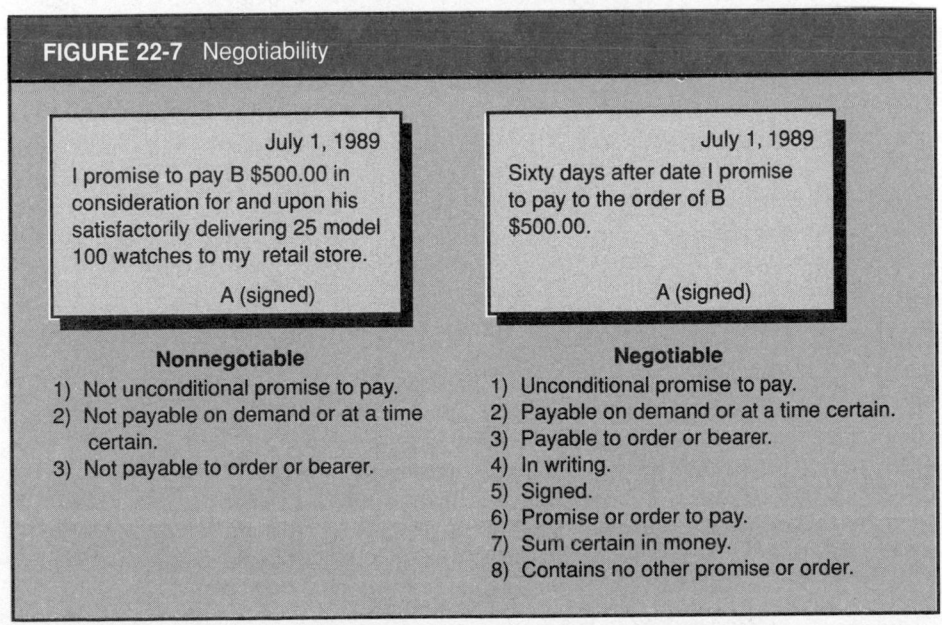

FIGURE 22-7 Negotiability

> July 1, 1989
>
> I promise to pay B $500.00 in consideration for and upon his satisfactorily delivering 25 model 100 watches to my retail store.
>
> A (signed)

Nonnegotiable
1) Not unconditional promise to pay.
2) Not payable on demand or at a time certain.
3) Not payable to order or bearer.

> July 1, 1989
>
> Sixty days after date I promise to pay to the order of B $500.00.
>
> A (signed)

Negotiable
1) Unconditional promise to pay.
2) Payable on demand or at a time certain.
3) Payable to order or bearer.
4) In writing.
5) Signed.
6) Promise or order to pay.
7) Sum certain in money.
8) Contains no other promise or order.

CHAPTER SUMMARY

Negotiability	**Rule** Invests instruments (commercial paper, documents of title, investment securities) with a high degree of marketability and commercial utility by conferring upon certain good faith transferees immunity from most defenses to the instrument **Formal Requirements** negotiability is wholly a matter of form, and all the requirements for negotiability must be met within the four corners of the instrument

Types of Commercial Paper	**Orders to Pay** ■ *Drafts* a draft involves three parties: the drawer orders the drawee to pay a sum certain in money to the payee ■ *Checks* a specialized form of draft that is drawn on a bank and payable on demand; the drawer orders the drawee (bank) to pay the payee on demand (upon the request of the holder) **Promises to Pay** ■ *Notes* a written promise by a maker (issuer) to pay a payee ■ *Certificates of Deposit* a specialized form of note that is given by a bank or thrift association

Form of Commercial Paper	**Writing** any reduction to tangible form is sufficient **Signed** any symbol executed or adopted by a party with the intention to validate a writing **Promise or Order to Pay** ■ *Promise to Pay* an undertaking to pay, which must be more than a mere acknowledgment or recognition of, an existing debt ■ *Order to Pay* direction or command to pay **Unconditional** an absolute promise to pay that is not subject to any contingencies ■ *Reference to Other Agreements* does not destroy negotiability unless the recital makes the instrument subject to or governed by the terms of another agreement ■ *The Particular Fund Doctrine* an order or promise to pay only out of a particular fund is conditional and destroys negotiability **Sum Certain in Money** ■ *Money* legal tender authorized or adopted by a sovereign government as part of its currency ■ *Sum Certain* the holder must be assured of a determinable minimum payment although provisions in the instrument may increase the amount of recovery under certain circumstances **No Other Promise or Order** a promise or order to do an act in addition to the payment of money destroys negotiability **Payable on Demand or at a Definite Time** an instrument is demand paper if it must be paid upon request; an instrument is time paper if it is payable at a definite time which includes the following: "on or before" clauses, at a fixed period after a stated date, at a fixed period after sight, at a definite time subject to acceleration

> Payable to Order or to Bearer   a negotiable instrument must contain words indicating that the maker or drawer intends that it pass into the hands of someone other than the payee
> - ■ *Payable to Order*   payable to the "order of" (or other words which mean the same) a named person or anyone designated by that person
> - ■ *Payable to Bearer*   payable to the holder of the instrument and includes instruments payable (1) to bearer or the order of bearer; (2) to a specified person or to bearer; or (3) to "cash" or to order of "cash"

QUESTIONS

1. Discuss the concept and importance of negotiability.
2. Identify and discuss the types of commercial paper involving an order to pay.
3. Identify and discuss the types of commercial paper involving a promise to pay.
4. List and discuss the formal requirements that an instrument must meet in order to be negotiable.
5. Discuss the effect on the negotiability of an instrument of (1) the absence of a statement of consideration, (2) the absence of a statement of when the instrument is payable, (3) the undated, antedated, or postdated instrument, (4) the lack of completion of an instrument, and (5) an ambiguous instrument.

PROBLEMS

1. State whether the following provisions impair or preclude negotiability if the instruments are otherwise in proper form. Answer each statement with either the word "Negotiable" or "Nonnegotiable," and explain why.
(a) A note for $2,000 payable in twenty monthly installments of $100 each, providing: "In case of death of maker, all payments not due at date of death are canceled."
(b) A note stating: "This note is secured by a mortgage of even date herewith on personal property located at 351 Maple Street, Smithton, Illinois."
(c) A certificate of deposit reciting: "June 6, 1990, John Jones has deposited in the Citizens Bank of Emanon, Illinois, Two Thousand Dollars, to the credit of himself, payable upon the return of this instrument properly indorsed, with interest at the rate of 12¾ percent per annum from date of issue

upon ninety days' written notice. Signed Jill Crystal, President."
(d) An instrument reciting "I.O.U., Mark Noble, $1,000.00."
(e) A note stating: "In accordance with our contract of December 13, 1990, I promise to pay to the order of Sam Stone $100 on March 13, 1991."
(f) A draft drawn by Brown on the Acme Publishing Company for $500, payable to the order of the Sixth National Bank of Erehwon, directing the bank to "Charge this draft to my royalty account."
(g) A note executed by Pierre Janvier, a resident of Chicago, for $2,000, payable in Swiss francs.
(h) An undated note for $1,000 payable "six months after date."
(i) A note for $500 payable to the order of Ray Rodes six months after the death of Albert Olds.
(j) A note for $500 payable to the assigns of Levi Lee.

2. State whether the following provisions in a note impair or preclude negotiability if the instruments are otherwise in proper form. Answer each statement with either the word "Negotiable" or "Nonnegotiable" and explain why.
(a) A note signed by Henry Brown in the trade name of the Quality Store.
(b) A note for $450, payable to the order of TV Products Company, "If, but only if, the color television set for which this note is given proves entirely satisfactory to me."
(c) A note executed by Adams, Burton, and Cady Company, a partnership, for $1,000 payable to the order of Davis, payable only out of the assets of the partnership.
(d) A note promising to pay $500 to the order of Leigh and to deliver ten tons of coal to Leigh.
(e) A note for $10,000 executed by Eaton, payable to the order of the First National Bank of Emanon, in which Eaton promises to give additional collateral if the bank deems itself insecure and demands additional security.

478

PART 4 COMMERCIAL PAPER

(f) A note reading, "I promise to pay to the order of Richard Roe $2,000 on January 31, 1990, but it is agreed that if the crop of Blackacre falls below ten bushels per acre for the 1989 season, this note shall be extended indefinitely."

(g) A note payable to the order of Ray Rogers fifty years from date but providing that payment shall be accelerated by the death of Silas Hughes to a point of time four months after his death.

(h) A note for $4,000 calling for payments of installments of $250 each and stating: "In the event any installment hereof is not paid when due, this note shall immediately become due at the holder's option."

(i) An instrument dated September 17, 1990 in the handwriting of John Henry Brown, which reads in full: "Sixty days after date, I, John Henry Brown, promise to pay to the order of William Jones $500."

(j) A note reciting: "I promise to pay Ray Reed $100 on December 24, 1990."

3. On March 10, Tolliver Tolles, also known as Thomas Towle, delivered to Alonzo Craig and Abigail Craig the following instrument, written by him in pencil:

> For value received, I, Thomas Towle, promise to pay to the order of Alonzo Craig or Abigail Craig One Thousand Seventy-Five ($1,000.75) Dollars six months after my mother, Alma Tolles, dies with interest at the rate of 9 percent from date of maturity and after maturity at the rate of 10 percent. I hereby waive the benefit of all laws exempting real or personal property from levy or sale.

Is this instrument negotiable? Explain.

4. Henry Hughes, who operates a department store, executed the following instrument:

> $2,600   Chicago, March 5, 1990
> On July 1, 1990, I promise to pay Daniel Dalziel, or order, the sum of Twenty-Six Hundred Dollars for the privilege of one framed advertising sign, size 24 × 36 inches, at one end of each of two hundred sixty motor coaches of the New Omnibus Company for a term of three months from May 15, 1990.
>   Henry Hughes.

Is this instrument negotiable? Explain.

5. Pablo agreed to lend Marco $500. Marco made and delivered his note for $500 payable to Pablo or order "ten days after my marriage." Shortly thereafter Marco was married. Is the instrument negotiable? Explain.

6. Maria employs Crystal to work for her for one year from January 1, 1990, to December 31, 1990, at a salary of $1,000 a month payable monthly. On January 2, Maria delivers to Crystal twelve promissory notes in otherwise negotiable form, maturing respectively on the last day of successive calendar

months throughout the year 1990. On the first note there is the statement: "For January 1990 salary;" on the second note "For February 1990 salary;" and so on for each note. On January 3, 1990, Crystal sold and indorsed the twelve notes to Citibank and on January 4, 1990 quit work. Are these notes negotiable? Explain.

7. For the balance due on the purchase of a tractor, Henry Brown executed and delivered to Jane Jones his promissory note containing the following language:

> January 1, 1990, I promise to pay to the order of Jane Jones the sum of $7,000 to be paid only out of my checking account at the Columbia National Bank in Pinckard, Illinois, in two installments of $3,500 each, payable on May 1, 1990, and on July 1, 1990, provided that if I fail to pay the first installment on the due date, the entire sum shall become immediately due. (Signed) Henry Brown.

Is this note negotiable? Explain.

8. Sam Sharpe executed and delivered to Don Dole the following instrument:

>   Knoxville, Tennessee
>   May 29, 1990
> Thirty days after date I promise to pay Don Dole or order, Five Thousand Dollars. The holder of this instrument shall have the election to require the assignment and delivery to him of my 100 shares of Brookside Iron Works Corporation stock in lieu of the payment of Five Thousand Dollars in money.
>   (Signed) Sam Sharpe.

Is this instrument negotiable? Explain.

9. Is the following instrument negotiable?

>   March 1, 1990
> One month from date, I, James Jimson, hereby promises to pay Edmund Edwards Six thousand seven hundred Fifty ($6,750.00) dollars, plus 8¾ percent interest. Payment for cutting machines to be delivered on March 15, 1990. To be charged against garment sales account.
>   James Jimson

10. Broadway Management Corporation obtained a judgment against Briggs. The note on which the judgment was based reads in part: "Ninety Days after date, I, we, or either of us, promise to pay to the order of Three Thousand Four Hundred Ninety Eight and 45/100------------Dollars." (The underlined words and symbols were typed in; the remainder was printed.) There were no blanks on the face of the instrument, any unused space having been filled in with hyphens. The note contains clauses permitting acceleration in the event the holder deems itself insecure and authorizes judgment "if this note is not paid at any stated or accelerated maturity." Briggs appeals, claiming that the note is not negotiable order paper. Decision?

ENDNOTES

1. Uniform Commercial Code, Section 3–104(2), "Draft"; "Check"; "Certificate of Deposit"; "Note".

2. Uniform Commercial Code, Section 3–104(1), Form of Negotiable Instruments.

3. Uniform Commercial Code, Section 1–201(46), Definitions: Writing.

4. Uniform Commercial Code, Section 1–201(39), Definitions: Signed.

5. Uniform Commercial Code, Section 3–102, Definitions and Index of Definitions.

6. Uniform Commercial Code, Section 3–105, When Promise or Order Unconditional.

7. Uniform Commercial Code, Sections 1–201(24), Definitions: Money; 3–107, Money.

8. Uniform Commercial Code, Section 3–106, Sum Certain.

9. Uniform Commercial Code, Section 3–112, Terms and Omissions Not Affecting Negotiability.

10. Uniform Commercial Code, Section 3–108, Payable on Demand.

11. Uniform Commercial Code, Section 3–109, Definite Time.

12. Uniform Commercial Code, Section 3–110, Payable to Order.

13. Uniform Commercial Code, Section 3–111, Payable to Bearer.

14. Uniform Commercial Code, Section 3–118, Ambiguous Terms and Rules of Construction.

15. Uniform Commercial Code, Section 3–113, Seal.

16. Uniform Commercial Code, Section 3–114, Date, Antedating, Postdating.

17. Uniform Commercial Code, Section 3–115, Incomplete Instruments.

23 TRANSFER

The primary advantage of commercial paper is its ease of transferability. Both negotiable and nonnegotiable instruments are transferable by assignment, but only a transferee of a negotiable instrument can become a holder. This distinction is highly significant. If the transferee of a negotiable instrument is entitled to payment by the terms of the instrument, he is a holder of the instrument. Only holders may be holders in due course and thus entitled to greater rights in the instrument than the transferor may have possessed. These rights are discussed in the next chapter and are the reason why negotiable instruments move freely in the marketplace. The transfer of a nonnegotiable instrument operates as an assignment as does the transfer of a negotiable instrument by a means that does not render the transferee a holder. In this chapter we discuss the methods by which commercial paper may be transferred.

TRANSFER AND NEGOTIATION

Whether a transfer is by *assignment* or *negotiation*, the transferee acquires the rights his transferor had.[1] The transfer need not be for value; if the instrument is transferred as a gift, the donee acquires all the rights of the donor. If the transferor was a holder in due course, the transferee acquires the rights of a holder in due course, which he in turn may transfer. This rule, which is sometimes referred to as the **shelter rule,** existed at common law and exists under the Uniform Commercial Code. The shelter rule is discussed more fully in Chapter 24.

Negotiation is the transfer of a negotiable instrument in such a manner that the transferee becomes a holder.[2] A **holder** is defined as "a person who is in possession of an instrument drawn, issued or indorsed to him or to his order or to bearer or in blank."[3] Accordingly, to qualify as a holder, a person must have possession of an instrument that runs to him. Because *bearer paper* (an instrument payable to bearer) runs to whoever is in possession of it, a finder or a thief of bearer paper would be a holder even though he did not receive possession by voluntary transfer. For example, P loses an instrument payable to bearer that I issued to him. F finds it and sells and delivers it to B, who thus receives it by negotiation and is a holder. F also qualified as a holder because he was in possession of bearer paper. As a holder, F had the power to negotiate the instrument, and the transferee (B) may be a holder in due course if he meets the Code's requirements for such a holder. See Figure 23–1 for an illustration of this example.

Thus, a *bearer instrument* is transferred by mere *possession* and is therefore comparable to cash. On the other hand, if the instrument is *order paper* (an instrument payable to order), both *possession* and *indorsement* by the appropriate parties are necessary for the transferee to become a holder. Figure 23–2 compares bearer and order paper.

Any transfer for value of an instrument not payable to bearer gives the transferee the specifically enforceable right to have the unqualified indorsement of the transferor, unless the parties otherwise agreed.[1] The parties may agree that the transfer is to be an assignment

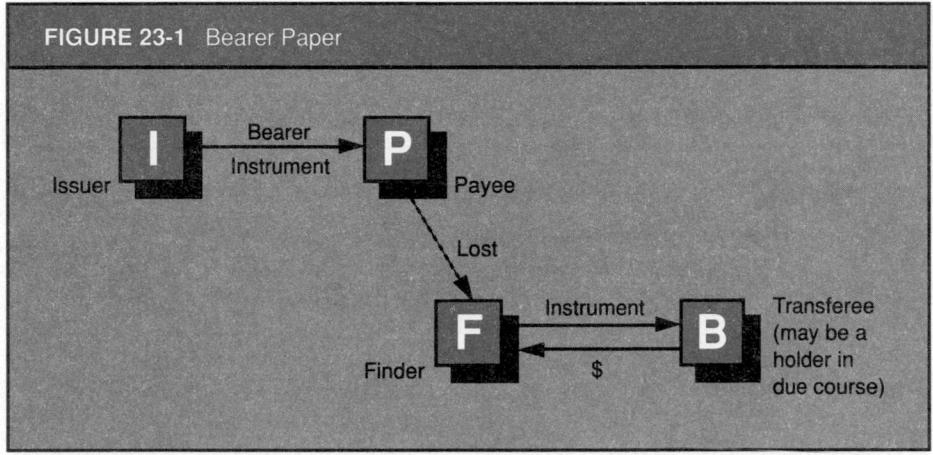

FIGURE 23-1 Bearer Paper

rather than a negotiation, in which case no indorsement is required. If there is no such agreement, the courts presume that negotiation was intended when value is given, and if the instrument is not payable to bearer, the right of the transferee to an unqualified indorsement is enforceable by court order. Where a transfer is not for value, the transaction is normally not commercial; thus the courts do not make such a presumption.

Until the necessary indorsement has been supplied, the transferee has nothing more than the contract rights of an assignee. Negotiation takes effect only when a proper indorsement is made, because it is not until then, notwithstanding possession, that the transferee of order paper becomes a holder of the instrument.

INDORSEMENTS

An **indorsement** is the signature of a payee, drawee, accommodation indorser, or holder of an instrument. An indorsement must be written on the instrument or on a paper, called an **allonge,** so firmly affixed to the instrument as to become a part of it. The use of an allonge is required when there are so many indorsements that there is no room for additional signatures or when the indorsement is too lengthy to fit on the instrument. A purported indorsement on a separate piece of paper, clipped or pinned to the instrument, is not valid, while a piece of paper stapled to the instrument is generally valid.

Customarily, indorsements are made on the back or reverse side of the instrument, starting

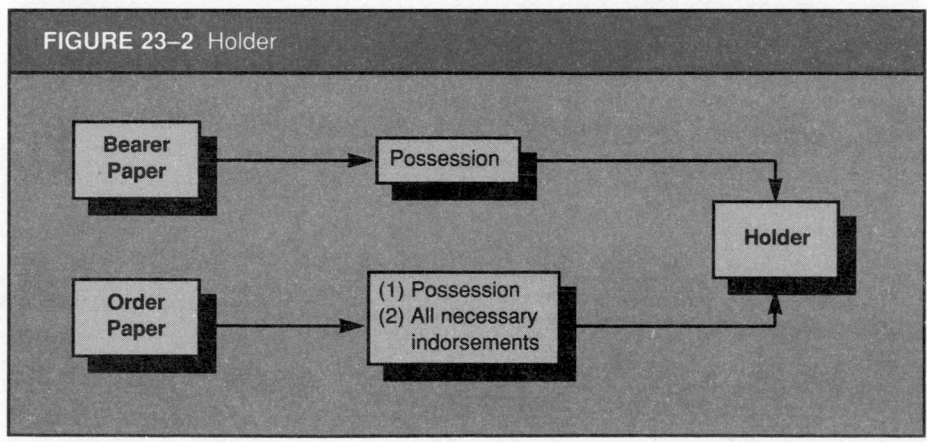

FIGURE 23–2 Holder

LAMSON v. COMMERCIAL CREDIT CORP.
Supreme Court of Colorado, 1975.
187 Colo. 382, 531 P.2d 966.

Facts: The drawer, Commercial Credit Corporation, issued two checks payable to Rauch Motor Company. Rauch indorsed the checks in blank, deposited them to its account in University National Bank, and received a corresponding amount of money. The bank stamped "pay any bank" on the checks and initiated collection. The checks were dishonored and returned to the bank with the notation "payment stopped." Rauch, through subsequent deposits, repaid the bank. Later, to compromise a lawsuit, the bank executed a special two-page indorsement of the two checks to Lamson. Lamson then sued the corporation for the face value of the checks, plus interest. The corporation contends that Lamson was not a holder of the checks because the indorsement was not in conformity with the UCC in that it was stapled to the checks. The trial court ruled in favor of Lamson, but the Court of Appeals reversed.

Decision: Judgment of the Court of Appeals reversed and the judgment of the trial court in favor of Lamson reinstated.

Opinion: **Day, J.**   When Rauch deposited the checks, it indorsed them in blank, transforming them into bearer paper. Sections 1–201(5) and 3–204(2). The Bank in turn indorsed the checks "pay any bank." That is a restrictive indorsement. Section 3–205(c). After a check has been restrictively indorsed, "only a bank may acquire the rights of a holder * * * [u]ntil the item has been specially indorsed by a bank to a person who is not a bank." Section 4–201(2)(b).

There is no question that the checks were indorsed to Lamson by name, thus qualifying as a special indorsement. Section 3–204(1). The problem is whether the special indorsement was correctly and properly affixed to the checks under section 3–202(2). It provides that "[a]n indorsement must be written * * * on behalf of the holder and on the instrument or on a paper so firmly affixed thereto as to become a part thereof."

The subject indorsement was typed on two legal size sheets of paper. It would have been physically impossible to place all of the language on the two small checks. Therefore, the indorsement had to be "affixed" to them in some way. Such a paper is called an allonge. In this case the allonge was affixed by stapling it to the checks.

We agree with the Court of Appeals' statement that a separate paper pinned or paperclipped to an instrument is not sufficient for negotiation. Section 3–202(2), comment 3. However, we hold, *contra* to its decision, that the section does permit stapling as an adequate method of firmly affixing the indorsement. Stapling is the modern equivalent of gluing or pasting. Certainly as a physical matter it is just as easy to cut by scissors a document pasted or glued to another as it is to detach the two by unstapling. Therefore we hold that under the circumstances described, stapling an indorsement to a negotiable instrument is a permanent attachment to the checks so that it becomes "a part thereof."

Section 1–201(20) defines a holder as "a person who is in possession of * * * an instrument * * * indorsed to him * * * ." The Bank's special indorsement, stapled to the two checks, effectively made Lamson a holder, although not a holder in due course.

> Once signatures are proven, Lamson, as a holder was entitled to payment by mere production of the instrument unless the Corporation established a defense. Sections 3–301 and 3–307(2).
>
> * * *
>
> Since we decide that Lamson became a holder by special indorsement, we do not have to consider whether he acquired rights as an assignee.

at the top and continuing down. For the proper placement of an indorsement see the Law in the News article on page 484. The order of the indorsement and the liability of indorsers, unless otherwise agreed, is presumed to be the order in which their signatures appear.[4] Occasionally, however, a signature may appear on an instrument in such a way that it is impossible to tell with certainty the nature of the liability undertaken by the signer. In such an event, the Code specifies the signer is to be treated as an indorser.[5] In keeping with the rule that a transferee must be able to determine her rights from the face of the instrument, the person who signed in an ambiguous capacity may not introduce parol evidence to establish that she intended to be something other than an indorser.

An indorsement showing that the signer is not in the chain of title is notice of its accommodation character.[6] An **accommodation indorser** signs in order to add her liability and thereby accommodate, or assist, another party who might otherwise be unable to obtain funds.

An indorsement may be complex or simple. It may be dated and may indicate where it is made, but neither date nor place is required. The simplest type is merely the signature of the indorser. Since the indorser undertakes certain obligations, as explained later, an indorsement consisting of merely a signature may be said to be the shortest contract known to the law. A forged or otherwise unauthorized signature necessary to negotiation is inoperative and thus breaks the chain of title to the instrument.[7]

An indorsement conveying less than the entire instrument or any unpaid balance is not a nego-

tiation, but operates as a partial assignment.[2] For example, an indorsement containing a direction to pay Ann "one-half of the note" or "$500 of the note," or "two-thirds to Ann, one-third to Bob" constitutes only a partial assignment, and neither Ann nor Bob becomes a holder. But an indorsement "to Art and Bess" is effective as a negotiation because it transfers the entire interest to Art and Bess. Words such as "I hereby assign all my right, title, and interest in the within note" are also sufficient as a negotiation.

The type of indorsement used in negotiating an instrument affects its subsequent negotiation. Every indorsement is (1) either blank or special, (2) either restrictive or nonrestrictive, and (3) either qualified or unqualified. These indorsements are not mutually exclusive. Indeed, all indorsements may be sorted into three of these six categories, because all indorsements disclose three things: (1) the method to be employed in making subsequent negotiations (this depends on whether the indorsement is blank or special); (2) the kind of interest that is being transferred (this depends on whether the indorsement is restrictive or nonrestrictive); and (3) the liability of the indorser (this depends on whether the indorsement is qualified or unqualified). For instance, an indorser who merely signs her name on the back of an instrument is making a blank, nonrestrictive, unqualified indorsement. See Figure 23–3 at the end of this chapter for further illustrations.

Blank Indorsements

A **blank indorsement** specifies no indorsee and may consist of merely the signature of the indorser or her authorized agent.[8] A blank

LAW IN THE NEWS

A Diagram Might Be Helpful When You Need to Cash a Check

New York—A simple "John Hancock" scribbled across the back of your paycheck might not be enough to get it cashed in a timely fashion. But a diagram could sure help.

The new federal regulations that guarantee customers of banks, savings associations and credit unions faster access to their deposits also include uniform standards for endorsing checks that many people—and a few of the smaller financial institutions—are just coming to grips with.

Under the guidelines, which took effect Thursday [September 1, 1988] along with the speedier check-holding policies, signatures must be made within a 1 1/2-inch section along the edge of the back of the check, so they don't interfere with endorsements from the bank at which the check is deposited.

The bank endorsements should be in "appropriate color ink," such as blue and black, according to the Federal Reserve Board, which is administering the guidelines.

Many financial institutions say they have been training their employees and are mailing out brochures with detailed diagrams to educate customers.

The Fed says that all checks are negotiable regardless of what might appear on the back, and there are no penalties for failing to abide by the standards.

The Fed has defended the new endorsement requirements as necessary to speed the check clearing process so that bounced checks can be returned quickly to the institution where they were cashed.

The Associated Press

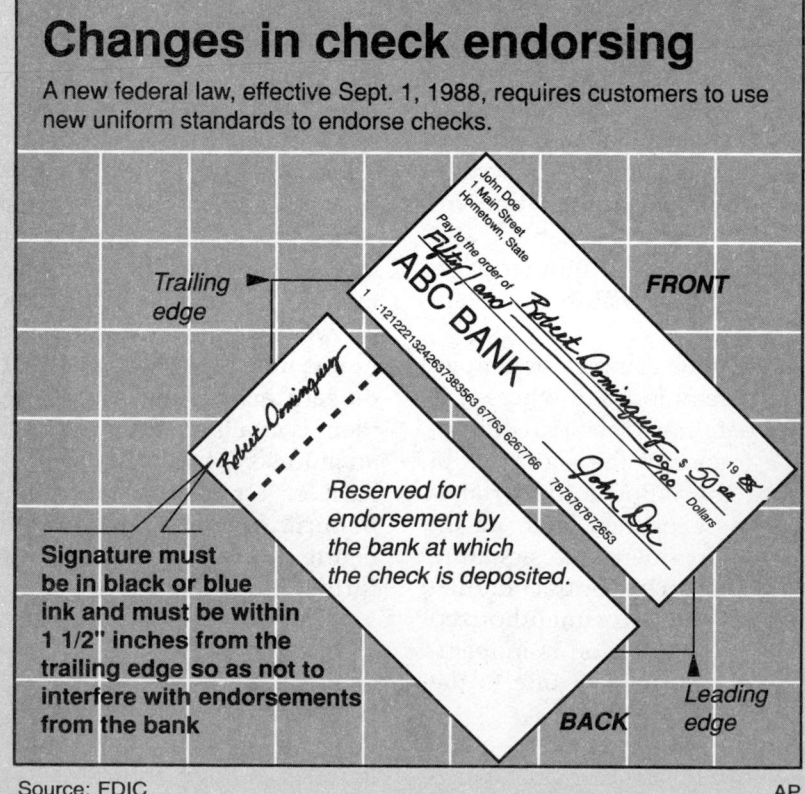

Changes in check endorsing

A new federal law, effective Sept. 1, 1988, requires customers to use new uniform standards to endorse checks.

Trailing edge

FRONT

Signature must be in black or blue ink and must be within 1 1/2" inches from the trailing edge so as not to interfere with endorsements from the bank

Reserved for endorsement by the bank at which the check is deposited.

BACK

Leading edge

Source: FDIC

AP

indorsement converts order paper into **bearer paper.** Thus, an instrument indorsed in blank may be negotiated by delivery alone without further indorsement. Hence, the holder should treat it with the same care as cash. See *Palmer & Ray Dental Supply of Abilene, Inc. v. First National Bank* at page 487.

Special Indorsements

A **special indorsement** specifically designates the person to whom or to whose order the instrument is to be payable (**order paper**).[8] Thus, if Peter, the payee of a note, indorses it "Pay to the order of Andrea," or even "Pay Andrea," the indorsement is special because it names the transferee. Words of negotiability— payable to order or bearer—are *not* required in

an indorsement. Thus, an indorsement reading "Pay Edward" is interpreted as meaning "Pay to the order of Edward." Any further negotiation of the instrument would require Edward's indorsement.

Moreover, a holder of an instrument with a blank indorsement may protect himself by converting the blank indorsement to a special indorsement by writing over the signature of the indorser any contract consistent with the character of the indorsement. For example, on the back of a negotiable instrument appears the blank indorsement "Sally Seller." Harry Holder, who received the instrument from Seller, may convert this bearer instrument into order paper by inserting above Seller's signature "Pay Harry Holder" or other similar words.

CASAREZ v. GARCIA
Court of Appeals of New Mexico, 1983.
99 N.M. 500, 660 P.2d 598

Facts: Arthur and Lucy Casarez contracted with Blas Garcia, who purported to be a representative of the Albuquerque Fence Company, for the construction of a new home. Blas introduced the Casarezes to Cecil Garcia, who agreed to make a loan to them to be used as a down payment on the project. Cecil then obtained a loan from Rio Grande Valley Bank in the form of a $25,000 cashier's check payable to himself, which he indorsed over to Lucy Casarez. Lucy indorsed the check: "Pay to the order of Albuquerque Fence Company, Lucy N. Casarez," and delivered it to Blas Garcia. Claiming he was following Cecil's instructions, Blas indorsed the check: "Alb. Fence Co." and gave the check to Cecil. Cecil signed his own name under "Alb. Fence Co." and presented the check to the bank in exchange for $25,000. The Casarezes soon learned that Blas and Cecil Garcia had never been in any way affiliated or employed by the Albuquerque Fence Company. Lucy then brought suit against the bank, claiming that the unauthorized signatures of Blas and Cecil Garcia invalidated the special indorsement to Albuquerque Fence Company and that therefore the bank negligently cashed the check, rendering the bank liable to Lucy for the amount of the check. The court granted the bank's motion for directed verdict and Casarez appeals.

Decision: Judgment granting bank's motion for directed verdict reversed.

Opinion: Donnelly, J.   The plaintiffs contend that the language placed on the check by Lucy Casarez, "Pay to the order of Albuquerque Fence Co.", preceding her signature constituted a special indorsement and that the check could be further negotiated only by a proper indorsement by an authorized representative of the company. Because of the special indorsement, plaintiffs argue, the action of the Bank in cashing the check without investigating or verifying the authority of Cecil

Garcia to negotiate the check on behalf of Albuquerque Fence Company was sufficient to raise an issue as to negligence on the part of the Bank. The plaintiffs further assert that the writing of the words "Alb. Fence Co." by Blas Garcia and the signature thereafter by Cecil Garcia amounted to an unauthorized signature of indorsement which invalidated the lawful negotiation of the check and rendered the Bank liable to the plaintiffs for the amount of the check.

* * *

Since the plaintiff Lucy Casarez specially indorsed the cashier's check "Pay to the order of Albuquerque Fence Co., Lucy N. Casarez," and purportedly without authority, Blas Garcia placed the indorsement of "Alb. Fence Co." thereon, the indorsement, if unauthorized, was inoperative to pass title to the instrument to Cecil Garcia. A special indorsement specifies to whom or to whose order it makes the instrument payable; it becomes payable to the order of the special indorsee and may be further negotiated only by his indorsement. [U.C.C.] § 3—204. As stated in the Official Comment to U.C.C. § 3—204, "The principle here adopted is that a special indorser, as the owner even of a bearer instrument, has the right to direct the payment and to require the indorsement of his indorsee as evidence of the satisfaction of own obligation." Under the Uniform Commercial Code, a "person" includes an individual or an organization. §—201(30).

* * *

As between the plaintiff Lucy Casarez, and Cecil Garcia, the plaintiff remained the owner of the check until the designated special indorsee indorsed the instrument. The unauthorized signature of the special indorsee rendered that signature inoperative under § 3—404(1) and prevented the further negotiation of the check since negotiation requires the proper indorsement of all special indorsees.

As noted in [citation], "when a bank pays on an instrument bearing a forged indorsement, the owner of the instrument may sue the drawee . . . or drawer. . . ." The plaintiff as the true owner of the cashier's check had a right to bring an action for conversion or negligence against the Bank as drawee when it paid on the unauthorized indorsement of Albuquerque Fence Company. [Citations.]

Restrictive Indorsements

As the term implies, a **restrictive indorsement** attempts to restrict the rights of the indorsee in some fashion. The UCC defines four kinds of indorsements as restrictive: conditional indorsements, indorsements prohibiting further transfer, indorsements for deposit or collection, and indorsements in trust.[9] An **unrestrictive indorsement** does not attempt to restrict the rights of the indorsee.

Conditional Indorsements In a conditional indorsement, the indorser makes the rights of the indorsee subject to the happening or nonhappening of a specified event. Suppose Mark makes a note payable to Pat's order. Pat indorses it "Pay Adam, but only if the good ship Jolly Jack arrives in Chicago harbor by November 15, 1990." If Mark had used this language in the instrument, it would be nonnegotiable, because his promise to pay must be unconditional to satisfy the formal requisites of negotiability. But indorsers *are* permitted to condition the rights of their indorsees without destroying negotiability.

If the good ship Jolly Jack does not arrive in Chicago harbor by November 15, 1990, Adam has no rights in the instrument. If he presents the instrument to Mark for payment, Mark must dishonor the instrument or be required to pay it again to Pat. Mark is not discharged when he pays an instrument that has been restrictively indorsed, unless he pays in a manner consistent with the indorsement.

Indorsements Prohibiting Further Transfer An indorsement may by its express terms prohibit further transfer, such as an indorsement stating "Pay only Tom Thomas." Such indorsements, or any other purporting to prohibit further transfer, are designed to be a restriction on the rights of the indorsee. To remove any doubt as to the effect of such a provision, the Code provides that *no* restrictive indorsement prevents further transfer or negotiation of the instrument. The net result of this provision is that an indorsement that purports to *prohibit* further transfer of the instrument is given the same effect as an unrestricted indorsement.

Indorsements for Deposit or Collection The most frequently used form of restrictive indorsement is that designed to lodge the instrument in the banking system for deposit or collection. Indorsements of this type include those "for collection," "for deposit," and "pay any bank." Such indorsements *effectively limit* further negotiation to those consistent with its limitation and put all nonbanking persons on notice as to who has a valid interest in the paper. The following two cases should be contrasted.

PALMER & RAY DENTAL SUPPLY OF ABILENE, INC. v. FIRST NATIONAL BANK
Court of Civil Appeals of Texas, 1972.
477 S.W.2d 954.

Facts: Mrs. Wilson was employed as the office manager of Palmer & Ray Dental Supply. Soon after an auditor discovered a discrepancy in the company's inventory, Mrs. Wilson confessed to cashing thirty-five checks that she was supposed to deposit on behalf of the company. Palmer & Ray Dental Supply used a rubber stamp to indorse checks. The stamp listed the company's name and address but did not read "for deposit only." Mrs. Wilson was authorized by the company's president, James Ray, to indorse checks with this stamp. All checks were cashed at First National Bank. Palmer & Ray Dental Supply now claims that First National converted the company's funds by giving Mrs. Wilson cash instead of depositing the checks into the company's bank account. Summary judgment was granted in favor of First National, and Palmer & Ray brought this appeal.

Decision: Judgment for the First National Bank affirmed.

Opinion: Walter, J. Article 3—204, Tex. Uniform Commercial Code, * * *, defines a blank endorsement as one that specifies no particular endorsee and may consist of a mere signature. Article 3—205 of the U.C.C. defines a restrictive endorsement to include one that uses the words "for deposit". Section 1—201(43), U.C.C., defines an unauthorized signature or endorsement as one made without actual implied or apparent authority and includes a forgery.

The summary judgment proof establishes that each of the checks has affixed thereto the blank rubber stamp endorsement of the appellant [Palmer & Ray]. We hold that such blank endorsement constitutes an authorized endorsement. When the Bank delivered cash to Mrs. Wilson instead of depositing the proceeds from the checks to appellant's account, the Bank [acted in accordance with the blank endorsement and therefore] was not guilty of conversion. [Citation.]

FULTZ v. FIRST NATIONAL BANK IN GRAHAM

Supreme Court of Texas, 1965.

388 S.W.2d 405.

Facts: Mrs. McCoy, as an employee of Fultz, secured cash in the amount of $13,060 from checks she deposited on Fultz's behalf and misappropriated the funds to her personal use. The full indorsement stamped on the back of each check read "Pay to order of the First National Bank, Graham, Texas—For deposit only—W. B. Fultz." Mrs. McCoy had not signed a signature card at the bank and was not authorized by Fultz to indorse checks or to withhold cash amounts from the deposits made on his behalf. Fultz now brings this suit against First National to recover the cash received by Mrs. McCoy on the "for deposit only" transactions. Both parties moved for summary judgment and the trial court granted Fultz's motion. The court of appeals reversed, holding that there were triable issues of fact, and Fultz appeals.

Decision: Judgment of the court of appeals reversed and trial court's grant of Fultz's motion for summary judgment affirmed.

Opinion: **Steakley, J.**   The key to the problem is the undisputed fact that the bank violated the written instructions of Fultz, and hence breached its deposit contract with him in each deposit transaction. In the exercise of care by Fultz, all of the checks which were deposited were endorsed "For Deposit Only." This was an unqualified direction to the bank to place the full amount of the checks to the account of Fultz. This instruction was violated when part of the amount of the checks were paid to Mrs. McCoy in cash. The bank had knowledge of its acts in violation of the instruction. Fultz as a depositor had the right to rely on the bank to honor the "For Deposit Only" instructions he had established as the regular deposit routine for his employee and the bank to follow; he was under no duty to exercise further care to ascertain if the bank had followed his instructions, and it is not asserted that Fultz had actual knowledge that the bank had not done so. The instruction carried in the restricted endorsement, "For Deposit Only," if followed, afforded absolute protection to both the bank and the depositor in the check deposit transactions and would have rendered the misappropriations impossible. The bank was in no way misled. Fultz had not filed a signature card for his defalcating employee and had not authorized his employee to sign checks on his account or make cash withdrawals in connection with deposits to his account. The "For Deposit Only" endorsements in the latter transactions were positively to the contrary.

The decisions which consider the question of the liability of a bank for the payment of forged checks recognize the principle stated by the Supreme Court of the United States in *Leather Manufacturers' National Bank v. Morgan*, [citation], that "If the bank's officers, before paying forged or altered checks, could by proper care and skill have detected the forgeries, then it cannot receive a credit for the amount of these checks, even if the depositor omitted all examination of his account."

So it is here. The Respondent bank had only to exercise proper care by following the specific instructions of Fultz, the depositor, the doing of this required no skill. Its course of action in failing to do so resulted in liability to Fultz. * * *

Indorsements in Trust Another common kind of restrictive indorsement is that in which the indorser creates a trust for the benefit of himself or others. If an instrument is indorsed "Pay Trish in trust for Boris" or "Pay Trish for Boris" or "Pay Trish for account of Boris" or "Pay Trish as agent for Boris," Trish is a fiduciary (trustee), subject to liability for any breach of her obligation. Trustees commonly and legitimately sell trust assets, and as a consequence, a trustee has power to negotiate an instrument. The first taker under an indorsement to her in trust (Trish in the above examples) is under the duty to pay or apply all funds given by her consistently with the indorsement or risk having to pay twice. Subsequent indorsees or transferees are not bound by such indorsement *unless* they have knowledge that the trustee negotiated the instrument for her own benefit or otherwise in breach of her fiduciary duty.

Qualified Indorsements

Unqualified indorsers promise that they will pay the instrument according to its terms at the time of their indorsement to the holder or to any subsequent indorser who pays the instrument.[4] In short, an unqualified indorser guarantees payment of the instrument if certain conditions are met.

An indorser may disclaim her liability on the contract of indorsement, but only if the indorsement so declares and the disclaimer is written on the instrument. The customary manner of disclaiming an indorser's liability is to add the words **without recourse,** either before or after her signature. A "without recourse" indorsement is called a **qualified indorsement.**

A qualified indorsement, however, does not eliminate all liability of an indorser. As discussed in Chapter 25, a qualified indorsement does disclaim contract liability, but it does not remove the warranty liability of the indorser (it slightly modifies transferor's warranties). A qualified indorsement and delivery is a negotiation and transfers legal title to the indorsee, but the indorser does *not* guarantee payment of the instrument. A qualified indorsement does not destroy negotiability or prevent further negotiation of the instrument. For example, assume that an attorney receives a check payable to her order in payment of a client's claim. She may indorse the check to the client without recourse, thereby disclaiming liability as a guarantor of payment of the check. The qualified indorsement plus delivery would transfer title to the client.

Negotiations Subject to Rescission

If a negotiation conforms to the requirements discussed above, it is effective to transfer the instrument even if it is

1. made by an infant, a corporation exceeding its powers, or any other person without capacity; or

---

FIGURE 23-3 Indorsements

Indorsement	Type of Indorsement	Interest Transferred	Liability of Indorser
1. "John Doe"	Blank	Nonrestrictive	Unqualified
2. "Pay to Richard Roe, John Doe"	Special	Nonrestrictive	Unqualified
3. "Without recourse, John Doe"	Blank	Nonrestrictive	Qualified
4. "Pay to Richard Roe in trust for John Roe, without recourse, John Doe"	Special	Restrictive	Qualified
5. "For collection only, without recourse, John Doe"	Blank	Restrictive	Qualified
6. "Pay to XYZ Corp., on the condition that it delivers goods ordered this date, John Doe"	Special	Restrictive	Unqualified

2. obtained by fraud, duress, or mistake of any kind; or

3. part of an illegal transaction; or

4. made in breach of a duty.[10]

Thus, a negotiation is valid even though the transaction in which it occurs is voidable or even void. For example, Margaret issues a promissory note to the order of Mustafa, a minor. Mustafa indorses the instrument to Helen. Mustafa's negotiation is effective and makes Helen a holder upon her obtaining possession. Likewise, if Mustafa had indorsed and delivered the instrument to Helen under the threat of death, Helen would nonetheless be a holder. This results from the basic principle of negotiable instruments that a transferee in possession of an instrument that by its terms runs to him is a holder.

In all of these instances, the transferor loses all rights in the instrument until he regains possession of it. The transferor's right to do so is determined by State law. This right is valid against the immediate transferee and all subsequent holders but not against a subsequent holder in due course. Therefore, in the above examples, Mustafa would be able to reclaim the note from Helen.

CHAPTER SUMMARY

Transfer and Negotiation	**Negotiation** transfer such that the transferee becomes a holder ■ *Bearer Instrument* transferred by mere possession ■ *Order Instrument* transferred by possession and indorsement by all appropriate parties **Holder** possessor of an instrument with all necessary indorsements **Shelter Rule** transferee gets rights of transferor
Indorsement	**Definition** signature on the instrument of a payee, drawee, accommodation party, or holder of an instrument **Accommodation Indorser** signer not in the chain of title who signs to add her liability **Blank Indorsement** one specifying no indorsee and making the instrument bearer paper **Special Indorsement** one designating an indorsee to be paid and making the instrument order paper **Restrictive Indorsement** one attempting to limit the rights of the indorsee ■ *Conditional Indorsement* indorsee's right to payment is made subject to the happening or nonhappening of a specified event ■ *Indorsements Prohibiting Further Transfer* are ineffective and operate as unrestrictive indorsements ■ *Indorsements for Deposit or Collection* effectively limit further negotiation to those consistent with the indorsement ■ *Indorsements in Trust* effectively limit the rights of the indorsee to pay or apply all funds in accordance with the indorsement **Unrestrictive Indorsement** one that does not attempt to restrict the rights of the indorsee **Qualified Indorsement** without recourse, one that limits the indorser's liability **Unqualified Indorsement** one that imposes liability on the indorser **Negotiations Subject to Rescission** negotiation is valid even though transaction is void or voidable

QUESTIONS

1. Distinguish among (1) transfer, (2) negotiation, and (3) assignment.
2. What is necessary to become a holder of an instrument?
3. Distinguish between a blank and a special indorsement.
4. Distinguish between a qualified and an unqualified indorsement.
5. Discuss the various types of restrictive indorsements.

PROBLEMS

1. Roy Rand executed and delivered the following note to Sue Sims: "Chicago, Illinois, June 1, 1990. I promise to pay to Sue Sims or bearer, on or before July 1, 1990, the sum of $7,000. This note is given in consideration of Sims's transferring to the undersigned title to her 1987 Buick automobile. (signed) Roy Rand." Rand and Sims agreed that delivery of the car be deferred to July 1, 1990. On June 15, Sims sold and delivered the note, without indorsement, to Karl Kaye for $6,200. What rights, if any, has Kaye acquired?
2. Lavinia Lane received a check from Wilmore Enterprises, Inc., drawn on the Citizens Bank of Erehwon, in the sum of $10,000. Mrs. Lane indorsed the check "Mrs. Lavinia Lane for deposit only, Account of Lavinia Lane," placed it in a "bank by mail" envelope addressed to the First National Bank of Emanon, where she maintained a checking account, and placed the envelope over a tier of mailboxes in her apartment building along with other letters to be picked up by the postman the next day.

Flora Fain stole the check, went to the Bank of Altoona, where Mrs. Lane was unknown, represented herself to be Lavinia Lane, and cashed the check. Has the Bank of Altoona taken the check by negotiation? Why or why not?
3. What types of indorsements are the following:
(a) "Pay to M without recourse."
(b) "Pay to A for collection."
(c) "I hereby assign all my rights, title, and interest in this note to F in full."
(d) "Pay to the Southern Trust Company."
(e) "Pay to the order of the Farmers Bank of Nicholasville for deposit only."

Indicate whether the indorsement is: (1) blank or special, (2) restrictive or nonrestrictive, and (3) qualified or unqualified.
4. Explain whether the following transactions result in a valid negotiation:
(a) A gives a negotiable check payable to bearer to B without indorsing it.
(b) G indorses a negotiable promissory note payable to the order of G, "Pay to M and N, (signed) G."
(c) X lost a negotiable check payable to his order. Y found it and indorsed the back of the check: "Pay to Z, (signed) Y."
(d) C indorsed a negotiable promissory note payable to the order of C, "(signed) C," and delivered it to D. D then wrote above C's signature, "Pay to D."
5. Alpha issues a negotiable check to Beta payable to the order of Beta in payment of an obligation Alpha owed Beta. Beta delivers the check to Gamma without indorsing it in exchange for 100 shares of General Motors stock owned by Gamma. How has Beta transferred the check? What rights, if any, does Gamma have against Beta?
6. Margarita executed and delivered to Poncho a negotiable promissory note payable to the order of Poncho as payment for 100 bushels of wheat Poncho had sold to Margarita. Poncho indorsed the note "Pay to Randy only, (signed) Poncho" and sold it to Randy. Randy then sold the note to Stephanie after indorsing it "Pay to Stephanie, (signed) Randy." What rights, if any, does Stephanie acquire in the instrument?
7. Simon Sharpe executed and delivered to Ben Bates a negotiable promissory note payable to the order of Ben Bates for $500. Bates indorsed the note, "Pay to Carl Cady upon his satisfactorily repairing the roof of my house, (signed) Ben Bates," and delivered it to Cady as a downpayment on the contract price of the roofing job. Cady then indorsed the note and sold it to Timothy Tate for $450. What rights, if any, does Tate acquire in the promissory note?
8. Debbie Dean issued a check to Betty Brown payable to the order of Cathy Cain and Betty Brown. Betty indorsed the check "Pay to Elizabeth East, (signed) Betty Brown." What rights, if any, does Elizabeth acquire in the check?
9. Triplett attempted to arrange a $2,850,000 loan through Meyer Rabin and his Consumer's Investment Company (CIC). CIC issued a commitment letter conditioned on the payment of a $14,250 commitment fee and the personal guarantee of C. D. Wyche. Triplett sought an additional loan from E. S. Tubin to cover the commitment fee. Tubin agreed to provide the $14,250 if the money would be "safe" pending the closing of the

$2,850,000 loan and if he would receive $4,500 for the use of his money. Triplett agreed, and Tubin purchased a $14,250 cashier's check payable to Melvin Rueckhaus, his attorney. Rueckhaus typed the following indorsement on the back of the check: "PAY TO THE ORDER—CONSUMERS INVESTMENT CO. and CHARLES D. WYCHE, SR . . ."

Rabin presented the check to Fair Park National Bank for immediate credit to CIC's account. Now knowing that Wyche's signature had been forged by Rabin, the bank complied, and Rabin subsequently depleted CIC's account. The loan was never closed, and the $14,250 was never returned to Tubin. Tubin then brought this suit against Fair Park National Bank. Decision?

ENDNOTES

1. Uniform Commercial Code, Section 3—201, Transfer: Right to Indorsement.

2. Uniform Commercial Code, Section 3—202, Negotiation.

3. Uniform Commercial Code, Section 1—201(20), Holder.

4. Uniform Commercial Code, Section 3—414, Contract of Indorser; Order of Liability.

5. Uniform Commercial Code, Section 3—402, Signature in Ambiguous Capacity.

6. Uniform Commercial Code, Section 3—415, Contract of Accommodation Party.

7. Uniform Commercial Code, Section 3—404, Unauthorized Signatures.

8. Uniform Commercial Code, Section 3—204, Special Indorsement; Blank Indorsement.

9. Uniform Commercial Code, Section, 3—205, Restrictive Indorsements and Section 3—206, Effect of Restrictive Indorsement.

10. Uniform Commercial Code, Section 3—207, Negotiations Effective Although It May Be Rescinded.

24 HOLDER IN DUE COURSE

The unique and most significant aspect of negotiability is the concept of the holder in due course. While a mere holder acquires a negotiable instrument subject to all claims and defenses to it, a holder in due course, in a **nonconsumer** credit transaction, takes the instrument free of all claims of other parties and free of all defenses to the instrument except for a very limited number specifically set forth in the Uniform Commercial Code. The law has conferred this preferred position on the holder in due course to encourage the free negotiability of commercial paper by minimizing the risks assumed by an innocent purchaser of the instrument. The transferee of a negotiable instrument wants payment for it; he does not want to be subject to any dispute between the obligor and the obligee (generally the original payee). In this chapter we discuss how a transferee becomes a holder in due course and the benefits conferred on a holder in due course.

REQUIREMENTS OF A HOLDER IN DUE COURSE

To acquire the preferential rights of a holder in due course, a person must meet the requirements of the Code[1] or must "inherit" these rights under the shelter rule.[2] To satisfy the requirements, a transferee must:

1. be a holder of a negotiable instrument;
2. take it for value;
3. take it in good faith; and
4. take it without notice
   (a) that it is overdue or has been dishonored, or
   (b) of any defense against or claim to it on the part of any person.

Figure 24–1 illustrates the various requirements of becoming a holder in due course and the consequences of meeting or not meeting them.

Holder

The transferee must be a holder before he can become a holder in due course. As previously discussed, a **holder** is a person who is in possession of a negotiable instrument (1) issued to his order, (2) issued to bearer, (3) indorsed to him, or (4) indorsed in blank. In other words, a holder is a person who has both possession of an instrument and all necessary indorsements. Whether or not the holder is the owner of the instrument, he may transfer it, negotiate it, enforce payment of it (subject to claims and defenses), or, with certain exceptions, discharge it.

The significance of being a holder is brought out in the following factual situation, which is illustrated in Figure 24–2. Poe indorsed her paycheck in blank and cashed it at a tavern where she was a well-known customer. Shortly thereafter, a burglar stole the check from the tavern. The owner of the tavern immediately notified Poe's employer, who gave the drawee bank a stop payment order (a command not to pay the instrument). The burglar indorsed the check in a false name and transferred it to a grocer, who took it in good faith and for value. The check was dishonored (not paid) when presented for payment to the drawee bank. The paycheck became bearer paper when Poe indorsed it in blank. It retained this character in the hands of the tavern owner, in the hands of the burglar, and in the

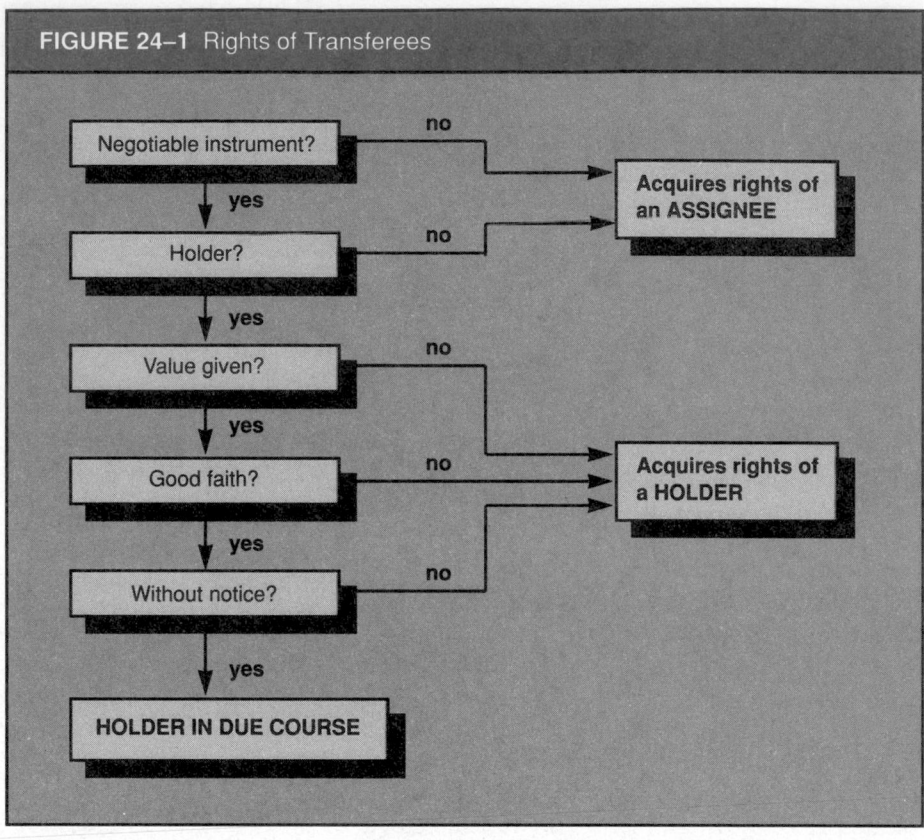

FIGURE 24-1 Rights of Transferees

hands of the grocer, who became a holder in due course even though he had received it from a thief who had indorsed it with a false name. Because an indorsement is not necessary to negotiate bearer paper, the forged indorsement was immaterial. The thief was a holder of the check[3] and as such could negotiate it.[4] Accordingly, one who, like the grocer, takes from a holder for value, in good faith, and without notice becomes a holder in due course and can collect the amount of the check from the drawer. Thus, in the absence of a real

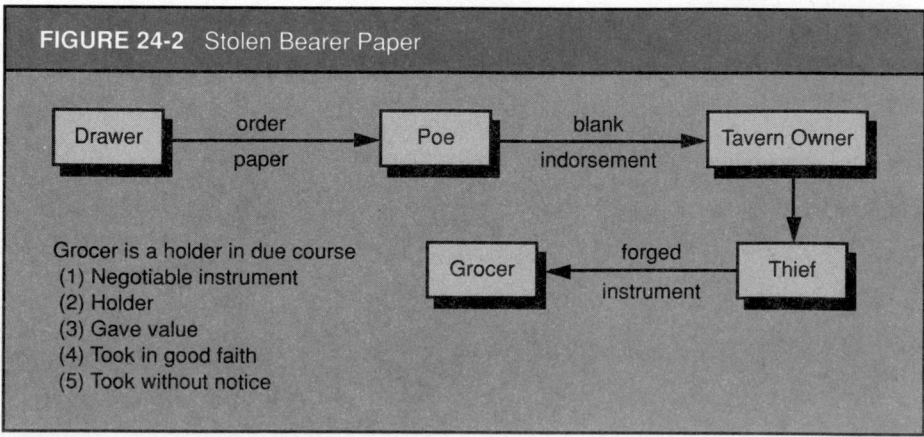

FIGURE 24-2 Stolen Bearer Paper

defense, discussed later in this chapter, the grocer will be entitled to payment from the drawer.

This rule does not apply to a stolen order instrument. In the example above, assume that the thief had stolen the paycheck from Poe prior to indorsement. The thief then forged Poe's signature and transferred the check to the grocer, who again took it in good faith, for value, and without notice. Negotiation of an order instrument requires a valid indorsement by the person to whose order the instrument is payable, in this case Poe. A forged indorsement is not valid. Consequently, the grocer has not taken the instrument with all necessary indorsements, and he could not be a holder or a holder in due course. The grocer's only recourse would be to collect the amount of the check from the thief. Figure 24–3 illustrates this example.

Value

The law requires a holder in due course to have given value. An obvious case of failure to give value is where the holder makes a gift of the instrument to a third person.

The concept of value in the law of negotiable instruments is not the same as that of consideration under the law of contracts. **Value,** for purposes of negotiable instruments, is defined as: (1) the timely *performance* of legal consideration (thus, executory promises are excluded since they have not been performed); (2) the

acquisition of a security interest or a lien on the instrument; (3) taking the instrument in payment of or as security for an antecedent debt; (4) the giving of a negotiable instrument; or (5) the giving of an irrevocable commitment to a third party.[5]

An **executory promise,** an unperformed obligation, clearly valid consideration to support a contract, is not the giving of value to support holder-in-due-course status. A purchaser of a note or draft who has not yet given value may rescind the transaction and avoid it through a valid defense. A person who has given value, however, needs and deserves the protection given to a holder in due course.

For example, Mike executes and delivers a $1,000 note payable to the order of Pat, who negotiates it to Henry, who promises to pay Pat for it a month later. During the month, Henry learns that Mike has a defense against Pat. Henry can rescind the agreement with Pat and return the note to Pat. This makes him whole, and he has no need to cut off Mike's defense. Assume, on the other hand, that Henry has paid Pat for the note before he learns of Mike's defense. It may not be possible for Henry to recover his money from Pat. Henry then needs the holder-in-due-course protection that permits him to recover on the instrument from Mike.

A holder, as demonstrated in *Korzenik v. Supreme Radio, Inc.,* therefore takes an instrument for value to the extent that the agreed consideration has been *given*, provided the

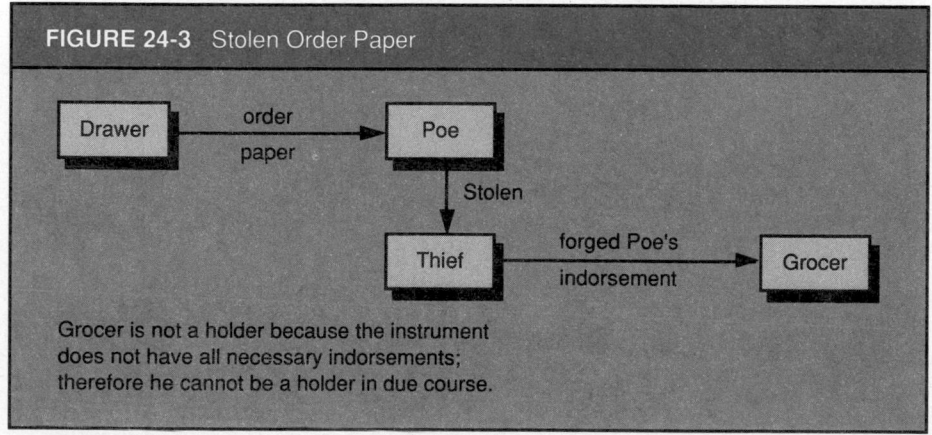

FIGURE 24-3 Stolen Order Paper

Drawer — order paper → Poe

Poe — Stolen → Thief

Thief — forged Poe's indorsement → Grocer

Grocer is not a holder because the instrument does not have all necessary indorsements; therefore he cannot be a holder in due course.

consideration was given prior to the holder's learning of any defense or claim to the instrument. Asume that in the previous example Henry had agreed to pay Pat $900 for the note. If Henry had paid Pat $600, he could be a holder in due course to the extent of $600 (a number of courts would allow Henry to recover $666.67: the $600 paid plus his *pro rata* share of the discount: 600/900 × $100 or 66.67), and if a defense were available, it would be valid against him only to the extent of the balance.

When Henry paid the $300 balance to Pat, he would become a holder in due course as to the full $1,000 face value of the note, provided payment was made prior to Henry's discovery of Mike's defense. If the $300 payment was made after discovery of the defense or claim, Henry would be a holder in due course only to the extent of $600 (or possibly $666.67). A holder in due course, to give value, is not required to pay the face amount of the instrument but only the amount he agreed to pay.

KORZENIK v. SUPREME RADIO, INC.
Supreme Judicial Court of Massachusetts, 1964.
347 Mass. 309, 197 N.E.2d 702.

Facts: Supreme Radio, Inc., issued to Southern New England Distributing Corporation two notes worth $1,900. The two notes and others, all of a total face value of about $15,000, were transferred to Korzenik, an attorney, by his client Southern "as a retainer for services to be performed" by Korzenik. Although Korzenik was unaware of the fact, Southern had obtained the notes by fraud. Southern retained Korzenik on October 25 in connection with certain antitrust litigation, and the notes were transferred on October 31. The value of the services performed by Korzenik during that time is unclear. Korzenik brought this action against Supreme Radio to recover $1,900 on the notes.

Decision: Judgment for Supreme Radio affirmed.

Opinion: Whittemore, J.   Decisive of the case, as the Appellate Division held, is the correct ruling that the plaintiffs are not holders in due course under * * * § 3–302; they have not shown to what extent they took for value under § 3–303. That section provides: "A holder takes the instrument for value (a) to the extent that the agreed consideration has been performed or that he acquires a security interest in or a lien on the instrument otherwise than by legal process; or (b) when he takes the instrument in payment of or as security for an antecedent claim against any person whether or not the claim is due; or (c) when he gives a negotiable instrument for it or makes an irrevocable commitment to a third person."

Under clause (a) of § 3–303 the "agreed consideration" was the performance of legal services. It is often said that a lawyer is "retained' when he is engaged to perform services, and we hold that the judge spoke of "retainer" in this sense. The phrase that the judge used, "retainer *for services*" (emphasis supplied), shows his meaning as does the finding as to services already performed by Korzenik at the time of the assignments. Even if the retainer had been only a fee to insure the attorney's availability to perform future services [citation] there is no basis in the record for determining the value of this commitment for one week.

The Uniform [U.C.C.] Laws Comment to § 3–303 points out that in this article "value is divorced from consideration" and that except as provided in paragraph (c) "[a]n executory promise to give value is not * * * value. * * * The underlying reason for policy is that when the purchaser learns of a defense * * * he is not required to enforce the instrument, but is free to rescind the transaction for breach of the transferor's warranty."

[U.C.C.] § 3–307(3), provides: "After it is shown that a defense exists a person claiming the rights of a holder in due course has the burden of establishing that he or some person under whom he claims is in all respects a holder in due course." The defense of fraud having been established this section puts the burden on the plaintiffs. The plaintiffs have failed to show "the extent * * * [to which] the agreed consideration * * * [had] been performed."

The Code, as noted in the above case, provides an exception to the executory promise rule in two situations: (1) the giving of a negotiable instrument, and (2) the making of an irrevocable commitment to a third party.[5] Suppose that Maurice issues a note for $1,000 payable to the order of Pamela, which Pamela indorses and delivers to Hillary, who gives Pamela her personal check for $1,000 in exchange for it. Hillary met the requirement of giving value for the note when she gave Pamela her check, not when the check was paid by the drawee bank. Value would likewise be given if Hillary made any other irrevocable commitment, if the commitment was to a *third party* rather than to Pamela.

Where an instrument is given as security for an obligation, the lender is also regarded as having given value to the extent of his security interest.[5] For example, Phillip is the holder of a $1,000 note payable to his order, executed by Mina, and due in twelve months. Phillip uses the note as security for a $700 loan made to him by Hilda. Because Hilda has advanced $700, she has met the requirement of value to the extent of $700.

Likewise, a bank gives value when a depositor is allowed to withdraw funds against a deposited item. The provisional or temporary crediting of a depositor's account (discussed in Chapter 26) is not sufficient. If a number of checks have been deposited, and some but not all of the funds have been withdrawn, the Code traces the deposit by following the "FIFO" or "first-in, first-out" method of accounting.

Finally, under general contract law, an **antecedent debt** (preexisting obligation) is not sufficient consideration to support a promise to pay the debt or a lesser amount in full satisfaction. Under the Code, however, a holder does give value when she takes an instrument in payment of or as security for an antecedent debt.[5] Thus, Martha makes and delivers a note for $1,000 to the order of Penny. Penny indorses the instrument and delivers it to Howes in payment of an outstanding debt of $970 that Penny owes Howes. Howes has given value. Similarly, see *St. Paul Fire & Marine Ins. Co. v. State Bank of Salem* on page 499.

Good Faith

The Code defines **good faith** as "honesty in fact in the conduct or transaction concerned."[6] The test is **subjective:** it determines good faith by what the purchaser knows or believes. He may be empty-headed, but if his heart is pure, he can pass muster on good faith grounds. Under this test, if the purchaser was actually innocent, he is held to have bought the instrument in good faith, even though a prudent man under the circumstances would have known that something was wrong.

Lack of Notice

To become a holder in due course, a holder must also take the instrument without notice that it is (1) overdue, (2) dishonored, or (3) subject to any defense or claim. Notice of any of these matters should alert the purchaser that she may be buying a lawsuit and therefore should not be accorded the favored position of a holder in due course. "Notice" is defined by the Code as: "A person has 'notice' of a fact when (a) he has actual knowledge of it; or (b) he has received a notice or notification of it; or (c) from all of the facts and circumstances known to him at the time in question he has reason to know that it exists."[7] The first two clauses of this definition impose a wholly subjective standard. The last clause provides a partially objective one: the fact that suspicious circumstances are present does not adversely affect the purchaser, unless he has reason to recognize them as suspicious. Since the applicable standard is "actual notice," "notice received," or "reason to know," constructive notice through public filing or recording is not of itself sufficient notice to prevent a person from being a holder in due course. To be effective, notice must be received at such a time and way that will give the recipient a reasonable opportunity to act on it.[8]

Buying an instrument at a discount less than face value does not mean that the buyer had notice of any defense or claim against the instrument. Likewise, buying an instrument at a discounted price does not demonstrate lack of good faith. Nonetheless, an unusually large discount may be construed by a court to indicate notice of a defense or claim.

Notice an Instrument Is Overdue To be a holder in due course, the purchaser must take the instrument without notice that it is overdue.[1] This requirement is based on the idea that overdue paper conveys a suspicion that something is wrong. Thus, if an instrument is payable on July 1, a purchaser cannot become a holder in due course by buying it on July 2, provided that July 1 was a business day. **Time paper** is due on its stated due date if the stated date is a business day or, if not, on the next business day.

Demand paper is not overdue for purposes of preventing one from becoming a holder in due course unless the purchaser has notice that she is taking it after demand has been made or until it has been outstanding an unreasonable length of time.[8] Although the Code does not state what a reasonable time is, in the case of a demand note, it is usually about sixty days. The time is somewhat shorter for drafts, and with regard to checks, a reasonable time is *presumed* to be thirty days after issuance. Nonetheless, the particular situa-

tion, business custom, and other relevant factors must be considered in making the determination, and no hard and fast rules are possible.

Notice an Instrument Has Been Dishonored **Dishonor** is the refusal to pay or accept an instrument when it becomes due. If a transferee has notice that an instrument has been dishonored, he cannot become a holder in due course. He knows the instrument may not be paid.

Notice of a Claim or Defense A purchaser of an instrument cannot become a holder in due course if he purchases it with notice of a defense or claim to it.[1] A **defense** to the instrument is a justification or shield protecting a person from liability on it, whereas a **claim** to the instrument is an assertion of ownership of it. Defenses to negotiable instruments are discussed below. Claims to negotiable instruments are generally made by a person contending that he is the rightful owner of the instrument. Claims may be made against thieves, finders, or possessors with voidable or void title. In many instances, both a defense and a claim will be involved. For example, Donna is fraudulently induced to draw a check to Pablo. Donna has a claim to ownership of the instrument as well as a defense to Pablo's demand for payment.

A purchaser has notice of a claim or defense if the instrument bears visible evidence of forgery or alteration or is so irregular as to call its validity into question.[8] For example, Deva draws a check on the First National Bank for $100, payable to the order of Penelope. Penelope crudely raises the amount of the check to $1,000 and negotiates it to Hiram. Hiram cannot be a holder in due course. The instrument is irregular, and the alteration is so obvious that Hiram would be held to have notice of it. Nonetheless, as the case on page 499 demonstrates, the courts vary greatly on how irregular the alteration must be to rule that a holder had notice of it.

Suppose there is an obvious change on the face of the instrument that does not normally indicate wrongdoing. For instance, the date may be changed from January 2, 1990, to

ST. PAUL FIRE AND MARINE INSURANCE CO. v. STATE BANK OF SALEM

Court of Appeals of Indiana, First District, 1980.
412 N.E.2d 103.

Facts: Stephens delivered 184 bushels of corn to Aubrey for which he was to receive $478.23. Aubrey issued a check with $478.23 typewritten in numbers, and on the line customarily used to express the amount in words appeared "$100478 and 23 cts" imprinted in red with a check-writing machine. Before Stephens cashed the check, someone crudely typed "100" in front of the typewritten $478.23. When Stephens presented this check to the State Bank of Salem, Anderson, the manager, questioned Stephens. Anderson knew that Stephens had just declared bankruptcy and was not accustomed to making such large deposits. Stephens told Anderson he had bought and sold a large quantity of corn at a great profit. Anderson accepted the explanation, applied the monies to nine promissory notes, an installment payment, and accrued interest owed by Stephens. Stephens also received $2,000 in cash, with the balance deposited in his checking account.

Later that day, Anderson reexamined the check and discovered the suspicious appearance of the typewriting. He then contacted Aubrey who said a check in that amount was suspicious, whereupon Anderson froze the transaction. When Aubrey stopped payment on the check, the bank sustained a $28,193.91 loss because Stephens could not be located. The bank then sued Aubrey for the loss. As defenses, Aubrey claims that: (1) the bank did not take the check for value and (2) the typed "100" put the bank on notice of Aubrey's defense. Thus, Aubrey contended that the bank was not a holder in due course and could not collect on the check from Aubrey. The trial court ruled in favor of the bank and Aubrey appeals.

Decision: Judgment for State Bank of Salem affirmed.

Opinion: Neal, J.   We think the only issue dispositive of Aubrey's appeal is whether the trial court could rightfully have found on the evidence that the Bank was a holder in due course of the Aubrey check under the Uniform Commercial Code (UCC) as adopted in Indiana. * * *

The Bank's right to recover on the check is conditioned upon its status as a holder in due course of the check. Section 3–305 states in part:

"To the extent that a holder is a holder in due course he takes the instrument free from

   "(1) all claims to it on the part of any person; and

   "(2) all defenses of any party to the instrument with whom the holder has not dealt except * * * "

Assuming, without presently deciding, that Aubrey showed the existence of a defense, the burden was on the Bank to prove by a preponderance of the evidence that it was in all respects a holder in due course of the check. § 3–307(3).

* * *

There is no contention on appeal, and there was none at trial, that the Bank did not take the Aubrey check in good faith, which means honesty in fact in the transaction concerned. [Citation.] There is also no question that the Bank was a holder of the instrument, as it was in possession of the check indorsed by the payee Stephens in blank. See § 1–204(20).

We initially consider whether the Bank took the Aubrey check for value. The Bank contends that it gave value for the check to the extent that it (a) acquired a security interest in the instrument under §§ 3–303(a), 4–208, and 4–209; and (b) took the check in payment of an antecedent claim under § 3–303(b). Aubrey contends that the Bank did not take the check for value since it immediately froze Stephen's account upon apprisal that the validity of the check was suspect and cancelled the amounts it had credited against Stephen's debt. Aubrey considers that the Bank's action in crediting Stephens's debt on the notes merely constituted a bookkeeping procedure and the Bank did not change its position by doing so, particularly since the Bank could still maintain an action against Stephens on the notes. Finally, Aubrey maintains that general principles of law and equity render the UCC provisions relied on by the Bank inapplicable.

We are of the opinion that the Bank took the check for value. The issue is most readily resolved by § 3–303(b) which states in part:

"A holder takes the instrument for value

* * *

"(b) when he takes the instrument in payment of or as security for an antecedent claim against any person whether or not the claim is due; * * * "

The statute [U.C.C.] plainly states that value is given for an instrument when the instrument is taken in payment for an antecedent debt not yet due. The statute contains no provision precluding application of the rule when fraud is exercised by the presenter of the instrument, as Aubrey would have us find.

While this section has not been construed in Indiana, an examination of authorities from other jurisdictions lends support to the Bank's position that the application of funds made available by the Aubrey check to Stephens's indebtedness and the surrender of the notes constituted taking the instrument for value.

Further, we believe that the Bank gave value for the check under §§ 4–208(1) and 4–209, in that it acquired a security interest in the check to the extent funds represented thereby were applied to Stephens's debt. Section 4–208(1)(a) states in part:

"(1) A bank has a security interest in an item and any accompanying documents or the proceeds of either

"(a) in case of an item deposited in an account to the extent to which credit given for the item has been withdrawn or applied; . . ."

Section 4–209 provides:

"For purposes of determining its status as a holder in due course, the bank has given value to the extent that it has a security interest in an item provided that the bank otherwise complies with the requirements of § 3–302 on what constitutes a holder in due course."

We find no support for Aubrey's argument that the Bank did not give value since it did not change its position vis-a-vis Stephens and made a bookkeeping entry only of the credit given Stephens. * * * Official Comment 3 to § 3–303 states that it is not necessary to give holder in due course status to one who has not actually paid value, and cites as illustration "the bank credit not drawn upon, which can be and is revoked when a claim or defense appears." [Citation.] When the credit is drawn upon, however, value is given to that extent. § 4–208(1)(a). Further, if the depositor's account is overdrawn at the time the check is taken, and funds represented thereby are applied to the overdrawal by way of set-off, value is given to that extent if the check is later dishonored. [Citation.]

* * *

As the section makes clear, in the event of an ambiguity between printed terms and typewritten terms, the latter would control. We do not consider the impressions made by the check imprinter to be "printed" terms under this section. [Citation.]

A conflict between the two amounts on a check would be resolved by § 3–118(c) which states that words control figures. Arguably, the amount imprinted by the checkwriting machine upon the line customarily expressing the amount in words, is expressed in figures. (Recall that the entry reads: "The sum of $100478 and 23 cts.") We think , however, that the purposes of the UCC are best served by considering an amount imprinted by a checkwriting machine as "words" for the purpose of resolving an ambiguity between that amount and an amount entered upon the line usually used to express the amount in figures.

Two purposes behind the rule that words control figures have been expressed which support the proposition expressed here, i.e., that impressions made by checkwriting machines upon the "words" line control typed or written figures. In *United States Fidelity and Guaranty Company v. First National Bank of South Carolina of Columbia*, it is stated:

> "A prime purpose, as we see it, of making a sum payable when expressed in words controlling over the sum payable expressed in figures is the very fact that words are much more difficult to alter. The perforated imprinting by a checkwriting machine, while expressing the sum payable in figures, is even more difficult to successfully alter than a sum payable in written words."

* * *

We cannot say as a matter of law that the bank acted unreasonably in relying upon the amount expressed by the checkwriting machine. Aubrey presented no evidence that customary banking standards require a bank to closely examine and compare the two amounts on the check, and it was Aubrey's burden to prove the existence of such custom. [Citation.] The issue of the Bank's constructive knowledge of any defense Aubrey may have had to the check, based on the alleged irregularity on the face of the check, was a question of fact for the trial court to determine. It was not error for the court to have determined that the Bank acted reasonably in relying on the amount imprinted by the checkwriting machine and took the check without notice, actual or constructive, of a defense thereto.

Aubrey further argues that the circumstances surrounding the transaction were so irregular as to put a reasonably prudent banker on notice of a defense to Aubrey's check. Aubrey directs us to no cases in which a holder was denied holder in due course status because of its knowledge of the questionable general financial position of the presenter of the instrument. Our research reveals such knowledge is not sufficient in itself to defeat holder in due course status. * * *

The only knowledge the Bank had concerning the transaction underlying the issue of the Aubrey check to Stephens, and thus the only knowledge relevant to the issue of Bank's notice of a possible defense to the check, grew out of Stephens's explanation to Anderson of how the check came into his hands. This was not sufficient to call into question the integrity of the Aubrey check.

We therefore hold that the evidence supports the trial court's determination that the Bank was a holder in due course of the Aubrey check. Since Aubrey has not shown a "real defense" under § 3–305(2) the Bank may enforce the check against Aubrey to the extent it gave value therefor, and we shall not disturb the trial court's award of that amount.

January 2, 1991. It would be reasonable to assume that the drawer, out of force of habit, wrote "1990" rather than "1991." This would not be considered a material alteration that would give notice of a defense or claim.

A purchaser has notice of a claim or defense if the purchaser has notice that the obligation of any party is **voidable** or that *all* parties to the instrument have been discharged. An obligation by a party that is **void** is a real defense and, as is discussed below, may be asserted against a holder in due course whether or not he has notice of it. The fact that the holder knows that one or more but not all the parties have been discharged does not prevent the holder from being a holder in due course with respect to the nondischarged parties. For example, Michael issues a negotiable promissory note to Percy, who indorses it in blank and delivers it to Arthur. The instrument then passes by blank indorsements to Bob, Clara, and Diane. Diane strikes out Clara's indorsement and negotiates it for value to Herb. Herb would have notice that Clara's liability had been discharged. This would not prevent Herb from being a holder in due course with respect to Michael, Percy, Arthur, Bob, and Diane, because their liability is not discharged.

HOLDER IN DUE COURSE STATUS

A holder who meets the requirements discussed in the previous sections enjoys the preferred position of holder in due course status. In this section, we discuss how any transferee of a holder in due course also acquires this status. We also address the question of whether or not a payee may become a holder in due course.

A Payee May Be a Holder in Due Course

The Code provides that a payee may be a holder in due course.[1] This does not mean that the payee will always be a holder in due course but merely that he *may* if he satisfies all the requirements for a holder to become a holder in due course. For example, if a seller delivers goods to a buyer and accepts a current check in payment, the seller will be a holder in due

course if he acted in good faith and had no notice of defenses or claims. The seller, however, takes the check *subject to* all claims and defenses because a holder in due course takes instruments free of defenses only from persons he has *not* dealt with.[9]

In some situations the payee is not an immediate party to the transaction and therefore will not be subject to any claims and most defenses if he meets the requirements of a holder in due course. For example, Robin, after purchasing goods from Paul, fraudulently obtains a check from Chris payable to the order of Paul and forwards it to Paul. Paul takes it for value and without any knowledge that Robin had defrauded Chris into issuing the check. In such a case, the payee, Paul, is held to be a holder in due course and takes the instrument free and clear of Chris's defense of fraud in the inducement. There are a number of other ways in which a payee may benefit from being a holder in due course, but they are rather infrequent. In each instance, there are three parties involved in the transaction, and the defense exists between the parties other than the payee.

The Shelter Rule

The transferee of an instrument, through the operation of the **shelter rule,** as previously noted, acquires the *same* rights in the instrument that the transferor had.[2] Therefore, even if a holder does not comply with all the requirements for being a holder in due course, she nevertheless acquires all the rights of that status if some previous holder of the instrument had been a holder in due course. Thus, Pauline induces Myrna, by fraud, to make a note payable to her order and then negotiates it to Asher, a holder in due course. After the note is overdue, Asher gives it to Berne, who has notice of the fraud. Berne is not a holder in due course, since he has taken the instrument when overdue, did not pay value, and has notice of Myrna's defense. Nonetheless, due to the shelter rule Berne acquires Asher's rights as a holder in due course, and Myrna cannot successfully assert her defense against Berne. The purpose of the shelter provision is not to benefit the transferee but to assure the holder in due course of a free market for negotiable instruments he acquires.

The shelter rule, however, provides that a transferee (1) who has himself been a party to any fraud or illegality affecting the instrument, or (2) who as a prior holder had notice of a claim or defense, cannot wash the paper clean by later reacquiring it from a subsequent holder in due course or person having the rights of one.[2] For example, Parker induces Miles, by fraud, to make an instrument payable to the order of Parker. Parker subsequently negotiates the instrument to Henson, a holder in due course, and later reacquires it from Henson. Parker does not succeed to Henson's rights as a holder in due course and remains subject to the defense of fraud.

THE PREFERRED POSITION OF A HOLDER IN DUE COURSE

In a **nonconsumer transaction,** a holder in due course takes the instrument (1) free from all claims on the part of any person and (2) free from all defenses of any party with whom he has not dealt except for a limited number of defenses that are available against anyone, including a holder in due course. Such defenses are referred to as **real defenses,** as opposed to defenses that may not be asserted against a holder in due course, which are referred to as **personal** or contractual **defenses** (see Figure 24–4).

Real Defenses

The real defenses available against *all* assignees and holders, including holders in due course, are

1. minority, to the extent that it is a defense to a simple contract,
2. any incapacity, duress, or illegality of the transaction that renders the obligation void,
3. fraud in the execution,
4. discharge in insolvency proceedings;
5. any other discharge of which the holder has notice when he takes the instrument;
6. unauthorized signature; and
7. material alteration.

Minority All States have a firmly entrenched public policy of protecting minors from persons who might take advantage of them through contractual dealings. The Code does not state when minority is available as a defense or the conditions under which it may be asserted. Rather, it provides that minority is a defense available against a holder in due course to the extent that it is a defense to a simple contract under the laws of the State involved.[9]

Void Obligations Where the obligation on an instrument originates in such a way that under the law of the State involved it is *void*, the Code authorizes the use of this defense against a holder in due course.[9] This follows from the fact that where the party was never obligated, it is

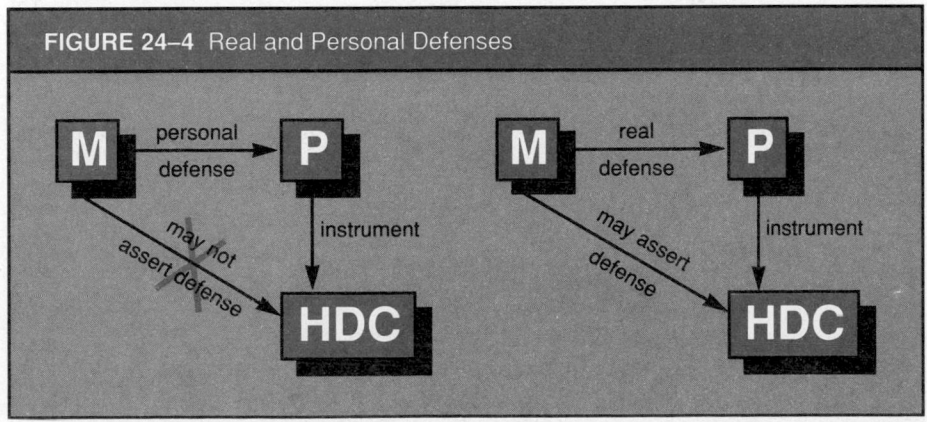

FIGURE 24–4 Real and Personal Defenses

unreasonable to permit an event over which he has no control—negotiation to a holder in due course—to make a void obligation into a valid claim against him.

Incapacity, duress, and illegality of the transaction are defenses that may render the obligation of a party voidable or void, depending on the law of the State and how it is applied to the facts of a transaction. To the extent the obligation is rendered void, the defense may be asserted against a holder in due course. To the extent it is voidable, which is generally the case, the defense (other than minority) is not effective against a holder in due course.

BANKERS TRUST COMPANY v. LITTON SYSTEMS, INC.
United States Court of Appeals, Second Circuit, 1979.
599 F.2d 488.

Facts: Litton Systems, Inc., sought to obtain photocopiers for some of its branch offices. Angelo Buquicchio, an employee of Royal (a division of Litton), suggested that the machines be leased from Regent Leasing Corporation. Unknown to Litton or Royal, Buquicchio was to receive secret "service fees" or bribes from Regent in exchange for his influence. Litton and Regent entered into a lease agreement. Regent borrowed from Bankers Trust Company and Chemical Bank to finance its purchases of the necessary equipment. Regent transferred its leases with Litton to the two banks, who became holders in due course, as security for the loans. Litton subsequently defaulted on the leases, and the banks brought an action against Litton and moved for summary judgment. Litton claimed that Regent's bribery of Buquicchio made its obligations to the banks null and void and claimed a real defense against the banks. The trial court, however, concluded otherwise and entered summary judgment for the banks. Litton appealed.

Decision: Judgment for Bankers Trust Company and Chemical Bank affirmed.

Opinion: **Moore, J.** *That the alleged service fee payments were illegal.* This defense goes to the heart of this appeal and constitutes the main portion of appellant's argument. In sum, it is that the alleged kickbacks to Buquicchio rendered the leases between Regent and Litton so utterly void that they became nullities, never to have any legal validity even for bona fide holders in due course without notice of the side deal Buquicchio made for his own benefit.

Buquicchio's conduct was arguably illegal under New York Penal Law which declares commercial bribery to be a criminal offense. Litton claims that the bribes were such "illegality of the transaction, as renders the obligation of the party a nullity . . ." and that, therefore, the leases were unenforceable even by a holder in due course. U.C.C. § 3–305(2)(b).

The court carefully analyzed the New York cases on the subject and concluded that whereas "such payments could constitute a defense as against Regent . . . the making of such payments could not be asserted against a holder in due course. . . ." Accordingly, it granted the banks' motions for summary judgment.

* * *

The court concluded that

"(I)n using the term 'nullity' the Legislature intended to provide a defense against a holder in due course only in cases where the obligation sued upon is void on its face (e.g., a wagering contract or a contract to perform an illegal act), and was not intended to provide a defense against such a holder where one of the parties to the original contract might have an option to declare it void because some illegal conduct in which the other party may have engaged in the course of the negotiations which gave rise to the contract."

There is a distinction here which should be preserved: the lease contracts for photocopiers were not themselves illegal; the contract to bribe a person in connection with those contracts was illegal.

* * *

The illegality defense under U.C.C. § 3–305(2)(b) is available only if under the applicable state law the effect of the illegality is to make the obligation entirely null and void; the defense is ineffective against a holder in due course if the illegality causes the contract to be merely voidable. Official Comment 6, U.C.C. § 3–305.

* * *

The problems and consequences of using the terms "void" and "voidable" were recognized by the Restatement of Contracts:

"Confusion in the use of the words 'void' and 'voidable' is common, chiefly because it frequently makes no difference whether a contract is void or voidable. In either event the injured party can usually escape liability, and in most cases that is the only question involved. The difference becomes important, however, where property is transferred and subsequently passes to a bona fide purchaser for value. If the original transfer is Voidable the innocent purchaser acquires an indefeasible title. A similar consequence follows the negotiation of a negotiable instrument that is Voidable. Furthermore, a contract which is Voidable may be ratified while a Void transaction cannot be." Restatement of Contracts § 475, Comment b.

Bribery which induces the making of a contract is much like a fraud which has the same result. The bribery of a contracting party's agent or employee is, in effect, a fraud on that party. See Restatement of Contracts § 577, Illustrations 4 & 11. Inasmuch as the New York Uniform Commercial Code allows a holder in due course to enforce a contract induced by fraud, § 3–305(2), the same treatment should be given to a contract induced by bribery. The result ought not be changed by the additional fact that commercial bribery is a criminal offense in New York.

Finally, it would be poor policy for courts to transform banks and other finance companies into policing agents charged with the responsibility of searching out commercial bribery committed by their [transferors]. We doubt that denying recovery to holders in due course would have an appreciable effect on the frequency of commercial bribery. Moreover, the holder in due course concept embodies important policies which must be weighed against the policy of holding void contracts induced by bribery. To paraphrase Professor Gilmore, the holder in due course is protected not because of his praiseworthy character, but to the end that commercial transactions may be engaged in without elaborate investigation of the process leading up to the contract or instrument and in reliance on the contract rights of one who offers them for sale or to secure a loan. [Citation.] Abrogation of the rights of a holder in due course is not warranted in this case.

Fraud in the Execution Fraud in the execution of the instrument renders the instrument void and therefore is a defense valid against a holder in due course. The Code describes this type of fraud as a misrepresentation that in-duced the party to sign the instrument with neither knowledge nor reasonable opportunity to obtain knowledge of its character or its essential terms.[9] For example, Mary is asked to sign a receipt and does so without realizing or having the opportunity of learning that her signature is going on a promissory note cleverly concealed under the receipt. Mary's signature has been obtained by fraud in the execution, and Mary would have a valid defense against a holder in due course. The fraud, however, as previously indicated and as shown in the following case, must preclude the deceived party from knowing or having a reasonable opportunity to know what she was signing.

EXCHANGE INTERNATIONAL LEASING CORP. v. CONSOLIDATED BUSINESS FORMS CO.

United States District Court, W.D. Pennsylvania, 1978.
462 F.Supp. 626.

Facts: Consolidated Business Forms leased a Phillips business computer from Benchmark. Benchmark subsequently transferred the lease and promissory note to Exchange International Leasing Corporation. Consolidated stopped making rental payments when the computer malfunctioned, and Exchange International brought this suit to recover the payments due on the promissory note. Consolidated defends on the grounds that Benchmark prevented its agent, Mr. Spohn, from examining the contents of the agreement between the two companies and further represented that the computer would be removed with a complete refund if it failed to operate properly.

Decision: Judgment for Exchange International; Exchange International, by virtue of the negotiation of the instrument, attained the status of a holder in due course.

Opinion: Diamond, J. It has been established * * * that the aforesaid assignment conferred upon plaintiff [Exchange International] the status of a holder in due course under § 3–302 of the Uniform Commercial Code (hereinafter UCC), and that the defendant's [Consolidated's] only plausible defense was misrepresentation under § 3–305(2)(c) of the UCC. The matter now before the court is plaintiff's * * * motion for summary judgment in which it claims that no genuine issue of misrepresentation exists. For the reasons set forth below, we conclude that there is no genuine issue of a material fact regarding the misrepresentations defense and that the defendant was not the victim of misrepresentation within the meaning of § 3—305(2)(c) and, therefore, grant the [plaintiff's] motion.

In order to rule on the instant motion we must consider (1) the meaning of "misrepresentation" under § 3—305(2)(c); (2) the factual basis in support of the allegations of misrepresentation relied on by Consolidated; and (3) whether or not there exists a genuine issue of a material fact which if true would constitute a defense.

Turning first to the meaning of "misrepresentation," § 3—305(2)(c) states:

To the extent that a holder is a holder in due course he takes the instrument free from

* * *

(2) all defenses of any party to the instrument with whom the holder has not dealt except

* * *

(c) such misrepresentation as has induced the party to sign the instrument with neither knowledge nor reasonable opportunity to obtain knowledge of its character or its essential terms * * *

Thus, to establish the defense, one must not only have had no knowledge of a document's character or essential terms, but also have had no "reasonable opportunity" to acquire such knowledge. Comment 7 to § 3–305 elaborates by stating that in determining what constitutes a "reasonable opportunity" factors such as the age, intelligence, and business experience of the signator, his ability to read English, and the representations made to him and his reason to rely on them are to be considered.

The reported Pennsylvania decisions interpreting § 3–305(2)(c) while few in number are nonetheless uniform in holding that only fraud in the [execution] as opposed to fraud in the inducement, is a defense under § 3–305. [Citations.] This view is in accord with comment 7 and also the view expressed by certain scholars in the area. [Citations.]

As comment 7 notes, the classic example of fraud in the [execution] is that of a person who is tricked into signing a note on the pretense that it is a mere receipt of some sort. Pennsylvania is apparently hesitant to expand the defense and afford relief to less obvious victims. For example, in [citation], defendants agreed to permit a company to install and demonstrate a water softening machine in defendants' home in order to promote sales to defendants' neighbors. The defendants signed a document which was represented by the company to be a bond securing the purchase price of the equipment. The court refused to hold that defendants had been the victims of misrepresentation within the purview of § 3–305(2)(c), for the reason that defendants had established no basis from which it could be concluded that they had reason to rely on the statements of the company's representative and, that they had the opportunity, time, and ability to read the document before signing it. * * *

With the foregoing in mind we consider the specific misrepresentations relied on by Consolidated. In its brief Consolidated contends that "Mr. Spohn was precluded from examining the contents of the agreement by the representations made to him" by employees of Phillips and Benchmark. Although defendant's brief does not disclose the specifics of those representations, Spohn's deposition indicates that they were in the nature of assurances that the computer would be removed with a complete refund if it failed to function properly. * * *

Assuming without deciding that the statements referred to by Spohn could form the basis of a misrepresentation, nevertheless the court is of the opinion that no genuine issue exists as to the presence of a § 3–305(2)(c) defense. For, even if it be true that Spohn did not have actual knowledge of the essential terms of the lease, it can hardly be said that he lacked a "reasonable opportunity" to acquire that knowledge—an essential element of a § 3–305(2)(c) defense. Spohn testified unequivocally that O'Connor in no way prevented him from reading the instrument before he signed it, that he could have read the document in its entirety had he so desired, and that he was not busy or otherwise distracted at the time of execution. Spohn further testified that he read part of the lease but simply chose not to read the "fine print" because he had trust in O'Connor.

Consolidated argues for a contrary result by emphasizing that portion of [U.C.C. § 3–305] comment 7 which states that in determining what constitutes a "reasonable opportunity" one is to consider the representations made to the signator and "his reason to rely on them or to have confidence in the person making them." The court does not find this argument persuasive because it simply ignores the other facts to be considered in determining whether one had reasonable opportunity to obtain knowledge of the instrument's character and essential terms. When these other factors; viz., age, intelligence, business experience, ability to read the document, necessity for acting speedily, are considered in the light of Spohn's deposition it is clear that there is no legal justification for the blind reliance which Spohn contends he had on the statements of O'Connor.

Discharge in Insolvency Proceedings If a party's obligation on an instrument is discharged in a bankruptcy or any other insolvency proceeding, he has a valid defense in any action brought against him on the instrument, including one by a holder in due course.[9] Thus, a debtor whose obligation on a negotiable instrument is discharged in an insolvency proceeding is relieved of payment, even to a holder in due course.

Discharge of Which the Holder Has Notice Any holder, including a holder in due course, takes the instrument subject to *any* discharge of which she has notice when she takes the instrument.[9] As previously noted, if a holder acquires an instrument with notice that *all* prior parties have been discharged, she cannot become a holder in due course.[1,8] If only some, but not all, of the parties to the instrument have been discharged, the purchaser can still become a holder in due course. The discharged parties, however, have a real defense against a holder in due course who had notice of their discharge. For example, Harris, who is in possession of a negotiable instrument, strikes out the indorsement of Jones. The instrument is subsequently negotiated to Stephen, a holder in due course. Jones has a real defense against Stephen.

Unauthorized Signature A person's signature on an instrument is unauthorized when it is made without express, implied, or apparent authority. A person whose signature is unauthorized or forged cannot be held liable on the instrument in the absence of estoppel or ratification, even if the instrument is negotiated to a holder in due course.[10] He has not made a contract. Similarly, if Frank's signature were forged on the back of an instrument, Frank

could not be held as an indorser. Frank has not made a contract. Thus, any unauthorized signature is totally invalid as that of the person whose name is signed unless he ratifies it or is precluded from denying it; the unauthorized signature operates only as the signature of the unauthorized signer.

It is well settled that a person may be *estopped* or prevented from asserting a defense because his conduct in the matter has caused reliance by a third party to her loss or damage. Suppose Don's son forges Don's name to a check, which the drawee bank cashes. When the returned check reaches Don, he learns of the forgery. Rather than subject his son to trouble, possibly criminal prosecution, Don says nothing. Thereafter, Don's son continues to forge checks and cash them at the drawee bank. The bank may be suspicious of the signature, but the fact that Don has not complained may induce it to believe that the signatures are proper. Finally, Don does complain, seeking to compel the bank to recredit his account for all the forged checks. Don will not succeed, because he is estopped by his conduct from denying that his son had authority to sign his name.

A party is similarly precluded from denying the validity of his signature if his *negligence* substantially contributes to the making of the unauthorized signature. The most obvious case is that of the drawer who makes use of a mechanized or other automatic signing device and is negligent in safeguarding it. In such an instance, the drawer would not be permitted to assert the unauthorized signature as a defense against a holder in due course.

An unauthorized signature may be *ratified* and thereby become valid as a signature. Thus, Oscar forges Sarah's indorsement on a promissory note and negotiates it to Rachel. Sarah subsequently ratifies Oscar's indorsement. As a result, Oscar is no longer liable to Rachel on the note, although Sarah is liable. Nonetheless, Sarah's ratification does *not* relieve Oscar from civil liability to Sarah, nor does it in any way affect Oscar's criminal liability for the forgery.

Material Alteration Any alteration that changes the contract of any party to the instrument in any way is a **material alteration**. Against any person *other* than a subsequent holder in due course

1. an alteration by the holder that is *both* fraudulent and material discharges any party whose contract is thereby changed, unless that party assents to the change or is precluded from asserting the defense;
2. no other alteration discharges any party, and the instrument may be enforced according to its original tenor (that is, its terms as initially written) or for incomplete instruments according to the authority given to the holder by the issuing party (e.g., an authorization to fill in an amount on a check for the amount of a purchase).[11]

A subsequent holder in due course may always enforce the instrument according to its original tenor, and when an incomplete instrument has been completed, she may enforce it as completed.[11]

Because an alteration is material only when it changes the contract of a party to the instrument, the addition or deletion of words that do not in any way affect the contract of any previous signer is not material. For example, where there is a discrepancy between words and figures on a check, the words stating "twenty-five hundred dollars" and the figures "$25," a correction of the figures to $2,500 is not a material change since words control figures. But even a slight change in the contract of a party is a material alteration; the addition of one cent to the amount payable or an advance of one day in the date of payment will operate as a discharge if it is fraudulent.

A material alteration, as previously stated, does not discharge any party unless it is made for a fraudulent purpose. Thus, there is no discharge where a blank is filled in with the honest belief that it is as authorized. Likewise, if the alteration is not material, there is no discharge, and the instrument may be enforced according to its original tenor. Where blanks are filled in or an incomplete instrument is otherwise completed, there are no original terms, but the instrument may be enforced according to the authority actually given.

To summarize, a party is discharged from liability on a negotiable instrument to any holder, other than a holder in due course, by an alteration if the alteration is (1) made by a holder, (2) with fraudulent intent, and (3) is material. If any of these requirements is not met, no party is discharged, and a holder may recover the original tenor of the altered instrument or the authorized amount where the instrument was incomplete. In keeping with the preferential position accorded a holder in due course, he may enforce any altered instrument according to its original terms and may enforce an incomplete instrument as completed (see Figure 24–5).

Material alterations frequently are made possible by the *negligent* manner in which the instrument is drawn or made. Suppose that Marie makes a note, writing it out in pencil. A party raises the amount. Against a holder in due course or other good faith payor, Marie will be precluded from raising the defense of material alteration because her own negligence allowed the alteration. Assent to an alteration given before or after it is made also prevents the party from asserting the defense.

The following examples, illustrated in Figure 24–6, may explain the operation of these rules.

1. M executes and delivers a note to P for $2,000, which P subsequently indorses and transfers to A for $1,900. A intentionally and skillfully raises the note to $20,000 and then negotiates it to B, who takes it in good faith and without notice of any wrongdoing, for $19,000. B is a holder in due course and therefore can collect the amount of the original tenor ($2,000) from M or P and the full amount ($20,000) from A, less the amount paid by the other parties.

FIGURE 24–5 Effects of Alterations

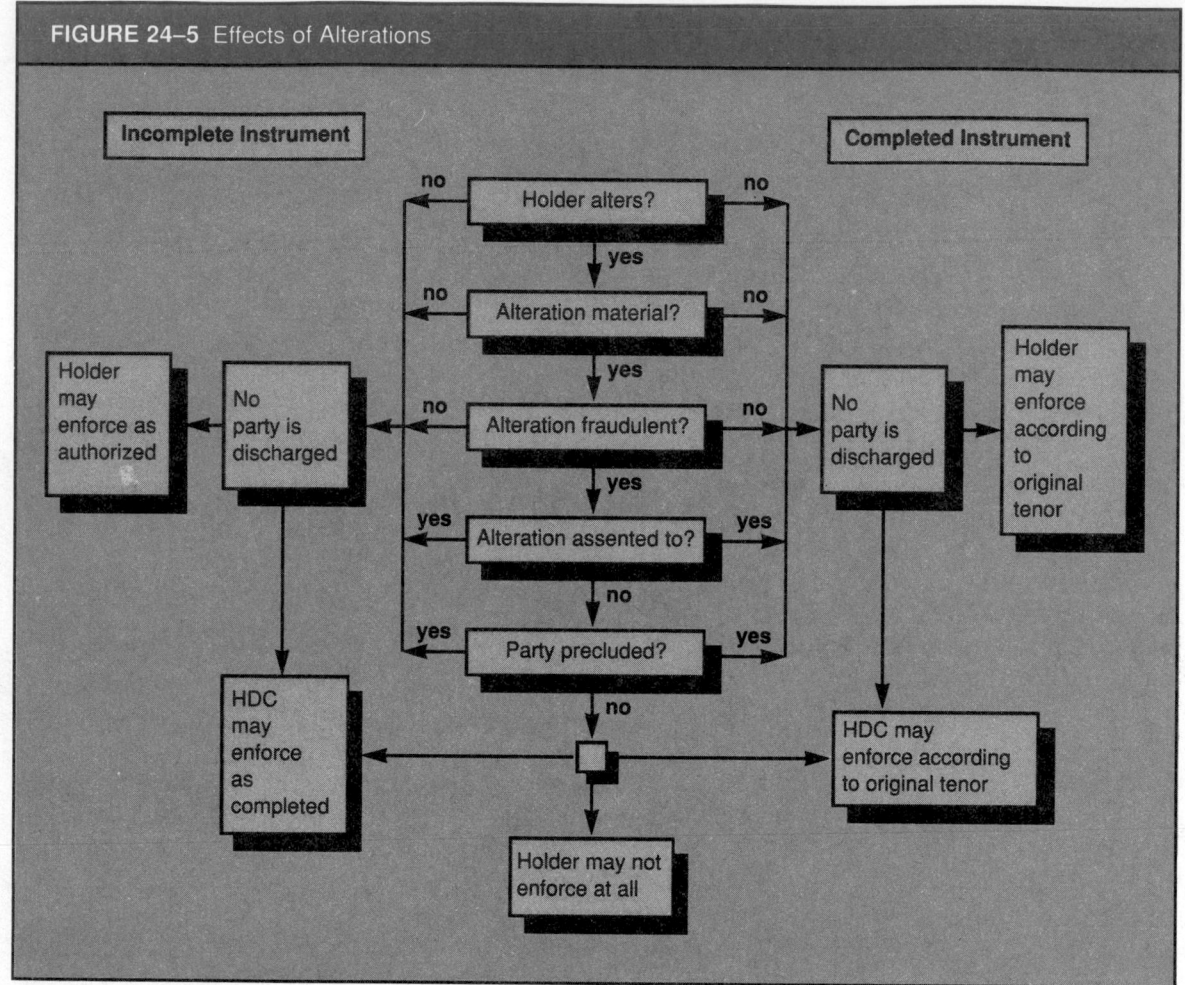

2. Assume the facts in (1) except that B is not a holder in due course. M and P are both discharged by A's fraudulent and material alteration. B's only recourse is against A for the full amount ($20,000).

3. Assume the facts in (1) except that A steals the note from P before P indorsed the instrument. After altering the instrument, A forges P's signature and transfers the note to B. A is not a holder, and therefore B can be neither a holder nor a holder in due course. P is entitled to recover the instrument or its value from B or anyone in possession of it. Moreover, because A was not a holder, his alteration of the instrument does not discharge M. Therefore, if P recovers the note he may enforce it against M.

4. M issues his blank check to P, who is to complete it when the exact amount is determined. P fraudulently fills in $4,000 when the correct amount should be $2,000. P then negotiates the check to T. If T is a holder in due course, she can collect the amount as completed ($4,000) from either M or P. If T is not a holder in due course, however, she has no recourse against M but may recover the full amount ($4,000) from P.

5. Assume the facts in (4) except that P filled in the amount of $4,000 in good faith. No party is discharged from liability on the instrument because the alteration was not fraudulent. If T is not a holder in due course, M is liable for the correct amount ($2,000). If T is a holder in due

FIGURE 24-6 Material Alteration

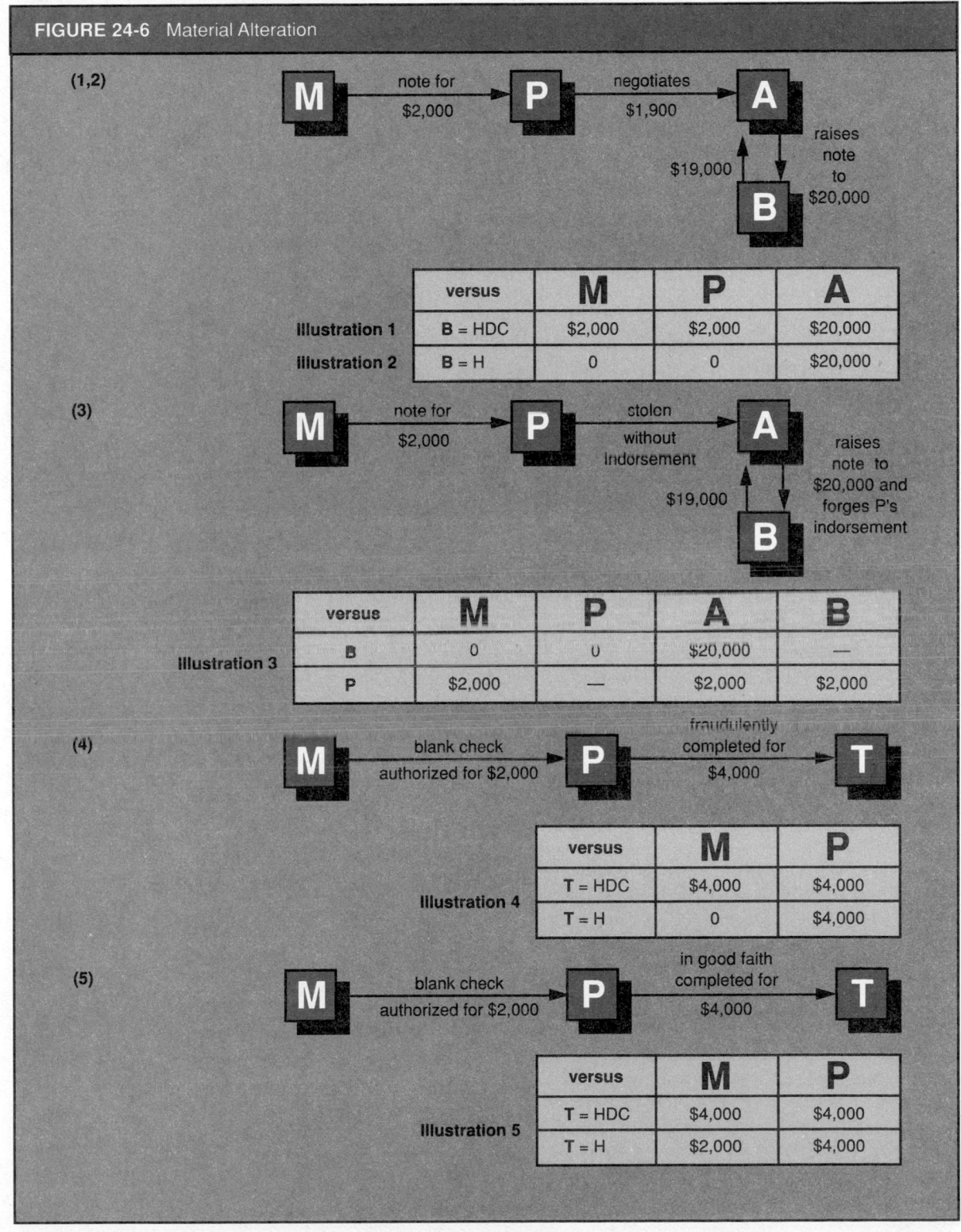

course, T is entitled to receive $4,000 from M because she can enforce an incomplete instrument as completed. Whether or not T is a holder in due course, T may recover $4,000 from P.

Personal Defenses

Defenses to an instrument may arise in many ways, either at the time it is issued or later. In general, defenses to liability on a negotiable instrument are similar to those that may be raised in the case of any action for breach of contract. They are numerous and are available against any possessor of the instrument unless he has the rights of a holder in due course. Among the personal defenses are (1) lack of consideration; (2) failure of consideration; (3) breach of contract; (4) fraud in the inducement; (5) illegality that does not render the transaction void; (6) duress, undue influence, mistake, misrepresentation, or incapacity that does not render the transaction void; (7) setoff or counterclaim; (8) discharge of which the holder in due course does not have notice; (9) nondelivery of an instrument, whether complete or incomplete; (10) unauthorized completion of an incomplete instrument; (11) payment without obtaining surrender of the instrument; (12) theft of a bearer instrument or a properly indorsed order instrument; (13) lack

of authority of a corporate officer or an agent or partner as to the particular instrument, where such officer, agent, or partner had general authority to issue negotiable paper for his principal or firm.

These thirteen situations are the most common examples, but others exist. Indeed, the Code does not attempt to detail defenses that may be cut off. It is content to state that a holder in due course takes free and clear of all defenses except those listed as real defenses (see Figure 24–7).

LIMITATIONS ON RIGHTS OF HOLDER IN DUE COURSE

The preferential position enjoyed by a holder in due course has been severely limited by a Federal Trade Commission rule restricting the rights of a holder in due course of an instrument concerning a debt arising out of a *consumer credit contract*, which includes negotiable instruments. The rule, entitled ''Preservation of Consumers' Claims and Defenses,'' applies to sellers and lessors of consumer goods, which are goods for personal, household, or family use. It also applies to lenders who advance money to finance the consumer's purchase of consumer goods or services. The rule is intended to prevent situations in which consumer purchase transactions have been fi-

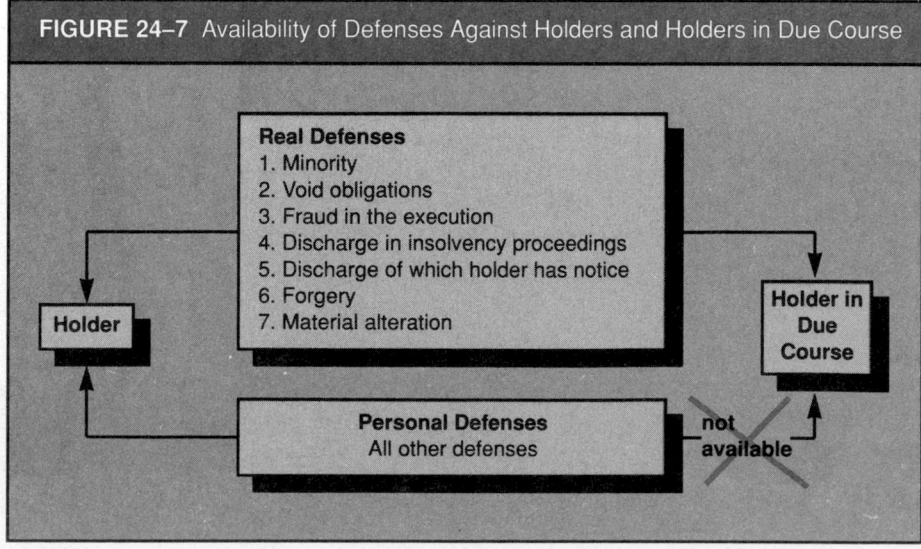

FIGURE 24–7 Availability of Defenses Against Holders and Holders in Due Course

Real Defenses
1. Minority
2. Void obligations
3. Fraud in the execution
4. Discharge in insolvency proceedings
5. Discharge of which holder has notice
6. Forgery
7. Material alteration

Holder

Holder in Due Course

Personal Defenses
All other defenses

not available

nanced in such manner that the purchaser is legally obligated to make full payment of the price to a third party, even though the dealer from whom she bought the goods committed fraud or the goods were defective. This occurs when the purchaser executes and delivers to the seller a negotiable instrument that the seller negotiates to a holder in due course. The buyer's defense that the goods were defective or that the seller committed fraud, although valid against the seller, is not valid against a holder in due course of the instrument.

In order to correct this situation, the Federal Trade Commission rule preserves claims and defenses of consumer buyers and borrowers against holders in due course. The rule states that no seller or creditor can take or receive a consumer credit contract unless the contract contains this conspicuous (boldface) provision:

This credit contract finances a purchase. All legal rights which the buyer has against the seller arising out of this transaction, including all claims and defenses, are also valid against any holder of this contract. The right to recover money from the holder under this provision is limited to the amount paid by the buyer under this contract.

A claim is a legally valid reason for suing the seller. A defense is a legally valid reason for not paying the seller. A holder is anyone trying to collect for the purchase.

The purpose of this conspicuous notice is to inform any holder that he takes the instrument subject to all claims and defenses that the buyer could assert against the seller. See *Jefferson Bank & Trust Co. v. Stamatiou*, which follows. The effect of the rule is to place a holder in due course of the paper or negotiable instrument in the position of an assignee. Figure 24–8 illustrates the rights of holders in due course under the FTC rule.

JEFFERSON BANK & TRUST CO. v. STAMATIOU
Supreme Court of Louisiana, 1980.
384 So.2d 388

Facts: Stamatiou purchased a truck from Key Dodge, Inc., apparently for use in his tow truck business. Stamatiou and an agent of Key Dodge signed an instrument designated "Sale and Chattel Mortgage" with a promissory note at the bottom of the same page. The note portion contained an unconditional promise to pay the entire purchase price on prescribed terms. The Sale and Chattel Mortgage portion included a provision preserving for the purchaser his defenses against a future holder of the note. Also included was a provision by which the purchaser acknowledged that the note secured by the Sale and Chattel Mortgage would be assigned to Jefferson Bank & Trust Company "as assignee and CREDITOR within the meaning of the applicable Federal law." Nowhere did the instrument designate the intended purpose for which the truck was purchased. Finally, Stamatiou signed the instrument at the end of the Sale and Chattel Mortgage and again at the end of the promissory note.

Key Dodge did, in fact, transfer the contract to Jefferson Bank & Trust Company. Stamatiou ceased making payments a short time later and notified both Key Dodge and Jefferson that the truck had become inoperable and unusable, and he demanded rescission of the contract. Jefferson Bank brought this action to collect on Stamatiou's promissory note. The trial court ruled in favor of the bank and the court of appeal affirmed.

Decision: Judgment reversed and remanded to the trial court.

Opinion: Calogero, J. Our [decision to review this case] requires that we determine whether the inclusion of the preservation of defenses language (federally required in all "consumer credit contracts") in a contract which is not a consumer credit contract, allows the defendant [Stamatiou] to present his defense against a party who would otherwise be a holder in due course; in effect, whether the language, specifically countering the primary effect of holder in due course status is applicable to this holder, Jefferson Bank.

Under authority of [federal statute] the Federal Trade Commission, a United States regulatory agency, requires the inclusion of the exact same language as was included in the present contract in all "consumer credit contracts" for the sale of goods or services. [Citation.] The federal regulations define a consumer as "a natural person who seeks or acquires goods or services for *personal, family or household use.*" Therefore in any contract for the sale of goods or services where credit is being extended to the purchaser, and the purchaser is acquiring the item for personal, family, or household use, * * * language identical to that language used in the contract and quoted above, must be contained in the contract.

* * *

The express purpose of the FTC regulation is to prevent the seller, in a consumer credit transaction, from separating the buyer's duty to pay from the seller's duty to perform as promised, by the seller's assigning the buyer's promissory note to a financing institution, as against whom, because of holder status, defenses would otherwise not be available.

Plaintiff makes the following argument; that the preservation of defenses language is included in all credit contracts to insure compliance with federal regulations but is only intended to apply to the appropriate transactions even though there is no notation to the effect that the clause is possibly inapplicable; absent inclusion in all credit contracts, the vendor and/or finance company would be required to have two different forms and to hire a staff attorney to instruct them each time which to use; and that the sale of the truck to defendant for use in his tow truck business takes the transaction out of the consumer credit contract category as defined by the FTC, and thus the provision, although there in the contract, was not applicable to this transaction and should be ignored.

Defendant on the other hand claims that the preservation of defenses language (whether federally required in this contract or not) was included in the contract and as such becomes a part of that contract.

* * *

We conclude that defendant's argument is the more persuasive and is more supported by the law. * * *, parties are free to govern their relationships through their contracts, and the contractual provisions have the effect of law on the parties. The contract between Stamatiou and Key Dodge, as assigned to plaintiff, provided "Any holder of this * * * contract is subject to all claims and defenses which the debtor could assert against the seller." That the parties to the contract mistakenly asserted that it was a consumer credit contract ("any holder of this consumer credit contract") is of little consequence. In looking at the contract, there was nothing on the face of the instrument to indicate that this was not a "consumer contract." The assignee/holder was put on notice that all defenses were available to the buyer against him at the time he acquired the instrument. In looking at the face of the instrument, plaintiff could not have expected to be a holder in due course, and is not now entitled to be so treated. At best the contract is ambiguous and is surely not to be construed against the purchaser who did not confect it. [Citations.]

* * *

For these reasons we conclude that the preservation of defenses language is applicable to the contract. Plaintiff bank is subject to defendant purchaser's claims or defenses and the contract provision takes precedence over the rights plaintiff would otherwise have been legally entitled to under [U.C.C.] 3–305 as holder in due course.

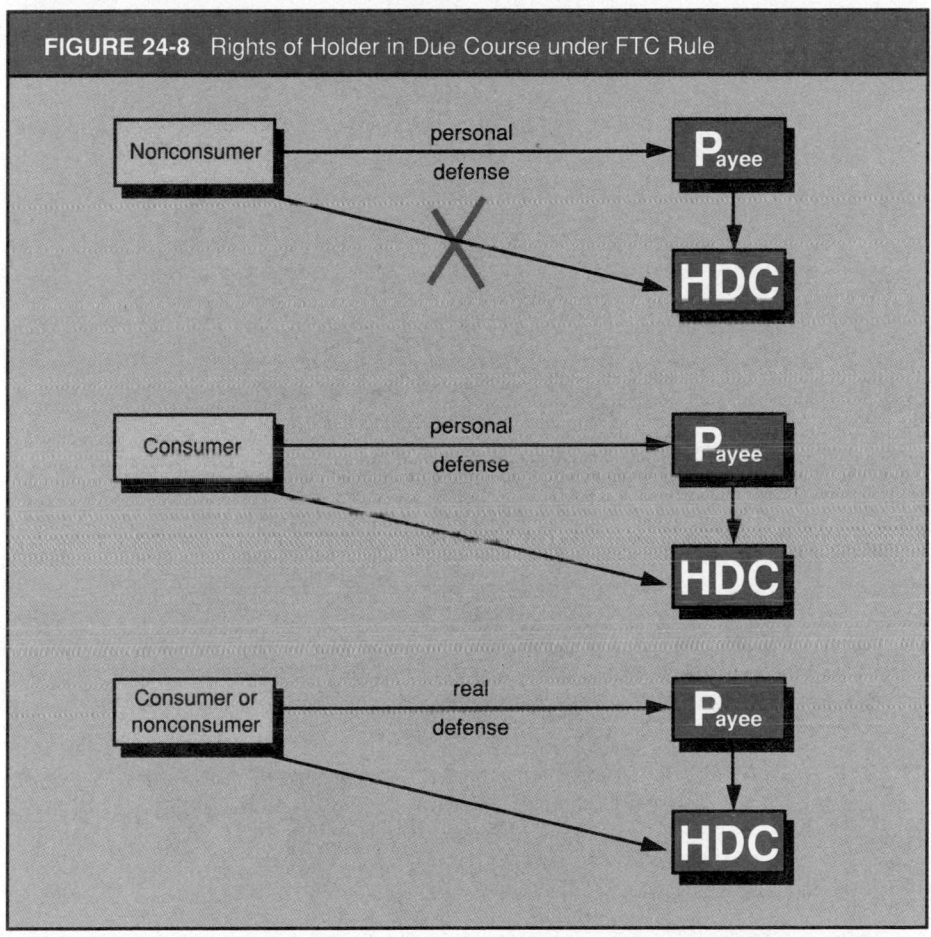

FIGURE 24-8   Rights of Holder in Due Course under FTC Rule

CHAPTER SUMMARY

Requirements of Holder in Due Course	**Holder** a person who has both possession of an instrument and all necessary indorsements **Value** differs from contractual consideration and consists of any of the following: ■ the timely performance of legal consideration (which excludes executory promises); ■ the acquisition of a security interest or a lien on the instrument; ■ taking the instrument in payment of or as security for an antecedent debt; ■ the giving of a negotiable instrument; or ■ the giving of an irrevocable commitment to a third party **Good Faith** honesty in fact in the conduct or transaction concerned as determined by what the purchaser knows or believes (subjective test) **Lack of Notice** ■ *Notice an Instrument Is Overdue* time paper is overdue after its stated date; demand paper is overdue after demand has been made or after it has been outstanding an unreasonable period of time ■ *Notice an Instrument Has Been Dishonored* dishonor is the refusal to pay or accept an instrument when it becomes due ■ *Notice of Claim or Defense* a defense protects a person from liability while a claim is an assertion of ownership
Holder in Due Course Status	**A Payee May Be a Holder in Due Course** the payee's rights as a holder in due course are limited to defenses of persons with whom he has not dealt **The Shelter Rule** the transferee of an instrument acquires the same rights in the instrument that the transferor had
The Preferred Position of a Holder in Due Course	**Real Defenses** real defenses are available against all holders, including holders in due course; the real defenses are as follows: ■ *Minority* ■ *Void Obligations* ■ *Fraud in the Execution* ■ *Discharge in Insolvency Proceedings* ■ *Discharge of Which the Holder Has Notice* ■ *Unauthorized Signature* ■ *Material Alteration* **Personal Defenses** all other defenses that might be asserted in the case of any action for breach of contract **Limitations on Rights of Holder in Due Course** the preferential position of a holder in due course has been severely limited by a Federal Trade Commission rule that applies to consumer credit contracts: under this rule a transferee of consumer credit contracts cannot take as a holder in due course

QUESTIONS

1. Discuss the requirements of becoming a holder in due course.
2. Discuss (a) the shelter rule, and (b) the rights of a payee.
3. Define a real defense. Identify and discuss the real defenses.
4. Define and discuss personal defenses.
5. Discuss the limitations upon the rights of a holder in due course imposed by the Federal Trade Commission.

PROBLEMS

1. On November 1 Perkins installed a burglar alarm system in Moore's store. Moore executed and delivered to Perkins a negotiable promissory note payable to the order of Perkins for $1,100, the purchase price, due on December 1. On November 8 Perkins returned to Moore's store and told Moore that he needed money and would accept $1,000 as payment in full. Moore immediately paid Perkins $1,000 but forgot to obtain the note from Perkins.

On November 10 Perkins indorsed the note in blank and transferred it to Harris for value. Two days later, Harris learned that Moore had already paid Perkins for the note, whereupon he gave the note to Valerie, his mother in law, as a going away present, without further indorsement. Valerie was not aware of Moore's prior payment of the note.

What are the rights of Valerie, if any, against Moore? Explain.

2. Marcus issues a negotiable promissory note payable to the order of Parish for the amount of $3,000. Parish raises the amount to $13,000 and negotiates it to Hilda for $12,000.

(a) If Hilda is a holder in due course, how much can she recover from Marcus? How much from Parish? If Marcus's negligence substantially contributed to the making of the alteration, how much can Hilda recover from Marcus and Parish respectively?

(b) If Hilda is not a holder in due course, how much can she recover from Marcus? How much from Parish? If Marcus's negligence substantially contributed to the making of the alteration, how much can Hilda recover from Marcus and Parish respectively?

3. On December 2, 1990, Miles executed and delivered to Proctor a negotiable promissory note for $1,000, payable to Proctor or order, due March 2, 1991, with interest at 12 percent from maturity, in partial payment of a printing press. On January 3, 1991, Proctor, in need of ready cash, indorsed and sold the note to Hughes for $800. Hughes paid $600 in cash to Proctor on January 3 and agreed to pay the balance of $200 one week later, namely, on January 10. On January 6 Hughes learned that Miles claimed a breach of warranty by Proctor and, for this reason, intended to refuse to pay the note when it matured. On January 10 Hughes paid Proctor $200 in conformity with their agreement of January 3. Following Miles's refusal to pay the note on March 2, 1991, Hughes sues Miles for $1,000. Decision?

4. Thornton fraudulently represented to Daye that he would obtain for her a new car to be used in Daye's business for $7,800 from Pennek Motor Company. Daye thereupon executed her personal check for $7,800 payable to the order of Pennek Motor Company and delivered the check to Thornton, who immediately delivered it to the motor company in payment of his own prior indebtedness. The motor company had no knowledge of the representations made by Thornton to Daye. Daye now brings an action to recover the amount of the check from Pennek Motor Company, contending a failure of consideration on Pennek's part. Decision?

5. Adams reads with difficulty. He arranged to borrow $200 from Bell. Bell prepared a note, which Adams read laboriously. As Adams was about to sign it, Bell diverted Adams's attention and substituted the following paper, which was identical to the note Adams had read except that the amounts were different:

On June 1, 1990, I promise to pay Ben Bell or order Two Thousand Dollars with interest from date at 11 percent. This note is secured by certificate No. 13 for 100 shares of stock of Brookside Mills, Inc.

Adams did not detect the substitution, signed as maker, handed the note and stock certificate to Bell and received from Bell $200. Bell indorsed and sold the paper to Fore, a holder in due course, who paid him $1,800. Fore presented the note at maturity to Adams, who refused to pay. What are Fore's rights, if any, against Adams?

6. On January 2, 1991, Martin, seventeen years of age, as a result of Dealer's fraudulent misrepresentation, bought a used motorboat to use in his fishing business for $2,000 from Dealer, signed an installment contract for $1,500, and gave Dealer the following instrument as down payment:

Dated:. 1991
I promise to pay to the order of Dealer, six months after date, the sum of $500 without interest. This is given as a down payment on an installment contract for a motorboat.

(signed) Martin

Dealer, on July 1, sold his business to Henry and included this note in the transaction. Dealer indorsed the note in blank and handed it to Henry. Henry left the note in his office safe. On July 10 Sharpie, an employee of Henry, stole the note and sold it to Bert for $300, indorsing the note "Sharpie." At the time, in Bert's presence, Sharpie filled in the date on the note as February 2, 1991. Bert demanded payment from Martin, who refused to pay.

What are Bert's rights against Martin?

7. McLaughlin borrowed $1,000 from Adler. Adler, disturbed about McLaughlin's ability to pay, demanded security. McLaughlin indorsed and delivered to Adler a negotiable promissory note executed by Topping for $1,200 payable to McLaughlin's order in twelve equal monthly installments. The note did not contain an acceleration clause, but it recited that the consideration for the note was McLaughlin's promise to paint and shingle Topping's barn. At the time McLaughlin transferred the note to Adler, the first installment was overdue and unpaid. Adler was unaware that the installment had not been paid. Topping did not pay any of the installments on the note. When the last installment became due, Adler presented the note to Topping for payment. Topping refused on the ground that McLaughlin had not painted or reshingled her barn.

What are Adler's rights, if any, against Topping on the note?

8. McEnolly purchased a refrigerator for his home from Perreault Appliance Store for $700. McEnolly paid $200 in cash and signed an installment contract for $500, which in its entirety stated:

> January 15, 1990
> I promise to pay to the order of Perreault Appliance Store the sum of $500 in ten equal monthly installments.
>
> (signed) McEnolly

Perreault negotiated the installment contract to Hughes, who took the instrument for value, in good faith, and without notice of any claim or defense of any party. After McEnolly had paid two installments, the refrigerator ceased operating. McEnolly wishes to recover his down payment, his first two monthly payments, and to discontinue further payments. What outcome?

9. Joseph Higbee executed and delivered to Robert Dudley the following instrument:

> On September 19, 1990, I promise to pay $15,000 to Robert Dudley.
>
> (signed) Joseph Higbee

This note was secured by a mortgage on Higbee's real property. Dudley altered the note and mortgage by changing the amount to $25,000 and the date to September 17, 1990. Dudley then sold the note and mortgage for $25,000 less 2 percent discount to Citizens Bank, which was unaware of the alterations. Dudley assigned the mortgage to Citizens Bank and signed the reverse side of the note as follows: "I hereby assign this note to the order of Citizens Bank. (signed) Robert Dudley."

On September 18, 1990, Citizens Bank demanded payment of the note from Higbee. Higbee refused. On September 22 Citizens Bank notified Higbee that the note was in default and demanded payment from him. Higbee again refused. Citizens Bank thereupon brought an action against Higbee to recover $25,000 on the note. No action was taken by Citizens Bank to foreclose the mortgage.

What defenses, if any, may Higbee properly assert in this action?

10. Adams, by fraudulent representations, induced Barton to purchase 100 shares of the capital stock of the Evermore Oil Company. The shares were worthless. Barton executed and delivered to Adams a negotiable promissory note for $5,000 dated May 5, in full payment for the shares, due six months after date. On May 20 Adams indorsed and sold the note to Cooper for $4,800. On October 21 Barton, having learned that Cooper now held the note, notified Cooper of the fraud and stated he would not pay the note. On December 1 Cooper negotiated the note to Davis, who, while not a party, had full knowledge of the fraud perpetrated on Barton. When Barton refused to pay the note, Davis sued Barton for $5,000. Decision?

11. Donna gives Peter a check for $50,000 in return for a personal computer. The check is dated December 2. Peter transfers the check for value to Howard on December 14, and Howard deposits it in his bank on December 20. In the meantime, Donna has discovered that the personal computer is not what was promised and has stopped payment on the check. If Peter and Howard disappear, may the bank recover from Donna notwithstanding her defense of failure of consideration? What will be the bank's cause of action?

12. Eldon's Super Fresh Stores, Inc., is a corporation engaged in the retail grocery business. William Drexler was the attorney for and the corporate secretary of Eldon's and was also the personal attorney of Eldon Prinzing, the corporation's president and sole shareholder. From January 1989 through January 1990, Drexler maintained an active stock trading account in his name with Merrill Lynch. Eldon's had no such account. On August 12, 1989, Drexler purchased 100 shares of Clark Oil & Refining Company stock through his Merrill Lynch

stockbroker. He paid for the stock with a check drawn by Eldon's made payable to Merrill Lynch and signed by Prinzing. On August 15, 1989, Merrill Lynch accepted the check as payment for Drexler's stock purchase. There was no communication between Eldon's and Merrill Lynch until November 1990, fifteen months after the issuance of the check. At that time Eldon's inquired of Merrill Lynch as to the whereabouts of the stock certificate and asserted a claim to its ownership. It then brought this action, claiming that it gave the check to Drexler to be delivered to Merrill Lynch for Eldon's benefit. Decision?

ENDNOTES

1. Uniform Commercial Code, Section 3—302, Holder in Due Course.

2. Uniform Commercial Code, Section 3—201, Transfer: Right to Indorsement.

3. Uniform Commercial Code, Section 1—201(20), Holder.

4. Uniform Commercial Code, Section 3—301, Rights of a Holder.

5. Uniform Commercial Code, Section 3—303, Taking for Value.

6. Uniform Commercial Code, Section 1—201(19), Good Faith.

7. Uniform Commercial Code, Section 1—201(25), Notice.

8. Uniform Commercial Code, Section 3—304, Notice to Purchaser.

9. Uniform Commercial Code, Section 3—305, Rights of a Holder in Due Course.

10. Uniform Commercial Code, Section 3—404, Unauthorized Signatures.

11. Uniform Commercial Code, Section 3—407, Alteration.

25 LIABILITY OF PARTIES

In the preceding chapters we discussed the negotiability of commercial paper, the transfer of negotiable instruments, and the preferred position of a holder in due course. When parties issue negotiable instruments, they do so with the expectation that they, whether directly or indirectly, will satisfy their obligations under the instrument. Likewise, when a person accepts, indorses, or transfers an instrument, he incurs liability for the instrument under certain circumstances. In this chapter we examine the liability of parties arising out of negotiable instruments and the ways in which liability may be terminated.

Two types of potential liability are associated with commercial paper: contractual liability and warranty liability. The law imposes **contractual liability** on those who sign a negotiable instrument. Because some parties to a negotiable instrument never sign it, they never assume contractual liability. As the Code provides: "[N]o person is liable on an instrument unless his signature appears thereon."[1]

Warranty liability, on the other hand, is not based on a signature; thus it may be imposed on both signers and nonsigners. **Warranty liability** applies (1) to persons who transfer an instrument, and (2) to persons who receive payment or acceptance of an instrument.

CONTRACTUAL LIABILITY

All parties whose *signatures* appear on a negotiable instrument incur certain contractual liabilities, unless they disclaim liability. The *maker* of a promissory note and the *acceptor* of a draft assume an absolute obligation **(primary liability)**, subject to valid claims and defenses, to pay according to the tenor of the instrument at the time they sign it or as completed according to the rules discussed in Chapter 24 for incomplete instruments. *Drawers* of drafts and checks and *indorsers* of all instruments incur **secondary liability** and thus are liable if the instrument is not paid. A *drawee* has **no** liability on the instrument until he *accepts* it. The contractual obligations of the maker, drawer, drawee, indorser and acceptor are illustrated in Figure 25–1.

SIGNATURE

The word "signature," as discussed in Chapter 22, is broadly defined to include any name, word, or mark, whether handwritten, typed, printed, or in any other form, made with the intention of authenticating the instrument.[2] The signature may be made by the individual

---

FIGURE 25–1 Contractual Liability

	Maker	Drawee	Acceptor	Drawer	Indorser
Primary Liability	●		●		
Secondary Liability				●	●

herself or on her behalf by the individual's authorized agent.

Authorized Signatures

Authorized agents often execute negotiable instruments on behalf of their principals. The agent is not liable if the instrument is executed properly (e.g., "P, principal, by A, agent") and the agent is authorized to execute the instrument. If these two conditions are met, then only the principal is liable on the instrument. (For a comprehensive discussion of the principal-agent relationship see Chapters 27 and 28.)

Occasionally, however, the agent, although fully authorized, uses an inappropriate form of signature, and holders or prospective holders may be misled as to the identity of the obligor. Although there are many incorrect forms of signatures by agents, they can be conveniently sorted into three groups. The first type occurs when an agent signs only his own name to an instrument. He does not indicate that he is signing in a representative capacity and he does not state the name of the principal. For example, Adams, the agent of Prince, makes a note on behalf of Prince but signs it "Adams." The signature does not indicate that Adams has signed in a representative capacity nor that he has made the instrument on behalf of Prince. In this situation, only the agent is liable on the instrument; Prince is not liable on the instrument because his name does not appear on it. Prince may be liable to Adams or a third party, however, on the basis of contract or agency law.

The second type of incorrect form occurs when an authorized agent indicates that he is signing in a representative capacity but does not disclose the name of his principal. For example, Adams, executing an instrument on behalf of Prince, merely signs it "Adams, agent." In this situation, Prince is liable if the payee is an immediate party to the instrument and knows that Adams represents Prince. But as to any subsequent party, and as to the payee if he does not know that Adams represents Prince, Prince is not liable on the instrument; Adams alone is liable.

The third type of inappropriate signature occurs when an agent reveals both her name and her principal's name, but does not indicate that she has signed in a representative capacity. For example, Adams, signing an instrument on behalf of Prince, signs it "Adams and Prince." Because a subsequent holder might reasonably believe that Adams and Prince were co-makers, both are fully liable. But if the party who dealt with Adams knew or should have known that Adams was acting on behalf of Prince without intending to incur personal liability, Adams may prove this fact by parol evidence and avoid liability to this immediate party.

VALLEY NATIONAL BANK, SUNNYMEAD v. COOK
Arizona Court of Appeals, Division One, 1983.
136 Ariz. 232, 665 P.2d 576.

Facts: On October 21, 1977, Cook, the treasurer of Arizona Auto Auction and R. V. Center, Inc., issued three corporate checks to Central Motors Company. The checks were boldly imprinted at the top "Arizona Auto Auction, Inc." Also, "Arizona Auto Auction, Inc.," was imprinted above the signature line appearing at the lower right-hand corner. Cook's signature appeared under the imprinted name of Arizona Auto Auction without any designation of her office or capacity. Central Motors deposited these three checks in its corporate account held by Valley National Bank, Sunnymead (the bank). Pursuant to a stop payment order, however, Arizona Auto Auction's drawee bank dishonored each of these checks. The checks were returned to the bank, and the account of Central Motors was charged back for the amount of the checks—$9,795. The bank, unable to recover this amount from Central Motors, brought suit against Arizona Auto Auction,

Cook, and her spouse. The bank claims that Cook is personally liable for the checks. The trial court held that Arizona Auto was liable as drawer for the amount of the checks ($9,795) but that Cook was not personally liable for the checks.

Decision: Judgment of the trial court affirmed.

Opinion: Corcoran, J.   The question of whether Cook signed in her individual or representative capacity is governed by § 3–403 of the Uniform Commercial Code (UCC) as adopted in this state. [§ 3–403] provides:

(1) A signature may be made by an agent or other representative, and his authority to make it may be established as in other cases of representation. No particular form of appointment is necessary to establish such authority.
(2) An authorized representative who signs his own name to an instrument:
(a) Is personally obligated if the instrument neither names the person represented nor shows that the representative signed in a representative capacity;
(b) Except as otherwise established between the immediate parties, is personally obligated if the instrument names the person represented but does not show that the representative signed in a representative capacity, or if the instrument does not name the person represented but does show that the representative signed in a representative capacity.
(3) Except as otherwise established the name of an organization preceded or followed by the name and office of an authorized individual is a signature made in a representative capacity.

The Bank argues that this section conclusively establishes Cook's personal liability on the checks. We do not agree. Admittedly, the checks fail to specifically show the office held by Cook. However, we do not find that this fact conclusively establishes liability, since [§ 3–403(2)(b)] imposes personal liability on an agent who signs his or her own name to an instrument only "if the instrument * * * does not show that the representative signed in a representative capacity." Thus, we must look to the entire instrument for evidence of the capacity of the signer. [Citations.]

The checks are in evidence and are boldly imprinted at the top "Arizona Auto Auction, Inc." and also "Arizona Auto Auction, Inc." is imprinted above a signature line appearing at the lower right-hand corner. Under the imprinted name of the corporate defendant appears the signature of appellee Cook without any designation of office or capacity on each of the checks before us on appeal. Appellee Cook did not endorse the checks on the back. The record does not reflect appellee Cook made any personal guaranty of these checks or any other corporate obligation.

* * *

The Superior Court of Pennsylvania was confronted with a similar situation in *Pollin v. Mindy Mfg. Co., Inc.* There the court denied recovery by a third party endorsee against one who affixed his signature to a payroll check directly beneath the printed corporate name without indicating his representative capacity. In *Pollin* the checks were boldly imprinted at the top with the corporate name, address, and appropriate check number. The printed name of the drawee bank appeared in the lower lefthand corner of the instrument and the corporate name was imprinted in the lower righthand corner. Directly beneath the corporate name were two blank lines. The defendant-appellant had signed the top line without any designation of office or capacity. Pointing out that the Code imposes liability on the individual only when the instrument controverts any showing of representative capacity, the court considered the instrument in its entirety. The court in *Pollin* held that disclosure on the face of the instrument that the checks were payable from a special payroll account of the corporation over which the appellant had no control as an individual negated any contention that appellant intended to make the instrument his own order to pay money to the payee.

The difference in outcome in the *Pollin* case and the cases cited by the Bank in which corporate agents were held liable for failing to show a corporate title reflects the *Pollin* court's emphasis on *business expectations*, an emphasis which is proper and entirely consistent with the spirit of UCC § 3–403. [Citation.] In determining what these expectations might be, it is important to draw a distinction between a check and a note:

> The payee of a corporate check with the corporate name imprinted on its face probably expects less from the individual drawer than the payee of a corporate note may, where both the corporate name and the maker's name may be either handwritten or typewritten. Further, it is common for creditors to demand the individual promise of officers on corporate promissory notes, specially in the case of small corporations. Thus, we think a court should be more reluctant to find an agent personally liable who has signed a corporate check than in the case of a similar indorsement of a corporate note. This does not mean that the drawer of a corporate check will never be personally liable; indeed, more than a few have been stuck. Rather, we hope that courts will be more conscious of differences in business practices with respect to different types of instruments when they evaluate the extrinsic evidence presented by the parties. [Citation.]

Thus, while it may be common for creditors of small corporations to demand that corporate officers personally obligate themselves on corporate notes, it would be most unusual to demand the individual obligation of an officer on corporate checks.

Unauthorized Signatures

Unauthorized signatures include both forgeries and signatures made by an agent without proper power to do so. An unauthorized signature is generally not binding on the person whose name appears on the instrument, but it is binding on the unauthorized signer whether or not her own name appears on the instrument.[3] Thus, if Adams, without authority, signed Prince's name to an instrument, Adams, not Prince, would be liable on the instrument. The rule, therefore, is an exception to the principle that only those whose names appear on a negotiable instrument can be liable on it.

There is an important exception to this rule that an unauthorized signature does not bind the person whose name is signed: any person who by his **negligence** substantially contributes to the making of an unauthorized signature may not assert the lack of authority as a defense against a holder in due course or a person who pays for the instrument in good faith and according to reasonable commercial standards.[4] For example, Jones employs a signature stamp to sign his checks and carelessly leaves it accessible to third parties. Brown discovers the stamp and uses it to write a number of checks with Jones's unauthorized signature as the drawer. Howard, a subsequent holder in due course of one the checks, will *not* be subject to Jones's defense of unauthorized signature and will be able to recover the amount of the check from Jones.

LIABILITY OF PRIMARY PARTIES

There is a primary party on every note: the *maker*. The maker's commitment is unconditional. No one, however, is primarily liable on a draft or check as issued. The *drawee* is *not* liable on the instrument unless he accepts it. He is free to pay or accept it as he sees fit. If, on the other hand, the drawee accepts the draft, after which he is known as the *acceptor*, he becomes primarily liable on the instrument. **Acceptance,** or in the case of a check, certification, is the drawee's signed promise to pay the draft as presented to him.

If the drawee refuses to accept or pay the instrument, he may be liable to the drawer for breach of contract. For example, a bank is not obligated to pay any check drawn on it. To do so would be to obligate a bank to pay an instrument regardless of whether the drawer had an account at that bank or sufficient funds in his account. On the other hand, if the drawer does have sufficient funds to cover the check, the drawee may still refuse to honor the instrument, but this would constitute a breach of its contract of deposit with the drawer. The drawee's refusal to pay or accept the draft causes the *drawer* to become liable on the instrument after receiving proper notice of dishonor (the contingent or secondary liability of the drawer will be discussed in the next section).

Makers

Makers guarantee that they will pay the instrument according to its terms when made, if the instrument is complete.[5] If an incomplete instrument is completed as authorized, the maker is liable for the amount as completed.[5,6] If the completion of an incomplete instrument is unauthorized (1) a holder in due course may recover from the maker as completed, (2) a holder of an incomplete instrument that has been materially and fraudulently completed may not recover anything, and (3) a holder of an incomplete instrument that has not been materially and fraudulently completed may collect the amount actually authorized.[7]

Acceptors

A drawee has no liability on the instrument until she accepts it, at which time she becomes an **acceptor** and, like a maker, primarily liable. The acceptor becomes liable on the draft ac-

cording to its terms at the time of the acceptance or as completed according to the rules for incomplete instruments.[5,6]

An acceptance must be written on the instrument.[8] No writing separate from the draft and no oral statement or conduct of the drawee will convert the drawee into an acceptor. The acceptance may take many forms. It may be printed on the face of the draft, ready for the drawee's signature. It may consist of a rubber stamp, with the signature of the drawee added. It may be the drawee's signature, preceded by a word or phrase such as "Accepted," "Certified," or "Good." It may consist of nothing more than the drawee's signature. Normally, but by no means necessarily, an acceptance is written vertically across the face of the draft. It must not, however, contain any words indicating an intent to refuse to honor the draft. Accepted checks are said to be certified. **Certification** is the drawee bank's promise to pay the check when presented for payment.[9,5] The bank, however, has no obligation to certify a check. The order on the bank is to *pay* the check, and if the bank is willing to pay, refusal to certify is not a dishonor of the check.

Where a check is certified at the request of the **holder,** the drawer and all prior indorsers are discharged. The liability of indorsers after certification is not affected. When the bank certifies an instrument, it should withhold sufficient funds from the drawer's account to pay the check. Because the bank is primarily liable on its certification and has the funds and the drawer does not, the discharge is reasonable.

Certification at the request of the **drawer** does not, however, relieve the drawer of secondary liability on the instrument. For example, the drawer may have a check certified before using it to close a business transaction, such as the purchase of a house. Because the drawer is then obtaining the benefit of the transaction, she should bear the risk of the bank's credit, rather than the payee.

Assume that Moe, a depositor in the Last National Bank, had $3,000 on deposit when the bank ceased operations because of insolvency. The bank proved to be 60 percent solvent. Two weeks prior to the bank's closing,

Hume received two checks for $1,000 each from Moe drawn on the bank. Check number 1 was certified by the bank at the request of Moe prior to Moe's delivery of the check to Hume. Check number 2 was taken by Hume to the bank which certified it at Hume's request. When the bank went into receivership, Hume was the holder of both checks.

Since check number 1 was certified at the request of Moe, the drawer, he remains secondarily liable on the instrument. The bank having certified the instrument is primarily liable. Hume may recover judgment against Moe for $1,000. Either Hume or Moe, or both, may file a claim in the insolvency proceedings against the bank for $1,000 upon which $600 will ultimately be distributed. If Moe pays the judgment he is entitled to the $600 distribution. If he fails to do so, Hume will receive it and credit the amount against the unpaid judgment.

Since Hume, the holder, obtained the bank's certification of check number 2, the drawer, Moe, is released from liability on that check. The bank is primarily liable. Hume is a general creditor of the bank to the extent of $1,000 and his only right is to file a claim and recover through the insolvency proceedings 60 percent of his claim ($600).

LIABILITY OF SECONDARY PARTIES

The drawer and indorsers (including the payee if he indorses) of an instrument are secondarily liable, because their liability is subject to the conditions of presentment, dishonor, notice of dishonor, and sometimes protest. Secondary parties do not unconditionally promise to pay the instrument but expect the drawee-acceptor or maker to pay.

Indorsers and Drawers

If the instrument is not paid by a primary party and the conditions precedent to the liability of secondary parties are satisfied (as discussed below), a secondary party is liable, unless he has disclaimed his liability or he possesses a valid defense to the instrument. Thus, as discussed in the case below, the **drawer** engages that she will pay the amount of the draft to the holder or any indorser who takes it up, unless she has disclaimed this liability by drawing it without recourse.[5] Unless the indorsement otherwise specifies, as by using such words as "without recourse," every indorser promises that she will pay the holder or any subsequent indorser of the instrument according to its tenor at the time of her indorsement.[10]

DAVIS v. WATSON BROTHERS PLUMBING, INC.
Court of Civil Appeals of Texas, Dallas, 1981.
615 S.W.2d 844.

Facts: Arnett Lee presented a $152.38 check for cashing to plaintiff, liquor store operator Troy Davis. After Davis gave Lee the cash, Lee requested a bottle of scotch and a six-pack of beer. As Davis turned to fill the order, a thief stole $110.00 of the $152.38. Lee immediately contacted the defendant—drawer of the check, Watson Brothers Plumbing, Inc., and notified them of the loss. Defendant then issued another check for $152.38 and stopped payment on the first check held by Davis. Davis brought this action against defendant for the full face amount of the check. The trial court rendered judgment for Davis for $40.88 (the amount Lee received from Davis: $152.38 minus the $110.00 that the thief took less the $1.50 check-cashing fee) and Davis brings this appeal.

Decision: Judgment for Davis for $152.38.

Opinion: Akin, J. The county court rendered judgment for plaintiff for the $40.88 that Lee actually received from plaintiff [after the robbery.] Plaintiff, as appellant, asserts that since he proved that he was the holder of the check and since defendant failed to raise any valid defenses, defendant was liable to him for the full face value of the check, $152.38. We agree.

"Holder" is defined in Tex Bus & Com Code Ann [U.C.C.] § 1.201(20) as: "[A] *person who is in possession of* a document of title or *an instrument* or an investment security drawn, issued or *indorsed to him* or to his order or to bearer or *in blank.*" Under the undisputed facts, Lee, the payee endorsed the check in blank to plaintiff, who is now in possession of the check. Thus, as a matter of law, plaintiff is a "holder" under the code § 3.413(b), which sets forth the rights of a holder, provides, in pertinent part, that: "The drawer engages that upon dishonor of the draft * * * *he will pay the amount of the draft to the holder* or to any indorser who takes it up." Thus, the defendant is liable to the holder of the dishonored check unless the defendant has raised a valid defense against the holder.

The rights of a holder not in due course are subject to the defenses specified in § 3.306, which provides:

"Unless he has the rights of a holder in due course any person takes the instrument subject to

"(1) all valid claims to it on the part of any person; and

"(2) all defenses of any party which would be available in an action on a simple contract; and

"(3) *the defenses of want or failure of consideration,* non-performance of any condition precedent, non-delivery, or delivery for a special purpose (Section 3.408); and

"(4) the defense that he or a person through whom he holds the instrument acquired it by theft, or that payment or satisfaction to such holder would be inconsistent with the terms of a restrictive indorsement. *The claim of any third person to the instrument is not otherwise available as a defense to any party liable thereon unless the third person himself defends the action for such party.*"

Defendant here asserts that it may raise want or failure of consideration in the transaction between *plaintiff and Lee,* its payee, as a defense to plaintiff's enforcement of the instrument against it. We disagree.

[U.C.C.] § 3.408 provides, in pertinent part that: "Want or failure of consideration is a defense against any person not having the rights of a holder in due course * * * " The comments to § 3.408 provide that: " 'Consideration' refers to what the obligor has received for his obligation, and is important only on the question of whether his obligation can be enforced against him." Thus, any holder can enforce the obligation of a draft against the drawer regardless of whether the holder gave anything in consideration for the draft to his endorser. The drawer can assert as a defense to enforcement of the draft want or failure of consideration only to the extent such defense lies against the payee of the draft. Thus, the fact that a holder remote to the drawer's transaction with the payee did not give full consideration for the draft is not a defense available to the drawer. [Citation.]

This is true because the drawer's sole obligation on the check is to pay it according to its tenor. Consequently, the fact that the transfer of the check by the payee to the transferee is without consideration is immaterial to the drawer's obligation and is not a defense available to the drawer against the holder. A similar conclusion was reached in [Citation.] In that case the court held that a defendant maker was not the proper party to raise as a defense that the transfer of the note to the holder was void. Consequently, that court concluded that the maker could not assert the defense that the equitable ownership of the instrument was in someone other than the holder-plaintiff.

> The rationale of this, and other decisions, reaching the same conclusion, is that the maker or drawer of an instrument admittedly owes the money and he should not be permitted to bring into the controversy equities of parties with which he has no connection. [Citation.] Furthermore, if the drawer or maker is permitted to assert the defense of another party such as the payee, the judgment on that issue would not be binding on the third party claimant who is not a party to the suit. [Citation.]
>
> Because defendant here may not assert want or failure of consideration in the transaction between plaintiff and Lee, and because defendant has asserted no other defense against plaintiff, plaintiff is entitled to recover the full face value of the check under § 3.413(b) of the Texas Uniform Commercial Code. * * *

Conditions Precedent to Liability

Conditions precedent to the liability of secondary parties are presentment, dishonor, notice of dishonor, and in some situations, protest. But noncompliance with the conditions precedent has a different effect on the liability of drawers than on indorsers' liability.

Presentment   Presentment is a demand for acceptance or payment made by the holder on the maker, acceptor, or drawee.[11] If there are two or more makers, acceptors, or drawees, presentment to one is sufficient. Presentments are of two kinds: presentment for acceptance and presentment for payment.

Presentment of a draft for **acceptance** is necessary to hold secondary parties liable on the instrument where (1) the draft so provides, (2) it is payable elsewhere than at the residence or place of business of the drawee, or (3) its date of payment depends on such presentment,[12] as in the case of a draft providing: "Seven days after acceptance pay. . . . " Presentment for acceptance is also authorized in the case of any other time draft, although it is not required.[12] Unless a draft must be presented for acceptance or is payable at a stated date, a drawee's refusal to accept the draft is not a dishonor of the instrument. Thus, a drawee bank's refusal to certify a check for the holder does not constitute a dishonor of the instrument, because a bank has no obligation to certify a check.[9] The distinction made between a time draft and demand draft is that with the latter the holder is entitled to

immediate payment, while with the former the holder is not entitled to payment until the due date but may by presentment for acceptance determine whether the drawer will honor it.

Presentment of any instrument for **payment** is necessary to charge any indorser, although an exception exists in the case of an instrument indorsed after maturity. Failure to present for payment does not discharge the drawer, however, except to the extent that there was an unreasonable delay in presenting a draft to a bank where funds were available for its payment and the bank became insolvent in the interim.

Presentment may be made in any reasonable manner. An instrument with a specified maturity date is due for presentment on that date or, if the specified date is not a full business day, on the next full business day. In any other case, presentment is due within "a reasonable time." What is "a reasonable time" depends on all the facts of the particular case. For an uncertified check, a reasonable time for presentment for payment is *presumed* to be (a) with respect to the liability of the *drawer, thirty days* after date or issue, whichever is later; and (b) with respect to the liability of an *indorser, seven days* after his indorsement.[13]

An unexcused delay in presentment *discharges* the **indorsers**. The **drawer** is discharged only to the extent of any *loss* suffered because of the delay.[14] The discharge of one indorser, of course, does not mean that all are discharged. Assume that Donald draws a check payable to the order of Paula on March 1. Paula indorses it to Ann on March 3, and Ann indorses it to Barry on March 6. Barry must present the check by March 10 to hold Paula liable and must present it by the thirteenth to hold Ann liable. If he waits until after the thirteenth, both indorsers are discharged unless Barry can show that the presentment was made within a reasonable time. Barry, however, has until March 31 to present the check to hold Donald liable, because a reasonable time for presentment with regard to the drawer is presumed to be thirty days. If Barry did not present the check for payment until after March 31, Donald would be discharged *only* to the extent of any loss he might have suffered as the result of the delay, but not otherwise. The indorsers Paula and Ann, however, would be completely discharged by Barry's failure to make presentment within a reasonable time, whether or not they had any loss.

Dishonor   An instrument is **dishonored** when (1) presentment has been duly made, and acceptance or payment is refused or cannot be obtained within the prescribed time, or (2) presentment is excused and the instrument is not duly accepted or paid.[15] Return for lack of a proper indorsement is not dishonor.

Notice of Dishonor   On proper presentment and dishonor, and subject to any necessary notice of protest, the holder has an immediate right of recourse against drawers and indorsers after giving them timely notice of the dishonor. Such notice is necessary to charge any indorser. Notice also must be made to the drawer, the acceptor of a draft payable at a bank, or the maker of a note payable at a bank, but failure to give such notice discharges these parties only if the bank becomes insolvent, thus depriving them of funds they maintained at the bank to cover the instrument.[14]

Notice of dishonor is normally given by the holder or by an indorser who has himself received notice. For example, Michael makes a note payable to the order of Phyllis; Phyllis indorses it to Arthur; Arthur indorses it to Bambi; and Bambi indorses it to Hershey, the last holder. Hershey presents the note to Michael within a reasonable time, but Michael refuses to pay. Hershey may give notice of dishonor to all the secondary parties: Phyllis, Arthur, and Bambi. If he is satisfied that Bambi will pay him, he may only notify Bambi. Bambi then must see to it that Arthur or Phyllis is notified, or Bambi will have no recourse. Bambi may notify either or both. If she notifies Arthur only, Arthur will have to see to it that Phyllis is notified, or Arthur will have no recourse. When notice is properly given, it benefits all parties who have rights on the instrument against the party notified. Thus, Hershey's notification to Phyllis operates as notice to Phyllis by both Arthur and Bambi. Likewise, if Hershey notifies only Bambi and Bambi notifies Arthur and Phyllis, then Hershey has the benefit of Bambi's notification of Arthur and Phyllis. Nonetheless, it would be advisable for Hershey to give notice to all prior parties because Bambi may be insolvent and thus not bother to notify Arthur or Phyllis.

If, in this hypothetical problem, Hershey notifies Phyllis alone, Arthur and Bambi are discharged. Phyllis cannot complain, because she has no claim against Arthur or Bambi, who indorsed the note after she did. It cannot matter to Phyllis that she is compelled to pay Hershey rather than Arthur. Therefore, subsequent parties are permitted to skip intermediate indorsers if they want to discharge them and are willing to look solely to prior indorsers for recourse.

Any necessary notice must be given by a *bank* before midnight on the first banking day after the banking day when it receives notice of dishonor. Any *nonbank* must give notice before midnight of the third business day after dishonor or receipt of notice of dishonor.[16] Written notice is effective when sent, regardless of whether it is received. For instance, Davis draws a check on Youngstown Bank payable to the order of Parker; Parker indorses it to Abrams; Abrams deposits it to her account in Lincoln Bank; and Lincoln Bank properly presents it to Youngstown Bank, the drawee. Youngstown Bank dishonors the check because the drawer, Davis, has insufficient funds on deposit to cover it. Youngstown Bank has until midnight of the following day to notify Lincoln Bank, Abrams, Parker, or Davis of the dishonor.

Lincoln Bank has until midnight of the day after receipt of notice of dishonor to notify Abrams, Parker, or Davis of the dishonor. That is, if Lincoln Bank received the notice of dishonor on Monday, it would have until midnight on Tuesday to notify Abrams, Parker, or Davis. If it failed to notify Abrams, it could not charge the item back to her. Abrams has until midnight of the third business day after receipt of notice of dishonor to notify Parker or Davis. If she received notice on Tuesday, she would have until midnight on Friday to notify Parker or Davis. Parker would also have three business days in which to notify Davis.

HANE v. EXTEN
Court of Appeals of Maryland, 1969.
255 Md. 668, 259 A.2d 290.

Facts: On August 10, 1964, Theta Electronic Laboratories, Inc., executed a promissory note to George and Marguerite Thomson. Three other individuals, Gerald Exten, Emil O'Neil, and James Hane, and their wives also indorsed the note. The note was then transferred to Hane by the Thomsons on November 26, 1965. Although a default occurred at this time, it was not until April 1967, eighteen months later, that Hane gave notice of the dishonor and made a demand for payment on the Extens as indorsers. Hane appeals from a judgment in favor of the Extens.

Decision: Judgment for the Extens affirmed.

Opinion: Singley, J.   This case raises the familiar question: Must Hane show that the Extens were given notice of presentment and dishonor before he can hold them on their indorsement?

The court below, in finding for the Extens, relied on the provisions of Uniform Commercial Code (the U.C.C.), § 3–414(1) of the U.C.C. provides:

"Unless the indorsement otherwise specifies (as by such words as 'without recourse') every indorser engages that upon dishonor and any necessary notice of dishonor and protest he will pay the instrument according to its tenor at the time of his indorsement to the holder or to any subsequent indorser who takes it up, even though the indorser who takes it up was not obligated to do so.

§ 3–501(1)(b) provides that "Presentment for payment is necessary to charge any indorser" and § 3–501(2)(a) that "Notice of any dishonor is necessary to charge any indorser," in each case subject, however, to the provisions of § 3–511 which recite the circumstances under which notice of dishonor may be waived or excused, none of which is here present. § 3–502(1)(a) makes it clear that unless presentment or notice of dishonor is waived or excused, unreasonable delay will discharge an indorser. [Citations.]

There was testimony from which the trier of the facts could find as he did that presentment and notice of dishonor were unduly delayed.

It is clear that Hane held the note from November, 1965, until some time in April 1967 before he made demand for payment. U.C.C. § 3–503(1)(d) provides that "Where an instrument is accelerated presentment for payment is due within a reasonable time after the acceleration." "Reasonable time" is not defined in § 3–503, except that § 3–503(2) provides, "A reasonable time for presentment is determined by the nature of the instrument, any usage of banking or trade and the facts of the particular case." But § 1–204(2) characterizes it. "What is a reasonable time for taking any action depends on the nature, purpose and circumstances of such action."

Reasonableness is primarily a question for the fact finder. [Citations.] We see no reason to disturb the lower court's finding that Hane's delay of almost 18 months in presenting the note "was unreasonable from any viewpoint." [Citation.]

As regards notice of dishonor, § 3–508(2) requires that notice be given by persons other than banks "before midnight of the third business day after dishonor or receipt of notice of dishonor." Exten, called as an adverse witness by Hane, testified that his first notice that the note had not been paid was * * * on 7 June 1967. Hane's brother testified that demand had been made about 15 April 1967. He was uncertain as to when he had given Exten notice of dishonor, but finally conceded that it was "within a week." The lower court found that the ambiguity of this testimony, coupled with Exten's denial that he had received *any* notice before 7 June fell short of meeting the three day notice requirement of the U.C.C. The date of giving notice of dishonor is a question of fact, solely for determination by the trier of facts. [Citation.] We cannot say that the court erred in its finding.

In the absence of evidence that presentment and notice of dishonor were waived or excused, Hane's unreasonable delay discharged the Extens, § 3–501(1)(a).

Frequently, notice of dishonor is given by returning the unpaid instrument with a stamp, ticket, or memorandum attached stating that the item was not paid and requesting that the recipient make good on it. But since the purpose of notice is to give knowledge of dishonor and to inform the secondary party that he may be held liable on the instrument, any kind of notice informing the recipient of his potential liability is sufficient. No formal requisites are imposed—notice may be given in any reasonable manner. An oral notice is sufficient, but is inadvisable because it may be difficult to

Protest Protest is required only if the draft is drawn or payable *outside* the United States. A **protest** is a certificate of dishonor made under the hand and seal of a United States consul or vice-consul or a notary public or other person authorized to certify to a dishonor by the law of the place where the dishonor occurred.[17] It must identify the instrument and certify either that due presentment has been made or the reason why it is excused and that the instrument has been dishonored by nonacceptance or nonpayment. The protest may also certify that notice of dishonor has been given to all parties or to specified parties. Protest, or the noting for protest, must be made within the time allowed for giving notice of dishonor.

Delay in Presentment, Notice, or Protest Excused The Code excuses a *delay* in presentment, notice, or protest in two situations.[18] The first excuses a delay where the holder does not have notice that the instrument is due; for example, an instrument may provide that its maturity shall be automatically accelerated on the happening of a particular event. If the holder does not know that this event has happened, she is excused from presentment until she learns of the acceleration, and secondary parties are not discharged because of the delay. Once the holder learns that the event has occurred, she must present the note within a reasonable time and give prompt notice of dishonor to hold the indorsers liable.

The second situation excuses the holder's delay where it is caused by circumstances beyond his control. For example, suppose the holder cannot present the instrument to the primary party because a storm has disrupted all means of communication and transportation. The circumstances need not make presentment impossible. It is enough if they are of the degree and character that would deter persons of ordinary prudence, energy, and courage from encountering them in the pursuit of business.

Presentment, Notice, or Protest Excused The Code *entirely* excuses the holder from presentment, notice, or protest if the party to be charged has himself dishonored the instrument or has countermanded payment or if the holder otherwise has no reason to expect the instrument to be accepted or paid.[18] If, for example, Dennis draws a check on a bank where he has no account, or if he has closed his account or stopped payment on the check, he is not entitled to a due presentment and notice of dishonor. These matters are entirely excused so far as he is concerned. But they would not be excused for intermediate indorsers who did not have any reason to expect that the instrument would not be accepted or paid.

The Code also entirely excuses a presentment, notice, or protest, as the case may be, if these things cannot be accomplished by reasonable diligence.[18] For example, if the maker of a note has "departed for places unknown" and cannot be located by reasonable diligence, the holder has no way of making a presentment to him. In such case, presentment is entirely excused, and the holder should treat the instrument as dishonored and give prompt notice of dishonor to the indorsers. Likewise, if one of the indorsers cannot be located by reasonable diligence, notice of dishonor would not have to be given to him—it would be entirely excused.

Presentment Excused The Code sets out some other specific situations in which only presentment is *entirely* excused.[18] These situations, which do not excuse notice or protest, include the following: (1) the maker, acceptor, or drawee is dead or in insolvency proceedings; or (2) payment of acceptance is refused for reasons not relating to proper presentment, making it clear that a subsequent presentment would be useless.

Waiver of Presentment, Notice, or Protest Presentment, notice, or protest may also be waived either before or after it is due.[18] Waivers are of two types, express and implied.

Disclaimer of Liability by Secondary Parties

Both drawers and indorsers *may* disclaim their normal secondary liability by drawing or indorsing instruments **"without recourse."** [5,10] The use of the qualifying words "without recourse" is understood in commercial circles to place purchasers on notice that they may not rely on the credit of the person using this language. A person drawing or indorsing an instrument in this manner does not incur the normal contractual liability of a drawer or indorser to pay the instrument, but he may nonetheless be liable for breach of warranty.

LIABILITY OF OTHER PARTIES

Accommodation Parties

Accommodation parties are those who sign a negotiable instrument for the purpose of lending their credit to another party. See *Oak Park Currency Exchange, Inc., v. Maropoulos* at page 535. They may be makers or co-makers, drawers or co-drawers, or indorsers. An indorsement indicating that the party is not in the chain of title is notice of the party's accommodation.

Frequently, one or more persons indorse an instrument to accommodate another party, rather than sign as maker or drawer. Suppose Marsha wants to borrow money from Peter, and Peter insists that Marsha procure the signatures of Ari, Benite, Clem, and Dixie before the loan is made. Marsha asks these parties to accommodate her and makes the note, and Ari, Benite, Clem, and Dixie sign their names on the back of it in that order. Because Ari, Benite, Clem, and Dixie have signed the note, they are liable to Peter as indorsers. Marsha is liable to Peter and to Ari, Benite, Clem, and Dixie, if these accommodating parties pay the instrument.

Suppose Marsha becomes insolvent so that the reimbursement rights that Ari, Benite, Clem, and Dixie have against her are meaningless. Suppose further that Peter enforces the note against Dixie. Can Dixie pass the loss on to Clem? May Clem shift it to Benite? Would Ari ultimately be out-of-pocket simply because he signed first? Parol evidence would be admissible to show that the indorsers had agreed to share the loss equally or in some other proportion, if that is the case. If they made no agreement among themselves, the rule that indorsers are liable in the order in which they signed does *not* apply. The law of suretyship, which applies to accommodation parties, is based on concepts of equity and fairness that would not be consistent with having the rights of these sureties among themselves depend on the order in which they signed the instrument. Although each is liable to the holder for the full amount, they should share the loss equally, and one who is required to pay more than his share is entitled to recover proportionately from the others. See Chapter 38 for a further discussion of suretyship.

Liability for Conversion

Conversion is a **tort** whereby a person becomes liable in damages because of his wrongful control over the personal property of another. The Code provides that a conversion occurs in three situations: (a) when a drawee to whom a draft is delivered for acceptance refuses to return it on demand; (b) when any person to whom an instrument is delivered for payment refuses on demand either to pay or to return it; and (c) when an instrument is paid on a forged indorsement. Situations (a) and (b) involve willful action on the part of the party guilty of the conversion, whereas in situation (c) the payor's action was in all probability completely innocent—his dominion over the instrument resulted from an unrecognized break in the chain of title. Nevertheless, liability is the same in all three cases. Good faith is completely immaterial, and the person wrongfully exercising dominion over the instrument is liable for damages.

SPECIAL SITUATIONS AFFECTING LIABILITY

If a drawee pays an instrument, the drawer is generally under a duty to make reimbursement. Usually, the drawer has funds in the hands of the drawee, and the drawee, honoring a draft or check, reimburses itself immediately by charging the drawer's account or her funds. The drawee can be reimbursed, however, only if it acts in accordance with the drawer's *order* as it appears on the instrument. Thus, if Davis draws a check to the order of Jones, the drawee bank to whom the instru-

ment is addressed acquires no right or reimbursement by paying Roe, unless Jones has indorsed the check to Roe. In short, the drawee must determine whether the person presenting the item for payment or acceptance has rights in it. If it pays the wrong party, it is the drawee's loss and not the drawer's. Two situations involving these principles that are especially troublesome have been specifically modified by the Code.

The Impostor Rule

Usually, the impostor rule comes into play in situations involving a confidence man who impersonates a respected citizen and who deceives a third party into delivering a negotiable instrument to the impostor in the name of the respected citizen. For instance, John Doe, falsely representing himself as Richard Roe, a creditor of Ray Davis, induces Davis to draw a check payable to the order of Richard Roe and to deliver it to him. Doe then forges Roe's name to the check and presents it to the drawee for payment. The drawee pays it. Subsequently, the drawer denies the drawee's right of reimbursement on the ground that the drawee did not pay in accordance with his order: the drawer ordered payment to Roe or to Roe's order. Roe did not order payment to anyone; therefore, the drawee would not acquire a right of reimbursement against the drawer Davis. This is the argument in favor of the drawer and is supported by the general rule governing unauthorized signatures.

Nevertheless, the Code provides that the indorsement of the impostor or of any other person in the name of the named payee is **effective** if the impostor has induced the maker or drawer to issue the instrument to him or his confederate using the name of the payee.[19] It is as if the named payee had indorsed the instrument. The reason for this rule is that the drawer or maker is to blame for failing to detect the impersonation by the impostor. Thus, as in the above example and the case that follows, the drawee would be able to debit the drawer's account.

PHILADELPHIA TITLE INSURANCE CO. v. FIDELITY-PHILADELPHIA TRUST CO.

Supreme Court of Pennsylvania, 1965.
419 Pa. 78, 212 A.2d 222.

Facts: Edmund Jezemski, estranged and living apart from his wife, Paula, was administrator and sole heir-at-law of his deceased mother's estate, one asset of which was real estate in Philadelphia. Without Edmund's knowledge or consent, and with the assistance of John M. McAllister, an attorney, and Anthony DiBenedetto, a real estate broker, Paula arranged for a mortgage on the property through Philadelphia Title Insurance Company. Shortly before settlement, Paula represented to McAllister and DiBenedetto that her husband would be unable to attend the closing on the mortgage. She appeared at McAllister's office in advance of the closing, accompanied by a man, whom she introduced to McAllister and DiBenedetto as her husband. She and this man, in the presence of McAllister and DiBenedetto, executed a deed conveying the property from the estate to her husband and herself as tenants by the entireties and also executed the mortgage. McAllister and DiBenedetto were witnesses. Thereafter, McAllister, DiBenedetto, and Paula met at the office of the title company on the closing date, produced the signed deed and mortgage, and Paula obtained from the title company its check for the mortgage loan proceeds of $15,640.82, payable to the order of Edmund Jezemski and Paula Jezemski individually and to Edmund as administrator.

Paula cashed the check, bearing the purported indorsements of all the payees, at Penns Grove National Bank and Trust Company. Edmund received none of the proceeds, either individually or as administrator. His purported indorsements were forgeries. In the collection process, the check was presented to and paid by the drawee bank, Fidelity-Philadelphia Trust Company, and charged against the drawer title company's account. Upon discovery of the existence of the mortgage, Edmund brought an action that resulted in the setting aside of the deed and mortgage and the repayment of the amount advanced by the mortgagee. The Title Company thereupon sued the drawee bank to recover the amount of the check, $15,640.82. Judgment was entered against the Title Company and in favor of Fidelity-Philadelphia.

Decision: Judgment for drawee, Fidelity-Philadelphia Trust Co., affirmed.

Opinion: Cohen, J. The complaint alleged that the endorsement of one of the payees had been forged and that, therefore, Fidelity should not have paid the check. * * * By way of defense all of the banks asserted that none of them were liable because the issuance of the check by the Title Company was induced by an imposter and delivered by the Title Company to a confederate of the imposter thereby making the forged endorsement effective.

* * * Judgment was entered against the Title Company and in favor of the banks.

* * *

"There is no question that the man whom Mrs. Jezemski introduced to McAllister and DiBenedetto was not Edmund Jezemski, her husband. It was sometime later that Edmund Jezemski, when he tried to convey the real estate, discovered the existence of the mortgage. When he did so he instituted an action in equity which resulted in the setting aside of the deed and mortgage and the repayment of the fund advanced by the mortgagee."

The parties do not dispute the proposition that as between the [drawee] bank (Fidelity-Philadelphia) and its customer (Title Company), ordinarily, the former must bear the loss occasioned by the forger of a payee's endorsement (Edmund Jezemski) upon a check drawn by its customer and paid by it. [Citations.] Uniform Commercial Code [citation] § 3–404. The latter provides . . . that "(1) Any unauthorized signature [Edmund Jezemski's] is wholly inoperative as that of the person whose name is signed unless he ratifies it or is precluded from denying * * *."

However, the banks argue that this case falls within an exception to the above rule, making the forged indorsement of Edmund Jezemski's name effective so that Fidelity-Philadelphia was entitled to charge the account of its customer, the Title Company, who was the drawer of the check. The exception asserted by the banks is found in § 3–405(1)(a) of the Uniform Commercial Code—Commercial Paper which provides:

"An endorsement by any person in the name of a named payee is effective if (a) an imposter by use of the mails or otherwise has induced the maker or drawer to issue the instrument to him or his confederate in the name of the payee; * * *."

The lower court found and the Title Company does not dispute that an imposter appeared before McAllister and DiBenedetto, impersonated Mr. Jezemski, and, in their presence, signed Mr. Jezemski's name to the deed, bond and mortgage; that Mrs. Jezemski was a confederate of the imposter; that the drawer, Title Company, issued the check to Mrs. Jezemski naming her and Mr. Jezemski as payees; and that some person other than Mr. Jezemski indorsed his name on the check. In effect, the only argument made by the Title Company to prevent the applicability of Section 3–405(1)(a) is that the imposter, who admittedly played a part in the swindle, *did not "by the mails or otherwise" induce the Title Company* to issue the check within the meaning of Section 3–405(1)(a). The argument must fail.

* * *

Both the words of Section 3–405(1)(a) and the official Comment thereto leave no doubt that the imposter can induce the drawer to issue him or his confederate a check within the meaning of the section even though he does not carry out his impersonation before the very eyes of the drawer. Section 3–405(1)(a) says the inducement might be by "the mails or otherwise." The comment elaborates:

"2. Subsection (1)(a) is new. It rejects decisions which distinguish between face-to-face imposture and imposture by mail and hold that where the parties deal by mail the dominant intent of the drawer is to deal with the name rather than with the person so that the resulting instrument may be negotiated only by indorsement of the payee whose name has been taken in vain. The result of the distinction has been under some prior law, to throw the loss in the mail imposture forward to a subsequent holder or to the drawee. Since the drawer believes the two to be one and the same, the two intentions cannot be separated, and the 'dominant intent' is a fiction. The position here taken is that the loss, regardless of the type of fraud which the particular imposter has committed, should fall upon the drawer."

* * * For purposes of imposing the loss on one of two "innocent" parties, either the drawer who was defrauded or the drawee bank which paid out on a forged indorsement, we see no reason for distinguishing between the drawer who is duped by an impersonator communicating indirectly with him through third persons. Thus, both the language of the Code and common sense dictates that the drawer must suffer the loss in both instances.

The Fictitious Payee Rule

The second situation is similar to the impostor situation, but it involves a faithless agent rather than an impostor. For instance, the drawer's agent falsely tells the drawer that money is owed to Leah, and the drawer writes a check payable to the order of Leah and hands it to the agent for delivery to her. The agent forges Leah's name on the check and obtains payment from the drawee bank. The drawer then denies the bank's claim to reimbursement on the ground that the bank did not comply with his order; that the drawer had ordered payment to Leah on order; that the drawee did not make payment either to Leah or as ordered by her, inasmuch as the forgery of Leah's signature is wholly inoperative; and that the drawee paid in accordance with the scheme of the faithless agent and not in compliance with the drawer's order.

Once again, the drawee bank will be able to debit the drawer's account. An indorsement by any person in the name of a named payee is **effective** if an agent or employee of the maker or drawer has supplied her with the name of the payee for fraudulent purposes.[19] The risk of employee fraud presents business risks that the Code imposes on the party employing the agent.

The rule also applies to the similar situation in which a person signs as or on behalf of a maker or drawer and does not intend the payee to have an interest in the instrument. In such situations, any person's indorsement in the name of the named payee is effective.[19]

LIABILITY BASED ON WARRANTY

A negotiable instrument is not only the written evidence of contract liability but also a kind of property intended for trading and having marketability. Just as the Code imposes certain implied warranties to the sale of goods, it also imposes certain warranties to the *sale* of commercial paper. There are two types of warranties to the transfer of commercial paper: (a) transferor's warranties, and (b) presenter's warranties. These warranties are effective whether or *not* the transferor or presenter signs the instrument, although, as you will see, the extent of the warranty to subsequent holders does depend on whether they have indorsed the instrument. Like other warranties, these may be disclaimed by agreement between immediate parties. In the case of an indorser, his disclaimer of transfer warranties must appear in the indorsement itself.

WARRANTIES ON TRANSFER

Any person who transfers an instrument, whether by negotiation or assignment, and receives **consideration** makes certain **transferor's warranties.**[20] If transfer is by delivery alone, warranties on transfer run only to the immediate transferee. If the transfer is made by indorsement, whether qualified or unqualified, the warranty runs to "any subsequent holder who takes the instrument in good faith" (see Figure 25–2).

OAK PARK CURRENCY EXCHANGE, INC. v. MAROPOULOS
Appellate Court of Illinois, First District, First Division, 1977.
48 Ill.App.3d 437, 6 Ill.Dec. 525, 363 N.E.2d 54.

Facts: James Maropoulos went to Oak Park Currency Exchange, Inc., to cash a check for $3,564 for his friend John Bugay. The check was a certified check drawn on American National Bank payable to the order of "Henry Sherman, Inc.," and indorsed "Henry Sherman" on the reverse side. Maropoulos had frequently transacted business at the currency exchange and was recognized by the clerk, Jacqueline Panveno. Maropoulos indorsed the check, and Panveno gave him the money. He immediately handed the money to Bugay, who had accompanied him to the currency exchange. Although Panveno stated that she saw Bugay hand Maropoulos some money after the two men had turned away from her, Maropoulos testified that he received no money from Bugay in exchange for his help. Some time later, Belmont National Bank, where Oak Park had deposited the check, filed a claim against Oak Park because the indorsement "Henry Sherman" had been forged. Oak Park paid the claim and brought an action against Maropoulos. The trial court directed a jury verdict for Maropoulos, and Oak Park appealed.

Decision: Judgment for Maropoulos affirmed.

Opinion: **Goldberg, J.**   In its judgment order directing the verdict, the trial court found that defendant was an accommodation indorser and as such made no warranty to defendant under the Uniform Commercial Code (§ 3–417(1)) and that payment of the check discharged all indorsers so that defendant was not liable to plaintiff on his indorsement.

In this court, plaintiff urges that defendant breached his warranty of good title when he obtained payment of a check on which the payee's indorsement was forged and that there was sufficient evidence to support a directed verdict in favor of plaintiff. Plaintiff's contentions are based exclusively on section 3–417(1) of the Code. Defendant contends that an accommodation indorser does not make warranties under § 3–417(1) and that the trial court properly directed a verdict for defendant.

A party who signs an instrument "for the purpose of lending his name to another party to . . . " that instrument is an accommodation party. (§ 3–415(1).) [Citation.] Such a party "is liable in the capacity in which he has signed. . . . " (§ 3–415(2).) Therefore defendant is an accommodation indorser and would be liable to plaintiff under his indorser's contract, provided that he had received timely notice that the check had been presented to the drawee bank and dishonored. (§ 3–414.) Because these conditions precedent to the contractual liability of an indorser have not been met, defendant is not liable on his contract as an accommodation indorser.

Furthermore, the drawee bank, American National, did not dishonor the check but paid it. This operated to discharge the liability of defendant as an accommodation indorser. [Citation.]

The portion of the Code upon which plaintiff seeks to hold defendant liable is section 3–417 entitled "Warranties on Presentment and Transfer." As shown above, the parties both confine their arguments to subsection 3–417(1) of the Code and the judgment order refers specifically thereto. Section 3–417(1) sets out warranties which run only to a party who "pays or accepts" an instrument upon presentment. We note that presentment is defined as "a demand for acceptance or payment made upon the maker, acceptor, drawee or other payor. . . . " (§ 3–504(1).) As applied to the instant case, the warranties contained in section 3–417(1) are limited to run only to the payor bank and not to any other transferee who acquired the check. In the case before us, plaintiff is not a payor or acceptor of the draft. This interpretation is strongly supported by the official comment which details the reasons for distinguishing warranties made to a payor or acceptor of an instrument from those made to a transferee. The case before us involves a transferee, not a party who paid or accepted the instrument. Thus it appears that reliance by plaintiff upon subsection 3–417(1) was misplaced. The authorities cited by plaintiff do not support its contention as all of these cases were decided before the effective date of the Code.

* * *

An additional theory requires affirmance of the judgment appealed from. Subsection 3–417(2) of the Code provides that one "who transfers an instrument and receives consideration warrants to his transferee . . . '' that he has good title. (§ 3–417(2).) The Illinois comments to this portion of the Code confirm that this warranty is made only by any party who transfers an instrument for consideration. In [Citation], the court noted the presence of the phrase "and receives consideration" in this subsection of the Code.

The evidence presented in the case at bar establishes that defendant received no consideration for his indorsement. Though Mrs. Panveno testified that she saw Bugay hand defendant some money as the two left the currency exchange, she also testified that defendant stated that he was doing a favor for his friend; that she was not paying close attention to the two men and that she did not watch them as they walked away from her. Thus her testimony was considerably weakened by her own qualifying statements and it was strongly and directly contradicted by the positive and unshaken testimony of defendant that he received nothing in return for his assistance. The simple fact standing alone that this witness saw Bugay hand some money to defendant, even if proved, would have no legal significance without additional proof of some type showing that the payment was consideration for defendant's indorsement.

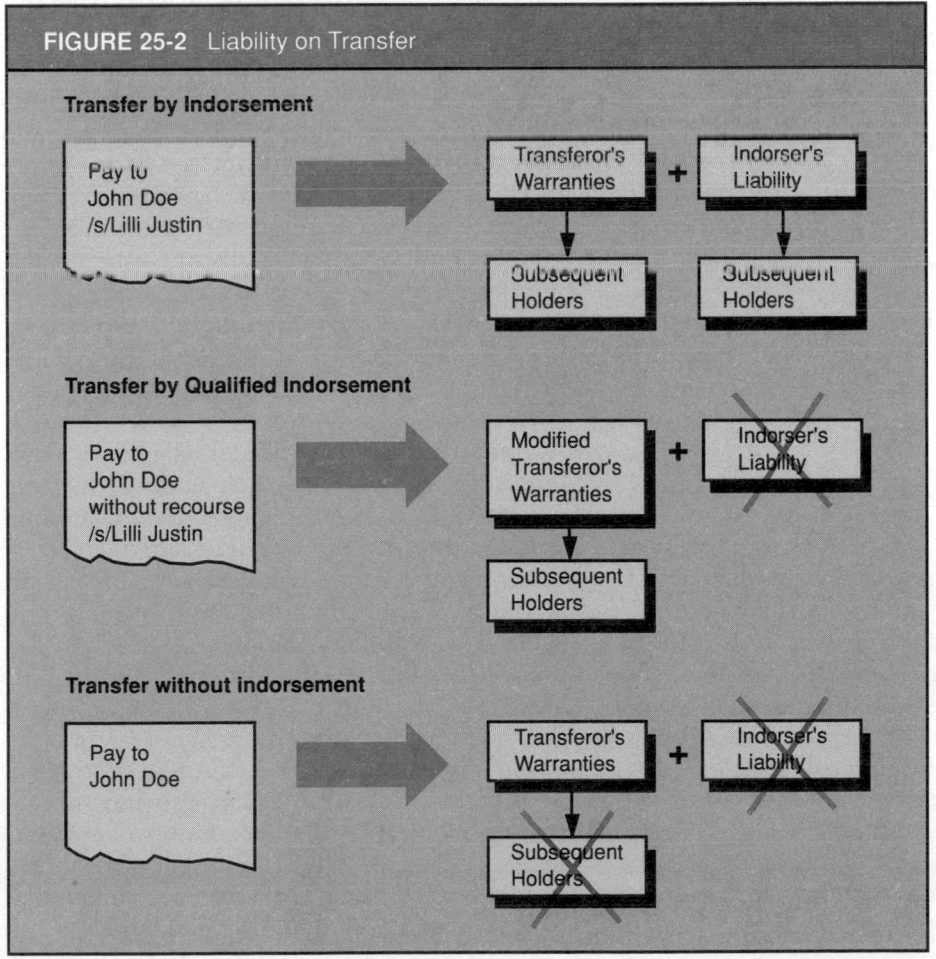

FIGURE 25-2 Liability on Transfer

The warranties of the transferor are as follows.

Good Title

The first warranty that the Code imposes on a transferor is that the transferor has good title to the instrument or is authorized to obtain payment or acceptance on behalf of one who has good title and the transfer is otherwise rightful. We illustrate this rule with the following example. Mitchell makes a note payable to the order of Penelope. A thief steals the note from Penelope, forges Penelope's indorsement, and sells the instrument to Karen. Karen does not have good title because the break in the indorsement chain prevents her from acquiring title. If Karen indorses the instrument to Ben for value, Ben can hold Karen liable for breach of warranty. The warranty action is important to Ben because it enables him to hold Karen liable, even if Karen indorsed the note "without recourse."

Signatures Genuine

In the example above, the second warranty imposed by the Code, that *all* signatures are genuine or authorized, would also be breached. If the signature of a maker, drawer, drawee, acceptor, or indorser not in the chain of title is unauthorized, there is a breach of this warranty but no breach of the warranty of good title.

No Material Alteration

A third warranty is the warranty against material alteration. Suppose that Mark makes a note payable to the order of the payee in the amount of $100. The payee, without authority, alters the note so that it appears to be drawn for $1,000 and negotiates the instrument to Alice, who buys it without knowing of the alteration. Alice, indorsing "without recourse," negotiates the instrument to Barry for value. Barry presents the instrument to Mark, who refuses to pay more than $100 on it. Barry can collect the difference from Alice. Although Alice is not liable to Barry on the indorsement contract because of her qualified indorsement, she is liable to him for breach of warranty. If Alice had not qualified her indorsement, Barry would be able to recover against Alice on the basis of either warranty or the indorsement contract.

No Defenses

The fourth transferor's warranty imposed by the Code is that *no defense* of any party is good against the transferor. Under this warranty, a transferor who indorses "without recourse" stands in a better position than an unqualified indorser. His warranty is only that he has *no knowledge* of any such defense. Suppose that Madeline, a minor, a resident of a State where minors' contracts for nonnecessaries are void, makes a note payable to bearer in payment of a motorcycle. Paul, the first holder, negotiates it to Alan by mere delivery. Alan indorses it "without recourse" (qualified indorsement) and negotiates it to Betty, and Betty unqualifiedly indorses it to Henry. Henry cannot recover on the instrument against Madeline because of Madeline's minority (a real defense). Henry therefore recovers against Betty on either the breach of warranty that no valid defense exists to the instrument or the indorsement contract, provided Henry gave Betty prompt notice of dishonor. Betty cannot recover against Alan on the instrument because of Alan's qualified indorsement. Can Betty hold Alan for breach of warranty? Because Alan indorsed without recourse, he does not warrant that the instrument is without defense; he only warrants that he knows of no defense that is good against him. Assuming that Alan did not know that Madeline was a minor, Betty cannot hold Alan for breach of warranty. Can Betty hold Paul? Paul is not liable as an indorser, because he did not indorse the instrument. Although Paul, as a transferor, warrants that there are no defenses good against him, this warranty extends only to his immediate transferee, Alan. Therefore, Betty cannot hold Paul liable. This illustration shows the interplay between indorsement and warranty liability. It also shows the relationship between the liability imposed under the various warranties and the individuals who can or cannot claim protection under a particular warranty.

No Knowledge of Insolvency

Any person who transfers a negotiable instrument warrants that he has no knowledge of any insolvency proceedings instituted by the maker, acceptor, or drawer of an unaccepted instrument. Thus, if Madge makes a note payable to bearer, and the first holder, Porter, negotiates it without indorsement to Adelle, who then negotiates it by qualified indorsement to Blanche, both Porter and Adelle make a warranty that they do not know that Madge is in bankruptcy. Blanche could not hold Porter for breach of warranty, however, because Porter's warranty runs only in favor of his immediate transferee, Adelle, since Porter transferred the instrument without indorsement. If Blanche should hold Adelle liable on her warranty, Adelle could then hold Porter, her immediate transferor, liable.

WARRANTIES ON PRESENTMENT

All parties called on to pay or accept an instrument must do so strictly in compliance with the order given. The drawee bank agrees to pay checks as ordered by the drawer so long as his account is sufficient to cover them. If the bank pays without the drawer's order, it cannot charge the payment to the drawer's account.

If a drawee pays an instrument that has been forged or altered, he has the initial loss, for he cannot charge this amount to the drawer. May the drawee shift this loss to the person who received the payment? For instruments on which the drawer's signature has been forged, the general answer is no, provided that the presenting party is a holder in due course or a person who in good faith has changed her position in reliance on the payment or acceptance. The drawee can, however, recover from a person to whom it made payment for any loss incurred because of a forged indorsement or material alteration of the instrument.

For example, suppose Donna's (drawer's) name is forged to a check, making it appear

that it was drawn by her. If the bank pays this check, it cannot charge Donna's account and cannot recover from a *holder in due course* or a person who in *good faith* has changed his position in reliance on the payment or acceptance. Similarly, if a drawee pays a draft purportedly drawn by Donna, it cannot seek reimbursement from Donna if Donna's signature is forged. The justification for the rule is that the drawee is supposed to know the drawer's signature. On the other hand, if Donna draws a check to Pablo or order, and Pablo's indorsement is forged, the bank does not follow Donna's order in paying such an item, and hence cannot charge her account (except in the impostor or fictitious payee situations discussed above). The bank, however, can recover from the person who obtained payment of the check from it. The bank should not be required to bear this loss, because it should not be expected to know the signature of payees of checks, although it should know the signatures of its own customers.

The same rationale applies to raised instruments. If Derek makes a check to Pierre's order in the amount of $3 and it is raised so as to appear to be in the amount of $300, the bank cannot charge the $300 it pays out on such an item to the drawer's account. It can charge the account only $3, because that is all the drawer ordered it to pay. Nonetheless, the bank can collect the difference against the presenting party who received payment.

The examples to this point have involved drawees. The maker of a note cannot recover payment he made on a forged maker's signature to a holder in due course or a good faith taker who changed his position in reliance; he should know his own signature. But suppose that the maker of a note pays on a forged indorsement. The maker, like the drawee, cannot know everyone's signature, and where the indorser's signature is forged, the maker can recover any money paid to the presenting party. The situation is different where the amount of the note has been raised. Suppose that the maker makes a note in the amount of $300, and it is raised to $3,000. If he pays this note, he is not permitted to recover from an innocent presenting party, because the maker—unlike a drawee—has a way of knowing the original amount of the instrument. Similarly, suppose that a check or draft is raised *after* it has been accepted or certified by the drawee. If the acceptor pays the raised amount to an innocent presenting party, the acceptor is not entitled to recover the amount by which the instrument was raised because the innocent holder has no way of knowing the proper amount while the acceptor does.

Presenter's warranties run not only *from* the person who obtains payment or acceptance, but also from *all* prior transferors. The presenter's warranties run to any person who in good faith pays or accepts the instrument. These presentment warranties[20] are as follows.

Good Title

Presenters give the same warranty of good title to persons who pay or accept that is granted to transferees under the transferor's warranty. As explained above, the warranty extends to the genuineness of the indorser's signatures but *not* to the signature of the drawer or maker.

Genuineness of Signature of Maker and Drawer

Presenters warrant that they have no *knowledge* that the signature of the maker or drawer is unauthorized. To protect a person who takes an instrument in good faith and later learns it was forged, certain exceptions to this warranty are specified in the Code. A holder in due course acting in good faith does not give such a warranty to (1) the maker with respect to his own signature; (2) the drawer with respect to his own signature; and (3) an acceptor of a draft with respect to the drawer's signature if such holder took the draft after acceptance or obtained the acceptance without knowledge of the unauthorized signature. These exceptions are available only to a holder in due course.

No Material Alteration

Presenters, as shown above, also give a warranty against material alteration, but again it is not given by a holder in due course acting in good faith to a maker or drawer, whether or not the drawer is also the drawee. Further, the holder in due course does not give this warranty to the acceptor of a draft or check when an alteration was made before it was accepted if the holder received the instrument after acceptance, even though the acceptance included a term such as "payable as originally drawn." The acceptor had the first opportunity to detect the alteration. To permit the acceptor to shift the responsibility for a prior material alteration to a subsequent party would defeat the entire purpose of acceptance and certification. An acceptance or certification must constitute a definite commitment to honor a definite instrument.

This rule should not be confused with that which applies where the alteration is made *after* the acceptance or certification. In such a situation, the drawee knows the amount of the original acceptance or certification, and she should not be able to charge back against an innocent party if she pays out more than that amount. Hence, a holder in due course does not warrant against alterations made after acceptance.

Figure 25–3 illustrates the various types of liability based on warranty.

TERMINATION OF LIABILITY

Eventually, every commercial transaction must end, with the potential liabilities of the parties to the instrument terminated. The Code specifies the various methods by and extent to which the liability of *any* party, primary or secondary, is discharged.[21] It also specifies when the liability of *all* parties is discharged. No discharge of a party is effective against a subsequent holder in due course unless she has knowledge of the discharge when she takes the instrument.[22]

DISCHARGE BY PERFORMANCE

The most obvious way for a party to discharge liability on an instrument is to pay the holder. Such a payment results in a discharge even though it is made with knowledge of the claim of another person to the instrument, unless such other person either supplies adequate

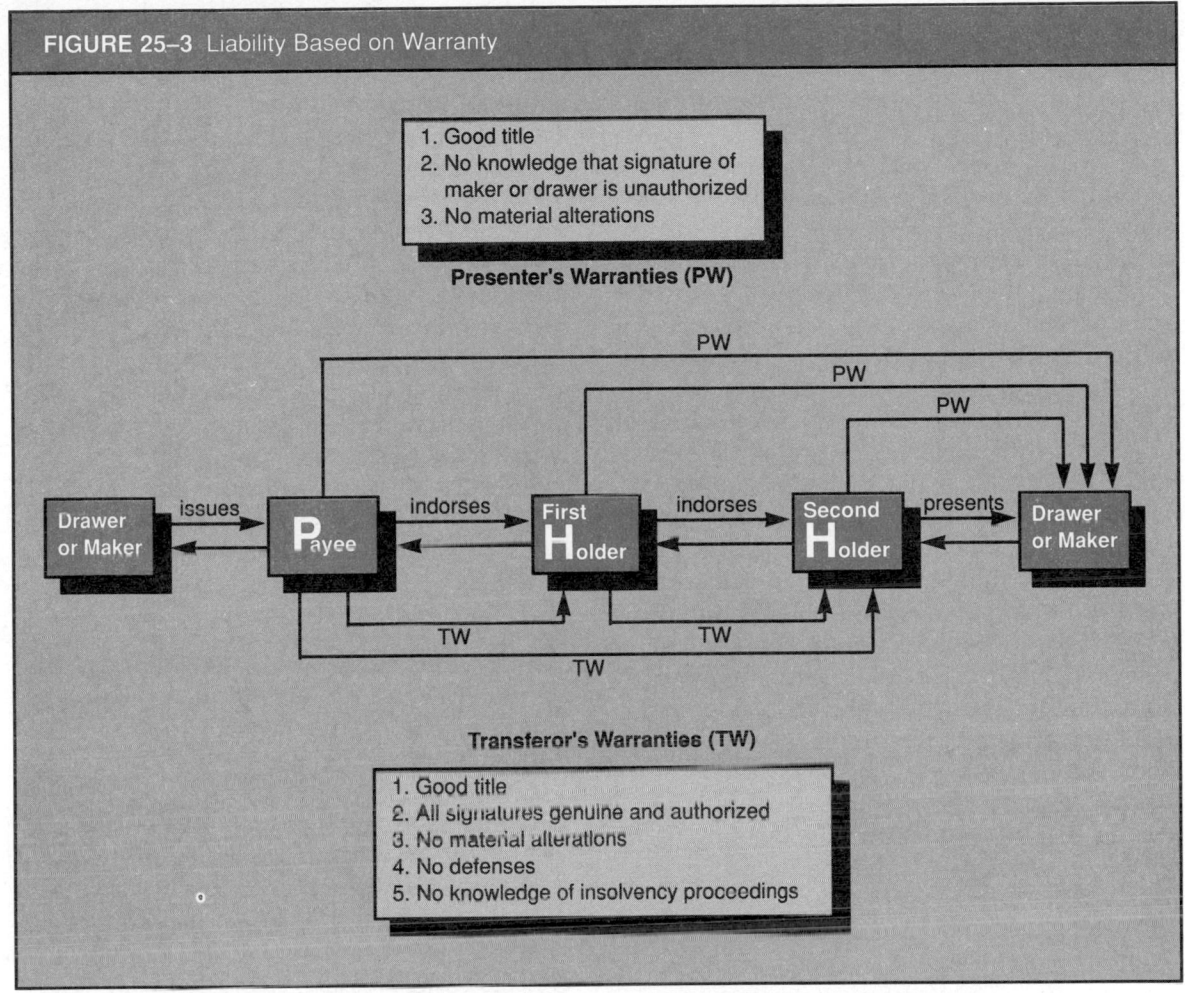

FIGURE 25-3 Liability Based on Warranty

1. Good title
2. No knowledge that signature of maker or drawer is unauthorized
3. No material alterations

Presenter's Warranties (PW)

Transferor's Warranties (TW)

1. Good title
2. All signatures genuine and authorized
3. No material alterations
4. No defenses
5. No knowledge of insolvency proceedings

indemnity or obtains an injunction in a proceeding to which the holder is made a party.[23] The person making payment is not required to decide at his peril whether the claim to the instrument is valid or not. Such a claim may arise, for example, where the prior holder contends the instrument was stolen from him.

The person making payment should, of course, take the instrument or have it canceled —marked "paid" or "canceled"—so that it cannot pass into the hands of a subsequent holder in due course against whom his discharge would not be effective.

TENDER OF PAYMENT

Any party liable on an instrument who makes tender of full payment to a holder when or

after payment is due is discharged from all subsequent liability for interest, costs, and attorney's fees.[24] Her tender does not relieve her of her liability for the face amount of the instrument or any interest accrued until the time of tender. The holder's refusal of full tender has the effect of wholly discharging every party who has a right of recourse against the party making tender.[24] For example, a note executed by Meghan in favor of Paloma is negotiated by indorsement successively to Aaron, Babs, and Helga. Meghan defaults, and Helga asserts her rights against indorsers Paloma, Aaron, and Babs. If Paloma tenders full payment to Helga and Helga refuses to accept it, desiring to collect from Meghan, Aaron and Babs are wholly discharged. The reason is that both Aaron and Babs would have rights of recourse against Paloma if they were required to pay.

CANCELLATION AND RENUNCIATION

A holder may discharge the liability of any party to an instrument in any manner apparent on the face of the instrument or the indorsement, such as by canceling the instrument or the signature of the party or parties to be discharged by destruction or mutilation or by striking out a party's signature.[25]

Because the instrument itself constitutes the obligation, intentional cancellation of it by the holder results in a discharge of all parties. Accidental destruction of an instrument does not have such an effect, nor does cancellation in any form by anyone other than the holder.

If the holder wishes to discharge one, but not all parties, he may merely strike out that party's signature. He must be careful, however, that he does not also discharge other parties by impairing their rights of recourse, as discussed below.

A holder may also renounce his rights by a writing, signed and delivered, or by surrender of the instrument to the party to be discharged. As in the case of other discharges, however, a written renunciation is of no effect against a subsequent holder in due course who has no knowledge of the renunciation.

Cancellation or renunciation is effective even without consideration.

IMPAIRMENT OF RECOURSE OR COLLATERAL

If the holder collects the amount of an instrument from an indorser, the indorser normally has a right of recourse against parties primarily liable, prior indorsers, if any, and the drawer in the case of a draft or check. At the time the indorser acquired the instrument, she relied on the credit of the prior parties, the strict nature of their liability, and, in the case of an instrument secured by collateral, on the value of that collateral.

If any of these rights is adversely affected by the action or inaction of the holder, the indorser should not be required to pay the instrument because when she subsequently seeks reimbursement, she will not possess the rights she bargained for when she acquired the instrument. The same rule applies to an accommodation party or acceptor who is known by the holder as an acceptor.

The Code, therefore, provides that the holder discharges any party to the instrument to the extent that without her consent the holder

1. releases or agrees not to sue any person against whom such party, to the knowledge of the holder, has a right of recourse;
2. agrees to suspend the right to enforce the instrument or collateral against such person;
3. otherwise discharges such person; or
4. unjustifiably impairs any collateral for the instrument given by or on behalf of the party or any person against whom such party has a right of recourse.[26]

OTHER METHODS OF DISCHARGE

As we discussed earlier, other methods by which a party's liability may be discharged include (1) fraudulent and material alteration;[7] (2) discharge of the drawer and prior indorsers by certification of a check procured by a holder;[9] and (3) unexcused delay in presentment, notice of dishonor, or protest.[14] Also, any party may be discharged from liability against another party by agreeing to pay money in exchange for discharge.[21]

CHAPTER SUMMARY

CONTRACTUAL LIABILITY

| **General Principles** | **Liability on the Instrument** no person has contractual liability on an instrument unless their signature appears on it |

Signature a signature may be made by the individual herself or by her authorized agent
- *Authorized Signatures* an agent who executes a negotiable instrument on behalf of his principal is not liable if the instrument is executed properly and as authorized
- *Unauthorized Signatures* include forgeries and signatures made by an agent without proper power; are generally not binding on the person whose name appears on the instrument but are binding on the unauthorized signer

Liability of Primary Parties

Primary Liability absolute obligation to pay a negotiable instrument
Makers the maker guarantees that he will pay the note according to its original terms
Acceptors a drawee has no liability on the instrument until she accepts it and then she becomes primarily liable
- *Acceptance* a drawee's signed engagement to honor the instrument
- *Certification* acceptance of a check by a bank

Liability of Secondary Parties

Secondary Liability obligation to pay a negotiable instrument that is subject to conditions precedent
Indorsers and Drawers if the instrument is not paid by a primary party and the conditions precedent to the liability of secondary parties are satisfied, then indorsers and drawers are secondarily liable unless they have disclaimed their liability or have a valid defense to the instrument
Conditions Precedent to Liability
- *Presentment* demand for acceptance or payment made by the holder on the maker, acceptor, or drawee
- *Dishonor* an instrument is dishonored when (1) presentment has been made and acceptance or payment is refused or cannot be obtained, or (2) presentment is excused and the instrument is not accepted or paid
- *Notice of Dishonor* must be given by a bank within one business day and by a nonbank within three business days
- *Protest* a certificate of dishonor; required only if the draft is drawn or payable outside the United States
- *Effect of Unexcused Delay in Presentment or Notice* indorsers are discharged; the drawer is discharged only to the extent of any loss suffered because of the delay

Disclaimer by Secondary Parties a drawer or indorser may disclaim liability by a qualified drawing or indorsing ("without recourse")

Liability of Other Parties

Accommodation Parties are liable as a maker, drawer, or indorser depending upon the manner in which they sign
Liability for Conversion conversion occurs: (a) when a drawee refuses to return a draft that was presented for acceptance, (b) when any person refuses to return an instrument after they dishonor it, or (c) when an instrument is paid on a forged indorsement

| **Special Situations Affecting Liability** | The Impostor Rule   an indorsement of an impostor or of any other person in the name of the named payee is effective if the impostor has induced the maker or drawer to issue the instrument to him using the name of the payee
The Fictitious Payee Rule   an indorsement by any person in the name of the named payee is effective if an agent of the maker or drawer has supplied her with the name of the payee for fraudulent purposes |

LIABILITY BASED UPON WARRANTY

| **Warranties on Transfer** | Parties
■ *Warrantor*   any person who transfers an instrument and receives consideration gives the transferor's warranties
■ *Beneficiary*   if the transfer is by delivery, the warranties run only to the immediate transferee; if the transfer is by indorsement the warranties run to any subsequent holder who takes the instrument in good faith
Warranties
■ *Good Title*
■ *All Signatures Genuine*
■ *No Material Alteration*
■ *No Defenses*
■ *No Knowledge of Insolvency* |

| **Warranties on Presentment** | Parties
■ *Warrantor*   all people who obtain payment or acceptance of an instrument as well as all prior transferors give the presenter's warranties
■ *Beneficiary*   the presenter's warranties run to any person who in good faith pays or accepts an instrument
Warranties
■ *Good Title*
■ *Genuineness of Signature of Maker and Drawer*
■ *No Material Alteration* |

TERMINATION OF LIABILITY

| **Special Rights of Holder in Due Course** | No discharge is effective against a holder in due course unless she has knowledge of the discharge when she takes the instrument |

| **Discharge** | Performance
Tender of Payment   for interest, costs, and attorney's fees
Cancellation
Renunciation
Impairment of Recourse or Collateral   to the extent any of the party's rights of recourse as to collateral are adversely affected |

> Other Methods of Discharge
> ■ *Fraudulent and material alteration*
> ■ *Discharge by certification of a check*
> ■ *Unexcused delay in presentment, notice of dishonor, or protest*
> ■ *Agreement of the parties*

QUESTIONS

1. Discuss contractual liability, warranty liability, and liability for conversion.
2. Discuss the liability of makers, acceptors, drawees, drawers, indorsers, and accommodation parties.
3. Discuss the conditions precedent to the liability of secondary parties.
4. Compare the warranties on transfer with the warranties on presentment.
5. Discuss the methods by which liability on an instrument may be terminated.

PROBLEMS

1. $800.00   Smalltown, Illinois

November 15, 1990
The undersigned promises to pay to the order of John Doe, Nine Hundred Dollars with interest from date of note. Payment to be made in five monthly installments of One Hundred Eighty Dollars, plus accrued interest beginning on December 1, 1990. In the event of default in the payment of any installment or interest on installment date, the holder of this instrument may declare the entire obligation due and owing and proceed forthwith to collect the balance due on this instrument.

(signed) Acton, agent

On December 18, no payment having been made on the note, Doe indorsed and deliverd the instrument to Todd to secure a preexisting debt in the amount of $800.

On January 18, 1991, Todd brought an action against Acton and Phi Corporation, Acton's principal, to collect the full amount of the instrument with interest. Acton defended on the basis that he signed the instrument in a representative capacity and that Doe had failed to deliver the consideration for which the instrument had been issued. Phi Corporation defended on the basis that it did not sign the

instrument and that its name does not appear on the instrument.

For what amount, if any, are Acton and Phi Corporation liable?

2. Cole was supervisor of the shipping department of Machine Mfg., Inc. In February Cole found herself in need of funds and at the end of that month submitted to Ames, the treasurer of the corporation, a payroll listing including the name, Ben Day, to whom was allegedly owed $800 for services rendered during February. Actually, there was no employee named Day. Relying on the word of Cole, Ames drew and delivered to her a series of corporate payroll checks drawn on the corporate account in the Capital Bank, one of which was made payable to the order of Ben Day for $800. Cole took the check, indorsed on its back "Ben Day," cashed it at the Capital Bank, and pocketed the proceeds. She repeated the same procedure at the end of March, April, and May. In mid-June, Machine Mfg., Inc., learned of Cole's fraudulent conduct, fired her, and brought an appropriate action against Capital Bank seeking a judgment for $3,200. Decision?

3. While employed as a night watchman at the place of business of A. B. Cate Trucking Company, Fred Fain observed that the office safe had been left unlocked. It contained fifty payroll checks that were ready to be distributed to employees two days later. The checks had all been signed by the sole proprietor, Cate. Fain removed five of the checks and also took two blank checks that were in the safe. Fain forged the indorsements of the payees on the five payroll checks and cashed them at local supermarkets. He then filled out one of the blank checks, making himself payee, and forged Cate's signature as drawer. After cashing that check at a supermarket, Fain departed by airplane to Jamaica. The six checks were promptly presented for payment to the drawee bank, the Bank of Emanon, which paid each of the checks. Shortly thereafter, Cate learned about the missing payroll checks and forgeries, and demanded that the Bank of Emanon credit his account with the amount of the six checks.

Must the bank comply with Cate's demand? What are the bank's rights, if any, against the supermarkets? You may assume that the supermarkets cashed all of the checks in good faith.

4. A negotiable promissory note executed and delivered by B to C passed in due course to and was indorsed in blank by C, D, E, and F. G, the present holder, strikes out D's indorsement. What is the liability of C, D, E, and F on their respective indorsements?

5. On June 15, 1986, Joanne, for consideration, executed a negotiable promissory note for $10,000 payable to Robert on or before June 15, 1991. Joanne subsequently suffered financial reverses. During January 1989, Robert, on two occasions told Joanne that he knew that Joanne was having a difficult time and that he, Robert, did not need the money and the debt should be considered as completely canceled, with no other act or payment being required. These conversations were witnessed by three persons, including Larry. On March 15, 1991, Robert changed his mind and indorsed the note for value to Larry. The note was not paid by June 15, 1991, and Larry sued Joanne for the amount of the note. Joanne defended on the ground that Robert had canceled the debt and renounced all rights against Joanne and that Larry had notice of this fact. Decision?

6. Tate and Fitch were longtime friends. Tate was a man of considerable means; Fitch had encountered financial difficulties. In order to bolster his failing business, Fitch desired to borrow $6,000 from Farmers Bank of Erehwon. To accomplish this, he persuaded Tate to help him make a promissory note by which it would appear that Tate had the responsibility of maker, but with Fitch agreeing to pay the instrument when due. Accordingly, they executed the following instrument:

December 1, 1990
Thirty days after date and for value received, I promise to pay to the order of Frank Fitch the sum of $6,600.   /s/ Timothy Tate

On the back of the note, Fitch indorsed, "Pay to the order of Farmers Bank of Erehwon /s/ Frank Fitch" and delivered it to the bank in exchange for $6,000.

When the note was not paid at maturity, the bank, without first demanding payment by Fitch, brought an action on the note against Tate. (a) Decision? (b) If Tate voluntarily pays the note to the bank, may he then recover on the note against Fitch, who appears as an indorser?

7. Alpha orally appointed Omega as his agent to find and purchase for him a 1930 Dodge automobile in good condition. Omega located such a car. The car's owner, Roe, agreed to sell and deliver the car on January 10, 1990, for $9,000. To evidence the purchase price, Omega mailed to Roe the following instrument:

December 1, 1990
$9,000.00
We promise to pay to the order of bearer Nine Thousand Dollars with interest from date of this instrument on or before January 10, 1990. This note is given in consideration of John Roe's transferring title to and possession of his 1930 Dodge automobile.   (signed) Omega, agent

Smith stole the note from Roe's mailbox, indorsed Roe's name on the note, and promptly discounted it with Sunset Bank for $8,700. Not having received the note, Roe sold the car to a third party. On January 10, 1991, the bank, having discovered all the facts, demanded payment of the note from Alpha and Omega. Payment was refused by both.

What are Sunset Bank's rights with regard to Omega? Its rights with regard to Roe and Smith?

8. In payment of the purchase price of a used motorboat that had been fraudulently misrepresented, Young signed and delivered to Armstrong his negotiable note in the amount of $2,000 due October 1, with Selby as an accommodation co-maker. Young intended to use the boat for his fishing business. Armstrong indorsed the note in blank preparatory to discounting it. Tillman stole the note from Armstrong and delivered it to McGowan on July 1 in payment of a past-due debt owing by Tillman to McGowan in the amount of $600, with McGowan making up the difference by giving Tillman his check for $800 and an oral promise to pay Tillman an additional $600 on October 1.

When McGowan demanded payment of the note on December 1, both Young and Selby refused to pay the note because it had not been presented for payment on its due date and because Armstrong had fraudulently misrepresented the motorboat for which the note had been executed.

What are McGowan's rights, if any, against Young, Selby, Tillman, and Armstrong, respectively?

9. On July 1 Anderson sold D'Aveni, a jeweler, a necklace containing imitation gems that Anderson fraudulently represented to be diamonds. In payment for the necklace D'Aveni executed and delivered to Anderson her promissory note for $25,000 dated July 1 and payable on December 1 to Anderson's order with interest at 14 percent per annum.

The note was thereafter successively indorsed in blank and delivered by Anderson to Bylinski, Bylinski to Conrad, and Conrad to Shapiro, who became a holder in due course on August 10. On November 1 D'Aveni discovered Anderson's fraud and immediately notified Anderson, Bylinski, Conrad, and Shapiro that she would not pay the note when it became due. Bylinski, a friend of Shapiro, requested that Shapiro release him from liability on the note, and Shapiro, as a favor to Bylinski and for no other consideration, struck out Bylinski's indorsement.

On November 15, Shapiro, who was solvent and had no creditors, indorsed the note to the order of Frederick, his father, and delivered it to Frederick as a gift. At the same time, Shapiro told Frederick of D'Aveni's statement that D'Aveni would not pay the note when it became due. Frederick presented the note to D'Aveni for payment on December 1, but D'Aveni refused to pay. Thereafter Frederick gave due notice of dishonor to Anderson, Bylinski, and Conrad.

What are Frederick's rights, if any, against Anderson, Bylinski, Conrad, and D'Aveni on the note?

10. Saul sold goods to Bruce, warranting that the goods were of a specified quality. The goods were not of the quality warranted, and Saul knew this at the time of the sale. Bruce drew and delivered a check payable to Saul and drawn on Third National Bank in the amount of the purchase price. Bruce subsequently discovered the goods were faulty and stopped payment on the check. Saul brings a suit against Bruce. Decision?

11. While assistant treasurer of Travco Corporation, Frank Mitchell caused two checks, each payable to a fictitious company, to be drawn on Travco's account with Brown City Savings Bank. In each case, Mitchell indorsed the check in his own name and then cashed it at Citizens Federal Savings & Loan Association of Port Huron. Both checks were cleared through normal banking channels and charged against Travco's account with Brown City. Travco subsequently discovered the embezzlement, and after its demand for reimbursement was denied, it brought this suit against Citizens. Decision?

12. R&A Concrete Contractors, Inc., executed a promissory note that identifies both R&A Concrete and Grover Roberts as its makers. On the reverse side of the note, the following appears: "X John Ament Sec. & Treas." National Bank of Georgia, the payee, now sues both R&A Concrete and Ament on the note. Decision?

ENDNOTES

1. Uniform Commercial Code, Section 3—401, Signature.

2. Uniform Commercial Code, Section 1—201(39), Definitions: Signed.

3. Uniform Commercial Code, Section 3—404, Unauthorized Signatures.

4. Uniform Commercial Code, Section 3—406, Negligence Contributing to Alteration or Unauthorized Signature.

5. Uniform Commercial Code, Section 3—413, Contract of Maker, Drawer and Acceptor.

6. Uniform Commercial Code, Section 3—115, Incomplete Instruments.

7. Uniform Commercial Code, Section 3—407, Alteration.

8. Uniform Commercial Code, Section 3—410, Definition and Operation of Acceptance.

9. Uniform Commercial Code, Section 3—411, Certification of a Check.

10. Uniform Commercial Code, Section 3—414, Contract of Indorser; Order of Liability.

11. Uniform Commercial Code, Section 3—504, How Presentment Made.

12. Uniform Commercial Code, Section 3—501, When Presentment, Notice of Dishonor, and Protest Necessary or Permissible.

13. Uniform Commercial Code, Section 3—503, Time of Presentment.

14. Uniform Commercial Code, Section 3—502, Unexcused Delay; Discharge.

15. Uniform Commercial Code, Section 3—507, Dishonor; Holder's Right of Recourse; Term Allowing Re-Presentment.

16. Uniform Commercial Code, Section 3—508, Notice of Dishonor.

17. Uniform Commercial Code, Section 3—509, Protest; Noting for Protest.

18. Uniform Commercial Code, Section 3—511, Waived or Excused Presentment, Protest or Notice of Dishonor or Delay Therein.

19. Uniform Commercial Code, Section 3—405, Impostors; Signature in Name of Payee.

20. Uniform Commercial Code, Section 3—417, Warranties on Presentment and Transfer.

21. Uniform Commercial Code, Section 3—601, Discharge of Parties.

22. Uniform Commercial Code, Section 3—602, Effect of Discharge Against Holder in Due Course.

23. Uniform Commercial Code, Section 3—603, Payment or Satisfaction.

24. Uniform Commercial Code, Section 3—604, Tender of Payment.

25. Uniform Commercial Code, Section 3—605, Cancellation and Renunciation.

26. Uniform Commercial Code, Section 3—606, Impairment of Recourse or of Collateral.

26 BANK DEPOSITS AND COLLECTIONS

In today's society, most goods and services are bought and sold without a physical transfer of cash. Credit cards, charge accounts, and various deferred payment plans have made cash sales increasingly rare. But even credit sales ultimately must be settled. When they are, payment is usually made by check rather than cash. If the parties to a sales transaction happen to have accounts at the same bank, a transfer of credit is easily accomplished. In most cases, however, the parties do business at different banks. Then the buyer's check must journey from the seller-payee's bank (the depositary bank), where the check is deposited by the seller for credit to his account, to the buyer-drawer's bank (the payor bank) for payment. In this collection process, the check frequently passes through one or more other banks (intermediary banks) so that it may be collected and the appropriate entries recorded. Any bank handling the item for collection other than the payor bank (that is, any intermediary or depositary bank) is also referred to as a collecting bank.

Our banking system has developed a network to handle the collection of checks and other instruments. Article 4 of the Uniform Commercial Code, entitled "Bank Deposits and Collections," provides the principal rules governing the bank collection process. Since items in the bank collection process are essentially those covered by Article 3, "Commercial Paper," and to a lesser extent by Article 8, "Investment Securities," these articles may apply to a bank collection problem.

COLLECTION OF ITEMS

When a person deposits a check in his bank (the **depositary bank**), the bank credits his account by the amount of the check. This is **provisional credit.** Normally, a bank does not permit a customer to draw funds against a provisional credit, but if it does permit its customer to draw against the credit, it has given *value* and, provided it meets the other requirements, will be a holder in due course. Under the customer's contract with his bank, the bank must make a reasonable effort to obtain payment of all checks deposited for collection. When the amount of the check has been collected from the payor bank (the drawee), the credit becomes final (**final credit**).

The Competitive Equality Banking Act of 1987 has expedited the availability of funds by establishing maximum time periods for a bank to hold (not permit a customer access to her funds) various types of instruments. As of September 1, 1988: (1) cash deposits, wire transfers, government checks, the first $100 of a day's check deposits, cashier's checks, and checks deposited in one branch of a depositary institution and drawn on the same or another branch of the same institution must clear by the next business day; (2) local checks must clear within two intervening business days; and (3) nonlocal checks must clear in no more than six intervening business days. Effective September 1, 1990, a bank has only one intervening business day between the day a local check is deposited and the day that the funds from the check are available for withdrawal; for nonlocal checks, the time period is four intervening business days. See Law in the News at page 550 for the banking community's reaction to this act.

If the **payor bank** (the drawee bank) does not pay the check for some reason, such as a stop payment order or insufficient funds in the drawer's account, the depositary bank reverses the provisional credit to the customer's account, debits his account for that amount, and returns the check to him with a statement of the reason for nonpayment. If, in the meantime, he has been permitted to draw against the provisional credit, the bank may recover the payment from him.

In some cases, the bank involved is both the depositary bank and the payor bank. In most cases, however, the depositary and payor banks are different, and the bank collection aspects of Article 4 come into play. Where the depositary and payor banks are different, a check must pass from one bank to the other, either directly through a clearinghouse or through one or more **intermediary banks** (a bank involved in the collection process other than the depositary or payor bank,[1] such as one of the twelve Federal Reserve Banks) as illustrated in Figure 26–1. A **clearinghouse** is an association of banks or other payors for the purpose of settling accounts with each other on a daily basis.[2] Each member of the clearing house forwards all deposited checks drawn on other members and receives from the clearinghouse all checks drawn on it. Balances are adjusted and settled each day.

Collecting Banks

As previously mentioned, a **collecting bank** is any bank handling the item for payment other than the payor bank.[1] In other words, a collecting bank is any intermediary or depositary bank. In the usual situation where the depositary and payor banks are different, the depositary bank gives a provisional credit to its customer, transfers the item to the next bank in the chain, receiving a provisional credit or "settlement" from it, and so on to the payor bank, which then debits the drawer's account. When the check is paid, all the provisional settlements given by the respective banks in the chain become final, and the transaction has been completed. No adjustment is necessary on the books of any of the banks involved. This procedure simplifies the bookkeeping processes of all the banks involved because only one entry is necessary if the check is paid.

If the payor bank does not pay the check, however, it returns the check, and each intermediary or collecting bank reverses the provisional settlement or credit it previously gave to its forwarding bank. Ultimately, the depositary bank will charge the account of its customer who deposited the item, and he

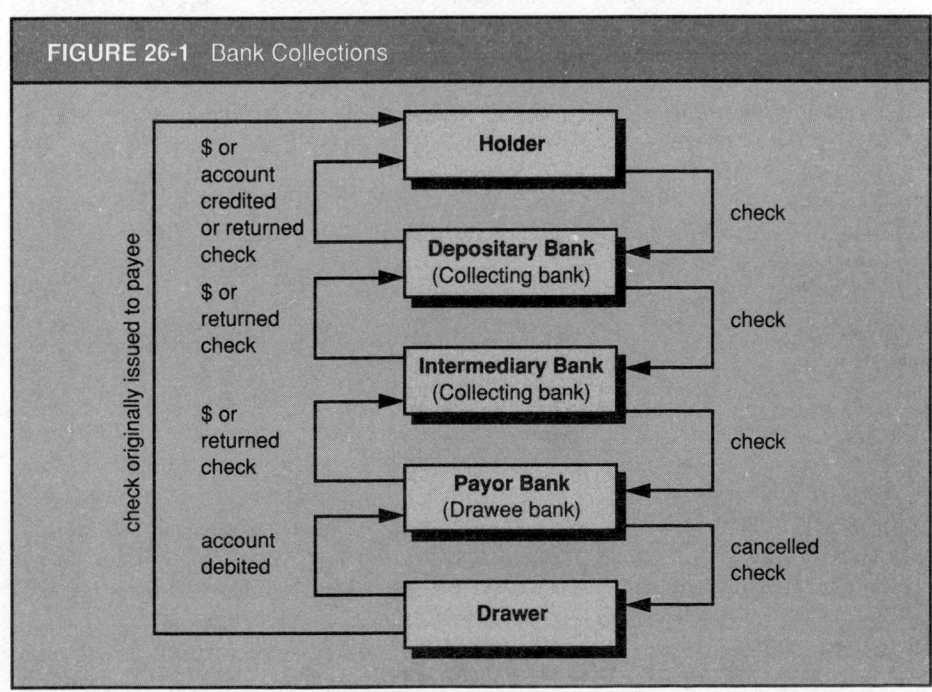

FIGURE 26-1 Bank Collections

LAW IN THE NEWS

Banks Are Waging Last-Ditch Bid to Ease New Rules That Speed Up Check Clearing

This fall, bank customers will gain quicker access to their money. But not as fast as new rules specify if bankers have their way.

Financial institutions have deluged the Federal Reserve Board with complaints and are lobbying Congress in a last-ditch effort to loosen rules taking effect Sept. 1 that require banks, thrifts and credit unions to make deposited funds available within one, three or seven business days, depending on the type of check deposited.

For years, consumers have complained that financial institutions, trying to assure that funds are collectible, place unduly long holds on checks (except for certain personal and payroll checks). A 1986 survey by the U.S. Public Interest Research Group, Washington, D.C., found that 53% of 458 banks and savings and loan associations held local checks for three to five business days and that 76% held out-of-state checks for more than a week.

But in coming to the aid of depositors, bankers assert, Congress has taken away important defenses against fraud. One banker half-jokingly refers to the new law—the Expedited Funds Availability Act—as the Check-Kiters Enrichment Act, because institutions will have to make funds available in many cases before they know whether a check is collectible. On average, it takes 6.8 days for a bank to learn that a check is uncollectible.

Some Bankers' Fear

Here's a scenario some bankers fear: A customer of a West Coast credit union deposits a $6,000 certified check drawn on a big New York bank.

Because of the time difference, the New York bank has closed, making verification impossible until the next day. But under the new law, funds on certified and government checks must be available for withdrawal the next business day, which is when the customer takes out his money. Only later does the credit union learn the check is counterfeit.

Even under the present law, variations of this scam have occurred. Robert Hutchinson, vice president of Manufacturers Hanover Trust Co. in New York says, "If dishonest people have found ways to cheat banks under the current law, what is the potential for fraud under this new law?"

Consumer activists counter that banks haven't demonstrated that fraud is a serious threat. If financial institutions are truly worried about fraud, they should speed up the check-return system rather than saddle consumers with lengthy delays, the activists argue.

Automation and special couriers have shortened the time it takes a check to get from the depositor's bank to the payor's bank—to a day and a half on average. But the process of returning insufficient checks to the institutions where they were deposited is far slower, requiring 10 days or longer for 15% of returned bad checks.

Returns of bad checks are lengthy because of their comparatively low volume and labor-intensive nature. Each year, only 1% of checks are returned for insufficient funds, but they total about $47 billion. Adding to the delay, institutions choose to return them by mail rather than special courier. And as anyone who has ever examined the bank stamps on a canceled check

must seek recovery from the indorsers or the drawer.

A collecting bank is an **agent** or subagent of the owner of the check until the settlement becomes final.[3] Clearly then, unless otherwise provided, any credit given for the item initially is provisional. Once it is finally settled, the agency relationship changes to one of **debtor-creditor.** The effect of this agency rule is that

the risk of loss remains with the owner and any chargebacks go to her, not to the collecting bank.

All collecting banks have certain responsibilities and duties in collecting checks and other items. We discuss these below.

Duty of Care   A collecting bank must use ordinary care in handling an item transferred

can attest, it can be difficult to tell where the check was initially deposited. Consequently, the process is done by hand rather than machine.

The Fed is considering steps to speed up the return of insufficient-funds checks. Paul M. Connolly, senior vice president of the Federal Reserve Bank of Boston, says, "A likely outcome is that there are going to be a number of improvements made to the return process."

Bankers say, however, that the potential for fraud under the new law isn't limited to bad checks. For instance, they point to the problems posed by automated teller machines. A customer could claim to be depositing $500 cash at an ATM and actually deposit nothing. Under the availability schedule for the new law, the customer could withdraw $500 the next business day before the bank has had a chance to verify the deposit, bankers argue.

Consumer activists say that banks can resolve that problem by speeding up their verification procedures. In addition, they say that the new law also allows financial institutions eight days to make funds available in new accounts and an added four days on deposits in excess of $5,000, on accounts with repeated overdrafts or on checks of dubious collectibility.

Broader Exceptions

Bankers complain that the exceptions need to be broader. For example, they want to lengthen the time an account is considered new, to 90 days from 30 days. New accounts are the ones most frequently involved in fraud, they say. And bankers want leeway to make ATM deposits available only after two business days.

Bankers say the rule permitting longer holds on checks greater than $5,000 doesn't apply to government and cashier's checks. And with recent advances in photocopying technology, counterfeit checks are becoming a bigger headache, bankers assert. Holding government and cashier's checks longer would allow them to be studied more carefully to determine whether they are counterfeit, bankers say.

Some of the protection in the new law is illusory, bankers say. For example, the provision that allows an extended hold for doubtful collectibility can be used only if a bank tells a depositor that it suspects fraud or insolvency. Marcia Z. Sullivan of the Consumer Bankers Association, an Arlington, Va., trade group, says this protection is not more than a fig leaf: "No bank is going to tell a depositor that it thinks he is involved in a check-kiting scheme or is going bankrupt."

Access to Deposited Funds Will Improve in Two Steps

The Expedited Funds Availability Act takes effect in two stages. The first, effective Sept. 1, sets a tight schedule for when deposited funds must be available for withdrawal:

■ Funds deposited in the form of cashier's checks, certified checks and government checks must be available to depositors the next business day.
■ "Local" checks written on an institution in the same metropolitan area or within the same Federal Reserve check-processing region must be available within three business days.
■ Banks, thrifts and credit unions are permitted to hold funds written on out-of-town institutions for as many as seven business days after deposit.

In 1990, the maximum hold periods shrink to two days for local checks and to five days for out-of-town checks. For cashiers' and other official checks, the rule will remain at one business day.

By Robert Guenther Staff Reporter of the *Wall Street Journal* Reprinted by permission of the *Wall Street Journal*, © Dow Jones & Company, Inc. 1988. All Rights Reserved Worldwide.

to it for collection.[4] The steps it takes in presenting an item or sending it for presentment are particularly important. It must act within a reasonable time after receipt of the item and must choose a reasonable method of forwarding the item for presentment. It is also responsible for using care in routing and selecting intermediary banks or other agents.

Duty to Act Seasonably Closely related to the collecting bank's duty of care is its duty to act seasonably. A collecting bank acts seasonably in any event if it takes proper action, such as forwarding or presenting an item before its "midnight deadline" following receipt of the item, notice, or payment. If the bank adheres to this standard, the timeliness of its action cannot be challenged. Although a reasonably longer time may be seasonable, the bank bears the burden of proof in such cases.[4] The **midnight deadline** means midnight of the banking day following the banking day on which the bank receives the item or notice.[2] Thus, if a bank receives a check on Monday, it must take proper action by midnight on the next banking day, or Tuesday. A banking day means that part of any day on which a bank is open to the public for carrying on its primary banking functions.

WELLS FARGO BANK v. HARTFORD NAT'L BANK & TRUST CO.
United States District Court, District of Connecticut, 1980.
484 F.Supp. 817.

Facts: On November 22, 1971, a $25,000 check drawn on the First National Bank of Nevada was deposited with Lincoln First Bank-Central. Lincoln forwarded the check to Nevada via Hartford National Bank and Trust Company and Wells Fargo Bank. Nevada received the check on Friday, December 10, and discovered that it was drawn on insufficient funds. That same day, Nevada informed Wells Fargo by telephone that the check had been dishonored. On Monday, December 13, Nevada mailed the check to Wells Fargo, which received it on Friday, December 17. Upon receiving the check, Wells Fargo promptly wired notice of the dishonor to Hartford and mailed the check to Hartford. Hartford received the check on December 21 and mailed it to Lincoln, which received it on December 27. Lincoln refused to accept the check, claiming that the notice of dishonor had arrived too late. Wells Fargo eventually ended up with the check and the $25,000 loss and brought an action to reverse the $25,000 credit it had given to Hartford in the course of handling the check.

Decision: Hartford's motion for summary judgment against Wells Fargo and Lincoln's motion for summary judgment against Hartford are granted.

Opinion: **Blumerfeld, J.:** UCC § 3–508(2) provides that "[a]ny necessary notice must be given by a bank before its midnight deadline." "Midnight deadline," in turn, is defined as "midnight on [the bank's] next banking day following the banking day on which it receives the relevant item or notice . . . " UCC § 4–104(1)(h). Thus, in order to determine whether Wells Fargo gave HNBT a timely notice of Nevada's dishonor, it is first necessary to establish "the banking day on which [Wells Fargo received] the relevant item or notice . . . "

As indicated above, Wells Fargo received a notice of Nevada's dishonor by telephone on Friday afternoon, December 10, 1971. It sent no notice to HNBT before the midnight deadline on its next banking day, Monday, December 13. Wells Fargo first received written notice from Nevada on Friday, December 17, when the dishonored check arrived in the mail. Notice of dishonor was then sent to HNBT prior to midnight on Monday, December 21, the next banking day following receipt of the *written* notice. Therefore, the first question this court must decide is whether oral notice from the payor bank, Nevada, can trigger the obligation of the collecting bank, Wells Fargo, to give notice to its customer, HNBT.

At first reading, Section 3–508(3) would seem to resolve this question. That section provides, "Notice may be given in any reasonable manner. It may be oral or written . . . " by virtue of Section 4–102(1), § 3–508(3) applies to bank collections unless it conflicts with a specific provision of Article 4. In such a case, the Article 4 provision governs the transaction.

Wells Fargo argues that Section 4–301 supersedes § 3–508 with respect to notice from payor banks and that therefore only written notice from such banks triggers the presenting bank's obligation to pass the notice of dishonor down through the chain of collection. This position appears to be meritorious and has been adopted by several courts. This court, however, need not rule on the specific question.

* * *

Lincoln has raised an issue which dispenses with the need to determine whether oral or written notification is required by the terms of the statute itself. In an introductory section to Article 4, the UCC provides:

"The effect of the provisions of this article may be varied by agreement except that no agreement can disclaim a bank's responsibility for its own lack of good faith or failure to exercise ordinary care or can limit the measure of damages for such lack or failure; but the parties may by agreement determine the standards by which such responsibility is to be measured if such standards are not manifestly unreasonable.

"Federal reserve regulations and operating letters, clearing house rules, and the like, have the effect of agreements under subsection (1), whether or not specifically assented to by all parties interested in items handled." UCC § 4–103(1), (2).

In its affidavits, Lincoln established that the transaction in question was governed by the terms of the Federal Reserve Operating Circular No. 6. At the time of the transaction this operating circular provided that payor banks can—in fact, must—give notice by "wire" when they dishonor items with values in excess of $1,000. "Wire" is expressly defined to include "telephonic" notices. Thus, since this operating circular governed the transaction here in dispute, it is clear that Nevada's telephonic notice was an adequate notice of dishonor, and Wells Fargo was not entitled to wait for written notice.

As is indicated above, Wells Fargo's failure to give timely notice essentially precludes it from prevailing under any of the three counts in its complaint.

Because it takes time to process an item through a bank—whether depositary, intermediary, or payor bank—the midnight deadline presents a problem. If the various steps involved in a day's transaction are to be completed without overtime work, the bank must either close early or fix an earlier cutoff time for the day's work. Accordingly, the Code provides that for the purpose of allowing time to process items, prove balances, and make the necessary entries on its books to determine its position for the day, a bank may fix an afternoon hour of 2:00 P.M. or later as a cutoff hour for the handling of money and items and the making of entries on its books.[5] Items received after the cutoff hour fixed as the close of the banking day are considered to have been received at the opening of the next banking day, and the time for taking action and for determining the bank's midnight deadline begins to run from that point.

Recognizing that if an item is not paid, everyone involved will be greatly inconvenienced, the Code provides that unless otherwise instructed, a collecting bank in a good faith effort to secure payment may, in the case of specific items, waive, modify, or extend the time limits, but not in excess of one additional banking day.[6]

Indorsements When an item is restrictively indorsed with words such as "pay any bank," it is locked into the bank collection system, and only a bank may acquire the rights of a holder.

When a bank forwards an item for collection, it normally indorses it "pay any bank," irrespective of the type of indorsement, if any, that the item carried at the time of receipt. This serves to protect the collecting bank by making it impossible for the item to stray from regular collection channels.

If the item had no indorsement when received by the depositary bank, it may supply any indorsement of its customer that is necessary to title unless the item contains the words "payee's indorsement required" or the equivalent.[7] The depositary bank must examine the item for prior restrictive indorsements. Subsequent intermediary banks and the payor bank need check only the indorsement of its transferor and may rely on the fact that the depositary bank performed its required function.

Warranties Customers and collecting banks give basically the same warranties as those given by parties under Article 3 of the Code on presentment and transfer which were discussed in Chapter 25. Each customer or collecting bank who **transfers** an item and receives a settlement or consideration warrants to his transferee and subsequent transferees that (1) he has good title (that is, the transferor is the true owner or is an authorized agent of the owner); (2) *all* signatures are genuine or authorized; (3) the item has not been materially altered; (4) no defense of any party is good against him; and (5) he has no knowledge of any insolvency proceeding involving the maker or acceptor or the drawer of an unaccepted instrument. Moreover, each customer or collecting bank who obtains payment or acceptance, as well as all prior customers and collecting banks, warrants to the *payor* bank on **presentment** that: (1) she has good title or is authorized to obtain payment; (2) she has no knowledge that the signature of the maker or drawer is unauthorized; and (3) the item has not been materially altered.[8]

Final Payment The provisional settlements made in the collection chain are all directed toward final payment of the item by the payor bank. This is one end of the collection process—the turnaround point from which the

proceeds of the item begin the return flow and provisional settlements become final. For example, a customer of the California Country State Bank may deposit a check drawn on the State of Maine Country National Bank. The check may then take a course such as: from the California Country State Bank to a correspondent bank in San Francisco, to the Federal Reserve Bank of San Francisco, to the Federal Reserve Bank of Boston, to the payor bank. Provisional settlements are made at each step. When the payor bank finally pays the item, the proceeds begin a return flow over the same course.

The critical question, then, is the point in time when the item has been **paid** by the payor bank, because this not only starts the payment process but also affects questions of priority between the item on the one hand and actions such as the filing of a stop payment order against the item. It is clear that final payment occurs at some moment during the processing of the item by the payor bank; however, this moment may be difficult to ascertain.

Under the Code, final payment occurs when the payor bank does any of the following, whichever happens first: (1) pays an item in cash; (2) settles and does not reserve the right to revoke the settlement, or does not have such right through agreement, statute, or clearinghouse rule; (3) makes a provisional settlement and does not revoke it in the time and manner permitted by statute, clearinghouse rule, or agreement; or (4) completes the process of posting the item to the account of the drawer.[9] Posting is normally completed after the following steps have been taken: (a) verifying any signature; (b) ascertaining that sufficient funds are available; (c) affixing a "paid" or other stamp; (d) entering a charge or entry to a customer's account; and (e) correcting or reversing an entry or erroneous action on the item.[10]

Payor Banks

The payor bank or drawee, under its contract of deposit with the drawer, agrees to pay to the payee or his order checks issued by the drawer provided the order is not countermanded and that there are sufficient funds in the drawer's account.

Due to the tremendous increase in volume of bank collections as well as the improved methods of processing items by payor banks, it has become necessary to adopt production-line methods for handling checks to assure an even flow of items on a day-to-day basis. This is necessary if work is to be conducted without abnormal peak loads and overtime. The solution has been the institution of deferred posting procedures whereby items are sorted and proved on the day they are received, but are not posted to customers' accounts or returned until the next banking day. The Code not only approves this procedure but also sets up specific standards to govern its application to the actions of payor banks.

When a payor bank that is not also a depositary bank receives a demand item other than for immediate payment over the counter, it must either return the item or give its transferor a provisional settlement before midnight of the banking day on which the item is received. Otherwise it becomes liable to its transferor for the amount of the item unless it has a valid defense.[11]

If it gives the provisional settlement as required, it then has until its midnight deadline to return the item or, if it is held for protest or is otherwise unavailable for return, to send written notice of dishonor or nonpayment.[12] After doing this, it is entitled to revoke the settlement and recover any payment made. If the payor bank fails to return the item or send notice before its midnight deadline, it becomes accountable for the amount of the item unless it has a valid defense for its inaction.

There are many reasons why a bank may dishonor an item and return it or send notice. The following situations are the most common: the drawer or maker may have no account or may have insufficient funds to cover the item; a signature on the item may be forged; or payment of the item may have been stopped by the drawer or maker.

If a customer's account does not have sufficient funds to pay all items that the bank receives on that account on any given day, the bank may charge them against the account in any order it deems convenient. Items against an account may reach the bank in several different ways on the same day, and it would be unreasonable to require the bank to determine their order of arrival. Items received at the same time but passing through different channels may be posted to the customer's account hours apart. Consequently, a person presenting an item to a payor bank may not object that the bank paid other items received the same day and left his unpaid. His only recourse is to seek remedy against the maker, drawer, or other secondary parties. The owner of the account from which the item was payable also has no basis for complaint that one item rather than another was paid. It is his responsibility to have enough funds on deposit to pay all items chargeable to his account at any time.

RELATIONSHIP BETWEEN PAYOR BANK AND ITS CUSTOMER

The relationship between a payor bank and its checking account customer is primarily the product of their contractual arrangement. Although the parties have relatively broad latitude in establishing the terms of their agreement and altering the provisions of the Code, a bank may not validly (1) disclaim responsibility for its lack of good faith, (2) disclaim responsibility for its failure to exercise ordinary care, or (3) limit its damages for a breach of such lack or failure.[13] The parties may by agreement, however, determine the standards by which such responsibility is to be measured if these standards are not clearly unreasonable.

Payment of an Item

When a payor bank receives an item properly payable from a customer's account but there are insufficient funds in the account to pay it, the bank may (1) dishonor the item and return it, or (2) pay the item and charge its customer's account even though an overdraft is created as a result. The item authorized or directed the bank to make the payment and hence carries with it an enforceable implied promise to reimburse the bank. Further, the customer may be liable to the bank to pay a service charge for the bank's handling of the overdraft or may be liable to pay interest on the amount of the overdraft.

A check or draft, however, is not an assignment of the drawer's funds that are in the possession of the drawee.[14] Moreover, as discussed in Chapter 25, the drawee is not liable on an instrument until he accepts the item. Therefore, the *holder* of a check has no right to require the drawee bank to pay it, whether or not there are sufficient funds in the drawer's account. But if an item is presented to a payor bank and the bank improperly refuses payment, it will incur a liability to its *customer* from whose account the item should have been paid.[15] If the item is not more than six months old, is regular in form, the customer has ade- quate funds on deposit, and there is no other valid basis for the refusal to pay, the bank is liable to its customer for damages proximately caused by the wrongful dishonor. If the dishonor occurs through mistake, liability is limited to actual damages proved, including damages for arrest, prosecution, or other consequential damages.

A payor bank is under no obligation to its customer to pay an uncertified check that is over six months old. This rule reflects the usual banking practice of consulting a depositor before paying an old item on her account. The bank, as shown in the case that follows, is not required to dishonor such an item, and if payment is made in good faith, the bank may charge the amount of the item to its customer's account.

ADVANCED ALLOYS, INC. v. SERGEANT STEEL CORP.
Civil Court of the City of New York, Queens County, 1973.
72 Misc.2d 614, 340 N.Y.S.2d 266.

Facts: Advanced Alloys, Inc., issued a check in the amount of $2,500 to Sergeant Steel Corporation. The check was presented for payment fourteen months later to the Chase Manhattan Bank. Chase Manhattan made payment on the check and charged Advanced Alloy's account. Advanced Alloy now seeks to recover the payment made on the check.

Decision: Judgment for Chase Manhattan granted.

Opinion: **Cohen, J.**   The question presented is whether a bank has a duty of inquiry before paying a check which is stale in that it was presented for payment 14 months after issuance. Prior to the enactment of the Uniform Commercial Code, such a duty existed. [Citation.] However, U.C.C. 4–404 states that:

> A bank is under no obligation to a customer having a checking account to pay a check, other than a certified check, which is presented more than six months after its date, but it may charge its customer's account for a payment made thereafter in good faith.

* * *

Under this statute, it must be determined whether this payment was made "in good faith." Since no evidence was presented on this point and since both plaintiff and defendant The Chase Manhattan Bank, N.A. agree that there are no issues of fact—the case having been presented to the Court on affidavits prepared for a summary judgment motion—the Court must simply decide whether a payment of a check by a drawee bank 14 months after issuance is a payment "in good faith" when made without inquiry of the depositor. U.C.C. 1–201(19) defines "good faith" as "honesty in fact in the conduct or transaction concerned." Under this definition, to which the Official Comment to U.C.C. 4–404 makes reference, it appears that the payment of the stale check, without making such inquiry constitutes a payment "in good faith." [Citation.]

Apparently, when the Code intends to apply a concept of "good faith" beyond "honesty in fact", a broader definition is provided. Thus, with respect to dealings of merchants, U.C.C. 2–103(1)(b) states:

'Good faith' in the case of a merchant means honesty in fact and the observance of reasonable commercial standards of fair dealing in the trade.

Presumably, if it were intended to place a duty of inquiry upon a bank before it could safely pay a stale check, a broader definition of "good faith" would have been made applicable to this situation. It may very well be that in enacting the Code consideration was given, as defendant [Chase] argues, to the vast number of checks being issued and the requirement that a bank accept or refuse to honor a check within a short, prescribed time limit (U.C.C. 4–301, 302), leading to the conclusion that a bank should not be liable for paying stale checks as long as the bank was honest in fact. * * *

The Court realizes that a determination that there is not duty of inquiry puts a substantial burden upon one who issues a check, and then, even for a good reason—as in this case—does not want it to be paid. Since a stop payment order is good for only six months (U.C.C. 4–403(2)), it means that the issuer must, in order to protect himself, either continue to renew the stop payment order every six months or close the account. Apparently, in balancing the problems of the issuer and the bank in this situation, the Code resolved the matter in favor of the bank.

The Court notes the statement in the Official Comment [citation] that normally a bank will not pay a stale check without consulting the depositor and, further that U.C.C. 4–404 does not require a bank to pay a stale check but the bank " * * * is given the option to pay because it may be in a position to know, as in the case of dividend checks, that the drawer wants payment made." Plaintiff argues that this option to pay is given only when the drawee bank is in a position to know that the drawer wants the check to be paid; and in this case the bank could only know this if it made inquiry—something it did not do. However, the language of the Code itself, as indicated above, does not support this argument and does not impose a duty of inquiry upon the bank in the situation presented herein.

Stop Payment Orders

A check drawn on a bank is an order to pay a sum of money and an authorization to charge the amount to the drawer's account. The drawer may countermand this order, however, by means of a **stop payment order.** If the order does not come too late, the bank is bound by it.[16] If the bank inadvertently pays a check over a valid stop order, it is liable to the customer, but only to the extent of the customer's loss resulting from the payment. The bur-

den of establishing the fact and amount of loss is on the customer.

To be effective, a stop payment order must be received by the bank in time to give it a reasonable opportunity to act on it.[16] See *Siniscalchi v. Valley Bank New York*, which follows. An oral stop order is binding on the bank for only fourteen calendar days. Therefore, the normal practice is for a customer to confirm an oral stop order in writing; this order is effective for six months and may be renewed in writing.

SINISCALCHI v. VALLEY BANK OF NEW YORK
District Court, Nassau County, Second District, 1974.
79 Misc.2d 64, 359 N.Y.S.2d 173.

Facts: On Tuesday, June 11, Siniscalchi issued a $200 check on the drawee, Valley Bank. On Saturday morning, June 15, the check was cashed. This transaction, as well as others taking place on that Saturday morning, was not recorded or processed through the bank's bookkeeping system until Monday, June 17. On that date, Siniscalchi arrived at the bank at 9:00 A.M. and asked to place a stop payment order on the check. A bank employee checked the bank records, which at that time indicated the instrument had not cleared the bank. At 9:45 A.M. she gave him a printed notice confirming his request to stop payment. Siniscalchi now seeks to recover the $200 paid on the check.

Decision: Judgment for Valley Bank granted.

Opinion: Mellan, J.   The testimony shows that on Saturday morning, June 15, 1974, the check had been cashed so that the cashing of the check preceded the actual stop order. It is significant that the check was outstanding for nearly a full week before the stop order payment came in.

Section 4–403 of the Uniform Commercial Code provides for the customer's right to stop payment on a check, but specifically provides that the stop payment order must be received at such time and in such manner as to afford the bank a reasonable opportunity to act on the stop payment order prior to other action normally taken by the bank as described in Section 4—303 of the Uniform Commercial Code. Furthermore, the law thus provides that the burden is upon the depositor or customer of the bank to establish the amount of loss which may result from the payment by the bank of an item contrary to a binding stop payment order.

A payment in violation of an effective direction to stop payment is an improper payment even though it is made by mistake or inadvertence. This, however, does not appear to have been the case in this instance since the payment actually anteceded the stop payment order.

It may have been difficult for most depositors without special knowledge of banking practices to realize the multiple details involved in the handling of checks and other banking instruments, but it is clear that the bank must have a reasonable opportunity to act upon stop payment orders. [Citation.] In the case of knowledge, notice and stop orders the effective time for determining whether they were received too late to affect the payment of an item and a charge to the customer's account by reason of such payment is receipt plus a reasonable time for the bank to act on any of these communications. Usually a relatively short time is required to communicate to the bookkeeping department advice of these specific notices, but certainly some time is necessary. In the instant case with the weekend activities all being reflected on the records on the Monday following, the bank certainly did not have a reasonable time to act upon the plaintiff's stop payment order. [Citation.]

Under Section 4–303 of the Uniform Commercial Code a stop payment order comes too late to modify the bank's right of duty to pay a check after the bank has already paid the item in cash. Such is the case in the instant matter and for these reasons I find that the defendant is entitled to judgment.

The fact that a drawer has filed a stop payment order does not automatically relieve her of liability. If the bank honors the stop payment order and returns the check, the holder may bring an action against the drawer. If the holder qualifies as a holder in due course, personal defenses that the drawer might have to such an action would be of no avail.

Bank's Right to Subrogation on Improper Payment

If a payor bank pays an item over a stop payment order or otherwise in violation of its contract with the drawer or maker, the payor bank is subrogated to (obtains) the rights of (a) any holder in due course on the item against the drawer or maker, (b) the payee or any other holder against the drawer or maker, and (c) the drawer or maker against the payee or any other holder.[17] For instance, a bank pays a check over the drawer's stop payment order. The check was presented to the drawee bank by a holder in due course. The drawer's defense is that the check was obtained by fraud in the inducement. The drawee bank is subrogated to the rights of the holder in due course, who would not be subject to the drawer's personal defense and thus can debit the drawer's account. The same would be true if the presenter was the payee against whom the drawer did not have a valid defense.

Customer's Duties

The Code imposes certain affirmative duties on bank customers and fixes time limits within which they must assert their rights.[18] The duties arise and the time starts to run from the time the bank either sends or makes available to its customer a statement of account accompanied by the items paid against the account. The customer is required to exercise reasonable care and promptness to examine the bank statement and items to discover his **unauthorized signature** or any **alteration** on an item. Because he is not presumed to know the signatures of payees or indorsers, this duty of prompt and careful examination applies only to his own signature and alterations, both of which he should be able to detect immediately. If he discovers an unauthorized signature or an alteration, he must notify the bank promptly.

If the customer fails to carry out these duties of prompt examination and notice, he may not assert against the bank his unauthorized signature or any alteration if the bank can show that it suffered a loss because of the customer's failure to carry out these duties promptly.[18]

Furthermore, the customer will lose his rights in a potentially more important situation. Occasionally a forger carries out a series of transactions involving the account of the same individual. Perhaps he is an employee who has access to his employer's checkbook. He may forge one or more checks each month until he is finally detected. The bank, on the other hand, having paid, without objection, one or more of the customer's checks with the false signatures, may be lulled into a false sense of security. Suddenly the forgery is detected by the customer after many months or even years. Under the Code, the bank is not held liable for all such items. The customer must examine the statement and items within a reasonable period, which in no event may exceed fourteen calendar days and may, under the circumstances, be less, and notify the bank. Any alterations or unauthorized signatures on instruments by the same wrongdoer and paid by the bank during that period will still be the responsibility of the bank, but any paid thereafter but before the customer notifies the bank may not be asserted against it. This rule is based on the concept that the loss involved is directly traceable to the customer's negligence, and as a result he should stand the loss.

The bank must, of course, exercise ordinary care in paying the items involved. If it does not, it loses its right to require prompt action on the part of its customer. But, as shown in the case that follows, whether the bank exercised due care or not, the customer must always report an alteration or his unauthorized signature within one year from the time the statement and items were made available to him or be barred from asserting them against the bank. Any **unauthorized indorsement** must be asserted within three years from the time the bank statements and items containing such indorsements are made available to the customer.[18]

TALLY v. AMERICAN SECURITY BANK
United States District Court, District of Columbia, 1982.
355 U.C.C.R.S. 215.

Facts: Tally held a savings account with American Security Bank. On seven occasions, Tally's personal secretary, who received his bank statements and had custody of his passbook, forged Tally's name on withdrawal slips that she then presented to the bank. The secretary obtained $52,825 in this manner. She confessed this to Tally after avoiding detection for several years. Tally brought an action against American Security Bank to recover the funds. The bank moved for partial summary judgment.

Decision: Partial summary judgment for American Security Bank granted.

Opinion: **Greene, J.** § 4–406(1) . . . establishes the duty of a bank customer to review promptly a "statement and items" sent to him or made available to him "in a reasonable manner." Subsection (4) provides that "a customer who does not within one year from the time the statement and items are made available to the customer (subsection (1)) discover and report his unauthorized signature . . . on the face or back of the item . . . is precluded from asserting against the bank such unauthorized signature. . . . " The issue is whether subsection (4) applies when the "item," here a savings withdrawal order, is made available to the customer not through the mail but upon the customer's request.

The U.S. Court of Appeals for this Circuit recently decided that § 4–406 applies to savings as well as checking accounts. *Boutros v. Riggs National Bank* [citation.] *Boutros* also held that savings withdrawal slips are "items" within the meaning of § 4–406. Subsection (4), however, was not in issue in *Boutros*, and the plaintiff urges first, that it is not applicable to savings accounts even if the other subsections are, and second, if the subsection is applicable, the one-year time bar attaches only when the savings statements sent to the customer are accompanied by the negotiated items supporting the statement's entries. The court rejects both contentions.

In order to hold that subsections (2) and (3) were applicable to allegedly unauthorized savings withdrawal orders, the Court of Appeals in *Boutros* necessarily had to find that when banks send periodic statements to savings customers while keeping the withdrawal orders on file they are "mak[ing] the statement and items available to the customer" within the meaning of § 4–406(1). No reason is apparent from the face of § 4–406 or from the comments to it to suspect that subsection (1) and subsection (4) apply to different kinds of banking transactions. Indeed, subsection (4) expressly incorporates subsection (1) by reference. It is not illogical to suppose that the drafters of the UCC expected a customer to make inquiries of his bank if his savings account balance, as stated on the mailed statement, appeared inexplicably low. Upon these inquiries, the savings withdrawal slips would then be "made available."

It is not necessary now to decide whether the one year should run from the time the customer receives his statement or from the time the slips are made available for inspection. If the appropriate starting point were the latter, the law would have to require that the request for the items be made reasonably promptly after issuance of the statement, or the objective of finality would be undermined. In the instant case, the last allegedly wrongful savings withdrawal took place over three years before the plaintiff notified the bank that his account was awry. It is unclear whether he asked to see the withdrawal orders at this time, but even if he did so, it was too late to fall within a reasonable interpretation of § 4–406(4).

The court is mindful that § 4–406 should not be interpreted so as to give banks more protection than was intended by the drafters of the UCC or by Congress when it adopted the provision for the District of Columbia. [Citation.] It is this court's view, however, that if § 4–406 is to be segmented into subsections that apply to checking accounts and subsections that apply to savings accounts, it is for the legislating body to do. The court holds, therefore, that subsection (4) bars assertion of the savings account claims as the bank was not notified of the irregularities until over three years after the last withdrawal was effected.

* * *

Ordered That said motion be and it is hereby granted. The court dismisses with prejudice that portion of the plaintiff's claim based on allegedly forged . . . savings withdrawal orders paid by defendant. . . .

ELECTRONIC FUND TRANSFERS

We mentioned earlier that the use of commercial paper for payment has transformed the United States into a virtually cashless society. The advent and technological advances of computers make it likely that in the foreseeable future electronic fund transfer systems (EFTs) will bring about a checkless society. Financial institutions seek to substitute EFTs for checks for two principal reasons. The first is to eliminate the ever-increasing paperwork involved in processing the billions of checks that are issued annually. The second is to eliminate the "float" that a drawer of a check currently enjoys as a result of maintaining the use of his funds during the check processing period between issuing the check and final payment.

An **electronic fund transfer** has been defined as "any transfer of funds, other than a transaction originated by check, draft, or similar paper instrument, which is initiated through an electronic terminal, telephonic instrument, or computer or magnetic tape so as to order, instruct, or authorize a financial institution to debit or credit an account." For example, with EFTs, Carl in New York would be able to pay a debt he owes to Joanne in Illinois by entering into his computer an order to his bank to pay Joanne. The drawee bank would then instantly debit Carl's account and transfer the credit to Joanne's bank, where Joanne's account would immediately be credited in that amount. The entire transaction would be completed in minutes. The following case presents the issue of whether an informal telephone conversation with a bank official to pay a named party constitutes an EFT.

KASHANCHI v. TEXAS COMMERCE MEDICAL BANK, N.A.
United States Court of Appeals, Fifth Circuit, 1983.
703 F.2d 936.

Facts: Morvarid Kashanchi and her sister, Firoyeh Paydar, held a savings account with Texas Commerce Medical Bank. An unauthorized withdrawal of $4,900 from the account was allegedly made by means of a telephone conversation between some other unidentified individual and a bank employee. Paydar learned of the transfer of funds when she received her bank statement and notified the bank that the withdrawal was unauthorized. The bank, however, declined to recredit the account for the $4,900 transfer. Kashanchi brought an action against the bank, claiming that the bank had violated the Electronic Fund Transfer Act. The district court dismissed the complaint for lack of subject matter jurisdiction, finding that the transaction in question was not governed by the Act. Kashanchi appealed.

Decision: Judgement affirmed.

Opinion: **Randall, J.** This is apparently the first case in which we have been called upon to interpret any of the substantive provisions of the EFTA. . . .

The parties agree that the telephonic transfer that allegedly occurred in this case falls within the broad definition of "electronic fund transfers" in the Act:

(T)he term "electronic fund transfer" means any transfer of funds, other than a transaction originated by check, draft, or similar paper instrument, which is initiated through an electronic terminal, telephonic instrument, or computer or magnetic tape so as to order, instruct, or authorize a financial institution to debit or credit an account. Such term includes, but is not limited to, point-of-sale transfers, automated teller machine transactions, direct deposits or withdrawals of funds, and transfers initiated by telephone.

[Citation.] Some of what Congress has given, however, it has also taken away. Excluded from the definition of an electronic fund transfer is

any transfer of funds which is initiated by a telephone conversation between a consumer and an officer or employee of a financial institution which is not pursuant to a prearranged plan and under which periodic or recurring transfers are not contemplated. . . .

[Citation.] The plaintiff concedes that the unauthorized transfer of her funds was not made "pursuant to any prearranged plan," and that it was made by an employee of the bank.

* * *

Many aspects of electronic fund transfer systems are undergoing evolutionary changes and, thus, projections about future events necessarily involve a degree of speculation. Consequently, the appropriate approach to those new financial service concepts is, in general, to permit further development in a free market environment and, to the extent possible, in a manner consistent with the nature and purpose of existing law and regulations governing financial services. [Citation.] The absence of discussion about informal personal phone transfers would seem to indicate an intent not to cover these transfers, or at least an absence of congressional concern about them, in light if the extensive discussion throughout the hearings and reports of the other existing types of electronic transfers. It is highly unlikely that this silence was a result of congressional ignorance of the problem since these informal phone withdrawals presumably had been occurring since shortly after the time of Alexander Graham Bell.

* * *

Finally, we note that the EFTA was passed because "(e)xisting law and regulations in the consumer protection area are not appliable to some aspects of the new financial service concepts." [Citations.] The plaintiff suggests in her reply brief that she would have no adequate legal remedy for the wrong she has suffered if she were denied relief under the EFTA. While she conceded at oral argument that she might have an action under state law for conversion or breach of contract (her deposit agreement with the bank), she maintained that a person suffering a loss resulting from the abuse of one of the other electronic fund transfer systems would also have such an action under state law.

The plaintiff ignores the essential difference between electronic fund transfer systems and personal transfers by phone or by check. When the bank employee allegedly agreed to withdraw funds from the plaintiff's account, he or she presumably could have asked some questions to ascertain whether the caller was one of the account holders. The failure to attempt to make a positive identification of the caller might be considered negligence or a breach of the deposit agreement under state law. When someone makes an unauthorized use of an electronic fund transfer system, however, the financial institution often has no way of knowing that the transfer is unauthorized. For example, in order to make a transfer at an automatic teller machine, a person need only possess the machine card and know the correct personal identification number. The computer cannot determine whether the person who has inserted the card and typed in the magic number is authorized to use the system. What might be a withdrawal negligently permitted by the financial institution in one situation might not be a negligent action in the other.

Our analysis of both the language of the EFTA and the legislative history of the Act leads us to conclude that Congress intended to exclude from the Act's coverage any transfer of funds initiated by a phone conversation between any natural person and an officer or employee of a financial institution, which was not made pursuant to a prearranged plan and under which periodic and recurring transfers were not contemplated. Accordingly, we hold that the withdrawal of funds from the plaintiff's account is not covered by the Act even though said withdrawal allegedly was not made by either the plaintiff or her sister.

Although EFTs are still fairly new, their use has brought about considerable confusion concerning the legal rights of customers and financial institutions. A partial solution to these legal issues was provided in 1978 by Congress when it enacted the Electronic Fund Transfer Act, which we discuss below. But, many important legal problems remain. A committee of the Permanent Editorial Board of the Uniform Commercial Code is in the process of drafting a New Payments Code to deal with EFTs.

Types of Electronic Fund Transfers

Although it is highly probable that a number of new EFTs will appear in the coming years, at the moment there are principally four EFTs in use: (1) automated teller machines, (2) point-of-sale systems, (3) direct deposit and withdrawal of funds, and (4) pay-by-phone systems.

Automated Teller Machines Automated teller machines (ATMs) are rapidly becoming available throughout the country. ATMs permit customers to conduct various transactions with their bank through the use of electronic terminals. After activating an ATM with a plastic identification card and a secret number, customers can deposit and withdraw funds from their accounts, transfer funds between accounts, obtain cash advances from bank credit card accounts, and make payments on loans.

Point-of-Sale Systems Point-of-sale (POS) systems permit consumers to transfer funds from their bank accounts to a merchant automatically. The POS machines are located within the merchant's store and are activated by the consumer's identification card and code. The computer will then instantaneously debit the consumer's account and credit the merchant's account.

Direct Deposits and Withdrawals Another type of EFT involves direct deposits made to a customer's account through an electronic terminal when the deposit has been authorized in advance by the consumer. Examples include direct payroll deposits, deposits of Social Security payments, and deposits of pension payments. Conversely, automatic withdrawals are preauthorized electronic fund transfers from the customer's account for regular payments to some party other than the financial institution where the funds are deposited. Automatic withdrawals to pay insurance premiums, utility bills, or automobile loan payments are common examples of this type of EFT.

Pay-by-Phone Systems Recently some financial institutions have instituted a service that permits customers to pay bills by telephoning the bank's computer system and directing transfer of funds to a designated third party. This service also permits customers to transfer funds between accounts.

Electronic Fund Transfer Act

In 1978 Congress determined that the use of electronic systems to transfer funds provided the potential for substantial benefits to consumers. But because of the unique characteristics of such systems, the application of existing consumer protection legislation was unclear, leaving the rights and obligations of consumers and financial institutions undefined. Accordingly, Congress enacted Title IX of the Consumer Protection Act, called the Electronic Fund Transfer Act, to "provide a basic framework establishing the rights, liabilities, and responsibilities of participants in electronic fund transfers" with primary emphasis on "the provision of individual consumer rights." Because the act deals exclusively with the protection of consumers, it does not govern electronic transfers between financial institutions, between financial institutions and businesses, and between businesses. The act is similar in many respects to the Fair Credit Billing Act (see Chapter 41), which applies to credit card transactions. The Electronic Fund Transfer Act is administered by the Board of Governors of the Federal Reserve System, which is authorized to make regulations to carry out the purposes of the act.

Disclosure The act is primarily a disclosure statute and as such requires that the terms and conditions of electronic fund transfers involving a consumer's account be disclosed in readily understandable language at the time the consumer contracts for such services. Included among the required disclosures are the consumer's liability for unauthorized transfers, the kinds of EFTs allowed, any charges for transfers or the right to make transfers, the consumer's right to stop payment of preauthorized EFTs, the consumer's right to receive documentation of EFTs, and the financial institution's liability to the consumer under the act.

Documentation and Periodic Statements The act requires the financial institution to provide the consumer with written documentation of each transfer made from an electronic terminal at the time of the transfer. The documentation must clearly state the amount involved, the date, the type of transfer, the identity of the consumer's accounts involved, the identity of any third party involved, and the location of the terminal involved. In addition, the financial institution must provide each consumer with a periodic statement for each account of the consumer that may be accessed by means of an EFT.

Preauthorized Transfers A preauthorized transfer *from* a consumer's account must be authorized in advance by the consumer in *writing*, and a copy of the authorization must be provided to the consumer when made. A consumer may stop payment of a preauthorized EFT by notifying the financial institution orally or in writing at any time up to three business days before the scheduled date of the transfer. The financial institution may require the consumer to provide written confirmation within fourteen days of an oral notification.

Error Resolution The consumer has sixty days after the financial institution sends a periodic statement in which to notify the financial institution of any errors that appear on that statement. The financial institution is required to investigate and report the results within ten business days. If the financial institution needs more than ten days to investigate, it may take up to forty-five days, provided it recredits the consumer's account for the amount alleged to be in error. If it determines that an error did occur, it must properly correct the error. Failure to investigate in good faith makes the financial institution liable to the consumer for treble damages (that is, three times the amount of provable damages).

Consumer Liability A consumer's liability for unauthorized electronic fund transfer is limited to a maximum of $50 if the consumer notifies the financial institution within *two days* after he learns of the loss or theft. If the consumer does not report the loss or theft within two days, he is liable for losses up to $500. If the consumer fails to report the unauthorized use within *sixty days* of transmittal of a periodic statement, he is liable for losses resulting from *any* unauthorized EFT that appeared on the statement if the financial institution can show that the loss would not have

occurred but for the failure of the consumer to report the loss within sixty days.

Liability of Financial Institution A financial institution is liable to a consumer for all damages proximately caused by its failure to make an EFT according to the terms and conditions of an account, in the correct amount or in a timely manner when properly instructed to do so by the consumer. There are, however, some exceptions. The financial institution will not be liable if

1. the consumer's account has insufficient funds through no fault of the financial institution,
2. the funds are subject to legal process,
3. such transfer would exceed an established credit limit,
4. an electronic terminal has insufficient cash, or
5. circumstances beyond the financial institution's control prevent the transfer.

The financial institution is also liable for failure to stop payment of a preauthorized transfer from a consumer's account when instructed to do so in accordance with the terms and conditions of the account.

CHAPTER SUMMARY

Collection of Items	**Depositary Bank** the bank in which the payee or holder deposits a check for credit
	Provisional Credit tentative credit for the deposit of an instrument until final credit is given
	Final Credit payment of the instrument by the payor bank; if the payor bank (drawee) does not pay the check the depositary bank reverses the provisional credit
	Intermediary Bank a bank involved in the collection process other than the depositary or payor bank
	Collecting Bank any bank handling the item for payment other than the payor bank
	■ *Agency* a collecting bank is an agent or subagent of the owner of the check until the settlement becomes final
	■ *Duty of Care* a collecting bank must exercise ordinary care in handling an item
	■ *Duty to Act Seasonably* a collecting bank acts seasonably if it takes proper action before its midnight deadline (midnight of the next banking day)

- *Indorsements*   if an item is restrictively indorsed "for deposit only," only a bank may be a holder
- *Warranties*   customer and collecting banks give warranties on transfer and presentment
- *Final Payment*   occurs when the payor bank does any of the following, whichever happens first: (1) pays an item in cash; (2) settles and does not have the right to revoke the settlement; (3) makes a provisional settlement and does not properly revoke it; or (4) completes the process of posting the item to the account of the drawer

Payor Bank   under its contract with the drawer, the payor or drawee bank agrees to pay to the payee or his order checks that are issued by the drawer, provided the order is not countermanded by a stop payment order and provided there are sufficient funds in the drawer's account

Relationship between Payor Bank and Its Customer

Contractual Relationship   the relationship between a payor bank and its checking account customer is primarily the product of their contractual arrangement

Payment of an Item   when a payor receives an item for which there are insufficient funds in the account, the bank may either dishonor the item and return it or pay the item and charge the customer's account even though an overdraft is created

Stop Payment Orders   an oral stop payment order (a command from a drawer to a drawee not to pay an instrument) is binding for fourteen calendar days; a written order is effective for six months and may be renewed in writing

Bank's Right to Subrogation on Improper Payment   if a payor bank pays an item over a stop payment order or otherwise in violation of its contract, the payor bank is subrogated to (obtains) the right of (a) any holder in due course on the item against the drawer or maker; (b) the payee or any other holder against the drawer or maker; and (c) the drawer or maker against the payee or any other holder

Customer's Duties   the customer must exercise reasonable care and promptness in examining the bank statement and items to discover any unauthorized signatures or alterations

Electronic Fund Transfers

Definition   any transfer of funds, other than a transaction originated by check, draft, or similar paper instrument, which is initiated through an electronic terminal, telephonic instrument, or computer or magnetic tape so as to order, instruct, or authorize a financial institution to debit or credit an account

Purpose   to eliminate the paperwork involved in processing checks and the "float" of a drawer of a check

Types of Electronic Fund Transfers

- *Automatic teller machines*
- *Point-of-sale systems*
- *Direct deposits and withdrawals*
- *Pay-by-phone systems*

Electronic Fund Transfer Act   provides a basic framework establishing the rights, liabilities, and responsibilities of participants in consumer electronic fund transfers

QUESTIONS

1. Distinguish among depositary, payor, intermediary, and collecting banks.
2. Define provisional credit and discuss when the credit becomes final.
3. Discuss the duties of collecting banks.
4. Discuss the obligations between a customer and the drawee bank.
5. Define electronic fund transfer and outline the major provisions of the Electronic Fund Transfer Act.

PROBLEMS

1. On December 9 Jane Jones writes a check for $500 payable to Ralph Rodgers in payment for goods to be received later in the month. Before the close of business on the ninth, Jane notifies the bank by telephone to stop payment on the check. On Monday, December 19, Ralph gives the check to Bill Briggs for value and without notice. On the twentieth, Bill deposits the check in his account at Bank A. On the twenty first, Bank A sends the check to its correspondent, Bank B. On the twenty-second, Bank B presents the check through the clearinghouse to Bank C. On the twenty-third, Bank C presents the check to Bank P, the payor bank. On December 28 the payor bank makes payment of the check final. Jane Jones sues the payor bank. Decision?

2. Howard Harrison, a long-time customer of Western Bank, operates a small department store, Harrison's Store. Because his store has few experienced employees, Harrison frequently travels throughout the United States on buying trips, although he also runs the financial operations of the business. On one of his buying trips, Harrison purchased a gross of sport shirts from Well-Made Shirt Company and paid for the transaction with a check on his store account with Western Bank in the amount of $1,000. Adams, an employee of Well-Made who deposits its checks in Security Bank, sloppily raised the amount of the check to $10,000 and indorsed the check, "Pay to the order of Adams from Pension Plan benefits, Well-Made Shirt Company by Adams." He cashes the check and cannot be found. The check is processed and paid by the Western Bank and is sent to Harrison's Store with the monthly statement. After brief examination of the statement, Harrison leaves on another buying trip for three weeks.

(a) Assuming the bank acted in good faith and the alteration is not discovered and reported to the bank until an audit conducted thirteen months after the statement was received by Harrison's Store, who must bear the loss on the raised check?

(b) Assuming that Harrison, because he was unable to examine his statement promptly because of his buying trips, left instructions with the bank to carefully examine and to notify him of any item over $5,000 to be charged to his account, and the bank paid the item anyway in his absence, who bears the loss if (a) the alteration is discovered one month after the statement was received by Harrison's Store, (b) the alteration is discovered thirteen months later?

3. Tom Jones owed Bank of Cleveland $10,000 on a note due November 17, with 1 percent interest due the bank for each day delinquent in payment. Tom Jones issued a $10,000 check to Bank of Cleveland and deposited it in the night vault the evening of November 17. Several days later, he received a letter saying he owed one day's interest on the payment because of one day delinquency in payment. Jones refused because he said he had put it in the vault on November 17. Decision?

4. Assume that Davis draws a check on Dallas Bank payable to the order of Perkins; that Perkins indorses it to Cooper; that Cooper deposits it to her account in Houston Bank; that Houston Bank presents it to Dallas Bank, the drawee; and that Dallas Bank dishonors it because of insufficient funds. Houston Bank receives notification of the dishonor on Monday. Houston Bank fails to notify Cooper until Wednesday. What result?

5. Jones, a food wholesaler whose company has an account with B Bank in New York City, is traveling in California on business. He finds a particularly attractive offer and decides to buy a carload of oranges, for delivery in New York. He gives Smith, the seller, his company's check for $25,000 to pay for the purchase. Smith deposits the check, with others he received that day, with his bank, the C Bank. C Bank sends the check to D Bank in Los Angeles which in turn deposits it with the Los Angeles Federal Reserve Bank. The L.A. Fed. sends the check, with others, to the N.Y. Fed. The N.Y. Fed. forwards the check to B Bank, Jones's bank, for collection.

(a) Is B Bank a depositary bank? A collecting bank? A payor bank?

(b) Is C Bank a depositary bank? A collecting bank?

(c) Is the N.Y. Fed. an intermediary bank?

(d) Is D Bank a collecting bank?
   Explain.

6. On April 1, Moore gave Pipkin a check properly drawn by Moore on Zebra Bank for $500 in payment of a painting to be framed and delivered the next day. Pipkin immediately indorsed the check and gave it to Yeager Bank as payment in full of his indebtedness to the bank on a note he previously had signed. Yeager Bank canceled the note and returned it to Pipkin.

On April 2, on learning that the painting had been destroyed in a fire at Pipkin's studio, Moore promptly went to Zebra Bank, signed a printed form of stop payment order, and gave it to the cashier. Zebra Bank refused payment on the check on proper presentment by Yeager Bank.

(a) What are the rights of Yeager Bank against Zebra Bank?

(b) What are the rights of Yeager Bank against Moore?

(c) Assuming that Zebra Bank, by inadvertence, had paid the amount of the check to Yeager Bank and debited Moore's account, what are the rights of Moore against Zebra Bank?

7. As payment in advance for services to be performed, Acton signed and delivered the following instrument:

December 2, 1990

LAST NATIONAL BANK
MONEYVILLE, ILLINOIS

Pay to the order of Olaf Owen $1,500.00 _____ Fifteen Hundred Dollars _____ For services to be performed by Olaf Owen starting on December 7, 1990.

(signed) Arthur Acton

Owen requested and received Last National Bank's certification of the check even though Acton had only $900 on deposit. Owen indorsed the check in blank and delivered it to Dan Doty in payment of a pre-existing debt.

When Owen failed to appear for work, Acton gave a written stop payment order to the bank ordering the bank not to pay the check. Doty presented the check to Last National Bank for payment. The bank refused payment.

What are the bank's rights and liabilities relating to the transactions described?

8. Jones drew a check for $1,000 on The First Bank and mailed it to the payee, Thrift, Inc. Caldwell stole the check from Thrift, Inc., chemically erased the name of the payee, and inserted the name of Henredon as payee. Caldwell also increased the amount of the check to $10,000 and, by using the name of Henredon, negotiated the check to Willis. Willis then took the check to The First Bank and obtained its certification on the check. Willis then negotiated the check to Griffin, who deposited the

check in The Second National Bank for collection. The Second National forwarded the check to the Detroit Trust Company for collection from The First Bank, which honored the check. Griffin exhausted her account in the Second National Bank, and the account was closed. Shortly thereafter, The First Bank learned that it had paid an altered check.

What are the rights of each of the parties? Assume that all parties (except Caldwell) are respectively holders in due course.

9. On July 21, Boehmer, a customer of Brimingham Trust, secured a loan from that bank for the principal sum of $5,500 in order to purchase a boat allegedly being built for him by A. C. Manufacturing Company, Inc. After Boehmer signed a promissory note, Birmingham Trust issued a cashier's check to Boehmer and A. C. Manufacturing Company as payees. The check was given to Boehmer, who then forged A. C. Manufacturing Company's indorsement and deposited the check in his own account at Central Bank. Central Bank credited Boehmer's account and then placed the legend "P.I.G.," meaning "Prior Indorsements Guaranteed," on the check. The check was presented to and paid by Birmingham Trust on July 22. When the loan became delinquent in March of the following year, Birmingham Trust contacted A. C. Manufacturing Company to learn the location of the boat. They were informed that it had never been purchased, and they soon after learned that Boehmer had died on January 24 of that year. On May 1 Birmingham Trust sought reimbursement from Central Bank under the latter's warranty of prior indorsements. Decision?

10. Jason, who has extremely poor vision, went to an ATM to withdraw $200 on February 1. Joshua saw that Jason was having great difficulty reading the computer screen and offered to help. Joshua obtained Jason's secret pass number and secretly exchanged one of his old credit cards for Jason's ATM card. Between February 1 and February 15, Joshua withdrew $1,600 from Jason's account. On February 15 Jason discovered that his ATM card was missing and immediately notified his bank. The bank closed Jason's ATM account on February 16, by which time Joshua had withdrawn another $150. What is Jason's liability, if any, for the unauthorized use of his account?

<hr>

ENDNOTES

1. Uniform Commercial Code, Section 4—105, "Depository Bank"; "Intermediary Bank"; "Collect-

ing Bank"; "Payor Bank"; "Presenting Bank"; "Remitting Bank".

2. Uniform Commercial Code, Section 4—104, Definitions and Index of Definitions.

3. Uniform Commercial Code, Section 4—201, Presumption and Duration of Agency Status of Collecting Banks and Provisional Status of Credits; Applicability of Article; Item Indorsed "Pay Any Bank".

4. Uniform Commercial Code, Section 4—202, Responsibility for Collection; When Action Seasonable.

5. Uniform Commercial Code, Section 4—107, Time of Receipt of Items.

6. Uniform Commercial Code, Section 4—108, Delays.

7. Uniform Commercial Code, Section 4—205, Supplying Missing Indorsement; No Notice from Prior Indorsement.

8. Uniform Commercial Code, Section 4—207, Warranties of Customer and Collecting Bank on Transfer or Presentment of Items; Time for Claims.

9. Uniform Commercial Code, Section 4—213, Final Payment of Item by Payor Bank; When Provisional Debits and Credits Become Final; When Certain Credits Become Available for Withdrawal.

10. Uniform Commercial Code, Section 4—109, Process of Posting.

11. Uniform Commercial Code, Section 4—302,, Payor Bank's Responsibility for Late Return of Item.

12. Uniform Commercial Code, Section 4—301, Deferred Posting: Recovery of Payment by Return of Items; Time of Dishonor.

13. Uniform Commercial Code, Section 4—103, Variation by Agreement; Measure of Damages; Certain Action Constituting Ordinary Care.

14. Uniform Commercial Code, Section 3—409, Draft Not an Assignment.

15. Uniform Commercial Code, Section 4—402, Bank's Liability to Customer for Wrongful Dishonor.

16. Uniform Commercial Code, Section 4—403, Customer's Right to Stop Payment; Burden of Proof of Loss.

17. Uniform Commercial Code, Section 4—407, Payor Bank's Right to Subrogation on Improper Payment.

18. Uniform Commercial Code, Section 4—406, Customer's Duty to Discover and Report Unauthorized Signature or Alteration.

PART 5
AGENCY

In considering Part Five, Agency, you should keep in mind the importance of the agency relationship in permitting business enterprises—proprietorships, partnerships, and corporations—to expand their business activities. Agency, as we fully explore in the next two chapters, is a relationship between two persons whereby one of them (the agent) is authorized to act for and on behalf of the other (principal). Within the scope of the authority granted to her by her principal, the agent may negotiate the terms of contracts with others and bind her principal to such contracts. An agent may be an employee of the principal, but this is not necessary.

If the law were to require each party to a business transaction to participate personally and directly in carrying out the transaction, the ability of any person to conduct a business enterprise would be limited by the number of transactions that he could *personally* negotiate. This would severely curtail the size and operation of every business unit and practically paralyze commercial activity. Furthermore, it would make the conduct of business by a corporation impossible, because as an artificial legal entity a corporation can act only through its agents, officers, and employees. Moreover, it would radically change the fundamental rule of the law of partnership that every partner is an agent of the partnership with respect to the conduct of its business. The agency concept is therefore indispensable to modern trade and commerce. Through the use of agents, one person may enter into any number of business transactions with the same effect as if done by him personally and in no more time than he would normally require to negotiate a single contract. A person may thus multiply and expand his business activities.

Because of the enormous economic significance of agency, it is important to consider the social costs that may be imposed by the use of agents and the public policy considerations that determine the allocation of these costs among those who use agents, the agents themselves, third parties with whom they deal, and society at large.

Because of the power an agent has to bind her principal in contracts, the law imposes a number of obligations on the agent, including the duties of loyalty, diligence, and obedience. For example, the duty of loyalty requires an agent to act exclusively for her principal and to promote the interests of her principal. But what if her principal is engaged in unlawful conduct such as selling adulterated food or polluting a stream? Should the agent's duty of loyalty to her principal control, or is there a higher duty owed to society that requires the agent to disclose the criminal activities? If the agent does disclose publicly, may the principal discharge the agent? The long-standing rule has been that if the agency or employment relationship is not for a definite term, the principal or employer is free to terminate the relationship for cause, no cause, or "bad" cause. Some courts, however, have made an exception to this rule where the agent's disclosure protects the public interest, especially where there is a definite violation of a criminal statute by the principal or employer.

What if an agent, while pursuing her principal's business, tortiously injures a third party? Who should bear the responsibility for the loss? The principal would argue that he did not cause the harm and that the responsibility is solely the agent's. The third party would assert that the agent would not have caused the harm had she not been engaged in carrying on the principal's business. The law has imposed civil liability for the loss on the agent *and*, when the agent was an employee acting within the scope of her employment, *also* on the principal. The liability of the principal is vicarious and called *respondeat superior*. William Prosser and W. Page Keeton, eminent authorities on the law of torts, have explained the policy reasons for this doctrine:

> What has emerged as the modern justification for vicarious liability is a rule of policy, a deliberate allocation of a risk. The losses caused by the torts of employees, which as a practical matter are sure to occur in the conduct of the employer's enterprise, are placed upon that enterprise itself, as a required cost of doing business. They are placed upon the employer because, having engaged in an enterprise, which will on the basis of all past experience involve harm to others through the torts of employees, and sought to profit by it, it is just that he, rather than the innocent injured plaintiff, should bear them; and because he is better able to absorb them, and to distribute them, through prices, rates or liability insurance, to the public, and so to shift them to society, to the community at large. Added to this is the makeweight argument that an employer who is held strictly liable is under the greatest incentive to be careful in the selection, instruction and supervision of his servants, and to take every precaution to see that the enterprise is conducted safely. Notwithstanding the occasional condemnation of the entire doctrine which used to appear in the past, the tendency is clearly to justify it on such grounds, and gradually to extend it. Keeton, *Prosser and Keeton on Torts*, 5th ed. 500–501 (footnotes omitted).

Similar issues are raised by the question of whether a principal should be held *criminally* liable for an agent's violation of the criminal law. When the principal has actually authorized the agent to commit the crime, the answer is simple: both the principal and the agent are criminally liable. But when the principal has not expressly authorized the criminal act, the question is much more difficult, because imposing vicarious criminal liability raises distinctly different policy considerations than imposing vicarious civil liability. The purposes of the criminal law are to punish and deter offensive conduct; tort law attempts to compensate injured parties and redistribute loss. Accordingly, as a general rule, a principal is not ordinarily liable for the unauthorized criminal acts of his agents. There has been a trend, however, to impose a criminal penalty on an employer where the criminal act is that of an advisory or managerial person acting in the scope of employment. Moreover, where a crime does not require intent, an employer may be held subject to a penalty for acts of employees acting within the scope of employment.

Finally, to what extent should an agent have the power to bind his principal contractually to third parties? The answer to this question constitutes the keystone of the law of agency and is addressed in detail in Chapter 28. The competing policy interests are clear: the principal wishes to be bound only to those contracts he actually authorized the agent to form, whereas third parties want the principal bound to all contracts that the agent negotiates on the principal's behalf. The law of agency has chosen an intermediate outcome—the principal is bound to those contracts he actually authorized *plus* those the principal has by word or conduct *apparently* authorized the agent to negotiate.

27 RELATIONSHIP OF PRINCIPAL AND AGENT

The law of agency, like the law of contracts, is basic to almost every other branch of business law. Practically every type of contract or business transaction can be created or conducted through an agent. Therefore, the place and importance of agency in the practical conduct and operation of business cannot be overemphasized, particularly in the case of partnerships and corporations. Partnership is founded on the agency of the partners. Each partner is an agent of the partnership and as such has the authority to represent and bind the partnership in all usual transactions pertaining to the partnership business. Corporations must function through the agency of its officers and employees. Thus, practically and legally, agency is an integral part of partnerships and corporations. Agency, however, is not limited to these business associations. Sole proprietors may also employ agents in the operations of their businesses. Business, therefore, is very largely conducted, not by the proprietors of business, but by their representatives or agents.

By using agents, one person (the principal) may enter into any number of business transactions as though he had carried them out personally. A person may thus multiply and expand his business activities. Although there is some overlap, the law of agency divides broadly into two main parts: the internal and external parts. An agent functions as an agent by dealing with third persons. It is in this way that legal relations are established between the principal and third persons. These relations are the external part of agency law, which we discuss in the next chapter. In this chapter, however, we consider the nature and function of agency, as well as other topics of the internal part of the law of agency.

Agency is primarily governed by State common law. An orderly presentation of this law is found in the Restatements of the Law of Agency. The first Restatement was adopted on June 30, 1933, by the American Law Institute. On April 11, 1958, the institute adopted a revised edition of the Restatement, the Restatement, Second, Agency, which will be referred to as the Restatement. The Restatements have been regarded as a valuable authoritative reference work and are extensively cited and quoted in reported judicial opinions.

NATURE OF AGENCY

Agency is the relation existing between two persons known as **principal** and **agent** through which the agent is authorized to act for and on behalf of the principal.[1] An agent is therefore one who represents another, the principal, in business dealings with third persons. Three persons are involved in the operation of **agency:** the principal, the agent, and a third person. In dealings with a third person, the agent acts for and in the name and place of the principal. The parties to the transaction, which is usually contractual, are the principal and the third person. The agent is not a party but simply an intermediary. The result of the agent's functioning is exactly the same as if the principal had dealt directly with the third person and without the intervention of an agent. When the agent is dealing with the third person, the principal, in legal effect, is present in the person of the agent.

Within the scope of the authority granted to her by her principal, the agent may negotiate the terms of contracts with others and bind her principal to such contracts. Moreover, the negligence of an agent who is an employee in conducting the business of her principal exposes the principal to tort liability for injury and loss to third persons. A duly authorized agent may effect a transfer of her principal's title to real estate or personal property. The old maxim "*Qui facet per alium, facet per se*" ("Who acts through another, acts himself") accurately describes the relationship between principal and agent.

Scope of Agency Purposes

As a general rule, whatever business activity a person may accomplish personally, he may do through an agent. Conversely, whatever he cannot legally do himself, he cannot authorize another to do for him. Thus a person may not validly authorize another to commit on his behalf an illegal act or crime. Any such agreement is illegal and therefore unenforceable.[2] Also, a person may not appoint an agent to perform acts that are so personal that their performance may not be delegated to another, as in the case of a contract for personal services.[3] For example, Howard, a painter, contracts to paint a portrait of Doris. Howard has one of his students execute the painting and tenders it to Doris. This is not a valid tender, as the duty to paint Doris's portrait is not delegable.

Other Legal Relations

Two other legal relationships are closely related to agency: employer-employee and principal-independent contractor. In the **employment relationship** (historically referred to as the master-servant relationship), the employer has the right to *control* the physical conduct of the employee.[4] In contrast, a person who engages an **independent contractor** to do a specific job does *not* have the right to control the conduct and activities of the independent contractor in the performance of his contract.[4] The latter simply contracts to do a job and is free to choose the method and manner to perform the job. For example, a full-time chauffeur is an employee, whereas a taxicab driver hired to carry a person to the airport is an independent contractor of the passenger.

Although all employees are agents, not all agents are employees. Agents who are not employees are independent contractors. For instance, an attorney retained to handle a particular transaction would be an independent contractor-agent regarding that particular transaction. Finally, not all independent contractors are agents. For example, if Pam hires Bill to build a stone wall around her property, Bill is an independent contractor who is not an agent.

The distinction between employee and independent contractor has a number of important legal consequences. As we discuss in the next chapter, a principal is liable for the torts committed by an employee within the scope of his employment but ordinarily is not liable for torts committed by an independent contractor. To illustrate: Post, owner, and Ingram, a building contractor, enter into a contract under which Ingram agrees to build a house for Post, in accordance with certain plans and specifications, at an agreed cost. If, in the course of the work, one of Ingram's workers, Walters, injured Tiffany, a third person, Tiffany may recover from Walters, because a person is always liable for his own torts, whether he commits them in the capacity of an employee, agent, or otherwise. Tiffany could also trace liability through Walters to Ingram because of their relationship of employer and employee. Tiffany cannot recover damages from Post because Walters is not an employee of Post. Moreover, because Ingram is neither the agent nor the employee of Post, Tiffany cannot trace liability through Ingram to Post. Ingram, as an independent contractor, insulates Post from liability.

The following case further explains the differences between an employee and an independent contractor.

In addition, the obligations of a principal under numerous Federal and State statutes apply only to agents who are employees. Examples of these statutes are the Social Security Act, the National Labor Relations Act, and Workers' Compensation Acts. We discuss these and other statutory enactments affecting the employment relationship in Chapter 42.

MASSEY v. TUBE ART DISPLAY, INC.
Court of Appeals of Washington, Division 1, 1976.
15 Wash.App. 782, 551 P.2d 1387.

Facts: Tube Art was involved in moving a reader board sign to a new location. Tube Art's service manager and another employee went to the proposed site and took photographs and measurements. Later, a Tube Art employee laid out the exact size and location for the excavation by marking a four-by-four-foot square on the asphalt surface with yellow paint. The dimensions of the hole, including its depth of six feet, were indicated with spray paint inside the square. After the layout was painted on the asphalt, Tube Art engaged a backhoe operator, Richard F. Redford, to dig the hole. Redford began digging in the early evening hours at the location designated by Tube Art. At approximately 9:30 P.M., the bucket of Redford's backhoe struck a small natural gas pipeline. After examining the pipe and finding no indication of a break or leak, he concluded that the line was not in use and left the site. Shortly before 2:00 A.M. on the following day, an explosion and fire occurred in the building serviced by that gas pipeline. As a result, two people in the building were killed and most of its contents were destroyed.

Massey and his associates, as tenants of the building, brought an action against Tube Art and Richard Redford for the total destruction of drawings, plans, sketches, prototype machine components, castings, and other work products. The trial court entered judgment on a jury verdict awarding $143,000 in damages to Massey. Tube Art appeals.

Decision: Judgment for Massey affirmed.

Opinion: Swanson, J.   Traditionally, servants and non-servant agents have been looked upon as persons employed to perform services in the affairs of others under an express or implied agreement, and who, with respect to physical conduct in the performance of those services, is [sic] subject to the other's control or right of control. [Citations.]

An independent contractor, on the other hand, is generally defined as one who contracts to perform services for another, but who is not controlled by the other nor subject to the other's right to control with respect to his physical conduct in performing the services. [Citations], Restatement (Second) of *Agency* § 2(3) (1958).

In determining whether one acting for another is a servant or independent contractor, several factors must be taken into consideration. These are listed in Restatement (Second) of *Agency* § 220(2)(1958), as follows:

(a) the extent of control which, by the agreement, the master may exercise over the details of the work;

(b) whether or not the one employed is engaged in a distinct occupation or business;

(c) the kind of occupation, with reference to whether, in the locality, the work is usually done under the direction of the employer or by a specialist without supervision;

(d) the skill required in the particular occupation;

(e) whether the employer or the workman supplies the instrumentalities, tools, and the place of work for the person doing the work;

(f) the length of time for which the person is employed;

(g) the method of payment, whether by the time or by the job;

(h) whether or not the work is a part of the regular business of the employer;

(i) whether or not the parties believe they are creating the relation of master and servant; and

(j) whether the principal is or is not in business.

All of these factors are of varying importance in determining the type of relationship involved and, with the exception of the element of control, not all the elements need be present. [Citation.] It is the right to control another's physical conduct that is the essential and oftentimes decisive factor in establishing vicarious liability whether the person controlled is a servant or a non-servant agent. [Citation.]

In discussing the actual extent to which the element of control must be exercised, we pointed out in [citation], that the plaintiff need not show that the principal controlled or had the right to control every aspect of the agent's operation in order to incur vicarious liability. Rather,

[i]t should be sufficient that plaintiff present substantial evidence of . . . control or right to control over those activities from whence the actionable negligence flowed. If the rule were otherwise, then a person wishing to accomplish a certain result through another could declare the other to be an independent contractor generally, and yet retain control over a particularly hazardous part of the undertaking without incurring liability for acts arising out of that part. Such a result would effectively thwart the purpose of the rule of vicarious liability. [Citations.]

In the recent case of [citation], we stated:

In this regard, it may be emphasized that it is not de facto control nor actual exercise of a right to interfere with or direct the work which constitutes the test, but rather, the *right to control* the negligent actor's physical conduct in the performance of the service. (Citations omitted.)

In making his ruling that Tube Art was responsible as a matter of law for Redford's actions the trial judge stated,

I think that under the undisputed evidence in this case they not only had the right to control, but they did control. They controlled the location of the spot to dig. They controlled the dimensions. They controlled the excavation and they got the building permits. They did all of the discretionary work that was necessary before he started to operate. They knew that the method of excavation was going to be by use of a backhoe rather than a pick and shovel which might have made a little difference on the exposure in this situation. They in effect created the whole atmosphere in which he worked. And the fact that even though he did not work for them all of the time and they paid him on a piece-work basis for the individual job didn't impress me particularly when they used him the number of times they did. Most of the time they used him for this type of work. So I am holding as a matter of law that Redford's activities are the responsibility of Tube Art.

Our review of the evidence supports the trial court's evaluation of both the right and exercise of control even though Redford had been essentially self-employed for about 5 years at the time of trial, was free to work for other contractors, selected the time of day to perform the work assigned, paid his own income and business taxes and did not participate in any of Tube Art's employee programs. The testimony advanced at trial, which we find determinative, established that during the previous 3 years Redford had worked exclusively for sign companies and 90 percent of his time for Tube Art. He had no employees, was not registered as a contractor or subcontractor, was not bonded, did not himself obtain permits or

> licenses for his jobs, and dug the holes at locations and in dimensions in exact accordance with the instructions of his employer. In fact, Redford was left no discretion with regard to the placement of the excavations that he dug. Rather, it was his skill in digging holes pursuant to the exact dimensions prescribed that caused him to be preferred over the other backhoe operators. We therefore find no disputed evidence of the essential factor—the right to control, nor is there any dispute that control was exercised over the most significant decisions—the size and location of the hole. Consequently, only one conclusion could reasonably be drawn from the facts presented. In such a circumstance, the nature of the relationship becomes a question of law. [Citation.] We find no error.

CREATION OF AGENCY

Agency is a **consensual** relationship that may be formed by contract or agreement between the principal and agent.[5] Because the relationship of principal and agent is consensual and not necessarily contractual, it may exist without consideration.[6] Agency by contract, however, is the most usual method of creating the relationship and must satisfy all of the requirements of a contract.

Formalities

As a general rule, no particular formality is required in a contract of agency. In most cases, the contract may be oral. In some cases, however, the contract must be in writing. The appointment of an agent for a period of more than a year comes within the one-year clause of the Statute of Frauds and thus must be in writing. In some States, the authority of an agent to sell land must be in writing and signed by the principal. Where the authority of an agent will require him to execute an instrument under seal, this authority must be granted in an instrument executed under seal by the principal.[7]

A **power of attorney** is a formal appointment of an agent who is known as an attorney in fact. Under a power of attorney, for example, a principal may appoint an agent not only to execute a contract for the sale of the principal's real estate but also to execute the deed conveying title to the real estate to the third party. In such cases, the agent executes the contract, deed, or other instrument in the following manner: John Preston, by Peter Ames, his attorney in fact.

Capacity

The capacity to be a principal and thus to act through an agent depends on the capacity of the principal to do the act herself. For example, contracts entered into by a minor or an incompetent not under a guardianship are voidable. Consequently, the appointment of an agent by a minor or an incompetent not under a guardianship and any resulting contracts are voidable, regardless of the agent's contractual capacity.

Because the act of the agent is considered the act of the principal, the incapacity of an agent to bind himself by contract does *not* disqualify him from making a contract that is binding on his principal. Thus, minors and incompetents not under a guardianship may act as agents. Although the contract of agency may be voidable, the contract between the principal and the third person who dealt with the agent is valid. Nonetheless, some mental capacity is necessary in an agent; therefore, very young minors and mental incompetents may not have the capacity to act as agents in certain situations.

DUTIES OF AGENT TO PRINCIPAL

Because the relationship of principal and agent is ordinarily created by contract, the duties of the agent to the principal are determined by the provisions of the contract. In addition to the contractual duties assumed by the agent, he is subject to various other duties imposed by law. Normally, a principal selects an agent based on the agent's ability, skill, and integrity. Moreover, the principal not only authorizes and empowers the agent to bind him on contracts with third persons, but in many cases he also places the agent in possession of his money and other property. As a result, the agent is in a position, either through negligence or dishonesty, to injure the principal by involving him in detrimental liabilities or obligations to third persons or by wrongfully using or disposing of the property committed to his care. Accordingly, an agent owes his principal the duties of obedience, diligence, providing information, providing an accounting, and loyalty as a fiduciary (a person in a position of trust and confidence). Moreover, an agent is liable for any loss caused to the principal for breach of any of these duties.[8]

Duty of Obedience

The duty of obedience requires the agent to act in the principal's affairs only as authorized by the principal and to obey all reasonable instructions and directions of the principal.[9] The agent may be subject to liability to his principal for breach of this duty (1) because he entered into an unauthorized contract for which his principal is liable; (2) because he has improperly delegated his authority, or (3) because he has committed a tort for which the principal is liable. Thus, if an agent sells on credit in violation of the explicit instructions of the principal, the agent has breached the duty of obedience and is liable to the principal for any amounts not paid by the purchaser. Moreover, an agent who is disobedient loses the right to compensation.[10]

Duty of Diligence

An agent must act with reasonable care and skill in performing the work for which he is employed. He must also exercise any special skill that he may have.[11] If an agent does not exercise the required care and skill, he is liable to the principal for any resulting loss. For example, Peg appoints Alvin as her agent to sell goods in markets where the highest price can be obtained. Alvin sells goods in a market that is glutted and obtains a low price, although a higher price would have been obtained in a nearby market if Alvin had used care in obtaining information available to him. Alvin is subject to liability to Peg for breach of the duty of diligence. See *F. W. Myers & Company v. Hunter Farms* below.

Duty to Inform

An agent must use reasonable efforts to give the principal information that is relevant to the affairs entrusted to her and that, as the agent knows or should know, the principal would desire to have.[12] This duty is made essential by the rule of agency providing that notice to an agent is notice to his principal. Some examples of information that an agent has been held under a duty to communicate to his principal are that a customer of the principal has become insolvent; that a debtor of the principal has become insolvent; that one of the partners of a firm with which the principal has previously dealt, and with which the principal or agent is about to deal, has withdrawn from the firm; or that the principal's property that the principal has authorized the agent to sell at a specified price can be sold at a higher price. The following case addresses both the duty of diligence and the duty to inform.

F. W. MYERS & COMPANY v. HUNTER FARMS
Supreme Court of Iowa, 1982.
319 N.W.2d 186.

Facts: Hunter Farms contracted with Petrolia Grain & Feed Company, a Canadian company, to purchase a large supply of the farm herbicide Sencor from Petrolia for resale. Petrolia learned from the U.S. Customs Service that the import duty for the Sencor would be 5 percent but that the final rate could only be determined upon an inspection of the Sencor at the time of importation. Petrolia forwarded this information to Hunter. Meanwhile, Hunter employed F. W. Myers & Company, an import broker, to assist in moving the herbicide through customs. When customs later determined that certain chemicals in the herbicide, not listed on its label, would increase the customs duty from $30,000 to $128,000, Myers paid the additional amount under protest and turned to Hunter for indemnification. Hunter refused to pay Myers, claiming that Myers breached its duty of care as an import broker in failing to inform Hunter that the 5 percent duty rate was subject to increase. Myers brought an action against Hunter, arguing that it was not employed to give advice to Hunter on matters of importation. Hunter appeals from the trial court's judgment for Myers.

Decision: Judgment for Myers affirmed.

Opinion: Larson, J. The right of indemnity under such circumstances is clear: If one is compelled to pay sums which another ought to pay, he is entitled to indemnity. [Citations.] Although Hunter does not challenge the general right of an agent to indemnity under such circumstances, it claims Myers had breached a concomitant duty of disclosure, thus precluding its recovery.

An agent is required to exercise such skill as is required to accomplish the object of his employment. If he fails to exercise reasonable care, diligence, and judgment under the circumstances, he is labile to his principal for any loss or damage resulting. [Citation.] Thus,

> [u]nless otherwise agreed, a paid agent is subject to a duty to the principal to act with standard care and with the skill which is standard in the locality for the kind of work which he is employed to perform and, in addition, to exercise any special skill that he has.

Restatement (Second) of Agency, § 379(1), at 177 (1958).

We believe there was substantial evidence, [citation], to support the trial court's finding there was no breach of duty by Myers. Evidence was presented that the standard of care for import brokers did not include a special duty to render advice to the importer unless requested to do so. Expert testimony showed such brokers are basically involved in drafting the necessary papers, arranging for the necessary bonds, and actual forwarding of the duty payment. There was no evidence of a request to advise Hunter on import law, nor was there any evidence Myers was advised that Hunter was new in the import business.

Hunter contends, however, Myers had a special duty of disclosure to advise Hunter the five-percent figure was advisory or only an estimate. It claims the trial court erred in failing to recognize and apply such duty of care.

The scope of an agent's duty to disclose is explained by the *Restatement* in this manner:

> Unless otherwise agreed, an agent is subject to a duty to use reasonable efforts to give his principal information which is relevant to affairs entrusted to him and which, as the agent has notice, the principal would desire to have and which can be communicated without violating a superior duty to a third person.

Restatement, supra § 381, at 182. This standard requires that the agent have notice the principal would desire to have the relevant information. In this case there was evidence the open-ended nature of an initial duty assessment was widely known and understood by importers. Myers was never informed of the need to convey this information to Hunter which, it could reasonably presume, possessed the fundamental knowledge of an importer. Myers was never advised of Hunter's lack of experience in the business, nor was it aware of the problem in labeling the herbicide which caused the increase in the duty charged. Absent knowledge of Hunter's

> special need for advice and of the circumstances which might give rise to the additional importation fees, there was no special duty on Myers to advise Hunter of the tentative nature of the assessment. Accordingly, it was not error for the trial court to refuse to recognize such a duty.

Duty to Account

The agent is under a duty to maintain and provide the principal with a true and complete account of money or other property that the agent has received or expended on behalf of the principal.[13] An agent must also keep the principal's property separate from his own.

Fiduciary Duty

A fiduciary duty is one that arises out of a relationship of trust and confidence. It is a duty imposed by law and is owed by a trustee to a beneficiary of a trust, an officer or director of a corporation to the corporation and its shareholders, a lawyer to his clients, an employee to his employer, and an agent to his principal. Fiduciary duties are not limited to these situations but exist in every relationship where the law authorizes one person to place trust and confidence in another.

The **fiduciary duty** is one of **utmost loyalty and good faith.** An agent must act solely in the interest of his principal and not in his own interest or in the interest of another.[1] An agent may not represent his principal in any transaction in which he has a personal interest. An agent may not take a position in conflict with the interest of his principal, unless the principal, with full knowledge of all of the facts, consents. The agent owes his principal at all times the duty of full disclosure. He does not deal with his principal at arm's length.

The fiduciary duty of an agent prevents him from competing with his principal or acting on behalf of a competitor or for persons whose interests conflict with those of the principal. Moreover, an agent who is employed to buy may not buy from himself without the principal's consent. Thus, Penelope employs Alexander to purchase for her a site suitable for a shopping center. Alexander owns one that is suitable and sells it to Penelope at the fair market value. Alexander does not disclose to Penelope that Alexander had owned the land. Penelope may rescind the transaction. An agent who is employed to sell may not become the purchaser, nor may he act as agent for the purchaser. The agent's loyalty must be undivided, and his actions must be devoted exclusively to represent and promote the interests of his principal.

An agent may not use information obtained in the course of the agency for his own benefit or against the interest of his principal. For example, if an agent, in the course of his employment, discovers a defect in his principal's title to certain property, he may not use the information to acquire the title for himself. Or if an employee, prior to the expiration of his employer's lease, secretly obtains a lease of the property for his own benefit, he may be compelled to transfer it to his employer. This rule also applies to unique business methods of the employer, trade secrets, and customer lists. After termination of the agency, unless otherwise agreed, the agent may compete with his former principal but may not use or disclose to third persons trade secrets, customer lists, or other similar confidential matters. The agent, however, is entitled to use skill, knowledge, and general information acquired during the agency relationship. A contractual agreement by the agent not to compete with the principal after termination of the agency will be enforced if the restriction is reasonable as to time and place and necessary to protect the principal's legitimate interest. Contractual agreements not to compete are discussed in Chapter 11.

An agent is not permitted to make a secret profit out of any transaction subject to the agency. All such profits belong to the principal. Thus, if an agent, authorized to sell certain property of his principal for $1,000, sells it for

$1,500, he may not secretly pocket the additional $500. Further, suppose Michael employs real estate broker Doris to sell his land for a commission of 6 percent of the sale price. Doris, knowing that Michael is willing to sell for $20,000, agrees secretly with a prospective buyer who is willing to pay $22,000 for the land that she will endeavor to obtain the consent of Michael to sell for $20,000, in which event the buyer will pay Doris $1,000, or one-half of the amount the buyer believes she is saving on the price. The broker has violated her fiduciary duty, and she must pay the $1,000 to Michael. Furthermore, Doris loses the right to any commission on the transaction. The result is that the seller, who willingly sold the land for $20,000, expecting to pay a commission of $1,200 and net $18,800, receives $21,000 free of commission. Doris's breach of fiduciary duty produces an unexpected windfall for Michael. This, however, is incidental to the deterrent purpose of the rule that requires a faithless fiduciary to account for any gain or profit from his acts of disloyalty.

DETROIT LIONS, INC. v. ARGOVITZ

United States District Court, Eastern District of Michigan, 1984.
580 F.Supp. 542.

Facts: Jerry Argovitz was employed as an agent of Billy Sims, a professional football player. Early in 1983, Argovitz informed Sims that he was awaiting the approval of his application for a United States Football League franchise in Houston. Sims was unaware, however, of Argovitz's extensive ownership interest in the new Houston Gamblers organization. Meanwhile, during the spring of 1983, Argovitz continued contract negotiations on behalf of Sims with the Detroit Lions of the National Football League. By June 22 Argovitz and the Lions were very close to an agreement, although Argovitz represented to Sims that the negotiations were not proceeding well. Argovitz then sought an offer for Sims's services from the Gamblers. The Gamblers offered Sims a $3.5 million five-year deal. Argovitz told Sims that he thought the Lions would match this figure; however, he did not seek a final offer from the Lions and then present the terms of both packages to Sims. Sims, convinced that the Lions were not negotiating in good faith, signed with the Gamblers on July 1, 1983. On December 16, 1983, Sims signed a second contract with the Lions. The Lions and Sims brought an action against Argovitz, seeking to invalidate Sims's contract with the Gamblers on the ground that Argovitz breached his fiduciary duty when negotiating the contract with the Gamblers.

Decision: Judgment for the Lions and Sims rescinding the Gamblers' contract with Sims.

Opinion: DeMascio, J. The relationship between a principal and agent is fiduciary in nature, and as such imposes a duty of loyalty, good faith, and fair and honest dealing on the agent. [Citation.]

A fiduciary relationship arises not only from a formal principal-agent relationship, but also from informal relationships of trust and confidence. [Citations.]

In light of the express agency agreement, and the relationship between Sims and Argovitz, Argovitz clearly owed Sims the fiduciary duties of an agent at all times relevant to this lawsuit.

An agent's duty of loyalty requires that he not have a personal stake that conflicts with the principal's interest in a transaction in which he represents his principal. As stated in [citation]:

(T)he principal is entitled to the best efforts and unbiased judgment of his agent. . . . (T)he law denies the right of an agent to assume any relationship that is antagonistic to his duty to his principal, and it has many times been held that the agent cannot be both buyer and seller at the same time nor connect his own interests with property involved in his dealings as an agent for another.

A fiduciary violates the prohibition against self-dealing not only by dealing with himself on his principal's behalf, but also by dealing on his principal's behalf with a third party in which he has an interest, such as a partnership in which he is a member. . . .

Where an agent has an interest adverse to that of his principal in a transaction in which he purports to act on behalf of his principal, the transaction is voidable by the principal unless the agent disclosed all material facts within the agent's knowledge that might affect the principal's judgment. [Citation.]

The mere fact that the contract is fair to the principal does not deny the principal the right to rescind the contract when it was negotiated by an agent in violation of the prohibition against self-dealing. . . .

Once it has been shown that an agent had an interest in a transaction involving his principal antagonistic to the principal's interest, fraud on the part of the agent is presumed. The burden of proof then rests upon the agent to show that his principal had full knowledge, not only of the fact that the agent was interested, but also of every material fact known to the agent which might affect the principal and that having such knowledge, the principal freely consented to the transaction.

It is not sufficient for the agent merely to inform the principal that he has an interest that conflicts with the principal's interest. Rather, he must inform the principal "of all facts that come to his knowledge that are or may be material or which might affect his principal's rights or interests or influence the action he takes." [Citation.]

Argovitz clearly had a personal interest in signing Sims with the Gamblers that was adverse to Sims' interest—he had an ownership interest in the Gamblers and thus would profit if the Gamblers were profitable, and would incur substantial personal liabilities should the Gamblers not be financially successful. Since this showing has been made, fraud on Argovitz's part is presumed, and the Gamblers' contract must be rescinded unless Argovitz has shown by a preponderance of the evidence that he informed Sims of every material fact that might have influenced Sims' decision whether or not to sign the Gamblers' contract.

We conclude that Argovitz has failed to show by a preponderance of the evidence either: 1) that he informed Sims of the [material] facts, or 2) that these facts would not have influenced Sims' decision whether to sign the Gamblers' contract. . . .

As a court sitting in equity, we conclude that rescission is the appropriate remedy. We are dismayed by Argovitz's egregious conduct. The careless fashion in which Argovitz went about ascertaining the highest price for Sims' service convinces us of the wisdom of the maxim: no man can faithfully serve two masters whose interests are in conflict.

DUTIES OF PRINCIPAL TO AGENT

Although both principal and agent have rights and duties arising out of the agency relationship, more emphasis is placed on the duties of the agent. This is necessarily so because of the nature of the agency relationship. First, the acts and services to be performed, both under the agency contract and as may be required by law, are to be performed mostly by the agent. Second, the agent is a fiduciary and is subject to the duties of loyalty and good faith, as discussed earlier. Nonetheless, an agent has certain rights against the principal, both under the contract and by the operation of law. Connected to these rights are certain duties that the principal owes to the agent. The duties are based in contract and tort law.

Contractual Duties

As with any party to a contract, a principal is under a duty to perform his part of the contract according to its terms. The most important duty of the principal, from the standpoint of the agent, is to compensate the agent as specified in the contract. It is also the duty of the principal not to terminate the agency wrongfully. Whether the principal must furnish the means of employment or opportunity for work will depend on the particular case. A principal who employs an agent to sell his goods must supply the agent with the goods. If the contract specifies the quality of the goods, the principal must not furnish inferior or defective goods. In other cases, the agent must create his own opportunity for work, as in the case of a broker employed to procure a buyer for his principal's house. How far, if at all, the principal must assist or cooperate with the agent will depend on the particular agency. Usually, cooperation on the part of the principal is more necessary where the agent's compensation is contingent on the success of his efforts than where the agent is paid a fixed salary regularly over a period of permanent employment.

Compensation   A principal has a duty to compensate her agent unless the agent has agreed to serve gratuitously. If the agreement does not specify a definite amount or rate of compensation, a principal is under a duty to pay the reasonable value of authorized services performed for her by her agent.[14] A principal also has a duty to maintain and provide the agent a true and complete account of money or property due the agent.[13] Although a gratuitous agent is not owed a duty of compensation, she is entitled to reimbursement and indemnification as discussed below.

Reimbursement   A principal is under a duty to **reimburse** his agent for authorized payments made by the agent on behalf of the principal and for authorized expenses incurred by the agent.[15] For example, an agent who reasonably and properly pays a fire insurance premium for the protection of her principal's property is entitled to reimbursement for the payment.

Indemnification   The principal is under a duty to **indemnify** the agent for losses incurred or suffered while acting as directed by the principal in a transaction that is not illegal or not known by the agent to be wrongful.[15] To indemnify is to make good or pay a loss. Suppose that Perry, the principal, has in his possession goods belonging to Margot. Perry directs Alma, his agent, to sell these goods. Alma, believing Perry to be the owner, sells the goods to Turner. Margot then sues Alma for the conversion of her goods and recovers a judgment, which Alma pays to Margot. Alma is entitled to payment from Perry for her loss, including the amount reasonably expended by Alma in defense of the lawsuit brought by Margot.

Tort Duties

A principal owes to any agent the same duties under tort law that the principal owes to all parties. Moreover, a principal is under a duty to disclose to an agent those risks involved in the agency, of which the principal knows or should know, if the principal should realize that the agent is unaware of these risks. For instance, if a principal directs his agent to collect rent from a tenant who is known to have assaulted rent collectors, the principal has a duty to warn the agent of this risk.

Where the agent is an employee, the principal owes the employee additional duties. Among these is the duty to provide an employee with reasonably safe conditions of employment and to warn the employee of any unreasonable risk involved in the employment. An employer is also liable to his employees for injury caused by the negligence of other employees and of other agents doing work for him. We discuss the tort duties owed by an employer to an employee more fully in Chapter 42.

TERMINATION OF AGENCY

Because the authority of an agent is based on the consent of the principal, the agency is terminated when such consent is withdrawn or otherwise ceases to exist. On termination of the agency, the agent's actual authority ends, and she is not entitled to compensation for services subsequently rendered, although her fiduciary duties may continue. Termination may take place by the acts of the parties or by operation of law.

Acts of the Parties

Termination by the acts of the parties may occur by the acts of both principal and agent or by the act of either one of them. The methods of termination by acts of the parties are as follows.

Lapse of Time   Authority conferred upon an agent for a specified time terminates at the expiration of that period. If no time is specified, authority terminates at the end of a reasonable period. For example, Palmer authorizes Avery to sell a tract of land for him. Ten years pass without communication between Palmer and Avery. Avery purports to sell the tract. Avery's authorization has terminated due to lapse of time, and the purported sale is not binding upon Palmer.

Mutual Agreement of the Parties   The agency relationship is created by agreement and may be terminated at any time by mutual agreement of the principal and the agent.

Fulfillment of Purpose   The authority of an agent to perform a specific act or to accomplish a particular result is terminated when the act is performed or the result is accomplished by the agent. Thus, if Porter authorizes Alford to sell or lease Porter's land, and Alford leases the land to Taft, Alford's authority is terminated, and he may not thereafter sell or lease the land without new authorization.

Revocation of Authority   A principal may revoke an agent's authority at any time. But if such revocation constitutes a breach of contract by the principal, as in the next case, the agent may recover damages from the principal.

HILGENDORF v. HAGUE
Supreme Court of Iowa, 1980.
293 N.W.2d 272.

Facts: Harvey Hilgendorf was a licensed real estate broker acting as the agent of the Hagues in the sale of eighty acres of farmland. The Hagues, however, terminated Hilgendorf's agency before the expiration of the listing contract when they encountered financial difficulties and decided to liquidate their entire holdings of land at one time. Hilgendorf brought this action for breach of the listing contract. The Hagues maintain that Hilgendorf's duty of loyalty requires him to give up the listing contract. The Hagues appealed from the trial court's judgment in favor of Hilgendorf.

Decision: Judgment for Hilgendorf affirmed.

Opinion: **Uhlenhopp, J.**   I. *Right to terminate listing.* Since agency is a consensual relationship, a principal has *power* to terminate an agency which is not coupled with an interest [where the agent has an ownership interest in the subject matter of the agency], although the contract is for a period which has not expired. Ordinarily the agent's authority thereupon ceases. Absent some legal ground, however, the principal does not have a *right* to terminate an unexpired agency contract, and may subject himself to damages by doing so. [Citations.]

The whole question regarding liability here turns on whether the Hagues had a legal ground for terminating Hilgendorf's agency before the expiration of the year. All agree that they had power to terminate, but they contend they also had a right to do so. They say PCA [Hagues' principal creditor] would not renew their loan, they had to sell the 80 acres in addition to their other land, and the best way to sell the 80 acres was with the 160 acres. Did these circumstances given them a "right" to terminate the listing contract they had signed and cast on Hilgendorf a "duty" to give up his listing contract as a matter of an agent's loyalty to his principal?

The Hagues appear to confuse the two roles an agent occupies. In performing agency functions for the principal an agent does indeed occupy a fiduciary position, and his duty of loyalty requires him to place the principal's interests first. Restatement (Second) of Agency § 387. But in the contract of agency itself between the agent and principal, neither of the parties is acting for the other; each is acting for himself.

This case involve the latter role. * * *

* * *

Several circumstances are given in the texts as grounds for terminating fixed-term agencies, but coming upon hard times is not among them. [Citations.] We agree with the trial court that the Hagues did not have a right to terminate the one-year listing contract . . . and that Hilgendorf did not have a duty to give up his listing contract.

II. *Damages*. Hague terminated the listing on August 13, 1976. Since Hague had the power to do so, Hilgendorf no longer had authority to sell the . . . parcel. For that reason, he cannot recover a commission *as such*, although he thereafter and within the year produced a ready, willing, and able buyer for the price in the listing. Nonetheless, since Hague breached the listing agreement by terminating it, Hilgendorf can recover damages. [Citation.]

The question here relates to the *measure* of damages Hilgendorf is entitled to *recover*. The editors state the measure thus in [citation]:

> The courts generally support the principle that a broker whose employment or authority is wrongfully revoked may consider his contract of employment as rescinded and sue for damages, in which event he is entitled to have his recovery include the value of the services he has already rendered, his disbursements, and *such prospective profits as he can establish would have been his but for such revocation.* . . .

* * *

Where as here the principal terminates an exclusive listing within the term, the agent may endeavor to show that he would, but for the termination, have sold the property within the unexpired period at the listed price. If he is successful in his proof, his lost profits are ordinarily measured by the commission he would have earned. He does not recover the commission itself, but his damages are measured by the commission.

* * *

Here Hilgendorf proceeded on the damage issue by showing "the gains prevented" by Hague's breach of the listing contract. He established beyond question that he would have sold the . . . parcel for the full asking price within the listing period. His lost profit was the offered price times the six percent commission rate, and this is the amount the trial court allowed him.

We agree with the trial court's decision.

Renunciation by the Agent The agent also has the power to put an end to the agency by notice to the principal that she renounces the authority given her by the principal. If the parties have contracted that the agency continue for a specified time, an unjustified renunciation prior to the expiration of the time is a breach of contract.

Operation of Law

An agency relationship may also be terminated by operation of law. Although one of the parties may suffer a loss, in any such case he has no rights against the other regarding the loss, because the agency was terminated by law. Thus, where the agency is terminated by the death of the principal, the agent has no claim against the deceased principal's estate for any loss he suffers because the agency was terminated. As a matter of law, agency is ordinarily terminated by the occurrence of any of the following events.

Bankruptcy Bankruptcy is a proceeding in a Federal court affording relief to financially troubled debtors. The filing of the petition in bankruptcy, which initiates the proceedings, usually terminates all the debtor's existing agency relationships. The trustee in bankruptcy, however, may assume an executory contract of agency unless under State law the contract is not assignable. If the credit standing of the agent is important to the agency relationship, then it will be terminated by the bankruptcy of the agent. Thus, Arnold is appointed by Pacific Securities, Inc., an investment house, to act as its agent in advising Pacific's local clients as to investments. Arnold becomes bankrupt. Arnold is no longer authorized to act for Pacific.

Death The death of the principal terminates the authority of the agent. For example, Polk employs Allison to sell Polk's line of goods under a contract that specifies Allison's commission and that the employment is to continue for a year even if Polk should die before then. Without Allison's knowledge Polk dies. Allison has no authority to sell Polk's goods. Similarly, the authority given to an agent by a principal is strictly personal, and the agent's death terminates the agency.

Incapacity Incapacity of the principal that occurs after the formation of the agency terminates the agent's authority. To illustrate: Powell authorizes Anna to sell in the next ten months an apartment complex for not less than $2 million. Powell is adjudicated incompetent two months later without Anna's knowledge. Anna's authority to sell the apartment complex is terminated. Likewise, subsequent incapacity of an agent to perform the acts authorized by the principal terminates the agent's authority.

Change in Business Conditions The authority of an agent is terminated by notice or knowledge of a change in the value of the subject matter or of a change in business conditions from which the agent should reasonably infer that the principal would not consent to an exercise of the authority given him. For example, Patricia authorizes Aaron to sell her eighty acres of farmland for $800 per acre. Subsequently, oil is discovered on nearby land and Patricia's land greatly increases in value. Aaron knows of this, but Patricia does not. Aaron's authority to sell the land is terminated.

Loss or Destruction of the Subject Matter Where the authority of the agent relates to a specific subject matter that becomes lost or destroyed, her authority is thereby terminated. This corresponds to the rule that loss or destruction of the subject matter of an offer terminates the offer. For example, Pauline authorizes Abraham to make a contract for the sale of Pauline's residence. The next week the residence burns completely, as Abraham is aware. Abraham's authority is terminated.

Loss of Qualification of Principal or Agent When the authority given the agent relates to the conduct of a certain business for which a license from the government or a regulatory agency is required, the failure to acquire or the loss of this license terminates the authority of the agent. Thus, Paine, who holds a retail liquor license, employs Adrian to sell liquor at retail in Paine's store. Paine's license is revoked. Adrian's authority to sell Paine's liquor at retail is terminated.

Disloyalty of Agent   If an agent, without the knowledge of her principal, acquires interests that are adverse to those of the principal or otherwise breaches her duty of loyalty to the principal, her authority to act on behalf of the principal is terminated.[16] Thus, Parker employs Agnes, a realtor, to sell Parker's land. Unknown to Parker, Agnes has been authorized by Trent to purchase this land from Parker. Agnes is not authorized to sell the land to Trent.

Change of Law   A change in the law that takes effect after the employment of the agent may cause the performance of the authorized act to be illegal or criminal. Such a change in the law terminates the authority of the agent. Thus, Paul directs his agent Allan to ship young elm trees from State X to State Y. In order to control elm disease, a quarantine is established by State X on the shipment of elm trees to any other State, and any such shipment is punishable by fine. Allan's authority to ship the elm trees is terminated.

Outbreak of War   Where the outbreak of war places the principal and agent in the position of alien enemies, the authority of the agent is terminated because its exercise is illegal. Where the principal and agent are citizens of the same country and the outbreak of war or revolution makes the originally authorized transaction unexpectedly hazardous or impracticable, the agent's authority is terminated.

Irrevocable Agencies

In the foregoing discussion of the various ways in which the authority of an agent may be terminated, the agency relationship was assumed to be the ordinary one in which the agent does not have a security interest in the power conferred on him by the principal. Where the **agency is coupled with an interest** of the agent in the subject matter, as where the agent has advanced funds on behalf of the principal and his power to act is given as security for the loan, the authority of the agent may *not* be revoked by the principal.[17] In addition, incapacity or bankruptcy of the principal will not terminate the authority or power of the agent. The death of the principal also will not terminate the agency unless the duty for which the security was given terminates with the death of the principal.

CHAPTER SUMMARY

Nature of Agency	**Definition of Agency** relationship authorizing one party (the agent) to act for and on behalf of the other party (the principal)
	Scope of Agency Purposes whatever business activity a person may accomplish personally he generally may do through an agent
	Other Legal Relations
	■ *Employment Relationship* one in which the employer has the right to control the physical conduct of the employee
	■ *Independent Contractor* a person who contracts with another to do a particular job and is *not* subject to the control of the other

Creation of Agency	**Formalities** agency is a consensual relationship that may be formed by contract or agreement between the principal and agent but agency may exist without consideration

- *Requirements*   no particular formality is usually required in a contract of agency although appointments of agents for a period of more than one year must be in writing
- *Power of Attorney*   written, formal appointment of an agent

Capacity

- *Principal*   if the principal is a minor or an incompetent not under a guardianship, then his appointment of another to act as an agent is voidable
- *Agent*   minors or incompetents not under a guardianship may act as agents since the act of the agent is considered the act of the principal

Duties of Agent to Principal	**Duty of Obedience** an agent must act in the principal's affairs only as authorized by the principal and obey all reasonable instructions and directions **Duty of Diligence** an agent must act with reasonable care and skill in performing the work for which he is employed **Duty to Inform** an agent must use reasonable efforts to give the principal information that is relevant to the affairs entrusted to her **Duty to Account** an agent must maintain and provide the principal with a true and complete account of money or other property that the agent has received or expended on behalf of the principal **Fiduciary Duty** an agent owes a duty of utmost loyalty and good faith to the principal

Duties of Principal to Agent	**Contractual Duties**

- *Compensation*   a principal must compensate the agent as specified in the contract, or for the reasonable value of the services provided, if no amount is specified
- *Reimbursement*   the principal must pay back to the agent authorized payments the agent has made on the principal's behalf
- *Indemnification*   the principal must pay the agent for losses incurred by the agent while acting as directed by the principal

Tort Duties   include the duty to provide an employee with reasonably safe conditions of employment and to warn the employee of any unreasonable risk involved in the employment

Termination of Agency	**Acts of Parties**

- *Lapse of Time*
- *Mutual Agreement of the Parties*
- *Fulfillment of Purpose*
- *Revocation of Authority*
- *Renunciation by the Agent*

Operation of Law
- *Bankruptcy*   the bankruptcy of the principal usually terminates all of the principal's agency relationships; if the credit of the agent is important to the agency relationship, then it will be terminated by the bankruptcy of the agent
- *Death*   of either the principal or the agent
- *Incapacity*   of either the principal or the agent
- *Change in Business Conditions*
- *Loss or Destruction of the Subject Matter*
- *Loss of Qualification of Principal or Agent*
- *Disloyalty of Agent*
- *Change in Law*
- *Outbreak of War*

Irrevocable Agencies   an agency coupled with an interest is irrevocable and occurs where the agent has a security interest in the subject matter of the agency

QUESTIONS

1. Distinguish among the following relationships: (a) agency, (b) employment, and (c) independent contractor.
2. Discuss the requirements for creating an agency relationship.
3. Discuss the duties owed by an agent to her principal.
4. Discuss the duties owed by a principal to his agent.
5. Identify the ways in which an agency relationship may be terminated.

PROBLEMS

1. Parker, the owner of certain unimproved real estate in Chicago, employed Adams, a real estate agent, to sell the property for a price of $25,000 or more and agreed to pay Adams a commission of 6 percent for making a sale. Adams negotiated with Turner, who was interested in the property and willing to pay as much as $28,000 for it. Adams made an agreement with Turner that if Adams could obtain Parker's signature to a contract to sell the property to Turner for $25,000, Turner would pay Adams a bonus of $1,000. Adams prepared and Parker and Turner signed a contract for the sale of the property to Turner for $25,000. Turner refuses to pay Adams the $1,000 as promised. Parker refuses to pay Adams the 6 percent commission. In an action by Adams against Parker and Turner, what judgment.

2. Perry employed Alice to sell a parcel of real estate at a fixed price without knowledge that David had previously employed Alice to purchase the same property for him. Perry gave Alice no discretion as to price or terms, and Alice entered into a contract of sale with David on the exact terms authorized by Perry. After accepting a partial payment, Perry discovered that Alice was employed by David and brought an action to rescind. David resisted on the ground that Perry had suffered no damage because Alice had been given no discretion and the sale was made on the exact basis authorized by Perry. Decision?

3. Packer owned and operated a fruit cannery in Southton, Illinois. He stored a substantial amount of finished canned goods in a warehouse in East St. Louis, Illinois, owned and operated by Alden, in order to have goods readily available for the St. Louis market. On March 1 he had 10,000 cans of peaches and 5,000 cans of apples in storage with Alden. On the day named, he borrowed $5,000 from Alden, giving Alden his promissory note for this amount due June 1 together with a letter authorizing Alden, in the event the note was not paid at maturity, to sell any or all of his goods in storage, pay the indebtedness, and account to him for any surplus. Packer died on June 2 without having paid the note. On June 8 Alden told Taylor, a wholesale food distributor, that he had for sale, as agent of the owner, 10,000 cans of peaches and 5,000 cans of apples. Taylor said he would take the peaches and would decide later about the apples. A contract for the sale of 10,000 cans of peaches for $6,000 was thereupon signed. "Alden, agent for Packer, seller; Taylor, buyer." Both Alden and Taylor knew of the death of Packer. Delivery of the peaches

and payment were made on June 10. On June 11 Alden and Taylor signed a similar contract covering the 5,000 cans of apples, delivery and payment to be made June 30. On June 23 Packer's executor, having learned of these contracts, wrote Alden and Taylor stating that Alden had no authority to make the contracts, demanding that Taylor return the peaches, and directing Alden not to deliver the apples. Discuss the correctness of the contentions of Packer's executor.

4. Green, a licensed real estate broker in Illinois, and Jones, also an Illinois resident, while both in New York, signed a contract whereby Green agreed to endeavor to find a buyer for certain real estate located in Illinois owned by Jones, who agreed to pay Green a commission of $10,000 in the event of a sale. Green found a buyer, a resident of New York, to whom the land was sold. Thereafter, Jones refused to pay the commission. Green commenced an action in Illinois to recover the commission. Jones defended on the sole ground that the brokerage contract was unenforceable because Green was not a licensed real estate broker in New York. Relevant provisions of the applicable New York statute forbid any person from holding himself out or acting temporarily as a real estate broker or salesman without first procuring a license. A violation is declared to be a misdemeanor, and the commission of a single prohibited act is a violation for which the statute provides a penalty. For whom should judgment be rendered?

5. Palmer made a valid contract with Ames under which Ames was to sell Palmer's goods on commission during the period from January 1 to June 30. Ames made satisfactory sales up to May 15 and was then about to close an unusually large order when Palmer suddenly and without notice revoked Ames's authority to sell. Can Ames continue to sell Palmer's goods during the unexpired term of her contract?

6. Piedmont Electric Co. gave a list of delinquent accounts to Alexander, an employee, with instructions to discontinue electric service to delinquent customers. Among those listed was Todd Hatchery, which was then in the process of hatching chickens in a large, electrically heated incubator. Todd Hatchery told Alexander that it did not consider its account delinquent, but Alexander nevertheless cut the wires leading to the hatchery. Subsequently, Todd Hatchery recovered a judgment of $5,000 against Alexander in an action brought against Alexander for the loss resulting from the interruption of the incubation process. Alexander has paid the judgment and brings a cause of action against Piedmont Electric Co. Decision?

7. In October 1985, Black, the owner of the Grand Opera House, and Harvey entered into a written agreement leasing the opera house to Harvey for five years at a rental of $30,000 a year. Harvey engaged Day as manager of the theater at a salary of $175 per week plus 10 percent of the profits. One of Day's duties was to determine the amounts of money taken in each night and, after deducting expenses, to divide the profits between Harvey and the manager of the particular attraction playing at the theater. In September 1990, Day went to Black and offered to rent the opera house from Black at a rental of $37,500 per year, whereupon Black entered into a lease with Day for five years at this figure. When Harvey learned of and objected to this transaction, Day offered to assign the lease to him for $60,000 per year. Harvey refused and brought an appropriate action seeking to have Day declared a trustee of the opera house lease on behalf of Harvey. Decision?

8. Timothy retains Cynthia, an attorney, to bring a lawsuit upon a valid claim against Vincent. Recently enacted legislation has shortened the statute of limitations for this type of legal action. Cynthia fails to make herself aware of this new statute. Consequently, she files the complaint after the statute of limitations has run. As a result, the lawsuit is dismissed. What rights, if any, does Timothy have against Cynthia?

9. Wilson engages Ruth to sell Wilson's antique walnut chest to Harold for $2,500. The next day, Ruth learns that Sandy is willing to pay $3,000 for Wilson's chest. Ruth nevertheless sells the chest to Harold. Wilson then discovers these facts. What are Wilson's rights, if any, against Ruth?

10. Morris is a salesman for Acme, Inc., a manufacturer of household appliances. Morris receives a commission on all sales made and no further compensation. He drives his own automobile and pays his own expenses. Morris calls on whom he pleases. While driving to make a call on a potential customer, Morris negligently collides with Hudson. Hudson sues Acme and Morris. Who should be held liable?

11. Sierra Pacific Industries purchased various areas of timber and six other pieces of real property, including a ten-acre parcel on which five duplexes and two single-family units were located. Sierra Pacific requested the assistance of Joseph Carter, a licensed real estate broker, in selling the nontimberland properties. It commissioned him to sell the property for an asking price of $85,000, of which Sierra Pacific would receive $80,000 and Carter would receive $5,000 as a commission. Carter was unable to find a prospective buyer, and finally he

sold the property to his daughter and son-in-law for $85,000 and retained the $5,000 commission without informing Sierra Pacific of his relationship to the buyers. After learning of these facts, Sierra Pacific brought an action for breach of fiduciary duty against Carter. Decision?

ENDNOTES

1. Restatement, Second, Agency, Section 1, Agency; Principal; Agent.

2. Restatement, Second, Agency, Section 19, Appointment to Perform Illegal Acts.

3. Restatement, Second, Agency, Section 17, What Acts are Delegable.

4. Restatement, Second, Agency, Section 2, Master; Servant; Independent Contractor.

5. Restatement, Second, Agency, Section 15, Manifestations of Consent.

6. Restatement, Second, Agency, Section 16, Consideration.

7. Restatement, Second, Agency, Section 28, Authority to Execute Sealed Instruments.

8. Restatement, Second, Agency, Section 401, Liability for Loss Caused.

9. Restatement, Second, Agency, Section 383, Duty to Act Only as Authorized; Section 385, Duty to Obey.

10. Restatement, Second, Agency, Section 469, Disloyalty or Insubordination as Defense.

11. Restatement, Second, Agency, Section 379, Duty of Care and Skill.

12. Restatement, Second, Agency, Section 381, Duty to Give Information.

13. Restatement, Second, Agency, Section 382, Duty to Keep and Render Accounts.

14. Restatement, Second, Agency, Section 443, Amount of Compensation.

15. Restatement, Second, Agency, Section 438, Duty of Indemnity; the Principle; Section 439, When Duty of Indemnity Exists.

16. Restatement, Second, Agency, Section 112, Disloyalty of Agent.

17. Restatement, Second, Agency, Section 138, Definition; Section 139, Termination of Powers Given as Security.

28 RELATIONSHIP WITH THIRD PARTIES

The purpose of an agency relationship is to allow the principal to extend his business activities by authorizing agents to enter into contracts with third persons on the principal's behalf. Accordingly, it is important that the law balance the competing interests of principals and third persons. The principal wants to be liable *only* for those contracts he actually authorized the agent to make for him. On the other hand, the third party wishes the principal bound on *all* contracts that the agent negotiates on the principal's behalf. As this chapter discusses, the law has adopted an intermediate outcome: the principal and the third party are bound to those contracts the principal *actually* authorizes *plus* those the principal has *apparently* authorized.

While pursuing her principal's business, an agent may tortiously injure third parties, who may seek to hold the principal personally liable. Under what circumstances should the principal be held liable? Similar questions arise concerning the criminal liability of a principal for an agent's violation of the criminal law. The law of agency has established rules to determine when the principal is liable for the torts and crimes committed by his agents. We discuss these rules in this chapter.

Finally, what liability to the third party should the agent incur and what rights should she acquire against the third party? Usually, the agent has no liability for, or rights under, contracts made on behalf of a principal. As we discuss in this chapter, however, in some situations the agent has contractually created obligations or rights or both.

RELATIONSHIP OF PRINCIPAL AND THIRD PERSONS

In this section, we first consider the contract liability of the principal; then we examine the principal's potential tort liability.

CONTRACT LIABILITY OF THE PRINCIPAL

The **authority** of an agent is his power or capacity to change the legal status of his principal. Thus, whenever an agent, acting within his authority, makes a contract for his principal, he creates new rights or liabilities of his principal and thus changes his principal's legal status. This authority of an agent to act for his principal in business transactions is the basis of agency. Without it, the agency relation could not exist.

The contract liability of a principal also depends upon whether the principal is disclosed, partially disclosed, or undisclosed. The principal is a **disclosed principal** if at the time of a transaction conducted by an agent, the other party has notice that the agent is acting for a principal and of the principal's identity.[1] The principal is a **partially disclosed principal** if at the time of the transaction conducted by the agent, the other party has notice that the agent is or may be acting for a principal but has no notice of the principal's identity.[1] The principal is an **undisclosed principal** if the other party has no notice that the agent is acting for a principal.[1]

Types of Authority

There are two basic types of authority: actual and apparent. **Actual authority** occurs when the principal gives actual consent to the agent. It may be either express or implied. In either case, it is binding and gives the agent both the power and the right to create or affect legal relations of the principal with third persons. **Apparent authority** is based on acts or conduct of the principal that show a third person that the agent has actual authority and on which the third person *justifiably* relies. This manifestation may consist of words or actions of the principal as well as other facts and circumstances that induce the third person reasonably to rely on the existence of an agency relationship. To the extent that things are as represented, there is both actual and apparent authority.

Actual Express Authority The **express authority** of an agent is found in the words of the principal, spoken or written, and communicated to the agent. It is actual authority embodied in language directing or instructing the agent to do something specific. Thus, if Lee, orally or in writing, requests his agent Anita to sell Lee's automobile for $6,500, Anita's authority to sell the car for this sum is actual and express.

Actual Implied Authority **Implied authority** is not found in express or explicit words of the principal but is inferred from words or conduct manifested to the agent by the principal. Implied authority may arise from customs and usages of the business. In addition, authority granted to an agent to accomplish a particular purpose necessarily includes authority to employ means reasonably required for its accomplishment.[2] For example, Helen authorizes Clyde to manage her eighty-two-unit apartment complex. Nothing is said by Helen about expenses. In order to manage the building, however, Clyde must employ a janitor, purchase fuel for heating, and arrange for ordinary maintenance. The authority to incur these expenses, while not expressly granted, is implied from the express authority to manage the build-

ing because they are required for its proper management. The agent has implied authority to do what is reasonably necessary to complete the task assigned.

Unless otherwise agreed, authority to make a contract is inferred from authority to conduct a transaction, if the making of such a contract is incidental to the transaction, usually accompanies such a transaction, or is reasonably necessary to accomplish it.[3] Thus, Paragon, Inc. appoints Astor as the general manager of Paragon's manufacturing business. Astor's authority is interpreted as including authority to make contracts for the employment of necessary employees. On the other hand, suppose Paige employs Arthur, a real estate broker, to find a purchaser for her residence at a stated price. Arthur has no authority to contract for its sale.

Certain rules have been developed to determine what authority is implied in particular types of agencies. Unless otherwise agreed, authority to acquire or convey property for the principal includes authority to agree on the terms, to demand or make the usual representations and warranties, to receive or execute the instruments usually required, to pay or receive as much of the purchase price as is to be paid at the time of the transfer, and to receive possession of the goods if a buying agent or to surrender possession of them if a selling agent.

General authority to manage or operate a business for a principal confers, unless otherwise agreed, implied authority on the agent (1) to buy and sell property for the principal; (2) to make contracts that are incidental or reasonably necessary to such business; (3) to acquire equipment and supplies; (4) to make repairs; (5) to employ, supervise, and discharge employees; (6) to receive payments due the principal and to pay debts due from the principal; and (7) to direct the ordinary operations of the business.[4]

Apparent Authority Apparent authority is authority that arises out of words or conduct of a disclosed or partially disclosed principal manifested to third persons by which they are reasonably induced to rely upon the assumption that actual authority exists.[5] Apparent authority confers upon the agent or supposed agent the **power** to bind the disclosed or partially disclosed principal in contracts with third persons and prevents the principal from denying the existence of actual authority. Thus, when there is apparent authority but not actual authority, the disclosed or partially disclosed principal is nonetheless bound by the act of the agent. By exceeding his actual authority, however, the agent has violated his duty of obedience and is liable to the principal for any loss suffered as a result of his acting in excess of his actual authority. See Figures 28–1 and 28–2.

For example, Peter writes a letter to Alice authorizing her to sell his automobile and sends a copy of the letter to Thomas, a prospective purchaser. On the following day, Peter writes a letter to Alice revoking the authority to sell the car but does not send a copy of the second letter to Thomas, who is not otherwise informed of the revocation. Although Alice has no actual authority to sell the car, she continues to have apparent authority with respect to Thomas. Or, suppose that Arlene, in the presence of Polly, tells Thad that Arlene is Polly's agent to buy lumber. Although this statement is not true, Polly does not deny it, as she could easily have done. Thad, in reliance upon the statement, ships lumber to Polly on Arlene's order. Polly is obligated to pay for the lumber because Arlene had apparent authority to act on Polly's behalf. This apparent author-

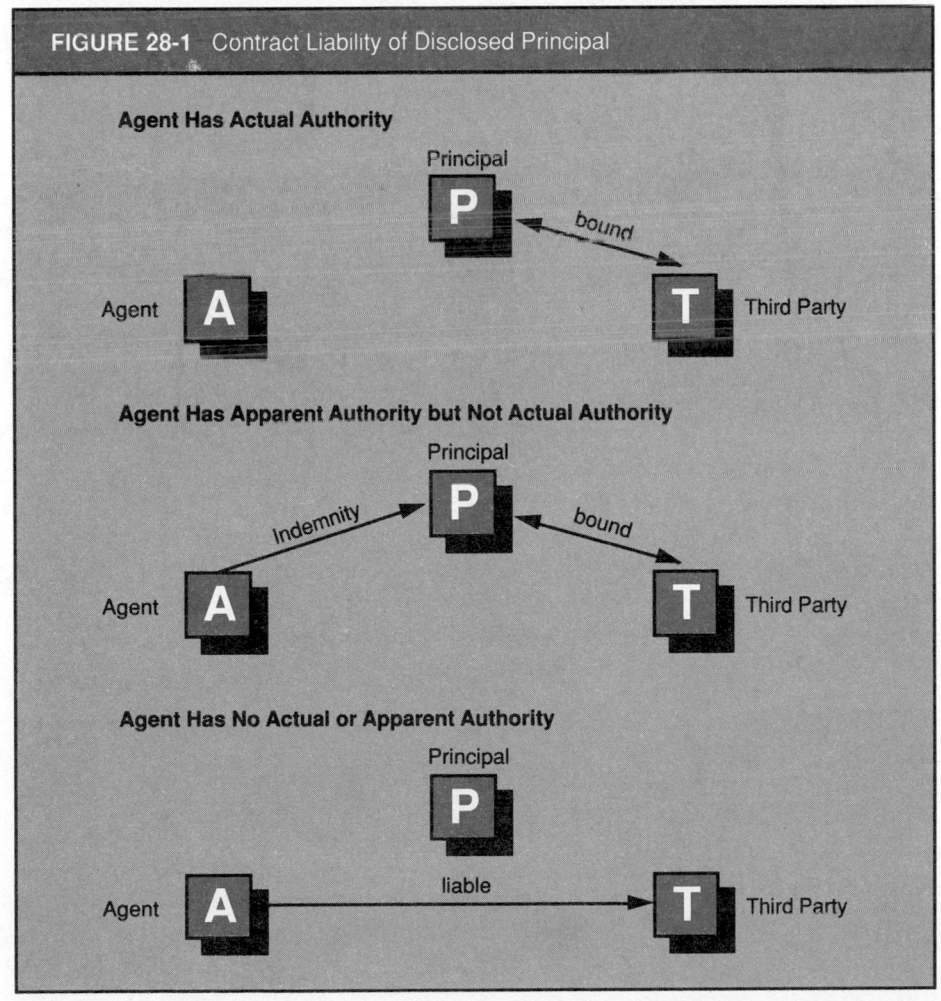

FIGURE 28-1   Contract Liability of Disclosed Principal

Agent Has Actual Authority

Principal

P

bound

Agent   A

T   Third Party

Agent Has Apparent Authority but Not Actual Authority

Principal

P

Indemnity   *bound*

Agent   A

T   Third Party

Agent Has No Actual or Apparent Authority

Principal

P

liable

Agent   A   T   Third Party

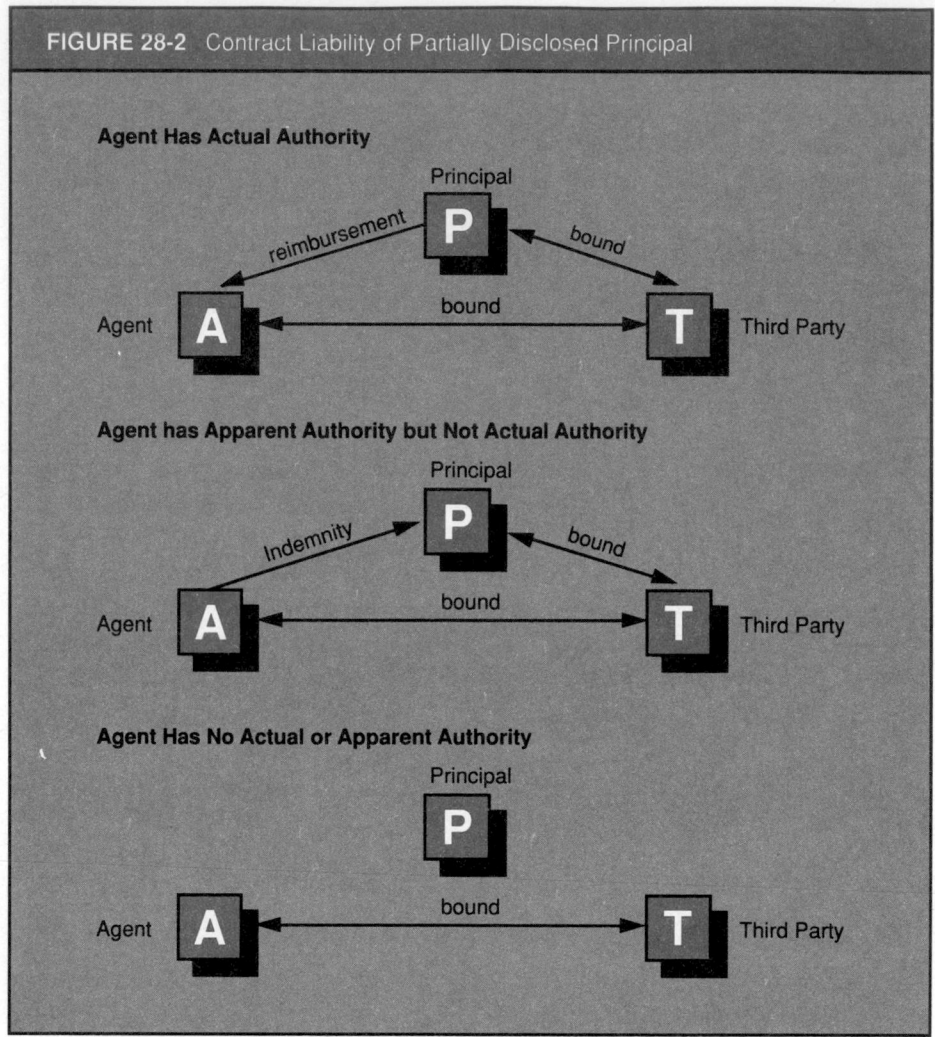

FIGURE 28-2   Contract Liability of Partially Disclosed Principal

ity of Arlene exists only with respect to Thad. If Arlene were to give David an order for a shipment of lumber to Polly, David would not be able to hold Polly liable. No actual authority existed, and as to David there was no apparent authority.

Since apparent authority is the power resulting from acts that appear to the third party to be authorized by the principal, there can be no apparent authority where the principal is *undisclosed*. See Figure 28–3.

SCHOENBERGER v. CHICAGO TRANSIT AUTHORITY
Appellate Court of Illinois, First District, First Division, 1980.
84 Ill.App.3d 1132, 39 Ill.Dec. 941, 405 N.E.2d 1076.

Facts: Schoenberger applied for and interviewed concerning a position with the Chicago Transit Authority (C.T.A.). He met several times with Frank ZuChristian, who was in charge of recruiting for the C.T.A. Data Center. At the third of these meetings, ZuChristian informed Schoenberger that he wanted to employ him at a salary of $19,800 and that he was making a recommendation to that effect. When the formal offer was made by the placement department, however, the salary was stated at $19,300. Schoenberger did not accept the offer immediately but instead called ZuChristian for an explanation of the salary difference. After making inquiries, ZuChristian informed Schoenberger that a clerical error had been made and that it would take some time to correct. He urged Schoenberger to accept the job at $19,300 and said that he would see that the $500 was made up to him at one of the salary reviews in the following year. When the increase was not given, Schoenberger resigned and filed this suit to recover damages. The trial court ruled in favor of C.T.A. and Schoenberger appeals.

Decision: Judgment for Chicago Transit Authority affirmed.

Opinion: Campbell, J. The main question before us is whether ZuChristian, acting as an agent of the C.T.A., orally contracted with Schoenberger for $500 in compensation in addition to his $19,300 salary. The authority of an agent may only come from the principal and it is therefore necessary to trace the source of an agent's authority to some word or act of the alleged principal. [Citations.] The authority to bind a principal will not be presumed, but rather, the person alleging authority must prove its source unless the act of the agent has been ratified. [Citations.] Moreover, the authority must be founded upon some word or act of the principal, not on the acts or words of the agent. [Citations.]

* * * Both Hogan and Bonner, ZuChristian's superiors, testified that ZuChristian had no actual authority to either make an offer of a specific salary to Schoenberger or to make any promise of additional compensation. Furthermore, ZuChristian's testimony corroborated the testimony that he lacked the authority to make formal offers. From this evidence, it is clear that the trial court properly determined that ZuChristian lacked the actual authority to bind the C.T.A. for the additional $500 in compensation to Schoenberger.

Nor can it be said that the C.T.A. clothed ZuChristian with the apparent authority to make Schoenberger a promise of compensation over and above that formally offered by the Placement Department. The general rule to consider in determining whether an agent is acting within the apparent authority of his principal was stated in [citation] in this way:

Apparent authority in an agent is such authority as the principal knowingly permits the agent to assume or which he holds his agent out as possessing—it is such authority as a reasonably prudent man, exercising diligence and discretion, in view of the principal's conduct, would naturally suppose the agent to possess.

* * *

Here, Schoenberger's initial contact with the C.T.A. was with the Placement Department where he filled out an application and had his first interview. There is no evidence that the C.T.A. did anything to permit ZuChristian to assume authority nor did they do anything to hold him out as having the authority to hire and set salaries. ZuChristian was not at a management level in the C.T.A. nor did his job title of Principal Communications Analyst suggest otherwise. The mere fact that he was allowed to interview prospective employees does not establish that the C.T.A. held him out as possessing the authority to hire employees or set salaries. Moreover, ZuChristian did inform Schoenberger that the formal offer of employment would be made by the Placement Department.

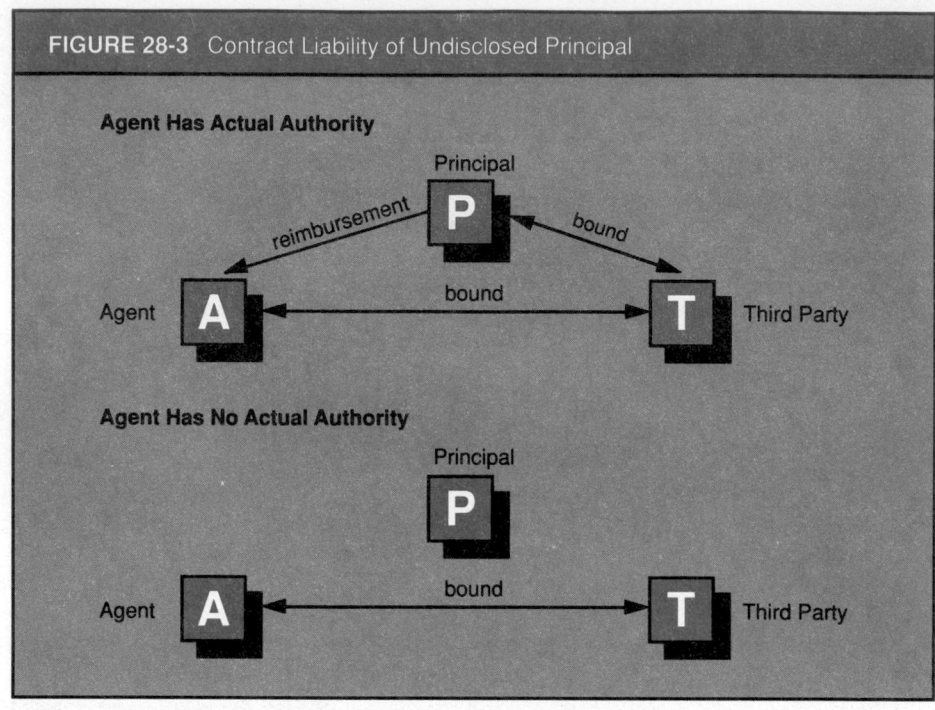

FIGURE 28-3 Contract Liability of Undisclosed Principal

Delegation of Authority

The appointment of an agent reflects the confidence and reliance of the principal on the agent's personal skill, integrity, and other qualifications. The agent has been selected because of her fitness to perform the task assigned to her and therefore ordinarily has no power to delegate her authority or to appoint a subagent.[6] Thus, Donna employs Harold to collect her accounts. Harold may not delegate this authority to Davis, as Donna reposed trust and confidence in Harold and not in Davis.

In certain situations it is clear that the principal intended to permit the agent to delegate the authority granted to her. Such an intention may be gathered from the express authorization of the principal, the character of the business, the usages of trade, or the prior conduct of the parties.[7] For example, if a check is deposited in a bank for collection at a distant place, the bank is impliedly authorized to employ another bank at the place of payment.

If an agent is authorized to appoint or select other persons, called **subagents,** to perform or assist in the performance of the agent's duties, the acts of the subagent are binding on the principal to the same extent as if they had been done by the agent. The subagent is an agent of both the principal and the agent and owes a fiduciary duty to both.

If no authority exists to delegate the agent's authority, but the agent nevertheless does so, the acts of the subagent do not impose on the principal any obligations or liability to third persons. Likewise, the principal acquires no rights against such third persons.

Effect of Termination of Agency on Authority

On the termination of an agency, the agent's actual authority ceases. When the termination is by death or incapacity of the principal or agent, the agent's apparent authority also expires.[8] Notice of such termination to third persons is *not* required. Thus, in a case where Thomas, a tenant of the principal, Perry, paid rent to Perry's agent, Augustus, in ignorance of Perry's death, and Augustus failed to account for the payment, Thomas is liable to Perry's estate for payment of the amount of the rent. The same holds where an authorized transaction is made impossible of performance,[8] such as where the subject matter of the transaction is destroyed or the transaction is made illegal.

In other cases, apparent authority continues until the third party has knowledge or receives actual notice, if the third party is one (1) with whom the agent had previously dealt on credit, (2) to whom the agent has been specially accredited, or (3) with whom the agent has begun to deal.[9] **Actual notice** requires a communication to the third party, either oral or written. All other third parties must have knowledge or be given **constructive notice,** such as publication in a newspaper of general circulation in the area where the agency is regularly carried on.[9] To illustrate: Alfred is the general agent of Pace, who carries on business in Chicago. Carol knows of the agency, but has never dealt with Alfred. Daphne sells goods on credit to Alfred, as agent of Pace. Pace revokes Alfred's authority and publishes a statement to that effect in a newspaper of general circulation published in Chicago. Carol does not see the statement and deals with Alfred in reliance upon the former agency. Daphne also does not see the statement and has no knowledge of the revocation. Daphne sells more goods to Alfred, as the agent of Pace. Pace has given sufficient notice of revocation as to Carol and, therefore, Alfred's apparent authority has terminated with respect to Carol. On the other hand, Pace has not given sufficient notice of revocation as to Daphne, and Pace is bound to Daphne by the contract of sale made on Pace's behalf by Alfred.

ZUKAITIS v. AETNA CASUALTY AND SURETY CO.
Supreme Court of Nebraska, 1975.
195 Neb. 59, 236 N.W.2d 819.

Facts: Raymond Zukaitis was a physician practicing medicine in Douglas County, Nebraska. Aetna issued a policy of professional liability insurance to Zukaitis through its agent, the Ed Larsen Insurance Agency. The policy covered the period from August 31, 1969, through August of the following year. On August 7, 1971, Dr. Zukaitis received a written notification of a claim for malpractice that occurred on September 27, 1969. Dr. Zukaitis notified the Ed Larsen Insurance Agency immediately and forwarded the written claim to them. The claim was then mistakenly referred to St. Paul Fire and Marine Insurance Company, the company that currently insured Dr. Zukaitis. Apparently without notice to Dr. Zukaitis, the agency contract between Larsen and Aetna had been canceled on August 1, 1970, and St. Paul had been replaced as the insurance carrier. When St. Paul discovered it was not the carrier on the date of the alleged wrongdoing, it notified Aetna and withdrew from Dr. Zukaitis's defense. Aetna, however, refused to represent Dr. Zukaitis, contending that it was relieved of its obligation to Dr. Zukaitis because he had not notified Aetna immediately of the claim. Dr. Zukaitis then secured his own attorney to defend against the malpractice claim and brought this action against Aetna to recover the attorney's fees and other expenses incurred in the defense. The trial court found for Aetna and Dr. Zukaitis appeals.

Decision: Judgment for Aetna reversed and remanded.

Opinion: Blue, J. Ordinarily notice to a soliciting agent who countersigns and issues policies of insurance is notice to the insurance company. [Citations.] This is also true even if the agent forwards the notice to the wrong company. * * *

* * *

The question then is whether this is true after the agency contract between the insurance company and the agent has been terminated as it was in this case. To answer this, it is necessary to refer to the general law of agency.

The rule is that a revocation [by agreement of the principal and agent] of the agent's authority does not become effective as between the principal and third persons until they receive [actual] notice of the termination. [Citations.]

Here, Dr. Zukaitis did what most reasonable persons would do in this situation; he notified the agent who sold him the policy. There is no evidence that notice of the termination was sent to him or that he knew the agency contract has been canceled.

"When the insurer terminates the agency contract, it is its duty to notify third persons, such as the insureds with whom the agent dealt, and inform them of such termination. If it does not so notify and such third persons or insureds deal with the agent without notice or knowledge of the termination, and in reliance on the apparently continuing authority of the agent, the insurer is bound by the acts of the former agent." [Citation.]

"The principle of the carrying over of the authority of an agent after termination with respect to third persons having no notice or knowledge thereof has been applied so as to bind the insurer when the third person dealt with the apparent agent by contracting with him, or by forwarding or delivering to him suit papers and proofs of loss." [Citation.]

Ratification

Ratification is the confirmation or affirmance by one person of a prior act that another, without authority, has done as his agent. The ratification of such act or contract binds the principal and the third party as if the agent had been initially authorized.[10]

Ratification may relate to the acts of an agent that have exceeded the authority granted to him, as well as to acts that a person without any authority makes on behalf of an alleged principal. The actor, however, must have indicated to the third person that he was acting on behalf of a principal in order that the act may be ratified. There can be no ratification by a principal who is undisclosed. Thus, Archie, without any authority, contracts to sell to Tina an automobile belonging to Pierce. Archie states that the auto is Pierce's and that Archie is acting on Pierce's behalf. Tina promises to pay $5,500 for the automobile. Pierce subsequently learns of the agreement and affirms. Pierce's ratification of Archie's action is effective. On the other hand, if Archie had stated to Tina that the automobile was his, then Pierce's

affirmation would *not* be a ratification because Archie did not purport to act on Pierce's behalf.

To effect a ratification, the principal must show an intent to do so with knowledge of all material facts concerning the transaction.[11] The principal does not need to communicate this intent either to the purported agent or to the third person. It may be manifested by express language or implied from conduct of the principal. Thus, if Amanda, without authority contracts in Penelope's name for the purchase of goods from Tate on credit, and Penelope, having learned of Amanda's unauthorized act, accepts the goods from Tate, she thereby impliedly ratifies the contract and is bound on the contract. In express ratification, the principal gives notice of affirmance of the unauthorized act to the third person. In any event, the principal must ratify the entire act or contract.[12]

A ratification relates back to the time of performance of the unauthorized act. For example, Jeffrey, without authority from Robin, represents to Bart that he is Robin's agent and on June 1 enters into a bilateral executory contract with Bart on behalf of Robin. Because Jeffrey acted without authority neither Robin nor Bart is bound to the supposed contract. On June 15 Robin ratifies the act of Jeffrey. Both Robin and Bart thereupon become bound to the contract, effective as of June 1, to which date the ratification relates. Suppose, however, that on June 12 Bart learned of Jeffrey's lack of authority and notified Robin that he withdrew from the contract. Robin's ratification of June 15 would not cause a contract to be formed. To be effective, ratification must occur before the third person gives notice to the principal or agent of his withdrawal.[13]

If the affirmance of a transaction occurs at a time when the situation has so materially changed that it would be inequitable to subject the third party to liability on the transaction, the third party may elect to avoid liability. For example, Alex has no authority but, purporting to act for Penny, Alex contracts to sell Penny's house to Taylor. The next day the house burns down. Penny then affirms. Taylor is not bound.

Finally, for ratification to be effective, the purported principal must have been in existence when the act was done. For example, a promoter of a corporation not yet in existence may enter into contracts on behalf of the corporation. In the vast majority of States, these acts cannot be *ratified* by the corporation because it did not exist when the contracts were made.

Once made, a valid ratification is irrevocable. Ratification is equivalent to prior authority, which means that the effect of ratification is substantially the same as though the purported agent had been a duly authorized agent when he performed the act. The respective rights, duties, and remedies of the principal and the third party are the same as if the agent had originally possessed due authority. Both the principal and the agent are in the same position as they would have been if the act had been originally authorized by the principal. The agent is entitled to her due compensation. Moreover, the agent is freed from liability to the principal for acting as his agent without authority or for exceeding her authority, as the case may be. Between the agent and the third party, the agent is released from any liability she may have been under to the third party by reason of her having induced the third party to enter into the contract without the principal's authority.

BRADSHAW v. McBRIDE
Supreme Court of Utah, 1982.
649 P.2d 74.

Facts: Aretta J. Parkinson owned a 200-acre farm. Prior to her death on December 23, 1976, Parkinson deeded a one-eighth undivided interest in the farm to each of her eight children as tenants in common. On January 15, 1977, one of the daughters, Roma Funk, approached Barbara Bradshaw about purchasing the Parkinson farm. They orally agreed to a selling price of $33,000. After this meeting, Funk contacted Bryant Hansen, a real estate broker, to assist her in completing the transaction. Hansen prepared an earnest money agreement that was signed by the Bradshaws but by none of the Parkinson children. Hansen also prepared warranty deeds, which were signed by three of the children. Several of the children subsequently refused to convey their interests in the farm to the Bradshaws. The Bradshaws brought an action against the defendants, seeking specific performance of the oral contract of sale. The trial court ruled for the Bradshaws, finding that the defendants ratified the oral contract by their knowledge of and failure to repudiate it. The defendants appealed.

Decision: Judgment for Bradshaws reversed.

Opinion: Stewart, J.   A principal may impliedly or expressly ratify an agreement made by an unauthorized agent. Ratification of an agent's acts relates back to the time the unauthorized act occurred and is sufficient to create the relationship of principal and agent. [Citations.] A deliberate and valid ratification with full knowledge of all the material facts is binding and cannot afterward be revoked or recalled. [Citation.] However, a ratification requires the principal to have knowledge of all material facts and an intent to ratify. [Citation.] Under some circumstances failure to disaffirm may constitute ratification of the agent's acts. In [citation]:

> Ratification like original authority need not be express. Any conduct which indicates assent by the purported principal to become a party to the transaction or which is justifiable only if there is ratification is sufficient. Even silence with full knowledge of the facts may manifest affirmance and thus operate as a ratification. The person with whom the agent dealt will so obviously be deceived by assuming the professed agent was authorized to act as such, that the principal is under a duty to undeceive him. . . . So a purported principal may not be wilfully ignorant, nor may he purposely shut his eyes to means of information within his possession and control and thereby escape ratification 'if the circumstances are such that he could reasonably have been expected to dissent unless he were willing to be a party to the transaction.'. . .

The trial court found that the defendants other than Funk had ratified the Funk-Bradshaw agreement, in part, by their knowledge and acceptance of the agreement. This finding, however, is clearly not supported by the evidence in the record as to two defendants who were not notified of the agreement until receipt of the warranty deeds prepared by Hansen. Funk testified that she did not contact her brother Foch or John Lister, the administrator of Annabelle Lister's estate. At trial, Foch testified that when he first learned of the agreement he was opposed to it, but was willing to go along with the agreement only if the court found it enforceable. Foch attempted to determine the validity of the contract by meeting with his attorney and Ron Bradshaw in his attorney's office. He continually stated his objection to the agreement, and his actions cannot be interpreted as ratification. John Lister testified that he did not become aware of the agreement until he received the real estate documents from Hansen. Lister did not sign the documents and did nothing to ratify the agreement between Funk and Bradshaw. When presented with a writing to convey ownership in property, Lister had no duty to disavow any putative agreement. On the contrary, his failure to sign is evidence of rejection. It is clear that neither Foch nor Lister in fact ratified the agreement.

Furthermore, as to all defendants, there was no ratification as a matter of law because the Utah statute of frauds requires that any agent executing an agreement conveying an interest in land on behalf of his principal must be authorized in writing. [Citation.] In order to enforce an oral agreement, the same kind of authorization that is required to clothe an agent initially with authority to contract must be given by the principal to constitute a ratification of an unauthorized act. Where the law requires the authority to be given in writing, the ratification must also generally be in writing. [Citations.] There was, therefore, no ratification in this case.

Fundamental Rules of Contractual Liability

The following rules summarize the contractual relations between the principal and the third party:

1. A disclosed principal and the third party are contractually bound if the agent acts within her *actual* or *apparent* authority in making the contract. See Figure 28–1.

2. A partially disclosed principal and the third party are contractually bound if the agent acts within her *actual* or *apparent* authority in making the contract. See Figure 28–2.

3. An undisclosed principal and the third party are contractually bound if the agent acts within her *actual* authority in making the contract unless (a) the principal is excluded by the terms of the contract, or (b) his existence is fraudulently concealed. See Figure 28–3.

4. No principal is contractually bound to a third party if the agent acts *without* any authority unless a disclosed or partially disclosed principal ratifies the contract.

TORT LIABILITY OF THE PRINCIPAL

In addition to contract liability to third persons, a principal may be liable in tort to third persons as a consequence of the acts of her agent. Tort liability may arise directly or indirectly (vicariously) from authorized or unauthorized acts of the agent. Also, a principal is liable for the unauthorized torts committed by an agent in connection with a transaction that the purported principal, with full knowledge of the tort, subsequently ratifies.[14] Needless to say, cases involving unauthorized but ratified torts are extremely rare.

Direct Liability of Principal

All individuals are liable for their own tortious conduct. Consequently, a principal may be held liable in damages for his own negligence or recklessness in carrying on an activity through employees or agents. Such negligence or recklessness may result from giving improper or ambiguous orders, using improper persons or instruments, or providing inadequate supervision.[15] For example, if Larry lends to his employee, Molly, a company car to run a business errand knowing that Molly is incapable of driving the vehicle, Larry would be liable for his own negligence to anyone injured by Molly's negligent driving.

Vicarious Liability of Principal for Authorized Acts of Agent

A principal who authorizes his agent to commit a tortious act concerning the property or person of another is **vicariously liable** for the injury or loss sustained by that person.[16] The authorized act is that of the principal. Thus, if Phillip directs his agent, Anthony, to enter on Clark's land and cut timber, which neither Phillip nor Anthony has any right to do, the cutting of the timber is a trespass, and Phillip is liable to Clark. Or, suppose Phillip instructs his agent, Anthony, to make certain representations as to Phillip's property that Anthony is authorized to sell. Phillip knows these representations are false, but Anthony does not. Such representations by Anthony to Dryden, who buys the property in reliance on them, is a deceit for which Phillip is liable to Dryden.

Vicarious Liability of Principal for Unauthorized Acts of Agent

The liability of a principal for unauthorized torts by an agent depends primarily on whether the agent is an employee or not. An employee is an agent employed to perform services for the principal-employer and whose physical conduct in the performance of the service is controlled or subject to the right to control by the principal. If the agent's physical conduct is not controlled or subject to the control of the principal, then the agent is not an employee but is an independent contractor. The general rule is that a principal is *not* liable for physical harm caused by the tortious conduct of an agent who is an independent contractor if the principal did not intend or authorize the result or the manner of performance.[17] Conversely, a principal is liable for an unauthorized tort committed by an employee in the course of his employment.[18] See *Massey v. Tube Art Display, Inc.* in Chapter 27.

On the other hand, if an agent makes an unauthorized yet tortious **misrepresentation,** the principal's liability does not depend upon whether the agent is an employee. A principal is liable for loss caused to another who relies upon a tortious representation made by an agent (whether an employee or an independent contractor) if the representation is *apparently* authorized.[19] For example, Adams is an agent of Pillsbury engaged to sell some land owned by Pillsbury. While negotiating with Trent, Adams states that a stream running through the property had not overflowed its banks during the past ten years. Adams knows that this is false. In reliance upon this false statement, Trent purchases the land. Pillsbury is liable to Trent for fraudulent misrepresentation.

Respondeat Superior An employer may be liable for an unauthorized tort committed by his employee, even one that is in flagrant disobedience of his instructions, if the tort was committed by the employee in the course of her employment. This is a form of liability without fault and is based on the doctrine of **respondeat superior,** ("let the superior respond"). The rationale of this doctrine is that a person who carries out his business activities through the use of employees should be liable for their tortious conduct in carrying out the business purposes for which they were employed. It is the price the employer pays for enlarging the scope of his business activities. It does not matter how carefully the employer selected the employee, if in fact that latter tortiously injured a third person while engaged in the business of the employer. Moreover, an undisclosed principal-employer is liable for the torts committed by his employee within the scope of employment.[20]

The liability of the principal under *respondeat superior* is vicarious or derivative and depends on proof of wrongdoing by the employee *in the course of his employment.*[18] Frequently, both principal and employee are defendants in the same suit. If the employee is not held liable, the principal is not liable. A principal who is held liable for her employee's tort has a right of **indemnification** against the employee, which is the right to be reimbursed for the amount that she was required to pay as a result of the employee's wrongful act. See Figure 28–4. Frequently an employee is not able to reimburse his employer, and the principal must bear the brunt of the liability.

The wrongful act of the employee must be connected with his employment and within its scope if the principal is to be held liable for resulting injuries or damage to third persons.[21] For example, Hal is delivering gasoline for Martha. He lights his pipe and negligently throws the blazing match into a pool of gasoline that has dripped on the ground during the delivery. The gasoline ignites. For the resulting harm, Martha is subject to liability because the negligence of the employee delivering the gasoline relates directly to the manner in which he is handling the goods in his custody. But if a chauffeur, while driving his employer's car on an errand for his employer, suddenly decided to use his pistol and shoot at pedestrians on the sidewalk for target practice, the employer would not be liable to the pedestrians. This willful and intentional misconduct is not related to the performance of the services for which the chauffeur was employed.

The same rule applies to tortious conduct of an employee unrelated to his employment. If Page employs Earl to deliver merchandise to Page's customers in a given city, and while driving a delivery truck in going to or returning from a place of delivery Earl negligently causes the truck to hit and injure Fred, Page is liable to Fred for injuries sustained. But if, after making the scheduled deliveries, Earl drives the truck to a neighboring city to visit a friend and while so doing negligently causes the truck to hit and injure Dottie, Page is not liable. In such case, Earl is said to be on a "frolic of his own." He has deviated from the purpose of his employment and was using Page's truck to accomplish his own purposes, not those of his employer. Of course, in all of these situations the wrongdoing agent is personally liable to the injured persons because he committed a tort. See *Austen v. Sherwood* on page 606.

Torts of Independent Contractor An independent contractor is not the employee of the person for whom he is performing work or rendering services. Hence, the doctrine of *respondeat superior* does not apply to torts committed by an independent contractor such as an attorney, broker, or rental agent. For example, Parnell authorizes Bob, his broker, to sell land for him. Parnell, Teresa, and Bob meet in Teresa's office. Bob arranges the sale to Teresa. While Bob is preparing a deed for Parnell to sign, he negligently knocks over an inkstand and ruins a valuable rug belonging to Teresa. Bob but *not* Parnell is liable to Teresa. Similarly,

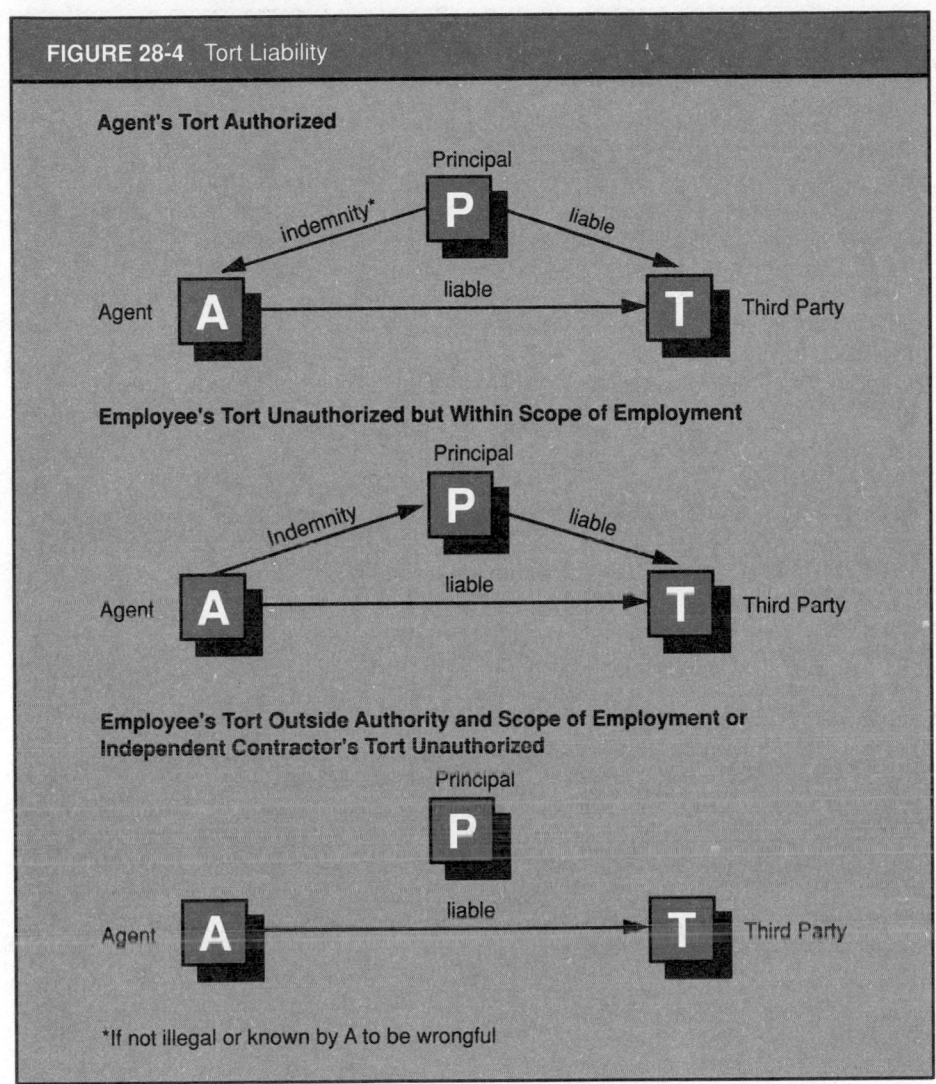

FIGURE 28-4 Tort Liability

Agent's Tort Authorized

Principal

indemnity*   liable

Agent

liable

Third Party

Employee's Tort Unauthorized but Within Scope of Employment

Principal

Indemnity   liable

Agent

liable

Third Party

Employee's Tort Outside Authority and Scope of Employment or Independent Contractor's Tort Unauthorized

Principal

Agent

liable

Third Party

*If not illegal or known by A to be wrongful

Patty employs Igor, a roofer, as an independent contractor to repair Patty's roof. Igor drops a hammer upon Wanda, a pedestrian walking by on the public sidewalk. Igor but not Patty is liable to Wanda.

Nevertheless, certain duties imposed by law are nondelegable, and a person may not escape the consequences of their nonperformance by contracting with an independent contractor. For example, a landowner who permits an independent contractor to maintain a dangerous condition on his premises, such as an excavation that adjoins a public sidewalk and is unprotected by a guard rail or by lights at night, is liable to a member of the public who is injured as a result of falling into the excavation.

Moreover, the principal may be liable if he should know that there is an undue risk that the agent will be negligent and harm others. Thus, Melanie employs Gordon as an independent contractor to repair her roof. Melanie knows that Gordon is an alcoholic. Gordon attempts the repairs while heavily intoxicated and drops a fifty-pound bundle of shingles upon Eric, a pedestrian walking by on the public sidewalk. Both Gordon and Melanie are liable to Eric.

AUSTEN v. SHERWOOD
Court of Appeals of Louisiana, Fifth Circuit, 1983.
425 So.2d 818.

Facts: Sherwood negligently ran into the rear of Austen's car, which was stopped at a stoplight. As a result, Austen received bodily injuries and her car was damaged. Sherwood, arts editor for the *Mississippi Press Register,* was en route from a Louis Armstrong concert he had covered for the newspaper. When the accident occurred he was on his way to spend the night at a friend's house. Austen sued Sherwood and—under the doctrine of *respondeat superior*—Sherwood's employer, the *Mississippi Press Register.* The trial court found for Austen against Sherwood and the *Mississippi Press Register.* The *Mississippi Press Register* brings this appeal.

Decision: Judgment for Austen against the *Mississippi Press Register* reversed.

Opinion: Grisbaum, J. The issue on appeal is whether Sherwood was acting within the course and scope of his employment with Mississippi Press Register at the time of the collision. The trial judge, in his reasons for judgment, was satisfied by the testimony at trial and by the depositions introduced into evidence that the defendant, Wallace Sherwood, was acting within the course and scope of his employment. The trial judge stated that although Mr. Sherwood did attend the concert partly for personal reasons, that fact did not mean his attendance was not in the course and scope of his employment.

However, although Mr. Sherwood may have attended the concert within the scope of his employment, the accident occurred on his way to a friend's house to sleep for the night. The negligent acts of an employee on his way to or from work are not generally imputable to an employer under [Louisiana law]. [Citation.] The inquiry is whether the employee's tortious conduct was so closely connected in time, place and causation to his employment duties as to be regarded a risk of harm fairly attributable to the employer's business, as compared with conduct motivated by purely personal considerations entirely extraneous to the employer's interests. [Citation.] In the instant case Sherwood was clearly on his own time which in no way benefited his employer nor was related to the service of his employer. [Citation.] The accident did not occur within the course and scope of Sherwood's employment.

CRIMINAL LIABILITY OF THE PRINCIPAL

A principal is liable for the authorized criminal acts of his agents only if the principal directed, participated in, or approved of the acts. For example, if an agent, at his principal's direction or with his principal's knowledge, fixes prices with the principal's competitors, both the agent and the principal have criminally violated the antitrust laws. Otherwise, a principal is not ordinarily liable for the unauthorized criminal acts of his agents. One of the elements of a crime is mental fault, and this element is not present, so far as criminal responsibility of the principal is concerned, where the act of the agent was not authorized.

An employer may, nevertheless, be subject to a criminal penalty for the act of an advisory or managerial person acting in the scope of employment. Moreover, an employer may be criminally liable under liability without fault statutes for certain unauthorized acts of his employees, whether the employee is managerial or not. These statutes are usually regulatory statutes and do not require mental fault.

For example, many States have statutes that punish "every person who by himself or his employee or agent sells anything at short weight," or "whoever sells liquor to a minor and any sale by an employee shall be deemed the act of the employer as well." Another example is a statute prohibiting the sale of unwholesome or adulterated food. See Chapter 4 for a more detailed discussion of this topic. Also, see Law in the News on page 608.

RELATIONSHIP OF AGENT AND THIRD PERSONS

The function of an agent is to assist in the conduct of the principal's business by carrying out his orders. Generally, the agent acquires no rights against third parties and likewise incurs no liabilities to them. There are, however, several exceptions to this proposition. In certain instances, an agent may become personally liable to the third party for contracts she made on behalf of a principal. In some of these situations, the agent may also acquire rights against the third party. In addition, an agent who commits a tort is personally liable to the injured third party. In this section, we cover these circumstances involving the personal liability of an agent, as well as those under which an agent may acquire rights against third persons.

CONTRACT LIABILITY OF AGENT

The agent is not normally a party to the contract he makes with a third person on behalf of a disclosed principal. If the agent exceeds his actual and apparent authority, however, he may be personally liable to the third party. In addition, an agent acting for a disclosed principal may become liable if he guarantees performance of the contract by the principal. When an agent enters into a contract on behalf of a partially disclosed principal or an undisclosed principal, the agent also becomes personally liable to the third party on the contract. Furthermore, an agent who knowingly enters into a contract on behalf of a nonexistent or incompetent principal is per-

sonally liable to the third party on that contract.

Disclosed Principal

As we explained earlier, an agent acts for a disclosed principal when at the time of the transaction the other party has notice that the agent is acting for a principal and of the principal's identity. The agent is not normally a party to the contract she makes with a third person on behalf of a disclosed principal. The third person is on notice that he is transacting business with an agent who is acting for an identified principal and that the agent is not personally undertaking to perform the contract, but that she is simply negotiating on behalf of her principal. The resulting contract, if within the agent's actual or apparent authority, is between the third person and the principal. The agent ordinarily incurs no liability on the contract to either party.[22] Thus, Angela who has actual authority to sell circuit boards manufactured by Pinter, writes to Toni: "On behalf of Pinter, I offer to sell you 5,000 circuit boards for $15,000." Toni accepts. There is a contract between Toni and Pinter. Angela is not a party to that contract and has no liability to Pinter or Toni. See Figure 28–1.

Unauthorized Contracts   If an agent exceeds his actual and apparent authority, the principal is not bound. The fact that the principal is not bound does not make the agent a party to the contract. The agent's liability, if any, arises from express or implied representations about his authority that he makes to the third party. An agent may **expressly warrant** that he has authority. For example, the agent may state that he has authority and that he will be personally liable to the third party if he does not have the authority to bind his principal.

Moreover, a person who undertakes to make a contract on behalf of another gives an **implied warranty** that he is in fact authorized to make the contract on behalf of the party whom he purports to represent. If the agent does not have authority to bind the principal, the agent is liable to the third party for damages unless the principal ratifies the contract or the third

Murder in the Front Office

Corporate crime has never provoked the same indignation as street violence; it seemed a little roguish, perhaps but nothing that actually hurt anyone. But if last week was an indication, that image is about to change. In suburban Chicago, a judge prepared to sentence three corporate executives to jail terms of up to 40 years. Their crime: on-the-job homicide. Meanwhile, in a courtroom in Toms River, N.J., the trial of Great Adventure Inc. amusement park completed its seventh week on charges stemming from a fire last year that killed eight teen-agers. And in Los Angeles, investigators from the district attorney's office seized the records of the Jalisco Mexican Products Co., whose tainted cheese has allegedly killed 48 people since mid-March. That fishing expedition aims to net any corporate officer who looked away while contaminated goods went to market.

For the moment, criminal prosecution of corporations and their executives may be a growth industry. As work-safety agents have retreated in the name of deregulation, local prosecutors are forcing managers to review their health-and-safety policies. "Any businessman who isn't more careful is foolish," says Richard Kissell, a corporate lawyer in Chicago. "Now a wrong decision could lose them money [and] land them in jail."

It still takes an especially sloppy executive and an unusually vigorous prosecutor to put a corporation in the dock. According to legal doctrine, corporations are regarded as individuals and can be held accountable for their officers' actions; if the executives are sufficiently reckless, then their actions—or failures to act in the face of danger—can be prosecuted as well. But there is "very seldom a smoking gun" in these cases, says William J. Maakestad, a Western Illinois University professor who has served as an aide to Cook County prosecutors. As a result, they may be very difficult to prove.

'Indignant'

That was certainly true in Elk Grove Village, Ill., where Stefan Golab worked for Film Recovery Systems Corp. Golab's job was cleaning the barrels of cyanide into which exposed X-rays were dunked, a necessary step in recovering silver from the film. In February 1983 he collapsed on the job; the county coroner ruled that the cyanide fumes had killed him. Yet it took months for state investigators to piece together a sturdy case. Managers failed to caution workers about the lethal cyanide—although the cyanide suppliers repeat-

party knew that the agent was unauthorized. No implied warranty exists, however, if the contract expressly provides that the agent shall not be responsible for any lack of authority or if the agent, acting in good faith, discloses to the third person all of the facts upon which his authority rests. For example, agent Larson has received an ambiguous letter of instruction from his principal, Dan. Larson shows it to Carol stating that it represents all of the authority that he has to act, and both Larson and Carol rely upon its sufficiency. In this case, there is no implied or express warranty by Larson to Carol of his authority.

If a purported agent **misrepresents** to a third person that he has authority to make a contract

on behalf of a principal whom he has no power to bind, he is liable in a tort action to the third person for the loss sustained in reliance upon the misrepresentation. If the third party, however, knows that the representations are false, then the agent is not liable.

Agent Assumes Liability   An agent may agree to become liable on a contract between the principal and the third party. She may do this by making the contract in her own name or by co-making the contract with the principal. Or she may guarantee that the principal will perform the contract between the third party and the principal. In all of these situations, the agent's liability is separate unless the parties

edly warned the firm—and provided only cotton gloves, no match for the corrosive chemicals. Uncovered tanks spewed fumes into the factory, and managers ignored complaints of illness. The investigation led to charges of murder against corporate owners and managers for having "knowingly created a strong probability of death," a statute normally reserved for an arsonist who torches an occupied building.

After an eight-week trial, Judge Ronald J. P. Banks, sitting without a jury, convicted former FRS president Steven O'Neil, plant foreman Daniel Rodriguez and plant manager Charles Kirschbaum—the first time in the nation's history that a murder charge had been sustained against an employer. "I'm more indignant about this case than other murders," says prosecutor Jay Maguson. "We're talking about educated, privileged people taking advantage of the poor." The three defendants plan to appeal, arguing that at worst they were no more than negligent. They insist they didn't know the plant was dangerous; the officers say they worked near the vats themselves. "If we find them guilty of murder," says defense lawyer Ronald Menaker, "we may as well find them guilty of attempted suicide."

Reckless

Sometimes managers can talk themselves out of a case, leaving the corporation to face the rap. New Jersey prosecutors originally charged two corporate officers with manslaughter after part of Great Adventure burned down last May. Instead of standing trial, the two agreed to perform several hundred hours of community service, after which the charges will be dropped. But the state is pursuing aggravated manslaughter charges against the park and its parent, Six Flags Corp. The prosecutors charge that the company recklessly ignored warnings that it needed more fire-prevention devices; the defense says the park believed it had complied with local building and fire codes and the recommendations of safety consultants. If convicted, the corporations face fines of up to $600,000. But where's the logic in convicting a firm for acts committed by senior officers who get off with barely a wrist slap? That's an anomaly that the law has learned to live with, says Kathleen Brickey, a Washington University law professor. Juries are often reluctant to convict corporate officers even when they're willing to throw the book at the company. And sometimes, opting for collective guilt is equitable because no one can tell just who, if anyone, is individually responsible.

It's unclear whether holding corporations criminally liable is more than a passing fad; these high-profile cases may well remain isolated phenomena. But the specter of punishment may be the sort of short-term incentive that no M.B.A. could afford to ignore.

ARIC PRESS with SHAWN DOHERTY in Chicago. MADLYN RESENER in New York and bureau reports. From *Newsweek*, July 8, 1985. © 1985, Newsweek, Inc. All rights reserved. Reprinted by permission.

---

agree otherwise. Therefore, the third party may sue the agent separately without joining the principal. The third party may obtain a judgment against either the principal or the agent or both. If the principal satisfies the judgment, then the agent is discharged. If the agent pays the judgment, he will usually have a right of reimbursement from the principal. This right is based upon principles of suretyship discussed in Chapter 38.

Partially Disclosed Principal

An agent, as we previously discussed, acts for a partially disclosed principal if the third party has notice that the agent is acting for a principal but has no notice of the principal's identity. Thus, the third person is aware that the agent is acting on behalf of another, but he is not informed of the name or identity of the principal. The use of partially disclosed principals may be helpful where the third party might inflate the price of property he was selling if he knew the identity of the principal.

Unless, otherwise agreed, an agent making a contract for a partially disclosed principal is a party to the contract.[23] For example, Ashley writes to Terrence offering to sell a rare painting on behalf of its owner, who wishes to remain unknown. Terrence accepts. Ashley is a party to the contract.

Whether the particular transaction is authorized or not, an agent for a partially disclosed principal is liable on the contract to the third party. See Figure 28–2. If the agent is actually authorized to make the contract, then both the agent and the partially disclosed principal are liable. In any event, the agent is separately liable and may be sued individually without joining the principal. The third party may obtain a judgment against either the principal or the agent or both. If the principal satisfies the judgment, then the agent is discharged. If the agent pays the judgment, he has the right to be reimbursed by the principal.

VAN D. COSTAS, INC. v. ROSENBERG
District Court of Appeals of Florida, Second District, 1983.
432 So.2d 656.

Facts: Costas entered into a contract to remodel the entrance of the Magic Moment Restaurant owned by Seascape Restaurants, Inc. Rosenberg, part owner and president of Seascape, signed the contract on the line under which was typed "Jeff Rosenberg, The Magic Moment." When a dispute arose over the performance and payment of the contract, Costas brought suit against Rosenberg for breach of contract. Rosenberg contends that he has no personal liability for the contract and that only Seascape, the owner of the restaurant, is liable. Costas claims that Rosenberg signed for an undisclosed principal and, therefore, is individually liable. The trial court held that Rosenberg was not liable on the contract. Costas appeals.

Decision: Reversed. Rosenberg is individually liable.

Opinion: **Grimes, J.**   It is well settled that where one enters into a contract as agent for an undisclosed principal, he may be held individually liable on the contract. [Citations.] The extent to which an agent must make disclosure of his principal in order to avoid personal liability is explained in 3 Am.Jur.2d *Agency* § 320 (1962):

> In order for an agent to avoid personal liability on a contract negotiated in his principal's behalf, he must disclose not only that he is an agent but also the identity of his principal, regardless of whether the third person might have known that the agent was acting in a representative capacity. It is not the third person's duty to seek out the identity of the principal; rather, the duty to disclose the identity of the principal is on the agent. The disclosure of an agency is not complete for the purpose of relieving the agent from personal liability unless it embraces the name of the principal; without that, the party dealing with the agent may understand that he intended to pledge his personal liability and responsibility in support of the contract and for its performance. Furthermore, the use of a tradename is not necessarily a sufficient disclosure of the identity of the principal and the fact of agency so as to protect the agent against personal liability.

Section 321 of the Restatement (Second) of the Law of Agency (1957) discusses the liability of the agent under circumstances in which it appears that he is acting for someone else but the identity of his principal is unknown to the other party.

§ 321. Principal Partially Disclosed
Unless otherwise agreed, a person purporting to make a contract with another for a partially disclosed principal is a party to the contract.
Comment:

a. A principal is a partially disclosed principal when, at the time of making the contract in question, the other party thereto has notice that the agent is acting for a principal but has no notice of the principal's identity. See § 4. The fact that, to the knowledge of the agent, the other party does not know the identity of the principal is of great weight in ascribing to the other party the intention to hold the agent liable either solely, or as a surety or co-promisor with the principal. The inference of an understanding that the agent is a party to the contract exists unless the agent gives such complete information concerning his principal's identity that he can be readily distinguished. If the other party has no reasonable means of ascertaining the principal, the inference is almost irresistible and prevails in the absence of an agreement to the contrary.

Restatement (Second) of Agency § 321, at 70.

In view of the contractual reference to the Magic Moment trade name, the annotation at 150 A.L.R. 1303 (1944) entitled "Use of trade name in connection with contract executed by agent as sufficient disclosure of agency or principal to protect agent against personal liability" is directly on point. The annotator points out that with the possible exception of a single decision, all of the prior cases on the subject have held that the use of a trade name is not a sufficient disclosure of the identity of the principal so as to eliminate the liability of the agent.

* * *

Of course, if the contracting party knows the identity of the principal for whom the agent purports to act, the principal is deemed to be disclosed. [Citation.] A dispute concerning such knowledge presents an issue of fact. [Citation.] Here, however, nothing indicates that appellant had ever heard of Seascape at the time the contract was signed. Subsequent knowledge of the true principal is irrelevant where performance of an indivisible contract has commenced. [Citation.] The trial court emphasized that Costas drafted the contract. However, it was not incumbent upon him to ferret out the record ownership of the Magic Moment when he had every reason to believe that one of the owners was signing the contract. Jeff knew that the owner was Seascape, and he had it within his power to avoid personal liability by properly disclosing his principal. Since there is no evidence that the appellant knew or should have known the true principal, the law holds Jeff legally responsible.

Undisclosed Principal

An agent acts for an undisclosed principal when she appears to be acting in her own behalf and the third person with whom she is dealing has no knowledge that she is acting as an agent. The instructions of the principal to the agent are to conceal not only the identity of the principal but also the agency relationship. Thus, the third person is dealing with the agent as though she were a principal.

The agent is personally liable upon a contract she enters into with a third person on behalf of an undisclosed principal, unless the third person, after discovering the existence and identity of the principal, elects to hold the principal to the contract. The reason for the liability of the agent is that the third person has placed reliance upon the agent individually and has accepted the agent's personal undertaking to perform the contract. Obviously, where the principal is undisclosed, the third person does not know of the interest of anyone in the contract other than himself and the agent. The reason for the liability of the undisclosed principal is that the concealment by the agent is pursuant to the instructions of the principal, and having received the benefits of the agent's acts, she should also assume and be responsible for the burdens.

After the third person has become informed of the identity of the undisclosed principal, he may hold either the principal or the agent to performance of the contract, but not both. Having once made an election, he is irrevocably bound by it. The third person, however, may bring suit against both the principal and agent so that he does not incur the risk that in a trial the evidence may fail to establish the agency relationship. In most States, bringing suit and proceeding to trial against both is not an election, but before the entry of any judgment, the third person is compelled to make an election because he is not entitled to a judgment against both. A judgment against the agent by a third party who knows the identity of the previously undisclosed principal discharges the liability of the principal. In this case, the agent would have the right to be reimbursed by the principal. If the third party obtains a judgment against the agent before learning the identity of the principal, then the principal is not discharged. Finally, the agent is discharged from liability if the third party gets a judgment against the principal.

Nonexistent or Incompetent Principal

A person who purports to act as agent for a principal, whom both the agent and the third party know to be nonexistent or incompetent, is personally liable on a contract entered into with a third person on behalf of such a principal.[24] For example, a promoter of a corporation who enters into contracts with third persons in the name of a corporation to be organized is personally liable on such contracts. The corporation is not liable because it did not authorize the contracts. If the corporation, after coming into existence, affirmatively adopts a preincorporation contract made on its behalf, it becomes bound in addition to the promoter. If the corporation enters into a new contract with such a third person, however, the prior contract between the promoter and the third person is discharged, and the liability of the promoter is terminated. This is a novation. See Figure 33–3 in Chapter 33.

TORT LIABILITY OF AGENT

An agent is personally liable for his tortious acts that injure third persons, whether or not such acts are authorized by the principal and whether or not the principal may also be liable.[25] For example, an agent is personally liable if he converts the goods of a third person to his principal's use. An agent is also liable for making representations that he knows to be fraudulent to a third person who in reliance sustains a loss.

RIGHTS OF AGENT AGAINST THIRD PERSON

An agent who makes a contract with a third person on behalf of a disclosed principal usually has no right of action against the third person for breach of contract.[26] The agent is not a party to the contract. An agent for a disclosed principal may sue on the contract, however, if it provides that the agent is a party to the contract. An agent for an undisclosed principal or a partially disclosed principal may maintain in her own name an action against the third person for breach of contract.

CHAPTER SUMMARY

PRINCIPAL AND THIRD PARTIES

Contract Liability of Principal	Types of Principals ■ *Disclosed Principal* principal whose existence and identity are known ■ *Partially Disclosed Principal* principal whose existence is known but whose identity is not known ■ *Undisclosed Principal* principal whose existence and identity are not known

Authority power of an agent to change the legal status of the principal
- *Actual Authority* power conferred upon the agent by actual consent given by the principal
- *Actual Express Authority* actual authority derived from written or spoken words of the principal
- *Actual Implied Authority* actual authority inferred from words or conduct manifested to the agent by the principal
- *Apparent Authority* power conferred upon the agent by acts or conduct of the principal that reasonably lead a third party to believe that the agent has such power

Delegation of Authority is usually not permitted unless expressly or impliedly authorized by the principal; if the agent is authorized to appoint other subagents, the acts of these subagents are as binding on the principal as if they were done by the agent

Effect of Termination of Agency upon Authority ends actual authority
- *Termination by Operation of Law* apparent authority also ends without notice to third parties
- *Termination by Act of Parties* apparent authority ends when third parties have knowledge or appropriate notice is given to third parties: actual notice must be given to third parties with whom the agent had previously dealt on credit, has been specially accredited, or has begun to deal; all other third parties need only be given constructive notice

Ratification affirmation by one person of a prior act that another, without authority, has done as her agent

Fundamental Rules of Contractual Liability
- *Disclosed Principal* is contractually bound with the third party if the agent acts within her actual or apparent authority in making the contract
- *Partially Disclosed Principal* is contractually bound with the third party if the agent acts within her actual or apparent authority in making the contract
- *Undisclosed Principal* is contractually bound with the third party if the agent acts within her actual authority in making the contract

Tort Liability of Principal

Direct Liability of Principal a principal may be held liable for his own negligence or recklessness in carrying out an activity through employees or agents

Vicarious Liability of Principal for Authorized Act of Agent a principal is vicariously (indirectly) liable for torts she authorizes another to commit

Vicarious Liability of Principal for Unauthorized Acts of Agent
- *Respondeat Superior* an employer is liable for unauthorized torts committed by an employee in the course of his employment
- *Independent Contractor* a principal is not liable for the unauthorized torts of an independent contractor

Criminal Liability of Principal

Authorized Acts the principal is liable if he directed, participated in, or approved the criminal act of his agents

Unauthorized Acts the principal may be liable for a criminal act of a managerial person or under liability without fault statutes

AGENTS AND THIRD PARTIES

Contract Liability of Agent	**Disclosed Principals** the agent is not normally a party to the contract she makes with a third person ■ *Unauthorized Contracts* if an agent exceeds her actual and apparent authority, the principal is not bound but the agent may be liable for breach of warranty or misrepresentation ■ *Agent Assumes Liability* an agent may agree to become liable on a contract between the principal and the third party **Partially Disclosed Principal** an agent who acts for a partially disclosed principal is a party to the contract with the third party unless otherwise agreed **Undisclosed Principal** an agent who acts for an undisclosed principal is personally liable on the contract to the third party **Nonexistent or Incompetent Principal** a person who purports to act as agent for a principal, whom both the agent and the third party know to be nonexistent or incompetent, is personally liable on a contract entered into with a third person on behalf of such a principal
Tort Liability of Agent	**Authorized Acts** the agent is liable to the third party for his own torts **Unauthorized Acts** the agent is liable to the third party for his own torts
Rights of Agent	**Disclosed Principal** the agent usually has no rights against the third party **Partially Disclosed Principal** the agent may enforce the contract against the third party **Undisclosed Principal** the agent may enforce the contract against the third party

QUESTIONS

1. Distinguish among actual express authority, actual implied authority, and apparent authority.
2. Discuss the contractual liability of the principal, agent, and third party when the principal is (a) disclosed, (b) partially disclosed, and (c) undisclosed.
3. Distinguish between actual and constructive notice.
4. Discuss the doctrine of ratification.
5. Discuss the tort liability of a principal for the (a) authorized acts of agents, (b) unauthorized acts of employees, and (c) unauthorized acts of independent contractors.

PROBLEMS

1. Alice was Peter's traveling salesperson and was also authorized to collect accounts. Before the agreed termination of the agency, Peter wrongfully discharged Alice. Alice then called on Tom, an old customer, and collected an account from Tom. She also called on Laura, a new prospect, as Peter's agent, secured a large order, collected the price of the order, sent the order to Peter, and disappeared with the collections. Peter delivered the goods to Laura per the order.

(a) Peter sues Tom for his account. Decision?
(b) Peter sues Laura for the agreed price of the goods. Decision?

2. Paula instructed Alvin, her agent, to purchase a quantity of hides. Alvin order the hides from Ted in his own (Alvin's) name and delivered the hides to Paula. Ted, learning later that Paula was the principal, sends the bill to Paula, who refuses to pay Ted. Ted sues Paula and Alvin. Decision?

3. Stan sold goods to Bill in good faith, believing him to be a principal. Bill in fact was acting as agent for Nancy and within the scope of his authority. The goods were charged to Bill, and on his refusal to pay, Stan sued Bill for the purchase price. While this

action was pending, Stan learned of Bill's relationship with Nancy. Nevertheless, thirty days after learning of that relationship, Stan obtained judgment against Bill and had an execution issued that was never satisfied. Three months after the judgment was made, Stan sued Nancy for the purchase price of the goods. Decision?

4. Green Grocery Company employed Jones as its manager and gave her authority to purchase supplies and goods for resale. Jones had conducted business for several years with Brown Distributing Company, although her purchases had been limited to groceries. Jones contacted Brown Distributing Company and had it deliver a color television set to her house. She told Brown Company that the set was to be used in promotional advertising to increase Green Grocery Company's business. The advertising did not develop. Jones disappeared from the area, taking the television set with her. Brown Company sued Green Grocery Company for the purchase price of the set. Decision?

5. Stone was the authorized agent to sell stock of the Turner Company at $10 per share and was authorized in case of sale to fill in the blanks in the certificates with the name of the purchaser, the number of shares, and the date of sale. He sold 100 shares to Barrie, and without the knowledge or consent of the company and without reporting to the company, he endorsed on the back of the certificate the following:

"It is hereby agreed that Turner Company shall, at the end of three years after the date, repurchase the stock at $11 per share on thirty days' notice. Turner Company, by Stone."

After three years, demand was made on Turner Company to repurchase, which was refused, and the company repudiated the agreement on the ground that the agent had no authority to make the agreement for repurchase. Barrie sued Turner Company. Decision?

6. Helper, a delivery boy for Gunn, delivered two heavy packages of groceries to Reed's porch. As instructed by Gunn, Helper rang the bell to let Reed know the groceries had arrived. Mrs. Reed came to the door and asked Helper if he would deliver the groceries into the kitchen because the bags were heavy. Helper did so, and on leaving he observed Mrs. Reed having difficulty in moving a cabinet in the dining room. He undertook to assist her, but being more interested in watching Mrs. Reed than the cabinet, he failed to observe a small, valuable antique table, which he smashed into with the cabinet and totally destroyed. Does Reed have a cause of action against Gunn for the value of the destroyed antique?

7. Driver picked up Friend to accompany him on an out-of-town delivery for his employer, Speedy Service. A "No Riders" sign was prominently displayed on the windshield of the truck, and Driver violated specific instructions of his employer by permitting an unauthorized person to ride in the vehicle. While discussing a planned fishing trip with Friend, Driver ran a red light and collided with an automobile driven by Motorist. Both Friend and Motorist were injured. Is Speedy Service liable to either Friend or Motorist for the injuries they sustained?

8. Cook's Department Store advertises that it maintains a barber shop in its store managed by Hunter. Actually, Hunter is not an employee of the store but merely rents space in the store. Hunter, while shaving Jordan in the barber shop, negligently puts a deep gash, requiring ten stitches, into one of Jordan's ears. Jordan sues Cook's Department Store for damages. Decision?

9. The following contract was executed on August 22:

Ray agrees to sell and Shaw, the representative of Todd and acting on his behalf, agrees to buy 10,000 pounds of 0.32 x 1-5/8 stainless steel strip type 410.
(signed) Ray
(signed) Shaw

On August 26 Ray informs Shaw and Todd that the contract was in reality signed by him as agent for Upson. What are the rights of Ray, Shaw, Todd, and Upson in the event of a breach of the contract?

10. Harris, owner of certain land known as Red Bank, mailed a letter to Byron, a real estate broker in City X, stating: "I have been thinking of selling Red Bank. I have never met you, but a friend has advised me that you are an industrious and honest real estate broker. I therefore employ you to find a purchaser for Red Bank at a price of $35,000." Ten days after receiving the letter, Byron mailed the following reply to Harris: "Acting pursuant to your recent letter requesting me to find a purchaser for Red Bank, this is to advise that I have sold the property to Sims for $35,000. I enclose your copy of the contract of sale signed by Sims. Your name was signed to the contract by me as your agent." Is Harris obligated to convey Red Bank to Sims?

11. While crossing a public highway in the city, Joel was struck by a horse-drawn cart driver by Morison's agent. The agent was traveling between Burton Crescent Mews and Finchley on his employer's business and was not supposed to go into the city at all. Apparently, the agent was on a detour to visit a friend when the accident occurred. Joel brought this action against Morison for the injuries sustained as a result of the agent's negligence. Morison argues that he is not liable for his agent's negligence because the agent had strayed from his assigned path. Decision?

12. Serges is the owner of a retail meat marketing business. His managing agent borrowed $3,500 from David on Serges's behalf and for use in Serges's business. Serges paid $200 on the alleged loan and on several other occasions told David that the full balance owed would eventually be paid. He then disclaimed liability on the debt, asserting that he had not authorized his agent to enter into the loan agreement. David brought this action to collect on the loan. Decision?

ENDNOTES

1. Restatement, Second, Agency, Section 4, Disclosed Principal; Partially Disclosed Principal; Undisclosed Principal.

2. Restatement, Second, Agency, Section 35, When Incidental Authority is Inferred.

3. Restatement, Second, Agency, Section 50, When Authority to Contract Inferred.

4. Restatement, Second, Agency, Section 73, What Authority is Inferred.

5. Restatement, Second, Agency, Section 27, Creation of Apparent Authority: General Rule.

6. Restatement, Second, Agency, Section 18, Delegation of Powers Held by Agent.

7. Restatement, Second, Agency, Section 79, When Authority to Appoint an Agent is Inferred.

8. Restatement, Second, Agency, Section 133, Incapacity of Parties or Other Impossibility.

9. Restatement, Second, Agency, Section 136, Notification Terminating Apparent Authority.

10. Restatement, Second, Agency, Section 82, Ratification.

11. Restatement, Second, Agency, Section 91, Knowledge of Principal at Time of Affirmance.

12. Restatement, Second, Agency, Section 96, Effect of Affirming Part of a Transaction.

13. Restatement, Second, Agency, Section 88, Affirmance after Withdrawal of Other Party or Other Termination of Original Transaction.

14. Restatement, Second, Agency, Section 218, Effect of Ratification.

15. Restatement, Second, Agency, Section 213, Principal Negligent or Reckless.

16. Restatement, Second, Agency, Section 212, Principal Intends Conduct or Consequences.

17. Restatement, Second, Agency, Section 250, Non-liability for Physical Harm by Non-Servant Agents.

18. Restatement, Second, Agency, Section 219, When Master is Liable for Torts of His Servants.

19. Restatement, Second, Agency, Section 257, Misrepresentations; in General.

20. Restatement, Second, Agency, Section 222, Servants of Agent of Undisclosed Principal.

21. Restatement, Second, Agency, Section 228, General Statement.

22. Restatement, Second, Agency, Section 320, Principal Disclosed.

23. Restatement, Second, Agency, Section 321, Principal Partially Disclosed.

24. Restatement, Second, Agency, Section 326, Principal Known to be Nonexistent or Incompetent.

25. Restatement, Second, Agency, Section 343, General Rule.

26. Restatement, Second, Agency, Section 363, Contracts; General Rule.

PART 6
PARTNERSHIPS

Owners of businesses frequently decide to join forces with one or more associates, usually to gain additional and otherwise unavailable capital or expertise. Once this decision has been made, a second and just as significant decision must be reached—what form of business organization should be used? There are two general types of business associations: unincorporated and incorporated. In Part Six we discuss the three most common forms of unincorporated business associations: general partnerships, joint ventures, and limited partnerships. In Part Seven we cover incorporated business associations, which are usually referred to simply as corporations.

Although corporations today outnumber unincorporated business associations by about two to one and generate greater revenues by over twenty to one, unincorporated business associations are widely used in a number of areas. General partnerships have been used principally in finance, insurance, accounting, real estate, wholesale and retail trade, law, and other services. Joint ventures have enjoyed popularity among major corporations planning to engage in cooperative research; in the exploitation of land and mineral rights; in the development, promotion, and sale of patents, trade names, and copyrights; and in manufacturing operations in foreign countries. Limited partnerships have been widely used for enterprises such as real estate investment and development, motion picture and theater productions, oil and gas ventures, and equipment leasing.

Regardless of the particular form of business organization, three sets of basic policy issues are important. First, what rights and responsibilities should owners and managers have among themselves? Second, what should be the rights and responsibilities of the business unit and its members with respect to the rest of society? Third, what should be the rights and responsibilities between the business organization and its employees? Unlike the first two policy issues, which vary considerably with the form of business organization, employee relations is independent of the type of business entity, as we discuss in Chapter 42.

The first issue—the relationship of the owners and managers among themselves—involves several policy questions. For example, what limitations, if any, should be placed on the number or type of associates, the name they may use for the business, the purposes for which the business may be formed, the size of the entity, the powers it may exercise, or the property it may own? In addition, to what extent should the associates be allowed to vary by contract their rights and responsibilities? Conversely, how much automatic protection should the law provide for business associates who fail to make their own arrangements to set forth each associate's rights and responsibilities?

In the operation of the business, to what extent may the associates exert control over the management of the enterprise? How far may the majority go in advancing its own interests? May the minority have veto power over the will of the majority? What remedies should be available to the minority and to the majority? How should the financial gains and losses be divided among the owners?

When changes are made in the organization, should all the owners have control over choosing new associates and making fundamental changes in the business? Should a member be permitted to transfer his interest to outsiders or to withdraw his capital contribution? How long should the enterprise be permitted to exist, and who may bring about its termination?

The second set of basic policy issues involves the relationship of the business unit and its members to the rest of society—suppliers, customers, creditors, parties injured by civil wrongs committed by members, employees and agents of the business, and society at large if the enterprise or one of its members commits a crime. How these issues of external liability are resolved affects the ease by which capital can be raised and the extent to which financially risky enterprises use a particular form of business organization. External liability for a business arises in a variety of ways, but for most enterprises the crucial and most commonly occurring causes of loss consist of tort and contract liability. The first results from some act or omission that falls below the standard of care that society demands of all its members. Losses from contract liability can occur as a result of incorrect judgments about market conditions or constrictions in cash flow that render the firm unable to meet its debt service, as well as any number of other problems.

A critical social issue is whether a person with a tort or contract claim should be limited to proceeding against the property of the enterprise or whether he may seek satisfaction of his court judgment from property of the individual members of the business organization. A less common but still important issue is the extent to which the organization and its members should be held accountable for the criminal conduct of the business's employees, members, and agents.

As we indicated above, the resolution of these questions varies considerably among the different kinds of business organizations. Consequently, when choosing which form of organization is most appropriate, business associates should consider these factors as well as questions of taxation. This decision, however, cannot be made in any general way. It depends entirely on the particular circumstances of the given group of associates:

Apart from the ever changing problems of taxation, . . . there are certain ponderables and imponderables which must be weighed in the choice of a business association. Continuity of existence of the business, centralization of control, legitimate devices to obtain and keep control, limited or unlimited liability of the associates, the possibility of death, bankruptcy, insanity, inadequate performance or poor health and old age of the associates, probability of expansion and the necessity of obtaining capital from outside sources, the ease or difficulty of holding and disposing of property both personal and real, of bringing suit and defending the same, of the use of authority or the abuse of it by the associates, of the amount of "red tape" involved in making reports to governmental agencies, of complying with state and federal securities acts, and of the expense involved in setting up the particular business association, should be analyzed and weighed before determining what business form should be recommended. N. Lattin, *The Law of Corporations* 3–4 (1971).

In Part Six we examine how the law resolves these public policy issues for unincorporated business associations. These legal resolutions have a significant impact on business persons in organizing, financing, operating, and dissolving their business organizations.

29 NATURE AND FORMATION

A business enterprise may be operated or conducted by a sole proprietor, a general partnership, a limited partnership, a corporation, or by some other form of business organization. The owner or owners of the enterprise determine which form of business unit to use. Various factors, not the least of which are Federal and State income tax laws, affect the decision to use one medium rather than another. Other factors include ease of formation, capital requirements, flexibility of management and control, extent of external liability, and the duties imposed by law on management. For a concise comparison of general partnerships, limited partnerships, and corporations, see Figure 33–2 in Chapter 33.

In Chapters 29 through 31 we examine general partnerships, commonly called simply partnerships; in Chapter 32 we discuss limited partnerships and other types of unincorporated business associations. Part Seven covers corporations.

NATURE OF PARTNERSHIP

Partnership is an extremely old form of business association known to have been used in ancient Babylonia, classical Greece, and the Roman Empire. It was also used in Europe and England during the Middle Ages. Eventually the English common law recognized partnerships. In the nineteenth century, partnerships were widely used in England and the United States and the common law of partnership developed considerably during this period. Partnerships are extremely important in that they allow individuals with different expertise, backgrounds, resources, and interests to bring their various skills together to form a more competitive enterprise.

In 1914 the National Conference of Commissioners on Uniform State Laws promulgated the Uniform Partnership Act (UPA). Since then it has been adopted in all States except Louisiana and also has been adopted by the District of Columbia, the Virgin Islands, and Guam. The UPA is reprinted in Appendix D. Although the UPA is rather comprehensive, it does not cover all legal issues concerning partnerships. Accordingly, the UPA provides that any situation not provided for by the act shall be governed by the rules of law and equity.

Definition of Partnership

A **partnership,** or copartnership as it is sometimes called, has been defined in various ways. The standard definition, however, is contained in the UPA: "A partnership is an association of two or more persons to carry on as co-owners a business for profit."[1] The UPA broadly defines "person" to include "individuals, partnerships, corporations, and other associations."[2] A business is defined by the UPA to include every trade, occupation, or profession.[2]

Entity Theory

A **legal entity** is an organization having a separate legal existence from its members. It therefore is a unit with the capacity of possessing legal rights and being subject to legal duties. A legal entity may acquire, own, and dispose of property. It may enter into contracts, commit wrongs, sue, and be sued. Each business corporation is a legal entity having a distinct legal existence separate from its shareholders.

A partnership was regarded by the common law as a **legal aggregate,** a group of individuals not having a legal existence separate from its members. The UPA, however, has partially rejected the common law view of partnerships. It treats partnerships as a legal entity for some purposes, although for other purposes it still treats them as a legal aggregate.

Partnership as a Legal Entity   The UPA recognizes a partnership as an entity distinct from its members in several ways: (1) the assets of the firm are treated as those of the business and are considered separate and distinct from the individual assets of its members; (2) title to real estate may be acquired by a partnership in the partnership name; (3) a partner is accountable as a fiduciary to the partnership; (4) every partner is considered an agent of the partnership; and (5) under the doctrine of marshaling of assets—which applies in cases of insolvency administered by a State court of equity—partnership creditors have a prior right to partnership assets, while creditors of the individual members have a prior right to the separate assets of their individual debtors. Some States have modified the UPA to recognize a partnership as an entity in additional respects. Moreover, some courts have extended entity treatment to matters not addressed by the UPA.

Partnership as a Legal Aggregate   Because a partnership is considered an aggregate for some purposes, it can neither sue nor be sued in the firm name unless a statute specifically allows it. Similarly, the debts of the partnership are ultimately the debts of the individual partners, and any one partner may be held liable for the partnership's entire indebtedness.[3] Thus, if Meg and Mike enter into a partnership that becomes insolvent, as does Meg, Mike is fully liable for the debts of the partnership.

In addition, a partnership generally lacks continuity of existence: whenever any partner ceases to be associated with the partnership, it is dissolved.[4] Likewise, a partner's interest in the partnership may be assigned, but the assignee does not become a partner without the consent of all the partners.[5]

Finally, the Internal Revenue Code treats a partnership as an aggregate. A partnership is not required to pay Federal income tax but must file an information return stating the name of each partner and the amount of income derived from the partnership. It is the responsibility of each partner to include his share of partnership income in his individual tax return and to pay the tax on his share. Partnership income is taxed to the individual partners regardless of whether the income is actually distributed.

PEOPLE v. SMITHTOWN GENERAL HOSPITAL
Supreme Court, Criminal Term, Suffolk County, Part II, 1977.
92 Misc.2d 144, 399 N.Y.S.2d 993.

Facts: Smithtown General Hospital was operated as a forty-two-member general partnership. The hospital was criminally indicted for (1) allowing an unauthorized individual to take part in a surgical procedure on an uninformed, nonconsenting patient, and (2) falsifying records in an effort to conceal the offense. The partnership moved to dismiss the indictment, claiming that it was not an entity distinct from the aggregate of the forty-two individual partners and thus could not be indicted without a showing of culpable intent on the part of each partner.

Decision: Motion to dismiss denied.

Opinion: Jaspan, J.   The partnership can be either an entity or an aggregate of its members depending upon the nature of its activities and in the case of criminal law depending also upon the nature of the infraction.

* * *

The concept of a partnership as an entity liable for certain of its criminal activities independent of culpability by its respective members was expressly considered in *United States v. A & P Trucking Co.,*[citation]. Two partnerships were charged, as entities, with violations of [citation] which makes it a crime to knowingly violate some Interstate Commerce Commission regulations [citation].

The [U.S.] Supreme Court, relying upon a definition of person [citation] similar to that found in [the N.Y. statute], held that impersonal entities can be guilty of knowing or wilful violations of regulatory statutes through the doctrine of respondeat superior and that a partnership may be considered an entity separate and apart from the aggregate of its members.

* * *

The health care is provided by the facility and not necessarily by any of its proprietors. Accreditation, when given, is provided to the institution and not to the component members of the named proprietor. The hospital is in every sense an entity and not just an aggregate of the 42 individual partners.

The counts in the respective indictments relating first to the anesthetization of a patient without his consent for a purpose other than lawful medical or therapeutic treatment and secondly to the records maintained with respect thereto have that apparent nexus to the regulatory provisions controlling a hospital as to bring this case within the orbit of the principles enunciated in *United States v. A & P Trucking*, supra. * * *

* * * I now hold that this defendant may be charged in an indictment as an entity with the commission of crimes related to the discharge of its primary obligations as a general hospital even though there is no showing of culpability on the part of the individual's partners.

Types of Partners

Partners can be classified as either general or limited. In addition, a partner may be silent, secret, or dormant.

A **general partner** is a partner of either a general or limited partnership whose liability for partnership indebtedness is unlimited, who has full management powers, and who shares in the profits. Most partnerships consist of only general partners and are referred to as "general partnerships" or just "partnerships."

A special or **limited partner** is one who, as a member of a limited partnership, is liable for firm indebtedness only to the extent of the capital he has contributed or agreed to contribute. Limited partnerships are formed by compliance with a number of statutory requirements and are discussed in Chapter 32.

A **silent partner** is a partner who has no voice and elects to take no part in the partnership business.

A **secret partner** is a partner whose membership in the firm is not disclosed to the public.

A **dormant partner** is a partner who is both a silent and a secret partner.

FORMATION OF A PARTNERSHIP

The formation of a partnership is relatively simple and may be done consciously or unconsciously. A partnership may result from an oral or written agreement between the parties, from an informal arrangement, or from the conduct of the parties. Persons become partners by associating themselves in business together as co-owners. Consequently, if two or more individuals share the control and profits of a business, the law may deem them partners without regard to how they might characterize their relationship. Thus, associates frequently discover, to their displeasure, that they have inadvertently formed a partnership and have thereby subjected themselves to the duties and liabilities of partners. Whether their agreement is simple or elaborate, definite or indefinite, fully understood and fair, or obscure and inequitable is of importance principally to the partners. The legal existence of the relationship depends on the parties' explicit or implicit agreement and their association in business as co-owners and not on the degree of care, intelligence, study, or investigation that preceded its formation.

Articles of Partnership

In the interest of achieving a more clear, definite, and complete understanding between the partners, it is preferable, although not usually required, that partners put their agreement in writing. A written agreement creating a partnership is referred to as the partnership agreement or **articles of partnership.** Any partnership agreement should include:

1. the firm name and the identity of the partners;
2. the nature and scope of the partnership business;
3. the duration of the partnership;
4. the capital contributions of each partner;
5. the division of profits and sharing of losses;
6. the duties of each partner in the management;
7. a provision for salaries, if desired;
8. restrictions, if any, on the authority of particular partners to bind the firm;
9. the right, if desired, of a partner to withdraw from the firm, and the terms, conditions, and required notice in the event of such withdrawal; and
10. a provision for continuation of the business by the remaining partners, if desired, in the event of the death of a partner or other dissolution, and a statement of the method or formula for appraisal and payment of the interest of the deceased or former partner.

A well-drawn partnership agreement can provide almost any conceivable arrangement of capital investment, control sharing, and profit distribution that the partners desire. In addition, it can provide for continuity of the partnership in the event of one member's death or retirement.

Figure 29–1 shows a sample partnership agreement.

Statute of Frauds   The Statute of Frauds does not specifically apply to a contract for the formation of a partnership, and therefore no writing is required to create the relationship. A contract to form a partnership to continue for a period longer than one year is *within* the statute and requires a writing in order to be enforceable. Moreover, a contract for the transfer of an interest in real estate to or by a partnership is governed by the Statute of Frauds and requires a writing to be enforceable.

Firm Name   In the interest of acquiring and retaining good will, a partnership should have a firm name. The name selected by the partners should not be identical with or deceptively similar to the name of any other existing business concern. It may be the name of the partners or of any one of them, or the partners may decide to operate the business under a fictitious or assumed name, such as "Peachtree Restaurant" or "Globe Theater" or "Paradise Laundry." A partnership may not use a name that would be likely to indicate to the public that it is a corporation. Nearly all of the States have enacted statutes that require any persons conducting any business under an assumed or fictitious name to file in a designated public office a certificate setting forth the name under which the business is conducted and the real names and addresses of all persons conducting the business as partners or proprietors.

Tests of Partnership Existence

Partnerships can be formed without the slightest formality. Consequently, it is important that the law establish a test for determining whether a partnership has been formed. Two situations most often require this determination. The most common is a creditor who has dealt with one person but wants to hold another also liable by asserting that the two were partners. Less frequently, a person seeks to share profits and property held by another by claiming that they are partners.

FIGURE 29–1 Sample Partnership Agreement

This agreement, made and entered into as of the [*Date*], by and among [*Names*] (hereinafter collectively sometimes referred to as "Partners").

WITNESSETH:

Whereas, the Parties hereto desire to form a General Partnership (hereinafter referred to as the "Partnership"), for the term and upon the conditions hereinafter set forth;

Now, therefore, in consideration of the mutual covenants hereinafter contained, it is agreed by and among the Parties hereto as follows:

Article I
BASIC STRUCTURE

§ 1.1 Form

The Parties hereby form a General Partnership pursuant to the Laws of [*Name of State*].

§ 1.2 Name

The business office and place of business of the Partnership shall be conducted under the name of [*Name*].

§ 1.3 Place of Business

The principal office and place of business of the Partnership shall be located at [*Describe*], or such other place as the Partners may from time to time designate.

§ 1.4 Term

The Partnership shall commence on [*Date*], and shall continue for [*Number*] years, unless earlier terminated in the following manner:

(a) By the completion of the purpose intended, or

(b) Pursuant to this Agreement, or

(c) By applicable [*State*] law, or

(d) By death, insanity, bankruptcy, retirement, withdrawal, resignation, expulsion, or disability of all of the then Partners.

§ 1.5 Purpose —General

The purpose for which the Partnership is organized is _____.

Article II
FINANCIAL ARRANGEMENTS

§ 2.1 Initial Contributions of Partners

Each Partner has contributed to the initial capital of the Partnership property in the amount and form indicated on Schedule A attached hereto and made a part hereof. Capital contributions to the Partnership shall not earn interest. An individual capital account shall be maintained for each Partner.

§ 2.2 Additional Capital Contribution

If at any time during the existence of the Partnership it shall become necessary to increase the capital with which the said Partnership is doing business, then (upon the vote of the Managing Partner(s)):

Each party to this Agreement shall contribute to the capital of this Partnership within _____ days notice of such need in an amount according to his then Percentage Share of Capital as called for by the Managing Partner(s).

§ 2.3 Percentage Share of Profits and Capital

(a) The Percentage Share of Profits and Capital of each Partner shall be (unless otherwise modified by the terms of this Agreement) as follows:

Names	Initial Percentage Share of Profits and Capital

§ 2.4 Interest

No interest shall be paid on any contribution to the capital of the Partnership.

FIGURE 29–1 Continued

§ 2.5 Return of Capital Contributions
No Partner shall have the right to demand the return of his capital contributions except as herein provided.

§ 2.6 Rights of Priority
Except as herein provided, the individual Partners shall have no right to any priority over each other as to the return of capital contributions except as herein provided.

§ 2.7 Distributions
Distributions to the Partners of net operating profits of the Partnership, as hereinafter defined, shall be made at (*least monthly/such times as the Managing Partner(s) shall reasonable agree.*) Such distributions shall be made to the Partners simultaneously.

For the purpose of this Agreement, net operating profit for any accounting period shall mean the gross receipts of the Partnership for such period, less the sum of all cash expenses of operation of the Partnership, and such sums as may be necessary to establish a reserve for operating expenses.

§ 2.8 Compensation
No Partner shall be entitled to receive any compensation from the Partnership, nor shall any Partner receive any drawing account from the Partnership.

Article III
MANAGEMENT

§ 3.1 Managing Partners
The Managing Partner(s) shall be [*Names*] [*or* "all partners"].

§ 3.2 Voting
The Managing Partner(s) shall have the right to vote as to the management and conduct of the business of the Partnership as follows.

Names	**Vote**

Article IV
DISSOLUTION

§ 4.1 Dissolution
In the event that the Partnership shall hereinafter be dissolved for any reason whatsoever, a full and general account of its assets, liabilities and transactions shall at once be taken. Such assets may be sold and turned into cash as soon as possible and all debts and other amounts due the Partnership collected. The proceeds thereof shall thereupon be applied as follows:

(a) To discharge the debts and liabilities of the Partnership and the expenses of liquidation.

(b) To pay each Partner or his legal representative any unpaid salary, drawing account, interest or profits to which he shall then be entitled and in addition, to repay to any Partner his capital contributions in excess of his original capital contribution.

(c) To divide the surplus, if any, among the Partners or their representatives as follows:

   (1) First (to the extent of each partner's then capital account) in proportion to their then capital accounts.

   (2) Then according to each Partner's then Percentage Share of *Capital/Income*.

§ 4.2 Right To Demand Property
No Partner shall have the right to demand and receive property in kind for his distribution.

Witnesses	**Partners**
_____	_____
_____	_____

Dated: _____

Adopted from "West's Legal Forms," 2d ed. by Paul Lieberman. Copyright © 1981 by West Publishing Co. Reprinted with permission.

The UPA provides the basic definition of a partnership: an association of two or more persons to carry on as co-owners of a business for profit.[1] Thus, there are three components to this definition, all of which have to be met; (1) an association of two or more persons, (2) conducting a business for profit, (3) which they co-own.

Association A partnership must have two or more persons who agree to become partners. Any natural person having full *capacity* may enter into a partnership. To the extent that a minor has capacity to act as a principal or agent, she may become a partner, although she has the right both to disaffirm the partnership agreement at any time before reaching majority and to avoid personal liability to partnership creditors. On disaffirmance and withdrawal from the partnership, a minor is entitled to the return of her capital contribution and her accrued and unpaid share of the profits except to the extent that such funds are necessary to pay partnership creditors.

The position of a nonadjudicated incompetent is basically the same as that of a minor except that his incompetency may afford his copartners a ground for seeking dissolution by court decree. Since all contracts of an adjudicated incompetent are void, not voidable, a partnership agreement entered into by such an individual is void.

A corporation is defined as a "person" by the UPA[2] and is, therefore, legally capable of entering into a partnership in those States whose incorporation statutes authorize a corporation to do so. A partnership may be a member of other partnerships.[2]

Business for Profit The UPA provides that co-ownership does not of itself establish a partnership, even though the co-owners share the profits derived from use of the property.[6] For a partnership to exist, there must be a business in addition to the mere co-ownership of property. Moreover, to be a partnership, the business carried on by the association of two or more persons must be "for a profit." This requirement excludes social clubs, fraternal orders, civic societies, and charitable organizations from using the partnership form.

Where persons are associated together for mutual financial gain on a temporary or limited basis involving a single transaction or relatively few isolated transactions, no partnership results because the parties are not engaged in a continuous series of commercial activities necessary to constitute a business. Co-ownership of the means or instrumentality of accomplishing a single business transaction or a limited series of transactions may result in a **joint venture** but not a general partnership. (We discuss joint ventures in Chapter 32.)

For example, Emmett and Beth are joint owners of shares of the capital stock of a corporation, have a joint bank account, and have inherited or purchased real estate as joint tenants or tenants in common. They share the dividends paid on the stock, the interest on the bank account, and the net proceeds from the sale or lease of the real estate. Emmett and Beth are not partners. Although they are co-owners and share profits, they are not engaged in the carrying on of a business, and hence no partnership results. On the other hand, if Emmett and Beth were engaged in continuous transactions of buying and selling real estate over a period of time and were carrying on a business of trading in real estate, a partnership relation would exist between them, regardless of whether they considered one another as partners.

In another example, Alec, Laura, and Shirley each inherit an undivided one-third interest in a hotel and, instead of selling the property, decide by an informal agreement to continue operation of the hotel. The operation of a hotel is a business, and, as co-owners of a hotel business, Alec, Laura, and Shirley are partners and are subject to all of the rights, duties, and incidents arising from the partnership relation.

Co-ownership Although co-ownership of *property* used in a business is neither a necessary nor a sufficient condition for the existence of a partnership, the co-ownership of a *business* is essential. In determining the element of co-ownership of a business, the sharing of profits, the sharing of losses, and the right to manage and control the business are important.

The receipt by a person of a share of the **profits** of a business is *prima facie* evidence that he is a partner in the business. The UPA provides, however, that no inference of the existence of a partnership relation shall be drawn where such profits are received in payment:

1. of a debt by installments or otherwise;
2. of wages of an employee or rent to a landlord;
3. of an annuity to a widow or representative of a deceased partner;
4. of interest on a loan, though the amount of payment may vary with the profits of the business, or
5. as consideration for the sale of the good will of a business or other property by installments, or otherwise.[6]

These transactions do not give rise to a presumption that the party is a partner, because the law assumes it more likely that the creditor, employee, landlord, or other recipient of a share of the profits is not a co-owner. It is possible, however, to establish that such a person was a partner by proof of other facts and circumstances. For example, the payment of money or the transfer of title to property in exchange for a share of the profits may be (1) the capital contribution of a partner, or (2) a loan by a creditor or a sale on credit. Outside the usual incidents of a loan or a sale on credit, the test most frequently employed in doubtful situations is whether an obligation has been created to pay in any event for the property received or to repay the money advanced. If the party sought to be charged as a partner is entitled at some time to receive payment for the money or property that he advanced, he is generally not a partner but a creditor.

The sharing of *gross returns,* in contrast to profits, does *not* of itself establish a partnership.[6] This is so whether or not the persons sharing the gross returns have a joint or common interest in any property from which the returns are derived. Thus, two brokers who share commissions are not necessarily or even presumed partners. Similarly, an author who receives royalties (a share of gross receipts from the sales of a book) is not a partner with the publisher.

An agreement to share in or contribute to the *losses* of a business, however, affords strong evidence of an ownership interest. Few jurisdictions insist on an express agreement of loss sharing for a partnership to exist, but all consider such an agreement compelling proof of the existence of a partnership.

By itself, evidence as to participation in the *management* or **control** of a business is not conclusive proof of a partnership relation. A voice in management and control of a business may be given, in a limited degree, to an employee, a landlord, or a creditor. On the other hand, one who is actually a partner may take no active part in the affairs of the firm and may, by agreement with his copartners, forego all right to exercise any control over the ordinary affairs of the business. In any event, the right to participate in control is an important factor considered by the courts in conjunction with other factors, profit sharing in particular.

Figure 29–2 illustrates the tests for determining whether a partnership exists, as do the following two cases.

CHAIKEN v. EMPLOYMENT SECURITY COMMISSION
Superior Court of Delaware, 1971.
274 A.2d 707.

Facts: Chaiken entered into separate but nearly identical agreements with Strazella and Spitzer to operate a barber shop. Under the terms of the "partnership" agreements, Chaiken would provide barber chairs, supplies, and licenses, while the other two would provide tools of the trade. The agreements also stated that gross returns from the partnership were to be divided on a percentage basis among the three men and that Chaiken would decide all matters of partnership policy. Finally, the agreements stated hours of work and holidays for Strazella and

Spitzer and required Chaiken to hold and distribute all receipts. The Delaware Employment Security Commission, however, determined that Strazella and Spitzer were not partners of Chaiken but rather were his employees. The commission then brought this action to assess unemployment compensation contributions against Chaiken for the two barbers. Chaiken contends that they are not employees but partners pursuant to written partnership agreements. As partners, Chaiken would not be liable for unemployment compensation contributions.

Decision: Judgment for the commission.

Opinion: Storey, J.   Chaiken contends that he and his "partners":

(1) properly registered the partnership name and names of partners in the Prothonotary's office, in accordance with [citation],

(2) properly filed federal partnership information returns and paid federal taxes quarterly on an estimated basis, and

(3) duly executed partnership agreements.

Of the three factors, the last is most important. Agreements of "partnership" were executed between Chaiken and Mr. Strazella, a barber in the shop, and between Chaiken and Mr. Spitzer, similarly situated. The agreements were nearly identical. The first paragraph declared the creation of a partnership and the location of business. The second provided that Chaiken would provide barber chair, supplies, and licenses, while the other partner would provide tools of the trade. The paragraph also declared that upon dissolution of the partnership, ownership of items would revert to the party providing them. The third paragraph declared that the income of the partnership would be divided 30% for Chaiken, 70% for Strazella; 20% for Chaiken and 80% for Spitzer. The fourth paragraph declared that all partnership policy would be decided by Chaiken, whose decision was final. The fifth paragraph forbade assignment of the agreement without permission of Chaiken. The sixth paragraph required Chaiken to hold and distribute all receipts. The final paragraph stated hours of work for Strazella and Spitzer and holidays.

The mere existence of an agreement labeled "partnership" agreement and the characterization of signatories as "partners" does not conclusively prove the existence of a partnership. Rather, the intention of the parties, as explained by the wording of the agreement, is paramount. [Citation.]

A partnership is defined as an association of two or more persons to carry on as co-owners a business for profit. [Citation.] As co-owners of a business, partners have an equal right in the decision making process. [Citation.] But this right may be abrogated by agreement of the parties without destroying the partnership concept, provided other partnership elements are present. [Citation.]

Thus, while paragraph four reserves for Chaiken all right to determine partnership policy, it is not standing alone, fatal to the partnership concept. Co-owners should also contribute valuable consideration for the creation of the business. Under paragraph two, however, Chaiken provides the barber chair (and implicitly the barber shop itself), mirror, licenses and linen, while the other partners merely provide their tools and labor—nothing more than any barber-employee would furnish. Standing alone, however, mere contribution of work and skill can be valuable consideration for a partnership agreement. [Citations.]

Partnership interests may be assignable, although it is not a violation of partnership law to prohibit assignment in a partnership agreement. [Citation.] Therefore, paragraph five on assignment of partnership interests does not violate the partnership concept. On the other hand, distribution of partnership assets to the partners upon dissolution is only allowed after all partnership liabilities are satisfied. [Citation.] But paragraph two of the agreement, in stating the ground rules for dissolution, makes no declaration that the partnership assets will be utilized to pay partnership expenses before reversion to their original owners. This deficiency militates against a finding in favor of partnership intent since it is assumed Chaiken would have inserted such provision had he thought his lesser partners would accept such liability. Partners do accept such liability, employees do not.

Most importantly, co-owners carry on "a business for profit." The phrase has been interpreted to mean that partners share in the profits and the losses of the business. The intent to divide the profits is an indispensable requisite of partnership. [Citation.] Paragraph three of the agreement declares that each partner shall share in the income of the business. There is no sharing of the profits, and as the agreement is drafted, there are no profits. Merely sharing the gross returns does not establish a partnership.[Citation.] Nor is the sharing of profits prima facie evidence of a partnership where the profits received are in payment of wages.[Citation.]

The failure to share profits therefore, is fatal to the partnership concept here.

Evaluating Chaiken's agreement in the light of the elements implicit in a partnership, no partnership intent can be found. The absence of the important right of decision making or the important duty to share liabilities upon dissolution individually may not be fatal to a partnership. But when both are absent, coupled with the absence of profit sharing, they become strong factors in discrediting the partnership argument. * * *

In addition, the total circumstances of the case taken together indicate the employer-employee relationship between Chaiken and his barbers. The agreement set forth the hours of work and days off—unusual subjects for partnership agreements. The barbers brought into the relationship only the equipment required of all barber shop operators. And each barber had his own individual "partnership" with Chaiken. Furthermore, Chaiken conducted all transactions with suppliers, and purchased licenses, insurance, and the lease for the business property in his own name. Finally, the name "Richard's Barber Shop" continued to be used after the execution of the so called partnership agreements.

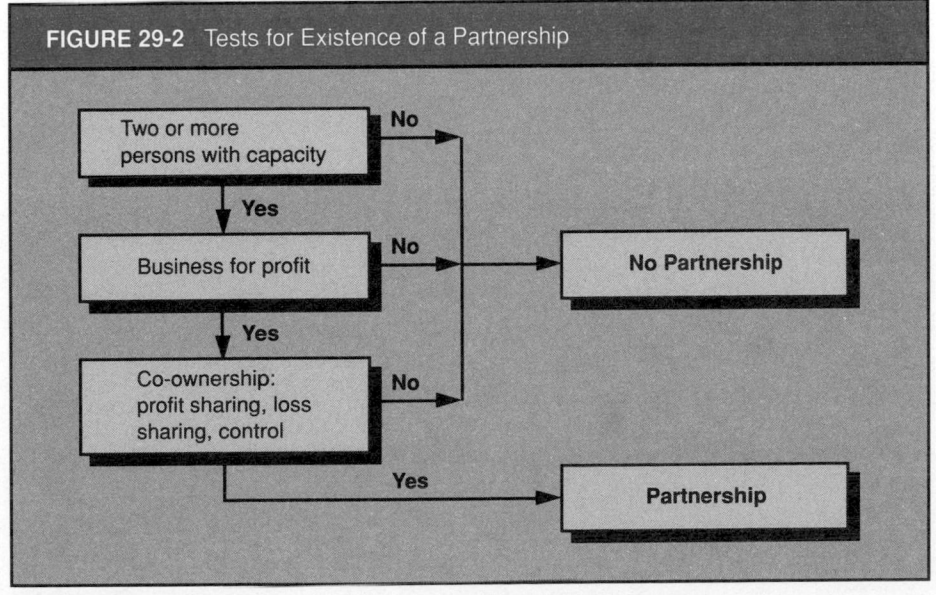

FIGURE 29-2 Tests for Existence of a Partnership

CUTLER v. BOWEN
Supreme Court of Utah, 1975.
543 P.2d 1349.

Facts: Cutler worked as a bartender for Bowen until they orally agreed that Bowen would have the authority and responsibility for the entire active management and operation of the tavern business known as the Havana Club. Each was to receive $100 per week plus half of the net profits. The business continued under this arrangement for four years until the building was taken over by Salt Lake City Redevelopment Agency. The agency paid $10,000 to Bowen as compensation for disruption. The business, however, was terminated after Bowen and Cutler failed to find a new, suitable location. Cutler, alleging a partnership with Bowen, then brought this action against him to recover one-half of the $10,000. Bowen contends that he is entitled to the entire $10,000 because he was the sole owner of the business and that Cutler was merely his employee. Cutler argues that although Bowen owned the physical assets of the business, she, as a partner in the business, is entitled to one-half of the compensation that was paid for the business's good will and going-concern value. The trial court entered judgment in favor of Cutler and Bowen appeals.

Decision: Judgment for Cutler affirmed.

Opinion: **Crockett, J.**   One of the primary matters to consider in determining whether a partnership exists is the nature of the contribution each party makes to the enterprise. It need not be in the form of tangible assets or capital, but, as is frequently done, one partner may make such a contribution, and this may be balanced by the other's performance of services and the shouldering of responsibility.

When parties join in an enterprise, it is usually in contemplation of success and making profits, and is often without much concern about who will bear losses. However, when they so engage in a venture for their mutual benefit or profit, that is generally held to be a partnership, in which the law imposes upon them both liability for debts or losses that may occur. This basic principle of partnership law is set forth in our Uniform Partnership Act, [Section 7]:

Rules for determining the existence of a partnership.—In determining whether a partnership exists these rules shall apply:

* * *

(4) The receipt by a person of a share of the profits of a business is prima facie evidence that he is a partner in the business, but no such inference shall be drawn if such profits were received in payment:

* * *

(b) As wages of an employee or rent to a landlord.

On the question whether profits shared should be regarded simply as wages, it is important to consider the degree to which a party participates in the management of the enterprise and whether the relationship is such that the party shares generally in the potential profits or advantages and thus should be held responsible for losses or liability incurred therein.

* * *

It is not shown here that any occasion arose where the plaintiff's responsibility for debts or other liabilities of the business was tested. However, throughout the four years in which she operated and managed the Club, apparently with competence and efficiency, it was her responsibility to see that all bills were paid, including the rental on the lease, employees' salaries, the costs of all purchases, licenses and other expenses of the business. During that time she saw the defendant Bowen only infrequently for the purpose of rendering an accounting and dividing the profits. It is further pertinent that the parties reported their income tax as a partnership.

Under the arrangement as shown and as found by the trial court, a good case can be made out that it was largely through the capability, experience, and efforts of the plaintiff that, in addition to the physical plant, there existed a separate asset in the value of the "going concern and goodwill" of the business, which was being lost by its displacement. On the basis of what has been said above, we see nothing to persuade us to disagree with the view taken by the trial court: that the plaintiff's involvement in this business was such that she would have been liable for any losses that might have occurred in its operation; and that, concomitantly, she was entitled to participate in any profits or advantages that inured to it.

* * *

From the circumstances shown in evidence as discussed herein, there appears to be a reasonable basis for the trial court's view that, except for the physical assets, which belonged to the defendant and to which the plaintiff makes no claim, the further asset of the business: that is, the value of what is called going concern and goodwill belonged to the two of them as partners in the enterprise; and that when the business could not be relocated, the $10,000 should properly be regarded as compensation for the loss by the forced relocation (which turned out to be a termination) of the business; and that the partners having lost their respective equal shares in the going business operation, they should also share equally in the compensation for its loss.

Partnership Capital and Property

The total money and property contributed by the partners and dedicated to permanent use in the enterprise is the **partnership capital.** A partnership is not required to have a minimum amount of capitalization before starting business. Nonetheless, no partner may withdraw any part of his capital contribution without the consent of all the partners, except when the partnership is dissolved.

Partnership property, on the other hand, is the sum of all of the partnership assets (including capital contributions), and it may vary in amount, whereas partnership capital is a fixed amount, changed only by an amendment to the articles of partnership. All property originally brought into the partnership or subse-quently acquired by the partnership is partnership property. Unless the contrary intention appears, property acquired with partnership funds is also partnership property.[7]

As we discuss later, who owns the property—an individual partner or the partnership— determines (1) who gets it upon dissolution of the partnership, (2) who shares in any loss or gain upon its sale, (3) who shares in income from it, (4) who may sell it or transfer it by will, and (5) whose creditors have a priority against it in satisfying their claims.

A partner, by the terms of the agreement, may contribute no capital but only his skill and services, or a partner may contribute the use of certain property rather than the property itself. For example, a partner who owns a store building may contribute to the partnership the use of the building but not the building itself. The building is therefore not partnership property, and the amount of capital contributed by this partner is the reasonable value of the rental of the building.

Although in accounting practice, partnership profits are frequently included in the capital amount, a clear differentiation should be made between capital and profits. Likewise, a loan by a partner to the firm should be distinguished from capital. A partner is entitled to her share of the profits and to repayment of money advanced as a loan without any new agreement with her copartners, but a withdrawal of capital requires a new agreement. Furthermore, on dissolution, a debt owed to a partner by the partnership has priority over the rights of partners to return of capital.

Title to real estate that is properly a partnership asset, as where purchased with partnership funds or specifically made a capital contribution, may stand in the name of the partnership, an individual partner, or a third party. The UPA alters the common law by permitting title to real estate to be conveyed to a partnership in the partnership name.[7] Title so acquired may be conveyed only in the partnership name.[8]

A question may arise whether property owned by a partner before formation of the partnership and used in the partnership business is a capital contribution and an asset of the partnership. Whether it is a partnership asset determines the rights of the creditors and partners in the property. The fact that legal title to the property remains unchanged is not conclusive evidence that it has not become a partnership asset. The intent of the partners controls the question of who owns the property. Where there is no express agreement, an intention that property is partnership property may be inferred from any of the following facts: (1) the property was improved with partnership funds; (2) the property was carried on the books of the partnership as an asset; (3) taxes, liens, or expenses, such as insurance or repairs, were paid by the partnership; (4) income or proceeds of the property were treated as partnership funds; or (5) admissions or declarations by the partners.

GAULDIN v. CORN
Court of Appeals of Missouri, Southern District, Division One, 1980.
595 S.W.2d 329.

Facts: In 1966 Gauldin and Corn entered into a partnership for the purpose of raising cattle and hogs. The two men were to share equally all costs, labor, losses, and profits. The business was started on land owned by Corn's parents but was later acquired by Corn and his wife. No rent was ever requested or paid for use of the land. Partnership funds were used to bulldoze and clear the land, to repair and build fences, and to seed and fertilize the land. In 1970, at a cost of $2,487.50, a machine shed was built on the land. In 1975 a Cargill unit was built on the land at a cost of $8,000. When the partnership dissolved in 1976, Gauldin paid Corn $7,500 for the "removable" assets; however, the two had no agreement regarding the distribution of the barn and the Cargill unit. Gauldin sues Corn, claiming he is entitled to one-half of the value of the two buildings. The trial court found for Corn and Gauldin appeals.

Decision: Judgment of trial court reversed and remanded with directions to the trial court to determine, from the record, the value of the Cargill unit and the barn at the time of dissolution of the partnership, that the trial court reopen the record for the purpose of hearing testimony on that issue only, and to thereafter enter a judgment awarding plaintiff his proportionate share (one-half) of their value.

Opinion: Greene, J. We agree that the rule is "well-established" that improvements made upon lands owned by one partner, if made with partnership funds for purposes of partnership business, are the personal property of the partnership, and the non-landowning partner is entitled to his proportionate share of their value. * * * [U.P.A. § 8] states, in part:

1. *All property* originally brought into the partnership stock or *subsequently acquired by purchase or otherwise, on account of the partnership is partnership property.*
2. *Unless the contrary intention appears,* property acquired with partnership funds is partnership property. (emphasis added)

It is clear * * * that the general rule, governing the disposition of improvements upon dissolution of a partnership, is activated only where, as here, there is no agreement between the partners which controls such disposition. It matters not that the landowning partner contributed the use of his land to the partnership, that the non-landowning partner knew that the improvements, when made, could not be removed from the land, or that a joint owner with the landowning partner was not joined in the suit for dissolution and accounting of the partnership. Thus the trial court, after finding that the partners had no agreement regarding the disposition of fixed assets upon dissolution of the partnership should have applied the rule that we have approved here, and should have awarded plaintiff his proportionate share of the value of the improvements at the time of dissolution of the partnership.

Rights in Specific Partnership Property

A partner's ownership interest in any specific item of partnership property is that of a **tenant in partnership**.[9] This type of ownership, which exists only in a partnership, has the following principal characteristics:

1. Each partner has an equal right with his copartners to possess partnership property for partnership purposes, but he has no right to possess it for any other purpose without the consent of his copartners.
2. A partner may not make an individual assignment of his right in specific partnership property.
3. A partner's interest in specific partnership property is not subject to attachment or execution by his individual creditors. It is subject to attachment or execution only on a claim against the partnership.
4. Upon the death of a partner, his right in specific partnership property vests in the surviving partner or partners. Upon the death of the last surviving partner, his right in such property vests in his legal representative.

Partner's Interest in the Partnership

In addition to owning as a tenant in partnership every specific item of partnership property, each partner has an **interest in the partnership** that is defined as his share of the profits and surplus and is expressly stated to be personal property.[10]

Assignability A partner may sell or assign his interest in the partnership, but this does not cause dissolution. The new owner does *not* become a partner, does not succeed to the partner's rights to participate in the management, and does not have access to the information available to a member of the firm as a matter of right. He is merely entitled to receive the share of profits and rights on liquidation to which the assigning partner would otherwise be entitled.[11] The assigning partner remains a partner with all the other rights and duties of a partner.

Creditor's Rights A partner's interest is subject to the claims of that partner's creditors who may obtain a **charging order** (a type of judicial lien) against the partner's interest.[12] A creditor who has charged the interest of a partner with a judgment debt may apply for the appointment of a receiver. The court may appoint a receiver for the partner's interest who will receive and hold for the benefit of the creditor the share of profits that ordinarily would be paid to the partner. Neither the judgment creditor nor the receiver becomes a partner, and neither is entitled to participate in the management or to have access to information.

Figure 29–3 compares a partner's rights in specific partnership property with his interest in the partnership.

FIGURE 29-3   Partnership Property Compared with Partner's Interest

	Partnership Property	Partner's Interest
Definition	Tenant in partnership	Share of profits and surplus
Possession	For partnership purposes and not for individual purposes	Intangible, personal property right
Assignability	NO: unless all other partners assign their rights in the property	YES: but the assignee does not become a partner
Attachment	YES: but only for a claim against the partnership	YES: by a charging order
Inheritance	NO: goes to surviving partner(s)	YES: passes to the personal representative

CHAPTER SUMMARY

Nature	**Definition of Partnership** an association of two or more persons to carry on as co-owners of a business for profit **Entity Theory** ■ *Legal Entity* an organization having a separate legal existence from its members; UPA considers a partnership a legal entity for some purposes ■ *Legal Aggregate* a group of individuals not having a legal existence separate from its members; the UPA considers a partnership a legal aggregate for some purposes

Types of Partners
- *General Partner*   member of either a general or limited partnership with unlimited liability for its debts, full management powers, and a right to share the profits
- *Limited Partner*   member of a limited partnership with liability for its debts only to the extent of her capital contribution
- *Silent Partner*   partner who takes no part in the partnership business
- *Secret Partner*   partner whose membership in the partnership is not disclosed to the public
- *Dormant Partner*   partner who is both a silent and secret partner

Formation

Articles of Partnership   it is preferable although not usually required that a written partnership agreement (articles of partnership) be entered into
Tests of Existence   the formation of a partnership requires all of the following:
- *Association*   two or more persons with legal capacity who agree to become partners
- *Business for Profit*
- *Co-Ownership*   includes sharing of profits, losses, and control of the business

Partnership Capital   total money and property contributed by the partners for permanent use by the partnership
Partnership Property   sum of all of the partnership's assets including all property brought into the partnership or subsequently acquired by it
Tenancy in Partnership   type of joint ownership that determines partners' rights in specific partnership property
Interest in Partnership   partner's share in the partnership's profits and surplus
- *Assignability*   a partner may sell or assign his interest in the partnership; the new owner does not become a partner but becomes entitled to the assigning partner's share of profits and surplus
- *Creditor's Rights*   a partner's interest is subject to the claims of creditors who may obtain a charging order (judicial lien) against the partner's interest

QUESTIONS

1. Distinguish between a legal entity and a legal aggregate. Identify those purposes for which a partnership is treated as a legal entity and those purposes for which it is treated as a legal aggregate.
2. List the main provisions that should be included in a partnership agreement.
3. Discuss the tests for the existence of a partnership.
4. Distinguish between partnership capital and partnership property.
5. Distinguish between a partner's rights in specific partnership property and a partner's interest in the partnership.

PROBLEMS

1. Lynn and Jack are joint owners of shares of stock of a corporation, have a joint bank account, and have purchased and own as tenants in common a piece of real estate. They share equally the dividends paid on the stock, the interest on the bank account, and the rent from the real estate. Without

the knowledge of Lynn, Jack makes a trip to inspect the real estate and on his way runs over Samuel. Samuel sues Lynn and Jack for his personal injuries, joining Lynn as defendant on the theory that Lynn was Jack's partner. Is Lynn liable?

2. Smith, Jones, and Brown were creditors of White, who operated a grain elevator known as White's Elevator. White was heavily involved and about to fail when the three creditors mentioned agreed to take title to his elevator property and pay all the debts. It was also agreed that White should continue as manager of the business at a salary of $1,500 per month and that all profits of the business were to be paid to Smith, Jones, and Brown. It was further agreed that they could dispense with White's services at any time, and he was also at liberty to quit when he pleased. White accepted the proposition and continued to operate the business as before, buying and selling grain, incurring obligations, and borrowing money at the bank in his own name for the business. He did, however, tell the banker of the transaction with Smith, Jones, and Brown, and other former creditors of the business knew of it. It worked successfully and for several years paid substantial profits, enough so that Smith, Jones, and Brown had received back nearly all that they had originally advanced. Were Smith, Jones, and Brown partners? Explain.

3. James and Suzanne engaged in the grocery business as partners. In one year they earned considerable money, and at the end of the year, they invested a part of the profits in oil land. Title to the land was taken in their names as tenants in common. The investment was fortunate, for oil was discovered near the land, and its value increased many times. Who owns the land? Why?

4. Sheila owned an old roadside building that she believed could be easily converted into an antique shop. She talked to her friend Barbara, an antique fancier, and they executed the following written agreement:

(a) Sheila would supply the building, all utilities, and $10,000 capital for purchasing antiques.

(b) Barbara would supply $3,000 for purchasing antiques, Sheila to repay her at the time the business terminates.

(c) Barbara would manage the shop, make all purchases, and receive a salary of $100 per week plus 5 percent of the gross receipts.

(d) Fifty percent of the net profits would go into the purchase of new stock. The balance of the net profits would go to Sheila.

(e) The business would operate under the name Roadside Antiques.

Business went poorly, and the result after one year is a debt of $4,000 owing to Old Fashioned, Inc., the principal supplier of antiques purchased by Barbara in the name of Roadside Antiques. Old Fashioned, Inc., sues Roadside Antiques, and Sheila and Barbara as partners. Decision?

5. Clark owned a vacant lot. Bird was engaged in building houses. An oral agreement was entered into between Clark and Bird by which Bird was to erect a house on the lot. When the house and lot were sold, Bird was to have his money first. Clark was then to have the agreed value of the lot, and the profits were to be equally divided. Did a partnership exist?

6. Grant, Arthur, and David formed a partnership for the purpose of betting on boxing matches. Grant and Arthur would become friendly with various boxers and offer them bribes to lose certain bouts. David would then place large bets, using money contributed by all three, and would collect the winnings. After David had accumulated a large sum of money, Grant and Arthur demanded their share, but David refused to make any split. Grant and Arthur then brought suit in a court of equity to compel David to account for the profits of the partnership. What decision?

7. Virginia, Georgia, Caroline, and Louis, residents of State X, were partners doing business under the trade name of Morning Glory Nursery. Virginia owned a one-third interest and Georgia, Caroline, and Louis two-ninths each. The partners acquired three tracts of land in State X for the purpose of the partnership. Two of the tracts were acquired in the names of the four partners, "trading and doing business as Morning Glory Nursery." The third tract was acquired in the names of the individuals, the trade name not appearing in the deed. This third tract was acquired by the partnership out of partnership funds and for partnership purposes. Who owns each of the three tracts? Why?

8. Teresa, Peter, and Walker were partners under a written agreement that it should continue for ten years. During the seventh year, Walker, being indebted to Rebecca, sold and conveyed his interest in the partnership to Rebecca. Teresa and Peter paid Rebecca $5,000 as Walker's share of the profits for that year but refused Rebecca permission to inspect the books or to come into the managing office of the partnership. Rebecca brings an action setting forth the above facts and asks for an account of partnership transactions and an order to inspect the books and to participate in the management of the partnership business.

(a) Does Walker's action dissolve the partnership?

(b) To what is Rebecca entitled with respect to (1) partnership profits, (2) inspection of partnership books, (3) an account of partnership transactions, and (4) participation in the partnership management?

9. Horn's Crane Service furnished supplies and services under a written contract to a partnership engaged in operating a quarry and rock-crushing business. Horn brought this action against Prior and Cook, the individual members of the partnership, to recover a personal judgment against them for the partnership's liability under that contract. Horn has not sued the partnership itself, nor does he claim that the partnership property is insufficient to satisfy its debts. Decision?

ENDNOTES

1. Uniform Partnership Act, Section 6, Partnership Defined.

2. Uniform Partnership Act, Section 2, Definition of Terms.

3. Uniform Partnership Act, Section 15, Nature of Partner's Liability.

4. Uniform Partnership Act, Section 29, Dissolution Defined.

5. Uniform Partnership Act, Section 18(g), Rules Determining Rights and Duties of Partners.

6. Uniform Partnership Act, Section 7, Rules for Determining the Existence of a Partnership.

7. Uniform Partnership Act, Section 8, Partnership Property.

8. Uniform Partnership Act, Section 10, Conveyance of Real Property of the Partnership.

9. Uniform Partnership Act, Section 25, Nature of a Partner's Right in Specific Partnership Property.

10. Uniform Partnership Act, Section 26, Nature of Partner's Interest in the Partnership.

11. Uniform Partnership Act, Section 27, Assignment of Partner's Interest.

12. Uniform Partnership Act, Section 28, Partner's Interest Subject to Charging Order.

30 RIGHTS AND DUTIES

The operation and management of a partnership involve interactions among the partners as well as with third persons. In this chapter we consider both of these relationships. The first part of the chapter focuses on the rights and duties of the partners among themselves, which are determined by the partnership agreement, the common law, and the Uniform Partnership Act. The second part of the chapter focuses on the relations of partners to third persons dealing with the partnership, which are governed by the laws of agency, contracts, and torts as well as by the UPA.

RELATIONSHIPS OF PARTNERS TO ONE ANOTHER

When parties enter into a partnership, the law imposes certain obligations on the parties and also gives them specific rights. So long as the rights of third parties are not affected and standards of fairness are maintained, the parties may, by agreement, vary these rights and obligations.

DUTIES AMONG PARTNERS

The legal duties imposed upon partners in their relationship among themselves are (1) the fiduciary duty (the duty of loyalty), (2) the duty of obedience, and (3) the duty of care. In addition, each partner has a duty to inform his copartners and a duty to account to the partnership. These additional duties are discussed later in the section covering rights of partners. All of these duties correspond precisely with those duties owed by an agent to his principal

and reflect the fact that a large part of the law of partnership is the law of agency.

Fiduciary Duty

A fiduciary relationship exists among the members of a partnership based on the high standard of trust and confidence that they place in one another. Each partner owes a duty of absolute and **utmost good faith** and **loyalty** to his partners. It is only on such basis that so intimate a business relationship can function.

The law of partnership has adopted as part of the fiduciary duty the requirement that a partner shall not make a profit other than his agreed compensation, shall not compete with the partnership, and shall not otherwise profit from the relationship at the expense of the partnership. The UPA states that every partner must account to the partnership for any benefit and hold as trustee for it any profits he made without the consent of the other partners from any transaction connected with the formation, conduct, or liquidation of the partnership or from any use by him of its property.[1] He may not prefer himself over the firm, nor may he even deal at arm's length with his partners. His duty is one of undivided and continuous loyalty to his partners.

The extent of this fiduciary duty, which binds all fiduciaries and not just partners, has been most eloquently expressed by the often quoted words of Judge (later Justice) Cardozo:

> Joint adventurers, like copartners, owe to one another, while the enterprise continues, the duty of *finest loyalty.* Many forms of conduct permissible in a workaday world for those acting at arm's length, are forbidden to those bound by

fiduciary ties. A trustee is held to something stricter than the morals of the market place. *Not honesty alone, but the punctilio of an honor the most sensitive, is then the standard of behavior.* As to this there has developed a tradition that is unbending and inveterate. Uncompromising rigidity has been the attitude of courts of equity when petitioned to undermine the rule of undivided loyalty by the ''disintegrating erosion'' of particular exceptions. Only thus has the level of conduct for fiduciaries been kept at a level higher than that trodden by the crowd. It will not consciously be lowered by any judgment of this court [emphasis added].

A partner cannot acquire for himself a partnership asset or opportunity without the consent of all the partners. Thus, a partner may not renew a partnership lease in his name alone. The fiduciary duty also applies to the purchase of a partner's interest from another partner. Each partner owes the highest duty of honesty and fair dealing to the other partners, including the obligation to disclose fully and accurately all material facts.

The next case illustrates how rigorously the courts enforce the fiduciary duty.

CLEMENT v. CLEMENT
Supreme Court of Pennsylvania, 1970.
436 Pa. 466, 260 A.2d 728.

Facts: Charles and L. W. Clement are brothers who had formed a partnership lasting forty years. In 1964 Charles discovered that his brother, who was the brighter of the two and kept the partnership's books, had made several substantial personal investments with funds improperly withdrawn from the partnership. He then brought an action in equity seeking dissolution of the partnership, appointment of a receiver, and an accounting. The chancellor of the court of equity issued a decree in favor of Charles but the court *en banc* reversed his decision. Charles brings this appeal.

Decision: Order of the court *en banc* reversed and case remanded.

Opinion: Roberts, J.   We disagree with the court en banc's statement of the applicable law and therefore reverse. Our theory is simple. There is a fiduciary relationship between partners. Where such a relationship exists actual fraud need not be shown. There was ample evidence of self-dealing and diversion of partnership assets on the part of L. W.—more than enough to sustain the chancellor's conclusion that several substantial investments made by L. W. over the years were bankrolled with funds improperly withdrawn from the partnership. * * * In all this we are strongly motivated by the fact that the chancellor saw and heard the various witnesses for exhausting periods of time and was in a much better position than we could ever hope to be to taste the flavor of the testimony.

[U.P.A.] § 21 very simply and unambiguously provides that partners owe a fiduciary duty one to another. [Citation.] One should not have to deal with his partner as though he were the opposite party in an arms-length transaction. One should be allowed to trust his partner, to expect that he is pursuing a common goal and not working at cross-purposes. * * *

It would be unduly harsh to require that one must prove actual fraud before he can recover for a partner's derelictions. Where one partner has so dealt with the partnership as to raise the probability of wrongdoing it ought to be his responsibility to negate that inference. It has been held that ''where a partner fails to keep a record of partnership transactions, and is unable to account for them, every presumption will be made against him.'' [Citation.] Likewise, where a partner commingles partnership funds with his own assets he ought to have to shoulder the task of demonstrating the probity of his conduct.

In the instant case L. W. dealt loosely with partnership funds. At various times he made substantial investments in his own name. He was totally unable to explain where he got the funds to make these investments. The court en banc held that Charles had no claim on the fruits of these investments because he could not trace the money that was invested therein dollar for dollar from the partnership. Charles should not have had this burden. He did show that his brother diverted substantial sums from the partnership funds under his control. The inference that these funds provided L. W. with the wherewithal to make his investments was a perfectly reasonable one for the chancellor to make and his decision should have been allowed to stand.

Duty of Obedience

A partner owes his partners a duty to act in obedience to the partnership agreement and to any business decisions properly made by the partnership. A partner who violates this duty is individually liable for any resulting loss. For example, a partner who violates a specific agreement not to extend credit to relatives and advances money from partnership funds and sells good on credit to an insolvent relative is personally liable to his partners for the unpaid debt.

Duty of Care

A partner must manage the partnership affairs without culpable negligence. **Culpable negligence** is something more than ordinary negligence, yet short of gross negligence. Thus, a partner does not breach her duty of care if she makes honest errors of judgment or fails to use ordinary skill in transacting partnership business so long as she is not culpably negligent. For example, a partner assigned to keep the partnership books uses a complicated system of bookkeeping and produces numerous mistakes. Since these errors result simply from poor judgment rather than fraud and are not intended to and do not operate to the personal advantage of the bookkeeping partner, the negligent partner is *not* liable to her copartners for any resulting loss.

RIGHTS AMONG PARTNERS

The law provides partners with certain rights, which include the following: (1) their rights in specific partnership property as a tenant in partnership; (2) their interest in the partnership; (3) their right to share in distributions; (4) their right to participate in management; (5) their right to choose associates; and (6) their right of enforcement.[2] We discussed the first two of these rights in Chapter 29. The four remaining rights among partners are discussed in this section.

Right to Share in Distributions

A **distribution** is a transfer of partnership property from the partnership to a partner. Distributions include a division of profits, a return of capital contributions, a repayment of a loan or advance made by a partner to the partnership, and a payment made to compensate a partner for services rendered to the partnership.

Right to Share in Profits   Because a partnership is an association to carry on a business for profit, each partner is entitled, unless otherwise agreed, to a share of the profits. Conversely, each partner must contribute toward any losses sustained by the partnership.[3] If the partners do not have an agreement about dividing the profits, the partners share the profits *equally,* regardless of the ratio of their financial contributions or their degree of participation in the management. Unless the partnership agreement provides otherwise, the partners bear losses in the *same proportion* in which they share profits. The agreement may, however, validly provide for bearing losses in a different proportion than that in which profits are shared.

For example, Alice, Betty, and Carol form a partnership, with Alice contributing $1,000, Betty, $2,000, and Carol, $3,000. They could agree that Alice would receive 20 percent of the profits and assume 30 percent of the losses; that Betty would receive 30 percent of the profits and assume 50 percent of the losses; and that Carol would receive 50 percent of the profits and assume 20 percent of the losses. If their agreement is silent as to the sharing of profits and losses, however, each would have a one-third share of both profits and losses.

Right to Return of Capital After all partnership creditors have been paid, each partner is entitled to be repaid his capital contribution when the firm is terminated.[3] Unless otherwise agreed, a partner is not entitled to interest on his capital contribution. If there is a delay in return of his capital contribution, however, he is entitled to interest at the legal rate from the date when it should have been repaid.[3]

Right to Return of Advances If a partner makes advances (loans) over and above his agreed capital contribution, he is entitled to repayment of the advance plus interest on it.[3] His position as a creditor of the firm, however, is subordinate to the claims of creditors who are not partners but is superior to the partners' right to return of capital. In addition, a partner who has incurred personal liabilities in the ordinary and proper conduct of the business of the firm or who has made payments on behalf of the partnership is entitled to indemnification or repayment on equal footing with an advance made by a partner.[3]

Right to Compensation The UPA provides that, unless otherwise agreed, *no* partner is entitled to remuneration (payment) for acting in the partnership business.[3] Even if one partner performs a substantial or disproportionate share of the work of conducting the business, he is entitled to no salary but only his share of the profits. A partner may, however, by agreement among all of the partners, receive a salary or a disproportionate percentage of the profits. Moreover, a surviving partner is entitled to reasonable compensation for his services in winding up the partnership affairs.[3]

Right to Participate in Management

Although each of the partners may have responsibility for a certain area of the business, they all, unless otherwise agreed, have an *equal* voice in its management.[3] The majority generally governs the actions and decisions of the partnership, except that *all* the partners must consent to any actions that are contrary to the partnership agreement.[3] In their partnership agreement, the partners may provide for unequal voting rights. For example, Jones, Smith, and Williams form a partnership, agreeing that Jones will have two votes, Smith four votes, and Williams five votes. It is common for large partnerships to concentrate most or all management authority in a committee of a few partners or even in just one partner. Different classes of partners may also be created with different management rights. This is a common practice in accounting and law firms, which may have two classes (junior and senior partners) or three classes (junior, senior, and managing partners).

Right to Choose Associates

No partner may be forced to accept any person as a partner whom she does not choose. This is because of the fiduciary relationship between the parties and because each partner has a right to take part in the management of the business, to handle the partnership assets for partnership purposes, and to act as an agent of the partnership. It is possible that a partner, by her negligence, poor judgment, or dishonesty, may bring financial loss or ruin to her copartners. Because of the close relationship involved, partnerships must necessarily be founded on mutual trust and confidence. All this finds expression in the term *delectus personae,* which literally means, "choice of the person" and indicates the right one has to choose or select her partners. This principle is embodied in the UPA, which provides: "No person can become a member of a partnership without the consent of *all* the partners" (emphasis added).[3] It is a consequence of *delectus personae* that when a partner sells her interest, the purchaser does not become a partner and is not entitled to participate in the management.

Enforcement Rights

As we have discussed, the partnership relationship creates a number of duties and rights among the partners. Accordingly, partnership law provides the partners with the means to enforce these rights and duties. First, each partner is allowed to have access to all information concerning the partnership and its books. Second, under certain circumstances, a partner may obtain a judicially ordered and supervised accounting (a detailed statement of financial transactions, including a balance owed) in an action brought in a court of equity against the partnership or his partners.

Right to Information and Inspection of the Books   Each partner may demand to have full information about all partnership matters. Each partner has a duty to supply other partners with full and accurate information of all things affecting the partnership.[4] The right to demand information extends also to the legal representative of a deceased partner for a

reasonable time following the dissolution of the partnership.

Unless the partners agree otherwise, the books of the partnership are to be kept at the principal place of business at all times, and each partner has a right to have access to them, to inspect them, and to copy any of them.[5] This right may also be exercised by a duly authorized agent on behalf of a partner.

Right to an Accounting   At common law and under the UPA, a partner is entitled to an **accounting,** which is an equitable proceeding for a comprehensive and effective settlement of all partnership affairs. An accounting is designed to produce and evaluate all testimony relevant to the various claims of the partners. A partner may invoke the power of a court of equity to decree an accounting whenever (1) he is wrongfully excluded from the partnership business or possession of its property by his copartners, (2) the partnership agreement provides, (3) a partner makes a profit in violation of his fiduciary duty, or (4) other circumstances render it just and reasonable.[6] A partner is not permitted to sue the partnership at law, but he may sue in equity in an action for an accounting.

CENTRAL TRUST & SAFE DEPOSIT CO. v. RESPASS
Court of Appeals of Kentucky, 1902.
112 Ky. 606, 66 S.W. 421.

Facts: Respass and Sharp, as partners, owned and managed a racing stable and, in addition, were engaged in bookmaking, that is, accepting bets on race horses. When Sharp died, $4,724—representing the undistributed profits of the bookmaking business—was on deposit in Sharp's personal bank account. Respass brought suit against Central Trust & Safe Deposit Co., the executor of Sharp's will, for an accounting of profits from their gambling business. Respass claims he is entitled to one-half of those profits. The trial court awarded Respass one-half of the profits and the executor appeals.

Decision: Judgment reversed and remanded with directions to enter a judgment for Central Trust.

Opinion: Durelle, J.   A closer question is presented by the claim for a division of the "bank roll." This $4,724 was, as found by the chancellor, earned by the firm composed of Respass and Sharp in carrying on an illegal business—that of "bookmaking"—in the State of Illinois. But though this amount had been won upon horse races in Chicago, it is claimed that, though secured illegally, "the transaction has been closed, and the appellee Respass is only seeking his share from the realized profits from the illegal contracts, if they are illegal." On the other hand, it is claimed for appellant, the executor, that, as to the bank roll, this proceeding is a bill for an accounting of profits from the business of gambling.

It does not seem to be seriously contended that the business of "bookmaking," whether carried on in Chicago or in this Commonwealth, was legal, for by the common law of this country all wagers are illegal. [Citation.] One of the most interesting cases upon this subject is that of Everet v. Williams—the celebrated Highwaymen's Case—an account of which is given in 9 Law Quart. Rev., 197 [England]. That was a bill for an accounting of a partnership in the business of highwaymen, though the true nature of the partnership was veiled in ambiguous language. The bill set up the partnership between defendant and plaintiff, who was "skilled in dealing with several sorts of commodities," that they "proceeded jointly in the said dealing with good success on Hounslow Heath, where they dealt with a gentleman for a gold watch," that defendant had informed plaintiff that Finchley "was a good and convenient place to deal in," such commodities being "very plenty" there, and if they were to deal there "it would be almost all gain to them"; that they accordingly "dealt with several gentlemen for divers watches, rings, swords, canes, hats, cloaks, horses, bridles, saddles, and other things, to the value of £2,000 and upwards"; that a gentleman of Blackheath had several articles which defendant thought "might be had for a little or no money in case they could prevail on the said gentleman to part with the same things," and that, "after some small discourse with the said gentlemen," the said things were dealt for "at a very cheap rate." The dealings were alleged to have amounted to £2,000 and upward. This case, while interesting, from the views it gives of the audacity of the parties and their solicitors, sheds little light upon the legal questions involved, for the bill was condemned for scandal and impertinence; the solicitors were taken into custody, and "fyned" £50 each for "reflecting upon the honor and dignity of this court"; the counsel whose name was signed to the bill was required to pay the costs; and both the litigants were subsequently hanged, at Tyburn and Maidstone, respectively, while one of the solicitors was transported. [Citations.] * * *

In Watson v. Fletcher, [citation], the business of the firm had been the operation of a faro bank. One of the partners having died, the survivor sought an accounting of profits earned. The syllabus reads: "A court of equity will not lend its aid for the settlement and adjustment of the transactions of a partnership for gambling. Nor will it give relief to either partner against the other, founded on transactions arising out of such partnership, whether for profits, losses, expenses, contribution, or reimbursement. * * * "

We conclude that in this country, in the case of a partnership in a business confessedly illegal, whatever may be the doctrine where there has been a new contract in relation to, or a new investment of, the profits of such illegal business, and whatever may be the doctrine as to the rights or liabilities of a third person who assumes obligations with respect to such profits, or by law becomes responsible therefor, the decided weight of authority is that a court of equity will not entertain a bill for an accounting.

RELATIONSHIP BETWEEN PARTNERS AND THIRD PARTIES

In the course of doing business, partners may also acquire rights and incur duties to third parties. Under the law of agency, a principal is liable on contracts made on his behalf by his duly authorized agents and is liable in tort for the wrongful acts his employees commit in the course of their employment. A large part of the law of partnership is the law of agency, and most problems arising between partners and third persons require the application of principles of agency law. This relationship is made explicit by the UPA, which states, "The law of agency shall apply under this act,"[7] and "Every partner is an agent of the partnership for the purpose of its business."[8]

CONTRACTS OF PARTNERSHIP

The act of every partner binds the partnership on transactions *within* the scope of the partnership business unless the partner does not have actual or apparent authority to so act.[8] If the partnership is bound, then each partner has **unlimited personal liability** for that partnership obligation. The UPA provides that partners are jointly liable on all debts and contract obligations of the partnership.[9] Under **joint liability,** a creditor must bring suit against all of the partners as a group. As a consequence, any suit against the partners must name all the partners as defendants.

Authority to Bind Partnership

A partner may bind the partnership by her act (a) if she has actual authority, express or implied, to perform the act, or (b) if she has apparent authority to perform the act.[8] If the act is not apparently within the scope of the partnership business, then the partnership is bound only where the partner has actual authority. In these cases, the third person dealing with the partner assumes the risk of the existence of such actual authority. Where there is no actual authority and no apparent authority, the partnership is bound only if it ratifies the act. Ratification is discussed in Chapter 28. See Figure 30–1.

Actual Express Authority   The actual express authority of partners may be specifically set forth in the partnership agreement or in an additional agreement between the partners and may be written or oral. In addition, it may arise from decisions made by a majority of the partners regarding ordinary matters connected with the partnership business.

The UPA provides that the following acts do *not* bind the partnership unless authorized by *all* of the partners:

1. assignment of partnership property for the benefit of its creditors,
2. disposal of the good will of the business;
3. any act that would make it impossible to carry on the ordinary business of the partnership;
4. confession of a judgment (written agreement by debtor authorizing creditor to obtain a court judgment in the event debtor defaults);
5. submission of a partnership claim or liability to arbitration.[8]

In addition, a partner who does not have actual authority from all of her partners may not bind the partnership by any act that is not apparently for the carrying on of the business of the partnership in the usual way. This would include the following acts, which under ordinary circumstances are clearly outside the scope of the partnership: (1) execution of contracts of guaranty and suretyship in the firm name; (2) sale of partnership property not held for sale in the usual course of business; and (3) payment of individual debts out of partnership assets.

Actual Implied Authority   Actual implied authority is authority that is neither expressly granted nor expressly denied but is reasonably deduced from the nature of the partnership, the terms of the partnership agreement, or the relations of the partners. For example, a partner has implied authority to hire and fire employees whose services are necessary to carry on the business of the partnership. In addition, a partner has implied authority to purchase property necessary for the business.

Apparent Authority   Apparent authority (which may or may not be actual) is authority that may, in view of the circumstances and the conduct of the parties, be reasonably considered to exist by a third person who has no knowledge or notice of the lack of actual authority. For example, a partner has apparent authority to indorse checks and notes, to make representations and warranties in selling goods, and to enter into contracts for advertising. A third person may not rely on apparent authority in any situation where he is put on notice or already knows that the partner does

FIGURE 30-1   Contract Liability

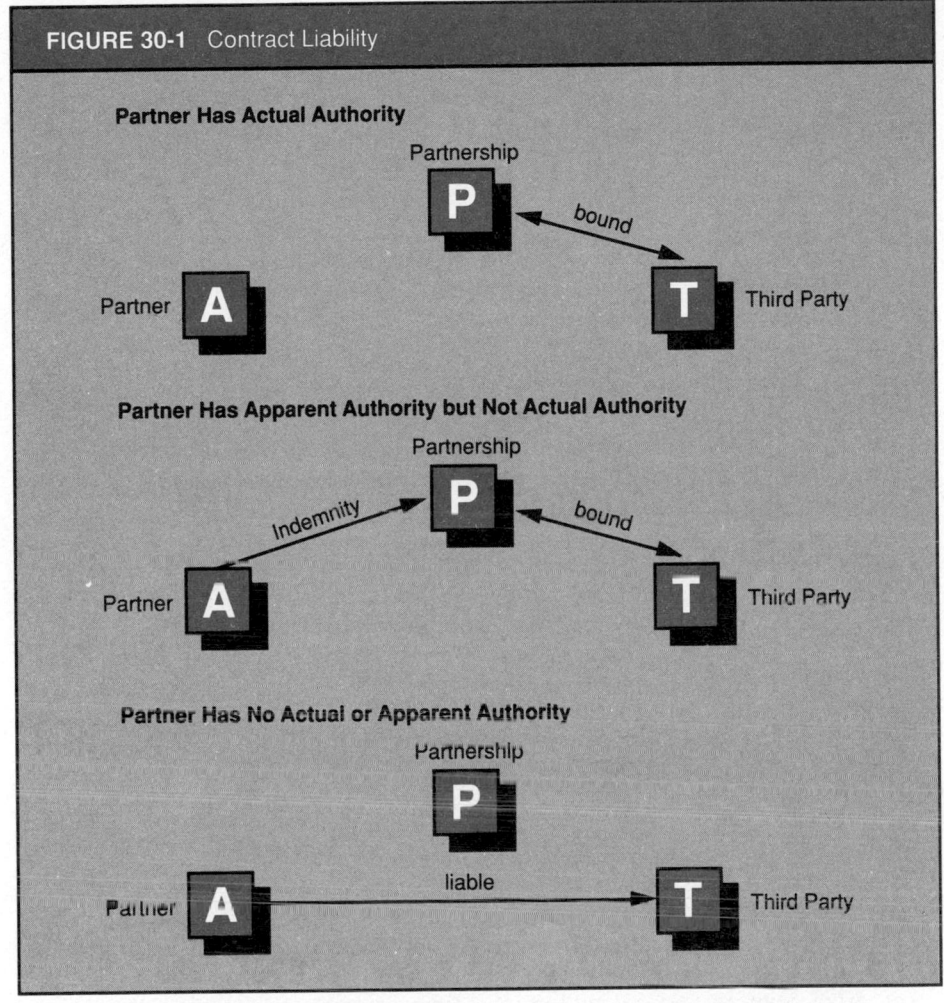

Partner Has Actual Authority

Partner Has Apparent Authority but Not Actual Authority

Partner Has No Actual or Apparent Authority

not, or may not, have actual authority.[8] In these situations, the third person must make sure of the actual authority of the partner or assume the risk of its absence.

HODGE v. GARRETT
Supreme Court of Idaho, 1980.
101 Idaho 397, 614 P.2d 420.

Facts: Hodge and Voeller, the managing partner of the Pay-Ont Drive-In Theatre, signed a contract for the sale of a small parcel of land belonging to the partnership. The parcel was not used in theater operations except for the last twenty feet, which was necessary for the theater's driveway. The agreement stated that it was between Hodge and the partnership, with Voeller signing for the partnership. Voeller claims that he told Hodge before signing that a plat plan would have to be approved by the other partners before the sale. Hodge denies this and sues for specific performance, claiming that Voeller had actual and apparent authority to bind the partnership.

The partners argue that Voeller had no such authority and that Hodge knew this. The trial court granted specific performance to Hodge and the partners appeal.

Decision: Judgment reversed.

Opinion: Bristline, J.   At common law one partner could not, "without the concurrence of his copartners, convey away the real estate of the partnership, bind his partners by a deed, or transfer the title and interest of his copartners in the firm real estate." [Citation.] This rule was changed by the adoption of the Uniform Partnership Act. The relevant provisions are currently embodied in [U.P.A. §§ 9(1) and 10(1)] as follows:

[U.P.A. § 10(1)]: Where title to real property is in the partnership name, any partner may convey title to such property by a conveyance executed in the partnership name; but the partnership may recover such property unless the partner's act binds the partnership under the provisions of paragraph 1 of section [9] unless such property has been conveyed by the grantee or a person claiming through such grantee to a holder for value without knowledge that the partner, in making the conveyance, has exceeded his authority.

[U.P.A. § 9(1)]: Every partner is an agent of the partnership for the purpose of its business, and the act of every partner, including the execution in the partnership name of any instrument, for apparently carrying on in the usual way the business of the partnership of which he is a member binds the partnership, unless the partner so acting has in fact no authority to act for the partnership in the particular matter, and the person with whom he is dealing has knowledge of the fact that he has no such authority.

The meaning of these provisions was stated in one text as follows:

If record title is in the partnership and a partner conveys in the partnership name, legal title passes. But the partnership may recover the property (except from a bona fide purchaser from the grantee) if it can show (A) that the conveying partner was not apparently carrying on business in the usual way or (B) that he had in fact no authority and the grantee had knowledge of that fact. The burden of proof with respect to authority is thus on the partnership. Crane and Bromburg [sic] on Partnership § 50A (1968) (footnotes omitted).

Thus this contract is enforceable if Voeller had the actual authority to sell the property, or, even if Voeller did not have such authority, the contract is still enforceable if the sale was in the usual way of carrying on the business and Hodge did not know that Voeller did not have this authority.

As to the question of actual authority, such authority must affirmatively appear, "for the authority of one partner to make and acknowledge a deed for the firm will not be presumed. . . . " [Citation.] Although such authority may be implied from the nature of the business, *id.*, or from similar past transactions, [citation], nothing in the record in this case indicates that Voeller had express or implied authority to sell real property belonging to the partnership. There is no evidence that Voeller had sold property belonging to the partnership in the past, and obviously the partnership was not engaged in the business of buying and selling real estate.

The next question, since actual authority has not been shown, is whether Voeller was conducting the partnership business in the usual way in selling this parcel of land such that the contract is binding under [U.P.A. §§ 10(1) and 9(1)], *i.e.*, whether Voeller had apparent authority. Here the evidence showed and the trial court found:

* * *

> That at the inception of the partnership, and at all times thereafter, Rex E. Voeller was the exclusive, managing partner of the partnership and had the full authority to make all decisions pertaining to the partnership affairs, including paying the bills, preparing profit and loss statements, income tax returns and the ordering of any goods or services necessary to the operation of the business.

The court made no finding that it was customary for Voeller to sell real property, or even personal property, belonging to the partnership. Nor was there any evidence to this effect. Nor did the court discuss whether it was in the usual course of business for the managing partner of a theater to sell real property. Yet the trial court found that Voeller had apparent authority to sell the property. From this it must be inferred that the trial court believed it to be in the usual course of business for a partner who has exclusive control of the partnership business to sell real property belonging to the partnership, where that property is not being used in the partnership business. We cannot agree with this conclusion. For a theater, "carrying on in the usual way the business of the partnership," [U.P.A. § 9(1)], means running the operations of the theater; it does not mean selling a parcel of property adjacent to the theater. Here the contract of sale stated that the land belonged to the partnership, and, even if Hodge believed that Voeller as the exclusive manager had authority to transact all business for the firm, Voeller still could not bind the partnership through a unilateral act which was not in the usual business of the partnership. We therefore hold that the trial court erred in holding that this contract was binding on the partnership.

Partnership by Estoppel

Partnership by estoppel imposes partnership duties and liabilities on a nonpartner who has either represented himself or consented to be represented as a partner. It extends to a third person to whom such a representation is made and who gives credit to the partnership in justifiable reliance on the representation.[10]

For example, Marks and Saunders are partners doing business as Marks and Company. Marks introduces Patterson to Taylor, describing Patterson as a member of the partnership. Believing that Patterson is a member of the partnership and relying on Patterson's good credit standing, Taylor sells goods on credit to Marks and Company. In an action by Taylor against Marks, Saunders, and Patterson as partners to recover the price of the goods, Patterson is liable even though he is not a partner in Marks and Company. Taylor had justifiably relied on the representation that Patterson was a partner in Marks and Company, to which Patterson, by his silence, consented. If Taylor, at the time, knew that Patterson was not a partner, however, his reliance on the representation would not have been justified, and Patterson would not be liable.

TORTS OF PARTNERSHIP

The UPA provides that a partnership is liable for loss or injury caused by any wrongful act or omission of any partner while acting within the ordinary course of the business of the partnership or with the authority of his copartners.[11] If the partnership is liable, then each partner has **unlimited personal liability** for the partnership obligation. The liability of partners for a tort or breach of trust[12] committed by any partner or by an employee of the firm in the course of partnership business is **joint and several,**[9] which means that all of the partners may be sued jointly in one action or separate actions may be maintained against each of them and separate judgments obtained. Judgments obtained are enforceable only against property of the defendant or defendants named in the suit. Payment of any one of the judgments, however, satisfies all of them.

LAW IN THE NEWS

Grant Thornton Finds Itself in Disarray
Suit Over ESM Shows Partners' Vulnerability

When Steve L. Hipp was invited early last year to join Alexander Grant & Co., he jumped at the chance. Mr. Hipp had been a partner at the troubled accounting firm of Fox & Co. which was being absorbed by Grant. Chicago-based Grant, now known as Grant Thornton, was a bigger firm and long regarded as the Mr. Clean of the accounting profession.

But a few months later, Mr. Hipp received a rude shock. Jose Gomez, Grant's managing partner for southern Florida, was accused of taking a $125,000 bribe from E.S.M. Government Securities Inc. in return for certifying false financial statements for at least four years. Mr. Gomez later pleaded guilty. Grant was sued for $300 million in actual damages and as much as $1 billion in punitive damages by parties that said they lost money in transactions with the now collapsed Fort Lauderdale securities firm.

The total damages sought are more than five times Grant's malpractice insurance coverage and almost 50 times partners' capital.

Aware that a partner in a profession firm can be held liable for frauds proven against other partners, Mr. Hipp chose to become a manager in Grant rather than a partner. While he won't disclose the loss in potential income, he acknowledges, the step-down is a "big sacrifice." But he adds, "It will save me a lot of liability worries."

Turmoil at Firm

Grant itself is in turmoil. The nation's 11th-largest accounting frim is having problems obtaining new clients and partners, retaining current clients and keeping its executive suite intact. Recently, Grant's top partner said he will step down, and the No. 2 partner already left. "It's been rough times," says Peter Skomorowsky, regional managing partner in New York and the firm's official spokesman.

The firm's travail illustrates the pressures on a professional firm—whether it be in accounting, law, architecture or another field—when its reputation is threatened by a major liability suit. The

problem is particularly significant for an accounting firm because, as an auditor, it is expected to be its clients' financial conscience.

"The E.S.M. case is the most dramatic example of how vulnerable professional partners are to mistakes made by colleagues in their firm," says Newton Minow, a partner in the Chicago law firm of Sidley & Austin, and a former adviser to Arthur Andersen & Co., the biggest U.S. accounting firm. "This suit could be severely damaging to the firm."

To add to Grant's woes, the plaintiffs are suing more than 400 Grant partners who were served with court papers saying that their personal assets could be attached by the court in any settlement of the E.S.M. case. Some Grant partners considered shifting personal assets to wives or relatives, but Grant told them this isn't necessary.

"As far as I'm concerned, there's a better chance their wives will file for divorce than that they will lose their shirts because of E.S.M.," says Alvin Stein, a New York lawyer representing Grant.

Since E.S.M., Grant has found it difficult to attract new tax partners in south Florida and Washington, D.C., two important areas for its practice, says Grant's Mr. Skomorowsky. In recent months, Grant has lost a dozen public clients, compared with only two or three for firms of comparable size, says Arthur Bowman, editor of Public Accounting Report, a newsletter.

Mr. Skomorowsky insists that any loss of clients hasn't been because of the E.S.M. case. A half dozen former clients confirm this, including one of the biggest: Baxter Travenol Laboratories Inc., a Grant client for 32 years that moved to Price Waterhouse in September.

But Mr. Skomorowsky concedes that the firm is "getting somewhat fewer opportunities for new business." He says, "There's no question that E.S.M. was a disaster for our image. But as Mark Twain said, 'The reports of our death are premature.'"

However, the E.S.M. case caused Grant to lose some Fox business and partners that it otherwise would have picked up in the combination. Walter Knepper, who ran Fox's office in St. Louis, says that "as a result of the E.S.M. case, we lost a big client" just before the Grant Fox combination May 1. He says the loss cut the office's annual revenues 20% and spurred Fox's St. Louis office to join Houston-based Pannell Kerr Forster, the 14th biggest accounting firm. "We're working hard to regain the reputation we lost when Fox had so many audit failures," says Mr. Knepper. "Why should I move from one firm with problems into another firm with problems?"

The Securities and Exchange Commission in mid-1983 prohibited Fox from accepting new publicly held clients until early 1984 because of problems with certain audits.

Grant Thornton (formerly Alexander Grant & Co.)	
Headquarters	Chicago
U.S. offices	77
U.S. partners	450
U.S. revenues	$175 million*
Major clients include	Sundstrand Corp., Southmark Corp., Republic Airlines Inc., Orange & Rockland Utilities Inc.

*Year ended July 31, 1985

Early Departure

In Grant's executive suite, Robert Kleckner decided to step down as executive partner this year instead of in 1988, as he had told other partners when the Fox combination was announced in late 1984. And Herbert Dooskin, named Grant's chairman several months ago, recently resigned to take a post in industry.

Both men maintain that the E.S.M. case didn't influence their actions, and they insist that Grant's future is bright. "Our standards of quality and performance are still outstanding, and from the 25 phone calls I've personally received from clients, they're all standing behind us," says Mr. Kleckner.

Mr. Dooskin says he's leaving the firm because a Grant client, Ply-Gem Industries Inc., a New York-based maker of specialty wood products, "made me an offer I couldn't refuse;" he says Ply-Gem will pay him a higher salary. "It was a difficult decision," Mr. Dooskin says, "I've been with Grant for 22 years and it's been like family."

Grant was founded in 1924 by Alexander Grant, an accountant from Cameron, Mo. Last January, Grant and its British affiliate, Thornton Baker, adopted the uniform Grant Thornton name.

"Grant was once considered one of the best-run firms in the profession," says James Emerson, publisher of the Big Eight Review, a Bellevue, Wash., newsletter, "Since E.S.M., it has come down several pegs."

A former Grant partner, who requests anonymity because he hasn't recovered all his capital from the firm, says he joined another firm in mid-1985 because he felt "it would be difficult to continue to try to sell my services after E.S.M." He adds, "Clients were already beginning to ask me embarrassing questions."

Counterattacking

Grant is counterattacking. Mr. Stein, the firm's New York attorney, says he is confident that Grant can reduce the impact of the E.S.M. claims because some of the parties suing Grant were themselves involved in the E.S.M. fraud. Mr. Stein recently filed a 200-page third-party complaint in a federal court in Fort Lauderdale claiming unspecified damages from eight entities and 22 people.

And in an unusual step for an accounting firm, Grant named another accounting firm, Arthur Andersen, in its third-party suit. Arthur Andersen was auditor of Home State Savings Bank, a Cincinnati thrift put up for sale after a run on its deposits spurred by its investment in E.S.M. Home State had sued Grant for more than $117 million for money allegedly lost in government securities trading with E.S.M. Grant claims Arthur Andersen conspired with Home State to withhold information from Grant that would have been damaging to E.S.M. Arthur Andersen denies this.

Harold Cunningham, Andersen's partner for legal affairs, says the Grant suit is "a desperation move" and that "Grant is groping for anything to get another accounting firm or other people involved to ease the claim against themselves."

Mr. Stein says he is telling executives at Grant that he can keep awards against Grant below the firm's liability insurance coverage because a lot of the parties didn't exercise sufficient diligence in transactions with E.S.M. And he is trying to reach a settlement before the trial starts Oct. 1.

'Strong Medicine'

Dan L. Goldwasser, a special counsel for the New York State Society of Certified Public Accountants, says the E.S.M. liability suit could cripple Grant. "A partner admitting to a payoff is awfully strong medicine for any judge or jury," he says.

Some Grant partners continue to worry that the E.S.M. case can do long-term damage to the firm's image and financial outlook. "Two clients have asked me if the firm will continue to be in existence," says Ronald Berman, a Grant tax partner in Madison, Wis., who has been with the firm a dozen years. "It's not a happy question to have to answer."

And Norman Essman, a Grant partner in St. Louis since 1969, says that while the E.S.M. case probably won't sink Grant. "It'll cost us a hell of a lot of money to defend. I'd like clients to call and hire us because Grant Thornton is as well known as a Big Eight firm, but that just isn't happening. As partners, we have to establish our own reputations."

By LEE BERTON
Reprinted by permission of The Wall Street Journal, © Dow Jones & Company, Inc. 1986. All Rights Reserved Worldwide.

This liability is comparable to the vicarious liability imposed on a principal for the torts of an agent by the doctrine of *respondeat superior*. The partner committing the tort is directly liable to the third party and must also **indemnify** the partnership for any damages it pays to the third party (see Figure 30–2). Tort liability of the partnership may include not only the negligence of the partners but also trespass, fraud, defamation, and breach of fiduciary duty, so long as the tort is committed in the course of partnership business. Moreover, the fact that a tort is intentional does not necessarily remove it from the course of business, but it is a factor to be considered.

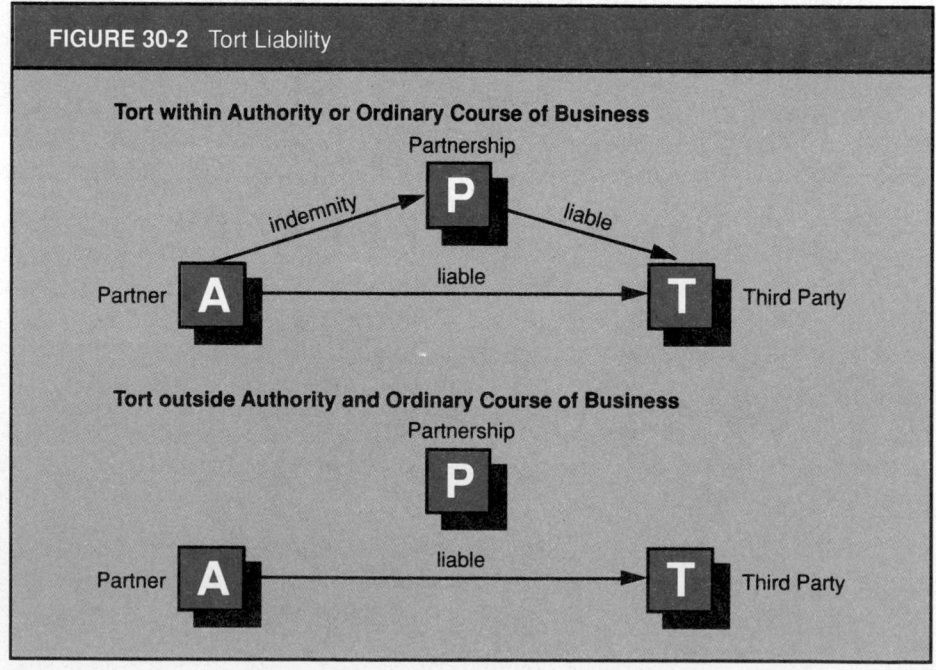

FIGURE 30-2 Tort Liability

HUSTED v. McCLOUD
Supreme Court of Indiana, 1983.
450 N.E.2d 491.

Facts: Herman McCloud retained the firm of Husted and Husted, a partnership consisting of Selwyn and Edgar Husted, to act as attorneys for his mother's estate. After the estate was closed, an additional estate tax liability of $18,006.73 was assessed by the IRS. Edgar falsely represented to McCloud that the precise amount of this liability was unknown. Edgar then induced McCloud to issue a check for $18,800 to the fictitious Husted and Husted trust account. Edgar indicated that he would pay the tax liability out of this sum and keep the remainder as his fee. Instead, Edgar converted all of McCloud's funds to his own use, convincing local bank officials to issue a check from another estate for the McCloud estate tax liability. When Edgar's illegal conduct was subsequently discovered, the IRS cancelled the satisfaction of the McCloud estate tax liability and reassessed the additional tax due with additional interest, which McCloud then paid. Edgar Husted was sentenced to prison, and McCloud brought an action against the partnership of Husted and Husted, seeking compensatory and punitive damages. The trial court awarded compensatory and punitive damages against Edgar Husted and the partnership. The Court of Appeals affirmed the decision.

Decision: Punitive damages awarded against Edgar Husted and the partnership set aside.

Opinion: Pivarnik, J. On the foregoing basis, the punitive damage award against Edgar Husted should be set aside. The public interest in punishing Husted and in deterring him from such misconduct was fully satisfied by the sentence Husted received. Accordingly, punitive damages are inappropriate. [Citation.] The award of punitive damages against Edgar Husted is set aside.

The trial court relied upon the provisions of Indiana's Uniform Partnership Act, [citation], when it entered judgment against the partnership for both punitive and compensatory damages. The trial court particularly relied upon the following sections of the Uniform Partnership Act which state:

"[§] 13. Partnership bound by partner's wrongful act.—Where, by any wrongful act or omission of any partner acting in the ordinary course of the business of the partnership or with the authority of his copartners, loss or injury is caused to any person, not being a partner in the partnership, or any penalty is incurred, the partnership is liable therefore to the same extent as the partner so acting or omitting to act.

[§] 14. Partnership bound by partner's breach of trust.—The partnership is bound to make good the loss:

(a) Where one partner acting within the scope of his apparent authority receives money or property of a third person and misapplies it; and

(b) Where the partnership in the course of its business receives money or property of a third person and the money or property so received is misapplied by any partner while it is in the custody of the partnership."

The trial court and the Court of Appeals determined that § 13 required that the partnership be liable to the same extent as Edgar Husted for any civil penalty imposed in this case. The partnership claims that Edgar's criminal acts were not within the ordinary course of partnership business. Furthermore, the partnership claims that it never had possession of the certain funds converted and therefore the partnership cannot be held liable for Edgar's acts with respect to said funds. There were two partners in the partnership law firm, Edgar Husted and Selwyn Husted, Edgar's father. McCloud clearly was a client of the partnership since McCloud dealt with both Selwyn and Edgar on his estate case. In fact, Selwyn was the partner who first brought McCloud's case into the partnership's office. Edgar was acting within the ordinary course of the partnership's business and with apparent authority since Edgar's request for and acceptance of money from McCloud to pay McCloud's estate tax liability was well within the work parameters of an attorney properly handling a decedent's estate. We therefore find that even though fraud and conversion of a client's funds are not part of the ordinary course of a law partnership's business, the trial court correctly found pursuant to § 14 that the partnership was responsible for partner Edgar in taking money entrusted to him and misapplying it. We also find that the trial court was justified in finding that McCloud's money was in the partnership's possession when it was in Edgar's possession since Edgar deviated from McCloud's plan and converted the money to his own use only after he received it in the ordinary course of the partnership's business. Accordingly, the trial court did not err by holding the partnership responsible to McCloud for compensatory damages.

Whether Appellant partnership is liable for punitive damages, however, is another story. Husted & Husted argues that the cases decided under § 13 or its counterpart in other jurisdictions as well as the earlier cases decided under the common law of agency and partnership have generally held that where a partnership is sued for a partner's intentional tort, the partnership's liability turns on whether the purpose or effect of the tortious act was to benefit the partnership's business or whether the tort was so removed from the ordinary course of that business that it could not be considered within the implicit authorization of the copartners. . . .

We accept Appellant's contention that § 13 is the only section by which punitive damages can be imposed against a partnership since § 14 merely limits a partnership's liability to restitution. We further agree with Appellant partnership that the rationale behind punitive damages in Indiana prohibits awarding such damages against an individual who is personally innocent of any wrongdoing. Punitive damages are not intended to compensate a plaintiff but rather are intended to punish the wrongdoer and thereby deter others from engaging in similar conduct in the future. [Citations.] Accordingly, we now hold that the trial court erred by adjudging the innocent partners in this case responsible for punitive damages.

ADMISSIONS OF AND NOTICE TO A PARTNER

An admission or representation by any partner about partnership affairs, within the scope of his authority, may be used as evidence against the partnership.[13] One person's admission that a partnership exists does not prove its existence. But once the partnership is established by competent evidence, the admission of one partner may be used against the partnership, provided the partner is acting within the scope of the partnership business.

A partnership is bound (1) by notice to any partner of any matter relating to partnership affairs, (2) by the knowledge of the partner acting in a particular matter acquired while he was a partner, and (3) by the knowledge of any other partners who reasonably could and should have communicated it to the acting partner.[14]

A demand on one partner as a representative of the firm is a demand on the partnership.

LIABILITY OF INCOMING PARTNER

A person admitted as a partner into an existing partnership is liable for *all* of the obligations of the partnership arising before his admission as though he had been a partner when such obligations were incurred, although this liability may be satisfied *only* out of partnership property.[15] This means that the liability of an incoming partner for preexisting debts and obligations of the firm is limited to his capital contribution. This restriction does not apply, of course, to obligations that arise after his admission into the partnership. His liability for these obligations is *unlimited*. For example, Nash is admitted to Higgins, Cooke and White Co., a partnership. Nash's capital contribution is $7,500, which was paid in cash upon her admission to the partnership. A year later, the partnership is dissolved when liabilities of the firm exceed its assets by $40,000. Porter had lent the firm $15,000 eight months before Nash was admitted; Skinner lent the firm $20,000 two months after Nash was admitted. Nash has no liability to Porter *except* to the extent of her capital contribution. Nash is *personally* liable to Skinner.

CHAPTER SUMMARY

RELATIONSHIP AMONG PARTNERS

Duties among Partners	**Fiduciary Duty** duty of utmost loyalty and good faith owed by partners to each other and to the partnership **Duty of Obedience** duty to act in accordance with the partnership agreement and any business decisions properly made by the partners **Duty of Care** duty owed by partners to manage the partnership affairs without culpable negligence, which is greater than ordinary negligence but less than gross negligence
Rights among Partners	**Tenancy in Partnership** **Interest in Partnership** **Distributions** transfer of partnership property from the partnership to a partner ■ *Profits* each partner is entitled to an equal share of the profits unless otherwise agreed ■ *Capital* after all partnership creditors have been paid, each partner is entitled to be repaid his capital contribution when the firm is terminated ■ *Advances* if a partner makes an advance (loan) to the firm, he is entitled to repayment of the advance plus interest, but subordinate to nonpartner creditors ■ *Compensation* unless otherwise agreed, no partner is entitled to payment for acting in the partnership business **Management** each partner has an equal voice in management unless otherwise agreed **Choice of Associates** under the doctrine of *delectus personae*, no person can become a member of a partnership without the consent of all of the partners

Enforcement Rights
- *Information*   each partner may demand full information about all partnership matters and each partner has a duty to supply other partners with full and accurate information
- *Accounting*   a partner is entitled to an accounting, which is an equitable proceeding for a complete settlement of all partnership affairs

RELATIONSHIP BETWEEN PARTNERS AND THIRD PARTIES

Contracts

Authority to Bind Partnership   a partner may bind the partnership if she has actual authority (express or implied) or apparent authority
- *Actual Express Authority*   authority set forth in the partnership agreement, in additional agreements among the partners, or in decisions made by a majority of the partners regarding the ordinary business of the partnership
- *Actual Implied Authority*   authority that is reasonably deduced from the nature of the partnership, the terms of the partnership agreement, or the relations of the partners
- *Apparent Authority*   authority that a third person may reasonably assume to exist in light of the conduct of the partners so long as that third person has no knowledge or notice of the lack of actual authority

Partners' Liability
- *Personal Liability*   if the partnership is contractually bound, each partner has joint, unlimited personal liability
- *Joint Liability*   a creditor must sue all of the partners as a group

Partnership by Estoppel   imposes partnership duties and liabilities on a nonpartner who has either represented himself or consented to be represented as a partner

Torts

Respondeat Superior   the partnership is liable for loss or injury caused by any wrongful act or omission of any partner while acting within the ordinary course of the business or with the authority of his copartners

Joint and Several Liability   the partners are jointly and severally liable for a tort or breach of trust committed by any partner or by an employee of the firm in the course of partnership business; means that the creditors may sue the partners jointly as a group or separately as individuals

Other Powers

Admissions   an admission by one partner within the scope of his authority may be used as evidence against the partnership

Notice   a partnership is bound by notice to and knowledge of a partner

Demand   a demand on one partner is a demand on the partnership

Liability of Incoming Partner

Antecedent Debts   the liability of an incoming partner for antecedent debts of the partnership is limited to his capital contribution

Subsequent Debts   the liability of an incoming partner for subsequent debts of the partnership is unlimited

QUESTIONS

1. Discuss the three principal duties owed by a partner to her copartners.
2. Identify and discuss the principal rights of partners (four are discussed in this chapter and two in the previous chapter).
3. Discuss the contract liability of a partnership and the partners.
4. Discuss the tort liability of a partnership and the partners.
5. Distinguish between the liability of an incoming partner for debts arising before his admission and those arising after his admission.

PROBLEMS

1. Albert, Betty, and Carol own and operate the Roy Lumber Company. Each contributed one-third of the capital, and they share equally in the profits and losses. Their partnership agreement states that all purchases over $500 must be authorized in advance by two partners and that only Albert is authorized to draw checks. Unknown to Albert or Carol, Betty purchases on the firm's account a $2,500 diamond bracelet and a $5,000 forklift and orders $2,000 worth of logs, all from Doug, who operates a jewelry store and is engaged in various activities connected with the lumber business. Before Betty made these purchases, Albert told Doug that Betty is not the log buyer. Albert refuses to pay Doug for Betty's purchases. Doug calls at the mill to collect, and Albert again refuses to pay him. Doug calls Albert an unprintable name, and Albert then punches Doug in the nose. While Doug is lying unconscious on the ground, an employee of Roy Lumber Company negligently drops a log on Doug's leg, breaking three bones. The firm and the three partners are completely solvent.

What are the rights of Doug?

2. Paula, Fred, and Stephanie agree that Paula and Fred will form and conduct a partnership business and that Stephanie will become a partner in two years. Stephanie agrees to lend the firm $5,000 and take 10 percent of the profits in lieu of interest. Without Stephanie's knowledge, Paula and Fred tell Harold that Stephanie is a partner, and Harold, relying on Stephanie's sound financial status, gives the firm credit. Later the firm becomes insolvent, and Harold seeks to hold Stephanie liable as a partner. Should Harold succeed?

3. Anita and Duncan had been partners for many years in a mercantile business. Their relationship deteriorated to the point where Anita threatened to bring an action for an accounting and dissolution of the firm. Duncan then offered to buy Anita's interest in the partnership for $25,000. Anita refused the offer and told Duncan that she would take no less than $36,000. A short time later, James approached Duncan and informed him he had inside information that a proposed street change would greatly benefit the business and that he, James, would buy the entire business for $100,000 or buy a one-half interest for $50,000. Duncan made a final offer of $35,000 to Anita for her interest. Anita accepted this offer, and the transaction was completed. Duncan then sold the one-half interest to James for $50,000. Several months later, Anita learned for the first time of the transaction between Duncan and James.

What rights, if any, does Anita have against Duncan?

4. Anthony and Karen were partners doing business as the Petite Garment Company. Leroy owned a dye plant that did much of the processing for the company. Anthony and Karen decided to offer Leroy an interest in their company in consideration for which Leroy would contribute his dye plant to the partnership. Leroy accepted the offer and was duly admitted as a partner. At the time he was admitted as a partner, Leroy did not know that the partnership was on the verge of insolvency.

About three months after Leroy was admitted to the partnership, a textile firm obtained a judgment against the partnership in the amount of $50,000. This debt represented an unpaid balance that had existed before Leroy was admitted as a partner. The textile firm brought an action to subject the partnership property, including the dye plant, to the satisfaction of its judgment. The complaint also requested that, in the event the judgment was unsatisfied by sale of the partnership property, Leroy's home be sold and the proceeds applied to the balance of the judgment. Anthony and Karen own nothing but their interest in the partnership property.

What should be the result (a) with regard to the dye plant, and (b) with regard to Leroy's home?

5. Jones and Ray formed a partnership on January 1, known as JR Construction Co., to engage in the construction business, each partner owning a one-half interest. On February 10, while conducting partnership business, Jones negligently injured Ware, who brought an action against Jones, Ray, and JR Construction Co. and obtained judgment for $25,000 against them on March 1. On April 15, Muir joined the partnership by contributing $10,000 cash,

and by agreement each partner was entitled to a one-third interest. In July the partners agreed to purchase new construction equipment for the partnership, and Muir was authorized to obtain a loan from XYZ Bank in the partnership name for $20,000 to finance the purchase. On July 10, Muir signed a $20,000 note on behalf of the partnership, and the equipment was purchased. In November the partnership was in financial difficulty, its total assets amounting to $5,000. The note was in default, with a balance of $15,000 owing to XYZ Bank. Muir has substantial resources, while Jones and Ray each individually have assets of $2,000.

What is the extent of Muir's personal liability and the personal liability of Jones and Ray as to (a) the judgment obtained by Ware, and (b) the debt owing to XYZ Bank?

6. Apex Company is a general partnership organized under the UPA. It consists of Dianne, Greg, Knox, and Laura, whose capital contributions were: Dianne = $5,000, Greg = $7,500, Knox = $10,000, and Laura = $5,000. The partnership agreement provided that the partnership would continue for a three-year period and that no withdrawals of capital were to be made without the consent of all the partners. The agreement also provided that all advances would be entitled to interest at 10 percent per year. Six months after the partnership was formed, Dianne made an advance to the partnership of $10,000. At the end of the first year, net profits were realized in the amount of $11,000 before any monies had been distributed to partners. How should the $11,000 be allocated to Dianne, Greg, Knox, and Laura? Explain.

7. Adams, a consulting engineer, entered into a partnership with three others for the practice of their profession. The only written partnership agreement is a brief document specifying that Adams is entitled to 55 percent of the profits and the others to 15 percent each.

The venture is a total failure. Creditors are pressing for payment, and some have filed suit. The partners are in fundamental disagreement as to their future course of action.

How many of the partners must agree to achieve each of the following objectives:

(a) To add Jones, also an engineer, as a partner, Jones being willing to contribute a substantial amount of new capital.
(b) To sell a vacant lot held in the partnership name, which had been acquired as the site of a future office for the partnership.
(c) To move the offices of the partnership to less expensive quarters.
(d) To demand a formal accounting.
(e) To dissolve the partnership.
(f) To agree to submit certain disputed claims to arbitration, which Adams believes will prove less expensive than litigation.
(g) To sell all of the partnership personal property, Adams having what he believes to be a good offer for the property from a newly formed engineering firm.
(h) To alter the respective interests of the parties in the profits and losses by decreasing Adams's share to 40 percent and increasing the others' shares accordingly.
(i) To assign all the assets to a bank in trust for the benefit of creditors, hoping to work out satisfactory arrangements without formal bankruptcy.

8. Charles and Jack orally agreed to become partners in a small tool and die business. Charles, who had experience in tool and die work, was to operate the business. Jack was to take no active part but was to contribute the entire $50,000 capitalization. Charles worked ten hours a day at the plant, for which he was paid nothing. Despite Charles's best efforts, the business failed. The $50,000 capital was depleted, and the partnership owed $50,000 in debts. Before the business failed, Jack became personally insolvent so that the creditors of the partnership collected the entire $50,000 indebtedness from Charles, who was forced to sell his home and farm to satisfy the debt. Jack later regained his financial responsibility, and Charles brought an appropriate action against Jack for (a) one-half of the $50,000 he had paid to partnership creditors, and (b) one-half of $18,000, the reasonable value of Charles's services during the operation of the partnership. Decision?

9. Glenn refuses an invitation to become a partner of Dorothy and Cynthia in the retail grocery business. Nevertheless, Dorothy inserts an advertisement in the local newspaper representing Glenn as their partner. Glenn takes no steps to deny the existence of a partnership between them. Ron, who extended credit to the firm, seeks to hold Glenn liable as a partner. Decision?

10. Hanover leased a portion of his farm to Brown and Black, doing business as the Colorite Hatchery. Brown went on the premises to remove certain chicken sheds that he and Black had placed there for hatchery purposes. Hanover thought Brown intended to remove certain other sheds that were Hanover's property, and an altercation occurred between them. Brown willfully struck Hanover and knocked him down. Then Brown ran to the Colorite truck, which he had previously loaded with chicken

coops, and drove back to the hatchery. On the way, he picked up George, who was hitchhiking to the city to look for a job. Brown was in a hurry and was driving at seventy miles per hour down the highway. At an open intersection with another highway, Brown ran a stop sign and struck another vehicle at the intersection. The collision caused severe injuries to George. Brown and Black's partnership was dissolved directly after these incidents, and Brown was insolvent. Hanover and George each bring separate actions against Black as copartner for the alleged tort committed by Brown against each.

What judgments as to each?

11. Phillips and Harris are partners in a used car business. Under their oral partnership, each has an equal voice in the conduct and management of the business. Because of the irregular business hours kept by the two, it was further agreed that they could use any partnership vehicle as desired. This includes use for transportation to and from work, even though the vehicles are for sale at all times. While driving a partnership vehicle home from the used car lot, Harris hit a car driven by Cook. Cook brought this action against Harris and Phillips individually and as copartners for his injuries. Decision?

ENDNOTES

1. Uniform Partnership Act, Section 21, Partner Accountable as a Fiduciary.

2. Uniform Partnership Act, Section 24, Extent of Property Rights of a Partner.

3. Uniform Partnership Act, Section 18, Rules Determining Rights and Duties of Partners.

4. Uniform Partnership Act, Section 20, Duty of Partners to Render Information.

5. Uniform Partnership Act, Section 19, Partnership Books.

6. Uniform Partnership Act, Section 22, Right to an Account.

7. Uniform Partnership Act, Section 4, Rules of Construction.

8. Uniform Partnership Act, Section 9, Partner Agent of Partnership as to Partnership Business.

9. Uniform Partnership Act, Section 15, Nature of Partner's Liability.

10. Uniform Partnership Act, Section 16, Partner by Estoppel.

11. Uniform Partnership Act, Section 13, Partnership Bound by Partner's Wrongful Act.

12. Uniform Partnership Act, Section 14, Partnership Bound by Partner's Breach of Trust.

13. Uniform Partnership Act, Section 11, Partnership Bound by Admission of Partner.

14. Uniform Partnership Act, Section 12, Partnership Charged with Knowledge of or Notice to Partner; Section 3, Interpretation of Knowledge and Notice.

15. Uniform Partnership Act, Section 17, Liability of Incoming Partner.

31 DISSOLUTION, WINDING UP, AND TERMINATION

Three stages lead to the extinguishment of a partnership: (1) dissolution, (2) winding up or liquidation, and (3) termination. Dissolution occurs when the partners cease to carry on the business together. Upon dissolution, the partnership is not terminated but continues until the winding up of the partnership affairs is completed. During winding up, the business affairs are put in order, receivables are collected, payments are made to creditors, and distribution of the remaining assets is made to the partners. Termination occurs when the process of winding up has been completed.

DISSOLUTION

The Uniform Partnership Act (UPA) defines **dissolution** as the change in the relation of the partners caused by any partner's ceasing to be associated in the carrying on, as distinguished from the winding up, of the business.[1] In this section we discuss the causes and effects of dissolution.

Causes of Dissolution

Dissolution may be brought about by (1) an act of the partners, (2) operation of law, or (3) court order. A number of events that were considered causes of dissolution under the common law are no longer considered so under the UPA. For example, the assignment of a partner's interest, a creditor's charging order on a partner's interest, and an accounting do *not* cause a dissolution.

Dissolution by Act of the Partners A partnership is a personal relationship, and a partner always has the *power* to dissolve it by his own actions, but whether he has the *right* to do so is determined by the partnership agreement. A partner who has withdrawn in violation of the partnership agreement is liable to the remaining partners for damages resulting from the wrongful dissolution.

A partnership is **rightfully dissolved,** that is, without violation of the agreement between the partners, by the act of the partners:

1. when they specifically agree to dissolve the partnership;
2. when the period of time provided in the agreement has ended or the purpose for which the partnership was formed has been accomplished;
3. when a partner withdraws from a **partnership at will,** that is, one with no definite term or specific undertaking; or

   when a partner is expelled in accordance with a power to expel conferred by the partnership agreement.[2]

Dissolution by Operation of Law A partnership is dissolved by operation of law upon (1) the death of a partner; (2) the bankruptcy of a partner or of the partnership; or (3) the subsequent illegality of the partnership, which includes any event that makes it unlawful for the business of the partnership to be carried on or for the members to carry on the business in partnership form.[2] For example, a partnership formed to manufacture liquor would be dissolved by a law prohibiting the production and sale of alcoholic beverages. A partnership of lawyers would be dissolved if one of its members was disbarred from the practice of law.

Dissolution by Court Order After application by a partner, a court will order a dissolution if it finds that (1) a partner is incompetent or suffers some other incapacity that prevents him from functioning as a partner; (2) a partner is guilty of conduct prejudicial to the business or has willfully and persistently breached the partnership agreement; (3) the business can be carried on only at a loss; or (4) other circumstances render a dissolution equitable.[3]

An assignee of a partner's interest or a partner's personal creditor who has obtained a charging order (judicial lien) against the partner's interest is entitled to a dissolution by court decree. If the partnership is not at will, however, the partnership will not be dissolved until after the specified term or particular undertaking.

Effects of Dissolution

On dissolution, the partnership is *not* terminated but continues until the winding up of partnership affairs is completed.[4] Moreover, dissolution does *not* discharge the existing liability of any partner. Dissolution *does* bring about restrictions on the authority of partners to act for the partnership.

Authority On dissolution, the *actual authority* of a partner to act for the partnership terminates, except so far as may be necessary to wind up partnership affairs.[5] Actual authority to wind up includes completing existing contracts, reducing partnership assets to cash, and paying partnership obligations.

Although actual authority terminates on dissolution, *apparent authority* persists and binds the partnership for acts within the scope of the partnership business unless notice of the dissolution is given to the thirty party.[6] A third party who had extended credit to the partnership before dissolution may hold the partnership liable for any transaction that would bind the partnership if dissolution had not taken place, unless the third party has knowledge or actual notice of the dissolution. **Actual notice** requires a verbal statement to the third party or actual delivery of a written statement.[7] On the other hand, a third party who knew of the partnership, but had not extended credit to it

before its dissolution can hold the partnership liable unless he has knowledge, actual notice, or constructive notice of dissolution. **Constructive notice** consists of advertising a notice of dissolution in a newspaper of general circulation in the places at which partnership business was regularly conducted.[6] *No* notice need be given to third parties who had no knowledge of the partnership before its dissolution.

Existing Liability The dissolution of the partnership does not by itself discharge the existing liability of any partner.[8] But in some instances the cause of dissolution may result in discharging an executory contract. For example, if the contract called for the personal services of one of the partners, the death of that partner usually will discharge the contract and also bring about the dissolution of the partnership.

A retiring partner may be discharged from his existing liabilities by a **novation** entered into with the continuing partners and the creditors. A creditor must agree to the novation, although his consent may be inferred from his course of dealing with the partnership after dissolution.[8] Whether such dealings with the continuing partnership constitutes an implied novation is a factual question of intent.

WINDING UP

Whenever a dissolved partnership is not to be continued, the partnership must be liquidated. The process of **liquidation** is called **winding up** and involves completing unfinished business, collecting debts, taking inventory, reducing assets to cash, auditing the partnership books, paying creditors, and distributing the remaining assets to the partners. During this period, the fiduciary duties of the partners continue in effect.

The Right to Wind Up

On dissolution, any partner has the right to insist on the winding up of the partnership unless the partnership agreement provides otherwise. A partner who has wrongfully dissolved the partnership or who has been rightfully expelled according to the terms of the partnership agreement cannot force the liquidation of the partnership. Unless otherwise agreed, all nonbankrupt partners who have not wrongfully dissolved the partnership have the right to wind up the partnership affairs,[9] as illustrated in the next case. A court, on the petition of a partner, may appoint a receiver of all of the property and assets of the partnership. The receiver has authority to operate the business under the court's direction for such time as may be reasonably necessary. The appointment of a receiver is discretionary with the court, and its discretion may be exercised on such grounds as dissension among the partners or waste, fraud, mental incompetence, misconduct, or other breach of duty by a partner.

STARK v. UTICA SCREW PRODUCTS, INC.
City Court of Utica, 1980.
103 Misc.2d 163, 425 N.Y.S.2d 750.

Facts: Stark, Henning & Co., a partnership formed by Stark and Henning for the purpose of acting as sales representatives for various firms in upstate New York, contracted with Utica Screw Product, Inc., on June 19, 1975, to act as its sales representative for most of New York State. On October 22, 1976, Stark sent a letter to Henning terminating the partnership. A copy of this letter was also sent to the president of Utica. When Utica refused to pay commissions owed to the partnership for orders the partnership had obtained for Utica between February 10, 1976, and October 20, 1976, Stark brought this action on behalf of the partnership to recover the commissions due. Utica contended that Stark had no standing to sue because he had not received authority from his partner, Henning, to institute this action.

Decision: Judgment for Stark.

Opinion: **Hymes, J.** Upon dissolution of a partnership, any partner has the right to participate in the winding up of a partnership. He needs no authority from his co-partners. An unilateral letter of dissolution does not cut off the partnership relationship. On dissolution the partnership continues until the winding up of the partnership affairs is completed. [Citation.] The only way in which a partnership is wound up is through an accounting. [Citations.]

The duty imposed upon the partner who is engaged in winding up the partnership business is one of agency. [Citations.] The general agency of one partner . . . ceases, but each partner then has the equal duty and power to do whatever is necessary to collect the debts of the partnership. [Citations.]

After the dissolution of a partnership, a partner may bind the partnership by any appropriate action necessary to wind up the partnership affairs or to complete transactions unfinished at the time of dissolution. [Citation.] While a partner would not be entitled to remuneration for winding up the partnership affairs, he would be allowed reasonable expenses incurred in performing the services. [Citations.]

* * *

A partner cannot bar his co-partner from suing to collect debts due the partnership. Any judgment recovered by Stark would be for the benefit of the partnership and not for himself individually. It would then be up to the partners to wind up the partnership through an accounting.

* * *

The defendant [Utica] was incorrect in assuming that the dissolution of the partnership voided the contract with the plaintiff [Stark.] The dissolution of a partnership operates only with respect to future transactions. All past transactions and obligations of the partnership continue until all pre-existing matters are terminated. The partnership continues to be responsible for its obligations and debts, and third parties are responsible to the partnership for obligations which they owe said partnership.

* * *

Under the terms of the agreement, both written and oral, the plaintiff had performed all that was required of him. * * *

"Where the major consideration in the earning of commissions is procurement of orders for the defendant, the employee is entitled to commissions on the sales he obtained during the period of employment." [Citations.]

Distribution of Assets

After all the partnership assets have been collected and reduced to cash, they are then distributed to the creditors and partners. When the partnership has been profitable, the order of distribution is not critical; however, when liabilities are greater than assets, the order of distribution has great importance.

The UPA sets forth the rules to be observed in settling accounts between the parties after dissolution.[10] It states that the liabilities of a partnership are to be paid out of partnership assets in the following order:

1. amounts owing to creditors other than partners;
2. amounts owing to partners other than for capital and profits;
3. amounts owing to partners for capital contributions;
4. amounts owing to partners for profits.

The partners may, by agreement, change the internal priorities of distribution (numbers 2, 3, and 4) but not the preferred position of third parties (number 1). This is the situation in the *Petersen* case on page 663. The UPA defines partnership assets to include all partnership property as well as the contributions necessary for the payment of all partnership liabilities, which consist of numbers 1, 2, and 3.

In addition, the UPA provides that, in the absence of any contrary agreement, each partner shall share equally in the profits and surplus remaining after all liabilities (numbers 1, 2, and 3) are satisfied and must contribute towards the losses, whether capital or otherwise, sustained by the partnership according to his share in the profits.[11] Thus, the proportion in which the partners bear losses, whether capital or otherwise, does not depend on their relative capital contributions. Rather, it is determined by their agreement. If there is no specific agreement, losses are borne in the same proportion in which profits are shared.

If the partnership is insolvent, the partners individually must contribute their respective share of the losses in order to pay the creditors. Furthermore, if one or more of the partners is insolvent or bankrupt or is out of the jurisdiction and refuses to contribute, the other partners must contribute the additional amount necessary to pay the firm's liabilities in the relative proportions in which they share the profits.[10] When any partner has paid an amount in excess of his proper share of the losses, he has a right of contribution against the partners who have not paid their share.[10]

The following examples illustrate the operation of these rules.

Solvent Partnership Assume that A, B, and C form the ABC Company, a partnership, with A contributing $6,000 capital, B contributing $4,000 capital, and C contributing services but no capital. A also loaned the partnership $3,000, which has not been repaid. There is no agreement as to the proportions in which profits and losses are to be shared. After a few years of operation, the partnership is liquidated. At this time, the assets of ABC Company are $54,000, and its liabilities to creditors are $26,000. The partnership is thus solvent and has enjoyed a profit of $15,000, which is calculated by subtracting the total liabilities ($39,000) from the total assets ($54,000). The total liabilities consist of the amount owed to creditors ($26,000), the amount owed to partners other than for capital and profits ($3,000 owed to A for his loan), and the capital contributions of the partners ($10,000: i.e., $6,000 from A and $4,000 from B). Because A, B, and C have not explicitly agreed on a profit-sharing ratio, they share the profits equally, in this case receiving $5,000 ($15,000 ÷ 3). After the creditors have been paid in full, A will receive $14,000 ($3,000 for repayment of the loan, $6,000 for capital, and $5,000 for share of profits); B will receive $9,000 ($4,000 for capital and $5,000 for share of profits); and C will receive $5,000 (for share of profits).

Insolvent Partnership Assume the same partnership had experienced financial adversity. It still owes creditors $26,000, but its total assets only amount to $12,000. In this case the partnership has sustained an aggregate loss of $27,000, which is calculated by subtracting the total liabilities ($39,000, calculated as in the example above) from the total assets ($12,000). If the agreement makes no other arrangement, the losses are shared as are the profits, which in this case is equally. Accordingly, each partner's share of the loss will be $9,000 ($27,000 ÷ 3). After the creditors are paid ($26,000), A will receive nothing ($3,000 owed for the loan plus $6,000 for capital *minus* $9,000 for his share of losses); B must make an additional *contribution* of $5,000 to make good his share of the loss ($4,000 owed for capital *minus* $9,000 for his share of losses); and C must contribute $9,000 (his share of losses). See chart below.

Contribution of Partner on Insolvency In the insolvent partnership example above, if A were individually insolvent, the results would not be changed, because A was not required to contribute any additional moneys. If A and B were solvent and C were individually insolvent, C would be unable to pay any of his share of the loss. Then A and B must contribute equally, because that is the relative proportion in which they share profits, in order to make good the amount of C's share. C's share of the loss is $9,000, and therefore A and B must each contribute an additional $4,500. This means that in total A will have to contribute $4,500 and B $9,500 in order to satisfy the unpaid claims of partnership creditors. On the other hand, if A and C were individually insolvent and B was solvent, B would be required to pay the entire balance of $14,000 due to partnership creditors, representing his unpaid share of the loss plus a contribution of the full amount of C's unpaid share of the loss.

	Loans	+	Capital Contribution	−	Share of Loss	=	Share of Assets or (Additional Contributions Owed)
A	$3,000		$ 6,000		−$ 9,000		$ 0
B	0		$ 4,000		−$ 9,000		($ 5,000)
C	0		0		−$ 9,000		($ 9,000)
Total	$3,000		$10,000		−$27,000		($14,000)

PETERSEN v. PETERSEN
Supreme Court of Minnesota, 1969.
284 Minn. 61, 169 N.W.2d 228.

Facts: In 1946 Donald Petersen joined his father, William Petersen, in a chicken hatchery business William had previously operated as a sole proprietorship. When the partnership was formed, William contributed the assets of the proprietorship, which included cash, equipment, and inventory having a total value of $41,000. Donald contributed nothing. From 1946 until Donald's death in 1964, Donald took over the operation of the hatchery. This suit was brought on behalf of Donald's estate when William refused to distribute any of the partnership assets to the estate. William contended that the total value of the partnership property at the time of Donald's death was $18,572. He claimed the full amount on the theory that he was entitled to the return of his capital investment of $41,000 before Donald's estate could recover anything. The trial court entered a judgment in favor of Donald's estate and William appeals.

Decision: Judgment for Donald's estate affirmed.

Opinion: Gallagher, J.   The law in Minnesota on the distribution of the partnership property upon dissolution of the partnership is governed by [§ 40] of the Uniform Partnership Act, which establishes the following priority: (1) Payment of debts to creditors other than partners; (2) payment of debts to partners for other than capital contributions; (3) payment to partners for capital contributions; and (4) payment to partners of their share of the profit. It is established beyond question in this state, as elsewhere, that the capital contributed by a partner is a debt of the partnership which must be paid after the outside creditors but before there is any division of the profits. [Citations.] However, the above-cited authorities, including § [40], make it equally clear that the right of a partner to receive back the capital he contributed is subject to a contrary agreement among the partners. Before setting out the rules for distribution of assets, § [40] provides:

"In settling accounts between the partners after dissolution, the following rules shall be observed, subject to any agreement to the contrary * * * ." (Italics supplied.)

It is also clear from past cases that a contrary agreement of the type referred to above need not be in writing. Where it is not written it is in effect an implied-in-fact contract and may be established in the same manner as any other such contract. [Citation.]

* * *

While the deceased did not contribute any capital to the business, for all but the very early years of the partnership, he operated it with very little help from his father. Although contributing nothing more than occasional assistance during this period, William continued to receive half of the income. The conduct of the parties makes it entirely reasonable to infer that William put up the capital and Donald provided the labor under an agreement by which each was to own half of the business, including both capital and profits.

FELTON INVESTMENT GROUP v. TAURMAN
Supreme Court of Montana, 1986.
722 P.2d 1135.

Facts: Wayne Taurman and Derrold Paige, employees of Felton Construction Company (FCC), were members of Felton Investment Group (FIG), a partnership of employee contributors to a retirement fund. The partnership agreement included a provision "that if a member ceases employment or is discharged for misconduct, his interest shall be returned in an amount equal to contributions paid into the fund plus 4% simple interest." In December 1978 Paige decided that his investment in FIG was in jeopardy and stopped contributing to the fund; however, he remained an employee of FCC. About a year later, Paige received a check from FIG, reflecting his contributions to the fund plus interest, in satisfaction of his claim in the partnership. He refused to indorse and cash the check. Taurman continued to invest in FIG until July 1980. At that time, he and Paige were both terminated by FCC for refusing to accept nonunion work. Taurman was then offered by FIG an amount equal to his contribution plus interest in satisfaction of his claim in the partnership, but he too refused to indorse and cash the check. FIG filed a complaint requesting that Taurman and Paige be ordered to accept the amounts offered in satisfaction of their claims in the partnership. Taurman and Paige filed a complaint seeking the judicial dissolution of FIG, a formal accounting of the partnership, and *pro rata* shares in the partnership's assets. FIG appealed from a trial court judgment for Taurman and Paige.

Decision: Judgment for Taurman and Paige affirmed.

Opinion: Morrison, J. Finally, we find no error in the trial court's decision that pursuant to [UPA § 18], Taurman and Paige must be repaid their contributions into the partnership and receive their pro rata share of the assets of the partnership. [UPA § 18] states at the outset that "[t]he rights and duties of the partners in relation to the partnership shall be determined, subject to any agreement between them, by the following rules." The agreement between the partners covers the voluntary termination of a partner's employment with FCC as well as his discharge for misconduct. It also covers involuntary termination caused by disability, death or retirement. However, there is nothing in the partnership agreement concerning the effect of a partner's involuntary termination from FCC absent misconduct. Numerous members of FIG, including its controller, testified that this contingency was not covered in FIG's partnership agreement. Since the rights of partners of FIG who were involuntarily terminated from FCC without cause were not expressed in the agreement, [UPA § 18] controls.

(1) Each partner shall be repaid his contributions whether by way of capital or advances to the partnership property and share equally in the profits and surplus remaining after all liabilities, including those to partners, are satisfied . . .

Taurman and Paige are entitled to receive their pro rata shares of the fair market value of the assets of FIG as of the date their employment with FCC terminated.

Marshaling of Assets

The doctrine of **marshaling of assets** applies *only* when the assets of a partnership and of its members are administered by a court of equity.

Marshaling means segregating and considering the assets and liabilities of the partnership separately from the respective assets and liabilities of the individual partners. Partnership creditors are entitled to be satisfied first out of partnership assets. They have a right to recover any deficiency out of the individually owned assets of the partners, subordinate, however, to the rights of nonpartnership creditors to those assets. Conversely, the nonpartnership creditors have first claim to the individually owned assets of their respective debtors; their claims to partnership assets are subordinate to claims of partnership creditors.

When a partner is insolvent, the order of distribution of his assets is as follows: (1) debts and liabilities owing to nonpartnership creditors; (2) debts and liabilities owing to partnership creditors; and (3) contributions owing to other partners who have paid more than their respective shares of the firm's liabilities to partnership creditors.

This rule, however, is *no longer* followed if the partnership is a debtor under the Bankruptcy Act. In a proceeding under the Federal bankruptcy law, a trustee is appointed to administer the estate of the debtor. If the partnership property is insufficient to pay all the claims against the partnership, then the trustee is directed by the act to seek recovery of the deficiency first from the general partners who are not bankrupt. The trustee may then seek recovery against the estates of bankrupt partners on the same basis as other creditors of the bankrupt partner. This provision, although contrary to the UPA's doctrine of marshaling of assets, governs whenever the assets of a partnership are being administered by a bankruptcy court.

CONTINUATION AFTER DISSOLUTION

After a partnership has been dissolved, one of two outcomes must follow: either the partnership is liquidated or the remaining partners continue the partnership. When a partnership is liquidated, the value of a going concern is sacrificed. On the other hand, continuation of the partnership after dissolution avoids this loss. The UPA nonetheless gives each partner the right to have the partnership liquidated except in a limited number of instances where the partners have the right to continue the partnership.[12]

Right to Continue Partnership

After dissolution, the remaining partners have the right to continue the partnership: (1) when the partnership has been dissolved in violation of the partnership agreement, (2) when a partner has been expelled in accordance with the partnership agreement, or (3) when all the partners agree to continue the business.

Continuation after Wrongful Dissolution A partner who wrongfully withdraws cannot force the liquidation of the firm. The aggrieved partners have the option of either liquidating the firm and recovering damages for the breach of the partnership agreement or continuing the partnership by buying out the withdrawing partner. The withdrawing partner is entitled to realize his interest in the partnership less the amount of the damages that the other partners have sustained as the result of his breach. The withdrawing partner's interest is computed without considering the good will of the business. In addition, the remaining partners may use the capital contributions of the wrongdoing partner for the unexpired period of the partnership agreement. They must, however, indemnify the former partner against all present and future partnership liabilities.[12]

Continuation after Expulsion A partner expelled according to the partnership agreement cannot force the liquidation of the partnership. He is entitled only to be discharged from all partnership liabilities by either payment or a novation with the creditors and to receive in cash the net amount due him from the partnership.[12]

Continuation Agreement of the Partners By far the best and most reliable way of assuring the preservation of a partnership business after dissolution is a continuation agreement. Continuation agreements are frequently used to ensure continuity in the event of death or retirement of one of the partners. A continuation agreement permits the remaining partners to keep the partnership property, carry on its business, and provide a specified settlement with the outgoing partners, as in the next case. Otherwise, when a partner dies or retires and the business is continued by the surviving partners, the retired partner or legal representative of the deceased partner is entitled to be paid the value of his interest as of the date of the dissolution as an ordinary creditor of the partnership. In addition, he is entitled to receive interest on this amount or, at his option, in lieu of interest, the profits of the business attributable to the use of his right in the property of the dissolved partnership. His rights, however, are subordinate to those of creditors of the dissolved partnership.[13]

McCLENNEN v. COMMISSIONER OF INTERNAL REVENUE
United States Court of Appeals, First Circuit, 1943.
131 F.2d 165.

Facts: George Nutter was a partner in the law firm of Nutter, McClennen & Fish. The partnership agreement provided that he was entitled to receive 8 percent of the firm's net profits and that on his death or retirement payments in the same percentage of net profits would continue to be made to Nutter or his estate for a period of eighteen months. The agreement expressly stated that the payments would be in full satisfaction of the deceased or retiring partner's interest in the capital, the assets, the receivables, and the good will of the firm.

When Nutter died in 1937, his partners continued the business and made the required payments, totaling $34,070, to Nutter's estate, but the Federal estate tax return filed for the estate did not include an amount representing the value of Nutter's interest in the partnership. As a result, the commissioner of internal revenue filed this notice of deficiency for taxes due on $34,070, the value of Nutter's partnership interest. The trial court found for the commissioner and Nutter appeals.

Decision: Judgment for the commissioner affirmed.

Opinion: Magruder, J.   In his notice of deficiency the Commissioner determined that $34,069.99 should have been included in the gross estate as the value of decedent's "interest in partnership Nutter, McClennen & Fish." The Board had upheld the Commissioner in this determination. We think the Board was right.

In the absence of a controlling agreement in the partnership articles the death of a partner dissolves the partnership. The survivors have the right and duty, with reasonable dispatch, to wind up the partnership affairs, to complete transactions begun but not then finished, to collect the accounts receivable, to pay the firm debts, to convert the remaining firm assets into cash, and to pay in cash to the partners and the legal representative of the deceased partner the net amounts shown by the accounts to be owing to each of them in respect of capital contributions and in respect of their shares of profits and surplus. The representative of a deceased partner does not succeed to any right to specific partnership property. In substance the deceased partner's interest, to which his representative succeeds, is a chose in action, a right to receive in cash the sum of money shown to be due him upon a liquidation and accounting. These substantive results may be rationalized upon a theory of the partnership "entity." [Citation.] The same substantive results are reached under the Uniform Partnership Act which, in form at least, proceeds on the aggregate theory. [Citation.] That act, which is law in Massachusetts, conceives of the partner as a "co-owner with his partners of specific partnership property holding as a tenant in partnership;" but provides that on the death of a partner "his right in specific partnership property vests in the surviving partner or partners." Another enumerated property right of a partner, "his interest in the partnership," is described as "his share of the profits and surplus, and the same is personal property," regardless of whether the firm holds real estate or personalty or both. [Citations.] * * *

In the case at bar, if there had not been the controlling provision in the partnership articles, above quoted, or if the survivors had not come to some agreement otherwise with the executors of Mr. Nutter, the survivors would have had to proceed to wind up the affairs of the partnership, to conclude all unfinished legal business on hand at the date of the death, to realize upon all of the assets of the firm, tangible or intangible, to pay the debts, to return to Mr. Nutter's estate his contribution of capital, if any, and to pay to his estate in cash the amount shown to be due in respect of his "interest in the partnership," that is, his "share of the profits and surplus", as determined upon an accounting. Among other things to be taken into account, "the earned proportion of the unfinished business" would have had "to be valued to determine the decedent's interest in the partnership assets." [Citations.]

To obviate the necessity of a liquidation, or to eliminate accounting difficulties in determining the value of the deceased partner's interest, partners often make specific provision in the partnership articles.

* * *

In the case at bar the partnership agreement contains another familiar arrangement, whereby no liquidation and final accounting will ever be necessary in order to satisfy the claim of the deceased partner. In place of the chose in action to which Mr. Nutter's executor would have succeeded in the absence of specific provision in the partnership articles, that is, a right to receive payment in cash of the amount shown to be due the deceased partner upon a complete liquidation and accounting, a different right is substituted, a right of the estate to receive a share of the net profits of the firm for 18 calendar months after the partner's death.

The language of the partnership agreement in the present case is couched in terms of a purchase of the deceased partner's interest. What the estate is to receive "shall be in full of the retiring or deceasing member's interest in the capital, the assets, the receivables, the possibilities and the good will of the Firm." There is to be an extinguishment of the decedent's interest in the totality of the firm assets, tangible and intangible, as they stood at the moment of death, and the interests therein of the surviving partners are to be correspondingly augmented. Decision in the estate tax case now before us does not turn on the question whether the effect of the partnership agreement may be characterized with entire accuracy as a "purchase" and "sale" of the deceased partner's interest in the partnership.

Rights of Creditors

Whenever a partnership is continued after dissolution, a new partnership is formed even though a majority of the old partners are present in the new combination. The creditors of the old partnership have claims against the new partnership and may also proceed to hold all of the members of the dissolved partnership personally liable.[14] If a withdrawing partner has made arrangements with those who continue the business whereby they assume and pay all debts and obligations of the firm, the withdrawing partner is still liable to creditors whose claims arose prior to the dissolution. If she is compelled to pay such debts, the withdrawing partner has a right of indemnity against her former partners, who had agreed to pay the debts but failed to do so.

A withdrawing partner may protect herself against liability on contracts entered into by the firm after her withdrawal by giving notice that she is no longer a member of the firm. Otherwise, she is liable for debts thus incurred to a creditor who had no notice or knowledge of the partner's having withdrawn from the firm. Actual notice must be given to persons who had extended credit to the partnership prior to its dissolution. Constructive notice by newspaper publication will be sufficient for those who knew of the partnership but had not extended credit to it before its dissolution.[6]

Figure 31–1 summarizes the causes and consequences of dissolution of a partnership.

CREDIT BUREAUS OF MERCED COUNTY, INC. v. SHIPMAN
District Court of Appeal, Third District, California, 1959.
334 P.2d 1036.

Facts: Davis and Shipman founded a partnership in 1954 under the name of Shipman & Davis Lumber Company. On September 20, 1955, the partnership was dissolved by written agreement. Notice of the dissolution was published in a newspaper of general circulation in Merced County, where the business was conducted. No actual notice of dissolution was given to firms that had previously extended credit to the partnership. By the dissolution agreement, Shipman, who was to continue the business, was to pay all of the partnership's debts. He continued the business as a sole proprietorship for a short time until he formed a successor corporation, Shipman Lumber Servaes Co. After the partnership's dissolution, two firms that had previously done business with the partnership extended credit to Shipman for certain repair work and merchandise. The partnership also had a balance due to Valley Typewriter Company for the prior purchase of a calculator. In 1956 two checks were drawn by Shipman Lumber Servaes Co. and accepted by Valley Typewriter as partial payment on this debt. Credit Bureaus of Merced County, as assignee of these three accounts, sued the partnership as well as Shipman and Davis individually. Davis argues that the dissolution of the partnership relieved him of personal liability for the accounts. Judgment in favor of the Credit Bureaus for all three accounts was entered by the trial court.

Decision: Judgment for the Credit Bureaus affirmed.

Opinion: Schottky, J.   As to the repair item incurred on November 3, 1955, which was after the date of the dissolution, appellant [Davis] would not be liable therefor if Laird Welding & Manufacturing Works had notice of the dissolution. While the evidence is conflicting as to whether the Welding Works had notice of the dissolution at the time the repairs were made, it is sufficient to support the finding of the court that the company did not have notice. The burden is on a defendant relying on dissolution to prove notice of dissolution. [Citation.] Appellant cannot rely on the provisions of [citation] to show actual knowledge. This section provides for publication of notice of dissolution of a partnership. However, as to firms having prior credit dealings with the partnership, actual notice of dissolution is necessary. While publication may be evidence from which actual knowledge could be inferred, publication alone would not compel a finding of actual knowledge. A retiring partner is not justified in placing sole reliance upon the publication of notice of dissolution, but should assure himself that existing creditors who have extended credit to the partnership receive actual notice of such dissolution.

As to the Merced Hardware account it is clear that the debt for the items sued upon were all incurred after February, 1956. Appellant contends that he is not liable for these items of debt because they were incurred after the dissolution of the partnership. Respondent in reply points out that [citation] provides that after a dissolution a partner can bind the partnership "By any transaction which would bind the partnership if dissolution had not taken place, provided, the other party to the transaction: I. Had extended credit to the partnership prior to dissolution and had no knowledge or notice of the dissolution." Here again the evidence is conflicting as to whether Merced Hardware & Implement Company had notice of dissolution of the partnership, and we are bound by the court's finding that it did not. There is also evidence that Merced Hardware & Implement Company had previously extended credit to the partnership. The credit reference on the contract on the Shipman & Davis Lumber Company with Valley Typewriter Company, dated March 15, 1955, and signed by Russell C. Shipman, lists Merced Hardware Company; and the items in dispute were charged to Shipman & Davis Lumber Company on the books of Merced Hardware & Implement Company. The evidence supports the implied finding that Merced Hardware & Implement Company had previously extended credit to Shipman & Davis Lumber Company.

As to the Valley Typewriter Company account, the record shows that five payments were made on this account after the date of the dissolution of the partnership. Two checks in favor of Valley Typewriter Company, both signed by Shipman Lumber Servaes Co., one dated June 20, 1956, for $76.20 and one dated October 26, 1956, for $38.10. Appellant contends that this is overwhelming evidence of a novation and conclusive proof that he was discharged from the obligation under [citation] which reads: "(2) A partner is discharged from any existing liability upon dissolution of the partnership by an agreement to that effect between himself, the partnership creditor and the person or partnership continuing the business; and such agreement may be inferred from the course of dealing between the creditor having knowledge of the dissolution and the person or partnership continuing the business." We are unable to agree with this contention. Whether or not there was a novation was a question of fact and conflicting inferences can be drawn from the evidence. The manager of Valley Typewriter Company testified that he had no actual knowledge of the dissolution of the partnership. The checks themselves would not necessarily compel a finding of actual knowledge since the inference appellant seeks to draw is dispelled by the testimony that the creditor had no knowledge. There can be no novation where the creditor testified he had no knowledge of dissolution and such testimony is believed by the trier of the fact.

Appellant also argues that he is entitled to a reversal of the judgment as to the Valley Typewriter account under the following provision of [citation]: "(3) Where a person agrees to assume the existing obligations of a dissolved partnership, the partners whose obligations have been assumed shall be discharged from any liability to any creditor of the partnership who, knowing of the agreement, consents to a material alteration in the nature or time of payment of such obligations." But here again knowledge of the dissolution of the partnership is required, and the court found upon sufficient evidence that none of the creditors here involved had notice or knowledge of the dissolution of the partnership. Furthermore, the fact that the Valley Typewriter Company accepted delayed payments under the contract does not compel a finding in accordance with appellant's argument that the creditor had consented to a material alteration in the nature or time of payment of the obligation.

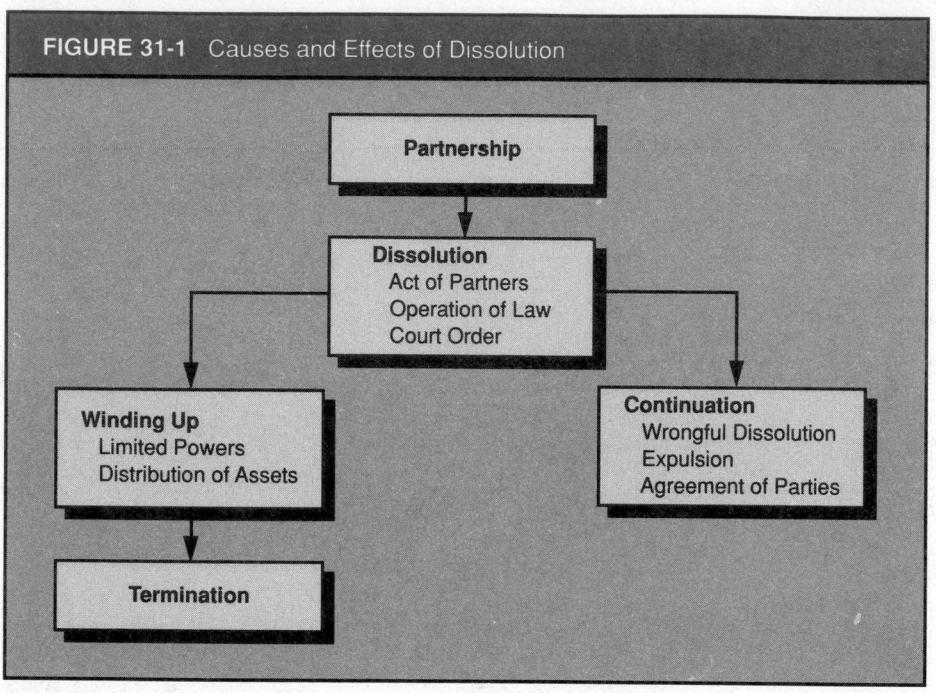

FIGURE 31-1   Causes and Effects of Dissolution

CHAPTER SUMMARY

Dissolution	**Definition of Dissolution** the change in the relation of partners caused by any partner's ceasing to be associated with the carrying on of the business

Causes of Dissolution

- *Dissolution by Act of the Partners*   a partner always has the power to dissolve a partnership, but whether he has the right to do so is determined by the partnership agreement
- *Dissolution by Operation of Law*   a partnership is dissolved by operation of law upon: (1) the death of a partner, (2) the bankruptcy of a partner or of the partnership, or (3) the subsequent illegality of the partnership
- *Dissolution by Court Order*   a court will order dissolution of a partnership under certain conditions

Effects of Dissolution   upon dissolution a partnership is not terminated but continues until the winding up is completed

- *Authority*   a partner's actual authority to act for the partnership terminates, except so far as may be necessary to wind up partnership affairs; apparent authority continues unless notice of the dissolution is given to a third party
- *Existing Liability*   dissolution does not by itself discharge the existing liability of any partner

Winding Up	**Definition of Winding Up** completion of unfinished business, collecting debts, and distributing assets to creditors and partners; also called liquidation
	Right to Wind Up on dissolution any partner has the right to insist on the winding up of the partnership unless the partnership agreement provides otherwise; however, a partner who has wrongfully dissolved the partnership or who has been properly expelled cannot force the liquidation of the partnership
	Distribution of Assets the liabilities of a partnership are to be paid out of partnership assets in the following order: (1) amounts owing to creditors other than partners, (2) amounts owing to partners other than for capital and profits, (3) amounts owing to partners for capital contributions, and (4) amounts owing to partners for profits
	Marshaling of Assets only applies when the assets of a partnership and of its members are administered by a State court of equity; means segregating and considering the assets and liabilities of the partnership separately from the respective assets and liabilities of the individual partners
	▪ *Partnership Creditors* are entitled to be first satisfied out of partnership assets
	▪ *Nonpartnership Creditors* have first claim to the individually owned assets of their respective debtor-partners
	▪ *Federal Bankruptcy* marshaling of assets is *not* followed if the partnership is a debtor

Continuation after Dissolution	**Right to Continue Partnership** the remaining partners have the right to continue the partnership in the following situations:
	▪ *Continuation after Wrongful Dissolution* the aggrieved partners can continue the firm by paying the withdrawing partner the value of his interest less the amount of damages they sustained as a result of the breach
	▪ *Continuation after Expulsion* the expelled partner is entitled to discharge from partnership liabilities and to receive cash in the net amount due him from the partnership
	▪ *Continuation Agreement of the Partners* permits the remaining partners to keep partnership property and to carry on its business; provides a specified settlement to the departing partner
	Rights of Creditors the creditors of the old partnership have claims against the continuing (new) partnership and may also proceed against all the members of the dissolved partnership

QUESTIONS

1. Identify the causes of dissolution of a partnership.
2. Explain the effect of dissolution upon the authority and liability of the partners.
3. Explain the order in which the assets of a partnership are distributed to creditors and partners.
4. Distinguish between the relative rights of partnership creditors and partners' creditors under the UPA and the Bankruptcy Act.

5. Identify and discuss when partners have the right to continue the partnership after dissolution.

PROBLEMS

1. Simmons, Hoffman, and Murray were partners doing business under the firm name of Simmons & Co. The firm borrowed money from a bank and gave the bank the firm's note for the loan. In addition, each partner guaranteed the note individ-

ually. The firm became insolvent, and a receiver was appointed. The bank claims that it has a right to file its claim as a firm debt and also that it has a right to participate in the distribution of the assets of the individual partners before partnership creditors receive any payment from such assets.

(a) Explain the principle involved in this case.

(b) Is the bank correct?

2. Lauren, Matthew, and Susan form a partnership, Lauren contributing $10,000, Matthew $5,000, and Susan her time and skill. Nothing was said as to the division of profits. The firm becomes insolvent, and after payment of all firm debts owed to third parties, $6,000 is left. Lauren claims that she is entitled to the entire $6,000. Matthew contends that the distribution should be $4,000 to Lauren and $2,000 to Matthew. Susan claims the $6,000 should be divided equally among the partners. Who is correct? Explain.

3. Martin, Mark, and Marvin formed a retail clothing partnership named M Clothiers and conducted a business for many years, buying most of their clothing from Hill, a wholesaler. On January 15 Marvin retired from the business, but Martin and Mark decided to continue it. As part of the retirement agreement, Martin and Mark agreed in writing with Marvin that Marvin would not be responsible for any of the partnership debts, either past or future. A news item concerning Marvin's retirement appeared in the local newspaper on January 15.

Before January 15 Hill was a creditor of M Clothiers to the extent of $10,000, and on January 30 he extended additional credit of $5,000. Hill was not advised and did not in fact know of Marvin's retirement and the change of the partnership. On January 30 Ray, a competitor of Hill, extended credit for the first time to M Clothiers in the amount of $3,000.

On February 1 Martin and Mark departed for parts unknown and left no partnership assets with which to pay the described debts. What is Marvin's liability, if any, (a) to Hill, and (b) to Ray?

4. Ben, Dan and Lilli were partners sharing profits in proportions of one-fourth, one-third, and five-twelfths, respectively. Their business failed, and the firm was dissolved. At the time of dissolution, no financial adjustments between the partners were necessary with reference to their respective capital contributions, but the firm's liabilities to creditors exceeded its assets by $24,000. Without contributing any amount toward the payment of the liabilities, Dan moved to a destination unknown. Ben and Lilli are financially responsible. How much must each contribute?

5. Indicate which of the following statements are true and which are false:

(a) Creditors having claims based on torts committed by partners in the course of business of the partnership are preferred over creditors with claims based on contracts.

(b) Partners who wish to continue the business have a prior right to purchase the assets.

(c) In the absence of a contract providing otherwise, the distribution to partners of accrued profits should be in equal parts, regardless of the fact that the partners had contributed to the firm unequally.

(d) Advances in the nature of loans made by the various partners to the partnership share in the firm assets on the same basis as debts due other creditors.

(e) Between the partners, the assets of the partnership must be applied to pay the claims of partners with respect to capital ahead of the claims of partners with respect to profits.

(f) Debts owing to partners (other than for capital and profits) rank ahead of debts owing to partners with respect to capital and profits.

6. Ames, Bell, and Cole were equal partners in the ABC Construction Company. They had no formal or written partnership agreement. Cole died on June 30, and his widow, Cora Cole, qualified as executor of his will. Ames and Bell continued the business of the partnership until December 31, when they sold all of the assets of the partnership. After paying all partnership debts, they distributed the balance equally among themselves and Mrs. Cole as executor.

Subsequently, Mrs. Cole learned that Ames and Bell had made and withdrawn a net profit of $20,000 during the period July 1 to December 31. The profit was made through new contracts using the partnership name and assets. Ames and Bell had concealed from Mrs. Cole the fact of such contracts and profit, and she learned about it from other sources. Immediately after acquiring this information, Mrs. Cole demanded one-third of the profit of $20,000 from Ames and Bell. They rejected her demand. What are the rights and remedies, if any, of Cora Cole as executor?

7. David and Barbara were partners in Miami. Steven, a traveling salesman for Karen, called on them and on January 14 received from them an order for merchandise. The order was forwarded by Steven to Karen in New York on January 15; the partnership of David and Barbara was dissolved by agreement between the partners on January 18. On January 19 Karen, without knowledge of the dissolution, acknowledged receipt of the order, accepted

it, and shipped the goods the next day. Barbara received them on January 23. On January 25 notice of dissolution of the partnership of David and Barbara was duly published. Karen sues David and Barbara for the purchase price of the merchandise sold. Decision?

8. The articles of partnership of the firm of Wilson and Company provide:

> William Smith to contribute $50,000; to receive interest thereon at 13 percent per annum and to devote such time as he may be able to give; to receive 30 percent of the profits.
> John Jones to contribute $50,000; to receive interest on same at 13 percent per annum; to give all of his time to the business and to receive 30 percent of the profits.
> Henry Wilson to contribute all of his time to the business and to receive 20 percent of the profits.
> James Brown to contribute all of his time to the business and to receive 20 percent of the profits.

There is no provision for sharing losses. After six years of operations, the firm has assets of $400,000 and liabilities to creditors of $420,000. Upon dissolution and winding up, what are the rights and liabilities of the respective parties?

9. Harold Fuller, Mary Warner, and Tom Clardy were copartners in a cattle-raising operation. Fuller and Clardy were both killed as the result of a common disaster. Mary Warner took charge of the partnership business and spent considerable time and effort in winding it up. In a suit brought for an accounting, Mary Warner made a claim for a reasonable allowance for services rendered in winding up the affairs of the partnership. The partnership agreement contained no provision for payment for services rendered in connection with the winding up of partnership affairs. What decision?

10. Adam, Stanley, and Rosalind formed a partnership in State X to distribute beer and wine. Their agreement provided that the partnership would continue until December 31, 1994. Which of the following events would cause the partnership to dissolve? If so, when would the partnership be dissolved?

(a) Rosalind assigns her interest in the partnership to Mary on April 1, 1990.

(b) Stanley dies on June 1, 1994.

(c) Adam withdraws from the partnership on September 15, 1993.

(d) A creditor of Stanley obtains a charging order against Stanley's interest on October 9, 1991.

(e) In 1992 the legislature of State X enacts a statute making the sale or distribution of alcoholic beverages illegal.

(f) Stanley has a formal accounting of partnership affairs on September 19, 1991.

ENDNOTES

1. Uniform Partnership Act, Section 29, Dissolution Defined.
2. Uniform Partnership Act, Section 31, Causes of Dissolution.
3. Uniform Partnership Act, Section 32, Dissolution by Decree of Court.
4. Uniform Partnership Act, Section 30, Partnership not Terminated by Dissolution.
5. Uniform Partnership Act, Section 33, General Effect of Dissolution on Authority of Partner.
6. Uniform Partnership Act, Section 35, Power of Partner to Bind Partnership to Third Persons After Dissolution.
7. Uniform Partnership Act, Section 3, Interpretation of Knowledge and Notice.
8. Uniform Partnership Act, Section 36, Effect of Dissolution on Partner's Existing Liability.
9. Uniform Partnership Act, Section 37, Right to Wind Up.
10. Uniform Partnership Act, Section 40, Rules for Distribution.
11. Uniform Partnership Act, Section 18, Rules Determining Rights and Duties of Partners.
12. Uniform Partnership Act, Section 38, Rights of Partners to Application of Partnership Property.
13. Uniform Partnership Act, Section 42, Rights of Retiring or Estate of Deceased Partner When the Business is Continued.
14. Uniform Partnership Act, Section 41, Liability of Persons Continuing the Business in Certain Cases.

32 LIMITED PARTNERSHIPS

In this chapter we consider limited partnerships and other types of unincorporated business associations, including joint ventures and business trusts. These forms of organizations have developed to meet special business and investment needs. Each has its own set of characteristics that make it most appropriate for certain purposes.

LIMITED PARTNERSHIPS

The limited partnership has proved itself to be an attractive vehicle for a variety of investments because of its tax advantages and the limited liability it confers upon the limited partners. Unlike general partnerships, limited partnerships are statutory creations. Before 1976 the governing statute in all States except Louisiana was the Uniform Limited Partnership Act (ULPA), which was promulgated in 1916. At this time, most limited partnerships were small and had only a few limited partners. Today, many limited partnerships are much larger, typically involving a small number of major investors and a relatively large group of widely distributed investors who purchase limited partnership interests. This type of limited partnership has evolved to attract substantial amounts of investment capital. Limited partnerships have been used for investments in real estate, oil and gas, motion pictures, and research and development. The large scale and multistate operations of the modern limited partnership, however, have severely burdened the framework established by the ULPA.

These shortcomings prompted the National Conference of Commissioners on Uniform State Laws to develop a Revised Uniform Limited Partnership Act (RULPA), which was promulgated in 1976. According to its preface, the RULPA is "intended to modernize the prior uniform law while retaining the special character of limited partnerships as compared with corporations." More than forty States have adopted the 1976 RULPA, which appears in Appendix E of this text. In 1985 the National Conference revised the RULPA "for the purpose of more effectively modernizing, improving and establishing uniformity in the law of limited partnerships." The 1985 Act makes almost no change in the basic structure of the 1976 RULPA and does not alter the underlying philosophy or thrust of that Act. This chapter will discuss the 1976 RULPA and the significant changes made by the 1985 Act. Appendix F of this text contains those provisions of the 1985 Act cited in this book. The ULPA, RULPA, and the 1985 Act are supplemented by the Uniform Partnership Act, which applies to limited partnerships except where it is inconsistent with the Limited Partnership Act.[1] For a concise comparison of general and limited partnerships, see Figure 33–2 in Chapter 33.

In addition, limited partnership interests are almost always considered to be securities, and their sale is therefore subject to State and Federal regulation as discussed in Chapter 43.

Definition

A **limited partnership** is a partnership formed by two or more persons under the laws of a State and has one or more general partners and one or more limited partners.[2] A *person* includes a natural person, partnership, limited partnership, trust, estate, association, or corporation.[3] It differs from a general partnership in several respects, three of which are fundamental:

1. there must be a statute in effect providing for the formation of limited partnerships;
2. the limited partnership must substantially comply with the requirements of such statute; and
3. the **liability** of a *limited* partner for partnership debts or obligations is **limited** to the extent of the capital he has contributed or agreed to contribute.

Formation

Although the formation of a *general* partnership may be accomplished without special procedures, the formation of a *limited* partnership requires substantial compliance with the limited partnership statute. Failure to do so may result in the limited partners not obtaining limited liability.

Filing of Certificate   The RULPA provides that two or more persons desiring to form a limited partnership shall file in the office of the Secretary of State of the State in which the limited partnership has its principal office a signed certificate of limited partnership.[4] The certificate must include the following information:

1. the name of the limited partnership;
2. the general character of its business;
3. the address of the office and the name and address of the agent for service of process;
4. the name and the business address of each partner, listing general partners and limited partners separately;
5. the amount of cash, and a description and statement of the value of the other property or services, contributed by each partner;
6. the times at which, or events on the happening of which, additional contributions are to be made by each partner;
7. any power of a limited partner to make an assignee of his partnership interest a limited partner;
8. the events permitting a partner to withdraw from the partnership;
9. the rights of partners to receive distributions of limited partnership property;

10. the rights of partners to receive a return of their capital contributions; and
11. the time or events upon which the limited partnership is to be dissolved.

Figure 32–1 shows a sample certificate of limited partnership.

The certificate of limited partnership must be amended if a new partner is admitted, a partner withdraws, or the capital contribution of any partner is changed as to amount or character.[5] In addition, the certificate may be amended at any time for any other proper purpose as determined by the general partners.

The 1985 Act requires the certificate to include far fewer matters. It need only provide the name of the limited partnership, the address of its office, the name and address of the agent for service of process, the name and business address of each general partner, and the latest date upon which the limited partnership is to dissolve. Limited partners need not be named and need not sign the certificate.[6] These changes reflect a policy underlying the 1985 Act that the partnership agreement, not the certificate of limited partnership, should be the comprehensive document for limited partnerships. Therefore, third parties dealing with the partnership should examine the limited partnership agreement.

Name   The inclusion of the surname of a limited partner in the partnership name is prohibited unless it is also the surname of a general partner or unless the business had been carried on under that name before the admission of that limited partner. A limited partner who knowingly permits his name to be used in violation of this provision is liable to any creditor who did not know that he was a limited partner.[7] The RULPA prohibits a name that is deceptively similar to any corporation or other limited partnership.[8] Finally, the name of the limited partnership must contain, without abbreviation, the words "limited partnership."

Contributions   Under the RULPA, the contribution of a partner may be cash, property, or services rendered or a promissory note or other obligation to contribute cash or property

FIGURE 32–1 Sample Limited Partnership Certificate

CERTIFICATE OF LIMITED PARTNERSHIP

The undersigned, desiring to form a Limited Partnership under the Limited Partnership Act of the State of _____, make this certificate for that purpose.

§ 1. Name. The name of the Limited Partnership shall be "_____."

§ 2. Purpose. The business of the Limited Partnership shall be to [*describe*].

§ 3. Location. The location of the Limited Partnership's principal place of business is _____ County, _____ .

§ 4. Agent for Service of Process. The agent for service of process on the Limited Partnership in the State of _____ shall be _____, whose business address is _____ .

§ 5. Members and Designation. The names and business addresses of the members, and their designation as General or Limited Partners, are

_____	[*Address*]	General Partner
_____	[*Address*]	General Partner
_____	[*Address*]	Limited Partner
_____	[*Address*]	Limited Partner

§ 6. Term. The term for which the Limited Partnership is to exist is _____ .

§ 7. Initial Contributions of Partners. The amount of cash and a description and statement of the agreed value of the other property or services contributed by each Partner are

[*Name*]	[*Describe*]
[*Name*]	[*Describe*]
[*Name*]	[*Describe*]
[*Name*]	[*Describe*]

§ 8. Subsequent Contributions of Partners. Each Partner may (but shall not be obliged to) make additional contributions to the capital of the Limited Partnership as follows:

§ 9. Profit Shares of Partners. The share of the profits that each Partner shall receive by reason of his contribution is

[*Name*]	_____ %
[*Name*]	_____ %
[*Name*]	_____ %
[*Name*]	_____ %

Signed _____, 19_____

_____

_____

_____

_____

or to perform services.[9] A partner is liable to the partnership for the difference between the contribution actually made and the amount stated in the certificate as having been made. Under the 1985 amendments, a promise by a limited partner to contribute to the limited partnership is not enforceable unless it is in a signed writing.[10]

Defective Formation   A limited partnership is formed when the certificate of limited partnership is filed if it substantially complies with the requirements of the statute. Therefore, there is a defective formation if no certificate is filed or if the certificate filed does not substantially meet the statutory requirements. In either case, the limited liability of limited partners is jeopardized. The RULPA provides that a person who has contributed to the capital of a business (an "equity participant"), erroneously and in good faith believing that he has become a limited partner in a limited partnership, is not liable as a general partner provided that on ascertaining the mistake he either (1) withdraws from the business and renounces *future* profits, or (2) files an amendment curing the defect.[11] The equity participant, however, will be liable to any third party who transacted business with the enterprise before the withdrawal or amendment and in good faith believed that the equity participant was a general partner at the time of the transaction.

The 1985 Act does not require that the limited partners be named in the certificate. This greatly reduces the risk that a limited partner would be exposed to liability because of an inadvertent omission of that information from the certificate.

IN RE WESTOVER HILL LTD.
United States Bankruptcy Court, District of Wyoming, 1985.
46 B.R. 300.

Facts: Dale Fullerton was chairman of the board of Enviroscarch and the sole stockholder in Westover Hills Management. James Anderson was president of AGFC. Fullerton and Anderson agreed to form a limited partnership to purchase certain property from WYORCO, a joint venture of which Fullerton was a member. The parties intended to form a limited partnership with Westover Hills Management as the sole general partner and AGFC and Envirosearch as limited partners. The certificate filed with the Wyoming Secretary of State, however, listed all three companies as both general and limited partners of Westover Hills Ltd. Anderson and Fullerton later became aware of this error and filed an amended certificate of limited partnership, which correctly named Envirosearch and AGFC as limited partners only. When Westover Hills Ltd. became bankrupt, the court sought to determine whether the enterprise was a general or limited partnership for the purposes of determining eligibility of relief under the Bankruptcy Code.

Decision: Westover Hills Ltd. held to be a limited partnership for purposes of bankruptcy.

Opinion: Mai, Bkrtcy. J.   The question of existence of a limited partnership is to be determined by state law. [Citation.]

In 1979, Wyoming adopted the Revised Uniform Limited Partnership Act. [Citation.]

The revised Act has in common with its predecessor, the Uniform Limited Partnership Act, the fundamental assumption that the limited partners are not general partners who secure limited liability by simply filing a certificate. The official comment to Section 1 of the Uniform Limited Partnership Act states this basic assumption.

"(t)he person who contributes the capital, though in accordance with custom called a limited partner, is not in any sense a partner. He is, however, a member of the association."

The official comment further states,

"The limited partner not being in any sense a principal in the business, failure to comply with the requirements of the act in respect to the certificate, while it may result in the nonformation of the association, does not make him a partner or liable as such. The exact nature of his liability in such cases is set forth in Sec. 11."

Thus, if the parties intend to form a limited partnership, the failure to comply with the Wyoming Limited Partnership Act would not, as petitioners argue, result in the formation of a general partnership. Rather, under the theory of the Uniform Act, such noncompliance would result only in the nonformation of the limited partnership.

It is clear that the parties at all times intended to form a limited partnership. However, the original certificate of limited partnership did not correctly reflect their intentions. In such a situation, the Revised Uniform Act provides a remedy to cure such defective compliance with the requirements for Limited Partnership. The applicable Wyoming Statute provides,

"Person Erroneously Believing Himself Limited Partner.

"(a) Except as provided in subsection (b) of this section, a person who makes a contribution to a business enterprise and erroneously but in good faith believes that he has become a limited partner in the enterprise is not a general partner in the enterprise and is not bound by its obligations by reason of making the contribution, receiving distributions from the enterprise, or exercising any rights of a limited partner, if, on ascertaining the mistake, he:

"(i) Causes an appropriate certificate of limited partnership or a certificate of amendment to be executed and filed; or

"(ii) Withdraws from future equity participation in the enterprise." [RULPA § 304.]

Thus, under Wyoming law, an intended limited partner who realizes that a limited partnership has been imperfectly formed, may take either alternative provided in subsection (a) to insure the retention of limited partnership status.

In the present case, when AGFC realized that the certificate of limited partnership had erroneously listed them as a general, rather than as a limited, partner they caused an appropriate certificate of amendment to be executed and filed. Thus, AGFC did not lose its intended status as a limited partner, having corrected the defect in accordance with [citation]. In view of these considerations, the court concludes, without difficulty, that the debtor is a limited partnership. [Citations.]

In deciding that the debtor is a limited partnership for purposes of filing a voluntary Chapter 11 case, the court does not reach the issue of whether, under Wyoming law, the individual limited partners may be liable to third parties in connection with their involvement in the debtor's business and financial affairs.

Although an intended limited partner does not become a general partner by reason of noncompliance with the Act alone, such a limited partner may, by reason of other factors, lose his limited liability and become "liable as" a general partner.

If a limited partner is found to be "liable as" a general partner to third parties, it does not change the fundamental relations of the partners inter se. It is the status of the partners inter se and not their potential liability to third parties that determines the existence of a general partnership or a limited partnership, for the purposes of determining eligibility of relief under the Bankruptcy Code. [Citations.]

Foreign Limited Partnerships A limited partnership is considered "foreign" in any State in which it has not been formed. The RULPA establishes that the laws of the State under which a foreign limited partnership is organized govern its organization, its internal affairs, and the liability of its limited partners.[12] At the same time, it requires all foreign limited partnerships to register with the Secretary of State before transacting any business in the State.[13] Any foreign limited partnership transacting business without so registering may not bring enforcement actions in the State's courts until it registers, although it may defend itself in the State's courts.

Rights

Because limited partnerships are organized pursuant to statute, the rights of the parties are usually set forth in the articles of limited partnership. A general partner of a limited partnership has all the rights and powers of a partner in a partnership without limited partners.[14]

Control The general partners of a limited partnership have almost exclusive control and management of the limited partnership. A limited partner, on the other hand, cannot share in the management or control of the association; if he does so, he forfeits his limited liability. If the limited partner's participation in control is substantially the same as the exercise of the powers of a general partner, then the limited partner assumes the liability of a general partner to *all* third parties who transact business with the partnership. If, however, the limited partner's participation in control of the business is *not* substantially the same as the exercise of the powers of a general partner, he is liable as a general partner for the obligations of the limited partnership *only* to those persons who transact business with the limited partnership *with actual knowledge* of his participation in control.[7] This approach recognizes the difficulty of determining when the control line has been overstepped and that the purpose of imposing general partner's liability is the protection of creditor's expectations.

The 1985 Act has eliminated the broader liability of a limited partner whose participation is substantially the same as a general partner. Under the 1985 Act, a limited partner who participates in the control of the business is liable only to those persons who transact business with the limited partnership reasonably believing, based upon the limited partner's conduct, that the limited partner is a general partner.[15]

Moreover, the RULPA provides a "safe harbor" by enumerating certain activities, any or all of which a limited partner may carry on without being deemed to have taken part in control of the business.[7] They are the following:

1. being a contractor for, or an agent or employee of the limited partnership or of a general partner;
2. consulting with and advising a general partner with respect to the business of the limited partnership;
3. acting as surety for the limited partnership;
4. approving or disapproving an amendment to the partnership agreement; and
5. voting on one or more of the following matters:
   a. the dissolution and winding up of the partnership;
   b. the sale, exchange, lease, mortgage, pledge, or other transfer of all or substantially all of the assets of the limited partnership other than in the ordinary course of its business;
   c. the incurrence of indebtedness by the limited partnership other than in the ordinary course of its business;
   d. a change in the nature of the business; or
   e. the removal of a general partner.

The RULPA provides that this listing is nonexclusive: there may be other permissible powers for a limited partner to exercise. The 1985 amendments have expanded the safe harbor list by adding the following:

1. winding up the partnership;
2. exercising any right or power granted by the Act;
3. voting on an amendment to the partnership agreement or certificate;

Sales Climbed for Partnerships in 2nd Quarter
Your Money Matters

Sales of public limited partnerships rose 7.3% in the second quarter from the first quarter but trailed the year-earlier period by 42.3%.

The quarter-to-quarter rise cheered some sponsors, but some partnership analysts and financial planners remain unimpressed.

"The increase is significant, since it's been a steady upward trend since March," says Fuhrman Nettles, vice president of Robert A. Stanger & Co., a Shrewsbury, N.J., firm that tracks partnerships. Steven Insel, a lawyer for financial planner Christopher Weil & Co. in Glendale, Calif., says he believes the partnership market will "continue to strengthen as people move some of their money out of cash equivalents into alternative investments to diversify."

'Hard Market'

But William G. Brennan, a Valley Forge, Pa., partnership analyst and investment adviser, says, "It's still a hard market to sell partnerships in. . . . Because of past problems, partnerships have gotten a bad press, and they're illiquid."

Second-quarter sales totaled $2.32 billion, up from $2.16 billion in the previous quarter but down from $4.02 billion in the year-earlier quarter. According to a survey by the Stanger company, the virtual disappearance of master limited partnerships—those traded on stock exchanges—accounted for more than half of the drop from a year earlier. Sales of master limited partnerships almost ground to a halt after a law passed late last year stipulated that new publicly traded partnerships, except those involved in oil and gas or real estate, will be taxed as corporations, eliminating a big advantage.

Equipment leasing was the only major partnership sector to show both quarter-to-quarter and year-to-year increases. Sales rose 12.8% from the first quarter and 16.2% from a year earlier.

Analysts say high current cash distributions are the main reason for rising sales of equipment-leasing partnerships. "But people don't realize they are getting a partial return of their capital with each cash payment, because at the end of

Public Limited Partnership Sales (Dollar amounts in millions)			
	1988 2nd QTR.	1987 2nd QTR.	PERCENT CHANGE
Real Estate	$1,310.5	$2,121.0	−38.2%
Oil and Gas	155.6	305.1	−49.0
Equipment Leasing	335.0	288.4	+16.2
Other	516.3	1,303.9	−60.4
TOTAL	**$2,317.4**	**$4,018.4**	**−42.3%**
NONTRADED	$2,251.4	$2,934.3	−23.2
MLPs	66.0	1,084.1	−93.9

MLPs = Master limited partnerships
Source: Robert A. Stanger & Co.

their partnership, their equipment may not be worth much," Mr. Brennan says.

Inflation Jitters

Sales of real-estate partnerships, the largest category, jumped 17.8% from the first quarter but fell 38.2% from a year earlier. Particularly significant was a 45.5% increase from the first quarter in sales of high-leverage real-estate partnerships, Mr. Nettles says. The surge reflects worries "about inflation, since high-leveraged real estate is one of the best protections against inflation," he adds.

Another positive indicator for partnership sales is a drop in the Stanger firm's market-clearing index, which measures how long it takes to sell unsold partnerships. The index declined to 1.28 years in June from 1.35 in April. The real-estate market-clearing index fell to 1.17 years in June from 1.48 in April.

—By Earl C. Gottschalk Jr.

4. voting on the admission of a general partner;

5. voting on the admission or removal of a limited partner; or

6. voting on any matter relating to the business of the limited partnership that the partnership agreement makes subject to the approval or disapproval of the limited partners.[15]

WEIL v. DIVERSIFIED PROPERTIES, INC.
United States District Court, District of Columbia, 1970.
319 F.Supp. 778.

Facts: Weil organized Diversified Properties as a limited partnership with varying degrees of ownership in several apartment complexes and other real estate located in Maryland. The parties signed a formal written agreement in July 1967, and the partnership was properly registered in the District of Columbia. Weil was the only general partner and managed the partnership's affairs until May 1, 1968. At that time, the partnership encountered cash flow problems, and to help matters, Weil gave up both his office and his salary. At a partnership meeting held the following week, two third parties, Rubenstein and Tempchin, were selected by the limited partners to manage the partnership properties on a commission basis in accordance with a proposal that Weil had advanced earlier. Weil began working for another real estate company as a vice-president, but he remained a general partner of Diversified Properties. Creditors of the partnership, therefore, turned to him with demands for payment of the partnership debts that had not been met. Weil claims that after he surrendered his office and his salary, he remained as the general partner but that his directions were ignored. He also claims that the limited partners at various times gave direct orders to Rubenstein and Tempchin as to how to manage the partnership's affairs. Accordingly, he brings this action seeking to have the limited partners declared general partners.

Decision: Judgment for the limited partners granted.

Opinion: Gesell, J.   Cases relating to whether or not limited partners have taken part in control of the business and are thus to be treated as general partners involve claims by creditors against the partners. [Citations.] No case has been found where a general partner has invoked Section 7 of the [Uniform Limited Partnership] Act against his own limited partners. The purpose of Section 7 is to protect creditors:

> The Act proceeds on the assumption that no public policy requires a person who contributes to the capital of a business, acquires an interest in its profits, and some degree of control over the conduct of the business to become bound for the obligations of the business, provided creditors have no reason to believe that when their credits were extended that such persons were so bound. [Citations.]

* * *

The remedy of a general partner who faces interference from his limited partners is to dissolve the partnership under Section 31 of the Uniform Partnership Act. So long as the partnership continues, he is in a relationship of trust with his colleagues. [Citation.] He may not invoke the provisions of the Act to enlarge the liability of his partners.

Even if a general partner might hold his limited partners to account as general partners under certain circumstances, Weil cannot do so on the facts of this case. Weil considers himself still a general partner and recognizes that the written partnership agreement by its terms is a bona fide limited partnership under the [U.L.P.A.] As between themselves, partners may make any agreement they wish which is not barred by prohibitory provisions of statutes, by common law, or by consideration of public policy. [Citation.] Whatever may be the obligations of the limited partners as against creditors or third parties, Weil may not prevail against them if they have not breached the terms of the agreement. * * * Accordingly, the initial inquiry must be to determine whether the limited partners have in any way violated the terms of the written agreement.

* * *

A limited partner under the [U.L.P.A.] has the right to require that the books and records be kept at a designated place for inspection and copying and he may at any time demand "true and full information of all things affecting the partnership". It is well established that just because a man is a limited partner in an enterprise he is not by reason of that status precluded from continuing to have an interest in the affairs of the partnership, from giving advice and suggestions to the general partner or his nominees, and from interesting himself in specific aspects of the business. Such casual advice as limited partners may have given to Rubenstein and Tempchin can hardly be said to be interference in day-to-day management. Certainly common sense dictates that in times of severe financial crisis all partners in such an enterprise, limited or general, will become actively interested in any effort to keep the enterprise afloat and many abnormal problems will arise that are not under any stretch of the imagination mere day-to-day matters of managing the partnership business. This is all that occurred in this instance.

* * *

Weil has not by a preponderance of the evidence established any violation by the limited partners of terms of the agreement with him, which at the very most is all that Weil can complain of in his effort to have the limited partners declared general partners. Since the partnership agreement was not violated by the limited partners. Weil has no cause of action and his request for the appointment of a receiver and an accounting will be denied. The provisions of the Limited Partnership Act were primarily designed to protect creditors. So long as the provisions of the agreement were followed, no partner can complain. Weil's complaint is dismissed.

Choice of Associates No person may be added as a general partner or a limited partner without the consent of *all* partners. After the formation of a limited partnership, the admission of additional limited partners requires the written consent of all partners unless the partnership agreement provides otherwise.[16] The admission of the new limited partner is not effective until the certificate of limited partnership has been amended to reflect that fact. After the formation of a limited partnership, new general partners may be admitted *only* with the specific written consent of *all* partners.[17]

The 1985 Act provides that the written partnership agreement determines the procedure for authorizing the admission of additional general partners.[18] The written consent of all partners is required only if the partnership agreement fails to deal with this issue.

Withdrawal A general partner may withdraw from a limited partnership at any time by giving written notice to the other partners.[19] If the withdrawal violates the partnership agreement, the limited partnership may recover damages from the withdrawing general partner. A limited partner may withdraw as provided in the limited partnership certificate or, under the 1985 Act, the written partnership agreement. If the certificate (or written partnership agreement under the 1985 Act) does not specify when a limited partner may withdraw, she may do so upon giving at least six months' prior written notice to each general partner.[20] Upon withdrawal, a withdrawing partner is entitled to receive any distribution to which she is entitled under the partnership agreement, subject to the restrictions discussed below on the amount of distributions. If the partnership agreement makes no provision, the partner is entitled to receive the fair value of her interest in the limited partnership as of the date of withdrawal based upon her right to share in distributions from the limited partnership.

Assignment of Partnership Interest A partnership interest is a partner's share of the profits and losses of a limited partnership and the right to receive distributions of partnership assets. A partnership interest is personal property. Unless otherwise provided in the partnership agreement, a partner may assign his partnership interest. An assignment does not dissolve the limited partnership. The assignee does not become a partner and may not exercise any rights of a partner. The assignment only entitles the assignee to receive, to the extent of the assignment, the assigning partner's share of distributions. Except as otherwise provided in the partnership agreement, a partner ceases to be a partner upon assignment of all his partnership interest.[21]

An assignee of a partnership interest, including an assignee of a general partner, may become a substituted *limited* partner if all the other partners consent or if the assigning partner, having such power provided in the certificate (or in the partnership agreement under the 1985 amendments), grants the assignee this right.[22] Upon the death of a partner, her executor or administrator has all the rights of the partner for the purpose of settling her estate, including any power the deceased partner had to make her assignee a substituted limited partner.

Profit and Loss Sharing The profits and losses are allocated among the partners as provided in the partnership agreement. If the partnership agreement does not make such a provision, then the profits and losses are allocated on the basis of the value of contributions actually made by each partner.[23] Nonetheless, limited partners are usually not liable for losses beyond their capital contribution. The 1985 Act requires the agreement sharing profits and losses to be in writing.[24]

Distributions The partners share distributions of cash or other assets of a limited partnership as provided in the partnership agreement. (The 1985 Act requires such agreement to be written.) The RULPA allows partners to share in distributions in a different proportion than they share in profits. If the partnership agreement does not allocate distributions, then distributions are made on the basis of the value of contributions actually made by each partner. Unless otherwise provided, a partner has no right to demand a distribution in any form other than cash. Once a partner becomes entitled to a distribution, he has the status of a creditor with respect to that distribution. A partner may not receive a distribution from a limited partnership unless there are sufficient assets after the distribution to pay all liabilities of the partnership other than liabilities to partners on account of their partnership interests.[25]

Loans Both general and limited partners may be secured or unsecured creditors of the partnership with the same rights as a person who is not a partner,[26] subject to applicable State and Federal bankruptcy and fraudulent conveyance statutes.

Information The RULPA requires that the partnership continuously maintain within the State an office at which basic organizational and financial records are kept.[27] Each limited partner has the right to inspect and copy any of the partnership records. She also may obtain the following from the general partners upon reasonable demand: (1) complete and accurate information regarding the business and financial condition of the limited partnership, (2) a copy of the limited partnership's Federal, State, and local income tax return for each year, and (3) any other reasonable information regarding the affairs of the limited partnership.

Derivative Actions   The RULPA recognizes the right of a limited partner to bring an action on behalf of a limited partnership to recover a judgment in its favor if the general partners having authority to do so have refused to bring the action.[28] The RULPA also establishes standing and pleading requirements similar to those imposed in shareholder's derivative actions, as well as permitting the court to award reasonable expenses, including attorney's fees, to a successful plaintiff.

Duties and Liabilities

The duties and liabilities of general partners in a limited partnership are quite different from those of a limited partner. A general partner is subject to all the duties and restrictions of a partner in a partnership without limited partners, whereas a limited partner is subject to few, if any, duties and enjoys limited liability.

Duties   A *general partner* of a limited partnership has a **fiduciary** relationship to her limited partners. This fiduciary duty imposed upon the general partner has extreme importance to the limited partners because of the circumscribed role that a limited partner may play in the control and management of the business enterprise. Conversely, it remains unclear whether a limited partner stands in a fiduciary relationship to his general partners or the limited partnership. Very limited judicial authority on this question exists, but it seems to point towards not placing such a duty on the limited partner.

As with fiduciary duty, the law does not distinguish between the duty of care owed by a general partner to a general partnership and that owed by a general partner to a limited partnership. This results in part from the UPA, which provides that it will apply to limited partnerships except insofar as it is inconsistent with the statutes relating to such partnerships.[1] On the other hand, a limited partner owes no duty of care to a limited partnership as long as she remains a limited partner.

WYLER v. FEUER

California Court of Appeals, Second District, Division 2, 1978.
85 Cal.App.3d 392, 149 Cal.Rptr. 626.

Facts: Feuer and Martin, associated as Feuer and Martin Productions, Inc. (FMPI), had been successful producers of Broadway musical comedies. Their first motion picture, "Cabaret," received eight Academy Awards in 1973. In 1972 FMPI bought the motion picture and television rights to Simone Berteaut's best-selling books about her life with her half-sister Edith Piaf. To finance a movie based on this novel, FMPI sought a substantial private investment from Wyler. In July 1973 Wyler signed a final limited partnership agreement with FMPI. The agreement stated that Wyler would provide, interest free, 100 percent financing for the proposed $1.6 million project in return for a certain portion of the profits, not to exceed 50 percent. In addition, FMPI would obtain $850,000 in production financing by September 30, 1973. The contract specifically provided that FMPI's failure to raise this amount by September 30, 1973, "shall not be deemed a breach of this agreement" and that Wyler's sole remedy would be a reduction in the producer's fee.

A year after its release in 1974, the motion picture proved less than an overwhelming success—costing $1.5 million with total receipts only $478,000. From the receipts, Wyler received $313,500 for his investment. FMPI had failed to obtain an amount even close to the required $850,000 for production financing. Wyler then sued Feuer, Martin, and FMPI for mismanagement of the business of the limited partnership and to recover his $1.5 million as damages. The trial court found in favor of Feuer, Martin, and FMPI.

Decision: Judgment for Feuer, Martin, and FMPI affirmed.

Opinion: **Fleming, J.**   A limited partnership affords a vehicle for capital investment whereby the limited partner restricts his liability to the amount of his investment in return for surrender of any right to manage and control the partnership business. [Citation.] In a limited partnership the general partner manages and controls the partnership business. [Citation.] In exercising his management functions the general partner comes under a fiduciary duty of good faith and fair dealing toward other members of the partnership. [Citations.]

These characteristics—limited investor liability, delegation of authority to management, and fiduciary duty owed by management to investors—are similar to those existing in corporate investment, where it has long been the rule that directors are not liable to stockholders for mistakes made in the exercise of honest business judgment [citations], or for losses incurred in the good faith performance of their duties when they have used such care as an ordinarily prudent person would use. [Citation.] By this standard a general partner may not be held liable for mistakes made or losses incurred in the good faith exercise of reasonable business judgment.

According all due inferences to plaintiff's evidence, as we do on review of a nonsuit, we agree with the trial court that plaintiff did not produce sufficient evidence to hold defendants liable for bad business management. Plaintiff's evidence showed that the Piaf picture did not make money, was not sought after by distributors, and did not live up to its producers' expectations. The same could be said of the majority of motion pictures made since the invention of cinematography. No evidence showed that defendants' decisions and efforts failed to conform to the general duty of care demanded of an ordinarily prudent person in like position under similar circumstances. The good faith business judgment and management of a general partner need only satisfy the standard of care demanded of an ordinarily prudent person, and will not be scrutinized by the courts with the cold clarity of hindsight.

Liabilities   One of the most appealing features of a limited partnership is the limited personal liability it offers to limited partners. **Limited liability** means that once a limited partner has paid her contribution she has no further liability to the limited partnership or its creditors. Thus, if a limited partner buys a 25 percent share of a limited partnership for $50,000 and does not forfeit her limited liability, her liability is limited to the $50,000 contributed even if the limited partnership suffers losses of $500,000. This protection is subject to three conditions discussed earlier:

1. that there is substantial compliance in good faith with the requirement that a certificate of limited partnership be filed;
2. that the surname of the limited partner does not appear in the partnership name; and

3. that the limited partner does not take part in control of the business.

In addition, if the certificate contains a false statement, anyone who suffers loss by reliance on that statement may hold liable any party to the certificate who knew the statement to be false when the certificate was executed.[29] As long as the limited partner abides by these conditions, his liability for any and all obligations of the partnership is limited to his capital contribution.

At the same time, the general partners of a limited partnership have unlimited external liability. Also, any general partner who knew or *should have known* that the limited partnership certificate contained a false statement is liable to anyone who suffers loss by reliance on that false statement. Moreover, a general partner is liable if he knows or should know that a statement in the certificate has *become* false and he has not amended the certificate within a reasonable time.

See Figure 32–2 for a comparison of general and limited partners.

Dissolution

As with a general partnership, there are three steps involved in the extinguishment of a limited partnership: (1) dissolution, (2) winding up or liquidation, and (3) termination. The causes of dissolution and the priorities in the distribution of the assets, however, are somewhat different than in a general partnership.

Causes   In a limited partnership, the limited partners do *not* have the right or the power to dissolve the partnership, except by decree of the court. The death or bankruptcy of a limited partner does *not* dissolve the partnership. The RULPA specifies those events that will trigger a dissolution, after which the affairs of the partnership must be liquidated:

1. the expiration of the time period, or the happening of the events specified in the certificate;
2. the unanimous written consent of all the partners;
3. the withdrawal of a general partner, unless all partners agree to continue the business; or

4. a decree of judicial dissolution, which may be granted whenever it is not reasonably practicable to carry on the business in conformity with the partnership agreement.[30]

Winding Up   Unless otherwise provided in the partnership agreement, the general partners who have not wrongfully dissolved the limited partnership may wind up the limited partnership's affairs.[31] The limited partners may wind up the limited partnership if there are no general partners who have not wrongfully dissolved the partnership. But any partner, his legal representative, or his assignee may obtain a winding up by court if cause is shown.

Distribution of Assets   The priorities in distributing the assets of a limited partnership are as follows:

1. to creditors, including partners who are creditors except with respect to liabilities for distributions;
2. to partners and ex-partners in satisfaction of liabilities for unpaid distributions;
3. to partners for the return of their contributions except as otherwise agreed; and
4. to partners for their partnership interests in the proportions in which they share in distributions, except as otherwise agreed.[32]

FIGURE 32-2   Comparison of General and Limited Partners

	General Partner	Limited Partner
Control	Has all the rights and powers of a partner in a partnership without limited partners	Has no right to take part in management or control
Liability	Unlimited	Limited, unless takes part in control or name used
Agency	Is an agent of the partnership	Is not an agent of the partnership
Fiduciary Duty	Yes	No
Duty of Care	Yes	No

OTHER TYPES OF UNINCORPORATED BUSINESS ASSOCIATIONS

Joint Ventures

A **joint venture** or joint adventure is a form of temporary partnership organized to carry out a particular business enterprise for profit. Usually, although not necessarily, it is of short duration. It is an association of persons who combine their property, money, efforts, skill, and knowledge for the purpose of carrying out a single business operation for profit. An example is a securities underwriting syndicate or a syndicate formed to acquire a certain tract of land for subdivision and resale. Other common examples include joint research conducted by corporations, exploitation of mineral rights, and manufacturing operations in foreign countries.

A joint venture differs from a partnership, which is formed to carry on a business over a considerable or indefinite period of time. A joint venturer is *not* an agent of her co-venturers and does not necessarily have authority to bind them, although in a given case a joint venturer may have actual or apparent authority to bind her co-venturers. Usually the management and operation of the enterprise is placed by agreement in the hands of one member designated as manager. The death of a partner dissolves the partnership, while the death of a joint venturer does not necessarily dissolve the joint venture. A partner cannot sue a copartner or the firm at law, but must go into equity for relief. On the other hand, a court of law will take jurisdiction over disputes between joint venturers. Except for these principal differences, a joint venture is generally governed by the law of partnerships.

FLORIDA TOMATO PACKERS, INC. v. WILSON
District Court of Appeals of Florida, Third District, 1974.
296 So.2d 536.

Facts: On September 23, 1971, Campbell was driving a farm vehicle owned by Lytton and struck an automobile owned and operated by Willie Wilson. When the accident occurred, Campbell was employed as a farmhand by Lytton. Prior to the accident, Lytton, a tomato farmer, had entered into an arrangement with Florida Tomato Packers, Inc., a corporation engaged in the business of packing, selling, wholesaling, and distributing tomatoes. According to this agreement, Lytton planted and raised the tomatoes and transported them to Florida Tomato Packers' warehouse. Florida Tomato Packers paid all of Lytton's farming bills, including land and equipment rentals, equipment repair, gasoline and oil, seeds and fertilizer, and all labor. The corporation also packed, crated, shipped, and sold the crop after it arrived at the packing house. Any profits from the sale of the tomatoes were equally divided between Lytton and the corporation. The Wilsons sued Florida Tomato Packers for the damages caused by the accident with Campbell. The trial court entered judgment on a jury verdict for the Wilsons.

Decision: Judgment for the Wilsons affirmed.

Opinion: **Richardson, J.** A partnership is usually defined as a voluntary contractual relationship between two or more competent persons to place their money, effects, labor and/or skill in lawful commerce or business, with the understanding that there shall be a communion of profits between them. [Citation.]

A joint venture, although a less formal relationship, partakes of many of the characteristics of a partnership. A joint venture has been defined as a special combination of two or more persons, who, in some specific venture, seek a profit jointly without the existence between them of any actual partnership, corporation, or other business entity. It is an association of persons or legal entities to carry out a single business enterprise for profit. [Citations.] Corporations may be members of a joint venture. [Citations.]

It has been held that as between the parties the existence of a contract is essential to the creation of the relationship of joint venturers. However, it is well established that the contract need not be express or embodied in a formal written agreement specifically defining the rights and duties of the parties. The existence of such a contract—and hence a joint venture—may be implied or inferred from the conduct of the parties or from acts and circumstances which in fact make it appear that they are participants in a joint venture. The courts of Florida have not hesitated to imply the existence of a contract. [Citations.] The Florida courts have held that to create a joint venture relationship, there must be concurrence of the following elements: (1) a community of interest in the performance of the common purpose; (2) joint control or right of control; (3) a joint proprietary interest in the subject matter; (4) a right to share in the profits; and (5) a duty to share in any losses which may be sustained. [Citations.]

In Florida a duty to share in losses actually and impliedly exists as a matter of law in a situation where one party supplies the labor, experience and skill, and the other the necessary capital since in the event of a loss, the party supplying the know-how would have exercised his skill in vain and the party supplying the capital investment would have suffered a diminishment thereof. [Citation.]

Participants in a joint venture are each liable for the torts of the other or of the servants of the joint undertaking committed within the course and scope of the undertaking, without regard to which of the joint venturers actually employed the servant. [Citations.]

This court finds the record contains more than ample evidence to provide the legal predicate for the jury finding that a partnership and/or joint venture relationship existed between George F. Lytton and Florida Tomato Packers, Inc.

Joint Stock Companies

A **joint stock company,** or joint stock association as it is sometimes called, is technically a form of general partnership that has some of the characteristics of a corporation and differs in several important ways from the ordinary partnership. It is unlike a partnership in that:

1. its capital is divided into shares represented by transferable certificates;
2. its business and affairs are managed by directors or managers elected by the members, who alone have the authority to represent and bind it;
3. its members are not its agents; and
4. a transfer of shares by a member or his death, insanity, or other incapacity does not dissolve it or give grounds for dissolution.

It is similar to a partnership but unlike a corporation in that it is formed by contract and not by State authority.

Mining Partnerships

A **mining partnership** is an association of the several owners of the mineral rights in land for the purpose of operating a mine and extracting minerals of economic value for their mutual profit. Although mining partnerships are governed to a considerable extent by the law of general partnerships, there are certain important differences between them. For example, a mining partner has the right to sell his interest in the partnership, and the death of a partner does not dissolve a mining partnership.

Limited Partnership Associations

Limited partnership associations are permitted by statute in certain States. This type of organization is a legal hybrid. Although called a partnership association, it closely resembles a corporation. It is a legal entity separate and distinct from its members, who are not personally responsible for its debts, their liabilities being limited to their capital contribution, except in the event of violation of some statutory provision. An important difference between this kind of association and a corporation pertains to the transfer of shares. Although the shares in a limited partnership association are freely transferable, the transferee does not become a member in the association unless so elected by the other members. If membership is refused, he may recover the value of his shares from the association.

Business Trusts

A trust is a transfer of the legal title to certain specific property to one person for the use and benefit of another. Where an express trust results from contract, the agreement is commonly known as a declaration of trust. It customarily sets forth a designation of the property, the duration of the trust, the exact functions and duties of the trustees concerning the management of the property, the persons to whom the income of the trust is to be paid and the share to be received by each, the method of winding up the trust, and the person or persons entitled to share in the trust property on termination. See Chapter 48 for a discussion of trusts.

Although trusts are almost as old as the law of equity itself, it was not until late in the nineteenth century that the trust concept was used as a method of conducting a commercial enterprise. The business trust, sometimes called a Massachusetts trust, was devised to avoid the burdens of corporate regulation and particularly the formerly widespread prohibition denying to corporations the power to own and deal in real estate. Like an ordinary trust between natural persons, a business trust may be created by a voluntary agreement without authorization or consent of the State.

A **business trust** has three distinguishing characteristics: (1) the trust estate is devoted to the conduct of a business; (2) by the terms of the agreement, each beneficiary is entitled to a certificate evidencing his ownership of a beneficial interest in the trust that he is free to sell or otherwise transfer; and (3) the trustees must have the exclusive right to manage and control the business free from control of the beneficiaries. If the third condition is not met, the trust may fail; the beneficiaries would then become personally liable for the obligations of the business as partners.

The trustees are personally liable for the debts of the business unless, in entering into contractual relations with others, it is expressly stated or definitely understood between the parties that the obligation is incurred solely on the responsibility of the trust estate. To escape personal liability on the contractual obligations of the business, the trustee must obtain the agreement or consent of the other contracting party to look solely to the assets of the trust. The personal liability of the trustees for their own torts or the torts of their agents and servants employed in the operation of the business stands on a different footing. While this liability cannot be avoided, the risk involved may be reduced substantially or eliminated altogether by insurance.

CHAPTER SUMMARY

Limited Partnership	**Definition of a Limited Partnership** a partnership formed by two or more persons under the laws of a State and having one or more general partners and one or more limited partners

Formation a limited partnership can only be formed by substantial compliance with a State limited partnership statute

- *Filing of Certificate* two or more persons must file a signed certificate of limited partnership
- *Name* inclusion of a limited partner's surname in the partnership name in most instances will result in the loss of the limited partner's limited liability
- *Contributions* may be cash, property, services, or a promise to contribute cash, property, or services
- *Defective Formation* if no certificate is filed or if one is filed but does not substantially meet the statutory requirements, the formation is defective and the limited liability of the limited partners is jeopardized
- *Foreign Limited Partnerships* a limited partnership is considered "foreign" in any State in which it has not been formed

Rights a general partner has all the rights and powers of a partner in a general partnership

- *Control* the general partners have almost exclusive control and management of the limited partnership; if a limited partner takes part in the control of the limited partnership, she may lose her limited liability
- *Choice of Associates* no person may be added as a general partner or a limited partner without the consent of all partners
- *Withdrawal* a general partner may withdraw from a limited partnership at any time by giving written notice to the other partners; a limited partner may withdraw as provided in the limited partnership certificate
- *Assignment of Partnership Interest* unless otherwise provided in the partnership agreement, a partner may assign his partnership interest; an assignee may become a substituted limited partner if all other partners consent
- *Profit and Loss Sharing* profits and losses are allocated among the partners as provided in the partnership agreement; if the partnership agreement has no such provision, then profits and losses are allocated on the basis of the value of contributions actually made by each partner
- *Distributions* the partners share distributions of cash or other assets of a limited partnership as provided in the partnership agreement
- *Loans* both general and limited partners may be secured or unsecured creditors of the partnership
- *Information* each partner has the right to inspect and copy the partnership records
- *Derivative Actions* a limited partner may sue on behalf of a limited partnership if the general partners refuse to bring the action

Duties and Liabilities

- *Duties* general partners owe a duty of care and loyalty (fiduciary duty) to the limited partners and the limited partnership; limited partners do not owe either of these duties
- *Liabilities* the general partners have unlimited liability; the limited partners have limited liability (liability for partnership obligations only to the extent of the capital that the limited partner contributed or agreed to contribute)

	Dissolution ■ *Causes* the limited partners do not have the right or the power to dissolve the partnership, except by decree of the court; the following events trigger a dissolution: (1) the expiration of the time period; (2) the withdrawal of a general partner, unless all partners agree to continue the business; or (3) a decree of judicial dissolution ■ *Winding Up* unless otherwise provided in the partnership agreement, the general partners who have not wrongfully dissolved the partnership may wind up its affairs ■ *Distribution of Assets* the priorities for distribution are as follows: (1) creditors including partners who are creditors; (2) partners and ex-partners in satisfaction of liabilities for unpaid distributions; (3) partners for the return of contributions except as otherwise agreed; and (4) partners for their partnership interests in the proportions in which they share in distributions, except as otherwise agreed
Other Unincorporated Business Associations	Joint Venture association of two or more persons to engage in a single business transaction for a profit Joint Stock Company a general partnership with some corporate attributes Mining Partnership a specific type of partnership for the purpose of extracting raw minerals Limited Partnership Association a partnership that closely resembles a corporation Business Trust a trust (managed by a trustee for the benefit of a beneficiary) established to conduct a business for a profit

QUESTIONS

1. Distinguish between a general partnership and a limited partnership.
2. Discuss the consequences of defective formation of a limited partnership.
3. Identify those activities in which a limited partner may engage without forfeiting limited liability.
4. Explain the order in which the assets of a limited partnership are distributed to creditors, limited partners, and general partners.
5. Distinguish among (a) joint ventures, (b) joint stock companies, (c) mining partnerships, (d) limited partnership associations, and (e) business trusts.

PROBLEMS

1. John Palmer and Henry Morrison formed the partnership of Palmer & Morrison for the management of the Huntington Hotel. The partnership agreement provided that Palmer would contribute $40,000 and be a general partner and Morrison would contribute $30,000 and be a limited partner. Palmer was to manage the dining and cocktail rooms, and Morrison was to manage the rest of the hotel. Nanette, a popular French singer, who knew nothing of the partnership affairs, appeared for four weeks in the Blue Room at the hotel and was not paid her fee of $8,000. Subsequently, Palmer and Morrison had a difference of opinion, and Palmer bought Morrison's interest in the partnership for

$20,000. Palmer later went into bankruptcy. Nanette sued Morrison for $8,000. For how much, if anything, is Morrison liable?

2. A limited partnership was formed consisting of Webster as the general partner and Stevens and Stewart as the limited partners. The limited partnership was organized in strict compliance with the limited partnership statute. Stevens was employed by the partnership as a purchasing agent. Stewart personally guaranteed a loan made to the partnership. Both Stevens and Stewart consulted with Webster about partnership business, voted on a change in the nature of the partnership business, and disapproved an amendment to the partnership agreement proposed by Webster. The partnership experienced serious financial difficulties and its creditors seek to hold Webster, Stevens, and Stewart personally liable for the debts of the partnership. Decision?

3. Fox, Dodge, and Gilbey agreed to become limited partners in Palatine Ventures, a limited partnership. The certificate of limited partnership stated that each would contribute $20,000. Fox's contribution consisted entirely of cash; Dodge contributed $12,000 in cash and gave the partnership her promissory note for $8,000; and Gilbey's contribution was his promise to perform 500 hours of legal services for the partnership. What liability, if any, do Fox, Dodge, and Gilbey have to the partnership by way of capital contribution?

4. Madison and Tilson agree to form a limited partnership with Madison as general partner and Tilson as the limited partner, each to contribute $12,500 as capital. No papers are ever filed, and after ten months the enterprise fails with liabilities exceeding assets by $30,000. Creditors of the partnership seek to hold Madison and Tilson personally liable for the $30,000. Decision?

5. Kraft is a limited partner of Johnson Enterprises, a limited partnership. As provided in the limited partnership agreement, Kraft decided to leave the partnership and demanded that her capital contribution of $20,000 be returned. At this time, the partnership assets were $150,000 and liabilities to all creditors totaled $140,000. The partnership returned to Kraft her capital contribution of $20,000. What liability, if any, does Kraft have to the creditors of Johnson Enterprises?

6. Gordon is the only limited partner in a limited partnership whose general partners are Daniels and McKenna. Gordon contributed $10,000 for his limited partnership interest and loaned the partnership $7,500. Daniels and McKenna each contributed $5,000 by way of capital. After a year, the partnership is dissolved, at which time it owes $12,500 to its only creditor, Dickel, and has assets of $30,000. How should these assets be distributed?

7. A limited partner has which of the following rights or powers: (a) to assign his interest in the limited partnership, (b) to receive repayment of loans made to the partnership on a *pro rata* basis with general creditors, (c) to manage the affairs of the limited partnership, (d) to receive his share of the profits before the general partners receive their share of the profits, (e) to dissolve the partnership if he withdraws from the partnership.

8. In January, Dr. Vidricksen contributed $25,000 to become a limited partner in a Chevrolet car agency business with Thom, the general partner. Articles of limited partnership were drawn up, but no effort was made to comply with the State's statutory requirement of recording the certificate of limited partnership. In March Vidricksen learned that he may not have formed a limited partnership because of the failure to file. At this time, the business developed financial difficulties and went into bankruptcy on September 11 of that year. Eight days later Vidricksen filed a renunciation of the business's profits. The trustee in bankruptcy now seeks to have Dr. Vidricksen adjudged a general partner for bankruptcy purposes. Decision?

ENDNOTES

1. Uniform Partnership Act, Section 6, Partnership Defined.

2. 1976 Revised Uniform Limited Partnership Act, Section 101(7), Definitions: Limited Partnership.

3. 1976 Revised Uniform Limited Partnership Act, Section 101(1), Definitions: Person.

4. 1976 Revised Uniform Limited Partnership Act, Section 201, Certificate of Limited Partnership.

5. 1976 Revised Uniform Limited Partnership Act, Section 202, Amendment to Certificate.

6. 1985 Revised Uniform Limited Partnership Act, Section 201, Certificate of Limited Partnership.

7. 1976 Revised Uniform Limited Partnership Act, Section 303, Liability to Third Parties.

8. 1976 Revised Uniform Limited Partnership Act, Section 102, Name.

9. 1976 Revised Uniform Limited Partnership Act, Section 501, Form of Contribution.

10. 1985 Revised Uniform Limited Partnership Act, Section 502, Liability for Contribution.

11. 1976 Revised Uniform Limited Partnership Act, Section 304, Person Erroneously Believing Himself Limited Partner.

12. 1976 Revised Uniform Limited Partnership Act, Section 901, Law Governing.

13. 1976 Revised Uniform Limited Partnership Act, Section 902, Registration.

14. 1976 Revised Uniform Limited Partnership Act, Section 403, General Powers and Liabilities.

15. 1985 Revised Uniform Limited Partnership Act, Section 303, Liability to Third Parties.

16. 1976 Revised Uniform Limited Partnership Act, Section 301, Admission of Additional Limited Partners.

17. 1976 Revised Uniform Limited Partnership Act, Section 401, Admission of Additional General Partners.

18. 1985 Revised Uniform Limited Partnership Act, Section 401, Admission of Additional General Partners.

19. 1976 Revised Uniform Limited Partnership Act, Section 602, Withdrawal of General Partner.

20. 1976 and 1985 Revised Uniform Limited Partnership Act, Section 603, Withdrawal of Limited Partner.

21. 1976 Revised Uniform Limited Partnership Act, Section 702, Assignment of Partnership Interest.

22. 1976 and 1985 Revised Uniform Limited Partnership Act, Section 704, Right of Assignee to Become Limited Partner.

23. 1976 Revised Uniform Limited Partnership Act, Section 503, Sharing of Profits and Losses.

24. 1985 Revised Uniform Limited Partnership Act, Section 503, Sharing of Profits and Losses.

25. 1976 Revised Uniform Limited Partnership Act, Section 607, Limitations on Distribution.

26. 1976 Revised Uniform Limited Partnership Act, Section 107, Business Transactions of Partner with the Partnership.

27. 1976 Revised Uniform Limited Partnership Act, Section 105, Records to Be Kept.

28. 1976 Revised Uniform Limited Partnership Act, Section 1001, Right of Action.

29. 1976 Revised Uniform Limited Partnership Act, Section 207, Liability for False Statement in Certificate.

30. 1976 Revised Uniform Limited Partnership Act, Section 801, Nonjudicial Dissolution.

31. 1976 Revised Uniform Limited Partnership Act, Section 803, Winding Up.

32. 1976 Revised Uniform Limited Partnership Act, Section 804, Distribution of Assets.

PART 7
CORPORATIONS

Corporations are without question the major form of business organization in the United States. Corporate assets currently exceed $5 trillion, corporate revenues are almost $7 trillion annually, and about thirty million persons directly own shares in corporations. In addition, more than 100 million persons own shares indirectly through institutional investors, such as banks, insurance companies, pension funds, and investment companies. Moreover, corporations employ three-fourths of the nation's labor force.

There are two basic types of corporations—closely held and publicly held. Harry Henn and John Alexander describe the two forms in *Laws of Corporations:*

> The closely-held corporation desires to function and does function very differently from the larger corporations with public shareholders. In the closely-held corporation, there are usually no public investors; its shareholders are active in the conduct and management of the business (with resulting coincidence of control and management); the insiders want to keep out outsiders (delectus personae), and the emphasis is on simplified and informal procedures with all participating, with attendant possible risk of deadlock. In short, its member or members desire to gain certain corporate advantages, such as limited liability and certain corporate tax consequences (with minimization of double taxation), at the same time preserving many of the internal attributes of an individual proprietorship or partnership.
>
> In contrast with the closely-held corporation, larger corporations with public shareholders and other investors necessarily involve substantial separation of ownership and control, have a form of representative government-by-the-majority, with management delegated to a board of directors, following rather formal procedures, and operate in a relatively institutionalized and depersonalized manner, which is not susceptible to deadlock. The transfer of its shares is usually not only free from transfer restrictions but is facilitated by securities exchange listing or an active over-the-counter market. H. Henn and J. Alexander, *Laws of Corporations* 696 (1983).

Most incorporated business entities in the United States are closely held. Nonetheless, their special needs, which in many instances differ from those of publicly held corporations, have not until recently received any specific statutory attention. One of the difficulties in drafting such legislation is the great diversity of closely held corporations. Nevertheless, they do have one common problem: minority shareholders in closely held corporations are especially in need of protection from oppression exerted by other shareholders. Because the typical shareholder has a relatively large investment of his time and financial assets committed to the closely held corporation, the need to protect his reasonable expectations is greater than that of a shareholder in a publicly held corporation. Although many forms of unfair treatment exist, there are two basic types of oppression in a closely held corporation. First, and probably most widespread, is the oppression of the minority shareholders by the majority shareholders. Without specific legal protection, the minority shareholders are essentially subject to the good will of the majority. The second type of oppression is that exercised by the minority on the majority shareholders, which can occur when minority shareholders who have a veto power over action desired by the majority misuse their power. Under these circumstances, the majority needs an adequate remedy to resolve the deadlock. In the absence of special statutes for closely held corporations (only some States have such legislation), the shareholders must provide their own protection through carefully drawn shareholder agreements and bylaws. While studying the corporate legal norms in the next four chapters, you should be alert to their failure to address the special requirements of the most common of corporations, the closely held corporation.

Whereas the shareholders of a closely held corporation need protection from oppression by other *shareholders*, those who own shares in a publicly held corporation need protection from unfair treatment by *management*, that is, the officers of the corporation who are supposedly selected by the board of directors who are elected by the shareholders. "In reality, this legal image is virtually a myth. In nearly every large American business corporation, there exists a management autocracy. One man—variously titled the President, or the Chairman of the Board, or the Chief Executive Officer—or a small coterie of men rule the corporation. Far from being chosen by the directors to run the corporation, this chief executive or executive clique chooses the board of directors and, with the acquiescence of the board, controls the corporation." R. Nader, M. Green, and J. Seligman, *Taming the Giant Corporation* 75–76 (1976). In a classic study published in 1932, Adolf Berle and Gardner Means concluded that great amounts of economic power had been concentrated in a relatively few large corporations, that the ownership of these corporations had become widely dispersed, and that the shareholders of these corporations had become far removed from active participation in management. Since their original study, these trends have steadily continued, and the 500 largest U.S. industrial corporations have sales of around $2,000 billion, profits of about $100 billion, assets of over $1,000 billion, and more than fifteen million employees.

Thus, vast amounts of wealth and power are now controlled by a small number of corporations, which are in turn controlled by a small group of corporate officers. In fact, the separation of ownership and control has widened so far that Myles Mace, a leading scholar in this area, has stated that boards of directors are so reluctant to discharge ineffective management that they fire a chief executive only when "the leadership of the [chief executive] was so unsatisfactory that even his mother thought he ought [to be removed] for the good of the company . . . before the board [of directors] reluctantly moved." Testimony before the SEC, September 30, 1977.

These developments raise a large number of social, policy, and ethical issues about how large publicly owned corporations are governed. These issues include the following: Who is actually running these corporations, and who should run them? To whom are they accountable, and to whom should they be accountable? What role should employees and shareholders have in corporate governance? Should the existing system of governance be changed, and if so, how? Is chartering by the States effective, or should these corporations be Federally chartered? The resolution of these and other issues is critical to dealing with a number of national policy issues affecting business, such as long-term economic prospects, employment policies, health and safety in the workplace, the quality of products, the effects of overseas operations, and environmental decisions. While reading the chapters on corporations, keep in mind the social, policy, and ethical concerns that have an impact on the operations of the large publicly held American business corporation.

33 NATURE AND FORMATION

A corporation is an entity created by law that exists separately and distinctly from the individuals whose contributions of initiative, property, and control enable it to function. The corporation is the dominant form of business organization in the United States, accounting for 90 percent of the gross revenues of all business entities (see Figure 33–1). Domestic corporations currently doing business in the United States number over three million, with annual revenues and assets in the trillions of dollars. Approximately thirty million Americans own shares of stock, while more than one hundred million additional people own stock indirectly through institutional investors such as banks, insurance companies, pension funds, and investment companies. Corporations have achieved this dominance because their attributes of limited liability, free transferability of shares, and continuity enabled them

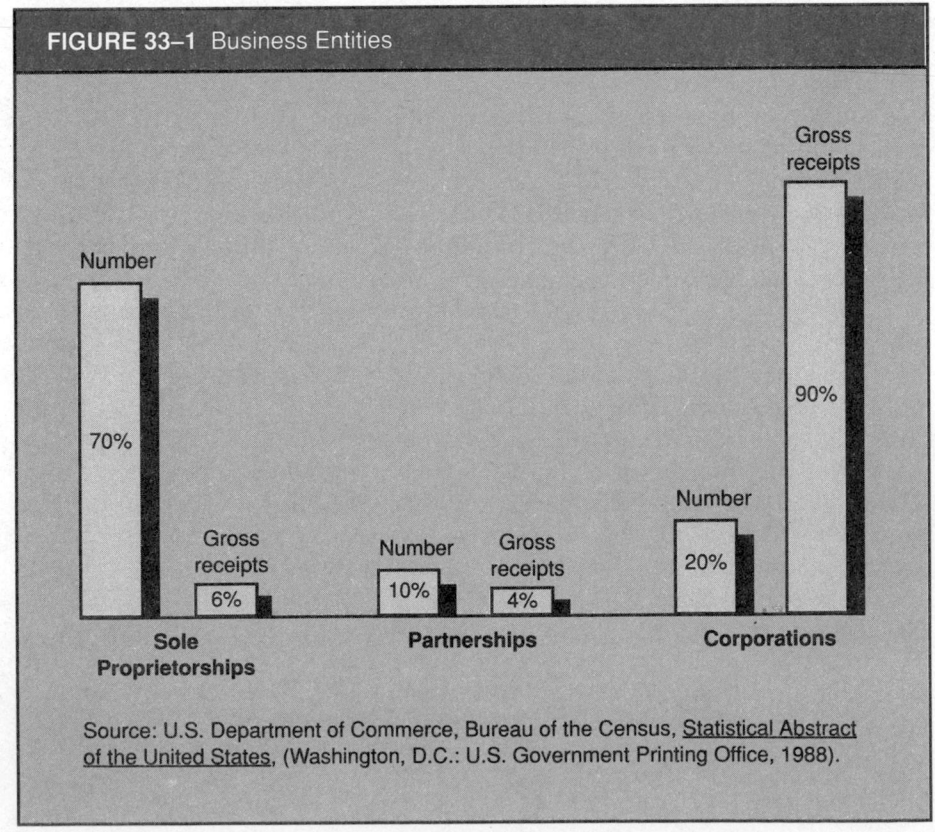

FIGURE 33–1 Business Entities

Number
70%

Gross receipts
6%

Sole Proprietorships

Number
10%

Gross receipts
4%

Partnerships

Number
20%

Gross receipts
90%

Corporations

Source: U.S. Department of Commerce, Bureau of the Census, Statistical Abstract of the United States, (Washington, D.C.: U.S. Government Printing Office, 1988).

to attract great numbers of widespread investors. Moreover, corporations' centralized management facilitated development of large organizations that could employ great quantities of invested capital so as to take advantage of economies of scale.

Use of the corporation as an instrument of commercial enterprise has made possible the vast concentrations of wealth and capital that have largely transformed this country from an agrarian to an industrial economy. Due to its size, power, and impact, the business corporation is a key institution not only in the American economy but also in the world power structure.

In 1946 a committee of the American Bar Association, after careful study and research, submitted a draft of a Model State Business Corporation Act (MBCA). The Model Act has been amended frequently since then. The provisions of the Model Act do not become law until enacted by a State, but its influence has been widespread, and it has been adopted in whole or in part by a majority of the States. As a recommended model statute, it sets a standard for the statutory law of business corporations, and we will use it throughout the chapters on corporations in this text. Because a number of States have not amended their versions of the MBCA, the text will discuss the Model Act in both its amended and unamended forms. Appendix G of this text contains selected provisions of the MBCA as amended.

In 1984 the Committee on Corporate Laws of the Section of Corporation, Banking, and Business Law of the American Bar Association approved a Revised Model Business Corporation Act (RMBCA). The Revised Act is the first complete revision of the Model Act in over thirty years, although there had been numerous statutory amendments to it since it was first published. One of the tasks of the revision was to reorganize the provisions of the Model Act more logically and to revise the language to make the act more consistent. In addition, substantive changes were made in a number of areas. We will discuss those provisions of the Revised Act that have made significant changes in the Model Act as amended. The revision will be referred to as the Revised Act

or the RMBCA. Appendix H of this text contains selected provisions of the RMBCA.

NATURE OF CORPORATIONS

Corporations can be most readily understood by examining the common attributes and the various types of corporations. We discuss both of these topics in this section.

CORPORATE ATTRIBUTES

The principal attributes of a corporation are that (1) it is a legal entity; (2) it owes its existence to a State, which also regulates it; (3) it provides limited liability to its shareholders; (4) its shares of stock are freely transferable; (5) it may have perpetual existence; (6) its management is centralized; and it is considered, for some purposes, (7) a person, and (8) a citizen.

Legal Entity

A corporation is a **legal entity** separate and apart from its shareholders, with rights and liabilities entirely distinct from theirs. It may sue or be sued by, as well as contract with, any other party, including any one of its shareholders. A transfer of stock in the corporation from one individual to another has no effect on the legal existence of the corporation. Title to corporate property belongs not to the shareholders but to the corporation. Even where a single individual owns all of the stock of the corporation, the shareholder and the corporation are not the same but have separate and distinct existences.

Creature of the State

A corporation may be formed only by compliance with a State incorporation statute. A corporation's charter and the provisions of the statute under which it is formed constitute a contract between it and the State. Article I, Section 10, of the United States Constitution provides that no State shall pass any law "impairing the obligation of contracts," and this prohibition applies to contracts between a State and a corporation.

To avoid the impact of this provision, incorporation statutes reserve to the State the power to prescribe such regulations, provisions, and limitations as it deems advisable and to amend, repeal, or modify the statute at its pleasure.[1] This reservation is a material part of the contract between the State and a corporation formed under the statute, and amendments or modifications regulating or altering the structure of the corporation do not impair the obligation of contract because they are expressly permitted by the contract.

Limited Liability

A corporation is a legal entity and is therefore liable out of its own assets for its debts. Generally, the shareholders have **limited liability** for the corporation's debts—their liability does not extend beyond the amount of their investment—although later in this chapter we discuss certain circumstances under which a shareholder may be personally liable.

Free Transferability of Corporate Shares

In the absence of contractual restrictions, shares in a corporation may be freely transferred by sale, gift, or pledge. The ability to transfer shares is a valuable right and may enhance their market value. Transfers of shares of stock are governed by Article 8 of the Uniform Commercial Code, Investment Securities, and are discussed in Chapter 34.

Perpetual Existence

A corporation has perpetual existence unless otherwise stated in its articles of incorporation.[2] As a consequence, the death, withdrawal, or addition of a shareholder, director, or officer does not terminate the existence of a corporation.

Centralized Management

The shareholders of a corporation elect the board of directors, which manages the business affairs of the corporation. The board must then appoint officers to run the day-to-day operations of the business. Because neither the directors nor the officers (collectively referred to as "management") need be shareholders, it is entirely possible, and in large corporations quite typical, for the ownership of the corporation to be separated from the management of the corporation. We discuss the management structure of corporations in Chapter 35.

As a Person

Whether a corporation is a "person" within the meaning of a constitution or statute is a matter of construction based on the intent of the lawmakers in using the word. For example, a corporation is considered a person within the provision in the Fifth and Fourteenth Amendments to the Federal Constitution that no "person" shall be "deprived of life, liberty or property without due process of law" and in the provision in the Fourteenth Amendment that no State shall "deny to any person within its jurisdiction the equal protection of the laws." A corporation also enjoys the right of a person to be secure against unreasonable searches and seizures, as provided for in the Fourth Amendment. On the other hand, a corporation is not considered to be a person within the clause of the Fifth Amendment that protects a "person" against self-incrimination.

As a Citizen

A corporation is considered a citizen for some purposes but not for others. A corporation is not a citizen as the term is used in the Fourteenth Amendment, which provides "No state shall make or enforce any law which shall abridge the privileges or immunities of citizens of the United States."

A corporation, however, is regarded as a citizen of the State of its incorporation and of the State in which it has its principal office for the purpose of determining whether diversity of citizenship exists between the parties to a lawsuit as a basis for jurisdiction of the Federal courts.

Corporations differ from partnerships because of these and other attributes. Figure 33–2 further outlines the differences and sim-

FIGURE 33–2 General Partnership, Limited Partnership, and Corporation Compared

	Partnership	Limited Partnership*	Corporation
Creation	By agreement of the parties	By statutory authorization	By statutory authorization
Entity	A legal entity for some but not all purposes	A legal entity for some but not all purposes	A legal entity
Duration	Dissolved by death, bankruptcy, or withdrawal of a partner	Limited partner may dissolve partnership only by decree of court	May be perpetual
Liability	Partners are subject to unlimited liability upon the contracts, debts, and torts of the partnership	Limited partners are not generally liable for the contracts, debts, or torts of the partnership	Shareholders are not generally liable for the contracts, debts, or torts of the corporation
Transferability	Interest of a partner in a partnership may be assigned; but the assignee does not become a partner	Interest of a limited partner may be assigned and assignee may become a substituted limited partner if all members consent	Shares of stock in a corporation are freely transferable
Management	Each partner is entitled to an equal voice in the management and control of the business	Limited partner may not take part in control of the business	The business of the corporation is managed by a board of directors elected by the shareholders
Agency	Each partner is an agent of the partnership	Limited partner is not an agent of the partnership	A shareholder is neither a principal nor an agent of the corporation
Suits	In actions brought by or against the partnership all partners are generally necessary parties	Limited partners are not a necessary party except where suit is to enforce their rights against or liability to the partnership	The corporation may sue and be sued in its own name

*A general partner of a limited partnership has all the rights, powers, and liabilities of a partner in a general partnership.

ilarities of general partnerships, limited partnerships, and corporations.

CLASSIFICATION OF CORPORATIONS

Corporations may be classified as public or private, profit or nonprofit, domestic or foreign, closely held, and professional. As you will see, these classifications are not mutually exclusive. For example, a corporation may be a closely held, professional, private, profit, domestic corporation.

Public or Private

A **public corporation** is one that is created to administer a unit of local civil government, such as a county, city, town, village, school district, or park district or one created by the United States to conduct public business, such as the Tennessee Valley Authority or the Federal Deposit Insurance Corporation. A public corporation is usually created by specific legislation, which determines the corporation's purpose and powers. Many public corporations are also referred to as municipal corporations.

A **private corporation** is one organized to conduct either a privately owned business enterprise for profit or a nonprofit corporation organized for community benefit or enjoyment.

Profit or Nonprofit

A **profit corporation** is one founded for the purpose of operating a business for profit from which payments are made to its shareholders in the form of dividends.

Although a **nonprofit** (or not-for-profit) **corporation** may make a profit, the profit may not be distributed to its members, directors, or officers but must be used exclusively for the charitable, educational, or scientific purpose for which it was organized. Examples of nonprofit corporations include private schools, library clubs, athletic clubs, fraternities, sororities, and hospitals. Most States have special incorporation statutes governing nonprofit corporations, some of which are patterned after the Model Nonprofit Corporation Act.

Domestic or Foreign

A corporation is a **domestic corporation** in the State in which it is incorporated. It is a **foreign corporation** in every other State or jurisdiction. A corporation may not do business, except for acts in interstate commerce, in a State other than the State of its incorporation without the permission and authorization of the other State.[3] Every State, however, provides for the issuance to foreign corporations of a certificate to do business within its borders and for the taxation of such foreign businesses. Obtaining a certificate (called "qualifying") usually involves filing certain information with the Secretary of State,[4] the payment of prescribed fees, and designation of a resident agent.[5] Conduct typically requiring a certificate of authority includes maintaining an office to conduct local intrastate business, selling personal property not in interstate commerce, entering into contracts relating to local business or sales, and owning or using real estate for general corporate purposes. A single agreement or isolated transaction within a State does not constitute doing business, as in the next case.

A foreign corporation that transacts business without having first qualified may be subject to a number of penalties. Most statutes provide that an unlicensed foreign corporation doing business in the State shall not be entitled to maintain a suit in the State courts until it has obtained a certificate of authority.[6] Failure to obtain a certificate of authority to transact business in the State, however, does not impair the validity of a contract entered into by the corporation and does not prevent it from defending any action or proceeding brought against it in the State.[6] In addition, many States impose fines on corporations that do not obtain certificates, and a few States also impose fines on the corporation's officers and directors as well as holding them personally liable on contracts made within the State.

A State also may specify conditions under which a license or certificate of authority shall be revoked. In general, the statutes provide that a failure to pay taxes, file reports, or maintain a registered agent or registered office in the State will justify revocation of a license.

JOHNSON v. MPL LEASING CORP.
Supreme Court of Alabama, 1983.
441 So.2d 904.

Facts: MPL Leasing Corporation is a California corporation that provides financing plans to dealers of Saxon Business Products. MPL invited Jay Johnson, a Saxon dealer in Alabama, to attend a sales seminar in Atlanta. MPL and Johnson entered into an agreement under which Johnson was to lease Saxon copiers with an option to buy. MPL shipped the equipment into Alabama and filed a financing statement with the Secretary of State. When Johnson became delinquent with his payments to MPL, MPL brought an action against Johnson in an Alabama court. Johnson moved to dismiss the action, claiming that MPL was not qualified to conduct business in Alabama and was thus barred from enforcing its contract with Johnson in an Alabama court. The trial court entered judgment in favor of MPL.

Decision: Judgment for MPL affirmed.

Opinion: **Torbert, C. J.** Section 232 of the Alabama Constitution and § 10-2A-247, Code 1975, bar foreign corporations not qualified to do business in this state from enforcing their contracts through our courts. These laws only come into play "when the business conducted in the state by non-qualified corporations is considered 'intrastate' in nature." [Citations.] MPL's activities within Alabama are limited to (1) delivering copying machines by common carrier and (2) filing this action. This Court has never held previously that contacts as minimal as those of MPL constitute "intrastate business."

For example, in [citation], this Court considered whether the foreign, non-qualifying corporation's contacts were sufficient to constitute "intrastate" business. The facts in [citation] are indistinguishable from those in this case. The corporation's activities in Alabama were "simply solicitation of orders and delivery incident to that solicitation." [Citation.] This Court held that "[the plaintiff], conducting business in interstate commerce, is justified and welcomed to use the state courts of Alabama to enforce its claim against those who defaulted on payment of an order which was delivered here." [Citation.]

* * *

The appellant cites several cases for the proposition that solicitation of sales constitutes "doing business." [Citation] held that a foreign, non-qualifying corporation (SAR) could not sue on a promissory note against an Alabama co-maker. Unlike MPL, SAR expanded its operation by purchasing a warehouse in Alabama, maintaining two vehicles in Alabama, and employing seven Alabama residents full-time. These factors were "localized enough to easily fall under the ambit of a series of transactions which are primarily intrastate and concomitantly the corporation falls under the satrapy of the qualification statutes. . . ." [Citation.]

In [citation], the Court confused the test for minimum contacts for service of process with the test for determining whether a foreign corporation must qualify to do business in order to sue in state court. The minimum contacts test for service of process protects defendants against the burden of litigating in a distant forum. The doing business test for qualifying foreign corporations is governed by the limits on state regulation inherent in the Commerce Clause of the United States Constitution. [Citations.] As these decisions make clear, it is far easier to find that a foreign corporation is "doing business" for service of process than it is to find that the corporation is conducting intrastate business subject to state regulation in view of the Commerce Clause.

* * *

Therefore, we hold that MPL is welcome to use Alabama courts to enforce rights arising from the agreement with Johnson. The judgment is affirmed.

Closely Held

A **corporation** is described as **closely held** when its outstanding shares of stock are held by a small number of persons, frequently family relatives or friends. In most closely held corporations, the shareholders are active in the management and control of the business. Accordingly, the shareholders are concerned with who their fellow shareholders are, and therefore they typically enter into a buy-sell agreement with one another at the time of incorporation in order to prevent the stock from getting into the hands of persons outside the original group of shareholders. Although most corporations in the United States are closely held, they account for only a small fraction of corporate revenues and assets.

In most States, closely held corporations are subject to the general incorporation statute that governs all corporations. The 1969 amendments to the MBCA included a number of liberalizing provisions for closely held corporations. These amendments were carried over to the RMBCA. Some States, however, have enacted special legislation to accommodate the needs of closely held corporations, and a Statutory Close Corporation Supplement to the MBCA (Supplement) has recently been promulgated.

The Supplement applies only to those eligible corporations that elect statutory close corporation status. To be eligible, a corporation must have fewer than fifty shareholders. A corporation may voluntarily terminate statutory close corporation status. We will discuss other provisions of the Supplement in this and other chapters.

Professional Corporations

All of the States have professional association or corporation statutes that permit the practice of professions by duly licensed individuals in the corporate form. Some statutes apply to all professions licensed to practice within the State, whereas others apply only to specified professions. There is a Model Professional Corporation Supplement to the MBCA.

FORMATION OF A CORPORATION

Incorporation involves greater expense and formality than the formation of any other form of business organization. The formation of a corporation under a general incorporation statute requires the performance of several acts by various groups, individuals, and State officials. The procedure to organize a corporation begins with the promotion of the proposed corporation by its organizers, also known as promoters, who procure offers by interested persons known as subscribers to buy stock in the corporation when created and who also prepare the necessary incorporation papers. The articles of incorporation are then executed by the incorporators and filed with the Secretary of State, who issues the charter or certificate of incorporation. Finally, an organization meeting is held by the incorporators, shareholders, or directors.

ORGANIZING THE CORPORATION

Promoters

A **promoter** is a person who brings about the "birth" of a corporation. The promoter arranges for the capital and financing of the corporation as well as assembling the necessary assets, equipment, licenses, personnel, leases, and services. He will also attend to the actual legal formation of the corporation. On incorporation, the promoter's organizational task is finished.

Promoters' Contracts In addition to procuring subscriptions and preparing the incorporation papers, promoters often enter into contracts in anticipation of the creation of the corporation. The contracts may be ordinary agreements necessary for the eventual operation of the business, such as leases, purchase orders, employment contracts, sales contracts, or franchises. If these contracts are executed by the promoter in her own name and there is no further action, the promoter is liable on such contracts, and the corporation, when created, is not liable. Moreover, a preincorporation contract made by promoters in the name of the corporation and on its behalf does not bind the corporation, except where so provided by statute. The promoter, in executing such contracts, may do so in the corporate name even though incorporation has not yet taken place. Before its formation, a corporation has no capacity to enter into contracts or to employ agents or representatives. After its formation, it is not liable at common law on any prior contract, even one made in its name, unless it adopts or ratifies the contract expressly, impliedly, or by knowingly accepting benefits under it.

A promoter who enters into a preincorporation contract in the name of the corporation usually remains liable on that contract even if the corporation adopts or ratifies the contract. This results from the rule of agency law that a principal must be in existence at the time a contract is made in order to ratify it. A promoter will be relieved of liability, however, if the contract itself provides that adoption shall terminate the promoter's liability or if the promoter, the third party, and the corporation enter into a novation substituting the corporation for the promoter.

Figure 33–3 summarizes the liability of the promoter and the corporation for preincorporation contracts.

Promoters' Fiduciary Duty The promoters of a corporation have a fiduciary relationship

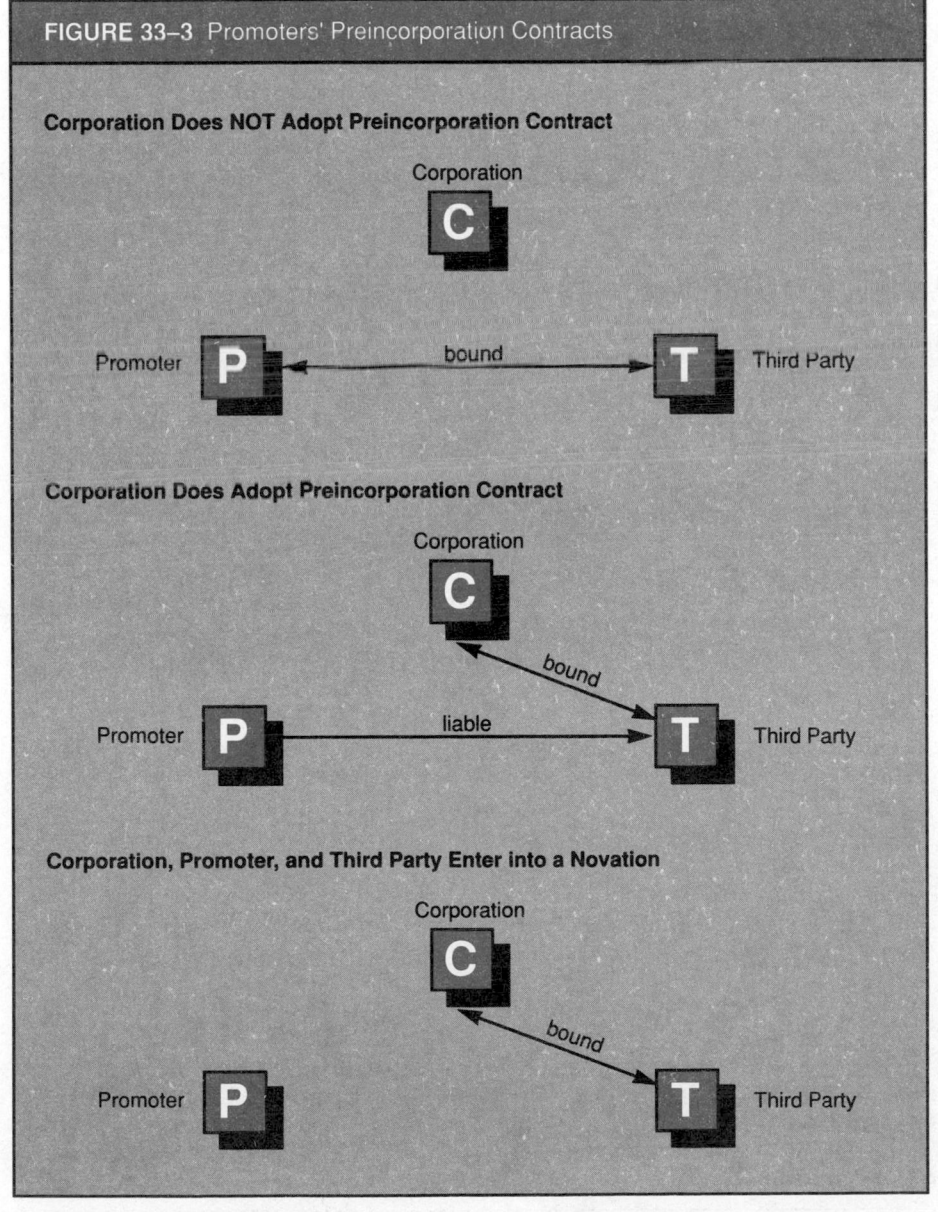

FIGURE 33–3 Promoters' Preincorporation Contracts

Corporation Does NOT Adopt Preincorporation Contract

Corporation

Promoter   bound   Third Party

Corporation Does Adopt Preincorporation Contract

Corporation

Promoter   bound   liable   Third Party

Corporation, Promoter, and Third Party Enter into a Novation

Corporation

Promoter   bound   Third Party

among themselves as well as with the corporation, its subscribers, and its initial shareholders. This duty requires good faith, fair dealing, and full disclosure to an independent board of directors. If an independent board has not been elected, then full disclosure must be made to all shareholders. Accordingly, the promoters are under a duty to account for any secret profit realized by them at the expense of those to whom this duty is owing. Failure to disclose may also violate Federal or State securities laws, discussed in Chapter 43.

GOLDEN v. OAHE ENTERPRISES, INC.
Supreme Court of South Dakota, 1980.
295 N.W.2d 160.

Facts: Oahe Enterprises was formed by the efforts of Emmick, who acted as a promoter and contributed shares of Colonial Manors, Inc. (CM), stock in exchange for stock in Oahe. The CM stock had been valued by CM's directors for internal stock-option purposes at $19 per share. One month prior to Emmick's incorporation of Oahe Enterprises, however, CM's board reduced the stock value to $9.50 per share. Although Emmick knew of this reduction prior to the meeting to form Oahe Enterprises, he did not disclose this information to the Morrises, the other shareholders of the new corporation. Oahe Enterprises then brought this action to recover the shortfall. The trial court found for Emmick.

Decision: Judgment for Emmick reversed and case remanded to the trial court with directions to redetermine the fair market value of the CM stock exchanged by Emmick for Oahe stock.

Opinion: **Wollman, C. J.**   Courts faced with the situation in which a promoter benefits from a violation of his fiduciary duty at the expense of the corporation or its members often characterize the promoter's gain as "secret profit." Such profit is not secret if all interested parties know of and assent to it. But where a promoter through, for example, overvaluation of property exchanged for stock and failure to disclose all material facts regarding such exchange, takes more from the corporation than he transfers in, he is held liable for what courts term secret profit. [Citations.]

  As a promoter of Oahe, Emmick stood in a fiduciary relationship to both the corporation and its stockholders and was bound to deal with them in the utmost good faith. "The obtaining of a secret profit by a promoter through the sale of property to a corporation is uniformly held to be a fraud on the corporation and stockholders, and the promoter may be required to account for such profit." [Citation.]

  The valuation of the CM stock was based on Emmick's self-serving estimate of matters well known to him as a CM insider and was warped by Emmick's self-interest. Emmick was not trading stock that had an easily ascertainable value; he was not dealing with people experienced in transactions of this type. He failed to make known facts of which he, as an insider of CM, was aware. It is true that Emmick was not the only member of the Oahe board of directors. He was, however, the controlling member and the one in possession of information pertinent to the value of his CM stock not generally available to the public or to the other Oahe board members. In addition to being an insider of CM, he was both a director of and the dominant and controlling force in Oahe. We hold, therefore, that he failed in his duty to the corporation to disclose information regarding stock he intended to transfer into Oahe for Oahe shares and is therefore liable for the shortfall to the corporation therefrom.

***

Because the total value of the CM stock Emmick transferred to Oahe was less than the value Emmick received in Oahe stock, the difference can be equalized by canceling the number of Oahe shares held by Emmick that is proportional to the overevaluation. [Citations.] We note that this Court has upheld the cancellation of stock under circumstances where original issue stock was transferred for the worthless stock of another corporation or for services to be performed in the future.

Subscribers

A **preincorporation subscription** is an offer to purchase capital stock in a corporation yet to be formed. The offeror is called a **subscriber.** Courts have traditionally viewed subscriptions in two ways. The majority regards a subscription as a continuing offer to purchase stock from a nonexisting entity, which is incapable of accepting the offer until created. Under this view, a subscription may be revoked at any time prior to its acceptance. A minority of jurisdictions treat a subscription as a contract among the various subscribers, which makes it irrevocable except with the consent of all of the subscribers. Modern incorporation statutes have taken an intermediate position in resolving this issue. The MBCA provides that a subscription is irrevocable for a period of six months, unless otherwise provided in the subscription agreement or unless all of the subscribers consent to the revocation of the subscription.[7] If the corporation accepts the subscription during the period of irrevocability, the subscription becomes a contract binding on both the subscriber and the corporation.

Selection of State for Incorporation

A corporation is usually incorporated in the State in which it intends to be located and transact all or the principal part of its business. A corporation may be formed in one State, however, and have its principal place of business and conduct all or most of its operations in another State or States by duly qualifying and obtaining a certificate of authority to transact business in the other States. The principal criteria useful in selecting a State for incorporation include the flexibility accorded management, the rights granted to shareholders, the

limitations imposed on the issuance of shares, the restrictions placed on the payment of dividends, and the organizational costs such as fees and taxes.

FORMALITIES OF INCORPORATION

Although the procedure involved in organizing a corporation varies to some extent from State to State, typically the incorporators execute and deliver to the Secretary of State or another designated official, articles of incorporation in duplicate, which in effect are an application for a charter. The Model Act provides that after issuance of the certificate of incorporation, an organizational meeting of the board of directors named in the articles of incorporation shall be held for the purpose of adopting bylaws, electing officers, and transacting such other business as may come before the meeting.[8] After completion of these organizational details, the corporation's business and affairs are managed by its board of directors and by its officers.

Selection of Name

Most general incorporation laws require that the name contain a word or words that clearly indicate that it is a corporation, such as "corporation," "company," "incorporated," "limited," "Corp.," "Co.," "Inc.," or "Ltd."[9] No corporate name may be the same as, or deceptively similar to, the name of any domestic corporation or any foreign corporation authorized to do business within the State.

Incorporators

The incorporators are the persons who sign the articles of incorporation filed with the Secretary of State of the State of incorporation.

Although they perform a necessary function, their services as incorporators are perfunctory and short-lived, ending with the organizational meeting of the initial board of directors following the issuance of the certificate of incorporation. Accordingly, modern statutes have greatly relaxed the qualifications of incorporators and reduced the number required. The Model Act, for example, provides that one or more persons or a domestic or foreign corporation may act as incorporators.[10]

Articles of Incorporation

The articles of incorporation or **charter** is generally a rather simple document that includes:

1. the name of the corporation;
2. the address of the corporation's registered office and the name of its registered agent;
3. the purpose for which the corporation is organized;
4. the period of duration, which may be perpetual;
5. the number of authorized shares and designations of classes of shares;
6. the number and names of the initial directors;
7. the name and address of each incorporator; and
8. the preemptive rights of shareholders, if any.[11]

In addition, the articles of incorporation *may* include provisions consistent with the incorporation statute and other law regarding the management of the corporation, limitations of the powers of the corporation and its director and shareholders, restrictions on the transfer of shares, and the par value of shares, as well as any provision permitted or required to be included in the bylaws.

The Revised Act requires even less information: the name of the corporation; the number of authorized shares; the street address of the registered office and the name of the registered agent; and the name and address of each incorporator.[12] The Revised Act permits optional information to be included in the charter, such as the initial directors, corporate purposes, management of internal affairs, powers of the corporation, authority of officers and directors, par value of shares, and any provision required or permitted to be set forth in the bylaws.

Figure 33–4 shows a sample charter. After the charter is drawn up, it must be signed and filed with the Secretary of State.[13] The articles of incorporation then become the basic governing document of the corporation, so long as its provisions are consistent with State and Federal law.

Organizational Meeting

The Model Act requires that an organizational meeting be held to adopt the bylaws, elect officers, and transact "such other business as may come before the meeting."[8] Such business typically includes authorization to issue shares of stock, approval of preincorporation contracts made by promoters, and selection of a bank, as well as approval of a corporate seal and the form of stock certificates.

Bylaws

The **bylaws** of a corporation are the rules and regulations that govern its internal management. They are necessary to its organization, and the adoption of bylaws is one of the first items of business at the organizational meeting held promptly after incorporation.[8] The bylaws may not contain anything contrary to or inconsistent with any provision in the incorporation statute or in the articles of incorporation.[14] In contrast to the certificate of incorporation, which embodies the articles of incorporation, the bylaws do not have to be publicly filed and in many States may be changed without shareholder approval. Under the Revised Act, the shareholders may amend or repeal the bylaws.[15] In addition, the board of directors may also amend or repeal the bylaws unless the articles of incorporation or other sections of the RMBCA reserve that power exclusively to the shareholders in whole or in part.[15]

The Statutory Close Corporation Supplement permits close corporations *not* to adopt any bylaws if all information required to be stated in corporate bylaws is included either in a shareholder agreement or in the articles of incorporation.

RECOGNITION OR DISREGARD OF CORPORATENESS

Business associates choose to incorporate to obtain one or more of the corporate attributes,

---

FIGURE 33-4 Sample Articles of Incorporation

ARTICLES OF INCORPORATION OF [CORPORATE NAME]

The undersigned, acting as incorporator(s) of a corporation under the _____ Business Corporation Act, adopt(s) the following Articles of Incorporation for such corporation:

First: The name of the corporation is _____

_____

Second: The period of its duration is _____

Third: The purpose or purposes for which the corporation is organized are: _____

_____

Fourth: The aggregate number of shares which the corporation shall have authority to issue is _____

_____

Fifth: Provisions granting preemptive rights are:

Sixth: Provisions for the regulation of the internal affairs of the corporation are: _____

Seventh: The address of the initial registered office of the corporation is _____ and the name of its initial registered agent at such address is _____

_____

Eighth: The number of directors constituting the initial board of directors of the corporation is _____, and the names and addresses of the persons who are to serve as directors until the first annual meeting of share holders or until their successors are elected and shall qualify are:

Name	Address
_____	_____
_____	_____
_____	_____

Ninth: The name and address of each incorporator is:

Name	Address
_____	_____
_____	_____

Dated _____, 19___ .

_____
_____
_____

Incorporator(s)

Source: Reprinted with permission from Henn & Alexander, Corporations, 3rd ed. Copyright © 1983 by West Publishing Company.

primarily limited liability and perpetual existence. Because a corporation is a creature of the State, such corporate attributes are recognized when the enterprise complies with the State's requirements for incorporation. Although the formal procedures are relatively simple, errors or omissions sometimes occur. In some cases the mistakes may be trivial, such as an incorrect address of an incorporator; in other instances the error may be more significant, such as a complete failure to file the articles of incorporation. The consequences of noncompliance with the statutory incorporation procedure depend on the seriousness of the error. Conversely, even when a corporation has been formed in strict compliance with the incorporation statute, a court may disregard the corporateness of the enterprise if justice requires. In this section we address these two complementary issues.

DEFECTIVE INCORPORATION

The frequency of defective attempts to incorporate has been greatly reduced by the simplified incorporation procedures of modern corporation statutes. Nonetheless, defective incorporations do occur. The possible consequences of a defective incorporation include the following: (1) the State brings an action against the association for involuntary dissolution; (2) the associates are held personally liable to a third party; (3) the association asserts that it is not liable on an obligation; or (4) a third party asserts that it is not liable to the association. Corporate statutes addressing this issue have taken a considerably different approach from the common law.

Common Law Approach

Under the common law, a defectively formed corporation was, under certain circumstances,

accorded corporate attributes. The courts developed a set of doctrines granting corporateness to *de jure* (of right) corporations, *de facto* (of fact) corporations, and corporations by estoppel but denying corporateness to corporations that were too defectively formed. Figure 33–5 illustrates the common law approach to defective formation.

Corporation *de Jure* A **corporation** *de jure* is one that has been formed in substantial compliance with the incorporation statute and the required organizational procedure. Once formed, the existence of a *de jure* corporation may not be challenged by anyone, even the State in a direct proceeding for this purpose.

Corporation *de Facto* A **corporation** *de facto* is a corporation that is not *de jure* because of a failure to comply substantially with the incorporation statute but nevertheless is recognized for most purposes as a corporation. A failure to form a *de jure* corporation may result in the formation of a *de facto* corporation if the following requirements are met: (1) the existence of a general corporation statute, (2) a *bona fide* attempt to comply with that law in organizing a corporation under the statute, and (3) the actual exercise of corporate power by conducting a business in the belief that a corporation has been formed. The existence of a *de facto*

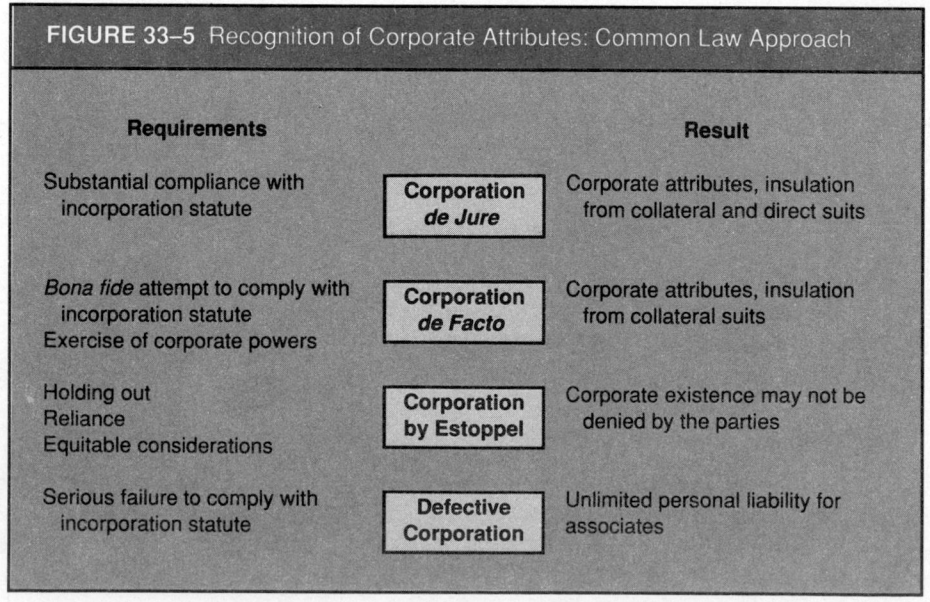

FIGURE 33–5 Recognition of Corporate Attributes: Common Law Approach

Requirements		Result
Substantial compliance with incorporation statute	Corporation de Jure	Corporate attributes, insulation from collateral and direct suits
Bona fide attempt to comply with incorporation statute / Exercise of corporate powers	Corporation de Facto	Corporate attributes, insulation from collateral suits
Holding out / Reliance / Equitable considerations	Corporation by Estoppel	Corporate existence may not be denied by the parties
Serious failure to comply with incorporation statute	Defective Corporation	Unlimited personal liability for associates

corporation can be challenged only by the State. If the corporation sues to collect a debt, it is no defense to such a suit that the plaintiff corporation is not *de jure*. Not even the State can collaterally (in a proceeding involving some other issue) question the *de facto* corporation's existence. The State must bring an independent suit against the corporation for this express purpose, known as an action of *quo warranto* ("by what right").

Corporation by Estoppel

The doctrine of corporation by estoppel is separate and distinct from that of corporation *de facto*. Estoppel does not create a corporation. It operates only to prevent a person or persons under the facts and circumstances of a particular case from raising the question of a corporation's existence or its capacity to act or to own property. Corporation by estoppel requires a holding out and reliance. In addition, application of the doctrine depends on equitable considerations. A person who has dealt with a defectively organized corporation may be precluded or estopped from denying its corporate existence where the necessary elements of holding out and reliance are present. The doctrine can be applied not only to third parties but also to the purported corporation as well as the associates who held themselves out as a corporation.

CRANSON v. INTERNATIONAL BUSINESS MACHINES CORP.

Court of Appeals of Maryland, 1964.
234 Md. 477, 200 A.2d 33.

Facts: In April 1961, Cranson was asked to invest in a new business corporation that was about to be created. He agreed to purchase stock and become an officer and director. After his attorney advised him that the corporation had been formed under the laws of Maryland, Cranson paid for and received a stock certificate evidencing his ownership of shares. The business of the new venture was conducted as if it were a corporation. Cranson was elected president, and all transactions conducted by him for the corporation, including those with I.B.M., were made as an officer of the corporation. At no time did he assume any personal obligation or pledge his individual credit to I.B.M. As a result of an oversight of the attorney, of which Cranson was unaware, the certificate of incorporation, which had been signed and acknowledged prior to May 1, 1961, was not filed until November 24, 1961. Between May 1 and November 8, the "corporation" purchased eight typewriters from I.B.M. After the corporation made only partial payment, I.B.M. brought suit against Cranson seeking to hold him personally liable for the balance due of $4,333.40. The trial court found for I.B.M. and Cranson appeals.

Decision: Judgment for I.B.M. reversed.

Opinion: **Horney, J.** The fundamental question presented by the appeal is whether an officer of a defectively incorporated association may be subjected to personal liability under the circumstances of this case. We think not.

Traditionally, two doctrines have been used by the courts to clothe an officer of a defectively incorporated association with the corporate attribute of limited liability. The first, often referred to as the doctrine of *de facto* corporations, has been applied in those cases where there are elements showing: (1) the existence of law authorizing incorporation; (2) an effort in good faith to incorporate under the existing law; and (3) actual user or exercise of corporate powers. [Citations.] The second, the doctrine of estoppel to deny the corporate existence, is generally employed where the person seeking to hold the officer personally liable has contracted or otherwise dealt with the association in such a manner as to recognize and in effect admit its existence as a corporate body. [Citations.]

* * * There is, as we see it, a wide difference between creating a corporation by means of the *de facto* doctrine and estopping a party, due to his conduct in a particular case, from setting up the claim of no incorporation. Although some cases tend to assimilate the doctrines of incorporation *de facto* and by estoppel, each is a distinct theory and they are not dependent on one another in their application. [Citations.] Where there is a concurrence of the three elements necessary for the application of the *de facto* corporation doctrine, there exists an entity which is a corporation *de jure* against all persons but the state. On the other hand, the estoppel theory is applied only to the facts of each particular case and may be invoked even where there is no corporation *de facto*. Accordingly, even though one or more of the requisites of a *de facto* corporation are absent, we think that this factor does not preclude the application of the estoppel doctrine in a proper case, such as the one at bar.

I.B.M. contends that the failure of the Bureau to file its certificate of incorporation debarred *all* corporate existence. But, in spite of the fact that the omission might have prevented the Bureau from being either a corporation *de jure* or *de facto*, [citation] supra, we think that I.B.M. having dealt with the Bureau as if it were a corporation and relied on its credit rather than that of Cranson, is estopped to assert that the Bureau was not incorporated at the time the typewriters were purchased. [Citations.] In 1 Clark and Marshall, Private Corporations, § 89, it is stated:

> The doctrine in relation to estoppel is based upon the ground that it would generally be inequitable to permit the corporate existence of an association to be denied by persons who have represented it to be a corporation, or held it out as a corporation, or by any persons who have recognized it as a corporation by dealing with it as such; and by the overwhelming weight of authority, therefore, a person may be estopped to deny the legal incorporation of an association which is not even a corporation *de facto*.

In cases similar to the one at bar, involving a failure to file articles of incorporation, the courts of other jurisdictions have held that where one has recognized the corporate existence of an association, he is estopped to assert the contrary with respect to a claim arising out of such dealings. [Citations.]

Since I.B.M. is estopped to deny the corporate existence of the Bureau, we hold that Cranson was not liable for the balance due on account of the typewriters.

Defective Corporation If the associates who purported to form a corporation fail to comply with the requirements of the incorporation statute to such an extent that neither a *de jure* nor a *de facto* corporation is formed and the circumstances do not justify the application of the corporation by estoppel doctrine, then the courts generally deny the associates the benefits of incorporation. This results in the associates being held unlimitedly liable as though they were partners.

Statutory Approach

The common law approach is cumbersome in both theory and application. The Model Act and many States provide that a "certificate of incorporation shall be conclusive evidence that all conditions precedent required to be performed by the incorporators have been complied with and that the corporation has been incorporated under this Act, except as against this State . . ."[16] With respect to the attribute of limited liability, the Model Act provides that all persons who assume to act as a corporation without authority to do so shall have joint and several unlimited liability for all debts and liabilities incurred as a result of so acting.[17] Some courts have interpreted these sections to mean that the Model Act has abolished both the *de facto* and corporation by estoppel doctrines.

Under the Revised Act, the *filing* of the articles of incorporation by the Secretary of State is conclusive proof that the incorporators have satisfied all conditions precedent to incorporation except in a proceeding brought by the State.[18] The Revised Act imposes liability only on persons who purport to act as or on behalf of a corporation, *knowing that there was no incorporation*.[19] This provision is analogous to the approach of the Revised Uniform Limited Partnership Act discussed in Chapter 32. Consider the following two illustrations: First, Smith had been shown executed articles of incorporation some months before he invested in the corporation and became an officer and director. He was also told by the corporation's attorney that the articles had been filed, but in fact they had not been filed because of confusion in the attorney's office. Under the Revised Act and many court decisions, Smith would not be held liable for the obligations of the defective corporation. Second, Jones represents that a corporation exists and enters into a contract in the corporate name when she knows that no corporation has been formed because no attempt has been made to file articles of incorporation. Jones would he held liable for the obligations of the defective corporation under the Model Act, the Revised Act, and most court decisions involving similar situations.

Figure 33–6 illustrates the approach to defective incorporation taken by the Model Act and the Revised Act.

PIERCING THE CORPORATE VEIL

If a corporation is formed by substantial compliance with the incorporation statute so that a *de jure* or *de facto* corporation results, the general rule is that corporateness and its attendant attributes—including limited liability—will be recognized. Nonetheless, the courts will disregard the corporate entity when it is used to defeat public convenience, commit a wrongdoing, protect fraud, or circumvent the law. Going behind the corporate entity in order to prevent its use by individuals seeking to insulate themselves from personal accountability and the consequences of their wrongdoing is referred to as piercing the corporate veil. Courts will pierce the corporate veil where deemed necessary to remedy wrongdoing. They have done so most frequently with closely held corporations and in parent-subsidiary relationships.

FIGURE 33–6 Recognition of Corporate Attributes: Statutory Approach

	No Certificate Issued	Certificate Issued
MBCA Approach	No corporate attributes Joint and several liability for all who assume to act as a corporation	Corporate attributes Limited liability Insulation from collateral suits
	No Filing of Articles of Incorporation	**Filing of Articles of Incorporation**
RMBCA Approach	No corporate attributes Joint and several liability for those who act knowing that there was no incorporation	Corporate attributes Limited liability Insulation from collateral suits

Closely Held Corporations

The joint and active management by all the shareholders of closely held corporations frequently results in a tendency to forgo adherence to all of the niceties of corporate formalities, such as holding meetings of the board and shareholders, while the small size of close corporations often results in creditors who are unable to satisfy fully their claims against the corporation. Accordingly, the frustrated creditor will likely invoke the court to disregard the organization's corporateness and impose personal liability for the corporate obligations on the shareholders. Courts have responded by piercing the corporate veil where the shareholders (1) have not conducted the business on a corporate basis, (2) have not provided an adequate financial basis for the business, or (3) have used the corporation to defraud. Conducting the business on a corporate basis involves maintaining the corporation's funds separate from the shareholders' funds, maintaining separate financial records, holding regular directors' meetings, and generally observing corporate formalities. Adequate capitalization requires that the shareholders invest sufficient capital to meet the reasonably anticipated requirements of the enterprise.

UNITED STATES v. HEALTHWIN-MIDTOWN CONVALESCENT HOSPITAL
United States District Court, Central District of California, 1981.
511 F.Supp. 416.

Facts: On September 14, 1971, Healthwin-Midtown Convalescent Hospital, Inc., was incorporated in California for the purpose of operating a health care facility. From that date until November 30, 1974, it participated as a provider of services under the Federal Medicare Act and received periodic payments from the United States Department of Health, Education and Welfare. Undisputed audits revealed that a series of overpayments had been made to Healthwin in the total amount of $30,481.00. The United States brought an action to recover this sum from the defendants, Healthwin and Zide. Zide was a member of the board of directors of the Healthwin corporation, the administrator of its health care facility, its president, and owner of 50 percent of its stock. Only Zide could sign the corporation's checks without prior approval of another corporate officer. In addition, Zide had a 50 percent interest in a partnership that owned both the realty in which Healthwin's health care facility was located and the furnishings used at that facility. The corporation was initially undercapitalized, and the liabilities of the corporation continued to exceed substantially its assets. Zide exercised control over Healthwin, causing its finances to become inextricably intertwined with both his personal finances and his other business holdings. The United States contends that the corporate veil should be pierced and that Zide should be held personally liable for the Medicare overpayments made to Healthwin.

Decision: Judgment for the United States granted.

Opinion: Maletz, J.   Against this background, the issue here is whether defendant Zide is personally liable for the Medicare overpayments to Healthwin. As a basis for such liability, plaintiff [United States] first argues that the corporate entity should be disregarded under the *alter ego* theory of liability. * * *
   We note at the outset that plaintiff's *alter ego* claim must be analyzed in accordance with state law. [Citation.] And under California law, "[i]ssues of *alter ego* do not lend themselves to strict rules and *prima facie* cases. Whether the corporate veil should be pierced depends upon the innumerable individual equities of each

case." [Citation.] Generally, however, the corporate veil may be pierced when it is shown:

> (1) that there . . . [is] such unity of interest and ownership that the separate personalities of the corporation and the individual no longer exist and (2) that if the acts are treated as those of the corporation alone, an inequitable result will follow.

[Citation.]

With regard to the "unity of interest and ownership" text, . . . the evidence at trial showed that at all times relevant here, Zide was a fifty percent shareholder of the Healthwin corporation. In addition, Zide had a fifty percent interest in a partnership which owned both the realty in which Healthwin's health care facility was located and the furnishings used at that facility.

Zide was also president of the Healthwin corporation as well as member of its board of directors and the administrator of its health care facility. While there were other members of the board, they usually did not attend board meetings. Further, only Zide could sign the corporation's checks without the prior approval of another corporate officer, and virtually all the corporation's checks were in fact signed by him. Thus, Zide alone controlled the corporation's operations. Although not dispositive, substantial ownership of a corporation and dominance of its management, as has been shown here, are factors favoring the piercing of the corporate veil. [Citations.]

Other factors the courts consider in determining whether the corporate veil should be pierced include: the inadequacy of the corporation's capitalization or its insolvency; the failure to observe corporate formalities; the absence of regular board meetings; the nonfunctioning of corporate directors; the commingling of corporate and noncorporate assets; the diversion of assets from the corporation to the detriment of creditors; and the failure of an individual to maintain an arm's length relationship with the corporation. [Citations.]

All these factors are present here. Zide himself testified that the corporation was undercapitalized. This testimony was confirmed by further evidence which established that although Healthwin consistently had outstanding liabilities in excess of $150,000, its initial capitalization was only $10,000. * * * In 1974 and 1975 the liabilities of the corporation continued substantially to exceed its assets.

The evidence also established that Zide exercised his control over Healthwin so as to cause its finances to become inextricably intertwined with both his personal finances and his other business holdings. * * *

* * *

The necessary conclusion from all this is that Zide handled Healthwin's finances so as to accommodate his own business interests. Treatment of corporate assets in this fashion has long been considered a significant factor supporting the piercing of the corporate veil. [Citations.]

Another factor present here is that the operations of Healthwin were marked by an essential disregard of corporate formalities. [Citation.] Thus board meetings were not regularly held and with the exception of the first board meeting Zide and his wife were the only directors or shareholders present.

There is the final consideration that the court should not pierce the corporation's veil unless necessary to prevent an inequitable result. [Citations.] As to this, it is not necessary that plaintiff prove actual fraud; it is enough if the failure to pierce the corporation's veil would result in an injustice. [Citations.] Given the situation present here, the court must conclude that it would be unjust not to pierce the corporate veil. For one thing, Healthwin's undercapitalization subjected all its creditors, including plaintiff, to inequitable risks regarding Healthwin's obligations to them. [Citations.] Further, the court finds it particularly inequitable that in 1974 Healthwin, though insolvent, paid back to the Zide partnership some $109,000 it had previously borrowed from the partnership leaving a balance due the partnership of only $164.06. What is more, the record indicates that during 1975 Healthwin repaid Zide at least $39,384 on loans he had made to it.

In view of the foregoing considerations, the court holds that Healthwin's corporate entity should be disregarded under the *alter ego* theory of liability.

The Statutory Close Corporation Supplement validates a number of arrangements whereby the shareholders may relax the traditional corporate formalities. The Supplement is intended to prevent a court from holding the shareholders in a statutory close corporation individually liable for the debts and torts of the business because the corporation does not follow the traditional model of a corporation. Courts may still pierce the corporate veil of a statutory close corporation if the same circumstances would justify imposing personal liability on the shareholders of a general business corporation. The Supplement simply prevents a court from piercing the corporate veil just because the corporation is a statutory close corporation.

Parent-Subsidiary

A corporation may choose to risk only a portion of its assets in a particular enterprise by forming a subsidiary corporation. A **subsidiary corporation** is one in which another corporation, the **parent corporation,** owns at least a majority of the subsidiary's shares and therefore has control over the subsidiary corporation. Courts will pierce the corporate veil and hold the parent liable for the debts of its subsidiary if

1. both corporations are not adequately capitalized, *or*
2. the formalities of separate corporate procedures are not observed, *or*
3. each corporation is not held out to the public as separate enterprises, *or*
4. the funds of the two corporations are commingled, *or*
5. the parent corporation completely dominates the operation of the subsidiary to advance only the parent's own interests.

So long as these pitfalls are avoided, the courts will generally recognize the separateness of the subsidiary even though the parent owns all the stock of the subsidiary and the two corporations have common directors and officers.

BERGER v. COLUMBIA BROADCASTING SYSTEM, INC.
United States Court of Appeals, Fifth Circuit, 1972.
453 F.2d 991.

Facts: Berger was planning to produce a fashion show in Las Vegas. In April 1965 Berger entered into a written licensing agreement with CBS Films, Inc., a wholly owned subsidiary of CBS, for presentation of the show. In 1966 Stewart Cowley decided to produce a fashion show similar to Berger's and entered into a contract with CBS. CBS broadcast Cowley's show and not Berger's show, and Berger brought this action against CBS to recover damages for breach of his contract with CBS Films. Berger claims that CBS is liable because CBS Films is its instrumentality or *alter ego*, and that the court should disregard the parent-subsidiary form. In support of this claim, Berger has shown that CBS Films' directors are employees of

CBS, that CBS's organizational chart includes CBS Films, and that all lines of employee authority from CBS Films pass through employees of CBS to the chairman of the board of CBS. CBS, in turn, argues that Berger has failed to justify piercing the corporate veil and disregarding the corporate identity of CBS Films in order to hold CBS liable. The trial court found for Berger.

Decision: Judgment of the trial court reversed.

Opinion: Goldberg, J.   It is elemental jurisprudence that a corporation is a creature of the law, endowed with a personality separate and distinct from that of its owners, and that one of the principal purposes for legal sanctioning of a separate corporate personality is to accord stockholders an opportunity to limit their personal liability. There does exist, however, a large class of cases in which the separateness of a corporate entity has been disregarded and a parent corporation held liable for the acts of its subsidiary because the subsidiary's affairs had been so controlled as to render its merely an instrument or agent of its parent. [Citation.] But the dual personality of parent and subsidiary is not lightly disregarded, since application of the instrumentality rule operates to defeat one of the principal purposes for which the law has created the corporation. [Citation.] Therefore, to justify judicial derogation of the separateness of a corporate creature, an aggrieved party must prove something more than a parent's mere ownership of a majority or even all of the capital stock and the parent's use of its power as an incident of its stock ownership to elect officers and directors of the subsidiary. [Citations.]

In formulating a basis for predicating liability of a parent corporation for the acts of its subsidiary, courts have developed various legal theories and descriptive terms to explain the relationship between a subsidiary and its dominating parent. For example, under the "identity" theory the separate corporate entity of the dominated subsidiary is disregarded and the parent and subsidiary are treated as one corporation. [Citation.] Furthermore, a dominated subsidiary has been labeled an instrument, agent, adjunct, branch, dummy, department, or tool of the parent corporation. [Citation.] In Lowendahl v. Baltimore & O.R.R., [citation], a New York court analyzed the various terms and legal theories and concluded that the instrumentality rule furnished the most practical theory for toppling a parent corporation's immunity. The court in *Lowendahl* then postulated the following three elements as the quantum of proof necessary to sustain application of the instrumentality rule:

> (1) Control, not mere majority or complete stock control, but complete domination, not only of finances, but of policy and business practice in respect to the transaction attacked so that the corporate entity as to this transaction had at the time no separate mind, will or existence of its own; and (2) Such control must have been used by the defendant to commit fraud or wrong, to perpetrate the violation of a statutory or other positive legal duty, or a dishonest and unjust act in contravention of plaintiff's legal rights; and (3) The aforesaid control and breach of duty must proximately cause the injury or unjust loss complained of.

Applying these three elements to the relationship between the defendant and Films in the case at bar, we first turn to the lower court's factual determinations. The district court held that at all relevant times Films was merely an instrumentality of the defendant based on the following findings: (1) the board of directors of Films consisted solely of employees of the defendant; (2) the organization chart of CBS, Inc. included Films; and (3) all lines of employee authority from Films, passed through employees of the defendant and other subsidiaries to the chairman of the board of CBS, Inc. In addition, the trial judge was greatly influenced by the fact that several witnesses, including a comptroller of one of the defendant's subsidiaries, testified that Films was a "division" of CBS, Inc. Comparing these several facts to the requisite quantum of proof necessary to satisfy *Lowendahl's* "control" element, we think it is obvious that these factual determinations, standing alone, are insufficient to sustain application of the instrumentality rule. Moreover, an independent examination of the record in this case convinces us that the evidence adduced below concerning the relationship between the defendant and Films could not sustain any finding that the defendant completely dominated not only the finances, but the policy and business practice of Films.

* * * In our opinion complete stock ownership, common officers and directors, and the use of organizational charts illustrating lines of authority are all business practices common to most parent-subsidiary relationships, and such proof of a parent's potential to dominate its subsidiary is precisely the kind of evidence that New York courts have consistently rejected as insufficient in proving a community of management between corporations. [Citations.] Furthermore, with respect to the testimony concerning Films' status as a division of the defendant, we think this evidence under New York law is equally unpersuasive. Affixing labels to corporate relationships for purposes of showing a parent's complete domination of a subsidiary is a dangerous business. As Justice Cardozo, speaking for the New York Court of Appeals [citation], stated: * * *

> Metaphors in law are to be narrowly watched, for starting as devices to liberate thought, they end often by enslaving it. We say at times that the corporate entity will be ignored when the parent corporation operates a business through a subsidiary which is characterized as an "alias" or a "dummy." All this is well enough if the picturesqueness of the epithets does not lead us to forget that the essential term to be defined is the act of operation.

* * * But when a lay witness testifies that one corporation is a division of another, then individual thought indeed becomes enslaved for a court to assume that the use of a descriptive term, by some process of testimonial osmosis, automatically introduces into evidence a composite of facts tending to show a community of management. Just as siamesing is a biological fact, so must corporate umbilication be anatomically demonstrated under New York law. For purposes of application of the instrumentality rule, descriptive characterization is simply not an adequate alternative to a factual showing of the essential "act of operation."

Our prerequisition of the record in this case reveals that the evidence concerning the defendant's "act of operation" is totally insufficient to sustain any possible finding that, with respect to the transaction attacked, Films possessed at the time no separate mind, will, or existence of its own.

* * *

Faced with both testimony and the total absence of any evidence showing the defendant's actual domination of its subsidiary Films during the period in which the plaintiff's contract was executed and allegedly breached, this court has no alternative but to reverse the decision of the district court on the simple basis that plaintiff has failed to prove, in accordance with New York law, that Films was the alter ego of the defendant. We reiterate that under the substantive law of the State of New York a parent's potential to dominate its subsidiary is insufficient to justify application of the instrumentality rule. New York law respects corporate identity, and its destruction by piercing or surrogation requires substantiation of facts, not just organizational charts and labels. The instrumentality referred to in New York cases requires a specific kinetic result, and muscularity to effectuate such result must be demonstrated. Plaintiff's omission in proving such muscularity constitutes his failing.

CORPORATE POWERS

Because a corporation derives its existence and all of its powers from the State of incorporation, it has only those powers that the State has conferred on it. These powers are those expressly set forth in the statute and articles of incorporation and powers reasonably implied from them.

SOURCES OF CORPORATE POWERS

Statutory Powers

Typical of the general powers granted by incorporation statutes are those provided by the Model Act, which include the following:

1. to have perpetual succession
2. to sue and be sued in its corporate name
3. to acquire, own, mortgage, and dispose of real and personal property
4. to lend money and use its credit to assist its employees
5. to acquire, own, vote, and dispose of shares or obligations of other business entities
6. to make contracts, incur liabilities, and issue notes, bonds, or other obligations
7. to invest surplus funds and acquire its own shares
8. to conduct its business and carry on its operations within or outside the State of incorporation
9. to elect or appoint officers and agents, define their duties, and fix their compensation
10. to make and alter bylaws for the administration and regulation of its affairs
11. to make donations for the public welfare or for charitable, scientific, or educational purposes
12. to establish pension, profit-sharing, and other incentive plans for its directors, officers, and employees
13. to be a promoter, partner, member, associate, or manager of any partnership, joint venture, trust, or other enterprise
14. to amend its articles of incorporation
15. to merge or consolidate with one or more other corporations
16. to indemnify against personal liability officers, directors, employees, and agents of the corporation who act on behalf of the corporation in good faith and without negligence[20]

The Revised Act broadens the statutory powers by permitting corporations to lend money to directors;[21] to establish benefit plans for both current and former directors, officers, and employees; and to donate money for the public welfare.[22] The Revised Act also makes a general grant to all corporations of the same powers as an individual to do all things necessary or convenient to carry out its business and affairs.

Express Charter Powers

The objects or purposes for which a corporation is formed are stated in its articles of incorporation, which outline in general language the type of business activities in which the corporation proposes to engage. This serves (1) to advise the shareholders of the nature and kind of particular business activity in which their investment is being risked; (2) to advise the officers, directors, and management of the extent of the corporation's authority to act; and (3) to inform any person who may contemplate dealing with the corporation of the extent of its legally authorized power. The express powers must relate to a legitimate business activity or industry within the purview of the general statute.

Implied Powers

A corporation has the authority to take any action that is necessary or convenient to and consistent with the execution of any of its express powers and the operation of the business that it was formed to conduct. This power exists by implication and does not depend on express language in the charter or statute but on reasonable inference as to the proper scope and content of such language, taking into consideration the facts and circumstances of the particular case.

The express powers of a corporation may and should be stated in general language, and it is not necessary to set forth in detail every particular type of act that the corporation has authority to perform. A general statement of corporate purpose or object is sufficient to give rise to all of the powers necessary, incidental, or convenient to accomplish that purpose. For instance, a corporation organized "to buy and sell goods, wares, and merchandise" has implied power to (a) purchase or lease store premises, (b) employ salespersons, (c) buy or rent trucks, (d) spend money for advertising, (e) open and manage a bank account, (f) employ buyers and pay their salaries and traveling expenses, and (g) purchase insurance on the lives of officers, as well as other powers necessary or incidental to the stated purpose.

ULTRA VIRES ACTS

Because a corporation has authority to act only within the limitation of its express and implied powers, any action taken or contract made by it that goes beyond these powers is *ultra vires*. *Ultra vires* does not mean without power or capability but rather without legal authorization because the act is not within the scope and type of acts that the corporation is legally empowered to perform.

The doctrine of *ultra vires* is of less significance today because modern statutes permit incorporation for any lawful purpose and most articles of incorporation do not limit the powers of the corporation. As a consequence, far fewer acts are *ultra vires*.

Effect of *Ultra Vires* Acts

Traditionally, *ultra vires* contracts were unenforceable as null and void. Under the modern approach, courts allow the *ultra vires* defense where the contract is wholly executory on both sides. A corporation having received full performance from the other party to the contract is not permitted to escape liability by a plea of *ultra vires*. Conversely, where a corporation is suing for breach of a contract that has been fully performed on its side, the other party may not use the defense of *ultra vires*. In any event, an illegal contract, whether *ultra vires* or not, is unenforceable on the basis of illegality.

Most statutes now have abolished the defense of *ultra vires* in an action by or against a corporation. The MBCA provides that "no act of a corporation and no conveyance or transfer of real or personal property to or by a corporation shall be invalid by reason of the fact that the corporation was without capacity or power to do such act or to make or receive such conveyance or transfer."[23] This provision extends beyond contract actions and covers any corporate action including conveyances of property. Thus, it is not necessary for persons dealing with a corporation to examine its charter to discover any limitations upon its purposes or powers that may appear there. The provision does not, however, validate illegal corporate actions.

Remedies for *Ultra Vires* Acts

Although *ultra vires* under modern statutes may no longer be used defensively as a shield against liability, corporate activities that are *ultra vires* may be redressed in any of the three following ways, as provided by the Model Act:

1. in an injunction proceeding brought by a shareholder against the corporation to restrain and enjoin the commission of the *ultra vires* act if equitable and if all affected persons are party to the proceeding;
2. in a suit by the corporation or through shareholders in a representative suit against the officers or directors of the corporation for causing the corporation to engage in an *ultra vires* act; or
3. in a proceeding by the attorney general of the State of incorporation to dissolve the corporation or to enjoin it from the transaction of unauthorized business.[23]

LIABILITY FOR TORTS AND CRIMES

A corporation is liable for the torts and crimes committed by its agents in the course of their employment. The doctrine of *ultra vires*, even in those jurisdictions where it is permitted as a defense, has no application to wrongdoing by the corporation. The doctrine of *respondeat superior* imposes full liability on a corporation for the torts committed by its agents and employees during the course of their employment. For example, Robert, a truck driver employed by the Webster Corporation, while on a business errand, negligently runs over Pamela, a pedestrian. Both Robert and the Webster Corporation are liable to Pamela in an action by her to recover damages for the injuries sustained. A corporation may also be found liable for fraud, false imprisonment, malicious prosecution, libel, and other torts, but some States hold the corporation liable for *punitive* damages only if it authorized or ratified the act of the agent.

Historically, corporations were not held criminally liable because, under the traditional view, a corporation could not possess the requisite criminal intent and, therefore, was incapable of committing a crime. The dramatic growth in size and importance of corporations has brought about a change in this view. Under the modern approach, a corporation may be liable for violation of statutes imposing liability without fault. In addition, a corpora-

tion may be liable where the offense is perpetrated by a high corporate officer or the board of directors. The Model Penal Code provides that a corporation may be convicted of a criminal offense for the conduct of its employees if

1. the legislative purpose of the statute defining the offense is to impose liability on corporations and the conduct is within the scope of the agent's office or employment;
2. the offense consists of an omission to discharge a specific, affirmative duty imposed on corporations by law; *or*
3. the offense was authorized, requested, commanded, performed, or recklessly tolerated by the board of directors or by a high managerial agent of the corporation.

Punishment of a corporation for crimes is necessarily by fine and not imprisonment.

CHAPTER SUMMARY

NATURE OF CORPORATIONS

Corporate Attributes	**Legal Entity** a corporation is an entity separate and apart from its shareholders with entirely distinct rights and liabilities **Creature of the State** a corporation may be formed only by compliance with a State incorporation statute **Limited Liability** a shareholder's liability is limited to the amount invested in the business enterprise **Free Transferability of Corporate Shares** **Perpetual Existence** **Centralized Management** shareholders of a corporation elect the board of directors to manage its business affairs; the board appoints officers to run the day-to-day operations of the business **As a Person** a corporation is considered a person for some but not all purposes **As a Citizen** a corporation is considered a citizen for some but not all purposes

Classification of Corporations	**Public or Private**
	  ■ *Public Corporation* one that is created to administer a unit of local civil government or one created by the U.S. to conduct public business
	  ■ *Private Corporation* one organized to conduct either a privately owned business enterprise for profit or a nonprofit corporation
	Profit or Nonprofit
	  ■ *Profit Corporation* one founded to operate a business for profit
	  ■ *Nonprofit Corporation* one whose profits must be used exclusively for charitable, educational, or scientific purposes

	Domestic or Foreign
	■ *Domestic Corporation* one created under the laws of a given State
	■ *Foreign Corporation* one created under the laws of any other State or jurisdiction
	Closely Held corporation that is owned by few shareholders and whose shares are not actively traded
	Professional Corporations corporate form under which duly licensed individuals may practice their professions

FORMATION OF A CORPORATION

Organizing the Corporation	Promoter person who takes the preliminary steps to organize a corporation
	Subscribers persons who agree to purchase the initial stock in a corporation

Formalities of Incorporation	Selection of Name the name must clearly indicate it is a corporation
	Incorporators the persons who sign the articles of incorporation
	Articles of Incorporation the charter or basic organizational document of a corporation
	Organizational Meeting first meeting held for directors to adopt the bylaws and elect officers
	Bylaws rules governing a corporation's internal management

RECOGNITION OR DISREGARD OF CORPORATENESS

Defective Incorporation	Common Law Approach
	■ *Corporation de Jure* one formed in substantial compliance with the incorporation statute and having all corporate attributes
	■ *Corporation de Facto* one not formed in compliance with the statute but recognized for most purposes as a corporation
	■ *Corporation by Estoppel* prevents a person from raising the question of a corporation's existence
	■ *Defective Corporation* the associates are denied the benefits of incorporation
	Statutory Approach the filing of the articles of incorporation is generally conclusive proof of proper incorporation
	■ *MBCA* unlimited personal liability is imposed on all persons who act on behalf of a defectively formed corporation
	■ *RMBCA* liability is imposed only on persons who act on behalf of a defectively formed corporation knowing that there was no incorporation

Piercing the Corporate Veil	General Rule the courts will disregard the corporate entity when it is used to defeat public convenience, commit a wrongdoing, protect fraud, or circumvent the law
	Application most frequently applied to
	■ *Closely held corporations*
	■ *Parent-subsidiary*

CORPORATE POWERS

Sources of Corporate Powers	**Statutory Powers** typically include perpetual existence, right to hold property in the corporate name, and all powers necessary or convenient to effect the corporation's purposes **Express Charter Powers** those stated in the articles of incorporation **Implied Powers** those necessary or convenient to and consistent with the express powers
***Ultra Vires* Acts**	**Definition of *Ultra Vires* Acts** any action taken or contract made by a corporation that goes beyond its express and implied powers **Effect of *Ultra Vires* Acts** under MBCA *ultra vires* acts and conveyances are not invalid **Remedies for *Ultra Vires* Acts** the MBCA provides three possible remedies
Liability for Torts and Crimes	**Torts** under the doctrine of *respondeat superior* a corporation is liable for torts committed by its employees within the course of their employment **Crimes** a corporation may be criminally liable for violations of statutes imposing liability without fault or where the offense is perpetrated by a high corporate officer or the board of directors

QUESTIONS

1. Identify the principal attributes of a corporation and explain how these distinguish it from a partnership and a limited partnership.
2. Discuss (a) the liability of promoters on preincorporation contracts, and (b) the nature of their fiduciary duty.
3. Distinguish between the common law and the statutory approaches to defective formation of a corporation.
4. Explain how the doctrine of piercing the corporate veil applies to (a) closely held corporations, and (b) parent-subsidiary corporations.
5. Distinguish between the common law and statutory approaches to the effect of *ultra vires* acts.

PROBLEMS

1. After part of the shares of a proposed corporation had been successfully subscribed, one of the promoters hired a carpenter to repair a building. The promoters subsequently secured subscriptions to the balance of the shares and completed the organization, but the corporation declined to use the building or pay the carpenter for the reason that it was not suitable to the purposes of the company. The carpenter brought suit against the corporation for the amount that the promoter agreed would be paid to him. Decision?

2. C. A. Nimocks was a promoter engaged in organizing the Times Printing Company. On September 12, on behalf of the proposed corporation, he made a contract with McArthur for her services as comptroller for the period of one year beginning October 1. The Times Printing Company was incorporated October 16, and on that date McArthur commenced her duties as comptroller. No formal action on her employment was taken by the board of directors or by any officer, but all the shareholders, directors, and officers knew of the contract made by Nimocks. On December 1 McArthur was discharged without cause. Has she a cause of action against the Times Printing Company?

3. Todd and Elaine obtained an option on a building that was used for manufacturing pianos. They acted as the promoters for a corporation and turned the building over to the new corporation for $500,000 worth of stock. As a matter of fact, their option on the building called for a purchase price of only $300,000. The other shareholders desire to have $200,000 of the common stock canceled. Can they succeed in this action?

4. Wayne signed a subscription agreement for ten shares of stock having a value of $100 per share of the proposed ABC Company. Two weeks later the company was incorporated. A certificate was duly tendered to Wayne, but he refused to accept it. He was notified of all shareholders' meetings, but he never attended. A dividend check was sent to him, but he returned it. ABC Company brings a legal action against Wayne to recover $1,000. He defends on the ground that his subscription agreement was an unaccepted offer, that he had done nothing to ratify it, and that he was therefore not liable on it. Decision?

5. Julian, Cornelia, and Sheila petitioned for a corporate charter for the purpose of conducting a retail shoe business. All the statutory provisions were complied with, except that they failed to have their charter recorded. This was an oversight on their part, and they felt that they had fully complied with the law. They operated the business for three years, after which time it became insolvent. The creditors desire to hold the members personally and individually liable. May they do so?

6. Arthur, Barbara, Carl, and Debra decided to form a corporation for bottling and selling apple cider. Arthur, Barbara, and Carl were to operate the business, and Debra was to supply the necessary capital but was to have no voice in the management. They went to Jane, a lawyer, who agreed to organize a corporation for them under the name A-B-C Inc., and sufficient funds were paid to her to accomplish the incorporation. Jane promised that the corporation would definitely be formed by May 3. On April 27 Arthur telephoned Jane to inquire how the incorporation was progressing, and Jane said she had drafted the articles of incorporation and would send them to the Secretary of State that very day. She assured Arthur that incorporation would occur before May 3.

Relying on Jane's assurance, Arthur, with the approval of Barbara and Carl, on May 4 entered into a written contract with Grower for his entire apple crop. The contract was executed by Arthur on behalf of "A-B-C Inc." Grower delivered the apples as agreed. Unknown to Arthur, Barbara, Carl, Debra, or Grower, the articles of incorporation were never filed, through Jane's negligence. The business subsequently failed.

What are Grower's rights, if any, against Arthur, Barbara, Carl, and Debra as individuals?

7. The Pyro Corporation has outstanding 20,000 shares of common stock, of which 19,000 are owned by Peter B. Arson, 500 shares are owned by Elizabeth Arson, his wife, and 500 shares are owned by Joseph Q. Arson, his brother. These three individuals are the officers and directors of the corporation. The Pyro Corporation obtained a $250,000 fire insurance policy covering a certain building owned by it. Thereafter, Peter B. Arson set fire to the building, and it was totally destroyed. The corporation now brings an action against the fire insurance company to recover on the $250,000 fire insurance policy. What judgment?

8. A Corporation is formed for the purpose of manufacturing, buying, selling, and dealing in drugs, chemicals, and similar products. The corporation, under authority of its board of directors, contracted to purchase the land and building occupied by it as a factory and store. Collins, a shareholder, sues in equity to restrain the corporation from completing the contract, claiming that as the certificate of incorporation contained no provision authorizing the corporation to purchase real estate, the contract was *ultra vires*. Decision?

9. Amalgamated Corporation, organized under the laws of State S, sends traveling salespersons into State M to solicit orders, which are accepted only at the Home Office of Amalgamated Corporation in State S. Riley, a resident of State M, places an order that is accepted by Amalgamated Corporation in State S. The Corporation Act of State M provides that "no foreign corporation transacting business in this state without a certificate of authority shall be permitted to maintain an action in any court of this state until such corporation shall have obtained a certificate of authority." Riley fails to pay for the goods, and when Amalgamated Corporation sues Riley in a court of State M, Riley defends on the ground that Amalgamated Corporation does not possess a certificate of authority from State M. Result?

10. Dr. North, a surgeon practicing in Georgia, engaged an Arizona professional corporation consisting of twenty lawyers to represent him in a dispute with a Georgia hospital. West, a member of the law firm, flew to Atlanta and hired local counsel with Dr. North's approval. West represented Dr. North in two hearings before the hospital and one court proceeding, as well as negotiating a compromise between Dr. North and the hospital. The total bill for the law firm's travel costs and professional services was $21,000, but Dr. North refused to pay $6,000 of it. The law firm brought an action against Dr. North for the balance owed. Dr. North argued that the action should be dismissed because the law firm failed to register as a foreign corporation in accordance with the Georgia Corporation Statute. Decision?

11. An Arkansas statute provides that if any foreign corporation authorized to do business in the State should remove to the Federal court any suit brought against it by a citizen of Arkansas or initiate any suit in the Federal court against a local citizen, without the consent of the other party, Arkansas's Secretary of State should revoke all authority of the corporation to do business in the State. The Burke Construction Company, a Missouri corporation authorized to do business in Arkansas, has brought a suit in and has removed a State suit brought against it to the Federal court. Burke now seeks to enjoin the Secretary of State from revoking its authority to do business in Arkansas. Burke contends that the Arkansas statute is unconstitutional. Decision?

ENDNOTES

1. Model Business Corporation Act, Section 149, Reservation of Power.
2. Model Business Corporation Act, Section 4(a), General Powers.
3. Model Business Corporation Act, Section 106, Admission of Foreign Corporation.
4. Model Business Corporation Act, Section 110, Application for Certificate of Authority.
5. Model Business Corporation Act, Section 113, Registered Office and Registered Agent of Foreign Corporation.
6. Model Business Corporation Act, Section 124, Transacting Business Without Certificate of Authority.
7. Model Business Corporation Act, Section 17, Subscriptions for Shares.
8. Model Business Corporation Act, Section 57, Organization Meeting of Directors.
9. Model Business Corporation Act, Section 8, Corporate Name.
10. Model Business Corporation Act, Section 53, Incorporators.
11. Model Business Corporation Act, Section 54, Articles of Incorporation.
12. Revised Model Business Corporation Act, Section 2.02, Articles of Incorporation.
13. Model Business Corporation Act, Section 55, Filing of Articles of Incorporation.
14. Model Business Corporation Act, Section 27, By-Laws.
15. Revised Model Business Corporation Act, Section 10.20, Amendment by Board of Directors or Shareholders.
16. Model Business Corporation Act, Section 56, Effect of Issuance of Certificate of Incorporation.
17. Model Business Corporation Act, Section 146, Unauthorized Assumption of Corporate Powers.
18. Revised Model Business Corporation Act, Section 2.03, Incorporation.
19. Revised Model Business Corporation Act, Section 2.04, Liability for Preincorporation Transactions.
20. Model Business Corporation Act, Section 4, General Powers.
21. Revised Model Business Corporation Act, Section 8.32, Loans to Directors.
22. Revised Model Business Corporation Act, Section 3.02, General Powers.
23. Model Business Corporation Act, Section 7, Defense of Ultra Vires.

34 FINANCIAL STRUCTURE

Capital is necessary for any business to function. Two of the principal sources for financing corporations involve debt and equity investment securities. Equity securities represent an ownership interest in the corporation and include both common and preferred stock. In addition, corporations finance much of their continued operations through debt securities. Debt securities, or bonds, do not represent an ownership interest in the corporation but rather create a debtor-creditor relationship between the corporation and the bondholder. The third principal way in which a corporation may meet its financial needs is through retained earnings.

In this chapter we discuss debt and equity securities as well as the payment of dividends and other distributions to shareholders. In addition, we examine the manner in which debt and equity investment securities are transferred.

DEBT SECURITIES

Corporations frequently find it advantageous to use debt as a source of funds. **Debt securities** (also called **bonds**) generally involve the corporation's promise to repay the principal amount of the loan at a stated time and to pay interest, usually at a fixed rate, while the debt is outstanding. In addition to bonds, a corporation may finance its operations through the use of other forms of debt, such as credit extended by its suppliers and short-term commercial paper.

AUTHORITY TO ISSUE DEBT SECURITIES

The Model Act provides that "[e]ach corporation shall have power to . . . borrow money at such rates of interest as the corporation may determine, issue its notes, bonds and other obligations, and secure any of its obligations by mortgage or pledge of all or any of its property, franchise and income."[1] The board of directors may issue bonds without the authorization or consent of the shareholders.

TYPES OF DEBT SECURITIES

Debt securities can be classified into various types depending on their characteristics. There are a great number of variants and combinations of each type, limited only by the ingenuity of the corporation. Debt securities are typically issued under an **indenture** or debt agreement, which specifies in great detail the terms of the loan.

Unsecured Bonds

Unsecured bonds, usually called **debentures,** have only the obligation of the corporation behind them. Debenture holders are thus unsecured creditors and rank equally with other general creditors. To protect the unsecured bondholders, debenture agreements frequently impose limitations on the corporation's borrowing, its payment of dividends, and its redemption and reacquisition of its own shares. They also may require the maintenance of specified minimum reserves.

Secured Bonds

A secured creditor is one whose claim against the corporation not only is enforceable against the general assets of the corporation but also is a lien on specific property. Thus, **secured** or mortgage **bonds** provide the security of specific corporate property in addition to the general obligation of the corporation. After resorting to the specified security, the holder of secured bonds becomes a general creditor for any unsatisfied amount of the debt.

Income Bonds

Traditionally, debt securities bear a fixed interest rate that is payable without regard to the financial condition of the corporation. **Income bonds,** on the other hand, condition the payment of interest to some extent on corporate earnings. This provision lessens the burden of the debt on the issuer during periods of financial adversity. Nonetheless, some income bonds call for a stated percentage of return regardless of earnings, with additional payments dependent on earnings.

Convertible Bonds

Convertible bonds may be exchanged, usually at the option of the holder, for other securities of the corporation at a specified ratio. For example, a convertible bond may provide that the bondholder shall have the right for a specified time to exchange each bond for twenty shares of common stock.

Callable Bonds

Callable bonds are bonds that are subject to a redemption provision that permits the corporation to redeem or call (pay off) all or part of the issue before maturity at a specified redemption price. This provision enables the corporation to reduce fixed costs, to improve its credit rating, to refinance at a lower interest rate, to free mortgaged property, or to reduce its proportion of debt.

EQUITY SECURITIES

The shareholders of a corporation, as owners of **equity securities,** occupy a position of greater financial risk than creditors, and changes in the corporation's fortunes and general economic conditions have a greater effect on shareholders than on any other class of investor. The market value of shares of stock should proportionately advance more in times of prosperity and decline more in times of adversity, and do either more rapidly, than should the market value of bonds, debentures, or any type of debt security.

Shares are a method of describing a proportionate proprietary interest in a corporate enterprise, but they do not in any way vest their owner with title to any property of the corporation. Shares do confer on their owner, however, a threefold interest in the corporation: (1) the right to participate in control, (2) the right to participate in the earnings of the corporation, and (3) the right to participate in the residual assets of the corporation on dissolution. The shareholder's interest is usually represented by a certificate of ownership and is recorded by the corporation.

ISSUANCE OF SHARES

Authority to Issue

The initial amount of shares to be issued is determined by the promoters or incorporators and is generally governed by practical business considerations and financial needs. A corporation is limited, however, to selling only the amount of shares that has been authorized in the articles of incorporation.[2] Unauthorized shares of stock that are purportedly issued by a corporation are void. The rights of parties entitled to these overissued shares are governed by Article 8 of the Uniform Commercial Code. The Code provides that the corporation must either obtain an identical security, if it is reasonably available, for the person entitled to the security or pay that person the price with interest he (or the last purchaser for value) paid for it.[3]

Once the amount of shares that the corporation is authorized to issue has been established and specified in the charter, it cannot be increased or decreased without amendment to the charter.[4] This means that the shareholders have the residual authority over increases or decreases in the amount of authorized capital stock, because they must approve any amendment to the articles of incorporation. Consequently, it is common for articles of incorporation to specify more shares than are to be issued immediately.

Qualification of Stock

All States now have statutes regulating the issuance and sale of corporate shares and other securities, popularly known as **Blue Sky Laws**. These statutes typically have provisions prohibiting fraud in the sale of securities. In addition, a number of States require the registration of securities, and some States also regulate brokers, dealers, and others who engage in the securities business.

In 1933 Congress passed the first Federal statute providing regulation of securities offered for sale and sold through the use of the mails or other instrumentalities of interstate commerce. This statute, often called the **Truth in Securities Act,** is administered by the Securities and Exchange Commission (SEC). The basic objectives of the statute are (1) to provide investors with relevant information about securities offered to the public, and (2) to prevent misrepresentations in the sale of securities. The statute requires corporations to disclose certain information about a proposed security in a registration statement and in their **prospectus** (an offer made by corporations to interest people in buying stock). The SEC does not examine the merits of the proposed security, and registration does not guarantee the accuracy of the facts presented in the registration statement or prospectus. The law does prohibit false and misleading statements under penalty of fine or imprisonment or both.

Under certain conditions, a corporation may receive an exemption from the requirement of registration under the Blue Sky Laws of most States and the Securities Act of 1933. If no exemption is available, a corporation offering for sale or selling its shares of stock or other securities, as well as any person selling such securities, is subject to court injunction, possible criminal prosecution, and civil liability in damages to the persons to whom securities are sold in violation of the regulatory statute. A discussion of Federal regulation of securities appears in Chapter 43.

Preemptive Rights

A shareholder's proportionate interest in the corporation can be changed by either a nonproportionate issuance of additional shares or a nonproportionate reacquisition of outstanding shares. Management is subject to fiduciary duties in both types of transactions. Moreover, when additional shares are issued, a shareholder may have the **preemptive right** to purchase a proportionate part of the new issue. Preemptive rights are used far more frequently in closely held corporations than in publicly traded corporations. In the absence of preemptive rights, a shareholder may be unable to prevent a dilution of his ownership interest in the corporation. For example, Leonard owns 200 shares of stock of the Fordham Company, which has a total of 1,000 shares outstanding. The company decides to increase its capital stock by issuing 1,000 additional shares of stock. If Leonard has preemptive rights, he and every other shareholder will be offered one share of the newly issued stock for every share they own. If he accepts the offer and buys the stock, he will have 400 shares out of a total of 2,000 outstanding, and his relative interest in the corporation will be unchanged. Without preemptive rights, however, he would have only 200 out of the 2,000 shares outstanding and, instead of owning 20 percent of the stock, would own 10 percent.

At common law, shareholders have preemptive rights to the issuance of additionally authorized shares. Preemptive rights do not apply to the reissue of previously issued shares, shares issued for noncash consideration, or shares issued in connection with a merger or consolidation. There is a division among the jurisdictions whether preemptive rights apply to the issuance of unissued shares that were originally authorized.

Modern statutes expressly authorize the articles of incorporation to deny or limit preemptive rights. In some States, preemptive rights exist unless denied by the charter; in others, they do not exist unless the charter so provides. The Model Act provides the States with a choice of either alternative.[5]

Amount of Consideration for Shares

Shares are deemed fully paid and nonassessable when the corporation receives full payment of the lawful consideration for which the shares are issued.[6] The amount of consideration depends on the kind of shares being issued.

Par Value Stock Par value shares may be issued for any amount, not less than par, set by the board of directors or shareholders. The par value of a share of stock can be an arbitrary value selected by the corporation and may or may not reflect either the actual value of the share or the actual price paid to the corporation. It indicates only the *minimum price* that the corporation must receive for it. The par value of stock must be stated in the articles of incorporation. The consideration received constitutes *stated capital* to the extent of the par value of the shares; any consideration in excess of par value constitutes *capital surplus*.

The 1980 amendments to the MBCA eliminated the concepts of par value, stated capital, and capital surplus. Under the MBCA as amended, *all* shares may be issued for such consideration as authorized by the board of directors.[7]

No Par Value Stock Shares without par value may be issued for any amount set by the board of directors or shareholders. The entire consideration received constitutes *stated capital* unless the board of directors allocates a portion of the consideration to capital surplus within sixty days after the stock is issued. The directors are free to allocate any or all of the consideration received, unless the no par stock has a liquidation preference. In that event, only the con-

sideration in excess of the amount of liquidation preference may be allocated to capital surplus. No par shares provide the directors with great latitude in establishing capital surplus, which can, in some jurisdictions, provide greater flexibility for subsequent distributions to shareholders.

Treasury Stock Treasury stock are shares that a corporation buys back after it has issued them. Treasury shares are *issued but not outstanding*, in contrast to shares owned by shareholders, which are deemed issued *and* outstanding. A corporation may sell treasury shares for any amount the board of directors determines, even if the shares have a par value that is more than the sale price. Treasury shares do not have voting rights or preemptive rights. In addition, no dividend is paid on treasury stock.

The 1980 amendments to the MBCA eliminated the concept of treasury shares. Under the MBCA as amended, all shares reacquired by a corporation are authorized but unissued shares, unless the articles of incorporation prohibit reissue, in which event the authorized shares are reduced by the number of shares reacquired.[8]

Figure 34–1 illustrates the way authorized shares are categorized.

Payment for Shares

There are two major issues regarding payment for shares. First, what type of consideration may be validly accepted in payment for shares? Second, who shall determine the value to be placed upon the consideration received in payment for shares?

Type of Consideration Consideration for the issuance of capital stock is defined in a more limited fashion than it is under contract law. In most States, cash, property, and services actually rendered to the corporation are generally acceptable as valid consideration, but promissory notes and future services are not.[6] The next case illustrates this requirement. Some States permit shares to be issued for preincorporation services while other States do not.

FIGURE 34-1 Issuance of Shares

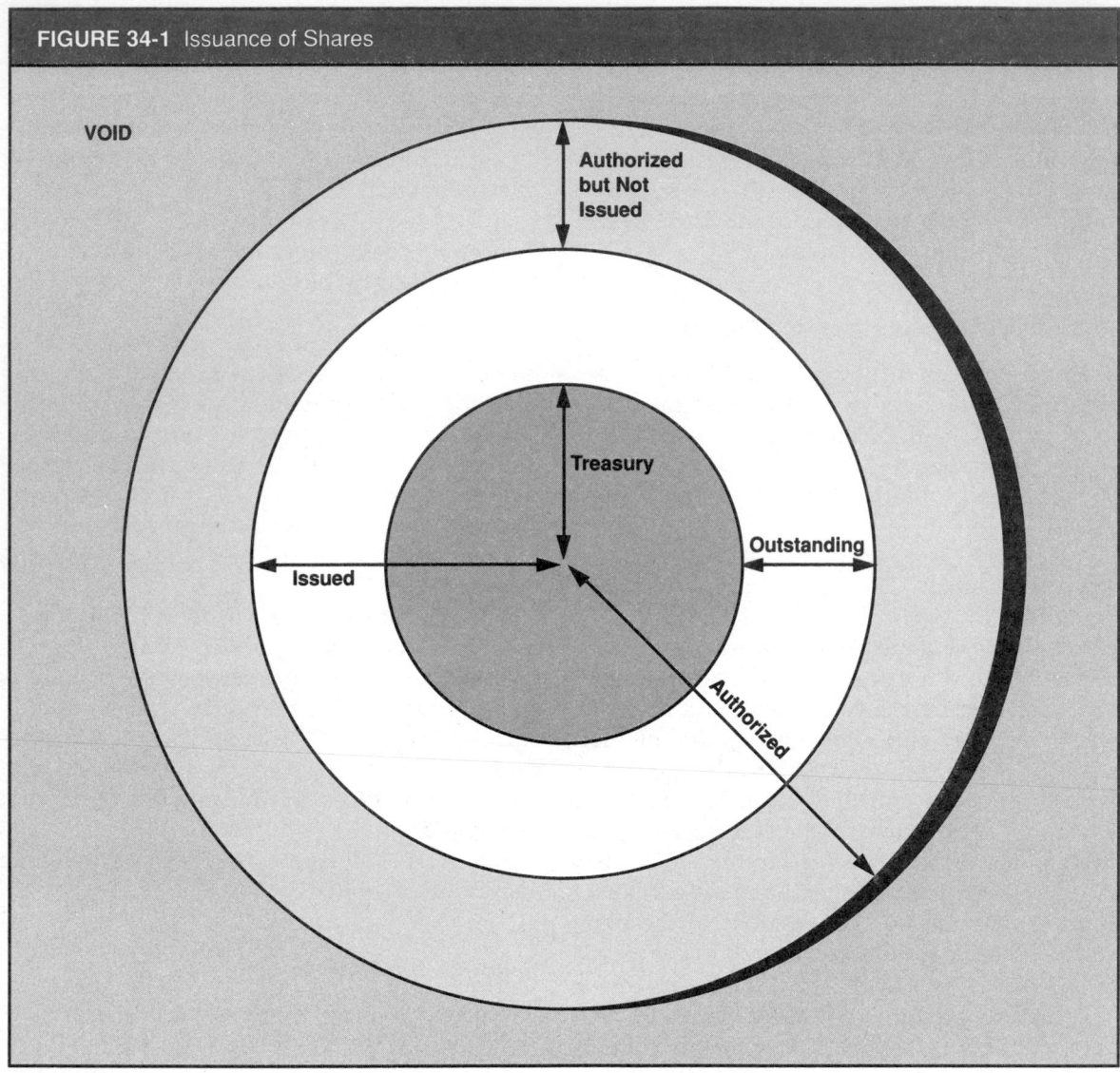

The Revised Act has greatly liberalized these rules by also specifically validating contracts for future services and promissory notes as consideration for the issuance of shares.[9] To guard against possible abuse, the Revised Act requires that corporations annually inform shareholders of all shares issued during the previous year for promissory notes or promises of future services.[10]

Valuation of Consideration   The determination of the value to be placed on the consideration

exchanged for shares is the responsibility of the directors. The majority of jurisdictions hold that this valuation is a matter of opinion and that, in the absence of fraud in the transaction, the judgment of the board of directors as to the value of the consideration received for shares shall be conclusive.[6] For example, assume that the directors of Elite Corporation authorize the issuance of 2,000 shares of common stock for $5 per share to Kramer for property the directors value at $10,000. The valuation is fraudulent and the property is actually worth $5,000. Kramer is liable to Elite

Corporation and its creditors for $5,000. If, on the other hand, the valuation had been made by the directors without fraud and in good faith, Kramer would not be liable, even though the property is actually worth less than $10,000.

UNITED STEEL INDUSTRIES, INC. v. MANHART
Court of Civil Appeals of Texas, 1966.
405 S.W.2d 231.

Facts: United Steel issued stock to Hurt in exchange for future accounting services. United also issued shares to Griffitts in return for Griffitts's promise to convey land to United. Manhart, a shareholder of United, brought this action against the corporation, Hurt, and Griffitts, claiming that the shares were not issued for valid consideration and asking that the shares be declared void and canceled. The trial court entered judgment for Manhart.

Decision: Judgment for Manhart affirmed.

Opinion: **McDonald, C. J.** The trial court found (on ample evidence) that the incorporators of the Corporation made an agreement with Hurt to issue him 5000 shares in consideration of Hurt's agreement to perform bookkeeping and accounting services for the Corporation for the first year of its operation. The Corporation minutes reflect the 5000 shares issued to Hurt "in consideration of labor done, services in the incorporation and organization of the Corporation." The trial court found (on ample evidence) that such minutes do not reflect the true consideration agreed upon, and that Hurt performed no services for the Corporation prior to February 1, 1965. The Articles of Incorporation were filed on January 28, 1965, and the 5000 shares were issued to Hurt on May 29, 1965. There is evidence that Hurt performed some services for the Corporation between January and May 29, 1965; but Hurt himself testified the "5000 (shares) were issued to me for services rendered or to be rendered for the first year in keeping the books * * *."

The situation is thus one where the stock was issued to Hurt both for services already performed and for services to be rendered in the future.

The trial court concluded the promise of future services was not a valid consideration for the issuance of stock under Article 2.16 Business Corporation Act; that the issuance was void; and that since there was no apportionment of the value of future services from the value of services already rendered, the entire 5000 shares were illegally issued and void.

Article 12, Section 6, Texas Constitution, Vernon's Ann. St. provides: "No corporation shall issue stock * * * except for money paid, labor done, or property actually received * * *." And Article 2.16 Texas Business Corporation Act provides: "Payment for Shares.

"A. The consideration paid for the issuance of shares shall consist of money paid, labor done, or property actually received. Shares may not be issued until the full amount of the consideration, fixed as provided by law, has been paid. * * *

"B. Neither promissory notes nor the promise of future services shall constitute payment or part payment for shares of a corporation.

"C. In the absence of fraud in the transaction, the judgment of the board of directors * * * as to the value of the consideration received for shares shall be conclusive."

* * *

The 5000 shares were issued before the future services were rendered. Such stock was illegally issued and void.

Griffitts was issued 10,000 shares partly in consideration for legal services to the Corporation and partly in exchange for the 5 acres of land. The stock was valued at $1 per share and the land had an agreed value of $4000. The trial court found (upon ample evidence) that the 4000 shares of stock issued to Griffitts was in consideration of his promise to convey the land to the Corporation; that Griffitts never conveyed the land; and the issuance of the stock was illegal and void.

The judgment of the board of directors "as to the value of consideration received for shares" is conclusive, but such does not authorize the board to issue shares contrary to the Constitution, for services to be performed in the future (as in the case of Hurt), or for property not received (as in the case of Griffitts).

Liability for Shares

A shareholder has no liability to the corporation or its creditors with respect to shares other than to pay the corporation in full consideration for which the shares were issued.[11] When the corporation receives payment of that consideration, the shares are fully paid and nonassessable.[6]

If shares are issued before they have been fully paid for, the shareholder is liable to the corporation and its creditors for the unpaid amount. A transferee who acquires these shares in good faith and without knowledge or notice that the full consideration had not been paid is *not* personally liable to the corporation or its creditors for the unpaid portion of the consideration.[11]

CLASSES OF SHARES

Corporations are generally authorized by statute to issue two or more classes of stock, which may vary with respect to their rights to dividends, their voting rights, and their right to share in the assets of the corporation on liquidation. The most usual classification of stock is common and preferred shares. Although the Revised Act has eliminated the terms preferred and common, it permits the issuance of classes of shares with different preferences, limitations, and relative rights.[12]

Common Stock

Common stock does not have any special contract rights or preferences. Frequently, it is the only class of stock outstanding. It generally represents the greatest proportion of the corporation's capital structure and bears the greatest risk of loss in the event of failure of the enterprise.

Preferred Stock

Stock is generally considered **preferred stock** if it has contractual rights superior to common stock with regard to dividends or assets on liquidation or both. Other kinds of special rights or privileges are not generally considered to remove a class of stock from the classification of common stock. The contractual rights and preferences of an issue of preferred stock must be provided for in the articles of incorporation.[13]

Notwithstanding the special rights and preferences that distinguish preferred from common stock, both represent a contribution of capital. Preferred stock is no more a debt than common, and until a dividend is declared, the holder of preferred shares is not a creditor of the corporation. Furthermore, the rights of preferred shareholders are subordinate to the rights of all of the creditors of the corporation.

Dividend Preferences No dividend is payable on any class of stock, common or preferred, unless it has been declared by the board of directors. An issue of preferred stock with a dividend preference means that its holders will receive full dividends before any dividend may be paid to holders of common stock. Preferred stock may provide that dividends are cumulative, noncumulative, or cumulative to the extent earned.

For **cumulative** dividends, if the board does not declare regular dividends on the preferred stock, such omitted dividends cumulate, and no dividend may be declared on the common stock until all dividend arrearages on the preferred stock are declared and paid. If **noncumulative,** regular dividends do not cumulate on failure of the board to declare them, and all rights to a dividend for the period omitted are gone forever. Accordingly, noncumulative stock has a priority over common only in the fiscal period a dividend on common stock is declared. Unless the dividends on preferred stock are made expressly noncumulative, the courts generally hold them to be cumulative. **Cumulative-to-the-extent-earned** shares cumulate unpaid dividends only to the extent funds were legally available to pay such dividends in that fiscal period.

Preferred stock also may be **participating**. The nature and extent of such participation on a specified basis with the common stock must be stated in the articles of incorporation. For example, a class of participating preferred stock could be entitled to share at the same rate with the common in any additional distribution of earnings for a given year *after* provision has been made for payment of the prior preferred dividend and payment of dividends on the common at a rate equal to the fixed rate of the preferred.

Liquidation Preferences When a corporation is dissolved, its assets liquidated, and claims of all of its creditors have been satisfied, the remaining assets are to be distributed *pro rata* among the shareholders according to their priority as provided in the articles of incorporation. If preferred stock does not expressly provide for a preference of any kind on dissolution and liquidation, the holders of the preferred stock share *pro rata* with the common shareholders.

When a liquidation preference is provided, preferred stock usually has priority over common to the extent of the par value of the stock. In addition, if specified, preferred shares may participate beyond the liquidation preference in a stated ratio with other classes of shares. Such shares are called participating preferred with reference to liquidation. If not so specified, preferred shares do not participate beyond the liquidation preference.

ROTHSCHILD INTERNATIONAL CORP. v. LIGGETT GROUP, INC.
Court of Chancery of Delaware, 1983.
463 A.2d 642.

Facts: GM Sub Corporation ("GM Sub"), a subsidiary of Grand Metropolitan Limited, acquired all outstanding shares of Liggett Group, Inc., a Delaware corporation. Rothschild International Corporation ("Rothschild") was the owner of 650 shares of the 7 percent cumulative preferred stock of Liggett Group, Inc. According to Liggett's certificate of incorporation, the holders of the 7 percent preferred were to receive $100 per share "in the event of any liquidation of the assets of the Corporation." GM Sub had offered $70 per share for the 7 percent preferred, $158.63 for another class of preferred stock, and $69 for each common stock share. Liggett's board of directors approved the offer as fair and recommended acceptance by Liggett's shareholders. As a result, 39.8 percent of the 7 percent preferred shares was sold to GM Sub. In addition, GM Sub acquired 75.9 percent of the other preferred stock and 87.4 percent of the common stock. The acquisition of the overwhelming majority of these classes of stock—coupled with the fact that the 7 percent preferred shareholders could not vote as a class on the merger proposal—gave GM Sub sufficient voting power to approve a follow-up merger. As a result, all remaining shareholders other than GM Sub were eliminated in return for payment of cash for their shares. These shareholders received the same consideration ($70 per share) as offered in the tender offer.

Rothschild brought suit against Liggett and Grand Metropolitan, charging each with a breach of its duty of fair dealing owed to the 7 percent preferred shareholders. Rothschild based both claims on the contention that the merger was a liquidation of Liggett insofar as the rights of the 7 percent preferred stockholders were concerned. Therefore, those preferred shareholders were entitled to the liquidation preference of $100 per share, not $70 per share.

Decision: Judgment for Liggett and Grand Metropolitan granted.

Opinion: **Brown, Chancellor**   Quite simply, no liquidation of Liggett occurred here. It still existed as a corporate entity following the tender offer and merger. It still retained shareholder status even though all shares merged in one owner. What happened was that all of its outstanding shares were acquired by a single owner. The corporation did not sell off all of its assets, pay its obligations, distribute the remaining proceeds to its shareholders, and cease to exist as a corporate entity. The fact that the practical effect of the transaction as to the 7% Preferred shareholders may have been similar to the result that would have followed from a liquidation does not make the transaction a liquidation.

The Delaware General Corporation law recognizes the concept of a merger. It is separate and distinct from a liquidation or a sale of assets. Indeed, the argument that a good faith merger is essentially a sale of assets when it suits a plaintiff to view it as such has long since been put to rest. [Citation.] Moreover, it has been held that preference rights of preferred stock can be eliminated legally through the merger process.

Consequently, in a case where a merger of corporations is permitted by law and is accomplished in accordance with the law, the holder of cumulative preference stock as to which dividends have accumulated may not insist that his right to the dividends is a fixed contractual right in the nature of a debt, in that sense vested and, therefore, secure against attack. Looking at the law which is a part of the corporate charter, and, therefore, a part of the shareholder's contract, he has not been deceived nor lulled into the belief that the right to such dividends is firm and stable. On the contrary, his contract has informed him that the right is defeasible; and with that knowledge the stock was acquired.

So here, the merger provisions of the Delaware General Corporation Law necessarily form a part of Liggett's charter. Thus, the liquidation preference given the 7% Preferred under Liggett's restated certificate of incorporation, * * * was always subject to the possibility of defeasance by merger, and the 7% Preferred shareholders were necessarily charged with knowledge of this at the time that they acquired their shares.

The preferential rights attaching to shares of preferred stock are contractual in nature and are governed by the express provisions of a corporation's charter. [Citations.] Nothing is to be presumed in favor of preferences attached to stock, but rather they must be expressed in clear language. [Citations.]

Under the express language of Liggett's charter the holders of the 7% Preferred were entitled to be paid the $100 par value of the shares only in the event of "any liquidation of the assets of the Corporation (whether voluntary or involuntary)." From this there can be no presumption that they would also be paid the par value under other circumstances. The total transfer of the ownership of the stock of the corporation through the tender offer and the follow-up merger was not a "liquidation of the assets" of the corporation, and, I think it fair to say, was never

> intended to be by either Liggett or by GM Sub. Therefore, no contractual liquidation right of the 7% Preferred shareholders was activated by the combined transaction, and thus no contractual right of the 7% Preferred shareholders was violated by either Liggett or by GM Sub as a result of the payment to the 7% Preferred shareholders of something less than $100 per share.

Additional Rights and Limitations Preferred stock may have additional rights, designations, and limitations. For instance, it may be expressly denied voting rights if permitted by the incorporation statute, it may be redeemable by the corporation, or it may be convertible into shares of another class.

Stock Rights and Options

A corporation may create and issue stock rights or **stock options** entitling the holders of them to purchase from the corporation shares of a specified class or classes.[14] Such rights or options state the terms, the time, and the price at which the shares may be purchased from the corporation. In the absence of fraud in the transaction, the judgment of the board of directors as to the adequacy of the consideration received for rights or options is conclusive. One of the uses of stock options is incentive compensation plans for directors, officers, and employees. Another is to assist in raising capital by making one class of securities more attractive by including rights to purchase shares in another class.

DIVIDENDS AND OTHER DISTRIBUTIONS

The board of directors, in its discretion, determines when to declare distributions and dividends and in what amount. The corporation's working capital requirements, expectations of shareholders, tax consequences, and other factors influence the board in its formation of distribution policy. In addition, the conditions under which the earnings of a business may be paid out in the form of dividends or other distributions of corporate assets will depend upon the contractual rights of the holders of the particular shares involved, the provisions in the charter and bylaws of the corporation, and the statute of the State of incorporation, which is designed to protect creditors and shareholders from dissipation of corporate assets. More significant protection of creditors is provided by contractual restrictions typically included in their loan agreements, as well as by State fraudulent conveyance laws and Federal bankruptcy law.

TYPES OF DIVIDENDS AND OTHER DISTRIBUTIONS

The Model Act defines a **distribution** as "a direct or indirect transfer of money or other property (except its own shares) or incurrence of indebtedness, by a corporation to or for the benefit of any of its shareholders in respect of any of its shares, whether by dividend or by purchase, redemption or other acquisition of its shares, or otherwise."[15] We will discuss these distributions, as well as stock dividends and stock splits, which are not included in this definition.

Cash Dividends

The most customary type of dividend is the cash dividend, declared and paid at regular intervals from legally available funds. These dividends may vary in amount depending on the policy of the board of directors and the earnings of the enterprise.

Property Dividends

Although dividends are almost always paid in cash, in a few instances a distribution of earnings has been made to shareholders in the form of property and has been termed a property dividend. On one occasion, a distillery declared and paid a dividend in bonded whiskey.

Stock Dividends

A stock or share dividend is a ratable distribution of additional shares of the capital stock of the corporation to its shareholders. The practical and legal significance of a stock dividend differs greatly from a dividend payable in cash or property. Following the payment of a stock dividend, the assets of the corporation are no less than they were before, and the shareholder does not have any greater relative interest in the net worth of the corporation than he had before, except possibly where the dividend is paid in shares of a different class. His shares will each represent a smaller proportionate interest in the assets of the corporation, but by reason of the increase in the number of shares, his total investment will remain the same. Accordingly, a stock dividend is not considered a distribution.

Stock Splits

In a stock split, each of the issued and outstanding shares is simply broken up into a greater number of shares, each representing a proportionately smaller interest in the corporation. The usual purpose of a stock split is to lower the price per share to a more marketable price and thus increase the number of potential shareholders. As with a stock dividend, a stock split is *not* a distribution.

Liquidating Dividends

Although dividends are ordinarily identified with the distribution of profits, a distribution of capital assets to shareholders on termination of the business is referred to as a liquidating dividend. A distribution to common shareholders of paid-in surplus or capital surplus is also a liquidating dividend and should be specifically identified as such. Incorporation statutes usually require that the shareholder be informed when a distribution is a liquidating dividend.

Redemption of Shares

Redemption is the repurchase by the corporation of its own shares, usually at its own option. The Model Act and the statutes of many States permit preferred shares to be redeemed but do not allow common stock to be redeemed. The Revised Act does not prohibit redeemable common stock. The power of redemption must be expressly provided for in the articles of incorporation.[13]

Acquisition of Shares

A corporation may acquire its own shares by purchase, gift, or otherwise. Such shares, unless canceled, are referred to as treasury shares. Under the MBCA as amended, such shares are considered authorized but unissued.[8] As with redemptions, the acquisition of shares is a distribution to shareholders and has an effect similar to a dividend.

LEGAL RESTRICTIONS ON DIVIDENDS AND OTHER DISTRIBUTIONS

A number of legal restrictions limit the amount of distributions the board of directors may declare. All States have statutes restricting the funds that are legally available for dividends and other distributions of corporate assets. In many instances, contractual restrictions imposed by lenders provide even more stringent limitations on the declaration of dividends and distributions.

States restrict the payment of dividends and other distributions in order to protect creditors. All States impose the **equity insolvency test,** which prohibits the payment of any dividend or other distribution when the corporation is insolvent or when payment of the dividend or distribution would make the corporation insolvent. **Insolvent** means the inability of a corporation to pay its debts as they become due in the usual course of its business. In addition, each State imposes further restrictions on what funds are legally available to pay dividends and other distributions. These additional restrictions are based upon the corporation's assets, whereas the equity insolvency test is based upon the corporation's cash flow.

Definitions

The legal, asset-based restrictions on the payment of dividends or other distributions involve the concepts of earned surplus, surplus, net assets, stated capital, and capital surplus (see Figure 34–2).

Earned surplus consists of the undistributed net profits, income, gains, and losses from the date of incorporation.

Surplus means the excess of the net assets of a corporation over its stated capital.

Net assets are the amount by which the total assets of a corporation exceed the total debts of the corporation.

Stated capital is the sum of the consideration received by the corporation for its issued stock, except that part of the consideration properly allocated to capital surplus, and including any amount transferred to stated capital when stock dividends are declared. In the case of par value shares, the amount of stated capital is the total par value of all the issued shares. In the case of no par stock, it is the consideration received by the corporation for all the no par shares that have been issued, except that amount allocated to an account designated as capital surplus or paid-in surplus in a manner permitted by law.

Capital surplus means the entire surplus of a corporation other than its earned surplus. It may result from an allocation of part of the consideration received for no par shares, or from any consideration in excess of par value received for par shares, or from a higher reappraisal of certain corporate assets.

Legal Restrictions on Cash Dividends

Earned Surplus Test Unreserved and unrestricted earned surplus is available for dividends in all jurisdictions. Some States permit dividends to be paid *only* from earned surplus; dividends in these jurisdictions may not be paid out of capital surplus or stated capital. In addition, dividends may not be paid if the corporation is or would be rendered insolvent in the equity sense by the payment. The MBCA used this test until 1980.

Surplus Test A number of States are less restrictive and permit dividends to be paid out of any surplus—earned or capital. Some of these States express this test by prohibiting dividends that impair stated capital. Moreover, dividends may not be paid if the corporation is or would be rendered insolvent in the equity sense by the payment.

Net Asset Test The MBCA as amended in 1980[16] and the Revised Act[17] have adopted a net asset test. They permit dividends to be

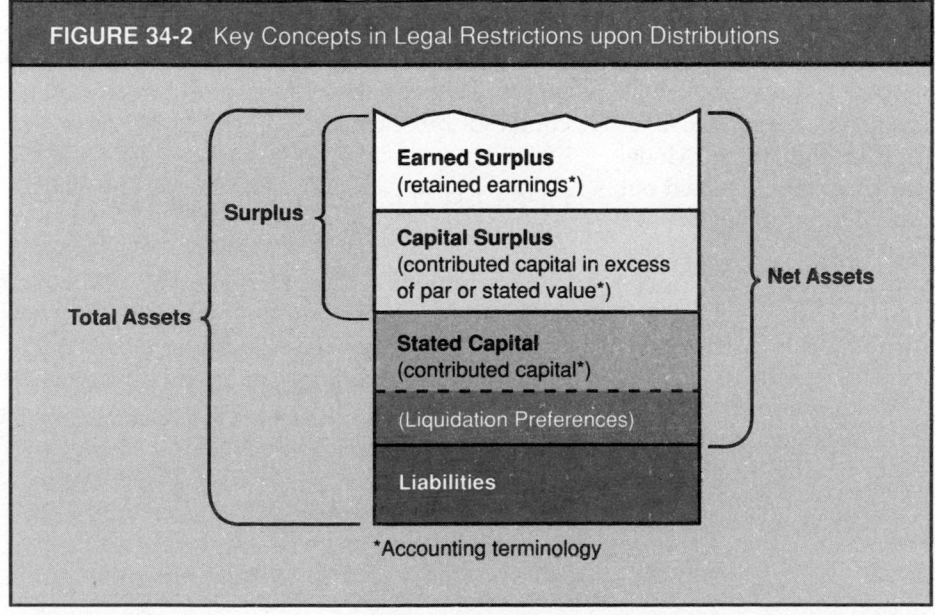

FIGURE 34-2 Key Concepts in Legal Restrictions upon Distributions

Total Assets

Surplus
- **Earned Surplus** (retained earnings*)
- **Capital Surplus** (contributed capital in excess of par or stated value*)
- **Stated Capital** (contributed capital*)

Net Assets

(Liquidation Preferences)

Liabilities

*Accounting terminology

paid unless the corporation's total assets after payment of the dividend would be less than the sum of its total liabilities and the maximum amount that then would be payable for all outstanding shares having preferential rights in liquidation. In addition, a dividend may not be paid if the corporation would not be able to pay its debts as they became due in the usual course of business.

Nimble Dividends Although dividends in many States are properly payable only out of earnings or earned surplus and are generally not payable when the corporation has an accrued earned deficit, the statutes of a number of these States permit payment of dividends out of current earnings notwithstanding the existence of such deficit. Some States permit dividends to be paid out of earnings of the current or next preceding year, but shares having a liquidation preference may not be thus impaired. A board of directors in these States is permitted by timely action to declare a dividend in a year when the corporation has no earnings, provided it had earnings for the year immediately preceding. Because of the time limitation within which such dividends must be declared, they are sometimes called "nimble dividends."

Legal Restrictions on Liquidating Distributions

Even those States that do not permit cash dividends to be paid from capital surplus usually will permit distributions, or dividends, in partial liquidation from that source. Prior to 1980, the Model Act had such a provision. A distribution paid out of such surplus is a return to the shareholders of a part of their investment.

No such distribution may be made, however, when the corporation is insolvent or would become insolvent by the distribution. Distributions from capital surplus are also restricted to protect the liquidation preference of preferred shareholders. Unless provided for in the articles of incorporation, a liquidating dividend must be authorized not only by the board of directors but also by the affirmative vote of the holders of a majority of the outstanding shares of stock of each class.

The Model Act as amended and the Revised Act do not distinguish between cash and liquidating dividends but impose the same limitations discussed above under cash dividends.[16,17]

Legal Restrictions on Redemption and Acquisition of Shares

To protect creditors and holders of other classes of shares, most States have statutory restrictions on redemption. A corporation may not redeem or purchase its redeemable shares when insolvent or when such redemption or purchase would render it insolvent or reduce its net assets below the aggregate amount payable on shares having prior or equal rights to the assets of the corporation on involuntary dissolution.

A corporation may purchase its own shares only out of earned surplus or, if the articles of incorporation permit or if the shareholders approve, out of capital surplus. As with redemption, no purchase of shares may be made at a time when the corporation is insolvent or when such purchase would make it insolvent.

The Model Act as amended and the Revised Act permit the purchase, redemption, or other acquisition by a corporation of its own shares unless (1) the corporation's total assets after the distribution would be less than the sum of its total liabilities and the maximum amount that then would be payable for all outstanding shares having preferential rights in liquidation, or (2) the corporation would be unable to pay its debts as they become due in the usual course of business.[16,17]

DECLARATION AND PAYMENT OF DIVIDENDS

The board of directors of a corporation declares dividends, and this power may not be delegated.[16,18] If the charter clearly and expressly provides for mandatory dividends, however, the board must comply with the provision. Nonetheless, such provisions are extremely infrequent, and any other attempt by shareholders to take over this power is ineffective, although it is in the shareholders' power to elect a new board. Moreover, it is well settled that there can be no discrimination in the declaration of dividends among shareholders of the same class.

A shareholder may not maintain an action at law against the corporation to recover a dividend until and unless the dividend has been formally declared by a resolution of the board of directors. A proper dividend so declared becomes a debt of the corporation and enforceable at law as any other debt.

Where the directors have failed to declare a dividend, a shareholder may bring a suit in equity against them and the corporation seeking a mandatory injunction requiring the directors to declare a dividend. Courts of equity are reluctant to order an injunction of this kind, which involves substituting the business judgment of the court for that of the directors elected by the shareholders. A court of equity will, however, grant an injunction and require the directors to declare a dividend where

1. a demand has been made on the directors before the suit was brought;
2. corporate earnings or surplus are available out of which a dividend may be legally declared;
3. the earnings or surplus are in the form of available cash; and
4. the directors have acted so unreasonably in withholding a dividend that their conduct clearly amounts to an abuse of discretion.

The existence of a large accumulated surplus does not by itself justify compelling the directors to distribute funds that, in their opinion, should be retained for *bona fide* corporate purposes. Where the evidence shows noncorporate motives or personal animosity as the basis for a refusal to declare dividends, however, a court may require the directors to distribute what appears to be a reasonable portion of the earnings. This is not a frequent occurrence; the following case is a landmark example.

DODGE v. FORD MOTOR CO.
Supreme Court of Michigan, 1919.
204 Mich. 459, 170 N.W. 668.

Facts: Ford Motor Company had made large profits for several years. Henry Ford, Ford's president and the dominant figure on the board of directors, declared that although it had paid special dividends in the past, Ford would not, as a matter of policy, pay any special dividends in the future but instead would reinvest the profits in the proposed expansion of the company. At the conclusion of Ford's most prosperous year, John and Horace Dodge, minority shareholders in Ford, brought this action against Ford's directors to compel the declaration of dividends and to enjoin the expansion of the business. The Dodges complain that the reinvestment of the profits is not in the best interests of Ford and its shareholders and that it is an arbitrary action of the directors. The trial court entered a decree requiring the directors to declare and pay a dividend of $19,275,385.96.

Decision: The decree of the trial court fixing and determining the specific amount to be distributed to stockholders affirmed; in other respects, the decree is reversed.

Opinion: Ostrander, J. The case for plaintiffs must rest upon the claim, and the proof in support of it, that the proposed expansion of the business of the corporation involving the further use of profits as capital, ought to be enjoined because inimical to the best interests of the company and its shareholders, and upon the further claim that in any event the withholding of the special dividend asked for by plaintiffs is arbitrary action of the directors requiring judicial interference.

The rule which will govern courts in deciding these questions is not in dispute. * * * In [citation], it is stated:

Profits earned by a corporation may be divided among its shareholders; but it is not a violation of the charter if they are allowed to accumulate and remain invested in the company's business. The managing agents of a corporation are impliedly invested with a discretionary power with regard to the time and manner of distributing its profits. They may apply profits in payment of floating or funded debts, or in development of the company's business; and so long as they do not abuse their discretionary powers, or violate the company's charter, the courts cannot interfere.

But it is clear that the agents of a corporation, and even the majority, cannot arbitrarily withhold profits earned by the company, or apply them to any use which is not authorized by the company's charter. The nominal capital of a company does not necessarily limit the scope of its operations; a corporation may borrow money for the purpose of enlarging its business, and in many instances it may use profits for the same purpose. * * *

When plaintiffs made their complaint and demand for further dividends the Ford Motor Company had concluded its most prosperous year of business. The demand for its cars at the price of the preceding year continued. It could make and could market in the year beginning August 1, 1916, more than 500,000 cars. Sales of parts and repairs would necessarily increase. The cost of materials was likely to advance, and perhaps the price of labor, but it reasonably might have expected a profit for the year of upwards of $60,000,000. It had assets of more than $132,000,000, a surplus of almost $112,000,000, and its cash on hand and municipal bonds were nearly $54,000,000. Its total liabilities, including capital stock, was a little over $20,000,000. It had declared no special dividend during the business year except the October, 1915, dividend. It had been the practice, under similar circumstances, to declare larger dividends. Considering only these facts, a refusal to declare and pay further dividends appears to be not an exercise of discretion on the part of the directors, but an arbitrary refusal to do what the circumstances required to be done. These facts and others call upon the directors to justify their action, or failure or refusal to act. In justification, the defendants have offered testimony tending to prove, and which does prove, the following facts. It had been the policy of the corporation for a considerable time to annually reduce the selling price of cars, while keeping up, or improving, their quality. As early as in June 1915 a general plan for the expansion of the productive capacity of the concern by a practical duplication of its plant had been talked over by the executive officers and directors and agreed upon, not all of the details having been settled and no formal action of directors having been taken. The erection of a smelter was considered, and engineering and other data in connection therewith secured. In consequence, it was determined not to reduce the selling price of cars for the year beginning August 1, 1915, but to maintain the price and to accumulate a large surplus to pay for the proposed expansion of plant and equipment, and perhaps to build a plant for smelting ore. It is hoped, by Mr. Ford, that eventually 1,000,000 cars will be annually produced. The contemplated changes will permit the increased output.

The plan, as affecting the profits of the business for the year beginning August 1, 1916, and thereafter, calls for a reduction in the selling price of cars. * * * In short, the plan does not call for and is not intended to produce immediately a more profitable business but a less profitable one; not only less profitable than formerly but less profitable than it is admitted it might be made. The apparent immediate effect will be to diminish the value of shares and the return to shareholders.

It is the contention of plaintiffs that the apparent effect of the plan is intended to be the continued and continuing effect of it and that it is deliberately proposed, not of record and not by official corporate declaration, but nevertheless proposed, to continue the corporation henceforth as a semi-eleemosynary institution and not as a business institution. In support of this contention they point to the attitude and to the expressions of Mr. Henry Ford.

Mr. Henry Ford is the dominant force in the business of the Ford Motor Company. No plan of operations could be adopted unless he consented, and no board of directors can be elected whom he does not favor. One of the directors of the company has no stock. One share was assigned to him to qualify him for the position, but it is not claimed that he owns it. A business, one of the largest in the world, and one of the most profitable, has been built up. It employs many men, at good pay.

"My ambition," said Mr. Ford, "is to employ still more men, to spread the benefits of this industrial system to the greatest possible number, to help them build up their lives and their homes. To do this we are putting the greatest share of our profits back in the business." * * *

The record, and especially the testimony of Mr. Ford, convinces that he has to some extent the attitude towards shareholders of one who has dispensed and distributed to them large gains and that they should be content to take what he chooses to give. His testimony creates the impression, also, that he thinks the Ford Motor Company has made too much money, has had too large profits, and that although large profits might still be earned, a sharing of them with the public, by reducing the price of the output of the company, ought to be undertaken. We have no doubt that certain sentiments, philanthropic and altruistic, creditable to Mr. Ford, had large influence in determining the policy to be pursued by the Ford Motor Company—the policy which has been herein referred to. * * *

These cases, after all, like all others in which the subject is treated, turn finally upon the point, the question, whether it appears that the directors were not acting for the best interest of the corporation. * * * The difference between an incidental humanitarian expenditure of corporate funds for the benefit of the employees, like the building of a hospital for their use and the employment of agencies for the betterment of their condition, and a general purpose and plan to benefit mankind at the expense of others, is obvious. * * * A business corporation is organized and carried on primarily for the profit of the stockholders. The powers of the directors are to be employed for that end. The discretion of directors is to be exercised in the choice of means to attain that end and does not extend to a change in the end itself, to the reduction of profits or to the nondistribution of profits among stockholders in order to devote them to other purposes. * * *

We are not, however, persuaded that we should interfere with the proposed expansion of the business of the Ford Motor Company. In view of the fact that the selling price of products may be increased at any time, the ultimate results of the larger business cannot be certainly estimated. The judges are not business experts. It is recognized that plans must often be made for a long future, for expected competition, for a continuing as well as an immediately profitable venture. The experience of the Ford Motor Company is evidence of capable management of its affairs. * * *

The fact that a preferred shareholder has prior rights with respect to dividends does not make her position different from that of the holder of common shares with respect to the discretion of the directors as to the declaration of dividends. The holders of preferred stock, in the absence of special contractual or statutory rights, must likewise abide by the decision of the directors.

Once lawfully and properly declared, a cash dividend is considered a debt owing by the corporation to the shareholders. It follows from the debtor-creditor relationship created by the declaration of a cash dividend that, once declared, it cannot be rescinded against nonassenting shareholders: however, a stock dividend may be revoked unless actually distributed.

The time, place, and manner of payment of dividends are at the discretion of the directors. It is not uncommon for the resolution declaring a dividend to fix a cutoff date by providing that the dividend shall be paid to the shareholders of record as of the close of business on a specified future date, usually about two weeks earlier than the date fixed for payment. Where the resolution declaring a dividend fixes a cutoff date, the shareholder of record as of that date is entitled to the dividend.

LIABILITY FOR IMPROPER DIVIDENDS AND DISTRIBUTIONS

The Model Act[19] and the Revised Act[20] impose joint and several liability on the directors of a corporation who vote for or assent to the declaration of a dividend or other distribution of corporate assets contrary to the incorporation statute or the articles of incorporation. The measure of damages is the amount of the dividend or distribution in excess of the amount that may have been lawfully paid. The directors may not escape liability by delegation of the power to declare dividends to an executive committee. The directors are not liable, however, if they rely in good faith on financial statements presented by the corporation's officers, public accountants, or finance committee.

The liability of directors is generally to the corporation or to its creditors. The Model Act and the Revised Act expressly provide that the directors who vote for or assent to an illegal dividend or distribution are jointly and severally liable to the corporation.[19,20]

The obligation of a shareholder to repay an illegally declared dividend depends on a variety of factors, which may include the good or bad faith on the part of the shareholder in accepting the dividend, his knowledge of the facts, the solvency or insolvency of the corporation, and, in some instances, special statutory provisions. The existence of statutory liability on the part of directors does not relieve shareholders from the duty to make repayment.

A shareholder who receives illegal dividends, either as a result of his own fraudulent act or with knowledge of their unlawful character, is under a duty to refund them to the corporation. Where the corporation is insolvent, a dividend may not be retained by the shareholder even though received by him in good faith. Where an unsuspecting shareholder receives an illegal dividend from a solvent corporation, the majority rule is that he cannot be compelled to make a refund.

FRIED v. CANO
United States District Court, Southern District of New York, 1958.
167 F.Supp. 625.

Facts: International Distributing Export Company (I.D.E.) was organized as a corporation on September 7, 1948 , under the laws of New York and commenced business on November 1, 1948. I.D.E. formerly had been in existence as an individual proprietorship. On October 31, 1948, the newly organized corporation had liabilities of $64,084. Its only assets, in the sum of $33,042, were those of the former sole proprietorship. The corporation, however, set up an asset on its balance sheet in the amount of $32,000 for good will. As a result of this entry, I.D.E. had a surplus at the end of each of its fiscal years from 1949 until 1954. Cano, a shareholder, received $7,144 in dividends from I.D.E. during the period from 1950 to 1955. Fried, the trustee in bankruptcy of I.D.E., brought an action against Cano to recover the amount of these dividends paid to Cano, alleging that they had been paid when I.D.E. was insolvent or when its capital was impaired.

> **Decision:** Judgment for Cano granted.
>
> **Opinion: Dawson, J.** The Minute Book shows that when dividends were declared the accountant reported that the surplus was sufficient to allow the declaration of the dividend. The income tax returns of the corporation for the years in which dividends were paid showed that the corporation, at least from a book standpoint, had a surplus out of which dividends could be paid. It is true that this might have been a fictitious surplus, if the good will was not of the value attributed to it, or if certain accounts receivable carried on the books were not collectible. However, no proof was offered that the defendant had knowledge at the time that he received the dividends that they were being paid out of capital or that the corporation was insolvent. There was no evidence produced that the corporation was not paying its debts as they matured.
>
> The law is clear that wrongful declaration of a dividend out of capital, in violation of [the incorporation statute] is a wrong of those committing it and innocent participants are not accomplices to its commission; and in order to hold the stockholder who received the dividend liable it is necessary positively to allege and prove the stockholder's complicity in and knowledge of the wrong. [Citations.]
>
> The Court holds that the plaintiff has not established by a fair preponderance of the evidence that the defendant had knowledge that the dividends received by him were paid out of capital of I.D.E., or that the dividends which were paid impaired the capital of I.D.E. The Court concludes that the plaintiff has not established a cause of action against the defendant, in so far as the defendant received dividends from I.D.E.

TRANSFER OF INVESTMENT SECURITIES

Any investor has the right to transfer her securities by sale, gift, or pledge, just as she has the inherent right to transfer any other properties she may own. The right to transfer securities is a valuable one, and the ease with which it may be done adds to their value and marketability. The availability of a ready market for any security affords liquidity and makes the security attractive to investors and useful as collateral.

The statutory rules applicable to transfers of securities are contained in the Uniform Commercial Code, Article 8, Investment Securities, which establishes rules similar to those in Article 3, which concerns commercial paper. Article 8 applies not only to shares but also to bonds, debentures, voting trust certificates, certificates of beneficial interest in business trusts, and any other "interest in property of or an enterprise of the issuer or an obligation of the issuer" that is of a "class or series" and "issued or dealt in as a medium for investment."[21]

A number of aspects of the transfer of securities are also regulated by Federal securities laws, which we discuss in Chapter 43.

OWNERSHIP OF SECURITIES

Record Ownership

A security is intangible personal property and exists independently of a certificate. Article 8 permits the issuance and transfer of **certificated securities** and **uncertificated securities**. The transfer of uncertificated securities is registered on books maintained for that purpose by or on behalf of the issuer.[21]

The 1980 amendments to the MBCA provide that "the shares of a corporation shall be represented by certificates or shall be uncertificated shares."[22] The rights and obligations of holders of uncertificated shares and certificated shares of the same class and series are identical.

Duty of Issuer to Register
Transfer of Security

The issuing corporation is under a duty to register transfer of its certificated securities and issue new certificates to the new owner. The owner or purchaser is entitled to registration in order to vote and to receive dividends, notices, periodic reports of the corporation, and a new certificate, because the only way that he can sell or pledge or dispose of the certificated securities is by a transfer of the certificate.

Lost, Destroyed, or Stolen
Certificated Securities

If a certificated security has been lost, destroyed, or stolen, the owner is entitled to a new certificate to replace the missing one, provided she (1) requests it before the issuer has notice that the "missing" certificate has been acquired by a *bona fide* purchaser, (2) files a sufficient indemnity bond with the issuer, and (3) satisfies other reasonable requirements of the issuer, such as furnishing a sworn statement of the facts in connection with the loss.[23]

The owner of a lost, destroyed, or stolen certificate may be deprived of the right to a replacement certificate by failing to notify the issuing corporation within a reasonable time after learning of the loss, if the corporation has registered a transfer of the certificate before receiving such notification.[23]

TRANSFER OF SECURITIES

Restrictions on Transfer

In the absence of a specific agreement, shares of stock are freely transferable. Although free transferability of shares is usually considered an advantage of the corporate form, in some situations the shareholders prefer to restrict the transfer of shares. In closely held corporations, stock transfer restrictions are used to control who may become shareholders. They are also used to restrict the number of persons who may become shareholders in order to maintain statutory close corporation status. In

publicly held corporations, restrictions on the transfer of shares are used to preserve exemptions under State and Federal securities laws. (These are discussed in Chapter 43.)

Most incorporation statutes have no provisions governing share transfer restrictions. The common law validates these restrictions if they are adopted for a lawful purpose and do not unreasonably restrain or prohibit transferability. In addition, the UCC provides that an otherwise valid share transfer restriction is ineffective against a person without actual knowledge of it unless the restriction is conspicuously noted on the share certificate or in the initial transaction statement for an uncertificated security.[24]

The Revised Act and the statutes of a few States permit transfer restrictions to be imposed in the articles of incorporation, bylaws, or a shareholder agreement but require that the restriction be noted conspicuously on the certificate or be contained in the information statement for uncertificated securities.[25] The Revised Act authorizes restrictions for any reasonable purpose. See the case on page 745.

Statute of Frauds

A contract for the sale of securities is not enforceable unless one of the following conditions is satisfied:

1. a writing is signed by the party against whom enforcement is sought and indicating that a contract has been made for sale of a stated quantity of described securities at a defined or stated price;
2. performance, as evidenced by acceptance of delivery or acceptance of payment, but only to the extent of such delivery or payment;
3. failure to object in writing within ten days to a written confirmation binding on the sender; or
4. an admission in pleading, testimony, or otherwise in court that a contract was made.[26]

Manner of Transfer

Under the Code, a transfer of certificated securities is made by delivery of the certificate

MATTER OF ESTATE OF SPAZIANI
Surrogate's Court of New York, Jefferson County, 1984.
125 Misc.2d 901, 480 N.Y.S.2d 854.

Facts: Vincent Spaziani was one of the five original subscribers to the certificate of incorporation of Spaziani Bakeries, Inc. The certificate provided that "[n]o certificate of stock or any interest therein of this corporation shall be transferred . . . until it has first been offered for sale . . . to this Corporation." Upon the death of Spaziani, his heirs demanded distribution of the stock to them in equal shares by the administrator of the estate. Spaziani Bakeries, Inc., sought to enforce the clause restricting the transferability of the stock and to require the administrator to offer the stock back to the corporation.

Decision: Administrator not required to offer the stock back to Spaziani Bakeries, Inc.

Opinion: Gilbert, J.   A common objective of incorporation, especially in a closely held corporation, is the avoidance of personal liability. [Citations.] Another primary objective is to guarantee and define the continuation of a family business, including the parties who are to be shareholders. [Citation.] Clauses * * * are inserted in the certificate of incorporation to accomplish this latter objective. However, it appears that draftsmen must pay particular attention to the language used in such a clause if it is to be binding upon the estate of a deceased shareholder.

The ownership of stock vests in a person an interest or right in the management, profits and assets of that corporation. [Citation.] The stockholder has basic ownership rights to such stock, including the right to dispose of it as his self-interest dictates. [Citations.] A close corporation generally will seek to define or limit such right of disposition in its certificate of incorporation. [Citation.] As selected herein, one of the common methods of limiting such right of disposition is by requiring the stockholders to offer the stock first to the corporation or by giving it a right of refusal, before transferring the stock to another party. [Citation.] Such restriction is pursuant to the objective of a close corporation to determine "the selection of a particular plan of ownership and classification of the interests of security holders." [Citation.]

Therefore, there has evolved in the law a general principle that the courts will uphold and enforce restrictions on a stockholder's right of disposition of his stock, or his right of alienability, if reasonable and for a valid business purpose. [Citations.] A first option restricting, or right of first refusal, on behalf of the corporation or other stockholders has been determined to be a reasonable and valid business purpose. [Citations.]

Consequently, such a clause, as has been adopted by the incorporators of Spaziani Bakeries, Inc. herein, is valid and enforceable. [Citations.]

The draftsman of such a clause, however, must be very careful if it is the intention of the incorporators to bind the estate of a stockholder with such a clause. In order to bind the estate the restriction must not only be reasonable but must also be clearly expressed as intended to bind the estate. [Citations.] The restriction concerning a "transfer" of stock has generally been held not to include the passing of title by operation of law through a personal representative to the distributees or beneficiaries of a deceased stockholder. [Citations.] The application of such restrictions is limited by the principle "that death would not be presumed to trigger the operation of a repurchase option which did not mention death as a specified contingency." [Citations.] If the certificate of incorporation specifically excludes

> stock passing by will or intestacy, the restrictive clause will not be applicable to such passage by will or intestacy. [Citation.] If silent as to the contingency of death such a restrictive clause is not valid and enforceable against the estate. [Citations.]
>
> Therefore, the administratrix herein is not required to offer the stock back to the corporation. She may distribute it in kind to the distributees of Vincent Spaziani, since the contingency of death was not specifically referred to in the certificate of incorporation. [Citations.]

alone, if it is in bearer form or indorsed in blank, or, if in registered form, which is more usual, by delivery of the certificate with either (1) the indorsement on it by "an appropriate person," or (2) a separate document of assignment and transfer signed by "an appropriate person." The term "appropriate person" includes the person specified in the certificate or entitled to it by special indorsement, their successors in interest, or the authorized agent of a person so specified or so entitled.[27] A transfer of uncertificated securities occurs at the time the transfer is registered.

Prior to presentment for registration of transfer of a certificated security in registered form, the corporation may treat the registered owner as the person entitled to vote, to receive notices, and otherwise to exercise all of the rights and powers of the owner.[28]

The delivery of an unindorsed certificate by the owner with the intention of transferring title to the securities represented thereby gives the intended transferee as against the transferor complete rights in the certificate and in the certificated securities, including the right to compel indorsement. He becomes a *bona fide* purchaser of the certificated securities, however, only as of the time the indorsement is supplied.[29]

Bona Fide Purchasers

A "*bona fide* purchaser" is a purchaser for value in good faith and without notice of any adverse claim who takes delivery of a certificated security in bearer form or in registered form issued to her or indorsed to her or in blank.[30] The negotiation and transfer of a security to a *bona fide* purchaser passes title to her free of all adverse claims not conspicuously noted on the certificate.[24] Adverse claims include a claim that a transfer was or would be wrongful or that a particular adverse person is the owner of or has an interest in the security.[30] Thus, the *bona fide* purchaser from a thief, finder, or other unauthorized person is protected.

Transfer Warranties

A person transferring certificated securities to a purchaser for value warrants that

1. the transfer is effective and rightful;
2. the security is genuine and has not been materially altered; and
3. he knows of no fact that might impair the validity of the security.[31]

A person who presents a certificated security for registration of transfer or for payment or exchange warrants to the issuer that he is entitled to the registration, payment, or exchange, but a purchaser for value and without notice of adverse claims who receives a new, reissued, or registered certificated security on registration of transfer warrants only that he has no knowledge of any unauthorized signature in a necessary indorsement.[31]

Forged or Unauthorized Indorsement

The owner of securities represented by a certificate is not deprived of his title by a transfer of the certificate bearing a forged or unauthorized indorsement. The purchaser of a security bearing a forged or unauthorized indorsement who resells and transfers it to a *bona fide* purchaser is liable to him for the value of the securities at the time of sale because he has breached his warranty that the transfer is effective and rightful.[31] Neither party is owner of the securities, as title cannot be transferred through a forged or unauthorized indorsement.

Unless the owner has ratified an unauthorized indorsement or is otherwise prevented from asserting its ineffectiveness, he may assert its ineffectiveness against the issuer and against any purchaser other than a *bona fide* purchaser who has in good faith received a new, reissued, or reregistered certificated security on registration of transfer.[32] An issuer who registers the transfer of a certificated security on an unauthorized indorsement is subject to liability for improper registration.[32]

CHAPTER SUMMARY

DEBT SECURITIES

Authority to Issue Debt Securities	**Definitions** ■ *Debt Security* source of capital creating no ownership interest and involving the corporation's promise to repay funds lent to it ■ *Bond* a debt security **Rule** each corporation has the power to issue debt securities as determined by the board of directors
Types of Debt Securities	**Unsecured Bonds** called debentures; have only the obligation of the corporation behind them **Secured Bonds** are claims against a corporation's general assets and also a lien on specific property **Income Bonds** condition the payment of interest to some extent on corporate earnings **Convertible Bonds** may be exchanged for other securities **Callable Bonds** bonds subject to redemption

EQUITY SECURITIES

| Issuance of Shares | **Definitions**
■ *Equity Security*   source of capital creating an ownership interest in the corporation
■ *Share*   a proportionate ownership interest in a corporation
■ *Treasury Stock*   shares reacquired by a corporation
Authority to Issue   only those shares authorized in the articles of incorporation may be issued
Preemptive Rights   right to purchase a pro rata share of new stock offerings
Amount of Consideration for Shares   shares are deemed fully paid and nonassessable when a corporation receives full payment of the lawful consideration for which the shares are issued, which in the case of par value stock must be at least par
Payment for Newly Issued Shares   may be cash, property, and services actually rendered as determined by the board of directors |

Classes of Shares	**Common Stock** stock not having any special contract rights
	Preferred Stock stock having contractual rights superior to those of common stock
	■ *Dividend Preferences* must receive full dividends before any dividend may be paid on common stock
	■ *Liquidation Preferences* priority over common stock in corporate assets upon liquidation
	Stock Rights and Options contractual right to purchase stock from a corporation

DIVIDENDS AND OTHER DISTRIBUTIONS

Types of Dividends and Other Distributions	**Distributions** a transfer of property by a corporation to any of its shareholders; must be declared by the board and then becomes a debt of the corporation
	Cash Dividends the most common type of distribution
	Property Dividends distribution in form of property
	Stock Dividends a ratable distribution of additional shares of stock
	Stock Splits each of the outstanding shares is broken into a greater number of shares
	Liquidating Dividends a distribution of capital assets to shareholders on termination of the corporation
	Redemption of Shares a corporation's exercise of the right to repurchase its own shares

Legal Restrictions on Dividends and Other Distributions	**Legal Restrictions on Cash Dividends** dividends may be paid only if the cash flow and applicable balance sheet tests are satisfied
	■ *Cash Flow Test* a corporation must not be or become insolvent (unable to pay its debts as they become due in the usual course of business)
	■ *Balance Sheet Test* varies among the States and includes the earned surplus test (available in all States), the surplus test, and the net assets test (used by the Model Act)
	Legal Restrictions on Liquidating Distributions States usually permit distribution in partial liquidation from capital surplus unless the company is insolvent
	Legal Restrictions on Redemptions of Shares in most States, a corporation may not redeem shares when insolvent or when such redemption would render it insolvent
	Legal Restrictions on Acquisition of Shares similar restrictions to those on cash dividends usually apply

Liability for Improper Dividends and Distributions	**Directors** the directors who assent to an improper dividend are liable for the unlawful amount of the dividend
	Shareholders a shareholder must return illegal dividends if he knew of the illegality, if the dividend resulted from his fraud, or if the corporation is insolvent

Transfer of Securities	**Restrictions on Transfer** must be reasonable and conspicuously noted on stock certificate
	Statute of Frauds a contract for the sale of securities must be in writing or otherwise satisfy the statute of frauds
	Manner of Transfer made by delivery of the certificate if it is in bearer form or indorsed in blank, or if in registered form with either an indorsement or a separate assignment, each signed by an appropriate person
	Transfer Warranties a person by transferring securities represented by a certificate gives certain warranties
	Forged or Unauthorized Indorsement the owner of securities represented by a certificate is not deprived of his title by a transfer of the certificate bearing a forged or unauthorized indorsement

QUESTIONS

1. Distinguish between equity and debt securities.
2. Identify and describe the principal kinds of equity and debt securities.
3. Explain what type and amount of consideration may be validly received for shares issued by a corporation.
4. Explain the legal restrictions imposed upon dividends and other distributions.
5. Identify the warranties a person transferring investment securities makes to a purchaser for value.

PROBLEMS

1. Frank McAnarney and Joseph Lemon entered into an agreement to promote a corporation to engage in the manufacture of farm implements. Before the corporation was organized, McAnarney and Lemon solicited subscriptions to the stock of the corporation and presented a written agreement for signatures of the subscribers.

The agreement provided that subscribers pay $100 per share for stock in the corporation in consideration of McAnarney's and Lemon's agreement to organize the corporation and advance the preincorporation expenses. Thomas Jordan signed the agreement, making application for 100 shares of stock. After the filing of the articles of incorporation with the Secretary of State, but before the charter to the corporation was issued, Jordan died. The administrator of Jordan's estate notified McAnarney and Lemon that the estate would not honor Jordan's subscription.

After the formation of the corporation, Franklin Adams signed a subscription agreement making

application for 100 shares of stock. Before acceptance by the corporation, Adams informed the corporation that he was canceling his subscription.

(a) The corporation brings an appropriate action against Jordan's estate to enforce Jordan's stock subscription. Decision?

(b) The corporation brings an appropriate action to enforce Adams's stock subscription. Decision?

2. The XYZ Corporation was duly organized on July 10. Its certificate of incorporation provides for a total authorized capital of $100,000, consisting of 1,000 shares of common stock with a par value of $100 per share. The corporation issues for cash a total of fifty certificates, numbered one to fifty inclusive, representing various amounts of shares in the names of various individuals. The shares were all paid for in advance, so the certificates are all dated and mailed on the same day. The fifty certificates of stock represent a total of 1,050 shares. Certificate 49 for thirty shares was issued to Jane Smith. Certificate 50 for twenty-five shares was issued to William Jones. Is there any question concerning the validity of any of the stock thus issued? What are the rights of Smith and Jones?

3. Doris subscribed for 200 shares of 12 percent cumulative, participating, redeemable, convertible, preferred shares of the Ritz Hotel Company with a par value of $100 per share. The subscription agreement provided that she was to receive a bonus of one share of common stock of $100 par value for each share of preferred stock. Doris fully paid her subscription agreement of $20,000 and received the 200 shares of preferred and the bonus stock of 200 shares of the par value common. The Ritz Hotel Company later becomes insolvent. Ronald, the receiver of the corporation, brings suit for $20,000, the par value of the common stock. What judgment?

4. The Hyperion Company has an authorized capital stock of 1,000 shares with a par value of $100 per

share, of which 900 shares, all fully paid, are outstanding. Having an ample surplus, the Hyperion Company purchases from its shareholders 100 shares at par. Subsequently, the Hyperion Company, needing additional working capital, issues the 200 shares in question to Alexander at $80 per share. Two years later the Hyperion Company is forced into bankruptcy. The trustee in bankruptcy now sues Alexander for $4,000. Decision?

5. For five years, Henry and James had been engaged as partners in building houses. They owned the necessary equipment to conduct the business and had an excellent reputation. In March, Joyce, who had previously been in the same kind of business, proposed that Henry, James, and Joyce form a corporation for the purpose of constructing medium-priced houses. They engaged attorney Portia, who did all the work required and caused the business to be incorporated under the name of Libra Corp.

The certificate of incorporation authorized one hundred shares of $100 par value stock. At the organizational meeting of the incorporators, Henry, James, and Joyce were elected directors, and Libra Corp. issued a total of sixty-five shares of its stock. Henry and James each received twenty shares in consideration for transferring to Libra Corp. the equipment and good will of their partnership, which together had a value of over $4,000. Joyce received twenty shares as an inducement to work for Libra Corp. in the future, and Portia received five shares as compensation for the legal services rendered in forming Libra Corp.

Later that year, Libra Corp. had a number of financial setbacks and in December ceased operations. What rights, if any, does Libra Corp. have against Henry, James, Joyce, and Portia in connection with the original issuance of its shares?

6. Paul Bunyan is the owner of noncumulative 8 percent preferred stock in the Broadview Corporation, which had no earnings or profits in 1988. In 1989 the corporation had large profits and a surplus from which it might properly have declared dividends. The directors refused to do so, but instead used the surplus to purchase goods necessary for their expanding business.

In view of the large profits made in 1989, the directors at the end of 1990 declared a 10 percent dividend on the common stock and an 8 percent dividend on the preferred stock without paying preferred dividends for 1989. The corporation earned a small profit in 1990.

(a) Is Bunyan entitled to dividends for 1988? For 1989?

(b) Is Bunyan entitled to a dividend of 10 percent rather than 8 percent in 1990?

7. Alpha Corporation has outstanding 400 shares of $100 par value common stock, which has been issued and sold at $105 per share for a total of $42,000. Alpha is incorporated in State X, which has adopted the earned surplus test for all distributions. At a time when the assets of the corporation amount to $65,000 and the liabilities to creditors total $10,000, the directors learn that Rachel, who holds 100 of the 400 shares of stock, is planning to sell her shares on the open market for $10,500. Believing that this will not be in the best interest of the corporation, the directors enter into an agreement with Rachel to buy the shares for $10,500. About six months later, when the assets of the corporation have decreased to $50,000 and its liabilities, not including its liability to Rachel, have increased to $20,000, the directors use $10,000 to pay a dividend to all of the shareholders. The corporation later becomes insolvent.

(a) Does Rachel have any liability to the corporation or its creditors in connection with the corporation's reacquisition of the 100 shares?

(b) Was the payment of the $10,000 dividend proper?

8. Almega Corporation, organized under the laws of State S, has outstanding 20,000 shares of $100 par value nonvoting preferred stock calling for noncumulative dividends of $5 per year; 10,000 shares of voting preferred stock of par $50 value, calling for cumulative dividends of $2.50 per year; and 10,000 shares of no par common stock. State S has adopted the earned surplus test for all distributions. As of the end of 1985 the corporation had no earned surplus. In 1986 the corporation had net earnings of $170,000; in 1987, $135,000; in 1988, $60,000; in 1989, $210,000; and in 1990, $120,000. The board of directors passed over all dividends during the four years 1986–1989, since the company needed working capital for expansion purposes. In 1990 the directors declared a dividend of $5 per share on the noncumulative preferred shares, a dividend of $12.50 per share on the cumulative preferred shares, and a dividend of $30 per share on the common stock. The board submitted its declaration to the voting shareholders, and they ratified it. Before the dividends were paid, Payne, the record holder of 500 shares of the noncumulative preferred stock, brought an appropriate action to restrain any payment to the cumulative preferred or common shareholders until a full dividend for 1986–1990 was paid to noncumulative preferred shareholders. Decision?

9. Sayre learned that Adams, Boone, and Chase were planning to form a corporation for the purpose of manufacturing and marketing a line of novelties to wholesale outlets. Sayre had patented a self-locking gas tank cap but lacked the financial backing to market it profitably. He negotiated with Adams, Boone, and Chase, who agreed to purchase the patent rights for $5,000 in cash and 200 shares of $100 par value preferred stock in a corporation to be formed.

The corporation was formed and Sayre's stock issued to him, but the corporation has refused to make the cash payment. It has also refused to declare dividends, although the business has been very profitable because of Sayre's patent and has a substantial earned surplus with a large cash balance on hand. It is selling the remainder of the originally authorized issue of preferred shares, ignoring Sayre's demand to purchase a proportionate number of these shares. What are Sayre's rights, if any?

10. A bylaw of Betma Corporation provides that no shareholder can sell his shares unless he first offers them for sale to the corporation or its directors. The bylaw also states that this restriction shall be printed or stamped on each stock certificate and binds all present or future owners or holders. Betma Corporation did not comply with this latter provision. Shaw, having knowledge of the bylaw restriction, nevertheless purchased twenty shares of the corporation's stock from Rice, without having Rice first offer them for sale to the corporation or its directors. When Betma Corporation refused to effectuate a transfer of the shares to her, Shaw sued to compel a transfer and the issuance of a new certificate to her. Decision?

11. Wood, the receiver of Stanton Oil Company, sued Stanton's shareholders to recover dividends paid to them for three years, claiming that at the time these dividends were declared, Stanton was in fact insolvent. Wood did not allege that the present creditors were also creditors when the dividends were paid. Decision?

12. Olympic National Agencies was organized with an authorized capitalization of preferred stock and common stock. The articles of incorporation provided for a 7 percent annual dividend for the preferred stock. The articles further stated that the preferred stock would be given priority interests in the corporation's assets up to the par value of the stock. In 1965 the shareholders voted to dissolve Olympic. Because the assets of Olympic greatly exceeded its liabilities, the liquidating trustee petitioned the court for instructions on the respective rights of the shareholders in the assets of the corporation upon dissolution. Decision?

ENDNOTES

1. Model Business Corporation Act, Section 4(h), General Powers.
2. Model Business Corporation Act, Section 15, Authorized Shares.
3. Uniform Commercial Code, Section 8–104, Effect of Overissue.
4. Model Business Corporation Act, Section 58(d), Right to Amend Articles of Incorporation.
5. Model Business Corporation Act, Sections 26, 26A, Shareholders' Preemptive Rights.
6. Model Business Corporation Act, Section 19, Payment for Shares.
7. Model Business Corporation Act, Section 18, Issuance of Shares.
8. Model Business Corporation Act, Section 6, Power of Corporation to Acquire Its Own Shares.
9. Revised Model Business Corporation Act, Section 6.21, Issuance of Shares.
10. Revised Model Business Corporation Act, Section 16.21(b), Other Reports to Shareholders.
11. Model Business Corporation Act, Section 25, Liability of Subscribers and Shareholders.
12. Revised Model Business Corporation Act, Section 6.01, Authorized Shares.
13. Model Business Corporation Act, Section 15, Authorized Shares.
14. Model Business Corporation Act, Section 20, Stock Rights and Options.
15. Model Business Corporation Act, Section 2(i), Definitions.
16. Model Business Corporation Act, Section 45, Distributions to Shareholders.
17. Revised Model Business Corporation Act, Section 6.40, Distributions to Shareholders.
18. Model Business Corporation Act, Section 42, Executive and Other Committees.
19. Model Business Corporation Act, Section 48, Liability of Directors in Certain Cases.
20. Revised Model Business Corporation Act, Section 8.33, Liability for Unlawful Distributions.
21. Uniform Commercial Code, Section 8–102, Definitions and Index of Definitions.
22. Model Business Corporation Act, Section 23, Shares Represented by Certificates and Uncertificated Shares.
23. Uniform Commercial Code, Section 8—405, Lost, Destroyed, and Stolen Certificated Securities.
24. Uniform Commercial Code, Section 8–204, Effect of Issuer's Restrictions on Transfer.
25. Revised Model Business Corporation Act, Section 6.27, Restrictions on Transfer of Shares and Other Securities.

26. Uniform Commercial Code, Section 8–319, Statute of Frauds.

27. Uniform Commercial Code, Section 8–308, Indorsements; Instructions.

28. Uniform Commercial Code, Section 8–207, Rights and Duties of Issuer With Respect to Registered Owners and Registered Pledgees.

29. Uniform Commercial Code, Section 8–307, Effect of Delivery Without Indorsement; Right to Compel Indorsement.

30. Uniform Commercial Code, Section 8–302, "Bona Fide Purchaser"; "Adverse Claim"; Title Acquired by Bona Fide Purchaser.

31. Uniform Commercial Code, Section 8—306, Warranties on Presentment and Transfer of Certificated Securities; Warranties of Originators of Instructions.

32. Uniform Commercial Code, Section 8–311, Effect of Unauthorized Indorsement or Instruction.

35 MANAGEMENT STRUCTURE

The corporate management structure, as required by State incorporation statutes, is pyramidal. At the base of the pyramid are the *shareholders*, who are the residual owners of the corporation. Basic to their role in controlling the corporation is the right to elect representatives to manage the ordinary business matters of the corporation and the right to approve all extraordinary matters.

The *board of directors*, as the shareholders' elected representatives, are delegated the power to manage the business of the corporation. Directors exercise dominion and control over the corporation, hold positions of trust and confidence, and determine questions of operating policy. Directors are not expected to devote full time to the affairs of the corporation and have broad authority to delegate power to officers and agents. The *officers* of the corporation hold their offices at the will of the board. The officers, in turn, hire and fire all necessary operating personnel and run the day-to-day affairs of the corporation. The pyramid structure of corporate management is illustrated in Figure 35–1.

CORPORATE GOVERNANCE

The statutory model of corporate management, although required by most States, accurately describes the actual governance of only a few corporations. The great majority of corporations are closely held; they have a small number of stockholders, no ready market for their shares, and most of the shareholders take an active part in the management of the business. Typically, the shareholders of a closely

held corporation are also its directors and officers. Figure 35–2 depicts the actual management structure of a typical closely held corporation.

Although the statutory model and the actual governance of closely held corporations diverge, in most States closely held corporations must adhere to the general corporate statutory model. One of the greatest burdens conventional general business corporation statutes impose on closely held corporations is the rigid formalities that they require of corporations. Although these formalities may be necessary and desirable in publicly held corporations whose management and ownership have been separated, in a closely held corporation, where the owners are usually the managers, many of these formalities are unnecessary and without meaning. Consequently, shareholders in closely held corporations tend to disregard the formalities with the result that limited liability may be forfeited. In response to this problem, the 1969 amendments to the MBCA included several liberalizing provisions for closely held corporations. The amendments were carried over to the RMBCA. Moreover, some States have enacted special legislation to accommodate the needs of closely held corporations and, as noted in Chapter 33, a Statutory Close Corporation Supplement (Supplement) to the MBCA was recently promulgated.

The Supplement has relaxed most of the nonessential formalities. It permits operation without a board of directors, authorizes broad use of shareholder agreements (including using them instead of bylaws), makes annual meetings optional, and authorizes the execution of documents by one person in more than one capacity.

Most importantly, it prevents courts from denying limited liability simply because the corporation is a statutory close corporation. The general incorporation statute applies to closely held corporations except to the extent it is inconsistent with the Supplement.

In sharp contrast is the large, publicly held corporation with a vast market for its shares. These shares are typically widely dispersed, and very few are owned by management. Approximately one-third of these shares are held by institutional investors (such as insurance companies, pension funds, mutual funds, and trusts), which manage funds for individual investors; the remainder are owned directly by individual investors. The great majority of institutional investors exercise their right to vote their shares, whereas a relatively small percentage of individual investors exercise their right to vote. Nonetheless, virtually all shareholders who vote for the directors do so through the use of a **proxy**— an authorization by a shareholder to an agent (usually the chief executive officer of the corporation) to vote his shares. The majority of shareholders who return their proxies vote as management advises. As a result, management prevails in nearly all elections and actually determines who will be directors. Figure 35–3 illustrates the actual management structure of a typical large, publicly held corporation.

Thus, the 500 to 1,000 large, publicly held corporations—which own the great bulk of the industrial wealth of the United States—are controlled by a small group of corporate officers. This great concentration of control over wealth, and the power that results from it, raises social, policy, and ethical issues concerning the governance of these corporations and the accountability of their management. The actions (or inactions) of these powerful corporations greatly affect the national economy, employment policies, health and safety of the workplace and the environment, the quality of products, and the effects of overseas operations.

Accordingly, the accountability of management is a critical issue. In particular, what obligations should the large, publicly held corporation and its management have to (1) the corporation's shareholders, (2) its employees, (3) its customers, (4) its suppliers, (5) the communities in which the corporation is located, and (6) the rest of society? For the most part, these critical questions are unanswered. Some corporate statutes now provide that the board of directors, committees of the board, individual directors, and individual officers *may*, in determining the best interests of the corporation, consider the effects of any action upon employees, suppliers, creditors, and customers of the corporation, communities in which offices or other establishments of the corporation are located, the economy of the State and nation, societal considerations, and all other pertinent factors.

The structure and governance of corporations, nevertheless, must adhere to the requirements of the incorporation statutes. Therefore, in this chapter we discuss the rights, duties, and liabilities of shareholders, directors, and officers.

ROLE OF SHAREHOLDERS

The role of the shareholders in management is generally restricted to the election of directors, approval of certain extraordinary matters, and the right to bring suits to enforce these rights. At the same time, shareholders assume potential personal liability for defective incorporation, disregard of corporateness, and receipt of improper distributions.

VOTING RIGHTS OF SHAREHOLDERS

The shareholder's right to vote is fundamental to the concept of the corporation and its management structure. In most States today, a shareholder is entitled to one vote for each share of stock that he owns, unless the articles of incorporation provide otherwise. In addition, incorporation statutes generally permit the issuance of one or more classes of nonvoting stock, as long as at least one class of shares has voting rights. The articles of incorporation may provide for more or less than one vote for any share.[1]

Shareholders may exercise their voting rights at both annual and special shareholder

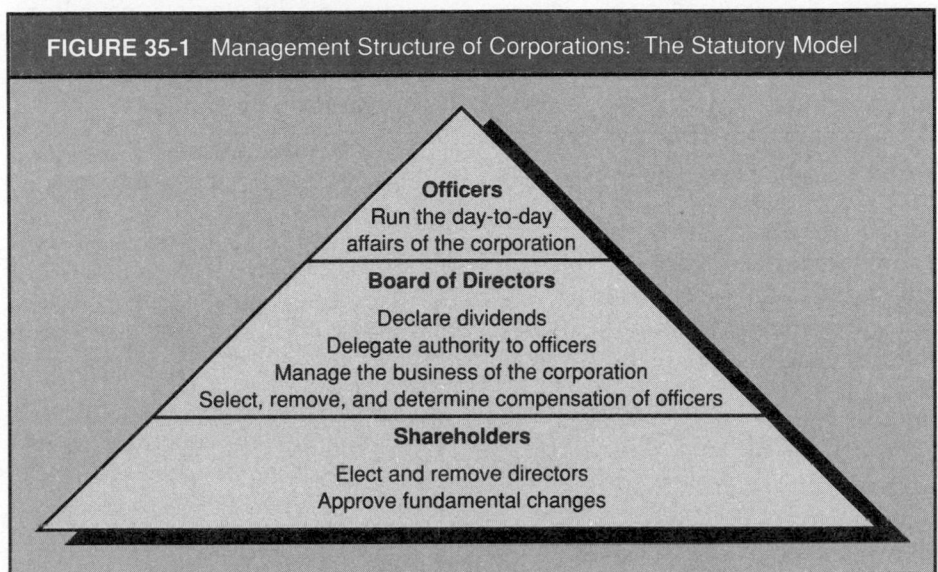

FIGURE 35-1 Management Structure of Corporations: The Statutory Model

Officers
Run the day-to-day
affairs of the corporation

Board of Directors

Declare dividends
Delegate authority to officers
Manage the business of the corporation
Select, remove, and determine compensation of officers

Shareholders

Elect and remove directors
Approve fundamental changes

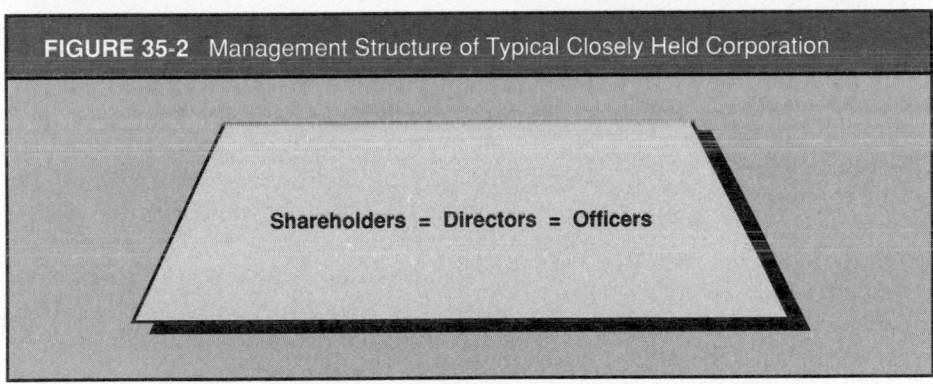

FIGURE 35-2 Management Structure of Typical Closely Held Corporation

Shareholders = Directors = Officers

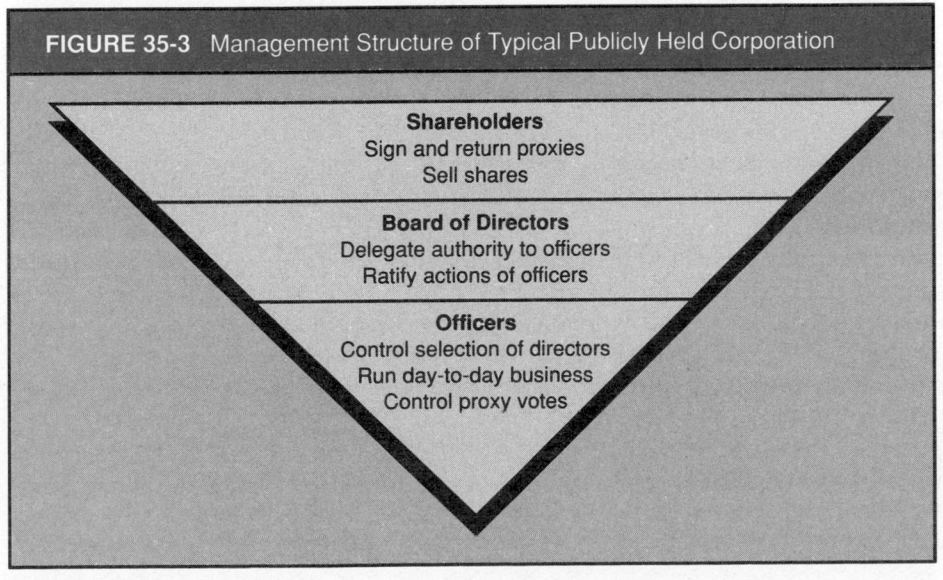

FIGURE 35-3 Management Structure of Typical Publicly Held Corporation

Shareholders
Sign and return proxies
Sell shares

Board of Directors
Delegate authority to officers
Ratify actions of officers

Officers
Control selection of directors
Run day-to-day business
Control proxy votes

meetings. **Annual meetings** are required and must be held at a time fixed by the bylaws.[2] If the annual shareholder meeting is not held within a thirteen-month period, any shareholder may petition and obtain a court order requiring that a meeting be held.[2] The Revised Act provides this right if the annual meeting is not held within the earlier of six months after the end of the corporation's fiscal year or fifteen months after its last annual meeting.[3] The Close Corporation Supplement provides that no annual meeting of shareholders need be held unless a written request is made by a shareholder at least thirty days in advance of the date specified for the meeting. The date may be established in the articles of incorporation, bylaws, or in a shareholder's agreement.

Special meetings may be called by the board of directors, holders of at least 10 percent of the shares, or such other persons authorized in the articles of incorporation.[2] Written notice, stating the place, day, and hour of the meeting and, in the case of a special meeting, the purposes for which it is called, must be given in advance. Notice, however, may be waived in writing by any shareholder entitled to notice.[4]

A **quorum** of shares must be represented at the meeting, either in person or by proxy. Unissued shares and treasury stock may not be voted or counted in determining whether a quorum exists. Decisions made at the meeting will have no effect if a quorum is not present. Once a quorum is present at a meeting, it is deemed present for the rest of the meeting despite the withdrawal of shareholders in an effort to break quorum. Unless otherwise provided in the articles of incorporation, a majority of shares entitled to vote constitutes a quorum, but under no circumstances may a quorum consist of less than one-third of the shares entitled to vote.[5] The Revised Act does not contain a statutory minimum for a quorum.

Most States require shareholder actions to be approved by a majority of shares represented at the meeting and entitled to vote. Nonetheless, many States permit the articles of incorporation to increase the percentage of shares required to take any action that is subject to shareholder approval.[6] A provision which increases the voting requirements is usually referred to as a "supermajority provision". The Revised Act has added an additional requirement to supermajority provisions:

> An amendment to the articles of incorporation that adds, changes, or deletes a greater quorum or voting requirement must meet the same quorum requirement and be adopted by the same vote and voting groups required to take action under the quorum and voting requirement then in effect or proposed to be adopted, whichever is greater.[6]

Thus, this section protects a supermajority requirement for shareholder action from elimination by a simple majority vote generally required for amendments. For example, a supermajority provision requiring a 75 percent affirmative vote may not be deleted from the articles of incorporation or reduced except by a 75 percent affirmative vote. A proposal to increase the 75 percent voting requirement to 90 percent must be approved by a 90 percent affirmative vote.

A number of States permit shareholders to conduct business without a meeting if all the shareholders consent in writing to the action taken.[7] A few States have further relaxed the formalities of shareholder action by permitting shareholders to act without a meeting with written consent of only the number of shares required to act on the matter.

Election and Removal of Directors

Directors are elected each year at the annual meeting of the shareholders. Most States provide that where the board consists of nine or more directors, the charter or bylaws may provide for a **classification** of directors, that is, a division into two or three classes to be as nearly equal in number as possible.[8] If the directors are divided into two classes, the members of each class are elected once a year in alternate years for a two-year term; if into three classes, for three-year terms. This permits one-half of the board to be elected every two years, or one-third to be elected every three years, thus providing an element of continuity in the membership of the board. Moreover, where there are two or more classes of shares, each class may elect a specified number of directors if provided for in the articles of incorporation.

Normally, each shareholder has one vote for each share owned, and directors are elected by a *plurality* of the votes. In certain States, however, shareholders have the right of cumulative voting for the election of directors of the corporation. In most States, and under the Model Act, cumulative voting is permissive and not mandatory.[1] **Cumulative voting** entitles each shareholder who has one vote for each share owned to cumulate his votes and give one candidate as many votes as the number of directors to be elected multiplied by the number of shares owned or to distribute his votes among as many candidates as he wishes. Cumulative voting permits a minority shareholder, or group of minority shareholders acting together, to obtain minority representation on the board if they own a certain minimum number of shares. Without cumulative voting, the holder or holders of 51 percent of the voting shares can elect all of the members of the board.

The formula for determining how many shares a minority shareholder with cumulative voting rights must own, or have proxies to vote, in order to secure representation on the board is as follows:

$$X = \frac{ac}{b + 1} + 1$$

a = number of shares voting

b = number of directors to be elected

c = number of directors desired to be elected

X = number of shares necessary to elect the number of directors desired to be elected

For example, Gray Corporation has two shareholders, Stephanie with sixty-four shares and Thomas with thirty-six shares. The board of directors of Gray Corporation consists of three directors. Under "straight" or noncumulative voting, Stephanie could cast sixty-four votes for each of her three candidates, and Thomas could cast thirty-six votes for his three candidates. As a result, all three of Stephanie's candidates would be elected. On the other hand, if cumulative voting were in force, Thomas could elect one director:

$$X = \frac{ac}{b + 1} + 1$$

$$X = \frac{100\ (1)}{3 + 1} + 1 = 26 \text{ shares}$$

Since Thomas has the right to vote more than twenty-six shares, he would be able to elect one director. Stephanie, of course, with her sixty-four shares, could elect the remaining two directors:

$$X = \frac{ac}{b + 1} + 1$$

$$X = \frac{100\ (2)}{3 + 1} + 1 = 51 \text{ shares}$$

To elect all three directors, Stephanie would need seventy-six shares:

$$X = \frac{100\ (3)}{3 + 1} + 1 = 76 \text{ shares}$$

The effect of cumulative voting for directors may be diluted by classification or staggered election of the board of directors or reducing the size of the board. For example, if nine directors are each elected annually, only 11 percent of the shares are needed to elect one director; if the nine directors are classified and three are elected annually, 26 percent of the shares are required to elect one director.

Shareholders may, by a majority vote, remove, with or without cause, any director or the entire board of directors in a meeting called for that purpose. In the case of a corporation having cumulative voting, however, removal of a director requires sufficient votes to prevent his election.[9] We discuss removal of directors more fully later in this chapter.

Approval of Fundamental Changes

The board of directors manages the ordinary business affairs of the corporation. Extraordinary matters involving fundamental changes in the corporation require shareholder approval and include such matters as amendments to the articles of incorporation, a sale or lease of all or substantially all of the corporate assets not in the regular course of business, most mergers, consolidations, compulsory share exchanges, and dissolution. We discuss fundamental changes in Chapter 36.

LAW IN THE NEWS

The Return of the Proxy Fight
Will Icahn's Strike at Texaco Help All Shareholders?

Normally, an annual stockholders meeting has all the spectator appeal of a tiddlywinks match. But public interest in Texaco Inc.'s gathering in Tulsa, Okla., last week was so high that a company spokesman went on a local radio show urging everyone except shareholders to stay away. The meeting still drew an overflow crowd of about 1,000, all eager for a showdown between management and raider Carl Icahn. They weren't disappointed. Texaco president James Kinnear belittled Icahn's bid to take over Texaco. Icahn, whose sales pitch ran past the allotted 10 minutes, said he was battling the "corporate welfare state." Speeches concluded, the election inspectors began to count the ballots, a process proxy experts call "entering the snake pit." Kinnear said it was "likely" management had won. But key ballots were certain to be challenged by the opposing sides, and the official verdict could be weeks away.

The struggle over Texaco is only the latest—and by far the biggest—in a recent wave of corporate proxy fights. At stake are five seats on the 14-man Texaco board of directors; Icahn hopes that by winning those spots he can convince Texaco to put his $60-a-share offer for the giant oil company to a shareholders' vote. If he succeeds, his foray may help increase the power of shareholders in general. Since most big corporations now have "poison pill" takeover defenses in place, often the only way a raider can seize a company is to solicit proxies from shareholders and win seats on its board of directors. The Investor Responsibility Research Center in Washington says there have been at least 44 proxy fights so far in 1988, mostly seeking board control. That's up from an annual average of 26 in recent years. Raiders-by-proxy have tried to take over such companies as Irving Bank Corp., USG Corp. and Media General. All have failed.

Making Headway

That's par for the course: dissidents usually lose proxy fights. But they are clearly gaining ground. Coniston Partners didn't win the board seats it sought at Gillette Co., but it pushed through a nonbinding resolution urging the company not to pay greenmail to get rid of annoying stockholders. Bank of New York narrowly lost its proxy bid for control of Irving Bank and may yet win the prize through a tender offer. Institutional investors, who often own as much as 50 percent of the shares

Concentrations of Voting Power

Proxies   A shareholder may vote either in person or by written proxy. A proxy is simply the authorization by a shareholder to an agent to vote his shares at a particular meeting or on a particular question. Generally, proxies must be in writing to be effective. The duration of proxies is typically limited by statute to no more than eleven months, unless the proxy specifically provides otherwise.[1] Since a proxy is the appointment of an agent, it is revocable, as all agencies are, unless coupled with an interest, such as when shares are held as collateral. The solicitation of proxies by publicly held corporations is also regulated by the Securities Exchange Act of 1934 as we discuss in Chapter 43.

Voting Trusts   Voting trusts, which are devices designed to concentrate corporate control in one or more persons, have been used in both publicly held and closely held corporations. A **voting trust** is a device by which one or more shareholders separate the voting rights of their shares from the ownership of

in big companies, now frequently support dissidents and may be nudged further in that direction. The Department of Labor is investigating whether pension-fund managers—who as fiduciaries are bound to make independent voting judgments—submit to pressure from corporate clients and vote for management proposals. Corporate brass are also paying more attention to their big stockholders. Kinnear wooed some institutions before last week's vote by saying he might even put them on the board. (Icahn called that "boardmail.")

Management still holds the balance of power in most cases. Astute companies always know who their stockholders are—even though many hold shares in the names of brokers—and can solicit them quickly if a proxy fight breaks out. Dissidents, on the other hand, must painstakingly figure out who the shareholders are before they swing into action. Some dissident victories prove hollow. Santa Fe Southern Pacific's owners recently approved a nonbinding resolution to repeal the company's poison-pill provisions, but management is recommending against the board adopting the proposal.

Call-In Votes

Shareholders who launch a proxy war must steel themselves against other frustrations. In both the Gillette and Western Union fights, dissidents had trouble getting their message out. Brokers in charge of some mailings ran out of proxy materials and didn't ask for more. Mutual Shares, a mutual fund, says it cast 400,000 votes in favor of Bank of New York's takeover of Irving Bank. "But somewhere along the way, our vote didn't get counted," says Mutual Shares executive vice president Peter Langerman. "It was a breakdown in the system." Proxy fights are tough on small shareholders, too. Texaco owners were deluged with mailings and solicited via full-page newspaper ads from both sides. Even those who didn't attend the meeting were urged to switch their votes at the last minute, either by calling an 800 number or by transmitting their proxy cards through facsimile machines.

Both Icahn and Texaco had strong cases. Many analysts say Texaco has been poorly managed for years. But some think that Kinnear deserves more time to complete a restructuring effort. Just last week he announced plans to sell a half interest in Texaco's East and Gulf Coast refining and marketing operations to Saudi Arabia for $1.3 billion. Many stockholders were attracted to Icahn's takeover price, but some wondered about his strategy for the company. George Friesen of Dean Witter Reynolds Inc. disagrees, for instance, with Icahn's plan to sell Texaco's half interest in Caltex, a Far East operator. If management does win the proxy fight, it won't have much time to relax. Icahn has promised to dump his 14.8 percent stake if he loses. That could send Texaco's stock into a nose dive. Then it might simply be a matter of time before another raider emerges and takes Texaco back into the snake pit.

DAVID PAULY and CAROLYN FRIDAY in New York

them. Under a voting trust, all or part of the stock of a corporation may, by written agreement among the shareholders, be issued to a trustee or trustees who then holds legal title to the stock and has all of the voting rights possessed by the stock. In most States, voting trusts are permitted by statute but are usually limited in duration to ten years.[10]

Shareholder Agreements In most jurisdictions, shareholders may agree in advance to vote in a specified manner for the election or removal of directors or on any matter subject to shareholder approval.[10] Unlike voting trusts, shareholder agreements are not limited in duration. Shareholder agreements are used frequently in closely held corporations, especially in conjunction with restrictions on the transfer of shares, in order to provide each of the shareholders with greater control and *delectus personae* (the right to choose who become shareholders).

Even under modern general incorporation statutes, however, two major obstacles prevent the full and effective use of shareholder agreements: (1) in many States, contractual terms restricting the discretion of directors may not be valid, and (2) in some States, certain types of control arrangements must be contained in the articles of incorporation. The Close Corporation Supplement addresses both of these obstacles. It provides that the shareholders of a statutory closely held corporation may, by unanimous action, enter in written agreements to regulate the exercise of the corporate powers, the management of the business and affairs of the corporation, or the relations among the shareholders of the corporation. The Supplement also provides that any authorized agreement shall be valid and enforceable even if the agreement eliminates the board of directors, restricts the discretion or power of the board of directors, or gives proxy or weighted voting rights to the directors. It also makes shareholder agreements valid even if they result in the business being operated essentially as a partnership. Shareholder agreements can include provisions regarding the payment of dividends, employment of officers and other employees, selection of directors and officers, arbitration of disagreements, allocation of voting power between shareholders and directors, and the shareholder's right of dissolution.

GALLER v. GALLER
Supreme Court of Illinois, 1965.
32 Ill.2d 16, 203 N.E.2d 577.

Facts: In 1927 two brothers, Benjamin and Isadore Galler, incorporated the Galler Drug Co., a wholesale drug business that they had operated as equal partners since 1919. The company continued to grow, and in 1955 the two brothers and their wives, Emma and Rose Galler, entered into a written shareholder agreement to leave the corporation in equal control of each family after the death of either brother. Specifically, the agreement provided for the corporation to continue to provide income for the support and maintenance of their immediate families and for the parties to vote for directors so as to give the estate and heirs of a deceased shareholder the same representation as before.

Benjamin died in 1957, and shortly thereafter his widow, Emma, requested that Isadore, the surviving brother, comply with the terms of the agreement. When he refused and proposed that certain changes be made in the agreement, Emma brought this action seeking specific performance of the agreement. Isadore and his wife, Rose, defend on the ground that the shareholder agreement was against public policy and the State's corporation law. The trial court entered a decree of specific performance in favor of Emma. On appeal the decree was reversed.

Decision: Judgment of appellate court reversed.

Opinion: Underwood, J. At this juncture it should be emphasized that we deal here with a so-called close corporation. Various attempts at definition of the close corporation have been made. [Citation.] For our purposes, a close corporation is one in which the stock is held in a few hands, or in a few families, and wherein it is not at all, or only rarely, dealt in by buying or selling. [Citation.] Moreover, it should be recognized that shareholder agreements similar to that in question here are often, as a practical consideration, quite necessary for the protection of those financially interested in the close corporation. While the shareholder of a public-issue corporation may readily sell his shares on the open market should management fail to use, in his opinion, sound business judgment, his counterpart of the close corporation often has a large total of his entire capital invested in the business and has no ready market for his shares should he desire to sell. He feels, understandably, that he is more than a mere investor and that his voice should be heard concerning all corporate activity. Without a shareholder agreement, specifically enforceable by the courts, insuring him a modicum of control, a large minority shareholder might find himself at the mercy of an oppressive or unknowledgeable majority. Moreover, as in the case at bar, the shareholders of a close corporation are often also the directors and officers thereof. With substantial shareholding interests abiding in each member of the board of directors, it is often quite impossible to secure, as in the large public-issue corporation, independent board judgment free from personal motivations concerning corporate policy. For these and other reasons too voluminous to enumerate here, often the only sound basis for protection is afforded by a lengthy, detailed shareholder agreement securing the rights and obligations of all concerned.

* * *

* * * While limiting voting trusts in 1947 to a maximum duration of 10 years, the legislature has indicated no similar policy regarding straight voting agreements although these have been common since prior to 1870. In view of the history of decisions of this court generally upholding, in the absence of fraud or prejudice to minority interests or public policy, the right of stockholders to agree among themselves as to the manner in which their stock will be voted, we do not regard the period of time within which this agreement may remain effective as rendering the agreement unenforceable.

The clause that provides for the election of certain persons to specified offices for a period of years likewise does not require invalidation. * * *

We turn next to a consideration of the effect of the stated purpose of the agreement upon its validity. The pertinent provision is: "The said Benjamin A. Galler and Isadore A. Galler desire to provide income for the support and maintenance of their immediate families." Obviously, there is no evil inherent in a contract entered into for the reason that the persons originating the terms desired to so arrange their property as to provide post-death support for those dependent upon them. Nor does the fact that the subject property is corporate stock alter the situation so long as there exists no detriment to minority stock interests, creditors or other public injury.

* * *

The terms of the dividend agreement require a minimum annual dividend of $50,000, but this duty is limited by the subsequent provision that it shall be operative only so long as an earned surplus of $500,000 is maintained. It may be noted that in 1958, the year prior to commencement of this litigation, the corporation's net earnings after taxes amounted to $202,759 while its earned surplus was $1,543,270, and this was increased in 1958 to $1,680,079 while earnings were $172,964. The minimum earned surplus requirement is designed for the protection of the corporation and its creditors, and we take no exception to the contractual dividend requirements as thus restricted. [Citation.]

The salary continuation agreement is a common feature, in one form or another, of corporate executive employment. It requires that the widow should receive a total benefit, payable monthly over a five-year period, aggregating twice the amount paid her deceased husband in one year. This requirement was likewise limited for the protection of the corporation by being contingent upon the payments being income tax-deductible by the corporation. The charge made in those cases which have considered the validity of payment to the widow of an officer and shareholder in a corporation is that a gift of its property by a noncharitable corporation is in violation of the rights of its shareholders and *ultra vires*. Since there are no shareholders here other than the parties to the contract, this objection is not here applicable, and its effect, as limited, upon the corporation is not so prejudicial as to require its invalidation.

[Judgment for Emma Galler.]

ENFORCEMENT RIGHTS OF SHAREHOLDERS

To protect a shareholder's interests in the corporation, the law provides shareholders with certain enforcement rights. These include the right to obtain information, the right to sue the corporation directly or to sue on the corporation's behalf, and the right to dissent.

Right to Inspect Books and Records

Most States have enacted statutory provisions granting shareholders the right to inspect for a *proper purpose* books and records in person or by an agent and to copy parts of them. A number of States, however, limit this right to shareholders who own a minimum number of shares or have been a shareholder for a minimum period of time. For example, the MBCA requires that a shareholder either must own 5 percent of the outstanding shares or must have owned his shares for at least six months, but a court may, nevertheless, order an inspection even when neither condition is met.[11] The Revised Act relaxes this rule and provides that *every* shareholder is entitled to examine specified corporate records upon prior written request if the demand is made in good faith, for a proper purpose, and during regular business hours at the corporation's principal office.[12]

Proper purpose for inspection means a purpose that is reasonably relevant to that shareholder's interest in the corporation. Proper purposes include determining the financial condition of the corporation, the value of shares, the existence of mismanagement, or the names of other shareholders in order to communicate with them about corporate affairs. The right of inspection is subject to abuse and will be denied a shareholder who is seeking information for an im-

proper purpose. Examples of improper purpose are obtaining information for use by a competing company or obtaining a list of shareholders in order to offer it for sale.

Shareholder Suits

The ultimate recourse of a shareholder, short of selling his shares, is to bring suit against or on behalf of the corporation. Shareholder suits are essentially of two kinds: direct suits or derivative suits.

Direct Suits   A **direct suit** may be brought by a shareholder to enforce a claim that the shareholder has *against* the corporation based on his ownership of shares. Any recovery in a direct suit goes to the shareholder plaintiff. Examples of direct suits include actions by a shareholder to compel payment of dividends properly declared, to enforce the right to inspect corporate records, to enforce the right to vote, to protect preemptive rights, and to compel dissolution.

Derivative Suits   A **derivative suit** is a cause of action brought by one or more shareholders on *behalf* of the corporation to enforce a right belonging to the corporation. It is brought when the board of directors refuses to take such action on behalf of the corporation. Recovery usually goes to the corporation's treasury so that all shareholders can benefit proportionately. Examples of derivative suits are actions to recover damages from management for an *ultra vires* act, to recover damages for a breach of duty by management, and to recover improper dividends. In many such situations, the board of directors may be hesitant to bring suit against the corporation's officers or directors. Consequently, a shareholder derivative suit is the only recourse.

In most States, a shareholder must have owned his shares at the time the transaction complained of occurred in order to bring a derivative suit.[13] In addition, the shareholder must first make demand on the board of directors to enforce the corporate right. The Revised Act does not require that such demand be made if circumstances indicate that a demand would be useless.[14]

The statutes of many States require a plaintiff to give security for reasonable expenses, including attorneys' fees, if his holdings of shares are not of a specified size or value. Before amendment in 1982, Section 49 of the Model Act required 5 percent of the outstanding shares or a value of $25,000. The Revised Act and the 1982 Amendments to the MBCA have deleted this requirement. Both Acts provide that upon termination of a proceeding the court may require the plaintiff to pay the defendants' reasonable expenses, including attorneys' fees, if it finds that the proceeding was brought without reasonable cause.[13, 14] The Revised Act and the statutes of a number of States require that all proposed settlements and discontinuances receive judicial approval.[14]

RICHARDSON v. ARIZONA FUELS CORP.
Supreme Court of Utah, 1980.
614 P.2d 636.

Facts: Donald J. Richardson, Grove L. Cook, and Wayne Weaver are stockholders of Major Oil. They brought an action, individually and on behalf of all other stockholders of Major, against certain directors and other officers of the corporation. In all, the complaint stated twelve causes of action. The first eight causes of action alleged some misappropriation of Major's assets by the defendants and sought to require the defendants to return the assets to Major. Three of the remaining four causes alleged breaches of fiduciary duty implicit in those fraudulent acts and sought compensatory or punitive damages for the injury that resulted. The final cause sought the appointment of a receiver. Richardson, Cook, and Weaver moved for an order certifying the suit as a class action. The motion was granted by the district court, and the defendants appeal.

Decision: Judgment certifying the suit as a class action reversed and remanded.

Opinion: **Stewart, J.** A class action and a derivative action rest upon fundamentally different principles of substantive law; to ignore those differences is not a minor procedural solecism. A derivative action must necessarily be based on a claim for relief which is owned by the stockholders' corporation. Indeed, a prerequisite for filing a derivative action is the failure of the corporation to initiate the action in its own name. The stockholder, as a nominal party, has no right, title or interest whatsoever in the claim itself—whether the action is brought by the corporation or by the stockholder on behalf of the corporation.

A class action, on the other hand, is predicated on ownership of the claim for relief sued upon in the representative of the class and all other class members in their capacity *as individuals*. Shareholders of the corporation may, of course, have claims for relief directly against their corporation because the corporation itself has violated rights possessed by the shareholders, and a class action would be an appropriate means for enforcing their claims. A recovery in a class action is a recovery which belongs directly to the shareholders. However, in a derivative action, the plaintiff shareholder recovers nothing and the judgment runs in favor of the corporation.

The difference in the two procedures and their relationship to underlying substantive law has been stated as follows:

> Suits which are said to be derivative, and therefore come within the rule, are those which seek to enforce any right which belongs to the corporation and is not being enforced, such as the liability of corporate officers or majority shareholders for mismanagement, to recover corporate assets and related claims, to enforce rights of the corporation by virtue of its contract with a third person, and to enjoin those in charge of the corporation from causing it to commit an ultra vires act. [Citation.]

On the other hand,

> [i]f the injury is one to the plaintiff as a stockholder and to him individually, and not to the corporation, as where the action is based on a contract to which he is a party, or on a right belonging severally to him, or on a fraud affecting him directly, it is an individual action. [Citation.]

* * *

The amended complaint states twelve causes of action, the first eight of which allege some fraudulent appropriation of or scheme to appropriate Major's assets by defendants. These causes of action seek to require the defendants to disgorge and return to Major the assets wrongfully obtained. Of the remaining four causes, three seek compensatory or punitive damages for injury attributable to alleged breaches of fiduciary duty implicit in the fraudulent acts enumerated in the first eight causes. The final cause of action seeks appointment of a receiver.

There is no doubt that the first eight causes of action allege injury to the corporation only. The injury alleged can be asserted by plaintiffs only derivatively as stockholders on behalf of the corporation. This leaves the ninth, tenth and eleventh causes of action to be analyzed to determine if they state claims which may be pursued by the stockholders as a class to redress injuries to the stockholders as individuals.

The ninth cause of action alleges initially that the defendants "breached their fiduciary duties to Major Oil and to its stockholders. . . ." As a general rule, directors and other officers of a corporation stand in a fiduciary relation to the corporation. [Citation.] While the statement is made that directors and officers stand in a like relation to the stockholders of the corporation, [citation], in Utah it is clear that that relation is to the stockholders collectively. [Citations.] The distinction between a fiduciary duty owed to the corporation as a whole as opposed to the stockholders collectively does not appear to be one of substance in this case. There is no important issue as to whether the cause of action states a corporate claim. Although plaintiff frames this claim, in the alternative, as one belonging to the shareholders, the claim for relief belongs to the corporation.

The ninth cause of action then goes on to allege that the defendants "mismanaged the corporate and prudential affairs of Major Oil. . . ." The rule in Utah is that mismanagement of the corporation gives rise to a cause of action in the corporation, even if the mismanagement results in damage to stockholders by depreciating the value of the corporation's stock. [Citation.] Therefore, any compensatory damages which may be recovered on account of any breach by defendants of their fiduciary duty as directors and officers or arising as a result of mismanagement of the corporation by defendants belong to the corporation and not to the stockholders individually.

Shareholder's Right to Dissent

A shareholder has the right to dissent from certain corporate actions that require shareholder approval. These actions include most mergers, consolidations, compulsory share exchanges, and a sale or exchange of all or substantially all the assets of the corporation not in the usual and regular course of business. We discuss the shareholder's right to dissent in Chapter 36.

ROLE OF DIRECTORS AND OFFICERS

Management of a corporation is vested by statute in its board of directors, which determines general corporate policy and appoints officers to execute that policy and to administer the day-to-day operations of the corporation. Both the directors and officers of the corporation owe certain duties to the corporate entity as well as to the corporation's shareholders and are liable for breaching these duties.

In the following sections we discuss the role of directors and officers of a corporation. Shareholders who own a sufficient number of shares to have effective control over the corporation are called "controlling shareholders." In some instances, controlling shareholders are held to the same duties as directors and officers, which we discuss later in this chapter. Moreover, in close corporations, some courts impose upon *all* the shareholders a fiduciary duty similar to that imposed upon partners.

DONAHUE v. RODD ELECTROTYPE CO., INC.
Massachusetts Supreme Court, 1974.
367 Mass. 578, 328 N.E.2d 505.

Facts: Euphemia Donahue is a minority stockholder in the Rodd Electrotype Company of New England, Inc. Rodd Electrotype is, by definition, a close corporation. Members of the Rodd and Donahue families are the sole owners of the corporate stock, and no ready market for the shares exists. Moreover, the Rodds have effectively controlled the corporation through their control of the chief management positions and their ownership of the majority of the stock. When Harry Rodd, a director, officer, and controlling stockholder of Rodd Electrotype, retired from the business, Rodd Electrotype purchased his shares in the corporation for $36,000. Donahue was not offered an equal opportunity to sell her shares to the corporation. Donahue brought an action against Rodd Electrotype, Harry Rodd, and the present directors of the corporation, claiming that the defendants breached their fiduciary duty to her in causing the corporation to purchase the shares of Harry Rodd. She sought rescission of the purchase and repayment by Harry Rodd to Rodd Electrotype of the purchase price of the shares plus interest. The trial court dismissed the case and the appellate court affirmed.

Decision: Judgment reversed and relief granted to the plaintiff.

Opinion: **Tauro, C. J.** . . . We deem a close corporation to be typified by: (1) a small number of stockholders; (2) no ready market for the corporate stock; and (3) substantial majority stockholder participation in the management, direction and operations of the corporation.

As thus defined, the close corporation bears striking resemblance to a partnership. Commentators and courts have noted that the close corporation is often little more than an "incorporated" or "chartered" partnership. . . . Just as in a partnership, the relationship among the stockholders must be one of trust, confidence and absolute loyalty if the enterprise is to succeed. Close corporations with substantial assets and with more numerous stockholders are no different from smaller close corporations in this regard. All participants rely on the fidelity and abilities of those stockholders who hold office. Disloyalty and self-seeking conduct on the part of any stockholder will engender bickering, corporate stalemates, and perhaps, efforts to achieve dissolution. . . .

* * *

Although the corporate form provides . . . advantages for the stockholders (limited liability, perpetuity, and so forth), it also supplies an opportunity for the majority stockholders to oppress or disadvantage minority stockholders. The minority is vulnerable to a variety of oppressive devices, termed "freeze-outs," which the majority may employ. [Citation.] An authoritative study of such "freeze-outs" enumerates some of the possibilities: "The squeezers [those who employ the freeze-out techniques] may refuse to declare dividends; they may drain off the corporation's earnings in the form of exorbitant salaries and bonuses to the majority shareholder-officers and perhaps to their relatives, or in the form of high rent by the corporation for property leased from majority shareholders . . .; they may deprive minority shareholders of corporate offices and of employment by the company; they may cause the corporation to sell its assets at an inadequate price to the majority shareholders. . . ." [Citation.] In particular, the power of the board of directors, controlled by the majority, to declare or withhold dividends and to deny the minority employment is easily converted to a device to disadvantage minority stockholders. . . .

The minority can, of course, initiate suit against the majority and their directors. Self-serving conduct by directors is proscribed by the director's fiduciary obligation to the corporation. [Citation.] However, in practice, the plaintiff will find difficulty in challenging dividend or employment policies. Such policies are considered to be within the judgment of the directors. This court has said: "The courts prefer not to interfere . . . with the sound financial management of the corporation by its directors, but declare as a general rule that the declaration of dividends rests within the sound discretion of the directors, refusing to interfere with their determination unless a plain abuse of discretion is made to appear." . . .

Thus, when these types of "freeze-outs" are attempted by the majority stockholders, the minority stockholders, cut off from all corporation-related revenues, must either suffer their losses or seek a buyer for their shares. Many minority stockholders will be unwilling or unable to wait for an alteration in majority policy. Typically, the minority stockholder in a close corporation has a substantial percentage of his personal assets invested in the corporation. [Citation.] The stockholder may have anticipated that his salary from his position with the corporation would be his livelihood. Thus, he cannot afford to wait passively. He must liquidate his investment in the close corporation in order to reinvest the funds in income-producing enterprises.

At this point, the true plight of the minority stockholder in a close corporation becomes manifest. He cannot easily reclaim his capital. In a large public corporation, the oppressed or dissident minority stockholder could sell his stock in order to extricate some of his invested capital. By definition, this market is not available for shares in the close corporation. In a partnership, a partner who feels abused by his fellow partners may cause dissolution by his "express will . . . at any time" [citation] and recover his share of partnership assets and accumulated profits. . . .

To secure dissolution of the ordinary close corporation subject to [citation], the stockholder, in the absence of corporate deadlock, must own at least fifty per cent of the shares [citation] or have the advantage of a favorable provision in the articles of organization [citation]. The minority stockholder, by definition lacking fifty per cent of the corporate shares, can never "authorize" the corporation to file a petition for dissolution under [citation], by his own vote. He will seldom have at his disposal the requisite favorable provision in the articles of organization.

Thus, in a close corporation, the minority stockholders may be trapped in a disadvantageous situation. No outsider would knowingly assume the position of the disadvantaged minority. The outsider would have the same difficulties. To cut losses, the minority stockholder may be compelled to deal with the majority. This is the capstone of the majority plan. Majority "freeze-out" schemes which withhold dividends are designed to compel the minority to relinquish stock at inadequate prices. . . . When the minority stockholder agrees to sell out at less than fair value, the majority has won.

Because of the fundamental resemblance of the close corporation to the partnership, the trust and confidence which are essential to this scale and manner of enterprise, and the inherent danger to minority interests in the close corporation, we hold that stockholders in the close corporation owe one another substantially the same fiduciary duty in the operation of the enterprise that partners owe to one another. In our previous decisions, we have defined the standard of duty owed by partners to one another as the "utmost good faith and loyalty." [Citations.] Stockholders in close corporations must discharge their management and stockholder responsibilities in conformity with this strict good faith standard. They may not act out of avarice, expediency or self-interest in derogation of their duty of loyalty to the other stockholders and to the corporation.

We contrast this strict good faith standard with the somewhat less stringent standard of fiduciary duty to which directors and stockholders of all corporations must adhere in the discharge of their corporate responsibilities. Corporate directors are held to a good faith and inherent fairness standard of conduct [citation] and are not "permitted to serve two masters whose interests are antagonistic." [Citation.] "Their paramount duty is to the corporation, and their personal pecuniary interests are subordinate to that duty." [Citation.]

The more rigorous duty of partners and participants in a joint adventure, here extended to stockholders in a close corporation, was described by then Chief Judge Cardozo of the New York Court of Appeals in [citation]: "Joint adventurers, like copartners, owe to one another, while the enterprise continues, the duty of the finest loyalty. Many forms of conduct permissible in a workaday world for those acting at arm's length, are forbidden to those bound by fiduciary ties. . . . Not honesty alone, but the punctilio of an honor the most sensitive, is then the standard of behavior."

Application of this strict standard of duty to stockholders in close corporations is a natural outgrowth of the prior case law. In a number of cases involving close corporations, we have held stockholders participating in management to a standard of fiduciary duty more exacting than the traditional good faith and inherent fairness standard because of the trust and confidence reposed in them by the other stockholders. . . .

* * *

Under settled Massachusetts law, a domestic corporation, unless forbidden by statute, has the power to purchase its own shares. When the corporation reacquiring its own stock is a close corporation, the purchase is subject to the additional requirement, in the light of our holding in this opinion, that the stockholders, who, as directors or controlling stockholders, caused the corporation to enter into the stock purchase agreement, must have acted with the utmost good faith and loyalty to the other stockholders.

To meet this test, if the stockholder whose shares were purchased was a member of the controlling group, the controlling stockholders must cause the corporation to offer each stockholder an equal opportunity to sell a ratable number of his shares to the corporation at an identical price. . . .

The benefits conferred by the purchase are twofold: (1) provision of a market for shares; (2) access to corporate assets for personal use. By definition, there is no ready market for shares of a close corporation. The purchase creates a market for shares which previously had been unmarketable. It transforms a previously illiquid investment into a liquid one. If the close corporation purchases shares only from a member of the controlling group, the controlling stockholder can convert his shares into cash at a time when none of the other stockholders can. Consistent with its strict fiduciary duty, the controlling group may not utilize its control of the corporation to establish an exclusive market in previously unmarketable shares from which the minority stockholders are excluded. . . .

The purchase also distributes corporate assets to the stockholder whose shares were purchased. Unless an equal opportunity is given to all stockholders, the purchase of shares from a member of the controlling group operates as a *preferential* distribution of assets. In exchange for his shares, he receives a percentage of the contributed capital and accumulated profits of the enterprise. The funds he so receives are available for his personal use. The other stockholders benefit from no such access to corporate property and cannot withdraw their shares of the corporate profits and capital in this manner unless the controlling group acquiesces. Although the purchase price for the controlling stockholder's shares may seem fair to the corporation and other stockholders under the tests established in the prior case law, the controlling stockholder whose stock has been purchased has still received a relative advantage over his fellow stockholders, inconsistent with his strict fiduciary duty—an opportunity to turn corporate funds to personal use.

The rule of equal opportunity in stock purchases by close corporations provides equal access to these benefits for all stockholders. We hold that, in any case in which the controlling stockholders have exercised their power over the corporation to deny the minority such equal opportunity, the minority shall be entitled to appropriate relief. . . .

* * *

On its face, then, the purchase of Harry Rodd's shares by the corporation is a breach of the duty which the controlling stockholders, the Rodds, owed to the minority stockholders, the plaintiff and her son. The purchase distributed a portion of the corporate assets to Harry Rodd, a member of the controlling group, in exchange for his shares. The plaintiff and her son were not offered an equal opportunity to sell their shares to the corporation. In fact, their efforts to obtain an equal opportunity were rebuffed by the corporate representative. As the trial judge found, they did not, in any manner, ratify the transaction with Harry Rodd.

FUNCTION OF THE BOARD OF DIRECTORS

Although the directors are elected by the shareholders to manage the corporation, they are neither trustees nor agents of the shareholders or the corporation. They are, however, fiduciaries who must perform their duties in good faith, in the best interests of the corporation, and with due care.

The Model Act states that "[a]ll corporate powers shall be exercised by or under authority of, and the business and affairs of a corporation shall be managed under the direction of, a board of directors."[15] In some corporations, the board consists of members all of whom are actively involved in the management of the business. In these cases, the corporate powers are exercised *by* the board of directors. On the other hand, in publicly held corporations, a majority of the board members frequently are not actively involved in management. Here, the corporate powers are exercised *under* the authority of the board, which formulates major management policy but does not involve itself in the day-to-day management. Under the Revised Act, a corporation having fifty or fewer shareholders may dispense with or limit the authority of a board of directors by describing in its articles of incorporation who will perform some or all of the duties of a board.[16]

The board determines corporate policy in a number of areas, including (1) selecting and removing officers, (2) determining the capital structure, (3) initiating fundamental changes, (4) declaring dividends, and (5) selling management compensation.

Selection and Removal of Officers

In most States, the board of directors has the responsibility to choose the corporate officers and may remove any officer at any time.[17] Officers are agents of the corporation and are delegated their responsibilities by the board of directors.

Capital Structure

The board of directors determines the capital structure and financial policy of the corporation. For example, the board of directors has the power to

1. fix the selling price of newly issued par value shares at not less than par;
2. fix the stated value and selling price of no par shares, unless the power to do so is reserved to the shareholders by the articles of incorporation;
3. determine the value of the consideration in the form of property, labor, or services re-

ceived by the corporation in payment for shares issued;
4. purchase, redeem, or otherwise acquire shares of the corporation's equity securities;
5. borrow money, issue notes, bonds, and other obligations, and secure any of the corporation's obligations by mortgage or pledge of any or all of the corporation's property; and
6. sell, lease, or mortgage assets of the corporation in the *usual* and *regular* course of business.

Fundamental Changes

The board of directors has the power to make, alter, amend, or repeal the bylaws, unless this power is reserved to the shareholders by the articles of incorporation.[18] In addition, the board initiates a number of actions that are beyond its powers and require shareholder approval. For instance, the board must initiate proceedings to amend the articles of incorporation; to effect a merger, consolidation, compulsory share exchange, or the sale or lease of all or substantially all of the assets of the corporation other than in the usual and regular course of business; and to dissolve the corporation.

Dividends

The board of directors declares the amount and type of dividends, subject to restrictions in the State incorporation statute, the articles of incorporation, and corporate loan and preferred stock agreements.[19] The board also provides for closing of stock transfer books and fixes a record date for the purpose of determining the shareholders who are entitled to receive dividends.[20]

Management Compensation

The board of directors usually determines the compensation of officers. In addition, a number of States allow the board to fix the compensation of board members.

ELECTION AND TENURE OF DIRECTORS

The governing incorporation statute, articles of incorporation, and the bylaws determine the qualifications that individuals must possess in order to be eligible as directors of the corporation. They also determine the election, number, tenure, and compensation of directors.

Election, Number, and Tenure of Directors

The initial board of directors is generally named in the articles of incorporation and serves until the first meeting of the shareholders. Thereafter, directors are elected at annual meetings of the shareholders and hold office for one year or until their successors are duly elected and qualified. If the shares represented at a meeting in person or by proxy are not sufficient to constitute a quorum, the incumbent board continues in office as "holdover" directors until a valid election can be held. State statutes traditionally required that each corporation have three or more directors, although the modern trend is to permit the board to consist of one or more members.[21]

Moreover, the number of directors may be increased or decreased, within statutory limits, by amendment to the bylaws or charter. The Revised Act permits the board of directors, if it has the power to fix or change the number of directors, to increase or decrease its own size by up to 30 percent without shareholder approval.[22] For example, in a board fixed or approved by the shareholders at 15 members, the board may, without shareholder approval, change the size of the board to as few as 11 or as many as 19. A board of 5 may be changed by the board to as few as 4 or as many as 6. The Revised Act authorizes the articles of incorporation or bylaws to establish a variable range for the size of the board by fixing a minimum and maximum number of directors.[22]

Vacancies and Removal of Directors

The Model Act provides that a vacancy in the board may be filled by the affirmative vote of a majority of the remaining directors, even though they constitute less than a quorum of the board, and the director so elected shall hold office for the unexpired term of his predecessor.[23] A directorship to be filled because of an increase in the number of directors may be filled by the board for a term continuing until the next election of directors by the shareholders.

Some States have no statutory provision for removal of directors, although a common law rule permits removal for cause by action of the shareholders. The Model Act and an increasing number of other statutes permit removal of one or more of the directors or of the entire board by the shareholders, with or without cause, at a special meeting called for that purpose, subject to cumulative voting rights, if applicable.[9] The Revised Act permits the articles of incorporation to provide that directors may be removed only for cause.[24]

Compensation of Directors

Traditionally, directors did not receive salaries for their services as directors, although it was usual for them to be paid a fee or honorarium for attendance at meetings. The Model Act and other incorporation statutes now specifically authorize the board of directors to fix the compensation of directors unless there is a contrary provision in the articles of incorporation.[15]

EXERCISE OF DIRECTORS' FUNCTIONS

Directors do not have the power to bind the corporation when acting individually but only when acting as a board. The board may act only at a meeting of the directors or by written consent by all of the directors, if written consent without a meeting is authorized by the incorporation statute and not contrary to the charter or bylaws.

Meetings are held either at a regular time and place fixed in the bylaws or at special times as they are called. Notice of meetings must be given as prescribed in the bylaws. A director's attendance at any meeting is a waiver of such notice, unless the director attends for the express purpose of objecting to the transaction of any business on the ground that the meeting is not lawfully called or convened. Most modern statutes provide that meetings of the board may be held either in or out of the State of incorporation.[25]

Quorum and Voting

A majority of the members of the board of directors constitutes a quorum, the minimum number of members necessary to be present at a meeting in order to transact business. The articles of incorporation or bylaws may, however, require a number greater than a simple majority. If a quorum is present at any meeting, the act of a majority of the directors in attendance at such meeting is the act of the board, unless the act of a greater number is required by the articles of incorporation or bylaws.[26]

Closely held corporations sometimes use supermajority or unanimous quorum requirements. In addition, they may require a supermajority or unanimous vote of the board for some or all matters.

The Revised Act requires a quorum to be present when "a vote is taken," making it clear that the board may act only when a quorum is present.[27] This rule is in contrast to the rule governing shareholder meetings: once a quorum of shareholders is obtained it *cannot* be broken by the withdrawal of shareholders. In any event, directors may not vote by proxy, although a number of States permit directors to participate in meetings by means of conference telephones.

If a director is present at a meeting of the board at which action on any corporate matter is taken, he is presumed to have assented to such action unless, in addition to dissenting from it, he (1) has his dissent entered in the minutes of the meeting, or (2) files his written dissent to such action with the person acting as secretary before the meeting adjourns, or (3) forwards his written dissent by registered mail to the secretary of the corporation immediately after the adjournment of the meeting.[15]

Action Taken without a Meeting

The Model Act provides that, unless otherwise provided by the articles of incorporation or bylaws, any action required by the statute to be taken at a meeting of the board may be taken without a meeting if a consent in writing is signed by all of the directors.[28] Such consent has the same effect as a unanimous vote.

Delegation of Board Powers

If provided for by the articles of incorporation or bylaws, the board of directors may, by majority vote of the full board, appoint executive and other committees, all of whose members must be directors.[29] The Revised Act provides that the "creation of a committee and appointment of members to it must be approved by the greater of (1) a majority of all the directors in office when the action is taken or (2) the number of directors required by the articles of incorporation or bylaws to take action."[30] Committees may exercise all of the authority of the board except for certain matters specified in the incorporation statute, such as the declaration of dividends and other distributions, filling vacancies on the board of directors, amending the bylaws, recommending fundamental changes to the shareholders, approving a merger not requiring shareholder approval, and authorizing the sale of stock.[29] Delegation of authority to a committee does not relieve any board member of his duties to the corporation. Commonly used committees include executive committees, audit committees (to recommend and oversee independent public accountants), compensation committees, finance committees, nominating committees, and investment committees.

Directors' Inspection Rights

Directors have the right to inspect corporate books and records so they can competently and fully perform their duties.

OFFICERS

The officers of a corporation are appointed by the board of directors to hold the offices provided in the bylaws, which set forth the respective duties of each officer. Statutes generally require as a minimum that officers consist of a president, one or more vice-presidents as prescribed by the bylaws, a secretary, and a treasurer.[17] A person may hold more than one office, except that the same person may not hold the office of president and secretary at the same time.

The Revised Act permits every corporation to designate whatever officers it wants. Although no particular number of officers is specified, one of the officers must be delegated responsibility for preparing the minutes of directors' and shareholders' meetings and authenticating records of the corporation. The Revised Act permits the same individual to hold *all* of the offices of a corporation.[31]

Selection and Removal of Officers

Most State statutes provide that the officers are appointed by the board of directors and serve at the pleasure of the board.[17] Accordingly, officers may be removed by the board with or without cause. Of course, if the officer has a valid employment contract for a specified period of time, removal of the officer without cause before the contract expires would constitute a breach of the employment contract. The board also determines the compensation of officers.

Role of Officers

The officers are, like the directors, fiduciaries to the corporation. On the other hand, unlike the directors, they are agents of the corporation. The roles of officers are set forth in the corporate bylaws. The following is a typical description drawn from model bylaws:

President The president is the principal executive officer of the corporation and, subject to the control of the board of directors, in general supervises and controls all of the business and affairs of the corporation. He presides at all meetings of the shareholders and of the board of directors. He may sign for the corporation any deeds, mortgages, bonds, contracts, or other instruments that the board of directors has authorized to be executed.

Vice-President In the absence of the president or in the event of his death, inability, resignation, or refusal to act, the vice-president performs the duties of the president and, when so acting, has all the powers of and is subject to all the restrictions on the president.

Secretary The secretary keeps the minutes of the proceedings of the shareholders and of the board of directors; sees that all notices are duly given; is custodian of the corporate records and of the seal of the corporation; signs with the president certificates for shares of the corporation, the issuance of which has been authorized by resolution of the board of directors; and has general charge of the stock transfer books of the corporation.

Treasurer The treasurer has charge and custody of and is responsible for all funds and securities of the corporation; he receives and gives receipts for and deposits money due and payable to the corporation.

Authority of Officers

The Model Act provides that all officers of the corporation shall have such authority as may be provided in the bylaws or as may be determined by resolution of the board of directors not inconsistent with the bylaws.[17] As with other agents, the authority of an officer to bind the corporation may be (1) actual express, (2) actual implied, or (3) apparent.

Actual Express Authority Actual express authority results from the manifestation of assent by the corporation to the officer that the officer should act on the behalf of the corporation. Actual express authority arises from the incorporation statute, the articles of incorporation, the bylaws, and resolutions of the board of directors. The principal source of actual express authority is the resolutions of the board of directors.

Actual Implied Authority Officers, as agents of the corporation, have implied authority to do what is reasonably necessary to perform their actual, delegated authority. In addition, the question arises whether officers possess implied authority merely by virtue of their positions. The courts have been cautious in granting such implied or inherent authority. Traditionally, the courts tended to hold that the president had no implied authority by virtue of his office, although the more recent decisions tend to recognize his authority to bind the corporation in ordinary business transactions. Any act requiring board approval, such as issuing stock, however, is clearly beyond the implied authority of the president or any other officer. In most jurisdictions, implied authority of position does not extend to any officer other than the president.

Apparent Authority Apparent authority arises from acts of the principal that lead third parties to believe reasonably and in good faith that an officer has the required authority. Apparent authority might arise when a third party relies on the fact that an officer has exercised the same authority in the past with the consent of the board of directors.

Ratification A corporation may ratify the unauthorized acts of its officers. Ratification is equivalent to having granted the officer prior authority. Ratification relates back to the original transaction and may be express or implied from the corporation's acceptance of the benefits of the contract with full knowledge of the facts

DUTIES OF DIRECTORS AND OFFICERS

A corporation may not recover damages from its directors and officers for losses resulting from their poor business judgments or honest mistakes of judgment. The directors and officers are not insurers of business success. They are required only to be obedient, reasonably diligent, and completely loyal. These duties of obedience, diligence, and loyalty are for the most part judicially imposed. State and Federal statutes supplement the common law by imposing liability on directors and officers for specific acts, but the common law still remains the most significant source of duties.

Duty of Obedience

Directors and officers must act within their respective authority. For any loss resulting to the corporation from their unauthorized acts, they are held absolutely liable in some jurisdictions; in others they are held liable only if they intentionally or negligently exceeded their authority.

Duty of Diligence

In the discharge of their duties, directors and officers must exercise ordinary care and prudence. Some States interpret this standard to mean that directors and officers must exercise "the same degree of care and prudence that men promoted by self-interest generally exercise in their own affairs." Most States, as well as the MBCA, hold that the test requires that "[a] director shall perform his duties as a director . . . with such care as an ordinarily prudent person in a like position would use under similar circumstances."[15]

So long as the directors and officers act in good faith and with due care, the courts will not substitute their judgment for the board's or officer's judgment—the so-called business judgment rule. Directors and officers will nevertheless be held liable for bad faith or negligent conduct. Moreover, they may be liable for failing to act. In one instance, a director of a bank, who in the five-and-one-half years that he had been on the board had never attended a board meeting or made any examination of the books and records, was held liable for the losses resulting from the unsupervised acts of the president and cashier, who had made various improper loans and had permitted large overdrafts.

Reliance on Others Directors and officers, however, are permitted to entrust important work to others, and if they have selected employees with care, they are not personally liable for the negligent acts or willful wrongs of the employees. A reasonable amount of supervision is required, and an officer or director will be held liable for the losses resulting from an employee's carelessness, theft, or embezzlement if he knew or ought to have known or suspected that such losses were being incurred.

Directors may also rely on information provided them by officers and employees of the corporation. The Model Act provides:

In performing his duties, a director shall be entitled to rely on information, opinions, reports or statements, including financial statements and other financial data, in each case prepared or presented by:

(a) one or more officers or employees of the corporation whom the director reasonably believes to be reliable and competent in the matters presented,

(b) counsel, public accountants or other persons as to matters which the director reasonably believes to be within such person's professional or expert competence, or

(c) a committee of the board upon which he does not serve, duly designated in accordance with a provision of the articles of incorporation or the bylaws, as to matters within its designated authority, which committee the director reasonably believes to merit confidence

but he shall not be considered to be acting in good faith if he has knowledge concerning the matter in question that would cause such reliance to be unwarranted.[15]

An officer is also entitled to rely upon this information, but this right may, in many circumstances, be more limited than a director's because of the officer's greater familiarity with the affairs of the corporation.[32]

Business Judgment Rule Directors are continuously called on to make decisions that require balancing the benefits and risks for the corporation. Although hindsight may reveal that some of these decisions were not the best, the **business judgment rule** precludes imposing liability on the directors for honest mistakes of judgment. To benefit from the business judgment rule, a director must discharge his duties

1. in good faith;
2. with the care an ordinarily prudent person

in a like position would exercise under similar circumstances; and

3. in a manner he reasonably believes to be in the best interests of the corporation.[15,33]

This requires that the director make an informed decision without any conflict of interests and have a rational basis for making it. Moreover, where there is a failure to satisfy this standard of conduct, it must be shown that the director's actions (or inaction) is the proximate cause of damage to the corporation. The business judgment rule also applies to officers.[32]

The fourth tentative draft of Section 4.01(c) of the American Law Institute's Corporate Governance Project provides:

A director or officer who makes a business judgment in good faith fulfills his duty under this Section if:

(1) he is not interested in the subject of his business judgment;

(2) he is informed with respect to the subject of his business judgment to the extent he reasonably believes to be appropriate under the circumstances; and

(3) he rationally believes that his business judgment is in the best interests of the corporation.

Hasty or ill-advised action can also cause directors to be held liable. In a recent Delaware case, the Supreme Court of Delaware held the directors liable for approving the terms of a cash-out merger. The court found that the directors did not adequately inform themselves of the company's intrinsic value and were grossly negligent in approving the terms of the merger upon two hours' consideration and without prior notice. The next case is an example of a director being held liable for negligence.

FRANCIS v. UNITED JERSEY BANK
Supreme Court of New Jersey, 1981.
87 N.J. 15, 432 A.2d 814.

Facts: Pritchard & Baird was a reinsurance broker. A reinsurance broker arranges contracts between insurance companies so companies that have sold large policies may sell participations in these policies to other companies in order to share the risks. Pritchard & Baird was controlled for many years by Charles Pritchard, who died in December 1973. Prior to his death, he brought his two sons, Charles Jr. and William, into the business. The pair assumed an increasingly dominant role in the affairs of the business during the elder Charles's later years. Starting in 1970, Charles Jr. and William began to withdraw ever-increasing sums from the corporation account that were designated as "loans" on the balance sheet. These "loans," however, represented a significant misappropriation of funds belonging to the clients of the corporation. By late 1975, Charles Jr. and William had plunged the corporation into hopeless bankruptcy. A total of $12,333,514.47 in "loans" had accumulated by October of that year. Mrs. Lillian Pritchard, the widow of the elder Charles, was a member of the corporation's board of directors during this period until her resignation on December 3, 1975, the day before the corporation filed for bankruptcy. Francis, as trustee in the bankruptcy proceeding, brought suit against United Jersey Bank, the administrator of the estate of Charles Sr. He also charged that Lillian Pritchard, as a director of the corporation, was personally liable for the misappropriated funds on the basis of negligence in discharging her duties as director. The trial court found Lillian Pritchard liable and the appellate court affirmed.

Decision: Judgment for Francis affirmed.

Opinion: **Pollock, J.**   Individual liability of a corporate director for acts of the corporation is a prickly problem. Generally directors are accorded broad immunity and are not insurers of corporate activities. The problem is particularly nettlesome when a third party asserts that a director, because of nonfeasance, is liable for losses caused by acts of insiders, who in this case were officers, directors and shareholders. Determination of the liability of Mrs. Pritchard requires findings that she had a duty to the clients of Pritchard & Baird, that she breached that duty and that her breach was a proximate cause of their losses.

The New Jersey Business Corporation Act, which took effect on January 1, 1969, was a comprehensive revision of the statutes relating to business corporations. One section, [citation], concerning a director's general obligation had no counterpart in the old Act. That section makes it incumbent upon directors to

discharge their duties in good faith and with that degree of diligence, care and skill which ordinarily prudent men would exercise under similar circumstances in like positions.

* * *

As a general rule, a director should acquire at least a rudimentary understanding of the business of the corporation. Accordingly, a director should become familiar with the fundamentals of the business in which the corporation is engaged. [Citation.] Because directors are bound to exercise ordinary care, they cannot set up as a defense lack of the knowledge needed to exercise the requisite degree of care. If one "feels that he has not had sufficient business experience to qualify him to perform the duties of a director, he should either acquire the knowledge by inquiry, or refuse to act." [Citation.]

Directors are under a continuing obligation to keep informed about the activities of the corporation. Otherwise, they may not be able to participate in the overall management of corporate affairs. [Citations.] Directors may not shut their eyes to corporate misconduct, and then claim that because they did not see the misconduct, they did not have a duty to look. The sentinel asleep at his post contributes nothing to the enterprise he is charged to protect. [Citation.]

Directorial management does not require a detailed inspection of day-to-day activities, but rather a general monitoring of corporate affairs and policies.

[Citation.] Accordingly, a director is well advised to attend board meetings regularly. Indeed, a director who is absent from a board meeting is presumed to concur in action taken on a corporate matter, unless he files a "dissent with the secretary of the corporation within a reasonable time after learning of such action." [Citation.] Regular attendance does not mean that directors must attend every meeting, but that directors should attend meetings as a matter of practice. A director of a publicly held corporation might be expected to attend regular monthly meetings, but a director of a small, family corporation might be asked to attend only an annual meeting. The point is that one of the responsibilities of a director is to attend meetings of the board of which he or she is a member. That burden is lightened by [citation], which permits board action without a meeting if all members of the board consent in writing.

While directors are not required to audit corporate books, they should maintain familiarity with the financial status of the corporation by a regular review of financial statements. [Citations.] In some circumstances, directors may be charged with assuring that bookkeeping methods conform to industry custom and usage. [Citation.] The extent of review, as well as the nature and frequency of financial statements, depends not only on the customs of the industry, but also on the nature of the corporation and the business in which it is engaged. Financial statements of some small corporations may be prepared internally and only on an annual basis; in a large publicly held corporation, the statements may be produced monthly or at some other regular interval. Adequate financial review normally would be more informal in a private corporation than in a publicly held corporation.

Of some relevance in this case is the circumstance that the financial records disclose the "shareholders' loans". Generally directors are immune from liability if, in good faith,

> they rely upon the opinion of counsel for the corporation or upon written reports setting forth financial data concerning the corporation and prepared by an independent public accountant or certified public accountant or firm of such accountants or upon financial statements, books of account or reports of the corporation represented to them to be correct by the president, the officer of the corporation having charge of its books of account, or the person presiding at a meeting of the board. [Citation.]

The review of financial statements, however, may give rise to a duty to inquire further into matters revealed by those statements. [Citations.] Upon discovery of an illegal course of action, a director has a duty to object and, if the corporation does not correct the conduct, to resign. [Citations.]

In certain circumstances, the fulfillment of the duty of a director may call for more than mere objection and resignation. Sometimes a director may be required to seek the advice of counsel. * * *

A director is not an ornament, but an essential component of corporate governance. Consequently, a director cannot protect himself behind a paper shield bearing the motto, "dummy director." [Citations.] The New Jersey Business Corporation Act, in imposing a standard of ordinary care on all directors, confirms that dummy, figurehead and accommodation directors are anachronisms with no place in New Jersey law. * * * Thus, all directors are responsible for managing the business and affairs of the corporation. [Citations.]

* * *

A director's duty of care does not exist in the abstract, but must be considered in relation to specific obligees. In general, the relationship of a corporate director to the corporation and its stockholders is that of a fiduciary. [Citation.] Shareholders have a right to expect that directors will exercise reasonable supervision and control over the policies and practices of a corporation. The institutional integrity of a corporation depends upon the proper discharge by directors of those duties.

* * *

As a director of a substantial reinsurance brokerage corporation, she should have known that it received annually millions of dollars of loss and premium funds which it held in trust for ceding and reinsurance companies. Mrs. Pritchard should have obtained and read the annual statements of financial condition of Pritchard & Baird. Although she had a right to rely upon financial statements prepared in accordance with [citation], such reliance would not excuse her conduct. The reason is that those statements disclosed on their face the misappropriation of trust funds.

From those statements, she should have realized that, as of January 31, 1970, her sons were withdrawing substantial trust funds under the guise of "Shareholders' Loans." The financial statements for each fiscal year commencing with that of January 31, 1970, disclosed that the working capital deficits and the "loans" were escalating in tandem. Detecting a misappropriation of funds would not have required special expertise or extraordinary diligence; a cursory reading of the financial statements would have revealed the pillage. Thus, if Mrs. Pritchard had read the financial statements, she would have known that her sons were converting trust funds. When financial statements demonstrate that insiders are bleeding a corporation to death, a director should notice and try to stanch the flow of blood.

In summary, Mrs. Pritchard was charged with the obligation of basic knowledge and supervision of the business of Pritchard & Baird. Under the circumstances, this obligation included reading and understanding financial statements, and making reasonable attempts at detection and prevention of the illegal conduct of other officers and directors. She had a duty to protect the clients of Pritchard & Baird against policies and practices that would result in the misappropriation of money they had entrusted to the corporation. She breached that duty.

Nonetheless, the negligence of Mrs. Pritchard does not result in liability unless it is a proximate cause of the loss. * * * Thus, the plaintiff must establish not only a breach of duty, "but in addition that the performance by the director of his duty would have avoided loss, and the amount of the resulting loss." [Citation.]

* * *

Within Pritchard & Baird, several factors contributed to the loss of the funds: comingling of corporate and client monies, conversion of funds by Charles, Jr. and William and dereliction of her duties by Mrs. Pritchard. The wrongdoing of her sons, although the immediate cause of the loss, should not excuse Mrs. Pritchard from her negligence which also was a substantial factor contributing to the loss. [Citation.] Her sons knew that she, the only other director, was not reviewing their conduct; they spawned their fraud in the backwater of her neglect. Her neglect of duty contributed to the climate of corruption; her failure to act contributed to the continuation of that corruption. Consequently, her conduct was a substantial factor contributing to the loss.

Analysis of proximate cause is especially difficult in a corporate context where the allegation is that nonfeasance of a director is a proximate cause of damage to a third party. Where a case involves nonfeasance, no one can say "with absolute certainty what would have occurred if the defendant had acted otherwise." [Citation.] Nonetheless, where it is reasonable to conclude that the failure to act would produce a particular result and that result has followed, causation may be inferred. [Citation.] We conclude that even if Mrs. Pritchard's mere objection had not stopped the depredations of her sons, her consultation with an attorney and the threat of suit would have deterred them. That conclusion flows as a matter of common sense and logic from the record. Whether in other situations a director has a duty to do more than protest and resign is best left to case-by-case determinations. In this case, we are satisfied that there was a duty to do more than object and resign. Consequently, we find that Mrs. Pritchard's negligence was a proximate cause of the misappropriations.

To conclude, by virtue of her office, Mrs. Pritchard had the power to prevent the losses sustained by the clients of Pritchard & Baird. With power comes responsibility. She had a duty to deter the depredation of the other insiders, her sons. She breached that duty and caused plaintiffs to sustain damages.

Duty of Loyalty

The officers and directors of a corporation owe a duty of loyalty (**fiduciary duty**) to the corporation and to its shareholders. The essence of a fiduciary duty is the subordination of self-interest to the interest of the person or persons to whom the duty is owing. It requires undeviating loyalty on the part of officers and directors to the corporation, which they both serve and control.

An officer or director is required to make full disclosure to the corporation of any financial interest that he may have in any contract or transaction to which the corporation is a party. This is a corollary to the rule that forbids fiduciaries from making secret profits. His business conduct must be insulated from self-interest, and he may not take advantage of opportunities to advance his personal interest at the expense of the corporation. Moreover, he may not represent conflicting interests; his duty is one of strict allegiance to the corporation.

The remedy for breach of fiduciary duty is a suit in equity by the corporation, or more often a derivative suit instituted by a shareholder, to require the fiduciary to pay to the corporation the profits that he obtained through breach of his fiduciary duty. It need not be shown that the corporation could otherwise have made the profits that the fiduciary realized. The object of the rule is to discourage breaches of duty by a fiduciary, and this is achieved by taking from the fiduciary all of the profits he has made. The enforcement of the rule may result in a windfall to the corporation, but this is incidental to the deterrent effect of the rule. Whenever a director or officer breaches his fiduciary duty, he forfeits his right to compensation during the period he engaged in the breach.

WILSHIRE OIL CO. OF TEXAS v. RIFFE
United States Court of Appeals, Tenth Circuit, 1969.
406 F.2d 1061.

Facts: Riffe, while serving as an officer of Wilshire Oil Company, received a secret commission for work done on behalf of a competing corporation. Wilshire Oil brings this action against Riffe to recover these secret profits and, in addition, to recover the compensation paid to Riffe by Wilshire Oil during the period that he acted on behalf of the competitor. The trial court entered judgment for Wilshire Oil Company for the profits but denied recovery of compensation.

Decision: The case is reversed and remanded to the trial court with directions to enter judgment for Wilshire Oil Company against Riffe in an amount equal to seven-twelfths of all compensation (both salary and bonus) paid to Riffe for services during the calendar year 1962.

Opinion: **Seth, C. J.**   This is an appeal by the plaintiff-appellant from a portion of the judgment of the trial court in this action which was commenced by the plaintiff corporation against one of its former corporate officers. The suit was to recover profits made by the corporate officer by participating in competitive enterprises, in receiving personally commissions for corporate construction work, and to recover the compensation paid to the officer by the corporation during the period he was interested in a competitive corporation.

This is the second appeal. This court on the first appeal reversed and remanded the case, holding that the defendant had breached his duty to the corporation and had engaged in activities contrary to the terms of his contract of employment (Wilshire Oil Co. of Texas v. Riffe, 381 F.2d 646). On remand the trial court entered judgment on the claims for recovery of the profits made through participating in a competitive corporation, but denied the corporation recovery of the compensation it paid to the defendant for this period.

The nature and extent of the fiduciary duties owed by a corporate officer to the corporation he serves have been long established. This matter was considered at some length in the previous opinion in this case as it related to these facts and need not be repeated here. As stated in the first opinion the acts of the appellee also constituted a breach of his contract of employment. On the prior appeal all the basic and determinative issues were thus decided.

When a corporate officer engages in activities which constitute a breach of his duty of loyalty or if it is a wilful breach of his contract of employment, he is not entitled to compensation for services during such a period of time although part of his services may have been properly performed. In the Restatement (Second), Agency § 469 the above doctrine is set forth, and this is followed by the comment which states in part:

"An agent, who, without the acquiescence of his principal, acts for his own benefit or for the benefit of another in antagonism to or in competition with the principal in a transaction is not entitled to compensation which otherwise be due him."

The comment continues and states that the agent is not entitled to compensation although the acts may not actually harm his principal and even if he thinks his actions will benefit the principal or he is otherwise "justified" in "so acting." [Citations.]

This rule is applicable to the case before us, and it it not necessary to again describe the several breaches of duty involved which were clearly established in the record. The record shows, as to one of the principal events, that the failure commenced on or before May 31, 1962, and continued to the end of the year when the officer's employment terminated. It was then also that the particular division which he was responsible for was sold by the corporation. The record thus sets out the period of this violation, and this is sufficient to apply the above doctrine. Thus we hold that the appellee was not entitled to compensation of any kind from May 31, 1962, to December 31, 1962.

The appellee argues that the corporate division he was responsible for made money during the period in question, and that the division was itself sold at a profit to appellant corporation. However, under the authorities or on any other basis, this is no answer to the established violation of duty. The fact that the division may have made money does not prove that no breach took place nor does it excuse one any more than a failure to make money demonstrates a breach of du' . The same may be said about whether the officer considered that he was acting properly or in good faith.

Conflict of Interests   A contract between an officer or a director and the corporation is not void, but voidable. A rule that would not allow such a contract would be unreasonable because it would prevent directors from entering into contracts that are beneficial to the corporation. Therefore, if such a contract is honest and fair, it will be upheld.

In the case of contracts between corporations having an interlocking directorate, or having one or more persons who are members of both boards of directors, the courts subject the contracts to scrutiny and will set them aside unless the transaction is shown to have been entirely fair and entered into in good faith.

The Model Act and most States address both of these related problems by providing that such transactions are neither void nor voidable if, after full disclosure, they are approved by either the board of disinterested directors or the shareholders or if they are fair and reasonable to the corporation.[34]

Loans to Directors   The Model Act does not permit a corporation to lend money to its directors without authorization in each instance by its shareholders.[35] The Revised Act permits such loans if the particular loan is approved (1) by a majority of disinterested shareholders, or (2) by the board of directors after determining that the loan benefits the corporation.[36]

Corporate Opportunity   Directors and officers may not usurp any corporate opportunity that in all fairness should belong to the corporation. A corporate opportunity is an opportunity in which the corporation has a right, property interest, or expectancy, and it depends on the facts and circumstances of each case. The American Law Institute's *Principles of Corporate Governance*, defines a corporate opportunity broadly as including any proposed acquisition of contract rights or other property that is communicated or made available to the officer or director (1) in connection with the performance of his obligations or under cir-

cumstances that should reasonably lead him to believe that the person offering the opportunity expects him to offer it to the corporation, or (2) through the use of corporate information or property, if the resulting opportunity is one that he should reasonably be expected to believe would be of interest to the corporation. In the case of an officer, an opportunity is a corporate opportunity if it is one that she knows or reasonably should know is closely related to the business in which the corporation is engaged or may reasonably be expected to engage. A corporate opportunity must be promptly offered to the corporation, which should promptly accept or reject the opportunity. Rejection may be based on one or more of a number of factors, such as lack of interest of the corporation in the opportunity, its financial inability to acquire the opportunity, legal restrictions on its ability to accept the opportunity, or unwillingness of a third party to deal with the corporation.

For instance, a party proposes a business arrangement to a corporation through its vice-president, who personally accepts it without offering it to the corporation. The vice-president has usurped a corporate opportunity. On the other hand, it generally would not include an opportunity that the corporation was unable to accept or one that the corporation specifically rejected by a vote of disinterested directors after full disclosure. In both of these instances, a director or officer can take personal advantage of the opportunity.

Transactions in Shares   The issuance of shares at favorable prices to management by excluding other shareholders will normally constitute a violation of the fiduciary duty. So might the issuance of shares to a director at a fair price if the purpose of the issuance is to perpetuate corporate control rather than to raise capital or serve some other interest of the corporation. Officers and directors have access to inside advance information not available to the public that may affect the future market value of the shares of the corporation. Federal statutes have attempted to deal with this trading advantage by prohibiting officers and directors from purchasing or selling shares of stock of their corporation without adequate disclosure of all material facts in their possession that may affect the value or potential value of the stock. Under the Securities Exchange Act of 1934, the Securities and Exchange Commission adopted Rule 10b-5, which requires disclosure in such purchases or sales where use has been made of the mails or an instrumentality of interstate commerce, such as the telephone or telegraph. In addition, Section 16(b) of the same statute requires insiders to give to the corporation any profit realized by their short-swing speculation in its stock. In addition, the SEC is authorized by the Insider Trading Sanctions Act of 1984 to bring an action in a U.S. district court to have a civil penalty (of up to three times the profit gained or loss avoided) imposed upon any person who purchases or sells a security while in possession of material nonpublic information. We discuss these matters more fully in Chapter 43.

Although State law has not consistently imposed liability on officers and directors for secret, profitable use of inside information, the trend is toward holding them liable for breach of fiduciary duty to shareholders from whom they purchase stock without making disclosure to them of facts that give the stock added potential value. They are also held liable to the corporation for profits realized on a sale of the stock when undisclosed conditions of the corporation make a substantial decline in value practically inevitable.

Duty Not to Compete   As fiduciaries, directors and officers owe to the corporation the duty of undivided loyalty, which means that they may not compete with the corporation. A director or officer who breaches his fiduciary duty by competing with the corporation is liable for damages caused to the corporation. Although directors and officers may engage in their own business interests, courts will closely scrutinize any interest that competes with the business of the corporation. Moreover, an officer or director may not use corporate personnel, fa-

cilities, or funds for his own benefit or disclose trade secrets of the corporation to others.

Indemnification of Directors and Officers

Directors and officers incur personal liability for breaching any of the duties they owe to the corporation and shareholders. Under many modern incorporation statutes, a corporation may indemnify a director or officer for liability incurred if he acted in good faith and in a manner he reasonably believed to be in the best interests of the corporation, so long as he has not been judged negligent or liable for misconduct. The Model Act and the Revised Act also provide for *mandatory* indemnification of directors and officers for reasonable expenses incurred by them in the wholly successful defense of any proceeding brought against them because they are or were a director or officer.[37,38] These provisions, however, may be limited by the articles of incorporation. In addition, a corporation may purchase insurance to indemnify officers and directors for liability arising out of their corporate activities, including liabilities against which the corporation is not empowered to indemnify directly.

Over one-half of the States, including Delaware, have recently enacted legislation authorizing corporations—with shareholder approval—to limit or eliminate the liability of directors for some breaches of duty. A few States permit shareholders to limit the liability of officers. The Delaware statute provides that the articles of incorporation may contain a provision eliminating or limiting the personal liability of a director to the corporation or its stockholders for monetary damages for breach of duty as a director, provided that such provision may not eliminate or limit the liability of a director (1) for any breach of the director's duty of loyalty to the corporation or its stockholders, (2) for acts or omissions not in good faith or that involve intentional misconduct or a knowing violation of law, (3) for liability for unlawful dividend payments or redemptions, or (4) for any transaction from which the director derived an improper personal benefit.

CHAPTER SUMMARY

ROLE OF SHAREHOLDERS

Voting Rights of Shareholders	**Management Structure of Corporations** See Figures 35-1, 2, and 3 for illustrations of the statutory model of corporate governance, the structure of the typical closely held corporation, and the structure of the typical publicly held corporation **Quorum** minimum number necessary to be present at a meeting in order to transact business **Election of Directors** the shareholders elect the board at the annual meeting of the corporation 　■ *Straight Voting* directors are elected by a plurality of votes 　■ *Cumulative Voting* entitles each shareholder to give one candidate as many votes as the number of directors to be elected multiplied by the number of shares owned **Removal of Directors** the shareholders may by majority vote remove directors with or without cause subject to cumulative voting rights **Approval of Fundamental Changes** shareholder approval is required for charter amendments, most acquisitions, and dissolution **Concentrations of Voting Power** 　■ *Proxy* authorization to vote another's shares at a shareholder meeting 　■ *Voting Trust* transfer of corporate shares' voting rights to a trustee 　■ *Shareholder Agreement* used to provide shareholders with greater control

Enforcement Rights of Shareholders	**Right to Inspect Books and Records** if the demand is made in good faith and for a proper purpose **Shareholder Suits** 　■ *Direct Suits* brought by a shareholder against the corporation based upon his ownership of shares 　■ *Derivative Suits* brought by a shareholder on behalf of the corporation to enforce a right belonging to the corporation

ROLE OF DIRECTORS AND OFFICERS

Function of the Board of Directors	**Selection and Removal of Officers** **Capital Structure** **Fundamental Changes** the directors have the power to make, amend, or repeal the bylaws, unless this power is reserved to the shareholders **Dividends** directors declare the amount and type of dividends **Management Compensation** **Vacancies in the Board** may be filled by the vote of a majority of the remaining directors

Exercise of Director's Function	**Meeting** directors have the power to bind the corporation only when acting as a board **Action Taken Without a Meeting** permitted if a consent in writing is signed by all of the directors

Delegation of Board Powers committees may be appointed to perform some but not all of the board's functions

Directors' Inspection Rights directors have the right to inspect corporate books and records

Officers

Role of Officers

- *President* supervises and controls the affairs of the corporation
- *Vice-President* serves in the absence of the president
- *Secretary* keeps the minutes
- *Treasurer* has custody of and is responsible for all funds and securities of the corporation

Authority of Officers

- *Actual Express Authority* arises from the incorporation statute, the charter, the bylaws, and resolutions of the directors
- *Actual Implied Authority* authority to do what is reasonably necessary to perform actual authority
- *Apparent Authority* acts of the principal that lead a third party to believe reasonably and in good faith that an officer has the required authority
- *Ratification* a corporation may ratify the unauthorized acts of its officers

Duties of Officers and Directors

Duty of Obedience must act within their respective authority

Duty of Diligence must exercise ordinary care and prudence

Duty of Loyalty requires undeviating loyalty to the corporation; the duty prohibits:

- *Conflicts of interest*
- *Loans to directors*
- *Usurpation of corporate opportunities*
- *Competition with the corporation*

Business Judgment Rule precludes imposing liability on directors and officers for honest mistakes in judgment if they act with due care, in good faith, and in a manner reasonably believed to be in the best interests of the corporation

Indemnification a corporation may indemnify a director or officer for liability incurred if he acted in good faith and he was not adjudged negligent or liable for misconduct

QUESTIONS

1. Compare the actual governance of closely held corporations, the actual governance of publicly held corporations, and the statutory model of corporate governance.
2. Distinguish between (a) straight and cumulative voting; (b) proxies and voting trusts; and (c) direct suits and derivative suits.
3. Identify the areas of corporate policy determined by the board of directors.
4. Discuss the business judgment rule.
5. Identify and discuss the most important situations involved in management's duties of loyalty, obedience, and diligence.

PROBLEMS

1. Brown was the president and director of a corporation engaged in owning and operating a chain of motels. Brown was advised, on what seemed to be good authority, that a superhighway

was to be constructed through the town of X, which would be a most desirable location for a motel. Brown presented these facts to the board of directors of the motel corporation and recommended that the corporation build a motel in the town of X at the location described. The board of directors agreed, and the new motel was constructed. It developed that the superhighway plans were changed after the motel was constructed. The highway was never built. Later, a packing house was built on property adjoining the motel, and as a result the corporation sustained a considerable loss.

The shareholders brought an appropriate action against Brown, charging that his proposal had caused a substantial loss to the corporation. Decision?

2. A, B, C, D, and E constituted the board of directors of the X Corporation. While D and E were out of town, A, B, and C held a special meeting of the board. Just as the meeting began, C became ill. He then gave a proxy to A and went home. A resolution was then adopted directing and authorizing the purchase by the X Corporation of an adjoining piece of land owned by S as a site for an additional factory building. A and B voted for the resolution, and A, as C's proxy, cast C's vote in favor of the resolution. A contract was then made by the X Corporation with S for the purchase of the land. After the return of D and E, another special meeting of the board was held with all five directors present. A resolution was then unanimously adopted to cancel the contract with S. S was so notified and now sues X Corporation for damages for breach of contract. Decision?

3. Bernard Koch was president of United Corporation, a closely held corporation. Koch, James Trent, and Henry Phillips made up the three-person board of directors. At a meeting of the board of directors, Trent was elected president, replacing Koch. At the same meeting, Trent attempted to have the salary of the president increased. He was unable to obtain board approval of the increase because, although Phillips voted for the increase, Koch voted against it. Trent was disqualified from voting by charter.

As a result, the directors, by a two-to-one vote, amended the bylaws to provide for the appointment of an executive committee composed of three reputable business persons to pass upon and fix all matters of salary for employees of the corporation. Subsequently, the executive committee, consisting of Jane Jones, James Black, and William Johnson, increased the salary of the president.

Koch brought an appropriate action against the corporation, Trent, and Phillips to enjoin them from paying the increased compensation to the president above that fixed by the board of directors. What decision?

4. Zenith Steel Company operated a prosperous business. In January its president, Roe, who is also a director, was voted a $100,000 bonus by the board of directors for valuable services he provided to the company during the previous year. Roe received an annual salary of $85,000 from the company. Black, a minority shareholder in Zenith Steel Company, brings an appropriate action to enjoin the payment by the company of the $100,000 bonus. Decision?

5. (a) Smith, a director of the Sample Corporation, sells a piece of vacant land to the Sample Corporation for $50,000. The land cost him $20,000.
(b) Jones, a shareholder of the Sample Corporation, sells a used truck to the Sample Corporation for $8,400, although the truck was worth $6,000.

Raphael, a minority shareholder of the Sample Corporation, claims that these sales are void and should be annulled. Is he correct? Why?

6. The X Corporation manufactures machine tools. Its two principal competitors are Y Corporation and Z Corporation. The five directors of X Corporation are Black, White, Brown, Green, and Crimson. At a duly called meeting of the board of directors of X Corporation in January, all five directors were present. They transacted the following business and voted as indicated.

A contract for the purchase of $1 million worth of steel from the D Company, of which Black, White, and Brown are directors, was discussed and approved by a unanimous vote. There was a lengthy discussion about entering into negotiations for the purchase of Q Corporation, which allegedly was about to be sold for around $15 million. By a three-to-two vote, it was decided not to open such negotiations.

Three months later, Green purchased Q Corporation for $15 million. Shortly thereafter, a new board of directors for X Corporation took office.

X Corporation now brings actions to rescind its contract with D Company and to compel Green to assign to X Corporation his contract for the purchase of Q Corporation. Decisions as to each action?

7. Gore had been the owner of 1 percent of the outstanding shares of the Webster Company, a corporation, since its organization ten years ago. Ratliff, the president of the company, was the owner of 70 percent of the outstanding shares. Ratliff used the shareholders' list to submit to the shareholders an offer of $50 per share for their stock. Gore, on receiving the offer, called Ratliff and told him that the offer was inadequate and advised that she was willing to offer $60 per share and for

that purpose demanded a shareholders' list. Ratliff knew that Gore was willing and able to supply the funds necessary to purchase the stock, but he nevertheless refused to supply the list to Gore. Further, he did not offer to transmit Gore's offer to the shareholders of record. Gore then brought an action to compel the corporation to make the shareholders' list available to her. Decision?

8. Mitchell, Nelson, Olsen, and Parker, experts in manufacturing baubles, each owned fifteen out of one hundred authorized shares of Baubles, Inc., a corporation of State X that does not permit cumulative voting. On July 7, 1984, the corporation sold forty shares to Quentin, an investor, for $1,500,000, which it used to purchase a factory building. On July 8, 1984, Mitchell, Nelson, Olsen, and Parker contracted as follows:

> All parties will act jointly in exercising voting rights as shareholders. In the event of a failure to agree, the question shall be submitted to George Yost, whose decision shall be binding upon all parties.

Until a meeting of shareholders on April 17, 1990, when a dispute arose, all parties to the contract had consistently and regularly voted for Nelson, Olsen, and Parker as directors. At that meeting, Yost considered the dispute and decided and directed that Mitchell, Nelson, Olsen, and Parker vote their shares for the latter three as directors. Nelson, Olsen, and Parker so voted. Mitchell and Quentin voted for themselves and Olsen as directors.

(a) Is the contract of July 8, 1984, valid, and, if so, what is its effect?
(b) Who were elected directors of Baubles, Inc., at the meeting of its shareholders on April 17, 1990?

9. Acme Corporation's articles of incorporation require cumulative voting for the election of its directors. The board of directors of Acme Corporation consists of nine directors, each elected annually.

(a) Peter owns 25 percent of the outstanding shares of Acme Corporation. How many directors can he elect with his votes?
(b) If Acme Corporation were to classify its board into three classes, each consisting of three directors elected every three years, how many directors would Peter be able to elect?

10. Neese, trustee in bankruptcy for First Trust Company, brings a suit against the directors of the company for losses sustained by the company as a result of the failure of the directors to use due care and diligence in the discharge of their duties. The specific acts of negligence alleged are: (1) failure to give as much time and attention to the affairs of the company as its business interests required; (2) abdication of their control of the corporation by turning the entire management of the corporation over to its president, Brown; (3) failure to keep informed as to the affairs, condition, and management of the corporation; (4) taking no action to direct or control the corporation's affairs; (5) permitting large, open, unsecured loans to affiliated but financially unsound companies that were owned and controlled by Brown; (6) failure to examine financial reports that would have shown illegal diversions and waste of the corporation's funds; and (7) failure to supervise properly the corporation's officers and directors. Decision?

11. Minority shareholders of Midwest Technical Institute Development Corporation, a closed-end investment company owning assets consisting principally of securities of companies in technological fields, brought a shareholder derivative suit against officers and directors of Midwest. The shareholders sought to recover on Midwest's behalf the profits realized by the officers and directors through dealings in stock held in Midwest's portfolio in breach of their fiduciary duty. Approximately three years after commencement of the action, a new corporation, Midtex, was organized to acquire Midwest's assets. The shareholders now seek to add Midtex as a party defendant to their suit. Decision?

12. Litton, an officer and the dominant shareholder of Dixie Splint Coal Company, transferred the company's remaining assets to himself when the company came to the verge of bankruptcy. The transfer allegedly was in satisfaction of an accrued salary claim that Litton had not enforced until the company came into financial difficulty. The trustee in bankruptcy seeks to have Litton's claim disallowed. Decision?

ENDNOTES

1. Model Business Corporation Act, Section 33, Voting of Shares.
2. Model Business Corporation Act, Section 28, Meetings of Shareholders.
3. Revised Model Business Corporation Act, Section 7.03, Court-Ordered Meeting.
4. Model Business Corporation Act, Section 144, Waiver of Notice.
5. Model Business Corporation Act, Section 32, Quorum of Shareholders.
6. Model Business Corporation Act, Section 143, Greater Voting Requirements; Revised Model Business Corporation Act, Section 7.27, Greater Quorum or Voting Requirements.

7. Model Business Corporation Act, Section 145, Action by Shareholders Without a Meeting.

8. Model Business Corporation Act, Section 37, Classification of Directors.

9. Model Business Corporation Act, Section 39, Removal of Directors.

10. Model Business Corporation Act, Section 34, Voting Trusts and Agreements Among Shareholders.

11. Model Business Corporation Act, Section 52, Books and Records: Financial Reports to Shareholders; Examination of Records.

12. Revised Model Business Corporation Act, Section 16.02, Inspection of Records by Shareholders.

13. Model Business Corporation Act, Section 49, Provisions Relating to Actions by Shareholders.

14. Revised Model Business Corporation Act, Section 7.40, Procedure in Derivative Proceedings.

15. Model Business Corporation Act, Section 35, Board of Directors.

16. Revised Model Business Corporation Act, Section 8.01, Requirement for and Duties of Board of Directors.

17. Model Business Corporation Act, Sections 50, Officers; 51, Removal of Officers.

18. Model Business Corporation Act, Section 27, By-Laws.

19. Model Business Corporation Act, Section 45, Distributions to Shareholders.

20. Model Business Corporation Act, Section 30, Closing of Transfer Books and Fixing Record Date.

21. Model Business Corporation Act, Section 36, Number and Election of Directors.

22. Revised Model Business Corporation Act, Section 8.03, Number and Election of Directors.

23. Model Business Corporation Act, Section 38, Vacancies.

24. Revised Model Business Corporation Act, Section 8.08, Removal of Directors by Shareholders.

25. Model Business Corporation Act, Section 43, Place and Notice of Directors' Meetings; Committee Meetings.

26. Model Business Corporation Act, Section 40, Quorum of Directors.

27. Revised Model Business Corporation Act, Section 8.24, Quorum and Voting.

28. Model Business Corporation Act, Section 44, Action by Directors Without a Meeting.

29. Model Business Corporation Act, Section 42, Executive and Other Committees.

30. Revised Model Business Corporation Act, Section 8.25, Committees.

31. Revised Model Business Corporation Act, Section 8.40, Required Officers.

32. Revised Model Business Corporation Act, Section 8.42, Standards of Conduct for Officers.

33. Revised Model Business Corporation Act, Section 8.30, General Standards for Directors.

34. Model Business Corporation Act, Section 41, Director Conflicts of Interest.

35. Model Business Corporation Act, Section 47, Loans to Employees and Directors.

36. Revised Model Business Corporation Act, Section 8.32, Loans to Directors.

37. Model Business Corporation Act, Section 5, Indemnification of Officers, Directors, Employees and Agents.

38. Revised Model Business Corporation Act, Sections 8.25, Mandatory Indemnification; 8.56, Indemnification of Officers, Employees, and Agents.

36 FUNDAMENTAL CHANGES

Certain extraordinary changes affect a corporation in such a fundamental manner that they are outside the authority of the board of directors and require shareholder approval. Charter amendments, a sale or lease of all or substantially all the corporation's assets, mergers, consolidations, compulsory share exchanges, and dissolution are fundamental changes because they alter the basic structure of the corporation. Although each of these actions is authorized by State incorporation statutes that impose specific procedural requirements, they are also subject to equitable limitations imposed by the courts.

Since shareholder approval for fundamental changes does not usually need to be unanimous, such changes frequently will be approved despite opposition by minority shareholders. Shareholder approval means a majority (or some other specified fraction) of *all* votes entitled to be cast rather than a majority (or other fraction) of votes represented at a shareholders' meeting at which a quorum is present. In some instances, minority shareholders have the right to dissent and recover the fair value of their shares if they follow the prescribed procedure. This right is called the appraisal remedy. We discuss the legal aspects of fundamental changes in this chapter.

CHARTER AMENDMENTS

Modern statutes permit the articles of incorporation to be amended freely. The amended articles of incorporation, however, may contain only those provisions that might be lawfully contained in the original articles of incorporation. The Model Act is comprehensive in its authorization for amendments and includes very broad powers. Several of the powers that the Model Act grants to corporations are the following:

1. to change its corporate name;
2. to change its period of duration;
3. to change, enlarge, or diminish its corporate purposes;
4. to increase or decrease the number or par value of shares;
5. to reclassify shares and change the preferential rights of shares;
6. to create new classes of shares; and
7. to limit, deny, or grant preemptive rights.[1]

Today, articles of incorporation rarely limit the duration or powers of the corporation, so the most common amendments relate to changes in the capital structure of the corporation.

Under modern statutes, the typical procedure for amending the articles of incorporation requires the board of directors to adopt a resolution setting forth the proposed amendment, which must then be approved by a majority vote of the shareholders entitled to vote, although some older statutes require a two-thirds shareholder vote. After the amendment is approved by the shareholders, articles of amendment are executed and filed with the Secretary of State. The amendment becomes effective on the issuance of the certificate of amendment by the Secretary of State but does not affect the existing rights of nonshareholders.

The Revised Act permits the board of directors to adopt certain amendments without shareholder action unless the articles of incorporation provide otherwise.[2] These amendments include (1) extending the duration of the corporation if it was incorporated when limited duration was required by law, (2) changing each issued and unissued authorized share of an outstanding class into a greater number of whole shares if the corporation has only one class of shares, and (3) making minor name changes.[2]

Under the Model Act, *dissenting shareholders* are given an appraisal remedy *only* if an amendment materially and adversely affects the rights attached to the shares owned by the dissenting shareholders in one of the following ways:

1. the amendment alters or abolishes a preferential right of such shares;
2. the amendment creates, alters, or abolishes a right involving the redemption of such shares;
3. the amendment alters or abolishes a preemptive right of the holder of such shares; or
4. the amendment excludes or limits the right of the holder of such shares to vote on any matter or to cumulate his votes.[3]

Under the Revised Act, the required shareholder approval for an amendment depends upon the nature of the amendment.[4] If the amendment would give rise to dissenters' rights, the amendment must be approved by a majority of all votes *entitled* to be cast on the amendment unless the act or the charter requires a greater vote. All other amendments must be approved by a majority of all votes *cast* on the amendment unless the act or the charter requires a greater vote.

COMBINATIONS

It may be desirable and profitable for a corporation to acquire all or substantially all of the assets of another corporation or corporations.

This may be accomplished by (1) purchase or lease of the assets, (2) purchase of a controlling stock interest in other corporations, (3) merger with other corporations, or (4) consolidation with other corporations. In 1986 there were more than three thousand mergers and acquisitions involving almost $200 billion. In 1988 there were at least one hundred merger and acquisition transactions, each of which exceeded $500 million.

When any of these methods of combination involves the issuance of shares, proxy solicitations, or tender offers, it may be subject to Federal securities regulation, as discussed in Chapter 43. Moreover, when a combination may have a detrimental effect on competition, Federal antitrust laws, as discussed in Chapter 41, may apply.

Purchase or Lease of All or Substantially All of the Assets

When one corporation purchases or leases all or substantially all of the assets of another corporation, there is no change in the legal personality of either corporation. The purchaser or lessee corporation has simply acquired ownership or control of additional physical assets. The selling or lessor corporation, in exchange for its physical properties, receives cash, other property, or a stipulated rental. Each corporation continues its separate existence with only the form or extent of its assets altered (see Figure 36–1).

Generally, a corporation that purchases the assets of another corporation does not assume the other's liabilities unless (1) the purchaser expressly or impliedly agrees to assume the liabilities of the seller; (2) the transaction amounts to a consolidation or merger of the

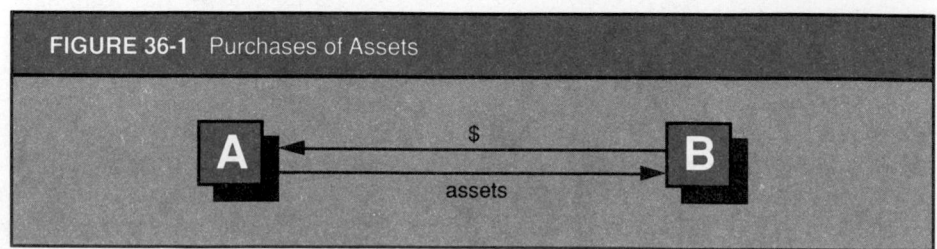

FIGURE 36-1 Purchases of Assets

two corporations; (3) the purchaser is a mere continuation of the seller; or (4) the sale is for the fraudulent purpose of avoiding the liabilities of the seller. Some courts, as in the next case, recognize a fifth exception (called the "product line" exception), which imposes strict tort liability upon the purchaser for defects in products manufactured and distributed by the seller corporation when the purchaser corporation continues the product line.

RAY v. ALAD CORP.
Supreme Court of California, 1977.
19 Cal.3d 22, 136 Cal.Rptr. 574, 560 P.2d 3.

Facts: On March 24, 1969, Ray fell from a defective ladder while working for his employer. Ray brought suit in strict tort liability against the Alad Corporation (Alad II), which neither manufactured nor sold the ladder to Ray's employer. Prior to the accident, Alad II succeeded to the business of the ladder's manufacturer, the now dissolved "Alad Corporation" (Alad I), through a purchase of Alad I's assets for an adequate cash consideration. Alad II acquired Alad I's plant, equipment, inventory, trade name, and good will and continued to manufacture the same line of ladders under the "Alad" name, using the same equipment, designs, and personnel. In addition, Alad II solicited through the same sales representatives with no outward indication of any change in the ownership of the business. The parties had no agreement, however, concerning Alad II's assumption of Alad I's tort liabilities. Ray appealed from a judgment for Alad II.

Decision: Judgment reversed.

Opinion: Wright, J. Our discussion of the law starts with the rule ordinarily applied to the determination of whether a corporation purchasing the principal assets of another corporation assumes the other's liabilities. As typically formulated the rule states that the purchaser does not assume the seller's liabilities unless (1) there is an express or implied agreement of assumption, (2) the transaction amounts to a consolidation or merger of the two corporations, (3) the purchasing corporation is a mere continuation of the seller, or (4) the transfer of assets to the purchaser is for the fraudulent purpose of escaping liability for the seller's debts. [Citations.]

If this rule were determinative of Alad II's liability to plaintiff it would require us to affirm the summary judgment. None of the rule's four stated grounds for imposing liability on the purchasing corporation is present here. There was no express or implied agreement to assume liability for injury from defective products previously manufactured by Alad I. Nor is there any indication or contention that the transaction was prompted by any fraudulent purpose of escaping liability for Alad I's debts.

With respect to the second stated ground for liability, the purchase of Alad I's assets did not amount to a consolidation or merger. This exception has been invoked where one corporation takes all of another's assets without providing any consideration that could be made available to meet claims of the other's creditors [citation] or where the consideration consists wholly of shares of the purchaser's stock which are promptly distributed to the seller's shareholders in conjunction with the seller's liquidation [citation]. In the present case the sole consideration given for Alad I's assets was cash in excess of $207,000. * * * There is no contention that this consideration was inadequate or that the cash and promissory note given to Alad I were not included in the assets available to meet claims of Alad I's creditors at the time of dissolution. Hence the acquisition of Alad I's assets was not in the nature of a merger or consolidation for purposes of the aforesaid rule.

Plaintiff contends that the rule's third stated ground for liability makes Alad II liable as a mere continuation of Alad I in view of Alad II's acquisition of all Alad I's operating assets, its use of those assets and of Alad I's former employees to manufacture the same line of products, and its holding itself out to customers and the public as a continuation of the same enterprise. However, California decisions holding that a corporation acquiring the assets of another corporation is the latter's mere continuation and therefore liable for its debts have imposed such liability only upon a showing of one or both of the following factual elements: (1) no adequate consideration was given for the predecessor corporation's assets and made available for meeting the claims of its unsecured creditors; (2) one or more persons were officers, directors, or stockholders of both corporations. [Citations.] There is no showing of either of these elements in the present case.

We therefore conclude that the general rule governing succession to liabilities does not require Alad II to respond to plaintiff's claim. * * * We must decide whether the policies underlying strict tort liability for defective products call for a special exception to the rule that would otherwise insulate the present defendant from plaintiff's claim. [Citations.]

The purpose of the rule of strict tort liability "is to insure that the costs of injuries resulting from defective products are borne by the manufacturers that put such products on the market rather than by the injured persons who are powerless to protect themselves." [Citation.] However, the rule "does not rest on the analysis of the financial strength or bargaining power of the parties to the particular action. It rests, rather, on the proposition that '[t]he cost of an injury and the loss of time or health may be an overwhelming misfortune to the person injured, and a needless one, for the risk of injury can be insured by the manufacturer and distributed among the public as a cost of doing business.' [Citations.]" Thus, "the paramount policy to be promoted by the rule is the protection of otherwise defenseless victims of manufacturing defects and the *spreading throughout society* of the cost of compensating them." (Italics added.) [Citation.] Justification for imposing strict liability upon a *successor* to a manufacturer under the circumstances here presented rests upon (1) the virtual destruction of the plaintiff's remedies against the original manufacturer caused by the successor's acquisition of the business, (2) the successor's ability to assume the original manufacturer's risk-spreading rule, and (3) the fairness of requiring the successor to assume a responsibility for defective products that was a burden necessarily attached to the original manufacturer's good will being enjoyed by the successor in the continued operation of the business. We turn to a consideration of each of these aspects in the context of the present case.

We must assume for purposes of the present proceeding that plaintiff was injured as a result of defects in a ladder manufactured by Alad I and therefore could assert strict tort liability against Alad I under the rule of [citation.] However, the practical value of this right of recovery against the original manufacturer was vitiated by the purchase of Alad I's tangible assets, trade name and good will on behalf of Alad II and the dissolution of Alad I within two months thereafter in accordance with the purchase agreement. The injury giving rise to plaintiff's claim against Alad I did not occur until more than six months after the filing of the dissolution certificate declaring that Alad I's "known debts and liabilities have been actually paid" and its "known assets have been distributed to its shareholders." This distribution of assets was perfectly proper as there was no requirement that provision be made for claims such as plaintiff's that had not yet come into existence. Thus, even if plaintiff could obtain a judgment on his claim against the dissolved and assetless Alad I he would face formidable and probably insuperable obstacles in attempting to obtain satisfaction of the judgment from former stockholders or directors. [Citations.]

* * *

While depriving plaintiff of redress against the ladder's manufacturer, Alad I, the transaction by which Alad II acquired Alad I's name and operating assets had the further effect of transferring to Alad II the resources that had previously been available to Alad I for meeting its responsibilities to persons injured by defects in ladders it had produced. These resources included not only the physical plant, the manufacturing equipment, and the inventories of raw material, work in process, and finished goods, but also the know-how available through the records of manufacturing designs, the continued employment of the factory personnel, and the consulting services of Alad I's general manager. With these facilities and sources of information, Alad II had virtually the same capacity as Alad I to estimate the risks of claims for injuries from defects in previously manufactured ladders for purposes of obtaining insurance coverage or planning self-insurance. [Citation.] Moreover, the acquisition of the Alad enterprise gave Alad II the opportunity formerly enjoyed by Alad I of passing on to purchasers of new "Alad" products the costs of meeting these risks. Immediately after the takeover it was Alad II, not Alad I, which was in a position to promote the "paramount policy" of the strict products liability rule by "spreading throughout society . . . the cost of compensating (otherwise defenseless victims of manufacturing defects)." [Citation.]

Finally, the imposition upon Alad II of liability for injuries from Alad I's defective products is fair and equitable in view of Alad II's acquisition of Alad I's trade name, good will, and customer lists, its continuing to produce the same line of ladders, and its holding itself out to potential customers as the same enterprise. This deliberate albeit legitimate exploitation of Alad I's established reputation as a going concern manufacturing a specific product line gave Alad II a substantial benefit which its predecessor could not have enjoyed without the burden of potential liability for injuries from previously manufactured units. Imposing this liability upon successor manufacturers in the position of Alad II not only causes the one "who takes the benefit (to) bear the burden" [citation] but precludes any windfall to the predecessor that might otherwise result from (1) the reflection of an absence of such successor liability in an enhanced price paid by the successor for the business assets and (2) the liquidation of the predecessor resulting in avoidance of its responsibility for subsequent injuries from its defective products. [Citations.] By taking over and continuing the established business of producing and distributing Alad ladders, Alad II became "an integral part of the overall producing and marketing enterprise that should bear the cost of injuries resulting from defective products" [Citation.]

We therefore conclude that a party which acquires a manufacturing business and continues the output of its line of products under the circumstances here presented assumes strict tort liability for defects in units of the same product line previously manufactured and distributed by the entity from which the business was acquired. * * *

Regular Course of Business If the sale or lease of all or substantially all of its assets is in the usual and regular course of business of the selling or lessor corporation, approval by its board of directors is required but shareholder authorization is not. In addition, a mortgage or pledge of any or all of the property and assets of a corporation—whether or *not* in the usual or regular course of business—also requires approval by just the board of directors.[5] The

Revised Act considers a transfer of any or all of a corporation's assets to a wholly owned subsidiary to be a sale in the regular course of business.[5] Under the Revised Act, a sale of assets in the regular course of business does not require shareholder approval unless the articles of incorporation provide otherwise.

Other Than in Regular Course of Business Shareholder approval is necessary only if a sale or lease of all or substantially all of the assets is *not* in the usual and regular course of business. The selling corporation, by liquidation of its assets, or the lessor corporation, by placing its physical assets beyond its control, has significantly changed its position and perhaps its ability to carry on the type of business contemplated by its charter. For this reason, such sale or lease must be approved not only by action of the directors but also by the affirmative vote of the holders of a majority of its shares entitled to vote at a meeting of shareholders called for this purpose.[6] In most States, *dissenting shareholders* of the selling corporation are given an appraisal remedy.[3]

Purchase of Shares

An alternative to the purchase of the assets of another corporation is the purchase of its stock. When one corporation acquires all or a controlling interest of the stock of another corporation, there is no change in the legal existence of either corporation. The acquiring corporation acts through its board of directors, while the corporation that becomes a subsidiary does not act at all, because the sale of stock is a decision made by the individual shareholders. The capital structure of the subsidiary remains unchanged, and that of the parent is usually not altered unless required in connection with financing the acquisition of the stock. Because no formal shareholder approval of either corporation is required, there is *no* appraisal remedy (see Figure 36–2).

Sale of Control When a controlling interest is owned by one or a few shareholders, a privately negotiated transaction is possible. The courts require that these sales be made with due care. The controlling shareholders must make a reasonable investigation so as not to transfer control to purchasers who wrongfully plan to steal or "loot" the assets of the corporation or to act contrary to the best interests of the corporation. In addition, purchasers are frequently willing to pay a premium for a block of shares that conveys control. Although some courts have required that this so-called "control premium" inure to the benefit of the corporation, today virtually all courts permit the controlling shareholders to retain the full amount of the control premium.

Tender Offer When a controlling interest is not held by one or a few shareholders, acquisition of a corporation by the purchase of shares may take the form of a tender offer. A **tender offer** is a general invitation to all of the shareholders of a target company to tender their shares for sale at a specified price. The offer may be for all of the target company's

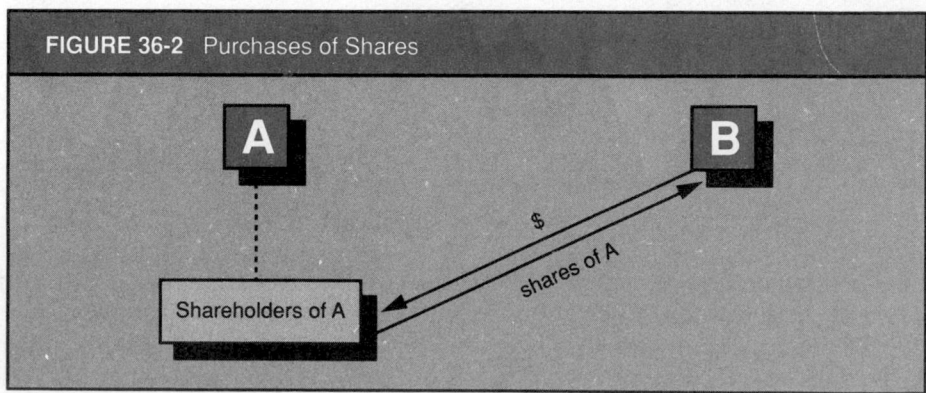

FIGURE 36-2 Purchases of Shares

A

B

Shareholders of A

$

shares of A

shares or just for a controlling interest. Tender offers for publicly held companies, which are subject to Federal securities regulation, are discussed in Chapter 43.

Compulsory Share Exchange

The Model Act provides different procedures, however, where the share acquisition is through a compulsory share exchange, which is a transaction by which a corporation becomes the owner of *all* the outstanding shares of one or more classes of another corporation by an exchange that is *compulsory* on *all* owners of the acquired shares.[7] The shares may be acquired with shares, obligations, or other securities of the acquiring corporation or with other consideration. For example, if B Corporation acquires all of the outstanding shares of A Corporation through a compulsory exchange, then A becomes a wholly owned subsidiary of B. In all compulsory share exchanges, the separate existence of both corporate parties to the transaction is not affected by the exchange. Although producing results similar to a merger, as discussed below, compulsory share exchanges are used instead of mergers where it is desirable that the acquired corporation does not go out of existence as, for example, in the formation of holding company systems for insurance companies and banks.

A compulsory share exchange requires approval of the board of directors of each corporation and approval by the shareholders of the corporation whose shares are being acquired.[7,8] The transaction need *not* be approved by the shareholders of the corporation acquiring the shares. After the compulsory share exchange plan is adopted and approved by the shareholders, it is binding on all holders of shares of the class to be acquired. Dissenting shareholders of the corporation whose shares are acquired are given an appraisal remedy.[3]

Merger

A **merger** of two or more corporations is the combination of all of their assets. One of the corporations, known as the **surviving corporation,** receives title to all the assets. The other party or parties to the merger, known as the **merged corporation** or corporations, is merged into the surviving corporation and ceases to exist as a separate entity. Thus, if A Corporation and B Corporation combine into the A Corporation, A is the surviving corporation and B the merged corporation (see Figure 36-3). The shareholders of the merged corporation may receive stock or other securities issued by the surviving corporation or other consideration, as provided in the plan of merger. All debts and other liabilities of the merged corporation are assumed by the surviving corporation by operation of law.[9]

A merger requires the approval of the board of directors of each corporation, as well as the affirmative vote of the holders of a majority of the shares entitled to vote of each corporation that is involved in the merger.[8,10] In a **short-**

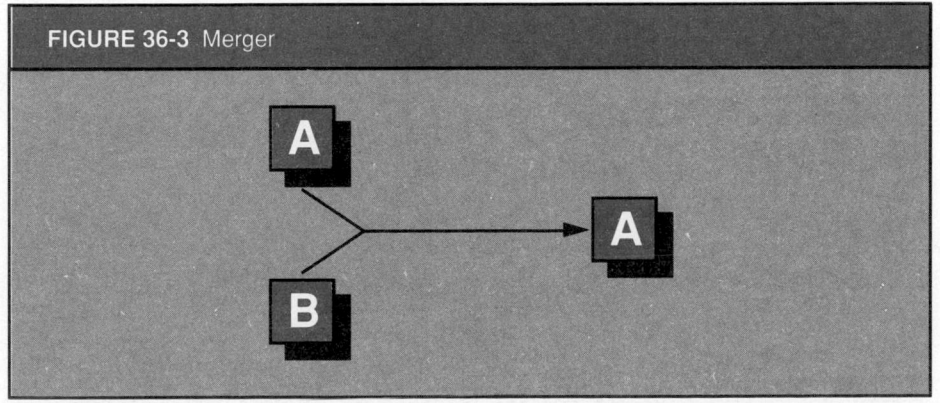

FIGURE 36-3 Merger

form merger, however, a corporation that owns at least *90 percent* of the outstanding shares of a subsidiary may merge the subsidiary into itself without approval by the shareholders of either corporation.[11] Requiring the approval of the shareholders or board of directors of the subsidiary is unnecessary because the parent's 90 percent ownership assures that the plan of merger would be approved. All that is required is a resolution by the board of directors of the parent corporation.

The dissenting shareholders of the subsidiary have the right to obtain payment from the parent for their shares.[3] The shareholders of the parent do not have this appraisal remedy because the transaction has not materially changed their rights. Instead of indirectly owning 90 percent of the subsidiary's assets, the parent now directly owns 100 percent of the same assets.

Consolidation

A **consolidation** of two or more corporations is the combination of all of their assets, title to which is taken by a newly created corporation known as the **consolidated corporation** (see Figure 36–4). Each of the constituent corporations ceases to exist, and all of their debts and liabilities are assumed by the new corporation.[9] The shareholders of each of the constituent corporations receive stock or other securities, not necessarily of the same class, issued to them by the new corporation or other consideration provided in the plan of consolidation. A consol-

idation requires the approval of the boards of directors of each constituent corporation as well as the affirmative vote of the holders of a majority of the shares entitled to vote of each constituent corporation.[8,12] Dissenting shareholders have an appraisal remedy.[3] The Revised Act, however, has deleted all references to consolidations.

Going Private Transactions

Corporate combinations are sometimes used to take a publicly held corporation private in order to eliminate minority interests, to reduce the burdens of certain provisions of the Federal securities laws, or both. One method of going private is for the corporation or the majority shareholder to acquire the corporation's shares through purchases on the open market or through a tender offer for the shares. Other methods include a cash-out combination (merger or sale of assets) with a corporation controlled by the majority shareholder. If the majority shareholder is a corporation, it may arrange a cash-out combination with itself or, if it owns enough shares, use a short-form merger. In recent years, a new type of going private transaction—a management buyout—has become much more frequent. In this section we examine cash-out combinations and management buyouts.

Cash-out Combinations Cash-out combinations are used to eliminate minority shareholders by forcing them to accept cash or property for their shares. A cash-out combination is often used after a person, group, or

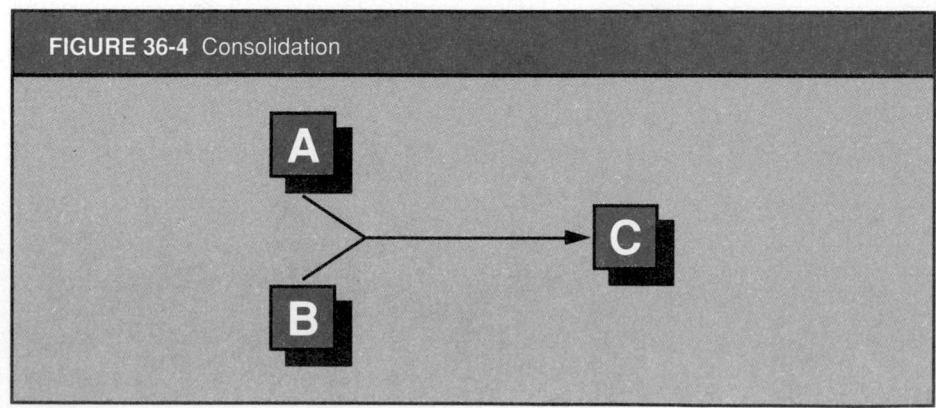

FIGURE 36-4 Consolidation

company has acquired a large interest in a target company (T) through a tender offer. The tender offeror (TO) then seeks to eliminate all other shareholders, thereby achieving complete control of T. To do so, TO might form a new corporation (Corporation N) and take 100 percent of its stock. A cash-out merger of T into N is then arranged with all the shareholders of T other than TO to receive cash for their shares. Since TO owns all the stock of N and a controlling interest in T, the merger will be approved by the shareholders of both companies. Alternatively, TO could purchase for cash or notes the assets of T,

leaving the minority shareholders with only an interest in the proceeds of the sale. The use of cash-out combinations has raised questions concerning their purpose and their fairness to the minority shareholders. Some States require that cash-out combinations have a valid business purpose and that they are fair to all concerned. Fairness, in this context, includes both fair dealing (which involves the procedural aspects of the transaction) and fair price (which involves the financial considerations of the merger). Other States require only that the transaction is fair.

ALPERT v. 28 WILLIAMS ST. CORP.

New York Court of Appeals, 1984.
63 N.Y.2d 557, 483 N.Y.S.2d 667, 473 N.E.2d 19

Facts: 79 Realty Corporation owned a valuable seventeen-story office building in Manhattan. The plaintiffs in this action held 26 percent of the outstanding shares of 79 Realty Corporation. The defendants formed a limited partnership, Madison 28 Associates, to buy the building. This limited partnership created 28 Williams Street Corporation to act as the nominal purchaser. The defendants planned to achieve the purchase by means of a "two-step" merger in which Madison Associates would buy control of the majority shares of Realty Corporation and then merge Realty Corporation with Williams Street, "freezing out" the minority shareholders of Realty Corporation through a cash buyout. All shareholders of Realty Corporation were sent a statement of intent explaining the details of the proposed merger. Soon after the merger was approved, and in accordance with the merger plan, Realty Corporation, the surviving corporation, was dissolved, and title to the building passed to Madison Associates. The plaintiffs brought an action for equitable relief in the form of rescission of the merger. The trial court found for 28 Williams Street Corporation and the appellate court affirmed.

Decision: Judgment for 28 Williams Street Corporation affirmed.

Cooke, C. J. In New York, two or more domestic corporations are authorized to "merge into a single corporation which shall be one of the constituent corporations", known as the "surviving corporation" [citation]. The statute does not delineate substantive justifications for mergers, but only requires compliance with certain procedures: the adoption by the boards of each corporation of a plan of merger setting forth, among other things, the terms and conditions of the merger; a statement of any changes in the certificate of incorporation of the surviving corporation; the submission of the plan to a vote of shareholders pursuant to notice to all shareholders; and adoption of the plan by a vote of two thirds of the shareholders entitled to vote on it [citation].

Generally, the remedy of a shareholder dissenting from a merger and the offered "cash-out" price is to obtain the fair value of his or her stock through an appraisal proceeding [citation]. This protects the minority shareholder from being forced to sell at unfair values imposed by those dominating the corporation while allowing the majority to proceed with its desired merger [citations]. The pursuit of an appraisal proceeding generally constitutes the dissenting stockholder's exclusive remedy [citations]. An exception exists, however, when the merger is unlawful or fraudulent as to that shareholder, in which event an action for equitable relief is authorized [citations]. Thus, technical compliance with the Business Corporation Law's requirements alone will not necessarily exempt a merger from further judicial review.

Because the power to manage the affairs of a corporation is vested in the directors and majority shareholders, they are cast in the fiduciary role of "guardians of the corporate welfare" * * *

The fiduciary must treat all shareholders, majority and minority, fairly . . . Moreover, all corporate responsibilities must be discharged in good faith and with "conscientious fairness, morality and honesty in purpose" [citation]. Also imposed are the obligations of candor [citation] and of good and prudent management of the corporation [citations].

* * * In reviewing a freeze-out merger, the essence of the judicial inquiry is to determine whether the transaction, viewed as a whole, was "fair" as to all concerned. This concept has two principal components: the majority shareholders must have followed "a course of fair dealing toward minority holders" . . . and they must also have offered a fair price for the minority's stock. * * *

Generally, the plaintiff has the burden of proving that the merger violated the duty of fairness, but when there is an inherent conflict of interest, the burden shifts to the interested directors or shareholders to prove good faith and the entire fairness of the merger. * * * The interested parties may attempt to establish this element of fair dealing by introducing evidence of efforts taken to simulate arm's length negotiations. Such steps may have included the appointment of an independent negotiating committee made up of neutral directors or of an independent board to evaluate the merger proposal and to oversee the process of its approval. * * *

Fair dealing is also concerned with the procedural fairness of the transaction, such as its timing, initiation, structure, financing, development, disclosure to the independent directors and shareholders, and how the necessary approvals were obtained. * * * Basically, the courts must look for complete and candid disclosure of all the material facts and circumstances of the proposed merger known to the majority or directors, including their dual roles and events leading up to the merger proposal. * * *

The fairness of the transaction cannot be determined without considering the component of the financial remuneration offered the dissenting shareholders. * * *

In determining whether there was a fair price, the court need not ascertain the precise "fair value" of the shares as it would be determined in an appraisal proceeding. It should be noted, however, that the factors used in an appraisal proceeding are relevant here . . . This would include but would not be limited to net asset value, book value, earnings, market value, and investment value. * * * Elements of future value arising from the accomplishment or expectation of the merger which are known or susceptible of proof as of the date of the merger and not the product of speculation may also be considered. * * *

Fair dealing and fair price alone will not render the merger acceptable. As mentioned, there exists a fiduciary duty to treat all shareholders equally. [Citation.] This duty arises as a concomitant to the power reposed in the majority over corporate governance. [Citation]. The fact remains, however, that in a freeze-out merger the minority shareholders are being treated in a different manner: the majority is permitted continued participation in the equity of the surviving corporation while the minority has no choice but to surrender their shares for cash. On its face, the majority's conduct would appear to breach this fiduciary obligation.

* * *

In the context of a freeze-out merger, variant treatment of the minority shareholders—i.e., causing their removal—will be justified when related to the advancement of a general corporate interest. The benefit need not be great, but it must be for the corporation. For example, if the sole purpose of the merger is reduction of the number of profit sharers—in contrast to increasing the corporation's capital or profits, or improving its management structure—there will exist no "independent corporate interest" [citation]. All of these purposes ultimately seek to increase the individual wealth of the remaining shareholders. What distinguishes a proper corporate purpose from an improper one is that, with the former, removal of the minority shareholders furthers the objective of conferring some general gain upon the corporation. Only then will the fiduciary duty of good and prudent management of the corporation serve to override the concurrent duty to treat all shareholders fairly [citation]. We further note that a finding that there was an independent corporate purpose for the action taken by the majority will not be defeated merely by the fact that the corporate objective could have been accomplished in another way, or by the fact that the action chosen was not the best way to achieve the bona fide business objective.

In sum, in entertaining an equitable action to review a freeze-out merger, a court should view the transaction as a whole to determine whether it was tainted with fraud, illegality, or self-dealing, whether the minority shareholders were dealt with fairly, and whether there exists any independent corporate purpose for the merger.

* * *

Without passing on all of the business purposes cited by Supreme Court as underlying the merger, it is sufficient to note that at least one justified the exclusion of plaintiffs' interests: attracting additional capital to effect needed repairs of the building. There is proof that there was a good-faith belief that additional, outside capital was required. Moreover, this record supports the conclusion that this capital would not have been available through the merger had not plaintiffs' interest in the corporation been eliminated. Thus, the approval of the merger, which would extinguish plaintiffs' stock, was supported by a bona fide business purpose to advance this general corporate interest of obtaining increased capital.

Management Buyout   A management buyout is a transaction by which existing management increases its ownership of a corporation and eliminates its public shareholders. The typical procedure is as follows. Management of an existing company (Corporation A) forms a new corporation (Corporation B) in which management owns some of the stock and institutional investors own the rest. Corporation B issues bonds to institutional investors to raise cash with which it purchases the assets or stock of Corporation A. The assets of Corporation A are used as security for the bonds issued by Corporation B. (Because of the extensive use of borrowed funds, management buyouts are commonly called **leveraged buyouts** (LBO).) The result of this transaction is twofold: the public shareholders of Corporation A no longer have any proprietary interest in the assets of Corporation A, and management's equity interest in Corporation B is greater than its interest was in Corporation A.

In recent years, leveraged buyouts have become more frequent, and some have involved large, well-known companies. In 1986 Beatrice Foods went private for $6.2 billion, all of which was financed by debt. In the same year, Safeway Stores (the largest supermarket chain in the United States) went private for $4.3 billion, as did Macy's for $3.6 billion. In 1989 the largest LBO ever occured: Kohlberg Kravis Roberts and Co. acquired RJR Nabisco for $24.53 billion.

A critical issue raised by a management buyout is its fairness to the shareholders of Corporation A. The transaction inherently places management in a potential conflict of interest because management owes a fiduciary duty to represent the interests of the shareholders of Corporation A. As substantial shareholders of Corporation B, however, management has a personal and probably adverse financial interest in the transaction.

Dissenting Shareholders

The **shareholder's** right to **dissent** is a statutory right to obtain payment for his shares and is accorded to shareholders who object to certain fundamental changes in the corporation. Most States grant a right to dissent to any plan of *merger* or *consolidation* to which the corporation is a party as well as to a *sale* or *lease* of all or substantially all of the property or assets of the corporation not made in the usual or regular course of business. In addition to these three fundamental changes, the Model Act also provides a right to dissent to (1) any plan of compulsory share exchange to which the corporation is a party as the corporation the shares of which are to be acquired, (2) any amendment of the articles of incorporation that materially and adversely affects the rights appurtenant to the shares of the dissenting shareholder, and (3) any other corporate action taken pursuant to a shareholder vote with respect to which the articles of incorporation, the bylaws, or a resolution of the board of directors directs that dissenting shareholders shall have a right to obtain payment for their shares.[3]

A number of States have a stock market exception to the appraisal remedy. Under these statutes, there is no right to dissent if an established market, such as the New York Stock Exchange, exists for the shares. The Model Act and the Revised Act do not contain this exception.

The Introductory Comment to Chapter 13 of the Revised Act explains the purpose of dissenters' rights:

> Chapter 13 deals with the tension between the desire of the corporate leadership to be able to enter new fields, acquire new enterprises, and rearrange investor rights and the desire of investors to adhere to the rights and the risks on the basis of which they invested. Most contemporary corporation codes in the United States attempt to resolve this tension through a combination of two devices. On the one hand, the majority is given an almost unlimited power to change the nature and shape of the enterprise and the rights of its members. On the other hand, the members who dissent from these changes are given a right to withdraw their investment at a fair value.

The corporation must notify the shareholders of the existence of dissenters' rights before the vote is taken on the corporate action. If a shareholder dissents and strictly complies with the provisions of the statute, he is entitled to receive the fair value of his shares.[13] In order to perfect his right to payment for his shares, a dissenting shareholder must:

1. file with the corporation a written objection to the proposed corporate action before the vote of the shareholders;
2. refrain from voting in favor of the proposed corporate action either in person or by proxy; and
3. make a written demand on the corporation on a form provided by that corporation within the time period set by the corporation, which may not be less than thirty days after the corporation mails the form.

Unless written demand is made within the prescribed time period, the dissenting shareholder is not entitled to payment for his shares.

A dissenting shareholder who complies with all of these requirements is entitled to an appraisal remedy, which is payment by the corporation of the fair value of his shares with accrued interest. The Model Act defines **fair value** to mean their value immediately before the corporate action to which the dissenter objects takes place, excluding any appreciation or depreciation in anticipation of such corporate action unless such exclusion would be inequitable.[13] The next case explains how fair value is determined.

ENDICOTT JOHNSON CORP. v. BADE
Court of Appeals of New York, 1975.
37 N.Y.2d 585, 376 N.Y.S.2d 103, 338 N.E.2d 614.

Facts: The shareholders of Endicott Johnson who had dissented from a proposed merger of Endicott with McDonough Corporation brought this proceeding to fix the fair value of their stock. At issue is the proper weight required to be given to the market price of the stock in fixing its fair value. The shareholders argue that the market value should not be considered because of McDonough's control of Endicott's stock and the stock's subsequent delisting from the New York Stock Exchange. The trial court fixed the fair value of the shares at $45.75 and the appellate court modified the order by reducing the value to $42.77. Both sides appealed.

Decision: Order of the appellate court affirmed.

Opinion. Fuchsberg, J. The general principles applicable here are clear. Dissenting stockholders were entitled to be paid the "fair value" of their Endicott common stock, excluding any appreciation or depreciation due to the merger or its proposal. [Citation.] Although the statute itself is silent as to how fair value is to be determined, it is well established by case law that, in our State, the elements which are to enter into such an appraisal are net asset value, investment value and market value. [Citations.] While, in order to provide the elasticity deemed necessary to reach a just result, all three factors are to be considered, the weight to be accorded to each varies with the facts and circumstances in a particular case. [Citations.]

* * *

It follows that all three elements do not have to influence the result in every valuation proceeding. It suffices if they are all considered. Compelling the consideration of all of them, including those which may turn out to be unreliable in a particular case, has the salutary effect of assuring more complete justification by the appraiser of the conclusion he reaches. It also provides a more concrete basis for court review.

The three elements are not always discrete: definitionally, they may even flow into one another. For instance, in this very case, by their general concurrence that it would here be inappropriate, no estimation of net asset value was attempted by the parties or the appraiser. Since the corporation was not being liquidated, but was to continue to operate as part of the surviving parent McDonough Corporation, that made business and legal sense. For, in cases of nonliquidation, to the extent that the net asset value might include elements such as good will and potential earnings, these are invariably taken into account, in any event, among the numerous tangible and intangible factors that enter into judgment of the investment value of going concerns, whether by experienced appraisers or prudent investors. [Citations.]

Indeed, in this case investment value, for all practical purposes, became the sole determinant of fair value when the appraiser eliminated market value as a meaningful factor by reporting as follows:

"My opinion is that little weight should be given to the past history of market value prior to 1969 because I believe that there was a radical enough change in the management of the company so that it had 'turned around,' and that the pre–1969 market is not particularly helpful.

"I agree with the thinking of the text writers that a dramatic change in leadership for the good may be valid grounds for disregarding company's [sic] past history of weakness.

"Subsequent to 1969 I believe the market became so thin because of the control of McDonough and the subsequent delisting that it is fairly meaningless."

Endicott, pointing to an average market price of $26.25 per share in public trading of the stock for the six months immediately preceding the announcement of the merger, argues that market value was required to be given substantial weight and that the lower courts acted contrary to law in adopting that part of the appraiser's report which had failed to do so. In further support of its position, Endicott, among other things, asserts that, during the pre-merger period it regards as relevant, McDonough controlled only 31.8% of the common shares, the remainder constituting a large enough public float in the hands of over two thousand stockholders to ensure a free and active market. On the other hand, the stockholders, relying heavily on such facts as the stock's delisting from the New York Stock Exchange, its relegation for a year before the merger to being traded on the over-the-counter market and, by then, the ownership by McDonough of 70% of the stock, claim the marketplace was no longer "a fair reflection of the judgment of the buying and selling public" as to Endicott common. [Citation.]

Under the circumstances, the weight of market value, whether great or small or none, was for the fact-finding tribunals, and there is no reason to disturb the Appellate Division's conclusion, on the facts and in its discretion, that in this case the appraiser was not required to rely "to any large degree" on the market value of Endicott's common stock.

* * *

In addition, the right of dissenting stockholders to obtain fair value rather than market value for their stock protects them from being forced to sell at unfair values arbitrarily and unilaterally fixed by those who may dominate a corporation. The obligation to accept fair value is an accepted risk of public stock ownership for, in some instances market price at the time of a merger may have been pushed to levels in excess of fair value, and the automatic right to it in a valuation proceeding could bring a windfall. Either way, market price is but an ingredient that must enter into the calculation for what it is worth, no more or no less. [Citation.]

The purpose of the statutory procedure is to fix a reasonable time in which the corporation may know the number of shares for which it is required to pay cash in order to carry through the proposed corporate action. If enough dissenting shareholders demand to be paid, the lack of sufficient cash or the inability of the surviving or new corporation to raise funds for this purpose may mean that the proposed corporate action cannot be carried out at that time.

A shareholder of a corporation who has a right to obtain payment for his shares does not have the right to attack the validity of the corporate action that gives rise to his right to obtain payment or to have the action set aside or rescinded, except when the corporate action is unlawful or fraudulent with regard to the complaining shareholders or to the corporation.[3] Where the corporate action is not unlawful or fraudulent, the appraisal remedy is exclusive, and the shareholder may not challenge the action.

DISSOLUTION

Although a corporation may have perpetual existence, its life may be terminated in a number of ways. Incorporation statutes usually provide both for dissolution without judicial proceedings and for dissolution with judicial proceedings. Dissolution does not terminate the corporation's existence but does require that the corporation *wind up* its affairs and *liquidate* its assets.

Nonjudicial Dissolution

Nonjudicial dissolution may be brought about by

1. an act of the legislature of the State of incorporation;
2. expiration of the period of time provided for in the articles of incorporation;
3. voluntary action on the part of all of the holders of all of the outstanding shares of stock;[14] or
4. voluntary action by the corporation, pursuant to a resolution of the board of directors approved by the affirmative vote of the holders of a majority of the shares of the corporation entitled to vote at a meeting of the shareholders duly called for this purpose.[15] No right to dissent and recover the fair value of shares is usually provided to shareholders objecting to dissolution. The Model Act, however, grants dissenters' rights in connection with a sale or exchange of all or substantially all the assets not made in the usual or regular course of business, *including* a sale in dissolution, but *excludes* such rights in sales by court order and sales for cash on terms requiring that all or substantially all of the net proceeds be distributed to the shareholders within one year.[3]

The Statutory Close Corporation Supplement to the MBCA gives the shareholders, if they elect in the articles of incorporation, the power to dissolve the corporation. Unless the charter specifies otherwise, an amendment to include, modify, or delete a power to dissolve must be approved by *all* the shareholders. The power to dissolve may be conferred upon any shareholder or holders of a specified number or percentage of shares of any class and may be exercised at will or upon the occurrence of a specified event or contingency.

Judicial Dissolution

Involuntary dissolution by judicial proceeding may be instituted by the State, the shareholders, or the creditors.

1. The attorney general of the State of incorporation may bring a court action to dissolve the corporation when it is established that the corporation has failed to file its annual report with the Secretary of State, failed to pay its annual franchise tax, procured its articles of incorporation through fraud, continued to exceed or abuse the authority conferred upon it by law, failed for thirty days to appoint and maintain a registered agent in the State, or failed for thirty days after a change of its registered office or registered agent to file a statement of such change.[16]
2. Shareholders may bring a court action to dissolve the corporation when it is established that the directors are deadlocked in the management of the corporate affairs and the shareholders are unable to break the deadlock and that irreparable injury to the corporation is being suffered or is threatened; that the acts of the directors or those in control of the corporation are illegal, oppressive, or fraudulent; that the corporate assets are being misapplied or wasted; or that the shareholders are deadlocked and cannot elect directors.[17]
3. A creditor may bring a court action to dissolve the corporation on showing that the corporation has become unable to pay its debts and obligations as they mature in the regular course of its business and either (a) the creditor has reduced his claim to a judgment and an execution issued on it has been returned unsatisfied; or (b) that the corporation has admitted in writing that the claim of the creditor is due and owing.[17]

FIGURE 36-5 Fundamental Changes

Change	Board of Director Resolution Required	Shareholder Approval Required	Shareholders' Appraisal Remedy Available
A amends its articles of incorporation	A: Yes	A: Yes	A: No, unless amendment materially and adversely affects rights of shares
A sells its assets in usual and regular course of business to B	A: Yes	A: No	A: No
A sells its assets not in usual and regular course or business to B	A: Yes	A: Yes	A: Yes
A voluntarily purchases shares of B	A: Yes B: No	A: No B: No, individual shareholders decide	A: No B: No
A acquires shares of B through a compulsory exchange	A: Yes B: Yes	A: No B: Yes	A: No B: Yes
A and B merge	A: Yes B: Yes	A: Yes B: Yes	A: Yes B: Yes
A merges its 90% subsidiary B into A	A: Yes B: No	A: No B: No	A: No B: Yes
A and B consolidate	A: Yes B: Yes	A: Yes B: Yes	A: Yes B: Yes
A voluntarily dissolves	A: Yes, unless unanimous shareholder consent	A: Yes	A: No usually

CALLIER v. CALLIER

Appellate Court of Illinois, Fifth District, 1978.
61 Ill.App.3d 1011, 18 Ill.Dec. 941, 378 N.E.2d 405.

Facts: All Steel Pipe and Tube is a closely held corporation engaged in the business of selling steel pipes and tubes. Leo and Scott Callier are its two equal shareholders. Leo, Scott's uncle, is one of the company's two directors and is president of the corporation. Scott is the general manager. Scott's father and Leo's grandfather, Felix, is the other director. Over the years, Scott and Leo have had differences of opinion about various aspects of the operation of the business. Despite the deterioration of their relationship, the company nonetheless flourished. Negotiations aimed at the redemption of Scott's shares by Leo began, but the parties could not reach an agreement. The discussion then turned to voluntary dissolution and liquidation of the corporation, but still no agreement could be reached. Finally, Leo fired Scott and began to wind down All Steel's business and form a new corporation, Callier Steel Pipe and Tube. Leo then brought this action seeking a dissolution and liquidation of All Steel. The trial court ordered liquidation.

Decision: Judgment reversed and remanded for further proceeding.

Opinion: **Wineland, J.**   Corporations, which are creatures of statute, can only be dissolved according to statute. [Citation.] As our Supreme Court said in [citation], "Corporate dissolution is a drastic remedy, and the teachings of generations of chancellors admonish us that it must not be lightly invoked." [Citations.]

The statute at issue here is as follows:

Circuit courts have full power to liquidate the assets and business of a corporation:

(a) In an action by a shareholder when it appears:

(1) That the directors are deadlocked in the management of the corporate affairs and the shareholders are unable to break the deadlock, and that irreparable injury to the corporation is suffered or threatened by reason thereof * * *. [Citation.]

[This] section has not been a frequently used basis for dissolution, presumably because of the "substantial problems of interpretation" connected with its provisions. [Citation.] The terms *deadlock* and *irreparable injury* are both undefined and troublesome. It has been said that mere dissension among stockholders is not a ground for dissolution unless it is of such serious proportions as to defeat the end for which the corporation is organized. [Citations.] * * *

After a careful review of the entire record, we have concluded that plaintiff's proof was insufficient to show either deadlock in the management of corporate affairs or the threat of irreparable injury to the corporation. What the evidence shows, instead, is two equal shareholders who were unable to get along and unable to reach agreement within a four-month period as to the redemption of one's shares by the other or to the terms of voluntary dissolution. This is not equivalent to an inability of the corporation to perform the functions for which it was created. Without adopting the position of the defendants that the threat of irreparable injury can never be shown under this statute so long as a corporation is making a profit, we must agree with defendants that such a threat was not proved here.

It appears to us that Leo Callier simply decided that he was not going to have anything more to do with Scott Callier, and when their redemption-liquidation negotiations stalled, he made a unilateral decision—without consulting the other director or shareholder—to shut down the corporation. On the day that he informed the employees of the closing of the corporation, corporate affairs were being managed, and quite successfully. In fact, the company appeared on its way to the second best year of its history, despite a general downturn in the pipe industry. Neither Scott not Felix Callier was interfering with the management of the corporation; Scott had in fact intentionally stayed away from the company and allowed Leo to run things alone while the redemption discussions were going on.

Thus, absent sufficient proof of the jurisdictional facts of deadlock and irreparable injury, the court below erred in ordering liquidation of the corporate assets.

Liquidation

Dissolution does not terminate the corporation's existence but does require that the corporation devote itself to winding up its affairs and liquidating its assets. After dissolution, the corporation must cease carrying on its business except as is necessary to wind up.[18] When a corporation is dissolved, its assets are liquidated and used first to pay the expenses of liquidation and its creditors according to their respective contract or lien rights. Any remainder is distributed to shareholders proportionately according to their respective contract rights, and stock with a liquidation preference has priority over common stock. When liquidation is voluntary, it is carried out by the board of directors, who serve as trustees; when liquidation is involuntary, it is conducted by a receiver appointed by the court.[19]

Protection of Creditors

The statutory provisions governing dissolution and liquidation usually prescribe procedures to safeguard the interests of creditors of the corporation. Such procedures typically include required mailing of notice to known creditors, general publication of notice, and preservation of claims against the corporation. For example, the Model Act provides that the dissolution of a corporation shall not impair any remedy available to or against the corporation, its directors, officers, or shareholders for any right or claim existing or any liability incurred before dissolution if suit is brought within two years after the date of dissolution.[20] The Revised Act provides a five-year period for (1) a claimant who did not receive notice, (2) a claimant whose timely claim was not acted on, or (3) a claimant whose claim is contingent on an event occurring after dissolution.[21]

CHAPTER SUMMARY

Charter Amendments	**Authority to Amend** statutes permit charters to be amended freely **Procedure** the board of directors must adopt a resolution which must be approved by a majority vote of the shareholders
Combinations	**Purchase or Lease of All or Substantially All of the Assets** results in no change in the legal personality of either corporation ■ *Regular Course of Business* approval by the selling corporation's board of directors is required, but shareholder authorization is not ■ *Other Than in Regular Course of Business* approval by the board of directors and shareholders of selling corporation is required **Purchase of Shares** a transaction by which one corporation acquires all or a controlling interest of the stock of another corporation; there is no change in the legal existence of either corporation and no formal shareholder approval of either corporation is required **Compulsory Share Exchange** a transaction by which a corporation becomes the owner of all of the outstanding shares of one or more classes of stock of another corporation by an exchange that is compulsory on all owners of the acquired shares; the board of directors of each corporation and the shareholders of the corporation whose shares are being acquired must approve

Merger   the combination of the assets of two or more corporations into one of the corporations
- *Procedure*   requires approval by the board of directors and shareholders of each corporation
- *Short-Form Merger*   a corporation that owns at least 90 percent of the outstanding shares of a subsidiary may merge the subsidiary into itself without approval by the shareholders of either corporation
- *Effect*   the surviving corporation receives title to all of the assets of the merged corporation and assumes all of its liabilities; the merged corporation ceases to exist

Consolidation   the combination of two or more corporations into a new corporation
- *Procedure*   requires approval of the board of directors and shareholders of each corporation
- *Effect*   each of the constituent corporations ceases to exist; all of their debts and liabilities are assumed by the new corporation

Going Private Transactions   a combination that makes a publicly held corporation a private one; includes cash-out combinations and management buyouts

Dissenting Shareholder   one who opposes a fundamental change and has the right to receive the fair value of her shares
- *Fair Value*   value of shares immediately before the corporate action to which the dissenter objects takes place, excluding any appreciation or depreciation in anticipation of such corporate action unless such exclusion would be inequitable
- *Availability*   dissenters' rights arise in (1) mergers, (2) consolidations, (3) sales or leases of all or substantially all of the assets of a corporation not in the regular course of business, (4) compulsory share exchanges, and (5) amendments that materially and adversely affect the rights of shares

Dissolution

Nonjudicial Dissolution   may be brought about by (1) act of the legislature, (2) expiration of the period of time provided for in the articles of incorporation, or (3) voluntary action by the corporation with the approval of the board of directors and the shareholders

Judicial Dissolution   may occur by court action taken (1) by the attorney general, (2) by shareholders under certain circumstances, and (3) by a creditor on a showing that the corporation has become unable to pay its debts and obligations as they mature in the regular course of its business

Liquidation   when a corporation is dissolved, its assets are liquidated and used first to pay the expenses of liquidation and its creditors according to their respective contract or lien rights, and then any remainder is distributed to shareholders proportionately according to their respective contract rights

QUESTIONS

1. Which charter amendments (a) do not require shareholder approval, and (b) give dissenting shareholders an appraisal remedy?

2. Which combinations (a) do not require shareholder approval, and (b) give dissenting shareholders an appraisal remedy?

3. Distinguish between a tender offer and a compulsory share exchange.

4. Compare and contrast a cash-out combination and a management buyout.

5. Identify the ways by which nonjudicial and judicial dissolution may occur.

PROBLEMS

1. The stock in Hotel Management, Inc., a hotel management corporation, was divided equally between two families. For several years, the two families had been unable to agree or cooperate in the management of the corporation. As a result, no meeting of shareholders or directors had been held for five years. There had been no withdrawal of profits for five years, and last year the hotel operated at a loss. Although the corporation was not insolvent, such a state was imminent because the business was poorly managed and its properties were in need of repair. As a result, the owners of half the stock brought an action in equity for dissolution of the corporation. What decision?

2. (a) When may a corporation sell, lease, exchange, mortgage, or pledge all or substantially all of its assets in the usual and regular course of its business?

(b) When may a corporation sell, lease, exchange, mortgage, or pledge all or substantially all of its assets other than in the usual and regular course of its business?

(c) What are the rights of a shareholder who dissents from a proposed sale or exchange of all or substantially all of the assets of a corporation other than in the usual and regular course of its business?

3. The Cutler Company was duly merged into the Stone Company. Yetta, a shareholder of the former Cutler Company, having paid only one-half of her subscription, is now sued by the Stone Company for the balance of the subscription. Yetta, who took no part in the merger proceedings, denied liability on the ground that, inasmuch as the Cutler Company no longer exists, all her rights and obligations in connection with the Cutler Company have been terminated. Decision?

4. Smith, while in the course of his employment with the Bee Corporation, negligently ran the company's truck into Williams, injuring him very severely. Subsequently, the Bee Corporation and the Sea Corporation consolidated, forming the SeaBee Corporation. Williams filed suit against the SeaBee Corporation for damages, and the SeaBee Corporation argued the defense that the injuries sustained by Williams were not caused by any of SeaBee's employees, that SeaBee was not even in existence at the time of the injury, and that the SeaBee Corporation was therefore not liable. What decision?

5. The Johnson Company, a corporation organized under the laws of State X, after proper authorization by the shareholders, sold its entire assets to the Samson Company, also a State X corporation. Ellen, an unpaid creditor of the Johnson Company, sues the Samson Company on her claim. Decision?

6. Zenith Steel Company operates a prosperous business. The board of directors voted to spend $20 million of the surplus funds of the company to purchase a majority of the stock of two other companies—the Green Insurance Company and the Blue Trust Company. The Green Insurance Company is a thriving business whose stock is an excellent investment at the price at which it will be sold to Zenith Steel Company. The principal reasons for Zenith's purchase of the Green Insurance stock are as an investment of surplus funds and as a diversification of its business. The Blue Trust Company owns a controlling interest in Zenith Steel Company. The main purpose for Zenith's purchase of the Blue Trust Company stock is to enable the present management and directors of Zenith Steel Company to continue their management of the company. Jones, a minority shareholder in Zenith Steel Company, brings an appropriate action to enjoin the purchase by Zenith Steel Company of the stock of either the Green Insurance Company or of the Blue Trust Company. Decision?

7. Mildred, Deborah, and Bob each own one-third of the stock of Nova Corporation. On Friday, Mildred received an offer to merge Nova into Buyer Corporation. Mildred agreed to call a shareholders' meeting to discuss the offer on the following Tuesday. Mildred telephoned Deborah and Bob and informed them of the offer and the scheduled meeting. Deborah agreed to attend. Bob was unable to attend because he was leaving on a trip on Saturday and asked if the three of them could meet Friday night to discuss the offer. Mildred and Deborah agreed. The three shareholders met informally Friday night and agreed to accept the offer only if they received preferred stock of Buyer Corporation for their shares. Bob then left on his trip. On Tuesday, at the time and place appointed by Mildred, Mildred and Deborah convened the shareholders' meeting. After discussion, they concluded that the preferred stock payment limitation was unwise and passed a formal resolution to accept Buyer Corporation's offer without any such condition. Bob files suit to enjoin Mildred, Deborah, and the Nova Corporation from implementing this resolution. Decision?

8. Tretter alleged that his exposure over the years to asbestos products manufactured by Philip Carey Manufacturing Corporation caused him to contract asbestosis. Tretter brought an action against Rapid American Corporation, which was the surviving corporation of a merger between Philip Carey and Rapid American. Rapid American denied liability, claiming that immediately after the merger it had transferred its asbestos operations to a newly formed subsidiary corporation. Decision?

9. Wilcox was chief executive officer, chairman of the board of directors, and owned 60 percent of the shares of Sterling Corporation. When the market price of Sterling's shares was $22 per share, Wilcox sold all of his shares in Sterling to Conrad for $29 per share. The minority shareholders of Sterling brought suit against Wilcox demanding a portion of the amount Wilcox received in excess of the market price. Decision?

ENDNOTES

1. Model Business Corporation Act, Section 58, Right to Amend Articles of Incorporation.

2. Revised Model Business Corporation Act, Section 10.02, Amendment by Board of Directors.

3. Model Business Corporation Act, Section 80, Right of Shareholders to Dissent and Obtain Payment for Shares.

4. Revised Model Business Corporation Act, Sections 10.03, Amendment by Board of Directors and Shareholders; 7.25, Quorum and Voting Requirements for Voting Groups; 7.26, Action by Single and Multiple Voting Groups.

5. Model Business Corporation Act, Section 78, Sale of Assets in Regular Course of Business and Mortgage or Pledge of Assets; Revised Model Business Corporation Act, Section 12.01, Sale of Assets in Regular Course of Business and Mortgage of Assets.

6. Model Business Corporation Act, Section 79, Sale of Assets Other Than in Regular Course of Business.

7. Model Business Corporation Act, Section 72A, Procedure for Share Exchange.

8. Model Business Corporation Act, Section 73, Approval for Shareholders.

9. Model Business Corporation Act, Section 76, Effect of Merger, Consolidation or Exchange.

10. Model Business Corporation Act, Section 71, Procedure for Merger.

11. Model Business Corporation Act, Section 75, Merger of Subsidiary Corporation.

12. Model Business Corporation Act, Section 72, Procedure for Consolidation.

13. Model Business Corporation Act, Section 81, Procedures for Protection of Dissenters' Rights.

14. Model Business Corporation Act, Section 83, Voluntary Dissolution by Consent of Shareholders.

15. Model Business Corporation Act, Section 84, Voluntary Dissolution by Act of Corporation.

16. Model Business Corporation Act, Section 94, Involuntary Dissolution.

17. Model Business Corporation Act, Section 97, Jurisdiction of Court to Liquidate Assets and Business of Corporation.

18. Model Business Corporation Act, Section 86, Effect of Statement of Intent to Dissolve.

19. Model Business Corporation Act, Section 98, Procedure in Liquidation of Corporation by Court.

20. Model Business Corporation Act, Section 105, Survival of Remedy after Dissolution.

21. Revised Model Business Corporation Act, Section 14.07, Unknown Claims Against Dissolved Corporation.

PART 8
DEBTOR AND CREDITOR RELATIONS

In Part Eight we discuss debtor and creditor relations, an area of business that has assumed great importance. Today our economy literally runs on borrowed funds. As of 1986, $724 billion of consumer installment credit was outstanding and mortgage debt outstanding exceeded $2,500 billion.

This extensive use of credit is a relatively recent phenomenon. Shakespeare's well-known lines in *Hamlet* reflect the earlier view of debt: "Neither a borrower nor a lender be; For loan oft loses both itself and friend, And borrowing dulls the edge of husbandry." Professors Speidel, Summers, and White, in *Commercial Transactions*, have explained the long-standing historical opposition to debt:

> It was once thought bad for a person to incur debts. In Plato's ideal legal system, debts were not to be incurred at all. It was thought even worse not to repay a debt. In early Rome, debtors who did not repay were dismembered: deprived of arms and legs and more. Not too long ago in Anglo-American law, they were thrown in jail where they might well rot. This was known as body execution on a live body. Even corpses were in jeopardy. Thus on July 7, 1816, Richard Brinsley Sheridan expired at the age of 65. "As his body lay in state in Great George Street, London, a bailiff, disguised as a mourner was admitted to have a last look. Once entered, he served the corpse with a warrant arresting it in the King's name for a debt of five hundred pounds. Only when Mr. Carring and Lord Sidmouth each satisfied the bailiff with a check for two-hundred and fifty pounds did he release the body, so that the funeral could proceed."

Over time this attitude has changed dramatically, and today under our economic system's borrowed funds are absolutely essential and entirely honorable. Without them units of production would be severely restricted in the goods and services they could provide, and consumers would be greatly limited in the quantities they could afford to purchase. The public policy and social issues to which the enormous use of debt gives rise are essentially fourfold. First, the means by which debt is created and transferred should be as simple and inexpensive as possible. Second, the risks to lenders should be reduced to the minimum level possible. Third, the lenders should have adequate means for collecting unpaid debts. Finally, debtors should have protection from overreaching and deception by lenders and, in some instances, from their own foolhardiness. The legal system's response to these needs constitutes the law of debtor and creditor relations.

The law governing the creation and transfer of debt is designed to make it as expeditious and efficient as possible. For the most part, this area of the law has been discussed elsewhere. For example, Article 3 of the Uniform Commercial Code (discussed in Part Four) deals with debt evidenced by commercial paper, and Article 8 (discussed in Chapter 34) governs debt evidenced by investment securities such as bonds. The issuance and transfer of investment securities is also subject to State and Federal securities regulation, which we discuss in Chapter 43. In addition, the common law of contracts and sales law under Article 2 of the UCC provides simple methods of creating debt, although it does not provide very efficient means by which to transfer such debt. See Chapter 14 for a discussion of the assignment of contract rights.

A lender typically incurs two basic collection risks. The first is that the borrower is unwilling to repay the loan even though he is able to do so. The law has provided the lender with a considerable number of collection remedies that significantly reduce this risk, although these remedies are by no means without cost. We discuss a number of these remedies in Chapter 37.

The law has also sought to deal with the second and more significant collection risk: that the borrower may be *unable* to repay the loan. In addition to the remedies just mentioned, the law has developed several devices to maximize the likelihood that the loan will be repaid. The two most important of these are consensual security interests and sureties. A consensual security interest is an agreement by the borrower granting to the lender the right to reach specified property of the borrower to pay off the debt if the borrower fails to do so. If the property used as collateral is real property, the security is called a mortgage or a deed of trust, which we discuss in Chapter 50. If the property is personal property, the security interest is governed by Article 9 of the Uniform Commercial Code, which we cover in Chapter 37.

The Official Comment to UCC Section 9–101 states: "The aim of this Article is to provide a simple and unified structure within which the immense variety of present-day secured financing transactions can go forward with less cost and with greater certainty." Article 9 establishes a comprehensive scheme for the regulation of security interests in personal property that supersedes prior law, which, although it had recognized a wide variety of security devices, did not keep pace with new types of collateral and financing that had developed. Moreover, the recognition of so many inconsistent devices had not only increased the costs to both lender and debtor but had also increased the uncertainty as to their rights. Article 9 replaced these distinct and diverse devices with a single "generic" security interest that applies to all transactions intended to create

security interests in personal property. By doing so, Article 9 has radically simplified the formal requirements for creating a security interest and has substituted a more rational system for the multiple filing systems of previous law. Both of these changes have reduced the cost of acquiring a security interest in personal property.

The other common device to reduce the risk of default is a *surety*, the subject of Chapter 38. A surety is a person who promises the creditor that he will pay the debtor's obligation to the creditor if the debtor does not. If the debtor defaults, the creditor may proceed directly against the surety. The use of a surety, with or without security, can significantly reduce the collection risk to the lender.

The last important policy objective of debtor-creditor law is the protection of debtors against the overreaching of creditors as well as from the debtor's own foolhardiness. This problem is most acute where the creditor is a professional and the debtor is a consumer. Both State and Federal legislation have been enacted to address many of the particular problems faced by consumer debtors. We discuss these statutes in Chapter 45.

In some instances, debtors of all sorts—wage earners, sole proprietorships, partnerships, and corporations—accumulate debts far in excess of their assets or suffer financial reverses that make it impossible for them to meet their obligations as they become due. In such an event, it is an important policy of the law to treat all creditors fairly and equitably. It is also necessary to provide the debtor with relief from these debts so that he may continue to function and contribute to society. These are the two basic purposes of the Federal bankruptcy law, which we discuss in Chapter 39.

37 SECURED TRANSACTIONS

A secured transaction includes two elements: (1) a debt or obligation to pay money, and (2) an interest of the creditor in specific property of the debtor that secures performance of the obligation. An obligation or debt can exist without security; in fact, a vast amount of indebtedness is unsecured. The integrity, reputation, and net worth of the debtor are deemed adequate by the creditor.

In many situations, however, businesses or other individuals cannot obtain credit without giving adequate security. In other cases, an unsecured loan can be obtained, but giving security results in a lower interest rate. Financing transactions involving security in personal property are governed by *Article 9* of the Uniform Commercial Code, Secured Transactions. This article provides a simple and unified structure within which the tremendous variety of current secured financing transactions can take place with less cost and with greater certainty. Moreover, the article's flexibility and simplified formalities make it possible for new forms of secured financing to fit comfortably under its provisions. In the first part of this chapter we discuss secured transactions in personal property. Article 9 does not cover secured transactions involving real property, which we discuss in Chapter 50.

ESSENTIALS OF SECURED TRANSACTIONS

Secured transactions in personal property are governed by Article 9 if the debtor *consents* to provide a security interest in personal property to secure the payment of a debt. Article 9 does *not* apply to security interests without consent that arise by operation of law, such as mechanics' or landlords' liens. A common type of consensual secured transaction covered by Article 9 occurs when a person who wants to buy goods does not have either the cash or sufficient credit standing to obtain the goods on open credit. The seller obtains a security interest in the goods to secure payment of all or part of the price. Alternatively, the buyer may borrow the purchase price from a third party and pay the seller in cash. The third-party lender may then take a security interest in the goods to secure repayment of the loan.

In every consensual secured transaction there is a debtor, a secured party, collateral, a security agreement, and a security interest. As defined in the Code[1], a **debtor** is a person who owes payment or performance of an obligation. A **secured party** is the creditor-lender, seller, or other person who possesses the security interest in the collateral. **Collateral** is the property subject to the security interest. A **security agreement** is the agreement that creates or provides for a **security interest,** which in its broadest sense is an interest in personal property or fixtures that secures payment or performance of an obligation.[2] A seller of goods who retains a security interest in them by a security agreement has a **purchase money security interest** (PMSI). Similarly, a third-party lender who advances funds to enable the debtor to purchase goods has a purchase money security interest if she has a security agreement and the debtor in fact uses the funds to purchase the goods.[3]

Thus, a security interest is created when an automobile dealer sells and delivers a car to an individual *(debtor)* under a retail installment contract *(security agreement)* through which the dealer *(secured party)* obtains a *security interest (purchase money security interest)* in the car *(collateral)* until the price is paid. A security interest in property cannot exist apart from the debt it secures, and once the debt is discharged in any way, the security interest in the property is terminated. Figure 37–1 illustrates the fundamental rights of the debtor and the secured party in a secured transaction.

CLASSIFICATION OF COLLATERAL

Although most of the provisions of Article 9 apply to all kinds of personal property, some provisions state special rules that apply only to particular kinds of collateral. Under the Code, collateral is classified according to its nature and its use. The classifications according to nature are: (a) goods, (b) indispensable paper, and (c) intangibles.

Goods

Goods are tangible personal property that can be moved when the security interest in them becomes enforceable.[1] Goods are subdivided into (1) consumer goods, (2) farm products, (3) inventory, and (4) equipment.[4] Goods that become so affixed to real estate are called fixtures.[4] An item of goods may fall into different classifications depending on its use or purpose. For example, a refrigerator purchased by a physician to store medicines in his office is classified as equipment, but the same refrigerator would be classified as consumer goods if it was purchased for use in his home.

The refrigerator would be classified as inventory in the hands of a refrigerator dealer or manufacturer.

Consumer Goods   Goods are **consumer goods** if they are used or bought for use primarily for personal, family, or household purposes.[4] Thus, Amos purchases a television set for use in his house from an appliance dealer under a retail installment contract and grants the dealer a security interest in the television. This is an example of consumer goods.

Farm Products   The Code defines **farm products** as ''crops or livestock or supplies used or produced in farming operations or if they are products of crops or livestock in their unmanufactured states.''[4] Thus, farm products would include wheat growing on the farmer's land, the farmer's pigs, cows, hens, and the hen's eggs.

Inventory   **Inventory** includes goods held for sale or lease and raw materials, work in process, or materials used or consumed in a business.[4] Thus, a retailer's or wholesaler's merchandise as well as a manufacturer's materials are inventory.

Equipment   Goods are classified as **equipment** if they are used or purchased for use primarily in business (including farming or a profession), provided they are not included in the definition of inventory, farm products, or consumer goods.[4] This category is broad enough to include a lawyer's library, a physician's office furniture, or machinery in a factory.

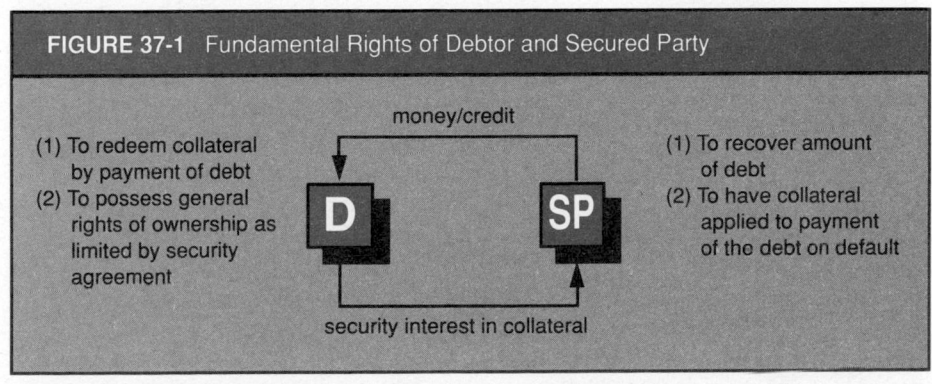

FIGURE 37-1   Fundamental Rights of Debtor and Secured Party

money/credit

D   SP

security interest in collateral

(1) To redeem collateral by payment of debt
(2) To possess general rights of ownership as limited by security agreement

(1) To recover amount of debt
(2) To have collateral applied to payment of the debt on default

Fixtures Goods or personal property that have become so related to particular *real property* that an interest in them arises under real estate law are called **fixtures**.[5] Thus, State law other than the Code determines whether and when goods become fixtures. In general terms, goods become fixtures when they are so firmly affixed or attached to real estate in such a way that they are considered part of the real estate. Examples are furnaces, air-conditioning units, and plumbing fixtures. See Chapter 47 for a further discussion of fixtures. A security interest under Article 9 may be created in goods that are fixtures, and under certain circumstances a perfected security interest in fixtures will have priority over a conflicting security interest or mortgage in the real property to which the goods have been attached.

Indispensable Paper

Three kinds of collateral involve rights evidenced by indispensable paper: (1) chattel paper, (2) instruments, and (3) documents.

Chattel Paper **Chattel paper** is a writing or writings that evidence both a monetary obligation and a security interest in or a lease of specific goods.[1] Frequently, a secured party may borrow against or sell the security agreement of his debtor along with his interest in the collateral. The secured party's collateral in this type of transaction is chattel paper. The Code provides the following illustration:

> A dealer sells a tractor to a farmer on conditional sales contract or purchase money security interest. The conditional sales contract is a "security agreement," the farmer is the debtor, the dealer is the "secured party" and the tractor is the type of "collateral" defined . . . as "equipment." But now the dealer transfers the contract to his bank either by outright sale or to secure a loan. Since the conditional sales contract is a security agreement relating to specific equipment, the conditional sales contract is now the type of collateral called "chattel paper." In this transaction between the dealer and his bank, the bank is the "secured party," the dealer is the "debtor," and the farmer is the "account debtor."[6]

Instruments **Instruments** include negotiable instruments, stocks, bonds, and other investment securities. An instrument is any writing that evidences a right to payment of money, that is transferable by delivery with any necessary indorsement or assignment, and that is not of itself a security agreement or lease.[1]

Documents The term **document** includes documents of title, such as bills of lading and warehouse receipts, that may be either negotiable or nonnegotiable.[1, 7] A document of title is negotiable if by its terms the goods it covers are deliverable to bearer or to the order of a named person. Any other document is nonnegotiable.

Intangibles

The Code also recognizes two kinds of collateral that are neither goods nor indispensable paper, namely, accounts and general intangibles. These types of **intangible** collateral are not evidenced by any indispensable paper, such as a stock certificate or a negotiable bill of lading.

Accounts The term **account** or *account receivable* refers to the right to payment for goods sold or leased or for services rendered that is not evidenced by an instrument or chattel paper, whether or not it has been earned by performance.[8] The 1972 Code deletes the term "contract right" but includes contract rights in its expanded definition of account.

General Intangibles The term **general intangibles** applies to any personal property other than goods, accounts, chattel paper, documents, instruments, and money.[8] This is a catchall category for interests not otherwise covered unless they are specifically excluded. It leaves room for the use of new kinds of collateral for financing purposes. It includes good will, literary rights, rights to performance of a contract, and interests in patents, trademarks, and copyrights to the extent they are not regulated by Federal statute.

ATTACHMENT

Attachment is the Code's terminology to describe a security interest that is *enforceable* against the debtor.[9] Attachment is also a prerequisite to a security interest's enforceability against parties other than the debtor. Enforceability against third parties is called perfection and is discussed below. Until a security interest "attaches," it is ineffective against the debtor. The security interest created by a security agreement attaches to the described collateral once the following events have taken place:

1. the giving of value by the secured party,
2. the debtor's acquiring rights in the collateral; and
3. either the collateral is in the possession of the secured party according to agreement *or* the security agreement is in a writing that contains a reasonable description of the collateral and is signed by the debtor.[9]

Value

The term **value** is broadly defined and includes consideration under contract law, a binding commitment to extend credit, and an antecedent debt.[10] For example, Buyer purchases goods from Seller on credit. When Buyer fails to make timely payment, Seller and Buyer enter into a security agreement under which Seller is granted a security interest in the goods. Value has been given by the Seller, even though he does not provide any new consideration but instead relies on an antecedent debt—the original transfer of goods to Buyer. Moreover, Seller is not limited to acquiring a security interest in the goods he sold to Buyer but may also obtain a security interest in other personal property of the Buyer.

Debtor's Rights in Collateral

The concept of the debtor's rights in collateral is elusive and not specifically defined by the Code. Before 1972 the UCC attempted to provide rules for determining when a debtor acquired rights in certain types of collateral. The 1972 amendments eliminated these provisions because they were considered unnecessary, arbitrary, and confusing. It was decided that such questions were best left for the courts to determine. As a general rule, the debtor is deemed to have **rights in collateral** he owns or is in possession of as well as those items that he is in the process of acquiring from the seller. For example, if Julia borrows money from Nick and grants him a security interest in corporate stock that Julia owns, then Julia had rights in the collateral before entering into the secured transaction. If Susan sells goods to Peter on credit and Peter provides Susan a security interest in the goods, Peter will acquire rights in the collateral on identification of the goods to the contract.

Security Agreement

A security interest cannot attach unless there is an agreement between the debtor and creditor granting, creating, or providing the creditor a security interest in the debtor's collateral. With the exception of pledges, the agreement must (1) be *in writing*, (2) be *signed* by the *debtor*, and (3) contain a *reasonable description* of the collateral.[9] See *Matter of Amex-Protein Dev. Corp.* below. In addition, if the collateral is crops growing or to be grown or timber to be cut, the agreement must contain a reasonable description of the land. A sample security agreement is provided as Figure 37–2.

MATTER OF AMEX-PROTEIN DEV. CORP.
United States Court of Appeals, Ninth Circuit, 1974.
504 F.2d 1056.

Facts: Plant Reclamation Company sold equipment to Amex-Protein Development Corporation on an open account. Later Plant Reclamation substituted a promissory note for the open account indebtedness and caused a financing statement to be signed and filed that provided notice of the parties' intention to create a security interest in the property sold as collateral for the note. The note stated that it was secured by a security interest in the property "as per invoices." Amex-Protein subsequently declared bankruptcy, and the validity of Plant Reclamation's security interest in the property is now in issue. The trustee asserts that the promissory note does not constitute a valid security agreement and questions the adequacy of the description of the collateral contained in that instrument. The district court ruled in favor of Plant Reclamation, holding that an enforceable security interest had been created.

Decision: Judgment for Plant Reclamation Corporation affirmed.

Opinion: Per Curiam   The financing statement names Plant Reclamation as the secured party and recited that it covered the following types or items of property:

> 1—Door Oliver 100 Sq. Ft. Vacuum Filter
> 1—Chicago Pheumatic [sic] Vacuum Compression
> 1—Stainless Steel Augar [sic] and Drive
> 1—Nichols micro 7" dryer
> 1—Tolhurst Centerfuge [sic] 26 inch

Discussion
I. Did the Promissory Note 'Create or Provide for' a Security Interest?

* * *

No magic words or precise form are necessary to create or provide for a security interest so long as the minimum formal requirements of the Code are met. [Citations.]

This liberal approach is mandated by an expressed purpose of the secured transaction provisions of the Code:

> The aim of this Article is to provide a simple and unified structure within which the immense variety of present-day secured financing transactions can go forward with less cost and with greater certainty.

* * *

The Article's flexibility and simplified formalities should make it possible for new forms of secured financing, as they develop, to fit comfortably under its provisions * * *. Comment to U.C.C.

The court in *In re Center Auto Parts*, [citation] upheld the validity of a promissory note as a security agreement by reading the two together. The promissory note merely recited that, 'This note is secured by a certain financing statement,' and the court found that such was sufficient to 'create or provide for' a security interest within the meaning of § 9–105(1)(h).

* * *

Accordingly, the promissory note herein qualifies as a security agreement which by its terms 'creates or provides for' a security interest.
II. Adequacy of Description of the Collateral
The trustee urges a second ground for sustaining the Order of the Referee complained of here, namely the inadequacy of the description of the collateral in the promissory note and hence the failure to comply with [U.C.C.] § 9–203(1)(b) [citation].

* * *

Although the promissory note does not describe the collateral within the four corners of the document such description is provided (1) through incorporation by reference of the subject invoices, as well as (2) through reference to the more specific description of the collateral contained in the financing statement.

The use of such extrinsic aids is clearly permissible to identify the collateral:

Under the Uniform Commercial Code there is no reason why parol evidence may not be admitted in aid of the description of the collateral, even where the collateral has been reasonably and sufficiently identified in the security agreement. In many instances, a description in a security agreement may be in general terms; parol evidence should therefore be admissible to explain or supplement the general description, or to resolve ambiguities. [Citations.]

The doctrine of incorporation by reference is likewise available in this area:

There is nothing in the Uniform Commercial Code to prevent reference in the security agreement to another writing for particular terms and conditions of the transaction. There is also nothing in the Uniform Commercial Code to prevent reference in the Security Agreement to another writing for a description of the collateral, so long as the reference in the security agreement is sufficient to identify reasonably what it described. In other words, it will at times be expedient to give a general description of the collateral in the security agreement and refer to a list or other writing for more exact description. In addition, the security agreement could itself consist of separate parts, one a general description of the obligation secured and the rights and duties of the parties, and the other a description of the collateral, both such writings being signed by the debtor and stated to comprise a single security agreement or referring to each other. [Citations.]

Thus there is no requirement that the description of the collateral be complete within the four corners of the security agreement or other single document. The description in the security agreement is sufficient, however, if it provides such information as would lead a reasonable inquirer to the identity of the collateral. [Citations.]

It is manifest that the reference to the invoices in the subject promissory note, coupled with the existence of a financing statement containing a more specific description, satisfies the requirements of [U.C.C.] §§ 9–203(1)(b) and 9–110.

Under the Code, no written security agreement is required when the collateral is pledged or in the possession of the secured party pursuant to an agreement.[9] A **pledge** is the delivery of personal property to a creditor as security for the payment of a debt. A pledge requires that the secured party (the pledgee) and the debtor agree to the pledge of the collateral and that the collateral is delivered to the pledgee.

Consumer Goods Federal regulation prohibits a credit seller or lender from obtaining a consumer's grant of a nonpossessory security interest in household goods. This rule does not apply to purchase money security interests or to pledges. Household goods are defined to include clothing, furniture, appliances, kitchenware, personal effects, one radio, and one television. Works of art, other electronic entertainment equipment, antiques, and jewelry are specifically excluded from being considered household goods. This rule prevents a lender or seller from obtaining a nonpurchase money security interest covering the consumer's household goods.

After-Acquired Property A security agreement may provide a secured party with a security interest in after-acquired property.[11]

FIGURE 37–2 Sample Security Agreement

SECURITY AGREEMENT

August 22, 1989

Daniel Debtor of 113 Hillsborough Street, City of Raleigh, County of Wake, State of North Carolina, hereinafter called the "Debtor," does hereby grant to S.P. & Assoc., Inc., of Raleigh, North Carolina, hereinafter called "S.P.," its successors and assigns, a security interest in the following described property, hereinafter called the "Collateral," to-wit:

> One (1) Deluxe Microcomputer
> Serial number VDL 16794321
> Manufacturer: Apex Mechanical
>   Equipment Co.
> Model 420A

to secure the payment of Debtor's note or notes of even date herewith in the aggregate principal or aggregate face amount of Seven Thousand Five Hundred Dollars ($7,500.00), together with interest and any renewal or extension thereof, in whole or in part, and any and all other debts, obligations, and liabilities of any kind of Debtor to S.P., however created, arising, or evidenced, whether direct or indirect, joint or several, whether as maker, indorser, surety, guarantor or otherwise, whether now or hereafter existing, whether due or not due, and however acquired by S.P. (all hereinafter called the "Obligations").

DEBTOR WARRANTS AND AGREES THAT:

1. Except for the security interest hereby granted, the Debtor will use the proceeds of advances made hereunder, which proceeds may be paid by the S.P. directly to the seller of the Collateral, to become the owner of marketable title to the Collateral free from any prior lien, security interest or encumbrance, and the Debtor will defend the Collateral against all claims and demands of all persons at any time claiming an interest therein.

2. The Collateral is and will be used primarily for personal, family, or household purposes, and the Debtor's residence is that shown at the beginning of this Agreement.

3. The Collateral will be kept at the Debtor's address shown at the beginning of this Agreement.

4. There are no financing statements covering any of the Collateral on file in any public office, and the Debtor has not executed in favor of other secured parties financing statements that could be placed on file prior to any of S.P.'s financing statements.

5. DEBTOR AGREES THAT:
A.   He will pay to S.P. all amounts due on the note or notes mentioned above and the other Obligations secured hereby as and when same shall be due and payable, whether by maturity, acceleration, or otherwise, and will pay to S.P. reasonable attorney's fees incurred by S.P. in collection of said Obligations or enforcement of this Security Agreement.
B.   He will maintain all mechanical equipment and machinery hereby covered in sound and efficient operating condition, including the procurement and installation of such

After-acquired property is property the debtor does not own or have rights to but may acquire at some time in the future. For example, after-acquired property clauses in a security agreement may include all present and subsequently acquired inventory, accounts, or equipment of the debtor. For example, this clause would provide the secured party with a valid security interest not only in the debtor's presently existing typewriter, desk, and file

FIGURE 37–2 Continued

new parts, attachments, and replacements as may be necessary or desirable to maintain said Collateral in proper operating condition.

C. He will maintain such insurance upon all of the Collateral as S.P. may requir, payable to Debtor and S.P. as their interest may appear, in an amount not less than the actual value of the Collateral.

D. He will pay all insurance premiums and taxes, licenses, or other charges assessed against the Collateral or required to be paid in connection with the use and ownership of the Collateral. If Debtor shall fail to pay such insurance premiums, taxes, licenses, or other charges when they are due, S.P. at its option, may pay the cost thereof, and the amounts so paid and advanced shall be added to the indebtedness secured hereby and shall bear interest at the maximum rate permitted by Law.

E. He will not (a) permit any liens or security interest to attach to any of the Collateral; (b) permit any of the Collateral to be levied upon under any legal process; (c) sell or dispose of any of the Collateral without prior written consent of S.P.; (d) permit anything to be done that may impair the value of the Collateral or the security intended to be afforded by this Agreement.

F. He will immediately notify S.P. in writing of any change of the Debtor's place of residence, place or places of business, or the location of the Collateral.

G. He will not remove the Collateral from the State of North Carolina without prior written consent by S.P.

6. IT IS FURTHER AGREED THAT THE DEBTOR SHALL BE IN DEFAULT UNDER THIS AGREEMENT:

A. If the Debtor uses any of the Collateral in violation of any statute or ordinance or the Debtor is found to have a record or reputation for violating the laws of the United States or any State relating to liquor or narcotics; or

B. If the Debtor shall fail to perform any covenant or Agreement made by him herein; or

C. If the Debtor shall fail to make due and punctual payment of any of the Obligations secured hereby when and as any part or all of such Obligation becomes due and payable; or

D. If any warranty, representation, or statement made or furnished to S.P. by or on behalf of the Debtor in connection with this Agreement proves to have been false in any material respect when made or furnished; or

E. If the Collateral suffers material damage or destruction; or

F. If any bankruptcy or insolvency proceedings are commenced by or against the Debtor or any guarantor or surety for the Debtor; or

G. If the Debtor dies, becomes incompetent, is dissolved, or the Debtor's existence otherwise terminates.

Upon the happening of any of the above events of default or in the event that S.P., in good faith, deems itself insecure, S.P. may at its option, declare all Obligations secured hereby due and payable immediately and have, in addition to other rights and remedies, the rights and remedies of a secured party upon default under the North Carolina Uniform Commercial Code.

The waiver of any particular default of the Debtor hereunder shall not be a waiver of any other or subsequent default of the Debtor.

Any requirement of the North Carolina Uniform Commercial Code of reasonable notification of time and place of public sale, or the time on or after which private sale may be held, may be met by sending written notice by registered or certified mail to the above address of the Debtor at least five (5) days prior to public sale or the date after which private sale may be made.

The Debtor shall be and remain liable for any deficiency remaining after applying the proceeds of disposition of the Collateral first to the reasonable expenses of re-taking, holding, preparing for sale, selling, and the like, including the reasonable attorney's fees, incurred by S.P. in connection therewith, and then to satisfaction of the Obligations

---

FIGURE 37–2 Continued

secured hereby.

This Agreement and all rights, remedies, and duties hereunder, including matters of construction, shall be governed by the laws of North Carolina.

This Agreement shall apply to, inure to the benefit of, and be binding upon the heirs, administrators, executors, and assigns of S.P. and the Debtor. This is the entire agreement of the parties, and no amendment, alteration, deletion, or addition hereto shall be effective and binding unless it is in writing and signed by the parties.

Debtor acknowledges that this Agreement is and shall be effective upon execution by the Debtor and delivery hereof to S.P., and it shall not be necessary for S.P. to execute or otherwise signify its acceptance hereof.

Signed and delivered on the day first above written.

_____(SEAL)
Daniel Debtor

S.P. & Assoc., Inc.
(Secured Party)
By:_____

---

cabinet, but also in a personal computer subsequently purchased by the debtor. The concept of a "continuing general lien" or a *floating lien* is therefore accepted by Article 9. The Code, however, limits the operation of an after-acquired property clause against *consumers*. No such interest can be claimed as additional security in consumer goods, except accessions, if the goods are acquired more than ten days after the secured party gives value.[11] An *accession* is property installed in or affixed to other property.[12] For example, a new engine placed in an old automobile is an accession.

Proceeds A secured party is necessarily interested in the use and control of the **proceeds,** which includes whatever is received upon the sale, exchange, collection, or other disposition of the collateral.[13] These proceeds may be in the form of money, checks, deposit accounts, promissory notes, or other types of personal property. Unless otherwise agreed, a security agreement gives the secured party rights to proceeds.[9]

Future Advances The obligations covered by a security agreement may include future advances.[11] Frequently, a debtor will obtain a line of credit from a creditor for advances to be made at some later time. For instance, a manufacturer may provide a retailer with a $60,000 line of credit although the retailer initially uses only $20,000 of the credit. Nevertheless, the manufacturer may enter into a security agreement with the retailer granting the manufacturer a security interest in the retailer's inventory to secure not only the initial $20,000 advance but also any future advances.

PERFECTION

To be effective against third parties (including other creditors of the debtor, the debtor's trustee in bankruptcy, and transferees of the debtor), the security interest must be perfected. **Perfection** of a security interest occurs when it has attached *and* when all the applicable steps required for perfection have been taken.[14] If these steps are taken before the security interest attaches, it is perfected at the time it attaches. Once a security interest becomes perfected, as the official comments to the Code provide, it "may still be or become subordinate to other interests but in general after perfection the secured party is protected against creditors and transferees of the debtor and in particular against any representative of creditor in insolvency proceedings instituted by or against the debtor."[15]

Depending upon the type of collateral, a security interest may be perfected:

1. by the secured party's filing a financing statement in the designated public office;
2. by the secured party's taking or retaining possession of the collateral;
3. automatically on the attachment of the security interest; or
4. temporarily for a period of time specified by the Code.

Figure 37–3 lists the requirements for enforceability of security interests.

Filing a Financing Statement

Filing a financing statement is the general method of perfecting a security interest under Article 9. Filing may be used to perfect a security interest in any kind of collateral with the *exception* of instruments. The form of the **financing statement,** which is filed to give public notice of the security interest, may vary from State to State. The financing statement does not contain details, but the names and addresses of the secured party and the debtor, a reasonable description of the collateral, and the signature of the debtor are required.[16] Figure 37–4 shows a sample financing statement.

So that the terms of secured transaction between the parties can be determined, the security agreement or the collateral note or preferably both must be available. It is possible that neither the maturity date of the obligation nor the amount of the obligation secured will appear on the financing statement. Where no maturity date is stated on a financing statement, the statement is effective for *five years* from the date of filing.[17] If a **continuation statement** is filed by the secured party within six months prior to expiration, the effectiveness of the filing will be extended for another five-year period.[17]

In most States, security interests in **motor vehicles** must be perfected by a notation on the certificate of title rather than by filing a financing statement.

A **certificate of title** is an official representation of ownership. Nevertheless, in most States, certificate of title laws do not apply to motor vehicles that are held as inventory for sale by a dealer.

Where to File The Code provides three alternative provisions regarding the proper place to file a financing statement.[18] The alternatives differ as to which types of collateral are to be filed *locally* (in the county) or *centrally* (with the Secretary of State or another designated State official).

FIGURE 37-3 Requisites for Enforceability of Security Interests

I. Attachment
(enforceable against debtor)

A. Agreement
   1. in writing (unless SP has possession)
   2. providing a security interest
   3. in described collateral
   4. signed by debtor,

B. Value given by secured party, and

C. Debtor has rights in collateral.

II. Perfection
(enforceable against third parties)

A. Filing a financing statement, or

B. SP takes possession, or

C. Automatically, or

D. Temporarily

FIGURE 37-4 Sample Financing Statement

UNIFORM COMMERCIAL CODE—FINANCING STATEMENT
APPROVED FOR USE IN NORTH CAROLINA AND THE FOLLOWING STATES

Alabama	Delaware	Maine	New Jersey	Tennessee
Alaska	Hawaii	Maryland	New Mexico	Virginia
Arkansas	Idaho	Massachusetts	North Dakota	West Virginia
Arizona	Indiana	Mississippi	Ohio	Wyoming
Colorado	Kansas	Montana	Oklahoma	District of Columbia
Connecticut	Kentucky	New Hampshire	South Carolina	

UCC-1

This FINANCING STATEMENT is presented to a Filing Officer for filing pursuant to the Uniform Commercial Code.

No. of Additional Sheets Presented:

(1) Debtor(s) (Last Name First) and Address(es):

(2) Secured Party(ies) Name(s) and Address(es):

(3) (a)☐ Collateral is or includes fixtures.
  (b)☐ Timber, Minerals or Accounts Subject to UCC-9-103
(5) are covered
  (c)☐ Crops Are Growing Or To Be Grown On Real Property Described in Section (5).
If either block 3(a) or block 3(b) applies describe real estate, including record owner(s) in section (5).

(4) Assignee(s) of Secured Party, Address(es):

For
Filing
Officer

(5) This Financing Statement Covers the Following types [or items] of property.

☐ Products of the Collateral Are Also Covered.

(6) Signatures: Debtor(s)   Secured Party(ies) [or Assignees]

(By) _____   (By) _____
Standard Form Approved by N.C. Sec. of State   Signature of Secured Party Permitted in Lieu of
  and other states shown above.   Debtor's Signature:
                                                   (1) Collateral is subject to Security Interest In
  (1) Filing Officer Copy—Numerical   Another Jurisdiction and☐
                                                       ☐ Collateral Is Brought Into This State
                                                       ☐ Debtor's Location Changed To This State
                                                   (2) For Other Situations See: UCC-9-402 (2)

UCC-1

NATIONAL CASH REGISTER CO. v. FIRESTONE & CO.
Supreme Judicial Court of Massachusetts, 1963.
346 Mass. 255, 191 N.E.2d 471.

Facts: National Cash Register Company (NCR), a manufacturer of cash registers, entered into a sales contract for a cash register with Edmund Carroll. On November 18, 1960, Firestone and Company made a loan to Carroll, who conveyed certain property to Firestone as collateral under a security agreement. The property outlined in the security agreement included "[a]ll contents of luncheonette including equipment such as . . . " twenty-five different listed items, " . . . together with all property and articles now, and which may hereafter be, used . . . with, [or] added . . . to . . . any of the foregoing described property." A similarly detailed description of the property conveyed as collateral appeared in Firestone's financing statement, but the financing statement made no mention of property to be acquired thereafter, and neither document made a specific reference to a cash register. NCR delivered the cash register to Carroll in Canton between November 19 and November 25 and filed a financing statement with the town clerk of Canton on December 20 and with the Secretary of State on December 21. Carroll subsequently defaulted both on the contract with NCR and on the security agreement with Firestone. Firestone took possession of the cash register and sold it at auction. NCR brought an action against Firestone for conversion of the cash register. The trial court and the appellate court ruled in favor of NCR. Firestone appeals.

Decision: Judgment reversed and new judgment issued in favor of Firestone.

Opinion: Wilkins, C. J. Under the Uniform Commercial Code, after-acquired property, such as this cash register, might become subject to the defendant's security agreement when delivered, [UCC], § 9–204(3); and likewise its delivery under a conditional sale agreement with retention of title in the plaintiff would not, in and of itself, affect the rights of the defendant. [UCC] § 9–202. Although the plaintiff could have completely protected itself by perfecting its interest before or within ten days of the delivery of the cash register to Carroll, it did not try to do so until more than ten days after delivery. Thus the principal issue is whether the defendant's earlier security interest effectively covers the cash register.

* * *

Contrary to the plaintiff's contention, we are of opinion that the security agreement is broad enough to include the cash register, which concededly did not have to be specifically described. The agreement covers "All contents of luncheonette including equipment such as," which we think covers all those contents and does not mean "equipment, to wit." There is a reference to "all property and articles now, and which may hereafter be, used . . . with, [or] added . . . to . . . any of the foregoing described property." . . .

We now come to the question whether the defendant's financing statement should have mentioned property to be acquired thereafter before a security interest in the cash register could attach. The Code [UCC], § 9–402(1), reads in part: "A financing statement is sufficient if it is signed by the debtor . . . , gives an address of the secured party from which information concerning the security interest may be obtained, gives a mailing address of the debtor and contains a statement indicating the types, or describing the items, of collateral."

In the official comment to this section appears the following: "2. This Section adopts the system of 'notice filing' which has proved successful under the Uniform

Trust Receipts Act. What is required to be filed is not, as under chattel mortgage and conditional sales acts, the security agreement itself, but only a simple notice which may be filed before the security interest attaches or thereafter. The notice itself indicates merely that the secured party who has filed may have a security interest in the collateral described. Further inquiry from the parties concerned will be necessary to disclose the complete state of affairs. Section 9–208 provides a statutory procedure under which the secured party, at the debtor's request, may be required to make disclosure. Notice filing has proved to be of great use in financing transactions involving inventory, accounts and chattel paper, since it obviates the necessity of refiling on each of a series of transactions in a continuing arrangement where the collateral changes from day to day. Where other types of collateral are involved, the alternative procedure of filing a signed copy of the security agreement may prove to be the simplest solution." [Citation.]

The framers of the Uniform Commercial Code, by adopting the "notice filing" system, had the purpose to recommend a method of protecting security interests which at the same time would give subsequent potential creditors and other interested persons information and procedures adequate to enable the ascertainment of the facts they needed to know. In this respect the completed Code reflects a decision of policy reached after several years' study and discussion by experts. We conceive our duty to be the making of an interpretation which will carry out the intention of the framers of uniform legislation which already has been enacted in twenty-five States. That the result of their policy decision may be asserted to favor certain types of creditors as against others or that a different policy could have been decided upon is quite beside the point.

The case at bar is, for all practical purposes, one of first impression under the Code. There seem to be no decisions anywhere which specifically deal with the situation presented to us.

* * *

The words, "All contents of luncheonette," including, as we have held, all equipment, were enough to put the plaintiff on notice to ascertain what those contents were. This is not a harsh result as to the plaintiff, to which, as we have indicated, § 9–312(4) made available a simple and sure procedure for completely protecting its purchase money security interest.

The first alternative, which has been adopted in only a few States, provides that where the collateral is fixtures, timber to be cut, or minerals to be extracted, then the financing statement should be filed locally in the office where a mortgage on real estate would be filed or recorded. All other filings are to be made centrally with the Secretary of State or another designated State official.

The second alternative, which is the most widely adopted, stipulates local filing for fixtures, farm products, consumer goods, timber, minerals, and farming equipment. All other filings are to be made in the office of the Secretary of State or another designated State official.

The third alternative is the same as the second except that where central filing is required, the secured party must *also* file locally if the debtor has a place of business in only one county or if the debtor has no place of business in the State but resides in the State.

Improper Filing   If a secured party fails to file the financing statement in the proper location or fails to file it in all the required locations, the filing is *ineffective*, subject to two exceptions. First, if the filing is made in good faith, it is effective for any collateral for which the filing complied with the requirements of Article 9.[18] This exception applies to situations in which the filing covers a number of different kinds of collateral and is proper for some but not all of the collateral listed. Second, a filing made in good faith is also effective for collateral covered by the financing statement against any person who has knowledge of the contents of that financing statement.[18] This exception has been limited by the 1972 amendments, which give a lien creditor priority over an unperfected security interest without regard to whether the lien creditor knew of the unperfected security interest.[19]

Possession

Possession by the secured party may be used to perfect a security interest in goods (e.g., pawnbrokers), instruments, negotiable documents, or chattel paper.[20, 21] A pledge cannot be used with items that are intangible (accounts and general intangible). Subject to the limited exception of the twenty-one-day temporary period of perfection discussed later in this chapter, possession is the *only* way to perfect a security interest in instruments.[22] In addition, the usual and advisable method of perfecting a security interest in both negotiable documents and chattel paper is by possession. Although both of these types of collateral may be perfected by filing, it is not advisable to rely on filing because (a) the holder of a negotiable document of title that has been duly negotiated to him takes priority in the goods over an earlier security interest perfected by filing,[23] and (b) a good faith purchaser in the ordinary course of business of chattel paper takes priority over an earlier security interest perfected by filing.[24]

A pledge or possessory security interest is the delivery of personal property to a creditor, or to a third party acting as an agent for the creditor, as security for the payment of a debt. Perhaps the most common pledge is that of a borrower who pledges corporate stock by delivery of the certificates to a bank in order to secure a loan. The delivery of the stock certificates (collateral) to the bank (secured party) is the essential element of the pledge. Since *delivery* is made, the security interest is "perfected" without filing.[20] There is no pledge where the debtor retains possession of the collateral. In a pledge, the debtor is not legally required to sign a written security agreement; an oral agreement granting the secured party a security interest is sufficient. In any situation other than a pledge, the Code requires a written security agreement.[9]

One kind of pledge is the **field warehouse.** This common arrangement for financing inventory allows the debtor access to the pledged goods and at the same time gives the secured party control over the pledged property. In this arrangement, a professional warehouseman generally establishes a warehouse on the debtor's premises—usually by enclosing a portion of the premises and posting appropriate signs—to store the debtor's unsold inventory. Nonnegotiable receipts for the goods are then typically issued by the warehouseman to the secured party. The secured party may then authorize the warehouseman to release a portion of the goods to the debtor as the goods are sold, at a specified quantity per week, or at any rate agreed on by the parties. Thus, the secured party legally possesses the goods but allows the debtor easy access to the inventory.

Automatic Perfection

In some situations, a security interest is automatically perfected on attachment. The most important situation to which **automatic perfection** applies is a purchase money security interest in consumer goods. In addition, a partial or isolated assignment of accounts that does not transfer a significant part of the oustanding accounts of the assignor is also automatically perfected.

As previously mentioned, a seller of goods who retains a security interest in them by a security agreement has a purchase money security interest (PMSI). Similarly, a third party who advances funds to enable the debtor to purchase goods has a purchase money security interest if he has a security agreement and the debtor in fact uses the funds to purchase the goods.[3] A purchase money security interest in consumer goods, with the exception of motor vehicles, is perfected automatically on attachment without the necessity of filing a financing statement.[20] For example, Don purchases a refrigerator from Carol on credit for Don's own personal family, or household use. Don takes possession of the refrigerator and then grants Carol a security interest in the refrigerator according to a written security agreement. On Don's granting Carol the security interest in the refrigerator, Carol's security interest attaches and is automatically perfected. The same is also true if Don purchased the refrigerator for cash but borrowed the money from Laura, to whom Don granted a written security interest in the refrigerator. Laura's security interest attached and was automatically perfected when Laura received the security interest from Don. Because an automatically perfected PMSI in consumer goods does not protect the secured party as fully as a filed PMSI, secured parties do not always rely on automatic perfection but frequently file a financing statement.

Temporary Perfection

A security interest in certain collateral is automatically perfected but only for a temporary period of time depending on the type of collateral. After that period expires, the security interest becomes unperfected unless it is perfected by other available means of perfection. A security interest in *negotiable documents* or *instruments* is automatically perfected without filing or taking possession for **twenty-one days** from the time it attaches, to the extent that it arises for new value given under a written security agreement.[22] The secured party, however, runs the risk of loss or impairment of his security interest during the twenty-one-day period, for although his interest is temporarily perfected, a holder in due course of a negotiable instrument or a holder to whom a document has been duly negotiated will take priority over the security interest.[24, 23]

The Code further provides that a security interest remains perfected for **twenty-one days** where a secured party, who already has a perfected security interest in an instrument, negotiable document, or goods in possession of a bailee (provided he has not issued a negotiable document for the goods), under certain circumstances delivers the instrument to the debtor, releases the document to him, or makes the goods available to him.[22] Moreover, a security interest in proceeds is automatically perfected for **ten days** after receipt of the proceeds if the security interest in the original collateral was perfected.[13]

Figure 37–5 shows the methods of perfecting security interests.

FIGURE 37-5 Methods of Perfecting Security Interests

Collateral		Applicable Method of Perfection		
	Filing	Possession	Automatic	Temporary
Goods				
Consumer	•	•	PMSI	
Equipment	•	•		
Farm products	•	•		
Inventory	•	•		
Fixtures	•	•		
Indispensable Paper				
Chattel paper	•	•		
Instrument		•		21 days
Document	•	•		21 days
Intangibles				
Account	•		Isolated Assignment	
General Intangibles	•			

PRIORITIES OF SECURED CREDITORS

As we previously noted, a security interest must be perfected to be effective against other creditors of the debtor, the debtor's trustee in bankruptcy, and transferees of the debtor. Nonetheless, perfection of a security interest does *not* provide the secured party with a **priority** over *all* third parties with an interest in the collateral. On the other hand, even an unperfected security interest has priority over a limited number of third parties and is enforceable against the debtor. Article 9 establishes a complex set of rules that determine the relative priorities among these parties.

Figure 37–6 below summarizes the priorities among selected parties who have competing interests in collateral.

Against Unsecured Creditors

Once a security interest **attaches**, it has priority over claims of other creditors who do not have a security interest or a lien. This priority does not depend upon perfection. If a security interest does not attach, the creditor is merely an unsecured or general creditor of the debtor.

Against Other Secured Creditors

The rights of a secured creditor against other secured creditors depends upon which secu-

FIGURE 37-6 Priorities

VS	Unsecured Creditor	Creditor with Unperfected Security Interest	Creditor with Perfected Security Interest	Creditor with Perfected Purchase Money Security Interest
Unsecured Creditor	=	↑	↑	↑
Creditor with unperfected security interest	←	first to attach	↑	↑
Creditor with perfected security interest—noninventory	←	←	first to file or perfect	↑ if PMSI perfected within ten days
Creditor with perfected security interest—inventory	←	←	first to file or perfect	↑ if PMSI gives notice and perfects by time debtor gets possession
Buyer in ordinary course of business	←	←	← if created by immediate seller	←
Consumer buyer of consumer goods	←	←	↑	← if not filed
Lien creditor (including trustee in bankruptcy)	←	←	first in time	first time but PMSI has ten-day grace period
Trustee in bankruptcy—voidable preferences	←	←	↑ if secured party perfects within ten days	↑ if PMSI perfects within ten days

rity interests are perfected, when they are perfected, and the type of collateral. Notwithstanding the rules of priority, it is possible for a secured party entitled to priority to subordinate her interest to that of another secured creditor. This may be done by agreement between the secured parties, and nothing need be filed.

Perfected versus Unperfected A creditor with a **perfected** security interest has greater rights in the collateral than a creditor with an unperfected security interest, whether or not the unperfected security interest has attached.[19]

Perfected versus Perfected If two parties each have a **perfected** security interest, they rank according to priority in *time of filing or perfection.*[25] Priority dates from the time a filing is first made covering the collateral or the time the security interest is first perfected, whichever is earlier, provided that there is no subsequent period when there is neither filing nor perfection.[25] This rule gives special treatment to filing because it can occur prior to attachment and thus grants priority from a time that may precede perfection.

For example, Darwin Store and Surety Bank enter into a loan agreement under the terms of which Surety agrees to lend $6,000 on the security of Darwin's existing store equipment. A financing statement is filed, but no funds are advanced. One week later, Darwin enters into a loan agreement with Reserve Bank, and Reserve Bank agrees to lend $6,000 on the security of the same store equipment. The funds are advanced, and a financing statement is filed. One week later, Surety Bank advances the agreed sum of $6,000. Darwin Store defaults on both loans. Between Surety Bank and Reserve Bank, Surety has priority. When both security interests are perfected by filing, priority is determined in the order of filing. Reserve Bank could have checked the financing statements on file and would have learned that Surety Bank claimed a security interest in the equipment. Once Surety's financing statement was on file, with no prior secured party of record, Surety was not required to check the files prior to advancing funds to Darwin Store in accordance with its loan commitment.

To illustrate further, assume that Marc grants a security interest in a Chagall painting to Miro Bank, and according to the loan agreement the bank advances funds to Marc. A financing statement is filed. Later Marc wishes more money and goes to Braque, an art dealer, who advances funds to Marc on a pledge of the painting. Marc defaults on both loans. Between Miro and Braque, Miro has priority because its security interest was filed before Braque's perfection by possession. By checking the financing statements on file, Braque could have discovered that Miro had a prior security interest in the painting.

Where there is a **purchase money security interest** in the collateral, the rules vary depending on whether the collateral is noninventory or inventory.

1. A purchase money security interest in **noninventory** collateral takes priority over a conflicting security interest if the purchase money security interest is perfected at the time the debtor receives possession of the collateral *or* within *ten days* of receipt.[25] Thus, the secured party has a ten-day grace period.

For example, Dykstic Manufacturing Co. entered into a loan agreement with Smith Bank, which loaned money to Dykstic on the security of Dykstic's existing and future equipment. A financing statement was filed stating that the collateral is "all equipment presently owned and subsequently acquired" by Dykstic. At a later date, Dykstic buys new equipment from Hernandez Supply Co., paying 25 percent of the purchase price, with Hernandez retaining a security interest in the equipment to secure the remaining balance. If Hernandez files a financing statement within ten days of Dykstic's obtaining possession of the equipment, Hernandez's purchase money security interest in the new equipment has priority over Smith's interest. If Hernandez files on the eleventh day after Dykstic receives the equipment, Hernandez's interest is subordinate to Smith's interest.

MATTER OF ULTRA PRECISION INDUSTRIES, INC.
United States Court of Appeals, Ninth Court, 1974.
503 F.2d 414.

Facts: National Acceptance Company loaned Ultra Precision Industries $692,000, and to secure repayment of the loan Ultra executed a chattel mortgage security agreement on National's behalf on March 7, 1967. National perfected the security interest by timely filing a financing statement. Although the security interest covered specifically described equipment of Ultra, both the security agreement and the financing statement contained an after-acquired property clause that did not refer to any specific equipment.

Later in 1967 and 1968, Ultra placed three separate orders for machines from Wolf Machinery Company. In each case it was agreed that after the machines had been shipped to Ultra and installed, Ultra would be given an opportunity to test them in operation for a reasonable period. If the machines passed inspection, Wolf would then provide financing that was satisfactory to Ultra. In all three cases, financing was arranged with Community Bank (Bank) and accepted, and a security interest was given in the machines. Furthermore, in each case a security agreement was entered into, and a financing statement was then filed by the secured parties within ten days. Ultra became bankrupt on October 7, 1969. National now claims that its security interest in the after-acquired machines should take priority over those of Wolf and Bank because their interests were not perfected by timely filed financing statements. The district court affirmed the referee's ruling in favor of Wolf and Bank. National appeals.

Decision: Judgment for Wolf and Bank affirmed.

Opinion: **East, J.** The priorities among the three security interests involved are determined by the application of § 9–312(4), which reads:

A purchase money security interest in collateral other than inventory has priority over a conflicting security interest in the same collateral *if the purchase money security interest is perfected at the time the debtor receives possession of the collateral or within 10 days thereafter. (Emphasis added.)*

The sole issue presented by the facts and the contention of the parties on appeal is: On what dates did Ultra become "the debtor [receiving] possession of the collateral [the three respective machines]" within the meaning of § 9–312(4)?

Discussion: Briefly stated, National contends that Ultra was its "debtor" in "possession of the collateral" at the moment it received physical delivery of the respective three machines, without regard to any agreement to the contrary between Wolf and Ultra as to the terms and conditions of the ultimate sale and purchase of the machines respectively; hence, the machines were within the grasp of the after-acquired property clause. Since the Security Interest Agreements held by Bank and Wolf were not perfected within ten days "thereafter" as commanded by § 9–312(4), they are unenforceable as against National's perfected security interest.

Bank and Wolf each contend that Ultra did not become their "debtor" in "possession of the collateral" (the three respective machines) until the terms and conditions of the proposed sales and the purchases thereof had been met and the

Security Interest Agreement had been executed and delivered. We subscribe to that contention.

Section 9–105(1) of the Code provides:

(1) In this division unless the context otherwise requires:

(d) "Debtor" means the person who owes payment or other performance of the obligation secured * * *.

National urges that the term "debtor" as used in § 9–312(4) means the debtor under its "conflicting security interest." Such an interpretation does violence to the clear language of the section, and such a thesis is inherently rejected under the rationale and holdings in [citation]. To us, the word "debtor" in § 9–312(4) means the debtor of the seller or holder of the "purchase money security interest in collateral" (the thing sold).

It is manifest that Ultra was not a "debtor" of Wolf and did not owe payment or other performance of the obligation secured unto Wolf until the moment of the execution and delivery of the Security Interest Agreements on July 31, 1968, and October 23, 1968, respectively. Suffice to say that prior to those dates, (a) Wolf held no definitive security interest in the machines which could be perfected by the filing of a Financing Statement, and (b) Ultra held no assignable legal interest in the machines which could fall into the grasp of National's after-acquired property security clause.

We hold that Ultra became the purchase money security interest "debtor [receiving] possession of the collateral [the three respective machines]" at the instant of the execution and delivery of the Security Interest Agreements, respectively, and not before; and, further, that since each of the Security Interest Agreements were timely perfected, the security interests of Wolf and Bank, respectively, are each prior and superior to the conflicting security interest held by National. [Citation.]

* * *

The record as a whole reveals good faith, above board, uninvolved commercial credit transactions, without any withholding on the part of or secret equities among the parties. National was in no way misled by any acts of Wolf or Bank giving rise to an estoppel, and National advanced no money or credit on the strength of Ultra's pre-Security Interest Agreement possession of the machines. Wolf was entitled to abide with the terms and conditions of the proposed sales and purchases of its machines and to perfect its ultimate Security Interest Agreements in accordance with § 9–312(4).

2. A purchase money security interest in **inventory** has priority over conflicting security interests if the following requirements are met. The purchase money security holder must perfect his interest in the inventory at the time the debtor receives the inventory. Also, he must notify, in writing, all holders of conflicting security interests who have filed a financing statement covering the same type of inventory of his acquisition of a purchase money security interest and must give a description of the secured inventory.[25]

For example, Dodel Store and San Diego Bank enter into a loan agreement in which San Diego agrees to finance Dodel's entire inventory of stoves, refrigerators, and other kitchen appliances. A financing statement is filed, and San Diego advances funds to Dodel. Subsequently, Dodel enters into an agreement in which Regina Stove Co. will supply Dodel with stoves, retaining a purchase money security interest in this inventory. Regina will have priority on the inventory it supplies to Dodel provided that a financing statement is filed and Regina notifies San Diego that it is going to engage in this purchase money financing of the described stoves. If Regina fails to give the required notice or fails to file a financing statement, San Diego will have priority over Regina on the stoves it supplies to Dodel. The Code adopts a system of notice filing, and secured parties proceed at their peril in failing to check the financing statements on file.

Unperfected versus Unperfected   If neither security interest is perfected, then the first to attach has priority.[25] If neither attaches, both of the creditors are general, unsecured creditors.

Against Buyers

A security interest continues in collateral even though it is sold, unless the secured party authorizes the sale.[13] The security interest also continues in any identifiable proceeds from the sale of the collateral. In some instances, however, buyers of collateral sold without the secured party's authorization take it free of the security interest. Some of these purchasers take the collateral free of even a perfected security interest; others take it free of only an unperfected security interest.

Buyers in the Ordinary Course of Business   A **buyer in the ordinary course of business** takes collateral free of any security interest created by *her* seller, even if the security interest is perfected and the buyer knows of its existence.[26] A buyer in the ordinary course of business is a person who buys in good faith, without knowledge that the sale violates a security interest of a third party, and who buys from a person in the business of selling goods of that kind.[27] Thus, this rule applies primarily to purchasers of inventory. For example, a consumer who purchases a sofa from a furniture dealer and the dealer who purchases the sofa from another dealer are both buyers in the ordinary course of business. On the other hand, a person who purchases a sofa from a dentist who used the sofa in his waiting room or from an individual who used the sofa in his home is not a buyer in the ordinary course of business.

To illustrate further: a buyer in the ordinary course of business of an automobile from an automobile dealership will take free and clear of a security interest created by the dealer from whom he purchased the car. That same buyer, in the ordinary course of business, will *not* take clear of a security interest created by any person who owned the automobile prior to the dealer. In the leading case on this point, Wever bought a Dodge Dart from Wentworth Motor Company for his own personal use and granted a security interest in the car to Wentworth. Wentworth later assigned the security interest to National Shawmut Bank, which properly perfected it. Without Shawmut's consent, Wever sold the car to Hanson-Rock, another automobile dealer. Hanson-Rock then sold the car to Jones. Even though Jones is a buyer in the ordinary course of business from Hanson-Rock, he took the automobile subject to Shawmut's security interest since that interest had not been created by Jones's seller, Hanson-Rock. See also *Exchange Bank of Osceola v. Jarrett,* which follows.

EXCHANGE BANK OF OSCEOLA v. JARRETT
Supreme Court of Montana, 1979.
588 P.2d 1006.

Facts: On September 8, 1976, Daniel Holland purchased for his own use a tractor-scraper through the Exchange Bank of Osceola located in Kissimmee, Florida. The bank retained a security interest in the tractor for the full $13,000 purchase price and then perfected that security interest in Florida.

On February 1, 1977, Holland sold the tractor, without the Exchange Bank's permission, to C. B. and O. Equipment Company, a Council Bluffs, Iowa, farm implements merchant. The tractor arrived in Iowa on February 7, 1977, and on February 21, 1977, Jarrett, a Montana contractor, purchased it and transported it to Montana. Exchange Bank then properly filed a financing statement in both Iowa and Montana. When Holland subsequently defaulted on his obligation to Exchange Bank, the bank brought this action to foreclose on its security interest in the tractor. Exchange Bank brings this appeal from a judgment granting the defendant's motion to dismiss for failure to state a cause of action.

Decision: Judgment reversed and remanded.

Opinion: Sheehy, J. The sole issue for our determination is whether Spencer Jarrett purchased the tractor-scraper "free of" or "subject to" the bank's security interest.

It is agreed that the bank perfected its security interest in the tractor-scraper by filing the financing statement required by [U.C.C.] § 9–302. The Uniform Commercial Code contemplates the continued perfection of a security interest if there has been no intervening period when it was unperfected. [U.C.C.] § 9–303. A perfected security interest is generally not destroyed by the sale, exchange or other disposition of the collateral:

> (2) Except where this chapter otherwise provides, a security interest continues in collateral notwithstanding sale, exchange or other disposition thereof by the debtor unless his action was authorized by the secured party in the security agreement or otherwise, and also continues in any identifiable proceeds including collections received by the debtor. [U.C.C.] § 9–306(2).

Since Daniel Holland sold the tractor without plaintiff's permission and in violation of the security agreement, it is clear that C. B. and O. purchased the tractor-scraper "subject to" the bank's security interest.

When C. B. and O. transported the tractor from Florida to Iowa, the continued existence of the bank's security interest was contingent on the provisions of Iowa's Commercial Code.

* * *

The Courts uniformly hold that Section 9–103 gives a secured party a four-month grace period during which his security interest is protected without any further action on his part. * * *

Applying the provisions of Iowa Code § 9–103 to our fact pattern, it is obvious that the bank's security interest was viable at the time defendant purchased the tractor-scraper from C. B. and O. Equipment Company. The bank fully complied with section 9–103 by filing its financing statement in Iowa on April 4, 1977, well within the four-month period. Therefore, plaintiff's security interest continued unless Article 9 provides otherwise.

Defendant contends that Iowa Code § 9–307 allowed him to purchase the tractor-scraper "free of" plaintiff's security interest. Section 9–307 provides:

> *Protection of buyers of goods.* 1. A buyer in ordinary course of business (subsection 9 of Section 1–201) other than a person buying farm products from a person engaged in farming operations takes free of a security interest *created by his seller* even though the security interest is perfected and even though the buyer knows of its existence.

In the present case, defendant Jarrett purchased in good faith and without knowledge that the sale to him was in violation of the bank's security interest. Defendant also purchased the tractor in the ordinary course from a person in the business of selling tractors, therefore, he was a "buyer in the ordinary course of business". Iowa Code § 1–201(9).

However, section 9–307 contains the further limitation that the security interest must be "created by his [defendant's] seller". This Court has never interpreted the "created by his seller" limitation. However, the landmark case in this area is *National Shawmut Bank of Boston v. Jones* [citation].

Shawmut was a replevin action instituted to recover possession of a 1964 Dodge station wagon. The station wagon was originally purchased by a man named Robert Wever. To obtain the car, Wever had secured a loan from the plaintiff bank and had executed a security agreement using the car as collateral. Sometime thereafter, Wever traded or sold the wagon to a reputable dealer engaged in the business of selling new and used cars to the public. The dealer then sold the car to defendant. Neither the dealer nor the defendant knew of plaintiff's security interest.

While the defendant in Shawmut was obviously a "buyer in the ordinary course," the Court nonetheless allowed the bank to recover the automobile from him. The Shawmut court held:

* * * defendant purchased in good faith without knowledge that the sale was in violation of the security interest of another and bought in the ordinary course from a person in the business of selling automobiles, he was a "buyer in the ordinary course of business" * * * However, 9–307(1) permits him to take free only of "a security interest created by his seller". The security interest of the plaintiff was not created by * * * the defendant's seller, but by Wentworth Motor Co., Inc. *Defendant, therefore, does not take free of the plaintiff's security interest under this section.* [Citation.]

As in Shawmut, defendant's seller *did not* create plaintiff's security interest, therefore, defendant does not take the tractor "free of" plaintiff's security interest under Iowa Code § 9–307.

* * *

This Court recognizes that this is a harsh result, since the purchaser, on the date of purchase in Iowa, had no means to learn in Iowa that the property he purchased was subject to a security interest. It may be that legislative action is necessary to prevent such results in the future. Since we are bound by the enacted laws, and must give full faith and credit to the laws of our sister states, no other course is open to us here.

Buyers of Consumer Goods   In the case of consumer goods, a buyer who buys without knowledge of a security interest, for value, and for his own personal, family, or household use takes the goods free of any purchase money security interest automatically perfected, but takes the goods subject to a security interest perfected by filing.[26] For example, Ann purchases on credit a refrigerator from Steve for use in her home and grants Steve a security interest in the refrigerator. Steve does not file a financing statement but has a perfected security interest by attachment. Ann subsequently sells the refrigerator to her neighbor, Nick, for use in Nick's home. Nick did not have knowledge of Steve's security interest and therefore takes the refrigerator free of Steve's interest. If Steve had filed a financing statement, however, Steve's security interest would continue in the collateral in the hands of Nick.

Other Buyers An unperfected security interest is subordinate to the following rights: (1) in the case of goods, instruments, documents, and chattel paper, of a purchaser who gives value for the collateral, takes it without knowledge of the existing security interest, and before it is perfected;[19] and (2) in the case of accounts and general intangibles, of a purchaser who takes the collateral for value, without knowledge of the security interest, and before perfection.[19] If either of these purchasers has knowledge of the unperfected security interest, he takes the collateral subject to the security interest.

A purchaser of chattel paper or an instrument who gives new value and takes possession of it in the ordinary course of his business has priority over a perfected security interest in the chattel paper or instrument if he acts without knowledge that the specific paper or instrument is subject to a security interest.[24] A holder in due course of a negotiable instrument, a holder to whom a negotiable document of title has been duly negotiated, and a *bona fide* purchaser of an investment security take priority over an earlier security interest even though perfected. Filing under Article 9 does *not* constitute notice of the security interest to such holders or purchasers.[23]

Against Lien Creditors

A **lien creditor** means a creditor who has acquired a lien in the property by judicial decree *and* includes an assignee for the benefit of creditors, a receiver in equity, as well as a trustee in bankruptcy.[19] A **trustee in bankruptcy** is a representative of the estate in bankruptcy who is responsible for collecting, liquidating, and distributing the debtor's assets. A **perfected** security interest has priority over lien creditors who acquire their lien after perfection. An **unperfected** security interest is subordinate to the rights of a person who beomes a lien creditor before the security interest is perfected.[19] If a secured party files with respect to a *purchase money security interest* within ten days after the debtor receives poses-

sion of the collateral, however, the secured party takes priority over the rights of a lien creditor that arise between the time the security interest attaches and the time of filing.[19] Approximately half of the States have expanded the ten-day grace period to twenty days.

Nonetheless, a lien securing claims arising from services or materials furnished with respect to goods (an artisan's or mechanic's lien) "takes priority over a perfected security interest unless the lien is statutory and the statute specifically provides otherwise."[28]

Against Trustee in Bankruptcy

The Bankruptcy Act empowers a trustee in bankruptcy to invalidate secured claims in certain instances. It also imposes some limitations on the rights of secured parties. In this section we will examine the power of a trustee in bankruptcy to (a) take priority over an unperfected security interest, and (b) avoid preferential transfers.

Priority over Unperfected Security Interest A trustee in bankruptcy may invalidate any security interest that is voidable by a creditor who obtained a judicial lien on the date of the filing of the bankruptcy petition. Under the Code and the Bankruptcy Act, the trustee, as a hypothetical **lien creditor,** has priority over a creditor with a security interest that was not perfected when the bankruptcy petition was filed. A creditor with a purchase money security interest who files within ten days after the debtor receives the collateral will defeat the trustee, even if the petition is filed before the creditor perfects and after the creation of the security interest. For example, David borrowed $5,000 from Cynthia on September 1 and gave her a security interest in the equipment he purchased with the borrowed funds. On October 3, before Cynthia perfected her security interest, David filed for bankruptcy. The trustee in bankruptcy can invalidate Cynthia's security interest because it was unperfected when the bankruptcy petition was filed. If, however, David had filed for bankruptcy on September 8 and Cynthia had perfected the security interest on September 9, Cynthia would prevail because her purchase money security interest was perfected within ten days after David received the equipment.

Avoidance of Preferential Transfers The Bankruptcy Act provides that a trustee in bankruptcy may invalidate any transfer of property—including the granting of a security interest—from the debtor, provided that the transfer (1) was to or for the benefit of a creditor; (2) was made on account of an antecedent debt; (3) was made at a time the debtor was insolvent; (4) was made on or within ninety days before the filing of the bankruptcy petition, or if made to an insider, was made within one year before the date of the filing; and (5) enabled the transferee to receive more than he would have received in bankruptcy. (An insider includes a relative or general partner of a debtor, as well as a partnership in which the debtor is a general partner or a corporation of which the debtor is a director, officer, or person in control.) In determining whether the debtor is insolvent, the act establishes a rebuttable presumption of insolvency for the ninety days prior to the filing of the bankruptcy petition. In order to avoid a transfer to an insider that occurred more than ninety days before bankruptcy, the trustee must prove the debtor's insolvency. If a security interest is invalidated as a preferential transfer, the creditor may still make a claim for the unpaid debt, but the creditor's claim is unsecured.

To illustrate the operation of this rule, consider the following. On May 1 Debra bought and received merchandise from Stuart and gave him a security interest in the goods for the unpaid price of $20,000. On May 20 Stuart filed a financing statement. On August 1 Debra filed a petition for bankruptcy. The trustee in bankruptcy may avoid the perfected security interest as a preferential transfer. The transfer of the perfected security interest on May 20 was (1) to benefit a creditor (Stuart); (2) was on account of an antecedent debt (the $20,000 owed from the sale of the merchandise); (3) the debtor was insolvent at the time (it is presumed that the debtor is insolvent for the ninety days preceding the filing of the bankruptcy petition—August 1); (4) the trans-

fer was made within ninety days of bankruptcy (May 20 is less than ninety days before August 1); and (5) the transfer enabled the creditor to receive more than he would have received in bankruptcy (Stuart would have a secured claim on which he would recover more than on an unsecured claim).

For the purposes of the voidable preference section, the Bankruptcy Act deems a transfer of a security interest to be made when it is *perfected*. If it is perfected within ten days after attachment, however, the transfer is deemed to be made at the actual time of transfer; consequently, security interests perfected within ten days of attachment will not be preferential since they are not made for antecedent debt. This ten-day "grace" period applies to both purchase money and nonpurchase money security interests. Thus, in the example above, if Stuart had filed the financing statement by May 11, the security interest would not be a preferential transfer. Alternatively, if the goods had been consumer goods, the transaction would not be a preferential transfer because the security interest would have been automatically perfected upon attachment, and thus there would not be a transfer for an antecedent debt.

On the other hand, consider the following example. On January 6 Dawn purchases fifty refrigerators from Chad on credit. Dawn grants Chad a security interest in the inventory on January 6, and Chad perfects it on November 15. On December 15 Dawn files a petition in bankruptcy. The transfer of the security interest will be deemed to have been made on November 15, not on January 6. Thus, the security interest would be held to be within the ninety-day period and for an antecedent debt—the credit sale made on January 6. The trustee in bankruptcy would therefore be able to invalidate Chad's perfected security interest as a preferential transfer.

After-acquired property clauses, called floating liens, as previously discussed, are expressly permitted by the Code[11] and are frequently used in financing inventory and accounts. Such clauses, however, may give the floating lien creditor an unfair advantage over other creditors if a debtor accumulates property subject to the after-acquired property clause. The Bankruptcy Act addresses this problem by allowing a trustee in bankruptcy to invalidate any improvement in a creditor's position in inventory, receivables, or proceeds to the extent it occurs during the ninety-day (one year for insiders) period immediately preceding the filing of the bankruptcy petition. The amount of the voidable preference equals:

[Amount of secured debt 90 days prior to bankruptcy–
Amount of collateral available 90 days prior to bankruptcy]–
[Amount of debt on date of bankruptcy–
Amount of collateral available on date of bankruptcy]

To illustrate: at the time of bankruptcy, Dan owes Claudia $100,000 and has inventory valued at $90,000. Ninety days prior to bankruptcy Dan owed Claudia $120,000 and had inventory valued at $60,000. Dan has a security interest in all of Claudia's presently existing and future acquired inventory. In this situation, the trustee in bankruptcy can reduce Claudia's secured claim from $90,000 to $40,000: voidable preference = (120,000 − 60,000) − ($100,000 − $90,000) = $50,000.

DEFAULT

Afer default, the rights and remedies of the parties are governed by the security agreement and by the applicable provisions of the Code. In general, the secured party may ask for a judgment or foreclosure or otherwise enforce the security interest by available judicial procedure.[29] Unless the parties have agreed otherwise, the secured party may take possession of the collateral on default without judicial process if it can be done without a breach of the peace.[30]

After default, instead of repossessing the collateral, the secured party may leave it on the debtor's premises and render it unusable until disposing of it.[30] Unless the debtor has waived his rights in the collateral after default, he has a right of **redemption** (to free the collateral of the security interest by paying off the loan) at any time before the secured party has disposed of the collateral, entered into a contract to dispose of it, or discharged the obligation by retention of the collateral.[31, 32]

Sale of Collateral

The secured party may sell, lease, or otherwise dispose of any collateral in its existing condition at the time of default or following any commercially reasonable preparation or processing.[33] The debtor is entitled to any surplus and is liable for any deficiency, except that in the case of a sale of accounts or chattel paper, he is not entitled to any surplus or liable for a defiency unless the security agreement so provides.[33]

The collateral, as demonstrated in the case that follows, may be disposed of at *public* or *private* sale, so long as all aspects of its disposition are "commercially reasonable." Unless the collateral is perishable or threatens to decline speedily in value or is of a type customarily sold on a recognized market, reasonable *notice* must be given to the debtor of a public sale or of the time after which a private disposition will be made and, except in the case of consumer goods, to other secured parties who have filed or who are known by the secured party to have security interests in the collateral.

The secured party may buy at a public sale and at a private sale if the collateral is customarily sold in a recognized market or is the subject of widely distributed standard price quotations.[33]

EGGEMAN v. WESTERN NATIONAL BANK
Supreme Court of Wyoming, 1979.
596 P.2d 318.

Facts: Eggeman and his wife gave Western National Bank a $41,000 promissory note, securing the debt by a mortgage on two adjoining tracts of land. Some time later, Eggeman gave the bank an additional $8,625 note, which was secured by "inventory and accounts receivable" described more fully in the security agreement. When Eggeman defaulted on both notes, Western National filed a complaint against Eggeman requesting the sale of the mortgaged land in satisfaction of the balance due on the first note and the sale of the collateral in satisfaction of the balance due on the second note. The judgment authorizing the foreclosure sale provided, with respect to the second note, "that the collateral listed in the security agreement be sold under and pursuant to the judgment of this Court." The inventory and accounts receivable were not listed or itemized in the judgment or at the sale. When the sale was held, both tracts of land, the inventory, and the accounts receivable were offered only as a whole and in one group. They were purchased by James T. Frost for $67,500. Eggeman moved to vacate the sale, claiming that the remedy taken by Western National with reference to the second note was not pursuant to law. Western National countered that the sale was proper as a judicial sale. The motion to vacate the sale was denied, and Eggeman appealed.

Decision: Judgment reversed and remanded.

Opinion: Rooney, J. Under law, there are five principal remedies given to the secured party on default of the terms of a security agreement by the debtor. Since none of the remedies were properly used in this case, the sale of the personal property was not proper. The five remedies are:

1. Use of the real estate mortgage foreclosure procedures if the security agreement covers both real and personal property. [Section 9–501(4).] Although both real and personal property were involved in this action, the security agreement does not cover real property. Therefore, this remedy is not available to plaintiff.
2. With reference to accounts receivable, as here, collect the same from those obligated thereon. [Section 9–502(1).] Plaintiff did not choose to pursue this remedy.
3. Any special remedy provided in the security agreement. [Section 9–501(2).] This security agreement did not set forth any special remedy.
4. Take possession of the collateral without judicial process [Section 9–503] and either accept it in full satisfaction [Section 9–505(2)] or sell it. [Section 9–504(1).] The notice required for acceptance in full satisfaction was not here given. Here possession was not taken without judicial process, and the sale was made before plaintiff took possession. A sale under this remedy must be commercially reasonable. Section 9–504(3). This is the remedy most commonly used. The usual reasons for not using it are: (a) inability to secure peaceable possession of the collateral, and (b) desire to be able to proceed against assets of the debtor, other than the collateral. Plaintiff did not use this remedy.
5. Take a judgment on the underlying obligation, and proceed under the judgment. [Section 9–501(1).] This seems to be the remedy attempted in this case. The procedure for this remedy is not set out in the Uniform Commercial Code, i.e., § 1–101, et seq. The usual procedure for enforcement of judgments for money is set out in [Citation]. Usually the judgment is executed on by issuance of a writ of execution. The sheriff levies the writ upon the goods and chattels of the debtor, taking them actually or constructively into his possession. The various items levied upon are then identified and are subject to valuation and inspection. If necessary, the sheriff then holds an execution sale. Such procedure is anticipated by the Uniform Commercial Code. [Section 9–501(5).

A writ of execution was not issued or levied in this case. The sheriff did not take possession of the goods, actually or constructively, and they were not otherwise specifically identified or evaluated. The usual execution and levy procedure was not followed.

But plaintiff contends that a judicial sale, as distinguished from an execution sale, was here held. A judicial sale is proper under the Code [Section 9–501(5)] and under the remedy here under discussion. However, the judicial sale attempted in this case was not properly mandated or conducted. Inasmuch as the property to be sold was not definitely or accurately described in the judgment and at the sale; inasmuch as it was not taken into the sheriff's possession prior to the sale or was not otherwise specifically identified or made subject to evaluation as to quantity and quality prior to the sale, a jurisdictional defect existed and the sale was void.

* * *

The judgment in this case only directed that the sale be "pursuant to judgment of this court." It did not prescribe the terms and mode of sale as is required for a fair and proper judicial sale.

The distinctive characteristics of a judicial sale are that it must be the result of a judicial proceeding; it must be based upon an order, decree, or judgment directing that the property be sold, as distinguished from a judicial assent to the sale of property under statutory provisions authorizing certain sales by fiduciaries; and it must be made by the court or by its direction upon the terms and in the mode provided by the decree or order, which of course must conform with any pertinent statutory provisions regulating judicial sales. . . .

* * *

A judicial sale cannot be held in a "grab bag" fashion. Such would not be commercially reasonable. All parties to the sale must have an opportunity to see and evaluate the goods being sold. [Citations.] The judgment can direct that the sale be held at the place where the items are located, or it can direct a time and place before the sale at which the items can be inspected. Some means must be provided by which the items to be sold can be identified specifically, or the items must be identified specifically and not generically in the judgment.

Since this judgment and the sale resulting therefrom were deficient in these respects, the sale of personal property was void and must be vacated.

Retention of Collateral

The secured party may, after default and repossession, send written notice to the debtor and, except in the case of consumer goods, to other secured parties that he proposes to retain the collateral in satisfaction of the obligation, and if no objection is received within twenty-one days, the secured party may retain the collateral. If there is objection within this period, however, the collateral must be disposed of as provided in the Code.[31] In the case of *consumer* goods, if the debtor has paid *60 percent* of the obligation and has not, after default, signed a statement renouncing his rights, the secured party who has taken possession of the collateral must dispose of it by sale within ninety days after repossession or the debtor may recover, in conversion or under the Code, not less than the credit service charge plus 10 percent of the principal amount of the debt or the time price differential plus 10 percent of the cash price.[31, 34]

CHAPTER SUMMARY

Essentials of Secured Transactions	**Definition of Secured Transaction** an agreement by which one party obtains a security interest in the personal property of another to secure the payment of a debt
	■ *Debtor* person who owes payment or performance of an obligation
	■ *Secured Party* creditor who possesses a security interest in collateral
	■ *Collateral* property subject to a security interest
	■ *Security Agreement* agreement that grants a security interest
	■ *Security Interest* right in personal property to insure payment of an obligation
	■ *Purchase Money Security Interest* security interest in goods purchased; interest is retained either by the seller of the goods or by a lender who advances the purchase price
	■ *Financing Statement* document filed to provide notice of a security interest
	Fundamental Rights of Debtor
	■ to redeem collateral by payment of the debt
	■ to possess general rights of ownership
	Fundamental Rights of Secured Party
	■ to recover amount of debt
	■ to have collateral applied to payment of debt upon default

Classification of Collateral	**Goods** movable, tangible personal property
	■ *Consumer Goods* goods bought or used primarily for personal, family, or household purposes
	■ *Farm Products* crops, livestock, or supplies used or produced in farming
	■ *Inventory* goods held for sale or lease and raw materials used in business
	■ *Equipment* goods used primarily in business
	■ *Fixtures* goods that are so firmly attached to real property that they are considered part of the real estate
	Indispensable Paper
	■ *Chattel Paper* writing that evidences both a debt and a security interest
	■ *Instruments* negotiable instruments and investment securities
	■ *Documents* documents of title
	Intangibles
	■ *Accounts* right to payment for goods sold or leased or for services rendered
	■ *General Intangibles* catchall category of collateral not otherwise covered

Attachment	**Definition** security interest that is enforceable against the debtor
	Value consideration under contract law, a binding commitment to extend credit, or an antecedent debt

Debtor's Rights in Collateral   personal property the debtor owns, possesses, or is in the process of acquiring, including:

- *After-Acquired Property*   property the debtor may acquire sometime in the future
- *Proceeds*   consideration received for the sale, exchange, or other disposition of the collateral

Security Agreement   agreement between debtor and creditor creating a security interest

- must be in writing, unless the secured party has possession of the collateral
- signed by the debtor
- contain a reasonable description of the collateral

Perfection

Definition   attachment plus any steps required for perfection

Effect   enforceable against third parties

Methods of Perfecting

- *Filing a Financing Statement*   may be used for all collateral except instruments
- *Possession*   by the secured party (a pledge); may be used for goods, instruments, documents, or chattel paper
- *Automatic Perfection*   perfection upon attachment; applies to a purchase money security interest in consumer goods
- *Temporary Perfection*   a security interest in certain collateral is automatically perfected for a limited period of time depending upon the collateral

---

Priorities of Secured Parties

See Figure 37-6 for a summary of the priority rules

Default

Repossession of Collateral   the secured party may take possession of the collateral on default without judicial process if it can be done without a breach of peace

Sale of Collateral   the secured party may sell, lease, or otherwise dispose of any collateral

Retention of Collateral   secured party, unless the debtor objects, may (with the exception of the compulsory disposition of some consumer goods) retain the collateral in satisfaction of the obligation

---

QUESTIONS

1. Name and define the various kinds of collateral.
2. Define attachment, its purpose, and its requirements.
3. Define perfection and the various methods of perfecting.
4. Discuss the priorities among the various parties who may have competing interests in collateral.
5. Discuss the rights and remedies of the parties to a security agreement after default by the debtor.

PROBLEMS

1. Victor sells to Bonnie a refrigerator under a conditional sales contract for $600 payable in monthly installments of $30 for twenty months. The refrigerator is installed in the kitchen of Bonnie's

apartment. No financing statement is filed. Assume that after Bonnie has made the first three monthly payments:

(a) Bonnie moves from her apartment and sells the refrigerator in place to the new occupant for $350 cash. What are the rights of Victor?

(b) Bonnie is adjudicated bankrupt, and her trustee in bankruptcy claims the refrigerator. What are the rights of the parties?

2. On January 2 Burt asked Logan to loan him money "against my diamond ring." Logan agreed to do so. To guard against intervening liens, Logan received permission to record his interest, and Burt and Logan signed a security agreement giving Logan an interest in the ring. Burt also signed a financing statement, which Logan properly filed on January 3. On January 4 Burt borrowed money from Tillo, pledging his ring to secure the debt. Tillo took possession of the ring and paid Burt the money on the same day. The next day, January 5, Logan loaned Burt the money under the assumption that Burt still had the ring.

Who has priority, Logan or Tillo?

3. Joanna takes a security interest in the equipment in Jason Store and files a financing statement claiming "equipment and all after-acquired equipment." Berkeley later sells Jason Store a cash register on conditional sale and (a) files nine days after Jason receives the register, or (b) files fifteen days after Jason receives the register. If Jason fails to pay both Joanna and Berkeley and they foreclose their security interests, who has priority on the cash register?

4. Finley Motor Company sells an automobile to Sara and retains a security interest in it. The automobile is insured, and Finley is named beneficiary. The automobile is totally destroyed in an accident, and three days later Sara files a petition in bankruptcy. Who is entitled to the insurance proceeds, Finley or Sara's trustee in bankruptcy?

5. On September 5 Wanda, a widow who occasionally teaches piano and organ in her home, purchased an electric organ from Murphy's music store for $4,800, trading in her old organ for $1,200 and promising in writing to pay the balance at $120 per month and granting to Murphy a security interest in the property in terms consistent with and incorporating provisions of the UCC. A financing statement covering the transaction was also properly filled out and signed, and Murphy properly filed it. Wanda did not make the December or January payments, and Murphy went to her home to collect the payments or take the organ. Finding no one home and the door unlocked, he went in and took the organ. Two hours later, Tia a third

party and the present occupant of the house who had purchased the organ for her own use, stormed into Murphy's store demanding return of the organ and exhibited a bill of sale from Wanda to Tia dated December 15 that listed the organ and other furnishings in the house.

(a) What are the rights of Murphy, Tia, and Wanda?

(b) Would your answer change if Murphy did not file a financing statement? Why?

(c) Would your answer change if the piano was principally used to give lessons? Explain?

6. On May 1 Lincoln lends Donaldson $20,000 and receives from Donaldson his promissory note for this amount due in two years and takes a security interest in the machinery and equipment in Donaldson's factory. A proper financing statement is filed with respect to the security agreement. On August 1 on Lincoln's request, Donaldson executes an addendum to the security agreement covering after-acquired machinery and equipment in Donaldson's factory. A second financing statement is filed covering the addendum. In September Donaldson acquires $5,000 worth of new equipment from Thompson, which Donaldson installs in his factory. In December Carter, a judgment creditor of Donaldson, causes an attachment to issue against the new equipment. What are the rights of Lincoln, Donaldson, Carter, and Thompson? What can the parties do to best protect themselves?

7. Anita bought a television set from Bertrum for her own personal use. Bertrum was out of conditional sales contracts and showed Anita a form Bertrum had executed with Clarkson, another consumer. Anita and Bertrum orally agreed to the terms of the form. Anita subsequently defaults on payment, and Bertrum seeks to repossess the television. Decision? Would the result differ if Bertrum had filed a financing statement?

8. Aaron bought a television set for his own personal use from Penny. Aaron properly signed a security agreement and paid Penny $25 down as required by their agreement. Penny did not file a financing statement, and subsequently Aaron sells the television to Nathaniel, Aaron's neighbor, for $300 for Nathaniel to use in his hotel lobby.

(a) When Aaron fails to make the January and February payments, may Penny repossess the television from Nathaniel?

(b) What if, instead of Aaron's selling the television set to Nathaniel, a judgment creditor levied (sought possession) on the television? Who would prevail?

(c) What if Nathaniel intended to use the television set in her home? Who would prevail?

9. Standridge purchased a 1965 Chevrolet automobile from Billy Deavers, an agent of Walker Motor

Company. According to the sales contract, the balance due after trade-in allowance was $282.50, to be paid in twelve weekly installments. Standridge's version is that he was unable to make the second payment and that Billy Deavers orally agreed that he could make two payments the next week. The day after the double payment was due, Standridge still had not paid. That day, Ronnie Deavers, Billy's brother, went to Standridge's place of employment to repossess the car. Rather than consenting to the repossession, Standridge drove the car to the Walker Motor Company's place of business and tendered the overdue payments. The Deavers refused to accept the late payment and instead demanded the entire unpaid balance. Standridge could not do so. The Deavers therefore "blocked-in" Standridge's car with another car and told him he could just "walk his _____ home." Standridge then brought suit, seeking damages for the Deavers' wrongful reposession of his car. The Deavers deny that they granted Standridge permission to make a double payment; that Standridge tendered the double payment; and that they rejected it. They claim that he made no payment and, therefore, they were entitled to repossess the car. Decision?

10. Jones bought a used car from the A-Herts Car Rental System, who regularly sold its used equipment at the end of its fiscal year. First National Bank of Roxboro had previously obtained a perfected security interest in the car based upon its financing of A-Herts' automobiles. Upon A-Herts failure to pay, First National is seeking to repossess the car from Jones. Decision?

11. On May 1, Anson purchased on credit a refrigerator for his own personal use from XYZ for $600 and gave XYZ a security interest in the refrigerator. On May 5, Anson borrowed $500 from the Friendly Finance Company and gave Friendly a security interest in the refrigerator. Friendly properly perfected its security interest by filing. On May 15, one of Anson's creditors obtained a judgment lien against Anson and properly recorded the lien. On May 20th, after Anson had failed to make his payment on the refrigerator, XYZ properly filed a financing statement. On May 30, Anson sold the refrigerator at a yard sale to one of his neighbors for $200. All are claiming priority to the refrigerator. Who will prevail? Why?

ENDNOTES

1. Uniform Commercial Code, Section 9-105, Definitions and Index of Definitions.

2. Uniform Commercial Code, Section 1-201(37), General Definitions: "Security Interest."

3. Uniform Commercial Code, Section 9-107, Definitions: "Purchase Money Security Interest."

4. Uniform Commercial Code, Section 9-109, Classification of Goods; "Consumer Goods"; "Equipment"; "Farm Products"; "Inventory."

5. Uniform Commercial Code, Section 9-313, Priority of Security Interests in Fixtures.

6. Uniform Commercial Code, Section 9-105, Comment 4.

7. Uniform Commercial Code, Section 1-201(15), General Definitions: "Document of Title."

8. Uniform Commercial Code, Section 9-106, Definitions: "Account"; "General Intangibles."

9. Uniform Commercial Code, Section 9-203, Attachment and Enforceability of Security Interest; Proceeds; Formal Requisites.

10. Uniform Commercial Code, Section 1-201(44), General Definitions: "Value."

11. Uniform Commercial Code, Section 9-204, After-Acquired Property; Future Advances.

12. Uniform Commercial Code, Section 9-314, Accessions.

13. Uniform Commercial Code, Section 9-306, "Proceeds"; Secured Party's Rights on Disposition of Collateral.

14. Uniform Commercial Code, Section 9-303, When Security Interest Is Perfected; Continuity of Perfection.

15. Uniform Commercial Code, Section 9-303, Comment 1.

16. Uniform Commercial Code, Section 9-402, Formal Requisites of Financing Statement; Amendments; Mortgage as Financing Statement.

17. Uniform Commercial Code, Section 9-403, What Constitutes Filing; Duration of Filing; Effect of Lapsed Filing; Duties of Filing Officer.

18. Uniform Commercial Code, Section 9-401, Place of Filing; Erroneous Filing; Removal of Collateral.

19. Uniform Commercial Code, Section 9-301, Persons Who Take Priority Over Unperfected Security Interests; Rights of "Lien Creditor."

20. Uniform Commercial Code, Section 9-302, When Filing Is Required to Perfect Security Interest; Security Interests to Which Filing Provisions of This Article Do Not Apply.

21. Uniform Commercial Code, Section 9-305, When Possession by Secured Party Perfects Security Interest Without Filing.

22. Uniform Commercial Code, Section 9-304, Perfection of Security Interest in Instruments, Documents, and Goods Covered by Documents; Perfec-

tion by Permissive Filing; Temporary Perfection Without Filing or Transfer of Possession.

23. Uniform Commercial Code, Section 9–309, Protection of Purchasers of Instruments, Documents and Securities.

24. Uniform Commercial Code, Section 9–308, Purchase of Chattel Paper and Instruments.

25. Uniform Commercial Code, Section 9–312, Priorities among Conflicting Security Interests in the Same Collateral.

26. Uniform Commercial Code, Section 9–307, Protection of Buyers of Goods.

27. Uniform Commercial Code, Section 1–201(9), General Definitions: "Buyer in Ordinary Course of Business."

28. Uniform Commercial Code, Section 9–310, Priority of Certain Liens Arising by Operation of Law.

29. Uniform Commercial Code, Section 9–501, Default; Procedure When Security Agreement Covers Both Real and Personal Property.

30. Uniform Commercial Code, Section 9–503, Secured Party's Right to Take Possession After Default.

31. Uniform Commercial Code, Section 9–505, Compulsory Disposition of Collateral; Acceptance of the Collateral as Discharge of Obligation.

32. Uniform Commercial Code, Section 9–506, Debtor's Right to Redeem Collateral.

33. Uniform Commercial Code, Section 9–504, Secured Party's Right to Dispose of Collateral After Default; Effect of Disposition.

34. Uniform Commercial Code, Section 9–507, Secured Party's Liability for Failure to Comply with This Part.

38 SURETYSHIP

It is common in many business transactions involving the extension of credit for the creditor to require that someone in addition to the debtor promise to fulfill the obligation. This promisor generally is known as a surety. Sureties are commonly used in contracts involving minors so that there is a party with full contractual capacity responsible for the obligations arising from the contract. Sureties are often used in *addition to* security to reduce further the risks involved in the extension of credit. Sureties are used *instead of* security interests when security is not available or use of a secured transaction is too expensive or inconvenient. Sureties are also frequently used by employers to protect against losses caused by embezzlement by employees, as well as in construction contracts for commercial buildings to bond the performance of the contract. Similarly, it is commonly required by statute that many contracts for work to be done for governmental entities have the added protection of a surety. Premiums for compensated sureties exceed $1 billion annually in the United States.

NATURE AND FORMATION

A **surety** promises to answer for the payment of a debt or the performance of a duty owed to one person (called the **creditor**) by another (the **principal debtor**) on the *failure* of the principal debtor to make payment or otherwise perform the obligation. Thus, the suretyship relationship involves three parties—the principal debtor, the creditor, and the surety—and three contractual obligations, as illustrated by Figure 38–1. When there is more than one person bound for the same debt of a principal debtor, they are **cosureties.**

The creditor's rights against the principal debtor are determined by the contract between them. The creditor may also take action on any collateral securing the principal debtor's performance that the creditor or the surety holds. In addition, the creditor may proceed against the surety if the principal debtor defaults. If the surety is an **absolute surety,** then the creditor may hold the surety liable as soon as the principal debtor defaults. The creditor need *not* first proceed against the principal debtor. If the surety is a **conditional guarantor of collection,** he is liable only when the creditor exhausts his legal remedies against the principal debtor. Thus, a conditional guarantor of collection is liable if the creditor first obtains a judgment against the principal debtor and is unable to collect under the judgment.

A surety who is required to pay the creditor for the principal debtor's obligation is entitled to be exonerated (relieved of liability) and reimbursed by the principal debtor. In addition, the surety is subrogated to (assumes) the rights of the creditor and has a right of contribution from cosureties (see Figure 38–1). The rights of sureties are discussed more fully below.

Although in theory a distinction is drawn between a surety and a guarantor, the two terms are used almost synonymously in common usage. Strictly speaking, a surety is bound with the principal debtor as a primary obligor and usually, although not necessarily, on the same instrument, whereas the guarantor is separately or collaterally bound to pay if the principal debtor does not. For convenience, the term ''surety'' will be used to include both of these terms, because the rights and duties of a surety and a guarantor are almost indistinguishable.

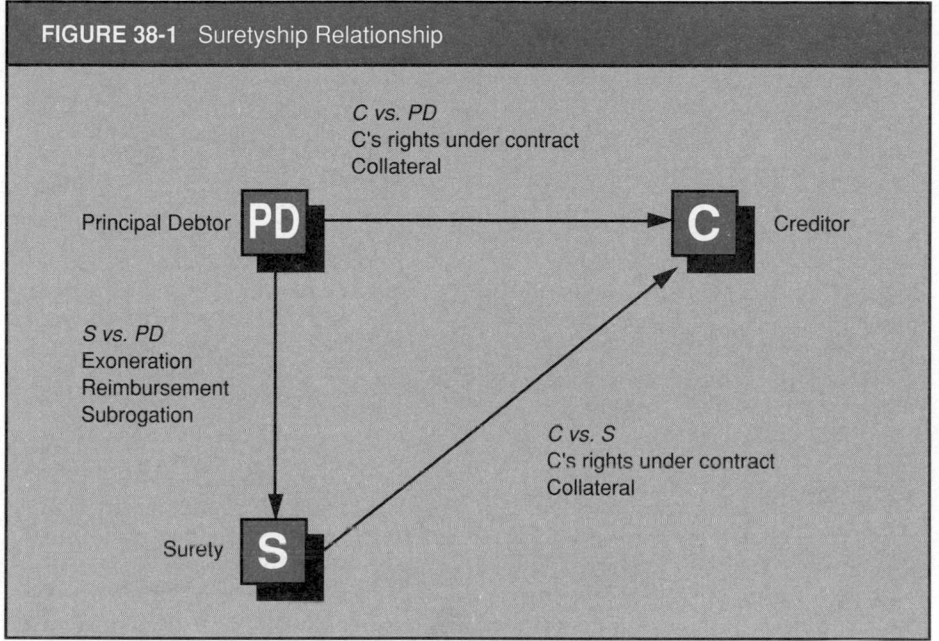

FIGURE 38-1 Suretyship Relationship

UNITED STATES v. TILLERAAS
United States Court of Appeals, Sixth Circuit, 1983.
709 F.2d 1088.

Facts: Elizabeth Tilleraas received three student loans totaling $3,500 under the Federal Insured Student Loan Program (FISLP) of the Higher Education Act of 1965. These loans were secured by three promissory notes executed in favor of Dakota National Bank & Trust Co., Fargo, North Dakota. Under the terms of these student loans, periodic payments were required beginning twelve months after Tilleraas ceased to carry at lease one-half of a full-time academic workload at an eligible institution. Her student status terminated on January 28, 1971, and the first installment payment thus became due January 28, 1972. She never made any payment on any of her loans. Under the provisions of the FISLP, the United States assured the lender bank repayment in event of any failure to pay by the borrower.

The first payment due on the loans was in "default" on July 27, 1972, 180 days after the failure to make the first installment payment. On December 17, 1973, Dakota National Bank & Trust sent notice of its election under the provisions of the loan to accelerate the maturity of the note. The bank demanded payment in full by December 27, 1973. It then filed FISLP insurance claims against the United States on May 6, 1974, and assigned the three Tilleraas notes to the United States on May 10, 1974. The government, in turn, paid the bank's claim in full on July 5, 1974. On June 4, 1980, the government filed suit against Tilleraas. The district court found for the United States.

Decision: Judgment for the United States affirmed.

Opinion: **Wellford, J.** The government's suit was met in the trial court by defendant-appellant's [Tilleraas'] motion for a summary judgment based on her contention that the action of the United States was barred by the six year statute of limitations set forth in [citation.] The complaint in the cause alleged that the government paid the Bank's insurance claim and was assigned title to the notes after default on the loan and payment by the government pursuant to [citation.]

* * *

* * * The government argues, however, that it is not limited to assignee status, since it may also rely on its common law right as a surety to bring an action against the principal for reimbursement. Since a surety's or guarantor's cause of action for indemnity does not accrue until payment of the principal's liability [citations], the government claims that it *also* has a cause of action which accrued on the date it paid the lender, July 6, 1974, a cause which was timely when this action was filed.

* * *

The use of the word "insurance" in the statute is not determinative in light of the realities existing between the relevant parties. The nature of the substantive rights and duties among the parties clearly reflects a surety-principal-lender relationship. Insurance is a contract where one undertakes to indemnify another against loss, damage or liability caused by an unknown or contingent event. Since the insured pays the insurer for the promise of indemnity, the insurer benefits to the extent that a contingency never occurs. Where a contingency does occur, the insurer can still be made whole, by virtue of subrogation, to the extent that the insured would be able to recover damages from a third party. Despite the presence of this right of subrogation it is clear that *when the contract is formed* all legal rights and obligations flow between the insurer and the insured. At this initial stage, there is no legal obligation owing from the third party to the insurer. In fact, it is unknown at that stage whether such a third party obligation will ever arise and, if so, who that third party will be.

A surety, on the other hand, promises to assume the responsibility for the payment of a debt incurred by another should he or she fail to repay the creditor. The arrangement is made to induce the creditor to deal with the borrower where there might otherwise be a reluctance to do so. Under this arrangement, the nature, size, and source of the possible loss to the creditor is known from the start. In addition, there is no payment from the creditor to the surety or guarantor for this "insured" payment. Rather, a kind of tripartite relationship is formed. The consideration running from the creditor to the debtor is deemed sufficient to support the surety's promise to make the debt good. In turn, the benefit flowing to the debtor by virtue of the surety's promise places the debtor under an implied legal obligation to make good any loss incurred by any payment the surety must ultimately make to the creditor. [Citation.] It is clear then that the two contracts are materially distinguishable, as are the rights and duties of the parties involved. [Citations.]

Under the FISLP the student contracts to borrow money with no collateral and upon favorable interest and repayment terms. The lender, in turn, contracts with the Department of Education to insure repayment should the student default. This has consistently been interpreted as creating a third-party surety contract, despite its nomenclature. [Citations.] The only possible "contingency" from which the government protects the lending institution is the possibility that the named student (in this case Tilleraas) may ultimately default on all or part of the designated loan amount. The interdependencies between the three parties, in this case the Dakota National Bank & Trust Co., Tilleraas, and the United States government, "are a situational adaptation of long-recognized principles of guar-

> anty." [Citation.] At common law the nature of the relationship would have undoubtedly given rise to an implied obligation on the part of Tilleraas to make good the loss incurred by the government when forced to satisfy her debt, a loss arising when the monies were paid to the Dakota National Bank & Trust Co.
>
> * * *
>
> We conclude, therefore, that the United States in this instance stands in the position of a surety-guarantor, and therefore it may pursue its right as a surety under FISLP. As pointed out, it was not until July of 1974 that the government paid the Bank's claim and obtained its right to sue the defaulting appellant on the underlying loan. Under the realities of the FISLP, the government is a surety of the borrower and is entitled to its rights as such. This is the position supported by the other Courts of Appeals that have considered the same issue under this law. [Citations.]

Types of Sureties

A suretyship arrangement is frequently used by creditors seeking to reduce the risk of default by their debtors. For example, Philco Developers, a closely held corporation, applies to Caldwell Bank, a lending institution, for a loan. After scrutinizing the assets and financial prospects of Philco, the lender refuses to extend credit unless Simpson, the sole shareholder of Philco, promises to repay the loan if Philco does not. Simpson agrees and Caldwell Bank makes the loan. Simpson's undertaking is that of a surety. Similarly, Philco Developers wishes to purchase goods on credit from Bird Enterprises, the seller, who agrees to extend credit to Philco Developers only if it obtains an acceptable surety. Simpson agrees to pay Bird Enterprises for the goods if Philco Developers does not. Simpson is a surety. In each of these examples, the effect of the surety's promise is to give the creditor recourse for payment against two persons—the principal debtor and the surety—instead of one, thereby reducing the creditor's risk of loss.

Another common instance of a suretyship relation arises when an owner of property subject to a mortgage sells the property to a purchaser who **assumes the mortgage.** By assuming the obligation, the purchaser becomes the principal debtor and is personally obligated to pay the seller's debt to the lender. The seller nevertheless remains liable to the lender and is a surety on the obligation assumed by the purchaser (see Figure 38–2). If the purchaser does *not* assume the mortgage but simply takes the property *subject to* the mortgage, the purchaser is *not* personally liable for the mortgage, nor is he a surety for the mortgage obligation. In this case, the purchaser's exposure to loss is limited to the value of the property. Although the mortgagee creditor may foreclose against the property, he may not hold the purchaser personally liable for the debt.

In addition to the more general kinds of sureties, there are numerous specialized kinds of suretyship, the most important of which are (1) fidelity, (2) performance, (3) official, and (4) judicial. **Fidelity bonds** are undertakings by a surety to protect an employer against the dishonesty of an employee. **Performance bonds** guarantee the performance of the terms and conditions of a contract. These bonds are used frequently in the construction industry to protect the owner from losses that may result from the contractor's failure to perform the building contract. Statutes commonly require that a public officer furnish a bond for the faithful performance of her duties. Such bonds are called **official bonds** and obligate the surety for all losses caused by the officer's negligence or nonperformance of her duties. **Judicial bonds** are provided on behalf of a party to a judicial proceedings to cover losses caused by delay or deprivation of use of property resulting from

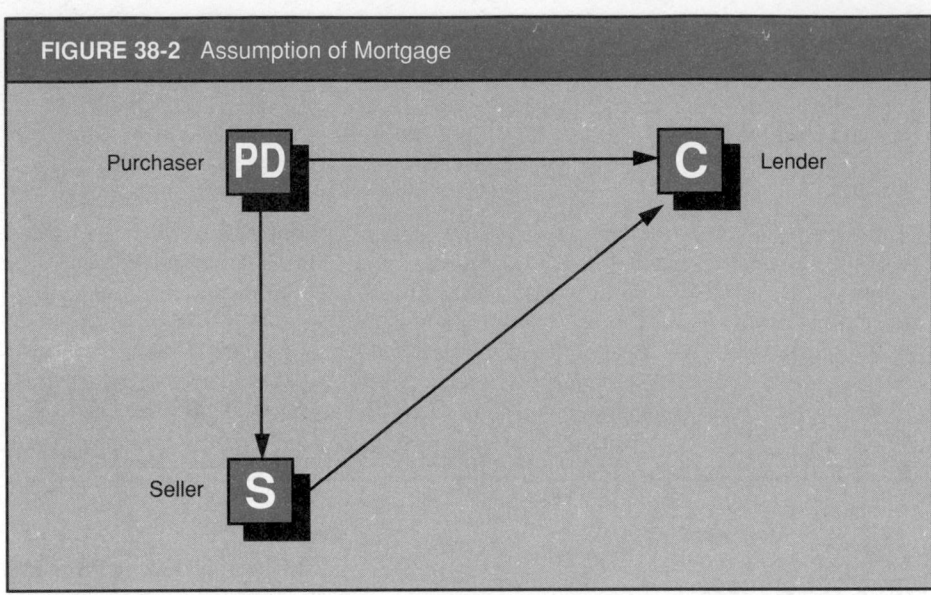

FIGURE 38-2   Assumption of Mortgage

the institution of the action. In criminal proceedings, the purpose of a judicial bond, called a **bail bond,** is to assure the appearance of the defendant in court.

Formation

The suretyship and guaranty relationship is contractual and must satisfy all the usual elements of a contract, including offer and acceptance, consideration, capacity of the parties, and legality of object, and it must also come within the provisions of the Statute of Frauds. Nonetheless, no particular words are required to constitute a contract of suretyship or guaranty.

As we discussed in Chapter 13, the contractual promise of a surety to the creditor must be in writing to be enforceable under the **Statute of Frauds.** This requirement applies only to collateral promises and is subject to the exception called the *main purpose doctrine.* Under this doctrine, if the leading object, or main purpose, of the promisor (surety) is to obtain an economic benefit that he did not previously enjoy, then the promise is *not* within the Statute of Frauds.

The promise of a surety is *not* binding without **consideration.** The surety's promise is usually supported by the same consideration that supports the principal debtor's promise because the surety's promise is generally made

to induce the creditor to confer a benefit on the principal debtor. Thus, if Constance lends money to Philip Drake on Sally's promise to act as a surety, Constance's extension of credit is the consideration to support not only Drake's promise to repay the loan but also Sally's suretyship undertaking. If the surety's promise is made *after* the principal debtor's receipt of the creditor's consideration, however, the surety's promise must be supported by new consideration. Accordingly, if Constance has already sold goods on credit to Drake, a subsequent guaranty by Sally will not be binding unless new consideration is given.

RIGHTS OF SURETY

If the principal debtor defaults, the surety has a number of rights against the principal debtor, third parties, and cosureties. These rights include (1) exoneration, (2) reimbursement, (3) subrogation, and (4) contribution. As discussed above, a surety or absolute guarantor has *no* right to compel the creditor to collect from the principal debtor or to take action on collateral provided by the principal debtor. Unless the contract of suretyship provides otherwise, the creditor is *not* required to give the surety notice of the principal debtor's default. A conditional guarantor of collection, on the other hand, has the right that the creditor first sue the principal debtor and exhaust his legal remedies of collection before resorting to the surety.

Exoneration

The ordinary expectation in a suretyship relation is that the principal debtor will perform the obligation and the surety will not be required to perform. Therefore, the surety has the right to require that his principal debtor pay the creditor when the obligation is due. This right of the surety against the principal debtor is called the right of **exoneration** and is enforceable at equity. If the principal debtor fails to pay the creditor when the debt is due, the surety may obtain a decree ordering the principal debtor to pay the creditor. The surety's remedy of exoneration is against the principal debtor and in no way affects the creditor's right to proceed against the surety.

A surety also has a right of exoneration against his cosureties. When the principal debtor's obligation becomes due, each surety owes every other cosurety the duty to pay her proportionate share of the principal debtor's obligation to the creditor. Accordingly, a surety may bring an action in equity against his cosureties to obtain an order requiring them to pay their share of the debt to the creditor.

Reimbursement

When a surety pays the creditor on the default of the principal debtor, the surety has the right of reimbursement against the principal debtor. The surety, however, has no right to reimbursement until he actually has made payment, and then only to the extent of the payment. Thus, if a surety makes an advantageous negotiation of a defaulted obligation and settles it at a compromise figure less than the original sum, he may not recover from the principal debtor any more than he had to pay.

Subrogation

On the surety's payment of the principal debtor's *entire* obligation, the surety "steps into the shoes" of the creditor. This is called **subrogation** and confers on the surety all the rights the creditor has against or through the principal debtor. These include the creditor's rights

1. against the principal debtor, including the creditor's priorities in a bankruptcy proceeding;
2. in security of the principal debtor;
3. against third parties who are also obligated on the principal debtor's obligation, such as co-makers; and
4. against cosureties.

Contribution

When there is more than one surety, the cosureties are *jointly and severally* liable for the principal debtor's default up to the amount of each surety's undertaking. The creditor may proceed against any or all of the cosureties and collect the entire amount of the default from any of them, limited to the amount that surety has agreed to guarantee. As a result, it is possible that one cosurety may pay the creditor the entire amount of the principal debtor's obligation.

When a surety pays her principal debtor's obligation, she is entitled to have her cosureties pay to her their proportionate share of the obligation paid. This right of **contribution** arises when a surety has paid more than her proportionate share of the debt, even though the cosureties originally were not aware of each other or were bound on separate instruments. All that is required is that they are sureties for the same principal debtor and the same obligation. The right and extent of contribution is determined by the contractual agreement among the cosureties. If there is no such agreement, sureties obligated for equal amounts share equally; where they are obligated for varying amounts, the proportion of the debt that each surety must contribute is determined by proration according to each surety's undertaking. For example, if X, Y, and Z are cosureties for PD to C in the amounts of $5,000, $10,000, and $15,000 respectively, which totals $30,000, then X's share of the total is one-sixth ($5,000/$30,000), Y's share is one-third ($10,000/$30,000), and Z's share is one-half ($15,000/$30,000). The following case presents another example of contribution.

COLLINS v. THROCKMORTON
Supreme Court of Delaware, 1980.
425 A.2d 146.

Facts: Throckmorton and Collins were the sole stockholders (as well as the officers and directors) in Central Ceilings, Inc. ("Central"). On March 26, 1973, Central borrowed $10,000 from the Wilmington Trust Company ("the bank"); a demand note was therefore executed by the corporate officers. On the back of the note, Throckmorton, Collins, and their wives unconditionally guaranteed payment of the note. In August 1973 Collins left the employ of Central and ceased to be actively involved in management. By mid-1975 Central became insolvent. Central made no payments on the note after 1973, and the bank became concerned about Central's ability to repay. On May 30, 1975, Throckmorton and his wife took out a $15,402 loan, using $9,668.73 to satisfy the 1973 note. In return, the bank assigned its rights to Throckmorton. Throckmorton then sued both Collins and his wife, each for one-quarter of the $9,668.73 plus interest and attorney's fees. The Collinses claim that Throckmorton's wife paid half of the total, or $4,834.16. Of the half that he paid, Throckmorton was only personally liable for half, $2,417.18, or one-quarter of the total. Therefore, he can recover only $2,417.18 total from the Collinses—the excess of the amount he personally paid—not $2,417.18 from each. The trial court entered judgment against each defendant for $2,417.18.

Decision: Judgment of trial court affirmed.

Opinion: McNeilly, J. In order to understand the defendants' argument, it is necessary to state the general rule governing contribution rights among co-guarantors. The Restatement of the Law of Security, *supra*, § 154 provides in pertinent part:

(1) A surety who has discharged more than his proportionate share of the principal's duty is entitled to contribution from a co-surety.

  (a) who has consented to the surety's becoming bound, in the proportionate amount of the net outlay properly expended. . .

[Citations.]

The undisputed facts show that the 1973 note was guaranteed by four persons. Consequently, each was potentially liable for one-quarter of Central's default on the note. [Citation.] Although the complaint alleged the plaintiff personally satisfied Central's default by paying the entirety of the principal and interest owed on the note in May, 1975, the defendants argue that the trial proofs show that the plaintiff's wife, the fourth co-guarantor, contributed equally with the plaintiff to this satisfaction. Thus, of the $9,668.73 paid to satisfy the 1973 note, the defendants claim the plaintiff contributed only half ($4,834.36). Of that amount the plaintiff was personally liable for half, which constituted one-quarter of Central's total default ($2,417.18). Thus argue the defendants, the maximum amount of contribution which the plaintiff could recover from the two defendants was $2,417.18, *i.e.* the amount in excess of his share of Central's default which the plaintiff personally paid to satisfy the 1973 note. Therefore, the defendants argue that the Trial Court's decision, which was premised on the assumption that the plaintiff satisfied the entire default by Central (or at least three-quarters thereof), erroneously awarded judgment against each defendant in the amount of $2,417.18, double the excess amount which the plaintiff allegedly paid in satisfaction of the note and, thus, double the total amount of contribution which he was entitled to recover from the defendants collectively.

* * *

Even considering the evidentiary aspect of the argument on the merits, we are not persuaded that the defendants are entitled to appellate relief. Although there was no direct testimony concerning the respective amounts which the plaintiff and his wife contributed to satisfaction of the 1973 note, the bank's assignment of the note to the plaintiff, individually, gives rise to a reasonable inference that, as between the plaintiff and his wife, the plaintiff alone was entitled to seek contribution from the defendants. While it would obviously be desirable to have a more detailed and explicit factual record on this point, the failure to so develop the record must be laid at the defendants' doorstep.

DEFENSES OF SURETY

The obligations owed to the creditor by the principal debtor and the surety both arise out of contracts. Accordingly, the usual contractual defenses are applicable, such as those that result from (1) the nonexistence of the principal debtor's obligation, (2) a discharge of the principal debtor's obligation, (3) a modification of the principal debtor's contract, or (4) a variation of the surety's risk. Some of these defenses are available only to the principal debtor, some only to the surety, and others to both parties (see Figure 38–3).

Personal Defenses of Principal Debtor

Some defenses that a principal debtor may assert against the creditor are available *only* to him and thus are called personal defenses of the principal debtor. The principal debtor's **incapacity** due to infancy or mental incompetency is a defense for the principal debtor but may *not* be used by the surety. If, however, the principal debtor disaffirms the contract *and* returns the consideration he received from the creditor, then the surety is discharged from his liability. A discharge of the principal debtor's obligation in **bankruptcy** also does not discharge the surety's liability to the creditor on that obligation. In addition, the surety may not use as a **setoff** any claim that the principal debtor has against the creditor.

Personal Defenses of Surety

Those defenses that only the surety may assert are called personal defenses of the surety. The surety may use as a defense, his own **incapacity**, noncompliance with the **Statute of Frauds,** the absence of mutual assent, or consideration to support the surety's obligation. **Fraud** or **duress** practiced by the creditor on the surety is a defense for the surety. Although, as a general rule, nondisclosure of material facts by the creditor to the surety is not fraud, there are two important exceptions. If the prospective surety requests information, the creditor must disclose it, and concealment of material facts will constitute fraud. Second, if the creditor knows, or should know, that the surety is being deceived, the creditor is under a duty to disclose this information, and nondisclosure is considered fraud upon the surety. Fraud on the part of the principal debtor may *not* be asserted against the creditor if the creditor is unaware of the fraud. Similarly, duress exerted by the principal debtor on the surety is not a defense against the creditor.

A surety is not liable if an intended cosurety, as shown by the contract instrument, does not sign. A surety may **set off** his claims against the creditor if the creditor is solvent. If the creditor is insolvent, then the surety may use his claim against the creditor only if the principal debtor is also insolvent.

If the principal debtor and the creditor enter into a binding **modification** of their contract, the surety is discharged unless he assents to the modification. Most courts hold that even a modification that does not materially affect the surety's risk will discharge the surety. This rule applies to valid and binding extensions of the time of payment *unless* the creditor expressly reserves his rights against the surety. An extension of time with reservation is construed

FIGURE 38-3 Defense of Surety

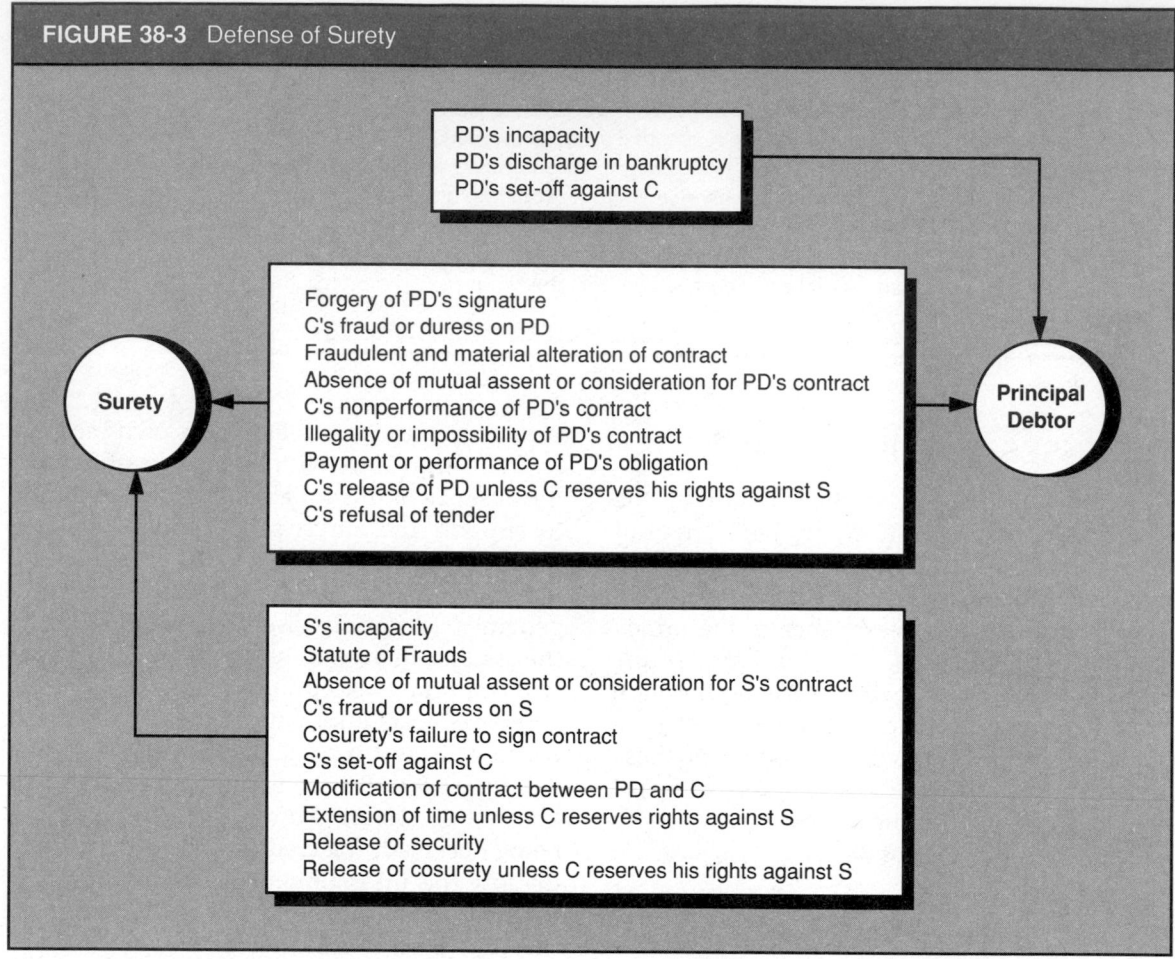

PD's incapacity
PD's discharge in bankruptcy
PD's set-off against C

Forgery of PD's signature
C's fraud or duress on PD
Fraudulent and material alteration of contract
Absence of mutual assent or consideration for PD's contract
C's nonperformance of PD's contract
Illegality or impossibility of PD's contract
Payment or performance of PD's obligation
C's release of PD unless C reserves his rights against S
C's refusal of tender

Surety

Principal Debtor

S's incapacity
Statute of Frauds
Absence of mutual assent or consideration for S's contract
C's fraud or duress on S
Cosurety's failure to sign contract
S's set-off against C
Modification of contract between PD and C
Extension of time unless C reserves rights against S
Release of security
Release of cosurety unless C reserves his rights against S

as only an agreement by the creditor not to sue the principal debtor for the period of the extension. Accordingly, the surety's rights of exoneration, reimbursement, and subrogation are *not* postponed. Thus, the surety's risk is not changed and he is not discharged.

As shown in the case below, if the creditor releases or impairs the value of the security, the surety is discharged to the extent of the value of the security released or impaired. Similarly, if the creditor releases a cosurety, the other cosureties are discharged to the extent of the contributive share of the surety released. If the creditor reserves his rights against the remaining cosureties, however, the release is considered a promise not to sue. As a result, the remaining cosureties are not discharged.

LANGEVELD v. L.R.Z.H. CORPORATION
Supreme Court of New Jersey, 1977.
74 N.J. 45, 376 A.2d 931.

Facts: On March 10, 1972, L.R.Z.H. Corporation made and delivered to Langeveld its promissory note in the sum of $57,500. The indebtedness evidenced by the note was secured by a mortgage in the same amount on real property owned by the corporation. By an instrument of guaranty set forth at the bottom of the note,

Higgins guaranteed performance of all obligations of the corporation under the note. The note became due on February 15, 1973, and was not paid. At this time, Higgins discovered that Langeveld had never recorded the mortgage securing the note. Langeveld then recorded the mortgage on March 1, 1973. In the intervening year between execution of the mortgage and recordation, another mortgage and two liens in substantial amounts had been filed. Langeveld brought suit against Higgins on the guaranty. Higgins argues that the creditor, Langeveld, owed a duty to him as surety for the debt to protect the security and allow nothing to occur to impair its value. Since Langeveld failed to fulfill this duty, Higgins should be released from all liability on his guaranty. The trial court granted summary judgment in favor of Langeveld and the appellate court affirmed. Higgins appeals.

Decision: Judgment reversed and remanded.

Opinion: Mountain, J.   On March 8, 1973 plaintiff instituted this suit on the guaranty. In defense of the claim thus asserted against him, defendant pointed out that there existed here the triparite arrangement typical of a suretyship relationship. L.R.Z.H. Corporation was principal debtor. Plaintiff was its creditor; defendant stood in the position of a guarantor or surety. He further called attention to the fact that plaintiff, as such creditor, held the mortgage from L.R.Z.H. Corporation as collateral security for the corporate obligation and that it owed a duty to him, as surety for the same debt, to protect this security and allow nothing to occur to impair its value and worth that reasonable effort and foresight on plaintiff's part could prevent or avoid. Failure to record the mortgage for about a year, predictably followed by the intervention of recorded liens in substantial amounts, constituted, he argued, a failure on plaintiff's part to fulfill this duty. Accordingly, concluded defendant, he should be *released from all liability* on his guaranty.

* * *

It is a well-recognized principle of law of suretyship that a release of collateral held by a creditor, or its impairment by improper action or inaction on his part, will extinguish the obligation of the surety, at least to the extent of the value of the security released or impaired. This rule has come to be accepted as the law of our State. [Citations.] * * *

The doctrine is an equitable one, designed to protect the surety's right of subrogation. Upon paying the debt, the surety is, as a matter of law, subrogated to all the creditor's rights against the principal debtor and is entitled to all benefits derivable from any security of the principal debtor that may be in the creditor's hands. The rule forbidding impairment of collateral has as its chief aim the protection of these potential benefits made available through subrogation.

Defendant has made out a prima facie case to support his contention that he comes within the favor of the rule. * * * A failure to record a mortgage held as collateral security—absent waiver, estoppel, or the like—seems clearly to be an instance of unjustifiable impairment. Common law authorities so held, almost without exception. [Citations.]

* * *

The point is that defendant appears to have been deprived of the opportunity effectively to exploit his right of subrogation to unimpaired collateral by the failure of plaintiff to record the mortgage given him by L.R.Z.H. Corporation.

* * *

> * * * If the impairment of collateral can be measured in monetary terms, then the calculated amount of the impairment will ordinarily measure the extent of the surety's discharge. But there are factual situations—this may or may not be one of them—where a surety may be able to establish that he has sustained prejudice, but be unable to measure the extent of the prejudice in terms of monetary loss. Where such a situation is presented the surety will normally be completely discharged.
>
> * * * The effect of the impairment upon one secondarily liable may or may not be translatable into dollars. There may be clear prejudice without precisely calculable loss. This will normally result in the discharge of the surety. To the extent that such impairment is found, defendant, Higgins will stand discharged of his obligation as guarantor.

Defenses of Both Surety and Principal Debtor

A number of defenses are available to both the surety and the principal debtor. Where the principal debtor's signature on an instrument is **forged** or the creditor has exerted **fraud** or **duress** on the principal debtor, neither the principal debtor nor the surety are liable. Likewise, if the contract instrument is fraudulently and **materially altered** by the creditor, both the principal debtor and the surety are discharged.

The absence of mutual assent or consideration to support the principal debtor's obligation is a defense for both the principal debtor and the surety. In addition, **illegality** and **impossibility** of performance of the principal debtor's contract are also defenses to both the surety and the principal debtor.

Payment or **performance** of the principal debtor's obligation discharges both the principal debtor and the surety. If the principal debtor owes several debts to the creditor and makes a payment to the creditor without directions as to which debt to apply payment, the creditor is free to apply it to any debt. For example, Pam Davis owes Charles two debts, one for $5,000 and another for $10,000. Susan is a surety on the $10,000 debt. Davis sends Charles a payment in the amount of $3,500. If Davis directs Charles to apply the payment to the $10,000 debt, Charles must apply it accordingly. Otherwise Charles may, if he pleases, apply the payment to the $5,000 debt.

If the creditor **releases** the principal debtor, then the surety is also discharged unless the surety consents to the release. If the creditor reserves his rights against the surety, however, the surety is *not* discharged. The release with reservation is construed as a promise not to sue, which leaves the surety's rights against the principal debtor unimpaired. Therefore, the surety is not discharged.

The creditor's refusal to accept **tender** of payment or performance by either the principal debtor or the surety completely discharges the surety. Tender of payment by the principal debtor refused by the creditor, however, does *not* discharge the principal debtor. The effect of such refusal is to stop further accrual of interest on the debt and to deprive the creditor of court costs on a subsequent suit by him to recover the amount due.

CHAPTER SUMMARY

Nature and Formation	**Definition of Surety** a person who promises to answer for the payment of a debt or the performance of a duty owed to the creditor by the principal debtor upon the failure of the principal debtor to perform
	■ *Principal Debtor* the party primarily liable on the obligation
	■ *Cosurety* each of two or more sureties who are liable for the same debt of the principal debtor
	■ *Absolute Surety* surety liable to a creditor immediately upon the default of a principal debtor
	■ *Conditional Guarantor of Collection* surety liable to a creditor only after the creditor has exhausted his legal remedies against the principal debtor
	Types of Sureties
	■ *Party Assuming a Mortgage*
	■ *Fidelity Bonds*
	■ *Performance Bonds*
	■ *Official Bonds*
	■ *Judicial Bonds*
	Formation the promise of the surety must satisfy all of the elements of a contract and also be in writing

Rights of Surety	**Exoneration** the right of a surety to be relieved of his obligation to the creditor by having the principal debtor perform the obligation
	Reimbursement the right of a surety who has paid the creditor to be repaid by the principal debtor
	Subrogation the right of a surety who has paid the creditor to assume all the rights the creditor has against the principal debtor
	Contribution payment owing from each cosurety of his proportionate share of the amount paid to the creditor

Defenses of Surety	**Personal Defenses of Principal Debtor** defenses available only to the principal debtor, including her incapacity, discharge in bankruptcy, and setoff
	Personal Defenses of Surety defenses available only to the surety including her own incapacity, the Statute of Frauds, contract defenses to his suretyship undertaking, his setoff, modification of the contract between the creditor and the principal debtor, and the creditor's release of security or a cosurety
	Defenses of Both Surety and Principal Debtor include contract defenses to the contract between the creditor and the principal debtor

QUESTIONS

1. Identify five types of sureties.
2. Explain the requirements for the formation of a suretyship relationship.
3. Explain the rights of a creditor against a surety.
4. Explain the rights of a surety including those of a cosurety.
5. Identify (a) the personal defenses of the principal debtor, (b) the personal defenses of the surety, and (c) the defenses of both the surety and the principal debtor.

PROBLEMS

1. Allen, Barker, and Cooper are cosureties on a $750,000 loan by Durham National Bank to Kingston Manufacturing Co., Inc. The maximum liability of the sureties is as follows: Allen, $750,000, Barker, $300,000, and Cooper, $150,000. If Kingston defaults on the entire $750,000 loan, what is the liability of Allen, Barker, and Cooper?

2. Peter Diamond owes Carter $500,000 secured by a first mortgage on Diamond's plant and land. Stephens is a surety on this obligation in the amount of $250,000. After Diamond defaulted on the debt, Carter demanded and received payment of $250,000 from Stephens. Carter then foreclosed on the mortgage and sold the property for $375,000. What rights, if any, does Stephens have in the proceeds from the sale of the property?

3. Adams sold his house to Baldwin for $80,000 with Baldwin expressly assuming a mortgage held by Evans on the property in the amount of $60,000. The property has a fair market value of $140,000. Six months later Baldwin defaulted in his payments to Evans on the mortgage.
(a) What are Evans's rights, if any, against Baldwin?
(b) What are Evans's rights, if any, against Adams?
(c) What are Adams's rights, if any, against Baldwin?

4. Paula Daniels purchased an automobile from Carey on credit. At the time of the sale Scott agreed to be a surety for Paula, who is sixteen years old. The automobile's odometer stated 52,000 miles, but Carey had turned it back from 72,000 miles. Paula refuses to make any payments due on the car. Carey proceeds against Paula and Scott. What defenses, if any, are available to (a) Paula and (b) Scott?

5. Stafford Surety Co. agreed to act as the conditional guarantor of collection on a debt owed by Preston Decker to Cole. Stafford was paid a premium by Preston to serve as surety. Preston defaults on the obligation. What are Cole's rights against Stafford Surety Co.?

6. Campbell loaned Perry Dixon $7,000, which was secured by a possessory security interest in stock owned by Perry. The stock had a market value of $4,000. In addition, Campbell insisted that Perry obtain a surety. For a premium, Sutton Surety Co. agreed to act as a surety for the full amount of the loan. Prior to the due date of the loan, Perry convinced Campbell to return the stock because its value had increased and he wished to sell it in order to realize the gain. Campbell released the stock and Perry subsequently defaulted. Campbell proceeds against Sutton. Decision?

7. Pamela Darden owed Clark $5,000 on an unsecured loan. On May 1, Pamela approached Clark for an additional loan of $3,000. Clark agreed to make the loan only if Pamela could obtain a surety. On May 5, Simpson agreed to be a surety on the $3,000 loan, which was granted that day. Both loans were due on October 1. On June 15, Pamela sent $1,000 to Clark but did not provide any instructions.
(a) What are Clark's rights?
(b) What are Simpson's rights?

8. Patrick Dillon applied for a $10,000 loan from Carlton Savings & Loan. Carlton required him to obtain a surety. Patrick approached Sinclair Surety Co., which insisted that Patrick provide it with a financial statement. Patrick did so, but the statement was materially false. In reliance upon the financial statement and in return for a premium, Sinclair agreed to act as surety. Upon Sinclair's commitment to act as surety, Carlton loaned Patrick the $10,000. After one payment of $400, Patrick defaulted. Patrick then filed a voluntary petition in bankruptcy. Carlton proceeds against Sinclair. Decision?

9. On June 1, Smith contracted with Martin d/b/a Martin Publishing Company to distribute Martin's newspapers and to account for the proceeds. As part of the contract, Smith agreed to furnish Martin a bond in the amount of $10,000 guaranteeing the payment of the proceeds. At the time the contract was executed and the credit extended, the bond was not furnished and no mention was made as to the prospective sureties. On July 1, Smith signed the bond with Black and Blue signing as sureties. The bond recited the awarding of the contract for distribution of the newspapers as consideration for the bond. On December 1, there was due from Smith to Martin the sum of $3,600 under the distributor's contract. Demand for payment was made, but Smith failed to make payment. As a result, Martin brought an appropriate action against Black and Blue to recover the $3,600. What decision?

10. Diggitt Construction Company was the low bidder on a well digging job for the Village of Drytown. On April 15, Diggitt signed a contract with Drytown for the job at a price of $40,000. At the same time, pursuant to the notice of bidding, Diggitt prevailed upon Ace Surety Company to execute a performance bond indemnifying Drytown on the contract. On May 1, after having put in three days on the job, the president of Diggitt refigured his bid and realized that if his company were to complete the job, it would lose $10,000. Accordingly, Diggitt notified Drytown that it was canceling the contract, effective immediately. What are the rights and duties of Ace Surety Company?

39 BANKRUPTCY

A debt is an obligation to pay money owed by a debtor to a creditor. Debts are created daily in countless purchases of goods at the consumer level; by retailers of goods in buying merchandise from a manufacturer, wholesaler, or distributor; by borrowers of funds from various lending institutions; and through the issuance and sale of debentures, corporate mortgage bonds, and other types of debt securities. An enormous volume of business transactions is entered into daily on a credit basis. Commercial activity would be restricted and greatly diminished if credit were not readily obtainable or needed funds not available for lending.

Fortunately, most debts are paid when due, thus justifying the extension of credit and encouraging its continuation. Defaults may create credit and collection problems, but normally the total amount in default represents a very small percentage of the total amount of outstanding indebtedness. Nevertheless, both individuals and corporations encounter financial crises and business misfortune. An individual or a business may be confronted by an accumulation of debts that exceeds total assets. Or he may have assets in excess of total indebtedness but have the assets in such non-cash form that the debtor is unable to pay his debts as they mature. Relief from pressing debt and from the threat of impending lawsuits by creditors is frequently necessary for economic survival.

Various solutions to the conflict between creditor rights and debtor relief have developed, such as voluntary adjustments and compromises requiring payment in installments to creditors over a period of time during which they agree to withhold legal action. Other voluntary methods include compositions and assignments of assets by a debtor to a trustee or assignee for the benefit of creditors. Equity receiverships or insolvency proceedings are sometimes filed by creditors in a State court according to statute. Nonetheless, the most adaptable and frequently used method of debtor relief—one that also affords protection to creditors—is by a proceeding in a Federal court under the Bankruptcy Act.

FEDERAL BANKRUPTCY LAW

Bankruptcy legislation serves a dual purpose: (1) to bring about an **equitable distribution** of the debtor's property among her creditors, and (2) to **discharge** the debtor from her debts and enable her to rehabilitate herself and start afresh. Other purposes are to provide uniform treatment of similarly situated creditors, preserve existing business relations, stabilize commercial usages, and bring about a speedy, equitable distribution of the debtor's assets.

Article I of the Constitution of the United States states: "The Congress shall have power . . . to establish . . . uniform Laws on the subject of Bankruptcies throughout the United States." Under this power, Congress has enacted or substantially revised bankruptcy acts in 1800, 1841, 1867, 1898, and 1938. Federal bankruptcy law has generally superseded State insolvency laws.

In 1978 Congress again enacted a major revision of the Bankruptcy Act, which was amended in several important respects in 1984 and 1986. The Bankruptcy Act consists of eight odd-numbered chapters and one even-numbered chapter (Chapter 12, which was added in 1986):

CHAPTER TITLE

1   General Provisions
3   Case Administration
5   Creditors, the Debtor, and the Estate
7   Liquidation
9   Adjustment of Debts of a Municipality
11 Reorganization
12 Adjustments of Debts of a Family Farmer
    with Regular Annual Income
13 Adjustment of Debts of an Individual
    with Regular Income
15 United States Trustees

Chapters 7, 9, 11, 12 and 13 provide five different types of proceedings, whereas Chapters 1, 3 and 5 apply to all five proceedings. **Straight,** or ordinary, **bankruptcy** (Chapter 7) provides for liquidation and termination of the business of the debtor, whereas the other proceedings provide for **reorganization** and adjustment of the debts of the debtor and the continuance of the debtor's business.

Chapter 7 applies to *all* debtors, with the exception of railroads, insurance companies, banks, savings and loan associations, homestead associations, and credit unions. More-

over, Chapter 7 has special provisions for the liquidation of the estates of stockbrokers and commodity brokers. Any person who may be a debtor under Chapter 7 (except stockbrokers and commodity brokers), and railroads may be debtors under Chapter 11. Chapter 9, however, applies only to a municipality that is generally authorized to be a debtor under that chapter, that is insolvent, and that desires to effect a plan to adjust its debts. Chapter 12 applies to an individual, or individual and spouse, engaged in farming if 50 percent of their gross income is from farming, their aggregate debts do not exceed $1.5 million, and at least 80 percent of their debts arise out of the farming operation. A corporation or partnership may also qualify for Chapter 12. Chapter 13 applies to individuals with regular income who owe liquidated unsecured debts of less than $100,000 and secured debts of less than $350,000. See Figure 39–1.

The Bankruptcy Act established a new bankruptcy court system that was held by the United States Supreme Court to have powers in violation of Article III of the U.S. Constitution. *Northern Pipeline Co. v. Marathon Pipe Line Co.*, 458 U.S. 50 (1982). The Bankruptcy

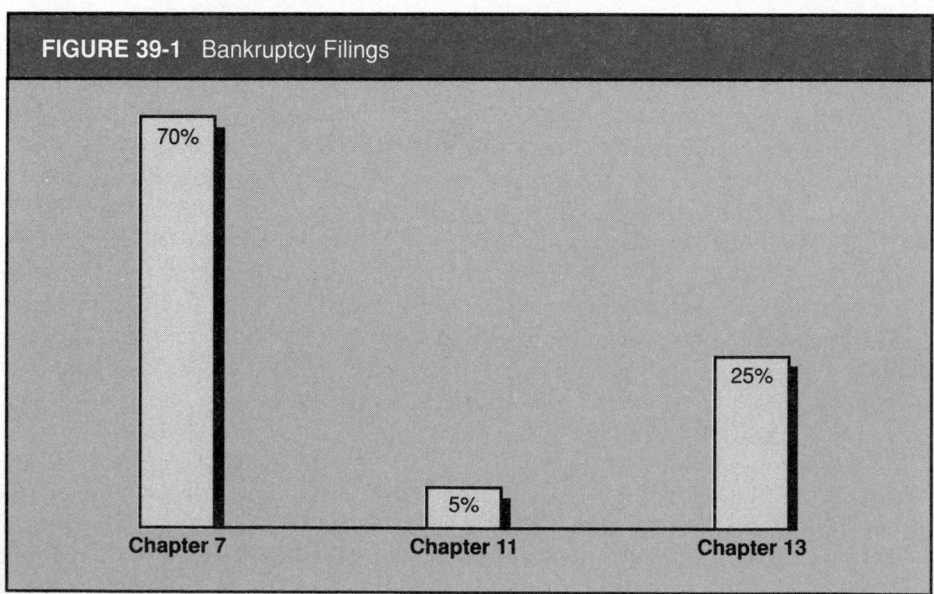

FIGURE 39-1 Bankruptcy Filings

Source: U.S. Department of Commerce, Bureau of the Census, *Statistical Abstract of the United States* (Washington, D.C.: U.S. Government Printing Office, 1988.)

Amendments Act of 1984 restructured the bankruptcy court system in an attempt to satisfy the constitutional considerations raised by the *Marathon* case. As amended, the Bankruptcy Act grants to U.S. District Courts original and exclusive jurisdiction over all bankruptcy cases and original, but not exclusive, jurisdiction over civil proceedings arising under bankruptcy cases. The district court must abstain from related matters that, but for bankruptcy, could not have been brought in a Federal court. The district court in which a bankruptcy case is commenced has exclusive jurisdiction over all of the debtor's property. In addition, a bankruptcy court staffed by bankruptcy judges is established as a unit of each Federal district court. Bankruptcy courts are authorized to hear certain matters specified by the act and to enter appropriate orders and judgments subject to review by the district court, or where established, a panel of three bankruptcy judges. The circuit court of appeals has jurisdiction over appeals from the district court or panel. In all other matters, unless the parties assent, only the district court may issue a final order or judgment that is based upon proposed findings of fact and conclusions of law submitted to the district court by the bankruptcy judge.

CASE ADMINISTRATION— CHAPTER 3

Chapter 3 of the Bankruptcy Act contains provisions dealing with the commencement of the case, the officers who administer the case, the meetings of creditors, and the administrative powers of the various officers.

Commencement of the Case

The jurisdiction of the bankruptcy court and the operation of the bankruptcy laws are begun by the filing of a voluntary or involuntary petition.

Voluntary Petitions More than 99 percent of all petitions are filed voluntarily. Any person eligible to be a debtor under a given bankruptcy proceeding may file a voluntary peti-

tion under that chapter. Moreover, the debtor need *not* be insolvent to file the petition. The commencement of a voluntary case constitutes an automatic **order for relief.** The petition must include a list of all creditors (secured and unsecured), a list of all property owned by the debtor, a list of property claimed by the debtor to be exempt, and a statement of the debtor's affairs.

Involuntary Petitions An involuntary petition in bankruptcy may be filed only under Chapter 7 (liquidation) or 11 (reorganization). It may be filed (1) by three or more creditors who have unsecured claims that total $5,000 or more, or (2) if there are fewer than twelve creditors of the debtor, by one or more creditors whose total claims equal $5,000 or more. An involuntary petition may not be filed against a farmer or a banking, insurance, or nonprofit corporation.

If the debtor does not contest the involuntary petition, the court will enter an order for relief against the debtor. If the debtor opposes the petition, the court may enter an order of relief only if (1) the debtor is generally not paying his debts as they become due, or (2) within 120 days before the filing of the petition a custodian or receiver took possession of substantially all of the debtor's property to enforce a lien against that property.

If an involuntary petition is contested successfully by the debtor and dismissed by the court, the Bankruptcy Act empowers the court to grant a judgment in favor of the debtor against the petitioning creditors for (1) costs, (2) reasonable attorney's fees, and (3) damages proximately caused by the trustee's taking possession of the debtor's property. Moreover, if the petition was filed in bad faith the court may award damages proximately caused by the filing or punitive damages.

If the court orders relief the debtor must provide the court with the same schedules as those provided by a voluntary petitioner.

Automatic Stays

The filing of a voluntary or involuntary petition operates as a stay against (that is, it prevents) attempts by creditors to begin or continue to

LAW IN THE NEWS

For Small Firms, Perils Lie in Chapter 11
Going to Court Often Hastens a Firm's Demise

Thousands of small companies are rushing into bankruptcy court these days.

Many of them probably shouldn't be in such a hurry.

Spurred by the publicity of big bankruptcy filings from the likes of Texaco Inc. and LTV Corp., a record number of small companies have sought protection from creditors under Chapter 11 of the Federal Bankruptcy Code in recent years. Many see Chapter 11 as the best way to address their business problems when creditors come knocking; under Chapter 11, they get protection from creditors while working out a plan of reorganization.

For many of them, that's no doubt true. They are in such dire straits that nothing short of bankruptcy protection can save them; or creditors force them into it.

But for others, Chapter 11 is a big mistake. In fact, rather than preventing small companies from failing, Chapter 11 often hastens their collapse.

Don't Copy the Big Boys

Small companies "read about Continental Airlines and Braniff and Storage Technology, and they think that it works for them, too," says Hugh Ray, a Houston bankruptcy attorney. "The truth is Chapter 11 doesn't work for them."

Moreover, says Joseph F. Finn Jr., a Boston accountant and consultant to distressed businesses, small firms "are not aware of alternatives" to Chapter 11. "I do everything I can to keep a company out of an Eleven. I'm fanatical about it."

He should be. The chances of a small or medium-sized company successfully emerging from a Chapter 11 are abysmal—less than one in 10, some bankruptcy experts say. Of the companies with less than $25 million in sales that filed for Chapter 11 last year, only 30% are still in business under the same ownership today, according to the Turnaround Management Association, a Chapel Hill, N.C., organization of professionals involved in turning around troubled companies. Nearly half have been liquidated and the remainder have been wholly or partially sold. By contrast, 69% of com-

panies with more than $100 million in sales are still in business after filing for Chapter 11 in 1987, the association says.

Nevertheless, 17,142 companies filed for Chapter 11 last year—nearly triple the 6,298 companies that filed in 1980, says the Administrative Office of the U.S. Courts. And most were small and medium-sized: About 41% had sales of $25 million or less and 71% had sales of $50 million or less, says Turnaround Management.

Why is Chapter 11 less successful for small companies than it is for big companies? Experts cite a number of factors:

High Costs: For corporate giants, Chapter 11 is expensive but manageable. But for small companies, the costs eat up a much larger percentage of revenue.

For a company with annual sales of about $5 million, fees for lawyers, accountants, consultants and court costs range from $50,000 to $250,000—depending on the complexity of the bankruptcy, says Edmond P. Freiermuth, a Santa Monica, Calif., financial consultant.

"Small companies can't withstand that kind of financial buffeting," says Gary Brooks of Allomet Partners, a New York consulting firm.

Indeed, 64% of the 61,209 companies that failed in the U.S. last year owed less than $100,000 to creditors when they failed, according to Dun & Bradstreet Corp., the New York credit-rating firm.

Shallow Management: Large companies have the management depth to assign a number of executives to spend most of their time on the bankruptcy. In small companies, though, owners usually handle the bankruptcy themselves, forcing them to neglect the root causes of the company's business problems at a time when they can least afford to be ignored.

"In a big company, the CEO may not have to get involved in an everyday basis," with the Chapter 11, says Robert Seidemann, a Cleveland consultant. "In a small company, the CEO and his people become so absorbed in the Eleven that it dominates the existence of the company."

Ken Hrovat, president of Cleveland-based George Worthington Co., says managing the company's Chapter 11 took up 50% to 80% of his time during the 1 1/2 years that the hardware and industrial supply concern was under court protection. "It's a huge administrative burden," says Mr. Hrovat. He says it was nearly impossible to oversee the bankruptcy while trying to cut costs and revive business. "What is a very simple task becomes very complicated" in Chapter 11, he says. "It comes at you from all sides."

Bargaining Power: A small company has a minimal amount of bargaining power with creditors, and a Chapter 11 filing can weaken its position still further. That's because the Bankruptcy Code gives creditors specific legal rights. Outside of a bankruptcy court setting, for example, creditors are cautious about doing anything that might force a company out of business and provoke lender-liability lawsuits. But once a company files for Chapter 11, creditors can seek a court-imposed liquidation to protect their investments—and they frequently do so.

Moreover, because a small company usually has only a handful of secured creditors, it is easier for them to take control of a bankruptcy than it is in the case of a big firm, where hundreds of creditors must agree on a single plan of action.

Michael Lissner, a Chicago consultant, learned that lesson the hard way. In 1985, he put his family's metals-refining company into Chapter 11, "thinking it would do some good" in working out a reorganization plan. Instead, he says, he "lost control" of the company in Chapter 11 and creditors liquidated the company. Mr. Lissner says the bankruptcy filing diminished his control of the company by adding layers of bureaucracy. "The judge called the shots and the attorneys called the shots," he says.

Market Disruption: Big companies face limited disruption in their businesses when they file for Chapter 11; customers kept flying Continental Airlines, for instance, and buying Texaco gas.

But for small companies, the negative publicity can create major problems because customers, suppliers and executives are quicker to jump ship. "The smaller, more closely held company's business is fragile, and its customer base is fragile," says Michael Silverman, a Skokie, Ill., consultant. "It breaks—and a Chapter 11 can be the thing that breaks it."

Mike Marcucci, president of Alpha Banking Co., says when the Chicago banking concern was struggling in 1979, he persuaded creditors to give Alpha time to reorganize out of court because filing for Chapter 11 would have done irreparable damage to the company. "Half of the business would have left," says Mr. Marcucci. By getting creditors to agree to stretch out repayment terms, Alpha returned to profitability and "no one realized how close to going under we were," he says.

More Options: The reasons small companies shouldn't file for bankruptcy aren't all negative,

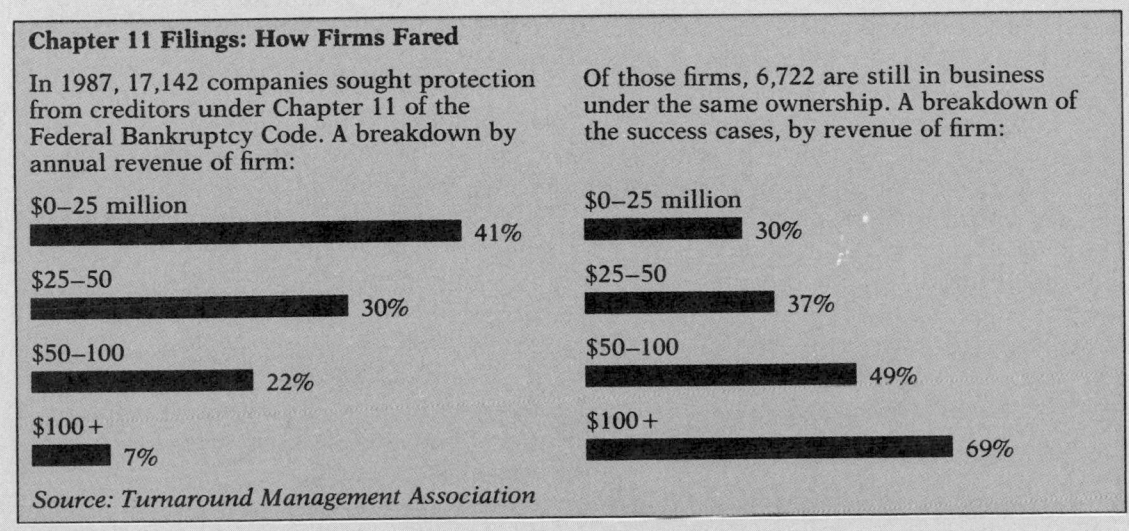

Chapter 11 Filings: How Firms Fared

In 1987, 17,142 companies sought protection from creditors under Chapter 11 of the Federal Bankruptcy Code. A breakdown by annual revenue of firm:

$0–25 million — 41%
$25–50 — 30%
$50–100 — 22%
$100+ — 7%

Of those firms, 6,722 are still in business under the same ownership. A breakdown of the success cases, by revenue of firm:

$0–25 million — 30%
$25–50 — 37%
$50–100 — 49%
$100+ — 69%

Source: Turnaround Management Association

however. Small-business specialists also say they have more options than their bigger brethren.

That's because big public companies—with hundreds of creditors, thousands of employees, and perhaps hundreds of thousands of shareholders—often have no choice but to seek court protection to sort out everyone's claims.

But for small companies, an out-of-court settlement is a viable alternative. For one thing, small companies have a more personal relationship with creditors and suppliers, making it easier to reach an agreement. Moreover, creditors frequently are more willing to gamble on a small company because they know a Chapter 11 filing could force the company out of business or could end up costing them as much as they would recover.

Still, many small companies won't make the sacrifices necessary to reorganize out of court.

Creditors may insist on the company seeking professional management help—a move that forces a small-business owner to admit his own management deficiencies. Moreover, many owners are reluctant to reveal financial and other business information even to other family members—let alone to creditors.

"If we have a customer coming to us with the problems, rather than us having to unearth the problems, that makes for a vast difference" in whether the bank is willing to work out problem loans, says Richard Sullivan, senior vice president of Shawmut Worcester County Bank in Worcester, Mass.

By BUCK BROWN
Reprinted by permission of The Wall Street Journal, © Dow Jones & Company, Inc. 1988. All Rights Reserved Worldwide.

recover claims against the debtor, to enforce judgments against the debtor, or to create or enforce liens against property of the debtor. This stay applies to both secured and unsecured creditors, although a secured creditor may petition the court to terminate the stay as to her security on showing that she lacks adequate protection in the secured property.

Trustees

The trustee is the representative of the estate and has the capacity to sue and be sued. In proceedings under Chapter 7, trustees are selected by a vote of the creditors; in all other proceedings, the trustee is appointed. The trustee is responsible for collecting, liquidating, and distributing the debtor's estate. The duties and powers of the trustee include: (1) to use, sell, or lease property of the estate; (2) to deposit or invest money of the estate; (3) to employ attorneys, accountants, appraisers, or auctioneers; and (4) to assume or reject any executory contract or unexpired lease of the debtor.

Meetings of Creditors

Within a reasonable time after relief is ordered, a meeting of creditors must be held. The court

may not attend this meeting. The debtor must appear and submit to an examination by creditors and the trustee of his financial situation. In a proceeding under Chapter 7, qualified creditors at this meeting elect the permanent trustee.

CREDITORS, THE DEBTOR, AND THE ESTATE—CHAPTER 5

Creditors

The Bankruptcy Act defines a **creditor** as any entity that has a claim against the debtor that arose at the time of or before the order for relief. A **claim** means a right to payment.

Proofs of Claim   Creditors may file a proof of claim. If a creditor does not do so in a timely manner, then the debtor or trustee may file a proof of such claim. Claims that are filed are allowed unless a party who has an interest objects. If an objection to a claim is made, the court determines, after a hearing, the amount and validity of the claim. The court will not allow any claim that (1) is unenforceable against the debtor or his property, (2) is for unmatured interest, (3) may be offset against a debt owing the debtor, or (4) is for services of an insider or attorney in excess of the reasonable value of such services. An **insider** includes a relative or general partner of a debtor as well as a partnership in which the debtor is a general partner or a corporation of which the debtor is a director, officer, or person in control.

Secured Claims   An allowed claim of a creditor who has a lien on property of the estate is a **secured claim** to the extent of the value of the creditor's interest in the property. The creditor's claim is unsecured to the extent that the value of his secured interest is less than the allowed amount of his claim. Thus, if Alice has an allowed claim of $5,000 against the estate of debtor Bart and has a security interest in property of the estate that is valued at $3,000, Alice has a secured claim in the amount of $3,000 and an unsecured claim for $2,000.

Priority of Claims   After secured claims have been satisfied, the remaining assets are distributed among creditors with unsecured claims. Certain classes of unsecured claims, however, have a **priority,** which means that they must be paid in full before any distribution is made to claims of lesser rank. The claims having a priority and the order of their priority are as follows:

1. expenses of administration of the debtor's estate, including the filing fees paid by creditors in involuntary cases; the expenses of creditors in recovering concealed assets for the benefit of the bankrupt's estate; the trustee's necessary expenses; and reasonable compensation to receivers, trustees, and their attorneys as allowed by the court;

2. unsecured claims in an involuntary case arising in the ordinary course of the debtor's business after the commencement of the case but before the earlier of the appointment of the trustee or the order for relief (such claimants are referred to as "**gap**" **creditors**);

3. allowed, unsecured claims up to $2,000 for **wages, salaries, or commissions** earned within ninety days before the filing of the petition or the date of cessation of the debtor's business, whichever comes first;

4. allowed, unsecured claims for contributions to **employee benefit plans** arising from services rendered within 180 days before the filing of the petition or the cessation of the

debtor's business, whichever occurs first, but limited to $2,000 multiplied by the number of employees covered by the plan;

5. allowed, unsecured claims up to $2,000 for **grain** or **fish producers** against a storage facility;

6. allowed, unsecured claims up to $900 for **consumer deposits;** that is, moneys deposited in connection with the purchase, lease, or rental of property or the purchase of services for personal, family, or household use;

7. specified income, property, employment, or excise **taxes owed to governmental units.**

After creditors with secured claims and creditors with claims having a priority have been satisfied, creditors with allowed, unsecured claims share proportionately in any remaining assets.

Subordination of Claims   In addition to statutory and contract priorities, the bankruptcy court itself can, at its discretion in proper cases, apply equitable priorities. This is accomplished through the doctrine of subordination of claims, whereby, assuming two claims of equal statutory priority, the bankruptcy court declares that one claim must be paid in full before the other claim can be paid anything. Subordination is applied in cases where allowing a claim in full would be unfair and inequitable to other creditors, such as to allow the inflated salary claims of officers in closely held corporations. In such cases, the court does not disallow the claim but merely orders it paid after all other claims are paid in full.

The claim of a parent corporation against its bankrupt subsidiary corporation may be subordinated to the claims of other creditors of the subsidiary in cases where the parent has been guilty of mismanaging the subsidiary to the detriment of its innocent creditors in a manner so unconscionable as to preclude the parent from seeking the aid of a bankruptcy court. For example, assume that Stanford Corporation owns all of the capital stock of Drexel Corporation. Assume further that whenever Drexel shows a profit, the profit is taken out of Drexel and transferred to Stanford by means of questionable intercorporate transactions; whenever Drexel shows a loss and Stanford is required to put some money back into Drexel, it does so by "lending" the money to Drexel. Over a period of time, Stanford takes $500,000 out of Drexel and puts $100,000 back. When Drexel goes into bankruptcy, Stanford has a claim of $100,000, while outside creditors have claims aggregating $100,000. Under the general rule of distribution, if the assets total $100,000, Stanford will receive $50,000 and the other creditors $50,000. Since Stanford has already received $500,000, it is clearly unfair for it to receive an additional $50,000 at the expense of the other creditors. The bankruptcy court can exercise its equity power of subordinating claims and subordinate Stanford's claim to that of the other creditors, so that the other creditors will receive the entire $100,000 and Stanford will receive nothing until the prior claims are paid in full.

Debtors

As indicated, the purpose of the Bankruptcy Act is to bring about an equitable distribution of the debtor's assets and to provide a discharge to the debtor. Accordingly, the act explicitly subjects the debtor to specified duties while exempting some of his property and discharging most of his debts.

Debtor's Duties   Under the Bankruptcy Act, the debtor must file a list of creditors, a schedule of assets and liabilities, and a statement of her financial affairs. In any case in which a trustee is serving, the debtor must cooperate with the trustee and surrender to the trustee all property of the estate and all records relating to property of the estate.

Debtor's Exemptions   The Bankruptcy Act exempts specified property of an individual debtor from the bankruptcy proceedings, including the following:

1. up to $7,500 in equity in property used as a residence or burial plot,
2. up to $1,200 in equity in one motor vehicle,
3. up to $200 for any particular item of household furnishings, household goods, wearing apparel, appliances, books, animals, crops, or musical instruments that are primarily for personal, family, or household use;
4. up to $500 in jewelry;
5. any property up to $400 plus any unused amount of the first exemption;
6. up to $750 in implements, professional books, or tools of the debtor's trade;
7. unmatured life insurance contracts owned by the debtor other than a credit life insurance contract;
8. professionally prescribed health aids;
9. social security, veteran's, and disability benefits;
10. unemployment compensation,
11. alimony and support payments, including child support;
12. payments from pension, profit-sharing, and annuity plans; and
13. payments from an award under a crime victim's reparation law, a wrongful death award, and up to $7,500, not including pain and suffering or compensation for actual pecuniary loss, from a personal injury award.

In addition, the debtor may avoid judicial liens on any exempt property and nonpossessory, nonpurchase money security interest on household goods, tools of the trade, and professionally prescribed health aids.

The debtor has the option of using either the exemptions provided by the Bankruptcy Act or those available under State law. Nevertheless, a State may, by specific legislative action, deny to its citizens the use of the Federal exemptions and limit them to the exemptions provided by State law. More than two-thirds of the States have enacted such legislation.

Discharge   **Discharge** relieves the debtor from liability for all dischargeable debts of the debtor. Certain debts, however, are nondischargeable under the act. A discharge of a debt voids any judgment obtained at any time concerning that debt and operates as an injunction against the commencement or continuation of any action to recover that debt.

No private employer may terminate the employment of, or discriminate with respect to employment against, an individual who is or has been a debtor under the Bankruptcy Act solely because such debtor (1) is or has been a debtor under the Bankruptcy Act; (2) has been insolvent before the commencement of a case or during the case; or (3) has not paid a debt that is dischargeable in a case under the Bankruptcy Act.

An agreement between a debtor and a creditor permitting the creditor to enforce a discharged debt is enforceable to the extent State law permits but only if (1) the agreement was made before the discharge has been granted; (2) the debtor has not rescinded the agreement within thirty days after it becomes enforceable; (3) the court has informed a debtor who is an individual that he is not required to enter into such an agreement and has explained the legal effect of the agreement; and (4) if the debt is a consumer debt, the court has approved the agreement as not imposing an undue hardship on the debtor and as being in the debtor's best interest.

The following debts are **not dischargeable** in bankruptcy:

1. certain taxes and customs duties;
2. legal liabilities for obtaining money or property by false pretenses or false representations;
3. legal liability for willful and malicious injuries to the person or property of another;
4. alimony and support of spouse or child;
5. debts not scheduled, unless the creditor knew of the bankruptcy;
6. debts created by the fraud or embezzlement of the debtor while acting in a fiduciary capacity;
7. student loans that first became due less than five years before the filing of the petition, unless the debt would impose undue hardship;
8. debts that were or could have been listed in a previous bankruptcy in which the debtor waived or was denied a discharge;
9. consumer debts for luxury goods in excess of $500 per creditor if incurred by an individual debtor on or within forty days before the order for relief;
10. cash advances aggregating more than $1,000 obtained by an individual debtor under

an open-end credit plan within twenty days before the order for relief; and
11. liability for a court judgment based upon the debtor's operation of a motor vehicle while legally intoxicated.

The following illustrates the operation of discharge: D files a petition in bankruptcy. D owes A $1,500, B $2,500, and C $3,000. Assume that A's claim is not dischargeable in bankruptcy while B's and C's claims are. A receives $180 from the liquidation of D's bankruptcy estate, B receives $300, and C receives $360. If D receives a bankruptcy discharge, B and C will be precluded from pursuing D for the remainder of their claims ($2,200 and $2,640 respectively). A, on the other hand, because his debt is not dischargeable, may pursue D for the remaining $1,320 subject to the applicable statute of limitations. If D does *not* receive a discharge, A, B and C may all pursue D for the unpaid portion of their claims.

The Estate

The commencement of a bankruptcy case creates an **estate** consisting of all legal and equitable interests of the debtor in nonexempt property at that time. The estate also includes property that the debtor acquires, within 180 days after the filing of the petition, by inheritance, by property settlement, by divorce decree, or as a beneficiary of a life insurance policy. In addition, property of the estate includes proceeds, rents, and profits from property of the estate. Finally, the estate includes property that the trustee recovers under her powers (1) as a lien creditor, (2) to avoid voidable preferences, (3) to avoid fraudulent transfers, and (4) to avoid statutory liens.

Trustee as Lien Creditor   When the case commences, the trustee gains the rights and powers of any creditor with a judicial lien against the debtor that is returned unsatisfied, whether or not such a creditor exists. A **judicial lien** is a charge or interest in property to secure payment of a debt or performance of an obligation that is obtained by a judgment, a levy, or some other legal or equitable process. The trustee is made an ideal creditor possessing every right and power conferred by the law of the State on its most favored creditor who has acquired a lien by legal or equitable proceedings. The trustee does not need to locate an actual existing lien creditor, for the trustee assumes the rights and powers of a purely hypothetical lien creditor.

Thus, under the Uniform Commercial Code and the Bankruptcy Act, the trustee, as a hypothetical lien creditor, has priority over a creditor with a security interest that was not perfected when the bankruptcy petition was filed. A creditor with a purchase money security interest who files within ten days of the debtor's receiving the collateral, however, will defeat the trustee, even if the petition is filed before the creditor perfects and after the creation of the security interest (gap filing). For example, Donald borrowed $5,000 from Cathy on September 1 and gave her a security interest in the equipment he purchased with the borrowed funds. On October 3, before Cathy perfected her security interest, Donald filed for bankruptcy. The trustee in bankruptcy can invalidate Cathy's security interest because it was unperfected when the bankruptcy petition was filed. Cathy would be able to assert a claim as an unsecured creditor. If, however, Donald had filed for bankruptcy on September 8 and Cathy had perfected the security interest on September 9, Cathy would prevail, because her purchase money security interest was perfected within ten days after Donald received the equipment.

Voidable Preferences   The Bankruptcy Act invalidates certain preferential transfers from the debtor to favored creditors before the date of bankruptcy. If a transfer is invalidated as preferential, the creditor may still make a claim for the unpaid debt, but the property he received from the debtor becomes a part of the debtor's estate to be shared by all creditors. The trustee may recover any *transfer* of property of the debtor

1. to or for the benefit of a creditor;
2. for or on account of an antecedent debt owed by the debtor before the transfer was made;

3. made while the debtor was insolvent;
4. made on or within ninety days before the date of the filing of the petition; or, if the creditor was an "insider" (as previously defined), within one year of the date of the filing of the petition; *and*
5. that enables such creditor to receive more than he would have received under Chapter 7.

A transfer is any means, whether direct or indirect, voluntary or involuntary, of disposing of property or an interest in property, including the retention of title as a security interest. It is presumed that the debtor has been insolvent on and during the ninety days immediately preceding the date of the filing of the petition. **Insolvency** is a financial condition of a debtor such that the sum of his debts is greater than all of his property at fair valuation.

For example, on March 3 David borrows $15,000 from Carla and promises to repay the loan on April 3. David repays Carla on April 3 as he promised. On June 1 David files a petition in bankruptcy. His assets are sufficient to pay general creditors only $.40 on the dollar. David's repayment of the loan is a voidable preference, which the trustee may recover from Carla. The transfer (repayment) on April 3 (1) was to a creditor (Carla); (2) was on account of an antecedent debt (the $15,000 loan made on March 3); (3) was made while the debtor was insolvent (it is presumed that a debtor is insolvent for the ninety days preceding the filing of the bankruptcy petition—June 1); (4) was made within ninety days of bankruptcy (April 3 is less than ninety days before June 1); and (5) enabled the creditor to receive more than she would have received under Chapter 7 (Carla received $15,000; she would have received .40 × $15,000 = $6,000 in bankruptcy). After returning the property to the trustee, Carla would have an unsecured claim of $15,000 against David's estate in bankruptcy for which she would receive $6,000.

To illustrate further, consider the following example. On May 1 Debra bought and received merchandise from Stuart and gave him a security interest in the goods for the unpaid price of $20,000. On May 20 Stuart filed a financing statement. On August 1 Debra filed a petition for bankruptcy. The trustee in bankruptcy may avoid the perfected security interest as a preferential transfer. The transfer of the perfected security interest on May 20 (1) was to benefit a creditor (Stuart); (2) was on account of an antecedent debt (the $20,000 owed from the sale of the merchandise); (3) the debtor was insolvent at the time (it is presumed that the debtor is insolvent for the ninety days preceding the filing of the bankruptcy petition—August 1); (4) the transfer was made within ninety days of bankruptcy (May 20 is less than ninety days before August 1); and (5) the transfer enabled the creditor to receive more than he would have received in bankruptcy (Stuart would have a secured claim, on which he would recover more than on an unsecured claim).

Nevertheless, not all transfers made within ninety days of bankruptcy are voidable. For example, if sixty days before the petition is filed, the debtor purchases an automobile for $9,000, this transfer of property (i.e., the $9,000) is *not* voidable because it was not made for an antecedent debt but rather as a contemporaneous exchange for new value. Similarly, if, within ninety days of the filing of the petition, the debtor purchases a refrigerator on credit and grants the seller or lender a security interest in the refrigerator, the transfer of that interest is not voidable if the secured party perfects within ten days after the debtor receives possession of the property. In addition, the trustee may *not* avoid a transfer made (1) in payment of a debt incurred in the ordinary course of business of the debtor and the transferee, (2) not later than forty-five days after the debt was incurred, and (3) according to ordinary business terms. Another exception was added in 1984: if the debtor is an individual whose debts are primarily consumer debts, then the trustee may not avoid any transfer of property valued at less than $600.

IN RE CONN

United States Bankruptcy Court, N.D. Ohio, 1981.
9 B.R. 431.

Facts: Freelin Conn filed a voluntary petition under Chapter 7 of the Bankruptcy Act on September 30, 1980. Conn listed BancOhio National Bank as having a claim incurred in October of 1979 in the amount of $4,000 secured by a 1978 Oldsmobile Omega. The car is listed as having a market value of $3,500. During the period from June 30, 1980, to September 30, 1980, Conn made three payments totaling $439.17 to BancOhio. The net payoff balance on the installment loan was $4,015.91 on September 30 when the bankruptcy petition was filed. The trustee in bankruptcy now seeks to set aside those three payments as voidable preferences.

Decision: Judgment for BancOhio granted.

Opinion: White, Bkrtcy. J. A trustee may avoid a transfer of property of the debtor to a creditor as a preference if the trustee proves that the five elements of a preference under 11 U.S.C. § 547(b) are met. 11 U.S.C. § 547(b) provides that:

the trustee may avoid any transfer of property of the debtor—
    (1) to or for the benefit of a creditor;
    (2) for or on account of an antecedent debt owed by the debtor before such transfer was made;
    (3) made while the debtor was insolvent;
    (4) made—
        (A) on or within 90 days before the date of the filing of the petition; or
        (B) between 90 days and one year before the date of the filing of the petition, if such creditor at the time of such transfer—

> (i) was an insider; and
>
> (ii) had reasonable cause to believe the debtor was insolvent at the time of such transfer; and
>
> (5) that enables such creditor to receive more than such creditor would receive if—
>
> (A) the case were a case under Chapter 7 of this title;
>
> (B) the transfer had not been made; and
>
> (C) such creditor received payment of such debt to the extent provided by the provisions of this title.
>
> In the instant case, debtor, during the period from June 30, 1980 to September 30, 1980, made three transfers of property to creditor. Creditor admits that said transfers meet the first four elements of a preference under § 547(b).
>
> The existence of the fifth and final element of a preferential transfer is denied by creditor. * * *
>
> In order to determine whether a transfer allows a creditor to receive a greater percentage of his claim than otherwise receivable under the distributive provisions of the Code, the court must determine the status of the creditor's claim; i.e., whether the creditor's claim is a secured claim or an undersecured claim. The Court must also consider the classes of creditors as provided for under Sections 507 and 506. The provision of the Bankruptcy Code that governs the determination of secured status is 11 U.S.C. § 506(a). Under § 506(a), a creditor's claim is secured to the extent of the value of his collateral. If the amount of a creditor's claim is greater than the value of his collateral, the creditor is undersecured and his claim is broken down into two parts: he has a secured claim to the extent of the value of his collateral; and he has an unsecured claim for the balance of his claim. [Citations.]

The claim of the creditor herein was secured by a 1978 Oldsmobile Omega automobile. The amount of creditor's claim on the date of the filing of debtor's petition was $4,015.91. The market value of creditor's collateral was listed by debtor on his Schedule A-2 at $3,500.00 At the trial upon the instant matter, debtor testified that he did not believe that $3,500.00 was a fair value of what the car was worth at the time he filed bankruptcy.

Debtor testified that the car was in excellent condition, except for a few stone marks around the rear wheel wells, at the time he filed his petition in bankruptcy. Debtor had purchased the car in October of 1979 for $4,250.00.

Trustee failed to carry his burden of establishing what the value of the collateral car was on the date of the filing of debtor's petition. There was no evidence presented by the trustee to prove that the amount of creditor's claim was greater than the value of creditor's collateral. Therefore, the court finds that the amount of creditor's claim was equivalent to the value of the collateral car and thus, creditor had a fully secured claim.

A trustee may only avoid as a preference a pre-bankruptcy transfer which enables one creditor to recover more on his claim than other creditors of the same class. The greater percentage test under § 547(b)(5) serves the prime bankruptcy policy of equality of distribution among creditors of the debtor. The legislative history describes the purpose of the preference section as follows:

> The purpose of the preference section is two-fold. First, by permitting the trustee to avoid pre-bankruptcy transfers that occur within a short period before bankruptcy, creditors are discouraged from racing to the courthouse to dismember the debtor during his slide into bankruptcy * * * Second, and more important, the preference provisions facilitate the prime bankruptcy policy of equality of distribution among creditors of the debtor. Any creditor that received a greater

payment than others of his class is required to disgorge so that all may share equally * * * [Citation.]

Trustee, herein, has failed to carry his burden of proving that the effect of the payments was to enable creditor to obtain a greater percentage of its debt than it would receive under the distributive provisions of the Code. If any one of the elements of a preference under § 547(b), is wanting, a preference has not been established. [Citation.]

Therefore, it is the conclusion of this Court that the transfers of property of the debtor to the creditor do not constitute voidable preferences under 11 U.S.C. § 547(b) as the trustee failed to prove that the effect of the transfers was to enable the creditor to obtain a greater percentage of its debt than it would receive under the distributive provisions of the Code. Trustee's complaint to recover the amount of the August 9, 1980, August 22, 1980, and September 10, 1980 payments in the total sum of $439.17 should be denied as said payments do not meet all five elements necessary for a preference under 11 U.S.C. § 547(b).

Fraudulent Transfers   The trustee may avoid fraudulent transfers made on or within one year before the date of the filing of the petition. One type of fraudulent transfer consists of the debtor's transferring property with the actual intent to hinder, delay, or defraud any of her creditors. Another type of fraudulent transfer is the transfer by the debtor of property for less than a reasonably equivalent consideration while she is insolvent or would become insolvent because of the transfer. For example, Carol, who is in debt, transfers title to her house to Wallace, her father, without any payment by Wallace to Carol and with the understanding that when the house is no longer in danger of seizure by creditors, Wallace will reconvey it to Carol. The transfer of the house by Carol to Wallace is a fraudulent transfer.

Statutory Liens   The trustee may avoid a statutory lien on property of the debtor if the lien (1) first becomes effective when the debtor becomes insolvent, *or* (2) is not perfected or enforceable on the date of the filing of the petition against a *bona fide* purchaser. A **statutory lien** is a lien that arises solely by a force of a statute and does *not* include a security interest or judicial lien.

LIQUIDATION—CHAPTER 7

To accomplish its dual goals of distributing the debtor's property fairly and providing the debtor with a fresh start, the Bankruptcy Act has established two approaches: liquidation and adjustment of debts. Chapter 7 uses liquidation, whereas Chapters 11, 12, and 13, discussed below, use the adjustment of debts. Liquidation involves the termination of the business of the debtor, distribution of his nonexempt assets, and usually a discharge of all dischargeable debts of the debtor.

Proceedings

Proceedings under Chapter 7 apply to all debtors except railroads, insurance companies, banks, savings and loan associations, homestead associations, and credit unions. Once a voluntary or involuntary petition has been filed, the court must determine whether to enter an order for relief. If an order is entered, an interim trustee is appointed, who serves until a permanent trustee is selected by the creditors. If the creditors do not elect a trustee, the interim trustee becomes the permanent trustee. Under Chapter 7, the trustee collects and reduces to money the property of the estate; accounts for all property received; investigates the financial affairs of the debtor; examines and, if appropriate, challenges proofs of claim; opposes, if advisable, the discharge of the debtor; and makes a final report of the administration of the estate.

The creditors may also elect a committee of not fewer than three and not more than eleven unsecured creditors to consult with the trustee, make recommendations to him, and submit questions to the court.

Distribution of the Estate

After the trustee has collected all the assets of the debtor's estate, she distributes them to the creditors and, if any assets remain, to the debtor in the following order:

1. Secured creditors are paid on their security interests.
2. Creditors entitled to a priority are paid in the order provided.
3. Unsecured creditors who filed their claims on time are paid.
4. Unsecured creditors who filed their claims late are paid.
5. Claims for multiple, exemplary, or punitive damages are paid.
6. Interest at the legal rate from the date of the filing of the petition is paid to all of the above claimants.
7. Whatever property remains is distributed to the debtor.

Claims of the same rank are paid proportionately. For example: D has filed a petition for a Chapter 7 proceeding. The total value of D's estate *after* paying the expenses of administration is $25,000. E, who is owed $15,000, has a security interest in property valued at $10,000. F has an unsecured claim of $6,000, which is entitled to a priority of $2,000. The United States has a claim for income taxes of $4,000. G has an unsecured claim of $9,000 that was filed on time. H has an unsecured claim of $12,000 that was filed on time. J has a claim of $8,000 that was not filed on time. The distribution would be as follows:

1. E receives $11,500
2. F receives $3,200
3. United States receives $4,000
4. G receives $2,700
5. H receives $3,600
6. J receives $0

E receives $10,000 as a secured creditor and has an unsecured claim of $5,000. F receives $2,000 on the portion of his claim entitled to a priority and has an unsecured claim of $4,000. The United States has a priority of $4,000. After paying $10,000 to E, $2,000 to F, and $4,000 to the United States, there remains $9,000 ($25,000 − $10,000 − $2,000 − $4,000) to be distributed *pro rata* to unsecured creditors who filed on time. Their claims total $30,000 (E = $5,000, F = $4,000, G = $9,000 and H = $12,000). Therefore, each will receive $\frac{\$\,9,000}{\$30,000}$ or $.30 on the dollar. Accordingly, E receives an additional $1,500, F receives an additional $1,200, G receives $2,700, and H receives $3,600. Because there were insufficient assets to pay all unsecured claimants who filed on time, J, who filed tardily, receives nothing. If J's claim were not timely filed because D had failed to schedule J's claim, then D's debt to J would not be discharged unless J knew or had notice of the bankruptcy.

Figure 39–2 summarizes the collection and distribution of the debtor's estate.

Discharge

A discharge under Chapter 7 relieves the debtor of all debts that arose before the date of the order for relief, except for those debts that are not dischargeable. After distribution of the estate, the court will grant the debtor a discharge unless the debtor

1. is not an individual (partnerships and corporations may *not* receive a discharge under Chapter 7);
2. has destroyed, falsified, concealed, or failed to keep books of account and records;
3. has knowingly and fraudulently made a false oath or account, presented or used a false claim, or given or received bribes;
4. has transferred, removed, destroyed, or concealed any of his property with intent to hinder, delay, or defraud his creditors within twelve months before the filing of the bankruptcy petition;
5. has within six years before the bankruptcy been granted a discharge;
6. has refused to obey any lawful order of the court or to answer any question approved by the court;

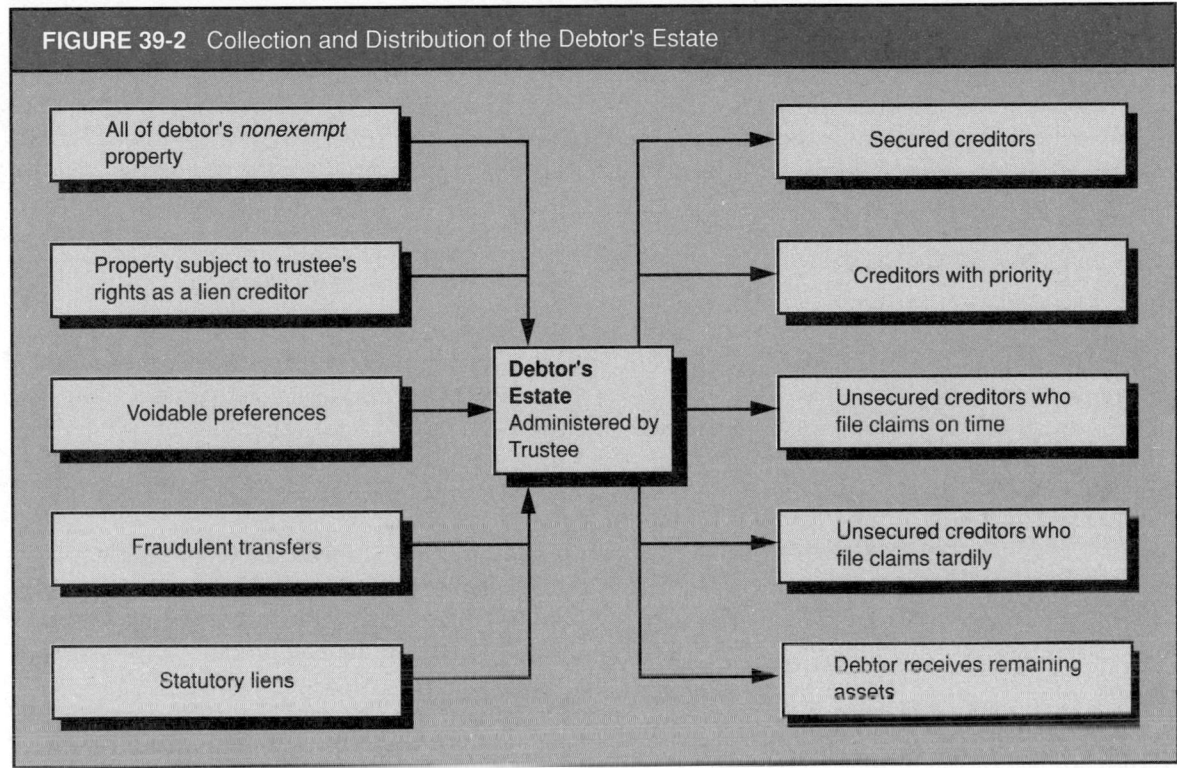

FIGURE 39-2 Collection and Distribution of the Debtor's Estate

7. has failed to explain satisfactorily any losses of assets or deficiency of assets to meet his liabilities; or

8. has executed a written waiver of discharge approved by the court.

On request of the trustee or a creditor and after notice and a hearing, the court may revoke a discharge within one year if it was obtained through the fraud of the debtor.

REORGANIZATION—CHAPTER 11

Reorganization is the means by which a distressed business enterprise and its value as a going concern are preserved through the correction or elimination of the factors that brought about its distress. Chapter 11 of the Bankruptcy Act governs reorganization of eligible debtors, including partnerships and corporations, and permits restructuring of their capital structure. The main objective of the reorganization proceeding is to develop and carry out a fair, equitable, and feasible (workable) plan of reorganization. After a plan has been prepared and filed, a hearing is held before the court to determine whether or not it will be confirmed.

Proceedings

Any person who may be a debtor under Chapter 7 (except stockbrokers and commodity brokers), and railroads may be debtors under Chapter 11. Petitions may be voluntary or involuntary. See *In Re Johns-Manville Corp.* at page 873.

As soon as possible after the order for relief, a committee of unsecured creditors is appointed. This committee usually consists of persons who hold the seven largest unsecured claims against the debtor. In addition, the court may order the appointment of additional committees of creditors or of equity security holders, if necessary, to assure adequate representation. The committee may, with the court's approval, employ attorneys, accountants, and other agents to represent or perform services for the committee. The committee should consult with the debtor or trustee concerning the administration of the case and may investigate the debtor's affairs and participate in formulating a reorganization plan.

The debtor will remain in possession and management of the property of the estate unless the court appoints a trustee, who may then operate the debtor's business. The court will appoint a trustee only for cause (including fraud, dishonesty, incompetence, or gross mismanagement of the debtor's affairs) or if the appointment is in the interests of creditors or equity security holders.

The duties of a trustee in a case under Chapter 11 are:

1. to be accountable for all property received;
2. to examine proofs of claim;
3. to furnish information to all parties with an interest;
4. to provide the court and taxing authorities with financial reports of the business operations;
5. to make a final report and account of the administration of the estate;
6. to investigate the financial condition of the debtor and the desirability of the continuance of the debtor's business; and
7. to file a plan or a report on why there will be no plan or to recommend conversion of the case to Chapter 7.

At any time before confirmation of a plan, the court may terminate the trustee's appointment and restore the debtor to possession and management of the property of the estate and operation of the debtor's business.

The Bankruptcy Amendments Act added a new provision dealing with the rejection of collective bargaining agreements. It provides that subsequent to filing and prior to seeking such rejection, the trustee or debtor-in-possession must make a proposal for the necessary modifications of the labor contract that will enable reorganization of the debtor and also provide for the fair and equitable treatment of all of the parties concerned. The provision also requires that good faith meetings to reach a mutually satisfactory agreement be held between management and the union.

It authorizes the court to approve rejection of the collective bargaining agreement only if the court finds that the proposal was made in accordance with these conditions, that the union refused the proposal without good cause, and that the balance of equities clearly favors rejection of such agreement.

Plan of Reorganization

The debtor may file a plan at any time and has the exclusive right to file a plan during the 120 days after the order for relief, unless a trustee has been appointed. Then other parties in interest, including the trustee, if a trustee has been appointed, or a creditors' committee, may file a plan.

A plan of reorganization must divide creditors' claims and shareholders' interests into classes, specify how each class will be treated, and deal with each class equally. After a plan has been filed, the plan and a written disclosure statement approved by the court as containing adequate information must be transmitted to each holder of a claim before seeking acceptance or rejection of the plan. Adequate information means information of a kind and in sufficient detail that would enable a hypothetical reasonable investor to make an informed judgment about the plan.

Acceptance of Plan

Each class of claims and interests has the opportunity to accept or reject the proposed plan. A **class of claims** has accepted a plan if it has been accepted by creditors that hold at least two-thirds in amount and more than one-half of the allowed claims of such class. Acceptance of a plan by a **class of interests,** such as shareholders, requires acceptance by holders of at least two-thirds in amount of the allowed interest of such class.

A class that is not impaired under a plan is deemed to have accepted the plan. Basically, a class is not impaired if the plan leaves unaltered the legal, equitable, and contractual rights to which such claim or interest entitles the holder of that claim or right.

Confirmation of Plan

A plan must be confirmed by the court before it is binding on any parties. A court will confirm a plan only if it meets all of the requirements of the Bankruptcy Act. The most important of these requirements are the following.

Good Faith The plan must have been proposed in good faith and not by any means forbidden by law.

Feasibility The court must find that confirmation of the plan is not likely to be followed by the liquidation or the need for further financial reorganization of the debtor. The essence of feasibility is that the reorganized entity will be able to operate economically and efficiently, will be able to compete on fairly equal terms with other companies within the industry, and is not likely to require liquidation or a second reorganization within the foreseeable future.

Cash Payments Certain classes of creditors must have their allowed claims paid in full in cash immediately or, in some instances, on a deferred basis. These classes include the expenses of administration, gap creditors, claims for wages and salaries, and employee benefits and consumer deposits.

Acceptance by Creditors To be confirmed, the plan must be accepted by at least *one* class of claims, and with respect to *each* class, each holder must either accept the plan *or* receive not less than the amount he would have received under Chapter 7. In addition, each class

must accept the plan or be unimpaired by the plan. Nonetheless, under certain circumstances, the court may confirm a plan that is not accepted by all impaired classes. The court must determine that the plan does not discriminate unfairly and that it is fair and equitable. Under these circumstances, a class of claims or interests may, over its objections, be involuntarily subjected to the provisions of a plan.

"Fair and equitable" with respect to secured creditors requires that they either retain their security interest and receive deferred cash payments at least equal to their claims or that they realize the "indubitable equivalent" of their claims. Fair and equitable with respect to unsecured creditors means that such creditors receive property of value equivalent to the full amount of their claim *or* that no junior claim or interest receive anything at all. With respect to a class of interests, a plan is fair and equitable if the holders receive full value or if no junior interest receives anything at all.

Effect of Reorganization

After confirmation of the plan, the debtor's performance obligations are governed by the plan. The plan binds the debtor and any creditor, equity security holder, or general partner of the debtor. After the entry of a final decree closing the proceedings, the debtor is discharged from all of its debts and liabilities that arose before the date of confirmation of the plan except as otherwise provided in the plan, the order of confirmation, or the Bankruptcy Act. The confirmation of a plan does not discharge an *individual* debtor from debts that are not dischargeable.

IN RE JOHNS-MANVILLE CORPORATION
United States Bankruptcy Court, Southern District of New York, 1984.
36 B.R. 727.

Facts: Johns-Manville Corporation and its affiliated companies (Manville) were highly successful, industrial enterprises among the nation's "Fortune 500." As of August 26, 1982, Manville had some 16,000 asbestos health suits pending against it because of its long-time use of products containing this deadly substance. The number of lawsuits was expected to multiply over the next two or three decades as individuals who had been exposed to asbestos began to develop asbestos-related diseases. Moreover, the insurance industry had generally disclaimed any liability to Manville on policies written for this purpose. Therefore, as a result of this mammoth economic burden, Manville filed for protection under Chapter 11 of the Bankruptcy Code on August 26, 1982. Four separate motions to dismiss Manville's petition were lodged before the court.

Decision: Motions to dismiss the Manville petition denied.

Opinion: **Lifland, Bkrtcy, J.**   * * * Preliminarily, it must be stated that there is no question that Manville is eligible to be a debtor under the Code's statutory requirements. * * *

* * *

   Moreover, it should also be noted that [no] . . . provision relating to voluntary petitions by companies contains any insolvency requirement. * * *

* * *

   Accordingly, it is abundantly clear that Manville has met all of the threshold eligibility requirements for filing a voluntary petition under the Code. This Court will now turn to the issue of whether any of the movants have demonstrated sufficient "cause" . . . to warrant the dismissal of Manville's petition.

* * *

   In determining whether to dismiss . . ., a court is not necessarily required to consider whether the debtor has filed in "good faith" because that is not a specified predicate under the Code for filing. Rather, according to [the] Code . . ., good faith emerges as a requirement for the confirmation of a plan. The filing of a Chapter 11 case creates an estate for the benefit of all creditors and equity holders of the debtor wherein all constituencies may voice their interests and bargain for their best possible treatment. [Citation.] It is thus logical that the good faith of the debtor be deemed a predicate primarily for emergence out of a Chapter 11 case. It is after confirmation of a concrete and immutable reorganization plan that creditors are foreclosed from advancing their distinct and parochial interests in the debtor's estate.
   A "principal goal" of the Bankruptcy Code is to provide "open access" to the "bankruptcy process". [Citation.] The rationale behind this "open access" policy is to provide access to bankruptcy relief which is as "open" as "access to the credit economy." [Citation.] Thus, Congress intended that "there should be no legal barrier to voluntary petitions." [Citation.] Another major goal of the Code, that of "rehabilitation of debtors", requires that relief for debtors must be "timely". [Citation.] * * *
   Accordingly, the drafters of the Code envisioned that a financially beleaguered debtor with real debt and real creditors should not be required to wait until the economic situation is beyond repair in order to file a reorganization petition. The "Congressional purpose" in enacting the Code was to encourage resort to the bankruptcy process. [Citation.] This philosophy not only comports with the elimination of an insolvency requirement, but also is a corollary of the key aim of Chapter 11 of the Code, that of avoidance of liquidation. The drafters of the Code announced this goal, declaring that reorganization is more efficient than liquidation

because "assets that are used for production in the industry for which they were designed are more valuable than those same assets sold for scrap." [Citation.] Moreover, reorganization also fosters the goals of preservation of jobs in the threatened entity. [Citation.]

In the instant case, not only would liquidation be wasteful and inefficient in destroying the utility of valuable assets of the companies as well as jobs, but, more importantly, liquidation would preclude just compensation of some present asbestos victims and all future asbestos claimants. This unassailable reality represents all the more reason for this Court to adhere to this basic potential liquidation avoidance aim of Chapter 11 and deny the motions to dismiss. Manville must not be required to wait until its economic picture has deteriorated beyond salvation to file for reorganization.

* * *

In [this case] it is undeniable that there has been no sham or hoax perpetrated on the Court in that Manville is a real business with real creditors in pressing need of economic reorganization. Indeed, the Asbestos Committee has belied its own contention that Manville has no debt and no real creditors by quantifying a benchmark settlement demand approaching one billion dollars for compensation of approximately 15,500 prepetition asbestos claimants, during the course of negotiations pitched toward achieving a consensual plan. This huge asserted liability does not even take into account the estimated 6,000 new asbestos health claims which have arisen in only the first 16 months since the filing date. The number of post-filing claims increases each day as "future claims back into the present." . . .

Moreover, asbestos related property damage claims present another substantial contingent and unliquidated liability. Prior to the filing date, various schools initiated litigation seeking compensatory and punitive damages from . . . Manville for their unknowing use of asbestos-containing products in ceilings, walls, structural members, piping, ductwork and boilers in school buildings. * * *

* * *

Accordingly, it is clear that Manville's liability for compensatory, if not punitive, damages to school authorities is not hypothetical, but real and massive debt. A range of $500 million to $1.4 billion is the total projected amount of Manville's real debt to the school creditors.

In addition, claims of $425 million of liquidated commercial debt have been filed in this proceeding. The filing also triggered the acceleration of more than $275 million in unsecured public and institutional debt which had not been due prior to the filing. Upon a dismissal of this petition, Manville may be liable in the amount of all of the above-described real debts, plus interest. Manville's present holdings of cash and liquid assets would be insufficient to pay these obligations and, as noted above, its insurance carriers have repeatedly expressed their unwillingness to contribute to the payment of this debt. Thus, upon dismissal, Manville would become a target for economic dismemberment, liquidation, and chaos, which would benefit no one except the few winners of the race to the courthouse. The economic reality of Manville's highly precarious financial position due to massive debt sustains its eligibility and candidacy for reorganization.

In short, there was justification for Manville to elect a course contemplating a viable court-supervised rehabilitation of the real debt owed by Manville to its real creditors. Manville's filing did not in the appropriate sense abuse the jurisdiction of this Court and it is indeed, like the debtor in (citation), a "once viable business supporting employees and unsecured creditors (which) has more recently been

> burdened with judgments (and suits) that threaten to put it out of existence."
> * * * [Citation.] Thus, its petition must be sustained.
>
> * * *
>
> In sum, Manville is a financially beseiged enterprise in desperate need of reorganization of its crushing real debt, both present and future. The reorganization provisions of the Code were drafted with the aim of liquidation avoidance by great access to Chapter 11. Accordingly, Manville's filing does not abuse the jurisdictional integrity of this Court, but rather presents the same kinds of reasons that were present in [citation], for awaiting the determination of Manville's good faith until it is considered . . . as a prerequisite to confirmation or as a part of the cadre of motions before me which are scheduled to be heard subsequently.

ADJUSTMENT OF DEBTS OF INDIVIDUALS—CHAPTER 13

To encourage debtors to pay their debts wherever possible, Congress enacted Chapter 13 of the Bankruptcy Act. This chapter permits an individual debtor to file a repayment plan that, if confirmed by the court, will discharge him from almost all of his debts when he completes his payments under the plan.

Proceedings

Chapter 13 provides a procedure for the adjustment of debts of an *individual* with regular income who owes liquidated, unsecured debts of less than $100,000 and secured debts of less than $350,000. Sole proprietorships are also eligible if these debt limitations are met. A case under Chapter 13 may be initiated *only* by a voluntary petition. A trustee is appointed in every Chapter 13 case.

The Plan

The debtor files the plan and may modify it at any time before confirmation. The plan must meet three requirements:

1. It must provide for submission of all or any portion of future earnings or income of the debtor, as is necessary for the execution of the plan, to the supervision and control of the trustee.
2. It must provide for full payment on a deferred basis of all claims entitled to a priority unless a holder of a claim agrees to a different treatment of such claim.
3. If the plan classifies claims, it must provide the same treatment for each claim in the same class.

In addition, the plan *may* modify the rights of unsecured creditors and the rights of secured creditors except those secured only by a security interest in the debtor's principal residence. A plan may provide for payments on any unsecured claim to be made at the same time as payments on any secured claim.

The plan may *not* provide for payments over a period longer than three years, unless the court approves for cause a longer period not to exceed five years.

Confirmation

The plan will be confirmed by the court if certain requirements have been met. First, the plan must comply with applicable law and be proposed in good faith. Second, the value of the property to be distributed to unsecured creditors must be not less than the amount that would be paid them under Chapter 7. Third, either the secured creditors must accept the plan *or* the plan must provide that the debtor will surrender to the secured creditors the collateral *or* the plan must permit the secured creditors to retain their security interest and the value of property to be distributed to them is not less than the allowed amount of their claim. Fourth, the debtor must be able to make all payments and comply with the plan. Fifth, if the trustee or holder of an unsecured claim objects to the confirmation of a plan, then the plan must either provide for payment in full of that claim or provide that all of the debtor's disposable income for three years be applied to payments under the plan. For purposes of this provision, *disposable income* means income received by the debtor that is not reasonably necessary for the maintenance or support of the debtor or a dependent of the debtor, or if the debtor is engaged in business, for the payment of expenditures necessary for the continuation, preservation, and operation of the business.

Discharge

After a debtor completes all payments under the plan, the court will grant him a discharge of all debts provided for by the plan except the nondischargeable debts for alimony, maintenance, and support. This discharge is considerably more extensive than that granted under Chapter 7. Moreover, a debtor who receives a discharge under Chapter 7 cannot obtain a discharge again under that chapter for six years, although a debtor discharged under Chapter 13 is not subject to that limitation if payments under the plan totaled at least (1) 100 percent of unsecured claims, or (2) 70 percent of such claims *and* the plan was the debtor's best effort.

Even if all payments have *not* been made, the court may, after a hearing, grant a discharge if the debtor's failure to complete such payments is due to circumstances for which the debtor should not justly be held accountable, the value of property actually distributed is not less than what would have been received under Chapter 7, and modification of the plan is not practicable. This discharge, however, is subject to the same exceptions for nondischargeable debts as a discharge under Chapter 7.

IN RE JONSON
United States Bankruptcy Court, S.D. Indiana, 1981
17 B.R. 78.

Facts: The debtor, Jonson, is a single, thirty-five-year-old male with no dependents. He works as an administrative assistant for a medical doctor and has a net income of $755 per month. Jonson received a master of music degree from Indiana University and is only two courses short of receiving his doctorate. His only indebtedness is a student loan in the amount of $10,250 from Indiana University. Jonson has made no payments on his loan, which became due and payable two years ago with monthly payments of $98.98. Jonson filed an amended plan under Chapter 13 in which he proposed to make payments to the trustee of $140 per month for thirty-six months. Jonson's proposed plan would result in a total payment of $4,036 to Indiana University for a $10,250 loan. The plaintiff, Indiana University, objected to the confirmation of Jonson's Chapter 13 plan, raising the question of "good faith" on the part of Jonson.

Decision: Judgment for Indiana University granted.

Opinion: Bayt, Bkrtcy. J. Before a bankruptcy court can confirm a Chapter 13 plan it must make certain findings. *See* 11 U.S.C. § 1325(a)(3). "In this respect, Chapter 13 differs markedly from Chapter 7 [since] [t]he court has virtually no role to play in straight bankruptcy or liquidation under Chapter 7." [Citation.]

One of the findings that the court must make is whether the "plan has been proposed in good faith. . . ." 11 U.S.C. § 1325(a)(3). The term "good faith", as used in 11 U.S.C. § 1325(a)(3), is not defined in the Code, nor can one look to the legislative history for a definition or a clarification of that term. Therefore, it is the court's duty "to fashion the meaning of that term." [Citation.]

This court is of the opinion that the major purpose of the court's discretion under § 1325 to scrutinize a Chapter 13 plan prior to confirmation, is to prevent debtor abuse of Chapter 13, and to insure that the distinction between Chapter 7 and Chapter 13, as well as the basic and underlying purpose of Chapter 13, is maintained. [Citation.]

A review of the legislative history unmistakably leads to the conclusion that the purpose of a Chapter 13 plan is to enable a debtor to pay either in full or in part, "debts which have become too burdensome to meet without the help of the bankruptcy laws." [Citations.] The purpose of Chapter 13 is not to allow a debtor to discharge a debt or debts which would not be dischargeable under Chapter 7, [citation], without substantial payment by the debtor to the creditor or creditors. To be sure, "the drafters [of the Code] did not intend the liberal provisions of Chapter 13 to be used as a disguised Chapter 7 liquidation. The drafters intended debtors to deal fairly and justly with their creditors." [Citation.] If a debtor is not dealing in such a manner, the court cannot find that the plan was proposed in good faith.

It is the court's opinion that the debtor's plan was not proposed in good faith. It appears that the debtor's sole purpose is to avoid the provisions of Chapter 7 which would not allow a discharge of the debtor's only debt, a student loan. [Citation.] This court does not mean to say, however, that a debtor's use of the liberal discharge provisions of Chapter 13 is *per se* bad faith. [Citation.] "But it may be bad faith to utilize these provisions without a corresponding attempt to repay creditors a meaningful [or substantial] amount. [Citation.] To allow confirmation of debtor's plan would in effect sanction "an abuse of the provisions, purpose and spirit of Chapter 13." [Citation.]

According to the terms of his plan, debtor would pay $140.00 per month for 36 months. At the end of 36 months debtor would have paid approximately $4,036.00 on a $10,250.00 student loan. The court notes that debtor's proposed payment is $41.00 more than the monthly payment of the student loan itself. Debtor's proposed payment is not a meaningful or substantial one. If he is able to pay more under the plan for three years than is required under the terms of his agreement with Indiana University, the court wonders why he should not continue to pay until the entire amount is paid off, particularly in view of the fact that he will earn more money as time passes.

In his Response, debtor maintains that a 39% dividend is a substantial payment, thus warranting confirmation of his plan. Such a dividend may well be substantial in other situations, but it is not so in the instant one, in which the debtor has only one debt and that debt is a student loan.

Given the nature of the debt, public policy should demand that the plan not be confirmed. Student loans serve an important and useful purpose. If a debtor fails to repay a student loan, a loan used to better oneself through higher education, such action by the debtor diminishes the amount that others may borrow.

The court CONCLUDES that debtor's Chapter 13 plan was not filed in good faith and, therefore, should not be confirmed by the court.

ADJUSTMENT OF DEBTS OF A FAMILY FARMER—CHAPTER 12

In 1986 Congress amended the Bankruptcy Act by adding Chapter 12, which provides for the adjustment of debts of a family farmer with regular annual income. Chapter 12 has a "sunset" provision: it will expire in 1993 unless Congress reenacts it. Its purpose is to provide a proceeding for family farmers who do not qualify for Chapter 13 and find Chapter 11 proceedings overly burdensome.

Proceedings

A family farmer is defined as an individual, or individual and spouse, who are engaged in farming and receive 50 percent of their gross income from farming. Their aggregate debts may not exceed $1.5 million, and at least 80 percent of the debts must arise out of the farming operation. A corporation or partnership may also qualify as a family farmer if, in addition to meeting the requirements just mentioned, 50 percent of the stock or equity is held by one family, and more than 80 percent of the assets of the corporation or partnership are related to the farming operation.

The debtor usually remains in possession of all property of the estate. A debtor-in-possession has the rights, powers, and performs many of the duties of a trustee serving in a case under Chapter 11. At the request of a party in interest and after notice and a hearing, the court shall remove a debtor-in-possession if cause is shown. Cause includes fraud, dishonesty, incompetence, or gross mismanagement. Upon removal, the trustee performs the duties of the debtor-in-possession as well as the duties of a trustee under Chapter 12.

The Plan

The debtor is required to file a plan within ninety days after the order for relief, unless the court grants an extension. The debtor may modify the plan at any time before confirmation. The plan must meet three requirements.

1. It must provide for submission of all or any portion of future earnings or income of the debtor, as necessary for the execution of the plan, to the supervision and control of the trustee.
2. It must provide for full payment on a deferred basis of all claims entitled to a priority, unless a holder of a claim agrees to a different treatment of that claim.
3. If the plan classifies claims, it must provide the same treatment for each claim in the same class.

In addition, the plan *may* modify the rights of unsecured creditors and the rights of secured creditors. A plan may provide for payments on any unsecured claim to be made concurrently with payments on any secured claim.

The plan may *not* provide for payments over a period that is longer than three years, unless the court approves for a cause a longer period not to exceed five years.

Confirmation

The plan will be confirmed by the court if certain requirements have been met. First, the plan must comply with applicable law and be proposed in good faith. Second, the value of the property to be distributed to unsecured creditors must not be less than the amount that would be paid them under Chapter 7. Third, either the secured creditors must accept the plan *or* the plan must provide that the debtor will surrender to the secured creditors the collateral *or* the plan must permit the secured creditors to retain their security interest and the value of property to be distributed to them is not less than the allowed amount of their claim. Fourth, the debtor must be able to make all payments and comply with the plan. Fifth, if the trustee or holder of an unsecured claim objects to the confirmation of a plan, then the plan must either provide for payment in full of that claim or provide that all of the debtor's disposable income for three years apply to payments under the plan. Once the plan is confirmed, it binds the debtor, each creditor, each equity security holder, and each general partner of the debtor.

Discharge

After a debtor completes all payments under the plan, the court will grant him a discharge of all debts provided for by the plan except the nondischargeable debts for alimony, maintenance, and support. Even if all payments have *not* been made, the court may, after a hearing, grant a discharge if the debtor's failure to complete such payments is due to circumstances for which the debtor should not justly be held accountable, the value of property actually distributed is not less than what would have been received under Chapter 7, and modification of the plan is not practicable. This discharge, however, is subject to the same exceptions for nondischargeable debts as a discharge under Chapter 7.

CREDITORS' RIGHTS AND DEBTOR RELIEF OUTSIDE OF BANKRUPTCY

The rights and remedies of debtors and creditors outside of bankruptcy are principally governed by State law. Because of the expense and notoriety associated with bankruptcy, it is often in the best interests of both debtor and creditor to resolve their claims outside of a bankruptcy proceeding. Accordingly, bankruptcy is usually viewed as the last resort.

The rights and remedies of creditors outside of bankruptcy are varied. In the first part of this section we examine the basic right of *all* creditors to pursue their overdue claims to judgment and to satisfy that judgment out of property belonging to the debtor. Other rights and remedies are discussed elsewhere in this book. The second part of this section describes the various forms of nonbankruptcy compromises that have developed to provide relief to debtors who have become overextended and are unable to pay all of their creditors.

CREDITORS' RIGHTS

When a debtor fails to pay a debt, the creditor may file suit to collect the debt owed. The ultimate objective is to obtain a judgment against the debtor and then to collect on that judgment.

Prejudgment Remedies

Because litigation takes time, a creditor attempting to collect on a claim through the judicial process will almost always experience delay in obtaining judgment. To protect against the debtor's disposing of his assets, the creditor may use, when available, certain prejudgment remedies. The most important of these is **attachment,** which is the process of

seizing property, by virtue of a writ, summons, or other judicial order, and bringing the property into the custody of the court for the purpose of securing satisfaction of the judgment ultimately to be entered in the action. At common law, the main objective was to coerce the defendant debtor to appear in court; today the writ of attachment is statutory and is used primarily to seize the debtor's property in the event a judgment is rendered. Most States limit attachment to specified grounds and require the opportunity for a hearing before a judge prior to the issuance of a writ of execution. Generally, attachment is limited to situations in which (a) the defendant cannot be personally served; (b) the claim is based upon fraud or the equivalent; or (c) the defendant has or is likely to transfer his property. In addition, the plaintiff must generally post a bond to compensate the defendant for loss should the plaintiff not prevail in the cause of action.

Similar in purpose is the remedy of prejudgment **garnishment,** which is a statutory proceeding directed at a third person who owes a debt to the debtor or has property belonging to the debtor. Garnishment is most commonly used against the employer of the debtor and the bank in which the debtor has a savings or checking account. Property garnished remains in the hands of the third party pending the outcome of the suit. For example, Calvin brings an action against Daisy to collect a debt that is past due. Alvin has property belonging to Daisy. Calvin might garnish this property so that if Calvin is successful in his action against Daisy, Calvin's judgment could be satisfied out of that property held by Alvin. If Alvin no longer had the property when Calvin obtained judgment, Calvin could recover from Alvin.

Postjudgment Remedies

If the debtor still has not paid the claim, the creditor may proceed to trial and try to obtain a court judgment against the debtor. Obtaining a judgment, however, is only the first, although necessary, step in collecting the debt. If the debtor does not voluntarily pay the judgment, the creditor will have to take additional steps to collect on the judgment. These steps are called "postjudgment remedies."

First, the judgment creditor will have the clerk issue a **writ of execution,** which is served by the sheriff upon the defendant/debtor demanding payment of the judgment. Upon return of the writ "unsatisfied," the judgment creditor may post bond or other security and order a levy on and sale of specified nonexempt property belonging to the defendant/debtor, which is then seized by the sheriff, advertised for sale, and sold at public sale under the writ of execution.

The writ of execution is limited to property of the debtor that is not exempt. All States restrict creditors from recourse to certain property, the type and amount of which varies greatly from State to State.

If the proceeds of the sale do not produce sufficient funds to pay the judgment, the creditor may institute a **supplementary proceeding** in an attempt to locate money or other property belonging to the defendant. He may also proceed by **garnishment** against the debtor's employer or a bank in which the debtor has an account in an attempt to collect the judgment.

DEBTOR'S RELIEF

There are several inherent conflicts between creditors' rights and debtor relief, including: (1) the right of diligent creditors to pursue their claims to judgment and to satisfy their judgments by sale of property of the debtor; (2) the right of unsecured creditors who have refrained from suing the debtor; and (3) the social policy of giving relief to a debtor who has contracted debts beyond his ability to pay and who may be confronted by a lifetime burden. Resolving these conflicts necessarily involves a compromise under which the debtor will disclose and surrender all his assets to a trustee or other person for the benefit of his creditors and the creditors will receive fair and equal treatment.

Various forms of nonbankruptcy compromises have been developed to provide relief to debtors, some of which are less formal, such as those offered by credit agencies and adjustment bureaus. Some are founded in common

law and involve simple contract and trust principles, such as compositions and assignments; others are statutory, such as statutory assignments. Some involve the intervention of a court and its officers, such as equity receiverships, and others do not.

Compositions

A common law or nonstatutory **composition** is an ordinary contract or agreement between the debtor and her creditors under which the creditors receive a proportional part of their claims and the debtor is discharged from the balance of the claims. As a contract, it requires the formalities of a contract, such as offer, acceptance, and consideration. For example, debtor D, owing debts of $5,000 to A, $2,000 to B, and $1,000 to C, offers to settle these claims by paying a total of $4,000 to A, B, and C. If A, B, and C accept the offer, a composition results, with A receiving $2,500, B $1,000, and C $500. The consideration for the promise of A to forgive the balance of his claim consists of the promises of B and C to forgive the balance of their claims. All the creditors benefit because a conflict among creditors to obtain the debtor's limited assets is avoided.

It should be noted, however, that the debtor in a composition is discharged from liability only on the claims of creditors who voluntarily consent to the composition. If, in the illustration above, C had refused to accept the offer of composition and had refused to take the $500, he could attempt to collect the full $1,000 claim. Likewise, if D owed additional debts to X, Y, and Z, these creditors would not be bound by the agreement between D and A, B, and C. Another disadvantage of the composition is the fact that any creditor can attach the assets of the debtor during the usual period of bargaining and negotiation that precedes the execution of the composition agreement. For instance, once D advised A, B and C that he was offering to compose the claims, any one of the creditors could seize D's property.

A variation of the composition is an extension agreement worked out by the debtor with her creditor providing for payment of her debts either in full or proportionately scaled down over a period of time.

Assignments for Benefit of Creditors

A common law or nonstatutory assignment for the benefit of creditors, or a general assignment, as it is sometimes called, is a voluntary transfer by the debtor of some or all of his property to a trustee, who applies the property to the payment of all of the debtor's debts. For instance, debtor D transfers title to his property to trustee T, who converts the property into money and pays it to all of the creditors on a *pro rata* basis.

The advantage of the assignment over the composition is that it prevents the debtor's assets from being attached or executed and halts the race of diligent creditors to attach. On the other hand, the common law assignment does not require the consent of the creditors, and payment by the trustee of part of the claims does not discharge the debtor from the balance of them. Thus, in the previous example, even after T pays A $2,500, B $1,000 and C $500 (and appropriate payments to all other creditors), A, B, and C and the other creditors may still attempt to collect the balance of their claims.

Statutory Assignments

Because assignments benefit creditors by protecting the debtor's assets from attachment, there have been many statutory attempts to combine the idea of the assignment with a corresponding benefit to the debtor by discharging him from the balance of his debts. Since the United States Constitution prohibits

a State from impairing the obligation of a contract between private citizens, it is impossible for a State to force all creditors to discharge a debtor on a *pro rata* distribution of assets, although, as previously discussed, the Federal government *does* have such power and exercises it in the Bankruptcy Act. Accordingly, the States have generally enacted assignment statutes permitting the debtor to obtain *voluntary* releases of the balance of claims from creditors who accept partial payments, thus combining the advantages of common law compositions and assignments.

Equity Receiverships

One of the oldest remedies in equity is the appointment of a receiver by the court. The receiver is a disinterested (unbiased) person appointed by the court who collects and preserves the debtor's assets and income and disposes of them at the direction of the court. The court may instruct her (1) to liquidate the assets by public or private sale; (2) to operate the business as a going concern temporarily; or (3) to conserve the assets until final disposition of the matter before the court.

A receiver will be appointed on the petition (1) of a secured creditor seeking foreclosure of his security; (2) of a judgment creditor after exhausting legal remedies to satisfy the judgment; or (3) of a shareholder of a corporate debtor where it appears that the assets of the corporation will be dissipated by fraud or mismanagement. The receiver is always appointed at the discretion of the court. Insolvency, in the equity sense of inability by the debtor to pay his debts as they mature, is one of the factors considered by the court in appointing a receiver.

CHAPTER SUMMARY

FEDERAL BANKRUPTCY LAW

Case Administration— Chapter 3	**Commencement of the Case** jurisdiction of the bankruptcy court is begun by the filing of a voluntary or involuntary petition ■ *Voluntary Petitions* available to any debtor even if solvent ■ *Involuntary Petitions* may be filed only under Chapter 7 or 11 if the debtor is generally not paying his debts as they become due

Automatic Stays prevents attempts by creditors to recover claims against the debtor

Trustee responsible for collecting, liquidating, and distributing the debtor's estate

Meeting of Creditors

Creditors, the Debtor, and the Estate— Chapter 5

Creditors any entity that has a claim against the debtor
- *Claim* a right to payment
- *Secured Claims* claim with a lien on property of the debtor
- *Unsecured Claims* portion of a claim that exceeds the value of any property securing that claim
- *Priority of Claims* the right of a claim to be paid before claims of lesser rank

Debtors
- *Debtor's Duties* the debtor must file specified information, cooperate with the trustee, and surrender all property of the estate
- *Debtor's Exemptions* determined by State or Federal law depending upon the State
- *Discharge* relief from liability for all debts except those the Bankruptcy Act specifies are not dischargeable

The Estate all legal and equitable interests of a debtor in nonexempt property
- *Trustee as Lien Creditor* trustee gains the rights and powers of a creditor with a judicial lien (which is an interest in property to secure payment of a debt that is obtained by court action)
- *Voidable Preferences* Bankruptcy Act invalidates certain preferential transfers made before the date of bankruptcy from the debtor to favored creditors
- *Fraudulent Transfers* trustee may avoid fraudulent transfers made on or within one year before the date of bankruptcy

Liquidation— Chapter 7

Purpose to distribute the debtor's nonexempt assets equitably and usually to discharge all dischargeable debts of the debtor

Proceedings applies to most debtors

Distribution of the Estate in the following order: (1) secured creditors, (2) creditors entitled to a priority, (3) unsecured creditors, and (4) the debtor

Discharge granted by the court unless the debtor has committed an offense under the Bankruptcy Act or has received a discharge within six years

Reorganization— Chapter 11

Purpose to preserve a distressed business enterprise and its value as a going concern

Proceedings debtor usually remains in possession of the property of the estate

Acceptance of Plan requries a specified proportion of creditors to approve the plan

Confirmation of Plan requires (1) good faith, (2) feasibility, (3) cash payments to certain creditors, and usually (4) acceptance by creditors

Effect of Reorganization binds the debtor and creditors

Adjustment of Debts of Individuals— Chapter 13	**Purpose** to permit an individual debtor to file a repayment plan which will discharge him from most debts **Confirmation of Plan** requires (1) good faith, (2) value of property distributed to creditors must not be less than the amount that would be paid them under Chapter 7, (3) secured creditors must accept the plan, and (4) the debtor must be able to make all payments and comply with the plan **Discharge** after a debtor completes all payments under the plan

Adjustment of Debts of a Family Farmer— Chapter 12	**Purpose** to permit a family farmer to file a repayment plan which will discharge him from most debts **Proceedings** available to a farmer who receives at least 50 percent of his income from farming and meets certain debt limitations **Confirmation of Plan** same as a Chapter 13 proceeding **Discharge** after a debtor completes all payment under the plan

CREDITORS' RIGHTS AND DEBTOR RELIEF OUTSIDE OF BANKRUPTCY

Creditors' Rights	**Prejudgment Remedies** include attachment and garnishment **Postjudgment Remedies** include writ of execution and garnishment

Debtor's Relief	**Compositions** agreement between debtor and two or more of her creditors that each will take a portion of his claim as full payment **Assignment for Benefit of Creditors** voluntary transfer by the debtor of some or all of his property to a trustee, who applies the property to the payment of all of the debtor's debts **Statutory Assignments** provides a voluntary release of balance of claims from creditors who accept partial payments made by the trustee for the debtor **Equity Receiverships** receiver is a disinterested person appointed by the court to collect and preserve the debtor's assets and income and dispose of them at the direction of the court

QUESTIONS

1. List (a) the priorities of creditors' claims, (b) the debtor's exemptions, and (c) the debts that are not dischargeable in bankruptcy.
2. Discuss the rights of a trustee (a) as a lien creditor, (b) to avoid preferential transfers, (c) to avoid fraudulent transfers, and (d) to avoid statutory liens.
3. State the order in which the debtor's estate is distributed under Chapter 7.
4. List those acts of a debtor that will prevent him from receiving a discharge under Chapter 7.
5. Compare the adjustment of debt proceedings under Chapters 11, 12, and 13.
6. Identify and define the nonbankruptcy compromises between debtors and creditors.

PROBLEMS

1. (a) Benson goes into bankruptcy. His estate has no assets. Are Benson's taxes discharged by the proceedings? Why or why not?

(b) Benson obtains property from Anderson on credit by representing that he is solvent when in fact he knows he is insolvent. Is Benson's debt to Anderson discharged by Benson's discharge in bankruptcy?

2. Bradley goes into bankruptcy owing $5,000 as wages to his four employees. There is enough in his estate to pay all costs of administration and enough to pay his employees, but nothing will be left for general creditors. Do the employees take all the estate? Under what conditions? If the general creditors received nothing at all, would these debts be discharged?

3. Jessica sold goods to Stacy for $2,500 and retained a security interest in them. Three months later, Stacy filed a petition in bankruptcy under Chapter 7. At this time Stacy still owed Jessica $2,000 for the purchase price of the goods, whose value was $1,500.

(a) May the trustee invalidate Jessica's security interest? If so, under what provision?

(b) If the security interest is invalidated, what is Jessica's status in the bankruptcy proceeding?

(c) If the security interest is *not* invalidated, what is Jessica's status in the bankruptcy proceeding?

4. A debtor went through bankruptcy and received his discharge. Which of the following debts were completely discharged, and which remain debts against him in the future?

(a) A claim of $900 for wages earned within three months immediately prior to bankruptcy.

(b) A judgment of $3,000 against the debtor for breach of contract.

(c) Sales taxes of $1,800.

(d) $1,000 in past alimony and support money owed to his divorced wife for herself and their child.

(e) A judgment of $4,000 for injuries received because of the debtor's negligent operation of an automobile.

5. Rosinoff and his wife, who were business partners, entered bankruptcy. Objection was made to their discharge in bankruptcy by a creditor, Baldwin, on the grounds that:

(a) the partners had obtained credit from Baldwin on the basis of a false financial statement;

(b) the partners had failed to keep books of account and records from which their financial conditions could be determined; and

(c) Rosinoff had falsely sworn that he had taken $70 from the partnership account when the correct amount was $700.

Were the debtors entitled to a discharge?

6. X Corporation is a debtor in a reorganization proceeding under Chapter 11 of the Bankruptcy Act. By fair and proper valuation, its assets are worth $100,000. The indebtedness of the corporation is $105,000, it has outstanding preferred stock of par value of $20,000, and common stock of par value of $75,000. The plan of reorganization submitted by the trustees would eliminate the common shareholders and give bonds of the face amount of $5,000 to the creditors and common stock in the ratio of 84 percent to the creditors and 16 percent to the preferred shareholders. Should this plan be confirmed?

7. Alex is a wage earner with a regular income. He has unsecured debts of $42,000 and secured debts owing to Betty, Connie, David, and Eunice totaling $120,000. Eunice's debt is secured only by a mortgage on Alex's house. Alex files a petition under Chapter 13 and a plan providing payment as follows: (a) 60 percent of all taxes owed, (b) 35 percent of all unsecured debts, and (c) $100,000 in total to Betty, Connie, David, and Eunice. Should the court confirm the plan? If not, how must the plan be modified or what other conditions must be satisfied?

8. John Bunker has assets of $130,000 and liabilities of $185,000 owed to nine creditors. Nonetheless, his cash flow is positive and he is making payment on all of his obligations as they become due. I. M. Flintheart, who is owed $22,000 by Bunker, files an involuntary petition in bankruptcy against Bunker. Bunker contests the petition. Decision?

9. Karen has filed a petition for a Chapter 7 proceeding. The total value of Karen's estate is $35,000. Ben, who is owed $18,000, has a security interest in property valued at $12,000. Lauren has an unsecured claim of $9,000, which is entitled to a priority of $2,000. The United States has a claim for income taxes of $7,000. Steve has an unsecured claim of $10,000 that was filed on time. Sarah has an unsecured claim of $17,000 that was filed on time. Wally has a claim of $14,000 that was not filed on time even though Wally was aware of the bankruptcy proceedings.

What should each of the creditors receive in a distribution under Chapter 7?

10. Landmark at Plaza Park, Ltd., filed a plan of reorganization under Chapter 11 of the Bankruptcy Code. Landmark is a limited partnership whose only substantial asset is a 200-unit garden apartment complex. City Federal holds the first mortgage on the property in the face amount of $2,250,000. The mortgage bears an interest rate of 9.5 percent and is due and payable six years from now.

Landmark has proposed a plan of reorganization under which the property now in possession of City Federal would be returned. Landmark will then deliver a nonrecourse note, payable in three years, in the face amount of $2,705,820.31 to City Federal in substitution of all of the partnership's existing liabilities. On the sixteenth month through the thirty-sixth month after the effective date of the plan, Landmark will make monthly interest payments at a rate of 12.5 percent computed on the value of the property of $2,260,000. Finally, the note will be secured by the existing mortgage. Landmark's theory is that the note will be paid off at the end of thirty-six months by a combination of refinancing and accumulation of cash from the project. The key is Landmark's proposal to obtain a new first mortgage in three years in the face amount of $2,400,000.

City Federal is a first mortgagee without recourse that has been collecting rents pursuant to a rent assignment agreement since the default on the mortgage eleven months ago. City Federal is impaired by the plan, has rejected the plan, and seeks to complete its foreclosure action. Decision?

PART 9
REGULATION OF BUSINESS

40
UNFAIR COMPETITION

41
ANTITRUST

42
EMPLOYMENT LAW

43
SECURITIES REGULATION

44
ACCOUNTANTS' LEGAL LIABILITY

45
CONSUMER PROTECTION

46
INTERNATIONAL BUSINESS LAW

Part Nine addresses the role of government in regulating business, a role that has grown in this country to great proportions during the twentieth century. It is theoretically possible to have an economic system in which government plays no part at all; it is also conceivable to have an economy in which government exercises a totally dominant role by owning all productive property as well as deciding what is produced, where it is produced, who shall produce it, and who shall consume it. In practice, however, economic systems fall somewhere between these two extremes: our economy has less governmental involvement than the Soviet Union's or China's but more than Hong Kong's.

Our economic system is thus a "mixed economy" that has evolved from capitalism. As explained and justified by Adam Smith in *The Wealth of Nations* (1776), the capitalistic system is composed of six "institutions": economic motivation, private productive property, free enterprise, free markets, competition, and limited government. Economic motivation assumes that a person will work harder if he receives an economic return for his effort; therefore the economic system should provide greater economic rewards for those who work harder. Private property (which we discuss in Part Ten of this book) is the means by which economic motivation is exercised. It permits individuals to innovate and produce while securing to them the fruits of their efforts. Jack Behrman has described how the four other institutions combine with these two to bring about industrialized capitalism:

> Free enterprise permits the combination of properties so people can do things together that they can't do alone. Free enterprise means a capitalistic combination of factors of production under decisions of free individuals. Free enter-prise is the group expression of the use of private property, and it permits greater efficiency in an industrial setting through variation in the levels and kinds of production.
>
> . . . The free market operates to equate supply and demand—supply reflecting the ability and willingness to offer certain goods or services, and demand reflecting the consumer's *ability* and *willingness* to pay. Price is adjusted to include the maximum number of *both* bids and offers. The market, therefore, is *the* decision-making mechanism outside of the firm. It is the *means* by which basic decisions are made about the use of resources, and all factors are supposed to respond to it, however they wish.
>
> . . . Just in case it doesn't work out that way, there is one more institution—the *Government*—which is supposed to set rules and provide protection for the society and its members. That's all, said Smith, that it should do: it should set the rules, enforce them, and stand aside. J. Behrman, *Discourses on Ethics and Business*, 25–29 (1981).

As long as all these constituent institutions continued to exist and operate in a balanced manner, the factors of production—land, capital, and labor—would combine to produce an efficient allocation of resources for individual consumers and for the economy as a whole. For this outcome to succeed, however, Smith's model required that a number of conditions be satisfied: "standardized products, numerous firms in markets, each firm with a small share and unable by its actions alone to exert significant influence over price, no barriers to entry, and output carried to the point where each seller's marginal cost equals the going market price." E. Singer, *Antitrust Economics and Legal Analysis* 2 (1981).

History has demonstrated that almost all of these assumptions have *not* been satisfied by the actual operation of the economy. More specifically, the actual competitive process falls considerably short of the assumptions of the classic economic model of perfect competition:

> Competitive industries are never perfectly competitive in this sense. Many of the resources they employ cannot be shifted to other employments without substantial cost and delay. The allocation of those resources, as between industries or as to relative proportions within a single industry, is unlikely to have been made in a way that affords the best possible expenditure of economic effort. Information is incomplete, motivation confused, and decision therefore ill informed and often unwise. Variations in efficiency are not directly reflected in variations of profit. Success is derived in large part from competitive selling efforts, which in the aggregate may be wasteful, and from differentiation of products, which may be undertaken partly by methods designed to impair the opportunity of the buyer to compare quality and price.
> C. Edwards, *Maintaining Competition* 7 (1964).

In addition to capitalism's failure to accomplish its objective of efficient resource allocation, it cannot be relied on to achieve all of the social and public policy objectives required by a pluralistic democracy. For example, equitable distribution of wealth, national defense, conservation of natural resources, full employment, stability in economic cycles, protection against economic dislocations, health and safety, social security, and other important social and economic goals are simply not comprehended or addressed by the free enterprise model. As a consequence, increased governmental intervention has occurred not only to preserve the competitive process in our mixed economic system but also to achieve social goals extrinsic to the efficient allocation of resources. Such intervention attempts (1) to regulate both "legal" monopolies such as those conferred by law through copyrights, patents, and trade symbols and "natural" monopolies such as utilities, transportation, and communications; (2) to correct imperfections in the market system to preserve competition; (3) to protect specific groups from failures of the marketplace, the most important example being labor; and (4) to promote other social goals. Successful government regulation involves a delicate balance between regulations that attempt to preserve competition and those that attempt to advance other social objectives. The latter must not undermine the basic competitive processes that are relied on to bring about an efficient allocation of economic resources.

In Part Nine we examine a number of critical areas of governmental intervention. The chapters on Unfair Competition and Antitrust address the ways in which the government has sought to preserve a free and fair competitive system. The chapter on Employment Law covers the various regulatory efforts protecting one of the productive factors in capitalism: labor. Governmental regulation of another key factor—capital—is discussed in the chapters on Securities Regulation and Accountants' Legal Liability. In the chapter on consumer protection, we deal with the attempts by government to ensure that, as Adam Smith said, "the consumer is King." Finally, the chapter on international law examines the legal environment of international business transactions. In studying these chapters, you should keep in mind the goals and objectives of the capitalistic system, the failures of the system in actual operation, the abuses of the system, and the economic and social reasons underlying government's intervention.

40 UNFAIR COMPETITION

The law of unfair competition has been developed to prevent businesses from taking unfair advantage of their competitors. An important part of this area of law is the protection of intellectual property, which includes trade secrets, trade symbols, copyrights, and patents. These interests are protected from **infringement,** or unauthorized use, by others. Such protection is essential to the conduct of business. For example, business would be far less willing to invest considerable resources in research and development unless the resulting discoveries, inventions, and processes were protected by patents and trade secrets. Similarly, business would not be secure in devoting time and money to the marketing of its products and services if its trade symbols and trade names were not protected. Moreover, without copyright protection, the publishing, entertainment, and computer software industries would be vulnerable to having their efforts pirated by competition. In this chapter we discuss the law protecting (1) trade secrets; (2) trade symbols, including trademarks, service marks, certification marks, collective marks, and trade names; (3) copyrights; and (4) patents.

TRADE SECRETS

Every business has secret information, including lists of customers, as well as contracts with suppliers and customers. Some have secret formulas, processes, and methods used in the production of goods that are vital to successful operation of the business. This information is considered a protected **trade secret** if it is a *commercially valuable secret* (guarded from disclosure), and not common knowledge. A trade secret may be disclosed in confidence to an employee with the understanding that the employee will not disclose the information. To the extent the owner of the information obtains a patent on it, then it is no longer a trade secret, but is protected by patent law.

If a person **misappropriates** (wrongfully uses) a trade secret, the owner of the information may obtain damages and, where appropriate, injunctive relief. Basically, trade secrets are misappropriated in two ways: (1) an employee wrongfully uses or discloses it, or (2) a competitor wrongfully obtains it.

An employee is under a duty of loyalty to his employer, which includes the nondisclosure of trade secrets to competitors. It is wrongful for a competitor to obtain vital secret trade information of this type from an employee by bribery or other means. The faithless employee also commits a tort by divulging secret trade information. In the absence of contract restriction, an employee is under no duty upon termination of his employment to refrain from competing or working for a competitor of his former employer. After termination of the employment, unless otherwise agreed, the employee may compete with his former employer, but he may not use trade secrets or disclose them to third persons. The employee, however, is entitled to use skill, knowledge, and general information acquired during the employment relationship. For example, Woodrow and Gail, who have been employees of the High Tech Company for fifteen years, have developed in the course of their employment highly specialized knowledge and skills in the manufacture of space suits for astronauts. There are few, if any, persons who have equivalent skill and knowledge. Low Tech Company, desirous of obtaining a contract with the government for the manufacture of space suits, approaches Woodrow and Gail and offers them employment. There is no contract prohibiting Woodrow and Gail from leaving the High Tech Company and going to work for the Low Tech Company. If they do so, however, the High Tech Company is entitled to an injunction restraining Woodrow, Gail, and the Low Tech Company from the use of trade secrets and methods for manufacturing space suits that were developed by Woodrow and Gail while in the employ of the High Tech Company.

Another improper method of acquiring trade secrets is industrial espionage such as electronic surveillance or spies. In the broadest sense, discovery of another's trade secrets by any means other than one's own independent research efforts or inspection of the finished product is improper unless the other party voluntarily discloses the secret or fails to take reasonable precautions to protect its secrecy.

TRADE SYMBOLS

One of the earliest forms of unfair competition is the fraudulent marketing of one person's goods as those of another. This unlawful practice is sometimes referred to as "passing off" or "palming off." It is basically a "cashing in" on the good will, good name, and reputation of a competitor and of his products. It results in deception of the public and loss of trade by honest businesses. Section 43(a) of the Federal Trademark Act (the Lanham Act) is a statutory descendant of palming off. It provides protection against the use of a false designation of origin in connection with any goods or services. This section also prohibits false descriptions or representations of a person's own goods and services. In 1988 this section was amended to prohibit misrepresentations of *another* persons's goods, services, or commercial activities. See Law in the News at page 892.

The Lanham Act also established Federal registration of trade symbols and protection against misuse or infringement by injunctive relief and a right of action for damages against the infringer. An infringement is a form of passing off one's goods or services as those of the owner of the mark, is deceptive of the public, and constitutes unfair competition.

Types of Trade Symbols

The Lanham Act recognizes four types of trade symbols or **marks.** A **trademark** is a *distinctive* mark, word, letter, number, design, picture, or combination in any form of arrangement that is adopted or used by a person identifying goods he manufactures or sells.

Similar in function to the trademark, which identifies tangible goods and products, a **service mark** is used to identify and distinguish the services of one person from those of others. For example, the titles, character names, and other distinctive features of radio and television shows may be registered as service marks.

A **certification mark** is a mark used upon or in connection with goods or services to certify regional or other origin, material, mode of manufacture, quality, accuracy, or other characteristics of the goods or services or that the work or labor in the goods or services were performed by members of a union or other organization. The marks "Good Housekeeping Seal of Approval" and "Underwriter's Laboratory" are examples of certification marks. The owner of the certification mark may *not* be the producer or provider of the goods or services with which the mark is used.

A **collective mark** is a distinctive mark or symbol used to indicate either membership in a trade union, trade association, fraternal society, or other organization or that the goods or services are produced by members of a collective group. As in the case of a certification mark, the owner of a collective mark is not the producer or provider but rather is the group of which the producer or provider is a member. An example of a collective mark is the union mark attached to many products to indicate they were made by a unionized company.

Registration

To be protected by the Lanham Act, a mark must be distinctive so that it identifies the

LAW IN THE NEWS

New Law Adds Risk to Comparative Ads

It's getting nasty out there. Makers of everything from jam to air fresheners to bug killers have launched ad campaigns that mimic or attack their competitors with a zeal that industry veterans say they have never seen before.

"Comparative advertising has become really pointed and mean," says Bob Wolf, vice chairman, Chiat/Day Advertising Inc. "One of the reasons is that manufacturers no longer compete for every consumer in a category. Now it's very precise, niche marketing."

It's also about to become more dangerous. In an article in the current issue of the Harvard Business Review, authors Bruce Buchanan and Doron Goldman write that the little-noticed Trademark Law Revision Act of 1988, which becomes effective this November, makes it easier for victims of attack advertising to sue.

Under the old Lanham Act, advertisers were prohibited from misrepresenting their own products. The new act prevents them from misrepresenting the qualities or characteristics of "another person's goods, services, or commercial activities."

This means companies that believe their brand names have been unfairly tarnished by attack advertising have protection under federal law, a significant change. Not only does the new act close a loophole often used by the defense, but it also covers all states.

"It's definitely pro-plaintiff," says Michael Epstein, a partner at Weil, Gotshal & Manges. "If you feel your company has been misrepresented, it will be easier to sue. I don't think there's going to be a tenfold increase in suits, but companies will have to be more careful about their advertising."

There are numerous examples of advertising that might be affected by the new act. Consider **Sorrell Ridge,** a maker of spreadable fruit jams and jellies. In Sorrell Ridge's TV campaign, created by **Follis & Verdi,** viewers are told that preserves made by **J. M. Smucker** Co. are mostly corn syrup, refined sugar, and just some fruit. Sorrell Ridge products, in comparison, are presented as consisting of all fruit and fruit juice.

Some viewers might take that to mean that Sorrell Ridge products are healthier than Smuck-

er's. Although Sorrell Ridge's chief executive officer, Fred Ross, says the company doesn't see any problem with the commercials, he concedes the new law gives him pause. "We'll have to reconsider the direction we've taken," he says, even though he credits the campaign with boosting the company's sales by 50%.

Another recent example of tough comparative advertising is the fight between Lysol, made by Sterling Drug Inc., and Glade, which is made by **S.C. Johnson & Son** Inc. Last month Glade aired a commercial suggesting that the air doesn't smell good for Lysol users because Lysol is 75% alcohol. In turn, viewers recently saw a TV commercial for Lysol contending that Glade is more than 97% water and gas.

A Sterling Drug spokesman says the Lysol ad "was completely accurate." But under the new act, being accurate may not be total protection from a lawsuit.

"You can make a true statement but still give a false impression to a consumer," notes Daniel Ebenstein, a partner with the law firm of Amster, Rothstein & Ebenstein in New York. Without commenting on the merits of the Lysol ad, he says, "A product may contain mostly water, for example. But the remaining ingredients may be very significant. One issue is what you say, but a separate issue is the message you communicate."

Regarding the Sorrell Ridge ads, Richard Smucker, president of Smucker's, said, "We do make an all-fruit product, but their comparisons are against our traditional fruit line." Mr. Smucker said his company won't bring suit. S. C. Johnson officials declined comment.

Mr. Ebenstein doesn't think the new act will drastically change the body of law that has been written around the Lanham Act. But, he says, "This is a congressional acknowledgement that there ought to be a national remedy for false and misleading advertising, and that is likely to create more litigation."

By Jeffrey A. Trachtenberg
Reprinted by permission of the Wall
Street Journal, © Dow Jones & Company, Inc. 1989. All Rights
Reserved Worldwide.

origin of the goods or services. Marks that are fanciful or arbitrary satisfy the distinctiveness requirement, whereas generic or descriptive designations do not. For example, a word describing the ingredients, quality, purpose, function, or uses of a product may not be monopolized as a mark. Thus, the word *Plow* cannot be a trademark for plows, although it may be a trademark for shoes. A descriptive mark is entitled to protection, however, if it has acquired a secondary meaning by "becoming distinctive" of the goods or services. A mark acquires a **secondary meaning** when it is associated by a substantial number of purchasers with the product or service.

Federal registration is denied to marks that are immoral, deceptive, or scandalous. Marks may not be registered if they disparage or falsely suggest a connection with persons, living or dead, institutions, beliefs, or national symbols. In addition, a trademark may not consist of the flag, coat of arms, or other insignia of the United States, any State, municipality, or any foreign nations.

To obtain Federal protection, the mark must be registered with the Patent and Trademark Office. Registration provides numerous advantages. It gives nationwide constructive notice of the mark to all later users. It permits the registrant to use the Federal courts to enforce the mark. It constitutes *prima facie* evidence of the registrant's exclusive right to use the mark. (This right becomes incontestable, subject to certain specified limitations, after five years.) Finally, it gives the registrant protection by the Bureau of Customs against imports infringing upon the mark.

MILLER BREWING COMPANY v. G. HEILEMAN BREWING COMPANY, INC.

United States Court of Appeals, Seventh Circuit, 1977.
561 F.2d 75.

Facts: In 1967 a Chicago brewer, Meister Brau, Inc., began making and selling a reduced calorie, reduced carbohydrate beer under the name "LITE." Late in 1968 that company filed applications for registration of "LITE" as a trademark in the United States Patent Office, which ultimately approved three registrations of labels containing the name "LITE" for "beer with no available carbohydrates." In 1972 Meister Brau sold its interest in the "LITE" trademarks and the accompanying goodwill to Miller Brewing Company. Miller decided to expand its marketing of beer under the brand "LITE." It developed a modified recipe, which resulted in a beer lower in calories than Miller's regular beer but not without available carbohydrates. The label was revised and one of the registrations was amended to show "LITE" printed rather than in script. In addition, an extensive advertising campaign was undertaken. From 1973 through 1976, Miller expanded its annual sales of "LITE" from 50,000 barrels to 4,000,000 barrels and increased its annual advertising expenditures from $500,000 to more than $12,000,000.

Since early 1975 a number of other brewers, including G. Heileman Brewing Company, have introduced reduced calorie beers labeled or described as "light." Miller began filing trademark infringement actions against competitors to enjoin the use of the word "light". The District Court enjoined Heileman from continuing to sell, advertise, and distribute beer anywhere in the United States under the brand name incorporating the word 'Light'. Heileman appeals.

Decision: Preliminary injunction reversed.

Opinion: Tone, J. **The Effect of Registration** Miller claims the benefit of [citation], which provides that registration on the principal register "shall be prima facie evidence of registrant's exclusive right to use the registered mark in commerce on the goods or services specified in the registration subject to any conditions or limitation stated therein. . . ."

The three registrations on which Miller relies specify "beer with no available carbohydrates" as the goods on which the registered mark is to be used. This limitation came about because the Patent Office refused registration on the applications as initially filed, which described the goods as "beer," on the ground that "LITE" was "merely descriptive" and therefore not registerable because of [citation]. In response to this action, Meister Brau offered evidence of secondary meaning, but in addition its attorney stated that "the beer in connection with which Applicant uses this mark is no-available carbohydrates beer . . ." and also had "one-third less calories than ordinary draft beer," and that "LITE" was suggestive rather than merely descriptive of these qualities. The examiner then required that the applications be amended to describe the goods to which the mark applied as "beer with no available carbohydrates" and they were so amended. We hold that the statute means what it says. The registrations are prima facie evidence of Miller's exclusive right to use the word "LITE" for beer with no available carbohydrates, not for any beer, a breadth of coverage which the applicant disclaimed by amending its applications. Inasmuch as the beer marketed by Heileman as its "Light" beer contains available carbohydrates, as indeed does Miller's "LITE," the registrations are not prima facie evidence of Miller's exclusive right to use the mark on that beer. Thus, although we think the result would be the same whether or not [citation] applied, Miller's brand name "LITE" must be evaluated under the common law of trademarks without the benefit of registration.

General Principles   The basic principles of trademark law which are applicable here have often been stated, [citations], and may be briefly summarized. A term for which trademark protection is claimed will fit somewhere in the spectrum which ranges through (1) generic or common descriptive and (2) merely descriptive to (3) suggestive and (4) arbitrary or fanciful. As the ease with which hues in the solar spectrum may be classified on the basis of perception will depend upon where they fall in that spectrum, so it is with a term on the trademark spectrum.

A generic or common descriptive term is one which is commonly used as the name or description of a kind of goods. It cannot become a trademark under any circumstances. [Citations.] Using the phonetic equivalent of a common descriptive word, *i.e.*, misspelling it, is of no avail. [Citation.]

A merely descriptive term specifically describes a characteristic or ingredient of an article. It can, by acquiring a secondary meaning, *i.e.*, becoming "distinctive of the applicant's goods" [citation], become a valid trademark. [Citation.]

A suggestive term suggests rather than describes an ingredient or characteristic of the goods and requires the observer or listener to use imagination and perception to determine the nature of the goods. Such a term can be protected without proof of a secondary meaning. [Citation.]

An arbitrary or fanciful term enjoys the same full protection as a suggestive term but is far enough removed from the merely descriptive not to be vulnerable to possible attack as being merely descriptive rather than suggestive. [Citation.]

Miller's Position   Although Miller argued in the District Court that "LITE" was suggestive, and persuaded the District Court that this was so with respect to the quality of being reduced in calories, it conceded in oral argument before us that the choice is between (1) generic or common descriptive and (2) merely descriptive. Miller argues that light beer is not a "genus," indeed that "light," as an adjective, cannot be a generic or common descriptive term, and that it is a merely descriptive term that has acquired a secondary meaning.

An Adjective as a Generic Term   The fact that "light" is an adjective does not prevent it from being a generic or common descriptive word. [Citations.] This must be the law, given the reason for the rule that precludes appropriation of a common descriptive word, *viz.*, otherwise "a competitor could not describe his goods as what they are." [Citation]. Ordinarily, as here, the adjective which is sought to be appropriated in its generic sense as a trademark will be a part of a name. [Citation.] If "light beer" is a generic name, then "light" is a generic word when used as part of that name.

"Light" Is Generic   The record before us (although less complete than that in at least one of the other pending cases) and facts of which we may take judicial notice, including generally accepted English usage, enable us to conclude that "light" is a generic or common descriptive term when used with "beer."

"Light" has been widely used in the beer industry for many years to describe a beer's color, flavor, body, or alcoholic content, or a combination of these or similar characteristics. The use of that word by Heileman and other brewers long antedated either Miller's or Meister Brau's use of "LITE." The definition given in *Webster's Third New International Dictionary, supra,* at 1308, of "light" as an adjective includes the following:

> "10 *of a beverage* a. having a comparatively low alcoholic content ([light] wines and beers) b. having a low concentration of flavoring congenerics: characterized by a relatively mild flavor: not heavy 11a: capable of being easily digested (a [light] soup). . . ."

* * *

Similar definitions and usage are found in reference works on chemical technology, industry publications, and magazines and newspapers generally. Indeed, state statutes even use "light beer" as a generic or common descriptive term. "Light" is clearly a common descriptive word when used with beer.

"Light" is also a common descriptive word in other similar contexts. Miller's president testified in a deposition which has been made part of this record that Miller chose the word "LITE" for its low-calorie beer because of its desire to capitalize on the trend of "consumer products going lighter all over the world, be it foods, be it whiskeys, be it cigarettes," as well as to "convey the message that it would be lighter in taste" and to communicate "the conception of a less filling product." Miller's parent company, Philip Morris, Inc., registered "Light" (Registration No. 878,062) and used that word as a brand name for cigarettes (Marlboro Light). Judge Stewart held the word to be descriptive and ordered the registration cancelled in [citation], a decision from which no appeal was taken. The word is also used by Pepsico, Inc. for "Pepsi Light" a soft drink described as having "half the calories out."

Miller argues that it uses the word as the name for "less filling, low calorie" beer, and that "light" has not heretofore been used in that sense. This argument fails for two reasons. First, "less filling" means essentially light in body and taste and not oppressive to the stomach, which is a common descriptive meaning of "light"; and, as Miller conceded in its brief, the caloric content of beer depends primarily on alcoholic content. Second, even if Miller had given its light beer a characteristic not found in other light beers, it could not acquire the exclusive right to use the common descriptive word "light" as a trademark for that beer. Other brewers

> whose beers have qualities that make them "light" as that word has commonly been used remain free to call their beer "light." Otherwise a manufacturer could remove a common descriptive word from the public domain by investing his goods with an additional quality, thus gaining the exclusive right to call his wine "rose," his whiskey "blended," or his bread "white."
>
> The word "light," including its phonetic equivalent "lite," being a generic or common descriptive term as applied to beer, could not be exclusively appropriated by Miller as a trademark, "despite whatever promotional effort [Miller] may have expended to exploit it." [Citations.] Because probability of success cannot be established, other issues argued by the parties need not be decided, and the preliminary injunction must be reversed.

Infringement and Remedies

Infringement of a mark occurs when a person without authorization uses an identical or substantially indistinguishable mark that is likely to cause confusion, to cause mistake, or to deceive. Intent to cause confusion among purchasers is not required, nor is proof of actual confusion. Infringement occurs if an appreciable number of ordinarily prudent purchasers are *likely* to be misled or confused as to the source of the goods or services. In deciding whether infringement has occurred, the courts consider various factors, including the strength of the mark, the intent of the unauthorized user, the degree of similarity between the two marks, the relation between the two products or services identified by the marks, and the marketing channels through which the goods or services are purchased.

The Lanham Act provides several remedies for infringement: (1) injunctive relief, (2) an accounting for profits, (3) damages, (4) attorney's fees in exceptional cases, and (5) costs. In assessing profits, the plaintiff has to prove only the gross sales made by the defendant; the defendant has the burden of proving any costs to be deducted in determining profits. If the court finds that the amount of recovery based on profits is either inadequate or excessive, the court may, in its discretion, award an amount it determines to be just. In assessing damages, the court *may* award up to three times the actual damages according to the circumstances of the case.

When an infringement is knowing and intentional, the court *shall* award attorneys' fees plus the greater of treble profits or treble damages, unless there are extenuating circumstances. Moreover, where a *counterfeit* mark is intentionally and knowingly used, criminal sanctions may be imposed, and goods bearing the counterfeit mark may be destroyed. Criminal sanctions include a fine of up to $250,000, imprisonment of up to five years, or both. If the offense is a repeat offense, the limits are $1 million and fifteen years, respectively. If the person infringing is not an individual, such as a corporation, the fine may be up to $1 million for a first offense and up to $5 million for a repeat offense.

TRADE NAMES

A **trade name** is any name used to identify a business, vocation, or occupation. Descriptive and generic words, and personal and generic names, although not proper trademarks, may become protected as trade names upon acquiring a special significance in the trade. This special significance is frequently referred to as a "secondary meaning" of the name acquired as the result of continuing and extended use in connection with specific goods or services whereby the name has lost its primary meaning to a substantial number of purchasers or users of the goods or services. Although trade names may *not* be federally registered under the Lanham Act, trade names are protected, and a person who palms off his goods or services by using the trade name of another is liable in damages and also may be enjoined from doing so.

COPYRIGHTS

Copyright is a form of protection provided by Federal law to authors of original works which, under Section 102 of the Copyright Act, include literary works, musical works, dramatic works, pantomimes, choreographic works, pictorial, graphic and sculptural works, motion picture and other audiovisual works, and sound recordings. This listing is illustrative and not exhaustive, as the act extends copyright protection to "original works of authorship in any tangible medium of expression, now known or later developed." In 1980 the Copyright Act was amended to extend copyright protection to computer programs. On May 1, 1989, the United States joined the Berne Convention, which is an international treaty protecting copyrighted works.

In no case does copyright protection for an original work of authorship include any idea, procedure, process, system, method of operation, concept, principle, or discovery, regardless of the form in which it is described, explained, illustrated, or embodied in such work. Copyright protection extends to an *original expression* of an idea. For example, the idea of interfamily feuding cannot be copyrighted, but a particular expression of that idea in the form of a novel, drama, movie, or opera may be copyrighted.

Procedure

Applications for copyright are filed with the Register of Copyrights, Copyright Office, Library of Congress, Washington, D.C. Registra-

tion of the copyright is not required, as copyright protection begins as soon as the work is fixed in a tangible medium. Registration is, nonetheless, advisable, as it is a condition of certain remedies for copyright infringement and some rights can be permanently lost by failure to register soon enough. When a work is published, a notice of copyright should be placed on all publicly distributed copies so as to give reasonable notice of the claim of copyright.

Rights

Copyright protection subsists in most instances for a period of the author's life plus an additional fifty years. The Copyright Act gives the owner of the copyright the exclusive right, and to authorize others, to reproduce the copyrighted work, prepare derivative works based upon the copyrighted work, distribute copies or phonorecords of the copyrighted work, perform the copyrighted work publicly, and display the copyrighted work publicly.

These broad rights are subject, however, to several limitations, the most important of which are "compulsory licenses" and "fair use." **Compulsory licenses** permit certain limited uses of copyrighted material upon the payment of specified royalties and compliance with statutory conditions. The Copyright Act provides that the fair use of a copyrighted work for purposes such as criticism, comment, news reporting, teaching (including multiple copies for classroom use), scholarship, or research, is *not* an infringement of copyright. In determining whether the use made of a work in any particular case is a fair use, the following factors are considered: (1) the purpose and character of the use including whether such use is of a commercial nature or is for nonprofit educational purposes; (2) the nature of the copyrighted work; (3) the amount and substantiality of the portion used in relation to the copyrighted work as a whole; and (4) the effect of the use upon the potential market for or value of the copyrighted work.

SONY CORP. OF AMERICA v. UNIVERSAL CITY STUDIOS, INC.
Supreme Court of the United States, 1984.
464 U.S. 417, 104 S.Ct. 774, 78 L.Ed.2d 574.

Facts: Sony Corporation manufactures and sells home video recorders, specifically the Betamax video tape recorders (VTRs). Universal City Studios, Inc. (Universal), owns the copyrights on some programs aired on commercially sponsored television. Individual Betamax owners frequently used the device to record some of Universal's copyrighted television programs for their own noncommercial use. Universal brought suit, claiming that the sale of the Betamax VTRs to the general public violated its rights under the Copyright Act. It sought no relief against any Betamax consumer. Instead, Universal sued Sony for contributory infringement of its copyrights, seeking money damages, an equitable accounting of profits, and an injunction against the manufacture and sale of Betamax VTRs. The district court entered judgment for Sony. The appellate court reversed and held Sony liable for contributory infringement.

Decision: Judgment of appellate court reversed.

Opinion: **Stevens, J.**   Article I, Sec 8 of the Constitution provides that:

> The Congress shall have Power . . . to Promote the Progress of Science and useful Arts, by securing for limited Times to Authors and Inventors the exclusive Right to their respective Writing and Discoveries.

The monopoly privileges that Congress may authorize are neither unlimited nor primarily designed to provide a special private benefit. Rather, the limited grant is a means by which an important public purpose may be achieved. It is intended to motivate the creative activity of authors and inventors by the provision of a special reward and to allow the public access to the products of their genius after the limited period of exclusive control has expired.

* * *

As the text of the Constitution makes plain, it is Congress that has been assigned the task of defining the scope of the limited monopoly that should be granted to authors or to inventors in order to give the public appropriate access to their work product. * * *

* * *

The judiciary's reluctance to expand the protections afforded by the copyright without explicit legislative guidance is a recurring theme. [Citations.] * * *

In a case like this, in which Congress has not plainly marked our course, we must be circumspect in construing the scope of rights created by a legislative enactment which never contemplated such a calculus of interests. * * *

Copyright protection "subsists . . . in original works of authorship fixed in any tangible medium of expression." [Citation.] This protection has never accorded the copyright owner complete control over all possible uses of his work. Rather, the Copyright Act grants the copyright holder "exclusive" rights to use and to authorize the use of his work in five qualified ways, including reproduction of the copyrighted work in copies. [Citation.] All reproductions of the work, however, are not within the exclusive domain of the copyright owner; some are in the public domain. Any individual may reproduce a copyrighted work for a "fair use;" the copyright owner does not possess the exclusive right to such a use. [Citation.]

"Anyone who violates any of the exclusive rights of the copyright owner," that is, anyone who trespasses into his exclusive domain by using or authorizing the use of the copyrighted work in one of the five ways set forth in the statute, "is an infringer of the copyright." [Citation.] Conversely, anyone who is authorized by the copyright owner to use the copyrighted work in a way specified in the statute or who makes a fair use of the work is not an infringer of the copyright with respect to such use.

The Copyright Act provides the owner of a copyright with a potent arsenal of remedies against an infringer of his work, including an injunction to restrain the infringer from violating his rights, the impoundment and destruction of all reproductions of his work made in violation of his rights, a recovery of his actual damages and any additional profits realized by the infringer or a recovery of statutory damages, and attorney's fees. [Citation.]

The two respondents in this case do not seek relief against the Betamax users who have allegedly infringed their copyrights. * * * It is, however, the taping of respondents' own copyrighted programs that provides them with standing to charge Sony with contributory infringement. To prevail, they have the burden of proving that users of the Betamax have infringed their copyrights and that Sony should be held responsible for that infringement.

The Copyright Act does not expressly render anyone liable for infringement committed by another. * * * The absence of such express language in the copyright statute does not preclude the imposition of liability for copyright infringements on certain parties who have not themselves engaged in the infringing activity. For vicarious liability is imposed in virtually all areas of the law, and the concept of contributory infringement is merely a species of the broader problem of identifying the circumstances in which it is just to hold one individual accountable for the actions of another.

* * *

* * * [A]nd the label "contributory infringement" has been applied in a number of lower court copyright cases involving an ongoing relationship between the direct infringer and the contributory infringer at the time the infringing conduct occurred. In such cases, as in other situations in which the imposition of vicarious liability is manifestly just, the "contributory" infringer was in a position to control the use of copyrighted works by others and had authorized the use without permission from the copyright owner. This case, however, plainly does not fall in that category. The only contact between Sony and the users of the Betamax that is disclosed by this record occurred at the moment of sale. * * *

If vicarious liability is to be imposed on petitioners in this case, it must rest on the fact that they have sold equipment with constructive knowledge of the fact that their customers may use that equipment to make unauthorized copies of copyrighted material. There is no precedent in the law of copyright for the imposition of vicarious liability on such a theory. * * *

* * *

* * * Accordingly, the sale of copying equipment, like the sale of other articles of commerce, does not constitute contributory infringement if the product is widely used for legitimate, unobjectionable purposes. Indeed, it need merely be capable of substantial noninfringing uses.

* * *

* * * In this case, the record makes it perfectly clear that there are many important producers of national and local television programs who find nothing objectionable about the enlargement in the size of the television audience that results from the practice of time-shifting for private home use.

Even authorized uses of a copyrighted work are not necessarily infringing. An unlicensed use of the copyright is not an infringement unless it conflicts with one of the specific exclusive rights conferred by the copyright statute. [Citation.] Moreover, the definition of exclusive rights in § 106 of the present Act is prefaced by the words "subject to sections 107 through 118." Those sections describe a variety of uses of copyrighted material that "are not infringements of copyright notwithstanding the provisions of § 106." The most pertinent in this case is § 107, the legislative endorsement of the doctrine of "fair use."

That section identifies various factors that enable a Court to apply an "equitable rule of reason" analysis to particular claims of infringement. * * *

* * *

* * * A challenge to a noncommercial use of a copyrighted work requires proof either that the particular use is harmful, or that if it should become widespread, it would adversely affect the potential market for the copyrighted work.

* * *

When these factors are all weighed in the "equitable rule of reason" balance, we must conclude that this record amply supports the District Court's conclusion that home time-shifting is fair use. In light of the findings of the District Court regarding the state of the empirical data, it is clear that the Court of Appeals erred in holding that the statute as presently written bars such conduct.

In summary, the record and findings of the District Court lead us to two conclusions. First, Sony demonstrated a significant likelihood that substantial numbers of copyright holders who license their works for broadcast on free television would not object to having their broadcasts time-shifted by private viewers. And second, respondents failed to demonstrate that time-shifting would cause any likelihood of non-minimal harm to the potential market for, or the value of, their copyrighted works. The Betamax is, therefore, capable of substantial noninfringing uses. Sony's sale of such equipment to the general public does not constitute contributory infringement of respondent's copyrights.

> The direction of Art I is that *Congress* shall have the power to promote the progress of science and the useful arts. When, as here, the Constitution is permissive, the sign of how far Congress has chosen to go can come only from Congress. Deepsouth Packing Co. v. Laitram Corp., [citation.]

One may search the Copyright Act in vain for any sign that the elected representatives of the millions of people who watch television every day have made it unlawful to copy a program for later viewing at home, or have enacted a flat prohibition against the sale of machines that make such copying possible.

It may well be that Congress will take a fresh look at this new technology, just as it so often has examined other innovations in the past. But it is not our job to apply laws that have not yet been written. Applying the copyright statute, as it now reads, to the fact as they have been developed in this case, the judgment of the Court of Appeals must be reversed.

Ownership

The ownership of a copyright may be transferred in whole or in part by conveyance, will, or intestate succession. A transfer of copyright ownership, other than by operation of law, is not valid unless a note or memorandum of the transfer is in writing and signed by the owner of the rights conveyed or the owner's duly authorized agent.

Ownership of a copyright, or of any of the exclusive rights under a copyright, is distinct from ownership of any material object in which the work is embodied. Transfer of ownership of any material object, including the copy or phonorecord in which the work is first fixed, does not of itself convey any rights in the copyrighted work embodied in the object; nor, in the absence of an agreement, does transfer of ownership of a copyright or of any exclusive rights under a copyright convey property rights in any material object. Thus, the purchase of this textbook does not affect the publisher's copyright nor does it authorize the purchaser to make and sell copies of the book.

Infringement and Remedies

Infringement occurs whenever somebody exercises the rights exclusively reserved for the copyright owner without authorization. Infringement need *not* be intentional. To prove infringement, the plaintiff must establish that he owns the copyright and that the defendant violated one or more of the plaintiff's exclusive rights under the copyright.

In order to sue for infringement, the copyright must be registered with the Copyright Office. If an infringement occurs *after* registration, the following remedies are available(1) injunction; (2) impoundment and possible destruction of infringing articles; (3) actual damages plus profits made by the infringer that are additional to those damages *or* statutory damages of at least $500 but no more than $20,000 ($100,000 if the infringement is willful) according to what the court determines to be just; (4) costs and, in the court's discretion, reasonable attorney's fees to the prevailing party; or (5) criminal penalties of a fine of up to $10,000 or up to one year's imprisonment for willful infringement for purposes of commercial advantage or private gain. The Piracy and Counterfeiting Amendments Act of 1982 imposes harsher punishments for large-scale piracy: $250,000 fine and five years for pirating 1,000 phonorecords or 65 films within 180 days.

PATENTS

A **patent** is a grant by the Federal government of a monopoly right to an inventor to make, use, or sell the invention to the absolute exclusion of others for the period of the patent, which currently is seventeen years. The owner of the patent may also profit by licensing others to use the patent on a royalty basis. The patent may not be renewed, and upon expiration the invention enters the "public domain" and anyone may then use it.

Patentability

The Patent Act specifies those inventions that may be patented: any new and useful process, machine, manufacture, or composition of matter or any new and useful improvement thereof. Thus, naturally occurring substances are not patentable, as the invention must be made or modified by humans. For example, the discovery of an existing bacteria with useful properties is *not* patentable, whereas the manufacture of a human-made, genetically engineered bacterium is patentable. By the same token, laws of nature, principles, systems of bookkeeping, fundamental truths, methods of calculation, and ideas are not patentable. Accordingly, Einstein could not patent his law that $E = mc^2$, nor could Newton have patented the law of gravity. Similarly, isolated computer programs are not patentable, although, as we mentioned above, they may be copyrighted.

To be patentable, the process, machine, manufacture, or composition of matter must meet three criteria:

1. novelty,
2. utility, and
3. nonobviousness.

DIAMOND, COMMISSIONER OF PATENTS AND TRADEMARKS v. CHAKRABARTY

Supreme Court of the United States, 1980.
447 U.S. 303, 100 S.Ct. 2204, 65 L.Ed.2d 144.

Facts: In 1972, Chakrabarty, a microbiologist, filed a patent application, assigned to the General Electric Co., for an invention of a bacterium. This human-made, genetically engineered bacterium is capable of breaking down multiple components of crude oil. Because of this property, which is possessed by no naturally occurring bacteria, Chakrabarty's invention was believed to have significant value for the treatment of oil spills.

Chakrabarty's patent claims were of three types: first, process claims for the method of producing the bacteria; second, claims for an inoculum, and third, claims to the bacteria themselves. The patent examiner allowed the claims falling into the first two categories, but rejected claims for the bacteria. His decision rested on two grounds: (1) that micro-organisms are "products of nature," and (2) that as living things they are not patentable subject matter under Section 101 of the Patent Act. Chakrabarty appealed to the Patent Office Board of Appeals, which affirmed the examiner. The Court of Customs and Patent Appeals reversed.

Decision: The decision of the Court of Customs and Patent Appeals affirmed.

Opinion: **Burger, C. J.**   The Constitution grants Congress broad power to legislate to "promote the Progress of Science and useful Arts, by securing for limited Times to Authors and Inventors the exclusive Right to their respective Writings and Discoveries." Art. I, § 8, cl. 8. The patent laws promote this progress by offering inventors exclusive rights for a limited period as an incentive for their inventiveness and research efforts. [Citations.] The authority of Congress is exercised in the hope that "[t]he productive effort thereby fostered will have a positive effect on society through the introduction of new products and processes of manufacture into the economy, and the emanations by way of increased employment and better lives for our citizens." [Citation.]

The question before us in this case is a narrow one of statutory interpretation requiring us to construe § 101 [of the Patent Act], which provides:

> Whoever invents or discovers any new and useful process, machine, manufacture, or composition of matter, or any new and useful improvement thereof, may obtain a patent therefor, subject to the conditions and requirements of this title.

Specifically, we must determine whether respondent's micro-organism constitutes a "manufacture" or "composition of matter" within the meaning of the statute.

In cases of statutory construction we begin, of course, with the language of the statute. [Citation.] And "unless otherwise defined, words will be interpreted as taking their ordinary, contemporary, common meaning." [Citation.] We have also cautioned that courts "should not read into the patent laws limitations and conditions which the legislature has not expressed." [Citation.]

Guided by these canons of construction, this Court has read the term "manufacture" in § 101 in accordance with its dictionary definition to mean "the production of articles for use from raw or prepared materials by giving to these materials new forms, qualities, properties, or combinations, whether by handlabor or by machinery." [Citation.] Similarly, "composition of matter" has been construed consistent with its common usage to include "all compositions of two or more substances and . . . all composite articles, whether they be the results of chemical union, or of mechanical mixture, or whether they be gases, fluids, powders or solids." [Citation.] In choosing such expansive terms as "manufacture" and "composition of matter," modified by the comprehensive "any," Congress plainly contemplated that the patent laws would be given wide scope.

* * *

This is not to suggest that § 101 has no limits or that it embraces every discovery. The laws of nature, physical phenomena, and abstract ideas have been held not patentable. [Citations.] Thus, a new mineral discovered in the earth or a new plant found in the wild is not patentable subject matter. Likewise, Einstein could not patent his celebrated law that $E = mc^2$; nor could Newton have patented the law of gravity. Such discoveries are "manifestations of . . . nature, free to all men and reserved exclusively to none." [Citation.]

Judged in this light, respondent's micro-organism plainly qualifies as patentable subject matter. His claim is not to a hitherto unknown natural phenomenon, but to a nonnaturally occurring manufacture or composition of matter—a product of human ingenuity "having a distinctive name, character [and] use." [Citation.] The point is under-scored dramatically by comparison of the invention here with that in *Funk*. There, the patentee had discovered that there existed in nature certain species of root-nodule bacteria which did not exert a mutually inhibitive effect on each other. He used that discovery to produce a mixed culture capable of inoculating the seeds of leguminous plants. Concluding that the patentee had discovered "only some of the handiwork of nature," the Court ruled the product nonpatentable:

Each of the species of root-nodule bacteria contained in the package infects the same group of leguminous plants which it always infected. No species acquires a different use. The combination of species produces no new bacteria, no change in the six species of bacteria, and no enlargement of the range of their utility. Each species has the same effect it always had. The bacteria perform in their natural way. Their use in combination does not improve in any way their natural functioning. They serve the ends nature originally provided and act quite independently of any effort of the patentee." [Citation.]

Here, by contrast, the patentee has produced a new bacterium with markedly different characteristics from any found in nature and one having the potential for significant utility. His discovery is not nature's handiwork, but his own; accordingly it is patentable subject matter under § 101.

* * *

We have emphasized in the recent past that "[o]ur individual appraisal of the wisdom or unwisdom of a particular [legislative] course . . . is to be put aside in the process of interpreting a statute." [Citation.] Our task, rather, is the narrow one of determining what Congress meant by the words it used in the statute; once that is done our powers are exhausted. Congress is free to amend § 101 so as to exclude from patent protection organisms produced by genetic engineering. Cf. 42 U.S.C. § 2181(a), exempting from patent protection inventions "useful solely in the utilization of special nuclear material or atomic energy in an atomic weapon." Or it may choose to craft a statute specifically designed for such living things. But, until Congress takes such action, this Court must construe the language of § 101 as it is. The language of that section fairly embraces respondent's invention.

LAW IN THE NEWS

A Not-So-Nice Greeting
Hallmark Challenges Competitors with Look-alikes

In the early '70s, as the hippie era drew to a close, Susan Polis Schutz and her husband, Stephen, decided to translate the flowery sentiments of the peace movement into greeting cards. Today, Blue Mountain Arts, Inc., in Boulder, Colo., makes some of the industry's top-selling cards. Its Water-Color Feelings and Airebrush Feelings designs, featuring poetry by Susan and pastel illustrations by Stephen, pioneered a new greeting-card category: the "nonoccasion, highly emotional message." Last April, while visiting a California gift shop, Susan was surprised to discover so few of her cards in the racks. She picked up one card, only to discover it wasn't a Blue Mountain Arts product but a Hallmark look-alike. "That's when I went into shock," she says.

Blue Mountain Arts didn't stay in shock for long; the company filed a $50 million lawsuit against Hallmark charging copyright infringement and unfair competition. Last week in federal court Blue Mountain asked for a restraining order preventing Hallmark from marketing look-alike cards—a decision will be issued shortly. Two other card manufacturers have also filed multimillion-dollar suits. These small companies argue that their very survival is at stake. With more than $1.5 billion in revenues, Kansas City-based Hallmark Card Inc. controls 40 percent of the greeting-card industry. But the company lost out on the fast growth of the "alternative" market—the contemporary, humorous and emotional cards favored by the baby-boom generation and developed by smaller companies. Recently Hallmark struck back with its largest card introduction ever, flooding the market with more than 800 alternative-style designs under the names Personal Touch and Shoebox Greetings (which the company labels "a tiny little division of Hallmark").

For its part, Hallmark denies that it copies any designs. In any case, sales of its new cards far exceed projections. No wonder. Through its Gold Crown program, the company offers special incentives, such as interest-free loans, to Hallmark retailers who agree not to display competitors' cards on racks purchased from Hallmark. Some card companies say Hallmark even bought up rival cards in order to make room for its own lines. (Hallmark will not comment on the charge.) In Denver three Hallmark shops filed lawsuits alleging the company threatened to end their licensing agreements if they did not remove all rival products from their stores. Recycled Paper Products, makers of a popular card line designed by Sandra Boynton, ran ads in the trade press denouncing the incentives and the imitative products as "The Hallmark Hall of Shame."

Others view Hallmark's program as smart business strategy. "Hallmark has successfully recaptured market share," says analyst E. Gray Glass III of Kidder Peabody. American Greetings and Gibson Greetings, the other big players in the industry, agree: they have plans for their own new card lines. Glass predicts a shakeout among smaller companies, but he expects them to respond quickly with new card designs. Even so, the bitter feelings created by Hallmark's strategy may outlast its retail sentiments. Diane Pell, owner of a gift store in Kansas City, sold samples of her offbeat cards to Hallmark employees for years. Today she has a sign outside her shop that warns: "Hallmark researchers and other Hallmark departments not appreciated in this store."

Penelope Wang
From *Newsweek*, Nov. 3, 1986. © 1986, Newsweek, Inc. All rights reserved. Reprinted by permission.

FIGURE 40-1 Intellectual Property

	Trade Secrets	Trade Symbols	Copyright	Patents
What is Protected	information	mark	work of authorship	invention
Rights Protected	use or sell	use or sell	reproduce, prepare derivative works, distribute, perform, and display	make, use, or sell
Duration	until disclosed	until abandoned	usually author's life plus 50 years	17 years
Federally Protected	no	yes	yes	yes
Requirements for Protection	valuable secret	distinctive	original and fixed	novel, useful, and nonobvious

Procedure

A patent is issued by the United States Patent and Trademark Office upon the basis of a patent application containing a *specification*, which describes how the invention works, and *claims*, which describe the features of the invention that make it patentable. The applicant must be the inventor. Before granting a patent, the Patent Office makes a careful and thorough examination of the prior art and determines whether the submitted invention has novelty (does not conflict with a prior pending application or a previously issued patent), utility, and is nonobvious. An application for a patent is confidential and its contents will not be divulged by the Patent Office. This confidentiality ends upon the granting of the patent.

If the application is rejected, the applicant may apply for reexamination. If the application is again rejected, the applicant may appeal to the Patent and Trademark Office's Board of Appeals, and from there to the Federal courts.

Infringement

Anyone who, without permission, makes, uses, or sells a patented invention is a **direct infringer**. Good faith or ignorance is *not* a defense to direct infringement. A person who actively encourages another to make, use, or sell a patented invention without permission is an **indirect infringer**. A person is a **contributory infringer** if he knowingly sells or supplies a part or component of a patented invention, unless the component is a staple or commodity or it is suitable for a substantial noninfringing use. Good faith and ignorance *are* defenses to contributory infringement.

Remedies

The remedies for infringement under the Patent Act are (1) injunctive relief; (2) damages adequate to compensate the plaintiff but "in no event less than a reasonable royalty for the use made of the invention by the infringer"; (3) treble damages when appropriate; (4) attorney's fees in exceptional cases such as knowing infringement; and (5) costs.

CHAPTER SUMMARY

Trade Secrets	**Definition of Trade Secret** commercially valuable, secret information **Protection** owner of a trade secret may obtain damages or injunctive relief when it is misappropriated (wrongfully used) by an employee or a competitor

Trade Symbols	**Types of Trade Symbols** 　■ *Trademark* distinctive symbol, word, or design on a good that is used to identify the manufacturer 　■ *Service Mark* distinctive symbol, word, or design that is used to identify the services of a provider 　■ *Certification Mark* distinctive symbol, word, or design used with goods or services to certify specific characteristics 　■ *Collective Mark* distinctive symbol used to indicate membership in an organization **Registration** to be registered and thus protected by the Lanham Act, a mark must be distinctive and not immoral, deceptive, or scandalous **Infringement** occurs when a person without authorization uses a substantially indistinguishable mark that is likely to cause confusion, mistake, or deception **Remedies** the Lanham Act provides the following remedies for infringement: injunctive relief, profits, damages, costs, and in exceptional cases, attorney's fees

Trade Names	**Definition of Trade Name** any name used to identify a business, vocation, or occupation **Protection** may not be registered under the Lanham Act but infringement is prohibited **Remedies** damages and injunctions are available if infringement occurs

Copyrights	**Definition of Copyright** exclusive right, usually for the author's life plus 50 years, to original works of authorship **Procedure** registration is not required but provides additional remedies for infringement **Rights** copyright protection gives the exclusive right to (1) reproduce the copyrighted work (2) prepare derivative works based on the work, (3) distribute copies of the work, and (4) perform or display the work publicly **Infringement** occurs when someone exercises the copyright owner's rights without authorization **Remedies** if infringement occurs after registration, the following remedies are available: (1) injunction, (2) impoundment and possible destruction of infringing articles, (3) actual damages plus profits or statutory damages, (4) costs, and (5) criminal penalties

Patents	Definition of Patent the exclusive right for 17 years to an invention
	Patentability to be patentable, the invention must be (1) novel, (2) useful, and (3) not obvious
	Procedure patents are issued upon application to and after examination by the U.S. Patent and Trademark Office
	Infringement occurs when anyone without permission makes, uses, or sells a patented invention
	Remedies for infringement of a patent are (1) injunctive relief, (2) damages, (3) treble damages where appropriate, (4) attorney's fees, and (5) costs

QUESTIONS

1. Explain what is protected by trade secrets and how they may be infringed.
2. Distinguish among the various types of trade symbols.
3. Explain the extent to which trade names are protected.
4. Explain what is protected by copyrights and the remedies for infringement.
5. Explain what is protected by patents and the remedies for infringement.

PROBLEMS

1. Keller, a professor of legal studies at Rhodes University, is a diligent instructor. Late one night while reading a newly published, copyrighted treatise of 1800 pages written by Gilbert, he came across a three-page section discussing the subject matter he was going to cover in class the next day. Keller considered the treatment to be illuminating and therefore photocopied the three pages and distributed the copies to his class. One of Keller's students is a second cousin of Gilbert, the author of the treatise, and she showed Gilbert the copies. Instead of being flattered, Gilbert sued Keller for copyright infringement. Decision?

2. A conceived a secret process for the continuous freeze drying of food stuffs and related products and constructed a small pilot plant which practiced the process. A lacked the financing necessary to develop the commercial potential of the process and in hopes of obtaining a contract for its development and the payment of royalties, disclosed it in confidence to B, a coffee manufacturer, who signed an agreement not to disclose it to anyone else. At the same time, A signed an agreement not to disclose the process to any other person as long as A and B were considering a contract for its development.

Upon disclosure, B became extremely interested and offered to pay A the sum of $1,750,000 if, upon further development, the process proved to be commercially feasible. While negotiations between A and B were in progress, C, a competitor of B, learned of the existence of the process and requested a disclosure from A who informed C that the process could not be disclosed to anyone unless negotiations with B were broken off. C offered to pay A $2,500,000 for the process provided it met certain defined objective performance criteria. A contract was prepared and executed between A and C on this basis without any prior disclosure of the process to C. Upon the making of this contract, A rejected the offer of B. The process was thereupon disclosed to C and demonstration runs of the pilot plant in the presence of representatives of C were conducted under varying conditions. After three weeks of experimental demonstrations, compiling of data and analyses of results, C informed A that the process did not meet the performance criteria in the contract and that for this reason C was rejecting the process. Two years later C placed on the market freeze-dried coffee which resembled in color, appearance, and texture the product of A's pilot plant. What are the rights of the parties?

3. B, a chemist, was employed by A, a manufacturer, to work on a secret process for A's product under an exclusive three-year contract. C, a salesman, was employed by A on a week-to-week basis. B and C resigned the employment with A and accepted employment in their respective capacities with D, a rival manufacturer. C began soliciting patronage from A's former customers whose names he had memorized. What are the rights of the parties in (a) a suit by A to enjoin B from working for D; and (b) a suit by A to enjoin C from soliciting A's customers?

4. Conrad and Darby were competitors in the business of dehairing raw cashmere, the fleece of certain Asiatic goats. Dehairing is the process of separating the commercially valuable soft down from the matted mass of raw fleece which also contains long

coarse guard hairs and other impurities. Machinery for this process is not readily available on the open market. Each company in the business designed and built its own machinery and kept the nature of its process secret. Conrad contracted with Lawton, owner of a small machine shop, to build and install new improved dehairing machinery of increased efficiency for which Conrad furnished designs, drawings, and instructions. Lawton knew that the design of the machinery was confidential, and agreed that he would manufacture the machinery exclusively for plaintiff and that he would not reproduce the machinery or any of its essential parts for any one else. Darby purchased from Lawton a copy of the dehairing machinery which Conrad had specially designed. Decision?

5. X, having filed locally an affidavit required under the "Assumed Name" statute, has been operating and advertising his exclusive toy store for 20 years in Centerville, Illinois. His advertising has consisted of large signs on his premises reading "The Toy Mart". B, after operating a store in Chicago under the name of "The Chicago Toy Mart" relocated in Centerville, Illinois, and erected a large sign reading "TOY MART" with the word "Centerville" being written underneath in substantially smaller letters. Thereafter, the sales of X declined, and many of X's customers patronized B's store thinking it to be a branch of B's business. What are the rights of the parties?

6. (a) Ryan Corporation manufactures and sells a variety of household cleaning products in interstate commerce. On national television Ryan falsely advertises that its laundry liquid is biodegradable. Has Ryan violated the Lanham Act?

(b) Gibbons, Inc. and Marvin Corporation are manufacturers who sell a variety of household cleaning products in interstate commerce. On national television Gibbons states that its laundry liquid is biodegradable and that Marvin's is not. In fact, both products are biodegradable. Has Gibbons violated the Lanham Act?

7. George McCoy of Florida has been manufacturing and distributing a cheese cake for over five years, labeling his product with a picture of a cheese cake which serves as a background for a Florida bathing beauty under which is written the slogan "McCoy All Spice Florida Cheese Cake." George McCoy has not registered his trademark. Subsequently, Leo McCoy of California begins manufacturing a similar product on the West coast using a label in appearance similar to that of George McCoy, containing a picture of a Hollywood star, and the words "McCoy's All Spice Cheese Cake." Leo McCoy begins marketing his products in the Eastern United States, using labels with the word "Florida" added as in George McCoy's label. Leo McCoy has registered his product under the Federal Trademark Act. To what relief, if any, is George McCoy entitled?

COMPUTER RESEARCH PROBLEMS

1. The Coca-Cola Company manufactures a carbonated beverage, Coke, made from coca leaves and cola nuts. The Koke Company of America introduced a similar product into the beverage market named Koke. The Coca-Cola Company brought a trade-mark infringement action against Koke. Coke claimed unfair competition within the beverage business due to Koke's imitation of the Coca-Cola product and Koke's attempt to reap the benefit of consumer identification with the Coke name. Decision?

2. Vuitton, a French corporation, manufactures high quality handbags, luggage, and accessories. Crown Handbags, a New York corporation, manufactures and distributes ladies' handbags. Vuitton handbags are sold exclusively in expensive department stores and distribution is strictly controlled to maintain a certain retail selling price. The Vuitton bags bear a registered trademark and a distinctive design. Crown's handbags appear identical to the Vuitton bags but are of inferior quality. Vuitton sues Crown for manufacturing counterfeit handbags and selling them at a discount. Decision?

3. T.G.I. Friday's, a New York corporation and registered service-mark, entered into an exclusive licensing agreement with Tiffany which allowed Tiffany to open a Friday's restaurant in Jackson, Mississippi. International Restaurant Group, operated by the owners of Tiffany, applied for a license to open a Friday's in Baton Rouge, Louisiana but was refused. International then opened another restaurant, called E.L. Saturday's or Ever Lovin' Saturday's, in Baton Rouge which had the same type of menu and decor as Friday's. Friday's sues International for trademark infringement. Decision?

41 ANTITRUST

The economic community is best served in normal times by free competition in trade and industry. It is in the public interest that quality, price, and service in an open, competitive market for goods and services be determining factors in the business rivalry for the customer's dollar. Antitrust law attempts to assure such free and fair competition.

The common law has traditionally favored free and open competition in the marketplace and has held agreements and contracts in restraint of trade illegal and unenforceable. In addition, some States during the 1800s had enacted antitrust statutes but in the latter half of the nineteenth century it became apparent that concentrations of economic power in the form of "trusts" and "combinations" were too powerful and widespread to be effectively curbed and controlled by State action. This prompted the Congress in 1890 to enact the Sherman Antitrust Act, which was the first Federal statute in this field. Since then, Congress has enacted other antitrust statutes, including the Clayton Act, the Robinson-Patman Act, and the Federal Trade Commission Act. These statutes prohibit anticompetitive practices and seek to prevent unreasonable concentration of economic power because they stifle or weaken competition.

SHERMAN ANTITRUST ACT

Section 1 of the Sherman Act prohibits contracts, combinations, and conspiracies that restrain trade, while Section 2 outlaws monopolies and attempts to monopolize. Failure to comply with either section is a criminal violation and subjects the offender to fine or impris-

onment or both. Individual offenders are subject to imprisonment of up to three years and fines of up to $100,000, while corporate offenders are subject to fines of up to $1,000,000. Moreover, the Federal district courts are empowered to issue injunctions restraining violations, and anyone injured by a violation is entitled to recover in a civil action **treble damages** (that is, three times the amount of the actual loss sustained). It is the duty of United States Department of Justice and the Federal Trade Commission to institute appropriate enforcement proceedings other than treble damage actions.

Restraint of Trade

Section 1 of the Sherman Act provides that "[e]very contract, combination in the form of trust or otherwise, or conspiracy, in restraint of trade or commerce among the several states, or with foreign nations is hereby declared to be illegal." Taken literally, this prohibition would invalidate every unperformed contract. To avoid such a broad and impractical application, the courts have interpreted this section to invalidate only *unreasonable* restraints of trade:

> The true test of legality is whether the restraint imposed is such as merely regulates and perhaps thereby promotes competition or whether it is such as may suppress or even destroy competition. To determine that question the courts must ordinarily consider the facts peculiar to the business to which the restraint is applied; its condition before and after the restraint was imposed; the nature of the restraint and its effect, actual or probable. The history of the restraint, the evil believed to exist, the reason for adopting the

particular remedy, the purpose or end sought to be attained, are all relevant facts. This is not because a good intention will save an otherwise objectionable regulation or the reverse; but because knowledge of intent may help the court to interpret facts and to predict consequences. *Chicago Board of Trade v. United States*, 246 U.S. 231 (1918).

This standard, known as the **rule of reason** test, however, presented several problems of its own. By mandating that courts balance the *anticompetitive* effects against the *procompetitive* effects of every questioned restraint, this standard placed a substantial burden upon the judicial system. The United States Supreme Court responded by declaring certain categories of restraints to be unreasonable by their very nature and thus **illegal per se:**

> [T]here are certain agreements or practices which because of their pernicious effect on competition and lack of any redeeming virtue are conclusively presumed to be unreasonable and therefore illegal without elaborate inquiry as to the precise harm they have caused or the business excuse for their use. This principle of *per se* unreasonableness not only makes the type of restraints which are proscribed by the Sherman Act more certain to the benefit of everyone concerned, but it also avoids the necessity for an incredibly complicated and prolonged economic investigation into the entire history of the industry involved, as well as related industries, in an effort to determine at large whether a particular restraint has been unreasonable—an inquiry so often wholly fruitless when undertaken. *Northern Pacific Railway Co. v. United States*, 356 U.S. 1 (1958).

Those restraints not categorized as illegal *per se* are judged by the rule of reason test.

In addition, restraints may be classified as either horizontal or vertical. A **restraint** is **horizontal** if it involves collaboration among competitors at the same level in the chain of distribution (see Figure 41–1). For example, an agreement among manufacturers or among wholesalers or among retailers would be horizontal.

On the other hand, an agreement is a **vertical restraint** if it is made by parties that are not in direct competition at the same level of distribution (see Figure 41–2). Thus an agreement between a manufacturer and a wholesaler is vertical. Although the distinction between horizontal and vertical restraints can become blurred, it often determines whether a restraint is illegal *per se* or should be judged by the rule of reason test. For instance, horizontal market allocations are illegal *per se*, whereas vertical market allocations are not illegal *per se* but are subject to the rule of reason test.

Finally, Section 1 does not prohibit *unilateral* conduct; rather, it forbids *concerted* action. Thus, one person or business by itself cannot violate the section. As recently held by the United States Supreme Court, an organization has the "right to deal, or refuse to deal, with whomever it likes, as long as it does so independently." *Monsanto Corp. v. Spray-Rite Service Corp.*, 465 U.S. 752 (1984). Moreover, agreements within a single firm do not fall within the reach of Section 1. Therefore, a conspiracy may not be based on an agreement among officers or employees of the same firm, or between the firm and its officers or employees. Furthermore, the United States Supreme Court has also held that an agreement between a corporation and its wholly owned subsidiary was not a conspiracy or combination. *Copperwald Corp. v. Independence Tube Corp.*, 467 U.S. 752 (1984). The Court did not, however, extend

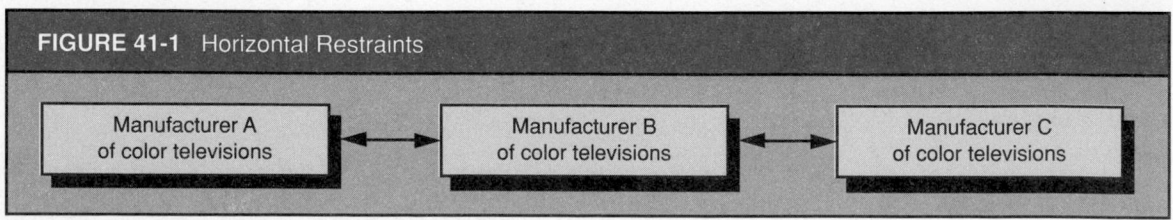

FIGURE 41-1 Horizontal Restraints

Manufacturer A of color televisions ⟷ Manufacturer B of color televisions ⟷ Manufacturer C of color televisions

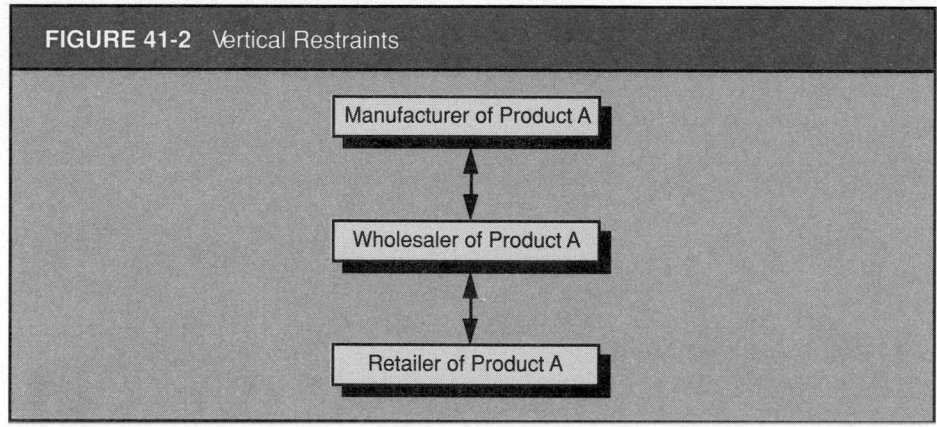

FIGURE 41-2 Vertical Restraints

Manufacturer of Product A

Wholesaler of Product A

Retailer of Product A

the decision to subsidiaries that are not wholly owned and indicated that ownership of 30 percent to 50 percent would allow a finding of conspiracy. Thus, the degree of control appears to be the determining factor.

Although concerted action usually takes the form of explicit agreements, combinations, or conspiracies, less obvious conduct has on occasion been found to violate Section 1 where there is sufficient circumstantial evidence to warrant such a finding. Nonetheless, similar patterns of conduct among competitors, called *conscious parallelism*, are not sufficient by themselves to infer a conspiracy in violation of Section 1. There must also be an *additional* factor, such as (1) complex action taken by each competitor that would only benefit each competitor if all of them took similar action, (2) indications of a traditional conspiracy such as identical sealed bids from each competitor, or (3) the presence of a motive or reason to conspire.

In 1984, the United States Supreme Court addressed the type and amount of evidence necessary to infer a conspiracy. In determining whether a vertical conspiracy existed, the Court held that:

There must be evidence that tends to exclude the possibility that the manufacturer and nonterminated distributors were acting independently. . . . [T]he antitrust plaintiff should present direct or circumstantial evidence that reasonably tends to prove that the manufacturer and others "had a conscious commitment to a common scheme designed to achieve an unlawful objective." *Monsanto Corp. v. Spray-Rite Service Corp.*, 465 U.S. at 764.

The lower courts, however, have not been consistent in interpreting this language. Some courts emphasize that the evidence must "tend to exclude the possibility" of independent action whereas others emphasize the requirement of a "conscious commitment to a common scheme."

Price Fixing   **Price fixing** is an agreement with the purpose or effect of inhibiting price competition and includes agreements raising, depressing, fixing, pegging, or stabilizing prices. Price fixing is the primary and most serious example of a *per se* violation under the Sherman Act. As held in *United States v. Socony-Vacuum Oil Co.*, all **horizontal** price-fixing agreements are illegal *per se*. This prohibition covers any agreement between sellers to establish *maximum* prices at which certain commodities or services are offered for sale as well as *minimum* prices. The law also prohibits sellers' agreements to change the prices of certain commodities or services simultaneously or not to advertise their prices.

UNITED STATES v. SOCONY-VACUUM OIL CO.
United States Supreme Court, 1940.
310 U.S. 150, 60 S.Ct. 811, 84 L.Ed. 1129.

Facts: In the early 1930s, intense price competition characterized both the retail and the wholesale oil markets. At times, prices in the wholesale market fell below the manufacturer's cost. One cause of the volatile situation was the supply of "distress gasoline" placed on the market by seventeen independent refiners. These independent refiners had no retail sales outlets and little storage capacity, so they were forced to sell it at "distress prices." In spite of their unprofitable operations, they could not afford to shut down, for if they did so, they would be apt to lose their oil connections in the field and their regular customers.

In an attempt to remedy this problem, the major oil companies entered into an informal agreement whereby each selected one or more independent refiners having distress gasoline as its "dancing partner." The major oil company would then assume responsibility for purchasing the independent's distress supply at the "fair going market price." As a result, the market price of oil rose in 1935 and 1936, and the spot market became stable. The United States then brought this criminal action against the companies, charging them with horizontal price fixing in violation of the Sherman Act. The defendants were convicted by a jury but on appeal the Circuit Court reversed the conviction and remanded for a new trial.

Decision: Judgment of the Circuit Court reversed.

Opinion: **Douglas, J.**   The [trial] court charged the jury that it was a violation of the Sherman Act for a group of individuals or corporations to act together to raise the prices to be charged for the commodity which they manufactured where they controlled a substantial part of the interstate trade and commerce in that commodity. The court stated that where the members of a combination had the power to raise prices and acted together for that purpose, the combination was illegal; and that it was immaterial how reasonable or unreasonable those prices were or to what extent they had been affected by the combination. It further charged that if such illegal combination existed, it did not matter that there may also have been other factors which contributed to the raising of the prices. * * * The court then charged that, unless the jury found beyond a reasonable doubt that the price rise and its continuance were "caused" by the combination and not caused by those other factors, verdicts of "not guilty" should be returned. It also charged that there was no evidence of governmental approval which would exempt the buying programs from the prohibitions of the Sherman Act; and that knowledge or acquiescence of officers of the government or the good intention of the members of the combination would not give immunity from prosecution under that Act.

The Circuit Court of Appeals held this charge to be reversible error, since it was based upon the theory that such a combination was illegal per se. In its view respondents' activities were not unlawful unless they constituted an unreasonable restraint of trade.

* * *

In United States v. Trenton Potteries Co., [citation], this Court sustained a conviction under the Sherman Act where the jury was charged that an agreement on the part of the members of a combination, controlling a substantial part of an industry, upon the prices which the members are to charge for their commodity is in itself an unreasonable restraint of trade without regard to the reasonableness of the prices or the good intentions of the combining units.

* * *

Therefore the sole remaining question of this phase of the case is the applicability of the rule of the Trenton Potteries case to these facts. Respondents seek to distinguish the Trenton Potteries case from the instant one.

* * *

But we do not deem those distinctions material. In the first place, there was abundant evidence that the combination had the purpose to raise prices. And likewise, there was ample evidence that the buying programs at least contributed to the price rise and the stability of the spot markets, and to increases in the price of gasoline sold in the Mid-Western area during the indictment period. That other factors also may have contributed to that rise and stability of the markets is immaterial. * * *

Secondly, the fact that sales on the spot markets were still governed by some competition is of no consequence. For it is indisputable that the competition was restricted through the removal by respondents of a part of the supply which but for the buying programs would have been a factor in determining the going prices on those markets. * * *

The elimination of so-called competitive evils is no legal justification for such buying programs. The elimination of such conditions was sought primarily for its effect on the price structures. Fairer competitive prices, it is claimed, resulted when distress gasoline was removed from the market. But such defense is typical of the protestations usually made in price-fixing cases. Ruinous competition, financial disaster, evils of price cutting and the like appear throughout our history as ostensible justifications for price-fixing. If the so-called competitive abuses were to be appraised here, the reasonableness of prices would necessarily become an issue in every price-fixing case. In that event the Sherman Act would soon be emasculated; its philosophy would be supplanted by one which is wholly alien to a system of free competition; it would not be the charter of freedom which its framers intended.

The reasonableness of prices has no constancy due to the dynamic quality of the business facts underlying price structures. Those who fixed reasonable prices today would perpetuate unreasonable prices tomorrow, since those prices would not be subject to continuous administrative supervision and readjustment in light of changed conditions. Those who controlled the prices would control or effectively dominate the market. And those who were in that strategic position would have it in their power to destroy or drastically impair the competitive system. But the thrust of the rule is deeper and reaches more than monopoly power. Any combination which tampers with price structures is engaged in an unlawful activity. Even though the members of the price-fixing group were in no position to control the market, to the extent that they raised, lowered, or stabilized prices they would be directly interfering with the free play of market forces. The Act places all such schemes beyond the pale and protects that vital part of our economy against any degree of interference. Congress has not left us the determination of whether or not particular price-fixing schemes are wise or unwise, healthy or destructive. It has not permitted the age-old cry of ruinous competition and competitive evils to be a defense to price-fixing conspiracies. * * *

Nor is it important that the prices paid by the combination were not fixed in the sense that they were uniform and inflexible. * * *

* * *

Under the Sherman Act a combination formed for the purpose and with the effect of raising, depressing, fixing, pegging, or stabilizing the price of a commodity in interstate or foreign commerce is illegal per se. * * *

LAW IN THE NEWS

Protect the Full Service Retailer
Doom for Discounters?

For those who have followed the development of antitrust law in the courts, the Supreme Court's decision in Business Electronics Corp. v. Sharp Electronics Corp. came as little surprise. The decision simply made explicit what has been implicit under the antitrust law for over a decade. The decision stands for the unremarkable proposition that because most agreements between manufacturers and their dealers, involving terms other than prices and price levels, may actually benefit consumers, the courts should not automatically condemn them.

To understand why the court declined to expand the group of agreements between manufacturers and dealers (referred to in antitrust cases as "vertical restraints") that are conclusively presumed illegal (or illegal per se) under antitrust law, it is necessary to understand how such restraints can benefit consumers.

To compete with other brands, a manufacturer often may need to induce its dealers to make its product more attractive to consumers by investing in services and promoting its brand. Vertical restraints can provide the incentive for such investments by protecting full-service dealers from "free riders"—that is, dealers who do not make such investments and are able to undercut full-service dealers.

In the short run free riders will increase the sales of a manufacturer's product, but the manufacturer may determine that in the long run free riding will mean that full-service dealers will be unwilling to service and promote its brand. Without such service and promotion by dealers, the manufacturer may be unable to compete with rival manufacturers.

Recognizing that vertical restraints may increase competition among brands, the Supreme Court in 1977 held that non-price vertical restraints are not illegal unless they actually threaten competition in the particular circumstances. There is a separate rule for resale price maintenance, which, since 1911, has been per se illegal.

In the Sharp decision all that the Court did was to announce a clear line between resale price maintenance and all other restrictions in distribution agreements. The Supreme Court held that a distribution restraint can be labeled resale price maintenance only if it "includes some agreement

Similarly, it is illegal *per se* for a seller to fix the price at which its purchasers must resell the product. This **vertical** form of price fixing—usually called **retail price maintenance**—is considered a *per se* violation of Section 1. It is believed that the seller has no interest sufficient to outweigh the buyer's right to resell at a price that is responsive to the buyer's competitive conditions. Nevertheless, in 1988 the Supreme Court held that a company can terminate price discounters without violating the Sherman Act so long as the distribution restraint does not "include some agreement on price or price levels." See Law in the News on this page and page 918.

Market Allocations　Direct price fixing is not the only method by which prices can be con-

trolled. Another way is by **market allocation** whereby competitors agree not to compete with each other in specific markets, which may be defined by geographic area, type of customer, or class of product. Because their effects are similar to price fixing, all **horizontal** agreements to divide markets have been declared illegal *per se*. Thus, if RAC and Sonny, both manufacturers of color televisions, agree that RAC shall have the exclusive right to sell color televisions in Illinois and Iowa and that Sonny shall have the exclusive right in Minnesota and Wisconsin, RAC and Sonny have committed a *per se* violation of Section 1 of the Sherman Act. Likewise, if RAC and Sonny agree that RAC shall have the exclusive right to sell color televisions to Sears and Sonny to J. C. Penney on price or price levels." The Court rejected the plaintiff's arguments that agreements to terminate "price cutters" should, without regard to all of the facts, always and automatically be unlawful. One man's price cutter is another man's free rider. If a price cutter is simply a free rider who is frustrating the effective distribution of the manufacturer's product, terminating the price cutter may benefit consumers and competition.

After the Sharp decision, as before, resale price maintenance is per se illegal. On the other hand, vertical restraints falling outside the Court's definition of resale price maintenance are not automatically legal. Rather, such vertical restraints will still be illegal if on balance they actually harm competition.

The Sharp decision does not threaten the discounters. Under the decade-old approach to vertical restraints that the Sharp decision clarified but did not change, discounters have flourished and grown dramatically. That growth results from consumers voting with their dollars. If consumers want to shop at the discounters, that is where manufacturers will sell their products. Otherwise, customers will quickly switch to other brands.

Indeed, the very idea that full-service retailers will somehow coerce manufacturers to eliminate discounters as a force in the market, is ludicrous. Discounters, like K Mart, Wal-Mart, Zayre and others, are generally large national chains that have little to fear from small locally owned full-service dealers.

On the other hand, significant numbers of consumers still like shopping at full-service retailers, and some products, particularly complex and technological novel consumer electronics, might never reach the market if not for full service retailers. The Sharp decision allows manufacturers to choose a method or methods of distribution that are most effective in selling their products—whether through full-service dealers, discounters, or both.

In the Sharp decision, the Court merely refused to load the dice in favor of discounters by threatening automatic treble-damage liability whenever a manufacturer chooses the full service route. Obviously, discounters and plaintiff's attorneys would have preferred a different outcome. But as six Supreme Court Justices, including Justices William J. Brennan Jr. and Thurgood Marshall, concluded, the result in the Sharp decision preserves freedom of choice and diversity for consumers.

—By Charles F. Rule and David L. Meyer

Charles F. Rule is the assistant attorney general in charge of the antitrust division at the Department of Justice. David L. Meyer is special assistant to the assistant attorney general. Copyright © 1988/89 by The New York Times Company. Reprinted by permission.

or that RAC shall have exclusive rights to manufacture nineteen-inch color televisions and Sonny to manufacture fifteen-inch sets, they are also in *per se* violation of Section 1 of the Sherman Antitrust Act. Horizontal market allocations may be found not only on the manufacturing level but also on the wholesale or retail level.

Vertical territorial and customer restrictions are no longer illegal *per se* but are now judged by the rule of reason. This change in approach has resulted from the United States Supreme Court decision in *Continental T.V., Inc. v. GTE Sylvania, Inc.*, which mandated the lower Federal courts to balance the positive effect of vertical market restrictions on interbrand competition against the negative effects on intraband competition. Consequently, in some situations, vertical territorial restrictions will be found legitimate if they, on balance, do not have an anticompetitive impact on the relevant market.

In 1985 the United States Department of Justice issued a "market structure screen." Under this screen, the Justice Department will not challenge restraints by a firm having less than 10 percent of the relevant market or a "Vertical Restraint Index" (a measure of relative market share) indicating that neither collusion nor exclusion is possible. We discuss the concept of relevant market later in the section on monopolization.

CONTINENTAL T.V., INC. v. GTE SYLVANIA, INC.
United States Supreme Court, 1977.
433 U.S. 36, 97 S.Ct. 2549, 53 L.Ed.2d 568.

Facts: As part of a corporate plan to stimulate sagging color television sales, GTE Sylvania began to phase out its wholesale distributors and began to sell its television sets directly to a smaller and more select group of franchised retailers. To this end, Sylvania limited the number of franchises granted for any given area and required each franchisee to sell Sylvania products only from the location or locations at which he was franchised. A franchise did not constitute an exclusive territory, and Sylvania retained sole discretion to increase the number of retailers in an area in light of the success or failure of existing retailers. The strategy apparently was successful, as Sylvania's national market share increased from less than 2 percent to 5 percent.

In the course of carrying out its plan, Sylvania franchised Young Brothers as a retailer of televisions at a location in San Francisco one mile from that of Continental T.V., Inc., one of Sylvania's most successful franchisees. A course of feuding began between Sylvania and Continental that reached a head when Continental requested permission to open a store in Sacramento, but Sylvania refused. Continental opened a Sacramento store anyway and began shipping merchandise there from its San Jose warehouse. Shortly thereafter, Sylvania terminated Continental's franchise.

Continental brought this action against Sylvania, claiming that the franchise location restriction is *per se* violative of the Sherman Act. The jury found for Continental and assessed damages at $591,505, which were trebled. On appeal, the Court of Appeals for the Ninth Circuit, sitting *en benc,* reversed the judgment.

Decision: Judgment of the Court of Appeals for Sylvania affirmed.

Opinion: **Powell, J.**   We turn first to Continental's contention that Sylvania's restriction on retail locations is a per se violation of § 1 of the Sherman Act as interpreted in Schwinn. [Schwinn, decided in 1967 by the United States Supreme Court, held vertical market restraints imposed by sellers was a violation of § 1, regardless of the reasonableness of the restrictions.] Sylvania argues that if Schwinn cannot be distinguished, it should be reconsidered. * * *

The traditional framework of analysis under § 1 of the Sherman Act is familiar and does not require extended discussion. * * * [The "rule of reason" is] the prevailing standard of analysis. [Citation.] Under this rule, the factfinder weighs all of the circumstances of a case in deciding whether a restrictive practice should be prohibited as imposing an unreasonable restraint on competition. Per se rules of illegality are appropriate only when they relate to conduct that is manifestly anticompetitive. As the Court explained in *Northern Pac. R. Co. v. United States,* [citation], "there are certain agreements or practices which because of their pernicious effect on competition and lack of redeeming virtue are conclusively presumed to be unreasonable and therefore illegal without elaborate inquiry as to the precise harm they have caused or the business excuse for their use."

In essence, the issue before us is whether Schwinn's per se rule can be justified under the demanding standards of Northern Pac. R. Co. * * *

The market impact of vertical restrictions is complex because of their potential for a simultaneous reduction of intrabrand competition and stimulation of interbrand competition. Significantly, the Court in Schwinn did not distinguish among the challenged restrictions on the basis of their individual potential for intrabrand harm or interbrand benefit. Restrictions that completely eliminated intrabrand competition among Schwinn distributors were analyzed no differently than those that merely moderated intrabrand competition among retailers.

* * *

Vertical restrictions reduce intrabrand competition by limiting the number of sellers of a particular product competing for the business of a given group of buyers. Location restrictions have this effect because of practical constraints on the effective marketing area of retail outlets. Although intrabrand competition may be reduced, the ability of retailers to exploit the resulting market may be limited both by the ability of consumers to travel to other franchised locations and, perhaps more importantly, to purchase the competing products of other manufacturers. * * *

Vertical restrictions promote interbrand competition by allowing the manufacturer to achieve certain efficiencies in the distribution of his products. These "redeeming virtues" are implicit in every decision sustaining vertical restrictions under the rule of reason. Economists have identified a number of ways in which manufacturers can use such restrictions to compete more effectively against other manufacturers. [Citation.] For example, new manufacturers and manufacturers entering new markets can use the restrictions in order to induce competent and aggressive retailers to make the kind of investment of capital and labor that is often required in the distribution of products unknown to the consumer. Established manufacturers can use them to induce retailers to engage in promotional activities or to provide service and repair facilities necessary to the efficient marketing of their products. Service and repair are vital for many products, such as automobiles and major household appliances. The availability and quality of such services affect a manufacturer's good will and the competitiveness of his product. Because of market imperfections such as the so-called "free rider" effect, these services might not be provided by retailers in a purely competitive situation, despite the fact that each retailer's benefit would be greater if all provided the services than if none did. [Citation.]

* * *

Certainly, there has been no showing in this case, either generally or with respect to Sylvania's agreements, that vertical restrictions have or are likely to have a "pernicious effect on competition" or that they "lack * * * any redeeming virtue." Accordingly, we conclude that the per se rule stated in Schwinn must be overruled. In so holding we do not foreclose the possibility that particular applications of vertical restrictions might justify per se prohibition under Northern Pac. R. Co. But we do make clear that departure from the rule of reason standard must be based upon demonstrable economic effect rather than—as in Schwinn—upon formalistic line drawing.

* * *

Boycotts As we noted above, Section 1 of the Sherman Act does not apply to unilateral action but only to agreements or combinations. Accordingly, the refusal of a seller to deal with any particular buyer does not violate the Act. Thus a manufacturer can refuse to sell to a retailer who persists in selling below the manufacturer's suggested retail price. On the other hand, concerted refusals to deal—group boycotts—are prohibited. A **boycott** is an agreement among competitors not to deal with a supplier or customer. Therefore, a manufacturer would violate Section 1 if it were to induce other manufacturers to refuse to deal

LAW IN THE NEWS

The Court Is Winking at 'Price Fixing'

Price competition is the basis of the American retail economy and a first principle of the antitrust laws. Yet the Supreme Court's recent decision in Business Electronics Corp. v. Sharp Electronics Corp. threatens to erode that competitive system by weakening protection for price cutting and discounters. Unless Congress acts to restore strong anti-price-fixing laws, the country will suffer an erosion in price competition.

At stake is the practice of price competition among retailers—which enormously benefits consumers and the economy as a whole. Independent pricing allows even young businesses to go head-to-head with established stores by offering the public lower prices. In the past decade, a $125 billion discount industry has emerged, stocking quality products ranging from designer clothes to electronics and computers. A study by Public Citizen's Congress Watch showed that comparison shopping for typical Christmas gifts could save families between 10 percent and 45 percent. Estimates vary, but failure to enforce the antitrust laws cost consumers at least $23 billion.

The antitrust laws have long encouraged and protected this full-throated price competition. Since the Court's 1911 Dr. Miles decision, both "horizontal price fixing"—agreements among competitors—and "vertical price fixing"—agreements between manufacturers and dealers—have been deemed illegal.

But the antitrust policy makers within the Reagan Administration have a fervent ideological aversion to traditional antitrust enforcement. Since 1981, the Justice Department has not prosecuted a single vertical price fixing case. In the 1984 Monsanto v. Spray-Rite case, the Justice Department intervened on behalf of a price fixer and urged the Court to reverse the rule that price-fixing is automatically illegal. The Administration was partly successful. In that case, the Court erected a virtually impenetrable evidentiary barrier to keep discounters who have been terminated as a result of a price complaint from a competitor from taking their case to a jury. Since the Monsanto case, according to a pleased National Association of Manufacturers, "most lower courts have issued summary dismissals of suits involving allegations of price fixing."

Now, with the Sharp decision, the Court has again assaulted price competition. In that case, a

---

with retailers that disobeyed suggested retail prices.

For example, assume that GE wishes to establish set prices for the resale of its products by both wholesalers and retailers and indicates that it will cease to deal with any wholesaler who resells at a different price. GE has *not* violated the Sherman Act; it has merely exercised its right to deal with whomever it pleases. On the other hand, if GE were to join with Whirlpool and Fridgidaire (competing manufacturers) in refusing to deal with any wholesaler who does not follow their pricing policy, GE and the other manufacturers have entered into an illegal concerted refusal to deal as well as an illegal vertical price-fixing scheme. Moreover, the illegality of the conduct does not depend on the express agreement of GE and the other manufacturers but may be implied from the conduct of the parties. Finally, it should be noted that GE would violate the Sherman Act by engaging in horizontal price fixing if it obtained an agreement from the other manufacturers that they will sell at prices set by GE.

Finally, most courts hold that the *per se* rule of illegality for concerted refusals to deal extends only to horizontal boycotts and not to vertical refusals to deal. Most courts have interpreted *Sylvania* to hold that a rule of reason test should govern all nonprice vertical restraints, including concerted refusals to deal.

Tying Arrangements A **tying arrangement** occurs when a seller of a product, service, or intangible (the "tying" product) conditions its sale on the buyer's purchasing a second product, service, or intangible (the "tied" product)

retailer had complained to a manufacturer about the price cutting of a competitor, and demanded that the manufacturer terminate the retailer's rival. The manufacturer agreed. The Court found no price fixing. There must be agreement on a price or price level, it held, for there to be price fixing. In effect, the Court held that there must be a stated agreement on the price level to be charged in order for there to be price fixing. A full-price store and a manufacturer can now agree in writing to cut off a discounter expressly to eliminate price cutting without falling under the rule of illegality. Under the new rule, any businessman who actually agrees on the price he will charge should be convicted of stupidity as well as price fixing.

Defenders of price fixing assert that a higher resale price gives retailers a guaranteed margin that might be used to provide more elaborate service (such as, say, point-of-sale service for computers). Yet a manufacturer can easily require service, floor space, repairs or any other feature by contract—without fixing the price. Letting retailers fix prices in the hope they will use the profits to bolster service is like throwing paint at a wall and hoping it will result in a Renoir. Moreover, consumers are fully capable of deciding whether to shop at a full-service showroom or at a discounter.

Congress has responded to the Administration's assault on antitrust by seeking to enact legislation to strengthen the laws against price fixing. Last year, the House passed a bill introduced by Representative Peter W. Rodino, Jr., Democrat of New Jersey, and Representative Henry J. Hyde, Republican of Illinois, that writes the per se standard into the United States Code and provides for fairer evidentiary standards. The Senate Judiciary Committee has approved similar legislation, introduced by Senator Howard M. Metzenbaum, Democrat of Ohio, and others.

But the National Association of Manufacturers and the United States Chamber of Commerce and their allies have mounted a fierce effort to block the bill on the Senate floor. And, the Justice Department has threatened a Presidential veto.

That would be a shame. Unless Congress acts soon, there will be a seismic shift from vigorous competition toward a marketplace dominated by full-price retailers. Only restoration and enforcement of anti-price-fixing laws will prevent retailing from becoming yet another American "competitiveness" problem.

By Michael Waldman and Jonathan W. Cuneo
Michael Waldman is legislative director of Public Citizen's Congress Watch. Jonathan W. Cuneo is counsel to the Committee to Support the Antitrust Laws.
Copyright © 1988/89 by The New York Times Company. Reprinted by permission.

from the seller. For example, assume that Xerox, a major manufacturer of photocopying equipment, were to require that all purchasers of its photocopiers also purchase from Xerox all of the paper they use with the copier. Xerox has tied the sale of its photocopier—the *tying* product—to the sale of paper—the *tied* product. Because tying arrangements limit the freedom of choice of buyers and may exclude competitors, the law closely scrutinizes such agreements. A tying arrangement exists where a seller exploits its economic power in one market to expand its empire into another market. When the seller has considerable economic power in the tying product *or* when a not insubstantial amount of interstate commerce is affected in the tied product, the tying arrangement will be *per se* illegal. Otherwise, tying arrangements are judged by the rule of reason standard.

Economic power may be demonstrated by showing that (1) the seller occupied a dominant position in the tying market, (2) the seller's product is sufficiently unique in having some advantage not shared by its competitors in the tying market, or (3) a substantial number of customers have accepted the tying arrangement and there are no explanations for their willingness to comply, other than the seller's economic power in the tying market.

Figure 41–3 summarizes how these restraints on trade are judged under Section 1.

Monopolies

Economic analysis indicates that a monopolist will use its power to limit production and increase prices. Therefore, a monopolistic market will produce fewer goods at a higher price

FIGURE 41-3 Restraints of Trade

Restraint	Standard
Price fixing	*Per se* illegal
Market allocations	Horizontal: *per se* illegal Vertical: rule of reason
Group boycotts	*Per se* illegal
Tying arrangements	*Per se* illegal*

*If seller has power in tying product or a not insubstantial amount of interstate commerce is affected in the tied product.

than a competitive market. Addressing the problem of monopolization, Section 2 of the Sherman Act prohibits monopolization, attempts to monopolize, and conspiracies to monopolize. Thus, Section 2 prohibits both agreements among businesses and, unlike Section 1, unilateral conduct by one firm.

Monopolization Although the language of Section 2 appears to prohibit *all* monopolies, the courts have not interpreted it in that manner. Rather, they have required that in addition to the mere possession of market power there also must be either the unfair attainment of the monopoly power or the abusive use of that power once attained.

It is extremely rare to find an unregulated industry with only one firm, so the issue of monopoly power involves defining what degree of market dominance constitutes monopoly power. **Monopoly power** is the ability to control price or to exclude competitors from the marketplace. The courts have grappled

with this question of monopoly power and have developed a number of approaches, but the most common test is market share. A market share greater than 75 percent generally indicates monopoly power, while a share less than 50 percent does not. A 50 to 75 percent share is inconclusive.

Market share is the fractional share possessed by a firm of the total relevant product and geographic markets, but defining the relevant markets is often a difficult and subjective project for the courts. The relevant *product market*, as demonstrated in the case that follows, includes products that are substitutable for the firm's product on the basis of price, quality, and adaptability for other purposes. For example, although brick and wood siding are both used in buildings as exteriors, it is not likely that they would be considered as part of the same product market. On the other hand, Coca-Cola and Seven-Up are both soft drinks and would be considered part of the same product market.

UNITED STATES v. E. I. du PONT De NEMOURS & CO.
United States Supreme Court, 1956.
351 U.S. 377, 76 S.Ct. 994, 100 L.Ed. 1264.

Facts: In 1923 du Pont was granted the exclusive right to make and sell cellophane in North America. In 1927 the company introduced a moistureproof brand of cellophane that was ideal for various wrapping needs. Although more expensive than most competing wrapping, it was favored for many uses because it offered a desired combination of transparency, strength, and cost. Except permeability to gases, however, cellophane had no qualities that were not possessed by a number of competing materials. Cellophane sales increased dramatically, and by 1950 du Pont produced almost 75 percent of the cellophane sold in the United States. Nevertheless, sales of the material constituted less than 20 percent of the sales of "flexible packaging materials."

The United States brought this action contending that by so dominating cellophane production, du Pont had monopolized a part of trade or commerce in violation of the Sherman Act. Du Pont argued that it had not monopolized in violation of the Sherman Act because it did not have the power to control the price of cellophane or to exclude competitors from the market for flexible wrapping materials. The government takes a direct appeal from a ruling in favor of du Pont.

Decision: Judgment for du Pont affirmed.

Opinion: Reed, J. Our cases determine that a party has monopoly power if it has, over "any part of the trade or commerce among the several states," a power of controlling prices or unreasonably restricting competition. * * *

If cellophane is the "market" that du Pont is found to dominate, it may be assumed it does have monopoly power over that "market." Monopoly power is the power to control prices or exclude competition. It seems apparent that du Pont's power to set the price of cellophane has been limited only by the competition afforded by other flexible packaging materials.

* * *

Determination of the competitive market for commodities depends on how different from one another are the offered commodities in character or use, how far buyers will go to substitute one commodity for another. For example, one can think of building materials as in commodity competition but one could hardly say that brick competed with steel or wood or cement or stone in the meaning of Sherman Act litigation; the products are too different. This is the interindustry competition emphasized by some economists. * * * On the other hand, there are certain differences in the formulae for soft drinks but one can hardly say that each one is an illegal monopoly. Whatever the market may be, we hold that control of price or competition establishes the existence of monopoly power under § 2. Section 2 requires the application of a reasonable approach in determining the existence of monopoly power just as surely as did § 1. This of course does not mean that there can be a reasonable monopoly. Our next step is to determine whether du Pont has monopoly power over cellophane: that is, power over its price in relation to or competition with other commodities. The charge was monopolization of cellophane. The defense, that cellophane was merely a part of the relevant market for flexible packaging materials.

* * *

But where there are market alternatives that buyers may readily use for their purposes, illegal monopoly does not exist merely because the product said to be monopolized differs from others. If it were not so, only physically identical products would be a part of the market. To accept the Government's argument, we would have to conclude that the manufacturers of plain as well as moistureproof cellophane were monopolists, and so with films such as Pliofilm, foil, glassine, polyethylene, and Saran, for each of these wrapping materials is distinguishable. These were all exhibits in the case. New wrappings appear, generally similar to cellophane: is each a monopoly? What is called for is an appraisal of the "cross-elasticity" of demand in the trade. * * * In considering what is the relevant market for determining the control of price and competition, no more definite rule can be declared than that commodities reasonably interchangeable by consumers for the same purposes make up that "part of the trade or commerce," monopolization of which may be illegal. As respects flexible packaging materials, the market geographically is nationwide.

* * *

An element for consideration as to cross-elasticity of demand between products is the responsiveness of the sales of one product to price changes of the other. If a slight decrease in the price of cellophane causes a considerable number of customers of other flexible wrappings to switch to cellophane, it would be an indication that a high cross-elasticity of demand exists between them; that the products compete in the same market. The court below held that the "[g]reat sensitivity of customers in the flexible packaging markets to price or quality changes" prevented du Pont from possessing monopoly control over price. The record sustains these findings.

We conclude that cellophane's interchangeability with the other materials mentioned suffices to make it a part of this flexible packaging material market.

* * *

[T]he trial court found that du Pont could not exclude competitors even from the manufacture of cellophane, an immaterial matter if the market is flexible packaging material. Nor can we say that du Pont's profits, while liberal (according to the Government 15.9% net after taxes on the 1937–1947 average), demonstrate the existence of a monopoly without proof of lack of comparable profits during those years in other prosperous industries. Cellophane was a leader, over 17%, in the flexible packaging materials market. There is no showing that du Pont's rate of return was greater or less than that of other producers of flexible packaging materials.

The "market" which one must study to determine when a producer has monopoly power will vary with the part of commerce under consideration. The tests are constant. That market is composed of products that have reasonable interchangeability for the purposes for which they are produced—prices, use and qualities considered. While the application of the tests remains uncertain, it seems to us that du Pont should not be found to monopolize cellophane when that product has the competition and interchangeability with other wrappings that this record shows.

The relevant *geographic market* is the territory in which the firm sells its products or services. This may be at the local, regional, or national level. For instance, the relevant geographic market for the manufacture and sale of aluminum might be national, whereas that of a taxi company would be local. The scope of the relevant geographic market will depend on such factors as transportation costs, the type of product or services, and the location of competitors and customers.

If sufficient monopoly power has been proved, it must then be shown that the firm has engaged in **unfair conduct.** The courts have not yet agreed on what constitutes unfair conduct. One judicial approach is that a firm possessing monopoly power has the burden of proving that it acquired such power passively or that it had the power "thrust" upon it. An alternative view is that monopoly power, when combined with conduct designed to exclude competitors, violates Section 1. A third approach requires monopoly power plus some type of predatory practice, such as pricing below marginal costs. For example, one case that adopted the third approach held that a firm does not violate Section 2 of the Sherman Act if it attained its market share by either (1) research, technical innovation, or a superior product, or (2) ordinary marketing methods available to all. *Telex Corp. v. IBM*, 510 F.2d 894 (10th Cir. 1975). A recent Supreme Court decision appears to adopt a combination of these approaches. The Court held that "[i]f a firm has been attempting to exclude rivals on some basis other than efficiency, it is fair to characterize its behavior as predatory." *Aspen Skiing Co. v. Aspen Highlands Skiing Co.*, 472 U.S. 585 (1985).

To date, however, the United States Supreme Court has not provided a definitive answer to the basic question of exactly what conduct, beyond the mere possession of monopoly power, violates Section 2. To do so, the Court must resolve the complex and conflicting policies involved. On the one hand, condemning fairly acquired monopoly power—that acquired "merely by virtue of superior skill, foresight and industry"—penalizes firms that compete effectively. On the other hand, permitting firms with monopoly power to continue provides them the opportunity to lower output and raise prices, thereby injuring consumers.

Attempts to Monopolize Section 2 also prohibits attempts to monopolize. As with monopolization, the courts have experienced difficulty in developing a standard that distinguishes undesirable conduct likely to lead to monopoly from healthy, competitive conduct. The standard test applied by the courts requires proof of a specific intent to monopolize plus a dangerous probability of success. This standard leaves numerous questions unanswered, such as what conduct constitutes an attempt and how much power must be achieved. Recent cases suggest that the greater the power acquired, the less fla-

grant the conduct must be to constitute an attempt. These cases, however, do not specify any threshold level of market power.

CLAYTON ACT

In 1914 Congress strengthened the Sherman Act by adopting the Clayton Act, which was expressly designed "to supplement existing laws against unlawful restraints and monopolies." The Clayton Act does not provide for criminal penalties but only for civil actions. Civil actions may be brought by private parties in Federal court for *treble* damages and attorneys' fees. In addition, the Justice Department and the Federal Trade Commission are authorized to bring civil actions, including proceedings in equity, to prevent and restrict violations of the act.

The major provisions of the Clayton Act deal with price discrimination, tying contracts, exclusive dealing, and mergers. Section 2, which deals with price discrimination, was amended and rewritten by the Robinson-Patman Act, which we discuss below. The Clayton Act exempts labor, agricultural, and horticultural organizations from all antitrust laws.

Tying Contracts and Exclusive Dealing

Section 3 of the Clayton Act prohibits tying arrangements and exclusive dealing, selling, or leasing arrangements that prevent purchasers from dealing with the seller's competitors where the effect *may* be substantially to lessen competition or *tend* to create a monopoly. This section is intended to attack anticompetitive practices when they start, before they ripen into violations of Section 1 or 2 of the Sherman Act. Unlike the Sherman Act, however, Section 3 applies only to leases or sales of goods, wares, merchandise, machinery, supplies, or other commodities and *not* to services or intangibles.

Tying arrangements, which we discussed above, have been labeled by the Supreme Court as serving "hardly any purpose beyond the suppression of competition." Exclusive dealing arrangements are agreements by which the seller or lessor of a product conditions the agreement on the buyer's or lessor's promise not to deal in the goods of a competitor. For example, a manufacturer of razors might require that retailers wishing to sell its line of shaving equipment agree not to carry competing merchandise. Such conduct will violate Section 3 if it tends to create a monopoly or may substantially lessen competition.

Mergers

Corporate mergers have played a significant role in reshaping the structure of both corporations in the United States and our economic system. We are currently in the midst of the fourth major wave of mergers in United States history. In 1986 there were 3,336 mergers. The total value of all mergers in 1986 exceeded 173 billion. In 1988 the largest acquisition took place when Philip Morris acquired Kraft for $12.6 billion. Figure 41–4 lists the largest acquisitions from 1985 through 1988.

Mergers may be classified as horizontal, vertical, or conglomerate. A **horizontal merger** involves the acquisition by a company of all or

---

FIGURE 41-4   Largest Acquisitions from 1985 through 1988

RANK*	ACQUIRING COMPANY	ACQUIRED/MERGED COMPANY	PRICE PAID (millions of dollars)
		1985	
1	Royal Dutch	Shell Oil	$5,700.1
2	Phillip Morris	General Foods	5,627.7
3	Allied	Signal Cos.	4,955.0
4	R.J. Reynolds	Nabisco	4,889.1
5	General Motors	Hugh's Aircraft	4,712.5
		1986	
1	General Electric	RCA	$6,406.0
2	Captial Cities	ABC	3,509.0
3	Campeau	Allied Stores	3,505.7
4	Cleveland Electric	Toledo Edison	3,140.5
5	USX	Texas Oil & Gas	2,996.6
		1987	
1	British Petroleum	Standard Oil	$7,564.7
2	National Amusements	Viacom International	3,299.1
3	Unilever	Chesebrough–Pond's	3,095.2
4	Hoechst AG	Celanese Corp.	2,723.5
5	JMB Realty	Cadillac Fairview	1,973.6
		1988	
1	Phillip Morris	Kraft	$12,644.2
2	Campeau	Federated Department Stores	6,506.2
3	BAT Industries	Farmers Group	5,168.7
4	Eastman Kodak	Sterling Drug	5,093.1
5	Amoco	Dome Petroleum	3,766.1

*Excluding Leveraged Buyouts

part of the stock or assets of a competing company. For example, if IBM were to acquire Apple, this would be a horizontal merger. A **vertical merger** is the acquisition by a company of one of its customers or suppliers. A vertical merger is a *forward* merger if the acquiring company purchases a *customer*, such as the purchase of Revco Discount Drug Stores by Procter & Gamble. A vertical merger is a *backward* merger if the acquiring company purchases a supplier; for example, IBM's purchase of a manufacturer of microchips. The third type of merger, the **conglomerate merger,** is a catchall category that covers all acquisitions not involving a competitor, customer, or supplier. Many of the recent mergers have been horizontal, as was the first merger wave (late 1800s until approximately 1904) and the second merger wave (from the end of World War I through the 1920s). The third merger wave (1945 until the late 1960s) was primarily conglomerate in nature.

Section 7 of the Clayton Act prohibits the merger or acquisition by a corporation of stock in another corporation or assets of another corporation where the effect may be substantially to lessen competition or tend to create a monopoly. The current state of the law regarding horizontal, vertical, and conglomerate mergers is, particularly with respect to the last two, in a state of flux.

The principal objective of antitrust law governing mergers is to maintain competition. Accordingly, horizontal mergers are scrutinized most carefully. Factors that the courts consider in reviewing the legality of a horizontal merger include the market share of each of the merging firms, the degree of industry concentration, the number of firms in the industry, entry barriers, market trends, the vigor and strength of other competitors in the industry, the character and history of the merging firms, market demand, and the extent of industry price competition. See *United States v. Von's Grocery Co.* below. Vertical mergers, which are far less likely to be challenged by the Justice Department or the FTC, will be attacked if the merger is likely to raise entry barriers in the industry or is likely to shut out other firms in the industry of the acquiring firm from competitively significant customers or suppliers. Finally, conglomerate mergers have been challenged only (1) where one of the merging firms is a highly likely entrant into the market of the other firm, or (2) where the merged company would be disproportionately large compared with the largest competitors in its industry.

UNITED STATES v. VON'S GROCERY CO.
Supreme Court of the United States, 1966.
384 U.S. 270, 86 S.Ct. 1478, 16 L.Ed.2d 555.

Facts: Von's Grocery, a large retail grocery chain in Los Angeles, sought to acquire Shopping Bag Food Stores, a direct competitor. At the time of the proposed merger, Von's sales ranked third in the Los Angeles area and Shopping Bag's ranked sixth. Both chains were increasing their number of stores. The merger would have resulted in the creation of the second largest grocery chain in Los Angeles, with total sales in excess of $170 million. Prior to the proposed merger, the number of owners operating single stores declined from 5,365 in 1950 to 3,590 by 1963. During this same period, the number of chains with two or more stores rose from 96 to 150. The United States brought suit against Von's to prevent the merger. It claimed that the proposed merger violated Section 7 of the Clayton Act in that it may result in the substantial lessening of competition or tend to create a monopoly. The district court entered judgment for the defendant and the United States took direct appeal to the U.S. Supreme Court.

Decision: Judgment reversed and remanded.

Opinion: Black, J. From this country's beginning there has been an abiding and widespread fear of the evils which flow from monopoly—that is the concentration of economic power in the hands of a few. On the basis of this fear, Congress in 1890, when many of the Nation's industries were already concentrated into what it deemed too few hands, passed the Sherman Act in an attempt to prevent further concentration and to preserve competition among a large number of sellers. Several years later, in 1897, this Court emphasized this policy of the Sherman Act by calling attention to the tendency of powerful business combinations to restrain competition "by driving out of business the small dealers and worthy men whose lives have been spent therein, and who might be unable to readjust themselves in their altered surroundings." *United States v. Trans-Missouri Freight Assn.*, [citation]. The Sherman Act failed to protect the smaller businessmen from elimination through the monopolistic pressures of large combinations which used mergers to grow ever more powerful. As a result in 1914 Congress, viewing mergers as a continuous, pervasive threat to small business, passed § 7 of the Clayton Act which prohibited corporations under most circumstances from * * *. [In 1950] to arrest this "rising tide" toward concentration into too few hands and to halt the gradual demise of the small businessman, Congress decided to clamp down with vigor on mergers. It both revitalized § 7 of the Clayton Act by "plugging its loophole" and broadened its scope so as not only to prohibit mergers between competitors, the effect of which "may be substantially to lessen competition, or to tend to create a monopoly" but to prohibit all mergers having that effect. By using these terms in § 7 which look not merely to the actual present effect of a merger but instead to its effect upon future competition, Congress sought to preserve competition among many small businesses by arresting a trend toward concentration in its incipiency before that trend developed to the point that a market was left in the grip of a few big companies. Thus, where concentration is gaining momentum in a market, we must be alert to carry out Congress' intent to protect competition against ever-increasing concentration through mergers.

The facts of this case present exactly the threatening trend toward concentration which Congress wanted to halt. The number of small grocery companies in the Los Angeles retail grocery market had been declining rapidly before the merger and continued to decline rapidly afterwards. This rapid decline in the number of grocery store owners moved hand in hand with a large number of significant absorptions of the small companies by the larger ones. In the midst of this steadfast trend toward concentration, Von's and Shopping Bag, two of the most successful and largest companies in the area, jointly owning 66 grocery stores merged to become the second largest chain in Los Angeles. This merger cannot be defended on the ground that one of the companies was about to fail or that the two had to merge to save themselves from destruction by some larger and more powerful competitor. What we have on the contrary is simply the case of two already powerful companies merging in a way which makes them even more powerful than they were before. If ever such a merger would not violate § 7, certainly it does when it takes place in a market characterized by a long and continuous trend toward fewer and fewer owner-competitors which is exactly the sort of trend which Congress, with power to do so, declared must be arrested.

Appellees' primary argument is that the merger between Von's and Shopping Bag is not prohibited by § 7 because the Los Angeles grocery market was competitive before the merger, has been since, and may continue to be in the future. Even so, § 7 "requires not merely an appraisal of the immediate impact of the merger upon competition, but a prediction of its impact upon competitive conditions in the future; this is what is meant when it is said that the amended § 7 was intended to arrest anticompetitive tendencies in their incipiency." [Citation.] It is enough for us that Congress feared that a market marked at the same time by both a continuous decline in the number of small businesses and a large number of mergers would slowly but inevitably gravitate from a market of many small competitors to one dominated by one or a few giants, and competition would thereby be destroyed. Congress passed the Celler-Kefauver Act to prevent such a destruction of competition. Our cases since the passage of that Act have faithfully endeavored to enforce this Congressional command. We adhere to them now.

The Justice Department and the FTC have both indicated that they will be primarily concerned with horizontal mergers in highly or moderately concentrated industries and that they question the benefits of challenging vertical and conglomerate mergers. Both have justified this policy on the basis that the latter two types of mergers are necessary to transfer assets to their most productive use and that any challenge to them would impose costs on consumers without corresponding benefits.

Antitrust law, as currently applied, deals with mergers by focusing on the size of the merged firm in relation to the relevant market and not on the absolute size of the resulting entity. The focus of the Justice Department Guidelines (issued in 1982 and amended in 1984) is that "mergers should not be permitted to create or enhance market power or to facilitate its exercise." The Guidelines seek to detect and prevent the use of "market power" by quantifying market concentration using the **Herfindahl-Hirschman Index (HHI)** and by measuring a horizontal merger's impact on the Index. This concentration index is calculated by summing the squares of the individual market shares of all firms in the market. An industry with only one firm would have an HHI of 10,000 (100^2). With two firms of equal size it would be 5,000 ($50^2 + 50^2$), with five firms of equal size the result would be 2,000 ($20^2 + 20^2 + 20^2 + 20^2 + 20^2$). The increase in the Index caused by any merger is calculated by doubling the product of the market shares of the merging firms. For example, the merger of two firms with market shares of 5 percent and 10 percent respectively would increase the Index by 100 ($5 \times 10 \times 2 = 100$).

The Guidelines use three categories of market concentration to analyze horizontal mergers and to determine the likelihood of governmental opposition based on the increase in the Index caused by the proposed merger. The three categories are classified according to the postmerger HHI. If the postmerger figure is below 1,000, then the Department is unlikely to challenge the merger without regard to the increase in the Index caused by the merger. For postmerger HHIs between 1,000 and 1,800 the Department will examine the increase in HHI due to the merger. Increases less than 100 are unlikely to generate a challenge, but those greater than 100 probably will. When the postmerger HHI is above 1800, the Department will look closely at the effects of the merger if the increase is above 50, and is likely to challenge any merger contributing an increase of more than 100.

Interlocking Directorates

Section 8 prohibits interlocking directorates in competing corporations engaged in interstate commerce (except banks, banking associations, trust companies, and common carriers) where the total capital of the corporations is a million dollars or more.

The broad purposes of Congress are unmistakably clear. Section 8 was but one of a series of measures which finally emerged as the Clayton Act, all intended to strengthen the Sherman Act, which, through the years, had not proved entirely effective. Congress had been aroused by the concentration of control by a few individuals or groups over many gigantic corporations which in the normal course of events should have been in active and unrestrained competition. Instead, and because of such control, the healthy competition of the free enterprise system had been stifled or eliminated. Interlocking directorships on rival corporations had been the instrumentality of defeating the purpose of the antitrust laws. They had tended to suppress competition or to foster joint action against third party competitors. The continued potential threat to the competitive system resulting from these conflicting directorships was the evil aimed at. Viewed against this background, a fair reading of the legislative debates leaves little room for doubt that, in its efforts to strengthen the antitrust laws, what Congress intended by § 8 was to nip in the bud incipient violations of the antitrust laws by removing the opportunity or temptation to such violations through interlocking directorates. The legislation was essentially preventative. *United States v. Sears, Roebuck & Co.*, 111 F.Supp. 14 (S.D.N.Y.1953).

Since Section 8 of the Clayton Act prohibits interlocking directorships in *competing* corporations, it does not apply to a director who serves on the board of two firms that are vertically associated. Moreover, it has been held that the section does not apply to an individual who is an officer of two corporations or an officer of one corporation and a director of another.

ROBINSON-PATMAN ACT

The Robinson-Patman Act amended the Clayton Act to prohibit buyers from inducing and sellers from granting **price discrimination** in interstate commerce of commodities of similar grade and quality. To be a violation, the price discrimination must substantially lessen competition or tend to create a monopoly.

Under this Act, sellers of goods are prevented from granting discounts to buyers, including allowances for advertisements, counter displays, and samples, unless the same discounts are offered to all other purchasers on proportionately equal terms. The Act also prohibits other types of discounts, rebates, and allowances and makes it unlawful to sell goods at unreasonably low prices for the purpose of destroying competition or eliminating a competitor. The Act further makes it unlawful for a person knowingly to "induce or receive" an illegal discrimination in price, thus imposing liability on the buyer as well as the seller. Violation of the Robinson-Patman Act, with limited exceptions, is a civil rather than a criminal wrong.

Price differentials are permitted when justified by proof of either a cost savings to the seller or a good faith price reduction to meet the lawful price of a competitor. The following case discusses the legality of functional discounts, which are different prices charged to wholesalers or other middlemen than those charged to retailers.

IN RE BOISE CASCADE CORP.
Federal Trade Commission, 1986.
50 ATRR 335.

Facts: Boise Cascade Corporation is a wholesaler and retailer of office products. The Federal Trade Commission issued a complaint charging that Boise had violated the Robinson-Patman Act by receiving a wholesaler's discount from certain suppliers on products that Boise resold at retail, in competition with other retailers that could not obtain wholesale discounts.

Decision: Judgment for FTC granted.

Opinion: Calvani, Acting Chairman. Thus, this case deals with claims about functional discounts. A functional discount occurs when a seller permits one buyer, *e.g.*, a wholesaler, to purchase a product at a lower price than another buyer, *e.g.*, a retailer, because of the marketing functions that the favored buyer performs for the seller's product. If the wholesaler does not sell to end-user customers in competition with the retailer, the difference in the prices that the wholesaler and the retailer pay cannot support a claim of secondary line competitive injury under the Act. But the differing discounts may have legal consequences where the "wholesaler," or the favored buyer, sells not as a middleman reselling to retailers, but acts itself as a retailer in selling to end-user customers, in competition with other retailers that could not obtain wholesaler discounts. Here, Boise is both a wholesaler and retailer, but receives a wholesaler discount on all the goods it buys. In evaluating the effects on competition, does the Act require that an integrated entity's distribution level be determined by its buying function or by its selling function? Put differently, if a retail chain has its own wholesale unit, does the Act require—or permit—a supplier to give the chain a wholesaler discount or a retailer discount?

* * *

We adopt the Administrative Law Judge's findings and conclusions, and thus affirm that Boise knowingly received unlawful discounts in violation of Section 2(f) of the Act.

II. KNOWING RECEIPT OF PRICE DISCRIMINATION

Other than the determination of injury under the Act and the establishment of the Act's affirmative defenses, the basic elements of liability under Section 2(f) are not seriously in dispute. Boise does not challenge the ALJ's findings on the various jurisdictional interstate commerce requirements. Boise does not deny that it received wholesaler discounts on office products, both on merchandise that it resold to other dealers and on merchandise that it sold to end-user customers in competition with them.

* * *

Moreover, the record clearly discloses that Boise was aware that it was receiving discriminatory preferences. A common difficulty in buyer liability cases under Section 2(f) of the Act is proving that the buyer knowingly received favored treatment.

* * *

IV. TREATMENT OF FUNCTIONAL DISCOUNTS

Boise's major argument against liability is the claim that the prices it pays include a discount that represents the value of distributional functions it performs. The discounts in question are the ones Boise receives as a wholesaler. There is no dispute that Boise performs wholesaler functions in its middleman capacity, such as warehousing inventory, handling credit and bookkeeping, publishing product catalogs, and providing sales assistance to dealers in promotional activities. Discounts to compensate Boise for its performance of these functions as a wholesaler are not at issue here.

However, about half of Boise's sales are at retail, not at wholesale. In purchasing these goods that it resells at retail, Boise still gets the wholesaler discount. Those retail sales are made in competition with dealers who generally cannot get the wholesaler discount because they do not make wholesale sales. Yet the record shows that the dealers, many of which are substantial operations, also perform distributional functions similar to Boise. They thus incur distributional costs, but cannot obtain the discounts Boise receives to compensate for them, and thus cannot price competitively with Boise at retail.

This disparate treatment is the gravamen of the complaint. The fundamental question presented is whether the "functional" discounts Boise receives on the goods it resells at retail are illegal because they cause injury to competing retailers who are denied these discounts.

* * *

In the absence of an explicit instruction from the legislature on this issue, the general terms of the Act's text, understood in the context of the Act's purposes, must be applied. The major legislative purpose behind the Robinson-Patman Act was to prove some measure of protection to small independent retailers and their independent suppliers from what was thought to be unfair competition from vertically integrated, multi-location chain stores, [citation]. Accomplishing this purpose can be inconsistent with the goals of the other antitrust laws, so the Commission will eschew efforts to broaden the Act's application beyond that established by law [citation], where such inconsistencies would result. But the Commission may not refuse to apply the Act to accomplish Congress' purposes where the law is well established.

* * *

A. The Mueller Rule

Mueller holds that a favored distributor cannot avoid the inference of competitive injury by claiming that its costs equal its discriminatory advantage. The Commission in *Mueller* rejected the contention that functional discounts to a distributor no greater than the distributor's cost of providing middleman services could never cause competitive injury to other distributors not receiving the same discount. * * * Instead, the Commission explained that a favored distributor could have a competitive advantage over its competitors even if the price impact of its favored purchasing position were consumed by its cost of handling the items sold in competition with them. * * *

* * *

Under *Mueller*, if the costs of sale or delivery being compensated by the discount are truly the supplier's own costs, then those cost savings could support a cost justification defense. Thus, Boise's reliance on showing its *own* costs of performing services to avoid the inference of injury is not probative. Boise sells to end-user customers in competition with other dealers, yet purchases at lower prices than are available to those dealers. Its claim that the price difference is no greater than its costs of performing services and therefore that there can be no competitive injury due to its discriminatory advantage is rejected by *Mueller*, and by this Commission.

* * *

C. The "Availability" Defense

Boise argues that the prices it receives are available to dealers and therefore there is no statutory injury. In this context, Boise really makes two arguments. First, it urges that wholesale functional discounts are available to all purchasers that perform the wholesale function. In other words, a retailer who feels disadvantaged can simply become a wholesaler too. Boise's suggestion that all dealers could become dual distributors or wholesalers is impractical on its face, and contradicted by the record. The courts and the Commission have long required that availability be practical. [Citations.] Lower prices are "unavailable" where a purchaser must alter his purchasing status before receiving them. [Citation.]

* * *

The second prong of Boise's argument is that equally low prices were available to competing retail dealers from other suppliers. In essence, respondent urges an "alternative source" defense. The defense "has not been successful in any of the dual function buyer cases." [Citation.] The alternative source defense presumes that businessmen act irrationally, by choosing to pay more to a supplier that discriminates against them than they could pay to an alternative source for the same goods. Instead, the continued purchases even in the face of discriminatory prices suggest that the alleged alternative sources are not competitive. If an alternative source defense is legally recognized, despite its presumption of buyer irrationality, it is critical to examine whether the alternative sources are, in fact, competitively equivalent.

We need not reach the issue of whether an available alternative source negates a finding of price discrimination. The record shows that equivalent goods were not available on equivalent terms from alternative suppliers.

Cost Justification

If a seller can show that it costs less to sell a product to a particular buyer, the seller may lawfully pass along the cost savings. For example, if Sears orders goods from Wrangler by the carload, whereas retailer B orders in small quantities, Wrangler, who delivers F.O.B. buyer's warehouse, may pass along the transportation savings to Sears. Nonetheless, although it is possible to pass along transportation savings, it is extremely difficult to pass along alleged savings in manufacturing or distribution because of the complexity involved in calculating and proving such savings. Therefore, sellers rarely rely on the defense of cost justification.

Meeting Competition

A seller may lower his price in a good faith attempt to meet competition. To illustrate:

1. Manufacturer X sells its motor oil to retail outlets for $.65 per can. Manufacturer Y approaches A, one of manufacturer X's customers, and offers to sell a comparable type of motor oil for $.60 per can. Manufacturer X will be permitted to lower its price to A to $.60 per can and need not lower its price to its other retail customers—B, C, and D. Manufacturer X, however, may *not* lower its price to A to $.55 unless it also lowers its price to B, C, and D.
2. Manufacturer X will not be permitted to lower its price to A without also lowering its price to B, C, and D in order to allow A to meet the lower price charged by A's competitor, N, selling manufacturer Y's oil. The meeting competition defense is available only to meet the competition of the seller and does not extend to the price of a competitor to a specific, individual *purchaser*. See Figure 41–5.

A seller may beat its competitor's price if it does not know the competitor's price, cannot reasonably determine the competitor's price, and acts reasonably in setting its own price.

FEDERAL TRADE COMMISSION ACT

In 1914 Congress enacted the Federal Trade Commission Act, creating the Federal Trade Commission (FTC), which is charged with the duty to prevent unfair methods of competition in commerce and unfair or deceptive acts or practices in commerce. To this end, the five-member commission is empowered to conduct appropriate investigations and hearings. It may issue cease and desist orders against violators that are enforceable in the Federal courts. Its broad power has been described by the United States Supreme Court:

The "unfair methods of competition," which are condemned by . . . the Act, are not confined to those that were illegal at common law or that were condemned by the Sherman Act. . . . It is also clear that the Federal Trade Commission Act was designed to supplement and bolster the Sherman Act and the Clayton Act . . . *to stop in*

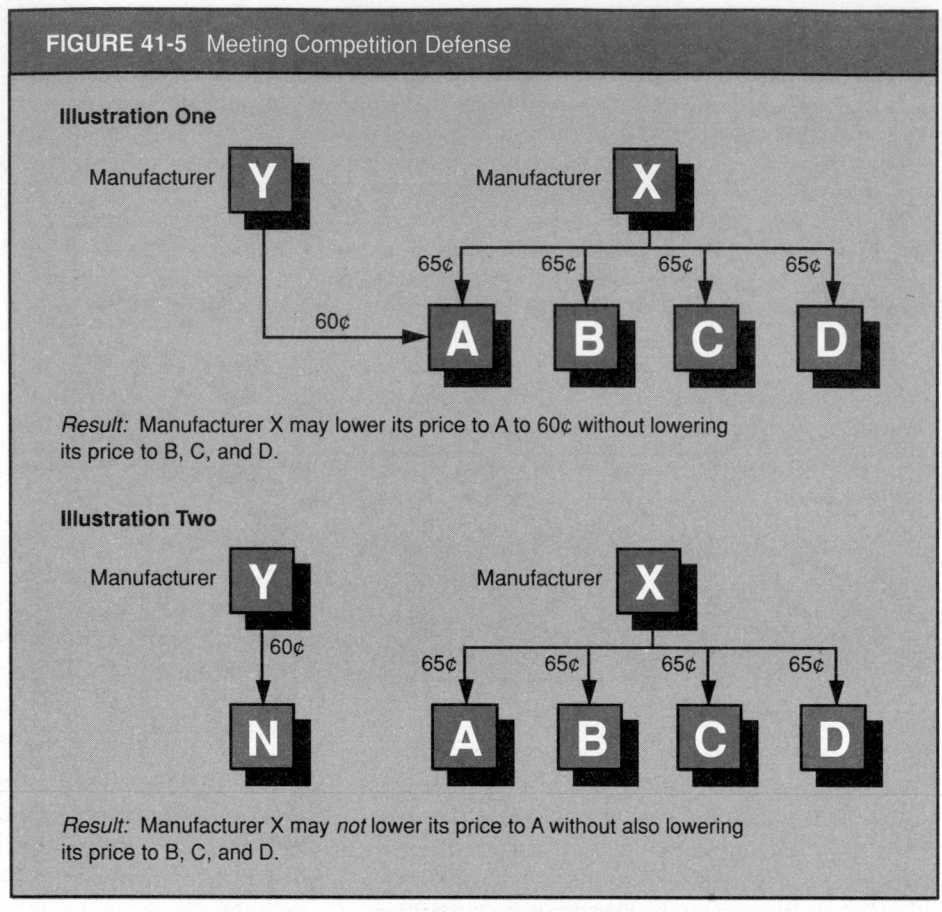

FIGURE 41-5 Meeting Competition Defense

Illustration One

Result: Manufacturer X may lower its price to A to 60¢ without lowering its price to B, C, and D.

Illustration Two

Result: Manufacturer X may *not* lower its price to A without also lowering its price to B, C, and D.

their incipiency acts and practices which, when full blown, would violate those Acts. (Emphasis added.) *F.T.C. v. Motion Picture Advertising Service Co.,* 344 U.S. 392 (1953).

Complaints may be instituted by the FTC, which, after a hearing, "has wide latitude for judgment and the courts will not interfere except where the remedy selected has no reasonable relation to the unlawful practices found to exist." Although the FTC most frequently enters a cease and desist order having the effect of an injunction, it may order other relief, such as affirmative disclosure, corrective advertising, and the granting of licenses to patents on a reasonable royalty basis. (See *Warner-Lambert Co. v. Federal Trade Commission,* in Chapter 45.) Appeals may be taken from orders of the FTC to the United States Courts of Appeals, which have exclusive jurisdiction to enforce, set aside, or modify orders of the FTC.

The work of the FTC includes not only investigation of possible violations of the antitrust laws but also unfair methods of competition, such as false and misleading advertisements, false or inadequate labeling of products, passing or palming off goods as those of a competitor, lotteries, gambling schemes, discriminatory offers of rebates and discounts, false disparagement of a competitor's goods, false or misleading descriptive names of products, use of false testimonials, and other unfair trade practices. For a more detailed discussion of the FTC and its powers see Chapter 45.

CHAPTER SUMMARY

Sherman Antitrust Act	**Restraint of Trade** Section 1 prohibits contracts, combinations, and conspiracies that restrain trade

- *Rule of Reason*   standard that balances the anticompetitive effects against the procompetitive effects of the restraint
- *Per Se*   conclusively presumed unreasonable and therefore illegal
- *Horizontal Restraints*   agreements among competitors
- *Vertical Restraints*   agreements among parties at different levels in the chain of distribution

Application of Section 1

- *Price Fixing*   an agreement with the purpose or effect of inhibiting price competition; both horizontal and vertical agreements are *per se* illegal
- *Market Allocation*   division of markets by customers, geography, or products; horizontal agreements are *per se* illegal, while vertical agreements are judged by the rule of reason standard
- *Boycott*   agreement among competitors not to deal with a supplier or customer; *per se* illegal
- *Tying Arrangement*   conditioning a sale of a desired product (tying product) on the buyer purchasing a second product (tied product); *per se* illegal if the seller has considerable power in the tying product or a not insubstantial amount of interstate commerce is affected in the tied product

Monopolies   Section 2 prohibits monopolization, attempts to monopolize, and conspiracies to monopolize

- *Monopolization*   requires market power (ability to control price or exclude others from the marketplace) plus either the unfair attainment of the power or the abusive use of the power
- *Attempt to Monopolize*   specific intent to monopolize plus a dangerous probability of success

Sanctions

- *Treble Damages*   three times actual loss
- *Criminal Penalties*

Clayton Act	**Tying Arrangement** prohibited if it tends to create a monopoly or may substantially lessen competition

Exclusive Dealing   arrangement where a party has sole right to a market; prohibited if it tends to create a monopoly or may substantially lessen competition

Merger   prohibited if it tends to create a monopoly or may substantially lessen competition

- *Horizontal Merger*   acquisition by one company of a competing company
- *Vertical Merger*   acquisition by one company of one of its suppliers or customers
- *Conglomerate Merger*   an acquisition by one company of another that is not a competitor, customer, or supplier

	Interlocking Directorates prohibited in competing corporations engaged in interstate commerce where the total capital is $1 million or more **Sanctions** treble damages

Robinson-Patman Act	**Price Discrimination** the Act prohibits buyers from inducing or sellers from giving different prices to buyers of commodities of similar grade and quality **Defenses** (1) cost justification, (2) meeting competition, and (3) functional discounts **Sanctions** civil (treble damages); criminal in limited situations

Federal Trade Commission Act	**Purpose** to prevent unfair methods of competition and unfair or deceptive practices **Sanctions** actions may be brought by the FTC and not by private individuals

QUESTIONS

1. Discuss horizontal restraints of trade.
2. Discuss vertical restraints of trade.
3. Discuss monopolization.
4. Discuss the Clayton Act and its rules governing (a) tying contracts, (b) exclusive dealing, (c) vertical mergers, (d) horizontal mergers, and (e) conglomerate mergers.
5. Discuss the Robinson-Patman Act and the various defenses to it.

PROBLEMS

1. Discuss the validity and effect of each of the following situations:
(a) A, B, and C, manufacturers of radios, orally agree that due to the disastrous, cutthroat competition in the market, they would establish a reasonable price to charge their purchasers.
(b) A, B, C, and D, newspaper publishers, agree not to charge their customers more than thirty cents per newspaper.
(c) A, a distiller of liquor, and B, A's retail distributor, agree that B should charge a price of $5 per bottle.
2. Discuss the validity of the following:
(a) An agreement between two manufacturers of the same type of products to allocate territories whereby neither will sell its products in the area allocated to the other.

(b) An agreement between manufacturer and distributor not to sell a dealer a particular product or parts necessary for repair of the product.
3. Universal Video sells $40 million worth of video recording equipment in the United States. The total sales of such equipment in the United States is $100 million. One-half of Universal's sales are to Giant Retailer, a company that possesses 50 percent of the retail market. Giant is presently seeking (1) to obtain an exclusive dealing arrangement with Universal, or (2) to acquire Universal. Advise Giant as to the validity of its alternatives.
4. Z sells cameras to A, B, C, and D for $60 per camera. Y, one of Z's competitors, sells a comparable camera to A for $58.50. Z, in response to this competitive pressure from Y, lowers its price to A to $58.50. B, C, and D insist that Z lower its price to them to $58.50, but Z refuses. B, C, and D sue Z for unlawful price discrimination. Decision? Would your answer differ if Z reduced its price to A to $58?
5. Discount is a discount appliance chain store that continually sells goods at a price below the manufacturers' suggested retail prices. A, B, and C, the three largest manufacturers of appliances, agree that unless Discount ceases its discount pricing, they will no longer sell to Discount. Discount refuses, and A, B, and C refuse to sell to Discount. Discount sues A, B, and C. Decision?
6. Taylor Company produces 77 percent of all of the coal used in the United States. Coal provides 25 percent of all of the energy used in the United States. In a suit brought by the United States against Taylor for violation of the antitrust laws, what result?

7. Whirlpool Corporation manufactured vacuum cleaners under both its own name and under the Kenmore name. Oreck exclusively distributed the vacuum cleaners sold under the Whirlpool name. Sears, Roebuck & Co. exclusively distributed the Kenmore vacuum cleaners. Oreck alleged that its exclusive distributorship agreement with Whirlpool was not renewed because of the existence of an unlawful conspiracy between Whirlpool and Sears. Oreck further contended that a *per se* rule was applicable because the agreement was (a) price fixing, or (b) a group boycott or both. Decision?

8. Indian Coffee of Pittsburgh, Pennsylvania, marketed vacuum-packed coffee under the brand name, Breakfast Cheer, in the Pittsburgh and Cleveland, Ohio, areas. Later Folger Coffee, a leading coffee seller, began selling coffee in Pittsburgh. In order to make inroads into the new territory, Folger sold its coffee at greatly reduced prices. At first, Indian Coffee met Folger's prices but could not continue operating at such a reduced price and was forced out of the market. Indian Coffee brings an antitrust action. Decision?

9. Justin Manufacturing Company sells high fashion clothing under the prestigious "Justin" label. The company has a firm policy that it will not deal with any company that sells below its suggested retail price. Justin is informed by one of its customers, XYZ, that its competitor, Duplex, is selling the "Justin" line at a great discount. Justin now demands that Duplex comply with their agreement that they will not sell the "Justin" line below the suggested retail price. Discuss the implications of this situation.

10. Jay Corporation, the largest manufacturer of bicycles in the United States with 40 percent of the market, has recently entered into an agreement with Retail Bike, the largest retailer of bicycles in the United States with 37% of the market, under which Jay will furnish its bicycles only to Retail and Retail will sell only Jay's bicycles. The government is now questioning this agreement. Discuss.

COMPUTER RESEARCH PROBLEMS

1. Great Atlantic and Pacific Tea Company desired to achieve cost savings by switching to the sale of "private label" milk. A&P asked Borden company, its longtime supplier of "brand label" milk to submit a bid to supply certain of A&P's private label dairy products. A&P was not satisfied with Borden's bid, however, and it solicited other offers. Bowman Dairy, a competitor of Borden's, submitted a lower bid. At this point, A&P contacted Borden and asked it to rebid on the private label contract. A&P included a warning that Borden would have to substantially lower its original bid in order to undercut Bowman's bid. Borden offered a bid that doubled A&P's potential annual cost savings. A&P accepted Borden's bid. The Federal Trade Commission then brought this action, charging that A&P had violated the Robinson-Patman Act by knowingly inducing or receiving illegal price discrimination from Borden. Decision?

2. Clorox is the nation's leading manufacturer of household liquid bleach (accounting for 49%—40,000,000—of sales) and is the only brand sold nationally. Clorox and its next largest competitor Purex hold 65% of national sales, and the top four bleach manufacturers control 80% of sales. Since all bleach is chemically identical, Clorox spends over $5,000,000 each year in advertising to attract and keep customers.

Proctor & Gamble is the dominant national manufacturer of household cleaning products, with yearly sales of $1.1 billion. Just as with bleach, advertising is vital in the household cleaning products industry. Proctor & Gamble spends over $127,000,000 in advertising and promotions. Proctor & Gamble decided to diversify into the bleach business, since its household cleaning products and bleach are both low-cost, high-turnover consumer goods, dependent on mass advertising, sold to the same customers at the same stores, by the same merchandising methods. Proctor & Gamble decided to merge with Clorox, rather than starting their own bleach division, in order to secure the dominant position in the bleach market immediately. Should the FTC take action against this merger, and if so, what decision?

3. In 1981 the NCAA adopted a plan for televising college football games in order to reduce the adverse effect of TV coverage on spectator attendance. The plan limited the total number of televised intercollegiate football games, and also limited the number of games any one school could televise. No member of the NCAA was permitted to sell any television rights except in accordance with the plan. As part of the plan, the NCAA had agreements with the American Broadcasting Company (ABC) and the Columbia Broadcasting System (CBS) to pay to each school at least a specified minimum price for televising football games. Several member universities join to bring suit against the NCAA claiming the new plan is a horizontal price fixing agreement and output limitation and as

such is illegal *per se*. The NCAA counters that the existence of the product, college football, depends upon member compliance with restrictions and regulations. According to the NCAA its restrictions have a pro-competitive effect, including the TV plan. Is the TV plan valid? Explain.

4. The National Society of Professional Engineers (Society) had an ethical rule that prohibited member engineers from disclosing or discussing price/fee information with customers until after the customer had hired a particular engineer. This rule against competitive bidding was designed to maintain high standards in the field of engineering. The Society felt that competitive pressure to offer engineering services at the lowest possible price would encourage engineers to design and specify inefficient, unsafe, and unnecessarily expensive structures and construction methods. According to the Society, awarding engineering contracts to the lowest bidder, regardless of quality, would be dangerous to the public health, safety, and welfare. The Society emphasizes that the rule is not an agreement to fix prices. Rather, it claims the rule was drafted by experienced, highly trained professional engineers to prevent public harm and is therefore reasonable. The Government contends that the rule unreasonably restrains trade and thus violates §1 of the Sherman \ct. Decision?

42 EMPLOYMENT LAW

The common law governed the relationship between employer and employee in terms of tort and contract duties. These rules are a part of the law of agency and are discussed in Chapter 27—Relationship of Principal and Agent. This common law has been supplemented—and in some instances replaced—by statutory enactments, principally at the Federal level. In fact, the balance and working relationship between employers and employees are now greatly affected by government regulation. First, the general framework in which management and labor negotiate and bargain over the terms of employment is regulated by Federal statutes designed to promote both labor-management harmony and the welfare of society at large. Second, Federal law has been enacted to prohibit discrimination in employment based upon race, sex, religion, age, handicap, or national origin. Finally, Congress, in response to the changing nature of American industry and the tremendous number of industrial accidents, has intervened by mandating that employers provide their employees with a safe and healthy work environment. Moreover, all of the States have adopted workers' compensation acts to provide compensation to employees injured during the course of employment.

In this chapter, we focus upon these three categories of government regulation of the employment relationship: (1) labor law, (2) employment discrimination law, and (3) employee protection.

LABOR LAW

Traditionally, labor law did not favor concerted activities by workers (such as strikes, picketing, and refusals to deal) to obtain higher wages and better working conditions. At various times, these concerted activities were found to constitute criminal conspiracy, tortious conduct, and violation of antitrust law. Eventually, public pressure in response to the adverse treatment accorded labor forced Congress to intervene.

Norris-La Guardia Act

The Norris-LaGuardia Act was enacted in 1932 in response to the growing criticism of the use of injunctions in peaceful labor disputes. The Act withdrew from the Federal courts the power to issue injunctions in nonviolent labor disputes. The term **labor dispute** was broadly defined to include any controversy concerning terms or conditions of employment or union representation, regardless of whether the parties stood in an employer-employee relationship. More significantly, the Act declared it to be the policy of the United States that labor was to have full freedom to form labor unions without interference by the employer. Accordingly, the act prohibited the so-called "yellow dog" contracts by which employers required their employees to promise that they would not join a union.

National Labor Relations Act

The National Labor Relations Act (NLRA), or **Wagner Act,** was enacted in 1935 and marked an affirmative effort by the Federal government to support collective bargaining and unionization. Section 7 of the Act provides that "the right to self-organization, to form, join or assist labor organizations, to bargain collectively through representatives of their own choosing, and to engage in concerted activities for the purpose of collective bargaining or other mutual aid or protection" is a Federally protected right. Thus, the Act gave employees the right to be represented by a union in their negotiations with their employer concerning terms of employment. Moreover, the Act seeks to enforce this right by prohibiting certain conduct by employers and unions as unfair

labor practices. Under Section 8(a) of the Act, the following activities by employers are unfair employer practices: (1) to interfere with the employees' rights to unionize and bargain collectively; (2) to dominate the union; (3) to discriminate against union members; (4) to discriminate against an employee because he has filed charges or testified under the NLRA; and (5) to refuse to bargain in good faith with the duly established representatives of the employees.

NATIONAL LABOR RELATIONS BOARD v. BERGER TRANSFER & STORAGE
United States Court of Appeals, Seventh Circuit, 1982.
678 F.2d 679.

Facts: The defendant, Berger Transfer and Storage, operates a national moving and transfer business employing approximately forty persons. In May and June of 1979, Local 705 of the International Bortherhood of Teamsters Union spoke with a number of Berger employees, obtaining twenty-eight cards signed in support of the union. The management of Berger, unwilling to work with the union, attempted to prevent it from representing its employees. The company first assigned all work to those with high seniority, in effect temporarily laying off low seniority employees. The management then threatened to lay off permanently those with low seniority and threatened all employees with a total closedown of the palnt. The management interrogated several employees about their union involvement and attempted to extract information about other employees' activities. When the union presented the company the signed cards and recognition agreement, Berger refused to acknowledge the union's existence or right to bargain on behalf of the employees. The union then called a strike, with employees picketing the warehouse. During the picketing, the company threatened to terminate the picketers if they did not return to work. Later, one manager, on two occasions, recklessly drove a truck through the picket line, striking employees. Finally, the company contacted several of the employees and offered them the "grievance procedures and job security" the union would provide. The employees refused the offer. On June 15 the strike ended, with most of the picketers returning to work. Local 705 of the International Brotherhood of Teamsters filed a complaint with the National Labor Relations Board that the defendant is guilty of unfair labor practices by violating Sections 8(a)(1), (3), and (5) of the National Labor Relations Act. The Board upheld the administrative law judge's determination that the Company had violated Sections 8(a)(1), (3), and (5). Berger appeals.

Decision: NLRB order in favor of the union affirmed.

Opinion: Baker, J. (A) Section 8(a)(1) Violations.
   The Board found the Company had committed eighteen independent 8(a)(1) violations which can be divided into six basic categories: (1) interrogating employees about union activities; (2) threatening employees with discharge, layoff and plant closure; (3) creating the impression of surveillance; (4) making promises to

redress employees' complaints; (5) assaulting employees, and (6) actual layoff and discharge of employees.

Section 8(a)(1) makes it an unfair labor practice for an employer to interfere with, restrain, or coerce employees in the exercise of their rights to organize and bargain collectively through representatives of their own choosing. [Citation.] The test of interference with the right of self-organization is not whether an attempt at coercion has succeeded or failed, but whether the employer engaged in conduct which reasonably tends to interfere with, restrain, or coerce employees in the free exercise of their section 7 rights. [Citation.]

(1) Interrogation of employees.

Section 8(a)(1) does not prohibit all employer questioning of employees about union activities. However, when the questions asked "viewed and interpreted as the employee must have understood the questioning and its ramifications, could reasonably coerce or intimidate the employee with regard to union activities," a violation has been established. [Citation.]

* * *

(2) Threats to close the plant, discharge and layoff employees.

An employer violates section 8(a)(1) when he threatens employees with reprisals or other unfavorable consequences as a result of their union activities. [Citation.] Here the evidence shows that the Company began a campaign of threatened reprisals immediately following the Union's organizational drive. In particular, the Company: (1) informed the employees that if the Union succeeded there would be less work, smaller crews; (2) told the employees that no work would be booked for Mondays and Tuesdays; (3) emphasized that layoffs would be controlled by seniority; (4) threatened to discharge employees if they continued to participate in the strike; and (5) threatened to close the warehouse if employees continued to support the Union.

* * *

(3) Impressions of surveillance.

An employer violates section 8(a)(1) when it conveys to employees the impression that it is engaged in surveillance of their union activities. [Citation.] Here the Company: (1) made it known to employees that the Company was aware of employees signing authorization cards, (2) made notes on a list of employees during an interrogation, and (3) suggested that York and Roesecke were the instigators. * * *

(4) Solicitation of grievances, implied promises or redress.

An employer violates section 8(a)(1) of the Act by soliciting grievances when such solicitation is " 'accompanied by an express or implied promise of benefits specifically aimed at interfering with, restraining, and coercing employees in their organizational effort.' " [Citation.] Here the Company repeatedly approached employees to determine how differences could be reconciled. On one occasion, Vice-President Goodwin told employee Overton that the Company would give him "basically the same thing" as the Union, and suggested a meeting with the "top guys." * * *

(5) Assaults.

The evidence shows that on two occasions, Manager Harris recklessly drove his truck through the picket line. The first incident occurred on May 23, when Harris drove a Company truck through the picket line striking picketers Most and Gocha. He later stated that he hit the picketers both "intentionally and unintentionally." A similar incident occurred on June 6. Although there was testimony that the picketers were inebriated and blocking the Company driveway on that occasion, the Board found that the assaults were connected to the employees' union activity. * * *

* * *

(B) Section 8(a)(3) Violations—Layoffs, Demotions & Discharges.

Section 8(a)(3) of the Act makes it an unfair labor practice for an employer to discriminate against an employee "in regard to hire or tenure of employment or any term or condition of employment to encourage or discourage membership in any labor organization * * *." [Citation.] For example, an employer violates section 8(a)(3) when it discharges an employee because of his union activities. [Citation.]

The critical issue in a section 8(a)(3) claim is whether the employer's actions are motivated by anti-union considerations. [Citation.] * * * If a causal relationship between the discharge and protected activity is established, the employer is responsible under the Act unless he sustains his burden of proof. Furthermore, an employer's explanation need not be accepted if there is a reasonable basis for believing the explanation is a pretext for the retaliatory action. [Citation.]

The evidence shows that Company officials made numerous unlawful threats of discharge, layoff, plant shutdown, together with unlawful interrogations, solicitation of grievances, promises of redress and assaults. Such conduct is a significant factor in determining motive [Citation.] * * *

(1) Discharges.

One of the protected rights of employees under section 7 of the Act is the right to strike. * * *

Although the Company asserts that the employees "quit," the total atmosphere of hostility promoted by the Company supports the inference of a section 8(a)(3) violation and discredits the Company's argument * * *

(2) Layoffs.

Where anti-union considerations result in the layoff of employees, the employer has violated section 8(a)(3) of the Act. [Citation.] The testimony before the ALJ established that during the week of May 21, several employees were laid off when the Company failed to book jobs on Mondays and Tuesdays. Furthermore employee Redman testified that he overheard Manager Harris state that he had work for "thirty guys" but was not using them because of the organizational drive. * * *

(3) Demotion of Gocha.

The demotion of an employee for engaging in protected union activities is a violation of section 8(a)(3) of the Act. [Citation.] Although there was testimony that Gocha was demoted because of customer complaints, the Board found the claimed justification to be a pretext, citing Harris' explanation that Gocha was no longer warehouse foreman because of his union sympathy. * * *

Section 8(a)(5) Violation.

The evidence shows that on May 23 the Union had collected signed authorization cards from twenty-eight employees. The Board found that the appropriate unit consisted of forty-two employees, giving the Union majority status. It is well established that the National Labor Relations Act authorizes two methods for the confirmation of a binding bargaining relationship between an employer and a labor union. Generally, Board certification of a union's election success is the prevalent and preferred practice, but it is not the only one; an employer may voluntarily recognize the union upon some demonstrable showing of majority status, i.e., union authorization cards.

> Although an employer generally has the right to refuse to recognize a card based majority and to demand an election, en employer who engages in unfair labor practices "likely to destroy the union's majority and seriously impede the election" may not insist that before it bargains an election be held. [Citation.] Therefore, when a union requests recognition and bargaining from an employer which has been presented with cards showing a majority support for the union, and the employer subsequently engages in unfair labor practices which destroy the "laboratory conditions" needed for a fair election, the employer forfeits any right to an election and must bargain with the union or violate section 8(a)(5) of the Act. Whether or not the union maintains majority status in the face of the employer's unfair labor practices is irrelevant to such a violation finding. [Citation.]
>
> The evidence is clear that the Union had valid authorization cards from twenty-eight of the forty-two employees within the bargaining unit and properly requested recognition by the Company. The Company's response was an onslaught of flagrant, unfair labor practices. * * *

The United States Supreme Court has interpreted the Act to include as an unfair labor practice conduct by the employer that improves employment conditions or benefits that are being criticized by the union as part of its organizing drive.

Moreover, the Act established the **National Labor Relations Board** (NLRB) to monitor and administer these employee rights. The NLRB is empowered to order employers to remedy their unfair labor practices and to supervise elections by secret ballot so that employees can freely select a representative organization.

Labor-Management Relations Act

Following the passage of the National Labor Relations Act, the country underwent a tremendous increase in union membership and labor unrest. In response to this trend, Congress passed the Labor-Management Relations Act (**LMRA or Taft-Hartley Act**) in 1947. The Act prohibits certain **unfair union** practices and separates the NLRB's prosecutorial and adjudicative functions. More specifically, the Act amended the NLRA by declaring the following seven union activities to be **unfair labor practices:** (1) coercing an employee to join a union, (2) causing an employer to discharge or discriminate against a non-union employee, (3) refusing to bargain in good faith, (4) levying excessive or discriminatory dues or fees, (5) causing an employer to pay for work not performed (featherbedding), (6) picketing an employer to require it to recognize an uncertified union, and (7) engaging in secondary activities. (Section 8(b).) A secondary activity is a boycott, strike, or picketing of an employer with whom a union has no labor dispute in order to persuade the employer to cease doing business with the company that is the target of the labor dispute. For example, a labor union is engaged in a labor dispute with Company A. To coerce Company A into resolving the dispute favorably for the labor union, the union organizes a strike against Company B, with which the union has no labor dispute. The union agrees to cease striking Company B if Company B agrees to cease doing business with Company A. The strike against Company B is a secondary activity prohibited as an unfair labor practice.

In addition to prohibiting unfair union practices, the Act also limits the scope of employer unfair labor practice in order to foster employer free speech. The Act declares that no *employer* unfair labor practice could be based on any statement of opinion or argument that contained no threat of reprisal.

The LMRA also prohibits the closed shop, although it permits the existence of union shops, unless union shops are prohibited by a

State right-to-work law. A **closed shop** contract requires the employer to hire only union members. A **union shop** contract permits the employer to hire nonunion members but requires that the employee must become a member of the union within a specified period of time after gaining employment and must remain a member in good standing as a condition of employment. A **right-to-work law** is a State statute that prohibits union shop contracts. Most States permit the existence of union shops.

Finally, the Act reinstates the availability of civil injunctions in labor disputes if requested of the NLRB in order to prevent an unfair labor practice. The Act also grants the President of the United States the power to obtain an injunction for an eighty-day cooling-off period if the strike is likely to endanger the national health or safety.

Labor-Management Reporting and Disclosure Act

The Labor-Management Reporting and Disclosure Act, also known as the **Landrum-Griffin Act,** is aimed at eliminating corruption in labor unions. The Act, which was passed in 1959, attempts to deal with the problem of corruption by establishing an elaborate reporting system and the enactment of a union "bill of rights" designed to make unions more democratic. The latter provides union members with the right to nominate candidates for union offices, to vote in elections, to attend membership meetings, to participate in union business, to have free expression at union meetings and conventions, and to be accorded a full and fair hearing before any disciplinary action is taken by the union against them.

EMPLOYMENT DISCRIMINATION LAW

A number of Federal statutes prohibit discrimination in employment on the basis of race, sex, religion, national origin, age, and handicap. The cornerstone of Federal employment discrimination law is Title VII of the 1964 Civil Rights Act, but also of significance are the Equal Pay Act, the Age Discrimination in Employment Act of 1967, the Rehabilitation Act of 1973, and various Executive Orders. In addition, most States have enacted similar laws prohibiting discrimination based on race, sex, religion, national origin, and handicap.

Equal Pay Act

The **Equal Pay** Act prohibits an employer from discriminating between employees on the basis of **sex** by paying unequal wages for the same work. The Act forbids an employer from paying wages at a rate less than the rate at which he pays wages to employees of the opposite sex for equal work at the same establishment. Once the employee has demonstrated that the employer pays unequal wages for *equal* work to members of the opposite sex, the burden shifts to the employer to prove that the pay differential is based on:

1. a seniority system;
2. a merit system;
3. a system that measures earnings by quantity or quality of production; or
4. any factor except sex.

Remedies include recovery of back pay and enjoining the employer from further unlawful conduct. The Department of Labor is the Federal agency designated by the statute to interpret and enforce the Act. In 1979 these functions were transferred to the Equal Employment Opportunity Commission.

Civil Rights Act of 1964

Title VII of the Civil Rights Act of 1964 prohibits **employment discrimination** on the basis of race, color, sex, religion, or national origin in hiring, firing, compensating, promoting, training, or otherwise. The Act applies to employers engaged in an industry affecting commerce and having fifteen or more employees.

The enforcement agency for Title VII is the **Equal Employment Opportunity Commission (EEOC).** The EEOC is charged with the responsibility and empowered to (1) file legal actions in its own name or to intervene in actions filed by third parties; (2) to attempt to resolve alleged violations through informal means prior to bringing suit; (3) to investigate all charges of discrimination; and (4) to issue guidelines and regulations concerning enforcement policy.

The Act provides three basic defenses: (1) a *bona fide* seniority or merit system, (2) a professionally developed ability test, and (3) a *bona fide* occupational qualification. Remedies for violation of the Act include enjoining the employer from engaging in the unlawful behavior, appropriate affirmative action, and reinstatement of employees and award of back pay from a date not more than two years prior to the filing of the charge with the EEOC. **Affirmative action** generally means the active recruitment of a designated group of applicants, although courts have used the remedy of affirmative action to impose numerical hiring ratios (quotas).

Discrimination   Each of the following constitutes discriminatory conduct prohibited by the act:

1. Disparate Treatment. An individual shows that an employer used a proscribed criteria in making an employment decision. The Supreme Court has held that a *prima facie* case of discrimination would be shown if the plaintiff (a) is within a protected class, (b) applied for an open position, (c) was qualified for the position, (d) was denied the job, and (e) the employer continued to try to fill the position. Once the plaintiff establishes a *prima facie* case, the burden shifts to the defendant to "articulate legitimate and non-discriminatory reasons for the plaintiff's rejection." *McDonnell Douglas Corp. v. Green*, 411 U.S. 792 (1973).

2. Present Effects of Past Discrimination. An employer engages in conduct that on its face is "neutral," that is, nondiscriminatory, but nonetheless continues to perpetuate past discriminatory practices. For example, it has been held illegal for a union that had previously limited membership to whites to adopt a requirement that new members be related to or recommended by existing members. *Local 53 of International Association of Heat and Frost Insulators and Asbestos Workers v. Vogler*, 407 F.2d 1047 (5th Cir. 1969).

3. Disparate Impact. An employer adopts "neutral" rules that have an adverse impact on a protected class and that are not justified as being necessary to the business. The following case illustrates this point, but for a more recent and limiting case, holding that an employer merely had to show that the personnel practices were reasonable in order to rebut statistical proof of bias, see Law in the News at page 948.

 GRIGGS v. DUKE POWER CO.
Supreme Court of the United States, 1971.
401 U.S. 424, 91 S.Ct. 849, 28 L.Ed.2d 158.

Facts: During the years prior to the passage of the Civil Rights Act of 1964, Duke Power openly discriminated against blacks by allowing them to work only in the labor department of the plant's five departments. The highest paying job in the labor department paid less than the lowest paying jobs in the other four "operating" departments in which only whites were employed. In 1955 the company began requiring a high school education for initial assignment to any department except labor. When Duke Power stopped restricting Negroes to the labor department in 1965, it made completion of high school a prerequisite to transfer from labor to any other department. White employees hired before the high school education requirement was adopted continued to perform satisfactorily and achieve promotions in the "operating' departments.

In 1965 the company also began requiring new employees in the departments other than labor to register satisfactory scores on two professionally prepared aptitude tests, in addition to having a high school education. In September 1965

Duke Power began to permit employees to qualify for transfer to another department from labor by passing two tests, neither of which was directed or intended to measure the ability to learn to perform a particular job or category of jobs. Griggs brought suit against Duke Power, claiming that the high school education and testing requirements were discriminatory and therefore prohibited by the Civil Rights Act of 1964. The district court held that Title VII was prospective only and thus Duke's earlier policy of racial discrimination was beyond the reach of the Act. The Court of Appeals rejected the district court's holding that residual discrimination from previous employment practices was beyond the scope of the Act, but it held the district court was correct in its conclusion that there was no showing of a racial purpose or invidious intent in the promulgation of its new hiring requirements. The Court of Appeals, therefore, held that the use of such standards was not prohibited by the Act.

Decision: Judgment of the Court of Appeals in favor of Duke Power reversed.

Opinion: **Burger, C. J.**   The objective of Congress in the enactment of Title VII is plain from the language of the statute. It was to achieve equality of employment opportunities and remove barriers that have operated in the past to favor an identifiable group of white employees over other employees. Under the Act, practices, procedures, or tests neutral on their face and even neutral in terms of intent, cannot be maintained if they operate to "freeze" the status quo of prior discriminatory employment practices.

The Court of Appeals' opinion, and the partial dissent, agreed that, on the record in the present case, "whites register far better on the Company's alternative requirements" than Negroes. [Footnote 6. In North Carolina, 1960 census statistics show that, while 34% of white males had completed high school, only 12% of Negro males had done so. Similarly, with respect to standardized tests, the EEOC in one case found that use of a battery of tests, including the Wonderlic and Bennett tests used by the Company in the instant case, resulted in 58% of whites passing the tests, as compared with only 6% of the blacks. [Citations.]] This consequence would appear to be directly traceable to race. Basic intelligence must have the means of articulation to manifest itself fairly in a testing process. Because they are Negroes, petitioners have long received inferior education in segregated schools and this Court expressly recognized these differences in [citation]. There, because of the inferior education received by Negroes in North Carolina, this Court barred the institution of a literacy test for voter registration on the ground that the test would abridge the right to vote indirectly on account of race. Congress did not intend by Title VII, however, to guarantee a job to every person regardless of qualifications. In short, the Act does not command that any person be hired simply because he was formerly the subject of discrimination, or because he is a member of a minority group. Discriminatory preference for any group, minority or majority, is precisely and only what Congress has proscribed. What is required by Congress is the removal of artificial, arbitrary, and unnecessary barriers to employment when the barriers operate invidiously to discriminate on the basis of racial or other impermissible classification.

* * *

The Act proscribes not only overt discrimination but also practices that are fair in form, but discriminatory in operation. The touchstone is business necessity. If an employment practice which operates to exclude Negroes cannot be shown to be related to job performance, the practice is prohibited.

On the record before us, neither the high school completion requirement nor the general intelligence test is shown to bear a demonstrable relationship to successful performance of the jobs for which it was used. Both were adopted, as the Court of Appeals noted, without meaningful study of their relationship to job-performance ability. * * *

The evidence, however, shows that employees who have not completed high school or taken the tests have continued to perform satisfactorily and make progress in departments for which the high school and test criteria are now used.

* * *

The facts of this case demonstrate the inadequacy of broad and general testing devices as well as the infirmity of using diplomas or degrees as fixed measures of capability. History is filled with examples of men and women who rendered highly effective performance without the conventional badges of accomplishment in terms of certificates, diplomas, or degrees. Diplomas and tests are useful servants, but Congress has mandated the commonsense proposition that they are not to become masters of reality.

* * *

Nothing in the Act precludes the use of testing or measuring procedures; obviously they are useful. What Congress has forbidden is giving these devices and mechanisms controlling force unless they are demonstrably a reasonable measure of job performance. Congress has not commanded that the less qualified be preferred over the better qualified simply because of minority origins. Far from disparaging job qualifications as such, Congress has made such qualifications the controlling factor, so that race, religion, nationality, and sex become irrelevant. What Congress has commanded is that any tests used must measure the person for the job and not the person in the abstract.

Reverse Discrimination A major controversy has arisen over the equality of the use of reverse discrimination in achieving affirmative action. In this context, **reverse discrimination** refers to affirmative action that directs an employer to take the race or sex of an individual into account when hiring or promoting for the purpose of remedying underrepresentation of that race or sex in traditionally segregated jobs. An example would be an employer who discriminates against white males in order to increase the proportion of females or members of a racial minority. This question is presented in the following case and in Law in the News at page 948.

UNITED STEELWORKERS OF AMERICA v. WEBER
Supreme Court of the United States, 1979.
443 U.S. 193, 99 S.Ct. 2721, 61 L.Ed.2d 480.

Facts: In 1974 the United Steelworkers of America and Kaiser Aluminum entered into a master collective bargaining agreement covering terms and conditions of employment at fifteen Kaiser plants. The agreement contained an affirmative action plan designed to eliminate conspicuous racial imbalances in Kaiser's then almost exclusively white craftwork forces. Black craft-hiring goals were set for each Kaiser plant equal to the percentage of blacks in the respective local labor forces. To meet these goals, on-the-job training programs were established to teach unskilled production workers—blacks and whites—the skills necessary to become craftworkers. The plan reserved for black employees 50 percent of the openings in these newly created inplant training programs.

Pursuant to the national agreement, Kaiser altered its craft-hiring practice in its Gramercy, Louisiana, plant by establishing a program to train its production workers to fill craft openings. Selection of craft trainees was made on the basis of seniority. At least 50 percent of the new trainees were to be black until the percentage of black skilled craftworkers in the Gramercy plant approximated the percentage of blacks in the local force. During the first year of the operation of this affirmative action plan, thirteen craft trainees (seven black, six white) were selected from Gramercy's productions work force. The most senior black selected had less seniority than several white production workers who were denied admission to the program. Weber, one of these white employees, brought suit claiming that the affirmative action plan discriminated against white employees and therefore violated the Civil Rights Act of 1964. The district court held that the affirmative action plan of Kaiser did violate Title VII and entered judgment for the plaintiff. The Court of Appeals for the Fifth Circuit affirmed the decision.

Decision: Judgment of the Court of Appeals in favor of Weber reversed.

Opinion: **Brennan, J.**   We emphasize at the outset the narrowness of our inquiry. Since the Kaiser-USWA plan does not involve state action, this case does not present an alleged violation of the Equal Protection Clause of the Fourteenth Amendment. Further, since the Kaiser-USWA plan was adopted voluntarily, we are not concerned with what Title VII requires or with what a court might order to remedy a past proved violation of the Act. The only question before us is the narrow statutory issue of whether Title VII *forbids* private employers and unions from voluntarily agreeing upon *bona fide* affirmative action plans that accord racial preferences in the manner and for the purpose provided in the Kaiser-USWA plan. That question was expressly left open in *MacDonald v. Santa Fe Trail Transp. Co.,* [citation], which held, in a case not involving affirmative action Title VII protects whites as well as blacks from certain forms of racial discrimination.

Respondent argues that Congress intended in Title VII to prohibit all race-conscious affirmative action plans. Respondent's argument rests upon a literal interpretation of [two sections] of the Act. Those sections make it unlawful to "discriminate * * * because of * * * race" in hiring and in the selection of apprentices for training programs. Since, the argument runs, *McDonald v. Santa Fe Trail Transp. Co.* settled that Title VII forbids discrimination against whites as well as blacks, and since the Kaiser-USWA affirmative action plan operates to discriminate against white employees solely because they are white, it follows that the Kaiser-USWA plan violates Title VII.

Respondent's argument is not without force. But it overlooks the significance of the fact that the Kaiser-USWA plan is an affirmative action plan voluntarily adopted by private parties to eliminate traditional patterns of racial segregation. * * *

Congress' primary concern in enacting the prohibition against racial discrimination in Title VII of the Civil Rights Act of 1964 was with "the plight of the Negro in our economy." [Citation.] Before 1964, blacks were largely relegated to "unskilled and semi-skilled jobs." [And, the situation was worsening.] "In 1947 the nonwhite unemployment rate was only 64 percent higher than the white rate; in 1962 it was 124 percent higher" (remarks of Sen. Humphrey). [Citation.] Congress considered this a serious social problem. As Senator Clark told the Senate:

The rate of Negro unemployment has gone up consistently as compared with white unemployment for the past 15 years. This is a social malaise and a social situation which we should not tolerate. That is one of the principal reasons why the bill should pass. [Citation.]

Congress feared that the goals of the Civil Rights Act—the integration of blacks into the mainstream of American society—could not be achieved unless this trend were reversed. And Congress recognized that that would not be possible unless blacks were able to secure jobs "which have a future."

* * *

Accordingly, it was clear to Congress that "[t]he crux of the problem [was] to open employment opportunities for Negroes in occupations which have been traditionally closed to them," [citation], and it was to this problem that Title VII's prohibition against racial discrimination in employment was primarily addressed.

* * *

Given this legislative history, we cannot agree with respondent that Congress intended to prohibit the private sector from taking effective steps to accomplish the goal that Congress designed Title VII to achieve. The very statutory words intended as a spur or catalyst to cause "employers and unions to self-examine and to self-evaluate their employment practices and to endeavor to eliminate, so far as possible, the last vestiges of an unfortunate and ignominious page in this country's history," [citation], cannot be interpreted as an absolute prohibition against all private, voluntary, race-conscious affirmative action efforts to hasten the elimina tion of such vestiges. It would be ironic indeed if a law triggered by a Nation's concern over centuries of racial injustice and intended to improve the lot of those who had "been excluded from the American dream for so long," [citation], constituted the first legislative prohibition of all voluntary, private, race-conscious efforts to abolish traditional patterns of racial segregation and hierarchy.

* * *

We need not today define in detail the line of demarcation between permissible and impermissible affirmative action plans. It suffices to hold that the challenged Kaiser-USWA affirmative action plan falls on the permissible side of the line. The purposes of the plan mirror those of the statute. Both were designed to break down old patterns of racial segregation and hierarchy. Both were structured to "open employment opportunities for Negroes in occupations which have been tradition-ally closed to them. [Citation.]

At the same time, the plan does not unnecessarily trammel the interests of the white employees. The plan does not require the discharge of white workers and their replacement with new black hirees. [Citation.] Nor does the plan create an absolute bar to the advancement of white employees; half of those trained in the program will be white. Moreover, the plan is a temporary measure; it is not intended to maintain racial balance, but simply to eliminate a manifest racial imbalance. Preferential selection of craft trainees at the Gramercy plant will end as soon as the percentage of black skilled craftworkers in the Gramercy plant approximates the percentage of blacks in the local labor force. [Citation.]

We conclude, therefore, that the adoption of the Kaiser-USWA plan for the Gramercy plant falls within the area of discretion left by Title VII to the private sector voluntarily to adopt affirmative action plans designed to eliminate conspic-uous racial imbalance in traditionally segregated job categories.

LAW IN THE NEWS

A Changed Court Revises Rules on Civil Rights

With a recent burst of discrimination rulings, the Supreme Court did something more than provide newly confining definitions to widely used civil rights laws. The Court all but guaranteed that civil rights would leap to the forefront of domestic politics.

Three decisions this month, each by the same 5-to-4 conservative majority that now dominates the Court on civil rights issues, rewrote long-settled ground rules of proof and procedure in employment discrimination cases. The decisions, plus a fourth that set strict time limits on challenges to discriminatory seniority systems, make discrimination suits harder to bring, harder to win and more vulnerable to attack if successfully concluded.

The decisions left no doubt that Ronald Reagan, out of office five months, finally succeeded in a goal that had appeared to elude him for much of his eight years in the White House: to shift the Supreme Court's direction on civil rights. The new majority consists of his three appointees, Justices Sandra Day O'Connor, Antonin Scalia and Anthony M. Kennedy; Chief Justice William H. Rehnquist, whom he elevated to that position; and Justice Byron R. White, who started taking conservative positions on civil rights years ago.

Civil rights leaders, reeling from the string of defeats, turned immediately to Congress, where liberals vowed to restore what had been lost. That worked earlier in the decade, when Congress overturned a Supreme Court ruling on voting rights and another concerning discrimination by institutions that receive Federal funds.

But such efforts rarely prove as straightforward or cost-free as they might appear at the start. For example, it took four years for Congress to overturn the 1984 decision on Federal funds. The Congressional effort to overturn that decision, Grove City College v. Bell, became mired in a debate over its possible impact on abortion rights, opening painful fissures in the civil rights coalition before the Civil Rights Restoration Act finally became law over President Reagan's veto in 1988.

A brief filed on behalf of 66 Senators and 145 Representatives in one of the cases decided last week, Patterson v. McLean Credit Union, noted, in asking the Court not to tamper with the precedent, that "any congressional effort to change a decision of this Court could prove divisive" and could "confront grave difficulties in addressing the nuances that have arisen from case-by-case elaboration of the statute."

The point is telling because it was the superstructure of judicial interpretation, not the statutory foundations, that the majority knocked loose in the recent decisions.

Filling in the Law

For example, Title VII of the Civil Rights Act of 1964 forbids, in rather spare language, discrimination in employment on the basis of race, sex and some other categories. It was the Court that gave life and force to the statute's words. In a 1971 case called Griggs v. Duke Power, the Court ruled unanimously that Title VII prohibited not just purposeful discrimination but also job requirements and practices that had the effect of discriminating. In those kinds of cases, the Griggs opinion said, employers had the burden of justifying the necessity for such practices.

In its June 5 opinion in Wards Cove Packing v. Antonio, written by Justice White, the Court shifted that burden to employees, who must now prove that the challenged practices are in fact not necessary. The shift might appear to be a technical matter, but the outcome of lawsuits is often determined by standards and burdens of proof.

Lawyers representing blacks and women in job discrimination suits said the Wards Cove decision gave plaintiffs an onerous burden, while employer groups greeted the result as overdue relief from a set of rules that they veiwed as stacked against them. Charles Fried, the Solicitor General during the last four years of the Reagan Administration, called the decision a welcome development that would help end the "sinister pressure" for quotas.

Wards Cove may be the most difficult of the decisions for Congress to overrule, because any debate over the structure of Title VII almost inevitably invites messy debate about affirmative action.

Congress is much more comfortable painting with a broad brush—"discrimination is forbidden"—than in filling in the details. The Court's approach this month was essentially the opposite: to rearrange the details while leaving the broad image, at least at first glance, untouched.

In the Patterson case, decided on Thursday, the Court unanimously did what the 211 Senators and Representatives who filed the brief had asked it to do: retained its decision in a 1976 case, Runyon v. McCrary, that interpreted a Reconstruction-era civil rights law to bar private as well as officially sponsored acts of racial discrimination.

But then a 5-to-4 majority revisited the old law, known as Section 1981, giving it a new interpretation that civil rights leaders said would severely weaken it as a tool against job discrimination. Justice Kennedy's majority opinion said that Section 1981 covered discrimination in the initial hiring process but not discriminatory treatment on the job. The Congressional brief, aimed at preserving the law, did not focus on its particular application, but that must now be the focus of any Congressional debate to overturn the ruling.

Of all the decisions, the ruling last Monday in Martin v. Wilks may be the most unsettling for civil rights leaders. The Court ruled that white firefighters in Birmingham, Ala., could sue to reopen an affirmative-action settlement, approved by the Federal District Court there eight years ago to remedy discrimination that had kept blacks out of all senior positions in the department. Because Chief Justice Rehnquist's majority opinion was based not on a particular statute but on an interpretation of the procedural rules that govern the Federal courts, it may have the effect of reopening many cases long believed closed.

The timing of the decisions in a two-week period, while perhaps coincidental, gave an added sense of drama to the Court's shift. "The second Reconstruction period has ended," Richard Cohen, a Washington Post columnist, wrote on Friday, dating the period from the Court's 1954 school desegregation ruling until this month.

The new majority appeared to be aware of a firestorm of criticism. "Neither our words nor our decisions should be interpreted as signaling one inch of retreat from Congress' policy to forbid discrimination," Justice Kennedy wrote at the end of his opinion in the Patterson case. From one perspective it was a statement of the obvious. Others, hearing a defensive tone in Justice Kennedy's words, pre-pared to do uncertain battle to hold Congress, if not the Court, to their promise.

Language of the Law

As recent decisions have made clear, the Burger and Rehnquist courts have looked at similar civil rights cases from different angles. The following excerpts, from some of the Court's principal cases, show the Justices' changing observations about the purpose and scope of the laws.

Unequal Opportunity

In this term, the Court effectively shifted the burden of proof in suits alleging discriminatory patterns in hiring and promotion.

1971: [The Civil Rights Act of 1964] proscribes not only overt discrimination but also practices that are fair in form, but discriminatory in operation. . . . Congress directed the thrust of the Act to the consequences of employment practices, not simply their motivation.
Griggs v. Duke Power Co.
Chief Justice Burger

1989: The plaintiff bears the burden of disproving an employer's assertion that the adverse employment action or practice was based solely on a legitimate neutral consideration.
Wards Cove Packing Co. v. Atonio
Justice White

Affirmative Action

Ten years ago, the Court found that an affirmative action plan agreed upon in labor negotiations did not violate whites' civil rights; this year, it held that whites affected by a court-ordered affirmative action plan could sue to reopen the case.

1979: It would be ironic indeed if a law triggered by a Nation's concern over centuries of racial injustice and intended to improve the lot of those who had "been excluded from the American dream for so long," constituted the first legislative prohibition of all voluntary, private, race-conscious efforts to abolish traditional patterns of racial segregation and hierarchy. . . . We need not today define in detail the line of demarcation between permissible and impermissible affirmative actions plans. . . . The challenged Kaiser-

U.S.W.A. affirmative action plan falls on the permissible side of the line.

United Steelworkers v. Weber
Justice Brennan

1989: A voluntary settlement in the form of a consent decree between one group of employees and their employer cannot possibly "settle," voluntarily or otherwise, the conflicting claims of . . . employees who do not join in the agreement.

Martin v. Wilks
Chief Justice Rehnquist

Minority Set-Asides

The Court has outlined limits on set-asides of public-works funds for minority contractors, an arrangement approved in 1980.

1980: Congress, after due consideration, perceived a pressing need to move forward with new approaches in the continuing effort to achieve the goal of equality of economic opportunity. In this effort, Congress has necessary latitude to try new techniques such as the limited use of racial and ethnic criteria to accomplish remedial objectives.

Fullilove v. Klutznick
Chief Justice Burger

1989: While there is no doubt that the sorry history of both private and public discrimination in this country has contributed to a lack of opportunities for black entrepreneurs, this observation, standing alone, cannot justify a rigid racial quota in the awarding of public contracts in Richmond, Va.

Richmond v. Croson
Justice O'Connor

by Linda Greenhouse
Copyright © 1989 by the New York Times Company.
Reprinted by permission.

Similarly, in 1987 the United States Supreme Court upheld the employer's right to promote a female employee instead of a white male employee with higher test scores on the qualifying examination:

In making our decision, we find that the employment decision was justified by the existence of a "manifest imbalance" that reflected underrepresentation of women in "traditionally segregated job categories." The Agency's [employer's] Plan did not authorize such blind hiring but expressly directed that numerous factors be taken into account in making employment decisions. Furthermore, the Plan did not trammel male employee's rights or create a bar to their advancement as it set aside no positions for women. Substantial evidence shows that the Agency has sought to take a moderate, gradual approach to eliminating the imbalance in its work force, one which establishes realistic guidance for employment decisions. Given this fact, as well as the Agency's express commitment to "attain" a balanced work force, there is ample assurance that the Agency does not seek to use its Plan to "maintain" a permanent racial and sexual balance. Thus, we do not find the Agency in violation of Title VII. *Johnson v. Transportation Agency,* 480 U.S. 616 (1987).

Sexual Harassment   In 1980 the EEOC issued a definition of sexual harassment:

Unwelcome sexual advances, requests for sexual favors, and other verbal or physical conduct of a sexual nature constitute sexual harassment when

(1) submission to such conduct is made either explicitly or implicitly a term or condition of an individual's employment.

(2) submission to or rejection of such conduct by an individual is used as the basis for employment decisions affecting such individual, or

(3) such conduct has the purpose or effect of reasonably interfering with an individual's work performance or creating an intimidating, hostile or offensive working environment.

The courts, including the United State Supreme Court, have held that sexual harassment may constitute illegal sexual discrimination in violation of Title VII. Moreover, an employer will be held liable for sexual harassment committed by one of its employees if it does not take immediate action when it knows or should have known of the harassment. When the employee engaging in sexual harassment is an agent of the employer or is in a supervisory position over the victim, the employer may be liable without knowledge or reason to know.

MERITOR SAVINGS BANK, FSB v. VINSON
Supreme Court of the United States, 1986.
477 U.S. 57, 106 S.Ct. 2399, 91 L.Ed.2d 49.

Facts: Mechelle Vinson was an employee of Meritor Savings Bank for approximately four years. Beginning as a teller-trainee, she ultimately advanced to the position of assistant branch manager. Her promotions were based solely upon merit. Sidney Taylor, a vice-president of the bank and manager of the branch office in which Vinson worked, was Vinson's supervisor throughout her employment with the bank. After the bank fired Vinson for her abusive use of sick leave, Vinson brought an action against Taylor and the bank, alleging that during her employment she had "constantly been subjected to sexual harassment" by Taylor in violation of Title VII of the Civil Rights Act of 1964. At trial, Vinson stated that Taylor repeatedly demanded sexual favors from her, fondled her in front of other employees, and forcibly raped her on a number of occasions. Taylor and the bank categorically denied Vinson's allegations. The district court denied relief to Vinson, finding that any sexual relationship between Vinson and Taylor "was a voluntary one having nothing to do with her continued employment . . . or her advancement or promotions at that institution." Notwithstanding this conclusion, the district court went on to determine that "the bank was without notice [of Taylor's alleged conduct] and cannot be held liable for the alleged actions of Taylor." The Court of Appeals reversed.

Decision: Judgment of Court of Appeals affirmed and the case remanded.

Opinion: Rehnquist, J. Respondent argues, and the Court of Appeals held, that unwelcome sexual advances that create an offensive or hostile working environment violate Title VII. Without question, when a supervisor sexually harasses a subordinate because of the subordinate's sex, that supervisor "discriminate(s)" on the basis of sex. Petitioner apparently does not challenge this proposition.

* * *

First, the language of Title VII is not limited to "economic" or "tangible" discrimination. The phrase "terms, conditions, or privileges of employment" evinces a congressional intent " 'to strike at the entire spectrum of disparate treatment of men and women' " in employment. . . .

Second, in 1980 the EEOC issued guidelines specifying that "sexual harassment," as there defined, is a form of sex discrimination prohibited by Title VII. As an "administrative interpretation of the Act by the enforcing agency," [citation], these guidelines, " 'while not controlling upon the courts by reason of their authority, do constitute a body of experience and informed judgment to which courts and litigants may properly resort for guidance,' " [citation].

The EEOC guidelines fully support the view that harassment leading to noneconomic injury can violate Title VII.

In defining "sexual harassment," the guidelines first describe the kinds of workplace conduct that may be actionable under Title VII. These include "(u)nwelcome sexual advances, requests for sexual favors, and other verbal or physical conduct of a sexual nature." [Citation.] Relevant to the charges at issue in this case, the guidelines provide that such sexual misconduct constitutes prohibited "sexual harassment," whether or not it is directly linked to the grant or denial of an economic quid pro quo, where "such conduct has the purpose or effect of unreasonably interfering with an individual's work performance or creating an intimidating, hostile, or offensive working environment."

* * *

The question remains, however, whether the District Court's ultimate finding that respondent "was not the victim of sexual harassment," [citation], effectively disposed of respondent's claim. The Court of Appeals recognized, we think correctly, that this ultimate finding was likely based on one or both of two erroneous views of the law. First, the District Court apparently believed that a claim for sexual harassment will not lie absent an economic effect on the complainant's employment. . . . Since it appears that the District Court made its findings without ever considering the "hostile environment" theory of sexual harassment, the Court of Appeals' decision to remand was correct.

Second, the District Court's conclusion that no actionable harassment occurred might have rested on its earlier "finding" that "(i)f (respondent) and Taylor did engage in an intimate or sexual relationship . . ., that relationship was a voluntary one." But the fact that sex-related conduct was "voluntary," in the sense that the complainant was not forced to participate against her will, is not a defense to a sexual harassment suit brought under Title VII. The gravamen of any sexual harassment claim is that the alleged sexual advances were "unwelcome."

* * *

III

Although the District Court concluded that respondent had not proved a violation of Title VII, it nevertheless went on to consider the question of the bank's liability. Finding that "the bank was without notice" of Taylor's alleged conduct, and that notice to Taylor was not the equivalent of notice to the bank, the court concluded that the bank therefore could not be held liable for Taylor's alleged actions. The Court of Appeals took the opposite view, holding that an employer is strictly liable for a hostile environment created by a supervisor's sexual advances, even though the employer neither knew nor reasonably could have known of the alleged misconduct. The court held that a supervisor, whether or not he possesses the authority to hire, fire, or promote, is necessarily an "agent" of his employer for all Title VII purposes, since "even the appearance" of such authority may enable him to impose himself on his subordinates.

* * *

This debate over the appropriate standard for employer liability has a rather abstract quality about it given the state of the record in this case. We do not know at this stage whether Taylor made any sexual advances toward respondent at all, let alone whether those advances were unwelcome, whether they were sufficiently pervasive to constitute a condition of employment, or whether they were "so pervasive and so long continuing . . . that the employer must have become conscious of (them)," [citation].

We therefore decline the parties' invitation to issue a definitive rule on employer liability, but we do agree with the EEOC that Congress wanted courts to look to agency principles for guidance in this area. While such common-law principles may not be transferable in all their particulars to Title VII, Congress' decision to define "employer" to include any "agent" of an employer, [citation], surely evinces an intent to place some limits on the acts of employees for which employers under Title VII are to be held responsible. For this reason, we hold that the Court of Appeals erred in concluding that employers are always automatically liable for sexual harassment by their supervisors. [Citation.] For the same reason, absence of notice to an employer does not necessarily insulate that employer from liability. [Citation.]

Finally, we reject petitioner's view that the mere existence of a grievance procedure and a policy against discrimination, coupled with respondent's failure to invoke that procedure, must insulate petitioner from liability.

* * *

IV

In sum, we hold that a claim of "hostile environment" sex discrimination is actionable under Title VII, that the District Court's findings were insufficient to dispose of respondent's hostile environment claim, and that the District Court did not err in admitting testimony about respondent's sexually provocative speech and dress. As to employer liability, we conclude that the Court of Appeals was wrong to entirely disregard agency principles and impose absolute liability on employers for the acts of their supervisors, regardless of the circumstances of a particular case.

Comparable Worth Industrial statistics indicate that women earn approximately two-thirds of the salaries of men. Studies have suggested that between one-third and one-half of the disparity in earnings results from sexual discrimination. Other probable causes for the gap include (1) males and females have different education and job skills, (2) females are employed in lower-paying occupations, and (3) females are more likely to interrupt their careers to raise families.

Because the Equal Pay Act only requires equal pay for equal work, it does not apply to different jobs even if they are comparable. Thus, that statute provides no remedy for women whose traditional jobs have been systematically undervalued and underpaid. As a result, women sought redress under Title VII by arguing that failure to pay comparable worth is discrimination on the basis of sex. The concept of **comparable worth** provides that the relative values to an employer of different jobs should be measured through a rating system or job evaluation that is free of any potential sex bias. Theoretically, all employees will be fairly paid if objective weights are attached consistently across job categories, using such factors as skill, effort, working conditions, responsibility, and mental demands. For example, if under such a system the jobs of truck

driver and nurse are evaluated at the same level, then both jobs should receive the same pay.

In 1981 the United States Supreme Court held that a claim of discriminatory undercompensation based on sex may be brought under Title VII, even where the plaintiffs were performing different jobs from their male counterparts. As the Court noted, however, the case involved a situation in which the defendant intentionally discriminated in wages; and the defendant, not the courts, had compared the jobs in terms of value. *County of Washington v. Gunther*, 452 U.S. 161 (1981). The Court also held that the four defenses available under the Equal Pay Act would apply to a Title VII claim. Since this decision, the concept of comparable worth has met with limited success in the courts. Nonetheless, more than a dozen States have legislatively adopted requirements that public and private employers pay equally for comparable work.

Age Discrimination in Employment Act of 1967

The Age Discrimination in Employment Act prohibits discriminating in hiring, firing, compensating, or otherwise on the basis of age. Originally, the Act applied the substantive language of Title VII to benefit individuals between the ages of forty and sixty-five. In 1978 the upper age limit was raised from sixty-five to seventy, and finally, in 1986, the upper age limit was eliminated. The Act applies to private employers having twenty or more employees and to all governmental units regardless of size. The Act also prohibits the mandatory retirement of most employees under the age of seventy.

The major statutory defenses include (1) a *bona fide* occupational qualification, (2) a *bona fide* seniority system, and (3) any other reasonable action. Remedies include back pay, injunctive relief, and affirmative action.

Rehabilitation Act of 1973

The Rehabilitation Act of 1973 attempts to provide assistance to the handicapped in obtaining rehabilitation training, access to public facilities, and employment. The act requires Federal contractors and Federal agencies to take affirmative action to hire qualified handicapped persons. It also prohibits discrimination on the basis of handicap in Federal programs and programs receiving Federal financial assistance.

A handicapped person is defined as an individual who (1) has a physical or mental impairment that substantially affects one or more of her major life activities; (2) has a history of major life activity impairment; *or* (3) is regarded as having such an impairment. Major life activities include such functions as caring for oneself, seeing, speaking, or walking. Alcohol and drug abuses are not considered handicapping conditions for the purposes of this statute.

Executive Order

In 1965 President Johnson issued an Executive Order that prohibited discrimination by Federal contractors on the basis of race, color, sex, religion, or national origin in employment on *any work* performed by the contractor during the period of the Federal contract. Federal contractors are also required to take affirmative action in recruiting. The Secretary of Labor, **Office of Federal Contract Compliance Pro-**

grams (OFCCP) administers enforcement of the program.

The program applies to all contractors who enter into a contract to be performed in the United States with the Federal government and all of their subcontractors in excess of $10,000. Compliance with the affirmative action requirement differs for construction and nonconstruction contractors. All **nonconstruction** contractors with fifty or more employees or with contracts for more than $50,000 must have a written affirmative action plan in order to be in compliance. The plan must include a work force analysis, planned corrective action, if necessary, with specific goals and timetables, and procedures for auditing and reporting. The Director of the OFCCP periodically issues goals and timetables for each segment of the **construction** industry for each region of the country. As a condition precedent to bidding on the Federal contract, the contractor must agree to make a good faith effort to achieve current published goals.

EMPLOYEE PROTECTION

Employees are accorded a number of protections relating to their jobs. These include a limited right not to be unfairly dismissed, a right to a safe and healthy workplace, compensation for injuries sustained in the workplace, and some financial security upon retirement or loss of employment. This section discusses (1) employee termination at will, (2) occupational safety and health, (3) workers' compensation, (4) Social Security and unemployment insurance, and (5) the Fair Labor Standard Act.

Employee Termination at Will

Under the common law, a contract of employment for other than a definite term is terminable at will by either party. Accordingly, under the common law, employers may "dismiss their employees at will for good cause, for no cause or even for cause morally wrong, without being thereby guilty of legal wrong." In recent years, however, a growing number of judicial exceptions to the rule have developed based on implied contract, tort, and public policy. A number of Federal and State statutes enacted in the last fifty years also limit the rule. Finally, the rule may be restricted by contractual agreement between employer and employee. In particular, most collective bargaining agreements negotiated through union representatives contain a provision prohibiting dismissal "without cause."

Statutory Limitations In 1934, as previously discussed, Congress enacted the National Labor Relations Act, which provided employees with the right to unionize free of intimidation or coercion from their employers, including freedom from dismissal for engaging in union activities. Since the enactment of the NLRA, additional Federal legislation has been passed that limits the employer's right to discharge. These statutes fall into three categories: (1) those protecting certain employees from discriminatory discharge; (2) those protecting certain employees in their exercise of statutory rights; and (3) those protecting certain employees from discharge without cause.

An example is Title VII of the Civil Rights Act of 1964, discussed above. Although its primary focus is on hiring, promotion, and seniority practices, this statute has been used in challenging the employer's right to discharge employees for discriminatory reasons. Another example is the Consumer Credit Protection Act, discussed in Chapter 45, under which an employer may not dismiss an employee whose wages have been garnished for indebtedness. Additional Federal statutes protect other categories of employees such as the handicapped, public employees serving jury duty, and the aged.

At the State level there are statutes protecting workers from discriminatory discharge for filing workers' compensation claims. There are also many State statutes that parallel Federal legislation. Some States have adopted statutes similar to the NLRA, and many States prohibit discrimination in employment on the basis of such factors as race, creed, nationality, sex, or age. In addition, some States have statutes prohibiting discharge or other punitive actions taken for the purpose of influencing voting or, in some States, political activity.

Judicial Limitations Judicial limitations on the employment-at-will doctrine have been based on contract law, tort law, and public policy. Cases founded in contract theory have relied on various arguments, including (1) the dismissal was improper because the employee had detrimentally relied on the employer's promise of work for a reasonable period of time; (2) the employment was not at will because of implied-in-fact promises of employment for a specific duration, which meant that the employer could not terminate the employee without just cause; (3) the employment contract contained express or implied provisions that the employee would not be dismissed so long as he satisfactorily performed his work; (4) the employer had assured the employee that he would not be dismissed except for cause; or (5) that, upon entering into the employment contract, the employee gave consideration over and above the performance of services to support a promise of job security.

Cases applying implied contract theory frequently involve reliance by an employee on personnel manuals containing some assurance of job security, often in the form of a provision stating that employees shall be discharged only for "cause." Some courts have circumvented the common law at-will doctrine under implied contract theories by finding that contracts of employment contain an implied promise to deal in good faith, including a duty on the part of the employer to terminate only in good faith. These cases provide a remedy for an employee whose discharge was motivated by bad faith, malice, or retaliation.

Courts have also created exceptions to the employment-at-will doctrine by imposing tort obligations on employers with respect to the employment relationship. In particular, the torts of intentional infliction of emotional distress and of interference with employment relations have been used.

The most frequent basis for wrongful discharge is that the discharge violates statutory or other established public policy. In general, these cases involve dismissal for (1) refusing to violate a statute, (2) exercising a statutory right, (3) performing a statutory obligation, or (4) reporting an alleged violation of a statute of public interest.

NOVOSEL v. NATIONWIDE INSURANCE CO.
United States Court of Appeals, Third Circuit, 1983.
721 F.2d 894.

Facts: John Novosel was employed by Nationwide Insurance Company from December 1966 until November 1981. Novosel had been a model employee and, at the time of discharge, was a district claims manager and a candidate for the position of division claims manager. In October 1981 Nationwide circulated a memorandum requesting the participation of all employees in an effort to lobby the Pennsylvania state legislature for the passage of a certain bill before the body. Novosel, who had privately indicated his disagreement with Nationwide's political views, refused to lend his support to the lobby, and his employment with Nationwide was terminated. Novosel brought two separate claims against Nationwide, arguing, first, that his discharge for refusing to lobby the State legislature on behalf of Nationwide constituted the tort of wrongful discharge in that it was arbitrary, malicious, and contrary to public policy. Novosel also contended that Nationwide breached an implied contract guaranteeing continued employment so long as his job performance was satisfactory. The district court dismissed both claims and Novosel appealed.

Decision: Judgment of district court vacated and case remanded.

Opinion: Adams, J. Considerable ferment surrounds the doctrine of employment-at-will. Once the common-law cornerstone of employment relations not covered by either civil service laws or the National Labor Relations Act, the at-will doctrine has been significantly eroded by both tort and contract theories similar to those propounded by appellant in this case. Already 29 states have granted some form of common-law exceptions to the at-will doctrine; in addition, the courts of five other states as well as the District of Columbia have indicated their willingness to do so.

* * *

III

A

The circumstances of the discharge presented by Novosel fall squarely within the range of activity embraced by the emerging tort case law. As one commentator has written:

> The factual pattern alleged in these cases seldom varies. The employee objects to work that the employee believes is violative of state or federal law or otherwise improper; the employee protests to his employer that the work should not be performed; the employee expresses his intention not to assist the employer in the furtherance of such work and/or engages in "selfhelp" activity outside the work place to halt the work; and the employer discharges the employee for refusal to work or incompatibility with management. [Citation.]

* * *

B

[W]e find that Pennsylvania law permits a cause of action for wrongful discharge where the employment termination abridges a significant and recognized public policy. The district court did not consider the question whether an averment of discharge for refusing to support the employer's lobbying efforts is sufficiently violative of such public policy as to state a cause of action. Nationwide, however, now proposes that "the only prohibition on the termination of an employee is that the termination cannot violate a statutorily recognized public policy."

* * *

The key question in considering the tort claim is therefore whether a discharge for disagreement with the employer's legislative agenda or a refusal to lobby the state legislature on the employer's behalf sufficiently implicate a recognized facet of public policy. The definition of a "clearly mandated public policy" as one that "strikes at the heart of a citizen's social right, duties and responsibilities," [citation], appears to provide a workable standard for the tort action. While no Pennsylvania law directly addresses the public policy question at bar, the protection of an employee's freedom of political expression would appear to involve no less compelling a societal interest than the fulfillment of jury service or the filing of a workers' compensation claim.

* * *

IV

Employment-at-will has long been a major tenet of American contract law. Numerous proposals for statutory protection from arbitrary discharge have come from commentators concerned by the absence of job security for over 60 percent of the American workforce. Legislative proposals extending a "just cause" discharge requirement to all employees regardless of coverage or lack of it under the National Labor Relations Act have been considered in Pennsylvania as well as Colorado, Connecticut, Michigan, New Jersey and Wisconsin.

Novosel concedes that there is no statutory basis at present in Pennsylvania for a just cause requirement for discharges and, in fact, "the case law favoring someone like plaintiff under a breach of contract theory has been sparse." Instead, we are urged to fashion a common-law just cause standard premised primarily on the critical treatment of at-will discharges by the commentaries. Whatever the merits of such a standard, it is not the role of a federal court sitting in diversity to create its own common law.

The absence of a uniform just cause requirement for discharge, however, does not conclude the contractual issue presented here. As with the wrongful discharge tort doctrine, the contractual claims of non-union employees have been the subject of rapidly evolving judicial developments. . . .

Thus, Novosel's allegation that Nationwide's custom, practice or policy created either a contractual just cause requirement or contractual procedures by which defendant failed to abide is a factual matter that should survive a motion to dismiss.

Occupational Safety and Health Act

In 1970 Congress enacted the Occupational Safety and Health Act to assure, as far as possible, every worker a safe and healthful working environment. The Act established the **Occupational Safety and Health Administra-** **tion (OSHA)** to develop standards, conduct inspections, monitor compliance, and institute enforcement actions against those who are not in compliance.

The Act imposes upon each employer a general duty to provide a work environment that is "free from recognized hazards that are causing or likely to cause death or serious physical harm to his employees." In addition to this general duty, the employer is required to comply with specific safety rules promulgated by OSHA. The Act also requires employees to comply with all OSHA rules and regulations. Finally, the Act prohibits any employer from discharging or discriminating against an employee who exercises his rights under the Act, as in the following case.

WHIRLPOOL CORP. v. MARSHALL
Supreme Court of the United States, 1980.
445 U.S. 1, 100 S.Ct. 883, 63 L.Ed.2d 154.

Facts: At Whirlpool's manufacturing plant in Ohio, overhead conveyors transported household appliance components throughout the plant. A wire mesh screen was positioned below the conveyors in order to catch falling components and debris. Maintenance employees, frequently had to stand on the screens to clean them. In 1973 Whirlpool began installing heavier wire because several employees had fallen partly through the old screens and one had fallen completely through to the plant floor. At this time, the company warned workers to walk only on the frames beneath the wire but not on the wire itself. Before the heavier wire had been completely installed, a worker fell to his death through the old screen. A short time after this incident, Deemer and Cornwell, two plant employees, met with the plant safety director to discuss the mesh, to voice their concerns, and to obtain the name, address, and telephone number of the local Occupational Safety and Health Administration (OSHA) representative. The next day, the two employees refused to clean a portion of the old screen. They were then ordered to punch out for the remainder of the shift without pay and also received written reprimands, which were placed in their employment files. Secretary of Labor Marshall brought suit, claiming that Whirlpool's actions against Deemer and Cornwell constituted discrimination in violation of the Occupational Safety and Health Act. The district court ruled in favor of Whirlpool. The Court of Appeals reversed the decision and Whirlpool appeals.

Decision: Judgment of the Court of Appeals affirmed.

Opinion: Stewart, J.   The Act itself creates an express mechanism for protecting workers from employment conditions believed to pose an emergent threat of death or serious injury. Upon receipt of an employee inspection request stating reasonable grounds to believe that an imminent danger is present in a workplace, OSHA must conduct an inspection. [Citation.] In the event this inspection reveals workplace conditions or practices that "could reasonably be expected to cause death or serious physical harm immediately or before the imminence of such danger can be eliminated through the enforcement procedures otherwise provided by" the Act, [citation], the OSHA inspector must inform the affected employees and the employer of the danger and notify them that he is recommending to the Secretary that injunctive relief be sought. [Citation.] At this juncture, the Secretary can petition a federal court to restrain the conditions or practices giving rise to the imminent danger. By means of a temporary restraining order or preliminary injunction, the court may then require the employer to avoid, correct, or remove the danger or to prohibit employees from working in the area. [Citation.]

  To ensure that this process functions effectively, the Act expressly accords to every employee several rights, the exercise of which may not subject him to discharge or discrimination. An employee is given the right to inform OSHA of an imminently dangerous workplace condition or practice and request that OSHA inspect that condition or practice. [Citation.] He is given a limited right to assist the OSHA inspector in inspecting the workplace, [citation], and the right to aid a court in determining whether or not a risk of imminent danger in fact exists. [Citation.] Finally, an affected employee is given the right to bring an action to compel the Secretary to seek injunctive relief if he believes the Secretary has wrongfully declined to do so. [Citation.]

In the light of this detailed statutory scheme, the Secretary is obviously correct when he acknowledges in his regulation that, "as a general matter, there is no right afforded by the Act which would entitle employees to walk off the job because of potential unsafe conditions at the workplace." By providing for prompt notice to the employer of an inspector's intention to seek an injunction against an imminently dangerous condition, the legislation obviously contemplates that the employer will normally respond by voluntarily and speedily eliminating the danger. And in the few instances where this does not occur, the legislative provisions authorizing prompt judicial action are designed to give employees full protection in most situations from the risk of injury or death resulting from an imminently dangerous condition at the worksite.

As this case illustrates, however, circumstances may sometimes exist in which the employee justifiably believes that the express statutory arrangement does not sufficiently protect him from death or serious injury. Such circumstances will probably not often occur, but such a situation may arise when (1) the employee is ordered by his employer to work under conditions that the employee reasonably believes pose an imminent risk of death or serious bodily injury, and (2) the employee has reason to believe that there is not sufficient time or opportunity either to seek effective redress from his employer or to apprise OSHA of the danger.

Nothing in the Act suggests that those few employees who have to face this dilemma must rely exclusively on the remedies expressly set forth in the Act at the risk of their own safety. But nothing in the Act explicitly provides otherwise. Against this background of legislative silence, the Secretary has exercised his rulemaking power [citation] and has determined that, when an employee in good faith finds himself in such a predicament, he may refuse to expose himself to the dangerous condition, without being subjected to "subsequent discrimination" by the employer.

* * *

The regulation clearly conforms to the fundamental objective of the Act—to prevent occupational deaths and serious injuries. The Act, in its preamble, declares that its purpose and policy is "to assure so far as possible every working man and woman in the Nation safe and healthful working conditions and to *preserve* our human resources. * * * " [Citation.]

To accomplish this basic purpose, the legislation's remedial orientation is prophylactic in nature. [Citation]. The Act does not wait for an employee to die or become injured. It authorizes the promulgation of health and safety standards and the issuance of citations in the hope that these will act to prevent deaths or injuries from ever occurring. It would seem anomalous to construe an Act so directed and constructed as prohibiting an employee, with no other reasonable alternative, the freedom to withdraw from a workplace environment that he reasonably believes is highly dangerous.

Moreover, the Secretary's regulation can be viewed as an appropriate aid to the full effectuation of the Act's "general duty" clause. That clause provides that "[e]ach employer * * * shall furnish to each of his employees employment and a place of employment which are free from recognized hazards that are causing or are

> likely to cause death or serious physical harm to his employees." [Citation.] As the legislative history of this provision reflects, it was intended itself to deter the occurrence of occupational deaths and serious injuries by placing on employers a mandatory obligation independent of the specific health and safety standards to be promulgated by the Secretary. Since OSHA inspectors cannot be present around the clock in every workplace, the Secretary's regulation ensures that employees will in all circumstances enjoy the rights afforded them by the "general duty" clause.
>
> The regulation thus on its face appears to further the overriding purpose of the Act, and rationally to complement its remedial scheme.

The enforcement of the Act generally involves OSHA inspections and citations of employers, if appropriate, for: (1) breach of the general duty obligation; (2) breach of specific safety and health standards; or (3) failure to keep records, make reports, or post notices required by the Act.

When a violation is discovered, a written citation, proposed penalty, and correction date are given to the employer. Citations may be contested, and in such cases, administrative law judges are assigned by the Occupational Safety and Health Review Commission to hold hearings. The Commission, at its discretion, may grant review of an administrative law judge's decision; review is not a matter of right. If Commission review is not undertaken, then the judge's decision becomes the final order of the Commission thirty days after receipt, and the order may be appealed by the aggrieved party to the appropriate United States Circuit Court of Appeals.

Penalties for violations are both civil and criminal and may be as high as $1,000 per violation per day, while a $10,000 criminal penalty may be imposed for certain willful violations. In cases involving civil penalties, serious violations require that a penalty be proposed, while in nonserious violation cases, penalties are rarely proposed. The Secretary of Labor is further empowered by the Act to obtain temporary restraining orders in situations where regular OSHA procedures cannot be effective to shut down business operations that create imminent dangers of death or serious injury.

One stated purpose of the Act is to encourage State participation in regulating safety and health. The Act therefore permits the States to regulate the safety and health of the work environment, provided that OSHA approves the plan. The Act sets minimum acceptable standards for the States to impose, but it does not require that the State plan be identical to OSHA. More than one-half of the States have adopted some form of State regulation of health and safety in the workplace.

Workers' Compensation

At common law, the basis of most actions by an injured employee against his employer was the failure of the employer to use reasonable care under the circumstances for the safety of the employee. In such an action, the employer had several well-established defenses available to him at common law. These included the defense of the fellow servant rule; contributory negligence on the part of the employee; and the doctrine of assumption of risk by the employee.

The **fellow servant rule** is that an employer is not liable for injuries sustained by an employee caused by the negligence of a fellow employee. Another common-law defense is **contributory negligence.** If an employer establishes that the negligence of an injured employee contributed to the injury he sustained in the course of his employment, in many jurisdictions the employee cannot recover damages from the employer. At common law, an employer was not liable to an employee for harm or injury caused by the unsafe condition of the premises if the employee, with knowledge of the facts and understanding the risks involved, voluntarily enters into or continues in the employment. This is regarded as a **voluntary assumption of risk** by the employee.

In order to provide speedier and more certain relief to injured employees, all States have adopted statutes providing for **workers' compensation.** These statutes create commissions or boards that determine whether an injured employee is entitled to receive compensation and, if so, how much. The common law defenses discussed above are *not* available to employers in proceedings under these statutes. Such defenses are *abolished.* The *only* requirement is that the employee be injured and that the injury arise out of and in the course of his employment. The amounts recoverable are fixed by statute for each type of injury and are on a scale less than a court or jury would probably award in an action at common law. Actions at law, however, are not permitted against employers to injured employees who come within the workers' compensation acts. The courts do not have jurisdiction over such cases except to review decisions of the board or commission, and then only to determine whether such decisions are in accordance with the statute. If a third party causes the injury, however, the employee may bring a tort action against that third party.

Early workers' compensation laws did not provide coverage for occupational disease, and most courts held that occupational injury did not include disease. Today, virtually all States provide general compensation coverage for occupational diseases, although the coverage varies greatly from State to State.

Social Security and Unemployment Insurance

Social Security was enacted in 1935 in an attempt to provide limited retirement and death benefits to certain employees. Since then, the Federal Social Security system has expanded to cover almost all employees and to increase greatly the benefits offered. The system now contains four major benefit programs: (1) Old-Age and Survivors Insurance (OASI) (providing retirement and survivor benefits); (2) Disability Insurance (DI); (3) Hospitalization Insurance (Medicare); and (4) Supplemental Security Income (SSI).

The system is financed by contributions (taxes) paid by employers, employees, and self-employed individuals. Employees and employers pay matching contributions. These contributions are calculated by multiplying the Social Security tax (a fixed percentage) times the employee's wages up to a specified maximum. Both the base tax rate and the maximum dollar amount are subject to change by Congress. It is the employer's responsibility to withhold the employee's contribution and to forward the full amount of the tax to the Internal Revenue Service. Contributions made by the employee are not tax deductible by the employee, while those made by the employer are tax deductible.

Self-employed persons are also required to report their own taxable income and pay the Social Security tax. Currently, the tax paid by self-employed individuals is greater than that paid by either the employer or employee, but less than the combined employer/employee contribution. Starting in 1990, the tax paid by a self-employed individual will be equal to the combined employer/employee contribution.

Benefits vary greatly depending on the particular program and whether the beneficiary is "fully" insured, "currently" insured, or a dependent. To be *fully insured* a person must be credited with forty quarters of coverage: a quarter of coverage is received for each $370 of earnings in a year up to a maximum of four quarters per year. An individual is *currently insured* if he has been credited with at least six quarters of coverage in the last three years. In addition, dependents (spouses and children) are also eligible for certain Social Security benefits. Finally, benefits received are tax free unless the individual receiving benefits under OASI has income in excess of a specified amount, which in 1987 was $25,000 for single persons and $32,000 for married couples.

The Federal unemployment insurance system was initially created by Title IX of the Social Security Act of 1935. Subsequently, Title IX was supplemented by the Federal Unemployment Tax Act as well as numerous other

Federal statutes. This complex system depends upon the cooperation of State and Federal programs. Federal law provides the general guidelines, standards, and requirements, while the States handle the administration of the program under their own employment laws. The system is funded by taxes imposed on employers, with Federal taxes generally paying the administrative costs of the program and State contributions paying for the actual benefits.

Under the Federal Unemployment Tax Act, an employer must pay unemployment tax if (1) he employs one or more persons for some portion of a day in each of twenty weeks in the current or preceding calendar year, or (2) he pays $1,500 or more in wages in any calendar quarter. The employee does not pay any unemployment tax. The tax, like the Social Security tax, is calculated as a fixed percentage of an employee's salary up to a stated maximum. The purpose of the tax is to provide **unemployment compensation** to workers who have lost their jobs and cannot find other employment. Payments generally are made weekly and are based on the particular State's formula.

Fair Labor Standards Act

The Fair Labor Standards Act (FLSA) regulates the employment of child labor outside of agriculture. The Act prohibits the employment of anyone under fourteen years in nonfarm work except for newspaper deliverers and child actors. Fourteen- and fifteen-year-olds may be employed for a limited number of hours outside of school hours, under specific conditions, in certain *nonhazardous* occupations. Sixteen- and seventeen-year-olds may work in any *nonhazardous* job, while persons eighteen-years-old or older may work in *any* job whether it is hazardous or not. The Secretary of Labor determines which occupations are considered hazardous.

In addition, the FLSA imposes wage and hour requirements upon covered employers. The Act provides for a minimum hourly wage (currently $3.35) and overtime pay of time-and-a-half for hours worked in excess of forty hours per week. Certain jobs are exempted from both the FLSA's minimum wage and overtime provisions, including the following: professionals, managers, and outside sales persons.

CHAPTER SUMMARY

Labor Law	**Purpose** to provide the general framework in which management and labor negotiate terms of employment
	Norris-LaGuardia Act established as the policy of the United States that labor was to have full freedom to form labor unions without interference by the employer and withdrew from the Federal courts the power to issue injunctions in nonviolent labor disputes (any controversy concerning terms or conditions of employment or union representation)
	National Labor Relations Act
	■ *Right to Unionize* declares it a Federally protected right of employees to unionize and to bargain collectively
	■ *Prohibits Unfair Employer Practices* the Act identifies five unfair labor practices by an employer
	■ *National Labor Relations Board (NLRB)* created to administer these rights
	Labor-Management Relations Act
	■ *Prohibits Unfair Union Practices* the Act identifies seven unfair labor practices by a union
	■ *Prohibits Closed Shops* agreement that mandates that an employer can only hire union members
	■ *Allows Union Shops* an employer can hire nonunion members, but the employee must join the union

Labor-Management Reporting and Disclosure Act aimed at eliminating corruption in labor unions

Employment Discrimination Law

Equal Pay Act prohibits an employer from discriminating between employees on the basis of sex by paying unequal wages for the same work

Civil Rights Act of 1964 prohibits employment discrimination on the basis of race, color, sex, religion, or national origin

- *Equal Employment Opportunity Commission (EEOC)* enforcement agency for the Act
- *Affirmative Action* the active recruitment of a designated group of applicants
- *Discrimination* prohibited by the Act, includes (1) using proscribed criteria to produce disparate treatment, (2) engaging in nondiscriminatory conduct that perpetuates past discrimination, and (3) adopting neutral rules that have a disparate impact
- *Reverse Discrimination* affirmative action that directs an employer to take the race or sex of an individual into account when hiring or promoting for the purpose of remedying underrepresentation of that race or sex in traditionally segregated jobs
- *Sexual Harassment* is an illegal form of sexual discrimination and includes unwelcome sexual advances, requests for sexual favors, and other verbal or physical conduct of a sexual nature
- *Comparable Worth* equal pay for jobs of equal value to the employer

Age Discrimination in Employment Act prohibits discrimination in hiring, firing, or compensating on the basis of age

Rehabilitation Act attempts to provide assistance to the handicapped in obtaining rehabilitation training, access to public facilities, and employment

Executive Order prohibits discrimination by Federal contractors on the basis of race, color, sex, religion, or national origin on any work performed by the contractors during the period of the Federal contract

Employee Protection

Employee Termination at Will under the common law, a contract of employment for other than a definite term is terminable at will by either party

- *Statutory Limitations* have been enacted by the Federal government and some States
- *Judicial Limitations* based on contract law, tort law, or public policy
- *Limitations Imposed by Union Contract*

Occupational Safety and Health Act enacted to assure workers of a safe and healthful work environment

Workers' Compensation compensation awarded to an employee who is injured in the course of his or her employment

Social Security measures by which the government provides economic assistance to disabled or retired employees and their dependents

Unemployment Compensation compensation awarded to workers who have lost their jobs and cannot find other employment

Fair Labor Standard Act regulates the employment of child labor outside of agriculture

QUESTIONS

1. List and briefly discuss the major labor law statutes.
2. Distinguish between the prohibited unfair labor practices that apply to employers and those that apply to unions.
3. Discuss the defenses available to an employer under (1) the Equal Pay Act, and (b) the Civil Rights Act of 1964.
4. Discuss (a) the various types of conduct prohibited as employment discrimination, (b) reverse discrimination, (c) sexual harassment, and (d) comparable worth.
5. Discuss the traditional common law, the statutory, and the recent judicial approaches to the termination-at-will doctrine.

PROBLEMS

1. Gooddecade manufactures and sells automobile parts throughout the eastern part of the United States. Among its full-time employees are 220 fourteen- and fifteen-year-olds. These teenagers are employed throughout the company and are paid at an hourly wage rate of $3 per hour. Discuss the legality of this arrangement.

2. Janet, a twenty-year-old-woman, applied for a position driving a truck for Federal Trucking, Inc. Janet, who is 5'4'' tall and weighs 135 lbs, was denied the job because the company requires that all employees be at least 5'6'' tall and weigh at least 150 lbs. Federal justified this requirement on the basis that its drivers frequently were forced to move heavy loads in order to make pickups and deliveries. Janet brings a cause of action. Decision?

3. N.I.S. promoted, John, a forty-two-year-old employee, to a foreman's position while passing over James, a fifty-eight-year-old employee. N.I.S. told James he was too old for the job and it preferred a younger man. James brings a cause of action. Decision?

4. Anthony was employed as a forklift operator for Blackburn Construction Company. While on the job, Anthony carelessly and in direct violation of Blackburn's procedure manual operated the forklift and caused himself severe injury. Blackburn now denies liability based on Anthony's (a) gross negligence, (b) disobedience of the procedural manual, and (c) written waiver of liability. Anthony now brings a cause of action. Decision?

5. Hazelwood School District is located in Sleepy Hollow Township. It is being sued by applicants who applied for teaching positions with the school but were rejected. The plaintiffs are all black and produce the following evidence:

(a) 1.8 percent of the Hazelwood School District's teachers are black, whereas 15.4 percent of the teachers in Sleepy Hollow Township are black, and (b) the hiring decisions by Hazelwood School District are based solely on subjective criteria.

6. T.W.E., a larger manufacturer, prohibited its employees from distributing union leaflets to other employees while on the company's property. Richard, an employee of T.W.E., disregarded the prohibition and passed out the leaflets before his work shift began. T.W.E. discharged Richard for his actions. Has T.W.E. committed an unfair labor practice?

7. Erwick was dismissed from her job at the C & T Steel Company because she was "an unsatisfactory employee." At the time, Erwick was active in an effort to organize a union at C & T. Is the dismissal valid?

8. Johnson, president of the First National Bank of A, believes that it is only appropriate to employ female tellers. Hence, First National refuses to employ Ken Baker as a teller but does make him an offer to be a maintenance man at the same salary. Baker brings a cause of action against First National Bank. Decision?

9. Section 103 of the Federal Public Works Employment Act of 1977 establishes the MBE (Minority Business Enterprise) program and requires that, absent a waiver by the Secretary of Commerce, 10 percent of all Federal grants given by the Economic Development Administration must be used to purchase services or supplies from businesses owned and controlled by U.S. citizens belonging to one of six minority groups: Black, Spanish-speaking, Oriental, Indian, Eskimo, and Aleut. White owners of businesses contend the act constitutes illegal reverse discrimination. Discuss.

10. Worth H. Percivil, a mechanical engineer, was employed by General Motors and remained in their employment for twenty-six years until he was discharged. At the time his employment was terminated, Percivil was head of GM's Mechanical Development Department. Percivil sued GM for wrongful discharge. He contends that he was discharged as a result of a conspiracy among his fellow executives to force him out of his employment because of his age, because he had legitimately complained about certain deceptive practices of GM, because he had refused to give the government false information

although urged to do so by his superiors, and because he had, on the contrary, undertaken to correct certain alleged misrepresentations made to the government. General Motors claims that Percivil's employment was terminable at the will of GM for any reason and with or without cause, provided that the discharge was not prohibited by statute. Decision?

11. On May 26, the trial examiner issued his Intermediate Report finding that the Respondent (Sailers' Union) had not engaged in unfair union practice under Section 8(b) in their dispute with Samsoc. With respect to the unfair labor practices, the complaint alleged that the Respondent induced and encouraged employees of Moore to engage in a strike or concerted refusal in the course of their employment to perform services for Moore in connection with the conversion into a bulk gypsum carrier of the S.S. *Phopho*, a vessel owned by Samsoc, the object being to force Moore to cease doing business with Samsoc and thus force Samsoc to resolve its dispute with Respondent. The General Counsel and Moore Dry Dock Company appealed. Decision?

COMPUTER RESEARCH PROBLEMS

1. Burdine, a female, was hired by the Texas Department of Community Affairs as a clerk in the Public Service Careers Division (PSC). The PSC provides training and employment opportunities for unskilled workers. At the time she was hired, Burdine already had several years experience in employment training. She was soon promoted, and later when her supervisor resigned, she performed additional duties usually assigned to the supervisor. Burdine applied for the position of supervisor, but that position remained unfilled for six months, and a male from another division was eventually brought in as supervisor. Burdine alleges discrimination violating Title VII of the 1964 Civil Rights Act. The defendant Texas Department of Community Affairs responds that nondiscriminatory evaluation criteria were used to choose the new supervisor. In order to comply with Title VII, must the Texas Department of Community Affairs hire Burdine as supervisor if she and the male candidate are equally qualified? Explain.

2. Ms. Wise was fired from her job at the Mead Corporation after she was involved in a fight with another co-worker. In four other unrelated occasions fights occurred between male co-workers. Only one of the males was fired, but this was after his second fight in which he seriously injured another employee. There is no dispute that Ms. Wise was qualified and performed her duties adequately. Ms. Wise successfully establishes a *prima facie* case of discrimination. However, defendant Mead Corporation meets its burden to "articulate legitimate and nondiscriminatory reasons" for firing Ms. Wise. Can Ms. Wise prevail? Explain.

43 SECURITIES REGULATION

The primary purpose of Federal securities regulation is to prevent fraudulent practices in the sale of securities and thereby foster public confidence in the securities market. Federal securities law consists principally of two statutes: the Securities Act of 1933, which focuses on the issuance of securities, and the Securities Exchange Act of 1934, which deals mainly with trading in issued securities. Both statutes are administered by the Securities and Exchange Commission (SEC), an independent, quasi-judicial agency. The SEC has the power to seek civil injunctions against violation of the statutes, to recommend that the Justice Department bring criminal prosecution, and to issue orders suspending or expelling broker-dealers.

The 1933 Act has two basic objectives: (1) to provide investors with material information concerning securities offered for sale to the public, and (2) to prohibit misrepresentation, deceit, and other fraudulent acts and practices in the sale of securities generally, whether or not they are required to be registered.

The 1934 Act extends protection to investors trading in securities that are already issued and outstanding. The 1934 Act also imposes disclosure requirements on publicly held corporations and regulates tender offers and proxy solicitations.

In addition to the Federal laws regulating the sale of securities, the States have their own laws regulating such sales within the State, commonly called Blue Sky laws. These statutes all have provisions prohibiting fraud in the sale of securities. In addition, a number of States require the registration of securities, and some States also regulate brokers and dealers.

Any person who sells securities must comply with the Federal securities laws as well as with those of each State in which he intends to offer his securities. Because State securities laws vary greatly, we will discuss only the 1933 Act and the 1934 Act in this chapter.

THE SECURITIES ACT OF 1933

The 1933 Act, also called the "Truth in Securities Act," requires that a registration statement be filed with the SEC and become effective before any securities may be offered for sale to the public, unless either the securities or the transaction in which they are offered are exempt from registration. The purpose of registration is to disclose financial and other information about the issuer and those in control of it so that potential investors may consider the merits of the securities. The Act provides that potential investors must be furnished with a **prospectus** (a document offering the securities for sale to interested buyers) containing the important data set forth in the registration statement.

Regardless of whether the securities are exempt from the registration and disclosure requirements of the Act, the antifraud provisions of the Act apply to all sales of securities involving interstate commerce or the mails. Civil and criminal liability may be imposed for violations of the provisions of the Act.

Definition of a Security

The 1933 Act defines the term **security** to include any note, stock, bond, debenture, evidence of indebtedness, preorganization certificate or subscription, investment contract, voting-trust certificate, fractional undivided interest in oil, gas, or other mineral rights, or in general, any interest or instrument commonly known as a security. This definition broadly includes the many types of instruments that fall within the ordinary concept of a security. Nevertheless, even though a transaction is evidenced by an instrument labeled "stock," it may not be considered a security under the Securities Act. Accordingly, the ultimate task of determining which of the numerous financial transactions constitutes a security has fallen to the SEC and the Federal courts.

The courts have generally interpreted the statutory definition to include nontraditional forms of investments. For the purpose of the securities laws, as the following case demonstrates, a security is an investment of money, property, or other valuable consideration made in expectation of receiving a financial return solely from the efforts of others. Under this test, investments in limited partnership interests, citrus groves, whiskey warehouse receipts, real estate condominiums, cattle, franchises, and pyramid schemes have been held to be securities in certain circumstances.

SECURITIES AND EXCHANGE COMM'N v. W. J. HOWEY CO.
Supreme Court of the United States, 1970.
328 U.S. 293, 66 S.Ct. 1100, 90 L.Ed. 1244.

Facts: W. J. Howey Co. and Howey-in-the-Hills Service, Inc., are Florida corporations under direct common control and management. The Howey Company owns large tracts of citrus acreage in Florida. The service company cultivates, harvests, and markets the crops. During the past several years, Howey Company has offered one-half of its planted acreage to the public to help it "finance additional development." Each prospective customer is offered both a land sales contract and a service contract with Howey-in-the-Hills after having been told that it is not feasible to invest in the grove without a service arrangement. Upon payment of the purchase price, the land is conveyed by warranty deed. The service company is given full discretion over cultivation and marketing of the crop. The purchaser has no right of entry to market the crop. The service company is also accountable only for an allocation of the net profits after the produce is pooled by the companies. The purchasers are predominantly nonresident business persons attracted by the expectation of substantial profits. Contending that this arrangement is an investment contract within the coverage of the Securities Act of 1933, the Securities and Exchange Commission brought this action against the two companies to restrain them from using the mails and instrumentalities of interstate commerce in the offer and sale of unregistered and nonexempt securities. The District Court denied the injunction and the Court of Appeals affirmed.

Decision: Judgment reversed.

Opinion: Murphy, J.   Section 2(1) of the Act defines the term "security" to include the commonly known documents traded for speculation or investment. This definition also includes "securities" of a more variable character, designated by such descriptive terms as "certificate of interest or participation in any profit-sharing agreement," "investment contract" and "in general, any interest or instrument commonly known as a 'security.' " The legal issue in this case turns upon a determination of whether, under the circumstances, the land sales contract, the warranty deed and the service contract together constitute an "investment contract" within the meaning of § 2(1). An affirmative answer brings into operation the registration requirements of § 5(a), unless the security is granted an exemption under § 3(b). * * *

The term "investment contract" is undefined by the Securities Act or by relevant legislative reports. But the term was common in many state "blue sky" laws in existence prior to the adoption of the federal statute * * *.

By including an investment contract within the scope of § 2(1) of the Securities Act, Congress was using a term the meaning of which had been crystallized by this prior judicial interpretation. It is therefore reasonable to attach that meaning to the term as used by Congress, especially since such a definition is consistent with the statutory aims. In other words, an investment contract for purposes of the Securities Act means a contract, transaction or scheme whereby a person invests his money in a common enterprise and is led to expect profits solely from the efforts of the promoter or a third party, it being immaterial whether the shares in the enterprise are evidenced by formal certificates or by nominal interests in the physical assets employed in the enterprise. Such a definition * * * permits the fulfillment of the statutory purpose of compelling full and fair disclosure relative to the issuance of "the many types of instruments that in our commercial world fall within the ordinary concept of a security." [Citation.] It embodies a flexible rather than a static principle, one that is capable of adaptation to meet the countless and variable schemes devised by those who seek the use of the money of others on the promise of profits.

The transactions in this case clearly involve investment contracts as so defined. The respondent companies are offering something more than fee simple interests in land, something different from a farm or orchard coupled with management services. They are offering an opportunity to contribute money and to share in the profits of a large citrus fruit enterprise managed and partly owned by respondents. They are offering this opportunity to persons who reside in distant localities and who lack the equipment and experience requisite to the cultivation, harvesting and marketing of the citrus products. Such persons have no desire to occupy the land or to develop it themselves; they are attracted solely by the prospects of a return on their investment. Indeed, individual development of the plots of land that are offered and sold would seldom be economically feasible due to their small size. Such tracts gain utility as citrus groves only when cultivated and developed as component parts of a larger area. A common enterprise managed by respondents or third parties with adequate personnel and equipment is therefore essential if the investors are to achieve their paramount aim of a return on their investments. Their respective shares in this enterprise are evidenced by land sales contracts and warranty deeds, which serve as a convenient method of determining the investors' allocable shares of the profits. The resulting transfer of rights in land is purely incidental.

Thus all the elements of a profit-seeking business venture are present here. The investors provide the capital and share in the earnings and profits; the promoters manage, control and operate the enterprise. It follows that the arrangements whereby the investors' interests are made manifest involve investment contracts, regardless of the legal terminology in which such contracts are clothed. The investment contracts in this instance take the form of land sales contracts, warranty deeds and service contracts which respondents offer to prospective investors. And respondents' failure to abide by the statutory and administrative rules in making such offerings, even though the failure result from a bona fide mistake as to the law, cannot be sanctioned under the Act.

This conclusion is unaffected by the fact that some purchasers choose not to accept the full offer of an investment contract by declining to enter into a service contract with the respondents. The Securities Act prohibits the offer as well as the sale of unregistered, non-exempt securities. Hence it is enough that the respondents merely offer the essential ingredients of an investment contract.

Registration of Securities

The 1933 Act prohibits the offer or sale through the use of the mails or any means of interstate commerce of any security unless a registration statement for that security is in effect or an exemption from registration is secured. The purpose of registration is to provide adequate and accurate *disclosure* of financial and other information on which investors may judge the merits of the securities. Registration does not insure investors against loss—the SEC does *not* make any judgment on the financial merits of any security. Moreover, the SEC does *not* guarantee the accuracy of the information presented in the registration statement.

In general, registration calls for disclosure of such information as (1) a description of the registrant's properties and business, (2) a description of the significant provisions of the security to be offered for sale and its relationship to the registrant's other capital securities, (3) information about the management of the registrant, and (4) financial statements certified by independent public accountants. A company issuing not more than $7.5 million of securities for cash may use a shorter registration form.

The registration statement and prospectus become public immediately on filing with the SEC. The effective date of a registration statement is the twentieth day after filing, although the commission, at its discretion, may advance the effective date. It is unlawful to sell the securities until the effective date. After the filing of the registration statement, the securities may be *offered* orally or by certain summaries of the information in the registration statement as permitted by rules of the SEC.

Integrated Disclosure

The disclosure system under the 1933 Act developed independently of that required by the 1934 Act, which is discussed later in this chapter. As a result, issuers subject to both statutes were compelled to provide duplicative or overlapping disclosure. In 1982 the SEC adopted an integrated disclosure system in an effort to reduce or eliminate unnecessary duplication of corporate reporting. Under this system, there are three levels of disclosure, depending on the issuer's reporting history and market following. All issuers may use the detailed form described previously. Corporations that have continuously reported under the 1934 Act for at least three years are permitted to disclose less detailed information in the 1933 Act registration statement and to incorporate some information by reference to reports filed under the 1934 Act. Those corporations that have filed under the 1934 Act continuously for at least three years and also have a "market following" are permitted to disclose even less detail in the 1933 Act registration and to incorporate even more information by reference to 1934 Act reports. The SEC's rules establish a test for market following: a minimum market value of voting stock of $150 million (called the "float") or a float of $100 million and a minimum annual trading volume of three million shares.

Shelf Registrations

Shelf registrations permit certain qualified issuers to register securities that are to be offered and sold "off the shelf" on a delayed or continuous basis in the future. This is a departure from the requirement that an issuer must file a registration for *every* new distribution of nonexempt securities. **Rule 415** of the SEC, which governs shelf registrations, requires that the information in the original registration is kept accurate and current. Only companies eligible to use either of the shorter forms of registration qualify for shelf registrations. Shelf registrations allow issuers to respond more quickly to market conditions such as changes in stock prices and interest rates.

Exempt Securities

The 1933 Act exempts a number of specific securities from its registration requirements. **Exempt securities** include (1) those sold under Regulation A, (2) those sold in intrastate transactions, and (3) short-term commercial paper. Because these exemptions apply to the securities themselves, the securities may be resold without registration.

Regulation A

Regulation A permits an issuer to offer up to $1.5 million of securities in any twelve-month period without registering them provided that the issuer files a notification and an offering circular with the SEC's regional office prior to the sale of the securities. The circular must also be provided to offerees and purchasers. Regulation A filings are less detailed and time-consuming than full registration statements, and the required financial statements are simpler and do not need to be audited. Because each purchaser must be supplied with an offering circular, securities sold under Regulation A may be freely traded after they are issued.

Intrastate Issues   The 1933 Act also exempts from registration any security that is a part of an issue offered and sold *only* to persons who live in a single State where the issuer of such security is resident and doing business. This exemption is intended to apply to local issues representing local financing by local persons and carried out through local investments. The exemption does not apply if any offeree, who need not be a purchaser, is not a resident of the State in which the issuer is resident.

Rule 147, promulgated by the SEC, provides a "nonexclusive safe harbor" for securing the intrastate exemption. Satisfying the rule assures the exemption, but there is no presumption that the exemption is not available for transactions that do not comply with the rule. Rule 147 requires that:

1. the issuer is incorporated or organized in the State in which the issuance occurs;
2. the issuer is principally doing business in that State, which means that 80 percent of its gross revenues must be derived from that State, 80 percent of its assets must be located in that State, and 80 percent of the net proceeds from the issue must be used in that State;
3. all of the *offerees* and purchasers are residents of that State;
4. during the period of sale and for nine months after the last sale, no resales to nonresidents are made; and
5. precautions are taken against interstate distributions. Such precautions include (a) placing a legend on the certificate evidencing the security stating that the securities have not been registered and that resales can be made only to residents of the State, and (b) obtaining

a written statement of residence from each purchaser.

Short-Term Commercial Paper   The Act exempts any note, draft, or bankers' acceptance (a draft accepted by a bank) issued for working capital that has a maturity of not more than nine months when issued. The exemption is not available if the proceeds are to be used for permanent purposes, such as the acquisition of a plant, or if the paper is of a type not ordinarily purchased by the general public.

Other Exempt Securities   The 1933 Act also exempts the following kinds of securities from registration:

1. securities of domestic governments
2. securities of domestic banks and savings and loan associations
3. securities of nonprofit charitable organizations
4. securities of issuers where the issuance is regulated by the Interstate Commerce Commission
5. certificates issued by a receiver or trustee in bankruptcy with court approval
6. insurance policies and annuity contracts issued by State regulated insurance companies
7. securities issued solely for exchange by the issuer with its existing security holders where no commission is paid
8. reorganization securities issued and exchanged with court or other governmental approval

Exempt Transactions

In addition to the exemptions provided for specific types of securities, the 1933 Act also provides issuers with an exemption from the registration requirements for certain kinds of transactions. These **exempt transactions** include (1) private placements, (2) limited offers not exceeding $5 million, (3) limited offers not exceeding $1 million, and (4) limited offers solely to accredited investors. These exemptions from registration apply only to the transaction in which the securities are issued and not to the securities themselves. Securities sold according to these exemptions are considered **restricted securities** and may be resold only by registration or in another transaction exempt from registration.

An issuer who uses these exemptions must take reasonable care to assure against nonexempt, unregistered resales of restricted securities. Reasonable care includes but is not limited to the following: (a) making a reasonable inquiry to determine if the purchaser is acquiring the securities for herself or for other persons; (b) providing written disclosure, prior to the sale to each purchaser, that the securities have not been registered and therefore cannot be resold unless they are registered or an exemption from registration is available; and (c) placing a legend on the securities certificate stating that the securities have not been registered and that they are restricted securities.

Private Placements The most important exemption for issuers who wish to raise money without registration is the so-called private placement provision of the Act, which exempts "transactions by an issuer not involving any public offering." **Rule 506** of the SEC establishes a nonexclusive safe harbor for limited offers and sales without regard to the dollar amount of the offering. Securities sold under this exemption are restricted securities and may be resold only by registration or in a transaction exempt from registration. General advertising or general solicitation is not permitted. The issue may be purchased by an unlimited number of "accredited investors" and by no more than thirty-five other purchasers. **Accredited investors** include banks, insurance companies, investment companies, executive officers or directors of the issuer, business entities with total assets in excess of $5 million, and natural persons who have considerable net worth or large annual incomes. If the sale involves any nonaccredited investors, such purchasers must be given material information before the sale about the issuer, its business, and the securities being offered; otherwise such information is not required to be disclosed. The issuer must reasonably believe that each purchaser who is not an accredited investor has sufficient knowledge and experience in finan-

cial and business matters to be capable of evaluating the merits and risks of the investment or has the services of a representative who has the requisite knowledge and experience to make such an evaluation. The issuer must take precautions against nonexempt, unregistered resales and must notify the SEC of sales made under the exemption.

Limited Offers Not Exceeding $5 Million In order to facilitate capital formation for small businesses, the SEC promulgated **Rule 505,** which exempts from registration offerings by noninvestment company issuers that do not exceed $5 million over twelve months. Securities sold under this exemption are restricted securities and may be resold only by registration or in a transaction exempt from registration. General advertising or general solicitation is not permitted. The issue may be purchased by an unlimited number of accredited investors and by no more than thirty-five other purchasers. If the sale involves any nonaccredited investors, such purchasers must be given material information before the sale about the issuer, its business, and the securities being offered; otherwise, such information is not required to be disclosed. Unlike Rule 506, however, the issuer is *not* required to believe reasonably that each nonaccredited investor, either alone or with his representative, has sufficient knowledge and experience in financial matters to be capable of evaluating the merits and risks of the investment. The issuer must take precautions against nonexempt, unregistered resales and must notify the SEC of sales made under the exemption.

Limited Offers Not Exceeding $1 Million The SEC's **Rule 504** provides private, noninvestment company issuers with an exemption from registration for small issues not exceeding $1 million. The rule permits sales to an unlimited number of investors and does not require any information to be furnished to them. The exemption requires that:

1. the securities are offered and sold without general advertising;
2. the aggregate offering price within twelve months does not exceed $1 million;

3. the issuer takes precautions against nonexempt, unregistered resales; and

4. the issuer notifies the SEC of sales under the rule.

The limitations on general advertising do not apply, and unregistered resales are permitted if the offering is either (1) made exclusively in compliance with State registration provisions that require the delivery of a disclosure document before sale, or (2) made in at least one State requiring such registration and the disclosure document is delivered to all purchasers before sale. No more than $500,000 of securities, however, may be sold in States not requiring registration.

Limited Offers Solely to Accredited Investors

In 1980 Congress added **Section 4(6),** which provides an exemption for offers and sales by an issuer made *solely* to accredited investors if not in excess of $5 million. General advertising or public solicitation is not permitted. As with Rules 505 and 506, an unlimited number of accredited investors may purchase the issue; however, Section 4(6) is unlike these rules in that *no* unaccredited investors may purchase at all. No information is required to be furnished to the purchasers. Securities sold under this exemption are restricted securities and may be resold only by registration or in a transaction exempt from registration. The issuer must take precautions against nonexempt, unregistered resales and must notify the SEC of sales made under the exemption.

Resales of Restricted Securities   Transaction-based exemptions from registration do not necessarily exempt a later transaction in the same securities. Rather, those who acquire securities under Rule 506, Rule 505, Rule 504, or Section 4(6) must register any resales or find an exemption from registration, subject to the limited exception provided for some issuances under Rule 504.

   Rule 144 of the SEC sets forth conditions that, if met by any person selling restricted securities, exempt her from registering them. The rule requires that there must be adequate current public information about the issuer, that the person selling under the rule must

have owned the securities for at least two years, that she sell them only in limited amounts in unsolicited brokers' transactions, and that notice of the sale must be provided to the SEC. A person who is *not* an affiliate of the issuer at the time of sale of the restricted securities and who has owned the securities for at least three years, however, may sell them in unlimited amounts and is not subject to *any* of the other requirements of Rule 144. An **affiliate** is a person who controls, is controlled by, or is under common control with the issuer.

   Moreover, **Regulation A,** in addition to providing an exemption for issuers from registration for securities up to $1.5 million, also provides an exemption of up to $300,000 in any twelve-month period for all investors with a $100,000 limit for any one investor. Use of this exemption requires compliance with all of the conditions imposed on issuers by Regulation A, as we discussed above.

   Figure 43–1 summarizes the exemptions from registration available under the 1933 Act, and Figure 43–2 graphically illustrates the requirements for registration and the exemptions available for various transactions.

Liability

To implement the statutory objectives of providing full disclosure and preventing fraud in the sale of securities, the 1933 Act imposes a number of sanctions for noncompliance with its requirements. The sanctions include administrative remedies by the SEC, civil liability to injured investors, and criminal penalties.

Unregistered Sales   **Section 12(1)** of the Act imposes civil liability for the sale of an unregistered security that is required to be registered, the sale of a registered security without delivery of a prospectus, the sale of a security by use of a prospectus that is not current, or the offer of a sale before the filing of the registration statement. Liability is absolute, as there are no defenses. The person who purchases a security sold in violation of this provision of the Act has the right to tender it back to the seller and recover the purchase price. If

FIGURE 43-1   Exemptions under the 1933 Act

Exemption	Requirements	Result
Regulation A	1. Limited to $1.5 million of securities sold within 12 months 2. Proper notification and offering circular provided to SEC and offerees	Unrestricted resales
Intrastate sales	1. Issuer incorporated or organized in that State 2. Issuer principally doing business within that State 3. All offerees and purchasers are residents of that State 4. No resale for 9 months to nonresidents	Freely transferable to residents; transferable to nonresidents after 9 months
Private placement	1. No dollar limitation 2. Unlimited number of accredited investors 3. No more that 35 unaccredited but sophisticated investors 4. If any unaccredited investors, must disclose material information 5. Sold without advertising 6. SEC notified of sale	Restricted security
Limited offers not exceeding $5 million	1. Not to exceed $5 million over 12 months 2. Unlimited number of accredited investors 3. No more than 35 unaccredited investors 4. If any unaccredited investors, must disclose material information 5. Sold without advertising 6. SEC notified of sale	Restricted security
Limited offers not exceeding $1 million	1. Not to exceed $1 million over 12 months 2. Sold without advertising 3. SEC notified of sale	Restricted security
Limited offers solely to accredited investors	1. Not to exceed $5 million 2. Unlimited number of accredited investors 3. No unaccredited investors 4. No information required 5. Sold without advertising 6. SEC notified of sale	Restricted security

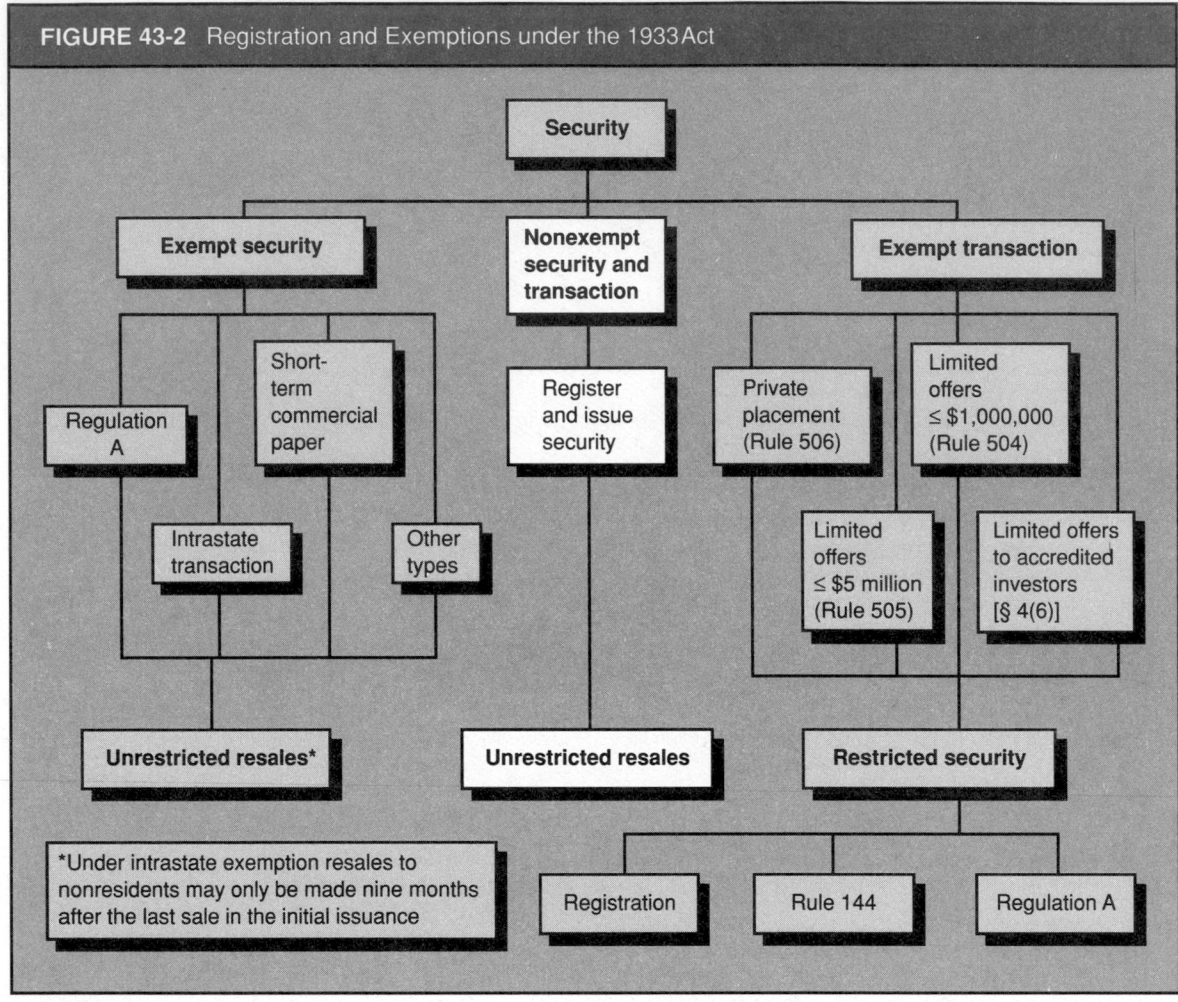

FIGURE 43-2 Registration and Exemptions under the 1933 Act

the purchaser no longer owns the security, he may recover monetary damages from the seller.

False Registration Statements When securities have been sold subject to a registration statement, **Section 11** of the Act imposes liability for the inclusion in the registration statement of any untrue statement or omission of material fact. **Material** refers to those matters to which there is a substantial likelihood that a reasonable investor would attach importance in determining whether to purchase the security registered. Liability is imposed on (1) the issuer; (2) all persons who signed the registration statement, including the principal executive officer, principal financial officer, and prin-

cipal accounting officer; (3) every person who was a director or partner; (4) every accountant, engineer, appraiser, or expert who prepared or certified any part of the registration statement; and (5) all underwriters. These persons are jointly and severally liable to any person who acquires the security without knowledge of the untruth or omission for the amount paid for the security less either its value at the time of suit or the price for which it was sold.

An expert is only liable for misstatements or omissions in the portion of the registration that he prepared or certified. Moreover, any defendant, other than the issuer, may assert the defense of due diligence. The **due diligence defense** generally requires showing that the defendant had reasonable grounds to believe that there were no untrue statements or material omissions. In some instances, due diligence requires that a reasonable investigation be made. In determining what constitutes a reasonable investigation and reasonable ground for belief, the standard of reasonableness is that required of a prudent man in the management of his own property.

ESCOTT v. BARCHRIS CONST. CORP.
United States District Court, Southern District of New York, 1968.
283 F.Supp. 643.

Facts: BarChris Construction Corporation sold shares of common stock to the public in December 1959. By early 1961 BarChris needed additional working capital and sold debentures to meet this need. A registration statement was filed with the SEC in March 1961, with amendments filed in May. By the time BarChris received the net proceeds of this sale, it was experiencing financial difficulties. Eventually BarChris filed for bankruptcy. Escott, a purchaser of the debentures, brought suit under the Securities Act of 1933 against BarChris, the underwriters, the company's auditors (Peat, Marwick, Mitchell & Co.), and the persons who signed the registration, alleging that the registration statement contained material false statements and material omissions. The defendants denied the falsity of the statements and their materiality. Furthermore, all of the defendants, except BarChris, claimed that they individually had exercised due diligence in connection with the statement so as to be free from liability under the statute.

Decision: Judgment for Escott granted.

Opinion: McLean, J.   *The "Due Diligence" Defenses*   Section 11(b) of the Act provides that:
"* * * no person, other than the issuer, shall be liable * * * who shall sustain the burden of proof—

* * *

"(3) that (A) as regards any part of the registration statement not purporting to be made on the authority of an expert * * * he had, after reasonable investigation, reasonable ground to believe and did believe, at the time such part of the registration statement became effective, that the statements therein were true and that there was no omission to state a material fact required to be stated therein or necessary to make the statements therein not misleading; * * * and (C) as regards any part of the registration statement purporting to be made on the authority of an expert (other than himself) * * * he had no reasonable ground to believe and did not believe, at the time such part of the registration statement became effective, that the statements therein were untrue or that there was an omission to state a material fact required to be stated therein or necessary to make the statements therein not misleading. * * * "
Section 11(c) defines "reasonable investigation" as follows:

"In determining, for the purposes of paragraph (3) of subsection (b) of this section, what constitutes reasonable investigation and reasonable ground for belief, the standard of reasonableness shall be that required of a prudent man in the management of his own property."

Every defendant, except BarChris itself, to whom, as the issuer, these defenses are not available, and except Peat, Marwick, whose position rests on a different statutory provision, has pleaded these affirmative defenses. Each claims that (1) as to the part of the registration statement purporting to be made on the authority of an expert (which, for convenience, I shall refer to as the "expertised portion"), he had no reasonable ground to believe and did not believe that there were any untrue statements or material omissions, and (2) as to the other parts of the registration statement, he made a reasonable investigation, as a result of which he had reasonable ground to believe and did believe that the registration statement was true and that no material fact was omitted. As to each defendant, the question is whether he has sustained the burden of proving these defenses. Surprising enough, there is little or no judicial authority on this question. No decisions directly in point under Section 11 have been found.

Before considering the evidence, a preliminary matter should be disposed of. The defendants do not agree among themselves as to who the "experts" were or as to the parts of the registration statement which were expertised.

* * *

* * * Neither the lawyer for the company nor the lawyer for the underwriters is an expert within the meaning of Section 11. The only expert, in the statutory sense, was Peat, Marwick, and the only parts of the registration statement which purported to be made upon the authority of an expert were the portions which purported to be made on Peat, Marwick's authority.

* * *

I turn now to the question of whether defendants have proved their due diligence defenses. The position of each defendant will be separately considered.

* * *

Kircher. Kircher was treasurer of BarChris and its chief financial officer. He is a certified public accountant and an intelligent man. He was thoroughly familiar with BarChris's financial affairs. * * *

Moreover, as a member of the executive committee, Kircher was kept informed as to those branches of the business of which he did not have direct charge.

* * *

Knowing the facts, Kircher had reason to believe that the expertised portion of the prospectus, *i.e.*, the 1960 figures, was in part incorrect. He could not shut his eyes to the facts and rely on Peat, Marwick for that portion.

As to the rest of the prospectus, knowing the facts, he did not have a reasonable ground to believe it to be true. On the contrary, he must have known that in part it was untrue. Under these circumstances, he was not entitled to sit back and place the blame on the lawyers for not advising him about it.

Kircher has not proved his due diligence defenses.

* * *

Birnbaum. Birnbaum was a young lawyer, admitted to the bar in 1957, who, after brief periods of employment by two different law firms and an equally brief period of practicing in his own firm, was employed by BarChris as house counsel and assistant secretary in October 1960. Unfortunately for him, he became secretary and a director of BarChris on April 17, 1961, after the first version of the registration statement had been filed with the Securities and Exchange Commission. He signed the later amendments, thereby becoming responsible for the accuracy of the prospectus in its final form.

Although the prospectus, in its description of "management," lists Birnbaum among the "executive officers" and devotes several sentences to a recital of his career, the fact seems to be that he was not an executive officer in any real sense. He did not participate in the management of the company. As house counsel, he attended to legal matters of a routine nature.

* * *

One of Birnbaum's more important duties, first as assistant secretary and later as fullfledged secretary, was to keep the corporate minutes of BarChris and its subsidiaries. This necessarily informed him to a considerable extent about the company's affairs. * * *

It seems probable that Birnbaum did not know of many of the inaccuracies in the prospectus. He must, however, have appreciated some of them. In any case, he made no investigation and relied on the others to get it right. * * * As a lawyer, he should have known his obligations under the statute. He should have known that he was required to make a reasonable investigation of the truth of all the statements in the unexpertised portion of the document which he signed. Having failed to make such an investigation, he did not have reasonable ground to believe that all these statements were true. Birnbaum has not established his due diligence defenses except as to the audited 1960 figures.

Auslander. Auslander was an "outside" director, *i.e.,* one who was not an officer of BarChris. He was chairman of the board of Valley Stream National Bank * * *

* * *

In considering Auslander's due diligence defenses, a distinction is to be drawn between the expertised and non-expertised portions of the prospectus. As to the former, Auslander knew that Peat, Marwick had audited the 1960 figures. He believed them to be correct because he had confidence in Peat, Marwick. He had no reasonable ground to believe otherwise.

As to the non-expertised portions, however, Auslander is in a different position. He seems to have been under the impression that Peat, Marwick was responsible for all the figures. This impression was not correct, as he would have realized if he had read the prospectus carefully. Auslander made no investigation of the accuracy of the prospectus. * * *

It is true that Auslander became a director on the eve of the financing. He had little opportunity to familiarize himself with the company's affairs. The question is whether, under such circumstances, Auslander did enough to establish his due diligence defense with respect to the nonexpertised portions of the prospectus.

* * *

Section 11 imposes liability in the first instance upon a director, no matter how new he is. He is presumed to know his responsibility when he becomes a director. He can escape liability only by using that reasonable care to investigate the facts which a prudent man would employ in the management of his own property. In my opinion, a prudent man would not act in an important matter without any knowledge of the relevant facts, in sole reliance upon representations of persons who are comparative strangers and upon general information which does not purport to cover the particular case. To say that such minimal conduct measures up to the statutory standard would to all intents and purposes, absolve new directors from responsibility merely because they are new. This is not a sensible construction of Section 11, when one bears in mind its fundamental purpose of requiring full and truthful disclosures for the protection of investors.

* * *

Grant. Grant became a director of BarChris in October 1960. His law firm was counsel to BarChris in matters pertaining to the registration of securities. Grant drafted the registration statement for the stock issue in 1959 and for the warrants in January 1961. He also drafted the registration statement for the debentures. In the preliminary division of work between him and Ballard, the underwriters' counsel, Grant took initial responsibility for preparing the registration statement, while Ballard devoted his efforts in the first instance to preparing the indenture.

Grant is sued as a director and as a signer of the registration statement. This is not an action against him for malpractice in his capacity as a lawyer. Nevertheless, in considering Grant's due diligence defense, the unique position which he occupied cannot be disregarded. As the director most directly concerned with writing the registration statement and assuring its accuracy, more was required of him in the way of reasonable investigation than could fairly be expected of a director who had no connection with this work.

* * *

Grant was entitled to rely on Peat, Marwick for the 1960 figures. He had no reasonable ground to believe them to be inaccurate. But the matters which * * * were not within the expertised portion of the prospectus * * * Grant was obliged to make a reasonable investigation. I am forced to find that he did not make one. * * *

The Underwriters. The underwriters other than Drexel made no investigation of the accuracy of the prospectus. * * * They all relied upon Drexel as the "lead" underwriter.

Drexel did make an investigation. The work was in charge of Coleman, a partner of the firm, assisted by Casperson, an associate. Drexel's attorneys acted as attorneys for the entire group of underwriters. Ballard did the work, assisted by Stanton.

* * *

The underwriters say that the prospectus is the company's prospectus, not theirs. Doubtless this is the way they customarily regard it. But the Securities Act makes no such distinction. The underwriters are just as responsible as the company if the prospectus is false. And prospective investors rely upon the reputation of the underwriters in deciding whether to purchase the securities.

* * *

The purpose of Section 11 is to protect investors. To that end the underwriters are made responsible for the truth of the prospectus. If they may escape that responsibility by taking at face value representations made to them by the company's management, then the inclusion of underwriters among those liable under Section 11 affords the investors no additional protection. To effectuate the statute's purpose, the phrase "reasonable investigation" must be construed to require more effort on the part of the underwriters than the mere accurate reporting in the prospectus of "data presented" to them by the company. It should make no difference that this data is elicited by questions addressed to the company officers by the underwriters, or that the underwriters at the time believe that the company's officers are truthful and reliable. In order to make the underwriters' participation in this enterprise of any value to the investors, the underwriters must make some reasonable attempt to verify the data submitted to them. They may not rely solely on the company's officers or on the company's counsel. A prudent man in the management of his own property would not rely on them.

It is impossible to lay down a rigid rule suitable for every case defining the extent to which such verification must go. It is a question of degree, a matter of judgment in each case. In the present case, the underwriters' counsel made almost no attempt to verify management's representations. I hold that that was insufficient.

On the evidence in this case, I find that the underwriters' counsel did not make a reasonable investigation of the truth of those portions of the prospectus which were not made on the authority of Peat, Marwick as an expert. Drexel is bound by their failure. It is not a matter of relying upon counsel for legal advice. Here the attorneys were dealing with matters of fact. Drexel delegated to them, as its agent, the business of examining the corporate minutes and contracts. It must bear the consequences of their failure to make an adequate examination.

The other underwriters, who did nothing and relied solely on Drexel and on the lawyers, are also bound by it. It follows that although Drexel and the other underwriters believed that those portions of the prospectus were true, they had no reasonable ground for that belief, within the meaning of the statute. Hence, they have not established their due diligence defense, except as to the 1960 audited figures.

[The decision with respect to the auditors Peat, Marwick is presented in the next chapter.]

Antifraud Provisions The 1933 Act also contains two broad antifraud provisions that apply to *all* securities, whether registered or exempt. The first, **Section 12(2)**, imposes liability on any person who offers or sells a security by means of a prospectus or oral communication that contains an untrue statement of material fact or an omission of a material fact. This liability extends only to the immediate purchaser, provided she did not know of the untruth or omission. The seller may avoid liability by proving that he did not know, and in the exercise of reasonable care could not have known, of the untrue statement or omission. The seller is liable to the purchaser for the amount paid on tender of the security. If the purchaser no longer owns the security, she may recover damages from the seller.

The second provision, **Section 17(a)**, makes it unlawful for any person in the offer or sale of any securities, whether registered or not, to do any of the following when using any means of transportation or communication in interstate commerce or the mails:

1. employ any device, scheme, or artifice to defraud, or
2. obtain money or property by means of any untrue statement of a material fact or any omission to state a material fact without which the information is misleading, or
3. engage in any transaction, practice, or course of business that operates or would operate as a fraud or deceit upon the purchaser.

There is some doubt whether the courts may imply a private right of action for persons injured by violations of this section. The Supreme Court has reserved this question and the lower courts are divided on the issue. The SEC may, however, bring enforcement actions under Section 17(a).

Criminal Sanctions The 1933 Act imposes criminal sanctions on any person who willfully violates any of the provisions of the Act or the rules and regulations promulgated by the SEC pursuant to the Act. Conviction may carry a fine of not more than $10,000 or imprisonment of not more than five years or both.

THE SECURITIES EXCHANGE ACT OF 1934

The Securities Exchange Act of 1934 deals mainly with the secondary distribution (resale) of securities. The Act seeks to ensure fair and orderly securities markets by establishing rules for the operation of the markets, and by prohibiting fraudulent and manipulative practices. It provides protection for holders of securities listed on national exchanges as well as for holders of equity securities of companies traded over the counter if their assets exceed $5 million and they have a class of equity securities with 500 or more shareholders. Companies must register such securities and are also subject to the Act's periodic reporting requirements, the short-swing profits provision, the tender offer provisions, the proxy solicitation provisions, and the internal control and recordkeeping requirements of the Foreign Corrupt Practices Act. In addition, issuers of securities, whether registered under the 1934 Act or not, must comply with the antifraud and the antibribery provisions of the Act. (See Figure 43–3.)

Registration and Periodic Reporting Requirements

The 1934 Act requires all regulated publicly held companies to register with the SEC.

These registrations are one-time registrations that apply to an entire class of securities. Thus, they differ from registrations under the Securities Act of 1933, which relate only to securities involved in a specific offering. Registration requires disclosure of such information as the organization, financial structure, and nature of the business; the terms, positions, rights, and privileges of the different classes of outstanding securities; the names of the directors, officers, and underwriters and each security holder owning more than 10 percent of any class of nonexempt equity security; bonus and profit-sharing arrangements; and balance sheets and profit and loss statements for the three preceding fiscal years. Following registration, an issuer must file specified annual and periodic reports to update the information contained in the original registration. The Act also requires that each director, officer, and any person who owns 10 percent or more of a registered equity security file monthly reports with the SEC stating any changes in his ownership of such equity securities.

Section 18 imposes express civil liability upon any person who makes or causes to be made any false or misleading statement with

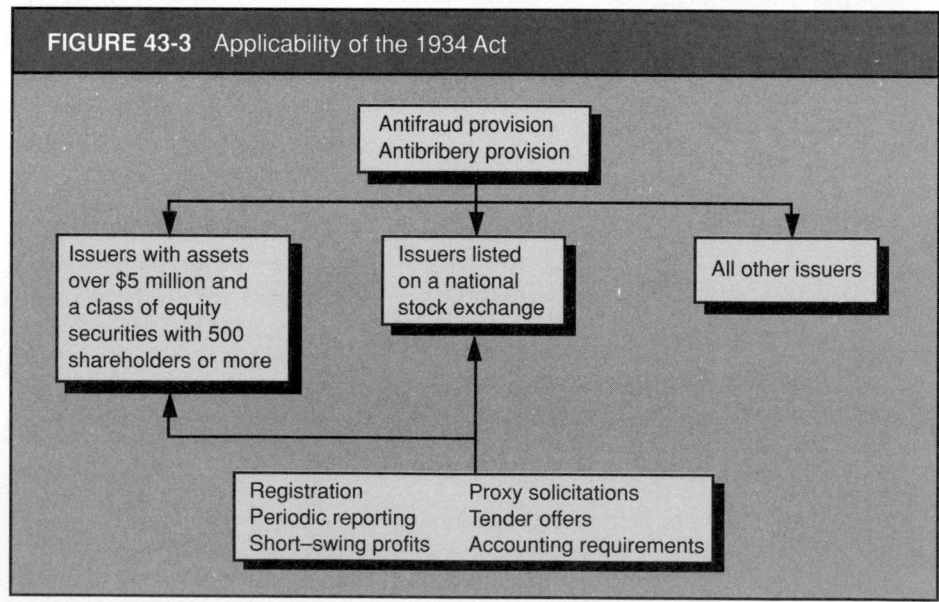

FIGURE 43-3 Applicability of the 1934 Act

respect to any material fact in any application, report, document, or registration filed with the SEC under the 1934 Act. Liability extends to any person who purchased or sold a security in reliance upon that false or misleading statement without knowing that it was false or misleading. A person is not liable, however, if she proves that she acted in good faith and had no knowledge that such statement was false or misleading.

Criminal Sanctions

The 1934 Act imposes criminal sanctions on any person who willfully violates any of the provisions of the Act (except the antibribery provision) or the rules and regulations promulgated by the SEC pursuant to the Act. For individuals, conviction may carry a fine of not more than $1 million or imprisonment of not more than 10 years or both, except no person is subject to *imprisonmnet* if he proves he had no knowledge of the rule or regulation. If the person, however, is not a natural person, such as a corporation, then a fine not exceeding $2.5 million may be imposed.

Antifraud Provisions

Section 10(b) of the 1934 Act and SEC **Rule 10b-5** make it unlawful for any person to do any of the following when using the mails or any other facilities of interstate commerce in connection with the purchase or sale of any security:

1. employ any device, scheme, or artifice to defraud;
2. make any untrue statement of a material fact;
3. omit to state a material fact without which the information is misleading; or
4. engage in any act, practice, or course of business that operates or would operate as a fraud or deceit on any person.

Rule 10b-5 applies to any purchase or sale of **any** security, whether it is registered under the 1934 Act or not, whether it is publicly traded or closely held, whether it is listed on an exchange or sold over the counter, or whether it is part of an initial issuance or a secondary distribution. There are **no** exemptions. Unlike the liability provisions of the 1933 Act, Rule 10b-5 applies to misconduct of purchasers as well as sellers and allows both defrauded sellers and buyers to recover.

Requisites of Rule 10b-5 Recovery of damages under Rule 10b-5 requires proof of several elements, including (1) a misstatement or omission (2) that is material, (3) made with *scienter*, and (4) relied on (5) in connection with the purchase or sale of a security. Violation of this rule is different from common law fraud because the rule imposes an affirmative duty of disclosure. A misstatement or omission is material if there is a substantial likelihood that a reasonable investor would consider it important in deciding whether to purchase or sell the security. In an action for damages under Rule 10b-5, it must be shown that the violation was committed with **scienter**, which is intentional misconduct. Negligence is not sufficient.

Insider Trading Rule 10b-5 applies to sales or purchases of securities made by an "insider" who possesses material information that is not available to the public. An insider is liable under Rule 10b-5 if he fails to disclose the material, nonpublic information before trading on the information unless he waits until the information becomes public. **Insiders,** for the purpose of Rule 10b-5, include directors, officers, employees, and agents of the issuer of the security as well as those with whom the issuer has entrusted information solely for corporate purposes, such as underwriters, accountants, lawyers, and consultants. In some instances, persons who receive material, nonpublic information from insiders—**tippees**—are also precluded from trading on that information. A tippee is under a duty not to trade on inside information when the insider has breached his fiduciary duty to the shareholders by disclosing the information to the tippee who knows or should know that there has been such a breach. See Law in the News on page 985.

DIRKS v. SECURITIES AND EXCHANGE COMMISSION
Supreme Court of the United States, 1983.
463 U.S. 646, 103 S.Ct. 3255, 77 L.Ed.2d 911.

Facts: In 1973 Dirks was an officer of a New York broker-dealer firm who specialized in providing investment analysis of insurance company securities to institutional investors. On March 6 Dirks received information from Ronald Secrist, a former officer of Equity Funding of America. Secrist alleged that the assets of Equity Funding, a diversified corporation primarily engaged in selling life insurance and mutual funds, were vastly overstated as the result of fraudulent corporate practices. Dirks decided to investigate the allegations. He visited Equity Funding's headquarters in Los Angeles and interviewed several officers and employees of the corporation. The senior management denied any wrongdoing, but certain corporation employees corroborated the charges of fraud. Neither Dirks nor his firm owned or traded any Equity Funding stock, but throughout his investigation he openly discussed the information he had obtained with a number of clients and investors. Some of these persons sold their holdings of Equity Funding securities, including five investment advisers who liquidated holdings of more than $16 million.

While Dirks was in Los Angeles, he was in touch regularly with William Blundell, the *Wall Street Journal's* Los Angeles bureau chief. Dirks urged Blundell to write a story on the fraud allegations. Blundell did not believe, however, that such a massive fraud could go undetected and declined to write the story. He feared that publishing such damaging hearsay might be libelous.

During the two-week period in which Dirks pursued his investigation and spread word of Secrist's charges, the price of Equity Funding stock fell from $26 per share to less than $15 per share. This led the New York Stock Exchange to halt trading on March 27. Shortly thereafter, California insurance authorities impounded Equity Funding's records and uncovered evidence of the fraud. Only then did the Securities and Exchange Commission (SEC) file a complaint against Equity Funding.

The SEC began an investigation into Dirks's role in the exposure of the fraud. After a hearing by an administrative law judge, the SEC found that Dirks had aided and abetted violations of § 10(b) of the Securities Exchange Act of 1934 and SEC Rule 10b-5 by repeating the allegations of fraud to members of the investment community who later sold their Equity Funding stock. Recognizing, however, that Dirks "played an important role in bringing Equity Funding's massive fraud to light," the SEC only censured him. The Court of Appeals affirmed the action of the SEC.

Decision: Judgment reversed.

Opinion: **Powell, J.**   In the seminal case of In re Cady, Roberts & Co., [citation] the SEC recognized that the common law in some jurisdictions imposes on "corporate 'insiders,' particularly officers, directors, or controlling stockholders" an "affirmative duty of disclosure * * * when dealing in securities." [Citation.] The SEC found that not only did breach of this common-law duty also establish the elements of a Rule 10b-5 violation, but that individuals other than corporate insiders could be obligated either to disclose material nonpublic information before trading or to abstain from trading altogether. [Citation.] In *Chiarella*, we accepted the two elements set out in *Cady, Roberts* for establishing a Rule 10b-5 violation: "(i) the existence of a relationship affording access to inside information intended to be available only for a corporate purpose, and (ii) the unfairness of allowing a corporate insider to take advantage of that information by trading without disclosure." [Citation.] In examining whether Chiarella had an obligation to disclose or abstain, the Court found that there is no general duty to disclose before trading on material nonpublic information, and held that "a duty to disclose under § 10(b) does not arise from the mere possession of nonpublic market information." [Citation.] Such a duty arises rather from the existence of a fiduciary relationship. [Citation.]

Not "all breaches of fiduciary duty in connection with a securities transaction," however, come within the ambit of Rule 10b-5. [Citation.] There must also be "manipulation or deception." [Citation.] In an inside-trading case this fraud derives from the "inherent unfairness involved where one takes advantage" of "information intended to be available only for a corporate purpose and not for the personal benefit of anyone." [Citation.] Thus, an insider will be liable under Rule 10b-5 for inside trading only where he fails to disclose material nonpublic information before trading on it and thus makes "secret profits." *Cady, Roberts* [citation.]

We were explicit in *Chiarella* in saying that there can be no duty to disclose where the person who has traded on inside information "was not [the corporation's] agent, * * * was not a fiduciary, [or] was not a person in whom the sellers [of the securities] had placed their trust and confidence." [Citation.] Not to require such a fiduciary relationship, we recognized, would "depar[t] radically from the established doctrine that duty arises from a specific relationship between two parties" and would amount to "recognizing a general duty between all participants in market transactions to forgo actions based on material, nonpublic information." [Citation.] This requirement of a specific relationship between the shareholders and the individual trading on inside information has created analytical difficulties for the SEC and courts in policing tippees who trade on inside information. Unlike insiders who have independent fiduciary duties to both the corporation and its shareholders, the typical tippee has no such relationships. In view of this absence, it has been unclear how a tippee acquires the *Cady, Roberts* duty to refrain from trading on inside information.

* * *

In effect, the SEC's theory of tippee liability . . . appears rooted in the idea that the antifraud provisions require equal information among all traders. This conflicts with the principle set forth in *Chiarella* that only some persons, under some circumstances, will be barred from trading while in possession of material nonpublic information. Judge Wright correctly read our opinion in *Chiarella* as repudiating any notion that all traders must enjoy equal information before trading: "[T]he 'information' theory is rejected. Because the disclose-or-refrain duty is extraordinary, it attaches only when a party has legal obligations other than a mere duty to comply with the general antifraud proscriptions in the federal securities laws." [Citation.] We reaffirm today that "[a] duty [to disclose] arises from the relationship between parties * * * and not merely from one's ability to acquire information because of his position in the market." [Citation.]

Imposing a duty to disclose or abstain solely because a person knowingly receives material nonpublic information from an insider and trades on it could have an inhibiting influence on the role of market analysts, which the SEC itself recognizes is necessary to the preservation of a healthy market. It is commonplace for analysis to "ferret out and analyze information," and this often is done by meeting with and questioning corporate officers and others who are insiders. And information that the analysts obtain normally may be the basis for judgments as to the market worth of a corporation's securities. The analyst's judgment in this respect is made available in market letters or otherwise to clients of the firm. It is the nature of this type of information, and indeed of the markets themselves, that such information cannot be made simultaneously available to all of the corporation's stockholders or the public generally.

The conclusion that recipients of inside information do not invariably acquire a duty to disclose or abstain does not mean that such tippees always are free to trade on the information. The need for a ban on some tippee trading is clear. Not only are insiders forbidden by their fiduciary relationship from personally using undisclosed corporate information to their advantage, but they may not give such information to an outsider for the same improper purpose of exploiting the information for their personal gain. * * *

Thus, some tippees must assume an insider's duty to the shareholders not because they receive inside information, but rather because it has been made available to them *improperly.* * * * Thus, a tippee assumes a fiduciary duty to the shareholders of a corporation not to trade on material nonpublic information only when the insider has breached his fiduciary duty to the shareholders by disclosing the information to the tippee and the tippee knows or should know that there has been a breach. * * *

* * * Whether disclosure is a breach of duty therefore depends in large part on the purpose of the disclosure. This standard was identified by the SEC itself in *Cady, Roberts:* a purpose of the securities laws was to eliminate "use of inside information for personal advantage." [Citation.] Thus, the test is whether the insider personally will benefit, directly or indirectly, from his disclosure. Absent some personal gain, there has been no breach of duty to stockholders. And absent a breach by the insider, there is no derivative breach.

* * *

Under the inside-trading and tipping rules set forth above, we find that there was no actionable violation by Dirks. It is undisputed that Dirks himself was a stranger to Equity Funding, with no pre-existing fiduciary duty to its shareholders. He took no action, directly or indirectly, that induced the shareholders or officers of Equity Funding to repose trust or confidence in him. There was no expectation by Dirks' sources that he would keep their information in confidence. Nor did Dirks misappropriate or illegally obtain the information about Equity Funding. Unless the insiders breached their *Cady, Roberts* duty to shareholders in disclosing the nonpublic information to Dirks, he breached no duty when he passed it on to investors * * *.

It is clear that neither Secrist nor the other Equity Funding employees violated their *Cady, Roberts* duty to the corporation's shareholders by providing information to Dirks. The tippers received no monetary or personal benefit for revealing Equity Funding's secrets, nor was their purpose to make a gift of valuable information to Dirks. As the facts of this case clearly indicate, the tippers were motivated by a desire to expose the fraud. In the absence of a breach of duty to shareholders by the insiders, there was no derivative breach by Dirks. * * *

We conclude that Dirks, in the circumstances of this case, had no duty to abstain from use of the inside information that he obtained.

LAW IN THE NEWS

Law Is Still a Bit Murky on Matter of What Constitutes Insider Trading

When does trading on a hot tip violate the law?

The question has prompted many suits, since insider trading isn't explicitly defined in the securities laws, and the law has evolved on a case-by-case basis over two decades. The topic has spawned lengthy analyses by legal experts. The Securities and Exchange Commission relies on recent Supreme Court rulings and has welcomed the flexibility to address problems as they arise.

In a landmark case, Dirks vs. SEC, the high court defined insider trading as buying or selling securities in breach of a fiduciary duty or other relationship of trust while possessing material, non-public information about an issuer.

That's relatively easy to spot when an obvious insider—an officer in a corporation, say—trades in the company's stock based on confidential information. But what happens when the investor isn't an insider, and has simply heard the information? Or what if the original source isn't an officer in the company but someone entrusted with the information, such as an investment banker or lawyer?

According to Joseph I. Goldstein, associate director of enforcement for the SEC, the agency applies a four-part test derived from the Dirks case. First it establishes, often through data from exchange surveillance operations, that there has been suspicious trading. Then it determines whether the trading was based on information that was material and non-public. Next it looks to the source of information to see if a duty has been breached. (It is now well established that such a duty is breached even if the source isn't a corporate insider but someone entrusted with confidential information.) Finally, the SEC asks whether the recipient of the information "knew or should have known" that the source of the information had breached a fiduciary duty or other relationship of trust and confidence. The SEC satisfies itself that all four tests are met before it brings charges.

Probably the most troublesome aspect of defining insider trading is the requirement that the recipient of a tip "knew" or "should have known" that his or her source breached a duty of confidentiality. Much depends on the circumstances. If the source is an investment banker working on a takeover deal, a recipient of information about the deal probably should have known it would be illegal to trade on the information. Generally, using a tip like "don't ask me why, but investing in stock XYZ is a sure thing" is no guarantee the recipient won't be deemed to have known that inside information was involved.

On the other hand, if a broker recommends a stock to a client, without elaborating on the basis or source of information, then the client probably wouldn't be expected to know that a breach had occurred. In one well known case, a football coach who overheard a tip while sitting in a stadium was found not to have engaged in insider trading because the source of the information didn't realize he was being overheard, and hence, didn't breach a duty of confidentiality.

Jonathan Eisenberg, a partner with Kirkpatrick & Lockhart in Washington, has a rough rule-of-thumb: "If you overhear it, it's legal. If someone who is an insider intentionally tells you, it's illegal."

Is being far down a chain of tips any protection? Theoretically, it is irrelevant, the SEC says. Practically speaking, this may make it harder for SEC to prove parts of the case, especially the "knew or should have known" element. As information is passed, it typically becomes less and less explicit.

As with many of the securities laws, insider trading can be a civil or criminal offense or both. While the elements of the offense are the same, a criminal case entails a higher standard of proof.

James B. Stewart The Wall Street Journal, July 21, 1989.
Reprinted by permission of the Wall Street Journal, © Dow Jones & Company, Inc. 1989. All Rights Reserved Worldwide.

Short-Swing Profits

Section 16(b) of the 1934 Act imposes liability on insiders—directors, officers, and any person owning 10 percent or more of the stock of a corporation listed on a national stock exchange or registered with the SEC—for all profits resulting from their short-swing trading in such stock. If any insider sells such stock within six months from the date of its purchase or purchases such stock within six months from the date of a sale of the stock, the corporation is entitled to recover any and all profit realized by the insider from these transactions. The "profit" recoverable is calculated by matching the highest sale price against the lowest purchase price within six months of each other. Losses cannot be offset against profits.

Although both Section 16(b) and Rule 10b-5 address the problem of insider trading and may apply to the same transaction, they differ in a number of respects. First, Section 16(b) applies only to transactions involving registered equity securities, whereas Rule 10b-5 applies to all securities. Second, the definition of "insider" is much broader under Rule 10b-5 and may extend beyond directors, officers, and owners of 10 percent or more of a company's stock, whereas Section 16(b) is limited to these persons. Third, Section 16(b) does *not* require that the insider possess material, nonpublic information; Rule 10b-5 applies only to insider trading where such information is not disclosed. Fourth, Section 16(b) applies only to transactions within six months of each other; Rule 10b-5 has no such limitation. Fifth, under Rule 10b-5, injured investors may recover damages on their own behalf, whereas under Section 16(b), although shareholders may bring suit, any recovery is on behalf of the corporation.

Insider Trading Acts

In addition to the remedies discussed above, the SEC is authorized by legislation enacted in 1984 and 1988 to bring an action in a U.S. district court to have a civil penalty imposed upon any person who purchases or sells a security while in possession of material, nonpublic information. Liability may also be imposed on any person who directly or indirectly controlled the person who committed a violation, if the controlling person knew or recklessly disregarded the fact that the controlled person was likely to commit a violation. The transaction must be on or through the facilities of a national securities exchange or from or through a broker or dealer. Purchases that are part of a public offering by an issuer of securities are not subject to this provision.

The amount of the civil penalty for the person who committed a violation by trading on inside information is determined by the court in light of the facts and circumstances but may not exceed three times the profit gained or loss avoided as a result of the unlawful purchase or sale. The maximum amount of the civil penalty which may be imposed upon a controlling person is the greater of $1 million or three times the profit gained or loss avoided as a result of the controlled person's violation. If the controlled person's violation consists of tipping inside information, then the liability of the controlling person is measured by the profit gained or loss avoided by the person to whom the controlled person directed the tip. For the purpose of this provision, "profit gained" or "loss avoided" is "the difference between the purchase or sale price of the security and the value of that security as measured by the trading price of the security a reasonable period after public dissemination of the nonpublic information."

The penalty is payable into the Treasury of the United States. The SEC is authorized to award bounties of up to ten percent of the penalty recovered to informants who provide information leading to the imposition of the penalty. An action must be brought within five years after the date of the purchase or sale.

In 1988 Congress amended the 1934 Act to impose express civil liability upon any person who violated the Act by purchasing or selling a security while in possession of material, nonpublic information. Any person who contemporaneously sold or purchased securities of the same class as persons who improperly traded may bring a private action to recover damages for the violation. The total amount of damages may not exceed the profit gained or loss avoided by the violation diminished by any amount disgorged to the SEC pursuant to a court order. The action must be brought within five years after the date of the last transaction that is the subject of the violation. Tippers are jointly and severally liable with their tippees, if the tippee commits a violation by trading on the inside information.

Proxy Solicitations

A **proxy** is a writing signed by a shareholder of a corporation authorizing a named person to vote his shares of stock at a specified meeting of the shareholders. To ensure that shareholders have adequate information upon which to vote, the 1934 Act regulates the proxy solicitation process. The Act makes it unlawful for any person to solicit any proxy concerning any registered security "in contravention of such rules and regulations as the Commission may prescribe." **Solicitation** includes any request for a proxy, any request not to execute a proxy, or any request to revoke a proxy. Solicitation of a proxy is prohibited unless each person solicited has been furnished with a written proxy statement containing specified information. In the case of solicitations by the issuer, the issuer must furnish security holders with a *proxy statement* describing all material facts concerning the matters being submitted to their vote, together with a *proxy form* on which the security holders can indicate their approval or disapproval of each proposal to be presented. Even if a company does not solicit proxies from its shareholders but submits a matter to a shareholder vote, it must provide them with information substantially equivalent to that which would appear in a proxy statement. In addition, in an election of directors, solicitations of proxies by a person other than the issuer are subject to similar disclosure requirements. The *issuer* in such an election also must include an annual report with the proxy statement.

Where management makes a solicitation, any security holder entitled to vote has the opportunity to communicate with other security holders. On written request, the corpora-

tion must mail the communication at the security holder's expense or, at its option, promptly furnish to that security holder a current list of security holders.

If an eligible security holder entitled to vote submits a timely proposal for action at a forthcoming meeting, management must include the proposal in its proxy statement and provide security holders with an opportunity to vote for or against it. If management opposes the proposal, it must include in its proxy materials a statement by the security holder of not more than 200 words. Management may omit a proposal if, among other things, (1) under State law it is not a proper subject for shareholder action, (2) it is not significantly related to the business of the issuer, (3) it is beyond the issuer's power to accomplish, or (4) it relates to the conduct of the ordinary business operations of the issuer.

Any person who distributes a materially false or misleading proxy statement may be liable to any person who suffers a loss caused by purchasing or selling a security in reliance on the statement. In this context, a misstatement or omission is material if there is a substantial likelihood that a reasonable shareholder would consider it important in deciding how to vote.

Tender Offers

A **tender offer** is a general invitation to all of the shareholders of a company to purchase their shares at a specified price. In 1968 Congress enacted the Williams Act, which amended the 1934 Act to extend reporting and disclosure requirements to tender offers and other block acquisitions. The purpose of the Williams Act is to provide public shareholders with full disclosure by both the bidder and the target so that the shareholders may make an informed decision.

The 1934 Act imposes disclosure requirements in three situations: (1) a person or group acquires more than 5 percent of a class of voting securities registered under the 1934 Act, (2) a person makes a tender offer for more than 5 percent of a class of registered equity securities, or (3) the issuer makes an offer to repurchase its own registered shares. Although each of these situations is governed by different rules, the disclosure required is substantially the same. A statement must be filed with the SEC containing (1) the person's background; (2) the source of the funds used to acquire the securities; (3) the purpose of the acquisition, including any plans to liquidate the company or make major changes in the corporate structure; (4) the number of shares owned; and (5) any relevant contracts, arrangements, or understandings. This disclosure is also required by anyone soliciting shareholders to accept or reject a tender offer. A copy of the statement must be furnished to each offeree and sent to the issuer.

The target company has ten days in which to respond to the bidder's tender offer by (1) recommending acceptance or rejection, (2) expressing no opinion and remaining neutral, or (3) stating it is unable to take a position. The target company's response must include the reasons for the position taken.

A tender offer must be kept open for at least twenty business days. Shareholders who tender their shares may withdraw them at any time during the offering period. Moreover, all shares tendered must be purchased for the same price; if an offering price is increased, those who have already tendered receive the benefit of the increase. A tender offeror who offers to purchase less than all of the outstanding securities of the target must accept, on a *pro rata* basis, securities tendered during the offer. During the tender offer, the bidder may buy shares of the target only through that tender offer.

It is unlawful for any person to make any untrue statement of material fact or omit to state any material fact or to engage in any fraudulent, deceptive, or manipulative practices in connection with any tender offer, even if the target company is not subject to the 1934 Act's reporting requirements.

SCHREIBER v. BURLINGTON NORTHERN, INC.
Supreme Court of the United States, 1985.
472 U.S. 1, 105 S.Ct. 2458, 86 L.Ed.2d 1.

Facts: On December 21, 1982, Burlington Northern, Inc., made a hostile tender offer for El Paso Gas Co., proposing to purchase 25.1 million El Paso shares at $24 per share. The shareholders of El Paso fully subscribed the offer by the December 30, 1982, deadline. Burlington refused to accept those tendered shares and instead announced the terms of a new and friendly takeover agreement on January 10, 1983. Under this agreement, Burlington withdrew the December tender offer and substituted a new tender offer for 21 million shares at $24 per share. Over 40 million shares were tendered in response to this offer. Thus, the new offer disadvantaged those shareholders who had tendered during the first offer, for those who retendered were subject to substantial proration and hence received a diminished payment. Barbara Schreiber, one of the disadvantaged shareholders, brought an action against Burlington, El Paso, and members of El Paso's board, claiming that Burlington's rescission of the first tender offer and substitution of the new one was a "manipulative" distortion of the market for El Paso stock prohibited by Section 14(e) of the Securities Exchange Act. The District Court dismissed the suit for failure to state a claim and the Court of Appeals affirmed.

Decision: Judgment of Court of Appeals affirmed.

Opinion: **Burger, C. J.** We are asked in this case to interpret § 14(e) of the Securities Exchange Act, [citation]. The starting point is the language of the statute. Section 14(e) provides:

"It shall be unlawful for any person to make any untrue statement of a material fact or omit to state any material fact necessary in order to make the statements made, in the light of the circumstances under which they are made, not misleading, or to engage in any fraudulent, deceptive or manipulative acts or practices, in connection with any tender offer or request or invitation for tenders, or any solicitation of security holders in opposition to or in favor of any such offer, request, or invitation. The Commission shall, for the purposes of this subsection, by rules and regulations define, and prescribe means reasonably designed to prevent, such acts and practices as are fraudulent, deceptive, or manipulative." [Citation.]

Petitioner relies on a construction of the phrase, "fraudulent, deceptive or manipulative acts or practices." Petitioner reads the phrase "fraudulent, deceptive or manipulative acts or practices" to include acts which, although fully disclosed, "artificially" affect the price of the takeover target's stock. Petitioner's interpretation relies on the belief that § 14(e) is directed at purposes broader than providing full and true information to investors.

Petitioner's reading of the term "manipulative" conflicts with the normal meaning of the term. We have held in the context of an alleged violation of § 10(b) of the Securities Exchange Act:

"Use of the word 'manipulative' is especially significant. It is and was virtually a term of art when used in connection with the securities markets. It connotes intentional or willful conduct *designed to deceive or defraud* investors by controlling or artificially affecting the price of securities." Ernst & Ernst v. Hochfelder. [see Chapter 44.]

Other cases interpreting the term reflect its use as a general term comprising a range of misleading practices:

"The term refers generally to practices, such as wash sales, matched orders, or rigged prices, that are intended to mislead investors by artificially affecting market activity. . . . Section 10(b)'s general prohibition of practices deemed by the SEC to be 'manipulative'—in this technical sense of artificially affecting market activity in order to mislead investors—is fully consistent with the fundamental purpose of the 1934 Act ' "to substitute a philosophy of full disclosure for the philosophy of *caveat emptor*. . . ." ' . . . Indeed, nondisclosure is usually essential to the success of a manipulative scheme. . . . No doubt Congress meant to prohibit the full range of ingenious devices that might be used to manipulate securities prices. But we do not think it would have chosen this 'term of art' if it had meant to bring within the scope of § 10(b) instances of corporate mismanagement such as this, in which the essence of the complaint is that shareholders were treated unfairly by a fiduciary." [Citation.]

The meaning the Court has given the term "manipulative" is consistent with the use of the term at common law, and with its traditional dictionary definition.

She argues, however, that the term manipulative takes on a meaning in § 14(e) that is different from the meaning it has in § 10(b). Petitioner claims that the use of the disjunctive "or" in § 14(e) implies that acts need not be deceptive or fraudulent to be manipulative. But Congress used the phrase "manipulative or deceptive" in § 10(b) as well, and we have interpreted "manipulative" in that context to require misrepresentation. Moreover, it is a " 'familiar principle of statutory construction that words grouped in a list should be given related meaning.' " [Citation.] All three species of misconduct, i.e., "fraudulent, deceptive or manipulative," listed by Congress are directed at failures to disclose. The use of the term "manipulative" provides emphasis and guidance to those who must determine which types of acts are reached by the statute; it does not suggest a deviation from the section's facial and primary concern with disclosure or Congressional concern with disclosure which is the core of the Act.

Our conclusion that "manipulative" acts under § 14(e) require misrepresentation or nondisclosure is buttressed by the purpose and legislative history of the provision. Section 14(e) was originally added to the Securities Exchange Act as part of the Williams Act, [citation]. "The purpose of the Williams Act is to insure that public shareholders who are confronted by a cash tender offer for their stock will not be required to respond without adequate information." [Citation.]

It is clear that Congress relied primarily on disclosure to implement the purpose of the Williams Act. Senator Williams, the Bill's Senate sponsor, stated in the debate:

"Today, the public shareholder in deciding whether to accept or reject a tender offer possess limited information. No matter what he does, he acts without adequate knowledge to enable him to decide rationally what is the best course of action. This is precisely the dilemma which our securities laws are designed to prevent." [Citation.]

The expressed legislative intent was to preserve a neutral setting in which the contenders could fully present their arguments. The Senate sponsor went on to say:

"We have taken extreme care to avoid tipping the scales either in favor of management or in favor of the person making the takeover bids. S. 510 is designed solely to require full and fair disclosure for the benefit of investors. The bill will at the same time provide the offeror and management equal opportunity to present their case." [Citation.]

To implement this objective, the Williams Act added §§ 13(d), 13(e), 14(d), 14(e), and 14(f) to the Securities Exchange Act. Some relate to disclosure; §§ 13(d), 14(d) and 14(f) all add specific registration and disclosure provisions. Others—§§ 13(e) and 14(d)—require or prohibit certain acts so that investors will possess additional time within which to take advantage of the disclosed information.

Section 14(e) adds a "broad antifraud prohibition," [citation], modeled on the antifraud provisions of § 10(b) of the Act and Rule 10b-5, [citation]. It supplements the more precise disclosure provisions found elsewhere in the Williams Act, while requiring disclosure more explicitly addressed to the tender offer context than that required by § 10(b).

While legislative history specifically concerning § 14(e) is sparse, the House and Senate Reports discuss the role of § 14(e). Describing § 14(e) as regulating "fraudulent transactions," and stating the thrust of the section:

"This provision would affirm the fact that persons engaged in making or opposing tender offers or otherwise seeking to influence the decision of investors or the outcome of the tender offer are under an obligation to make *full disclosure* of material information to those with whom they deal." [Citations.]

Nowhere in the legislative history is there the slightest suggestion that § 14(e) serves any purpose other than disclosure, or that the term "manipulative" should be read as an invitation to the courts to oversee the substantive fairness of tender offers; the quality of any offer is a matter for the marketplace.

To adopt the reading of the term "manipulative" urged by petitioner would not only be unwarranted in light of the legislative purpose but would be at odds with it. Inviting judges to read the term "manipulative" with their own sense of what constitutes "unfair" or "artificial" conduct would inject uncertainty into the tender offer process. An essential piece of information—whether the court would deem the fully disclosed actions of one side or the other to be "manipulative"—would not be available until after the tender offer had closed. This uncertainty would directly contradict the expressed Congressional desire to give investors full information.

Congress' consistent emphasis on disclosure persuades us that it intended takeover contests to be addressed to shareholders. In pursuit of this goal, Congress, consistent with the core mechanism of the Securities Exchange Act, created sweeping disclosure requirements and narrow substantive safeguards. The same Congress that placed such emphasis on shareholder choice would not at the same time have required judges to oversee tender offers for substantive fairness. It is even less likely that a Congress implementing that intention would express it only through the use of a single word placed in the middle of a provision otherwise devoted to disclosure.

We hold that the term "manipulative" as used in § 14(e) requires misrepresentation or nondisclosure. It connotes "conduct designed to deceive or defraud investors by controlling or artificially affecting the price of securities." Ernst & Ernst v. Hochfelder, [see Chapter 44.] Without misrepresentation or nondisclosure, § 14(e) has not been violated.

Applying that definition to this case, we hold that the actions of respondents were not manipulative. The amended complaint fails to allege that the cancellation of the first tender offer was accompanied by any misrepresentation, nondisclosure or deception. The District Court correctly found, "All activity of the defendants that could have conceivably affected the price of El Paso shares was done openly." [Citation.]

Defensive Tactics   When confronted with an uninvited takeover bid—or by a potential, uninvited bid—management of the target company may decide either to oppose the bid or to seek to prevent it. The defensive tactics employed by management to prevent or defend against undesired tender offers have developed into a highly ingenious, and metaphorically named, set of maneuvers, some of which require considerable planning. The tactics continue to evolve, and some of them are of questionable legality. The following excerpt describes most of the commonly used defensive tactics:

When faced with an outsider's attempt to take over the company, target management will frequently respond with a defensive tactic such as seeking a friendly suitor or "white knight." For example, the white knight may be granted a "lock-up" option which gives it an advantage in acquiring the target over other bidders, or the target may arrange to sell its "crown jewel," or most desirable asset, to the white knight, thereby diminishing the target's attractiveness to others. . . .

Common alternatives to finding a "white knight" as a defensive tactic include: the issuance of additional shares to dilute any holdings of the would-be acquiring company; stock repurchase programs to strengthen the control of "inside" or "friendly" shareholders; restrictive bylaw and charter provisions, (sometimes referred to as "porcupine provisions" or "shark repellent") such as extraordinarily high voting requirements for mergers with other corporations; staggering of directors' terms of office which necessarily increases the time it will take to effect a turnover in management; obligating the corporation to long-term salary or bonus contracts (known as "golden parachutes" or "silver wheel chairs") for top management in the event of a change in control; and using state tender offer statutes to introduce additional delays into the tender offer process. A similar move is for the target company to reincorporate in a state with more onerous antitakeover laws. Other defensive and preventive tactics used in recent years include: the acquisition of another business by the target company, creating a potential antitrust threat to impending tender offers; the purchase of a radio station or some other heavily regulated business to tie up the takeover attempt in administrative proceedings which may be needed to approve any change of ownership in the regulated business; and the "Pac-Man" defense, where the target company makes a tender offer for control of the original tender offeror. Defensive tactics continue to proliferate. Another recent defensive tactic is the "poison pill" which is a conditional stock right that is triggered by a hostile takeover and makes the takeover prohibitively expensive. The poison pill is a variation of the scorched earth defense whereby the target company prepares itself for self-destruction in the event of a hostile takeover. Another variation on the poison pill is the so-called "flipover" provisions in corporate charters which prohibit combinations with persons who have acquired more than a stated percentage of the issuer's stock without prior approval of the target company's directors. Under such flipover provisions, the shareholders receive rights in the acquiring company's shares for any takeover occurring within a predetermined period. Another device which has survived judicial challenge, but is now prohibited by a proposed SEC rule is the discriminatory issuer self-tender that excludes the hostile bidder from the offer's terms. Greenmail, which consists of target's management buying back the hostile bidder shares at a premium, has also been a widely used tactic. A common charter amendment has been the so-called "fair price" amendment under which all shareholders are guaranteed the best price paid to any one shareholder. Many states have adopted fair price statutes which are to the same effect. Still another approach has been the issuance of preferred shares with extraordinary voting power. Such unequal voting rights have been held to violate state law and also violate the New York Stock Exchange's one share/one vote rule, the enforcement of which has been suspended pending SEC reconsideration of the rule. The SEC has since proposed adoption of a uniform rule limiting dual class voting. Hazen, *The Law of Securities Regulation*, Section 11.20.

State Regulation More than two-thirds of the States have enacted statutes regulating tender offers. Although they vary greatly, most of them tend to protect the target company from an unwanted tender offer. Some give the State the power to review the merits of the offer or the adequacy of disclosure. Many impose waiting periods before the tender offer is effective. The State statutes generally require more detailed disclosures than the Williams Act requires. Many of them exempt tender offers supported by the target company's management.

Some of these statutes have been declared unconstitutional because of Federal preemption by the Williams Act. In 1987 the Supreme Court upheld Indiana's statute, which gave the majority of a target company's shareholders the right to determine whether a controlling block of shares acquired by a bidder would have voting rights. The Court validated the statute because it concluded that the statute was consistent with and furthered a basic purpose of the Williams Act, to place shareholders on an equal footing with the takeover bidder. *CTS Corp. v. Dynamics Corp.*, 481 U.S. 69 (1987). More than one-half of the States with tender offer regulations have adopted similar provisions.

Foreign Corrupt Practices Act

In 1977 Congress enacted the Foreign Corrupt Practices Act (FCPA) as an amendment to the 1934 Act. The Act imposes internal control requirements on companies with securities registered under the 1934 Act and prohibits all domestic concerns from bribing foreign governmental or political officials.

Accounting Requirements The accounting requirements of the FCPA reflect the principle that accurate record-keeping is essential for managerial responsibility and that investors should be able to rely on the financial reports they receive. Accordingly, the accounting requirements were enacted (1) to assure that an issuer's books accurately reflect financial transactions, (2) to protect the integrity of independent audits of financial statements, and (3) to promote the reliability of financial information required by the 1934 Act.

The FCPA requires every issuer that has a class of registered securities to

1. make and keep books, records, and accounts that, in reasonable detail, accurately and fairly reflect the transactions and disposition of the assets of the issuer; and

2. devise and maintain a system of internal controls to assure that transactions are executed as authorized and recorded in conformity with generally accepted accounting principles so as to provide accountability for assets and to assure that access to assets is permitted only with management's authorization.

It has been held that *scienter* is not required under this provision and that the issuer is responsible for even those errors that are small in dollar amount.

Antibribery Provisions The Foreign Corrupt Practices Act makes it unlawful for *any* domestic concern or any of its officers, directors, employees, or agents to offer or give anything of value directly or indirectly to any foreign official, political party, or political official for the purpose of (1) influencing any act or decision of that person or party in his or its official capacity, or (2) inducing that person or party to use his or its influence to affect a decision of a foreign government in order to assist the domestic concern in obtaining or retaining business. The term *foreign official* does *not* include any employee of a foreign government whose duties are essentially ministerial or clerical. An offer or promise to make a prohibited payment is a violation even if the offer is not accepted or the promise is not performed. Violations can result in fines of up to $1 million for companies; individuals may be fined a maximum of $10,000 and imprisoned up to five years or both. Fines imposed on individuals may not be paid directly or indirectly by the domestic concern on whose behalf they acted.

CHAPTER SUMMARY

Securities Act of 1933	**Definition of a Security** includes any note, stock, bond, preorganization subscription, and investment contract (any investment of money or property made in expectation of receiving a financial return solely from the efforts of others)
	Registration of Securities required to provide investors with disclosure of accurate material information regarding securities publicly offered
	Exempt Securities securities not subject to the registration requirements of the 1933 Act; see Figures 43-1 and 43-2
	Exempt Transactions issuance of securities (which become restricted securities) not subject to the registration requirements of the 1933 Act; see Figures 43-1 and 43-2
	Liability
	■ *Unregistered Sales* absolute civil liability is imposed as there are no defenses
	■ *False Registration Statements* liability is imposed on the issuer, all persons who signed the statement, every director or partner, experts who prepared or certified any part of the statement, and all underwriters; defendants, other than issuer, may assert the defense of due diligence
	■ *Antifraud Provision* liability is imposed upon the seller to the immediate purchaser, provided the purchaser did not know of the untruth or omission; the seller is not liable if he did not know, and in the exercise of reasonable care could not have known, of the untrue statement or omission
	■ *Criminal Sanctions* willful violations are subject to a fine of not more than $10,000 and/or imprisonment of not more than five years

Securities Exchange Act of 1934	**Applicability** some provisions apply to all issuers; others apply only to issuers who must register (see Figure 43-3)
	Criminal Sanctions willful violations are subject to a fine of not more than $1 million and/or imprisonment of not more than ten years
	Registration and Periodic Reporting Requirements apply to publicly held companies; Section 18 imposes civil liability for any false or misleading statement made in a registration or report filed with the SEC
	Antifraud Provision Rule 10b–5 makes it unlawful to (1) employ any device, scheme, or artifice to defraud; (2) make any untrue statement of a material fact; (3) omit to state a material fact; or (4) engage in any act that operates as a fraud
	■ *Requisites of Rule 10b-5* recovery requires (1) a misstatement or omission, (2) materiality, (3) scienter (intentional and knowing conduct), (4) reliance, and (5) connection with the purchase or sale of a security
	■ *Insider Trading* "insiders" (directors, officers, employees, and agents of the issuer as well as those entrusted by the issuer with information solely for corporate purposes) are liable under Rule 10b-5 if they fail to disclose material, nonpublic information before trading on the information
	Short-Swing Profits Section 16(b) imposes liability on certain insiders (directors, officers, and shareholders owning 10 percent or more of the stock of a corporation) for all profits made on sales and purchases within six months of each other with any recovery going to the issuer
	Insider Trading Acts authorize courts to impose a civil penalty of up to three times the profit gained or loss avoided upon persons who purchase or sell a security while in possession of material, nonpublic information
	Proxy Solicitations
	■ *Definition of a Proxy* a signed writing by a shareholder authorizing a named person to vote her stock at a specified meeting of shareholders
	■ *Regulation* proxy disclosure statements are required when proxies are solicited or an issuer submits a matter to a shareholder vote
	■ *Liability* imposed for false or misleading proxy statements
	Tender Offers
	■ *Definition of a Tender Offer* a general invitation to all shareholders to purchase their shares at a specified price
	■ *Regulation* a statement disclosing specified information must be filed with the SEC and furnished to each offeree
	■ *Liability* imposed for false and material statements or omissions or fraudulent, deceptive, or manipulative practices in connection with any tender offer
	Foreign Corrupt Practices Act imposes internal control requirements on companies with securities registered under the 1934 Act and prohibits all domestic concerns from bribing foreign governmental or political officials

QUESTIONS

1. Distinguish between exempt securities and exempt transactions under the 1933 Act. List four examples of each.

2. Discuss the potential civil liabilities under the 1933 Act.

3. Distinguish between publicly held companies under the 1934 Act and those that are not publicly held. Which provisions of the 1934 Act

apply only to publicly held and which apply to all companies?

4. Discuss the requirements and applications of Rule 10b-5.

5. Discuss (a) tender offers and (b) proxy solicitations.

PROBLEMS

1. Acme Realty, a real estate development company, is a limited partnership organized in Georgia. It is planning to develop a 200-acre parcel of land for a regional shopping center and needs to raise $1,250,000. As part of its financing, Acme plans to offer $1,250,000 worth of limited partnership interests to about 100 prospective investors in the southeastern United States. It anticipates that about forty to fifty private investors will purchase the limited partnership interests.

(a) Must Acme register this offering? Why or why not?

(b) If Acme must register but fails to do so, what are the legal consequences?

2. Bigelow Corporation has total assets of $850,000, sales of $1,350,000, one class of common stock with 375 shareholders, and a class of preferred stock with 250 shareholders, both of which are traded over the counter. Which provisions of the Securities Exchange Act of 1934 apply to Bigelow Corporation?

3. Capricorn, Inc., is planning to "go public" by offering its common stock, which had been previously owned by only three shareholders. The company intends to limit the number of purchasers to twenty-five persons resident in the State of its incorporation. All of Capricorn's business and all of its assets are located in the State of incorporation. Based on these facts, what exemptions from registration, if any, are available to Capricorn, and what conditions would each of these available exemptions impose on the terms of the offer?

4. The boards of directors of DuMont Corp. and Epsot, Inc., agreed to enter into a friendly merger, with DuMont Corp. to be the surviving entity. The stock of both corporations was listed on a national stock exchange. In connection with the merger, both corporations distributed to their shareholders proxy statements seeking approval of the proposed merger. The shareholders of both corporations voted to approve the merger. About three weeks after the merger was consummated, the price of DuMont Corp. stock fell from $25 to $13 as a result of the discovery that Epsot, Inc., had entered into several unprofitable long-term contracts two

months before the merger had been proposed. The contracts will result in substantial losses from Epsot's operations for at least the next four years. The existence and effect of these contracts, although known to both corporations at the time of the proposed merger, were not disclosed in the proxy statements of either corporation. Shareholders of DuMont Corp. bring suit against DuMont Corp. under the 1934 Act. Decision?

5. Farthing is a director and vice-president of Garp, Inc., whose common stock is listed on the New York Stock Exchange. Farthing engaged in the following transactions in the same calendar year: on January 2 Farthing sold 500 shares at $30 per share; on January 15 she purchased 300 shares at $30 per share; on February 1 she purchased 200 shares at $45 per share; on March 1 she purchased 300 shares at $60 per share; on March 15 she sold 200 shares at $55 per share; and on April 1 she sold 100 shares at $40 per share. Howell brings suit on behalf of Garp alleging that Farthing has violated the Securities Act of 1934. Farthing defends on the ground that she lost money on the transactions in question. Decision?

6. Intercontinental Widgets, Inc., had applied for a patent for a new state-of-the-art widget that, if patented, would significantly increase the value of Intercontinental's shares. On September 1 the Patent Office notified Jackson, the attorney for Intercontinental, that the patent application had been approved. After informing Kingsley, the company's president, of the good news, Jackson called his broker and purchased 1,000 shares of Intercontinental at $18 per share. He also told his partner, Lucas, who immediately proceeded to purchase 500 shares at $19 per share. Lucas then called his brother-in-law, Mammon, and told him the news. On September 3 Mammon bought 4,000 shares at $21 per share. On September 4 Kingsley issued a press release that accurately reported that a patent had been granted to Intercontinental. On the next day, Intercontinental's stock soared to $38 per share. A class action suit is brought against Jackson, Lucas, Mammon, and Intercontinental for violations of Rule 10b-5. Who, if anyone, is liable?

7. Nova, Inc., sought to sell a new issue of common stock. It registered the issue with the SEC but included false information in both the registration statement and the prospectus. The issue was underwritten by Omega & Sons and was sold in its entirety by Periwinkle, Rameses, and Sheffield, Inc., a securities broker-dealer. Telford purchased 500 shares at $6 per share. Three months later, the falsity of the information contained in the prospectus was made public, and the price of the shares fell

to $1 per share. The following week, Telford brought suit against Nova, Inc., Omega & Sons, and Periwinkle, Rameses and Sheffield, Inc., under the Securities Act of 1933.

(a) Who, if anyone, is liable under the Act?

(b) What defenses, if any, are available to the various defendants?

8. Tanaka, a director and officer of Deep Hole Oil Company, approached Romani for the purpose of buying 200 shares of Deep Hole Company stock owned by Romani. During the period of negotiations, Tanaka concealed his identity and did not disclose the fact that earlier in the day he had received a report of two rich oil strikes on the oil company's property. Romani sold his 200 shares to Tanaka for $10 per share. Taking into consideration the new strikes, the fair value of the stock was approximately $20 per share. Romani sues Tanaka to recover damages. Decision?

9. Venable Corporation has 750,000 shares of common stock outstanding, which is owned by 640 shareholders. The assets of Venable Corporation are valued at over $5 million dollars. In March Underhill began purchasing shares of Venable's common stock in the open market. By April he had acquired 40,000 shares at prices ranging from $12 to $14. Upon discovering Underhill's activities in late April, the directors of Venable had the corporation purchase the 40,000 shares from Underhill for $18 per share. Which provisions of the 1934 Act, if any, have been violated?

44 ACCOUNTANTS' LEGAL LIABILITY

Accountants perform a number of important roles in our business society. One of them is providing reliable financial information to facilitate the effective and efficient allocation of resources in the economy. As Harold M. Williams, former Chairman of the Securities and Exchange Commission, stated: "Obviously, if users of financial data, who often may have little or no contact with the business in question, could not trust in its financial statements, capital formation and lending could not be carried on as they are today."

An accountant is subject to potential civil liability arising from the professional services he provides to his clients and third parties. This legal liability is imposed by both the common law at the State level as well as Federal securities laws. In addition, an accountant may violate Federal and State criminal law in connection with the performance of his professional activities. In this chapter we discuss accountants' legal liability under both State and Federal law.

COMMON LAW

An accountant's legal responsibility under State law may be based on (1) contract law, (2) tort law, or (3) criminal law. In addition, the common law gives accountants certain rights and privileges: in particular, ownership of their working papers and, in some States, a limited accountant-client privilege.

Contract Liability

The employment contract between an accountant and her client is subject to the general principles of contract law. All of the requirements of a common law contract must be present for the contract to be binding, including offer and acceptance, capacity, consideration, legality, and a writing if, as is often the case, the agreement falls within the one-year provision of the Statue of Frauds.

On entering into a binding contract, the accountant is bound to perform all the duties she **explicitly** agrees to provide under the contract. For example, if an accountant agrees to complete her audit of the client by October 15 to enable the client to release its annual report on time, the accountant is under a contractual obligation to do so. Likewise, if an accountant contractually promises to conduct an audit for the client to detect possible embezzlement, the accountant is under a contractual obligation to provide an audit *beyond* Generally Accepted Auditing Standards (GAAS) and must conduct an expanded audit.

By entering into a contract, an accountant also **implicitly** agrees to perform the contract in a competent and professional manner. By agreeing to render professional services, an accountant is held to those standards that are generally accepted by the accounting profession.

If an accountant breaches his contract, he will incur liability not only to his client but also to certain third-party beneficiaries. A **third-party beneficiary** is a noncontracting party intended by the contracting parties to receive the *primary* benefit under the contract. For example, Otis Manufacturing Co. hires Adler, an accountant, to prepare Otis's financial statement for Otis to use to obtain a loan from Chemical Bank. Chemical Bank is a third-party beneficiary of the contract between Otis and Adler.

Following general contract principles, an accountant will not be entitled to any compensation if he *materially breaches* his contract. Thus, if an accountant does not perform his audit on time when time is of the essence, or if the accountant completes only 60 percent of the audit, he has materially breached the contract. On the other hand, if the accountant *substantially performs* his contractual duties, he is generally entitled to be compensated for the contractually agreed upon fee less any damages or loss his nonmaterial breach has caused the client.

Tort Liability

In performing his professional services, an accountant may incur tort liability to his client or third parties for negligence or fraud. A tort, as discussed in Chapters 5 and 6, is a private or civil wrong or injury, other than a breach of contract, for which the courts will provide a remedy in the form of an action for damages.

Negligence An accountant is negligent if she does not exercise the degree of care a reasonably competent accountant would exercise under the circumstances. For example, Arthur, an accountant, is engaged to audit the books of Zebra Corporation. During the audit, Olivia, an officer of Zebra Corporation, notifies Arthur that she suspects that Terrance, the company's treasurer, is engaged in a scheme to embezzle from the corporation. Arthur does not pursue the matter because he was previously informed that Olivia and Terrance are on

bad terms with each other. Terrance was, in fact, engaged in a commonly used scheme of embezzlement. Arthur is negligent for failing to conduct a reasonable investigation of the alleged defalcation. Nonetheless, an accountant is *not* liable for honest inaccuracies or errors of judgment so long as she exercises reasonable care in performing her duties. Moreover, an accountant is *not an insurer* of the accuracy of her reports provided she acts in a reasonably competent and professional manner.

Historically, an accountant's liability for negligence extended only to the client and to third-party beneficiaries. Under this view, *privity* of contract was a requirement to a cause of action based on negligence. This approach was established by the landmark case of *Ultramares Corp. v. Touche*, 255 N.Y. 170, 174 N.E. 441 (1931). In recent years the *Ultramares* doctrine has been eroded by most courts, which have in general extended the class of protected persons to include foreseen plaintiffs. This approach has also been adopted by the Restatement of Torts. Foreseen third parties are individuals who are members of a class that is known to the accountant or auditor to be intended recipients of the information provided or certified by the accountant. This class does not, however, include potential investors and the general public.

Some courts, as in the following case, have extended liability to benefit an even broader group: reasonably foreseeable plaintiffs who are neither known nor members of a class of intended recipients.

INTERNATIONAL MORTGAGE COMPANY v. JOHN P. BUTLER ACCOUNTANCY CORP.
Court of Appeals, Fourth District, Division 3, 1986.
177 Cal.App.3d 806, 223 Cal.Rptr. 218.

Facts: John P. Butler Accountancy Corporation agreed to audit the financial statements of Westside Mortgage, Inc., a mortgage company that arranges financing for real property, for the year ending December 31, 1978. On March 22, 1979, after completing the audit, Butler issued unqualified audited financial statements listing Westside's corporate net worth as $175,036. The primary asset on the balance sheet was a $100,000 note receivable that had, in reality, been rendered worthless in August 1977 when the trust deed on real property securing the note was wiped out by a prior foreclosure of a superior deed of trust. The note constituted 57 percent of Westside's net worth and was thus material to an accurate representation of Westside's financial position. In October 1979 International Mortgage Company (IMC) approached Westside for the purpose of buying and selling loans on the secondary market. IMC signed an agreement with Westside in December after reviewing Westside's audited financial statements. In June 1980 Westside issued a $475,293 promissory note to IMC on which it ultimately defaulted. IMC brought an action against Westside, its owners, principals, and Butler. IMC alleged negligence and negligent misrepresentation against Butler in auditing and issuing without qualification the defective financial statements of Westside on which IMC relied in deciding to do business with Westside. Butler moved for summary judgment, claiming that it owed no duty of care to IMC, a third party who was not specifically known to Butler as an intended recipient of the audited financial statements. The trial court granted Butler's motion and IMC appealed.

Decision: Judgment reversed.

Opinion: **Trotter, J.**   The application of the "duty" doctrine to the accounting profession has been unique. Beginning with Justice Cardozo's seminal opinion in Ultramares Corp. v. Touche [citation], certified public accountants have been shielded from liability for negligence in the preparation and issuance of unqualified audited financial statements when the plaintiff was only a member of a foreseeable class. Liability, based on a "duty" analysis, was limited to those "in privity" with the accountant and more recently to those "intended" recipients of the information. (E.g., Rest.2d Torts (1977) § 552.)

* * *

Even as he was limiting accountants liability by requiring privity before a duty could be found, Justice Cardozo recognized such a holding, even in 1931, was against the flow of the common law. For he observed "(t)he assault upon the citadel of privity is proceeding in these days apace. How far the inroads shall extend is now a favorite subject of juridical discussion." [Citation.]

Yet, the privity requirement in accountant malpractice suits has survived the shifting sands of time and remains relatively intact today in most jurisdictions. That the "citadel" has not been breached, insofar as certified public accountants' liability, may well be due to the reputation of the distinguished author of Ultramares. While we recognize his brilliance and the then compelling logic of Ultramares, we assert that, in light of other decisions (discussed, infra) and the role of an independent auditor in today's society, the rule of Ultramares is no longer consistent with the fundamental principles of California negligence law.

* * *

Thus, even as Ultramares was being articulated, the tide of precedent had already begun to move against the privity rule. The erosion continued, washing away the protection from all other professions, leaving accountancy as some ennobled species specially protected by the "citadel."

. . . Ultramares was clearly based upon a social utility rationale which has been followed under the privity doctrine or some modification thereof. Section 552 of the Restatement of Torts (Second) adopts a limited approach to liability; however, it rejects Ultramares' requirement of privity, settling instead on the reasoning of [citation] in requiring "knowing reliance." (See Rusch Factors, Inc. v. Levin (1968) 284 F.Supp. 85.) One of the bases for the Restatement rule as stated in the comment and by others is the reluctance of courts to impose liability for pecuniary loss alone absent privity. [Citations.]

* * *

Butler claims that basic differences between the accounting profession and others require a more limited rule of liability, whether it be the rule of Ultramares or the Restatement. While manufacturers, attorneys, architects, doctors, and the like control their products and their records, the accountant does not control his client's records, nor does the accountant control the client's use of the audit product. Further, other professionals do not expose themselves or their services to the public for review and possible reliance. He points out, in reality just the opposite occurs. The lawyer's duty generally is to his or her client only. . . . However, such duty is recognized in ethical as well as legal obligations of confidentiality. Further, an attorney's duty is to represent the client to the best of his or her ability without regard to public opinion; so too the medical practitioner, whose duty of care is easily traced to the patient. The same relationship generally exists between all other professionals and their clients. Not so an accountant. [Citations.]

This criticism seems to misunderstand the role of the accountant. An independent auditor (as opposed to an in-house accountant) is employed to analyze a client's financial status and make public the ultimate findings in accord with recognized accounting principles. Such an undertaking is imbued with considerations of public trust, for the accountant must well realize the finished product, the unqualified financial statement, will be relied upon by creditors, stockholders, investors, lenders or anyone else involved in the financial concerns of the audited client. As stated in the AICPA (American Institute of Certified Public Accountants), Professional Standards, Code of Professional Ethics [citation], "The ethical Code of the American Institute (of Certified Public Accountants) emphasizes the profession's responsibility to the public, a responsibility that has grown as the number of investors has grown, as the relationship between corporate managers and stockholders has become more impersonal, and as government increasingly relies on accounting information." Chief Justice Burger, writing for a unanimous United States Supreme Court in United States v. Arthur Young & Co. [see below], described the role of the independent auditor, "(a)n independent certified public accountant performs a different role. By certifying the public reports that collectively depict a corporation's financial status, the independent auditor assumes a public responsibility transcending any employment relationship with the client. The independent public accountant performing this special function owes ultimate allegiance to the corporation's creditors and stockholders, as well as to the investing public. This 'public watchdog' function demands that the accountant maintain total independence from the client at all times and requires complete fidelity to the public trust. To insulate from disclosure a certified public accountant's interpretations of the client's financial statements would be to ignore the significance of the accountant's role as a disinterested analyst charged with public obligations." [Citation.]

The auditor must, by necessity, be independent of the client. Unlike a manufacturer who guarantees a product's safety, the accountant does not guarantee that the client's financial statements are completely true and without fault. The accountant's audit certification merely guarantees that the financial statements fairly present the firm's financial position in compliance with generally accepted accounting principles ("GAAP"). The professional standards of the AICPA express the auditor's function as follows: "The objective of the ordinary examination of financial statements by the independent auditor is the expression of an opinion on the fairness with which they present financial position, results of operations, and changes in financial position in conformity with generally accepted accounting principles." [Citation.] The AICPA has promulgated reporting standards which govern the preparation of financial statements:

"1. The report shall state whether the financial statements are presented in accordance with generally accepted accounting principles.

"2. The report shall state whether such principles have been consistently observed in the current period in relation to the preceding period.

"3. Informative disclosures in the financial statements are to be regarded as reasonably adequate unless otherwise stated in the report.

"4. The report shall either contain an expression of opinion regarding the financial statements, taken as a whole, or an assertion to the effect that an opinion cannot be expressed. When an overall opinion cannot be expressed, the reasons therefor should be stated. In all cases where an auditor's name is associated with financial statements, the report should contain a clear-cut indication of the character of the auditor's examination, if any, and the degree of responsibility he is taking." [Citation.]

Thus, in issuing an opinion, the auditor is guaranteeing only that the numbers comply with the AICPA's standardized accounting rules and procedures, the GAAP. Further, the auditor is guaranteeing that he tested for GAAP compliance using generally accepted auditing standards ("GAAS"). The auditor is not guaranteeing the client's records and resulting financial statements are perfect; only that any errors which might exist could not be detected by an audit conducted under GAAS and GAAP. Thus, the auditor's degree of control over the client's records is unimportant; the auditor need only control his or her abilities to apply GAAS and GAAP to a given audit situation.

Under a foreseeability standard, the auditor would be liable only to those third parties who reasonably and foreseeably rely on the audited statements. The accountant's lack of control over ultimate users is not prejudicial; the foreseeability standard holds everyone, including accountants, liable to only reasonably foreseeable users. [Citations.] It is only reasonable that the same judicial criteria govern the imposition of negligence liability, regardless of the defendant's profession.

We note that other jurisdictions have already held accountants to the same standard of negligence liability as other professionals. In H. Rosenblum, Inc. v. Adler [citation], faced with almost the exact scenario before us, the Supreme Court of New Jersey stated, "(c)ertified financial statements have become the benchmark for various reasonably foreseeable business purposes and accountants have been engaged to satisfy those ends. In those circumstances accounting firms should no longer be permitted to hide within the citadel of privity and avoid liability for their malpractice. . . . Defendants' ignorance of the precise use to which the statements would be put does not eliminate their obligation. . . . (I)t is necessary only that Giant, the entity for whom the audit was being made, used it for a proper business purpose. There was no limitation in the accountants' opinion. They could reasonably expect that their client would distribute the statements in furtherance of matters relating to its business. Having inserted the audit in that economic stream, the defendants should be responsible for their careless misrepresentations to parties who justifiably relied upon their expert opinions." [Citation.] In Citizens State Bank v. Timm, Schmidt & Co. [citation], the court reversed a summary judgment granted on the basis no duty was owed by the defendant accountant to the unknown third party plaintiff who had relied on an audited financial statement prepared by the defendant. The court rejected defendant's reliance on the Restatement Second of Torts, section 552. "Although the absence of privity does not bar this action, the question remains as to the extent of an accountant's liability to injured third parties. Courts which have examined this question have generally relied upon section 552 of the Restatement to restrict the class of third persons who could sue accountants for their negligent acts. Under section 552(2)(a) and (b), liability is limited to loss suffered. . . . (Citation.) The fundamental principle of Wisconsin negligence law is that a tortfeasor is fully liable for all foreseeable consequences of his act except as those consequences are limited by policy factors. . . . (Citation.) The Restatement's statement of limiting liability to certain third parties is too restrictive a statement of policy factors for this Court to adopt." [Citation.]

* * *

We have determined the protectionist rule of privity announced in Ultramares is no longer viable, for the role of the accountant in our modern society has changed. At the time of Ultramares, the primary obligation of the auditor was to the client who hired him or her to detect fraud or embezzlement by the client's employees. As explained earlier, the accountant (independent auditor) today occupies a position of public trust. [Citation.] We also find the Restatement limitation of liability to those "he intends to supply the information or (to those he) knows that the recipient intends to supply it" (Rest.2d Torts, supra, § 552,), does not meet California's concept of tort liability for negligence.

* * *

An innocent plaintiff who forseeably relies on an independent auditor's unqualified financial statement should not be made to bear the burden of the professional's malpractice. The risk of such loss is more appropriately placed on the accounting profession which is better able to pass such risk to its customers and the ultimate consuming public. By doing so, society is better served; for such a rule provides a financial disincentive for negligent conduct and will heighten the profession's cautionary techniques.

Thus, we find no societal considerations sufficient to create an exception to California's well established general principles of tort liability. We hold an independent auditor owes a duty of care to reasonably foreseeable plaintiffs who rely on negligently prepared and issued unqualified audited financial statements. Having so determined, the summary judgment must be reversed. A question of fact exists as to whether IMC's reliance was reasonably foreseeable and, if so, whether Butler breached the resulting duty. That determination is for the trial court.

Fraud An accountant who commits a fraudulent act is liable to any person who the accountant *should have* reasonably foreseen would be injured by the misrepresentation and who justifiably relied on it. The required elements of fraud, which were more fully discussed in Chapter 9, are (1) a false representation (2) of fact (3) that is material (4) made with knowledge of its falsity and with the intention to deceive (5) is justifiably relied on, and (6) causes injury to the plaintiff. An accountant who commits fraud may be held liable for *both* compensatory and punitive damages.

Criminal Liability

An accountant's potential criminal liability in rendering professional services is primarily based on the Federal law of securities regulation and taxation. Nonetheless, an accountant would violate State criminal law if she knowingly and willfully certified false documents, altered or tampered with accounting records, used false financial reports, gave false testimony under oath, or committed forgery.

Criminal sanctions may be imposed under the Internal Revenue Code for knowingly preparing false or fraudulent tax returns or documents used in connection with a tax return. Such liability also extends to willfully assisting or advising a client or others to prepare a false return. Penalties may be a fine not to exceed $5,000 or three years imprisonment or both.

Client Information

In providing services for his client an accountant necessarily obtains information concerning the client's business affairs. Two legal issues arise concerning this client information: (1) who owns the working papers generated by the accountant and (2) whether the client information is privileged.

Working Papers   Audit working papers include the records kept by the auditor of the procedures followed, the tests performed, the information obtained, and the conclusions reached pertaining to the audit. All relevant information obtained in connection with the examination should be included in the working papers. An accountant is held to be the owner of his working papers and thus need not surrender them to his client. Nevertheless, the accountant may not disclose the contents of these papers unless (1) the client consents or (2) a court orders the disclosure.

Accountant-Client Privilege   The issue of confidentiality of communication between the accountant and his client is important for, if such information is considered to be privileged, it may not be admitted into evidence over the objection of the person possessing the privilege. The question of a possible accountant-client privilege frequently arises in tax disputes, criminal prosecution, and civil litigation.

Neither the common law nor Federal law recognizes such a privilege. Nevertheless, some States have adopted statutes granting some form of accountant-client privilege. Most of these statutes grant the privilege to the client, although a few extend the privilege to the accountant. Regardless of whether the privilege exists, it is generally considered to be professionally unethical for an accountant to disclose confidential communications from his client unless the disclosure is in accordance with (1) American Institute of Certified Public Accountants (AICPA) or GAAS requirements, (2) a court order, or (3) the client's request.

UNITED STATES v. ARTHUR YOUNG & COMPANY
Supreme Court of the United States, 1984.
465 U.S. 805, 104 S.Ct. 1495, 79 L.Ed.2d 826.

Facts: Arthur Young & Co., a firm of certified public accountants, is the independent auditor for Amerada Hess Corporation. During its review of Amerada's financial statements as required by Federal securities laws, Young confirmed Amerada's statement of its contingent tax liabilities and prepared tax accrual work papers. These work papers pertain to Young's evaluation of Amerada's reserves for contingent tax liabilities, and such work papers sometimes include discussions of questionable positions Amerada may have taken on its tax returns. The Internal Revenue Service initiated a criminal investigation of Amerada's tax returns when, during a routine audit, it discovered questionable payments made by Amerada from a "special disbursement account." The IRS summoned Young to make available all its information relating to Amerada, including the tax accrual work papers. Amerada instructed Young not to obey the summons. The IRS then brought an action against Young to enforce the administrative summons. The district court declined to recognize an accountant-client privilege that would protect the work papers from disclosure, but the Court of Appeals, holding that the work papers should be shielded by some form of work-product immunity, affirmed in part and reversed in part.

Decision: The judgment of the Court of Appeals affirmed in part and reversed in part, and the case remanded.

Opinion: Burger, C. J.   We now turn to consider whether tax accrual workpapers prepared by an independent auditor in the course of a routine review of corporate financial statements should be protected by some form of work-product immunity from disclosure under § 7602. Based upon its evaluation of the competing policies of the federal tax and securities laws, the Court of Appeals found it necessary to create a so-called privilege for the independent auditor's workpapers.

Our complex and comprehensive system of federal taxation, relying as it does upon self-assessment and reporting, demands that all taxpayers be forthright in the disclosure of relevant information to the taxing authorities. Without such disclosure, and the concomitant power of the Government to compel disclosure, our national tax burden would not be fairly and equitably distributed. In order to encourage effective tax investigations, Congress has endowed the IRS with expansive information-gathering authority; * * *

While § 7602 is "subject to the traditional privileges and limitations," [citation], any other restrictions upon the IRS summons power should be avoided "absent unambiguous directions from Congress." [Citation.] We are unable to discern the sort of "unambiguous directions from Congress" that would justify a judicially created work-product immunity for tax accrual workpapers summoned under § 7602. Indeed, the very language of § 7602 reflects precisely the opposite: a congressional policy choice in favor of disclosure of all information relevant to a legitimate IRS inquiry. In light of this explicit statement by the Legislative Branch, courts should be chary in recognizing exceptions to the broad summons authority of the IRS or in fashioning new privileges that would curtail disclosure under § 7602. [Citation.] If the broad latitude granted to the IRS by § 7602 is to be circumscribed, that is a choice for Congress, and not this Court, to make. [Citation.]

The Court of Appeals nevertheless concluded that "substantial countervailing policies," [citation], required the fashioning of a work-product immunity for an independent auditor's tax accrual workpapers. To the extent that the Court of Appeals, in its concern for the "chilling effect" of the disclosure of tax accrual workpapers, sought to facilitate communication between independent auditors and their clients, its remedy more closely resembles a testimonial accountant-client privilege than a work-product immunity for accountants' workpapers. But as this Court stated in [citation], "no confidential accountant-client privilege exists under federal law, and no state-created privilege has been recognized in federal cases." In light of [citation], the Court of Appeals' effort to foster candid communication between accountant and client by creating a self-styled work-product privilege was misplaced, and conflicts with what we see as the clear intent of Congress.

Nor do we find persuasive the argument that a work-product immunity for accountants' tax accrual workpapers is a fitting analogue to the attorney work-product doctrine established in [citation]. The . . . work-product doctrine was founded upon the private attorney's role as the client's confidential advisor and advocate, a loyal representative whose duty it is to present the client's case in the most favorable possible light. An independent certified public accountant performs a different role. By certifying the public reports that collectively depict a corporation's financial status, the independent auditor assumes a public responsibility transcending any employment relationship with the client. The independent public accountant performing this special function owes ultimate allegiance to the corporation's creditors and stockholders, as well as to the investing public. This "public watchdog" function demands that the accountant maintain total independence from the client at all times and requires complete fidelity to the public trust. To insulate from disclosure a certified public accountant's interpretations of the client's financial statements would be to ignore the significance of the accountant's role as a disinterested analyst charged with public obligations.

We cannot accept the view that the integrity of the securities markets will suffer absent some protection for accountants' tax accrual workpapers. The Court of Appeals apparently feared that, were the IRS to have access to tax accrual workpapers, a corporation might be tempted to withhold from its auditor certain information relevant and material to a proper evaluation of its financial statements. But the independent certified public accountant cannot be content with the corporation's representations that its tax accrual reserves are adequate; the auditor is ethically and professionally obligated to ascertain for himself as far as possible whether the corporation's contingent tax liabilities have been accurately stated. If the auditor were convinced that the scope of the examination had been limited by management's reluctance to disclose matters relating to the tax accrual reserves, the auditor would be unable to issue an unqualified opinion as to the accuracy of the corporation's financial statements. Instead, the auditor would be required to issue a qualified opinion, an adverse opinion, or a disclaimer of opinion, thereby notifying the investing public of possible potential problems inherent in the corporation's financial reports. Responsible corporate management would not risk a qualified evaluation of a corporate taxpayer's financial posture to afford cover for questionable positions reflected in a prior tax return. Thus, the independent auditor's obligation to serve the public interest assures that the integrity of the securities markets will be preserved, without the need for a work-product immunity for accountants' tax accrual workpapers.

We also reject respondents' position that fundamental fairness precludes IRS access to accountants' tax accrual workpapers. Respondents urge that the enforcement of an IRS summons for accountants' tax accrual workpapers permits the Government to probe the thought processes of its taxpayer citizens, thereby giving the IRS an unfair advantage in negotiating and litigating tax controversies. But if the SEC itself, or a private plaintiff in securities litigation, sought to obtain the tax accrual workpapers at issue in this case, they would surely be entitled to do so. In light of the broad congressional command of § 7602, no sound reason exists for conferring lesser authority upon the IRS than upon a private litigant suing with regard to transactions concerning which the public has no interest.

Congress has granted to the IRS "broad latitude to adopt enforcement techniques helpful in the performance of (its) tax collection and assessment responsibilities." [Citation.] Recognizing the intrusiveness of demands for the production of tax accrual workpapers, the IRS has demonstrated administrative sensitivity to the concerns expressed by the accounting profession by tightening its internal requirements for the issuance of such summonses. [Citation.] Although these IRS guidelines were not applicable during the years at issue in this case, their promulgation further refutes respondents' fairness argument and reflects an administrative flexibility that reinforces our decision not to reduce irrevocably the § 7602 summons power.

Beyond question it is desirable and in the public interest to encourage full disclosures by corporate clients to their independent accountants; if it is necessary to balance competing interests, however, the need of the Government for full disclosure of all information relevant to tax liability must also weigh in that balance. This kind of policy choice is best left to the Legislative Branch.

FEDERAL SECURITIES LAW

Accountants may be both civilly and criminally liable under provisions of the 1933 and 1934 Acts. This liability is more extensive and has fewer limitations than liability under the common law.

1933 Act

Accountants are subject to **civil** liability under Section 11 of the 1933 Act if the financial statements they prepare or certify for inclusion in a registration statement contain any untrue statement or omission of material fact. This liability extends to anyone who acquires the security without knowledge of the untruth or omission. Not only is there no requirement of privity between the accountant and the pur-

chasers, but proof of reliance on the financial statements is also usually not required under Section 11. An accountant will not be liable, however, if he can prove "due diligence." The defense of **due diligence** requires that the accountant had, after reasonable investigation, reasonable grounds to believe and did believe, at the *time* the registration statement became *effective*, that the financial statements were true, complete, and accurate. The standard of reasonableness is that required of a prudent man in the management of his own property. Thus, Section 11 imposes liability on accountants for **negligence** in the conduct of the audit or presentation of the information in the financial statements.

Moreover, if an accountant *willfully* violates this section, he may be held **criminally** liable for a fine of not more than $10,000 or imprisonment of not more than five years or both.

ESCOTT v. BARCHRIS CONST. CORP.
United States District Court, Southern District of New York, 1968.
283 F.Supp. 643.

Facts: BarChris Construction Corporation sold shares of common stock to the public in December 1959. By early 1961, BarChris needed additional working capital and sold debentures to meet this need. A registration statement was filed with the SEC in March 1961, with amendments filed in May. By the time BarChris received the net proceeds of this sale, it was experiencing financial difficulties. Eventually BarChris filed for bankruptcy. Escott, a purchaser of the debentures, brought suit under the Securities Act of 1933 against BarChris, the underwriters, the company's auditors (Peat, Marwick, Mitchell & Co.), and the persons who signed the registration statement, alleging that the registration statement contained material false statements and material omissions. The defendants denied the falsity of the statements and their materiality. Furthermore, all of the defendants, except BarChris, claimed that they individually had exercised due diligence in connection with the statement so as to be free from liability under the statute. The case against BarChris, the underwriters, and the persons who signed the registration statement was presented in Chapter 43. Additional facts relevant to the liability of the auditors Peat, Marwick, Mitchell & Co. are the following falsities and omissions found by the court:

1. *1960 Earnings*
  (a) *Sales*

As per prospectus	$9,165,320
Correct figure	8,511,420
Overstatement	$ 653,900

(b) *Net Operating Income*
    As per prospectus $1,742,801
    Correct figure   1,496,196

    Overstatement $ 246,605
(c) *Earnings per Share*
    As per prospectus $.75
    Correct figure   .65

    Overstatement $.10
2. *1960 Balance Sheet Current Assets*
  As per prospectus $4,524,021
  Correct figure   3,914,332

  Overstatement $ 609,689
3. *Contingent Liabilities as of December 31, 1960 on Alternative Method of Financing*
  As per prospectus $ 750,000
  Correct figure   1,125,795

  Understatement $ 375,795
  Capitol Lanes should have been shown as a direct liability $ 325,000
4. *Contingent Liabilities as of April 30, 1961*
  As per prospectus $ 825,000
  Correct figure   1,443,853

  Understatement $ 618,853
  Capitol Lanes should have been shown as a direct liability $ 314,166
5. *Earnings Figures for Quarter Ending March 31, 1961*
  (a) *Sales*
    As per prospectus $2,138,455
    Correct figure   1,618,645

    Overstatement $ 519,810
  (b) *Gross Profit*
    As per prospectus $ 483,121
    Correct figure   252,366

    Overstatement $ 230,755
6. *Backlog as of March 31, 1961*
  As per prospectus $6,905,000
  Correct figure   2,415,000

  Overstatement $4,490,000
7. *Failure to Disclose Officers' Loans Outstanding and Unpaid on May 16, 1961* $ 386,615
8. *Failure to Disclose Use of Proceeds in Manner Not Revealed in Prospectus*
  Approximately $1,160,000
9. *Failure to Disclose Customers' Delinquencies in May 1961 and BarChris's Potential Liability with Respect Thereto*   Over $1,350,000
10. *Failure to Disclose the Fact that BarChris Was Already Engaged and Was about to be More Heavily Engaged, in the Operation of Bowling Alleys*

Decision: Judgment for Escott.

Opinion: McLean, J.   Section 11(b) provides:

"Notwithstanding the provisions of subsection (a) no person * * * shall be liable as provided therein who shall sustain the burden of proof—

* * *

"(3) that * * * (B) as regards any part of the registration statement purporting to be made upon his authority as an expert * * * (i) he had, after reasonable investigation, reasonable ground to believe and did believe, at the time such part of the registration statement became effective, that the statements therein were true and that there was no omission to state a material fact required to be stated therein or necessary to make the statements therein not misleading * * *."

This defines the due diligence defense for an expert. Peat, Marwick has pleaded it.

The part of the registration statement purporting to be made upon the authority of Peat, Marwick as an expert was, as we have seen, the 1960 figures. But because the statute requires the court to determine Peat, Marwick's belief, and the grounds thereof, "at the time such part of the registration statement became effective," for the purposes of this affirmative defense the matter must be viewed as of May 16, 1961, and the question is whether at that time, Peat, Marwick, after reasonable investigation, had reasonable ground to believe and did believe that the 1960 figures were true and that no material fact had been omitted from the registration statement which should have been included in order to make the 1960 figures not misleading. In deciding this issue, the court must consider not only what Peat, Marwick did in its 1960 audit, but also what it did in its subsequent "S–1 review."

* * *

The 1960 Audit   Peat, Marwick's work was in general charge of a member of the firm, Cummings, and more immediately in charge of Peat, Marwick's manager, Logan. Most of the actual work was performed by a senior accountant, Berardi, who had junior assistants, one of whom was Kennedy.

Berardi was then about thirty years old. He was not yet a C.P.A. He had had no previous experience with the bowling industry. This was his first job as a senior accountant. He could hardly have been given a more difficult assignment.

After obtaining a little background information on BarChris by talking to Logan and reviewing Peat, Marwick's work papers on its 1959 audit, Berardi examined the results of test checks of BarChris's accounting procedures which one of the junior accountants had made, and he prepared an "internal control questionnaire" and an "audit program." Thereafter, for a few days subsequent to December 30, 1960, he inspected BarChris's inventories and examined certain alley construction. Finally, on January 13, 1961, he began his auditing work which he carried on substantially continuously until it was completed on February 24, 1961. Toward the close of the work, Logan reviewed it and made various comments and suggestions to Berardi. It is unnecessary to recount everything that Berardi did in the course of the audit. We are concerned only with the evidence relating to what Berardi did or did not do with respect to those items which I have found to have been incorrectly reported in the 1960 figures in the prospectus. More narrowly, we are directly concerned only with such of those items as I have found to be material.

Capitol Lanes   First and foremost is Berardi's failure to discover that Capitol Lanes had not been sold. The error affected both the sales figure and the liability side of the balance sheet. Fundamentally, the error stemmed from the fact that Berardi never realized that Heavenly Lanes and Capitol were two different names for the same alley.

* * *

In any case, he never identified this mysterious Capitol with the Heavenly Lanes which he had included in his sales and profit figures. The vital question is whether he failed to make a reasonable investigation which, if he had made it, would have revealed the truth.

Certain accounting records of BarChris, which Berardi testified he did not see, would have put him on inquiry. One was a job cost ledger card for job no. 6036, the job number which Berardi put on his own sheet for Heavenly Lanes. This card read "Capitol Theatre (Heavenly)." In addition, two accounts receivable cards each showed both names on the same card, Capitol and Heavenly. Berardi testified that he looked at the accounts receivable records but that he did not see these particular cards. He testified that he did not look on the job cost ledger cards because he took the costs from another record, the costs register.

The burden of proof on this issue is on Peat, Marwick. Although the question is a rather close one, I find that Peat, Marwick has not sustained that burden. Peat, Marwick has not proved that Berardi made a reasonable investigation as far as Capitol Lanes was concerned and that his ignorance of the true facts was justified.

Howard Lanes Annex   Berardi also failed to discover that this alley was not sold. Here the evidence is much scantier. Berardi saw a contract for this alley in the contract file. No one told him that it was to be leased rather than sold. There is no evidence to indicate that any record existed which would have put him on notice. I find that his investigation was reasonable as to this item.

* * *

The S–1 Review   The purpose of reviewing events subsequent to the date of a certified balance sheet (referred to as an S–1 review when made with reference to a registration statement) is to ascertain whether any material change has occurred in the company's financial position which should be disclosed in order to prevent the balance sheet figures from being misleading. The scope of such a review, under generally accepted auditing standards, is limited. It does not amount to a complete audit.

Peat, Marwick prepared a written program for such a review. I find that this program conformed to generally accepted auditing standards.

* * *

Berardi made the S–1 review in May 1961. He devoted a little over two days to it, a total of 20½ hours. He did not discover any of the errors or omissions pertaining to the state of affairs in 1961 * * *, all of which were material. The question is whether, despite his failure to find out anything, his investigation was reasonable within the meaning of the statute.

What Berardi did was to look at a consolidating trial balance as of March 31, 1961, which had been prepared by BarChris, compare it with the audited December 31, 1960, figures, discuss with Trilling [controller of BarChris] certain unfavorable developments which the comparison disclosed, and read certain minutes. He did not examine any "important financial records" other than the trial balance. As to minutes, he read only what minutes Birnbaum [BarChris's house counsel and secretary] gave him, which consisted only of the board of directors' minutes of BarChris. He did not read such minutes as there were of the executive committee. He did not know that there was an executive committee, hence he did not discover that Kircher [BarChris's treasurer] had notes of executive committee minutes which had not been written up. He did not read the minutes of any subsidiary.

> In substance, what Berardi did [was to ask] questions, he got answers which he considered satisfactory, and he did nothing to verify them.
>
> * * *
>
> Accountants should not be held to a standard higher than that recognized in their profession. I do not do so here. Berardi's review did not come up to that standard. He did not take some of the steps which Peat, Marwick's written program prescribed. He did not spend an adequate amount of time on a task of this magnitude. Most important of all, he was too easily satisfied with glib answers to his inquiries.
>
> This is not to say that he should have made a complete audit. But there were enough danger signals in the materials which he did examine to require some further investigation on his part. Generally accepted accounting standards required such further investigation under these circumstances. It is not always sufficient merely to ask questions.
>
> Here again, the burden of proof is on Peat, Marwick. I find that that burden has not been satisfied. I conclude that Peat, Marwick has not established its due diligence defense.

1934 Act

Section 18 of the 1934 Act imposes **civil** liability on an accountant if she makes or causes to be made any false or misleading statement about any material fact in any application, report, document, or registration filed with the SEC under the 1934 Act. Liability extends to any person who purchased or sold a security in reliance on that false or misleading statement without knowing that it was false or misleading. An accountant is not liable, however, if she proves that she acted in good faith and had no knowledge that such statement was false or misleading.

Accountants may also be held **civilly** liable for violations of **Rule 10b-5.** Their liability may be for direct participation in a violation of the rule or for indirect participation resulting from their aiding and abetting others to violate the rule. Rule 10b-5, as previously discussed in Chapter 43, is extremely broad in that it applies to *both* oral and written misstatements or omissions of material fact and to *all* securities. This liability extends to purchasers and sellers who rely on the misstatement or omission of material fact in connection with the purchase or sale of a security. Liability is imposed, however, only if the accountant acted with *scienter.* Therefore, accountants are not liable under Rule 10b-5 for mere negligence, although reckless disregard of the truth *may* constitute *scienter.*

Accountants may also be held *criminally* liable for any willful violation of Section 18 or Rule 10b-5. Conviction may carry a fine of not more than $1 million or imprisonment for not more than ten years or both.

ERNST & ERNST v. HOCHFELDER
Supreme Court of the United States, 1976.
425 U.S. 185, 96 S.Ct. 1375, 47 L.Ed.2d 668.

Facts: The defendant, Ernst & Ernst, is an accounting firm. From 1946 through 1967 it was retained by First Securities Company of Chicago, a small brokerage firm and member of the Midwest Stock Exchange and the National Association of Securities Dealers, to perform periodic audits of the firm's books and records. In connection with these audits, Ernst & Ernst prepared for filing with the Securities and Exchange Commission the annual reports required of First Securities under the 1934 Act. It also prepared for First Securities' responses to the financial question- naires of the Midwest Stock Exchange.

Hochfelder and others (plaintiffs) were customers of First Securities who in- vested in a fraudulent securities scheme perpetrated by Leston B. Nay, president of the firm and owner of 92 percent of its stock. This fraud came to light in 1968 when Nay committed suicide, leaving a note that described First Securities as bankrupt and the escrow accounts as "spurious." Plaintiffs subsequently filed this action for damages against Ernst & Ernst under § 10(b) of the 1934 Act. The complaint charged that Nay's escrow scheme violated § 10(b) and Commission Rule 10b-5 and that Ernst & Ernst had "aided and abetted" Nay's violations by its "failure" to conduct proper audits of First Securities. The plaintiffs' cause of action rests on a theory of negligent nonfeasance—that Ernst & Ernst had failed to use "appropriate auditing procedures" in its audits of First Securities, thereby failing to discover internal practices of the firm said to prevent an effective audit. The District Court dismissed the action but the Court of Appeals reversed and remanded.

Decision: The judgment of the Court of Appeals reversed.

Opinion: Powell, J.   Federal regulation of transactions in securities emerged as part of the aftermath of the market crash in 1929. The Securities Act of 1933 (1933 Act), [citation] was designed to provide investors with full disclosure of material information concerning public offerings of securities in commerce, to protect investors against fraud and, through the imposition of specified civil liabilities, to promote ethical standards of honesty and fair dealing. [Citation.] The 1934 Act was intended principally to protect investors against manipulation of stock prices through regulation of transactions upon securities exchanges and in over-the- counter markets, and to impose regular reporting requirements on companies whose stock is listed on national securities exchanges. [Citation.] Although the Acts contain numerous carefully drawn express civil remedies and criminal penalties, Congress recognized that efficient regulation of securities trading could not be accomplished under a rigid statutory program. As part of the 1934 Act Congress created the Commission, which is provided with an arsenal of flexible enforcement powers. [Citation.]

Section 10 of the 1934 Act makes it "unlawful for any person * * * (b) [t]o use or employ, in connection with the purchase or sale of any security * * * any manipulative or deceptive device or contrivance in contravention of such rules and regulations as the Commission may prescribe as necessary or appropriate in the public interest or for the protection of investors." [Citation.] In 1942, acting pursuant to the power conferred by § 10(b), the Commission promulgated Rule 10b-5.

* * *

Although § 10(b) does not by its terms create an express civil remedy for its violation, and there is no indication that Congress, or the Commission when adopting Rule 10b-5, contemplated such a remedy, the existence of a private cause of action for violations of the statute and the Rule is now well established. [Citation.] During the 30-year period since a private cause of action was first implied under § 10(b) and Rule 10b-5, a substantial body of case law and commentary has developed as to its elements. Courts and commentators long have differed with regard to whether scienter is a necessary element of such a cause of action, or whether negligent conduct alone is sufficient.

* * *

Although the extensive legislative history of the 1934 Act is bereft of any explicit explanation of Congress' intent, we think the relevant portions of that history support our conclusion that § 10(b) was addressed to practices that involve some element of scienter and cannot be read to impose liability for negligent conduct alone.

* * *

The section was described rightly as a "catchall" clause to enable the Commission "to deal with new manipulative [or cunning] devices." It is difficult to believe that any lawyer, legislative draftsman, or legislator would use these words if the intent was to create liability for merely negligent acts of omissions. Neither the legislative history nor the briefs supporting respondents identify any usage or authority for construing "manipulative [or cunning] devices" to include negligence.

* * *

The Commission argues that Congress has been explicit in requiring willful conduct when that was the standard of fault intended, * * *.

* * *

The structure of the Acts does not support the Commission's argument. In each instance that Congress created express civil liability in favor of purchasers or sellers of securities it clearly specified whether recovery was to be premised on knowing or intentional conduct, negligence, or entirely innocent mistake. [Citations.] For example, § 11 of the 1933 Act unambiguously creates a private action for damages when a registration statement includes untrue statements of material facts or fails to state material facts necessary to make the statements therein not misleading. Within the limits specified by § 11(e), the issuer of the securities is held absolutely liable for any damages resulting from such misstatement or omission. But experts such as accountants who have prepared portions of the registration statement are accorded a "due diligence" defense. In effect, this is a negligence standard. An expert may avoid civil liability with respect to the portions of the registration statement for which he was responsible by showing that "after reasonable investigation" he had "reasonable ground[s] to believe" that the statements for which he was responsible were true and there was no omission of a material fact. § 11(b)(3)(B)(i). See e.g., Escott v. BarChris Const. Corp. [citation.] The express recognition of a cause of action premised on negligent behavior in § 11 stands in sharp contrast to the language of § 10(b), and significantly undercuts the Commission's argument.

We also consider it significant that each of the express civil remedies in the 1933 Act allowing recovery for negligent conduct, see §§ 11, 12(2), 15, [citations] is subject to significant procedural restrictions not applicable under § 10(b). * * *

* * *

We have addressed, to this point, primarily the language and history of § 10(b). The Commission contends, however, that subsections (b) and (c) of Rule 10b-5 are cast in language which—if standing alone—could encompass both intentional and negligent behavior. These subsections respectively provide that it is unlawful "[t]o make any untrue statement of a material fact or to omit to state a material fact necessary in order to make the statements made, in the light of the circumstances under which they were made, not misleading * * * " and "[t]o engage in any act, practice, or course of business which operates or would operate as a fraud or deceit upon any person * * *."

Viewed in isolation the language of subsection (b), and arguably that of subsection (c), could be read as proscribing, respectively, any type of material misstatement or omission, and any course of conduct, that has the effect of defrauding investors, whether the wrongdoing was intentional or not.

We note first that such a reading cannot be harmonized with the administrative history of the Rule, a history making clear that when the Commission adopted the Rule it was intended to apply only to activities that involved scienter. More importantly, Rule 10b-5 was adopted pursuant to authority granted the Commission under § 10(b). The rulemaking power granted to an administrative agency charged with the administration of a federal statute is not the power to make law. Rather, it is " 'the power to adopt regulations to carry into effect the will of Congress as expressed by the statute.' " [Citations.] * * * When a statute speaks so specifically in terms of manipulation and deception, and of implementing devices and contrivances—the commonly understood terminology of intentional wrongdoing—and when its history reflects no more expansive intent, we are quite unwilling to extend the scope of the statute to negligent conduct.

CHAPTER SUMMARY

Common Law	Contract Liability the employment contract between an accountant and her client is subject to the general principles of contract law
	■ *Explicit Duties* the accountant is bound to perform all the duties she expressly agrees to provide
	■ *Implicit Duties* the accountant impliedly agrees to perform the contract in a competent and professional manner
	■ *Beneficiaries* contract liability extends to the client/contracting party and to third-party beneficiaries (noncontracting parties intended by the contracting parties to receive the primary benefit under the contract)
	■ *Breach of Contract* general contract law principles apply
	Tort Liability a tort is a private or civil wrong or injury other than a breach of contract
	■ *Negligence* an accountant is liable for failing to exercise the degree of care a reasonably competent accountant would exercise under the circumstances; most courts have extended an accountant's liability for negligence beyond the client and third-party beneficiaries to foreseen third parties
	■ *Fraud* an accountant who commits a fraudulent act is liable for both compensatory and punitive damages to any person who he should have reasonably foreseen would be injured; a fraudulent act is a false representation of fact that is material, made with knowledge of its falsity and with the intention to deceive, and is justifiably relied on
	Criminal Liability State law imposes criminal liability on accountants for willfully certifying false documents, altering or tampering with accounting records, using false financial reports, giving false testimony, and committing forgery

Client Information
- *Working Papers* an accountant is considered the owner of his working papers but may not disclose their contents unless the client agrees or a court orders the disclosure
- *Accountant-Client Privilege* not recognized by the common law or Federal law, although some States have adopted statutes granting some form of privilege

Federal Securities Law

1933 Act

- *Civil Liability* Section 11 imposes civil liability upon accountants if the financial statements they prepare or certify for a registration statement contain any untrue statement or omission of material fact unless the accountant proves his due diligence defense which requires that the accountant had, after reasonable investigation, reasonable grounds to believe and did believe that the financial statements were true, complete, and accurate
- *Criminal Liability* a willful violation of Section 11 is subject to fines of not more than $10,000 and/or imprisonment of not more than five years

1934 Act

- *Section 18* imposes civil liability on an accountant who knowingly makes any false or misleading statement about any material fact in any report, document, or registration filed with the SEC
- *Rule 10b-5* an accountant is civilly liable under this rule if he acts with *scienter* in making or aiding others to make oral or written misstatements or omissions of material fact in connection with the purchase or sale of a security
- *Criminal Liability* a willful violation of either Section 18 or Rule 10b-5 is subject to fines of not more than $1 million and/or imprisonment of not more than ten years

QUESTIONS

1. Explain the contract liability of an accountant to her client.
2. For what and to whom does an accountant have tort liability?
3. Explain who owns the working papers generated by an accountant and whether client information is privileged.
4. Discuss the potential civil and criminal liability of an accountant under the 1933 Act.
5. Discuss the potential civil and criminal liability of an accountant under the 1934 Act.

PROBLEMS

1. Baldwin Corporation made a public offering of $25,000,000 of convertible debentures. It registered the offering with the SEC. The registration statement contained financial statements certified by Adams and Allen, CPAs. The financial statements overstated Baldwin's net income and assets by 20 percent while it understated the company's liability by 15 percent. Because Adams and Allen did not carefully follow GAAS it failed to detect these inaccuracies, the discovery of which has caused the bond prices to drop from their original selling price of $1,000 per bond to $720. Conrad, who purchased $10,000 of the debentures, has brought suit against Adams and Allen. Decision?

2. Ingram is a CPA employed by Jordan, Keller and Lane, CPAs, to audit Martin Enterprises, Inc., a fast-growing service firm that had gone public two years earlier. The financial statements that were audited by Ingram were included in a proxy statement proposing a merger with several other firms. The proxy statement was filed with the SEC and included several inaccuracies. First, approximately $1 million, or more than 20 percent, of the previous

year's "net sales originally reported" had proven nonexistent by the time the proxy statement was filed and had been written off on Martin's own books. This was not disclosed in the proxy statement in violation of Accounting Board Opinion Number 9. Second, net sales of Martin for the current year were stated as $11,300,000 when they were less than $10,500,000. Third, net profits of Martin for the current year were reported as $700,000 when it had no earnings at all.

(a) What civil liability, if any, does Ingram have?

(b) What criminal liability, if any, does Ingram have?

3. Girard & Company, CPAs, audited the financial statements included in the annual report submitted by PMG Enterprises, Inc., to the SEC. The audit failed to detect numerous false and misleading statements contained in the financial statements.

(a) Investors who subsequently purchased PMG stock have brought suit against Girard under Section 18 of the 1934 Act. What defenses, if any, are available to Girard?

(b) The SEC has initiated criminal proceedings under the 1934 Act against Girard. What must be proven for Girard to be held criminally liable?

4. Dryden, a certified public accountant, audited the books of Elixir, Inc., and certified incorrect financial statements in a form that was filed with the SEC. Shortly thereafter Elixir, Inc., went bankrupt. Investigation into the bankruptcy disclosed that Kraft, the president of Elixir, had engaged in an intricate and clever embezzlement scheme that siphoned off substantial sums of money that now support Kraft in a luxurious life-style in South America. Investors who purchased shares of Elixir have brought suit against Dryden under Rule 10b–5. At the trial Dryden produces evidence which demonstrates that his failure to discover the embezzlements resulted merely from negligence on his part and that he had no knowledge of the fraudulent conduct. Decision?

5. Johnson Enterprises, Inc., contracted with the accounting firm of P, A. & E. to perform an audit of Johnson. The accounting firm performed its duty in a nonnegligent, competent manner but failed to discover a novel embezzlement scheme perpetrated by Johnson's treasurer. Shortly thereafter Johnson's treasurer disappeared with $75,000 of the company's money. Johnson now refuses to pay P, A. & E. its $20,000 audit fee and is seeking to recover $75,000 from P, A. & E.

(a) What are the rights and liabilities of P, A. & E. and Johnson? Explain.

(b) Would your answer to (a) differ if the scheme was a common embezzlement scheme which GAAS should have disclosed? Explain.

6. The accounting firm of T, W & S was engaged to perform an audit of Progate Manufacturing Company. During the course of its investigation T, W & S discovered that the inventory was overvalued by the company in that it was carried on the books at the previous year's prices, which were significantly higher than current prices. When T, W & S approached Progate's president, Lehman, about the improper valuation of inventory, Lehman became enraged and told T, W & S that unless the firm accepted the valuation Progate would sue T, W & S. Although T, W & S knew that Progate's suit was frivolous and unfounded it wished to avoid the negative publicity that would arise from any suit brought against it. Therefore, on the assumption that the overvaluation would not harm anybody T, W & S accepted Progate's inflated valuation of inventory, Progate subsequently went bankrupt and T, W & S is now being sued by (1) First National Bank, a bank that relied upon T, W & S's statement to loan money to Progate and (2) Thomas, an investor who purchased 20 percent of Progate's stock after receiving T, W & S's statement. What are the rights and liabilities of First National Bank, Thomas, and T, W & S?

7. J, B, and J, CPAs, has audited the Highcredit Corporation for the past five years. Recently the SEC has commenced an investigation against Highcredit for possible violations of the Federal securities law. The SEC has subpoenaed all of J, B, and J's working papers pertinent to the audit of Highcredit. Highcredit insists that J, B, and J not turn over the documents to the SEC. What action should J, B, and J take? Why?

8. On February 1, the Gazette Corporation hired Susan Sharp to conduct an audit of its books and to prepare financial statements for the corporation's annual meeting on July 1. Sharp made every reasonable attempt to comply with the deadline but could not finish the report on time due to delays in receiving needed information from Gazette. Gazette now refused to pay Sharp for her audit and is threatening to bring a cause of action against Sharp. What course of action should Sharp pursue? Why?

45 CONSUMER PROTECTION

Consumer transactions have increased enormously since World War II, and today they amount to hundreds of billions of dollars. Although the definition of a consumer transaction varies, it is generally considered one involving goods, credit, services, or land acquired for personal, household, or family purposes. Historically, consumers were subject to the rule of *caveat emptor*—let the buyer beware. In recent years, however, the law has abandoned this principle in most consumer transactions and has given greater protection to consumers. Most of this protection takes the form of statutory enactments at both the State and Federal levels, and a wide variety of governmental agencies are charged with enforcement of these statutes. Nonetheless, many contend that consumer fears and ignorance are all too frequently being exploited by charlatans and that more protection is needed.

In this chapter we examine consumer protection statutes that regulate (a) unfair and deceptive trade practices; (b) consumer purchases of goods, services, and land; (c) consumer credit obligations; and (d) consumer health and safety.

UNFAIR AND DECEPTIVE TRADE PRACTICES

In 1914 Congress enacted the **Federal Trade Commission Act** creating the Federal Trade Commission (FTC), which is charged with preventing unfair methods of competition in commerce, and unfair or deceptive acts or practices in commerce. To this end the five-member commission is empowered to issue substantive rules and to conduct appropriate investigations and hearings. The FTC may institute complaints and, after a hearing, may order appropriate relief, including cease and desist orders, and under certain circumstances, recovery of civil penalties and damages for persons injured by unfair or deceptive acts or practices. Appeals may be taken from orders of the FTC to the United States Courts of Appeals, which have exclusive jurisdiction to enforce, set aside, or modify orders of the Commission. Imprisonment may be imposed upon those who violate FTC orders. Numerous States have consumer protection statutes that are similar to the FTC Act and prohibit unfair and deceptive trade practices.

The Commission has established a Bureau of Consumer Protection, which investigates unfair methods of competition, such as false and misleading advertisements, false or inadequate labeling of products, passing or palming off goods as those of a competitor, lotteries, gambling schemes, discriminatory offers of rebates and discounts, false disparagement of a competitor's goods, false or misleading descriptive names of products, and use of false testimonials. See Law in the News at page 1028.

Standards

The FTC act does not define the words *unfair* or *deceptive*, and the Commission has long been criticized for its failure to do so. Partly in response to these criticisms and partly in response to Congressional pressure, the Commission issued three policy statements in the early 1980s. The first addressed the meaning of **unfairness** and provided:

To justify a finding of unfairness the injury must satisfy three tests. It must be substantial; it must not be outweighed by any countervailing benefits to consumers or competition that the practice produces; and it must be an injury that consumers themselves could not reasonably have avoided. The standard, therefore, applies a cost-benefit analysis to the issue of unfairness.

The second policy statement dealt with the meaning of **deception.** The formulation of this statement generated considerable disagreement among the Commissioners, and the statement was approved by a three to two vote. The dissenting Commissioners issued a minority statement. It is generally accepted that the minority position reflected previous FTC policy, whereas the majority position established new policy.

The majority position provides that "the Commission will find deception if there is a misrepresentation, omission or practice that is likely to mislead the consumer acting reasonably in the circumstances, to the consumer's detriment." Thus, the Commission will find an act or practice deceptive if it meets a three-prong test:

First, there must be a representation, omission, or practice that is likely to mislead the consumer. Second, we examine the practice from the perspective of a consumer acting reasonably in the circumstances. Third, the representation, omission, or practice must be a "material" one. The basic question is whether the act or practice is likely to affect the consumer's conduct or decision with regard to a product or service. If so, the practice is material, and consumer injury is likely because consumers are likely to have chosen differently but for the deception.

The following case applies the majority rewording of the traditional deception standard.

IN RE CLIFFDALE ASSOCIATES, INC.

Federal Trade Commission, 1984.
46 Antitrust and Trade Reg. Rep. 703.

Facts: The FTC brought this action, claiming that Cliffdale Associates engaged in unfair and deceptive trade practices by advertising its "new air bleed" engine attachment known as the Ball-Matic Gas Save Valve, as an "amazing automobile discovery" and as "the most significant breakthrough in the last ten years." The device was designed to allow more air to enter an automobile's engine and thus increase the automobile's efficiency and gas mileage. The Administrative Law Judge (ALJ) ruled in favor of the FTC and ordered Cliffdale to cease and desist from engaging in these unfair and deceptive trade practices.

Decision: Judgment for FTC.

Opinion: **Miller, Chairman.**

II. LEGAL STANDARD FOR DECEPTION

[The ALJ] concluded that "any advertising representation that has the tendency and capacity to mislead or deceive a prospective purchaser is an unfair and deceptive practice which violates the Federal Trade Commission Act." [Citations.] We find this approach to deception and violations of Section 5 to be circular and therefore inadequate to provide guidance on how a deception claim should be analyzed. Accordingly, we believe it appropriate for the Commission to articulate a clear and understandable standard for deception.

Consistent with its Policy Statement on Deception, issued on October 14, 1983, the Commission will find an act or practice deceptive if, first, there is a representation, omission, or practice that, second, is likely to mislead consumers acting reasonably under the circumstances, and third, the representation, omission, or practice is material. These elements articulate the factors actually used in most earlier Commission cases identifying whether or not an act or practice was deceptive, even though the language used in those cases was often couched in such terms as "a tendency and capacity to deceive."

The requirement that an act or practice be "likely to mislead," for example, reflects the long established principle that the Commission need not find *actual* deception to hold that a violation of Section 5 has occurred. This concept was explained as early as 1964, when the Commission stated:

> In the application of [the deception] standard to the many different factual patterns that have arisen in cases before the Commission, certain principles have been well established. One is that under Section 5 actual deception of particular consumers need not be shown.

Similarly, the requirement that an act or practice be considered from the perspective of a "consumer acting reasonably in the circumstances" is not new. Virtually all representations, even those that are true, can be misunderstood by some consumers. The Commission has long recognized that the law should not be applied in such a way as to find that honest representations are deceptive simply because they are misunderstood by a few. Thus, the Commission has noted that an advertisement would not be considered deceptive merely because it could be "unreasonably misunderstood by an insignificant and unrepresentative segment of the class of persons to whom the representation is addressed." In recent cases, this concept has been increasingly emphasized by the Commission.

The third element is materiality. As noted in the Commission's policy statement, a material representation, omission, act or practice involves information that is important to consumers and, hence, likely to affect their choice of, or conduct regarding, a product. Consumers thus are likely to suffer injury from a material misrepresentation. A review of past Commission deception cases shows that one of the factors usually considered, either directly or indirectly, is whether or not a claim is material.

Although the ALJ in this case used the phrase "tendency and capacity to deceive" in his initial decision, we find after reviewing the record that his underlying analysis shows that the three elements necessary for a finding of deception are present in this case.

III. THE QUESTION OF LIABILITY

The obvious first step in analyzing whether a claim is deceptive is for the Commission to determine what claim has been made. When the advertisement contains an express claim, the representation itself establishes its meaning. When the claim is implied, the Commission will often be able to determine the meaning through an examination of the representation, including an evaluation of such factors as the entire document, the juxtaposition of various phrases in the document, the nature of the claim, and the nature of the transaction.

In other situations, the Commission will require extrinsic evidence that reasonable consumers interpret the implied claims in a certain way. The evidence can consist of expert opinion, consumer testimony, copy tests, surveys, or any other reliable evidence of consumer interpretation. In all instances, the Commission will carefully consider any extrinsic evidence that is introduced.

A. *Descriptive Claims*

a. *Were the Claims Made?*

1. Important New Invention

Most of respondents' advertisements refer to the Ball-Matic as an "amazing automobile discovery." The same advertisements also describe the products as "the most significant automotive breakthrough in the last ten years." Other ads term the Ball-Matic an "important automobile invention" and a "unique, patented" valve. The Ball-Matic is even compared to a "mini-computer brain."

The ALJ found these advertisements expressly claim that the Ball-Matic is an important, significant, and unique new invention. We agree.

* * *

2. Were the Claims Deceptive?

* * *

a. *Ball-Matic as an Important New Invention*

The evidence presented at trial amply documented that the Ball-Matic is a simple air-bleed device similar to many other such devices that have been marketed over the years. Clearly the Ball-Matic is not new. In fact, the Commission has already issued cease and desist orders against various marketers of two such devices, the Albano Air Jet and the G. A. Valve, both of which are virtually identical in design to the Ball-Matic. Air bleed devices have been around a long time and, as the ALJ found, are considered to be of little value by the automobile industry.

The claim that the Ball-Matic was a new invention was expressly made. Having found such a claim to have been made, and that the claim is false, the Commission may infer, within the bounds of reason, that it is material. We therefore conclude that the ALJ was correct in holding that this claim was deceptive.

* * *

B. *Representation that Competent Scientific Tests Prove the Fuel Economy Claims Made for the Ball-Matic*

1. Was the Claim Made?

Most of respondents' advertisements refer to a "controlled, supervised test." The text of some ads details the procedure used in the test, *i.e.*, use of cars equipped with the Ball-Matic driven by non-professional drivers with mileage and fuel consumption monitored by "testers." We find that descriptions of these types of consumer "tests" in advertisements cannot, alone, reasonably be interpreted as representing that the device was tested scientifically.

However, other advertisements simply state that the Ball-Matic was "tested and proven (to yield) up to (a) 20 percent increase in fuel economy." Still other advertisements cite "field tests for over seven years and lab tests at an Accredited Eastern University." Additional tests results are suggested through respondents' invitation that consumers send for test reports if in doubt about the Ball-Matic's performance. These advertisements can be reasonably understood to imply that competent scientific tests support the performance claims made for the Ball-Matic.

2. Was the Claim Deceptive?

Respondents introduced a number of test results with varying evaluations of the Ball-Matic. These include a test conducted by the Vernon, California Emission Test Laboratory, an engine dynomometer test by a University of Bridgeport professor, and a series of tests by Scott Environmental Technology, Industries. However, the ALJ found the tests did not prove the fuel economy claims made for the Ball-Matic. We agree.

First, although the tests did indicate some improvement in fuel economy arguably attributable to the Ball-Matic, none revealed improvement even close to that claimed by respondents. While respondents claim up to 20 percent savings in fuel economy, the highest savings any of the "scientific" tests established was 11 percent. Thus, even assuming that respondents' tests were competent, the claim that they support the representation made for the Ball-Matic's performance is false.

Moreover, the evidence presented by complaint counsel casts serious doubt on the validity of the results obtained in respondent's tests.

* * *

C. *Representations Based on Consumer Endorsements*
1. Were the Claims Made?

* * *

The ALJ concluded, and we agree, that consumers could reasonably interpret these advertisements as claiming that the Ball-Matic would produce significant fuel economy improvement, that the testimonials were unrestrained and unbiased, that the endorsements were from recent or actual users of the Ball-Matic, and that the experiences were typical of all users.
2. Were the Claims Deceptive?
a. *Performance Claims in Testimonials*
By printing the testimonials, respondents implicitly made performance claims similar to those express claims found to be false and deceptive. Thus, irrespective of the veracity of the individual consumer testimonials, respondents' use of the testimonials to make underlying claims that were false and deceptive was, itself, deceptive. Accordingly, we agree with the ALJ that use of these endorsements constituted a law violation.
b. *Unrevealed Relationship of Endorsers to Seller*
The ALJ found that a good number of the testimonials used in the Ball-Matic advertisements were by business associates of the marketers of the product. Nevertheless, he concluded that the failure to disclose these relationships did not constitute either an unfair or a deceptive practice. Complaint counsel appeal from this holding, and we hold for complaint counsel on this issue.
In its "Guides Concerning the Use of Endorsements and Testimonials in Advertising," The Commission's policy is clear that whenever "there exists a connection between the endorser and the seller of the advertised product which might materially affect the weight or credibility of the endorsement" it should be disclosed. In a case such as this, where it is difficult for a consumer to evaluate the effectiveness of the product on his or her own, the consumer is likely to rely more heavily on endorsements by other users, particularly if the consumer believes such endorsements are independent and unbiased. Failure to disclose the relationship, and therefore the bias, will materially affect the weight given to the endorsement. Thus, having determined that the implied claim of impartiality is false and that the failure to disclose the relationship is a material fact to consumers, we conclude that respondents are guilty of making a deceptive claim.

Deception may occur by either false representation or material omission. Examples of deceptive practices include advertising that a certain product will save consumers 25 percent on their automotive motor oil where the product simply replaces a quart of oil in the engine (which normally contains four quarts of oil) and was more expensive than the replaced motor oil; placing marbles in a bowl of vegetable soup in order to displace the vegetables from the bottom of the soup and therefore make it appear that the soup had more vegetables; and claiming that a drug provides greater pain relief than another named drug when there is insufficient evidence to prove the claim to the medical community.

The third policy statement issued by the Commission involved **ad substantiation**. This policy requires that advertisers have a reasonable basis for their claims at the time their claims are made. Moreover, in determining the reasonableness of the claim, the Commission places great weight upon the cost and benefits of substantiation.

Remedies

In addition to the remedies discussed above, the FTC has employed three other potent remedies: (1) affirmative disclosure, (2) corrective advertising, and (3) multiple product orders. **Affirmative disclosure** is frequently employed by the FTC and requires the offender to provide certain information in its advertisement in order for the ad not to be considered deceptive. In ordering such remedial action, however, the Commission must be careful not to infringe upon the advertiser's constitutional rights. For instance, the National Commission on Egg Nutrition (NCEN), an egg producers' trade association, was organized in an attempt to combat the damage being done to the egg industry by the anticholesterol forces. The Federal Trade Commission alleged that in its attempt to achieve this goal the NCEN had made several false and misleading statements in its advertising campaign. Principally, the FTC contended and subsequently ruled that it was an unfair trade practice for NCEN to represent "that there is no scientific evidence that eating eggs increases the risk of . . . heart and [circulatory] disease. . . . " In addition to ordering the NCEN to cease and desist from this and other representations, the FTC also ordered that (1) any reference made to the relationship between cholesterol (and hence eggs) and circulatory disease be accompanied by a conspicuous statement that many medical authorities believe that eating cholesterol might increase the risk of heart or circulatory

disease, and (2) any representation disparaging the scientific evidence connecting cholesterol and heart and circulatory disease is forbidden. The United States Court of Appeals for the Seventh Circuit, however, amended the FTC's affirmative disclosure order on the ground that the order was an overly broad remedial decree. It held that the First Amendment prohibited a remedy "broader than that which is necessary." And, since the order directed NCEN to argue the other side of the issue rather than merely acknowledge the existence of the controversy, the order unduly infringed upon NCEN's freedom of speech. The court, nevertheless, held that: (1) the NCEN cannot disseminate any advertisement that represents that the consumption of eggs or cholesterol does not enhance the risk of heart or circulatory disease unless it conspicuously discloses that a controversy exists surrounding this connection and that the advertisement is merely stating its position, and (2) the NCEN cannot disseminate any advertisement that presents scientific evidence supporting the position that the consumption of eggs or cholesterol does not increase the consumer's risk of heart or circulatory disease unless it conspicuously discloses that many medical authorities are of the belief that the eating of eggs (cholesterol) does, based on scientific evidence, increase one's risk of heart or circulatory ailments. *National Commission on Egg Nutrition v. FTC*, 570 F.2d 157 (7th Cir., 1977).

Corrective advertising goes beyond affirmative disclosure and requires that the advertiser of a deceptive claim disclose in future advertisements that the deceptive claims made in the prior advertisements were in fact not true. The following case is an example of this remedy.

WARNER-LAMBERT CO. v. FTC
United States Court of Appeals, District of Columbia Circuit, 1977.
562 F.2d 749.

Facts: The FTC ordered Warner-Lambert to cease and desist from advertising that its product, Listerine antiseptic mouthwash, prevents, cures, or alleviates the common cold and sore throats. The order further required disclosure in future advertisements that: "Contrary to prior advertising, Listerine will not help prevent colds or sore throats or lessen their severity." Warner-Lambert contended that even if its past advertising claims were false, the corrective advertising portion of the order exceeds the FTC's statutory power. The FTC claims that corrective advertising is necessary in light of Warner-Lambert's 100 years of false claims and the resulting persistence of erroneous consumer beliefs.

Decision: Order of the FTC is affirmed as modified by this opinion.

Opinion: Wright, J. Background   The order under review represents the culmination of a proceeding begun in 1972, when the FTC issued a complaint charging petitioner with violation of Section 5(a)(1) of the Federal Trade Commission Act by misrepresenting the efficacy of Listerine against the common cold.

Listerine has been on the market since 1879. Its formula has never changed. Ever since its introduction it has been represented as being beneficial in certain respects for colds, cold symptoms, and sore throats. Direct advertising to the consumer, including the cold claims as well as others, began in 1921.

* * *

The Commission's Power   Petitioner [Warner-Lambert] contends that even if its advertising claims in the past were false, the portion of the commission's order requiring "corrective advertising" exceeds the Commission's statutory power. The argument is based upon a literal reading of Section 5 of the Federal Trade Commission Act, which authorizes the Commission to issue "cease and desist" orders against violators and does not expressly mention any other remedies. The Commission's position, on the other hand, is that the affirmative disclosure that Listerine will not prevent colds or lessen their severity is absolutely necessary to give effect to the prospective cease and desist order; a hundred years of false cold claims have built up a large reservoir or erroneous consumer belief which would persist, unless corrected, long after petitioner ceased making the claims.

The need for the corrective advertising remedy and its appropriateness in this case are important issues which we will explore. But the threshold question is whether the Commission has the authority to issue such an order. We hold that it does.

Petitioner's narrow reading of Section 5 was at one time shared by the Supreme Court. In FTC v. Eastman Kodak Co. the Court held that the Commission's authority did not exceed that expressly conferred by statute. The Commission has not, the Court said, "been delegated the authority of a court of equity."

But the modern view is very different.

* * *

"[W]here the problem lies within the purview of the [Commission], * * * Congress must have intended to give it authority that was ample to deal with the evil at hand. * * *   Authority to mold administrative decrees is indeed like the authority of courts to frame injunctive decrees * * *."

* * *

Thus it is clear that the Commission has the power to shape remedies which go beyond the simple cease and desist order. Our next inquiry must be whether a corrective advertising order is for any reason outside the range of permissible remedies. Petitioner * * * argue(s) that it is because (1) legislative history precludes it, (2) it impinges on the First Amendment, and (3) it has never been approved by any court.

Legislative History Petitioner relies on the legislative history of the 1914 Federal Trade Commission Act and the Wheeler-Lea amendments to it in 1938 for the proposition that corrective advertising was not contemplated. In 1914 and in 1938 Congress chose not to authorize such remedies as criminal penalties, treble damages, or civil penalties, but that fact does not dispose of the question of corrective advertising.

Petitioner's reliance on the legislative history of the 1975 amendments to the Act is also misplaced. The amendments added a new Section 19 to the Act authorizing the Commission to bring suits in federal District Courts to redress injury to consumers resulting from a deceptive practice. The section authorizes the court to grant such relief as it "finds necessary to redress injury to consumers or other persons, partnerships, and corporations resulting from the rule violation or the unfair or deceptive act or practice," including, but not limited to, rescission or reformation of contracts, the refund of money or return of property, the payment of damages, and public notification respecting the rule violation or the unfair or deceptive act or practice * * *.

* * *

The First Amendment Petitioner * * * further contends that corrective advertising is not a permissible remedy because it trenches on the First Amendment. Petitioner is correct that this triggers a special responsibility on the Commission to order corrective advertising only if the restriction inherent in its order is no greater than necessary to serve the interest involved. But this goes to the appropriateness of the order in this case.

* * *

The Supreme Court [has] expressly noted that the First Amendment presents "no obstacle" to government regulation of false or misleading advertising. The First Amendment, the Court said, as we construe it today, does not prohibit the State from insuring that the stream of commercial information flow[s] cleanly as well as freely.

* * *

Precedents According to petitioner, "The first reference to corrective advertising in Commission decisions occurred in 1970, nearly fifty years and untold number of false advertising cases after passage of the Act." In petitioner's view, the late emergence of this "newly discovered" remedy is itself evidence that it is beyond the Commission's authority. This argument fails on two counts. First the fact that an agency has not asserted a power over a period of years is not proof that the agency lacks such power. Second, and more importantly, we are not convinced that the corrective advertising remedy is really such an innovation. The label may be newly coined, but the concept is well established. It is simply that under certain circumstances an advertiser may be required to make affirmative disclosure of unfavorable facts.

* * *

The Remedy Having established that the Commission does have the power to order corrective advertising in appropriate cases, it remains to consider whether use of the remedy against Listerine is warranted and equitable. We have concluded that the order should be modified to delete the phrase "Contrary to prior advertising." With that modification, we approve the order.

Our role in reviewing the remedy is limited. The Supreme Court has set forth the standard:

The Commission is the expert body to determine what remedy is necessary to eliminate the unfair or deceptive trade practices which have been disclosed. It has wide latitude for judgment and the courts will not interfere except where the remedy selected has no reasonable relation to the unlawful practices found to exist.

The Commission has adopted the following standard for the imposition of corrective advertising:

[I]f a deceptive advertisement has played a substantial role in creating or reinforcing in the public's mind a false and material belief which lives on after the false advertising ceases, there is clear and continuing injury to competition and to the consuming public as consumers continue to make purchasing decisions based on the false belief. Since this injury cannot be averted by merely requiring respondent to cease disseminating the advertisement, we may appropriately order respondent to take affirmative action designed to terminate the otherwise continuing ill effects of the advertisement.

We think this standard is entirely reasonable.

Multiple product orders require that the deceptive advertisers cease and desist from any future deception not only in regard to the product in question but also to all products sold by the company. See *Sears, Roebuck and Co.* below. This remedy is particularly useful in dealing with companies that are repeated violators of the law.

SEARS, ROEBUCK AND CO. v. FTC
United States Court of Appeals, Ninth Circuit, 1982.
676 F.2d 385.

Facts: In the early 1970s, Sears formulated a plan to increase sales of its top of the line "Lady Kenmore" brand dishwasher. Sears's plan sought to change the Lady Kenmore's image, without the need for reengineering or any mechanical improvements in the dishwasher itself. To accomplish this, Sears undertook a four-year, $8 million advertising campaign that claimed that the Lady Kenmore completely eliminated the need for prerinsing and prescraping dishes. As a result of this campaign, sales rose by more than 300 percent. The "no scraping, no prerinsing" claim was not true, however, and Sears had no reasonable basis for asserting the claim. In addition, the owner's manual customers received after they purchased the dishwasher contradicted the claim.

After a thorough investigation, the Federal Trade Commission, in 1977, filed a complaint against Sears, alleging that the advertisements were false and misleading. The final FTC order required Sears to stop making the no scraping, no prerinsing claim. The order also prevented Sears from (1) making any "performance claims" for "major home appliances" without first possessing a reasonable basis consisting of substantiating tests or other evidence; (2) misrepresenting any test, survey, or demonstration regarding "major home appliances;" and (3) making any advertising statements not consistent with statements in postpurchase materials supplied to purchasers of "major home appliances." Sears contends the order is too broad, since it covers appliances other than dishwashers, as well as including "performance claims."

Decision: Order of the FTC enforced.

Opinion: Reinhardt, J. *1. Statutory Power.* Sears argues first that the language and legislative history of section 5(b) of the [FTC] Act, [citation], require the Commission to direct its cease and desist order only to those specific violations alleged in the complaint since only those violations have been litigated in the manner contemplated by the statute. From this doctrine, Sears seems to reason that since the complaint here describes dishwasher advertising, the Commission lacks the power to issue an order covering any product except dishwashers. Sears' conclusion is that to the extent that the order covers products other than dishwashers, it is invalid as a matter of law. We disagree.

It is too late to argue that when the Commission establishes a violation only as to one product, its power under the Act is limited to the issuance of a single product order. As the Second Circuit said in [citation] "[C]ourts have often upheld FTC orders encompassing all products or all products in a broad category, based on violations involving only a single product or group of products * * * ." The Supreme Court rendered this doctrine metaphorically in [citation]. There, the Court reminded the companies that objected to the breadth of the Commission's order that "those caught violating the Act must expect some *fencing in*." [Citation]. Allowance of this "fencing in" authority is based in part on our deference to the FTC's accumulated expertise in striking the proper relationship between violations found and effective orders, [citation], and in part on necessity since "there is no limit to human inventiveness in this field." [Citation.]

Accordingly, we reject Sears' argument here.

2. Rationality of the Remedy. Sears' next argument can be separated into * * * elements. First, the company says there is no reasonable relationship between the multi-product portion of the order and the violation found; second, that a multi-product order covering "performance claims" is unreasonably broad. * * *

* * *

The general principles governing objections to FTC orders are well known.

The Commission is the expert body to determine what remedy is necessary to eliminate the unfair or deceptive trade practices which have been disclosed. It has wide latitude for judgment and the courts will not interfere except where the remedy selected has no reasonable relation to the unlawful practices found to exist. [Citation.]

In addition,

Congress has placed the primary responsibility for fashioning orders on the Commission. *Federal Trade Comm'n v. National Lead Co.*, 352 U.S. 419, 429. For these reasons the courts should not "lightly modify" the Commission's orders. *Federal Trade Comm'n v. Cement Institute*, 333 U.S. 683, 726. However, this Court has also warned that an order's prohibitions "should be clear and precise in order that they may be understood by those against whom they are directed," *Federal Trade Comm'n v. Cement Institute, supra*, at 726 * * *. [Citation.]

A judgment regarding "reasonable relation" in multi-product order cases "depends upon the specific circumstances of the case." [Citation.] "[T]he ultimate question is the likelihood of the petitioner committing the sort of unfair practices [the order] prohibit[s]," [citation]. We answer that question by first examining the specific circumstances present in a particular case. Then, giving due deference to the Commission's expertise and judgment, we determine whether there is a "reasonable relation" between those circumstances and the concern regarding future violations manifested by the Commission's order.

Where a fair assessment of an advertiser's conduct shows a ready willingness to flout the law, sufficient cause for concern regarding further, additional violations exists. Two factors or elements frequently influence our decision—the deliberateness and seriousness of the present violation, and the violator's past record with respect to unfair advertising practices. [Citation.] Other circumstances may be weighed, including the adaptability or transferability of the unfair practice to other products. [Citation.] The weight given a particular factor or element will vary. The more egregious the facts with respect to a particular element, the less important it is that another negative factor be present. In the final analysis, we look to the circumstances as a whole and not to the presence or absence of any single factor. [Citations.]

* * *

We now consider the Commission's order in light of the specific circumstances of this case. This advertising campaign cost $8 million, ran for four years, and appeared in magazines, newspapers and on television throughout the country. The Commission found, and Sears does not dispute, that the campaign's central claim was false. Sears had no reasonable basis for making the claim, and the tests which Sears purportedly relied on showed, if anything, that the claim was false. Moreover, the Owner's Manual, which Sears furnished its customers after they purchased the Lady Kenmore, implicitly acknowledged the falsity of the claim and establishes that Sears knew it was false at all times. Under these circumstances, Sears' advertising campaign demonstrates "blatant and utter disregard" for the law. [Citation.] The Commission also considered petitioner's compliance record and concluded that it was "a wash." [Citation.] We see no reason to find otherwise.

Sears' advertisements were no accident or "isolated instance." [Citation] Rather, they were part of an advertising strategy, with attendant slogans, adopted without regard to the actual performance of the advertised machines. As the Commission pointed out, the covered machines are major ticket items generally purchased infrequently by any particular person. For that reason, their profitability does not depend on repeat purchases as is the case with frequently purchased, low-cost items. A selling strategy based on this purchasing fact, *e.g.*, the making of false and unsubstantiated performance claims as to a major ticket item, would be effective for a considerable period of time, with great benefit to the merchant but at great cost to consumers. This selling strategy could readily be transferred to the marketing of other machines in the home appliance category.

* * *

To prevent the false and unsubstantiated performance claims strategy from being used in connection with another major home appliance or from becoming Sears' general practice with respect to such appliances, the Commission deemed a broad order necessary. A judgment of this nature depends on detailed knowledge of the major home appliances business and its related advertising techniques. "[D]eceptive advertising cases necessarily require 'inference and pragmatic judgment.' " [Citations.] This sort of knowledge of the commercial world and the ability to make the type of judgment required lie in the realm of the Commission's greatest expertise.

> * * *
>
> In light of the flagrant and egregious nature of the violation found and the other circumstances present here, and giving the Commission's conclusions the required "great weight," [citations], we find no basis for substituting our judgment for the Commission's regarding the necessity for this multi-product order. We hold that the multi-product order is reasonably related to the petitioner's conduct, that a multi-product order is appropriate, and that the inclusion of the "performance claims" provision in that order is supported by the record before us and does not render the order overbroad.

CONSUMER PURCHASES

A number of State and Federal regulations protect consumers in their purchases of goods, services, and real property for personal, household, or family use. The Uniform Commercial Code, which we discussed more fully in Chapters 17–21, prohibits unconscionable contractual terms and imposes implied warranties for the protection of the purchaser.

Federal Warranty Protection

To protect buyers and to prevent deception in selling, in 1974 Congress enacted the Magnuson-Moss Warranty Act, which requires that sellers of consumer products give adequate information about warranties. The FTC administers and enforces the Act.

The **Magnuson-Moss Warranty Act** was enacted in order to alleviate certain reported warranty problems: (1) most warranties were not understandable; (2) most warranties disclaimed implied warranties; (3) most warranties were unfair; and (4) in some instances the warrantors did not live up to their warranties. The Act was Congress's attempt to make consumer product warranties more easily understood and to help consumers enforce their claims satisfactorily. To accomplish this purpose, the Act provides for:

1. disclosure in clear and understandable language of the warranty that is to be offered;
2. a description of the warranty as either "full" or "limited;"
3. a prohibition against disclaiming implied warranties if a written warranty is given; and

4. an optional informal settlement mechanism.

The Act applies to consumer products with *written warranties.* A **consumer product** is any item of tangible personal property that is *normally* used for family, household, or personal use and that is distributed in commerce. Commercial purchasers are *not* protected by the Act, partly because they are considered to have sufficient knowledge in contracting to protect themselves. Also, they are able to employ their own attorneys to protect themselves and can spread the cost of their injuries in the marketplace.

The Act contains *presale disclosure* provisions that are calculated to prevent confusion and deception and to enable purchasers to make educated product comparisons. A warrantor must, "to the extent required by the rules of the Commission [Federal Trade Commission], fully and conspicuously disclose in simple and readily understood language the terms and conditions of such warranty." When it implemented this requirement, the FTC adopted a rule that the text of the warranties must be accessible to the consumer. Under the rule, the warranty could be attached to the package, it could be placed on a visible sign, or it could be maintained in a binder. In 1986 the FTC relaxed this rule by permitting stores simply to make warranties available to consumers *upon request.* Retailers using this option, however, must post signs informing the consumer that the warranties are available. Separate rules apply to mail order, catalog, and door-to-door sales.

Dial M for Marketing Fraud
Regulators Are Fighting a Rise in Phone-Sale Scams

Milan F. Doering *thought* he was being careful. The psychologist from Logansport, Ind., says one day someone claiming to be from Schoolhouse Coins, Inc., called to suggest he buy English shillings. The caller spoke in "a pleasing, believable voice," Doering says. He also gave references, including a chamber of commerce and a better business bureau. When Doering inquired, neither had heard complaints about Schoolhouse Coins. In a sworn statement, Doering said the salesman spoke of the "trading room floor"; Doering imagined a busy room "with orders coming in and going out . . . like Wall Street." Several months after Doering started buying coins, he says the Schoolhouse people admitted that one of his investments wasn't doing as well as they had hoped. "Goodness, I thought, if they were dishonest everything would be moving up."

Doering says he invested $127,000 before concluding that Schoolhouse was not an operation "like Wall Street." The Federal Trade Commission last year brought suit against the operation. Schoolhouse, the FTC alleges, has defrauded an estimated 2,000 customers out of $6 million. A representative from Schoolhouse would not discuss the case. Con artists are nothing new, of course. But in recent years the trend toward selling over the telephone has provided them with a new hustle. Operating out of "boiler rooms" usually stocked with nothing more than desks, phones and scripts, fraudulent telemarketers earn from $1 billion to $20 billion a year.

Successful con artists are astute trend watchers. Greater airline competition spawned travel scams; the health craze gave rise to vitamin-pill ripoffs. FTC officials said telemarketers in one diamond scam capitalized on news stories about the appreciation of Elizabeth Taylor's jewels in their sales pitch. Recently telemarketers have peddled overseas jobs, AIDS cures, art, grandfather clocks and cellular-telephone franchises. The feds say the millions of victims include not just gullible recluses but a lieutenant governor, a federal judge and an FTC economist.

Fraudulent telemarketers owe their success in part to their legitimate counterparts. Salesmen for everything from news magazines to securities have learned that consumers who quickly toss junk mail or refuse to let in door-to-door salesmen will pick up a ringing phone. Still relatively rare in 1980, phone marketing now accounts for more than $100 billion in sales. As a result, consumers may have lowered their defenses against telephone fraud.

'Yakkers' and 'Moochers'

The anonymity of the phone allows skilled salesmen to conjure up images of reputable, profitable

The second major part of the Magnuson-Moss Warranty Act concerns the *labeling* requirement. The Act divides written warranties into two categories—limited and full—one of which, for any product costing more than $10, must be designated on the written warranty itself. The purpose of this provision is to alert the consumer to the legal rights under a certain warranty for purposes of initial comparison. If a **warranty** is designated as **full,** the warrantor must agree to repair the product without charge to conform with the warranty, no limitation may be placed on the duration of any implied warranty, the consumer must be given the option of a refund or replacement if repair is unsuccessful, and consequential damages may be excluded only if conspicuously noted. A limited warranty is any warranty not designated as full.

Most significantly, the Act provides that a *written* warranty, whether full or limited, may *not disclaim any implied* warranty. This provi-

companies. According to the Commodities Futures Trading Commission, one Florida boiler-room operation pushing precious metals had salesmen (known as "yakkers" in the trade) tell customers ("moochers") to phone a bogus reference (a "singer") called "The New York Metals Exchange." Customers who dialed the New York City phone number, said the CFTC, were transferred back to the Florida office, where another yakker pretended to be a metals-exchange official. In California, telemarketers often hire out-of-work actors to play the parts. Many operations manufacture TV commercials, brochures and newspaper ads boosting their "products." Diana Stewart of Fair Haven, N.J., claims she lost thousands of dollars to an operation she called after it advertised on cable TV. By gradually building her confidence, she says, salesmen persuaded her to buy cobalt, diamonds and coins." [One] called me once a week. He told me a lot about himself and his love life. I was kind of lonely. It seemed safe and he made me feel good."

Telemarketing con artists are adept at covering their tracks. Many use a variety of names. One male telemarketer pretended he was a woman so customers couldn't identify him. The operators usually tailor scams so that customers don't realize they've been had for months or years. Several oil and gas schemes gave out small payments over many months but stopped when customers didn't want to invest anymore. If authorities start to close in, the boiler rooms can shut down and move quickly.

The con artists have learned how to exploit legal loopholes. Because the CFTC has gone after illegal precious-metals trading, some telemarketers have modified their operations so that they won't fall under the agency's purview. Prosecutors are more likely to shut down boiler rooms if residents in their jurisdiction have been defrauded, so telemarketers often avoid bilking the locals. Since 1983 the FTC has brought 22 telemarketing-fraud cases and obtained $72 million in compensation for 6,500 victims. But that represents only a tiny part of the industry, and few victims get their money back. "Law enforcement generally has to catch up with this problem," concedes Michael McCarey, an FTC official.

'Data Bank' Network

Local and federal agencies have started making telefraud a higher priority. The FTC recently beefed up its "data bank" to help governments track complaints and coordinate prosecutions. State officials increasingly seek criminal charges because civil penalties can leave con artists free to open up elsewhere. A congressional panel last month approved legislation giving state officials more authority to pursue bogus telemarketers. Legitimate telemarketers complain that publicity about telephone fraud has hurt their sales and warn that too much caution (if people stopped giving credit-card numbers over the phone, for example) could also injure honest companies.

FTC chairman Daniel Oliver says government can do only so much. "People have this idea that if it were illegal, the government would be preventing it. That's a terrible impression for people to have." The safest route for consumers to take, he says, is to buy over the telephone only when *they're* making the call.

---

sion strikes at the heart of the problem, for a presidential task force report made before the Act was passed revealed that most written warranties gave limited protection but in return took away the more valuable implied warranties. Hence, consumers were led to believe that the warranties they received and the warranty registration cards they promptly returned to the manufacturer were to their benefit. The Act, on the other hand, provides that a full warranty must not disclaim, modify, or limit any implied warranty, and a limited warranty may not disclaim or modify any implied warranty but may limit its duration to that of the written warranty, provided that the limitation is reasonable, conscionable, and conspicuously displayed.

For example, GE sells consumer goods to Barry for $150 and provides a written warranty regarding the quality of the goods. GE must designate the warranty as full or limited, depending on the characteristics of the warranty, and may not disclaim or modify any implied warranty. On the other hand, if GE had not provided Barry with a written warranty, then the Magnuson-Moss Act would not apply, and GE could disclaim any and all implied warranties (see Figure 45–1).

Finally, the Act also contains a part dealing with *remedies* and the establishment, at the option of the warrantor, of an informal settlement procedure. The Act does not provide any new or expanded remedies.

Consumer Right of Rescission

In most cases, a consumer is legally obligated once he has signed a contract. Many States, however, have statutes allowing a consumer a brief period of time—generally two or three days—during which he may **rescind** an otherwise binding credit obligation if the solicitation of the sale occurred in his home. Moreover, the Federal Trade Commission has also set forth a trade regulation that applies to door-to-door sales of goods and services for $25 or more, whether the sale is for cash or on credit. The regulation permits a consumer to rescind the contract within *three days* of signing.

A consumer also has a right of rescission under the **Federal Consumer Credit Protection Act** (discussed more fully below), which allows a consumer three days during which he may withdraw from any credit obligation secured by a mortgage on his home, unless the extension of credit was made to acquire the dwelling. After the consumer rescinds, the creditor has twenty days to return any money or property he has received from the consumer.

The **Interstate Land Sales Full Disclosure Act** applies to sales or leases of one hundred or more lots of unimproved land as part of a common promotional plan in interstate commerce. The Act requires the developer to file a detailed statement of record containing specified information about the subdivision and the developer with the Department of Housing and Urban Development before offering the lots for sale or lease. The developer must provide a property report, which is a condensed version of the statement of record, to each prospective purchaser or lessee. The Act provides that any contract or agreement for sale or lease may be revoked at the option of the purchaser or lessee within seven days of signing the contract, and the contract must clearly provide this right. If the property report has not been given to the purchaser or lessee before the contract was signed, the contract may be revoked within two years from the date of signing.

CONSUMER CREDIT

In the absence of special regulation, consumer credit transactions are governed by laws regulating commercial transactions generally. A consumer credit transaction is customarily defined as any credit transaction involving

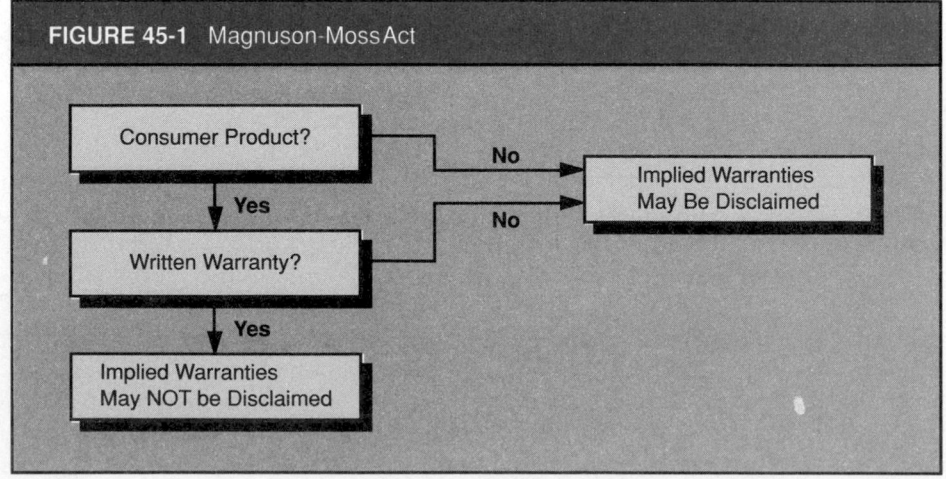

FIGURE 45-1 Magnuson-Moss Act

goods, services, or land acquired for personal, household, or family purposes. The following examples illustrate consumer credit transactions: Atkins borrows $600 from a bank to pay a dentist bill or to take a vacation; Bevins buys a refrigerator for her home from a department store and agrees to pay the purchase price in twelve equal monthly installments; Carpenter has an oil company credit card that he uses to purchase gasoline and tires for his family car.

Two significant developments have accelerated the legislative trend toward regulating consumer sales credit: (1) the enactment in 1968 of the **Federal Consumer Credit Protection Act** (FCCPA), and (2) the promulgation of the **Uniform Consumer Credit Code** (UCCC) in the same year. The FCCPA deals with effective disclosure of interest and finance charges, credit extension charges, and garnishment proceedings. The UCCC integrates into one document the regulation of all consumer credit transactions and gives substantially similar regulatory treatment to both credit sales and loan transactions.

Consumer credit protection has broadened considerably since the passage of the FCCPA and today includes the following areas: (1) access by creditors and consumers to the consumer credit market, (2) disclosure of information to the consumer, (3) regulation of contract terms, (4) regulation of consumer credit card fraud, (5) fair reportage of credit information concerning consumers, and (6) creditors' remedies.

Access to the Market

The **Equal Credit Opportunity Act,** enacted by Congress in 1974 and revised in 1985, prohibits all businesses that regularly extend credit from discriminating in extending credit on the basis of sex, marital status, race, color, religion, national origin, or age. Under the Act, creditors have thirty days after receipt of an application for credit to notify the applicant of action taken, and they must give specific reasons for a denial of credit. Although the Act is administered and enforced by several Federal agencies, the FTC has overall enforcement authority. Credit applicants who are aggrieved by a violation of the Act may recover actual and punitive damages, plus attorneys' fees.

Disclosure Requirements

Title One of the FCCPA, also known as the **Truth-in-Lending Act,** has superseded State disclosure requirements relating to credit terms for both consumer loans and credit sales. Federal disclosure standards must be complied with in every State except those specifically exempted by the Federal Reserve Board. Such an exemption is made only if the State disclosure requirements are substantially the same as the Federal requirements and enforcement is assured. The FCCPA does not eliminate the necessity for creditor compliance with State requirements not covered by, or more stringent than, the requirements of the FCCPA, so long as the State required disclosure is not inconsistent with the FCCPA.

A creditor is required, under both State and Federal statutes, to provide certain information about contract terms to the consumer before he formally incurs the obligation. This information must be provided in a written statement presented to the consumer. Generally, the required disclosure is associated with the cost of credit, that is, interest or sales finance charges. An important requirement in the Truth-in-Lending Act is that sales finance and interest rates must be quoted in terms of an **APR** (*annual percentage rate*) and must be calculated on a uniform basis. Congress required disclosure of this information to encourage comparison of credit terms by consumers, to increase competition among financial institutions, and to facilitate economic stability. Enforcement and interpretation of the Truth-in-Lending Act was assigned to the Federal Reserve Board, which issued **Regulation Z** to carry out this responsibility.

In addition to the cost of the credit, under the Truth-in-Lending Act a creditor must inform the consumers who open revolving or open-ended credit accounts how the finance charge is computed and when it is imposed, what other charges may be levied, and whether a security interest is retained or acquired by the creditor. An **open-ended credit** account is one that permits the debtor to enter into a series of credit transactions that he may pay off in installments or in a lump sum. Examples of this type of credit include most department store credit cards, many gasoline credit cards, Visa cards, and Mastercard. With this type of credit, the creditor is also required to provide a statement of account for each billing period.

Close-ended credit is credit extended for a specified period of time during which periodic payments are generally made in an amount and at a time agreed on in advance. For non-revolving or close-ended credit accounts, the creditor must provide the consumer with information about the total amount financed; the cash price; the number, amount, and due date of installments; delinquency charges; and a description of the security, if any. Examples of this type of transaction include most automobile financing agreements, most real estate purchases, and many other major purchases.

CHAPMAN v. MILLER
Court of Civil Appeals of Texas, 1978.
575 S.W.2d 581.

Facts: Miller purchased a used automobile from Chapman. The installment contract provided for a down payment, six weekly payments, and eighteen monthly payments. The contract, however, failed to describe the credit terms on the side of the contract on which Miller's signature appeared. The notices for Miller to read both sides of the contract were on the top and bottom of the front page, but there was no corresponding notice on the back page. Moreover, the space provided for Miller's signature was on the front page and, thus, did not follow the full content of the document. Miller made some of the payments on time but made five of the monthly payments late. Although Chapman had accepted Miller's late payments before, when the March 1975 payment became overdue, Chapman repossesed the car and notified Miller that the entire balance was then due and payable. When Miller did not pay the balance, Chapman sold the car and determined that Miller was entitled to a refund of $19.69. Miller then brought this action against Chapman for violation of the Federal Truth-in-Lending Act. The trial court found for Miller.

Decision: Judgment for Miller, as modified to $497.08 plus court costs and attorney's fees, is affirmed.

Opinion: Keith, J. Violation of Federal Regulation.   * * * defendant complains that the trial court erred   * * * by holding that his contract violated Regulation Z because the description of the security interest is not on the same side of the paper as the buyer's signature.

The cited section requires that all disclosures which must be made thereunder be made together on:

(1) The note or other instrument evidencing the obligation on the same side of the page and above or adjacent to the place for the customer's signature; or (2) One side of a separate statement which identifies the transaction.

Defendant chose to make his disclosures on the retail credit contract. However, he failed to put all the required disclosures on one side of the contract above plaintiff's signature, *i.e.*, the description of his retained security interest is located on the reverse side of the contract. Relying upon the language found in Southwestern Inv. Co. v. Mannix, [citation], we are of the opinion that the trial court correctly found a violation of Regulation Z.

Defendant claims that he did not have to make all required disclosures on the front side because of the Interpretive Ruling of the Federal Reserve Board, [citation], which allows the required disclosures to be made on both sides of a combination contract and security agreement. This interpretation, however, has a caveat:

> *Provided.* That the amount of the finance charge and the annual percentage rate shall appear on the face of the document, and, if the reverse side is used, the printing on both sides of the document shall be equally clear and conspicuous, both sides shall contain the statement, "NOTICE: See other side for important information," *and the place for the customer's signature shall be provided following the full content of the document.*

The space provided for the plaintiff's signature is on the front page of the contract only and does not follow "the full content of the document." Therefore, defendant has violated [this] Section. [Citation.]

Defendant rationalizes that his notices at the top and bottom of the front side allow him to incorporate by reference all disclosures and conditions from the reverse side into the front side above the signature. The notice at the top of the page provides:

BUYER HAS ELECTED TO PURCHASE FROM SELLER SUBJECT TO THE TERMS AND CONDITIONS AS SET FORTH BELOW AND UPON THE REVERSE SIDE HEREOF, THE FOLLOWING DESCRIBED MOTOR VEHICLE, WHICH BUYER HAS THOROUGHLY INSPECTED AND WHICH MEETS WITH BUYER'S APPROVAL IN ALL RESPECTS:

The notice at the bottom of the page provides: "NOTICE: SEE REVERSE SIDE FOR IMPORTANT INFORMATION, ALL TERMS OF WHICH ARE HEREBY INCORPORATED BY REFERENCE." However, this notice was below plaintiff's signature.

The Truth in Lending Act was enacted and Regulation Z was issued "to assure a meaningful disclosure of credit terms so that the consumer will be able to compare more readily the various credit terms available to him and avoid the uninformed use of credit * * *." [Citations.] Their provisions are detailed and explicit.

As noted in *Charles v. Drauss Co., Ltd.*, [citation]:

> Moreover, liability flows from even minute deviations from the requirements of the statute and of Regulation Z. The statute aims to assure a meaningful disclosure of credit terms so that consumers may shop comparatively for credit * * *. [Citations.] Therefore, the defendant may not escape liability by means of incorporation by reference. The line provided for plaintiff's signature should have been at the end of the contract; her signature so located would show that she knew to read the entire contract—front and back—for all important provisions before signing it. The fact that she did not read any of the contract is immaterial.   * * *

Finance Charge and Statutory Penalty.   * * * both parties contend that the trial court erred . . . by holding that the finance charge in this transaction was $326.99. Defendant claims the finance charge was $199.99, while plaintiff claims it was $423.46. We disagree with both parties.

[Regulation Z] gives instructions on how to determine a finance charge. Applying these rules to the contract before us, we hold that the finance charge is the sum of the time price differential and the official fees, or $249.04. We are not required to include the premiums for property insurance, credit life insurance, or health and accident insurance in the finance charge * * *.

The applicable statutory penalty . . . includes twice the amount of the finance charge, plus court costs and reasonable attorney's fees. [Citations.] In the present case, the proper statutory penalty would have been twice of $249.04, or $498.08, plus court costs and reasonable attorney's fees.

In 1975 the **Fair Credit Billing Act** went into effect to relieve some of the problems and abuses associated with billing errors. This Act sets forth procedures for the consumer to follow in making complaints about specified errors in billing and requires the creditor to explain or correct such errors. Billing errors are defined to include: (1) extensions of credit that were never made or were not made in the amount indicated on the billing statement; (2) undelivered or unaccepted goods or services; (3) incorrect recording of payments or credits; and (4) accounting or computational errors. Until the creditor responds to the complaint, it may not (1) take any action to collect the disputed amount, (2) restrict the use of an open-ended credit account because the disputed amount is unpaid, or (3) report the disputed amount as delinquent.

In 1974 Congress enacted the **Real Estate Settlement Procedures Act** (RESPA) to provide consumers who purchase a home with greater and more timely information on the nature and costs of the settlement process and to protect them from unnecessarily high settlement charges. This Act applies to all federally related mortgage loans and requires advance disclosure to home buyers and sellers of all settlement costs, including attorneys' fees, credit reports, and title insurance. Nearly all first mortgage loans fall within the scope of the Act. RESPA prohibits kickbacks and referral fees and limits the amount home buyers are required to place in escrow accounts to insure payment of real estate taxes and insurance. The Act is administered and enforced by the Secretary of Housing and Urban Development.

Contract Terms

Consumer credit is marketed on a mass basis. Contract documents are frequently printed forms containing blank spaces to be filled in by the creditor. These blank spaces relate to matters usually negotiated at the time of the extension of credit. Standardization and uniformity of contract terms facilitate transfer of the rights of the creditor (in most situations a seller) to a third party, which is usually a bank or finance company.

Almost all States impose statutory ceilings on the amount that may be charged for the extension of consumer credit. Statutes regulating rates also specify what other charges may be made. For example, charges for insurance, official fees, and taxes are usually not considered part of the finance charge. Charges that are incidental to the extension of credit are usually considered part of the finance charge; for example, a service charge or a commission for extending credit. Any charge that does not qualify as an authorized additional charge is treated as part of the finance charge and is subject to the statutory rate ceiling. Other special permitted charges include delinquency and default charges, charges incurred in connection with storing and repairing repossessed goods for sale, reasonable fees for a lawyer who is not a salaried employee of the creditor, and court costs.

Most statutes require a creditor to permit the debtor to pay her obligation in full at any time before the maturity date of the final installment. If the interest charge over the period of the loan was computed in advance and added to the principal of the loan, when making prepayment in full, the debtor is entitled to a refund of the unearned interest already paid.

Aside from provisions relating to cost, the balance of a credit contract deals with the terms of repayment and the remedies of the creditor if payments are delinquent. Usually, payments must be periodic and substantially equal in amount. Balloon payments (loans in which the final payment is much larger than the regular payments; for example, monthly installments of $50 and a final installment is $1,000) may be prohibited. If they are not prohibited, the creditor may be required to refinance the loan at the same rate and with installments in the same amount as the original loan without penalty to the borrower.

In the past, certain consumer purchase transactions were financed in such a way that the purchaser was legally obligated to make full payment of the price to a third party, even though the dealer from whom she bought the goods had committed fraud or the goods were defective. This occurred when the purchaser executed and delivered to the seller a negotiable instrument (promissory note, draft or check), and the seller negotiated it to a holder in due course, who purchased the note for value, in good faith, and without notice that it was overdue or had any defenses or claims attached to it. The buyer's defense that the goods were defective or that the seller had committed fraud, although valid against the seller, were not valid against a holder in due course of the note. To correct this situation by preserving and making available claims and defenses of consumer buyers and borrowers against holders in due course, the FTC adopted a rule that limits the rights of a holder in due course of an instrument evidencing a debt that arises out of a *consumer credit contract*. The rule applies to sellers and lessors of goods. We discuss this rule in Chapter 24.

A similar rule applies to credit card users under the **Fair Credit Billing Act.** The Act preserves a consumer's defense against the issuer provided the consumer had made a good faith attempt to resolve the dispute with the seller, but only if (1) the seller is controlled by the issuer or under common control with the issuer, (2) the card issuer included the seller's promotional literature in the monthly billing statement sent to the card holder, or (3) the sale involves more than $50 and the consumer's billing address is in the same State as or within one hundred miles of the seller's place of business.

Consumer Credit Card Fraud

Consumer credit card fraud has become an increasingly serious problem and now totals approximately $200 million per year. In 1984 Congress enacted the **Credit Card Fraud Act,** which closed many loopholes in prior law. The Act prohibits the following practices: (1) possessing unauthorized cards, (2) counterfeiting or altering credit cards, (3) using account numbers alone, and (4) using cards obtained from a third party with his consent, even if the third party conspires to report the cards as stolen. It also imposes stiffer, criminal penalties for violation.

The FCCPA provides protection to the *credit card holder* from loss by limiting the card hold-

er's liability for unauthorized use of a credit card to $50. The card issuer may collect up to that amount for unauthorized use only if (1) the card has been accepted; (2) the issuer has furnished adequate notice of potential liability to the card holder; (3) the issuer has provided the card holder with a statement of the means by which the card issuer may be notified of the loss or theft of the credit card; (4) the unauthorized use occurs before the card holder has notified the card issuer of the loss or theft; and (5) the card issuer has provided a method by which the user can be identified as the person authorized to use the card.

Fair Reportage

Because consumers are usually granted credit only after an investigation into the consumer's creditworthiness, it is essential that the information on which such decisions are made is accurate and current. To this end, in 1970 Congress enacted the **Fair Credit Reporting Act,** which applies to consumer reports used for purposes of securing employment, insurance, and credit. The Act prohibits including inaccurate or specified obsolete information in consumer reports. The Act requires consumer reporting agencies to give written advance notice to consumers that an investigative report may be made. The consumer may request information regarding the nature and substance of all information in the consumer reporting agency's files, the source of the information, and the names of all recipients of the consumer reports furnished for employment purposes within the preceding two years and for other purposes within the preceding six months.

If the consumer notifies the reporting agency of disagreement with the accuracy and completeness of information in the file, the agency must then reinvestigate the matter within a reasonable time unless the complaint is frivolous or irrelevant. If reinvestigation proves that the information is inaccurate, it must be promptly deleted. If the dispute remains unresolved after the reinvestigation, the consumer may submit a brief statement setting forth the nature of the dispute, and this must be incorporated into the report.

Creditors' Remedies

A primary concern of creditors is their rights if a debtor defaults or is late in payment. When the credit charge is precomputed, the creditor may impose a delinquency charge for late payments, subject to statutory limits for such charges. If instead of being delinquent, the consumer defaults, the creditor may declare the entire balance of the debt immediately due and payable and may sue on the debt. What other courses of action are open to the creditor depend on his security. Various security provisions included in consumer credit contracts are a co-signer, an assignment of wages, a security interest in the goods sold, a security interest in other real or personal property of the debtor, and a confession of judgment clause (i.e., a clause by the defendant giving the plaintiff power to enter judgment against the defendant). Wage assignments, however, are prohibited by some States. In most States and under the FCCPA, a limitation is imposed on the amount that may be deducted from an individual's wages during any pay period. In addition, the FCCPA prohibits an employer from discharging an employee solely because of a creditor's exercise of an assignment of wages in connection with any one debt.

Even where assignments of wages are prohibited, the creditor may still reach the wages of the consumer through garnishment. But garnishment is only available in a court proceeding to enforce the collection of a judgment. The FCCPA and State statutes contain exemption provisions that limit the amount of wages subject to garnishment.

In the case of credit sales, the seller may retain a security interest in the goods sold. Many States impose restrictions on other security the creditor may obtain. Where the debt is secured by property as collateral, the creditor, on default by the debtor, may take possession of the property and, subject to the provisions of the Uniform Commercial Code, either retain it in full satisfaction of the debt or sell it and, if the proceeds are less than the outstanding debt, sue the debtor for the balance and obtain a deficiency judgment. The UCC provides that where the buyer of goods has paid 60 percent of the purchase price of the goods or 60 percent of a loan secured by consumer goods, the secured creditor may not retain the property in full satisfaction but must sell the goods and pay to the buyer that part of the sale proceeds in excess of the balance due. Secured transactions are discussed in Chapter 37.

In addition, Federal regulation prohibits a credit seller or lender from obtaining a consumer's grant of a nonpossessory security interest in household goods. This rule does not apply to purchase money security interests or to pledges. Household goods include clothing, furniture, appliances, kitchenware, personal effects, one radio, and one television. Works of art, other electronic entertainment equipment, antiques, and jewelry are specifically excluded. This rule prevents a lender or seller from obtaining a nonpurchase money security interest covering the consumer's household goods.

In 1977 Congress enacted the **Fair Debt Collection Practices Act** to eliminate abusive, deceptive, and unfair practices in collecting consumer debts by debt collection agencies. The Act does not apply to the creditors themselves. Rather, the Act provides that any debt collector who communicates with a person other than the consumer for the purpose of acquiring information about the location of the consumer may not state that the consumer owes any debt. Moreover, the Act prohibits a number of abusive collection practices, including: (1) communication with the consumer at unusual or inconvenient hours; (2) communication with the consumer if she is represented by an attorney; (3) harassing, oppressive, or abusive conduct, such as threats of violence or obscene language; (4) false, deceptive, or misleading representations or means of collection; and (5) unfair or unconscionable means to collect any debt. The Act is enforced by the Federal Trade Commission, and consumers may recover damages from the collection agency for violations of the Act.

CONSUMER HEALTH AND SAFETY

In 1972 Congress enacted the **Consumer Product Safety Act,** which has the following purposes:

1. to protect the public against unreasonable risk of injury associated with consumer products;
2. to assist consumers in evaluating the comparative safety of consumer products;
3. to develop uniform safety standards for consumer products and to minimize conflicting State and local regulations; and
4. to promote research and investigation into the causes and prevention of product-related deaths, illnesses, and injuries.

The Act creates an independent regulatory Federal agency, the Consumer Product Safety Commission (CPSC), consisting of five commissioners, to carry out the Act's mandate.

To achieve its basic goal of reducing the number of injuries, deaths, or serious illnesses caused by products, the CPSC has authority to (1) work with consumers and industry to promote voluntary standards for product safety, (2) set and enforce mandatory standards, (3) ban unsafe products when a safety standard would not adequately protect the public, (4) order recalls of hazardous products, (5) provide information to help consumers select and properly use safe products, and (6) work with State and local governments to promote consumer safety.

The CPSC has jurisdiction over all consumer products except those specifically exempted. Exempted products include motor vehicles, aircraft, food, drugs, cosmetics, medical devices, boats, tobacco, firearms, meat, poultry, and eggs.

The most significant provision of the Act is the power it confers on the CPSC to issue and enforce mandatory product safety rules. First, the CPSC is empowered to promulgate *performance* and *descriptive standards* when it finds that these standards are reasonably necessary to prevent or reduce an unreasonable risk of injury associated with a specific product. Whenever possible, the standards should establish performance requirements rather than describing composition, design, construction, or packaging. Second, the CPSC may promulgate *labeling standards* for warnings or instructions when the risk of injury cannot be sufficiently reduced through performance or descriptive standards. Third, the CPSC may issue an order banning any *hazardous product* from the market whenever the Commission determines that a consumer product presents an unreasonable risk of injury and that no practicable safety standards would adequately protect the public. In the case of an *imminent hazard*, the CPSC may go directly to district court to obtain an injunction to stop the distribution of the product or for authorization to seize the product.

In addition, a number of Federal statutes impose labeling and packaging requirements designed to provide the consumer with accurate information and adequate warnings about specific products. These include the Fair Packaging and Labeling Act; the Food, Drugs, and Cosmetic Act; the Fur Products Labeling Act; the Wholesome Meat Act; the Flammable Fabrics Act; the Cigarette Labeling and Advertising Act; the Wool Products Labeling Act; the Wholesome Poultry Products Act; the Special Packaging of Household Substances for the Protection of Children Act; and the Refrigerator Safety Act.

CHAPTER SUMMARY

Federal Trade Commission	**Purpose** to prevent unfair methods of competition and unfair or deceptive acts or practices
	Standards
	■ *Unfairness* requries injury to be (1) substantial, (2) not be outweighed by any countervailing benefit, and (3) unavoidable by reasonable actions of consumers
	■ *Deception* misrepresentation, omission, or practice that is likely to mislead the consumer acting reasonably in the circumstances
	■ *Ad Substantiation* requires advertisers to have a reasonable basis for their claims
	Remedies
	■ *Cease and Desist Orders* command to stop doing the act in question
	■ *Affirmative Disclosure* requires an advertiser to include certain information in its ad so that it is not deceptive
	■ *Corrective Advertising* requires an advertiser to disclose that previous ads were deceptive
	■ *Multiple Product Order* requires an advertiser to cease and desist from deceptive statements regarding all products it sells

Consumer Purchases	**Uniform Commercial Code** prohibits unconscionable contracts and imposes implied warranties
	Federal Warranty Protection applies to sellers of consumer goods who give written warranties
	■ *Presale Disclosure* requires terms of warranty to be simple and readily understood and to be made available before the sale
	■ *Labeling Requirement* requires warrantor to inform consumers of their legal rights under a warranty (full or limited)
	■ *Disclaimer Limitation* prohibits a written warranty from disclaiming any implied warranty
	Consumer Right of Rescission in certain instances a consumer is granted a brief period of time during which she may rescind (cancel) an otherwise binding obligation

Consumer Credit	**Definition** any credit transaction involving goods, services, or land for personal, household, or family purposes
	Access to the Market discrimination in extending credit on the basis of sex, marital status, race, color, religion, national origin, or age is prohibited

	Disclosure Requirements
	■ *Truth-In-Lending Act* requires creditor to provide certain information including APR (annual percentage rate) about contract terms to the consumer before he formally incurs the obligation
	■ *Fair Credit Billing Act* establishes procedures for the consumer to follow in making complaints about specified errors in billing and requires the creditor to explain or correct such errors
	■ *Real Estate Settlement Procedures Act* provides consumers who purchase a home with greater and more timely information on the nature and costs of settlement and protects them from unnecessarily high settlement charges
	Contract Terms statutory and judicial limitations have been imposed on the obligations of a consumer
	Consumer Credit Card Fraud Act prohibits certain fraudulent practices and limits a card holder's liability for unauthorized use of a credit card to $50
	Fair Credit Reporting consumer credit reports are prohibited from containing inaccurate or obsolete information
	Creditors' Remedies Federal and State regulations govern creditors' remedies such as delinquency charges, acceleration clauses, taking possession of collateral, and assignment of wages

Consumer Health and Safety	**Consumer Product Safety Act** Federal statute enacted to:
	■ *Protect public against unsafe products*
	■ *Assist consumers in evaluating products*
	■ *Develop uniform safety standard*
	■ *Promote safety research*
	Other Federal Safety Statutes

QUESTIONS

1. Discuss the role of the FTC and the major enforcement sanctions that it may use.
2. Discuss the principal provisions of the Magnuson-Moss Act and distinguish between a full and a limited warranty.
3. Discuss what information a creditor must provide a consumer before the consumer incurs the obligation. Distinguish between open-ended and close-ended credit.
4. Outline the major remedies that are available to a creditor.
5. Discuss the role and workings of the CPSC.

PROBLEMS

1. The FTC brings a deceptive trade practice action against Beneficial Finance Company based on Beneficial's use of its "instant tax refund" slogan. The FTC argues that Beneficial's advertising a tax refund loan or instant tax refund is deceptive in that the loan is not in any way connected with a tax refund but is merely Beneficial's everyday loan based on the applicant's creditworthiness. Decision?

2. Brenda borrows $1,000 from Lincoln for one year. Brenda agrees to pay Lincoln $200 in interest on the loan and to repay the loan in twelve monthly installments of $100. The contract that Lincoln provides and Brenda signs specifies that the APR is 20 percent. Brenda now contends that the contract violates the FCCPA. Decision?

3. A consumer entered into an agreement with Rent-It Corporation for the rental of a television set at a charge of $17 per week. The agreement also provides that if the renter chooses to rent the set for seventy-eight consecutive weeks, title will be transferred. The consumer now contends that the agreement is really a sales agreement and not a lease and therefore is a credit sale subject to the Truth-in-Lending Act. Decision?

4. Central Adjustment Bureau allegedly threatened Consumer with a lawsuit, service at his office, and attachment and sale of his property in order to collect a debt, although it did not intend to carry out the threat and did not have the authority to commence litigation. On some notices sent to Consumer, Central failed to disclose that it was attempting to collect a debt. In addition, Central, it is charged, sent notices demanding payment that purported to be from attorneys but were written, signed, and sent by Central. Decision?

5. The Giant Development Company undertakes a massive real estate venture to sell 9,000 one-acre unimproved lots in Utah. The company advertises the project nationally. Arrington, a resident of New York, learns of the opportunity and requests information about the project. The company provides Arrington with a small advertising brochure that contains no information about the developer and the land. The brochure consists of vague descriptions of the joys of home ownership and nothing else. Arrington purchases a lot. Two weeks after entering into the agreement, Arrington wishes to rescind the contract. Will Arrington prevail?

6. Jane Jones, a married woman, applies for a credit card from Exxon but is refused credit. Jane is bewildered as to why she was turned down. What are her legal rights in this situation?

7. On a beautiful Saturday in October, Francie decides to take the twenty-mile ride from her home in New Jersey into New York City in order to do some shopping. Francie finds that Brown's Retail Sales, Inc., has a terrific sale on television sets and decides to surprise her husband with a new color TV. She purchases the set from Brown's on her American Express credit card for $450. When the set is delivered, Francie discovers that it does not work. Brown's refuses to repair or replace it or to refund the money. Francie therefore refuses to pay American Express for the television. American Express brings a suit against Francie. Decision?

8. Frank finds Thomas's wallet, which contains many credit cards and Thomas's identification. By using Thomas's identification and Visa card, Frank goes on a shopping spree and runs up $5,000 in charges. Thomas does not discover that he has lost his wallet until the following day, when he promptly notifies his Visa bank. How much can Visa collect from Thomas?

9. Robert applies to Northern National Bank for a loan. Before granting the loan, Northern requests that Callis Credit Agency provide it with a credit report on Robert. Callis reports that three years previously Robert had embezzled money from his employer. Based on this report, Northern rejects Robert's loan application.
(a) Robert demands to know why the loan was rejected, but Northern refuses to divulge the information, arguing that it is privileged. Is Robert entitled to the information?
(b) Assume that Robert obtains the information and alleges that it is inaccurate. What recourse does Robert have?

10. Colgate-Palmolive Co. produced a television advertisement that dramatically demonstrated the effectiveness of its Rapid Shave shaving cream. The ad purported to show the shaving cream used to shave sandpaper. But because actual sandpaper appeared on television to be regular colored paper, Colgate substituted a sheet of Plexiglas with sand sprinkled on it. The FTC brought an action against Colgate claiming that Colgate's ad was deceptive. Colgate defended on the ground that the consumer was merely being shown a representation of the actual test. Decision?

11. In 1982 several manufacturers introduced into the American market a product known as All-Terrain Vehicles (ATVs). ATVs are motorized bikes that sit on three or four low-pressure balloon tires and are meant to be driven off paved roads. Almost immediately, the Consumer Product Safety Commission began receiving reports of deaths and serious injuries. As the number of injuries and deaths increased, the CPSC began investigating ATV hazards. According to CPSC staff, children under the age of sixteen accounted for roughly half the deaths and injuries associated with this product.

What type of rule, if any, may the CPSC issue for ATVs?

COMPUTER RESEARCH PROBLEMS

1. William Thompson was denied credit based on an inaccurate credit report compiled by the San Antonio Retail Merchant's Association. The Association confused Thompson's credit history with that of another William Thomspon and failed to use social security numbers to distinguish the two men. The second Mr. Thompson had a poor credit history. Thompson made numerous attempts to have the Association correct its mistake, but the error was never corrected. Thompson sued the Association for violation of the Fair Credit Reporting Act. Decision?

2. Thompson Medical Company manufactures and sells Aspercreme, a topical analgesic. Aspercreme is a pain reliever which contains no

aspirin. Thompson's avertisements strongly suggest that Aspercreme is related to aspirin, however, by claiming that it "provided the strong relief of aspirin right where you hurt." The Federal Trade Commission brought a complaint against Thompson for false and misleading advertising of Aspercreme. Decision?

3. Mary Smith bought a car from Doug Chapman under an installment sales contract. Smith carried the insurance on the car, as required by the contract. Shortly after Smith purchased the car, it was wrecked in an accident. Smith's insurance company paid Chapman the installments still owed on the car as well as Smith's equity in the car. Smith requested a new car from Chapman under the same installment plan as the first car. Chapman refused claiming that the contract for the first car allowed him to retain the equity amount as security interest and that Smith understood this as a term of the contract. The provision relating to the security interest appeared on the back of the contract although the Truth in Lending Act required it to be on the front side. The front side had a notice referring to provisions on the back side. Smith sued Chapman for violation of the Truth in Lending Act. Decision?

46 INTERNATIONAL BUSINESS LAW

Today every aspect of business, including business law, requires some understanding of international business practices. Since World War II, the entire global economy has become increasingly interconnected. Many U.S. corporations now have investments or manufacturing facilities in other countries, while at the same time there is an increase in the number of foreign corporations with business operations in the United States. Furthermore, whether a domestic corporation exports goods or not, it competes with imports from many other countries. For example, U.S. firms face competition from Japanese electronics and automobiles, French wines and fashions, German machinery, and Taiwanese textiles. In order to compete effectively, U.S. firms need to be aware of international business practices and developments.

Laws vary greatly from country to country: what is required by law in one nation may be forbidden by law in another. To make matters more complicated, there is no single authority in international law that can compel countries to act. When the laws of two or more nations conflict, or when one party has violated an agreement and the other party wishes to enforce it or recover damages, it is often very confusing to establish who will adjudicate the matter, which laws will be applied, what remedies are available, or where the matter should be decided. Nonetheless, because of the growing impact of the global economy, it is important that you have a basic understanding of international business law.

THE INTERNATIONAL ENVIRONMENT

International law includes the law that deals with the conduct and relations of nation-states and international organizations as well as some of their relations with persons. Unlike domestic law, as a general rule international law cannot be enforced. International courts do not have compulsory jurisdiction to resolve international disputes. These courts, however, have authority to resolve a dispute if the parties to the dispute *accept* the court's jurisdiction over the matter. Furthermore, if an international law has been adopted as law by a sovereign nation, that law will be enforced by that country to the same extent as all of its domestic laws. In this section of the chapter we examine some of the sources and institutions of international law, including the International Court of Justice, regional trade communities, and international trade agreements.

International Court of Justice

The United Nations, which is probably the most famous international organization, has a judiciary branch called the International Court of Justice (ICJ). The ICJ consists of fifteen judges, no two of whom may be from the same sovereign state, elected for a nine-year term by a majority of both the U.N. General Assembly and the U.N. Security Council. The usefulness of the ICJ is limited, however, because only nations (not private individuals or corporations) may be parties to an action before the court. Furthermore, the ICJ has contentious jurisdiction only if the nations who are parties agree to allow the ICJ to decide the case and agree to be bound by its decision. Moreover, because the ICJ cannot enforce its rulings, countries that do not like a decision by the ICJ may choose to ignore it. Consequently, few nations choose to submit their disputes to the ICJ.

The ICJ also has advisory jurisdiction if requested by a U.N. organ or specialized U.N. agency. Neither sovereign states nor individuals have standing to request an advisory opinion. These opinions are nonbinding, and the requesting U.N. agency usually votes to decide whether to follow the opinion.

Regional Trade Communities

Of much greater significance are international organizations, conferences, and treaties that focus on business and trade regulation. Regional trade communities, such as the European Economic Community (EEC), promote common trade policies among member nations. The EEC, better known as the Common Market, was formed in 1957 by the Treaty of Rome in order to remove trade barriers between the member nations and to unify their economic policies. The EEC now has twelve members (Belgium, France, Italy, Luxemburg, the Netherlands, West Germany, Denmark, Ireland, the United Kingdom, Greece, Portugal, and Spain) with a combined annual gross product of around $3 trillion. The EEC is the largest importer of U.S. made goods. The EEC has the power to make rules that are binding on member nations and that preempt member nations' domestic laws. In order to achieve free movement of goods among member states, the EEC has committed to establishing a truly free trade market by 1992. Some of the other important regional trade communities include the Central American Common Market (CACM), the Caribbean Community (CARICOM), the Association of South East Asian Nations (ASEAN), the Andean Common Market (ANCOM), the Economic Community of West African States (ECOWAS), and the Union Douaniere et Economique et l'Afrique Centrale (UDEAC). There is also the Council for Mutual Economic Cooperation (COMECON) made up of the centrally planned economies of eastern Europe, including Bulgaria, Czechoslovakia, East Germany, Hungary, Poland, Romania, and the Soviet Union.

International Treaties

A **treaty** is an agreement between or among independent nations. As discussed in Chapter 1, the U.S. Constitution authorizes the president to enter into treaties with the advice and consent of the Senate "providing two-thirds of the Senators present concur." The U.S. Constitution provides that all valid treaties are "the law of the land," having the legal force of a Federal statute.

Nations have entered into bilateral and multilateral treaties in order to facilitate and regulate trade and to protect their national interests. In addition, treaties have been used to serve as constitutions of international organizations, to establish general international law, to transfer territory, to settle disputes, to secure human rights, and to protect investments. The Treaty Section of the Office of Legal Affairs within the United Nations Secretariat is responsible for registering and publishing treaties and agreements among member nations. Since its inception in 1946, the U.N. Secretariat has registered and published over 30,000 treaties that expressly or indirectly concern international business.

Probably the most important multilateral trade treaty is the General Agreement on Tariffs and Trade (GATT). With almost 100 participants, the signatories of GATT represent over four-fifths of world trade. The basic purpose of GATT is to facilitate the flow of trade by establishing agreements on potential trade barriers such as import quotas, customs, export regulations, antidumping restrictions (the prohibition against selling goods for less than their fair market value), subsidies, and import fees. This is accomplished by GATT's most favored nation provision, which states that all signatories must treat each other as favorably as they treat any other country. Thus, any privilege, immunity, or favor given to one country must be given to all. Nevertheless, nations may give preferential treatment to developing nations and may also enter into free trade areas with one or more other nations. A free trade area permits countries to discriminate in favor of their free trade partners provided that the agreement covers substantially all trade among the free trade partners. A second important principle adopted by GATT is that where protection is given to domestic industries, it should be in the form of a customs tariff as opposed to other more trade-inhibiting measures.

JURISDICTION OVER ACTIONS OF FOREIGN GOVERNMENTS

In this section we will focus upon the power, and the limits upon that power, of a sovereign nation to exercise jurisdiction over a foreign nation or to take over property owned by foreign citizens. More specifically, we will examine state immunities (the principle of sovereign immunity and the act of state doctrine) and the power of a state to take foreign investment property.

Sovereign Immunity

One of the oldest concepts in international law is that every nation has absolute and total authority over what goes on within its own territory. It has also been long recognized, however, that in order to maintain international relations and trade, a host country must refrain from imposing its laws on a foreign sovereign nation present in that host country. This principle of absolute immunity of a foreign sovereign from the courts of the host country is known as **sovereign immunity.** Originally, all acts of a foreign sovereign nation within a host country were considered immune from the host country's laws. In modern times, a distinction is made between public and commercial acts of a foreign nation. Only public acts, such as those concerning diplomatic activity, internal administration, or armed forces, will be granted sovereign immunity by the host country. When a foreign nation engages in trade or commercial activities, that nation subjects itself to the jurisdiction of the courts of the host country with respect to disputes arising out of those commercial activities.

In 1976 Congress enacted the Foreign Sovereign Immunities Act in order to establish legislatively when immunity will be extended to foreign nations. The Act specifically provides that a foreign state shall *not* be immune from the jurisdiction of courts of the United States or of the States if the suit is based upon (1) a commercial activity carried on in the United States by the foreign state, (2) an act performed in the United States in connection with a commercial activity of the foreign state carried on elsewhere, or (3) a commercial activity of a foreign state carried on outside the United States that causes a direct effect in the United States. Examples of commercial activities include a contract by a foreign government to buy provisions or equipment for its armed forces; a contract by a foreign government to construct or make repairs on a government building; and a sale of a service or a product by a foreign government or its leasing of property, borrowing money, or investing in a security of a U.S. corporation. Examples of public (noncommercial) activities to which sovereign immunity would extend include nationalizing a corporation, determining the limitations upon the use of natural resources, and granting licenses to export a natural resource.

TEXAS TRADING & MILLING CORPORATION v. FEDERAL REPUBLIC OF NIGERIA
United States Court of Appeals, Second Circuit, 1981.
647 F.2d 300.

Facts: Nigeria, experiencing an economic boom due to exports of high-grade oil, embarked on an infrastructure development plan. Accordingly, Nigeria entered into at least 109 contracts with 68 suppliers for the purchase of cement at a price of almost $1 billion. Among the contracting suppliers were four American corporations, including Texas Trading & Milling Corporation. Nigeria misjudged the cement market (having anticipated only a 20 percent fulfillment rate) and was forced to repudiate most of the contracts. Texas Trading & Milling Corporation and three other American companies brought suit alleging anticipatory breach of contract. Nigeria claimed immunity under the Foreign Sovereign Immunities Act of 1976. In three of the cases the district court held jurisdiction to be present and proceeded to trial. In one of the cases the district court dismissed for lack of jurisdiction.

Decision: The three cases finding jurisdiction affirmed; the case denying jurisdiction reversed and remanded.

Opinion: Kaufman, J.   [Section 1605 of the Foreign Sovereign Immunities Act of 1976 (FSIA)] provides, in part:

(a) A foreign state shall not be immune from the jurisdiction of courts of the United States or of the States in any case—

* * *

(2) in which the action is based upon a commercial activity carried on in the United States by the foreign state; or upon an act performed in the United States in connection with a commercial activity of the foreign state elsewhere; or upon an act outside the territory of the United States in connection with a commercial activity of the foreign state elsewhere and that act causes a direct effect in the United States.

Crucial to each of the three clauses of [this section] is the phrase "commercial activity." In it is lodged centuries of Anglo-American and civil law precedent construing the term "sovereign immunity." If the activity is not "commercial," but, rather, is "governmental," then the foreign state is entitled to immunity under [this section], and "original jurisdiction" is not present under [citation].

For the definition of "commercial activity," we turn to subsection 1603(d), which provides:

(d) A "commercial activity" means either a regular course of commercial conduct or a particular commercial transaction or act. The commercial character of an activity shall be determined by reference to the nature of the course of conduct or particular transaction or act, rather than by reference to its purpose.

If "commercial activity" under § 1603(d) is present, and if it bears the relation to the United States required by § 1605(a)(2), then the foreign state is "not entitled to immunity," and the district court has statutory subject matter jurisdiction over the claim through [citation]. And, if the exercise of that jurisdiction falls within the judicial power set forth by Article III of the Constitution, subject matter jurisdiction over the claim exists.

* * *

The determination of whether particular behavior is "commercial" is perhaps the most important decision a court faces in an FSIA suit. This problem is significant because the primary purpose of the Act is to "restrict" the immunity of a foreign state to suits involving a foreign state's public acts. [Citation.] If the activity is not "commercial," it satisfies none of the three clauses of § 1605(a)(2), and the foreign state is (at least under that subsection) immune from suit. Unfortunately, the definition of "commercial" is the one issue on which the Act provides almost no guidance at all. Subsection 1603(d) advances the inquiry somewhat, for it provides: "The commercial character of an activity shall be determined by reference to the nature of the course of conduct or particular transaction or act, rather than by reference to its purpose." No provision of the Act, however, defines "commercial."

Congress deliberately left the meaning open and, as noted above, "put [its] faith in the U.S. courts to work out progressively, on a case-by-case basis . . . the distinction between commercial and governmental." [Citations.] We are referred to no less than three separate sources of authority to resolve this fundamental definitional question.

* * *

Under each of these three standards, Nigeria's cement contracts and letters of credit qualify as "commercial activity." Lord Denning, writing in [citation], with his usual erudition and clarity, stated: "If a government department goes into the market places of the world and buys boots or cement—as a commercial transaction—that government department should be subject to all the rules of the marketplace." Nigeria's activity here is in the nature of a private contract for the purchase of goods. Its purpose—to build roads, army barracks, whatever—is irrelevant. Accordingly, courts in other nations have uniformly held Nigeria's 1975 cement purchase program and appurtenant letters of credit to be "commercial activity," and have denied the defense of sovereign immunity. We find defendants' activity here to constitute "commercial activity," . . .

* * *

Our rulings today vindicate more than Congressional intent. They affirm the right of all participants in the marketplace of the world to be treated as equals, and to ascribe to principles of trade which found their birth in the law merchant, centuries ago. Corporations can enter contracts without fear that the defense of sovereign immunity will be inequitably interposed, and foreign states can bargain without paying a premium required by a trader in anticipation of a judgment-proof client. Commerce is fostered, and all interests are advanced.

CAREY v. NATIONAL OIL CORPORATION
United States Court of Appeals, Second Circuit, 1979.
592 F.2d 673.

Facts: New England Petroleum Corporation (NEPCO), a New York corporation, was in the business of selling fuel oil in the United States. PETCO, a refinery incorporated in the Bahamas, was a wholly owned subsidiary of NEPCO. In 1968 PETCO entered into a long-term contract to purchase crude oil from Chevron Oil Trading (COT), which held 50 percent of an oil concession in Libya. In 1973 Libya nationalized COT and several other foreign-owned oil concessions. COT was thereby forced to terminate its contract with PETCO. In order to secure needed oil supplies, PETCO entered into a new contract with National Oil Corporation (NOC), which was wholly owned by the Libyan government. This contract was at a substantially higher price than the original contract with COT. The following month, Libya declared an oil embargo on exports to the United States, the Netherlands, and the Bahamas. Accordingly, NOC cancelled its contracts with PETCO. After oil prices rose dramatically, NOC accepted bids for new contracts to replace the ones inactivated by the embargo. Suit was brought by NEPCO against the Libyan government and NOC alleging breach of contract. The district court dismissed the case for lack of jurisdiction and the plaintiff appealed.

Decision: Judgment for Libya and NOC affirmed.

Opinion: Per Curiam Foreign states are immune from suit in the courts of the United States for many of their acts, and thus federal courts have no jurisdiction in disputes involving such public acts. Specific exceptions to this general grant of immunity were carefully mapped out by Congress in the Foreign Sovereign Immunities Act of 1976 [citation].

Appellants claim, most relevantly, that the events involved in this case come within the exception to immunity which allows U.S. jurisdiction where a claim is based on "an act outside the territory of the United States in connection with a commercial activity of the foreign state elsewhere and that act causes a direct effect in the United States." [Citation.] We find no direct effect in the United States here.

We assume that Congress chose the language in the act purposefully. Section 1605(a)(2) speaks of acts which have a "direct" effect in the United States. The legislative history of this section makes clear that it embodies the standard set out in *International Shoe Co. v. Washington*, [citation], that in order to satisfy due process requirements, a defendant over whom jurisdiction is to be exercised must have "certain minimum contacts with [the forum state] such that the maintenance of the suit does not offend 'traditional notions of fair play and substantive justice.' " That standard has not been met here.

PETCO is a Bahamian corporation. Though a subsidiary of NEPCO, it was a separate corporate entity, and we will not here "pierce the corporate veil" in favor of those who created that veil. The cancellation of the contracts between NOC and PETCO, and the overcharge on the charters, had a direct effect on PETCO as a party to those contracts, but not in the United States. Similarly, while there was an admitted effect on NEPCO, an American company, that effect can only be deemed indirect, through NEPCO's relations with PETCO and Antco, whose dealings with NOC were entirely outside the United States.

At no time did NOC or Libya "purposely avail itself of the privilege" of conducting business in the United States. The product which was destined for the United States, the refined oil, was a different substance than the crude oil sold by NOC to PETCO, so there was no real entering of the marketplace in the United States.

The appellants claim that the Libyan government and NOC were aware that the refineries in the Bahamas were being used primarily to channel oil into the United States. Appellants also contend that the Libyan oil embargo was expressly aimed at affecting the United States. Even if these allegations are true, they do not fulfill the "minimum contacts" requirement of *International Shoe*, and thus cannot reach the level of "direct" effects described in the statute. The claims concerning the charter parties fail for the same reason.

Act of State Doctrine

The **act of state doctrine** provides that the judicial branch of a nation should not question the validity of actions taken by a foreign government within that foreign sovereign's own borders. In 1897 the U.S. Supreme Court de-scribed the act of state doctrine in terms that remain valid today: "Every sovereign State is bound to respect the independence of every other sovereign State, and the courts of one country will not sit in judgment on the acts of the government of another done within its own territory."

UNITED STATES v. BELMONT
United States Supreme Court, 1937.
301 U.S. 324, 57 S.Ct. 758.

Facts: Prior to 1918 a Russian corporation had deposited sums of money with August Belmont, a private banker doing business in New York City. In 1918 the Soviet government nationalized the corporation and appropriated all of the corporation's property and assets, including the deposit account with Belmont. The deposit became the property of the Soviet government until 1933, when it was released and assigned to the U.S. government as part of an international compact between the United States and the Soviet Union. The purpose of this arrangement was to bring about a final settlement of the claims and counterclaims between the two countries. The United States brought an action to recover the deposit from Belmont. The district court held against the United States because the act of nationalization by the Soviets was a confiscation prohibited by the Fifth Amendment to the U.S. Constitution and also violated the public policy of New York. The Court of Appeals affirmed and the United States appealed.

Decision: Judgment reversed.

Opinion: Sutherland, J. First. We do not pause to inquire whether in fact there was any policy of the state of New York to be infringed, since we are of opinion that no state policy can prevail against the international compact here involved.

This court has held, [citation], that every sovereign state must recognize the independence of every other sovereign state; and that the courts of one will not sit in judgment upon the acts of the government of another, done within its own territory.

* * * This court held that the conduct of foreign relations was committed by the Constitution to the political departments of the government, and the propriety of what may be done in the exercise of this political power was not subject to judicial inquiry or decision; that who is the sovereign of a territory is not a judicial question, but one the determination of which by the political departments conclusively binds the courts; and that recognition by these departments is retroactive and validates all actions and conduct of the government so recognized from the commencement of its existence. "The principle," we said, [citation], "that the conduct of one independent government cannot be successfully questioned in the courts of another is as applicable to a case involving the title to property brought within the custody of a court, such as we have here, as it was held to be to the cases cited, in which claims for damages were based upon acts done in a foreign country, for it rests at last upon the highest considerations of international comity and expediency. To permit the validity of the acts of one sovereign state to be reëxamined and perhaps condemned by the courts of another would very certainly 'imperil the amicable relations between governments and vex the peace of nations.' " * * *

* * *

We take judicial notice of the fact that coincident with the assignment set forth in the complaint, the President recognized the Soviet government, and normal diplomatic relations were established between that government and the government of the United States, followed by an exchange of ambassadors. The effect of this was to validate, so far as this country is concerned, all acts of the Soviet government here involved from the commencement of its existence. The recognition, establishment of diplomatic relations, the assignment, and agreements with respect thereto, were all parts of one transaction, resulting in an international compact between the two governments. That the negotiations, acceptance of the assignment and agreements and understandings in respect thereof were within the competence of the President may not be doubted. Governmental power over internal affairs is distributed between the national government and the several states. Governmental power over external affairs is not distributed, but is vested exclusively in the national government. And in respect of what was done here, the Executive had authority to speak as the sole organ of that government. The assignment and the agreements in connection therewith did not, as in the case of treaties, as that term is used in the treaty making clause of the Constitution (article 2,§ 2), require the advice and consent of the Senate.

* * *

Plainly, the external powers of the United States are to be exercised without regard to state laws or policies. The supremacy of a treaty in this respect has been recognized from the beginning. Mr. Madison, in the Virginia Convention, said that if a treaty does not supersede existing state laws, as far as they contravene its operation, the treaty would be ineffective. "To counteract it by the supremacy of the state laws, would bring on the Union the just charge of national perfidy, and involve us in war." [Citations.] And while this rule in respect of treaties is established by the express language of clause 2, article 6, of the Constitution, the same rule would result in the case of all international compacts and agreements from the very fact that complete power over international affairs is in the national government and is not and cannot be subject to any curtailment or interference on the part of the several states. [Citation.] In respect of all international negotiations and compacts, and in respect of our foreign relations generally, state lines disappear. As to such purposes the state of New York does not exist. Within the field of its powers, whatever the United States rightfully undertakes, it necessarily has warrant to consummate. And when judicial authority is involved in aid of such consummation, State Constitutions, state laws, and state policies are irrelevant to the inquiry and decision. It is inconceivable that any of them can be interposed as an obstacle to the effective operation of a federal constitutional power. [Citations.]

Second. The public policy of the United States relied upon as a bar to the action is that declared by the Constitution, namely, that private property shall not be taken without just compensation. But the answer is that our Constitution, laws, and policies have no extraterritorial operation, unless in respect of our own citizens. [Citation.] What another country has done in the way of taking over property of its nationals, and especially of its corporations, is not a matter for judicial consideration here. Such nationals must look to their own government for any redress to which they may be entitled. So far as the record shows, only the rights of the Russian corporation have been affected by what has been done; and it will be time enough to consider the rights of our nationals when, if ever, by proper judicial proceeding, it shall be made to appear that they are so affected as to entitle them to judicial relief. The substantive right to the moneys, as now disclosed, became vested in the Soviet government as the successor to the corporation; and this right that government has passed to the United States. It does not appear that respondents have any interest in the matter beyond that of a custodian. Thus far no question under the Fifth Amendment is involved.

In the United States, there are several possible exceptions to the act of state doctrine. Some courts hold (1) that a sovereign may waive its right to raise the act of state defense, and (2) that the doctrine may be inapplicable to commercial activities of a foreign sovereign. In addition, by Federal statute, the act of state doctrine will not be applied to claims to specific property located in the United States based on the assertion that a foreign state confiscated the property in violation of international law, unless the president of the United States determines that the act of state doctrine should be applied in a particular case.

Taking of Foreign Investment Property

Investing in foreign states involves the risk that the investment property may be taken by the host nation's government. An **expropriation** or nationalization occurs when a government seizes foreign-owned property or assets for a public purpose and pays the owner just compensation for what is taken. **Confiscation** is the term used when no payment (or a highly inadequate payment) is given in exchange for the seized property, or it is seized for a non-public purpose. Confiscations violate generally observed principles of international law, whereas expropriations do not. In either case, there are few remedies available to injured parties. One precaution that can be taken by U.S. firms is to obtain insurance from a private insurer or the Overseas Private Investment Corporation (OPIC), which is an agency of the U.S. government.

TRANSACTING BUSINESS ABROAD

Transacting business abroad may involve such activities as selling goods, information, or services or investing capital or arranging for the movement of labor. Because these transactions may affect the national security, economy, foreign policy, and national interest of both the exporting and importing countries, nations have imposed measures to restrict or encourage such transactions. In this section we examine the legal controls imposed upon the flow of trade, labor, and capital across national borders.

Flow of Trade

Advances in modern technology, communication, transportation, and production methods have resulted in an enormous increase in goods flowing across national boundaries. The governments within each country are thereby faced with a dilemma. On the one hand, they want to protect and stimulate domestic industry. On the other hand, they want to provide their citizens with the best quality goods at the lowest possible prices and to encourage exports from their own countries.

Governments have used a variety of trade barriers to protect domestic businesses. A frequently applied device is the **tariff,** which is a duty or tax imposed on goods moving into or out of a country. Tariffs raise the price of imported goods, causing some consumers to purchase less expensive, domestically produced items. Governments can also use **nontariff barriers** to give a competitive advantage to local industries. Examples of nontariff barriers include unilateral or bilateral import quotas, import bans, overly restrictive safety or manufacturing standards, complicated and time-consuming customs procedures, and subsidies to local industry.

Governments also exercise control over the flow of some types of goods out of their countries by imposing quotas, tariffs, or total prohibitions. **Export controls** or restrictions usually result from important policy considerations, such as national defense, foreign policy, or protection of scarce national resources. For example, the United States passed the Export Administration Act of 1979, which imposes restrictions on the flow of technologically advanced goods and data from the United States to other countries. Nonetheless, countries generally encourage exports by the use of *export incentives* and *export subsidies* in order to assist domestic businesses.

Flow of Labor

The flow of labor across national borders generates policy questions involving the employment needs of local workers. Each country has its immigration policies and regulations. Almost all countries require that foreigners obtain valid passports before entering their borders. They also require their citizens to have a passport to leave or reenter the country. In addition, a country may issue visas to foreign citizens permitting them to enter the country for identified purposes or specific periods of time. For example, the U.S. Immigration and Naturalization Service issues various types of visas to persons who are temporarily visiting the United States for pleasure or business, to persons who enter the United States to perform services that the unemployed in this country cannot perform, and to persons who are transferred to the United States by their employers.

Flow of Capital

Multinational businesses frequently have the need to transfer funds to, and receive money from, operations in other countries. Because there is no international currency, nations have sought to ease the flow of capital among themselves. In 1945 the International Monetary Fund (IMF) was established to facilitate the expansion and balanced growth of international trade, to assist in the elimination of foreign exchange restrictions that hamper the growth of international trade, and to shorten the duration and lessen the disequilibrium in the international balance of payments of members. Currently, there are over 140 countries that are members of the IMF.

Nations have also joined to form international and regional banks to facilitate the flow of capital and trade. Such banks include the International Bank for Reconstruction and Development (part of the World Bank), the African Development Bank, the Asian Development Bank, the European Investment Bank, and the Inter-American Development Bank.

International trade involves a number of risks not usually created by domestic trade, especially governmental controls over the export or import of goods and currency. The most effective means of managing these risks—as well as the ordinary trade risks of

nonperformance by seller and buyer—is the irrevocable documentary letter of credit. A **letter of credit** is a promise by a buyer's bank to pay the seller provided certain conditions are met. The letter of credit transaction involves three or four different parties and three underlying contracts. To illustrate: a U.S. business wishes to sell computers to a Belgian company. The U.S. and Belgian firms enter into a sales agreement, including such details as how many computers, what features they will have, and when they will be shipped. The buyer then enters into a second contract with a local bank, called an **issuer,** calling for the bank to pay the agreed price upon presentation of specified documents. These documents normally include a bill of lading (proving that the seller has delivered the goods for shipment), a commercial invoice listing the terms of purchase, proof of insurance, and a customs certificate indicating that the goods have been cleared for export by customs officials. The buyer's bank's commitment to pay is the irrevocable letter of credit. Typically, a **correspondent** or **paying bank** located in the seller's country makes payment to the seller. Here, the Belgian issuing bank arranges to pay to the U.S. correspondent bank the agreed sum of money in exchange for the documents. The issuer then sends the U.S. computer firm the letter of credit. When the U.S. firm obtains all the necessary documents, it presents them to the U.S. correspondent bank. The correspondent bank verifies the documents, pays the computer company in U.S. dollars, and sends the documents to the Belgian issuing bank. Upon receiving the required documents, the issuing bank pays the correspondent bank and then presents the documents to the buyer. In our example, the Belgian buyer pays the issuing bank in Belgian francs for the letter of credit when the buyer receives the specified documents from the bank.

International Contracts

The legal issues inherent in domestic commercial contracts also arise in international contracts. Moreover, there are additional issues that are peculiar to international contracts, such as differences in language, legal systems, and currency. These issues should be addressed by the parties in a carefully drawn contract. The contract should specify the official language of the contract and include definitions of all significant legal terms used. In addition, the acceptable currency or currencies and method of payment should be specified. The contract should include a choice of law clause designating what law will govern any breach or dispute regarding the contract and whether disputes will be settled by arbitration. Finally, the contract should include a *force majeure* (unavoidable superior force) clause apportioning the liabilities and responsibilities of the parties in the event of an unforeseeable occurrence, such as a typhoon, tornado, flood, earthquake, war, or nuclear disaster.

The United Nations Convention on Contracts for the International Sales of Goods (CISG), which has been ratified by the United States, governs all contracts for the international sales of goods between parties located in different nations that have ratified the CISG. Since treaties are Federal law, the CISG supersedes the UCC whenever the CISG applies. The CISG includes provisions dealing with interpretation, trade usage, contract formation, obligations of sellers and buyers, remedies of sellers and buyers, and risk of loss. Parties to an international sales contract, however, may expressly exclude the CISG in their sales contract.

Antitrust Laws

Section 1 of the Sherman Act provides for a broad, extraterritorial reach of the U.S. antitrust laws. As discussed in Chapter 41, contracts, combinations, or conspiracies that restrain trade with foreign nations, as well as among the several states, are deemed illegal. Therefore, agreements among competitors to increase the cost of imports, as well as arrangements to exclude imports from U.S. domestic markets in exchange for not competing in other countries, clearly violate U.S. antitrust laws. The antitrust provisions are also de-

signed to provide protection for U.S. exports in situations where privately imposed restrictions seek to exclude U.S. competitors from foreign markets. Recent amendments to the Sherman Act and the Federal Trade Commission Act limit their application to unfair methods of competition that have a direct, substantial, and reasonably foreseeable effect on U.S. domestic commerce, U.S. import commerce, or U.S. export commerce.

FORMS OF MULTINATIONAL ENTERPRISES

The term **multinational enterprise** refers to any business that engages in transactions involving the movement of goods, information, money, people, or services across national borders. There are a number of business forms in which a multinational enterprise may conduct business: direct sales, foreign agents, distributorships, licensing, joint ventures, and wholly owned subsidiaries. A number of considerations affect the decision of which form of business organization to use in conducting international transactions. These factors include financing, tax consequences, legal restrictions imposed by the host country, and the degree of control over the business sought by the multinational enterprise. See Law in the News at page 1058.

Direct Export Sales

Under a direct export sale, the seller contracts directly with the buyer in the other country. This is the simplest and least involved multinational enterprise.

Foreign Agents

An agency relationship is often used by multinational enterprises that want a limited involvement in an international market. The principal firm will appoint a local agent, who is empowered to enter into contracts in the agent's country on behalf of the principal. The agent generally does not take title to the merchandise.

Distributorships

A commonly used form of multinational enterprise is the distributorship in which a foreign distributor is appointed. Unlike an agent, a distributor takes title to the merchandise it receives, which means that the distributor, not the producer, bears many of the risks connected with commercial sales. The distributorship format, however, is especially susceptible to antitrust violations. Therefore, special care must be taken to ensure that the antitrust laws of both the producer and distributor's governments are not violated.

Licensing

Multinational enterprises wishing to exploit an intellectual property right, such as a patent, trademark, trade secret, or unpatented but innovative production technology, may choose to sell the right to use such property to a foreign company instead of entering the foreign market itself. The sale of such rights, called licensing, is one of the major means by which technology and information are transferred among nations. Normally, the foreign firm will pay royalties in exchange for the information, technology, or patent. Franchising is a form of licensing in which the owner of intellectual property grants permission to a foreign business under carefully specified conditions.

Joint Ventures

In a joint venture, two or more independent businesses from different countries agree to coordinate their efforts to achieve a common result. The sharing of profits and liabilities, as well as the delegation of responsibilities, is fixed by contract. One of the advantages of the joint venture form is that each company can be assigned responsibility for that which it does best. In order to promote local ownership of investment, a number of developing nations and regional groups have enacted legislation that prohibits foreign businesses from owning more than 49 percent of any business enterprise in that country. In addition, the country may require that its citizens comprise a majority of the management of the enterprise.

Wholly Owned Subsidiaries

By far, wholly owned subsidiaries require the most active participation by the parent firm. The creation of a foreign wholly owned subsidiary corporation, however, can offer numerous advantages to a business, most significantly the opportunity to retain authority and control over all phases of operation. This is especially attractive to businesses wishing to safeguard their technology.

BULOVA WATCH COMPANY, INC. v. K. HATTORI & CO.
United States District Court, Eastern District of New York, 1981.
508 F.Supp. 1322.

Facts: Plaintiff Bulova Watch Company is a New York corporation with its principal place of business in Flushing, New York. As both a manufacturer and seller of watches, Bulova claims to have the largest direct sales marketing system in the watch business. Defendant Hattori, incorporated under the laws of Japan with its principal office in Tokyo, is the parent company of the wholly owned subsidiary Seiko Corporation of America (SCA), a New York corporation. SCA, in turn, owns all the stock of three "sub-subsidiaries," namely, Seiko Time Corp., Pulsar Time, and SPD Precision Inc., all of which are incorporated under New York law. While the United States is Hattori's largest market, accounting for over one-half billion dollars in sales, Hattori distributes its products in over one hundred countries, using wholly owned subsidiaries in ten of those countries. For the remaining countries, Hattori employs independent distributors who conduct their own marketing and advertising activities and maintain their own repair centers. Desiring to expand the markets of its U.S. based wholly owned subsidiaries, Hattori masterminded certain advertising campaigns and began recruiting and hiring several high-level direct sales marketing personnel from the Bulova company. Bulova filed this action against Hattori alleging unfair competition, disparagement, and conspiracy to raid the plaintiff's marketing personnel. The defendant moved to dismiss the case for lack of jurisdiction, claiming that the Japanese parent company Hattori was a distinct and separate entity from its American subsidiaries and therefore lacked sufficient control over the subsidiaries to satisfy jurisdictional requirements.

Decision: Motion to dismiss denied.

Opinion: Weinstein, C. J.   [The N.Y statute] permits the exercise of such jurisdiction over "persons, property, or status as might have been exercised heretofore." It confers personal jurisdiction over unlicensed foreign corporations that are "doing business" in New York. [Citations.]

The definition of "doing business" has been variously stated, but the common denominator is that the corporation is operating within the state "not occasionally or casually, but with a fair measure of permanence and continuity." [Citations.]

It is no longer a matter of doubt that a foreign corporation can do business in New York through its employees, [citations].

Equally settled is the concept that a corporation may be amenable to New York personal jurisdiction when the systematic activities of a subsidiary in this state may fairly be attributed to the parent. [Citations.]

* * *

When Cardozo enunciated the standard for doing business in New York, [citation], there would have been little need to consider how, or whether, a foreign-based multinational enterprise would be found to be doing business in New York. For one thing, the term "multinational firm," so common in today's parlance, was first used only in 1960. [Citation.] For another, it was not until after World War II that the phenomenon of the multinational enterprise, as we now know it, became a major factor in the world scene. [Citation.] Since then tens of thousands of subsidiaries have been created or acquired by parent enterprises located in other countries. [Citation.] By 1972 it was estimated that in a world that produced about $3,000 billion of goods and services a year, something like one-eighth of the output moved across international boundaries. [Citation.] In that same year the value of American investments abroad was $94 billion. [Citation.]

After the Second World War investment in the United States by foreign parent companies also expanded tremendously so that by the early 1970s non-United States corporations owned more than seven hundred "major manufacturing enterprises" in this country. [Citation.] Direct foreign investment, defined as ownership by foreign parents of at least ten percent of the equity of an American enterprise, was $3.4 billion at the start of the 1950s, $6.6 billion in 1959 and $26.5 billion by 1974. [Citation.] Total assets of foreign-owned affiliates in the United States in 1974 were $174.3 billion, of which more than one-fifth was Japanese-owned. [Citation.] These trends have accelerated.

The vehicles of this modern international economic growth were and are the multinational enterprises. Their size is often awesome: the annual sales of General Motors exceeded the gross national products of Switzerland, Pakistan, or South Africa. [Citation.]

The phenomenon of penetration into the economies of distant areas can be traced through artifacts back into pre-history. But the current situation is in many respects quite different in the sophisticated organizational and legal techniques utilized from even that of earlier periods in American history when foreign financing made so much of our industrial and commercial expansion possible and when American companies like Singer, the American sewing machine company, established manufacturing plants abroad. [Citations.] Aside from their magnitude, today's multinationals are unique in the way vast investments in myriad locations are made to serve the interests of a single organization. Large advantages lie in the possibility of making centralized management and investment decisions on the basis of the situations and opportunities prevailing in various host countries. [Citations.] Such an organization has the resources and scope to plan and to utilize world-wide markets and resources. [Citations.]

The profit motivation for international expansion is common to multinationals. [Citations.] Nevertheless, the means by which the multinational exercises control over its far-flung elements vary. The degree and nature of control may depend upon the nationality of the corporate parent. [Citations.] The formal structure of the parent's form of ownership also has control implications. Choice among the various corporate modes of entering a market, e. g., by means of licensing arrangement, joint venture, minority-, majority- or wholly-owned subsidiary, has very significant implications for the control exercised by the parent. [Citation.] Utilization of a wholly-owned marketing-based subsidiary is found where "the . . . retention of unambiguous control of foreign operations is critical to the firm's strategy." [Citation.] The decision of marketing-oriented firms to choose wholly-owned subsidiaries means that they can exercise more control over their foreign operation in subtle, indirect ways as well as directly. [Citation.]

Another criterion that will determine the "corporate intimacy" joining a parent and its subsidiary, [citation], is the type and range of products being sold. Enterprises with narrow product lines tend to organize their operations on a highly integrated basis, linking production and marketing into tight strategic patterns. [Citation.] While Hattori manufactures a number of products, the overwhelming concern of its American marketing operation is with its timepieces—constituting ninety percent of its total production by value.

Thus sales subsidiaries tend to be under especially close control where a company produces a limited number of products. In such a case the company has

> a higher stake in the maintenance of quality standards, a higher sense of risk in sharing its technology with others, a higher need for a centralized marketing strategy . . . . The strategy of [these] firms, therefore, requires relatively tight controls.

[Citation.]

Finally, a crucial factor in the degree of control over the subsidiary is the age of the subsidiary and the extent to which the subsidiary has been able to develop independently of its parent. A leading scholar of international trade distinguishes multinational firms from national firms with foreign operations: "A multinational firm starts out like a national firm with foreign operations, but after time each national operation takes on a life of its own." [Citation.] The history of modern international business enterprise is largely the history of just this development from a national firm with foreign sales operations, to the truly multinational firm with quasi-independent component entities. [Citation.]

An important question in assessing presence for jurisdictional purposes is whether a multinational has reached a state in its evolution when it can be said that its sales and marketing subsidiaries truly have a "life of their own." [Citation.] * * *

The expanding multinational generally traverses a number of stages. At first it exports its goods to markets abroad, next it establishes sales organizations abroad, then it may license the use of its patents, and finally it may establish foreign manufacturing facilities. At a later stage it may "multinationalize its management and, ultimately, multinationalize the ownership of its stock." [Citation.] While many thousands of corporations are at the first, export stage, only a handful have developed into advanced multinational enterprises each of whose elements can be said to be significant in its own right.

After World War II, foreign companies gained familiarity with the United States market "by first exporting to this country; then, after achieving acceptance for their products, foreign firms set up manufacturing or assembly plants here." [Citation.] As these later stages were reached, the businesses established came to have lives of their own. The "monocentric" enterprise gradually gave way to a polycentric one, with more autonomy in the different elements. Wilkins detects three stages: in the first stage, the firm "reached out to sell or to obtain and in doing so felt the necessity or saw the opportunity to cross over domestic boundaries." [Citation.] The relationship was "monocentric" with the center of operations clearly in the parent's home country. The external activities in a monocentric relationship were "spokes on a wheel, with the parent company at the hub." [Citation.] In stage two, the functions of the branches broadened. There might, for example, be investment by the subsidiary in a plant for local production or the subsidiary might sell products in third-country markets. "What characterizes stage two is the presence of foreign units that have developed their own separate histories and their own satellite activities." [Citation.] The final, third, stage is characteristic of the most advanced of these entities:

It garbles any chart's attempt to delineate international trade and control lines. The parent company comes to have a number of foreign multifunctional centers, serving overlapping geographical areas with various products. Supply and market lines cross international boundaries in . . . chaotic confusion . . . .

[Citation.]

Over time, certain foreign subsidiaries and affiliates have become full-fledged, fully integrated, multiprocess, multiproduct enterprises, with engineering, product planning and research staffs, with a continuity of employee, supplier, dealer, consumer and banking relationships with their own prominent role in foreign industries, with their own dealings with foreign governments and with their own third-country investments.

[Citation.] At this final stage, complicated, many-faceted relationships have replaced simple bilateral connections. [Citation.]

* * *

It is apparent that Hattori's international activities, large as they may be in terms of sales figures and associated product lines, are essentially akin to Wilkins' stage one "monocentric" export model and not to the much more complex multinationals to which defendants point. What is involved here is a series of relatively young sales and marketing subsidiaries abroad, whose purpose is to market a single product—timepieces. There is no manufacturing or product research done by any of these subsidiaries. They do not seem to have developed third-country trade except for the purpose of selling Hattori's Japanese manufactured goods. Only very recently have they begun to make some investments in third countries, again to produce further outlets for Hattori's factories in Japan. The use of the wholly-owned subsidiary form here reflects the desire for "unambiguous control" over sales and marketing subsidiaries to insure uniform quality and promotion of the product sold. [Citations.]

Hattori and its American subsidiaries do maintain some independence—about as much as the egg and vegetables in a western omelette. Just as, from a culinary point of view, we focus on the ultimate omelette and not its ingredients, so, too, from a jurisdictional standpoint, it is the integrated international operation of Hattori affecting activities in New York that is the primary focus of our concern.

Although with time the Hattori subsidiaries might well evolve, along with their parent, into the later stages of multinational development, today Hattori is a highly effective export manufacturer and not a fully developed multinational. It is monocentric more than polycentric. Large and sophisticated as it may be, it is very much the hub of a wheel with many spokes. It is appropriate, therefore, to look to the center of the wheel in Japan when the spokes violate substantive rights in other countries.

* * *

What is decisive is that at the time this complaint was filed, Hattori, through its American subsidiaries, continued to engage in the market penetration and expansion that are its corporate *raison d'être* and that are the grounds underlying this action. We have no doubt about the validity of an "inference as to the broad scope of the agency" linking Hattori to the activities of its subsidiaries in New York. [Citation.]

* * *

A court might well find substantial unfairness were it to drag a foreign parent into court to defend itself against actions completely unrelated to the subsidiary corporation's purposive activities on behalf of its parent. The holding in this case is simply that while a subsidiary establishes and expands a parent's market position then, so long as that activity is being conducted, and with respect to those activities furthering the parent's ends, the parent is doing business in New York. This is particularly true as to activities directly related to primary steps taken to ensure a place for its subsidiaries, as where action is taken to raid an established competitor's personnel in penetrating the American market.

LAW IN THE NEWS

Globalization: Corporate Strategy as the 1900s End

With a new surge of investment abroad, many American companies are shedding the banner of a national identity and proclaiming themselves to be global enterprises whose fortunes are no longer dependent on the U.S. economy.

Globalization is emerging as corporate America's strategy of choice for the 1990s, one heralded in the latest issue of The Harvard Business Review as a main road to industrial prowess.

In the name of globalization, American companies' overseas spending on plants and equipment has revived for the first time in a decade.

Executives increasingly speak as if the United States were no longer home port.

"The United States does not have an automatic call on our resources," said Cyrill Siewert, chief financial officer at the Colgate-Palmolive Co., which now sells more toothpaste, soaps and other toiletries outside the United States than inside.

"There is no mindset that puts this country first."

Inevitably, such views are putting American companies at odds with widely advocated national goals.

In a growing number of cases, high-paying jobs, including those for engineers and other professionals, are going abroad, instead of being kept at home.

Spending by American manufacturers on research—an important source of financing for universities and laboratories—is rising far more quickly overseas than at home, according to the National Science Foundation.

And American companies are increasingly supplying foreign markets from their overseas operations, rather than by exporting, a practice that makes this country's trade deficit hard to eliminate.

Perhaps the sharpest test of globalization would come in a recession, when the companies would face public pressure to preserve as many jobs as possible in the United States, thus holding down the unemployment rate.

One way to do this would be for them to close overseas operations and pull back production to the United States, exporting from this country to keep their American factories occupied.

But many executives say the global strategy supersedes preferential treatment for American employees.

Motorola Inc., for example, makes telephone pagers in Boyton Beach, Fla., and Kuala Lumpur, Malaysia—with the Malaysian plant now also the design and engineering center for these electronic beepers.

"We'd try to make a balanced decision that took everyone into consideration, Malaysians and Americans," said Robert H. Galvin, Motorola's chairman.

"We need our Far Eastern customers, and we cannot alienate the Malaysians. We must treat our employees all over the world equally."

Many global executives also distance themselves from the trade issues that are stirring so much concern in Congress and the Bush administration.

Motorola and the Hewlett-Packard Co. say they will not be directly affected if the United States fails to outdistance other countries in the development of high-definition television, a breakthrough technology that could require every household to buy a new television set.

"Whatever the technology that is developed, in whatever country, we'll be going after it for our products," said John Young, chief executive of Hewlett-Packard.

These products include semiconductors and electronic measuring instruments made in several countries.

To be sure, American companies still spend much more on plant and equipment in this country than they do abroad: $488 billion last year versus $42 billion overseas.

But the outlays have been rising since the mid-1980s.

In addition, companies like International Business Machines, Ford Motor, NCR, Motorola, Colgate-Palmolive and the Stanley Works now collect 30 percent or more of their revenues, and big chunks of their profit, from production outside the country, usually in high-tech factories far more sophisticated than the assembly plant operations that characterized earlier periods of overseas expansion.

Very slowly, corporate America is building up its holdings abroad.

Nearly 17 percent of total corporate assets are now overseas, up from 14.4 percent in 1984, according to data compiled by Robert Lipsey of the Nation Bureau of Economic Research.

This amount is greater than that for nearly every other industrial nation and more than three times the percentage of Japan's overseas holdings, although in every developed country the percentages are also rising.

The explanation of this trend is evident in the comments of many American executives, among them John A.M. Grant, executive director of corporate strategy at Ford Motor Co.

"In any country where Ford operates, the value added—the amount of manufacturing done in that country—should be as great as possible," he said.

True to this policy, Ford's automaking operation in Europe, among the largest on the Continent, now makes or buys 98 percent of its parts, supplies and machinery in Europe, building up to this level over more than a decade.

"The only thing we import from the United States is some machine tools," Grant said.

For Ford and many American companies, the big lure of globalization is the promise of Europe and Asia.

Sales of many products are growing more rapidly in these two markets than in the United States. Corporate America has decided that they must be served on the spot, not from home.

"You cannot really make a penetration with exports," said Ralph Hake, vice president of planning at Whirlpool Corp.

But the exodus abroad is raising the possibility that American companies, by expanding foreign production, are transferring too much wealth to other countries.

Not only are the factories as sophisticated as those back home, but much of the overseas investment today takes the form of joint production ventures with foreign companies, a rare practice before the 1980s.

According to a survey by the Conference Board, a business organization, 40 percent of the overseas investment last year was in such joint ventures, which spread technology quickly across borders.

"There is a decoupling of the corporation from the country; that is what is developing," said Gus Tyler, an official of the International Ladies Garment Workers Union.

"The country can be facing economic disaster, and the global corporation can avoid it."

Twenty years ago, in a period of overseas expansion that peaked in 1977, the trend was much less of a national problem.

For one thing, most American companies insisted on ownership control of their foreign operations, and they kept their best factories, their best jobs and their best technologies at home.

As Richard H. Ayers, chairman of Stanley Works, put it, the tendency was to equip foreign operations with hand-me-down machinery and technology, used first in this country and then sent abroad, often to make products from parts and material shipped from the United States.

But in those days, the American multinational company's foreign operations did not have to be as productive and modern as they must be today.

For one thing, low-wage foreign labor more than offset the extra cost of using older, less-efficient machinery.

Now, this advantage is gradually being lost as wages rise not only in Europe and Japan, but also in South Korea, Taiwan, Singapore, Indonesia and other Third World countries.

Finally, until the 1970s, many of the overseas operations served only one country's marketplace, a strategy often dictated by tariff barriers.

But as these barriers disappear and consumption rises abroad, American companies are closing their one-country factories.

In their place, regional operations are emerging that serve a host of countries and draw their parts and materials partly from the United States but increasingly from local suppliers.

The Stanley Works, based in New Britain, Conn., has gone through this conversion process.

A factory in Taiwan, originally opened because of the low-wage labor force, has been upgraded to production of quality wrenches, sockets and other tools for auto mechanics. The American market is supplied from this plant.

Most of Stanley's most sophisticated products are still made in the United States.

"But if the best markets for any product develop overseas, then I would not hesitate to switch the operation abroad," Ayers said.

Pursuing this strategy, Stanley's factory in Sheffield, England, has become the company's engineering, design and manufacturing center for wood planes, the metal hand tools used to shave wood.

All the world is served from this plant, which was placed in England because Europe has become the biggest market for wood planes and might grow even bigger after 1992, when the 12 members of the European Community plan to remove the last of the barriers that separate their marketplaces.

The leading critics of globalization are union leaders, trying to save American jobs, and some economists and politicians, who assert that any manufacturing operation creates wealth for the host country.

The argument is that industry is not only a source of jobs, but also of income for researchers who develop new products, for parts suppliers and for lawyers, accountants and many other service workers.

Realizing this, the Japanese and most European countries find ways to limit globalization and to keep industry at home, said Clyde V. Prestowitz, a trade negotiator in the Reagan administration and a frequent critic of the Japanese.

They do so through trade barriers, tax breaks and local-content laws that require foreign manufacturers, including Americans, to use locally made supplies, he said.

"My view is that globalization is not really taking place as a worldwide phenomenon," Prestowitz said.

"Only American companies are really doing it."

Whatever the case, American executives defend the practice with growing confidence.

Their survival depends on serving all the world's major markets, and this can be done efficiently in most cases only when production is near each market, they say.

Although globalization might deprive the United States of some factories, Ayers of the Stanley Works said, "wealth still comes back to the country in the form of dividends to shareholders, who are mostly Americans."

Americans do indeed hold 93.8 percent of all corporate stock, according to the Securities Industry Association.

But foreign ownership is creeping up, from 4.1 percent in 1980 to 6.2 percent through last year's first half.

And foreign ownership of corporate bonds has risen several fold in this decade, to 12.9 percent last year. The interest on these bonds is paid, like stock dividends, from company earnings.

Finally, executives and economists point out that, while American companies invested $42 billion in plant and equipment abroad last year, Japanese, European and other foreign companies invested as much here, creating jobs and other benefits for Americans.

"If the argument is that wealth is created where the production is done, then what difference does it make whether the factories are owned by Japanese or Americans, as long as they're here?" said Charles Wolf Jr., director of Rand Corp.'s international economic policy program.

CHAPTER SUMMARY

| The International Environment | **International Law** includes law that deals with the conduct and relations of nation-states and international organizations as well as some of their relations with persons; it is enforceable by the courts of a nation if that nation has adopted the international law as domestic law
International Court of Justice judicial branch of the United Nations having voluntary jurisdiction over nations
Regional Trade Communities international organizations, conferences, and treaties focusing on business and trade regulation; the EEC (the Common Market) is the most prominent of these
International Treaties agreements between or among independent nations such as the General Agreement on Tariffs and Trade (GATT) |

Jurisdiction over Actions of Foreign Governments	**Sovereign Immunity** foreign country's freedom from a host country's laws **Act of State Doctrine** rule that a court should not question the validity of actions taken by a foreign government in its own country **Taking of Foreign Investment Property** ■ *Expropriation* governmental taking of foreign-owned property for a public purpose and with payment of just compensation ■ *Confiscation* governmental taking of foreign-owned property without payment (or for a highly inadequate payment) or for a nonpublic purpose

Transacting Business Abroad	**Flow of Trade** controlled by trade barriers on imports and exports ■ *Tariff* duty or tax imposed on goods moving into or out of a country ■ *Nontariff Barriers* include quotas, bans, safety standards, and subsidies **Flow of Labor** controlled through passport, visa, and immigration regulations **Flow of Capital** ■ *International Monetary Fund* established to facilitate the expansion and balanced growth of international trade, to assist in eliminating foreign exchange restrictions, and to smooth out international balance of payments ■ *Letter of Credit* bank's promise to pay the seller provided certain conditions are met; used to manage the payment risks in international trade **International Contracts** involve additional issues beyond those in domestic contracts such as differences in language, legal systems, and currency **Antitrust Laws** of the U.S. apply to unfair methods of competition that have a direct, substantial, and reasonably foreseeable effect on the domestic, import, or export commerce of the U.S.

Forms of Multinational Enterprises	**Definition of Multinational Enterprise (MNE)** any business that engages in transactions involving the movement of goods, information, money, people, or services across national borders **Forms of MNE** the choice of form depends upon a number of factors including financing considerations, tax consequences, and degree of control ■ *Direct Export Sales* seller contracts directly with the buyer in the other country ■ *Foreign Agents* a local agent in the host country is used to provide limited involvement for an MNE ■ *Distributorship* MNE sells to a foreign distributor who takes title to the merchandise ■ *Licensing* MNE sells the right to use technology or information to a foreign company ■ *Joint Ventures* two independent businesses from different countries share profits, liabilities, and duties ■ *Wholly Owned Subsidiary* enables an MNE to retain control and authority over all phases of operation

QUESTIONS

1. Discuss the purpose and major provisions of GATT.
2. Discuss and compare the doctrines of sovereign immunity and act of state.
3. Contrast expropriation and confiscation.
4. Briefly discuss the legal controls imposed on the flow of trade, labor, and capital across national borders.
5. List and briefly describe the various forms a multinational enterprise may choose to conduct its business in a foreign country.

PROBLEMS

1. Three banks that are wholly owned by the Republic of Costa Rica had issued promissory notes, payable in U.S. dollars in New York City. The notes are now in default due solely to actions of the Costa Rican government, which had suspended all payments of external debt because of escalating economic problems. Efforts by Costa Rica to curb foreign debt payment difficulties conflicted with U.S. policy for debt resolution procedure as conducted under the auspices of the International Monetary Fund. A syndicate of U.S. banks brought suit to recover on the promissory notes. The three Costa Rican banks assert the act of state doctrine as a defense. Decision?
2. Six U.S. manufacturers of broad spectrum antibiotics derived a large percentage of their sales from overseas markets, including India, Iran, the Philippines, Spain, South Korea, West Germany, Colombia, and Kuwait. The manufacturers agreed to a common plan of marketing, whereby territories were divided and prices for products were set. The members of the plan also agreed not to grant foreign producers licenses to the manufacturing technology of any of their "big money" drugs. The above foreign countries bring suit for treble damages for violation of the U.S. antitrust laws. Decision?
3. After reading attractive brochures advertising a package tour of the Dominican Republic, a U.S. family decided to purchase tickets for the family vacation plan. The tour was a product of four different business entities, two domestic (U.S.) and two foreign. Sheraton Hotels & Inns, World Corporation, was to provide food and lodging; Dominicana Airlines, wholly owned by the government of the Dominican Republic, which routinely flew into Miami International Airport and sold tickets within

the United States, was to provide round-trip air transportation and "tourist cards" necessary for entry into the Dominican Republic; while two U.S. firms organized and sold the tour. Problems for the family began when their Dominicana flight landed in the Dominican Republic, and immigration officials denied them entry. Forced to leave, the family was shuttled first to Puerto Rico and then to Haiti, where they had to secure their own passage back to the United States at additional expense. The family brings suit against all four different business entities. Decision?
4. A privately owned business in a developing country determines that current computer technology could solve many of the problems faced by its country's private and public sectors. This business, however, lacks the capital resources necessary for research and development to acquire such computer technology, even if trained personnel were available. Furthermore, despite a sense of patriotism, the business concludes that its national government could not efficiently or effectively handle such a development project. What business forms are available to this business for acquiring sophisticated computer technology? What are the advantages and problems inherent in the various options?
5. King Faisal II of Iraq was killed on July 14, 1958, in the midst of a revolution in that country which led to the establishment of a republic subsequently recognized by the U.S. government. On July 19, 1958, the new republic issued a decree that all property of the former ruling dynasty, regardless of location, should be confiscated. Subsequently, the Republic of Iraq brought suit in the United States to obtain possession of money and stocks deposited in the deceased king's U.S. bank account in New York City. Decision?
6. A business entity incorporated under the laws of one of the EEC member nations contracts with the government of a developing nation to form a joint venture for the mining and refining of a scarce raw material used by several developed nations in the manufacture of highly sensitive weapons systems. The contract calls for the investment by the EEC-based corporation of money and technology that will be used to build permanent refinery plants that will eventually revert to the developing nation. The developing nation also reserves the right to set quotas on sales of this scarce resource and to choose the destination of exports. Due to political conflicts, the developing nation refuses to allow any exports of the scarce material to the United States. This causes a sharp price increase in exports to the United States by other suppliers. The United States asserts antitrust violations against the EEC-based

corporation for the effects produced within the United States. Decision?

7. A Panamanian corporation lends money to a Turkish enterprise, which issues a promissory note. The loan contract specifies that payment on the interest and principal shall be made to the Chemical Bank of New York City, where both parties maintain accounts. The loan contract contains no choice of law designation, but the Panamanian and Turkish companies have referred to the Chemical Bank in New York as their "legal address." As a result of a contractual performance dispute, the Turkish company has suspended payments on the loan. The Panamanian corporation then brings suit in the United States to recover the balance of the payments due. What possible options for choice of law apply?

PART 10
PROPERTY

The concept of property is fundamental to our economic system, which is based on exchanges between units of production and consumption. The significance of property nonetheless goes beyond its immeasurable economic importance. As the eminent English jurist, Blackstone, stated: "There is nothing which so generally strikes the imagination, and engages the affections of mankind, as the right of property; or that sole and despotic dominion which one man claims and exercises over the external things of the world, in total exclusion of the right of any other individual in the universe."

Before inquiring further into the social and public policy issues concerning the private and public ownership of property, we must first define "property." Jeremy Bentham, in explaining the advantages of law, stated: "Property is nothing but a basis of expectation; the expectation of deriving certain advantages from a thing which we are said to possess, in consequence of the relation in which we stand towards it. . . . Property and law are born together, and die together. Before laws were made there was no property; take away laws, and property ceases." More specifically, property consists of a set of *rights* entitling one person to use and exclusively enjoy some item. R. Ely stated:

By property we mean an exclusive right to control an economic good.

By private property we mean the exclusive right of a private person to control an economic good.

By public property we mean the exclusive right of a political unit (city, state, nation, etc.) to control an economic good. . . .

. . . Speaking accurately, then, property is not a thing but the rights which extend over a thing. A less strict use of the word property makes property include the things over which the right extends. We say of a farm, this is my property, meaning the land and improvements on it and not merely the right, or rather, the land and its improvements together with the right. But, strictly speaking, property is the right, and not the object over which the right extends. R. Ely, *Property and Contract in their Relation to the Distribution of Wealth.*

No matter which sense of the word is intended—the right over the object or the object itself—there is an enormous quantity of property in the Untied States today. It has been estimated that as of 1980 there was $4,247 billion of real estate, $1,381 billion of stock owned, $1,112 billion of bonds and other fixed income assets, $973 billion of durables, and $373 billion of cash.

The most obvious—and the most important—question regarding all of the wealth is: who should own it? This question has been answered quite differently at various times in history and today is answered just as diversely. Our economic and political system has provided for both private and public ownership of property. Moreover, it has established constitutional protections for the private ownership of property. As a result, private ownership is accepted as the norm in this country, and those who own property may assert: "To the world: Keep off unless you have my permission, which I may grant or withhold. Signed: Private citizen. Endorsed: The state." F. Cohen, "Dialogue on Private Property," 9 *Rutgers L. Rev.* (1954) 357, 374. Of course, there are other views regarding the propriety of private property. For example, Karl Marx and Friedrich Engels, in *The Communist*

Manifesto, maintained "The proletarians cannot become masters of the productive forces of society, except by abolishing their own previous mode of appropriation, and thereby also every other previous mode of appropriation. They have nothing of their own to secure and to fortify; their mission is to destroy all previous securities for, and insurances of, individual property."

Economists have set forth countless arguments supporting the notion of privately owned property. The basic one is that by allowing private property, the capitalistic system creates incentives for the efficient use and allocation of resources. The right to exclusive ownership of property encourages individuals to incur costs in order to make efficient use of their property, while the right to transfer ownership in their property provides an incentive for them to shift resources from less productive uses to more productive uses. Behrman has explained this concept as follows:

> An individual must have something to be creative with. Private property can be used for private benefit, but the society as a whole should benefit, too. Each individual will greedily use property for his greatest economic benefit: he would not use it as efficiently if someone else owned it and paid him part of the fruits of his labor. Private productive property assures that each person reaps the benefit of his own efforts. If everybody works for one man, who alone has all the property, he is the only one with the ability to create. The feudal lord who owned all of the land, the cattle, stables, and so forth—he told the serfs what to do. He could be creative. But the serf who was greedy—what happened to him? He got his hands cuffed! Private productive property is a necessary com-

plement to individual economic motivation. It is necessary for individuals to work effectively, doing the best they can with it, responsibly, and thereby improving the whole society. J. Behrman, *Discourses on Ethics and Business* (1981) 23.

Even in our society, which constitutionally recognizes the private ownership of property, such ownership is by no means absolute. The government imposes limitations on a number of the rights embodied in ownership:

> Our students of property law need, therefore, to be reminded that not only has the whole law since the industrial revolution shown a steady growth in ever new restrictions upon the use of private property, but that the ideal of absolute *laissez faire* has never in fact been completely operative. . . .
>
> . . . There must be restrictions on the use of property not only in the interests of other property owners but also in the interests of the health, safety, religion, morals, and general welfare of the whole community. No community can view with indifference the exploitation of the needy by commercial greed. As under the conditions of crowded life the reckless or unconscionable use of one's property is becoming more and more dangerous, enlightened jurists find new doctrines to limit the abuse of ancient rights. M. Cohen, "Property and Sovereignty," 13 *Cornell L. Q.* (1927) 8.

In the next six chapters we explore our legal system's answers to several questions of public policy regarding the private ownership of property. How freely should property rights be transferable? Should the government be permitted to seize privately owned property? To what extent should the government control the use of private property? Should individuals be allowed to restrict the use of property that they have transferred?

47 INTRODUCTION TO REAL AND PERSONAL PROPERTY

In our democratic and free enterprise society, the concept of property has an importance second only to the idea of liberty. Although many of our rules of property in the United States stem directly from English law, property in America occupies a unique status because of the protection expressly granted it by the Federal Constitution as well as by most State Constitutions. The Fifth Amendment to the Federal Constitution provides in part that "No person shall be . . . deprived of life, liberty, or property, without due process of law; nor shall private property be taken for public use, without just compensation." A similar requirement is contained in the Fourteenth Amendment: "No State shall . . .deprive any person of life, liberty, or property, without due process of law." This protection afforded to property owners is subject, however, to police regulation for the public good. In this chapter we introduce the law governing real and personal property and then discuss personal property more specifically.

INTRODUCTION TO PROPERTY

In spite of the unique place given to property in our society, uncertainties arise because the term is not easily defined. This is not all that surprising, because the term "property" includes almost every *right*, exclusive of personal liberty, that the law will protect. Property is valuable only because our law provides that certain consequences follow from the ownership of it. The right to use the property, to sell it, and to control to whom it shall pass on the death of the owner are all included within the term property. Accordingly, **property** is an interest or group of interests that is legally protected.

Thus, when a person speaks of "owning property," he may have two separate ideas in mind: (1) the *physical thing* itself, as when a homeowner says, "I just bought a piece of property in Oakland," meaning complete ownership of a physically identifiable parcel of land; or (2) a *right* or *interest* in the physical object, as, for example, with respect to land, a tenant under a lease has a property interest in the leased land, although he does not own the land.

KINDS OF PROPERTY

Property may be classified as (1) tangible or intangible, and (2) real or personal (see Figure 47–1). As you will see, these classifications are not mutually exclusive.

Tangible and Intangible Property

A forty-acre farm, a chair, and a household pet are *tangible* property. The group of rights or interests referred to as "title" or "ownership" to **tangible property** are embodied in each of these *physical* objects. On the other hand, **intangible property** is property that does *not* exist in a physical form. For example, a stock certificate, a promissory note, and a deed granting Jones a right-of-way over the land of Young are intangible property. Each represents and stands for certain rights that are not capable of reduction to physical possession but have a legal reality in the sense that they will be protected.

FIGURE 47-1 Kinds of Property

	Personal	Real
Tangible	Goods	Land Buildings Fixtures
Intangible	Commercial paper Stock certificates Contract rights Copyrights Patents	Leases Easements Mortgages

The same item may be the object of both tangible and intangible property rights. Suppose Ann purchases a book published by Broundson. On the first page, there is the statement "Copyright 1989, by Broundson." Ann owns the book she purchased. She has the right to exclusive physical possession and use of that particular copy. It is a tangible piece of property of which she is the owner. Broundson, however, has the exclusive right to publish copies of the book. This is a right granted it by the copyright laws. The courts will protect this intangible property of Broundson as well as Ann's right to the particular volume.

Real and Personal Property

The most significant practical distinction between types of property is the classification into real and personal property. A simple definition would be to say that land and all interests in it are **real property** (also called realty), and every other thing or interest identified as property is **personal property.** This description is adequate for most purposes, although certain physical objects that are personal property under most circumstances may, because of their attachment to land or their use in connection with land, become a form of real property called fixtures.

Fixtures

A **fixture**, as defined above, is an article or piece of personal property that has been so firmly attached to land or a building that an interest in it arises under *real* property law. For example, materials for a building are clearly personal property, but when worked into a building as its construction progresses, they become real property, since buildings are part of the land. Thus, clay in its natural state is, of course, real property; when made into bricks it becomes personal property, and if the bricks are then built into the wall of a house, the "clay" once again becomes real property.

Although the question whether various items are personal property or real property may in certain instances be difficult to answer, it is only by obtaining the answer that conflicting claims to their ownership may be determined. Unless otherwise provided by agreement, personal property remains the property of the person who placed it on the real estate. On the other hand, if the property has been affixed so as to become a fixture (an actual part of the real estate), it becomes the property of the owner of the real estate.

These questions affect many persons. The apartment dweller who puts a new chandelier or a bathroom cabinet in his landlord's apartment and the shoe repairman who attaches equipment to the floor of his leased premises will not be entitled to remove them when the lease expires *if* they are held to have become part of the real estate. Thus, if a seller of real estate has installed screens on the premises, the buyer is entitled to them as part of the real estate even though they were not specifically mentioned in the deed.

In determining whether personal property becomes a fixture, the intention of the parties with conflicting claims to the property as expressed in their agreement will control. Without the binding force of an agreement, the following factors are relevant in determining whether any particular item is a fixture: (1) the physical relationship of the item to the land or building; (2) the intention of the person who attaches the item to the land or building; (3) the purpose served by the item in relation to the land or building and in relation to the person who brought it there; and (4) the interest of that person in the land or building at the time of the attachment of the item.

Although physical attachment is significant, a more important test is whether the item can be removed without material injury to the land or building on the land. If it *cannot* be so removed, it is generally held that the item has become part of the realty. The opposite is also true but to a lesser degree. Where the item may be removed without material injury to the land or building, it is generally held that it has not become part of the realty. This test, however, is not conclusive.

Rather, the courts have searched for the answer in the intention of the person who attached the item to the realty. The tests of intention are objective. One of the tests developed has been to inquire into the purpose or use of the item in relation to the land and in relation to the person who brought it there. If the use or purpose of the item is unusual for the type of realty involved (e.g., a small crane in the backyard of a country house) or peculiar to the particular individual who brought it there, then it may be reasonably concluded that the individual intended to remove the item when he left.

The courts do not regard an item as part of the realty merely because its use or purpose is usual for the kind of realty involved. For example, it is usual to have beds and dressers in bedrooms and dining tables in dining rooms, but these items are not ordinarily part of the realty. The test of purpose or use applies only if the item both (a) is affixed to the realty in some way, and (b) can be removed without material injury to the realty. See *Sears, Roebuck & Co. v. Seven Palms Motor Inn, Inc.*, which follows. In such a situation, if the use or purpose of the item is peculiar to the particular owner or occupant of the premises, the courts will tend to let him remove the item when he leaves. Accordingly, in the law of landlord and tenant, it is settled that the tenant may remove **trade fixtures** (that is, items used in connection with his trade) provided that this can be done without material injury to the realty. On the other hand, doors may be removed without injury to the structure, yet because they are necessary to the ordinary use of the building and not peculiar to the use of the occupant, they are considered fixtures and thus part of the real property.

SEARS, ROEBUCK & CO. v. SEVEN PALMS MOTOR INN, INC.
Supreme Court of Missouri, 1975.
530 S.W.2d 695.

Facts: Sears had sold to and installed in Seven Palm Motor Inn a number of furnishings, including drapes and bedspreads, in connection with the construction of a motel on land Seven Palms owned. Sears did not receive payment in full for the materials and labor and brought suit to recover $8,357.49 with interest and to establish a mechanic's lien on the motel and land for the unpaid portion of the furnishings. Seven Palms asserts that neither the drapes nor bedspreads are fixtures and thus Sears cannot obtain a mechanic's lien on them. The trial court decided that Sears was entitled to recover $8,357.49 with interest and that it did have a mechanic's lien. The court of appeals affirmed the money judgment but reversed the mechanic's lien, holding that the bedspreads were not lienable items and their inclusion voided the entire lien.

Decision: Judgment for Sears, affirming the money judgment and granting a mechanic's lien for the draperies but not the bedspreads.

Opinion: Henley, J.   Missouri law provides in part: "Every mechanic or other person, who shall do or perform any work or labor upon, or furnish any material [or], fixtures * * * for any building * * * under or by virtue of any contract with the owner * * * shall have for his work or labor done, or materials [or], fixtures * * * furnished, a lien upon such building * * * and upon the land * * *"

Characterization of an item as a fixture, something otherwise personal but attached to realty under such circumstances as to become part of it, depends upon the finding of three elements: annexation to the realty, adaptation to the use to which the realty is devoted, and intent of the annexor that the object become a permanent accession to the freehold [realty]. Missouri cases are uniform in requiring each of these elements to be present in some degree, however slight, before an item may be considered a fixture. [Citations.]

Appellants [Seven Palms] contend that neither the drapes nor the bedspreads are fixtures * * * and therefore not lienable, because they are not annexed or attached to the building.

The purpose of attaching the traverse rods to the realty was to hang drapes therefrom which could be opened or drawn across a window by the motel's guest to control the light in his room or secure his privacy. Of itself, the traverse rod attached to the wall above the window in the room did not accomplish this purpose. To serve this purpose it was essential that the drapes be provided and attached to the rod. They were provided and attached, and became an integral part of the instrument designed for use in connection with the window in the guest's room. As such, the drapes were as much a fixture as the traverse rod itself. It is obvious that the rod and drapes, as a unit, were adapted to the proper use of rooms in a motel and were placed therein with the intent they would form a part of the special purpose for which the building was designed to be used.

Not so the bedspreads. Respondent [Sears] admits that those items are not physically attached to the realty in any way but insists that they have been "constructively annexed." In support of this proposition, respondent argues: the rods are physically fastened to the building; the drapes are affixed to the rods by hooks; the bedspreads match the drapes; a fortiori, the bedspreads "are at least 'constructively annexed' to the rooms * * * by their relationship with the drapes."

The doctrine of constructive annexation recognizes that a particular article, not physically attached to the land, "may be so adapted to the use to which the land is put that it may be considered an integral part of the land" and "constructively annexed" thereto. [Citation.] * * * The rule has not been applied to establishments such as hotels, restaurants, bars and apartment buildings. Thus, movable furniture, tableware and similar equipment, although necessary to the operation of a hotel, are generally not considered fixtures. [Citations.]

The bedspreads are not essential to the use of what is clearly a fixture, nor has it been shown that they cannot readily be used independently elsewhere. Respondent asserts that because the bedspreads "were designed to match and to coexist with the drapes" they must be considered part of a matched set which is essential to the use of rods which are clearly fixtures. Respondent seeks support for this contention in cases that have held easily removable parts of machines and other fixtures may not be considered as separate items. [Citations.] However, in each of these cases, the fixture would have been rendered absolutely useless by removal of the items in question, and such items could not readily be used independently elsewhere. There is no indication that the unit of rod and drapes could not serve its function, which respondent says is to "regulate the flow of light and serve the need for privacy," if the bedspreads were removed. That the decor of a guest room in a motel may be more aesthetically pleasing when bedspreads are made of the same material as drapes, falls far short of the functional relationship needed to justify "constructive annexation." Since the bedspreads were not annexed, physically or constructively, they cannot be characterized as fixtures and are, therefore, nonlienable items.

INCIDENTS OF PROPERTY OWNERSHIP

The importance of the distinction between real and personal property stems primarily from very practical legal consequences that follow from the distinction. Some of these consequences are transfer of property and taxation.

Transfer of Property

As we will discuss in Chapter 50, the transfer of real property during life can be accomplished only by certain formalities, including the execution and delivery of a written instrument known as a deed. Personal property, on the other hand, may be transferred with relative simplicity and informality.

Taxation

Most States levy taxes on the ownership of both real and personal property. The applicable tax rate depends on whether the property is classified as real or personal property.

PERSONAL PROPERTY

The law concerning personal property has been largely codified. The Uniform Commercial Code includes the law of sales of goods (Article 2), as well as the law governing the transfer and negotiation of commercial paper (Article 3), and of investment securities (Article 8). Nonetheless, a number of issues involving the ownership and transfer of title to personal property are not covered by the Code. We address these issues in the remainder of this chapter.

TRANSFER OF TITLE

The acquisition or transfer of title to real property is generally a formal affair. In contrast, title to personal property may be acquired and transferred with relative ease and with a minimum of formality. The facility with which personal property may be transferred is required by the demands of a society whose trade and industry is principally based on transactions in personal property. Stocks, bonds, merchandise, and intellectual property must be sold with a minimum of delay in a free economy. It is only natural that the law will reflect these needs.

By Sale

By definition, a **sale** of *tangible* personal property (goods) is a transfer of title to specified existing goods for a consideration known as the price. Title passes when the parties intend it to pass, and transfer of possession is not required for a transfer of title. For a discussion of this manner of transfer of title, see Chapter 18.

Sales of *intangible* personal property also involve the transfer of title. Many of these sales are also governed by provisions of the UCC, while some, such as copyrights and patents, are governed by specialized Federal legislation.

By Gift

A **gift** is a transfer of property from one person to another without consideration. The lack of any consideration is the basic distinction between a gift and a sale. Because a gift involves no consideration or compensation, it must be completed by delivery of the gift to be effective. A gratuitous promise to make a gift is not binding. In addition, there must be intent on the part of the maker (the **donor**) of the gift to make a present transfer, and there must be acceptance by the recipient (the **donee**) of the gift.

Delivery   Delivery is absolutely necessary to a valid gift. The term "delivery" has a very special meaning, including but not limited to manual transfer of the item to the donee. There can be "delivery" of a gift sufficient to

make it irrevocable if the item is turned over to a third person with instructions to give it to the donee. Frequently, an item, because of its size or location or because it is intangible, is incapable of immediate manual delivery. In such cases, an irrevocable gift may be effected by delivery of something symbolic of dominion over the item. This is referred to as **constructive delivery.** For example, if Joanne declares that she gives an antique desk and all its contents to Barry and hands Barry the key to the desk, in many States a valid gift has been made.

ESTATE OF ROSS v. ROSS
Supreme Court of Utah, 1981.
626 P.2d 489.

Facts: David E. Ross, his two brothers, and their families operated and owned the entire stock of five businesses. Ross had three children, Rod, David II, and Betsy. David II and Betsy were not involved in the operation of the companies, but Rod began working for one of the firms, Equitable Life and Casualty Insurance Company, in 1972. Between 1974 and 1978, the elder Ross informed a number of persons of his desire to reward Rod for his work with Equitable Life by giving him stock in addition to the stock he would inherit. He subsequently executed several stock transfers to Rod, representing shares in various family businesses, which were reflected by appropriate entries on the corporate books. Certificates were issued in Rod's name and placed in an envelope identified with the name of Rod Ross, but they were kept with the other family stock certificates in an office safe to which Rod did not have access. In all, one-fourth of the stock holdings of David E. Ross were transferred to Rod in this manner. This fact is consistent with the elder Ross's expressed intention that Rod should ultimately receive a total of one-half of the stock upon his father's death. David E. died in April 1978. His will divided the estate equally among the three children and made no reference to prior gifts of stock to Rod. David II and Betsy brought an action contesting the validity of the stock transfers. The district court held that the inter vivos (between the living) gifts of the stock were valid, and David II and Betsy appeal.

Decision: Judgment for Rod Ross affirmed.

Opinion: Howe, J.   Appellants assert that three elements must be proven for a person to claim valid title to property by inter vivos gift: a clear and unmistakable intention on the part of the donor to pass immediate ownership, an irrevocable delivery, and acceptance. They concede that there is substantial evidence in the record to support the lower court's conclusion that there was the necessary intent on the part of decedent to make a gift and that Rod "accepted" the stock transfer. They contend, however, that the court's decision was erroneous in that the element of irrevocable delivery was not established by clear and convincing evidence.

An important purpose of the delivery requirement is to avoid the hedging of a would-be donor who wishes to retain certain benefits of ownership, including the control of the gift property, while designating another as the recipient of the property during the donor's lifetime. If a gift is not completed before one's death, of course, it is subject to the formalities of testamentary disposition. In the instant case, therefore, the finding of a gift must be based on the decedent's voluntary parting with the control of the stock during his lifetime.

It is appellants' position that decedent should have parted with his dominion over the certificates by physically delivering them to Rod and that the transfer of ownership on the corporate records was insufficient to meet the requirement of delivery. Other courts have split on this issue, and the question has not been ruled on by this Court.

* * *

We . . . hold that manual delivery of the stock certificates personally to Rod was not a prerequisite to a valid gift.

Viewing the facts of this case in light of the requirements of inter vivos gifts, we find the gifts of stock to Rod were complete and valid. Evidence of decedent's intention that Rod be made the owner of the stock in question during his lifetime was uncontroverted. Appellants do not challenge the sufficiency of the evidence as to donative intent nor the finding of the trial court that the change in ownership was recorded on the corporate books. New certificates were issued in Rod's name. The decedent did not thereafter exercise control over the stocks. On the contrary, Rod voted the stock as its legal owner and received cash and stock dividends.

The fact that the stock certificates were kept in a safe to which decedent, but not Rod, had access is not fatal to the finding of a completed gift. The decedent had physical possession of stock certificates belonging to a number of other Ross family members. There was no assertion or evidence that he exerted control or possessory rights over any of that stock. His custody of Rod's stock was simply consistent with the practice within the family businesses of keeping the stock certificates in a central location clearly identified as to the owners of the shares. Individual envelopes carried owners' names, stock certificate numbers, and the number of shares represented by the certificates.

We find no error in the trial court's interpretation of the evidence or its application of Utah law in reaching the conclusion that the inter vivos gifts to Rod were valid.

Intent   The law is also clear that there must be an intent on the part of the donor to make a present gift of the property. Thus, if Joanne leaves a packet of stocks and bonds with Barry, Barry may or may not acquire good title to them, depending on whether Joanne intended to make a gift of them or simply to place them in Barry's hands for safekeeping. A voluntary, uncompensated delivery with intent to give the recipient title constitutes a gift when the donee accepts it. If these conditions are met, as shown in the following case, the donor has no further claim to the property.

COHEN v. BAYSIDE FEDERAL SAVINGS AND LOAN ASSOCIATION
Supreme Court of New York, Term, 1970.
62 Misc.2d 738, 309 N.Y.S.2d 980.

Facts: When Richard Rothchild became engaged to Carol Cohen, he gave her a diamond engagement ring valued at $1,000. Shortly before the wedding date, however, Richard was killed in an automobile accident. His estate then instituted this action to recover the ring.

Decision: Judgment for Carol Cohen.

Opinion: **Tessler, J.** Actions for return of engagement rings have had an interesting and confusing history in New York. These actions were permitted at common law prior to 1935. However, in 1935 the Legislature of this State enacted * * * (the heart balm statute) which was later interpreted by the courts so as to bar actions for the return of engagement rings in most instances. [Citations.] These results were widely criticized. [Citations.] In response to this criticism, in 1965 the Legislature amended * * * the Civil Rights Law to permit recovery of engagement rings where "justice so requires."

In Lowe v. Quinn, [citation] the Appellate Division, First Department, held that the common law rules formulated before 1935 would again be applicable.

* * *

However, reference to these common law rules formulated prior to 1935 is of little help in the present instance since this case appears to be one of first impression in this State. In the absence of any controlling authority, this court has sought help by looking to applicable decisional law in other jurisdictions, the general principles underlying engagement ring cases in general and, finally, to what justice requires in this situation.

An examination of the relevant authorities in other states indicates that they are split.

* * *

Nor does an examination of the principles underlying the gift of engagement ring cases in general clearly point the way to a particular result. The results set forth in the decisions in gift of engagement ring cases are usually predictable and understandable. However, the legal principles and rationales relied upon by the courts are often divergent and muddled. For example, it is settled that where a fiancee breaks an engagement without the fault of the donor, she must return the ring. [Citation.] It is also well settled that where the donor breaks the engagement, the ring may be kept by the donee [citation] and, generally, where the engagement is broken by mutual consent, the ring also goes back to the donor. [Citation.]

While these results are equitable, the various legal theories asserted are not always logical and persuasive. Some courts have propounded a pledge theory. [Citation.] Other courts state that principles of unjust enrichment govern [citation] and the most popular rationale is that the ring is given as a gift on condition subsequent. [Citation.] It is not always clear, however, whether it is the actual marriage of the parties or the donee's not performing any act that would prevent the marriage that is the actual condition of the "transaction."

Thus, a confusing body of law has grown up around the engagement ring and, after careful consideration of these principles, this court has decided that Carol should keep the ring because that result is equitable and because "justice so requires" for the following reasons:

While the engagement ring to some people in the "mod" world of today is just another material possession and while it has not been unknown in some circles for recipients of these rings to flaunt them, to compare their luster, number of carats, etc., with the rings of their friends, for the vast majority the ring still remains a hallowed symbol of the love and devotion that a prospective husband and wife bear for each other. In my judgment, no gift given during a lifetime can approach the meaningfulness and significance of the engagement ring. When Richard gave the ring to Carol, he obviously intended that she have it and keep it unless she affirmatively did something to prevent the marriage of the parties. While it is improbable that at the time of the gift either gave a thought to the consequences that would arise in the event of the death of one of the parties, I firmly believe that had Richard thought of these consequences he would have intended that in the event of his untimely death Carol should keep the ring as a symbol of his love and affection. There appears to be no reason, in logic or morals, to prevent such a result.

This court frankly acknowledges that implicit in this determination is a recognition that the gift of an engagement ring is a special occasion interwoven with romance and mutual love. It is a meaningful act symbolic of much more than the ordinary and usual business transaction. I am convinced that it is time for a change in our approach to this area. The traditional approach of applying the sound and settled principles of business law and the law of gifts to the giving of an engagement ring has resulted in a myriad of decisional law in this area, which is, to say the least, in much confusion and determinative of little.

I cannot believe that the age-old ritual of giving an engagement ring to bind the mutual premarital vows can be or is intended to be treated as an exchange of consideration as practical in the everyday market place. Can it be seriously urged that the giving of this ring by the decedent "groom" to his loved one and bride-to-be can be treated as the ordinary commercial or business transaction requiring the ultimate in consideration and payment? I think not. To treat this special and usually once in a lifetime occasion, one as requiring quid pro quo, is a mistake and unrealistic.

Acceptance   The final requirement of a valid gift is acceptance by the donee. In most instances, of course, the donee will accept the gift with gratitude. Accordingly, the law usually presumes that the donee has accepted. But there are situations in which a donee does not wish to accept a gift, such as when the gift imposes a burden on the donee. In such cases, the law will not require the recipient to accept an unwanted gift. For example, a gift of an elephant or a wrecked car in need of extensive repairs may be prudently rejected by a donee.

By Will or Descent

Title to personal property is frequently acquired by inheritance from a person who dies, either with or without a will. We discuss this method of acquiring title in Chapter 51.

By Accession

Many of the practical problems surrounding the title to personal property stem from its principal characteristic—movability. One of these problems is identified by the phrase "title by accession." **Accession,** in its strict sense, means the right of the owner of property to any increase in it, whether caused by natural or artificial means. For example, the owner of a cow requires title by accession to any calves born to that cow.

Problems arise, however, if David attaches an item of personal property to Timothy's property without Timothy's consent or if David improves by his labor the property of Timothy without Timothy's consent. For example, David takes lumber belonging to Timothy and without Timothy's consent builds it into a wagon. Or David takes a silver cup belonging to Timothy and without Timothy's consent melts it down into a tray. To whom does the "new" product belong? The material, or part of it, was originally the property of Timothy. The labor and skill necessary to create the new product were David's. Timothy, the owner of the property converted, will be entitled to one of the two forms of relief. He will be entitled either to a return of the item or to damages. Which of these two forms of relief he can claim depends on the facts of the case. If the taking was deliberate and with knowledge that the item was the property of another, the general rule is that the original owner can have the improved property returned to him.

The more difficult and frequent problem arises when the person making the improvement mistakenly believes that the property belongs to him. In this case, the law is not aided by a sense of punishing a wrongdoer. The law must attempt to reconcile the competing interests of two innocent parties. If there is an innocent taking and the identity of the converted item has changed or the value of the labor is greater than the value of the converted material in its original form, then title passes to the person who applied the labor. In such a case, the original owner will not be entitled to the new item; his only remedy will be an award of money damages for the value of the original article. Otherwise, the original owner may recover the property but must compensate the other party for the reasonable value of the benefits conferred by the improvements.

By Confusion

The basic problem of confusion is somewhat similar to the case of title by accession. **Confusion** arises when identical goods belonging to different people are so *commingled* (mixed) that the owners cannot identify their own property. For example, Hereford cattle belonging to Benton are mixed with Hereford cattle belonging to Armstrong, and neither person's herd can be specifically identified; or grain owned by Courts is combined with similar grain owned by Beck. Confusion may result from accident, mistake, willful act, or agreement of the parties. If the goods can be apportioned, each owner who proves his proportion of the whole is entitled to receive his share. If, however, the confusion results from the willful and wrongful act of one of the parties, he will lose his entire interest if he cannot prove his share. Frequently, the problem arises not because the original interest cannot be proved but because there is not enough left to distribute a full share to each owner. In such case, if the

confusion was due to mistake, accident, or agreement, the loss will be borne by each in proportion to his share. If caused by an intentional and unauthorized act, the wrongdoer will first bear any loss.

By Possession

In some instances a person may acquire title to movable personal property by taking possession of it. If the **property** has been intentionally **abandoned** (intentionally disposed of), a *finder* is entitled to the property. Moreover, under the general rule, a finder is entitled to **lost property** (unintentionally left) against everyone except the true owner. Suppose Karen, the owner of an apartment complex, leases a kitchenette apartment to Fountaine. One night Regina, Fountaine's mother-in-law, is invited to sleep in the convertible bed in the living room. In the course of preparing the bed, Regina finds an emerald ring caught on the springs under the mattress. The ring is turned over to the police, but diligent inquiry does not turn up the true owner. Regina will be entitled to the ring because she is considered the finder.

A different rule applies when the lost property is in the ground. Here, the owner of the land has a claim superior to that of the finder. For example, Jack employs Joseph to excavate a lateral sewer. Joseph uncovers old Indian relics. Jack, not Joseph, has the superior claim.

There is a further exception to the rule giving the finder first claim against all but the true owner. If property is intentionally placed somewhere by the owner, who then unintentionally leaves it, it is called **mislaid property.** Most courts hold that if property has been mislaid, not lost, then the owner of the premises, not the finder, has first claim if the true owner is not discovered. This doctrine is involved frequently in cases where items are found on trains, buses, airplanes, and in restaurants.

Many States, including Illinois, as shown in the following case, now have statutes that provide a means of vesting title to lost property in the finder when a prescribed search for the owner is fruitless. These statutes generally do not determine the right to possession against any party other than the true owner.

PASET v. OLD ORCHARD BANK AND TRUST CO.
Appellate Court of Illinois, First District, 1978.
62 Ill.App.3d 534, 19 Dec. 389, 378 N.E.2d 1264.

Facts: While in the examination booth in the safety deposit vault of Old Orchard Bank, Brenice Paset found $6,235 in currency in the seat of a chair that was partially under the table. She notified the bank officials and turned the money over to them. They told her that they would try to locate the owner but, if unsuccessful within one year, that she, Brenice, could have the money. The bank then sent a notice to all of its safety deposit box customers asking if they had lost some property. No response was received within a year, but the bank still refused to turn over the money, contending that it had to hold it for the true owner. Brenice then brought this action to establish herself as the owner of the money by her compliance with the requirements of the applicable State statute. The bank argues that the money was mislaid, and therefore the statute is not applicable. The trial court adopted the bank's argument and the plaintiff appeals.

Decision: Judgment reversed and remanded with directions to enter judgment for the finder, Brenice Paset.

Opinion: Simon, J. This appeal, then, requires a determination of whether a finder of cash in an examining booth in a safety deposit vault may be a keeper under the Illinois estray statute and an analysis of the extent to which the common law concepts of lost and mislaid property apply to the statute. * * * The Illinois estray statute's principal purposes are to encourage and facilitate the return of property to the true owner, and then to reward a finder for his honesty if the property remains unclaimed. The statute provides an incentive for finders to report their discoveries by making it possible for them, after the passage of the requisite time, to acquire legal title to the property they have found. [Citation.] By directing the county clerk to publicize and advertise the property, the statute further enhances the opportunity of the owner to recover what he has lost.

Traditionally, the common law has treated lost and mislaid property differently for the purposes of determining ownership of property someone has found. Mislaid property is that which is intentionally put in a certain place and later forgotten; at common law a finder acquires no rights to mislaid property. The element of intentional deposit present in the case of mislaid property is absent in the case of lost property, for property is deemed lost when it is unintentionally separated from the dominion of its owner. The general rule is that the finder is entitled to possession of lost property against everyone except the true owner. We are not concerned in this case with abandoned property where the owner, intending to relinquish all rights to his property, leaves it free to be appropriated by any other person. Although at common law the finder is entitled to keep abandoned property, the plaintiff has not taken the position that the money here was abandoned. [Citation.]

As is usual in cases involving a determination of whether property is lost or mislaid, this court is not here assisted by direct evidence, for, obviously, the true owner is not available to state what his intent was. Also, because all the evidence here has been presented by affidavit or stipulation, this court is in as advantageous a position as the trial judge to determine whether the money was lost or mislaid. Our conclusion is that the estray statute should be applied, and ownership of the money vested in the plaintiff finder.

Thus, we do not accept the bank's argument that the money was mislaid rather than lost. It is complete speculation to infer, as the bank urges, that the money was deliberately placed by its owner on the chair located partially under a table in the examining booth, and then forgotten. If the money was intentionally placed on the chair by someone who forgot where he left it, the bank's notice to safety deposit box subscribers should have alerted the owner. The failure of an owner to appear to claim the money in the interval since its discovery is affirmative evidence that the property was not mislaid. [Citations.]

Because the evidence, though ambiguous, tends to indicate that the money probably was not mislaid, and because neither party contends that the money was abandoned, we conclude that the ambiguity should, as a matter of public policy, be resolved in favor of the presumption that the money was lost. This conclusion is in harmony with the above mentioned purposes of the estray statute, for it construes the statute liberally rather then technically, with the result that the statute is brought into play rather than rejected. Such an application of the statute better effectuates the legislature's goal of restoring property to a true owner; it provides incentive for a finder to report his discovery by rewarding him if the true owner does not appear within the statutorily-determined time limit.

CONCURRENT OWNERSHIP

Real or personal property may be owned by one individual or by two or more persons concurrently. If title is held concurrently by two or more persons, they are generally referred to as *co-tenants*, each entitled to an undivided interest in the entire item and neither having a claim to any specific portion of it.

Each may have equal undivided interests or one may have a larger undivided share than the other.

There are four ways in which personal property may be owned concurrently: (1) joint tenancy, (2) tenancy in common, (3) tenancy by the entireties, and (4) community property. We discuss these forms of concurrent ownership in Chapter 49.

CHAPTER SUMMARY

INTRODUCTION TO PROPERTY

Property	**Definition** interest that is legally protected **Tangible Property** physical objects **Intangible Property** property that does not exist in a physical form **Real Property** land and interests in land **Personal Property** all property that is not real property **Fixture** personal property so firmly attached to real property that an interest in it arises under real property law
Incidents of Property Ownership	**Transfer of Property** ■ *Real Property* by formal procedure ■ *Personal Property* by simple and informal procedure **Taxation** taxability and tax rates often depend upon whether property is real or personal

PERSONAL PROPERTY

Transfer of Title	Sale transfer of property for consideration (price)
	Gift transfer of property without consideration

- *Delivery*   includes both manual transfer of the item and constructive delivery (delivery of something symbolic of control over the item)
- *Intent*
- *Acceptance*

Will   right acquired upon death of the owner

Accession   right of the owner of the property to any increase in it

Confusion   intermixing of goods belonging to two or more owners such that the property of all of them can no longer be identified except as part of a mass of like goods

- *If due to mistake, accident, or agreement, any loss will be shared proportionately*
- *If caused by an intentional or unauthorized act, the wrongdoer will bear any loss*

Possession   a person may acquire title by taking possession of property

- *Abandoned Property*   intentionally disposed of by the owner; the finder is entitled to the property
- *Lost Property*   unintentionally left by the owner; the finder is generally entitled to the property
- *Mislaid Property*   intentionally placed by the owner but unintentionally left; the owner of the premises is generally entitled to the property

QUESTIONS

1. Distinguish between (a) tangible and intangible property, and (b) real and personal property.
2. Define and give three examples of a fixture.
3. Identify and discuss the three elements for a valid gift.
4. Distinguish among the rights of a finder to abandoned, mislaid, and lost property.
5. Define and contrast the property rights created by accession and confusion.

PROBLEMS

1. In January, Roger Burke loaned his favorite nephew, Jimmy White, his valuable painting by Picasso. Knowing that Jimmy would celebrate his twenty-first birthday on May 15, Burke sent a letter to Jimmy on April 14 stating:

Dear Jimmy,
   Tomorrow I leave on my annual trip to Europe, and I want to make you a fitting birthday gift which I do by sending you my enclosed promissory note. Also I want you to keep the Picasso which I loaned you last January, and you may now consider it yours. Happy birthday!

Affectionately,
/s/ Uncle Roger

The negotiable promissory note for $5,000 sent with the letter was signed by Roger Burke, payable to Jimmy White or bearer, and dated May 15. On May 21 Burke was killed in an automobile accident while motoring in France.

First Bank was appointed administrator of Burke's estate. Jimmy presented the note to the administrator and demanded payment, which was refused. Jimmy brought an action against First Bank as administrator, seeking recovery on the note. The administrator brought an action against Jimmy seeking return of the painting by Picasso.

(a) What decision in the action on the note?
(b) What decision in the action to recover the painting?

2. Several years ago Pierce purchased a tract of land on which there was an old, vacant house. Recently, Pierce employed Fried, a carpenter, to repair and remodel the house. While Fried was tearing out a partition for the purpose of enlarging one of the rooms, he discovered a metal box hidden in the wall of the house. Fried broke open the box and discovered that it contained $2,000 in gold and

silver coins and old-style bills. Fried then took the box and its contents to Pierce and told her where he had found it. When Fried handed the box and the money over to Pierce, he said, "If you do not find the owner, I claim the money." Pierce placed the money in an envelope and deposited it in her safe deposit box, where it is at present. No one has ever claimed the money, but Pierce refuses to give it to Fried.

Fried brings an action against Pierce to recover the money. Decision?

3. Gable, the owner of a lumber company, was cutting trees over the boundary line of his property and property owned by Lane. Although he realized he had crossed onto Lane's property, Gable cut trees on Lane's property of the same kind as those he had cut on his own land. While on Lane's property, he found a diamond ring on the ground, which he took home. All of the timber cut that day by Gable was commingled.

What are Lane's rights, if any, (a) in the timber and (b) in the ring?

4. Decide each of the following problems.

(a) A chimney sweep found a jewel and took it to a goldsmith, whose apprentice took the stone out and refused to return it. The chimney sweep sues the goldsmith.

(b) One of several boys walking along a railroad track found an old stocking. All started playing with it until it burst in the hands of its discoverer, revealing several hundred dollars. The original discoverer claims it all; the other boys claim it should be divided equally.

(c) A traveling salesman notices a parcel of bank notes on the floor of a store as he is leaving. He picks them up and gives them to the owner of the store to keep for the true owner. After three years they have not been reclaimed, and the salesman sues the storekeeper.

(d) Frank is hired to clean out the swimming pool at the country club. He finds a diamond ring on the bottom of the pool. The true owner cannot be found. The country club sues Frank for possession of the ring.

(e) A customer found a pocketbook lying on a barber's table. He gave it to the barber to hold for the true owner, who failed to appear. The customer sues the barber.

5. Jones had fifty crates of oranges about equally divided between grades A, B, and C, grade A being the highest quality and C the lowest quality. Smith had 1,000 crates of oranges, about 90 percent of which were grade A, but some of them grades B and C, the exact quantity of each being unknown. Smith willfully mixed Jones's crates with his own so that it was impossible to identify any particular crate. Jones seized the whole lot. Smith demanded 900 crates of grade A and fifty each of grades B and C. Jones refused to give them up unless Smith could identify particular crates. This Smith could not do. Smith brought an action against Jones to recover what he demanded or its value. Judgment for whom, and why?

6. Bernes, the owner and operator of Blackacre, decided to cease farming operations and liquidate his holdings. Bernes sold fifty head of yearling Merino sheep to Billings and sold Blackacre to Clifton. He executed and delivered to Billings a bill of sale for the sheep and was paid for them. It was understood that Billings would send a truck for the sheep within a few days. At the same time, Bernes executed a warranty deed conveying Blackacre to Clifton. Clifton took possession of the farm and brought along 100 head of his yearling Merino sheep and turned them into the pasture, not knowing the sheep Bernes sold Billings were still in the pasture. After the sheep were mixed, it was impossible to identify the fifty head belonging to Billings. After proper demand, Billings sued Clifton to recover the fifty head of sheep. Decision?

7. Susan permitted Kevin to take her very old grandfather clock on the basis of Kevin's representations that he was skilled at repairing such clocks and restoring them to their original condition and could do the job for $60. The clock had been badly damaged for years. Kevin immediately sold the clock to Fixit Shop for $30. Fixit Shop was in the business of repairing a large variety of items and also sold used articles. Three months later, Susan was in the Fixit Shop and clearly established that a grandfather clock Fixit Shop had for sale was the one she had given Kevin to repair. Fixit Shop had replaced more than half of the moving parts by having exact duplicates custom made; the clock's exterior had been restored by a skilled cabinet-maker; and the clock's face had been replaced by a duplicate. All materials belonged to Fixit Shop, and the work was accomplished by its employees. Fixit Shop asserts it bought the clock in the normal course of business from Kevin, who represented that it belonged to him. The fair market value of the clock in its damaged condition was $30, and the value of repairs made is $220.

Susan sued Fixit Shop for return of the clock. Fixit Shop defended that it now had title to the clock and, in the alternative, that Susan must pay the value of the repairs if she is entitled to regain possession. Decision?

8. Hyer rented a vacant lot from Bateman for a filling station under an oral agreement and placed on it a lightly constructed building bolted to a concrete slab and storage tanks laid on the ground in a shallow excavation. Later, a lease was prepared by Hyer, providing that Hyer might remove the equipment at the termination of the lease. This lease was not executed, having been rejected by Bateman because of a renewal clause it contained, but several years later another lease was prepared that both Hyer and Bateman did sign. This lease did not mention removal of the equipment. At the termination of this lease Hyer removed the equipment, and Bateman brought an action to recover possession of the equipment. What judgment?

9. Elvers sold a parcel of real estate, describing it by its legal description and making no mention of any improvements or fixtures on it. The land had on it a residence, a barn, a rail fence, a stack of hay, some growing corn, and a windmill. The residence had a mirror built into the panel and a heating system consisting of a furnace and steam pipes and coils. There were chairs, beds, tables, and other furniture in the house. On the house was a lightning rod. In the basement were screens for the windows. Which of these things passed by the deed and which did not?

10. John Swan rented a safety deposit box at the Tenth Citizens Bank of Emanon, State of X. On December 17, 1989, Swan went to the bank with stock certificates to place in the safety deposit box. After he was admitted to the vault and had placed the stock certificates in the box, Swan found lying on the floor of the vault a $5,000 negotiable bearer bond issued by the State of Wisconsin with coupons attached, due June 30, 1995. Swan picked up the bond and, observing that it did not recite the name of the owner, left the vault and went to the office of the president of the bank. He told the president what had occurred and delivered the bond to the president only after obtaining his promise that, should the owner not call for the bond or become known to the bank by June 30, 1990, the bank would redeliver the bond to Swan. On July 1, 1990, Swan learned that the owner of the bond had not called for it, nor was his identity known to the bank. Swan then asked that the bond be returned to him. The bank refused, stating that it would continue to hold the bond until claimed by the owner. Swan brings an action against the bank to recover possession of the bond. Decision?

48 BAILMENTS AND DOCUMENTS OF TITLE

A bailment is the relationship created by the transfer by delivery of possession of personal property, without transfer of title, by one person called the bailor to another called the bailee for the accomplishment of a certain purpose, after which the property is to be returned by the bailee to the bailor or disposed of according to the bailor's directions. Unlike such well-known legal terms as contract, agent, sale, partnership, corporation, and insurance, the term *bailment* has not passed into common usage and thus is not familiar to many people. Nonetheless, the word *bailment* denotes a transaction that not only is of considerable antiquity but also is one of the most common occurrences in everyday life. It is not an exaggeration to say that practically every person, whether carrying on a business or not, becomes a party to a bailment. You will easily understand this from the following common examples of bailments: keeping a car in a public garage; leaving a car, a watch, or any other article to be repaired; renting a car or truck; checking a hat or coat at a theater or restaurant; leaving clothes to be laundered; delivery of jewelry, stocks, bonds, or other valuables to secure the payment of a debt; storage of goods in a warehouse; and the shipment of goods by public or private transportation.

Not only are bailments of common occurrence, but they are also of great commercial importance in their own right. As the above examples indicate, bailments include the transportation, storage, repairing, and renting of goods, which together involve billions of dollars worth of transactions each year.

Documents of title are commonly used in bailment transactions. The most frequently used documents of title are warehouse receipts issued by warehousers and bills of lading issued by carriers.

BAILMENTS

A **bailment** is the temporary transfer of possession without title of personal property by one party (the **bailor**) to another (the **bailee**). The benefit of a bailment may, by its terms, accrue solely to the bailor or solely to the bailee or may accrue to both parties. A bailment may be with or without compensation. On this basis, bailments are classified as follows.

1. *Bailments for the bailor's sole benefit* include the gratuitous custody of personal property and the gratuitous services that involve custody of personal property, such as repairs or transportation. For example, if Sherry stores, repairs, or transports Tim's goods without compensation, this is a bailment for the sole benefit of the bailor, Tim.
2. *Bailments for the bailee's sole benefit* are usually limited to the gratuitous loan of personal property for use by the bailee, as where Tim, without compensation, lends his car, lawn mower, or book to Sherry for her use.
3. *Bailments for the mutual benefit of both parties* include the ordinary commercial bailments, such as when goods are delivered to a repairman, jewels to a pawnbroker, or an automobile to a parking lot attendant.

ESSENTIAL ELEMENTS OF A BAILMENT

The basic and essential elements of a bailment are (1) delivery of possession by a bailor to a bailee; (2) delivery of personal property and not real property; (3) possession without ownership by the bailee; (4) a determinable period of time; and (5) an absolute duty on the bailee to return the property to the bailor or to dispose of it according to the bailor's directions.

In the great majority of cases, there are two simple tests by which the existence of a bailment can be determined: (1) a separation of ownership and possession of the property (possession without ownership), and (2) a duty on the party in possession to redeliver the identical property to the owner or to dispose of it according to his directions.

Delivery of Possession

The term *bailment* is derived from the French word *bailler*, meaning "to deliver." Possession by a bailee in a bailment relationship involves (1) the bailee's power to control, and (2) either an intention to control or an awareness on the part of the bailee that the rightful possessor has given up physical control of the personal property. Thus, for example, where a customer in a restaurant hangs her hat or coat on a hook furnished for that purpose, the hat or coat is within an area under the physical control of the restaurant owner. But the restaurant owner is not a bailee of the hat or coat unless he clearly signifies that he intends to exercise the power to control the hat or coat. On the other hand, where a clerk in a store helps a customer remove her coat in order to try on a new one, it is generally held that the owner of the store becomes a bailee of the old coat through the clerk, his employee. Here, the clerk has signified an intention to exercise control over the coat by taking it from the customer, and a bailment results.

Leaving a car in a commercial parking lot may be a bailment. The parking lot cases fall generally into three categories: (1) where an owner parks his car in a parking lot, pays a charge, and receives a claim check, but locks the car and takes the keys away. This class of cases is generally held to be a lease or license (a right to use the space); (2) where an owner leaves his car with an attendant who assumes control of the car and parks it, and the owner pays a charge and receives a ticket as a means of identifying the car on redelivery. This class is held to be a bailment; (3) where the status of the parties falls in between the above two categories and is controlled by the nature of the circumstances. The third class covers cases where, even though the owner parks his car and keeps the keys, the parking lot operator maintains sufficient control to constitute a bailment. In analyzing this third class of cases, the amount of free access permitted by the parking lot operator is crucial. The question is how much control does the parking lot operator hold himself out to the public to be exercising?

SEWALL v. FITZ-INN AUTO PARKS, INC.
Court of Appeals of Massachusetts, 1975.
3 Mass.App. 380, 330 N.E.2d 853.

Facts: Mr. Sewall left his car in a parking lot owned by Fitz-Inn Auto Parks, Inc. The lot is approximately 100 by 200 feet in size and has a chain link fence along the rear boundary to separate the lot from a facility of the Massachusetts Bay Transportation Authority. Although the normal entrance and exit are located at the front of the lot, it is also possible to leave by way of a small side street on each side of the lot. Upon entering the lot, the driver would pay the attendant on duty a fee of $.25 to park. The attendant's duties are limited to collecting money from patrons and directing them to parking spaces. Ordinarily, the attendant remained on duty until 11:00 A.M., after which time the lot was left unattended. Furthermore, a patron could remove his car from the lot at any time without interference by any employee of the parking lot.

On the morning of April 15, 1970, Sewall entered the lot, paid the $.25 fee, parked his car in a space designated by the attendant, locked it, and took the keys with him. This was a practice that he had followed routinely for several years. When he returned to the unattended lot that evening, however, he found that his car was gone, apparently having been stolen by an unidentified third person. He then brought this action against Fitz-Inn, the owner of the lot, to recover the value of the car. The trial court directed verdict for the defendant and Sewall appeals.

Decision: Judgment for Fitz-Inn Auto Parks, Inc. affirmed.

Opinion: **Armstrong, J.** The case turns on whether the facts warranted a finding that the transaction between the parties constituted a bailment for hire of the plaintiff's automobile, rather than a mere letting of parking space. [Citations.] The existence of a bailment is a prerequisite to the plaintiff's right to recover, either in contract or in tort, as the defendant would not otherwise be under any duty to safeguard the plaintiff's car against theft. [Citations.] We are of the opinion that no bailment has been shown and that the trial judge was correct in directing verdicts [in favor of Fitz-Inn Auto Parks.]

A bailment, by definition, arises only upon delivery of possession of the property sought to be bailed, and at least some degree of control over that property, to the putative bailee. [Citations.] Once possession and control of an automobile have been transferred to the operator of a parking facility for a fee, the owner (in the absence of any warning or understanding to the contrary) is justified in concluding that the operator has assumed responsibility to safeguard the automobile, and the operator has a legally enforceable duty to exercise reasonable care in the fulfillment of that responsibility. [Citation.] But if there has been no such delivery of possession or control to the operator, nor any acceptance thereof by him, he cannot, without more, be regarded as having undertaken to protect the car and owes the owner no duty to do so. [Citation.]

It has long been held that the surrender of the car keys to the parking facility attendant is a sufficient delivery of possession and control to create a bailment for hire, whether the keys are left at the attendant's request [citation] or with his knowledge and acquiescence in the absence of such a request. [Citation.] The same result has recently been reached where the owner parked and locked his car, without surrendering the keys, in an enclosed parking facility whose sole means of egress was manned by an attendant responsible for stopping and checking each car leaving the facility. [Citation.] * * *

The plaintiff in effect is asking us to extend the principle applied in [citations.] In those cases the garage, while not exercising the degree of control possible through possession of the keys, did exercise (or purport to exercise) control over the departure of vehicles from its facility. In the present case neither type of control was actually or apparently exercised or asserted by the defendant. The role of the attendant, so far as known to the plaintiff, was confined to collecting a uniform twenty-five cent fee from motorists as they entered the lot and directing them to parking spaces. The plaintiff knew that he could remove his car from the lot at any time without interference by an employee of the defendant. Indeed, it should have been obvious to him, because of the open character of the lot and the absence of any attendant on all the evenings when he had removed his car, that any control exercised by the defendant over his car, and any correlative responsibility assumed with respect thereto, came to an end once he had paid the fee and parked the car. [Citation.]

Personal Property

The bailment relationship can exist only with respect to personal property. The delivery of possession of real property by the owner to another is covered by real property law. It is not necessary that the bailed property be tangible. Intangible property such as promissory notes, corporate bonds, shares of stock, and life insurance policies that are evidenced by written instruments and thus capable of delivery may be and frequently are the subject matter of bailments.

Possession for a Determinable Time

To establish a bailment relationship, the person receiving possession must be under a duty to return the personal property and must not obtain title to it. Whether a particular transaction constitutes a bailment or a sale must be determined by the particular situation. A sale always involves a transfer to the buyer of *title* to specific property. If the identical property transferred is to be returned, even though in altered form, the transaction is a bailment; however, if other property of equal value or the money value may be returned, there is a transfer of title, and the transaction is a sale.

Restoration of Possession to the Bailor

The bailee is legally obligated to restore possession of the property when the period of the bailment ends. A bailment for the mutual benefit of both parties ordinarily terminates when the purpose of the bailment is fully accomplished or when the time for which the bailment was created expires. The bailment may, of course, be terminated earlier by mutual consent of the parties. A breach by the bailee of any of his obligations gives the bailor the privilege of terminating the bailment. A bailment is also terminated by destruction of the bailed property because there can be no bailment without the subject personal property.

Bailments for the benefit of the bailee alone or for the benefit of the bailor alone are ordinarily for a definite time or purpose. Such bailments do not terminate until the specified time expires or the purpose is accomplished.

In practice, however, these bailments are often terminated at will. For example, an individual who has gratuitously undertaken to store his neighbor's piano for six months will most likely be able to return the piano before the expiration of that period without liability.

Normally, the bailee is required to return the identical goods bailed, although the goods may be in a changed condition because of the work that the bailee was required to perform on them. An exception to this rule obtains in the case of **fungible goods,** such as grain, where, for all practical purposes, every particle is the equivalent of every other particle, and which the bailee is expected to mingle with other like goods during the bailment. In such a case, obviously the bailee cannot be required to return the identical goods bailed. His obligation is simply to return goods of the same quality and quantity.

RIGHTS AND DUTIES OF BAILOR AND BAILEE

The bailment relationship creates rights and duties on the part of the bailor and the bailee. The bailee is under a duty to exercise due care for the safety of the property and to return it to the right person. The bailee has the exclusive right to possess the property for the term of the bailment. Depending on the nature of the transaction, a bailee may have the right to compensation and reimbursement of expenses. The bailor has certain duties with respect to the condition of the bailed goods.

The law does not permit certain bailees, namely, common carriers, public warehousers, and innkeepers, to limit their liability for breach of their duties to the bailor, except as provided by statute. Other bailees, however, may vary their duties and liabilities by contract with the bailor. Where liability is limited by contract, the law requires that any such limitation be properly brought to the attention of the bailor before the property is bailed by her. This is especially true in the case of "professional bailees," such as repair garages, who make it their business to act as bailees and who deal with the public on a uniform rather than an individual basis. Thus, a variation or limitation in writing contained in a check or stub given to the bailor or posted on the walls of the bailee's place of business will ordinarily *not* bind the bailor unless the bailee (a) draws the bailor's attention to the writing, and (b) informs the bailor that it contains a limitation or variation of liability.

Bailee's Duty to Exercise Due Care

The bailee must exercise due care not to permit injury to or destruction of the property by him or third parties. The amount of recovery is discussed in *Mieske v. Bartell Drug Co.*, which follows. The degree of care depends on the nature of the bailment relationship and the character of the property. Ordinarily, a bailee is *not* an insurer of the subject of the bailment. Because the failure to exercise due care for the property or intentional wrongdoing is the basis of his liability, in the absence of fault, the bailee is not liable where the property is lost, stolen, or destroyed.

MIESKE v. BARTELL DRUG CO.
Supreme Court of Washington, 1979.
92 Wash.2d 40, 593 P.2d 1308.

Facts: Mrs. Mieske delivered thirty-two fifty-foot reels of developed movie film to the Bartell Drug Company to be spliced together into four reels for convenience of viewing. She placed the films, which contained irreplaceable pictures of her family activities over a period of years, into the order in which they were to be spliced and then delivered them to the manager of Bartell. The manager placed a film processing packet on the bag of films and gave Mrs. Mieske a receipt that stated that "We assume no responsibility beyond retail cost of film unless otherwise agreed to in writing." Although the disclaimer was not discussed, Mrs. Mieske's parting words to the store manager were "Don't lose these. They are my life."

Bartell sent the film to its processing agent, GAF Corporation, which intended to send them to another processing lab for splicing. While at the GAF laboratory, however, the film was accidently disposed of into the garbage dumpster and was never recovered. Upon learning of the loss of their film, the Mieskes brought this action to recover damages from Bartell and GAF. Defendants argue that their liability is limited to the cost of the unexposed film. A jury verdict was entered for the Mieskes for $7,500 and the defendants appeal.

Decision: Judgment for the Mieskes affirmed.

Opinion: Brachtenbach, J. Two main issues are raised: (1) the measure of damages and (2) the effect of the exclusionary clause appearing on the film receipt.

* * *

The standard of recovery for destruction of personal property was summarized in *McCurdy v. Union Pac. R.R.*, [Citation]. We recognized in *McCurdy* that (1) personal property which is destroyed may have a market value, in which case that market value is the measure of damages; (2) if destroyed property has no market value but can be replaced or reproduced, then the measure is the cost of replacement or reproduction; (3) if the destroyed property has no market value and cannot be replaced or reproduced, then the value to the owner is to be the proper measure of damages. However, while not stated in *McCurdy*, we have held that in the third *McCurdy* situation, damages are not recoverable for the sentimental value which the owner places on the property. [Citations.]

The defendants argue that plaintiffs' property comes within the second rule of *McCurdy, i.e.*, the film could be replaced and that their liability is limited to the cost of replacement film. Their position is not well taken. Defendants' proposal would award the plaintiffs the cost of acquiring film without pictures imposed thereon. That is not what plaintiffs lost. Plaintiffs lost not merely film able to capture images by exposure but rather film upon which was recorded a multitude of frames depicting many significant events in their lives. Awarding plaintiffs the funds to purchase 32 rolls of blank film is hardly a replacement of the 32 rolls of image which they had recorded over the years. Therefore the third rule of *McCurdy* is the appropriate measure of damages, *i.e.*, the property has no market value and cannot be replaced or reproduced.

The law, in those circumstances, decrees that the measure of damages is to be determined by the value to the owner, often referred to as the intrinsic value of the property. Restatement of Torts § 911.

Necessarily the measure of damages in these circumstances is the most imprecise of the three categories. Yet difficulty of assessment is not cause to deny damages to a plaintiff whose property has no market value and cannot be replaced or reproduced. [Citations.]

The fact that damages are difficult to ascertain and measure does not diminish the loss to the person whose property has been destroyed. Indeed, the very statement of the rule suggests the opposite. If one's destroyed property has a market value, presumably its equivalent is available on the market and the owner can acquire that equivalent property. However, if the owner cannot acquire the property in the market or by replacement or reproduction, then he simply cannot be made whole.

The problem is to establish the value to the owner. Market and replacement values are relatively ascertainable by appropriate proof. Recognizing that value to the owner encompasses a subjective element, the rule has been established that compensation for sentimental or fanciful values will not be allowed. [Citations.] That restriction was placed upon the jury in this case by the court's damages instruction.

* * *

The next issue is to determine the legal effect of the exclusionary clause which was on the film receipt given plaintiff wife by Bartell. As noted above, it read: "We assume no responsibility beyond retail cost of film unless otherwise agreed to in writing."

Is the exclusionary clause valid? Defendants rely upon 2–719(3), a section of the Uniform Commercial Code, which authorizes a limitation or exclusion of consequential damages unless the limitation is unconscionable.

Plaintiffs, on the other hand, argue that the Uniform Commercial Code is not applicable to this transaction. Their theory is that article 2 applies only to sales and not to a bailment as was present in this case. Plaintiffs read article 2 too narrowly. While article 2 is entitled "Sales," the declared scope is more comprehensive. 2–102 sets the parameters of the article by its declaration that it applies to *transactions in goods*, excluding security transactions. If article 2 were limited to sales it would not be directly applicable to this bailment transaction as 2–106(1) defines "Sales" as the passing of title from a seller to a buyer, a factor not present here. Obviously, "transactions in goods"—the scope of article 2—is broader than "sales." Had the drafters of the code intended to limit article 2 to sales they could have easily so stated. They did not.

* * *

In determining conscionability, the parties are to be provided "a reasonable opportunity to present evidence as to its commercial setting, purpose and effect to aid the court in making the determination." [U.C.C.] 2–302(2). Defendants concede that there was adequate compliance with that requirement in this case. The court had before it testimony and documents as to each element it was required to consider [and concluded that the exclusionary clause was unconscionable under the circumstances.]

In the context of a **commercial bailment,** from which both parties derive a mutual benefit, the law requires the bailee to exercise the care that a reasonably prudent person would exercise under the same circumstances. Where the bailment is one that benefits the bailee alone, as in the case of one who gratuitously borrows a truck from another, the law requires more than reasonable care of him. On the other hand, where the bailee accepts the property for the sole benefit of the bailor, the law requires a lesser degree of care (see Figure 48–1).

It should be remembered, however, that the amount of care required to satisfy any of the standards will vary with the character of the property. A bailee required to take only slight care under the general rules mentioned above may be liable if he does not take greater care of a $1,000 bracelet than he would have of a $20 watch. In practice, therefore, the distinctions are blurred by the fact that whatever degree of care is required in the abstract, a bailee must respond to the magnitude of the consequences that reasonably ought to have been foreseen if the property were lost or destroyed.

When the property is lost, damaged, or destroyed while in the possession of the bail-ee, it is often impossible for the bailor to obtain enough information to show that the loss or damage was due to the bailee's failure to exercise the required care. The law aids the bailor in this respect by *presuming* that the bailee was at fault. The bailor is merely required to show that certain property was delivered by way of bailment and that the bailee has failed to return it or that it was returned in damaged condition. The burden then rests on the bailee to prove that he exercised the degree of care required of him.

Bailee's Absolute Liability

As just discussed, the bailee is free from liability if she has exercised the degree of care required of her under the particular bailment while the property was within her control. This general rule has certain important exceptions that impose an absolute duty on the bailee to return the property undamaged to the proper person.

Where the bailee has an obligation by express *agreement* with the bailor or by *custom* to insure the property against certain risks but fails to do so, and the property is destroyed or damaged through such risks, she is liable for

FIGURE 48-1   Bailee's Duty of Care

Type of Bailment	Duty of Care	Liability For
For sole benefit of bailor	Slight	Gross negligence
For sole benefit of bailee	Utmost	Slight negligence
For mutual benefit	Ordinary	Ordinary negligence

the damage or nondelivery, even though she has exercised due care.

Where the bailee uses the bailed property in a manner *not* authorized by the bailor or by the character of the bailment, and during the course of such use the property is damaged or destroyed, without fault on the part of the bailee, the bailee is absolutely liable for the damage or destruction. The reason for this is that wrongful use by the bailee automatically terminates her lawful possession, and she becomes a trespasser as to the property. For example, suppose a garage mechanic, after repairing Brown's car, takes it out for a road test, and the car is damaged in an accident that is solely the fault of someone other than the mechanic. The proprietor of the garage will not be liable as bailee for such damage, because a road test is a normal incident to this type of bailment. But where the mechanic takes Brown's car for a joy ride or on independent business, and the car is damaged solely through the fault of someone other than the mechanic, the proprietor will be absolutely liable as bailee for the damage.

A bailee has a duty to return the property to the right person. She is not excused by delivering the property to the wrong person by mistake, even when the mistake is induced by negligence on the part of the bailor. If the bailee, by mistake or intentionally, *misdelivers* the property to someone other than the bailor and who has no right to its possession, she is guilty of conversion and is liable to the bailor.

Bailee's Right to Compensation

A bailee who by express or implied agreement undertakes to perform work on or render services in connection with the bailed goods is entitled to reasonable compensation for those services or work. In most cases, the agreement between bailor and bailee fixes the amount of compensation and provides how it shall be paid. In the absence of a contrary agreement, the compensation is payable on completion of the work or the performance of the services by the bailee. If, after such completion or performance, and before the goods are redelivered to the bailor, the goods are lost or damaged without fault on the part of the bailee, the bailee is still entitled to compensation for his work and services.

Most bailees who are entitled to compensation for work and services performed in connection with bailed goods acquire a possessory lien on the goods to secure the payment of such compensation. In most jurisdictions, the bailee has a statutory right to obtain a judicial foreclosure of his lien and sale of the goods. Many statutes also provide that the bailee does not lose his lien on redelivery of the goods to the bailor, as was the case at common law. Instead, the lien continues for a specified period after redelivery by timely recording with the proper authorities an instrument claiming such a lien.

Bailor's Duties

In a bailment for the sole benefit of the bailee, the bailor warrants that she is unaware of any defects in the bailed property. In all other instances, the bailor has a duty to warn the bailee of all defects she knows of or should have discovered upon a reasonable inspection of the bailed property. A number of courts have extended strict liability in tort and the implied warranties under Article 2 of the UCC to leases and bailments. Proposed Article 2A imposes implied warranties on the lease of goods.

CRAINE v. UNITED STATES
United States Court of Appeals, Eleventh Circuit, 1984.
722 F.2d 1523.

Facts: Robert L. Moore, a United States Army sergeant stationed at Fort Benning, Georgia, rented a fourteen-foot aluminum boat from the Fort Benning Morale Support Activities Division, Outdoor Rentals. The manager of the rentals section gave Moore general instructions concerning the use of the craft and provided Moore with a copy of the Fort Benning Boating Safety Rules. He also followed the routine procedure of examining the fuel line of the boat and starting the motor to insure its serviceability. Three days later, while Moore was operating the boat on the Chattahoochee River, the motor stalled, forcing Moore to row the boat back to shore. Later that same day, Moore took six minor children out in the boat to give them a ride on the river. At the time, Moore's blood alcohol level was .29 percent, a level that would have made it "extremely difficult to do it [operate a boat] with any type of proficiency." Moore recklessly moved into the swift current and headed toward a concrete dam and spillway. When he finally reversed course, the motor stalled again, and the boat and its occupants were swept over the dam. Juanita Craine and Nancy Brown, parents of four of the drowned children, brought an action against the United States, claiming that the government breached its duty to warn Moore and that the government is liable as the owner of a vessel that was negligently operated. The district court entered judgment in favor of the United States.

Decision: Judgment for the United States affirmed.

Opinion: Hill, J.   The appellants' first contention on appeal is that the Government had a duty to warn Sergeant Moore and breached that duty. The evidence showed that the Government agent discussed the operation of the motor with Moore as well as giving him a copy of the basic safety rules for operating a small craft. The appellants now contend that the Government agent should have warned Moore about operating the boat in rapid current or near a dam. The law imposes no requirement that one who rents equipment such as a boat or vehicle instruct the renter on every possible danger that could be faced. For example, one would not expect a car rental company to warn its customers about the dangers of reckless operation of a vehicle along hazardous roads during inclement weather.

Further, when there has intervened between the defendant's negligent act and the injury an independent illegal act of a third person producing the injury, and without which it would not have happened, the latter is properly held to be the proximate cause of the injury and the defendant is excused unless the defendant has reasonable grounds for apprehending that such criminal act would be committed. [Citations.]

* * *

The district court found that there was no negligence on the part of the employees of the Army facility which rented the boat to Moore.

SPECIAL TYPES OF BAILMENTS

Although pledgees, warehousemen, and safe deposit companies are ordinarily bailees and are subject to the general principles that apply to all ordinary bailees, there are some special features about the transactions in which they respectively engage that make it desirable they be given some further consideration. In addition, innkeepers and common carriers are known as *extraordinary* bailees, whereas all other bailees are known as *ordinary* bailees. This distinction is based on the character and extent of the liability of these two classes of bailees for loss of or injury to the bailed goods. As we have seen, an **ordinary bailee** is liable for such loss or injury only where it resulted from his failure to exercise ordinary or reasonable care. The liability of the **extraordinary bailee,** on the other hand, is, in general, *absolute.* In other words, the extraordinary bailee is liable to the bailor for any loss or injury to the goods without regard to the question of his care or negligence as to their safety. As it is frequently put, an extraordinary bailee is an insurer of the safety of the goods. This simply means that just as an insurer, in general, becomes automatically liable to the insured on the happening of the hazard insured against, regardless of the cause, so does the extraordinary bailee become liable to the bailor for any loss or injury to the goods, regardless of the cause.

Pledges

A **pledge** is a bailment for security in which the owner gives possession of her personal property to another (the secured party) to secure a debt or the performance of some obligation. The secured party does not have title to the property involved but merely a possessory interest to secure a debt or some other obligation. The secured party can usually transfer and assign his special interest in the property to others, even without the consent of the debtor. Pledges of most types of personal property for security purposes are governed by Article 9 of the Uniform Commercial Code, which is discussed in Chapter 37. In most respects, the secured party's duties and liabilities are the same as those of a bailee for compensation.

Warehousing

A **warehouser** is a bailee who receives goods to be stored in a warehouse for compensation. His duties and liabilities under the common law were in all ways the same as those of the ordinary bailee for compensation. Today, because the activities of warehousers are affected by a strong public interest, they are subject to extensive regulation by State and Federal authorities. Warehousers must also be distinguished from ordinary bailees in that the receipts they issue for storage have acquired a special status in commerce. These receipts are regarded as documents of title and are governed by Article 7 of the Uniform Commercial Code. We discuss documents of title later in this chapter.

Carriers of Goods

In the broadest sense of the term, anyone who transports good from one place to another, either gratuitously or for compensation, is a **carrier.** Normally, however, a carrier engages in the business of transportation for hire or reward. The delivery of goods to a carrier for shipment creates a bailment; the carrier has the exclusive possession of the goods without ownership and is under a duty to deliver them to the person designated by the shipper. Carriers of goods are by far the most important of all bailees. Not only are their transactions the most numerous and the largest in volume, but also their function in the movement of raw materials and the distribution of manufactured and other goods of every description is of enormous importance in our economic system.

Carriers are classified primarily as common carriers and private carriers. A **common carrier** offers its services and facilities to the public on terms and under circumstances indicating that the offering is made to all persons. Common carriers of goods include railroad, steamship, aircraft, public trucking, and pipeline companies. One who carries the goods of another on isolated occasions or who serves a limited number of customers under individual contracts without offering the same or similar contracts to the public at large is a **private** or **contract carrier**— not a common carrier. Stated somewhat differently, the criteria for determining whether a carrier is subject to the rules applicable to common carriers are (1) the carriage must be part of its business; (2) the carriage must be for remuneration; and (3) the carrier must represent to the general public that it is willing to serve the public in the transportation of property.

The person who delivers goods to a carrier for shipment is known as the **consignor** or shipper. The person to whom the goods are to be delivered by the carrier is known as the **consignee.** The instrument containing the terms of the contract of transportation, which the carrier issues to the shipper, is called a *bill of lading.*

Duty to Carry A common carrier is under a duty to serve the public to the limits of its capacity and, within those limits, to accept for carriage goods of the kind that it normally transports. A private carrier has no duty to accept goods for carriage except where it agrees to do so by contract.

Duty to Deliver to the Right Person The carrier is under an absolute duty to deliver the goods to the person to whom they are consigned by the shipper. This duty applies to both common and private carriers. Essentially, this is the duty that renders an ordinary bailee liable for misdelivery. The person to whom delivery must be made is controlled by the form of the bill of lading or other contract of carriage, as discussed later in this chapter.

Liability for Loss or Damage A private carrier, in the absence of special contract terms, is liable as a bailee for the goods it undertakes to carry. A common carrier, on the other hand, is under a stricter liability that approaches that of an insurer of the safety of the goods, except where loss or damage is caused by an act of God, an act of a public enemy, the acts or fault of the shipper, the inherent nature of or a defect in the goods, or an act of public authority.

In most jurisdictions the carrier is permitted to limit its liability by contract with the shipper. A carrier may not absolve itself of liability for its own negligence, however.[1]

Innkeepers

At common law, **innkeepers** (today better known as hotel and motel owners or operators) are held to the same *strict or absolute liability* for their guests' belongings as are common carriers for the goods they carry. This rule of strict liability applies only to those who furnish lodging to the public for compensation as a regular business, and liability extends only to the belongings of lodgers who are guests.

Today, in almost all jurisdictions, the old common law strict liability of the innkeeper has been substantially modified by case law and statute. Although the statutes vary in detail, they all have certain common features.

They provide that the innkeeper may avoid strict liability for loss of his guests' valuables or money by providing a safe where they may be kept and by posting adequate notice of its availability. For articles that are not placed in a safe provided for this purpose or that are not articles of the kind normally kept in a safe, the statutes often limit recovery to a maximum figure that, although it varies from State to State, is generally insubstantial. These statutory limitations do not apply where the loss is due to the fault of the innkeeper or his employees, in which case the innkeeper is liable for the full value of the lost property.

DOCUMENTS OF TITLE

A **document of title** is a warehouse receipt, bill of lading, or other document evidencing a right to receive, hold, and dispose of the document *and* the goods it covers. To be a document of title, a document must be issued by or addressed to a bailee and cover goods in the bailee's possession that are either identified or are fungible portions of an identified mass.

Briefly, a document of title is a symbol of ownership of the goods it describes. Because of the legal characteristics of a document of title, its ownership is equivalent to the ownership or control of the goods it represents, without the necessity of the actual or physical possession of the goods. Likewise, its transfer is a transfer of the ownership or control of the goods without the necessity or inconvenience of the physical transfer of the goods themselves. For these reasons, documents of title are a convenient means of dealing with the billions of dollars worth of goods that are transported by carriers or are stored with warehousers. Documents of title also serve a very important function in facilitating the transfer of title to goods and the creation of a security interest in goods. Article 7 of the UCC has consolidated and revised the Uniform Warehouse Receipts Act and the Uniform Bills of Lading Act and now governs the negotiation of documents of title.

TYPES OF DOCUMENTS OF TITLE

Warehouse Receipts

A **warehouse receipt** is a receipt issued by a person engaged in the business of *storing* goods for hire.[2]

Duties of Warehousers   A warehouser is liable for damages for loss or injury to the goods caused by his failure to exercise such care in regard to them as a reasonably careful man would exercise under the circumstances.[3] The warehouser must deliver the goods to the person entitled to receive them under the terms of the warehouse receipt.

The liability of a warehouser, however, *may* be limited by a provision in the warehouse receipt fixing a specific maximum liability per article or item or unit of weight.[3] This limitation, as shown in the following case, does not apply in the event of a conversion of the goods by the warehouseman to his own use.[3]

I.C.C. METALS, INC. v. MUNICIPAL WAREHOUSE CO.
Court of Appeals of New York, 1980.
50 N.Y.2d 657, 431 N.Y.S.2d 372, 409 N.E.2d 849.

Facts: In the fall of 1974, I.C.C. Metals, Inc., delivered three lots of indium, an industrial metal, to Municipal Warehouse Company for safekeeping. The indium had an aggregate weight of 845 pounds and was worth $100,000. The warehouse supplied I.C.C. with receipts for each lot. Printed on the back of these receipts were the terms and conditions of the bailment, including an exculpatory clause limiting the liability of the warehouse to a maximum of $50. For two years, the warehouse billed I.C.C. for storage of the indium, and I.C.C. paid each invoice. In 1976 I.C.C. requested the return of the indium. For the first time, the warehouse told I.C.C. it was unable to locate any of the indium. I.C.C. brought an action in conversion to recover the full value of the indium. The warehouse defended on the ground that the metal had been stolen through no fault of its own; and that its liability was limited to $50 in accordance with the terms of the warehouse receipts. The trial court granted summary judgment to I.C.C. for the full value of the stored property and the appellate court affirmed.

Decision: Judgment for I.C.C. affirmed.

Opinion: **Gabrielli, J.**   Absent an agreement to the contrary, a warehouse is not an insurer of goods and may not be held liable for any injury to or loss of stored property not due to some fault upon its part (Uniform Commercial Code, § 7–204, subd. [1]). As a bailee, however, a warehouse is required both to exercise reasonable care so as to prevent loss of or damage to the property [citation] and, a fortiori, to refrain from itself converting materials left in its care [citation.] If a warehouse does not convert the goods to its own use and does exercise reasonable care, it may not be held liable for any loss of or damage to the property unless it specifically agrees to accept a higher burden. If, however, the property is lost or damaged as a result of negligence upon the part of the warehouse, it will be liable in negligence. Similarly, should a warehouse actually convert stored property to its own use, it will be liable in conversion. Hence, a warehouse which fails to redeliver goods to the person entitled to their return upon a proper demand, may be liable for either negligence or conversion, depending upon the circumstances [Citation.]

A warehouse unable to return bailed property either because it has lost the property as a result of its negligence or because it has converted the property will be liable for the full value of the goods at the time of the loss or conversion [citations], unless the parties have agreed to limit the warehouse's potential liability. It has long been the law in this State that a warehouse, like a common carrier, may limit its liability for loss of or damage to stored goods even if the injury or loss is the result of the warehouse's negligence, so long as it provides the bailor with an opportunity to increase that potential liability by payment of a higher storage fee [Citations.] If the warehouse converts the goods, however, strong policy considerations bar enforcement of any such limitation upon its liability [Citations.] This rule, which has now been codified in subdivision (2) of section 7–204 of the Uniform Commercial Code, is premised on the distinction between an intentional and an unintentional tort. Although public policy will in many situations countenance voluntary prior limitations upon that liability which the law would otherwise impose upon one who acts carelessly [citations], such prior limitations may not properly be applied so as to diminish one's liability for injuries resulting from an affirmative and intentional act of misconduct (see, generally, Restatement, Torts 2d, § 500; Restatement, Contracts 2d, Tent Draft No. 12, § 337) such as a conversion. Any other rule would encourage wrongdoing by allowing the converter to retain the difference between the value of the converted property and the limited amount of liability provided in the agreement of storage. That result would be absurd. To avoid such an anomaly, the law provides that when a warehouse converts bailed property, it thereby ceases to function as a warehouse and thus loses its entitlement to the protections afforded by the agreement of storage [Citation.] In short, although the merely careless bailee remains a bailee and is entitled to whatever limitations of liability the bailor has agreed to, the converter forsakes his status as bailee completely and accordingly forfeits the protections of such limitations. Hence, in the instant case, whether defendant is entitled to the benefit of the liability limiting provision of the warehouse receipt turns upon whether plaintiff has proven conversion or merely negligence.

Plaintiff [I.C.C.] has proffered uncontroverted proof of delivery of the indium to defendant [Warehouse], of a proper demand for its return, and of defendant's failure to honor that demand. Defendant has failed to make a sufficient showing in support of its suggested explanation of the loss. * * * [Defendant's] unsupported claim that the metal was stolen does not suffice to raise any issue of fact on this point. Upon this record, it is beyond cavil that plaintiff would be entitled to judgment had it elected to sue defendant in negligence [Citations.] We now hold that such a record also suffices to sustain plaintiff's action in conversion, thereby rendering inapplicable the contractual limitation upon defendant's liability.

A warehouser is not required to keep the goods indefinitely. At the termination of the period of storage stated in the document, the warehouser may notify the person on whose account the goods are held to pay storage charges and remove the goods. If no period of time is stated in the document, the warehouser is required to give thirty days' notice to pay charges and remove the goods. A shorter time, which must be reasonable, is permitted if the goods are about to deteriorate or decline in value to less than the amount of the warehouser's lien, or if the quality or condition of the goods causes them to be a hazard to other property or to persons.[4]

Lien of Warehouser   To enforce the payment of his charges and necessary expenses in connection with keeping and handling the goods, a warehouser has a lien on the goods that enables him to sell them at public or private sale after notice and to apply the net proceeds of the sale to the amount of his charges. The Code, moreover, provides a definite procedure for enforcement of the lien of a warehouser against the goods stored and in his possession.[5]

Against the holder of a negotiable ware-house receipt to whom it has been duly nego-tiated, this lien is limited to charges at the rate specified in the receipt, and if none are speci-fied, to a reasonable charge for storage of the goods subsequent to the date of the receipt.[6]

Bills of Lading

A **bill of lading** is a document issued by a carrier on receipt of goods for *transportation.* It serves a threefold function: (1) as a receipt for the goods, (2) as evidence of the contract of carriage, and (3) as a document of title. A bill of lading is negotiable if, by its terms, the goods are de-liverable to bearer or to the order of a named per-son. Any other document is nonnegotiable.[7]

Under the Code, bills of lading may be issued not only by common carriers but also by contract carriers, freight forwarders, or any person engaged in the business of transporting or forwarding goods.[8]

Duties of Issuer of Bill of Lading   The carrier must deliver the goods to the person entitled to receive them under the terms of the bill of lading. The carrier's duty in this respect is similar to that of the warehouser. Common carriers of goods are extraordinary bailees un-der the law and are subject to a greater degree of liability than an ordinary bailee such as a warehouser.[1]

The Code allows a carrier to limit its liability by contract in all cases where its rates are dependent on value and the shipper is given an opportunity to declare a higher value. The limitation does not apply to a conversion of the goods by the carrier to its own use.[1]

Through Bills of Lading   A bill of lading may provide that the issuer deliver the goods to a *connecting* carrier for further transportation to a destination. A bill of lading that specifies one or more connecting carriers is called a **through bill of lading.**

The initial or *originating* carrier, which re-ceives the goods from the shipper and issues a through bill of lading, is liable to the holder of the document for loss or damage to the goods caused by any connecting or delivering carrier.[9] The initial carrier has a right of reim-bursement from the connecting or delivering carrier in possession of the goods when the loss or damage occurred. A carrier, however, is not required to issue through bills of lading.

Unlike the initial carrier, the liability of a connecting carrier is limited to the period the goods are in its possession.

Lien of Carrier   The carrier has a lien on goods in its possession covered by a bill of lading for its charges and expenses necessary for preser-vation of the goods. Against a purchaser for value of a negotiable bill of lading, this lien is limited to charges stated in the bill or in the applicable published tariff, and if no charges are so stated, to a reasonable charge.[10]

The enforcement of the lien of the carrier is by public or private sale of the goods after notice to all persons known to the carrier to claim an interest in them. The sale must be on terms that are "commercially reasonable" and must be conducted in a "commercially reason-able manner." [11]

A purchaser in good faith of goods sold to enforce the lien takes free of any rights of persons against whom the lien was valid, even though the enforcement of the lien does not comply with the requirements of the Code. This rule applies to both carrier's and ware-houser's liens.[11, 12]

NEGOTIABILITY OF DOCUMENTS OF TITLE

The concept of negotiability has long been established in law. It is important not only in connection with documents of title but also in connection with commercial paper and invest-ment securities treated in other chapters of this book.

Negotiability is a characteristic the law con-fers on instruments and documents that com-ply with the required statutory form. The magic words are "bearer" or "order." A prom-ise to deliver goods to a named person is manifestly different from a promise to deliver the goods to bearer or to the order of a named person. The first promise may be safely per-formed by the promisor by delivery of the goods to the person named in the promise. This is typical of a straight bill of lading; that is, one issued by a carrier that undertakes to deliver the goods to a named consignee at a specific destination. In this case it is not necessary for the carrier to obtain the bill of lading on delivery of the goods at destination. The only concern of the carrier is to make sure that the person to whom it delivers the goods at destination is the person named in the straight bill of lading as the consignee. Such a bill of lading is *nonnegotiable*.

If, on the other hand, the promise of the carrier in the bill of lading is to deliver the goods to *bearer* or to the *order* of a person named in the bill, the carrier may not safely deliver the goods to anyone at destination without obtaining surrender of the original bill of lading. Anyone in possession of a bearer form document is entitled to receive the goods from the carrier. Anyone in possession of an order form document, properly indorsed, is likewise entitled to receive possession of the goods from the carrier. A bearer or order form document of title is *negotiable*. By the terms of the promise contained on its face, it was intended to go to market, to pass from hand to hand, and to circulate freely through the channels of commerce.

The Code provides that a warehouse receipt, bill of lading, or other document of title is negotiable if, by its terms, the goods are to be delivered to bearer or to the order of a named person or where, in overseas trade, it runs to a named person or assigns. *Any* other document is nonnegotiable.[7]

A nonnegotiable document, such as a straight bill of lading or a warehouse receipt under which the goods are deliverable to a person named in the bill and not to the order of any person or to bearer, may be transferred by assignment but may not be negotiated. Only a negotiable document or instrument may be negotiated.

Due Negotiation

The manner in which a negotiable document of title may be negotiated and the requirements of due negotiation are set forth in the Code.[13] An order form negotiable document of title running to the order of named person is negotiated by her indorsement and delivery. After such indorsement in blank or to bearer, the document may be negotiated by delivery alone. A special indorsement by which the document is indorsed over to a specified person requires the indorsement of the special indorsee as well as delivery to accomplish a further negotiation.

The naming in a negotiable document of a person to be notified on the arrival of the goods does not limit the negotiability of the bill of lading or serve as a notice to any purchaser of the document that the named person has any interest in the goods.

Due negotiation is a term peculiar to Article 7 and requires not only that the purchaser of the negotiable document must take it in good faith without notice of any adverse claim or defense and pay value, but also that she must take it in the regular course of business or financing and not in settlement or payment of a money obligation. Thus, a transfer for value of a negotiable document of title to a nonbanker or person not in business, such as a college professor or student, would not be a due negotiation.

Rights Acquired by Due Negotiation Negotiation is a form of transfer in which the transferee acquires not only the rights that the transferor had but also direct rights based on the language of the promise contained in the instrument or document. Where a property right is merely assigned, the assignee takes only those rights that the assignor had. He stands in the shoes of the assignor, and his rights are subject to all defects and infirmities in the title of the assignor. Where a document is negotiable and is transferred by due negotiation, however, the transferee is one to whom the promise of the issuer runs, and he thereby acquires the direct obligation of the issuer.

The effect of due negotiation is that it creates new rights in the holder of the document. On due negotiation, the transferee does not stand in the shoes of his transferor. Defects and defenses available against the transferor are not available against the new holder. His rights are newly created by the negotiation and free of such defects and defenses. This enables bankers and business persons to extend credit on documents of title without concern about possible adverse claims or the rights of third parties.

The rights of a holder of a negotiable document of title to whom it has been duly negotiated are that he has (1) title to the document; (2) title to the goods; (3) all rights accruing under the law of agency or estoppel, including rights to goods delivered to the bailee after the document was issued; and (4) the direct obligation of the issuer to hold or deliver the goods according to the terms of the document.[14]

Rights Acquired in the Absence of Due Negotiation If a nonnegotiable document is transferred or a negotiable document is transferred without due negotiation, the transferee of the document acquires all of the title and rights that the transferor had or had actual authority to convey. Prior to notification received by the bailee of the transfer, the rights of the transferee may be defeated (1) by the creditors of the transferor, who could treat the sale as void; (2) by a buyer from the transferor in the ordinary course of business, if the bailee has delivered the goods to the buyer; or (3) against the bailee by good faith dealings of the bailee with the transferor.[15]

Warranties

A person who either negotiates or transfers a document of title for value other than a collecting bank or other intermediary incurs certain warranty obligations unless otherwise agreed.[16] Such transferor warrants to her immediate purchaser (1) that the document is genuine, (2) that she had no knowledge of any fact that would impair its validity or worth, and (3) that her negotiation or transfer is rightful and fully effective with respect to the title to the document and the goods it represents.

Ineffective Documents of Title

It is fundamental that a thief or finder of goods may not deliver them to a warehouser or carrier in return for a negotiable document of title and thus defeat the rights of the owner by a negotiation of the document. Although such a document would be genuine and its indorsement by the thief or finder would not be a forgery, it would not represent title to the goods.

In order for a person to obtain title to goods by a negotiation to him of a document, the goods must have been delivered to the issuer of the document by the owner of the goods or by one to whom the owner has delivered or entrusted them with actual or apparent authority to ship, store, or sell them.[17] A warehouser or carrier, however, may deliver goods according to the terms of the document that it has issued or otherwise dispose of the goods as provided in the Code without incurring liability, even though the document did not represent title to the goods. It must have acted in good faith and complied with reasonable commercial standards in both the receipt and delivery or other disposition of the goods. The bailee has no liability, even though the person from whom it received the goods had no authority to obtain the issuance of the document or dispose of the goods, and even though the person to whom it delivered the goods had no authority to receive them.[18]

Thus a carrier or warehouser who receives goods from a thief or finder and later delivers them to a person to whom the thief or finder ordered them to be delivered is not liable to the true owner of the goods. Even a sale of the goods by the carrier or warehouser to enforce a lien for transportation or storage charges and expenses would not subject it to liability.

Warehousers and carriers are regarded as furnishing a service necessary to trade and commerce. They are not a link in the chain of title and do not purport to represent the owner in transactions affecting title to the goods. Consequently, this is a justifiable rule to relieve them from liability on delivery of the goods according to their contract under the document of title even though the document is ineffective against the true owner of the goods.

Lost or Missing Documents of Title

If a document of title has been lost, stolen, or destroyed, a claimant of the goods may apply to a court for an order directing delivery of the

ervice to the general public; is
absolute liability and thus is
e)
s services and does not offer
dinary bailee (one who must

xtraordinary bailee except as

ent without a court order, it is
person who is thereby injured.
ch person in good faith is not a
the goods if security is posted in
least double the value of the
nify any person injured by the
iles notice of claim within one

rship of the document and the

y person storing goods
he shipper by the carrier (1) as a
of their carriage contract, and (3)

nal property by one party (the

if, by its terms, the goods are to
med person
ocument in the regular course of
, for value, and without notice of

on   rights of the transferor plus
rce of defects and defenses avail-

Negotiation   rights of transferor
transfers a document of title for
her intermediary, incurs certain
ed
erson to obtain title to goods by
have been delivered to the issuer
ds or by one to whom actual or
the owner

y commercial bailments

terminable time

ust exercise reasonable care
he proper person
e must exercise utmost care
st exercise ordinary care
e must exercise slight care
parties so agree, (2) the
e the property against the
e uses the bailed property

onable compensation for

or warrants that she is

of all known defects and
nable inspection

owner of a herd of twenty highly
s. He was a prosperous farmer, but
very poor. On the advice of his
ided to winter in Arizona. Before he
agreement with Freya under which
ep the cows on Freya's farm through
Phil the sum of $800, and return to
cows at the close of the winter. For
Freya thought were good farming,
of the cows and replaced them with

ehouser must exercise
and to deliver them to

	Carrier of Goods transporter of goods
	■ *Common Carrier* carrier that offers s
	an extraordinary bailee (one who has
	liable even if he exercises ordinary ca
	■ *Private Carrier* carrier that limits i
	them to the general public; is an or
	exercise ordinary care)
	Innkeeper hotel or motel operator; is an
	limited by statute or case law

DOCUMENTS OF TITLE

Nature of the Document of Title	Definition an instrument evidencing own goods it covers Types ■ *Warehouse Receipt* receipt issued ■ *Bill of Lading* document issued to receipt for the goods, (2) as evidence as a document of title

Negotiability	Definition a document of title is negotiabl be delivered to bearer or to the order of a n Due Negotiation transfer of a negotiable business to a holder, who takes in good fait any defense or claim ■ *Rights Acquired by Due Negotiati* the direct obligation of the issuer; f able against the transferor ■ *Rights Acquired in Absence of Due* Warranties a person who negotiates or value, other than a collecting bank or o warranty obligations unless otherwise agr Ineffective Documents in order for a negotiation of a document, the goods mus of the document by the owner of the go apparent authority has been entrusted by

QUESTIONS

1. Discuss the essential elements of a bailment.
2. Discuss the rights and duties of the bailor and bailee.
3. Discuss the duties of a (a) warehouser, (b) common carrier, and (c) innkeeper.
4. Define a document of title. Identify and discuss the various types of documents of title.
5. Discuss the negotiability of documents of title, the rights acquired by due negotiation, and the rights acquired in the absence of due negotiation.

PROBLEMS

1. Phil was th
bred dairy cow
his health wa
doctor, Phil de
left, he made a
Freya was to k
the winter, pa
Phil the twent
reasons that
Freya sold six

six other cows. After the winter was over, Phil returned from Arizona. When he saw that Freya had replaced six cows out of the twenty originally given, he sued Freya for the conversion of the original six cows. Decision?

2. Hines stored her furniture, including a grand piano, in Arnett's warehouse. Needing more space, Arnett stored Hines's piano in Butler's warehouse next door. As a result of a fire, which occurred without any fault of Arnett or Butler, both warehouses and contents were destroyed. Hines sues Arnett for the value of her piano and furniture. Decision?

3. Curtis rented a safe deposit box from Reliable Safe Deposit Company in which he deposited valuable securities and $4,000 in cash. Subsequently, Curtis went to the box and found that $1,000 was missing. Curtis brought an action against Reliable, and at the trial the company showed that its customary procedure was as follows: that there were two keys for each box furnished to each renter; that if a key was lost, the lock was changed; that new keys were provided for each lock each time a box was rented; that there were two clerks in charge of the vault; and that one of the clerks was always present to open the box. Reliable Safe Deposit Company also proved two keys were given to Curtis at the time he rented his box; that his box could not be opened without the use of one of the keys in his possession; and the company had issued no other keys to Curtis's box. Decision?

4. Adrian, Barney, and Chang each stored 5,000 bushels of yellow corn in the same bin in Kennedy's warehouse. Kennedy wrongfully sold 10,000 bushels of this corn to Johnson. Adrian contends that inasmuch as her 5,000 bushels of corn were placed in the bin first, the remaining 5,000 bushels belong to her. What are the rights of the parties?

5. (a) On April 1 Mary Rich, at the solicitation of Super Fur Company, delivered a $3,000 mink coat to the company at its place of business for storage in its vaults until November 1. On the same day, she paid the company its customary charge of $20 for such storage. After Mary left the store, the general manager of the company, on finding that its storage vaults were already filled to capacity, delivered Mary's coat to Swift Trucking Company for shipment to Fur Storage Company. En route, the truck in which Mary's coat was being transported was totally damaged by fire caused by negligence on the part of the driver of the truck, and Mary's coat was totally destroyed. Is Super Fur Company liable to Mary for the value of her coat? Why?

(b) Would your answer be the same if Mary's coat had been safely delivered to Fur Storage Company and had been stolen from its storage vaults without negligence on its part? Why?

6. Rich, a club member, left his golf clubs with Bogan, the pro at the Happy Hours Country Club, to be refinished at Bogan's pro shop. The refinisher employed by Bogan suddenly left town, taking Rich's clubs with him. The refinisher had previously been above suspicion, although Bogan had never checked on the man's character references. A valuable sand wedge that Bogan had borrowed from another member, Smith, for his own use in an important tournament match was also stolen by the refinisher, as well as several pairs of golf shoes that Bogan had checked for members without charge as an accommodation. The club members concerned each made claims against Bogan for their losses. Can (a) Rich, (b) Smith, and (c) the other members compel Bogan to make good their respective losses?

7. Donna drove an automobile into Terry's garage and requested him to make repairs for which the charge would be $125. Donna never returned to get the automobile, and two months later Carla saw it in Terry's garage. Carla claimed it as her own and asserted that it had been stolen from her. Terry told Carla that she could have the automobile if she paid for the repairs and storage. One week later Molly appeared and proved that the automobile was hers, that it had been stolen from her, and that neither Donna nor Carla had any rights in it.

Molly brings an action against Terry for conversion of the automobile. Decision?

8. On June 1 Cain delivered his 1984 automobile to Barr, the operator of a repair shop, for necessary repairs. Barr put the car in his lot on Main Street. The lot, which is fenced on all sides except along Main Street, holds one hundred cars and is unguarded at night, although the police make periodic checks. The lot is well lighted. The cars do not have the keys in them when left out overnight. At some time during the night of June 4, the hood, starter, alternator, and gear shift were stolen from Cain's car. The car remained on the lot, and during the evening of June 5, the transmission was stolen from the car. The cost of replacement of the parts stolen in the first theft was $600 and in the second theft $500.

Cain sued Barr to recover $1,100. Decision?

9. Seton, in Phoenix, according to a contract with Rider in New York, ships to Rider goods conforming to the contract and takes from the carrier a shipper's order bill of lading that Seton indorses in blank and forwards by mail to Clemson, his agent in New York, with instructions to deliver the bill of lading to Rider on receipt of payment of the price for the goods. Forest, a thief, steals the bill of lading

from Clemson and transfers it for value to Pace, a *bona fide* purchaser. Before the goods arrive in New York, Rider is petitioned into bankruptcy. What are the rights of the parties?

10. Rutger, a Philadelphia merchant, purchased merchandise from Washington in Chicago. The contract of sale provided that the merchandise was sold F.O.B., Chicago, payment to be made sixty days after delivery. Washington delivered the goods to the railroad carrier in Chicago, took an order bill of lading in the name of Rutger, and forwarded it to Rutger. Before the goods arrived in Philadelphia, Washington learned that Rutger had become insolvent and exercised a right of stoppage in transit by proper notice to the railroad company. Thereafter, and before the shipment reached Philadelphia, Rutger indorsed and delivered the bill of lading to Lee, an innocent purchaser for value. Lee claimed the goods by reason of holding the bill of lading. To whom should the goods be awarded?

11. Mrs. Laval was a patient of Dr. Leopold, a practicing psychiatrist. Dr. Leopold shared an office with two associates practicing in the same field. No receptionist or other employee attended the office. Mrs. Laval placed her coat in the clothes closet in the office reception room. Later, when she returned to retrieve the coat to leave, she found it missing. Mrs. Laval then brought this action to recover $1,725, the value of her coat. Decision? Explain.

ENDNOTES

1. Uniform Commercial Code, Section 7–309, Duty of Care; Contractual Limitation of Carrier's Liability.

2. Uniform Commercial Code, Section 1–201(45), General Definitions: Warehouse Receipt.

3. Uniform Commercial Code, Section 7–204, Duty of Care; Contractual Limitation of Warehouseman's Liability.

4. Uniform Commercial Code, Section 7–206, Termination of Storage at Warehouseman's Option.

5. Uniform Commercial Code, Section 7–210, Enforcement of Warehouseman's Lien.

6. Uniform Commercial Code, Section 7–209, Lien of Warehouseman.

7. Uniform Commercial Code, Section 7–104, Negotiable and Non-Negotiable Warehouse Receipt, Bill of Lading or Other Document of Title.

8. Uniform Commercial Code, Section 1–201(6), General Definitions: Bill or Lading.

9. Uniform Commercial Code, Section 7–302, Through Bills of Lading and Similar Documents.

10. Uniform Commercial Code, Section 7–307, Lien of Carrier.

11. Uniform Commercial Code, Section 7–308, Enforcement of Carrier's Lien.

12. Uniform Commercial Code, Section 7–210, Enforcement of Warehouseman's Lien.

13. Uniform Commercial Code, Section 7–501, Form of Negotiation and Requirements of "Due Negotiation."

14. Uniform Commercial Code, Section 7–502, Rights Acquired by Due Negotiation.

15. Uniform Commercial Code, Section 7–504, Rights Acquired in the Absence of Due Negotiation; Effect of Diversion; Seller's Stoppage of Delivery.

16. Uniform Commercial Code, Section 7–507, Warranties on Negotiation or Transfer of Receipt or Bill.

17. Uniform Commercial Code, Section 7–503, Document of Title to Goods Defeated in Certain Cases.

18. Uniform Commercial Code, Section 7–404, No Liability for Good Faith Delivery Pursuant to Receipt or Bill.

19. Uniform Commercial Code, Section 7–601, Lost and Missing Documents.

49 INTERESTS IN REAL PROPERTY

Interests in real property may be divided into ownership, possessory, and nonpossessory interests. Rights of ownership in real property are called estates and are classified to indicate the quantity, nature, and extent of the rights. The two major categories are freehold estates (those existing for an indefinite time or for the life of a person) and estates less than freehold (those that exist for a predetermined time), called leasehold estates. The ownership of property may be held by one individual or concurrently by two or more persons, each of whom is entitled to an undivided interest in the entire property. Both freehold estates and leasehold estates are regarded as possessory interests in property. In addition, there are several nonpossessory interests in property, including easements, *profits à prendre*, and licenses. We consider all of these topics in this chapter.

FREEHOLD ESTATES

A **freehold estate** is a right of ownership of real property for an indefinite time or for the life of a person. Of all the estates in real property, the most valuable are usually those that combine the enjoyment of immediate possession with ownership at least for life. These estates are either some form of fee estate or estates for life. In addition, it is possible that either type of estate may be created without immediate right to possession, called a future interest.

FEE ESTATES

Fee estates include both fee simple and qualified fee estates.

Fee Simple Estate

When a person says that he has "bought" a house, or a corporation informs its shareholders that it has "purchased" an industrial site, the property is generally held in fee simple. **Fee simple** means that the property is owned absolutely and can be sold or passed on at will. The absolute right of transferability and of transmitting by inheritance are basic characteristics of a fee simple estate. The estate signifies full control over the property, which is *owned absolutely* and can be sold or disposed of as desired.

A fee simple is created by any words that indicate an intent to convey absolute ownership. "To Barnes in fee simple" will accomplish the purpose, as will "to Barnes forever." The general presumption is that conveyance is intended to convey full and absolute title in the absence of a clear intent to the contrary.

A practical consequence of a fee simple title is that not only may it be voluntarily transferred, but it may also be levied on and sold at the insistence of judgment creditors of the fee simple holder (the owner).

Qualified or Base Fee Estate

It is possible to convey or will property to a person to enjoy it absolutely, *subject to* its being taken away at a later date if a certain event takes place. The estate thus created is known as a base fee, **qualified fee,** conditional fee or fee simple defeasible. For example, Abe may provide in his will that his widow is to have his house and lot in "fee simple forever so long as she does not remarry." If his widow dies without remarrying, the property is transferred to her heirs as if she owned it absolutely, because the condition of remarrying did not take place. If Abe's widow remarries or sells the land to Ben and then remarries, the widow and Ben would respectively lose their title to the land, and it would revert to the heirs of Abe.

LIFE ESTATES

By tradition, life estates are divided into two major classes: (1) conventional life estates or those created by voluntary act, and (2) those established by law, the most significant example of which is a wife's dower right in the property of her husband.

Conventional Life Estates

A grant or a devise (grant by will) "to Alex for life" creates in Alex an estate that terminates on his death. Such a provision may stand alone, in which case the property will revert to the grantor and his heirs, or, as is more likely, it will be followed by a subsequent grant to another party such as "to Alex for life and then to Mario and his heirs." Alex is the **life tenant,** and Mario is generally described as the **remainderman.** Alex's life, however, need not be the measure of his life estate, as where an estate is granted "to Alex for the life of Bob." On Bob's death, Alex's interest terminates, and if Alex dies before Bob, Alex's interest passes to his heirs or as he directs in his will for the remainder of Bob's life. Thus, a **life estate** is an ownership right in the property for the life of a designated individual, while the **remainder** is the ownership estate that takes effect when the prior life estate terminates.

No particular words are necessary to create a life estate. It is always a matter of determining the intent of the grantor. Life estates arise most frequently in connection with the creation of trusts, which we discuss in Chapter 51.

Generally, a life tenant may make reasonable use of the property as long as he does not commit "waste." Any action or omission that does permanent injury to the realty or unreasonably changes its characteristics or value constitutes **waste.** For example, the failure to make repairs on a building, the unreasonable cutting of timber, or the neglect of an adequate conservation policy may subject the life tenant to an action by the remainderman to recover damages for waste.

A conveyance by the life tenant passes only his interest. The life tenant and the remainderman may, however, join in a conveyance to pass the entire fee to the property, or the life tenant may terminate his interest by conveying it to the remainderman.

Life Estates Established by Law

Dower Under common law, **dower** is a life estate that a *wife* who survives her husband has in one-third of all the real property the husband owned during the marriage. It arises by operation of law and exists regardless of the intent or wishes of the parties.

Until the death of the husband, the wife's dower is contingent or inchoate. During his life, she cannot transfer or sell her dower interest. Dower can exist only in fee simple estates or in an estate that for practical purposes is equivalent to a fee simple estate. There is no dower in a life estate because it is not an estate of inheritance.

Although the widow does not realize her dower unless she survives her husband, her right to the dower is protected during the marriage. If the husband sells his property after he marries, the purchaser takes the property subject to the inchoate right of dower even if the purchaser did not know that the seller was married. Dower also takes precedence over any claims against the husband's estate that were not reduced to judgment or made a lien against his property before marriage. In most jurisdictions, the wife can relinquish her dower simply by joining in a conveyance with her husband.

The incidents of dower at common law have been substantially modified by statute in most jurisdictions. In some States, the widow may elect whether to take common law dower or an alternative amount given her by statute, and she has a certain period of time within which to make the election. In many jurisdictions, dower has been abolished, and a statutory share of the husband's property, generally including both real and personal, is substituted in place of it.

Curtesy At common law, the surviving *husband* had a life estate in the real property of his wife similar to, although not identical with, the widow's dower. This estate, known as **curtesy,** required a valid marriage and the death of the wife before the husband. As with dower, it existed only in estates of inheritance, and there was no curtesy in a life estate. Unlike dower, curtesy did not exist unless a child were born of the marriage. The child, however, did not need to survive the wife. But curtesy was like dower in that the wife could not bar the husband's claim to curtesy without his written waiver. In most States, the estate of curtesy has been substantially modified or entirely abolished, and in place of it the husband in some States is given a statutory share in the estate of his deceased wife.

FUTURE INTERESTS

Not all interests in property are subject to immediate use and possession, even though the right and title to the interest are absolute. Thus, where property is conveyed or devised by will "to Adam during his life and then to Barbara and her heirs," Barbara has a definite, existing *interest* in the property, but she is not entitled to immediate *possession*. This right and similar rights are generically referred to as future interests.

Reversions

If Anderson conveys property "to Benson for life" and makes no disposition of the remainder of the estate, Anderson holds the **reversion**— the grantor's right to the property on the death of the life tenant. Thus Anderson would regain ownership to the property when Benson dies. This result is not as apparent when Anderson conveys property "to Benson for life and then to my heirs." It is arguable that there is a remainder in the grantor's next of kin. The common law doctrine, however, was that such a reference to the heirs of the grantor placed a

reversion in the *grantor,* and his heirs took nothing except as they might inherit the reversion.

A **possibility of reverter** is a conditional reversionary interest and exists where property may return to the grantor or his successor in interest because of the happening of an event on which a fee simple estate was to terminate. It is the possibility of a reversion that is present in the grant of a base or qualified fee as previously discussed in this chapter. Thus Karlene has a possibility of reverter if she dedicates property to a public use "so long as it is used as a park." If, in one hundred years, the city ceases to use the property for a park, the heirs of Karlene will be entitled to the property. Unlike a reversion, which is a present estate to be enjoyed in the future, a possibility of reverter is simply an expectancy.

Remainders

A remainder, as previously discussed, is an estate in property that, like a reversion, will take effect in possession, if at all, on the termination of a prior estate created by the *same instrument.* Unlike a reversion, a remainder is held by a person other than the grantor or his successors. A grant from Gwen "to Lew for his life and then to Robert and his heirs" creates a remainder in Robert. On the termination of the life estate, Robert will be entitled to possession as remainderman. Robert takes his title not from Lew but from the original grantor, Gwen. There are two kinds of remainders, vested remainders and contingent remainders.

Vested Remainders A remainder is vested when the only contingency to the possession by the remainderman is the termination of the preceding estate. When Richard has a remainder in fee, subject only to a life estate in Laura, the only obstacle to the right of immediate possession by Robert or his heirs is Laura's life. Laura's death, no more, no less, is sufficient and necessary to place Robert in possession. The law considers this unconditional or **vested remainder** as a fixed, *present* interest to be enjoyed in the future. It is an interest in property that is transferable just as much as the preceding life estate, and it is characteristic of a vested remainder that the owner of the preceding estate can do nothing to defeat the remainder.

Contingent Remainders A remainder is contingent if the right to possession is dependent or conditional on the happening of some event *in addition to* the termination of the preceding estate. The remainder may be conditioned on the existence of some person who does not yet exist or on the happening of an event that may never occur. A **contingent remainder,** by definition and unlike a vested remainder, is *not* ready to take immediate possession simply on

the termination of the preceding estate. A provision in a will "to David for life and then to his children but if he has no children then to Julie" creates contingent remainders both as to the children and as to Julie. If David marries and has a child, the remainder then vests in that child, and Julie's expectancy is closed out. If David dies without having fathered a child, then and only then will an estate vest in Julie. It is, of course, possible for a contingent remainder to become vested while possession is still in the preceding life estate, as evidenced by the birth of a child to David in the above example. Another illustration is provided by the following case.

STRICKLAND v. JACKSON
Supreme Court of North Carolina, 1963.
259 N.C. 81, 130 S.E.2d 22.

Facts: In 1905 a deed for land in Pitt County was executed and delivered by Joel and Louisa Tyson "unto M. H. Jackson and wife Maggie Jackson, for and during the term of their natural lives and after their death to the children of the said M. H. Jackson and Maggie Jackson that shall be born to their inter-marriage as shall survive them to them and their heirs and assigns in fee simple forever." Thelma Jackson Vester, a daughter of M. H. and Maggie Jackson, died in 1957, survived by three children. M. H. Jackson, who survived his wife Maggie Jackson, died in 1958, survived by four sons. The children of Thelma Jackson Vester brought this action against M. P. Jackson, a son of and executor of the will of M. H. Jackson. The children of Vester contended that through their deceased mother they were entitled to one-fifth interest in the land conveyed by the deed of 1905. The executor contended that the deed conveyed a contingent remainder and only those children who survived the parents took an interest in the land. The trial court granted the executor's demurrer to the complaint for its failure to state a cause of action.

Decision: Judgment for executor affirmed.

Opinion: Rodman, J. The distinction between a vested and a contingent remainder is the capacity to take upon the termination of the preceding estate. Where those who are to take in remainder cannot be determined until the happening of a stated event, the remainder is contingent. Only those who can answer the roll immediately upon the happening of the event acquire any estate in the properties granted. [Citations.]
   Here the estate in remainder was not given to the children of M. H. Jackson and Maggie Jackson, but by clear and express language to those children and only those who survived their parents. Since Mrs. Vester did not survive her parents, there was nothing for her children, plaintiffs, to inherit. [Citations.]
   It affirmatively appears from the complaint that plaintiffs acquired no interest in the land by virtue of the deed from Tyson and wife to M. H. Jackson and others.

LEASEHOLD ESTATES

No part of the law of real property affects so many persons in their daily affairs as the law of the landlord and tenant. By virtue of a **leasehold estate,** a tenant has an estate in land, which is an interest in real property, and its primary characteristic is the right to possession. If Linda, the owner of a house and lot, rents it to Ted for a year, Linda, of course, still holds title to the property but she has sold the right to occupy the property to Ted. Ted's right to occupy the property is superior to that of Linda, and as long as Ted occupies the property according to the terms of the lease contract, he does, as a practical matter, have exclusive possession against all the world as though he were the actual owner.

CREATION AND DURATION

A lease is both a contract and a grant of an estate in land. It is a contract by which the owner of the land, the **landlord,** grants to another, the **tenant,** an exclusive right to use and possession of the land for a definite or ascertainable period of time or term. The possessory term thus granted is an estate in land called a leasehold. The landlord retains an interest in the property called a *reversion.* The principal characteristics of the leasehold estate are that it continues for a definite or ascertainable term and that it carries with it the obligation on the part of the tenant to pay rent to the landlord.

By statute, in most jurisdictions, leases for a term longer than a specified period of time must be in writing. The period is generally fixed at either one or three years.

Definite Term

A lease for a **definite term** automatically expires at the end of the term. Such a lease is frequently termed an *estate for years*, even though the duration may be for one year or shorter. No notice to terminate is required.

Periodic Tenancy

A **periodic tenancy** is a definite term lease of specified duration that is to be held over and

over in the same length of time in indefinite succession. For example, a lease "to Ted from month to month" or "from year to year" creates a periodic tenancy. Periodic tenancies arise frequently by implication. Laura leases to Ted without stating any term in the lease. This creates a tenancy at will. If Ted pays rent to Laura at the beginning of each month and Laura accepts such payments, most courts hold that the tenancy at will has been transformed into a tenancy from month to month.

A periodic tenancy may be terminated by either party at the expiration of any one period but only on adequate notice to the other party. If there is no specific agreement in the lease, the common law requires six months' notice in tenancies from year to year. This period has been shortened in most jurisdictions by statute to periods ranging between thirty and ninety days. In periodic tenancies involving periods of less than one year, the notice required at common law is one full period in advance, but, again, this may be subject to regulation by statute.

Tenancy at Will

A lease containing a provision that either party may terminate at any time creates a **tenancy at will.** A lease that does not specify any duration also creates a tenancy at will. At common law, such tenancies were terminable without any prior notice, but many jurisdictions now have statutes requiring a notice to terminate, usually thirty days.

Tenancy at Sufferance

One who is in possession without a valid lease is a **tenant at sufferance.** A tenant at sufferance is technically a trespasser, and the landlord owes him no duties except that, under the common law, a landowner has no right to willfully injure a trespasser. The most common case of a tenancy at sufferance arises when a tenant fails to vacate the premises at the expiration of the lease. The common law gives the landlord the right to elect either to dispossess such tenant or to hold him for another term. Until the landlord makes this election, a tenancy at sufferance exists.

TRANSFER OF INTERESTS

Both the tenant's interest in the leasehold and the landlord's reversionary interest in the property may be freely transferred in the absence of contractual or statutory prohibition. This general rule is subject to one major exception: the tenancy at will. Any attempt by either party to transfer her interest is usually considered as an expression of the intent to terminate the tenancy.

Transfers by Landlord

After conveying the leasehold interest, a landlord is left with a reversionary interest in the property plus the right to rent and other benefits acquired under the lease. The landlord may transfer either or both of these interests. The party to whom the reversion is transferred takes the property subject to the tenant's leasehold interest if the transferee has actual or constructive notice of the lease. For example, Linda leases Whiteacre to Tina for five years, and Tina records the lease with the register of deeds. Linda then sells Whiteacre to Arthur. Tina's lease is still valid and enforceable against Arthur, whose right to possession of Whiteacre begins only after the expiration of the lease.

Transfers by Tenant

A tenant may dispose of his interest either by (1) assignment, or (2) sublease. In the absence of a provision in his lease, both of these rights are available to him. As a consequence, most standard leases expressly require the consent of the landlord to an assignment or subletting of the premises.

Assignment   If a tenant transfers *all* his interest in the leasehold so that he has no reversionary rights, he has made an **assignment.** This complete transfer does not refer only to the length of the time involved in the transfer. A transfer of the entire remaining period may not be an assignment if the tenant retains any control over the premises. If there are no specific restrictions in the lease, leases are freely assignable. Many leases, however, prohibit assignment without the landlord's written consent. If the tenant assigns without such written consent, the assignment is not void, but it may be avoided by the landlord. In other words, the prohibition of assignment in a lease is only for the benefit of the landlord and cannot be relied on by the assignor to terminate an otherwise valid assignment on the ground that the landlord did not consent. If, however, the landlord accepts rent from the assignee, he will be held to have waived the restriction.

The agreement to pay rent and certain other contractual **covenants** (express promises) pass to and obligate the assignee of the lease as long as he remains in possession of the leasehold estate. Although the assignee of the lease is thus bound to pay rent, the original tenant is *not* relieved of his contractual obligation to pay rent. If the assignee fails to pay the stipulated rent, the original tenant will have to pay. He will have a right to be reimbursed by the assignee. Thus, after an assignment of a tenant's interest, *both* the original tenant and the assignee are liable to the landlord for failure to pay rent.

Sublease   A **sublease** differs from an assignment in that it involves the transfer by the tenant to another of *less* than all the tenant's rights in the lease. For example, Toni is a tenant under a lease from Lawrence that is to terminate on December 31, 1990. If Toni leases the premises to Sara Lindsey for a shorter period than that covered by her own lease, say, until November 30, 1990, Toni has subleased the premises because she has transferred less than her whole interest in the lease.

The legal effects of a sublease are entirely different from those of an assignment. In a sublease, the sublessee, Sara Lindsey in the example above, has no obligation to Toni's landlord, Lawrence. Sara Lindsey's obligations run solely to Toni, the original tenant, and Toni is not relieved of any of her obligations under the lease. Thus Lawrence has no right of action against Toni's sublessee Sara Lindsey under any covenants contained in the original lease between him and Toni, because the lease has not been assigned to Sara Lindsey. Toni, of course, remains liable to Lawrence for the rent and for all of the other covenants in the original lease between her and Lawrence. Under the majority view, a covenant against assignment of a lease does not prohibit the tenant from subleasing the premises. Conversely, a prohibition against subleasing is not considered a restriction on the right to assign the lease (see Figure 49–1).

TENANT'S OBLIGATIONS

Although the leasehold estate carries with it an implied obligation on the part of the tenant to pay reasonable rent, the contract of lease almost always contains an express promise or covenant by the tenant to pay rent in specified amounts at specified times. In the absence of a specific covenant providing the amount of rent and the times for payment, the rent is a *reasonable* amount and is *payable only at the end of the term.*

Most leases contain a provision to the effect that if the tenant breaches any of the covenants in the lease, the landlord is entitled to declare the lease at an end and may regain possession of the premises. The tenant's express undertaking to pay rent thus becomes one of the covenants on which this provision can operate. Where there is no such provision in the lease, at common law, the tenant's failure to pay rent when due gives the landlord only the right to recover a judgment for the amount of such rent; it does *not* give him the right to oust the tenant from the premises. In most jurisdictions, however, the common law rule has been changed by statute to give the landlord the right to dispossess the tenant for nonpayment of rent, even though there is no provision for this in the lease.

A tenant is under *no* duty to make any repairs to the leased premises, unless the lease has specific provisions to the contrary. He is not obliged to repair or restore substantial or extraordinary damage occurring without his fault, nor to repair damage caused by ordinary wear and tear. The tenant is obliged to use the premises so that no substantial injury is caused them. The law imposes this duty on him even though it is not expressly stated in the lease. For example, a tenant who overloads a barn

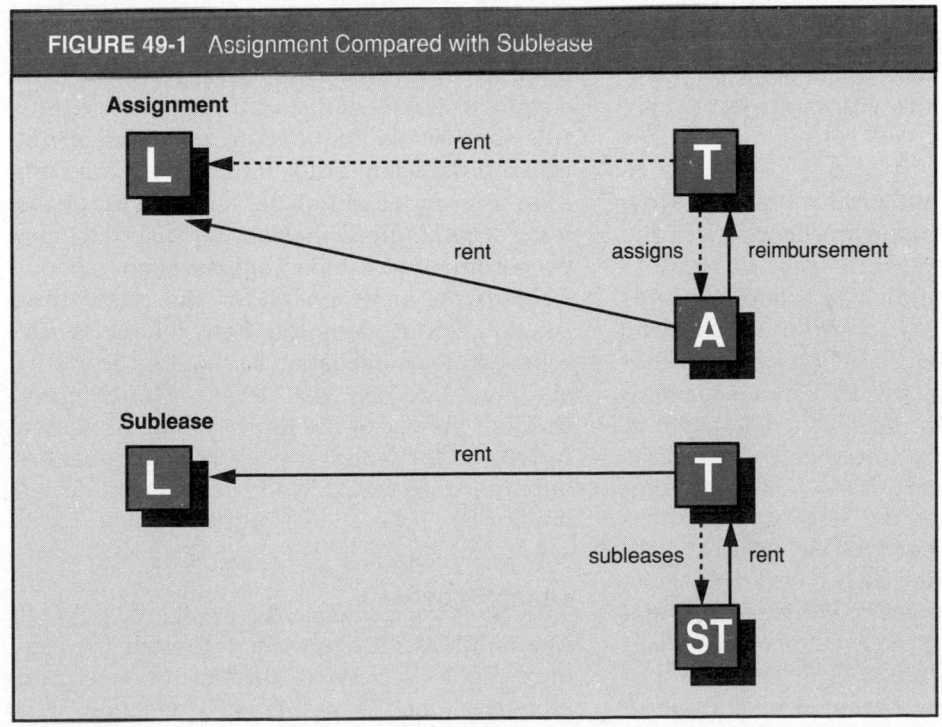

FIGURE 49-1 Assignment Compared with Sublease

and thus causes it to fall is liable to the landlord, and the overloading of an electrical connection that causes damage to a wiring system will entitle a landlord to maintain an action for damages.

Destruction of the Premises

The dual character of a lease as a contract and as a grant of an estate in land is particularly evident when considering the common law rule governing the destruction of the premises by fire or other cause. Where the tenant leases land together with a building, and the building is destroyed by fire or some other chance event, the common law does not relieve him of his obligation to pay rent or permit him to terminate the lease. The common law rule has been modified in some States by statute, and in most States it does not apply to tenants who occupy only a portion of the building and have no interest in the building as a whole, such as apartment tenants. Most leases contain clauses covering the fortuitous destruction of the premises.

Eviction or Abandonment

The tenant's obligations also depend on whether the landlord rightfully evicts the tenant, the tenant wrongfully abandons the premises, or the landlord wrongfully evicts the tenant.

Dispossession by Landlord for Breach of Covenant When the tenant breaches one of the covenants in her lease, such as the covenant to pay rent, and the landlord **evicts** or removes her from the premises according to a specific provision in the lease or under a statute authorizing him to do so, the lease is terminated. Because the breach of the covenant to pay rent does not involve any injury to the premises and because the landlord's action in evicting the tenant terminates the lease, the tenant is not liable to the landlord for any future installments of the rent after such an eviction. Most long-term leases, however, contain a *survival clause* providing that the eviction of the tenant for nonpayment of rent will not relieve her of liability for damages measured by the differ-

ence between the rent specified in the lease and the rent the landlord is able to obtain when reletting the premises.

Wrongful Abandonment by Tenant If the tenant wrongfully abandons the premises before the expiration of the term of the lease and the landlord reenters the premises or relets them to another, a majority of the courts hold that the tenant's obligation to pay rent after reentry terminates. ("Reenter" in this case means to occupy the premises.) The landlord, if he desires to hold the tenant to his obligation to pay rent, must either leave the premises vacant or must have another "survival clause" in the lease that covers this situation.

Wrongful Eviction by Landlord If the tenant is wrongfully evicted by the landlord, the tenant's obligations under the lease are terminated, and as discussed below, the landlord is liable for breach of the tenant's right of quiet enjoyment.

LANDLORD'S OBLIGATIONS

Unless there are specific provisions in the lease, the landlord, under the common law, has few obligations to her tenant. At the beginning of the lease, she must give the tenant a right to possession, but under the majority rule, she is not required to give the tenant actual possession. Thus, if the previous tenant refuses to move out at the termination of the lease, the landlord must bring dispossession proceedings to oust him, but she is not responsible to the new tenant for the delay thus brought about, and the new tenant is not relieved of the obligation to pay rent from the starting date of the lease. Nonetheless, through the use of the court system, as shown in Law in the News at page 1114, tenants are attempting to broaden the responsibilities of landlords.

Quiet Enjoyment

The landlord may not interfere with the tenant's right to physical possession, use, and enjoyment of the premises. The landlord is bound to provide the tenant with quiet and peaceful enjoyment. This duty arises by implication and is known as the landlord's covenant of **quiet enjoyment.** The landlord breaches this covenant whenever he wrongfully evicts the tenant. The law also regards the landlord as having breached this covenant if the tenant is evicted by someone having a better title than the landlord. The landlord is not responsible, however, for the wrongful acts of third parties unless they are done with his assent and under his direction.

Fitness for Use

Unless there is a specific provision in the lease, the landlord, under the common law, is under *no* obligation to maintain the premises in a livable condition or to make them fit for any purpose since the primary value of the lease to the tenant is land. Some courts, however, have abandoned this rule in residential leases by imposing an implied warranty that the leased premises are habitable, that is, fit for ordinary residential purposes. These courts have also held that the covenant to pay rent is conditioned on the landlord's performance of the **implied warranty of habitability.** Courts, as in *Javins v. First National Realty Corp.*, reaching these results have emphasized that the tenant's interest is in a place to live and not merely in the land. The common law assumption that the value of the leasehold is the land may have been valid in an agricultural society and may even be valid in some farm leases, but it is not true in the case of a modern apartment rental.

JAVINS v. FIRST NATIONAL REALTY CORP.
United States Court of Appeals, District of Columbia Circuit, 1970.
428 F.2d 1071.

Facts: By separate leases, Javins and a few others rented an apartment at the Clifton Terrace apartment complex. When they had defaulted on their rent payments, the landlord, First National Realty, brought an action to evict them. The tenants admitted to the default but defended on the ground that the landlord had failed to maintain the premises in compliance with the Washington, D.C., Housing Code. They alleged that approximately 1,500 violations of this code had arisen since the term of their lease began. The Landlord and Tenant Branch of the District of Columbia Court of General Sessions ruled the evidence of the housing code violations inadmissible and the appellate court affirmed.

Decision: Judgment reversed and case remanded for proceedings consistent with this opinion.

Opinion: Wright, J. II Since, in traditional analysis, a lease was the conveyance of an interest in land, courts have usually utilized the special rules governing real property transactions to resolve controversies involving leases. However, as the Supreme Court has noted in another context, "the body of private property law * * *, more than almost any other branch of law, has been shaped by distinctions whose validity is largely historical." Courts have a duty to reappraise old doctrines in the light of the facts and values of contemporary life—particularly old common law doctrines which the courts themselves created and developed. As we have said before, "[T]he continued validity of the common law * * * depends upon its ability to reflect contemporary community values and ethics."

The assumption of landlord-tenant law, derived from feudal property law, that a lease primarily conveyed to the tenant an interest in land may have been reasonable in a rural, agrarian society; it may continue to be reasonable in some leases involving farming or commercial land. In these cases, the value of the lease to the tenant is the land itself. But in the case of the modern apartment dweller, the value of the lease is that it gives him a place to live. The city dweller who seeks to lease an apartment on the third floor of a tenement has little interest in the land 30 or 40 feet below, or even in the bare right to possession within the four walls of his apartment. When American city dwellers, both rich and poor, seek "shelter" today, they seek a well known package of goods and services—a package which includes not merely walls and ceilings, but also adequate heat, light and ventilation, serviceable plumbing facilities, secure windows and doors, proper sanitation, and proper maintenance.

* * *

Ironically, however, the rules governing the construction and interpretation of "predominantly contractual" obligations in leases have too often remained rooted in old property law.

Some courts have realized that certain of the old rules of property law governing leases are inappropriate for today's transactions. In order to reach results more in accord with the legitimate expectations of the parties and the standard of the community, courts have been gradually introducing more modern precepts of contract law in interpreting leases. Proceeding piecemeal has, however, led to confusion where "decisions are frequently conflicting, not because of a healthy disagreement on social policy, but because of the lingering impact of rules whose policies are long since dead."

In our judgment the trend toward treating leases as contracts is wise and well considered. Our holding in this case reflects a belief that leases of urban dwelling units should be interpreted and construed like any other contract.

III   Modern contract law has recognized that the buyer of goods and services in an industrialized society must rely upon the skill and honesty of the supplier to assure that goods and services purchased are of adequate quality. In interpreting most contracts, courts have sought to protect the legitimate expectations of the buyer and have steadily widened the seller's responsibility for the quality of goods and services through implied warranties of fitness and merchantability.

* * *

The rigid doctrines of real property law have tended to inhibit the application of implied warranties to transactions involving real estate. Now, however, courts have begun to hold sellers and developers of real property responsible for the quality of their product. For example, builders of new homes have recently been held liable to purchasers for improper construction on the ground that the builders had breached an implied warranty of fitness. In other cases courts have held builders of new homes liable for breach of an implied warranty that all local building regulations had been complied with. And following the developments in other areas, very recent decisions and commentary suggest the possible extension of liability to parties other than the immediate seller for improper construction of residential real estate.

Despite this trend in the sale of real estate, many courts have been unwilling to imply warranties of quality, specifically a warranty of habitability, into leases of apartments. Recent decisions have offered no convincing explanation for their refusal; rather they have relied without discussion upon the old common law rule that the lessor is not obligated to repair unless he covenants to do so in the written lease contract. However, the Supreme Courts of at least two states, in recent and well reasoned opinions, have held landlords to implied warranties of quality in housing leases. [Citations.] In our judgment, the old no-repair rule cannot coexist with the obligations imposed on the landlord by a typical modern housing code, and must be abandoned in favor of a implied warranty of habitability. In the District of Columbia, the standards of this warranty are set out in the Housing Regulations.

IV A. In our judgment the common law itself must recognize the landlord's obligation to keep his premises in a habitable condition. This conclusion is compelled by three separate considerations. First, we believe that the old rule was based on certain factual assumptions which are no longer true; on its own terms, it can no longer be justified. Second, we believe that the consumer protection cases discussed above require that the old rule be abandoned in order to bring residential landlord-tenant law into harmony with the principles on which those cases rest. Third, we think that the nature of today's urban housing market also dictates abandonment of the old rule.

* * *

Today's urban tenants, the vast majority of whom live in multiple dwelling houses, are interested, not in the land, but solely in "a house suitable for occupation." Furthermore, today's city dweller usually has a single, specialized skill unrelated to maintenance work; he is unable to make repairs like the "jack-of-all-trades" farmer who was the common law's model of the lessee. Further, unlike his agrarian predecessor who often remained on one piece of land for his entire life, urban tenants today are more mobile than ever before. A tenant's tenure in a specific apartment will often not be sufficient to justify efforts at repairs. In addition, the increasing complexity of today's dwellings renders them much more difficult to repair than the structures of earlier times. In a multiple dwelling repair may require access to equipment and areas in control of the landlord. Low and middle income tenants, even if they were interested in making repairs, would be unable to obtain any financing for major repairs since they have no long-term interest in the property.

* * *

Since a lease contract specifies a particular period of time during which the tenant has a right to use his apartment for shelter, he may legitimately expect that the apartment will be fit for habitation for the time period for which it is rented. We point out that in the present cases there is no allegation that appellants' [lessees'] apartments were in poor condition or in violation of the housing code at the commencement of the leases. Since the lessees continue to pay the same rent, they were entitled to expect that the landlord would continue to keep the premises in their beginning condition during the lease term. It is precisely such expectations that the law now recognizes as deserving of formal, legal protection.

* * *

We follow the Illinois court in holding that the housing code must be read into housing contracts—a holding also required by the purposes and the structure of the code itself. The duties imposed by the Housing Regulations may not be waived or shifted by agreement if the Regulations specifically place the duty upon the lessor.

* * *

V In the present cases, the landlord sued for possession for nonpayment of rent. Under contract principles, however, the tenant's obligation to pay rent is dependent upon the landlord's performance of his obligations, including his warranty to maintain the premises in habitable condition.

Tenant Suits May Broaden the Liability of Landlords

Jerry Warshaw, an Atlanta apartment owner, is being sued in state court in DeKalb County for $1 million by a tenant raped by a man who broke into her apartment. The tenant contends that Mr. Warshaw failed to warn her that the neighborhood is a high-crime area.

Mr. Warshaw is also being threatened with a $1 million suit by another woman raped by a man who wandered off the street into an apartment while she was looking at it as a possible rental. And he faces four more suits from tenants victimized by other crimes, all committed by third parties.

"All of this scares me," he says.

It scares a lot of landlords these days. Tenants are increasingly suing apartment owners, developers and management companies in cases that are threatening to broaden landlord liability to more areas than ever before. Some of the suits involve crimes committed by people who walk into buildings and shoot, rape or burglarize tenants. Others involve mishaps such as attacks on tenants by pets owned by other residents. Some tenants, apartment owners say, may even be concocting accidents in order to sue their landlords.

As a result of the litigation, "the sphere of liability for apartment owners is definitely growing. There's no doubt about it," says Charles Fritts, general counsel and a lobbyist for the National Apartment Association, a Washington, D.C.-based trade group of apartment owners.

Insurance Claims

There are no figures showing how many, and what type, of tenant lawsuits have been filed and won. But apartment executives say they believe that a rise in apartment claims paid by insurers partly reflects damages paid to tenants. According to the Insurance Services Office, a New York group that provides statistical data to property casualty insurers, apartment claims paid by insurers rose to $127.5 million in 1985, the latest year available, from $44.2 million in 1980.

Landlords insist that tenants perceive them as having unlimited financial resources and sue them to reap some satisfaction in a dispute, "It's the deep-pocket theory," says Max Lewels, risk manager for Lincoln Property Co., Dallas.

For instance, landlords point to a case involving Plaza Realty Co., owner of a New York City apartment building, and Douglaston Realty Corp., which manages the building. Three years ago, Myrna Tarter, a tenant, was shot by a jilted boyfriend in the building's lobby.

Ms. Tarter, who is paralyzed from the waist down as a result of the shooting, sued Plaza and Douglaston in New York State Supreme Court, claiming they had failed to secure the lobby. Earlier this month, a jury agreed and awarded her $4.5 million in damages, one of the largest awards ever against a landlord. Lawyers for Plaza say they

---

A few States have statutes requiring landlords, specifically apartment landlords, to keep the premises fit for occupation. Zoning ordinances and health and safety regulations may also impose certain duties on the landlord.

Repair

Unless there is a specific provision in the lease or a statutory duty to do so, the landlord has *no* obligation to repair or restore the premises. The landlord does, however, have a duty to maintain, repair, and keep in safe condition those parts of the premises that remain under her control. For example, an apartment house owner who controls the stairways, elevators, lobbies, and other common areas is liable for their maintenance and repair and is responsible for injuries that occur as a result of her failure to do so. With respect to apartment buildings, the courts presume that any portion of the premises that is not specifically leased to the tenants remains under the landlord's control. Thus, in such cases, the landlord is liable

plan to appeal; Douglaston officials didn't return phone calls.

Even the usual category of tenant-landlord litigation—accidents—is being stretched by cases that sometimes border on the bizarre. John Gil, a San Diego landlord, and Mike Black, an apartment manager, were sued in state Superior Court in San Diego by a tenant who was assaulted by a pet monkey owned by two other renters. Mr. Gil and Mr. Black won the case, but an appellate court reversed the decision and ordered a new trial. Before a new trial, the case was settled out of court for an undisclosed amount.

As described in the appellate court's decision, the tenant, Angela Jendralski, said that she had warned the apartment manager weeks before the attack that she had heard "screeching, screaming, cheeping, howling, squealing and cooing" sounds coming from a neighboring apartment. Ms. Jendralski alleged in the decision that she was attacked during a visit to the apartment, where there were "hundreds" of birds, as well as squirrels and a monkey, all in apparent violation of the lease.

Fraudulent Suits?

Landlords say that some of the tenant suits are fraudulent. Last year, a tenant in a unit owned by de Mirada Property Inc., Torrance, Calif., complained that a chunk of ceiling in his apartment fell on his head. A company-hired investigator confirmed that a piece of the ceiling had fallen, but added that it appeared to have been cut away by a sharp object.

Suspecting fraud, Shirley Rearick, the company's vice president, said she alerted her insurer, to no avail. The carrier paid the tenant $18,000. Apartment executives say that paying claims suspected as fraudulent merely increases the potential for fraudulent suits. But insurers counter that it's often cheaper to pay the claim, which is usually lower than the legal expenses incurred by a trial. What's more, insurers say, the risk of a big judgment against the company is increased by going to trial.

In response to the increased threat of litigation, landlords are taking a variety of steps to bolster their defense against potential suits. For instance, at a 7,000-unit complex in Dallas, Lincoln Property has initiated private security patrols, including some mounted on horseback, and has received an increased local police presence. The company also has scheduled free self-defense clinics for tenants and has started installing electronic gates to parking areas that are accessible only by using plastic key cards issued to tenants.

In Houston, DMC Management is stopping previous claims touting their buildings as secure. The company, which owns and manages 12,000 apartments in Texas, New Mexico and Florida, coaches its staff to tell prospective tenants that security is the responsibility of the tenant and local police. Says Gary B. Blumberg, president of the firm: "We just aren't going to say the word 'security' anymore."

By William Celis III
Staff Reporter of The Wall Street Journal
Reprinted by permission of The Wall Street Journal, © Dow Jones & Company, Inc. 1988. All Rights Reserved Worldwide.

for making external repairs, including repairs to the roof.

While at common law the landlord is under no duty to repair, restore, or keep the premises in a livable condition, she may and often does assume those duties in the lease. When she does, her breach of any of these obligations under the lease does *not* entitle the tenant to abandon the premises and refuse to pay rent. Unless a specific provision in the lease gives the tenant this right, the common law allows him only an action for damages.

Under the doctrine of **constructive eviction,** however, a failure by the landlord in any of her undertakings under the lease that causes a substantial and lasting injury to the tenant's beneficial enjoyment of the premises is regarded as being, in effect, an eviction of the tenant. Under such circumstances, the courts permit the tenant to abandon the premises and terminate the lease. The tenant must abandon possession within a reasonable time in order to claim that there was a constructive eviction.

COLONIAL COURT APARTMENTS, INC. v. KERN
282 Minn. 533, 163 N.W.2d 770 (1968).

Facts: On January 1, Mrs. Irene Kern leased an apartment from Colonial Court Apartments, Inc., for a one-year term. When the lease was entered into, Mrs. Kern asked for a quiet apartment, and Colonial assured her that the assigned apartment was in a quiet, well-insulated building. In fact, however, the apartment above Mrs. Kern's was occupied by a young couple, the Lindgrens. From the start of her occupancy, Mrs. Kern complained of their twice-weekly parties and other actions that so disturbed her sleep she had to go elsewhere for rest. After Mrs. Kern had lodged several complaints, Colonial terminated the Lindgrens' lease effective February 28. The termination of the Lindgrens' lease was put off, however, and Mrs. Kern vacated her apartment, claiming that she was no longer able to endure the continued disturbances. Colonial then brought this action to recover rent owed by Mrs. Kern. Colonial appeals from a judgment for Mrs. Kern.

Decision: Judgment for Mrs. Kern affirmed.

Opinion: **Per Curiam**   A constructive eviction is said to occur when the beneficial enjoyment of an apartment by the lessee is so interfered with by the landlord as to justify an abandonment. It does not suppose an actual ouster or dispossession by the landlord. [Citation.] Ordinarily, the rule is that the acts of one tenant do not constitute a constructive eviction of another tenant of the same landlord unless they materially disturb the latter tenant in the use, occupancy, and enjoyment of the demised premises or the natural consequence thereof is to injure the other tenant. [Citations.]

* * *

In fairness it should be said that the trial court could well have found that the landlord took such reasonable measures as were warranted under the circumstances to correct the conditions of which defendant complained. He might also have found that the landlord's letter to the tenants that their "first possibility to vacate, according to law, will be June 30," referred to liability for rent rather than a requirement to remain in possession. Nevertheless, we are not warranted in making an exception to our well-established rule that in reviewing the record the testimony must be considered in the light most favorable to the prevailing party, and if support for the findings may be found in the evidence as a whole, such findings will not be disturbed. The findings of fact by the trial court and the jury stand on equal footing and are entitled to the same weight and will not be reversed on appeal unless they are manifestly and palpably contrary to the evidence. [Citation.]

"The definition of what constitutes constructive eviction does not get us far. Usually the question whether there is a constructive eviction is one of fact with each case largely dependent upon its particular circumstances."

CONCURRENT OWNERSHIP

As we have mentioned before, property may be owned by one individual or by two or more persons concurrently. Two or more persons who hold title concurrently are generally referred to a **co-tenants.** Each is entitled to an undivided interest in the entire property, and neither has a claim to any specific part of it. Each may have equal undivided interests, or one may have a larger undivided share than the other. Regardless of the particular relationships between the co-tenants, this form of ownership must be carefully distinguished from the separate ownership of specific parts of property by different persons. Thus, it is possible, for example, for Ann, Barbara, and Carol each to own distinct and separate parts of Blackstone Manor, or they may each own, as co-tenants, an undivided one-third interest in all of Blackstone Manor. Whether they are co-tenants or owners of specific portions depends on the manner and form in which they acquired their interests.

The two major types of concurrent ownership are joint tenancy and tenancy in common. They both have the characteristics of an undivided interest in the whole, the right of both tenants to possession, and the right of either to sell his interest during life and thus terminate the original relationship. Other forms of concurrent ownership of real estate are tenancy by the entireties, community property, condominiums, and cooperatives.

Joint Tenancy

The most significant feature of joint tenancy is the right of **survivorship.** On the death of one of the joint tenants, title to the entire property passes by operation of law to the survivor or survivors. Neither the heirs of the deceased joint tenant nor his general creditors have a claim to his interest, and a joint tenant cannot transfer his interest by executing a will. Any joint tenant may sever the joint tenancy, however, by conveying or mortgaging his interest to a third party. Further, the interest of either co-tenant is subject to levy and sale on execution. **Sever** means the right of survivorship is lost, and the tenancy becomes a tenancy in common among the remaining joint tenants and the transferee.

HENDRICKSON v. MINNEAPOLIS FEDERAL SAVINGS & LOAN ASSOCIATION
Supreme Court of Minnesota, 1968.
281 Minn. 462, 161 N.W.2d 688.

Facts: On June 30, 1956, Martin Hendrickson and Solveig Hendrickson were married, and on January 3, 1957, a home previously owned by Martin was conveyed to them as joint tenants and not as tenants in common. No part of the consideration for the premises was paid by Mrs. Hendrickson.

On August 3, 1964, Martin Hendrickson duly executed a Declaration of Election to Sever Survivorship of Joint Tenancy by which he endeavored to preserve an interest in the premises for Ruth Halbert, appellant, his daughter by a previous marriage. On the same day, he executed his last will and testament, by the terms of which he directed that his wife, Solveig M. Hendrickson, receive the minimum amount to which she was entitled under the laws of the State of Minnesota. Mr. Hendrickson died testate on October 9, 1964. The trial court found that Martin Hendrickson did not terminate the joint tenancy and thus Solveig Hendrickson became the owner of the entire property through survivorship.

Decision: Judgment reversed.

Opinion: Sheran, J. The Issue The issue for decision is this: Did the declaration have the effect of severing the joint tenancy, creating a tenancy in common? If it did, Ruth Halbert is the owner of an undivided one-half interest in said real estate subject to the life estate therein of Solveig M. Hendrickson. If it did not, Solveig M. Hendrickson owns the realty in fee simple absolute.

The Decision Under the common law, there were three types of concurrent ownership: tenancy in common, joint tenancy, and tenancy by the entirety. A joint tenancy is distinguished from a tenancy in common by the fact that a surviving joint tenant succeeds to the person with whom he shared the joint tenancy. A tenancy by the entirety, which can exist only between husband and wife, is like a joint tenancy in that survivorship exists, but is distinguished from the joint tenancy by the fact that there can be no partition, and it cannot be converted into a tenancy in common. [Citations.]

As the common law of property developed during feudal times, there was a presumption in favor of joint tenancy due to reasons related to feudalism. As the age of feudalism ended, the reasons for this presumption also ended and survivorship came to be regarded "as an 'odious thing' that too often deprived a man's heirs of their rightful inheritance." [Citations.]

In Minnesota, the original presumption in favor of joint tenancy has been reversed by [statute], which provides: "All grants and devises of lands, made to two or more persons, shall be construed to create estates in common, and not in joint tenancy, unless expressly declared to be in joint tenancy." Disfavor for survivorship in Minnesota is also shown by the fact that in this state the estate of tenancy by the entirety, with its indestructible survivorship, is not recognized. [Citations.]

For a joint tenancy to exist, unity of time, title, interest, and possession must concur. [Citations.] Traditionally, the survivorship feature could be destroyed and the joint tenancy converted into a tenancy in common if one of the unities was destroyed. [Citations.] This would result, for example, if one of the joint tenants conveyed his interest to a third party. [Citation.] The common-law lawyer used this principle to enable one joint tenant to unilaterally eliminate the survivorship feature and yet retain ownership in the property. A conveyance would be made to a third party or strawman, thus destroying the joint tenancy. Immediately thereafter the property would be reconveyed to the original owner. A tenancy in common would thus be created because the unities of time and interest would no longer be present. More recently the courts have come to allow joint tenants to convert their estate into a tenancy in common without the ritual of conveyance and reconveyance. It is only necessary for the joint tenants to mutually agree to sever the joint tenancy. [Citations.] We are now asked to allow one joint tenant to do unilaterally that which we allow joint tenants acting in concert to do, i.e., terminate the joint tenancy by declaration without being required to go through the ceremony of a conveyance to a strawman and a reconveyance back again.

* * *

We hold that the method chosen here is sufficient to sever a joint tenancy. Had the property involved been any property other than a homestead, the decedent could have unilaterally severed the joint tenancy. [Minnesota Statutes] establish a public policy to protect for the wife the continued occupancy of the place of joint abode. However, this public policy does not necessarily apply to the remainder interest, which can be disposed of without adversely affecting the right of the surviving spouse to continue in possession and enjoyment for so long as she might live. Putting the property into joint tenancy was apparently an estate-planning device. If the decedent had kept title to this real estate in his own name and executed a will by the terms of which it was devised to his wife in fee simple absolute, he would have been free at any time to revoke the will unilaterally. His wife would nevertheless have the right to a life estate in the homestead upon his death, but her right would be based on the statute and not the will. [Citation.]

* * *

> If the survivor had taken some irrevocable action in reliance upon the creation or existence of the joint tenancy, or if some consideration was given or received when the joint tenancy was created, it would seem reasonable to insist that unilateral action would not be effective to deprive the passive joint tenant of the rights so created. But this is not such a case.

A joint tenancy may be terminated by partition of the property among the tenants, making each the exclusive owner of a specific part of the entire property. **Partition** is a physical division of the property, changing undivided interests into smaller parcels owned by each person individually. The size of individual parcels is based upon the size of the owners' prior share of the undivided interest.

By statute in most States, certain words must be used to create a joint tenancy in real property. Some of those statutes provide that a grant of an estate to two or more persons in their own right is a tenancy in common unless it is specifically declared to be in joint tenancy. Thus, if a deed of conveyance is not drafted properly, the resulting ownership would be a tenancy in common.

To sustain a **joint tenancy,** the common law requires the presence of what are known as the **four unities** of time, title, interest, and possession. The unity of time means that the interest of all the tenants must take effect at the same time; the unity of title means that all the tenants must acquire title by the same instrument; the unity of interest means that all the tenants must have identical interests as to duration and scope; and the unity of possession means that all the tenants have the same right of possession and enjoyment. The absence of any one of these four unities will prevent the creation of a joint tenancy. A failure of any one of the first three unities will result in the creation of a tenancy in common, because the only unity required of a tenancy in common is the unity of possession.

Tenancy in Common

Tenancy in common, like joint tenancy, is an undivided interest in the same property, each person having the right to possession but none claiming any specific portion of the property. But unlike joint tenants, tenants in common do not have the right of survivorship. Also, unlike joint tenancy, the only prerequisite for tenancy in common is the unity of possession. By statute in many States, a transfer of title to two or more persons is presumed to create a tenancy in common. A tenancy in common may be terminated either by transfer of all the co-interests to one person or by partition of the property among the tenants, making each the exclusive owner of a specific part of the entire property.

Tenancy by the Entireties

Tenancy by the entireties, which is recognized in some States, is created only by a conveyance to a *husband and wife.* It is distinguished from joint tenancy by the inability of either spouse to convey separately his or her interest during life and thus destroy the right of survivorship. Likewise, the interest of either spouse cannot be attached by creditors. By the nature of the tenancy, a divorce terminates the relationship, and partition would then be available as a method of creating separate interests in the property.

Figure 49–2 compares the right of concurrent owners in joint tenancy, tenancy in common, and tenancy by the entireties.

Community Property

In Arizona, California, Idaho, Louisiana, Nevada, New Mexico, Texas, and Washington, one-half of any property acquired by the efforts of either the husband or the wife belongs to each spouse. This system, known as **community property,** originated in the civil law of continental Europe but has been modified and

FIGURE 49-2 Rights of Concurrent Owners

	Undivided Interest	Right to Possession	Right to Sell	Right to Mortgage	Levy by Creditors	Right to Will	Right of Survivorship
Joint Tenancy	YES	YES	YES	YES	YES	NO	YES
Tenancy in Common	YES	YES	YES	YES	YES	YES	NO
Tenancy by Entireties	YES	YES	NO	NO	NO	NO	YES

affected by the common law as well as by statutes in this country.

In most instances, the only property that belongs separately to either spouse is that acquired before the marriage or acquired after it by gift or inheritance. On the death of either spouse, one-half of the community property belongs outright to the survivor, and the interest of the deceased spouse in the other half may go to the heirs of the decedent or as directed by will. Under some conditions in a few jurisdictions, however, the surviving spouse may also claim an interest in the decedent's one-half share of the property.

Condominiums

Condominiums are a form of concurrent ownership that have become commonplace in the United States. All States have enacted statutes authorizing the use of this form of ownership. The purchaser of a condominium acquires separate ownership to the unit and becomes a tenant in common with respect to the common facilities, such as the land on which the project is built, recreational facilities, hallways, parking areas, and spaces between the units. The common elements are maintained by a condominium association funded by assessments levied on each unit. The transfer of a condominium conveys both the separate ownership of the unit and the share in the common elements.

Cooperatives

Cooperatives involve an indirect form of common ownership. A cooperative, usually a cor-poration, purchases or constructs the dwelling units. The cooperative then leases the units to its shareholders as tenants, who acquire the right to use and occupy their units.

NONPOSSESSORY INTERESTS

Nonpossessory interests include easements, *profits à prendre*, and licenses.

EASEMENTS

An **easement** is a *limited right* to make use of the land of another in a specific manner that is created by the acts of the parties or by operation of law and that has all the attributes of an estate in the land itself. For example, a typical easement exists where Liz sells a part of her land to Bill and expressly provides in the same or a separate document that Bill, as the adjoining landowner, shall have a right-of-way over a strip of Liz's remaining parcel of land. Bill's land is said to be the **dominant** parcel (land whose owner has rights in other land), and Liz's land, which is subject to the easement, is the **servient** parcel. Easements may, of course, exist for many different types of uses, as, for example, the right to run a ditch across another's land, to lay pipe under the surface, to erect power lines, or in the case of adjacent buildings, to use a stairway or a common or "party" wall.

Because the owner of the entire servient tract retains the title to the servient parcel, she may make any use of or allow others the use of the tract as long as this use does not interfere with the easement. Thus, crops may be grown over an easement for a pipeline, but livestock could not be pastured on an easement for a driveway. Although it is the duty of the owner of the servient parcel not to interfere with the use of the easement, it is generally the responsibility of the owner of the dominant parcel to maintain the easement and keep it in repair.

Types of Easements

Easements fall into two classes: easements appurtenant and easements in gross. **Appurtenant** easements are by far the more common, and, as the name indicates, the rights and duties created by such easements pertain to the land itself and not to the particular individuals who may have created them. See *Nelson v. Johnson* at page 1122. Therefore the easement usually stays with the land when it is sold. For example, continuing with the illustration of Liz and Bill above, if Liz sells her servient parcel to Kyle, who has actual notice of the easement for the benefit of Bill's land or constructive notice by means of the local recording act, Kyle takes the parcel subject to the easement. Likewise, if Bill sells his dominant parcel to Daniel, it is not necessary to refer specifically to the easement in the deed from Bill to Daniel in order to give to Daniel, as the new owner of the dominant parcel, the right to use the right-of-way over the servient parcel. Because Bill no longer owns the dominant parcel, he has no further right to use the right-of-way. Bill could not, however, transfer the benefit of the easement to a party who did not acquire an interest in the dominant parcel of land. Most frequently, a deed conveying the land "together with all appurtenances" is sufficient to transfer the easement. This characteristic of an appurtenant easement is described by the statement that both the burden and the benefit of an appurtenant easement pass with the land.

The second type of easement is an easement **in gross,** which is personal to the particular individual who received the right. It does not depend on the ownership of land and actually amounts to little more than an irrevocable personal right to use.

Creation of Easements

Easements may be created by (1) express grant or reservation, (2) implied grant or reservation, (3) necessity, (4) dedication, and (5) prescription.

Express Grant or Reservation   The most common way to create an easement is to convey it by deed. For example, when Amy sells part of her land to Robert, she may, in the same deed, expressly grant an easement to Robert over Amy's remaining property. Alternatively, Amy may grant an easement to Robert in a separate document. This document must comply with all the formalities of a deed. An easement is an interest in land subject to the Statute of Frauds.

In other instances, when an owner of land transfers it, she may wish to retain certain rights in it. In the example given, Amy may want to "reserve" an easement in favor of the land retained by her over the land granted to Robert. Amy may do this by specific words reserving that right to her in the deed of conveyance to Robert.

Implied Grant or Reservation   Easements by implied grant or implied reservation arise whenever an owner of adjacent properties establishes an *apparent* and *permanent* use in the nature of an easement, and then conveys one of the properties without mention of any easement. For example, suppose that Anita owns two adjacent lots, 1 and 2. There is a house on each lot. Behind each house is a garage. Anita has constructed a driveway along the boundary between the two lots, partly on lot 1 and partly on lot 2, which leads from the street in front of the houses to the two garages in the rear. Anita sells lot 2 to Michael without any mention of the driveway. Anita is held to have *impliedly granted* an easement to Michael over that portion of the driveway that lies on Anita's lot 1, and she is held to have *impliedly reserved* an easement over that portion of the driveway that lies on Michael's lot 2.

Necessity   If Andrew conveys part of his land to Sharon, and the part conveyed to Sharon is so situated that Sharon would have no access to it except across Andrew's remaining land, the law implies a grant by Andrew to Sharon of an easement by necessity across Andrew's remaining land. An easement by necessity will not usually arise if an alternative but circuitous approach to Sharon's land is available.

An easement by necessity may also arise by implied reservation. This would be the case where Andrew conveys part of his land to Sharon, and Andrew's remaining property would be wholly landlocked unless he is given a right-of-way across the land conveyed to Sharon.

Dedication When an owner of land subdivides it into lots and records the plan or plat of the subdivision, she is held, both by common law and now more frequently by statute, to have dedicated *to the public* all of the streets, alleys, parks, playgrounds, and beaches shown on the plat. In addition, when the subdivider sells the lots by reference to the plat, it is now generally recognized that the purchasers acquire easements by implication over the areas shown dedicated to the public.

Prescription An easement may arise by prescription in most States if certain required conditions are met. To obtain an easement by prescription, a person must use a portion of land owned by another in a way (1) that is adverse to the rightful owner's use, (2) that is open and generally known, and (3) that is continuous and uninterrupted for a specific period of time that varies from State to State. If the owner gives the claimant permission to use the land, no easement by prescription is acquired.

NELSON v. JOHNSON
Supreme Court of Idaho, 1984.
106 Idaho 385, 679 P.2d 662.

Facts: Robert and Majorie Wake owned land that they used as both a cattle ranch and a farm. Each spring and autumn the Wakes would drive their cattle from the ranch portion of the operation across an access road on the farmland to Butler Springs, which was also on the farmland.

In December 1956, the Wakes sold the farm to Jesse and Maud Hess but retained for themselves a right-of-way over the farm access road and the right to use Butler Springs for watering their livestock. In 1963 the Hesses sold the farm to the Johnsons, granting them uninterrupted possession of the property "excepting only that permissive use of the premises" owned by the Wakes.

The Wakes continued to use the access road and Butler Springs until 1964 when they sold their ranch and granted the new owners "their rights to the water of Butler Springs . . .," but they said nothing about the access road. The ranch was subsequently sold several times and all the owners used the access road and watering hole. In 1978 the Nelsons purchased the ranch. Shortly thereafter the Johnsons notified the Nelsons that they had revoked the Nelsons' right to use the access road and Butler Springs. In 1979 the Johnsons closed the access road by locking the gates across the road. The Nelsons brought this action, claiming easements to both the access road and Butler Springs. The trial court ruled in favor of the Nelsons and the Johnsons appeal.

Decision: Judgment of the district court affirmed.

Opinion: Huntley, J.

I. BUTLER SPRINGS EASEMENT
In construing an easement in a particular case, the instrument granting the easement is to be interpreted in connection with the intention of the parties, and

the circumstances in existence at the time the easement was granted and utilized. [Citation.] The trial court in this case determined that the easement reserved in the 1956 Wake-Hess contract was appurtenant in nature, with a dominant estate in the cattle ranch and a servient estate in the farm, and that the easement had consequently passed with the dominant estate upon each transfer of title. The evidence fully supports that interpretation. The language of the reservation clause in the contract, as well as the established pattern of use of the Butler Springs area, indicate a clear intention by the parties that the easement be for the benefit of the cattle ranch. There is no showing that the parties intended it to be a mere personal right.

The definitions of "appurtenant" and "in gross" further make it clear that the easement is appurtenant. The primary distinction between an easement in gross and an easement appurtenant is that in the latter there is, and in the former there is not, a dominant estate to which the easement is attached. [Citation.] An easement in gross is merely a personal interest in the land of another, [citation]; whereas an easement appurtenant is an interest which is annexed to the possession of the dominant tenement and passes with it. [Citation.] An appurtenant easement must bear some relation to the use of the dominant estate and is incapable of existence separate from it; any attempted severance from the dominant estate must fail. [Citation.] The easement in the Butler Springs area is a beneficial and useful adjunct of the cattle ranch, and it would be of little use apart from the operations of the ranch. Moreover, in case of doubt, the weight of authority holds that the easement should be presumed appurtenant. [Citation.] * * *

II. THE ACCESS ROAD EASEMENT

"A prescriptive easement must be established by open notorious use of the servient property with the actual or imputed knowledge thereof by the owner of the servient tenement. The use must be continuous for a prescriptive period of five years and must be done under a claim of right." [Citation.]

The use of the access road was open and known to both the Hesses and the Johnsons. The Nelsons and their predecessors in interest claimed a right of way in the access road, and no permission was given for such use until Johnson purported to do so in 1978. In fact, Mr. Johnson testified at trial that he believed the ranch owners had driven the cattle over the road by right. These facts established a prescriptive use of the road for the period between 1956 and 1978, at a minimum, which clearly meets the five-year requirement.

PROFITS À PRENDRE

The phrase **profit à prendre** comes from the French and means the right to remove the produce of another's land. An example would be the grant by B to A, an adjoining land-owner, of the right to remove coal or fish or timber from B's land or to graze his cattle on B's land. Like an easement, a **profit à prendre** may arise by prescription, but if it comes about by an act of the parties, it must be created with all the formalities of a grant of an estate in real property. Unless the right is clearly designated as exclusive, it is always subject to a similar use by the owner of the land. The right to take profits is frequently held even without the ownership of other land. Thus, A may have a right to remove crushed gravel from B's acreage even though A lives in another part of the country.

LICENSES

It it not always easy to distinguish such real interests in property as easements or *profits à prendre* from an equally common right of use designated as a **license.** Permission to make use of one's land generally constitutes a license that creates no interest in the property and is usually exercised only at the will of and subject to revocation by the owner at any time. For example, if Adam tells Brenda she may cut across Adam's land to pick hickory nuts, Brenda has nothing but a license subject to revocation at any time. It is possible that, on the basis of a license, Brenda may expend funds to exercise the right, and the courts may prevent Adam from revoking the license simply because it would be unfair to penalize Brenda under the circumstances. In such a case, Brenda's interest is in practice indistinguishable from an easement.

A common illustration of a license is a theater ticket or the use of a hotel or motel room. No interest is acquired in the premises; there is simply a right of use for a given length of time, subject to good behavior. No formality is required to create a license; a shopkeeper licenses persons to enter his establishment merely by being open for business.

CHAPTER SUMMARY

FREEHOLD ESTATES

Fee Estates	**Freehold Estate Defined** ownership of real property for an indefinite time or for the life of a person **Fee Simple** absolute ownership of property **Qualified Fee** ownership subject to its being taken away upon the happening of an event

Life Estates	**Conventional Life Estates** ■ *Life Estate* ownership right for the life of a designated person ■ *Remainder* ownership estate that takes effect when the prior estate terminates **Established by Law** ■ *Dower* wife's estate in the real property of her husband ■ *Curtesy* husband's estate in the real property of his wife

Future Interests	**Reversion** grantor's right to property upon termination of another estate **Remainders** ■ *Vested Remainder* unconditional remainder that is a fixed, present interest to be enjoyed in the future ■ *Contingent Remainder* remainder interest conditional upon the happening of an event in addition to the termination of the preceding estate

LEASEHOLD ESTATES

Nature	**Lease** Both (1) a contract for use and possession of land and (2) a grant of an estate in land ■ *Landlord* owner of land who grants a leasehold interest to another while retaining a reversionary interest in the property ■ *Tenant* possessor of the leasehold interest in the land

Duration of Leases
- ■ *Definite Term* lease that automatically expires at the end of the term
- ■ *Periodic Tenancy* lease with a definite term that is to be continued for the same length of time in indefinite succession
- ■ *Tenancy at Will* lease that is terminable at any time
- ■ *Tenancy at Sufferance* possession of real property without a lease

Transfer of Tenant's Interests
- ■ *Assignment* transfer of all of the tenant's interest in the leasehold
- ■ *Sublease* transfer of less than all of the tenant's interest in the leasehold

Tenant's Obligations	**Rent** the tenant has an obligation to pay a specified rent at specified times or, if none is specified, to pay a reasonable amount at the end of the term **Destruction of the Premises** under the common law, if the premises are destroyed the tenant is not relieved of his obligation to pay rent and cannot terminate the lease **Eviction for Breach of Covenant** if the tenant breaches one of the covenants of her lease, the landlord may terminate the lease and evict (remove) her from the premises

Landlord's Obligations	**Quiet Enjoyment** the right of a tenant not to have his physical possession of the premises interfered with by the landlord **Fitness for Use** ■ *Common Law Rule* the landlord has no obligation to maintain the premises in a livable condition ■ *Implied Warranty of Habitability* for residential leases some courts impose a warranty that the leased premises are fit for the ordinary residential purposes **Repair** ■ *Common Law* unless there is a statute or a specific provision in the lease, the landlord has no duty to repair or restore the premises ■ *Constructive Eviction* failure by the landlord in any obligation under the lease that causes a substantial and lasting injury to the tenant's enjoyment of the premises; permits the tenant to abandon the premises and terminate the lease

OTHER INTERESTS

Concurrent Ownership	**Joint Tenancy** co-owners with the right of survivorship; requires the presence of the four unities (time, title, interest, and possession) **Tenancy in Common** co-ownership in which each tenant holds an undivided interest with no right of survivorship **Tenancy by the Entireties** co-ownership by spouses in which neither may convey his or her interest during life **Community Property** rights by spouses in property acquired by the other during their marriage **Condominium** separate ownership of an individual unit with tenancy in common with respect to common areas

	Cooperative the corporate owner of the property leases units to its share-holders as tenants

| **Nonpossessory Interests** | **Easement**   limited right to use the land of another in a specified manner
■ *Appurtenant*   rights and duties created by the easement pertain to and run with the land of the owner of the easement (dominant parcel) and the land subject to the easement (servient parcel)
■ *In Gross*   rights and duties created by the easement are personal to the individual who received the right
■ *Creation of Easements*   easements may be created by (1) express grant, (2) implied grant, (3) necessity, (4) dedication, and (5) pre-scription (adverse use)
Profits à Prendre   right to remove the produce from the land of another
Licenses   permission to use the land of another |

QUESTIONS

1. Define and discuss the following feehold interests: (a) fee simple, (b) qualified fee, (c) life estate, (d) remainder interest, (e) dower, (f) curtesy, and (g) reversionary interest.
2. Distinguish between a vested and a contingent remainder.
3. Discuss the primary rights and obligations of landlords and tenants.
4. Identify and discuss the various forms of concurrent ownership of real property.
5. Identify and discuss the various ways in which an easement may be created.

PROBLEMS

1. Kirkland conveyed a farm to Sandler to have and to hold for and during his life and on Sandler's death to Rubin. Some years thereafter, oil was discovered in the vicinity. Sandler thereupon made an oil and gas lease, and the oil company set up its machinery to begin drilling operations. Rubin then filed suit to enjoin the operations. Assuming an injunction to be the proper form of remedy, what decision?

2. Smith owned Blackacre in fee simple. In section 3 of a properly executed will, Smith devised Blackacre as follows: "I devise my farm Blackacre to my son Darwin so long as it is used as a farm." Sections 5 and 6 of the will made gifts to persons other than Darwin. The last clause of Smith's will provided: "All the remainder of my real and personal property not disposed of heretofore in this will, I devise and bequeath to Stanford University."

Smith died, survived by her son Darwin. Smith's estate has been administered. Darwin has been offered $100,000 for Blackacre if he can convey title to it in fee simple.

What interests in Blackacre were created by Smith's will?

3. Panessi leased to Barnes, for a term of ten years beginning May 1 certain premises located at 527–529 Main Street in the City of Cleveland. The premises were improved with a three-story building, the first floor being occupied by stores and the upper stories by apartments. On May 1 of the following year, Barnes leased one of the apartments to Clinton for one year. On July 5 a fire destroyed the second and third floors of the building. The first floor was not burned but was rendered unusable. Neither the lease from Panessi to Barnes nor the lease from Barnes to Clinton contained any provision in regard to the fire loss. Discuss the liability of Barnes and Clinton to continue to pay rent.

4. Ames leased an apartment to Boor for $200 a month payable the last day of each month. The term of the written lease was from January 1, 1989, through April 30, 1990. On March 15, 1989, Boor moved out, telling Ames that he disliked all the other tenants. Ames replied: "Well, you are no prize as a tenant; I probably can get more rent from someone more agreeable than you." Ames and Boor then had a minor physical altercation in which neither was injured. Boor sent the keys to the apartment to Ames by mail. Ames wrote Boor, "It will be my pleasure to hold you for every penny you owe me. I am renting the apartment on your behalf to Clay until April 30, 1990 at $175 a month." Boor

CHAPTER 49 INTERESTS IN REAL PROPERTY

had paid his rent through February 28, 1989. Clay entered the premises on April 1, 1989.

How much rent, if any, may Ames recover from Boor?

5. Jay signed a two-year lease containing a clause that expressly prohibited subletting. After six months, Jay asked the landlord for permission to sublet the apartment for one year. The landlord refused. This angered Jay, and he immediately assigned his right under the lease to Kay. Kay was a distinguished gentlemen, and Jay knew that everyone would consider him a desirable tenant. Is Jay's assignment of his lease to Kay valid?

6. In 1977 Roy Martin and his wife Alice, their son, Hiram, and Hiram's wife Myrna acquired title to a 240-acre farm. The deed ran to Roy Martin and Alice Martin, the father and mother, as joint tenants with the right of survivorship, and to Hiram Martin and Myrna Martin, the son and his wife, as joint tenants with the right of survivorship. Alice Martin died in 1985, and in 1988 Roy Martin married Agnes Martin. By his will, Roy Martin bequeathed and devised his entire estate to Agnes Martin. When Roy Martin died in 1990, Hiram and Myrna Martin assumed complete control of the farm.

State the interest in the farm, if any, of Agnes, Hiram, and Myrna Martin on the death of Roy Martin.

7. In her will, Teressa granted a life estate to Amos in certain real estate, with remainder to Brenda and Clive in joint tenancy. All the rest of Teressa's estate was left to Hillman College. While going to Teressa's funeral, the car in which Amos, Brenda, and Clive were driving was wrecked. Brenda was killed, Clive died a few minutes later, and Amos died on his way to the hospital. Who is entitled to the real estate in question?

8. Otis Olson, the owner of two adjoining city lots, A and B, built a house on each. He laid a drainpipe from lot B across lot A to the main sewer pipe under the alley beyond lot A. Olson then sold and conveyed lot A to Fred Ford. The deed, which made no mention of the drainpipe, was promptly recorded. Ford had no actual knowledge or notice of the drainpipe, although it would have been apparent to anyone making an inspection of the premises because it was only partially buried. Later, Olson sold and conveyed lot B to Luke Lane. This deed also made no reference to the drainpipe and was promptly recorded.

A few weeks, later, Ford discovered the drainpipe across lot A and removed it. Did he have the right to do so?

9. At the time of his marriage to Ann, Robert owned several parcels of real estate in joint tenancy with his brother, Sam. During his marriage, Robert purchased a house and put the title in his name and his wife's name as joint tenants and not as tenants in common. Robert died; within a month of his death, Smith obtained a judgment against Robert's estate. What are the relative rights of Sam, Smith, and Ann?

10. In 1964, Ogle owned two adjoining lots numbered 6 and 7 fronting at the north on a city street. In that year, she laid out and built a concrete driveway along and two feet in front of what she erroneously believed to be the west boundary of lot 7. Ogle used the driveway for access to buildings situated at the southern end of both lots. Later in the same year, she conveyed lot 7 to Dale, and thereafter in the same year, she conveyed lot 6 to Pace. Neither deed made any reference to the driveway, and after the conveyance Dale used it exclusively for access to lot 7. In 1990 a survey by Pace established that the driveway overlapped six inches on lot 6, and he brought an appropriate action to establish his lawful ownership of the strip on which the driveway approaches, to enjoin its use by Dale, and to require Dale to remove the overlap. Decision?

11. Temco, Inc., conveyed to the Wynns certain property adjoining an apartment complex being developed at that time by Sonnett Realty Company. Although nothing to this effect was contained in the deed, the sales contract gave the purchaser of the property use of the apartment's swimming pool. Temco's sales agent also emphasized that the use of the pool would be a desirable feature in the event that the Wynns decided to sell the property.

Seven years later, the Bunns contracted to buy the property from the Wynns through the latter's agent, Sonnett Realty. Although both the Wynns and Sonnett Realty's agent told the Bunns that the use of the apartment's pool went with the purchased property, neither the contract nor the deed subsequently conveyed to the Bunns so provided. When the Bunns requested passes from Temco and Offutt, the company that owned the apartments, their request was refused. The Bunns then brought this action. Decision?

50 TRANSFER AND CONTROL OF REAL PROPERTY

The law has always been, and is still today, extremely cautious about the transfer of title to real estate. Personal property may, for the most part, be easily and informally passed from owner to owner, but real property can be transferred only in compliance with a variety of formalities. This tendency is apparent in the transfer of real property at death, where the strict formalities are relaxed only with respect to personal property, and this attitude of care and formality is most evident in a transfer of land during the lifetime of the owner.

Title to land may be transferred in three principal ways: (1) by deed; (2) by will or by the law of descent on the death of the owner; and (3) by open, continuous, and adverse possession by a nonowner for a statutorily prescribed period of time. In this chapter we discuss the first and third methods of transfer, while we cover the second method in Chapter 51.

In addition to the legal restrictions placed on the transfer of real property, a number of other controls apply to the use of privately owned property. Some of these are imposed by governmental units and include zoning and eminent domain. Others are imposed by private parties through restrictive covenants. We consider these three controls in the second part of this chapter.

TRANSFER OF REAL PROPERTY

The most common way in which real property is transferred is by deed. Such transfers usually involve a contract for the sale of the land and the subsequent delivery of the deed and payment of the agreed upon consideration. In most cases, the purchase of real estate requires borrowing a part of the purchase price secured by the real property. A far less common method of transfer is called adverse possession. This unusual means of transfer of title requires no contract, deed, or other formality.

CONTRACT OF SALE

Formation

Because an oral agreement for the sale of an interest in land is not enforceable under the Statute of Frauds, the buyer and seller must put their agreement in *writing*. Neither party can enforce the agreement unless it is signed by the other party. The simplest agreement should contain (1) the names and addresses of the parties, (2) a description of the property to be conveyed, (3) the time for the conveyance (called the closing), (4) the type of deed to be given, and (5) the price and manner of payment. To avoid dispute and to assure adequate protection of the rights of both parties, many other points should also be covered by a properly drawn contract for the sale of land. For example, the contract should contain carefully written provisions for any and all fixtures intended to be included in the sale.

The great majority of the jurisdictions adhere to the common law rule that the risk of loss or destruction of the property is on the purchaser after the contract is formed. The contract of sale may, of course, provide that the risk of loss or destruction shall remain on the seller until conveyance of the deed to the purchaser, or it may provide that the seller will restore any structures destroyed before the deed is conveyed, that the seller will obtain insurance for the benefit of the purchaser, or any other allocation of risk agreed on by the parties.

Marketable Title

It is firmly established in the law of conveyancing that a contract for the sale of land carries with it an *implied* obligation on the part of the seller to transfer marketable title. **Marketable title** means that the title is free from (1) encumbrances (such as mortgages, easements, liens, leases, and restrictive covenants); (2) defects in the chain of title appearing in the land records (such as a prior recorded conveyance of the same property by the seller); and (3) any other defects that, although they are not sufficient to amount to encumbrances, may subject the purchaser to the inconvenience of having to defend his title in court. The significance of the seller's obligation to convey marketable title is that if the title search reveals any defect that has not been *specifically* excepted in the contract, the purchaser may refuse to take the conveyance on the date set for closing and may sue and recover damages from the seller unless the defect in title is promptly remedied.

There are two important exceptions to this rule, however. First, most courts hold that the seller's implied or express obligation to convey marketable title does not require him to convey title free from existing zoning restrictions. Second, some courts also hold that the seller's implied or express obligation to convey marketable title does not require him to convey title free from open and visible public rights-of-way or easements such as public roads and sewers.

Implied Warranty of Habitability

The obligation of marketable title deals with the title to the property conveyed and has nothing to do with the quality of any improvements to the land. The traditional common law rule is *caveat emptor*—let the buyer beware. Under the rigid common law rule, the buyer has to inspect the property before the sale is completed. Any undiscovered defect would not be the seller's responsibility. The seller is liable only for any misrepresentations or *express* warranties he may have made about the property.

An increasing number of States have relaxed the harshness of the common law in sales by the builder of residential dwellings. In such a sale, the builder-seller *impliedly* warrants that a newly constructed house is free of latent defects, that is, those defects not visible or apparent upon a reasonable inspection of the house at the time of the sale. In some States, this implied warranty of habitability benefits only the original purchaser. In other States, the warranty has been extended to subsequent purchasers for a reasonable period of time.

GAITO v. AUMAN
Supreme Court of North Carolina, 1985.
313 N.C. 243, 327 S.E.2d 870.

Facts: Sam and Eleanor Gaito purchased a home from Howard Frank Auman Jr. in the spring of 1978. The construction of the house had been completed by Auman in November 1973. In the interim, three different parties had lived in the house for brief periods, but Auman had retained ownership. The last tenants, the Ashleys, experienced difficulties with the home's air conditioning system. Repairs were attempted, but no effort was made to change the capacity of the air conditioning unit.

When the Gaitos moved into the house in June 1978, they too had problems with the air conditioning. The system created only a ten-degree difference between the outside and inside temperatures. The Gaitos complained to Auman on a number of occasions, but extensive repairs failed to correct the cooling problem. In May 1981 the Gaitos brought an action against Auman, alleging that the purchase price of the home included central air conditioning and that Auman had breached the implied warranty of habitability. At trial, an expert in the field of heating and air conditioning testified that a four-ton air conditioning system rather than the three-and-one-half-ton system originally installed was appropriate for the Gaitos' house. The jury returned a verdict in favor of the Gaitos in the amount of $3,655 and the court of appeals affirmed.

Decision: Judgment for Gaitos affirmed.

Opinion: Branch, C. J.   The essence of defendant's arguments, however, is that plaintiffs' claim was not cognizable under an implied warranty theory because of the age of the house and its occupation by tenants prior to its purchase by the plaintiffs. Although we held in [citation], that the implied warranty of habitability arises by operation of law, we hold that the applicability of the warranty is to be determined on a case by case basis and that under these facts, plaintiffs presented a legally cognizable claim under a theory of implied warranty of habitability.

The trend of recent judicial decisions has been to invoke the doctrine of implied warranty of habitability or fitness in cases involving the sale of a new house by the builder. [Citations.] The rigid common law rule of *caveat emptor* in the sale of recently completed dwellings was relaxed in this state by this Court's opinion in *Hartley v. Ballou*, [citation]. In *Hartley*, the plaintiffs purchased a "recently" constructed house from defendants. Although they inspected the house prior to moving in, plaintiffs observed nothing amiss. Shortly after moving in the house showed signs of substantial water leakage and insufficient waterproofing in the basement. This Court, in an opinion authored by Chief Justice Bobbitt, concluded that the defendant builder-vendor had an obligation to perform work in a proper, workmanlike and ordinarily skillful manner. Chief Justice Bobbitt then stated the rule as follows:

> [I]n every contract for the sale of a recently completed dwelling, and in every contract for the sale of a dwelling then under construction, the vendor, if he be in the business of building such dwellings, shall be held to impliedly warrant to the initial vendee that, at the time of the passing of the deed or the taking of possession by the initial vendee (whichever first occurs), the dwelling, together with all its fixtures, is sufficiently free from major structural defects, and is constructed in a workmanlike manner, so as to meet the standard of workmanlike quality then prevailing at the time and place of construction; and that this implied warranty in the contract of sale survives the passing of the deed or the taking of possession by the initial vendee.

The doctrine recited in *Hartley* is known as an implied warranty of habitability and represents a growing trend in the jurisprudence of our states. An implied warranty of habitability is limited to latent defects—those not visible or apparent to a reasonable person upon inspection of a dwelling. [Citation.]

The relaxing of the rigid rule of *caveat emptor* in *Hartley* is based on a policy which holds builder-vendors accountable beyond the passage of title or the taking of possession by the initial vendee for defects which are not apparent to the purchaser at that time. This policy is justified because the innocent purchaser is often making one of the largest investments of a lifetime from one whose experience and expertise places him in a dominating position in that sale. [Citation.]

Defendant appellant argues that the facts of this case are legally insufficient to support a verdict for the plaintiff because the facts do not fall within the exception to the rule of *caveat emptor* established by *Hartley*. Defendant contends that an implied warranty of habitability is inapplicable because both the pretrial pleadings and evidence at trial show that the house was not "recently completed" or under construction at the time of the passing of the deed; the plaintiff claims and the evidence shows instead that the house was built four and one-half years earlier. Defendant also argues that the previous occupancy by tenants invalidated any implied warranty which may have arisen.

We first consider defendant's argument that he must prevail because the house was built four and one-half years before the plaintiffs received a deed or took possession. Our cases do not address the precise limits of our requirement in *Hartley* that a house be "recently completed." We therefore turn to other jurisdictions for instruction on this question.

A number of courts have established a standard of reasonableness in determining how the age of a house affects the application of the warranty. [Citation.]

* * *

We are persuaded that the reasoning of these courts is sound and that the standard of reasonableness is the appropriate standard for determining whether a dwelling has been recently completed. Thus, under the facts of this case, it was a question of fact for the fact finder to determine whether the house was "recently completed."Among some of the factors which may be considered in determining this question are the age of the building, the use to which it has been put, its maintenance, the nature of the defects and the expectations of the parties. This standard allows extension of the warranty to vary in lengths of time, depending on the nature of the defect and whether the warranty should reasonably be expected to apply. [Citation.]

Even so, defendant argues that the tenancies which intervened between construction and purchase by plaintiffs rendered the warranty inapplicable. We disagree. We note that the purpose of the warranty is to protect homeowners from defects which can only be within the knowledge of vendors. There are many kinds of major structural defects upon which the presence of tenants can have little or no effect. In other cases intervening tenants may contribute to or directly cause major defects in a dwelling's structure. We hold that the effect of occupation by tenants prior to the passage of the deed to the initial vendee is but one of the factors which a fact finder should consider in determining whether defendant is liable for breach of an implied warranty of habitability. [Citation.]

At this point we note that *Hartley* limits the implied warranty of habitability to *initial vendees* at the time of the taking of possession or the passing of the deed. Here plaintiff was an initial vendee and therefore it is unnecessary for us to discuss the applicability of the implied warranty to subsequent purchasers.

* * *

[B]uilders are still accorded substantial protection by the requirement that the defect in a dwelling or its fixtures be latent or not reasonably discoverable at the time of sale or possession. Claimants must also show that structural defects had their origin in the builder-seller and in construction which does not meet the standard of workmanlike quality then prevailing at the time and place of construction. [Citation.] We have also made it clear that the implied warranty falls short of "an absolute guarantee." [Citation.] In regard to this argument we wish to make it clear that the test of reasonableness to determine whether a dwelling is "recently completed" does not affect the relevant statutes of limitation and repose.

Although defendant did not raise the argument at the Court of Appeals level, he now argues that an implied warranty is inapplicable to an air conditioning unit because it is not "an absolute essential utility to a dwelling house." In *Hartley* we held that the builder of a recently completed dwelling impliedly warrants that "the dwelling, *together with all its fixtures,* is sufficiently free from major structural defects and is constructed in a workmanlike manner, so as to meet the standard of workmanlike quality then prevailing at the time and place of construction." [Citation.]

* * *

The test of a breach of an implied warranty of habitability in North Carolina is not whether a fixture is an "absolute essential utility to a dwelling house." The test is whether there is a failure to meet the prevailing standard of workmanship quality. [Citation.] We hold that under the facts of this case, a jury may properly find a defective air conditioning system in a "recently completed dwelling" to be a major structural defect as between an initial vendee and a builder-vendor.

DEEDS

Types of Deeds

A **deed** is a formal document transferring any interest in land. The modern deed authorized in American jurisdictions is a somewhat simplified version of an early English deed known as a "grant." Originally, a grant was used to transfer intangible interests in land, but its use was gradually expanded to include transfers of any type of interest in land.

Warranty Deed By a **warranty deed,** the **grantor** (seller) promises the **grantee** (buyer) that she has a valid title to the property. In addition, under a warranty deed, the grantor, either expressly or implicitly, obliges herself to make the grantee whole if the grantee suffers any damage because the grantor's title was defective. Aside from the grantor's liability for any defects in her title, a distinct characteristic of the general warranty deed is that it will convey after-acquired title. For example, on January 30 Andrea conveys Blackacre by warranty deed to Barry. On January 30 Andrea's title to Blackacre is defective, but by February 14 Andrea has acquired a good title. Without further formalities, Barry has acquired Andrea's good title under the January 30 warranty deed.

Special Warranty Deed Whereas a warranty deed contains a general warranty of title, a **special warranty deed** warrants only that the title has not been impaired, encumbered, or made defective because of any act or omission *of the grantor.* The grantor merely warrants the title so far as acts or omissions of the grantor are concerned. He does *not* warrant that the title may be defective because of the acts or omissions of others.

Quitclaim Deed By a **quitclaim deed,** the grantor says no more, in effect, than "I make no promise as to what interest I do have in this land, but whatever it is I convey it to you." Quitclaim deeds are used most frequently when it is desired that persons who appear to have an interest in land release their interest.

Formal Requirements

As previously noted, any transfer of an interest in land is within the Statute of Frauds if it is an interest of more than a limited duration. The transfer must therefore be in writing. Nearly all deeds, whatever the type, follow nearly the same pattern. Statutes in most States suggest that certain words of conveyance be used to make the deed effective. The words used will vary depending on whether the instrument is a warranty deed, special warranty deed, or a quitclaim deed. A common phrase for a warranty deed is "convey and warrant," although in a number of States the phrase "grant, bargain, and sell" is used together with a covenant by the seller appearing later in the deed that she will "warrant and defend the title." A quitclaim deed will generally provide that the grantor "conveys and quitclaims" or more simply "quitclaims all interest" in the property.

Consideration In most instances, the law does not require consideration for a valid deed. A grantor may be bound by his gift of land if the deed is properly executed and delivered.

Description of the Land The primary requirement of any description is that it is sufficiently clear and certain to permit identification of the property conveyed. The test is frequently applied in terms of whether a subsequent purchaser or a surveyor employed by him could mark off the land from the description.

Quantity of the Estate After the property has been described, the deed will generally proceed to describe the quantity of estate conveyed to the grantee. Thus, either "to have and to hold to himself and his heirs forever" or "to have and to hold in fee simple" would vest the grantee with absolute title to the land. A deed conveying title to "George for life and to Francis on George's death" would grant a life estate to George and a remainder interest to Francis.

Covenants of Title It is the practice in deeds for the grantor to make certain promises concerning her title to the land. If any one of these promises or covenants is breached, the grantee is entitled to be compensated. There are a number of these covenants, the most usual of which are *title, against encumbrances, quiet enjoyment*, and *warranty*. These various covenants add up to an assurance that the grantee will have undisturbed possession of the land and will, in turn, be able to transfer it without adverse claims of third parties. In many States, all or many of these covenants are implied from the words of conveyance themselves— for example, "warrants" or "grant, bargain, and sell."

Execution Deeds generally end with the signature of the grantor, a seal, and an acknowledgment before a notary public or other official authorized to verify the authenticity of documents. The signature can be made by an agent of the grantor if the agent has written authority from the grantor in a form required by law. Today, the seal has lost most of its former significance, and in those jurisdictions where it is required, the seal is sufficient if the word "Seal" or the letters "L. S." appear next to the signature.

Although the notary public's acknowledgment may not be required to bind the parties to the deed, it is generally a prerequisite to recording the deed, and without an acknowledgment, a deed may not be effective against third parties. In most jurisdictions, a special form of acknowledgment for deeds is specified by statute.

Delivery of Deeds

A deed does not transfer title to land until it is delivered. **Delivery** means an *intent* that the deed is to take effect and is evidenced by the acts or statements of the grantor. Manual or physical transfer of the deed is usually the best evidence of this intent, but it is not necessary. For example, the act of the grantor in placing a deed in a safe deposit box may or may not constitute delivery, depending on whether the grantee did or did not have access to the box and whether the grantor acts as if the property were the grantee's. A deed conceivably may be "delivered" even when kept in the possession of the grantor, just as it would be possible that physical delivery of the deed to the grantee would not transfer title. Delivery, as shown in the case that follows, is not an exact ceremony to be done in one particular way. A deed is frequently turned over to a third party to hold until the grantee performs certain conditions. This is called an **escrow,** and the third party is the escrow agent. When the grantee performs the condition, the escrow agent must turn the deed over to the grantee.

PARRAMORE v. PARRAMORE
Court of Appeals of Florida, 1978.
371 So.2d 123.

Facts: In May 1963 Fred Parramore executed four deeds, each conveying a life estate in his land to him and his wife and a remainder interest in one-fourth of his land to each of his four children: Alney, Eudell, Bernice, and Iris. Although Fred executed and acknowledged the four deeds as part of his plan to distribute his estate at his death, he did not deliver them to his children at this time. Instead, he placed the deeds with his will in a safe deposit box and instructed the children to pick up their deeds at his death. Fred later conveyed Alney's deed to Alney, thereby vesting Alney's interest in that parcel, but Eudell, Bernice, and Iris's deeds were never handed over to them during Fred's lifetime. Fred, however, acted as if the land was beyond his control, and on one occasion told a prospective buyer that the land had already been deeded away. When Fred died in November 1974, Alney brought this action, claiming that the deeds to Eudell, Bernice, and Iris were ineffective because they had never been handed over during Fred's lifetime. Accordingly, Alney argued the remaining land should pass in equal shares to each of the four children under the residuary clause of Fred's will. Alney appeals from a judgment in favor of Eudell, Bernice, and Iris.

Decision: Judgment for Eudell, Bernice, and Iris affirmed.

Opinion: **Smith, C. J.**   Delivery is "the life of a deed"; without it no deed is good, though "the intent to deliver is clear and failure to deliver due to accident." [Citation.] Yet delivery is not an exact ceremony, to be done invariably in a particular way. The clearest delivery is by "a manual tradition of the prepared deed with accompanying words or circumstances showing an appropriate intent." [Citation.] But a grantor may fully relinquish a deed, signifying a conveyance, otherwise than by placing it in the grantee's hands. The grantor may hand his deed to a person not the grantee, with directions to deliver it; and, if an intent to relinquish the deed is shown, and the grantor's directions eventually are carried out, delivery is regarded as having been accomplished even though it cannot be proved absolutely that the grantor could never have retrieved the deed. [Citations.]

* * *

We believe there is substantial competent evidence to support the trial court's decision that Fred Parramore, during his life, vested remainder interests in his children [Eudell, Bernice, and Iris] by conduct recognizable as delivery of the deeds. * * * It is enough that Fred Parramore, unsophisticated in such matters, signed deeds creating remainder interests in his several children and put the deeds beyond his immediate reach in a place which he understandably regarded and verbally identified as the appropriate depository for instruments having practical effect at life's end; that he invariably spoke and acted to indicate that he considered the children's remainder interests vested, even to the point of declaring to a prospective buyer that he could not convey the land because it had been deeded away; and that he did not again take the deeds into his more immediate possession or otherwise disturb them. There is no reason why the grantor's evident intent, as discerned by the trial court, should not be regarded as effectuated by his conduct; nor any reason to doubt that his deeds were thereby delivered by all ceremonies that the law may sensibly require.

Recordation

In almost all States it is not necessary to record deeds in order to pass title from grantor to grantee. Unless the grantee has the deed recorded, however, a subsequent good faith purchaser of the property will acquire superior title to the grantee. Recordation consists of delivery of a duly executed and acknowledged deed to the recorder's office in the county where the property is located. There a copy of the instrument is made and inserted in the current deed book and indexed.

In some States, called *notice* States, unrecorded instruments are invalid against any subsequent purchaser without notice. In other States, called *notice-race* States, an unrecorded deed is invalid against any subsequent purchaser without notice of who records first. Finally, in a few States, called *race* States, an unrecorded deed is invalid against any deed recorded before it.

SECURED TRANSACTIONS

The purchase of real estate usually involves a relatively large outlay of money, and few people pay cash for a house or business real estate. Most people must borrow part of the purchase price or defer payment over a period of time. In these cases, the real estate itself is used to secure the obligation, which is evidenced by a note and either a mortgage or deed of trust. The debtor is referred to as the **mortgagor** and the creditor as the **mortgagee.**

A secured transaction includes two elements: (1) a debt or obligation to pay money, and (2) an interest of the creditor in specific property that secures performance of the obligation. A security interest in property cannot exist apart from the debt it secures. When the debt is discharged in any manner, the security interest in the property is terminated. Transactions involving the use of real estate as security for a debt are subject to real estate law, which consists of statutes and rules developed by the common law regarding mortgages and trust deeds. The Uniform Commercial Code does *not* apply to real estate mortgages or deeds of trust.

Form of Mortgages

The instrument creating a mortgage is in the form of a conveyance from the *mortgagor* to the *mortgagee* and must meet all the necessary requirements for such documents—it must be in writing, it must contain an adequate description of the property, and it must be signed, sealed, acknowledged, and delivered. The usual mortgage, however, differs from an outright conveyance of the property because it contains a provision that, on the performance of the promise by the mortgagor, the conveyance is void and of no effect. This condition is referred to as the "defeasance," and although it normally appears on the face of the mortgage, it may be in a separate document.

The concept of a **mortgage** as a lien on real property as security for the payment of a debt applies with equal force to transactions having the same purpose but under a different name and form. A **deed of trust** is nearly identical to a mortgage, the most striking difference being that, under a deed of trust, the property is conveyed not to the creditor as security but to a third person as trustee for the benefit of the creditor. The deed of trust creates rights almost the same as those created by a mortgage. In some States, it is customary to use a deed of trust in lieu of the ordinary form of mortgage.

As with all interests in realty, the mortgage or deed of trust should be promptly recorded to protect the mortgagee's rights against third persons who acquire an interest in the mortgaged property without knowledge of the mortgage.

Rights and Duties

The rights and duties of the parties to a mortgage may depend on whether it is viewed as creating a lien or as transferring legal title to the mortgagee. Most States have adopted the **lien** theory. The mortgagor retains title and, even in the absence of any stipulation in the mortgage, is entitled to possession of the premises to the exclusion of the mortgagee even in the event of default by the mortgagor. Only by foreclosure (sale) or court appointment of a receiver can the right of possession be taken from the mortgagor. Other States have adopted the common law **title** theory, which gives the right of ownership and possession to the mortgagee. In most cases, as a practical matter, the mortgagor retains possession because the mortgagee does not care about possession unless the mortgagor defaults.

If the mortgagor is in possession, he is entitled to the rents and profits from the land. His obligation to the mortgagee is to pay the interest and principal when due. It is occasionally stipulated in a mortgage, however, that rents and profits will be assigned to the mortgagee as additional security for the debt.

Even though the mortgagor is generally entitled to possession and to many of the attributes of unrestricted ownership, he has a responsibility to deal with the property in such a manner as not to impair the security. In most instances, *"waste"* (impairment of the security) results from the mortgagor's failure to prevent the action or threatened action of third parties against the land. For example, a failure by the debtor to pay taxes or to discharge a prior lien may seriously impair the security of the mortgagee. In such cases, the mortgagee is generally permitted to pay the obligation and add it to his claim against the mortgagor.

The mortgagor has the right to relieve his mortgaged property from the lien of a mortgage by payment of the indebtedness that it secures. This right of **redemption** is characteristic of a mortgage and cannot be defeated except by operation of law. The right to redeem carries with it the obligation to pay the debt, and payment in full with interest is prerequisite to redemption.

Transfer of the Interests Under the Mortgage

The interests of the original mortgagor and mortgagee can be transferred, and the rights and obligations of the assignees will depend primarily on (1) the agreement of the parties to the assignment, and (2) the rules of law protecting the interest of the one who is party to the mortgage but not to the transfer.

If the mortgagor conveys the land, the purchaser is *not* personally liable for the mortgage debt unless she expressly assumes the mortgage. If she **assumes the mortgage,** she is personally obligated to pay the mortgagor's debt owing to the mortgagee. Furthermore, the mortgagee can also hold the mortgagor on his promise to pay. A transfer of mortgaged property **"subject to" the mortgage** does *not* personally obligate the transferee to pay the mortgage debt. In such a case, the transferee's risk of loss is limited to the property.

A mortgagee has the right to assign the mortgage to another person without the consent of the mortgagor. An assignee of a mortgage is well advised to obtain the assignment in writing duly executed by the mortgagee and to record it promptly with the proper public official. This will protect her rights against persons who subsequently acquire an interest in the mortgaged property without knowledge of the assignment. Failure to record an assignment may cause an assignee of a mortgage note to lose her security. For example, Dylan buys land from Owen, relying on a release executed and recorded by the mortgagee, Kristi. However, Kristi had previously assigned the mortgage to Ali, who had failed to have her assignment recorded. If Dylan had no actual knowledge of Kristi's assignment to Ali, Ali has no claim against the property.

Foreclosure

The right to foreclose usually arises upon default by the mortgagor. **Foreclosure** is an action by the mortgage holder to take the property away from the mortgagor, to end the mortgagor's rights in the property, and to sell the property to pay the mortgage debt. The mortgagor's default by nonperformance of other promises in the mortgage may also give the mortgagee this right. For example, a mortgage may provide that failure of the mortgagor to pay taxes is a default that permits foreclosure. It is also a common provision in mortgages that default in payment of an installment of the debt makes the entire unpaid balance of the indebtedness immediately due and payable, permitting foreclosure for the entire amount.

The most general method of terminating the mortgagor's right to redeem the property is by a suit in equity to obtain a judicial decree directing the sale of the property by an officer of the court, the debt being paid out of the proceeds of the sale and the excess, if any, paid to the mortgagor. In some jurisdictions, the mortgagor is given a statutory right to redeem from the foreclosure sale within a specified period of time after the sale. In effect, this right is a second "right of redemption" and should not be confused with the customary right of redemption before foreclosure. In most jurisdictions, a foreclosure sale is subject to approval by the court.

In States where foreclosure is not limited to a sale under judicial decree, a clause may be inserted in mortgages permitting the mortgagee to foreclose by a sale without obtaining an order of court. This power of sale is considerably less time-consuming than a judicial proceeding. The power of sale usually provides for a public auction with published notice, and frequently the mortgagee is forbidden by statute to purchase at the sale on the theory that he occupies a fiduciary relation to the mortgagor that would be breached by buying the property at a sale conducted by him.

Whether foreclosure is by sale under judicial proceeding or by grant of power in the mortgage itself, the transaction retains its character of a procedure to obtain satisfaction of a debt. If the proceeds are insufficient to satisfy the debt in full, the debtor-mortgagor remains liable for payment of the balance of the debt. Generally, the mortgagee will obtain a *deficiency judgment* for any unsatisfied balance of the debt and may proceed to enforce payment of this amount out of other assets of the mortgagor.

ADVERSE POSSESSION

It is possible, although very rare, that title to land may be transferred **involuntarily** without any deed or other formality by adverse possession. In most States, if a person openly and continuously occupies the land of another for a statutorily prescribed period of time, typically twenty years, that person will gain title to the land by **adverse possession**. The possession must be actual. Courts have held that living on land, farming it, building on it, or maintaining structures on it are sufficient to constitute possession. The possession must be adverse, however. This means that any act of dominion by the true owner will stop the period from running. Her entry on the land or assertion of ownership will break the period. The statutory period would then have to begin again from that time.

GERWITZ v. GELSOMIN
Supreme Court, Appellate Division, Fourth Department, 1979.
69 A.D.2d 992, 416 N.Y.S.2d 127.

Facts: The Gerwitz family resides on a piece of land known as Lot #24 of the Belleville tract, which they acquired by deed in 1957. Shortly thereafter, the Gerwitzes began to use the adjacent vacant Lot #25. At various times, they planted grass seed, flowers, and shrubs on the land and used it for picnics and cookouts. In 1977 Gelsomin acquired Lot #25 and constructed a foundation on it so that he could place a house there. The Gerwitzes then brought this action to stop him, claiming title to Lot #25 by adverse possession. The trial court found for Gelsomin.

Decision: Judgment for Gelsomin affirmed.

Opinion: Memorandum Before a claimant may acquire land by adverse possession, he must prove by clear and convincing evidence that his possession of the premises has been (1) hostile and under a claim of right, (2) actual, (3) open and notorious, (4) exclusive, and (5) continuous. [Citations.] The trial court found that plaintiffs had failed to prove that their occupation of these premises had been exclusive or continuous. We affirm because the possession was not hostile to the owner and under a claim of right.

The reasonable inference to be drawn from the evidence is that plaintiffs knew in 1957 that they did not own Lot #25 and they never intended to claim ownership of it. They entered the land to remedy an eyesore next to their home and use the land as they could. Thus, the proof establishes that plaintiffs had clear knowledge of the boundaries of their land by map and deed and because the other lots on the street were the same size. At the time of purchase, plaintiffs' Lot #24 was graded and improved by the contractor, but he did not grade or improve Lot #25. Plaintiffs were satisfied with this grading which established a clear boundary line between their improved property and the unimproved Lot #25 next door which was covered with debris. Plaintiffs paid the taxes on their own property regularly and received receipts for those payments. They have never paid or attempted to pay the taxes on Lot #25, even after defendant started his construction. While the failure to pay taxes is not conclusive evidence, it is a significant circumstance which weakens plaintiffs' claim that occupation of the land was under a claim of title, particularly when the failure continued for 20 years. [Citation.]

Finally, the proof establishes that at various times during the prospective period "For sale" signs were placed upon the vacant premises by the owner without objection or inquiry by plaintiffs. Upon this evidence, plaintiffs have failed to sustain their burden of proof that they occupied Lot #25 or any part of it under a claim of right.

In some jurisdictions, shorter periods of adverse possession have been established by statute where there is not only possession but also some other claim such as the payment of taxes for seven years and an apparent claim of title, even if it is not valid.

PUBLIC AND PRIVATE CONTROLS

In the exercise of its police power, the State can and does place controls on the use of privately owned land for the benefit of the community. Furthermore, the State does not pay the owner any compensation for loss or damage sustained by the owner because of such legitimate controls. The enforcement of zoning laws, which is a proper exercise of the police power, is not a taking of property but a regulation of its use. The taking of private property for a public use or purpose under the State's power of eminent domain is not, however, an exercise of police power, and the owners of the property so taken are entitled to be paid its fair and reasonable value.

There are also private controls of the use of privately owned property by means of restrictive covenants, which we also consider in this section.

ZONING

Zoning is the principal method of public control over *land use*. The validity of zoning is based on the police power of the State. The police power to provide for the public health, safety, morals, and welfare is one of the inherent powers of government. Police power can be used only to regulate private property, never to "take" it. It is firmly established that regulation that has no reasonable relation to public health, safety, morals, or welfare is unconstitutional because it is contrary to due process of law.

Enabling Acts and Zoning Ordinances

The power to zone is generally delegated to local city and village authorities by statutes known as enabling statutes. A typical enabling statute grants the following powers to municipalities: (1) to regulate and limit the height and bulk of buildings to be erected; (2) to establish, regulate, and limit the building or setback lines on or along any street, trafficway, drive, or parkway; (3) to regulate and limit the intensity of the use of lot areas and to regulate and determine the area of open spaces within and surrounding buildings; (4) to classify, regulate, and restrict the location of trades and industries and the location of buildings designated for specified industrial, business, residential, and other uses; (5) to divide the entire municipality into districts of such number, shape, area, and such different classes as may be deemed best suited to carry out the purposes of the statute; and (6) to set standards to which buildings or structures must conform.

Under these powers, the local authorities may enact zoning ordinances, which consist of a map and a text. The map divides the municipality into districts that are designated principally as industrial, commercial, or residential, with possible subclassifications. A well-drafted zoning ordinance will carefully define the uses permitted in each area.

Variance

Enabling statutes provide that the zoning authorities shall have power to grant **variances** in cases of "particular hardship," which is caused by the application of the zoning ordinance to the property and is unique or peculiar to the property. Special circumstances applicable to the particular property include such matters as its unusual shape, topography, size, location, or surroundings. A variance is not available if the hardship is caused by conditions general to the neighborhood or by the actions of the property owner. It must affirmatively appear that the property as presently zoned cannot yield a reasonable return on the owner's investment.

Nonconforming Uses

A zoning ordinance may not immediately terminate a lawful use that existed before it was enacted. This use must be permitted to continue as a **nonconforming use** for at least a reasonable time. Most ordinances provide for the elimination of nonconforming uses (1) when the use is discontinued, (2) when a nonconforming structure is destroyed or substantially damaged, or (3) when a nonconforming structure has been permitted to exist for the period of its useful life as fixed by municipal authorities.

Judicial Review of Zoning

Although the zoning process is traditionally viewed as legislative, it is subject to judicial review on a number of grounds, including (1) that the zoning ordinance is invalid, and (2) that the zoning ordinance amounts to a confiscation or taking of property.

Subdivision Master Plans

A growing municipality has a special interest in regulating new housing developments so that they will harmonize with the rest of the community; so that streets within the development are integrated with existing streets or planned roads; so that adequate provision is made for open spaces for traffic, recreation, light, and air; and so that adequate provision is made for water, drainage, and sanitary facilities. Accordingly, most States have legislation enabling local authorities to require municipality approval of every land subdivision plat. These enabling statutes provide penalties for failure to secure such approval where required by local ordinance. Some statutes make it a criminal offense to sell lots by reference to unrecorded plats and provide that such plats may not be recorded unless approved by the local planning board. Other statutes provide that building permits will not be issued unless the plat is approved and recorded.

EMINENT DOMAIN

The power to take private property for public use, known as the power of **eminent domain,** is recognized as one of the inherent powers of government in the U.S. Constitution and in State constitutions. At the same time, however, the power is carefully circumscribed and controlled. The Fifth Amendment to the Federal Constitution provides, ''Nor shall private property be taken for public use without just compensation.'' Similar or identical provisions are to be found in the constitutions of the States. There is, therefore, a direct constitutional prohibition against taking private property without just compensation and implicit prohibition against taking private property for other than public use. Moreover, under both Federal and State constitutions, the individual is entitled to due process of law in connection with the taking.

Public Use

As noted, there is an implicit constitutional prohibition against taking private property for other than public use. Most States interpret public use to mean ''public advantage.'' Thus, the power of eminent domain may be delegated to railroad and public utility companies. The reasonable exercise of this power by such companies to enable them to offer continued and improved service to the public is upheld as a public advantage. As society grows more complex, other public purposes are accepted as legitimate grounds for exercise of the power of eminent domain. One is in the area of urban renewal. Most States have legislation permitting the establishment of housing authorities with power to condemn slum, blighted, and vacant areas and to finance, construct, and maintain housing projects.

Just Compensation

When the power of eminent domain is exercised, the owners of the property taken must receive just compensation. The measure of compensation is the fair market value of the property as of the time of taking. The compensation goes to holders of vested interests in the condemned property.

FIRST ENGLISH EVANGELICAL LUTHERAN CHURCH OF GLENDALE v. LOS ANGELES COUNTY, CALIFORNIA
Supreme Court of the United States, 1987.
482 U.S. 304, 107 S.Ct. 2378, 96 L.Ed.2d 250.

Facts: First English Evangelical Lutheran Church purchased a twenty one-acre tract of land in a canyon along the banks of Mill Creek in the Angeles National Forest. The church operated a campground, known as ''Lutherglen,'' on the site as a retreat and recreational center for handicapped children. In July 1977 a forest fire destroyed approximately 3,860 acres upstream from Lutherglen, resulting in a serious flood hazard. Indeed, the next February, after a severe rainstorm, Mill Creek overflowed its banks, flooding Lutherglen and destroying its buildings. The county of Los Angeles responded to the flooding of the canyon in January 1979 by adopting an interim ordinance, effective immediately, that established a flood protection area on either side of Mill Creek within which no building, construction, or reconstruction could occur. This interim flood protection area included the areas on which Lutherglen stood. The church brought an action againt the county, claiming that the ordinance denied the church all use of Lutherglen and seeking compensation for the loss of such use. The California Court of Appeals held that the church was unable to recover damages.

Decision: Judgment of Court of Appeals reversed, and case remanded for further proceedings consistent with this opinion.

Opinion: Rehnquist, C. J. Appellant asks us to hold that the Supreme Court of California erred in Agins v. Tiburon in determining that the Fifth Amendment, as made applicable to the States through the Fourteenth Amendment, does not require compensation as a remedy for "temporary" regulatory takings—those regulatory takings which are ultimately invalidated by the courts.

* * *

Consideration of the compensation question must begin with direct reference to the language of the Fifth Amendment, which provides in relevant part that "private property (shall not) be taken for public use, without just compensation." As its language indicates, and as the Court has frequently noted, this provision does not prohibit the taking of private property, but instead places a condition on the exercise of that power. [Citations.] This basic understanding of the Amendment makes clear that it is designed not to limit the governmental interference with property rights per se, but rather to secure compensation in the event of otherwise proper interference amounting to a taking. Thus, government action that works a taking of property rights necessarily implicates the "constitutional obligation to pay just compensation." [Citation.]

We have recognized that a landowner is entitled to bring an action in inverse condemnation as a result of " 'the self-executing character of the constitutional provision with respect to compensation. . . .' " . . .

* * *

It has also been established doctrine at least since Justice Holmes' opinion for the Court in [citation] that "(t)he general rule at least is, that while property may be regulated to a certain extent, if regulation goes too far it will be recognized as a taking." [Citation.] While the typical taking occurs when the government acts to condemn property in the exercise of its power of eminent domain, the entire doctrine of inverse condemnation is predicated on the proposition that a taking may occur without such formal proceedings. . . .

While the Supreme Court of California may not have actually disavowed this general rule in Agins, we believe that it has truncated the rule by disallowing damages that occurred prior to the ultimate invalidation of the challenged regulation. The Supreme Court of California justified its conclusion at length in the Agins opinion, concluding that:

"In combination, the need for preserving a degree of freedom in the land-use planning function, and the inhibiting financial force which inheres in the inverse condemnation remedy, persuade us that on balance mandamus or declaratory relief rather than inverse condemnation is the appropriate relief under the circumstances." Agins v. Tiburon, [citation].

We, of course, are not unmindful of these considerations, but they must be evaluated in the light of the command of the Just Compensation Clause of the Fifth Amendment. The Court has recognized in more than one case that the government may elect to abandon its intrusion or discontinue regulations. [Citations.] Similarly, a governmental body may acquiesce in a judicial declaration that one of its ordinances has affected an unconstitutional taking of property; the landowner has no right under the Just Compensation Clause to insist that a "temporary" taking be deemed a permanent taking. But we have not resolved whether abandonment by the government requires payment of compensation for the period of time during which regulations deny a landowner all use of his land.

In considering this question, we find substantial guidance in cases where the government has only temporarily exercised its right to use private property. . . .

These cases reflect the fact that "temporary" takings which, as here, deny a landowner all use of his property, are not different in kind from permanent takings, for which the Constitution clearly requires compensation. [Citation.] ("Nothing in the Just Compensation Clause suggests that 'takings' must be permanent and irrevocable".) It is axiomatic that the Fifth Amendment's just compensation provision is "designed to bar Government from forcing some people alone to bear public burdens which, in all fairness and justice, should be borne by the public as a whole." [Citations.] In the present case the interim ordinance was adopted by the county of Los Angeles in January 1979, and became effective immediately. Appellant filed suit within a month after the effective date of the ordinance and yet when the Supreme Court of California denied a hearing in the case on October 17, 1985, the merits of appellant's claim had yet to be determined. The United States has been required to pay compensation for leasehold interests of shorter duration than this. The value of a leasehold interest in property for a period of years may be substantial, and the burden on the property owner in extinguishing such an interest for a period of years may be great indeed. [Citation.] Where this burden results from governmental action that amounted to a taking, the Just Compensation Clause of the Fifth Amendment requires that the government pay the landowner for the value of the use of the land during this period. [Citation.] ("It is the owner's loss, not the taker's gain, which is the measure of the value of the property taken".) Invalidation of the ordinance or its successor ordinance after this period of time, though converting the taking into a "temporary" one, is not a sufficient remedy to meet the demands of the Just Compensation Clause.

* * *

Nothing we say today is intended to abrogate the principle that the decision to exercise the power of eminent domain is a legislative function, " 'for Congress and Congress alone to determine.' " [Citations.] Once a court determines that a taking has occurred, the government retains the whole range of options already available—amendment of the regulation, withdrawal of the invalidated regulation, or exercise of eminent domain. Thus we do not, as the Solicitor General suggests, "permit a court, at the behest of a private person, to require the . . . Government to exercise the power of eminent domain. . . ." [Citation.] We merely hold that where the government's activities have already worked a taking of all use of property, no subsequent action by the government can relieve it of the duty to provide compensation for the period during which the taking was effective.

We also point out that the allegation of the complaint which we treat as true for purposes of our decision was that the ordinance in question denied appellant all use of its property. We limit our holding to the facts presented, and of course do not deal with the quite different questions that would arise in the case of normal delays in obtaining building permits, changes in zoning ordinances, variances, and the like which are not before us. We realize that even our present holding will undoubtedly lessen to some extent the freedom and flexibility of land-use planners and governing bodies of municipal corporations when enacting land-use regulations. But such consequences necessarily flow from any decision upholding a claim of constitutional right; many of the provisions of the Constitution are designed to limit the flexibility and freedom of governmental authorities and the Just Compensation Clause of the Fifth Amendment is one of them. As Justice Holmes aptly noted more than 50 years ago, "a strong public desire to improve the public condition is not enough to warrant achieving the desire by a shorter cut than the constitutional way of paying for the change." [Citation.]

Here we must assume that the Los Angeles County ordinances have denied appellant all use of its property for a considerable period of years, and we hold that invalidation of the ordinance without payment of fair value for the use of the property during this period of time would be a constitutionally insufficient remedy.

PRIVATE RESTRICTIONS ON LAND USE

The owners of lots are subject to restrictive covenants that, if actually brought to the attention of subsequent purchasers or recorded by original deed or by means of a recorded plat or separate agreement, bind purchasers of lots in the subdivision as though the restriction had been inserted in their own deed.

For example, suppose Becker owns a lot in a residential subdivision of a suburban community. On the lot are a house and a garage, and the remainder of the subdivision is either similarly improved or vacant. Becker decides to enlarge his living room and to extend the front of the house to within twenty feet of the front line of the lot. He knows that this is not prohibited by the zoning ordinance and that there is no limitation in the deed from his seller limiting the area of the house. He will, indeed, be astounded when a neighbor, observing the excavation, informs him that he cannot build to within twenty feet of the front line. He will be only slightly less surprised to hear that the reason he cannot do so is because of a provision in the recorded deed from the original subdivider to the original purchasers of lots in the subdivision requiring front yards of at least thirty-foot depth.

Becker will discover on further investigation that the entire subdivision has been subjected to a general building plan designed to benefit all the lots, and any lot owner in the subdivision has the right to enforce the restriction against a purchaser whose title descends from a common grantor.

Nature of Restrictive Covenants

Restrictive covenants of the type mentioned above are, in a sense, easements—or at least *negative* easements—to the extent that they impose a limitation on the use of the land. But, unlike most easements, they are not directly based on any formal grant, and the ability of any number of property owners to enforce them does not suggest the usual easement that normally is enforceable by an adjoining landowner.

If there is a clear intent that a restriction is intended to benefit an entire tract, the fact that the covenant is not formally executed will not prevent it being enforced against a subsequent purchaser of one of the lots in the tract. As long as both of the following requirements are met, the restriction will be enforced: first, that it is apparent that the restriction was intended to benefit the purchaser of any lot in the tract, and second, that the restriction appears somewhere in the chain of title to which the lot is subject.

Types of Restrictive Covenants

There are many types of restrictive covenants. The more common ones limit the use of property to residential purposes, restrict the area of the lot on which a structure can be built, or provide for a special type of architecture. Frequently a subdivider will specify a minimum size for each house in an attempt to maintain a minimum standard in the neighborhood.

Restrictive covenants, however, are construed strictly against the party asserting their applicability.

Termination of Restrictive Covenants

A restrictive covenant may end by the terms of the original agreement. For example, the developer of a subdivision may provide that the restrictive covenant will terminate after thirty-five years unless a specified majority of the property owners reaffirm the covenant. In addition, a court will not enforce a restrictive covenant if changed circumstances make enforcement inequitable and oppressive. Evidence of *changed conditions* may be found either within the tract covered by the original covenant or within the area adjacent to or surrounding the tract.

Validity of Restrictive Covenants

Although restrictions on the use of land have never been popular in the law, if it appears that the restriction will operate to the general benefit of the owners of all the land intended to be affected, the restriction will be enforced.

The usual method of enforcing such agreements is by injunction to restrain a violation.

It has been the law for many years, however, that a State or municipality cannot, under the Fourteenth Amendment to the Constitution, impose any such restrictions by statute or ordinance. In 1947 the Supreme Court held that private racial restrictive covenants cannot be enforced by State courts because the courts are an arm of the State government. This effectively invalidated private racial restrictive covenants.

CHAPTER SUMMARY

TRANSFER

Contract of Sale	**Formation** a contract to transfer any interest in land must be in writing to be enforceable **Marketable Title** the seller must transfer marketable title which is a title free from any defects or encumbrances **Quality of Improvements** ■ *Common Law Rule* under *caveat emptor* ("let the buyer beware") the seller is not liable for any undiscovered defects ■ *Implied Warranty of Habitability* in a number of States the builder-seller of a dwelling impliedly warrants that a newly constructed house is free from latent defects
Deeds	**Definition** a formal document transferring any type of interest in land **Types** ■ *Warranty Deed* the grantor (seller) promises the grantee (buyer) that she has a valid title to the property without defect ■ *Special Warranty Deed* the seller promises that he has not impaired the title ■ *Quitclaim Deed* the seller transfers whatever interest she has in the property **Requirements** the deed must (1) be written; (2) contain certain words of conveyance and a description of the property; (3) end with the signature of the grantor, a seal, and an acknowledgment before a notary public; and (4) be delivered **Delivery** intent that the deed take effect as evidenced by acts or statements of the grantor **Recordation** required to protect the buyer's interest against third parties; consists of delivery of a duly executed and acknowledged deed to the appropriate recorder's office
Secured Transactions	**Elements** a secured transaction involves (1) a debt or obligation to pay money, (2) an interest of the creditor in specific property that secures performance, and (3) the right of the debtor to redeem the property (remove the security interest) by payment of the debt **Mortgage** interest in land created by a written document that provides security to the mortgagee (secured party) for payment of the mortgagor's debt **Deed of Trust** an interest in real property which is conveyed to a third person as trustee for the benefit of the creditor

	Transfer ■ *Assumes the Mortgage* the purchaser of mortgaged property becomes personally liable to pay the debt ■ *Subject to the Mortgage* purchaser is not personally liable to pay the debt, but the property remains subject to the mortgage Foreclosure sale of the mortgaged property upon default to satisfy the debt
Adverse Possession	**Definition** acquisition of title to land by open, continuous, and adverse occupancy for a statutorily prescribed period **Possession** must be actual and without intervening dominion by true owner

PUBLIC AND PRIVATE CONTROLS

Zoning	**Definition** principal method of public control over private land use, involving regulation of land but may not constitute a taking of the property **Authority** the power to zone is generally delegated to local authorities by statutes known as *enabling acts* **Variance** a use differing from that provided in the zoning ordinance granted in order to avoid undue hardship **Nonconforming Use** a use not in accordance with, but existing prior to, a zoning ordinance which is permitted to continue for at least a reasonable period of time **Judicial Review** zoning ordinances may be reviewed to determine if they are invalid or a confiscation of property
Eminent Domain	**Definition** the power of a government to take (buy) private land for public use **Just Compensation** the owner of the property taken by eminent domain must be paid the fair market value of the property
Restrictive Covenants	**Definition** private restrictions on property contained in a conveyance **Types** the most common types limit the use of property to residential purposes, restrict the area of the lot on which a structure can be built, or provide for a special type of architecture **Validity** restrictive covenants are enforced when they are to the general benefit of the owners of all the land affected

QUESTIONS

1. Distinguish among warranty, special warranty, and quitclaim deeds.
2. Distinguish between the obligations of a purchaser who assumes a mortgage and one who buys the property subject to the mortgage.
3. Describe the fundamental requirements of a valid deed.
4. Define and give an example of (a) a variance, and (b) a nonconforming use.
5. Describe the nature and types of restrictive covenants.

PROBLEMS

1. A was the father of B, C and D and the owner of Redacre, Blackacre, and Greenacre.

A made and executed a warranty deed conveying Redacre to B. The deed provided that "this deed shall only become effective on the death of the grantor." A retained possession of the deed and died leaving the deed in his safe deposit box.

A made and executed a warranty deed conveying Blackacre to C. The deed provided "this deed shall only become effective on the death of the grantor." A delivered the deed to C. After A died, C recorded the deed.

A made and executed a warranty deed conveying Greenacre to D. A delivered the deed to X with specific instructions to deliver the deed to D on A's death. X duly delivered the deed to D when A died.

(a) What is the interest of B in Redacre, if any?
(b) What is the interest of C in Blackacre, if any?
(c) What is the interest of D in Greenacre, if any?

2. Arkin, the owner of Redacre, executed a real estate mortgage to the Shawnee Bank and Trust Company for $10,000. After the mortgage was executed and recorded, Arkin constructed a dwelling on the premises and planted a corn crop. After default in the payment of the mortgage debt, the bank proceeded to foreclose the mortgage. At the time of the foreclosure sale, the corn crop was mature and unharvested. Arkin contends (a) that the value of the dwelling should be credited to him, and (b) that he is entitled to the corn crop. Decision?

3. Robert and Stanley held legal title of record to adjacent tracts of land, each consisting of eighty acres. Stanley fenced his eighty acres in 1966. He placed his east fence fifteen feet onto Robert's property. Thereafter, he was in possession of this fifteen-foot strip of land and kept it fenced and cultivated continuously until he sold his tract of land to Nathan on March 1, 1971. Nathan took possession under deed from Stanley, and continued possession and cultivation of the fifteen-foot strip until May 27, 1990, when Robert, having on several occasions strenuously objected to Nathan's possession, brought suit against Nathan for trespass.

What decision?

4. Marcia executed a mortgage of Blackacre to secure her indebtedness to Ajax Savings and Loan Association in the amount of $25,000. Later, Marcia sold Blackacre to Morton. The deed contained the following provision: "This deed is subject to the mortgage executed by the Grantor herein to Ajax Savings and Loan Association."

The sale price of Blackacre to Morton was $50,000. Morton paid $25,000 in cash, deducting the $25,000 mortgage debt from the purchase price. On default in the payment of the mortgage debt, Ajax brings an action against Marcia and Morton to recover a judgment for the amount of the mortgage debt and to foreclose the mortgage. Decision?

5. On January 1, 1989, Davis and Hershey owned Blackacre as tenants in common. On July 1, 1989, Davis made a written contract to sell Blackacre to Dibbert for $25,000. Pursuant to this contract, Dibbert paid Davis $25,000 on August 1, 1989, and Davis executed and delivered to Dibbert a warranty deed to Blackacre. On May 1, 1990, Hershey quitclaimed his interest in Blackacre to Davis. Dibbert brings an action against Davis for breach of warranty of title. What judgment?

6. John Doe, for valuable consideration, agreed to convey to Richard Roe eighty acres of land. He delivered a deed, the material portions of which read:

"I, John Doe, grant and convey to Richard Roe eighty acres of land [land description]: To have and to hold unto Richard Roe, his heirs, and assigns forever.

"I, John Doe, covenant to warrant and defend the premises hereby conveyed against all persons claiming the same or any part thereof by or through me."

Thereafter, Roe conveyed "all my right, title, and interest" in the eighty acres to Paul Poe. It develops that Doe had no title to the land when he conveyed it to Roe. Subsequently, Doe inherited an undivided one-half interest in the property.

What rights, if any, does Poe have against Doe and Roe?

7. Barker operated a retail bakery, Davidson a drugstore, Farrell a food store, Gibson a gift shop, and Harper a hardware store in adjoining locations along one side of a single suburban village block. As the population grew, the business section developed at the other end of the village, and the establishments of Barker, Davidson, Farrell, Gibson, and Harper were surrounded for at least a mile in each direction solely by residences. A zoning ordinance with the usual provisions was adopted by the village, and the area including the five stores was declared to be a "residential district for single-family dwellings." Thereafter, Barker tore down the frame building that housed the bakery and began to construct a modern brick bakery. Davidson found her business increasing to such an extent that she began to build an addition on the drugstore to extend it to the rear alley. Farrell's building was destroyed by fire, and he started to reconstruct it to restore it to its former condition. Gibson changed the gift shop into a sporting goods store and after six months of operation decided to go back into the gift shop business. Harper sold his hardware store to Hempstead.

The village building commission brings an action under the zoning ordinance to enjoin the construction work of Barker, Davidson, and Farrell and to enjoin the carrying on of any business by Gibson and Hempstead. Assume the ordinance is valid. What result?

8. Alda and Mattingly are residents of Unit I of Chimney Hills Subdivision. The lots owned by Alda and Mattingly are subject to the following restrictive covenant: "Lots shall be for single-family residence puposes only." Alda intends to convert the interior of her carport into a beauty shop, and Mattingly brings suit against Alda to enjoin her from doing so. Alda argues that the covenant restricts only the type of building that can be constructed, not the incidental use to which residential structures are put. Decision?

9. The city of Boston sought to condemn land in fee simple for use in constructing an entrance to an underground terminal for a subway. The owners of the land contend that no more than surface and subsurface easements are necessary for the terminal entrance and seek to retain air rights above thirty-six feet. The city argues that any building using this air space would require structural supports that would interfere with the city's plan for the terminal. The city concedes that the properties around the condemned property could be assembled and structures could be designed to span over the condemned property, in which case the air rights would be quite valuable. Decision?

10. For seven years, Desford Potts has owned a six-acre tract of land within the corporate limits of the city of Franklin. The tract contained a livestock barn in which Potts stored lumber and other building materials. Bricks were also stored in stacks four or five feet high outside and behind the barn. Franklin passed a zoning ordinance by virtue of which Pott's lot was classified as residential property. Soon afterward, Potts moved some saw logs onto his back lot, and the city complained that Pott's use of his property for storage of building materials is a "nonconforming use." Potts then brought an action to enjoin interference by the city of Franklin. Decision?

51 TRUSTS AND WILLS

In previous chapters we have seen that real and personal property may be transferred in a number of ways, including by sale and by gift. Another important way in which a person may convey property or allow others to use or benefit from it is through trusts and wills. Trusts may take effect during the transferor's lifetime, or, when used in a will, they may become effective upon his death. Wills enable individuals to control the transfer of their property at their death. Upon a person's death, his or her property must pass to someone. It is almost always the best policy for individuals to decide how their property should be distributed and, except for the limitations of dower and curtesy, the law permits individuals to do so by sale, gift, trust, and will. If, however, an individual dies without a will—that is, *intestate*—State law prescribes who shall be entitled to the property owned by that individual at death. In this chapter we will examine both trusts and wills, as well as the manner in which property descends when a person dies intestate.

TRUSTS

A **trust** arises when legal title to property is held by one or more persons while its use, enjoyment, and benefit belong to another. A trust may be created by agreement of the parties, by a grant in a will, or by a court decree. However created, the relationship is known as a trust. The party creating the trust is the **creator** or **settlor,** the party holding the legal title to the property is the **trustee** of the trust, and the person who receives the benefit of the trust is the **beneficiary** (see Figure 51–1).

TYPES OF TRUSTS

Although there are many varieties of trusts, all trusts may be divided into two major groups:

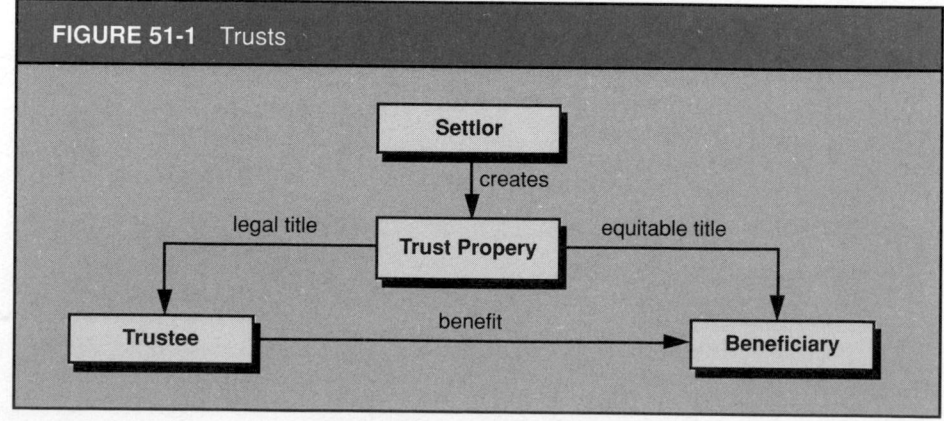

FIGURE 51-1 Trusts

Settlor

creates

legal title

Trust Propery

equitable title

Trustee

benefit

Beneficiary

express and implied. The implied trusts, which are imposed upon property by court order, are known as either "constructive" or "resulting" trusts.

Express Trusts

The express trust is, as the name indicates, a trust established by voluntary action and is represented by a written document or, under some conditions, an oral statement. In a majority of jurisdictions, an express trust of real property must be in writing to meet the requirements of the Statute of Frauds. No particular words are necessary to create a trust, provided that the intent of the settlor to establish a trust is unmistakable. It is not always easy to tell whether a settlor really intended to create a trust. Sometimes, words of request or recommendation are used in connection with a gift, implying or hoping that the gift will be used for the purpose stated. Thus, instead of leaving property "to Kathy for the benefit and use of Matthew," a settlor may leave property to Kathy "in full confidence and with hope that she will care for Matthew." Such a **precatory** (wishful) expression may be so definite and certain as to impose a trust upon the property for the benefit of Matthew. Whether it creates a trust or is nothing more than a gratuitous wish will depend on whether the court believes from all the facts that the settlor genuinely intended a trust. Generally, courts view such words as "request," "hope," and "rely" as imposing no legal obligation upon the recipient of the gift and therefore do not create a trust.

Charitable Trusts Almost any trust that has for its purpose the improvement of humankind or a class of humankind is a **charitable trust,** unless it is so vague and indefinite that it cannot be enforced. Gifts for public museums, upkeep of parks, and to further a particular political doctrine or religious belief have been upheld as charitable.

There are practical differences in the law depending on whether a trust is for charitable or private purposes. In general, the rule against perpetuities (that an interest in prop-

erty must vest within 21 years plus a period of gestation after some life or lives in being) does not apply to charitable trusts. For example, it is valid to provide for a gift in trust to the Middlesex Hospital, a nonprofit corporation, with a provision that if the Hospital ceased to maintain free wards the property should go to the Town of Middlesex for care of the poor. If the trust had been noncharitable, the contingent gift to the town would have violated the rule against perpetuities.

Spendthrift Trusts A settlor frequently does not believe that a beneficiary can be relied on to preserve even the limited rights granted her as beneficiary. He may then provide in the trust instrument that the beneficiary cannot, by assignment or otherwise, impair her rights to receive principal or income and that creditors of the beneficiary cannot attach the fund or the income. The term *spendthrift*, as used in connection with spendthrift trusts, refers to a provision in a trust instrument under which the trust estate is removed from the beneficiary's control and disposition and from liability for her individual debts. Spendthrift provisions are generally valid. Of course, once income from the trust is actually received by the beneficiary, creditors may seize it or the beneficiary may use it as she pleases.

Totten Trusts A **totten trust** involves a joint bank account opened by the settlor of the trust. For example, Sally deposits a sum of money in a savings account in a bank in the name of "Sally, in trust for Justin." Sally may make additional deposits in the account from time to time and may withdraw money from it whenever she pleases. The courts have held this to be a tentative trust that Sally may revoke by withdrawing the funds or changing the form of the account. The transfer of ownership becomes complete only on the depositor's death.

Implied Trusts

In some cases, the courts, in the absence of any expressed intent to create a trust, will impose a trust on property because the acts of the parties appear to call for such a construction. An implied trust owes its existence to the law. As previously stated, implied trusts are usually divided into two classes, constructive trusts and resulting trusts.

Constructive Trusts   A **constructive trust** covers those instances where a court will impose a trust on property to rectify fraud or to prevent unjust enrichment. A constructive trust will be established where there has been abuse of a confidential relationship or where actual fraud or duress is considered an equitable ground for creating the trust. The mere existence of a confidential relationship prohibits the trustee from seeking any personal benefit for himself during the course of the relationship. Business and personal affairs provide many potential situations in which constructive trusts may be implied. For example, a director of a corporation who takes advantage of a "corporate opportunity" or who makes an undisclosed profit in a transaction with the corporation will be treated as a trustee for the corporation with respect to the property or profits he acquires. Likewise, a trustee under an express trust who permits a lease held by the trust to expire and then acquires a new lease of the property in his individual capacity will be required to hold the new lease in a confidential trust for the beneficiary.

As previously indicated, constructive trusts are also invoked in situations where persons use their positions of friendship or marriage to their unjust advantage.

SHARP v. KOSMALSKI
Court of Appeals of New York, 1976.
40 N.Y.S.2d 119, 386 N.Y.S.2d 72, 351 N.E.2d 721.

Facts: Rodney Sharp is a fifty-six-year-old dairy farmer whose education did not go beyond the eighth grade. Upon the death of his wife of thirty-two years, Sharp developed a very close relationship with Jean Kosmalski, a school teacher sixteen years his junior. Sharp eventually proposed to Kosmalski, but when she refused, he continued to make gifts to her in hopes of changing her mind. He also gave her access to his bank account from which she withdrew substantial amounts of money, made a will naming her as sole beneficiary, and executed a deed naming her as a joint owner of his farm. Then, in September 1971, Sharp transferred his remaining joint interest in the farm to Kosmalski. In February 1973 Kosmalski ordered Sharp to move out of his home and to vacate the farm. She then took possession of both, leaving Sharp with assets of $300. Sharp brought this action to impose a constructive trust on the property transferred to Kosmalski. The trial court dismissed plaintiff's complaint and the decision was affirmed by the appellate court.

Decision: Judgment reversed and remanded.

Opinion: Gabrielli, J.   Generally, a constructive trust may be imposed "[w]hen property has been acquired in such circumstances that the holder of the legal title may not in good conscience retain the beneficial interest" [citation]. In the development of the doctrine of constructive trust as a remedy available to courts of equity, the following four requirements were posited: (1) a confidential or fiduciary relation, (2) a promise, (3) a transfer in reliance thereon and (4) unjust enrichment. [Citations.]

Most frequently, it is the existence of a confidential relationship which triggers the equitable considerations leading to the imposition of a constructive trust. [Citation.] Although no marital or other family relationship is present in this case, such is not essential for the existence of a confidential relation. [Citations.] The record in this case clearly indicates that a relationship of trust and confidence did exist between the parties and, hence, the defendant must be charged with an obligation not to abuse the trust and confidence placed in her by the plaintiff. The disparity in education between the plaintiff and defendant highlights the degree of dependence of the plaintiff upon the trust and honor of the defendant.

Unquestionably, there is a transfer of property here, but the Trial Judge found that the transfer was made "without a promise or understanding of any kind." Even without an express promise, however, courts of equity have imposed a constructive trust upon property transferred in reliance upon a confidential relationship. In such a situation, a promise may be implied or inferred from the very transaction itself. As Judge Cardozo so eloquently observed: "Though a promise in words was lacking, the whole transaction, it might be found, was 'instinct with an obligation' imperfectly expressed." [Citations.] In deciding that a formal writing or express promise was not essential to the application of the doctrine of constructive trust, Judge Cardozo further observed in language that is most fitting in the instant case:

"Here was a man transferring to his sister the only property he had in the world * * * He was doing this, as she admits, in reliance upon her honor. Even if we were to accept her statement that there was no distinct promise to hold for his benefit, the exaction of such a promise, in view of the relation, might well have seemed to be superfluous." [Citation].

* * *

Indeed in the case before us, it is inconceivable that plaintiff would convey all of his interest in property which was not only his abode but the very means of his livelihood without at least tacit consent upon the part of the defendant that she would permit him to continue to live on and operate the farm. I would therefore reject the Trial Judge's conclusion, erroneously termed a finding of fact, that no agreement or limitation may, as a matter of law, be implied from the circumstances surrounding the transfer of plaintiff's farm.

The statutory purpose of the constructive trust remedy is to prevent unjust enrichment and it is to this requirement that I now turn. The Trial Judge in his findings of fact, concluded that the transfer did not constitute unjust enrichment. In this instance also, a legal conclusion was mistakenly labeled a finding of fact. A person may be deemed to be unjustly enriched if he (or she) has received a benefit, the retention of which would be unjust (Restatement, Restitution, § 1, Comment *a*). A conclusion that one has been unjustly enriched is essentially a legal inference drawn from the circumstances surrounding the transfer of property and the relationship of the parties. It is a conclusion reached through the application of principles of equity. Having determined that the relationship between plaintiff and defendant in this case is of such a nature as to invoke consideration of the equitable remedy of constructive trust, it remains to be determined whether defendant's conduct following the transfer of plaintiff's farm was in violation of that relationship and, consequently, resulted in the unjust enrichment of the defendant. This must be determined from the circumstances of the transfer since there is no express promise concerning plaintiff's continued use of the land. Therefore, the case should be remitted to the Appellate Division for a review of the facts. In so doing I would emphasize that the conveyance herein should be interpreted "not literally or irrespective of its setting, but sensibly and broadly with all its human implications." [Citation.] This case seems to present the classic example of a situation where equity should intervene to scrutinize a transaction pregnant with opportunity for abuse and unfairness. It was for just this type of case that there evolved equitable principles and remedies to prevent injustices. Equity still lives. To suffer the hands of equity to be bound by misnamed "findings of fact" which are actually conclusions of law and legal inferences drawn from the facts is to ignore and render impotent the rich and vital impact of equity on the common law and, perforce, permit injustice. Universality of law requires equity.

Resulting Trusts A **resulting trust** is different from a constructive trust in that it serves to carry out the true *intent* of the parties in those cases where the intent was inadequately expressed rather than to rectify fraud, duress, or a breach of confidence. The most common example of a resulting trust is where Joel pays the purchase price for property and title is taken in the name of Ellen. The presumption here is that the parties intended Ellen to hold the property for the benefit of Joel, and Ellen will be treated as a trustee. The difficulty is that, in many cases, it may be equally reasonable to presume that Joel intended to make a gift to Ellen.

A resulting trust does not depend on contract or agreement but is founded on presumed intent that arises out of the acts of the parties. Since a resulting trust is created by implication and operation of law, it does not need to be evidenced in writing. If, however, a reasonable explanation of the evidence may be made on any theory other than the existence of a resulting trust, a trust will not be declared and enforced.

CREATION OF TRUSTS

Each trust has (1) a creator or settlor, (2) a "corpus" or trust property, (3) a trustee, and (4) a beneficiary. Duane may convey property in trust to Sam for the benefit of Clara, Duane may declare himself trustee of the property for the benefit of Clara, or Duane may convey property in trust to Sam for the benefit of himself.

No particular words are necessary to create a trust, provided that the intent of the settlor to establish a trust is unmistakable. Consideration is not essential to an enforceable trust. In this respect, a trust is more like a conveyance than a contract. Trusts employed in wills are known as **testamentary trusts** because they become effective after the death of the settlor. Frequently, individuals establish trusts during their lifetimes, in which case they are referred to as **inter vivos** or "living" **trusts.**

Settlor

Any person legally capable of making a contract may create a trust. But if the settlor's conveyance would be voidable or void because of infancy, incompetency, or some other reason, a declaration of trust is also voidable or void.

Subject Matter

One of the main characteristics that sets a trust apart from other relationships, such as a debtor-creditor relationship, is the requirement of a trust corpus or **res**, which must be property that is definite and specific. A trust cannot be effective immediately for property not yet in existence or to be acquired at a later date. The requirement of a definite and certain subject matter is, however, satisfied by the creation of a testamentary trust. Donna's will provides that she leaves to Terry, as trustee, sufficient funds to pay $300 a month to Barbara. The will takes effect on the death of Donna, and provides the corpus for the trust.

Trustee

Anyone legally capable of holding title to and dealing with property may be a trustee. The lack of a trustee will not destroy the trust. If the settlor neglects to appoint one, if the named trustee does not qualify, or if the named trustee declines to serve, the court will appoint an individual or institution to act as trustee.

Duties of the Trustee A trustee has three primary duties: (1) to carry out the purposes of the trust; (2) to act with prudence and care in the administration of the trust; and (3) to exercise a high degree of loyalty toward the beneficiary.

No special skills are required of a trustee under ordinary circumstances. He is required to act with the same degree of care that a **prudent man** would use to carry out his personal affairs. What constitutes the care of a "prudent man" is, of course, not easy to classify in any particular case.

WITMER v. BLAIR
Missouri Court of Appeals, Western District, 1979.
588 S.W.2d 222.

Facts: By his last will and testament, Nussbaum made a residual bequest and devise of his estate to his niece, Jane Blair, as trustee, in trust for the education of his grandchildren. If the trust could not be fulfilled, the residue would revert to Dorothy Witmer, Nussbaum's daughter. Nussbaum died in 1960. Janice Witmer, Dorothy's daughter, was the only grandchild who became a beneficiary of the trust. She was born in September 1953. At the time of the trial she was twenty-three years old and had not attended a college or university. When the trustee, Blair, acquired the trust in 1961, it consisted of $1,905 in checking and savings accounts, $5,700 in certificates of deposit, and a house valued at $6,000. In 1962 the house was sold for $4,467, which was deposited in the trust checking account, a noninterest-bearing account. A considerable portion of the trust funds were held in the checking account from 1962–1971. In 1972 Blair reduced the checking account balance by transfers to the savings account. The Witmers sued Blair, claiming she breached her beneficiary duty by failing to invest properly the trust corpus. Blair argues that the will failed to specify when and what investments were to be made. Thus, such matters were left to her good faith discretion. Also, she explained the large checking account balances by the fact that college for Janice "was talked about throughout high school." The trial court entered judgment against defendant for $309 for unaccounted for funds but found against the Witmers on their claim for breach of fiduciary duty. The Witmers appeal.

Decision: Judgment for $309 affirmed; judgment against Witmers on their claim of fiduciary duty reversed.

Opinion: Welborn, J. In this court, appellants contend that the respondent as trustee was bound to comply with the directions of the trust that she "invest the principal and reinvest the same" and that her failure to invest the trust corpus constituted a breach of her fiduciary duty for which she is liable. The respondent answers that inasmuch as the will failed to specify when and what investments were to be made, such matters were left to the discretion of the trustee and that she exercised such discretion honestly, with ordinary prudence and within the limits of the trust and is not liable for damages.

A concise summary of the law applicable in this situation appears in [citation]:

"It is a general power and duty of a trustee, implied if not expressed, at least in the case of an ordinary trust, to keep trust funds properly invested. Having uninvested funds in his hands, it is his duty to make investments of them, where at least they are not soon to be applied to the purposes and objects or turned over to the beneficiaries of the trust. Generally, he cannot permit trust funds to lie dormant or on deposit for a prolonged period, but he may keep on hand a fund sufficient to meet expenses, including contingent expenses, and he need not invest a sum too small to be prudently invested. A trustee ordinarily may not say in excuse of a failure to invest that he kept the funds on hand to pay the beneficiaries on demand."

"The trustee is under a duty to the beneficiary to use reasonable care and skill to make the trust property productive." Restatement (Second) of Trusts § 181. Comment c to this section states:

"*Money.* In the case of money, it is normally the duty of the trustee to invest it so that it will produce an income. The trustee is liable if he fails to invest trust funds which it is his duty to invest for a period which is under all the circumstances unreasonably long. If, however, the delay is not unreasonable, he is not liable."

"A breach of trust is a violation by the trustee of any duty which as trustee he owes to the beneficiary." Restatement (Second) of Trusts § 201. Comment b to this section states:

"*Mistake of law as to existence of duties and powers.* A trustee commits a breach of trust not only where he violates a duty in bad faith, or intentionally although in good faith, or negligently, but also where he violates a duty because of a mistake as to the extent of his duties and powers. This is true not only where his mistake is in regard to a rule of law, whether a statutory or common-law rule, but also where he interprets the trust instrument as authorizing him to do acts which the court determines he is not authorized by the instrument to do. In such case, he is not protected from liability merely because he acts in good faith, nor is he protected merely because he relies upon the advice of counsel. [Citation.] If he is in doubt as to the interpretation of the instrument, he can protect himself by obtaining instructions from the court. The extent of his duties and powers is determined by the trust instrument and the rules of law which are applicable, and not by his own interpretation of the instrument or his own belief as to the rules of law."

Under the above rules, there has been a breach of trust by the trustee in this case and her good faith is not a defense to appellants' claim.

* * *

The accountant who testified for appellants calculated that between the opening of the Trust and 1971, when college for Marguerite would have been a realistic possibility, had the trust funds, in excess of $100 checking account and approximately $800–1,000 savings account, been invested in one-year certificates of deposit, the trust would have earned additional interest of $2,840.00. In view of the trustee's transfer of a substantial portion of the checking account balance to savings in 1971 and 1972 and in view of the relatively small difference between the return from savings and what might have been earned from certificates of deposit (1/2% to 1 1/2%), no damages should be assessed against the trustee for the handling of the estate during that period. However, the trustee should be held liable for the $2,840 which, according to the measure of damages, invoked by appellants, might have been earned by investment of the trust between 1962 and 1971.

The duty of loyalty arises out of and illustrates the fiduciary character of the relationship between the trustee and the beneficiary. In all his dealings with the trust property, the beneficiary, and third parties, the trustee must act in the exclusive interest of the beneficiary. Lack of loyalty may arise from obvious self-interest, or it may be entirely innocent; in either event, the trustee can be charged with lack of loyalty.

Powers of the Trustee The powers of a trustee are determined by (1) the authority granted him by the settlor in the instrument creating the trust, and (2) the rules of law in the jurisdiction in which the trust is established. State laws affecting the powers of trustees have their greatest impact on the investments a trustee may make with trust funds. Most States prescribe a list of types of securities qualified for trust investment. In some jurisdictions this list is permissive; in others it is mandatory. If the list is permissive, the trustee may invest in types of securities not listed, but he carries the burden of showing that he made a prudent choice. The trust instrument may give the trustee wide discretion as to investments, and in such an event the trustee is not bound to adhere to the list deemed advisable under the statute.

Allocation of Principal and Income Trusts often settle a life estate in the trust corpus on one beneficiary and a remainder interest on another beneficiary. For example, on his death, a man leaves his property to trustees who are instructed to pay the income from the property to his widow during her life and to distribute the property to his children when she dies. In these instances, the trustee must distribute the principal to one party (the remainderman) and the income to another (the life tenant or income beneficiary). The trustee must also allocate receipts and charge expenses between the income beneficiary and the remainderman. If the trust agreement does not specify how the funds should be allocated, the trustee is provided guidance by statute, which in most States is the **Uniform Principal and Income Act.** A trustee who fails to comply with the trust agreement or the statute is personally liable for any loss.

The general rule in allocating benefits and burdens between income beneficiaries and remaindermen is that *ordinary* or current receipts and expenses are chargeable to the income beneficiary, whereas *extraordinary* receipts and expense are allocated to the remainderman. Figure 51–2 illustrates these four types of allocations.

Beneficiary

There are very few restrictions on who (or what) may be a beneficiary. Dogs, cats, horses, and a multitude of other pets have at one time or another been held to be the proper objects of a settlor's bounty. Charitable uses are a common purpose of trusts, and if the settlor's object does not outrage public policy or morals, almost any purpose that happens to strike the fancy of a settlor will be upheld.

In the absence of restrictive provisions in the trust instrument such as a spendthrift clause, a beneficiary's interest may be reached by his

---

FIGURE 51-2 Allocation of Principal and Income

	Receipts	Expenses

**Ordinary—
Income Beneficiary**
	Rents
	Royalties
	Cash dividends
	  (regular and
	  extraordinary)
	Interest
		Interest payments
		Insurance
		Ordinary taxes
		Ordinary repairs
		Depreciation

**Extraordinary—
Remainderman**
	Stock dividends
	Stock splits
	Proceeds from sale or
	  exchange of corpus
	Settlement of claims for
	  injury to corpus
		Extraordinary repairs
		Long-term improvements
		Principal amortization
		Costs incurred in the sale or
		  purchase of corpus

creditors, or the beneficiary may sell or dispose of his interest. If he held more than a life estate in the trust, his interest upon his death, unless disposed of by his will, passes to his heirs or personal representatives.

TERMINATION OF A TRUST

Unless a power of revocation is reserved by the settlor, the general rule is that a trust, once validly created, is *irrevocable*. If so reserved, the trust may be terminated at the discretion of the settlor.

Normally, the instrument creating a trust establishes a termination date, and the trust terminates at the time stated without complication. A period of years may be specified, or the settlor may provide that the trust shall continue during the life of a named individual. The death of the trustee or beneficiary does not terminate the trust if neither of their lives is the measure of the duration of the trust.

Occasionally, the purpose for which a trust has been established may be regarded as fulfilled before the specified termination date. In such a case, on petition by the trustee or beneficiary, the court may decree a termination of the trust. A court will usually decree a trust terminated if the beneficiary acquires legal title to the trust assets, but courts will not order the termination of a trust simply because all of the beneficiaries petition the court to do so. The court will be governed by the purposes set forth in the trust instrument by the settlor, not by the wishes of the beneficiaries.

DECEDENT'S ESTATES

The assets (the estate) of a person who dies leaving a valid will are to be distributed according to the directions contained in the will. A will is also called a **testament;** the maker of a will is called a testator; and gifts made in a will are called devises or bequests. If a person dies without leaving a will, her property will pass to her heirs and next of kin in the proportions provided in the applicable State statute. This is known as **intestate** (dying without a will) succession. If a person dies without a will and leaves no heirs or next of kin, her property **escheats** (reverts) to the State. Nonetheless, not all of the decedent's property will pass through the probate estate (the distribution of a decedent's estate to her successors). Certain property will pass outside of the estate as a result of arrangements that are not affected by the distribution of the decedent's estate. For instance, the decedent's life insurance policy or pension plan will pass to the beneficiary of the policy or plan, property the decedent jointly owned with a right of survivorship will pass to the survivor, and property subject to a trust will be governed by the trust instrument.

WILLS

A **will** is a written instrument executed with the formalities required by statutes, whereby a person makes a disposition of his property to take effect after his death. One major characteristic of a will sets it apart from other transactions such as deeds and contracts: a will is revocable at any time during life. There is no such thing as an irrevocable will. A document binding during life may be a contract (such as a promise to make a will) or a deed (conveying a vested remainder after a life estate in the grantor), but it is not a will. Even if a testator contractually promises not to revoke her will, such as with joint or mutual wills, she retains the power to revoke the will. Nonetheless, the testator may be liable for breach of contract, and a constructive trust may be imposed upon the beneficiaries of the estate. A will takes effect only on the death of the testator.

Mental Capacity

In order to make a valid will, the testator must have both the "power" and the "capacity" to do so. The requisite testamentary intent must always be present to create a valid will.

Testamentary Capacity and Power   The *power* to make a will is granted by the State to persons who are of a class believed generally able to handle their affairs without regard to personal limitations. Thus, in most States, children under a certain age cannot make valid wills.

The *capacity* to make a will refers to the limits placed on particular persons in the class generally granted the power to make wills because of personal mental deficiencies. Underlying the notion of capacity is the premise that, for a will to be valid, a testator must *intend* a document to be his will. This required intent will be lacking if he is incompetent or suffers from delusions.

Conduct Invalidating a Will Any document appearing to be a will that reflects an intent other than the testator's is not a valid will. This is the basis for the rule that a will that transmits property as a result of *duress, undue influence,* or *fraud* is no will at all.

The great difficulty in this area is what constitutes "undue influence" cannot be generally defined. Certainly, a wife can urge her husband to leave all his property to her and, out of love and affection, he will probably accede. This influence is not "undue." Nor is a general influence over the testator sufficient to make a case of improper pressure. The influence must be directed specifically to the act of making the will. Most frequently, the charge of undue influence is made when a testator leaves his property to a person who is not a blood relative, such as a friend who took care of the testator in his last illness or during his last years. If the evidence demonstrates that the beneficiary under the will was in close contact with the testator and that natural objects of his bounty are ignored in the will, there is a suggestion of undue influence. But see *In Re Estate of Hobelsberger* below for the necessity of supporting evidence.

The charge of fraud can also be used to invalidate a will. For example, Brian dies, leaving all his property to Mark upon the representation by Mark that he is Brian's long-lost son. Mark in fact is not Brian's son. In such a case, the will may be set aside because the misrepresentation was made with the intent to deceive and that Brian relied upon it.

The law is generally not as ready to invalidate or partially revise a will because of *mistake* as it is to adjust a contract based on an error. A mistake as to the identity of the instrument voids a will. But a stenographic error or a mistake in drafting may be corrected by clear evidence of the testator's intent.

Formal Requirements of a Will

By statute in all jurisdictions, a will, to be valid, must comply with certain formalities. These are necessary not only to indicate that the testator understood what she was doing but also to help prevent fraud.

Writing A basic requirement to a valid will is that it be in writing. The writing may be informal, as long as the basic formalities required by the statute are substantially met. Pencil, ink, and mimeograph are equally valid methods, and valid wills have been made on scratch paper and on an envelope.

It is also valid to incorporate into a will by reference another document that in itself is not a will because it was not properly executed. To incorporate a memorandum in a will by reference, the following four conditions must exist: (1) the memorandum must be in writing; (2) it must be in existence when the will is executed; (3) it must be adequately described in the will; and (4) it must be described in the will as being in existence.

Signature A will must be signed by the testator. The signature verifies that the will has been executed and is a fundamental requirement in almost all jurisdictions. The initials "A. H.," the word "father," or a mark (as indicated in the case that follows) at the end of a will in the handwriting of the testator are adequate if intended as an execution.

IN RE ESTATE OF HOBELSBERGER
Supreme Court of South Dakota, 1970.
181 N.W.2d 455.

Facts: John Hobelsberger lived alone on his farm near Kranzburg, South Dakota. A grandniece, Phyllis Raml, and her husband Ralph lived on and operated a farm about two miles away. Hobelsberger and the Ramls had a friendly and cordial relationship. The Ramls visited him rather frequently and largely cared for him during his later years. Hobelsberger was hospitalized on October 23, 1966, and his condition was diagnosed as intermittent cerebral insufficiency. During his hospitalization, he requested that the Ramls send an attorney to see him about the preparation of a will. Thomas Green, an attorney, interviewed the testator on or about November 10 and prepared a will in compliance with his instructions.

Hobelsberger was transferred to a nursing home on November 19. On November 22 Green and a secretary went to the nursing home and witnessed his signing of the will. Hobelsberger was then eighty years old. He subscribed the will with a mark because he was having trouble with his hands. Hobelsberger died on July 19, 1967, survived by twenty-seven nieces and nephews and seven grandnieces and grand-nephews. The will, after providing for the payment of debts and funeral expenses, left Hobelsberger's entire estate to Phyllis Raml. Nine of the nieces and nephews contested the will, claiming lack of testamentary capacity, undue influence by the Ramls, and improper execution. The county court admitted the will to probate, the circuit court affirmed, and the contestants appealed.

Decision: Decree affirmed.

Opinion: **Rentto, J.**   The matter in issue is the condition of [the testator's] mind when the will was executed. One may be physically weak and aged and still possess a sound mind. [Citation.]

* * *

It was for the trial judge to select from the conflicting evidence that which he would believe. He, not this court, is the trier of the facts. Obviously he chose the proponent's version. From it he found that on the date of executing the will in question "the said John Hobelsberger was of sound and disposing mind and memory, competent and had testamentary capacity to execute a Last Will and Testament." Contestants challenge this finding. On review the successful party is entitled to the benefit of his version of the evidence, and of all favorable inferences fairly deducible therefrom. [Citation.]

* * *

In support of their claim of undue influence the contestants urge that the disposition made by the will is unnatural. If it is subject to reasonable explanation even though apparently unnatural, it becomes understandable. [Citations.] Accepting the evidence of the proponent, the will merely prefers a grandniece and her husband who have been helpful to him during the years when he had need of such concern. [Citation.] Such recognition is not necessarily improper.

What could be more natural in view of his feeling that he did not have enough to remember all of his heirs? Moreover, his nieces, nephews, grandnieces, and grandnephews because of such relationship alone, are not the natural objects of his bounty. [Citation.] Our law does not require that a testator recognize his relatives equally or at all. [Citation.] In any event it is only a circumstance to be considered with the other evidence bearing on the issue. [Citation.]

Contestants seize on the fact that the Ramls had a motive and the opportunity to exert an undue influence on the testator. These factors alone are not sufficient to invalidate the will. To accomplish that result there must be evidence that they did exert such influence. [Citations.] Here there is none. That the Ramls were provided for in the will and had an opportunity to influence him does not prove that they did. [Citations.] Nor is it alone sufficient to warrant an inference of undue influence. [Citation.]

* * *

They also urge that between the Ramls and the testator there existed a confidential relationship which has a bearing on this issue. Such relationship exists whenever trust and confidence is reposed by the testator in the integrity and fidelity of another. [Citations.] Even if the relationship between them rose to that level, which appears doubtful, it would not require a finding of undue influence nor raise a presumption of such which the beneficiary has the burden of disproving. Its existence, however, may demand close judicial scrutiny and is another item for the court to ponder in deciding the issue. [Citation.]

* * *

In subscribing the will testator did so with a mark. [A South Dakota statute] provides:

" 'Signature or subscription' includes mark, when the person cannot write, his name being written near such mark, and written by a person who writes his own name as a witness;"

It appears that he was a person who was able to write and had signed checks before and after the execution of the will with the help of Mrs. Raml. It is fair to infer that at earlier times he had been able to do so without any help. Contestants argue that because of this he is not one authorized to sign with a mark. It is their only complaint as to the execution of the instrument. This we think is a too restricted view of our statute.

* * *

It appears that at the time of subscribing the will the testator said he could not write because he had trouble with his hands. That this was so becomes apparent on examination of the checks that he had attempted to sign, with the help of others, shortly before and after that occasion. It follows the trial court did not err in holding that the will under attack had been validly executed.

Most statutes require the signature to be at the end of the will, and even in jurisdictions where this is not specified, a signature at the end will prevent the charge that the portions of a will coming after a signature were written after its execution and therefore do not have the necessary formality of a signature.

Attestation With the exception of a few isolated types of wills noted later that are valid in a limited number of jurisdictions, a written will must be attested, or certified, by witnesses. The number and qualification of witnesses and the manner of attestation are generally set out by statute. Usually two or three witnesses are required.

The function of witnesses is to acknowledge that the testator did execute the will and that she had the required intent and capacity. It is important that the testator sign first in the presence of all the witnesses, and it is usually essential that each witness sign in her presence and in the presence of the other witness.

The most common restriction is that a witness must not have any interest under the will. This requirement takes at least two forms under statutes. One type of statute disqualifies a witness who is also a beneficiary under the will. The other type voids the bequest or devise to the interested witness, thus making him a disinterested and qualified witness.

Revocation of a Will

By definition, a will is revocable by the testator. Under certain circumstances, a will may be revoked by operation of law. This does not mean that certain formalities are not necessary to effect a revocation. In most jurisdictions, the methods by which a will is revoked are specified by statute.

Destruction or Alteration Tearing, burning, or otherwise destroying a will is a strong sign that the testator intended to revoke it, and, unless it can be shown that the destruction was inadvertent, it is an effective way of revoking a will. In some States, partial revocation of a will may be accomplished by erasure or obliteration of a part of the will. But substituted or additional bequests made by insertions between the written or printed lines of a will are not effective without reexecution and reattestation.

Courts are occasionally faced with the difficult question of determining whether a will was revoked by destruction or simply mislaid. The following case deals with this problem.

BARKSDALE v. PENDERGRASS
Supreme Court of Alabama, 1975.
294 Ala. 526, 319 So.2d 267.

Facts: Mamie Henry, a widow, died on October 18, 1972. She had no children, but was survived by several nieces and nephews. At first no will was found, and Joe Barksdale, a nephew, was appointed administrator of Mrs. Henry's estate. Later, Rita Pendergrass produced a copy of a will allegedly made by Mrs. Henry. The will left all of Mrs. Henry's property to Mrs. Pendergrass and appointed her as executrix. She now seeks to have the will admitted to probate. Joe Barksdale and Olen Barksdale file a contest on the grounds that the purported will was never duly executed, or, if executed, was destroyed by Mrs. Henry prior to her death. The jury found in favor of Rita Pendergrass and judgment was entered ordering the admission of the will to probate.

Decision: Judgment affirmed.

Opinion: **Merrill, J.** In a proceeding to probate an alleged lost or destroyed will, the burden is on the proponent to establish, to the reasonable satisfaction of the judge or jury trying the facts:

(1) The existence of a will—an instrument in writing, signed by the testator or some person in his presence, and by his direction, and attested by at least two witnesses, who must subscribe their names thereto in the presence of the testator. [Citations.]

* * *

(3) The nonrevocation of the instrument by the testator. [Citations.]
(4) The contents of the will in substance and effect. [Citations.]

The first question then is whether there was a validly executed will. It is not necessary that the attestation be at the personal request of the testator. It is sufficient if done in testator's presence with his knowledge and consent expressed or implied. [Citations.]

The testator does not have to tell the subscribing witnesses that the instrument is his will, or to inform them of its contents. [Citations.]

It is not necessary for the witnesses to actually see the testator sign his name. [Citations.] The testator may acknowledge to the subscribing witnesses that it is his signature on the instrument by his express words or by implication from his conduct and from the surrounding circumstances. [Citations.]

* * *

The evidence produced at trial showed that Charles M. Scott, a Ft. Payne attorney, prepared a will for Mrs. Henry in November of 1963. She did not execute the will in Scott's office because she wanted to "get her own witnesses" in Collinsville where she lived. Scott subsequently made several minor changes in the will and mailed her a final version in January of 1964. Rita Jan Gray [Pendergrass] was named as beneficiary in every version of the will.

The evidence also showed that sometime around 1964, Bill Cook, Jack Farmer and Cecil Sharp met at Sharp's funeral home and witnessed Mrs. Henry's signature on a document. The testimony adduced at trial indicated that there was some doubt as to whether each of the witnesses knew that the document was a will. Jack Farmer was deceased at the time of the trial. Witness Bill Cook thought that Mrs. Henry mentioned that the document was a will at some time, but Cecil Sharp could only say that Mrs. Henry wanted him to witness a signature. Nevertheless it is apparent that the requirements of [citation], were met since both Cook and Sharp witnessed a signature which Mrs. Henry acknowledged as her own.

The second thing which the proponent must prove is the loss or destruction of the instrument. Billy McDowell, who rented an apartment from Mrs. Henry between 1967 and 1969, testified that Mrs. Henry showed him a will; that she said Charles M. Scott prepared it; that Cecil Sharp's name was on the will as a witness; and that Rita Jan Gray [Pendergrass] was the sole beneficiary. He also said that Mrs. Henry kept the will in a purse under a mattress in a spare room. Floyd Gray, the father of the beneficiary, testified that he saw one of Mrs. Henry's nephews at her house shortly after her death. Willard Reaves, an employee of the funeral home, testified that several of Mrs. Henry's relatives visited her house that day after she died. There was also an abundance of testimony that the will might have been lost or destroyed by accident. Finally, attorney Scott testified that several weeks after Mrs. Henry's death he searched the house himself. Proponent Rita Jan Gray Pendergrass subsequently filed an application to compel production of the will. Appellant Barksdale responded "That the said purported will, if executed, has been destroyed prior to the death of the Testatrix, and was not found in her possession nor among has [sic] effects at the time of her death, and is presumed, if ever executed, to have been destroyed in accordance with law."

The third element of proof involved the presumption of revocation. When the will is shown to have been in the possession of the testator, and is not found at his death, the presumption arises that he destroyed it for the purpose of revocation; but the presumption may be rebutted, and the burden of rebutting it is on the proponent. [Citations.]

Billy McDowell, attorney Scott, and Mildred Johnson, a former neighbor of Mrs. Henry, testified that Mrs. Henry said that she did not want her nieces and nephews to have anything she had; that she had always made it abundantly clear that she wanted to select somebody other than her nieces and nephews; that she was afraid

> they were going to get her property; that she knew that her nieces and nephews would get her property if she died intestate; that she wanted Rita to have it, and that this was her fixed opinion.
>
> Finally, proponent offered the copy of the will in evidence as proof of its contents.
>
> A jury question was adequately presented * * * and the jury found for the proponent.

Subsequent Will The execution of a second will does not in itself constitute a revocation of an earlier will. The first will is revoked only to the extent that the second will is inconsistent with the first. The most certain manner of revocation is the execution of a later will containing a declaration that all former wills are revoked. In some but not all jurisdictions, a will may be revoked by a written declaration to this effect in a subsequent document, such as a letter, even though the document does not meet the formal requirements of a will.

Operation of Law A **marriage** generally revokes a will executed before the marriage. **Divorce,** on the other hand, generally, does *not* revoke a provision in the will of one of the parties for the benefit of the other party.

The **birth** of a child after execution of a will may revoke a will at least as far as that child is concerned if it appears that the testator omitted a provision for the child. In some jurisdictions, the subsequent birth of a child will not revoke the will, but the child is entitled to the same share as though the testator died without a will, unless it appears from the will that the omission was intentional.

Renunciation by the Surviving Spouse Statutes generally provide for a right of renunciation of the will by a surviving spouse and set forth the method of accomplishing it. The purpose of such statutory provisions is to enable the spouse to elect which method of taking—under the will or under intestate succession—would be more advantageous to him or her. Where a spouse dies owning real and personal property, the surviving spouse has an interest in the decedent's estate that cannot be divested by will without the surviving spouse's consent. The right to renounce a will may be exercised only by persons designated by the statute, and the right conferred on the surviving spouse is personal. On renunciation of the will, the law of intestate succession determines the share of the estate taken by the surviving spouse.

Abatement and Ademption of a Bequest

In his will, Adam leaves $5,000 to Bernice, $5,000 to Chloe, and "my faithful collie, Rex," to Don. At the time of Adam's death, after payment of his debts, there is only $5,000 in his estate and a Siamese cat by the name of Queenie, faithful Rex having been disposed of after biting his master. Bernice and Chloe will each receive $2,500, and Don will receive nothing, Queenie going to whomever takes the residue of Adam's estate. The gifts to Bernice and Chloe are said to have abated, and the gift to Don, not being in existence at the time of Adam's death, has adeemed.

Abatement is the reduction or elimination of gifts by category upon the reduction in the value of the estate of the testator after the execution of his will. It can have serious implications. The first items to abate in a will are all the *residue* or remainder after provisions for *specific devises* and legacies. Specific gifts must be satisfied first. For example, if John, a widower, after making specific gifts, leaves "all the rest, residue, and remainder of my estate to my daughter, Mary," Mary may receive a great deal less than her deceased father intended. For example, suppose at the time John exe-

ed "intestate," and the State prescribes
all be entitled to the property. The
y laws also apply to property that is not
by a will. See *Ferguson v. Croom* below.
rules set forth in statutes for determin-
case of intestacy, to whom the dece-
property shall be distributed not only
assure an orderly transfer of title to property but also attempt to carry out what would probably be the wishes of the decedent. Nonetheless, the distribution of the estate is according to the statute and may be contrary to the clear intentions of the decedent.

FERGUSON v. CROOM
Court of Appeals of North Carolina.
326 S.E.2d 373 (N.C.App. 1985).

Facts: On June 21, 1983, George W. Croom died testate. In his will, Croom left various bequests of real and personal property to his children and a grandchild. Also in his will, Croom stated: "I leave nothing whatsoever to my daughter Kathryn Elizabeth Turner and my son Ernest Edward Croom." At his death, Croom left three optional share certificates in Carolina Savings & Loan Association issued to George Croom or Kimberly Croom, his minor daughter. Each of these certificates purported to create a joint account with a right of survivorship. Two of them were signed by George Croom only and the third agreement was not signed at all. None of these certificates were specifically devised by Croom's will, and the will contained no residuary clause. Ferguson, as administrator of George's will, brought suit seeking a determination as to who is entitled to these certificates. Kimberly Croom contends that the share certificates should pass to her by right of survivorship. Kathryn and Ernest argue that, regardless of George's intent to leave them nothing, they are entitled to a portion of the certificates under the laws of intestate succession. The trial court entered judgment for Kimberly Croom.

Decision: Judgment reversed and case remanded for entry of judgment consistent with this opinion.

Opinion: Arnold, J. By their appeal, Ernest Edward Croom and Kathryn Elizabeth Turner contend the court erred by concluding that they were not to share in the property which passed by partial intestacy because the deceased's will evidenced an intent that they should be disinherited. We agree, therefore, we reverse.

[North Carolina statute] states: "If part but not all of the estate of a decedent is validly disposed of by his will, the part not disposed of by such will *shall* descend and *be distributed as intestate property.*" [This statute] creates a mandatory plan for disposing of a decedent's property which does not pass by will. It directs that the property pass by intestate succession without regard to the intent expressed by a testator in a will. The statute, which was adopted in 1959, was a codification of our common law. [Citation] (where our Supreme Court held that property not disposed of by will passes as directed by the law regardless of attempts by the testator to disinherit the lawful takers). The rule adopted by [the Statute] is also in accordance with the rule followed by a majority of our sister states. [Citation.]

Under the Intestate Succession Act each of testator's children is entitled to take an equal share of the property not disposed of by his will. [Citation.] Thus, the trial court erred in excluding Kathryn Elizabeth Turner and Ernest Edward Croom from taking a share of the intestate property.

cutes his will, he estimates his worth at $150,000. He leaves $20,000 to his church and $20,000 to the Salvation Army and assumes that Mary will receive approximately $110,000. John dies five years later without changing his will but having suffered substantial business and market reverses. His executor reports that there is only $50,000 in the estate. Mary will receive $10,000.

Ademption is the removal or extinction of a devise by act of the testator. Ademption may not be as serious as abatement, but its consequences may be regrettable. It occurs when a testator neglects to change his will after changed circumstances have made the performance of a provision in the will impossible. For example, Hope buys a farm, Blackacre, and wants it to go on her death to a favorite nephew who is studying agriculture at college. After so providing in her will, she sells Blackacre and uses the money to buy Greenacre. The general rule is that the nephew will not be entitled to Greenacre. Nonetheless, the courts have sometimes limited this doctrine based upon the perceived intent of the decedent.

Special Types of Wills

There are many special types of wills, including nuncupative wills, holographic wills, soldiers' and sailors' wills, conditional wills, and joint and reciprocal wills.

Nuncupative Wills   A nuncupative will is an oral declaration made before witnesses without any writing. In the few jurisdictions where authorized, it can usually be made only when the testator is in his last illness. Under most statutes permitting nuncupative wills, only limited amounts of personal property, generally under $1,000, may be passed by such wills.

Holographic Wills   In some jurisdictions, a will entirely in the handwriting of the testator is a valid testamentary document even if the will is *not* witnessed. Such an instrument is referred to as a holographic will. A holo-

graphic will must co___
statutory requirements

Soldiers' and Sailors'
soldiers on active servic___
sea, most statutes rela___
ments and permit a vali___
sition regardless of the i___
ument. In most jurisdicti___
will cannot pass title to r___

Conditional Wills   A cont___
will is one that takes effect___
happening of a specified c___
called a *condition precedent___*
the will.

Joint and Mutual or Recipr___
will is one where the same i___
the will of two or more per___
by them jointly. Mutual or r___
separate instruments with___
made by two or more perso___
makes a testamentary dispo___
the other.

Codicils

A codicil is an addition to or ___
will, generally by a separate ___
which the will is expressly refe___
effect, incorporated into the c___
ence. Codicils must be execute___
formal requirements of a will. ___
quent problem raised by codicil___
to which their terms, if not ab___
revoke or alter provisions in the ___
purpose of determining the test___
the codicil and the will are regard___
instrument.

INTESTATE SUCCESSION

When a person dies, the title to h___
must pass to someone. If the decede___
valid will, his property will pass as ___
subject only to certain limitations in___
the State, such as the widow's right___
discussed in Chapter 49. If, howevei___
will has been executed, the decedent___

have d___
who s___
intesta___
devise___

The ___
ing, in___
dent's ___

Course of Descent

The rules of descent vary widely from State to State, but as a general rule and except for the specific statutory or dower rights of the widow, the intestate property passes in equal shares to each child of the decedent living at the time of his death, with the share of any child who dies before the decedent to be divided equally among that child's children. For example, if A dies intestate, leaving a widow and children, the widow will generally receive one-third of his real estate and personal property, and the remainder will pass to his children in the manner stated above. If the wife does not survive A, his entire estate passes to the children. If A dies and leaves two surviving children, B and C, and two grandchildren, D_1 and D_2, the children of a predeceased child D, the estate will go one-third to B, one-third to C, and one-sixth each to D_1 and D_2, the grandchildren dividing equally their parent's one-third share. This result is legally described by the statement that *lineal* descendants of predeceased children take property **per stirpes,** or by representation of their parent. If A had executed a will, he may have provided that all his lineal descendants, regardless of generation, would share equally. In that case, A's estate would be divided into four equal parts, and his descendants would be said to take the property **per capita** (see Figure 51–3).

If no children but only the widow and other relatives survive the decedent, a larger share is generally allotted the widow. She may receive all the personal property and one-half the real estate or, in some States, the entire estate.

At common law, property could not lineally ascend; parents of an intestate decedent did not share in his estate. Today, in many States, if there are no lineal descendants, the statute provides that parents are the next to share.

Most statutes make some provision for brothers and sisters in the event that no spouse, parents, or children survive the dece-

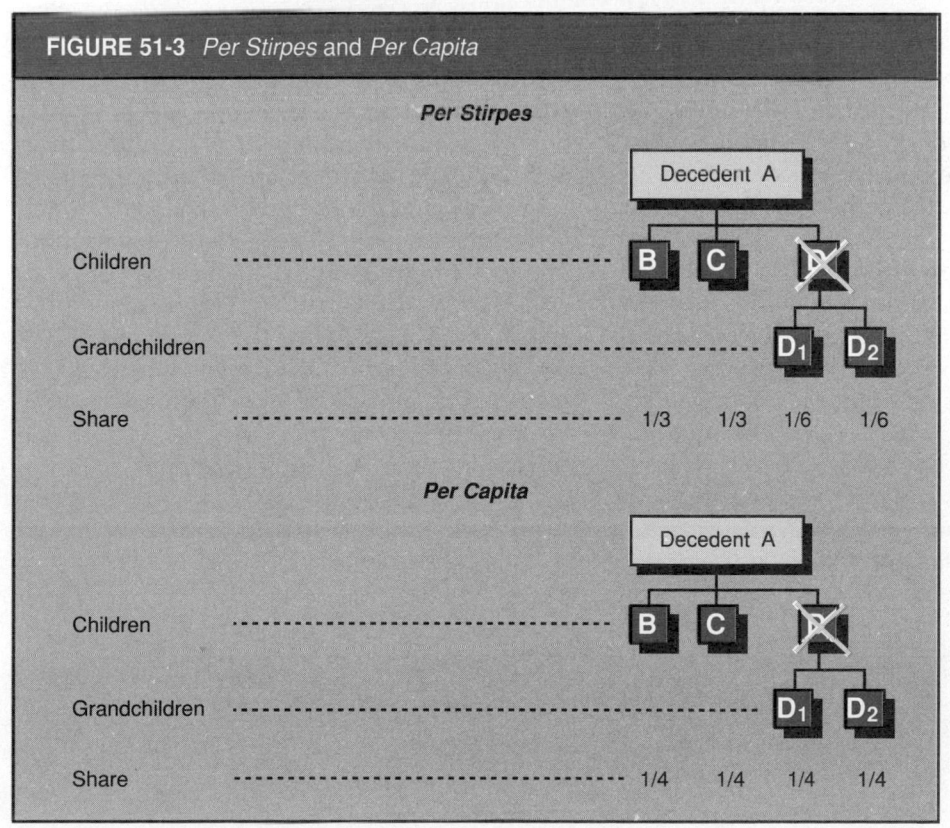

FIGURE 51-3 *Per Stirpes* and *Per Capita*

dent. Brothers and sisters, together with nieces, nephews, aunts, and uncles, are termed *collateral* heirs. Beyond these limits, most statutes provide that, if there are no survivors of the named classes, the property shall be distributed equally among the next of kin in equal degree.

The common law did not consider a *stepchild* as an heir or next of kin, that is, as one to whom property would descend by operation of law, and this rule prevails today. Legally *adopted* children are, however, recognized as lawful heirs of their adopting parents.

These generalities should be accepted as such; few fields of the law of property are so strictly a matter of statute, and the rights of heirs cannot be reasonably predicted without a knowledge of the exact terms of the applicable statute.

ADMINISTRATION OF ESTATES

The rules and procedures controlling the management of the estate of a deceased are statutory and therefore vary somewhat from State to State. In all jurisdictions, the estate is managed and finally disbursed under the supervision of a court. The procedure of managing the distribution of decedents' estates is referred to as **probate,** and the court that supervises the procedure is often designated as the probate court.

The first legal step after death is usually to determine whether or not the deceased left a will. If a will exists, it is probable that the testator named her executor in it. If there is no will or if there is a will that fails to name an executor, the court will, on petition, appoint an administrator. The closest adult relative who is a resident of the State is entitled to this appointment.

Once approved or appointed by the court, the **executor** or **administrator** holds title to all the personal property of the deceased and accounts to the creditors and the beneficiaries. The estate is his responsibility.

If there is a will, it must be proved before the court by the witnesses. They will testify to the signing of the will by all signatories and as to the mental condition of the testator at the time of the execution of the will. If the witnesses are dead, proof of their handwriting is necessary. If the court is satisfied that the will is proved, a formal decree will be entered admitting the will to probate.

Soon after the admission of the will to probate, the personal representative of the decedent—the executor or administrator—must file an inventory of the estate. The personal representative will then begin her duties of collecting the assets, paying the debts, and disbursing the remainder. The executor or administrator occupies a *fiduciary* position not unlike that of a trustee, and her responsibility for investing proceeds and otherwise managing the estate is equally demanding.

In the administration of every estate, there are probate expenses as well as fees to be paid to the executor or administrator and the attorney who handles the estate. In addition, taxes are imposed at death by both the Federal and State governments. The Federal government imposes an **estate tax** on the transfer of property at death. Most State governments impose an **inheritance tax** on the privilege of an heir or beneficiary to receive the property. These taxes are separate and apart from the basic income tax that the estate must pay on income received during estate administration.

CHAPTER SUMMARY

Trusts	**Definition** the transfer of legal title to property from the creator or settlor to one party (the trustee) for the use, enjoyment, and benefit of another (the beneficiary)

Express Trusts a trust established by voluntary action; generally in writing although it may be oral
- *Charitable Trust* a trust that has as its purpose the benefit of humankind
- *Spendthrift Trust* a trust designed to remove the trust estate from the beneficiary's control and from liability for his individual debts
- *Totten Trust* a tentative trust consisting of a joint bank account opened by the settlor

Implied Trusts a trust created by operation of law
- *Constructive Trust* an implied trust imposed to rectify fraud or to prevent unjust enrichment
- *Resulting Trust* an implied trust imposed to fulfill the presumed intent of the settlor

Trustee anyone legally capable of holding title to and dealing with property may be a trustee
- *Duties* the three primary duties of a trustee are to (1) carry out the purposes of the trust, (2) act prudently, and (3) act with utmost loyalty
- *Powers* generally established by the trust instrument and State law
- *Allocation of Principal and Income* see Figure 51-2

Termination the general rule is that the trust is irrevocable unless a power of revocation is reserved in the trust instrument

---

Wills

Definition a Will (or Testament) is a written instrument executed with the formalities required by statute whereby a person makes a disposition of his property to take effect after his death

Mental Capacity
- *Testamentary Capacity* for a will to be valid the testator must be sufficiently competent so as to intend the document to be her will
- *Conduct Invalidating a Will* a will that is the product of duress, undue influence, or fraud is invalid and of no effect

Formal Requirements a will must be (1) in writing, (2) signed, and (3) attested to by witnesses

Revocation a will is revocable by the testator and under certain circumstances may be revoked by operation of law
- *Destruction or Alteration* revokes a will
- *Subsequent Will* revokes prior wills to the extent they are inconsistent
- *Marriage* generally revokes a will executed before the marriage
- *Birth of a Child* may revoke a will at least as far as that child is concerned
- *Renunciation by Surviving Spouse* surviving spouse may elect to take under laws of descent

Abatement and Ademption of a Bequest
- *Abatement* reduction or elimination of gifts by category upon the reduction in value of the estate
- *Ademption* the removal or extinction of a devise by act of the testator

Special Types of Wills generally binding only in specific situations and may have limitations upon their use

Codicil an addition to or revision of a will executed with all the formalities of a will

Intestate Successor	Intestate person who dies without a valid will Course of Descent each State prescribes rules for the passage of property not governed by a valid will; as a general rule the property passes in equal shares to each child after the widow's statutory or dower rights have been settled

Administration of Estates	Probate the court's supervision of the management and distribution of the estate Executor or Administrator a person who is responsible for collecting the assets, paying the debts, and disbursing the remainder according to the will or intestate statute ■ *Executor* the person named in the will and appointed by the court to administer the will ■ *Administrator* a person appointed by the court to administer the estate when there is no will or the person named in the will fails to qualify

QUESTIONS

1. Define the following types of trusts: (a) express, (b) charitable, (c) spendthrift, (d) totten, (e) implied, (f) constructive, and (g) resulting.
2. Describe the powers and duties of a trustee.
3. Discuss the formal requirements of making a valid will and the various ways in which a will may be revoked.
4. Define the following types of wills: (a) nuncupative, (b) holographic, (c) soldiers' and sailors', (d) conditional, (e) joint, and (f) reciprocal.
5. Discuss intestate succession.

PROBLEMS

1. State whether or not a trust is created in each of the following situations.
(a) A declares herself trustee of "the bulk of my securities" in trust for B.
(b) A, the owner of Blackacre, purports to convey to B in trust for C "a small part" of Blackacre.
(c) A orders B, a stockbroker, to buy 2,000 shares of American Steel or any part thereof at $20 per share. After the broker has bought 500 shares but before A knows whether any shares have been bought for him, A declares himself trustee for C of such shares of American Steel as B has bought.
(d) A owns ten bonds. He declares himself trustee for B of such five of the bonds as B may select at any time within a month.
(e)A deposits $1,000 in a savings bank. He declares himself trustee of the deposit in trust to pay B $500

out of the deposit, reserving the power to withdraw from the deposit any amounts not in excess of $500.
2. Testator gives property to Timothy in trust for Barney's benefit, providing that Barney cannot anticipate the income by assignment or pledge. Barney borrows money from Linda, assigning his future income under the trust for a stated period. Can Linda obtain any judicial relief to prevent Barney from collecting this income?
3. Collins was trustee for Indolent under the will of Indolent's father. Indolent, a middle-aged doctor, gave little concern to the management of the trust fund, contenting himself with receiving the income paid to him by the trustee. Among the assets of the trust were 100 shares of ABC Corporation and 100 shares of XYZ Corporation. About two years before the termination of the trust, Collins purchased the ABC stock from the trust at a fair price and after a full explanation to Indolent. At the same time but without saying anything to Indolent, he purchased the XYZ stock at a price above its market value at the time. At the termination of the trust, both stocks had advanced in market value well beyond the prices paid by Collins, and Indolent demanded that Collins either account for this advance in the value of both stocks or replace the stocks. What are Indolent's rights?
4. On September 1, 1979, Joe Brown gave $35,000 to his wife Mary with which to buy real property. They orally agreed that title to the real property should be taken in the name of Mary Brown but that she should hold the property in trust for Joe Brown. There were two witnesses to the oral agreement, both of whom are still living. Mary purchased the property on September 2, and a deed to it with Mary Brown as the grantee was delivered.

Mary died on October 5, 1990, without a will. The real property is now worth $100,000. Joe Brown is claiming the property as the beneficiary of a trust. Mary's children are claiming that the property belongs to Mary's estate and have pleaded the statute of limitations and the statute of frauds as defenses to Joe's claim. There is no evidence one way or the other whether Mary would have conveyed the property to Joe during her lifetime if she had been requested to do so.

What are Joe's ownership rights to this particular real property?

5. On March 10, 1990, John Carver executed his will, which was witnessed by William Hobson and Sam Witt. By his will, Carver devised his farm, Stonecrest, to his nephew, Roy White. The residue of his estate was given to his sister, Florence Carver.

A codicil to his will executed April 15, 1990, provided that $5,000 be given to Carver's niece, Mary Jordan, and $5,000 to Wanda White, Roy White's wife. The codicil was witnessed by Roy White and Harold Brown. John Carver died September 1, 1990, and the will and codicil were admitted to probate.

How should Carver's estate be distributed?

6. Edwin Fuller, a bachelor, prepared his will in his office. The will, which contained no residuary clause, provided that one-third of his estate would go to his nephew, Tom Fuller, one-third to the city of Emanon to be used for park improvements, and one-third to his brother, Kurt.

He signed the will in his office and then went to the office of his nephew, Tom Fuller, who signed the will as a witness at Edwin's request. No other persons were available in Tom's office, so Edwin then went to the bank, where Frank Cash, the cashier, also signed as a witness at Edwin's request. In each instance Edwin stated that he had signed the document but did not state that it was his will.

Edwin returned to his office and placed the will in his safe. Subsequently, Edwin died, survived by Kurt, his only heir-at-law. How should the estate be distributed?

7. Arnold executed a one-page will in which he devised his farm to Burton. Later, after a quarrel with Burton, Arnold wrote the words "I hereby cancel and revoke this will /s/Arnold" in the margin of the will but did not destroy the will. Arnold then executed a deed to the farm, naming Connie as grantee, and placed the deed and will in his safe. Shortly afterward, Arnold married Donna, with whom he had one child, Ernest. Arnold died some time later, and the deed and will were found in his safe. Burton, Connie, and Ernest claim the farm, and Donna claims dower. Discuss the validity of each claim.

8. John Walker, a widower, made a will containing the following provisions:

"I give and bequeath my piano to my daughter Nancy. I give and bequeath to my daughter Jennifer the sum of $1,000. I give and bequeath to my son John the sum of $1,000 to be paid out of my account at the Tenth National Bank in the city of Erehwon. All the rest and residue of my estate I give to Nancy, Jennifer, and John, share and share alike."

After the will was executed, Walker sold his piano for $2,300 and deposited the proceeds in the Citizens bank of Erehwon. He withdrew the money he had on deposit in the Tenth National Bank and purchased a new automobile.

When Walker died, he had no debts. The account in the Citizens Bank of Erehwon had a balance of $2,300, which constituted his entire net estate after all expenses of administration were paid. How should Walker's estate be distributed?

9. The validly executed will of John Dane contained the following provision: "I give and devise to my daughter, Mary, Redacre for and during her natural life and, at her death, the remainder to go to Wilmore College." The will also provided that the residue of his estate should go to Wilmore College. Thereafter, Dane sold Redacre and then added a validly executed codicil to his will, "Due to the fact that I have sold Redacre, which I previously gave to my daughter, Mary, I now give and devise Blackacre to Mary in place and instead of Redacre."

Another clause of the codicil provided: "I give my one-half interest in the oil business that I own in common with William Steele to my son, Henry." Subsequently, Dane acquired all of the interest in the oil business from his partner, Steele, and, at the time of his death, Dane owned the entire oil business. The will and codicil have been admitted to probate.

(a) What interest, if any, does Mary acquire in Blackacre?

(b) What interest, if any, does Henry acquire in the oil business?

10. Leonard Wolfe was killed in an automobile accident while driving his 1969 Buick Electra automobile. The car was rendered a total loss, and Wolfe's insurance carrier paid his estate $3,550 for damage to the vehicle. Under the terms of Wolfe's will, any car owned at his death was to be given to his brother, David. Wolfe's daughter, Carol, however, brought an action, claiming that the gift of the car to David was adeemed by its total destruction and that she, as the residuary legatee under the will, was entitled to the insurance proceeds. Decision?

52 INSURANCE

Insurance covers a vast range of contracts, all of which distribute risk among a large number of members (the **insureds**) through an insurance company (the **insurer**). It is a contractual undertaking by the insurer to pay a sum of money or give something of value to the insured or a beneficiary on the happening of a contingency or fortuitous event that is beyond the control of the contracting parties.

It is impossible to name a commercial activity not affected by insurance coverage of one form or other. Tangible assets of a business can be the subject of insurance protecting it against almost any form of damage or destruction, whether from natural causes or from the accidental or improper actions of another. Insurance may also protect a business from virtually any type of liability that may be asserted against it through strict liability or through the negligent or intentional act of any of its representatives that in any way might be deemed to be the act of the business. A business may procure credit insurance to protect against losses from poor credit risks and fidelity bonds to protect it against losses incurred through defalcations of employees. If a business hires a famous pianist, it may insure the latter's hands; if it decides to present an outdoor concert, it may insure against the possibility of rain. A business may purchase life insurance on its key executives to reimburse it for the financial loss arising from their deaths, or it may purchase such life insurance payable to the families of the executives as part of an incentive compensation. A recent development of growing importance is the use of insurance to carry out pension commitments arising from bargaining agreements with unions.

The McCarran-Ferguson Act, enacted by Congress in 1945, left the regulation of insurance to the States. Each State has its own statutes that regulate its domestic insurance companies and also set forth standards that foreign (out-of-state) insurance companies must meet if they wish to do business within the State. Most State legislation relates to the incorporation, licensing, supervision, and liquidation of insurers and to the licensing and supervision of agents and brokers.

Because the insurance relationship arises from a contract of insurance between the insurer and the insured, the law of insurance is a branch of contract law. For this reason, the doctrines of offer and acceptance, consideration, and other rules that apply to contracts in general also apply to insurance contracts. Beyond that, however, insurance law, like the law of sales, bailments, negotiable instruments, or other specialized types of contracts, contains many modifications of fundamental contract law. We discuss the basics of insurance law in this chapter.

FORMS OF ORGANIZATION

Perhaps the oldest kind of insurance organization is the fraternal society, which existed in many ancient civilizations. There are still many fraternal benefit societies that write insurance only for members of their groups.

The oldest continuously operating form of insurer is Lloyd's of London. Although originally Lloyd's was restricted to marine insurance, the organization now writes every form of insurance except ordinary life, and the form of organization remains basically unchanged; the insurance is written by syndicates of individuals who are personally liable to the extent of the risk they have assumed.

Most insurance is written either by mutual corporations or by stock corporations. In theory, **mutual** corporations are aggregations of individuals, each of whom is both insurer and insured; if there is a surplus, it is divided among the members by way of a dividend; and if there is insolvency, the members are required to contribute their appropriate shares. The contribution requirement may be restricted by statute so that a member's liability is limited or may not exist at all.

Stock insurance corporations are organized along the lines of ordinary corporations and are intended to make a profit for their shareholders, although many stock life insurance companies issue participating policies by which surplus is shared with the policyholders. There is no call, however, on policyholders for contribution in the event of insolvency. Stock companies generally operate through agents who are paid commissions on insurance sold, whereas mutual companies often operate through salaried employees.

KINDS OF INSURANCE

There are many kinds of insurance and many kinds of insurance policies. Although the listing that follows is not complete, it contains the most common kinds of insurance.

Life Insurance

Life insurance might be more accurately called "death insurance," because it is a contract by the terms of which the insurer will pay a specified sum of money on the death of the insured, provided the required premiums have been paid. The payment is made either to a named beneficiary, ordinarily a third-party donee or creditor, or to the estate of the deceased. The naming of a beneficiary is a privilege of the *owner* of the policy, but unless the right to do so is reserved in the policy, the owner has no right to change the beneficiary. Most modern policies, as part of the standard form, reserve to the owner of the policy the right to change beneficiaries. One person may occupy one or more of these three roles (insured, owner, and beneficiary) or each may be held by a different party.

Ordinary Life Ordinary life, or whole life, insurance is often considered a form of savings or investment, because the insured has a right to borrow from the insurer an amount not to exceed the **cash surrender value** of the policy, which increases the longer the policy is in force. Such a loan generally bears a low interest rate and is secured by an assignment to the insurer of the policy proceeds to the extent necessary to pay the loan in the event of death, with the remainder going to the beneficiary.

Ordinary life insurance is designed to run for the entire life of the insured and generally requires, under a **straight life** policy, the payment of premiums until his death. **Limited payment life** policies require the payment of premiums only for a fixed number of years, thus eliminating the duty of paying premiums through the later years of life when such payments may be burdensome. With **single premium life** insurance, the entire premium is prepaid in one lump sum.

Term Life **Term life** insurance is issued for a limited number of years, with premiums payable during the period of coverage. The insurance proceeds are paid only if the insured dies within the specified time period. Term insurance, moreover, does not build up any cash surrender value or loan value, and thus the insurer may not be obligated to pay out anything on the policy. Frequently, this type of life insurance carries with it a provision to renew the policy without regard to the state of the insured's health.

Universal Life **Universal life** insurance is a form of ordinary life, which was first sold in 1979. Universal life divides the whole-life contract into two components: life insurance protection and savings. The life insurance protection is provided by renewable term insurance to the end of one's life. The savings component is the extra portion of the premium, beyond what is necessary to buy term life, which is invested and accumulated.

Endowment and Annuity Contracts

An **endowment contract** is basically an agreement by the insurer to pay a lump sum of money to the insured when she reaches a certain age or to a beneficiary in the event of premature death. An **annuity contract** is an agreement by the insurer to pay fixed sums to the insured at periodic intervals after the insured reaches a designated age. Strictly speaking, endowment and annuity policies are not insurance contracts; however, many endowment and annuity contracts contain various provisions that are customarily found in life insurance contracts, and thus the contracts are subject to regulation by State insurance departments.

Accident and Health Insurance

Accident and **health insurance** is really insurance against losses due to accidents and sickness and provides for the payment of certain benefits or the reimbursement of specified expenses in the event of illness or accidental injury, within the limits set forth in the policies.

Fire and Property Insurance

Fire and **property insurance** protects the owner (or another person with an insurable interest such as a secured creditor or mortgagee) of real or personal property against loss resulting from damage to or destruction of the property by fire and certain related perils. Most fire insurance policies cover damage caused by lightning, explosion, earthquake, water, wind, rain, collision, and riot.

Fire insurance policies are standardized in the United States, either by statute or by order of the State insurance departments, but their coverage is frequently enlarged by an "endorsement" or "rider" to include other perils or to benefit the insured in ways not provided

in the standard form. These policies are normally written for periods of one or three years.

Fire insurance policies are generally held to cover damage from "hostile" fires, but do not cover losses caused by "friendly" fires. A **friendly** fire is one that is contained where it is intended to be, for instance, a fire in a fireplace, furnace, or stove. A **hostile** fire is all other fires—any fire outside of where it is intended or is usual. Thus, a friendly fire will be hostile once it escapes from its usual confines. A standard insurance policy therefore will not cover damage to a fireplace from its continual use or damage done to personal property accidentally thrown into a stove. Damages caused by smoke, soot, water, and heat from a hostile fire are covered by the standard fire insurance policy, whereas such damages caused by a friendly fire are generally not covered. Moreover, most policies do not cover recovery for business interruption unless there is a special indorsement covering such loss.

Co-insurance is common in property insurance and is a means of sharing the risk between insurer and insured. For example, under the typical 80 percent co-insurance clause, the insured may recover the full amount of loss not to exceed the face amount of the policy, provided the policy is for an amount not less than 80 percent of the insurable value of the property. If the policy is for less than 80 percent, the insured recovers that proportion of the loss that the amount of the policy bears up to 80 percent of the insurable value. The formula for recovery is as follows: Recovery =

$$\frac{\text{Face value of policy}}{\text{Fair market value of property} \times \text{co-insurance \%}} \times \text{Loss}$$

Thus, if the co-insurance percentage is 80 percent, the value of the property is $100,000, and the policy is for $80,000 or more, the insured is protected against loss not to exceed the amount of the policy. If the amount of the policy is less than 80 percent of the value of the property, however, the insured does not receive the full amount of loss but only the proportion as determined in the formula above. Thus, in the example above, if the fire policy was for $60,000 and the property was 50 percent destroyed, the loss would be $50,000, of which the insurer would pay $37,500, which is 60,000/(100,000 × 80%) × $50,000. On a total loss, the recovery could not, of course, exceed the face amount of the policy. Some States, as shown in the following case, do not favor co-insurance clauses and strictly construe the applicable statute against their validity.

SURRANT v. GRAIN DEALERS MUTUAL INSURANCE COMPANY
Court of Appeals of North Carolina, 1985.
74 N.C.App. 288, 328 S.E.2d 16.

Facts: The Surrants lost their home and personal property by fire. They sought to recover under their homeowner's insurance policy with Grain Dealers Mutual Insurance Company. The face amount of the policy was $30,000 for loss to the dwelling, $15,000 for personal property loss, and $6,000 for living expenses. The replacement cost provisions of the policy allowed the Surrants to collect the full repair or replacement costs only if they had insured their home for at least 80 percent of the full replacement cost. In addition, if the insurance was for less than the 80 percent, the Surrants were required to pay the difference between the amount of coverage and 80 percent of the full replacement costs. Based on these replacement provisions, Grain Dealers Mutual contends that the Surrants were underinsured. Therefore, they contend that they are only liable for the cost to repair the dwelling minus the amount the Surrants were underinsured. Judgment was entered for the Surrants in the amount of $30,000 and Grain Dealers Mutual appeals.

Decision: Judgment for the Surrants affirmed.

Opinion: Whichard, J.   [North Carolina Statute] provides that fire insurance policies issued on property within this State may contain replacement cost provisions.

* * *

[North Carolina Statute], however, specifically prohibits the inclusion of coinsurance clauses in insurance policies covering property in this State.

* * *

Coinsurance has been defined as a relative division of risk between the insurer and the insured, dependent upon the relative amount of the policy and the actual value of the property insured. [Citations.] "Coinsurance clauses in substance require the insured to maintain insurance on the property covered by the policy in a certain amount, and stipulate that upon his failure to do so, the insured shall be a coinsurer and bear his proportionate part of the loss on the deficit." [Citations.] For example, [i]nsurance policies that protect against hazards such as fire or water damage often specify that the owner of the property may not collect the full amount of insurance for a loss unless the insurance policy covers at least some specified percentage, usually about 80 percent, of the replacement cost of the property. [Citation.]

Coinsurance clauses are designed to induce the insured to carry full, or nearly full coverage, [citation], and are generally held enforceable unless they are specifically prohibited by statute in the jurisdiction. [Citation.]

> Under the replacement cost provisions of the policy here, plaintiffs could only collect the full cost of repair or replacement of their dwelling if they had insured the dwelling for at least 80 percent of its full replacement cost. If the insurance maintained on the dwelling was for less than 80 percent of its full replacement cost, defendant admits that under the policy plaintiffs become coinsurers or self-insurers for the difference between the amount of coverage and 80 percent of the full replacement cost. Thus, the policy's replacement cost provisions are essentially coinsurance provisions as defined in [the Statute]. The words "coinsurance contract" are not printed or stamped on the policy; therefore, the coinsurance provisions are not allowable under the proviso in [the Statute]. We conclude that to the extent the policy's replacement cost provisions provide for coinsurance they are null and void, and that defendant was not entitled to any reduction of its liability pursuant to those provisions in the event plaintiffs were underinsured. [Citation.]

Recovery under nonlife insurance policies is typically limited by *other insurance clauses.* These clauses generally require that liability be distributed *pro rata* among the various insurers. Thus, Johnson insured his $120,000 building with Atlas Insurance Co. for $60,000 and Broker Insurance Co. for $90,000. Johnson's building is partially destroyed by fire, causing Johnson $20,000 in damages. Johnson will collect ⅖ (60,000 ÷ 150,000) of his damages from Atlas ($8,000) and ⅗ (90,000 ÷ 150,000) from Broker ($12,000).

Casualty Insurance

Casualty insurance is broad in scope but usually covers loss due to the damage or destruction of personal property by various causes other than fire or the elements. It is sometimes applied to personal injury or death or property loss due to accident.

Collision Insurance

Collision insurance protects the owner of an automobile against the risk of loss or damage due to contact with other vehicles or objects, usually subject to a deductibility clause.

Liability Insurance

Liability insurance provides indemnification against loss by reason of liability of the insured for damages resulting from injuries to another's person or property. Although this kind of insurance is usually thought of in connection with automobiles, where it is often of greater interest to the injured person than to the driver who caused the injury, it is customarily carried by owners and lessees of real property to protect against public liability for injuries arising on the premises.

No-fault insurance

A few States have legislatively adopted a system of **no-fault insurance,** which compensates victims of automobile accidents regardless of liability. Generally, coverage is provided to the named insured, members of his household, authorized operators of the vehicle, passengers, and pedestrians for personal injury caused by a motor vehicle accident involving the insured's vehicle.

Group Insurance

Group insurance covers a number of individuals, all with some common interest, under a blanket or single policy. This insurance is usually either life or accident and health insurance. The term "group" insurance simply refers to the method of selling standard types of insurance.

Title Insurance

Title insurance is issued in the amount of the purchase price of the property and guarantees the owner against any loss due to defects in the title to the property or due to liens or encumbrances, except for those stated in the policy as existing at the time the policy is issued. Such policies may also be issued to mortgagees or to tenants of property to protect their interests.

NATURE OF INSURANCE CONTRACTS

The basic principles of **contract** law apply to insurance policies. Insurance companies engage in a large volume of business over wide areas, however, and therefore their policies are standardized. In some States, standardization is required by statute. This usually means that the insured must accept a given policy or do without the desired insurance.

Offer and Acceptance

No matter how aggressively a life insurance agent has solicited a person to take out a policy, it is generally true that it is the applicant who makes the offer, and the contract is created when that offer is accepted by the company. The company's acceptance may be conditioned, for instance, on payment of the premium or delivery of the policy while the insured is in good health. If the company writes a policy that differs from the application, then it is the company that makes a counteroffer that the applicant may or may not choose to accept. This situation arises most frequently where the company is unwilling to write the policy that the agent proposed because of the results of a physical examination of the applicant but is willing to write a different policy based on the particular risk involved.

Life insurance agents, therefore, usually cannot bind the company to a contract with the insured, although on occasion an authorized agent may issue a **binding receipt** acknowledging payment of the premium and providing for the issuance of a standard policy effective from the date of the medical examination so long as the company has no *bona fide* reason to reject the application. In fire and casualty insurance, agents often have authority to make the insurance effective immediately, when needed, by means of a **binder.** In the event of a loss before the company has actually issued a policy, the binder will be effective on the same terms and conditions the policy would have had if it had been issued.

Insurable Interest

The concept of insurable interest has been developed over many years, primarily to eliminate gambling and to lessen the moral hazard. If a person could obtain an enforceable insurance policy on the life of anyone or a fire insurance policy on property that he did not own or in which he had no interest, he would be in a position to profit by the death of a stranger or the destruction of property that represented no loss to him. An **insurable interest** is a relationship that a person has to the insured person or with respect to certain property such that the happening of a possible, specific, damage-causing contingency would result in direct loss or injury to the first person. The purpose of insurance is protection against the risk of loss resulting from such a happening, not the realization of gain or profit.

Property Insurance Ownership obviously creates an insurable interest in the property, whether the ownership is sole or concurrent. Moreover, a right deriving from a contract concerning the property also gives rise to an insurable interest. See *Butler v. Farmers Insurance Co. of Arizona* below. For instance, shareholders in a closely held corporation have been held to have an insurable interest in the corporation's property. Lessees of property also have insurable interests, as do holders of security interests, such as mortgagees or conditional sellers. The insurable interest must exist at the time the property *loss* occurs. Property insurance policies are not assignable before loss occurs but are freely assignable after the loss.

BUTLER v. FARMERS INSURANCE COMPANY OF ARIZONA
Supreme Court of Arizona, 1980.
126 Ariz. 371, 616 P.2d 46.

Facts: In 1976 Butler purchased a 1967 Austin-Healy for $3,500. He received an Arizona certificate of title and was unaware that the vehicle had been previously stolen. Two years later, Tucson police seized the automobile and returned it to its lawful owner. Butler was insured against loss of the vehicle by Farmers Insurance Company of Arizona. When Farmers Insurance denied his claim for benefits, Butler brought suit. Farmers Insurance based its refusal to reimburse Butler upon a lack of insurable interest. Both parties moved for summary judgment and the trial court granted the motion of Farmer Insurance. The court of appeals reversed.

Decision: Judgment of the court of appeals reversed and cause remanded for proceedings consistent with this opinion.

Opinion: Hays, J. Any analysis of the insurable interest principle in Arizona must focus initially upon the language of our statutes. The governing standard is set forth in [Arizona Statute].

> "Insurable interest" means any actual, lawful and substantial economic interest in the safety or preservation of the subject of the insurance free from loss, destruction or pecuniary damage or impairment.

We believe that the innocent purchaser of stolen property falls within this protection and reject any construction to the contrary.

Initially, examination of identical circumstances reveals that appellant's interest in conservation of the vehicle was both "lawful" and "substantial." The law is clear that a bona fide purchaser of stolen commodities inherits title defeasible by none other than the rightful owner. [Citations.] S/he possesses a valid legal claim to the property which will be given full force and effect in a court of law. Even as against the true owner, moreover, the innocent purchaser may, upon loss or destruction of the illicit merchandise, be held liable in tort for conversion, and therefore has an interest in maintaining the property in an undamaged condition. [Citations.]

In addition, the rule above stated is not only sustained by the authorities, but is in accord with justice and common sense. Among the vices sought to be discouraged by the insurable interest requirement is the intentional destruction of the covered property in order to profit from the insurance proceeds. We believe this purpose will be furthered where the insured has a financial investment in the property and believes him or herself to be in lawful possession. We see no greater risk of illicit activity under these circumstances than where the insured is, in actuality, the rightful owner.

Life Insurance Only close relatives, creditors, and business associates or employers, depending generally on the particular facts involved, may take out insurance on another's life. An insured, however, may take out a policy on her own life and name anyone she chooses as beneficiary, even though that particular beneficiary may have no insurable interest in the insured's life. The insurable interest must exist at the time the *policy* is taken out and need not exist at the time of death. An insured-owner may assign the life policy proceeds to a third person who has no insurable interest.

Premiums

Premiums are the consideration paid for an insurance policy. Life insurance companies usually receive premiums from insured parties over periods of years. These premiums are fixed in amount and are such that the company will be able to pay the principal sum when the policy matures on the death of the insured through the accumulation of reserves. Life insurance premiums are calculated on the basis of (1) mortality rates, (2) interest, and (3) expense.

Casualty insurance policies are written only for periods of a few years at most. Long, continued liability on this type of policy is the exception rather than the rule. The rates that may be charged for fire and various kinds of casualty insurance are regulated by State law. The regulatory authorities are under a duty to require that the companies' rates be reasonable, not unfairly discriminatory, and neither excessively high nor inadequately low.

Double Indemnity

A provision found in some life insurance contracts provides for the recovery of "double indemnity," or twice the face amount of the policy, in the event of accidental death or death that results "directly and independently of all other causes from bodily injuries sustained solely from external, violent, and accidental means."

Defenses of the Insurer

In addition to the ordinary defenses to a contract, the insurer may assert the closely related defenses of misrepresentation, breach of warranty, and concealment.

Misrepresentations A representation is a statement made by or on behalf of an applicant for insurance to induce an insurer to enter into a contract. The representation is not a part of the insurance contract, but if the application containing the representation is incorporated by reference into the contract, as in liability or burglary insurance, the representation becomes a warranty. For a representation to have legal consequences, it must have been relied on by the insurer as an inducement to enter into the contract and it must have been substantially false when made or must have become so, to the insured's knowledge, before the contract was created. For an example see *Hawkeye-Security Insurance Co. v. Government Employees Insurance Co.,* which follows. The principal remedy of the insurer on discovery of the material **misrepresentation** is rescission of the contract. To rescind the contract, the insurer must return to the insured all premiums that have been paid, because a rescission restores the parties to the position they were in before the contract was made. To be effective, rescission must be made as soon as possible after discovery of the misrepresentation.

HAWKEYE-SECURITY INSURANCE COMPANY v. GOVERNMENT EMPLOYEES INSURANCE CO.
Supreme Court of Virginia, 1967.
207 Va. 944, 154 S.E.2d 173.

Facts: On August 18, 1962, Einer Mattson Jr. was involved in a collision with an automobile driven by William Droughn. At the time, Mattson Jr. was operating a car owned by his father, Einer Mattson Sr., and with his father's consent. Mattson Sr. reported the accident to Government Employees Insurance Company (GEICO), the company that had issued Mattson Sr. the liability policy on which his son was an additional insured. On November 20, 1962, GEICO wrote Mattson Sr. advising him that his policy was null and void because of a material misrepresentation in his application as well as sending a refund of the premiums paid to date. Then, on September 22, 1964, Droughn recovered a judgment for $2,000 against Mattson Jr. for injuries suffered in the wreck.

The alleged misrepresentation concerned Mattson's denial that any insurance company had ever refused to issue, cancelled, or refused to renew a policy of insurance. In fact, a policy that Mattson Sr. had with State Farm Mutual Insurance Company prior to the GEICO policy in question here had been cancelled for "general underwriting reasons." The trial court entered judgment for GEICO, and Hawkeye appeals.

Decision: Judgment for GEICO affirmed.

Opinion: Snead, J. The crucial issue presented in this appeal is whether the insurance policy issued to Mattson, Sr. by Government Employees was in full force and effect on August 18, 1962, the date Droughn was injured, or whether it was void *ab initio* because of an alleged material misrepresentation made by Mattson, Sr. in the procurement of the policy.

The record shows that Mattson, Sr. was insured under an automobile liability policy issued by State Farm Mutual Insurance Company from January 29, 1959, until it was cancelled by the company on August 5, 1959. Douglas R. Mays, an underwriter for State Farm, testified that the policy was cancelled for "general underwriting reasons" and that Mattson, Sr. was notified of the Company's action by registered mail.

Thereafter, Mattson, Sr. obtained another policy from Home Indemnity Insurance Company which he retained until October 20, 1960 when he was issued the policy here involved by Government Employees. This policy was twice renewed with coverage extending through October 20, 1963. All premiums were duly paid.

Mattson, Sr. testified that he contacted Government Employees by mail for the insurance and was mailed an application for him to complete and return. Above the space for his signature and the questions to be answered the application read:

"I understand and agree that if the answers to questions 7, 8, 9 or 10, or any of them are other than 'No,' the insurance requested will not be effective until approved by the Company. * * * The Company agrees that * * * if the true answers to questions 7, 8, 9 or 10 are 'No,' the insurance applied for will be effective as of: postmarked time and date * * *

* * *

"IMPORTANT ISSUANCE OF A VALID POLICY IS DEPENDENT UPON YOUR TRUE ANSWERS."

We are concerned only with question No. 7, which follows:

"7. Has any insurance company (including this company) ever refused, cancelled, refused to renew, or given notice of intention to cancel or refuse, any automobile insurance for you or any member of your household? * * * If 'yes' see above (the quoted statement) (Give full information on separate sheet)"

The application which Mattson, Sr. admitted that he himself completed and signed, contained a "No" answer in response to question No. 7. * * *

Gerald T. Jackson, underwriting manager for Government Employees, testified that he had the responsibility of deciding whether a policy should or should not be issued by his Company to an applicant. He said that if question No. 7 had been answered "yes" without elaboration, the application of Mattson, Sr. would have been rejected; * * *

Jackson, on the other hand, testified that when an application contained a "No" answer to question No. 7, and the rest of the application showed no accidents or violations, the answer would be accepted as true and no investigation would be made.

Hawkeye concedes that the answer "No" to question No. 7 was untrue, but contends Government Employees did not clearly prove that such answer was material to the risk when assumed.

"A fact is material to the risk to be assumed by an insurance company if the fact would reasonably influence the company's decision whether or not to issue a policy." [Citations.]

* * *

We have repeatedly held that a misrepresentation of a fact material to the risk when assumed renders an insurance contract void. [Citations.]

Here, Government Employees carried its burden of clearly proving that the untrue answer to question No. 7 in the application for insurance made by Mattson, Sr. was material to the risk when assumed. * * *

Government Employees was entitled to know the whole truth. The false answer ("No") to question No. 7 caused the Company to forego an opportunity to investigate why the State Farm policy was cancelled and to determine whether or not the risk should be assumed as well as the premium rate applicable to the risk in the event the policy was issued. [Citation.]

* * *

Under the evidence adduced, the trial court properly held that the misrepresentation was material to the risk when assumed and that the policy was null and void *ab initio* for that reason.

Rescission may or may not be available to the life insurer, however, because of the **incontestability clause,** which generally makes the life insurance policy incontestable by the insurer after a specified period of time, generally two years, after the policy has been in effect. The incontestability clause, however, does not prevent the insurer from contesting the policy for failure to pay the premiums, for misrepresentation of age, for lack of an insurable interest by the policy owner, or for false impersonation, as, for example, when the physical examination is taken by another person. If the applicant for insurance *misstates his age,* the amount of insurance is simply reduced to that sum that the premiums paid would have purchased at the insured's correct age.

An innocent misrepresentation of a material fact (not opinion) before the running of the incontestability clause is a sufficient ground for avoidance of a policy by the insurer. Whether the fact is material or not usually depends on whether the policy would have been issued if the truth had been known. An immaterial misrepresentation, even though fraudulently made, is not a ground for avoidance of the policy.

Breach of Warranty Warranties are of great importance in insurance contracts because they operate as conditions that *must* exist before the contract is effective or before the insurer's promise to pay is enforceable. Failure of the condition to exist or to occur relieves the insurer form any obligation to perform its promise. Broadly speaking, a condition is simply an event whose happening or failure to happen precedes the existence of a legal relationship or terminates one previously existing. Conditions are either precedent or subsequent. For example, payment of the premium is a condition precedent to the enforcement of the insurer's promise, as is the happening of the insured event. A condition subsequent is an event that ends an existing legal obligation. A provision in a policy to the effect that the insured shall not be liable unless suit is brought within twelve months from the date of the occurrence of the loss is an example of a condition subsequent.

Usually, the statements in policies that the insurer considers as express warranties can be identified by the use of such words as "warrant" or "on condition that" or "provided that." Other statements that are important to the risk assumed, such as the building address in the case where personal property at a particular location is insured against fire, are sometimes held to be informal warranties. Generally, the trend is away from allowing an insurer to avoid liability on the policy for *any* breach of a warranty by an insured; the breach usually must be material to have such an effect.

Concealment   Although rarely relied upon in life insurance, the doctrine of concealment has vitality in other fields of insurance. **Concealment** is simply the failure of an applicant for insurance to disclose material facts that the insurer does not know. The nondisclosure must normally be fraudulent as well as material to invalidate the policy; the applicant must have had reason to believe that the fact was material, and its disclosure must have affected the acceptance of the risk by the insurer.

Waiver and Estoppel   In certain instances, an insurer who normally would be entitled to deny liability under a policy because of a misrepresentation, breach of condition, or concealment is "estopped" from taking advantage of the defense or else is said to have "waived" the right to rely on it because of other facts.

The terms "waiver" and "estoppel" are used interchangeably, but by definition they are not synonymous. As generally defined, **waiver** is the intentional relinquishment of a known right, and **estoppel** means that a person is prevented by his own conduct from asserting a position that is inconsistent with acts of his on which another person justifiably relied.

Because a corporation such as an insurance company can act only through agents, situations involving waiver invariably are based on an agent's conduct. The higher the agent's position in the company's organization, the more likely is his conduct to bind the company, since an agent acting within the scope of his authority binds the principal. Insureds have the right to rely on representations made by the insurer's employees, and where such representations reasonably induce or cause a change of position by the insured or prevent the insured from causing a condition to occur,

the insurer may not assert the failure of the condition to occur, whether the term applied to the situation is "waiver" or "estoppel." Companies have tried in many ways to limit the authority of local selling agents to bind the company through waiver or estoppel, but this is difficult to do effectively.

As a general rule, when a local agent delivers a policy with knowledge of the nonoccurrence of a condition precedent to the company's liability that would make the policy void or voidable at the company's option, the condition is waived. Although there is always a question about whether the agent had authority to waive the condition, most courts will find an effective waiver even though the condition is a delivery-in-good-health clause of the medical treatment clause in a life insurance policy. These clauses provide that a life insurance policy shall not take effect unless delivered to the applicant while his insurability or good health continues and that the policy shall not take effect if the applicant has been treated by a physician or has been hospitalized between the date of the application and the date of delivery of the policy.

Performance and Termination

Most contracts of insurance are performed according to their terms, and due performance terminates the insurer's obligation. Normally, the insurer pays the principal sum due and the contract is thereby performed and discharged.

Cancellation   Cancellation of an insurance contract by mutual consent is another way of terminating it. Cancellation by the insurer alone means that the insurer is liable according to the terms of the policy until the time that the cancellation is effective. The right of cancellation is not always available to insurers, but where available, it is sometimes mistakenly used where rescission is preferable from the insurer's point of view. If an insurer under an accident policy elects to cancel after the occurrence of an insured event where a right of rescission existed because of material misrepresentation, this will be taken as an admission of liability for events that occurred before cancellation. To cancel a policy, the insurer must return the unearned portion of the premium to the insured. To rescind a policy, the insurer must return all premiums received to the insured.

Notice After the occurrence of the insured event, the owner of the policy or the insured is required to give notice to the insurer and, in the case of property insurance, proof of loss within a specified time, such as sixty days for fire insurance. In liability policies, the requirement of immediate notice is construed by the courts as notice within a "reasonable" time.

Automobile liability policies require that the insured immediately notify the insurer of any accident or occurrence that may involve liability. Notice requirements are conditions precedent to the insurer's contractual liability but may be waived by the insurer.

CHAPTER SUMMARY

Insurance	**Definition** contractual arrangement that distributes risk of loss among a large number of members (the insureds) through an insurance company (the insurer)
	Forms of Organizations
	■ *Mutual Companies* aggregations of individuals, each of whom is both insurer and insured
	■ *Stock Companies* organized along the lines of ordinary corporations and are intended to make a profit for their shareholders

Kinds of Insurance	**Life Insurance** contract for the payment of a specific sum of money to a designated beneficiary upon the death of the insured
	■ *Ordinary Life* life insurance with a savings component that runs for the life of the insured
	■ *Term Life* life insurance for a limited number of years that does not have a savings component
	■ *Universal Life* ordinary life insurance divided into two components: a renewable term policy and an investment portfolio
	Endowment Contract agreement to pay the insured a lump sum upon reaching a specified age or to a beneficiary in the event of premature death
	Annuity Contract agreement to pay fixed sums at periodic intervals to insured upon his reaching a designated age
	Accident and Health Insurance insurance against losses due to accidents and sickness
	Property Insurance fire and property insurance provides protection against loss due to fire or other related perils
	■ *Related Perils Covered* most property insurance policies cover damage caused by lightning, explosion, earthquake, water, wind, rain, smoke, soot, and heat
	■ *Co-Insurance* insurance in which a person insures property for less than its full or stated value and agrees to share the risk of loss
	Casualty Insurance covers property loss due to causes other than fire or the elements
	Liability Insurance covers liability to others by reason of damage resulting from injuries to another's person or property
	Collision Insurance protects the owner of an automobile against damage due to contact with other vehicles or objects

> **No-Fault Insurance**   compensates victims of automobile accidents regardless of fault
> **Title Insurance**   provides protection against defects in title to real property

Nature of Insurance Contracts	**General Contract Law** basic principles of contract law apply **Insurable Interest** a financial interest or close personal relationship in someone's life or property that justifies insuring the life or property ■ *Property Insurance* insurable interest must exist at the time the property loss occurs ■ *Life Insurance* insurable interest must exist at the time the policy is taken out **Premiums** amount to be paid for an insurance policy **Defenses of the Insurer** ■ *Misrepresentation* false representation of a material fact made by the insured that is justifiably relied upon by the insurer; enables the insurer to rescind the contract unless an incontestability clause (the prohibition of an insurer to avoid a life insurance policy after a specified period of time) is applicable ■ *Breach of Warranty* the failure of a required condition; generally an insurer may avoid liability for a breach of warranty only if the breach is material ■ *Concealment* fraudulent failure of an applicant for insurance to disclose material facts that the insurer does not know; allows the insurer to rescind the contract ■ *Waiver* an insurer intentionally relinquishes the right to deny liability ■ *Estoppel* an insurer is prevented by its own conduct from asserting a defense **Termination** an insurance contract may be terminated by due performance or cancellation

QUESTIONS

1. Distinguish among ordinary life, term life, and universal life insurance.
2. Discuss (a) an annuity contract, (b) an endowment contract, (c) accident and health insurance, (d) fire and property insurance, (e) casualty insurance, (f) automobile insurance, (g) title insurance, (h) liability insurance, and (i) group insurance.
3. Explain the co-insurance clause in property insurance contracts.
4. Explain an insurable interest. Distinguish between an insurable interest in life insurance and property insurance.
5. Compare the defenses of misrepresentation, concealment, breach of warranty, waiver, and estoppel.

PROBLEMS

1. Lile, an insurance broker, handled all insurance for Tempo Co. Lile purchased a fire policy from Insurance Company insuring Tempo Co.'s factory against fire in the amount of $150,000. Before the policy was delivered to Tempo Co., and while it was still in Lile's hands, Tempo Co. advised Lile to cancel the policy. But before the cancellation took effect, Tempo Co. suffered a loss. Now Tempo Co. makes a claim against Insurance Company on the policy. The premium had been billed to Lile but was unpaid at the time of loss. In an action by Tempo Co. against Insurance Company, what judgment?
2. On July 15 Adler purchased in Chicago a Buick sedan, intending to drive it that day to St. Louis, Missouri. He telephoned a friend, Maruchek, who was in the insurance business and told him that he

wanted liability insurance on the automobile, limited in amount to $50,000 for injuries to one person and $100,000 for any one accident. Maruchek took the order and told Adler over the telephone that he was covered and that his policy would be written by the Young Insurance Company. Later that same day and before Maruchek had informed the Young Insurance Company of Adler's application, Adler negligently operated the automobile and seriously injured Barry, who brings suit against Adler. Is Adler covered by liability insurance?

3. Graham owns a building having a fair market value of $120,000. She takes out a fire insurance policy with an 80 percent co-insurance clause from the Bentley Insurance Company for $72,000. The building is damaged by fire to the extent of $48,000. How much insurance is Graham entitled to collect?

4. The Best Automobile Insurance Company issues to Ravenscraft, the owner of a Mercury automobile, a liability policy with $30,000–$60,000 limits. On April 3, as the result of Ravenscraft's negligent operation of his car, Clarke, Dawson, and Ernst are injured in a collision. Clarke, Dawson, and Ernst sue Ravenscraft and recover judgments of $45,000, $9,000, and $6,000 respectively. To what extent is the Best Company liable?

5. Arthur Heartburn, having knowledge of a bad heart condition, arranges to have his friend, Ira Impostor, represent himself as Heartburn to the medical examiner of the Taken Life Insurance Company. Impostor, posing as Heartburn, is found to be physically sound, and the insurance company issues a $75,000 life insurance policy to Heartburn. The policy contains a two-year incontestable clause. Twenty-six months after the policy is issued, Heartburn suffers a heart attack and dies. Before paying off the claim of Heartburn's widow, the beneficiary under the policy, the insurance company learns about Impostor's actions in helping Heartburn procure the policy. When the Taken Insurance Company refuses to pay the claim, the widow files suit on the policy. Decision?

6. Wiley, an insurance salesman, induces Glutz to purchase a $60,000 life insurance policy on the life of his best friend, Doe, and at the same time sells a policy to Doe insuring Glutz's life. After ten years, Doe dies, and on due proof of death the insurance company denies liability. Glutz sues the company. Decision?

7. Kay was issued a $30,000 life insurance policy by Atlantic Bell Life Insurance Company. In her application, Kay truthfully warranted that she was a professional actress ant that she was not engaged in the employ of a railroad company or an airplane

company. The policy provided that the company insured "the life of Kay so long as she engaged solely in the business of a professional actress." The policy also provided:

> This policy shall be incontestable for any cause after it shall have been in force during the life of the insured for two years from its date.

After the policy had been in effect for three years, Kay was killed while employed as a brakeman by a railroad company. Kay was so employed without the knowledge and consent of the insurance company. The beneficiary of the policy sued the company to recover the face amount of the policy. The company defended, denying liability on the ground that Kay was employed by a railroad company at the time of her death and had been so employed for six months previously. Decision?

8. Paul Poe purchased a life insurance policy in the sum of $100,000. The policy provided: "The proceeds of this policy are payable upon the death of the insured to Penelope Poe, wife of the insured." The policy also provided that Poe had the right to change the name of the beneficiary. Four years after he purchased the policy, Poe obtained a divorce from Penelope. One year later, Poe married Dora Doe, and this marriage continued until Poe's death two years later. At Poe's death, the policy remained in its original form. Penelope demanded that the insurance company pay her the proceeds of the policy. When it refused, she brought an action against the company to recover $100,000. Decision?

9. Day had for some time been seeking out Short to "teach him a lesson" for taking out Day's girlfriend, and Day carried a pistol for this purpose. Eventually, Day caught up with Short at a local beer parlor and without warning fired a shot at Short. Day's aim was not too good, for the shot only creased Short's head. Short dove at Day, and a scuffle ensued. During the scuffle, Day fell to the floor, hitting his head on the bar railing. As a direct result of this blow to his head, Day died. At the time of his death, Day had in effect a policy of accidental death insurance in which the insurance company had agreed to pay the named beneficiary, Day's mother, $70,000 on the death of Day if the death were "effected solely through external, violent, and accidental means." The insurance company refused to pay the beneficiary. What are the beneficiary's rights, if any?

10. Scarola purchased an automobile for value and without knowledge that it was stolen. After he insured the car with Insurance Company of North America (INA), the car was stolen once again.

When INA refused to reimburse for the loss, contending that Scarola did not have an insurable interest in the car, Scarola brought an action. Decision?

11. Pioneer Foundry Company employed Jack Secor for a period of nine years. In the fifth year of employment, Pioneer Foundry obtained a $50,000 insurance policy on his life; Pioneer was the applicant, the owner, and the beneficiary, and it paid the premiums on the policy. After the employment relationship ended, Pioneer Foundry paid the annual premium of $5,625 for the next year. Secor died the following month. Pioneer Foundry had paid over $28,000 in premiums before he died. The insurer paid the proceeds of the policy to Pioneer Foundry. Jack's widow, Florence, sued Pioneer Foundry to recover these proceeds. She contends that after the termination of Secor's employment, Pioneer Foundry lost whatever insurable interest it had in Secor's life. Furthermore, she contended that to pay the insured's former employer violates the public policy against speculation on the life of another. Decision?

THE CONSTITUTION OF THE UNITED STATES OF AMERICA

We the People of the United States, in Order to form a more perfect Union, establish Justice, insure domestic Tranquility, provide for the common defense, promote the general Welfare, and secure the Blessings of Liberty to ourselves and our Posterity, do ordain and establish this Constitution for the United States of America.

Article I

Section 1

All legislative Powers herein granted shall be vested in a Congress of the United States, which shall consist of a Senate and House of Representatives.

Section 2

The House of Representatives shall be composed of Members chosen every second Year by the People of the several States, and the Electors in each State shall have the Qualifications requisite for Electors of the most numerous Branch of the State Legislature.

No Person shall be a Representative who shall not have attained to the Age of twenty five Years, and been seven Years a Citizen of the United States, and who shall not, when elected, be an Inhabitant of that State in which he shall be chosen.

Representatives and direct Taxes shall be apportioned among the several States which may be included within this Union, according to their respective Numbers, which shall be determined by adding to the whole Number of free Persons, including those bound to Service for a Term of Years, and excluding Indians not taxed, three fifths of all other Persons. The actual Enumeration shall be made within three Years after the first Meeting of the Congress of the United States, and within every subsequent Term of ten Years, in such Manner as they shall by Law direct. The number of Representatives shall not exceed one for every thirty Thousand, but each State shall have at Least one Representative; and until such enumeration shall be made, the State of New Hampshire shall be entitled to chuse three, Massachusetts eight, Rhode Island and Providence Plantations one, Connecticut five, New-York six, New Jersey four, Pennsylvania eight, Delaware one, Maryland six, Virginia ten, North Carolina five, South Carolina five, and Georgia three.

When vacancies happen in the Representation from any State, the Executive Authority thereof shall issue Writs of Election to fill such vacancies.

The House of Representatives shall chuse their Speaker and other Officers; and shall have the sole Power of Impeachment.

Section 3

The Senate of the United States shall be composed of two Senators from each State, chosen by the Legislature thereof, for six Years; and each Senator shall have one Vote.

Immediately after they shall be assembled in Consequence of the first Election, they shall be divided as equally as may be into three Classes. The Seats of the Senators of the first Class shall be vacated at the Expiration of the second Year, of the second Class at the Expiration of the fourth Year, and of the third Class at the Expiration of the sixth Year, so that one third may be chosen every second Year; and if Vacancies happen by Resignation or otherwise, during the Recess of the Legislature of any State, the Executive thereof may make temporary Appointments until the next Meeting of the Legislature, which shall then fill such Vacancies.

No Person shall be a Senator who shall not have attained to the Age of thirty Years, and been nine Years a Citizen of the United States, and who shall not, when elected, be an Inhabitant of that State for which he shall be chosen.

The Vice President of the United States shall be President of the Senate, but shall have no Vote, unless they be equally divided.

The Senate shall chuse their other Officers, and also a President pro tempore, in the Absence of the Vice President, or when he shall exercise the Office of President of the United States.

The Senate shall have the sole power to try all Impeachments. When sitting for that Purpose, they shall be an Oath or Affirmation. When the President of the United States is tried, the Chief Justice shall preside: And no Person shall be convicted without the Concurrence of two thirds of the Members present.

Judgment in Cases of Impeachment shall not extend further than to removal from Office, and disqualification to hold and enjoy any Office of honor, Trust or Profit under the United States: but the Party convicted shall nevertheless be liable and subject to Indictment, Trial, Judgment and Punishment, according to Law.

Section 4

The Times, Places and Manner of holding Elections for Senators and Representatives, shall be prescibed in each State by the Legislature thereof: but the Congress may at any time by Law make or alter such Regulations, except as to the Places of chusing Senators.

The Congress shall assemble at least once in every Year, and such Meeting shall be on the first Monday in December, unless they shall by Law appoint a different Day.

Section 5

Each House shall be the Judge of the Elections, Returns and Qualifications of its own Members, and a Majority of each shall constitute a Quorum to do Business; but a smaller Number may adjourn from day to day, and may be authorized to compel the Attendance of absent Members, in such Manner, and under such Penalties as each House may provide.

Each House may determine the Rules of its Proceedings, punish its Members for disorderly Behaviour, and, with the Concurrence of two thirds, expel a Member.

Each House shall keep a Journal of its Proceedings, and from time to time publish the same, excepting such Parts as may in their Judgment require Secrecy; and the Yeas and Nays of the Members of either House on any question shall, at the Desire of one fifth of those Present, be entered on the Journal.

Neither House, during the Session of Congress, shall, without the Consent of the other, adjourn for more than three days, nor to any other Place than that in which the two Houses shall be sitting.

Section 6

The Senators and Representatives shall receive a Compensation for their Services, to be ascertained by Law, and paid out of the Treasury of the United States. They shall in all Cases, except Treason, Felony and Breach of the Peace, be privileged from Arrest during their Attendance at the Session of their respective Houses, and in going to and returning from the same; and for any Speech or Debate in either House, they shall not be questioned in any other Place.

No Senator or Representative shall, during the Time for which he was elected, be appointed to any civil Office under the Authority of the United States, which shall have been created, or the Emoluments whereof shall have been encreased during such time; and no Person holding any Office under the United States, shall be a Member of either House during his Continuance in Office.

Section 7

All Bills for raising Revenue shall originate in the House of Representatives; but the Senate may propose or concur with Amendments as on other Bills.

Every Bill which shall have passed the House of Representatives and the Senate, shall, before it become a Law, be presented to the President of the United States; If he approve he shall sign it, but if not he shall return it, with his Objections to that House in which it shall have originated, who shall enter the Objections at large on their Journal, and proceed to reconsider it. If after such Reconsideration two thirds of that House shall agree to pass the Bill, it shall be sent, together with the Objections, to the other House, by which it shall likewise be reconsidered, and if approved by two thirds of that House, it shall become a Law. But in all such Cases the Votes of both Houses shall be determined by Yeas and Nays, and the Names of the Persons voting for and against the Bill shall be entered on the Journal of each House respectively. If any Bill shall not be returned by the President within ten Days (Sundays excepted) after it shall have been presented to him, the Same shall be a Law, in like Manner as if he had signed it, unless the Congress by their Adjournment prevent its Return, in which Case it shall not be a Law.

Every Order, Resolution, or Vote to which the Concurrence of the Senate and House of Representatives may be necessary (except on a question of Adjournment) shall be presented to the President of the United States; and before the Same shall take Effect, shall be approved by him, or being disapproved by him, shall be repassed by two thirds of the Senate and House of Representatives, according to the Rules and Limitations prescribed in the Case of a Bill.

Section 8

The Congress shall have Power to lay and collect Taxes, Duties, Imposts and Excises, to pay the Debts and provide for the common Defence and general Welfare of the United States; but all Duties, Imposts and Excises shall be uniform throughout the United States;

To borrow Money on the credit of the United States;

To regulate Commerce with foreign Nations, and among the several States, and with the Indian Tribes;

To establish an uniform Rule of Naturalization, and uniform Laws on the subject of Bankruptcies throughout the United States;

To coin Money, regulate the Value thereof, and of foreign Coin, and fix the Standard of Weights and Measures;

To provide for the Punishment of counterfeiting the Securities and current Coin of the United States;

To establish Post Offices and post Roads;

To promote the Progress of Science and useful Arts, by securing for limited Times to Authors and Inventors the exclusive Right to their respective Writings and Discoveries;

To constitute Tribunals inferior to the supreme Court;

To define and punish Piracies and Felonies committed on the high Seas, and Offenses against the Law of Nations;

To declare War, grant Letters of Marque and Reprisal, and make Rules concerning Captures on Land and Water;

To raise and support Armies, but no Appropriation of Money to that Use shall be for a longer Term than two Years;

To provide and maintain a Navy;

To make Rules for the Government and Regulation of the land and naval Forces;

To provide for calling forth the Militia to execute the Laws of the Union, suppress Insurrections and repel Invasions;

To provide for organizing, arming, and disciplining, the Militia, and for governing such Part of them as may be employed in the Service of the United States, reserving to the States respectively, the Appointment of the Officers, and the Authority of training the Militia according to the discipline described by Congress;

To exercise exclusive Legislation in all Cases whatsoever, over such District (not exceeding ten Miles square) as may, by Cession of particular States, and the Acceptance of Congress, become the Seat of the Government of the United States, and to exercise like Authority over all Places purchased by the Consent of the Legislature of the State in which the Same shall be, for the Erection of Forts, Magazines, Arsenals, dock-Yards, and other needful Buildings;—And

To make all Laws which shall be necessary and proper for carrying into Execution the foregoing Powers, and all other Powers vested by this Constitution in the Government of the United States, or in any Department or Officer thereof.

Section 9

The Migration or Importation of such Persons as any of the States now existing shall think proper to admit, shall not be prohibited by the Congress prior to the Year one thousand eight hundred and eight, but a Tax or Duty may be imposed on such Importation, not exceeding ten dollars for each Person.

The Privilege of the Writ of Habeas Corpus shall not be suspended, unless when in Cases of Rebellion or Invasion the public Safety may require it.

No Bill of Attainder or ex post facto Law shall be passed.

No Capitation, or other direct, Tax shall be laid, unless in Proportion to the Census or Enumeration herein before directed to be taken.

No Tax or Duty shall be laid on Articles exported from any State.

No Preference shall be given by any Regulation of Commerce or Revenue to the Ports of one State over those of another; nor shall Vessels bound to, or from, one State, be obliged to enter, clear, or pay Duties in another.

No Money shall be drawn from the Treasury, but in Consequence of Appropriations made by Laws; and a regular Statement and Account of the Receipts and Expenditures of all public Money shall be published from time to time.

No Title of Nobility shall be granted by the United States: And no Person holding any Office of Profit or Trust under them, shall, without the Consent of the Congress, accept of any present, Emolument, Office, or Title, of any kind whatever, from any King, Prince, or foreign State.

Section 10

No State shall enter into any Treaty, Alliance, or Confederation; grant Letters of Marque and Reprisal; coin Money; emit Bills of Credit; make any Thing but gold and silver Coin a Tender in Payment of Debts; pass any Bill of Attainder, ex post facto Law, or Law impairing the Obligation of Contracts, or grant any Title of Nobility.

No State shall, without the Consent of the Congress, lay any Imposts or Duties on Imports or Exports, except what may be absolutely necessary for executing its inspection Laws: and the net Produce of all Duties and Imposts, laid by any State on Imports or Exports, shall be for the Use of the Treasury of the United States; and all such Laws shall be subject to the Revision and Controul of the Congress.

No State shall, without the Consent of Congress, lay any Duty of Tonnage, keep Troops, or Ships of War in time of Peace, enter into any Agreement or Compact with another State, or with a foreign Power, or engage in War, unless actually invaded, or in such imminent Danger as will not admit of delay.

Article II

Section 1

The executive Power shall be vested in a President of the United States of America. He shall hold his Office during the Term of four Years, and, together with the Vice President, chosen for the same Term, be elected, as follows:

Each State shall appoint, in such Manner as the Legislature thereof may direct, a Number of Electors, equal to the whole Number of Senators and Representatives to which the State may be entitled in the Congress: but no Senator or Representative, or Person holding an Office of Trust or Profit under the United States, shall be appointed an Elector.

The Electors shall meet in their respective States, and vote by Ballot for two Persons, of whom one at least shall not be an Inhabitant of the same State with themselves. And they shall make a list of all the Persons voted for, and of the Number of Votes for each; which List they shall sign and certify, and transmit sealed to the Seat of the Government of the United States, directed to the President of the Senate. The President of the Senate shall, in the presence of the Senate and House of Representatives, open all the Certificates, and the Votes shall be counted. The Person having the greatest Number of Votes shall be the President, if such Number be a Majority of the whole Number of Electors appointed; and if there be more than one who have such Majority, and have an equal Number of Votes, then the House of Representatives shall immediately chuse by Ballot one of them for President; and if no Person have a Majority, then from the five highest on the List the said House shall in like Manner chuse the President. But in chusing the President, the Votes shall be taken by States, the Representation from each State having one Vote; A quorum for this Purpose shall consist of a Member or Members from two thirds of the States, and a Majority of all the States shall be necessary to a Choice. In every Case, after the Choice of the President, the Person having the greatest Number of Votes of the Electors shall be the Vice President. But if there should remain two or more who have equal Votes, the Senate shall chuse from them by Ballot the Vice President.

The Congress may determine the Time of Chusing the Electors, and the Day on which they shall give their Votes; which Day shall be the same throughout the United States.

No Person except a natural born Citizen, or a Citizen of the United States, at the time of the Adoption of this Constitution, shall be eligible to the Office of President; neither shall any Person be eligible to that Office who shall not have attained to the Age of thirty five Years, and been fourteen Years a Resident within the United States.

In Case of the Removal of the President from Office, or of his Death, Resignation, or Inability to discharge the Powers and Duties of the said Office, the Same shall devolve on the Vice President, and the Congress may by Law provide for the Case of Removal, Death, Resignation or Inability, both of the President and Vice President, declaring what Officer shall then act as President, and such Officer shall act accordingly, until the Disability be removed, or a President shall be elected.

The President shall, at stated Times, receive for his Services, a Compensation, which shall neither be encreased nor diminished during the Period for which he shall have been elected, and he shall not receive within that Period any other Emolument from the United States, or any of them.

Before he enter on the Execution of his Office, he shall take the following Oath or Affirmation:—"I do solemnly swear (or affirm) that I will faithfully execute the Office of President of the United States, and will to the best of my Ability, preserve, protect and defend the Constitution of the United States."

Section 2

The President shall be Commander in Chief of the Army and Navy of the United States, and of the Militia of the several States, when called into the actual Service of the United States; he may require the Opinion, in writing, of the principal Officer in each of the executive Departments, upon any Subject relating to the Duties of their respective Offices, and he shall have Power to grant Reprieves and Pardons for Offences against the United States, except in Cases of Impeachment.

He shall have Power, by and with the Advice and Consent of the Senate, to make Treaties, providing two thirds of the Senators present concur; and he shall nominate, and by and with the Advice and Consent of the Senate, shall appoint Ambassadors, other public Ministers and Consuls, Judges of the supreme Court, and all other Officers of the United States, whose Appointments are not herein otherwise provided for, and which shall be estab-

lished by Law: but the Congress may by Law vest the Appointment of such inferior Officers, as they think proper, in the President alone, in the Courts of Law, or in the Heads of Departments.

The President shall have Power to fill up all Vacancies that may happen during the Recess of the Senate, by granting Commissions which shall expire at the End of their next Session.

Section 3

He shall from time to time give to the Congress Information of the State of the Union, and recommend to their Consideration such Measures as he shall judge necessary and expedient; he may, on extraordinary Occasions, convene both Houses, or either of them, and in Case of Disagreement between them, with Respect to the Time of Adjournment, he may adjourn them to such Time as he shall think proper, he shall receive Ambassadors and other public Ministers; he shall take Care that the Laws be faithfully executed, and shall Commission all the Offices of the United States.

Section 4

The President, Vice President and all civil Officers of the United States, shall be removed from Office on Impeachment for, and Conviction of, Treason, Bribery, or other high Crimes and Misdemeanors.

Article III

Section 1

The judicial Power of the United States, shall be vested in one supreme Court, and in such inferior Courts as the Congress may from time to time ordain and establish. The Judges, both of the supreme and inferior Courts, shall hold their Offices during good Behaviour, and shall, at Times, receive for their Services, a Compensation, which shall not be diminished during their Continuance in Office.

Section 2

The judicial Power shall extend to all Cases, in Law and Equity, arising under this Constitution, the Laws of the United States, and Treaties made, or which shall be made, under their Authority;—to all Cases affecting Ambassadors, other public Ministers and Consuls;—to all Cases of admiralty and maritime Jurisdiction;—to Controversies to which the United States shall be a Party;—to controversies between two or more States;—between a State and Citizens of another State;—between Citizens of different States;—between Citizens of the same State claiming Lands under Grants of different States; and between a State, or the Citizens thereof, and foreign States, Citizens or Subjects.

In all Cases affecting Ambassadors, other public Ministers and Consuls, and those in which a State shall be Party, the supreme Court shall have original Jurisdiction. In all the other Cases before mentioned, the supreme Court shall have appellate Jurisdiction, both as to Law and Fact, with such Exceptions, and under such Regulations as the Congress shall make.

The Trial of all Crimes, except in Cases of Impeachment, shall be by Jury; and such Trial shall be held in the State where the said Crimes shall have been committed; but when not committed within any State, the Trial shall be at such Place or Places as the Congress may by Law have directed.

Section 3

Treason against the United States, shall consist only in levying War against them, or in adhering to their Enemies, giving them Aid and Comfort. No Person shall be convicted of Treason unless on the Testimony of two Witnesses to the same overt Act, or on Confession in open Court.

The Congress shall have Power to declare the Punishment of Treason, but no Attainder of Treason shall work Corruption of Blood, or Forfeiture except during the Life of the Person attainted.

Article IV

Section 1

Full Faith and Credit shall be given in each State to the public Acts, Records, and judicial Proceedings of every other State. And the Congress may by general Laws prescribe the Manner in which such Arts, Records and Proceedings shall be proved, and the Effect thereof.

Section 2

The Citizens of each State shall be entitled to all Privileges and Immunities of Citizens in the several States.

A Person charged in any State with Treason, Felony, or other Crime, who shall flee from Justice, and be found in another State, shall on Demand of the executive Authority of the State from which he fled, be delivered up, to be removed to the State having Jurisdiction of the Crime.

No Person held to Service or Labour in one State, under the Laws thereof, escaping into another, shall, in Consequence of any Law or Regulation therein, be discharged from such Service or Labour, but shall be delivered up on Claim of the Party to whom such Service or Labour may be due.

Section 3

New States may be admitted by the Congress into this Union; but no new State shall be formed or erected within the Jurisdiction of any other State; nor any State be formed by the Junction of two or more States, or Parts of States, without the Consent of the Legislatures of the States concerned as well as the Congress.

The Congress shall have Power to dispose of and make all needful Rules and Regulations respecting the Territory or other Property belonging to the United States; and nothing in this Constitution shall be so construed as to Prejudice any Claims of the United States, or of any particular State.

Section 4

The United States shall guarantee to every State in this Union a Republican Form of Government, and shall protect each of them against Invasion; and on Application of the Legislature, or of the Executive (when the Legislature cannot be convened) against domestic Violence.

Article V

The Congress, whenever two thirds of both Houses shall deem it necessary, shall propose Amendments to this Constitution, or, on the Application of the Legislatures of two thirds of the several States, shall call a Convention for proposing Amendments, which, in either Case, shall be valid to all Intents and Purposes, as Part of this Constitution, when ratified by the Legislatures of three fourths of the several States, or by Conventions in three fourths thereof, as the one or the other Mode of Ratification may be proposed by the Congress; Provided that no Amendment which may be made prior to the Year One thousand eight hundred and eight shall in any Manner affect the first and fourth Clauses in the Ninth Section of the first Article; and that no State, without its Consent, shall be deprived of its equal Suffrage in the Senate.

Article VI

All Debts contracted and Engagements entered into, before the Adoption of this Constitution, shall be as valid against the United States under this Constitution, as under the Confederation.

This Constitution, and the Laws of the United States which shall be made in Pursuance thereof; and all Treaties made, or which shall be made, under the Authority of the United States, shall be the supreme Law of the Land; and the Judges in every State shall be bound thereby, any Thing in the Constitution or Laws of any State to the Contrary notwithstanding.

The Senators and Representatives before mentioned, and the Members of the several State Legislatures, and all executive and judicial Officers, both of the United States and of the Several States, shall be bound by Oath or Affirmation, to support this Constitution; but no religious Test shall ever be required as a Qualification to any Office or public Trust under the United States.

Article VII

The Ratification of the Conventions of nine States, shall be sufficient for the Establishment of this Constitution between the States so ratifying the Same.

Amendment I [1791]

Congress shall make no law respecting an establishment of religion, or prohibiting the free exercise thereof; or abridging the freedom of speech, or the press; or the right of the people peaceably to assemble, and to petition the Government for a redress of grievances.

Amendment II [1791]

A well regulated Militia, being necessary to the security for a free State, the right of the people to keep and bear Arms, shall not be infringed.

Amendment III [1791]

No Soldier shall, in time of peace be quartered in any house, without the consent of the Owner, nor in time of war, but in a manner to be prescribed by law.

Amendment IV [1791]

The right of the people to be secure in their persons, houses, papers, and effects, against unreasonable searches and seizures, shall not be violated, and no Warrants shall issue, but upon probable cause, supported by Oath or Affirmation, and particularly describing the place to be searched, and the persons or things to be seized.

Amendment V [1791]

No person shall be held to answer for a capital, or otherwise infamous crime, unless on a presentment or indictment of a Grand Jury, except in cases arising in the land or naval forces, or in the Militia, when in actual service in time of War or public danger; nor shall any person be subject for the same offense to be twice put in jeopardy of life or limb; nor shall be compelled in any criminal case to be a witness against himself, nor be deprived of life, liberty, or property, without due process of law; nor shall private property be taken for public use, without just compensation.

Amendment VI [1791]

In all criminal prosecutions, the accused shall enjoy the right to a speedy and public trial, by an impartial jury of the State and district wherein the crime shall have been committed, which district shall have been previously ascertained by law, and to be informed of the nature and cause of the accusation; to be confronted with the Witnesses against him; to have compulsory process for obtaining witnesses in his favor, and to have the Assistance of counsel for his defence.

Amendment VII [1791]

In suits at common law, where the value in controversy shall exceed twenty dollars, the right of trial by jury shall be preserved, and no fact tried by a jury, shall be otherwise re-examined in any Court of the United States, than according to the rules of the common law.

Amendment VIII [1791]

Excessive bail shall not be required, no excessive fines imposed, nor cruel and unusual punishments inflicted.

Amendment IX [1791]

The enumeration in the Constitution, of certain rights, shall not be construed to deny or disparage others retained by the people.

Amendment X [1791]

The powers not delegated to the United States by the Constitution, nor prohibited by it to the States, are reserved to the States respectively, or to the people.

Amendment XI [1798]

The judicial power of the United States shall not be construed to extend to any suit in law or equity, commenced or prosecuted against one of the United States by Citizens of another State, or by Citizens or Subjects of any Foreign State.

Amendment XII [1804]

The Electors shall meet in their respective states and vote by ballot for President and Vice-President, one of whom, at least, shall not be an inhabitant of the same state with themselves; they shall name in their ballots the person voted for as President, and in distinct ballots the person voted for as Vice-President, and they shall make distinct lists of all persons voted for as President, and of all persons voted for as Vice-President, and of the number of votes for each, which lists they shall sign and certify, and transmit sealed to the seat of the government of the United States, directed to the President of the Senate;—The President of the Senate shall, in the presence of the Senate and House of Representatives, open all the certificates and the votes shall then be counted;—The person having the greatest number of votes for President, shall be the President, if such number be a majority of the whole number of Electors appointed; and if no person have such majority, then from the persons having the highest numbers not exceeding three on the list of those voted for as President, the House of Representatives shall choose immediately, by ballot, the President. But in choosing the President, the votes shall be taken by states, the representation from each state having one vote; a quorum for this purpose shall consist of a member or members from two-thirds of the states, and a majority of all the states shall be necessary to a choice. And if the House of Representatives shall not choose a President whenever the right of choice shall devolve upon them, before the fourth day of March next following, then the Vice-President shall act as President, as in the case of the death or other constitutional disability of the President. The person having the greatest number of votes as Vice-President, shall be the Vice-President, if such number be a majority of the whole number of Electors appointed, and if no person have a majority, then from the two highest numbers on the list, the Senate shall choose the Vice-President; a quorum for the purpose shall consist of two-thirds of the whole number of Senators, and a majority of the whole number shall be necessary to a choice. But no person constitutionally ineligible to the office of President shall be eligible to that of the Vice-President of the United States.

Amendment XIII [1865]

Section 1

Neither slavery nor involuntary servitude, except as a punishment for crime whereof the party shall have been duly convicted, shall exist within the United States, or any place subject to their jurisdiction.

Section 2

Congress shall have power to enforce this article by appropriate legislation.

Amendment XIV [1868]

Section 1

All persons born or naturalized in the United States, and subject to the jurisdiction thereof, are citizens of the United States and of the State wherein they reside. No State shall make or enforce any law which shall abridge the privileges or immunities of citizens of the United States; nor shall any State deprive any person of life, liberty, or property, without due process of law; nor deny to any person within its jurisdiction the equal protection of the laws.

Section 2

Representatives shall be appointed among the several States according to their respective numbers, counting the whole number of persons in each State, excluding Indians not taxed. But when the right to vote at any election for the choice of electors for President and Vice President of the United States, Representatives in Congress, the Executive and Judicial officers of a State, or the members of the Legislature thereof, is denied to any of the male inhabitants of such State, being twenty one years of age, and citizens of the United States, or in any way abridged, except for participation in rebellion, or other crime, the basis of representation therein shall be reduced in the proportion which the number of such male citizens shall bear the whole number of male citizens twenty-one years of age in such State.

Section 3

No person shall be a Senator or Representative in Congress, or elector of President and Vice President, or hold any office, civil or military, under the United States, or under any State, who, having previously taken an oath, as a member of Congress, or as an officer of the United States, or as a member of any State legislature, or as an executive or judicial officer of any State, to support the Constitution of the United States, shall have engaged in insurrection or rebellion against the same, or given aid or comfort to the enemies thereof. But Congress may by a vote of two-thirds of each House, remove such disability.

Section 4

The validity of the public debt of the United States, authorized by law, including debts incurred for payment of pensions and bounties for services in suppressing insurrection or rebellion, shall not be questioned. But neither the United States nor any State shall assume or pay any debt or obligation incurred in aid of insurrection of rebellion against the United States, or any claim for the loss or emancipation of any slave; but all such debts, obligations and claims shall be held illegal and void.

Section 5

The Congress shall have power to enforce, by appropriate legislation, the provisions of this article.

Amendment XV [1870]

Section 1

The right of citizens of the United States to vote shall not be denied or abridged by the United States or by any State on account of race, color, or previous condition of servitude.

Section 2

The Congress shall have power to enforce this article by appropriate legislation.

Amendment XVI [1913]

The Congress shall have power to lay and collect taxes on incomes, from whatever source derived, without apportionment among the several States, and without regard to any census or enumeration.

Amendment XVII [1913]

The Senate of the United States shall be composed of two Senators from each State, elected by the people thereof, for six years; and each Senator shall have one vote. The electors in each State shall have the qualifications requisite for electors of the most numerous branch of the State legislatures.

When vacancies happen in the representation of any State in the Senate, the executive authority of each State shall issue writs of election to fill such vacancies; *Provided*, That the legislature of any State may empower the executive thereof to make temporary appointments until the people fill the vacancies by election as the legislature may direct.

This amendment shall not be construed as to affect the election or term of any Senator chosen before it becomes valid as part of the Constitution.

Amendment XVIII [1919]

Section 1

After one year from the ratification of this article the manufacture, sale, or transportation of intoxicating liquors within, the importation thereof into, or the exportation thereof from the United States and all territory subject to the jurisdiction thereof for beverage purposes is hereby prohibited.

Section 2

The Congress and the several States shall have concurrent power to enforce this article by appropriate legislation.

Section 3

This article shall be inoperative unless it shall have been ratified as an amendment to the Constitution by the legislatures of the several States, as provided in the Constitution, within seven years from the date of the submission hereof to the States by the Congress.

Amendment XIX [1920]

The right of citizens of the United States to vote shall not be denied or abridged by the United States or by any State on account of sex.

Congress shall have power to enforce this article by appropriate legislation.

Amendment XX [1933]

Section 1

The terms of the President and Vice President shall end at noon on the 20th day of January, and the terms of Senators and Representatives at noon on the 3d day of January, of the years in which such terms would have ended if this article had not been ratified; and the terms of their successors shall then begin.

Section 2

The Congress shall assemble at least once in every year, and such meeting shall begin at noon on the 3d day of January, unless they shall by law appoint a different day.

Section 3

If, at the time fixed for the beginning of the term of the President, the President elect shall have died, the Vice President elect shall become President. If a President shall not have been chosen before the time fixed for the beginning of his term, or if the President elect shall have failed to qualify, then the Vice President elect shall act as President until a President shall have qualified; and the Congress may by law provide for the case wherein neither a President elect nor a Vice President elect shall have qualified, declaring who shall then act as President, or the manner in which one who is to act shall be selected, and such person shall act accordingly until a President or Vice President shall have qualified.

Section 4

The Congress may by law provide for the case of the death of any of the persons from whom the House of Representatives may choose a President whenever the right of choice shall have devolved upon them, and for the case of the death of any of the persons from whom the Senate may choose a Vice President whenever the right of choice shall have devolved upon them.

Section 5

Sections 1 and 2 shall take effect on the 15th day of October following the ratification of this article.

Section 6

This article shall be inoperative unless it shall have been ratified as an amendment to the Constitution by the legislatures of three-fourths of the several States within seven years from the date of its submission.

Amendment XXI [1933]

Section 1

The eighteenth article of amendment to the Constitution of the United States is hereby repealed.

Section 2

The transportation or importation into any State, Territory, or possession of the United States for delivery or use therein of intoxicating liquors, in violation of the laws thereof, is hereby prohibited.

Section 3

This article shall be inoperative unless it shall have been ratified as an amendment to the Constitution by conventions in the several States, as provided in the Constitution, within seven years from the date of the submission hereof to the States by the Congress.

Amendment XXII [1951]

Section 1

No person shall be elected to the office of the President more than twice, and no person who has held the office of President, or acted as President, for more than two years of a term to which some other person was elected President shall be elected to the office of the President more than once. But this Article shall not apply to any person holding the office of President when this Article was proposed by the Congress, and shall not prevent any person who may be holding the office of President, or acting as President, during the term within which this Article becomes operative from holding the office of President, or acting as President during the remainder of such term.

Section 2

This article shall be inoperative unless it shall have been ratified as an amendment to the Constitution by the legislatures of three-fourths of the several States within seven years from the date of its submission to the States by the Congress.

Amendment XXIII [1961]

Section 1

The District constituting the seat of Government of the United States shall appoint in such manner as the Congress may direct:

A number of electors of President and Vice President equal to the whole number of Senators and Representatives in Congress to which the District would be entitled if it were a State, but in no event more than the least populous State; they shall be in addition to those appointed by the States, but they shall be considered, for the purposes of the election of President and Vice President, to be electors appointed by a State; and they shall meet in the District and perform such duties as provided by the twelfth article of amendment.

Section 2

The Congress shall have power to enforce this article by appropriate legislation.

Amendment XXIV [1964]

Section 1

The right of citizens of the United States to vote in any primary or other election for President or Vice President, for electors for President or Vice President, or for Senator or Representative in Congress, shall not be denied or abridged by the United States or any State by reason of failure to pay any poll tax or other tax.

Section 2

The Congress shall have power to enforce this article by appropriate legislation.

Amendment XXV [1967]

Section 1

In case of the removal of the President from office or of his death or resignation, the Vice President shall become President.

Section 2

Whenever there is a vacancy in the office of the Vice President, the President shall nominate a Vice President who shall take office upon confirmation by a majority vote of both Houses of Congress.

Section 3

Whenever the President transmits to the President pro tempore of the Senate and the Speaker of the House of Representatives his written declaration that he is unable to discharge the powers and duties of his office, and until he transmits to them a written declaration to the contrary, such powers and duties shall be discharged by the Vice President as Acting President.

Section 4

Whenever the Vice President and a majority of either the principal officers of the executive departments or of such other body as Congress may by law provide, transmit to the President pro tempore of the Senate and the Speaker of the House of Representatives their written declaration that the President is unable to discharge the powers and duties of his office, the Vice President shall immediately assume the powers and duties of the office as Acting President.

Thereafter, when the President transmits to the President pro tempore of the Senate and the Speaker of the House of Representatives his written declaration that no inability exists, he shall resume the powers and duties of his office unless the Vice President and a majority of either the principal officers of the executive department or of such other body as Congress may by law provide, transmit within four days to the President pro tempore of the Senate and the Speaker of the House of Representatives their written declaration that the President is unable to discharge the powers and duties of his office. Thereupon Congress shall decide the issue, assembling within forty-eight hours for that purpose if not in session. If the Congress, within twenty-one days after receipt of the latter written declaration, or, if Congress is not in session, within twenty-one days after Congress is required to assemble, determines by two-thirds vote of both Houses that the President shall continue to discharge the same as Acting President; otherwise, the President shall resume the powers and duties of his office.

Amendment XXVI [1971]

Section 1

The right of citizens of the United States, who are eighteen years of age or older, to vote shall not be denied or abridged by the United States or by any State on account of age.

Section 2

The Congress shall have power to enforce this article by appropriate legislation.

SELECTED PROVISIONS OF RESTATEMENTS

Restatement, Second, of Torts [13]
Restatement, Second, of Contracts [15]
Restatement, Second, of Agency [18]

RESTATEMENT, SECOND, OF TORTS*

§ 8A. Intent

The word "intent" is used throughout the Restatement of this Subject to denote that the actor desires to cause consequences of his act, or that he believes that the consequences are substantially certain to result from it.

§ 46. Outrageous Conduct Causing Severe Emotional Distress

(1) One who by extreme and outrageous conduct intentionally or recklessly causes severe emotional distress to another is subject to liability for such emotional distress, and if bodily harm to the other results from it, for such bodily harm.

(2) Where such conduct is directed at a third person, the actor is subject to liability if he intentionally or recklessly causes severe emotional distress

(a) to a member of such person's immediate family who is present at the time, whether or not such distress results in bodily harm, or
(b) to any other person who is present at the time, if such distress results in bodily harm.

§ 63. Self-Defense by Force Not Threatening Death or Serious Bodily Harm

(1) An actor is privileged to use reasonable force, not intended or likely to cause death or serious bodily harm, to defend himself against unprivileged harmful or offensive contact or other bodily harm which he reasonably believes that another is about to inflict intentionally upon him.

(2) Self-defense is privileged under the conditions stated in Subsection (1), although the actor correctly or reasonably believes that he can avoid the necessity of so defending himself,

(a) by retreating or otherwise giving up a right or privilege, or
(b) by complying with a command with which the actor is under no duty to comply or which the other is not privileged to enforce by the means threatened.

§ 76. Defense of Third Person

The actor is privileged to defend a third person from a harmful or offensive contact or other invasion of his interests of personality under the same conditions and by the same means as those under and by which he is privileged to defend himself if the actor correctly or reasonably believes that

(a) the circumstances are such as to give the third person a privilege of self-defense, and
(b) his intervention is necessary for the protection of the third person.

§ 164. Intrusions Under Mistake

One who intentionally enters land in the possession of another is subject to liability to the possessor of the land as a trespasser, although he acts under a mistaken belief of law or fact, however reasonable, not induced by the conduct of the possessor, that he

(a) is in possession of the land or entitled to it, or
(b) has the consent of the possessor or of a third person who has the power to give consent on the possessor's behalf, or
(c) has some other privilege to enter or remain on the land.

§ 218. Liability to Person in Possession

One who commits a trespass to a chattel is subject to liability to the possessor of the chattel if, but only if,

(a) he dispossesses the other of the chattel, or
(b) the chattel is impaired as to its condition, quality, or value, or
(c) the possessor is deprived of the use of the chattel for a substantial time, or
(d) bodily harm is caused to the possessor, or harm is caused to some person or thing in which the possessor has a legally protected interest.

§ 286. When Standard of Conduct Defined by Legislation or Regulation Will Be Adopted

The court may adopt as the standard of conduct of a reasonable man the requirements of a legislative enactment or an administrative regulation whose purpose is found to be exclusively or in part

(a) to protect a class of persons which includes the one whose interest is invaded, and
(b) to protect the particular interest which is invaded, and
(c) to protect that interest against the kind of harm which has resulted, and
(d) to protect that interest against the particular hazard from which the harm results.

§ 296. Emergency

(1) In determining whether conduct is negligent toward another, the fact that the actor is confronted with a sudden emergency which requires rapid decision is a factor in determining the reasonable character of his choice of action.
(2) The fact that the actor is not negligent after the emergency has arisen does not preclude his liability for his tortious conduct which has produced the emergency.

§ 314. Duty to Act for Protection of Others

The fact that the actor realizes or should realize that action on his part is necessary for another's aid or protection does not of itself impose upon him a duty to take such action.

§ 328D. Res Ipsa Loquitur

(1) It may be inferred that harm suffered by the plaintiff is caused by negligence of the defendant when

(a) the event is of a kind which ordinarily does not occur in the absence of negligence;
(b) other responsible causes, including the conduct of the plaintiff and third persons, are sufficiently eliminated by the evidence; and
(c) the indicated negligence is within the scope of the defendant's duty to the plaintiff.

(2) It is the function of the court to determine whether the inference may reasonably be drawn by the jury, or whether it must necessarily be drawn.
(3) It is the function of the jury to determine whether the inference is to be drawn in any case where different conclusions may reasonably be reached.

§ 342. Dangerous Conditions Known to Possessor

A possessor of land is subject to liability for physical harm caused to licensees by a condition on the land if, but only if,

(a) the possessor knows or has reason to know of the condition and should realize that it involves an unreasonable risk of harm to such licensees, and should expect that they will not discover or realize the danger, and
(b) he fails to exercise reasonable care to make the condition safe, or to warn the licensees of the condition and the risk involved, and
(c) the licensees do not know or have reason to know of the condition and the risk involved.

§ 343. Dangerous Conditions Known to or Discoverable by Possessor

A possessor of land is subject to liability for physical harm caused to his invitees by a condition on the land if, but only if, he

(a) knows or by the exercise of reasonable care would discover the condition, and should realize that it involves an unreasonable risk of harm to such invitees, and
(b) should expect that they will not discover or realize the danger, or will fail to protect themselves against it, and
(c) fails to exercise reasonable care to protect them against the danger.

§ 402A. Special Liability of Seller of Product for Physical Harm to User or Consumer

(1) One who sells any product in a defective condition unreasonably dangerous to the user or consumer or to his property is subject to liability for physical harm thereby caused to the ultimate user or consumer, or to his property, if

(a) the seller is engaged in the business of selling such a product, and
(b) it is expected to and does reach the user or consumer without substantial change in the condition in which it is sold.

(2) The rule stated in Subsection (1) applies although

(a) the seller has exercised all possible care in the preparation and sale of his product, and
(b) the user or consumer has not bought the product from or entered into any contractual relation with the seller.

§ 432. Negligent Conduct as Necessary Antecedent of Harm

(1) Except as stated in Subsection (2), the actor's negligent conduct is not a substantial factor in bringing about harm to another if the harm would have been sustained even if the actor had not been negligent.
(2) If two forces are actively operating, one because of the actor's negligence, the other not because of any misconduct on his part, and each of itself is sufficient to bring

about harm to another, the actor's negligence may be found to be a substantial factor in bringing it about.

§ 435. Foreseeability of Harm or Manner of Its Occurrence

(1) If the actor's conduct is a substantial factor in bringing about harm to another, the fact that the actor neither foresaw nor should have foreseen the extent of the harm or the manner in which it occurred does not prevent him from being liable.

(2) The actor's conduct may be held not to be a legal cause of harm to another where after the event and looking back from the harm to the actor's negligent conduct, it appears to the court highly extraordinary that it should have brought about the harm.

§ 442. Considerations Important in Determining Whether an Intervening Force is a Superseding Cause

The following considerations are of importance in determining whether an intervening force is a superseding cause of harm to another:

(a) the fact that its intervention brings about harm different in kind from that which would otherwise have resulted from the actor's negligence;

(b) the fact that its operation or the consequences thereof appear after the event to be extraordinary rather than normal in view of the circumstances existing at the time of its operation;

(c) the fact that the intervening force is operating independently of any situation created by the actor's negligence, or, on the other hand, is or is not a normal result of such a situation;

(d) the fact that the operation of the intervening force is due to a third person's act or to his failure to act;

(e) the fact that the intervening force is due to an act of a third person which is wrongful toward the other and as such subjects the third person to liability to him;

(f) the degree of culpability of a wrongful act of a third person which sets the intervening force in motion.

§ 463. Contributory Negligence Defined

Contributory negligence is conduct on the part of the plaintiff which falls below the standard to which he should conform for his own protection, and which is a legally contributing cause co-operating with the negligence of the defendant in bringing about the plaintiff's harm.

§ 509. Harm Done by Abnormally Dangerous Domestic Animals

(1) A possessor of a domestic animal that he knows or has reason to know has dangerous propensities abnormal to its class, is subject to liability for harm done by the animal to another, although he has exercised the utmost care to prevent it from doing the harm.

(2) This liability is limited to harm that results from the abnormally dangerous propensity of which the possessor knows or has reason to know.

§ 549. Measure of Damages for Fraudulent Misrepresentation

(1) The recipient of a fraudulent misrepresentation is entitled to recover as damages in an action of deceit against the maker the pecuniary loss to him of which the misrepresentation is a legal cause, including

(a) the difference between the value of what he has received in the transaction and its purchase price or other value given for it; and

(b) pecuniary loss suffered otherwise as a consequence of the recipient's reliance upon the misrepresentation.

(2) The recipient of a fraudulent misrepresentation in a business transaction is also entitled to recover additional damages sufficient to give him the benefit of his contract with the maker, if these damages are proved with reasonable certainty.

§ 552B. Damages for Negligent Misrepresentation

(1) The damages recoverable for a negligent misrepresentation are those necessary to compensate the plaintiff for the pecuniary loss to him of which the misrepresentation is a legal cause, including

(a) the difference between the value of what he has received in the transaction and its purchase price or other value given for it; and

(b) pecuniary loss suffered otherwise as a consequence of the plaintiff's reliance upon the misrepresentation.

(2) the damages recoverable for a negligent misrepresentation do not include the benefit of the plaintiff's contract with the defendant.

§ 552C. Misrepresentation in Sale, Rental or Exchange Transaction

(1) One who, in a sale, rental or exchange transaction with another, makes a misrepresentation of a material fact for the purpose of inducing the other to act or to refrain from acting in reliance upon it, is subject to liability to the other for pecuniary loss caused to him by his justifiable reliance upon the misrepresentation, even though it is not made fraudulently or negligently.

(2) Damages recoverable under the rule stated in this section are limited to the difference between the value of what the other has parted with and the value of what he has received in the transaction.

§ 580A. Defamation of Public Official or Public Figure

One who publishes a false and defamatory communication concerning a public official or public figure in regard to his conduct, fitness or role in that capacity is subject to liability, if, but only if, he

(a) knows that the statement is false and that it defames the other person, or

(b) acts in reckless disregard of these matters.

§ 623A. Liability for Publication of Injurious Falsehood—General Principle

One who publishes a false statement harmful to the interests of another is subject to liability for pecuniary loss resulting to the other if

(a) he intends for publication of the statement to result in harm to interests of the other having a pecuniary value, or either recognizes or should recognize that it is likely to do so, and

(b) he knows that the statement is false or acts in reckless disregard of its truth or falsity.

§ 652B. Intrusion upon Seclusion

One who intentionally intrudes, physically or otherwise, upon the solitude or seclusion of another or his private affairs or concerns, is subject to liability to the other for invasion of his privacy, if the intrusion would be highly offensive to a reasonable person.

§ 652C. Appropriation of Name or Likeness

One who appropriates to his own use or benefit the name or likeness of another is subject to liability to the other for invasion of his privacy.

§ 652E. Publicity Placing Person in False Light

One who gives publicity to a matter concerning another that places the other before the public in a false light is subject to liability to the other for invasion of his privacy, if

(a) the false light in which the other was placed would be highly offensive to a reasonable person, and

(b) the actor had knowledge of or acted in reckless disregard as to the falsity of the publicized matter and the false light in which the other would be placed.

§ 766. Intentional Interference with Performance of Contract by Third Person

One who intentionally and improperly interferes with the performance of a contract (except a contract to marry) between another and a third person by inducing or otherwise causing the third person not to perform the contract, is subject to liability to the other for the pecuniary loss resulting to the other from the failure of the third person to perform the contract.

---

*Copyright 1965 by The American Law Institute. Reprinted with the permission of The American Law Institute.

§ 908. Punitive Damages

(1) Punitive damages are damages, other than compensatory or nominal damages, awarded against a person to punish him for his outrageous conduct and to deter him and others like him from similar conduct in the future.

(2) Punitive damages may be awarded for conduct that is outrageous, because of the defendant's evil motive or his reckless indifference to the rights of others. In assessing punitive damages, the trier of fact can properly consider the character of the defendant's act, the nature and extent of the harm to the plaintiff that the defendant caused or intended to cause and the wealth of the defendant.

RESTATEMENT, SECOND, OF CONTRACTS**

§ 1. Contract Defined

A contract is a promise or a set of promises for the breach of which the law gives a remedy, or the performance of which the law in some way recognizes as a duty.

§ 2. Promise; Promisor; Promisee; Beneficiary

(1) A promise is a manifestation of intention to act or refrain from acting in a specified way, so made as to justify a promisee in understanding that a commitment has been made.

(2) The person manifesting the intention is the promisor.

(3) The person to whom the manifestation is addressed is the promisee.

(4) Where performance will benefit a person other than the promisee, that person is a beneficiary.

§ 3. Agreement Defined; Bargain Defined

An agreement is a manifestation of mutual assent on the part of two or more persons. A bargain is an agreement to exchange promises or to exchange a promise for a performance or to exchange performances.

§ 7. Voidable Contracts

A voidable contract is one where one or more parties have the power, by a manifestation of election to do so, to avoid the legal relations created by the contract, or by ratification of the contract to extinguish the power of avoidance.

§ 8. Unenforceable Contracts

An unenforceable contract is one for the breach of which neither the remedy of damages nor the remedy of specific performance is available, but which is recognized in some other way as creating a duty of performance, though there has been no ratification.

§ 12. Capacity to Contract

(1) No one can be bound by contract who has not legal capacity to incur at least voidable contractual duties. Capacity to contract may be partial and its existence in respect of a particular transaction may depend upon the nature of the transaction or upon other circumstances.

(2) A natural person who manifests assent to a transaction has full legal capacity to incur contractual duties thereby unless he is

(a) under guardianship, or

(b) an infant, or

(c) mentally ill or defective, or

(d) intoxicated.

§ 13. Persons Affected by Guardianship

A person has no capacity to incur contractual duties if his property is under guardianship by reason of an adjudication of mental illness or defect.

§ 14. Infants

Unless a statute provides otherwise, a natural person has the capacity to incur only voidable contractual duties until the beginning of the day before the person's eighteenth birthday.

§ 15. Mental Illness or Defect

(1) A person incurs only voidable contractual duties by entering into a transaction if by reason of mental illness or defect

(a) he is unable to understand in a reasonable manner the nature and consequences of the transaction, or

(b) he is unable to act in a reasonable manner in relation to the transaction and the other party has reason to know of his condition.

(2) Where the contract is made on fair terms and the other party is without knowledge of the mental illness or defect, the power of avoidance under Subsection (1) terminates to the extent that the contract has been so performed in whole or in part or the circumstances have so changed that avoidance would be unjust. In such a case a court may grant relief as justice requires.

§ 16. Intoxicated Persons

A person incurs only voidable contractual duties by entering into a transaction if the other party has reason to know that by reason of intoxication

(a) he is unable to understand in a reasonable manner the nature and consequences of the transaction, or

(b) he is unable to act in a reasonable manner in relation to the transaction.

§ 20. Effect of Misunderstanding

(1) There is no manifestation of mutual assent to an exchange if the parties attach materially different meanings to their manifestations and

(a) neither party knows or has reason to know the meaning attached by the other; or

(b) each party knows or each party has reason to know the meaning attached by the other.

(2) The manifestations of the parties are operative in accordance with the meaning attached to them by one of the parties if

(a) that party does not know of any different meaning attached by the other, and the other knows the meaning attached by the first party; or

(b) that party has no reason to know of any different meaning attached by the other, and the other has reason to know the meaning attached by the first party.

§ 24. Offer Defined

An offer is the manifestation of willingness to enter into a bargain, so made as to justify another person in understanding that his assent to that bargain is invited and will conclude it.

§ 30. Form of Acceptance Invited

(1) An offer may invite or require acceptance to be made by an affirmative answer in words, or by performing or refraining from performing a specified act, or may empower the offeree to make a selection of terms in his acceptance.

(2) Unless otherwise indicated by the language or the circumstances, an offer invites acceptance in any manner and by any medium reasonable in the circumstances.

§ 33. Certainty

(1) Even though a manifestation of intention is intended to be understood as an offer, it cannot be accepted so as to form a contract unless the terms of the contract are reasonably certain.

(2) The terms of a contract are reasonably certain if they provide a basis for determining the existence of a breach and for giving an appropriate remedy.

(3) The fact that one or more terms of a proposed bargain are left open or uncertain may show that a manifestation of intention is not intended to be understood as an offer or as an acceptance.

§ 34. Certainty and Choice of Terms; Effect of Performance or Reliance

(1) The terms of a contract may be reasonably certain even though it empowers one or both parties to make a selection of terms in the course of performance.

(2) Part performance under an agreement may remove uncertainty and establish that a contract enforceable as a bargain has been formed.

(3) Action in reliance on an agreement may make a contractual remedy appropriate even though uncertainty is not removed.

§ 43. Indirect Communication of Revocation

An offeree's power of acceptance is terminated when the offeror takes definite action inconsistent with an intention to enter into the proposed contract and the offeree acquires reliable information to that effect.

§ 45. Option Contract Created by Part Performance or Tender

(1) Where an offer invites an offeree to accept by rendering a performance and does not invite a promissory acceptance, an option contract is created when the offeree tenders or begins the invited performance or tenders a beginning of it.

(2) The offeror's duty of performance under any option contract so created is conditional on completion or tender of the invited performance in accordance with the terms of the offer.

§ 54. Acceptance by Performance; Necessity of Notification to Offeror

(1) Where an offer invites an offeree to accept by rendering a performance, no notification is necessary to make such an acceptance effective unless the offer requests such a notification.

(2) If an offeree who accepts by rendering a performance has reason to know that the offeror has no adequate means of learning of the performance with reasonable promptness and certainty, the contractual duty of the offeror is discharged unless

(a) the offeree exercises reasonable diligence to notify the offeror of acceptance, or
(b) the offeror learns of the performance within a reasonable time, or
(c) the offer indicates that notification of acceptance is not required.

§ 67. Effect of Receipt of Acceptance Improperly Dispatched

Where an acceptance is seasonably dispatched but the offeree uses means of transmission not invited by the offer or fails to exercise reasonable diligence to insure safe transmission, it is treated as operative upon dispatch if received within the time in which a properly dispatched acceptance would normally have arrived.

§ 71. Requirement of Exchange; Types of Exchange

(1) To constitute consideration, a performance or a return promise must be bargained for.

(2) A performance or return promise is bargained for if it is sought by the promisor in exchange for his promise and is given by the promisee in exchange for that promise.

(3) The performance may consist of

(a) an act other than a promise, or
(b) a forbearance, or
(c) the creation, modification, or destruction of a legal relation.

(4) The performance or return promise may be given to the promisor or to some other person. It may be given by the promisee or by some other person.

§ 77. Illusory and Alternative Promises

A promise or apparent promise is not consideration if by its terms the promisor or purported promisor reserves a choice of alternative performances unless

(a) each of the alternative performances would have been consideration if it alone had been bargained for; or
(b) one of the alternative performances would have been consideration and there is or appears to the parties to be a substantial possibility that before the promisor exercises his choice events may eliminate the alternatives which would not have been consideration.

§ 82. Promise to Pay Indebtedness; Effect on the Statute of Limitations

(1) A promise to pay all or part of an antecedent contractual or quasi-contractual indebtedness owed by the promisor is binding if the indebtedness is still enforceable or would be except for the effect of a statute of limitations.

(2) The following facts operate as such a promise unless other facts indicate a different intention:

(a) A voluntary acknowledgment to the obligee, admitting the present existence of the antecedent indebtedness; or
(b) A voluntary transfer of money, a negotiable instrument, or other thing by the obligor to the obligee, made as interest on or part payment of or collateral security for the antecedent indebtedness; or
(c) A statement to the obligee that the statute of limitations will not be pleaded as a defense.

§ 89. Modification of Executory Contract

A promise modifying a duty under a contract not fully performed on either side is binding

(a) if the modification is fair and equitable in view of circumstances not anticipated by the parties when the contract was made; or
(b) to the extent provided by statute; or
(c) to the extent that justice requires enforcement in view of material change of position in reliance on the promise.

§ 90. Promise Reasonably Inducing Action or Forbearance

(1) A promise which the promisor should reasonably expect to induce action or forbearance on the part of the promisee or a third person and which does induce such action or forbearance is binding if injustice can be avoided only by enforcement of the promise. The remedy granted for breach may be limited as justice requires.

(2) A charitable subscription or a marriage settlement is binding under Subsection (1) without proof that the promise induced action or forbearance.

§ 110. Classes of Contracts Covered

(1) The following classes of contracts are subject to a statute, commonly called the Statute of Frauds, forbidding enforcement unless there is a written memorandum or an applicable exception:

(a) a contract of an executor or administrator to answer for a duty of his decedent (the executor-administrator provision);
(b) a contract to answer for the duty of another (the suretyship provision);
(c) a contract made upon consideration of marriage (the marriage provision);
(d) a contract for the sale of an interest in land (the land contract provision);
(e) a contract that is not to be performed within one year from the making thereof (the one-year provision).

(2) The following classes of contracts, which were traditionally subject to the Statute of Frauds, are now governed by Statute of Frauds provisions of the Uniform Commercial Code:

(a) a contract for the sale of goods for the price of $500 or more (Uniform Commercial Code § 2–201);
(b) a contract for the sale of securities (Uniform Commercial Code § 8–319);
(c) a contract for the sale of personal property not otherwise covered, to the extent of enforcement by way of action or defense beyond $5,000 in amount or value of remedy (Uniform Commercial Code § 1–206).

(3) In addition the Uniform Commercial Code requires a writing signed by the debtor for an agreement which creates or provides for a security interest in personal property or fixtures not in the possession of the secured party.

(4) Statutes in most states provide that no acknowledgment or promise is sufficient evidence of a new or continuing contract to take a case out of the operation of a statute of limitations unless made in some writing signed by the party to be charged, but that the statute does not alter the effect of any payment of principal or interest.

(5) In many states other classes of contracts are subject to a requirement of a writing.

§ 111. Contract of Executor or Administrator

A contract of an executor or administrator to answer personally for a duty of his decedent is within the Statute of Frauds if a similar contract to answer for the duty of a living person would be within the Statute as a contract to answer for the duty of another.

§ 116. Main Purpose; Advantage to Surety

A contract that all or part of a duty of a third person to the promisee shall be satisfied is not within the Statute of Frauds as a promise to answer for the duty of another if the consideration for the promise is in fact or apparently desired by the promisor mainly for his own economic advantage, rather than in order to benefit the third person. If, however, the consideration is merely a premium for insurance, the contract is within the Statute.

§ 124. Contract Made Upon Consideration of Marriage

A promise for which all or part of the consideration is either marriage or a promise to marry is within the Statute of Frauds, except in the case of an agreement which consists only of mutual promises of two persons to marry each other.

§ 125. Contract to Transfer, Buy, or Pay for an Interest in Land

(1) A promise to transfer to any person any interest in land is within the Statute of Frauds.
(2) A promise to buy any interest in land is within the Statute of Frauds, irrespective of the person to whom the transfer is to be made.
(3) When a transfer of an interest in land has been made, a promise to pay the price, if originally within the Statute of Frauds, ceases to be within it unless the promised price is itself in whole or in part an interest in land.
(4) Statutes in most states except from the land contract and one-year provisions of the Statute of Frauds short-term leases and contracts to lease, usually for a term not longer than one year.

§ 129. Action in Reliance; Specific Performance

A contract for the transfer of an interest in land may be specifically enforced notwithstanding failure to comply with the Statute of Frauds if it is established that the party seeking enforcement, in reasonable reliance on the contract and on the continuing assent of the party against whom enforcement is sought, has so changed his position that injustice can be avoided only by specific enforcement.

§ 130. Contract Not to Be Performed Within a Year

(1) Where any promise in a contract cannot be fully performed within a year from the time the contract is

made, all promises in the contract are within the Statute of Frauds until one party to the contract completes his performance.

(2) When one party to a contract has completed his performance, the one-year provision of the Statute does not prevent enforcement of the promises of other parties.

§ 132. Several Writings

The memorandum may consist of several writings if one of the writings is signed and the writings in the circumstances clearly indicate that they relate to the same transaction.

§ 157. Effect of Fault of Party Seeking Relief

A mistaken party's fault in failing to know or discover the facts before making the contract does not bar him from avoidance or reformation under the rules stated in this Chapter, unless his fault amounts to a failure to act in good faith and in accordance with reasonable standards of fair dealing.

§ 163. When a Misrepresentation Prevents Formation of a Contract

If a misrepresentation as to the character or essential terms of a proposed contract induces conduct that appears to be a manifestation of assent by one who neither knows nor has reasonable opportunity to know of the character or essential terms of the proposed contract, his conduct is not effective as a manifestation of assent.

§ 174. When Duress by Physical Compulsion Prevents Formation of a Contract

If conduct that appears to be a manifestation of assent by a party who does not intend to engage in that conduct is physically compelled by duress, the conduct is not effective as a manifestation of assent.

§ 175. When Duress by Threat Makes a Contract Voidable

(1) If a party's manifestation of assent is induced by an improper threat by the other party that leaves the victim no reasonable alternative, the contract is voidable by the victim.

(2) If a party's manifestation of assent is induced by one who is not a party to the transaction, the contract is voidable by the victim unless the other party to the transaction in good faith and without reason to know of the duress either gives value or relies materially on the transaction.

§ 176. When a Threat Is Improper

(1) A threat is improper if

(a) what is threatened is a crime or a tort, or the threat itself would be a crime or a tort if it resulted in obtaining property,

(b) what is threatened is a criminal prosecution,

(c) what is threatened is the use of civil process and the threat is made in bad faith, or

(d) the threat is a breach of the duty of good faith and fair dealing under a contract with the recipient.

(2) A threat is improper if the resulting exchange is not on fair terms, and

(a) the threatened act would harm the recipient and would not significantly benefit the party making the threat,

(b) the effectiveness of the threat in inducing the manifestation of assent is significantly increased by prior unfair dealing by the party making the threat, or

(c) what is threatened is otherwise a use of power for illegitimate ends.

§ 177. When Undue Influence Makes a Contract Voidable

(1) Undue influence is unfair persuasion of a party who is under the domination of the person exercising the persuasion or who by virtue of the relation between them is justified in assuming that that person will not act in a manner inconsistent with his welfare.

(2) If a party's manifestation of assent is induced by undue influence by the other party, the contract is voidable by the victim.

(3) If a party's manifestation of assent is induced by one who is not a party to the transaction, the contract is voidable by the victim unless the other party to the transaction in good faith and without reason to know of the undue influence either gives value or relies materially on the transaction.

§ 181. Effect of Failure to Comply with Licensing or Similar Requirement

If a party is prohibited from doing an act because of his failure to comply with a licensing, registration or similar requirement, a promise in consideration of his doing that act or of his promise to do it is unenforceable on grounds of public policy if

(a) the requirement has a regulatory purpose, and

(b) the interest in the enforcement of the promise is clearly outweighed by the public policy behind the requirement.

§ 186. Promise in Restraint of Trade

(1) A promise is unenforceable on grounds of public policy if it is unreasonably in restraint of trade.

(2) A promise is in restraint of trade if its performance would limit competition in any business or restrict the promisor in the exercise of a gainful occupation.

§ 187. Non-Ancillary Restraints on Competition

A promise to refrain from competition that imposes a restraint that is not ancillary to an otherwise valid transaction or relationship is unreasonably in restraint of trade.

§ 188. Ancillary Restraints on Competition

(1) A promise to refrain from competition that imposes a restraint that is ancillary to an otherwise valid transaction or relationship is unreasonably in restraint of trade if

(a) the restraint is greater than is needed to protect the promisee's legitimate interest, or
(b) the promisee's need is outweighed by the hardship to the promisor and the likely injury to the public.

(2) Promises imposing restraints that are ancillary to a valid transaction or relationship include the following:

(a) a promise by the seller of a business not to compete with the buyer in such a way as to injure the value of the business sold;
(b) a promise by an employee or other agent not to compete with his employer or other principal;
(c) a promise by a partner not to compete with the partnership.

§ 192. Promise Involving Commission of a Tort

A promise to commit a tort or to induce the commission of a tort is unenforceable on grounds of public policy.

§ 201. Whose Meaning Prevails

(1) Where the parties have attached the same meaning to a promise or agreement or a term thereof, it is interpreted in accordance with that meaning.
(2) Where the parties have attached different meanings to a promise or agreement or a term thereof, it is interpreted in accordance with the meaning attached by one of them if at the time the agreement was made

(a) that party did not know of any different meaning attached by the other, and the other knew the meaning attached by the first party; or
(b) that party had no reason to know of any different meaning attached by the other, and the other had reason to know the meaning attached by the first party.

(3) Except as stated in this Section, neither party is bound by the meaning attached by the other, even though the result may be a failure of mutual assent.

§ 202. Rules in Aid of Interpretation

(1) Words and other conduct are interpreted in the light of all the circumstances, and if the principal purpose of the parties is ascertainable it is given great weight.
(2) A writing is interpreted as a whole, and all writings that are part of the same transaction are interpreted together.
(3) Unless a different intention is manifested,

(a) where language has a generally prevailing meaning, it is interpreted in accordance with that meaning;
(b) technical terms and words of art are given their technical meaning when used in a transaction within their technical field.

(4) Where an agreement involves repeated occasions for performance by either party with knowledge of the nature of the performance and opportunity for objection to it by the other, any course of performance accepted or acquiesced in without objection is given great weight in the interpretation of the agreement.
(5) Wherever reasonable, the manifestations of intention of the parties to a promise or agreement are interpreted as consistent with each other and with any relevant course of performance, course of dealing, or usage of trade.

§ 203. Standards of Preference in Interpretation

In the interpretation of a promise or agreement or a term thereof, the following standards of preference are generally applicable:

(a) an interpretation which gives a reasonable, lawful, and effective meaning to all the terms is preferred to an interpretation which leaves a part unreasonable, unlawful, or of no effect;
(b) express terms are given greater weight than course of performance, course of dealing, and usage of trade, course of performance is given greater weight than course of dealing or usage of trade, and course of dealing is given greater weight than usage of trade;
(c) specific terms and exact terms are given greater weight than general language;
(d) separately negotiated or added terms are given greater weight than standardized terms or other terms not separately negotiated.

§ 208. Unconscionable Contract or Term

If a contract or term thereof is unconscionable at the time the contract is made a court may refuse to enforce the contract, or may enforce the remainder of the contract without the unconscionable term, or may so limit the application of any unconscionable term as to avoid any unconscionable result.

§ 213. Effect of Integrated Agreement on Prior Agreements (Parol Evidence Rule)

(1) A binding integrated agreement discharges prior agreements to the extent that it is inconsistent with them.
(2) A binding completely integrated agreement discharges prior agreements to the extent that they are within its scope.
(3) An integrated agreement that is not binding or that is voidable and avoided does not discharge a prior agreement. But an integrated agreement, even though not binding, may be effective to render inoperative a term which would have been part of the agreement if it had not been integrated.

§ 214. Evidence of Prior or Contemporaneous Agreements and Negotiations

Agreements and negotiations prior to or contemporaneous with the adoption of a writing are admissible in evidence to establish

(a) that the writing is or is not an integrated agreement;
(b) that the integrated agreement, if any, is completely or partially integrated;
(c) the meaning of the writing, whether or not integrated;
(d) illegality, fraud, duress, mistake, lack of consideration, or other invalidating cause;
(e) ground for granting or denying rescission, reformation, specific performance, or other remedy.

§ 216. Consistent Additional Terms

(1) Evidence of a consistent additional term is admissible to supplement an integrated agreement unless the court finds that the agreement was completely integrated.
(2) An agreement is not completely integrated if the writing omits a consistent additional agreed term which is

(a) agreed to for separate consideration, or
(b) such a term as in the circumstances might naturally be omitted from the writing.

§ 217. Integrated Agreement Subject to Oral Requirement of a Condition

Where the parties to a written agreement agree orally that performance of the agreement is subject to the occurrence of a stated condition, the agreement is not integrated with respect to the oral condition.

§ 235. Effect of Performance as Discharge and of Non-Performance as Breach

(1) Full performance of a duty under a contract discharges the duty.
(2) When performance of a duty under a contract is due any non-performance is a breach.

§ 241. Circumstances Significant in Determining Whether a Failure Is Material

In determining whether a failure to render or to offer performance is material, the following circumstances are significant:

(a) the extent to which the injured party will be deprived of the benefit which he reasonably expected;
(b) the extent to which the injured party can be adequately compensated for the part of that benefit of which he will be deprived;
(c) the extent to which the party failing to perform or to offer to perform will suffer forfeiture;
(d) the likelihood that the party failing to perform or to offer to perform will cure his failure, taking account of all the circumstances including any reasonable assurances;
(e) the extent to which the behavior of the party failing to perform or to offer to perform comports with standards of good faith and fair dealing.

§ 261. Discharge by Supervening Impracticability

Where, after a contract is made, a party's performance is made impracticable without his fault by the occurrence of an event the non-occurrence of which was a basic assumption on which the contract was made, his duty to render that performance is discharged, unless the language or the circumstances indicate the contrary.

§ 279. Substituted Contract

(1) A substituted contract is a contract that is itself accepted by the obligee in satisfaction of the obligor's existing duty.
(2) The substituted contract discharges the original duty and breach of the substituted contract by the obligor does not give the obligee a right to enforce the original duty.

§ 280. Novation

A novation is a substituted contract that includes as a party one who was neither the obligor nor the obligee of the original duty.

§ 281. Accord and Satisfaction

(1) An accord is a contract under which an obligee promises to accept a stated performance in satisfaction of the obligor's existing duty. Performance of the accord discharges the original duty.
(2) Until performance of the accord, the original duty is suspended unless there is such a breach of the accord by the obligor as discharges the new duty of the obligee to accept the performance in satisfaction. If there is such a breach, the obligee may enforce either the original duty or any duty under the accord.
(3) Breach of the accord by the obligee does not discharge the original duty, but the obligor may maintain a suit for specific performance of the accord, in addition to any claim for damages for partial breach.

§ 286. Alteration of Writing

(1) If one to whom a duty is owed under a contract alters a writing that is an integrated agreement or that satisfies the Statute of Frauds with respect to that contract, the duty is discharged if the alteration is fraudulent and material.
(2) An alteration is material if it would, if effective, vary any party's legal relations with the maker of the alteration or adversely affect that party's legal relations with a third person. The unauthorized insertion in a blank space in a writing is an alteration.

§ 317. Assignment of a Right

(1) An assignment of a right is a manifestation of the assignor's intention to transfer it by virtue of which the assignor's right to performance by the obligor is extin-

guished in whole or in part and the assignee acquires a right to such performance.

(2) A contractual right can be assigned unless

(a) the substitution of a right of the assignee for the right of the assignor would materially change the duty of the obligor, or materially increase the burden or risk imposed on him by his contract, or materially impair his chance of obtaining return performance, or materially reduce its value to him, or

(b) the assignment is forbidden by statute, or is otherwise inoperative on grounds of public policy, or

(c) assignment is validly precluded by contract.

§ 318. Delegation of Performance of Duty

(1) An obligor can properly delegate the performance of his duty to another unless the delegation is contrary to public policy or the terms of his promise.

(2) Unless otherwise agreed, a promise requires performance by a particular person only to the extent that the obligee has a substantial interest in having that person perform or control the acts promised.

(3) Unless the obligee agrees otherwise, neither delegation of performance nor a contract to assume the duty made with the obligor by the person delegated discharges any duty or liability of the delegating obligor.

§ 328. Interpretation of Words of Assignment; Effect of Acceptance of Assignment

(1) Unless the language or the circumstances indicate the contrary, as in an assignment for security, an assignment of "the contract" or of "all my rights under the contract" or an assignment in similar general terms is an assignment of the assignor's rights and a delegation of his unperformed duties under the contract.

(2) Unless the language or the circumstances indicate the contrary, the acceptance by an assignee of such an assignment operates as a promise to the assignor to perform the assignor's unperformed duties, and the obligor of the assigned rights is an intended beneficiary of the promise.

Caveat: The Institute expresses no opinion as to whether the rule stated in Subsection (2) applies to an assignment by a purchaser of his rights under a contract for the sale of land.

§ 342. Successive Assignees from the Same Assignor

Except as otherwise provided by statute, the right of an assignee is superior to that of a subsequent assignee of the same right from the same assignor, unless

(a) the first assignment is ineffective or revocable or is voidable by the assignor or by the subsequent assignee; or

(b) the subsequent assignee in good faith and without knowledge or reason to know of the prior assignment gives value and obtains

(i) payment or satisfaction of the obligation,

(ii) judgment against the obligor,

(iii) a new contract with the obligor by novation, or

(iv) possession of a writing of a type customarily accepted as a symbol or as evidence of the right assigned.

§ 346. Availability of Damages

(1) The injured party has a right to damages for any breach by a party against whom the contract is enforceable unless the claim for damages has been suspended or discharged.

(2) If the breach caused no loss or if the amount of the loss is not proved under the rules stated in this Chapter, a small sum fixed without regard to the amount of loss will be awarded as nominal damages.

§ 350. Avoidability as a Limitation on Damages

(1) Except as stated in Subsection (2), damages are not recoverable for loss that the injured party could have avoided without undue risk, burden or humiliation.

(2) The injured party is not precluded from recovery by the rule stated in Subsection (1) to the extent that he has made reasonable but unsuccessful efforts to avoid loss.

§ 351. Unforeseeability and Related Limitations on Damages

(1) Damages are not recoverable for loss that the party in breach did not have reason to foresee as a probable result of the breach when the contract was made.

(2) Loss may be foreseeable as a probable result of a breach because it follows from the breach

(a) in the ordinary course of events, or

(b) as a result of special circumstances, beyond the ordinary course of events, that the party in breach had reason to know.

(3) A court may limit damages for foreseeable loss by excluding recovery for loss of profits, by allowing recovery only for loss incurred in reliance, or otherwise if it concludes that in the circumstances justice so requires in order to avoid disproportionate compensation.

§ 352. Uncertainty as a Limitation on Damages

Damages are not recoverable for loss beyond an amount that the evidence permits to be established with reasonable certainty.

§ 355. Punitive Damages

Punitive damages are not recoverable for a breach of contract unless the conduct constituting the breach is also a tort for which punitive damages are recoverable.

§ 356. Liquidated Damages and Penalties

(1) Damages for breach by either party may be liquidated in the agreement but only at an amount that is reasonable in the light of the anticipated or actual loss caused by the breach and the difficulties of proof of loss. A term fixing unreasonably large liquidated damages is unenforceable on grounds of public policy as a penalty.

(2) A term in a bond providing for an amount of money as a penalty for non-occurrence of the condition of the bond is unenforceable on grounds of public policy to the extent that the amount exceeds the loss caused by such non-occurrence.

§ 360. Factors Affecting Adequacy of Damages

In determining whether the remedy in damages would be adequate, the following circumstances are significant:

(a) the difficulty of proving damages with reasonable certainty,

(b) the difficulty of procuring a suitable substitute performance by means of money awarded as damages, and

(c) the likelihood that an award of damages could not be collected.

§ 367. Contracts for Personal Service or Supervision

(1) A promise to render personal service will not be specifically enforced.

(2) A promise to render personal service exclusively for one employer will not be enforced by an injunction against serving another if its probable result will be to compel a performance involving personal relations the enforced continuance of which is undesirable or will be to leave the employee without other reasonable means of making a living.

RESTATEMENT, SECOND, OF AGENCY***

§ 1. Agency; Principal; Agent

(1) Agency is the fiduciary relation which results from the manifestation of consent by one person to another that the other shall act on his behalf and subject to his control, and consent by the other so to act.

(2) The one for whom action is to be taken is the principal.

(3) The one who is to act is the agent.

§ 2. Master; Servant; Independent Contractor

(1) A master is a principal who employs an agent to perform service in his affairs and who controls or has the right to control the physical conduct of the other in the performance of the service.

(2) A servant is an agent employed by a master to perform service in his affairs whose physical conduct in the performance of the service is controlled or is subject to the right to control by the master.

(3) An independent contractor is a person who contracts with another to do something for him but who is not controlled by the other nor subject to the other's right to control with respect to his physical conduct in the performance of the undertaking. He may or may not be an agent.

§ 4. Disclosed Principal; Partially Disclosed Principal; Undisclosed Principal

(1) If, at the time of a transaction conducted by an agent, the other party thereto has notice that the agent is acting for a principal and of the principal's identity, the principal is a disclosed principal.

(2) If the other party has notice that the agent is or may be acting for a principal but has no notice of the principal's identity, the principal for whom the agent is acting is a partially disclosed principal.

(3) If the other party has no notice that the agent is acting for a principal, the one for whom he acts is an undisclosed principal.

§ 15. Manifestations of Consent

An agency relation exists only if there has been a manifestation by the principal to the agent that the agent may act on his account, and consent by the agent so to act.

§ 16. Consideration

The relation of principal and agent can be created although neither party receives consideration.

§ 17. What Acts are Delegable

A person privileged, or subject to a duty, to perform an act or accomplish a result can properly appoint an agent to perform the act or accomplish the result, unless public policy or the agreement with another requires personal performance; if personal performance is required, the doing of the act by another on his behalf does not constitute performance by him.

§ 18. Delegation of Powers Held by Agent

Unless otherwise agreed, an agent cannot properly delegate to another the exercise of discretion in the use of a power held for the benefit of the principal.

§ 19. Appointment to Perform Illegal Acts

The appointment of an agent to do an act is illegal if an agreement to do such an act or the doing of the act itself would be criminal, tortious, or otherwise opposed to public policy.

§ 27. Creation of Apparent Authority: General Rule

Except for the execution of instruments under seal or for the conduct of transactions required by statute to be authorized in a particular way, apparent authority to do an act is created as to a third person by written or spoken words or any other conduct of the principal which, reasonably interpreted, causes the third person to believe that the principal consents to have the act done on his behalf by the person purporting to act for him.

§ 28. Authority to Execute Sealed Instruments

(1) Except as stated in Subsection (2), an instrument executed by an agent as a sealed instrument does not operate as such unless authority or apparent authority to execute it has been conferred by an instrument under seal.

(2) Sealed authority is not necessary to execute an instrument under seal where:

(a) the instrument is executed in the principal's presence and by his direction;

(b) the instrument is authorized by a corporation or partnership in accordance with the rules relating to the authorization of such instruments by such associations; or

(c) a statute deprives seals of their legal significance.

§ 35. When Incidental Authority is Inferred

Unless otherwise agreed, authority to conduct a transaction includes authority to do acts which are incidental to it, usually accompany it, or are reasonably necessary to accomplish it.

§ 50. When Authority to Contract Inferred

Unless otherwise agreed, authority to make a contract is inferred from authority to conduct a transaction, if the making of such a contract is incidental to the transaction, usually accompanies such a transaction, or is reasonably necessary to accomplish it.

§ 73. What Authority is Inferred

Unless otherwise agreed, authority to manage a business includes authority:

(a) to make contracts which are incidental to such business, are usually made in it, or are reasonably necessary in conducting it;

(b) to procure equipment and supplies and to make repairs reasonably necessary for the proper conduct of the business;

(c) to employ, supervise, or discharge employees as the course of business may reasonably require;

(d) to sell or otherwise dispose of goods or other things in accordance with the purposes for which the business is operated;

(e) to receive payment of sums due the principal and to pay debts due from the principal arising out of the business enterprise; and

(f) to direct the ordinary operations of the business.

§ 79. When Authority to Appoint an Agent is Inferred

Unless otherwise agreed, an agent is authorized to appoint another agent for the principal if:

(a) the agent is appointed to a position which, in view of business customs, ordinarily includes authority to appoint other agents; or

(b) the proper conduct of the principal's business in the contemplated manner reasonably requires the employment of other agents; or

(c) the agent is employed to act at a place where or in a business in which it is customary to employ other agents for the performance of such acts; or

(d) an unforeseen contingency arises making it impracticable to communicate with the principal and making such an appointment reasonably necessary for the protection of the interests of the principal entrusted to the agent.

§ 82. Ratification

Ratification is the affirmance by a person of a prior act which did not bind him but which was done or professedly done on his account, whereby the act, as to some or all persons, is given effect as if originally authorized by him.

§ 88. Affirmance after Withdrawal of Other Party or Other Termination of Original Transaction

To constitute ratification, the affirmance of a transaction must occur before the other party has manifested his withdrawal from it either to the purported principal or to the agent, and before the offer or agreement has otherwise terminated or been discharged.

§ 91. Knowledge of Principal at Time of Affirmance

(1) If, at the time of affirmance, the purported principal is ignorant of material facts involved in the original transaction, and is unaware of his ignorance, he can thereafter avoid the effect of the affirmance.

(2) Material facts are those which substantially affect the existence or extent of the obligations involved in the transaction, as distinguished from those which affect the values or inducements involved in the transaction.

§ 96. Effect of Affirming Part of a Transaction

A contract or other single transaction must be affirmed in its entirety in order to effect its ratification.

§ 112. Disloyalty of Agent

Unless otherwise agreed, the authority of an agent terminates if, without knowledge of the principal, he acquires adverse interests or if he is otherwise guilty of a serious breach of loyalty to the principal.

§ 133. Incapacity of Parties or Other Impossibility

The apparent authority of an agent terminates upon the happening of an event which destroys the capacity of the principal to give the power, or an event which otherwise makes the authorized transaction impossible.

§ 136. Notification Terminating Apparent Authority

(1) Unless otherwise agreed, there is a notification by the principal to the third person of revocation of an agent's authority or other fact indicating its termination:

(a) when the principal states such fact to the third person; or
(b) when a reasonable time has elapsed after a writing stating such fact has been delivered by the principal

(i) to the other personally;
(ii) to the other's place of business;
(iii) to a place designated by the other as one in which business communications are received; or
(iv) to a place which, in view of the business customs or relations between the parties is reasonably believed to be the place for the receipt of such communications by the other.

(2) Unless otherwise agreed, a notification to be effective in terminating apparent authority must be given by the means stated in Subsection (1) with respect to a third person:

(a) who has previously extended credit to or received credit from the principal through the agent in reliance upon a manifestation from the principal of continuing authority in the agent;
(b) to whom the agent has been specially accredited;
(c) with whom the agent has begun to deal, as the principal should know; or
(d) who relies upon the possession by the agent of indicia of authority entrusted to him by the principal.

(3) Except as to the persons included in Subsection (2), the principal can properly give notification of the termination of the agent's authority by:

(a) advertising the fact in a newspaper of general circulation in the place where the agency is regularly carried on; or

(b) giving publicity by some other method reasonably adapted to give the information to such third person.

§ 138. Definition

A power given as security is a power to affect the legal relations of another, created in the form of an agency authority, but held for the benefit of the power holder or a third person and given to secure the performance of a duty or to protect a title, either legal or equitable, such power being given when the duty or title is created or given for consideration.

§ 139. Termination of Powers Given as Security

(1) Unless otherwise agreed, a power given as security is not terminated by:

(a) revocation by the creator of the power;
(b) surrender by the holder of the power, if he holds for the benefit of another;
(c) the loss of capacity during the lifetime of either the creator of the power or the holder of the power; or
(d) the death of the holder of the power, or, if the power is given as security for a duty which does not terminate at the death of the creator of the power, by his death.

(2) A power given as security is terminated by its surrender by the beneficiary, if of full capacity; or by the happening of events which, by its terms, discharges the obligations secured by it, or which makes its execution illegal or impossible.

§ 212. Principal Intends Conduct or Consequences

A person is subject to liability for the consequences of another's conduct which results from his directions as he would be for for his own personal conduct if, with knowledge of the conditions, he intends the conduct, or if he intends its consequences, unless the one directing or the one acting has a privilege or immunity not available to the other.

§ 213. Principal Negligent or Reckless

A person conducting an activity through servants or other agents is subject to liability for harm resulting from his conduct if he is negligent or reckless:

(a) in giving improper or ambiguous orders of in failing to make proper regulations; or
(b) in the employment of improper persons or instrumentalities in work involving risk of harm to others:
(c) in the supervision of the activity; or
(d) in permitting, or failing to prevent, negligent or other tortious conduct by persons, whether or not his servants or agents, upon premises or with instrumentalities under his control.

§ 218. Effect of Ratification

Upon ratification, a purported master or other principal becomes subject to liability for injuries caused by the tortious act of one acting or purporting to act as his agent as if the act had been authorized, if there has been no loss of capacity by the principal.

§ 219. When Master is Liable for Torts of His Servants

(1) A master is subject to liability for the torts of his servants committed while acting in the scope of their employment.

(2) A master is not subject to liability for the torts of his servants acting outside the scope of their employment, unless:

(a) the master intended the conduct or the consequences, or

(b) the master was negligent or reckless, or

(c) the conduct violated a non-delegable duty of the master, or

(d) the servant purported to act or to speak on behalf of the principal and there was reliance upon apparent authority, or he was aided in accomplishing the tort by the existence of the agency relation.

§ 222. Servants of Agent of Undisclosed Principal

An undisclosed principal is subject to liability to third persons for conduct within the scope of employment of servants and of subservants employed for him by a servant or other agent empowered to employ them.

§ 228. General Statement

(1) Conduct of a servant is within the scope of employment if, but only if:

(a) it is of the kind he is employed to perform;

(b) it occurs substantially within the authorized time and space limits;

(c) it is actuated, at least in part, by a purpose to serve the master; and

(d) if force is intentionally used by the servant against another, the use of force is not unexpectable by the master.

(2) Conduct of a servant is not within the scope of employment if it is different in kind from that authorized, far beyond the authorized time or space limits, or too little actuated by a purpose to serve the master.

§ 250. Non-liability for Physical Harm by Non-Servant Agents

A principal is not liable for physical harm caused by the negligent physical conduct of a non-servant agent during the performance of the principal's business, if he neither intended nor authorized the result nor the manner of performance, unless he was under a duty to have the act performed with due care.

§ 257. Misrepresentations; in General

A principal is subject to liability for loss caused to another by the other's reliance upon a tortious representation of a servant or other agent, if the representation is:

(a) authorized;

(b) apparently authorized; or

(c) within the power of the agent to make for the principal.

§ 320. Principal Disclosed

Unless otherwise agreed, a person making or purporting to make a contract with another as agent for a disclosed principal does not become a party to the contract.

§ 321. Principal Partially Disclosed

Unless otherwise agreed, a person purporting to make a contract with another for a partially disclosed principal is a party to the contract.

§ 326. Principal Known to be Nonexistent or Incompetent

Unless otherwise agreed, a person who, in dealing with another, purports to act as agent for a principal whom both know to be nonexistent or wholly incompetent, becomes a party to such a contract.

§ 343. General Rule

An agent who does an act otherwise a tort is not relieved from liability by the fact that he acted at the command of the principal or on account of the principal, except where he is exercising a privilege of the principal, or a privilege held by him for the protection of the principal's interests, or where the principal owes no duty or less than the normal duty of care to the person harmed.

§ 363. Contracts; General Rule

An agent who makes a contract on behalf of a principal cannot maintain an action thereon in his own name on behalf of the principal although authorized by the principal to bring suit, unless the agent is a promisee or transferee.

§ 379. Duty of Care and Skill

(1) Unless otherwise agreed, a paid agent is subject to a duty to the principal to act with standard care and with the skill which is standard in the locality for the kind of work which he is employed to perform and, in addition, to exercise any special skill that he has.

(2) Unless otherwise agreed, a gratuitous agent is under a duty to the principal to act with the care and skill which is required of persons not agents performing similar gratuitous undertakings for others.

§ 381. Duty to Give Information

Unless otherwise agreed, an agent is subject to a duty to use reasonable efforts to give his principal information which is relevant to affairs entrusted to him and which, as the agent has notice, the principal would desire to have and which can be communicated without violating a superior duty to a third person.

§ 382. Duty to Keep and Render Accounts

Unless otherwise agreed, an agent is subject to a duty to keep, and render to his principal, an account of money or other things which he has received or paid out on behalf of the principal.

§ 383. Duty to Act Only as Authorized

Except when he is privileged to protect his own or another's interests, an agent is subject to a duty to the principal not to act in the principal's affairs except in accordance with the principal's manifestation of consent.

§ 385. Duty to Obey

(1) Unless otherwise agreed, an agent is subject to a duty to obey all reasonable directions in regard to the manner of performing a service that he has contracted to perform.
(2) Unless he is privileged to protect his own or another's interests, an agent is subject to a duty not to act in matters entrusted to him on account of the principal contrary to the directions of the principal, even though the terms of the employment prescribe that such directions shall not be given.

§ 401. Liability for Loss Caused

An agent is subject to liability for loss caused to the principal by any breach of duty.

§ 438. Duty of Indemnity; the Principle

(1) A principal is under a duty to indemnify the agent in accordance with the terms of the agreement with him.
(2) In the absence of terms to the contrary in the agreement of employment, the principal has a duty to indemnify the agent where the agent

(a) makes a payment authorized or made necessary in executing the principal's affairs or, unless he is officious, one beneficial to the principal, or
(b) suffers a loss which, because of their relation, it is fair that the principal should bear.

§ 439. When Duty of Indemnity Exists

Unless otherwise agreed, a principal is subject to a duty to exonerate an agent who is not barred by the illegality of his conduct to indemnify him for:

(a) authorized payments made by the agent on behalf of the principal;
(b) payments upon contracts upon which the agent is authorized to make himself liable, and upon obligations arising from the possession or ownership of things which he is authorized to hold on account of the principal;
(c) payments of damages to third persons which he is required to make on account of the authorized performance of an act which constitutes a tort or a breach of contract;
(d) expenses of defending actions by third persons brought because of the agent's authorized conduct, such actions being unfounded but not brought in bad faith; and
(e) payments resulting in benefit to the principal, made by the agent under such circumstances that it would be inequitable for indemnity not to be made.

§ 443. Amount of Compensation

If the contract of employment provides for compensation to the agent, he is entitled to receive for the full performance of the agreed service:

(a) the definite amount agreed upon and no more, if the agreement is definite as to amount; or
(b) the fair value of his services, if there is no agreement for a definite amount.

§ 469. Disloyalty or Insubordination as Defense

An agent is entitled to no compensation for conduct which is disobedient or which is a breach of his duty of loyalty; if such conduct constitutes a wilful and deliberate breach of his contract or service, he is not entitled to compensation even for properly performed services for which no compensation is apportioned.

APPENDIX C
THE UNIFORM COMMERCIAL CODE

The Code consists of 10 Articles as follows:
1. GENERAL PROVISIONS
2. Sales
3. Commercial Paper
4. Bank Deposits and Collections
5. Letters of Credit
6. Bulk Transfers
7. Warehouse Receipts, Bills of Lading and Other Documents of Title
8. Investment Securities
9. Secured Transactions: Sales of Accounts, Contract Rights and Chattel Paper
10. Effective Date and Repealer

Article 1

GENERAL PROVISIONS

Part 1 Short Title, Construction, Application and Subject Matter of the Act

§ 1–101. Short Tile.

This Act shall be known and may be cited as Uniform Commercial Code.

§ 1–102. Purposes; Rules of Construction; Variation by Agreement.

(1) This Act shall be liberally construed and applied to promote its underlying purposes and policies.
(2) Underlying purposes and policies of this Act are

(a) to simplify, clarify and modernize the law governing commercial transactions;
(b) to permit the continued expansion of commercial practices through custom, usage and agreement of the parties;
(c) to make uniform the law among the various jurisdictions.

(3) The effect of provisions of this Act may be varied by agreement, except as otherwise provided in this Act and except that the obligations of good faith, diligence, reasonableness and care prescribed by this Act may not be disclaimed by agreement but the parties may by agreement determine the standards by which the performance of such obligations is to be measured if such standards are not manifestly unreasonable.
(4) The presence in certain provisions of this Act of the words "unless otherwise agreed" or words of similar import does not imply that the effect of other provisions may not be varied by agreement under subsection (3).
(5) In this Act unless the context otherwise requires

(a) words in the singular number include the plural, and in the plural include the singular;
(b) words of the masculine gender include the feminine and the neuter, and when the sense so indicates words of the neuter gender may refer to any gender.

§ 1–103. Supplementary General Principles of Law Applicable.

Unless displaced by the particular provisions of this Act, the principles of law and equity, including the law merchant and the law relative to capacity to contract, principal and agent, estoppel, fraud, misrepresentation, duress, coercion, mistake, bankruptcy, or other validating or invalidating cause shall supplement its provisions.

§ 1–104. Construction Against Implicit Repeal.

This Act being a general act intended as a unified coverage of its subject matter, no part of it shall be deemed to be impliedly repealed by subsequent legislation if such construction can reasonably be avoided.

§ 1–105. Territorial Application of the Act; Parties' Power to Choose Applicable Law.

(1) Except as provided hereafter in this section, when a transaction bears a reasonable relation to this state and also to another state or nation the parties may agree that the law either of this state or of such other state or nation shall govern their rights and duties. Failing such agreement this Act applies to transactions bearing an appropriate relation to this state.
(2) Where one of the following provisions of this Act specifies the applicable law, that provision governs and a contrary agreement is effective only to the extent permitted by the law (including the conflict of laws rules) so specified:

Rights of creditors against sold goods. Section 2–402.
Applicability of the Article on Bank Deposits and Collections. Section 4–102.

Bulk transfers subject to the Article on Bulk Transfers. Section 6–102.

Applicability of the Article on Investment Securities. Section 8–106.

Perfection provisions of the Article on Secured Transactions. Section 9–103.

§ 1–106. Remedies to Be Liberally Administered.

(1) The remedies provided by this Act shall be liberally administered to the end that the aggrieved party may be put in as good a position as if the other party had fully performed but neither consequential or special nor penal damages may be had except as specifically provided in this Act or by other rule of law.

(2) Any right or obligation declared by this Act is enforceable by action unless the provision declaring it specifies a different and limited effect.

§ 1–107. Waiver or Renunciation of Claim or Right After Breach.

Any claim or right arising out of an alleged breach can be discharged in whole or in part without consideration by a written waiver or renunciation signed and delivered by the aggrieved party.

§ 1–108. Severability.

If any provision or clause of this Act or application thereof to any person or circumstances is held invalid, such invalidity shall not affect other provisions or applications of the Act which can be given effect without the invalid provision or application, and to this end the provisions of this Act are declared to be severable.

§ 1–109. Section Captions.

Section captions are parts of this Act.

Part 2 General Definitions and Principles of Interpretation

§ 1–201. General Definitions.

Subject to additional definitions contained in the subsequent Articles of this Act which are applicable to specific Articles or Parts thereof, and unless the context otherwise requires, in this Act:

(1) "Action" in the sense of a judicial proceeding includes recoupment, counterclaim, set-off, suit in equity and any other proceedings in which rights are determined.

(2) "Aggrieved party" means a party entitled to resort to a remedy.

(3) "Agreement" means the bargain of the parties in fact as found in their language or by implication from other circumstances including course of dealing or usage of trade or course of performance as provided in this Act (Sections 1–205 and 2–208). Whether an agreement has legal consequences is determined by the provisions of this Act, if applicable; otherwise by the law of contracts (Section 1–103). (Compare "Contract".)

(4) "Bank" means any person engaged in the business of banking.

(5) "Bearer" means the person in possession of an instrument, document of title, or certificated security payable to bearer or indorsed in blank.

(6) "Bill of lading" means a document evidencing the receipt of goods for shipment issued by a person engaged in the business of transporting or forwarding goods, and includes an airbill. "Airbill" means a document serving for air transportation as a bill of lading does for marine or rail transportation, and includes an air consignment note or air waybill.

(7) "Branch" includes a separately incorporated foreign branch of a bank.

(8) "Burden of establishing" a fact means the burden of persuading the triers of fact that the existence of the fact is more probable than its non-existence.

(9) "Buyer in ordinary course of business" means a person who in good faith and without knowledge that the sale to him is in violation of the ownership rights or security interest of a third party in the goods buys in ordinary course from a person in the business of selling goods of that kind but does not include a pawnbroker. All persons who sell minerals or the like (including oil and gas) at wellhead or minehead shall be deemed to be persons in the business of selling goods of that kind. "Buying" may be for cash or by exchange of other property or on secured or unsecured credit and includes receiving goods or documents of title under a pre-existing contract for sale but does not include a transfer in bulk or as security for or in total or partial satisfaction of a money debt.

(10) "Conspicuous": A term or clause is conspicuous when it is so written that a reasonable person against whom it is to operate ought to have noticed it. A printed heading in capitals (as: NON- NEGOTIABLE BILL OF LADING) is conspicuous. Language in the body of a form is "conspicuous" if it is in larger or other contrasting type or color. But in a telegram any stated term is "conspicuous". Whether a term or clause is "conspicuous" or not is for decision by the court.

(11) "Contract" means the total legal obligation which results from the parties' agreement as affected by this Act and any other applicable rules of law. (Compare "Agreement".)

(12) "Creditor" includes a general creditor, a secured creditor, a lien creditor and any representative of creditors, including an assignee for the benefit of creditors, a trustee in bankruptcy, a receiver in equity and an executor or administrator of an insolvent debtor's or assignor's estate.

(13) "Defendant" includes a person in the position of defendant in a cross-action or counterclaim.

(14) "Delivery" with respect to instruments, documents of title, chattel paper, or certificated securities means voluntary transfer of possession.

(15) "Document of title" includes bill of lading, dock warrant, dock receipt, warehouse receipt or order for the delivery of goods, and also any other document which in the regular course of business or financing is treated as adequately evidencing that the person in possession of it is entitled to receive, hold and dispose of the document and the goods it covers. To be a document of title a document must purport to be issued by or addressed to a bailee and purport to cover goods in the bailee's possession which are either identified or are fungible portions of an identified mass.

(16) "Fault" means wrongful act, omission or breach.

(17) "Fungible" with respect to goods or securities means goods or securities of which any unit is, by nature or usage of trade, the equivalent of any other like unit. Goods which are not fungible shall be deemed fungible for the purposes of this Act to the extent that under a particular agreement or document unlike units are treated as equivalents.

(18) "Genuine" means free of forgery or counterfeiting.

(19) "Good faith" means honesty in fact in the conduct or transaction concerned.

(20) "Holder" means a person who is in possession of a document of title or an instrument or a certificated investment security drawn, issued, or indorsed to him or his order or to bearer or in blank.

(21) To "honor" is to pay or to accept and pay, or where a credit so engages to purchase or discount a draft complying with the terms of the credit.

(22) "Insolvency proceedings" includes any assignment for the benefit of creditors or other proceedings intended to liquidate or rehabilitate the estate of the person involved.

(23) A person is "insolvent" who either has ceased to pay his debts in the ordinary course of business or cannot pay his debts as they become due or is insolvent within the meaning of the federal bankruptcy law.

(24) "Money" means a medium of exchange authorized or adopted by a domestic or foreign government as a part of its currency.

(25) A person has "notice" of a fact when

(a) he has actual knowledge of it; or
(b) he has received a notice or notification of it; or
(c) from all the facts and circumstances known to him at the time in question he has reason to know that it exists.

A person "knows" or has "knowledge" of a fact when he has actual knowledge of it. "Discover" or "learn" or a word or phrase of similar import refers to knowledge rather than to reason to know. The time and circumstances under which a notice or notification may cease to be effective are not determined by this Act.

(26) A person "notifies" or "gives" a notice or notification to another by taking such steps as may be reasonably required to inform the other in ordinary course whether or not such other actually comes to know of it. A person "receives" a notice or notification when

(a) it comes to his attention; or
(b) it is duly delivered at the place of business through which the contract was made or at any other place held out by him as the place for receipt of such communications.

(27) Notice, knowledge or a notice or notification received by an organization is effective for a particular transaction from the time when it is brought to the attention of the individual conducting that transaction, and in any event from the time when it would have been brought to his attention if the organization had exercised due diligence. An organization exercises due diligence if it maintains reasonable routines for communicating significant information to the person conducting the transaction and there is reasonable compliance with the routines. Due diligence does not require an individual acting for the organization to communicate information unless such communication is part of his regular duties or unless he has reason to know of the transaction and that the transaction would be materially affected by the information.

(28) "Organization" includes a corporation, government or governmental subdivision or agency, business trust, estate, trust, partnership or association, two or more persons having a joint or common interest, or any other legal or commercial entity.

(29) "Party", as distinct from "third party", means a person who has engaged in a transaction or made an agreement within this Act.

(30) "Person" includes an individual or an organization (See Section 1–102).

(31) "Presumption" or "presumed" means that the trier of fact must find the existence of the fact presumed unless and until evidence is introduced which would support a finding of its non-existence.

(32) "Purchase" includes taking by sale, discount, negotiation, mortgage, pledge, lien, or re-issue, gift or any other voluntary transaction creating an interest in property.

(33) "Purchaser" means a person who takes by purchase.

(34) "Remedy" means any remedial right to which an aggrieved party is entitled with or without resort to a tribunal.

(35) "Representative" includes an agent, an officer of a corporation or association, and a trustee, executor or administrator of an estate, or any other person empowered to act for another.

(36) "Rights" includes remedies.

(37) "Security interest" means an interest in personal property or fixtures which secures payment or performance of an obligation. The retention or reservation of title by a seller of goods notwithstanding shipment or delivery to the buyer (Section 2–401) is limited in effect to a reservation of a "security interest". The term also

includes any interest of a buyer of accounts or chattel paper which is subject to Article 9. The special property interest of a buyer of goods on identification of such goods to a contract for sale under Section 2–401 is not a "security interest", but a buyer may also acquire a "security interest" by complying with Article 9. Unless a lease or consignment is intended as security, reservation of title thereunder is not a "security interest" but a consignment is in any event subject to the provisions on consignment sales (Section 2–326). Whether a lease is intended as security is to be determined by the facts of each case; however, (a) the inclusion of an option to purchase does not of itself make the lease one intended for security, and (b) an agreement that upon compliance with the terms of the lease the leasee shall become or has the option to become the owner of the property for no additional consideration or for a nominal consideration does make the lease one intended for security.

(38) "Send" in connection with any writing or notice means to deposit in the mail or delivery for transmission by any other usual means of communication with postage or cost of transmission provided for and properly addressed and in the case of an instrument to an address specified thereon or otherwise agreed, or if there be none to any address reasonable under the circumstances. The receipt of any writing or notice within the time at which it would have arrived if properly sent has the effect of a proper sending.

(39) "Signed" includes any symbol executed or adopted by a party with present intention to authenticate a writing.

(40) "Surety" includes guarantor.

(41) "Telegram" includes a message transmitted by radio, teletype, cable, any mechanical method of transmission, or the like.

(42) "Term" means that portion of an agreement which relates to a particular matter.

(43) "Unauthorized" signature or indorsement means one made without actual, implied or apparent authority and includes a forgery.

(44) "Value". Except as otherwise provided with respect to negotiable instruments and bank collections (Sections 3–303, 4–208 and 4–209) a person gives "value" for rights if he acquires them

(a) in return for a binding commitment to extend credit or for the extension of immediately available credit whether or not drawn upon or whether or not a chargeback is provided for in the event of difficulties in collection; or

(b) as security for or in total or partial satisfaction of a pre-existing claim; or

(c) by accepting delivery pursuant to a pre-existing contract for purchase; or

(d) generally, in return for any consideration sufficient to support a simple contract.

(45) "Warehouse receipt" means a receipt issued by a person engaged in the business of storing goods for hire.

(46) "Written" or "writing" includes printing, typewriting or any other intentional reduction to tangible form. Amended in 1962, 1972 and 1977.

§ 1–202. Prima Facie Evidence by Third Party Documents.

A document in due form purporting to be a bill of lading, policy or certificate of insurance, official weigher's or inspector's certificate, consular invoice, or any other document authorized or required by the contract to be issued by a third party shall be prima facie evidence of its own authenticity and genuineness and of the facts stated in the document by the third party.

§ 1–203. Obligation of Good Faith.

Every contract or duty within this Act imposes an obligation of good faith in its performance or enforcement.

§ 1–204. Time; Reasonable Time; "Seasonably".

(1) Whenever this Act requires any action to be taken within a reasonable time, any time which is not manifestly unreasonable may be fixed by agreement.

(2) What is a reasonable time for taking any action depends on the nature, purpose and circumstances of such action.

(3) An action is taken "seasonably" when it is taken at or within the time agreed or if no time is agreed at or within a reasonable time.

§ 1–205. Course of Dealing and Usage of Trade.

(1) A course of dealing is a sequence of previous conduct between the parties to a particular transaction which is fairly to be regarded as establishing a common basis of understanding for interpreting their expressions and other conduct.

(2) A usage of trade is any practice or method of dealing having such regularity of observance in a place, vocation or trade as to justify an expectation that it will be observed with respect to the transaction in question. The existence and scope of such a usage are to be proved as facts. If it is established that such a usage is embodied in a written trade code or similar writing the interpretation of the writing is for the court.

(3) A course of dealing between parties and any usage of trade in the vocation or trade in which they are engaged or of which they are or should be aware give particular meaning to and supplement or qualify terms of an agreement.

(4) The express terms of an agreement and an applicable course of dealing or usage of trade shall be construed wherever reasonable as consistent with each other, but when such construction is unreasonable express terms control both course of dealing and usage of trade and course of dealing controls usage of trade.

(5) An applicable usage of trade in the place where any part of performance is to occur shall be used in interpreting the agreement as to that part of the performance.

(6) Evidence of a relevant usage of trade offered by one party is not admissible unless and until he has given the other party such notice as the court finds sufficient to prevent unfair surprise to the latter.

§ 1–206. Statute of Frauds for Kinds of Personal Property Not Otherwise Covered.

(1) Except in the cases described in subsection (2) of this section a contract for the sale of personal property is not enforceable by way of action or defense beyond five thousand dollars in amount or value of remedy unless there is some writing which indicates that a contract for sale has been made between the parties at a defined or stated price, reasonably identifies the subject matter, and is signed by the party against whom enforcement is sought or by his authorized agent.

(2) Subsection (1) of this section does not apply to contracts for the sale of goods (Section 2–201) nor of securities (Section 8–319) nor to security agreements (Section 9–203).

§ 1–207. Performance or Acceptance Under Reservation of Rights.

A party who with explicit reservation of rights performs or promises performance or assents to performance in a manner demanded or offered by the other party does not thereby prejudice the rights reserved. Such words as "without prejudice", "under protest" or the like are sufficient.

§ 1–208. Option to Accelerate at Will.

A term providing that one party or his successor in interest may accelerate payment or performance or require collateral or additional collateral "at will" or "when he deems himself insecure" or in words of similar import shall be construed to mean that he shall have power to do so only if he in good faith believes that the prospect of payment or performance is impaired. The burden of establishing lack of good faith is on the party against whom the power has been exercised.

§ 1–209. Subordinated Obligations.

An obligation may be issued as subordinated to payment of another obligation of the person obligated, or a creditor may subordinate his right to payment of an obligation by agreement with either the person obligated or another creditor of the person obligated. Such a subordination does not create a security interest as against either the common debtor or a subordinated creditor. This section shall be construed as declaring the law as it existed prior to the enactment of this section and not as modifying it. Added 1966.

Note: *This new section is proposed as an optional provision to make it clear that a subordination agreement does not create a security interest unless so intended.*

Article 2

SALES

Part 1 Short Title, Construction and Subject Matter

§ 2–101. Short Title.

This Article shall be known and may be cited as Uniform Commercial Code—Sales.

§ 2–102. Scope; Certain Security and Other Transactions Excluded From This Article.

Unless the context otherwise requires, this Article applies to transactions in goods; it does not apply to any transaction which although in the form of an unconditional contract to sell or present sale is intended to operate only as a security transaction nor does this Article impair or repeal any statute regulating sales to consumers, farmers or other specified classes of buyers.

§ 2–103. Definitions and Index of Definitions.

(1) In this Article unless the context otherwise requires

(a) "Buyer" means a person who buys or contracts to buy goods.

(b) "Good faith" in the case of a merchant means honesty in fact and the observance of reasonable commercial standards of fair dealing in the trade.

(c) "Receipt" of goods means taking physical possession of them.

(d) "Seller" means a person who sells or contracts to sell goods.

(2) Other definitions applying to this Article or to specified Parts thereof, and the sections in which they appear are:

"Acceptance". Section 2–606.
"Banker's credit". Section 2–325.
"Between merchants". Section 2–104.
"Cancellation". Section 2–106(4).
"Commercial unit". Section 2–105.
"Confirmed credit". Section 2–325.
"Conforming to contract". Section 2–106.
"Contract for sale". Section 2–106.
"Cover". Section 2–712.
"Entrusting". Section 2–403.
"Financing agency". Section 2–104.
"Future goods". Section 2–105.
"Goods". Section 2–105.
"Identification". Section 2–501.
"Installment contract". Section 2–612.
"Letter of Credit". Section 2–325.
"Lot". Section 2–105.
"Merchant". Section 2–104.
"Overseas". Section 2–323.

"Person in position of seller". Section 2–707.
"Present sale". Section 2–106.
"Sale". Section 2–106.
"Sale on approval". Section 2–326.
"Sale or return". Section 2–326.
"Termination". Section 2–106.

(3) The following definitions in other Articles apply to this Article:

"Check". Section 3–104.
"Consignee". Section 7–102.
"Consignor". Section 7–102.
"Consumer goods". Section 9–109.
"Dishonor". Section 3–507.
"Draft". Section 3–104.

(4) In addition Article 1 contains general definitions and principles of construction and interpretation applicable throughout this Article.

§ 2–104. Definitions: "Merchant"; "Between Merchants"; "Financing Agency".

(1) "Merchant" means a person who deals in goods of the kind or otherwise by his occupation holds himself out as having knowledge or skill peculiar to the practices or goods involved in the transaction or to whom such knowledge or skill may be attributed by his employment of an agent or broker or other intermediary who by his occupation holds himself out as having such knowledge or skill.

(2) "Financing agency" means a bank, finance company or other person who in the ordinary course of business makes advances against goods or documents of title or who by arrangement with either the seller or the buyer intervenes in ordinary course to make or collect payment due or claimed under the contract for sale, as by purchasing or paying the seller's draft or making advances against it or by merely taking it for collection whether or not documents of title accompany the draft. "Financing agency" includes also a bank or other person who similarly intervenes between persons who are in the position of seller and buyer in respect to the goods (Section 2–707).

(3) "Between merchants" means in any transaction with respect to which both parties are chargeable with the knowledge or skill of merchants.

§ 2–105. Definitions: Transferability; "Goods"; "Future" Goods; "Lot"; "Commercial Unit".

(1) "Goods" means all things (including specially manufactured goods) which are movable at the time of identification to the contract for sale other than the money in which the price is to be paid, investment securities (Article 8) and things in action. "Goods" also includes the unborn young of animals and growing crops and other identified things attached to realty as described in the section on goods to be severed from realty (Section 2–107).

(2) Goods must be both existing and identified before any interest in them can pass. Goods which are not both existing and identified are "future" goods. A purported present sale of future goods or of any interest therein operates as a contract to sell.

(3) There may be a sale of a part interest in existing identified goods.

(4) An undivided share in an identified bulk of fungible goods is sufficiently identified to be sold although the quantity of the bulk is not determined. Any agreed proportion of such a bulk or any quantity thereof agreed upon by number, weight or other measure may to the extent of the seller's interest in the bulk be sold to the buyer who then becomes an owner in common.

(5) "Lot" means a parcel or a single article which is the subject matter of a separate sale or delivery, whether or not it is sufficient to perform the contract.

(6) "Commercial unit" means such a unit of goods as by commercial usage is a single whole for purposes of sale and division of which materially impairs its character or value on the market or in use. A commercial unit may be a single article (as a machine) or a set of articles (as a suite of furniture or an assortment of sizes) or a quantity (as a bale, gross, or carload) or any other unit treated in use or in the relevant market as a single whole.

§ 2–106. Definitions: "Contract"; "Agreement"; "Contract for Sale"; "Sale"; "Present Sale"; "Conforming" to Contract; "Termination"; "Cancellation".

(1) In this Article unless the context otherwise requires "contract" and "agreement" are limited to those relating to the present or future sale of goods. "Contract for sale" includes both a present sale of goods and a contract to sell goods at a future time. A "sale" consists in the passing of title from the seller to the buyer for a price (Section 2–401). A "present sale" means a sale which is accomplished by the making of the contract.

(2) Goods or conduct including any part of a performance are "conforming" or conform to the contract when they are in accordance with the obligations under the contract.

(3) "Termination" occurs when either party pursuant to a power created by agreement or law puts an end to the contract otherwise than for its breach. On "termination" all obligations which are still executory on both sides are discharged but any right based on prior breach or performance survives.

(4) "Cancellation" occurs when either party puts an end to the contract for breach by the other and its effect is the same as that of "termination" except that the cancelling party also retains any remedy for breach of the whole contract or any unperformed balance.

§ 2–107. Goods to Be Severed From Realty: Recording.

(1) A contract for the sale of minerals or the like (including oil and gas) or a structure or its materials to be

removed from realty is a contract for the sale of goods within this Article if they are to be severed by the seller but until severance a purported present sale thereof which is not effective as a transfer of an interest in land is effective only as a contract to sell.

(2) A contract for the sale apart from the land of growing crops or other things attached to realty and capable of severance without material harm thereto but not described in subsection (1) or of timber to be cut is a contract for the sale of goods within this Article whether the subject matter is to be severed by the buyer or by the seller even though it forms part of the realty at the time of contracting, and the parties can by identification effect a present sale before severance.

(3) The provisions of this section are subject to any third party rights provided by the law relating to realty records, and the contract for sale may be executed and recorded as a document transferring an interest in land and shall then constitute notice to third parties of the buyer's rights under the contract for sale.

Part 2 Form, Formation and Readjustment of Contract

§ 2–201. Formal Requirements; Statute of Frauds.

(1) Except as otherwise provided in this section a contract for the sale of goods for the price of $500 or more is not enforceable by way of action or defense unless there is some writing sufficient to indicate that a contract for sale has been made between the parties and signed by the party against whom enforcement is sought or by his authorized agent or broker. A writing is not insufficient because it omits or incorrectly states a term agreed upon but the contract is not enforceable under this paragraph beyond the quantity of goods shown in such writing.

(2) Between merchants if within a reasonable time a writing in confirmation of the contract and sufficient against the sender is received and the party receiving it has reason to know its contents, it satisfies the requirements of subsection (1) against such party unless written notice of objection to its contents is given within ten days after it is received.

(3) A contract which does not satisfy the requirements of subsection (1) but which is valid in other respects is enforceable

(a) if the goods are to be specially manufactured for the buyer and are not suitable for sale to others in the ordinary course of the seller's business and the seller, before notice of repudiation is received and under circumstances which reasonably indicate that the goods are for the buyer, has made either a substantial beginning of their manufacture or commitments for their procurement; or
(b) if the party against whom enforcement is sought admits in his pleading, testimony or otherwise in court that a contract for sale was made, but the contract is not

enforceable under this provision beyond the quantity of goods admitted; or
(c) with respect to goods for which payment has been made and accepted or which have been received and accepted (Sec. 2–606).

§ 2–202. Final Written Expression: Parol or Extrinsic Evidence.

Terms with respect to which the confirmatory memoranda of the parties agree or which are otherwise set forth in a writing intended by the parties as a final expression of their agreement with respect to such terms as are included therein may not be contradicted by evidence of any prior agreement or of a contemporaneous oral agreement but may be explained or supplemented

(a) by course of dealing or usage of trade (Section 1–205) or by course of performance (Section 2–208); and
(b) by evidence of consistent additional terms unless the court finds the writing to have been intended also as a complete and exclusive statement of the terms of the agreement.

§ 2–203. Seals Inoperative.

The affixing of a seal to a writing evidencing a contract for sale or an offer to buy or sell goods does not constitute the writing a sealed instrument and the law with respect to sealed instruments does not apply to such a contract or offer.

§ 2–204. Formation in General.

(1) A contract for sale of goods may be made in any manner sufficient to show agreement, including conduct by both parties which recognizes the existence of such a contract.
(2) An agreement sufficient to constitute a contract for sale may be found even though the moment of its making is undetermined.
(3) Even though one or more terms are left open a contract for sale does not fail for indefiniteness if the parties have intended to make a contract and there is a reasonably certain basis for giving an appropriate remedy.

§ 2–205. Firm Offers.

An offer by a merchant to buy or sell goods in a signed writing which by its terms gives assurance that it will be held open is not revocable, for lack of consideration, during the time stated or if no time is stated for reasonable time, but in no event may such period of irrevocability exceed three months; but any such term of assurance on a form supplied by the offeree must be separately signed by the offeror.

§ 2–206. Offer and Acceptance in Formation of Contract.

(1) Unless other unambiguously indicated by the language or circumstances

(a) an offer to make a contract shall be construed as inviting acceptance in any manner and by any medium reasonable in the circumstances;

(b) an order or other offer to buy goods for prompt or current shipment shall be construed as inviting acceptance either by a prompt promise to ship or by the prompt or current shipment of conforming or nonconforming goods, but such a shipment of non-conforming goods does not constitute an acceptance if the seller seasonably notifies the buyer that the shipment is offered only as an accommodation to the buyer.

(2) Where the beginning of a requested performance is a reasonable mode of acceptance an offeror who is not notified of acceptance within a reasonable time may treat the offer as having lapsed before acceptance.

§ 2–207. Additional Terms in Acceptance or Confirmation.

(1) A definite and seasonable expression of acceptance or a written confirmation which is sent within a reasonable time operates as an acceptance even though it states terms additional to or different from those offered or agreed upon, unless acceptance is expressly made conditional on assent to the additional or different terms.

(2) The additional terms are to be construed as proposals for addition to the contract. Between merchants such terms become part of the contract unless:

(a) the offer expressly limits acceptance to the terms of the offer;

(b) they materially alter it; or

(c) notification of objection to them has already been given or is given within a reasonable time after notice of them is received.

(3) Conduct by both parties which recognizes the existence of a contract is sufficient to establish a contract for sale although the writings of the parties do not otherwise establish a contract. In such case the terms of the particular contract consist of those terms on which the writings of the parties agree, together with any supplementary terms incorporated under any other provisions of this Act.

§ 2–208. Course of Performance or Practical Construction.

(1) Where the contract for sale involves repeated occasions for performance by either party with knowledge of the nature of the performance and opportunity for objection to it by the other, any course of performance accepted or acquiesced in without objection shall be relevant to determine the meaning of the agreement.

(2) The express terms of the agreement and any such course of performance, as well as any course of dealing and usage of trade, shall be construed whenever reasonable as consistent with each other; but when such construction is unreasonable, express terms shall control course of performance and course of performance shall control both course of dealing and usage of trade (Section 1–205).

(3) Subject to the provisions of the next section on modification and waiver, such course of performance shall be relevant to show a waiver or modification of any term inconsistent with such course of performance.

§ 2–209. Modification, Rescission and Waiver.

(1) An agreement modifying a contract within this Article needs no consideration to be binding.

(2) A signed agreement which excludes modification or rescission except by a signed writing cannot be otherwise modified or rescinded, but except as between merchants such a requirement on a form supplied by the merchant must be separately signed by the other party.

(3) The requirements of the statute of frauds section of this Article (Section 2–201) must be satisfied if the contract as modified is within its provisions.

(4) Although an attempt at modification or rescission does not satisfy the requirements of subsection (2) or (3) it can operate as a waiver.

(5) A party who has made a waiver affecting an executory portion of the contract may retract the waiver by reasonable notification received by the other party that strict performance will be required of any term waived, unless the retraction would be unjust in view of a material change of position in reliance on the waiver.

§ 2–210. Delegation of Performance; Assignment of Rights.

(1) A party may perform his duty through a delegate unless otherwise agreed or unless the other party has a substantial interest in having his original promisor perform or control the acts required by the contract. No delegation of performance relieves the party delegating of any duty to perform or any liability for breach.

(2) Unless otherwise agreed all rights of either seller or buyer can be assigned except where the assignment would materially change the duty of the other party, or increase materially the burden or risk imposed on him by his contract, or impair materially his chance of obtaining return performance. A right to damages for breach of the whole contract or a right arising out of the assignor's due performance of his entire obligation can be assigned despite agreement otherwise.

(3) Unless the circumstances indicate the contrary a prohibition of assignment of "the contract" is to be construed as barring only the delegation to the assignee of the assignor's performance.

(4) An assignment of "the contract" or of "all my rights under the contract" or an assignment in similar general terms is an assignment of rights and unless the language or the circumstances (as in an assignment for security) indicate the contrary, it is a delegation of performance of the duties of the assignor and its acceptance by the

assignee constitutes a promise by him to perform those duties. This promise is enforceable by either the assignor or the other party to the original contract.

(5) The other party may treat any assignment which delegates performance as creating reasonable grounds for insecurity and may without prejudice to his rights against the assignor demand assurances from the assignee (Section 2–609).

Part 3 General Obligation and Construction of Contract

§ 2–301. General Obligations of Parties.

The obligation of the seller is to transfer and deliver and that of the buyer is to accept and pay in accordance with the contract.

§ 2–302. Unconscionable Contract or Clause.

(1) If the court as a matter of law finds the contract or any clause of the contract to have been unconscionable at the time it was made the court may refuse to enforce the contract, or it may enforce the remainder of the contract without the unconscionable clause, or it may so limit the application of any unconscionable clause as to avoid any unconscionable result.

(2) When it is claimed or appears to the court that the contract or any clause thereof may be unconscionable the parties shall be afforded a reasonable opportunity to present evidence as to its commercial setting, purpose and effect to aid the court in making the determination.

§ 2–303. Allocation or Division of Risks.

Where this Article allocates a risk or a burden as between the parties "unless otherwise agreed", the agreement may not only shift the allocation, but may also divide the risk or burden.

§ 2–304. Price Payable in Money, Goods, Realty, or Otherwise.

(1) The price can be made payable in money or otherwise. If it is payable in whole or in part in goods each party is a seller of the goods which he is to transfer.

(2) Even though all or part of the price is payable in an interest in realty the transfer of the goods and the seller's obligations with reference to them are subject to this Article, but not the transfer of the interest in realty or the transferor's obligations in connection therewith.

§ 2–305. Open Price Term.

(1) The parties if they so intend can conclude a contract for sale even though the price is not settled. In such a case the price is a reasonable price at the time for delivery if

(a) nothing is said as to price; or
(b) the price is left to be agreed by the parties and they fail to agree; or

(c) the price is to be fixed in terms of some agreed market or other standard as set or recorded by a third person or agency and it is not so set or recorded.

(2) A price to be fixed by the seller or by the buyer means a price for him to fix in good faith.

(3) When a price left to be fixed otherwise than by agreement of the parties fails to be fixed through fault of one party the other may at his option treat the contract as cancelled or himself fix a reasonable price.

(4) Where, however, the parties intend not to be bound unless the price be fixed or agreed and it is not fixed or agreed there is no contract. In such a case the buyer must return any goods already received or if unable so to do must pay their reasonable value at the time of delivery and the seller must return any portion of the price paid on account.

§ 2–306. Output, Requirements and Exclusive Dealings.

(1) A term which measures the quantity by the output of the seller or the requirements of the buyer means such actual output or requirements as may occur in good faith, except that no quantity unreasonably disproportionate to any stated estimate or in the absence of a stated estimate to any normal or otherwise comparable prior output or requirements may be tendered or demanded.

(2) A lawful agreement by either the seller or the buyer for exclusive dealing in the kind of goods concerned imposes unless otherwise agreed an obligation by the seller to use best efforts to supply the goods and by the buyer to use best efforts to promote their sale.

§ 2–307. Delivery in Single Lot or Several Lots.

Unless otherwise agreed all goods called for by a contract for sale must be tendered in a single delivery and payment is due only on such tender but where the circumstances give either party the right to make or demand delivery in lots the price if it can be apportioned may be demanded for each lot.

§ 2–308. Absence of Specified Place for Delivery.

Unless otherwise agreed

(a) the place for delivery of goods is the seller's place of business or if he has none his residence; but
(b) in a contract for sale of identified goods which to the knowledge of the parties at the time of contracting are in some other place, that place is the place for their delivery; and
(c) documents of title may be delivered through customary banking channels.

§ 2–309. Absence of Specific Time Provisions; Notice of Termination.

(1) The time for shipment or delivery or any other action under a contract if not provided in this Article or agreed upon shall be a reasonable time.

(2) Where the contract provides for successive performances but is indefinite in duration it is valid for a reasonable time but unless otherwise agreed may be terminated at any time by either party.

(3) Termination of a contract by one party except on the happening of an agreed event requires that reasonable notification be received by the other party and an agreement dispensing with notification is invalid if its operation would be unconscionable.

§ 2–310. Open Time for Payment or Running of Credit; Authority to Ship Under Reservation.

Unless otherwise agreed

(a) payment is due at the time and place at which the buyer is to receive the goods even though the place of shipment is the place of delivery; and

(b) if the seller is authorized to send the goods he may ship them under reservation, and may tender the documents of title, but the buyer may inspect the goods after their arrival before payment is due unless such inspection is inconsistent with the terms of the contract (Section 2–513); and

(c) if delivery is authorized and made by way of documents of title otherwise than by subsection (b) then payment is due at the time and place at which the buyer is to receive the documents regardless of where the goods are to be received; and

(d) where the seller is required or authorized to ship the goods on credit the credit period runs from the time of shipment but post-dating the invoice or delaying its dispatch will correspondingly delay the starting of the credit period.

§ 2–311. Options and Cooperation Respecting Performance.

(1) An agreement for sale which is otherwise sufficiently definite (subsection (3) of Section 2–204) to be a contract is not made invalid by the fact that it leaves particulars of performance to be specified by one of the parties. Any such specification must be made in good faith and within limits set by commercial reasonableness.

(2) Unless otherwise agreed specifications relating to assortment of the goods are at the buyer's option and except as otherwise provided in subsections (1)(c) and (3) of Section 2–319 specifications or arrangements relating to shipment are at the seller's option.

(3) Where such specification would materially affect the other party's performance but is not seasonably made or where one party's cooperation is necessary to the agreed performance of the other but is not seasonably forthcoming, the other party in addition to all other remedies

(a) is excused for any resulting delay in his own performance; and

(b) may also either proceed to perform in any reasonable manner or after the time for a material part of his own performance treat the failure to specify or to cooperate as a breach by failure to deliver or accept the goods.

§ 2–312. Warranty of Title and Against Infringement; Buyer's Obligation Against Infringement.

(1) Subject to subsection (2) there is in a contract for sale a warranty by the seller that

(a) the title conveyed shall be good, and its transfer rightful; and

(b) the goods shall be delivered free from any security interest or other lien or encumbrance of which the buyer at the time of contracting has no knowledge.

(2) A warranty under subsection (1) will be excluded or modified only by specific language or by circumstances which give the buyer reason to know that the person selling does not claim title in himself or that he is purporting to sell only such right or title as he or a third person may have.

(3) Unless otherwise agreed a seller who is a merchant regularly dealing in goods of the kind warrants that the goods shall be delivered free of the rightful claim of any third person by way of infringement or the like but a buyer who furnishes specifications to the seller must hold the seller harmless against any such claim which arises out of compliance with the specifications.

§ 2–313. Express Warranties by Affirmation, Promise, Description, Sample.

(1) Express warranties by the seller are created as follows:

(a) Any affirmation of fact or promise made by the seller to the buyer which relates to the goods and becomes part of the basis of the bargain creates an express warranty that the goods shall conform to the affirmation or promise.

(b) Any description of the goods which is made part of the basis of the bargain creates an express warranty that the goods shall conform to the description.

(c) Any sample or model which is made part of the basis of the bargain creates an express warranty that the whole of the goods shall conform to the sample or model.

(2) It is not necessary to the creation of an express warranty that the seller use formal words such as "warrant" or "guarantee" or that he have a specific intention to make a warranty, but an affirmation merely of the value of the goods or a statement purporting to be merely the seller's opinion or commendation of the goods does not create a warranty.

§ 2–314. Implied Warranty: Merchantability; Usage of Trade.

(1) Unless excluded or modified (Section 2–316), a warranty that the goods shall be merchantable is implied in a contract for their sale if the seller is a merchant with respect to goods of that kind. Under this section the serving for value of food or drink to be consumed either on the premises or elsewhere is a sale.

(2) Goods to be merchantable must be at least such as

(a) pass without objection in the trade under the contract description; and
(b) in the case of fungible goods, are of fair average quality within the description; and
(c) are fit for the ordinary purpose for which such goods are used; and
(d) run, within the variations permitted by the agreement, of even kind, quality and quantity within each unit and among all units involved; and
(e) are adequately contained, packaged, and labeled as the agreement may require; and
(f) conform to the promises or affirmations of fact made on the container or label if any.

(3) Unless excluded or modified (Section 2–316) other implied warranties may arise from course of dealing or usage of trade.

§ 2–315. Implied Warranty: Fitness for Particular Purpose.

Where the seller at the time of contracting has reason to know any particular purpose for which the goods are required and that the buyer is relying on the seller's skill or judgment to select or furnish suitable goods, there is unless excluded or modified under the next section an implied warranty that the goods shall be fit for such purpose.

§ 2–316. Exclusion or Modification of Warranties.

(1) Words or conduct relevant to the creation of an express warranty and words or conduct tending to negate or limit warranty shall be construed wherever reasonable as consistent with each other, but subject to the provisions of this Article on parol or extrinsic evidence (Section 2–202) negation or limitation is inoperative to the extent that such construction is unreasonable.
(2) Subject to subsection (3), to exclude or modify the implied warranty of merchantability or any part of it the language must mention merchantability and in case of a writing must be conspicuous, and to exclude or modify any implied warranty of fitness the exclusion must be by a writing and conspicuous. Language to exclude all implied warranties of fitness is sufficient if it states, for example, that "There are no warranties which extend beyond the description on the face hereof."
(3) Notwithstanding subsection (2)

(a) unless the circumstances indicate otherwise, all implied warranties are excluded by expressions like "as is", "with all faults" or other language which in common understanding calls the buyer's attention to the exclusion of warranties and makes plain that there is no implied warranty; and
(b) when the buyer before entering into the contract has examined the goods or the sample or model as fully as he desired or has refused to examine the goods there is no implied warranty with regard to defects which an examination ought in the circumstances to have revealed to him; and

(c) an implied warranty can also be excluded or modified by course of dealing or course of performance or usage of trade.

(4) Remedies for breach of warranty can be limited in accordance with the provisions of this Article on liquidation or limitation of damages and on contractual modification of remedy (Sections 2–718 and 2–719).

§ 2–317. Cumulation and Conflict of Warranties Express or Implied.

Warranties whether express or implied shall be construed as consistent with each other and as cumulative, but if such construction is unreasonable the intention of the parties shall determine which warranty is dominant. In ascertaining that intention the following rules apply:

(a) Exact or technical specifications displace an inconsistent sample or model or general language of description.
(b) A sample from an existing bulk displaces inconsistent general language of description.
(c) Express warranties displace inconsistent implied warranties other than an implied warranty of fitness for a particular purpose.

§ 2–318. Third Party Beneficiaries of Warranties Express or Implied.

Note: If this Act is introduced in the Congress of the United States this section should be omitted. (States to select one alternative.)

Alternative A

A seller's warranty whether express or implied extends to any natural person who is in the family or household of his buyer or who is a guest in his home if it is reasonable to expect that such person may use, consume or be affected by the goods and who is injured in person by breach of the warranty. The seller may not exclude or limit the operation of this section.

Alternative B

A seller's warranty whether express or implied extends to any natural person who may reasonably be expected to use, consume or be affected by the goods and who is injured in person by breach of the warranty. A seller may not exclude or limit the operation of this section.

Alternative C

A seller's warranty whether express or implied extends to any person who may reasonably be expected to use, consume or be affected by the goods and who is injured by breach of the warranty. A seller may not exclude or limit the operation of this section with respect to injury to the person of an individual to whom the warranty extends. As amended 1966.

§ 2–319. F.O.B. and F.A.S. Terms.

(1) Unless otherwise agreed the term F.O.B. (which means "free on board") at a named place, even though used only in connection with the stated price, is a delivery term under which

(a) when the term is F.O.B. the place of shipment, the seller must at that place ship the goods in the manner provided in this Article (Section 2–504) and bear the expense and risk of putting them into the possession of the carrier; or
(b) when the term is F.O.B. the place of destination, the seller must at his own expense and risk transport the goods to that place and there tender delivery of them in the manner provided in this Article (Section 2–503);
(c) when under either (a) or (b) the term is also F.O.B. vessel, car or other vehicle, the seller must in addition at his own expense and risk load the goods on board. If the term is F.O.B. vessel the buyer must name the vessel and in an appropriate case the seller must comply with the provisions of this Article on the form of bill of lading (Section 2–323).

(2) Unless otherwise agreed the term F.A.S. vessel (which means "free alongside") at a named port, even though used only in connection with the stated price, is a delivery term under which the seller must

(a) at his own expense and risk deliver the goods alongside the vessel in the manner usual in that port or on a dock designated and provided by the buyer; and
(b) obtain and tender a receipt for the goods in exchange for which the carrier is under a duty to issue a bill of lading.

(3) Unless otherwise agreed in any case falling within subsection (1)(a) or (c) or subsection (2) the buyer must seasonally give any needed instructions for making delivery, including when the term is F.A.S. or F.O.B. the loading berth of the vessel and in an appropriate case its name and sailing date. The seller may treat the failure of needed instructions as a failure of cooperation under this Article (Section 2–311). He may also at his option move the goods in any reasonable manner preparatory to delivery or shipment.
(4) Under the term F.O.B. vessel or F.A.S. unless otherwise agreed the buyer must make payment against tender of the required documents and the seller may not tender nor the buyer demand delivery of the goods in substitution for the documents.

§ 2–320. C.I.F. and C. & F. Terms.

(1) The term C.I.F. means that the price includes in a lump sum the cost of the goods and the insurance and freight to the named destination. The term C. & F. or C.F. means that the price so includes cost and freight to the named destination.
(2) Unless otherwise agreed and even though used only in connection with the stated price and destination, the term C.I.F. destination or its equivalent requires the seller at his own expense and risk to

(a) put the goods into the possession of a carrier at the port for shipment and obtain a negotiable bill or bills of lading covering the entire transportation to the named destination; and
(b) load the goods and obtain a receipt from the carrier (which may be contained in the bill of lading) showing that the freight has been paid or provided for; and
(c) obtain a policy or certificate of insurance, including any war risk insurance, of a kind and on terms then current at the port of shipment in the usual amount, in the currency of the contract, shown to cover the same goods covered by the bill of lading and providing for payment of loss to the order of the buyer or for the account of whom it may concern; but the seller may add to the price the amount of premium for any such war risk insurance; and
(d) prepare an invoice of the goods and procure any other documents required to effect shipment or to comply with the contract; and
(e) forward and tender with commercial promptness all the documents in due form and with any indorsement necessary to perfect the buyer's rights.

(3) Unless otherwise agreed the term C. & F. or its equivalent has the same effect and imposes upon the seller the same obligations and risks as a C.I.F. term except the obligation as to insurance.
(4) Under the term C.I.F. or C. & F. unless otherwise agreed the buyer must make payment against tender of the required documents and the seller may not tender nor the buyer demand delivery of the goods in substitution for the documents.

§ 2–321. C.I.F. or C. & F.: "Net Landed Weights"; "Payment on Arrival"; Warranty of Condition on Arrival.

Under a contract containing a term C.I.F. or C. & F.

(1) Where the price is based on or is to be adjusted according to "net landed weights", "delivered weights", "out turn" quantity or quality or the like, unless otherwise agreed the seller must reasonably estimate the price. The payment due on tender of the documents called for by the contract is the amount so estimated, but after final adjustment of the price a settlement must be made with commercial promptness.
(2) An agreement described in subsection (1) or any warranty of quality or condition of the goods on arrival places upon the seller the risk of ordinary deterioration, shrinkage and the like in transportation but has no effect on the place or time of identification to the contract for sale or delivery or on the passing of the risk of loss.
(3) Unless otherwise agreed where the contract provides for payment on or after arrival of the goods the seller must before payment allow such preliminary inspection as is feasible; but if the goods are lost delivery of the documents and payment are due when the goods should have arrived.

§ 2–322. Delivery "Ex-Ship".

(1) Unless otherwise agreed a term for delivery of goods "ex-ship" (which means from the carrying vessel) or in equivalent language is not restricted to a particular ship and requires delivery from a ship which has reached a place at the named port of destination where goods of the kind are usually discharged.

(2) Under such a term unless otherwise agreed

(a) the seller must discharge all liens arising out of the carriage and furnish the buyer with a direction which puts the carrier under a duty to deliver the goods; and

(b) the risk of loss does not pass to the buyer until the goods leave the ship's tackle or are otherwise properly unloaded.

§ 2–323. Form of Bill of Lading Required in Overseas Shipment; "Overseas".

(1) Where the contract contemplates overseas shipment and contains a term C.I.F. or C. & F. or F.O.B. vessel, the seller unless otherwise agreed must obtain a negotiable bill of lading stating that the goods have been loaded on board or, in the case of a term C.I.F. or C. & F., received for shipment.

(2) Where in a case within subsection (1) a bill of lading has been issued in a set of parts, unless otherwise agreed if the documents are not to be sent from abroad the buyer may demand tender of the full set; otherwise only one part of the bill of lading need be tendered. Even if the agreement expressly requires a full set

(a) due tender of a single part is acceptable within the provisions of this Article on cure of improper delivery (subsection (1) of Section 2–508); and

(b) even though the full set is demanded, if the documents are sent from abroad the person tendering an incomplete set may nevertheless require payment upon furnishing an indemnity which the buyer in good faith deems adequate.

(3) A shipment by water or by air or a contract contemplating such shipment is "overseas" insofar as by usage of trade or agreement it is subject to the commercial, financing or shipping practices characteristic of international deep water commerce.

§ 2–324. "No Arrival, No Sale" Term.

Under a term "no arrival, no sale" or terms of like meaning, unless otherwise agreed,

(a) the seller must properly ship conforming goods and if they arrive by any means he must tender them on arrival but he assumes no obligation that the goods will arrive unless he has caused the non-arrival; and

(b) where without fault of the seller the goods are in part lost or have so deteriorated as no longer to conform to the contract or arrive after the contract time, the buyer may proceed as if there had been casualty to identified goods (Section 2–613).

§ 2–325. "Letter of Credit" Term; "Confirmed Credit".

(1) Failure of the buyer seasonably to furnish an agreed letter of credit is a breach of the contract for sale.

(2) The delivery to seller of a proper letter of credit suspends the buyer's obligation to pay. If the letter of credit is dishonored, the seller may on seasonable notification to the buyer require payment directly from him.

(3) Unless otherwise agreed the term "letter of credit" or "banker's credit" in a contract for sale means an irrevocable credit issued by a financing agency of good repute and, where the shipment is overseas, of good international repute. The term "confirmed credit" means that the credit must also carry the direct obligation of such an agency which does business in the seller's financial market.

§ 2–326. Sale on Approval and Sale or Return; Consignment Sales and Rights of Creditors.

(1) Unless otherwise agreed, if delivered goods may be returned by the buyer even though they conform to the contract, the transaction is

(a) a "sale on approval" if the goods are delivered primarily for use, and

(b) a "sale or return" if the goods are delivered primarily for resale.

(2) Except as provided in subsection (3), goods held on approval are not subject to the claims of the buyer's creditors until acceptance; goods held on sale or return are subject to such claims while in the buyer's possession.

(3) Where goods are delivered to a person for sale and such person maintains a place of business at which he deals in goods of the kind involved, under a name other than the name of the person making delivery, then with respect to claims of creditors of the person conducting the business the goods are deemed to be on sale or return. The provisions of this subsection are applicable even though an agreement purports to reserve title to the person making delivery until payment or resale or uses such words as "on consignment" or "on memorandum". However, this subsection is not applicable if the person making delivery

(a) complies with an applicable law providing for a consignor's interest or the like to be evidenced by a sign, or

(b) establishes that the person conducting the business is generally known by his creditors to be substantially engaged in selling the goods of others, or

(c) complies with the filing provisions of the Article on Secured Transactions (Article 9).

(4) Any "or return" term of a contract for sale is to be treated as a separate contract for sale within the statute of frauds section of this Article (Section 2–201) and as contradicting the sale aspect of the contract within the provisions of this Article on parol or extrinsic evidence (Section 2–202).

§ 2–327. Special Incidents of Sale on Approval and Sale or Return.

(1) Under a sale on approval unless otherwise agreed

(a) although the goods are identified to the contract the risk of loss and the title do not pass to the buyer until acceptance; and

(b) use of the goods consistent with the purpose of trial is not acceptance but failure seasonably to notify the seller of election to return the goods is acceptance, and if the goods conform to the contract acceptance of any part is acceptance of the whole; and

(c) after due notification of election to return, the return is at the seller's risk and expense but a merchant buyer must follow any reasonable instructions.

(2) Under a sale or return unless otherwise agreed

(a) the option to return extends to the whole or any commercial unit of the goods while in substantially their original condition, but must be exercised seasonably; and

(b) the return is at the buyer's risk and expense.

§ 2–328. Sale by Auction.

(1) In a sale by auction if goods are put up in lots each lot is the subject of a separate sale.

(2) A sale by auction is complete when the auctioneer so announces by the fall of the hammer or in other customary manner. Where a bid is made while the hammer is falling in acceptance of a prior bid the auctioneer may in his discretion reopen the bidding or declare the goods sold under the bid on which the hammer was falling.

(3) Such a sale is with reserve unless the goods are in explicit terms put up without reserve. In an auction with reserve the auctioneer may withdraw the goods at any time until he announces completion of the sale. In an auction without reserve, after the auctioneer calls for bids on an article or lot, that article or lot cannot be withdrawn unless no bid is made within a reasonable time. In either case a bidder may retract his bid until the auctioneer's announcement of completion of the sale, but a bidder's retraction does not revive any previous bid.

(4) If the auctioneer knowingly receives a bid on the seller's behalf or the seller makes or procures such a bid, and notice has not been given that liberty for such bidding is reserved, the buyer may at his option avoid the sale or take the goods at the price of the last good faith bid prior to the completion of the sale. This subsection shall not apply to any bid at a forced sale.

Part 4 Title, Creditors and Good Faith Purchasers

§ 2–401. Passing of Title; Reservation for Security; Limited Application of This Section.

Each provision of this Article with regard to the rights, obligations and remedies of the seller, the buyer, purchasers or other third parties applies irrespective of title to the goods except where the provision refers to such title. Insofar as situations are not covered by the other provisions of this Article and matters concerning title became material the following rules apply:

(1) Title to goods cannot pass under a contract for sale prior to their identification to the contract (Section 2–501), and unless otherwise explicitly agreed the buyer acquires by their identification a special property as limited by this Act. Any retention or reservation by the seller of the title (property) in goods shipped or delivered to the buyer is limited in effect to a reservation of a security interest. Subject to these provisions and to the provisions of the Article on Secured Transactions (Article 9), title to goods passes from the seller to the buyer in any manner and on any conditions explicitly agreed on by the parties.

(2) Unless otherwise explicitly agreed title passes to the buyer at the time and place at which the seller completes his performance with reference to the physical delivery of the goods, despite any reservation of a security interest and even though a document of title is to be delivered at a different time or place; and in particular and despite any reservation of a security interest by the bill of lading

(a) if the contract requires or authorizes the seller to send the goods to the buyer but does not require him to deliver them at destination, title passes to the buyer at the time and place of shipment; but

(b) if the contract requires delivery at destination, title passes on tender there.

(3) Unless otherwise explicitly agreed where delivery is to be made without moving the goods,

(a) if the seller is to deliver a document of title, title passes at the time when and the place where he delivers such documents; or

(b) if the goods are at the time of contracting already identified and no documents are to be delivered, title passes at the time and place of contracting.

(4) A rejection or other refusal by the buyer to receive or retain the goods, whether or not justified, or a justified revocation of acceptance revests title to the goods in the seller. Such revesting occurs by operation of law and is not a "sale".

§ 2–402. Rights of Seller's Creditors Against Sold Goods.

(1) Except as provided in subsections (2) and (3), rights of unsecured creditors of the seller with respect to goods which have been identified to a contract for sale are subject to the buyer's rights to recover the goods under this Article (Sections 2–502 and 2–716).

(2) A creditor of the seller may treat a sale or an identification of goods to a contract for sale as void if as against him a retention of possession by the seller is fraudulent under any rule of law of the state where the goods are situated, except that retention of possession in good faith and current course of trade by a merchant-seller for a

commercially reasonable time after a sale or identification is not fraudulent.

(3) Nothing in this Article shall be deemed to impair the rights of creditors of the seller

(a) under the provisions of the Article on Secured Transactions (Article 9); or

(b) where identification to the contract or delivery is made not in current course of trade but in satisfaction of or as security for a pre-existing claim for money, security or the like and is made under circumstances which under any rule of law of the state where the goods are situated would apart from this Article constitute the transaction a fraudulent transfer or voidable preference.

§ 2–403. Power to Transfer; Good Faith Purchase of Goods; "Entrusting".

(1) A purchaser of goods acquires all title which his transferor had or had power to transfer except that a purchaser of a limited interest acquires rights only to the extent of the interest purchased. A person with voidable title has power to transfer a good title to a good faith purchaser for value. When goods have been delivered under a transaction of purchase the purchaser has such power even though

(a) the transferor was deceived as to the identity of the purchaser, or

(b) the delivery was in exchange for a check which is later dishonored, or

(c) it was agreed that the transaction was to be a "cash sale", or

(d) the delivery was procured through fraud punishable as larcenous under the criminal law.

(2) Any entrusting of possession of goods to a merchant who deals in goods of that kind gives him power to transfer all rights of the entruster to a buyer in ordinary course of business.

(3) "Entrusting" includes any delivery and any acquiescence in retention of possession regardless of any condition expressed between the parties to the delivery or acquiescence and regardless of whether the procurement of the entrusting or the possessor's disposition of the goods have been such as to be larcenous under the criminal law.

(4) The rights of other purchasers of goods and of lien creditors are governed by the Articles on Secured Transactions (Article 9), Bulk Transfers (Article 6) and Documents of Title (Article 7).

Part 5 Performance

§ 2–501. Insurable Interest in Goods; Manner of Identification of Goods.

(1) The buyer obtains a special property and an insurable interest in goods by identification of existing goods as goods to which the contract refers even though the goods so identified are nonconforming and he has an option to return or reject them. Such identification can be made at any time and in any manner explicitly agreed to by the parties. In the absence of explicit agreement identification occurs

(a) when the contract is made if it is for the sale of goods already existing and identified;

(b) if the contract is for the sale of future goods other than those described in paragraph (c), when goods are shipped, marked or otherwise designated by the seller as goods to which the contract refers;

(c) when the crops are planted or otherwise become growing crops or the young are conceived if the contract is for the sale of unborn young to be born within twelve months after contracting or for the sale of crops to be harvested within twelve months or the next normal harvest season after contracting whichever is longer.

(2) The seller retains an insurable interest in goods so long as title to or any security interest in the goods remains in him and where the identification is by the seller alone he may until default or insolvency or notification to the buyer that the identification is final substitute other goods for those identified.

(3) Nothing in this section impairs any insurable interest recognized under any other statute or rule of law.

§ 2–502. Buyer's Right to Goods on Seller's Insolvency.

(1) Subject to subsection (2) and even though the goods have not been shipped a buyer who has paid a part or all of the price of goods in which he has a special property under the provisions of the immediately preceding section may on making and keeping good a tender of any unpaid portion of their price recover them from the seller if the seller becomes insolvent within ten days after receipt of the first installment on their price.

(2) If the identification creating his special property has been made by the buyer he acquires the right to recover the goods only if they conform to the contract for sale.

§ 2–503. Manner of Seller's Tender of Delivery.

(1) Tender of delivery requires that the seller put and hold conforming goods at the buyer's disposition and give the buyer any notification reasonably necessary to enable him to take delivery. The manner, time and place for tender are determined by the agreement and this Article, and in particular

(a) tender must be at a reasonable hour, and if it is of goods they must be kept available for the period reasonably necessary to enable the buyer to take possession; but

(b) unless otherwise agreed the buyer must furnish facilities reasonably suited to the receipt of the goods.

(2) Where the case is within the next section respecting shipment tender requires that the seller comply with its provisions.

(3) Where the seller is required to deliver at a particular destination tender requires that he comply with subsection (1) and also in any appropriate case tender documents as described in subsections (4) and (5) of this section.

(4) Where goods are in the possession of a bailee and are to be delivered without being moved

(a) tender requires that the seller either tender a negotiable document of title covering such goods or procure acknowledgment by the bailee of the buyer's right to possession of the goods; but

(b) tender to the buyer of a non-negotiable document of title or of a written direction to the bailee to deliver is sufficient tender unless the buyer seasonably objects, and receipt by the bailee of notification of the buyer's rights fixes those rights as against the bailee and all third persons; but risk of loss of the goods and of any failure by the bailee to honor the non-negotiable document of title or to obey the direction remains on the seller until the buyer has had a reasonable time to present the document or direction, and a refusal by the bailee to honor the document or to obey the direction defeats the tender.

(5) Where the contract requires the seller to deliver documents

(a) he must tender all such documents in correct form, except as provided in this Article with respect to bills of lading in a set (subsection (2) of Section 2–323); and

(b) tender through customary banking channels is sufficient and dishonor of a draft accompanying the documents constitutes non-acceptance or rejection.

§ 2–504. Shipment by Seller.

Where the seller is required or authorized to send the goods to the buyer and the contract does not require him to deliver them at a particular destination, then unless otherwise agreed he must

(a) put the goods in the possession of such a carrier and make such a contract for their transportation as may be reasonable having regard to the nature of the goods and other circumstances of the case; and

(b) obtain and promptly deliver or tender in due form any document necessary to enable the buyer to obtain possession of the goods or otherwise required by the agreement or by usage of trade; and

(c) promptly notify the buyer of the shipment.

Failure to notify the buyer under paragraph (c) or to make a proper contract under paragraph (a) is a ground for rejection only if material delay or loss ensues.

§ 2–505. Seller's Shipment Under Reservation.

(1) Where the seller has identified goods to the contract by or before shipment:

(a) his procurement of a negotiable bill of lading to his own order or otherwise reserves in him a security interest in the goods. His procurement of the bill to the order of a financing agency or of the buyer indicates in addition only the seller's expectation of transferring that interest to the person named.

(b) a non-negotiable bill of lading to himself or his nominee reserves possession of the goods as security but except in a case of conditional delivery (subsection (2) of Section 2–507) a non-negotiable bill of lading naming the buyer as consignee reserves no security interest even though the seller retains possession of the bill of lading.

(2) When shipment by the seller with reservation of a security interest is in violation of the contract for sale it constitutes an improper contract for transportation within the preceding section but impairs neither the rights given to the buyer by shipment and identification of the goods to the contract nor the seller's powers as a holder of a negotiable document.

§ 2–506. Rights of Financing Agency.

(1) A financing agency by paying or purchasing for value a draft which relates to a shipment of goods acquires to the extent of the payment or purchase and in addition to its own rights under the draft and any document of title securing it any rights of the shipper in the goods including the right to stop delivery and the shipper's right to have the draft honored by the buyer.

(2) The right to reimbursement of a financing agency which has in good faith honored or purchased the draft under commitment to or authority from the buyer is not impaired by subsequent discovery of defects with reference to any relevant document which was apparently regular on its face.

§ 2–507. Effect of Seller's Tender; Delivery on Condition.

(1) Tender of delivery is a condition to the buyer's duty to accept the goods and, unless otherwise agreed, to his duty to pay for them. Tender entitles the seller to acceptance of the goods and to payment according to the contract.

(2) Where payment is due and demanded on the delivery to the buyer of goods or documents of title, his right as against the seller to retain or dispose of them is conditional upon his making the payment due.

§ 2–508. Cure by Seller of Improper Tender or Delivery; Replacement.

(1) Where any tender or delivery by the seller is rejected because non-conforming and the time for performance has not yet expired, the seller may seasonably notify the buyer of his intention to cure and may then within the contract time make a conforming delivery.

(2) Where the buyer rejects a non-conforming tender which the seller had reasonable grounds to believe would be acceptable with or without money allowance the seller may if he seasonably notifies the buyer have a further reasonable time to substitute a conforming tender.

§ 2–509. Risk of Loss in the Absence of Breach.

(1) Where the contract requires or authorizes the seller to ship the goods by carrier

(a) if it does not require him to deliver them at a particular destination, the risk of loss passes to the buyer when the goods are duly delivered to the carrier even though the shipment is under reservation (Section 2–505); but

(b) if it does require him to deliver them at a particular destination and the goods are there duly tendered while in the possession of the carrier, the risk of loss passes to the buyer when the goods are there duly so tendered as to enable the buyer to take delivery.

(2) Where the goods are held by a bailee to be delivered without being moved, the risk of loss passes to the buyer

(a) on his receipt of a negotiable document of title covering the goods; or

(b) on acknowledgment by the bailee of the buyer's right to possession of the goods; or

(c) after his receipt of a non-negotiable document of title or other written direction to deliver, as provided in subsection (4)(b) of Section 2–503.

(3) In any case not within subsection (1) or (2), the risk of loss passes to the buyer on his receipt of the goods if the seller is a merchant; otherwise, the risk passes to the buyer on tender of delivery.

(4) The provisions of this section are subject to contrary agreement of the parties and to the provisions of this Article on sale on approval (Section 2–327) and on effect of breach on risk of loss (Section 2–510).

§ 2–510. Effect of Breach on Risk of Loss.

(1) Where a tender or delivery of goods so fails to conform to the contract as to give a right of rejection the risk of their loss remains on the seller until cure or acceptance.

(2) Where the buyer rightfully revokes acceptance he may to the extent of any deficiency in his effective insurance coverage treat the risk of loss as having rested on the seller from the beginning.

(3) Where the buyer as to conforming goods already identified to the contract for sale repudiates or is otherwise in breach before risk of their loss has passed to him, the seller may to the extent of any deficiency in his effective insurance coverage treat the risk of loss as resting on the buyer for a commercially reasonable time.

§ 2–511. Tender of Payment by Buyer; Payment by Check.

(1) Unless otherwise agreed tender of payment is a condition to the seller's duty to tender and complete any delivery.

(2) Tender of payment is sufficient when made by any means or in any manner current in the ordinary course of business unless the seller demands payment in legal tender and gives any extension of time reasonably necessary to procure it.

(3) Subject to the provisions of this Act on the effect of an instrument on an obligation (Section 3–802), payment by check is conditional and is defeated as between the parties by dishonor of the check on due presentment.

§ 2–512. Payment by Buyer Before Inspection.

(1) Where the contract requires payment before inspection non-conformity of the goods does not excuse the buyer from so making payment unless

(a) the non-conformity appears without inspection; or

(b) despite tender of the required documents the circumstances would justify injunction against honor under the provisions of this Act (Section 5–114).

(2) Payment pursuant to subsection (1) does not constitute an acceptance of goods or impair the buyer's right to inspect or any of his remedies.

§ 2–513. Buyer's Right to Inspection of Goods.

(1) Unless otherwise agreed and subject to subsection (3), where goods are tendered or delivered or identified to the contract for sale, the buyer has a right before payment or acceptance to inspect them at any reasonable place and time and in any reasonable manner. When the seller is required or authorized to send the goods to the buyer, the inspection may be after their arrival.

(2) Expenses of inspection must be borne by the buyer but may be recovered from the seller if the goods do not conform and are rejected.

(3) Unless otherwise agreed and subject to the provisions of this Article on C.I.F. contracts (subsection (3) of Section 2–321), the buyer is not entitled to inspect the goods before payment of the price when the contract provides

(a) for delivery "C.O.D." or on other like terms; or

(b) for payment against documents of title, except where such payment is due only after the goods are to become available for inspection.

(4) A place or method of inspection fixed by the parties is presumed to be exclusive but unless otherwise expressly agreed it does not postpone identification or shift the place for delivery or for passing the risk of loss. If compliance becomes impossible, inspection shall be as provided in this section unless the place or method fixed was clearly intended as an indispensable condition failure of which avoids the contract.

§ 2–514. When Documents Deliverable on Acceptance; When on Payment.

Unless otherwise agreed documents against which a draft is drawn are to be delivered to the drawee on acceptance of the draft if it is payable more than three days after presentment; otherwise, only on payment.

§ 2–515. Preserving Evidence of Goods in Dispute.

In furtherance of the adjustment of any claim or dispute

(a) either party on reasonable notification to the other and for the purpose of ascertaining the facts and preserving evidence has the right to inspect, test and sample the goods including such of them as may be in the possession or control of the other; and
(b) the parties may agree to a third party inspection or survey to determine the conformity or condition of the goods and may agree that the findings shall be binding upon them in any subsequent litigation or adjustment.

Part 6 Breach, Repudiation and Excuse

§ 2–601. Buyer's Rights on Improper Delivery.

Subject to the provisions of this Article on breach in installment contracts (Section 2–612) and unless otherwise agreed under the sections on contractual limitations of remedy (Sections 2–718 and 2–719), if the goods or the tender of delivery fail in any respect to conform to the contract, the buyer may

(a) reject the whole; or
(b) accept the whole; or
(c) accept any commercial unit or units and reject the rest.

§ 2–602. Manner and Effect of Rightful Rejection.

(1) Rejection of goods must be within a reasonable time after their delivery or tender. It is ineffective unless the buyer seasonably notifies the seller.
(2) Subject to the provisions of the two following sections on rejected goods (Sections 2–603 and 2–604),

(a) after rejection any exercise of ownership by the buyer with respect to any commercial unit is wrongful as against the seller; and
(b) if the buyer has before rejection taken physical possession of goods in which he does not have a security interest under the provisions of this Article (subsection (3) of Section 2–711), he is under a duty after rejection to hold them with reasonable care at the seller's disposition for a time sufficient to permit the seller to remove them; but
(c) the buyer has no further obligations with regard to goods rightfully rejected.

(3) The seller's rights with respect to goods wrongfully rejected are governed by the provisions of this Article on seller's remedies in general (Section 2–703).

§ 2–603. Merchant Buyer's Duties as to Rightfully Rejected Goods.

(1) Subject to any security interest in the buyer (subsection (3) of Section 2–711), when the seller has no agent or place of business at the market of rejection a merchant buyer is under a duty after rejection of goods in his possession or control to follow any reasonable instructions received from the seller with respect to the goods and in the absence of such instructions to make reasonable efforts to sell them for the seller's account if they are perishable or threaten to decline in value speedily. Instructions are not reasonable if on demand indemnity for expenses is not forthcoming.
(2) When the buyer sells goods under subsection (1), he is entitled to reimbursement from the seller or out of the proceeds for reasonable expenses of caring for and selling them, and if the expenses include no selling commission then to such commission as is usual in the trade or if there is none to a reasonable sum not exceeding ten per cent on the gross proceeds.
(3) In complying with this section the buyer is held only to good faith and good faith conduct hereunder is neither acceptance nor conversion nor the basis of an action for damages.

§ 2–604. Buyer's Options as to Salvage of Rightfully Rejected Goods.

Subject to the provisions of the immediately preceding section on perishables if the seller gives no instructions within a reasonable time after notification of rejection the buyer may store the rejected goods for the seller's account or reship them to him or resell them for the seller's account with reimbursement as provided in the preceding section. Such action is not acceptance or conversion.

§ 2–605. Waiver of Buyer's Objections by Failure to Particularize.

(1) The buyer's failure to state in connection with rejection a particular defect which is ascertainable by reasonable inspection precludes him from relying on the unstated defect to justify rejection or to establish breach

(a) where the seller could have cured it if stated seasonably; or
(b) between merchants when the seller has after rejection made a request in writing for a full and final written statement of all defects on which the buyer proposes to rely.

(2) Payment against documents made without reservation of rights precludes recovery of the payment for defects apparent on the face of the documents.

§ 2–606. What Constitutes Acceptance of Goods.

(1) Acceptance of goods occurs when the buyer

(a) after a reasonable opportunity to inspect the goods signifies to the seller that the goods are conforming or that he will take or retain them in spite of their nonconformity; or
(b) fails to make an effective rejection (subsection (1) of Section 2–602), but such acceptance does not occur until the buyer has had a reasonable opportunity to inspect them; or

(c) does any act inconsistent with the seller's ownership; but if such act is wrongful as against the seller it is an acceptance only if ratified by him.

(2) Acceptance of a part of any commercial unit is acceptance of that entire unit.

§ 2–607. Effect of Acceptance; Notice of Breach; Burden of Establishing Breach After Acceptance; Notice of Claim or Litigation to Person Answerable Over.

(1) The buyer must pay at the contract rate for any goods accepted.

(2) Acceptance of goods by the buyer precludes rejection of the goods accepted and if made with knowledge of a non-conformity cannot be revoked because of it unless the acceptance was on the reasonable assumption that the non-conformity would be seasonably cured but acceptance does not of itself impair any other remedy provided by this Article for non-conformity.

(3) Where a tender has been accepted

(a) the buyer must within a reasonable time after he discovers or should have discovered any breach notify the seller of breach or be barred from any remedy; and
(b) if the claim is one for infringement or the like (subsection (3) of Section 2–312) and the buyer is sued as a result of such a breach he must so notify the seller within a reasonable time after he receives notice of the litigation or be barred from any remedy over for liability established by the litigation.

(4) The burden is on the buyer to establish any breach with respect to the goods accepted.

(5) Where the buyer is sued for breach of a warranty or other obligation for which his seller is answerable over

(a) he may give his seller written notice of the litigation. If the notice states that the seller may come in and defend and that if the seller does not do so he will be bound in any action against him by his buyer by any determination of fact common to the two litigations, then unless the seller after seasonable receipt of the notice does come in and defend he is so bound.
(b) if the claim is one for infringement or the like (subsection (3) of Section 2–312) the original seller may demand in writing that his buyer turn over to him control of the litigation including settlement or else be barred from any remedy over and if he also agrees to bear all expense and to satisfy any adverse judgment, then unless the buyer after seasonable receipt of the demand does turn over control the buyer is so barred.

(6) The provisions of subsections (3), (4) and (5) apply to any obligation of a buyer to hold the seller harmless against infringement or the like (subsection (3) of Section 2–312).

§ 2–608. Revocation of Acceptance in Whole or in Part.

(1) The buyer may revoke his acceptance of a lot or commercial unit whose non-conformity substantially impairs its value to him if he has accepted it

(a) on the reasonable assumption that its non-conformity would be cured and it has not been seasonably cured; or
(b) without discovery of such non-conformity if his acceptance was reasonably induced either by the difficulty of discovery before acceptance or by the seller's assurances.

(2) Revocation of acceptance must occur within a reasonable time after the buyer discovers or should have discovered the ground for it and before any substantial change in condition of the goods which is not caused by their own defects. It is not effective until the buyer notifies the seller of it.

(3) A buyer who so revokes has the same rights and duties with regard to the goods involved as if he had rejected them.

§ 2–609. Right to Adequate Assurance of Performance.

(1) A contract for sale imposes an obligation on each party that the other's expectation of receiving due performance will not be impaired. When reasonable grounds for insecurity arise with respect to the performance of either party the other may in writing demand adequate assurance of due performance and until he receives such assurance may if commercially reasonable suspend any performance for which he has not already received the agreed return.

(2) Between merchants the reasonableness of grounds for insecurity and the adequacy of any assurance offered shall be determined according to commercial standards.

(3) Acceptance of any improper delivery or payment does not prejudice the aggrieved party's right to demand adequate assurance of future performance.

(4) After receipt of a justified demand failure to provide within a reasonable time not exceeding thirty days such assurance of due performance as is adequate under the circumstances of the particular case is a repudiation of the contract.

§ 2–610. Anticipatory Repudiation.

When either party repudiates the contract with respect to a performance not yet due the loss of which will substantially impair the value of the contract to the other, the aggrieved party may

(a) for a commercially reasonable time await performance by the repudiating party; or
(b) resort to any remedy for breach (Section 2–703 or Section 2–711), even though he has notified the repudiating party that he would await the latter's performance and has urged retraction; and
(c) in either case suspend his own performance or proceed in accordance with the provisions of this Article on the seller's right to identify goods to the contract notwithstanding breach or to salvage unfinished goods (Section 2–704).

§ 2–611. Retraction of Anticipatory Repudiation.

(1) Until the repudiating party's next performance is due he can retract his repudiation unless the aggrieved party has since the repudiation cancelled or materially changed his position or otherwise indicated that he considers the repudiation final.

(2) Retraction may be by any method which clearly indicates to the aggrieved party that the repudiating party intends to perform, but must include any assurance justifiably demanded under the provisions of this Article (Section 2–609).

(3) Retraction reinstates the repudiating party's rights under the contract with due excuse and allowance to the aggrieved party for any delay occasioned by the repudiation.

§ 2–612. "Installment Contract"; Breach.

(1) An "installment contract" is one which requires or authorizes the delivery of goods in separate lots to be separately accepted, even though the contract contains a clause "each delivery is a separate contract" or its equivalent.

(2) The buyer may reject any installment which is nonconforming if the non-conformity substantially impairs the value of that installment and cannot be cured or if the non-conformity is a defect in the required documents; but if the non-conformity does not fall within subsection (3) and the seller gives adequate assurance of its cure the buyer must accept that installment.

(3) Whenever non-conformity or default with respect to one or more installments substantially impairs the value of the whole contract there is a breach of the whole. But the aggrieved party reinstates the contract if he accepts a non-conforming installment without seasonably notifying of cancellation or if he brings an action with respect only to past installments or demands performance as to future installments.

§ 2–613. Casualty to Identified Goods.

Where the contract requires for its performance goods identified when the contract is made, and the goods suffer casualty without fault of either party before the risk of loss passes to the buyer, or in a proper case under a "no arrival, no sale" term (Section 2–324) then

(a) if the loss is total the contract is avoided; and

(b) if the loss is partial or the goods have so deteriorated as no longer to conform to the contract the buyer may nevertheless demand inspection and at his option either treat the contract as avoided or accept the goods with due allowance from the contract price for the deterioration or the deficiency in quantity but without further right against the seller.

§ 2–614. Substituted Performance.

(1) Where without fault of either party the agreed berthing, loading, or unloading facilities fail or an agreed type of carrier becomes unavailable or the agreed manner of delivery otherwise becomes commercially impractica-

ble but a commercially reasonable substitute is available, such substitute performance must be tendered and accepted.

(2) If the agreed means or manner of payment fails because of domestic or foreign governmental regulation, the seller may withhold or stop delivery unless the buyer provides a means or manner of payment which is commercially a substantial equivalent. If delivery has already been taken, payment by the means or in the manner provided by the regulation discharges the buyer's obligation unless the regulation is discriminatory, oppressive or predatory.

§ 2–615. Excuse by Failure of Presupposed Conditions.

Except so far as a seller may have assumed a greater obligation and subject to the preceding section on substituted performance:

(a) Delay in delivery or non-delivery in whole or in part by a seller who complies with paragraphs (b) and (c) is not a breach of his duty under a contract for sale if performance as agreed has been made impracticable by the occurrence of a contingency the non-occurrence of which was a basic assumption on which the contract was made or by compliance in good faith with any applicable foreign or domestic governmental regulation or order whether or not it later proves to be invalid.

(b) Where the causes mentioned in paragraph (a) affect only a part of the seller's capacity to perform, he must allocate production and deliveries among his customers but may at his option include regular customers not then under contract as well as his own requirements for further manufacture. He may so allocate in any manner which is fair and reasonable.

(c) The seller must notify the buyer seasonably that there will be delay or non-delivery and, when allocation is required under paragraph (b), of the estimated quota thus made available for the buyer.

§ 2–616. Procedure on Notice Claiming Excuse.

(1) Where the buyer receives notification of a material or indefinite delay or an allocation justified under the preceding section he may by written notification to the seller as to any delivery concerned, and where the prospective deficiency substantially impairs the value of the whole contract under the provisions of this Article relating to breach of installment contracts (Section 2–612), then also as to the whole,

(a) terminate and thereby discharge any unexecuted portion of the contract; or

(b) modify the contract by agreeing to take his available quota in substitution.

(2) If after receipt of such notification from the seller the buyer fails so to modify the contract within a reasonable time not exceeding thirty days the contract lapses with respect to any deliveries affected.

(3) The provisions of this section may not be negated by agreement except in so far as the seller has assumed a greater obligation under the preceding section.

Part 7 Remedies

§ 2–701. Remedies for Breach of Collateral Contracts Not Impaired.

Remedies for breach of any obligation or promise collateral or ancillary to a contract for sale are not impaired by the provisions of this Article.

§ 2–702. Seller's Remedies on Discovery of Buyer's Insolvency.

(1) Where the seller discovers the buyer to be insolvent he may refuse delivery except for cash including payment for all goods theretofore delivered under the contract, and stop delivery under this Article (Section 2–705).

(2) Where the seller discovers that the buyer has received goods on credit while insolvent he may reclaim the goods upon demand made within ten days after the receipt, but if misrepresentation of solvency has been made to the particular seller in writing within three months before delivery the ten day limitation does not apply. Except as provided in this subsection the seller may not base a right to reclaim goods on the buyer's fraudulent or innocent misrepresentation of solvency or of intent to pay.

(3) The seller's right to reclaim under subsection (2) is subject to the rights of a buyer in ordinary course or other good faith purchaser under this Article (Section 2–403). Successful reclamation of goods excludes all other remedies with respect to them.

§ 2–703. Seller's Remedies in General.

Where the buyer wrongfully rejects or revokes acceptance of goods or fails to make a payment due on or before delivery or repudiates with respect to a part or the whole, then with respect to any goods directly affected and, if the breach is of the whole contract (Section 2–612), then also with respect to the whole undelivered balance, the aggrieved seller may

(a) withhold delivery of such goods;

(b) stop delivery by any bailee as hereafter provided (Section 2–705);

(c) proceed under the next section respecting goods still unidentified to the contract;

(d) resell and recover damages as hereafter provided (Section 2–706);

(e) recover damages for non-acceptance (Section 2–708) or in a proper case the price (Section 2–709);

(f) cancel.

§ 2–704. Seller's Right to Identify Goods to the Contract Notwithstanding Breach or to Salvage Unfinished Goods.

(1) An aggrieved seller under the preceding section may

(a) identify to the contract conforming goods not already identified if at the time he learned of the breach they are in his possession or control;

(b) treat as the subject of resale goods which have demonstrably been intended for the particular contract even though those goods are unfinished.

(2) Where the goods are unfinished an aggrieved seller may in the exercise of reasonable commercial judgment for the purposes of avoiding loss and of effective realization either complete the manufacture and wholly identify the goods to the contract or cease manufacture and resell for scrap or salvage value or proceed in any other reasonable manner.

§ 2–705. Seller's Stoppage of Delivery in Transit or Otherwise.

(1) The seller may stop delivery of goods in the possession of a carrier or other bailee when he discovers the buyer to be insolvent (Section 2–702) and may stop delivery of carload, truckload, planeload or larger shipments of express or freight when the buyer repudiates or fails to make a payment due before delivery or if for any other reason the seller has a right to withhold or reclaim the goods.

(2) As against such buyer the seller may stop delivery until

(a) receipt of the goods by the buyer; or

(b) acknowledgment to the buyer by any bailee of the goods except a carrier that the bailee holds the goods for the buyer; or

(c) such acknowledgment to the buyer by a carrier by reshipment or as warehouseman; or

(d) negotiation to the buyer of any negotiable document of title covering the goods.

(3) (a) To stop delivery the seller must so notify as to enable the bailee by reasonable diligence to prevent delivery of the goods.

(b) After such notification the bailee must hold and deliver the goods according to the directions of the seller but the seller is liable to the bailee for any ensuing charges or damages.

(c) If a negotiable document of title has been issued for goods the bailee is not obliged to obey a notification to stop until surrender of the document.

(d) A carrier who has issued a non-negotiable bill of lading is not obliged to obey a notification to stop received from a person other than the consignor.

§ 2–706. Seller's Resale Including Contract for Resale.

(1) Under the conditions stated in Section 2–703 on seller's remedies, the seller may resell the goods concerned or the undelivered balance thereof. Where the resale is made in good faith and in a commercially reasonable manner the seller may recover the difference between the resale price and the contract price together with any incidental damages allowed under the provisions of this Article (Section 2–710), but less expenses saved in consequence of the buyer's breach.

(2) Except as otherwise provided in subsection (3) or unless otherwise agreed resale may be at public or private

sale including sale by way of one or more contracts to sell or of identification to an existing contract of the seller. Sale may be as a unit or in parcels and at any time and place and on any terms but every aspect of the sale including the method, manner, time, place and terms must be commercially reasonable. The resale must be reasonably identified as referring to the broken contract, but it is not necessary that the goods be in existence or that any or all of them have been identified to the contract before the breach.

(3) Where the resale is at private sale the seller must give the buyer reasonable notification of his intention to resell.

(4) Where the resale is at public sale

(a) only identified goods can be sold except where there is a recognized market for a public sale of futures in goods of the kind; and

(b) it must be made at a usual place or market for public sale if one is reasonably available and except in the case of goods which are perishable or threaten to decline in value speedily the seller must give the buyer reasonable notice of the time and place of the resale; and

(c) if the goods are not to be within the view of those attending the sale the notification of sale must state the place where the goods are located and provide for their reasonable inspection by prospective bidders; and

(d) the seller may buy.

(5) A purchaser who buys in good faith at a resale takes the goods free of any rights of the original buyer even though the seller fails to comply with one or more of the requirements of this section.

(6) The seller is not accountable to the buyer for any profit made on any resale. A person in the position of a seller (Section 2–707) or a buyer who has rightfully rejected or justifiably revoked acceptance must account for any excess over the amount of his security interest, as hereinafter defined (subsection (3) of Section 2–711).

§ 2–707. "Person in the Position of a Seller".

(1) A "person in the position of a seller" includes as against a principal an agent who has paid or become responsible for the price of goods on behalf of his principal or anyone who otherwise holds a security interest or other right in goods similar to that of a seller.

(2) A person in the position of a seller may as provided in this Article withhold or stop delivery (Section 2–705) and resell (Section 2–706) and recover incidental damages (Section 2–710).

§ 2–708. Seller's Damages for Non-Acceptance or Repudiation.

(1) Subject to subsection (2) and to the provisions of this Article with respect to proof of market price (Section 2–723), the measure of damages for non-acceptance or repudiation by the buyer is the difference between the market price at the time and place for tender and the unpaid contract price together with any incidental damages provided in this Article (Section 2–710), but less expenses saved in consequence of the buyer's breach.

(2) If the measure of damages provided in subsection (1) is inadequate to put the seller in as good a position as performance would have done then the measure of damages is the profit (including reasonable overhead) which the seller would have made from full performance by the buyer, together with any incidental damages provided in this Article (Section 2–710), due allowance for costs reasonably incurred and due credit for payments or proceeds of resale.

§ 2–709. Action for the Price.

(1) When the buyer fails to pay the price as it becomes due the seller may recover, together with any incidental damages under the next section, the price

(a) of goods accepted or of conforming goods lost or damaged within a commercially reasonable time after risk of their loss has passed to the buyer; and

(b) of goods identified to the contract if the seller is unable after reasonable effort to resell them at a reasonable price or the circumstances reasonably indicate that such effort will be unavailing.

(2) Where the seller sues for the price he must hold for the buyer any goods which have been identified to the contract and are still in his control except that if resale becomes possible he may resell them at any time prior to the collection of the judgment. The net proceeds of any such resale must be credited to the buyer and payment of the judgment entitles him to any goods not resold.

(3) After the buyer has wrongfully rejected or revoked acceptance of the goods or has failed to make a payment due or has repudiated (Section 2–610), a seller who is held not entitled to the price under this section shall nevertheless be awarded damages for non-acceptance under the preceding section.

§ 2–710. Seller's Incidental Damages.

Incidental damages to an aggrieved seller include any commercially reasonable charges, expenses or commissions incurred in stopping delivery, in the transportation, care and custody of goods after the buyer's breach, in connection with return or resale of the goods or otherwise resulting from the breach.

§ 2–711. Buyer's Remedies in General; Buyer's Security Interest in Rejected Goods.

(1) Where the seller fails to make delivery or repudiates or the buyer rightfully rejects or justifiably revokes acceptance then with respect to any goods involved, and with respect to the whole if the breach goes to the whole contract (Section 2–612), the buyer may cancel and whether or not he has done so may in addition to recovering so much of the price as has been paid

(a) "cover" and have damages under the next section as to all the goods affected whether or not they have been identified to the contract; or

(b) recover damages for non-delivery as provided in this Article (Section 2–713).

(2) Where the seller fails to deliver or repudiates the buyer may also

(a) if the goods have been identified recover them as provided in this Article (Section 2–502); or
(b) in a proper case obtain specific performance or replevy the goods as provided in this Article (Section 2–716).

(3) On rightful rejection or justifiable revocation of acceptance a buyer has a security interest in goods in his possession or control for any payments made on their price and any expenses reasonably incurred in their inspection, receipt, transportation, care and custody and may hold such goods and resell them in like manner as an aggrieved seller (Section 2–706).

§ 2–712. "Cover"; Buyer's Procurement of Substitute Goods.

(1) After a breach within the preceding section the buyer may "cover" by making in good faith and without unreasonable delay any reasonable purchase of or contract to purchase goods in substitution for those due from the seller.
(2) The buyer may recover from the seller as damages the difference between the cost of cover and the contract price together with any incidental or consequential damages as hereinafter defined (Section 2–715), but less expenses saved in consequence of the seller's breach.
(3) Failure of the buyer to effect cover within this section does not bar him from any other remedy.

§ 2–713. Buyer's Damages for Non-Delivery or Repudiation.

(1) Subject to provisions of this Article with respect to the proof of market price (Section 2–723), the measure of damages for non-delivery or repudiation by the seller is the difference between the market price at the time when the buyer learned of the breach and the contract price together with any incidental and consequential damages provided in this Article (Section 2–715), but less expenses saved in consequence of the seller's breach.
(2) Market price is to be determined as of the place for tender or, in cases of rejection after arrival or revocation of acceptance, as of the place of arrival.

§ 2–714. Buyer's Damages for Breach in Regard to Accepted Goods.

(1) Where the buyer has accepted goods and given notification (subsection (3) of Section 2–607) he may recover as damages for any non-conformity of tender the loss resulting in the ordinary course of events from the seller's breach as determined in any manner which is reasonable.
(2) The measure of damages for breach of warranty is the difference at the time and place of acceptance between

the value of the goods accepted and the value they would have had if they had been as warranted, unless special circumstances show proximate damages of a different amount.
(3) In a proper case any incidental and consequential damages under the next section may be recovered.

§ 2–715. Buyer's Incidental and Consequential Damages.

(1) Incidental damages resulting from the seller's breach include expenses reasonably incurred in inspection, receipt, transportation and care and custody of goods rightfully rejected, any commercially reasonable charges, expenses or commissions in connection with effecting cover and any other reasonable expense incident to the delay or other breach.
(2) Consequential damages resulting from the seller's breach include

(a) any loss resulting from general or particular requirements and needs of which the seller at the time of contracting had reason to know and which could not reasonably be prevented by cover or otherwise; and
(b) injury to person or property proximately resulting from any breach of warranty.

§ 2–716. Buyer's Right to Specific Performance or Replevin.

(1) Specific performance may be decreed where the goods are unique or in other proper circumstances.
(2) The decree for specific performance may include such terms and conditions as to payment of the price, damages, or other relief as the court may deem just.
(3) The buyer has a right of replevin for goods identified to the contract if after reasonable effort he is unable to effect cover for such goods or the circumstances reasonably indicate that such effort will be unavailing or if the goods have been shipped under reservation and satisfaction of the security interest in them has been made or tendered.

§ 2–717. Deduction of Damages From the Price.

The buyer on notifying the seller of his intention to do so may deduct all or any part of the damages resulting from any breach of the contract from any part of the price still due under the same contract.

§ 2–718. Liquidation or Limitation of Damages; Deposits

(1) Damages for breach by either party may be liquidated in the agreement but only at an amount which is reasonable in the light of the anticipated or actual harm caused by the breach, the difficulties of proof of loss, and the inconvenience or nonfeasibility of otherwise obtaining an adequate remedy. A term fixing unreasonably large liquidated damages is void as a penalty.
(2) Where the seller justifiably withholds delivery of goods because of the buyer's breach, the buyer is entitled

to restitution of any amount by which the sum of his payments exceeds

(a) the amount to which the seller is entitled by virtue of terms liquidating the seller's damages in accordance with subsection (1), or
(b) in the absence of such terms, twenty per cent of the value of the total performance for which the buyer is obligated under the contract or $500, whichever is smaller.

(3) The buyer's right to restitution under subsection (2) is subject to offset to the extent that the seller establishes

(a) a right to recover damages under the provisions of this Article other than subsection (1), and
(b) the amount or value of any benefits received by the buyer directly or indirectly by reason of the contract.

(4) Where a seller has received payment in goods their reasonable value or the proceeds of their resale shall be treated as payments for the purposes of subsection (2); but if the seller has notice of the buyer's breach before reselling goods received in part performance, his resale is subject to the conditions laid down in this Article on resale by an aggrieved seller (Section 2–706).

§ 2–719. Contractual Modification or Limitation of Remedy.

(1) Subject to the provisions of subsection (2) and (3) of this section and of the preceding section on liquidation and limitation of damages,

(a) the agreement may provide for remedies in addition to or in substitution for those provided in this Article and may limit or alter the measure of damages recoverable under this Article, as by limiting the buyer's remedies to return of the goods and repayment of the price or to repair and replacement of non-conforming goods or parts; and
(b) resort to a remedy as provided is optional unless the remedy is expressly agreed to be exclusive, in which case it is the sole remedy.

(2) Where circumstances cause an exclusive or limited remedy to fail of its essential purpose, remedy may be had as provided in this Act.
(3) Consequential damages may be limited or excluded unless the limitation or exclusion is unconscionable. Limitation of consequential damages for injury to the person in the case of consumer goods is prima facie unconscionable but limitation of damages where the loss is commercial is not.

§ 2–720. Effect of "Cancellation" or "Rescission" on Claims for Antecedent Breach.

Unless the contrary intention clearly appears, expressions of "cancellation" or "rescission" of the contract or the like shall not be construed as a renunciation or discharge of any claim in damages for an antecedent breach.

§ 2–721. Remedies for Fraud.

Remedies for material misrepresentation or fraud include all remedies available under this Article for non-fraudulent breach. Neither rescission or a claim for rescission of the contract for sale nor rejection or return of the goods shall bar or be deemed inconsistent with a claim for damages or other remedy.

§ 2–722. Who Can Sue Third Parties for Injury to Goods.

Where a third party so deals with goods which have been identified to a contract for sale as to cause actionable injury to a party to that contract

(a) a right of action against the third party is in either party to the contract for sale who has title to or a security interest or a special property or an insurable interest in the goods; and if the goods have been destroyed or converted a right of action is also in the party who either bore the risk of loss under the contract for sale or has since the injury assumed that risk as against the other;
(b) if at the time of the injury the party plaintiff did not bear the risk of loss as against the other party to the contract for sale and there is no arrangement between them for disposition of the recovery, his suit or settlement is subject to his own interest, as a fiduciary for the other party to the contract;
(c) either party may with the consent of the other sue for the benefit of whom it may concern.

§ 2–723. Proof of Market Price: Time and Place

(1) If an action based on anticipatory repudiation comes to trial before the time for performance with respect to some or all of the goods, any damages based on market price (Section 2–708 or Section 2–713) shall be determined according to the price of such goods prevailing at the time when the aggrieved party learned of the repudiation.
(2) If evidence of a price prevailing at the times or places described in this Article is not readily available the price prevailing within any reasonable time before or after the time described or at any other place which in commercial judgment or under usage of trade would serve as a reasonable substitute for the one described may be used, making any proper allowance for the cost of transporting the goods to or from such other place.
(3) Evidence of a relevant price prevailing at a time or place other than the one described in this Article offered by one party is not admissible unless and until he has given the other party such notice as the court finds sufficient to prevent unfair surprise.

§ 2–724. Admissibility of Market Quotations.

Whenever the prevailing price or value of any goods regularly bought and sold in any established commodity market is in issue, reports in official publications or trade journals or in newspapers or periodicals of general circulation published as the reports of such market shall be admissible in evidence. The circumstances of the preparation of such a report may be shown to affect its weight but not its admissibility.

§ 2-725. Statute of Limitations in Contracts for Sale.

(1) An action for breach of any contract for sale must be commenced within four years after the cause of action has accrued. By the original agreement the parties may reduce the period of limitation to not less than one year but may not extend it.

(2) A cause of action occurs when the breach occurs, regardless of the aggrieved party's lack of knowledge of the breach. A breach of warranty occurs when tender of delivery is made, except that where a warranty explicitly extends to future performance of the goods and discovery of the breach must await the time of such performance the cause of action accrues when the breach is or should have been discovered.

(3) Where an action commenced within the time limited by subsection (1) is so terminated as to leave available another remedy by another action for the same breach such other action may be commenced after the expiration of the time limited and within six months after the termination of the first action unless the termination resulted from voluntary discontinuance or from dismissal for failure or neglect to prosecute.

(4) This section does not alter the law on tolling of the statute of limitations nor does it apply to causes of action which have accrued before this Act becomes effective.

Article 3

COMMERCIAL PAPER

Part 1 Short Title, Form and Interpretation

§ 3-101. Short Title.

This Article shall be known and may be cited as Uniform Commercial Code—Commercial Paper.

§ 3-102. Definitions and Index of Definitions.

(1) In this Article unless the context otherwise requires

(a) "Issue" means the first delivery of an instrument to a holder or a remitter.

(b) An "order" is a direction to pay and must be more than an authorization or request. It must identify the person to pay with reasonable certainty. It may be addressed to one or more such persons jointly or in the alternative but not in succession.

(c) A "promise" is an undertaking to pay and must be more than an acknowledgment of an obligation.

(d) "Secondary party" means a drawer or endorser.

(e) "Instrument" means a negotiable instrument.

(2) Other definitions applying to this Article and the sections in which they appear are:

"Acceptance". Section 3-410.
"Accommodation party". Section 3-415.
"Alteration". Section 3-407.
"Certificate of deposit". Section 3-104.
"Certification". Section 3-411.
"Check". Section 3-104.
"Definite time". Section 3-109.
"Dishonor". Section 3-507.
"Draft". Section 3-104.
"Holder in due course". Section 3-302.
"Negotiation". Section 3-202.
"Note". Section 3-104.
"Notice of dishonor". Section 3-508.
"On demand". Section 3-108.
"Presentment". Section 3-504.
"Protest". Section 3-509.
"Restrictive Indorsement". Section 3-205.
"Signature". Section 3-401.

(3) The following definitions in other Articles apply to this Article:

"Account". Section 4-104.
"Banking Day". Section 4-104.
"Clearing House". Section 4-104.
"Collecting Bank". Section 4-105.
"Customer". Section 4-104.
"Depositary Bank". Section 4-105.
"Documentary Draft". Section 4-104.
"Intermediary Bank". Section 4-105.
"Item". Section 4-104.
"Midnight deadline". Section 4-104.
"Payor Bank". Section 4-105.

(4) In addition Article 1 contains general definitions and principles of construction and interpretation applicable throughout this Article.

§ 3-103. Limitations on Scope of Article.

(1) This Article does not apply to money, documents of title or investment securities.

(2) The provisions of this Article are subject to the provisions of the Article on Bank Deposits and Collections (Article 4) and Secured Transactions (Article 9).

§ 3-104. Form of Negotiable Instruments; "Draft"; "Check"; "Certificate of Deposit"; "Note".

(1) Any writing to be a negotiable instrument within this Article must

(a) be signed by the maker or drawer; and

(b) contain an unconditional promise or order to pay a sum certain in money and no other promise, order, obligation or power given by the maker or drawer except as authorized by this Article; and

(c) be payable on demand or at a definite time; and

(d) be payable to order or to bearer.

(2) A writing which complies with the requirements of this section is

(a) a "draft" ("bill of exchange") if it is an order;
(b) a "check" if it is a draft drawn on a bank and payable on demand;
(c) a "certificate of deposit" if it is an acknowledgment by a bank of receipt of money with an engagement to repay it;
(d) a "note" if it is a promise other than a certificate of deposit.

(3) As used in other Articles of this Act, and as the context may require, the terms "draft", "check", "certificate of deposit" and "note" may refer to instruments which are not negotiable within this Article as well as to instruments which are so negotiable.

§ 3–105. When Promise or Order Unconditional.

(1) A promise or order otherwise unconditional is not made conditional by the fact that the instrument

(a) is subject to implied or constructive conditions; or
(b) states its consideration, whether performed or promised, or the transaction which gave rise to the instrument, or that the promise or order is made or the instrument matures in accordance with or "as per" such transaction; or
(c) refers to or states that it arises out of a separate agreement or refers to a separate agreement for rights as to prepayment or acceleration; or
(d) states that it is drawn under a letter of credit; or
(e) states that it is secured, whether by mortgage, reservation of title or otherwise; or
(f) indicates a particular account to be debited or any other fund or source from which reimbursement is expected; or
(g) is limited to payment out of a particular fund or the proceeds of a particular source, if the instrument is issued by a government or governmental agency or unit; or
(h) is limited to payment out of the entire assets of a partnership, unincorporated association, trust or estate by or on behalf of which the instrument is issued.

(2) A promise or order is not unconditional if the instrument

(a) states that it is subject to or governed by any other agreement; or
(b) states that it is to be paid only out of a particular fund or source except as provided in this section.

§ 3–106. Sum Certain.

(1) The sum payable is a sum certain even though it is to be paid

(a) with stated interest or by stated installments; or
(b) with stated different rates of interest before and after default or a specified date; or

(c) with a stated discount or addition if paid before or after the date fixed for payment, or
(d) with exchange or less exchange, whether at a fixed rate or at the current rate; or
(e) with costs of collection or an attorney's fee or both upon default.

(2) Nothing in this section shall validate any term which is otherwise illegal.

§ 3–107. Money.

(1) An instrument is payable in money if the medium of exchange in which it is payable is money at the time the instrument is made. An instrument payable in "currency" or "current funds" is payable in money.
(2) A promise or order to pay a sum stated in a foreign currency is for a sum certain in money and, unless a different medium of payment is specified in the instrument, may be satisfied by payment of that number of dollars which the stated foreign currency will purchase at the buying sight rate for that currency on the day on which the instrument is payable or, if payable on demand, on the day of demand. If such an instrument specifies a foreign currency as the medium of payment the instrument is payable in that currency.

§ 3–108. Payable on Demand.

Instruments payable on demand include those payable at sight or on presentation and those in which no time for payment is stated.

§ 3–109. Definite Time.

(1) An instrument is payable at a definite time if by its terms it is payable

(a) on or before a stated date or at a fixed period after a stated date; or
(b) at a fixed period after sight; or
(c) at a definite time subject to any acceleration; or
(d) at a definite time subject to extension at the option of the holder, or to extension to a further definite time at the option of the maker or acceptor or automatically upon or after a specified act or event.

(2) An instrument which by its terms is otherwise payable only upon an act or event uncertain as to time of occurrence is not payable at a definite time even though the act or event has occurred.

§ 3–110. Payable to Order.

(1) An instrument is payable to order when by its terms it is payable to the order or assigns of any person therein specified with reasonable certainty, or to him or his order, or when it is conspicuously designated on its face as "exchange" or the like and names a payee. It may be payable to the order of

(a) the maker or drawer; or

(b) the drawee; or

(c) a payee who is not maker, drawer or drawee; or

(d) two or more payees together or in the alternative; or

(e) an estate, trust or fund, in which case it is payable to the order of the representative of such estate, trust or fund or his successors; or

(f) an office, or an officer by his title as such in which case it is payable to the principal but the incumbent of the office or his successors may act as if he or they were the holder; or

(g) a partnership or unincorporated association, in which case it is payable to the partnership or association and may be indorsed or transferred by any person thereto authorized.

(2) An instrument not payable to order is not made so payable by such words as "payable upon return of this instrument properly indorsed."

(3) An instrument made payable both to order and to bearer is payable to order unless the bearer words are handwritten or typewritten.

§ 3–111. Payable to Bearer.

An instrument is payable to bearer when by its terms it is payable to

(a) bearer or the order of bearer; or

(b) a specified person or bearer; or

(c) "cash" or the order of "cash", or any other indication which does not purport to designate a specific payee.

§ 3–112. Terms and Omissions Not Affecting Negotiability.

(1) The negotiability of an instrument is not affected by

(a) the omission of a statement of any consideration or of the place where the instrument is drawn or payable; or

(b) a statement that collateral has been given to secure obligations either on the instrument or otherwise of an obligor on the instrument or that in case of default on those obligations the holder may realize on or dispose of the collateral; or

(c) a promise or power to maintain or protect collateral or to give additional collateral; or

(d) a term authorizing a confession of judgment on the instrument if it is not paid when due; or

(e) a term purporting to waive the benefit of any law intended for the advantage or protection of any obligor; or

(f) a term in a draft providing that the payee by indorsing or cashing it acknowledges full satisfaction of an obligation of the drawer; or

(g) a statement in a draft drawn in a set of parts (Section 3–801) to the effect that the order is effective only if no other part has been honored.

(2) Nothing in this section shall validate any term which is otherwise illegal.

§ 3–113. Seal.

An instrument otherwise negotiable is within this Article even though it is under a seal.

§ 3–114. Date, Antedating, Postdating.

(1) The negotiability of an instrument is not affected by the fact that it is undated, antedated or postdated.

(2) Where an instrument is antedated or postdated the time when it is payable is determined by the stated date if the instrument is payable on demand or at a fixed period after date.

(3) Where the instrument or any signature thereon is dated, the date is presumed to be correct.

§ 3–115. Incomplete Instruments.

(1) When a paper whose contents at the time of signing show that it is intended to become an instrument is signed while still incomplete in any necessary respect it cannot be enforced until completed, but when it is completed in accordance with authority given it is effective as completed.

(2) If the completion is unauthorized the rules as to material alteration apply (Section 3–407), even though the paper was not delivered by the maker or drawer; but the burden of establishing that any completion is unauthorized is on the party so asserting.

§ 3–116. Instruments Payable to Two or More Persons.

An instrument payable to the order of two or more persons

(a) if in the alternative is payable to any one of them and may be negotiated, discharged or enforced by any of them who has possession of it;

(b) if not in the alternative is payable to all of them and may be negotiated, discharged or enforced only by all of them.

§ 3–117. Instruments Payable With Words of Description.

An instrument made payable to a named person with the addition of words describing him

(a) as agent or officer of a specified person is payable to his principal but the agent or officer may act as if he were the holder;

(b) as any other fiduciary for a specified person or purpose is payable to the payee and may be negotiated, discharged or enforced by him;

(c) in any other manner is payable to the payee unconditionally and the additional words are without effect on subsequent parties.

§ 3–118. Ambiguous Terms and Rules of Construction.

The following rules apply to every instrument:

(a) Where there is doubt whether the instrument is a draft or a note the holder may treat it as either. A draft drawn on the drawer is effective as a note.

(b) Handwritten terms control typewritten and printed terms, and typewritten control printed.

(c) Words control figures except that if the words are ambiguous figures control.

(d) Unless otherwise specified a provision for interest means interest at the judgment rate at the place of payment from the date of the instrument, or if it is undated from the date of issue.

(e) Unless the instrument otherwise specifies two or more persons who sign as maker, acceptor or drawer or indorser and as a part of the same transaction are jointly and severally liable even though the instrument contains such words as "I promise to pay."

(f) Unless otherwise specified consent to extension authorizes a single extension for not longer than the original period. A consent to extension, expressed in the instrument, is binding on secondary parties and accommodation makers. A holder may not exercise his option to extend an instrument over the objection of a maker or acceptor or other party who in accordance with Section 3–604 tenders full payment when the instrument is due.

§ 3–119. Other Writings Affecting Instrument.

(1) As between the obligor and his immediate obligee or any transferee the terms of an instrument may be modified or affected by any other written agreement executed as a part of the same transaction, except that a holder in due course is not affected by any limitation of his rights arising out of the separate written agreement if he had no notice of the limitation when he took the instrument.

(2) A separate agreement does not affect the negotiability of an instrument.

§ 3–120. Instruments "Payable Through" Bank.

An instrument which states that it is "payable through" a bank or the like designates that bank as a collecting bank to make presentment but does not of itself authorize the bank to pay the instrument.

§ 3–121. Instruments Payable at Bank.

Note: If this Act is introduced in the Congress of the United States this section should be omitted. (States to select either alternative)

Alternative A—

A note or acceptance which states that it is payable at a bank is the equivalent of a draft drawn on the bank payable when it falls due out of any funds of the maker or acceptor in current account or otherwise available for such payment.

Alternative B—

A note or acceptance which states that it is payable at a bank is not of itself an order or authorization to the bank to pay it.

§ 3–122. Accrual of Cause of Action.

(1) A cause of action against a maker or an acceptor accrues

(a) in the case of a time instrument on the day after maturity;

(b) in the case of a demand instrument upon its date or, if no date is stated, on the date of issue.

(2) A cause of action against the obligor of a demand or time certificate of deposit accrues upon demand, but demand on a time certificate may not be made until on or after the date of maturity.

(3) A cause of action against a drawer of a draft or an indorser of any instrument accrues upon demand following dishonor of the instrument. Notice of dishonor is a demand.

(4) Unless an instrument provides otherwise, interest runs at the rate provided by law for a judgment

(a) in the case of a maker, acceptor or other primary obligor of a demand instrument, from the date of demand;

(b) in all other cases from the date of accrual of the cause of action.

Part 2 Transfer and Negotiation

§ 3–201. Transfer: Right to Indorsement.

(1) Transfer of an instrument vests in the transferee such rights as the transferor has therein, except that a transferee who has himself been a party to any fraud or illegality affecting the instrument or who as a prior holder had notice of a defense or claim against it cannot improve his position by taking from a later holder in due course.

(2) A transfer of a security interest in an instrument vests the foregoing rights in the transferee to the extent of the interest transferred.

(3) Unless otherwise agreed any transfer for value of an instrument not then payable to bearer gives the transferee the specifically enforceable right to have the unqualified indorsement of the transferor. Negotiation takes effect only when the indorsement is made and until that time there is no presumption that the transferee is the owner.

§ 3–202. Negotiation.

(1) Negotiation is the transfer of an instrument in such form that the transferee becomes a holder. If the instrument is payable to order it is negotiated by delivery with any necessary indorsement; if payable to bearer it is negotiated by delivery.

(2) An indorsement must be written by or on behalf of the holder and on the instrument or on a paper so firmly affixed thereto as to become a part thereof.

(3) An indorsement is effective for negotiation only when it conveys the entire instrument or any unpaid residue. If it purports to be of less it operates only as a partial assignment.

(4) Words of assignment, condition, waiver, guaranty, limitation or disclaimer of liability and the like accompanying an indorsement do not affect its character as an indorsement.

§ 3–203. Wrong or Misspelled Name.

Where an instrument is made payable to a person under a misspelled name or one other than his own he may indorse in that name or his own or both; but signature in both names may be required by a person paying or giving value for the instrument.

§ 3–204. Special Indorsement; Blank Indorsement.

(1) A special indorsement specifies the person to whom or to whose order it makes the instrument payable. Any instrument specially indorsed becomes payable to the order of the special indorsee and may be further negotiated only by his indorsement.

(2) An indorsement in blank specifies no particular indorsee and may consist of a mere signature. An instrument payable to order and indorsed in blank becomes payable to bearer and may be negotiated by delivery alone until specially indorsed.

(3) The holder may convert a blank indorsement into a special indorsement by writing over the signature of the indorser in blank any contract consistent with the character of the indorsement.

§ 3–205. Restrictive Indorsements.

An indorsement is restrictive which either

(a) is conditional; or

(b) purports to prohibit further transfer of the instrument; or

(c) includes the words "for collection", "for deposit", "pay any bank", or like terms signifying a purpose of deposit or collection; or

(d) otherwise states that it is for the benefit or use of the indorser or of another person.

§ 3–206. Effect of Restrictive Indorsement.

(1) No restrictive indorsement prevents further transfer or negotiation of the instrument.

(2) An intermediary bank, or a payor bank which is not the depositary bank, is neither given notice nor otherwise affected by a restrictive indorsement of any person except the bank's immediate transferor or the person presenting for payment.

(3) Except for an intermediary bank, any transferee under an indorsement which is conditional or includes the words "for collection", "for deposit", "pay any bank", or like terms (subparagraphs (a) and (c) of Section 3–205) must pay or apply any value given by him for or on the security of the instrument consistently with the indorsement and to the extent that he does so he becomes a holder for value. In addition such transferee is a holder in due course if he otherwise complies with the requirements of Section 3–302 on what constitutes a holder in due course.

(4) The first taker under an indorsement for the benefit of the indorser or another person (subparagraph (d) of Section 3–205) must pay or apply any value given by him for or on the security of the instrument consistently with the indorsement and to the extent that he does so he becomes a holder for value. In addition such taker is a holder in due course if he otherwise complies with the requirements of Section 3–302 on what constitutes a holder in due course. A later holder for value is neither given notice nor otherwise affected by such restrictive indorsement unless he has knowledge that a fiduciary or other person has negotiated the instrument in any transaction for his own benefit or otherwise in breach of duty (subsection (2) of Section 3–304).

§ 3–207. Negotiation Effective Although It May Be Rescinded.

(1) Negotiation is effective to transfer the instrument although the negotiation is

(a) made by an infant, a corporation exceeding its powers, or any other person without capacity; or

(b) obtained by fraud, duress or mistake of any kind; or

(c) part of an illegal transaction; or

(d) made in breach of duty.

(2) Except as against a subsequent holder in due course such negotiation is in an appropriate case subject to rescission, the declaration of a constructive trust or any other remedy permitted by law.

§ 3–208. Reacquisition.

Where an instrument is returned to or reacquired by a prior party he may cancel any indorsement which is not necessary to his title and reissue or further negotiate the instrument, but any intervening party is discharged as against the reacquiring party and subsequent holders not in due course and if his indorsement has been cancelled is discharged as against subsequent holders in due course as well.

Part 3 Rights of a Holder

§ 3–301. Rights of a Holder.

The holder of an instrument whether or not he is the owner may transfer or negotiate it and, except as otherwise provided in Section 3–603 on payment or satisfaction, discharge it or enforce payment in his own name.

§ 3–302. Holder in Due Course.

(1) A holder in due course is a holder who takes the instrument

  (a) for value; and
  (b) in good faith; and
  (c) without notice that it is overdue or has been dishonored or of any defense against or claim to it on the part of any person.

(2) A payee may be a holder in due course.
(3) A holder does not become a holder in due course of an instrument:

  (a) by purchase of it at judicial sale or by taking it under legal process; or
  (b) by acquiring it in taking over an estate; or
  (c) by purchasing it as part of a bulk transaction not in regular course of business of the transferor.

(4) A purchaser of a limited interest can be a holder in due course only to the extent of the interest purchased.

§ 3–303. Taking for Value.

A holder takes the instrument for value

  (a) to the extent that the agreed consideration has been performed or that he acquires a security interest in or a lien on the instrument otherwise than by legal process; or
  (b) when he takes the instrument in payment of or as security for an antecedent claim against any person whether or not the claim is due; or
  (c) when he gives a negotiable instrument for it or makes an irrevocable commitment to a third person.

§ 3–304. Notice to Purchaser.

(1) The purchaser has notice of a claim or defense if

  (a) the instrument is so incomplete, bears such visible evidence of forgery or alteration, or is otherwise so irregular as to call into question its validity, terms or ownership or to create an ambiguity as to the party to pay; or
  (b) the purchaser has notice that the obligation of any party is voidable in whole or in part, or that all parties have been discharged.

(2) The purchaser has notice of a claim against the instrument when he has knowledge that a fiduciary has negotiated the instrument in payment of or as security for his own debt or in any transaction for his own benefit or otherwise in breach of duty.
(3) The purchaser has notice that an instrument is overdue if he has reason to know

  (a) that any part of the principal amount is overdue or that there is an uncured default in payment of another instrument of the same series; or
  (b) that acceleration of the instrument has been made; or
  (c) that he is taking a demand instrument after demand has been made or more than a reasonable length of time

after its issue. A reasonable time for a check drawn and payable within the states and territories of the United States and the District of Columbia is presumed to be thirty days.

(4) Knowledge of the following facts does not of itself give the purchaser notice of a defense or claim

  (a) that the instrument is antedated or postdated;
  (b) that it was issued or negotiated in return for an executory promise or accompanied by a separate agreement, unless the purchaser has notice that a defense or claim has arisen from the terms thereof;
  (c) that any party has signed for accommodation;
  (d) that an incomplete instrument has been completed, unless the purchaser has notice of any improper completion;
  (e) that any person negotiating the instrument is or was a fiduciary;
  (f) that there has been default in payment of interest on the instrument or in payment of any other instrument, except one of the same series.

(5) The filing or recording of a document does not of itself constitute notice within the provisions of this Article to a person who would otherwise be a holder in due course.
(6) To be effective notice must be received at such time and in such manner as to give a reasonable opportunity to act on it.

§ 3–305. Rights of a Holder in Due Course.

To the extent that a holder is a holder in due course he takes the instrument free from

(1) all claims to it on the part of any person; and
(2) all defenses of any party to the instrument with whom the holder has not dealt except

  (a) infancy, to the extent that it is a defense to a simple contract; and
  (b) such other incapacity, or duress, or illegality of the transaction, as renders the obligation of the party a nullity; and
  (c) such misrepresentation as has induced the party to sign the instrument with neither knowledge nor reasonable opportunity to obtain knowledge of its character or its essential terms; and
  (d) discharge in insolvency proceedings; and
  (e) any other discharge of which the holder has notice when he takes the instrument.

§ 3–306. Rights of One Not Holder in Due Course.

Unless he has the rights of a holder in due course any person takes the instrument subject to

  (a) all valid claims to it on the part of any person; and
  (b) all defenses of any party which would be available in an action on a simple contract; and
  (c) the defenses of want or failure of consideration, non-performance of any condition precedent, non-

THE UNIFORM COMMERCIAL CODE

A-57

delivery, or delivery for a special purpose (Section 3–408); and

(d) the defense that he or a person through whom he holds the instrument acquired it by theft, or that payment or satisfaction to such holder would be inconsistent with the terms of a restrictive indorsement. The claim of any third person to the instrument is not otherwise available as a defense to any party liable thereon unless the third person himself defends the action for such party.

§ 3–307. Burden of Establishing Signatures, Defenses and Due Course.

(1) Unless specifically denied in the pleadings each signature on an instrument is admitted. When the effectiveness of a signature is put in issue

(a) the burden of establishing it is on the party claiming under the signature; but
(b) the signature is presumed to be genuine or authorized except where the action is to enforce the obligation of a purported signer who has died or become incompetent before proof is required.

(2) When signatures are admitted or established, production of the instrument entitles a holder to recover on it unless the defendant establishes a defense.
(3) After it is shown that a defense exists a person claiming the rights of a holder in due course has the burden of establishing that he or some person under whom he claims is in all respects a holder in due course

Part 4 Liability of Parties

§ 3–401. Signature.

(1) No person is liable on an instrument unless his signature appears thereon.
(2) A signature is made by use of any name, including any trade or assumed name, upon an instrument, or by any word or mark used in lieu of a written signature.

§ 3–402. Signature in Ambiguous Capacity.

Unless the instrument clearly indicates that a signature is made in some other capacity it is an indorsement.

§ 3–403. Signature by Authorized Representative.

(1) A signature may be made by an agent or other representative, and his authority to make it may be established as in other cases of representation. No particular form of appointment is necessary to establish such authority.
(2) An authorized representative who signs his own name to an instrument

(a) is personally obligated if the instrument neither names the person represented nor shows that the representative signed in a representative capacity;
(b) except as otherwise established between the immediate parties, is personally obligated if the instrument

names the person represented but does not show that the representative signed in a representative capacity, or if the instrument does not name the person represented but does show that the representative signed in a representative capacity.

(3) Except as otherwise established the name of an organization preceded or followed by the name and office of an authorized individual is a signature made in a representative capacity.

§ 3–404. Unauthorized Signatures.

(1) Any unauthorized signature is wholly inoperative as that of the person whose name is signed unless he ratifies it or is precluded from denying it; but it operates as the signature of the unauthorized signer in favor of any person who in good faith pays the instrument or takes it for value.
(2) Any unauthorized signature may be ratified for all purposes of this Article. Such ratification does not of itself affect any rights of the person ratifying against the actual signer.

§ 3–405. Impostors; Signature in Name of Payee.

(1) An indorsement by any person in the name of a named payee is effective if

(a) an imposter by use of the mails or otherwise has induced the maker or drawer to issue the instrument to him or his confederate in the name of the payee; or
(b) a person signing as or on behalf of a maker or drawer intends the payee to have no interest in the instrument; or
(c) an agent or employee of the maker or drawer has supplied him with the name of the payee intending the latter to have no such interest.

(2) Nothing in this section shall affect the criminal or civil liability of the person so indorsing.

§ 3–406. Negligence Contributing to Alteration or Unauthorized Signature.

Any person who by his negligence substantially contributes to a material alteration of the instrument or to the making of an unauthorized signature is precluded from asserting the alteration or lack of authority against a holder in due course or against a drawee or other payor who pays the instrument in good faith and in accordance with the reasonable commercial standards of the drawee's or payor's business.

§ 3–407. Alteration.

(1) Any alteration of an instrument is material which changes the contract of any party thereto in any respect, including any such change in

(a) the number or relations of the parties; or
(b) an incomplete instrument, by completing it otherwise than as authorized; or

(c) the writing as signed, by adding to it or by removing any part of it.

(2) As against any person other than a subsequent holder in due course

(a) alteration by the holder which is both fraudulent and material discharges any party whose contract is thereby changed unless that party assents or is precluded from asserting the defense;

(b) no other alteration discharges any party and the instrument may be enforced according to its original tenor, or as to incomplete instruments according to the authority given.

(3) A subsequent holder in due course may in all cases enforce the instrument according to its original tenor, and when an incomplete instrument has been completed, he may enforce it as completed.

§ 3–408. Consideration.

Want or failure of consideration is a defense as against any person not having the rights of a holder in due course (Section 3–305), except that no consideration is necessary for an instrument or obligation thereon given in payment of or as security for an antecedent obligation of any kind. Nothing in this section shall be taken to displace any statute outside this Act under which a promise is enforceable notwithstanding lack or failure of consideration. Partial failure of consideration is a defense pro tanto whether or not the failure is in an ascertained or liquidated amount.

§ 3–409. Draft Not an Assignment.

(1) A check or other draft does not of itself operate as an assignment of any funds in the hands of the drawee available for its payment, and the drawee is not liable on the instrument until he accepts it.

(2) Nothing in this section shall affect any liability in contract, tort or otherwise arising from any letter of credit or other obligation or representation which is not an acceptance.

§ 3–410. Definition and Operation of Acceptance.

(1) Acceptance is the drawee's signed engagement to honor the draft as presented. It must be written on the draft, and may consist of his signature alone. It becomes operative when completed by delivery or notification.

(2) A draft may be accepted although it has not been signed by the drawer or is otherwise incomplete or is overdue or has been dishonored.

(3) Where the draft is payable at a fixed period after sight and the acceptor fails to date his acceptance the holder may complete it by supplying a date in good faith.

§ 3–411. Certification of a Check.

(1) Certification of a check is acceptance. Where a holder procures certification the drawer and all prior indorsers are discharged.

(2) Unless otherwise agreed a bank has no obligation to certify a check.

(3) A bank may certify a check before returning it for lack of proper indorsement. If it does so the drawer is discharged.

§ 3–412. Acceptance Varying Draft.

(1) Where the drawee's proffered acceptance in any manner varies the draft as presented the holder may refuse the acceptance and treat the draft as dishonored in which case the drawee is entitled to have his acceptance cancelled.

(2) The terms of the draft are not varied by an acceptance to pay at any particular bank or place in the United States, unless the acceptance states that the draft is to be paid only at such bank or place.

(3) Where the holder assents to an acceptance varying the terms of the draft each drawer and indorser who does not affirmatively assent is discharged.

§ 3–413. Contract of Maker, Drawer and Acceptor.

(1) The maker or acceptor engages that he will pay the instrument according to its tenor at the time of his engagement or as completed pursuant to Section 3–115 on incomplete instruments.

(2) The drawer engages that upon dishonor of the draft and any necessary notice of dishonor or protest he will pay the amount of the draft to the holder or to any indorser who takes it up. The drawer may disclaim this liability by drawing without recourse.

(3) By making, drawing or accepting the party admits as against all subsequent parties including the drawee the existence of the payee and his then capacity to indorse.

§ 3–414. Contract of Indorser; Order of Liability.

(1) Unless the indorser otherwise specifies (as by such words as "without recourse") every indorser engages that upon dishonor and any necessary notice of dishonor and protest he will pay the instrument according to its tenor at the time of his indorsement to the holder or to any subsequent indorser who takes it up, even though the indorser who takes it up was not obligated to do so.

(2) Unless they otherwise agree indorsers are liable to one another in the order in which they indorse, which is presumed to be the order in which their signatures appear on the instrument.

§ 3–415. Contract of Accommodation Party.

(1) An accommodation party is one who signs the instrument in any capacity for the purpose of lending his name to another party to it.

(2) When the instrument has been taken for value before it is due the accommodation party is liable in the capacity in which he has signed even though the taker knows of the accommodation.

(3) As against a holder in due course and without notice of the accommodation oral proof of the accommodation is

not admissible to give the accommodation party the benefit of discharges dependent on his character as such. In other cases the accommodation character may be shown by oral proof.

(4) An indorsement which shows that it is not in the chain of title is notice of its accommodation character.

(5) An accommodation party is not liable to the party accommodated, and if he pays the instrument has a right of recourse on the instrument against such party.

§ 3–416. Contract of Guarantor.

(1) "Payment guaranteed" or equivalent words added to a signature mean that the signer engages that if the instrument is not paid when due he will pay it according to its tenor without resort by the holder to any other party.

(2) "Collection guaranteed" or equivalent words added to a signature mean that the signer engages that if the instrument is not paid when due he will pay it according to its tenor, but only after the holder has reduced his claim against the maker or acceptor to judgment and execution has been returned unsatisfied, or after the maker or acceptor has become insolvent or it is otherwise apparent that it is useless to proceed against him.

(3) Words of guaranty which do not otherwise specify guarantee payment.

(4) No words of guaranty added to the signature of a sole maker or acceptor affect his liability on the instrument. Such words added to the signature of one of two or more makers or acceptors create a presumption that the signature is for the accommodation of the others.

(5) When words of guaranty are used presentment, notice of dishonor and protest are not necessary to charge the user.

(6) Any guaranty written on the instrument is enforcible notwithstanding any statute of frauds.

§ 3–417. Warranties on Presentment and Transfer.

(1) Any person who obtains payment or acceptance and any prior transferor warrants to a person who in good faith pays or accepts that

(a) he has a good title to the instrument or is authorized to obtain payment or acceptance on behalf of one who has a good title; and

(b) he has no knowledge that the signature of the maker or drawer is unauthorized, except that this warranty is not given by a holder in due course acting in good faith

(i) to a maker with respect to the maker's own signature; or

(ii) to a drawer with respect to the drawer's own signature, whether or not the drawer is also the drawee; or

(iii) to an acceptor of a draft if the holder in due course took the draft after the acceptance or obtained the acceptance without knowledge that the drawer's signature was unauthorized; and

(c) the instrument has not been materially altered, except that this warranty is not given by a holder in due course acting in good faith

(i) to the maker of a note; or

(ii) to the drawer of a draft whether or not the drawer is also the drawee; or

(iii) to the acceptor of a draft with respect to an alteration made prior to the acceptance if the holder in due course took the draft after the acceptance, even though the acceptance provided "payable as originally drawn" or equivalent terms; or

(iv) to the acceptor of a draft with respect to an alteration made after the acceptance.

(2) Any person who transfers an instrument and receives consideration warrants to his transferee and if the tranfer is by indorsement to any subsequent holder who takes the instrument in good faith that

(a) he has a good title to the instrument or is authorized to obtain payment or acceptance on behalf of one who has a good title and the transfer is otherwise rightful; and

(b) all signatures are genuine or authorized; and

(c) the instrument has not been materially altered; and

(d) no defense of any party is good against him; and

(e) he has no knowledge of any insolvency proceeding instituted with respect to the maker or acceptor or the drawer of an unaccepted instrument.

(3) By transferring "without recourse" the transferor limits the obligation stated in subsection (2)(d) to a warranty that he has no knowledge of such a defense.

(4) A selling agent or broker who does not disclose the fact that he is acting only as such gives the warranties provided in this section, but if he makes such disclosure warrants only his good faith and authority.

§ 3–418. Finality of Payment or Acceptance.

Except for recovery of bank payments as provided in the Article on Bank Deposits and Collections (Article 4) and except for liability for breach of warranty on presentment under the preceding section, payment or acceptance of any instrument is final in favor of a holder in due course, or a person who has in good faith changed his position in reliance on the payment.

§ 3–419. Conversion of Instrument; Innocent Representative.

(1) An instrument is converted when

(a) a drawee to whom it is delivered for acceptance refuses to return it on demand; or

(b) any person to whom it is delivered for payment refuses on demand either to pay or to return it; or

(c) it is paid on a forged indorsement.

(2) In an action against a drawee under subsection (1) the measure of the drawee's liability is the face amount of the instrument. In any other action under subsection

(1) the measure of liability is presumed to be the face amount of the instrument.

(3) Subject to the provisions of this Act concerning restrictive indorsements a representative, including a depositary or collecting bank, who has in good faith and in accordance with the reasonable commercial standards applicable to the business of such representative dealt with an instrument or its proceeds on behalf of one who was not the true owner is not liable in conversion or otherwise to the true owner beyond the amount of any proceeds remaining in his hands.

(4) An intermediary bank or payor bank which is not a depositary bank is not liable in conversion solely by reason of the fact that proceeds of an item indorsed restrictively (Sections 3–205 and 3–206) are not paid or applied consistently with the restrictive indorsement of an indorser other than its immediate transferor.

Part 5 Presentment, Notice of Dishonor and Protest

§ 3–501. When Presentment, Notice of Dishonor, and Protest Necessary or Permissible.

(1) Unless excused (Section 3–511) presentment is necessary to charge secondary parties as follows:

(a) presentment for acceptance is necessary to charge the drawer and indorsers of a draft where the draft so provides, or is payable elsewhere than at the residence or place of business of the drawee, or its date of payment depends upon such presentment. The holder may at his option present for acceptance any other draft payable at a stated date;

(b) presentment for payment is necessary to charge any indorser;

(c) in the case of any drawer, the acceptor of a draft payable at a bank or the maker of a note payable at a bank, presentment for payment is necessary, but failure to make presentment discharges such drawer, acceptor or maker only as stated in Section 3–502(1)(b).

(2) Unless excused (Section 3–511)

(a) notice of any dishonor is necessary to charge any indorser;

(b) in the case of any drawer, the acceptor of a draft payable at a bank or the maker of a note payable at a bank, notice of any dishonor is necessary, but failure to give such notice discharges such drawer, acceptor or maker only as stated in Section 3–502(1)(b).

(3) Unless excused (Section 3–511) protest of any dishonor is necessary to charge the drawer and indorsers of any draft which on its face appears to be drawn or payable outside of the states, territories, dependencies, and possessions of the United States, the District of Columbia and the Commonwealth of Puerto Rico. The holder may at his option make protest of any dishonor of any other instrument and in the case of a foreign draft may on insolvency of the acceptor before maturity make protest for better security.

(4) Notwithstanding any provision of this section, neither presentment nor notice of dishonor nor protest is necessary to charge an indorser who has indorsed an instrument after maturity.

§ 3–502. Unexcused Delay; Discharge.

(1) Where without excuse any necessary presentment or notice of dishonor is delayed beyond the time when it is due

(a) any indorser is discharged; and

(b) any drawer or the acceptor of a draft payable at a bank or the maker of a note payable at a bank who because the drawee or payor bank becomes insolvent during the delay is deprived of funds maintained with the drawee or payor bank to cover the instrument may discharge his liability by written assignment to the holder of his rights against the drawee or payor bank in respect of such funds, but such drawer, acceptor or maker is not otherwise discharged.

(2) Where without excuse a necessary protest is delayed beyond the time when it is due any drawer or indorser is discharged.

§ 3–503. Time of Presentment.

(1) Unless a different time is expressed in the instrument the time for any presentment is determined as follows:

(a) where an instrument is payable at or a fixed period after a stated date any presentment for acceptance must be made on or before the date it is payable;

(b) where an instrument is payable after sight it must either be presented for acceptance or negotiated within a reasonable time after date or issue whichever is later;

(c) where an instrument shows the date on which it is payable presentment for payment is due on that date;

(d) where an instrument is accelerated presentment for payment is due within a reasonable time after the acceleration;

(e) with respect to the liability of any secondary party presentment for acceptance or payment of any other instrument is due within a reasonable time after such party becomes liable thereon.

(2) A reasonable time for presentment is determined by the nature of the instrument, any usage of banking or trade and the facts of the particular case. In the case of an uncertified check which is drawn and payable within the United States and which is not a draft drawn by a bank the following are presumed to be reasonable periods within which to present for payment or to initiate bank collection:

(a) with respect to the liability of the drawer, thirty days after date or issue whichever is later; and

(b) with respect to the liability of an indorser, seven days after his indorsement.

(3) Where any presentment is due on a day which is not a full business day for either the person making present-

ment or the party to pay or accept, presentment is due on the next following day which is a full business day for both parties.

(4) Presentment to be sufficient must be made at a reasonable hour, and if at a bank during its banking day.

§ 3–504. How Presentment Made.

(1) Presentment is a demand for acceptance or payment made upon the maker, acceptor, drawee or other payor by or on behalf of the holder.

(2) Presentment may be made

(a) by mail, in which event the time of presentment is determined by the time of receipt of the mail; or
(b) through a clearing house; or
(c) at the place of acceptance or payment specified in the instrument or if there be none at the place of business or residence of the party to accept or pay. If neither the party to accept or pay nor anyone authorized to act for him is present or accessible at such place presentment is excused.

(3) It may be made

(a) to any one of two or more makers, acceptors, drawees or other payors; or
(b) to any person who has authority to make or refuse the acceptance or payment.

(4) A draft accepted or a note made payable at a bank in the United States must be presented at such bank.

(5) In the cases described in Section 4–210 presentment may be made in the manner and with the result stated in that section.

§ 3–505. Rights of Party to Whom Presentment Is Made.

(1) The party to whom presentment is made may without dishonor require

(a) exhibition of the instrument; and
(b) reasonable identification of the person making presentment and evidence of his authority to make it if made for another; and
(c) that the instrument be produced for acceptance or payment at a place specified in it, or if there be none at any place reasonable in the circumstances; and
(d) a signed receipt on the instrument for any partial or full payment and its surrender upon full payment.

(2) Failure to comply with any such requirement invalidates the presentment but the person presenting has a reasonable time in which to comply and the time for acceptance or payment runs from the time of compliance.

§ 3–506. Time Allowed for Acceptance or Payment.

(1) Acceptance may be deferred without dishonor until the close of the next business day following presentment. The holder may also in a good faith effort to obtain acceptance and without either dishonor of the instrument

or discharge of secondary parties allow postponement of acceptance for an additional business day.

(2) Except as a longer time is allowed in the case of documentary drafts drawn under a letter of credit, and unless an earlier time is agreed to by the party to pay, payment of an instrument may be deferred without dishonor pending reasonable examination to determine whether it is properly payable, but payment must be made in any event before the close of business on the day of presentment.

§ 3–507. Dishonor; Holder's Right of Recourse; Term Allowing Re-Presentment.

(1) An instrument is dishonored when

(a) a necessary or optional presentment is duly made and due acceptance or payment is refused or cannot be obtained within the prescribed time or in case of bank collections the instrument is seasonably returned by the midnight deadline (Section 4–301); or
(b) presentment is excused and the instrument is not duly accepted or paid.

(2) Subject to any necessary notice of dishonor and protest, the holder has upon dishonor an immediate right of recourse against the drawers and indorsers.

(3) Return of an instrument for lack of proper indorsement is not dishonor.

(4) A term in a draft or an indorsement thereof allowing a stated time for re-presentment in the event of any dishonor of the draft by nonacceptance if a time draft or by nonpayment if a sight draft gives the holder as against any secondary party bound by the term an option to waive the dishonor without affecting the liability of the secondary party and he may present again up to the end of the stated time.

§ 3–508. Notice of Dishonor.

(1) Notice of dishonor may be given to any person who may be liable on the instrument by or on behalf of the holder or any party who has himself received notice, or any other party who can be compelled to pay the instrument. In addition an agent or bank in whose hands the instrument is dishonored may give notice to his principal or customer or to another agent or bank from which the instrument was received.

(2) Any necessary notice must be given by a bank before its midnight deadline and by any other person before midnight of the third business day after dishonor or receipt of notice of dishonor.

(3) Notice may be given in any reasonable manner. It may be oral or written and in any terms which identify the instrument and state that it has been dishonored. A misdescription which does not mislead the party notified does not vitiate the notice. Sending the instrument bearing a stamp, ticket or writing stating that acceptance or payment has been refused or sending a notice of debit with respect to the instrument is sufficient.

(4) Written notice is given when sent although it is not received.

(5) Notice to one partner is notice to each although the firm has been dissolved.

(6) When any party is in insolvency proceedings instituted after the issue of the instrument notice may be given either to the party or to the representative of his estate.

(7) When any party is dead or incompetent notice may be sent to his last known address or given to his personal representative.

(8) Notice operates for the benefit of all parties who have rights on the instrument against the party notified.

§ 3–509. Protest; Noting for Protest.

(1) A protest is a certificate of dishonor made under the hand and seal of a United States consul or vice consul or a notary public or other person authorized to certify dishonor by the law of the place where dishonor occurs. It may be made upon information satisfactory to such person.

(2) The protest must identify the instrument and certify either that due presentment has been made or the reason why it is excused and that the instrument has been dishonored by nonacceptance or nonpayment.

(3) The protest may also certify that notice of dishonor has been given to all parties or to specified parties.

(4) Subject to subsection (5) any necessary protest is due by the time that notice of dishonor is due.

(5) If, before protest is due, an instrument has been noted for protest by the officer to make protest, the protest may be made at any time thereafter as of the date of the noting.

§ 3–510. Evidence of Dishonor and Notice of Dishonor.

The following are admissible as evidence and create a presumption of dishonor and of any notice of dishonor therein shown:

(a) a document regular in form as provided in the preceding section which purports to be a protest;

(b) the purported stamp or writing of the drawee, payor bank or presenting bank on the instrument or accompanying it stating that acceptance or payment has been refused for reasons consistent with dishonor;

(c) any book or record of the drawee, payor bank, or any collecting bank kept in the usual course of business which shows dishonor, even though there is no evidence of who made the entry.

§ 3–511. Waived or Excused Presentment, Protest or Notice of Dishonor or Delay Therein.

(1) Delay in presentment, protest or notice of dishonor is excused when the party is without notice that it is due or when the delay is caused by circumstances beyond his control and he exercises reasonable diligence after the cause of the delay ceases to operate.

(2) Presentment or notice or protest as the case may be is entirely excused when

(a) the party to be charged has waived it expressly or by implication either before or after it is due; or

(b) such party has himself dishonored the instrument or has countermanded payment or otherwise has no reason to expect or right to require that the instrument be accepted or paid; or

(c) by reasonable diligence the presentment or protest cannot be made or the notice given.

(3) Presentment is also entirely excused when

(a) the maker, acceptor or drawee of any instrument except a documentary draft is dead or in insolvency proceedings instituted after the issue of the instrument; or

(b) acceptance or payment is refused but not for want of proper presentment.

(4) Where a draft has been dishonored by nonacceptance a later presentment for payment and any notice of dishonor and protest for nonpayment are excused unless in the meantime the instrument has been accepted.

(5) A waiver of protest is also a waiver of presentment and of notice of dishonor even though protest is not required.

(6) Where a waiver of presentment or notice or protest is embodied in the instrument itself it is binding upon all parties; but where it is written above the signature of an indorser it binds him only.

Part 6 Discharge

§ 3–601. Discharge of Parties.

(1) The extent of the discharge of any party from liability on an instrument is governed by the sections on

(a) payment or satisfaction (Section 3–603); or

(b) tender of payment (Section 3–604); or

(c) cancellation or renunciation (Section 3–605); or

(d) impairment of right of recourse or of collateral (Section 3–606); or

(e) reacquisition of the instrument by a prior party (Section 3–208); or

(f) fraudulent and material alteration (Section 3–407); or

(g) certification of a check (Section 3–411); or

(h) acceptance varying a draft (Section 3–412); or

(i) unexcused delay in presentment or notice of dishonor or protest (Section 3–502).

(2) Any party is also discharged from his liability on an instrument to another party by any other act or agreement with such party which would discharge his simple contract for the payment of money.

(3) The liability of all parties is discharged when any party who has himself no right of action or recourse on the instrument

(a) reacquires the instrument in his own right; or

(b) is discharged under any provision of this Article, except as otherwise provided with respect to discharge for impairment of recourse or of collateral (Section 3–606).

§ 3–602. Effect of Discharge Against Holder in Due Course.

No discharge of any party provided by this Article is effective against a subsequent holder in due course unless he has notice thereof when he takes the instrument.

§ 3–603. Payment or Satisfaction.

(1) The liability of any party is discharged to the extent of his payment or satisfaction to the holder even though it is made with knowledge of a claim of another person to the instrument unless prior to such payment or satisfaction the person making the claim either supplies indemnity deemed adequate by the party seeking the discharge or enjoins payment or satisfaction by order of a court of competent jurisdiction in an action in which the adverse claimant and the holder are parties. This subsection does not, however, result in the discharge of the liability

  (a) of a party who in bad faith pays or satisfies a holder who acquired the instrument by theft or who (unless having the rights of a holder in due course) holds through one who so acquired it; or
  (b) of a party (other than an intermediary bank or a payor bank which is not a depositary bank) who pays or satisfies the holder of an instrument which has been restrictively indorsed in a manner not consistent with the terms of such restrictive indorsement.

(2) Payment or satisfaction may be made with the consent of the holder by any person including a stranger to the instrument. Surrender of the instrument to such a person gives him the rights of a transferee (Section 3–201).

§ 3–604. Tender of Payment.

(1) Any party making tender of full payment to a holder when or after it is due is discharged to the extent of all subsequent liability for interest, costs and attorney's fees.
(2) The holder's refusal of such tender wholly discharges any party who has a right of recourse against the party making the tender.
(3) Where the maker or acceptor of an instrument payable otherwise than on demand is able and ready to pay at every place of payment specified in the instrument when it is due, it is equivalent to tender.

§ 3–605. Cancellation and Renunciation.

(1) The holder of an instrument may even without consideration discharge any party

  (a) in any manner apparent on the face of the instrument or the indorsement, as by intentionally cancelling the instrument or the party's signature by destruction or mutilation, or by striking out the party's signature; or

  (b) by renouncing his rights by a writing signed and delivered or by surrender of the instrument to the party to be discharged.

(2) Neither cancellation nor renunciation without surrender of the instrument affects the title thereto.

§ 3–606. Impairment of Recourse or of Collateral.

(1) The holder discharges any party to the instrument to the extent that without such party's consent the holder

  (a) without express reservation of rights releases or agrees not to sue any person against whom the party has to the knowledge of the holder a right of recourse or agrees to suspend the right to enforce against such person the instrument or collateral or otherwise discharges such person, except that failure or delay in effecting any required presentment, protest or notice of dishonor with respect to any such person does not discharge any party as to whom presentment, protest or notice of dishonor is effective or unnecessary; or
  (b) unjustifiably impairs any collateral for the instrument given by or on behalf of the party or any person against whom he has a right of recourse.

(2) By express reservation of rights against a party with right of recourse the holder preserves

  (a) all his rights against such party as of the time when the instrument was originally due; and
  (b) the right of the party to pay the instrument as of that time; and
  (c) all rights of such party to recourse against others.

Part 7 Advice of International Sight Draft

§ 3–701. Letter of Advice of International Sight Draft.

(1) A "letter of advice" is a drawer's communication to the drawee that a described draft has been drawn.
(2) Unless otherwise agreed when a bank receives from another bank a letter of advice of an international sight draft the drawee bank may immediately debit the drawer's account and stop the running of interest pro tanto. Such a debit and any resulting credit to any account covering outstanding drafts leaves in the drawer full power to stop payment or otherwise dispose of the amount and creates no trust or interest in favor of the holder.
(3) Unless otherwise agreed and except where a draft is drawn under a credit issued by the drawee, the drawee of an international sight draft owes the drawer no duty to pay an unadvised draft but if it does so and the draft is genuine, may appropriately debit the drawer's account.

Part 8 Miscellaneous

§ 3–801. Drafts in a Set.

(1) Where a draft is drawn in a set of parts, each of which is numbered and expressed to be an order only if no other

part has been honored, the whole of the parts constitutes one draft but a taker of any part may become a holder in due course of the draft.

(2) Any person who negotiates, indorses or accepts a single part of a draft drawn in a set thereby becomes liable to any holder in due course of that part as if it were the whole set, but as between different holders in due course to whom different parts have been negotiated the holder whose title first accrues has all rights to the draft and its proceeds.

(3) As against the drawee the first presented part of a draft drawn in a set is the part entitled to payment, or if a time draft to acceptance and payment. Acceptance of any subsequently presented part renders the drawee liable thereon under subsection (2). With respect both to a holder and to the drawer payment of a subsequently presented part of a draft payable at sight has the same effect as payment of a check notwithstanding an effective stop order (Section 4–407).

(4) Except as otherwise provided in this section, where any part of a draft in a set is discharged by payment or otherwise the whole draft is discharged.

§ 3–802. Effect of Instrument on Obligation for Which It Is Given.

(1) Unless otherwise agreed where an instrument is taken for an underlying obligation

(a) the obligation is pro tanto discharged if a bank is drawer, maker or acceptor of the instrument and there is no recourse on the instrument against the underlying obligor; and

(b) in any other case the obligation is suspended pro tanto until the instrument is due or if it is payable on demand until its presentment. If the instrument is dishonored action may be maintained on either the instrument or the obligation; discharge of the underlying obligor on the instrument also discharges him on the obligation.

(2) The taking in good faith of a check which is not postdated does not of itself so extend the time on the original obligation as to discharge a surety.

§ 3–803. Notice to Third Party.

Where a defendant is sued for breach of an obligation for which a third person is answerable over under this Article he may give the third person written notice of the litigation, and the person notified may then give similar notice to any other person who is answerable over to him under this Article. If the notice states that the person notified may come in and defend and that if the person notified does not do so he will in any action against him by the person giving the notice be bound by any determination of fact common to the two litigations, then unless after seasonable receipt of the notice the person notified does come in and defend he is so bound.

§ 3–804. Lost, Destroyed or Stolen Instruments.

The owner of an instrument which is lost, whether by destruction, theft or otherwise, may maintain an action in his own name and recover from any party liable thereon upon due proof of his ownership, the facts which prevent his production of the instrument and its terms. The court may require security indemnifying the defendant against loss by reason of further claims on the instrument.

§ 3–805. Instruments Not Payable to Order or to Bearer.

This Article applies to any instrument whose terms do not preclude transfer and which is otherwise negotiable within this Article but which is not payable to order or to bearer, except that there can be no holder in due course of such an instrument.

Article 4

BANK DEPOSITS AND COLLECTIONS

Part 1 General Provisions and Definitions

§ 4–101. Short Title.

This Article shall be known and may be cited as Uniform Commercial Code—Bank Deposits and Collections.

§ 4–102. Applicability.

(1) To the extent that items within this Article are also within the scope of Articles 3 and 8, they are subject to the provisions of those Articles. In the event of conflict the provisions of this Article govern those of Article 3 but the provisions of Article 8 govern those of this Article.

(2) The liability of a bank for action or non-action with respect to any item handled by it for purposes of presentment, payment or collection is governed by the law of the place where the bank is located. In the case of action or non-action by or at a branch or separate office of a bank, its liability is governed by the law of the place where the branch or separate office is located.

§ 4–103. Variation by Agreement; Measure of Damages; Certain Action Constituting Ordinary Care.

(1) The effect of the provisions of this Article may be varied by agreement except that no agreement can disclaim a bank's responsibility for its own lack of good faith or failure to exercise ordinary care or can limit the measure of damages for such lack or failure; but the parties may by agreement determine the standards by which such responsibility is to be measured if such standards are not manifestly unreasonable.

(2) Federal Reserve regulations and operating letters, clearing house rules, and the like, have the effect of

agreements under subsection (1), whether or not specifically assented to by all parties interested in items handled.

(3) Action or non-action approved by this Article or pursuant to Federal Reserve regulations or operating letters constitutes the exercise of ordinary care and, in the absence of special instructions, action or nonaction consistent with clearing house rules and the like or with a general banking usage not disapproved by this Article, prima facie constitutes the exercise of ordinary care.

(4) The specification or approval of certain procedures by this Article does not constitute disapproval of other procedures which may be reasonable under the circumstances.

(5) The measure of damages for failure to exercise ordinary care in handling an item is the amount of the item reduced by an amount which could not have been realized by the use of ordinary care, and where there is bad faith it includes other damages, if any, suffered by the party as a proximate consequence.

§ 4–104. Definitions and Index of Definitions.

(1) In this Article unless the context otherwise requires

(a) "Account" means any account with a bank and includes a checking, time, interest or savings account;
(b) "Afternoon" means the period of a day between noon and midnight;
(c) "Banking day" means that part of any day on which a bank is open to the public for carrying on substantially all of its banking functions;
(d) "Clearing house" means any association of banks or other payors regularly clearing items;
(e) "Customer" means any person having an account with a bank or for whom a bank has agreed to collect items and includes a bank carrying an account with another bank;
(f) "Documentary draft" means any negotiable or non-negotiable draft with accompanying documents, securities or other papers to be delivered against honor of the draft;
(g) "Item" means any instrument for the payment of money even though it is not negotiable but does not include money;
(h) "Midnight deadline" with respect to a bank is midnight on its next banking day following the banking day on which it receives the relevant item or notice or from which the time for taking action commences to run, whichever is later;
(i) "Properly payable" includes the availability of funds for payment at the time of decision to pay or dishonor;
(j) "Settle" means to pay in cash, by clearing house settlement, in a charge or credit or by remittance, or otherwise as instructed. A settlement may be either provisional or final;
(k) "Suspends payments" with respect to a bank means that it has been closed by order of the supervisory authorities, that a public officer has been appointed to take it over or that it ceases or refuses to make payments in the ordinary course of business.

(2) Other definitions applying to this Article and the sections in which they appear are:

"Collecting bank" Section 4–105.
"Depositary bank" Section 4–105.
"Intermediary bank" Section 4–105.
"Payor bank" Section 4–105.
"Presenting bank" Section 4–105.
"Remitting bank" Section 4–105.

(3) The following definitions in other Articles apply to this Article:

"Acceptance" Section 3–410.
"Certificate of deposit" Section 3–104.
"Certification" Section 3–411.
"Check" Section 3–104.
"Draft" Section 3–104.
"Holder in due course" Section 3–302.
"Notice of dishonor" Section 3–508.
"Presentment" Section 3–504.
"Protest" Section 3–509.
"Secondary party" Section 3–102.

(4) In addition Article 1 contains general definitions and principles of construction and interpretation applicable throughout this Article.

§ 4–105. "Depositary Bank"; "Intermediary Bank"; "Collecting Bank"; "Payor Bank"; "Presenting Bank"; "Remitting Bank".

In this Article unless the context otherwise requires:

(a) "Depositary bank" means the first bank to which an item is transferred for collection even though it is also the payor bank;
(b) "Payor bank" means a bank by which an item is payable as drawn or accepted;
(c) "Intermediary bank" means any bank to which an item is transferred in course of collection except the depositary or payor bank;
(d) "Collecting bank" means any bank handling the item for collection except the payor bank;
(e) "Presenting bank" means any bank presenting an item except a payor bank;
(f) "Remitting bank" means any payor or intermediary bank remitting for an item.

§ 4–106. Separate Office of a Bank.

A branch or separate office of a bank [maintaining its own deposit ledgers] is a separate bank for the purpose of computing the time within which and determining the place at or to which action may be taken or notices or orders shall be given under this Article and under Article 3.

Note: *The brackets are to make it optional with the several states whether to require a branch to maintain its own deposit ledgers in order to be considered to be a separate bank for certain purposes under Article 4. In some states "maintaining its own deposit ledgers" is a satisfactory test. In others branch banking practices are such that this test would not be suitable.*

§ 4–107. Time of Receipt of Items.

(1) For the purpose of allowing time to process items, prove balances and make the necessary entries on its books to determine its position for the day, a bank may fix an afternoon hour of two P.M. or later as a cut-off hour for the handling of money and items and the making of entries on its books.

(2) Any item or deposit of money received on any day after a cut-off hour so fixed or after the close of the banking day may be treated as being received at the opening of the next banking day.

§ 4–108. Delays.

(1) Unless otherwise instructed, a collecting bank in a good faith effort to secure payment may, in the case of specific items and with or without the approval of any person involved, waive, modify or extend time limits imposed or permitted by this Act for a period not in excess of an additional banking day without discharge of secondary parties and without liability to its transferor or any prior party.

(2) Delay by a collecting bank or payor bank beyond time limits prescribed or permitted by this Act or by instructions is excused if caused by interruption of communication facilities, suspension of payments by another bank, war, emergency conditions or other circumstances beyond the control of the bank provided it exercises such diligence as the circumstances require.

§ 4–109. Process of Posting.

The "process of posting" means the usual procedure followed by a payor bank in determining to pay an item and in recording the payment including one or more of the following or other steps as determined by the bank:

(a) verification of any signature;
(b) ascertaining that sufficient funds are available;
(c) affixing a "paid" or other stamp;
(d) entering a charge or entry to a customer's account;
(e) correcting or reversing an entry or erroneous action with respect to the item.

Part 2 Collection of Items: Depositary and Collecting Banks

§ 4–201. Presumption and Duration of Agency Status of Collecting Banks and Provisional Status of Credits; Applicability of Article; Item Indorsed "Pay Any Bank".

(1) Unless a contrary intent clearly appears and prior to the time that a settlement given by a collecting bank for an item is or becomes final (subsection (3) of Section 4–211 and Sections 4–212 and 4–213) the bank is an agent or sub-agent of the owner of the item and any settlement given for the item is provisional. This provision applies regardless of the form of indorsement or lack of indorsement and even though credit given for the item is subject to immediate withdrawal as of right or is in fact withdrawn; but the continuance of ownership of an item by its owner and any rights of the owner to proceeds of the item are subject to rights of a collecting bank such as those resulting from outstanding advances on the item and valid rights of setoff. When an item is handled by banks for purposes of presentment, payment and collection, the relevant provisions of this Article apply even though action of parties clearly establishes that a particular bank has purchased the item and is the owner of it.

(2) After an item has been indorsed with the words "pay any bank" or the like, only a bank may acquire the rights of a holder

(a) until the item has been returned to the customer initiating collection; or
(b) until the item has been specially indorsed by a bank to a person who is not a bank.

§ 4–202. Responsibility for Collection; When Action Seasonable.

(1) A collecting bank must use ordinary care in

(a) presenting an item or sending it for presentment; and
(b) sending notice of dishonor or non-payment or returning an item other than a documentary draft to the bank's transferor [or directly to the depositary bank under subsection (2) of Section 4–212] (*see note to Section 4–212*) after learning that the item has not been paid or accepted as the case may be; and
(c) settling for an item when the bank receives final settlement; and
(d) making or providing for any necessary protest; and
(e) notifying its transferor of any loss or delay in transit within a reasonable time after discovery thereof.

(2) A collecting bank taking proper action before its midnight deadline following receipt of an item, notice or payment acts seasonably; taking proper action within a reasonably longer time may be seasonable but the bank has the burden of so establishing.

(3) Subject to subsection (1)(a), a bank is not liable for the insolvency, neglect, misconduct, mistake or default of another bank or person or for loss or destruction of an item in transit or in the possession of others.

§ 4–203. Effect of Instructions.

Subject to the provisions of Article 3 concerning conversion of instruments (Section 3–419) and the provisions of both Article 3 and this Article concerning restrictive indorsements only a collecting bank's transferor can give instructions which affect the bank or constitute notice to it and a collecting bank is not liable to prior parties for any action taken pursuant to such instructions or in accordance with any agreement with its transferor.

§ 4–204. Methods of Sending and Presenting; Sending Direct to Payor Bank.

(1) A collecting bank must send items by reasonably prompt method taking into consideration any relevant instructions, the nature of the item, the number of such items on hand, and the cost of collection involved and the method generally used by it or others to present such items.

(2) A collecting bank may send

(a) any item direct to the payor bank;

(b) any item to any non-bank payor if authorized by its transferor; and

(c) any item other than documentary drafts to any non-bank payor, if authorized by Federal Reserve regulation or operating letter, clearing house rule or the like.

(3) Presentment may be made by a presenting bank at a place where the payor bank has requested that presentment be made.

§ 4–205. Supplying Missing Indorsement; No Notice from Prior Indorsement.

(1) A depository bank which has taken an item for collection may supply any indorsement of the customer which is necessary to title unless the item contains the words "payee's indorsement required" or the like. In the absence of such a requirement a statement placed on the item by the depository bank to the effect that the item was deposited by a customer or credited to his account is effective as the customer's indorsement.

(2) An intermediary bank, or payor bank which is not a depository bank, is neither given notice nor otherwise affected by a restrictive indorsement of any person except the bank's immediate transferor.

§ 4–206. Transfer Between Banks.

Any agreed method which identifies the transferor bank is sufficient for the item's further transfer to another bank.

§ 4–207. Warranties of Customer and Collecting Bank on Transfer or Presentment of Items; Time for Claims.

(1) Each customer or collecting bank who obtains payment or acceptance of an item and each prior customer and collecting bank warrants to the payor bank or other payor who in good faith pays or accepts the item that

(a) he has a good title to the item or is authorized to obtain payment or acceptance on behalf of one who has a good title; and

(b) he has no knowledge that the signature of the maker or drawer is unauthorized, except that this warranty is not given by any customer or collecting bank that is a holder in due course and acts in good faith

(i) to a maker with respect to the maker's own signature; or

(ii) to a drawer with respect to the drawer's own signature, whether or not the drawer is also the drawee; or

(iii) to an acceptor of an item if the holder in due course took the item after the acceptance or obtained the acceptance without knowledge that the drawer's signature was unauthorized; and

(c) the item has not been materially altered, except that this warranty is not given by any customer or collecting bank that is a holder in due course and acts in good faith

(i) to the maker of a note; or

(ii) to the drawer of a draft whether or not the drawer is also the drawee; or

(iii) to the acceptor of an item with respect to an alteration made prior to the acceptance if the holder in due course took the item after the acceptance, even though the acceptance provided "payable as originally drawn" or equivalent terms; or

(iv) to the acceptor of an item with respect to an alteration made after the acceptance.

(2) Each customer and collecting bank who transfers an item and receives a settlement or other consideration for it warrants to his transferee and to any subsequent collecting bank who takes the item in good faith that

(a) he has a good title to the item or is authorized to obtain payment or acceptance on behalf of one who has a good title and the transfer is otherwise rightful; and

(b) all signatures are genuine or authorized; and

(c) the item has not been materially altered; and

(d) no defense of any party is good against him; and

(e) he has no knowledge of any insolvency proceeding instituted with respect to the maker or acceptor or the drawer of an unaccepted item.

In addition each customer and collecting bank so transferring an item and receiving a settlement or other consideration engages that upon dishonor and any necessary notice of dishonor and protest he will take up the item.

(3) The warranties and the engagement to honor set forth in the two preceding subsections arise notwithstanding the absence of indorsement or words of guaranty or warranty in the transfer or presentment and a collecting bank remains liable for their breach despite remittance to its transferor. Damages for breach of such warranties or engagement to honor shall not exceed the consideration received by the customer or collecting bank responsible plus finance charges and expenses related to the item, if any.

(4) Unless a claim for breach of warranty under this section is made within a reasonable time after the person claiming learns of the breach, the person liable is discharged to the extent of any loss caused by the delay in making claim.

§ 4–208. Security Interest of Collecting Bank in Items, Accompanying Documents and Proceeds.

(1) A bank has a security interest in an item and any accompanying documents or the proceeds of either

(a) in case of an item deposited in an account to the extent to which credit given for the item has been withdrawn or applied;
(b) in case of an item for which it has given credit available for withdrawal as of right, to the extent of the credit given whether or not the credit is drawn upon and whether or not there is a right of charge-back; or
(c) if it makes an advance on or against the item.

(2) When credit which has been given for several items received at one time or pursuant to a single agreement is withdrawn or applied in part the security interest remains upon all the items, any accompanying documents or the proceeds of either. For the purpose of this section, credits first given are first withdrawn.
(3) Receipt by a collecting bank of a final settlement for an item is a realization on its security interest in the item, accompanying documents and proceeds. To the extent and so long as the bank does not receive final settlement for the item or give up possession of the item or accompanying documents for purposes other than collection, the security interest continues and is subject to the provisions of Article 9 except that

(a) no security agreement is necessary to make the security interest enforceable (subsection (1)(b) of Section 9–203); and
(b) no filing is required to perfect the security interest; and
(c) the security interest has priority over conflicting perfected security interests in the item, accompanying documents or proceeds.

§ 4–209. When Bank Gives Value for Purposes of Holder in Due Course.

For purposes of determining its status as a holder in due course, the bank has given value to the extent that it has a security interest in an item provided that the bank otherwise complies with the requirements of Section 3–302 on what constitutes a holder in due course.

§ 4–210. Presentment by Notice of Item Not Payable by, Through or at a Bank; Liability of Secondary Parties.

(1) Unless otherwise instructed, a collecting bank may present an item not payable by, through or at a bank by sending to the party to accept or pay a written notice that the bank holds the item for acceptance or payment. The notice must be sent in time to be received on or before the day when presentment is due and the bank must meet any requirement of the party to accept or pay under Section 3–505 by the close of the bank's next banking day after it knows of the requirement.
(2) Where presentment is made by notice and neither honor nor request for compliance with a requirement under Section 3–505 is received by the close of business on the day after maturity or in the case of demand items by the close of business on the third banking day after notice was sent, the presenting bank may treat the item as dishonored and charge any secondary party by sending him notice of the facts.

§ 4–211. Media of Remittance; Provisional and Final Settlement in Remittance Cases.

(1) A collecting bank may take in settlement of an item

(a) a check of the remitting bank or of another bank on any bank except the remitting bank; or
(b) a cashier's check or similar primary obligation of a remitting bank which is a member of or clears through a member of the same clearing house or group as the collecting bank; or
(c) appropriate authority to charge an account of the remitting bank or of another bank with the collecting bank; or
(d) if the item is drawn upon or payable by a person other than a bank, a cashier's check, certified check or other bank check or obligation.

(2) If before its midnight deadline the collecting bank properly dishonors a remittance check or authorization to charge on itself or presents or forwards for collection a remittance instrument of or on another bank which is of a kind approved by subsection (1) or has not been authorized by it, the collecting bank is not liable to prior parties in the event of the dishonor of such check, instrument or authorization.
(3) A settlement for an item by means of a remittance instrument or authorization to charge is or becomes a final settlement as to both the person making and the person receiving the settlement

(a) if the remittance instrument or authorization to charge is of a kind approved by subsection (1) or has not been authorized by the person receiving the settlement and in either case the person receiving the settlement acts seasonably before its midnight deadline in presenting, forwarding for collection or paying the instrument or authorization,—at the time the remittance instrument or authorization is finally paid by the payor by which it is payable;
(b) if the person receiving the settlement has authorized remittance by a non-bank check or obligation or by a cashier's check or similar primary obligation of or a check upon the payor or other remitting bank which is not of a kind approved by subsection (1)(b),—at the time of the receipt of such remittance check or obligation; or
(c) if in a case not covered by sub-paragraphs (a) or (b) the person receiving the settlement fails to seasonably present, forward for collection, pay or return a remittance instrument or authorization to it to charge before its midnight deadline,—at such midnight deadline.

§ 4–212. Right of Charge-Back or Refund.

(1) If a collecting bank has made provisional settlement with its customer for an item and itself fails by reason of dishonor, suspension of payments by a bank or otherwise to receive a settlement for the item which is or becomes final, the bank may revoke the settlement given by it, charge-back the amount of any credit given for the item to its customer's account or obtain refund from its customer whether or not it is able to return the items if by its midnight deadline or within a longer reasonable time

after it learns the facts it returns the item or sends notification of the facts. These rights to revoke, charge-back and obtain refund terminate if and when a settle-ment for the item received by the bank is or becomes final (subsection (3) of Section 4–211 and subsections (2) and (3) of Section 4–213).

[(2) Within the time and manner prescribed by this section and Section 4–301, an intermediary or payor bank, as the case may be, may return an unpaid item directly to the depositary bank and may send for collec-tion a draft on the depositary bank and obtain reimburse-ment. In such case, if the depositary bank has received provisional settlement for the item, it must reimburse the bank drawing the draft and any provisional credits for the item between banks shall become and remain final.]

Note: *Direct returns is recognized as an innovation that is not yet established bank practice, and therefore, Paragraph 2 has been bracketed. Some lawyers have doubts whether it should be included in legislation or left to development by agreement.*

(3) A depositary bank which is also the payor may charge-back the amount of an item to its customer's account or obtain refund in accordance with the section governing return of an item received by a payor bank for credit on its books (Section 4–301).

(4) The right to charge-back is not affected by

(a) prior use of the credit given for the item; or
(b) failure by any bank to exercise ordinary care with respect to the item but any bank so failing remains liable.

(5) A failure to charge-back or claim refund does not affect other rights of the bank against the customer or any other party.

(6) If credit is given in dollars as the equivalent of the value of an item payable in a foreign currency the dollar amount of any charge-back or refund shall be calculated on the basis of the buying sight rate for the foreign currency prevailing on the day when the person entitled to the charge-back or refund learns that it will not receive payment in ordinary course.

§ 4–213. Final Payment of Item by Payor Bank; When Provisional Debits and Credits Become Final; When Certain Credits Become Available for Withdrawal.

(1) An item is finally paid by a payor bank when the bank has done any of the following, whichever happens first:

(a) paid the item in cash; or
(b) settled for the item without reserving a right to revoke the settlement and without having such right under statute, clearing house rule or agreement; or
(c) completed the process of posting the item to the indicated account of the drawer, maker or other person to be charged therewith; or
(d) made a provisional settlement for the item and failed to revoke the settlement in the time and manner permitted by statute, clearing house rule or agreement.

Upon a final payment under subparagraphs (b), (c), or (d) the payor bank shall be accountable for the amount of the item.

(2) If provisional settlement for an item between the presenting and payor banks is made through a clearing house or by debits or credits in an account between them, then to the extent that provisional debits or credits for the item are entered in accounts between the presenting and payor banks or between the presenting and successive prior collecting banks seriatim, they become final upon final payment of the item by the payor bank.

(3) If a collecting bank receives a settlement for an item which is or becomes final (subsection (3) of Section 4–211, subsection (2) of Section 4–213) the bank is accountable to its customer for the amount of the item and any provisional credit given for the item in an account with its customer becomes final.

(4) Subject to any right of the bank to apply the credit to an obligation of the customer, credit given by a bank for an item in an account with its customer becomes available for withdrawal as of right

(a) in any case where the bank has received a provi-sional settlement for the item,—when such settlement becomes final and the bank has had a reasonable time to learn that the settlement is final;
(b) in any case where the bank is both a depositary bank and a payor bank and the item is finally paid,—at the opening of the bank's second banking day following receipt of the item.

(5) A deposit of money in a bank is final when made but, subject to any right of the bank to apply the deposit to an obligation of the customer, the deposit becomes available for withdrawal as of right at the opening of the bank's next banking day following receipt of the deposit.

§ 4–214. Insolvency and Preference.

(1) Any item in or coming into the possession of a payor or collecting bank which suspends payment and which item is not finally paid shall be returned by the receiver, trustee or agent in charge of the closed bank to the presenting bank or the closed bank's customer.

(2) If a payor bank finally pays an item and suspends payments without making a settlement for the item with its customer or the presenting bank which settlement is or becomes final, the owner of the item has a preferred claim against the payor bank.

(3) If a payor bank gives or a collecting bank gives or receives a provisional settlement for an item and thereaf-ter suspends payments, the suspension does not prevent or interfere with the settlement becoming final if such finality occurs automatically upon the lapse of certain time or the happening of certain events (subsection (3) of Section 4–211, subsections (1)(d), (2) and (3) of Section 4–213).

(4) If a collecting bank receives from subsequent parties settlement for an item which settlement is or becomes final and suspends payments without making a settle-ment for the item with its customer which is or becomes final, the owner of the item has a preferred claim against such collecting bank.

Part 3 Collection of Items: Payor Banks

§ 4–301. Deferred Posting; Recovery of Payment by Return of Items; Time of Dishonor.

(1) Where an authorized settlement for a demand item (other than a documentary draft) received by a payor bank otherwise than for immediate payment over the counter has been made before midnight of the banking day of receipt the payor bank may revoke the settlement and recover any payment if before it has made final payment (subsection (1) of Section 4–213) and before its midnight deadline it

(a) returns the item; or
(b) sends written notice of dishonor or nonpayment if the item is held for protest or is otherwise unavailable for return.

(2) If a demand item is received by a payor bank for credit on its books it may return such item or send notice of dishonor and may revoke any credit given or recover the amount thereof withdrawn by its customer, if it acts within the time limit and in the manner specified in the preceding subsection.
(3) Unless previous notice of dishonor has been sent an item is dishonored at the time when for purposes of dishonor it is returned or notice sent in accordance with this section.
(4) An item is returned:

(a) as to an item received through a clearing house when it is delivered to the presenting or last collecting bank or to the clearing house or is sent or delivered in accordance with its rules; or
(b) in all other cases, when it is sent or delivered to the bank's customer or transferor or pursuant to his instructions.

§ 4–302. Payor Bank's Responsibility for Late Return of Item.

In the absence of a valid defense such as breach of a presentment warranty (subsection (1) of Section 4–207), settlement effected or the like, if an item is presented on and received by a payor bank the bank is accountable for the amount of

(a) a demand item other than a documentary draft whether properly payable or not if the bank, in any case where it is not also the depositary bank, retains the item beyond midnight of the banking day of receipt without settling for it or, regardless of whether it is also the depositary bank, does not pay or return the item or send notice of dishonor until after its midnight deadline; or
(b) any other properly payable item unless within the time allowed for acceptance or payment of that item the bank either accepts or pays the item or returns it and accompanying documents.

§ 4–303. When Items Subject to Notice, Stop-Order, Legal Process or Setoff; Order in Which Items May Be Charged or Certified.

(1) Any knowledge, notice or stop-order received by, legal process served upon or setoff exercised by a payor bank, whether or not effective under other rules of law to terminate, suspend or modify the bank's right or duty to pay an item or to charge its customer's account for the item, comes too late to so terminate, suspend or modify such right or duty if the knowledge, notice, stop-order or legal process is received or served and a reasonable time for the bank to act thereon expires or the setoff is exercised after the bank has done any of the following:

(a) accepted or certified the item;
(b) paid the item in cash;
(c) settled for the item without reserving a right to revoke the settlement and without having such right under statute, clearing house rule or agreement;
(d) completed the process of posting the item to the indicated account of the drawer, maker, or other person to be charged therewith or otherwise has evidenced by examination of such indicated account and by action its decision to pay the item; or
(e) become accountable for the amount of the item under subsection (1)(d) of Section 4–213 and Section 4–302 dealing with the payor bank's responsibility for late return of items.

(2) Subject to the provisions of subsection (1) items may be accepted, paid, certified or charged to the indicated account of its customer in any order convenient to the bank.

Part 4 Relationship Between Payor Bank and Its Customer

§ 4–401. When Bank May Charge Customer's Account.

(1) As against its customer, a bank may charge against his account any item which is otherwise properly payable from that account even though the charge creates an overdraft.
(2) A bank which in good faith makes payment to a holder may charge the indicated account of its customer according to

(a) the original tenor of his altered item; or
(b) the tenor of his completed item, even though the bank knows the item has been completed unless the bank has notice that the completion was improper.

§ 4–402. Bank's Liability to Customer for Wrongful Dishonor.

A payor bank is liable to its customer for damages proximately caused by the wrongful dishonor of an item. When the dishonor occurs through mistake liability is limited to actual damages proved. If so proximately caused and proved damages may include damages for an arrest or prosecution of the customer or other consequential damages. Whether any consequential damages are proximately caused by the wrongful dishonor is a question of fact to be determined in each case.

§ 4–403. Customer's Right to Stop Payment; Burden of Proof of Loss.

(1) A customer may by order to his bank stop payment of any item payable for his account but the order must be received at such time and in such manner as to afford the bank a reasonable opportunity to act on it prior to any action by the bank with respect to the item described in Section 4–303.
(2) An oral order is binding upon the bank only for fourteen calendar days unless confirmed in writing within that period. A written order is effective for only six months unless renewed in writing.
(3) The burden of establishing the fact and amount of loss resulting from the payment of an item contrary to a binding stop payment order is on the customer.

§ 4–404. Bank Not Obligated to Pay Check More Than Six Months Old.

A bank is under no obligation to a customer having a checking account to pay a check, other than a certified check, which is presented more than six months after its date, but it may charge its customer's account for a payment made thereafter in good faith.

§ 4–405. Death or Incompetence of Customer.

(1) A payor or collecting bank's authority to accept, pay or collect an item or to account for proceeds of its collection if otherwise effective is not rendered ineffective by incompetence of a customer of either bank existing at the time the item is issued or its collection is undertaken if the bank does not know of an adjudication of incompetence. Neither death nor incompetence of a customer revokes such authority to accept, pay, collect or account until the bank knows of the fact of death or of an adjudication of incompetence and has reasonable opportunity to act on it.
(2) Even with knowledge a bank may for ten days after the date of death pay or certify checks drawn on or prior to that date unless ordered to stop payment by a person claiming an interest in the account.

§ 4–406. Customer's Duty to Discover and Report Unauthorized Signature or Alteration.

(1) When a bank sends to its customer a statement of account accompanied by items paid in good faith in support of the debit entries or holds the statement and items pursuant to a request or instructions of its customer or otherwise in a reasonable manner makes the statement and items available to the customer, the customer must exercise reasonable care and promptness to examine the statement and items to discover his unauthorized signature or any alteration on an item and must notify the bank promptly after discovery thereof.
(2) If the bank establishes that the customer failed with respect to an item to comply with the duties imposed on the customer by subsection (1) the customer is precluded from asserting against the bank

(a) his unauthorized signature or any alteration on the item if the bank also establishes that it suffered a loss by reason of such failure; and
(b) an unauthorized signature or alteration by the same wrongdoer on any other item paid in good faith by the bank after the first item and statement was available to the customer for a reasonable period not exceeding fourteen calendar days and before the bank receives notification from the customer of any such unauthorized signature or alteration.

(3) The preclusion under subsection (2) does not apply if the customer establishes lack of ordinary care on the part of the bank in paying the item(s).
(4) Without regard to care or lack of care of either the customer or the bank a customer who does not within one year from the time the statement and items are made available to the customer (subsection (1)) discover and report his unauthorized signature or any alteration on the face or back of the item or does not within three years from that time discover and report any unauthorized indorsement is precluded from asserting against the bank such unauthorized signature or indorsement or such alteration.
(5) If under this section a payor bank has a valid defense against a claim of a customer upon or resulting from payment of an item and waives or fails upon request to assert the defense the bank may not assert against any collecting bank or other prior party presenting or transferring the item a claim based upon the unauthorized signature or alteration giving rise to the customer's claim.

§ 4–407. Payor Bank's Right to Subrogation on Improper Payment.

If a payor bank has paid an item over the stop payment order of the drawer or maker or otherwise under circumstances giving a basis for objection by the drawer or maker, to prevent unjust enrichment and only to the extent necessary to prevent loss to the bank by reason of its payment of the item, the payor bank shall be subrogated to the rights.

(a) of any holder in due course on the item against the drawer or maker; and
(b) of the payee or any other holder of the item against the drawer or maker either on the item or under the transaction out of which the item arose; and

(c) of the drawer or maker against the payee or any other holder of the item with respect to the transaction out of which the item arose.

Part 5 Collection of Documentary Drafts

§ 4–501. Handling of Documentary Drafts; Duty to Send for Presentment and to Notify Customer of Dishonor.

A bank which takes a documentary draft for collection must present or send the draft and accompanying documents for presentment and upon learning that the draft has not been paid or accepted in due course must seasonably notify its customer of such fact even though it may have discounted or bought the draft or extended credit available for withdrawal as of right.

§ 4–502. Presentment of "On Arrival" Drafts.

When a draft or the relevant instructions require presentment "on arrival", "when goods arrive" or the like, the collecting bank need not present until in its judgment a reasonable time for arrival of the goods has expired. Refusal to pay or accept because the goods have not arrived is not dishonor; the bank must notify its transferor of such refusal but need not present the draft again until it is instructed to do so or learns of the arrival of the goods.

§ 4–503. Responsibility of Presenting Bank for Documents and Goods; Report of Reasons for Dishonor; Referee in Case of Need.

Unless otherwise instructed and except as provided in Article 5 a bank presenting a documentary draft

(a) must deliver the documents to the drawee on acceptance of the draft if it is payable more than three days after presentment; otherwise, only on payment; and
(b) upon dishonor, either in the case of presentment for acceptance or presentment for payment, may seek and follow instructions from any referee in case of need designated in the draft or if the presenting bank does not choose to utilize his services it must use diligence and good faith to ascertain the reason for dishonor, must notify its transferor of the dishonor and of the results of its effort to ascertain the reasons therefor and must request instructions.

But the presenting bank is under no obligation with respect to goods represented by the documents except to follow any reasonable instructions seasonably received; it has a right to reimbursement for any expense incurred in following instructions and to prepayment of or indemnity for such expenses.

§ 4–504. Privilege of Presenting Bank to Deal With Goods; Security Interest for Expenses.

(1) A presenting bank which, following the dishonor of a documentary draft, has seasonably requested instructions but does not receive them within a reasonable time may store, sell, or otherwise deal with the goods in any reasonable manner.
(2) For its reasonable expenses incurred by action under subsection (1) the presenting bank has a lien upon the goods or their proceeds, which may be foreclosed in the same manner as an unpaid seller's lien.

Article 5

LETTERS OF CREDIT

§ 5–101. Short Title.

This Article shall be known and may be cited as Uniform Commercial Code—Letters of Credit.

§ 5–102. Scope.

(1) This Article applies

(a) to a credit issued by a bank if the credit requires a documentary draft or a documentary demand for payment; and
(b) to a credit issued by a person other than a bank if the credit requires that the draft or demand for payment be accompanied by a document of title; and
(c) to a credit issued by a bank or other person if the credit is not within subparagraphs (a) or (b) but conspicuously states that it is a letter of credit or is conspicuously so entitled.

(2) Unless the engagement meets the requirements of subsection (1), this Article does not apply to engagements to make advances or to honor drafts or demands for payment, to authorities to pay or purchase, to guarantees or to general agreements.
(3) This Article deals with some but not all of the rules and concepts of letters of credit as such rules or concepts have developed prior to this act or may hereafter develop. The fact that this Article states a rule does not by itself require, imply or negate application of the same or a converse rule to a situation not provided for or to a person not specified by this Article.

§ 5–103. Definitions.

(1) In this Article unless the context otherwise requires

(a) "Credit" or "letter of credit" means an engagement by a bank or other person made at the request of a customer and of a kind within the scope of this Article (Section 5–102) that the issuer will honor drafts or other demands for payment upon compliance with the conditions specified in the credit. A credit may be either revocable or irrevocable. The engagement may be either an agreement to honor or a statement that the bank or other person is authorized to honor.

(b) A "documentary draft" or a "documentary demand for payment" is one honor of which is conditioned upon the presentation of a document or documents. "Document" means any paper including document of title, security, invoice, certificate, notice of default and the like.

(c) An "issuer" is a bank or other person issuing a credit.

(d) A "beneficiary" of a credit is a person who is entitled under its terms to draw or demand payment.

(e) An "advising bank" is a bank which gives notification of the issuance of a credit by another bank.

(f) A "confirming bank" is a bank which engages either that it will itself honor a credit already issued by another bank or that such a credit will be honored by the issuer or a third bank.

(g) A "customer" is a buyer or other person who causes an issuer to issue a credit. The term also includes a bank which procures issuance or confirmation on behalf of that bank's customer.

(2) Other definitions applying to this Article and the sections in which they appear are:

"Notation of Credit". Section 5–108.
"Presenter". Section 5–112(3).

(3) Definitions in other Articles applying to this Article and the sections in which they appear are:

"Accept" or "Acceptance". Section 3–410.
"Contract for sale". Section 2–106.
"Draft". Section 3–104.
"Holder in due course". Section 3–302.
"Midnight deadline". Section 4–104.
"Security". Section 8–102.

(4) In addition, Article 1 contains general definitions and principles of construction and interpretation applicable throughout this Article.

§ 5–104. Formal Requirements; Signing.

(1) Except as otherwise required in subsection (1)(c) of Section 5–102 on scope, no particular form of phrasing is required for a credit. A credit must be in writing and signed by the issuer and a confirmation must be in writing and signed by the confirming bank. A modification of the terms of a credit or confirmation must be signed by the issuer or confirming bank.

(2) A telegram may be a sufficient signed writing if it identifies its sender by an authorized authentication. The authentication may be in code and the authorized naming of the issuer in an advice of credit is a sufficient signing.

§ 5–105. Consideration.

No consideration is necessary to establish a credit or to enlarge or otherwise modify its terms.

§ 5–106. Time and Effect of Establishment of Credit.

(1) Unless otherwise agreed a credit is established.

(a) as regards the customer as soon as a letter of credit is sent to him or the letter of credit or an authorized written advice of its issuance is sent to the beneficiary; and

(b) as regards the beneficiary when he receives a letter of credit or an authorized written advice of its issuance.

(2) Unless otherwise agreed once an irrevocable credit is established as regards the customer it can be modified or revoked only with the consent of the customer and once it is established as regards the beneficiary it can be modified or revoked only with his consent.

(3) Unless otherwise agreed after a revocable credit is established it may be modified or revoked by the issuer without notice to or consent from the customer or beneficiary.

(4) Notwithstanding any modification or revocation of a revocable credit any person authorized to honor or negotiate under the terms of the original credit is entitled to reimbursement for or honor of any draft or demand for payment duty honored or negotiated before receipt of notice of the modification or revocation and the issuer in turn is entitled to reimbursement from its customer.

§ 5–107. Advice of Credit; Confirmation; Error in Statement of Terms.

(1) Unless otherwise specified an advising bank by advising a credit issued by another bank does not assume any obligation to honor drafts drawn or demands for payment made under the credit but it does assume obligation for the accuracy of its own statement.

(2) A confirming bank by confirming a credit becomes directly obligated on the credit to the extent of its confirmation as though it were its issuer and acquires the rights of an issuer.

(3) Even though an advising bank incorrectly advises the terms of a credit it has been authorized to advise the credit is established as against the issuer to the extent of its original terms.

(4) Unless otherwise specified the customer bears as against the issuer all risks of transmission and reasonable translation or interpretation of any message relating to a credit.

§ 5–108. "Notation Credit"; Exhaustion of Credit.

(1) A credit which specifies that any person purchasing or paying drafts drawn or demands for payment made under it must note the amount of the draft or demand on the letter or advice of credit is a "notation credit".

(2) Under a notation credit

(a) a person paying the beneficiary or purchasing a draft or demand for payment from him acquires a right to honor only if the appropriate notation is made and by transferring or forwarding for honor the documents under the credit such a person warrants to the issuer that the notation has been made; and

(b) unless the credit or a signed statement that an appropriate notation has been made accompanies the draft or demand for payment the issuer may delay honor until evidence of notation has been procured which is satisfactory to it but its obligation and that of its customer continue for a reasonable time not exceeding thirty days to obtain such evidence.

(3) If the credit is not a notation credit

(a) the issuer may honor complying drafts or demands for payment presented to it in the order in which they are presented and is discharged pro tanto by honor of any such draft or demand;

(b) as between competing good faith purchasers of complying drafts or demands the person first purchasing has priority over a subsequent purchaser even though the later purchased draft or demand has been first honored.

§ 5–109. Issuer's Obligation to Its Customer.

(1) An issuer's obligation to its customer includes good faith and observance of any general banking usage but unless otherwise agreed does not include liability or responsibility

(a) for performance of the underlying contract for sale or other transaction between the customer and the beneficiary; or

(b) for any act or omission of any person other than itself or its own branch or for loss or destruction of a draft, demand or document in transit or in the possession of others; or

(c) based on knowledge or lack of knowledge of any usage of any particular trade.

(2) An issuer must examine documents with care so as to ascertain that on their face they appear to comply with the terms of the credit but unless otherwise agreed assumes no liability or responsibility for the genuineness, falsification or effect of any document which appears on such examination to be regular on its face.

(3) A non-bank issuer is not bound by any banking usage of which it has no knowledge.

§ 5–110. Availability of Credit in Portions; Presenter's Reservation of Lien or Claim.

(1) Unless otherwise specified a credit may be used in portions in the discretion of the beneficiary.

(2) Unless otherwise specified a person by presenting a documentary draft or demand for payment under a credit relinquishes upon its honor all claims to the documents and a person by transferring such draft or demand or

causing such presentment authorizes such relinquishment. An explicit reservation of claim makes the draft or demand non-complying.

§ 5–111. Warranties on Transfer and Presentment.

(1) Unless otherwise agreed the beneficiary by transferring or presenting a documentary draft or demand for payment warrants to all interested parties that the necessary conditions of the credit have been complied with. This is in addition to any warranties arising under Articles 3, 4, 7 and 8.

(2) Unless otherwise agreed a negotiating, advising, confirming, collecting or issuing bank presenting or transferring a draft or demand for payment under a credit warrants only the matters warranted by a collecting bank under Article 4 and any such bank transferring a document warrants only the matters warranted by an intermediary under Articles 7 and 8.

§ 5–112. Time Allowed for Honor or Rejection; Withholding Honor or Rejection by Consent; "Presenter".

(1) A bank to which a documentary draft or demand for payment is presented under a credit may without dishonor of the draft, demand or credit

(a) defer honor until the close of the third banking day following receipt of the documents; and

(b) further defer honor if the presenter has expressly or impliedly consented thereto.

Failure to honor within the time here specified constitutes dishonor of the draft or demand and of the credit [except as otherwise provided in subsection (4) of Section 5–114 on conditional payment].

Note: *The bracketed language in the last sentence of subsection (1) should be included only if the optional provisions of Section 5–114(4) and (5) are included.*

(2) Upon dishonor the bank may unless otherwise instructed fulfill its duty to return the draft or demand and the documents by holding them at the disposal of the presenter and sending him an advice to that effect.

(3) "Presenter" means any person presenting a draft or demand for payment for honor under a credit even though that person is a confirming bank or other correspondent which is acting under an issuer's authorization.

§ 5–113. Indemnities.

(1) A bank seeking to obtain (whether for itself or another) honor, negotiation or reimbursement under a credit may give an indemnity to induce such honor, negotiation or reimbursement.

(2) An indemnity agreement inducing honor, negotiation or reimbursement

(a) unless otherwise explicitly agreed applies to defects in the documents but not in the goods; and

(b) unless a longer time is explicitly agreed expires at the end of ten business days following receipt of the documents by, the ultimate customer unless notice of objection is sent before such expiration date. The ultimate customer may send notice of objection to the person from whom he received the documents and any bank receiving such notice is under a duty to send notice to its transferor before its midnight deadline.

§ 5–114. Issuer's Duty and Privilege to Honor; Right to Reimbursement.

(1) An issuer must honor a draft or demand for payment which complies with the terms of the relevant credit regardless of whether the goods or documents conform to the underlying contract for sale or other contract between the customer and the beneficiary. The issuer is not excused from honor of such a draft or demand by reason of an additional general term that all documents must be satisfactory to the issuer, but an issuer may require that specified documents must be satisfactory to it.

(2) Unless otherwise agreed when documents appear on their face to comply with the terms of a credit but a required document does not in fact conform to the warranties made on negotiation or transfer of a document of title (Section 7–507) or of a certificated security (Section 8–306) or is forged or fraudulent or there is fraud in the transaction:

(a) the issuer must honor the draft or demand for payment if honor is demanded by a negotiating bank or other holder of the draft or demand which has taken the draft or demand under the credit and under circumstances which would make it a holder in due course (Section 3–302) and in an appropriate case would make it a person to whom a document of title has been duly negotiated (Section 7–502) or a bona fide purchaser of a certificated security (Section 8–302); and

(b) in all other cases as against its customer, an issuer acting in good faith may honor the draft or demand for payment despite notification from the customer of fraud, forgery or other defect not apparent on the face of the documents but a court of appropriate jurisdiction may enjoin such honor.

(3) Unless otherwise agreed an issuer which has duly honored a draft or demand for payment is entitled to immediate reimbursement of any payment made under the credit and to be put in effectively available funds not later than the day before maturity of any acceptance made under the credit.

[(4) When a credit provides for payment by the issuer on receipt of notice that the required documents are in the possession of a correspondent or other agent of the issuer

(a) any payment made on receipt of such notice is conditional; and

(b) the issuer may reject documents which do not comply with the credit if it does so within three banking days following its receipt of the documents; and

(c) in the event of such rejection, the issuer is entitled by charge back or otherwise to return of the payment made.]

[(5) In the case covered by subsection (4) failure to reject documents within the time specified in sub-paragraph (b) constitutes acceptance of the documents and makes the payment final in favor of the beneficiary.]

Amended in 1977.

Note: *Subsections (4) and (5) are bracketed as optional. If they are included the bracketed language in the last sentence of Section 5–112(1) should also be included.*

§ 5–115. Remedy for Improper Dishonor or Anticipatory Repudiation.

(1) When an issuer wrongfully dishonors a draft or demand for payment presented under a credit the person entitled to honor has with respect to any documents the rights of a person in the position of a seller (Section 2–707) and may recover from the issuer the face amount of the draft or demand together with incidental damages under Section 2–710 on seller's incidental damages and interest but less any amount realized by resale or other use or disposition of the subject matter of the transaction. In the event no resale or other utilization is made the documents, goods or other subject matter involved in the transaction must be turned over to the issuer on payment of judgment.

(2) When an issuer wrongfully cancels or otherwise repudiates a credit before presentment of a draft or demand for payment drawn under it the beneficiary has the rights of a seller after anticipatory repudiation by the buyer under Section 2–610 if he learns of the repudiation in time reasonably to avoid procurement of the required documents. Otherwise the beneficiary has an immediate right of action for wrongful dishonor.

§ 5–116. Transfer and Assignment.

(1) The right to draw under a credit can be transferred or assigned only when the credit is expressly designated as transferable or assignable.

(2) Even though the credit specifically states that it is nontransferable or nonassignable the beneficiary may before performance of the conditions of the credit assign his right to proceeds. Such an assignment is an assignment of an account under Article 9 on Secured Transactions and is governed by that Article except that

(a) the assignment is ineffective until the letter of credit or advice of credit is delivered to the assignee which delivery constitutes perfection of the security interest under Article 9; and

(b) the issuer may honor drafts or demands for payment drawn under the credit until it receives a notification of the assignment signed by the beneficiary which reasonably identifies the credit involved in the assignment and contains a request to pay the assignee; and

(c) after what reasonably appears to be such a notification has been received the issuer may without dishonor refuse to accept or pay even to a person otherwise entitled to honor until the letter of credit or advice of credit is exhibited to the issuer.

(3) Except where the beneficiary has effectively assigned his right to draw or his right to proceeds, nothing in this section limits his right to transfer or negotiate drafts or demands drawn under the credit.

§ 5–117. Insolvency of Bank Holding Funds for Documentary Credit.

(1) Where an issuer or an advising or confirming bank or a bank which has for a customer procured issuance of a credit by another bank becomes insolvent before final payment under the credit and the credit is one to which this Article is made applicable by paragraphs (a) or (b) of Section 5–102(1) on scope, the receipt or allocation of funds or collateral to secure or meet obligations under the credit shall have the following results:

(a) to the extent of any funds or collateral turned over after or before the insolvency as indemnity against or specifically for the purpose of payment of drafts or demands for payment drawn under the designated credit, the drafts or demands are entitled to payment in preference over depositors or other general creditors of the issuer or bank; and

(b) on expiration of the credit or surrender of the beneficiary's rights under it unused any person who has given such funds or collateral is similarly entitled to return thereof; and

(c) a charge to a general or current account with a bank if specifically consented to for the purpose of indemnity against or payment of drafts or demands for payment drawn under the designated credit falls under the same rules as if the funds had been drawn out in cash and then turned over with specific instructions.

(2) After honor or reimbursement under this section the customer or other person for whose account the insolvent bank has acted is entitled to receive the documents involved.

Article 6

BULK TRANSFERS

§ 6–101. Short Title.

This Article shall be known and may be cited as Uniform Commercial Code—Bulk Transfers.

§ 6–102. "Bulk Transfer"; Transfers of Equipment; Enterprises Subject to This Article; Bulk Transfers Subject to This Article.

(1) A "bulk transfer" is any transfer in bulk and not in the ordinary course of the transferor's business of a major part of the materials, supplies, merchandise or other inventory (Section 9–109) of an enterprise subject to this Article.

(2) A transfer of a substantial part of the equipment (Section 9–109) of such an enterprise is a bulk transfer if it is made in connection with a bulk transfer of inventory, but not otherwise.

(3) The enterprises subject to this Article are all those whose principal business is the sale of merchandise from stock, including those who manufacture what they sell.

(4) Except as limited by the following section all bulk transfers of goods located within this state are subject to this Article.

§ 6–103. Transfers Excepted From This Article.

The following transfers are not subject to this Article:

(1) Those made to give security for the performance of an obligation;

(2) General assignments for the benefit of all the creditors of the transferor, and subsequent transfers by the assignee thereunder;

(3) Transfers in settlement or realization of a lien or other security interest;

(4) Sales by executors, administrators, receivers, trustees in bankruptcy, or any public officer under judicial process;

(5) Sales made in the course of judicial or administrative proceedings for the dissolution or reorganization of a corporation and of which notice is sent to the creditors of the corporation pursuant to order of the court or administrative agency;

(6) Transfers to a person maintaining a known place of business in this State who becomes bound to pay the debts of the transferor in full and gives public notice of that fact, and who is solvent after becoming so bound;

(7) A transfer to a new business enterprise organized to take over and continue the business, if public notice of the transaction is given and the new enterprise assumes the debts of the transferor and he receives nothing from the transaction except an interest in the new enterprise junior to the claims of creditors;

(8) Transfers of property which is exempt from execution.

Public notice under subsection (6) or subsection (7) may be given by publishing once a week for two consecutive weeks in a newspaper of general circulation where the transferor had its principal place of business in this state an advertisement including the names and addresses of the transferor and transferee and the effective date of the transfer.

§ 6–104. Schedule of Property, List of Creditors.

(1) Except as provided with respect to auction sales (Section 6–108), a bulk transfer subject to this Article is ineffective against any creditor of the transferor unless:

(a) The transferee requires the transferor to furnish a list of his existing creditors prepared as stated in this section; and

Actions and Levies.

Article shall be brought nor levy
nonths after the date on which the
sion of the goods unless the transfer
If the transfer has been concealed,
ht or levies made within six months

on 6–106 is bracketed to indicate division
r or not it is a wise provision, and to
int on which State enactments may differ
to the principle of uniformity.
tion 6–106 is not enacted, the following
bracketed in the text, should also be

Section 6–106 is enacted, these other
lso.

RECEIPTS, BILLS OF
OTHER DOCUMENTS

e.

be known and may be cited as Uniform
—Documents of Title.

ns and Index of Definitions.

, unless the context otherwise requires:

eans the person who by a warehouse
ding or other document of title acknowl-
on of goods and contracts to deliver

" means the person named in a bill to
hose order the bill promises delivery.
r" means the person named in a bill as the
whom the goods have been received for

order" means a written order to deliver
d to a warehouseman, carrier or other
n the ordinary course of business issues
ceipts or bills of lading.
t" means document of title as defined in
efinitions in Article 1 (Section 1–201).
means all things which are treated as
the purposes of a contract of storage or
h.
means a bailee who issues a document
relation to an unaccepted delivery order it

val of uniformity. In any State where this
following parts of sections, also bracketed
to be omitted, namely:

this section is enacted, these other provi-

(4)

y within ten days after he takes pos-
y the consideration into the (specify
here the transferor had its principal
state and thereafter may discharge
tion by giving notice by registered
he persons to whom the duty runs
ıs been paid into that court and that
ims there. On motion of any inter-
y order the distribution of the con-
s entitled to it.]
(4) is recommended for those states
tatute providing for payment of money

s (Section 6–105) shall state:

s about to be made; and
ıess addresses of the transferor
other business names and ad-
ısferor within three years last
he transferee; and
debts of the transferor are to
fall due as a result of the
e address to which creditors

eror are not to be paid in full
ansferee is in doubt on that
tate further:

description of the property
timated total of the transfer-

chedule of property and list
nay be inspected;
pay existing debts and if so
d to whom owing;
r new consideration and if
leration and the time and

he time and place where
to file their claims.]

be delivered personally or
mail to all the persons
rnished by the transferor
persons who are known
sert claims against the

§ 6–108. Auction Sales; "Auctioneer".

(1) A bulk transfer is subject to this Article even though it is by sale at auction, but only in the manner and with the results stated in this section.

(2) The transferor shall furnish a list of his creditors and assist in the preparation of a schedule of the property to be sold, both prepared as before stated (Section 6–104).

(3) The person or persons other than the transferor who direct, control or are responsible for the auction are collectively called the "auctioneer". The auctioneer shall:

(a) receive and retain the list of creditors and prepare and retain the schedule of property for the period stated in this Article (Section 6–104);

(b) give notice of the auction personally or by registered or certified mail at least ten days before it occurs to all persons shown on the list of creditors and to all other persons who are known to him to hold or assert claims against the transferor; [and]

[(c) assure that the net proceeds of the auction are applied as provided in this Article (Section 6–106).]

(4) Failure of the auctioneer to perform any of these duties does not affect the validity of the sale or the title of the purchasers, but if the auctioneer knows that the auction constitutes a bulk transfer such failure renders the auctioneer liable to the creditors of the transferor as a class for the sums owing to them from the transferor up to but not exceeding the net proceeds of the auction. If the auctioneer consists of several persons their liability is joint and several.

§ 6–109. What Creditors Protected; [Credit for Payment to Particular Creditors].

(1) The creditors of the transferor mentioned in this Article are those holding claims based on transactions or events occurring before the bulk transfer, but creditors who become such after notice to creditors is given (Sections 6–105 and 6–107) are not entitled to notice.

[(2) Against the aggregate obligation imposed by the provisions of this Article concerning the application of the proceeds (Section 6–106 and subsection (3)(c) of 6–108) the transferee or auctioneer is entitled to credit for sums paid to particular creditors of the transferor, not exceeding the sums believed in good faith at the time of the payment to be properly payable to such creditors.]

§ 6–110. Subsequent Transfers.

When the title of a transferee to property is subject to a defect by reason of his non-compliance with the requirements of this Article, then:

(1) a purchaser of any such property from such transferee who pays no value or who takes with notice of such non-compliance takes subject to such defect, but

(2) a purchaser for value in good faith and without such notice takes free of such defect.

§ 6–111. Limitation o[f]

No action under thi[s] made more than six [months after the] transferee took posses[sion] has been concealed. [In cases of concealment,] actions may be broug[ht within...] after its discovery.

Note to Article 6: Sect[ions...] of opinion as to wheth[er...] suggest that this is a p[oint...] without serious damag[e...] In any State where Se[ction...] parts of sections, als[o...] omitted, namely:

Sec. 6–107(2)(e).
6–108(3)(c).
6–109(2).

In any State where [...] provisions should be a[...]

Article 7

WAREHOUSE [RECEIPTS, BILLS OF] LADING AND [OTHER DOCUMENTS] OF TITLE

Part 1 General

§ 7–101. Short Tit[le].

This Article shall [be known as Uniform] Commercial Code[—Documents of Title.]

§ 7–102. Definiti[ons.]

(1) In this Articl[e]

(a) "Bailee" m[eans the person who by a warehouse] receipt, bill of l[ading or other document of title acknowl-] edges possess[ion of goods and contracts to deliver] them.

(b) "Consigne[e"...] whom or to w[...]

(c) "Consigno[r"...] person from [whom...] shipment.

(d) "Delivery [order"...] goods directe[d...] person who i[...] warehouse re[...]

(e) "Docume[nt"...] the general d[...]

(f) "Goods" [...] movable for [...] transportatio[n...]

(g) "Issuer" [...] except that i[...]

means the person who orders the possessor of goods to deliver. Issuer includes any person for whom an agent or employee purports to act in issuing a document if the agent or employee has real or apparent authority to issue documents, notwithstanding that the issuer received no goods or that the goods were misdescribed or that in any other respect the agent or employee violated his instructions.

(h) "Warehouseman" is a person engaged in the business of storing goods for hire.

(2) Other definitions applying to this Article or to specified Parts thereof, and the sections in which they appear are:

"Duly negotiate". Section 7–501.
"Person entitled under the document". Section 7–403(4).

(3) Definitions in other Articles applying to this Article and the sections in which they appear are:

"Contract for sale". Section 2–106.
"Overseas". Section 2–323.
"Receipt" of goods. Section 2–103.

(4) In addition Article 1 contains general definitions and principles of construction and interpretation applicable throughout this Article.

§ 7–103. Relation of Article to Treaty, Statute, Tariff, Classification or Regulation.

To the extent that any treaty or statute of the United States, regulatory statute of this State or tariff, classification or regulation filed or issued pursuant thereto is applicable, the provisions of this Article are subject thereto.

§ 7–104. Negotiable and Non-Negotiable Warehouse Receipt, Bill of Lading or Other Document of Title.

(1) A warehouse receipt, bill of lading or other document of title is negotiable

(a) if by its terms the goods are to be delivered to bearer or to the order of a named person; or
(b) where recognized in overseas trade, if it runs to a named person or assigns.

(2) Any other document is non-negotiable. A bill of lading in which it is stated that the goods are consigned to a named person is not made negotiable by a provision that the goods are to be delivered only against a written order signed by the same or another named person.

§ 7–105. Construction Against Negative Implication.

The omission from either Part 2 or Part 3 of this Article of a provision corresponding to a provision made in the other Part does not imply that a corresponding rule of law is not applicable.

Part 2 Warehouse Receipts: Special Provisions

§ 7–201. Who May Issue a Warehouse Receipt; Storage Under Government Bond.

(1) A warehouse receipt may be issued by any warehouseman.
(2) Where goods including distilled spirits and agricultural commodities are stored under a statute requiring a bond against withdrawal or a license for the issuance of receipts in the nature of warehouse receipts, a receipt issued for the goods has like effect as a warehouse receipt even though issued by a person who is the owner of the goods and is not a warehouseman.

§ 7–202. Form of Warehouse Receipt; Essential Terms; Optional Terms.

(1) A warehouse receipt need not be in any particular form.
(2) Unless a warehouse receipt embodies within its written or printed terms each of the following, the warehouseman is liable for damages caused by the omission to a person injured thereby:

(a) the location of the warehouse where the goods are stored;
(b) the date of issue of the receipt;
(c) the consecutive number of the receipt;
(d) a statement whether the goods received will be delivered to the bearer, to a specified person, or to a specified person or his order;
(e) the rate of storage and handling charges, except that where goods are stored under a field warehousing arrangement a statement of that fact is sufficient on a non-negotiable receipt;
(f) a description of the goods or of the packages containing them;
(g) the signature of the warehouseman, which may be made by his authorized agent;
(h) if the receipt is issued for goods of which the warehouseman is owner, either solely or jointly or in common with others, the fact of such ownership; and
(i) a statement of the amount of advances made and of liabilities incurred for which the warehouseman claims a lien or security interest (Section 7–209). If the precise amount of such advances made or of such liabilities incurred is, at the time of the issue of the receipt, unknown to the warehouseman or to his agent who issues it, a statement of the fact that advances have been made or liabilities incurred and the purpose thereof is sufficient.

(3) A warehouseman may insert in his receipt any other terms which are not contrary to the provisions of this Act and do not impair his obligation of delivery (Section 7–403) or his duty of care (Section 7–204). Any contrary provisions shall be ineffective.

§ 7–203. Liability for Non-Receipt or Misdescription.

A party to or purchaser for value in good faith of a document of title other than a bill of lading relying in either case upon the description therein of the goods may recover from the issuer damages caused by the non-receipt or misdescription of the goods, except to the extent that the document conspicuously indicates that the issuer does not know whether any part or all of the goods in fact were received or conform to the description, as where the description is in terms of marks or labels or kind, quantity or condition, or the receipt or description is qualified by "contents, condition and quality unknown", "said to contain" or the like, if such indication be true, or the party or purchaser otherwise has notice.

§ 7–204. Duty of Care; Contractual Limitation of Warehouseman's Liability.

(1) A warehouseman is liable for damages for loss of or injury to the goods caused by his failure to exercise such care in regard to them as a reasonably careful man would exercise under like circumstances but unless otherwise agreed he is not liable for damages which could not have been avoided by the exercise of such care.

(2) Damages may be limited by a term in the warehouse receipt or storage agreement limiting the amount of liability in case of loss or damage, and setting forth a specific liability per article or item, or value per unit of weight, beyond which the warehouseman shall not be liable; provided, however, that such liability may on written request of the bailor at the time of signing such storage agreement or within a reasonable time after receipt of the warehouse receipt be increased on part or all of the goods thereunder, in which event increased rates may be charged based on such increased valuation, but that no such increase shall be permitted contrary to a lawful limitation of liability contained in the warehouseman's tariff, if any. No such limitation is effective with respect to the warehouseman's liability for conversion to his own use.

(3) Reasonable provisions as to the time and manner of presenting claims and instituting actions based on the bailment may be included in the warehouse receipt or tariff.

(4) This section does not impair or repeal . . .

Note: *Insert in subsection (4) a reference to any statute which imposes a higher responsibility upon the warehouseman or invalidates contractual limitations which would be permissible under this Article.*

§ 7–205. Title Under Warehouse Receipt Defeated in Certain Cases.

A buyer in the ordinary course of business of fungible goods sold and delivered by a warehouseman who is also in the business of buying and selling such goods takes free of any claim under a warehouse receipt even though it has been duly negotiated.

§ 7–206. Termination of Storage at Warehouseman's Option.

(1) A warehouseman may on notifying the person on whose account the goods are held and any other person known to claim an interest in the goods require payment of any charges and removal of the goods from the warehouse at the termination of the period of storage fixed by the document, or, if no period is fixed, within a stated period not less than thirty days after the notification. If the goods are not removed before the date specified in the notification, the warehouseman may sell them in accordance with the provisions of the section on enforcement of a warehouseman's lien (Section 7–210).

(2) If a warehouseman in good faith believes that the goods are about to deteriorate or decline in value to less than the amount of his lien within the time prescribed in subsection (1) for notification, advertisement and sale, the warehouseman may specify in the notification any reasonable shorter time for removal of the goods and in case the goods are not removed, may sell them at public sale held not less than one week after a single advertisement or posting.

(3) If as a result of a quality or condition of the goods of which the warehouseman had no notice at the time of deposit the goods are a hazard to other property or to the warehouse or to persons, the warehouseman may sell the goods at public or private sale without advertisement on reasonable notification to all persons known to claim an interest in the goods. If the warehouseman after a reasonable effort is unable to sell the goods he may dispose of them in any lawful manner and shall incur no liability by reason of such disposition.

(4) The warehouseman must deliver the goods to any person entitled to them under this Article upon due demand made at any time prior to sale or other disposition under this section.

(5) The warehouseman may satisfy his lien from the proceeds of any sale or disposition under this section but must hold the balance for delivery on the demand of any person to whom he would have been bound to deliver the goods.

§ 7–207. Goods Must Be Kept Separate; Fungible Goods.

(1) Unless the warehouse receipt otherwise provides, a warehouseman must keep separate the goods covered by each receipt so as to permit at all times identification and delivery of those goods except that different lots of fungible goods may be commingled.

(2) Fungible goods so commingled are owned in common by the persons entitled thereto and the warehouseman is severally liable to each owner for that owner's share. Where because of overissue a mass of fungible goods is insufficient to meet all the receipts which the warehouseman has issued against it, the persons entitled include all holders to whom overissued receipts have been duly negotiated.

§ 7–208. Altered Warehouse Receipts.

Where a blank in a negotiable warehouse receipt has been filled in without authority, a purchaser for value and without notice of the want of authority may treat the insertion as authorized. Any other unauthorized alteration leaves any receipt enforceable against the issuer according to its original tenor.

§ 7–209. Lien of Warehouseman.

(1) A warehouseman has a lien against the bailor on the goods covered by a warehouse receipt or on the proceeds thereof in his possession for charges for storages or transportation (including demurrage and terminal charges), insurance, labor, or charges present or future in relation to the goods, and for expenses necessary for preservation of the goods or reasonably incurred in their sale pursuant to law. If the person on whose account the goods are held is liable for like charges or expenses in relation to other goods whenever deposited and it is stated in the receipt that a lien is claimed for charges and expenses in relation to other goods, the warehouseman also has a lien against him for such charges and expenses whether or not the other goods have been delivered by the warehouseman. But against a person to whom a negotiable warehouse receipt is duly negotiated a warehouseman's lien is limited to charges in an amount or at a rate specified on the receipt or if no charges are so specified then to a reasonable charge for storage of the goods covered by the receipt subsequent to the date of the receipt.

(2) The warehouseman may also reserve a security interest against the bailor for a maximum amount specified on the receipt for charges other than those specified in subsection (1), such as for money advanced and interest. Such a security interest is governed by the Article on Secured Transactions (Article 9).

(3)(a) A warehouseman's lien for charges and expenses under subsection (1) or a security interest under subsection (2) is also effective against any person who so entrusted the bailor with possession of the goods that a pledge of them by him to a good faith purchaser for value would have been valid but is not effective against a person as to whom the document confers no right in the goods covered by it under Section 7–503.

(b) A warehouseman's lien on household goods for charges and expenses in relation to the goods under subsection (1) is also effective against all persons if the depositor was a legal possessor of the goods at the time of deposit. "Household goods" means furniture, furnishings and personal effects used by the depositor in a dwelling.

(4) A warehouseman loses his lien on any goods which he voluntarily delivers or which he unjustifiably refuses to deliver.

§ 7–210. Enforcement of Warehouseman's Lien.

(1) Except as provided in subsection (2), a warehouseman's lien may be enforced by public or private sale of the goods in bloc or in parcels, at any time or place and on any terms which are commercially reasonable, after notifying all persons known to claim an interest in the goods. Such notification must include a statement of the amount due, the nature of the proposed sale and the time and place of any public sale. The fact that a better price could have been obtained by a sale at a different time or in a different method from that selected by the warehouseman is not of itself sufficient to establish that the sale was not made in a commercially reasonable manner. If the warehouseman either sells the goods in the usual manner in any recognized market therefor, or if he sells at the price current in such market at the time of his sale, or if he has otherwise sold in conformity with commercially reasonable practices among dealers in the type of goods sold, he has sold in a commercially reasonable manner. A sale of more goods than apparently necessary to be offered to insure satisfaction of the obligation is not commercially reasonable except in cases covered by the preceding sentence.

(2) A warehouseman's lien on goods other than goods stored by a merchant in the course of his business may be enforced only as follows:

(a) All persons known to claim an interest in the goods must be notified.

(b) The notification must be delivered in person or sent by registered or certified letter to the last known address of any person to be notified.

(c) The notification must include an itemized statement of the claim, a description of the goods subject to the lien, a demand for payment within a specified time not less than ten days after receipt of the notification, and a conspicuous statement that unless the claim is paid within the time the goods will be advertised for sale and sold by auction at a specified time and place.

(d) The sale must conform to the terms of the notification.

(e) The sale must be held at the nearest suitable place to that where the goods are held or stored.

(f) After the expiration of the time given in the notification, an advertisement of the sale must be published once a week for two weeks consecutively in a newspaper of general circulation where the sale is to be held. The advertisement must include a description of the goods, the name of the person on whose account they are being held, and the time and place of the sale. The sale must take place at least fifteen days after the first publication. If there is no newspaper of general circulation where the sale is to be held, the advertisement must be posted at least ten days before the sale in not less than six conspicuous places in the neighborhood of the proposed sale.

(3) Before any sale pursuant to this section any person claiming a right in the goods may pay the amount necessary to satisfy the lien and the reasonable expenses incurred under this section. In that event the goods must not be sold, but must be retained by the warehouseman subject to the terms of the receipt and this Article.

(4) The warehouseman may buy at any public sale pursuant to this section.

(5) A purchaser in good faith of goods sold to enforce a warehouseman's lien takes the goods free of any rights of persons against whom the lien was valid, despite noncompliance by the warehouseman with the requirements of this section.

(6) The warehouseman may satisfy his lien from the proceeds of any sale pursuant to this section but must hold the balance, if any, for delivery on demand to any person to whom he would have been bound to deliver the goods.

(7) The rights provided by this section shall be in addition to all other rights allowed by law to a creditor against his debtor.

(8) Where a lien is on goods stored by a merchant in the course of his business the lien may be enforced in accordance with either subsection (1) or (2).

(9) The warehouseman is liable for damages caused by failure to comply with the requirements for sale under this section and in case of willful violation is liable for conversion.

Part 3 Bills of Lading: Special Provisions

§ 7–301. Liability for Non-Receipt or Misdescription; "Said to Contain"; "Shipper's Load and Count"; Improper Handling.

(1) A consignee of a non-negotiable bill who has given value in good faith or a holder to whom a negotiable bill has been duly negotiated relying in either case upon the description therein of the goods, or upon the date therein shown, may recover from the issuer damages caused by the misdating of the bill or the non-receipt or misdescription of the goods, except to the extent that the document indicates that the issuer does not know whether any part of all of the goods in fact were received or conform to the description, as where the description is in terms of marks or labels or kind, quantity, or condition or the receipt or description is qualified by "contents or condition of contents of packages unknown", "said to contain", "shipper's weight, load and count" or the like, if such indication be true.

(2) When goods are loaded by an issuer who is a common carrier, the issuer must count the packages of goods if package freight and ascertain the kind and quantity if bulk freight. In such cases "shipper's weight, load and count" or other words indicating that the description was made by the shipper are ineffective except as to freight concealed by packages.

(3) When bulk freight is loaded by a shipper who makes available to the issuer adequate facilities for weighing such freight, an issuer who is a common carrier must ascertain the kind and quantity within a reasonable time after receiving the written request of the shipper to do so. In such cases "shipper's weight" or other words of like purport are ineffective.

(4) The issuer may by inserting in the bill the words "shipper's weight, load and count" or other words of like purport indicate that the goods were loaded by the shipper; and if such statement be true the issuer shall not be liable for damages caused by the improper loading. But their omission does not imply liability for such damages.

(5) The shipper shall be deemed to have guaranteed to the issuer the accuracy at the time of shipment of the description, marks, labels, number, kind, quantity, condition and weight, as furnished by him; and the shipper shall indemnify the issuer against damage caused by inaccuracies in such particulars. The right of the issuer to such indemnity shall in no way limit his responsibility and liability under the contract of carriage to any person other than the shipper.

§ 7–302. Through Bills of Lading and Similar Documents.

(1) The issuer of a through bill of lading or other document embodying an undertaking to be performed in part by persons acting as its agents or by connecting carriers is liable to anyone entitled to recover on the document for any breach by such other persons or by a connecting carrier of its obligation under the document but to the extent that the bill covers an undertaking to be performed overseas or in territory not contiguous to the continental United States or an undertaking including matters other than transportation this liability may be varied by agreement of the parties.

(2) Where goods covered by a through bill of lading or other document embodying an undertaking to be performed in part by persons other than the issuer are received by any such person, he is subject with respect to his own performance while the goods are in his possession to the obligation of the issuer. His obligation is discharged by delivery of the goods to another such person pursuant to the document, and does not include liability for breach by any other such persons or by the issuer.

(3) The issuer of such through bill of lading or other document shall be entitled to recover from the connecting carrier or such other person in possession of the goods when the breach of the obligation under the document occurred, the amount it may be required to pay to anyone entitled to recover on the document therefor, as may be evidenced by any receipt, judgment, or transcript thereof, and the amount of any expense reasonably incurred by it in defending any action brought by anyone entitled to recover on the document therefor.

§ 7–303. Diversion; Reconsignment; Change of Instructions.

(1) Unless the bill of lading otherwise provides, the carrier may deliver the goods to a person or destination other than that stated in the bill or may otherwise dispose of the goods on instructions from

(a) the holder of a negotiable bill; or
(b) the consignor on a non-negotiable bill notwithstanding contrary instructions from the consignee; or

(c) the consignee on a non-negotiable bill in the absence of contrary instructions from the consignor, if the goods have arrived at the billed destination or if the consignee is in possession of the bill; or

(d) the consignee on a non-negotiable bill if he is entitled as against the consignor to dispose of them.

(2) Unless such instructions are noted on a negotiable bill of lading, a person to whom the bill is duly negotiated can hold the bailee according to the original terms.

§ 7-304. Bills of Lading in a Set.

(1) Except where customary in overseas transportation, a bill of lading must not be issued in a set of parts. The issuer is liable for damages caused by violation of this subsection.

(2) Where a bill of lading is lawfully drawn in a set of parts, each of which is numbered and expressed to be valid only if the goods have not been delivered against any other part, the whole of the parts constitute one bill.

(3) Where a bill of lading is lawfully issued in a set of parts and different parts are negotiated to different persons, the title of the holder to whom the first due negotiation is made prevails as to both the document and the goods even though any later holder may have received the goods from the carrier in good faith and discharged the carrier's obligation by surrender of his part.

(4) Any person who negotiates or transfers a single part of a bill of lading drawn in a set is liable to holders of that part as if it were the whole set.

(5) The bailee is obliged to deliver in accordance with Part 4 of this Article against the first presented part of a bill of lading lawfully drawn in a set. Such delivery discharges the bailee's obligation on the whole bill.

§ 7-305. Destination Bills.

(1) Instead of issuing a bill of lading to the consignor at the place of shipment a carrier may at the request of the consignor procure the bill to be issued at destination or at any other place designated in the request.

(2) Upon request of anyone entitled as against the carrier to control the goods while in transit and on surrender of any outstanding bill of lading or other receipt covering such goods, the issuer may procure a substitute bill to be issued at any place designated in the request.

§ 7-306. Altered Bills of Lading.

An unauthorized alteration or filling in of a blank in a bill of lading leaves the bill enforceable according to its original tenor.

§ 7-307. Lien of Carrier.

(1) A carrier has a lien on the goods covered by a bill of lading for charges subsequent to the date of its receipt of the goods for storage or transportation (including demur-

rage and terminal charges) and for expenses necessary for preservation of the goods incident to their transportation or reasonably incurred in their sale pursuant to law. But against a purchaser for value of a negotiable bill of lading a carrier's lien is limited to charges stated in the bill or the applicable tariffs, or if no charges are stated then to a reasonable charge.

(2) A lien for charges and expenses under subsection (1) on goods which the carrier was required by law to receive for transportation is effective against the consignor or any person entitled to the goods unless the carrier had notice that the consignor lacked authority to subject the goods to such charges and expenses. Any other lien under subsection (1) is effective against the consignor and any person who permitted the bailor to have control or possession of the goods unless the carrier had notice that the bailor lacked such authority.

(3) A carrier loses his lien on any goods which he voluntarily delivers or which he unjustifiably refuses to deliver.

§ 7-308. Enforcement of Carrier's Lien.

(1) A carrier's lien may be enforced by public or private sale of the goods, in bloc or in parcels, at any time or place and on any terms which are commercially reasonable, after notifying all persons known to claim an interest in the goods. Such notification must include a statement of the amount due, the nature of the proposed sale and the time and place of any public sale. The fact that a better price could have been obtained by a sale at a different time or in a different method from that selected by the carrier is not of itself sufficient to establish that the sale was not made in a commercially reasonable manner. If the carrier either sells the goods in the usual manner in any recognized market therefor or if he sells at the price current in such market at the time of his sale or if he has otherwise sold in conformity with commercially reasonable practices among dealers in the type of goods sold he has sold in a commercially reasonable manner. A sale of more goods than apparently necessary to be offered to ensure satisfaction of the obligation is not commercially reasonable except in cases covered by the preceding sentence.

(2) Before any sale pursuant to this section any person claiming a right in the goods may pay the amount necessary to satisfy the lien and the reasonable expenses incurred under this section. In that event the goods must not be sold, but must be retained by the carrier subject to the terms of the bill and this Article.

(3) The carrier may buy at any public sale pursuant to this section.

(4) A purchaser in good faith of goods sold to enforce a carrier's lien takes the goods free of any rights of persons against whom the lien was valid, despite noncompliance by the carrier with the requirements of this section.

(5) The carrier may satisfy his lien from the proceeds of any sale pursuant to this section but must hold the balance, if any, for delivery on demand to any person to whom he would have been bound to deliver the goods.

(6) The rights provided by this section shall be in addition to all other rights allowed by law to a creditor against his debtor.

(7) A carrier's lien may be enforced in accordance with either subsection (1) or the procedure set forth in subsection (2) of Section 7–210.

(8) The carrier is liable for damages caused by failure to comply with the requirements for sale under this section and in case of willful violation is liable for conversion.

§ 7–309. Duty of Care; Contractual Limitation of Carrier's Liability.

(1) A carrier who issues a bill of lading whether negotiable or non-negotiable must exercise the degree of care in relation to the goods which a reasonably careful man would exercise under like circumstances. This subsection does not repeal or change any law or rule of law which imposes liability upon a common carrier for damages not caused by its negligence.

(2) Damages may be limited by a provision that the carrier's liability shall not exceed a value stated in the document if the carrier's rates are dependent upon value and the consignor by the carrier's tariff is afforded an opportunity to declare a higher value or a value as lawfully provided in the tariff, or where no tariff is filed he is otherwise advised of such opportunity; but no such limitation is effective with respect to the carrier's liability for conversion to its own use.

(3) Reasonable provisions as to the time and manner of presenting claims and instituting actions based on the shipment may be included in a bill of lading or tariff.

Part 4 Warehouse Receipts and Bills of Lading: General Obligations

§ 7–401. Irregularities in Issue of Receipt or Bill or Conduct of Issuer.

The obligations imposed by this Article on an issuer apply to a document of title regardless of the fact that

(a) the document may not comply with the requirements of this Article or of any other law or regulation regarding its issue, form or content; or

(b) the issuer may have violated laws regulating the conduct of his business; or

(c) the goods covered by the document were owned by the bailee at the time the document was issued; or

(d) the person issuing the document does not come within the definition of warehouseman if it purports to be a warehouse receipt.

§ 7–402. Duplicate Receipt or Bill; Overissue.

Neither a duplicate nor any other document of title purporting to cover goods already represented by an outstanding document of the same issuer confers any right in the goods, except as provided in the case of bills in a set, overissue of documents for fungible goods and substitutes for lost, stolen or destroyed documents. But the issuer is liable for damages caused by his overissue or failure to identify a duplicate document as such by conspicuous notation on its face.

§ 7–403. Obligation of Warehouseman or Carrier to Deliver; Excuse.

(1) The bailee must deliver the goods to a person entitled under the document who complies with subsections (2) and (3), unless and to the extent that the bailee establishes any of the following:

(a) delivery of the goods to a person whose receipt was rightful as against the claimant;

(b) damage to or delay, loss or destruction of the goods for which the bailee is not liable [, but the burden of establishing negligence in such cases is on the person entitled under the document];

Note: *The brackets in (1)(b) indicate that State enactments may differ on this point without serious damage to the principle of uniformity.*

(c) previous sale or other disposition of the goods in lawful enforcement of a lien or on warehouseman's lawful termination of storage;

(d) the exercise by a seller of his right to stop delivery pursuant to the provisions of the Article on Sales (Section 2–705);

(e) a diversion, reconsignment or other disposition pursuant to the provisions of this Article (Section 7–303) or tariff regulating such right;

(f) release, satisfaction or any other fact affording a personal defense against the claimant;

(g) any other lawful excuse.

(2) A person claiming goods covered by a document of title must satisfy the bailee's lien where the bailee so requests or where the bailee is prohibited by law from delivering the goods until the charges are paid.

(3) Unless the person claiming is one against whom the document confers no right under Sec. 7–503(1), he must surrender for cancellation or notation of partial deliveries any outstanding negotiable document covering the goods, and the bailee must cancel the document or conspicuously note the partial delivery thereon or be liable to any person to whom the document is duly negotiated.

(4) "Person entitled under the document" means holder in the case of a negotiable document, or the person to whom delivery is to be made by the terms of or pursuant to written instructions under a non-negotiable document.

§ 7–404. No Liability for Good Faith Delivery Pursuant to Receipt or Bill.

A bailee who in good faith including observance of reasonable commercial standards has received goods and delivered or otherwise disposed of them according to the terms of the document of title or pursuant to this Article is not liable therefor. This rule applies even though the person from whom he received the goods had no authority to procure the document or to dispose of the goods and even though the person to whom he delivered the goods had no authority to receive them.

Part 5 Warehouse Receipts and Bills of Lading: Negotiation and Transfer

§ 7–501. Form of Negotiation and Requirements of "Due Negotiation."

(1) A negotiable document of title running to the order of a named person is negotiated by his indorsement and delivery. After his indorsement in blank or to bearer any person can negotiate it by delivery alone.

(2)(a) A negotiable document of title is also negotiated by delivery alone when by its original terms it runs to bearer.
(b) When a document running to the order of a named person is delivered to him the effect is the same as if the document had been negotiated.

(3) Negotiation of a negotiable document of title after it has been indorsed to a specified person requires indorsement by the special indorsee as well as delivery.
(4) A negotiable document of title is "duly negotiated" when it is negotiated in the manner stated in this section to a holder who purchases it in good faith without notice of any defense against or claim to it on the part of any person and for value, unless it is established that the negotiation is not in the regular course of business or financing or involves receiving the document in settlement or payment of a money obligation.
(5) Indorsement of a non-negotiable document neither makes it negotiable nor adds to the transferee's rights.
(6) The naming in a negotiable bill of a person to be notified of the arrival of the goods does not limit the negotiability of the bill nor constitute notice to a purchaser thereof of any interest of such person in the goods.

§ 7–502. Rights Acquired by Due Negotiation.

(1) Subject to the following section and to the provisions of Section 7–205 on fungible goods, a holder to whom a negotiable document of title has been duly negotiated acquires thereby:

(a) title to the document;
(b) title to the goods;
(c) all rights accruing under the law of agency or estoppel, including rights to goods delivered to the bailee after the document was issued; and
(d) the direct obligation of the issuer to hold or deliver the goods according to the terms of the document free of any defense or claim by him except those arising under the terms of the document or under this Article. In the case of a delivery order the bailee's obligation accrues only upon acceptance and the obligation acquired by the holder is that the issuer and any indorser will procure the acceptance of the bailee.

(2) Subject to the following section, title and rights so acquired are not defeated by any stoppage of the goods represented by the document or by surrender of such goods by the bailee, and are not impaired even though the negotiation or any prior negotiation constituted a breach of duty or even though any person has been deprived of possession of the document by misrepresentation, fraud, accident, mistake, duress, loss, theft or conversion, or even though a previous sale or other transfer of the goods or document has been made to a third person.

§ 7–503. Document of Title to Goods Defeated in Certain Cases.

(1) A document of title confers no right in goods against a person who before issuance of the document had a legal interest or a perfected security interest in them and who neither

(a) delivered or entrusted them or any document of title covering them to the bailor or his nominee with actual or apparent authority to ship, store or sell or with power to obtain delivery under this Article (Section 7–403) or with power of disposition under this Act (Sections 2–403 and 9–307) or other statute or rule of law; nor
(b) acquiesced in the procurement by the bailor or his nominee of any document of title.

(2) Title to goods based upon an unaccepted delivery order is subject to the rights of anyone to whom a negotiable warehouse receipt or bill of lading covering the goods has been duly negotiated. Such a title may be defeated under the next section to the same extent as the rights of the issuer or a transferee from the issuer.
(3) Title to goods based upon a bill of lading issued to a freight forwarder is subject to the rights of anyone to whom a bill issued by the freight forwarder is duly negotiated; but delivery by the carrier in accordance with Part 4 of this Article pursuant to its own bill of lading discharges the carrier's obligation to deliver.

§ 7–504. Rights Acquired in the Absence of Due Negotiation; Effect of Diversion; Seller's Stoppage of Delivery.

(1) A transferee of a document, whether negotiable or non-negotiable, to whom the document has been delivered but not duly negotiated, acquires the title and rights which his transferor had or had actual authority to convey.
(2) In the case of a non-negotiable document, until but not after the bailee receives notification of the transfer, the rights of the transferee may be defeated

(a) by those creditors of the transferor who could treat the sale as void under Section 2–402; or

(b) by a buyer from the transferor in ordinary course of business if the bailee has delivered the goods to the buyer or received notification of his rights; or

(c) as against the bailee by good faith dealings of the bailee with the transferor.

(3) A diversion or other change of shipping instructions by the consignor in a non-negotiable bill of lading which causes the bailee not to deliver to the consignee defeats the consignee's title to the goods if they have been delivered to a buyer in ordinary course of business and in any event defeats the consignee's rights against the bailee.

(4) Delivery pursuant to a non-negotiable document may be stopped by a seller under Section 2–705, and subject to the requirement of due notification there provided. A bailee honoring the seller's instructions is entitled to be indemnified by the seller against any resulting loss or expense.

§ 7–505. Indorser Not a Guarantor for Other Parties.

The indorsement of a document of title issued by a bailee does not make the indorser liable for any default by the bailee or by previous indorsers.

§ 7–506. Delivery Without Indorsement: Right to Compel Indorsement.

The transferee of a negotiable document of title has a specifically enforceable right to have his transferor supply any necessary indorsement but the transfer becomes a negotiation only as of the time the indorsement is supplied.

§ 7–507. Warranties on Negotiation or Transfer of Receipt or Bill.

Where a person negotiates or transfers a document of title for value otherwise than as a mere intermediary under the next following section, then unless otherwise agreed he warrants to his immediate purchaser only in addition to any warranty made in selling the goods

(a) that the document is genuine; and

(b) that he has no knowledge of any fact which would impair its validity or worth; and

(c) that his negotiation or transfer is rightful and fully effective with respect to the title to the document and the goods it represents.

§ 7–508. Warranties of Collecting Bank as to Documents.

A collecting bank or other intermediary known to be entrusted with documents on behalf of another or with collection of a draft of other claim against delivery of documents warrants by such delivery of the documents only its own good faith and authority. This rule applies even though the intermediary has purchased or made advances against the claim or draft to be collected.

§ 7–509. Receipt or Bill: When Adequate Compliance With Commercial Contract.

The question whether a document is adequate to fulfill the obligations of a contract for sale or the conditions of a credit is governed by the Articles on Sales (Article 2) and on Letters of Credit (Article 5).

Part 6 Warehouse Receipts and Bills of Lading: Miscellaneous Provisions

§ 7–601. Lost and Missing Documents.

(1) If a document has been lost, stolen or destroyed, a court may order delivery of the goods or issuance of a substitute document and the bailee may without liability to any person comply with such order. If the document was negotiable the claimant must post security approved by the court to indemnify any person who may suffer loss as a result of non-surrender of the document. If the document was not negotiable, such security may be required at the discretion of the court. The court may also in its discretion order payment of the bailee's reasonable costs and counsel fees.

(2) A bailee who without court order delivers goods to a person claiming under a missing negotiable document is liable to any person injured thereby, and if the delivery is not in good faith becomes liable for conversion. Delivery in good faith is not conversion if made in accordance with a filed classification or tariff or, where no classification or tariff is filed, if the claimant posts security with the bailee in an amount at least double the value of the goods at the time of posting to indemnify any person injured by the delivery who files a notice of claim within one year after the delivery.

§ 7–602. Attachment of Goods Covered by a Negotiable Document.

Except where the document was originally issued upon delivery of the goods by a person who had no power to dispose of them, no lien attaches by virtue of any judicial process to goods in the possession of a bailee for which a negotiable document of title is outstanding unless the document be first surrendered to the bailee or its negotiation enjoined, and the bailee shall not be compelled to deliver the goods pursuant to process until the document is surrendered to him or impounded by the court. One who purchases the document for value without notice of the process or injunction takes free of the lien imposed by judicial process.

§ 7–603. Conflicting Claims; Interpleader.

If more than one person claims title or possession of the goods, the bailee is excused from delivery until he has had a reasonable time to ascertain the validity of the adverse claims or to bring an action to compel all claimants to interplead and may compel such interpleader, either in defending an action for non-delivery of the goods, or by original action, whichever is appropriate.

Article 8

INVESTMENT SECURITIES

Part 1 Short Title and General Matters

§ 8–101. Short Title.

This Article shall be known and may be cited as Uniform Commercial Code—Investment Securities.

§ 8–102. Definitions and Index of Definitions.

(1) In this Article, unless the context otherwise requires:

(a) A "certificated security" is a share, participation, or other interest in property of or an enterprise of the issuer or an obligation of the issuer which is

(i) represented by an instrument issued in bearer or registered form;
(ii) of a type commonly dealt in on securities exchanges or markets or commonly recognized in any area in which it is issued or dealt in as a medium for investment; and
(iii) either one of a class or series or by its terms divisible into a class or series of shares, participations, interests, or obligations.

(b) An "uncertificated security" is a share, participation, or other interest in property or an enterprise of the issuer or an obligation of the issuer which is

(i) not represented by an instrument and the transfer of which is registered upon books maintained for that purpose by or on behalf of the issuer;
(ii) of a type commonly dealt in on securities exchanges or markets; and
(iii) either one of a class or series or by its terms divisible into a class or series of shares, participations, interests, or obligations.

(c) A "security" is either a certificated or an uncertificated security. If a security is certificated, the terms "security" and "certificated security" may mean either the intangible interest, the instrument representing that interest, or both, as the context requires. A writing that is a certificated security is governed by this Article and not by Article 3, even though it also meets the requirements of that Article. This Article does not apply to money. If a certificated security has been retained by or surrendered to the issuer or its transfer agent for reasons other than registration of transfer, other temporary purpose, payment, exchange, or acquisition by the issuer, that security shall be treated as an uncertificated security for purposes of this Article.

(d) A certificated security is in "registered form" if

(i) it specifies a person entitled to the security or the rights it represents; and
(ii) its transfer may be registered upon books maintained for that purpose by or on behalf of the issuer, or the security so states.

(e) A certificated security is in "bearer form" if it runs to bearer according to its terms and not by reason of any indorsement.

(2) A "subsequent purchaser" is a person who takes other than by original issue.

(3) A "clearing corporation" is a corporation registered as a "clearing agency" under the federal securities laws or a corporation:

(a) at least 90 percent of whose capital stock is held by or for one or more organizations, none of which, other than a national securities exchange or association, holds in excess of 20 percent of the capital stock of the corporation, and each of which is

(i) subject to supervision or regulation pursuant to the provisions of federal or state banking laws or state insurance laws,
(ii) a broker or dealer or investment company registered under the federal securities laws, or
(iii) a national securities exchange or association registered under the federal securities laws; and

(b) any remaining capital stock of which is held by individuals who have purchased it at or prior to the time of their taking office as directors of the corporation and who have purchased only so much of the capital stock as is necessary to permit them to qualify as directors.

(4) A "custodian bank" is a bank or trust company that is supervised and examined by state or federal authority having supervision over banks and is acting as custodian for a clearing corporation.

(5) Other definitions applying to this Article or to specified Parts thereof and the sections in which they appear are:

"Adverse claim". Section 8–302.
"Bona fide purchaser". Section 8–302.
"Broker". Section 8–303.
"Debtor". Section 9–105.
"Financial intermediary". Section 8–313.
"Guarantee of the signature". Section 8–402.
"Initial transaction statement". Section 8–408.
"Instruction". Section 8–308.
"Intermediary bank". Section 4–105.
"Issuer". Section 8–201.
"Overissue". Section 8–104.
"Secured Party". Section 9–105.
"Security Agreement". Section 9–105.

(6) In addition, Article 1 contains general definitions and principles of construction and interpretation applicable throughout this Article.

Amended in 1962, 1973 and 1977.

§ 8–103. Issuer's Lien.

A lien upon a security in favor of an issuer thereof is valid against a purchaser only if:

(a) the security is certificated and the right of the issuer to the lien is noted conspicuously thereon; or

(b) the security is uncertificated and a notation of the right of the issuer to the lien is contained in the initial transaction statement sent to the purchaser or, if his interest is transferred to him other than by registration of transfer, pledge, or release, the initial transaction statement sent to the registered owner or the registered pledgee.

Amended in 1977.

§ 8–104. Effect of Overissue; "Overissue".

(1) The provisions of this Article which validate a security or compel its issue or reissue do not apply to the extent that validation, issue, or reissue would result in overissue; but if:

(a) an identical security which does not constitute an overissue is reasonably available for purchase, the person entitled to issue or validation may compel the issuer to purchase the security for him and either to deliver a certificated security or to register the transfer of an uncertificated security to him, against surrender of any certificated security he holds; or
(b) a security is not so available for purchase, the person entitled to issue or validation may recover from the issuer the price he or the last purchaser for value paid for it with interest from the date of his demand.

(2) "Overissue" means the issue of securities in excess of the amount the issuer has corporate power to issue.

Amended in 1977.

§ 8–105. Certificated Securities Negotiable; Statements and Instructions Not Negotiable; Presumptions.

(1) Certificated securities governed by this Article are negotiable instruments.
(2) Statements (Section 8–408), notices, or the like, sent by the issuer of uncertificated securities and instructions (Section 8–308) are neither negotiable instruments nor certificated securities.
(3) In any action on a security:

(a) unless specifically denied in the pleadings, each signature on a certificated security, in a necessary indorsement, on an initial transaction statement, or on an instruction, is admitted;
(b) if the effectiveness of a signature is put in issue, the burden of establishing it is on the party claiming under the signature, but the signature is presumed to be genuine or authorized;
(c) if signatures on a certificated security are admitted or established, production of the security entitles a holder to recover on it unless the defendant establishes a defense or a defect going to the validity of the security;
(d) if signatures on an initial transaction statement are admitted or established, the facts stated in the statement are presumed to be true as of the time of its issuance; and

(e) after it is shown that a defense or defect exists, the plaintiff has the burden of establishing that he or some person under whom he claims is a person against whom the defense or defect is ineffective (Section 8–202).

Amended in 1977.

§ 8–106. Applicability.

The law (including the conflict of laws rules) of the jurisdiction of organization of the issuer governs the validity of a security, the effectiveness of registration by the issuer, and the rights and duties of the issuer with respect to:

(a) registration of transfer of a certificated security;
(b) registration of transfer, pledge, or release of an uncertificated security; and
(c) sending of statements of uncertificated securities.

Amended in 1977.

§ 8–107. Securities Transferable; Action for Price.

(1) Unless otherwise agreed and subject to any applicable law or regulation respecting short sales, a person obligated to transfer securities may transfer any certificated security of the specified issue in bearer form or registered in the name of the transferee, or indorsed to him or in blank, or he may transfer an equivalent uncertificated security to the transferee or a person designated by the transferee.
(2) If the buyer fails to pay the price as it comes due under a contract of sale, the seller may recover the price of:

(a) certificated securities accepted by the buyer;
(b) uncertificated securities that have been transferred to the buyer or a person designated by the buyer; and
(c) other securities if efforts at their resale would be unduly burdensome or if there is no readily available market for their resale.

Amended in 1977.

§ 8–108. Registration of Pledge and Release of Uncertificated Securities.

A security interest in an uncertificated security may be evidenced by the registration of pledge to the secured party or a person designated by him. There can be no more than one registered pledge of an uncertificated security at any time. The registered owner of an uncertificated security is the person in whose name the security is registered, even if the security is subject to a registered pledge. The rights of a registered pledgee of an uncertificated security under this Article are terminated by the registration of release.
Added in 1977.

Part 2 Issue—Issuer

§ 8–201. "Issuer".

(1) With respect to obligations on or defenses to a security, "issuer" includes a person who:

(a) places or authorizes the placing of his name on a certificated security (otherwise than as authenticating trustee, registrar, transfer agent, or the like) to evidence that it represents a share, participation, or other interest in his property or in an enterprise, or to evidence his duty to perform an obligation represented by the certificated security;

(b) creates shares, participations, or other interests in his property or in an enterprise or undertakes obligations, which shares, participations, interests, or obligations are uncertificated securities;

(c) directly or indirectly creates fractional interests in his rights or property, which fractional interests are represented by certificated securities; or

(d) becomes responsible for or in place of any other person described as an issuer in this section.

(2) With respect to obligations on or defenses to a security, a guarantor is an issuer to the extent of his guaranty, whether or not his obligation is noted on a certificated security or on statements of uncertificated securities sent pursuant to Section 8–408.

(3) With respect to registration of transfer, pledge, or release (Part 4 of this Article), "issuer" means a person on whose behalf transfer books are maintained.

Amended in 1977.

§ 8–202. Issuer's Responsibility and Defenses; Notice of Defect or Defense.

(1) Even against a purchaser for value and without notice, the terms of a security include:

(a) if the security is certificated, those stated on the security;

(b) if the security is uncertificated, those contained in the initial transaction statement sent to such purchaser or, if his interest is transferred to him other than by registration of transfer, pledge, or release, the initial transaction statement sent to the registered owner or registered pledgee; and

(c) those made part of the security by reference, on the certificated security or in the initial transaction statement, to another instrument, indenture, or document or to a constitution, statute, ordinance, rule, regulation, order or the like, to the extent that the terms referred to do not conflict with the terms stated on the certificated security or contained in the statement. A reference under this paragraph does not of itself charge a purchaser for value with notice of a defect going to the validity of the security, even though the certificated security or statement expressly states that a person accepting it admits notice.

(2) A certificated security in the hands of a purchaser for value or an uncertificated security as to which an initial transaction statement has been sent to a purchaser for value, other than a security issued by a government or governmental agency or unit, even though issued with a defect going to its validity, is valid with respect to the purchaser if he is without notice of the particular defect unless the defect involves a violation of constitutional provisions, in which case the security is valid with respect to a subsequent purchaser for value and without notice of the defect. This subsection applies to an issuer that is a government or governmental agency or unit only if either there has been substantial compliance with the legal requirements governing the issue or the issuer has received a substantial consideration for the issue as a whole or for the particular security and a stated purpose of the issue is one for which the issuer has power to borrow money or issue the security.

(3) Except as provided in the case of certain unauthorized signatures (Section 8–205), lack of genuineness of a certificated security or an initial transaction statement is a complete defense, even against a purchaser for value and without notice.

(4) All other defenses of the issuer of a certificated or uncertificated security, including nondelivery and conditional delivery of a certificated security, are ineffective against a purchaser for value who has taken without notice of the particular defense.

(5) Nothing in this section shall be construed to affect the right of a party to a "when, as and if issued" or a "when distributed" contract to cancel the contract in the event of a material change in the character of the security that is the subject of the contract or in the plan or arrangement pursuant to which the security is to be issued or distributed.

Amended in 1977.

§ 8–203. Staleness as Notice of Defects or Defenses.

(1) After an act or event creating a right to immediate performance of the principal obligation represented by a certificated security or that sets a date on or after which the security is to be presented or surrendered for redemption or exchange, a purchaser is charged with notice of any defect in its issue or defense of the issuer if:

(a) the act or event is one requiring the payment of money, the delivery of certificated securities, the registration of transfer of uncertificated securities, or any of these on presentation or surrender of the certificated security, the funds or securities are available on the date set for payment or exchange, and he takes the security more than one year after that date; and

(b) the act or event is not covered by paragraph (a) and he takes the security more than 2 years after the date set for surrender or presentation or the date on which performance became due.

(2) A call that has been revoked is not within subsection (1).

Amended in 1977.

§ 8–204. Effect of Issuer's Restrictions on Transfer.

A restriction on transfer of a security imposed by the issuer, even if otherwise lawful, is ineffective against any person without actual knowledge of it unless:

(a) the security is certificated and the restriction is noted conspicuously thereon; or
(b) the security is uncertificated and a notation of the restriction is contained in the initial transaction statement sent to the person or, if his interest is transferred to him other than by registration of transfer, pledge, or release, the initial transaction statement sent to the registered owner or the registered pledgee.

Amended in 1977.

§ 8–205. Effect of Unauthorized Signature on Certificated Security or Initial Transaction Statement.

An unauthorized signature placed on a certificated security prior to or in the course of issue or placed on an initial transaction statement is ineffective, but the signature is effective in favor of a purchaser for value of the certificated security or a purchaser for value of an uncertificated security to whom the initial transaction statement has been sent, if the purchaser is without notice of the lack of authority and the signing has been done by:

(a) an authenticating trustee, registrar, transfer agent, or other person entrusted by the issuer with the signing of the security, of similar securities, or of initial transaction statements or the immediate preparation for signing of any of them; or
(b) an employee of the issuer, or of any of the foregoing, entrusted with responsible handling of the security or initial transaction statement.

Amended in 1977.

§ 8–206. Completion or Alteration of Certificated Security or Initial Transaction Statement.

(1) If a certificated security contains the signatures necessary to its issue or transfer but is incomplete in any other respect:

(a) any person may complete it by filling in the blanks as authorized; and
(b) even though the blanks are incorrectly filled in, the security as completed is enforceable by a purchaser who took it for value and without notice of the incorrectness.

(2) A complete certificated security that has been improperly altered, even though fraudulently, remains enforceable, but only according to its original terms.

(3) If an initial transaction statement contains the signatures necessary to its validity, but is incomplete in any other respect:

(a) any person may complete it by filling in the blanks as authorized; and
(b) even though the blanks are incorrectly filled in, the statement as completed is effective in favor of the person to whom it is sent if he purchased the security referred to therein for value and without notice of the incorrectness.

(4) A complete initial transaction statement that has been improperly altered, even though fraudulently, is effective in favor of a purchaser to whom it has been sent, but only according to its original terms.

Amended in 1977.

§ 8–207. Rights and Duties of Issuer With Respect to Registered Owners and Registered Pledgees.

(1) Prior to due presentment for registration of transfer of a certificated security in registered form, the issuer or indenture trustee may treat the registered owner as the person exclusively entitled to vote, to receive notifications, and otherwise to exercise all the rights and powers of an owner.

(2) Subject to the provisions of subsections (3), (4), and (6), the issuer or indenture trustee may treat the registered owner of an uncertificated security as the person exclusively entitled to vote, to receive notifications, and otherwise to exercise all the rights and powers of an owner.

(3) The registered owner of an uncertificated security that is subject to a registered pledge is not entitled to registration of transfer prior to the due presentment to the issuer of a release instruction. The exercise of conversion rights with respect to a convertible uncertificated security is a transfer within the meaning of this section.

(4) Upon due presentment of a transfer instruction from the registered pledgee of an uncertificated security, the issuer shall:

(a) register the transfer of the security to the new owner free of pledge, if the instruction specifies a new owner (who may be the registered pledgee) and does not specify a pledgee;
(b) register the transfer of the security to the new owner subject to the interest of the existing pledgee, if the instruction specifies a new owner and the existing pledgee; or
(c) register the release of the security from the existing pledge and register the pledge of the security to the other pledgee, if the instruction specifies the existing owner and another pledgee.

(5) Continuity of perfection of a security interest is not broken by registration of transfer under subsection (4)(b) or by registration of release and pledge under subsection (4)(c), if the security interest is assigned.

(6) If an uncertificated security is subject to a registered pledge:

(a) any uncertificated securities issued in exchange for or distributed with respect to the pledged security shall be registered subject to the pledge;

(b) any certificated securities issued in exchange for or distributed with respect to the pledged security shall be delivered to the registered pledgee; and

(c) any money paid in exchange for or in redemption of part or all of the security shall be paid to the registered pledgee.

(7) Nothing in this Article shall be construed to affect the liability of the registered owner of a security for calls, assessments, or the like.

Amended in 1977.

§ 8–208. Effect of Signature of Authenticating Trustee, Registrar, or Transfer Agent.

(1) A person placing his signature upon a certificated security or an initial transaction statement as authenticating trustee, registrar, transfer agent, or the like, warrants to a purchaser for value of the certificated security or a purchaser for value of an uncertificated security to whom the initial transaction statement has been sent, if the purchaser is without notice of the particular defect, that:

(a) the certificated security or initial transaction statement is genuine;

(b) his own participation in the issue or registration of the transfer, pledge, or release of the security is within his capacity and within the scope of the authority received by him from the issuer; and

(c) he has reasonable grounds to believe the security is in the form and within the amount the issuer is authorized to issue.

(2) Unless otherwise agreed, a person by so placing his signature does not assume responsibility for the validity of the security in other respects.

Amended in 1962 and 1977.

Part 3 Transfer

§ 8–301. Rights Acquired by Purchaser.

(1) Upon transfer of a security to a purchaser (Section 8–313), the purchaser acquires the rights in the security which his transferor had or had actual authority to convey unless the purchaser's rights are limited by Section 8–302(4).

(2) A transferee of a limited interest acquires rights only to the extent of the interest transferred. The creation or release of a security interest in a security is the transfer of a limited interest in that security.

Amended in 1977.

§ 8–302. "Bona Fide Purchaser"; "Adverse Claim"; Title Acquired by Bona Fide Purchaser.

(1) A "bona fide purchaser" is a purchaser for value in good faith and without notice of any adverse claim:

(a) who takes delivery of a certificated security in bearer form or in registered form, issued or indorsed to him or in blank;

(b) to whom the transfer, pledge, or release of an uncertificated security is registered on the books of the issuer; or

(c) to whom a security is transferred under the provisions of paragraph (c), (d)(i), or (g) of Section 8–313(1).

(2) "Adverse claim" includes a claim that a transfer was or would be wrongful or that a particular adverse person is the owner of or has an interest in the security.

(3) A bona fide purchaser in addition to acquiring the rights of a purchaser (Section 8–301) also acquires his interest in the security free of any adverse claim.

(4) Notwithstanding Section 8–301(1), the transferee of a particular certificated security who has been a party to any fraud or illegality affecting the security, or who as a prior holder of that certificated security had notice of an adverse claim, cannot improve his position by taking from a bona fide purchaser.

Amended in 1977.

§ 8–303. "Broker".

"Broker" means a person engaged for all or part of his time in the business of buying and selling securities, who in the transaction concerned acts for, buys a security from, or sells a security to, a customer. Nothing in this Article determines the capacity in which a person acts for purposes of any other statute or rule to which the person is subject.

§ 8–304. Notice to Purchaser of Adverse Claims.

(1) A purchaser (including a broker for the seller or buyer, but excluding an intermediary bank) of a certificated security is charged with notice of adverse claims if:

(a) the security, whether in bearer or registered form, has been indorsed "for collection" or "for surrender" or for some other purpose not involving transfer; or

(b) the security is in bearer form and has on it an unambiguous statement that it is the property of a person other than the transferor. The mere writing of a name on a security is not such a statement.

(2) A purchaser (including a broker for the seller or buyer, but excluding an intermediary bank) to whom the transfer, pledge, or release of an uncertificated security is registered is charged with notice of adverse claims as to which the issuer has a duty under Section 8–403(4) at the time of registration and which are noted in the initial transaction statement sent to the purchaser or, if his interest is transferred to him other than by registration of transfer, pledge, or release, the initial transaction statement sent to the registered owner or the registered pledgee.

(3) The fact that the purchaser (including a broker for the seller or buyer) of a certificated or uncertificated security has notice that the security is held for a third person or is

registered in the name of or indorsed by a fiduciary does not create a duty of inquiry into the rightfulness of the transfer or constitute constructive notice of adverse claims. However, if the purchaser (excluding an intermediary bank) has knowledge that the proceeds are being used or the transaction is for the individual benefit of the fiduciary or otherwise in breach of duty, the purchaser is charged with notice of adverse claims.

Amended in 1977.

§ 8–305. Staleness as Notice of Adverse Claims.

An act or event that creates a right to immediate performance of the principal obligation represented by a certificated security or sets a date on or after which a certificated security is to be presented or surrendered for redemption or exchange does not itself constitute any notice of adverse claims except in the case of a transfer:

(a) after one year from any date set for presentment or surrender for redemption or exchange; or
(b) after 6 months from any date set for payment of money against presentation or surrender of the security if funds are available for payment on that date.

Amended in 1977.

§ 8–306. Warranties on Presentment and Transfer of Certificated Securities; Warranties of Originators of Instructions.

(1) A person who presents a certificated security for registration of transfer or for payment or exchange warrants to the issuer that he is entitled to the registration, payment, or exchange. But, a purchaser for value and without notice of adverse claims who receives a new, reissued, or re-registered certificated security on registration of transfer or receives an initial transaction statement confirming the registration of transfer of an equivalent uncertificated security to him warrants only that he has no knowledge of any unauthorized signature (Section 8–311) in a necessary indorsement.
(2) A person by transferring a certificated security to a purchaser for value warrants only that:

(a) his transfer is effective and rightful;
(b) the security is genuine and has not been materially altered; and
(c) he knows of no fact which might impair the validity of the security.

(3) If a certificated security is delivered by an intermediary known to be entrusted with delivery of the security on behalf of another or with collection of a draft or other claim against delivery, the intermediary by delivery warrants only his own good faith and authority, even though he has purchased or made advances against the claim to be collected against the delivery.
(4) A pledgee or other holder for security who redelivers a certificated security received, or after payment and on order of the debtor delivers that security to a third person, makes only the warranties of an intermediary under subsection (3).
(5) A person who originates an instruction warrants to the issuer that:

(a) he is an appropriate person to originate the instruction; and
(b) at the time the instruction is presented to the issuer he will be entitled to the registration of transfer, pledge, or release.

(6) A person who originates an instruction warrants to any person specially guaranteeing his signature (subsection 8–312(8)) that:

(a) he is an appropriate person to originate the instruction; and
(b) at the time the instruction is presented to the issuer:

(i) he will be entitled to the registration of transfer, pledge, or release; and
(ii) the transfer, pledge, or release requested in the instruction will be registered by the issuer free from all liens, security interests, restrictions, and claims other than those specified in the instruction.

(7) A person who originates an instruction warrants to a purchaser for value and to any person guaranteeing the instruction (Section 8–312(6)) that:

(a) he is an appropriate person to originate the instruction;
(b) the uncertificated security referred to therein is valid; and
(c) at the time the instruction is presented to the issuer

(i) the transferor will be entitled to the registration of transfer, pledge, or release;
(ii) the transfer, pledge, or release requested in the instruction will be registered by the issuer free from all liens, security interests, restrictions, and claims other than those specified in the instruction; and
(iii) the requested transfer, pledge, or release will be rightful.

(8) If a secured party is the registered pledgee or the registered owner of an uncertificated security, a person who originates an instruction of release or transfer to the debtor or, after payment and on order of the debtor, a transfer instruction to a third person, warrants to the debtor or the third person only that he is an appropriate person to originate the instruction and, at the time the instruction is presented to the issuer, the transferor will be entitled to the registration of release or transfer. If a transfer instruction to a third person who is a purchaser for value is originated on order of the debtor, the debtor makes to the purchaser the warranties of paragraphs (b), (c)(ii) and (c)(iii) of subsection (7).
(9) A person who transfers an uncertificated security to a purchaser for value and does not originate an instruction in connection with the transfer warrants only that:

(a) his transfer is effective and rightful; and

(b) the uncertificated security is valid.

(10) A broker gives to his customer and to the issuer and a purchaser the applicable warranties provided in this section and has the rights and privileges of a purchaser under this section. The warranties of and in favor of the broker, acting as an agent are in addition to applicable warranties given by and in favor of his customer.

Amended in 1962 and 1977.

§ 8–307. Effect of Delivery Without Indorsement; Right to Compel Indorsement.

If a certificated security in registered form has been delivered to a purchaser without a necessary indorsement he may become a bona fide purchaser only as of the time the indorsement is supplied; but against the transferor, the transfer is complete upon delivery and the purchaser has a specifically enforceable right to have any necessary indorsement supplied.

Amended in 1977.

§ 8–308. Indorsements; Instructions.

(1) An indorsement of a certificated security in registered form is made when an appropriate person signs on it or on a separate document an assignment or transfer of the security or a power to assign or transfer it or his signature is written without more upon the back of the security.

(2) An indorsement may be in blank or special. An indorsement in blank includes an indorsement to bearer. A special indorsement specifies to whom the security is to be transferred, or who has power to transfer it. A holder may convert a blank indorsement into a special indorsement.

(3) An indorsement purporting to be only of part of a certificated security representing units intended by the issuer to be separately transferable is effective to the extent of the indorsement.

(4) An "instruction" is an order to the issuer of an uncertificated security requesting that the transfer, pledge, or release from pledge of the uncertificated security specified therein be registered.

(5) An instruction originated by an appropriate person is:

(a) a writing signed by an appropriate person; or

(b) a communication to the issuer in any form agreed upon in a writing signed by the issuer and an appropriate person.

If an instruction has been originated by an appropriate person but is incomplete in any other respect, any person may complete it as authorized and the issuer may rely on it as completed even though it has been completed incorrectly.

(6) "An appropriate person" in subsection (1) means the person specified by the certificated security or by special indorsement to be entitled to the security.

(7) "An appropriate person" in subsection (5) means:

(a) for an instruction to transfer or pledge an uncertificated security which is then not subject to a registered pledge, the registered owner; or

(b) for an instruction to transfer or release an uncertificated security which is then subject to a registered pledge, the registered pledgee.

(8) In addition to the persons designated in subsections (6) and (7), "an appropriate person" in subsections (1) and (5) includes:

(a) if the person designated is described as a fiduciary but is no longer serving in the described capacity, either that person or his successor;

(b) if the persons designated are described as more than one person as fiduciaries and one or more are no longer serving in the described capacity, the remaining fiduciary or fiduciaries, whether or not a successor has been appointed or qualified;

(c) if the person designated is an individual and is without capacity to act by virtue of death, incompetence, infancy, or otherwise, his executor, administrator, guardian, or like fiduciary;

(d) if the persons designated are described as more than one person as tenants by the entirety or with right of survivorship and by reason of death all cannot sign, the survivor or survivors;

(e) a person having power to sign under applicable law or controlling instrument, and

(f) to the extent that the person designated or any of the foregoing persons may act through an agent, his authorized agent.

(9) Unless otherwise agreed, the indorser of a certificated security by his indorsement or the originator of an instruction by his origination assumes no obligation that the security will be honored by the issuer but only the obligations provided in Section 8–306.

(10) Whether the person signing is appropriate is determined as of the date of signing and an indorsement made by or an instruction originated by him does not become unauthorized for the purposes of this Article by virtue of any subsequent change of circumstances.

(11) Failure of a fiduciary to comply with a controlling instrument or with the law of the state having jurisdiction of the fiduciary relationship, including any law requiring the fiduciary to obtain court approval of the transfer, pledge, or release, does not render his indorsement or an instruction originated by him unauthorized for the purposes of this Article.

Amended in 1962 and 1977.

§ 8–309. Effect of Indorsement Without Delivery.

An indorsement of a certificated security, whether special or in blank, does not constitute a transfer until delivery of the certificated security on which it appears or, if the indorsement is on a separate document, until delivery of both the document and the certificated security.

Amended in 1977.

§ 8–310. Indorsement of Certificated Security in Bearer Form.

An indorsement of a certificated security in bearer form may give notice of adverse claims (Section 8–304) but does not otherwise affect any right to registration the holder possesses.

Amended in 1977.

§ 8–311. Effect of Unauthorized Indorsement or Instruction.

Unless the owner or pledgee has ratified an unauthorized indorsement or instruction or is otherwise precluded from asserting its ineffectiveness:

(a) he may assert its ineffectiveness against the issuer or any purchaser, other than a purchaser for value and without notice of adverse claims, who has in good faith received a new, reissued, or re-registered certificated security on registration of transfer or received an initial transaction statement confirming the registration of transfer, pledge, or release of an equivalent uncertificated security to him; and
(b) an issuer who registers the transfer of a certificated security upon the unauthorized indorsement or who registers the transfer, pledge, or release of an uncertificated security upon the unauthorized instruction is subject to liability for improper registration (Section 8–404).

Amended in 1977.

§ 8–312. Effect of Guaranteeing Signature, Indorsement or Instruction.

(1) Any person guaranteeing a signature of an indorser of a certificated security warrants that at the time of signing:

(a) the signature was genuine;
(b) the signer was an appropriate person to indorse (Section 8–308); and
(c) the signer had legal capacity to sign.

(2) Any person guaranteeing a signature of the originator of an instruction warrants that at the time of signing:

(a) the signature was genuine;
(b) the signer was an appropriate person to originate the instruction (Section 8–308) if the person specified in the instruction as the registered owner or registered pledgee of the uncertificated security was, in fact, the registered owner or registered pledgee of the security, as to which fact the signature guarantor makes no warranty;
(c) the signer had legal capacity to sign; and
(d) the taxpayer identification number, if any, appearing on the instruction as that of the registered owner or registered pledgee was the taxpayer identification number of the signer or of the owner or pledgee for whom the signer was acting.

(3) Any person specially guaranteeing the signature of the originator of an instruction makes not only the warranties of a signature guarantor (subsection (2)) but also warrants that at the time the instruction is presented to the issuer:

(a) the person specified in the instruction as the registered owner or registered pledgee of the uncertificated security will be the registered owner or registered pledgee; and
(b) the transfer, pledge, or release of the uncertificated security requested in the instruction will be registered by the issuer free from all liens, security interests, restrictions, and claims other than those specified in the instruction.

(4) The guarantor under subsections (1) and (2) or the special guarantor under subsection (3) does not otherwise warrant the rightfulness of the particular transfer, pledge, or release.
(5) Any person guaranteeing an indorsement of a certificated security makes not only the warranties of a signature guarantor under subsection (1) but also warrants the rightfulness of the particular transfer in all respects.
(6) Any person guaranteeing an instruction requesting the transfer, pledge, or release of an uncertificated security makes not only the warranties of a special signature guarantor under subsection (3) but also warrants the rightfulness of the particular transfer, pledge, or release in all respects.
(7) No issuer may require a special guarantee of signature (subsection (3)), a guarantee of indorsement (subsection (5)), or a guarantee of instruction (subsection (6)) as a condition to registration of transfer, pledge, or release.
(8) The foregoing warranties are made to any person taking or dealing with the security in reliance on the guarantee, and the guarantor is liable to the person for any loss resulting from breach of the warranties.

Amended in 1977.

§ 8–313. When Transfer to Purchaser Occurs; Financial Intermediary as Bona Fide Purchaser; "Financial Intermediary".

(1) Transfer of a security or a limited interest (including a security interest) therein to a purchaser occurs only:

(a) at the time he or a person designated by him acquires possession of a certificated security;
(b) at the time the transfer, pledge, or release of an uncertificated security is registered to him or a person designated by him;
(c) at the time his financial intermediary acquires possession of a certificated security specially indorsed to or issued in the name of the purchaser;
(d) at the time a financial intermediary, not a clearing corporation, sends him confirmation of the purchase

and also by book entry or otherwise identifies as belonging to the purchaser

(i) a specific certificated security in the financial intermediary's possession;
(ii) a quantity of securities that constitute or are part of a fungible bulk of certificated securities in the financial intermediary's possession or of uncertificated securities registered in the name of the financial intermediary; or
(iii) a quantity of securities that constitute or are part of a fungible bulk of securities shown on the account of the financial intermediary on the books of another financial intermediary;

(e) with respect to an identified certificated security to be delivered while still in the possession of a third person, not a financial intermediary, at the time that person acknowledges that he holds for the purchaser;
(f) with respect to a specific uncertificated security the pledge or transfer of which has been registered to a third person, not a financial intermediary, at the time that person acknowledges that he holds for the purchaser;
(g) at the time appropriate entries to the account of the purchaser or a person designated by him on the books of a clearing corporation are made under Section 8–320;
(h) with respect to the transfer of a security interest where the debtor has signed a security agreement containing a description of the security, at the time a written notification, which, in the case of the creation of the security interest, is signed by the debtor (which may be a copy of the security agreement) or which, in the case of the release or assignment of the security interest created pursuant to this paragraph, is signed by the secured party, is received by

(i) a financial intermediary on whose books the interest of the transferor in the security appears;
(ii) a third person, not a financial intermediary, in possession of the security, if it is certificated;
(iii) a third person, not a financial intermediary, who is the registered owner of the security, if it is uncertificated and not subject to a registered pledge; or
(iv) a third person, not a financial intermediary, who is the registered pledgee of the security, if it is uncertificated and subject to a registered pledge;

(i) with respect to the transfer of a security interest where the transferor has signed a security agreement containing a description of the security, at the time new value is given by the secured party; or
(j) with respect to the transfer of a security interest where the secured party is a financial intermediary and the security has already been transferred to the financial intermediary under paragraphs (a), (b), (c), (d), or (g), at the time the transferor has signed a security agreement containing a description of the security and value is given by the secured party.

(2) The purchaser is the owner of a security held for him by a financial intermediary, but cannot be a bona fide purchaser of a security so held except in the circumstances specified in paragraphs (c), (d)(i), and (g) of subsection (1). If a security so held is part of a fungible bulk, as in the circumstances specified in paragraphs (d)(ii) and (d)(iii) of subsection (1), the purchaser is the owner of a proportionate property interest in the fungible bulk.
(3) Notice of an adverse claim received by the financial intermediary or by the purchaser after the financial intermediary takes delivery of a certificated security as a holder for value or after the transfer, pledge, or release of an uncertificated security has been registered free of the claim to a financial intermediary who has given value is not effective either as to the financial intermediary or as to the purchaser. However, as between the financial intermediary and the purchaser the purchaser may demand transfer of an equivalent security as to which no notice of adverse claim has been received.
(4) A "financial intermediary" is a bank, broker, clearing corporation, or other person (or the nominee of any of them) which in the ordinary course of its business maintains security accounts for its customers and is acting in that capacity. A financial intermediary may have a security interest in securities held in account for its customer.

Amended in 1962 and 1977.

§ 8–314. Duty to Transfer, When Completed.

(1) Unless otherwise agreed, if a sale of a security is made on an exchange or otherwise through brokers:

(a) the selling customer fulfills his duty to transfer at the time he:

(i) places a certificated security in the possession of the selling broker or a person designated by the broker;
(ii) causes an uncertificated security to be registered in the name of the selling broker or a person designated by the broker;
(iii) if requested, causes an acknowledgment to be made to the selling broker that a certificated or uncertificated security is held for the broker; or
(iv) places in the possession of the selling broker or of a person designated by the broker a transfer instruction for an uncertificated security, providing the issuer does not refuse to register the requested transfer if the instruction is presented to the issuer for registration within 30 days thereafter; and

(b) the selling broker, including a correspondent broker acting for a selling customer, fulfills his duty to transfer at the time he:

(i) places a certificated security in the possession of the buying broker or a person designated by the buying broker;
(ii) causes an uncertificated security to be registered in the name of the buying broker or a person designated by the buying broker;
(iii) places in the possession of the buying broker or of a person designated by the buying broker a transfer

instruction for an uncertificated security, providing the issuer does not refuse to register the requested transfer if the instruction is presented to the issuer for registration within 30 days thereafter; or

(iv) effects clearance of the sale in accordance with the rules of the exchange on which the transaction took place.

(2) Except as provided in this section or unless otherwise agreed, a transferor's duty to transfer a security under a contract of purchase is not fulfilled until he:

(a) places a certificated security in form to be negotiated by the purchaser in the possession of the purchaser or of a person designated by the purchaser;

(b) causes an uncertificated security to be registered in the name of the purchaser or a person designated by the purchaser; or

(c) if the purchaser requests, causes an acknowledgment to be made to the purchaser that a certificated or uncertificated security is held for the purchaser.

(3) Unless made on an exchange, a sale to a broker purchasing for his own account is within subsection (2) and not within subsection (1).

Amended in 1977.

§ 8–315. Action Against Transferee Based Upon Wrongful Transfer.

(1) Any person against whom the transfer of a security is wrongful for any reason, including his incapacity, as against anyone except a bona fide purchaser, may:

(a) reclaim possession of the certificated security wrongfully transferred;

(b) obtain possession of any new certificated security representing all or part of the same rights;

(c) compel the origination of an instruction to transfer to him or a person designated by him an uncertificated security constituting all or part of the same rights; or

(d) have damages.

(2) If the transfer is wrongful because of an unauthorized indorsement of a certificated security, the owner may also reclaim or obtain possession of the security or a new certificated security, even from a bona fide purchaser, if the ineffectiveness of the purported indorsement can be asserted against him under the provisions of this Article on unauthorized indorsements (Section 8–311).

(3) The right to obtain or reclaim possession of a certificated security or to compel the origination of a transfer instruction may be specifically enforced and the transfer of a certificated or uncertificated security enjoined and a certificated security impounded pending the litigation.

Amended in 1977.

§ 8–316. Purchaser's Right to Requisites for Registration of Transfer, Pledge, or Release on Books.

Unless otherwise agreed, the transferor of a certificated security or the transferor, pledgor, or pledgee of an uncer-

tificated security on due demand must supply his purchaser with any proof of his authority to transfer, pledge, or release or with any other requisite necessary to obtain registration of the transfer, pledge, or release of the security; but if the transfer, pledge, or release is not for value, a transferor, pledgor, or pledgee need not do so unless the purchaser furnishes the necessary expenses. Failure within a reasonable time to comply with a demand made gives the purchaser the right to reject or rescind the transfer, pledge, or release.

Amended in 1977.

§ 8–317. Creditors' Rights.

(1) Subject to the exceptions in subsections (3) and (4), no attachment or levy upon a certificated security or any share or other interest represented thereby which is outstanding is valid until the security is actually seized by the officer making the attachment or levy, but a certificated security which has been surrendered to the issuer may be reached by a creditor by legal process at the issuer's chief executive office in the United States.

(2) An uncertificated security registered in the name of the debtor may not be reached by a creditor except by legal process at the issuer's chief executive office in the United States.

(3) The interest of a debtor in a certificated security that is in the possession of a secured party not a financial intermediary or in an uncertificated security registered in the name of a secured party not a financial intermediary (or in the name of a nominee of the secured party) may be reached by a creditor by legal process upon the secured party.

(4) The interest of a debtor in a certificated security that is in the possession of or registered in the name of a financial intermediary or in an uncertificated security registered in the name of a financial intermediary may be reached by a creditor by legal process upon the financial intermediary on whose books the interest of the debtor appears.

(5) Unless otherwise provided by law, a creditor's lien upon the interest of a debtor in a security obtained pursuant to subsection (3) or (4) is not a restraint on the transfer of the security, free of the lien, to a third party for new value; but in the event of a transfer, the lien applies to the proceeds of the transfer in the hands of the secured party or financial intermediary, subject to any claims having priority.

(6) A creditor whose debtor is the owner of a security is entitled to aid from courts of appropriate jurisdiction, by injunction or otherwise, in reaching the security or in satisfying the claim by means allowed at law or in equity in regard to property that cannot readily be reached by ordinary legal process.

Amended in 1977.

§ 8–318. No Conversion by Good Faith Conduct.

An agent or bailee who in good faith (including observance of reasonable commercial standards if he is in the business of buying, selling, or otherwise dealing with securities) has received certificated securities and sold, pledged, or delivered them or has sold or caused the transfer or pledge of uncertificated securities over which he had control according to the instructions of his principal, is not liable for conversion or for participation in breach of fiduciary duty although the principal had no right so to deal with the securities.

Amended in 1977.

§ 8–319. Statute of Frauds.

A contract for the sale of securities is not enforceable by way of action or defense unless:

(a) there is some writing signed by the party against whom enforcement is sought or by his authorized agent or broker, sufficient to indicate that a contract has been made for sale of a stated quantity of described securities at a defined or stated price;

(b) delivery of a certificated security or transfer instruction has been accepted, or transfer of an uncertificated security has been registered and the transferee has failed to send written objection to the issuer within 10 days after receipt of the initial transaction statement confirming the registration, or payment has been made, but the contract is enforceable under this provision only to the extent of the delivery, registration, or payment;

(c) within a reasonable time a writing in confirmation of the sale or purchase and sufficient against the sender under paragraph (a) has been received by the party against whom enforcement is sought and he has failed to send written objection to its contents within 10 days after its receipt; or

(d) the party against whom enforcement is sought admits in his pleading, testimony, or otherwise in court that a contract was made for the sale of a stated quantity of described securities at a defined or stated price.

Amended in 1977.

§ 8–320. Transfer or Pledge Within Central Depository System.

(1) In addition to other methods, a transfer, pledge, or release of a security or any interest therein may be effected by the making of appropriate entries on the books of a clearing corporation reducing the account of the transferor, pledgor, or pledgee and increasing the account of the transferee, pledgee, or pledgor by the amount of the obligation or the number of shares or rights transferred, pledged, or released, if the security is shown on the account of a transferor, pledgor, or pledgee on the books of the clearing corporation; is subject to the control of the clearing corporation; and

(a) if certificated,

(i) is in the custody of the clearing corporation, another clearing corporation, a custodian bank, or a nominee of any of them; and

(ii) is in bearer form or indorsed in blank by an appropriate person or registered in the name of the clearing corporation, a custodian bank, or a nominee of any of them; or

(b) if uncertificated, is registered in the name of the clearing corporation, another clearing corporation, a custodian bank, or a nominee of any of them.

(2) Under this section entries may be made with respect to like securities or interests therein as a part of a fungible bulk and may refer merely to a quantity of a particular security without reference to the name of the registered owner, certificate or bond number, or the like, and, in appropriate cases, may be on a net basis taking into account other transfers, pledges, or releases of the same security.

(3) A transfer under this section is effective (Section 8–313) and the purchaser acquires the rights of the transferor (Section 8–301). A pledge or release under this section is the transfer of a limited interest. If a pledge or the creation of a security interest is intended, the security interest is perfected at the time when both value is given by the pledgee and the appropriate entries are made (Section 8–321). A transferee or pledgee under this section may be a bona fide purchaser (Section 8–302).

(4) A transfer or pledge under this section is not a registration of transfer under Part 4.

(5) That entries made on the books of the clearing corporation as provided in subsection (1) are not appropriate does not affect the validity or effect of the entries or the liabilities or obligations of the clearing corporation to any person adversely affected thereby.

Added in 1962; amended in 1977.

§ 8–321. Enforceability, Attachment, Perfection and Termination of Security Interests.

(1) A security interest in a security is enforceable and can attach only if it is transferred to the secured party or a person designated by him pursuant to a provision of Section 8–313(1).

(2) A security interest so transferred pursuant to agreement by a transferor who has rights in the security to a transferee who has given value is a perfected security interest, but a security interest that has been transferred solely under paragraph (i) of Section 8–313(1) becomes unperfected after 21 days unless, within that time, the requirements for transfer under any other provision of Section 8–313(1) are satisfied.

(3) A security interest in a security is subject to the provisions of Article 9, but:

(a) no filing is required to perfect the security interest; and

(b) no written security agreement signed by the debtor is necessary to make the security interest enforceable, except as provided in paragraph (h), (i), or (j) of Section 8–313(1). The secured party has the rights and duties provided under Section 9–207, to the extent they are applicable, whether or not the security is certificated, and, if certificated, whether or not it is in his possession.

(4) Unless otherwise agreed, a security interest in a security is terminated by transfer to the debtor or a person designated by him pursuant to a provision of Section 8–313(1). If a security is thus transferred, the security interest, if not terminated, becomes unperfected unless the security is certificated and is delivered to the debtor for the purpose of ultimate sale or exchange or presentation, collection, renewal, or registration of transfer. In that case, the security interest becomes unperfected after 21 days unless, within that time, the security (or securities for which it has been exchanged) is transferred to the secured party or a person designated by him pursuant to a provision of Section 8–313(1).

Added in 1977.

Part 4 Registration

§ 8–401. Duty of Issuer to Register Transfer, Pledge, or Release.

(1) If a certificated security in registered form is presented to the issuer with a request to register transfer or an instruction is presented to the issuer with a request to register transfer, pledge, or release, the issuer shall register the transfer, pledge, or release as requested if:

(a) the security is indorsed or the instruction was originated by the appropriate person or persons (Section 8–308);
(b) reasonable assurance is given that those indorsements or instructions are genuine and effective (Section 8–402);
(c) the issuer has no duty as to adverse claims or has discharged the duty (Section 8–403);
(d) any applicable law relating to the collection of taxes has been complied with; and
(e) the transfer, pledge, or release is in fact rightful or is to a bona fide purchaser.

(2) If an issuer is under a duty to register a transfer, pledge, or release of a security, the issuer is also liable to the person presenting a certificated security or an instruction for registration or his principal for loss resulting from any unreasonable delay in registration or from failure or refusal to register the transfer, pledge, or release.

Amended in 1977.

§ 8–402. Assurance that Indorsements and Instructions Are Effective.

(1) The issuer may require the following assurance that each necessary indorsement of a certificated security or each instruction (Section 8–308) is genuine and effective:

(a) in all cases, a guarantee of the signature (Section 8–312(1) or (2)) of the person indorsing a certificated security or originating an instruction including, in the case of an instruction, a warranty of the taxpayer identification number or, in the absence thereof, other reasonable assurance of identity;

(b) if the indorsement is made or the instruction is originated by an agent, appropriate assurance of authority to sign;
(c) if the indorsement is made or the instruction is originated by a fiduciary, appropriate evidence of appointment or incumbency;
(d) if there is more than one fiduciary, reasonable assurance that all who are required to sign have done so; and
(e) if the indorsement is made or the instruction is originated by a person not covered by any of the foregoing, assurance appropriate to the case corresponding as nearly as may be to the foregoing.

(2) A "guarantee of the signature" in subsection (1) means a guarantee signed by or on behalf of a person reasonably believed by the issuer to be responsible. The issuer may adopt standards with respect to responsibility if they are not manifestly unreasonable.

(3) "Appropriate evidence of appointment or incumbency" in subsection (1) means:

(a) in the case of a fiduciary appointed or qualified by a court, a certificate issued by or under the direction or supervision of that court or an officer thereof and dated within 60 days before the date of presentation for transfer, pledge, or release; or
(b) in any other case, a copy of a document showing the appointment or a certificate issued by or on behalf of a person reasonably believed by the issuer to be responsible or, in the absence of that document or certificate, other evidence reasonably deemed by the issuer to be appropriate. The issuer may adopt standards with respect to the evidence if they are not manifestly unreasonable. The issuer is not charged with notice of the contents of any document obtained pursuant to this paragraph (b) except to the extent that the contents relate directly to the appointment or incumbency.

(4) The issuer may elect to require reasonable assurance beyond that specified in this section, but if it does so and, for a purpose other than that specified in subsection (3)(b), both requires and obtains a copy of a will, trust, indenture, articles of co-partnership, by-laws, or other controlling instrument, it is charged with notice of all matters contained therein affecting the transfer, pledge, or release.

Amended in 1977.

§ 8–403. Issuer's Duty as to Adverse Claims.

(1) An issuer to whom a certificated security is presented for registration shall inquire into adverse claims if:

(a) a written notification of an adverse claim is received at a time and in a manner affording the issuer a reasonable opportunity to act on it prior to the issuance of a new, reissued, or re-registered certificated security, and the notification identifies the claimant, the registered owner, and the issue of which the security is a part, and provides an address for communications directed to the claimant; or

(b) the issuer is charged with notice of an adverse claim from a controlling instrument it has elected to require under Section 8–402(4).

(2) The issuer may discharge any duty of inquiry by any reasonable means, including notifying an adverse claimant by registered or certified mail at the address furnished by him or, if there be no such address, at his residence or regular place of business that the certificated security has been presented for registration of transfer by a named person, and that the transfer will be registered unless within 30 days from the date of mailing the notification, either:

(a) an appropriate restraining order, injunction, or other process issues from a court of competent jurisdiction; or
(b) there is filed with the issuer an indemnity bond, sufficient in the issuer's judgment to protect the issuer and any transfer agent, registrar, or other agent of the issuer involved from any loss it or they may suffer by complying with the adverse claim.

(3) Unless an issuer is charged with notice of an adverse claim from a controlling instrument which it has elected to require under Section 8–402(4) or receives notification of an adverse claim under subsection (1), if a certificated security presented for registration is indorsed by the appropriate person or persons the issuer is under no duty to inquire into adverse claims. In particular:

(a) an issuer registering a certificated security in the name of a person who is a fiduciary or who is described as a fiduciary is not bound to inquire into the existence, extent, or correct description of the fiduciary relationship; and thereafter the issuer may assume without inquiry that the newly registered owner continues to be the fiduciary until the issuer receives written notice that the fiduciary is no longer acting as such with respect to the particular security;
(b) an issuer registering transfer on an indorsement by a fiduciary is not bound to inquire whether the transfer is made in compliance with a controlling instrument or with the law of the state having jurisdiction of the fiduciary relationship, including any law requiring the fiduciary to obtain court approval of the transfer; and
(c) the issuer is not charged with notice of the contents of any court record or file or other recorded or unrecorded document even though the document is in its possession and even though the transfer is made on the indorsement of a fiduciary to the fiduciary himself or to his nominee.

(4) An issuer is under no duty as to adverse claims with respect to an uncertificated security except:

(a) claims embodied in a restraining order, injunction, or other legal process served upon the issuer if the process was served at a time and in a manner affording the issuer a reasonable opportunity to act on it in accordance with the requirements of subsection (5);
(b) claims of which the issuer has received a written notification from the registered owner or the registered pledgee if the notification was received at a time and in

a manner affording the issuer a reasonable opportunity to act on it in accordance with the requirements of subsection (5);
(c) claims (including restrictions on transfer not imposed by the issuer) to which the registration of transfer to the present registered owner was subject and were so noted in the initial transaction statement sent to him; and
(d) claims as to which an issuer is charged with notice from a controlling instrument it has elected to require under Section 8–402(4).

(5) If the issuer of an uncertificated security is under a duty as to an adverse claim, he discharges that duty by:

(a) including a notation of the claim in any statements sent with respect to the security under Sections 8–408(3), (6), and (7); and
(b) refusing to register the transfer or pledge of the security unless the nature of the claim does not preclude transfer or pledge subject thereto.

(6) If the transfer or pledge of the security is registered subject to an adverse claim, a notation of the claim must be included in the initial transaction statement and all subsequent statements sent to the transferee and pledgee under Section 8–408.

(7) Notwithstanding subsections (4) and (5), if an uncertificated security was subject to a registered pledge at the time the issuer first came under a duty as to a particular adverse claim, the issuer has no duty as to that claim if transfer of the security is requested by the registered pledgee or an appropriate person acting for the registered pledgee unless:

(a) the claim was embodied in legal process which expressly provides otherwise;
(b) the claim was asserted in a written notification from the registered pledgee;
(c) the claim was one as to which the issuer was charged with notice from a controlling instrument it required under Section 8–402(4) in connection with the pledgee's request for transfer; or
(d) the transfer requested is to the registered owner.

Amended in 1977.

§ 8–404. Liability and Non-Liability for Registration.

(1) Except as provided in any law relating to the collection of taxes, the issuer is not liable to the owner, pledgee, or any other person suffering loss as a result of the registration of a transfer, pledge, or release of a security if:

(a) there were on or with a certificated security the necessary indorsements or the issuer had received an instruction originated by an appropriate person (Section 8–308); and
(b) the issuer had no duty as to adverse claims or has discharged the duty (Section 8–403).

(2) If an issuer has registered a transfer of a certificated security to a person not entitled to it, the issuer on

demand shall deliver a like security to the true owner unless:

(a) the registration was pursuant to subsection (1);
(b) the owner is precluded from asserting any claim for registering the transfer under Section 8–405(1); or
(c) the delivery would result in overissue, in which case the issuer's liability is governed by Section 8–104.

(3) If an issuer has improperly registered a transfer, pledge, or release of an uncertificated security, the issuer on demand from the injured party shall restore the records as to the injured party to the condition that would have obtained if the improper registration had not been made unless:

(a) the registration was pursuant to subsection (1); or
(b) the registration would result in overissue, in which case the issuer's liability is governed by Section 8–104.

Amended in 1977.

§ 8–405. Lost, Destroyed, and Stolen Certificated Securities.

(1) If a certificated security has been lost, apparently destroyed, or wrongfully taken, and the owner fails to notify the issuer of that fact within a reasonable time after he has notice of it and the issuer registers a transfer of the security before receiving notification, the owner is precluded from asserting against the issuer any claim for registering the transfer under Section 8–404 or any claim to a new security under this section.
(2) If the owner of a certificated security claims that the security has been lost, destroyed, or wrongfully taken, the issuer shall issue a new certificated security or, at the option of the issuer, an equivalent uncertificated security in place of the original security if the owner:

(a) so requests before the issuer has notice that the security has been acquired by a bona fide purchaser;
(b) files with the issuer a sufficient indemnity bond; and
(c) satisfies any other reasonable requirements imposed by the issuer.

(3) If, after the issue of a new certificated or uncertificated security, a bona fide purchaser of the original certificated security presents it for registration of transfer, the issuer shall register the transfer unless registration would result in overissue, in which event the issuer's liability is governed by Section 8–104. In addition to any rights on the indemnity bond, the issuer may recover the new certificated security from the person to whom it was issued or any person taking under him except a bona fide purchaser or may cancel the uncertificated security unless a bona fide purchaser or any person taking under a bona fide purchaser is then the registered owner or registered pledgee thereof.

Amended in 1977.

§ 8–406. Duty of Authenticating Trustee, Transfer Agent, or Registrar.

(1) If a person acts as authenticating trustee, transfer agent, registrar, or other agent for an issuer in the registration of transfers of its certificated securities or in the registration of transfers, pledges, and releases of its uncertificated securities, in the issue of new securities, or in the cancellation of surrendered securities:

(a) he is under a duty to the issuer to exercise good faith and due diligence in performing his functions; and
(b) with regard to the particular functions he performs, he has the same obligation to the holder or owner of a certificated security or to the owner or pledgee of an uncertificated security and has the same rights and privileges as the issuer has in regard to those functions.

(2) Notice to an authenticating trustee, transfer agent, registrar or other agent is notice to the issuer with respect to the functions performed by the agent.

Amended in 1977.

§ 8–407. Exchangeability of Securities.

(1) No issuer is subject to the requirements of this section unless it regularly maintains a system for issuing the class of securities involved under which both certificated and uncertificated securities are regularly issued to the category of owners, which includes the person in whose name the new security is to be registered.
(2) Upon surrender of a certificated security with all necessary indorsements and presentation of a written request by the person surrendering the security, the issuer, if he has no duty as to adverse claims or has discharged the duty (Section 8–403), shall issue to the person or a person designated by him an equivalent uncertificated security subject to all liens, restrictions, and claims that were noted on the certificated security.
(3) Upon receipt of a transfer instruction originated by an appropriate person who so requests, the issuer of an uncertificated security shall cancel the uncertificated security and issue an equivalent certificated security on which must be noted conspicuously any liens and restrictions of the issuer and any adverse claims (as to which the issuer has a duty under Section 8–403(4)) to which the uncertificated security was subject. The certificated security shall be registered in the name of and delivered to:

(a) the registered owner, if the uncertificated security was not subject to a registered pledge; or
(b) the registered pledgee, if the uncertificated security was subject to a registered pledge.

Added in 1977.

§ 8–408. Statements of Uncertificated Securities.

(1) Within 2 business days after the transfer of an uncertificated security has been registered, the issuer shall

send to the new registered owner and, if the security has been transferred subject to a registered pledge, to the registered pledgee a written statement containing:

(a) a description of the issue of which the uncertificated security is a part;

(b) the number of shares or units transferred;

(c) the name and address and any taxpayer identification number of the new registered owner and, if the security has been transferred subject to a registered pledge, the name and address and any taxpayer identification number of the registered pledgee;

(d) a notation of any liens and restrictions of the issuer and any adverse claims (as to which the issuer has a duty under Section 8–403(4)) to which the uncertificated security is or may be subject at the time of registration or a statement that there are none of those liens, restrictions, or adverse claims; and

(e) the date the transfer was registered.

(2) Within 2 business days after the pledge of an uncertificated security has been registered, the issuer shall send to the registered owner and the registered pledgee a written statement containing:

(a) a description of the issue of which the uncertificated security is a part;

(b) the number of shares or units pledged;

(c) the name and address and any taxpayer identification number of the registered owner and the registered pledgee;

(d) a notation of any liens and restrictions of the issuer and any adverse claims (as to which the issuer has a duty under Section 8–403(4)) to which the uncertificated security is or may be subject at the time of registration or a statement that there are none of those liens, restrictions, or adverse claims; and

(e) the date the pledge was registered.

(3) Within 2 business days after the release from pledge of an uncertificated security has been registered, the issuer shall send to the registered owner and the pledgee whose interest was released a written statement containing:

(a) a description of the issue of which the uncertificated security is a part;

(b) the number of shares or units released from pledge;

(c) the name and address and any taxpayer identification number of the registered owner and the pledgee whose interest was released;

(d) a notation of any liens and restrictions of the issuer and any adverse claims (as to which the issuer has a duty under Section 8–403(4)) to which the uncertificated security is or may be subject at the time of registration or a statement that there are none of those liens, restrictions, or adverse claims; and

(e) the date the release was registered.

(4) An "initial transaction statement" is the statement sent to:

(a) the new registered owner and, if applicable, to the registered pledgee pursuant to subsection (1);

(b) the registered pledgee pursuant to subsection (2); or

(c) the registered owner pursuant to subsection (3).

Each initial transaction statement shall be signed by or on behalf of the issuer and must be identified as "Initial Transaction Statement".

(5) Within 2 business days after the transfer of an uncertificated security has been registered, the issuer shall send to the former registered owner and the former registered pledgee, if any, a written statement containing:

(a) a description of the issue of which the uncertificated security is a part;

(b) the number of shares or units transferred;

(c) the name and address and any taxpayer identification number of the former registered owner and of any former registered pledgee; and

(d) the date the transfer was registered.

(6) At periodic intervals no less frequent than annually and at any time upon the reasonable written request of the registered owner, the issuer shall send to the registered owner of each uncertificated security a dated written statement containing:

(a) a description of the issue of which the uncertificated security is a part;

(b) the name and address and any taxpayer identification number of the registered owner;

(c) the number of shares or units of the uncertificated security registered in the name of the registered owner on the date of the statement;

(d) the name and address and any taxpayer identification number of any registered pledgee and the number of shares or units subject to the pledge; and

(e) a notation of any liens and restrictions of the issuer and any adverse claims (as to which the issuer has a duty under Section 8–403(4)) to which the uncertificated security is or may be subject or a statement that there are none of those liens, restrictions, or adverse claims.

(7) At periodic intervals no less frequent than annually and at any time upon the reasonable written request of the registered pledgee, the issuer shall send to the registered pledgee of each uncertificated security a dated written statement containing:

(a) a description of the issue of which the uncertificated security is a part;

(b) the name and address and any taxpayer identification number of the registered owner;

(c) the name and address and any taxpayer identification number of the registered pledgee;

(d) the number of shares or units subject to the pledge; and

(e) a notation of any liens and restrictions of the issuer and any adverse claims (as to which the issuer has a duty under Section 8–403(4)) to which the uncertificated security is or may be subject or a statement that there are none of those liens, restrictions, or adverse claims.

(8) If the issuer sends the statements described in subsections (6) and (7) at periodic intervals no less frequent than quarterly, the issuer is not obliged to send additional statements upon request unless the owner or pledgee requesting them pays to the issuer the reasonable cost of furnishing them.

(9) Each statement sent pursuant to this section must bear a conspicuous legend reading substantially as follows: "This statement is merely a record of the rights of the addressee as of the time of its issuance.

Delivery of this statement, of itself, confers no rights on the recipient. This statement is neither a negotiable instrument nor a security."

Added in 1977.

Article 9

SECURED TRANSACTIONS; SALES OF ACCOUNTS AND CHATTEL PAPER

Note: *The adoption of this Article should be accompanied by the repeal of existing statutes dealing with conditional sales, trust receipts, factor's liens where the factor is given a non-possessory lien, chattel mortgages, crop mortgages, mortgages on railroad equipment, assignment of accounts and generally statutes regulating security interests in personal property.*

Where the state has a retail installment selling act or small loan act, that legislation should be carefully examined to determine what changes in those acts are needed to conform them to this Article. This Article primarily sets out rules defining rights of a secured party against persons dealing with the debtor; it does not prescribe regulations and controls which may be necessary to curb abuses arising in the small loan business or in the financing of consumer purchases on credit. Accordingly there is no intention to repeal existing regulatory acts in those fields by enactment or re-enactment of Article 9. See Section 9–203(4) and the Note thereto.

Part 1 Short Title, Applicability and Definitions

§ 9–101. Short Title.

This Article shall be known and may be cited as Uniform Commercial Code—Secured Transactions.

§ 9–102. Policy and Subject Matter of Article.

(1) Except as otherwise provided in Section 9–104 on excluded transactions, this Article applies

(a) to any transaction (regardless of its form) which is intended to create a security interest in personal property or fixtures including goods, documents, instruments, general intangibles, chattel paper or accounts; and also

(b) to any sale of accounts or chattel paper.

(2) This Article applies to security interests created by contract including pledge, assignment, chattel mortgage, chattel trust, trust deed, factor's lien, equipment trust, conditional sale, trust receipt, other lien or title retention contract and lease or consignment intended as security. This Article does not apply to statutory liens except as provided in Section 9–310.

(3) The application of this Article to a security interest in a secured obligation is not affected by the fact that the obligation is itself secured by a transaction or interest to which this Article does not apply.

Amended in 1972.

§ 9–103. Perfection of Security Interest in Multiple State Transactions.

(1) Documents, instruments and ordinary goods.

(a) This subsection applies to documents and instruments and to goods other than those covered by a certificate of title described in subsection (2), mobile goods described in subsection (3), and minerals described in subsection (5).

(b) Except as otherwise provided in this subsection, perfection and the effect of perfection or non-perfection of a security interest in collateral are governed by the law of the jurisdiction where the collateral is when the last event occurs on which is based the assertion that the security interest is perfected or unperfected.

(c) If the parties to a transaction creating a purchase money security interest in goods in one jurisdiction understand at the time that the security interest attaches that the goods will be kept in another jurisdiction, then the law of the other jurisdiction governs the perfection and the effect of perfection or non-perfection of the security interest from the time it attaches until thirty days after the debtor receives possession of the goods and thereafter if the goods are taken to the other jurisdiction before the end of the thirty-day period.

(d) When collateral is brought into and kept in this state while subject to a security interest perfected under the law of the jurisdiction from which the collateral was removed, the security interest remains perfected, but if action is required by Part 3 of this Article to perfect the security interest,

(i) if the action is not taken before the expiration of the period of perfection in the other jurisdiction or the end of four months after the collateral is brought into this state, whichever period first expires, the security interest becomes unperfected at the end of that period and is thereafter deemed to have been unperfected as against a person who became a purchaser after removal;

(ii) if the action is taken before the expiration of the period specified in subparagraph (i), the security interest continues perfected thereafter;

(iii) for the purpose of priority over a buyer of consumer goods (subsection (2) of Section 9–307), the period of the effectiveness of a filing in the jurisdiction from which the collateral is removed is governed by the rules with respect to perfection in subparagraphs (i) and (ii).

(2) Certificate of title.

(a) This subsection applies to goods covered by a certificate of title issued under a statute of this state or of another jurisdiction under the law of which indication of a security interest on the certificate is required as a condition of perfection.

(b) Except as otherwise provided in this subsection, perfection and the effect of perfection or non-perfection of the security interest are governed by the law (including the conflict of laws rules) of the jurisdiction issuing the certificate until four months after the goods are removed from that jurisdiction and thereafter until the goods are registered in another jurisdiction, but in any event not beyond surrender of the certificate. After the expiration of that period, the goods are not covered by the certificate of title within the meaning of this section.

(c) Except with respect to the rights of a buyer described in the next paragraph, a security interest, perfected in another jurisdiction otherwise than by notation on a certificate of title, in goods brought into this state and thereafter covered by a certificate of title issued by this state is subject to the rules stated in paragraph (d) of subsection (1).

(d) If goods are brought into this state while a security interest therein is perfected in any manner under the law of the jurisdiction from which the goods are removed and a certificate of title is issued by this state and the certificate does not show that the goods are subject to the security interest or that they may be subject to security interests not shown on the certificate, the security interest is subordinate to the rights of a buyer of the goods who is not in the business of selling goods of that kind to the extent that he gives value and receives delivery of the goods after issuance of the certificate and without knowledge of the security interest.

(3) Accounts, general intangibles and mobile goods.

(a) This subsection applies to accounts (other than an account described in subsection (5) on minerals) and general intangibles (other than uncertificated securities) and to goods which are mobile and which are of a type normally used in more than one jurisdiction, such as motor vehicles, trailers, rolling stock, airplanes, shipping containers, road building and construction machinery and commercial harvesting machinery and the like, if the goods are equipment or are inventory leased or held for lease by the debtor to others, and are not covered by a certificate of title described in subsection (2).

(b) The law (including the conflict of laws rules) of the jurisdiction in which the debtor is located governs the perfection and the effect of perfection or non-perfection of the security interest.

(c) If, however, the debtor is located in a jurisdiction which is not a part of the United States, and which does not provide for perfection of the security interest by filing or recording in that jurisdiction, the law of the jurisdiction in the United States in which the debtor has its major executive office in the United States governs the perfection and the effect of perfection or non-

perfection of the security interest through filing. In the alternative, if the debtor is located in a jurisdiction which is not a part of the United States or Canada and the collateral is accounts or general intangibles for money due or to become due, the security interest may be perfected by notification to the account debtor. As used in this paragraph, "United States" includes its territories and possessions and the Commonwealth of Puerto Rico.

(d) A debtor shall be deemed located at his place of business if he has one, at his chief executive office if he has more than one place of business, otherwise at his residence. If, however, the debtor is a foreign air carrier under the Federal Aviation Act of 1958, as amended, it shall be deemed located at the designated office of the agent upon whom service of process may be made on behalf of the foreign air carrier.

(e) A security interest perfected under the law of the jurisdiction of the location of the debtor is perfected until the expiration of four months after a change of the debtor's location to another jurisdiction, or until perfection would have ceased by the law of the first jurisdiction, whichever period first expires. Unless perfected in the new jurisdiction before the end of that period, it becomes unperfected thereafter and is deemed to have been unperfected as against a person who became a purchaser after the change.

(4) Chattel paper.

The rules stated for goods in subsection (1) apply to a possessory security interest in chattel paper. The rules stated for accounts in subsection (3) apply to a nonpossessory security interest in chattel paper, but the security interest may not be perfected by notification to the account debtor.

(5) Minerals.

Perfection and the effect of perfection or non-perfection of a security interest which is created by a debtor who has an interest in minerals or the like (including oil and gas) before extraction and which attaches thereto as extracted, or which attaches to an account resulting from the sale thereof at the wellhead or minehead are governed by the law (including the conflict of laws rules) of the jurisdiction wherein the wellhead or minehead is located.

(6) Uncertificated securities.

The law (including the conflict of laws rules) of the jurisdiction of organization of the issuer governs the perfection and the effect of perfection or non-perfection of a security interest in uncertificated securities.

Amended in 1972 and 1977.

§ 9–104. Transactions Excluded From Article.

This Article does not apply

(a) to a security interest subject to any statute of the United States, to the extent that such statute governs the rights of parties to and third parties affected by transactions in particular types of property; or

(b) to a landlord's lien; or

(c) to a lien given by statute or other rule of law for services or materials except as provided in Section 9–310 on priority of such liens; or

(d) to a transfer of a claim for wages, salary or other compensation of an employee; or

(e) to a transfer by a government or governmental subdivision or agency; or

(f) to a sale of accounts or chattel paper as part of a sale of the business out of which they arose, or an assignment of accounts or chattel paper which is for the purpose of collection only, or a transfer of a right to payment under a contract to an assignee who is also to do the performance under the contract or a transfer of a single account to an assignee in whole or partial satisfaction of a preexisting indebtedness; or

(g) to a transfer of an interest in or claim in or under any policy of insurance, except as provided with respect to proceeds (Section 9–306) and priorities in proceeds (Section 9–312); or

(h) to a right represented by a judgment (other than a judgment taken on a right to payment which was collateral); or

(i) to any right of set-off; or

(j) except to the extent that provision is made for fixtures in Section 9–313, to the creation or transfer of an interest in or lien on real estate, including a lease or rents thereunder; or

(k) to a transfer in whole or in part of any claim arising out of tort; or

(l) to a transfer of an interest in any deposit account (subsection (1) of Section 9–105), except as provided with respect to proceeds (Section 9–306) and priorities in proceeds (Section 9–312).

Amended in 1972.

§ 9–105. Definitions and Index of Definitions.

(1) In this Article unless the context otherwise requires:

(a) "Account debtor" means the person who is obligated on an account, chattel paper or general intangible;

(b) "Chattel paper" means a writing or writings which evidence both a monetary obligation and a security interest in or a lease of specific goods, but a charter or other contract involving the use or hire of a vessel is not chattel paper. When a transaction is evidenced both by such a security agreement or a lease and by an instrument or a series of instruments, the group of writings taken together constitutes chattel paper;

(c) "Collateral" means the property subject to a security interest, and includes accounts and chattel paper which have been sold;

(d) "Debtor" means the person who owes payment or other performance of the obligation secured, whether or not he owns or has rights in the collateral, and includes the seller of accounts or chattel paper. Where the debtor and the owner of the collateral are not the same person, the term "debtor" means the owner of the collateral in any provision of the Article dealing with the collateral, the obligor in any provision dealing with the obligation, and may include both where the context so requires;

(e) "Deposit account" means a demand, time, savings, passbook or like account maintained with a bank, savings and loan association, credit union or like organization, other than an account evidenced by a certificate of deposit;

(f) "Document" means document of title as defined in the general definitions of Article 1 (Section 1–201), and a receipt of the kind described in subsection (2) of Section 7–201;

(g) "Encumbrance" includes real estate mortgages and other liens on real estate and all other rights in real estate that are not ownership interests;

(h) "Goods" includes all things which are movable at the time the security interest attaches or which are fixtures (Section 9–313), but does not include money, documents, instruments, accounts, chattel paper, general intangibles, or minerals or the like (including oil and gas) before extraction. "Goods" also includes standing timber which is to be cut and removed under a conveyance or contract for sale, the unborn young of animals, and growing crops;

(i) "Instrument" means a negotiable instrument (defined in Section 3–104), or a certificated security (defined in Section 8–102) or any other writing which evidences a right to the payment of money and is not itself a security agreement or lease and is of a type which is in ordinary course of business transferred by delivery with any necessary indorsement or assignment;

(j) "Mortgage" means a consensual interest created by a real estate mortgage, a trust deed on real estate, or the like;

(k) An advance is made "pursuant to commitment" if the secured party has bound himself to make it, whether or not a subsequent event of default or other event not within his control has relieved or may relieve him from his obligation;

(l) "Security agreement" means an agreement which creates or provides for a security interest;

(m) "Secured party" means a lender, seller or other person in whose favor there is a security interest, including a person to whom accounts or chattel paper have been sold. When the holders of obligations issued under an indenture of trust, equipment trust agreement or the like are represented by a trustee or other person, the representative is the secured party;

(n) "Transmitting utility" means any person primarily engaged in the railroad, street railway or trolley bus business, the electric or electronics communications transmission business, the transmission of goods by pipeline, or the transmission or the production and transmission of electricity, steam, gas or water, or the provision of sewer service.

(2) Other definitions applying to this Article and the sections in which they appear are:

"Account". Section 9–106.
"Attach". Section 9–203.
"Construction mortgage". Section 9–313(1).

"Consumer goods". Section 9–109(1).
"Equipment". Section 9–109(2).
"Farm products". Section 9–109(3).
"Fixture". Section 9–313(1).
"Fixture filing". Section 9–313(1).
"General intangibles". Section 9–106.
"Inventory". Section 9–109(4).
"Lien creditor". Section 9–301(3).
"Proceeds". Section 9–306(1).
"Purchase money security interest". Section 9–107.
"United States". Section 9–103.

(3) The following definitions in other Articles apply to this Article:

"Check". Section 3–104.
"Contract for sale". Section 2–106.
"Holder in due course". Section 3–302.
"Note". Section 3–104.
"Sale". Section 2–106.

(4) In addition Article 1 contains general definitions and principles of construction and interpretation applicable throughout this Article.

Amended in 1966, 1972 and 1977.

§ 9–106. Definitions: "Account"; "General Intangibles".

"Account" means any right to payment for goods sold or leased or for services rendered which is not evidenced by an instrument or chattel paper, whether or not it has been earned by performance. "General intangibles" means any personal property (including things in action) other than goods, accounts, chattel paper, documents, instruments, and money. All rights to payment earned or unearned under a charter or other contract involving the use or hire of a vessel and all rights incident to the charter or contract are accounts.

Amended in 1966, 1972.

§ 9–107. Definitions: "Purchase Money Security Interest".

A security interest is a "purchase money security interest" to the extent that it is

(a) taken or retained by the seller of the collateral to secure all or part of its price; or
(b) taken by a person who by making advances or incurring an obligation gives value to enable the debtor to acquire rights in or the use of collateral if such value is in fact so used.

§ 9–108. When After-Acquired Collateral Not Security for Antecedent Debt.

Where a secured party makes an advance, incurs an obligation, releases a perfected security interest, or otherwise gives new value which is to be secured in whole or in part by after-acquired property his security interest in the after-acquired collateral shall be deemed to be taken for new value and not as security for an antecedent debt if the debtor acquires his rights in such collateral either in the ordinary course of his business or under a contract of purchase made pursuant to the security agreement within a reasonable time after new value is given.

§ 9–109. Classification of Goods; "Consumer Goods"; "Equipment"; "Farm Products"; "Inventory".

Goods are

(1) "consumer goods" if they are used or bought for use primarily for personal, family or household purposes;
(2) "equipment" if they are used or bought for use primarily in business (including farming or a profession) or by a debtor who is a non-profit organization or a governmental subdivision or agency or if the goods are not included in the definitions of inventory, farm products or consumer goods;
(3) "farm products" if they are crops or livestock or supplies used or produced in farming operations or if they are products of crops or livestock in their unmanufactured states (such as ginned cotton, wool-clip, maple syrup, milk and eggs), and if they are in the possession of a debtor engaged in raising, fattening, grazing or other farming operations. If goods are farm products they are neither equipment nor inventory;
(4) "inventory" if they are held by a person who holds them for sale or lease or to be furnished under contracts of service or if he has so furnished them, or if they are raw materials, work in process or materials used or consumed in a business. Inventory of a person is not to be classified as his equipment.

§ 9–110. Sufficiency of Description.

For purposes of this Article any description of personal property or real estate is sufficient whether or not it is specific if it reasonably identifies what is described.

§ 9–111. Applicability of Bulk Transfer Laws.

The creation of a security interest is not a bulk transfer under Article 6 (see Section 6–103).

§ 9–112. Where Collateral Is Not Owned by Debtor.

Unless otherwise agreed, when a secured party knows that collateral is owned by a person who is not the debtor, the owner of the collateral is entitled to receive from the secured party any surplus under Section 9–502(2) or under Section 9–504(1), and is not liable for the debt or for any deficiency after resale, and he has the same right as the debtor.

(a) to receive statements under Section 9–208;
(b) to receive notice of and to object to a secured party's proposal to retain the collateral in satisfaction of the indebtedness under Section 9–505;

(c) to redeem the collateral under Section 9–506;

(d) to obtain injunctive or other relief under Section 9–507(1); and

(e) to recover losses caused to him under Section 9–208(2).

§ 9–113. Security Interests Arising Under Article on Sales.

A security interest arising solely under the Article on Sales (Article 2) is subject to the provisions of this Article except that to the extent that and so long as the debtor does not have or does not lawfully obtain possession of the goods

(a) no security agreement is necessary to make the security interest enforceable; and

(b) no filing is required to perfect the security interest; and

(c) the rights of the secured party on default by the debtor are governed by the Article on Sales (Article 2).

§ 9–114. Consignment.

(1) A person who delivers goods under a consignment which is not a security interest and who would be required to file under this Article by paragraph (3)(c) of Section 2–326 has priority over a secured party who is or becomes a creditor of the consignee and who would have a perfected security interest in the goods if they were the property of the consignee, and also has priority with respect to identifiable cash proceeds received on or before delivery of the goods to a buyer, if

(a) the consignor complies with the filing provision of the Article on Sales with respect to consignments (paragraph (3)(c) of Section 2–326) before the consignee receives possession of the goods; and

(b) the consignor gives notification in writing to the holder of the security interest if the holder has filed a financing statement covering the same types of goods before the date of the filing made by the consignor; and

(c) the holder of the security interest receives the notification within five years before the consignee receives possession of the goods; and

(d) the notification states that the consignor expects to deliver goods on consignment to the consignee, describing the goods by item or type.

(2) In the case of a consignment which is not a security interest and in which the requirements of the preceding subsection have not been met, a person who delivers goods to another is subordinate to a person who would have a perfected security interest in the goods if they were the property of the debtor.

Added in 1972.

Part 2 Validity of Security Agreement and Rights of Parties Thereto

§ 9–201. General Validity of Security Agreement.

Except as otherwise provided by this Act a security agreement is effective according to its terms between the parties, against purchasers of the collateral and against creditors. Nothing in this Article validates any charge or practice illegal under any statute or regulation thereunder governing usury, small loans, retail installment sales, or the like, or extends the application of any such statute or regulation to any transaction not otherwise subject thereto.

§ 9–202. Title to Collateral Immaterial.

Each provision of this Article with regard to rights, obligations and remedies applies whether title to collateral is in the secured party or in the debtor.

§ 9–203. Attachment and Enforceability of Security Interest; Proceeds; Formal Requisites.

(1) Subject to the provisions of Section 4–208 on the security interest of a collecting bank, Section 8–321 on security interests in securities and Section 9–113 on a security interest arising under the Article on Sales, a security interest is not enforceable against the debtor or third parties with respect to the collateral and does not attach unless:

(a) the collateral is in the possession of the secured party pursuant to agreement, or the debtor has signed a security agreement which contains a description of the collateral and in addition, when the security interest covers crops growing or to be grown or timber to be cut, a description of the land concerned;

(b) value has been given; and

(c) the debtor has rights in the collateral.

(2) A security interest attaches when it becomes enforceable against the debtor with respect to the collateral. Attachment occurs as soon as all of the events specified in subsection (1) have taken place unless explicit agreement postpones the time of attaching.

(3) Unless otherwise agreed a security agreement gives the secured party the rights to proceeds provided by Section 9–306.

(4) A transaction, although subject to this Article, is also subject to . . .*, and in the case of conflict between the provisions of this Article and any such statute, the provisions of such statute control. Failure to comply with any applicable statute has only the effect which is specified therein.

Amended in 1972 and 1977.

Note: *At * in subsection (4) insert reference to any local statute regulating small loans, retail installment sales and the like.*

The foregoing subsection (4) is designed to make it clear that certain transactions, although subject to this Article, must also comply with other applicable legislation.

This Article is designed to regulate all the "security" aspects of transactions within its scope. There is, however, much regulatory legislation, particularly in the consumer field, which supplements this Article and should not be repealed by its enactment. Examples are small loan acts, retail installment selling acts and the like. Such acts may provide for licensing and rate regulation and may prescribe particular forms of contract. Such provisions should remain in force despite the enactment of this Article. On the other hand if a retail installment selling act contains provisions on filing, rights on default, etc., such provisions should be repealed as inconsistent with this Article except that inconsistent provisions as to deficiencies, penalties, etc., in the Uniform Consumer Credit Code and other recent related legislation should remain because those statutes were drafted after the substantial enactment of the Article and with the intention of modifying certain provisions of this Article as to consumer credit.

§ 9–204. After-Acquired Property; Future Advances.

(1) Except as provided in subsection (2), a security agreement may provide that any or all obligations covered by the security agreement are to be secured by after-acquired collateral.

(2) No security interest attaches under an after-acquired property clause to consumer goods other than accessions (Section 9–314) when given as additional security unless the debtor acquires rights in them within ten days after the secured party gives value.

(3) Obligations covered by a security agreement may include future advances or other value whether or not the advances or value are given pursuant to commitment (subsection (1) of Section 9–105).

Amended in 1972.

§ 9–205. Use or Disposition of Collateral Without Accounting Permissible.

A security interest is not invalid or fraudulent against creditors by reason of liberty in the debtor to use, commingle or dispose of all or part of the collateral (including returned or repossessed goods) or to collect or compromise accounts or chattel paper, or to accept the return of goods or make repossessions, or to use, commingle or dispose of proceeds, or by reason of the failure of the secured party to require the debtor to account for proceeds or replace collateral. This section does not relax the requirements of possession where perfection of a security interest depends upon possession of the collateral by the secured party or by a bailee.

Amended in 1972.

§ 9–206. Agreement Not to Assert Defenses Against Assignee; Modification of Sales Warranties Where Security Agreement Exists.

(1) Subject to any statute or decision which establishes a different rule for buyers or lessees of consumer goods, an agreement by a buyer or lessee that he will not assert against an assignee any claim or defense which he may have against the seller or lessor is enforceable by an assignee who takes his assignment for value, in good faith and without notice of a claim or defense, except as to defenses of a type which may be asserted against a holder in due course of a negotiable instrument under the Article on Commercial Paper (Article 3). A buyer who as

part of one transaction signs both a negotiable instrument and a security agreement makes such an agreement.

(2) When a seller retains a purchase money security interest in goods the Article on Sales (Article 2) governs the sale and any disclaimer, limitation or modification of the seller's warranties.

Amended in 1962.

§ 9–207. Rights and Duties When Collateral is in Secured Party's Possession.

(1) A secured party must use reasonable care in the custody and preservation of collateral in his possession. In the case of an instrument or chattel paper reasonable care includes taking necessary steps to preserve rights against prior parties unless otherwise agreed.

(2) Unless otherwise agreed, when collateral is in the secured party's possession

(a) reasonable expenses (including the cost of any insurance and payment of taxes or other charges) incurred in the custody, preservation, use or operation of the collateral are chargeable to the debtor and are secured by the collateral;

(b) the risk of accidental loss or damage is on the debtor to the extent of any deficiency in any effective insurance coverage;

(c) the secured party may hold as additional security any increase or profits (except money) received from the collateral, but money so received, unless remitted to the debtor, shall be applied in reduction of the secured obligation;

(d) the secured party must keep the collateral identifiable but fungible collateral may be commingled;

(e) the secured party may repledge the collateral upon terms which do not impair the debtor's right to redeem it.

(3) A secured party is liable for any loss caused by his failure to meet any obligation imposed by the preceding subsections but does not lose his security interest.

(4) A secured party may use or operate the collateral for the purpose of preserving the collateral or its value or pursuant to the order of a court of appropriate jurisdiction or, except in the case of consumer goods, in the manner and to the extent provided in the security agreement.

§ 9–208. Request for Statement of Account or List of Collateral.

(1) A debtor may sign a statement indicating what he believes to be the aggregate amount of unpaid indebtedness as of a specified date and may send it to the secured party with a request that the statement be approved or corrected and returned to the debtor. When the security agreement or any other record kept by the secured party identifies the collateral a debtor may similarly request the secured party to approve or correct a list of the collateral.

(2) The secured party must comply with such a request within two weeks after receipt by sending a written correction or approval. If the secured party claims a

security interest in all of a particular type of collateral owned by the debtor he may indicate that fact in his reply and need not approve or correct an itemized list of such collateral. If the secured party without reasonable excuse fails to comply he is liable for any loss caused to the debtor thereby; and if the debtor has properly included in his request a good faith statement of the obligation or a list of the collateral or both the secured party may claim a security interest only as shown in the statement against persons misled by his failure to comply. If he no longer has an interest in the obligation or collateral at the time the request is received he must disclose the name and address of any successor in interest known to him and he is liable for any loss caused to the debtor as a result of failure to disclose. A successor in interest is not subject to this section until a request is received by him.

(3) A debtor is entitled to such a statement once every six months without charge. The secured party may require payment of a charge not exceeding $10 for each additional statement furnished.

Part 3 Rights of Third Parties; Perfected and Unperfected Security Interests; Rules of Priority

§ 9–301. Persons Who Take Priority Over Unperfected Security Interests; Rights of "Lien Creditor".

(1) Except as otherwise provided in subsection (2), an unperfected security interest is subordinate to the rights of

(a) persons entitled to priority under Section 9–312;
(b) a person who becomes a lien creditor before the security interest is perfected;
(c) in the case of goods, instruments, documents, and chattel paper, a person who is not a secured party and who is a transferee in bulk or other buyer not in ordinary course of business or is a buyer of farm products in ordinary course of business, to the extent that he gives value and receives delivery of the collateral without knowledge of the security interest and before it is perfected;
(d) in the case of accounts and general intangibles, a person who is not a secured party and who is a transferee to the extent that he gives value without knowledge of the security interest and before it is perfected.

(2) If the secured party files with respect to a purchase money security interest before or within ten days after the debtor receives possession of the collateral, he takes priority over the rights of a transferee in bulk or of a lien creditor which arise between the time the security interest attaches and the time of filing.
(3) A "lien creditor" means a creditor who has acquired a lien on the property involved by attachment, levy or the like and includes an assignee for benefit of creditors from the time of assignment, and a trustee in bankruptcy from

the date of the filing of the petition or a receiver in equity from the time of appointment.
(4) A person who becomes a lien creditor while a security interest is perfected takes subject to the security interest only to the extent that it secures advances made before he becomes a lien creditor or within 45 days thereafter or made without knowledge of the lien or pursuant to a commitment entered into without knowledge of the lien.

Amended in 1972.

§ 9–302. When Filing Is Required to Perfect Security Interest; Security Interests to Which Filing Provisions of This Article Do Not Apply.

(1) A financing statement must be filed to perfect all security interests except the following:

(a) a security interest in collateral in possession of the secured party under Section 9–305;
(b) a security interest temporarily perfected in instruments or documents without delivery under Section 9–304 or in proceeds for a 10 day period under Section 9–306;
(c) a security interest created by an assignment of a beneficial interest in a trust or a decedent's estate;
(d) a purchase money security interest in consumer goods; but filing is required for a motor vehicle required to be registered; and fixture filing is required for priority over conflicting interests in fixtures to the extent provided in Section 9–313;
(e) an assignment of accounts which does not alone or in conjunction with other assignments to the same assignee transfer a significant part of the outstanding accounts of the assignor;
(f) a security interest of a collecting bank (Section 4–208) or in securities (Section 8–321) or arising under the Article on Sales (see Section 9–113) or covered in subsection (3) of this section;
(g) an assignment for the benefit of all the creditors of the transferor, and subsequent transfers by the assignee thereunder.

(2) If a secured party assigns a perfected security interest, no filing under this Article is required in order to continue the perfected status of the security interest against creditors of and transferees from the original debtor.
(3) The filing of a financing statement otherwise required by this Article is not necessary or effective to perfect a security interest in property subject to

(a) a statute or treaty of the United States which provides for a national or international registration or a national or international certificate of title or which specifies a place of filing different from that specified in this Article for filing of the security interest; or
(b) the following statutes of this state; [list any certificate of title statute covering automobiles, trailers, mobile homes, boats, farm tractors, or the like, and any central filing statute.]; but during any period in which collateral

is inventory held for sale by a person who is in the business of selling goods of that kind, the filing provisions of this Article (Part 4) apply to a security interest in that collateral created by him as debtor; or

(c) a certificate of title statute of another jurisdiction under the law of which indication of a security interest on the certificate is required as a condition of perfection (subsection (2) of Section 9–103).

(4) Compliance with a statute or treaty described in subsection (3) is equivalent to the filing of a financing statement under this Article, and a security interest in property subject to the statute or treaty can be perfected only by compliance therewith except as provided in Section 9–103 on multiple state transactions. Duration and renewal of perfection of a security interest perfected by compliance with the statute or treaty are governed by the provisions of the statute or treaty; in other respects the security interest is subject to this Article.

Amended in 1972 and 1977.

§ 9–303. When Security Interest Is Perfected; Continuity of Perfection.

(1) A security interest is perfected when it has attached and when all of the applicable steps required for perfection have been taken. Such steps are specified in Sections 9–302, 9–304, 9–305 and 9–306. If such steps are taken before the security interest attaches, it is perfected at the time when it attaches.

(2) If a security interest is originally perfected in any way permitted under this Article and is subsequently perfected in some other way under this Article, without an intermediate period when it was unperfected, the security interest shall be deemed to be perfected continuously for the purposes of this Article.

§ 9–304. Perfection of Security Interest in Instruments, Documents, and Goods Covered by Documents; Perfection by Permissive Filing; Temporary Perfection Without Filing or Transfer of Possession.

(1) A security interest in chattel paper or negotiable documents may be perfected by filing. A security interest in money or instruments (other than certificated securities or instruments which constitute part of chattel paper) can be perfected only by the secured party's taking possession, except as provided in subsections (4) and (5) of this section and subsections (2) and (3) of Section 9–306 on proceeds.

(2) During the period that goods are in the possession of the issuer of a negotiable document therefor, a security interest in the goods is perfected by perfecting a security interest in the document, and any security interest in the goods otherwise perfected during such period is subject thereto.

(3) A security interest in goods in the possession of a bailee other than one who has issued a negotiable document therefor is perfected by issuance of a document in the name of the secured party or by the bailee's receipt of notification of the secured party's interest or by filing as to the goods.

(4) A security interest in instruments (other than certificated securities) or negotiable documents is perfected without filing or the taking of possession for a period of 21 days from the time it attaches to the extent that it arises for new value given under a written security agreement.

(5) A security interest remains perfected for a period of 21 days without filing where a secured party having a perfected security interest in an instrument (other than a certificated security), a negotiable document or goods in possession of a bailee other than one who has issued a negotiable document therefor

(a) makes available to the debtor the goods or documents representing the goods for the purpose of ultimate sale or exchange or for the purpose of loading, unloading, storing, shipping, transshipping, manufacturing, processing or otherwise dealing with them in a manner preliminary to their sale or exchange, but priority between conflicting security interests in the goods is subject to subsection (3) of Section 9–312; or

(b) delivers the instrument to the debtor for the purpose of ultimate sale or exchange or of presentation, collection, renewal or registration of transfer.

(6) After the 21 day period in subsections (4) and (5) perfection depends upon compliance with applicable provisions of this Article.

Amended in 1972 and 1977.

§ 9–305. When Possession by Secured Party Perfects Security Interest Without Filing.

A security interest in letters of credit and advices of credit (subsection (2)(a) of Section 5–116), goods, instruments (other than certificated securities), money, negotiable documents, or chattel paper may be perfected by the secured party's taking possession of the collateral. If such collateral other than goods covered by a negotiable document is held by a bailee, the secured party is deemed to have possession from the time the bailee receives notification of the secured party's interest. A security interest is perfected by possession from the time possession is taken without a relation back and continues only so long as possession is retained, unless otherwise specified in this Article. The security interest may be otherwise perfected as provided in this Article before or after the period of possession by the secured party.

Amended in 1972 and 1977.

§ 9–306. "Proceeds"; Secured Party's Rights on Disposition of Collateral.

(1) "Proceeds" includes whatever is received upon the sale, exchange, collection or other disposition of collateral or proceeds. Insurance payable by reason of loss or damage to the collateral is proceeds, except to the extent

that it is payable to a person other than a party to the security agreement. Money, checks, deposit accounts, and the like are "cash proceeds". All other proceeds are "non-cash proceeds".

(2) Except where this Article otherwise provides, a security interest continues in collateral notwithstanding sale, exchange or other disposition thereof unless the disposition was authorized by the secured party in the security agreement or otherwise, and also continues in any identifiable proceeds including collections received by the debtor.

(3) The security interest in proceeds is a continuously perfected security interest if the interest in the original collateral was perfected but it ceases to be a perfected security interest and becomes unperfected ten days after receipt of the proceeds by the debtor unless

(a) a filed financing statement covers the original collateral and the proceeds are collateral in which a security interest may be perfected by filing in the office or offices where the financing statement has been filed and, if the proceeds are acquired with cash proceeds, the description of collateral in the financing statement indicates the types of property constituting the proceeds; or

(b) a filed financing statement covers the original collateral and the proceeds are identifiable cash proceeds; or

(c) the security interest in the proceeds is perfected before the expiration of the ten day period.

Except as provided in this section, a security interest in proceeds can be perfected only by the methods or under the circumstances permitted in this Article for original collateral of the same type.

(4) In the event of insolvency proceedings instituted by or against a debtor, a secured party with a perfected security interest in proceeds has a perfected security interest only in the following proceeds:

(a) in identifiable non-cash proceeds and in separate deposit accounts containing only proceeds;

(b) in identifiable cash proceeds in the form of money which is neither commingled with other money nor deposited in a deposit account prior to the insolvency proceedings;

(c) in identifiable cash proceeds in the form of checks and the like which are not deposited in a deposit account prior to the insolvency proceedings; and

(d) in all cash and deposit accounts of the debtor in which proceeds have been commingled with other funds, but the perfected security interest under this paragraph (d) is

(i) subject to any right to set-off; and

(ii) limited to an amount not greater than the amount of any cash proceeds received by the debtor within ten days before the institution of the insolvency proceedings less the sum of (I) the payments to the secured party on account of cash proceeds received by the debtor during such period and (II) the cash proceeds received by the debtor during such period to which the secured party is entitled under paragraphs (a) through (c) of this subsection (4).

(5) If a sale of goods results in an account or chattel paper which is transferred by the seller to a secured party, and if the goods are returned to or are repossessed by the seller or the secured party, the following rules determine priorities:

(a) If the goods were collateral at the time of sale, for an indebtedness of the seller which is still unpaid, the original security interest attaches again to the goods and continues as a perfected security interest if it was perfected at the time when the goods were sold. If the security interest was originally perfected by a filing which is still effective, nothing further is required to continue the perfected status; in any other case, the secured party must take possession of the returned or repossessed goods or must file.

(b) An unpaid transferee of the chattel paper has a security interest in the goods against the transferor. Such security interest is prior to a security interest asserted under paragraph (a) to the extent that the transferee of the chattel paper was entitled to priority under Section 9–308.

(c) An unpaid transferee of the account has a security interest in the goods against the transferor. Such security interest is subordinate to a security interest asserted under paragraph (a).

(d) A security interest of an unpaid transferee asserted under paragraph (b) or (c) must be perfected for protection against creditors of the transferor and purchasers of the returned or repossessed goods.

Amended in 1972.

§ 9–307. Protection of Buyers of Goods.

(1) A buyer in ordinary course of business (subsection (9) of Section 1–201) other than a person buying farm products from a person engaged in farming operations takes free of a security interest created by his seller even though the security interest is perfected and even though the buyer knows of its existence.

(2) In the case of consumer goods, a buyer takes free of a security interest even though perfected if he buys without knowledge of the security interest, for value and for his own personal, family or household purposes unless prior to the purchase the secured party has filed a financing statement covering such goods.

(3) A buyer other than a buyer in ordinary course of business (subsection (1) of this section) takes free of a security interest to the extent that it secures future advances made after the secured party acquires knowledge of the purchase, or more than 45 days after the purchase, whichever first occurs, unless made pursuant to a commitment entered into without knowledge of the purchase and before the expiration of the 45 day period.

Amended in 1972.

§ 9–308. Purchase of Chattel Paper and Instruments.

A purchaser of chattel paper or an instrument who gives new value and takes possession of it in the ordinary course of his business has priority over a security interest in the chattel paper or instrument.

(a) which is perfected under Section 9–304 (permissive filing and temporary perfection) or under Section 9–306 (perfection as to proceeds) if he acts without knowledge that the specific paper or instrument is subject to a security interest; or

(b) which is claimed merely as proceeds of inventory subject to a security interest (Section 9–306) even though he knows that the specific paper or instrument is subject to the security interest.

Amended in 1972.

§ 9–309. Protection of Purchasers of Instruments, Documents and Securities.

Nothing in this Article limits the rights of a holder in due course of a negotiable instrument (Section 3–302) or a holder to whom a negotiable document of title has been duly negotiated (Section 7–501) or a bona fide purchaser of a security (Section 8–302) and the holders or purchasers take priority over an earlier security interest even though perfected. Filing under this Article does not constitute notice of the security interest to such holders or purchasers.

Amended in 1977.

§ 9–310. Priority of Certain Liens Arising by Operation of Law.

When a person in the ordinary course of his business furnishes services or materials with respect to goods subject to a security interest, a lien upon goods in the possession of such person given by statute or rule of law for such materials or services takes priority over a perfected security interest unless the lien is statutory and the statute expressly provides otherwise.

§ 9–311. Alienability of Debtor's Rights: Judicial Process.

The debtor's rights in collateral may be voluntarily or involuntarily transferred (by way of sale, creation of a security interest, attachment, levy, garnishment or other judicial process) notwithstanding a provision in the security agreement prohibiting any transfer or making the transfer constitute a default.

§ 9–312. Priorities Among Conflicting Security Interests in the Same Collateral.

(1) The rules of priority stated in other sections of this Part and in the following sections shall govern when applicable: Section 4–208 with respect to the security interests of collecting banks in items being collected, accompanying documents and proceeds; Section 9–103 on security interests related to other jurisdictions; Section 9–114 on consignments.

(2) A perfected security interest in crops for new value given to enable the debtor to produce the crops during the production season and given not more than three months before the crops become growing crops by planting or otherwise takes priority over an earlier perfected security interest to the extent that such earlier interest secures obligations due more than six months before the crops become growing crops by planting or otherwise, even though the person giving new value had knowledge of the earlier security interest.

(3) A perfected purchase money security interest in inventory has priority over a conflicting security interest in the same inventory and also has priority in identifiable cash proceeds received on or before the delivery of the inventory to a buyer if

(a) the purchase money security interest is perfected at the time the debtor receives possession of the inventory; and

(b) the purchase money secured party gives notification in writing to the holder of the conflicting security interest if the holder had filed a financing statement covering the same types of inventory (i) before the date of the filing made by the purchase money secured party, or (ii) before the beginning of the 21 day period where the purchase money security interest is temporarily perfected without filing or possession (subsection (5) of Section 9–304); and

(c) the holder of the conflicting security interest receives the notification within five years before the debtor receives possession of the inventory; and

(d) the notification states that the person giving the notice has or expects to acquire a purchase money security interest in inventory of the debtor, describing such inventory by item or type.

(4) A purchase money security interest in collateral other than inventory has priority over a conflicting security interest in the same collateral or its proceeds if the purchase money security interest is perfected at the time the debtor receives possession of the collateral or within ten days thereafter.

(5) In all cases not governed by other rules stated in this section (including cases of purchase money security interests which do not qualify for the special priorities set forth in subsections (3) and (4) of this section), priority between conflicting security interests in the same collateral shall be determined according to the following rules:

(a) Conflicting security interests rank according to priority in time of filing or perfection. Priority dates from the time a filing is first made covering the collateral or the time the security interest is first perfected, whichever is earlier, provided that there is no period thereafter when there is neither filing nor perfection.

(b) So long as conflicting security interests are unperfected, the first to attach has priority.

(6) For the purposes of subsection (5) a date of filing or perfection as to collateral is also a date of filing or perfection as to proceeds.

(7) If future advances are made while a security interest is perfected by filing, the taking of possession, or under Section 8–321 on securities, the security interest has the same priority for the purposes of subsection (5) with respect to the future advances as it does with respect to the first advance. If a commitment is made before or while the security interest is so perfected, the security interest has the same priority with respect to advances made pursuant thereto. In other cases a perfected security interest has priority from the date the advance is made.

Amended in 1972 and 1977.

§ 9–313. Priority of Security Interests in Fixtures.

(1) In this section and in the provisions of Part 4 of this Article referring to fixture filing, unless the context otherwise requires

(a) goods are "fixtures" when they become so related to particular real estate that an interest in them arises under real estate law
(b) a "fixture filing" is the filing in the office where a mortgage on the real estate would be filed or recorded of a financing statement covering goods which are or are to become fixtures and conforming to the requirements of subsection (5) of Section 9–402
(c) a mortgage is a "construction mortgage" to the extent that it secures an obligation incurred for the construction of an improvement on land including the acquisition cost of the land, if the recorded writing so indicates.

(2) A security interest under this Article may be created in goods which are fixtures or may continue in goods which become fixtures, but no security interest exists under this Article in ordinary building materials incorporated into an improvement on land.
(3) This Article does not prevent creation of an encumbrance upon fixtures pursuant to real estate law.
(4) A perfected security interest in fixtures has priority over the conflicting interest of an encumbrancer or owner of the real estate where

(a) the security interest is a purchase money security interest, the interest of the encumbrancer or owner arises before the goods become fixtures, the security interest is perfected by a fixture filing before the goods become fixtures or within ten days thereafter, and the debtor has an interest of record in the real estate or is in possession of the real estate; or
(b) the security interest is perfected by a fixture filing before the interest of the encumbrancer or owner is of record, the security interest has priority over any conflicting interest of a predecessor in title of the encumbrancer or owner, and the debtor has an interest of

record in the real estate or is in possession of the real estate; or
(c) the fixtures are readily removable factory or office machines or readily removable replacements of domestic appliances which are consumer goods, and before the goods become fixtures the security interest is perfected by any method permitted by this Article; or
(d) the conflicting interest is a lien on the real estate obtained by legal or equitable proceedings after the security interest was perfected by any method permitted by this Article.

(5) A security interest in fixtures, whether or not perfected, has priority over the conflicting interest of an encumbrancer or owner of the real estate where

(a) the encumbrancer or owner has consented in writing to the security interest or has disclaimed an interest in the goods as fixtures; or
(b) the debtor has a right to remove the goods as against the encumbrancer or owner. If the debtor's right terminates, the priority of the security interest continues for a reasonable time.

(6) Notwithstanding paragraph (a) of subsection (4) but otherwise subject to subsections (4) and (5), a security interest in fixtures is subordinate to a construction mortgage recorded before the goods become fixtures if the goods become fixtures before the completion of the construction. To the extent that it is given to refinance a construction mortgage, a mortgage has this priority to the same extent as the construction mortgage.
(7) In cases not within the preceding subsections, a security interest in fixtures is subordinate to the conflicting interest of an encumbrancer or owner of the related real estate who is not the debtor.
(8) When the secured party has priority over all owners and encumbrancers of the real estate, he may, on default, subject to the provisions of Part 5, remove his collateral from the real estate but he must reimburse any encumbrancer or owner of the real estate who is not the debtor and who has not otherwise agreed for the cost of repair of any physical injury, but not for any diminution in value of the real estate caused by the absence of the goods removed or by any necessity of replacing them. A person entitled to reimbursement may refuse permission to remove until the secured party gives adequate security for the performance of this obligation.

Amended in 1972.

§ 9–314. Accessions.

(1) A security interest in goods which attaches before they are installed in or affixed to other goods takes priority as to the goods installed or affixed (called in this section "accessions") over the claims of all persons to the whole except as stated in subsection (3) and subject to Section 9–315(1).
(2) A security interest which attaches to goods after they become part of a whole is valid against all persons

subsequently acquiring interests in the whole except as stated in subsection (3) but is invalid against any person with an interest in the whole at the time the security interest attaches to the goods who has not in writing consented to the security interest or disclaimed an interest in the goods as part of the whole.

(3) The security interests described in subsections (1) and (2) do not take priority over

(a) a subsequent purchaser for value of any interest in the whole; or

(b) a creditor with a lien on the whole subsequently obtained by judicial proceedings; or

(c) a creditor with a prior perfected security interest in the whole to the extent that he makes subsequent advances

if the subsequent purchase is made, the lien by judicial proceedings obtained or the subsequent advance under the prior perfected security interest is made or contracted for without knowledge of the security interest and before it is perfected. A purchaser of the whole at a foreclosure sale other than the holder of a perfected security interest purchasing at his own foreclosure sale is a subsequent purchaser within this section.

(4) When under subsections (1) or (2) and (3) a secured party has an interest in accessions which has priority over the claims of all persons who have interests in the whole, he may on default subject to the provisions of Part 5 remove his collateral from the whole but he must reimburse any encumbrancer or owner of the whole who is not the debtor and who has not otherwise agreed for the cost of repair of any physical injury but not for any diminution in value of the whole caused by the absence of the goods removed or by any necessity for replacing them. A person entitled to reimbursement may refuse permission to remove until the secured party gives adequate security for the performance of this obligation.

§ 9-315. Priority When Goods Are Commingled or Processed.

(1) If a security interest in goods was perfected and subsequently the goods or a part thereof have become part of a product or mass, the security interest continues in the product or mass if

(a) the goods are so manufactured, processed, assembled or commingled that their identity is lost in the product or mass; or

(b) a financing statement covering the original goods also covers the product into which the goods have been manufactured, processed or assembled.

In a case to which paragraph (b) applies, no separate security interest in that part of the original goods which has been manufactured, processed or assembled into the product may be claimed under Section 9-314.

(2) When under subsection (1) more than one security interest attaches to the product or mass, they rank equally according to the ratio that the cost of the goods to which each interest originally attached bears to the cost of the total product or mass.

§ 9-316. Priority Subject to Subordination.

Nothing in this Article prevents subordination by agreement by any person entitled to priority.

§ 9-317. Secured Party Not Obligated on Contract of Debtor.

The mere existence of a security interest or authority given to the debtor to dispose of or use collateral does not impose contract or tort liability upon the secured party for the debtor's acts or omissions.

§ 9-318. Defenses Against Assignee; Modification of Contract After Notification of Assignment; Term Prohibiting Assignment Ineffective; Identification and Proof of Assignment.

(1) Unless an account debtor has made an enforceable agreement not to assert defenses or claims arising out of a sale as provided in Section 9-206 the rights of an assignee are subject to

(a) all the terms of the contract between the account debtor and assignor and any defense or claim arising therefrom; and

(b) any other defense or claim of the account debtor against the assignor which accrues before the account debtor receives notification of the assignment.

(2) So far as the right to payment or a part thereof under an assigned contract has not been fully earned by performance, and notwithstanding notification of the assignment, any modification of or substitution for the contract made in good faith and in accordance with reasonable commercial standards is effective against an assignee unless the account debtor has otherwise agreed but the assignee acquires corresponding rights under the modified or substituted contract. The assignment may provide that such modification or substitution is a breach by the assignor.

(3) The account debtor is authorized to pay the assignor until the account debtor receives notification that the amount due or to become due has been assigned and that payment is to be made to the assignee. A notification which does not reasonably identify the rights assigned is ineffective. If requested by the account debtor, the assignee must seasonably furnish reasonable proof that the assignment has been made and unless he does so the account debtor may pay the assignor.

(4) A term in any contract between an account debtor and an assignor is ineffective if it prohibits assignment of an account or prohibits creation of a security interest in a general intangible for money due or to become due or requires the account debtor's consent to such assignment or security interest.

Amended in 1972.

Part 4 Filing

§ 9–401. Place of Filing; Erroneous Filing; Removal of Collateral.

First Alternative Subsection (1)

(1) The proper place to file in order to perfect a security interest is as follows:

(a) when the collateral is timber to be cut or is minerals or the like (including oil and gas) or accounts subject to subsection (5) of Section 9–103, or when the financing statement is filed as a fixture filing (Section 9–313) and the collateral is goods which are or are to become fixtures, then in the office where a mortgage on the real estate would be filed or recorded;
(b) in all other cases, in the office of the [Secretary of State].

Second Alternative Subsection (1)

(1) The proper place to file in order to perfect a security interest is as follows:

(a) when the collateral is equipment used in farming operations, or farm products, or accounts or general intangibles arising from or relating to the sale of farm products by a farmer, or consumer goods, then in the office of the _____ in the county of the debtor's residence or if the debtor is not a resident of this state then in the office of the _____ in the county where the goods are kept, and in addition when the collateral is crops growing or to be grown in the office of the _____ in the county where the land is located;
(b) when the collateral is timber to be cut or is minerals or the like (including oil and gas) or accounts subject to subsection (5) of Section 9–103, or when the financing statement is filed as a fixture filing (Section 9–313) and the collateral is goods which are or are to become fixtures, then in the office where a mortgage on the real estate would be filed or recorded;
(c) in all other cases, in the office of the [Secretary of State].

Third Alternative Subsection (1)

(1) The proper place to file in order to perfect a security interest is as follows:

(a) when the collateral is equipment used in farming operations, or farm products, or accounts or general intangibles arising from or relating to the sale of farm products by a farmer, or consumer goods, then in the office of the _____ in the county of the debtor's residence or if the debtor is not a resident of this state then in the office of the _____ in the county where the goods are kept, and in addition when the collateral is crops growing or to be grown in the office of the _____ in the county where the land is located;
(b) when the collateral is timber to be cut or is minerals or the like (including oil and gas) or accounts subject to

subsection (5) of Section 9–103, or when the financing statement is filed as a fixture filing (Section 9–313) and the collateral is goods which are or are to become fixtures, then in the office where a mortgage on the real estate would be filed or recorded;
(c) in all other cases, in the office of the [Secretary of State] and in addition, if the debtor has a place of business in only one county of this state, also in the office of _____ of such county, or, if the debtor has no place of business in this state, but resides in the state, also in the office of _____ of the county in which he resides.

Note: *One of the three alternatives should be selected as subsection (1).*

(2) A filing which is made in good faith in an improper place or not in all of the places required by this section is nevertheless effective with regard to any collateral as to which the filing complied with the requirements of this Article and is also effective with regard to collateral covered by the financing statement against any person who has knowledge of the contents of such financing statement.
(3) A filing which is made in the proper place in this state continues effective even though the debtor's residence or place of business or the location of the collateral or its use, whichever controlled the original filing, is thereafter changed.

Alternative Subsection (3)

[(3) A filing which is made in the proper county continues effective for four months after a change to another county of the debtor's residence or place of business or the location of the collateral, whichever controlled the original filing. It becomes ineffective thereafter unless a copy of the financing statement signed by the secured party is filed in the new county within said period. The security interest may also be perfected in the new county after the expiration of the four-month period; in such case perfection dates from the time of perfection in the new county. A change in the use of the collateral does not impair the effectiveness of the original filing.]
(4) The rules stated in Section 9–103 determine whether filing is necessary in this state.
(5) Notwithstanding the preceding subsections, and subject to subsection (3) of Section 9–302, the proper place to file in order to perfect a security interest in collateral, including fixtures, of a transmitting utility is the office of the [Secretary of State]. This filing constitutes a fixture filing (Section 9–313) as to the collateral described therein which is or is to become fixtures.
(6) For the purposes of this section, the residence of an organization is its place of business if it has one or its chief executive office if it has more than one place of business.

Amended in 1962 and 1972.
Note: *Subsection (6) should be used only if the state chooses the Second or Third Alternative Subsection (1).*

§ 9–402. Formal Requisites of Financing Statement; Amendments; Mortgage as Financing Statement.

(1) A financing statement is sufficient if it gives the names of the debtor and the secured party, is signed by the debtor, gives an address of the secured party from which information concerning the security interest may be obtained, gives a mailing address of the debtor and contains a statement indicating the types, or describing the items, of collateral. A financing statement may be filed before a security agreement is made or a security interest otherwise attaches. When the financing statement covers crops growing or to be grown, the statement must also contain a description of the real estate concerned. When the financing statement covers timber to be cut or covers minerals or the like (including oil and gas) or accounts subject to subsection (5) of Section 9–103, or when the financing statement is filed as a fixture filing (Section 9–313) and the collateral is goods which are or are to become fixtures, the statement must also comply with subsection (5). A copy of the security agreement is sufficient as a financing statement if it contains the above information and is signed by the debtor. A carbon, photographic or other reproduction of a security agreement or a financing statement is sufficient as a financing statement if the security agreement so provides or if the original has been filed in this state.

(2) A financing statement which otherwise complies with subsection (1) is sufficient when it is signed by the secured party instead of the debtor if it is filed to perfect a security interest in

(a) collateral already subject to a security interest in another jurisdiction when it is brought into this state, or when the debtor's location is changed to this state. Such a financing statement must state that the collateral was brought into this state or that the debtor's location was changed to this state under such circumstances; or
(b) proceeds under Section 9–306 if the security interest in the original collateral was perfected. Such a financing statement must describe the original collateral; or
(c) collateral as to which the filing has lapsed; or
(d) collateral acquired after a change of name, identity or corporate structure of the debtor (subsection (7)).

(3) A form substantially as follows is sufficient to comply with subsection (1):

Name of debtor (or assignor) _____
Address _____
Name of secured party (or assignee) _____
Address _____
1. This financing statement covers the following types (or items) of property:
    (Describe) _____
2. (If collateral is crops) The above described crops are growing or are to be grown on:
    (Describe Real Estate) _____
3. (If applicable) The above goods are to become fixtures on*
*Where appropriate substitute either "The above timber is standing on _____" or "The above minerals or the like (including oil and gas) or accounts will be financed

at the wellhead or minehead of the well or mine located on _____"
(Describe Real Estate) _____ and this financing statement is to be filed [for record] in the real estate records. (If the debtor does not have an interest of record) The name of a record owner is _____
4. (If products of collateral are claimed) Products of the collateral are also covered.

   (use   . . . .
whichever   Signature of Debtor (or Assignor)
   is   . . . .
applicable   Signature of Secured Party
               (or Assignee)

(4) A financing statement may be amended by filing a writing signed by both the debtor and the secured party. An amendment does not extend the period of effectiveness of a financing statement. If any amendment adds collateral, it is effective as to the added collateral only from the filing date of the amendment. In this Article, unless the context otherwise requires, the term "financing statement" means the original financing statement and any amendments.

(5) A financing statement covering timber to be cut or covering minerals or the like (including oil and gas) or accounts subject to subsection (5) of Section 9–103, or a financing statement filed as a fixture filing (Section 9–313) where the debtor is not a transmitting utility, must show that it covers this type of collateral, must recite that it is to be filed [for record] in the real estate records, and the financing statement must contain a description of the real estate [sufficient if it were contained in a mortgage of the real estate to give constructive notice of the mortgage under the law of this state]. If the debtor does not have an interest of record in the real estate, the financing statement must show the name of a record owner.

(6) A mortgage is effective as a financing statement filed as a fixture filing from the date of its recording if

(a) the goods are described in the mortgage by item or type; and
(b) the goods are or are to become fixtures related to the real estate described in the mortgage; and
(c) the mortgage complies with the requirements for a financing statement in this section other than a recital that it is to be filed in the real estate records; and
(d) the mortgage is duly recorded.

No fee with reference to the financing statement is required other than the regular recording and satisfaction fees with respect to the mortgage.

(7) A financing statement sufficiently shows the name of the debtor if it gives the individual, partnership or corporate name of the debtor, whether or not it adds other trade names or names of partners. Where the debtor so changes his name or in the case of an organization its name, identity or corporate structure that a filed financing statement becomes seriously misleading, the filing is not effective to perfect a security interest in collateral acquired by the debtor more than four months after the change, unless a new appropriate financing statement is filed before the expiration of that time. A

filed financing statement remains effective with respect to collateral transferred by the debtor even though the secured party knows of or consents to the transfer.

(8) A financing statement substantially complying with the requirements of this section is effective even though it contains minor errors which are not seriously misleading.

Amended in 1972.

Note: *Language in brackets is optional.*

Note: *Where the state has any special recording system for real estate other than the usual grantor-grantee index (as, for instance, a tract system or a title registration or Torrens system) local adaptations of subsection (5) and Section 9–403(7) may be necessary. See Mass. Gen.Laws Chapter 106, Section 9–409.*

§ 9–403. What Constitutes Filing; Duration of Filing; Effect of Lapsed Filing; Duties of Filing Officer.

(1) Presentation for filing of a financing statement and tender of the filing fee or acceptance of the statement by the filing officer constitutes filing under this Article.

(2) Except as provided in subsection (6) a filed financing statement is effective for a period of five years from the date of filing. The effectiveness of a filed financing statement lapses on the expiration of the five year period unless a continuation statement is filed prior to the lapse. If a security interest perfected by filing exists at the time insolvency proceedings are commenced by or against the debtor, the security interest remains perfected until termination of the insolvency proceedings and thereafter for a period of sixty days or until expiration of the five year period, whichever occurs later. Upon lapse the security interest becomes unperfected, unless it is perfected without filing. If the security interest becomes unperfected upon lapse, it is deemed to have been unperfected as against a person who became a purchaser or lien creditor before lapse.

(3) A continuation statement may be filed by the secured party within six months prior to the expiration of the five year period specified in subsection (2). Any such continuation statement must be signed by the secured party, identify the original statement by file number and state that the original statement is still effective. A continuation statement signed by a person other than the secured party of record must be accompanied by a separate written statement of assignment signed by the secured party of record and complying with subsection (2) of Section 9–405, including payment of the required fee. Upon timely filing of the continuation statement, the effectiveness of the original statement is continued for five years after the last date to which the filing was effective whereupon it lapses in the same manner as provided in subsection (2) unless another continuation statement is filed prior to such lapse. Succeeding continuation statements may be filed in the same manner to continue the effectiveness of the original statement. Unless a statute on disposition of public records provides otherwise, the filing officer may remove a lapsed statement from the files and destroy it immediately if he has retained a microfilm or other photographic record, or in other cases after one year after the lapse. The filing officer shall so arrange matters by physical annexation of financing statements to continuation statements or other related filings, or by other means, that if he physically destroys the financing statements of a period more than five years past, those which have been continued by a continuation statement or which are still effective under subsection (6) shall be retained.

(4) Except as provided in subsection (7) a filing officer shall mark each statement with a file number and with the date and hour of filing and shall hold the statement or a microfilm or other photographic copy thereof for public inspection. In addition the filing officer shall index the statement according to the name of the debtor and shall note in the index the file number and the address of the debtor given in the statement.

(5) The uniform fee for filing and indexing and for stamping a copy furnished by the secured party to show the date and place of filing for an original financing statement or for a continuation statement shall be $ if the statement is in the standard form prescribed by the [Secretary of State] and otherwise shall be $_____, plus in each case, if the financing statement is subject to subsection (5) of Section 9–402, $_____. The uniform fee for each name more than one required to be indexed shall be $_____. The secured party may at his option show a trade name for any person and an extra uniform indexing fee of $_____ shall be paid with respect thereto.

(6) If the debtor is a transmitting utility (subsection (5) of Section 9–401) and a filed financing statement so states, it is effective until a termination statement is filed. A real estate mortgage which is effective as a fixture filing under subsection (6) of Section 9–402 remains effective as a fixture filing until the mortgage is released or satisfied of record or its effectiveness otherwise terminates as to the real estate.

(7) When a financing statement covers timber to be cut or covers minerals or the like (including oil and gas) or accounts subject to subsection (5) of Section 9–103, or is filed as a fixture filing, [it shall be filed for record and] the filing officer shall index it under the names of the debtor and any owner of record shown on the financing statement in the same fashion as if they were the mortgagors in a mortgage of the real estate described, and, to the extent that the law of this state provides for indexing of mortgages under the name of the mortgagee, under the name of the secured party as if he were the mortgagee thereunder, or where indexing is by description in the same fashion as if the financing statement were a mortgage of the real estate described.

Amended in 1972.

Note: *In states in which writings will not appear in the real estate records and indices unless actually recorded the bracketed language in subsection (7) should be used.*

§ 9–404. Termination Statement.

(1) If a financing statement covering consumer goods is filed on or after _____, then within one month or within ten days following written demand by the debtor after

there is no outstanding secured obligation and no commitment to make advances, incur obligations or otherwise give value, the secured party must file with each filing officer with whom the financing statement was filed, a termination statement to the effect that he no longer claims a security interest under the financing statement, which shall be identified by file number. In other cases whenever there is no outstanding secured obligation and no commitment to make advances, incur obligations or otherwise give value, the secured party must on written demand by the debtor send the debtor, for each filing officer with whom the financing statement was filed, a termination statement to the effect that he no longer claims a security interest under the financing statement, which shall be identified by file number. A termination statement signed by a person other than the secured party of record must be accompanied by a separate written statement of assignment signed by the secured party of record complying with subsection (2) of Section 9–405, including payment of the required fee. If the affected secured party fails to file such a termination statement as required by this subsection, or to send such a termination statement within ten days after proper demand therefor, he shall be liable to the debtor for one hundred dollars, and in addition for any loss caused to the debtor by such failure.

(2) On presentation to the filing officer of such a termination statement he must note it in the index. If he has received the termination statement in duplicate, he shall return one copy of the termination statement to the secured party stamped to show the time of receipt thereof. If the filing officer has a microfilm or other photographic record of the financing statement, and of any related continuation statement, statement of assignment and statement of release, he may remove the originals from the files at any time after receipt of the termination statement, or if he has no such record, he may remove them from the files at any time after one year after receipt of the termination statement.

(3) If the termination statement is in the standard form prescribed by the [Secretary of State], the uniform fee for filing and indexing the termination statement shall be $, and otherwise shall be $_____, plus in each case an additional fee of $_____ for each name more than one against which the termination statement is required to be indexed.

Amended in 1972.

Note: *The date to be inserted should be the effective date of the revised Article 9.*

§ 9–405. Assignment of Security Interest; Duties of Filing Officer; Fees.

(1) A financing statement may disclose an assignment of a security interest in the collateral described in the financing statement by indication in the financing statement of the name and address of the assignee or by an assignment itself or a copy thereof on the face or back of the statement. On presentation to the filing officer of such a financing statement the filing officer shall mark the same as provided in Section 9–403(4). The uniform fee for filing, indexing and furnishing filing data for a financing statement so indicating an assignment shall be $_____ if the statement is in the standard form prescribed by the [Secretary of State] and otherwise shall be $_____, plus in each case an additional fee of $_____ for each name more than one against which the financing statement is required to be indexed.

(2) A secured party may assign of record all or part of his rights under a financing statement by the filing in the place where the original financing statement was filed of a separate written statement of assignment signed by the secured party of record and setting forth the name of the secured party of record and the debtor, the file number and the date of filing of the financing statement and the name and address of the assignee and containing a description of the collateral assigned. A copy of the assignment is sufficient as a separate statement if it complies with the preceding sentence. On presentation to the filing officer of such a separate statement, the filing officer shall mark such separate statement with the date and hour of the filing. He shall note the assignment on the index of the financing statement, or in the case of a fixture filing, or a filing covering timber to be cut, or covering minerals or the like (including oil and gas) or accounts subject to subsection (5) of Section 9–103, he shall index the assignment under the name of the assignor as grantor and, to the extent that the law of this state provides for indexing the assignment of a mortgage under the name of the assignee, he shall index the assignment of the financing statement under the name of the assignee. The uniform fee for filing, indexing and furnishing filing data about such a separate statement of assignment shall be $_____ if the statement is in the standard form prescribed by the [Secretary of State] and otherwise shall be $_____, plus in each case an additional fee of $_____ for each name more than one against which the statement of assignment is required to be indexed. Notwithstanding the provisions of this subsection, an assignment of record of a security interest in a fixture contained in a mortgage effective as a fixture filing (subsection (6) of Section 9–402) may be made only by an assignment of the mortgage in the manner provided by the law of this state other than this Act.

(3) After the disclosure or filing of an assignment under this section, the assignee is the secured party of record.

Amended in 1972.

§ 9–406. Release of Collateral; Duties of Filing Officer; Fees.

A secured party of record may by his signed statement release all or a part of any collateral described in a filed financing statement. The statement of release is sufficient if it contains a description of the collateral being released, the name and address of the debtor, the name and address of the secured party, and the file number of the financing statement. A statement of release signed by a person other than the secured party of record must be accompanied by a separate written statement of assignment signed by the secured party of record and complying with subsection (2) of Section 9–405, including payment of the required fee. Upon presentation of such a statement of release to the filing officer he shall mark the statement with the hour and date of filing and shall note the same upon the margin of the index of the filing of the financing statement. The uniform fee for filing and noting such a statement of release shall be $_____ if the statement is in the standard form prescribed by the [Secretary of State] and otherwise shall be $_____, plus in each case an additional fee of $ for each name more than one against which the statement of release is required to be indexed.

Amended in 1972.

[§ 9–407. Information From Filing Officer].

[(1) If the person filing any financing statement, termination statement, statement of assignment, or statement of release, furnishes the filing officer a copy thereof, the filing officer shall upon request note upon the copy the file number and date and hour of the filing of the original and deliver or send the copy to such person.]

[(2) Upon request of any person, the filing officer shall issue his certificate showing whether there is on file on the date and hour stated therein, any presently effective financing statement naming a particular debtor and any statement of assignment thereof and if there is, giving the date and hour of filing of each such statement and the names and addresses of each secured party therein. The uniform fee for such a certificate shall be $_____ if the request for the certificate is in the standard form prescribed by the [Secretary of State] and otherwise shall be $. Upon request the filing officer shall furnish a copy of any filed financing statement or statement of assignment for a uniform fee of $_____ per page.]

Amended in 1972.

Note: *This section is proposed as an optional provision to require filing officers to furnish certificates. Local law and practices should be consulted with regard to the advisability of adoption.*

§ 9–408. Financing Statements Covering Consigned or Leased Goods.

A consignor or lessor of goods may file a financing statement using the terms "consignor," "consignee," "lessor," "lessee" or the like instead of the terms specified in Section 9–402. The provisions of this Part shall apply as appropriate to such a financing statement but its filing shall not of itself be a factor in determining whether or not the consignment or lease is intended as security (Section 1–201(37)). However, if it is determined for other reasons that the consignment or lease is so intended, a security interest of the consignor or lessor which attaches to the consigned or leased goods is perfected by such filing.

Added in 1972.

Part 5 Default

§ 9–501. Default; Procedure When Security Agreement Covers Both Real and Personal Property.

(1) When a debtor is in default under a security agreement, a secured party has the rights and remedies provided in this Part and except as limited by subsection (3) those provided in the security agreement. He may reduce his claim to judgment, foreclose or otherwise enforce the security interest by any available judicial procedure. If the collateral is documents the secured party may proceed either as to the documents or as to the goods covered thereby. A secured party in possession has the rights, remedies and duties provided in Section 9–207. The rights and remedies referred to in this subsection are cumulative.

(2) After default, the debtor has the rights and remedies provided in this Part, those provided in the security agreement and those provided in Section 9–207.

(3) To the extent that they give rights to the debtor and impose duties on the secured party, the rules stated in the subsections referred to below may not be waived or varied except as provided with respect to compulsory disposition of collateral (subsection (3) of Section 9–504 and Section 9–505) and with respect to redemption of collateral (Section 9–506) but the parties may by agreement determine the standards by which the fulfillment of these rights and duties is to be measured if such standards are not manifestly unreasonable:

(a) subsection (2) of Section 9–502 and subsection (2) of Section 9–504 insofar as they require accounting for surplus proceeds of collateral;

(b) subsection (3) of Section 9–504 and subsection (1) of Section 9–505 which deal with disposition of collateral;

(c) subsection (2) of Section 9–505 which deals with acceptance of collateral as discharge of obligation;

(d) Section 9–506 which deals with redemption of collateral; and

(e) subsection (1) of Section 9–507 which deals with the secured party's liability for failure to comply with this Part.

(4) If the security agreement covers both real and personal property, the secured party may proceed under this Part as to the personal property or he may proceed as to both the real and the personal property in accordance with his rights and remedies in respect of the real property in which case the provisions of this Part do not apply.

(5) When a secured party has reduced his claim to judgment the lien of any levy which may be made upon his collateral by virtue of any execution based upon the judgment shall relate back to the date of the perfection of the security interest in such collateral. A judicial sale, pursuant to such execution, is a foreclosure of the security interest by judicial procedure within the meaning of this section, and the secured party may purchase at the

sale and thereafter hold the collateral free of any other requirements of this Article.

Amended in 1972.

§ 9–502. Collection Rights of Secured Party.

(1) When so agreed and in any event on default the secured party is entitled to notify an account debtor or the obligor on an instrument to make payment to him whether or not the assignor was theretofore making collections on the collateral, and also to take control of any proceeds to which he is entitled under Section 9–306.

(2) A secured party who by agreement is entitled to charge back uncollected collateral or otherwise to full or limited recourse against the debtor and who undertakes to collect from the account debtors or obligors must proceed in a commercially reasonable manner and may deduct his reasonable expenses of realization from the collections. If the security agreement secures an indebtedness, the secured party must account to the debtor for any surplus, and unless otherwise agreed, the debtor is liable for any deficiency. But, if the underlying transaction was a sale of accounts or chattel paper, the debtor is entitled to any surplus or is liable for any deficiency only if the security agreement so provides.

Amended in 1972.

§ 9–503. Secured Party's Right to Take Possession After Default.

Unless otherwise agreed a secured party has on default the right to take possession of the collateral. In taking possession a secured party may proceed without judicial process if this can be done without breach of the peace or may proceed by action. If the security agreement so provides the secured party may require the debtor to assemble the collateral and make it available to the secured party at a place to be designated by the secured party which is reasonably convenient to both parties. Without removal a secured party may render equipment unusable, and may dispose of collateral on the debtor's premises under Section 9–504.

§ 9–504. Secured Party's Right to Dispose of Collateral After Default; Effect of Disposition.

(1) A secured party after default may sell, lease or otherwise dispose of any or all of the collateral in its then condition or following any commercially reasonable preparation or processing. Any sale of goods is subject to the Article on Sales (Article 2). The proceeds of disposition shall be applied in the order following to

(a) the reasonable expenses of retaking, holding, preparing for sale or lease, selling, leasing and the like and, to the extent provided for in the agreement and not prohibited by law, the reasonable attorneys' fees and legal expenses incurred by the secured party;

(b) the satisfaction of indebtedness secured by the security interest under which the disposition is made;

(c) the satisfaction of indebtedness secured by any subordinate security interest in the collateral if written notification of demand therefor is received before distribution of the proceeds is completed. If requested by the secured party, the holder of a subordinate security interest must seasonably furnish reasonable proof of his interest, and unless he does so, the secured party need not comply with his demand.

(2) If the security interest secures an indebtedness, the secured party must account to the debtor for any surplus, and, unless otherwise agreed, the debtor is liable for any deficiency. But if the underlying transaction was a sale of accounts or chattel paper, the debtor is entitled to any surplus or is liable for any deficiency only if the security agreement so provides.

(3) Disposition of the collateral may be by public or private proceedings and may be made by way of one or more contracts. Sale or other disposition may be as a unit or in parcels and at any time and place and on any terms but every aspect of the disposition including the method, manner, time, place and terms must be commercially reasonable. Unless collateral is perishable or threatens to decline speedily in value or is of a type customarily sold on a recognized market, reasonable notification of the time and place of any public sale or reasonable notification of the time after which any private sale or other intended disposition is to be made shall be sent by the secured party to the debtor, if he has not signed after default a statement renouncing or modifying his right to notification of sale. In the case of consumer goods no other notification need be sent. In other cases notification shall be sent to any other secured party from whom the secured party has received (before sending his notification to the debtor or before the debtor's renunciation of his rights) written notice of a claim of an interest in the collateral. The secured party may buy at any public sale and if the collateral is of a type customarily sold in a recognized market or is of a type which is the subject of widely distributed standard price quotations he may buy at private sale.

(4) When collateral is disposed of by a secured party after default, the disposition transfers to a purchaser for value all of the debtor's rights therein, discharges the security interest under which it is made and any security interest or lien subordinate thereto. The purchaser takes free of all such rights and interests even though the secured party fails to comply with the requirements of this Part or of any judicial proceedings

(a) in the case of a public sale, if the purchaser has no knowledge of any defects in the sale and if he does not buy in collusion with the secured party, other bidders or the person conducting the sale; or

(b) in any other case, if the purchaser acts in good faith.

(5) A person who is liable to a secured party under a guaranty, indorsement, repurchase agreement or the like

and who receives a transfer of collateral from the secured party or is subrogated to his rights has thereafter the rights and duties of the secured party. Such a transfer of collateral is not a sale or disposition of the collateral under this Article.

Amended in 1972.

§ 9–505. Compulsory Disposition of Collateral; Acceptance of the Collateral as Discharge of Obligation.

(1) If the debtor has paid sixty per cent of the cash price in the case of a purchase money security interest in consumer goods or sixty per cent of the loan in the case of another security interest in consumer goods, and has not signed after default a statement renouncing or modifying his rights under this Part a secured party who has taken possession of collateral must dispose of it under Section 9–504 and if he fails to do so within ninety days after he takes possession the debtor at his option may recover in conversion or under Section 9–507(1) on secured party's liability.

(2) In any other case involving consumer goods or any other collateral a secured party in possession may, after default, propose to retain the collateral in satisfaction of the obligation. Written notice of such proposal shall be sent to the debtor if he has not signed after default a statement renouncing or modifying his rights under this subsection. In the case of consumer goods no other notice need be given. In other cases notice shall be sent to any other secured party from whom the secured party has received (before sending his notice to the debtor or before the debtor's renunciation of his rights) written notice of a claim of an interest in the collateral. If the secured party receives objection in writing from a person entitled to receive notification within twenty-one days after the notice was sent, the secured party must dispose of the collateral under Section 9–504. In the absence of such written objection the secured party may retain the collateral in satisfaction of the debtor's obligation.

Amended in 1972.

§ 9–506. Debtor's Right to Redeem Collateral.

At any time before the secured party has disposed of collateral or entered into a contract for its disposition under Section 9–504 or before the obligation has been discharged under Section 9–505(2) the debtor or any other secured party may unless otherwise agreed in writing after default redeem the collateral by tendering fulfillment of all obligations secured by the collateral as well as the expenses reasonably incurred by the secured party in retaking, holding and preparing the collateral for disposition, in arranging for the sale, and to the extent provided in the agreement and not prohibited by law, his reasonable attorneys' fees and legal expenses.

§ 9–507. Secured Party's Liability for Failure to Comply With This Part.

(1) If it is established that the secured party is not proceeding in accordance with the provisions of this Part disposition may be ordered or restrained on appropriate terms and conditions. If the disposition has occurred the debtor or any person entitled to notification or whose security interest has been made known to the secured party prior to the disposition has a right to recover from the secured party any loss caused by a failure to comply with the provisions of this Part. If the collateral is consumer goods, the debtor has a right to recover in any event an amount not less than the credit service charge plus ten per cent of the principal amount of the debt or the time price differential plus 10 per cent of the cash price.

(2) The fact that a better price could have been obtained by a sale at a different time or in a different method from that selected by the secured party is not of itself sufficient to establish that the sale was not made in a commercially reasonable manner. If the secured party either sells the collateral in the usual manner in any recognized market therefor or if he sells at the price current in such market at the time of his sale or if he has otherwise sold in conformity with reasonable commercial practices among dealers in the type of property sold he has sold in a commercially reasonable manner. The principles stated in the two preceding sentences with respect to sales also apply as may be appropriate to other types of disposition. A disposition which has been approved in any judicial proceeding or by any bona fide creditors' committee or representative of creditors shall conclusively be deemed to be commercially reasonable, but this sentence does not indicate that any such approval must be obtained in any case nor does it indicate that any disposition not so approved is not commercially reasonable.

Article 10

EFFECTIVE DATE AND REPEALER

§ 10–101. Effective Date.

This Act shall become effective at midnight on December 31st following its enactment. It applies to transactions entered into and events occurring after that date.

§ 10–102. Specific Repealer; Provision for Transition.

(1) The following acts and all other acts and parts of acts inconsistent herewith are hereby repealed: (Here should follow the acts to be specifically repealed including the following:

Uniform Negotiable Instruments Act
Uniform Warehouse Receipts Act
Uniform Sales Act

Uniform Bills of Lading Act
Uniform Stock Transfer Act
Uniform Conditional Sales Act
Uniform Trust Receipts Act
  Also any acts regulating:
Bank collections
Bulk sales
Chattel mortgages
Conditional sales
Factor's lien acts
Farm storage of grain and similar acts
Assignment of accounts receivable)

(2) Transactions validly entered into before the effective date specified in Section 10–101 and the rights, duties and interests flowing from them remain valid thereafter and may be terminated, completed, consummated or enforced as required or permitted by any statute or other law amended or repealed by this Act as though such repeal or amendment had not occurred.

Note: *Subsection (1) should be separately prepared for each state. The foregoing is a list of statutes to be checked.*

§ 10–103. General Repealer.

Except as provided in the following section, all acts and parts of acts inconsistent with this Act are hereby repealed.

§ 10–104. Laws Not Repealed.

(1) The Article on Documents of Title (Article 7) does not repeal or modify any laws prescribing the form or contents of documents of title or the services or facilities to be afforded by bailees, or otherwise regulating bailees' businesses in respects not specifically dealt with herein; but the fact that such laws are violated does not affect the status of a document of title which otherwise complies with the definition of a document of title (Section 1–201). [(2) This Act does not repeal _____*, cited as the Uniform Act for the Simplification of Fiduciary Security Transfers, and if in any respect there is any inconsistency between that Act and the Article of this Act on investment securities (Article 8) the provisions of the former Act shall control.]

Note: *At * in subsection (2) insert the statutory reference to the Uniform Act for the Simplification of Fiduciary Security Transfers if such Act has previously been enacted. If it has not been enacted, omit subsection (2).*

Article 11

(REPORTERS' DRAFT) EFFECTIVE DATE AND TRANSITION PROVISIONS

This material has been numbered Article 11 to distinguish it from Article 10, the transition provision of the 1962

Code, which may still remain in effect in some states to cover transition problems from pre-Code law to the original Uniform Commercial Code. Adaptation may be necessary in particular states. The terms "[old Code]" and "[new Code]" and "[old U.C.C.]" and "[new U.C.C.]" are used herein, and should be suitably changed in each state. Note: *This draft was prepared by the Reporters and has not been passed upon by the Review Committee, the Permanent Editorial Board, the American Law Institute, or the National Conference of Commissioners on Uniform State Laws. It is submitted as a working draft which may be adapted as appropriate in each state.*

§ 11–101. Effective Date.

This Act shall become effective at 12:01 A.M. on _____, 19___.

§ 11–102. Preservation of Old Transition Provision.

The provisions of [here insert reference to the original transition provision in the particular state] shall continue to apply to [the new U.C.C.] and for this purpose the [old U.C.C. and new U.C.C.] shall be considered one continuous statute.

§ 11–103. Transition to [New Code]—General Rule.

Transactions validly entered into after [effective date of old U.C.C.] and before [effective date of new U.C.C.], and which were subject to the provisions of [old U.C.C.] and which would be subject to this Act as amended if they had been entered into after the effective date of [new U.C.C.] and the rights, duties and interests flowing from such transactions remain valid after the latter date and may be terminated, completed, consummated or enforced as required or permitted by the [new U.C.C.]. Security interests arising out of such transactions which are perfected when [new U.C.C.] becomes effective shall remain perfected until they lapse as provided in [new U.C.C.], and may be continued as permitted by [new U.C.C.], except as stated in Section 11–105.

§ 11–104. Transition Provision on Change of Requirement of Filing.

A security interest for the perfection of which filing or the taking of possession was required under [old U.C.C.] and which attached prior to the effective date of [new U.C.C.] but was not perfected shall be deemed perfected on the effective date of [new U.C.C.] if [new U.C.C.] permits perfection without filing or authorizes filing in the office or offices where a prior ineffective filing was made.

§ 11–105. Transition Provision on Change of Place of Filing.

(1) A financing statement or continuation statement filed prior to [effective date of new U.C.C.] which shall not have lapsed prior to [the effective date of new U.C.C.]

which shall remain effective for the period provided in the [old Code], but not less than five years after the filing.

(2) With respect to any collateral acquired by the debtor subsequent to the effective date of [new U.C.C.], any effective financing statement or continuation statement described in this section shall apply only if the filing or filings are in the office or offices that would be appropriate to perfect the security interests in the new collateral under [new U.C.C.].

(3) The effectiveness of any financing statement or continuation statement filed prior to [effective date of new U.C.C.] may be continued by a continuation statement as permitted by [new U.C.C.], except that if [new U.C.C.] requires a filing in an office where there was no previous financing statement, a new financing statement conforming to Section 11–106 shall be filed in that office.

(4) If the record of a mortgage of real estate would have been effective as a fixture filing of goods described therein if [new U.C.C.] had been in effect on the date of recording the mortgage, the mortgage shall be deemed effective as a fixture filing as to such goods under subsection (6) of Section 9–402 of the [new U.C.C.] on the effective date of [new U.C.C.].

§ 11–106. Required Refilings.

(1) If a security interest is perfected or has priority when this Act takes effect as to all persons or as to certain persons without any filing or recording, and if the filing of a financing statement would be required for the perfection or priority of the security interest against those persons under [new U.C.C.], the perfection and priority rights of the security interest continue until 3 years after the effective date of [new U.C.C.]. The perfection will then lapse unless a financing statement is filed as provided in subsection (4) or unless the security interest is perfected otherwise than by filing.

(2) If a security interest is perfected when [new U.C.C.] takes effect under a law other than [U.C.C.] which requires no further filing, refiling or recording to continue its perfection, perfection continues until and will lapse 3 years after [new U.C.C.] takes effect, unless a financing statement is filed as provided in subsection (4) or unless the security interest is perfected otherwise than by filing, or unless under subsection (3) of Section 9–302 the other law continues to govern filing.

(3) If a security interest is perfected by a filing, refiling or recording under a law repealed by this Act which required further filing, refiling or recording to continue its perfection, perfection continues and will lapse on the date provided by the law so repealed for such further filing, refiling, or recording unless a financing statement is filed as provided in subsection (4) or unless the security interest is perfected otherwise than by filing.

(4) A financing statement may be filed within six months before the perfection of a security interest would otherwise lapse. Any such financing statement may be signed by either the debtor or the secured party. It must identify the security agreement, statement or notice (however denominated in any statute or other law repealed or modified by this Act), state the office where and the date when the last filing, refiling or recording, if any, was made with respect thereto, and the filing number, if any, or book and page, if any, of recording and further state that the security agreement, statement or notice, however denominated, in another filing office under the [U.C.C.] or under any statute or other law repealed or modified by this Act is still effective. Section 9–401 and Section 9–103 determine the proper place to file such a financing statement. Except as specified in this subsection, the provisions of Section 9–403(3) for continuation statements apply to such a financing statement.

§ 11–107. Transition Provisions as to Priorities.

Except as otherwise provided in [Article 11], [old U.C.C.] shall apply to any questions of priority if the positions of the parties were fixed prior to the effective date of [new U.C.C.]. In other cases questions of priority shall be determined by [new U.C.C.].

§ 11–108. Presumption that Rule of Law Continues Unchanged.

Unless a change in law has clearly been made, the provisions of [new U.C.C.] shall be deemed declaratory of the meaning of the [old U.C.C.].

APPENDIX D
THE UNIFORM PARTNERSHIP ACT

The Act consists of 7 Parts as follows:

I. Preliminary Provisions

II. Nature of Partnership

III. Relations of Partners to Persons Dealing with the Partnership

IV. Relations of Partners to One Another

V. Property Rights of a Partner

VI. Dissolution and Winding Up

VII. Miscellaneous Provisions

An Act to make uniform the Law of Partnerships Be it enacted, etc.:

Part I Preliminary Provisions

Sec. 1. Name of Act.

This act may be cited as Uniform Partnership Act.

Sec. 2. Definition of Terms.

In this act, "Court" includes every court and judge having jurisdiction in the case.

"Business" includes every trade, occupation, or profession.

"Person" includes individuals, partnerships, corporations, and other associations.

"Bankrupt" includes bankrupt under the Federal Bankruptcy Act or insolvent under any state insolvent act.

"Conveyance" includes every assignment, lease, mortgage, or encumbrance.

"Real property" includes land and any interest or estate in land.

Sec. 3. Interpretation of Knowledge and Notice.

(1) A person has "knowledge" of a fact within the meaning of this act not only when he has actual knowledge thereof, but also when he has knowledge of such other facts as in the circumstances shows bad faith.

(2) A person has "notice" of a fact within the meaning of this act when the person who claims the benefit of the notice

(a) States the fact to such person, or

(b) Delivers through the mail, or by other means of communication, a written statement of the fact to such person or to a proper person at his place of business or residence.

Sec. 4. Rules of Construction.

(1) The rule that statutes in derogation of the common law are to be strictly construed shall have no application to this act.

(2) The law of estoppel shall apply under this act.

(3) The law of agency shall apply under this act.

(4) This act shall be so interpreted and construed as to effect its general purpose to make uniform the law of those states which enact it.

(5) This act shall not be construed so as to impair the obligations of any contract existing when the act goes into effect, nor to affect any action or proceedings begun or right accrued before this act takes effect.

Sec. 5. Rules for Cases Not Provided for in this Act.

In any case not provided for in this act the rules of law and equity, including the law merchant, shall govern.

Part II Nature of Partnership

Sec. 6. Partnership Defined.

(1) A partnership is an association of two or more persons to carry on as co-owners a business for profit.

(2) But any association formed under any other statute of this state, or any statute adopted by authority, other than the authority of this state, is not a partnership under this act, unless such association would have been a partnership in this state prior to the adoption of this act; but this act shall apply to limited partnerships except in so far as the statutes relating to such partnerships are inconsistent herewith.

Sec. 7. Rules for Determining the Existence of a Partnership.

In determining whether a partnership exists, these rules shall apply:

(1) Except as provided by Section 16 persons who are not partners as to each other are not partners as to third persons.

(2) Joint tenancy, tenancy in common, tenancy by the entireties, joint property, common property, or part ownership does not of itself establish a partnership, whether such co-owners do or do not share any profits made by the use of the property.

(3) The sharing of gross returns does not of itself establish a partnership, whether or not the persons sharing them have a joint or common right or interest in any property from which the returns are derived.

(4) The receipt by a person of a share of the profits of a business is prima facie evidence that he is a partner in the business, but no such inference shall be drawn if such profits were received in payment:

(a) As a debt by installments or otherwise,

(b) As wages of an employee or rent to a landlord,

(c) As an annuity to a widow or representative of a deceased partner,

(d) As interest on a loan, though the amount of payment vary with the profits of the business,

(e) As the consideration for the sale of a good-will of a business or other property by installments or otherwise.

Sec. 8. Partnership Property.

(1) All property originally brought into the partnership stock or subsequently acquired by purchase or otherwise, on account of the partnership, is partnership property.

(2) Unless the contrary intention appears, property acquired with partnership funds is partnership property.

(3) Any estate in real property may be acquired in the partnership name. Title so acquired can be conveyed only in the partnership name.

(4) A conveyance to a partnership in the partnership name, though without words of inheritance, passes the entire estate of the grantor unless a contrary intent appears.

Part III Relations of Partners to Persons Dealing with the Partnership

Sec. 9. Partner Agent of Partnership as to Partnership Business.

(1) Every partner is an agent of the partnership for the purpose of its business, and the act of every partner, including the execution in the partnership name of any instrument, for apparently carrying on in the usual way the business of the partnership of which he is a member binds the partnership, unless the partner so acting has in fact no authority to act for the partnership in the particular matter, and the person with whom he is dealing has knowledge of the fact that he has no such authority.

(2) An act of a partner which is not apparently for the carrying on of the business of the partnership in the usual way does not bind the partnership unless authorized by the other partners.

(3) Unless authorized by the other partners or unless they have abandoned the business, one or more but less than all the partners have no authority to:

(a) Assign the partnership property in trust for creditors or on the assignee's promise to pay the debts of the partnership,

(b) Dispose of the good-will of the business,

(c) Do any other act which would make it impossible to carry on the ordinary business of a partnership,

(d) Confess a judgment,

(e) Submit a partnership claim or liability to arbitration or reference.

(4) No act of a partner in contravention of a restriction on authority shall bind the partnership to persons having knowledge of the restriction.

Sec. 10. Conveyance of Real Property of the Partnership.

(1) Where title to real property is in the partnership name, any partner may convey title to such property by a conveyance executed in the partnership name; but the partnership may recover such property unless the partner's act binds the partnership under the provisions of paragraph (1) of section 9 or unless such property has been conveyed by the grantee or a person claiming through such grantee to a holder for value without knowledge that the partner, in making the conveyance, has exceeded his authority.

(2) Where title to real property is in the name of the partnership, a conveyance executed by a partner, in his own name, passes the equitable interest of the partnership, provided the act is one within the authority of the partner under the provisions of paragraph (1) of section 9.

(3) Where title to real property is in the name of one or more but not all the partners, and the record does not disclose the right of the partnership, the partners in whose name the title stands may convey title to such property, but the partnership may recover such property if the partners' act does not bind the partnership under the provisions of paragraph (1) of section 9, unless the purchaser or his assignee, is a holder for value, without knowledge.

(4) Where the title to real property is in the name of one or more or all the partners, or in a third person in trust for the partnership, a conveyance executed by a partner in the partnership name, or in his own name, passes the equitable interest of the partnership, provided the act is one within the authority of the partner under the provisions of paragraph (1) of section 9.

(5) Where the title to real property is in the names of all the partners a conveyance executed by all the partners passes all their rights in such property.

Sec. 11. Partnership Bound by Admission of Partner.

An admission or representation made by any partner concerning partnership affairs within the scope of his authority as conferred by this act is evidence against the partnership.

Sec. 12. Partnership Charged with Knowledge of or Notice to Partner.

Notice to any partner of any matter relating to partnership affairs, and the knowledge of the partner acting in the particular matter, acquired while a partner or then present to his mind, and the knowledge of any other partner who reasonably could and should have communicated it to the acting partner, operate as notice to or knowledge of the partnership, except in the case of a fraud on the partnership committed by or with the consent of that partner.

Sec. 13. Partnership Bound by Partner's Wrongful Act.

Where, by any wrongful act or omission of any partner acting in the ordinary course of the business of the partnership or with the authority of his co-partners, loss or injury is caused to any person, not being a partner in the partnership, or any penalty is incurred, the partnership is liable therefor to the same extent as the partner so acting or omitting to act.

Sec. 14. Partnership Bound by Partner's Breach of Trust.

The partnership is bound to make good the loss:

(a) Where one partner acting within the scope of his apparent authority receives money or property of a third person and misapplies it; and
(b) Where the partnership in the course of its business receives money or property of a third person and the money or property so received is misapplied by any partner while it is in the custody of the partnership.

Sec. 15. Nature of Partner's Liability.

All partners are liable

(a) Jointly and severally for everything chargeable to the partnership under sections 13 and 14.
(b) Jointly for all other debts and obligations of the partnership; but any partner may enter into a separate obligation to perform a partnership contract.

Sec. 16. Partner by Estoppel.

(1) When a person, by words spoken or written or by conduct, represents himself, or consents to another representing him to any one, as a partner in an existing partnership or with one or more persons not actual partners, he is liable to any such person to whom such representation has been made, who has, on the faith of such representation, given credit to the actual or apparent partnership, and if he has made such representation or consented to its being made in a public manner he is liable to such person, whether the representation has or has not been made or communicated to such person so giving credit by or with the knowledge of the apparent partner making the representation or consenting to its being made.

(a) When a partnership liability results, he is liable as though he were an actual member of the partnership.
(b) When no partnership liability results, he is liable jointly with the other persons, if any, so consenting to the contract or representation as to incur liability, otherwise separately.

(2) When a person has been thus represented to be a partner in an existing partnership, or with one or more persons not actual partners, he is an agent of the persons consenting to such representation to bind them to the same extent and in the same manner as though he were a partner in fact, with respect to persons who rely upon the representation. Where all the members of the existing partnership consent to the representation, a partnership act or obligation results; but in all other cases it is the joint act or obligation of the person acting and the persons consenting to the representation.

Sec. 17. Liability of Incoming Partner.

A person admitted as a partner into an existing partnership is liable for all the obligations of the partnership arising before his admission as though he had been a partner when such obligations were incurred, except that this liability shall be satisfied only out of partnership property.

Part IV Relations of Partners to One Another

Sec. 18. Rules Determining Rights and Duties of Partners.

The rights and duties of the partners in relation to the partnership shall be determined, subject to any agreement between them, by the following rules:

(a) Each partner shall be repaid his contributions, whether by way of capital or advances to the partnership property and share equally in the profits and surplus remaining after all liabilities, including those to partners, are satisfied; and must contribute towards the losses, whether of capital or otherwise, sustained by the partnership according to his share in the profits.
(b) The partnership must indemnify every partner in respect of payments made and personal liabilities reasonably incurred by him in the ordinary and proper conduct of its business, or for the preservation of its business or property.
(c) A partner, who in aid of the partnership makes any payment or advance beyond the amount of capital which he agreed to contribute, shall be paid interest from the date of the payment or advance.

(d) A partner shall receive interest on the capital contributed by him only from the date when repayment should be made.

(e) All partners have equal rights in the management and conduct of the partnership business.

(f) No partner is entitled to remuneration for acting in the partnership business, except that a surviving partner is entitled to reasonable compensation for his services in winding up the partnership affairs.

(g) No person can become a member of a partnership without the consent of all the partners.

(h) Any difference arising as to ordinary matters connected with the partnership business may be decided by a majority of the partners; but no act in contravention of any agreement between the partners may be done rightfully without the consent of all the partners.

Sec. 19. Partnership Books.

The partnership books shall be kept, subject to any agreement between the partners, at the principal place of business of the partnership, and every partner shall at all times have access to and may inspect and copy any of them.

Sec. 20. Duty of Partners to Render Information.

Partners shall render on demand true and full information of all things affecting the partnership to any partner or the legal representative of any deceased partner or partner under legal disability.

Sec. 21. Partner Accountable as a Fiduciary.

(1) Every partner must account to the partnership for any benefit, and hold as trustee for it any profits derived by him without the consent of the other partners from any transaction connected with the formation, conduct, or liquidation of the partnership or from any use by him of its property.

(2) This section applies also to the representatives of a deceased partner engaged in the liquidation of the affairs of the partnership as the personal representatives of the last surviving partner.

Sec. 22. Right to an Account.

Any partner shall have the right to a formal account as to partnership affairs:

(a) If he is wrongfully excluded from the partnership business or possession of its property by his co-partners,

(b) If the right exists under the terms of any agreement,

(c) As provided by section 21,

(d) Whenever other circumstances render it just and reasonable.

Sec. 23. Continuation of Partnership Beyond Fixed Term.

(1) When a partnership for a fixed term or particular undertaking is continued after the termination of such term or particular undertaking without any express agreement, the rights and duties of the partners remain the same as they were at such termination, so far as is consistent with a partnership at will.

(2) A continuation of the business by the partners or such of them as habitually acted therein during the term, without any settlement or liquidation of the partnership affairs, is prima facie evidence of a continuation of the partnership.

Part V Property Rights of a Partner

Sec. 24. Extent of Property Rights of a Partner.

The property rights of a partner are (1) his rights in specific partnership property, (2) his interest in the partnership, and (3) his right to participate in the management.

Sec. 25. Nature of a Partner's Right in Specific Partnership Property.

(1) A partner is co-owner with his partners of specific partnership property holding as a tenant in partnership.

(2) The incidents of this tenancy are such that:

(a) A partner, subject to the provisions of this act and to any agreement between the partners, has an equal right with his partners to possess specific partnership property for partnership purposes; but he has no right to possess such property for any other purpose without the consent of his partners.

(b) A partner's right in specific partnership property is not assignable except in connection with the assignment of rights of all the partners in the same property.

(c) A partner's right in specific partnership property is not subject to attachment or execution, except on a claim against the partnership. When partnership property is attached for a partnership debt the partners, or any of them, or the representatives of a deceased partner, cannot claim any right under the homestead or exemption laws.

(d) On the death of a partner his right in specific partnership property vests in the surviving partner or partners, except where the deceased was the last surviving partner, when his right in such property vests in his legal representative. Such surviving partner or partners, or the legal representative of the last surviving partner, has no right to possess the partnership property for any but a partnership purpose.

(e) A partner's right in specific partnership property is not subject to dower, curtesy, or allowances to widows, heirs, or next of kin.

Sec. 26. Nature of Partner's Interest in the Partnership.

A partner's interest in the partnership is his share of the profits and surplus, and the same is personal property.

Sec. 27. Assignment of Partner's Interest.

(1) A conveyance by a partner of his interest in the partnership does not of itself dissolve the partnership,

nor, as against the other partners in the absence of agreement, entitle the assignee, during the continuance of the partnership to interfere in the management or administration of the partnership business or affairs, or to require any information or account of partnership transactions, or to inspect the partnership books; but it merely entitles the assignee to receive in accordance with his contract the profits to which the assigning partner would otherwise be entitled.

(2) In case of a dissolution of the partnership, the assignee is entitled to receive his assignor's interest and may require an account from the date only of the last account agreed to by all the partners.

Sec. 28. Partner's Interest Subject to Charging Order.

(1) On due application to a competent court by any judgment creditor of a partner, the court which entered the judgment, order, or decree, or any other court, may charge the interest of the debtor partner with payment of the unsatisfied amount of such judgment debt with interest thereon; and may then or later appoint a receiver of his share of the profits, and of any other money due or to fall due to him in respect of the partnership, and make all other orders, directions, accounts and inquiries which the debtor partner might have made, or which the circumstances of the case may require.

(2) The interest charged may be redeemed at any time before foreclosure, or in case of a sale being directed by the court may be purchased without thereby causing a dissolution:

(a) With separate property, by any one or more of the partners, or
(b) With partnership property, by any one or more of the partners with the consent of all the partners whose interests are not so charged or sold.

(3) Nothing in this act shall be held to deprive a partner of his right, if any, under the exemption laws, as regards his interest in the partnership.

Part VI Dissolution and Winding Up

Sec. 29. Dissolution Defined.

The dissolution of a partnership is the change in the relation of the partners caused by any partner ceasing to be associated in the carrying on as distinguished from the winding up of the business.

Sec. 30. Partnership Not Terminated by Dissolution.

On dissolution the partnership is not terminated, but continues until the winding up of partnership affairs is completed.

Sec. 31. Causes of Dissolution.

Dissolution is caused:

(1) Without violation of the agreement between the partners,

(a) By the termination of the definite term or particular undertaking specified in the agreement,
(b) By the express will of any partner when no definite term or particular undertaking is specified,
(c) By the express will of all the partners who have not assigned their interests or suffered them to be charged for their separate debts, either before or after the termination of any specified term or particular undertaking,
(d) By the expulsion of any partner from the business bona fide in accordance with such a power conferred by the agreement between the partners;

(2) In contravention of the agreement between the partners, where the circumstances do not permit a dissolution under any other provision of this section, by the express will of any partner at any time;
(3) By any event which makes it unlawful for the business of the partnership to be carried on or for the members to carry it on in partnership;
(4) By the death of any partner;
(5) By the bankruptcy of any partner or the partnership;
(6) By decree of court under section 32.

Sec. 32. Dissolution by Decree of Court.

(1) On application by or for a partner the court shall decree a dissolution whenever:

(a) A partner has been declared a lunatic in any judicial proceeding or is shown to be of unsound mind,
(b) A partner becomes in any other way incapable of performing his part of the partnership contract,
(c) A partner has been guilty of such conduct as tends to affect prejudicially the carrying on of the business,
(d) A partner wilfully or persistently commits a breach of the partnership agreement, or otherwise so conducts himself in matters relating to the partnership business that it is not reasonably practicable to carry on the business in partnership with him,
(e) The business of the partnership can only be carried on at a loss,
(f) Other circumstances render a dissolution equitable.

(2) On the application of the purchaser of a partner's interest under sections 27 or 28:

(a) After the termination of the specified term or particular undertaking,
(b) At any time if the partnership was a partnership at will when the interest was assigned or when the charging order was issued.

Sec. 33. General Effect of Dissolution on Authority of Partner.

Except so far as may be necessary to wind up partnership affairs or to complete transactions begun but not then finished, dissolution terminates all authority of any partner to act for the partnership,

(1) With respect to the partners,

(a) When the dissolution is not by the act, bankruptcy or death of a partner; or
(b) When the dissolution is by such act, bankruptcy or death of a partner, in cases where section 34 so requires.

(2) With respect to persons not partners, as declared in section 35.

Sec. 34. Right of Partner to Contribution From Copartners After Dissolution.

Where the dissolution is caused by the act, death or bankruptcy of a partner, each partner is liable to his copartners for his share of any liability created by any partner acting for the partnership as if the partnership had not been dissolved unless

(a) The dissolution being by act of any partner, the partner acting for the partnership had knowledge of the dissolution, or
(b) The dissolution being by the death or bankruptcy of a partner, the partner acting for the partnership had knowledge or notice of the death or bankruptcy.

Sec. 35. Power of Partner to Bind Partnership to Third Persons After Dissolution.

(1) After dissolution a partner can bind the partnership except as provided in Paragraph (3)

(a) By any act appropriate for winding up partnership affairs or completing transactions unfinished at dissolution;
(b) By any transaction which would bind the partnership if dissolution had not taken place, provided the other party to the transaction

(I) Had extended credit to the partnership prior to dissolution and had no knowledge or notice of the dissolution; or
(II) Though he had not so extended credit, had nevertheless known of the partnership prior to dissolution, and, having no knowledge or notice of dissolution, the fact of dissolution had not been advertised in a newspaper of general circulation in the place (or in each place if more than one) at which the partnership business was regularly carried on.

(2) The liability of a partner under paragraph (1b) shall be satisfied out of partnership assets alone when such partner had been prior to dissolution

(a) Unknown as a partner to the person with whom the contract is made; and
(b) So far unknown and inactive in partnership affairs that the business reputation of the partnership could not be said to have been in any degree due to his connection with it.

(3) The partnership is in no case bound by any act of a partner after dissolution

(a) Where the partnership is dissolved because it is unlawful to carry on the business, unless the act is appropriate for winding up partnership affairs; or
(b) Where the partner has become bankrupt; or
(c) Where the partner has no authority to wind up partnership affairs; except by a transaction with one who

(I) Had extended credit to the partnership prior to dissolution and had no knowledge or notice of his want of authority; or
(II) Had not extended credit to the partnership prior to dissolution, and, having no knowledge or notice of his want of authority, the fact of his want of authority has not been advertised in the manner provided for advertising the fact of dissolution in paragraph (1bII).

(4) Nothing in this section shall affect the liability under section 16 of any person who after dissolution represents himself or consents to another representing him as a partner in a partnership engaged in carrying on business.

Sec. 36. Effect of Dissolution on Partner's Existing Liability.

(1) The dissolution of the partnership does not of itself discharge the existing liability of any partner.
(2) A partner is discharged from any existing liability upon dissolution of the partnership by an agreement to that effect between himself, the partnership creditor and the person or partnership continuing the business; and such agreement may be inferred from the course of dealing between the creditor having knowledge of the dissolution and the person or partnership continuing the business.
(3) Where a person agrees to assume the existing obligations of a dissolved partnership, the partners whose obligations have been assumed shall be discharged from any liability to any creditor of the partnership who, knowing of the agreement, consents to a material alteration in the nature or time of payment of such obligations.
(4) The individual property of a deceased partner shall be liable for all obligations of the partnership incurred while he was a partner but subject to the prior payment of his separate debts.

Sec. 37. Right to Wind Up.

Unless otherwise agreed the partners who have not wrongfully dissolved the partnership or the legal representative of the last surviving partner, not bankrupt, has the right to wind up the partnership affairs; provided, however, that any partner, his legal representative or his assignee, upon cause shown, may obtain winding up by the court.

Sec. 38. Rights of Partners to Application of Partnership Property.

(1) When dissolution is caused in any way, except in contravention of the partnership agreement, each partner as against his co-partners and all persons claiming through them in respect of their interests in the partnership, unless otherwise agreed, may have the partnership property applied to discharge its liabilities, and the surplus applied to pay in cash the net amount owing to the respective partners. But if dissolution is caused by expulsion of a partner, bona fide under the partnership agreement and if the expelled partner is discharged from all partnership liabilities, either by payment or agreement under section 36(2), he shall receive in cash only the net amount due him from the partnership.

(2) When dissolution is caused in contravention of the partnership agreement the rights of the partners shall be as follows:

(a) Each partner who has not caused dissolution wrongfully shall have,

(I) All the rights specified in paragraph (1) of this section, and
(II) The right, as against each partner who has caused the dissolution wrongfully, to damages for breach of the agreement.

(b) The partners who have not caused the dissolution wrongfully, if they all desire to continue the business in the same name, either by themselves or jointly with others, may do so, during the agreed term for the partnership and for that purpose may possess the partnership property, provided they secure the payment by bond approved by the court, or pay to any partner who has caused the dissolution wrongfully, the value of his interest in the partnership at the dissolution, less any damages recoverable under clause (2aII) of the section, and in like manner indemnify him against all present or future partnership liabilities.

(c) A partner who has caused the dissolution wrongfully shall have:

(I) If the business is not continued under the provisions of paragraph (2b) all the rights of a partner under paragraph (1), subject to clause (2aII), of this section,
(II) If the business is continued under paragraph (2b) of this section the right as against his co-partners and all claiming through them in respect of their interests in the partnership, to have the value of his interest in the partnership, less any damages caused to his co-partners by the dissolution, ascertained and paid to him in cash, or the payment secured by bond approved by the court, and to be released from all existing liabilities of the partnership; but in ascertaining the value of the partner's interest the value of the good-will of the business shall not be considered.

Sec. 39. Rights Where Partnership is Dissolved for Fraud or Misrepresentation.

Where a partnership contract is rescinded on the ground of the fraud or misrepresentation of one of the parties thereto, the party entitled to rescind is, without prejudice to any other right, entitled,

(a) To a lien on, or right of retention of, the surplus of the partnership property after satisfying the partnership liabilities to third persons for any sum of money paid by him for the purchase of an interest in the partnership and for any capital or advances contributed by him; and
(b) To stand, after all liabilities to third persons have been satisfied, in the place of the creditors of the partnership for any payments made by him in respect of the partnership liabilities; and
(c) To be indemnified by the person guilty of the fraud or making the representation against all debts and liabilities of the partnership.

Sec. 40. Rules for Distribution.

In settling accounts between the partners after dissolution, the following rules shall be observed, subject to any agreement to the contrary:

(a) The assets of the partnership are:

(I) The partnership property,
(II) The contributions of the partners necessary for the payment of all the liabilities specified in clause (b) of this paragraph.

(b) The liabilities of the partnership shall rank in order of payment, as follows:

(I) Those owing to creditors other than partners,
(II) Those owing to partners other than for capital and profits,
(III) Those owing to partners in respect of capital,
(IV) Those owing to partners in respect of profits.

(c) The assets shall be applied in the order of their declaration in clause (a) of this paragraph to the satisfaction of the liabilities.
(d) The partners shall contribute, as provided by section 18(a) the amount necessary to satisfy the liabilities; but if any, but not all, of the partners are insolvent, or, not being subject to process, refuse to contribute, the other parties shall contribute their share of the liabilities, and, in the relative proportions in which they share the profits, the additional amount necessary to pay the liabilities.
(e) An assignee for the benefit of creditors or any person appointed by the court shall have the right to enforce the contributions specified in clause (d) of this paragraph.
(f) Any partner or his legal representative shall have the right to enforce the contributions specified in clause (d) of this paragraph, to the extent of the amount which he has paid in excess of his share of the liability.
(g) The individual property of a deceased partner shall be liable for the contributions specified in clause (d) of this paragraph.
(h) When partnership property and the individual properties of the partners are in possession of a court for distribution, partnership creditors shall have priority on

partnership property and separate creditors on individual property, saving the rights of lien or secured creditors as heretofore.

(i) Where a partner has become bankrupt or his estate is insolvent the claims against his separate property shall rank in the following order:

(I) Those owing to separate creditors,
(II) Those owing to partnership creditors,
(III) Those owing to partners by way of contribution.

Sec. 41. Liability of Persons Continuing the Business in Certain Cases.

(1) When any new partner is admitted into an existing partnership, or when any partner retires and assigns (or the representative of the deceased partner assigns) his rights in partnership property to two or more of the partners, or to one or more of the partners and one or more third persons, if the business is continued without liquidation of the partnership affairs, creditors of the first or dissolved partnership are also creditors of the person or partnership so continuing the business.

(2) When all but one partner retire and assign (or the representative of a deceased partner assigns) their rights in partnership property to the remaining partner, who continues the business without liquidation of partnership affairs, either alone or with others, creditors of the dissolved partnership are also creditors of the person or partnership so continuing the business.

(3) When any partner retires or dies and the business of the dissolved partnership is continued as set forth in paragraphs (1) and (2) of this section, with the consent of the retired partners or the representative of the deceased partner, but without any assignment of his right in partnership property, rights of creditors of the dissolved partnership and of the creditors of the person or partnership continuing the business shall be as if such assignment had been made.

(4) When all the partners or their representatives assign their rights in partnership property to one or more third persons who promise to pay the debts and who continue the business of the dissolved partnership, creditors of the dissolved partnership are also creditors of the person or partnership continuing the business.

(5) When any partner wrongfully causes a dissolution and the remaining partners continue the business under the provisions of section 38(2b), either alone or with others, and without liquidation of the partnership affairs, creditors of the dissolved partnership are also creditors of the person or partnership continuing the business.

(6) When a partner is expelled and the remaining partners continue the business either alone or with others, without liquidation of the partnership affairs, creditors of the dissolved partnership are also creditors of the person or partnership continuing the business.

(7) The liability of a third person becoming a partner in the partnership continuing the business, under this section, to the creditors of the dissolved partnership shall be satisfied out of partnership property only.

(8) When the business of a partnership after dissolution is continued under any conditions set forth in this section the creditors of the dissolved partnership, as against the separate creditors of the retiring or deceased partner or the representative of the deceased partner, have a prior right to any claim of the retired partner or the representative of the deceased partner against the person or partnership continuing the business, on account of the retired or deceased partner's interest in the dissolved partnership or on account of any consideration promised for such interest or for his right in partnership property.

(9) Nothing in this section shall be held to modify any right of creditors to set aside any assignment on the ground of fraud.

(10) The use by the person or partnership continuing the business of the partnership name, or the name of a deceased partner as part thereof, shall not of itself make the individual property of the deceased partner liable for any debts contracted by such person or partnership.

Sec. 42. Rights of Retiring or Estate of Deceased Partner When the Business is Continued.

When any partner retires or dies, and the business is continued under any of the conditions set forth in section 41(1, 2, 3, 5, 6), or section 38(2b), without any settlement of accounts as between him or his estate and the person or partnership continuing the business, unless otherwise agreed, he or his legal representative as against such persons or partnership may have the value of his interest at the date of dissolution ascertained, and shall receive as an ordinary creditor an amount equal to the value of his interest in the dissolved partnership with interest, or, at his option or at the option of his legal representative, in lieu of interest, the profits attributable to the use of his right in the property of the dissolved partnership; provided that the creditors of the dissolved partnership as against the separate creditors, or the representative of the retired or deceased partner, shall have priority on any claim arising under this section, as provided by section 41(8) of this act.

Sec. 43. Accrual of Actions.

The right to an account of his interest shall accrue to any partner, or his legal representative, as against the winding up partners or the surviving partners or the person or partnership continuing the business, at the date of dissolution, in the absence of any agreement to the contrary.

Part VII Miscellaneous Provisions

Sec. 44. When Act Takes Effect.

This act shall take effect on the _____ day of _____ one thousand nine hundred and _____.

Sec. 45. Legislation Repealed.

All acts or parts of acts inconsistent with this act are hereby repealed.

THE REVISED UNIFORM LIMITED PARTNERSHIP ACT

The Act consists of 11 Articles as follows:

1. General Provisions
2. Formation; Certificate of Limited Partnership
3. Limited Partners
4. General Partners
5. Finance
6. Distribution and Withdrawal
7. Assignment of Partnership Interests
8. Dissolution
9. Foreign Limited Partnerships
10. Derivative Actions
11. Miscellaneous

Article 1

GENERAL PROVISIONS

Sec. 101. Definitions.

As used in this Act:

(1) "Certificate of limited partnership" means the certificate referred to in Section 201, as that certificate is amended from time to time.

(2) "Contribution" means any cash, property, or services rendered, or a promissory note or other binding obligation to contribute cash or property or to perform services, which a partner contributes to a limited partnership in his capacity as a partner.

(3) "Event of withdrawal of a general partner" means an event that causes a person to cease to be a general partner as provided in Section 402.

(4) "Foreign limited partnership" means a partnership formed under the laws of any state other than this State and having as partners one or more general partners and one or more limited partners.

(5) "General partner" means a person who has been admitted to a limited partnership as a general partner in accordance with the partnership agreement and who is named in the certificate of limited partnership as a general partner.

(6) "Limited partner" means a person who has been admitted to a limited partnership as a limited partner in accordance with the partnership agreement and who is named in the certificate of limited partnership as a limited partner.

(7) "Limited partnership" and "domestic limited partnership" mean a partnership formed by 2 or more persons under the laws of this State and having one or more general partners and one or more limited partners.

(8) "Partner" means any limited partner or general partner.

(9) "Partnership agreement" means the agreement, written or, to the extent not prohibited by law, oral or both, of the partners as to the affairs of a limited partnership and the conduct of its business.

(10) "Partnership interest" has the meaning specified in Section 701.

(11) "Person" means a natural person, partnership, limited partnership (domestic or foreign), trust, estate, association, or corporation.

(12) "State" means a state, territory, or possession of the United States, the District of Columbia, or the Commonwealth of Puerto Rico.

Sec. 102. Name.

The name of each limited partnership as set forth in its certificate of limited partnership:

(1) shall contain the words "limited partnership" in full;
(2) may not contain the name of a limited partner unless

(i) it is also the name of a general partner or (ii) the business of the limited partnership had been carried on under that name before the admission of that limited partner;

(3) may not contain any word or phrase indicating or implying that it is organized other than for a purpose stated in its certificate of limited partnership;
(4) may not be the same as, or deceptively similar to, the name of any corporation or limited partnership organized

under the laws of this State or licensed or registered as a foreign corporation or limited partnership in this State; and

(5) may not contain the following words [here insert prohibited words].

Sec. 103. Reservation of Name.

(a) The exclusive right to the use of a name may be reserved by:

(1) any person intending to organize a limited partnership under this Act and to adopt that name;
(2) any domestic limited partnership or any foreign limited partnership registered in this State which, in either case, intends to adopt that name;
(3) any foreign limited partnership intending to register in this State and to adopt that name; and
(4) any person intending to organize a foreign limited partnership and intending to have it registered in this State and to adopt that name.

(b) The reservation shall be made by filing with the Secretary of State an application, executed by the applicant, to reserve a specified name. If the Secretary of State finds that the name is available for use by a domestic or foreign limited partnership, he shall reserve the name for the exclusive use of the applicant for a period of 120 days. Once having reserved a name, the same applicant may not again reserve the same name until more than 60 days after the expiration of the last 120-day period for which that applicant had reserved that name. The right to the exclusive use of a name so reserved may be transferred to any other person by filing in the office of the Secretary of State a notice of the transfer, executed by the applicant for whom the name was reserved and specifying the name and address of the transferee.

Sec. 104. Specified Office and Agent.

Each limited partnership shall continuously maintain in this State:

(1) an office, which may but need not be a place of its business in this State, at which shall be kept the records required to be maintained by Section 105; and
(2) an agent for service of process on the limited partnership, which agent must be an individual resident of this State, a domestic corporation, or a foreign corporation authorized to do business in this State.

Sec. 105. Records to be Kept.

Each limited partnership shall keep at the office referred to in Section 104(1) the following: (1) a current list of the full name and last-known business address of each partner set forth in alphabetical order, (2) a copy of the certificate of limited partnership and all certificates of amendment thereto, together with executed copies of any powers of attorney pursuant to which any certificate has been executed, (3) copies of the limited partnership's federal, state, and local income tax returns and reports, if any, for the 3 most recent years, and (4) copies of any then effective written partnership agreements and of any financial statements of the limited partnership for the 3 most recent years. These records shall be available for inspection and copying at the reasonable request, and at the expense, of any partner during ordinary business hours.

Sec. 106. Nature of Business.

A limited partnership may carry on any business that a partnership without limited partners may carry on except [here designate prohibited activities].

Sec. 107. Business Transactions of Partner with the Partnership.

Except as otherwise provided in the partnership agreement, a partner may lend money to and transact other business with the limited partnership and, subject to other applicable provisions of law, has the same rights and obligations with respect thereto as a person who is not a partner.

Article 2

FORMATION; CERTIFICATE OF LIMITED PARTNERSHIP

Sec. 201. Certificate of Limited Partnership.

(a) Two or more persons desiring to form a limited partnership shall execute a certificate of limited partnership. The certificate shall be filed in the office of the Secretary of State and shall set forth:

(1) the name of the limited partnership;
(2) the general character of its business;
(3) the address of the office and the name and address of the agent for service of process required to be maintained by Section 104;
(4) the name and the business address of each partner (specifying the general partners and limited partners separately);
(5) the amount of cash and a description and statement of the agreed value of the other property or services contributed by each partner and which each partner has agreed to contribute in the future;
(6) the times at which or events on the happening of which any additional contributions agreed to be made by each partner are to be made;
(7) any power of a limited partner to grant an assignee of any part of his partnership interest the right to become a limited partner, and the terms and conditions of the power;
(8) if agreed upon, the time at which or the events on the happening of which a partner may terminate his membership in the limited partnership and the amount of, or the method of determining, the distribution to

which he may be entitled respecting his partnership interest, and the terms and conditions of the termination and distribution;

(9) any right of a partner to receive distributions of property including cash from the limited partnership;

(10) any right of a partner to receive, or of a general partner to make, distributions to a partner which include a return of all or any part of the partner's contribution;

(11) any time at which or events upon the happening of which the limited partnership is to be dissolved and its affairs wound up;

(12) any right of the remaining general partners to continue the business on the happening of an event of withdrawal of a general partner; and

(13) any other matters the partners, in their sole discretion, determine to include therein.

(b) A limited partnership is formed at the time of the filing of the certificate of limited partnership in the office of the Secretary of State or at any later time specified in the certificate of limited partnership if, in each case, there has been substantial compliance with the requirements of this section.

Sec. 202. Amendments to Certificate.

(a) A certificate of limited partnership is amended by filing a certificate of amendment thereto in the office of the Secretary of State. The certificate shall set forth:

(1) the name of the limited partnership;
(2) the date of filing of the certificate; and
(3) the amendments to the certificate.

(b) Within 30 days after the happening of any of the following events an amendment to a certificate of limited partnership reflecting the occurrence of the event or events shall be filed:

(1) a change in the amount or character of the contribution of any partner, or in any partner's obligation to make a contribution;
(2) the admission of a new partner;
(3) the withdrawal of a partner; and
(4) the continuation of the business under Section 801 after an event of withdrawal of a general partner.

(c) A certificate of limited partnership must be amended promptly by any general partner upon becoming aware that any statement therein was false when made or that any arrangements or other facts described have changed, making the certificate inaccurate in any respect, but amendments to show changes of addresses of limited partners need be filed only once every 12 months.

(d) A certificate of limited partnership may be amended at any time for any other proper purpose the general partners may determine.

(e) No person shall have any liability because an amendment to a certificate of limited partnership has not been filed to reflect the occurrence of any event referred to in

subsection (b) of this section if the amendment is filed within the 30-day period specified in subsection (b).

Sec. 203. Cancellation of Certificate.

A certificate of limited partnership shall be cancelled upon the dissolution and the commencement of winding up of the limited partnership and at any other time there are no remaining limited partners. A certificate of cancellation shall be filed in the office of the Secretary of State and shall set forth:

(1) the name of the limited partnership;
(2) the date of filing of its certificate of limited partnership;
(3) the reason for filing the certificate of cancellation;
(4) the effective date (which shall be a date certain) of cancellation if it is not to be effective upon the filing of the certificate; and
(5) any other information the general partners filing the certificate may determine.

Sec. 204. Execution of Certificates.

(a) Each certificate required by this Article to be filed in the office of the Secretary of State shall be executed in the following manner:

(1) each original certificate of limited partnership must be signed by each partner named therein;
(2) each certificate of amendment must be signed by at least one general partner and by each other partner who is designated in the certificate as a new partner or whose contribution is described as having been increased; and
(3) each certificate of cancellation must be signed by each general partner.

(b) Any person may sign a certificate by an attorney-in-fact, but any power of attorney to sign a certificate relating to the admission or increased contribution of a partner must specifically describe the admission or increase.

(c) The execution of a certificate by a general partner constitutes an affirmation under the penalties of perjury that the facts stated therein are true.

Sec. 205. Amendment or Cancellation by Judicial Act.

If the persons required by Section 204 to execute any certificate of amendment or cancellation fail or refuse to do so, any other partner, and any assignee of a partnership interest, who is adversely affected by the failure or refusal, may petition the [here designate the proper court] to direct the amendment or cancellation. If the court finds that the amendment or cancellation is proper and that the persons so designated have failed or refused to execute the certificate, it shall order the Secretary of State to record an appropriate certificate of amendment or cancellation.

Sec. 206. Filing in the Office of the Secretary of State.

(a) Two signed copies of the certificate of limited partnership and of any certificates of amendment or cancellation (or of any judicial decree of amendment or cancellation) shall be delivered to the Secretary of State. A person who executes a certificate as an agent or fiduciary need not exhibit evidence of his authority as a prerequisite to filing. Unless the Secretary of State finds that any certificate does not conform to law, upon receipt of all filing fees required by law the Secretary of State shall:

(1) endorse on each duplicate original the word "Filed" and the day, month, and year of the filing thereof;
(2) file one duplicate original in his office; and
(3) return the other duplicate original to the person who filed it or his representative.

(b) Upon the filing of a certificate of amendment (or judicial decree of amendment) in the office of the Secretary of State, the certificate of limited partnership shall be amended as set forth therein, and upon the effective date of a certificate of cancellation (or a judicial decree thereof), the certificate of limited partnership shall be cancelled.

Sec. 207. Liability for False Statement in Certificate.

If any certificate of limited partnership or certificate of amendment or cancellation contains a false statement, one who suffers loss by reliance on the statement may recover damages for the loss from:

(1) any person actually executing, or causing another to execute on his behalf, the certificate who knew, and any general partner who knew or should have known, the statement to be false at the time the certificate was executed; and
(2) any general partner who thereafter knew or should have known that any arrangements or other facts described in the certificate have changed, making the statement inaccurate in any respect, within a sufficient time before the statement was relied upon to have reasonably enabled that general partner to cancel or amend the certificate, or to file a petition for its cancellation or amendment under Section 205.

Sec. 208. Constructive Notice.

The fact that a certificate of limited partnership is on file in the office of the Secretary of State is constructive notice that the partnership is a limited partnership and that the persons designated therein as limited partners are limited partners, but is not constructive notice of any other fact.

Sec. 209. Delivery of Certificates to Limited Partners.

Upon the return by the Secretary of State pursuant to Section 206 of any certificate marked "Filed," the general partners shall promptly deliver or mail a copy of the certificate to each limited partner unless the partnership agreement provides otherwise.

Article 3

LIMITED PARTNERS

Sec. 301. Admission of Additional Limited Partners.

(a) After the filing of a limited partnership's original certificate of limited partnership, a person may be admitted as a new limited partner:

(1) in the case of a person acquiring a partnership interest directly from the limited partnership, upon compliance with the partnership agreement or, if the partnership agreement does not so provide, upon the written consent of all partners; and
(2) in the case of an assignee of a partnership interest of a partner who has the power, as provided in Section 704, to grant the assignee the right to become a limited partner, upon the exercise of that power and compliance with any conditions limiting the grant or exercise of the power.

(b) In each case under subsection (a), the person acquiring the partnership interest becomes a limited partner only upon amendment of the certificate of limited partnership reflecting that fact.

Sec. 302. Voting.

Subject to the provisions of Section 303, the partnership agreement may grant to all or a specified group of the limited partners the right to vote (on a per capita or any other basis) upon any matter.

Sec. 303. Liability to Third Parties.

(a) Except as provided in subsection (d), a limited partner as such is not liable for the obligations of a limited partnership unless, in addition to the exercise of his rights and powers as a limited partner, he takes part in the control of the business. But the limited partner's participation in the control of the business is not substantially the same as the exercise of the powers of a general partner, he is liable only to persons who transact business with the limited partnership with actual knowledge of his participation in control.
(b) A limited partner does not participate in the control of the business within the meaning of subsection (a) solely by doing one or more of the following:

(1) being a contractor for or an agent or employee of the limited partnership or of a general partner;
(2) consulting with and advising a general partner with respect to the business of the limited partnership;
(3) acting as surety for the limited partnership;
(4) approving or disapproving an amendment to the partnership agreement; and
(5) voting on one or more of the following matters:

(i) the dissolution and winding up of the limited partnership;

(ii) the sale, exchange, lease, mortgage, pledge, or other transfer of all or substantially all of the assets of the limited partnership other than in the ordinary course of its business;

(iii) the incurrence of indebtedness by the limited partnership other than in the ordinary course of its business;

(iv) a change in the nature of the business; or

(v) the removal of a general partner.

(c) The enumeration in subsection (b) shall not be construed to mean that the possession or exercise of any other powers by a limited partner constitutes participation by him in the business of the limited partnership.

(d) A limited partner who knowingly permits his name to be used in the name of the limited partnership, except under circumstances permitted by Section 102(2)(i), is liable to creditors who extend credit to the limited partnership without actual knowledge that the limited partner is not a general partner.

Sec. 304. Person Erroneously Believing Himself a Limited Partner.

(a) Except as provided in subsection (b) a person who makes a contribution to a business enterprise and erroneously and in good faith believes that he has become a limited partner in the enterprise is not a general partner in the enterprise and is not bound by its obligations by reason of making the contribution, receiving distributions from the enterprise, or exercising any rights of a limited partner, if, on ascertaining the mistake, he:

(1) causes an appropriate certificate of limited partnership or a certificate of amendment to be executed and filed; or

(2) withdraws from future equity participation in the enterprise.

(b) Any person who makes a contribution of the kind described in subsection (a) is liable as a general partner to any third party who transacts business with the enterprise (i) before the person withdraws and an appropriate certificate if any is filed to show the withdrawal, or (ii) before an appropriate certificate is filed to show his status as a limited partner and, in the case of an amendment, after expiration of the 30-day period for filing an amendment relating to the person as a limited partner under Section 202, but in each case only if the third party actually believed in good faith that the person was a general partner at the time of the transaction.

Sec. 305. Information.

Each limited partner has the right to:

(1) inspect and copy any of the partnership records required to be maintained by Section 105; and

(2) obtain from the general partners from time to time upon reasonable demand (i) true and full information regarding the state of the business and financial condition of the limited partnership, (ii) promptly after becoming available, a copy of the limited partnership's federal, state, and local income tax return for each year, and (iii) any other information regarding the affairs of the limited partnership as is just and reasonable.

Article 4

GENERAL PARTNERS

Sec. 401. Admission.

After the filing of a limited partnership's original certificate of limited partnership, new general partners may be admitted only with the specific written consent of each partner.

Sec. 402. Events of Withdrawal.

Except as otherwise approved by the specific written consent at the time of all partners, a person ceases to be general partner of a limited partnership upon the happening of any of the following events:

(1) the general partner withdraws from the limited partnership as provided in Section 602;

(2) the general partner ceases to be a member of the limited partnership as provided in Section 702;

(3) the general partner is removed as a general partner in accordance with the partnership agreement;

(4) unless otherwise provided in the certificate of limited partnership, the general partner: makes an assignment for the benefit of creditors; files a voluntary petition in bankruptcy; is adjudicated a bankrupt or insolvent; files any petition or answer seeking for himself any reorganization, arrangement, composition, readjustment, liquidation, dissolution, or similar relief under any statute, law, or regulation; files any answer or other pleading admitting or failing to contest the material allegations of a petition filed against him in any proceeding of this nature; or seeks, consents to, or acquiesces in the appointment of any trustee, receiver, or liquidator of the general partner or of all or any substantial part of his properties;

(5) unless otherwise provided in the certificate of limited partnership, [120] days after the commencement of any proceeding against the general partner seeking any reorganization, arrangement, composition, readjustment, liquidation, dissolution, or similar relief under any statute, law, or regulation, the proceeding has not been dismissed, or if, within [90] days after the appointment without his consent or acquiescence of any trustee, receiver, or liquidator of the general partner or of all or any substantial part of his properties, the appointment is not vacated or stayed, or if, within [90] days after the expiration of any stay, the appointment is not vacated;

(6) in the case of a general partner who is a natural person

(i) his death; or

(ii) the entry by a court of competent jurisdiction adjudicating him incompetent to manage his person or his property;

(7) in the case of a general partner who is acting as such in the capacity of a trustee of a trust, the termination of the trust (but not merely the substitution of a new trustee);

(8) in the case of a general partner that is a partnership, the dissolution and commencement of winding up of the partnership;

(9) in the case of a general partner that is a corporation, the filing of a certificate of dissolution, or its equivalent, for the corporation or the revocation of its charter; and

(10) in the case of an estate, the distribution by the fiduciary of all the estate's interest in the partnership.

Sec. 403. General Powers and Liabilities.

Except as otherwise provided in this Act and in the partnership agreement, a general partner of a limited partnership has all the rights and powers and is subject to all the restrictions and liabilities of a partner in a partnership without limited partners.

Sec. 404. Contributions by a General Partner.

A general partner may make contributions to a limited partnership and share in the profits and losses of, and in distributions from, the limited partnership as a general partner. A general partner may also make contributions to and share in profits, losses, and distributions as a limited partner. A person who is both a general partner and a limited partner has all the rights and powers, and is subject to all the restrictions and liabilities, of a general partner and also has, except as otherwise provided in the partnership agreement, all powers, and is subject to the restrictions, of a limited partner to the extent he is participating in the partnership as a limited partner.

Sec. 405. Voting.

The partnership agreement may grant to all or a specified group of general partners the right to vote (on a per capita or any other basis), separately or with all or any class of the limited partners, on any matter.

Article 5

FINANCE

Sec. 501. Form of Contributions.

The contribution of a partner may be in cash, property, or services rendered, or a promissory note or other obligation to contribute cash or property or to perform services.

Sec. 502. Liability for Contributions.

(a) Except as otherwise provided in the certificate of limited partnership, a partner is obligated to the limited partnership to perform any promise to contribute cash or property or to perform services regardless of whether he is unable to perform because of death, disability or any other reason. If a partner does not make the required contribution of property or services, he is obligated at the option of the limited partnership to contribute cash equal to that portion of the value (as stated in the certificate of limited partnership) of the stated contribution that has not been made.

(b) Unless otherwise provided in the partnership agreement, the obligation of a partner to make a contribution or return money or other property paid or distributed in violation of this Act may be compromised only by consent of all of the partners. Notwithstanding a compromise so authorized, a creditor of a limited partnership who extends credit, or whose claim arises, after the filing of the certificate of limited partnership or an amendment thereto which, in either case, reflects the obligation and before the amendment or cancellation thereof to reflect the compromise may enforce the precompromise obligation.

Sec. 503. Sharing of Profits and Losses.

The profits and losses of a limited partnership shall be allocated among the partners, and among classes of partners, in the manner provided in the partnership agreement. If the partnership agreement does not so provide, profits and losses shall be allocated on the basis of the value (as stated in the certificate of limited partnership) of the contributions actually made by each partner to the extent they have not been returned.

Sec. 504. Sharing of Distributions.

Distributions of cash or other assets of a limited partnership shall be allocated among the partners, and among classes of partners, in the manner provided in the partnership agreement. If the partnership agreement does not so provide, distributions shall be made on the basis of the value (as stated in the certificate of limited partnership) of the contributions actually made by each partner to the extent they have not been returned.

Article 6

DISTRIBUTIONS AND WITHDRAWAL

Sec. 601. Interim Distributions.

Except as otherwise provided in this Article, a partner is entitled to receive distributions from a limited partnership before his withdrawal from the limited partnership and before the dissolution and winding up thereof:

(1) to the extent and at the times or upon the happening of the events specified in the partnership agreement; and (2) if any distribution constitutes a return of any part of his contribution under Section 608(b), to the extent and at the times or upon the happening of the events specified in the certificate of limited partnership.

Sec. 602. Withdrawal of General Partner.

A general partner may withdraw from a limited partnership at any time by giving written notice to the other partners, but if the withdrawal violates the partnership agreement, the limited partnership may recover from the withdrawing general partner damages for breach of the partnership agreement and offset the damages against the amount otherwise distributable to him.

Sec. 603. Withdrawal of Limited Partner.

A limited partner may withdraw from a limited partnership at the time or upon the happening of the events specified in the certificate of limited partnership and in accordance with any procedures provided in the partnership agreement. If the certificate of limited partnership does not specify the time or the events upon the happening of which a limited partner may withdraw from the limited partnership or a definite time for the dissolution and winding up of the limited partnership, a limited partner may withdraw from the limited partnership upon not less than 6 months' prior written notice to each general partner at his address on the books of the limited partnership at its office in this State.

Sec. 604. Distributions Upon Withdrawal.

Except as provided in this Article, upon withdrawal any withdrawing partner is entitled to receive any distributions to which he is entitled under the partnership agreement and, if not provided, he is entitled to receive, within a reasonable time after withdrawal, the fair value of his interest in the limited partnership as of the date of withdrawal, based upon his right to share in distributions from the limited partnership.

Sec. 605. Distributions in Kind.

Except as provided in the certificate of limited partnership, a partner, regardless of the nature of his contribution, has no right to demand and receive any distribution from a limited partnership in any form other than cash. Except as provided in the partnership agreement, a partner may not be compelled to accept a distribution of any asset in kind from a limited partnership to the extent that the percentage of the asset distributed to him exceeds a percentage of that asset which is equal to the percentage in which he shares in distributions from the limited partnership.

Sec. 606. Right to Distributions.

At the time a partner becomes entitled to receive a distribution, he has the status of, and is entitled to all of the remedies available to, a creditor of the limited partnership with respect to the distribution.

Sec. 607. Limitations on Distributions.

A partner may not receive a distribution from a limited partnership to the extent that, after giving effect to the distribution, all liabilities of the limited partnership other than liabilities to partners on account of their partnership interests, exceed the fair value of the partnership's assets.

Sec. 608. Liability Upon Return of Contributions.

(a) If a partner has received the return of any part of his contribution without violation of the partnership agreement or this Act, for a period of one year thereafter he is liable to the limited partnership for the amount of his contribution returned, but only to the extent necessary to discharge the limited partnership's liabilities to creditors who extended credit to the limited partnership during the period the contribution was held by the partnership. (b) If a partner has received the return of any part of his contribution in violation of the partnership agreement or this Act, for a period of 6 years thereafter he is liable to the limited partnership for the amount of the contribution wrongfully returned. (c) A partner has received a return of his contribution to the extent that a distribution to him reduces his share of the fair value of the net assets of the limited partnership below the value (as set forth in the certificate of limited partnership) of his contributions which have not theretofore been distributed to him.

Article 7

ASSIGNMENT OF PARTNERSHIP INTERESTS

Sec. 701. Nature of Partnership Interest.

A partnership interest is a partner's share of the profits and losses of a limited partnership and the right to receive distributions of partnership assets. A partnership interest is personal property.

Sec. 702. Assignment of Partnership Interest.

Except as otherwise provided in the partnership agreement, a partnership interest is assignable in whole or in part. An assignment of a partnership interest does not dissolve a limited partnership nor entitle the assignee to become a partner or to exercise any of the rights thereof. An assignment only entitles the assignee to receive, to the extent assigned, any distributions to which the assignor would be entitled. Except as otherwise provided in the partnership agreement, a partner ceases to be a partner upon assignment of all his partnership interest.

Sec. 703. Rights of Creditors.

On due application to a court of competent jurisdiction by any judgment creditor of a partner, the court may charge the partnership interest of the partner with payment of the unsatisfied amount of the judgment debt with interest thereon. To the extent so charged, the judgment creditor has only the rights of an assignee of the partnership interest. This Act shall not be construed to deprive any partner of the benefit of any exemption laws applicable to his partnership interest.

Sec. 704. Right of Assignee to Become Limited Partner.

(a) An assignee of a partnership interest, including an assignee of a general partner, may become a limited partner if and to the extent that (1) the assignor gives the assignee that right in accordance with authority described in the certificate of limited partnership or, (2) in the absence of that authority, all other partners consent.

(b) An assignee who has become a limited partner has, to the extent assigned, all the rights and powers, and is subject to all the restrictions and liabilities, of a limited partner under the partnership agreement and this Act. An assignee who becomes a limited partner is also liable for the obligations of his assignor to make and return contributions as provided in Article 6, but the assignee is not obligated for liabilities unknown to the assignee at the time he became a limited partner and which could not be ascertained from the certificate of limited partnership.

(c) If an assignee of a partnership interest becomes a limited partner, the assignor is not released from the liability to the limited partnership under Sections 207 and 502.

Sec. 705. Power of Estate of Deceased or Incompetent Partner.

If a partner who is a natural person dies or a court of competent jurisdiction adjudges him to be incompetent to manage his person or his property, the partner's executor, administrator, guardian, conservator, or other legal representative may exercise all of the partner's rights for the purpose of settling his estate or administering his property, including any power the partner had to give an assignee the right to become a limited partner. If a partner that is a corporation, trust, or other entity other than a natural person is dissolved or terminated, those powers may be exercised by the legal representative or successor of the partner.

Article 8

DISSOLUTION

Sec. 801. Nonjudicial Dissolution.

A limited partnership is dissolved and its affairs shall be wound up upon the happening of the first to occur of the following:

(1) at the time or upon the happening of the events specified in the certificate of limited partnership;

(2) upon the unanimous written consent of all partners;

(3) upon the happening of an event of withdrawal of a general partner unless at the time there is at least one other general partner and the certificate of limited partnership permits the business of the limited partnership to be carried on by the remaining general partner and he does so, but the limited partnership shall not be dissolved or wound up by reason of any event of withdrawal if, within 90 days after the withdrawal, all partners agree in writing to continue the business of the limited partnership and to the appointment of one or more new general partners if necessary or desired; or

(4) upon entry of a decree of judicial dissolution in accordance with Section 802.

Sec. 802. Dissolution by Decree of Court.

On application by or for a partner the [here designate the proper court] court may decree a dissolution of a limited partnership whenever it is not reasonably practicable to carry on the business in conformity with the partnership agreement.

Sec. 803. Winding Up.

Unless otherwise provided in the partnership agreement, the general partners who have not wrongfully dissolved the limited partnership or, if none, the limited partners, may wind up the limited partnership's affairs; but any partner, his legal representative or his assignee, upon cause shown, may obtain winding up by the [here designate the proper court] court.

Sec. 804. Distribution of Assets.

Upon the winding up of a limited partnership, the assets shall be distributed as follows:

(1) to creditors, including partners who are creditors (to the extent otherwise permitted by law), in satisfaction of liabilities of the limited partnership other than liabilities for distributions to partners pursuant to Section 601 or 604;

(2) except as otherwise provided in the partnership agreement, to partners and ex-partners in satisfaction of liabilities for distributions pursuant to Section 601 or 604; and

(3) except as otherwise provided in the partnership agreement, to partners *first* for the return of their contributions and *second* respecting their partnership interests, in the proportions in which the partners share in distributions.

Article 9

FOREIGN LIMITED PARTNERSHIPS

Sec. 901. Law Governing.

Subject to the constitution and public policy of this State, the laws of the state under which a foreign limited partnership is organized govern its organization and internal affairs and the liability of its limited partners, and a foreign limited partnership may not be denied registration by reason of any difference between those laws and the laws of this State.

Sec. 902. Registration.

Before transacting business in this State, a foreign limited partnership shall register with the Secretary of State. In order to register, a foreign limited partnership shall submit to the Secretary of State in duplicate an application for registration as a foreign limited partnership, signed and sworn to by a general partner and setting forth:

(1) the name of the foreign limited partnership and, if different, the name under which it proposes to transact business and register in this State;
(2) the state and date of its formation;
(3) the general character of the business it proposes to transact in this State;
(4) the name and address of any agent for service of process on the foreign limited partnership whom the foreign limited partnership desires to appoint, which agent must be an individual resident of this State, a domestic corporation, or a foreign corporation authorized to do business in this State; and with a place of business in this State;
(5) a statement that the Secretary of State is appointed the agent of the foreign limited partnership for service of process if no agent has been appointed pursuant to paragraph (4) or, if appointed the agent's authority has been revoked or the agent cannot be found or served with the exercise of reasonable diligence;
(6) the address of the office required to be maintained in the state of its organization by the laws of that state or, if not so required, of the principal office of the foreign limited partnership; and
(7) if the certificate of limited partnership filed in the foreign limited partnership's state of organization is not required to include the names and business addresses of the partners, a list of the names and addresses.

Sec. 903. Issuance of Registration.

(a) If the Secretary of State finds that an application for registration conforms to law and all requisite fees have been paid, he shall:

(1) endorse on the application the word "Filed", and the month, day, and year of the filing thereof;
(2) file in his office one of the duplicate originals of the application; and
(3) issue a certificate of registration to transact business in this State.

(b) The certificate of registration, together with one duplicate original of the application, shall be returned to the person who filed the application or his representative.

Sec. 904. Name.

A foreign limited partnership may register with the Secretary of State under any name (whether or not it is the name under which it is registered in its state of organization) that includes the words "limited partnership" and that could be registered by a domestic limited partnership.

Sec. 905. Changes and Amendments.

If any statement in a foreign limited partnership's application for registration was false when made or any arrangements or other facts described have changed, making the application inaccurate in any respect, the foreign limited partnership shall promptly file in the office of the Secretary of State a certificate, signed and sworn to by a general partner, correcting the statement.

Sec. 906. Cancellation of Registration.

A foreign limited partnership may cancel its registration by filing with the Secretary of State a certificate of cancellation signed and sworn to by a general partner. A cancellation does not terminate the authority of the Secretary of State to accept service of process on the foreign limited partnership with respect to [claims for relief] [causes of action] arising out of the transaction of business in this State.

Sec. 907. Transaction of Business Without Registration.

(a) A foreign limited partnership transacting business in this State without registration may not maintain any action, suit, or proceeding in any court of this State until it has registered.
(b) The failure of a foreign limited partnership to register in this State does not impair the validity of any contract or act of the foreign limited partnership, and does not prevent the foreign limited partnership from defending any action, suit, or proceeding in any court of this State.
(c) A limited partner of a foreign limited partnership is not liable as a general partner of the foreign limited

partnership solely by reason of the foreign limited partnership's transacting business in this State without registration.

(d) A foreign limited partnership, by transacting business in this State without registration, appoints the Secretary of State as its agent for service of process with respect to [claims for relief] [causes of action] arising out of the transaction of business in this State.

Sec. 908. Action by [Appropriate Official].

The [appropriate official] may bring an action to restrain a foreign limited partnership from transacting business in this State in violation of this Article.

Article 10

DERIVATIVE ACTIONS

Sec. 1001. Right of Action.

A limited partner may bring an action in the right of a limited partnership to recover a judgment in its favor if the general partners having authority to do so have refused to bring the action or an effort to cause those general partners to bring the action is not likely to succeed.

Sec. 1002. Proper Plaintiff.

In a derivative action, the plaintiff must be a partner at (1) the time of bringing the action, and (2) at the time of the transaction of which he complains or his status as a partner must have devolved upon him by operation of law or pursuant to the terms of the partnership agreement from a person who was a partner at the time of the transaction.

Sec. 1003. Pleading.

In any derivative action, the complaint shall set forth with particularity the effort of the plaintiff to secure initiation of the action by a general partner having authority to do so or the reasons for not making the effort.

Sec. 1004. Expenses.

If a derivative action is successful, in whole or in part, or anything is received by the plaintiff as a result of a judgment, compromise, or settlement of an action or claim, the court may award the plaintiff reasonable expenses, including reasonable attorney's fees, and shall direct him to account to the limited partnership for the remainder of the proceeds so received by him.

Article 11

MISCELLANEOUS

Sec. 1101. Savings Clause.

Sec. 1102. Name of Act.

This Act may be cited as the Uniform Limited Partnership Act.

Sec. 1103. Construction and Application.

This Act shall be so construed and applied to effect its general purpose to make uniform the law with respect to the subject of this Act among states enacting it.

Sec. 1104. Rules for Cases Not Provided for in This Act.

In any case not provided for in this Act the provisions of the Uniform Partnership Act govern.

Sec. 1105. Act Repealed.

Except as affecting existing limited partnerships to the extent set forth in Section _____, the Act of [here designate the existing limited partnership act or acts] is hereby repealed.

SELECTED PROVISIONS OF THE 1985 AMENDMENTS TO THE REVISED UNIFORM LIMITED PARTNERSHIP ACT

* * *

§ 201. Certificate of Limited Partnership

(a) In order to form a limited partnership, a certificate of limited partnership must be executed and filed in the office of the Secretary of State. The certificate shall set forth:

(1) the name of the limited partnership;
(2) the address of the office and the name and address of the agent for service of process required to be maintained by Section 104;
(3) the name and the business address of each general partner;
(4) the latest date upon which the limited partnership is to dissolve; and
(5) any other matters the general partners determine to include therein.

(b) A limited partnership is formed at the time of the filing of the certificate of limited partnership in the office of the Secretary of State or at any later time specified in the certificate of limited partnership if, in either case, there has been substantial compliance with the requirements of this section.

§ 202. Amendment to Certificate

(a) A certificate of limited partnership is amended by filing a certificate of amendment thereto in the office of the Secretary of State. The certificate shall set forth:

(1) the name of the limited partnership;
(2) the date of filing the certificate; and
(3) the amendment to the certificate.

(b) Within 30 days after the happening of any of the following events, an amendment to a certificate of limited partnership reflecting the occurrence of the event or events shall be filed:

(1) the admission of a new general partner;
(2) the withdrawal of a general partner; or
(3) the continuance of the business under Section 801 after an event of withdrawal of a general partner.

(c) A general partner who becomes aware that any statement in a certificate of limited partnership was false when made or that any arrangements or other facts described have changed, making the certificate inaccurate in any respect, shall promptly amend the certificate.

(d) A certificate of limited partnership may be amended at any time for any other proper purpose the general partners determine.

(e) No person has any liability because an amendment to a certificate of limited partnership has not been filed to reflect the occurrence of any event referred to in subsection (b) of this section if the amendment is filed within the 30-day period specified in subsection (b).

(f) A restated certificate of limited partnership may be executed and filed in the same manner as a certificate of amendment.

* * *

§ 303. Liability to Third Parties

(a) Except as provided in subsection (d), a limited partner is not liable for the obligations of a limited partnership unless he [or she] is also a general partner or, in addition to the exercise of his [or her] rights and powers as a limited partner, he [or she] participates in the control of the business. However, if the limited partner participates in the control of the business, he [or she] is liable only to persons who transact business with the limited partnership reasonably believing, based upon the limited partner's conduct, that the limited partner is a general partner.

(b) A limited partner does not participate in the control of the business within the meaning of subsection (a) solely by doing one or more of the following:

(1) being a contractor for or an agent or employee of the limited partnership or of a general partner or being an officer, director, or shareholder of a general partner that is a corporation;

(2) consulting with and advising a general partner with respect to the business of the limited partnership;

(3) acting as surety for the limited partnership or guaranteeing or assuming one or more specific obligations of the limited partnership;

(4) taking any action required or permitted by law to bring or pursue a derivative action in the right of the limited partnership;

(5) requesting or attending a meeting of partners;

(6) proposing, approving, or disapproving, by voting or otherwise, one or more of the following matters:

(i) the dissolution and winding up of the limited partnership;

(ii) the sale, exchange, lease, mortgage, pledge, or other transfer of all or substantially all of the assets of the limited partnership;

(iii) the incurrence of indebtedness by the limited partnership other than in the ordinary course of its business;

(iv) a change in the nature of the business;

(v) the admission or removal of a general partner;

(vi) the admission or removal of a limited partner;

(vii) a transaction involving an actual or potential conflict of interest between a general partner and the limited partnership or the limited partners;

(viii) an amendment to the partnership agreement or certificate of limited partnership; or

(ix) matters related to the business of the limited partnership not otherwise enumerated in this subsection (b), which the partnership agreement states in writing may be subject to the approval or disapproval of limited partners;

(7) winding up the limited partnership pursuant to Section 803; or

(8) exercising any right or power permitted to limited partners under this [Act] and not specifically enumerated in this subsection (b).

(c) The enumeration in subsection (b) does not mean that the possession or exercise of any other powers by a limited partner constitutes participation by him [or her] in the business of the limited partnership.

(d) A limited partner who knowingly permits his [or her] name to be used in the name of the limited partnership, except under circumstances permitted by Section 102(2), is liable to creditors who extend credit to the limited partnership without actual knowledge that the limited partner is not a general partner.

§ 304. Person Erroneously Believing Himself [or Herself] Limited Partner

(a) Except as provided in subsection (b), a person who makes a contribution to a business enterprise and erroneously but in good faith believes that he [or she] has become a limited partner in the enterprise is not a general partner in the enterprise and is not bound by its obligations by reason of making the contribution, receiving distributions from the enterprise, or exercising any rights of a limited partner, if, on ascertaining the mistake, he [or she]:

(1) causes an appropriate certificate of limited partnership or a certificate of amendment to be executed and filed; or

(2) withdraws from future equity participation in the enterprise by executing and filing in the office of the Secretary of State a certificate declaring withdrawal under this section.

(b) A person who makes a contribution of the kind described in subsection (a) is liable as a general partner to any third party who transacts business with the enterprise (i) before the person withdraws and an appropriate certificate is filed to show withdrawal, or (ii) before an appropriate certificate is filed to show that he [or she] is not a general partner, but in either case only if the third party actually believed in good faith that the person was a general partner at the time of the transaction.

* * *

§ 401. Admission of Additional General Partners

After the filing of a limited partnership's original certificate of limited partnership, additional general partners may be admitted as provided in writing in the partnership agreement or, if the partnership agreement does not provide in writing for the admission of additional general partners, with the written consent of all partners.

* * *

§ 502. Liability for Contribution

(a) A promise by a limited partner to contribute to the limited partnership is not enforceable unless set out in a writing signed by the limited partner.

(b) Except as provided in the partnership agreement, a partner is obligated to the limited partnership to perform any enforceable promise to contribute cash or property or to perform services, even if he [or she] is unable to perform because of death, disability, or any other reason. If a partner does not make the required contribution of property or services, he [or she] is obligated at the option of the limited partnership to contribute cash equal to that portion of the value, as stated in the partnership records required to be kept pursuant to Section 105, of the stated contribution which has not been made.

(c) Unless otherwise provided in the partnership agreement, the obligation of a partner to make a contribution or return money or other property paid or distributed in violation of this [Act] may be compromised only by consent of all partners. Notwithstanding the compromise, a creditor of a limited partnership who extends credit, or, otherwise acts in reliance on that obligation after the partner signs a writing which reflects the obligation and before the amendment or cancellation thereof to reflect the compromise may enforce the original obligation.

§ 503. Sharing of Profits and Losses

The profits and losses of a limited partnership shall be allocated among the partners, and among classes of partners, in the manner provided in writing in the partnership agreement. If the partnership agreement does not so provide in writing, profits and losses shall be allocated on the basis of the value, as stated in the partnership records required to be kept pursuant to Section 105, of the contributions made by each partner to the extent they have been received by the partnership and have not been returned.

§ 504. Sharing of Distributions

Distributions of cash or other assets of a limited partnership shall be allocated among the partners and among classes of partners in the manner provided in writing in the partnership agreement. If the partnership agreement does not so provide in writing, distributions shall be made on the basis of the value, as stated in the partnership records required to be kept pursuant to Section 105, of the contributions made by each partner to the extent they have been received by the partnership and have not been returned.

* * *

§ 603. Withdrawal of Limited Partner

A limited partner may withdraw from a limited partnership at the time or upon the happening of events specified in writing in the partnership agreement. If the agreement does not specify in writing the time or the events upon the happening of which a limited partner may withdraw or a definite time for the dissolution and winding up of the limited partnership, a limited partner may withdraw upon not less than six months' prior written notice to each general partner at his [other] address on the books of the limited partnership at its office in this State.

* * *

§ 704. Right of Assignee to Become Limited Partner

(a) An assignee of a partnership interest, including an assignee of a general partner, may become a limited partner if and to the extent that (i) the assignor gives the assignee that right in accordance with authority described in the partnership agreement, or (ii) all other partners consent.

(b) An assignee who has become a limited partner has, to the extent assigned, the rights and powers, and is subject to the restrictions and liabilities, of a limited partner under the partnership agreement and this [Act]. An assignee who becomes a limited partner also is liable for the obligations of his [or her] assignor to make and return contributions as provided in Articles 5 and 6. However, the assignee is not obligated for liabilities unknown to the assignee at the time he [or she] became a limited partner.

(c) If an assignee of a partnership interest becomes a limited partner, the assignor is not released from his [or her] liability to the limited partnership under Sections 207 and 502.

* * *

APPENDIX G
THE MODEL BUSINESS CORPORATION ACT

§ 1. Short Title*

This Act shall be known and may be cited as the "_____† Business Corporation Act."

§ 2. Definitions

As used in this Act, unless the context otherwise requires, the term:

(a) "Corporation" or "domestic corporation" means a corporation for profit subject to the provisions of this Act, except a foreign corporation.

(b) "Foreign corporation" means a corporation for profit organized under laws other than the laws of this State for a purpose or purposes for which a corporation may be organized under this Act.

(c) "Articles of incorporation" means the original or restated articles of incorporation or articles of consolidation and all amendments thereto including articles of merger.

(d) "Shares" means the units into which the proprietary interests in a corporation are divided.

(e) "Subscriber" means one who subscribes for shares in a corporation, whether before or after incorporation.

(f) "Shareholder" means one who is a holder of record of shares in a corporation. If the articles of incorporation or the by-laws so provide, the board of directors may adopt by resolution a procedure whereby a shareholder of the corporation may certify in writing to the corporation that all or a portion of the shares registered in the name of such shareholder are held for the account of a specified person or persons. The resolution shall set forth (1) the classification of shareholder who may certify, (2) the purpose or purposes for which the certification may be made, (3) the form of certification and information to be contained therein, (4) if the certification is with respect to a record date or closing of the stock transfer books within which the certification must be received by the corporation and (5) such other provisions with respect to the procedure as are deemed necessary or desirable. Upon receipt by the corporation of a certification complying with the procedure, the persons specified in the certification shall be deemed, for the purpose or purposes set forth in the certification, to be the holders of record of the number of shares specified in place of the shareholder making the certification.

(g) "Authorized shares" means the shares of all classes which the corporation is authorized to issue.

(h) "Employee" includes officers but not directors. A director may accept duties which make him also an employee.

(i) "Distribution" means a direct or indirect transfer of money or other property (except its own shares) or incurrence of indebtedness, by a corporation to or for the benefit of any of its shareholders in respect of any of its shares, whether by dividend or by purchase, redemption or other acquisition of its shares, or otherwise.

(j) "Stated capital" means, at any particular time, the sum of (1) the par value of all shares of the corporation having a par value that have been issued, (2) the amount of the consideration received by the corporation for all shares of the corporation without par value that have been issued, except such part of the consideration therefor as may have been allocated to capital surplus in a manner permitted by law, and (3) such amounts not

---

*[By the Editor] The Model Business Corporation Act prepared by the Committee on Corporate Laws (Section of Corporation, Banking and Business Law) of the American Bar Association was originally patterned after the Illinois Business Corporation Act of 1933. It was first published as a complete act in 1950. In subsequent years several revisions, addenda and optional or alternative provisions were added. The Act was substantially revised and renumbered in 1979.

This Act should be distinguished from the Model Business Corporation Act promulgated in 1928 by the Commissioners on Uniform State Laws under the name "Uniform Business Corporation Act" and renamed Model Business Corporation Act in 1943. This Uniform Act was withdrawn in 1957. The Model Business Corporation Act has been influential in the codification of corporation statutes in more than 35 states. However, there is no state that has totally adopted it in its current form. Moreover, since the Model Act itself has been substantially modified from time to time, there is considerable variation among the statutes of the states that used this Act as a model.

† Supply name of State.

included in clauses (1) and (2) of this paragraph as have been transferred to stated capital of the corporation, whether upon the issue of shares as a share dividend or otherwise, minus all reductions from such sum as have been effected in a manner permitted by law. Irrespective of the manner of designation thereof by the laws under which a foreign corporation is organized, the stated capital of a foreign corporation shall be determined on the same basis and in the same manner as the stated capital of a domestic corporation, for the purpose of computing fees, franchise taxes and other charges imposed by this Act.

(k) "Surplus" means the excess of the net assets of a corporation over its stated capital.

(l) "Earned surplus" means the portion of the surplus of a corporation equal to the balance of its net profits, income, gains and losses from the date of incorporation, or from the latest date when a deficit was eliminated by an application of its capital surplus or stated capital or otherwise, after deducting subsequent distributions to shareholders and transfers to stated capital and capital surplus to the extent such distributions and transfers are made out of earned surplus. Earned surplus shall include also any portion of surplus allocated to earned surplus in mergers, consolidations or acquisitions of all or substantially all of the outstanding shares or of the property and assets of another corporation, domestic or foreign.

(m) "Capital surplus" means the entire surplus of a corporation other than its earned surplus.

(n) "Insolvent" means inability of a corporation to pay its debts as they become due in the usual course of its business.

(o) "Employee" includes officers but not directors. A director may accept duties which make him also an employee.

§ 3. Purposes

Corporations may be organized under this Act for any lawful purpose or purposes, except for the purpose of banking or insurance.

§ 4. General Powers

Each corporation shall have power:

(a) To have perpetual succession by its corporate name unless a limited period of duration is stated in its articles of incorporation.

(b) To sue and be sued, complain and defend, in its corporate name.

(c) To have a corporate seal which may be altered at pleasure, and to use the same by causing it, or a facsimile thereof, to be impressed or affixed or in any other manner reproduced.

(d) To purchase, take, receive, lease, or otherwise acquire, own, hold, improve, use and otherwise deal in and with, real or personal property, or any interest therein, wherever situated.

(e) To sell, convey, mortgage, pledge, lease, exchange, transfer and otherwise dispose of all or any part of its property and assets.

(f) To lend money and use its credit to assist its employees.

(g) To purchase, take, receive, subscribe for, or otherwise acquire, own, hold, vote, use, employ, sell, mortgage, lend, pledge, or otherwise dispose of, and otherwise use and deal in and with, shares or other interests in, or obligations of, other domestic or foreign corporations, associations, partnerships or individuals, or direct or indirect obligations of the United States or of any other government, state, territory, governmental district or municipality or of any instrumentality thereof.

(h) To make contracts and guarantees and incur liabilities, borrow money at such rates of interest as the corporation may determine, issue its notes, bonds, and other obligations, and secure any of its obligations by mortgage or pledge of all or any of its property, franchises and income.

(i) To lend money for its corporate purposes, invest and reinvest its funds, and take and hold real and personal property as security for the payment of funds so loaned or invested.

(j) To conduct its business, carry on its operations and have offices and exercise the powers granted by this Act, within or without this State.

(k) To elect or appoint officers and agents of the corporation, and define their duties and fix their compensation.

(l) To make and alter by-laws, not inconsistent with its articles of incorporation or with the laws of this State, for the administration and regulation of the affairs of the corporation.

(m) To make donations for the public welfare or for charitable, scientific or educational purposes.

(n) To transact any lawful business which the board of directors shall find will be in aid of governmental policy.

(o) To pay pensions and establish pension plans, pension trusts, profit sharing plans, stock bonus plans, stock option plans and other incentive plans for any or all of its directors, officers and employees.

(p) To be a promoter, partner, member, associate, or manager of any partnership, joint venture, trust or other enterprise.

(q) To have and exercise all powers necessary or convenient to effect its purposes.

§ 5. Indemnification of Officers, Directors, Employees and Agents

(a) A corporation shall have power to indemnify any person who was or is a party or is threatened to be made a party to any threatened, pending or completed action, suit or proceeding, whether civil, criminal, administrative or investigative (other than an action by or in the right of the corporation) by reason of the fact that he is or was a director, officer, employee or agent of the corporation, or is or was serving at the request of the corporation as a director, officer, employee or agent of another corporation, partnership, joint venture, trust or other enterprise, against expenses (including attorney's fees), judgments, fines and amounts paid in settlement actually and reasonably incurred by him in connection with such action, suit or proceeding if he acted in good faith and in a manner he reasonably believed to be in or not opposed to the best interests of the corporation, and, with respect to any criminal action or proceeding, had no reasonable cause to believe his conduct was unlawful. The termination of any action, suit or proceeding by judgment, order, settlement, conviction, or upon a plea of nolo contendere or its equivalent, shall not, of itself, create a presumption that the person did not act in good faith and in a manner which he reasonably believed to be in or not opposed to the best interest of the corporation, and, with respect to any criminal action or proceeding, had reasonable cause to believe that his conduct was unlawful.

(b) A corporation shall have power to indemnify any person who was or is a party or is threatened to be made a party to any threatened, pending or completed action or suit by or in the right of the corporation to procure a judgment in its favor by reason of the fact that he is or was a director, officer, employee or agent of the corporation, or is or was serving at the request of the corporation as a director, officer, employee or agent of another corporation, partnership, joint venture, trust or other enterprise against expenses (including attorney's fees) actually and reasonably incurred by him in connection with the defense or settlement of such action or suit if he acted in good faith and in a manner he reasonably believed to be in or not opposed to the best interests of the corporation and except that no indemnification shall be made in respect of any claim, issue or matter as to which such person shall have been adjudged to be liable for negligence or misconduct in the performance of his duty to the corporation unless and only to the extent that the court in which such action or suit was brought shall determine upon application that, despite the adjudication of liability but in view of all circumstances of the case, such person is fairly and reasonably entitled to indemnity for such expenses which such court shall deem proper.

(c) To the extent that a director, officer, employee or agent of a corporation has been successful on the merits or otherwise in defense of any action, suit or proceeding referred to in subsections (a) or (b), or in defense of any claim, issue or matter therein, he shall be indemnified against expenses (including attorneys' fees) actually and reasonably incurred by him in connection therewith.

(d) Any indemnification under subsections (a) or (b) (unless ordered by a court) shall be made by the corporation only as authorized in the specific case upon a determination that indemnification of the director, officer, employee or agent is proper in the circumstances because he has met the applicable standard of conduct set forth in subsections (a) or (b). Such determination shall be made (1) by the board of directors by a majority vote of a quorum consisting of directors who were not parties to such action, suit or proceeding, or (2) if such a quorum is not obtainable, or, even if obtainable a quorum of disin-

terested directors so directs, by independent legal counsel in a written opinion, or (3) by the shareholders.

(e) Expenses (including attorneys' fees) incurred in defending a civil or criminal action, suit or proceeding may be paid by the corporation in advance of the final disposition of such action, suit or proceeding as authorized in the manner provided in subsection (d) upon receipt of an undertaking by or on behalf of the director, officer, employee or agent to repay such amount unless it shall ultimately be determined that he is entitled to be indemnified by the corporation as authorized in this section.

(f) The indemnification provided by this section shall not be deemed exclusive of any other rights to which those indemnified may be entitled under any by-law, agreement, vote of shareholders or disinterested directors or otherwise, both as to action in his official capacity and as to action in another capacity while holding such office, and shall continue as to a person who has ceased to be a director, officer, employee or agent and shall inure to the benefit of the heirs, executors and administrators of such a person.

(g) A corporation shall have power to purchase and maintain insurance on behalf of any person who is or was a director, officer, employee or agent of the corporation, or is or was serving at the request of the corporation as a director, officer, employee or agent of another corporation, partnership, joint venture, trust or other enterprise against any liability asserted against him and incurred by him in any such capacity or arising out of his status as such, whether or not the corporation would have the power to indemnify him against such liability under the provisions of this section.

§ 6. Power of Corporation to Acquire Its Own Shares

A corporation shall have the power to acquire its own shares. All of its own shares acquired by a corporation shall, upon acquisition, constitute authorized but unissued shares, unless the articles of incorporation provide that they shall not be reissued, in which case the authorized shares shall be reduced by the number of shares acquired.

If the number of authorized shares is reduced by an acquisition, the corporation shall, not later than the time it files its next annual report under this Act with the Secretary of State, file a statement of cancellation showing the reduction in the authorized shares. The statement of cancellation shall be executed in duplicate by the corporation by its president or a vice president and by its secretary or an assistant secretary, and verified by one of the officers signing such statement, and shall set forth:

(a) The name of the corporation.

(b) The number of acquired shares cancelled, itemized by classes and series.

(c) The aggregate number of authorized shares, itemized by classes and series, after giving effect to such cancellation.

Duplicate originals of such statement shall be delivered to the Secretary of State. If the Secretary of State finds that such statement conforms to law, he shall, when all fees and franchise taxes have been paid as in this Act prescribed:

(1) Endorse on each of such duplicate originals the word "Filed", and the month, day and year of the filing thereof.

(2) File one of such duplicate originals in his office.

(3) Return the other duplicate original to the corporation or its representative.

§ 7. Defense of Ultra Vires

No act of a corporation and no conveyance or transfer of real or personal property to or by a corporation shall be invalid by reason of the fact that the corporation was without capacity or power to do such act or to make or receive such conveyance or transfer, but such lack of capacity or power may be asserted:

(a) In a proceeding by a shareholder against the corporation to enjoin the doing of any act or the transfer of real or personal property by or to the corporation. If the unauthorized act or transfer sought to be enjoined is being, or is to be, performed or made pursuant to a contract to which the corporation is a party, the court may, if all of the parties to the contract are parties to the proceeding and if it deems the same to be equitable, set aside and enjoin the performance of such contract, and in so doing may allow to the corporation or to the other parties to the contract, as the case may be, compensation for the loss or damage sustained by either of them which may result from the action of the court in setting aside and enjoining the performance of such contract, but anticipated profits to be derived from the performance of the contract shall not be awarded by the court as a loss or damage sustained.

(b) In a proceeding by the corporation, whether acting directly or through a receiver, trustee, or other legal representative, or through shareholders in a representative suit, against the incumbent or former officers or directors of the corporation.

(c) In a proceeding by the Attorney General, as provided in this Act, to dissolve the corporation, or in a proceeding by the Attorney General to enjoin the corporation from the transaction of unauthorized business.

§ 8. Corporate Name

The corporate name:

(a) Shall contain the word "corporation," "company," "incorporated" or "limited," or shall contain an abbreviation of one of such words.

(b) Shall not contain any word or phrase which indicates or implies that it is organized for any purpose other than one or more of the purposes contained in its articles of incorporation.

(c) Shall not be the same as, or deceptively similar to, the name of any domestic corporation existing under the laws of this State or any foreign corporation authorized to transact business in this State, or a name the exclusive right to which is, at the time, reserved in the manner provided in this Act, or the name of a corporation which has in effect a registration of its corporate name as provided in this Act, except that this provision shall not apply if the applicant files with the Secretary of State either of the following: (1) the written consent of such other corporation or holder of a reserved or registered name to use the same or deceptively similar name and one or more words are added to make such name distinguishable from such other name, or (2) a certified copy of a final decree of a court of competent jurisdiction establishing the prior right of the applicant to the use of such name in this State.

A corporation with which another corporation, domestic or foreign, is merged, or which is formed by the reorganization or consolidation of one or more domestic or foreign corporations or upon a sale, lease or other disposition to or exchange with, a domestic corporation of all or substantially all the assets of another corporation, domestic or foreign, including its name, may have the same name as that used in this State by any of such corporations if such other corporation was organized under the laws of, or is authorized to transact business in, this State.

§ 9. Reserved Name

The exclusive right to the use of a corporate name may be reserved by:

(a) Any person intending to organize a corporation under this Act.

(b) Any domestic corporation intending to change its name.

(c) Any foreign corporation intending to make application for a certificate of authority to transact business in this State.

(d) Any foreign corporation authorized to transact business in this State and intending to change its name.

(e) Any person intending to organize a foreign corporation and intending to have such corporation make application for a certificate of authority to transact business in this State.

The reservation shall be made by filing with the Secretary of State an application to reserve a specified corporate name, executed by the applicant. If the Secretary of State finds that the name is available for corporate use, he shall reserve the same for the exclusive use of the applicant for a period of one hundred and twenty days.

The right to the exclusive use of a specified corporate name so reserved may be transferred to any person or corporation by filing in the office of the Secretary of State a notice of such transfer, executed by the applicant for whom the name was reserved, and specifying the name and address of the transferee.

§ 10. Registered Name

Any corporation organized and existing under the laws of any state or territory of the United States may register its corporate name under this Act, provided its corporate name is not the same as, or deceptively similar to, the name of any domestic corporation existing under the laws of this State, or the name of any foreign corporation authorized to transact business in this State, or any corporate name reserved or registered under this Act.

Such registration shall be made by:

(a) Filing with the Secretary of State (1) an application for registration executed by the corporation by an officer thereof, setting forth the name of the corporation, the state or territory under the laws of which it is incorporated, the date of its incorporation, a statement that it is carrying on or doing business, and a brief statement of the business in which it is engaged, and (2) a certificate setting forth that such corporation is in good standing under the laws of the state or territory wherein it is organized, executed by the Secretary of State of such state or territory or by such other official as may have custody of the records pertaining to corporations, and

(b) Paying to the Secretary of State a registration fee in the amount of _____ for each month, or fraction thereof, between the date of filing such application and December 31st of the calendar year in which such application is filed.

Such registration shall be effective until the close of the calendar year in which the application for registration is filed.

§ 11. Renewal of Registered Name

A corporation which has in effect a registration of its corporate name, may renew such registration from year to year by annually filing an application for renewal setting forth the facts required to be set forth in an original application for registration and a certificate of good standing as required for the original registration and by paying a fee of _____. A renewal application may be filed between the first day of October and the thirty-first day of December in each year, and shall extend the registration for the following calendar year.

§ 12. Registered Office and Registered Agent

Each corporation shall have and continuously maintain in this State:

(a) A registered office which may be, but need not be, the same as its place of business.
(b) A registered agent, which agent may be either an individual resident in this State whose business office is identical with such registered office, or a domestic corporation, or a foreign corporation authorized to transact business in this State, having a business office identical with such registered office.

§ 13. Change of Registered Office or Registered Agent

A corporation may change its registered office or change its registered agent, or both, upon filing in the office of the Secretary of State a statement setting forth:

(a) The name of the corporation.
(b) The address of its then registered office.
(c) If the address of its registered office is to be changed, the address to which the registered office is to be changed.
(d) The name of its then registered agent.
(e) If its registered agent is to be changed, the name of its successor registered agent.
(f) That the address of its registered office and the address of the business office of its registered agent, as changed, will be identical.
(g) That such change was authorized by resolution duly adopted by its board of directors.

Such statement shall be executed by the corporation by its president, or a vice president, and verified by him, and delivered to the Secretary of State. If the Secretary of State finds that such statement conforms to the provisions of this Act, he shall file such statement in his office, and upon such filing the change of address of the registered office, or the appointment of a new registered agent, or both, as the case may be, shall become effective.

Any registered agent of a corporation may resign as such agent upon filing a written notice thereof, executed in duplicate, with the Secretary of State, who shall forthwith mail a copy thereof to the corporation at its registered office. The appointment of such agent shall terminate upon the expiration of thirty days after receipt of such notice by the Secretary of State.

If a registered agent changes his or its business address to another place within the same _____,* he or it may change such address and the address of the registered office of any corporation of which he or it is registered agent by filing a statement as required above except that it need be signed only by the registered agent and need not be responsive to (e) or (g) and must recite that a copy of the statement has been mailed to the corporation.

§ 14. Service of Process on Corporation

The registered agent so appointed by a corporation shall be an agent of such corporation upon whom any process, notice or demand required or permitted by law to be served upon the corporation may be served.

Whenever a corporation shall fail to appoint or maintain a registered agent in this State, or whenever its registered agent cannot with reasonable diligence be found at the registered office, then the Secretary of State shall be an agent of such corporation upon whom any such process,

*Supply designation of jurisdiction, such as county, etc., in accordance with local practice.

notice, or demand may be served. Service on the Secretary of State of any such process, notice, or demand shall be made by delivering to and leaving with him, or with any clerk having charge of the corporation department of his office, duplicate copies of such process, notice or demand. In the event any such process, notice or demand is served on the Secretary of State, he shall immediately cause one of the copies thereof to be forwarded by registered mail, addressed to the corporation at its registered office. Any service so had on the Secretary of State shall be returnable in not less than thirty days.

The Secretary of State shall keep a record of all processes, notices and demands served upon him under this section, and shall record therein the time of such service and his action with reference thereto.

Nothing herein contained shall limit or affect the right to serve any process, notice or demand required or permitted by law to be served upon a corporation in any other manner now or hereafter permitted by law.

§ 15. Authorized Shares

Each corporation shall have power to create and issue the number of shares stated in its articles of incorporation. Such shares may be divided into one or more classes with such designations, preferences, limitations, and relative rights as shall be stated in the articles of incorporation. The articles of incorporation may limit or deny the voting rights of or provide special voting rights for the shares of any class to the extent not inconsistent with the provisions of this Act.

Without limiting the authority herein contained, a corporation, when so provided in its articles of incorporation, may issue shares of preferred or special classes:

(a) Subject to the right of the corporation to redeem any of such shares at the price fixed by the articles of incorporation for the redemption thereof.
(b) Entitling the holders thereof to cumulative, noncumulative or partially cumulative dividends.
(c) Having preference over any other class or classes of shares as to the payment of dividends.
(d) Having preference in the assets of the corporation over any other class or classes of shares upon the voluntary or involuntary liquidation of the corporation.
(e) Convertible into shares of any other class or into shares of any series of the same or any other class, except a class having prior or superior rights and preferences as to dividends or distribution of assets upon liquidation.

§ 16. Issuance of Shares of Preferred or Special Classes in Series

If the articles of incorporation so provide, the shares of any preferred or special class may be divided into and issued in series. If the shares of any such class are to be issued in series, then each series shall be so designated as to distinguish the shares thereof from the shares of all other series and classes. Any or all of the series of any such class

and the variations in the relative rights and preferences as between different series may be fixed and determined by the articles of incorporation, but all shares of the same class shall be identical except as to the following relative rights and preferences, as to which there may be variations between different series:

(A) The rate of dividend.
(B) Whether shares may be redeemed and, if so, the redemption price and the terms and conditions of redemption.
(C) The amount payable upon shares in the event of voluntary and involuntary liquidation.
(D) Sinking fund provisions, if any, for the redemption or purchase of shares.
(E) The terms and conditions, if any, on which shares may be converted.
(F) Voting rights, if any.

If the articles of incorporation shall expressly vest authority in the board of directors, then, to the extent that the articles of incorporation shall not have established series and fixed and determined the variations in the relative rights and preferences as between series, the board of directors shall have authority to divide any or all of such classes into series and, within the limitations set forth in this section and in the articles of incorporation, fix and determine the relative rights and preferences of the shares of any series so established.

In order for the board of directors to establish a series, where authority so to do is contained in the articles of incorporation, the board of directors shall adopt a resolution setting forth the designation of the series and fixing and determining the relative rights and preferences thereof, or so much thereof as shall not be fixed and determined by the articles of incorporation.

Prior to the issue of any shares of a series established by resolution adopted by the board of directors, the corporation shall file in the office of the Secretary of State a statement setting forth:

(a) The name of the corporation.
(b) A copy of the resolution establishing and designating the series, and fixing and determining the relative rights and preferences thereof.
(c) The date of adoption of such resolution.
(d) That such resolution was duly adopted by the board of directors.

Such statement shall be executed in duplicate by the corporation by its president or a vice president and by its secretary or an assistant secretary, and verified by one of the officers signing such statement, and shall be delivered to the Secretary of State. If the Secretary of State finds that such statement conforms to law, he shall, when all franchise taxes and fees have been paid as in this Act prescribed:

(1) Endorse on each of such duplicate originals the word "Filed," and the month, day, and year of the filing thereof.

(2) File one of such duplicate originals in his office.
(3) Return the other duplicate original to the corporation or its representative.

Upon the filing of such statement by the Secretary of State, the resolution establishing and designating the series and fixing and determining the relative rights and preferences thereof shall become effective and shall constitute an amendment of the articles of incorporation.

§ 17. Subscriptions for Shares

A subscription for shares of a corporation to be organized shall be irrevocable for a period of six months, unless otherwise provided by the terms of the subscription agreement or unless all of the subscribers consent to the revocation of such subscription.

Unless otherwise provided in the subscription agreement, subscriptions for shares, whether made before or after the organization of a corporation, shall be paid in full at such time, or in such installments and at such times, as shall be determined by the board of directors. Any call made by the board of directors for payment on subscriptions shall be uniform as to all shares of the same class or as to all shares of the same series, as the case may be. In case of default in the payment of any installment or call when such payment is due, the corporation may proceed to collect the amount due in the same manner as any debt due the corporation. The by-laws may prescribe other penalties for failure to pay installments or calls that may become due, but no penalty working a forfeiture of a subscription, or of the amounts paid thereon, shall be declared as against any subscriber unless the amount due thereon shall remain unpaid for a period of twenty days after written demand has been made therefor. If mailed, such written demand shall be deemed to be made when deposited in the United States mail in a sealed envelope addressed to the subscriber at his last post-office address known to the corporation, with postage thereon prepaid. In the event of the sale of any shares by reason of any forfeiture, the excess of proceeds realized over the amount due and unpaid on such shares shall be paid to the delinquent subscriber or to his legal representative.

§ 18. Issuance for Shares

Subject to any restrictions in the articles of incorporation:

(a) Shares may be issued for such consideration as shall be authorized by the board of directors establishing a price (in money or other consideration) or a minimum price or general formula or method by which the price will be determined; and
(b) Upon authorization by the board of directors, the corporation may issue its own shares in exchange for or in conversion of its outstanding shares, or distribute its own shares, pro rata to its shareholders or the shareholders of one or more classes or series, to effectuate stock dividends or splits, and any such transaction shall not require consideration; provided, that no such issuance of

shares of any class or series shall be made to the holders of shares of any other class or series unless it is either expressly provided for in the articles of incorporation, or is authorized by an affirmative vote or the written consent of the holders of at least a majority of the outstanding shares of the class or series in which the distribution is to be made.

§ 19. Payment for Shares

The consideration for the issuance of shares may be paid, in whole or in part, in cash, in other property, tangible or intangible, or in labor or services actually performed for the corporation. When payment of the consideration for which shares are to be issued shall have been received by the corporation, such shares shall be nonassessable.

Neither promissory notes nor future services shall constitute payment or part payment for the issuance of shares of a corporation.

In the absence of fraud in the transaction, the judgment of the board of directors or the shareholders, as the case may be, as to the value of the consideration received for shares shall be conclusive.

§ 20. Stock Rights and Options

Subject to any provisions in respect thereof set forth in its articles of incorporation, a corporation may create and issue, whether or not in connection with the issuance and sale of any of its shares or other securities, rights or options entitling the holders thereof to purchase from the corporation shares of any class or classes. Such rights or options shall be evidenced in such manner as the board of directors shall approve and, subject to the provisions of the articles of incorporation, shall set forth the terms upon which, the time or times within which and the price or prices at which such shares may be purchased from the corporation upon the exercise of any such right or option. If such rights or options are to be issued to directors, officers or employees as such of the corporation or of any subsidiary thereof, and not to the shareholders generally, their issuance shall be approved by the affirmative vote of the holders of a majority of the shares entitled to vote thereon or shall be authorized by and consistent with a plan approved or ratified by such a vote of shareholders. In the absence of fraud in the transaction, the judgment of the board of directors as to the adequacy of the consideration received for such rights or options shall be conclusive.

§ 21. Determination of Amount of Stated Capital [Repealed]

§ 22. Expenses of Organization, Reorganization and Financing

The reasonable charges and expenses of organization or reorganization of a corporation, and the reasonable expenses of and compensation for the sale or underwriting of its shares, may be paid or allowed by such corporation out of the consideration received by it in payment for its shares without thereby rendering such shares not fully paid or assessable.

§ 23. Shares Represented by Certificates and Uncertified Shares

The shares of a corporation shall be represented by certificates or shall be uncertificated shares. Certificates shall by signed by the chairman or vice-chairman of the board of directors or the president or a vice president and by the treasurer or an assistant treasurer or the secretary or an assistant secretary of the corporation, and may be sealed with the seal of the corporation or a facsimile thereof. Any of or all the signatures [of the president or vice president and the secretary or assistant secretary] upon a certificate may be a facsimile. [s if the certificate is manually signed on behalf of a transfer agent or a registrar, other than the corporation itself or an employee of the corporation.] In case any officer, transfer agent or registrar who has signed or whose facsimile signature has been placed upon such certificate shall have ceased to be such officer, transfer agent or registrar before such certificate is issued, it may be issued by the corporation with the same effect as if he were such officer, transfer agent or registrar at the date of its issue.

Every certificate representing shares issued by a corporation which is authorized to issue shares of more than one class shall set forth upon the face or back of the certificate, or shall state that the corporation will furnish to any shareholder upon request and without charge, a full statement of the designations, preferences, limitations, and relative rights of the shares of each class authorized to be issued, and if the corporation is authorized to issue any preferred or special class in series, the variations in the relative rights and preferences between the shares of each such series so far as the same have been fixed and determined and the authority of the board of directors to fix and determine the relative rights and preferences of subsequent series.

Each certificate representing shares shall state upon the face thereof:

(a) That the corporation is organized under the laws of this State.
(b) The name of the person to whom issued.
(c) The number and class of shares, and the designation of the series, if any, which such certificate represents.
(d) The par value of each share represented by such certificate, or a statement that the shares are without par value.

No certificate shall be issued for any share until such share is fully paid.

Unless otherwise provided by the articles of incorporation or by-laws, the board of directors of a corporation may provide by resolution that some or all of any or all classes and series of its shares shall be uncertificated shares, provided that such resolution shall not apply to shares represented by a certificate until such certificate is surrendered to the corporation. Within a reasonable time after the issuance or transfer of uncertificated shares, the corporation shall send to the registered owner thereof a written notice containing the information required to be set forth or stated on certificates pursuant to the second and third paragraphs of this section. Except as otherwise expressly provided by law, the rights and obligations of the holders of uncertificated shares and the rights and obligations of the holders of certificates representing shares of the same class and series shall be identical.

§ 24. Fractional Shares

A corporation may (1) issue fractions of a share, either represented by a certificate or uncertificated, (2) arrange for the disposition of fractional interests by those entitled thereto, (3) pay in money the fair value of fractions of a share as of a time when those entitled to receive such fractions are determined, or (4) issue scrip in registered or bearer form which shall entitle the holder to receive a certificate for a full share or an uncertificated full share upon the surrender of such scrip aggregating a full share. A certificate for a fractional share or an uncertificated fractional share shall, but scrip shall not unless otherwise provided therein, entitle the holder to exercise voting rights, to receive dividends thereon, and to participate in any of the assets of the corporation in the event of liquidation. The board of directors may cause scrip to be issued subject to the condition that it shall become void if not exchanged for certificates representing full shares or uncertificated full shares before a specified date, or subject to the condition that the shares for which scrip is exchangeable may be sold by the corporation and the proceeds thereof distributed to the holders of scrip, or subject to any other conditions which the board of directors may deem advisable.

§ 25. Liability of Subscribers and Shareholders

A holder of or subscriber to shares of a corporation shall be under no obligation to the corporation or its creditors with respect to such shares other than the obligation to pay to the corporation the full consideration for which such shares were issued or to be issued.

Any person becoming an assignee or transferee of shares or of a subscription for shares in good faith and without knowledge or notice that the full consideration therefor has not been paid shall not be personally liable to the corporation or its creditors for any unpaid portion of such consideration.

An executor, administrator, conservator, guardian, trustee, assignee for the benefit of creditors, or receiver shall not be personally liable to the corporation as a holder of or subscriber to shares of a corporation but the estate and funds in his hands shall be so liable.

No pledgee or other holder of shares as collateral security shall be personally liable as a shareholder.

§ 26. Shareholders' Preemptive Rights

The shareholders of a corporation shall have no preemptive right to acquire unissued shares of the corporation, or securities of the corporation convertible into or carrying a right to subscribe to or acquire shares, except to the extent, if any, that such right is provided in the articles of incorporation.

§ 26A. Shareholders' Preemptive Rights [Alternative]

Except to the extent limited or denied by this section or by the articles of incorporation, shareholders shall have a preemptive right to acquire unissued shares or securities convertible into such shares or carrying a right to subscribe to or acquire shares.

Unless otherwise provided in the articles of incorporation,

(a) No preemptive right shall exist

(1) to acquire any shares issued to directors, officers or employees pursuant to approval by the affirmative vote of the holders of a majority of the shares entitled to vote thereon or when authorized by and consistent with a plan theretofore approved by such a vote of shareholders; or

(2) to acquire any shares sold otherwise than for money.

(b) Holders of shares of any class that is preferred or limited as to dividends or assets shall not be entitled to any preemptive right.

(c) Holders of shares of common stock shall not be entitled to any preemptive right to shares of any class that is preferred or limited as to dividends or assets or to any obligations, unless convertible into shares of common stock or carrying a right to subscribe to or acquire shares of common stock.

(d) Holders of common stock without voting power shall have no preemptive right to shares of common stock with voting power.

(e) The preemptive right shall be only an opportunity to acquire shares or other securities under such terms and conditions as the board of directors may fix for the purpose of providing a fair and reasonable opportunity for the exercise of such right.

§ 27. By-Laws

The initial by-laws of a corporation shall be adopted by its board of directors. The power to alter, amend or repeal the by-laws or adopt new by-laws, subject to repeal or change by action of the shareholders, shall be vested in the board of directors unless reserved to the shareholders by the articles of incorporation. The by-laws may contain any provisions for the regulation and management of the affairs of the corporation not inconsistent with law or the articles of incorporation.

§ 27A. By-Laws and Other Powers in Emergency [Optional]

The board of directors of any corporation may adopt emergency by-laws, subject to repeal or change by action of the shareholders, which shall, notwithstanding any different provision elsewhere in this Act or in the articles of incorporation or by-laws, be operative during any emergency in the conduct of the business of the corporation resulting from an attack on the United States or any nuclear or atomic disaster. The emergency by-laws may make any provision that may be practical and necessary for the circumstances of the emergency, including provisions that:

(a) A meeting of the board of directors may be called by any officer or director in such manner and under such conditions as shall be prescribed in the emergency by-laws;

(b) The director or directors in attendance at the meeting, or any greater number fixed by the emergency by-laws, shall constitute a quorum; and

(c) The officers or other persons designated on a list approved by the board of directors before the emergency, all in such order of priority and subject to such conditions, and for such period of time (not longer than reasonably necessary after the termination of the emergency) as may be provided in the emergency by-laws or in the resolution approving the list shall, to the extent required to provide a quorum at any meeting of the board of directors, be deemed directors for such meeting.

The board of directors, either before or during any such emergency, may provide, and from time to time modify, lines of succession in the event that during such an emergency any or all officers or agents of the corporation shall for any reason be rendered incapable of discharging their duties.

The board of directors, either before or during any such emergency, may, effective in the emergency, change the head office or designate several alternative head offices or regional offices, or authorize the officers so to do.

To the extent not inconsistent with any emergency by-laws so adopted, the by-laws of the corporation shall remain in effect during any such emergency and upon its termination the emergency by-laws shall cease to be operative.

Unless otherwise provided in emergency by-laws, notice of any meeting of the board of directors during any such emergency may be given only to such of the directors as it may be feasible to reach at the time and by such means as may be feasible at the time, including publication or radio.

To the extent required to constitute a quorum at any meeting of the board of directors during any such emergency, the officers of the corporation who are present shall, unless otherwise provided in emergency by-laws, be deemed, in order of rank and within the same rank in order of seniority, directors for such meeting.

No officer, director or employee acting in accordance with any emergency by-laws shall be liable except for willful misconduct. No officer, director or employee shall be liable for any action taken by him in good faith in such an emergency in furtherance of the ordinary business affairs of the corporation even though not authorized by the by-laws then in effect.

§ 28. Meetings of Shareholders

Meetings of shareholders may be held at such place within or without this State as may be stated in or fixed in accordance with the by-laws. If no other place is stated or so fixed, meetings shall be held at the registered office of the corporation.

An annual meeting of the shareholders shall be held at such time as may be stated in or fixed in accordance with the by-laws. If the annual meeting is not held within any thirteen-month period the Court of _____ may, on the application of any shareholder, summarily order a meeting to be held.

A special meeting of the shareholders may be called by the board of directors, the holders of not less than one-tenth of all the shares entitled to vote at the meeting, or such other persons as may be authorized in the articles of incorporation or the by-laws.

§ 29. Notice of Shareholders' Meetings

Written notice stating the place, day and hour of the meeting and, in case of a special meeting, the purpose or purposes for which the meeting is called, shall be delivered not less than ten nor more than fifty days before the date of the meeting, either personally or by mail, by or at the direction of the president, the secretary, or the officer or persons calling the meeting, to each shareholder of record entitled to vote at such meeting. If mailed, such notice shall be deemed to be delivered when deposited in the United States mail addressed to the shareholder at his address as it appears on the stock transfer books of the corporation, with postage thereon prepaid.

§ 30. Closing of Transfer Books and Fixing Record Date

For the purpose of determining shareholders entitled to notice of or to vote at any meeting of shareholders or any adjournment thereof, or entitled to receive payment of any dividend, or in order to make a determination of shareholders for any other proper purpose, the board of directors of a corporation may provide that the stock transfer books shall be closed for a stated period but not to exceed, in any case, fifty days. If the stock transfer books shall be closed for the purpose of determining shareholders entitled to notice of or to vote at a meeting of shareholders, such books shall be closed for at least ten days immediately preceding such meeting. In lieu of closing the stock transfer books, the by-laws, or in the absence of an applicable by-law the board of directors, may fix in ad-vance a date as the record date for any such determination of shareholders, such date in any case to be not more than fifty days and, in case of a meeting of shareholders, not less than ten days prior to the date on which the particular action, requiring such determination of shareholders, is to be taken. If the stock transfer books are not closed and no record date is fixed for the determination of shareholders entitled to notice of or to vote at a meeting of shareholders, or shareholders entitled to receive payment of a dividend, the date on which notice of the meeting is mailed or the date on which the resolution of the board of directors declaring such dividend is adopted, as the case may be, shall be the record date for such determination of share-holders. When a determination of shareholders entitled to vote at any meeting of shareholders has been made as provided in this section, such determination shall apply to any adjournment thereof.

§ 31. Voting Record

The officer or agent having charge of the stock transfer books for shares of a corporation shall make a complete record of the shareholders entitled to vote at such meeting or any adjournment thereof, arranged in alphabetical order, with the address of and the number of shares held by each. Such record shall be produced and kept open at the time and place of the meeting and shall be subject to the inspection of any shareholder during the whole time of the meeting for the purposes thereof.

Failure to comply with the requirements of this section shall not affect the validity of any action taken at such meeting.

An officer or agent having charge of the stock transfer books who shall fail to prepare the record of shareholders, or produce and keep it open for inspection at the meeting, as provided in this section, shall be liable to any share-holder suffering damage on account of such failure, to the extent of such damage.

§ 32. Quorum of Shareholders

Unless otherwise provided in the articles of incorporation, a majority of the shares entitled to vote, represented in person or by proxy, shall constitute a quorum at a meeting of shareholders, but in no event shall a quorum consist of less than one-third of the shares entitled to vote at the meeting. If a quorum is present, the affirmative vote of the majority of the shares represented at the meeting and entitled to vote on the subject matter shall be the act of the shareholders, unless the vote of a greater number or voting by classes is required by this Act or the articles of incorporation or by-laws.

§ 33. Voting of Shares

Each outstanding share, regardless of class, shall be entitled to one vote on each matter submitted to a vote at a meeting of shareholders, except as may be otherwise provided in the articles of incorporation. If the articles of incorporation provide for more or less than one vote for any share, on any matter, every reference in this Act to a majority or other proportion of shares shall refer to such a majority or other proportion of votes entitled to be cast.

Shares held by another corporation if a majority of the shares entitled to vote for the election of directors of such other corporation is held by the corporation, shall not be voted at any meeting or counted in determining the total number of outstanding shares at any given time.

A shareholder may vote either in person or by proxy executed in writing by the shareholder or by his duly authorized attorney-in-fact. No proxy shall be valid after eleven months from the date of its execution, unless otherwise provided in the proxy.

[Either of the following prefatory phrases may be inserted here: "The articles of incorporation may provide that" or "Unless the articles of incorporation otherwise provide"] . . . at each election for directors every shareholder entitled to vote at such election shall have the right to vote, in person or by proxy, the number of shares owned by him for as many persons as there are directors to be elected and for whose election he has a right to vote, or to cumulate his votes by giving one candidate as many votes as the number of such directors multiplied by the number of his shares shall equal, or by distributing such votes on the same principle among any number of such candidates.

Shares standing in the name of another corporation, domestic or foreign, may be voted by such officer, agent or proxy as the by-laws of such other corporation may prescribe, or, in the absence of such provision, as the board of directors of such other corporation may determine.

Shares held by an administrator, executor, guardian or conservator may be voted by him, either in person or by proxy, without a transfer of such shares into his name. Shares standing in the name of a trustee may be voted by him, either in person or by proxy, but no trustee shall be entitled to vote shares held by him without a transfer of such shares into his name.

Shares standing in the name of a receiver may be voted by such receiver, and shares held by or under the control of a receiver may be voted by such receiver without the transfer thereof into his name if authority so to do be contained in an appropriate order of the court by which such receiver was appointed.

A shareholder whose shares are pledged shall be entitled to vote such shares until the shares have been transferred into the name of the pledgee, and thereafter the pledgee shall be entitled to vote the shares so transferred.

On and after the date on which written notice of redemption of redeemable shares has been mailed to the holders thereof and a sum sufficient to redeem such shares has been deposited with a bank or trust company with irrevocable instruction and authority to pay the redemption price to the holders thereof upon surrender of certificates therefor, such shares shall not be entitled to vote on any matter and shall not be deemed to be outstanding shares.

§ 34. Voting Trusts and Agreements Among Shareholders

Any number of shareholders of a corporation may create a voting trust for the purpose of conferring upon a trustee or trustees the right to vote or otherwise represent their shares, for a period of not to exceed ten years, by entering into a written voting trust agreement specifying the terms and conditions of the voting trust, by depositing a counterpart of the agreement with the corporation at its registered office, and by transferring their shares to such trustee or trustees for the purposes of the agreement. Such trustee or trustees shall keep a record of the holders of voting trust certificates evidencing a beneficial interest in the voting trust, giving the names and addresses of all such holders and the number and class of the shares in respect of which the voting trust certificates held by each are issued, and shall deposit a copy of such record with the corporation at its registered office. The counterpart of the voting trust agreement and the copy of such record so deposited with the corporation shall be subject to the same right of examination by a shareholder of the corporation, in person or by agent or attorney, as are the books and records of the corporation, and such counterpart and such copy of such record shall be subject to examination by any holder of record of voting trust certificates, either in person or by agent or attorney, at any reasonable time for any proper purpose.

Agreements among shareholders regarding the voting of their shares shall be valid and enforceable in accordance with their terms. Such agreements shall not be subject to the provisions of this section regarding voting trusts.

§ 35. Board of Directors

All corporate powers shall be exercised by or under authority of, and the business and affairs of a corporation shall be managed under the direction of, a board of directors except as may be otherwise provided in this Act or the articles of incorporation. If any such provision is made in the articles of incorporation, the powers and duties conferred or imposed upon the board of directors by this Act shall be exercised or performed to such extent and by such person or persons as shall be provided in the articles of incorporation. Directors need not be residents of this State or shareholders of the corporation unless the articles of incorporation or by-laws so require. The articles of incorporation or by-laws may prescribe other qualifications for directors. The board of directors shall have authority to fix the compensation of directors unless otherwise provided in the articles of incorporation.

A director shall perform his duties as a director, including his duties as a member of any committee of the board upon which he may serve, in good faith, in a manner he reasonably believes to be in the best interests of the corporation, and with such care as an ordinarily prudent person in a like position would use under similar circumstances. In performing his duties, a director shall be entitled to rely on information, opinions, reports or statements, including financial statements and other financial data, in each case prepared or presented by:

(a) one or more officers or employees of the corporation whom the director reasonably believes to be reliable and competent in the matters presented,

(b) counsel, public accountants or other persons as to matters which the director reasonably believes to be within such person's professional or expert competence, or

(c) a committee of the board upon which he does not serve, duly designated in accordance with a provision of the articles of incorporation or the by-laws, as to matters within its designated authority, which committee the director reasonably believes to merit confidence,

but he shall not be considered to be acting in good faith if he has knowledge concerning the matter in question that would cause such reliance to be unwarranted. A person who so performs his duties shall have no liability by reason of being or having been a director of the corporation.

A director of a corporation who is present at a meeting of its board of directors at which action on any corporate matter is taken shall be presumed to have assented to the action taken unless his dissent shall be entered in the minutes of the meeting or unless he shall file his written dissent to such action with the secretary of the meeting before the adjournment thereof or shall forward such dissent by registered mail to the secretary of the corporation immediately after the adjournment of the meeting. Such right to dissent shall not apply to a director who voted in favor of such action.

§ 36. Number and Election of Directors

The board of directors of a corporation shall consist of one or more members. The number of directors shall be fixed by, or in the manner provided in, the articles of incorporation or the by-laws, except as to the number constituting the initial board of directors, which number shall be fixed by the articles of incorporation. The number of directors may be increased or decreased from time to time by amendment to, or in the manner provided in, the articles of incorporation or the by-laws, but no decrease shall have the effect of shortening the term of any incumbent director. In the absence of a by-law providing for the number of directors, the number shall be the same as that provided for in the articles of incorporation. The names and addresses of the members of the first board of directors shall be stated in the articles of incorporation. Such persons shall hold office until the first annual meeting of shareholders, and until their successors shall have been elected and qualified. At the first annual meeting of shareholders and at each annual meeting thereafter the shareholders shall elect directors to hold office until the next succeeding annual meeting, except in case of the classification of directors as permitted by this Act. Each director shall hold office for the term for which he is elected and until his successor shall have been elected and qualified.

§ 37. Classification of Directors

When the board of directors shall consist of nine or more members, in lieu of electing the whole number of directors annually, the articles of incorporation may provide that the directors be divided into either two or three classes, each class to be as nearly equal in number as possible, the term of office of directors of the first class to expire at the first annual meeting of shareholders after their election, that of the second class to expire at the second annual meeting after their election, and that of the third class, if any, to expire at the third annual meeting after their election. At each annual meeting after such classification the number of directors equal to the number of the class whose term expires at the time of such meeting shall be elected to hold office until the second succeeding annual meeting, if there be two classes, or until the third succeeding annual meeting, if there be three classes. No classification of directors shall be effective prior to the first annual meeting of shareholders.

§ 38. Vacancies

Any vacancy occurring in the board of directors may be filled by the affirmative vote of a majority of the remaining directors though less than a quorum of the board of directors. A director elected to fill a vacancy shall be elected for the unexpired term of his predecessor in office. Any directorship to be filled by reason of an increase in the number of directors may be filled by the board of directors for a term of office continuing only until the next election of directors by the shareholders.

§ 39. Removal of Directors

At a meeting of shareholders called expressly for that purpose, directors may be removed in the manner provided in this section. Any director or the entire board of directors may be removed, with or without cause, by a vote of the holders of a majority of the shares then entitled to vote at an election of directors.

In the case of a corporation having cumulative voting, if less than the entire board is to be removed, no one of the directors may be removed if the votes cast against his removal would be sufficient to elect him if then cumulatively voted at an election of the entire board of directors, or, if there be classes of directors, at an election of the class of directors of which he is a part.

Whenever the holders of the shares of any class are entitled to elect one or more directors by the provisions of the articles of incorporation, the provisions of this section shall apply, in respect to the removal of a director or directors so elected, to the vote of the holders of the outstanding shares of that class and not to the vote of the outstanding shares as a whole.

§ 40. Quorum of Directors

A majority of the number of directors fixed by or in the manner provided in the by-laws or in the absence of a by-law fixing or providing for the number of directors, then of the number stated in the articles of incorporation, shall constitute a quorum for the transaction of business unless a greater number is required by the articles of incorporation or the by-laws. The act of the majority of the directors present at a meeting at which a quorum is present shall be the act of the board of directors, unless the act of a greater number is required by the articles of incorporation or the by-laws.

§ 41. Director Conflicts of Interest

No contract or other transaction between a corporation and one or more of its directors or any other corporation, firm, association or entity in which one or more of its directors are directors or officers or are financially interested, shall be either void or voidable because of such relationship or interest or because such director or directors are present at the meeting of the board of directors or a committee thereof which authorizes, approves or ratifies such contract or transaction or because his or their votes are counted for such purpose, if:

(a) the fact of such relationship or interest is disclosed or known to the board of directors or committee which authorizes, approves or ratifies the contract or transaction by a vote or consent sufficient for the purpose without counting the votes or consents of such interested directors; or

(b) the fact of such relationship or interest is disclosed or known to the shareholders entitled to vote and they authorize, approve or ratify such contract or transaction by vote or written consent; or

(c) the contract or transaction is fair and reasonable to the corporation.

Common or interested directors may be counted in determining the presence of a quorum at a meeting of the board of directors or a committee thereof which authorizes, approves or ratifies such contract or transaction.

§ 42. Executive and Other Committees

If the articles of incorporation or the by-laws so provide, the board of directors, by resolution adopted by a majority of the full board of directors, may designate from among its members an executive committee and one or more other committees each of which, to the extent provided in such resolution or in the articles of incorporation or the by-laws of the corporation, shall have and may exercise all the authority of the board of directors, except that no such committee shall have authority to (i) authorize distributions, (ii) approve or recommend to shareholders actions or proposals required by this Act to be approved by shareholders, (iii) designate candidates for the office of director, for purposes of proxy solicitation or otherwise, or fill vacancies on the board of directors or any committee thereof, (iv) amend the by-laws, (v) approve a plan of merger not requiring shareholder approval, (vi) authorize or approve the reacquisition of shares unless pursuant to a general formula or method specified by the board of directors, or authorize or approve the issuance or sale of, or any contract to issue or sell, shares or designate the terms of a series of a class of shares, provided that the

board of directors, having acted regarding general authorization for the issuance or sale of shares, or any contract, therefor, and, in the case of a series, the designation thereof, may, pursuant to a general formula or method specified by the board by resolution or by adoption of a stock option or other plan, authorize a committee to fix the terms of any contract for the sale of the shares and to fix the terms upon which such shares may be issued or sold, including, without limitation, the price, the dividend rate, provisions for redemption, sinking fund, conversion, voting or preferential rights, and provisions for other features of a class of shares, or a series of a class of shares, with full power in such committee to adopt any final resolution setting forth all the terms thereof and to authorize the statement of the terms of a series for filing with the Secretary of State under this Act.

Neither the designation of any such committee, the delegation thereto of authority, nor action by such committee pursuant to such authority shall alone constitute compliance by any member of the board of directors, not a member of the committee in question, with his responsibility to act in good faith, in a manner he reasonably believes to be in the best interests of the corporation, and with such care as an ordinarily prudent person in a like position would use under similar circumstances.

§ 43. Place and Notice of Directors' Meetings; Committee Meetings

Meetings of the board of directors, regular or special, may be held either within or without this State.

Regular meetings of the board of directors or any committee designated thereby may be held with or without notice as prescribed in the by-laws. Special meetings of the board of directors or any committee designated thereby shall be held upon such notice as is prescribed in the by-laws. Attendance of a director at a meeting shall constitute a waiver of notice of such meeting, except where a director attends a meeting for the express purpose of objecting to the transaction of any business because the meeting is not lawfully called or convened. Neither the business to be transacted at, nor the purpose of, any regular or special meeting of the board of directors or any committee designated thereby need be specified in the notice or waiver of notice of such meeting unless required by the by-laws.

Except as may be otherwise restricted by the articles of incorporation or by-laws, members of the board of directors or any committee designated thereby may participate in a meeting of such board or committee by means of a conference telephone or similar communications equipment by means of which all persons participating in the meeting can hear each other at the same time and participation by such means shall constitute presence in person at a meeting.

§ 44. Action by Directors Without a Meeting

Unless otherwise provided by the articles of incorporation or by-laws, any action required by this Act to be taken at a meeting of the directors of a corporation, or any action which may be taken at a meeting of the directors or of a committee, may be taken without a meeting if a consent in writing, setting forth the action so taken, shall be signed by all of the directors, or all of the members of the committee, as the case may be. Such consent shall have the same effect as a unanimous vote.

§ 45. Distributions to Shareholders

Subject to any restrictions in the articles of incorporation, the board of directors may authorize and the corporation may make distributions, except that no distribution may be made if, after giving effect thereto, either:

(a) the corporation would be unable to pay its debts as they become due in the usual course of its business; or
(b) the corporation's total assets would be less than the sum of its total liabilities and (unless the articles of incorporation otherwise permit) the maximum amount that then would be payable, in any liquidation, in respect of all outstanding shares having preferential rights in liquidation.

Determinations under subparagraph (b) may be based upon (i) financial statements prepared on the basis of accounting practices and principles that are reasonable in the circumstances, or (ii) a fair valuation or other method that is reasonable in the circumstances.

In the case of a purchase, redemption or other acquisition of a corporation's shares, the effect of a distribution shall be measured as of the date money or other property is transferred or debt is incurred by the corporation, or as of the date the shareholder ceases to be a shareholder of the corporation with respect to such shares, whichever is earlier. In all other cases, the effect of a distribution shall be measured as of the date of its authorization if payment occurs 120 days or less following the date of authorization, or as of the date of payment if payment occurs more than 120 days following the date of authorization.

Indebtedness of a corporation incurred or issued to a shareholder in a distribution in accordance with this Section shall be on a parity with the indebtedness of the corporation to its general unsecured creditors except to the extent subordinated by agreement.

§ 46. Distributions from Capital Surplus [Repealed]

§ 47. Loans to Employees and Directors

A corporation shall not lend money to or use its credit to assist its directors without authorization in the particular case by its shareholders, but may lend money to and use its credit to assist any employee of the corporation or of a subsidiary, including any such employee who is a director of the corporation, if the board of directors decides that such loan or assistance may benefit the corporation.

§ 48. Liability of Directors in Certain Cases

In addition to any other liabilities, a director who votes for or assents to any distribution contrary to the provi-

sions of this Act or contrary to any restrictions contained in the articles of incorporation, shall, unless he complies with the standard provided in this Act for the performance of the duties of directors, be liable to the corporation, jointly and severally with all other directors so voting or assenting, for the amount of such dividend which is paid or the value of such distribution in excess of the amount of such distribution which could have been made without a violation of the provisions of this Act or the restrictions in the articles of incorporation.

Any director against whom a claim shall be asserted under or pursuant to this section for the making of a distribution and who shall be held liable thereon, shall be entitled to contribution from the shareholders who accepted or received any such distribution, knowing such distribution to have been made in violation of this Act, in proportion to the amounts received by them.

Any director against whom a claim shall be asserted under or pursuant to this section shall be entitled to contribution from any other director who voted for or assented to the action upon which the claim is asserted and who did not comply with the standard provided in this Act for the performance of the duties of directors.

§ 49. Provisions Relating to Actions by Shareholders

No action shall be brought in this State by a shareholder in the right of a domestic or foreign corporation unless the plaintiff was a holder of record of shares or of voting trust certificates therefor at the time of the transaction of which he complains, or his shares or voting trust certificates thereafter devolved upon him by operation of law from a person who was a holder of record at such time.

In any action hereafter instituted in the right of any domestic or foreign corporation by the holder or holders of record of shares of such corporation or of voting trust certificates therefor, the court having jurisdiction, upon final judgment and a finding that the action was brought without reasonable cause, may require the plaintiff or plaintiffs to pay to the parties named as defendant the reasonable expenses, including fees of attorneys, incurred by them in the defense of such action.

In any action now pending or hereafter instituted or maintained in the right of any domestic or foreign corporation by the holder or holders of record of less than five per cent of the outstanding shares of any class of such corporation or of voting trust certificates therefor, unless the shares or voting trust certificates so held have a market value in excess of twenty-five thousand dollars, the corporation in whose right such action is brought shall be entitled at any time before final judgment to require the plaintiff or plaintiffs to give security for the reasonable expenses, including fees of attorneys, that may be incurred by it in connection with such action or may be incurred by other parties named as defendant for which it may become legally liable. Market value shall be determined as of the date that the plaintiff institutes the action or, in the case of an intervenor, as of the date that he becomes a party to the action. The amount of such security may from time to time be increased or decreased, in the discretion of the court, upon showing that the security provided has or may become inadequate or is excessive. The corporation shall have recourse to such security in such amount as the court having jurisdiction shall determine upon the termination of such action, whether or not the court finds the action was brought without reasonable cause.

§ 50. Officers

The officers of a corporation shall consist of a president, one or more vice presidents as may be prescribed by the by-laws, a secretary, and a treasurer, each of whom shall be elected by the board of directors at such time and in such manner as may be prescribed by the by-laws. Such other officers and assistant officers and agents as may be deemed necessary may be elected or appointed by the board of directors or chosen in such other manner as may be prescribed by the by-laws. Any two or more offices may be held by the same person, except the offices of president and secretary.

All officers and agents of the corporation, as between themselves and the corporation, shall have such authority and perform such duties in the management of the corporation as may be provided in the by-laws, or as may be determined by resolution of the board of directors not inconsistent with the by-laws.

§ 51. Removal of Officers

Any officer or agent may be removed by the board of directors whenever in its judgment the best interests of the corporation will be served thereby, but such removal shall be without prejudice to the contract rights, if any, of the person so removed. Election or appointment of an officer or agent shall not of itself create contract rights.

§ 52. Books and Records: Financial Reports to Shareholders; Examination of Records

Each corporation shall keep correct and complete books and records of account and shall keep minutes of the proceedings of its shareholders and board of directors and shall keep at its registered office or principal place of business, or at the office of its transfer agent or registrar, a record of its shareholders, giving the names and addresses of all shareholders and the number and class of the shares held by each. Any books, records and minutes may be in written form or in any form capable of being converted into written form within a reasonable time.

Any person who shall have been a holder of record of shares or of voting trust certificates therefor at least six months immediately preceding his demand or shall be the holder of record of, or the holder of record of voting trust certificates for, at least five percent of all the outstanding shares of the corporation, upon written demand stating the purpose thereof, shall have the right to examine, in person, or by agent or attorney, at any reasonable time or times, for any proper purpose its relevant books and records of accounts, minutes, and record of shareholders and to make extracts therefrom.

Any officer or agent who, or a corporation which, shall refuse to allow any such shareholder or holder of voting trust certificates, or his agent or attorney, so to examine and make extracts from its books and records of account, minutes, and record of shareholders, for any proper purpose, shall be liable to such shareholder or holder of voting trust certificates in a penalty of ten per cent of the value of the shares owned by such shareholder, or in respect of which such voting trust certificates are issued, in addition to any other damages or remedy afforded him by law. It shall be a defense to any action for penalties under this section that the person suing therefor has within two years sold or offered for sale any list of shareholders or of holders of voting trust certificates for shares of such corporation or any other corporation or has aided or abetted any person in procuring any list of shareholders or of holders of voting trust certificates for any such purpose, or has improperly used any information secured through any prior examination of the books and records of account, or minutes, or record of shareholders or of holders of voting trust certificates for shares of such corporation or any other corporation, or was not acting in good faith or for a proper purpose in making his demand.

Nothing herein contained shall impair the power of any court of competent jurisdiction, upon proof by a shareholder or holder of voting trust certificates of proper purpose, irrespective of the period of time during which such shareholder or holder of voting trust certificates shall have been a shareholder of record or a holder of record of voting trust certificates, and irrespective of the number of shares held by him or represented by voting trust certificates held by him, to compel the production for examination by such shareholder or holder of voting trust certificates of the books and records of account, minutes and record of shareholders of a corporation.

Each corporation shall furnish to its shareholders annual financial statements, including at least a balance sheet as of the end of each fiscal year and a statement of income for such fiscal year, which shall be prepared on the basis of generally accepted accounting principles, if the corporation prepares financial statements for such fiscal year on that basis for any purpose, and may consolidate statements of the corporation and one or more of its subsidiaries. The financial statements shall be mailed by the corporation to each of its shareholders within 120 days after the close of each fiscal year and, after such mailing and upon written request, shall be mailed by the corporation to any shareholder (or holder of a voting trust certificate for its shares) to whom a copy of the most recent annual financial statements has not previously been mailed. In the case of statements audited by a public accountant, each copy shall be accompanied by a report setting forth his opinion thereon; in other cases, each copy shall be accompanied by a statement of the president or the person in charge of the corporation's financial accounting records (1) stating his reasonable belief as to whether or not the financial statements were prepared in accordance with generally accepted accounting principles and, if not, describing the basis of presentation, and (2) describing any respects in which the financial statements were not prepared on a basis consistent with those prepared for the previous year.

§ 53. Incorporators

One or more persons, or a domestic or foreign corporation, may act as incorporator or incorporators of a corporation by signing and delivering in duplicate to the Secretary of State articles of incorporation for such corporation.

§ 54. Articles of Incorporation

The articles of incorporation shall set forth:

(a) The name of the corporation.
(b) The period of duration, which may be perpetual.
(c) The purpose or purposes for which the corporation is organized which may be stated to be, or to include, the transaction of any or all lawful business for which corporations may be incorporated under this Act.
(d) The aggregate number of shares which the corporation shall have authority to issue and, if such shares are to be divided into classes, the number of shares of each class.
(e) If the shares are to be divided into classes, the designation of each class and a statement of the preferences, limitations and relative rights in respect of the shares of each class.
(f) If the corporation is to issue the shares of any preferred or special class in series, then the designation of each series and a statement of the variations in the relative rights and preferences as between series insofar as the same are to be fixed in the articles of incorporation, and a statement of any authority to be vested in the board of directors to establish series and fix and determine the variations in the relative rights and preferences as between series.
(g) If any preemptive right is to be granted to shareholders, the provisions therefor.
(h) The address of its initial registered office, and the name of its initial registered agent at such address.
(i) The number of directors constituting the initial board of directors and the names and addresses of the persons who are to serve as directors until the first annual meeting of shareholders or until their successors be elected and qualify.
(j) The name and address of each incorporator.

In addition to provisions required therein, the articles of incorporation may also contain provisions not inconsistent with law regarding:

(1) the direction of the management of the business and the regulation of the affairs of the corporation;
(2) the definition, limitation and regulation of the powers of the corporation, the directors, and the shareholders, or any class of the shareholders, including restrictions on the transfer of shares;

(3) the par value of any authorized shares or class of shares;
(4) any provision which under this Act is required or permitted to be set forth in the by-laws;

It shall not be necessary to set forth in the articles of incorporation any of the corporate powers enumerated in this Act.

§ 55. Filing of Articles of Incorporation

Duplicate originals of the articles of incorporation shall be delivered to the Secretary of State. If the Secretary of State finds that the articles of incorporation conform to law, he shall, when all fees have been paid as in this Act prescribed:

(a) Endorse on each of such duplicate originals the word "Filed," and the month, day and year of the filing thereof.
(b) File one of such duplicate originals in his office.
(c) Issue a certificate of incorporation to which he shall affix the other duplicate original.

The certificate of incorporation, together with the duplicate original of the articles of incorporation affixed thereto by the Secretary of State, shall be returned to the incorporators or their representative.

§ 56. Effect of Issuance of Certificate of Incorporation

Upon the issuance of the certificate of incorporation, the corporate existence shall begin, and such certificate of incorporation shall be conclusive evidence that all conditions precedent required to be performed by the incorporators have been complied with and that the corporation has been incorporated under this Act, except as against this State in a proceeding to cancel or revoke the certificate of incorporation or for involuntary dissolution of the corporation.

§ 57. Organization Meeting of Directors

After the issuance of the certificate of incorporation an organization meeting of the board of directors named in the articles of incorporation shall be held, either within or without this State, at the call of a majority of the directors named in the articles of incorporation, for the purpose of adopting by-laws, electing officers and transacting such other business as may come before the meeting. The directors calling the meeting shall give at least three days' notice thereof by mail to each director so named, stating the time and place of the meeting.

§ 58. Right to Amend Articles of Incorporation

A corporation may amend its articles of incorporation, from time to time, in any and as many respects as may be desired, so long as its articles of incorporation as amended contain only such provisions as might be lawfully contained in original articles of incorporation at the time of making such amendment, and, if a change in shares or the rights of shareholders, or an exchange, reclassification or cancellation of shares or rights of shareholders is to be made, such provisions as may be necessary to effect such change, exchange, reclassification or cancellation.

In particular, and without limitation upon such general power of amendment, a corporation may amend its articles of incorporation, from time to time, so as:

(a) To change its corporate name.

(b) To change its period of duration.

(c) To change, enlarge or diminish its corporate purposes.

(d) To increase or decrease the aggregate number of shares, or shares of any class, which the corporation has authority to issue.

(e) To provide, change or eliminate any provision with respect to the par value of any shares or class of shares.

(f) To exchange, classify, reclassify or cancel all or any part of its shares, whether issued or unissued.

(g) To change the designation of all or any part of its shares, whether issued or unissued, and to change the preferences, limitations, and the relative rights in respect of all or any part of its shares, whether issued or unissued.

(h) To change the shares of any class, whether issued or unissued, into a different number of shares of the same class or into the same or a different number of shares of other classes.

(i) To create new classes of shares having rights and preferences either prior and superior or subordinate and inferior to the shares of any class then authorized, whether issued or unissued.

(j) To cancel or otherwise affect the right of the holders of the shares of any class to receive dividends which have accrued but have not been declared.

(k) To divide any preferred or special class of shares, whether issued or unissued, into series and fix and determine the designations of such series and the variations in the relative rights and preferences as between the shares of such series.

(l) To authorize the board of directors to establish, out of authorized but unissued shares, series of any preferred or special class of shares and fix and determine the relative rights and preferences of the shares of any series so established.

(m) To authorize the board of directors to fix and determine the relative rights and preferences of the authorized but unissued shares of series theretofore established in respect of which either the relative rights and preferences have not been fixed and determined or the relative rights and preferences theretofore fixed and determined are to be changed.

(n) To revoke, diminish, or enlarge the authority of the board of directors to establish series out of authorized but unissued shares of any preferred or special class and fix and determine the relative rights and preferences of the shares of any series so established.

(o) To limit, deny or grant to shareholders of any class the preemptive right to acquire additional shares of the corporation, whether then or thereafter authorized.

§ 59. Procedure to Amend Articles of Incorporation

Amendments to the articles of incorporation shall be made in the following manner:

(a) The board of directors shall adopt a resolution setting forth the proposed amendment and, if shares have been issued, directing that it be submitted to a vote at a meeting of shareholders, which may be either the annual or a special meeting. If no shares have been issued, the amendment shall be adopted by resolution of the board of directors and the provisions for adoption by shareholders shall not apply. If the corporation has only one class of shares outstanding, an amendment solely to change the number of authorized shares to effectuate a split of, or stock dividend in, the corporation's own shares, or solely to do so and to change the number of authorized shares in proportion thereto, may be adopted by the board of directors; and the provisions for adoption by shareholders shall not apply, unless otherwise provided by the articles of incorporation. The resolution may incorporate the proposed amendment in restated articles of incorporation which contain a statement that except for the designated amendment the restated articles of incorporation correctly set forth without change the corresponding provisions of the articles of incorporation as theretofore amended, and that the restated articles of incorporation together with the designated amendment supersede the original articles of incorporation and all amendments thereto.

(b) Written notice setting forth the proposed amendment or a summary of the changes to be effected thereby shall be given to each shareholder of record entitled to vote thereon within the time and in the manner provided in this Act for the giving of notice of meetings of shareholders. If the meeting be an annual meeting, the proposed amendment of such summary may be included in the notice of such annual meeting.

(c) At such meeting a vote of the shareholders entitled to vote thereon shall be taken on the proposed amendment. The proposed amendment shall be adopted upon receiving the affirmative vote of the holders of a majority of the shares entitled to vote thereon, unless any class of shares is entitled to vote thereon as a class, in which event the proposed amendment shall be adopted upon receiving the affirmative vote of the holders of a majority of the shares of each class of shares entitled to vote thereon as a class and of the total shares entitled to vote thereon.

Any number of amendments may be submitted to the shareholders, and voted upon by them, at one meeting.

§ 60. Class Voting on Amendments

The holders of the outstanding shares of a class shall be entitled to vote as a class upon a proposed amendment, whether or not entitled to vote thereon by the provisions of the articles of incorporation, if the amendment would:

(a) Increase or decrease the aggregate number of authorized shares of such class.

(b) Effect an exchange, reclassification or cancellation of all or part of the shares of such class.

(c) Effect an exchange, or create a right of exchange, of all or any part of the shares of another class into the shares of such class.

(d) Change the designations, preferences, limitations or relative rights of the shares of such class.

(e) Change the shares of such class, into the same or a different number of shares of the same class or another class or classes.

(f) Create a new class of shares having rights and preferences prior and superior to the shares of such class, or increase the rights and preferences or the number of authorized shares, of any class having rights and preferences prior or superior to the shares of such class.

(g) In the case of a preferred or special class of shares, divide the shares of such class into series and fix and determine the designation of such series and the variations in the relative rights and preferences between the shares of such series, or authorize the board of directors to do so.

(h) Limit or deny any existing preemptive rights of the shares of such class.

(i) Cancel or otherwise affect dividends on the shares of such class which have accrued but have not been declared.

§ 61. Articles of Amendment

The articles of amendment shall be executed in duplicate by the corporation by its president or a vice president and by its secretary or an assistant secretary, and verified by one of the officers signing such articles, and shall set forth:

(a) The name of the corporation.

(b) The amendments so adopted.

(c) The date of the adoption of the amendment by the shareholders, or by the board of directors where no shares have been issued.

(d) The number of shares outstanding, and the number of shares entitled to vote thereon, and if the shares of any class are entitled to vote thereon as a class, the designation and number of outstanding shares entitled to vote thereon of each such class.

(e) The number of shares voted for and against such amendment, respectively, and, if the shares of any class are entitled to vote thereon as a class, the number of shares of each such class voted for and against such amendment, respectively, or if no shares have been issued, a statement to that effect.

(f) If such amendment provides for an exchange, reclassification or cancellation of issued shares, and if the manner in which the same shall be effected is not set forth in the amendment, then a statement of the manner in which the same shall be effected.

§ 62. Filing of Articles of Amendment

Duplicate originals of the articles of amendment shall be delivered to the Secretary of State. If the Secretary of State finds that the articles of amendment conform to law, he shall, when all fees and franchise taxes have been paid as in this Act prescribed:

(a) Endorse on each of such duplicate originals the word "Filed," and the month, day and year of the filing thereof.

(b) File one of such duplicate originals in his office.

(c) Issue a certificate of amendment to which he shall affix the other duplicate original.

The certificate of amendment, together with the duplicate original of the articles of amendment affixed thereto by the Secretary of State, shall be returned to the corporation or its representative.

§ 63. Effect of Certificate of Amendment

Upon the issuance of the certificate of amendment by the Secretary of State, the amendment shall become effective and the articles of incorporation shall be deemed to be amended accordingly.

No amendment shall affect any existing cause of action in favor of or against such corporation, or any pending suit to which such corporation shall be a party, or the existing rights of persons other than shareholders; and, in the event the corporate name shall be changed by amendment, no suit brought by or against such corporation under its former name shall abate for that reason.

§ 64. Restated Articles of Incorporation

A domestic corporation may at any time restate its articles of incorporation as theretofore amended, by a resolution adopted by the board of directors.

Upon the adoption of such resolution, restated articles of incorporation shall be executed in duplicate by the corporation by its president or a vice president and by its secretary or assistant secretary and verified by one of the officers signing such articles and shall set forth all of the operative provisions of the articles of incorporation as theretofore amended together with a statement that the restated articles of incorporation correctly set forth without change the corresponding provisions of the articles of incorporation as theretofore amended and that the restated articles of incorporation supersede the original articles of incorporation and all amendments thereto.

Duplicate originals of the restated articles of incorporation shall be delivered to the Secretary of State. If the Secretary of State finds that such restated articles of incorporation conform to law, he shall, when all fees and franchise taxes have been paid as in this Act prescribed:

(1) Endorse on each of such duplicate originals the word "Filed," and the month, day and year of the filing thereof.

(2) File one of such duplicate originals in his office.

(3) Issue a restated certificate of incorporation, to which he shall affix the other duplicate original.

The restated certificate of incorporation, together with the duplicate original of the restated articles of incorporation affixed thereto by the Secretary of State, shall be returned to the corporation or its representative.

Upon the issuance of the restated certificate of incorporation by the Secretary of State, the restated articles of incorporation shall become effective and shall supersede the original articles of incorporation and all amendments thereto.

§ 65. Amendment of Articles of Incorporation in Reorganization Proceedings

Whenever a plan of reorganization of a corporation has been confirmed by decree or order of a court of competent jurisdiction in proceedings for the reorganization of such corporation, pursuant to the provisions of any applicable statute of the United States relating to reorganizations of corporations, the articles of incorporation of the corporation may be amended, in the manner provided in this section, in as many respects as may be necessary to carry out the plan and put it into effect, so long as the articles of incorporation as amended contain only such provisions as might be lawfully contained in original articles of incorporation at the time of making such amendment.

In particular and without limitation upon such general power of amendment, the articles of incorporation may be amended for such purpose so as to:

(A) Change the corporate name, period of duration or corporate purposes of the corporation;

(B) Repeal, alter or amend the by-laws of the corporation;

(C) Change the aggregate number of shares or shares of any class, which the corporation has authority to issue;

(D) Change the preferences, limitations and relative rights in respect of all or any part of the shares of the corporation, and classify, reclassify or cancel all or any part thereof, whether issued or unissued;

(E) Authorize the issuance of bonds, debentures or other obligations of the corporation, whether or not convertible into shares of any class or bearing warrants or other evidences of optional rights to purchase or subscribe for shares of any class, and fix the terms and conditions thereof; and

(F) Constitute or reconstitute and classify or reclassify the board of directors of the corporation, and appoint directors and officers in place of or in addition to all or any of the directors or officers then in office.

Amendments to the articles of incorporation pursuant to this section shall be made in the following manner:

(a) Articles of amendment approved by decree or order of such court shall be executed and verified in duplicate by such person or persons as the court shall designate or appoint for the purpose, and shall set forth the name of the corporation, the amendments of the articles of

incorporation approved by the court, the date of the decree or order approving the articles of amendment, the title of the proceedings in which the decree or order was entered, and a statement that such decree or order was entered by a court having jurisdiction of the proceedings for the reorganization of the corporation pursuant to the provisions of an applicable statute of the United States.

(b) Duplicate originals of the articles of amendment shall be delivered to the Secretary of State. If the Secretary of State finds that the articles of amendment conform to law, he shall, when all fees and franchise taxes have been paid as in this Act prescribed:

(1) Endorse on each of such duplicate originals the word "Filed," and the month, day and year of the filing thereof.

(2) File one of such duplicate originals in his office.

(3) Issue a certificate of amendment to which he shall affix the other duplicate original.

The certificate of amendment, together with the duplicate original of the articles of amendment affixed thereto by the Secretary of State, shall be returned to the corporation or its representative.

Upon the issuance of the certificate of amendment by the Secretary of State, the amendment shall become effective and the articles of incorporation shall be deemed to be amended accordingly, without any action thereon by the directors or shareholders of the corporation and with the same effect as if the amendments had been adopted by unanimous action of the directors and shareholders of the corporation.

§ 66. Restriction on Redemption or Purchase of Redeemable Shares [Repealed]

§ 67. Cancellation of Redeemable Shares by Redemption or Purchase [Repealed]

§ 68. Cancellation of Other Reacquired Shares [Repealed]

§ 69. Reduction of Stated Capital in Certain Cases [Repealed]

§ 70. Special Provisions Relating to Surplus and Reserves [Repealed]

§ 71. Procedure for Merger

Any two or more domestic corporations may merge into one of such corporations pursuant to a plan of merger approved in the manner provided in this Act.

The board of directors of each corporation shall by resolution adopted by each such board, approve a plan of merger setting forth:

(a) The names of the corporations proposing to merge, and the name of the corporation into which they propose to merge, which is hereinafter designated as the surviving corporation.

(b) The terms and conditions of the proposed merger.

(c) The manner and basis of converting the shares of each corporation into shares, obligations or other securities of the surviving corporation or of any other corporation or, in whole or in part, into cash or other property.

(d) A statement of any changes in the articles of incorporation of the surviving corporation to be effected by such merger.

(e) Such other provisions with respect to the proposed merger as are deemed necessary or desirable.

§ 72. Procedure for Consolidation

Any two or more domestic corporations may consolidate into a new corporation pursuant to a plan of consolidation approved in the manner provided in this Act.

The board of directors of each corporation shall, by a resolution adopted by each such board, approve a plan of consolidation setting forth:

(a) The names of the corporations proposing to consolidate, and the name of the new corporation into which they propose to consolidate, which is hereinafter designated as the new corporation.

(b) The terms and conditions of the proposed consolidation.

(c) The manner and basis of converting the shares of each corporation into shares, obligations or other securities of the new corporation or of any other corporation or, in whole or in part, into cash or other property.

(d) With respect to the new corporation, all of the statements required to be set forth in articles of incorporation for corporations organized under this Act.

(e) Such other provisions with respect to the proposed consolidation as are deemed necessary or desirable.

§ 72A. Procedure for Share Exchange

All the issued or all the outstanding shares of one or more classes of any domestic corporation may be acquired through the exchange of all such shares of such class or classes by another domestic or foreign corporation pursuant to a plan of exchange approved in the manner provided in this Act.

The board of directors of each corporation shall, by resolution adopted by each such board, approve a plan of exchange setting forth:

(a) The name of the corporation the shares of which are proposed to be acquired by exchange and the name of the corporation to acquire the shares of such corporation in the exchange, which is hereinafter designated as the acquiring corporation.

(b) The terms and conditions of the proposed exchange.

(c) The manner and basis of exchanging the shares to be acquired for shares, obligations or other securities of the acquiring corporation or any other corporation, or, in whole or in part, for cash or other property.

(d) Such other provisions with respect to the proposed exchange as are deemed necessary or desirable.

The procedure authorized by this Section shall not be deemed to limit the power of a corporation to acquire all or part of the shares of any class or classes of a corporation through a voluntary exchange or otherwise by agreement with the shareholders.

§ 73. Approval by Shareholders

(a) The board of directors of each corporation in the case of a merger or consolidation, and the board of directors of the corporation the shares of which are to be acquired in the case of an exchange, upon approving such a plan of merger, consolidation or exchange, shall, by resolution, direct that the plan be submitted to a vote at a meeting of its shareholders, which may be either an annual or a special meeting. Written notice shall be given to each shareholder of record, whether or not entitled to vote at such meeting, not less than twenty days before such meeting, in the manner provided in this Act for the giving of notice of meetings of shareholders, and, whether the meeting be an annual or a special meeting, shall state that the purpose or one of the purposes is to consider the proposed plan of merger, consolidation or exchange. A copy or a summary of the plan of merger, consolidation or exchange, as the case may be, shall be included in or enclosed with such notice.

(b) At each such meeting, a vote of the shareholders shall be taken on the proposed plan. The plan shall be approved upon receiving the affirmative vote of the holders of a majority of the shares entitled to vote thereon of each such corporation, unless any class of shares of any such corporation is entitled to vote thereon as a class, in which event, as to such corporation, the plan shall be approved upon receiving the affirmative vote of the holders of a majority of the shares of each class of shares entitled to vote thereon.

Any class of shares of any such corporation shall be entitled to vote as a class if any such plan contains any provision which, if contained in a proposed amendment to articles of incorporation, would entitle such class of shares to vote as a class and, in the case of an exchange, if the class is included in the exchange.

(c) After such approval by a vote of the shareholders of each such corporation, and at any time prior to the filing of the articles of merger, consolidation or exchange, the merger, consolidation or exchange may be abandoned pursuant to provisions therefor, if any, set forth in the plan.

(d)(1) Notwithstanding the provisions of subsections (a) and (b), submission of a plan of merger to a vote at a meeting of shareholders of a surviving corporation shall not be required if—

(i) the articles of incorporation of the surviving corporation do not differ except in name from those of the corporation before the merger,

(ii) each holder of shares of the surviving corporation which were outstanding immediately before the effective date of the merger is to hold the same number of shares with identical rights immediately after,

(iii) the number of voting shares outstanding immediately after the merger, plus the number of voting shares issuable on conversion of other securities issued by virtue of the terms of the merger and on exercise of rights and warrants so issued, will not exceed by more than 20 percent the number of voting shares outstanding immediately before the merger, and

(iv) the number of participating shares outstanding immediately after the merger, plus the number of participating shares issuable on conversion of other securities issued by virtue of the terms of the merger and on exercise of rights and warrants so issued, will not exceed by more than 20 percent the number of participating shares outstanding immediately before the merger.

(2) As used in this subsection—

(i) "voting shares" means shares which entitle their holders to vote unconditionally in elections of directors;

(ii) "participating shares" means shares which entitle their holders to participate without limitation in distribution of earnings or surplus.

§ 74. Articles of Merger, Consolidation or Exchange

(a) Upon receiving the approvals required by Sections 71, 72 and 73, articles of merger or articles of consolidation shall be executed in duplicate by each corporation by its president or a vice president and by its secretary or an assistant secretary, and verified by one of the officers of each corporation signing such articles, and shall set forth:

(1) The plan of merger or the plan of consolidation;

(2) As to each corporation, either (i) the number of shares outstanding, and, if the shares of any class are entitled to vote as a class, the designation and number of outstanding shares of each such class; or (ii) a statement that the vote of shareholders is not required by virtue of subsection 73(d);

(3) As to each corporation the approval of whose shareholders is required, the number of shares voted for and against such plan, respectively, and, if the shares of any class are entitled to vote as a class, the number of shares of each such class voted for and against such plan, respectively.

(b) Duplicate originals of the articles of merger, consolidation or exchange shall be delivered to the Secretary of State. If the Secretary of State finds that such articles conform to law, he shall, when all fees and franchise taxes have been paid as in this Act prescribed:

(1) Endorse on each of such duplicate originals the word "Filed," and the month, day and year of the filing thereof.

(2) File one of such duplicate originals in his office.

(3) Issue a certificate of merger, consolidation or exchange to which he shall affix the other duplicate original.

(c) The certificate of merger, consolidation or exchange together with the duplicate original of the articles affixed thereto by the Secretary of State, shall be returned to the surviving, new or acquiring corporation, as the case may be, or its representative.

§ 75. Merger of Subsidiary Corporation

Any corporation owning at least ninety per cent of the outstanding shares of each class of another corporation may merge such other corporation into itself without approval by a vote of the shareholders of either corporation. Its board of directors shall, by resolution, approve a plan of merger setting forth:

(A) The name of the subsidiary corporation and the name of the corporation owning at least ninety per cent of its shares, which is hereinafter designated as the surviving corporation.

(B) The manner and basis of converting the shares of the subsidiary corporation into shares, obligations or other securities of the surviving corporation or of any other corporation or, in whole or in part, into cash or other property.

A copy of such plan of merger shall be mailed to each shareholder of record of the subsidiary corporation.

Articles of merger shall be executed in duplicate by the surviving corporation by its president or a vice president and by its secretary or an assistant secretary, and verified by one of its officers signing such articles, and shall set forth:

(a) The plan of merger;

(b) The number of outstanding shares of each class of the subsidiary corporation and the number of such shares of each class owned by the surviving corporation; and

(c) The date of the mailing to shareholders of the subsidiary corporation of a copy of the plan of merger.

On and after the thirtieth day after the mailing of a copy of the plan of merger to shareholders of the subsidiary corporation or upon the waiver thereof by the holders of all outstanding shares duplicate originals of the articles of merger shall be delivered to the Secretary of State. If the Secretary of State finds that such articles conform to law, he shall, when all fees and franchise taxes have been paid as in this Act prescribed:

(1) Endorse on each of such duplicate originals the word "Filed," and the month, day and year of the filing thereof,

(2) File one of such duplicate originals in his office, and

(3) Issue a certificate of merger to which he shall affix the other duplicate original.

The certificate of merger, together with the duplicate original of the articles of merger affixed thereto by the Secretary of State, shall be returned to the surviving corporation or its representative.

§ 76. Effect of Merger, Consolidation or Exchange

Upon the issuance of the certificate of merger or the certificate of consolidation by the Secretary of State, the merger or consolidation shall be effected.

When such merger or consolidation has been effected:

(a) The several corporations parties to the plan of merger or consolidation shall be a single corporation, which, in the case of a merger, shall be that corporation designated in the plan of merger as the surviving corporation, and, in the case of a consolidation, shall be the new corporation provided for in the plan of consolidation.

(b) The separate existence of all corporations parties to the plan of merger or consolidation, except the surviving or new corporation, shall cease.

(c) Such surviving or new corporation shall have all the rights, privileges, immunities and powers and shall be subject to all the duties and liabilities of a corporation organized under this Act.

(d) Such surviving or new corporation shall thereupon and thereafter possess all the rights, privileges, immunities, and franchises, of a public as well as of a private nature, of each of the merging or consolidating corporations; and all property, real, personal and mixed, and all debts due on whatever account, including subscriptions to shares, and all other choses in action, and all and every other interest of or belonging to or due to each of the corporations so merged or consolidated, shall be taken and deemed to be transferred to and vested in such single corporation without further act or deed; and the title to any real estate, or any interest therein, vested in any of such corporations shall not revert or be in any way impaired by reason of such merger or consolidation.

(e) Such surviving or new corporation shall thenceforth be responsible and liable for all the liabilities and obligations of each of the corporations so merged or consolidated; and any claim existing or action or proceeding pending by or against any of such corporations may be prosecuted as if such merger or consolidation had not taken place, or such surviving or new corporation may be substituted in its place. Neither the rights of creditors nor any liens upon the property of any such corporation shall be impaired by such merger or consolidation.

(f) In the case of a merger, the articles of incorporation of the surviving corporation shall be deemed to be amended to the extent, if any, that changes in its articles of incorporation are stated in the plan of merger; and, in the case of a consolidation, the statements set forth in the articles of consolidation and which are required or permitted to be set forth in the articles of incorporation of corporations organized under this Act shall be deemed to be the original articles of incorporation of the new corporation.

§ 77. Merger, Consolidation or Exchange of Shares Between Domestic and Foreign Corporations

One or more foreign corporations and one or more domestic corporations may be merged or consolidated in the following manner, if such merger, consolidation or exchange is permitted by the laws of the state under which each such foreign corporation is organized:

(a) Each domestic corporation shall comply with the provisions of this Act with respect to the merger, consolidation or exchange, as the case may be, of domestic corporations and each foreign corporation shall comply with the applicable provisions of the laws of the state under which it is organized.

(b) If the surviving or new corporation in a merger or consolidation is to be governed by the laws of any state other than this State, it shall comply with the provisions of this Act with respect to foreign corporations if it is to transact business in this State, and in every case it shall file with the Secretary of State of this State:

(1) An agreement that it may be served with process in this State in any proceeding for the enforcement of any obligation of any domestic corporation which is a party to such merger or consolidation and in any proceeding for the enforcement of the rights of a dissenting shareholder of any such domestic corporation against the surviving or new corporation;

(2) An irrevocable appointment of the Secretary of State of this State as its agent to accept service of process in any such proceeding; and

(3) An agreement that it will promptly pay to the dissenting shareholders of any such domestic corporation, the amount, if any, to which they shall be entitled under provisions of this Act with respect to the rights of dissenting shareholders.

The effect of such merger or consolidation shall be the same as in the case of the merger or consolidation of domestic corporations, if the surviving or new corporation is to be governed by the laws of this State. If the surviving or new corporation is to be governed by the laws of any state other than this State, the effect of such merger or consolidation shall be the same as in the case of the merger or consolidation of domestic corporations except insofar as the laws of such other state provide otherwise.

At any time prior to the filing of the articles of merger or consolidation, the merger or consolidation may be abandoned pursuant to provisions therefor, if any, set forth in the plan of merger or consolidation.

§ 78. Sale of Assets in Regular Course of Business and Mortgage or Pledge of Assets

The sale, lease, exchange, or other disposition of all, or substantially all, the property and assets of a corporation in the usual and regular course of its business and the mortgage or pledge of any or all property and assets of a corporation whether or not in the usual and regular course of business may be made upon such terms and conditions and for such consideration, which may consist in whole or in part of cash or other property, including shares, obligations or other securities of any other corporation, domestic or foreign, as shall be authorized by its board of directors; and in any such case no authorization or consent of the shareholders shall be required.

§ 79. Sale of Assets Other Than in Regular Course of Business

A sale, lease, exchange, or other disposition of all, or substantially all, the property and assets, with or without the good will, of a corporation, if not in the usual and regular course of its business, may be made upon such terms and conditions and for such consideration, which may consist in whole or in part of cash or other property, including shares, obligations or other securities of any other corporation, domestic or foreign, as may be authorized in the following manner:

(a) The board of directors shall adopt a resolution recommending such sale, lease, exchange, or other disposition and directing the submission thereof to a vote at a meeting of shareholders, which may be either an annual or a special meeting.

(b) Written notice shall be given to each shareholder of record, whether or not entitled to vote at such meeting, not less than twenty days before such meeting, in the manner provided in this Act for the giving of notice of meetings of shareholders, and, whether the meeting be an annual or a special meeting, shall state that the purpose, or one of the purposes is to consider the proposed sale, lease, exchange, or other disposition.

(c) At such meeting the shareholders may authorize such sale, lease, exchange, or other disposition and may fix, or may authorize the board of directors to fix, any or all of the terms and conditions thereof and the consideration to be received by the corporation therefor. Such authorization shall require the affirmative vote of the holders of a majority of the shares of the corporation entitled to vote thereon, unless any class of shares is entitled to vote thereon as a class, in which event such authorization shall require the affirmative vote of the holders of a majority of the shares of each class of shares entitled to vote as a class thereon and of the total shares entitled to vote thereon.

(d) After such authorization by a vote of shareholders, the board of directors nevertheless, in its discretion, may abandon such sale, lease, exchange, or other disposition of assets, subject to the rights of third parties under any contracts relating thereto, without further action or approval by shareholders.

§ 80. Right of Shareholders to Dissent and Obtain Payment for Shares

(a) Any shareholder of a corporation shall have the right to dissent from, and to obtain payment for his shares in the event of, any of the following corporate actions:

(1) Any plan of merger or consolidation to which the corporation is a party, except as provided in subsection (c);

(2) Any sale or exchange of all or substantially all of the property and assets of the corporation not made in the usual or regular course of its business, including a sale in dissolution, but not including a sale pursuant to an order of a court having jurisdiction in the premises or a sale for cash on terms requiring that all or substantially all of the net proceeds of sale be distributed to the shareholders in accordance with their respective interests within one year after the date of sale;

(3) Any plan of exchange to which the corporation is a party as the corporation the shares of which are to be acquired;

(4) Any amendment of the articles of incorporation which materially and adversely affects the rights appurtenant to the shares of the dissenting shareholder in that it—

(i) alters or abolishes a preferential right of such shares;

(ii) creates, alters or abolishes a right in respect of the redemption of such shares, including a provision respecting a sinking fund for the redemption or repurchase of such shares;

(iii) alters or abolishes a preemptive right of the holder of such shares to acquire shares or other securities;

(iv) excludes or limits the right of the holder of such shares to vote on any matter, or to cumulate his votes, except as such right may be limited by dilution through the issuance of shares or other securities with similar voting rights; or

(5) Any other corporate action taken pursuant to a shareholder vote with respect to which the articles of incorporation, the bylaws, or a resolution of the board of directors directs that dissenting shareholders shall have a right to obtain payment for their shares.

(b)(1) A record holder of shares may assert dissenters' rights as to less than all of the shares registered in his name only if he dissents with respect to all the shares beneficially owned by any one person, and discloses the name and address of the person or persons on whose behalf he dissents. In that event, his rights shall be determined as if the shares as to which he has dissented and his other shares were registered in the names of different shareholders.

(2) A beneficial owner of shares who is not the record holder may assert dissenters' rights with respect to shares held on his behalf, and shall be treated as a dissenting shareholder under the terms of this section and Section 81 if he submits to the corporation at the time of or before the assertion of these rights a written consent of the record holder.

(c) The right to obtain payment under this section shall not apply to the shareholders of the surviving corporation in a merger if a vote of the shareholders of such corporation is not necessary to authorize such merger.

(d) A shareholder of a corporation who has a right under this section to obtain payment for his shares shall have no right at law or in equity to attack the validity of the corporate action that gives rise to his right to obtain payment, nor to have the action set aside or rescinded, except when the corporate action is unlawful or fraudulent with regard to the complaining shareholder or to the corporation.

§ 81. Procedures for Protection of Dissenters' Rights

(a) As used in this section:

(1) "Dissenter" means a shareholder or beneficial owner who is entitled to and does assert dissenters' rights under Section 80, and who has performed every act required up to the time involved for the assertion of such rights.

(2) "Corporation" means the issuer of the shares held by the dissenter before the corporate action, or the successor by merger or consolidation of that issuer.

(3) "Fair value" of shares means their value immediately before the effectuation of the corporate action to which the dissenter objects, excluding any appreciation or depreciation in anticipation of such corporate action unless such exclusion would be inequitable.

(4) "Interest" means interest from the effective date of the corporate action until the date of payment, at the average rate currently paid by the corporation on its principal bank loans, or, if none, at such rate as is fair and equitable under all the circumstances.

(b) If a proposed corporate action which would give rise to dissenters' rights under Section 80(a) is submitted to a vote at a meeting of shareholders, the notice of meeting shall notify all shareholders that they have or may have a right to dissent and obtain payment for their shares by complying with the terms of this section, and shall be accompanied by a copy of sections 80 and 81 of this Act.

(c) If the proposed corporate action is submitted to a vote at a meeting of shareholders, any shareholder who wishes to dissent and obtain payment for his shares must file with the corporation, prior to the vote, a written notice of intention to demand that he be paid fair compensation for his shares if the proposed action is effectuated, and shall refrain from voting his shares in approval of such action. A shareholder who fails in either respect shall acquire no right to payment for his shares under this section or section 80.

(d) If the proposed corporate action is approved by the required vote at a meeting of shareholders, the corporation shall mail a further notice to all shareholders who gave due notice of intention to demand payment and who refrained from voting in favor of the proposed action. If the proposed corporate action is to be taken without a vote of shareholders, the corporation shall send to all shareholders who are entitled to dissent and demand payment for their shares a notice of the adoption of the plan of corporate action. The notice shall (1) state where and when a demand for payment must be sent and certificates of certificated shares must be deposited in order to obtain payment, (2) inform holders of uncertificated shares to what extent transfer of shares will be restricted from the time that demand for payment is received, (3) supply a form for demanding payment which includes a request for certification of the date on which the shareholder, or the person on whose behalf the shareholder dissents, acquired beneficial ownership of the shares, and (4) be accompanied by a copy of sections 80 and 81 of this Act. The time set for the demand and deposit shall be not less than 30 days from the mailing of the notice.

(e) A shareholder who fails to demand payment, or fails (in the case of certificated shares) to deposit certificates, as required by a notice pursuant to subsection (d) shall have no right under this section or section 80 to receive payment for his shares. If the shares are not represented by certificates, the corporation may restrict their transfer from the time of receipt of demand for payment until effectuation of the proposed corporate action, or the release of restrictions under the terms of subsection (f). The dissenter shall retain all other rights of a shareholder until these rights are modified by effectuation of the proposed corporate action.

(f)(1) Within 60 days after the date set for demanding payment and depositing certificates, if the corporation has not effectuated the proposed corporate action and remitted payment for shares pursuant to paragraph (3), it shall return any certificates that have been deposited, and release uncertificated shares from any transfer restrictions imposed by reason of the demand for payment.

(2) When uncertificated shares have been released from transfer restrictions, and deposited certificates have been returned, the corporation may at any later time send a new notice conforming to the requirements of subsection (d), with like effect.

(3) Immediately upon effectuation of the proposed corporate action, or upon receipt of demand for payment if the corporate action has already been effectuated, the corporation shall remit to dissenters who have made demand and (if their shares are certificated) have deposited their certificates the amount which the corporation estimates to be the fair value of the shares, with interest if any has accrued. The remittance shall be accompanied by:

(i) the corporation's closing balance sheet and statement of income for a fiscal year ending not more than 16 months before the date of remittance, together with the latest available interim financial statements;

(ii) a statement of the corporation's estimate of fair value of the shares; and

(iii) a notice of the dissenter's right to demand supplemental payment, accompanied by a copy of sections 80 and 81 of this Act.

(g)(1) If the corporation fails to remit as required by subsection (f), or if the dissenter believes that the amount remitted is less than the fair value of his shares, or that the interest is not correctly determined, he may send the corporation his own estimate of the value of the shares or of the interest, and demand payment of the deficiency.

(2) If the dissenter does not file such an estimate within 30 days after the corporation's mailing of its remittance, he shall be entitled to no more than the amount remitted.

(h)(1) Within 60 days after receiving a demand for payment pursuant to subsection (g), if any such demands for payment remain unsettled, the corporation shall file in an appropriate court a petition requesting that the fair value of the shares and interest thereon be determined by the court.

(2) An appropriate court shall be a court of competent jurisdiction in the county of this state where the registered office of the corporation is located. If, in the case of a merger or consolidation or exchange of shares, the corporation is a foreign corporation without a registered office in this state, the petition shall be filed in the county where the registered office of the domestic corporation was last located.

(3) All dissenters, wherever residing, whose demands have not been settled shall be made parties to the proceeding as in an action against their shares. A copy of the petition shall be served on each such dissenter; if a dissenter is a nonresident, the copy may be served on him by registered or certified mail or by publication as provided by law.

(4) The jurisdiction of the court shall be plenary and exclusive. The court may appoint one or more persons as appraisers to receive evidence and recommend a decision on the question of fair value. The appraisers shall have such power and authority as shall be specified in the order of their appointment or in any amendment thereof. The dissenters shall be entitled to discovery in the same manner as parties in other civil suits.

(5) All dissenters who are made parties shall be entitled to judgment for the amount by which the fair value of their shares is found to exceed the amount previously remitted, with interest.

(6) If the corporation fails to file a petition as provided in paragraph (1) of this subsection, each dissenter who made a demand and who has not already settled his claim against the corporation shall be paid by the corporation the amount demanded by him, with interest, and may sue therefor in an appropriate court.

(i)(1) The costs and expenses of any proceeding under subsection (h), including the reasonable compensation and expenses of appraisers appointed by the court, shall be determined by the court and assessed against the corporation, except that any part of the costs and expenses may be apportioned and assessed as the court may deem equitable against all or some of the dissenters who are parties and whose action in demanding supplemental payment the court finds to be arbitrary, vexatious, or not in good faith.

(2) Fees and expenses of counsel and of experts for the respective parties may be assessed as the court may deem equitable against the corporation and in favor of any or all dissenters if the corporation failed to comply substantially with the requirements of this section, and may be assessed against either the corporation or a dissenter, in favor of any other party, if the court finds that the party against whom the fees and expenses are assessed acted arbitrarily, vexatiously, or not in good faith in respect to the rights provided by this section and section 80.

(3) If the court finds that the services of counsel for any dissenter were of substantial benefit to other dissenters similarly situated, and should not be assessed against the corporation, it may award to these counsel reasonable fees to be paid out the amounts awarded to the dissenters who were benefitted.

(j)(1) Notwithstanding the foregoing provisions of this section, the corporation may elect to withhold the remittance required by subsection (f) from any dissenter with respect to shares of which the dissenter (or the person on whose behalf the dissenter acts) was not the beneficial owner on the date of the first announcement to news media or to shareholders of the terms of the proposed corporate action. With respect to such shares, the corporation shall, upon effectuating the corporate action, state to each dissenter its estimate of the fair value of the shares, state the rate of interest to be used (explaining the basis thereof), and offer to pay the resulting amounts on receiving the dissenter's agreement to accept them in full satisfaction.

(2) If the dissenter believes that the amount offered is less than the fair value of the shares and interest determined according to this section, he may within 30 days after the date of mailing of the corporation's offer, mail the corporation his own estimate of fair value and interest, and demand their payment. If the dissenter fails to do so, he shall be entitled to no more than the corporation's offer.

(3) If the dissenter makes a demand as provided in paragraph (2), the provisions of subsections (h) and (i) shall apply to further proceedings on the dissenter's demand.

§ 82. Voluntary Dissolution by Incorporators

A corporation which has not commenced business and which has not issued any shares, may be voluntarily dissolved by its incorporators at any time in the following manner:

(a) Articles of dissolution shall be executed in duplicate by a majority of the incorporators, and verified by them, and shall set forth:

(1) The name of the corporation.
(2) The date of issuance of its certificate of incorporation.
(3) That none of its shares has been issued.
(4) That the corporation has not commenced business.
(5) That the amount, if any, actually paid in on subscriptions for its shares, less any part thereof disbursed for necessary expenses, has been returned to those entitled thereto.
(6) That no debts of the corporation remain unpaid.
(7) That a majority of the incorporators elect that the corporation be dissolved.

(b) Duplicate originals of the articles of dissolution shall be delivered to the Secretary of State. If the Secretary of State finds that the articles of dissolution conform to law, he shall, when all fees and franchise taxes have been paid as in this Act prescribed:

(1) Endorse on each of such duplicate originals the word "Filed," and the month, day and year of the filing thereof.
(2) File one of such duplicate originals in his office.
(3) Issue a certificate of dissolution to which he shall affix the other duplicate original.

The certificate of dissolution, together with the duplicate original of the articles of dissolution affixed thereto by the Secretary of State, shall be returned to the incorporators or their representative. Upon the issuance of such certificate of dissolution by the Secretary of State, the existence of the corporation shall cease.

§ 83. Voluntary Dissolution by Consent of Shareholders

A corporation may be voluntarily dissolved by the written consent of all of its shareholders.

Upon the execution of such written consent, a statement of intent to dissolve shall be executed in duplicate by the corporation by its president or a vice president and by its secretary or an assistant secretary, and verified by one of the officers signing such statement, which statement shall set forth:

(a) The name of the corporation.
(b) The names and respective addresses of its officers.
(c) The names and respective addresses of its directors.
(d) A copy of the written consent signed by all share-holders of the corporation.
(e) A statement that such written consent has been signed by all shareholders of the corporation or signed in their names by their attorneys thereunto duly authorized.

§ 84. Voluntary Dissolution by Act of Corporation

A corporation may be dissolved by the act of the corporation, when authorized in the following manner:

(a) The board of directors shall adopt a resolution recommending that the corporation be dissolved, and directing that the question of such dissolution be submitted to a vote at a meeting of shareholders, which may be either an annual or a special meeting.
(b) Written notice shall be given to each shareholder of record entitled to vote at such meeting within the time and in the manner provided in this Act for the giving of notice of meetings of shareholders, and, whether the meeting be an annual or special meeting, shall state that the purpose, or one of the purposes, of such meeting is to consider the advisability of dissolving the corporation.
(c) At such meeting a vote of shareholders entitled to vote thereat shall be taken on a resolution to dissolve the corporation. Such resolution shall be adopted upon receiving the affirmative vote of the holders of a majority of the shares of the corporation entitled to vote thereon, unless any class of shares is entitled to vote thereon as a class, in which event the resolution shall be adopted upon receiving the affirmative vote of the holders of a majority of the shares of each class of shares entitled to

vote thereon as a class and of the total shares entitled to vote thereon.
(d) Upon the adoption of such resolution, a statement of intent to dissolve shall be executed in duplicate by the corporation by its president or a vice president and by its secretary or an assistant secretary, and verified by one of the officers signing such statement, which statement shall set forth:

(1) The name of the corporation.
(2) The names and respective addresses of its officers.
(3) The names and respective addresses of its directors.
(4) A copy of the resolution adopted by the shareholders authorizing the dissolution of the corporation.
(5) The number of shares outstanding, and, if the shares of any class are entitled to vote as a class, the designation and number of outstanding shares of each such class.
(6) The number of shares voted for and against the resolution, respectively, and, if the shares of any class are entitled to vote as a class, the number of shares of each such class voted for and against the resolution, respectively.

§ 85. Filing of Statement of Intent to Dissolve

Duplicate originals of the statement of intent to dissolve, whether by consent of shareholders or by act of the corporation, shall be delivered to the Secretary of State. If the Secretary of State finds that such statement conforms to law, he shall, when all fees and franchise taxes have been paid as in this Act prescribed:

(a) Endorse on each of such duplicate originals the word "Filed," and the month, day and year of the filing thereof.
(b) File one of such duplicate originals in his office.
(c) Return the other duplicate original to the corporation or its representative.

§ 86. Effect of Statement of Intent to Dissolve

Upon the filing by the Secretary of State of a statement of intent to dissolve, whether by consent of shareholders or by act of the corporation, the corporation shall cease to carry on its business, except insofar as may be necessary for the winding up thereof, but its corporate existence shall continue until a certificate of dissolution has been issued by the Secretary of State or until a decree dissolving the corporation has been entered by a court of competent jurisdiction as in this Act provided.

§ 87. Procedure after Filing of Statement of Intent to Dissolve

After the filing by the Secretary of State of a statement of intent to dissolve:

(a) The corporation shall immediately cause notice thereof to be mailed to each known creditor of the corporation.

(b) The corporation shall proceed to collect its assets, convey and dispose of such of its properties as are not to be distributed in kind to its shareholders, pay, satisfy and discharge its liabilities and obligations and do all other acts required to liquidate its business and affairs, and, after paying or adequately providing for the payment of all its obligations, distribute the remainder of its assets, either in cash or in kind, among its shareholders according to their respective rights and interests.

(c) The corporation, at any time during the liquidation of its business and affairs, may make application to a court of competent jurisdiction within the state and judicial subdivision in which the registered office or principal place of business of the corporation is situated, to have the liquidation continued under the supervision of the court as provided in this Act.

§ 88. Revocation of Voluntary Dissolution Proceedings by Consent of Shareholders

By the written consent of all of its shareholders, a corporation may, at any time prior to the issuance of a certificate of dissolution by the Secretary of State, revoke voluntary dissolution proceedings theretofore taken, in the following manner:

Upon the execution of such written consent, a statement of revocation of voluntary dissolution proceedings shall be executed in duplicate by the corporation by its president or a vice president and by its secretary or an assistant secretary, and verified by one of the officers signing such statement, which statement shall set forth:

(a) The name of the corporation.
(b) The names and respective addresses of its officers.
(c) The names and respective addresses of its directors.
(d) A copy of the written consent signed by all shareholders of the corporation revoking such voluntary dissolution proceedings.
(e) That such written consent has been signed by all shareholders of the corporation or signed in their names by their attorneys thereunto duly authorized.

§ 89. Revocation of Voluntary Dissolution Proceedings by Act of Corporation

By the act of the corporation, a corporation may, at any time prior to the issuance of a certificate of dissolution by the Secretary of State, revoke voluntary dissolution proceedings theretofore taken, in the following manner:

(a) The board of directors shall adopt a resolution recommending that the voluntary dissolution proceedings be revoked, and directing that the question of such revocation be submitted to a vote at a special meeting of shareholders.
(b) Written notice, stating that the purpose or one of the purposes of such meeting is to consider the advisability of revoking the voluntary dissolution proceedings, shall be given to each shareholder of record entitled to vote at such meeting within the time and in the manner pro-

vided in this Act for the giving of notice of special meetings of shareholders.
(c) At such meeting a vote of the shareholders entitled to vote thereat shall be taken on a resolution to revoke the voluntary dissolution proceedings, which shall require for its adoption the affirmative vote of the holders of a majority of the shares entitled to vote thereon.
(d) Upon the adoption of such resolution, a statement of revocation of voluntary dissolution proceedings shall be executed in duplicate by the corporation by its president or a vice president and by its secretary or an assistant secretary, and verified by one of the officers signing such statement, which statement shall set forth:

(1) The name of the corporation.
(2) The names and respective addresses of its officers.
(3) The names and respective addresses of its directors.
(4) A copy of the resolution adopted by the shareholders revoking the voluntary dissolution proceedings.
(5) The number of shares outstanding.
(6) The number of shares voted for and against the resolution, respectively.

§ 90. Filing of Statement of Revocation of Voluntary Dissolution Proceedings

Duplicate originals of the statement of revocation of voluntary dissolution proceedings, whether by consent of shareholders or by act of the corporation, shall be delivered to the Secretary of State. If the Secretary of State finds that such statement conforms to law, he shall, when all fees and franchise taxes have been paid as in this Act prescribed:

(a) Endorse on each of such duplicate originals the word "Filed," and the month, day and year of the filing thereof.
(b) File one of such duplicate originals in his office.
(c) Return the other duplicate original to the corporation or its representative.

§ 91. Effect of Statement of Revocation of Voluntary Dissolution Proceedings

Upon the filing by the Secretary of State of a statement of revocation of voluntary dissolution proceedings, whether by consent of shareholders or by act of the corporation, the revocation of the voluntary dissolution proceedings shall become effective and the corporation may again carry on its business.

§ 92. Articles of Dissolution

If voluntary dissolution proceedings have not been revoked, then when all debts, liabilities and obligations of the corporation have been paid and discharged, or adequate provision has been made therefor, and all of the remaining property and assets of the corporation have been distributed to its shareholders, articles of dissolution shall be executed in duplicate by the corporation by its president or a vice president and by its secretary or an assistant secretary, and verified by one of the officers signing such statement, which statement shall set forth:

(a) The name of the corporation.

(b) That the Secretary of State has theretofore filed a statement of intent to dissolve the corporation, and the date on which such statement was filed.

(c) That all debts, obligations and liabilities of the corporation have been paid and discharged or that adequate provision has been made therefor.

(d) That all the remaining property and assets of the corporation have been distributed among its shareholders in accordance with their respective rights and interests.

(e) That there are no suits pending against the corporation in any court, or that adequate provision has been made for the satisfaction of any judgment, order or decree which may be entered against it in any pending suit.

§ 93. Filing of Articles of Dissolution

Duplicate originals of such articles of dissolution shall be delivered to the Secretary of State. If the Secretary of State finds that such articles of dissolution conform to law, he shall, when all fees and franchise taxes have been paid as in this Act prescribed:

(a) Endorse on each of such duplicate originals the word "Filed," and the month, day and year of the filing thereof.

(b) File one of such duplicate originals in his office.

(c) Issue a certificate of dissolution to which he shall affix the other duplicate original.

The certificate of dissolution, together with the duplicate original of the articles of dissolution affixed thereto by the Secretary of State, shall be returned to the representative of the dissolved corporation. Upon the issuance of such certificate of dissolution the existence of the corporation shall cease, except for the purpose of suits, other proceedings and appropriate corporate action by shareholders, directors and officers as provided in the Act.

§ 94. Involuntary Dissolution

A corporation may be dissolved involuntarily by a decree of the _____ court in an action filed by the Attorney General when it is established that:

(a) The corporation has failed to file its annual report within the time required by this Act, or has failed to pay its franchise tax on or before the first day of August of the year in which such franchise tax becomes due and payable; or

(b) The corporation procured its articles of incorporation through fraud; or

(c) The corporation has continued to exceed or abuse the authority conferred upon it by law; or

(d) The corporation has failed for thirty days to appoint and maintain a registered agent in this State; or

(e) The corporation has failed for thirty days after change of its registered office or registered agent to file in the office of the Secretary of State a statement of such change.

§ 95. Notification to Attorney General

The Secretary of State, on or before the last day of December of each year, shall certify to the Attorney General the names of all corporations which have failed to file their annual reports or to pay franchise taxes in accordance with the provisions of this Act, together with the facts pertinent thereto. He shall also certify, from time to time, the names of all corporations which have given other cause for dissolution as provided in this Act, together with the facts pertinent thereto. Whenever the Secretary of State shall certify the name of a corporation to the Attorney General as having given any cause for dissolution, the Secretary of State shall concurrently mail to the corporation at its registered office a notice that such certification has been made. Upon the receipt of such certification, the Attorney General shall file an action in the name of the State against such corporation for its dissolution. Every such certificate from the Secretary of State to the Attorney General pertaining to the failure of a corporation to file an annual report or pay a franchise tax shall be taken and received in all courts as prima facie evidence of the facts therein stated. If, before action is filed, the corporation shall file its annual report or pay its franchise tax, together with all penalties thereon, or shall appoint or maintain a registered agent as provided in this Act, or shall file with the Secretary of State the required statement of change of registered office or registered agent, such fact shall be forthwith certified by the Secretary of State to the Attorney General and he shall not file an action against such corporation for such cause. If, after action is filed, the corporation shall file its annual report or pay its franchise tax, together with all penalties thereon, or shall appoint or maintain a registered agent as provided in this Act, or shall file with the Secretary of State the required statement of change of registered office or registered agent, and shall pay the costs of such action, the action for such cause shall abate.

§ 96. Venue and Process

Every action for the involuntary dissolution of a corporation shall be commenced by the Attorney General either in the _____ court of the county in which the registered office of the corporation is situated, or the in the .... court of .... county. Summons shall issue and be served as in other civil actions. If process is returned not found, the Attorney General shall cause publication to be made as in other civil cases in some newspaper published in the county where the registered office of the corporation is situated, containing a notice of the pendency of such action, the title of the court, the title of the action, and the date on or after which default may be entered. The

Attorney General may include in one notice the names of any number of corporations against which actions are then pending in the same court. The Attorney General shall cause a copy of such notice to be mailed to the corporation at its registered office within ten days after the first publication thereof. The certificate of the Attorney General of the mailing of such notice shall be prima facie evidence thereof. Such notice shall be published at least once each week for two successive weeks, and the first publication thereof may begin at any time after the summons has been returned. Unless a corporation shall have been served with summons, no default shall be taken against it earlier than thirty days after the first publication of such notice.

§ 97. Jurisdiction of Court to Liquidate Assets and Business of Corporation

The _____ courts shall have full power to liquidate the assets and business of a corporation:

(a) In an action by a shareholder when it is established:

(1) That the directors are deadlocked in the management of the corporate affairs and the shareholders are unable to break the deadlock, and that irreparable injury to the corporation is being suffered or is threatened by reason thereof; or
(2) That the acts of the directors or those in control of the corporation are illegal, oppressive or fraudulent; or
(3) That the shareholders are deadlocked in voting power, and have failed, for a period which includes at least two consecutive annual meeting dates, to elect successors to directors whose terms have expired or would have expired upon the election of their successors; or
(4) That the corporate assets are being misapplied or wasted.

(b) In an action by a creditor:

(1) When the claim of the creditor has been reduced to judgment and an execution thereon returned unsatisfied and it is established that the corporation is insolvent; or
(2) When the corporation has admitted in writing that the claim of the creditor is due and owing and it is established that the corporation is insolvent.

(c) Upon application by a corporation which has filed a statement of intent to dissolve, as provided in this Act, to have its liquidation continued under the supervision of the court.
(d) When an action has been filed by the Attorney General to dissolve a corporation and it is established that liquidation of its business and affairs should precede the entry of a decree of dissolution.

Proceedings under clause (a), (b) or (c) of this section shall be brought in the county in which the registered office or the principal office of the corporation is situated.

It shall not be necessary to make shareholders parties to any such action or proceeding unless relief is sought against them personally.

§ 98. Procedure in Liquidation of Corporation by Court

In proceedings to liquidate the assets and business of a corporation the court shall have power to issue injunctions, to appoint a receiver or receivers pendente lite, with such powers and duties as the court, from time to time, may direct, and to take such other proceedings as may be requisite to preserve the corporate assets wherever situated, and carry on the business of the corporation until a full hearing can be had.

After a hearing had upon such notice as the court may direct to be given to all parties to the proceedings and to any other parties in interest designated by the court, the court may appoint a liquidating receiver or receivers with authority to collect the assets of the corporation, including all amounts owing to the corporation by subscribers on account of any unpaid portion of the consideration for the issuance of shares. Such liquidating receiver or receivers shall have authority, subject to the order of the court, to sell, convey and dispose of all or any part of the assets of the corporation wherever situated, either at public or private sale. The assets of the corporation or the proceeds resulting from a sale, conveyance or other disposition thereof shall be applied to the expenses of such liquidation and to the payment of the liabilities and obligations of the corporation, and any remaining assets or proceeds shall be distributed among its shareholders according to their respective rights and interests. The order appointing such liquidating receiver or receivers shall state their powers and duties. Such powers and duties may be increased or diminished at any time during the proceedings.

The court shall have power to allow from time to time as expenses of the liquidation compensation to the receiver or receivers and to attorneys in the proceeding, and to direct the payment thereof out of the assets of the corporation or the proceeds of any sale or disposition of such assets.

A receiver of a corporation appointed under the provisions of this section shall have authority to sue and defend in all courts in his own name as receiver of such corporation. The court appointing such receiver shall have exclusive jurisdiction of the corporation and its property, wherever situated.

§ 99. Qualifications of Receivers

A receiver shall in all cases be a natural person or a corporation authorized to act as receiver, which corporation may be a domestic corporation or a foreign corporation authorized to transact business in this State, and shall in all cases give such bond as the court may direct with such sureties as the court may require.

§ 100. Filing of Claims in Liquidation Proceedings

In proceedings to liquidate the assets and business of a corporation the court may require all creditors of the corporation to file with the clerk of the court or with the receiver, in such form as the court may prescribe, proofs under oath of their respective claims. If the court requires the filing of claims it shall fix a date, which shall be not less than four months from the date of the order, as the last day for the filing of claims, and shall prescribe the notice that shall be given to creditors and claimants of the date so fixed. Prior to the date so fixed, the court may extend the time for the filing of claims. Creditors and claimants failing to file proofs of claim on or before the date so fixed may be barred, by order of court, from participating in the distribution of the assets of the corporation.

§ 101. Discontinuance of Liquidation Proceedings

The liquidation of the assets and business of a corporation may be discontinued at any time during the liquidation proceedings when it is established that cause for liquidation no longer exists. In such event the court shall dismiss the proceedings and direct the receiver to redeliver to the corporation all its remaining property and assets.

§ 102. Decree of Involuntary Dissolution

In proceedings to liquidate the assets and business of a corporation, when the costs and expenses of such proceedings and all debts, obligations and liabilities of the corporation shall have been paid and discharged and all of its remaining property and assets distributed to its shareholders, or in case its property and assets are not sufficient to satisfy and discharge such costs, expenses, debts and obligations, all the property and assets have been applied so far as they will go to their payment, the court shall enter a decree dissolving the corporation, whereupon the existence of the corporation shall cease.

§ 103. Filing of Decree of Dissolution

In case the court shall enter a decree dissolving a corporation, it shall be the duty of the clerk of such court to cause a certified copy of the decree to be filed with the Secretary of State. No fee shall be charged by the Secretary of State for the filing thereof.

§ 104. Deposit with State Treasurer of Amount Due Certain Shareholders

Upon the voluntary or involuntary dissolution of a corporation, the portion of the assets distributable to a creditor or shareholder who is unknown or cannot be found, or who is under disability and there is no person legally competent to receive such distributive portion, shall be reduced to cash and deposited with the State Treasurer and shall be paid over to such creditor or shareholder or to his legal representative upon proof satisfactory to the State Treasurer of his right thereto.

§ 105. Survival of Remedy after Dissolution

The dissolution of a corporation either (1) by the issuance of a certificate of dissolution by the Secretary of State, or (2) by a decree of court when the court has not liquidated the assets and business of the corporation as provided in this Act, or (3) by expiration of its period of duration, shall not take away or impair any remedy available to or against such corporation, its directors, officers, or shareholders, for any right or claim existing, or any liability incurred, prior to such dissolution if action or other proceeding thereon is commenced within two years after the date of such dissolution. Any such action or proceeding by or against the corporation may be prosecuted or defended by the corporation in its corporate name. The shareholders, directors and officers shall have power to take such corporate or other action as shall be appropriate to protect such remedy, right or claim. If such corporation was dissolved by the expiration of its period of duration, such corporation may amend its articles of incorporation at any time during such period of two years so as to extend its period of duration.

§ 106. Admission of Foreign Corporation

No foreign corporation shall have the right to transact business in this State until it shall have procured a certificate of authority so to do from the Secretary of State. No foreign corporation shall be entitled to procure a certificate of authority under this Act to transact in this State any business which a corporation organized under this Act is not permitted to transact. A foreign corporation shall not be denied a certificate of authority by reason of the fact that the laws of the state or country under which such corporation is organized governing its organization and internal affairs differ from the laws of this State, and nothing in this Act contained shall be construed to authorize this State to regulate the organization or the internal affairs of such corporation.

Without excluding other activities which may not constitute transacting business in this State, a foreign corporation shall not be considered to be transacting business in this State, for the purposes of this Act, by reason of carrying on in this State any one or more of the following activities:

(a) Maintaining or defending any action or suit or any administrative or arbitration proceeding, or effecting the settlement thereof or the settlement of claims or disputes.
(b) Holding meetings of its directors or shareholders or carrying on other activities concerning its internal affairs.
(c) Maintaining bank accounts.
(d) Maintaining offices or agencies for the transfer, exchange and registration of its securities, or appointing and maintaining trustees or depositaries with relation to its securities.
(e) Effecting sales through independent contractors.
(f) Soliciting or procuring orders, whether by mail or through employees or agents or otherwise, where such orders require acceptance without this State before becoming binding contracts.
(g) Creating as borrower or lender, or acquiring, indebtedness or mortgages or other security interests in real or personal property.
(h) Securing or collecting debts or enforcing any rights in property securing the same.
(i) Transacting any business in interstate commerce.

(j) Conducting an isolated transaction completed within a period of thirty days and not in the course of a number of repeated transactions of like nature.

§ 107. Powers of Foreign Corporation

A foreign corporation which shall have received a certificate of authority under this Act shall, until a certificate of revocation or of withdrawal shall have been issued as provided in this Act, enjoy the same, but no greater, rights and privileges as a domestic corporation organized for the purposes set forth in the application pursuant to which such certificate of authority is issued; and, except as in this Act otherwise provided, shall be subject to the same duties, restrictions, penalties and liabilities now or hereafter imposed upon a domestic corporation of like character.

§ 108. Corporate Name of Foreign Corporation

No certificate of authority shall be issued to a foreign corporation unless the corporate name of such corporation:

(a) Shall contain the word "corporation," "company," "incorporated," or "limited," or shall contain an abbreviation of one of such words, or such corporation shall, for use in this State, add at the end of its name one of such words or an abbreviation thereof.

(b) Shall not contain any word or phrase which indicates or implies that it is organized for any purpose other than one or more of the purposes contained in its articles of incorporation or that it is authorized or empowered to conduct the business of banking or insurance.

(c) Shall not be the same as, or deceptively similar to, the name of any domestic corporation existing under the laws of this State or any foreign corporation authorized to transact business in this State, or a name the exclusive right to which is, at the time, reserved in the manner provided in this Act, or the name of a corporation which has in effect a registration of its name as provided in this Act, except that this provision shall not apply if the foreign corporation applying for a certificate of authority files with the Secretary of State any one of the following:

(1) a resolution of its board of directors adopting a fictitious name for use in transacting business in this State which fictitious name is not deceptively similar to the name of any domestic corporation or of any foreign corporation authorized to transact business in this State or to any name reserved or registered as provided in this Act, or

(2) the written consent of such other corporation or holder of a reserved or registered name to use the same or deceptively similar name and one or more words are added to make such name distinguishable from such other name, or

(3) a certified copy of a final decree of a court of competent jurisdiction establishing the prior right of such foreign corporation to the use of such name in this State.

§ 109. Change of Name by Foreign Corporation

Whenever a foreign corporation which is authorized to transact business in this State shall change its name to one under which a certificate of authority would not be granted to it on application therefor, the certificate of authority of such corporation shall be suspended and it shall not thereafter transact any business in this State until it has changed its name to a name which is available to it under the laws of this State or has otherwise complied with the provisions of this Act.

§ 110. Application for Certificate of Authority

A foreign corporation, in order to procure a certificate of authority to transact business in this State, shall make application therefor to the Secretary of State, which application shall set forth:

(a) The name of the corporation and the state or county under the laws of which it is incorporated.

(b) If the name of the corporation does not contain the word "corporation," "company," "incorporated," or "limited," or does not contain an abbreviation of one of such words, then the name of the corporation with the word or abbreviation which it elects to add thereto for use in this State.

(c) The date of incorporation and the period of duration of the corporation.

(d) The address of the principal office of the corporation in the state or country under the laws of which it is incorporated.

(e) The address of the proposed registered office of the corporation in this State, and the name of its proposed registered agent in this State at such address.

(f) The purpose or purposes of the corporation which it proposes to pursue in the transaction of business in this State.

(g) The names and respective addresses of the directors and officers of the corporation.

(h) A statement of the aggregate number of shares which the corporation has authority to issue, itemized by classes and series, if any, within a class.

(i) A statement of the aggregate number of issued shares itemized by class and by series, if any, within each class.

(j) An estimate, expressed in dollars, of the value of all property to be owned by the corporation for the following year, wherever located, and an estimate of the value of the property of the corporation to be located within this State during such year, and an estimate, expressed in dollars, of the gross amount of business which will be transacted by the corporation during such year, and an estimate of the gross amount thereof which will be transacted by the corporation at or from places of business in this State during such year.

(k) Such additional information as may be necessary or appropriate in order to enable the Secretary of State to determine whether such corporation is entitled to a certificate of authority to transact business in this State and to determine and assess the fees and franchise taxes payable as in this Act prescribed.

Such application shall be made on forms prescribed and furnished by the Secretary of State and shall be executed in duplicate by the corporation by its president or a vice president and by its secretary or an assistant secretary, and verified by one of the officers signing such application.

§ 111. Filing of Application for Certificate of Authority

Duplicate originals of the application of the corporation for a certificate of authority shall be delivered to the Secretary of State, together with a copy of its articles of incorporation and all amendments thereto, duly authenticated by the proper officer of the state or country under the laws of which it is incorporated.

If the Secretary of State finds that such application conforms to law, he shall, when all fees and franchise taxes have been paid as in this Act prescribed:

(a) Endorse on each of such documents the word "Filed," and the month, day and year of the filing thereof.

(b) File in his office one of such duplicate originals of the application and the copy of the articles of incorporation and amendments thereto.

(c) Issue a certificate of authority to transact business in this State to which he shall affix the other duplicate original application.

The certificate of authority, together with the duplicate original of the application affixed thereto by the Secretary of State, shall be returned to the corporation or its representative.

§ 112. Effect of Certificate of Authority

Upon the issuance of a certificate of authority by the Secretary of State, the corporation shall be authorized to transact business in this State for those purposes set forth in its application, subject, however, to the right of this State to suspend or to revoke such authority as provided in this Act.

§ 113. Registered Office and Registered Agent of Foreign Corporation

Each foreign corporation authorized to transact business in this State shall have and continuously maintain in this State:

(a) A registered office which may be, but need not be, the same as its place of business in this State.

(b) A registered agent, which agent may be either an individual resident in this State whose business office is identical with such registered office, or a domestic corporation, or a foreign corporation authorized to transact business in this State, having a business office identical with such registered office.

§ 114. Change of Registered Office or Registered Agent of Foreign Corporation

A foreign corporation authorized to transact business in this State may change its registered office or change its registered agent, or both, upon filing in the office of the Secretary of State a statement setting forth:

(a) The name of the corporation.

(b) The address of its then registered office.

(c) If the address of its registered office be changed, the address to which the registered office is to be changed.

(d) The name of its then registered agent.

(e) If its registered agent be changed, the name of its successor registered agent.

(f) That the address of its registered office and the address of the business office of its registered agent, as changed, will be identical.

(g) That such change was authorized by resolution duly adopted by its board of directors.

Such statement shall be executed by the corporation by its president or a vice president, and verified by him, and delivered to the Secretary of State. If the Secretary of State finds that such statement conforms to the provisions of this Act, he shall file such statement in his office, and upon such filing the change of address of the registered office, or the appointment of a new registered agent, or both, as the case may be, shall become effective.

Any registered agent of a foreign corporation may resign as such agent upon filing a written notice thereof, executed in duplicate, with the Secretary of State, who shall forthwith mail a copy thereof to the corporation at its principal office in the state or country under the laws of which it is incorporated. The appointment of such agent shall terminate upon the expiration of thirty days after receipt of such notice by the Secretary of State.

If a registered agent changes his or its business address to another place within the same _____*, he or it may change such address and the address of the registered office of any corporation of which he or it is registered agent by filing a statement as required above except that it need be signed only by the registered agent and need not be responsive to (e) or (g) and must recite that a copy of the statement has been mailed to the corporation.

§ 115. Service of Process on Foreign Corporation

The registered agent so appointed by a foreign corporation authorized to transact business in this State shall be an agent of such corporation upon whom any process, notice or demand required or permitted by law to be served upon the corporation may be served.

Whenever a foreign corporation authorized to transact business in this State shall fail to appoint or maintain a registered agent in this State, or whenever any such

---

*Supply designation of jurisdiction, such as county, etc. in accordance with local practice.

registered agent cannot with reasonable diligence be found at the registered office, or whenever the certificate of authority of a foreign corporation shall be suspended or revoked, then the Secretary of State shall be an agent of such corporation upon whom any such process, notice, or demand may be served. Service on the Secretary of State of any such process, notice or demand shall be made by delivering to and leaving with him, or with any clerk having charge of the corporation department of his office, duplicate copies of such process, notice or demand. In the event any such process, notice or demand is served on the Secretary of State, he shall immediately cause one of such copies thereof to be forwarded by registered mail, addressed to the corporation at its principal office in the state or country under the laws of which it is incorporated. Any service so had on the Secretary of State shall be returnable in not less than thirty days.

The Secretary of State shall keep a record of all processes, notices and demands served upon him under this section, and shall record therein the time of such service and his action with reference thereto.

Nothing herein contained shall limit or affect the right to serve any process, notice or demand, required or permitted by law to be served upon a foreign corporation in any other manner now or hereafter permitted by law.

§ 116. Amendment to Articles of Incorporation of Foreign Corporation

Whenever the articles of incorporation of a foreign corporation authorized to transact business in this State are amended, such foreign corporation shall, within thirty days after such amendment becomes effective, file in the office of the Secretary of State a copy of such amendment duly authenticated by the proper officer of the state or country under the laws of which it is incorporated; but the filing thereof shall not of itself enlarge or alter the purpose or purposes which such corporation is authorized to pursue in the transaction of business in this State, nor authorize such corporation to transact business in this State under any other name than the name set forth in its certificate of authority.

§ 117. Merger of Foreign Corporation Authorized to Transact Business in This State

Whenever a foreign corporation authorized to transact business in this State shall be a party to a statutory merger permitted by the laws of the state or country under the laws of which it is incorporated, and such corporation shall be the surviving corporation, it shall, within thirty days after such merger becomes effective, file with the Secretary of State a copy of the articles of merger duly authenticated by the proper officer of the state or country under the laws of which such statutory merger was effected; and it shall not be necessary for such corporation to procure either a new or amended certificate of authority to transact business in this State unless the name of such corporation be changed thereby or unless the corporation

desires to pursue in this State other or additional purposes than those which it is then authorized to transact in this State.

§ 118. Amended Certificate of Authority

A foreign corporation authorized to transact business in this State shall procure an amended certificate of authority in the event it changes its corporate name, or desires to pursue in this State other or additional purposes than those set forth in its prior application for a certificate of authority, by making application therefor to the Secretary of State.

The requirements in respect to the form and contents of such application, the manner of its execution, the filing of duplicate originals thereof with the Secretary of State, the issuance of an amended certificate of authority and the effect thereof, shall be the same as in the case of an original application for a certificate of authority.

§ 119. Withdrawal of Foreign Corporation

A foreign corporation authorized to transact business in this State may withdraw from this State upon procuring from the Secretary of State a certificate of withdrawal. In order to procure such certificate of withdrawal, such foreign corporation shall deliver to the Secretary of State an application for withdrawal, which shall set forth:

(a) The name of the corporation and the state or country under the laws of which it is incorporated.

(b) That the corporation is not transacting business in this State.

(c) That the corporation surrenders its authority to transact business in this State.

(d) That the corporation revokes the authority of its registered agent in this State to accept service of process and consents that service of process in any action, suit or proceeding based upon any cause of action arising in this State during the time the corporation was authorized to transact business in this State may thereafter be made on such corporation by service thereof on the Secretary of State.

(e) A post-office address to which the Secretary of State may mail a copy of any process against the corporation that may be served on him.

(f) A statement of the aggregate number of shares which the corporation has authority to issue, itemized by class and series, if any, within each class, as of the date of such application.

(g) A statement of the aggregate number of issued shares, itemized by class and series, if any, within each class, as of the date of such application.

(h) Such additional information as may be necessary or appropriate in order to enable the Secretary of State to determine and assess any unpaid fees or franchise taxes payable by such foreign corporation as in this Act prescribed.

The application for withdrawal shall be made on forms prescribed and furnished by the Secretary of State and shall be executed by the corporation by its president or a vice president and by its secretary or an assistant secretary, and verified by one of the officers signing the application, or, if the corporation is in the hands of a receiver or trustee, shall be executed on behalf of the corporation by such receiver or trustee and verified by him.

§ 120. Filing of Application for Withdrawal

Duplicate originals of such application for withdrawal shall be delivered to the Secretary of State. If the Secretary of State finds that such application conforms to the provisions of this Act, he shall, when all fees and franchise taxes have been paid as in this Act prescribed:

(a) Endorse on each of such duplicate originals the word "Filed," and the month, day and year of the filing thereof.
(b) File one of such duplicate originals in his office.
(c) Issue a certificate of withdrawal to which he shall affix the other duplicate original.

The certificate of withdrawal, together with the duplicate original of the application for withdrawal affixed thereto by the Secretary of State, shall be returned to the corporation or its representative. Upon the issuance of such certificate of withdrawal, the authority of the corporation to transact business in this State shall cease.

§ 121. Revocation of Certificate of Authority

The certificate of authority of a foreign corporation to transact business in this State may be revoked by the Secretary of State upon the conditions prescribed in this section when:

(a) The corporation has failed to file its annual report within the time required by this Act, or has failed to pay any fees, franchise taxes or penalties prescribed by this Act when they have become due and payable; or
(b) The corporation has failed to appoint and maintain a registered agent in this State as required by this Act; or
(c) The corporation has failed, after change of its registered office or registered agent, to file in the office of the Secretary of State a statement of such change as required by this Act; or
(d) The corporation has failed to file in the office of the Secretary of State any amendment to its articles of incorporation or any articles of merger within the time prescribed by this Act; or
(e) A misrepresentation has been made of any material matter in any application, report, affidavit, or other document submitted by such corporation pursuant to this Act.

No certificate of authority of a foreign corporation shall be revoked by the Secretary of State unless (1) he shall have given the corporation not less than sixty days' notice thereof by mail addressed to its registered office in this State, and (2) the corporation shall fail prior to revocation to file such annual report, or pay such fees, franchise taxes or penalties, or file the required statement of change of

registered agent or registered office, or file such articles of amendment or articles of merger, or correct such misrepresentation.

§ 122. Issuance of Certificate of Revocation

Upon revoking any such certificate of authority, the Secretary of State shall:

(a) Issue a certificate of revocation in duplicate.
(b) File one of such certificates in his office.
(c) Mail to such corporation at its registered office in this State a notice of such revocation accompanied by one of such certificates.

Upon the issuance of such certificate of revocation, the authority of the corporation to transact business in this State shall cease.

§ 123. Application to Corporations Heretofore Authorized to Transact Business in this State

Foreign corporations which are duly authorized to transact business in this State at the time this Act takes effect, for a purpose or purposes for which a corporation might secure such authority under this Act, shall, subject to the limitations set forth in their respective certificates of authority, be entitled to all the rights and privileges applicable to foreign corporations procuring certificates of authority to transact business in this State under this Act, and from the time this Act takes effect such corporations shall be subject to all the limitations, restrictions, liabilities, and duties prescribed herein for foreign corporations procuring certificates of authority to transact business in this State under this Act.

§ 124. Transacting Business Without Certificate of Authority

No foreign corporation transacting business in this State without a certificate of authority shall be permitted to maintain any action, suit or proceeding in any court of this State, until such corporation shall have obtained a certificate of authority. Nor shall any action, suit or proceeding be maintained in any court of this State by any successor or assignee of such corporation on any right, claim or demand arising out of the transaction of business by such corporation in this State, until a certificate of authority shall have been obtained by such corporation or by a corporation which has acquired all or substantially all of its assets.

The failure of a foreign corporation to obtain a certificate of authority to transact business in this State shall not impair the validity of any contract or act of such corporation, and shall not prevent such corporation from defending any action, suit or proceeding in any court of this State.

A foreign corporation which transacts business in this State without a certificate of authority shall be liable to this State, for the years or parts thereof during which it transacted business in this State without a certificate of authority, in an amount equal to all fees and franchise taxes which would have been imposed by this Act upon such corporation had it duly applied for and received a certificate of authority to transact business in this State as required by this Act and thereafter filed all reports required by this Act, plus all penalties imposed by this Act for failure to pay such fees and franchise taxes. The Attorney General shall bring proceedings to recover all amounts due this State under the provisions of this Section.

§ 125. Annual Report of Domestic and Foreign Corporations

Each domestic corporation, and each foreign corporation authorized to transact business in this State, shall file, within the time prescribed by this Act, an annual report setting forth:

(a) The name of the corporation and the state or country under the laws of which it is incorporated.

(b) The address of the registered office of the corporation in this State, and the name of its registered agent in this State at such address, and, in case of a foreign corporation, the address of its principal office in the state or country under the laws of which it is incorporated.

(c) A brief statement of the character of the business in which the corporation is actually engaged in this State.

(d) The names and respective addresses of the directors and officers of the corporation.

(e) A statement of the aggregate number of shares which the corporation has authority to issue, itemized by class and series, if any, within each class.

(f) A statement of the aggregate number of issued shares, itemized by class and series, if any, within each class.

(g) A statement, expressed in dollars, of the value of all the property owned by the corporation, wherever located, and the value of the property of the corporation located within this State, and a statement, expressed in dollars, of the gross amount of business transacted by the corporation for the twelve months ended on the thirty-first day of December preceding the date herein provided for the filing of such report and the gross amount thereof transacted by the corporation at or from places of business in this State. If, on the thirty-first day of December preceding the time herein provided for the filing of such report, the corporation had not been in existence for a period of twelve months, or in the case of a foreign corporation had not been authorized to transact business in this State for a period of twelve months, the statement with respect to business transacted shall be furnished for the period between the date of incorporation or the date of its authorization to transact business in this State, as the case may be, and such thirty-first day of December. If all the property of the corporation is located in this State and all of its business is transacted at or from places of business in this State, then the information required by this subparagraph need not be set forth in such report.

(h) Such additional information as may be necessary or appropriate in order to enable the Secretary of State to determine and assess the proper amount of franchise taxes payable by such corporation.

Such annual report shall be made on forms prescribed and furnished by the Secretary of State, and the information therein contained shall be given as of the date of the execution of the report, except as to the information required by subparagraphs (g) and (h) which shall be given as of the close of business on the thirty-first day of December next preceding the date herein provided for the filing of such report. It shall be executed by the corporation by its president, a vice president, secretary, an assistant secretary, or treasurer, and verified by the officer executing the report, or, if the corporation is in the hands of a receiver or trustee, it shall be executed on behalf of the corporation and verified by such receiver or trustee.

§ 126. Filing of Annual Report of Domestic and Foreign Corporations

Such annual report of a domestic or foreign corporation shall be delivered to the Secretary of State between the first day of January and the first day of March of each year, except that the first annual report of a domestic or foreign corporation shall be filed between the first day of January and the first day of March of the year next succeeding the calendar year in which its certificate of incorporation or its certificate of authority, as the case may be, was issued by the Secretary of State. Proof to the satisfaction of the Secretary of State that prior to the first day of March such report was deposited in the United States mail in a sealed envelope, properly addressed, with postage prepaid, shall be deemed a compliance with this requirement. If the Secretary of State finds that such report conforms to the requirements of this Act, he shall file the same. If he finds that it does not so conform, he shall promptly return the same to the corporation for any necessary corrections, in which event the penalties hereinafter prescribed for failure to file such report within the time hereinabove provided shall not apply, if such report is corrected to conform to the requirements of this Act and returned to the Secretary of State within thirty days from the date on which it was mailed to the corporation by the Secretary of State.

§ 127. Fees, Franchise Taxes and Charges to be Collected by Secretary of State

The Secretary of State shall charge and collect in accordance with the provisions of this Act:

(a) Fees for filing documents and issuing certificates.
(b) Miscellaneous charges.
(c) License fees.
(d) Franchise taxes.

§ 128. Fees for Filing Documents and Issuing Certificates

The Secretary of State shall charge and collect for:

(a) Filing articles of incorporation and issuing a certificate of incorporation, _____ dollars.

(b) Filing articles of amendment and issuing a certificate of amendment, _____ dollars.

(c) Filing restated articles of incorporation, _____ dollars.

(d) Filing articles of merger or consolidation and issuing a certificate of merger or consolidation, _____ dollars.

(e) Filing an application to reserve a corporate name, _____ dollars.

(f) Filing a notice of transfer of a reserved corporate name, _____ dollars.

(g) Filing a statement of change of address of registered office or change of registered agent, or both, _____ dollars.

(h) Filing a statement of the establishment of a series of shares, _____ dollars.

(i) Filing a statement of intent to dissolve, _____ dollars.

(j) Filing a statement of revocation of voluntary dissolution proceedings, _____ dollars.

(k) Filing articles of dissolution, _____ dollars.

(l) Filing an application of a foreign corporation for a certificate of authority to transact business in this State and issuing a certificate of authority, _____ dollars.

(m) Filing an application of a foreign corporation for an amended certificate of authority to transact business in this State and issuing an amended certificate of authority, _____ dollars.

(n) Filing a copy of an amendment to the articles of incorporation of a foreign corporation holding a certificate of authority to transact business in this State, _____ dollars.

(o) Filing a copy of articles of merger of a foreign corporation holding a certificate of authority to transact business in this State, _____ dollars.

(p) Filing an application for withdrawal of a foreign corporation and issuing a certificate of withdrawal, _____ dollars.

(q) Filing any other statement or report, except an annual report, of a domestic or foreign corporation, _____ dollars.

§ 129. Miscellaneous Charges

The Secretary of State shall charge and collect:

(a) For furnishing a certified copy of any document, instrument, or paper relating to a corporation, _____ cents per page and _____ dollars for the certificate and affixing the seal thereto.

(b) At the time of any service of process on him as agent of a corporation, _____ dollars, which amount may be recovered as taxable costs by the party to the suit or action causing such service to be made if such party prevails in the suit or action.

§ 130. License Fees Payable by Domestic Corporations

The Secretary of State shall charge and collect from each domestic corporation license fees, based upon the number of shares which it will have authority to issue or the increase in the number of shares which it will have authority to issue, at the time of:

(a) Filing articles of incorporation;

(b) Filing articles of amendment increasing the number of authorized shares; and

(c) Filing articles of merger or consolidation increasing the number of authorized shares which the surviving or new corporation, if a domestic corporation, will have the authority to issue above the aggregate number of shares which the constituent domestic corporations and constituent foreign corporations authorized to transact business in this State had authority to issue.

The license fees shall be at the rate of _____ cents per share up to and including the first 10,000 authorized shares, _____ cents per share for each authorized share in excess of 10,000 shares up to and including 100,000 shares, and _____ cents per share for each authorized share in excess of 100,000 shares, whether the shares are of par value or without par value.

The license fees payable on an increase in the number of authorized shares shall be imposed only on the increased number of shares, and the number of previously authorized shares shall be taken into account in determining the rate applicable to the increased number of authorized shares.

§ 131. License Fees Payable by Foreign Corporations

The Secretary of State shall charge and collect from each foreign corporation license fees, based upon the proportion represented in this State of the number of shares which it has authority to issue or the increase in the number of shares which it has authority to issue, at the time of:

(a) Filing an application for a certificate of authority to transact business in this State;

(b) Filing articles of amendment which increased the number of authorized shares; and

(c) Filing articles of merger or consolidation which increased the number of authorized shares which the surviving or new corporation, if a foreign corporation, has authority to issue above the aggregate number of shares which the constituent domestic corporations and constituent foreign corporations authorized to transact business in this State had authority to issue.

The license fees shall be at the rate of _____ cents per share up to and including the first 10,000 authorized shares represented in this State, _____ cents per share for each authorized share in excess of 10,000 shares up to and including 100,000 shares represented in this State, and _____ cents per share for each authorized share in excess of 100,000 shares represented in this State.

The license fees payable on an increase in the number of authorized shares shall be imposed only on the increased number of such shares represented in this State, and the number of previously authorized shares represented in this State shall be taken into account in determining the rate applicable to the increased number of authorized shares.

The number of authorized shares represented in this State shall be that proportion of its total authorized shares which the sum of the value of its property located in this State and the gross amount of business transacted by it at or from places of business in this State bears to the sum of the value of all of its property, wherever located, and the gross amount of its business, wherever transacted. Such proportion shall be determined from information contained in the application for a certificate of authority to transact business in this State until the filing of an annual report and thereafter from information contained in the latest annual report filed by the corporation.

§ 132. Franchise Taxes Payable by Domestic Corporations

The Secretary of State shall charge and collect from each domestic corporation an initial franchise tax at the time of filing its articles of incorporation at the rate of one-twelfth of one-half of the license fee payable by such corporation under the provisions of this Act at the time of filing its articles of incorporation, for each calendar month, or fraction thereof, between the date of the issuance of the certificate of incorporation by the Secretary of State and the first day of July of the next succeeding calendar year.

The Secretary of State shall charge and collect from each domestic corporation an annual franchise tax, payable in advance for the period from July 1 in each year to July 1 in the succeeding year, beginning July 1 in the calendar year in which such corporation is required to file its first annual report under this Act, (Alternative 1: at the rate of of _____ per cent of the amount represented in this State of the stated capital of the corporation, as determined in accordance with accounting practices and principles that are reasonable in the circumstances, as disclosed by the latest report filed by the corporation with the Secretary of State) (Alternative 2: at the rate of _____ cents per share up to and including the first 10,000 issued and outstanding shares, and _____ cents per share for each issued and outstanding share in excess of 10,000 shares up to and including 100,000 shares and _____ cents per share for each issued and outstanding share in excess of 100,000 shares).

[If Alternative 2 is enacted, the following paragraph should be deleted.]

The amount represented in this State of the stated capital of the corporation shall be that proportion of its stated capital which the sum of the value of its property located in this State and the gross amount of business transacted by it at or from places of business in this State bears to the sum of the value of all of its property, wherever located, and the gross amount of its business, wherever transacted.

§ 133. Franchise Taxes Payable by Foreign Corporations

The Secretary of State shall charge and collect from each foreign corporation authorized to transact business in this State an initial franchise tax at the time of filing its application for a certificate of authority at the rate of one-twelfth of one-half of the license fee payable by such corporation under the provisions of this Act at the time of filing such application, for each month, or fraction thereof, between the date of the issuance of the certificate of authority by the Secretary of State and the first day of July of the next succeeding calendar year.

The Secretary of State shall charge and collect from each foreign corporation authorized to transact business in this State an annual franchise tax, payable in advance for the period from July 1 in each year to July 1 in the succeeding year, beginning July 1 in the calendar year in which such corporation is required to file its first annual report under this Act, (Alternative 1: at the rate of _____ per cent of the amount represented in this State of the stated capital of the corporation, as determined in accordance with accounting practices and principles that are reasonable in the circumstances, as disclosed by the latest annual report filed by the corporation with the Secretary of State) (Alternative 2: at a rate of _____ cents per share up to and including the first 10,000 issued and outstanding shares represented in this State, and _____ cents per share for each issued and outstanding share in excess of 10,000 shares up to and including 100,000 shares represented in this State, and _____ cents per share for each issued and outstanding share in excess of 100,000 shares represented in this State).

[If Alternative 2 is enacted, the following paragraph should be deleted.]

The amount represented in this State of the stated capital of the corporation shall be that proportion of its stated capital which the sum of the value of its property located in this State and the gross amount of business transacted by it at or from places of business in this State bears to the sum of the value of all of its property, wherever located, and the gross amount of its business, wherever transacted.

§ 134. Assessment and Collection of Annual Franchise Taxes

It shall be the duty of the Secretary of State to collect all annual franchise taxes and penalties imposed by, or assessed in accordance with, this Act.

Between the first day of March and the first day of June of each year, the Secretary of State shall assess against each corporation, domestic and foreign, required to file an annual report in such year, the franchise tax payable by it for the period from July 1 of such year to July 1 of the succeeding year in accordance with the provisions of this Act, and, if it has failed to file its annual report within the time prescribed by this Act, the penalty imposed by this Act upon such corporation for its failure so to do; and shall mail a written notice to each corporation against which such tax is assessed, addressed to such corporation at its registered office in this State, notifying the corporation (1) of the amount of franchise tax assessed against it for the ensuing year and the amount of penalty, if any, assessed against it for failure to file its annual report; (2) that objections, if any, to such assessment will be heard by the officer making the assessment on or before the fifteenth day of June of such year, upon receipt of a request from the corporation; and (3) that such tax and penalty shall be payable to the Secretary of State on the first day of July next succeeding the date of the notice. Failure to receive such notice shall not relieve the corporation of its obligation to pay the tax and any penalty assessed, or invalidate the assessment thereof.

The Secretary of State shall have power to hear and determine objections to any assessment of franchise tax at any time after such assessment and, after hearing, to change or modify any such assessment. In the event of any adjustment of franchise tax with respect to which a penalty has been assessed for failure to file an annual report, the penalty shall be adjusted in accordance with the provisions of this Act imposing such penalty.

All annual franchise taxes and all penalties for failure to file annual reports shall be due and payable on the first day of July of each year. If the annual franchise tax assessed against any corporation subject to the provisions of this Act, together with all penalties assessed thereon, shall not be paid to the Secretary of State on or before the thirty-first day of July of the year in which such tax is due and payable, the Secretary of State shall certify such fact to the Attorney General on or before the fifteenth day of November of such year, whereupon the Attorney General may institute an action against such corporation in the name of this State, in any court of competent jurisdiction, for the recovery of the amount of such franchise tax and penalties, together with the cost of suit, and prosecute the same to final judgment.

For the purpose of enforcing collection, all annual franchise taxes assessed in accordance with this Act, and all penalties assessed thereon and all interest and costs that shall accrue in connection with the collection thereof, shall be a prior and first lien on the real and personal property of the corporation from and including the first day of July of the year when such franchise taxes become due and payable until such taxes, penalties, interest, and costs shall have been paid.

§ 135. Penalties Imposed upon Corporations

Each corporation, domestic or foreign, that fails or refuses to file its annual report for any year within the time prescribed by this Act shall be subject to a penalty of ten per cent of the amount of the franchise tax assessed against it for the period beginning July 1 of the year in which such report should have been filed. Such penalty shall be assessed by the Secretary of State at the time of the assessment of the franchise tax. If the amount of the franchise tax as originally assessed against such corporation be thereafter adjusted in accordance with the provisions of this Act, the amount of the penalty shall be likewise adjusted to ten per cent of the amount of the adjusted franchise tax. The amount of the franchise tax and the amount of the penalty shall be separately stated in any notice to the corporation with respect thereto.

If the franchise tax assessed in accordance with the provisions of this Act shall not be paid on or before the thirty-first day of July, it shall be deemed to be delinquent, and there shall be added a penalty of one per cent for each month or part of month that the same is delinquent, commencing with the month of August.

Each corporation, domestic or foreign, that fails or refuses to answer truthfully and fully within the time prescribed by this Act interrogatories propounded by the Secretary of State in accordance with the provisions of this Act, shall be deemed to be guilty of a misdemeanor and upon conviction thereof may be fined in any amount not exceeding five hundred dollars.

§ 136. Penalties Imposed upon Officers and Directors

Each officer and director of a corporation, domestic or foreign, who fails or refuses within the time prescribed by this Act to answer truthfully and fully interrogatories propounded to him by the Secretary of State in accordance with the provisions of this Act, or who signs any articles, statement, report, application or other document filed with the Secretary of State which is known to such officer or director to be false in any material respect, shall be deemed to be guilty of a misdemeanor, and upon conviction thereof may be fined in any amount not exceeding _____ dollars.

§ 137. Interrogatories by Secretary of State

The Secretary of State may propound to any corporation, domestic or foreign, subject to the provisions of this Act, and to any officer or director thereof, such interrogatories as may be reasonably necessary and proper to enable him to ascertain whether such corporation has complied with all the provisions of this Act applicable to such corporation. Such interrogatories shall be answered within thirty days after the mailing thereof, or within such additional time as shall be fixed by the Secretary of State, and the answers thereto shall be full and complete and shall be made in writing and under oath. If such interrogatories be directed to an individual they shall be answered by him, and if directed to a corporation they shall be answered by the president, vice president, secretary or assistant secretary thereof. The Secretary of State need not file any document to which such interrogatories relate until such interrogatories be answered as herein provided, and not then if the answers thereto disclose that such document is not in conformity with the provisions of this Act. The Secretary of State shall certify to the Attorney General, for such action as the Attorney General may deem appropriate, all interrogatories and answers thereto which disclose a violation of any of the provisions of this Act.

§ 138. Information Disclosed by Interrogatories

Interrogatories propounded by the Secretary of State and the answers thereto shall not be open to public inspection nor shall the Secretary of State disclose any facts or information obtained therefrom except insofar as his official duty may require the same to be made public or in the event such interrogatories or the answers thereto are required for evidence in any criminal proceedings or in any other action by this State.

§ 139. Powers of Secretary of State

The Secretary of State shall have the power and authority reasonably necessary to enable him to administer this Act efficiently and to perform the duties therein imposed upon him.

§ 140. Appeal from Secretary of State

If the Secretary of State shall fail to approve any articles of incorporation, amendment, merger, consolidation or dissolution, or any other document required by this Act to be approved by the Secretary of State before the same shall be filed in his office, he shall, within ten days after the delivery thereof to him, give written notice of his disapproval to the person or corporation, domestic or foreign, delivering the same, specifying the reasons therefor. From such disapproval such person or corporation may appeal to the _____ court of the county in which the registered office of such corporation is, or is proposed to be, situated by filing with the clerk of such court a petition setting forth a copy of the articles or other document sought to be filed and a copy of the written disapproval thereof by the Secretary of State; whereupon the matter shall be tried de novo by the court, and the court shall either sustain the action of the Secretary of State or direct him to take such action as the court may deem proper.

If the Secretary of State shall revoke the certificate of authority to transact business in this State of any foreign corporation, pursuant to the provisions of this Act, such foreign corporation may likewise appeal to the _____ court of the county where the registered office of such corporation in this State is situated, by filing with the clerk of such court a petition setting forth a copy of its certificate of authority to transact business in this State and a copy of the notice of revocation given by the Secretary of State; whereupon the matter shall be tried de novo by the court, and the court shall either sustain the action of the Secretary of State or direct him to take such action as the court may deem proper.

Appeals from all final orders and judgments entered by the _____ court under this section in review of any ruling or decision of the Secretary of State may be taken as in other civil actions.

§ 141. Certificates and Certified Copies to be Received in Evidence

All certificates issued by the Secretary of State in accordance with the provisions of this Act, and all copies of documents filed in his office in accordance with the provisions of this Act when certified by him, shall be taken and received in all courts, public offices, and official bodies as prima facie evidence of the facts therein stated. A certificate by the Secretary of State under the great seal of this State, as to the existence or non-existence of the facts relating to corporations shall be taken and received in all courts, public offices, and official bodies as prima facie evidence of the existence or non-existence of the facts therein stated.

§ 142. Forms to be Furnished by Secretary of State

All reports required by this Act to be filed in the office of the Secretary of State shall be made on forms which shall be prescribed and furnished by the Secretary of State. Forms for all other documents to be filed in the office of the Secretary of State shall be furnished by the Secretary of State on request therefor, but the use thereof, unless otherwise specifically prescribed in this Act, shall not be mandatory.

§ 143. Greater Voting Requirements

Whenever, with respect to any action to be taken by the shareholders of a corporation, the articles of incorporation require the vote or concurrence of the holders of a greater proportion of the shares, or of any class or series thereof, than required by this Act with respect to such action, the provisions of the articles of incorporation shall control.

§ 144. Waiver of Notice

Whenever any notice is required to be given to any shareholder or director of a corporation under the provisions of this Act or under the provisions of the articles of incorporation or by-laws of the corporation, a waiver thereof in writing signed by the person or persons entitled to such notice, whether before or after the time stated therein, shall be equivalent to the giving of such notice.

§ 145. Action by Shareholders Without a Meeting

Any action required by this Act to be taken at a meeting of the shareholders of a corporation, or any action which may be taken at a meeting of the shareholders, may be taken without a meeting if a consent in writing, setting forth the action so taken, shall be signed by all of the shareholders entitled to vote with respect to the subject matter thereof.

Such consent shall have the same effect as a unanimous vote of shareholders, and may be stated as such in any articles or document filed with the Secretary of State under this Act.

§ 146. Unauthorized Assumption of Corporate Powers

All persons who assume to act as a corporation without authority so to do shall be jointly and severally liable for all debts and liabilities incurred or arising as a result thereof.

§ 147. Application to Existing Corporations

The provisions of this Act shall apply to all existing corporations organized under any general act of this State providing for the organization of corporations for a purpose or purposes for which a corporation might be organized under this Act, where the power has been reserved to amend, repeal or modify the act under which such corporation was organized and where such act is repealed by this Act.

§ 148. Application to Foreign and Interstate Commerce

The provisions of this Act shall apply to commerce with foreign nations and among the several states only insofar as the same may be permitted under the provisions of the Constitution of the United States.

§ 149. Reservation of Power

The _____* shall at all times have power to prescribe such regulations, provisions and limitations as it may deem advisable, which regulations, provisions and limitations shall be binding upon any and all corporations subject to the provisions of this Act, and the _____* shall have power to amend, repeal or modify this Act at pleasure.

§ 150. Effect of Repeal of Prior Acts

The repeal of a prior act by this Act shall not affect any right accrued or established, or any liability or penalty

---

* Insert name of legislative body.

incurred, under the provisions of such act, prior to the repeal thereof.

§ 151. Effect of Invalidity of Part of this Act

If a court of competent jurisdiction shall adjudge to be invalid or unconstitutional any clause, sentence, paragraph, section or part of this Act, such judgment or decree shall not affect, impair, invalidate or nullify the remainder of this Act, but the effect thereof shall be confined to the clause, sentence, paragraph, section or part of this Act so adjudged to be invalid or unconstitutional.

§ 152. Exclusivity of Certain Provisions [Optional]

In circumstances to which section 45 and related sections of this Act are applicable, such provisions supersede the applicability of any other statutes of this state with respect to the legality of distributions.

§ 153. Repeal of Prior Acts

(insert appropriate provisions) _____

SELECTED PROVISIONS OF THE REVISED MODEL BUSINESS CORPORATION ACT

* * *

§ 2.02. Articles of Incorporation

(a) The articles of incorporation must set forth:

(1) a corporate name for the corporation that satisfies the requirements of section 4.01;
(2) the number of shares the corporation is authorized to issue;
(3) the street address of the corporation's initial registered office and the name of its initial registered agent at that office; and
(4) the name and address of each incorporator.

(b) The articles of incorporation may set forth:

(1) the names and addresses of the individuals who are to serve as the initial directors;
(2) provisions not inconsistent with law regarding:

(i) the purpose or purposes for which the corporation is organized;
(ii) managing the business and regulating the affairs of the corporation;
(iii) defining, limiting, and regulating the powers of the corporation, its board of directors, and shareholders;
(iv) a par value for authorized shares or classes of shares;
(v) the imposition of personal liability on shareholders for the debts of the corporation to a specified extent and upon specified conditions; and

(3) any provision that under this Act is required or permitted to be set forth in the bylaws.

(c) The articles of incorporation need not set forth any of the corporate powers enumerated in this Act.

§ 2.03. Incorporation

(a) Unless a delayed effective date is specified, the corporate existence begins when the articles of incorporation are filed.

(b) The secretary of state's filing of the articles of incorporation is conclusive proof that the incorporators satisfied all conditions precedent to incorporation except in a proceeding by the state to cancel or revoke the incorporation or involuntarily dissolve the corporation.

§ 2.04. Liability for Preincorporation Transactions

All persons purporting to act as or on behalf of a corporation, knowing there was no incorporation under this Act, are jointly and severally liable for all liabilities created while so acting.

* * *

§ 2.06. Bylaws

(a) The incorporators or board of directors of a corporation shall adopt initial bylaws for the corporation.
(b) The bylaws of a corporation may contain any provision for managing the business and regulating the affairs of the corporation that is not inconsistent with law or the articles of incorporation.

* * *

§ 3.02. General Powers

Unless its articles of incorporation provide otherwise, every corporation has perpetual duration and succession in its corporate name and has the same powers as an individual to do all things necessary or convenient to carry out its business and affairs, including without limitation power:

(1) to sue and be sued, complain and defend in its corporate name;
(2) to have a corporate seal, which may be altered at will, and to use it, or a facsimile of it, by impressing or affixing it or in any other manner reproducing it;
(3) to make and amend bylaws, not inconsistent with its articles of incorporation or with the laws of this state, for managing the business and regulating the affairs of the corporation;

(4) to purchase, receive, lease, or otherwise acquire, and own, hold, improve, use, and otherwise deal with, real or personal property, or any legal or equitable interest in property, wherever located;

(5) to sell, convey, mortgage, pledge, lease, exchange, and otherwise dispose of all or any part of its property;

(6) to purchase, receive, subscribe for, or otherwise acquire; own, hold, vote, use, sell, mortgage, lend, pledge, or otherwise dispose of; and deal in and with shares or other interests in, or obligations of, any other entity;

(7) to make contracts and guarantees, incur liabilities, borrow money, issue its notes, bonds, and other obligations, (which may be convertible into or include the option to purchase other securities of the corporation), and secure any of its obligations by mortgage or pledge of any of its property, franchises, or income;

(8) to lend money, invest and reinvest its funds, and receive and hold real and personal property as security for repayment;

(9) to be a promoter, partner, member, associate, or manager of any partnership, joint venture, trust, or other entity;

(10) to conduct its business, locate offices, and exercise the powers granted by this Act within or without this state;

(11) to elect directors and appoint officers, employees, and agents of the corporation, define their duties, fix their compensation, and lend them money and credit;

(12) to pay pensions and establish pension plans, pension trusts, profit sharing plans, share bonus plans, share option plans, and benefit or incentive plans for any or all of its current or former directors, officers, employees, and agents;

(13) to make donations for the public welfare or for charitable, scientific, or educational purposes;

(14) to transact any lawful business that will aid governmental policy;

(15) to make payments or donations, or do any other act, not inconsistent with law, that furthers the business and affairs of the corporation.

* * *

§ 6.01. Authorized Shares

(a) The articles of incorporation must prescribe the classes of shares and the number of shares of each class that the corporation is authorized to issue. If more than one class of shares is authorized, the articles of incorporation must prescribe a distinguishing designation for each class, and prior to the issuance of shares of a class the preferences, limitations, and relative rights of that class must be described in the articles of incorporation. All shares of a class must have preferences, limitations, and relative rights identical with those of other shares of the same class except to the extent otherwise permitted by section 6.02.

(b) The articles of incorporation must authorize (1) one or more classes of shares that together have unlimited voting rights, and (2) one or more classes of shares (which may be the same class or classes as those with voting rights) that together are entitled to receive the net assets of the corporation upon dissolution.

(c) The articles of incorporation may authorize one or more classes of shares that:

(1) have special, conditional, or limited voting rights, or no right to vote, except to the extent prohibited by this Act;

(2) are redeemable or convertible as specified in the articles of incorporation (i) at the option of the corporation, the shareholder, or another person or upon the occurrence of a designated event; (ii) for cash, indebtedness, securities, or other property; (iii) in a designated amount or in an amount determined in accordance with a designated formula or by reference to extrinsic data or events;

(3) entitle the holders to distributions calculated in any manner, including dividends that may be cumulative, noncumulative, or partially cumulative;

(4) have preference over any other class of shares with respect to distributions, including dividends and distributions upon the dissolution of the corporation.

(d) The description of the designations, preferences, limitations, and relative rights of share classes in subsection (c) is not exhaustive.

* * *

§ 6.21. Issuance of Shares

(a) The powers granted in this section to the board of directors may be reserved to the shareholders by the articles of incorporation.

(b) The board of directors may authorize shares to be issued for consideration consisting of any tangible or intangible property or benefit to the corporation, including cash, promissory notes, services performed, contracts for services to be performed, or other securities of the corporation.

(c) Before the corporation issues shares, the board of directors must determine that the consideration received or to be received for shares to be issued is adequate. That determination by the board of directors is conclusive insofar as the adequacy of consideration for the issuance of shares relates to whether the shares are validly issued, fully paid, and nonassessable.

(d) When the corporation receives the consideration for which the board of directors authorized the issuance of shares, the shares issued therefor are fully paid and nonassessable.

(e) The corporation may place in escrow shares issued for a contract for future services or benefits or a promissory note, or make other arrangements to restrict the transfer of the shares, and may credit distributions in respect of the shares against their purchase price, until the services are performed, the note is paid, or the benefits received. If the services are not performed, the note is not paid, or the benefits are not received, the shares escrowed or restricted and the distributions credited may be cancelled in whole or part.

* * *

§ 6.27. Restriction on Transfer or Registration of Shares and Other Securities

(a) The articles of incorporation, bylaws, an agreement among shareholders, or an agreement between shareholders and the corporation may impose restrictions on the transfer or registration of transfer of shares of the corporation. A restriction does not affect shares issued before the restriction was adopted unless the holders of the shares are parties to the restriction agreement or voted in favor of the restriction.

(b) A restriction on the transfer or registration of transfer of shares is valid and enforceable against the holder or a transferee of the holder if the restriction is authorized by this section and its existence is noted conspicuously on the front or back of the certificate or is contained in the information statement required by section 6.26(b). Unless so noted, a restriction is not enforceable against a person without knowledge of the restriction.

(c) A restriction on the transfer or registration of transfer of shares is authorized:

(1) to maintain the corporation's status when it is dependent on the number or identity of its shareholders;
(2) to preserve exemptions under federal or state securities law;
(3) for any other reasonable purpose.

(d) A restriction on the transfer or registration of transfer of shares may:

(1) obligate the shareholder first to offer the corporation or other persons (separately, consecutively, or simultaneously) an opportunity to acquire the restricted shares;
(2) obligate the corporation or other persons (separately, consecutively, or simultaneously) to acquire the restricted shares;
(3) require the corporation, the holders of any class of its shares, or another person to approve the transfer of the restricted shares, if the requirement is not manifestly unreasonable;
(4) prohibit the transfer of the restricted shares to designated persons or classes of persons, if the prohibition is not manifestly unreasonable.

(e) For purposes of this section, "shares" includes a security convertible into or carrying a right to subscribe for or acquire shares.

* * *

§ 6.40. Distributions to Shareholders

(a) A board of directors may authorize and the corporation may make distributions to its shareholders subject to restriction by the articles of incorporation and the limitation in subsection (c).

(b) If the board of directors does not fix the record date for determining shareholders entitled to a distribution (other than one involving a repurchase or reacquisition of shares), it is the date the board of directors authorizes the distribution.

(c) No distribution may be made if, after giving it effect:

(1) the corporation would not be able to pay its debts as they become due in the usual course of business; or
(2) the corporation's total assets would be less than the sum of its total liabilities plus (unless the articles of incorporation permit otherwise) the amount that would be needed, if the corporation were to be dissolved at the time of the distribution, to satisfy the preferential rights upon dissolution of shareholders whose preferential rights are superior to those receiving the distribution.

(d) The board of directors may base a determination that a distribution is not prohibited under subsection (c) either on financial statements prepared on the basis of accounting practices and principles that are reasonable in the circumstances or on a fair valuation or other method that is reasonable in the circumstances.

(e) The effect of a distribution under subsection (c) is measured:

(1) in the case of distribution by purchase, redemption, or other acquisition of the corporation's shares, as of the earlier of (i) the date money or other property is transferred or debt incurred by the corporation or (ii) the date the shareholder ceases to be a shareholder with respect to the acquired shares;
(2) in the case of any other distribution of indebtedness, as of the date the indebtedness is distributed;
(3) in all other cases, as of (i) the date the distribution is authorized if the payment occurs within 120 days after the date of authorization or (ii) the date the payment is made if it occurs more than 120 days after the date of authorization.

(f) A corporation's indebtedness to a shareholder incurred by reason of a distribution made in accordance with this section is at parity with the corporation's indebtedness to its general, unsecured creditors except to the extent subordinated by agreement.

* * *

§ 7.01. Annual Meeting

(a) A corporation shall hold annually at a time stated in or fixed in accordance with the bylaws a meeting of shareholders.

(b) Annual shareholders' meetings may be held in or out of this state at the place stated in or fixed in accordance with the bylaws. If no place is stated in or fixed in accordance with the bylaws, annual meetings shall be held at the corporation's principal office.

(c) The failure to hold an annual meeting at the time stated in or fixed in accordance with a corporation's bylaws does not affect the validity of any corporate action.

* * *

§ 7.03. Court-Ordered Meeting

(a) The [name or describe] court of the county where a corporation's principal office (or, if none in this state, its registered office) is located may summarily order a meeting to be held:

(1) On application of any shareholder of the corporation entitled to participate in an annual meeting if an annual meeting was not held within the earlier of 6 months after the end of the corporation's fiscal year or 15 months after its last annual meeting; or

(2) on application of a shareholder who signed a demand for a special meeting valid under section 7.02 if:

(i) notice of the special meeting was given within 30 days after the date the demand was delivered to the corporation's secretary; or

(ii) the special meeting was not held in accordance with the notice.

(b) The court may fix the time and place of the meeting, determine the shares entitled to participate in the meeting, specify a record date for determining shareholders entitled to notice of and to vote at the meeting, prescribe the form and content of the meeting notice, fix the quorum required for specific matters to be considered at the meeting (or direct that the votes represented at the meeting constitute a quorum for action on those matters), and enter other orders necessary to accomplish the purpose or purposes of the meeting.

* * *

§ 7.25. Quorum and Voting Requirements for Voting Groups

(a) Shares entitled to vote as a separate voting group may take action on a matter at a meeting only if a quorum of those shares exists with respect to that matter. Unless the articles of incorporation or this Act provide otherwise, a majority of the votes entitled to be cast on the matter by the voting group constitutes a quorum of that voting group for action on that matter.

(b) Once a share is represented for any purpose at a meeting, it is deemed present for quorum purposes for the remainder of the meeting and for any adjournment of that meeting unless a new record date is or must be set for that adjourned meeting.

(c) If a quorum exists, action on a matter (other than the election of directors) by a voting group is approved if the votes cast within the voting group favoring the action exceed the votes cast opposing the action, unless the articles of incorporation or this Act require a greater number of affirmative votes.

(d) An amendment of articles of incorporation adding, changing, or deleting a quorum or voting requirement for a voting group greater than specified in subsection (b) or (c) is governed by section 7.27.

(e) The election of directors is governed by section 7.28.

§ 7.27. Greater Quorum or Voting Requirements

(a) The articles of incorporation may provide for a greater quorum or voting requirement for shareholders (or voting groups of shareholders) than is provided by this Act.

(b) An amendment to the articles of incorporation that adds, changes, or deletes a greater quorum or voting requirement must meet the same quorum requirement and be adopted by the same vote and voting groups required to take action under the quorum and voting requirements then in effect or proposed to be adopted, whichever is greater.

* * *

§ 7.30. Voting Trusts

(a) One or more shareholders may create a voting trust, conferring on a trustee the right to vote or otherwise act for them, by signing an agreement setting out the provisions of the trust (which may include anything consistent with its purpose) and transferring their shares to the trustee. When a voting trust agreement is signed, the trustee shall prepare a list of the names and addresses of all owners of beneficial interests in the trust, together with the number and class of shares each transferred to the trust, and deliver copies of the list and agreement to the corporation's principal office.

(b) A voting trust becomes effective on the date the first shares subject to the trust are registered in the trustee's name. A voting trust is valid for not more than 10 years after its effective date unless extended under subsection (c).

(c) All or some of the parties to a voting trust may extend it for additional terms of not more than 10 years each by signing an extension agreement and obtaining the voting trustee's written consent to the extension. An extension is valid for 10 years from the date the first shareholder signs the extension agreement. The voting trustee must deliver copies of the extension agreement and list of beneficial owners to the corporation's principal office. An extension agreement binds only those parties signing it.

* * *

§ 7.40. Procedure in Derivative Proceedings

(a) A person may not commence a proceeding in the right of a domestic or foreign corporation unless he was a shareholder of the corporation when the transaction complained of occurred or unless he became a shareholder through transfer by operation of law from one who was a shareholder at that time.

(b) A complaint in a proceeding brought in the right of a corporation must be verified and allege with particularity the demand made, if any, to obtain action by the board of directors and either that the demand was refused or ignored or why he did not make the demand. Whether or not a demand for action was made, if the corporation commences an investigation of the changes made in the demand or complaint, the court may stay any proceeding until the investigation is completed.

(c) A proceeding commenced under this section may not be discontinued or settled without the court's approval. If the court determines that a proposed discontinuance or settlement will substantially affect the interest of the corporation's shareholders or a class of shareholders, the court shall direct that notice be given the shareholders affected.

(d) On termination of the proceeding the court may require the plaintiff to pay any defendant's reasonable expenses (including counsel fees) incurred in defending the proceeding if it finds that the proceeding was commenced without reasonable cause.

(e) For purposes of this section, "shareholder" includes a beneficial owner whose shares are held in a voting trust or held by a nominee on his behalf.

§ 8.01. Requirement for and Duties of Board of Directors

(a) Except as provided in subsection (c), each corporation must have a board of directors.

(b) All corporate powers shall be exercised by or under the authority of, and the business and affairs of the corporation managed under the direction of, its board of directors, subject to any limitation set forth in the articles of incorporation.

(c) A corporation having 50 or fewer shareholders may dispense with or limit the authority of a board of directors by describing in its articles of incorporation who will perform some or all the duties of a board of directors.

* * *

§ 8.03. Number and Election of Directors

(a) A board of directors must consist of one or more individuals, with the number specified in or fixed in accordance with the articles of incorporation or bylaws.

(b) If a board of directors has power to fix or change the number of directors, the board may increase or decrease by 30 percent or less the number of directors last approved by the shareholders, but only the shareholders may increase or decrease by more than 30 percent the number of directors last approved by the shareholders.

(c) The articles of incorporation or bylaws may establish a variable range for the size of the board of directors by fixing a minimum and maximum number of directors. If a variable range is established, the number of directors may be fixed or changed from time to time, within the minimum and maximum, by the shareholders or the board of directors. After shares are issued, only the shareholders may change the range for the size of the board or change from a fixed to a variable-range size board or vice versa.

(d) Directors are elected at the first annual shareholders' meeting and at each annual meeting thereafter unless their terms are staggered under section 8.06.

§ 8.04. Election of Directors by Certain Classes of Shareholders

If the articles of incorporation authorize dividing the shares into classes, the articles may also authorize the election of all or a specified number of directors by the holders of one or more authorized classes of shares. Each class (or

classes) of shares entitled to elect one or more directors is a separate voting group for purposes of the election of directors.

* * *

§ 8.08. Removal of Directors by Shareholders

(a) The shareholders may remove one or more directors with or without cause unless the articles of incorporation provide that directors may be removed only for cause.

(b) If a director is elected by a voting group of shareholders, only the shareholders of that voting group may participate in the vote to remove him.

(c) If cumulative voting is authorized, a director may not be removed if the number of votes sufficient to elect him under cumulative voting is voted against his removal. If cumulative voting is not authorized, a director may be removed only if the number of votes cast to remove him exceeds the number of votes cast not to remove him.

(d) A director may be removed by the shareholders only at a meeting called for the purpose of removing him and the meeting notice must state that the purpose, or one of the purposes, of the meeting is removal of the director.

§ 8.09. Removal of Directors by Judicial Proceeding

(a) The [name or describe] court of the county where a corporation's principal office (or, if none in this state, its registered office) is located may remove a director of the corporation from office in a proceeding commenced either by the corporation or by its shareholders holding at least 10 percent of the outstanding shares of any class if the court finds that (1) the director engaged in fraudulent or dishonest conduct, or gross abuse of authority or discretion, with respect to the corporation and (2) removal is in the best interest of the corporation.

(b) The court that removes a director may bar the director from reelection for a period prescribed by the court.

(c) If shareholders commence a proceeding under subsection (a), they shall make the corporation a party defendant.

* * *

§ 8.24. Quorum and Voting

(a) Unless the articles of incorporation or bylaws require a greater number, a quorum of a board of directors consists of:

(1) a majority of the fixed number of directors if the corporation has a fixed board size; or

(2) a majority of the number of directors prescribed, or if no number is prescribed the number in office immediately before the meeting begins, if the corporation has a variable range size board.

(b) The articles of incorporation or bylaws may authorize a quorum of a board of directors to consist of no fewer than one-third of the fixed or prescribed number of directors determined under subsection (a).

(c) If a quorum is present when a vote is taken, the affirmative vote of a majority of directors present is the act of the board of directors unless the articles of incorporation or bylaws require the vote of a greater number of directors.

(d) A director who is present at a meeting of the board of directors or a committee of the board of directors when corporate action is taken is deemed to have assented to the action taken unless: (1) he objects at the beginning of the meeting (or promptly upon his arrival) to holding it or transacting business at the meeting; (2) his dissent or abstention from the action taken is entered in the minutes of the meeting; or (3) he delivers written notice of his dissent or abstention to the presiding officer of the meeting before its adjournment or to the corporation immediately after adjournment of the meeting. The right of dissent or abstention is not available to a director who votes in favor of the action taken.

§ 8.25. Committees

(a) Unless the articles of incorporation or bylaws provide otherwise, a board of directors may create one or more committees and appoint members of the board of directors to serve on them. Each committee may have two or more members, who serve at the pleasure of the board of directors.

(b) The creation of a committee and appointment of members to it must be approved by the greater of (1) a majority of all the directors in office when the action is taken or (2) the number of directors required by the articles of incorporation or bylaws to take action under section 8.24.

(c) Sections 8.20 through 8.24, which govern meetings, action without meetings, notice and waiver of notice, and quorum and voting requirements of the board of directors, apply to committees and their members as well.

(d) To the extent specified by the board of directors or in the articles of incorporation or bylaws, each committee may exercise the authority of the board of directors under section 8.01.

(e) A committee may not, however:

(1) authorize distributions;
(2) approve or propose to shareholders action that this Act requires to be approved by shareholders;
(3) fill vacancies on the board of directors or on any of its committees;
(4) amend articles of incorporation pursuant to section 10.02;
(5) adopt, amend, or repeal bylaws;
(6) approve a plan of merger not requiring shareholder approval;
(7) authorize or approve reacquisition of shares, except according to a formula or method prescribed by the board of directors; or
(8) authorize or approve the issuance or sale or contract for sale of shares, or determine the designation and relative rights, preferences, and limitations of a class or series of shares, except that the board of directors may

authorize a committee (or a senior executive officer of the corporation) to do so within limits specifically prescribed by the board of directors.

(f) The creation of, delegation of authority to, or action by a committee does not alone constitute compliance by a director with the standards of conduct described in section 8.30.

§ 8.30. General Standards for Directors

(a) A director shall discharge his duties as a director, including his duties as a member of a committee:

(1) in good faith;
(2) with the care an ordinarily prudent person in a like position would exercise under similar circumstances; and
(3) in a manner he reasonably believes to be in the best interests of the corporation.

(b) In discharging his duties a director is entitled to rely on information, opinions, reports, or statements, including financial statements and other financial data, if prepared or presented by:

(1) one or more officers or employees of the corporation whom the director reasonably believes to be reliable and competent in the matters presented;
(2) legal counsel, public accountants, or other persons as to matters the director reasonably believes are within the person's professional or expert competence; or
(3) a committee of the board of directors of which he is not a member if the director reasonably believes the committee merits confidence.

(c) A director is not acting in good faith if he has knowledge concerning the matter in question that makes reliance otherwise permitted by subsection (b) unwarranted.

(d) A director is not liable for any action taken as a director, or any failure to take any action, if he performed the duties of his office in compliance with this section.

§ 8.31. Director Conflict of Interest

(a) A conflict of interest transaction is a transaction with the corporation in which a director of the corporation has a direct or indirect interest. A conflict of interest transaction is not voidable by the corporation solely because of the director's interest in the transaction if any one of the following is true:

(1) the material facts of the transaction and the director's interest were disclosed or known to the board of directors or a committee of the board of directors and the board of directors or committee authorized, approved, or ratified the transaction;
(2) the material facts of the transaction and the director's interest were disclosed or known to the shareholders entitled to vote and they authorized, approved, or ratified the transaction; or

(3) the transaction was fair to the corporation.

(b) For purposes of this section, a director of the corporation has an indirect interest in a transaction if (1) another entity in which he has a material financial interest or in which he is a general partner is a party to the transaction or (2) another entity of which he is a director, officer, or trustee is a party to the transaction and the transaction is or should be considered by the board of directors of the corporation.

(c) For purposes of subsection (a)(1), a conflict of interest transaction is authorized, approved, or ratified if it receives the affirmative vote of a majority of the directors on the board of directors (or on the committee) who have no direct or indirect interest in the transaction, but a transaction may not be authorized, approved, or ratified under this section by a single director. If a majority of the directors who have no direct or indirect interest in the transaction vote to authorize, approve, or ratify the transaction, a quorum is present for the purpose of taking action under this section. The presence of, or vote cast by, a director with a direct or indirect interest in the transaction does not affect the validity of any action taken under subsection (a)(1) if the transaction is otherwise authorized, approved, or ratified as provided in that subsection.

(d) For purposes of subsection (a)(2), a conflict of interest transaction is authorized, approved, or ratified if it receives the vote of a majority of the shares entitled to be counted under this subsection. Shares owned by or voted under the control of a director who has a direct or indirect interest in the transaction, and shares owned by or voted under the control of an entity described in subsection (b)(1), may not be counted in a vote of shareholders to determine whether to authorize, approve, or ratify a conflict of interest transaction under subsection (a)(2). The vote of those shares, however, shall be counted in determining whether the transaction is approved under other sections of this Act. A majority of the shares, whether or not present, that are entitled to be counted in a vote on the transaction under this subsection constitutes a quorum for the purpose of taking action under this section.

§ 8.32. Loans to Directors

(a) Except as provided by subsection (c), a corporation may not lend money to or guarantee the obligation of a director of the corporation unless:

(1) the particular loan or guarantee is approved by a majority of the votes represented by the outstanding voting shares of all classes, voting as a single voting group, except the votes of shares owned by or voted under the control of the benefited director; or
(2) the corporation's board of directors determines that the loan or guarantee benefits the corporation and either approves the specific loan or guarantee or a general plan authorizing loans and guarantees.

(b) The fact that a loan or guarantee is made in violation of this section does not affect the borrower's liability on the loan.
(c) This section does not apply to loans and guarantees authorized by statute regulating any special class of corporations.

§ 8.33. Liability for Unlawful Distributions

(a) Unless he complies with the applicable standards of conduct described in section 8.30, a director who votes for or assents to a distribution made in violation of this Act or the articles of incorporation is personally liable to the corporation for the amount of the distribution that exceeds what could have been distributed without violating this Act or the articles of incorporation.
(b) A director held liable for an unlawful distribution under subsection (a) is entitled to contribution:

(1) from every other director who voted for or assented to the distribution without complying with the applicable standards of conduct described in section 8.30; and
(2) from each shareholder for the amount the shareholder accepted knowing the distribution was made in violation of this Act or the articles of incorporation.

* * *

§ 8.40. Required Officers

(a) A corporation has the officers described in its bylaws or appointed by the board of directors in accordance with the bylaws.
(b) A duly appointed officer may appoint one or more officers or assistant officers if authorized by the bylaws or the board of directors.
(c) The bylaws or the board of directors shall delegate to one of the officers responsibility for preparing minutes of the directors' and shareholders' meetings and for authenticating records of the corporation.
(d) The same individual may simultaneously hold more than one office in a corporation.

* * *

§ 8.42. Standards of Conduct for Officers

(a) An officer with discretionary authority shall discharge his duties under that authority:

(1) in good faith;
(2) with the care an ordinarily prudent person in a like position would exercise under similar circumstances; and
(3) in a manner he reasonably believes to be in the best interests of the corporation.

(b) In discharging his duties an officer is entitled to rely on information, opinions, reports, or statements, including financial statements and other financial data, if prepared or presented by:

(1) one or more officers or employees of the corporation whom the officer reasonably believes to be reliable and competent in the matters presented; or

(2) legal counsel, public accountants, or other persons as to matters the officer reasonably believes are within the person's professional or expert competence.

(c) An officer is not acting in good faith if he has knowledge concerning the matter in question that makes reliance otherwise permitted by subsection (b) unwarranted.

(d) An officer is not liable for any action taken as an officer, or any failure to take any action, if he performed the duties of his office in compliance with this section.

* * *

§ 8.52. Mandatory Indemnification

Unless limited by its articles of incorporation, a corporation shall indemnify a director who was wholly successful, on the merits or otherwise, in the defense of any proceeding to which he was a party because he is or was a director of the corporation against reasonable expenses incurred by him in connection with the proceeding.

* * *

§ 8.56. Indemnification of Officers, Employees, and Agents

Unless a corporation's articles of incorporation provide otherwise:

(1) an officer of the corporation who is not a director is entitled to mandatory indemnification under section 8.52, and is entitled to apply for court-ordered indemnification under section 8.54, in each case to the same extent as a director;

(2) the corporation may indemnify and advance expenses under this subchapter to an officer, employee, or agent of the corporation who is not a director to the same extent as to a director; and

(3) a corporation may also indemnify and advance expenses to an officer, employee, or agent who is not a director to the extent, consistent with public policy, that may be provided by its articles of incorporation, bylaws, general or specific action of its board of directors, or contract.

* * *

§ 10.02. Amendment by Board of Directors

Unless the articles of incorporation provide otherwise, a corporation's board of directors may adopt one or more amendments to the corporation's articles of incorporation without shareholder action:

(1) to extend the duration of the corporation if it was incorporated at a time when limited duration was required by law;

(2) to delete the names and addresses of the initial directors;

(3) to delete the name and address of the initial registered agent or registered office, if a statement of change is on file with the secretary of state;

(4) to change each issued and unissued authorized share of an outstanding class into a greater number of whole shares if the corporation has only shares of that class outstanding;

(5) to change the corporate name by substituting the word "corporation," "incorporated," "company," "limited," or the abbreviation "corp.," "inc.," "co.," or "ltd.," for a similar word or abbreviation in the name, or by adding, deleting, or changing a geographical attribution for the name; or

(6) to make any other change expressly permitted by this Act to be made without shareholder action.

§ 10.03. Amendment by Board of Directors and Shareholders

(a) A corporation's board of directors may propose one or more amendments to the articles of incorporation for submission to the shareholders.

(b) For the amendment to be adopted:

(1) the board of directors must recommend the amendment to the shareholders unless the board of directors determines that because of conflict of interest or other special circumstances it should make no recommendation and communicates the basis for its determination to the shareholders with the amendment; and

(2) the shareholders entitled to vote on the amendment must approve the amendment as provided in subsection (e).

(c) The board of directors may condition its submission of the proposed amendment on any basis.

(d) The corporation shall notify each shareholder, whether or not entitled to vote, of the proposed shareholders' meeting in accordance with section 7.05. The notice of meeting must also state that the purpose, or one of the purposes, of the meeting is to consider the proposed amendment and contain or be accompanied by a copy or summary of the amendment.

(e) Unless this Act, the articles of incorporation, or the board of directors (acting pursuant to subsection (c)) require a greater vote or a vote by voting groups, the amendment to be adopted must be approved by:

(1) a majority of the votes entitled to be cast on the amendment by any voting group with respect to which the amendment would create dissenters' rights; and

(2) the votes required by sections 7.25 and 7.26 by every other voting group entitled to vote on the amendment.

§ 10.04. Voting on Amendments by Voting Groups

(a) The holders of the outstanding shares of a class are entitled to vote as a separate voting group (if shareholder voting is otherwise required by this Act) on a proposed amendment if the amendment would:

(1) increase or decrease the aggregate number of authorized shares of the class;

(2) effect an exchange or reclassification of all or part of the shares of the class into shares of another class;

(3) effect an exchange or reclassification, or create the right of exchange, of all or part of the shares of another class into shares of the class;

(4) change the designation, rights, preferences, or limitations of all or part of the shares of the class;

(5) change the shares of all or part of the class into a different number of shares of the same class;

(6) create a new class of shares having rights or preferences with respect to distributions or to dissolution that are prior, superior, or substantially equal to the shares of the class;

(7) increase the rights, preferences, or number of authorized shares of any class that, after giving effect to the amendment, have rights or preferences with respect to distributions or to dissolution that are prior, superior, or substantially equal to the shares of the class;

(8) limit or deny an existing preemptive right of all or part of the shares of the class; or

(9) cancel or otherwise affect rights to distributions or dividends that have accumulated but not yet been declared on all or part of the shares of the class.

(b) If a proposed amendment would affect a series of a class of shares in one or more of the ways described in subsection (a), the shares of that series are entitled to vote as a separate voting group on the proposed amendment.

(c) If a proposed amendment that entitles two or more series of shares to vote as separate voting groups under this section would affect those two or more series in the same or a substantially similar way, the shares of all the series so affected must vote together as a single voting group on the proposed amendment.

(d) A class or series of shares is entitled to the voting rights granted by this section although the articles of incorporation provide that the shares are nonvoting shares.

* * *

§ 10.20. Amendment by Board of Directors or Shareholders

(a) A corporation's board of directors may amend or repeal the corporation's bylaws unless:

(1) the articles of incorporation or this Act reserve this power exclusively to the shareholders in whole or part; or

(2) the shareholders in amending or repealing a particular bylaw provide expressly that the board of directors may not amend or repeal that bylaw.

(b) A corporation's shareholders may amend or repeal the corporation's bylaws even though the bylaws may also be amended or repealed by its board of directors.

* * *

§ 11.01. Merger

(a) One or more corporations may merge into another corporation if the board of directors of each corporation adopts and its shareholders (if required by section 11.03) approve a plan of merger.

(b) The plan of merger must set forth:

(1) the name of each corporation planning to merge and the name of the surviving corporation into which each other corporation plans to merge;

(2) the terms and conditions of the merger; and

(3) the manner and basis of converting the shares of each corporation into shares, obligations, or other securities of the surviving or any other corporation or into cash or other property in whole or part.

(c) The plan of merger may set forth:

(1) amendments to the articles of incorporation of the surviving corporation; and

(2) other provisions relating to the merger.

* * *

§ 12.01. Sale of Assets in Regular Course of Business and Mortgage of Assets

(a) A corporation may, on the terms and conditions and for the consideration determined by the board of directors:

(1) sell, lease, exchange, or otherwise dispose of all, or substantially all, of its property in the usual and regular course of business,

(2) mortgage, pledge, dedicate to the repayment of indebtedness (whether with or without recourse), or otherwise encumber any or all of its property whether or not in the usual and regular course of business, or

(3) transfer any or all of its property to a corporation all the shares of which are owned by the corporation.

(b) Unless the articles of incorporation require it, approval by the shareholders of a transaction described in subsection (a) is not required.

* * *

§ 14.07. Unknown Claims Against Dissolved Corporation

(a) A dissolved corporation may also publish notice of its dissolution and request that persons with claims against the corporation present them in accordance with the notice.

(b) The notice must:

(1) be published one time in a newspaper of general circulation in the county where the dissolved corporation's principal office (or, if none in this state, its registered office) is or was last located;

(2) describe the information that must be included in a claim and provide a mailing address where the claim may be sent; and

(3) state that a claim against the corporation will be barred unless a proceeding to enforce the claim is commenced within five years after the publication of the notice.

(c) If the dissolved corporation publishes a newspaper notice in accordance with subsection (b), the claim of each of the following claimants is barred unless the claimant commences a proceeding to enforce the claim against the dissolved corporation within five years after the publication date of the newspaper notice:

(1) a claimant who did not receive written notice under section 14.06;
(2) a claimant whose claim was timely sent to the dissolved corporation but not acted on;
(3) a claimant whose claim is contingent or based on an event occurring after the effective date of dissolution.

(d) A claim may be enforced under this section:

(1) against the dissolved corporation, to the extent of its undistributed assets; or
(2) if the assets have been distributed in liquidation, against a shareholder of the dissolved corporation to the extent of his pro rata share of the claim or the corporate assets distributed to him in liquidation, whichever is less, but a shareholder's total liability for all claims under this section may not exceed the total amount of assets distributed to him.

§ 14.20. Grounds for Administrative Dissolution

The secretary of state may commence a proceeding under section 14.21 to administratively dissolve a corporation if:

(1) the corporation does not pay within 60 days after they are due any franchise taxes or penalties imposed by this Act or other law;
(2) the corporation does not deliver its annual report to the secretary of state within 60 days after it is due,
(3) the corporation is without a registered agent or registered office in this state for 60 days or more;
(4) the corporation does not notify the secretary of state within 60 days that its registered agent or registered office has been changed, that its registered agent has resigned, or that its registered office has been discontinued; or
(5) the corporation's period of duration stated in its articles of incorporation expires.

* * *

§ 14.30. Grounds for Judicial Dissolution

The [name or describe court or courts] may dissolve a corporation:

(1) in a proceeding by the attorney general if it is established that:

(i) the corporation obtained its articles of incorporation through fraud; or

(ii) the corporation has continued to exceed or abuse the authority conferred upon it by law;

(2) in a proceeding by a shareholder if it is established that:

(i) the directors are deadlocked in the management of the corporate affairs, the shareholders are unable to break the deadlock, and irreparable injury to the corporation is threatened or being suffered, or the business and affairs of the corporation can no longer be conducted to the advantage of the shareholders generally, because of the deadlock;
(ii) the directors or those in control of the corporation have acted, are acting, or will act in a manner that is illegal, oppressive, or fraudulent;
(iii) the shareholders are deadlocked in voting power and have failed, for a period that includes at least two consecutive annual meeting dates, to elect successors to directors whose terms have expired; or
(iv) the corporate assets are being misapplied or wasted;

(3) in a proceeding by a creditor if it is established that:

(i) the creditor's claim has been reduced to judgment, the execution on the judgment returned unsatisfied, and the corporation is insolvent; or
(ii) the corporation has admitted in writing that the creditor's claim is due and owing and the corporation is insolvent; or

(4) in a proceeding by the corporation to have its voluntary dissolution continued under court supervision.

* * *

§ 15.01. Authority to Transact Business Required

(a) A foreign corporation may not transact business in this state until it obtains a certificate of authority from the secretary of state.
(b) The following activities, among others, do not constitute transacting business within the meaning of subsection (a):

(1) maintaining, defending, or settling any proceeding;
(2) holding meetings of the board of directors or shareholders or carrying on other activities concerning internal corporate affairs;
(3) maintaining bank accounts;
(4) maintaining offices or agencies for the transfer, exchange, and registration of the corporation's own securities or maintaining trustees or depositaries with respect to those securities;
(5) selling through independent contractors;
(6) soliciting or obtaining orders, whether by mail or through employees or agents or otherwise, if the orders require acceptance outside this state before they become contracts;
(7) creating or acquiring indebtedness, mortgages, and security interests in real or personal property;

(8) securing or collecting debts or enforcing mortgages and security interests in property securing the debts;
(9) owning, without more, real or personal property;
(10) conducting an isolated transaction that is completed within 30 days and that is not one in the course of repeated transactions of a like nature;
(11) transacting business in interstate commerce.

(c) The list of activities in subsection (b) is not exhaustive.

* * *

§ 16.02. Inspection of Records by Shareholders

(a) Subject to section 16.03(c), a shareholder of a corporation is entitled to inspect and copy, during regular business hours at the corporation's principal office, any of the records of the corporation described in section 16.01(e) if he gives the corporation written notice of his demand at least five business days before the date on which he wishes to inspect and copy.

(b) A shareholder of a corporation is entitled to inspect and copy, during regular business hours at a reasonable location specified by the corporation, any of the following records of the corporation if the shareholder meets the requirements of subsection (c) and gives the corporation written notice of his demand at least five business days before the date on which he wishes to inspect and copy:

(1) excerpts from minutes of any meeting of the board of directors, records of any action of a committee of the board of directors while acting in place of the board of directors on behalf of the corporation, minutes of any meeting of the shareholders, and records of action taken by the shareholders or board of directors without a meeting, to the extent not subject to inspection under section 16.02(a);
(2) accounting records of the corporation; and
(3) the record of shareholders.

(c) A shareholder may inspect and copy the records identified in subsection (b) only if:

(1) his demand is made in good faith and for a proper purpose;
(2) he describes with reasonable particularity his purpose and the records he desires to inspect; and
(3) the records are directly connected with his purpose.

(d) The right of inspection granted by this section may not be abolished or limited by a corporation's articles of incorporation or bylaws.

(e) This section does not affect:

(1) the right of a shareholder to inspect records under section 7.20 or, if the shareholder is in litigation with the corporation, to the same extent as any other litigant;
(2) the power of a court, independently of this Act, to compel the production of corporate records for examination.

§ 16.03. Scope of Inspection Right

(a) A shareholder's agent or attorney has the same inspection and copying rights as the shareholder he represents.
(b) The right to copy records under section 16.02 includes, if reasonable, the right to receive copies made by photographic, xerographic, or other means.
(c) The corporation may impose a reasonable charge, covering the costs of labor and material, for copies of any documents provided to the shareholder. The charge may not exceed the estimated cost of production or reproduction of the records.
(d) The corporation may comply with a shareholder's demand to inspect the record of shareholders under section 16.02(b)(3) by providing him with a list of its shareholders that was compiled no earlier than the date of the shareholder's demand.

* * *

§ 16.21. Other Reports to Shareholders

(a) If a corporation indemnifies or advances expenses to a director under section 8.51, 8.52, 8.53, or 8.54 in connection with a proceeding by or in the right of the corporation, the corporation shall report the indemnification or advance in writing to the shareholders with or before the notice of the next shareholder's meeting.
(b) If a corporation issues or authorizes the issuance of shares for promissory notes or for promises to render services in the future, the corporation shall report in writing to the shareholders the number of shares authorized or issued, and the consideration received by the corporation, with or before the notice of the next shareholders' meeting.

* * *

DICTIONARY OF LEGAL TERMS

abatement   Reduction or elimination of gifts by category upon the reduction in value of the estate.

absolute surety   Surety liable to a creditor immediately upon the default of the principal debtor.

acceptance   *Commercial paper*   Acceptance is the drawee's signed engagement to honor the draft as presented. It becomes operative when completed by delivery or notification. U.C.C. § 3–410.

Contracts   Compliance by offeree with terms and conditions of offer.

Sale of goods   U.C.C. § 2–606 provides three ways a buyer can accept goods: (1) by signifying to the seller that the goods are conforming or that he will accept them in spite of their nonconformity, (2) by failing to make an effective rejection, and (3) by doing an act inconsistent with the seller's ownership.

acceptor   Drawee who has accepted an instrument.

accession   An addition to one's property by increase of the original property or by production from such property. E.g., A innocently converts the wheat of B into bread. U.C.C. § 9–315 changes the common law where a perfected security interest is involved.

accident and health insurance   Provides protection from losses due to accident or sickness.

accommodation   An arrangement made as a favor to another, usually involving a loan of money or commercial paper. While a party's intent may be to aid a maker of note by lending his credit, if he seeks to accomplish thereby legitimate objects of his own, and not simply to aid the maker, the act is not for accommodation.

accommodation indorser   Signer not in the chain of title.

accommodation party   A person who signs commercial paper in any capacity for the purpose of lending his name to another party to an instrument. U.C.C. § 3–415.

accord and satisfaction   A method of discharging a claim whereby the parties agree to accept something in settlement, the "accord" being the agreement and the "satisfaction" its execution or performance. It is a new contract that

is substituted for an old contract, which is thereby discharged, or for an obligation or cause of action and that must have all of the elements of a valid contract.

account   Any account with a bank, including a checking, time, interest or savings account. U.C.C. § 4–194. Also, any right to payment, for goods or services, that is not evidenced by an instrument or chattel paper. E.g., account receivable.

accounting   Equitable proceeding for a complete settlement of all partnership affairs.

act of state doctrine   Rule that a court should not question the validity of actions taken by a foreign government in its own country.

actual authority   Power conferred upon agent by actual consent given by principal.

actual express authority   Actual authority derived from written or spoken words of principal.

actual implied authority   Actual authority inferred from words or conduct manifested to agent by principal.

actual notice   Knowledge actually and expressly communicated.

actus reas   Wrongful or overt act.

ademption   The removal or extinction of a devise by act of the testator.

adequacy of consideration   Not required where parties have freely agreed to the exchange.

adhesion contract   Standard "form" contract, usually between a large retailer and a consumer, in which the weaker party has no realistic choice or opportunity to bargain.

adjudication   The giving or pronouncing of a judgment in a case; also the judgment given.

administrative agency   Governmental entity (other than courts and legislatures) having authority to affect the rights of private parties.

administrative law   Law dealing with the establishment, duties and powers of agencies in the executive branch of government.

administrative process   Entire set of activities engaged in by administrative agencies while carrying out their rule-making, enforcement, and adjudicative functions.

---

*Many of the definitions are abridged and adapted from *Black's Law Dictionary*, 5th Edition.

administrator A person appointed by the court to manage the assets and liabilities of an intestate (person dying without a will). A person who is named in the will by testator (person dying with a will) is called the executor. Female designations are administratrix and executrix.

adversary system System in which opposing parties initiate and present their case.

adverse possession A method of acquisition of title to real property by possession for a statutory period under certain conditions. There may be different periods of time, depending on whether the adverse possessor has color of title.

affidavit A written statement of facts, made voluntarily, confirmed by oath or affirmation of party making it, and taken before an authorized officer.

affiliate Person who controls, is controlled by, or is under common control with the issuer.

affirm Uphold the lower court's judgment.

affirmative action Active recruitment of minority applicants.

affirmative defense A response that attacks the plaintiff's legal right to bring an action as opposed to attacking the truth of the claim. E.g., accord and satisfaction; assumption of risk; contributory negligence; duress; estoppel.

affirmative disclosure Requirement that an advertiser include certain information in its advertisement so that it is not deceptive.

after acquired property Property the debtor may acquire at some time after the security interest attaches.

agency Relation in which one person acts for or represents another by the latter's authority.
  Actual agency Exists where the agent is really employed by the principal.
  Agency by estoppel One created by operation of law and established by proof of such acts of the principal as reasonably lead to the conclusion of its existence.
  Implied agency One created by acts of parties and deduced from proof of other facts.

agent Person authorized to act on another's behalf.

allegation A statement of a party setting out what he expects to prove.

allonge Piece of paper firmly affixed to the instrument.

annuity contract Agreement to pay periodic sums to insured upon reaching a designated age.

annul To annul a judgment or judicial proceeding is to deprive it of all force and operation.

answer The answer is the formal written statement made by a defendant setting forth the ground of his defense.

antecedent debt Preexisting obligation.

anticipatory breach of contract (or **anticipatory repudiation**) The unjustified assertion by a party that he will not perform an obligation that he is contractually obligated to perform at a future time. See U.C.C. §§ 610 & 611.

apparent authority Such principal power that a reasonable person would assume an agent has in light of the principal's conduct.

appeal Resort to a superior (appellate) court to review the decision of an inferior (trial) court or administrative agency.

appeal by right Mandatory review by a higher court.

appellant A party who takes an appeal from one court to another. He may be either the plaintiff or defendant in the original court proceeding.

appellee The party in a cause against whom an appeal is taken; that is, the party who has an interest adverse to setting aside or reversing the judgment. Sometimes also called the "respondent."

appropriation Unauthorized use of another person's name or likeness for one's own benefit.

appurtenances Things appurtenant pass as incident to the principal thing. Sometimes an easement consisting of a right of way over one piece of land will pass with another piece of land as being appurtenant to it.

APR Annual percentage rate.

arbitration The reference of a dispute to an impartial (third) person chosen by the parties who agree in advance to abide by the arbitrator's award issued after a hearing at which both parties have an opportunity to be heard.

arraignment Accused is informed of the crime against him and enters a plea.

articles of incorporation (or **certificate of incorporation**) The instrument under which a corporation is formed. The contents are prescribed in the particular state's general incorporation statute.

articles of partnership A written agreement by which parties enter into a partnership, to be governed by the terms set forth therein.

as is Disclaimer of implied warranties.

assault Unlawful attempted battery; intentional infliction of apprehension of immediate bodily harm or offensive contact.

assignee Party to whom contract rights are assigned.

assignment A transfer of the rights to real or personal property, usually intangible property such as rights in a lease, mortgage, sale agreement or partnership.

assignment of rights Voluntary transfer to a third party of the rights arising from a contract.

assignor Party making an assignment.

assumes Delegatee agrees to perform the contractual obligation of the delegator.

assumes the mortgage Purchaser of mortgaged property becomes personally liable to pay the debt.

assumption of risk Plaintiff's express or implied consent to encounter a known danger.

attachment The process of seizing property, by virtue of a writ, summons, or other judicial order, and bringing the same into the custody of the court for the purpose of securing satisfaction of the judgment ultimately to be entered in the action. While formerly the main objective was to coerce the defendant debtor to appear in court, today the writ of attachment is used primarily to seize the debtor's property in the event a judgment is rendered.

Distinguished from execution See **execution.**

Also, the process by which a security interest becomes enforceable. Attachment may occur upon the taking of possession or upon the signing of a security agreement by the person who is pledging the property as collateral.

authority Power of an agent to change the legal status of his principal.

authorized means Any reasonable means of communication.

automatic perfection Perfection upon attachment.

award The decision of an arbitrator.

bad checks Issuing a check with insufficient funds to cover the check.

bailee The party to whom personal property is delivered under a contract of bailment.

Extraordinary bailee Absolutely liable for the safety of the bailed property without regard to the cause of the loss.

Ordinary bailee Must exercise due care.

bailment A delivery of personal property in trust for the execution of a special object in relation to such goods, beneficial either to the bailor or bailee or both, and upon a contract to either redeliver the goods to the bailor or otherwise dispose of the same in conformity with the purpose of the trust.

bailor The party who delivers goods to another in the contract of bailment.

bankrupt The state or condition of one who is unable to pay his debts as they are, or become, due.

bankruptcy act The Act was substantially revised in 1978, effective October 1, 1979. Straight bankruptcy is in the nature of a liquidation proceeding and involves the collection and distribution to creditors of all the bankrupt's non-exempt property by the trustee in the manner provided by the Act. The debtor rehabilitation provisions of the Act (Chapters 11, 12, and 13) differ however from straight bankruptcy in that the debtor looks to rehabilitation and reorganization, rather than liquidation, and the creditor looks to future earnings of the bankrupt, rather than property held by the bankrupt to satisfy their claims.

bargain Negotiated exchange.

bargained exchange Mutually agreed upon exchange.

basis of the bargain Part of the buyer's assumption underlying the sale.

battery Unlawful touching of another; intentional infliction of harmful or offensive bodily contact.

bearer Person in possession of an instrument.

bearer paper Payable to holder of the instrument.

beneficiary One who benefits from act of another. See also **third party beneficiary.**

Incidental A person who may derive benefit from performance on contract, though he is neither the promisee nor the one to whom performance is to be rendered. Since the incidental beneficiary is not a donee or creditor beneficiary (see **third party beneficiary**), he has no right to enforce the contract.

Intended beneficiary Third party intended by the two contracted parties to receive a benefit from their contract.

Trust As it relates to trust beneficiaries, includes a person who has any present or future interest, vested or contingent, and also includes the owner of an interest by assignment or other transfer and, as it relates to a charitable trust, includes any person entitled to enforce the trust.

beyond a reasonable doubt Proof that is entirely convincing, satisfied to a moral certainty; criminal law standard.

bilateral contract Contract in which both parties exchange promises.

bill of lading Document evidencing receipt of goods for shipment issued by person engaged in business of transporting or forwarding goods and it includes airbill. U.C.C. § 1–201(6).

Through bill of lading A bill of lading which specifies at least one connecting carrier.

bill of sale A written agreement, formerly limited to one under seal, by which one person assigns or transfers his right to or interest in goods to another.

binder A written memorandum of the important terms of contract of insurance which gives temporary protection to insured pending investigation of risk by insurance company or until a formal policy is issued.

blue law Prohibition of certain types of commercial activity on Sunday.

blue sky laws A popular name for state statutes providing for the regulation and supervision of securities offerings and sales, for the protection of citizen-investors from investing in fraudulent companies.

bona fide Latin. In good faith.

bond A certificate or evidence of a debt on which the issuing company or governmental body promises to pay the bondholders a specified amount of interest for a specified length of time, and to repay the loan on the expiration date. In every case a bond represents debt—its holder is a creditor of the corporation and not a part owner as is the shareholder.

boycott Agreement among parties not to deal with a third party.

breach Wrongful failure to perform the terms of a contract.

Material breach Nonperformance which significantly impairs the aggrieved party's rights under the contract.

bribery Offering property to a public official to influence the official's decision.

bulk transfer Transfer not in the ordinary course of the transferor's business of a major part of his inventory.

burglary Breaking and entering the home of another at night with intent to commit a felony.

business judgment rule Protects directors from liability for honest mistakes of judgment.

business trust A trust (managed by a trustee for the benefit of a beneficiary) established to conduct a business for a profit.

but for rule Conduct is a cause of an event if the event would not have occurred in the absence of the person's negligent conduct.

buyer in ordinary course of business Person who buys in ordinary course, in good faith, and without knowledge that the sale to him is in violation of anyone's ownership rights or of a security interest.

by-laws Regulations, ordinances, rules of laws adopted by an association or corporation for its government.

callable bond Bond that is subject to redemption (reacquisition) by the corporation.

cancellation Putting an end to a contract by one party because of a breach by other party.

capital Accumulated goods, possessions, and assets, used for the production of profits and wealth. Owners' equity in a business. Often used equally correctly to mean the total assets of a business. Sometimes used to mean capital assets.

capital surplus Surplus other than earned surplus.

carrier Transporter of goods.

casualty insurance Covers property loss due to causes other than fire or the elements.

cause of action The ground on which an action may be sustained.

caveat emptor Latin. Let the buyer beware. This maxim is more applicable to judicial sales, auctions, and the like, than to sales of consumer goods where strict liability, warranty, and other laws protect.

certificate of deposit A written acknowledgment by a bank or banker of a deposit with promise to pay to depositor, to his order, or to some other person or to his order. U.C.C. § 3–104(2)(c).

certificate of title Official representation of ownership.

certification Acceptance of a check by a drawee bank.

certification of incorporation See **articles of incorporation**.

certification mark Distinctive symbol, word, or design used with goods or services to certify specific characteristics.

certiorari Latin. To be informed of. A writ of common law origin issued by a superior to an inferior court requiring the latter to produce a certified record of a particular case tried therein. It is most commonly used to refer to the Supreme Court of the United States, which uses the writ of certiorari as a discretionary device to choose the cases it wishes to hear.

chancery Equity; equitable jurisdiction; a court of equity; the system of jurisprudence administered in courts of equity.

charging order Judicial lien against a partner's interest in the partnership.

charter An instrument emanating from the sovereign power, in the nature of a grant. A charter differs from a constitution in that the former is granted by the sovereign, while the latter is established by the people themselves.

Corporate law An act of a legislature creating a corporation, or creating and defining the franchise of a corporation. Also a corporation's constitution or organic law; that is to say, the articles of incorporation taken in connection with the law under which the corporation was organized.

chattel mortgage A pre-Uniform Commercial Code security device whereby a security interest was taken by the mortgagee in personal property of the mortgagor. Such security device has generally been superseded by other types of security agreements under U.C.C. Article 9 (Secured Transactions).

chattel paper Writings that evidence both a debt and a security interest.

check A draft drawn upon a bank and payable on demand, signed by the maker or drawer, containing an unconditional promise to pay a sum certain in money to the order of the payee. U.C.C. § 3–104(2)(b).

Cashier's check A bank's own check drawn on itself and signed by the cashier or other authorized official. It is a direct obligation of the bank.

C. & F. Cost and freight; a shipping contract.

C.I.F. Cost, insurance, and freight; a shipping contract.

civil law Laws concerned with civil or private rights and remedies, as contrasted with criminal laws.

The system of jurisprudence administered in the Roman empire, particularly as set forth in the compilation of Justinian and his successors, as distinguished from the common law of England and the canon law. The civil law (Civil Code) is followed by Louisiana.

claim A right to payment.

clearing house An association of banks for the purpose of settling accounts on a daily basis.

close corporation See **corporation**.

closed-ended credit Credit extended to debtor for a specific period of time.

closed shop   Employer can only hire union members.

C.O.D.   Collect on delivery; generally a shipping contract.

code   A compilation of all permanent laws in force consolidated and classified according to subject matter. Many states have published official codes of all laws in force, including the common law and statutes as judicially interpreted, which have been compiled by code commissions and enacted by the legislatures.

codicil   A supplement or an addition to a will; it may explain, modify, add to, subtract from, qualify, alter, restrain or revoke provisions in existing will. It must be executed with the same formalities as a will.

cognovit judgment   Written authority by debtor for entry of judgment against him in the event he defaults in payment. Such provision in a debt instrument on default confers judgment against the debtor.

collateral   Secondarily liable, only liable if the party with primary liability does not perform.

collateral (security)   Personal property subject to security interest. A security given in addition to the direct security, and subordinate to it, intended to guaranty its validity or convertibility or insure its performance.
   Banking   Some form of security in addition to the personal obligation of the borrower.

collateral promise   Undertaking to be secondarily liable, that is, liable if the principal debtor does not perform.

collecting bank   Any bank handling the item for collection except the payor bank. U.C.C.§ 4–105(d).

collective mark   Distinctive symbol used to indicate membership in an organization.

collision insurance   Protects the owner of an automobile against damage due to contact with other vehicles or objects.

commerce power   Exclusive power granted by the U.S. Constitution to the Federal government to regulate commerce with foreign countries and among the States.

commercial bailment   Bailment in which both parties derive a mutual benefit.

commercial impracticability   Performance can only be accomplished with unforeseen and unjust hardship.

commercial law   A phrase used to designate the whole body of substantive jurisprudence (*e.g.*, Uniform Commercial Code; Truth in Lending Act) applicable to the rights, intercourse, and relations of persons engaged in commerce, trade, or mercantile pursuits. See **Uniform Commercial Code.**

commercial paper   Bills of exchange (*i.e.*, drafts), promissory notes, bank-checks, and other negotiable instruments for the payment of money, which, by their form and on their face, purport to be such instruments. U.C.C. Article 3 is the general law governing commercial paper.

commercial reasonableness   Judgment of reasonable persons familiar with the business transaction.

commercial speech   Expression related to the economic interests of the speaker and its audience.

common carrier   Carrier open to the general public.

common law   Body of law originating in England and derived from judicial decisions. As distinguished from statutory law created by the enactment of legislatures, the common law comprises the judgments and decrees of the courts recognizing, affirming, and enforcing usages and customs of immemorial antiquity.

community property   Rights by spouses in property acquired by the other during marriage.

comparable worth   Equal pay for jobs of equal value to the employer.

comparative negligence   Under comparative negligence statutes or doctrines, negligence is measured in terms of percentage, and any damages allowed shall be diminished in proportion to amount of negligence attributable to the person for whose injury, damage or death recovery is sought.

complainant   One who applies to the courts for legal redress by filing complaint (*i.e.*, plaintiff).

complaint   The pleading which sets forth a claim for relief. Such complaint (whether it be the original claim, counterclaim, cross-claim, or third-party claim) shall contain: (1) a short and plain statement of the grounds upon which the court's jurisdiction depends, unless the court already has jurisdiction and the claim needs no new grounds of jurisdiction to support it, (2) a short and plain statement of the claim showing that the pleader is entitled to relief, and (3) a demand for judgment for the relief to which he deems himself entitled. Fed.R. Civil P. 8(a). The complaint, together with the summons, is required to be served on the defendant. Rule 4.

composition   Agreement between debtor and two or more of her creditors that each will take a portion of his claim as full payment.

compulsory arbitration   Arbitration required by statute for specific types of disputes.

computer crime   Crime by, with, or at a computer.

concealment   Fraudulent failure to disclose a material fact.

conciliation   Nonbinding process in which a third party acts as an intermediary between the disputing parties.

concurrent jurisdiction   Authority of more than one court to hear the same case.

condition   An uncertain event which affects the duty of performance.
   Concurrent conditions   Performance by the parties are to occur simultaneously.
   Express condition   Performance is contingent on the happening or nonhappening of a stated event.

condition precedent   An event which must occur or not occur before performance is due; event or events (presentment, dishonor, notice of dishonor) which must occur to hold a secondary party liable to commercial paper.

condition subsequent An event which terminates a duty of performance.

conditional acceptance An acceptance of an offer contingent upon the acceptance of an additional or different term.

conditional contract Obligations are contingent upon a stated event.

conditional guarantor of collection Surety liable to creditor only after creditor exhausts his legal remedies against the principal debtor.

confession of judgment Written agreement by debtor authorizing creditor to obtain a court judgment in the event debtor defaults. See also **cognovit judgment.**

confiscation Governmental taking of foreign-owned property without payment.

conflict of laws That branch of jurisprudence, arising from the diversity of the laws of different nations, states or jurisdictions, that reconciles the inconsistency, or decides which law is to govern in the particular case.

confusion Results when goods belonging to two or more owners become intermixed to the point where the property of any of them no longer can be identified except as part of a mass of like goods.

consanguinity Kinship; blood relationship; the connection or relation of persons descended from the same stock or common ancestor.

consensual arbitration Arbitration voluntarily entered into by the parties.

consent Voluntary and knowing willingness that an act should be done.

conservator Appointed by court to manage affairs of incompetent or to liquidate business.

consideration The cause, motive, price, or impelling influence which induces a contracting party to enter into a contract. Some right, interest, profit or benefit accruing to one party, or some forbearance, detriment, loss, or responsibility, given, suffered, or undertaken by the other.

consignee One to whom a consignment is made. Person named in bill of lading to whom or to whose order the bill promises delivery. U.C.C. § 7–102(b).

consignment Ordinarily implies an agency and denotes that property is committed to the consignee for care or sale.

consignor One who sends or makes a consignment; a shipper of goods. The person named in a bill of lading as the person from whom the goods have been received for shipment. U.C.C.§ 7–102(c).

consolidation In *corporate law,* the combination of two or more corporations into a newly created corporation. Thus, A Corporation and B Corporation combine to form C Corporation.

constitution Fundamental law of a government establishing its powers and limitations.

constructive That which is established by the mind of the law in its act of *construing* facts, conduct, circumstances, or instruments. That which has not the character assigned to it in its own essential nature, but acquires such character in consequence of the way in which it is regarded by a rule or policy of law; hence, inferred, implied, or made out by legal interpretation; the word "legal" being sometimes used here in lieu of "constructive."

constructive assent An assent or consent imputed to a party from a construction or interpretation of his conduct; as distinguished from one which he actually expresses.

constructive conditions Conditions in contracts which are neither expressed nor implied but are rather imposed by law to meet the ends of justice.

constructive delivery Term comprehending all those acts which, although not truly conferring a real possession of the vendee, have been held by construction of law to be the equivalent to acts of real delivery.

constructive eviction Failure by the landlord in any obligation under the lease that causes a substantial and lasting injury to the tenant's enjoyment of the premises.

constructive notice Knowledge imputed by law.

constructive trust Arising by operation of law to prevent unjust enrichment. See also **trustee.**

consumer goods Goods bought or used for personal, family, or household purposes.

consumer product Tangible personal property normally used for family, household, or personal purposes.

contingent remainder Remainder interest, conditional upon the happening of an event in addition to the termination of the preceding estate.

contract An agreement between two or more persons which creates an obligation to do or not to do a particular thing. Its essentials are competent parties, subject matter, a legal consideration, mutuality of agreement, and mutuality of obligation.

Destination contract Seller is required to tender delivery of the goods at a particular destination; seller bears the expense and risk of loss.

Executed contract Fully performed by all of the parties.

Executory contract Contract partially or entirely unperformed by one or more of the parties.

Express contract Agreement of parties that is expressed in words either in writing or orally.

Formal contract Agreement which is legally binding because of its particular form or mode of expression.

Implied in fact contract Contract where agreement of the parties is inferred from their conduct.

Informal contract All oral or written contracts other than formal contracts.

Installment contract Goods are delivered in separate lots.

Integrated contract Complete and total agreement.

Output contract A contract in which one party agrees to sell his entire output and the other agrees to buy it; it is not illusory, though it may be indefinite.

Quasi contract Obligation not based upon contract that is imposed to avoid injustice.

Requirements contract A contract in which one party agrees to purchase his total requirements from the other party and hence it is binding and not illusory.

Substituted contract An agreement between the parties to rescind their old contract and replace it with a new contract.

Unconscionable contract One which no sensible man not under delusion, duress, or in distress would make, and such as no honest and fair man would accept. A contract the terms of which are excessively unreasonable, overreaching and one-sided.

Unenforceable contract Contract for the breach of which the law does not provide a remedy.

Unilateral and bilateral A unilateral contract is one in which one party makes an express engagement or undertakes a performance, without receiving in return any express engagement or promise of performance from the other. Bilateral (or reciprocal) contracts are those by which the parties expressly enter into mutual engagements.

contract clause Prohibition against the states' retroactively modifying public and private contracts.

contractual liability Obligation on a negotiable instrument, based upon signing the instrument.

contribution Payment from cosureties of their proportionate share.

contributory negligence The act or omission amounting to want of ordinary care on part of complaining party, which, concurring with defendant's negligence, is proximate cause of injury.

The defense of contributory negligence is an absolute bar to any recovery in some states; because of this, it has been replaced by the doctrine of comparative negligence in many other states.

conversion Unauthorized and wrongful exercise of dominion and control over another's personal property, to exclusion of or inconsistent with rights of the owner.

convertible bond Bond that may be exchanged for other securities of the corporation.

copyright Exclusive right granted by Federal government to authors of original works including literary, musical, dramatic, pictorial, graphic, sculptural, and film works.

corporation A legal entity ordinarily consisting of an association of numerous individuals. Such entity is regarded as having a personality and existence distinct from that of its several members and is vested with the capacity of continuous succession, irrespective of changes in its membership, either in perpetuity or for a limited term of years.

Closely held or close corporation Corporation that is owned by few shareholders and whose shares are not actively traded.

Corporation de facto One existing under color of law and in pursuance of an effort made in good faith to organize a corporation under the statute. Such a corporation is not subject to collateral attack.

Corporation de jure That which exists by reason of full compliance with requirements of an existing law permitting organization of such corporation.

Domestic corporation Corporation created under the laws of a given State.

Foreign corporation Corporation created under the laws of any other State, government, or country.

Subchapter S corporation A small business corporation which, under certain conditions, may elect to have its undistributed taxable income taxed to its shareholders. I.R.C. § 1371 *et seq.* Of major significance is the fact that Subchapter S status usually avoids the corporate income tax, and corporate losses can be claimed by the shareholders.

Subsidiary and parent corporation Subsidiary corporation is one in which another corporation (called parent corporation) owns at least a majority of the shares, and thus has control.

corrective advertising Disclosure in an advertisement that previous ads were deceptive.

costs A pecuniary allowance, made to the successful party (and recoverable from the losing party), for his expenses in prosecuting or defending an action or a distinct proceeding within an action. Fed.R. Civil P. 54(d); Fed.R.App.P.39. Generally, "costs" do not include attorney fees unless such fees are by a statute denominated costs or are by statute allowed to be recovered as costs in the case.

cosureties Two or more sureties bound for the same debt of a principal debtor.

co-tenants Persons who hold title concurrently.

counter offer A statement by the offeree which has the legal effect of rejecting the offer and of proposing a new offer to the offeror. However, the provisions of U.C.C. § 2–207(2) modifies this principle by providing that the "additional terms are to be construed as proposals for addition to the contract."

counterclaim A claim presented by a defendant in opposition to or deduction from the claim of the plaintiff.

course of dealing A sequence of previous acts and conduct between the parties to a particular transaction which is fairly to be regarded as establishing a common basis of understanding for interpreting their expressions and other conduct. U.C.C. § 1–205(1).

course of performance Conduct between the parties concerning performance of the particular contract.

court above—court below In appellate practice, the "court above" is the one to which a cause is removed for review, whether by appeal, writ of error, or certiorari; while the "court below" is the one from which the case is being removed.

covenant Used primarily with respect to promises in conveyances or other instruments dealing with real estate.

Covenants against encumbrances A stipulation against all rights to or interests in the land which may subsist in third persons to the diminution of the value of the estate granted.

Covenant appurtenant A covenant which is connected with land of the grantor, and not in gross. A covenant running with the land and binding heirs, executors and assigns of the immediate parties.

Covenant for further assurance An undertaking, in the form of a covenant, on the part of the vendor of real estate to do such further acts for the purpose of perfecting the purchaser's title as the latter may reasonably require.

Covenant for possession A covenant by which the grantee or lessee is granted possession.

Covenant for quiet enjoyment An assurance against the consequences of a defective title, and of any disturbances thereupon.

Covenants for title Covenants usually inserted in a conveyance of land, on the part of the grantor, and binding him for the completeness, security, and continuance of the title transferred to the grantee. They comprise covenants for seisin, for right to convey, against incumbrances, or quiet enjoyment, sometimes for further assurance, and almost always of warranty.

Covenant in gross Such as do not run with the land.

Covenant of right to convey An assurance by the covenantor that the grantor has sufficient capacity and title to convey the *estate* which he by his deed undertakes to convey.

Covenant of seisin An assurance to the purchaser that the grantor has the very estate in quantity and quality which he purports to convey.

Covenant of warranty An assurance by the grantor of an estate that the grantee shall enjoy the same without interruption by virtue of paramount title.

Covenant running with land A covenant which goes with the land, as being annexed to the estate, and which cannot be separated from the land, and transferred without it. A covenant is said to run with the land when not only the original parties or their representatives, but each successive owner of the land, will be entitled to its benefit, or be liable (as the case may be) to its obligation. Such a covenant is said to be one which "touches and concerns" the land itself, so that its benefit or obligation passes with the ownership. Essentials are that the grantor and grantee must have intended that the covenant run with the land, the covenant must affect or concern the land with which it runs, and there must be privity of estate between party claiming the benefit and the party who rests under the burden.

covenant not to compete Agreement to refrain from entering into a competing trade, profession, or business.

cover Buyer's purchase of goods in substitution for those not delivered by breaching seller.

credit beneficiary See **third party beneficiary.**

creditor Any entity having a claim against the debtor.

crime An act or omission in violation of a public law and punishable by the government.

criminal duress Coercion by threat of serious bodily injury.

criminal intent Desired or virtually certain consequences of one's conduct.

criminal law The law that involves offenses against the entire community.

cure The right of a seller under U.C.C. to correct a non-conforming delivery of goods to buyer within the contract period. U.C.C. § 2–508.

curtsey Husband's estate in the real property of his wife.

cy-pres As near as (possible). Rule for the construction of instruments in equity, by which the intention of the party is carried out *as near as may be,* when it would be impossible or illegal to give it literal effect.

damage Loss, injury, or deterioration, caused by the negligence, design, or accident of one person to another, in respect of the latter's person or property. The word is to be distinguished from its plural, "damages", which means a compensation in money for a loss or damage.

damages Money sought as a remedy for breach of contract or for tortious acts.

Actual damages Real, substantial and just damages, or the amount awarded to a complainant in compensation for his actual and real loss or injury, as opposed on the one hand to "nominal" damages, and on the other to "exemplary" or "punitive" damages. Synonymous with "compensatory damages" and with "general damages."

Benefit-of-the-bargain damages Difference between the value received and the value of the fraudulent party's performance as represented.

Compensatory damages Compensatory damages are such as will compensate the injured party for the injury sustained, and nothing more; such as will simply make good or replace the loss caused by the wrong or injury.

Consequential damages Such damage, loss or injury as does not flow directly and immediately from the act of the party, but only from some of the consequences or results of such act. Consequential damages resulting from a seller's breach of contract include any loss resulting from general or particular requirements and needs of which the seller at the time of contracting had reason to know and which could not reasonably be prevented by cover or otherwise, and injury to person or property proximately resulting from any breach of warranty. U.C.C. § 2–715(2).

Exemplary or punitive damages Damages other than compensatory damages which may be awarded against person to punish him for outrageous conduct.

Expectancy damages Calculable by subtracting the injured party's actual dollar position as a result of the breach from that party's projected dollar position had performance occurred.

Foreseeable damages Loss that the party in breach had reason to know of when the contract was made.

Incidental damages Under U.C.C. § 2–710, such damages include any commercially reasonable charges, expenses or commissions incurred in stopping delivery, in the transportation, care and custody of goods after the buyer's breach, in connection with the return or resale of the goods or otherwise resulting from the breach. Also, such damages, resulting from a seller's breach of contract, include expenses reasonably incurred in inspection, receipt, transportation and care and custody of goods rightfully rejected, any commercially reasonable charges, expenses or commissions in connection with effecting cover and any other reasonable expense incident to the delay or other breach. U.C.C. § 2–715(1).

Irreparable damages   In the law pertaining to injunctions, damages for which no certain pecuniary standard exists for measurement.

Liquidated damages and penalties   Damages for breach by either party may be liquidated in the agreement but only at an amount which is reasonable in the light of the anticipated or actual harm caused by the breach, the difficulties of proof of loss, and the inconvenience or nonfeasibility of otherwise obtaining an adequate remedy. A term fixing unreasonably large liquidated damages is void as a penalty. U.C.C. § 2–718(1).

Mitigation of damages   A plaintiff may not recover damages for the effects of an injury which reasonably could have been avoided or substantially ameliorated. This limitation on recovery is generally denominated as "mitigation of damages" or "avoidance of consequences."

Nominal damages   A small sum awarded where a contract has been breached but the loss is negligible or unproven.

Out-of-pocket damages   Difference between the value received and the value given.

Reliance damages   Contract damages placing the injured party in as good a position as he would have been in had the contract not been made.

Treble damages   Three times actual loss.

de facto   In fact, in deed, actually. This phrase is used to characterize an officer, a government, a past action, or a state of affairs which must be accepted for all practical purposes, but is illegal or illegitimate. See also **corporation,** *corporation de facto.*

de jure   Descriptive of a condition in which there has been total compliance with all requirements of law. In this sense it is the contrary of *de facto.* See also **corporation,** *corporation de jure.*

de novo   Anew; afresh; a second time.

debenture   Unsecured bond.

debt security   Any form of corporate security reflected as debt on the books of the corporation in contrast to equity securities such as stock; *e.g.*, bonds, notes, and debentures are debt securities.

debtor   Person who owes payment or performance of an obligation.

deceit   A fraudulent and cheating misrepresentation, artifice, or device, used to deceive and trick one who is ignorant of the true facts, to the prejudice and damage of the party imposed upon. See also **fraud; misrepresentation.**

decree   Decision of a court of equity.

deed   A conveyance of realty; a writing signed by grantor, whereby title to realty is transferred from one to another.

deed of trust   Interest in real property which is conveyed to a third person as trustee for the creditor.

defamation   Injury of a person's reputation by publication of false statements.

default judgment   Judgment against a defendant who fails to respond to a complaint.

defendant   The party against whom legal action is sought.

definite term   Lease that automatically expires at end of the term.

delectus personae   Partner's right to choose who may become a member of the partnership.

delegatee   Third party to whom the delegator's duty is delegated.

delegation of duties   Transferring all or part of one's duties arising under a contract to another.

delegator   Party delegating his duty to a third party.

delivery   The physical or constructive transfer of an instrument or of goods from the hands of one person to those of another. See also **constructive delivery.**

demand   Request for payment made by the holder of the instrument.

demand paper   Payable on request.

demurrer   An allegation of a defendant that, even if the facts as stated in the pleading to which objection is taken be true, yet their legal consequences are not such as to put the demurring party to the necessity of answering them or proceeding further with the cause.

The Federal Rules of Civil Procedure do not provide for the use of a demurrer, but provide an equivalent to a general demurrer in the motion to dismiss for failure to state a claim on which relief may be granted. Fed.R. Civil P. 12(b).

deposition   The testimony of a witness taken upon interrogatories, not in court, but intended to be used in court. See also **discovery.**

depository bank   The first bank to which an item is transferred for collection even though it may also be the payor bank. U.C.C. § 4–105(a).

descent   Succession to the ownership of an estate by inheritance, or by any act of law, as distinguished from "purchase."

Descents are of two sorts, *lineal* and *collateral.* Lineal descent is descent in a direct or right line, as from father or grandfather to son or grandson. Collateral descent is descent in a collateral or oblique line, that is, up to the common ancestor and then down from him, as from brother to brother, or between cousins.

design defect   Inadequate plans or specifications to insure the products' safety.

devise A testamentary disposition of land or realty; a gift of real property by the last will and testament of the donor. When used as a noun, means a testamentary disposition of real or personal property and when used as a verb, means to dispose of real or personal property by will.

dictum Generally used as an abbreviated form of *obiter dictum*, "a remark by the way;" that is, an observation or remark made by a judge which does not embody the resolution or determination of the court and which is made without argument or full consideration of the point.

directed verdict In a case in which the party with the burden of proof has failed to present a prima facie case for jury consideration, the trial judge may order the entry of a verdict without allowing the jury to consider it, because, as a matter of law, there can be only one such verdict. Fed.R. Civil P. 50(a).

disaffirmance Avoidance of the contract.

discharge Termination of certain allowed claims against a debtor.

disclaimer Negation of warranty.

discount A discount by a bank means a drawback or deduction made upon its advances or loans of money, upon negotiable paper or other evidences of debt payable at a future day, which are transferred to the bank.

discovery The pre-trial devices that can be used by one party to obtain facts and information about the case from the other party in order to assist the party's preparation for trial. Under Federal Rules of Civil Procedure tools of discovery include: depositions upon oral and written questions, written interrogatories, production of documents or things, permission to enter upon land or other property, physical and mental examinations and requests for admission. Rules 26–37.

dishonor To refuse to accept or pay a draft or to pay a promissory note when duly presented. U.C.C. § 3–507(1); § 4–210. See also **protest**.

disparagement Publication of false statements resulting in harm to another's monetary interests.

disputed debt Obligation whose existence or amount is contested.

dissenting shareholder One who opposes a fundamental change and has the right to receive the fair value of her shares.

dissolution The dissolution of a partnership is the change in the relation of the partners caused by any partner ceasing to be associated in the carrying on as distinguished from the winding up of the business. See also **winding up**.

distribution Transfer of partnership property from the partnership to a partner; transfer of property from a corporation to any of its shareholders.

dividend The payment designated by the board of directors of a corporation to be distributed pro rata among a class or classes of the shares outstanding.

document Document of title.

document of title Instrument evidencing ownership of the document and the goods it covers.

domicile That place where a person has his true, fixed, and permanent home and principal establishment, and to which whenever he is absent he has the intention of returning.

dominant Land whose owner has rights in other land.

donee Recipient of a gift.

donee beneficiary See **third party beneficiary**.

donor Maker of a gift.

dormant partner One who is both a silent and a secret partner.

dower A species of life-estate which a woman is, by law, entitled to claim on the death of her husband, in the lands and tenements of which he was seised in fee during the marriage, and which her issue, if any, might by possibility have inherited.

Dower has been abolished in the majority of the states and materially altered in most of the others.

draft A written order by the first party, called the drawer, instructing a second party, called the drawee (such as a bank) to pay a third party, called the payee. An order to pay a sum certain in money, signed by a drawer, payable on demand or at a definite time, and to order or bearer. U.C.C. § 3–104.

drawee A person to whom a bill of exchange or draft is directed, and who is requested to pay the amount of money therein mentioned. The drawee of a check is the bank on which it is drawn.

When drawee accepts, he engages that he will pay the instrument according to its tenor at the time of his engagement or as completed. U.C.C. § 3–413(1).

drawer The person who draws a bill or draft. The drawer of a check is the person who signs it.

The drawer engages that upon dishonor of the draft and any necessary notice of dishonor or protest, he will pay the amount of the draft to the holder or to any indorser who takes it up. The drawer may disclaim this liability by drawing without recourse, U.C.C. § 3–413(2).

due negotiation Transfer of a negotiable document in the regular course of business to a holder, who takes in good faith, without notice of any defense or claim, and for value.

duress Unlawful constraint exercised upon a person, whereby he is forced to do some act against his will.
   Physical duress Coercion involving physical force or the threat of physical force.

duty Legal obligation requiring a person to perform or refrain from performing an act.

earned surplus Undistributed net profits, income, gains and losses.

earnest   The payment of a part of the price of goods sold, or the delivery of part of such goods, for the purpose of binding the contract.

easement   A right in the owner of one parcel of land, by reason of such ownership, to use the land of another for a special purpose not inconsistent with a general property in the owner. This right is distinguishable from a "license" which merely confers personal privilege to do some act on the land.

Affirmative easement   One where the servient estate must permit something to be done thereon, as to pass over it, or to discharge water on it.

Appurtenant easement   An incorporeal right which is attached to a superior right and inheres in land to which it is attached and is in the nature of a covenant running with the land.

Easement by necessity   Such arises by operation of law when land conveyed is completely shut off from access to any road by land retained by grantor or by land of grantor and that of a stranger.

Easement by prescription   A mode of acquiring title to property by immemorial or long-continued enjoyment, and refers to personal usage restricted to claimant and his ancestors or grantors.

Easement in gross   An easement in gross is not appurtenant to any estate in land or does not belong to any person by virtue of ownership of estate in other land but is mere personal interest in or right to use land of another; it is purely personal and usually ends with death of grantee.

Easement of access   Right of ingress and egress to and from the premises of a lot owner to a street appurtenant to the land of the lot owner.

ejectment   An action of which the purpose is to determine whether the title to certain land is in the plaintiff or is in the defendant.

electronic fund transfer   A transaction with a financial institution by means of computer, telephone, or electronic instrument.

emancipation   The act by which an infant is set at liberty from the control of parent or guardian and made his own master.

embezzlement   The taking in violation of a trust the property of one's employer.

emergency   Sudden, unexpected event calling for immediate action.

eminent domain   Right of the people or government to take private property for public use upon giving of a fair consideration.

employment discrimination   Hiring, firing, compensating, promoting, or training of employees based on race, color, sex, religion, or national origin.

employment relationship   One in which employer has right to control the physical conduct of employee.

endowment contract   Agreement to pay insured a lump sum upon reaching a specified age or in event of death.

entirety   Used to designate that which the law considers as one whole, and not capable of being divided into parts.

entrapment   Induced into committing a crime by a government official.

entrusting   Transfer of possession of goods to a merchant who deals in goods of that kind and who may in turn transfer valid title to a buyer in the ordinary course of business.

equal pay   Equivalent pay for the same work.

equal protection   Requirement that similarly situated persons be treated similarly by government action.

equipment   Goods used primarily in business.

equitable   Just, fair, and right. Existing in equity; available or sustainable only in equity, or only upon the rules and principles of equity.

equity   Justice administered according to fairness as contrasted with the strictly formulated rules of common law. It is based on a system of rules and principles which originated in England as an alternative to the harsh rules of common law and which were based on what was fair in a particular situation.

equity of redemption   The right of the mortgagor of an estate to redeem the same after it has been forfeited, at law, by a breach of the condition of the mortgage, upon paying the amount of debt, interest, and costs.

equity securities   Stock or similar security, in contrast to debt securities such as bonds, notes, and debentures.

error   A mistake of law, or false or irregular application of it, such as vitiates the proceedings and warrants the reversal of the judgment.

Harmless error   In appellate practice, an error committed in the progress of the trial below which was not prejudicial to the rights of the party assigning it and for which, therefore, the court will not reverse the judgment.

Reversible error   In appellate practice, such an error as warrants the appellate court in reversing the judgment before it.

escrow   A system of document transfer in which a deed, bond, or funds is delivered to a third person to hold until all conditions in a contract are fulfilled; *e.g.,* delivery of deed to escrow agent under installment land sale contract until full payment for land is made.

estate   The degree, quantity, nature, and extent of interest which a person has in real and personal property. An estate in lands, tenements, and hereditaments signifies such interest as the tenant has therein.

Also, the total property of whatever kind that is owned by a decedent prior to the distribution of that property in accordance with the terms of a will, or, when there is no will, by the laws of inheritance in the state of domicile of the decedent.

Future estate   An estate limited to commence in possession at a future day, either without the intervention of a precedent estate, or on the determination by lapse of time, or otherwise, of a precedent estate created at the same time. Examples include reversions and remainders.

estoppel A bar or impediment raised by the law, which precludes a man from alleging or from denying a certain fact or state of facts, in consequence of his previous allegation or denial or conduct or admission, or in consequence of a final adjudication of the matter in a court of law. See also **waiver**.

eviction Dispossession by process of law; the act of depriving a person of the possession of lands which he has held, in pursuance of the judgment of a court.

evidence Any species of proof, or probative matter, legally presented at the trial of an issue, by the act of the parties and through the medium of witnesses, records, documents, concrete objects, etc., for the purpose of inducing belief in the minds of the court or jury as to their contention.

exception A formal objection to the action of the court, during the trial of a cause, in refusing a request or overruling an objection; implying that the party excepting does not acquiesce in the decision of the court, but will seek to procure its reversal, and that he means to save the benefit of his request or objection in some future proceeding.

exclusionary rule Prohibition of illegally obtained evidence.

exclusive dealing Sole right to sell goods in a defined market.

exclusive jurisdiction Such jurisdiction that permits only one court (state or federal) to hear a case.

exculpatory clause Excusing oneself from fault or liability.

execution *Execution of contract* includes performance of all acts necessary to render it complete as an instrument and imports idea that nothing remains to be done to make complete and effective contract.

Execution upon a money judgment is the legal process of enforcing the judgment, usually by seizing and selling property of the debtor.

executive order Legislation issued by the President or a governor.

executor A person appointed by a testator to carry out the directions and requests in his will, and to dispose of the property according to his testamentary provisions after his decease. The female designation is executrix. A person appointed by the court in an intestacy situation is called the administrator (rix).

executory That which is yet to be executed or performed; that which remains to be carried into operation or effect; incomplete; depending upon a future performance or event. The opposite of executed.

executory contract See **contracts.**

executory promise Unperformed obligation.

exemplary damages See **damages.**

exoneration Relieved of liability.

express Manifested by direct and appropriate language, as distinguished from that which is inferred from conduct. The word is usually contrasted with "implied."

express warranty Explicitly made contractual promise regarding property or contract rights transferred; in a sale of goods affirmation of fact or promise about the goods or a description, including sample, of goods which becomes part of the basis of the bargain.

expropriation Governmental taking of foreign-owned property for a public purpose and with payment.

ex-ship Risk of loss passes to buyer upon the goods leaving the ship. See U.C.C. § 2–322. See also **F.A.S.**

extortion Making threats to obtain property.

fact An event that took place or a thing that exists.

false imprisonment Intentional interference with a person's freedom of movement by unlawful confinement.

false light Offensive publicity placing another in a false light.

false pretenses Intentional misrepresentation of fact for purpose to cheat.

farm products Crops, livestock, or stock used or produced in farming.

F.A.S. Free alongside. Term used in sales price quotations, indicating that the price includes all costs of transportation and delivery of the goods alongside the ship. See U.C.C. § 2–319(2).

federal preemption First right of the Federal government to regulate matters within its powers to the possible exclusion of State regulation.

federal question Any case arising under the Constitution, statutes, or treaties of the United States.

fee simple

Absolute A fee simple absolute is an estate that is unlimited as to duration, disposition, and descendibility. It is the largest estate and most extensive interest that can be enjoyed in land.

Conditional Type of transfer in which grantor conveys fee simple on condition that something be done or not done.

Defeasible Type of fee grant which may be defeated on the happening of an event. An estate which may last forever, but which may end upon the happening of a specified event, is a "fee simple defeasible".

Determinable Created by conveyance which contains words effective to create a fee simple and, in addition, a provision for automatic expiration of estate on occurrence of stated event.

fee tail An estate of inheritance, descending only to a certain class or classes or heirs; *e.g.*, an estate is conveyed or devised "to A. and the heirs of his body," or "to A. and the heirs male of his body," or "to A., and the heirs female of his body." State statutes have dealt variously with estates tail, some converting them into estates in fee simple.

fellow servant rule Common law defense relieving employer for liability to an employee for injuries caused by negligence of fellow employee.

felony Serious crime.

fiduciary A person or institution who manages money or property for another and who must exercise a standard of care in such management activity imposed by law or contract; *e.g.*, executor of estate; receiver in bankruptcy; trustee.

fiduciary duty Duty of utmost loyalty and good faith owed by a fiduciary such as an agent owes to her principal.

field warehouse Secured party takes possession of the goods but the debtor has access to the goods.

final credit Payment of the instrument by the payor bank.

financing statement Under the Uniform Commercial Code, a financing statement is used under Article 9 to reflect a public record that there is a security interest or claim to the goods in question to secure a debt. The financing statement is filed by the security holder with the Secretary of State, or similar public body, and as such becomes public record. See also **secured transaction.**

fire (property) insurance Provides protection against loss due to fire or other related perils.

firm offer Irrevocable offer to sell or buy goods by a merchant in a signed writing which gives assurance that it will not be rescinded for up to three months.

fitness for a particular purpose Goods are fit for a stated purpose provided the seller selects the product knowing the buyer's intended use and that the buyer is relying on the seller's judgment.

fixture An article in the nature of personal property which has been so annexed to realty that it is regarded as a part of the land. Examples include a furnace affixed to a house or other building, counters permanently affixed to the floor of a store, a sprinkler system installed in a building. U.C.C. § 9–313(1)(a).

 Trade fixtures Such chattels as merchants usually possess and annex to the premises occupied by them to enable them to store, handle, and display their goods, which are generally removable without material injury to the premises.

F.O.B. Free on board some location (for example, FOB shipping point; FOB destination); the invoice price includes delivery at seller's expense to that location. Title to goods usually passes from seller to buyer at the FOB location. U.C.C. § 2–319(1).

foreclosure Procedure by which mortgaged property is sold on default of mortgagor in satisfaction of mortgage debt.

forgery Intentional falsification of a document with intent to defraud.

four unities Time, title, interest, and possession.

franchise A privilege granted or sold, such as to use a name or to sell products or services. The right given by a manufacturer or supplier to a retailer to use his products and name on terms and conditions mutually agreed upon.

fraud Elements include: false representation; of a present or past fact; made by defendant; action in reliance thereon by plaintiff; damage resulting to plaintiff from such misrepresentation.

fraud in the execution Misrepresentation that deceives the other party as to the nature of a document evidencing the contract.

fraud in the inducement Misrepresentation regarding the subject matter of a contract and inducing the other party to enter into it.

fraudulent misrepresentation False statement made with knowledge of its falsity and intent to mislead.

freehold An estate for life or in fee. It must possess two qualities: (1) immobility, that is, the property must be either land or some interest issuing out of or annexed to land; and (2) indeterminate duration.

friendly fire Fire contained where it is intended to be.

frustration of purpose doctrine Excuses a promisor in certain situations when the objectives of contract have been utterly defeated by circumstances arising after formation of agreement, and performance is excused under this rule even though there is no impediment to actual performance.

full warranty One under which warrantor will repair the product and, if unsuccessful, will replace or refund.

fungibles With respect to goods or securities, those of which any unit is, by nature or usage of trade, the equivalent of any other like unit. U.C.C. § 1–201(17); *e.g.*, a bushel of wheat or other grain.

future estate See **estate**

garnishment A statutory proceeding whereby a person's property, money, or credits in the possession or control of another are applied to payment of the former's debt to a third person.

general intangible Catch-all category of collateral not otherwise covered.

general partner Member of either a general or limited partnership with unlimited liability for its debts, full management powers, and a right to share in the profits.

gift A voluntary transfer of property to another made gratuitously and without consideration. Essential requisites of "gift" are capacity of donor, intention of donor to make gift, completed delivery to or for donee, and acceptance of gift by donee.

gift causa mortis A gift in view of death is one which is made in contemplation, fear, or peril of death, and with intent that it shall take effect only in case of the death of the giver.

good faith Honesty in fact in conduct or a transaction.

good faith purchaser Buyer who acts honestly, gives value, and takes the goods without notice or knowledge of any defect in the title of his transferor.

goods A term of variable content and meaning. It may include every species of personal property or it may be given a very restricted meaning. Sometimes the meaning of "goods" is extended to include all tangible items, as in the phrase "goods and services."

All things (including specially manufactured goods) which are movable at the time of identification to the contract for sale other than the money in which the price is to be paid, investment securities and things in action. U.C.C. § 2–105(1).

grantee Transferee of property.

grantor A transferor of property. The creator of a trust is usually designated as the grantor of the trust.

gratuitous promise Promise made without consideration.

group insurance Covers a number of individuals.

guaranty A promise to answer for the payment of some debt, or the performance of some duty, in case of the failure of another person, who, in the first instance, is liable to such payment or performance.

The terms *guaranty* and *suretyship* are sometimes used interchangeably; but they should not be confounded. The distinction between contract of suretyship and contract of guaranty is whether or not the undertaking is a joint undertaking with the principal or a separate and distinct contract; if it is the former it is one of "suretyship", and if the latter, it is one of "guaranty". See also **surety**.

guardianship The relationship under which a person (the guardian) is appointed by a court to preserve and control the property of another (the ward).

heir A person who succeeds, by the rules of law, to an estate in lands, tenements, or hereditaments, upon the death of his ancestor, by descent and right of relationship.

holder Person who is in possession of a document of title or an instrument or an investment security drawn, issued or endorsed to him or to his order, or to bearer or in blank. U.C.C. § 1–201(20).

holder in due course A holder who takes an instrument for value, in good faith, and without notice that it is overdue or has been dishonored or of any defense against or claim to it on the part of any person.

holograph A will or deed written entirely by the testator or grantor with his own hand and not witnessed (attested). State laws vary with respect to the validity of the holographic will.

homicide Unlawful taking of another's life.

horizontal restraints Agreements among competitors.

horizontal privity Who may bring a cause of action.

hostile fire Any fire outside its intended or usual place.

identified goods Designated goods as part of a particular contract.

illegal per se Conclusively presumed unreasonable and therefore illegal.

illusory promise Promise imposing no obligation on the promisor.

implied-in-fact condition Contingencies understood but not expressed by the parties.

implied-in-law condition Contingency that arises from operation of law.

implied warranty Obligation imposed by law upon the transferor of property or contract rights; implicit in the sale arising out of certain circumstances.

implied warranty of habitability Leased premises are fit for ordinary residential purposes.

impossibility Performance that cannot be done.

in personam Against the person. Action seeking judgment against a person involving his personal rights and based on jurisdiction of his person, as distinguished from a judgment against property (*i.e.*, in rem).

in personam jurisdiction Jurisdiction based on claims against a person in contrast to jurisdiction over his property.

in re In the affair; in the matter of; concerning; regarding. This is the usual method of entitling a judicial proceeding in which there are not adversary parties, but merely some *res* concerning which judicial action is to be taken, such as a bankrupt's estate, an estate in the probate court, a proposed public highway, etc.

in rem A technical term used to designate proceedings or actions instituted *against the thing,* in contradistinction to personal actions, which are said to be *in personam.*

Quasi in rem A term applied to proceedings which are not strictly and purely *in rem,* but are brought against the defendant personally, though the real object is to deal with particular property or subject property to the discharge of claims asserted; for example, foreign attachment, or proceedings to foreclose a mortgage, remove a cloud from title, or effect a partition.

in rem jurisdiction Jurisdiction based on claims against property.

incidental beneficiary Third party whom the two parties to a contract have no intention of benefitting by their contract.

income bond Bond that conditions payment of interest on corporate earnings.

incontestability clause The prohibition of an insurer to avoid an insurance policy after a specified period of time.

indemnification Duty owed by principal to agent to pay agent for losses incurred while acting as directed by principal.

indemnify To reimburse one for a loss already incurred.

indenture A written agreement under which bonds and debentures are issued, setting forth maturity date, interest rate, and other terms.

independent contractor Person who contracts with another to do a particular job and is not subject to the control of the other.

indicia Signs; indications. Circumstances which point to the existence of a given fact as probable, but not certain.

indictment Grand jury charge that the defendant should stand trial.

indispensable paper Chattel paper, instruments, and documents.

indorsee The person to whom a negotiable instrument, promissory note, bill of lading, etc., is assigned by indorsement.

indorsement The act of a payee, drawee, accommodation indorser, or holder of a bill, note, check, or other negotiable instrument, in writing his name upon the back of the same, with or without further or qualifying words, whereby the property in the same is assigned and transferred to another. U.C.C. § 3–202 *et seq.*

Blank indorsement No indorsee is specified.

Qualified indorsement Without recourse, limiting one's liability of the instrument.

Restrictive indorsement Limits the rights of the indorser in some manner.

Special indorsement Designates an indorsee to be paid.

infliction of emotional distress Extreme and outrageous conduct intentionally or recklessly causing severe emotional distress.

information Formal accusation of a crime brought by a prosecutor.

infringement Unauthorized use.

injunction An equitable remedy forbidding the party defendant from doing some act which he is threatening or attempting to commit, or restraining him in the continuance thereof, such act being unjust and inequitable, injurious to the plaintiff, and not such as can be adequately redressed by an action at law.

innkeeper Hotel or motel operator.

inquisitorial system System in which the judiciary initiates, conducts and decides cases.

insider Relative or general partner of debtor, partnership in which debtor is a partner, or corporation in which debtor is an officer, director, or controlling person.

insiders Directors, officers, employees, and agents of the issuer as well as those the issuer has entrusted with information solely for corporate purposes.

insolvency Under U.C.C., a person is insolvent who either has ceased to pay his debts in the ordinary course of business or cannot pay his debts as they fall due or is insolvent within the meaning of the Federal Bankruptcy Law. U.C.C. § 1–201(23).

Insolvency (bankruptcy) Total liabilities exceed total value of assets.

Insolvency (equity) Inability to pay debts in ordinary course of business or as they become due.

inspection Examination of the goods to determine whether they conform to the contract.

instrument Negotiable instruments, stocks, bonds, and other investment securities.

insurable interest Exists where insured derives pecuniary benefit or advantage by preservation and continued existence of property or would sustain pecuniary loss from its destruction.

insurance A contract whereby, for a stipulated consideration, one party undertakes to compensate the other for loss on a specified subject by specified perils. The party agreeing to make the compensation is usually called the "insurer" or "underwriter"; the other, the "insured" or "assured"; the written contract, a "policy"; the events insured against, "risks" or "perils"; and the subject, right, or interest to be protected, the "insurable interest." Insurance is a contract whereby one undertakes to indemnify another against loss, damage, or liability arising from an unknown or contingent event.

Co-insurance A form of insurance in which a person insures property for less than its full or stated value and agrees to share the risk of loss.

Life insurance Payment of a specific sum of money to a designated beneficiary upon the death of the insured.

Ordinary life Life insurance with a savings component that runs for the life of the insured.

Term life Life insurance issued for a limited number of years that does not have a savings component.

intangible property Protected interests that are not physical.

intangibles Accounts and general intangibles.

intent Desire to cause the consequences of an act or knowledge that the consequences are substantially certain to result from the act.

inter alia Among other things.

inter se or **inter sese** Latin. Among or between themselves; used to distinguish rights or duties between two or more parties from their rights or duties to others.

interest in land Any right, privilege, power, or immunity in real property.

interest in partnership Partner's share in the partnership's profits and surplus.

interference with contractual relations Intentionally causing one of the parties to a contract not to perform the contract.

intermediary bank Any bank to which an item is transferred in the course of collection except the depositary or payor bank. U.C.C. § 4–105(c).

intermediate test Requirement that legislation have a substantial relationship to an important governmental objective.

international law Deals with the conduct and relations of nation-states and international organizations.

interpretation Construction or meaning of the contract.

interpretative rules Statements issued by an administrative agency indicating its construction of its governing statute.

intestate A person is said to die intestate when he dies without making a will. The word is also often used to signify the person himself. *Compare* **testator.**

intrusion Unreasonable and highly offensive interference with the seclusion of another.

inventory Goods held for sale or lease or consumed in a business.

invitee A person is an "invitee" on land of another if (1) he enters by invitation, express or implied, (2) his entry is connected with the owner's business or with an activity the owner conducts or permits to be conducted on his land and (3) there is mutuality of benefit or benefit to the owner.

joint and several liability Liability where creditor may sue partners jointly as a group or separately as individuals.

joint liability Liability where creditor must sue all of the partners as a group.

joint stock company A general partnership with some corporate attributes.

joint tenancy See **tenancy.**

joint venture An association of two or more persons to carry on a single business transaction for profit.

judgment The official and authentic decision of a court of justice upon the respective rights and claims of the parties to an action or suit therein litigated and submitted to its determination.

judgment in personam A judgment against a particular person, as distinguished from a judgment against a thing or a right or *status.*

judgment in rem An adjudication pronounced upon the status of some particular thing or subject matter, by a tribunal having competent authority.

judgment n. o. v. Judgment non obstante verdicto in its broadest sense is a judgment rendered in favor of one party notwithstanding the finding of a verdict in favor of the other party.

judgment notwithstanding the verdict A final binding determination on the merits made by the judge after and contrary to the jury's verdict.

judgment on the pleadings Final binding determination on the merits made by the judge after the pleadings.

judicial lien Interest in property that is obtained by court action to secure payment of a debt.

judicial review Power of the courts to determine the constitutionality of legislative and executive acts.

jurisdiction The right and power of a court to adjudicate concerning the subject matter in a given case.

jurisdiction over the parties Power of a court to bind the parties to a suit.

jury (From the Latin jurare, to swear.) A body of persons selected and summoned by law and sworn to try the facts of a case and to find according to the law and the evidence. In general, the province of the jury is to find the facts in a case, while the judge passes upon pure questions of law. As a matter of fact, however, the jury must often pass upon mixed questions of law and fact in determining the case, and in all such cases the instructions of the judge as to the law become very important.

justifiable reliance Reasonably influenced by the misrepresentation.

labor dispute Any controversy concerning terms or conditions of employment or union representation.

laches Based upon maxim that equity aids the vigilant and not those who slumber on their rights. It is defined as neglect to assert right or claim which, taken together with lapse of time and other circumstances causing prejudice to adverse party, operates as bar in court of equity.

landlord The owner of an estate in land, or a rental property, who has leased it to another person, called the "tenant." Also called "lessor."

larceny Trespassory taking and carrying away the goods of another with the intent to permanently deprive.

last clear chance Final opportunity to avoid an injury.

lease Any agreement which gives rise to relationship of landlord and tenant (real property) or lessor and lessee (real or personal property).
     The person who conveys is termed the "lessor," and the person to whom conveyed, the "lessee;" and when the lessor conveys land or tenements to a lessee, he is said to lease, demise, or let them.
     Sublease, or underlease One executed by the lessee of an estate to a third person, conveying the same estate for a shorter term than that for which the lessee holds it.

leasehold An estate in realty held under a lease. The four principal types of leasehold estates are the estate for years, periodic tenancy, tenancy at will, and tenancy at sufferance.

leasehold estate Right to possess real property.

legacy "Legacy" is a gift or bequest by will of personal property, whereas a "devise" is a testamentary disposition of real estate.
     Demonstrative legacy A bequest of a certain sum of money, with a direction that it shall be paid out of a particular fund. It differs from a specific legacy in this respect: that, if the fund out of which it is payable fails for any cause, it is nevertheless entitled to come on the estate as a general legacy. And it differs from a general legacy in this: that it does not abate in that class, but in the class of specific legacies.
     General legacy A pecuniary legacy, payable out of the general assets of a testator.

Residuary legacy   A bequest of all the testator's personal estate not otherwise effectually disposed of by his will.

Specific legacy   One which operates on property particularly designated. A legacy or gift by will of a particular specified thing, as of a horse, a piece of furniture, a term of years, and the like.

legal aggregate   A group of individuals not having a legal existence separate from its members.

legal benefit   Obtaining something one had no legal right to.

legal detriment   Doing an act not legally obligated to do or not doing an act which one has a legal right to do.

legal entity   An organization having a separate legal existence from its members.

legal sufficiency   Benefit to promisor or detriment to promisee.

legislative rules   Substantive rules issued by an administrative agency under the authority delegated to it by the legislature.

letter of credit   An engagement by a bank or other person made at the request of a customer that the issuer will honor drafts or other demands for payment upon compliance with the conditions specified in the credit.

letters of administration   Formal document issued by probate court appointing one an administrator of an estate.

letters testamentary   The formal instrument of authority and appointment given to an executor by the proper court, empowering him to enter upon the discharge of his office as executor. It corresponds to letters of administration granted to an administrator.

levy   To assess; raise; execute; exact; tax; collect; gather; take up; seize. Thus, to levy (assess, exact, raise, or collect) a tax; to levy an execution, *i.e.*, to levy or collect a sum of money on an execution.

liability insurance   Covers liability to others by reason of damage resulting from injuries to another's person or property.

liability without fault   Crime to do a specific act or cause a certain result without regard to the care exercised.

libel   Defamation communicated by writing, television, radio, or the like.

liberty   Ability of individuals to engage in freedom of action and choice regarding their personal lives.

license   License with respect to real property is a privilege to go on premises for a certain purpose, but does not operate to confer on, or vest in, licensee any title, interest, or estate in such property.

licensee   Person privileged to enter or remain on land by virtue of the consent of the lawful possessor.

lien   A qualified right of property which a creditor has in or over specific property of his debtor, as security for the debt or charge or for performance of some act.

lien creditor   A creditor who has acquired a lien on the property by attachment.

life estate   An estate whose duration is limited to the life of the party holding it, or some other person. Upon the death of the life tenant, the property will go to the holder of the remainder interest or to the grantor by reversion.

limited liability   Liability limited to amount invested in a business enterprise.

limited partner   Member of a limited partnership with liability for its debts only to the extent of her capital contribution.

limited partnership   See **partnership.**

limited partnership association   A partnership which closely resembles a corporation.

liquidated   Ascertained; determined; fixed; settled; made clear or manifest. Cleared away; paid; discharged.

liquidated damages   See **damages.**

liquidated debt   Obligation that is certain in amount.

liquidation   The settling of financial affairs of a business or individual, usually by liquidating (turning to cash) all assets for distribution to creditors, heirs, etc. It is to be distinguished from dissolution.

loss of value   Value of promised performance minus value of actual performance.

lost property   Property which the owner has involuntarily parted with and does not know where to find or recover it, not including property which he has intentionally concealed or deposited in a secret place for safekeeping. Distinguishable from mislaid property which has been deliberately placed somewhere and forgotten.

McNaughton test   Right/wrong test for criminal insanity.

main purpose rule   Where object of promisor/surety is to provide an economic benefit for herself, the promise is considered outside of the Statute of Frauds.

maker   One who makes or executes; as the maker of a promissory note. One who signs a check; in this context, synonymous with drawer. See **draft.**

mala in se   Morally wrong.

mala prohibita   Wrong by law.

mandamus   Latin, we command. A legal writ compelling the defendant to do an official duty.

manslaughter   Unlawful taking of another's life without malice.

Involuntary manslaughter   Taking the life of another by criminal negligence or during the course of a misdemeanor.

Voluntary manslaughter   Intentional killing of another under extenuating circumstances.

manufacturing defect   Not produced according to specifications.

mark   Trade symbol.

market allocations Division of market by customers, geographic location, or products.

marketable title Free from any defects, encumbrances or reasonable objections to one's ownership.

marshaling of assets Segregating the assets and liabilities of the partnership separately from the assets and liabilities of the individual partners.

master See **principal.**

material Matters to which a reasonable investor would attach importance in deciding whether to purchase a security.

material alteration Any change that changes the contract of any party to the instrument.

maturity The date at which an obligation, such as the principal of a bond or a note, becomes due.

maxim A general legal principle.

mechanic's lien A claim created by state statutes for the purpose of securing priority of payment of the price or value of work performed and materials furnished in erecting or repairing a building or other structure, and as such attaches to the land as well as buildings and improvements erected thereon.

mediation Nonbinding process in which a third party acts as an intermediary between the disputing parties and proposes solutions for them to consider.

mens rea Criminal intent.

mentally incompetent Unable to understand the nature and effect of one's acts.

mercantile law An expression substantially equivalent to commercial law. It designates the system of rules, customs, and usages generally recognized and adopted by merchants and traders, and which, either in its simplicity or as modified by common law or statutes, constitutes the law for the regulation of their transactions and the solution of their controversies. The Uniform Commercial Code is the general body of law governing commercial or mercantile transactions.

merchant A person who deals in goods of the kind or otherwise by his occupation holds himself out as having knowledge or skill peculiar to the practices or goods involved in the transaction or to whom such knowledge or skill may be attributed by his employment of an agent or broker or other intermediary who by his occupation holds himself out as having such knowledge or skill. U.C.C. § 2–104(1).

merchantability Merchant seller guarantees that the goods are fit for their ordinary purpose.

merger The fusion or absorption of one thing or right into another. In corporate law, the absorption of one company by another, latter retaining its own name and identity and acquiring assets, liabilities, franchises, and powers of former, and absorbed company ceasing to exist as separate business entity. It differs from a consolidation wherein all the corporations terminate their existence and become parties to a new one.

Conglomerate merger An acquisition by one company of another which is not horizontal or vertical.

Horizontal merger Merger between business competitors, such as manufacturers of the same type products or distributors selling competing products in the same market area.

Short-form merger Merger of a 90 percent subsidiary into its parent.

Vertical merger Union with corporate customer or supplier.

midnight deadline Midnight of the next banking day after receiving an item.

mining partnership A specific type of partnership for the purpose of extracting raw minerals.

minor Under full legal age (usually 18).

mirror image rule An acceptance cannot deviate from the terms of the offer.

misdemeanor Less serious crime.

mislaid property Property which an owner has put deliberately in a certain place but owner is unable to remember where he put it, as distinguished from lost property which the owner leaves unwittingly in a place, forgetting its location. See also **lost property.**

misrepresentation Any manifestation by words or other conduct by one person to another that, under the circumstances, amounts to an assertion not in accordance with the facts. A "misrepresentation" that justifies the rescission of a contract is a false statement of a substantive fact, or any conduct which leads to a belief of a substantive fact material to proper understanding of the matter in hand. See also **deceit; fraud.**

Fraudulent misrepresentation False statement made with knowledge of its falsity and intent to mislead.

Innocent misrepresentation Misrepresentation made without knowledge of its falsity but with due care.

Negligent misrepresentation Misrepresentation made without due care in ascertaining its falsity.

modify Change the lower court's judgment.

money Medium of exchange issued by government body.

monopoly Ability to control price or exclude others from the marketplace.

mortgage A mortgage is an interest in land created by a written instrument providing security for the performance of a duty or the payment of a debt.

mortgagor Debtor who uses real estate to secure an obligation.

multinational enterprise Business that engages in transactions involving the movement of goods, information, money, people, or services across national borders.

multiple product order Order requiring an advertiser to cease and desist from deceptive statements on all products it sells.

murder Unlawful and premeditated taking of another's life.

mutual mistake Where both parties have a common but erroneous belief forming the basis of a contract.

necessary Items needed to maintain a person's station in life.

negligence The omission to do something which a reasonable man, guided by those ordinary considerations which ordinarily regulate human affairs, would do, or the doing of something which a reasonable and prudent man would not do.

Culpable negligence Greater than ordinary negligence but less than gross negligence.

negligence *per se* Conclusive on the issue of negligence (duty of care and breach).

negotiable Legally capable of being transferred by endorsement or delivery. Usually said of checks and notes and sometimes of stocks and bearer bonds.

negotiable instrument Signed document (such as a check or promissory note) containing an unconditional promise to pay a "sum certain" of money at a definite time to order or bearer.

negotiation Transferee becomes a holder.

net assets Total assets minus total debts.

no arrival, no sale A destination contract, but if goods do not arrive, seller is excused from liability unless it is due to the seller's fault.

no-fault insurance Compensates victims of automobile accidents regardless of fault.

nonconforming use Pre-existing use not in accordance with the zoning ordinance.

nonprofit corporation One whose profits must be used exclusively for the charitable, educational, or scientific purpose for which it was formed.

nonsuit Action in form of a judgment taken against a plaintiff who has failed to appear to prosecute his action or failed to prove his case.

note See **promissory note.**

novation A novation substitutes a new party and discharges one of the original parties to a contract by agreement of all three parties. A new contract is created with the same terms as the original one but only the parties are changed.

nuisance Nuisance is that activity which arises from unreasonable, unwarranted or unlawful use by a person of his own property, working obstruction or injury to right of another, or to the public, and producing such material annoyance, inconvenience and discomfort that law will presume resulting damage.

obiter dictum See **dictum.**

objective fault Gross deviation from reasonable conduct.

objective manifestation What a reasonable man under the circumstances would believe.

objective satisfaction Approval based upon whether a reasonable person would be satisfied.

objective standard What a reasonable man under the circumstances would reasonably believe or do.

obligee Party to whom a duty of performance is owed (by delegator and delegatee).

obligor Party owing a duty (to the assignor).

offer A manifestation of willingness to enter into a bargain, so made as to justify another person in understanding that his assent to that bargain is invited and will conclude it. Restatement, Second, Contracts, § 24.

offeree Recipient of the offer.

offeror Person making the offer.

open-ended credit Credit arrangement under which debtor has rights to enter into a series of credit transactions.

opinion Belief in the existence of a fact or a judgment as to value.

option Contract that provides that an offer will stay open for a specified period of time.

order A final disposition made by an agency.

order paper Payable to a named person or anyone designated by that person.

order to pay Direction or command to pay.

original promise Promise to become primarily liable.

output contract See **contracts.**

palpable unilateral mistake Erroneous belief by one party that is recognized by the other.

parent corporation Corporation which controls another corporation.

parol evidence Literally oral evidence, but now includes prior to and contemporaneous, oral and written evidence.

parol evidence rule Under this rule, when parties put their agreement in writing, all previous oral agreements merge in the writing and a contract as written cannot be modified or changed by parol evidence, in the absence of a plea of mistake or fraud in the preparation of the writing. But rule does not forbid a resort to parol evidence not inconsistent with the matters stated in the writing. Also, as regards sales of goods, such written agreement may be explained or supplemented by course of dealing or usage of trade or by course of conduct, and by evidence of consistent additional terms unless the court finds the writing to have been intended also as a complete and exclusive statement of the terms of the agreement. U.C.C. § 2–202.

part performance In order to establish part performance taking an oral contract for the sale of realty out of the statute of frauds, the acts relied upon as part performance must be of such a character that they can reasonably be naturally accounted for in no other way than that they were performed in pursuance of the contract, and they must be in conformity with its provisions. See U.C.C. § 2–201(3).

partial assignment Transfer of a portion of contractual rights to one or more assignees.

partition The dividing of lands held by joint tenants, copartners, or tenants in common, into distinct portions, so that they may hold them in severalty.

partnership An association of two or more persons to carry on, as co-owners, a business for profit.

Partnerships are treated as a conduit and are, therefore, not subject to taxation. The various items of partnership income, gains, and losses, etc., flow through to the individual partners and are reported on their personal income tax returns.

Limited partnership Type of partnership comprised of one or more general partners who manage business and who are personally liable for partnership debts, and one or more limited partners who contribute capital and share in profits but who take no part in running business and incur no liability with respect to partnership obligations beyond contribution.

Partnership at will One with no definite term or specific undertaking.

partnership capital Total money and property contributed by partners for permanent use by the partnership.

partnership property Sum of all of the partnership's assets.

past consideration An act done before the contract is made.

patent Exclusive right to an invention.

payee The person in whose favor a bill of exchange, promissory note, or check is made or drawn.

payer, or **payor** One who pays, or who is to make a payment; particularly the person who is to make payment of a check, bill or note. Correlative to "payee."

payor bank A bank by which an item is payable as drawn or accepted. U.C.C. § 4–105(b). Drawee bank.

per capita This term, derived from the civil law, is much used in the law of descent and distribution, and denotes that method of dividing an intestate estate by which an equal share is given to each of a number of persons, all of whom stand in equal degree to the decedent, without reference to their stocks or the right of representation. It is the opposite of *per stirpes*.

per stirpes This term, derived from the civil law, is much used in the law of descents and distribution, and denotes that method of dividing an intestate estate where a class or group of distributees take the share which their deceased would have been entitled to, taking thus by their right of representing such ancestor, and not as so many individuals. It is the opposite of *per capita*.

perfect tender rule Seller's tender of delivery must conform exactly to the contract.

perfection of security interest Acts required of a secured party in the way of giving at least constructive notice so as to make his security interest effective at least against lien creditors of the debtor. See U.C.C. §§ 9–302 through 9–306. In most cases, the secured party may obtain perfection either by filing with Secretary of State or by taking possession of the collateral.

performance Fulfillment of one's contractual obligations. See also **part performance; specific performance.**

periodic tenancy Lease with a definite term that is to be continued.

personal defenses Contractual defenses which are good against holders but not holders in due course.

personal property Any property other than an interest in land.

petty crime Misdemeanor punishable by imprisonment of six months or less.

plaintiff The party who initiates a civil suit.

pleadings The formal allegations by the parties of their respective claims and defenses.

Rules or Codes of Civil Procedure Unlike the rigid technical system of common law pleading, pleadings under federal and state rules or codes of civil procedure have a far more limited function, with determination and narrowing of facts and issues being left to discovery devices and pretrial conferences. In addition, the rules and codes permit liberal amendment and supplementation of pleadings.

Under rules of civil procedure the pleadings consist of a complaint, an answer, a reply to a counterclaim, an answer to a cross-claim, a third party complaint, and a third party answer. Fed.R.Civil P. 7(a).

pledge A bailment of goods to a creditor as security for some debt or engagement.

Much of the law of pledges has been replaced by the provisions for secured transactions in Article 9 of the U.C.C.

possibility of reverter The interest which remains in a grantor or testator after the conveyance or devise of a fee simple determinable and which permits the grantor to be revested automatically of his estate on breach of the condition.

possibility test Under the Statute of Frauds the one year test is satisfied if performance possibly could be completed within one year.

power of appointment A power of authority conferred by one person by deed or will upon another (called the "donee") to appoint, that is, to select and nominate, the person or persons who are to receive and enjoy an estate or an income therefrom or from a fund, after the testator's death, or the donee's death, or after the termination of an existing right or interest.

power of attorney An instrument authorizing a person to act as the agent or attorney of the person granting it.

power of termination The interest left in the grantor or testator after the conveyance or devise of a fee simple on condition subsequent or conditional fee.

precatory Expressing a wish.

precedent An adjudged case or decision of a court, considered as furnishing an example or authority for an identical or similar case afterwards arising or a similar question of law. See also **stare decisis.**

pre-emptive right The privilege of a stockholder to maintain a proportionate share of ownership by purchasing a proportionate share of any new stock issues.

preference The act of an insolvent debtor who, in distributing his property or in assigning it for the benefit of his creditors, pays or secures to one or more creditors the full amount of their claims or a larger amount than they would be entitled to receive on a *pro rata* distribution. The treatment of such preferential payments in bankruptcy is governed by Bankruptcy Act, § 547.

preliminary hearing Determine whether there is probable cause.

premium The price for insurance protection for a specified period of exposure.

preponderance of the evidence Greater weight of the evidence; standard used in civil cases.

prescription Acquisition of a personal right to use a way, water, light, and air by reason of continuous usage. See also **easement.**

presenter's warranty Warranties given to any payor or acceptor of an instrument.

presentment The production of a negotiable instrument to the drawee for his acceptance, or to the drawer or acceptor for payment; or of a promissory note to the party liable, for payment of the same. U.C.C. § 3–504(1).

presumption A presumption is a rule of law, statutory or judicial, by which finding of a basic fact gives rise to existence of presumed fact, until presumption is rebutted. A presumption imposes on the party against whom it is directed the burden of going forward with evidence to rebut or meet the presumption, but does not shift to such party the burden of proof in the sense of the risk of nonpersuasion, which remains throughout the trial upon the party on whom it was originally cast.

price discrimination Price differential.

price fixing Any agreement for the purpose and effect of raising, depressing, fixing, pegging, or stabilizing prices.

prima facie Latin. At first sight; on the first appearance; on the face of it; so far as can be judged from the first disclosure; presumably; a fact presumed to be true unless disproved by some evidence to the contrary.

primary liability Absolute obligation to pay the negotiable instrument.

principal *Law of agency* The term "principal" describes one who has permitted or directed another (*i.e.*, agent or servant) to act for his benefit and subject to his direction and control. Principal includes in its meaning the term "master" or employer, a species of principal who, in addition to other control, has a right to control the physical conduct of the species of agents known as servants or employees, as to whom special rules are applicable with reference to harm caused by their physical acts.

Disclosed principal One whose existence and identity is known.

Partially disclosed principal One whose existence is known but whose identity is not known.

Undisclosed principal One whose existence and identity are not known.

principal debtor Person whose debt is being supported by a surety.

priority Precedence in order of right.

private carrier Carrier which limits its service and is not open to the general public.

private corporation One organized to conduct either a privately owned business enterprise for profit or a non-profit corporation.

private law The law involving relationships among individuals and legal entities.

privilege Immunity from tort liability.

privity Contractual relationship.

privity of contract That connection or relationship which exists between two or more contracting parties. The absence of privity as a defense in actions for damages in contract and tort actions is generally no longer viable with the enactment of warranty statutes (*e.g.*, U.C.C. § 2–318), acceptance by states of doctrine of strict liability and court decisions which have extended the right to sue to third party beneficiaries and even innocent bystanders.

probable cause Reasonable belief of the offense charged.

probate Court procedure by which a will is proved to be valid or invalid; though in current usage this term has been expanded to generally include all matters and proceedings pertaining to administration of estates, guardianships, etc.

procedural due process Requirement that governmental action depriving a person of life, liberty, or property be done through a fair procedure.

procedural law Rules for enforcing substantive law.

procedural rules Rules issued by an administrative agency establishing its organization, method of operation, and rules of conduct for practice before it.

procedural unconscionability Unfair or irregular bargaining.

proceeds Consideration for the sale, exchange or other disposition of the collateral.

process *Judicial process* In a wide sense, this term may include all the acts of a court from the beginning to the end of its proceedings in a given cause; but more specifically it means the writ, summons, mandate, or other process which is used to inform the defendant of the institution of proceedings against him and to compel his appearance, in either civil or criminal cases.

Legal process This term is sometimes used as equivalent to "lawful process." Thus, it is said that legal process means process not merely fair on its face, but in fact valid. But properly it means a summons, writ, warrant, mandate, or other process issuing from a court.

profit corporation One founded for the purpose of operating a business for profit.

profit à prendre Right to make some use of the soil of another, such as a right to mine metals, and it carries with it the right of entry and the right to remove.

promise to pay Undertaking to pay an existing obligation.

promisee Person to whom a promise is made.

promisor Person making a promise.

promissory estoppel Arises where there is a promise which promisor should reasonably expect to induce action or forbearance on part of promisee and which does induce such action or forbearance, and where injustice can be avoided only by enforcement of the promise.

promissory note An unconditional written promise to pay a specified sum of money on demand or at a specified date. Such a note is negotiable if signed by the maker and containing an unconditional promise to pay a sum certain in money either on demand or at a definite time and payable to order or bearer. U.C.C. § 3–104.

promoters In the law relating to corporations, those persons are called the "promoters" of a company who first associate themselves together for the purpose of organizing the company, issuing its prospectus, procuring subscriptions to the stock, securing a charter, etc.

property Interest that is legally protected.
Abandoned property Intentionally disposed of by the owner.
Lost property Unintentionally left by the owner.
Mislaid property Intentionally placed by the owner but unintentionally left.

prosecute To bring a criminal proceeding.

protest A formal declaration made by a person interested or concerned in some act about to be done, or already performed, whereby he expresses his dissent or disapproval, or affirms the act against his will. The object of such a declaration is generally to save some right which would be lost to him if his implied assent could be made out, or to exonerate himself from some responsibility which would attach to him unless he expressly negatived his assent.
Notice of protest A notice given by the holder of a bill or note to the drawer or indorser that the bill has been protested for refusal of payment or acceptance. U.C.C. § 3–509.

provisional credit Tentative credit for the deposit of an instrument until final credit is given.

proximate cause Where the act or omission played a substantial part in bringing about or actually causing the injury or damage and where the injury or damage was either a direct result or a reasonably probable consequence of the act or omission.

proxy (Contracted from procuracy.) Written authorization given by one person to another so that the second person can act for the first, such as that given by a shareholder to someone else to represent him and vote his shares at a shareholders' meeting.

public corporation One created to administer a unit of local civil government or one created by the United States to conduct public business.

public disclosure of private facts Offensive publicity given to private information about another person.

public law The law dealing with the relationship between government and individuals.

puffery Sales talk that is considered general bragging or overstatement.

punitive damages Damages awarded in excess of normal compensation to punish a defendant for a serious civil wrong.

purchase money security interest A seller of goods who retains a security interest in goods purchased with the loaned money.

qualified fee Ownership subject to its being taken away upon the happening of an event.

quantum meruit Expression "quantum meruit" means "as much as he deserves" and it is an expression that describes the extent of liability on a contract implied by law. Essential elements of recovery under quantum meruit are: (1) valuable services were rendered or materials furnished, (2) for person sought to be charged, (3) which services and materials were accepted by person sought to be charged, used and enjoyed by him, and (4) under such circumstances as reasonably notified person sought to be charged that plaintiff, in performing such services, was expected to be paid by person sought to be charged.

quasi Latin. As if; almost as it were; analogous to. It negatives idea of identity, but points out that the conceptions are sufficiently similar for one to be classed as the equal of the other.

quasi contract Legal fiction invented by common law courts to permit recovery by contractual remedy in cases where, in fact, there is no contract, but where circumstances are such that justice warrants a recovery as though there had been a promise.

quasi in rem See **in rem.**

quasi in rem jurisdiction Jurisdiction over property not based on claims against it.

quiet enjoyment Right of a tenant not to have his physical possession of premises interfered with by the landlord.

quitclaim deed A deed of conveyance operating by way of release; that is, intended to pass any title, interest, or claim which the grantor may have in the premises, but not professing that such title is valid, nor containing any warranty or covenants for title.

quorum When a committee, board of directors, meeting of shareholders, legislature, or other body of persons cannot act unless a certain number at least of them are present.

rape Unlawful and unconsented to sexual intercourse.

ratification In a broad sense, the confirmation of a previous act done either by the party himself or by another; as, confirmation of a voidable act.

In the law of principal and agent, the adoption and confirmation by one person with knowledge of all material facts, of an act or contract performed or entered into in his behalf by another who at the time assumed without authority to act as his agent.

rational relationship test Requirement that legislation bear a rational relationship to a legitimate governmental interest.

real defenses Defenses that are valid against all holders, including holders in due course.

real property Land, and generally whatever is erected or growing upon or affixed to land. Also rights issuing out of, annexed to, and exercisable within or about land. See also **fixture.**

reasonable man standard Duty of care required to avoid being negligent; one who is careful, diligent, and prudent.

receiver A fiduciary of the court, appointed as an incident to other proceedings wherein certain ultimate relief is prayed. He is a trustee or ministerial officer representing court, and all parties in interest in litigation, and property or fund intrusted to him.

recognizance Formal acknowledgment of indebtedness made in court.

redemption The realization of a right to have the title of property restored free and clear of the mortgage; performance of the mortgage obligation being essential for that purpose.

Repurchase by corporation of its own shares.

reformation Equitable remedy used to reframe written contracts to reflect accurately real agreement between contracting parties when, either through mutual mistake or unilateral mistake coupled with actual or equitable fraud by other party, the writing does not embody contract as actually made.

regulatory license Requirement to protect the public interest.

reimbursement Duty owed by principal to pay back authorized payments agent has made on principal's behalf. Duty owed by a principal debtor to repay surety who pays principal debtor's obligation.

rejection The refusal to accept an offer; manifestation of an unwillingness to accept the goods (sales).

release The relinquishment, concession, or giving up of a right, claim, or privilege, by the person in whom it exists or to whom it accrues, to the person against whom it might have been demanded or enforced.

remainder An estate limited to take effect and be enjoyed after another estate is determined.

remand To send back. The sending by the appellate court of the cause back to the same court out of which it came, for purpose of having some further action taken on it there.

remedy The means by which the violation of a right is prevented, redressed, or compensated. Though a remedy may be by the act of the party injured, by operation of law, or by agreement between the injurer and the injured, we are chiefly concerned with one kind of remedy, the judicial remedy, which is by action or suit.

rent Consideration paid for use or occupation of property. In a broader sense, it is the compensation or fee paid, usually periodically, for the use of any property, land, buildings, equipment, etc.

replevin An action whereby the owner or person entitled to repossession of goods or chattels may recover those goods or chattels from one who has wrongfully taken or who wrongfully detains such goods or chattels.

reply Plaintiff's pleading in response to the defendant's answer.

repudiation Repudiation of a contract means refusal to perform duty or obligation owed to other party.

requirements contract See **contracts.**

res ipsa loquitur "The thing speaks for itself"; permits the jury to infer both negligent conduct and causation.

rescission An equitable action in which a party seeks to be relieved of his obligations under a contract on the grounds of mutual mistake, fraud, impossibility, etc.

residuary Pertaining to the residue; constituting the residue; giving or bequeathing the residue; receiving or entitled to the residue. See also **legacy,** *residuary legacy.*

respondeat superior Latin. Let the master answer. This maxim means that a master or employer is liable in certain cases for the wrongful acts of his servant or employee, and a principal for those of his agent.

respondent In equity practice, the party who makes an answer to a bill or other proceeding in equity. In appellate practice, the party who contends against an appeal; *i.e.,* the appellee. The party who appeals is called the "appellant."

restitution An equitable remedy under which a person who has rendered services to another seeks to be reimbursed for the costs of his acts (but not his profits) even though there was never a contract between the parties.

restraint on alienation A provision in an instrument of conveyance which prohibits the grantee from selling or transferring the property which is the subject of the conveyance. Many such restraints are unenforceable as against public policy and the law's policy of free alienability of land.

restraint of trade Agreement that eliminates or tends to eliminate competition.

restrictive covenant Private restriction on property contained in a conveyance.

revenue license Measure to raise money.

reverse An appellate court uses the term "reversed" to indicate that it annuls or avoids the judgment, or vacates the decree, of the trial court.

reverse discrimination Employment decisions taking into account race or gender in order to remedy past discrimination.

reversion The term reversion has two meanings, first, as designating the estate left in the grantor during the continuance of a particular estate and also the residue left in grantor or his heirs after termination of particular estate. It differs from a remainder in that it arises by act of the law, whereas a remainder is by act of the parties. A reversion, moreover, is the remnant left in the grantor, while a remainder is the remnant of the whole estate disposed of, after a preceding part of the same has been given away.

revocation The recall of some power, authority, or thing granted, or a destroying or making void of some deed that had existence until the act of revocation made it void.

revocation of acceptance Rescission of one's acceptance of goods based upon the nonconformity of the goods which substantially impairs their value.

right Legal capacity to require another person to perform or refrain from performing an act.

right of entry The right of taking or resuming possession of land by entering on it in a peaceable manner.

right of redemption The right (granted by statute only) to free property from the encumbrance of a foreclosure or other judicial sale, or to recover the title passing thereby, by paying what is due, with interest, costs, etc. Not to be confounded with the "equity of redemption," which exists independently of statute but must be exercised before sale. See also **equity of redemption.**

right to work law State statute that prohibits union shop contracts.

rights in collateral Personal property the debtor owns, possesses, or is in the process of acquiring.

risk of loss Allocation of loss between seller and buyer where the goods have been damaged, destroyed, or lost.

robbery Larceny from a person by force or threat of force.

rule Agency statement of general or particular applicability designed to implement, interpret, or process law or policy.

rule against perpetuities Principle that no interest in property is good unless it must vest, if at all, not later than 21 years, plus period of gestation, after some life or lives in being at time of creation of interest.

rule of reason Balancing the anticompetitive effects against procompetitive effects of the restraint.

sale Transfer of title to goods from seller to buyer for a price.

sale on approval Transfer of possession without title to buyer for trial period.

sale or return Sale where buyer has option to return goods to seller.

sanction Means of enforcing legal judgments.

satisfaction The discharge of an obligation by paying a party what is due to him (as on a mortgage, lien, or contract) or what is awarded to him, by the judgment of a court or otherwise. Thus, a judgment is satisfied by the payment of the amount due to the party who has recovered such judgment, or by his levying the amount. See also **accord and satisfaction.**

scienter Latin. Knowingly.

seal Symbol that authenticates a document.

secondary liability Obligation to pay is subject to the conditions of presentment, dishonor, notice of dishonor, and sometimes protest.

secret partner Partner whose membership in the partnership is not disclosed.

Section 402A Strict liability in tort.

secured bond A bond having a lien on specific property.

secured claim Claim with a lien on property of the debtor.

secured party Creditor who possesses a security interest in collateral.

secured transaction A transaction which is founded on a security agreement. Such agreement creates or provides for a security interest. U.C.C. § 9–105(h).

securities Stocks, bonds, notes, convertible debentures, warrants, or other documents that represent a share in a company or a debt owed by a company.
Certificated security Security represented by a certificate.
Exempt security Security not subject to registration requirements of 1933 Act.
Exempt transaction Issuance of securities not subject to the registration requirements of 1933 Act.
Restricted securities Securities issued under an exempt transaction.
Uncertificated security Security not represented by a certificate.

security agreement Agreement that grants a security interest.

security interest Right in personal property securing payment or performance of an obligation.

seisin Possession with an intent on the part of him who holds it to claim a freehold interest.

self-defense Force to protect oneself against attack.

separation of powers Allocation of powers among the legislative, executive, and judicial branches of government.

service mark   Distinctive symbol, word, or design that is used to identify the services of a provider.

servient   Land subject to an easement.

set-off   A counterclaim demand which defendant holds against plaintiff, arising out of a transaction extrinsic of plaintiff's cause of action.

settlor   Creator of the trust.

severance   The destruction of any one of the unities of a joint tenancy. It is so called because the estate is no longer a joint tenancy, but is severed.

Term may also refer to cutting of the crops, such as corn, wheat, etc., or the separating of anything from the realty.

share   A proportionate ownership interest in a corporation.

Shelley's case, rule in   Where a person takes an estate of freehold, legally, or equitably, under a deed, will, or other writing, and in the same instrument there is a limitation by way of remainder of any interest of the same legal or equitable quality to his heirs, or heirs of his body, as a class of persons to take in succession from generation to generation, the limitation to the heirs entitles the ancestor to the whole estate.

The rule was adopted as a part of the common law of this country, though it has long since been abolished by most states.

shelter rule   Transferee gets rights of transferor.

shipment contract   Seller is authorized or required only to bear the expense of placing goods with the common carrier and bears the risk of loss only up to such point.

short swing profits   Profits made by insider through sale or other disposition of the corporate stock within six months after purchase.

sight draft   An instrument payable on presentment.

signature   Any symbol executed with intent to validate a writing.

silent partner   Partner takes no part in the partnership business.

slander   Oral defamation.

small claims courts   Inferior civil courts with jurisdiction limited by dollar amount.

social security   Measures by which the government provides economic assistance to disabled or retired employees and their dependents.

sole proprietorship   A form of business in which one person owns all the assets of the business in contrast to a partnership and corporation.

sovereign immunity   Foreign country's freedom from the host country's laws.

special warranty deed   Seller promises that he has not impaired title.

specific performance   The doctrine of specific performance is that, where damages would be an inadequate compensation for the breach of an agreement, the contractor or vendor will be compelled to perform specifically what he has agreed to do; *e.g.,* ordered to execute a specific conveyance of land.

With respect to sale of goods, specific performance may be decreed where the goods are unique or in other proper circumstances. The decree for specific performance may include such terms and conditions as to payment of the price, damages, or other relief as the court may deem just. U.C.C. §§ 2–711(2)(b), 2–716.

standardized business form   A preprinted contract.

stare decisis   Doctrine that, when court has once laid down a principle of law as applicable to a certain state of facts, it will adhere to that principle, and apply it to all future cases, where facts are substantially the same; regardless of whether the parties and property are the same.

state action   Actions by governments as opposed to actions taken by private individuals.

state of the art   Made in accordance with the level of technology at the time the product is made.

stated capital   Consideration received for issued stock other than that allocated to capital surplus.

Statute of Frauds   A celebrated English statute, passed in 1677, and which has been adopted, in a more or less modified form, in nearly all of the United States. Its chief characteristic is the provision that no action shall be brought on certain contracts unless there be a note or memorandum thereof in writing, signed by the party to be charged or by his authorized agent.

statute of limitation   A statute prescribing limitations to the right of action on certain described causes of action; that is, declaring that no suit shall be maintained on such causes of action unless brought within a specified period after the right accrued.

statutory lien   Interest in property to secure payment of a debt that arises solely by statute.

stock   "Stock" is distinguished from "bonds" and, ordinarily, from "debentures," in that it gives right of ownership in part of assets of corporation and right to interest in any surplus after payment of debt. "Stock" in a corporation is an equity, and it represents an ownership interest, and it is to be distinguished from obligations such as notes or bonds which are not equities and represent no ownership interest.

Capital stock   See **capital.**

Common stock   Securities which represent an ownership interest in a corporation. If the company has also issued preferred stock, both common and preferred have ownership rights. Claims of both common and preferred stockholders are junior to claims of bondholders or other creditors of the company. Common stockholders assume the greater risk, but generally exercise the greater control and may gain the greater reward in the form of dividends and capital appreciation.

Convertible stock   Stock which may be changed or converted into common stock.

Cumulative preferred   A stock having a provision that if one or more dividends are omitted, the omitted dividends must be paid before dividends may be paid on the company's common stock.

Preferred stock is a separate portion or class of the stock of a corporation, which is accorded, by the charter or by-laws, a preference or priority in respect to dividends, over the remainder of the stock of the corporation, which in that case is called *common stock.*

Stock warrant A certificate entitling the owner to buy a specified amount of stock at a specified time(s) for a specified price. Differs from a stock option only in that options are granted to employees and warrants are sold to the public.

Treasury stock Shares reacquired by a corporation.

stock option Contractual right to purchase stock from a corporation.

stop payment Order for a drawee not to pay an instrument.

strict liability A concept applied by the courts in product liability cases in which a seller is liable for any and all defective or hazardous products which unduly threaten a consumer's personal safety. This concept applies to all members involved in the manufacturing and selling of any facet of the product.

strict scrutiny test Requirement that legislation be necessary to promote a compelling governmental interest.

subagent Person appointed by agent to perform agent's duties.

subject matter jurisdiction Authority of a court to decide a particular kind of case.

subject to the mortgage Purchaser is not personally obligated to pay the debt, but the property remains subject to the mortgage.

subjective fault Desired or virtually certain consequences of one's conduct.

subjective satisfaction Approval based upon a party's honestly held opinion.

sublease Transfer of less than all of the tenant's interest in the leasehold.

subpoena A subpoena is a command to appear at a certain time and place to give testimony upon a certain matter. A subpoena duces tecum requires production of books, papers, and other things.

subrogation The substitution of one thing for another, or of one person into the place of another with respect to rights, claims, or securities.

Subrogation denotes the putting a third person who has paid a debt in the place of the creditor to whom he has paid it, so that he may exercise against the debtor all the rights which the creditor, if unpaid, might have done.

subscribe Literally to write underneath, as one's name. To sign at the end of a document. Also, to agree in writing to furnish money or its equivalent, or to agree to purchase some initial stock in a corporation.

subscriber Person who agrees to purchase initial stock in a corporation.

subsidiary corporation Corporation controlled by another corporation.

substantial performance Equitable doctrine protects against forfeiture for technical inadvertence or trivial variations or omissions in performance.

substantive due process Requirement that governmental action be compatible with individual liberties.

substantive law The basic law of rights and duties (contract law, criminal law, tort law, law of wills, etc.) as opposed to procedural law (law of pleading, law of evidence, law of jurisdiction, etc.).

substantive unconscionability Oppressive or grossly unfair contractual terms.

sue To begin a lawsuit in a court.

suit "Suit" is a generic term, of comprehensive signification, and applies to any proceeding in a court of justice in which the plaintiff pursues, in such court, the remedy which the law affords him for the redress of an injury or the recovery of a right.

Derivative suit Suit brought by a shareholder on behalf of the corporation to enforce a right belonging to the corporation.

Direct suit Suit brought by a shareholder against the corporation based upon his ownership of shares.

summary judgment Rule of Civil Procedure 56 permits any party to a civil action to move for a summary judgment on a claim, counterclaim, or cross-claim when he believes that there is no genuine issue of material fact and that he is entitled to prevail as a matter of law.

summons Writ or process directed to the sheriff or other proper officer, requiring him to notify the person named that an action has been commenced against him in the court from where the process issues, and that he is required to appear, on a day named, and answer the complaint in such action.

superseding cause Intervening event that occurs after the defendant's negligent conduct and relieves him of liability.

supreme law Law that takes precedence over all conflicting laws.

surety One who undertakes to pay money or to do any other act in event that his principal debtor fails therein.

suretyship A guarantee of debts of another.

surplus Excess of net assets over stated capital.

tangible property Physical objects.

tariff Duty or tax imposed on goods moving into or out of the country.

tenancy Possession or occupancy of land or premises under lease.

Joint tenancy Joint tenants have one and the same interest, accruing by one and the same conveyance, commencing at one and the same time, and held by one and the same undivided possession. The primary incident of joint tenancy is survivorship, by which the entire tenancy on the decease of any joint tenant remains to the survivors, and at length to the last survivor.

Tenancy at sufferance Only naked possession which continues after tenant's right of possession has terminated.

Tenancy at will Possession of premises by permission of owner or landlord, but without a fixed term.

Tenancy by the entirety A tenancy which is created between a husband and wife and by which together they hold title to the whole with right of survivorship so that, upon death of either, other takes whole to exclusion of deceased heirs. It is essentially a "joint tenancy," modified by the common law theory that husband and wife are one person.

Tenancy for a period A tenancy for years or for some fixed period.

Tenancy in common A form of ownership whereby each tenant (*i.e.*, owner) holds an undivided interest in property. Unlike a joint tenancy or a tenancy by the entirety, the interest of a tenant in common does not terminate upon his or her prior death (*i.e.*, there is no right of survivorship).

tenancy in partnership Type of joint ownership that determines partners' rights in specific partnership property.

tenant Possessor of the leasehold interest.

tender An offer of money; the act by which one produces and offers to a person holding a claim or demand against him the amount of money which he considers and admits to be due, in satisfaction of such claim or demand, without any stipulation or condition.

Also, there may be a tender of performance of a duty other than the payment of money.

tender of delivery Seller makes available to buyer goods conforming to the contract and so notifies the buyer.

tender offer General invitation to all shareholders to purchase their shares at a specified price.

testament Will.

testator One who makes or has made a testament or will; one who dies leaving a will.

third party beneficiary One for whose benefit a promise is made in a contract but who is not a party to the contract.

Creditor beneficiary Where performance of a promise in a contract will benefit a person other than the promisee, that person is a creditor beneficiary if no purpose to make a gift appears from the terms of the promise in view of the accompanying circumstances and performance of the promise will satisfy an actual or supposed or asserted duty of the promisee to the beneficiary.

Donee beneficiary The person who takes the benefit of the contract even though there is no privity between him and the contracting parties. A third party beneficiary who is not a creditor beneficiary. See also **beneficiary.**

time paper Payable at definite time.

time-price doctrine Permits sellers to have different prices for cash sales and credit sales.

title The means whereby the owner of lands or of personalty has the just possession of his property.

title insurance Provides protection against defect in title to real property.

tort A private or civil wrong or injury, other than breach of contract, for which the court will provide a remedy in the form of an action for damages.

Three elements of every tort action are: Existence of legal duty from defendant to plaintiff, breach of duty, and damage as proximate result.

tort-feasor One who commits a tort.

trade acceptance A draft drawn by a seller which is presented for signature (acceptance) to the buyer at the time goods are purchased and which then becomes the equivalent of a note receivable of the seller and the note payable of the buyer.

trade name Name used in trade or business to identify a particular business or manufacturer.

trade secrets Private business information.

trademark Distinctive insignia, word, or design of a good that is used to identify the manufacturer.

transferor's warranty Warranties given by any person who transfers an instrument and receives consideration.

treaty An agreement between or among independent nations.

treble damages Three times actual loss.

trespass At common law, trespass was a form of action brought to recover damages for any injury to one's person or property or relationship with another.

Trespass to chattels or personal property An unlawful and serious interference with the possessory rights of another to personal property.

Trespass to land At common law, every unauthorized and direct breach of the boundaries of another's land was an actionable trespass. The present prevailing position of the courts finds liability for trespass only in the case of intentional intrusion, or negligence, or some "abnormally dangerous activity" on the part of the defendant. Compare **nuisance.**

trespasser Person who enters or remains on the land of another without permission or privilege to do so.

trust Any arrangement whereby property is transferred with intention that it be administered by trustee for another's benefit.

A trust, as the term is used in the Restatement, when not qualified by the word "charitable," "resulting" or "constructive," is a fiduciary relationship with respect to property, subjecting the person by whom the title to the property is held to equitable duties to deal with the property for the benefit of another person, which arises as a result of a manifestation of an intention to create it. Restatement, Second, Trusts § 2.

Charitable trust To benefit humankind.

Constructive trust Wherever the circumstances of a transaction are such that the person who takes the legal estate in property cannot also enjoy the beneficial interest without necessarily violating some established principle of equity, the court will immediately raise a *constructive trust*, and fasten it upon the conscience of the legal owner, so as to convert him into a trustee for the parties who in equity are entitled to the beneficial enjoyment.

Intervivos trust Established during the settlor's lifetime.

Resulting trust One that arises by implication of law, where the legal estate in property is disposed of, conveyed, or transferred, but the intent appears or is inferred from the terms of the disposition, or from the accompanying facts and circumstances, that the beneficial interest is not to go or be enjoyed with the legal title.

Spendthrift trust Removal of the trust's estate from the beneficiary's control.

Testamentary trust Established by a will.

Totten trust A tentative trust which is a joint bank account opened by the settlor.

Voting trust A trust which holds the voting rights to stock in a corporation. It is a useful device when a majority of the shareholders in a corporation cannot agree on corporate policy.

trustee In a strict sense, a "trustee" is one who holds the legal title to property for the benefit of another, while, in a broad sense, the term is sometimes applied to anyone standing in a fiduciary or confidential relation to another, such as agent, attorney, bailee, etc.

trustee in bankruptcy Representative of the estate in bankruptcy who is responsible for collecting, liquidating, and distributing the debtor's assets.

tying arrangements Conditioning a sale of a desired product (tying product) on the buyer's purchasing a second product (tied product).

ultra vires Acts beyond the scope of the powers of a corporation, as defined by its charter or laws of state of incorporation. By doctrine of ultra vires a contract made by a corporation beyond the scope of its corporate powers is unlawful.

unconscionable Unfair or unduly harsh.

unconscionable contract See **contracts**.

underwriter Any person, banker, or syndicate that guarantees to furnish a definite sum of money by a definite date to a business or government in return for an issue of bonds or stock. In insurance, the one assuming a risk in return for the payment of a premium.

undisputed debt Obligation whose existence and amount is not contested.

undue influence Term refers to conduct by which a person, through his power over mind of testator, makes the latter's desires conform to his own, thereby overmastering the volition of the testator.

unemployment compensation Compensation awarded to workers who have lost their jobs and cannot find other employment.

unenforceable Neither party can recover under the contract.

unfair employer practice Conduct in which an employer is prohibited from engaging.

unfair labor practice Conduct in which an employer or union is prohibited from engaging.

unfair union practice Conduct in which a union is prohibited from engaging.

Uniform Commercial Code One of the Uniform Laws drafted by the National Conference of Commissioners on Uniform State Laws governing commercial transactions (sales of goods, commercial paper, bank deposits and collections, letters of credit, bulk transfers, warehouse receipts, bills of lading, investment securities, and secured transactions).

unilateral mistake Erroneous belief on the part of only one of the parties to a contract.

union shop Employer can hire nonunion members, but the employee must join the union.

universal life Ordinary life divided into two components, a renewable term insurance policy and an investment portfolio.

unliquidated debt Obligation that is uncertain or contested in amount.

unqualified indorsement (see Indorsement) One that imposes liability upon the indorser.

unreasonably dangerous Danger beyond that which the ordinary consumer contemplates.

unrestrictive indorsement (see Indorsement) One that does not attempt to restrict the rights of the indorsee.

usage of trade A usage of trade is any practice or method of dealing having such regularity of observance in a place, vocation, or trade as to justify an expectation that it will be observed with respect to the transaction in question.

usury Collectively, the laws of a jurisdiction regulating the charging of interest rates. A usurious loan is one whose interest rates are determined to be in excess of those permitted by the usury laws.

value The performance of legal consideration, the forgiveness of an antecedent debt, the giving of a negotiable instrument, or the giving of an irrevocable commitment to a third party. U.C.C. § 1–201(44).

variance A use differing from that provided in the zoning ordinance in order to avoid undue hardship.

vendee A purchaser or buyer; one to whom anything is sold. See also **vendor**.

vendor The person who transfers property by sale, particularly real estate; "seller" being more commonly used for one who sells personalty. See also **vendee**.

venue "Jurisdiction" of the court means the inherent power to decide a case, whereas "venue" designates the particular county or city in which a court with jurisdiction may hear and determine the case.

verdict The formal and unanimous decision or finding of a jury, impaneled and sworn for the trial of a cause, upon the matters or questions duly submitted to them upon the trial.

vertical privity Who is liable to the plaintiff.

vertical restraints Agreements among parties at different levels of the distribution chain.

vested Fixed; accrued; settled; absolute. To be "vested," a right must be more than a mere expectation based on an anticipation of the continuance of an existing law; it must have become a title, legal or equitable, to the present or future enforcement of a demand, or a legal exemption from the demand of another.

vested remainder Unconditional remainder that is a fixed, present interest to be enjoyed in the future.

vicarious liability Indirect legal responsibility; for example, the liability of an employer for the acts of an employee, or, a principal for torts and contracts of an agent.

void Null; ineffectual; nugatory; having no legal force or binding effect; unable, in law, to support the purpose for which it was intended.

There is this difference between the two words "void" and "voidable": *void* in the strict sense means that an instrument or transaction is nugatory and ineffectual so that nothing can cure it; *voidable* exists when an imperfection or defect can be cured by the act or confirmation of him who could take advantage of it.

Frequently the word "void" is used and construed as having the more liberal meaning of "voidable."

voidable Capable of being made void. See also **void**.

voir dire Preliminary examination of potential jurors.

voluntary Resulting from free choice. The word, especially in statutes, often implies knowledge of essential facts.

voting trust Transfer of corporate shares voting rights to a trustee.

wager (gambling) Agreement that one party will win or lose depending upon the outcome of an event in which the only interest is the gain or loss.

waiver Terms "estoppel" and "waiver" are not synonymous; "waiver" means the voluntary, intentional relinquishment of a known right, and "estoppel" rests upon principle that, where anyone has done an act, or made a statement, which would be a fraud on his part to controvert or impair, because other party has acted upon it in belief that what was done or said was true, conscience and honest dealing require that he not be permitted to repudiate his act or gainsay his statement. See also **estoppel**.

ward An infant or insane person placed by authority of law under the care of a guardian.

warehouse receipt Receipt issued by a person storing goods.

warehouser Storer of goods for compensation.

warrant, *v.* In contracts, to engage or promise that a certain fact or state of facts, in relation to the subject-matter, is, or shall be, as it is represented to be.

In conveyancing, to assure the title to property sold, by an express covenant to that effect in the deed of conveyance.

warranty A warranty is a statement or representation made by seller of goods, contemporaneously with and as a part of contract of sale, having reference to character, quality, or title of goods, and by which seller promises or undertakes to insure that certain facts are or shall be as he then represents them.

The general statutory law governing warranties on sales of goods is provided in U.C.C. § 2–312 *et seq*. The three main types of warranties are: (1) express warranty; (2) implied warranty of fitness; (3) implied warranty of merchantability.

warranty deed Deed in which grantor warrants good clear title. The usual covenants of title are warranties of seisin, quiet enjoyment, right to convey, freedom from encumbrances and defense of title as to all claims.

Special warranty deed Seller warrants that he has not impaired title.

warranty liability Applies to persons who transfer an instrument or receive payment or acceptance.

warranty of title Obligation to convey the right to ownership without any lien.

waste Any act or omission that does permanent injury to the realty or unreasonably changes its value.

white collar crime Corporate crime.

will A written instrument executed with the formalities required by statutes, whereby a person makes a disposition of his property to take effect after his death.

winding up To settle the accounts and liquidate the assets of a partnership or corporation, for the purpose of making distribution and terminating the concern.

without reserve Auctioneer may not withdraw the goods from the auction.

worker's compensation Compensation awarded to an employee who is injured when the injury arose out of and in the course of his employment.

writ of certiorari Discretionary review by a higher court. See also **certiorari**.

writ of execution Order served by sheriff upon debtor demanding payment of a court judgment against debtor.

zoning Public control over land use.

INDEX